A New Approach to

REASONING

Verbal, Non-Verbal & Analytical

A New Approach to

REASONING

Verbal, Non-Verbal & Analytical

Useful for

Management (CAT, XAT, MAT, CMAT, IIFT, SNAP & other), Bank (PO & Clerk), SSC (CGL, 10+2, Steno, FCI, CPO, Multitasking), LIC (AAO & ADO), CLAT, RRB, UPSC and Other State PSC Exams

BS Sijwali • Indu Sijwali

Arihant Publications (India) Ltd.

arihant

ARIHANT PUBLICATIONS (INDIA) LIMITED

Administrative & Production Offices

Regd. Office

'Ramchhaya' 4577/15, Agarwal Road, Darya Ganj, New Delhi -110002
Tele: 011- 47630600, 43518550

Head Office

Kalindi, TP Nagar, Meerut (UP) - 250002
Tel: 0121-7156203, 7156204

Sales & Support Offices

Agra, Ahmedabad, Bengaluru, Bareilly, Chennai, Delhi, Guwahati, Hyderabad, Jaipur, Jhansi, Kolkata, Lucknow, Nagpur & Pune.

ISBN 978-93-25299-47-4

PO No : TXT-XX-XXXXXXX-X-XX

Published by Arihant Publications (India) Ltd.

For further information about the books published by Arihant, log on to www.arihantbooks.com or e-mail at info@arihantbooks.com

Follow us on   

PREFACE

In any general, competitive or entrance examination, the section Reasoning and General Intelligence is equally weighted section in any question paper.

Reasoning basically tests candidates thinking power and mind applicability skills. Importance of reasoning is increasingly moving centre stage in today's competitive examinations. The questions that are asked in different examinations are not easy to solve and one cannot solve these problems without having prior knowledge and better practice. But if a candidate knows the basic concept behind the question, then he/she can solve it in no time.

This Book 'A New Approach to Reasoning is' the most appropriate and the best reference text book on reasoning as it caters to the needs of students who aspire to prepare and develop skills in Verbal, Non-Verbal and Analytical Reasoning for various competitive exams viz Management entrances (CAT, XAT, MAT, CMAT, IIFT & SNAP, etc.), SSC (10+2, CGL, CPO etc.), Bank (PO & Clerk), Railways, UPSC and other State PSCs entrance exams.

Above all, it can be said that the book at hand prove to be a real gem if studied with dedication and sincerity. We are sure that this book will add a new dimension to the preparation for every competitive examination and prove to be very helpful to all candidates.

However, we have put our best efforts in preparing this book, but if any error or whatsoever has been skipped out, we have welcomed your suggestions. A part from all those who helped in the compilation of this book a special note of thanks goes to Ms Garima Sharma without their support the book could not have come to its shape. Sandeep Saini has given their expertise in the layout of the book.

The contribution of Mr Amogh Goyal. Mr Rohit & Harvindar for this book is also very special and worthy of great applause.

Reader's recommendation will be highly treasured.

FEATURES OF REVISED & UPDATED EDITION

- The whole book is divided into three sections *viz.* **Verbal, Non-verbal and Analytical Reasoning.**
- Each chapter begins with a brief introduction about chapter and covers all possible **types** that are covered under it.
- Each type has its specific theory with supported **examples** and also has its separate exercise with detailed solutions.
- At the end of the chapter, there is a **Master Exercise** which covers questions based on all types and latest questions asked in **previous years' examinations**. Each question has its accurate and detailed answer.

Authors
BS Sijwali & Indu Sijwali

CONTENT

VERBAL REASONING

NON-VERBAL REASONING

ANALYTICAL REASONING

A New Approach to

REASONING

VERBAL REASONING

CHAPTER / 01

Alphabet and Number Test

Alphabet and Number Tests are based on arrangement of English letters/numbers in a certain defined pattern. These tests are also based on formation of new numbers/words and finding letter pairs and numbers between two specific letters and numbers.

In this chapter, we deal with the questions in which, a group or series of letters is given. This group can be a meaningful or in scrambled form. Based on that group, a candidate is asked to find a letters' pair between the words or form a meaningful word with different letters or find letter or number to the left or right of a particular letter. Before moving to the type of questions, first we should learn the letters' position of English alphabet and various other facts related to it.

There are 26 letters in English alphabetical series
A, B, C, D, E, F, G, H, I, J, K, L, M, N, O, P, Q, R, S, T, U, V, W, X, Y, Z.

The following diagram will give a better idea about English alphabet.

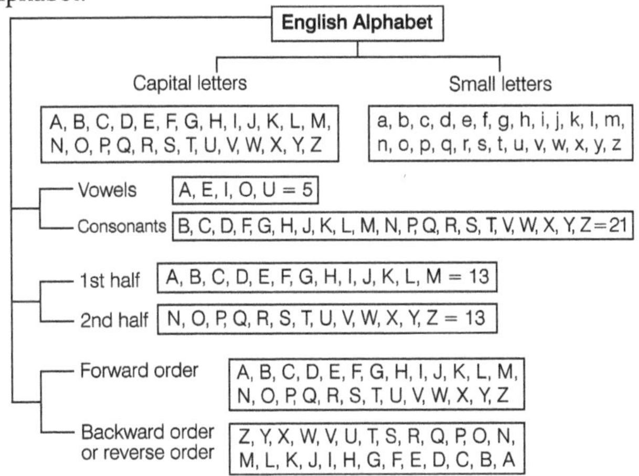

Positions

In English alphabet, each letter has its corresponding position and it is important to learn about the position or rank of the alphabets. Such positions of letters are of two types —

1. Forward Order Letter Position

In such order positions are counted from left to right. In other words, one starts counting from A and goes towards Z.

Left to Right

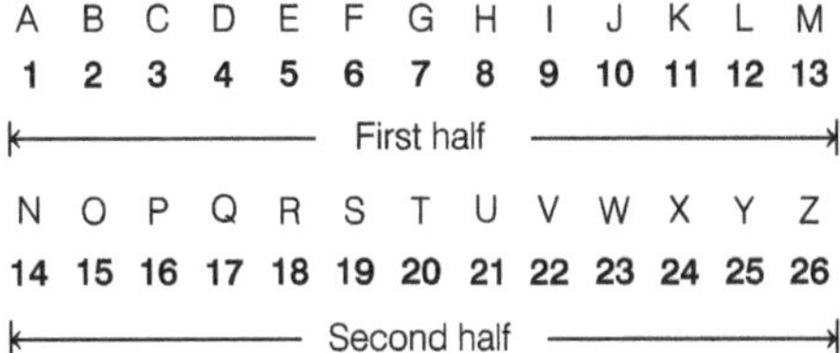

2. Backward Order Letter Position

In backward order position, counting is started from Z and is ended at A. In other words, counting is done from right to left.

Right to Left

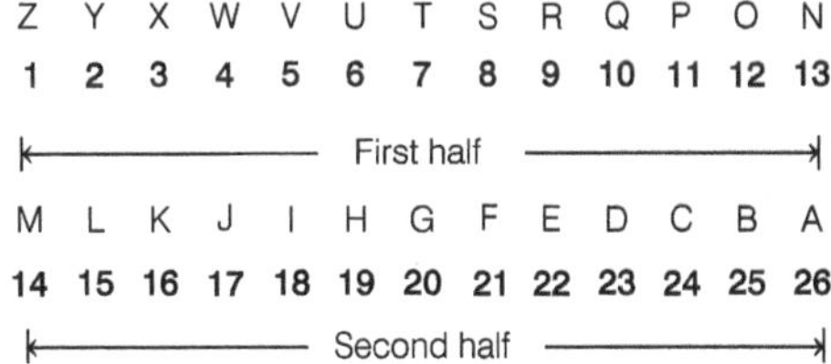

Trick to Learn Position/Rank of the Alphabets

We have already discussed that there are 26 letters in the alphabet series.

Now let us have a look at the tricks to learn the position of alphabets.

A to D First four letters A to D's, rank is 1 to 4 (easy to learn). No trick is required to learn them.

E For this you have to learn one word "EJOTY".

E	J	O	T	Y
5	10	15	20	25

Learning this word helps you to learn the position of 5 letters which are the multiple of 5.

F For this you have to learn another word "CFILORUX".

C	F	I	L	O	R	U	X
3	6	9	12	15	18	21	24

Learning this word helps you to learn the position of 8 letters which are the multiple of 3.

G Everybody know **G-7 Nations.**
The position of G is 7.

H If you join the 2 lines of H, it will become 8 or you can say H looks like 8. Thus, the position of H is "8".

I "I know (9) You". Learn this sentence and you will get position of "I".

J Remember the term "EJOTY".
The position of J is "10".

K K for **Kelvin** and which is similar to "**eleven**" in Pronunciation.
The position of K is "11".

L Remember the term "CFILORUX".
The position of L is "12".

M M looks like 3 (when we rotate M as 3)
The position of M is "13".

N N for November and November 14 is Children's day.
Thus, the position of N is "14".

O Again the term EJOTY. The position of O is "15".

P When we see water image of P, it look like Six (6). The position of P is "16".

Q Write Q like Q_7. Here, we can see "7" on right end of Q. The position of Q is "17".

R Remember the term CFILORUX or when we stretch R like R, it looks like 8. The position of R is "18".

S We write Nineteen, UNISSS in hindi. The position of S is "19". 19 (S)

T T-20 Match

Or

Remember the term EJOTY.
The position of T is "20".

U Again remember the term "CFILORUX". The position of U is 21.

V V for Victory.
You require two fingers to represent victory.
The position of "V" is "22".

W If you rotate anticlockwise the letter "W", it looks like 3, its position is 23.

X Remember the term CFILORUX.

Or

It is being divided into Four parts.

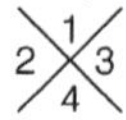

The position of X is 23.

Y Remember the term "EJOTY".
The position of Y is 25.

Z Last letter is Z. Its position is 26.
After the positional values of English letters are known, we should learn about the position of *Opposite* letters and *Left and Right* of a letter.

Opposite Letters

A letter is said to opposite of other when sum of their positional values is equal to 27.

e.g., Positional value of B = 2,
Positional value of Y = 25
Required sum = 2 + 25 = 27

Hence, they are opposite letter pair.

If we have to find the opposite letter of any letter, then corresponding position of that letter is subtracted from 27. *Let us see*

Opposite letter of A = 27 − Position of A
= 27 − 1 = 26th letter = Z

Opposite letter of B = 27 − Position of B
= 27 − 2 = 25th letter
= Y and so on.

Trick to Remember Opposite Letters

AZ	Remember (ZA) of 'go' in Hindi / AZad
BY	Remember the word 'by' / BoY
CX	Remember CIX (like 'Six') / CraX
DW	Remember DW of the word / DEW.
EV	Remember EV (Evening) / loVE
FU	Remember FU of 'Full' / ForU
GT	Remember GT Road (Built by Shershah)
HS	Higher Secondary / High School
IR	Indian Railway
JQ	Jack and Queen (in the game of cards)
KP	Kevin Peterson (England cricket player) / kal-Prso
LO	Remember LO of the word LOVE
MN	Remember MN of the word MAN

Left and Right of a Letter

Letters do not have their own left and right. We decide left and right of letters on the basis of ours left and right. In other words, the left of letters is towards our left and the right of letters is towards our right.

Let us see

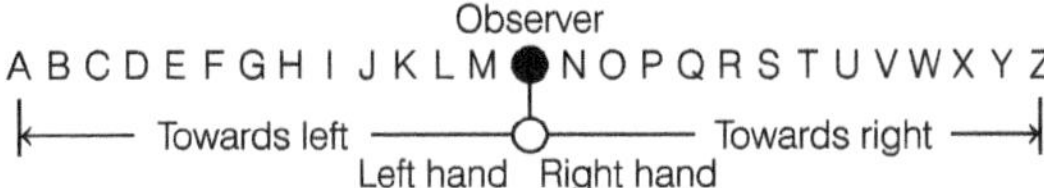

If you have to find out 4th letter to the left of T, then stand in front of T like below.

A B C D E F G H I J K L M N O P Q R S T U V W X Y Z

Observer

4th Towards left

So, 4th letter to the right of T is "X".

Clearly, 4th letter to the left of T is P.

And, if you have to find out 4th letter to the right of T, then stand in front of T and find required letter as below.

A B C D E F G H I J K L M N O P Q R S T U V W X Y Z

Towards right 4th

Some terms related to 'Left' and 'Right' are as follows

(i) **Just Left/Immediate left** It means just before. **e.g.,** G is the letter just left of H.

(ii) **Just right/immediate right** It means just after. **e.g.,** Q is the letter just right of P.

(iii) **From our Left** It means 'from our left to right' or we can say it as 'from letter A to Z'. *i.e.,*
$A \rightarrow B \rightarrow C \rightarrow \ldots\ldots \rightarrow Y \rightarrow Z$

(iv) **From our Right** It means 'from our right to left' or we can say it as 'from letter Z to A'. *i.e.,*
$A \leftarrow B \leftarrow C \leftarrow \ldots\ldots \leftarrow Y \leftarrow Z$

(v) **To the Left** It means 'from Z to A'. *i.e.,*
$A \leftarrow B \leftarrow C \leftarrow \ldots\ldots \leftarrow Y \leftarrow Z$

(vi) **To the Right** It means 'from A to Z'. *i.e.,*
$A \rightarrow B \rightarrow C \rightarrow \ldots\ldots \rightarrow Y \rightarrow Z$

Important formulae to find the position of letter in english alphabet

1. In english alphabet n+n letter to the right of m+n letter from your left = (m+n)+n letter from left.
2. In english alphabets n+n letter to the left of m+n letter from your right = (m+n)+n letter from right.
3. In english alphabet n+n letter to the left of m+n letter from your left = (m–n)+n letter from left.
4. In english alphabet n+n letter to the right of m+m letters from your right = (m–n)+n letter from right.
5. In backward order of english alphabet n+n letter to the right of m+n letter from your left = (m+n)+n letter from left.
6. In backward order of english alphabet n+n to the left of m+n letter from your right = (m+n)+n letter from right.
7. In backward order of english alphabet n+n letter to the left of m+n letter from your left (m–n)+n letter from left.
8. In backward order of english alphabet n+n letter to the right of m+n letter from your right = (m+n)+n letter from right.

Various types of questions asked in the examination are as follows.

TYPE 01

Alphabet Test

In this type, the questions asked are based on–finding the place of an English letter to the left or right of another English letter in the alphabetical order.

Sometimes the questions are based on

- finding the number of English letter(s) between two different English letters.
- finding the middle letter between two specified letters and in some questions it is asked that which letters do not change their places after alphabetical arrangement.

The detailed discussion with examples of the above mentioned types of questions are as follow

A. Place of a Letter in Forward Order

In this type of questions the exact letter has to be found out with the help of direction and place given in the question.

***Ex* 01** Find the 11th letter to the left of 20th letter from left in the English alphabet.

(a) D (b) J
(c) K (d) I

***Solution* (c)** Let us see

1 2 3 4 5 6 7 8 9 10 11 12 13 14 15 16 17 18 19 20 21 22 23 24 25 26
A B C D E F G H I J K L M N O P Q R S T U V W X Y Z

To the left

11th

From left 20th

Hence, 11th letter to the left of 20th letter from left is I.

Alternate Method (By formula 3)

In English alphabet 11th letter to the left of 20th letter from your left = (20 – 11)th letter from left = 9th letter from left = I

B. Place of Letter in Completely Backward Order

In such questions the order of letters is completely reversed or they are counted from Z to A and then the place of letter is asked with the help of direction.

Ex 02 If English alphabet is written in backward order, then what will be the 13th letter to the left of the 3rd letter from right?

(a) P (b) N
(c) R (d) Q

Solution (a) Backward order is written as

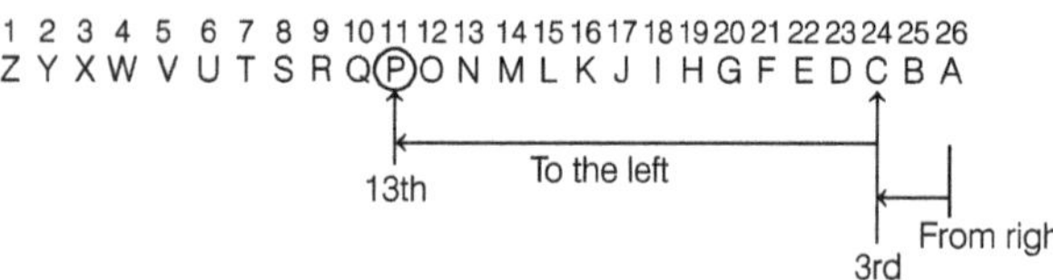

Now, the 13th letter to the left of the 3rd letter from right is P.

Alternate Method (By formula 6)

In backward order of alphabet, 13th letter to the left of 3rd letter from our right = (3 + 13)th letter from right
= 16th letter from right = P

C. Place of a Letter When First Half is in Backward Order

In such type of questions, only the 1st half of the order of alphabetical series is reversed and remaining are left unaltered *i.e.*, order of A to M is reversed and then questions related to position of letters are asked.

Ex 03 If 1st half of the English alphabet is written in backward order, then what will be the 7th letter to the left of the 10th letter from your right?

(a) C (b) E
(c) D (d) J

Solution (c) Let us see

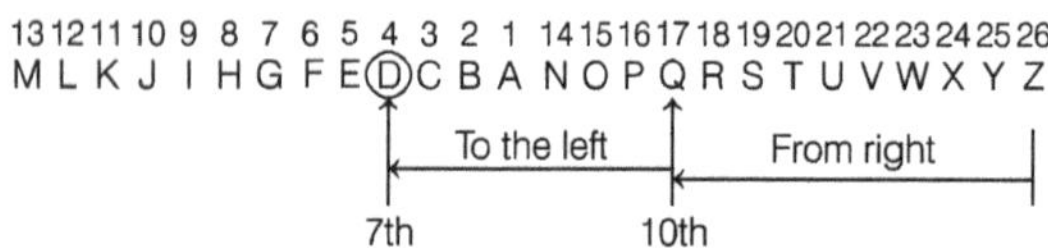

∴ The 7th letter to the left of 10th letter from our right is D.

D. Place of a Letter When Second Half is in Backward Order

In such type of questions the 2nd half is reversed *i.e.*, from N to Z and remaining are kept as it is and then questions related to place of English alphabet are asked.

Ex 04 If 2nd half of the English alphabet is written in backward order, then what will be the 7th letter to the right of 13th letter from your left?

(a) T (b) U (c) V (d) S

Solution (a) Let us see

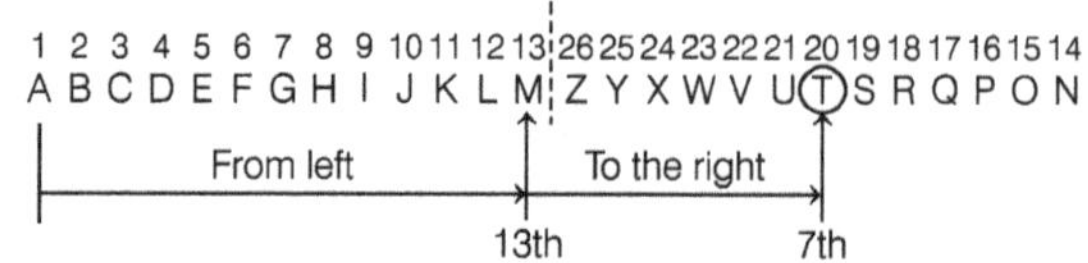

∴ The 7th letter to the right of 13th letter from our left is T.

E. Multiple Letter Segment in Backward Order

In such type of questions, no specified order of change is followed in alphabetical order. They are changed according to the condition given in a particular question.

Ex 05 If first four letters of the English alphabet are written in reverse order; again next 5 letters are written in reverse order; again next 6 letters are written in reverse order; again next 7 letters are written in reverse order and finally, the remaining letters are also written in reverse order, then what will be the 7th letter to the left of the 8th letter from right?

(a) M (b) N (c) O (d) L

Solution (a) Let us see the arrangement

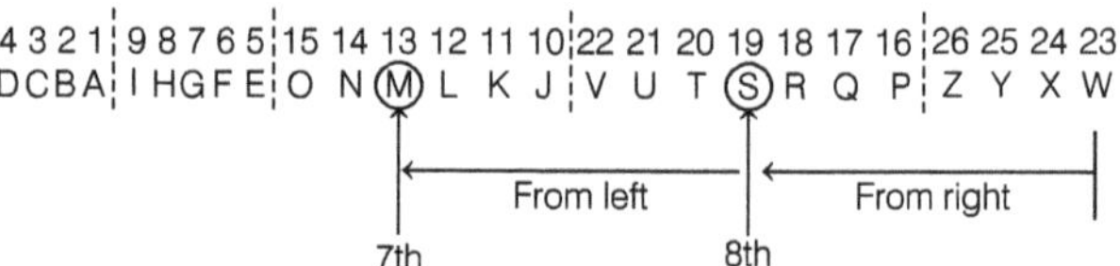

∴ The 7th letter to the left of the 8th letter from right is M.

F. Number of Letters Between Two Letters

In this particular type of questions the candidate is asked to calculate the total number of English letters between any two specified letters as directed in the question.

Four situations can be created under these types of problems

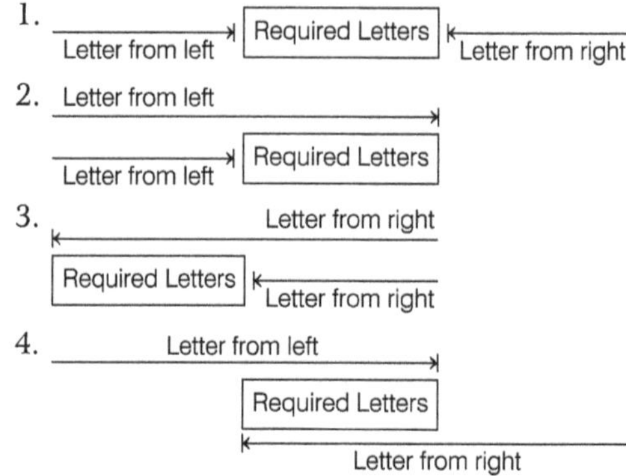

Ex 06 How many letters are there between 8th letter from left and 7th letter from right in the English alphabet?

(a) 7 (b) 11 (c) 8 (d) 9

Solution ***(b)*** Let us see

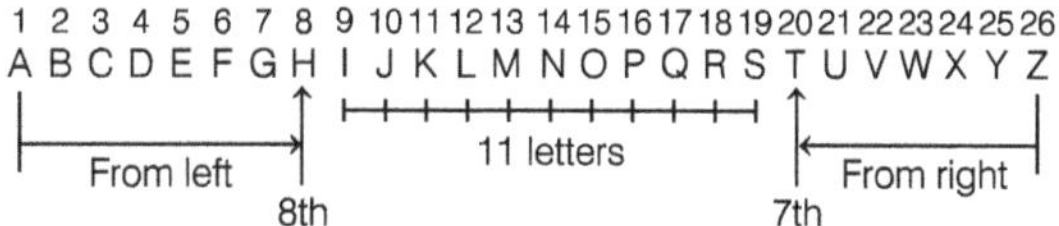

∴ There are 11 letters between 8th letter from left and 7th letter from right.

Alternate Method

Total number of letters in the English alphabet = 26

∴ Required number of letters = 26 – (8 + 7) = 26 – 15 = 11

Ex **07** How many number of letters are there between 22nd letter from left and 8th letter from left in the English alphabet?

(a) 12 (b) 15 (c) 11 (d) 13

Solution ***(d)*** Let us see there are 13 such letters

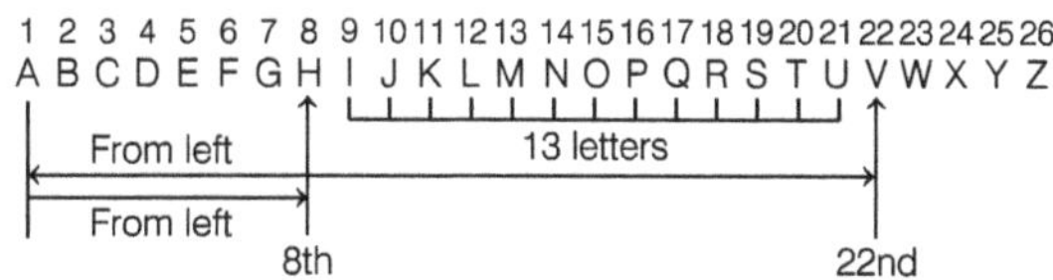

Alternate Method

22nd letter from left = (27 – 22) = 5th letter from right. Clearly, we have to find the number of letters between 8th letter from left and 5th letter from right.

∴ Required number of letters = 26 – (8 + 5) = 26 – 13 = 13

Ex **08** Find the number of letters between 20th letter from right and 10th letter from right in the English alphabet.

(a) 9 (b) 12 (c) 7 (d) 11

Solution ***(a)*** Let us see

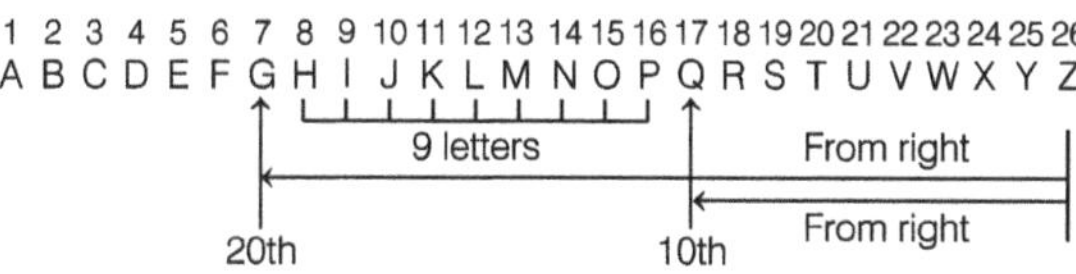

∴ There are 9 such letters.

Alternate Method

20th letter from right = (27 – 20) = 7th letter from left

Clearly, we have to find the number of letters between 7th letter from left and 10th letter from right.

∴ Required number of letters = 26 – (7 + 10) = 26 – 17 = 9

Ex **09** How many letters are there between 20th letter from left and 18th letter from right in the English alphabet?

(a) 15 (b) 6 (c) 10 (d) 12

Solution ***(c)*** Let us see

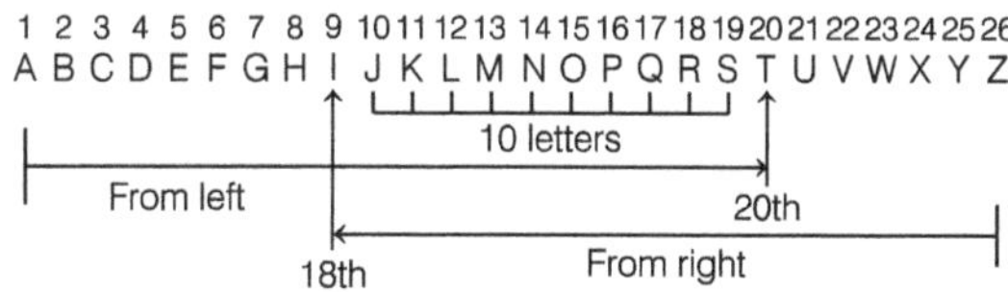

∴ There are 10 such letters.

Alternate Method

18th letter from right = (27 – 18) = 9th letter from left. And 20th letter from left = (27 – 20) = 7th letter from right.

Clearly, we have to find the number of letters between 9th letter from left and 7th letter from right.

∴ Required number of letters = 26 – (9 + 7)

= 26 – 16 = 10

G. Middle Letter between Two Letters

In these types of questions, the candidate is asked to find the middle letter between the two specified letters of English alphabet.

Ex **10** Which letter is in the middle of 7th letter from left and 10th letter from right in the English alphabet?

(a) L (b) P
(c) M (d) Q

Solution ***(a)*** Let us see

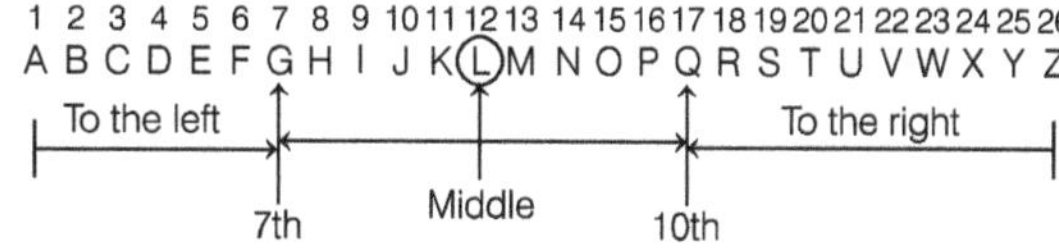

∴ Letter between G and Q is L.

Alternate Method

10th letter from right = 27 – 10 = 17th letter from left.

∴ Required middle letter $= \frac{7 + 17}{2} = \frac{24}{2}$

= 12th letter from left = L

H. Same Position of Alphabet after Arranging Alphabetically

In this type of questions, a word is given and then asked how many letters will remain at the same position, if they are arranged in alphabetical order.

Ex **11** How many letters will remain at the same position in the word 'SURFACE' when they are arranged in the alphabetical order from left to right? « IBPS Clerk 2017

(a) Four (b) Three
(c) One (d) Two
(e) None of these

Solution ***(c)***

S U R [F] A C E
A C E [F] R S U
[arranged in alphabetical order from left to right]

Only one letter 'F' remain at the same position.

Ex **12** If the vowels of the word 'ROUTINE' are 1st arranged in alphabetical order, followed by the consonants in the alphabetical order, which of the following will be 4th from the right end after the rearrangement?

(a) N (b) U (c) T (d) O

Solution ***(b)***

Original word, R O U T I N E
Rearrangement, E I O U N R T
4 3 2 1 (From right, under U N R T)

Hence, U is the correct answer.

Practice / CORNER 1.1

1. In the English alphabet, find the position of S from right.
(a) 8 (b) 5 (c) 4 (d) 9

2. In the English alphabet, find the position of L from left.
(a) 12 (b) 16 (c) 11 (d) 15

3. Which letter is 7th from right in the English alphabet?
(a) P (b) C (c) T (d) V

4. Find the letter which is 16th from right in the English alphabet.
(a) K (b) L (c) J (d) F

5. In the English alphabet, which letter is 10th from right? « UP B.Ed. 2011
(a) P (b) Q (c) R (d) S

6. If the English alphabet is written in backward order, then which letter will be 5th to the left of letter M? « MAT 2011
(a) G (b) H (c) S (d) R

7. Find the letter that comes 5th to the left of R in the English alphabet. SSC (CGL) 2009
(a) M (b) N (c) V (d) T

8. If English alphabet is written in the backward order, then which letter is 7th to the right of K? « UP B.Ed. 2011
(a) A (b) B (c) C (d) D

9. Which letter of the alphabet is 7th to the left of the 18th letter from the left in a forward alphabet series? « UPSSSC VDO 2018
(a) J (b) G (c) T (d) K

10. 4WXZ8QPOJ6GTMVEUH53B
In the above series, the 5th term to the left of the 8th term from the right is « RRB Group D 2018
(a) P (b) O (c) H (d) 5

11. Find the middle letter between K and V in the English alphabet.
(a) N (b) O
(c) Q (d) No letter possible

12. All the vowels are removed from the English alphabets. Remaining alphabets are arranged once in increasing order and once in decreasing. The letter (alphabet) whose position remains the same in both increasing and decreasing order is « CGPSC Pre 2016
(a) L (b) M (c) P (d) N
(e) None of these

13. Which letter is 10th to the left of 18th letter from left in the English alphabet? « UP B.Ed. 2010
(a) L (b) J (c) H (d) I

14. If the letters of English alphabet are written in reverse order, then find the 10th letter to the left of 10th letter from right? « UCO Bank (PO) 2010
(a) S (b) V (c) T (d) G (e) W

15. If the English alphabet is written in reverse order, then which letter is 7th to the left of 11th letter from right? « SSC (10+2) 2008
(a) W (b) H (c) R (d) D

16. If English alphabet is written in backward order, then find the 7th letter to the left of 11th letter from left.
(a) W (b) H (c) I (d) D

17. If 1st half of the English alphabet is written in reverse order, then find the 15th letter from right. « Canara Bank (Clerk) 2008
(a) A (b) B (c) C (d) D (e) E

18. If the 2nd half of the English alphabet is written in the reverse order, then find the 15th letter from right. « LIC (ADO) 2009
(a) M (b) L (c) K (d) J (e) O

19. If the 1st half of the English alphabet is written in the backward order, then find the 15th letter to the left of 20th letter from left. « Syndicate Bank (Clerk) 2010
(a) H (b) I (c) Y (d) X (e) N

20. If the 2nd half of the English alphabet is written in backward order, then which letter comes 5th to the left of the 20th letter from left? « PNB (PO) 2011
(a) J (b) H (c) Y (d) Z (e) X

21. Which letter will be midway between 6th letter from left and 14th letter from the left in the English alphabet?
(a) K (b) J
(c) I (d) L

22. Which letter comes in the middle of 20th letter from left and 21st letter from right? « PNB (PO) 2011
(a) L (b) M (c) N (d) O
(e) No letter possible

23. Find the middle letter between 7th letter from left and 14th letter from right in the English alphabet. « Allahabad Bank (Clerk) 2011
(a) H (b) I
(c) J (d) K
(e) No letter possible

24. All the English alphabets are arranged alphabetically in the reverse order. The difference of the positions of two vowels which appear in the beginning and in the end is « CGPSC Pre 2017
(a) 6 (b) 12
(c) 16 (d) 18
(e) None of these

25. Find the middle letter between 4th and 16th letters in the English alphabet. « SBI (PO) 2004
(a) J (b) K
(c) I (d) L
(e) None of these

DIRECTIONS ~ (Q.Nos. 26-28) *Study the following letter series and give the answer of following questions based on the letter series* « CGPSC Pre 2017

A B C F E D G H I L K J M N O R Q P S T U X W V Y Z

26. How many letters are not at their usual place in the alphabetical order?

(a) 7 (b) 9 (c) 8 (d) 10
(e) None of these

27. How many sets of two or more letters have letters in the alphabetical order?

(a) 4 (b) 5 (c) 6 (d) 7
(e) None of these

28. Some letters are preceded by and followed by wrong letters so far as their alphabetic order is concerned. What are these letters?

(a) G J P V (b) E K Q W (c) C H N T (d) B I O U
(e) None of these

29. How many such letters are there in the word 'CATEGORY' which remains same in its position, when they are arranged in alphabetical order?

(a) None (b) One (c) Two (d) Three

30. In the word CITRUS, the letter immediately before each vowel is replaced with the next alphabet (as per the English alphabetical order) and all other remain unchanged. Which of the following letters did not appear in the word thus formed? « RBI Assistant 2017

(a) I (b) V (c) T (d) S (e) D

31. In the given sequence, if every letter beginning from position 8 from the left is replaced by its next letter in the English alphabet, and Z is replaced by A, then how many V's will be there in the resulting sequence? « RRB ALP 2018

ZUDJKNCXVCSLLIEBSFJVATWQK

(a) 0 (b) 3 (c) 2 (d) 1

32. If all the letters in the word FIGURES are arranged in alphabetical order from left to right in such a way that vowels are arranged first followed by consonants, then how many letters are there in between U and R after the arrangement? « SBI Clerk 2018

(a) Two (b) One (c) None (d) Three
(e) Four

33. How many such letters are there in the word 'MONKEY' which remain at the same in its position, if the letters are arranged in descending order alphabetically?

(a) None (b) One (c) Two (d) Three

34. How many such letters are there in the word 'MARTINA'. Which remain same in its position, if they are arranged in alphabetical order?

(a) One (b) Two (c) Three (d) Four

35. If the last four letters of the word 'CONCENTRATION' are written in reverse order followed by next two in reverse order and next three in the reverse order. Counting from the end, which letter would be eighth in the new arrangement? « CMAT 2013

(a) O (b) I (c) N (d) T

36. If each alphabet in the word 'FRACTION' is arranged in alphabetical order and then each vowel is changed to the next letter in the English alphabetical series and each consonant is changed to previous letter in English alphabetical series, which of the following will be 4th from the right side of the new arrangement thus formed? « PNB (PO) 2010

(a) M (b) T
(c) P (d) E
(e) Q

37. Each vowel in the word 'TIRADES' is replaced by the previous letter and each consonant is replaced by the next letter in the English alphabet and the new letters are rearranged alphabetically, from right which of the following will be the fifth from the right end? « SBI (PO) 2011

(a) F (b) J (c) Q (d) C
(e) None of these

38. If each consonant in the word 'TOLERANT' is replaced by the previous letter in the English alphabet and each vowel in the word is replaced by the next letter in the English alphabet and a new set of letters is arranged alphabetically, which of the following will be the 6th from the left end after the replacement? « Andhra Bank (PO) 2009

(a) M (b) P
(c) B (d) Can't be determined
(e) None of these

39. In case of how many letters of the word 'RAIMENT' will their order in the word remains same when the letters are arranged in the alphabetical order ? « IDBI Bank (Clerk) 2010

(a) None (b) Three
(c) One (d) Two
(e) None of these

40. In the case of how many letters of the word 'FAINTS', will their order in the word not remain same when the letters are arranged in the alphabetical order? « Canara Bank (Clerk) 2011

(a) Two (b) One
(c) Three (d) None
(e) None of these

41. In the word 'Creation', if all the letters are arranged in alphabetical increasing order from left to right, then Which letter/letters remain/remains in the same position? « RBI Office Assistant 2020

(a) Only 'N'
(b) Both 'A' and 'T'
(c) Only 'E'
(d) Both 'C' and 'O'
(e) None of these

42. If the letters of the word 'DOLPHIN' are arranged as they appear in the English alphabetical order from right which of the following letters is preceded by the letter which is 5th from left? « UP B.Ed. 2011

(a) No such word (b) H
(c) I (d) None of these

43. The letters in the word 'MORTIFY' are changed in such a way that the vowels are replaced by the previous letter in the English alphabet and the consonants are replaced by the next letter in the English alphabet. Which of the following will be in the middle of the third letter from the right end and third letter from left end of the new set of letters?

(a) U (b) H (c) G (d) None of these

44. The position of first and the fourth letters of the word PRICED are interchanged, similarly, the positions of second and fifth letters and third and sixth letters. In new arrangement thus formed, how many letters are there in English alphabetical series between alphabets, which are at the extreme ends? « SBI Clerk 2016

(a) EDPI (b) EDCR (c) EDIR (d) EDPR

(e) None of these

45. Each vowel in the word 'JOURNEY' is replaced by the previous letter in the English alphabet and each consonant is replaced by the next letter in the English alphabet. Then, the substitute letters are arranged in alphabetical order. Which of the following will be the 5th from the left end? « PNB (PO) 2009

(a) S (b) T (c) N (d) O

(e) None of these

46. If all the letters of each given words are arranged in alphabetical order within the words, then in how many words third and fifth letter remains on the same position as earlier? « IBPS Clerk Mains 2018

I. MBEKTYD II. GPNAQUS

III. XCJRHO

(a) Only I (b) Only I and II

(c) All I, II and III (d) Only II

(e) None

47. The distinct letters of the word EXTRAORDINARY are arranged in alphabetic order. Then, the letter in the fifth position from left is « WBCS 2020

(a) N (b) O

(c) I (d) A

48. If in the English alphabet, all letters with odd numbered positions are written in serial order from right to left followed by the letters at even numbered positions written in reverse order, which letter will be 5th to the right of 18th letter from left?

(a) None (b) A

(c) S (d) Can't be determined

(e) None of these

Answers / WITH EXPLANATIONS

1. (*a*) Position of S from left = 19th

∴ Position of S from right = (27−19)th = 8th

2. (*a*) From CFILORUX, Position of L from left = 12th

3. (*c*) 7th letter from right = (27 − 7) th = 20th letter from left = T

4. (*a*) 16th letter from right = (27 − 16)th

= 11th letter from left = K

5. (*b*) Required letter = (27 − 10)th = 17th letter from left = Q

6. (*d*) 5th letter to the left of M in the backward order

= 5th letter to the right of M in forward order

= 5th letter after M in the forward order

= (13 + 5)th letter in the forward order

= 18th letter in the forward order

= R

Position of M in forward order alphabet = 13

7. (*a*) Position of R from left = 18

∴ 5th letter to the left of R = 5th letter before R

= (18 − 5)th = 13 th letter = M

8. (*d*) 7th letter to the right of K in backward order

= 7th letter to the left of K in forward order

= 7th letter before K in forward order

= (11 − 7)th letter in the forward order

= 4th letter in the forward order

= D

9. (*d*) The sequential order of Alphabets is as follows

Left A B C D E F G H I J K L M

N O P Q R S T U V W X Y Z Right

18th letter from left = R

7th letter from left of R = (18 − 7)th = 11th letter = K

10. (*b*) 8th term from the right is 'M' and 5th term to the left of 'M' is 'O'.

11. (*d*) Position of K = 11, Position of V = 22

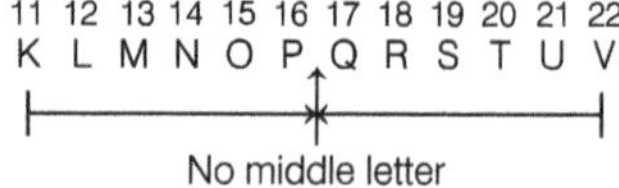

or Position of K = 11

Position of V = 22

As $\left(\frac{11+22}{2}\right) = \frac{33}{2}$ is not exactly divisible by 2.

Hence, no middle letter is possible.

12. (*d*) Correct letter is N as shown below

B C D F G H J K L M N P Q R S T V W X Y Z [increasing order]

Z Y X W V T S R Q P N M L K J H G F D C B [decreasing order]

13. (*c*) 18th letter from left = R

∴ 10th letter to the left of R = 10th letter before R

= (18 − 10)th = 8th letter from left = H

14. (*c*) 10th letter to the left of 10th letter from right in reverse order

= 10th letter to the right of 10th letter from left in forward order.

= 10th letter after, 10th letter in forward order

= (10 + 10)th letter = 20th letter from left in forward order = T

15. (*c*) 11th letter from right in reverse order

= 11th letter from left in forward order = K

Now, 7th letter to the left of K in reverse order

= 7th letter to the right of K in forward order

= 7th letter after K in forward order

= Position of K in forward order + 7

= (11 + 7) th letter in forward order

= 18th letter in forward order = R

16. (*a*) 11th letter form left in the reverse order
= (27 – 11)th letter from left in forward order
= 16th letter from left in forward order
= P
Now, 7th letter to the left of 16th letter from left in reverse order
= 7th letter to the right of 16th letter from left in forward order
= 7th letter after 16th letter from left in forward order
= (16 + 7)th letter from left in forward order
= 23rd letter in forward order = W

17. (*b*)

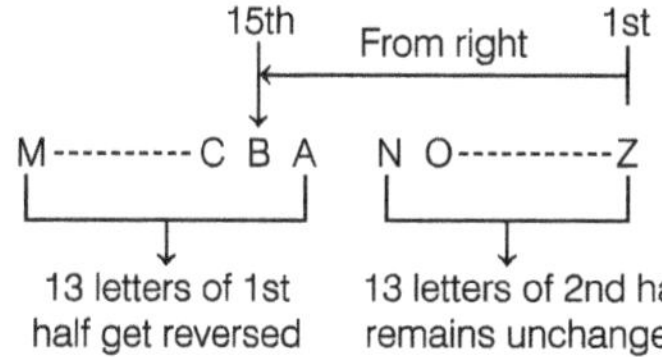

∴ 15th letter from right is B.

18. (*b*) 15th letter falls in the 1st half which remains unchanged. Hence, 15th letter has no relation with the change of 2nd half *i.e.*, reverse order of the last 13 letters of English alphabet.
∴ Required 15th letter from right = (27 – 15)th
= 12th letter from left = L

Or

Let us see

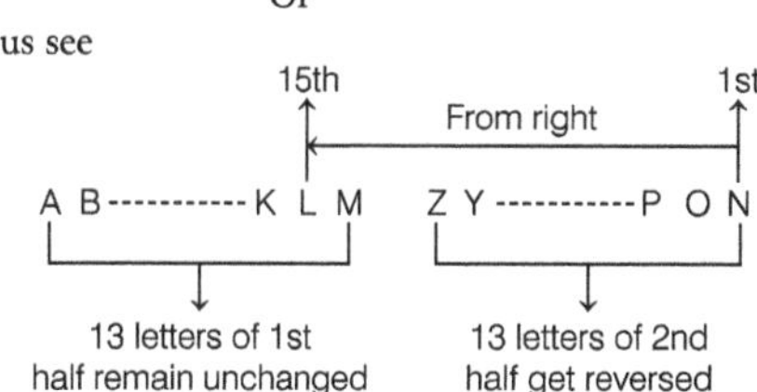

∴ The required letter is 'L'.

19. (*b*)

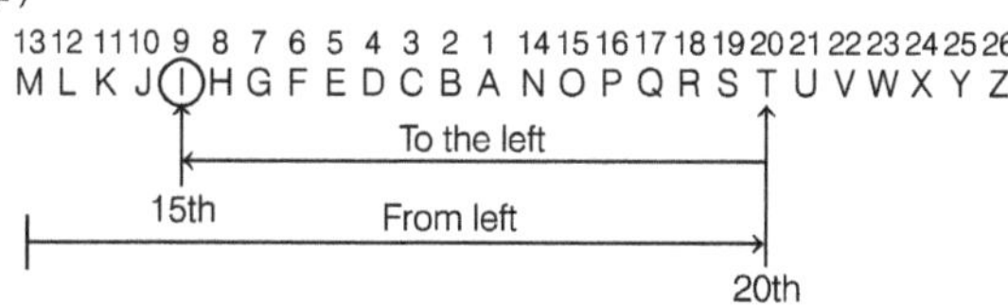

∴ The required letter is 'I'.

20. (*c*)

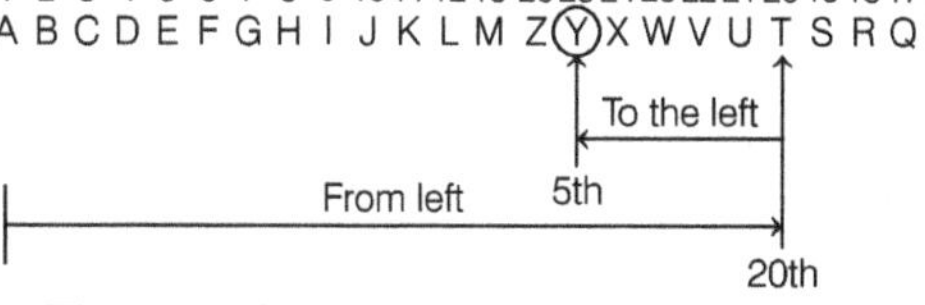

∴ The required letter is 'Y'.

21. (*b*) Middle letter between 6th and 14th letter from left

$= \left(\frac{6 + 14}{2}\right)$th letter from left

$= \left(\frac{20}{2}\right)$th = 10th letter from left = J

22. (*b*) 21st letter from right = (27 – 21) = 6th letter from left

∴ Required middle letter $= \frac{20 + 6}{2} = \frac{26}{2}$
= 13th letter from left = M

23. (*c*) 14th letter from right = (27 – 14) = 13th letter from left

∴ Required middle letter $= \frac{7 + 13}{2} = \frac{20}{2}$
= 10th letter from left = J

24. (*e*) Reverse order of an English alphabet is as follow

Z Y X W V [U] T S R Q P [O] N
(U = 6, O = 12)
M L K J [I] H G F [E] D C B [A]
(I = 18, E = 22, A = 26)

Vowel appear in beginning in new arrangement (U) = 6
and vowel appear in end in new arrangement (A) = 26
∴ Required difference = 26 – 6 = 20

25. (*a*) Required middle letter $= \frac{4 + 16}{2} = \frac{20}{2}$
= 10th letter from left = J

Solution (Q.Nos. 26-28)

Given Series : A B C [F] E [D] G H I [L] K [J] M N O [R] Q [P] S T U [X] W [V] Y Z

Alphabetical order: A B C [D] E [F] G H I [J] K [L] M N O [P] Q [R] S T U [V] W [X] Y Z

26. (*c*) For above it is clear that eight letters are not in their usual place in the alphabetical order which are F, D, L, R, P X, J, V.

27. (*b*) For above it is clear that five sets of two or more letters in the alphabetical order.

28. (*b*) The letters E, K, Q, W are preceded by and followed by wrong letters so far as their alphabetical order is concerned.

29. (*b*) Given word, C A T E G O R [Y]
Alphabetically, A C E G O R T [Y]
Clearly, only Y maintains its position when the letters of the word are arranged in alphabetical order.

30. (*b*) The new word formed is DITSUS. In this word letter 'V' will not appear.

31. (*a*) Given sequence
= Z U D J K N C X V C S L L I E B S F J V A T W Q K
New sequence
= A U D J K N C Y W D T M M J F C T G K W B U X R L
There is no 'V' in the resulting sequence.

32. (*a*) Given word ⇒ F I G U R E S
After rearrangement ⇒ EIUFGRS
Clearly, there are two letters between U and R which are F and G.

33. (*c*) M [O] [N] K E Y
Y [O] [N] M K E
The required letters are two in numbers, which are O and N.

34. (*a*) M [A] R T I N A
A [A] I M N R T
So, only one letter A will remain at the same position.

35. (*c*) Given words : C O N C E N T R A T I O N
After rearrangement : C O N C T [N] E A R N O I T
(8th from end ←)
∴ The required letter is N.

36. (*a*) Original word, F R A C T I O N
I. Change, A C F I N O R T
II. Change, B B E J (M) P Q S
Clearly, M will be fourth from the right.

37. (e) Original word, T I R A D E S
I. Change, U H S Z E D T
II. Change, B C F (J) Q R S
III. Change, Z U (T) S H E D
Hence, T will be fourth from the right.

38. (c) Original word, T O L E R A N T
I. Change, S P K F Q B M S
II. Change, B F K M (P) Q S S
III. Change, K M Q S S (B) F P
Clearly, B will be fourth from the right

39. (b) R A (I) (M) E N (T) ←Given word
A E (I) (M) N R (T) ←After rearrangement
Hence, there are three such type of letters, i.e. I, M and T.

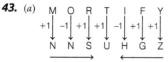

40. (a) [F] [A] I N [T] [S]
[A] [F] I N [S] [T]
Clearly, there are two letters of such type. i.e. I and N.

41. (c) Given word = C R [E] A T I O N
After arrangement = A C [E] I N O R T
Required letter = (E)

42. (d) Original word, D O L P H I N
New arrangement, P O N L I H D
Here, L is not present in any option, so (d) is the correct answer.

43. (a) M O R T I F Y
+1 −1 +1 +1 −1 +1 +1
N N S U H G Z
Third from left → ← Third from right
∴ The required letter is U.

44. (d) P R I C E D → C [E D P R] I

Letters at extreme end are C and I.
Alphabets between them are E, D, P, R.

45. (a) Given word,

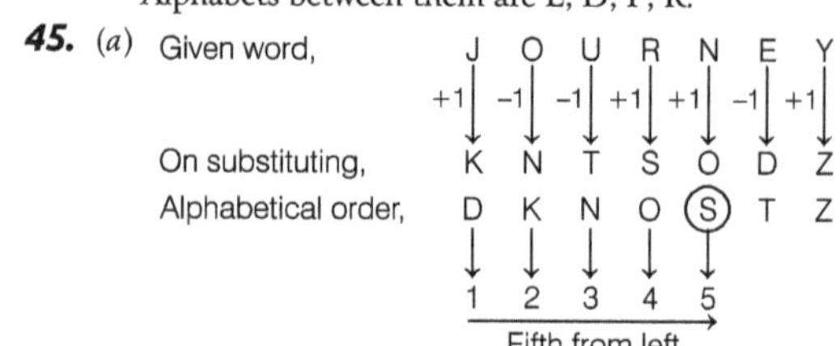

∴ The required letter is S.

46. (d) I. M B [E] [K] T Y D
B D [E] [K] M T Y
Here, third and fourth letters remain on the same position
II. G P [N] A [Q] U S
A G [N] P [Q] S U
Here, third and fifth letters remain on the same position
III. X C [J] R H O
C H [J] O R X
Here, only third letter remains on the same position.
Hence, option (d) is correct.

47. (c) Letters of the word EXTRAORDINARY in alphabetic order;
A A D E I N O R R R T X Y
From left (5) →
∴ Letter in the fifth position = I

48. (e) If all letters at odd positions are written in serial order from right to left, then the series will be
Y W U S Q O M K I G E C A
After this even positioned letters are written in reverse order, then the series will be

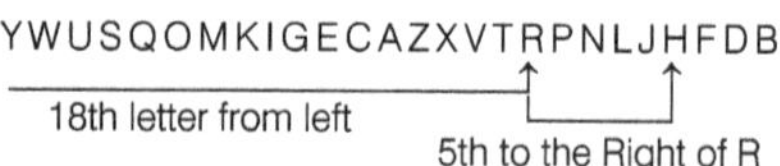

∴ Required letter is R.

TYPE 02

Letters Pair Problem

If between any two letters of a word, there exist same number of letters as in the English alphabetical series, then these two letters forms a letter pair. In this type of questions, a word is given and it is asked to find the different letter pair the word can have.

Chapter Tip

(i) A word may have more than one letter pair.
(ii) A letter in a word can make more than one letter pair.
(iii) If you are asked to find letter pairs, according to the English alphabet, you have to count both ways i.e., from left to right and from right to left or in forward and in backward order.
(iv) If you are asked to find letter pairs according to the sequence of alphabet, then you have to count only from left to right or in forward order.

Ex 13 How many pairs of letters are there in the word 'DECLARING' (both backward and forward), each of which has as many letters between them in the word as there are in the English alphabetical series? « IBPS Clerk 2018

(a) One (b) Three (c) Four (d) Five
(e) None of these

Solution (d)

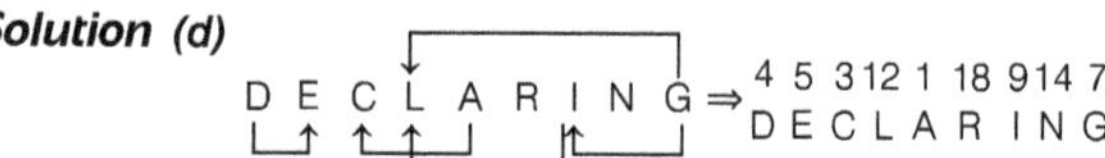

Clearly, there are five such pairs.

Practice / CORNER 1.2

DIRECTIONS ~ (Q. Nos. 1-28) *In each of the following questions a word is given. How many pairs of letters are there in these words which have as many letters between them as in the English alphabet?*

1. ABLE
(a) One (b) Two
(c) Nil (d) Cannot be determined

2. ACTION
(a) Three (b) Nil (c) One (d) Two

3. DELIBERATE
(a) One (b) Two (c) Four (d) Three

4. PLANTED « RBI Office Assistant 2020
(a) One (b) Two (c) Four (d) Three
(e) More than four

5. MATCHES « IBPS RRB (Office Assistant) 2020
(a) Two (b) One (c) More than three
(d) Three (e) None of these

6. CONFUSED « LIC (ADO) 2011
(a) Nil (b) One (c) Two (d) Three
(e) More than three

7. PREAMBLE « Syndicate Bank (Clerk) 2011
(a) Nil (b) One (c) Two (d) Three
(e) More than three

8. PRODUCE « SBI (Clerk) 2019
(a) Four (b) Two (c) One (d) Three
(e) More than three

9. STREAMING « IBPS (Clerk) 2011
(a) Nil (b) One (c) Two (d) Three
(e) More than three

10. CHRONICLE « PNB (PO) 2010
(a) Nil (b) One (c) Two (d) Three
(e) More than three

11. OBJECTIVE
(a) None (b) One
(c) Two (d) More than three

12. TRIBUNAL « IOB (PO) 2010
(a) None (b) One (c) Two (d) Three
(e) More than three

13. ADJUSTING
(a) None (b) One (c) Two (d) Three

14. SYSTEMATIC « IDBI Executive 2018
(a) None (b) One (c) Two (d) Three
(e) More than three

15. TERMINATE « PNB (PO) 2011
(a) None (b) One (c) Two (d) Three
(e) More than three

16. STATE « Allahabad Bank (Clerk) 2011
(a) None (b) One (c) Two (d) Three
(e) More than three

17. STONED « LIC (ADO) 2011
(a) None (b) One (c) Two (d) Three
(e) More than three

18. TERMITE
(a) None (b) One (c) Two (d) Three

19. RECRUIT « PNB (PO) 2011
(a) None (b) One (c) Two (d) Three
(e) More than three

20. ENGLISH « SBI (PO) 2011
(a) None (b) One (c) Two (d) Three
(e) More than three

21. CREDIBLE
(a) None (b) One
(c) Two (d) More than three

22. EDUCATION « IBPS RRB PO 2019
(a) One (b) Two (c) Three (d) Four
(e) More than four

23. CHANNEL « MP Patwari 2017
(a) None (b) One (c) Two (d) Three

24. STREAMING IBPS PO 2018
(a) Two (b) More than Three (c) Three
(d) One (e) None of these

25. APPLICATION « SBI Clerk 2016
(a) One (b) Two (c) Three (d) Four
(e) None of these

26. CLAYED « SBI Clerk 2015
(a) None (b) One (c) Two
(d) More than three (e) Three

27. SENATOR « IBPS Clerk 2017
(a) None (b) One (c) Two (d) Three
(e) Four

28. SUBSTANCE « IBPS (PO) 2012
(a) None (b) One (c) Two (d) Three
(e) More than three

29. Two words are given below. How many pairs of letters are there in these words which have as many letters between them as in the English alphabet respectively?

CHILDREN, BEHAVIOUR

(a) Two and Four (b) Three and Two
(c) Three and One (d) Four and Two
(e) Two and Three

30. Two words are given below.

DELUSION, FOREIGN

How many pairs of letters are there in these words which have as many letters between them as in the English alphabet respectively?

(a) Five and Three (b) Two and Five
(c) Five and Two (d) Four and Two
(e) None of these

Answers / WITH EXPLANATIONS

1. (*a*)

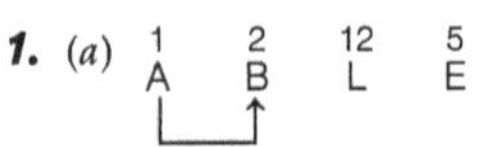

∴ Letter pair = AB ⇒ One

2. (*c*)

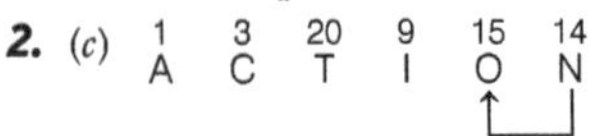

∴ Letter pair = NO ⇒ One

3. (*c*)

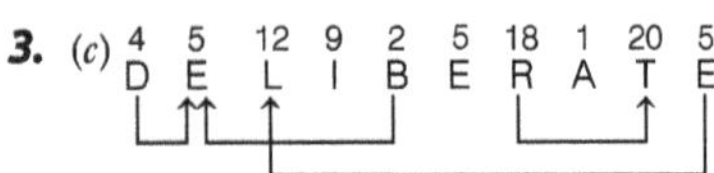

∴ Letter pairs = DE, BE, EL, RT

⇒ Four

4. (*d*) Given word

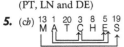

16 12 1 14 20 5 4
P L A N T E D

Hence, required number of pairs = 3 (PT, LN and DE)

5. (*cb*)

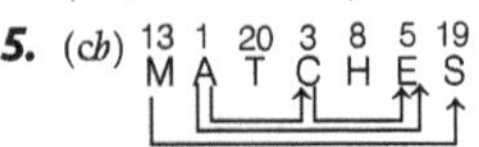

∴ Letter pairs = MS, AC, AE and CE

⇒ Four

6. (*e*)

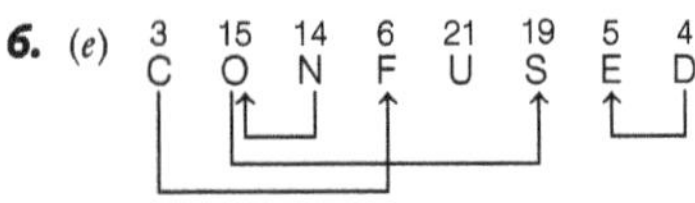

∴ Letter pairs = CF, NO, OS, ED

⇒ Four

7. (*c*)

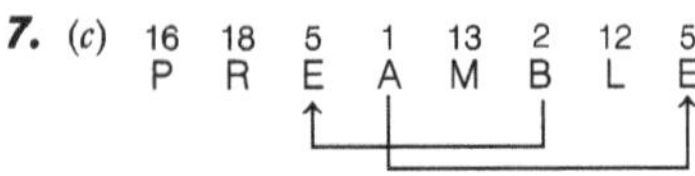

∴ Letter pairs = BE, AE

⇒ Two

8. (*c*) 16 18 15 4 21 3 5
P R O D U C E

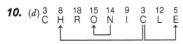

∴ Required pairs is RU i.e 1

9. (*d*)

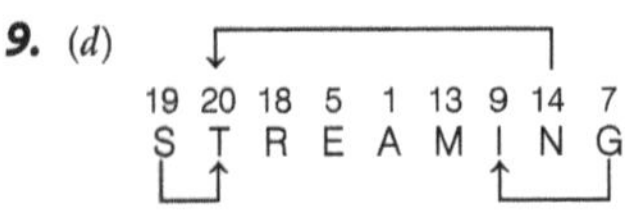

∴ Letter pairs = ST, GI, NT

⇒ Three

10. (*d*)

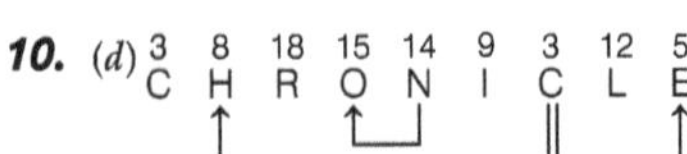

∴ Letter pairs = CH, CE, NO

⇒ Three

11. (*d*)

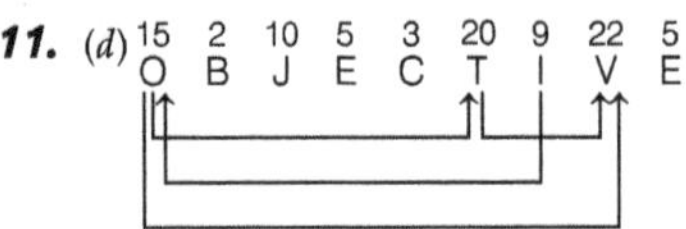

∴ Letter pairs = IO, OV, OT, TV

⇒ Four

12. (*e*)

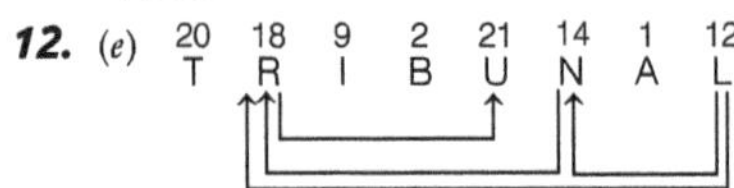

∴ Letter pairs = RU, NR, LN, LR

⇒ Four

13. (*d*)

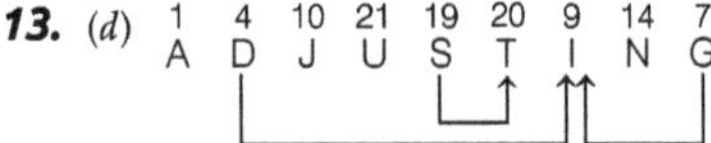

∴ Letter pairs = DI, GI, ST ⇒ Three

14. (*c*)

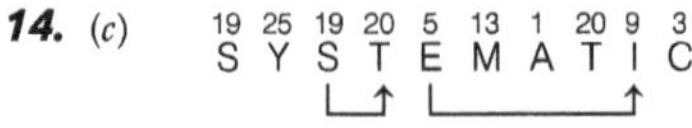

∴ There are two such pairs -SI and EI.

15. (*c*)

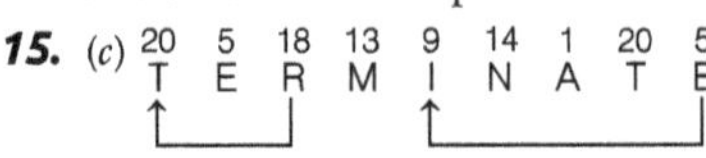

∴ Letter pairs = RT, EI ⇒ Two

16. (*b*) 19 20 1 20 5
S T A T E

∴ Letter pair = ST ⇒ One

17. (*d*) 19 20 15 14 5 4
S T O N E D

∴ Such pairs = ST, NO, DE ⇒ Three

18. (*b*) 20 5 18 13 9 20 5
T E R M I T E

∴ Letter pairs = RT

⇒ One

19. (*b*) 18 5 3 18 21 9 20
R E C R U I T

∴ Letter pair = EI

⇒ One

20. (*e*)

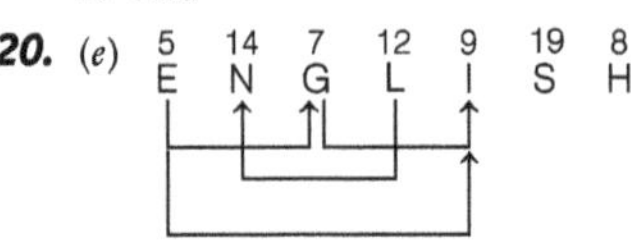

∴ Letter pairs = EG, GI, LN, EI

⇒ Four

21. (*d*)

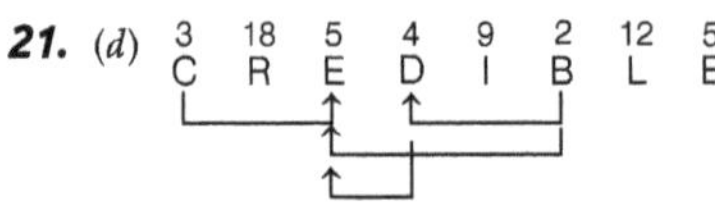

∴ Letter pairs = CE, BD, BE, DE

= Four

22. (*e*)

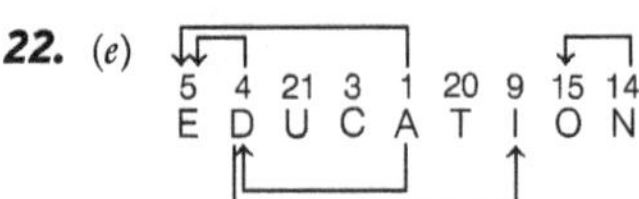

∴ Such pairs = DE, AE, AD, DI and NO ⇒ Five

23. (*c*) 3 8 1 14 14 5 12
C H A N N E L

So, such number of pairs are AC and LN i.e. two.

24. (c)

Clearly, there are three such pairs.

25. (*c*)

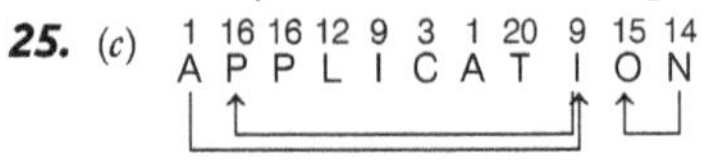

∴ Letter pairs = AI, IP and NO

⇒ Three

26. (*e*) 3 12 1 25 5 4
C L A Y E D

Hence, such number of pairs are AD, DE and AC ⇒ Three

27. (*c*)

Required pairs = NR and RT ⇒ Two

28. (*d*)

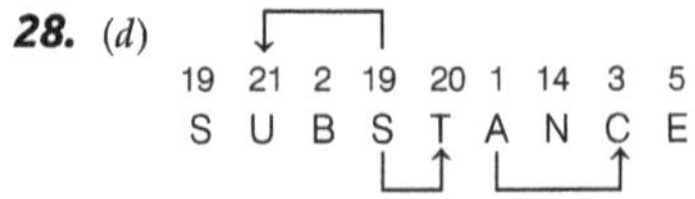

∴ Letter pairs = ST, AC, SU

⇒ Three

29. (*d*)

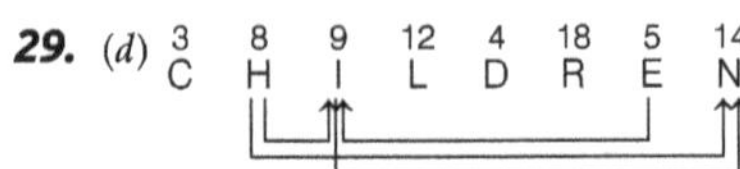

Required pairs = HI, HN, EI, IN ⇒ Four

and 2 5 8 1 22 9 15 21 18
B E H A V I O U R

Required pairs = EI, RV ⇒ Two

30. (*c*)

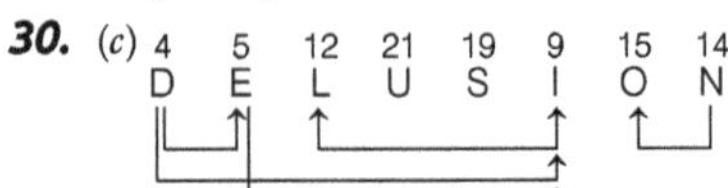

Letter pairs = DE, IL, DI, NO and EI ⇒ Five

Letter pairs = NR, EG ⇒ Two

TYPE 03

Word Formation and Letter Rearrangement

In this type, the questions asked can be further divided into four types which are explained as under

A. Changing Letters of a Meaningful Word

In this type of questions, a meaningful word is given followed by some directions. Based on these directions, we have to arrange the letters of that word and then it is asked to find a letter from left or right end.

The example which is given below will give a better idea about the type of questions asked in the exam.

***Ex* 14** If in the word 'CONGREGATION', 1st and 3rd letters are interchanged, 2nd and 4th letters are interchanged, 5th and 7th letters are interchanged and this interchange goes on in the same manner, then find the 10th letter from right in the new arrangement.

(a) E (b) C
(c) G (d) P

***Solution* (b)** The correct letter is C.

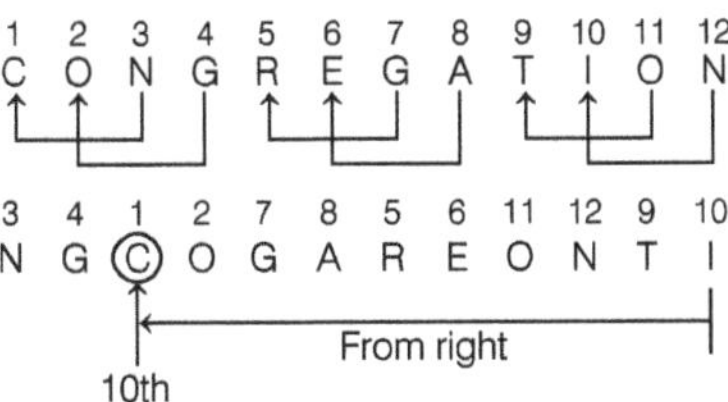

Alternate Method

10th letter from right in the original word = (13 – 10) = 3 rd letter from left in original word = N

As, N is interchanged with C in the new arrangement

∴ 10th letter from right in the new arrangement = C

B. Forming a Meaningful Word with Selected Letters of a Word

In this type of questions, it is asked whether a word can be formed or not from the selected letters of a meaningful word.

***Ex* 15** If only one meaningful English word can be made with the first, the fourth, the ninth and the tenth letters of the word CORRUPTION, using each letter only once, then which of the first letter of the word from the left. If no such word can be formed then your answer is X. If more than one such word can be formed then your answer is Z?

« IBPS RRB PO 2016

(a) X (b) Z (c) R (d) O
(e) C

***Solution* (e)**

C O R R U P T I O N
① 2 3 ④ 5 6 7 8 ⑨ ⑩

From letters C, R, O, N only one meaningful word can be formed 'CORN'.

∴ The first letter from left is 'C'.

C. Forming Meaningful Word(s) with the Different Letters of a Meaningful Word

Here, the question asked is based on formation of new word(s) from the different letters of a given words.

***Ex* 16** How many words can be formed using letters of the word 'DESIGN' unconditionally?

(a) More than 4 (b) Less than 3
(c) Exactly 4 (d) More than 8

***Solution* (d)** Let us see

Required words = DEN, DIG, DING, SIN, SING, SIGN, SIDE DIE, SEND, SIGNED, END, ENDS and many more.

***Ex* 17** How many meaningful English words can be formed by Using letters of the word 'ALEP'? « UKPSC 2016

(a) One (b) Two
(c) Three (d) More than three

***Solution* (d)** Such meaningful words are PEAL, LEAP, PALE and PLEA.

D. Suitable Word Formation

In this type of questions, a main/question word is given and candidate have to choose that word, which can or cannot be formed from the letters of the main/question word.

***Ex* 18** From the given alternative words, select the word which cannot be formed using the letters of the given word

ENVIRONMENT « SSC CGL Pre 2015

(a) ENTRANCE (b) MOVE
(c) EMINENT (d) ENTER

***Solution* (a)** The word ENTRANCE cannot be formed from the letters of the word ENVIRONMENT as letter 'A' and 'C' are missing in the given word.

***Ex* 19** From the given alternative words, select the words which cannot be formed using the letters of the given word.

INTERDEPENDENT « SSC GD Constable 2015

(a) REPENT (b) RETREAT
(c) DEPEND (d) DEEPEN

***Solution* (b)** Word 'RETREAT' cannot be formed because letter 'A' is not present in the given word. Therefore option (b) is correct.

DIRECTIONS ~ (Ex- 20-21) *In each of the following question, a word has been given, followed by four other words, one of which can be formed by using the letters of the given word. Find that word.*

***Ex* 20** DEMOCRACY « SSC (CGL) 2014

(a) SECRECY (b) MICRO
(c) MARCY (d) DEMON

Solution ***(c)*** MARCY—All the letters of this word are present in the main word.
Hence, 'MARCY' can be formed from the letters of the given word 'DEMOCRACY'.

***Ex* 21** COMPENSATION

(a) TINY (b) COPY
(c) MENTION (d) MOTIVE

Solution (c) MENTION—All the letters of this word are present in the main word. Hence, 'MENTION' can be formed from the letters of the given word 'COMPENSATION'.

E. Word Formation by Unscrambling Letters

In this type of questions, a set of English letters is given in a jumbled order. The candidate is required to arrange these letters to form a meaningful word.

Note *Always try to place the letters according to the numbers provided in options rather than doing it on the basis of your vocabulary knowledge.*

***Ex* 22** Select the combination of numbers that forms a meaningful word. « RRB NTPC 2016

N	P	O	A	C	L	M	I
1	2	3	4	5	6	7	8

(A) 5, 3, 2, 7, 6, 4, 8, 1
(B) 5, 3, 7, 2, 6, 4, 8, 1
(C) 4, 7, 5, 1, 6, 8, 2, 3
(D) 1, 7, 8, 6, 4, 3, 2, 5

(a) B (b) D
(c) C (d) A

Solution (a)

C	O	M	P	L	A	I	N
↓	↓	↓	↓	↓	↓	↓	↓
5	3	7	2	6	4	8	1

Clearly, the given letters, when arranged in the order of '5, 3, 7, 2, 6, 4, 8, 1,' form the word 'COMPLAIN'.

F. Formation of Meaningful Word by Adding Letters/words in the given Word(s)

In this type of questions, some words are given and the candidate has to either suffix or prefix same letter in each of the given words to make new meaningful words.

It also includes questions based on forming two meaningful words by inserting a word in between the given word.

***Ex* 23** Given below are some group of letters. Which of the options can be joined at the end of these letters to make them meaningful words? « SSC (CGL) 2015

LEN, SAN, WOR, SEE

(a) A (b) D (c) B (d) K

Solution (b) Letter D is suffixed to the given words

LEN + D = LEND
SAN + D = SAND
WOR + D = WORD
SEE + D = SEED

***Ex* 24** Which single letter can be prefixed to the following words to form entirely new words? « SSC (CGL) 2015

TILL, TABLE, PILE, TAB, PRING

(a) H (b) S (c) B (d) C

Solution (b) Letter S is prefixed to the given words

S + TILL = STILL
S + TABLE = STABLE
S + PILE = SPILE (SPILE means nail/Tip)
S + TAB = STAB
S + PRING = SPRING

G. Choosing the Different Word After Rearranging the Unorganised Letters

In this type of questions, groups of unorganised letters are given as options. The candidates are required to rearrange these letters to form meaningful words and then choose the word which is different from other words.

***Ex* 25** Rearrange the unorganised letters to create meaningful words and then choose one of them, which is different. « RRB NTPC 2016

(A) ANDOMY (B)STEAUDY
(C) DIARFY (D) DHAIOLY

(a) C (b) D
(c) B (d) A

Solution (b) Rearranging the unorganised letters,

ANDOMY – MONDAY
STEAUDY – TUESDAY
DIARFY – FRIDAY
DHAIOLY – HOLIDAY

Here, HOLIDAY is different, because all others are names of days of a week.

Practice / CORNER 1.3

1. If the positions of the letters in the word 'ORGANISE' are rearranged in such way that the position of the 1st and the 2nd letters are interchanged, similarly the position of the 3rd and the 4th letters are interchanged and so on, which of the following will be the 3rd from the right end after the rearrangement?
« Canara Bank (Clerk) 2010

(a) N (b) I (c) R (d) A
(e) None of these

2. If the first and last letters in the word 'COMMUNICATIONS' were interchanged, also the second and second from last letter, third and third from last, fourth and fourth from last and so on. Which letter would be the tenth letter counting from your right?

(a) C (b) A (c) N (d) S

3. If it is possible to make only one meaningful word with the 2nd, 4th, 6th and 7th letters of the word UNILATERAL using all the letters but each letter only once. Which would be the second letter of the word from the right end? If more than one such word can be formed give 'Y' as the answer. If no such word can be formed, give 'Z' as your answer. « SBI (Clerk) 2019

(a) Y (b) N (c) L (d) T (e) Z

4. If it is possible to make only one meaningful English word with the first, fourth, fifth and seventh letters from the left of the word EVACUATION, using all the letters but each letter only once, which would be the third letter of the word from your left? If more than one such word can be formed, give 'Z' as your answer. If no such word can be formed give 'Y' as your answer.
RBI Assistant 2017

(a) Y (b) Z (c) U (d) T
(e) C

5. If four letter word is formed from 1st, 3rd, and 6th letter of TRANSLATE using all the letters but each letter only once then what is the 3rd letter of newly formed word? If more than one meaningful word is formed, then the answer will be Z. « IBPS RRB (PO) 2019

(a) L (b) T (c) A (d) S (e) Z

6. Form a meaningful word with the first, fourth, seventh and eleventh letters of the word 'SUPERFLUOUS'. What is the first letter of that word?
« UPSSSC Junior Assistant 2020

(a) U (b) L (c) P (d) R

7. If it is possible to make only one meaningful word with the 3rd, 4th, 8th and 9th letters of the word 'CENTURIES' using all the letters but each letter only once. Which would be the 2nd letter of the word from left? If more than one such word can be formed, give 'A' as your answer. If no such word can be formed, give 'Z' as your answer. « SBI (PO) 2010

(a) T (b) N (c) A (d) E (e) Z

8. If it is possible to make only one meaningful word with the 1st, 2nd, 6th and 10th letters of the word 'DISCLAIMER', using all the letters but each letter only once. Which of the following will be the 3rd letter from left? If no such word can be formed, give 'X' as your answer and if more than one such word can be made give 'Y' as your answer. « CBI (Clerk) 2008

(a) I (b) R (c) D (d) X (e) Y

9. If it is possible to make only one meaningful word from the 1st, the 3rd, the 5th and the 8th letters of the word 'ENTERPRISE' using each letter only once, 1st letter of the word is your answer. If more than one such word can be made your answer is 'X' and if no such words can be made your answer is 'Y'. « Syndicate Bank (PO) 2009

(a) R (b) S (c) T (d) X (e) Y

10. If it is possible to make only one meaningful word with the first, fourth, sixth and eight letters of the word SENTENCE, using each letter only once. Which could be the second letter of the word from the right end? If more than one such word can be formed give X as the answer. If no such word can be formed given Z as your answer. « SBI Clerk 2015

(a) N (b) T (c) Z (d) X
(e) S

11. Select the second, fifth, tenth and twelfth letters of the word METROPOLITAN to form meaningful word (s). Using each letter only once if only one word can be formed, then select the third letter of that word as the answer. If more than one word can be formed, then select M as the answer. If no such word can be formed, then select X as the answer.
« UPSSSC Junior Assistant 2020

(a) T (b) N (c) M (d) X

12. If the below alphabets are formed as per the ascending order of their appearance in the standard alphabetical series, then which meaningful English word can be formed using the alphabets in 1st, 4th, 6th, 9th and 16th position from your left, When you use each letter only once.

XUIHQLETBWMRKSAGC
« UPSSSC Combined Lower Subordinate 2019

(a) STEAM (b) WHALE (c) MEANS (d) SHAME

13. How many meaningful English words can be made with the letters ESLA, using each letter only once in each word? « UCO Bank (Clerk) 2009

(a) None (b) One (c) Two (d) Three
(e) More than three

14. How many meaningful three letter words can be formed with the letters AER, using each letter only once in each word? « UCO Bank (Clerk) 2009

(a) None (b) One (c) Two (d) Three
(e) Four

15. How many meaningful English words can be made with the letters NREA, using each letter only once in each word?

(a) None (b) One (c) Two (d) Three

16. How many meaningful English words can be made with the letters NDOE using each letter only once in each word? « IOB (PO) 2009

(a) None (b) One (c) Two (d) Three
(e) More than three

17. How many meaningful English words can be made with letters TPSI, using each letter only once in each word?

(a) One (b) Two (c) Three (d) Four

18. How many meaningful three letters English words can be formed with the letters WNO using each letter only once in each word? « Syndicate Bank (Clerk) 2009

(a) None (b) One (c) Two (d) Three (e) Four

19. How many meaningful English words can be formed from the letters ADRW, using each letter only once in each word?

(a) None (b) One (c) Two (d) Three

20. How many meaningful words can be formed from the 1st, 6th, 8th and 9th letter of a word 'EMANICIPATE' by using each letter once in the word? « SBI Clerk 2018

(a) Two (b) One (c) None (d) Three
(e) More then three

21. How many meaningful English words can be formed with the letters LEGU, using each letter only once in each word? « PNB (PO) 2010

(a) None (b) One (c) Two (d) Three
(e) More than three

22. How many meaningful English words can be made with the letters DLEI, using each letter only once in each word? « UBI (PO) 2010

(a) None (b) One (c) Two (d) Three
(e) More than three

23. How many meaningful English words can be made with the letters DREO, using each letter only once in each word? « UBI (PO) 2010

(a) None (b) One (c) Two (d) Three
(e) More than three

24. How many meaningful English words can be made with the letters IFEL, using each letter only once in each word? « SBI (PO) 2010

(a) None (b) One (c) Two (d) Three
(e) More than three

25. How many meaningful English words can be formed with the letter ITRM, using each letter only once in each word? « SBI (PO) 2010

(a) None (b) One (c) Two (d) Three
(e) More than three

26. How many meaningful English words can be made with the letters ONDE, using each letter only once in each word?

(a) None (b) One (c) Two (d) Three

27. How many meaningful English words can be formed made with the letters ESTR, using each letter only once in each word?

(a) None (b) One
(c) Two (d) Three

28. How many meaningful words can be formed from the word ESRO without repeating any letter within that word?

(a) One (b) Three (c) Five (d) Two

29. How many meaningful four letter English words can be formed with the letters KEAB, using each letter only once in each word?

(a) One (b) Two
(c) Three (d) Four

30. How many meaningful English words can be made from the letters EOPR, using each letter only once? « SBI (PO) 2008

(a) None (b) One
(c) Two (d) Three
(e) More than three

31. How many three letter meaningful words can be formed from the word TEAR beginning with 'A' and without repeating any letter within that word?

(a) One (b) Three
(c) Five (d) Two

DIRECTIONS ~ (Q. Nos. 32-39) *In each of the following questions a word is given, followed by four other words, one of which can be formed by using the letters of given word, then find the word.*

32. RECOMMENDATION « SSC (FCI) 2012

(a) COMMUNICATE (b) REMINDER
(c) MEDICO (d) MEDIATES

33. MEASUREMENT « SSC (Steno) 2012

(a) ASSURE (b) MANTLE (c) MASTER (d) SUMMIT

34. MEASUREMENTED « SSC (Multitasking) 2012

(a) MASTERO (b) RENT
(c) TENANT (d) INSURANCE

35. CORRESPONDING

(a) DISCERN (b) RESPONSE
(c) REPENT (d) CORRECT

36. PREPARATION « SSC (10+2) 2013

(a) PAMPER (b) REPEAT
(c) PARTITION (d) PARROT

37. ULTRANATIONALISM « SSC (CPO) 2014

(a) ULTRAMONTANE (b) ULTRAMODERN
(c) ULTRAIST (d) ULULATE

38. PREMONITION « SSC (CGL) 2017

(a) ACTION (b) NATION (c) MONITOR (d) REMOVE

39. COMPANIONSHIP « SSC (10+2) 2013

(a) OPEN (b) OPIUM
(c) OPINION (d) NATION

DIRECTIONS ~ (Q. Nos. 40-54) *In each of the following questions a word is given followed by four other words, one of which cannot be formed by using the letters of the given word. Find that particular word.*

40. IMPOSSIONABLE « SSC (Multitasking) 2013
(a) IMPOSSIBE (b) POSSIBLE
(c) IMPOSE (d) IMPASSIVE

41. ECCENTRICITY « SSC CGL 2017
(a) NIECE (b) CREATE
(c) TRINITY (d) RETICENT

42. COURAGEOUS « SSC (CGL) 2013
(a) SECURE (b) ARGUE
(c) COURSE (d) GRACE

43. REPUTATION « SSC (CGL) April 2014
(a) TUTOR (b) PONDER
(c) PUTARION (d) RATION

44. MERCHANDISE « SSC (CGL) April 2014
(a) CHANGE (b) MESH
(c) DICE (d) CHARM

45. PORTFOLIO « SSC (Multitasking) 2014
(a) RIFT (b) ROOF
(c) FORT (d) PORTICO

46. INTERVENTION « SSC (10+2) 2013
(a) ENTER (b) INTENTION
(c) INVENTION (d) ENTERTAIN

47. COMMUNICATION « SSC (Multitasking) April 2014
(a) ACTION (b) UNION
(c) NATION (d) UNISON

48. LEGALIZATION « SSC (CPO) 2014
(a) ALERT (b) ALEGATION
(c) GALLANT (d) NATAL

49. CONTEMPTUOUS « SSC (10+2) 2018
(a) CON (b) TOM
(c) PRETTY (d) POST

50. INCARCERATION « SSC (CGL) 2014
(a) RELATION (b) TERRAIN
(c) INACTION (d) CREATION

51. BENEVOLENT « SSC (10+2) 2018
(a) BEEN (b) NEVIN (c) LENT (d) BEN

52. SEGREGATION « SSC (CGL) 2016
(a) EAGER (b) SEA (c) GATE (d) NATION

53. AUTOBIOGRAPHY Delhi Police (SI) 2016
(a) TROOP (b) BRIGHT (c) GRAPHIC (d) TROPHY

54. GEMDISTIONARY « Delhi Police (ASI) 2016
(a) MEGASITY (b) DISTART
(c) STAR (d) GAME

DIRECTIONS ~ (Q. Nos. 55-63) *Letters of the words given below have been jumbled up and you are required to construct the words. Each letter has been numbered and each word is followed by four options. Choose the option which gives the correct order of the letters as indicated by the numbers to form meaningful words.*

55. 1 2 3 4 5 6
G I C O D N « SSC (CGL) 2014
(a) 2, 1, 4, 3, 6, 5 (b) 4, 3, 2, 6, 5, 1
(c) 6, 5, 2, 3, 1, 4 (d) 3, 4, 5, 2, 6, 1

56. C E L S M U « UPSSSC Junior Assistant 2020
3 4 5 6 7 8
(a) 7, 4, 5, 3, 8, 6 (b) 6, 8, 7, 4, 5, 3
(c) 6, 8, 5, 7, 4, 3 (d) 7, 8, 6, 3, 5, 4

57. E M I H T R
1 2 3 4 5 6
(a) 1, 2, 3, 4, 5, 6 (b) 4, 1, 6, 2, 3, 5
(c) 5, 1, 6, 4, 3, 2 (d) 6, 1, 2, 3, 5, 4

58. R T A N U E
1 2 3 4 5 6
(a) 1, 3, 2, 6, 4, 5 (b) 3, 2, 4, 6, 1, 5
(c) 4, 3, 2, 5, 1, 6 (d) 4, 6, 5, 2, 3, 1

59. I A D O H E N S « UPSSSC 2018
1 2 3 4 5 6 7 8
(a) 3, 2, 5, 6, 8, 1, 4, 7 (b) 2, 3, 5, 6, 4, 8, 1, 7
(c) 2, 3, 5, 6, 8, 1, 4, 7 (d) 2, 3, 5, 6, 8, 4, 1, 7

60. E T C K O P « RRB ASM 2012
1 2 3 4 5 6
(a) 4, 1, 2, 3, 5, 6 (b) 2, 1, 6, 5, 3, 4
(c) 6, 5, 3, 4, 1, 2 (d) 3, 1, 4, 5, 6, 2

61. O R T C O B E
1 2 3 4 5 6 7
(a) 2, 3, 6, 7, 5, 1 (b) 3, 1, 4, 2, 6, 7, 5
(c) 7, 1, 2, 4, 5, 6, 3 (d) 5, 4, 3, 1, 6, 7, 2

62. A L I R E M C
1 2 3 4 5 6 7
(a) 6, 3, 4, 1, 7, 2, 5 (b) 6, 5, 1, 4, 7, 3, 2
(c) 7, 4, 5, 1, 6, 3, 2 (d) 7, 5, 4, 1, 6, 2, 3

63. C N A S P H I
1 2 3 4 5 6 7
(a) 5, 7, 4, 2, 6, 1, 3 (b) 2, 3, 7, 5, 4, 1, 6
(c) 4, 5, 7, 2, 3, 1, 6 (d) 7, 2, 3, 4, 5, 1, 6

64. Name a single letter that can be suffixed to the following words to form new words. « SSC (CPO) 2015
HAT BAR BAT PIN BATH
(a) A (b) E (c) B (d) D

65. Which single letter can be prefixed to the following words in order to obtain entirely new words?
(Same letter has to be prefixed in all five words) « SSC (CPO) 2015
EAT OUR IS AS AT
(a) S (b) H (c) C (d) B

DIRECTIONS ~ (Q. Nos. 66-72) *In each of the following questions, rearrange the unorganised letters to form an meaningful words and then choose that word which is odd/different from others.*

66. (A) ARC (B) USB « RRB NTPC 2016
(C) LACES (D) LECCY
(a) A (b) C (c) B (d) D

67. (A) LAFC (B) UKCGIDLN
(C) RILNIGHE (D) BCU
(a) D (b) B (c) C (d) A

68. (A) UTNA (B) EINEC
(C) OMEHRT (D) ROBEHRT
(a) C (b) D (c) B (d) A

69. (A) UNPE (B) ILOLSGNH
(C) OHALPB (D) ENANCIH
(a) D (b) C (c) B (d) A

70. (A) OLENV (B) EISTSH
(C) AGZEANIM (D) TCAYRIDION
(a) D (b) A (c) C (d) B

71. (A) KENAS (B) OFLG
(C) NNEIST (D) BLLOOTAF
(a) D (b) A
(c) C (d) B

72. (A) CEKRTCI (B) OHKCYE
(C) ESCSH (D) OTOLABLF
(a) B (b) D
(c) A (d) C

73. Seven letters are arranged in a linear arrangement to form a meaningful word. A is second to the left of I. L is to the left of N. Not more than two letters are placed between I and G. G is placed to the right of I. G is not neighbor of E and D. D and E are placed next to each other. Which letter is placed in exactly middle of the meaningful word so formed. If more than one word is formed mark your option as X? « IBPS Clerk Mains 2018
(a) N (b) L (c) X (d) E (e) G

74. If the word NUPKIPM is unscrambled, then the name of a fruit/vegetable is formed. What is the last letter of the word so formed? « UPSSSC Junior Assistant 2020
(a) K (b) U (c) N (d) M

Answers WITH EXPLANATIONS

1. (a)
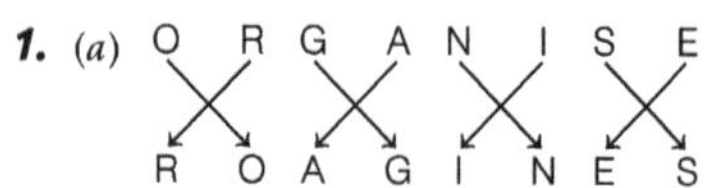

Hence, N is 3rd from right after rearrangement.

2. (b) According to the question,
Given word,
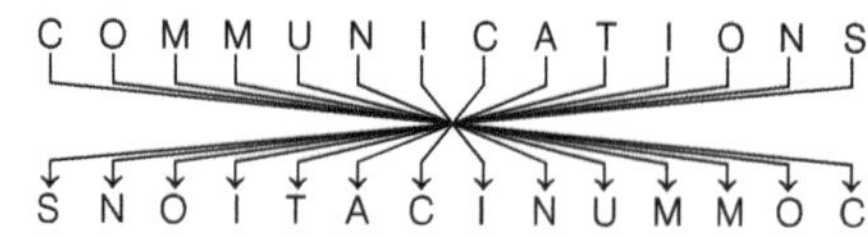

Hence, the required letter is A.

3. (b) Given word,
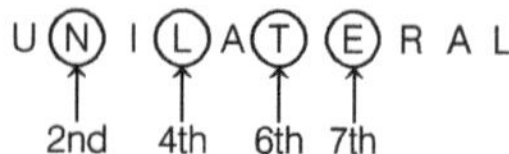

Now, meaningful word = LENT (Star vation, fast)
∴ Second letter from the right end of the word LENT = N

4. (d) The letters to be used are E, C, U, T.
The word formed is CUTE.

5. (e)
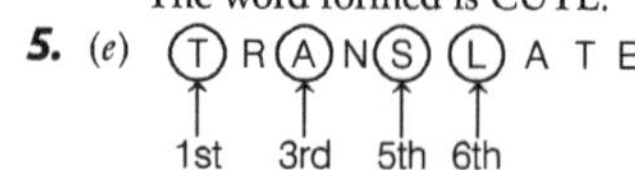

Words formed from TASL are SALT, LAST, and SLAT.

6. (b) The first, fourth, seventh and eleventh letters of the word 'SUPERFLUOUS' are S, E, L and S respectively. Meaningful word is LESS and the first letter of the word is L.

7. (c)
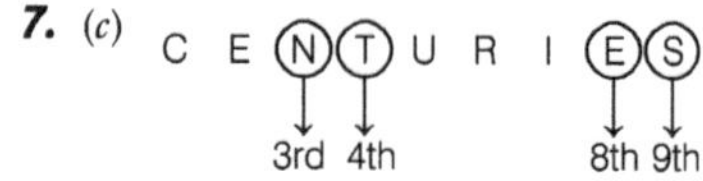

∴ Words formed = NEST, NETS, SENT, TENS

8. (e) D I S C L A I M E R
1st 2nd 6th 10th
Words formed = ARID, RAID

9. (d) E N T E R P R I S E
1st 3rd 5th 8th
Meaningful words = TIRE, TIER, RITE

10. (d) More than one word can be made by using the first, fourth, sixth and eight letters (i.e. S, T, N and E) and the words are NEST, SENT etc.

11. (c) The second, fifth, tenth and twelfth letters of the word METROPOLITAN are E, O, T and N respectively.
Two meaningful word can be formed with these letters, they are NOTE and TONE.
So, the required answer is M.

12. (b) Given order, X U I H Q L E T B W M R K S A G C
Arranging the series in alphabetical order we get,
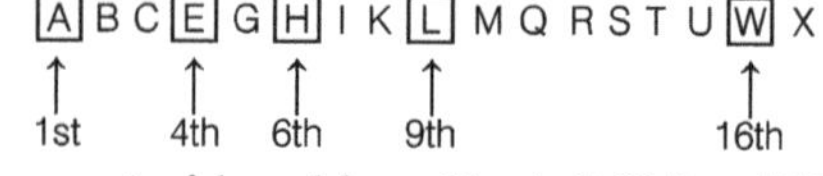

∴ The meaningful word formed by A, E, H, L and W is (WHALE).

13. (c) Required words = SALE, SEAL (Two meaningful words)

14. (d) Required words = ARE, EAR, ERA (Three meaningful words)

15. (c) Required words = NEAR, EARN (Two meaningful words)

16. (c) Required words = NODE, DONE (Two meaningful words)

17. (c) Required words = TIPS, PITS, SPIT (Three meaningful words)

18. (d) Required words = NOW, WON, OWN (Three meaningful words)

19. (c) Required words = DRAW and WARD (Two meaningful words)

20. (*a*) E M A N I C I P A T E
↓ ↓ ↓ ↓
1st 6th 8th 9th
Two meaningful words i.e., 'CAPE' and 'PACE' can be formed with the letters E, C, P and A.

21. (*b*) Required word = GLUE (Only one meaningful word)

22. (*c*) Required words = LIED, IDLE (Two meaningful words)

23. (*b*) Required word = RODE (one meaningful word)

24. (*c*) Required words = FILE, LIFE (Two meaningful words)

25. (*b*) Required word = TRIM (One meaningful word)

26. (*c*) Required words = NODE, DONE (Two meaningful words)

27. (*b*) Required word = REST (One meaningful word)

28. (*b*) Required words = EROS, ROSE, SORE (Three meaningful words)

29. (*b*) Required words = BEAK, BAKE (Two meaningful words)

30. (*c*) Required words = PORE, ROPE (Two meaningful words)

31. (*b*) Required words = ARE, ATE, ART (Three meaningful words)

32. (*c*) From the given word, 'MEDICO' is the only word which can be formed.

33. (*c*) By using the letters of the given word 'MEASUREMENT' we can form the word 'MASTER'.

34. (*b*) By using the letters of given word, 'RENT' is the only word which can be formed.

35. (*a*) By using the letters of given word 'CORRESPONDING', 'DISCERN', is the only word which can be formed.

36. (*d*) 'PARROT' can be formed from 'PREPARATION'.

37. (*c*) 'ULTRAIST' can be formed from 'ULTRANATIONALISM'.

38. (*c*) 'MONITOR' can be formed from 'PREMONITION'.

39. (*c*) 'OPINION' can be formed from 'COMPANIONSHIP'.

40. (*d*) Clearly, 'IMPASSIVE', cannot be formed by letters of the given word due to absence of letter 'V".

41. (*b*) From the letter of given word ECCENTRICITY, we cannot formed the word CREATE because in the given word letter A is not present.

42. (*a*) The word 'SECURE' cannot be formed from 'COURAGEOUS'.

43. (*b*) From the given word, 'PONDER' is the only word which can not be formed.

44. (*a*) From the given word, 'CHANGE' is the only word which cannot be formed due to the absence of letter 'G'.

45. (*d*) From the given word 'PORTICO' is the only word which cannot be formed due to the absence of letter 'C'.

46. (*d*) From the given word, 'ENTERTAIN' is the only word which cannot be formed due to the absence of letter 'A'.

47. (*d*) By using the letters of the given word, 'COMMUNICATION', 'UNISON' is the only word which cannot be formed due to the absence of letter 'S'.

48. (*a*) By using the letters of given word, 'ALERT' cannot be formed from 'LEGALIZATION' due to absence of letter 'R'.

49. (*c*) By using the letters of given word, 'PRETTY' cannot be formed because letters 'R' and 'Y' are not present in the given word.

50. (*a*) By using the letters of given word, 'RELATION' cannot be formed from 'INCARCERATION' due to absence of letter 'L'.

51. (*b*) By using the letters of given word, 'NEVIN' cannot be formed because letter 'I' is not present in the given word.

52. (*d*) By using the letters of the given word, 'NATION' cannot be formed because letter N' is used only once.

53. (*c*) By using the letters of given word, 'GRAPHIC' cannot be formed because letter 'C' is not present in the given word.

54. (*b*) By using the letters of given word, 'DISTART' cannot be formed because letter 'T' is used only once.

55. (*d*) CODING - (3, 4, 5, 2, 6, 1)

56. (*d*) MUSCLE - 7, 8, 6, 3, 5, 4

57. (*b*) HERMIT - (4, 1, 6, 2, 3, 5)

58. (*c*) NATURE - (4, 3, 2, 5, 1, 6)

59. (*c*) ADHESION - 2, 3, 5, 6, 8, 1, 4, 7

60. (*c*) POCKET - 6, 5, 3, 4, 1, 2

61. (*d*) OCTOBER - 5, 4, 3, 1, 6, 7, 2

62. (*a*) MIRACLE - 6, 3, 4, 1, 7, 2, 5

63. (*c*) SPINACH - 4, 5, 7, 2, 3, 1, 6

64. (*b*) Letter E is suffixed to the following words
HAT + E → HATE
BAR + E → BARE
BAT + E → BATE
PIN + E → PINE
BATH + E → BATHE

65. (*b*) Letter H is prefixed to the following words
H + EAT → HEAT
H + OUR → HOUR
H + IS → HIS
H + AS → HAS
H + AT → HAT

66. (*b*) ARC = CAR, USB = BUS
LACES = SCALE
LECCY = CYCLE
Hence, SCALE is different, as all others are transport vehicles

67. (*c*) LAFC = CALF
UKCGIDLN = DUCKLING
RILNIGHE = HIRELING
BCU = CUB
Hence, HIRELING is different as all others are name of animal kids.

68. (*b*) UTNA ⇒ AUNT
EINEC ⇒ NIECE
OMEHRT ⇒ MOTHER
ROBEHRT ⇒ BROTHER
Hence, Brother is different as all others are females.

69. (*d*) UNPE = PUNE
ILOLSGNH = SHILLONG
OHALPB = BHOPAL
ENANCIH = CHENNAI
Hence, PUNE is different as all others are capitals of different states.

70. (*d*) OLENV → NOVEL
EISTSH → THESIS
AGZEANIM → MAGAZINE
TCAYRIDION → DICTIONARY
Hence, THESIS is different as all others are available in the form of book.

71. (*b*) OFLG ⇒ GOLF
NNEIST ⇒ TENNIS
BLLOOTAF ⇒ FOOTBALL
KENAS ⇒ SNAKE
Hence, SNAKE is different as all others are different games.

72. (*d*) CEKRTCI → CRICKET
OHKCYE → HOCKEY
ESCSH → CHESS
OTOLABLF → FOOTBALL
Hence, CHESS is different as all others are outdoor games.

73. (*c*) The meaningful words are - ALIGNED, DEALING
Here, more than one word is formed. Hence, the correct answer is 'X '.

74. (*c*) If the word NUPKIPM is unscrambled, then the name of a Fruit/vegetable 'PUMPKIN' is formed. The last letter of the word is N.

TYPE 04

Questions Based on Letter's Group

In this type of questions, three, four or five groups of letters are given followed by some directions in each question. The candidates are required to rearrange the groups of letters according to the given directions and answer the question asked.

DIRECTIONS ~(Ex. Nos. 26-30) *These questions are based on five words given below.* « IBPS Clerk 2016

ROD ITS MUG RAY SEW

Ex 26 If the third alphabet in each of the words is changed to next alphabet according to the English alphabetical order, in how many words thus formed will an alphabet appear twice?

(a) One (b) Two (c) Four (d) Three
(d) None

Solution (a) According to the question, words are

ROE ITT MUH RAZ SEX

Only one word in which repetition of alphabet occurs i.e. ITT.

Ex 27 If the third letter in each of the words becomes the first letter, the first becomes the second and the second becomes the third letter, which of the following will form meaningful English words?

(a) Both MUG and RAY
(b) None of the given options will form a meaningful English word
(c) Both ROD and SEW
(d) Only RAY
(e) Only ITS

Solution (e) According to the condition given in question,

ROD ITS MUG RAY SEW

⇒ DRO [SIT] GMU YRA WSE

Ex 28 Which of the following represent the letters immediately following, (in the English alphabetical order) the third letter of the word which is third from the right and the second letter of the word which is second from the left of the given words? (the counting is done from left to right)

(a) H, U (b) F, R (c) R, H (d) K, N
(e) Y, T

Solution (a) Third letter of the word which is third from the right = 'G' (MUG), Second letter of the word which is second from the left = 'T' (ITS)

Letter immediately following G is H and letter immediately following T is U.

∴ H, U is the answer.

Ex 29 If the given words are arranged in the order as they would appear in the dictionary from left to right, the position of which of the following will not change when compared to the given positions?

(a) Both ITS and RAY
(b) The positions of all the given words would change
(c) Only MUG
(d) Only SEW
(e) Only ROD

Solution (d) According to the dictionary order, arrangement will be are as follows :

ITS MUG RAY ROD SEW

Only SEW will not change its position.

Ex 30 If in each of the given words, each of the consonant is changed to previous letter and each vowel is changed to next letter in the English alphabetical series, how many words thus formed will have at least one vowel?

(a) More than three (b) None
(c) Three (d) Two
(e) One

Solution (b) Given arrangement ROD ITS MUG RAY SEW

New arrangement QPC JSR LVF QBX RFV

No word formed.

Practice / CORNER 1.4

DIRECTIONS ~ (Q. Nos. 1-5) *These questions are based on five words given below.*

URN DEN MAT FOR SKI

(The new words formed after performing the mentioned operations below may or may not necessarily be meaningful English word).

1. If the position of the first and the second alphabet in each word is interchanged, which of the following will form a meaningful English word?

(a) Both SKI and MAT (b) Only URN
(c) Only DEN (d) Only FOR
(e) None of these

2. If the letters of given words and then those words themselves are arranged in the order as they would appear in dictionary from left to right, which of the following will be second from the right end?

(a) SKI (b) FOR (c) DEN (d) MAT
(e) None of these

3. If in each of the given words, each of the consonants is changed to previous letter and each vowel is changed to next letter according to the English alphabetical series, in how many words thus formed an alphabet will appear twice?

(a) Three (b) None (c) More than three
(d) One (e) Two

4. How many letters are there in the English alphabetical series between the first letter of the word which is second from the right end and first letter of the word which is second from left end of the given word series?

(a) Three (b) One (c) None (d) Two
(e) None of these

5. If the second alphabet in each of the words is changed to next alphabet according to the English alphabetical order, how many words will be formed with no vowel?

(a) Four (b) Two (c) Three (d) One
(e) None of these

DIRECTIONS ~(Q. Nos. 6-10) *The following questions are based on five words given below.*

RAT ONE BUT AND SAW

(The new words formed after performing the mentioned operations may or may not necessarily be meaningful English words).

6. If in each of the given words, each alphabet is changed to the next letter according to the English alphabetical series, how many words thus formed have the consonants changed from vowels?

(a) One (b) Two (c) Three (d) Four (e) Five

7. How many such pairs of letters are there in the word highlighted in **bold**, each of which has as many letters between them in the word (in both forward and backward directions) as they have between them in the English alphabetical order?

(a) None (b) One (c) Two (d) Three
(e) Four

8. If the first alphabet of each word is changed to the next alphabet according to English alphabetical series, how many meaningful English words will be formed?

(a) One (b) Two (c) Three (d) Four
(e) Five

9. If the given words are arranged in the order as they would appear in the dictionary from left to right, which of the following will be fourth from the left?

(a) RAT (b) ONE (c) BUT (d) AND
(e) SAW

10. If in each of the given words, only the consonants are changed to the next letter according to English alphabetical series and the vowels are retained, in how many words thus formed the vowel appear twice or more times? (same or different vowels)

(a) None (b) One (c) Two (d) Three
(e) Four

DIRECTIONS ~ (Q. Nos. 11-15) *Following questions are based on five words given below.*

MAN CAR WAR CAN HOT

(The new words formed after performing the mentioned operations may or may not necessarily be meaningful English words)

11. If in each of the words, all the alphabets are arranged in English alphabetical order within the word, how many words will NOT begin with a vowel?

(a) None (b) One (c) Two (d) Three
(e) More than three

12. How many letters are there in the English alphabetical series between second letter of the word which is second from the right and the third letter of the word which is third from the left of the given words?

(a) 14 (b) 15 (c) 16 (d) 17
(e) 18

13. If in each of the given words, each consonant is changed to previous letter and each vowel is changed to next letter according to the English alphabetical order, in how many words thus formed no vowels will appear?

(a) None (b) One (c) Two (d) Three
(e) More than three

14. If the last alphabet in each of the words is changed to the next alphabet in the English alphabetical order, how many words having two vowels (same or different vowels) will be formed?

(a) None (b) One (c) Two (d) Three
(e) Four

15. If the given words are arranged in the order as they would appear in the dictionary from left to right, which of the following will be fourth from the left?

(a) MAN (b) CAN (c) CAR (d) HOT
(e) WAR

DIRECTIONS ~(Q. Nos. 16-20) Study the following sequence carefully and answer the given questions.

COT IVY PEA FOX MRU

16. If we add 'L' after first letter in every word, then how many meaningful words will be formed?

(a) None (b) Three
(c) Two (d) One
(e) None of these

17. If third letter of each word is replaced by its succeeding letter according to English alphabetical order, then in how many words vowels will appear more than once?

(a) Two (b) One
(c) None (d) Three
(e) None of these

18. If all the words are arranged according to English alphabetical order from left to right, then which word will appear fourth from the left end?

(a) MRU (b) FOX
(c) PEA (d) IVY
(e) None of these

19. If all the letters are arranged according to English alphabetical order within each word, then in how many words vowel will appear at second position?

(a) One (b) None
(c) Two (d) Three
(e) None of these

20. How many letters are there in English alphabetical series between the first letter of the second word from the left end and third letter of the third word from the right end?

(a) Five (b) Six
(c) Seven (d) Four
(e) None of these

DIRECTIONS ~ (Q. Nos. 21-25) *Following questions are based on the five words given below*, study the following words and answer the following questions.

« RBI Office Assistant 2020

BOY CAT RAT MAT SIT PEN

21. If the vowel in each of the given words is changed to its next letter and each consonant is changed to its previous letter according to the English alphabetical series, then in how many words there are repeated letters?

(a) One (b) Two (c) Three (d) Four
(e) Five

22. How many letters are there between the first letter of the second word from left and first letter of the third word from right end in English alphabetical series?

(a) Eight (b) Six (c) Seven (d) Five
(e) More than eight

23. If the words are arranged according to the English dictionary from left to right then which of the following word is second from the left end?

(a) BOY (b) SIT
(c) CAT (d) RAT
(e) None of these

24. If all the letters in each word are arranged according to the English alphabetical series from left to right, then how many meaningful words are formed?

(a) One (b) Two
(c) Three (d) Four
(e) Five

25. If the first letter is interchanged with the third letter within the word then how many words starts with a vowel?

(a) None (b) One (c) Two (d) Three
(e) More than three

Answers / WITH EXPLANATIONS

1. (*b*) RUN EDN AMT OFR KSI
Only URN will form a meaningful word 'RUN'.

2. (*a*) AMT DEN FOR IKS NRU
SKI is the second word from the right end.

3. (*d*) VQM CFM LBS EPQ RJJ
Here, only in one word RJJ has an alphabet appear twice.

4. (*b*) [D] EN and [F] OR
Only one letter is there between D and F. i.e. E.

5. (*c*) There are three words which have no vowel.
USN [DFN] [MBT] [FPR] SLI

6. (*e*) RAT ⇒ SBU; ONE ⇒ POF;
BUT ⇒ CVU; AND ⇒ BOE;
SAW ⇒ TBX

7. (*b*)
18 1 20
R A T

8. (*b*) RAT ⇒ SAT; ONE ⇒ PNE;
BUT ⇒ CUT; AND ⇒ BND;
SAW ⇒ TAW
Meaningful Words ⇒ SAT, CUT

9. (*a*) AND, BUT, ONE, RAT, SAW

10. (*e*) RAT ⇒ SAU; ONE ⇒ OOE
BUT ⇒ CUU; AND ⇒ AOE
SAW ⇒ TAX

11. (*b*) Arranging the alphabets as per English alphabetical order, within the word.
AMN ACR ARW ACN HOT
four words begin with vowel.

12. (*c*) Second from the right = C [A] N
Third from the left = W A [R]
Alphabets between A and R = 16

13. (*a*) Changing the consonants to previous letter and vowels to the next letter as per English, alphabetical order.
LBM BBQ VBQ BBM GPS
All the words formed have no vowels.

14. (*d*) Changing the last alphabet to the next alphabet as per English alphabetical order.
MAO CAS WAS CAO HOU
Three words have two vowels.

15. (*a*) Arranging the words as per dictionary from left to right.
CAN CAR HOT MAN WAR
MAN is fourth from the left.

16. (*c*) There will be two meaningful words which are 'CLOT' and 'PLEA'.

17. (*b*) Given Words : COT, IVY, PEA, FOX, MRU.
After replacing third letter of each word by its succeeding letter we get,
<u>COU</u> IVZ PEB FOY MRV
In only one word vowel has appeared more than once i.e. COU.

18. (*a*) After arranging the given words in English alphabetical order, we get
COT FOX IVY MRU PEA
→ Fourth from the left end
Hence, 'MRU' is fourth from the left end.

19. (*d*) After arranging all the letters according to English alphabetical order within each word, we get
<u>COT</u> IVY <u>AEP</u> <u>FOX</u> MRU
Hence, in three words i.e. COT, AEP and FOX, vowels appear at second position

20. (*c*) First letter of the second word from the left end : I
Third letter of the third word from the right end : A
Hence, there are seven letters (B, C, D, E, F, G and H) between A and I

21. (*a*) New words after applying changes,
APX, BBS , QBS, LBS, RJS, OFM
Hence, required number of words having repeated letters
= 1 (BBS ⇔ CAT)

22. (*e*) First letter = First letter of the second word from left = C
And second letter = First letter of the third word from right = M
Required number of letters between C and M = 9 (More than eight)

23. (*c*) Rearranging the words from left to right as per dictionary, we get
BOY, CAT , MAT, PEN, RAT, SIT
Required word = CAT

24. (*c*) New words after applying changes,
[BOY], [ACT], [ART], AMT, IST, ENP
∴ Required number of meaningful words = 3

25. (*a*) New words after applying changes,
YOB, TAC, TAR, TAM, TIS NEP
Clearly, there are no words starting with vowel.

TYPE 05

Rule Detection

In this type of questions of alphabets, four options are given as the group of letters. Out of these four groups, candidates have to choose that one which follows a certain pattern in a particular manner. That pattern could be in increasing/decreasing order of same/different number.

***Ex* 31** Number of letters skipped in between adjacent letters in the series is two. Which of the following series observes this rule?

(a) MPSVYBE (b) QSVYZCF
(c) SVZCGJN (d) ZCGKMPR

***Solution* (a)** According to the question,

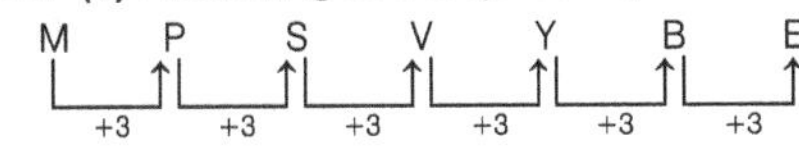

∴ Only option (a) is following the certain pattern in increasing order with same difference.

***Ex* 32** Number of letters skipped in between adjacent letters in the series decreases by one. Which of the following series is observing the rule?

(a) OUMYA (b) AEIKL (c) AZXUA (d) QUXZA

***Solution* (d)** According to the question

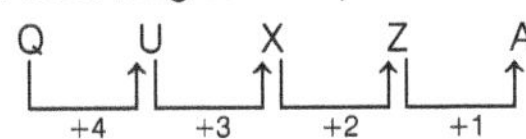

Therefore, option (d) is having the group of letters which follows the given rule.

Practice / CORNER 1.5

1. The letters skipped in between the adjacent letters in the series are followed by equal space. Which of the following series observes this rule? « SSC CGL 2013

(a) HKNGSW (b) RVZDFG
(c) RVZDHL (d) SUXADF

2. Number of letters skipped in between adjacent letters in the series is two. Which one of the following alternatives observes this rule?

(a) SPMLI (b) TSPNKH (c) UROLIF (d) WTQNKJ

3. Select that series in which letters are not according to a general rule.

(a) CEGIKM (b) MORTVX
(c) PRTVXZ (d) ZBDFHJ

4. Number of the letters skipped in between adjacent letters of the series are increased by one. Which of the following series observes this rule?

(a) OIGDC (b) OMJFA
(c) OMKIG (d) ONLKJ

5. Select the series in which the letters skipped in between adjacent letters decrease in order.

(a) AGMRV (b) HNSWA
(c) NSXCH (d) SYDHK

6. Number of letters skipped in between adjacent letters in the series starting from the end decreases by one. Which of the following series observes this rule? « SSC (10+2) 2014

(a) DBPUY (b) DBUYP
(c) DBPUY (d) DBYUP

7. Number of letters skipped in between adjacent letters in the series are increased by one. Which of the following alternatives observes this rule? « SSC Steno 2012

(a) KMPTY (b) IJKOT
(c) HJMQT (d) DFIJK

8. In which of the following letters sequences, there is a letter leaving three letters of the alphabet in order, after the letters placed at odd-numbered positions and leaving two letters of the alphabet in order after the letters placed at even-numbered positions?

(a) ADFIKN (b) BEGJLN (c) CFHKLO (d) DFIKNP

9. Select that series in which letters are according to a general rule.

(a) NQUXBE (b) NQUXAE (c) NRUXBE (d) NQUYBE

10. Which of the following series observes the rule, "Skip in between adjacent letters, increasing one letter more each time to build a set of letters"?

(a) SUXBGN (b) SUXBGM (c) SUYBGM (d) SVXBGN

11. Number of letters skipped in between adjacent letters in the series decreases by one. Which of the following series is observing the rule?

(a) BGKNPR (b) CINRTU
(c) EJNQST (d) LQUXAB

12. Number of letters skipped in between adjacent letters in the series increases by one. Which of the following series observes this rule?

(a) CPTOV (b) HCFKP
(c) HJHQV (d) IKNRW

13. Which of the following series observes the rule., "Skip in between adjacent letters, increasing one letter more each time to build a set of letters"?

(a) ACFJLQ (b) BDGKPV
(c) CEHLQV (d) HILPUZ

14. Number of letters skipped in between the adjacent letters in the series are consecutive odd number. Which of the following series observes this rule?

(a) FINUD (b) FHLRZ
(c) FINUC (d) FHLSZ

Answers WITH EXPLANATIONS

1. (*c*) Let us see

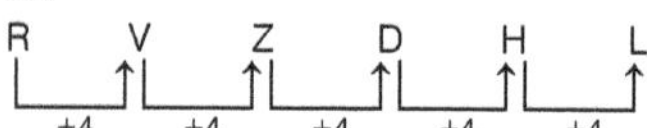

Now, it is clear that option (c) is correct answer.

2. (*c*) From the given question,

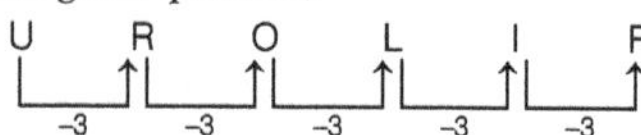

Clearly, only option (c) has the required group of letters.

3. (*b*) Let us see

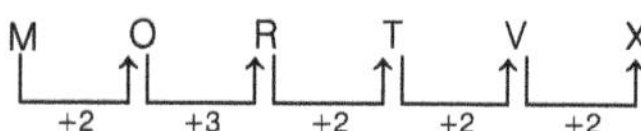

Clearly, only option (b) is having a group of letters which is not according to the general rule.

4. (*b*) As per the question,

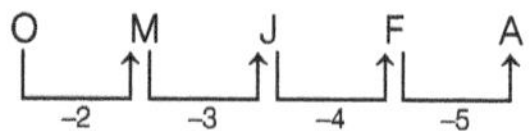

Clearly, only option (b) follows the given rule.

5. (*d*) According to the question,

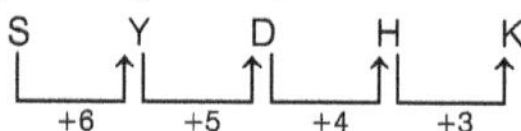

Clearly, only option (d) is having the letters according to the given rule.

6. (*d*) From the given question,

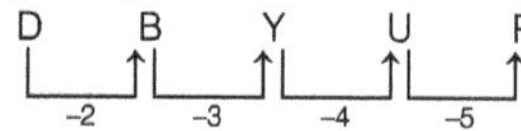

Now, it is clear that only DBYUP is a group of letters which follows the given rule.

7. (*a*) From the given question,

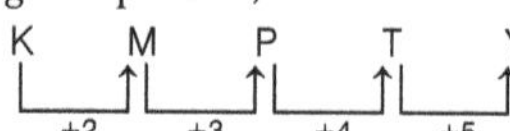

Clearly, only KMPTY having the series according to the given rule.

8. (*a*) From the given question,

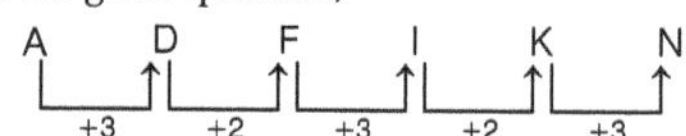

Clearly, only option (a) is having the given pattern in the question.

9. (*a*) According to the question,

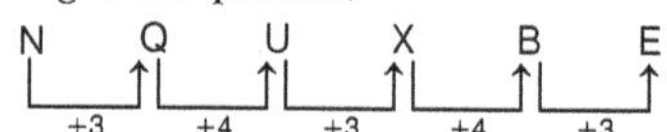

Here, general rule is followed by only option (a).

10. (*b*) From the given question,

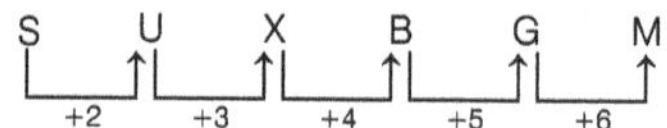

Clearly, only option (b) is having the series according to the given rule.

11. (*c*) According to the question,

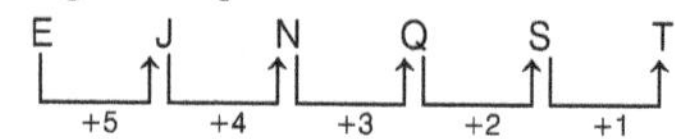

So, option (c) is having the group of letters which follows the given rule.

12. (*d*) Only option (d) is correct which follows the given pattern as given below

13. (*b*) According to the question,

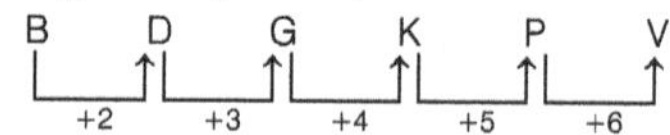

Hence, only option (b) is following the given pattern.

14. (*a*) As per the question given,

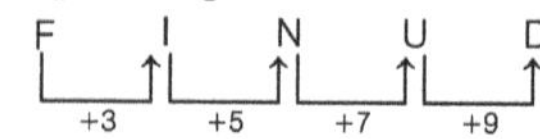

Hence, option (a) is having the series according to the given rule.

TYPE 06

Finding Digits After Rearrangement

In this type of questions, a specified order or pattern is used to rearrange the positions of digits of the number. Then, either the number of those digits is found whose positions remain unchanged after rearrangement or the digit at particular place from left or right of the number is to be found.

In some questions, generally five/six numbers of three digits are given and the digits of these numbers have to be rearranged according to the question.

Finally, the candidate is required to find out a certain number/digit on the basis of new arrangement.

Ex 33 In the number 7524693, how many digits will be as far away from beginning of the number, if arranged in ascending order as they are in the number?

« PNB (Clerk) 2010

(a) None
(b) One
(c) Two
(d) Three
(e) More than three

Solution (b) Let us see

Original number	7	5	2	4	6	9	3
Ascending order	2	3	4	5	6	7	9

Hence, only one digit (*i.e.*, 6) remains at the same place as in the original number.

Ex 34 In the number 53261489, if first and fifth digits interchange their positions, second and sixth digits interchange their positions and further changes keep going on in the same manner, then which digit will be 6th from the right in the rearrangement?

(a) 8 (b) 6 (c) 4 (d) 2

Solution (a) Let us see

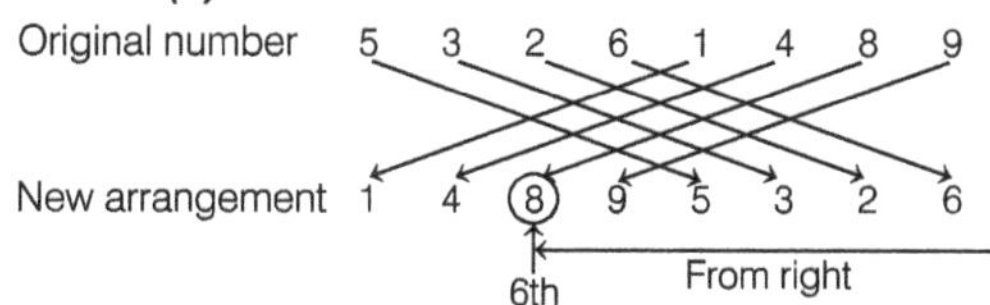

So, it is clear that 6th digit from the right after rearrangement is 8.

Ex 35 If in the number '35982476', 1 is added to each even digit and 2 is subtracted from each odd digit, then which digits will not appear twice in the number thus obtained? « SSC (Steno) 2012

(a) Only 1 (b) Only 9
(c) Both '1' and '9' (d) Only 5
(e) None of these

Solution (c) Given Number : 3 5 9 8 2 4 7 6

−2 −2 −2 +1 +1 +1 −2 +1

New Number : 1 3 7 9 3 5 5 7

Both '1' and '9' will not appear twice in the number thus obtained.

Ex 36 How many such pairs of digits are there in the number 75938462, each of which has as many digits between them in the number as they have between them when arranged in ascending order? « BOB PO 2000

(a) None (b) One (c) Two (d) Three
(e) More than three

Solution (e)

Given number 7 5 9 3 8 4 6 2

Arrange the digits in ascending order,

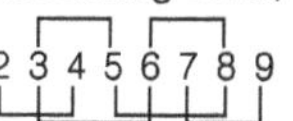

Therefore, such pair = six

i.e. (7,9), (5,8), (3,6), (8,6), (5,3) and (4,2).

Ex 37 The position of how many digits will remain the same if the digits in the number 297345618 are rearranged in the descending order with in the number, from left to right? « SBI Clerk 2015

(a) None (b) Two
(c) More than three (d) Three
(e) One

Solution (e)

Original Number ⟶ 2 9 [7] 3 4 5 6 1 8
New Number ⟶ 9 8 [7] 6 5 4 3 2 1

Only one digit '7' remains unchanged.

Ex 38 If in the following numbers, first and last digits are interchanged, then which one of the given options will be the least number?

418 319 179 589 409

(a) 179 (b) 589
(c) 319 (d) 418
(e) 409

Solution (d) Let us see

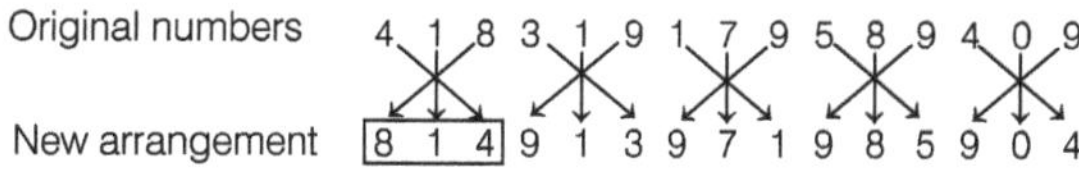

∴ Least number = 814 ⇒ 418

Practice / CORNER 1.6

1. The position of how many digits in the number 53269718 will remain unchanged, if the digits within the number are rearranged in ascending order?

(a) None (b) One (c) Two (d) Three

2. The position of how many digits in the number 59164823 will remain unchanged after the digits are rearranged in descending order within the number? Bank (PO) 2010

(a) None (b) One (c) Two (d) Three
(e) More than three

3. How many such digits are there in the number 62591483 each of which is as far away from the beginning of the number as when the digits are arranged in ascending order within the number?

(a) None (b) One
(c) Two (d) Three

4. How many such pairs of digits are there in the number 5234816 each of which has as many digits between them in the number as when the digits are arranged in descending order within the number?

(a) None (b) One
(c) Two (d) More than three

5. How many such pair of digits are there in the number 536142 each of which has as many digits between them in the number as when the digits are arranged in the ascending order within the number?

(a) None (b) One (c) Two (d) Three

6. How many such pairs are there in the number 6384257 each of which has as many digits between them in the number as they have between them in the number series both from backward and forward? « LIC AAO 2019

(a) None (b) One (c) Two (d) Three
(e) More than there

7. The position of how many digits in the number 8247531 will remain unchanged after the digits are rearranged in ascending order within the number? « K-MAT 2011

(a) None (b) One
(c) Two (d) Three
(e) More than three

8. If the digits in the number 86435192 are arranged in ascending order, what will be the difference between the digits which are second from the right and fourth from the left in the new arrangement? « PNB (Clerk) 2009

(a) One (b) Two
(c) Three (d) Four
(e) None of these

9. If each of the digits in the number 92581473 are arranged in ascending order, what will be the sum of the digits which are fourth from the right and third from the left in the new arrangement? « PNB (Clerk) 2011

(a) 8 (b) 7 (c) 6 (d) 11
(e) None of these

10. The positions of the first and fifth digits in the number 83146759 are interchanged. Similarly, the second and the sixth digits are interchanged and so on. Which of the following will be the third digit from the right end after the rearrangement?

(a) 3 (b) 1 (c) 6 (d) 7

11. In the number 3856490271, positions of the first and second digits are interchanged, positions of the third and fourth digits are interchanged and so on till the positions of 9th and 10th digits are interchanged, then which digit will be fifth from the left end and 7th from the right end respectively?

(a) 6,9 (b) 4,6 (c) 9,5 (d) 0,4

12. The positions of the first and the fifth digits of the number 81943275 are interchanged. Similarly, the positions of the second and the sixth digits are interchanged and so on till the fourth and the eighth digits. Which of the following will be the multiplication of fifth digit from the left end and third digit from the right end after the rearrangement? « IBPS (PO) 2012

(a) 5 (b) 35 (c) 7 (d) 28
(e) None of these

13. If in the number 39682147, 1 is added to each of the digit which is less than five and 1 is subtracted from each of the digit which is greater than five then how many digits are repeating in the number thus formed? « SBI Clerk 2018

(a) Two (b) One (c) None (d) Three
(e) Four

14. If 1 is subtracted from each even number and 2 is subtracted to each odd number in the number 5827936, then which digit/digits will appear twice in the new number thus formed? « CGPSC Pre 2017

(a) Only 7 (b) 5 and 7
(c) 1, 5 and 7 (d) 4, 5 and 9
(e) None of these

DIRECTIONS ~ (Q.Nos. 15-19) *Study the following arrangement carefully and answer the questions.* « SBI Clerk 2015

3 9 2 4 7 5 9 2 8 1 4 9 5 3 1 6 5 7 3 4 2 9 8 1 3 6 2 8 1 7 5 4 5

15. How many such 2s are there in the given arrangement, each of which is immediately followed by a perfect square?

(a) More than three (b) Three
(c) One (d) Two
(e) None

16. If all the even digits are deleted from the given arrangement, which of the following will be tenth from the right end of the arrangement?

(a) 3 (b) 1
(c) 5 (d) 7
(e) 9

17. How many such 4s are there in the given arrangement, each of which is immediately followed by a digit which has a numerical value of more than four?

(a) More than three (b) One
(c) None (d) Two
(e) Three

18. Which of the following is seventh to the left of the seventeenth digit from the left end of the given arrangement?

(a) 5 (b) 9 (c) 4 (d) 8
(e) 1

19. How many such 3s are there in the given arrangement, each of which immediately preceded by an odd digit and also immediately followed by an even digit?

(a) Three (b) None
(c) More than three (d) Two
(e) One

DIRECTIONS ~ (Q. Nos. 20-24) *The following questions are based on the three digits numbers given below.*

563 218 732 491 929 « SBI Clerk 2018

20. If 2 is subtracted from the second digit of all odd numbers and 2 is added in the first digits of all even numbers, then which number is lowest number after the arrangement?

(a) 218 (b) 732
(c) 491 (d) 929
(e) None of these

21. If third digit of highest number is divided by the first digit of lowest number, then what will be the resultant?

(a) 4 (b) 4.05 (c) 4.5 (d) 5
(e) None of these

22. If all the digits in each number are arranged in increasing order, then which number will be the highest number after the rearrangement?

(a) 218 (b) 732
(c) 491 (d) 563
(e) None of these

23. How many numbers will be there in the given series in which addition of first and third digit is greater than second digit?

(a) One (b) Two (c) Three (d) Four
(e) None of these

24. How many numbers will be there in the given series in which difference of first and third digit is greater than second digit?

(a) One (b) Two (c) Three (d) Four
(e) None of these

DIRECTIONS ~ (Q. Nos. 25-29) *Following questions are based on the five three-digit numbers given below.*

813 261 458 732 694 « Uttaranchal GBC 2012

25. If the positions of the first and the third digits are interchanged in each of these numbers, then which of these will be an odd number?

(a) 261 (b) 694 (c) 813 (d) 732

26. If all the three digits / numbers are rearranged in ascending order (from left to right) within the number, in each of these numbers, then which of these will be the second highest?

(a) 458 (b) 813 (c) 732 (d) 694

27. What is the difference between the sum of the three digits of the highest number and that of the second highest number?

(a) 5 (b) 8 (c) 12 (d) 0

28. If the positions of the second and the third digits are interchanged in each of these numbers, then which of these will be exactly divisible by 5?

(a) 694 (b) 458 (c) 261 (d) 732

29. If the first and the second digits are interchanged in each of these numbers, then which of the following will be the second smallest number?

(a) 732 (b) 261 (c) 458 (d) 813

DIRECTIONS ~ (Q.Nos. 30-31) *These questions are based on the following six numbers.* « SBI (Clerk) 2009

382 473 568 728 847 629

30. If the second and the third digits of each number are interchanged, which number will be the third lowest?

(a) 629 (b) 382
(c) 473 (d) 568
(e) None of these

31. If the first and the third digits of each number are interchanged, which number will be the third highest?

(a) 473 (b) 728
(c) 847 (d) 629
(e) None of these

DIRECTIONS ~ (Q.Nos. 32-36) *These questions are based on the following five numbers.*

834 427 563 649 975 « IBPS Clerk 2017

32. If all the digits of numbers are arranged in ascending order within the number, then which of the following is lowest number?

(a) 975 (b) 649 (c) 834 (d) 563
(e) 427

33. If 1st digit of highest number is divided by 2nd digit of 2nd highest number, then what will be the resultant?

(a) 2 (b) 4 (c) 3 (d) 5
(e) None of these

34. If 2 is subtracted from each even digit and 1 is subtracted from each odd digit number of each number, which number among them will be lowest number?

(a) 834 (b) 427 (c) 563 (d) 649
(e) 975

35. What is addition of 3rd digit of highest number and 2nd digit of lowest number?

(a) 7 (b) 6 (c) 4 (d) 3
(e) None of these

36. If 1st digit of 2nd highest number is divided by 1st digit of lowest number, then what will be the resultant?

(a) 5 (b) 3 (c) 2 (d) 4
(e) None of these

DIRECTIONS ~ (Q.Nos. 37-41) *The following questions are based on the five three-digit numbers given below*

684 512 437 385 296 « SBI Clerk 2016

37. If 2 is added to the first digit of each of the numbers how many numbers thus formed will be divisible by three?

(a) None (b) One
(c) Two (d) Three
(e) More than three

38. If all the digits in each of the numbers are arranged in descending order within the numbers, which of the following will be the highest number in the new arrangement of numbers?

(a) 684 (b) 385
(c) 296 (d) 437
(e) None of these

39. What will be the resultant number if the second digit of the second lowest number is divided by the third digit of the highest number?

(a) 2 (b) 3 (c) 0 (d) 1
(e) 4

40. If 1 is added to the first digit and 2 is added to the last digit of each of the numbers then which of the following numbers will be the second highest number?

(a) 385 (b) 684 (c) 437 (d) 296
(e) 512

41. If in each number the first and second digits are interchanged then which will be the highest number?

(a) 296 (b) 512 (c) 437 (d) 684
(e) 385

Answers WITH EXPLANATIONS

1. (*b*) Let us see

The given number 5 3 2 6 9 7 1 8
Ascending order arrangement 1 2 3 5 6 7 8 9

So, position of only one digit remains unchanged.

2. (*c*) Let us see

The given number 5 9 1 6 4 8 2 3
Descending order arrangement 9 8 6 5 4 3 2 1

So, position of two digits remain unchanged.

3. (*c*) Let us see

The given number 6 2 5 9 1 4 8 3
Ascending order arrangement 1 2 3 4 5 6 8 9

Hence, two digits remain at the same place from the beginning.

4. (*d*) Let us see

The given number 5 2 3 4 8 1 6
Descending order arrangement 8 6 5 4 3 2 1

∴ Required pairs = (53), (23), (34) and (24)

5. (*c*) Let us see

The given number 5 3 6 1 4 2
Ascending order arrangement 1 2 3 4 5 6

So, there are two required pair of digits.

6. (*e*) According to the given information,

6 3 8 4 2 5 7

There are four such pairs.

7. (*c*) Let us see

The given number 8 2 4 7 5 3 1
Ascending order arrangement 1 2 3 4 5 7 8

So, position of two digits remain unchanged.

8. (*d*) Original number 8 6 4 3 5 1 9 2
Ascending order 1 2 3 ④ 5 6 ⑧ 9

From left 4th; 2nd From right

∴ Required difference = 8 − 4 = 4

9. (*a*) Let us see

Original number 9 2 5 8 1 4 7 3
Ascending order 1 2 ③ 4 ⑤ 7 8 9

From left 3rd; 4th From right

∴ Required sum = 5 + 3 = 8

10. (*a*) Let us see

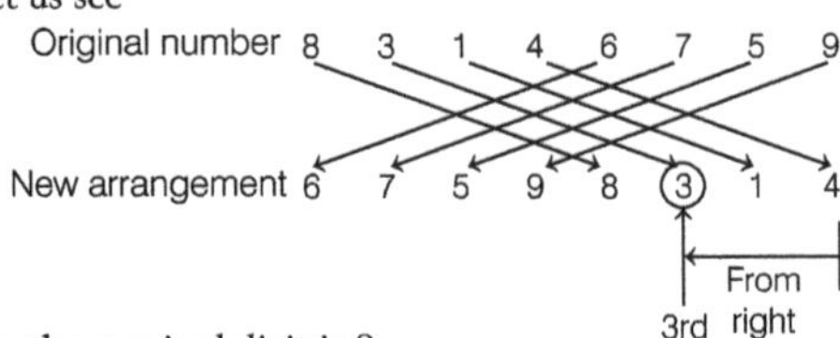

So, the required digit is 3.

11. (*c*) Let us see

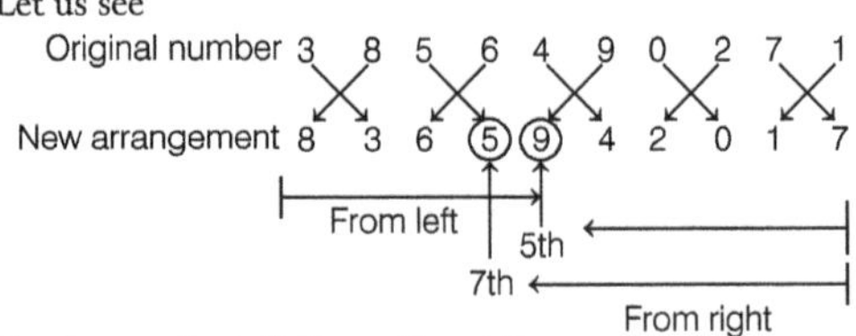

So, the required digits are 9 and 5.

12. (*a*) Let us see

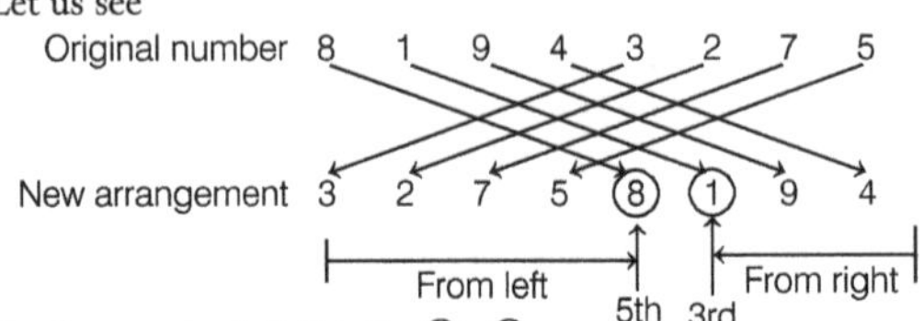

So, the required digit is 8 × ① = ⑧

13. (*b*) Given number ⇒ 3 9 6 8 2 ① 4 7
After adding and subtracting 1 according to the given condition
⇒ 4 8 ⑤ 7 3 2 ⑤ 6
Here, only one digit i.e., 5 repeats in the number.

14. (*c*) According to the question
One subtracted from even digit.
Two subtracted from odd digit.

5 8 2 7 9 3 6 → 3 7 1 5 7 1 5

1, 5 and 7 appear twice.

15. (*d*) 3 9 [2] 4 7 5 9 2 8 1 4 9 5 3 1 6 5 7 3 4 [2] 9 8 1 3 6 2 8 1 7 5 4 5
Thus, there are two required 2s.

16. (*c*) Deleting all the even digits,

3 9 7 5 9 1 9 5 3 1 5 7 3 9 1 3 1 7 5 5

Now, tenth digit from the right end = 5

17. (*e*) 3 9 2 [4] 7 5 9 2 8 1 [4] 9 5 3 1 6 5 7 3 4 2 9 8 1 3 6 2 8 1 7 [5] 4 5
There are three required 4s.

18. (*e*) Seventh to the left of the seventeenth digit from the left end
= (17 − 7)th digit from the left
= 10th digit from the left = 1

19. (*d*) 3 9 2 4 7 5 9 2 8 1 4 9 5 3 1 6 5 7 [3] 4 2 9 8 1 [3] 6 2 8 1 7 5 4 5
There are two 3s in the given arrangement, which are immediately preceded by an odd digit and also immediately followed by an even digit.

20. (*a*) Given numbers ⇒ 563 218 732 491 929
New numbers ⇒ 543 418 932 471 909
After arrangement the lowest number = 418
∴ Required number = 218

21. (*c*) Highest number = 929, Third digit = 9
Lowest number = 218, First digit = 2
∴ Resultant number = $\frac{9}{2} = 4.5$

22. (*d*) Given number ⇒ 563 218 732 491 929
New numbers ⇒ 356 128 237 149 299
∴ Highest number after arrangement = 356
∴ Required number = 563

23. (*d*) There are four numbers in which the addition of first and third digit is greater than second digit.
$563 \Rightarrow 5+3>6$ $218 \Rightarrow 2+8>1$
$732 \Rightarrow 7+2>3$ $929 \Rightarrow 9+9>2$ $491 \Rightarrow 4+1<9$

24. (*b*) There are two such digits in which the difference of first and third digit is greater than second digit.
$563 \Rightarrow 5 \sim 3 < 6$ $218 \Rightarrow 2 \sim 8 < 1$
$732 \Rightarrow 7 \sim 2 > 3$ $491 \Rightarrow 4 \sim 1 < 9$ $929 \Rightarrow 9 \sim 9 < 2$

25. (*d*) According to the question,

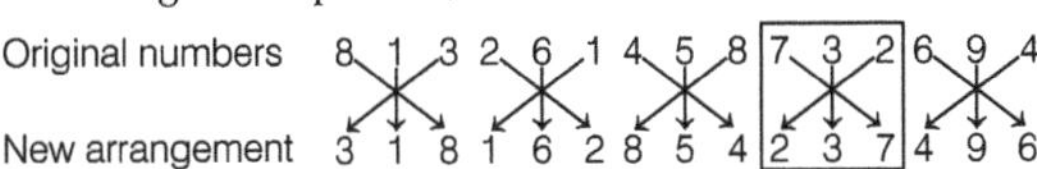

Here, only number 237 is odd.
∴ Required number = 732

26. (*a*) According to the question,

Original number	813	261	458	732	694
New arrangement	138	126	458	237	469
			2nd highest		

∴ Required number = 458

27. (*d*) Highest number = 813
Second highest number = 732
∴ Required difference = $(8+1+3)-(7+3+2)$
$= 12 - 12 = 0$

28. (*b*) According to the question,

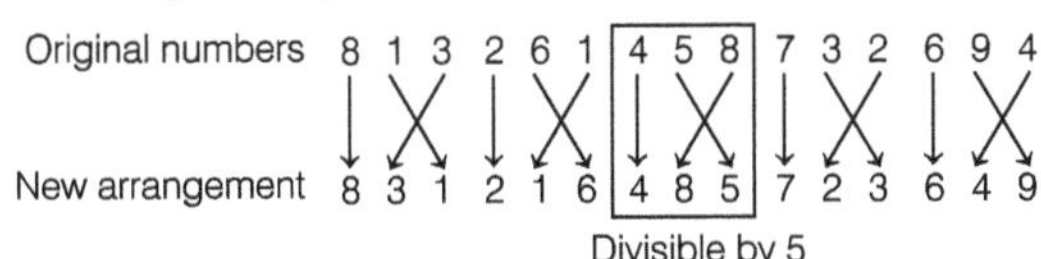

∴ Required number = 458.

29. (*a*) According to the question,

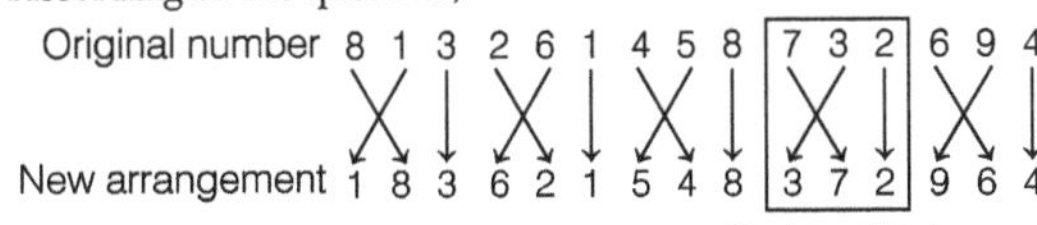

∴ Required number = 732

30. (*d*) According to the question,

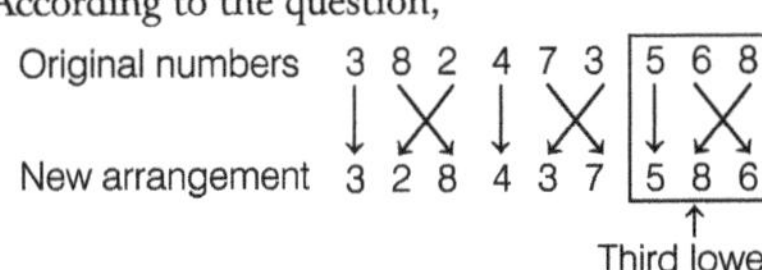

Original numbers	7 2 8	8 4 7	6 2 9
New arrangement	7 8 2	8 7 4	6 9 2

∴ Required number = 568

31. (*b*) According to the question,

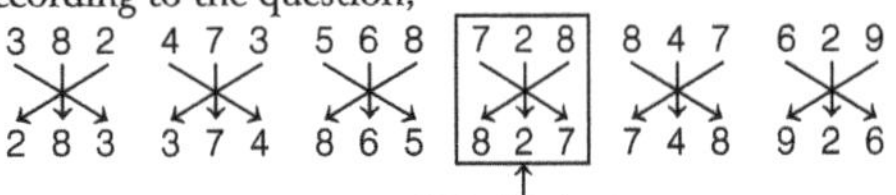

∴ Required number = 728

Solution (Q.Nos. 32-36)

32. (*e*)

834	427	563	649	975
348	247 (Lowest number)	356	469	579 – (ascending order of digits of numbers)

So, after arranging the digits of each number in ascending order, 427 in lowest numbers.

33. (*c*) 1st digit highest number = 9 7 5
2nd digit of 2nd highest number = 8 3 4
Resultant = 9 / 3 = 3

34. (*b*) According to the question,

834	427	563	649	975
622	206 (lowest number)	442	428	864

So, 427 is lowest number.

35. (*a*) 3rd digit of highest number = 9 7 [5]
2nd digit of lowest number = 4 [2] 7
Required addition = 5 + 2 = 7

36. (*c*) Ist digit of 2nd highest number = [8] 3 4
Ist digit of lowest number = [4] 2 7
Resultant = $\frac{8}{4} = 2$

37. (*b*) Arrangement of the given numbers as per instructions

684	512	437	385	296
+2	+2	+2	+2	+2
884	712	637	585	496

Now, number divisible by 3 from new formed numbers = 585
Hence, there is only one number is divisible by three from new formed numbers.

38. (*c*) Arrangement of numbers in descending order

684	512	437	385	296
864	521	743	853	(962)

Highest number in descending order = 962
∴ Required number = 296

39. (*a*) Highest number = 6 8 [4]
Second lowest number = 3 [8] 5
∴ Resultant = $\frac{8}{4} = 2$

40. (*e*)

6 8 4	5 1 2	4 3 7	3 8 5	2 9 6
+1 +2	+1 +2	+1 +2	+1 +2	+1 +2
7 8 6	6 1 4	5 3 9	4 8 7	3 9 8

Hence, second highest number in newly formed numbers = 614
∴ Required number = 512

41. (*a*)

6 8 4	5 1 2	4 3 7	3 8 5	2 9 6
8 6 4	1 5 2	3 4 7	8 3 5	9 2 6

Hence, highest number in newly formed numbers = 926
∴ Required number = 296

TYPE 07

Letter and Number Sequence Test

Letter and number sequence test is based on a sequence of letters and numbers in which a series of letters and/or numbers with or without repetitions are given. The candidates are required to find the total number of a particular number or letter in the series applying certain condition. Apart from that, the questions may be based on some series pattern, analogy, classification etc.

Sometimes, the given sequence also includes symbols along with numbers and letters. Such sequence is called 'Alphanumeric sequence'.

Let us see all types of sequence given below

(i) Number sequence, 4 9 6 9 4 4 6 2 2 1 5 0 3 0 3

(ii) A letter sequence B A B C D L L C L B A M A N

(iii) Alpha-numeric sequence, ϕ 4 3 θ A × * ↑ 1 J > + 5

Formats of the questions will give a better idea about such type of questions.

Ex 39 How many 7s immediately preceded by 6 but not immediately followed by 4 are there in the following series?

7 4 2 7 6 4 3 6 7 5 3 5 7 8 4 3 7 6 7 2 4 0 6 7 4 3

(a) One (b) Two
(c) Four (d) Six

Solution (b) Let us see

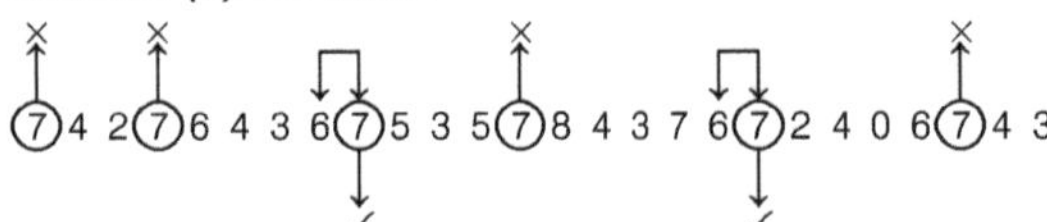

✓ = Condition fulfilled × = Condition not fulfilled.

Clearly, there are two such 7's.

DIRECTIONS ~ (Example Nos. 40-43) *Study the following sequence carefully and answer the questions that follow.*

B 5 R 1 @ E K 4 F 7 © D A M 2 P 3 % 9 H I W 8 * 6 U I $ V Q #

Ex 40 Which of the following is the 7th to the left of the 17th from the left end of the above arrangement?

(a) 7 (b) W (c) * (d) 4

Solution (a) Let us see

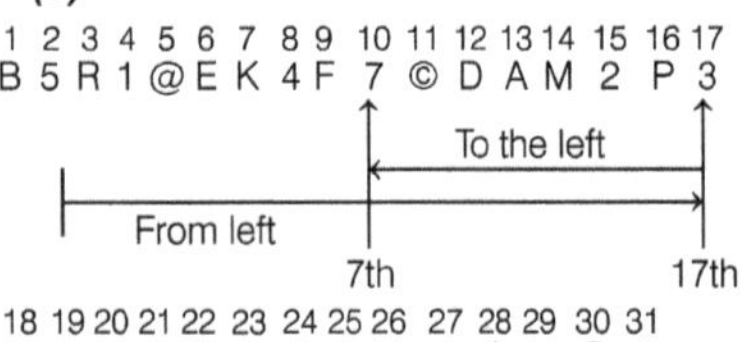

Note *7th to the left of 17th from the left end* = (17 − 7) = 10*th from left end* = 7

Ex 41 Which of the following is exactly in the middle between D and U in the given arrangement?

(a) % (b) H
(c) 9 (d) 3

Solution (c) Let us see

D = 12th from the left, U = 26th from the left

∴ Middle letter between D and U = $\frac{12+26}{2}$ = 19th from left = 9

Ex 42 Four of the following, three are alike in a certain way based on their position in the given arrangement and so form a group. Which is the one that does not belong to that group?

(a) P M 3 (b) K F E (c) 6 J * (d) 7 D 4

Solution (d) As in all others the first and the third elements are consecutive ones in the given arrangement.

Ex 43 How many such symbols are there in the given arrangement each of which is immediately preceded by a number but not immediately followed by a consonant?

(a) None (b) One (c) Two (d) Three

Solution (d) Let us see

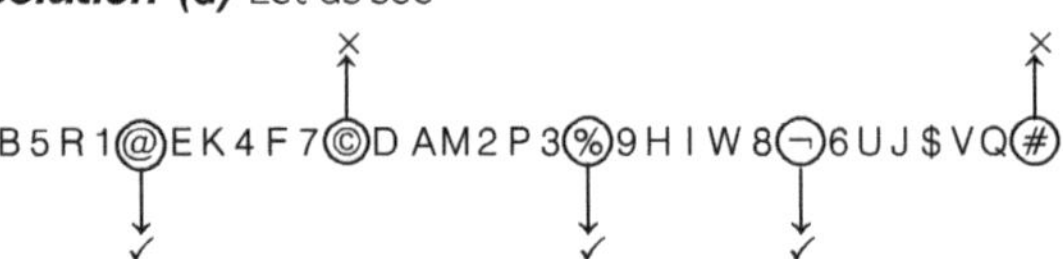

✓ = Condition fulfilled × = Condition not fulfilled

Clearly, there are three such symbols.

DIRECTIONS ~ (Example Nos. 44-48) *Study the following alphabetical sequence and answer the questions based on it.*

ABBCDEFEIBCAFECBBACAOBNUVW « IBPS Clerk 2017

Ex 44 How many Cs are there in the alphabetical series which are immediately preceded by a vowel and immediate followed by consonant?

(a) One (b) Two
(c) Three (d) More than three
(e) None of these

Solution (a) A B B C D E F E I B C A F [E C B] B A C A O B N U V W

Only one 'C' are there which is immediately preceded by a vowel and immediately followed by a consonant.

Ex 45 If all the vowels are dropped from the series, then which alphabet will be 8th from the left end?

(a) C (b) B (c) N (d) F
(e) None of these

Solution (d) B B C D F B C [F] C B B C B N V W

'F' is 8th from the left end.

Ex 46 How many vowels are there in the alphabetical series which are immediately preceded by a consonant?

(a) One (b) Two
(c) Four (d) More than five
(e) None

Solution (d) A B B C[D E][F E] I B[C A][F E] C B[B A][C A] O B[N U] V W

More than five vowels are there which is immediately preceded by a consonant.

Ex 47 If the position of the 1st and the 14th alphabets, 2nd and the 15th alphabets and so on up to the 13th and the 26th alphabets, are interchanged, Then which alphabets will be 7th to the right of 10th alphabets from the right end?

(a) A (b) C
(c) N (d) B
(e) None of these

Solution (b) According to the question,

E C B B A C A O B N U V W A B B

7th to the right

C D E F E I B C A F

10th from right end

Ex 48 How many total vowels in the alphabetical series?

(a) Five (b) Ten (c) Three (d) Nine
(e) None of these

Solution (b) A B B C D E F E I B C A F E C B B A C A O B N U V W

There are ten vowels in the given alphabetical series.

Practice / CORNER 1.7

1. Which number has come maximum time in the following number series?

5 4 3 3 5 4 8 8 3 2 5 3 6 5 5

(a) 5 (b) 4 (c) 3 (d) 2

2. Which number comes least in the given series?

8 4 6 7 3 4 3 7 8 3 4 4 5 6 3 4 6 4 3 4 8

« SSC (CGL) 2008

(a) 8 (b) 7 (c) 5 (d) 4

3. How many 4s are there in the series which comes between two 5s? « CBI (PO) 2011]

3 4 4 5 4 5 4 2 1 4 5 4 5 7 4 5 4 5

(a) 4 (b) 5 (c) 6 (d) 3
(e) None of these

4. In the sequence 1, 5, 7, 3, 5, 7, 4, 3, 5, 7 how many such 5s are there which are not immediately preceded by 3, but are immediately followed by 7? « UPSC CSAT 2019

(a) 1 (b) 2
(c) 3 (d) None of these

5. How many 7s are there in the given series which are immediately preceded by 6 but not immediately followed by 8? « SSC (CPO) 2008

3 4 8 7 6 1 5 6 7 8 4 9 6 7 5

(a) 1 (b) 2 (c) 3 (d) 4

6. Which digit comes in the middle of the given series?

2 4 3 5 4 4 5 6 7 8 8 9 5 6 7 1 7

(a) 5 (b) 7 (c) 6 (d) 9

7. In the given number series, how many 4s are there which are immediately preceded by a prime number but not immediately followed by a prime number?

« RBI Grade 'B' 2011

41 41 54 26 41 83 49 24 83 48 28 45 48 74 64 54

(a) 6 (b) 4 (c) 3 (d) 5
(e) None of these

8. How many letters are immediately followed by L in the given letter series? « UP B.Ed. 2011

C P M L M M B L T L D E S L

(a) 4 (b) 5
(c) 3 (d) 6

9. How many Ts are both immediately preceded and followed by 'E' in the following series?

« UP Police Constable 2018

E T E T T M E E E T E T E T E T E T T E E T T
T E E E T E T E T E T E T T E E T E

(a) 7 (b) 6 (c) 5 (d) 8

10. In the following series, how many Ks are there which are immediately preceded by N and immediately followed by U? « SSC (CGL) 2011

A B C D K N L J M N K S T R Z N K U A N K U B W X N K L S

(a) 6 (b) 2 (c) 3 (d) 4

DIRECTIONS ~ (Q. Nos 11-15) *Study the following sequence and answer the given questions.*

A @ 3 4 % E N M $ 8 6 & L D S # 9 8 6 Q Y Z 1 7 % R O G @ 2 1 B 2 U &

« SBI Clerk 2019

11. Which of the following element is sixth to the left of the fourteenth from the left end of the given arrangement?

(a) 6 (b) % (c) $ (d) M
(e) None of these

12. If all the symbols are dropped from the series, which element will be twelfth from the right end?

(a) 9 (b) Q (c) R (d) Y
(e) None of these

13. How many such numbers are there in the given series which are immediately preceded by a symbol and followed by a letter?

(a) None (b) One (c) Two (d) Three
(e) Four

14. How many such letters are there in the given series which are immediately preceded by number and immediately followed by a symbol?

(a) One (b) Two
(c) Three (d) More than three
(e) None of these

15. Find the odd one out.

(a) N64 (b) D86 (c) Y % 8 (d) R21
(e) 8EL

DIRECTIONS ~ (Q. Nos. 16-20) *To answer these questions study carefully the following arrangement of letters, digits and symbols.* « SBI Clerk 2016

M 7 Σ 8 L P @ ? 6 N B T Y 3 2 = E $ 4 9 © G H 5

16. How many such letters are there in the arrangement each of which is immediately followed by a number?
(a) Three (b) Four (c) One (d) Two
(e) None of these

17. How many such symbols are there in the arrangement each of which is immediately preceded by a number?
(a) Two (b) Three (c) Four (d) Nil
(e) None of these

18. If all the symbols are deleted from the arrangement, then which of the following will be fourth to the left of the 17th element from the left end?
(a) 9 (b) E (c) 2 (d) Y
(e) None of these

19. '78' is to 'P?6' and '?N' is to 'T32' in the same way as '2E' is to .... in the arrangement.
(a) 4©H (b) 49G (c) 4©G (d) 9GH
(e) None of these

20. If all the numbers are deleted from the arrangement then which of the following will be 4th to the right of the 14th element from the right end?
(a) B (b) N (c) Y (d) T
(e) None of these

21. In the following letter series, how many letters of K are preceded by G but not followed by P? « CG PSC Pre 2017

C L M G K P N M G K C L O G K L X G K B K G K A

(a) 1 (b) 2 (c) 3 (d) 4
(e) None of these

22. Which single letter is exactly between the two letters-one is 22nd from left side and the other is 19th from right side in the following? « CG PSC Pre 2017

ZYXWVUTSRQPONMLKJIHGFEDCBA

(a) M (b) N (c) L (d) K
(e) None of these

23. How many Ts are immediately followed by 'IE' in the following series? « UP Police Constable 2018

E T I E T T M E E E T E I T E T E T T I E E T T I E
T I E E E T E I T E T E T E I T E I E T I E

(a) 4 (b) 7 (c) 6 (d) 5

DIRECTIONS ~ (Q.Nos. 24-28) *Study the following arrangement carefully and answer the questions* « IBPS (Clerk) 2013

C E B A C D B C D A C E B E **D C A B A D A C** E D U B
A U B D B U

24. How many such pairs of alphabets are there in the series of alphabets given in BOLD (D to C) in the given arrangement each of which has as many letters between them (in both forward and backward directions) as they have between them in the English alphabetical series?
(a) Three (b) One (c) Two (d) None
(e) More than three

25. Which of the following is the ninth to the right of the twenty-second from the right end of the given arrangement?
(a) D (b) E (c) B (d) C
(e) U

26. If all the alphabets of the series are written in reverse order, then which of the following will be 8th to the right of the 7th from the left end of the series?
(a) A (b) B (c) C (d) D
(e) None of these

27. How many such As are there in the given arrangement each of which is immediately preceded by A 'B' and also immediately followed by a consonant?
(a) One (b) None (c) More than three
(d) Two (e) Three

28. How many such Ds are there in the given arrangement each of which is immediately preceded by a consonant and also immediately followed by a vowel?
(a) More than four (b) Four
(c) Two (d) Three
(e) One

29. In the following series of numbers, find out how many times 1, 3 and 7 have appeared together, 7 being in the middle and 1 and 3 on either side of 7? « CMAT 2013

2 9 3 1 7 3 7 7 7 1 3 3 1 7 3 8 5 7 1 3 7 7 1 7 3 9 0 6

(a) 3 (b) 4
(c) 5 (d) None of these

30. How many even numbers are there in the following sequence of numbers each of which is immediately followed by an odd number as well as immediately preceded by an even number? « CMAT 2013

8 6 7 6 8 9 3 2 7 5 3 4 2 2 3 5 5 2 2 8 1 1 9

(a) One (b) Three
(c) Five (d) None of these

31. How many such 6s are there in the following number series, each of which is immediately preceded by 1 or 5 and immediately following by 3 or 9?

2 6 3 7 5 6 4 2 9 6 1 3 4 1 6 3 9 1 5 6 9 2 3 1 6 5 4 3 2 1 9 6 7 1 6 3

(a) Nine (b) One (c) Two (d) Three

DIRECTIONS ~ (Q.Nos. 32-36) *Study the given information carefully to answer the given questions.* « RBI Assistant 2017

V J T & 9 H % # Y 5 @ 7 P * A 2 π M 4 φ K 6 F + 8 G

32. How many symbols are there between the fifth and the sixteenth elements from the left end?
(a) Five (b) Two (c) More than five
(d) Three (e) Four

33. If only one meaningful English word can be made using the letters between the seventh and the seventeenth elements from the left end, what will be the last letter of that word?
(a) Y (b) M (c) P
(d) More than one word can be formed using the given letters
(e) H

34. If all the symbols are deleted, then which of the following will be the tenth element from the right end?
(a) 5 (b) 7 (c) 2 (d) A (e) P

35. If all letters and symbols are deleted, then what will be the sum of the first, third and fifth elements from the left end?
(a) 17 (b) 10 (c) 8 (d) 14
(e) None of the given options

36. Which of the following is the 8th element to the right of 7?
(a) φ (b) F (c) π (d) 6 (e) M

37. In the following series, how many such odd numbers are there which are divisible by 3 or 5, then followed by odd numbers and then also followed by even numbers?
12, 19, 21, 3, 25, 18, 35, 20, 22, 21, 45, 46, 47, 48, 9, 50, 52, 54, 55, 56
(a) Three (b) One
(c) Two (d) None of these

DIRECTIONS ~ (Q.Nos. 38-42) *Study the following alphanumeric series carefully and answer the questions given below.* « IBPS Clerk 2017

7 A 6 P & R $ 4 Y Q % T @ 3 9 S I O 9 9 J L E U * K # 3

Step I The letters which are immediately preceded and immediately followed by a symbol are arranged in the end of the series in the alphabetical order. (They are arranged just after 3)

Step II The number which are immediately preceded by the letter and immediately followed by the symbol are arranged between 9 and S in the increasing order.

Step III The number which are immediately followed by letter are interchanged its position with respect to the element just after it.

(Step II is applied after Step I and Step III is applied after step II)

38. How many letters are arranged at the end of the series in the Step I?
(a) One (b) Three
(c) Four (d) Five
(e) More than five

39. Which among the following are the elements of the series which are second position from the left end and fifth position from the right end in Step III?
(a) 63 (b) 7# (c) P# (d) AK (e) 6#

40. How many symbols are immediately followed by numbers in Step III?
(a) One (b) Three (c) Four (d) Five (e) Two

41. Which of the following is the addition of 4th element from right end in Step II and 4th element from left in Step III?
(a) 7 (b) 10 (c) 9 (d) 18
(e) cannot be determine

42. Which of the following is 4th symbol from left end in Step II?
(a) % (b) & (c) * (d) #
(e) @

Answers / WITH EXPLANATIONS

1. (a) 5 4 3 3 5 4 8 8 3 2 5 3 6 5 5
8 = 2 times, 6 = 1 time, 5 = 5 times, 4 = 2 times
3 = 4 times, 2 = 1 time
Clearly, 5 has come maximum times.

2. (c) 8 4 6 7 3 4 3 7 8 3 4 4 5 6 3 4 6 4 3 4 8
8 = 3 times, 7 = 2 times, 6 = 3 times, 5 = 1 time
4 = 7 times, 3 = 5 times
Clearly, 5 comes least in the series.

3. (d)

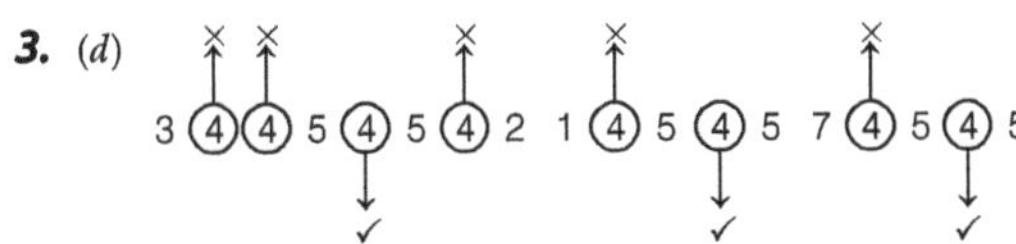

✓ = Condition fulfilled × = Condition not fulfilled
∴ Required 4s = 3 times

4. (a) 1 5 7 3 5 7 4 3 5 7
∴ Only one such 5 is possible which is not immediately preceded by 3, but immediately followed by 7.

5. (a)
3 4 8 7 6 1 5 6 7 8 4 9 6 7 5

✓ = Condition fulfilled × = Condition not fulfilled
∴ Required 7 = 1 time

6. (b) Total number of digits = 17
∴ Middle digit $= \frac{17+1}{2} = \frac{18}{2} = 9\text{th digit}$
∴ 9th digit in the given series = 7

7. (d)

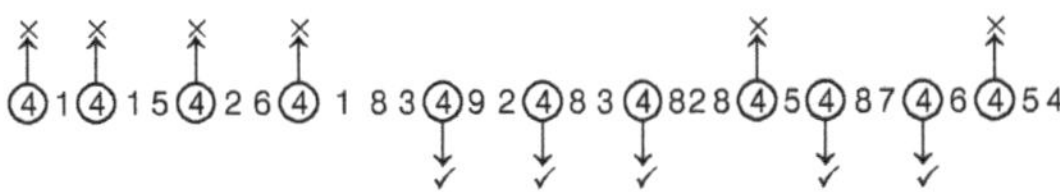

✓ = Condition fulfilled × = Condition not fulfilled
∴ Required 4s = 5 times

8. (a) C P M L M M B L T L D E S L
Clearly, M, B, T and S are immediately followed by L.

9. (*d*) There are '8' Ts here which are immediately preceded and followed by 'E' the given series.

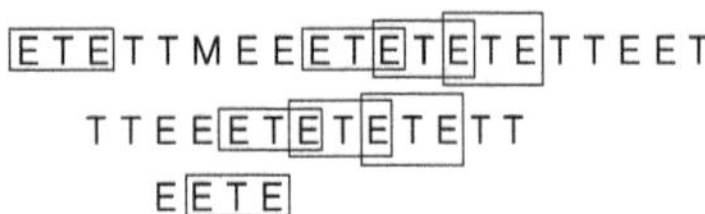

10. (*b*)

✓ = Condition fulfilled × = Condition not fulfilled

∴ Required number of K = 2 times

11. (*d*) A @ 3 4 % E N Ⓜ $ 8 6 & L D S # 9 8 6

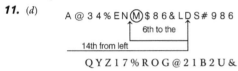

6th to the

14th from left

Q Y Z 1 7 % R O G @ 2 1 B 2 U &

∴ Required element = M

12. (*d*) After dropping all the symbols the series is as follows

A 3 4 E N M 8 6 L D S 9 8 6 Q Ⓨ Z 1 7 R O G 2 I B 2 U

12th from the right end

∴ Required element = Y

13. (*b*) Required combination =

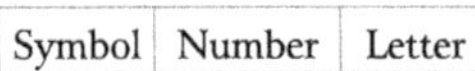

Symbol	Number	Letter

A @ 3 4 % ENM $ 8 6 & L D S # 9 8 6 Q Y Z 1 7 % R O G [@ 2 1] B 2 U &

∴ There is only one number which is immediately preceded by a symbol and followed by a letter i.e. @ 2 1

14. (*a*) Required combination =

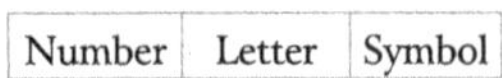

Number	Letter	Symbol

A @ 3 4 % ENM $ 8 6 & L D S # 9 8 6 Q Y Z 1 7 % R O G @ 2 1 B [2 U &]

∴ There is only one letter which is immediately preceded by number and immediately followed by symbol i.e. 2 U &

15. (*e*)

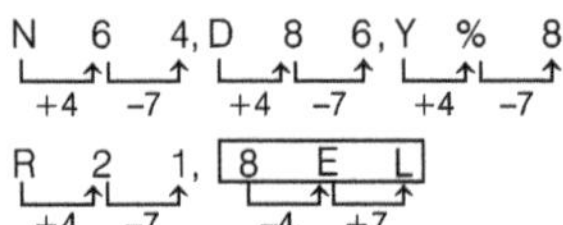

Clearly, '8 E L' is odd one out.

16. (*a*) The arrangement is as follows

[M] 7 Σ 8 L P @ ? 6 N B T [Y] 3 2 = E $ 4 9 © G [H] 5

It is clearly from above that there are three letters are immediately followed by a number.

17. (*b*) Given arrangement is as follows

M 7 [Σ] 8 L P @ ? 6 N B T Y 3 2 [=] E $ 4 9 [©] G H 5

It is clear from above that there are three such, symbols which are immediately preceded by a number.

18. (*b*) After deleting all the symbols from given arrangement, new arrangement is as follows

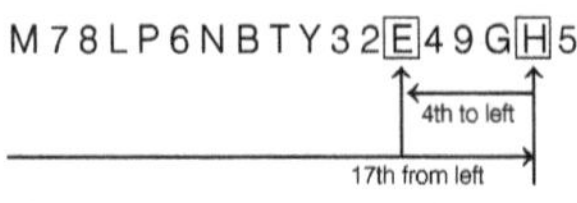

It is clear from above that required letter is E.

19. (*c*) As, '78' is related to 'P?6' and '?N' is related to 'T32', in the same way '2E' is related to '4©G' because all have the differences of one letter or symbol in between.

20. (*a*) After deleting all the numbers from given arrangement, new arrangement is as follows

M Σ L [P] @ ? N [B] T Y = E $ © G H 5

4th to right

14th from right

It is clear from above required element is B.

21. (*d*) Given series

C L M G K P N M G [K] C L O G [K] L X G [K] B K G [K] A

From above it is clear that four K are preceded by G but not followed by P.

22. (*c*) In the given series, 22nd letter from left = E

and 19th letter from right = S

Now, total number of letters between E and S with it = 15

∴ Letter exactly between E and S

$= \frac{15+1}{2} = \frac{16}{2} = 8\text{th letter} = \text{L}$

23. (*d*) There are 5 T's here which are immediately followed by IE in given series.

E [T I E] T T M E E E T E I T E T E T T

I E E T [T I E] [T I E] E E T E [I T E] T

E T E I T E I E [T I E]

24. (*e*) Series of alphabets given in BOLD

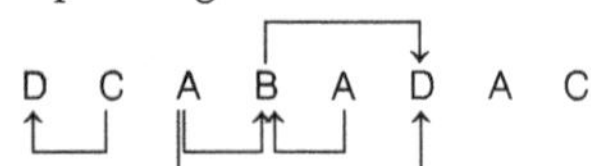

25. (*a*) Ninth to the right of the twenty second from the right end = (22 − 9) *i.e.*, 13th from the right end = D

26. (*b*) The given series of alphabets in reverse order

U B D B U A B U D E C A D A B A C D E B E C A D C B D C A B E C

Now, 8th to the right of the 7th from the left end = (8 + 7) th *i.e.*, 15th from the left end = Ⓑ

27. (*d*) C E [B A C] D B C D A C E B E D C A [B A D] A C E D U B A U B D B U

Thus, there are two such As.

28. (*e*) C E B A C D B [C D A] C E B E D C A B A D A C E D U B A U B D B U

Thus, there is only one such D.

29. (*a*) Clearly, the given number series is as follows

2 9 3 [1 7 3] 7 7 7 1 3 3 [1 7 3] 8 5 7 1 3 7 7 [1 7 3] 9 0 6

∴ Required pattern = $\frac{1/3}{\text{Preceding}}$ $\frac{7}{\text{Middle}}$ $\frac{1/3}{\text{Following}}$

Therefore, total number of such patterns = 3

30. (*d*) Clearly, the given sequence of numbers is as follows

[8 [6] 7] [6 [8] 9] 3 2 7 5 3 4 [2 [2] 3] 5 5 [2 [2] 8] 1 1 9

Required pattern = $\frac{\text{Even number}}{\text{Preceded}}$ $\frac{\text{Even number}}{\text{Middle}}$ $\frac{\text{Odd number}}{\text{Followed}}$

So, total number of such even numbers = Four

31. (*d*) Clearly, the given number series is as follows

2 6 3 7 5 6 4 2 9 6 1 3 4 [1 6 3] 9 1 [5 6 9] 2 3 1 6 5 4 3 2 1 9 6 7 [1 6 3]

Required pattern = $\frac{\text{1 or 5}}{\text{Preceded}}$ 6 $\frac{\text{3 or 9}}{\text{Followed}}$

Therefore, total number of such 6s = Three

Solutions (Q.Nos. 32-36) According to the given information

V J T & 9 H % # Y 5 @ 7 P * A 2 π M 4 Q K 6 F + B G

32. (*e*) Fifth element from the left end is 9.
Sixteenth element from left end is 2.
Symbols between them are % # @ *.

33. (*a*) Letters between seventh and seventeenth elements from left end are Y, P, A word formed is PAY last letter of the word is Y.

34. (*e*) If all the symbols are deleted, new series is V J T 9 H Y 5 7 P A 2 M 4 K 6 F 8 G

Tenth element from right end is P.

35. (*e*) New series after deleting all the letters and symbols are 9 5 7 2 4 6 8

Required sum = 9 + 7 + 4 = 20

36. (*a*) ϕ is 8th element to the right of 7.

37. (*c*) Clearly, the given number series is as follows

12, 19, 21, [3 , 25, 18,] 35, 20, 22, [21, 45, 46,] 47, 48, 9, 50, 52, 54, 55, 56

Required pattern

= $\frac{\text{Odd number divisible by 3 or 5}}{}$ $\frac{\text{Odd number}}{\text{Followed}}$ $\frac{\text{Even number}}{\text{Followed}}$

So, total number of such odd numbers = Two

Solutions (Q.Nos. 38-40)

Step I 7 A 6 P & $ 4 Y Q % @ 3 9 S I O 9 9 J L E U * # K R T

Step II 7 A 6 P & $ 4 Y Q % @ 3 9 S I O 9 9 J L E U * # K R T

Step III A 7 P6 & $ Y 4 Q % @ 3 S 9 I O 9 J 9 L E U * # K 3 R T

38. (*b*) There letters are arranged at the end of the series in the Step I.

39. (*b*) In Step III, element at second position from the left end = 7
In Step III, element at fifth position from the right end = #

40. (*a*) Required symbols = $ @ #

41. (*c*) 4th element from right in Step II ⇒ 3
4th element from left in step III ⇒ 6
∴ required sum = 6 + 3 ⇒ 9

42. (*e*) & $ % @ * #
∴ required symbol ⇒ @

Master Exercise

1. If the 1st half of the English alphabet is reversed and so is the 2nd half, then which letter is 7th to the right of the 12th letter from the left side?

(a) S (b) U (c) R (d) T

2. All the English alphabets are arranged alphabetically in the reverse order. The difference of the positions of two vowels which appear in the beginning and in the end, is « CGPSC 2014

(a) 6 (b) 12
(c) 16 (d) 18
(e) None of these

3. If the 1st half of the alphabets is written in the reverse order, which letter will be exactly middle between the 9th letter from the left and the 10th letter from the right end?

(a) B (b) A
(c) D (d) None of these

4. If the 2nd half of the letters of the word 'TRANSPORTATIONAL' are reversed and placed before 1st half of the letters, which letter will be the third to the right of the 13th letter from the right?

(a) R (b) N (c) L (d) A

5. If the last four letters of the word 'TABULATION' are written in reverse order followed by next two in reverse order and next three in the reverse order, counting from the end, which letter would be eighth in the new arrangement?

(a) N (b) T
(c) E (d) None of these

6. How many such letters are there in the word 'CREATIVE' which have as many letters between them in the word as in the alphabets?

(a) 1 (b) 2
(c) 3 (d) 4

7. How many such pairs of letters are there in the word JUMPING each of which has as many letters, between them in the word as in the English alphabet?

(a) None (b) One
(c) Two (d) Three

8. How many such pairs of letters are there in the word 'KINDNESS' each of which have as many letters between them in word as in the alphabets?

(a) Nil (b) One
(c) Two (d) Three

9. If the word 'FLOURISH', all the vowels are first arranged alphabetically and then all the consonants are arranged alphabetically and then all the vowels are replaced by the previous letter and all the consonants are replaced by the next letter from English alphabets. Which letter will be third from the right end?
« UCO Bank (Clerk) 2007

(a) I (b) S
(c) M (d) V
(e) None of these

10. If in the word 'DISTURBANCE', the first letter is interchanged with the last letter, the second letter is interchanged with the tenth letter and so on, which letter would come after the letter 'T' in the newly formed word?

(a) I (b) U
(c) N (d) S

11. If it is possible to make a meaningful word with the 2nd, the 6th, the 9th and the 12th letters of the word 'CONTRIBUTION', which of the following will be the last letter of that word? If more than one such word can be formed, give 'M' as the answer and if no such word is there, give 'X' as the answer. « CBI (PO) 2010

(a) T (b) O (c) N (d) M
(e) None of these

12. If the following scrambled letters are rearranged to form the name of city, which letter will appear in the middle?

AIDMURA

(a) M (b) R (c) U (d) D

13. If it is possible to make a meaningful word with the 1st, 4th, 7th and 11th letters of the word 'INTERPRETATION', which of the following will be the third letter of that word? If more than one such word can be made, give 'M' as the answer and if no such word can be formed, give 'X' as the answer.

(a) T (b) I (c) R (d) M

14. How many meaningful English words can be formed with the letters LBAE, using each letter only once in each word? « Andhra Bank (PO) 2010

(a) None (b) One (c) Two (d) Three
(e) More than three

15. How many meaningful English words can be made with 'EPRY' using each letter only once in each word?
« UPPSC (RO) 2014

(a) Two (b) One
(c) Three (d) More than four

16. How many meaningful English words can be made with the letters 'ERDU' using each letter only once in each word?

(a) None (b) One (c) Two (d) Three
(e) More than three

17. How many meaningful English words can be made with the letters 'NWTI' using each letter only once in each word? « Allahabad Bank (Clerk) 2012

(a) One (b) Two (c) None (d) Three
(e) More than three

18. How many meaningful English words can be made with the letters 'LAME' using each letter only once in each word?

(a) None (b) One (c) Two (d) Three
(e) More than three

DIRECTIONS ~ (Q. Nos. 19-21) *In the following questions, from the given alternatives words, select the word which cannot be formed using the letters of the given word.*
« SSC (Steno) 2013

19. Reasonable
(a) Bones (b) Brain (c) Arson (d) Noble

20. Attraction
(a) Caution (b) Traction (c) Ration (d) Carton

21. Workshop
(a) Show (b) Crow (c) Work (d) Pork

DIRECTIONS ~ (Q. Nos. 22-25) *In each of the following questions a word is given followed by four other words, one of which cannot be formed by using the letters of given word. Find that particular word.*

22. EDUCATIONAL « SSC (DEO) 2012
(a) NATIONAL (b) NEAT (c) DEAN (d) LION

23. PERMANENT « SSC (Multitasking) 2012
(a) REMNANT (b) TRAMP
(c) MENTOR (d) AMPERE

24. MORTGAGE « SSC FCI 2012
(a) AROMA (b) GEAR (c) ROAM (d) GRATE

25. SPECIFICATION « SSC (CGL) 2013
(a) PACIFIC (b) FACTION
(c) FAINTING (d) TONIC

26. In the following question a word is given followed by four different words, one of which can be formed by using the letter of the given word find the word.

'IMMEDIATELY' « LIC (ADO) 2012

(a) DIALECT (b) LIMITED
(c) DIAMETER (d) DICTATE
(e) None of these

DIRECTIONS ~ (Q. Nos. 27 and 28) *Letters of the words given here have been jumbled up and you are required to construct the words. Each letter has been numbered and each word is followed by four options. Choose the option which gives the correct order of the letters as indicated by the numbers to form meaningful words.*

27. G E D E M E N L C K N O W A T
1 2 3 4 5 6 7 8 9 10 11 12 13 14 15

(a) 14, 9, 10, 11, 12, 13, 8, 4, 3, 1, 2, 5, 6, 7, 15
(b) 2, 4, 6, 8, 10, 12, 14, 1, 3, 5, 7, 9, 11, 13, 15
(c) 8, 7, 5, 4, 3, 2, 1, 6, 9, 10, 11, 13, 12, 14, 15
(d) 6, 7, 8, 9, 10, 1, 2, 3, 4, 5, 15, 14, 13, 12, 11

28. E C O T I H T Y H O N P A
1 2 3 4 5 6 7 8 9 10 11 12 13

(a) 13, 7, 12, 6, 11, 5, 10, 4, 9, 3, 8, 2, 1
(b) 13, 12, 11, 10, 1, 2, 3, 4, 5, 6, 7, 8, 9
(c) 10, 9, 8, 7, 6, 5, 4, 3, 2, 11, 12, 13, 1
(d) 9, 8, 12, 3, 7, 6, 1, 2, 13, 4, 5, 10, 11

DIRECTIONS ~ (Q.Nos. 29-31) *In each of the following questions, there are a set of words. Choose the option which can be put before the set of words to make them meaningful words.*

29. CLOSE, MISS, ABLE, COUNT
(a) EN (b) DIS (c) FORE (d) RE

30. SULE, TAIN, ABLE, E
(a) SAG (b) MOV (c) MAN (d) CAP

31. MOVE, MARK, QUEST
(a) RE (b) MIS
(c) PRE (d) LESS

DIRECTIONS ~(Q.Nos. 32 and 33) *In each of the question given below, there are set of words. Choose the option which can be put after the set of words to make them meaningful words.*

32. ST, ENG, DAM, SEW
(a) EIL (b) ARM (c) AGE (d) RAP

33. H, CH, F, SW
(a) REE (b) ARM
(c) EAP (d) EART

DIRECTIONS ~ (Q.Nos. 34-37) *In each of the following questions two groups of letters are given on both sides of a bracket. Each question has four options. Which of the option has correct set of letters that will be brought inside the bracket so that two meaningful words are formed. The first word will be formed by including the bracket and the set of letters before the bracket. Whereas the second word will be formed by including the bracket and the letters after it.*

34. PLAT (?) ATION « SSC (Steno) 2013
(a) TENT (b) FORM
(c) TERR (d) EAU

35. REA ( ) URCH
(a) CT (b) DER
(c) SON (d) CH

36. PROFESS ( ) PHAN
(a) ION (b) OR
(c) ED (d) TION

37. PRACT ( ) BERG
(a) ICE (b) ICAL
(c) DNA (d) ORN

DIRECTIONS ~(Q.Nos. 38-41) *Rearrange the unorganised letters to create meaningful words and then choose the one which is different from others.* « RRB NTPC 2016

38. (A) LOWELY (B) IFER (C) THIWE (D) WRONB
(a) B (b) A (c) D (d) C

39. (A) DOGL (B) TSEVO (C) ENZROB (D) LVREIS
(a) B (b) C (c) A (d) D

40. (A) ORIN (B) NADS (C) POPCER (D) DLOG
(a) A (b) D (c) C (d) B

41. (A) ENNI (B) NEO (C) EPPI (D) REETH
(a) B (b) A (c) C (d) D

DIRECTIONS ~(Q.Nos. 42-45) *In each of these question, jumbled letters of a meaningful word are given. You are required to rearrange these letters and select from the given alternatives, the word which is almost similar in meaning to the rearranged word.* « LIC (ADO) 2011

42. DAXEPN
(a) INCREASE (b) REDUCE
(c) STILL (d) DECREASE
(e) None of these

43. HRADTE
(a) DECREASE (b) LOSS
(c) REDUCTION (d) SCARCITY
(e) None of these

44. DNHBEI
(a) FRONT (b) SIDE (c) BACK (d) LAST
(e) None of these

45. HNAGSRI
(a) DECORATE (b) COMPOSE
(c) IMPRESS (d) IMPOSE
(e) None of these

DIRECTIONS ~ (Q.Nos. 46-50) *Following questions are based on the five words given below, Study the following words and answer the following questions.* « IBPS Clerk 2018

TAP NOT MAT PQR STB

(The new words formed after performing the mentioned operations may not necessarily be a meaningful English word).

46. If the given words are arranged in the order as they appear in a dictionary from right to left, which of the following will be second from the left end?
(a) MAT (b) NOT (c) STB (d) TAP
(e) None of these

47. How many letters are there in the English alphabetical series between the third letter of the words which is second from the left end and the second letter of the word which is third from the right end?
(a) 20 (b) 19 (c) 18 (d) 17
(e) None of these

48. If in each of the word given, the second alphabet is replaced by its following alphabet and third alphabet is replaced by its preceding alphabet as per the English alphabetical order, then how many words thus formed will be without any **vowel**?
(a) None (b) One (c) Two (d) Three (e) Four

49. If the positions of the first and the third alphabet in each of the words given are interchanged, then how many meaningful word will be formed?
(a) Two (b) One (c) Four (d) Three
(e) None o these

50. If in each of the given words, every consonant is changed to its previous letter and every vowel is changed to its next letter according to the English alphabetical series, then in how many words, thus formed, at least one vowel will appear?
(a) None (b) One (c) Two (d) Three
(e) None of these

DIRECTIONS ~ (Q. Nos. 51-53) *The following questions are based on the given five three-letters words.* « SBI Clerk 2015

ACT SHY EON ACE WEB

51. If the letters F is added before each of the given words, how many of them will form meaningful English words?

(a) One (b) More than three
(c) None (d) Two
(e) Three

52. If the first and second letters of each of the given words are interchanged, then which of the following will become a meaningful English word?

(a) EON (b) ACE (c) SHY (d) ACT (e) WEB

53. If the first and third letters of each of the given words is changed to the next letters in the English alphabetical series, how many of them will have atleast two vowels (same or different vowels)?

(a) None (b) Two (c) Three (d) One
(e) Four

DIRECTIONS ~ (Q.Nos. 54-58) *In each of the following questions, find out which of the letter-series follows the given rule.*

54. Number of letters skipped in reverse order in between adjacent letters in the series is constant.

(a) SQOLJ (b) SPNLJ
(c) SPMJG (d) WUTRQ

55. Number of letters skipped in between the adjacent letters in the series is equal

(a) SUXADF (b) RVZDHL
(c) HKNGSW (d) RVZDFG

56. Number of letters skipped in between the adjacent letters in the series is one. SSC Matric Level 2011

(a) KMPQR (b) HJLMO
(c) PRSUW (d) EGIKM

57. In a series of letters, find the group in which the number of letters skipped in between the adjacent letters in the series is constant.

(a) ZXTN (b) EZUP
(c) PRTX (d) RSAB

58. In the series given below, find the group in which two letters are skipped in between adjacent letters.

(a) BEHKLM (b) LQRUXY
(c) EHKNQT (d) FHKOTZ

59. How many such numerals are there in the number 254136987 which will remain at the same position when arranged in ascending order from left to right? « IBPS RRB PO 2019

(a) one (b) two (c) three (d) four
(e) None of these

60. If '1' is added to all even digits of the number 4782659 and '2' is subtracted from all the odd digits, then which of the following digits will appear twice in the new number thus formed? « RBI Assistant 2017

(a) 7,2 (b) 1,5,9
(c) 7,9 (d) 1,9
(e) 5,3,7

DIRECTIONS ~ (Q. Nos. 61-63) The following questions are based on the five three-digit numbers given below.

684 512 437 385 296 « SBI Clerk 2016

61. If 2 is added to the first digit of each of the numbers how many numbers thus formed will be divisible by three?

(a) None (b) One
(c) Two (d) Three
(e) None of these

62. If all the digits in each of the numbers are arranged in descending order within the number, which of the following will be the highest number in the new arrangement of numbers?

(a) 684 (b) 385 (c) 296 (d) 437
(e) None of these

63. What will be the resultant number if the second digit of the second lowest number is divided by the third digit of the highest number?

(a) 2 (b) 3 (c) 0 (d) 1 (e) 4

64. When we arrange the letter of the words 'VRAKIE' in correct order, we get the name of a river. Fifth letter from left in that name, is « CG PSC Pre 2017

(a) R (b) E (c) I (d) K
(e) None of these

65. How many such pairs of letters are there in the word 'HOCKEY' each of which have as many letters between them in word as in the alphabets?

(a) Nil (b) One
(c) Two (d) Three

DIRECTIONS ~(Q. Nos. 66-68) *The following questions based on the five three digit numbers given below.* « IBPS Clerk 2017

374 659 821 945 247

66. If 1 is subtracted from the last digit of each of the numbers, how many numbers thus formed will be divisible by two?

(a) None (b) One
(c) Two (d) Three
(e) Four

67. If in each number, the first and the second digits are interchanged, which of the following will be the third lowest number?

(a) 374 (b) 659
(c) 821 (d) 945
(e) 247

68. If in each number, all the three digits are arranged in ascending order within the number, which of the following will be the second highest number?

(a) 374 (b) 659 (c) 821 (d) 945
(e) 247

69. In the following letter series, how many BCN occur in such a way, that C is in the middle and B and N are on any of the side? « SSC (10+2) 2013

B C M X N C X N B X N C B N C B Y B C X N B C N A B O N M Z C B

(a) 4 (b) 2 (c) 5 (d) 3

70. Study the number series given below and answer the question that follows.

7 8 9 7 6 5 3 4 2 8 9 7 2 4 5 9 2 9 7 6 4 7

How many 7s are preceded by 9 and followed by 6?

« CMAT 2013

(a) 2 (b) 3 (c) 4 (d) 5

71. How many Ms occur in the following series such that it is preceded by W and followed by V? « SSC (10+2) 2013

X U V M R S T M W N V M W O P M W U V M WA C W M V H P N V W M W T U N

(a) 3 (b) 2 (c) 1 (d) 5

72. How many 6s are there in the following number sequence which are immediately preceded by 9, but not immediately followed by 4? « FCI Watchman 2018

5 6 4 3 2 9 6 3 1 6 4 9 6 4 2 1 5 9 6 7 2 1 4 7 4 9 6 4 2

(a) Four (b) Three
(c) One (d) Two

DIRECTIONS ~ (Q. Nos. 73-77) *Answer these questions referring to the symbol letter number sequence given below.* « CMAT 2013

2 P J @ 8 $ L B 1 V # Q 6 δ G W 9 K C D 3 © • £ 5 F R 7 A γ 4

73. How many symbols and numbers are there in the sequence which are either immediately preceded or immediately followed by the letter which is from the first half of the English alphabet?

(a) 6 (b) 7 (c) 8 (d) 9

74. Four of the following five are similar in relation to their positions in the above sequence and hence from a group. Which one does not belong to that group?

(a) QK5 (b) L6D (c) PLδ (d) 1G©

75. Each symbol exchanges its position with its immediate right symbol/letter/number. Now, how many letters are there in the sequence which are immediately followed by a number and immediately preceded by a symbol?

(a) One (b) Two
(c) Three (d) None of these

76. P@L is to γ75 in the same way as $ B # is to

(a) R£© (b) 5£0
(c) F•3 (d) None of these

77. Which of the following indicates the total number of symbols, letters and numbers respectively, which get eliminated from the sequence when every second element of the sequence, from your left is dropped from the sequence?

(a) 5, 8, 2 (b) 6, 9, 1
(c) 5, 8, 1 (d) 6, 8, 1

DIRECTIONS ~(Q. Nos. 78-82) *Study the following arrangement carefully and answer the questions given below.* « IDBI Executive 2018

R 4 3 % M @ K E F 5 A # J N 1 8 U © D B P 6 1 W 7 δ Q H Z

78. If all the symbols are dropped from the above arrangement, which of the following will be fourth to the left of ninth from the left end?

(a) K (b) E (c) M (d) 3
(e) None of these

79. If all the numbers are dropped from the above arrangement, which of the following will be seventh to the right of eighteenth from the right end?

(a) J (b) # (c) U (d) N
(e) None of these

80. How many such consonants are there in the above arrangement, each of which is immediately preceded by a symbol and immediately followed by a letter?

(a) None (b) One (c) Two (d) Three
(e) More than three

81. Four of the following five are alike in a certain way based on their position in the above arrangement and so form a group, which is the one that does not belong to that group?

(a) J A 1 (b) 3 R % (c) 8 © 1 (d) # N A
(e) δ W Q

82. How many such numbers are there in the above arrangement, each of which is immediately followed by a letter, but not immediately preceded by an element?

(a) None (b) One (c) Two (d) Three
(e) More than three

DIRECTIONS ~ (Q. Nos. 83-87) *Study the following arrangement carefully and answer the questions given below.* « SBI Clerk 2018

B 5 R I @ E K 4 F 7 © D A M 2 P 3 % 9 H I W 8 6 U J $ V Q #

83. Which of the following is the fifth to the left of the seventeenth from the left end of the above arrangement?

(a) D (b) W (c) * (d) 4
(e) None of these

84. Which of the following is exactly in the middle between D and U in the above arrangement?

(a) % (b) H (c) 9 (d) 3
(e) None of these

85. Four of the following five are alike in a certain way base on their position in the above arrangement and so form a group. What is the one that does not belong to that group?

(a) RIE (b) F7D (c) M23 (d) 9HW
(e) UJ6

86. How many such symbols are there in the above arrangement each of which is immediately preceded by a number, but not immediately followed by a consonant?

(a) None (b) One (c) Two (d) Three
(e) More than three

87. Which of the following is the tenth to the left of the thirteenth from the right end?

(a) F (b) M (c) @ (d) % (e) 4

DIRECTIONS ~(Q.Nos. 88-91) *Study the following sequence of numbers and alphabets and answer the given questions.*

P 4 S A W 5 8 F 9 1 R E 7 2 O 3 7 5 1 B 6 K G N

88. How many numbers are there which are immediately preceded by a vowel?
(a) One (b) None
(c) Two (d) Three
(e) None of these

89. If all the numbers are removed from the given series, then which among the following element is seventh from the right end?
(a) E (b) O
(c) F (d) R
(e) None of these

90. If all the consonants are removed from the given series, then which among the following element is ninth from the left end?
(a) 2 (b) O (c) 3 (d) 7
(e) None of these

91. Which among the following element is fifth to the left of twelfth element from the left end?
(a) F (b) 8 (c) 9 (d) 1
(e) None of these

DIRECTIONS ~(Q. Nos. 92-96) *Study the following arrangement of letters, numbers and symbols carefully to answer the given questions.* « RBI Assistant Pre 2016

SR8%WP7$62NA3@M*D5UB49Ω1&l∠Y©E#K

92. As per the given arrangement, four of the following five are alike in a certain way and hence form a group. Which one of the following does not belong to the group?
(a) U*9 (b) EL#
(c) 32* (d) 14Y
(e) P86

93. If all the numbers from the given arrangement are deleted, then which of the following will represent fifth element to the right of '%' and the fourth element of the left of 'L' respectively?
(a) A, E (b) #, B
(c) #, Ω (d) A, U
(e) @, M

94. Which of the following will be sixth to the right of the fifteenth element from the right end in the given arrangement?
(a) Ω (b) B (c) 4 (d) &
(e) Y

95. What will be the sum of all the numbers between the eleventh element from the left end and sixth element from the right end of the given arrangement?
(a) 20 (b) 23 (c) 24 (d) 22
(e) 19

96. How many letters are there between the ninth element from the right end and the ninth element from the left end of the given arrangement?
(a) Five (b) Nine
(c) Ten (d) Eight
(e) Six

97. From the word 'LAPAROSCOPY', how many independent meaningful English words can be made without changing the order of the letters and using each letter only once?
(a) 1 (b) 2 (c) 3 (d) 4

98. Select the word that can be formed using the letters of the given word only as many times as the letters have been used in the word. « UPSSSC Junior Assistant 2020

AUDEFGRSA
(a) PSEUDO-GRADE (b) SAFEGUARD
(c) STAGNATION (d) GRANDSON

99. In the given number 69286257, if all digits are arranged in increasing and decreasing order in 1st and 2nd arrangement respectively from left to right, then how many digits remains at the same position in the new arrangement? « RBI Office Assistant 2020
(a) Three (b) Two
(c) None (d) One
(e) None of these

100. If every alternative letter of the English alphabet from B onwards (including B) is written in lower case (small letters) and the remaining letters are capitalised, then how is the first month of the second half of the year written? « UPSC CSAT 2019
(a) JuLY (b) jULy (c) jUly (d) jUlY

Answers / WITH EXPLANATIONS

1. (*b*) According to the question,

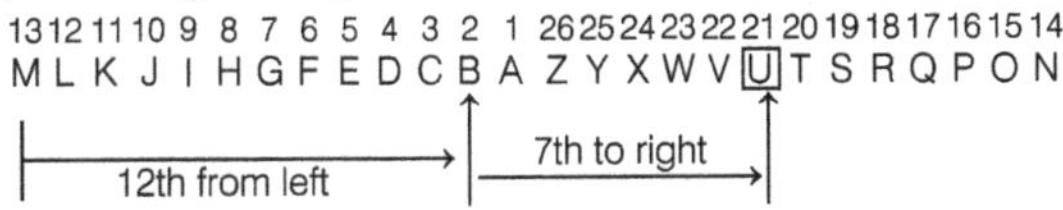

∴ Required letter = U

2. (*e*) Reverse order of an English alphabet is as follows

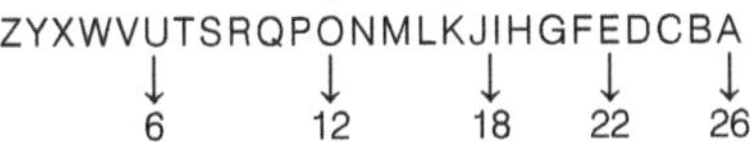

Vowel that appear in beginning in new arrangement = U
U's position in above arrangement = 6
and vowel that appear in end in new arrangement = A
A's position in the above arrangement = 26
∴ Required difference = 26 – 6 = 20

3. (*b*) M L K J I H G F (E) D C B A N O P (Q) R S T U V W X Y Z

9th from left → ← 10th from right

The 9th letter from the left is E and 10th letter from the right is Q and therefore we see that A lies exactly in middle between E and Q.

4. (*d*) 1 2 3 4 5 6 7 8 9 10 11 12 13 14 15 16
L A N O I T A T T R A N S P O R
13th letter from right = (16 + 1 – 13) = 4th letter from left
= O
∴ Required letter = 3rd to the right of O
= 4 + 3 = 7th from left = A

5. (*d*) The new word formed will be 'NOITALUBA', then eighth letter from the end would be O.

6. (*c*) There are three pairs C E, A E and TV in the word which have as many letters between them in the words as in the alphabetical order.

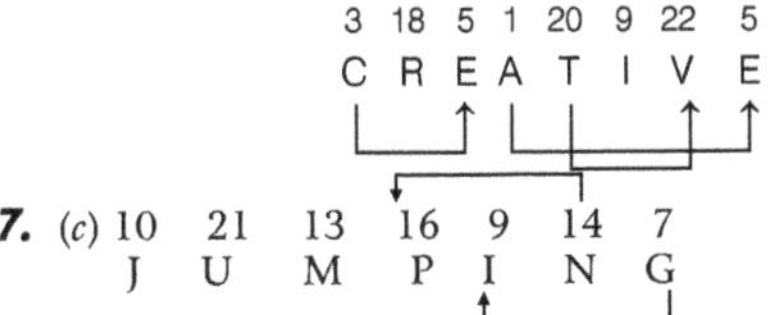

7. (*c*) 10 21 13 16 9 14 7
J U M P I N G

∴ Letter pairs = NP, GI ⇒ Two

8. (*c*) 11 9 14 4 14 5 19 19
K I N D N E S S

∴ Letter pairs = EI, NS ⇒ Two

9. (*c*) According to the question,

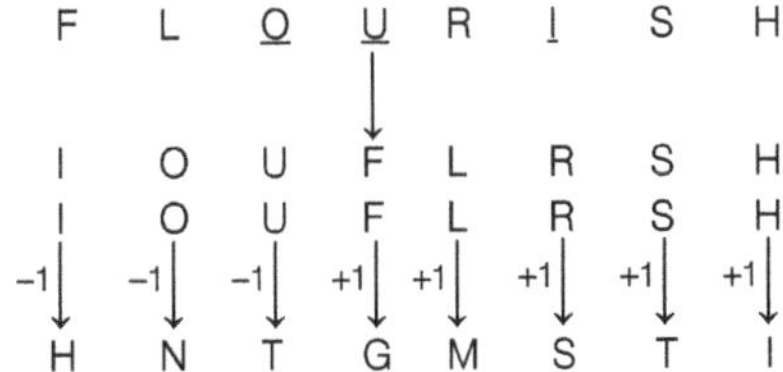

10. (*d*)

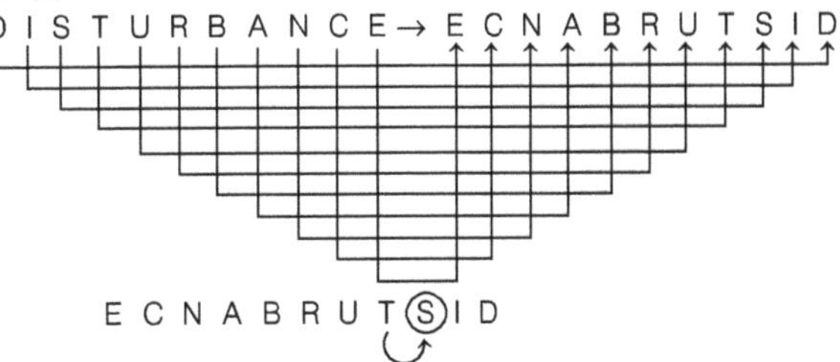

11. (*b*) From letters O, I, N, T, only one meaningful word 'INTO' can be formed and last letter of this word is O.

12. (*c*) The city name is 'MAD (U) RAI' and letter U exists exactly in the middle.

13. (*d*) Two meaningful words RITE and TIRE can be formed.

14. (*c*) Required words = ABLE, BALE.

15. (*b*) Only one meaningful word 'PREY' can be formed by using the letters of 'EPRY'.

16. (*b*) Only one meaningful word 'RUDE' can be formed by using the letters of 'ERDU'.

17. (*a*) Only one meaningful word 'TWIN' can be formed by using the letters of 'NWTI'.

18. (*d*) Three meaningful words 'LAME', 'MALE' and 'MEAL' can be formed by using the letters of 'LAME'.

19. (*b*) By using the letters of the given word 'Reasonable', 'Brain', is the only word which cannot be formed due to the absence of letter 'I'.

20. (*a*) By using the letters of the given word 'Attraction', 'Caution', is the only word which cannot be formed due to the absence of letter 'U'.

21. (*b*) By using the letters of the given word, 'Workshop', 'Crow', is the only word which cannot be formed due to the absence of letter 'C'.

22. (*a*) 'NATIONAL' is the only word which cannot be formed due to repetition of letter 'N'.

23. (*c*) Only 'MENTOR' is the word which cannot be formed due to absence of letter 'O'.

24. (*a*) The word 'AROMA' cannot be formed using the given letters because only one 'A' is present in the given word.

25. (*c*) The word which cannot be formed from 'SPECIFICATION' is FAINTING', because 'G' is not present in given word.

26. (*b*) 'LIMITED' is the only word which can be formed by using the letters of given word.

27. (*a*) According to the question,
14 9 10 11 12 13 8 4 3 1 2 5 6 7 15
↓ ↓ ↓ ↓ ↓ ↓ ↓ ↓ ↓ ↓ ↓ ↓ ↓ ↓ ↓
A C K N O W L E D G E M E N T

28. (*d*) According to the question,
9 8 12 3 7 6 1 2 13 4 5 10 11
↓ ↓ ↓ ↓ ↓ ↓ ↓ ↓ ↓ ↓ ↓ ↓ ↓
H Y P O T H E C A T I O N

29. (*b*)The meaningful words are 'DISCLOSE', 'DISMISS', 'DISABLE' and 'DISCOUNT'.

30. (*d*) The meaningful words are 'CAPSULE', 'CAPTAIN', 'CAPABLE' and 'CAPE'.

31. (*a*) The meaningful words are 'REMOVE', 'REMARK' and 'REQUEST'.

32. (*c*) The meaningful words are 'STAGE', 'ENGAGE', 'DAMAGE' and 'SEWAGE'

33. (*b*) The meaningful words are 'HARM', 'CHARM', 'FARM' and 'SWARM' SWARM means a large group of insects.

34. (*b*) 'FORM' completes the first word as PLATFORM and begin the second as 'FORMATION'.

35. (*d*) REA (CH) URCH

The meaningful words are 'REACH' and 'CHURCH'.

36. (*b*) PROFESS (OR) PHAN

The meaningful words are 'PROFESSOR' and 'ORPHAN'.

37. (*a*) PRACT (ICE) BERG

The meaningful words are 'PRACTICE' and 'ICEBERG'.

38. (*a*) LOWELY ⇒ YELLOW

THIWE ⇒ WHITE

WRONB ⇒ BROWN

IFER ⇒ FIRE

Hence, FIRE is different from others as all others are different colours.

39. (*a*) DOGL ⇒ GOLD, [TSEVO] ⇒ VOTES

ENZROB ⇒ BRONZE, LVREIS ⇒ SILVER

Hence, VOTES, is different from others as all others are metals.

40. (*d*) ORIN = IRON

[NADS] = SAND

POPCER = COPPER

DLOG = GOLD

Hence, SAND is different from others as all others are metals.

41. (*c*) ENNI ⇒ NINE, NEO = ONE,

[EPPI] = PIPE and REETH ⇒ THREE

Hence, PIPE is different from others as all others are numbers.

42. (*a*) The word is 'EXPAND' and the meaning is 'INCREASE'.

43. (*d*) The word is 'DEARTH' and the meaning is 'SCARCITY'.

44. (*c*) The word is 'BEHIND' and the meaning is 'BACK'.

45. (*a*) The word is 'GARNISH' and the meaning is 'DECORATE'.

46. (*c*) Rearranging the words from right to left as per dictionary. we get, TAP STB PQR NOT MAT

Clearly, STB is at second position from left.

47. (*c*) Word which is second from left-NOT

Third letter-T

Word which is third from right-MAT

Second letter-A

There are 18 letters between A and T.

48. (*d*) New words after applying changes,

TBO NPS MBS PRQ SUA

Clearly, there are three words without any vowel.

49. (*a*) New words after applying changes,

[PAT] [TON] TAM RQP BTS

Clearly, there are three meaningful words.

50. (*d*) New words after applying changes,

SBO MPS LBS OPQ RSA

Clearly, there are three words with vowels.

51. (*d*) FACT and FACE two words will be meaningful.

52. (*d*) After interchanging as per the questions, ACT will be CAT which is a meaningful word.

53. (*d*) According to the question, newly made words

ACT-BCU, SHY-THZ, EON-FOO, ACE-BCF, WEB-XEC

Hence, only one word EON has two vowels.

54. (*c*)

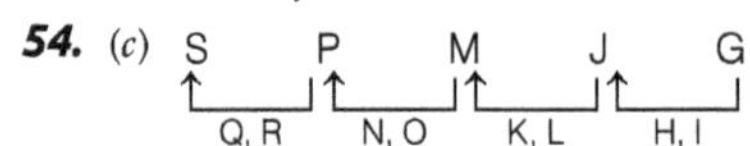

55. (*b*) R V Z D H L

S, T, U W, X, Y A, B, C E, F, G I, J, K

56. (*d*) 5 7 9 11 13

E G I K M

F H J L

57. (*b*) E Z U P

DCBA YXWV TSRQ

58. (*c*) E H K N Q T

FG IJ LM OP RS

59. (*b*) 2 5 4 1 3 [6] 9 [8] 7

1 2 3 4 5 [6] 7 [8] 9

60. (*e*) 4 7 8 2 6 5 9

+1 −2 +1 +1 +1 −2 −2

5 5 9 3 7 3 7

∴ 5, 7 and 3 will appear twice in the new number.

61. (*b*) Arrangement of the given numbers as per instructions

684 512 437 385 296

+2 +2 +2 +2 +2

884 712 637 585 496

Now, number divisible by 3 from new formed numbers = 585

Hence, there is only one number is divisible by three from new formed numbers.

62. (*c*) Arrangement of numbers in descending order

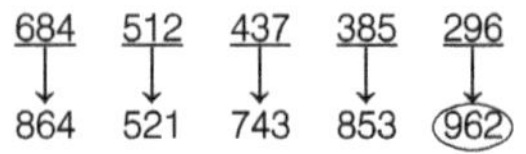

Highest number in descending order = 962

∴ Required number = 296

63. (*a*) Highest number = 684

Second lowest number = 3 8 5

∴ Resultant number = $\frac{8}{4} = 2$

64. (*a*) Arranged the given letters in proper sequence, we get the river name KAVERI and its fifth letter from left is R.

65. (*c*)

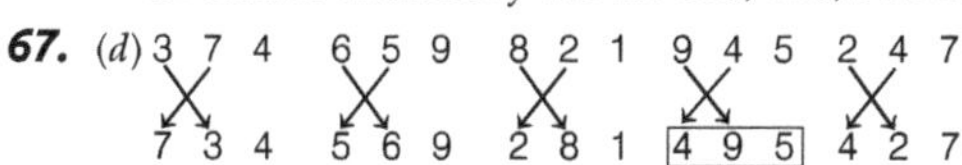

∴ Letter pairs = CE, HK

Solutions (Q.Nos. 66-68)

66. (*e*) 374 659 821 945 247 (−1 each) → 373 658 820 944 246

∴ Number divisible by two are 658, 820, 944 and 246.

67. (*d*) 3 7 4 → 7 3 4; 6 5 9 → 5 6 9; 8 2 1 → 2 8 1; 9 4 5 → 4 9 5; 2 4 7 → 4 2 7

∴ Third smallest number = 495 i.e., 945.

68. (*d*) Arranging in ascending order

347 569 128 459 247

∴ Second highest number = 459 i.e., 945

69. (*d*) B C M X N C X N B X (N C B)(N C B) Y B C X N (B C N) A B O N M Z C B

So, 3 'BCN' occur in such a way, that C is in the middle and B and N are on any of the side.

70. (*a*) 7 8 976 5 3 4 2 8 9 7 2 4 5 9 2 976 47

Clearly, there are two 7s following the rule.

71. (*c*) X U V M R S T M W N V M W O P M W U V M W A C (W M V) H P N V W M W T U N

Clearly, there is one M which is preceded by W and followed by V.

72. (*d*) Given, number sequence is as follows
5 6 4 3 2 9 6 3 1649642159672̲14749642

It is clear from above that the given number sequence has two 6 which are immediately preceded by 9 but not immediately followed by 4.

73. (*d*) Clearly, in the given arrangement, there are nine such symbols and numbers *i.e.*, @, $, 1, δ, 9, 3, 7 γ and 5.

74. (*c*) Clearly, the pattern is as follows

Q K 5; L 6 D; 1 G © (+6 +7, +6 +7, +6 +7) But P L δ (+5 +7)

75. (*b*) Clearly, the new alpha-numeric arrangement according to the question is

2 P J 8 @ L $ B 1 V Q # 6 G δ W 9 K C D 3 • £ 5 © F R 7 A 4 γ

So, in the given arrangement, there are two such letters *i.e.*, B and W.

76. (*d*) Clearly, the pattern is as follows

P @ L; γ 7 5; $ B #; F £ 3 (+2 +3, −2 −3, +2 +3, −2 −3)

77. (*d*) Clearly, the new alpha-numeric arrangement of eliminated element P @ $ B V Q δ W K D © £ F 7 γ

So, number of symbols = 6

Number of letters = 8, Number of numbers = 1

78. (*a*) According to the question,

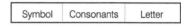

R 4 3 M (K) E F 5 A J N 1
8 U D B P 6 1 W 7 Q H Z

(4th to the left of 9th from left)

∴ Required answer = K

79. (*d*) According to the question,

R % M @ K E F A # J N U © D B P W δ Q H Z

(18 th from right; 7th letter to right)

∴ Required answer = N

80. (*d*) Required combination

Symbol	Consonants	Letter

R 4 3 % M @ K E F 5 A # J N 1 8 U © D B P 6 1 W 7 δ Q H Z

∴ Required answer = three

81. (*a*)

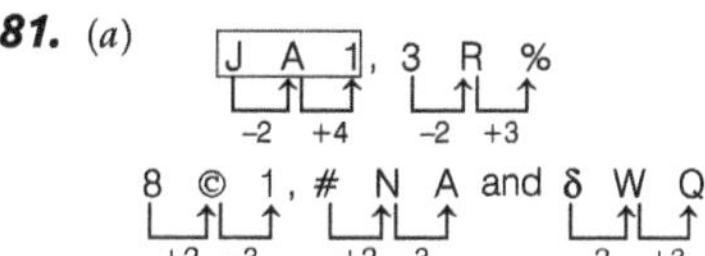

Clearly 'JA1' is different from others.

82. (*d*) Required answer

Element	Number	Letter

R 4 3 % M @ K E F 5 A # J
N 1 8 U © D B P 6 1 W 7
δ Q H Z

∴ Required answer = 3

83. (*a*) D is the required element.

84. (*c*) 9 is the required element.

85. (*e*) Except 'UJ6' in all other alternatives the first two elements are consecutive and the third element is second to the right of second element.

86. (*b*) There are only one such symbol which are preceded a number, but not followed by a consonant. viz 3 % 9.

87. (*e*) 4 is the required element.

Solutions (Q.Nos. 88-91) According to the given informations
P 4 S A W 5 8 F 9 1 R E 7 2 O 3 7 5 1 B 6 K G N

88. (*c*) There are two numbers (7 and 3) which are immediately preceded by a vowel. i.e. 'E 7' and 'O 3'.

89. (*d*) If all the numbers are removed from the series, then new series is

P S A W F R E O B K G N

(7th form the right end)

Hence, R is seventh from the right end.

90. (*a*) If all the consonants are removed from the given series, then new series is

4 A 5 8 9 I E 7 2 0 3 7 5 1 6
9th form the left end →

Hence, 2 will be 9th from the left end.

91. (*b*) P4SAW5⑧F91RE7203751B6KGN

5th to the left
12th form the left

Hence, element '8' is 5th to the left of 12th element form the left end.

92. (*b*) EL# does not belong to the group.

U * 9	→	* D 5 U	B 4 9
3 2 *	→	2 N A 3	@ M *
1 4 Y	→	4 9 Ω 1	& L Y
P B 6	→	8 % W P	7 $ 6
E L #	→	L Y © E	# K (×)

93. (*d*) If all the numbers are deleted from the given arrangement, then the arrangement will be are as follows.

S R % W P $ N A @ M * D U B Ω & L Y © E # K

A is the fifth element to the right of %, U is the fourth element to the left of L.

94. (*a*) Fifteenth elements from the right end is D. And sixth element from the right of D is Ω.

95. (*d*) Eleventh element from the left end is N and sixth element from the right end is L.

Sum of numbers between N and L = 3 + 5 + 4 + 9 + 1 = 22

96. (*e*) Ninth element from the right end is Ω and ninth element from the left end is 6.

Number of letters between 6 & Ω is five i.e., N, A, M, D, B and U.

97. (*b*) [LAP] A R O S [COPY]

Two meaningful words LAP and COPY can be formed.

98. (*b*) Word 'SAFEGUARD' can be formed by using the letters of the given word by only as many times as the letters have been used in the word 'AUDEFGRSA.'

99. (*b*) Given number = 6 9 2 8 6 2 5 7

After Ist arrangement = 2 2 5 [6] [6] 7 8 9

After IInd arrangement = 9 8 7 [6] [6] 5 2 2

∴ Required number of digits = 2

100. (*d*) According to the question, the English alphabet series is written as

A b C d E f G h I [j] K [l] M n O p Q r S t [U] v W x [Y] z

The first month of the second half of the year is July which will be written as jUlY.

CHAPTER / 02

Analogy

'Analogy' means 'similarity' or 'Resemblance' of an object to another in certain aspects. In these type of questions, a specific relationship is given to the candidate and he/she supposed to identify another similar relationship from the given alternatives.

The aim of analogy is to test overall logical understanding of the candidates and how coherently they understand different kinds of relationships among various elements.

To solve these questions, following two simple steps are to be followed

- Identify the relationship between the pair of elements.
- Complete the other pair.

Now, it is clear that analogy is established, when two pairs of elements bear the same relationship.

The questions based on analogy may be asked in various forms, it can be classified into following types.

TYPE 01

Word Analogy

In word analogy related problems, the candidate is required to identify the relationship between the given pair of words and then to find out the similar analogous pair or to complete the another analogous pair according to the relationship in the given pair.

The relationships can be of several types depending upon the kind of relationship between the two objects of a pair.

Some of the most common types of analogous relationships are as follows

Type of Relation

Synonymous words

- Kind : Benevolent
- Endless : Eternal
- Dearth : Scarcity
- Abduct : Kidnap
- Vacant : Empty

Antonymous words

- Deep : Shallow
- Lethargy : Alertness
- Notice : Ignore
- Create : Destroy

Country and Continent

- India : Asia
- France : Europe
- Brazil : South America
- Canada : North America

Country and Capital

- Japan : Tokyo
- Italy : Rome
- Nepal : Kathmandu
- Russia : Moscow

State : Capital

- Uttar Pradesh : Lucknow
- Gujarat : Gandhi Nagar
- Odisha : Bhuvneshwar
- Sikkim : Gangtok

Country and Currency

- USA : Dollar
- Thailand : Baht
- Greece : Euro
- Myanmar : Kyat

Country and Parliament

- India : Parliament
- Russia : Duma
- Iran : Majlis
- USA : Congress

Country and River

- India : Ganga
- Britain : Thames
- China : Hwang Ho
- Austria : Danube

Animal and Young One

- Cat : Kitten
- Tiger : Cub
- Stag : Fawn
- Sheep : Lamb

Animal/Things and their Keeping Place

- Birds : Aviary
- Bees : Apiary
- Aeroplane : Hanger
- Fish : Aquarium
- Animals : Zoo
- Weapons : Armoury

Male and Female

- Dog : Bitch
- Lion : Lioness
- Horse : Mare
- Stag : Doe

Worker and Tool

- Warrior : Sword
- Labourer : Spade
- Mason : Plumb line
- Carpenter : Saw

Product and Raw Material

- Paper : Pulp
- Furniture : Wood
- Fabric : Yarn
- Liven : Flax

Worker and Working Place

- Chef : Kitchen
- Astronomer : Observatory
- Waiter : Restaurant
- Lawyer : Court

Quantity and Unit

- Resistance : Ohm
- Pressure : Pascal
- Temperature : Degree
- Energy : Joule

Instrument and Measurement

- Thermometer : Temperature
- Anemometer : Wind
- Seismograph : Earthquake
- Odometer : Speed

Tool and Action

- Microscope : Magnify
- Shield : Guard
- Spoon : Feed
- Spade : Dig

Study and Topic

- Ornithology : Birds
- Palaeontology : Fossils
- Entomology : Insects
- Pedology : Soil
- Cardiology : Heart
- Hepatology : Liver

Individual and Dwelling Place

- Mouse : Hole
- Eskimo : Igloo
- Soldier : Barracks
- Eagle : Eyrie
- Horse : Stable
- Dog : Kennel

Games and Playing Place

- Cricket : Pitch
- Tennis : Court
- Skating : Rink
- Wrestling : Arena
- Boxing : Ring
- Kabaddi : Court

Sports and Players

- Tennis : Sania Mirza
- Badminton : Saina Nehwal
- Hockey : Sandeep Singh
- Cricket : Mithali Raj

Sports and Sports terms

- Smash : Badminton/Tennis
- Home run : Baseball
- Diamond : Baseball
- Free throw : Basketball
- Deuce : Tennis
- Dummy : Bridge
- Penalty Corner : Hockey
- Mallet : Pol

Sports and Cups/Trophies

- Golf : Ryder Cup
- Football : Durand Cup
- Badminton : Uber Cup
- Cricket : Duleep Trophy

Animals and Sound

- Lion : Roar
- Horse : Neigh
- Dog : Bark
- Frog : Croak
- Owl : Hoot
- Duck : Quack

Country and National Game

- Britain : Cricket
- India : Hockey
- USA : Baseball
- Japan : Judo
- China : Table Tennis
- Brazil : Football

Country and National Emblem

- India : Lion capital
- UK : Rose
- Canada : White Lily
- Spain : Eagle

Apart from these relations, there are many other types of relations that can also be possible. Such as

- Sports and Cups
- Awards
- Science and Technology
- History
- Politics
- Art and Culture
- Geography
- Social facts
- Monuments
- Famous personalities

Problems based on word analogy are asked in different formats in various competitive exams, where the candidate is required either to find out the similar analogous pair or to complete the given analogous pair. Based on this, we have classified word analogy into following types

A. Analogous Pair Completion

In such type of questions, the candidate will be provided with one pair of words and second pair of incomplete words. He/She supposed to find a relation between the first pair of words and then choose the correct alternative to complete the second pair.

Some solved examples given below will give you better idea about these type of questions.

DIRECTIONS ~ (Example Nos. 1-4) *Select the related word from the given alternative.*

Ex 01 Colour : Red :: Profession : ? « SSC MTS 2019

(a) Lawyer (b) Court (c) School (d) Black

Solution **(a)** As, Red is a colour. Similarly, Lawyer is a profession.

Ex 02 Tadpole : ? : : Caterpillar : Butterfly « SSC (Steno) 2013

(a) Crow (b) Goose (c) Fish (d) Frog

Solution **(d)** As 'Caterpillar' is the youngone or larvae of 'Butterfly'. Similarly, Tadpole is the youngone or larvae of 'Frog.'

Ex 03 Hongkong : China : : Vatican : ? « SSC (MTS) 2013

(a) France (b) Mexico (c) Canada (d) Rome

Solution **(d)** As, 'Hongkong' is in 'China' in the same way 'Vatican' is situated in 'Rome'.

Ex 04 Video player : Cassette : : Computer : ?

(a) Reels (b) CPU
(c) Files (d) Floppy
(e) Recordings

Solution **(d)** Data of the second are visualised on the first.

Ex 05 'Calm' is related to 'Cool' in the same way as 'Abandon' is related to

(a) Down (b) Leave (c) Attract (d) Clear

Solution **(b)** As, 'Calm' and 'Cool' are synonyms of each other in the same way synonym of 'Abandon' is 'Leave'.

Ex 06 'Cat' is related to 'Mew' in the same way as 'Horse' is related to

(a) Stable (b) Creep (c) Roar (d) Neigh

Solution **(d)** As, 'Mew' is the sound produced by 'Cat'. Similarly, 'Neigh' is the sound produced by 'Horse'.

B. Analogous Pair Selection

In such type of problems, a pair of words is given, followed by four pairs of words as options. The candidate is required to pick the pair in which the words bear the same relationship to each other as the words of the given pair bear.

DIRECTIONS ~ (Example Nos. 7 and 8) *Find out the pair in which the words bear the same relationship to each other as similar to the words of the given pair bear.*

***Ex* 07** Pig : Sty « SSC (CGL) 2015

(a) Donkey : Bray
(b) Hen : Chick
(c) Owl : Barn
(d) Bird : Asylum

Solution **(c)** A 'Pig' lives in a 'Sty' in the same way an 'Owl' lives in a 'Barn'.

***Ex* 08** Five : Pentagon « SSC MTS 2019

(a) Four : Rectangle
(b) Triangle : Three
(c) Square : Four
(d) Six : Septagon

Solution **(a)** As, a pentagon has five sides. Similarly, a rectangle has four sides.

C. Similar Word Selection

In such type of questions, a group of three/four words is given followed by four other words as options. The candidate is required to choose the alternative which is similar to the given words.

DIRECTIONS ~ (Example Nos. 9 and 10) *Out of the four given alternatives, choose that alternative as your answer which is similar to the given words.*

***Ex* 09** Which of the following is the same as 'India', 'Pakistan', Afghanistan'?

(a) Germany (b) England
(c) Sri Lanka (d) USA

Solution **(c)** India, Pakistan and Afghanistan all are Asian countries and so is 'Sri Lanka'.

***Ex* 10** Which of the following is the same as 'Dollar', 'Yen', 'Rupee'?

(a) Knessep (b) Shora
(c) Pound (d) Ground

Solution **(c)** 'Dollar', 'Yen' and 'Rupee' are the currencies of different countries and so is the 'Pound'.

D. Analogy Detection

In such type of questions, the candidate is required to find out the common feature among the given words and pick the alternative that mentions the properties/features common to the given words.

DIRECTIONS ~ (Example Nos. 11 and 12) *Find out the common feature among the given words and pick the alternative that mentions the properties/features common to the given words.*

***Ex* 11** Nose, Eyes, Ears

(a) They are internal part of human body
(b) They are not the external part of human body
(c) They are parts of the body below waist
(d) They are parts of the body above neck

Solution **(d)** 'Nose', 'Eyes' and 'Ears' are the parts of human body above neck.

***Ex* 12** Dhoni, Yuvraj, Dravid

(a) Cricketers (b) Athlete
(c) Politicians (d) Singers

Solution **(a)** It is clear that the common feature among Dhoni, Yuvraj and Dravid is that they all are cricketers.

E. Multiple Word Analogy

In such type of analogy a group of three/four inter-related words is given. The candidate is required to find out the relationship among these words and choose another group with similar relationship, from the options provided.

DIRECTIONS ~ (Example Nos. 13 and 14) *Find out the relationship among these words and choose another group with similar relationship from the options provided.*

***Ex* 13** Furniture, Table, Almirah

(a) Building, Wall, Brick
(b) Fruit, Orange, Apple
(c) Mother, Father, Sister
(d) Sea, Road, City

Solution **(b)** As, 'Table' and 'Almirah' are both 'Furniture' and similarly 'Orange' and 'Apple' are both 'Fruits'. Clearly, both second and third belong to the class denoted by the first.

***Ex* 14** Pink, Red, White

(a) Brown, Black, Blue
(b) Green, Blue, Yellow
(c) Orange, Yellow, Black
(d) Yellow, Red, Green

Solution **(b)** As, 'Pink' is obtained by the combination of 'Red' and 'White' and similarly 'Green' is obtained by the combination of 'Blue' and 'Yellow'.

F. Double Analogy

In such type of questions, the candidate will be provided with two sets of words. Both sets of words are seprated by double colon (::). Four/Five options are given to the candidate and he/she is supposed to identify the correct pair of words which will make an appropriate relationship between two words to the left of double colon and the same relationship for the words of right side.

Some solved examples given below will give you a better idea about these type of questions

DIRECTIONS ~ (Example Nos. 15 and 16) *Find out the correct pair of words which will make on appropriate analogical relationship between the two words to the left of the sign (::) and the same relationship between the two words to the right of the sign (::).*

Ex 15 A : Wheat : : Brick : B
(a) A. Bread , B. Clay
(b) A. Cereal, B. Clay
(c) A. Farmer, B. Mason
(d) A. Farmer, B. Clay

***Solution* (a)** As, 'Wheat' is used to make 'Bread'. Similarly, 'Clay' is used to make 'Brick'.

Ex 16 A : Sword : : Thread : B
(a) A. Dagger, B. Needle (b) A. Kill, B. Stitch
(c) A. Knife, B. Rope (d) A. Warrior, B. Tailor

***Solution* (c)** As, 'Sword' is the enlarged form of 'Knife'. Similarly, 'Rope' is the enlarged form of 'Thread'.

G. Analogy Based on Choosing Letters

In this type of analogy, the candidate is asked to find the word from the given alternatives which is having similar relations to the given word as in given pairs.

Ex 17 Select the related word from the given alternatives
Policeman, ice : Penniless, nil : Consonant, ?
(a) con (b) son
(c) ant (d) not

***Solution* (b)** As,

Policeman ⟶ ice ; Penniless ⟶ nil

Similarly,

Consonant ⟶ son

Practice /CORNER 2.1

DIRECTIONS ~ (Q. Nos. 1-28) *In each of the following questions, there is a certain relationship between two given words on one side of (::) and one word is given on another side (::) while another word is to be found from the given alternatives, having the same relation with this word as the words of the given pair bear. Choose the correct alternative.*

1. River : Stream :: Ocean: ? « SSC (CGL) 2017
(a) Current (b) Pond (c) Dam (d) Sea

2. Magazine : Editor :: Drama : ? « SSC (MTS) 2014
(a) Director (b) Player (c) Manager (d) Actor

3. Arc : Circle : : Line : ?
(a) Point (b) Rectangle (c) Ellipse (d) Sphere

4. French : France : : Dutch : ?
(a) Holland (b) Norway (c) Fiji (d) Sweden

5. Dress : Tailor : : ? : Carpenter
(a) Wood (b) Furniture (c) Leather (d) Cloth

6. Genuine : Authentic :: Mirage : ? « SSC MTS 2019
(a) Reflection (b) Image
(c) Illusion (d) Hideout

7. Prime facie : On the first view :: In part delicto : ?
(a) Both parties equally at fault
(b) While litigation is pending
(c) Aremedy for all disease
(d) Beyond powers

8. Nightingale : Warble : : Frog : ? « IBPS (Clerk) 2013
(a) Yelp (b) Croak (c) Cackle (d) Squeak
(e) None of these

9. Monotony : Variety : : Crudeness : ?
(a) Refinement (b) Raw
(c) Sobriety (d) Simplicity

10. Burglar : House : : Pirate : ?
(a) Sea (b) Ship (c) Sailor (d) Crew

11. Hill : Mountain : : Stream : ?
(a) River (b) Canal
(c) Glacier (d) Avalanche

12. Pyramid : Egypt : : Eiffel Tower : ?
(a) Spain (b) France (c) Canada (d) Japan

13. Foot : ? :: Hand : Wrist « SSC (10+2) 2013
(a) Length (b) Shoe (c) Ankle (d) Leg

14. Smell : Flower :: Taste : ? « SSC (10+2) 2013
(a) Water (b) Salt (c) Food (d) Sweet

15. Annihilation : Fire : : Cataclysm : ?
(a) Earthquake (b) Steam
(c) Emergency (d) Disaster

16. Smoke : Pollution :: War : ?
(a) Peace (b) Victory
(c) Treaty (d) Destruction

17. Wax : Candle : : ? : Paper
(a) Tree (b) Bamboo
(c) Pulp (d) Wood

18. Temperature : Thermometer :: Humidity : ?
« UPSSSC Combined Lower Subordinate 2019
(a) Spectrometer (b) Seismometer
(c) Hygrometer (d) Osmometer

19. Abduct : Kidnap : : Solicit : ? « SSC (CGL) 2009
(a) Request (b) Ban
(c) Squander (d) Allot

20. Work : Joule : : Area : ? « SSC (10+2) 2020
(a) Radian (b) Perimeter
(c) Length (d) Hectare

21. Cricket : Pitch : : Wrestling : ? « SBI (Clerk) 2007
(a) Rink (b) Wrestler (c) Ground (d) Arena
(e) None of these

22. Eye : Wink : : Heart : ? « CLAT 2014
(a) Throb (b) Move (c) Pump (d) Respirate

23. Pituitary : Brain : : Thymus : ?
(a) Larynx (b) Spinal Cord
(c) Throat (d) Chest

24. Field : Farmer :: Observatory : ? « SSC CPO 2019
(a) Stars (b) Astronomer (c) Telescope
(d) Astronaut

25. USA : Congress : : Iran : ?
(a) Althing (b) Storting (c) Majlis (d) Cortes

26. Ocean : Water : : Glacier : ? « CLAT 2014
(a) Cooling (b) Cave (c) Ice (d) Mountain

27. Ministers : Council : Sailors : ? « SSC CGL 2019
(a) Sea (b) Captain (c) Crew (d) Ship

28. Delusion : Hallucination :: Chagrin : ? « CLAT 2014
(a) Illusion (b) Ordered (c) Cogent (d) Annoyance

DIRECTIONS ~ (Q. Nos. 29-56) *In the following questions, two words are given which are related to each other in a particular manner and you have to find the word from the given alternatives which bears exactly same relationship to the third word, as the first two bear.*

29. 'Skating' is related to 'Rink' in the same way as 'Tennis' is related to « SSC CPO 2018
(a) Court (b) Arena (c) Pitch (d) Racket

30. Cup is related to 'Crockery' in the same way as 'Pen' is related to
(a) Paper (b) Books (c) Stationery (d) Ink
(e) Nib

31. 'Lion' is related to 'Cub' in the same way as 'Cow' is related to « SSC MTS 2019
(a) Calf (b) Lamb (c) Foal (d) Joey

32. 'Clock' is related to 'Time' in the same way as 'Metre' is related to
(a) Speed (b) Distance (c) Wrist (d) Sand

33. 'Museum' is related to 'Curator' in the same way as 'Prison' is related to
(a) Warden (b) Monitor (c) Manager (d) Jailor

34. 'Hour' is related to 'Second' in the same way as 'Tertiary' is related to
(a) Ordinary (b) Secondary
(c) Primary (d) Intermediary

35. 'Fire' is related to 'Ashes' in the same way as 'Explosion' is related to
(a) Sound (b) Debris (c) Explosive (d) Flame

36. 'Parliament' is related to 'Great Britain' in the same way as 'Congress' is related to
(a) Japan (b) India
(c) USA (d) Netherlands

37. 'Sports' is related to 'Logo' in the same way as 'Nation' is related to
(a) Emblem (b) Animal (c) Ruler (d) Anthem

38. 'Data Processing' is related to 'Raw Data' in the same way as 'University' is related to
(a) Teacher (b) Building
(c) Students (d) Principal

39. 'Braille' is related to 'Blindness' in the same way as 'Sign language' is related to
(a) Exceptional (b) Touch
(c) Deafness (d) Presentation

40. 'Boat' is related to 'Oar' in the same way as 'Bicycle' is related to
(a) Road (b) Wheel (c) Seat (d) Paddle

41. 'Match' is related to 'Victory' in the same way as 'Examination' is related to
(a) Write (b) Appear (c) Success (d) Attempt

42. 'Flower' is related to 'Essence' in the same way as 'Oven' is related to « LIC (ADO) 2006
(a) Vapour (b) Fire (c) Heat (d) Steam
(e) None of these

43. 'Major' is related to 'Lieutenant' in the same way as 'Squadron Leader' is related to « SSC (LDC) 2006
(a) Group Captain (b) Flying Attendant
(c) Flying Officer (d) Pilot Officer

44. 'Neck' is related to 'Tie' in the same way as 'Waist' is related to
(a) Watch (b) Belt (c) Ribbon (d) Shirt

45. 'Atom' is related to 'Molecule' in the same way as 'Cell' is related to
(a) Matter (b) Nucleus (c) Organism (d) Battery

46. 'Flower' is related to 'Petal' in the same way as 'Book' is related to
(a) Page (b) Content (c) Author (d) Library

47. 'Needle' is related to 'Sew' in the same way as 'Microscope' is related to '..........'. « SSC CPO 2019
(a) Science (b) Lens
(c) Laboratory (d) Magnify

48. 'Cardiologist' is related to 'Heart' in the same way as 'Neurologist' is related to '..........' . « SSC CGL 2020
(a) Ears (b) Brain (c) Lungs (d) Teeth

49. 'Grass' is related to 'Pasture' in the same way as 'Word' is related to
(a) Sentence (b) Spoken (c) Book (d) Write

50. 'Cell' is related to 'Tissue' in the same way as 'Tissue' is related to
(a) Object (b) Ear (c) Organ (d) Limb

51. 'Vendor' is related to 'Buyer' in the same way as 'Consultant' is related to
(a) Firm (b) Client
(c) Advice (d) Consult

52. 'Player' is related to 'Coach' in the same way as 'Pupil' is related to
(a) School (b) Academy (c) Teacher (d) Word

53. 'Save' is related to 'Rescue' in the same way as 'Severe' is related to
(a) Endure (b) Stern (c) Sever (d) Uneasy

54. 'Ignite' is to 'Combustion' as 'Trigger' is to
(a) Gun (b) War (c) Projectile (d) Reaction

55. 'Disease' is related to 'Medicine' in the same way as 'Famine' is related to
(a) Drought (b) River
(c) Waterfall (d) Rainfall

56. 'Go' is related to 'Come' in the same way as 'High' is related to « IBPS (Clerk) 2011
(a) Up (b) Low (c) Birth (d) Stand
(e) None of these

DIRECTIONS ~ (Q. Nos. 57-81) *The following questions consist of two words each, that have a certain relationship with each other, followed by four lettered pairs of words. Select the letter pair that has the same relationship as the original pair of words.*

57. Poverty : Prosperity « WBCS (Pre) 2018
(a) Love : Sorrow (b) Train : Cart
(c) Rain : Flood (d) Intelligence : Stupidity

58. Cow : Milk « SSC (10+2) 2020
(a) Bird : Fly (b) Hen : Egg
(c) Eagle : Clutch (d) Goat : Bleat

59. Book : Chapter
(a) Pen : Pencil (b) Computer : Calculator
(c) Mobile : Landline (d) House : Room

60. Chair : Wood :: ? « SSC (10+2) 2013
(a) Book : Print (b) Mirror : Glass
(c) Plate : Food (d) Purse : Money

61. Agra : Taj Mahal « UP B.Ed. 2011
(a) Delhi : Hawa Mahal (b) Patna : Red Fort
(c) Gaya : Golghar (d) Amritsar : Golden Temple

62. Animal : Zoology
(a) Body : Physiology (b) Disease : Bacteriology
(c) Poems : Anthology (d) Man : Philanthropy

63. Spider : Web « RRB (TC/CC) 2006
(a) Ink : Pen (b) Cock : Hen
(c) Teacher : Student (d) Poet : Poetry

64. Faculty : Teachers « SSC CGL 2020
(a) Ants : Flock (b) Galaxy : Apartments
(c) Colony : Wolves (d) Fleet : Trucks

65. Horse : Hoof « SSC (DEO) 2012
(a) Man : Foot (b) Dog : Black
(c) Paise : Rupee (d) Pen : Pencil

66. Tagore : Geetanjali
(a) Madam Curie : Radium (b) Shakespeare : Skylark
(c) Dickens : Oliver Twist (d) Nobel : Dynamite

67. Bud : Flower « IBPS (Clerk) 2013
(a) Clay : Mud (b) Sapling : Tree
(c) River : Glacier (d) Bird : Tree
(e) Paper : Book

68. Ideas : Brain
(a) Literature : Author (b) Clouds : Ocean
(c) Money : Bank (d) Planets : Earth

69. Frankness : Blunt
(a) Rise : Awake (b) Weep : Laugh
(c) Sickness : Death (d) Rest : Activity

70. Love : Hate « UP B.Ed. 2011
(a) Go : Do (b) Near : Where
(c) Up : Down (d) Come : Soon

71. Mendacity : Honesty « IB (ACIO) 2013
(a) Truth : Beauty
(b) Sportsmanship : Fortitude
(c) Courageous : Craven
(d) Turpitude : Depravity

72. Touch : Push « SSC CPO 2019
(a) Speak : Shout (b) Eat : Drink
(c) Refuse : Accept (d) Run : Walk

73. Capricious : Reliability
(a) Extemporaneous : Predictability
(b) Unreliable : Inhuman
(c) Tenacious : Practicality
(d) Arbitrary : Whimsical

74. Water : Oxygen
(a) Helium : Nitrogen (b) Salt : Sodium
(c) Tree : Plant (d) Food : Hunger

75. Geeta : Quran
(a) Orange : Mango (b) Temple : Worship
(c) Good : Man (d) Army : Defence

76. Sin : Crime « SSC (FCI) 2012
(a) Man : Animal (b) Home : Court
(c) Morality : Legality (d) Jury : Priest

77. Milk : Cream
(a) College : Students (b) Sugar : Sweet
(c) Clay : Pottery (d) Fruit : Glucose

78. Loathe : Coercion
(a) Detest : Caressing
(b) Irritate : Caressing
(c) Irate : Antagonism
(d) Reluctant : Persuasion

79. Players : Team « SSC CPO 2019
(a) Flowers : Bouquet (b) Grapes : Dozen
(c) Band : Musician (d) Class : Students

80. Umpire : Game
(a) Prodigy : Wonder (b) Chef : Banquet
(c) Legislator : Election (d) Moderator : Debate

81. Fly : Walk
(a) Sit : Sleep
(b) Roast : Bake
(c) Sky : Earth
(d) Pilot : Captain

DIRECTIONS ~ (Q. Nos. 82-111) *In the following questions, three words are given which have something in common among themselves. Out of the four given alternatives, choose that alternative as your answer which is similar to the given words.*

82. Bleat : Howl : Gibber : ?
(a) Grunt (b) Leap (c) Stuck (d) Duck

83. Iron : Copper : Zinc : ? « RRB (GG) 2005
(a) Ceramic (b) Carbon (c) Silver (d) Coke

84. Eyes : Tongue : Ear : ?
(a) Finger (b) Thumb (c) Knee (d) Nose

85. Intestine : Liver : Heart : ?
(a) Blood (b) Hand (c) Forehead (d) Kidney

86. Ohm : Watt : Ampere : ?
(a) Electricity (b) Volt (c) Hour (d) Light

87. Rice : Wheat : Maize : ? « RRB (TC/CC) 2005
(a) Jowar-Bajra (b) Tobacco
(c) Jute (d) Cotton

88. Branch : Stem : Leaf : ?
(a) Tree (b) Chair (c) Root (d) Glass

89. Neigh : Bray : Bark : ?
(a) Gibber (b) Peseta (c) Majlis (d) Leaf

90. Lion : Tiger : Bear : ? « UP B.Ed. 2009
(a) Cow (b) Cat (c) Panther (d) Buffalo

91. Calf : Kid : Pup : ?
(a) Infant (b) Young (c) Larva (d) Animal

92. Which of the following is same as 'Bhilai, Rourkela, Durgapur'? « RRB (TC/CC) 2005
(a) Chandigarh (b) Baroda
(c) Lucknow (d) Bokaro

93. Odissi : Kathak : Bharatnatyam : ?
(a) Kathakali (b) Gumar (c) Tamasha (d) Nautanki

94. Which of the following is the same as 'Sty', 'Stable', 'Kennel'? « UP B.Ed. 2009
(a) Whale (b) Horse (c) Burrow (d) Room

95. Which of the following is the same as 'Bitch', 'Mare', 'Doe'?
(a) Fox (b) Dog (c) Vixen (d) Horse

96. Which of the following is the same as 'Durga', 'Kali', 'Saraswati'?
(a) Ganesh (b) Worship (c) Laxmi (d) Shiv

97. Which of the following is the same as 'Varanasi', 'Kanpur', 'Lucknow'?
(a) Gaya (b) Jodhpur
(c) Ghaziabad (d) Bhagalpur

98. Which of the following is the same as 'Norway', 'Poland', 'Spain'?
(a) France (b) Rome (c) Kenya (d) Tokyo

99. Which of the following is the same as 'Flood', 'Fire', 'Cyclone'?
(a) Damage (b) Earthquake (c) Rain (d) Accident

100. Which of the following is the same as 'Count', 'List', 'Weight'?
(a) Compare (b) Sequence (c) Number (d) Measure

101. Which of the following is the same as 'Steel', 'Bronze', 'Brass'?
(a) Calcite (b) Magnalium
(c) Methane (d) Zinc

102. Rabbit : Rat : Mole : ?
(a) Mongoose (b) Frog
(c) Earthworm (d) Ant

103. Grunt : Bray : Bleat : ?
(a) Bark (b) Crock (c) Cry (d) Scream

104. Crocodile : Lizard : Chameleon : ?
(a) Whale (b) Lion (c) Snake (d) Hen

105. Pen : Pencil : Rubber : ?
(a) Page (b) Cell (c) Pillow (d) TV

106. Dhoni : Tendulkar : Sehwag : ?
(a) Saniya (b) Shahrukh (c) Dravid (d) Aadvani

107. Sapphire : Emerald : Diamond : ?
(a) Ruby (b) Bronze
(c) Gold (d) Silver

108. LBW : Slip : Cover : ?
(a) Dence (b) Dribble
(c) Corner (d) Chinaman

109. Lahore : Faislabad : Islamabad : ?
(a) Kabul (b) Ahmedabad
(c) Sialcot (d) Dhaka

110. Radiology : Pathology : Cardiology : ?
(a) Biology (b) Zoology
(c) Geology (d) Hematology

111. Release : Liberate : Emancipate : ?
(a) Pardon (b) Ignore
(c) Quit (d) Free

DIRECTIONS ~ (Q. Nos. 112-127) *Three words are given in each question, which have something in common among themselves. Out of the four given alternatives, choose the most appropriate description about these three words.*

112. Ganga : Narmada : Tapti
(a) They are name of rivers.
(b) They are dance form of India.
(c) They are the currency of different countries.
(d) They are the parliaments name of different countries.

113. Leap : Frisk : Trot
(a) They are youngone of animals.
(b) They are Indian monuments.
(c) They are movement of animals.
(d) They are the name of famous zoological parks.

114. Pen : Rubber : Pencil
(a) They are goods for all purpose.
(b) They are stationery goods.
(c) They are famous Indian sites.
(d) They are sports terms.

115. Sunday : Monday : Saturday
(a) They are name of the years.
(b) They are name of the months.
(c) They are name of the week days.
(d) They are name of the rivers.

116. Sale : Tale : Male
(a) They have 2 vowels.
(b) They have 4 consonants.
(c) The words have no vowels.
(d) The words have no consonants.

117. Peso : Won : Taka
(a) They are famous monuments.
(b) They are name of the young ones of animals.
(c) They are synonymous words.
(d) None of the above.

118. Jaipur : Bengaluru : Mumbai
(a) They are the cities in Rajasthan.
(b) They are the famous business cities of India.
(c) They are the three biggest villages of India.
(d) They are the capitals of Indian states.

119. Colombo : Kathmandu : Havana
(a) They are African cities.
(b) They are European cities.
(c) They are capitals of countries.
(d) They are sports cities.

120. Squeak : Hiss : Howl
(a) They are names of animals.
(b) They are currencies.
(c) They are biggest animals on earth.
(d) They are sound produced by animals.

121. Kathak : Bharatnatyam : Odissi
(a) They are the name of music instruments.
(b) They are the classical dance forms of India.
(c) They are the folk dance forms of India.
(d) They are the names of Indian tribes.

122. Indira : Nehru : Benazir
(a) They were Presidents.
(b) They were Prime Ministers.
(c) They were sports persons.
(d) They were Indian politicians.

123. Mohinder : Gavaskar : Azaharuddin
(a) They were Indian athletes.
(b) They were Indian foreign ministers.
(c) They were cricket umpires.
(d) They are former Indian cricketers.

124. Folketing : Stortling : Knesset
(a) They are the name of currencies.
(b) They are the name of rivers.
(c) They are the name of Parliaments.
(d) They are the name of cities.

125. Pitcher : Dusra : Bunker
(a) They are parliament's name.
(b) They are dwelling places of animals.
(c) They are sports terms.
(d) They are terms related to cricket.

126. Mamb : Krait : Viper
(a) They are insects.
(b) They are haunting spirits.
(c) These are boot polishes.
(d) These are snakes.

127. Metre : Mile : Kilometre
(a) They are units of electricity.
(b) They are units of measuring anything.
(c) They are units of distance.
(d) They are units of weight.

DIRECTIONS ~ (Q. Nos. 128-152) *Three words are given in each question below which have something in common among themselves. Choose one out of the four given alternatives, which mentions the quality common to the three given words.*

128. Chair : Table : Stool
(a) School (b) Office
(c) Company (d) Furniture

129. Pen : Pencil : Ink
(a) Education (b) Writing
(c) Teaching (d) Stationery

130. Snake : Crocodile : Lizard
(a) Animals (b) Insects (c) Reptiles (d) Domestic

131. New York : Washington : Orlando
(a) Australia (b) Germany (c) Sri Lanka (d) USA

132. Moscow : Paris : Athens
(a) Cities (b) Asia
(c) Capitals (d) Countries

133. Kohima : Lucknow : Chennai
(a) East (b) Capital (c) North (d) South

134. Kyat : Yuan : Baht
(a) Currency (b) Cities
(c) Monuments (d) Parliament

135. Minute : Hour : Second
(a) Distance (b) Weight (c) Time (d) Length

136. Crowd : Shoal : Team
(a) Individual (b) Fish (c) Woman (d) Group

137. Duma : Majlis : Khural
(a) Parliament (b) City
(c) Currency (d) Monuments

138. Lion : Tiger : Bear
(a) Child (b) Fawn (c) Cub (d) Foal

139. Rice : Barley : Wheat
(a) Fruits (b) Vegetables
(c) Cereals (d) Agriculture

140. Football : Hockey : Tennis
(a) Athletes (b) Indo (c) Games (d) Aquatic

141. Beetle : Grasshopper : Wasp
(a) Cricket (b) Insects (c) Pesticides (d) Butterfly

142. Mother : Sister : Daughter
(a) Relation (b) Aged (c) Females (d) Family

143. Doctor : Nurse : Compounder
(a) School (b) Hospital (c) Office (d) Shop

144. Volga : Seine : Nile
(a) Mountains (b) Rifts (c) Hills (d) Rivers

145. Shirt : Hat : Coat
(a) Dress (b) Trousers (c) Uniform (d) Tailor

146. Ant : Fly : Bee
(a) Termite (b) Insect (c) Lizard (d) Small

147. Kandla : Paradeep : Haldia
(a) Seas (b) Grounds (c) Ports (d) Industry

148. Pluto : Mercury : Saturn
(a) Marsh (b) Earth (c) Jupiter (d) Planets

149. Diesel : Kerosine : Petrol
(a) Coal (b) Fuel (c) Firework (d) Engine

150. Hat : Turban : Cap
(a) Finger (b) Legs (c) Head (d) Neck

151. Mustard : Groundnuts : Sesame
(a) Oil seeds (b) Roots (c) Fruits (d) Politicians

152. Amitabh : Shahrukh : Aamir
(a) Singers (b) Players (c) Actors (d) Politicians

DIRECTIONS ~ (Q. Nos. 153-167) *In each of the following questions, some words are given which are related in some way. The same relationship exists among the words in one of the four alternatives given under it. Find the correct alternatives.*

153. Correspondent : News : Newspaper « RRB (ASM) 2006
(a) Road : Vehicle : Destination
(b) Cloud : Water : Ponds
(c) Farmer : Crops : Food
(d) Mason : Cement : Construction

154. Iron : Silver : Gold
(a) Parents : Father : Mother
(b) Wheat : Barley : Cereal
(c) Tree : Brench : Fruit
(d) Deer : Lion : Wolf

155. Road : Bus : Driver
(a) Track : Train : Passenger (b) Watch : Ship : Driver
(c) Sky : Aeroplane : Pilot (d) Paper : Letters : Reader

156. Hand : Wrist : Bangle
(a) Neck : Head : Collar (b) Foot : Ankle : Anklet
(c) Foot : Socks : Toes (d) Toe : Foot : Knee

157. Music : Guitar : Performer
(a) Trick : Rope : Acrobat
(b) Dance : Tune : Instrument
(c) Food : Recipe : Cook
(d) Patient : Medicine : Doctor

158. Tragedy : Sadness : Tears
(a) Music : Emotion : Tune
(b) Game : Sound : Match
(c) Comedy : Humour : Laughter
(d) Dance : Rhythm : Grace

159. Ink : Pen : Paper
(a) Watch : Dial : Strip (b) Book : Paper : Words
(c) Farmer : Plough : Field (d) Colour : Brush : Canvas

160. Class : School : Student
(a) Ball : Bat : Pitch (b) Sister : Family : Brother
(c) Hand : Body : Finger (d) Leaf : Tree : Root

161. Bone : Skeleton : Nerve
(a) House : Door : Window (b) Spoke : Wheel : Handle
(c) Retina : Eye : Pupil (d) Snow : Cloud : Ice

162. Lion : Cow : Land
(a) Water : Land : Air
(b) Whale : Hippopotamus : Water
(c) Chair : Table : Stool
(d) England : Germany : USA

163. Stump : Cricket : Point
(a) Duce : Dribble : Racket (b) Diamond : Pitcher : Hit
(c) Dribble : Hockey : Corner (d) Penalty : Shoot : Boxing

164. Complexion : White : Black
(a) Alert : Intelligent : Babies
(b) Health : Disease : Hospital
(c) Train : Bus : Journey
(d) Officer : Honest : Corrupt

165. Talk : Whisper : Shout
(a) Boredom : Tiredness : Rest
(b) Touch : Hold : Embrace
(c) See : Look : Watch
(d) Create : Form : Make

166. Play : Win : Lose
(a) Accident : Death : Survive
(b) Examination : Success : Determination
(c) Read : Book : Magazine
(d) Music : Dance : Art

167. Clay : Potter : Pots
(a) Doctor : Injection : Pills
(b) Cloth : Tailor : Clothes
(c) Blackboard : Chalk : Teacher
(d) Electricity : Bulb : Light

DIRECTIONS ~ (Q. Nos. 168-180) *In the following questions, find out the correct pair of words which will make an appropriate analogical relationship between the two words to the left of the sign of double colon and the same relationship between the two words to the right of the sign of double colon (::).*

168. A : Ship :: Platform : B
(a) A. Caption, B. Coolie (b) A. Port, B. Station
(c) A. Quay, B. Train (d) A. Shore, B. Bench

169. A : Roots :: House : B
(a) A. Branches, B. Walls (b) A. Trunk, B. Floor
(c) A. Flower, B. Walls (d) A. Tree, B. Foundation

170. A : Square :: Arc : B
(a) A. Line, B. Circle
(b) A. Perimeter, B. Circumference
(c) A. Line, B. Diameter
(d) A. Rectangle, B. Chord

171. A : Flower :: Milky way : B
(a) A. Plant, B. Sky (b) A. Fruit, B. Planet
(c) A. Plant, B. Galaxy (d) A. Garden, B. Star

172. A : Water :: Thermometer : B
(a) A. Humidity, B. Fever
(b) A. Pitcher, B. Mercury
(c) A. Rain, B. Doctor
(d) A. Evaporation, B. Temperature

173. A : Winter :: B : Malaria
(a) A. Quilt, B. Quinine (b) A. Cold, B. Epidemic
(c) A. Cold, B. Mosquito (d) A. Wool, B. Fever

174. Explosion : I :: Locust : II
I. (A) Bomb (B) Ruin (C) debris (D) Smoke
II. (P) Crop (Q) Holocaust (R) Pest (S) Field
(a) AS (b) BR (c) CQ (d) DP

175. A : Dog :: B : Goat
(a) A. Puppy, B. Pony (b) A. Puppy, B. Lamb
(c) A. Bitch, B. Lamb (d) A. Colt, B. Pony

176. A : Gardening :: Bat : B
(a) A. Grass, B. Playing (b) A. Flowers, B. Ball
(c) A. Spade, B. Cricket (d) A. Gardner, B. Cricket

177. A : Prune :: Hair : B
(a) A. Wool, B. Shear (b) A. lawn, B. Mow
(c) A. Beard, B. Shave (d) A. Shrub, B. Trim

178. A : Herd :: Star : B
(a) A. Cattle, B. Constellation
(b) A. Wolves, B. Solar-System
(c) A. Sheep, B. Sum
(d) A. Fish, B. Planet

179. I. Canada :: Rangoon : II
I. (A) Detroit (B) Florida (C) Toronto (D) Alberta
II. (P) Indonesia (Q) Burma (R) East Pakistan (S) Ceylon
(a) BQ (b) CP (c) CQ (d) CS

180. I : Bird :: Shedding : II
I. (A) Calling (B) Flying (C) Migrating (D) Moulting
II. (P) Barn (Q) Dog (R) Hay (S) Farm
(a) BP (b) BR (c) DP (d) DS

DIRECTIONS ~ (Q. Nos. 181-185) *In the following questions, find out the correct word which will make an appropriate analogical relationship between the given words.*

181. Person, son : Forget, get : Engage,?
(a) eng (b) age (c) ganga (d) english

182. Doomday, Doom : Highest, High : Master,?
(a) Mastic (b) Mast (c) Star (d) Roster

183. Image, a : Hollywood, y : Calliness,?
(a) t (b) e (c) i (d) a

184. HAND, AND : TEAR, EAR : STAB,?
(a) TAB (b) STA (c) BAT (d) MAT

185. Coldly, old : Golden, old : Plastic,?
(a) stic (b) plas (c) last (d) tic

Answers / WITH EXPLANATIONS

1. (*a*) As, 'Stream' is produced by 'River', similarly 'Current' is produced by 'Ocean'.

2. (*a*) The role of a 'Editor' is publishing a 'Magazine', in the same way the role of a 'Director' is to direct a 'Drama'.

3. (*b*) Rectangle is formed by extending the line.

4. (*a*) Former is the language of the latter country.

5. (*b*) As, a 'Tailor' makes 'Dress', similarly a 'Carpenter' makes 'Furniture'.

6. (*c*) Genuine means Authentic. Similarly, Mirage means illusion.

7. (*a*) 'Prima facie', is a latin expression and the meaning of this is 'On the first view'. In the same way the meaning of 'In part delicto' is 'Both parties equally at fault'.

8. (*b*) As, sound of a 'Nightingale' is 'Warble', similarly, sound of a 'Frog' is 'Croak'.

9. (*a*) 'Monotony' is the antonym of 'Variety' and similarly, 'Crudeness' is the antonym of 'Refinement'.

10. (*b*) Second is robbed by the first.

11. (*a*) Second is the larger form of the first.

12. (*b*) 'Pyramid' is situated in 'Egypt' and 'Eiffel Tower' is situated in 'France'.

13. (*c*) As 'Wrist' is joined with the' Hand', similarly, 'Ankle' is joined with the foot.

14. (*c*) 'Smell' is found in 'flower' and 'Taste' is found in 'food'.

15. (*a*) As, 'Fire' can lead to 'Annihilation', similarly 'Earthquake' can lead to 'Cataclysm'.

16. (*d*) Second is result of the first.

17. (*c*) Former is used to manufacture the latter.

18. (*c*) As temperature is measured by 'thermometer', similarly humidity is measured by 'hygrometer'.

19. (*a*) Both, 'Abduct' and 'Kidnap' are synonyms to each other. In the same way, 'Solicit' and 'Request' are synonyms to each other.

20. (*d*) As, the work is measured in Joule. Similarly, the area is measured in Hectare.

21. (*d*) Second is the playing place of the first.

22. (*a*) Latter represents the movements of former.

23. (*d*) 'Pituitary' is the gland present in the 'Brain' and 'Thymus' is the gland present in the 'Chest'.

24. (*b*) As, farmer works in field. Similarly, Astronomer works in observatory.

25. (*c*) Latter is the Parliament of the country represented by former.

26. (*c*) As 'Ocean' is related to 'Water', in the same way 'Glacier' is related to 'Ice'.

27. (*c*) A group of ministers is called council. Similarly, a group of sailors is called crew.

28. (*d*) The words are synonyms of each other. So, synonym of Chagrin is Annoyance.

29. (*a*) As, Rink is the playing place of Skating. Similarly, Court is the playing place of Tennis.

30. (*c*) 'Cup' is related to 'Crockery' in the same way as 'Pen' is related to 'Stationery'.

31. (*a*) Cub is the young one of the lion, Similarly, Calf is the young one of the cow.

32. (*b*) As a 'Clock' measures 'Time', similarly 'Distance' is measured in 'Metres'.

33. (*d*) Person incharge of a 'Museum' is known as 'Curator'. Likewise person incharge of a 'Prison' is called 'Jailor'.

34. (*c*) 'Hour' is the third position after 'Second' in time measurement. Likewise 'Tertiary' is the third position after 'Primary' in the order of ranking.

35. (*b*) 'Fire' reduces anything to 'Ashes' in the same way as 'Explosion' reduces anything to 'Debris'.

36. (*c*) The supreme law making authority of 'Great Britain' is known as 'Parliament'. In the same way, law making supreme body of 'USA' is known as 'Congress'.

37. (*a*) The symbol 'Logo' is related to 'Sports'. Likewise 'Emblem' is related to a 'Nation'.

38. (*c*) 'Data Processing' is the process of using 'Raw Data' to shape it in the final product. Likewise 'University' is the place which shapes the 'Students' for their career.

39. (*c*) 'Braille' is the technique of reading and writing for the blind persons. Similarly, 'Sign language' is the technique of reading and writing for deaf persons.

40. (*d*) 'Oar' is a device used to push a 'Boat'. Likewise 'Paddle' is used to push the 'Bicycle'.

41. (*c*) One of the outcomes of a 'Match' is 'Victory'. Likewise 'Success' is one of the outcomes of 'Examination'.

42. (*c*) Second denotes the trait for which first is used.

43. (*c*) In army and air force 'Major' and 'Squadron Leader' are equivalent ranks and so are 'Lieutenant' and 'Flying Officer'.

44. (*b*) 'Tie' is worn on the 'Neck' and 'Belt' is worn on the 'Waist'.

45. (*c*) First constitutes the second.

46. (*a*) 'Petals' constitute a 'Flower', likewise 'Pages' constitute a 'Book'.

47. (*d*) As, Needle is used for sewing, similarly microscope is used for magnifying.

48. (*b*) As, 'Cardiologist' is a heart specialist, similarly 'Neurologist' is a brain specialist.

49. (*a*) 'Pasture' is collection of 'Grass' and 'Sentence' is a collection of 'Words'.

50. (*c*) 'Tissue' is made up of 'Cells' and 'Organ' is made up of 'Tissues'.

51. (*b*) 'Buyer' is the source of income for the 'Vendor'. Likewise 'Client' is the source of income for 'Consultant'.

52. (*c*) 'Coach' guides the 'Player'. In the same way, 'Teacher' guides the 'Pupil'.

53. (*b*) 'Save' and 'Rescue' are same in meaning and 'Severe' and 'Stern' are also same in meaning.

54. (*d*) 'Ignite' leads to 'Combustion' and 'Trigger' leads to violent 'Reaction'.

55. (*d*) As, 'Disease' can be cured by taking proper 'Medicine', similarly Famine can be avoided by adequate 'Rainfall'.

56. (*b*) As, 'Go' is opposite to 'Come', similarly 'High' is opposite to 'Low'.

57. (*d*) Poverty and Prosperity are antonyms to each other. Similarly, Intelligence and Stupidity are antonyms to each other.

58. (*b*) As, cow gives milk. Similarly, hen gives egg.

59. (*d*) As, 'Chapter' is a part of 'Book'. similarly, 'Room' is a part of 'House'.

60. (*b*) As, 'Chair' is made of 'Wood', similarly, 'Mirror' is made of 'Glass'.

61. (*d*) 'Taj Mahal' is located in 'Agra' and in the same way 'Golden Temple' is located in 'Amritsar'.

62. (*a*) As, 'Zoology' is the branch of science dealing with the study of 'Animals', similarly 'Physiology' is the branch of science dealing with the study of 'Body'.

63. (*d*) As, a 'Spider' makes 'Web', similarly a 'Poet' creates 'Poetry'.

64. (*d*) As, Group of academic staff (teachers) is called faculty, similarly, group of trucks is called fleet.

65. (*a*) 'Hoof ' is related to 'Horse', in the same way, 'Foot' is related to 'Man'.

66. (*c*) 'Geetanjali' is written by 'Tagore' and 'Oliver Twist' is written by 'Dickens'.

67. (*b*) As, 'Bud' grows and becomes a 'Flower'; similarly, 'Sapling' grows and becomes a 'Tree'.

68. (*c*) 'Ideas' are stored in 'Brain' and 'Money' is stored in 'Bank'.

69. (*a*) 'Frankness' and 'Blunt' are synonyms and so are 'Rise' and 'Awake'.

70. (*c*) As, 'Love' and 'Hate' are antonyms to each other, similarly up and down are antonyms of each other.

71. (*c*) They both are antonyms of each other 'Mendacity' means untruthfulness, which is the opposite of honesty. In the same way 'Craven' means coward which is antonym of 'Courageous'.

72. (*a*) As, Push in higher intensity of Touch. Similarly shout is higher intensity of speak.

73. (*c*) A person who is 'Capricious' loses 'Reliability'. In the same way, if a person is 'Tenacious', loses 'Practicality'.

74. (*b*) 'Water' contains 'Oxygen' in it and 'Salt' contains 'Sodium' in it.

75. (*a*) 'Geeta' and 'Quran' belong to the same class, *i.e.,* religious books and 'Orange' and 'Mango,' also belong to the same class, *i.e.,* fruits.

76. (*c*) 'Sin' is related to 'Crime', in the same way, 'Morality' is related to 'Legality'.

77. (*c*) 'Cream' is made from 'Milk'. Likewise, 'Pottery' is made from 'Clay'.

78. (*c*) 'Loathe' and 'Coercion' are related to each other. In the same way 'Irate' and 'Antagonism' are related to each other.

79. (*a*) As, a group of players is known as Team. Similarly, a group of flowers is known as Bouquet.

80. (*c*) As, 'Umpire' is in a 'Game', in the same way 'Legislator' is in an 'Election'.

81. (*c*) 'Sky' and 'Earth' are related to each another, in the same manner as 'Fly' and 'Walk'.

82. (*a*) All are the sounds produced by animals.

83. (*c*) All are metals.

84. (*d*) All are human sensory organs.

85. (*d*) All are internal organs of human body.

86. (*b*) All are the measuring units of electricity.

87. (*a*) All are food crops.

88. (*c*) All are parts of tree.

89. (*a*) All are sounds produced by animals.

90. (*c*) All are wild animals.

91. (*c*) All are young ones of animals.

92. (*d*) All are industrial towns famous for steel plants.

93. (*a*) All are classical forms of Indian dance.

94. (*c*) All are dwelling places of animals.

95. (*c*) All are female animals.

96. (*c*) All are the names of Hindu goddesses.

97. (*c*) All are the cities of Uttar Pradesh.

98. (*a*) All are European countries.

99. (*b*) All are natural calamities.

100. (*d*) All are terms related to quantitative measurement.

101. (*b*) All are alloys.

102. (*a*) All are rodents.

103. (*a*) All are the sounds produced by animals.
104. (*c*) All are reptiles.
105. (*a*) All are stationery items.
106. (*c*) All are Indian cricketers.
107. (*a*) All are precious stones.
108. (*d*) All are terms of cricket.
109. (*c*) All are Pakistani cities.
110. (*d*) All are branches of medical sciences.
111. (*d*) All are synonyms.
112. (*a*) All are the names of rivers.
113. (*c*) 'Leap' is the movement of rabbit; 'Frisk' is the movement of 'Lamb' and 'Trot' is the movement of 'Donkey'.
114. (*b*) All are stationery items.
115. (*c*) All are week days.
116. (*a*) They have two vowels 'a' and 'e'.
117. (*d*) None of the options is correct as they are the names of currencies.
118. (*d*) 'Jaipur' is the capital of 'Rajasthan'; 'Bengaluru' is the capital of 'Karnataka' and 'Mumbai' is the capital of 'Maharashtra'.
119. (*c*) 'Colombo' is the capital of Sri Lanka; 'Kathmandu' is the capital of 'Nepal' and 'Havana' is the capital of 'Cuba'.
120. (*d*) 'Squeak' is the sound produced by Mice; 'Hiss' is the sound produced by Snake and 'Howl' is the sound produced by Jackal.
121. (*b*) 'Kathak' is the classical dance of North India; 'Bharatnatyam' is the classical dance of Tamilnadu while 'Odissi' is the classical dance of Orissa.
122. (*b*) Indira and Nehru were the Prime Ministers of India, while Benazir was the Prime Minister of Pakistan.
123. (*d*) All are former Indian cricketers.
124. (*c*) 'Folketing' is the parliament of 'Denmark'; 'Stortling' is the parliament of 'Norway', 'Knesset' is the parliament of Israel.
125. (*c*) 'Pitcher' is a term used in Baseball; 'Dusra' is a term used in Cricket and 'Bunker' is a term used in Polo.
126. (*d*) These all are snakes.
127. (*c*) These all are units of distance.
128. (*d*) All are parts of furniture.
129. (*d*) All are stationery items.
130. (*c*) All creep and hence they come under the class of reptiles.
131. (*d*) All are the cities of USA.
132. (*c*) 'Moscow' is the capital of 'Russia', 'Paris' is the capital of France and 'Athens' is the capital of Greece.
133. (*b*) All are capital cities of India. 'Kohima' is the capital of Nagaland; 'Lucknow' is the capital of Uttar Pradesh; 'Chennai' is the capital of Tamil Nadu.
134. (*a*) 'Kyat' is the currency of Myanmar; 'Yuan' is the currency of China and 'Baht' is the currency of Thailand.
135. (*c*) All are the units of time.
136. (*d*) All represent group. 'Crowd' is a group of people; 'Shoal' is a group of fish and 'Team' is a group of players.
137. (*a*) All are the names of parliaments. 'Duma' is the parliament of Russia; Majlis is the parliament of Iran/Maldives/Malaysia and 'Khural' is the parliament of Mangolia.
138. (*c*) Young ones of given animals are called cub.
139. (*c*) All are cereals.
140. (*c*) All are games.
141. (*b*) All are insects.
142. (*c*) All are females.
143. (*b*) All work in the hospital.
144. (*d*) All are rivers.
145. (*a*) All are dress parts.
146. (*b*) All are insects.
147. (*c*) All the given names are port towns.
148. (*d*) All the given names are planets.
149. (*b*) All are the types of fuel.
150. (*c*) All are headwears.
151. (*a*) All are oil seeds.
152. (*c*) All are bollywood 'Actors'.
153. (*c*) A 'Correspondent' gathers and formats 'News' for 'Newspaper' and similarly a 'Farmer' grows and reaps 'Crops' for 'Food'.
154. (*d*) All the three belong to the same class. 'Iron', 'Silver' and 'Gold' are all metals and similarly 'Dear', 'Lion' and 'Wolf' are all wild animals.
155. (*c*) 'Bus' moves on 'Road' and is driven by 'Driver'. Likewise 'Aeroplane' flies in the 'Sky' and is driven by 'Pilot'.
156. (*b*) 'Bangle' is meant for 'Wrist' which is a part of 'Hand'. Similarly, Anklet is meant for 'Ankle' which is a part of 'Foot'.
157. (*a*) Music is performed with Guitar by the 'Performer'. Likewise, 'Trick' is performed with 'Rope' by the 'Acrobat'.
158. (*c*) 'Tragedy' has 'Sadness' and brings 'Tears'. Likewise 'Comedy' has 'Humour' and brings 'Laughter'.
159. (*d*) First is required to work with the second on the third.
160. (*c*) Third is a part of the first which, in turn, is a part of the second.
161. (*c*) First and third both are the parts of the second.
162. (*b*) 'Lion' and 'Cow' are 'land' animals and similarly 'Whale' and 'Hippopotamus' are 'water' animals.
163. (*c*) 'Stump' and 'Point' are the terms used in 'Cricket' and similarly 'Dribble' and 'Corner' are the terms used in 'Hockey'. Hence, first and last are the terms used in the second.
164. (*d*) As 'Complexion' may be 'White' or 'Black', similarly, 'Officer' can be 'Honest' or 'Corrupt'.
165. (*c*) 'Talk', 'Whisper' and 'Shout' are different terms related with speech. Likewise, 'See', Look' and 'Watch' are the different terms related with glance.
166. (*a*) As 'Win' and 'Lose' are the two outcomes of 'Play', similarly, 'Death' and 'Survival' are the two outcomes of 'Accident'.
167. (*b*) As 'Potter' uses 'Clay' to make 'Pots', similarly, 'Tailor' uses 'Cloth' to make Clothes.
168. (*c*) First is the place where second stops temporarily.
169. (*d*) Second is the lowest part of the first.
170. (*a*) First is a part of the second.
171. (*d*) Second is a part of first.
172. (*b*) First contains the second.
173. (*a*) First provides protection from second.
174. (*c*) Second is the left over after the action of first.
175. (*b*) First is the young one of second.
176. (*c*) First is used in the second.
177. (*d*) Second represents after cutting off the unnecessary parts of the first.
178. (*a*) Second is the collective group of first.
179. (*c*) Second denotes the country in which the city denoted by the first is located.
180. (*d*) Birds undergo moulting to shed feathers in changing plumage. Similarly, farms undergo shedding of leaves before a new growth.
181. (*b*) As,

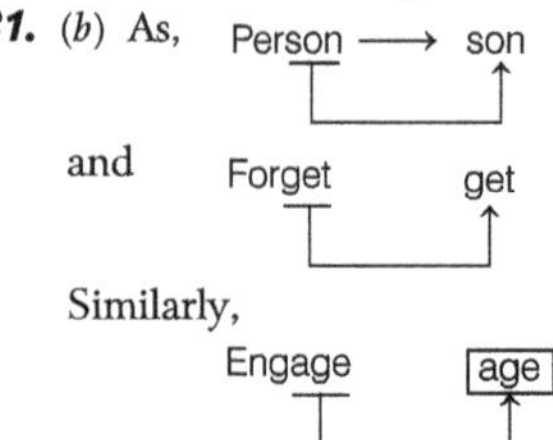

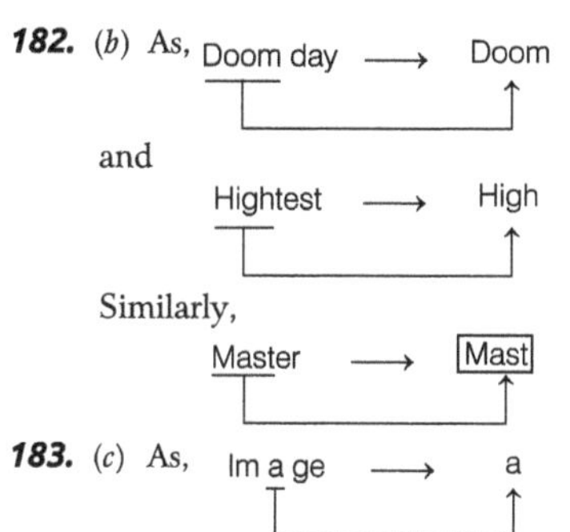

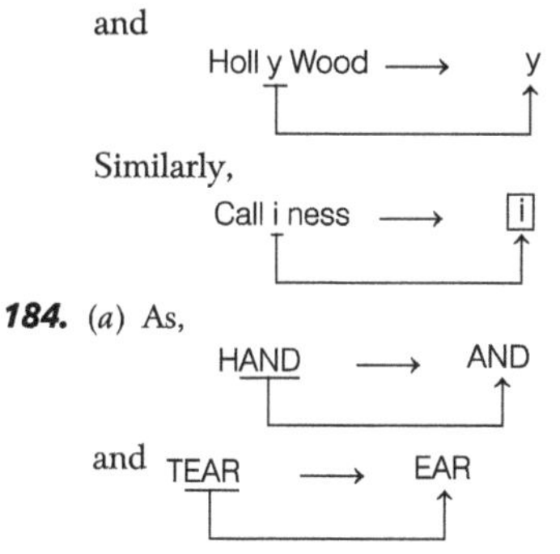

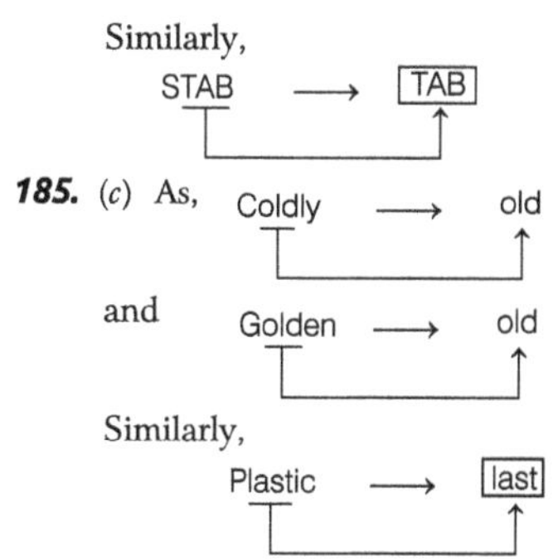

TYPE 02

Alphabet Analogy

In this type of analogy, there is a relationship between the given alphabets/letters or group of alphabets/letters. The candidate is required to find out the relationship between the given letters/alphabets or group of letters/alphabets then choose either a letter/alphabet group which is related in the same way to a third group provided in the question or a pair consisting of similarly related letter/alphabet groups.

To solve the problems based on alphabet analogy, the candidates are suggested to keep in mind the letters/alphabets position (forward and backward), opposite letters, vowels and consonants.

Forward Letter Positions (Left to Right)

A	B	C	D	E	F	G	H	I	J	K	L	M
1	2	3	4	5	6	7	8	9	10	11	12	13
N	O	P	Q	R	S	T	U	V	W	X	Y	Z
14	15	16	17	18	19	20	21	22	23	24	25	26

Backward Letter Positions (Right to Left)

A	B	C	D	E	F	G	H	I	J	K	L	M
26	25	24	23	22	21	20	19	18	17	16	15	14
N	O	P	Q	R	S	T	U	V	W	X	Y	Z
13	12	11	10	9	7	7	6	5	4	3	2	1

Opposite Letters

A	B	C	D	E	F	G	H	I	J	K	L	M
↕	↕	↕	↕	↕	↕	↕	↕	↕	↕	↕	↕	↕
Z	Y	X	W	V	U	T	S	R	Q	P	O	N

Vowels	A	E	I	O	U					
Consonants	B	C	D	F	G	H	J	K	L	M	N
	P	Q	R	S	T	V	W	X	Y	Z	

Below are some examples related to alphabet analogy

Ex 18 Select the related letters from the given alternatives.

EFG : HIJ : : PQR : ?

(a) STU (b) RST (c) TUS (d) SUT

Solution **(a)** Here, in both the pairs, each letter of the first letter group is replaced by the letter which is 3 positions ahead of that letter in the alphabetical series to obtain the second letter group.

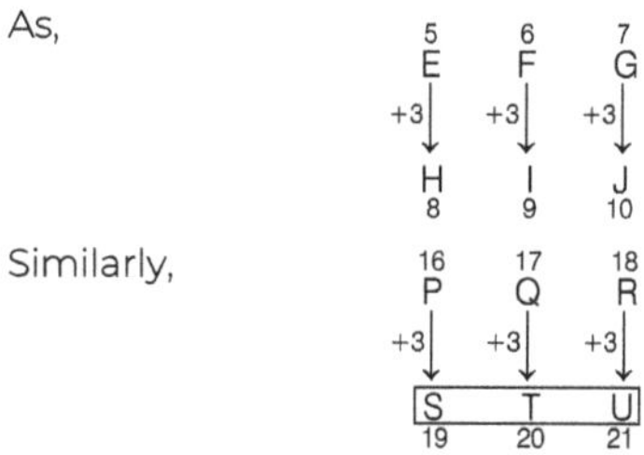

Ex 19 Select the related letters from the given alternatives.

UVW : RST : : MNO : ?

(a) OPR (b) LJK (c) JKL (d) KLM

Solution **(c)** Here, in both the pairs, each letter of the first letter group is replaced by the letter which is 3 positions behind of that letter in the alphabetical series to obtain the second letter group.

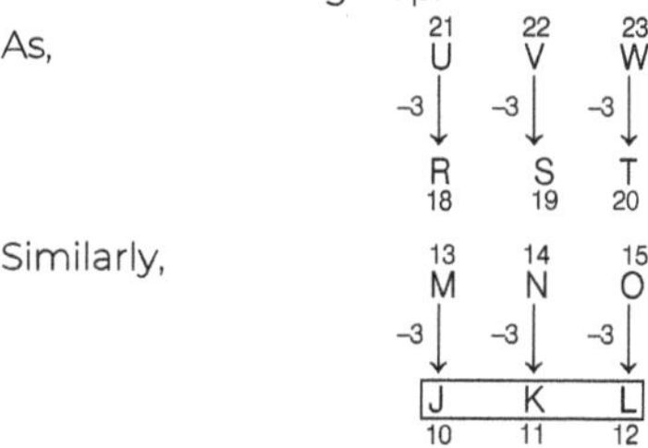

Ex 20 Select the related letters from the given alternatives.

VMR : ZIS : : AKT : ? « RRB ALP 2018

(a) HIR (b) EGU (c) FHS (d) EOU

Solution (b) The given pattern is as follows

As, V → (+4) → Z, M → (−4) → I, R → (+1) → S

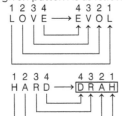

Similarly, A → (+4) → E, K → (−4) → G, T → (+1) → U

EGU

Ex 21 Select the related letters from the given alternatives.

LOVE : EVOL : : HARD : ?

(a) DARH (b) AHRD (c) DRAH (d) HDRA

Solution (c) The given pattern is as follows,

As, 1 2 3 4 → 4 3 2 1
L O V E → E V O L

Similarly, 1 2 3 4 → 4 3 2 1
H A R D → DRAH

Ex 22 Select the related letters from the given alternatives.

WUS : DFH : : MKI : ? « SSC (CGL) 2017

(a) LJH (b) GEC (c) OQS (d) NPR

Solution (d) Here, in both the pairs opposite letters in English alphabetical orders are given.

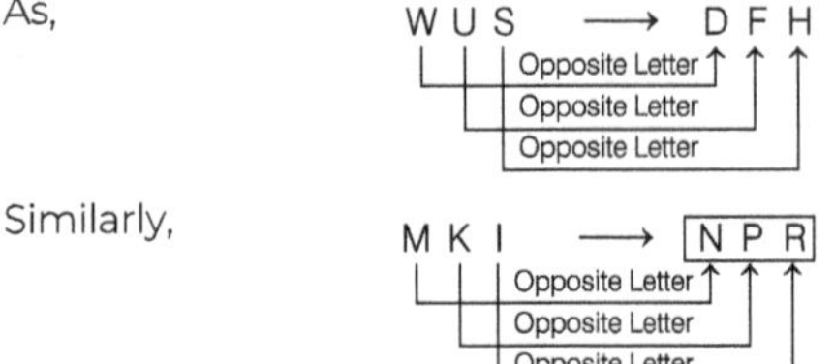

Ex 23 Select the related letters from the given alternatives.

NEUROTIC : TICRONEU : : PSYCHOTIC : ? « IBPS (Clerk) 2013

(a) TICCOHPSY (b) TICOCHPSY
(c) TICCHOPSY (d) TICHCOPSY
(e) None of these

Solution (c) As, NEU | RO | TIC → TIC | RO | NEU

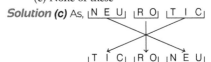

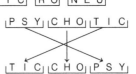

Similarly, PSY | CHO | TIC → TIC | CHO | PSY

Ex 24 Select the related letters from the given alternatives.

TSR : FED : : WVU : ? « SSC (Pre) 2016

(a) CAB (b) MLK (c) PQS (d) GFH

Solution (b) As,

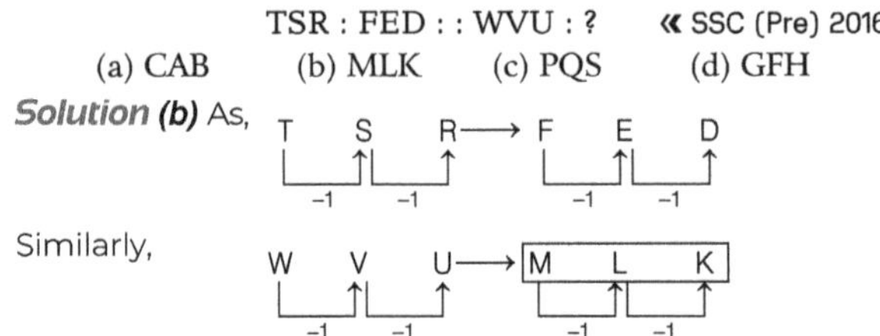

Ex 25 Select the related word which replace the question mark (?) from the given alternatives.

Fit, Feat, Sit, Seat, Bid, ?

(a) Bed (b) Beit (c) Beat (d) Bead

Solution (d) The given pattern is as follows,

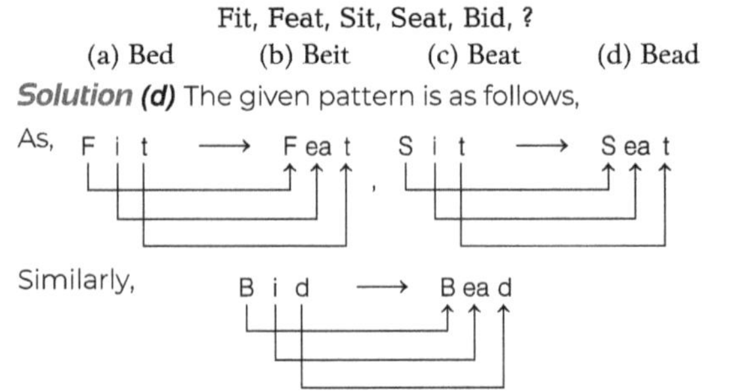

Practice CORNER 2.2

DIRECTIONS ~ (Q. Nos. 1-32) *In each of the following questions, there is some relationship between the two terms to the left of (::) and the same relationship holds between the two terms to its right. Also, in each question, one term either to the right of (::) or to the left of it is missing. This term is given as one of the alternatives given below each question. Find out this term.*

1. GIKM : HJLN : : PRTV : ? « RRB (ALP) 2018
(a) QSUW (b) QSUX (c) QSTU (d) NOSW

2. EGIK : LJHF : : SUWY : ? « SSC (10 + 2) 2015
(a) ZXVT (b) TVXZ (c) LNPR (d) MOQS

3. UHCDN : VIDEO : : OKZXDQ : ? « SSC (CGL) 2016
(a) REPLAY (b) REPOSE (c) PLAYER (d) OPPOSE

4. MN : OP : : QR : ?
(a) PR (b) TQ (c) ST (d) TV

5. HNP : JPR : : QRS : ? « SSC (10 + 2) 2017
(a) KNO (b) STU (c) NQR (D) TZA

6. CINQ : EXPS :: FRGS : ? « SSC MTS 2019
(a) HTIU (b) HITU (c) ITJU (d) HTUI

7. BFG : EIJ : : RVW : ? « SSC (MTS) 2014
(a) UWY (b) UYZ (c) SWX (d) QUV

8. ACPQ : BESU : : MNGI : ? « CSAT 2020
(a) NPJL (b) NOJM (c) NPIL (d) NPJM

9. TULIP : ZAROV : : SCALP : ? « SSC (Delhi Police Constable) 2017
(a) HRIGV (b) YIGRV (c) PRIHV (d) VHPRG

10. LMK : STR : : IJH : ? « SSC (Steno) 2016
(a) PQO (b) YAZ (c) VNM (d) WXZ

11. ACEG : IKMO : : PRTV : ?
(a) QRUW (b) JLMP (c) WXAC (d) XZBD

12. ABCDE : FGHIJ : : PQRST : ?
(a) TSRQP (b) UVWXY (c) KLMNO (d) EDCBA

13. QTU : ILM : : BEF : ?
(a) PSZ (b) CFH (c) WZA (d) UXB

14. RTU : SUW : : CEF : ? « SSC (10 + 2) 2018
(a) FGI (b) DGH (c) EGF (d) DFH

15. QPRS : TUWV : : JIKL : ?
(a) NMOP (b) NMPO (c) MNPO (d) MNOP

16. CLOSE : DNRWJ : OPEN : ?
(a) PRJO (b) RPJB (c) PRHR (d) RZWR

17. BOTTLE : CQWXQK : : FILLED : ? « SSC (Steno) 2016
(a) GKOPJJ (b) GKOPJK (c) GKPOJJ (d) GHOPJJ

18. HCM : FAK : : SGD : ?
(a) QEB (b) QIB (c) ESQ (d) GES

19. ENGINE : CLEGLC : : ? : KMRMP
(a) METER (b) ROTAR (c) MOTOR (d) GEARN

20. MAD : JXA : : RUN : ? « SSC (Steno) 2016
(a) OSQ (b) PRJ (c) UXQ (d) ORK

21. EJOT : ? : : YDIN : VAFK « SSC (Steno) 2016
(a) LQGB (b) BGLQ (c) QBGL (d) BGQL

22. FILM : ADGH : : MILK : ? « SSC (CGL) 2015)
(a) ADGF (b) HDGE (c) HDGF (d) HEGF

23. NEEDLE : MFDEKF :: BUCKET : ? « SSC CPO 2019
(a) AVBLDS (b) CVDLFS (c) AVBLDU (d) CVBLDU

24. GOAT : DQYW : : TRES : ? « SSC (10+2) 2020
(a) HUMO (b) PSBU (c) RSDW (d) QTCV

25. RMSK : SLUI : : KMFZ : ? « RRB (NTPC) 2016
(A) HKIB (B) LHKX (C) LIHB (D) LLHX
(a) C (b) B (c) D (d) A

26. AFHO : CHFM : : GBDJ : ?
(a) GBIM (b) GBLD (c) GPLD (d) IDBH

27. AZBY : CXDW : : EVFU : ? « SSC (Steno) 2016
(a) GHTS (b) TGSH (c) GTHS (d) GSTH

28. SAND : QCLF : : DUNE : ?
(a) BWLG (b) BWLH (c) BVLG (d) BWMG

29. PAN : TDM : : SIP : ?
(a) KMG (b) KLG (c) PAM (d) WLO

30. CFZ : HIU : : ...... : JLS « SSC (CPO) 2018
(a) EIX (b) EHW (c) FHX (d) EIY

31. ACB : GIH : : KML : ?
(a) TRS (b) RTS (c) RST (d) RTU

32. FGEHJ : BCADF : : VWUXZ : ?
(a) NKLMO (b) GFBAC (c) HIJKL (d) OPNQS

33. 'NQ' is related to SJ in the same way as 'DG' is related to
(a) JM (b) IK (c) IZ (d) HK

34. 'WT' is related to FQ in the same way as 'FC' is related to
(a) KH (b) OZ (c) ZW (d) GK

35. 'ERID' is related to 'DIRE' in the same way as 'RIPE' is related to
(a) EPIR (b) PERI (c) EPRI (d) PEIR
(e) IPRE

36. 'MORE' is related to 'EORM' in the same way as 'SUIT' is related to
(a) TIUS (b) IUST (c) ISTU (d) TUIS
(e) None of these

37. 'PURPLE' is related to 'LERPPU' in the same way as 'GARDEN' is related to
(a) ENRDBA (b) ENARGA (c) ENDRGA (d) ENRDGA

38. 'FG' is related to 'VU' in the same way as 'YZ' is related to
(a) CB (b) AC (c) WX (d) UV

DIRECTIONS ~ (Q. Nos. 39-54) *These questions are based on certain relation. Find out the particular letters which are related to the letters given in questions.*

39. MARKET : TEKRAM : : SATURN : ? « SSC (MTS) 2017
(a) NRUTAS (b) NRTUAS
(c) NRUATS (d) NURTAS

40. PARULK : APURKL : : BUFTGK : ?
(a) GKFUTB (b) UFGTKB
(c) UGFTBK (d) UBTFKG

41. FLOWER : REOWLF : : FRUITS : ?
(a) STRUIF (b) STUIRF (c) STIURF (d) STUIFR

42. REFORM : OREFRM : : ACTION : ? « SSC (CPO) 2018
(a) NOITCA (b) NOTICA (c) CTOINA (d) IOCTAN

43. NURTURE : ERUTRUN : : PRANK : ?
(a) KNARP (b) NKARP (c) KNPRA (d) PNARK

44. SNOP : ONSP : : CLAY : ? « SSC (CGL) 2017
(a) ALCY (b) LCYA (c) LYCA (d) ACLY

45. acme : mace : : face : ?
(a) cefa (b) cfae (c) cfea (d) afce

46. AB : ZY : : CD : ?
(a) VU (b) WX (c) UV (d) XW

47. WUS : DFH : : MKI : ? « SSC (CGL) 2017
(a) LJH (b) GEC (c) OQS (d) NPR

48. MGR : NTI : : SPQ : ?
(a) EFG (b) KRP (c) QRC (d) HKJ

49. ABCD : WXYZ : : EFGH : ?
(a) STUV (b) STOU (c) STUE (d) TSUV

50. SANDY : HZMWB : : CRATE : ? « RRB (Group-D) 2018
(a) XIZVG (b) XIZGV
(c) XIGZV (d) XZIGV

51. PALE : LEAP : : POSH : ? « RRB (NTPC) 2016
(A) HSPO (B) HSOP (C) POSH (D) SHOP
(a) B (b) D (c) C (d) A

52. JUMBUCKS : SKCUBMUJ : : SHIPJACK : ? « RRB (ALP) 2018
(a) KCASPHIS (b) KCAIJPHS
(c) KCAJIPSH (d) KCAJPIHS

53. $\frac{M}{AC} : \frac{N}{AD} :: \frac{O}{AE} : ?$
(a) $\frac{P}{AF}$ (b) $\frac{Q}{AB}$ (c) $\frac{P}{AC}$ (d) $\frac{R}{AD}$

54. $\frac{ABC}{F} : \frac{BCD}{I} :: \frac{CDE}{L} : ?$
(a) $\frac{DEF}{O}$ (b) $\frac{DEF}{N}$ (c) $\frac{EDF}{O}$ (d) $\frac{DEF}{M}$

DIRECTIONS ~ (Q. Nos. 55-57) *Each of the following questions consists of a pair of letter groups that have a certain relationship to each other, followed by four other pairs of letter groups given as options. The candidates are required to choose the pair in which the letter groups are similarly related as in the given pair.*

55. JT : NX « SSC MTS 2019
(a) TP : XT (b) RK : VG
(c) GS : KU (d) LD : PG

56. JKLM : NGPI
(a) ABCD : EFGH (b) PINK : NKIP
(c) PQRS : TMVO (d) SLOW : OHUX

57. WHITE : HWIET
(a) PRANK : KNPRA (b) BLACK : LBAKC
(c) BROWN : ORBWN (d) BOOK : OOBK

DIRECTIONS ~ (Q. Nos. 58-64) *In the following questions, given words are related to each other in a particular manner and you have to find the word from the given alternatives which bears exactly same relationship.*

58. POT → TOPE; FIN → NIFE; LIT → ?
(a) TILO (b) TILE (c) LITE (d) TILL

59. bit → tub; nib → bun; tin → ?
(a) nit (b) nut (c) int (d) nti

60. dam → mad; net → ten; drab → ?
(a) bread (b) bad (c) bard (d) drad

61. draw → ward; pots → stop; meat → ?
(a) taem (b) eatm (c) mate (d) team

62. tip → pit; gum → mug; pool → ?
(a) ploo (b) topo (c) lopo (d) loop

63. Bread → Bed; Flour → For; Wheat →?
(a) Wat (b) Wet (c) What (d) Whet

64. But → Tub; Sun → Nus; For → ?
(a) Orf (b) Rfo (c) Rof (d) Fro

Answers WITH EXPLANATIONS

1. (*a*) The given pattern is as follows,
As,
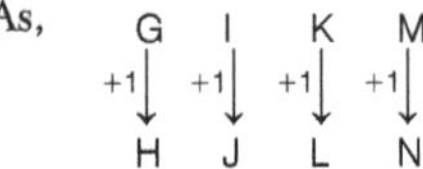
Similarly,
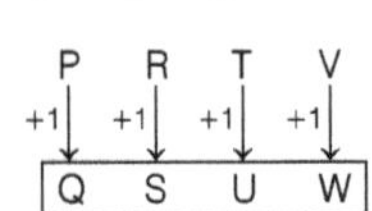

2. (*a*) As,
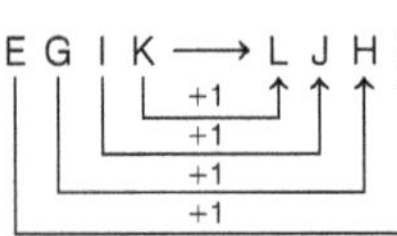
Similarly,
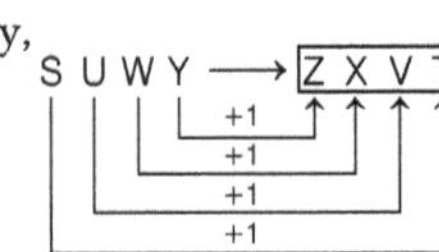

3. (*c*) As, U H C D N (+1 each) → V I D E O
Similarly,
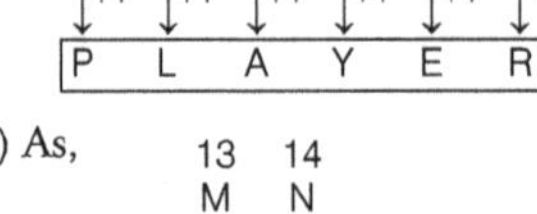

4. (*c*) As, 13 M, 14 N (+2 each) → O 15, P 16
Similarly,
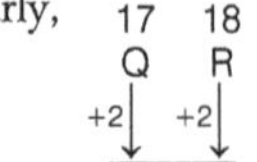

5. (*b*) As, H N P (+2 each) → J P R
Similarly, Q R S (+2 each) → S T U

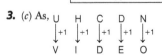

6. (*a*) As,
C —(+2)→ E
I —(+2)→ K
N —(+2)→ P
Q —(+2)→ S
Similarly,
F —(+2)→ H
R —(+2)→ T
G —(+2)→ I
S —(+2)→ U

7. (*b*) As,
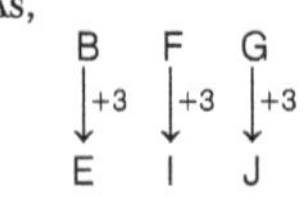
Similarly,
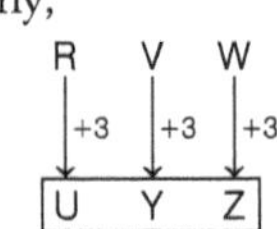

8. (*d*) As,

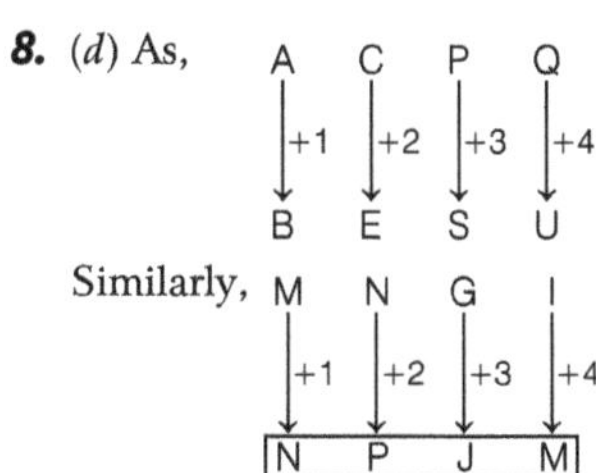

Similarly,

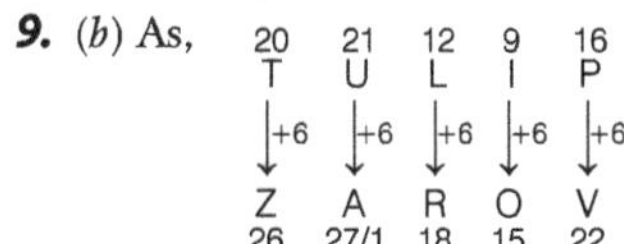

∴ ? ⇒ NPJM

9. (*b*) As,

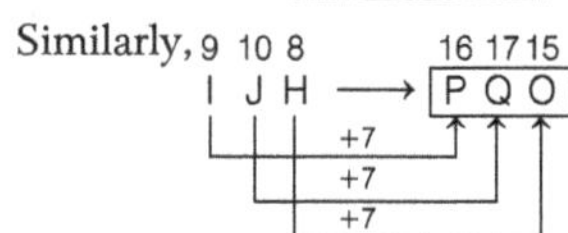

Similarly,

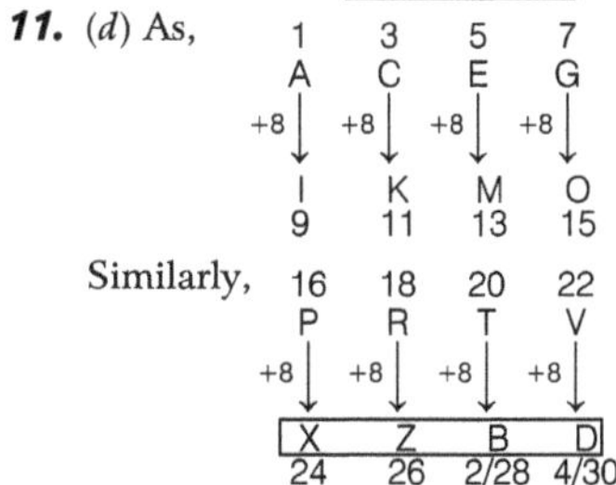

10. (*a*) As,

Similarly,

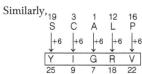

11. (*d*) As,

Similarly,

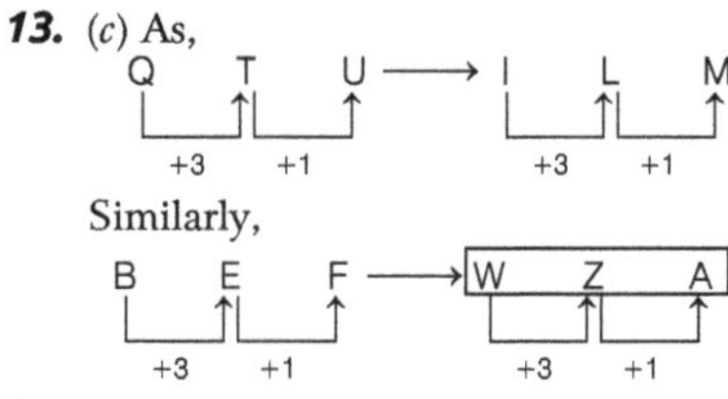

12. (*b*) ABCDE : FGHIJ :: PQRST : UVWXY

Letters of first and second parts are consecutive letters of english alphabet series.

13. (*c*) As,

Similarly,

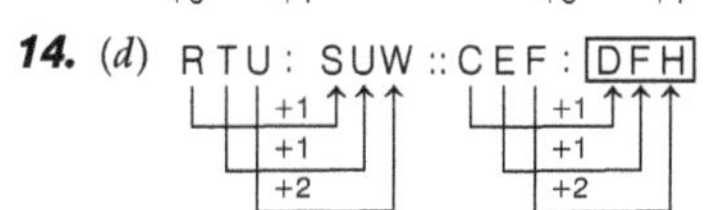

14. (*d*) RTU : SUW :: CEF : DFH

15. (*c*) As,

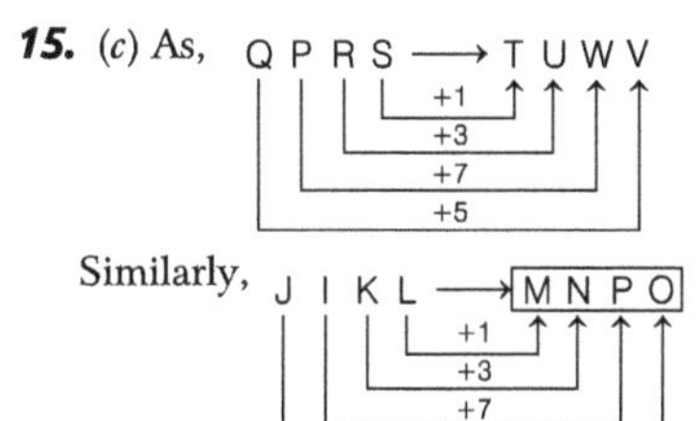

Similarly,

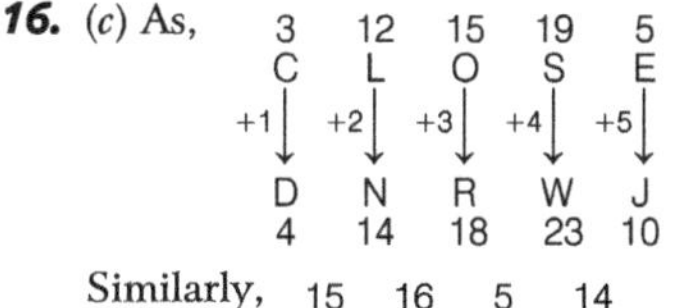

16. (*c*) As,

Similarly,

17. (*a*) As,

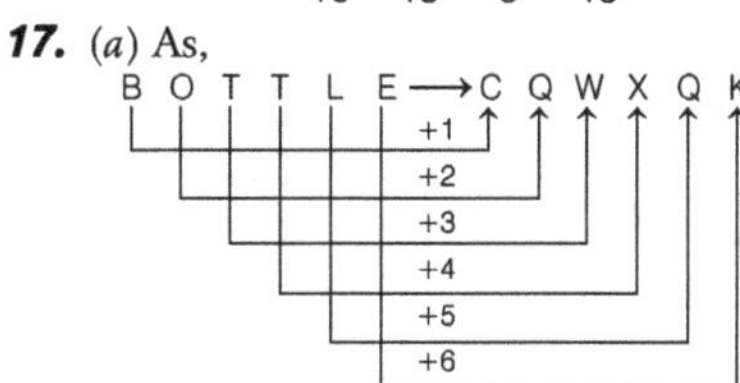

Similarly,

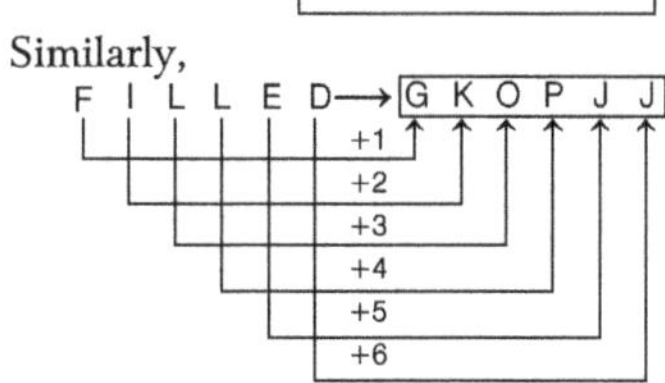

18. (*a*) As,

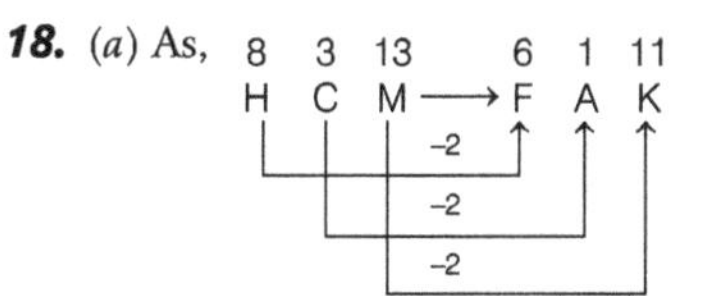

Similarly,

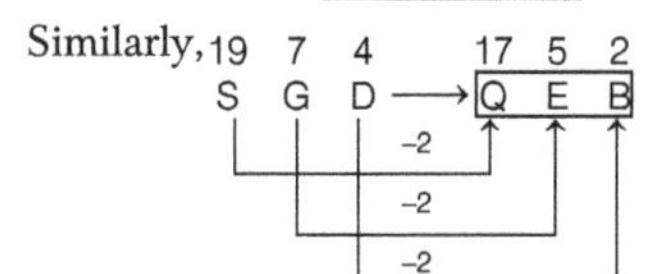

19. (*c*) As,

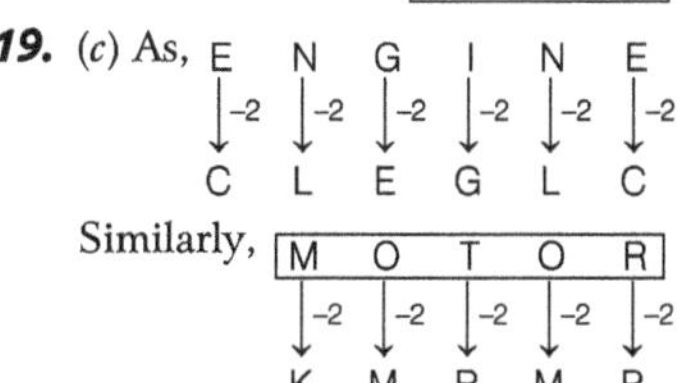

Similarly,

20. (*d*) As,

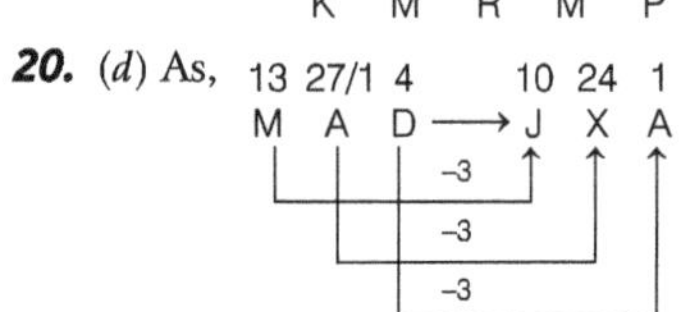

Similarly,

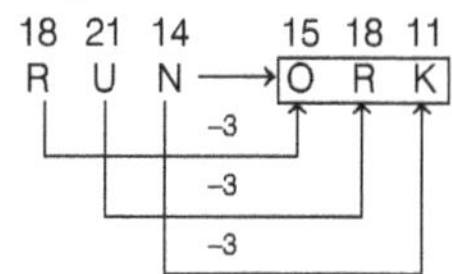

21. (*b*) As,

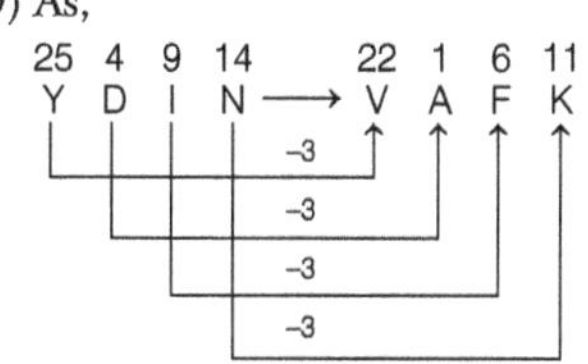

Similarly,

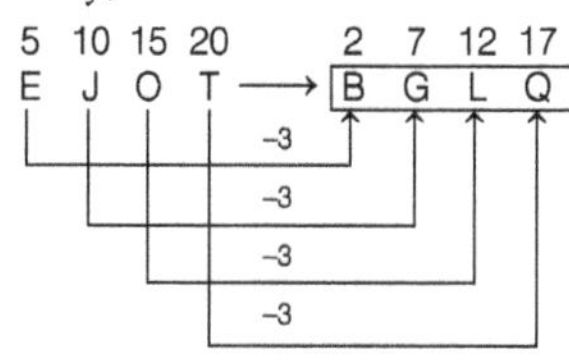

22. (*c*) As,

Similarly,

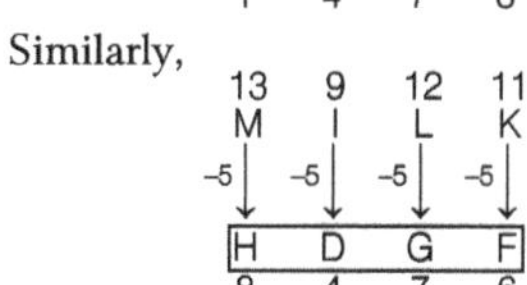

23. (*c*) As,

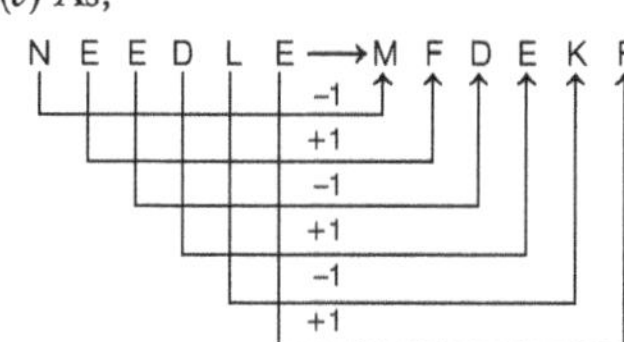

Similarly,

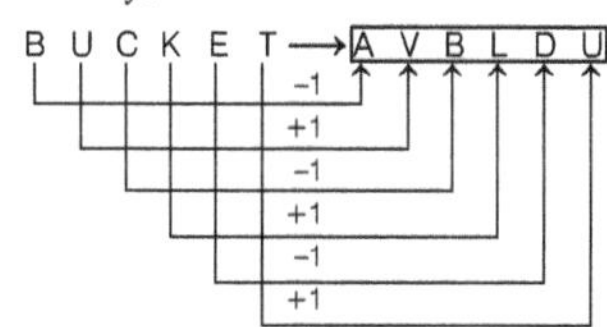

24. (*d*) As,

Similarly,

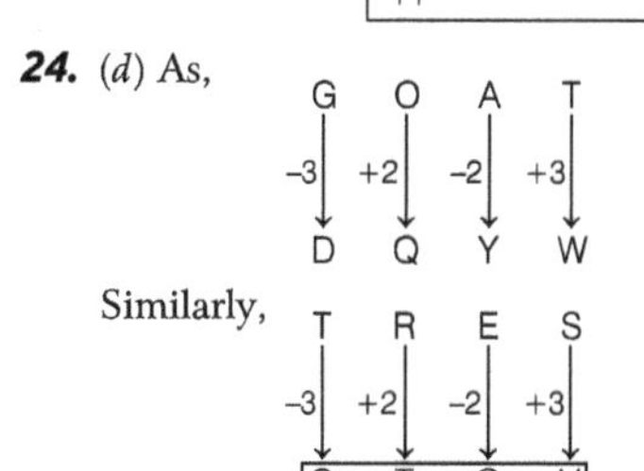

25. (*c*) As,

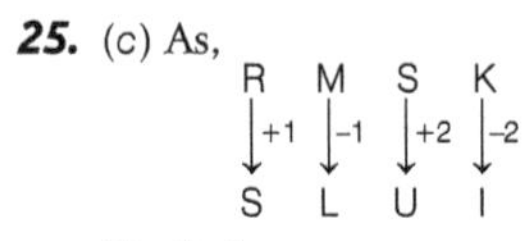

Similarly,

K M F Z → (+1, –1, +2, –2) → L L H X

26. (*d*) As,

A F H O → (+2, +2, –2, –2) → C H F M

Similarly,

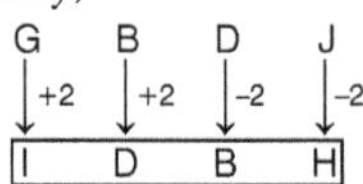

27. (*c*) As,

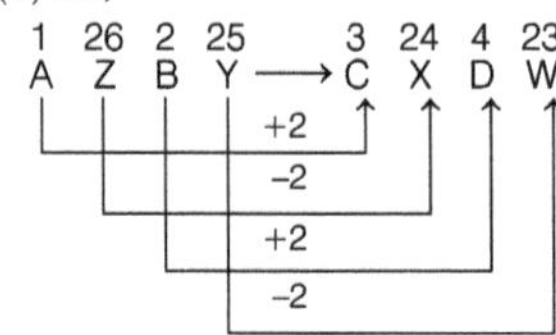

Similarly,

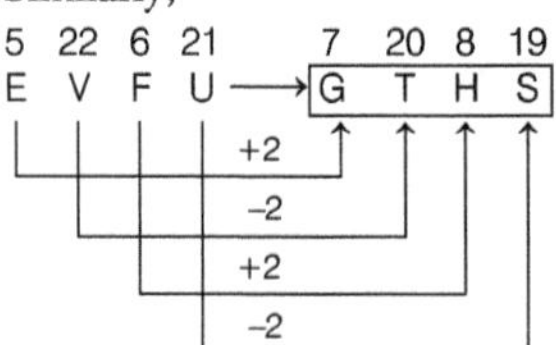

28. (*a*) As,

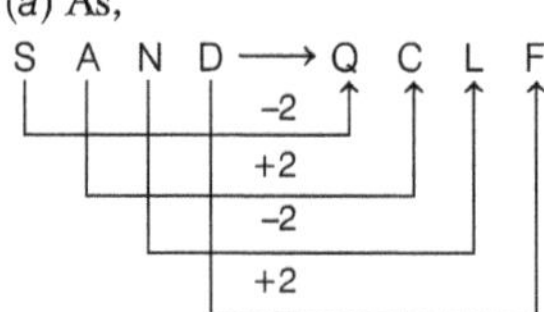

Similarly,

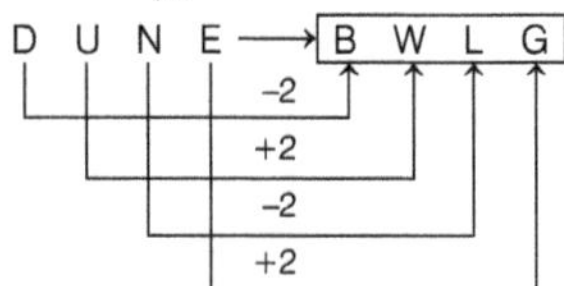

29. (*d*) As,

P A N → (+4, +3, –1) → T D M

Similarly,

S I P → (+4, +3, –1) → W L O

30. (*a*) As,

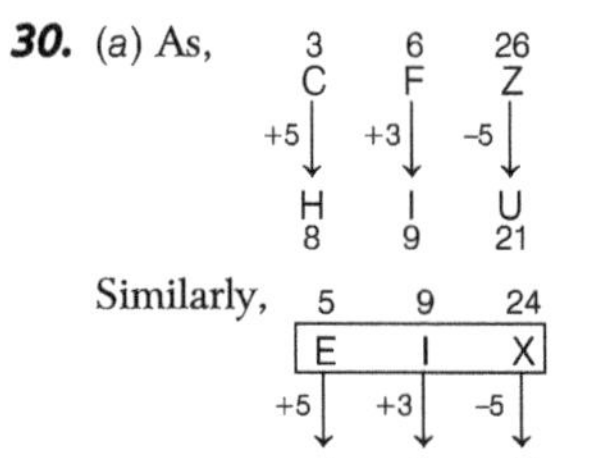

Similarly, 5 9 24 — E I X → (+5, +3, –5) → J L S (10 12 19)

31. (*b*) As,

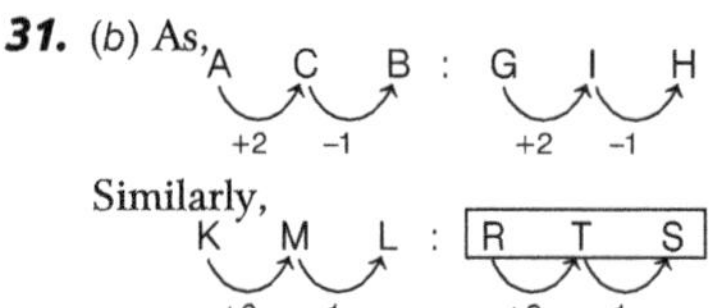

32. (*d*) As,

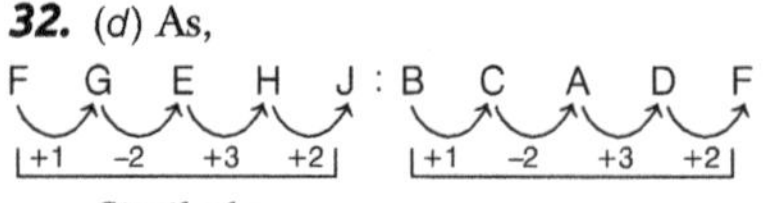

Similarly,

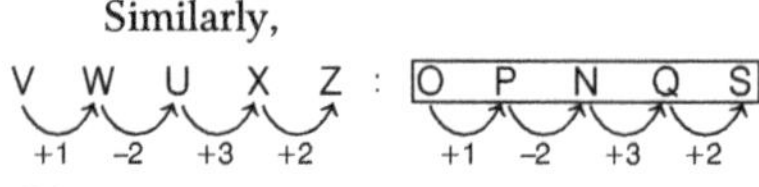

33. (*c*) As,

N —(+5)→ S

Q —(–7)→ J

Similarly,

D —(+5)→ I

G —(–7)→ Z

34. (*b*) As,

WT → FQ (+12, –6)

Similarly,

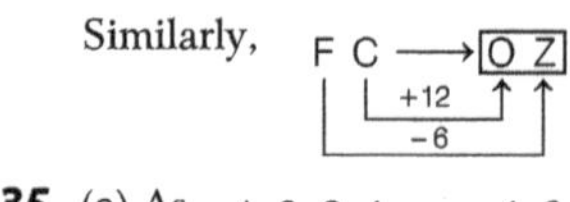

35. (*a*) As,

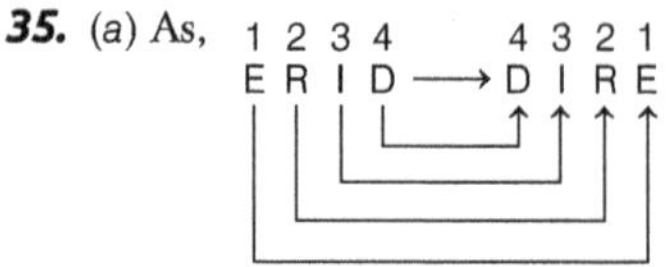

Similarly,

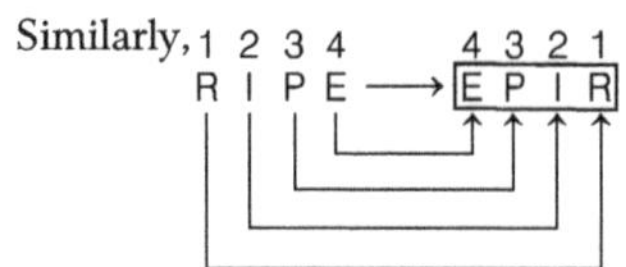

36. (*d*) As,

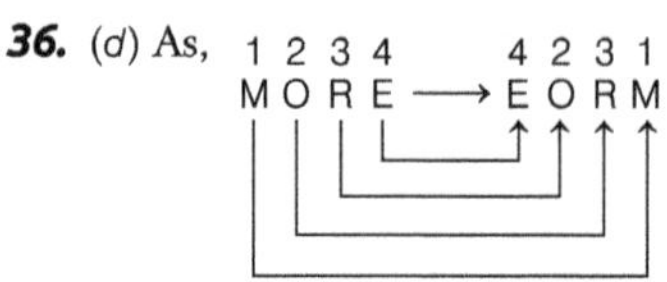

Similarly,

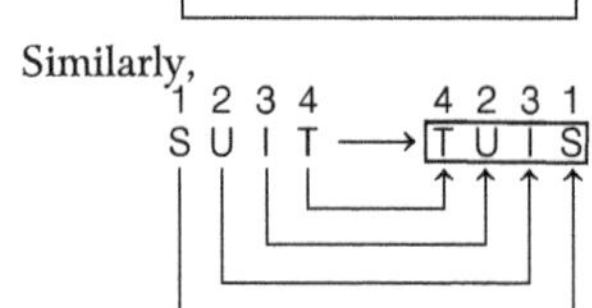

37. (*d*) As,

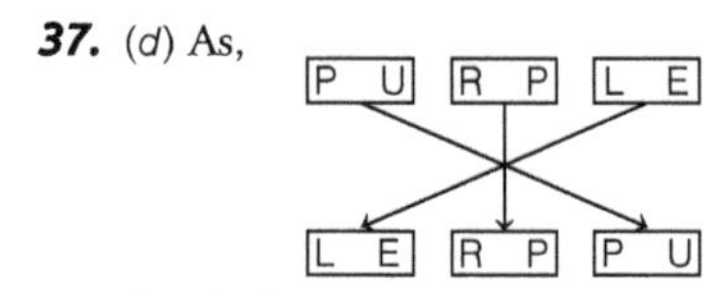

Similarly,

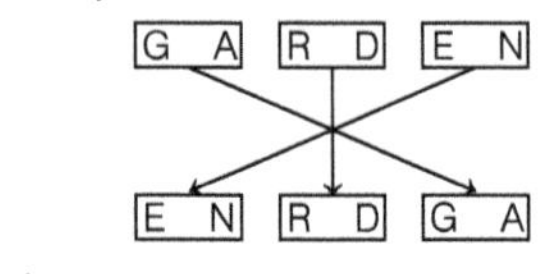

38. (*a*) As,

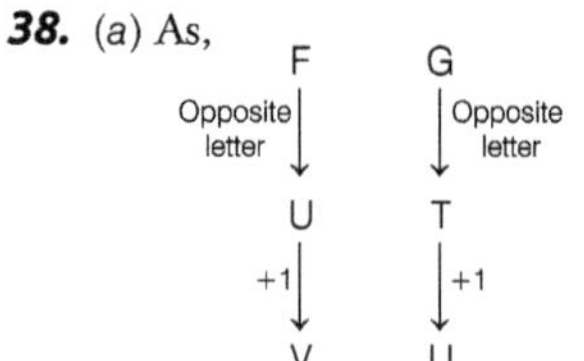

Similarly,

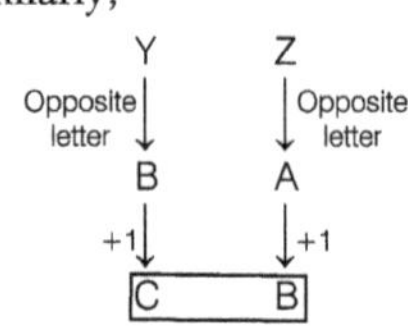

39. (*a*)

As, 1 2 3 4 5 6 MARKET → 6 5 4 3 2 1 TEKRAM

Similarly, 1 2 3 4 5 6 SATURN → 6 5 4 3 2 1 NRUTAS

40. (*d*)

As,

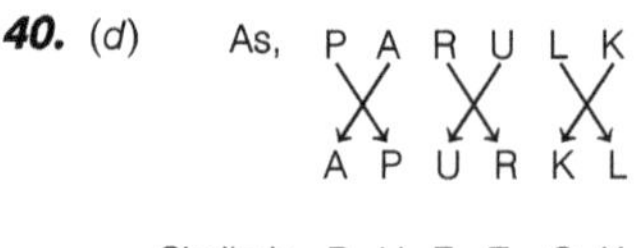

Similarly, B U F T G K → U B T F K G

41. (*b*) As,

1	2	3	4	5	6
F	L	O	W	E	R
R	E	O	W	L	F
6	5	3	4	2	1

Similarly,

1	2	3	4	5	6
F	R	U	I	T	S
S	T	U	I	R	F
6	5	3	4	2	1

42. (*d*) As,

1	2	3	4	5	6
R	E	F	O	R	M
O	R	E	F	R	M
4	5	2	3	1	6

Similarly,

1	2	3	4	5	6
A	C	T	I	O	N
I	O	C	T	A	N
4	5	2	3	1	6

43. (*a*) As,

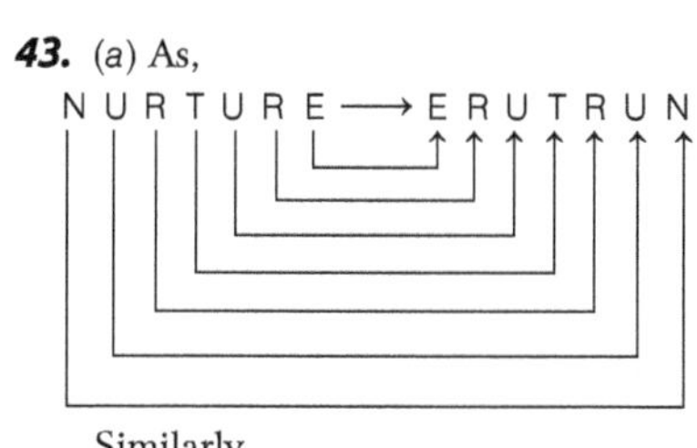

Similarly,

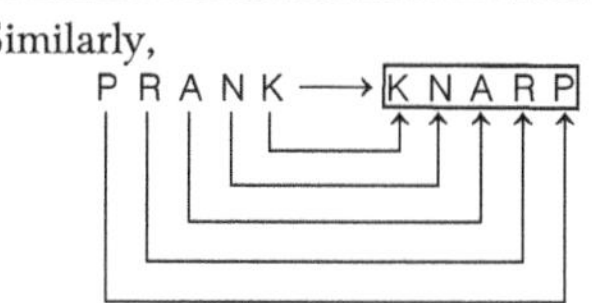

44. (*a*) As, 1 2 3 4 → 3 2 1 4
S N O P → O N S P
Similarly, 1 2 3 4 → 3 2 1 4
C L A Y → A L C Y

45. (*b*) As, a c m e → m a c e
1 2 3 4 → 3 1 2 4
Similarly, f a c e → c f a e
1 2 3 4 → 3 1 2 4

46. (*d*) As opposite letters of AB are ZY, similarly, opposite letters of CD are XW.

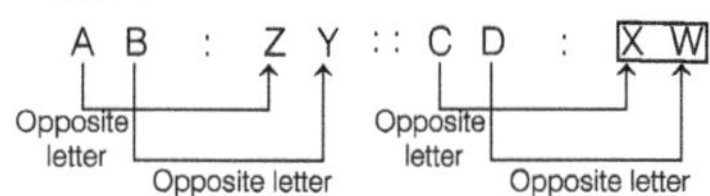

47. (*d*) As,

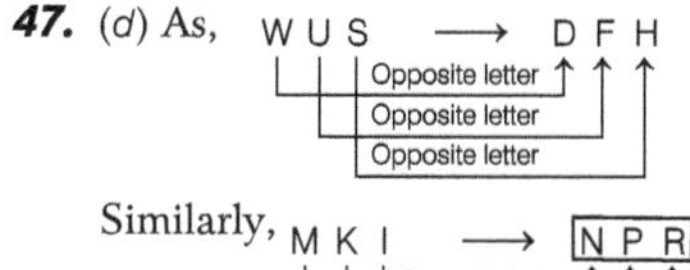

Similarly,

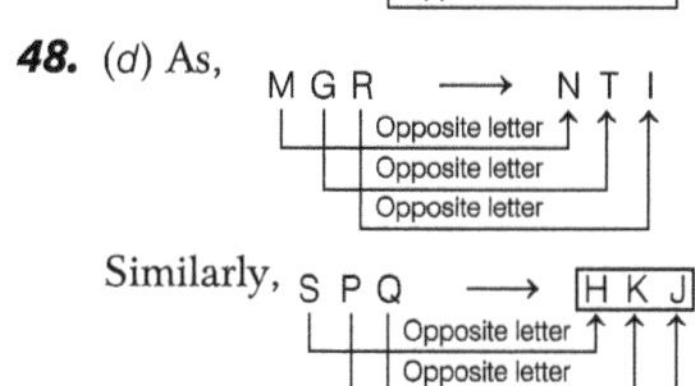

48. (*d*) As,

M G R → N T I (Opposite letter)

Similarly,

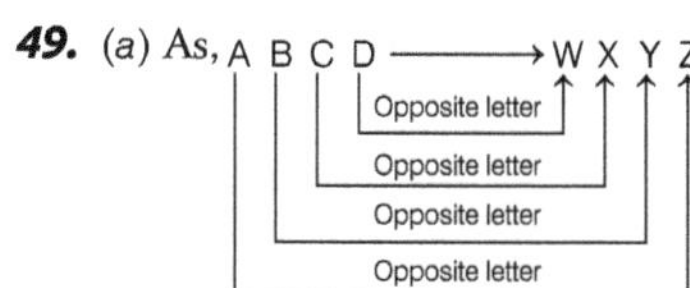

49. (*a*) As,

A B C D → W X Y Z (Opposite letter)

Similarly,

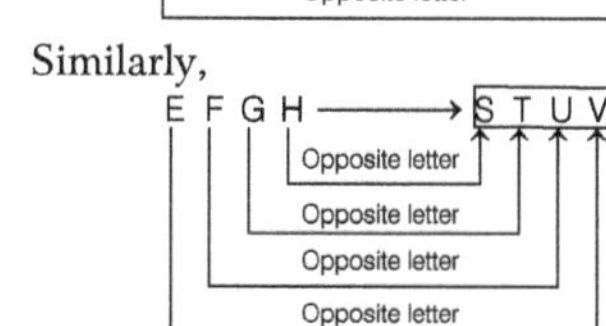

50. (*b*) As,

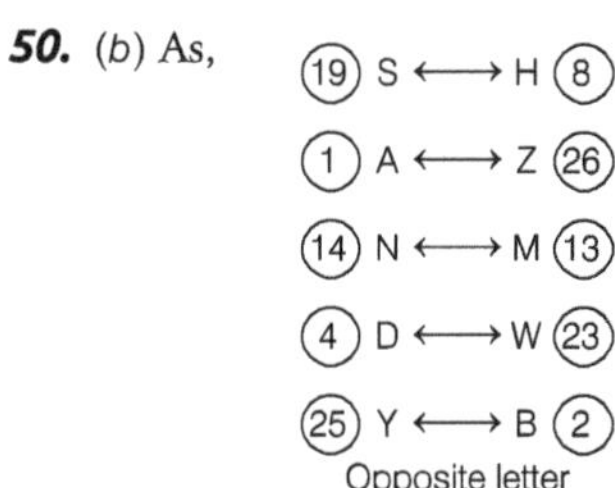

Similarly,

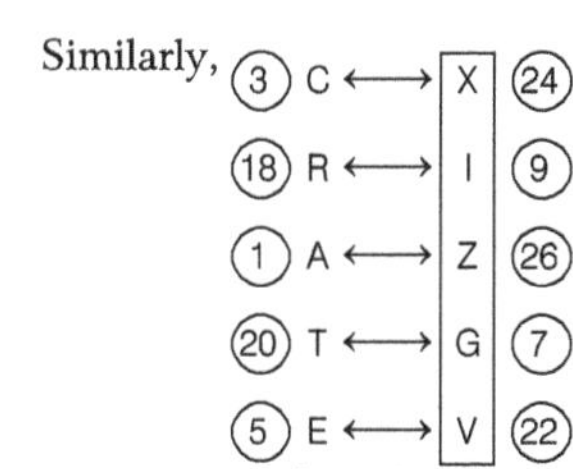

51. (*b*) As,

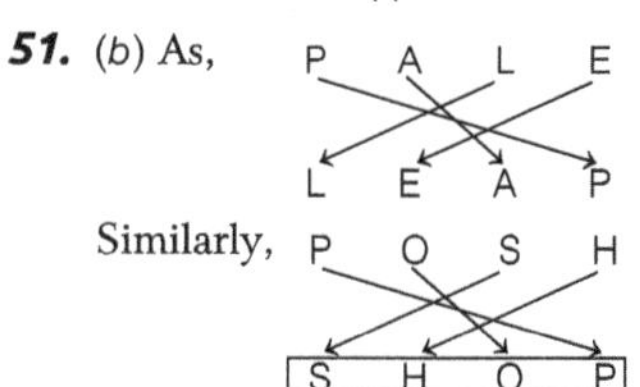

Similarly,

52. (*d*) The given pattern is as follows

As,

Similarly,

S H I P J A C K → K C A J P I H S

53. (*a*) As,

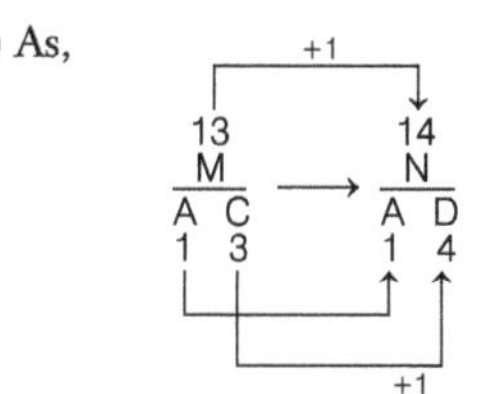

Similarly,

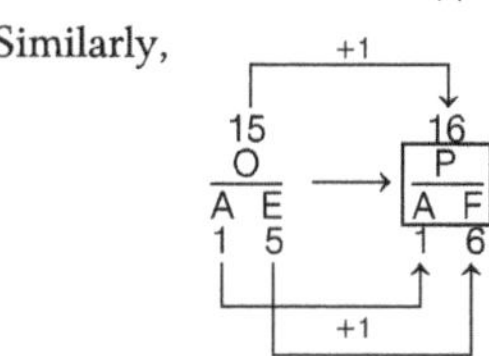

54. (*a*) As,

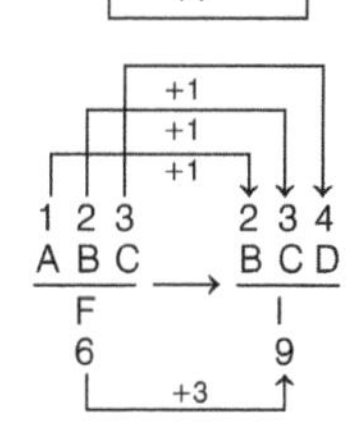

Similarly,

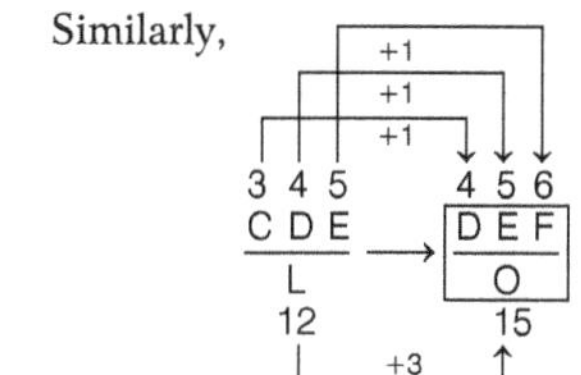

55. (*a*) As,

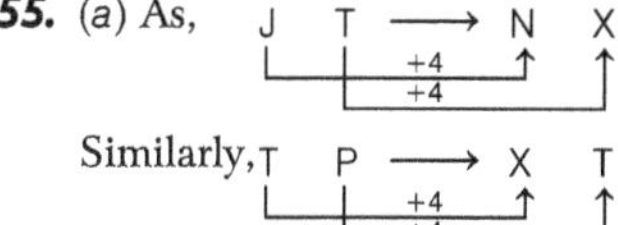

Similarly,

T P → X T (+4, +4)

56. (*c*) As,

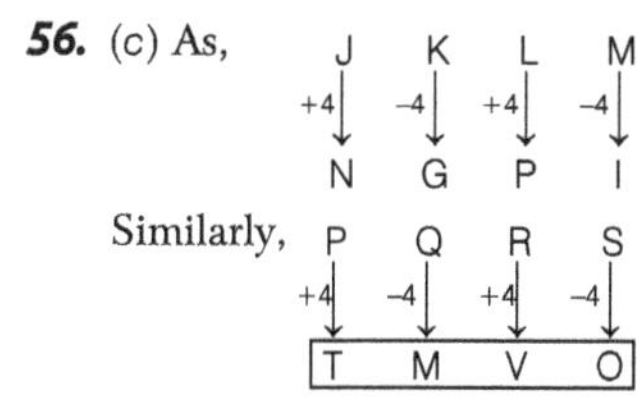

Similarly,

P Q R S (+4, −4, +4, −4) → T M V O

57. (*b*) As,

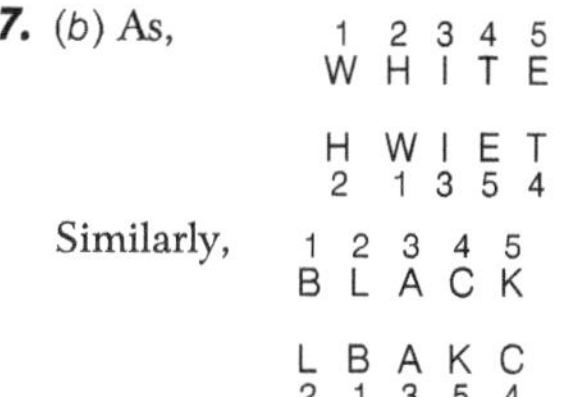

Similarly,

1 2 3 4 5
B L A C K

L B A K C
2 1 3 5 4

58. (*b*) As,

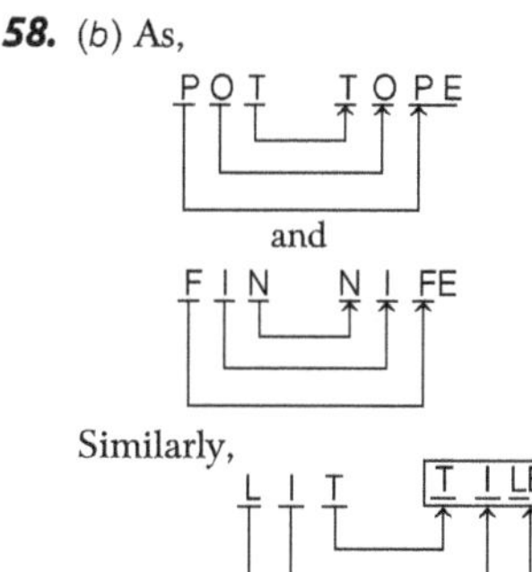

Similarly,

L I T → T I LE

59. (*b*) As,

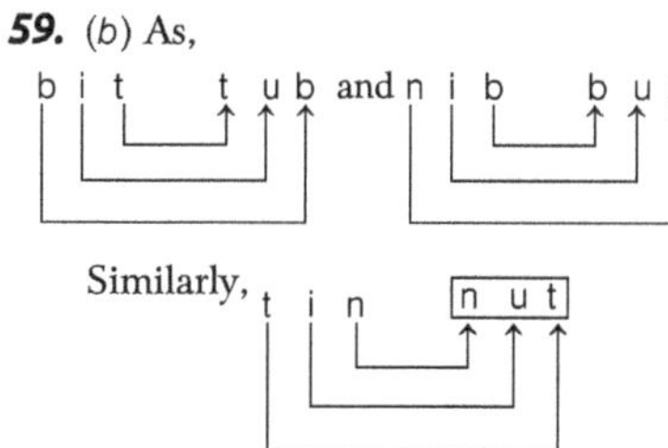

Similarly,

t i n → n u t

60. (*c*) As,

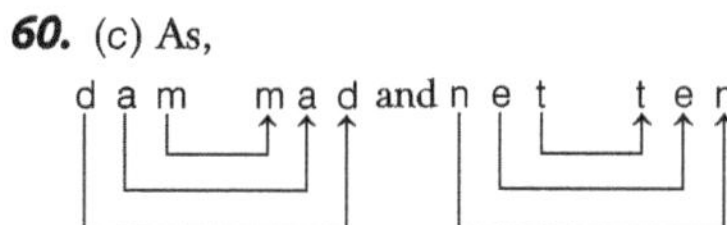

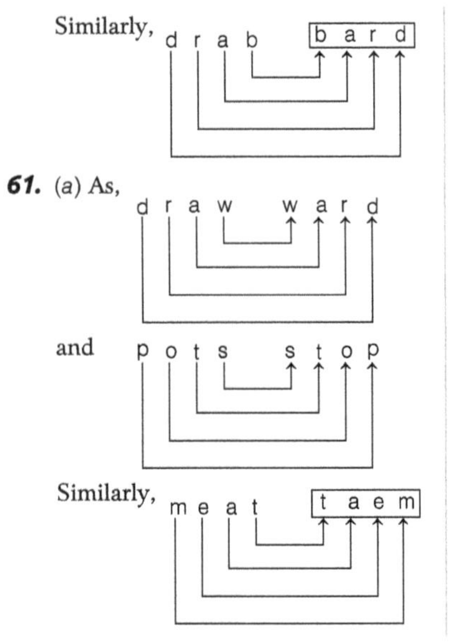

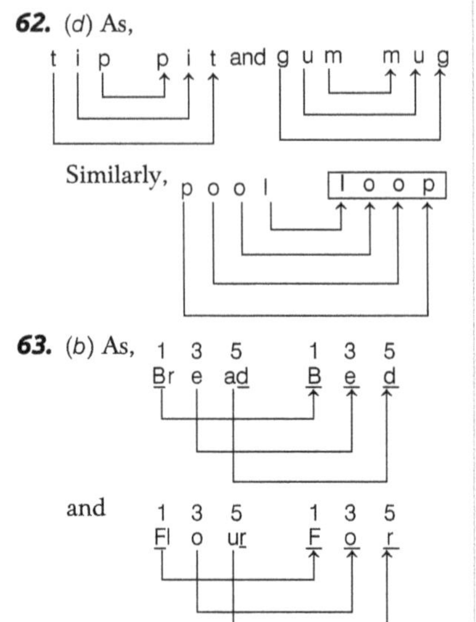

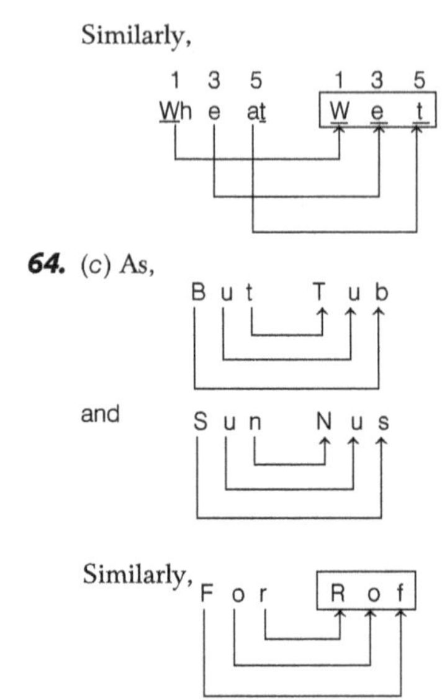

TYPE 03

Number Analogy

In the number analogy, numbers are given in a pair or in a group. The candidate is asked to find out the relationship between them and then find the number or group of numbers, which is having the same relation between/among them as in given pair. Such relationship is based on arithmetical operations like addition, subtraction, multiplication and division of numbers etc.

Number analogy based questions can be classified into following types

A. Choosing a Number

DIRECTIONS ~ (Example Nos. 26 and 27) *Choose a number which bears the same relationship with the third/four numbers as the first two bear.*

***Ex* 26** 8 : 56 : : 9 : ? « SSC (MTS) 2016

(a) 10 (b) 63 (c) 7 (d) 9

Solution ***(b)*** As, $8 \times 7 = 56$ Similarly, $9 \times 7 = \boxed{63}$

***Ex* 27** 386 : 383 : : 517 : ? « SSC (Steno) 2013

(a) 514 (b) 571 (c) 715 (d) 512

Solution ***(a)*** As, $386 - 3 = 383$ Similarly, $517 - 3 = \boxed{514}$

***Ex* 28** Select the option that is related to the third term in the same way as the second term is related to the first term.

6 : 18 : : 14 : ...... « SSC (CPO) 2018

(a) 64 (b) 98 (c) 108 (d) 70

Solution ***(b)*** As, $6 \times (6 \div 2) = 6 \times 3 = 18$

Similarly, $14 \times (14 \div 2) = 14 \times 7 = 98$

***Ex* 29** Select the missing number based on the given related pair of numbers. « RRB (ALP) 2018

27 : 65 : : 64 : ?

(a) 125 (b) 126 (c) 127 (d) 124

Solution ***(b)*** The given pattern is as follows

27 : 65 Similarly, 64 : ?

$(3)^3$ $(4)^3+1$ $(4)^3$ $(5)^3+1=\boxed{126}$

B. Choosing a Similarly Related Pair is the Given Number Pair

***Ex* 30** Choose the number pair which bears the same relationship.

3 : 27

(a) 2 : 8 (b) 3 : 9 (c) 4 : 36 (d) 5 : 120

Solution ***(a)***

As, 3 → 27 ($\times 3^2$) Similarly, 2 → 8 ($\times 2^2$)

OR As, $3 : 3^3$ so as $2 : 2^3$

C. Choosing a Number Similar to Set of Numbers

***Ex* 31** Choose one number which is similar to the numbers in the given set.

45, 54, 63

(a) 32 (b) 55 (c) 18 (d) 64

Solution ***(c)*** Digit sum of the given numbers are 9.

Let us see $45 = 4 + 5 = 9$, $54 = 5 + 4 = 9$, $63 = 6 + 3 = 9$

Hence, correct answer will be that alternative whose sum of digits is 9 and such alternative is 18 as $(1 + 8 = 9)$.

D. Choosing a Number Set Similar to a Given Number Set

Ex 32 Find out the set among the four sets which is like the given set (13 : 20 : 27). « SSC (10 + 2) 2013

(a) (3 : 11 : 18) (b) (18 : 25 : 32)
(c) (18 : 27 : 72) (d) (7 : 14 : 28)

Solution **(b)** As, 13 + 7 = 20 and 20 + 7 = 27
Similarly, 18 + 7 = 25 and 25 + 7 = 32

These are the indicative formats but number based analogy can be established based on several other patterns also.

Ex 33 Select the option in which the numbers are related in the same way as are the numbers in the given set.
(7, 15, 31) « SSC (10 + 2) 2020

(a) (6 : 13 : 21) (b) (5 : 625 : 6)
(c) (3 : 7 : 15) (d) (2 : 17 : 14)

Solution **(c)** As,

7 → 15 → 31 (×2+1, ×2+1)

Similarly,

3 → 7 → 15 (×2+1, ×2+1)

Practice / CORNER 2.3

DIRECTIONS ~ (Q. Nos. 1-38) *In each of the following questions, there is a certain relationship between two given numbers on one side of (::) and one number is given on another side of (::) where another number is to be found from the given alternatives, having the same relationship with this number as the numbers of the given pair bear. Choose the best alternative.*

1. 4 : 10 : : 8 : ? « IB (ACIO) 2017
(a) 10 (b) 13 (c) 17 (d) 14

2. 1, 2, 4, 7 : 3, 4, 6, 9 : : ? : 2, 3, 5, 8
(a) 0, 1, 3, 6 (b) 2, 4, 5, 8 (c) 1, 3, 4, 7 (d) 3, 5, 6, 8

3. 7 : 32 : : 28 : ? « SSC (CGL) 2016
(a) 126 (b) 136 (c) 116 (d) 128

4. 20 : 11 : : 102 : ?
(a) 49 (b) 52 (c) 61 (d) 98

5. 6 : 35: : 7 : ?
(a) 48 (b) 42 (c) 34 (d) 13

6. 14 : 9 : : 26 : ?
(a) 12 (b) 13 (c) 15 (d) 31

7. 100 : 121 : : 144 : ?
(a) 160 (b) 93 (c) 169 (d) 426

8. 3 : 27 : : 4 : ?
(a) 16 (b) 64 (c) 32 (d) 28

9. 7544 : 5322 : : 4673 : ?
(a) 2367 (b) 2451 (c) 2531 (d) 4472

10. 63 : 21 : : 27 :?
(a) 6 (b) 9 (c) 1 (d) 3

11. 64 : 144 : : 256 : ?
(a) 16 (b) 32 (c) 400 (d) 336

12. 35 : 66 :: 29 : ? « SSC MTS 2019
(a) 63 (b) 62 (c) 60 (d) 57

13. 11: 132 : : ? « SSC (CGL) 2014
(a) 15 : 250 (b) 10 : 100 (c) 9 : 90 (d) 13 : 169

14. $\frac{1}{9}:\frac{1}{81}::\frac{1}{13}:?$ « SSC (CGL) 2014
(a) $\frac{1}{127}$ (b) $\frac{1}{169}$ (c) $\frac{1}{125}$ (d) $\frac{1}{120}$

15. 25 : 625 :: 35 : ?
(a) 1575 (b) 1205 (c) 875 (d) 635

16. 1234 : 10 : : 6789 : ?
(a) 20 (b) 30 (c) 40 (d) 50

17. 08 : 66 :: ? : 38 « SSC (10+2) 2013
(a) 2 (b) 6 (c) 12 (d) 19

18. 583 : 488 :: 293 : ?
(a) 581 (b) 291 (c) 378 (d) 487

19. 428:717 :: 236 : ? « SSC CPO 2019
(a) 339 (b) 349 (c) 713 (d) 249

20. 64 : 216 : : 512 : ? « RRB (ALP) 2018
(a) 1331 (b) 700 (c) 1000 (d) 729

21. 2809 : 53 : : 1024 : ? « SSC (CGL) 2020
(a) 32 (b) 31 (c) 33 (d) 35

22. 6 : 180 : : 5 : ? « UPSSSC Vidhan Bhawan Rakshak/Vanrakshak 2018
(a) 25 (b) 125 (c) 115 (d) 325

23. 12 : 45 :: 175 : ? « SSC (Steno) 2016
(a) 608 (b) 697 (c) 659 (d) 579

24. 110 : 12100 : : 170 : ?
(a) 2890 (b) 28900 (c) 18900 (d) 36100

25. 8 : 63 : : 9 : ?
(a) 80 (b) 81 (c) 56 (d) 32

26. 08 : 28 : : 15 : ?
(a) 63 (b) 65 (c) 126 (d) 124

27. 236 : 4936 : : 724 : ? « SSC (Steno) 2017
(a) 49416 (b) 7416 (c) 49164 (d) 49464

28. 1245 : 3467 : : 1726 : ? « UP Police (SI) 2017
(a) 3498 (b) 3849 (c) 3948 (d) 3958

29. $-\frac{3}{7}:\frac{7}{3}::\frac{9}{2}:?$ « SSC (CGL) 2017

(a) $\frac{2}{9}$ (b) $-\frac{9}{2}$ (c) $\frac{7}{2}$ (d) $-\frac{2}{9}$

30. 8 : 24 : : ? : 32

(a) 5 (b) 6 (c) 10 (d) 8

31. 85 : 42 : : 139 : ? « SSC (CGL) 2016

(a) 68 (b) 69 (c) 70 (d) 67

32. 697 : 976 : 532 : ? « SSC (10+2) 2018

(a) 320 (b) 354
(c) 237 (d) 325

33. 147 : 159 :: 167 : ? « SSC MTS 2019

(a) 276 (b) 143 (c) 176 (d) 181

34. 14 : 225 :: 17 : ?

(a) 225 (b) 324 (c) 342 (d) 569

35. 697 : 976 : : 532 : ? « SSC (10+2) 2018

(a) 320 (b) 354 (c) 237 (d) 325

36. 63 : 36 : : ? : ? « SSC (10+2) 2018

(a) 94 : 49 (b) 35 : 54
(c) 47 : 72 (d) 73 : 39

37. 62 : 145 : : ? : ? « SSC (CPO) 2017

(a) 79 : 168 (b) 119 : 226
(c) 167 : 291 (d) 34 : 122

38. 11 : 132 : : ? : ?

(a) 10 : 100 (b) 9 : 90
(c) 13 : 169 (d) 15 : 250

DIRECTIONS ~ (Q. Nos. 39-43) *Each of the following questions consists of a pair of numbers that have a certain relationship to each other, followed by four other pair of numbers given as alternatives. Select the pair in which the numbers are similarly related as in the given pair.*

39. 8 : 49 « SSC (10+2) 2020

(a) 9 : 87 (b) 15 : 210 (c) 13 : 170 (d) 12 : 121

40. 55 : 10

(a) 15 : 5 (b) 18 : 1 (c) 16 : 75 (d) 88 : 16

41. 27 : 9

(a) 64 : 8 (b) 125 : 5 (c) 135 : 15 (d) 729 : 81

42. 36 : 49 « SSC (CPO) 2018

(a) 25 : 64 (b) 16 : 36 (c) 289 : 324 (d) 256 : 361

43. 56 : 63 « SSC CPO 2019

(a) 154 : 171 (b) 104 : 117
(c) 28 : 39 (d) 134 : 153

DIRECTIONS ~ (Q. Nos. 44-48) *In each of the following questions, choose one number which is similar to the numbers in the given set.*

44. 525, 813, 714

(a) 353 (b) 329 (c) 606 (d) 520

45. 94, 50, 61

(a) 75 (b) 91 (c) 81 (d) 72

46. 144, 256, 324

(a) 625 (b) 175 (c) 188 (d) 189

47. 29, 37, 43

(a) 45 (b) 80 (c) 40 (d) 47

48. 8, 1331, 4913

(a) 121 (b) 1330 (c) 64 (d) 9

DIRECTIONS ~ (Q. Nos. 49-60) *In each of the following questions, choose that set of numbers from the four alternative sets, which is similar to the given set.*

49. (32, 24, 8)

(a) (26, 32, 42) (b) (34, 24, 14)
(c) (24, 16, 0) (d) (42, 34, 16)

50. (3, 5, 7)

(a) (2, 3, 5) (b) (11, 15, 16)
(c) (29, 41, 43) (d) (4, 7, 9)

51. (12, 20, 28)

(a) (3, 15, 18) (b) (18, 27, 72)
(c) (18, 30, 42) (d) (7, 14, 28)

52. (3, 68, 5)

(a) (2, 72, 10) (b) (4, 64, 5)
(c) (5, 95, 8) (d) (2, 10, 1)

53. (2, 14, 16)

(a) (2, 7, 8) (b) (2, 9, 16)
(c) (3, 21, 24) (d) (4, 16, 18)

54. (4268, 8426, 8624)

(a) (3567, 7553, 4642) (b) (6824, 2468, 4862)
(c) (5687, 7691, 2525) (d) (4523, 5223, 4361)

55. (223, 324, 425)

(a) (225, 326, 437) (b) (451, 552, 636)
(c) (554, 655, 756) (d) (623, 723, 823)

56. (64, 48, 32) « UPSSSC 2015

(a) (96, 84, 60) (b) (48, 36, 27)
(c) (90, 72, 54) (d) (16, 12, 9)

57. (4, 10, 15)

(a) (3, 6, 12) (b) (2, 8, 10)
(c) (5, 12, 18) (d) (7, 10, 18)

58. (1050, 210, 42) « UPSSSC (Forest Guard) 2015

(a) 95, 19, 3 (b) 60, 12, 2
(c) 125, 25, 6 (d) 75, 15, 3

59. (101, 106, 131) « SSC CPO 2019

(a) (419, 424, 437) (b) (29, 34, 39)
(c) (123, 128, 153) (d) (170, 202, 137)

60. (13, 65, 117) « SSC CGL 2019

(a) (12, 55, 109) (b) (14, 70, 127)
(c) (17, 85, 163) (d) (15, 75, 135)

61. Select the option that is related to the third number in the same way as the second number is related to the first number and the sixth number is related to the fifth number.

72 : 108 :: 84 : ? :: 102 : 153 « SSC CGL 2019

(a) 135 (b) 126 (c) 144 (d) 117

Answers WITH EXPLANATIONS

1. (*d*) As, 4 : 10 ($+6$)

Similarly, 8 : 14 ($+6$)

$\therefore$? = 14

2. (*a*) As, 1 2 4 7 ($+2$, $+2$, $+2$, $+2$) → 3 4 6 9

Similarly, 0 1 3 6 ($+2$, $+2$, $+2$, $+2$) → 2 3 5 8

3. (*c*) As, 7 → 32 ($\times 4 + 4$)

Similarly, 28 → 116 ($\times 4 + 4$)

4. (*b*) As, 20 → 11 ($\div 2 + 1$)

Similarly, 102 → 52 ($\div 2 + 1$)

5. (*a*) As, 6 : 35 ($(6-1)\times(6+1)$)

Similarly, 7 : 48 ($(7-1)\times(7+1)$)

6. (*c*) As, $(9 \times 2) = 18$ and $(18 - 4) = 14$

Similarly, $(15 \times 2) = 30$

and $(30 - 4) = 26$

$\therefore$? = 15

7. (*c*) As, 100 : 121 or $10^2 : 11^2$

Similarly, 144 : 169

$\Rightarrow$ $12^2 : 13^2$

8. (*b*) As, cube of 3 is 27.

Similarly, cube of 4 is 64.

9. (*b*) As, 7544 : 5322 (-2222)

Similarly, 4673 : 2451 (-2222)

10. (*b*) As, $63 \div 3 = 21$

Similarly, $27 \div 3 = \boxed{9}$

11. (*c*) As, $8^2 = 64$

and $(8+4)^2 = 12^2 = 144$

Similarly, $16^2 = 256$

and $(16+4)^2 = 20^2 = \boxed{400}$

12. (*c*) As, $35 - 6 = 29$

Similarly, $66 - 6 = 60$

13. (*c*) As, $11 \times (11 + 1)$

$= 11 \times 12 = 132$

Similarly, $9 \times (9+1) = 9 \times 10 = 90$

$\therefore$? = 9 : 90

14. (*b*) As, $\left(\frac{1}{9}\right)^2 = \frac{1}{81}$

Similarly, $\left(\frac{1}{13}\right)^2 = \boxed{\frac{1}{169}}$

15. (*d*) As, $25 : 625 \rightarrow 25$ is common in both and 6 is added before it.

Similarly, $35 : \boxed{635} \rightarrow 35$ is common in both and 6 is added before it.

16. (*b*) As, 1234 : 10

$1 + 2 + 3 + 4 = 10$

Similarly, 6789 : 30

$6 + 7 + 8 + 9 = \boxed{30}$

17. (*b*) As, $66 - 2 = 64 \rightarrow \sqrt{64} = 8$

Similarly, $38 - 2 = 36 \rightarrow \sqrt{36} = 6$

18. (*c*) Taking option (c),

As sum of digits of

$583 = 5 + 8 + 3 = 16$

and sum of digits of

$488 = 4 + 8 + 8 = 20$

Similarly, sum of digits of

$293 = 2 + 9 + 3 = 14$

and sum of digits of

$\boxed{378} = 3 + 7 + 8 = 18$

Here, difference of both are

$(20 - 16) = (18 - 14) = 4$

$\therefore$? = 378

19. (*a*) As, $428 \Rightarrow 4 \times 2 = 8$

and $717 = 7 \times 1 = 7$

Similarly, $236 \Rightarrow 2 \times 3 = 6$

and $339 \Rightarrow 3 \times 3 = 9$

20. (*c*) The given pattern is as follows

As, 64 : 216 → $4^3 : 6^3$

Similarly, 512 : ? → $8^3 : 10^3 = \boxed{1000}$

21. (*a*) As, $\sqrt{2809} = 53$

Similarly, $\sqrt{1024} = \boxed{32}$

22. (*b*) As, $6^2 \times 5 = 36 \times 5 = 180$

Similarly, $5^2 \times 5 = 25 \times 5 = \boxed{125}$

23. (*b*) As, $12 \times 4 - 3 = 45$

Similarly, $175 \times 4 - 3 = \boxed{697}$

24. (*b*) As, $(110)^2 = 12100$

Similarly, $(170)^2 = \boxed{28900}$

25. (*a*) As, $8^2 - 1 = 64 - 1 = 63$

Similarly, $9^2 - 1 = 81 - 1 = \boxed{80}$

26. (*b*) As, 8 : 28 ← (3^2-1) (3^3+1)

Similarly, 15 : 65 ← (4^2-1) (4^3+1)

27. (*a*) As, $2^2 = 4$

$3^2 = 9$

$6^2 = 36 \Rightarrow 4936$

Similarly, $7^2 = 49$

$2^2 = 4$

$4^2 = 16$

$\Rightarrow$ $\boxed{49416}$

28. (*c*) As, $3467 - 1245 = 2222$

Similarly, $\boxed{3948} - 1726 = 2222$

29. (*d*) As, $\frac{-3}{7} \rightarrow \frac{7}{3}$

Similarly, $\frac{9}{2} \rightarrow \boxed{\frac{-2}{9}}$

30. (*b*) As,

(24) $\Rightarrow$ $\boxed{2 \times 4 = 8}$

Similarly,

(32) $\Rightarrow$ $\boxed{3 \times 2 = 6}$

31. (*b*) As,

85 → 42 ($\times \frac{1}{2} - \frac{1}{2}$)

Similarly, 139 → 69 ($\times \frac{1}{2} - \frac{1}{2}$)

32. (*d*) As, 6 9 7 → 9 7 6

Similarly, 5 3 2 → 3 2 5

33. (*d*) As, 147

$\Rightarrow 147 + (1 + 4 + 7) = 159$

Similarly,

$167 \Rightarrow 167 + (1 + 6 + 7) = 181$

34. (*b*) $(14 + 1)^2 = (15)^2 = 225$

$(17 + 1)^2 = (18)^2 = \boxed{324}$

35. (*d*) As, 697 ⟶ 976

Similarly, 532 ⟶ 325

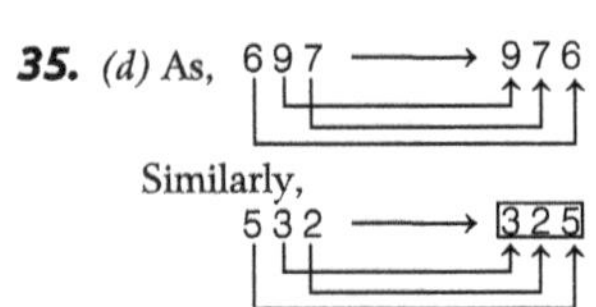

36. (*a*) As, 63 ⟶ 36

Similarly,

94 ⟶ 49

37. (*b*) As, 62 ⟶ 145

$(8)^2-2$ $(12)^2+1$

+4

Similarly,

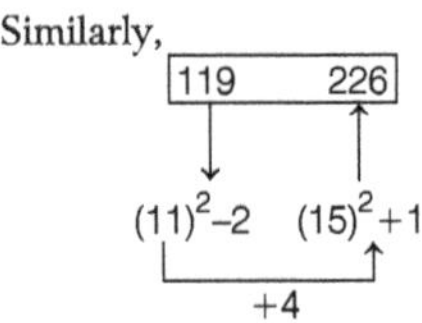

119 226

$(11)^2-2$ $(15)^2+1$

+4

38. (*b*) As, $(11)^2+11=121+11=132$

Similarly, $(9)^2+9=81+9=90$

39. (*d*) As, $8:49 \Rightarrow (8-1)^2=7^2=49$

Similarly,

$12:121 \Rightarrow (12-1)^2=11^2=121$

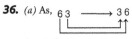

40. (*d*) Second number is the digit sum of the 1st number.

As, $5+5=10$

Similarly, $8+8=16$

41. (*d*) The relationship is $a^3:a^2$.

As, 27 : 9

3^3 3^2

Similarly, 729 : 81

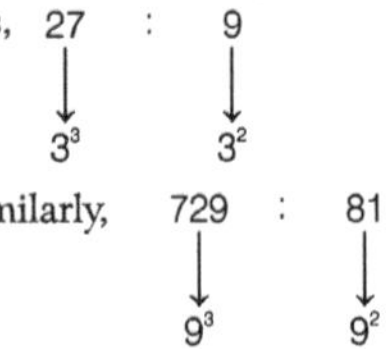

9^3 9^2

42. (*c*) As, $36:49 \Rightarrow 6^2:7^2$

+1

Similarly,

$289:324 \Rightarrow 17^2:18^2$

+1

43. (*b*) As, $8\times7=56$

$(8+1)\times7=9\times7=63$

Similarly, $8\times13=104$

$(8+1)\times13=9\times13=117$

44. (*c*) As, $5+2+5=12$

$8+1+3=12$

$7+1+4=12$

Similarly, $6+0+6=12$

45. (*d*) The difference between the 1st and 2nd digit of the numbers is 5.

46. (*a*) The numbers are perfect square.

Let us see

As, $144=12^2, 256=16^2, 324=18^2$

Similarly, $625=25^2$

47. (*d*) All are prime numbers.

48. (*c*) All the numbers are perfect cubes.

Let us see

As, $8=2^3$

$1331=11^3$ and $4913=17^3$

Similarly, $64=4^3$

49. (*c*) Here, 32 24 8

−8 −16

Similarly, 24 16 0

−8 −16

50. (*c*) All are set of consecutive odd prime numbers.

51. (*c*) In (12, 20, 28), every next number is obtained by adding 8 with the previous number and similarly, in (18, 30, 42), every next number is obtained by adding 12 with the previous number.

52. (*d*) As,

$\Rightarrow 3^2+5^2=9+25=34$

$\Rightarrow 34\times2=68$

Similarly,

$\Rightarrow 2^2+1^2=4+1=5$

$\Rightarrow 5\times2=10$

53. (*c*) In each set

2nd number = 1st number × 7

and 3rd number = 1st number × 8

Let us see

As, $14=2\times7$ and $16=2\times8$

Similarly, $21=3\times7$ and $24=3\times8$

54. (*b*) Each set is made of the digits 2, 4, 6, 8.

55. (*c*) In each set,

2nd number = 1st number + 101

3rd number = 2nd number + 101

Let us see

As, $223+101=324$

and $324+101=425$

Similarly, $554+101=655$

and $655+101=756$

56. (*c*) As, 64 48 32

−16 −16

Similarly,

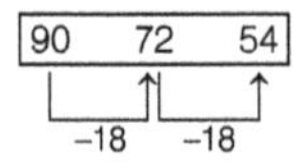

90 72 54

−18 −18

57. (*c*) As, 4 10 15

$\times2+2$ $\times\frac{3}{2}$

Similarly, 5 12 18

$\times2+2$ $\times\frac{3}{2}$

58. (*d*) As, 1050, (1050 ÷ 5); (1050 ÷ 25)

$\Rightarrow$ 1050, 210, 42

Similarly, 75, (75 ÷ 5), (75 ÷ 25)

$\Rightarrow$ 75, 15, 3

59. (*c*) As, $101 \xrightarrow{+5} 106 \xrightarrow{+25} 131$

Similarly,

$123 \xrightarrow{+5} 128 \xrightarrow{+25} 153$

60. (*d*) As, $13 \xrightarrow{13\times5} 65 \xrightarrow{13\times9} 117$

Similarly,

$15 \xrightarrow{15\times5} 75 \xrightarrow{15\times9} 135$

61. (*b*) In first pair, $8\times9=72$

$[8+(8\div2)]\times9$

$\Rightarrow (8+4)\times9 \Rightarrow 12\times9=108$

In third pair, $6\times17=102$

$[6+(6\div2)]\times17$

$\Rightarrow (6+3)\times17=9\times17=153$

Similarly, in third pair,

$12\times7=84$

$[12+(12\div2)]\times7$

$\Rightarrow (12+6)\times7=18\times7=126$

TYPE 04

Letter-Number Analogy

In such type of questions, the letters of English alphabetical series are related to numbers using some properties of the letters like sum, product or some other method based on letters positional values to form the analogy.

The candidate is asked to complete the given analogous pair, which has same relation as in the given pair.

Ex 34 Select the missing term based on the given related pair of terms.

NAME : 04 : : TRUMPET : ?

(a) 07 (b) 06 (c) 09 (d) 10

Solution ***(a)*** Here, 'NAME' has 4 letters and similarly, 'Trumpet' has 7.

Ex 35 Select the missing term based on the given related pair of terms.

NICE : 14935 : : PRICE : ?

(a) 1168935 (b) 1618953 (c) 1618935 (d) 1681935

Solution ***(c)*** Here, in each pair, every letter has been given its alphabetical position. Let us see

As, N I C E ⟶ 14 9 3 5

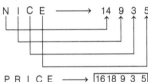

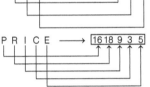

Similarly, P R I C E ⟶ 16 18 9 3 5

Ex 36 Select the missing term based on the given related pair of terms.

NICE : 13182422 : : PRICE : ?

(a) 119128422 (b) 119182422
(c) 111982224 (d) 119128242

Solution ***(b)*** As,

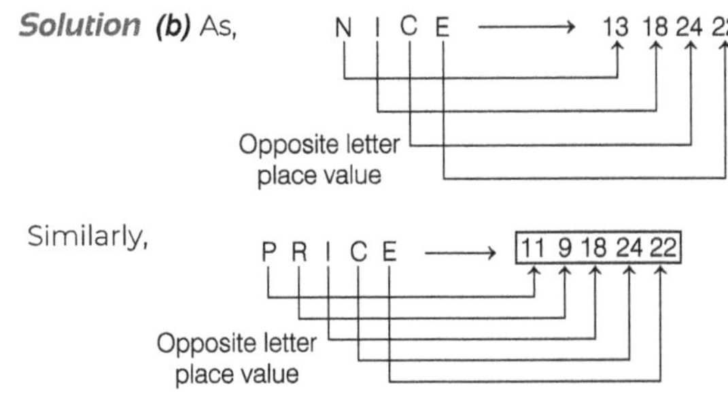

Similarly, P R I C E ⟶ 11 9 18 24 22

Opposite letter place value

Ex 37 Select the missing term based on the given related pair of terms.

COME : 36 : : PRANK : ?

(a) 70 (b) 50 (c) 55 (d) 60

Solution ***(d)*** Here, in both the pairs, alphabetical positions of letters have been added to establish analogy. Let us see

As, C O M E

3 + 15 + 13 + 5 = 36

Similarly, P R A N K

16 + 18 + 1 + 14 + 11 = 60

Ex 38 $\frac{V}{R} : \frac{18}{22} :: \frac{K}{P} : ?$

(a) $\frac{11}{16}$ (b) $\frac{15}{16}$

(c) $\frac{16}{11}$ (d) $\frac{13}{18}$

Solution ***(c)*** As, (22)V → 18, (18)R → 22 Based on place value

Similarly, (11)K → 16, (16)P → 11 Based on place value

Practice / CORNER 2.4

DIRECTIONS ~(Q. Nos. 1-23) *In each of the following questions, choose the missing term in place of question mark (?) on the basis of the relationship between the words given on the left/right side of the sign of analogy.*

1. NEWS : 14, 5, 23, 19 : : PAPER : ? « SSC (Steno) 2013

(a) 16, 5, 16, 1, 18 (b) 18, 5, 16, 1, 16
(c) 16, 1, 16, 5, 18 (d) 32, 2, 32, 10, 36

2. GREAT : 25 : : NUMBER : ? « SSC (FCI) 2012

(a) 36 (b) 38 (c) 27 (d) 24

3. STBP : 1920216 : : MNGO : ?

(a) 1314715 (b) 1413715
(c) 5173141 (d) 3114715

4. JPC : 10163 : : ? : ?

(a) TQG : 20177 (b) GQT : 20177
(c) TQG : 77102 (d) GOT : 20177

5. RAT : 18120 : : GOD : ? « RRB (ALP) 2018

(a) 7174 (b) 7144 (c) 7164 (d) 7154

6. ACE : 135 : : DFG : ? MP Police (SI) 2017

(a) 467 (b) 642 (c) 681 (d) 246

7. RAT : 912 : : UAM : ?

(a) 431 (b) 143 (c) 512 (d) 314

8. STAR : 1920118, MARS : 1311819, PARK : ?

(a) 1618111 (b) 1611811
(c) 1811611 (d) 1712812

9. SWETA : 05 : : YASSHI : ? « Delhi B.Ed 2008
(a) 04 (b) 06 (c) 08 (d) 09

10. ACE : 135 :: DFG : ? « MP Police (SI) 2017
(a) 467 (b) 642 (c) 681 (d) 246

11. NET : 13227 : : YAM : ?
(a) 22614 (b) 25614 (c) 25113 (d) 14520

12. MDNT : 1423137 : : KKGK : ?
(a) 16612016 (b) 16160216
(c) 16162016 (d) None of these

13. DUCK : 69 : : BEST : ?
(a) 68 (b) 64 (c) 82 (d) 62

14. JHBG : 9 : : IFKJ : ?
(a) 4 (b) 21 (c) 9 (d) 12

15. MAHESH : 154362 : : SHAME : ? « SSC (FCI) 2012
(a) 62513 (b) 62351 (c) 65231 (d) 65213

16. LPQ : 45 : : KAS : ? « SSC (CGL) 2008
(a) 103 (b) 31 (c) 13 (d) 23

17. MCTP : 8241511 : : XLDG : ? « SSC (CGL) 2009
(a) 197232 (b) 197252 (c) 197253 (d) 917252

18. INDIA : 95491 : : DELHI : ?
(a) 45289 (b) 45398 (c) 45389 (d) 45189

19. IC : 6 : : DP : ?
(a) 14 (b) 10 (c) 12 (d) 16

20. $L \times M : 12 \times 13 :: U \times W : ?$ « RRB (ASM) 2012
(a) 21×31 (b) 21×22 (c) 21×23 (d) 21×25

21. $P \times Q : 17 \times 18 :: L \times M : ?$
(a) 13×12 (b) 12×13
(c) 16×13 (d) 13×14

22. $\frac{G \times Q}{Q} : 20 :: \frac{B \times V}{V} : ?$
(a) 25 (b) 27
(c) 20 (d) 17

23. XMAE : 16 : : VTNG : ?
(a) 21 (b) 17 (c) 35 (d) 18

Answers / WITH EXPLANATIONS

1. (c) As,

N E W S ⟶ 14 5 23 19

Similarly,

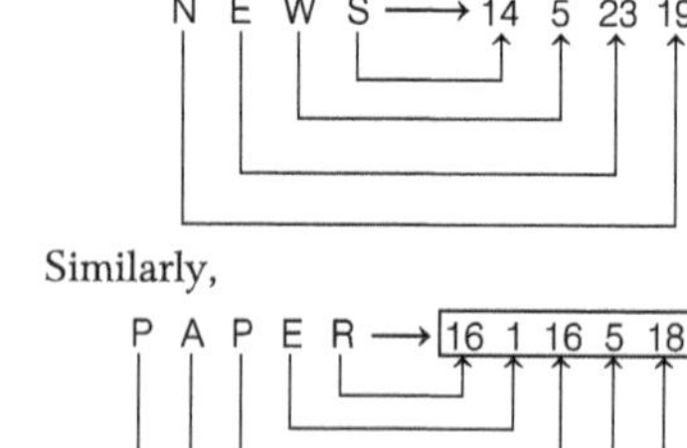

Second part is the positional values of the letters written in first part.

2. (a) As, 'GREAT' has 5 letters, it is represented by square of 5 i.e., 25. Similarly, 'NUMBER' has 6 letters it is represented by square of 6 i.e., 36.

3. (a) As,

S T B P ⟶ 19 20 2 16
Positional values

Similarly,

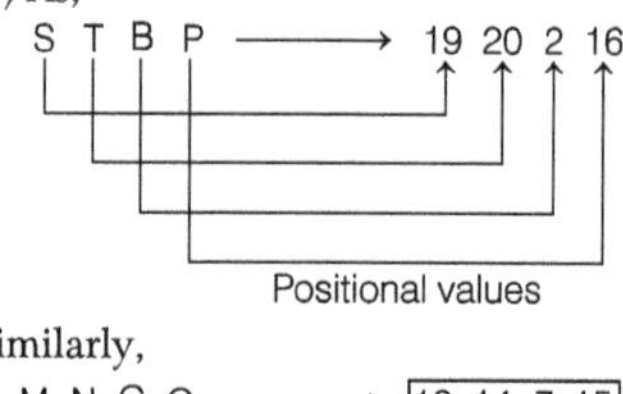

4. (a) As,

J P C ⟶ 10 16 3
Positional values

Similarly,

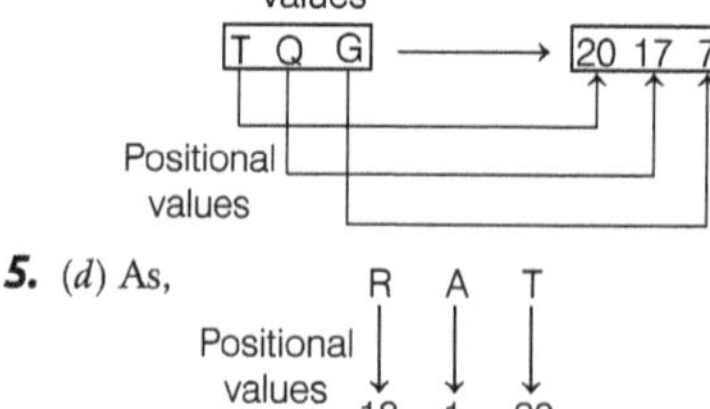

5. (d) As,

R A T
Positional values
18 1 20

Similarly,

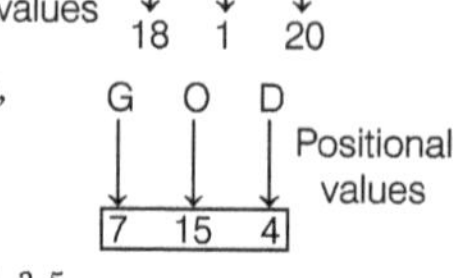

6. (a) As, $\overset{1\,3\,5}{\text{ACE}} \to 135$
Similarly, $\overset{4\,6\,7}{\text{DFG}} \to \boxed{467}$

7. (d) As,

18 1 20
R A T
1+8 1 2+0
9 1 2

Similarly,

21 1 13
U A M
2+1 1 1+3
3 1 4

8. (b) As, $\overset{19}{S}\ \overset{20}{T}\ \overset{1}{A}\ \overset{18}{R} \longrightarrow 19\ 20\ 1\ 18$
and $\overset{13}{M}\ \overset{1}{A}\ \overset{18}{R}\ \overset{19}{S} \longrightarrow 13\ 1\ 18\ 19$

Similarly, $\overset{16}{P}\ \overset{1}{A}\ \overset{18}{R}\ \overset{11}{K} \longrightarrow \boxed{16\ 1\ 18\ 11}$

9. (b) As, $\overset{1\,2\,3\,4\,5}{\text{SWETA}} \longrightarrow 05$
(Total number of the letter given in first part)
Similarly, $\overset{1\,2\,3\,4\,5\,6}{\text{YASSHI}} \longrightarrow \boxed{06}$

10. (a) As, $\overset{1\,3\,5}{\text{ACE}} \to 135$
Similarly, $\overset{4\,6\,7}{\text{DFG}} \to \boxed{467}$

11. (a) As,

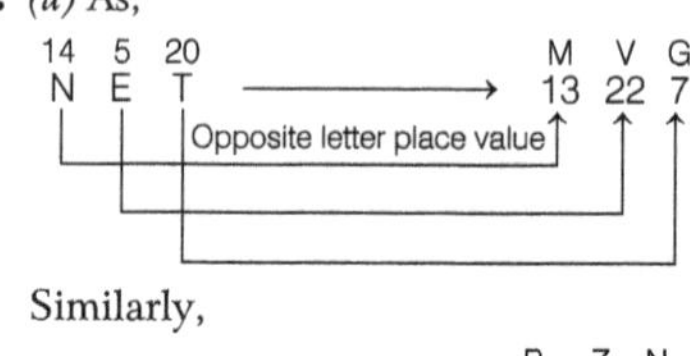

Similarly,

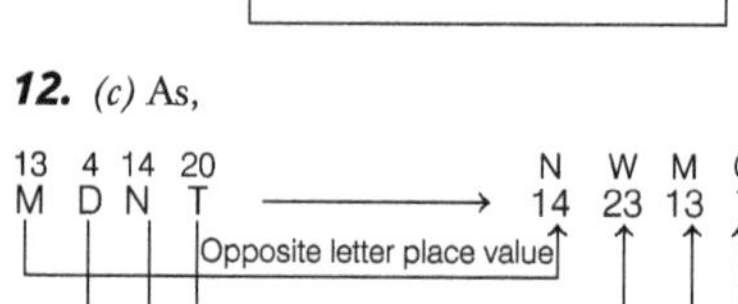

12. (c) As,

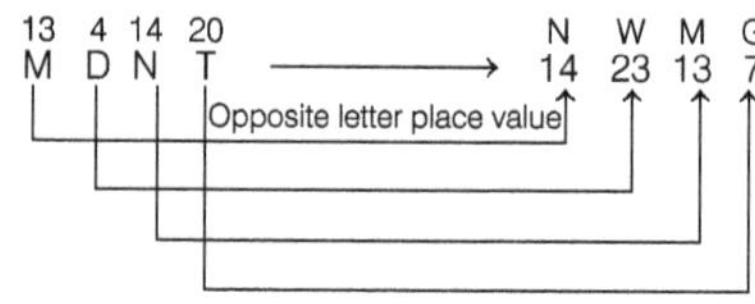

Similarly,

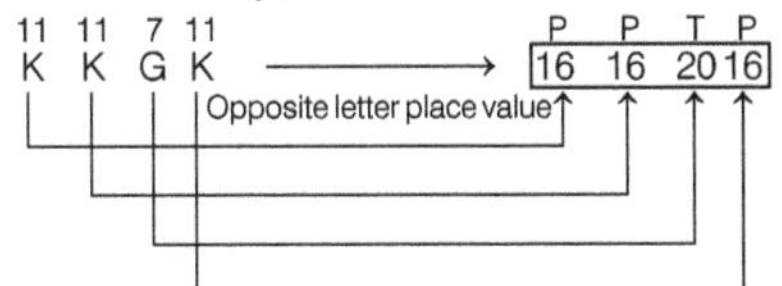

13. (*d*) As,

4 21 3 11 Opposite letter 23 6 24 16
D U C K ⟶ W F X P

23 6 24 16
W F X P ⇒ 23+6+24+16 = 69

Similarly,

2 5 14 20 Opposite letter 25 22 8 7
B E S T ⟶ Y V H G

25 22 8 7
Y V H G ⇒ 25+22+8+7 = 62

14. (*d*) As, J H B G (10 8 2 7)

⇒ $(10 + 8 + 2 + 7) \div 3 = 27 \div 3 = 9$

Similarly, I F K J (9 6 11 10)

⇒ $(9 + 6 + 11 + 10) \div 3 = 36 \div 3 = \boxed{12}$

15. (*a*) As,

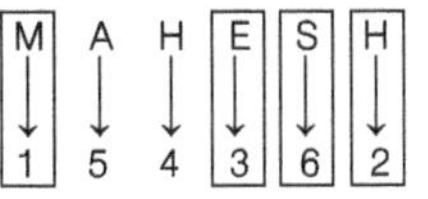

Similarly,

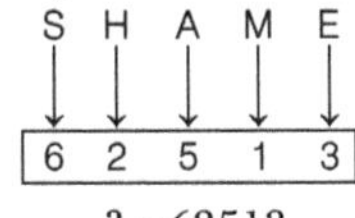

∴ ? = 62513

16. (*b*) As, L P Q (12 16 17)

⇒ $12 + 16 + 17 = 45$

Similarly, K A S (11 1 19)

⇒ $11 + 1 + 19 = \boxed{31}$

17. (*b*) As,

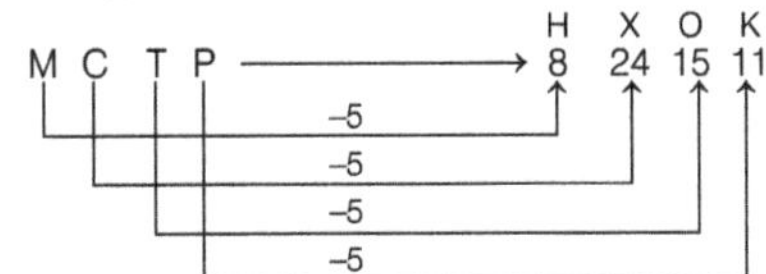

Similarly,

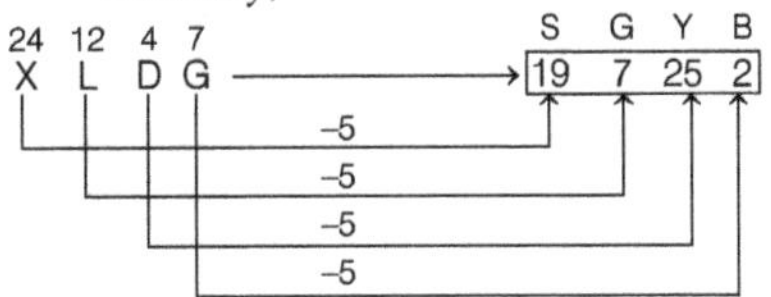

18. (*c*) As,

9 I ⇒ 9 + 0 = 9

14 N ⇒ 1 + 4 = 5

4 D ⇒ 4 + 0 = 4

9 I ⇒ 9 + 0 = 9

1 A ⇒ 1 + 0 = 1

Similarly,

4 D ⇒ 4 + 0 = 4

5 E ⇒ 5 + 0 = 5

12 L ⇒ 1 + 2 = 3

8 H ⇒ 8 + 0 = 8

9 I ⇒ 9 + 0 = 9

∴ ? = 45389

19. (*c*) As, I = 9; C = 3 ⇒ 9 − 3 = 6

Similarly, D = 4; P = 16

⇒ 16 − 4 = 12

20. (*c*) As, L × M ⟶ 12 × 13 (Positional values)

Similarly,

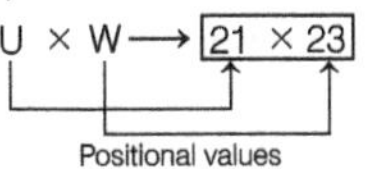

21. (*d*) In forward order letter sequence,

Position of P = (16) + 1

Position of Q = (17) + 1

∴ $P \times Q = 17 \times 18$

Similarly, Position of L = (12) + 1

Position of M = (13) + 1

∴ $L \times M = \boxed{13 \times 14}$

22. (*a*) In backward order letters sequence,

Position of G = 20

Position of Q = 10

∴ $\frac{G \times Q}{Q} = \frac{20 \times 10}{10} = 20$

Similarly, Position of B = 25

Position of V = 5

⇒ $\frac{B \times V}{V} = \frac{25 \times 5}{5} = \boxed{25}$

23. (*d*) As,

X	M	A	E
24	13	1	5
(2+4)	(1+3)	(0+1)	(0+5)
6 +	4 +	1 +	5 = 16

Similarly,

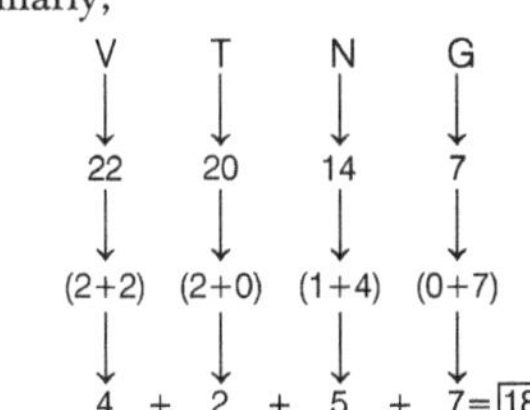

Master Exercise

DIRECTIONS ~ (Q. Nos. 1-13) *In each of the following questions, choose the missing word in place of question mark (?) on the basis of the relationship between the words given on the left/right hand side of the sign of analogy.*

1. Menu : Food : : Catalogue : ?
(a) Rack (b) Newspaper (c) Library (d) Books

2. Goat : Bleat : : Camel : ?
(a) Bleat (b) Howl (c) Bray (d) Grunt

3. Adult : Baby : : Flower : ?
(a) Seed (b) Bud (c) Fruit (d) Butterfly

4. Good : Bad : : Virtue : ?
(a) Blame (b) Sin (c) Despair (d) Vice

5. Bird : Fly : : Snake : ?
(a) Timid (b) Clatter (c) Crawl (d) Hole

6. STATUE : SIZE :: SONG : ? « UPSSSC Junior Assistant 2020
(a) POETRY (b) WORDS (c) SINGER (d) TUNE

7. Taka : Bangladesh : : Lira : ?
(a) Kuwait (b) Italy (c) Sri Lanka (d) Kenya

8. Doctor : Nurse : : ? : Follower
(a) Worker (b) Employer (c) Union (d) Leader

9. Food : Stomach : : Fuel : ?
(a) Engine (b) Automobile (c) Rail (d) Aeroplane

10. Water : Sand : : Ocean : ?
(a) Engine (b) River (c) Desert (d) Waves

11. Botany : Plants : : Entomology : ?
(a) Germs (b) Insects (c) Reptiles (d) Rodents

12. Radio : Listener : : Film : ?
(a) Producer (b) Actor (c) Viewer (d) Director

13. Igloos : Canada :: Rondavels : ? « WBCS (Pre) 2018
(a) Africa (b) Rangoon (c) Russia (d) Indonesia

14. Find the analogous pair.
Fetter : Liberate « UPSSSC (VDO) 2018
(a) Shackle : Loose (b) Common : Ghostly (c) Routine : Novel (d) Secular : Clerical

15. Select the option that is related to the third word on the same basis as the second word is related to the first word.
Ponder : Consider :: Pinnacle : ? « RRB Group D 2018
(a) Tackle (b) Peak (c) Low (d) Valley

16. 'Bank' is related to 'Money' in the same way as 'Transport' is related to
(a) Goods (b) Road (c) Movement (d) Traffic

17. 'Fan' is related to 'Wings' in the same way as 'Wheel' is related to
(a) Round (b) Cars (c) Spokes (d) Moves

18. 'Captain' is related to 'Soldier' in the same way as 'Leader' is related to
(a) Chair (b) Follower (c) Party (d) Minister

19. 'Skirmish' is related to 'War' in the same way as 'Disease' is related to
(a) Infection (b) Epidemic (c) Patient (d) Medicine

20. 'Tree' is related to 'Root' in the same way as 'Smoke' is related to
(a) Cigarette (b) Fire (c) Heat (d) Chimney

21. 'Good' is related to 'Bad' in the same way as 'Roof' is related to
(a) Wall (b) Pillar (c) Terrace (d) Floor

22. 'Oval' is related to 'Circle' in the same way as 'Rectangle' is related to
(a) Triangle (b) Square (c) Periphery (d) Diagonal

23. 'Umpire' is related to 'Match' in the same way as 'Judge' is related to
(a) Bar council (b) Lawyer (c) Judgement (d) Lawsuit

24. 'Thick' is related to 'Thin' in the same way as 'Idle' is related to
(a) Virtuous (b) Business (c) Industrious (d) Activity

25. 'Needle' is related to 'Thread' in the same way as 'Pen' is related to « IBPS (PO) 2012
(a) Ink (b) Cap (c) Paper (d) Word (e) Stationery

26. 'Marathon' is to 'Race' as 'Hibernation' is to « SSC (MTS) 2018
(a) Winter (b) Bear (c) Dream (d) Sleep

27. 'Blue' is related to 'Sky' in the same way as 'Brown' is related to « RRB Group D 2018
(a) Mud (b) Vessel (c) Wet (d) Board

28. 'Lion' is related to 'Roar' in the same way as 'Horse' is related to « RRB (Group D) 2018
(a) Bray (b) Neigh (c) Hiss (d) Hoot

DIRECTIONS ~(Q. Nos. 29-42) *The following questions consist of two words having a certain relationship to each other. Select the alternative whose words are having the same relationship amongst them.*

29. Umpire : Game
(a) Prodigy : Wonder (b) Chef : Banquet
(c) Legislator : Election (d) Moderator : Debate

30. Confession : Testimony
(a) Crime : Petition (b) Autobiography : Biography
(c) Edition : Correction (d) Witness : Judgement

31. Studious : Erudite
(a) Enterprising : Rich (b) Cupidity : Poor
(c) Virtuous : Judge (d) Ignorance : Illiterate

32. Action : Reaction
(a) Introvert : Extrovert (b) Assail : Defend
(c) Diseased : Treatment (d) Death : Rebirth

33. Triangle : Hexagon
(a) Cone : Sphere (b) Rectangle : Octagon
(c) Pentagon : Heptagon (d) Angle : Quadrilateral

34. Stare : Glance
(a) Gulp : Sip (b) Confide : Tell
(c) Hunt : Stalk (d) Step : Walk

35. Cloth : Texture
(a) Body : Weight (b) Silk : Cloth
(c) Wood : Grains (d) Ornaments : Gold

36. Nuts : Bolts
(a) Nitty : Gritty (b) Bare : Feet
(c) Naked : Clothes (d) Hard : Soft

37. Arrow : Bow « RRB NTPC 2016
(a) Football : Hand (b) Salad : Knife
(c) Bullet : Rifle (d) Smoke : Water

38. Annex : Lessening « UPSSSC Tech Assist. (Agri. service) 2018
(a) Affix : Ell (b) Jolly : Back-slapping
(c) Festal : Happy (d) Jocund : Serious

39. Heart : Cardiology « SSC (Constable) 2018
(a) Plants : Zoology (b) Phycology : Fungi
(c) Disease : Hospital (d) Virus : Virology

40. Binding : Book
(a) Criminal : Gang (b) Display : Museum
(c) Nail : Hammer (d) Frame : Picture

41. Gloves : Hand « SSC (MTS) 2018
(a) Neck : Collar (b) Tie : Shirt
(c) Socks : Feet (d) Coat : Pocket

42. Mammal : Bear « SSC (CPO) 2018
(a) Pen : Pencil (b) Player : Team
(c) Fruit : Mango (d) Plants : Food

DIRECTIONS ~ (Q. Nos. 43-57) *From the four given alternatives, select that word, which best completes the analogy (?) that exists among the three words.*

43. King : Royal : : ? : Religious
(a) Prayer (b) Saint
(c) Priesthood (d) Holy book

44. Hill : Mountain : : ? : Pain
(a) Distress (b) Discomfort (c) Headache (d) Fear

45. ? : ALKLO : : WOULD : TLRIA
(a) DONOR (b) CONES (c) BARGE (d) BLOCK

46. ? : DURXQG : : POLICE : SROLFH
(a) AROUND (b) SHOULD (c) ARMOUR (d) GROUND

47. Head : Hair : : Hand : ?
(a) Finger (b) Ear (c) Neck (d) Knee

48. Walking : Running : : Wind : ?
(a) Weather (b) Air (c) Rain (d) Storm

49. King : Throne : : Rider : ?
(a) Chair (b) Horse (c) Seat (d) Saddle

50. FILM : ADGH : : MILK : ?
(a) HEGF (b) ADGF (c) HDGE (d) HDGF

51. HCM : FAK : : SGD : ?
(a) QEB (b) QIB (c) ESQ (d) GES

52. Flow : River :: Stagnant : ? « SSC (MTS) 2018
(a) Rain (b) Stream (c) Pool (d) Canal

53. Contemporary : Historic :: ? : Ancient « RRB NTPC 2016
(a) Past (b) Classic (c) Modern (d) Future

54. Cheerful : Morose :: Valiant : ?
« UPSSSC Tech. Assist. (Agri. service) 2018
(a) Absurd (b) Ideal (c) Idle (d) Coward

55. Amusing : Delightful :: Weary : ?
« UPSSSC Tech. Assist. (Agri. Service) 2018
(a) Overdressed (b) Exhausted
(c) Greedy (d) Anxious

56. Barometer : Atmosphere :: Calorimeter :?
« UPSSSC Tech. Assist. (Agri. Service) 2018
(a) Calories (b) Heat (c) Sound (d) Humidity

57. Sphygmomanometer : Blood Pressure :: Pyrometer : ?
« CLAT 2018
(a) Temperature (b) Blood Flow
(c) Urine Flow (d) Atmospheric Pressure

58. Choose the option that expresses the same relationship as the word Tobacco : Cancer, has
(a) Milk : Food (b) Bud : Flower
(c) Soil : Erosion (d) Mosquito : Malaria

DIRECTIONS ~ (Q. Nos. 59-63) *Select the related word/letter/ number from the given alternatives.*

59. West : North-East : : South : ?
(a) North-West (b) South-East
(c) North (d) East

60. KNQT : LORU : : ADGJ : ?
(a) BEHK (b) FHLO (c) DGEF (d) MPVW

61. 401 : 19 :: 730 : ? « UPSSSC Tech. Asst. (Agri. Service) 2018
(a) 28 (b) 22 (c) 27 (d) 26

62. 42 : 56 : : 110 : ?
(a) 132 (b) 136 (c) 124 (d) 148

63. 5 : 100, 4 : 64 : : 4 : 80, 3 : ?
(a) 26 (b) 48 (c) 60 (d) 54

DIRECTIONS ~ (Q. Nos. 64-82) *In each of the following questions, there is a certain relationship between two given numbers/ group of letters on one side of (::) and one number/groups of letters is given on another side of (::) while another number/ group of letters is to be found from given options, having the same relationship with this number/group of letters as the numbers/groups of letters of the given pair bear. Choose the best option.*

64. WRITE : JEVGR : : WRONG : ?
(a) JEBAT (b) JECAT (c) JEDAT (d) JEDAD

65. TNGP : 2014716 : : LPDT : ?
(a) 2041612 (b) 1216204
(c) 2116420 (d) 1216420

66. PST : 01 : : NPR : ?
(a) 3 (b) 4 (c) 1 (d) 7

67. 212 : 436 : : 560 : ?
(a) 786 (b) 682 (c) 784 (d) 688

68. 63 : 9 : : ? : 14
(a) 68 (b) 48 (c) 98 (d) 108

69. 432 : 24 : : 735 : ?
(a) 105 (b) 25 (c) 73 (d) 81

70. DARE : ADER : : REEK : ?
(a) EEKR (b) EKER (c) ERKE (d) EERK

71. Silkworm : Silk : : Snake : ?
(a) Poisonless (b) Poison
(c) Death (d) Fear

72. L × M : 12 × 13 : : U × W : ?
(a) 21× 31 (b) 21× 22 (c) 21× 23 (d) 21× 25

73. a : One : : f : ?
(a) Property (b) Fail (c) E (d) Six

74. CEGI : RTVX : : IKMO : ?
(a) JKNP (b) MNQP (c) LNPR (d) DFHI

75. BFK : IMR :: DGP : ? « RRB (ALP) 2018
(a) KWN (b) WNK (c) KNU (d) KNW

76. GIK : FHJ :: OQS : ? « UPSSSC (Mandi Parishad) 2019
(a) MNO (b) NPR (c) LMN (d) KMO

77. DART : XGLZ :: SPIN : ?
« UPSSSC Tech. Asst. (Agri. Service) 2018
(a) MVOT (b) YVCT (c) YJCT (d) MVCT

78. MAKING : KGMANI :: CAPETO : ? « RRB (ALP) 2018
(a) POCATE (b) POACTE (c) POTECA (d) POCAET

79. CLOUD : COULD :: SMILE : ? « RRB (ALP) 2018
(a) MILSE (b) SLIME (c) SILME (d) MILES

80. EARTH : HDUWK :: VENUS : ? « RRB Group D 2018
(a) YQXHV (b) YHQXV (c) YQHXV (d) YQHVX

81. PURSE : UPRES :: RAZOR :? « SSC Constable 2018
(a) AROZR (b) AZROR (c) ARZRO (d) ARRZO

82. REASON : SFBTPO :: THINK : ? « SSC MTS 2018
(a) SGHMJ (b) UIJOL (c) UHNKI (d) UJKPM

DIRECTIONS ~ (Q. Nos. 83 and 84) *The pair of words in capitals is followed by four pairs of related words/phrases, which best expresses a relationship similar to that expressed in the original pair.*

83. Stygian : Dark
(a) Abysmal : Low (b) Cogent : Contentious
(c) Fortuitous : Accidental (d) Cataclysmic : Doomed

84. Contiguous : Abut
(a) Possible : Occur (b) Synthetic : Create
(c) Simultaneous : Coincide (d) Constant : Stabilise

DIRECTIONS ~ (Q. Nos. 85-89) *In each of the following questions, choose that set of numbers from the four alternative sets, which is similar to the given set.*

85. (15, 27, 39)
(a) (75, 27, 81) (b) (105, 125, 145)
(c) (77, 78, 85) (d) (57, 35, 65)

86. (49, 81, 25)
(a) (25, 45, 27) (b) (22, 37, 41)
(c) (17, 12, 9) (d) (100, 289, 4)

87. (12, 5, 7)
(a) (7, 4, 3) (b) (18, 21, 16)
(c) (19, 9, 11) (d) (50, 12, 16)

88. (23 : 30 : 37)
(a) (6 : 13 : 20) (b) (7 : 15 : 22)
(c) (21 : 28 : 34) (d) (12 : 19 : 25)

89. (7, 16, 34) « SSC (CPO) 2018
(a) (10, 19, 28) (b) (23, 31, 48)
(c) (29, 57, 96) (d) (49, 58, 76)

DIRECTIONS ~ (Q. Nos. 90-94) *For each of the following questions select the answer pair that expresses a relationship most similar to that expressed in the given pair.*

90. Omniscient : Knowledge
(a) Saturnine : Energy (b) Boundless : Expanse
(c) Inquisitive : Science (d) Complete : Retraction

91. Nebulous : Form
(a) Insincere : Misanthrope (b) Benevolent : Excellence
(c) Insipid : Taste (d) Composed : Innocence

92. Errors : Inexperience
(a) Skill : Mistake (b) Training : Economy
(c) Losses : Carelessness (d) News : Publication

93. Brain : Neurology
(a) Biology : Animals (b) Hydrology : Water
(c) Body : Physiology (d) Entomology : Plants

94. Duck : Quack
(a) Dog : Growl (b) Sparrow : Peck
(c) Snake : Creep (d) Camel : Desert

DIRECTIONS ~ (Q. Nos. 95-98) *In the following questions, select the related word/letters/number from the given alternatives.* « SSC (10+2) 2013

95. Picture : See : : Book : ?
(a) Buy (b) Read (c) Listen (d) Library

96. Dark : Light : : Hot : ?
(a) Contaminated (b) Accrued
(c) Diseased (d) Cold

97. Swimming : River : : Hiking : ?
(a) Road (b) Pond (c) Mountain (d) Sea

98. HOPEFUL : LUFEPOH : : ETHNICITY : ?
(a) YTICINHTE (b) TICINHTEY
(c) ICINHTEYT (d) CINHTEYTI

DIRECTIONS ~ (Q.Nos. 99-102) *In each of the following questions, two words are paired which have a certain relation. Select a correct option to substitute question mark, so as to make a similar relational pair with the word given after double colon (: :).* « CMAT 2011

99. Right : Duty : : Power : ?
(a) Wrong (b) Weak (c) Powerless (d) Liability

100. Elephant : Calf : : Tiger : ?
(a) Pup (b) Tigress (c) Cub (d) Baby Tiger

101. Patient : Doctor : : Litigant : ?
(a) Advisor (b) Help
(c) Legal aid (d) Lawyer

102. World War II : United Nations : : World War I : ?
(a) Treaty of Versailles
(b) International Commission of Jurists
(c) League of Nations
(d) International Court of Justice

DIRECTIONS ~ (Q. Nos. 103-113) *In the following questions, select the related word/letters/number from the given alternative.*

103. 841 : 29 : : 289 : ?
(a) 23 (b) 21 (c) 17 (d) 13

104. 8 : 28 : : 27 : ?
(a) 85 (b) 28 (c) 8 (d) 64

105. 11 : 120 :: 15 : ? « UPSSSC Junior Assist. 2017
(a) 224 (b) 225 (c) 242 (d) 252

106. 144 : 12 :: 576 : ? « SSC Constable 2017
(a) 36 (b) 26 (c) 34 (d) 24

107. 0.16 : 0.4 :: 1.21 : ? « UPSSSC Mandi Parishad 2019
(a) 0.11 (b) 1.1 (c) 0.011 (d) 11

108. 2264 : 7241 :: 3129 : ?
(a) 6342 (b) 2572 (c) 7132 (d) 9521

109. Tanning : Leather : : Pyrotechnics : ?
(a) Bombs (b) Fireworks (c) Wool (d) Machinery

110. F : 216 : : L : ?
(a) 1728 (b) 1700 (c) 1600 (d) 1723

111. MOUSE : KPSTC : : LIGHT : ?
(a) MGHFU (b) JGEFR (c) JJEIR (d) MJHIU

112. 584 : 488 : : 294 : ?
(a) 581 (b) 291 (c) 378 (d) 487

113. AHOP : CKSU : : BJMF : ?
(a) EZUQ (b) DMQK (c) DQKM (d) CJWM

DIRECTIIONS ~ (Q. Nos. 114-116) *Indicate the answer choice to the question mark(?).*

114. EDUCATION : NOITACUDE :: INTELLIGENCE : ? « SSC (10+2) 2013
(a) ECENGILLTEIN (b) ECNGEILLTENI
(c) ECNEGILLETNI (d) ECNEGILLTENI

115. BUCKET : ACTVBDJLDFSU : : BONUS : ?
(a) ACMNMOTVRT (b) SUNOB
(c) ACNPMOTVRT (d) ACMNMOTURT

116. Australia : Continent « UP PSC 2013
(a) Engine : Train (b) River : Coast
(c) Vikrant : Ship (d) Yuri Gagarin : Space

DIRECTIONS ~ (Q. Nos. 117-119) *Choose the option that best completes the relationship indicated in capitalised pair.* « JMET 2011

117. Criticise : Fulminate
(a) Tense : Assuage (b) Flail : Control
(c) Hurt : Torture (d) Land : Prevaricate

118. Poetry : Ballad
(a) Reptile : Snake (b) Bulb : Tube light
(c) Snake : Reptile (d) Life : Death

119. 5 : 35
(a) 7 : 77 (b) 9 : 45 (c) 11 : 55 (d) 3 : 24

DIRECTIONS ~ (Q. Nos. 120-131) *In each of the following questions, a related pairs of words is linked by a colon, followed by four pair of words. Choose the pair, which is most like the relationship expressed in the original pair in capital letters.* « FMS 2006

120. Impecunious : Mendicant
(a) Prodigal : Philanthropist (b) Petulant : Complainer
(c) Quizzical : Critic (d) Compulsive : Liar

121. Error : Infallible
(a) Emotion : Invulnerable (b) Defect : Intolerable
(c) Flaw : Impeccable (d) Cure : Irreversible

122. Tears : Lachrymose
(a) Words : Verbose (b) Speeches : Morose
(c) Jests : Ironic (d) Requests : Effusive

123. Authenticity : Apocryphal
(a) Wickedness : Nefarious (b) Artifice : Deceptive
(c) Assertiveness : Dogmatic (d) Integrity : Hypocritical

124. Servility : Grovel
(a) Arrogance : Titter (b) Modesty : Preen
(c) Hypocrisy : Snivel (d) Anger : Fume

125. 41537 is related to 4 in the same way as 421 is related to
(a) 50 (b) 137 (c) 2 (d) 49

126. If PUZZLE :: Solve, then Essay :: ?. Identify what can come in place of '?'.
(a) Resolve (b) Dictate
(c) Recite (d) Write

127. A : Transaction : : Language : B
(a) A. Agreement, B. Communication
(b) A. Business, B. Media
(c) A. Money, B. Conversation
(d) A. Contract, B. Scholar

128. A : Inert : : Active : B
(a) A. Statics, B. Gymnast
(b) A. Helium, B. Participation
(c) A. Air, B. Smart
(d) A. Static, B. Dynamic

129. A : Gum : : Worm : B
(a) A. Tree, B. Silk (b) A. Loaf, B. Tread
(c) A. Bottle, B. Insect (d) A. Brand, B. Cocoon

130. Lightning : A : : B : Sky
(a) A. Rain, B. Thunder (b) A. Rainbow, B. Wind
(c) A. Cloud, B. Rainbow (d) A. Sky, B. Rain

131. A : Ocean : : Stone : B
(a) A. Glacier, B. Granite
(b) A. River, B. Pebble
(c) A. Lake, B. Rock
(d) A. Continent, B. Mountain

DIRECTIONS ~ (Q. Nos. 132-135) *Select the option which is having similar analogy vis-a-vis the analogy given in the question.*

132. Communication : Message : :
(a) Humor : Delight (b) Expression : Words
(c) Clarification : Doubt (d) Emission : Cosmic

133. Activate : Detonate : :
(a) Deaden : Defuse (b) Expression : Words
(c) Connect : Detach (d) Inform : Deform

134. If 'Asinine' is for 'Donkey', then
(a) 'Vulpine' is for 'fox' (b) Vulpine is for 'Vulture'
(c) 'Avian' is for cow (d) 'Avian' is for 'Dove'

135. If 'Stallion' is for 'Mare', than
(a) 'Ewe' is for 'Ram' (b) 'Ram' is for 'Ewe'
(c) 'Goose' is for 'Gander' (d) 'Sow' is for 'Bear'

DIRECTIONS ~ (Q. Nos. 136-139) *In the following questions their words are given, first two words bear a certain relationship between them, based on that find a word from the option that will bear the same relation with the third word.*

136. Mycology : Fungi : : Pedology : ?
(a) Moon (b) Kidney (c) Child (d) Soil

137. Alleviate : Aggravate : : Elastic : ? « IIFT 2013
(a) Rigid (b) Flexible
(c) Malleable (d) Strong

138. Stag : Fawn : : Cockroach : ?
(a) Nymph (b) Cub (c) Larva (d) Colt

139. Benevolent : Kind : : Unclear : « IIFT 2013
(a) Bright (b) Thick (c) Luminous (d) Muddy

DIRECTIONS ~ (Q. Nos. 140-152) *A pair of word is given in each question bearing a certain relationship. Based on that find the pair from options that will bear the same relationship.*

140. Russia : Moscow
(a) India : Mumbai (b) Norway : Oslo
(c) China : Shanghai (d) Pakistan : Faislabad

141. Error : Mistake
(a) Connection : Retaliation
(b) Literature : Poetry
(c) Music : Art
(d) Doubt : Suspicion

142. Ass : Bray
(a) Flies : Squeak (b) Hen : Mew
(c) Fox : Snout (d) Sheep : Bleat

143. Cigarette : Tobacco
(a) Coffee : Caffeine (b) Milk : Bottle
(c) Cigar : Filter (d) Shoes : Socks

144. Traveller : Destination « MAT 2013
(a) Beggar : Donation (b) Accident : Hospital
(c) Teacher : Education (d) Refugee : Shelter

145. Apostate : Religion
(a) Teacher : Education (b) Traitor : Country
(c) Potentate : Kingdom (d) Jailer : Law

146. Light : Glint
(a) Tide : Wave (b) Scent : Whiff
(c) Colour : Shade (d) Sound : Blare

147. Racism : Apartheid
(a) Sexism : Chauvinism (b) Parochialism : Linguism
(c) Nationalism : Identity (d) Communalism : Religion

148. Patriotism : Citizens « MAT 2013
(a) Morality : Truthfulness (b) Character: Values
(c) Concentration : Students (d) Homage : Martyrs

149. Surgeon : Scalpel
(a) Musician : Instrument (b) Carpenter : Cabinet
(c) Sculptor : Chisel (d) Baker : Oven

150. Horns : Bull
(a) Mane : Lion (b) Wattles : Turkey
(c) Hoofs : Horse (d) Antlers : Stag

151. Spider : Web « MAT 2014
(a) Ink : Pen (b) Cock : Hen
(c) Teacher: Student (d) Poet : Poetry

152. Jew : Synagogue « MAT 2014
(a) Parsis : Temple (b) Jains : Fire Temple
(c) Buddhists : Pagoda (d) Hindus : Vedas

153. 'Steel' is related to 'Alloy' in the same way as 'Zinc' is related to
(a) Non-metal (b) Halogen
(c) Alloy (d) None of these

DIRECTIONS ~ (Q. Nos. 154 and 155) *Each question has four analogies from (a) to (d). Mark the incorrect analogy.*

154. (a) Murrey : Black : : Magenta : Red
(b) Inter : Exhume : : Piebald : Homogenous
(c) Effete : Fructuous : : Chapfallen : Depressed
(d) Selenology : Moon : : Epistemology : Knowledge

155. (a) Polyglot : Languages : : Polyphagous : Food
(b) Escutcheon : Scutcheon : : Fabulist : Liar
(c) Scurvy : Vitamin C : : Kwashiorkor : Protein
(d) Apothecary : Drugs : : Cruciverbalist : Crosswords

DIRECTIONS ~ (Q. Nos. 156-163) *Complete the analogy or find the pair or group of elements having same analogical relationship as given in the question.*

156. $\frac{M}{AC}:\frac{N}{AD}::\frac{O}{AE}:?$

(a) $\frac{P}{AF}$ (b) $\frac{Q}{AB}$ (c) $\frac{P}{AC}$ (d) $\frac{R}{AD}$

157. If IQS : LNV, then JRM : ?

(a) OKS (b) MOP (c) NIP (d) MOQ

158. 24 : 126 : : 48 : ?

(a) 433 (b) 192 (c) 240 (d) 344

159. (32, 24, 8)

(a) (26, 32, 42) (b) (34, 24, 14)
(c) (24, 16, 8) (d) (42, 34, 16)

160. (81, 77, 69)

(a) (56, 52, 44) (b) (64, 61, 53)
(c) (75, 71, 60) (d) (92, 88, 79)

161. 'Dubious : Indisputable' « UKPSC Assist. Conservator of Forest 2019

(a) Slander : Libel (b) Painful : Tormenting
(c) Perspicacious : Tenacit (d) Avaricious : Generous

162. Thrust : Spear « MAT 2014

(a) cabbard : Sword (b) Mangle : Iron
(c) Bow : Arrow (d) Fence : Epee

163. Money : Transaction « MAT 2014

(a) Life : Death (b) Water : Drink
(c) Ideas : Exchange (d) Language : Conversation

DIRECTIONS ~ (Q. Nos. 164-170) *Each of these questions, consists of a pair of words bearing a certain relationship. From amongst the alternative, pick up the pair that best illustrates a similar relationship.* « MAT 2013

164. Sunrise : Sunset

(a) Dawn : Twilight (b) Noon : Midnight
(c) Morning : Night (d) Energetic : Lazy

165. River : Ocean

(a) Child : School (b) Book : Library
(c) Lane : Road (d) Cloth : Body

166. Glove : Hand

(a) Neck : Collar (b) Tie : Shirt
(c) Socks : Feet (d) Coat : Pocket

167. $-\frac{3}{7}:\frac{7}{3}::\frac{9}{2}:?$ « SSC (CGL) 2017

(a) $\frac{2}{9}$ (b) $-\frac{9}{2}$ (c) $\frac{7}{2}$ (d) $-\frac{2}{9}$

168. ACAZX : DFDWU : : GIGTR : ?

(a) JKIQO (b) JLJQO (c) JKJOQ (d) JLJOP

169. $123 : 13^2 :: 235 : ?$

(a) 23^3 (b) 25^3 (c) 35^2 (d) 25^2

170. LOM : NMK : : PKI : ? « NIFT (UG) 2014

(a) RIH (b) SHG (c) RIG (d) RHG

171. 'Carnivorous is related to 'Panther' in the same way as 'Herbivorous' is related to

(a) Tiger (b) Lion (c) Leopard (d) Buffalo

172. ABCD is related to OPQR in the same way as WXYZ is related to

(a) EFGH (b) STUV (c) KLMN (d) QRST

173. Butter is related to Milk in the same way as Paper is related to « UPSSSC Junior Assist. 2017

(a) Write (b) Pen (c) Pulp (d) Eraser

174. 'Ocean' is related to 'Water' in the same way as 'Desert' is related to

(a) Sand (b) Wind (c) Wave (d) Mountain

DIRECTIONS ~ (Q. Nos. 175-178) *In each of the following questions there are two blanks marked* I *and* II. *The words to fill in these blanks are given against* I *as* (A,B,C,D) *and* II *as* (P,Q,R,S) *respectively. The right words to fill in these blanks are given as four alternatives. The words on either side of the sign* (: :) *have a similar relationship. The alternative which signifies this relationship is your answer.* « SNAP 2012, 2010, 2009

175. I : Increase : : Descend : II

I. (A) Grow (B) Ascend
(C) RISE (D) Price
II. (P) Reduce (Q) Down
(R) Decrease (S) Mountain

(a) AR (b) BR (c) CP (d) DQ

176. Modern : I : : II : Old

I. (A) Ancient (B) Death
(C) Famous (D) Civilization
II. (P) Industrialisation (Q) Young
(R) Fashion (S) Western

(a) AQ (b) AS (c) BP (d) CR

177. Part : I : : Class : II

I. (A) Section (B) Whole
(C) School (D) Student
II. (P) Student (Q) School
(R) Teachers (S) Rooms

(a) AR (b) BQ (c) CP (d) DS

178. Summit : Apex : : I : II

I. (A) Beautiful (B) Picture
(C) Attractive (D) Enchanting
II. (P) Comfortable (Q) Pretty
(R) Healthy (S) Brave

(a) AQ (b) BP (c) DS (d) CR

179. 'Jackal' is related to 'Carnivorous' in the same way as 'Horse' is related to

(a) Omnivorous (b) Carnivorous
(c) Herbivorous (d) Multivorous

180. RADIO : UCHKT : : AUDIO : ? « NIFT (PG) 2013

(a) CVHKT (b) BWHKT (c) DXHKT (d) DWHKT

DIRECTIONS ~ (Q. Nos. 181 and 182) *There are two pairs, the first pair follows some relationship. Use this relationship to find the analogy of the second pair.* « NIFT (PG) 2013

181. Rectangle : Pentagon

(a) Triangle : Rectangle (b) Diagonal : Perimeter
(c) Side : Angle (d) Circle : Square

182. Simmer : Boil

(a) Glide : Drift
(b) Drizzle : Downpour
(c) Gambol : Play
(d) Stagnate : Flow

DIRECTIONS ~ (Q. Nos. 183-186) *Select the pair of words/ numbers that has the same analogous relationship as the original pair of words/numbers.*

183. Propensity : Tendency

(a) Prologue : Epilogue
(b) Master : Slave
(c) Audacity : Impudence
(d) Conduct : Immortality

184. Intimidate : Wheedle

(a) Resolute : Impetuous
(b) Coordinate : Disinter
(c) Defile : Rebuke
(d) Extol : Disparage

185. Indefatigable : Inveterate « IIFT 2012

(a) Tireless : Tired
(b) Tired : Habitual
(c) Tireless : Habitual
(d) Impoverished : Habitual

186. Misanthrope : Humanity « IIFT 2012

(a) Chauvinist : Patriot
(b) Misogynist : Women
(c) Agnostic : God
(d) Witch : Magic

187. 'Celsius is related to 'Temperature' in the same way as 'Metre' is related to « MHA-CET 2011

(a) Depth (b) Square (c) Tall (d) Kilometer

188. 'Seed' is related to 'Fruit' in the same way as 'Fruit' is related to

(a) Tree (b) Branch (c) Flower (d) Petal

189. Choose the option that belongs to the same category as the below words:

Cinema, Actors, Director

« UPSSSC Junior Assist. 2017

(a) Book (b) Disease (c) Principal (d) Theatre

190. Select the option that is related to the fifth number in the same way as the second number is related to the first number and the fourth number is related to the third number.

19 : 23 :: 11 : 13 :: 7 : ? « SSC CPO 2019

(a) 3 (b) 9 (c) 5 (d) 11

DIRECTIONS ~ (Q. Nos. 191-195) *Select the related word from the given alternatives.*

191. Ornithology : Birds :: Mycology : ?

(a) Insects
(b) Mosquito
(c) Microbes
(d) Fungi

192. Paleontology : X :: Pedology : Y

X and Y = ?

(a) Primitive plants and teaching
(b) Fossils and soil
(c) Parenting and Nutrition
(d) Electrolytes and soil

193. Twitter : X :: Google : Y

X and Y = ?

(a) Palo Alto and Welwyn Garden city.
(b) Welwyn Garden city and London
(c) San Bruno and Milton Keynes
(d) San Francisco and Mountain view

194. Origami : Paper :: I ke bana : ?

(a) Tapertry
(b) Forest
(c) Plants
(d) Flowers

195. Chisel : Sculptor :: Harrow : ?

(a) Blacksmith
(b) Plumber
(c) Electrician
(d) Gardner

Answers / WITH EXPLANATIONS

1. (*d*) 'Menu' lists all the Food items in a restaurant and in the same way, a Catalogue is a list of all the Books in a library.

2. (*d*) 'Bleat' is the sound produced by Goat and in the same way 'Grunt' is the sound produced by a 'Camel'.

3. (*b*) Former is the grown up state of latter.

4. (*d*) Both the words are opposite in meaning to each other.

5. (*c*) Birds Fly while Snakes Crawl for movement.

6. (*d*) STATUE is related to SIZE in the same way as SONG is related to TUNE. Here, second is the criteria by which the quality of first is determined.

7. (*b*) Taka is the currency of Bangladesh. Similarly, Lira is the currency of Italy.

8. (*d*) 'Nurse' receives instructions from 'Doctor' and 'Follower' receives instructions from 'Leader'.

9. (*a*) 'Food' is consumed in the 'Stomach' and 'Fuel' is consumed in 'Engine'.

10. (*c*) Water' is contained in 'Ocean'. Likewise 'Sand' is contained in 'Desert'.

11. (*b*) 'Botany' is the branch of science which deals with the study of 'Plants'. Similarly, 'Entomology' is the branch of science which deals with the study of Insects.

12. (*c*) First is the meant for the second.

13. (*a*) As, Igloos are commonly found in Canada. Similarly, Rondavels are commonly found in Africa.

14. (*a*) As, Fetter means to bound and Liberated means to set free. In the same way, Shackle means as to arrest or to bound and Loose means as to set free.

15. (*b*) As, Ponder and Consider are synonym to each other, similarly, synonym of Pinnacle is Peak.

16. (*a*) A 'Bank' deals with transaction of 'Money'. Likewise 'Transport' deals with the movement of 'Goods'.

17. (*c*) 'Wings' are the parts of a 'Fan'. Likewise 'Spokes' are the parts of 'Wheel'.

18. (*b*) 'Captain' is supposed to lead the battalion of 'Soldiers' in the same way as 'Leader' is supposed to lead the 'Followers'.

19. (*b*) 'Skirmish', if uncontrolled gives rise to 'War'. In the same way, 'Disease', if uncontrolled gives rise to 'Epidemic'.

20. (*b*) 'Tree' originates from 'Root'. Likewise 'Smoke' originates from 'Fire'.

21. (*d*) As, 'Good' is antonym to 'Bad'. Similarly, 'Floor' is the antonym to 'Roof'.

22. (*b*) 'Oval' is the figure which is similar to the 'Circle'. Likewise 'Rectangle' is the figure which is similar to 'Square', as both of them have four corners.

23. (*d*) 'Umpire' is required to give decision in 'Match'. Likewise 'Judge' is required to give decision in a 'Lawsuit'.

24. (*c*) The given words in each pair are antonyms of each other.

25. (*a*) As, 'Needle' requires 'Thread' for stiching. Similarly, 'Pen' requires 'Ink' for writing.

26. (*d*) As, a Marathon is a long Race, Similarly, Hibernation is a lengthy period of Sleep.

27. (*a*) As, colour of the Sky is Blue. Similarly, colour of Mud is Brown.

28. (*b*) As, the sound produces by the Lion is called Roar. Similarly, the sound produces by the Horse is called Neigh.

29. (*c*) As, 'Umpire' is in the 'Game', in the same way, 'Legislator' is in the 'Election'.

30. (*a*) 'Confession' is made on the basis of 'Testimony', in the same way 'Crime' is decided on the basis of the 'Petition'.

31. (*a*) Person who is 'Studious' will be 'Erudite', similarly a person who is 'Enterprising' will be 'Rich'.

32. (*d*) As, 'Action' is followed by 'Reaction', in the same way 'Death' is followed by 'Rebirth'.

33. (*b*) Number of sides in figure second are double the number of sides of figure first.

34. (*a*) Both are synonyms of each other.

35. (*a*) As, 'Cloth' has 'Texture', in the same way 'Body' has 'Weight'.

36. (*c*) As, 'Nuts' are covered with 'Bolts', in the same way a 'Naked' is covered with 'Clothes'.

37. (*c*) As, an Arrow is fired from a Bow. Similarly, Bullet is fired from a Rifle.

38. (*d*) As, Annex and Lessening are antonym to each other. Similarly, Jocund and Serious are antonym to each other.

39. (*d*) As, Cardiology is the branch of medicine dealing with the Heart and its diseases. Similarly, Virology studies Viruses and viral diseases.

40. (*d*) As, Binding surrounds a Book. Similarly, a Frame surrounds a Picture.

41. (*c*) As, we wear Gloves on our Hands. Similarly, we wear Socks on our Feet.

42. (*c*) As, Bear comes under the category of Mammal. Similarly, Mango comes under the category of Fruit.

43. (*d*) Second shows the quality of first.

44. (*a*) Latter is the result of former.

45. (*a*) As,

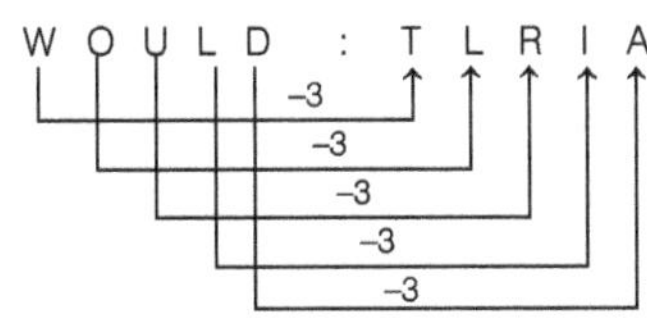

Similarly,

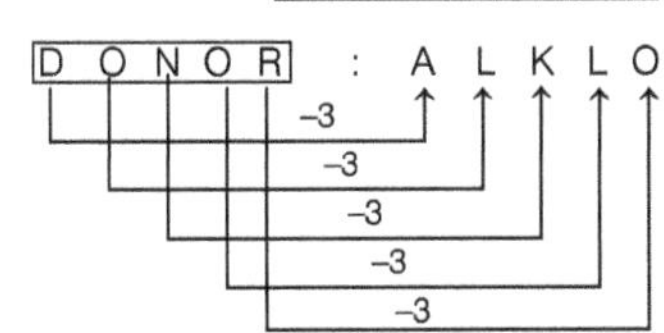

46. (*a*) As,

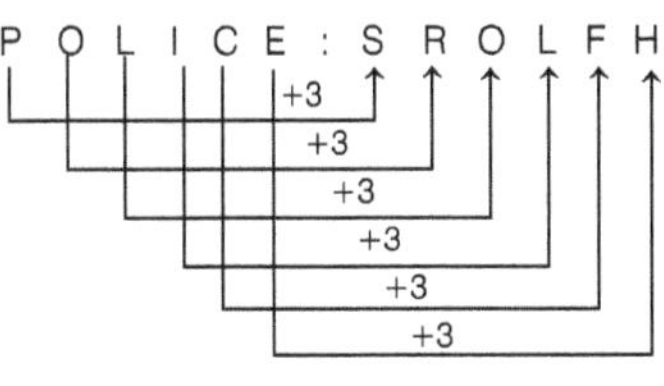

Similarly,

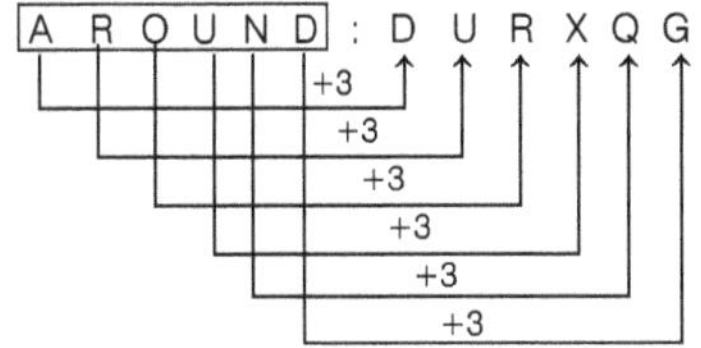

47. (*a*) As, 'Hair' are present on 'Head'. Similarly, Fingers are present in 'Hand.'

48. (*d*) As, 'Running' is the higher form of 'Walking'. Similarly, 'Storm' is the higher form of 'Wind'.

49. (*c*) As, 'King' sits on the 'Throne', in the same way 'Rider' sits on the 'Seat'.

50. (*d*)

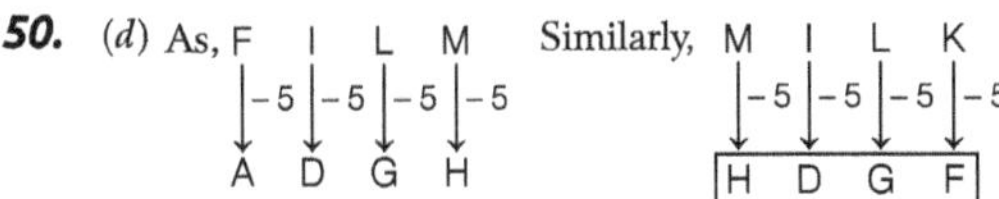

51. (*a*)

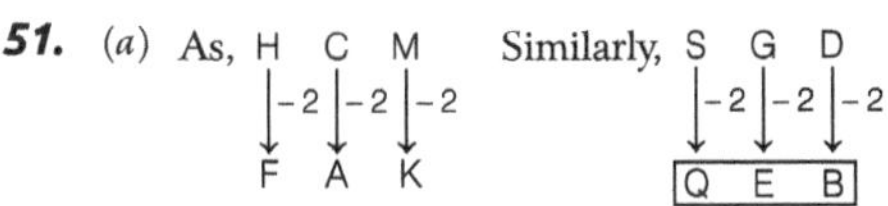

52. (*c*) As in the River, water Flows. Similarly, in the Pool, water is Stagnant.

53. (*c*) As, Contemporary is related to present time and Historic belonges to the past. Similarly, Modern is related to present time and Ancient belongs to the past or old.

54. (*d*) As, Cheerful and Morose are antonym to each other. Similarly, Valiant and Coward are antonym to each other.

55. (*b*) As, Amusing and Delightful are synonym to each other. Similarly, Weary and Exhausted are synonym to each other.

56. (*b*) As, Barometer is a measuring instrument used to determine the pressure of Atmosphere. Similarly, Calorimeter is used to measure the amount of heat involved in a chemical or physical process.

57. (*a*) As, Sphygmomanometer is used to measure Blood Pressure. Similarly, Pyrometer is used to measure high Temperature.

58. (*d*) As, 'Tobacco', causes 'Cancer', similarly 'Mosquito', causes 'Malaria'.

59. (*a*) If we move from West, clockwise through 135°, we get North-East direction. Similarly, if we move from South, clockwise through 135°, we get North-West direction.

60. (*a*) As,

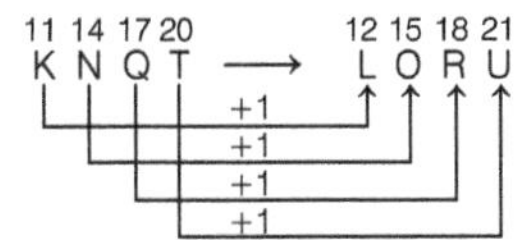

Similarly, 1 4 7 10 A D G J ⟶ 2 5 8 11 [B E H K] (+1, +1, +1, +1)

61. (*d*) As, 401 : 19 ⇒ $(19+1)^2+1=401$
Similarly, 730 : ? ⇒ $(26+1)^2+1=730$

62. (*a*) As, $42=(7)^2-7, 56=(8)^2-8$
Similarly, $110=(11)^2-11$ and $(12)^2-12=132$

63. (*b*) As, $5\times 20=100, 4\times 16=64$
Similarly, $4\times 20=80$ and $3\times 16=48$

64. (*a*) As, 23 18 9 20 5 W R I T E (+13 each) J E V G R 10 5 22 7 18
Similarly, 23 18 15 14 7 W R O N G (+13 each) [J E B A T] 10 5 2 1 20

65. (*d*) As, T N G P ⟶ 20 14 7 16
Similarly, L P D T ⟶ [12 16 4 20]

66. (*a*) As, P S T
16 + 19 + 20 = 55 (addition of place value)
and sum of the digits of 55 = 5 + 5 = 10
Sum of the digits of 10 = 1 + 0 = 1
Similarly, N P R
14 + 16 + 18 = 48 (addition of place value)
Sum of the digits of 48 = 4 + 8 = 12
Sum of the digits of 12 = 1 + 2 = [3]

67. (*c*) As, 212 : 436 (+224) Similarly, 560 : [784] (+224)

68. (*a*) As, 6 3 → 6 + 3 = 9 Similarly, 6 8 → 6 + 8 = 14

69. (*a*) As, 432 : 24 (4 × 3 × 2) Similarly, 735 : [105] (7 × 3 × 5)

70. (*c*)
As,

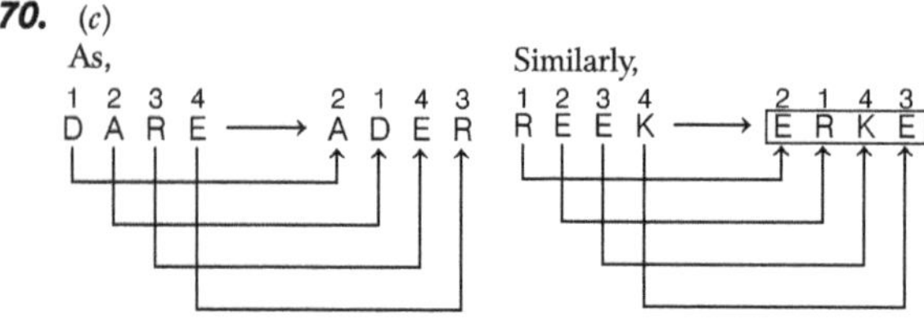

71. (*b*) We obtain Silk from Silkworm. Similarly, we can get Poison from Snake.

72. (*c*) As, L and M are 12th and 13th letters respectively in English alphabetical series, similarly as U and W are 21st and 23rd letters, respectively in English alphabetical series.

73. (*d*) As letter 'a' comes at first position in English alphabetical series, similarly, 'f' comes at sixth position in English alphabetical series.

74. (*c*) As,

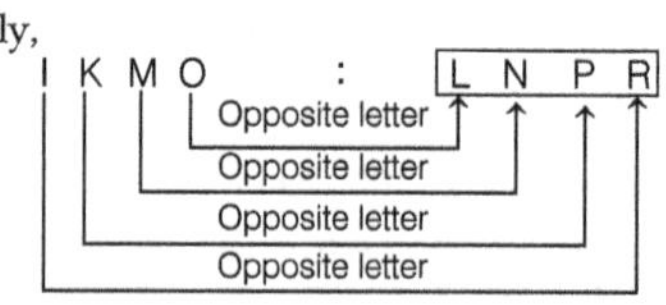

Similarly,
I K M O : [L N P R] (Opposite letter, Opposite letter, Opposite letter, Opposite letter)

75. (*d*) The given pattern is as follows
As, 2 6 11 B F K (+7 each) I M R 9 13 18
Similarly, 4 7 16 D G P (+7 each) [K N W] 11 14 23

76. (*b*) As, 7 9 11 G I K (−1 each) F H J 6 8 10
Similarly, 15 17 19 O Q S (−1 each) [N P R] 14 16 18

77. (*d*) As, 4 1 8 20 D A R T (−6, +6, −6, +6) X G L Z 24 7 12 26
Similarly, 19 16 9 14 S P I N (−6, +6, −6, +6) [M V C T] 13 22 3 20

78. (*a*) The given pattern is as follows
As, 13 1 11 9 14 7 M A K I N G → K G M A N I 11 7 13 1 14 9
Similarly, 3 1 16 5 20 15 C A P E T O → [P O C A T E] 16 15 3 1 20 5

79. (*d*) Second is the meaningful word from the letters of the first word.
As, CLOUD → COULD

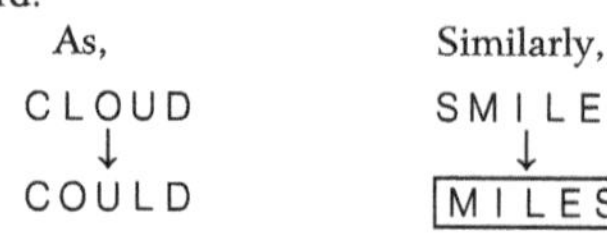

80. (b) As,

5	1	18	20	8
E	A	R	T	H
+3 ↓	+3 ↓	+3 ↓	+3 ↓	+3 ↓
H	D	U	W	K
8	4	21	23	11

Similarly,

22	5	14	21	19
V	E	N	U	S
+3 ↓	+3 ↓	+3 ↓	+3 ↓	+3 ↓
Y	H	Q	X	V
25	8	17	24	22

81. (c) As,

1	2	3	4	5
P	U	R	S	E
U	P	R	E	S
2	1	3	5	4

Similarly,

1	2	3	4	5
R	A	Z	O	R
A	R	Z	R	O
2	1	3	5	4

82. (b) As,

18	5	1	19	15	14
R	E	A	S	O	N
↓+1	↓+1	↓+1	↓+1	↓+1	↓+1
S	F	B	T	P	O
19	6	2	20	16	15

Similarly,

20	8	9	14	11
T	H	I	N	K
↓+1	↓+1	↓+1	↓+1	↓+1
U	I	J	O	L
21	9	10	15	12

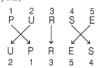

83. (c) Both the words are synonym of each other.

84. (c) Both the words are synonym of each other.

85. (b) As, $15 + 12 = 27$

$27 + 12 = 39$

Similarly, $105 + 20 = 125$

$125 + 20 = 145$

86. (d) Every number in each set is a perfect square

As, $49 = 7^2, 81 = 9^2, 25 = 5^2$

Similarly, $100 = 10^2, 289 = 17^2, 4 = 2^2$

87. (a) First number is the addition of the last two.

As, $5 + 7 = 12$

Similarly, $4 + 3 = 7$

88. (a) As, 23 : 30 : 37 = 23 : 30 : 37 (+7, +7)

Similarly, 6 : 13 : 20 = 6 : 13 : 20 (+7, +7)

89. (d) As, 7 16 34 (+9, +18)

Similarly, 49 58 76 (+9, +18)

90. (b) 'Omniscient' is an adjective used for someone who has the 'Knowledge' of all things. Similarly, 'Boundless' is an adjective used for 'Expanse'.

91. (c) A Nebulous Form means having an ambiguous form same as an Insipid Taste which is dull, boring, almost no taste.

92. (c) As 'Inexperience' causes 'Errors', similarly, 'Carelessness' causes 'Losses'.

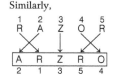

93. (c) As study of 'Brain' is called 'Neurology', similarly, study of 'Body' is called 'Physiology'.

94. (a) As 'Quack' is sound of 'Duck', similarly, 'Growl' is sound of 'Dog'.

95. (b) As 'Picture' is related to 'See', similarly the 'Book' is related to 'Read'.

96. (d) Both the words are opposite in meaning to each other.

97. (c) As, 'Swimming' takes place in 'River', similarly, 'Hiking' takes place on 'Mountain'.

98. (a) As, 1 2 3 4 5 6 7 HOPEFUL : 7 6 5 4 3 2 1 LUFEPOH

Similarly, 1 2 3 4 5 6 7 8 9 ETHNICITY : 9 8 7 6 5 4 3 2 1 YTICINHTE

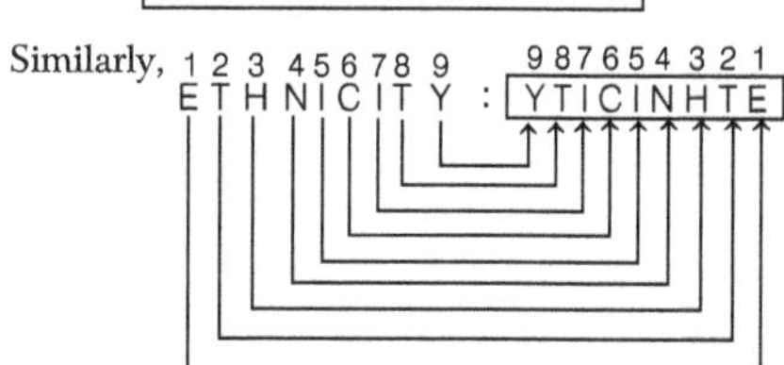

99. (d) As, with every 'Right' comes a 'Duty', similarly 'Power' invites 'Liability'.

100. (c) Young one of an 'Elephant' is 'Calf' and that of a 'Tiger' is 'Cub'.

101. (d) As, a 'Patient' goes to a 'Doctor' for medical help, similarly a 'Litigant' goes to a 'Lawyer' for legal help.

102. (c) United Nations was created after World War II and League of Nations was created after World War I.

103. (c) As, $841 = (29)^2$

Similarly, $289 = \boxed{(17)^2}$

104. (a) As, 8 : 28 ($\times 3 + 4$) Similarly, 27 : $\boxed{85}$ ($\times 3 + 4$)

105. (a) As, $11^2 - 1 = 121 - 1 = 120$

Similarly, $15^2 - 1 = 225 - 1 = \boxed{224}$

106. (d) As, $12^2 = 144$ Similarly, $\boxed{24^2} = 576$

107. (b) As, $0.16 = (0.4)^2$

Similarly, $1.21 = (1.1)^2$

108. (a) As, $2264 \Rightarrow 2 + 2 + 6 + 4 = 14$

$7241 \Rightarrow 7 + 2 + 4 + 1 = 14$

Similarly, $3129 \Rightarrow 3 + 1 + 2 + 9 = 15$

$\boxed{6342} \Rightarrow 6 + 3 + 4 + 2 = 15$

109. (b) As for finishing the 'Leather', 'Tanning' method is used, in the same way for 'Fireworks' 'Pyrotechnics' is used.

110. (a) As, $F = 6 \Rightarrow 6^3 = 216$

Similarly, $L = 12 \Rightarrow (12)^3 = \boxed{1728}$

111. (c) As, 13 15 21 19 5 MOUSE ⟶ 11 16 19 20 3 KPSTC (−2, +1, −2, +1, −2)

Similarly, 12 9 7 8 20 LIGHT ⟶ 10 10 5 9 18 JJEIR (−2, +1, −2, +1, −2)

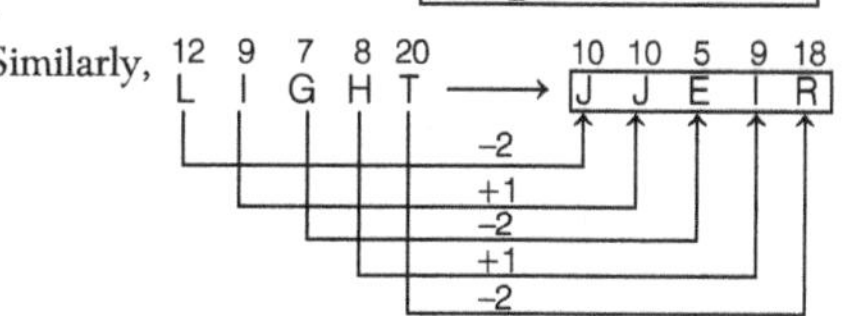

112. (c) As, sum of digits of $584 = 5 + 8 + 4 = 17$

and sum of digits of $488 = 4 + 8 + 8 = 20$

Similarly, sum of digits of $294 = 2 + 9 + 4 = 15$

$\therefore$ Sum of digits of $\boxed{378} = 3 + 7 + 8 = 18$

Here, difference of both are $(20 - 17) = (18 - 15) = 3$

113. (*b*) As,

1	8	15	16
A	H	O	P
↓ +2	↓ +3	↓ +4	↓ +5
C	K	S	U
3	11	19	21

Similarly,

2	10	13	6
B	J	M	F
↓ +2	↓ +3	↓ +4	↓ +5
D	M	Q	K
4	13	17	11

114. (*c*) As, NOITACUDE is made by reversing the order of the letters of the word EDUCATION, similarly reverse order of the letters of the word INTELLIGENCE is ECNEGILLETNI.

115. (*c*) Each letter in the word is replaced by the letter preceeding and following it in the alphabetical series.

116. (*c*) As, 'Australia' is a 'Continent', similarly, 'Vikrant' is a 'Ship'.

117. (*c*) The given pair contains synonymous words but the second word has a higher degree.

118. (*a*) 'Ballad' is a type of Poetry, in the same way as 'Snake' is a type of 'Reptile'.

119. (*a*) As, $5 \times 7 = 35$ i.e. 5 multiplied with next prime number i.e. 7.
Similarly, $7 \times 11 = 77$ i.e. 7 multiplied with next prime number i.e. 11.

120. (*b*) Relation – Condition : characteristic behavior.
'Impecunious' means 'Poor' and 'Mendicant' means 'Begging'. Petulant means bad tempered who is a Complainer.

121. (*c*) Relation – Noun : opposite adjective.
'Infallible' means never committing 'Error', 'Impeccable' means 'Flawless'.

122. (*a*) Relation – Factor : Something that causes it.
'Lachrymose' means causing 'Tears' while so many 'Words' makes a written matter 'Verbose'.

123. (*a*) Relation – Noun : opposite adjective.
Apocryphal means false, Nefarious means Wicked.

124. (*d*) Relation – Noun : verb.
Grovel means to be Servile, Fume means to show Anger.

125. (*d*) As, $41537 \Rightarrow 4 + 1 + 5 + 3 + 7 = 20$
$\Rightarrow 2 + 0 = 2 \Rightarrow (2)^2 = 4$
Similarly, $421 \Rightarrow 4 + 2 + 1 = 7 \Rightarrow (7)^2 = 49$

126. (*d*) As puzzle is need to be solved, similarly Essay is need to be written.

127. (*c*) First is required for the second.

128. (*d*) The words in each pair are synonyms.

129. (*a*) Second is obtained from the first.

130. (*c*) 'Lightning' occurs in 'Clouds' and 'Rainbow' is formed in the 'Sky'.

131. (*c*) Second is an enlarged form of the first.

132. (*a*) Both the words are opposite in meaning.

133. (*b*) Both the words are opposite in meaning.

134. (*a*) 'Asinine' means 'Foolish'; or like a Donkey. Similarly, 'Vulpine' means 'Cunning' or resembling a 'Fox'. 'Avian' means 'of or pertaining to birds' in general, and not specifically doves. Hence, the correct answer is option (a).

135. (*b*) A 'Stallion' is a male-horse while a 'Mare' is a female horse. Therefore, the relationship is Male : Female. In options (a), (c) and (d) this relationship is inverted. In option (b) 'Ram', a male sheep, proceeds 'Ewe' a female sheep.

136. (*d*) 'Mycology' is the study of 'Fungi'; in the same way 'Pedology' is the study of 'Soil'.

137. (*a*) 'Alleviate' means 'to reduce' and 'Aggravate' means 'to intensify'. So, it is a clear opposite analogy and it is similar to 'Elastic' and 'Rigid' which are mutually opposite.

138. (*a*) Second is the young-one of first.

139. (*d*) Benevolent and Kind are mutually synonyms, so Muddy is the best option which is similar to unclear in meaning.

140. (*b*) They are Country and capital pair.

141. (*d*) 'Error' and 'Mistake' are synonyms to each other and 'Doubt' and 'Suspicion' are also synonyms to each other.

142. (*d*) Second is the sound produced by the first.

143. (*a*) As, 'Tobacco' is the prime constituent of 'Cigarette'. Similarly, 'Caffeine' is the prime constituent of 'Coffee'.

144. (*d*) A 'Traveller' travels for reaching 'Destination', in the same way 'Refugee' travels for 'Shelter'.

145. (*b*) 'Apostate' is one who 'prsakes Religion', in the same way 'Traitor' is one who Betrays his Country.

146. (*d*) 'Glint' is a flash of 'Light'. Similarly, 'Blare' is a loud 'Sound'.

147. (*a*) Synonymous word relationship.

148. (*c*) A Citizen must be Patriotic to his country. Similarly, a Student should Concentrate on studies.

149. (*c*) A 'Surgeon' uses 'Scalpel' for doing operation, in the same way 'Sculptor' uses his 'Chisel' for making sculpture.

150. (*d*) A 'Bull' bears 'Horns' on its head, in the same way as a 'Stag' bears 'Antlers' on its head.

151. (*d*) As, 'Web' is made by 'Spider', in the same way 'Poetry' is made by 'Poet'.

152. (*c*) As, 'Synagogue' is the worship place of 'Jew', in the same way 'Pagoda' is the worship place of 'Buddhists'.

153. (*d*) 'Steel' is an 'Alloy' and 'Zinc' is a 'Metal'. Hence, none of the options gives the correct answer.

154. (*c*) In option (a) the relationship is – Derivative colour : Main colour; in option (b) there is relationship of opposite (Inter = to bury, Exhume = to dig out, Piebald = heterogeneous in hair colour); in option (c) the words in the first pairs are opposite to each other as effete means unproductive and fructuous means fertile but words in the second pair are similar to each other as chapfallen means depressed.
Hence, option (c) is wrong analogy; in option (d) the relationship is – Branch of study: Studied field.

155. (*d*) In option (a) the relationship is – Type of person using different types of something : The thing (Polyglot = one who uses different Languages, Polyphagous = one who uses different Foods); in option (b) there are synonyms (Escutcheon/Scutcheon = a shield, Fabulist = Liar); in option (c) the relationship is – Disease : Caused by the deficiency of.
In option (d) two unrelated analogies are given; Apothecary is one who sells Drugs and Cruciverbalist is one who is skillful in solving Crosswords.

156. (*a*) As,

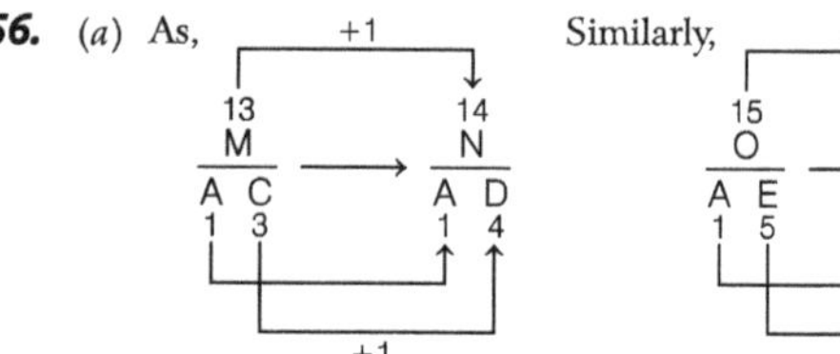

157. (*b*) As, 9 17 19 : 12 14 22 — I Q S : L N V (+3, −3, +3) Similarly, 10 18 13 : 13 15 16 — J R M : [M O P] (+3, −3, +3)

158. (*d*) As, 24 : 126 — $(5^2 - 1)$ $(5^3 + 1)$ Similarly, 48 : [344] — $(7^2 - 1)$ $(7^3 + 1)$

159. (*c*) In each set,

2nd number = (1st number − 3rd number)

As, 32 − 8 = 24

Similarly, 24 − 8 = 16

160. (*a*) In each set,

2nd number = 1st number − 4

3rd number = 2nd number − 8

As, 77 = 81 − 4

and 69 = 77 − 8

Similarly, 52 = 56 − 4

and 44 = 52 − 8

161. (*d*) As, Dubious and Indisputable are opposite to each other, similarly Avaricious and Generous are opposite to each other.

162. (*b*) As the 'Spear' is 'Thrust', in the same way 'Iron' is 'Mangle'.

163. (*d*) As 'Money' is a source of 'Transaction', in the same way 'Language' is a source of 'Conversation'.

164. (*d*) As, 'Sunrise' and 'Sunset' are opposite to each other, in the same manner 'Energetic' and 'Lazy' are opposite to each other.

165. (*c*) 'River' flows to meet the 'Ocean', in the same way 'Lane' goes onto meet the 'Road'.

166. (*c*) As 'Gloves' are worn on 'Hands', in the same way 'Socks' are worn on 'Feet'.

167. (*d*) As, $-\frac{3}{7} \times \frac{7}{3}$

Same as, $\frac{9}{2} \times \boxed{\frac{-2}{9}}$

Here, reciprocal of given number with opposite sign is written.

168. (*b*)

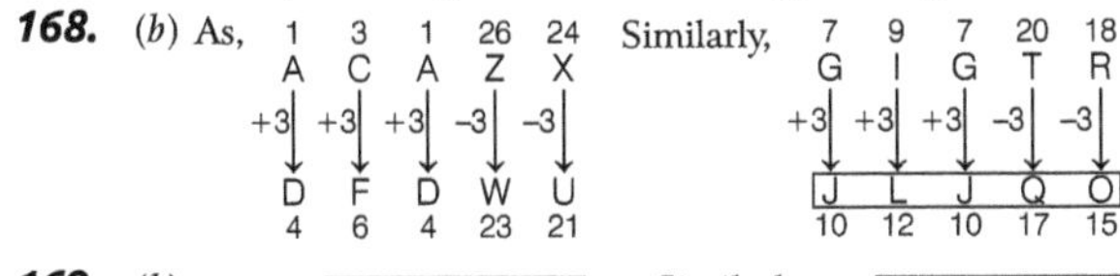

169. (*b*)

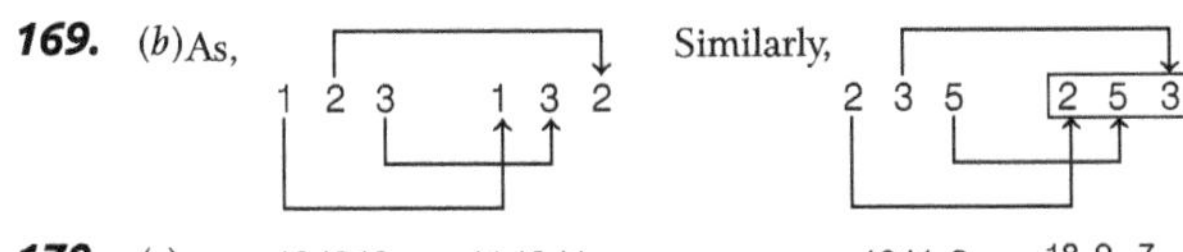

170. (*c*)

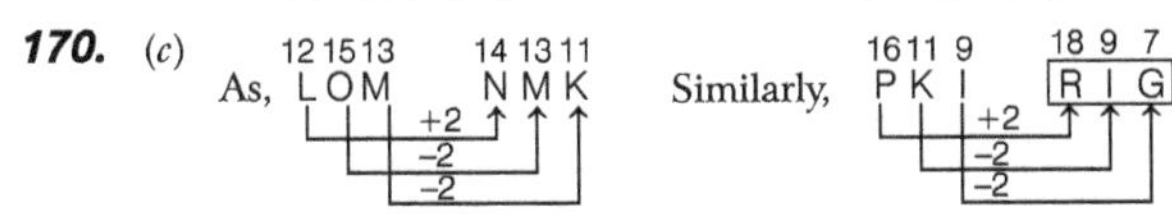

171. (*d*) As, 'Panther' is a flesh eating or 'Carnivorous' animal, similarly 'Buffalo' is a vegetarian or 'Herbivorous' animal.

172. (*c*)

As, 1 2 3 4 — A B C D : 15 16 17 18 — O P Q R (+14, +14, +14, +14) Similarly, 23 24 25 26 — W X Y Z : 11 12 13 14 — [K L M N] (+14, +14, +14, +14)

173. (*c*) As, Butter is the by product of Milk. Similarly, Paper is made of Pulp.

174. (*a*) As, Water flows in the Ocean. Similarly, Sand is in the Desert.

175. (*b*) BR shows the correct analogy with exact antonyms in both the pairs - Ascend : Increase : : Descend : Decrease. Here, ascent is the antonym of descent and increase is the antonym of decrease.

176. (*a*) AQ gives the perfect antonymous analogous relationship - Modern : Ancient : : Young : Old.

177. (*b*) Part : Whole : : Class : School.

178. (*a*) Summit and Apex are synonymous. The only option which comes close to being a synonym is AQ - Beautiful : Pretty.

179. (*c*) As, 'Jackal' is a flesh eating or 'Carnivorous' animal, similarly 'Horse' is a vegetarian or 'Herbivorous' animal.

180. (*d*)

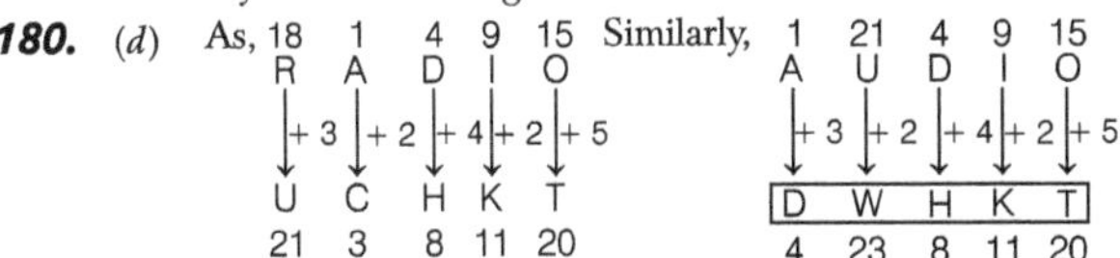

181. (*a*) Rectangle : Pentagon

As, rectangle has 4 sides and pentagon has 5 sides, one more side than rectangle, in the same way, triangle has 3 sides and rectangle has 4 sides, one more side than rectangle.

∵ Second analogy = Triangle : Rectangle

182. (*b*) Simmer is to cook slowly and Boil is when it is heated very heavily, in the same way Drizzle is raining slowly and Downpour is very heavy rainfall suddenly.

183. (*c*) Both the words are synonyms of each other.

184. (*d*) Both the words are antonyms. As, Wheedle means to flatter and Intimidate means giving threats, similarly, Disparage means to insult and Extol means to praise.

185. (*c*) As, Indefatigable means never giving up or getting tired of doing something and Inveterate means always doing something or unlikely to stop. Similarly, Tireless means putting a lot of effort and energy to do something over a long period of time and Habitual means doing something often and difficult to stop.

186. (*b*) As 'Misanthrope' means a person who hates and avoids 'Humanity' (people in general), similarly 'Misogynist' is a man who hates 'Women'.

187. (*c*) As 'Celsius' is the unit of measurement of 'Temperature', similarly 'Metre' is the unit of measurement of 'Tall'.

188. (*a*) 'Seed' is the part of 'Fruit', in the same way 'Fruit' is the part of 'Tree'.

189. (*d*) Cinema, Actors, and Director are related to Theatre.

190. (*d*) As, next prime number of 19 is 23 and next prime number of 11 is 13. Similarly, next prime number of 7 is 11.

191. (*d*) As, study of Birds is Ornithology, similarly, study of Fungi is Mycology.

192. (*b*) As, study of Fossils is Paleontology. Similarly, study of Soil is Pedology.

193. (*d*) Head office of Twitter and Google is situated in San Francisco and Mountain view.

194. (*d*) First is an art associated with the second.

195. (*d*) Chisel is the tool of Sculptor. Similarly, Harrow is the tool of Gardner.

CHAPTER / 03

Classification

Classification is the process of grouping various objects on the basis of their common properties like shape, size, category, colour, trait etc., and finding the odd object from the group.

In this chapter, the questions contain a set of different items and it is asked to find the odd item out of the given ones.

All the items except one, follow a certain rule or pattern or they possess some common quality or characteristics among them. The one, which is odd, does not possess the common quality or characteristics.

Let us take some examples

e.g. Find the odd word from the group.

(a) Apple (b) Grapes
(c) Banana (d) Potato

Solution (d) Now, when we closely observe the different words we find that all are edibles *i.e.,* consumed as food by human beings.

But apple, grapes and banana comes under the category of fruits and potato is a vegetable.

So, the odd word from the group is potato.

e.g. Find the odd word from the group.

(a) Dog (b) Cow
(c) Goat (d) Buffalo

Solution (a) All, are pet animals but we have to find the odd amongst them. Except dog, all are herbivorous animals *i.e.,* feed on green grass, whereas dog is an omnivorous animal *i.e.,* feeds on flesh and vegetarian food.

So, the odd word from the group is dog.

While solving these questions, the candidate should have basic awareness about general knowledge including Geography, Science, History and Mathematics etc.

There can be various types of patterns which can be found in these types of questions. Some of those classified group of patterns are given below to boost up your knowledge.

Group, Subgroups and their Units

Group	Subgroups	Units
World	• Continent	Asia, Africa, Europe, Australia, North America, South America, Antarctica
	• Ocean	Pacific Ocean, Atlantic Ocean
	• Country	India, Pakistan, China, Nepal, Sri Lanka, Myanmar, Bhutan, Japan, USA, Italy, France, Canada, Germany
	• Capital of Country	New Delhi, Kabul, Tokyo, Kathmandu, Moscow, London
	• Currency of Country	Rupee, Yen, Euro, Dollar, Yuan, Afghani, Rubal
	• Language of Country	Hindi, Arabi, English, Nepali, Mandarin
	• Parliament of Country	Congress, Duma, Diet, Shora, Parliament, Majlis
	• Rivers of Country	Ganga, Sindhu, Nile, Sin, Thames, Danube
	• Sports of Country	Hockey, Cricket, Rugby, Football, Baseball, Ice Hockey
	• Tribes of Country	Red Indians, Negro, Afridi, Kurd, Muri
India	• State	Uttar Pradesh, Madhya Pradesh, Arunachal Pradesh, Uttarakhand, Jharkhand
	• Union Territories	Delhi, Chandigarh, Puducherry, Lakshay dweep, Daman and Diu, Andaman and Nicobar Islands, Dadar and Nagar haveli
	• Capitals of State	Lucknow, Dehradun, Patna, Ranchi, Jaipur, Bhopal
	• City	New Delhi, Mumbai, Kolkata, Lucknow, Chennai, Allahabad
	• Rivers	Ganga, Yamuna, Saraswati, Narmada, Koshi, Sone
Planets	• Planet	Mercury, Venus, Earth, Mars, Jupiter, Saturn, Uranus, Neptune
Time	• Day	Monday, Tuesday, Wednesday, Thursday, Friday, Saturday, Sunday
	• Months	
	(i) 28 days	February
	(ii) 29 days	February (leap year)
	(iii) 30 days	April, June, September, November
	(iv) 31 days	January, March, May, July, August, October, December

Group	Subgroups	Units
Science	• Branch	Physics, Chemistry, Biology
	• Tools	Hygrometer, Lactometer, Aerometer, Fathometer
	• Unit	Jule, Watt, Newton, Dyne, Hertz, Calorie
	• Vitamin	A, B, C, D, E, K
	• Quantity	Force, Work, Energy, Power, Heat, Frequency
Person	• Profession	Doctor, Teacher, Writer, Carpenter, Barber
Parts of Body	• Above the Neck	Eyes, Ears, Nose, Mouth, Head, Face
	• Above the Waist	Neck, Shoulder, Hand, Chest, Back
	• Below the Waist	Heel, Leg, Thigh, Knee, Sole
	• Internal Parts	Heart, Kidney, Lungs, Small intestine, Large intestine, Liver, Brain
	• External Parts	Nose, Hand, Leg, Back
	• Sense Organs	Nose, Ears, Eyes, Tongue, Skin
Animals	• Herbivorous	Cow, Buffalo, Ass, Elephant, Horse, Zebra, Deer, Hippopotamus
	• Carnivorous	Lion, Tiger, Jackal, Fox
	• Omnivorous	Rat, Pig, Bear, Cat, Dog
	• Young One	Puppy (Dog), Lamb (Sheep), Calf (Cow), Piglet (Pig), Leveret (Rabbit), Pony (Horse), Cub (Lion)
	• Sound	Bark (Dog), Meow (Cat), Neigh (Horse), Roar (Lion)
Birds	• Flying Birds	Vulture, Crow, Pigeon
	• Non-flying Birds	Swan, Duck, Cock
	• Night flying Birds	Owl, Kakapo
	• Young One	Cygnet (Swan), Duckling (Duck), Eaglet (Eagle), Chicken (Hen), Owlet (Owl)
	• Sound	Quack (Duck), Caw (Crow), Ku-Ku (Cuckoo)
Crops	• Cereals	Wheat, Rice, Barley, Pulses, Corn, Millet
	• Cash Crops	Jute, Coffee, Sugarcane, Tobacco, Cotton
	• Rabi	Wheat, Barley, Gramme, Mustard, Rye, Soyabean
	• Kharif	Rice, Corn, Millet, Sugarcane, Cotton
	• Zaid	Watermelon, Cucumber, Muskmelon, Bitter gourd
Fruit	• Juicy Fruit	Mango, Orange, Pomegranate, Grapes
	• Dry Fruits	Cashew, Almond, Currant, Dates, Pea nuts, Chestnut, Wallnuts
Vegetables	• Green Vegetable	Cabbage, Cauliflower, Brinjal, Bitter gourd
	• Vegetable with Fibres	Beans, Ladyfinger
	• Salad	Tomato, Carrot, Radish, Onion
Spices	• Liquidy Spices	Onion, Ginger, Green chilly, Garlic, Coriander, Turmeric
	• Dry Spices	Bay leaf, Red chilly, Black Cardamom, White Pepper, Cumin seeds

Group	Subgroups	Units
Miscellaneous	• Furniture	Chair, Table, Sofa, Bed
	• Computer	Keyboard, Mouse, Motherboard
	• House	Window, Door, Roof
	• Academician	Professor, Teacher, Journalist, Editor, Writer
	• Sports	Cricket, Hockey, Chess, Football
	• Delhi	Red Fort, Qutub Minar, Chandni Chowk
	• Religious Books	Bhagwad Geeta, Quran, Mahabharata, Ramayana
	• Publication	Printing, Proofreading, Composing, Editing
	• Organs	Eyes, Ear, Nose, Mouth, Hand, Leg
	• Eatables/Grain	Cereal, Vegetable, Sweets, Fruits
	• Metals	Iron, Nickel, Cobalt, Copper, Zinc, Aluminium etc.
	• Non-Metals	Hydrogen, Chlorine, Fluorine, Carbon, Helium etc.
	• Gases	Oxygen, Nitrogen, Argon, Chlorine etc.
	• Alloys	Bronze, Alnico, Brass, Scandium etc.
	• In door Games	Chess, Table tennis, carrom, Ludo, Badminton, Playing card etc.
	• Out door Games	Cricket, Football, Hockey, Lawn tennis, etc.
	• Ranks — Army	General, Major General, Lieutenant General, Colonel, Major, Captain, Brigadier.
	— Navy	Admiral, Vice-Admiral, Commander, Captain etc.
	—Airforce	Air Chief Marshal, Group Captain, Air Marshal, Wing Commander, Air Commander etc.
	• Stationery	Pen, Pencil, Eraser, Sharpener, Paper etc.
	• Diseases caused by Virus	Small pox, Hepatitis, Measles Rabies, AIDS, Mumps etc.
	• Diseases caused by Bacteria	Leprosy, Cholera, Anthrax, Typhoid fever, Tuberculosis etc.

Types of Questions

From this chapter, several types of problems are asked in various competitive exams. So, we have classified these types of problems as follows

TYPE 01

Choosing the Odd Word

In this type of questions, four/five options are given and you have to select the odd word which does not possess the common property like the words given in other options. This odd word is your answer.

Word classification is based on some common properties of words.

Some of these common properties are given below

(i) Meaning based classification
(ii) Work based classification
(iii) Place based classification
(iv) Number based classification
(v) Technology based classification
(vi) Rank based classification
(vii) Area of usage related classification
(viii) Priority based classification
(ix) Category based classification
(x) Situation based classification, etc.

***Ex* 01** Find the odd word.

(a) Walking (b) Running (c) Moving (d) Reading

Solution (d) All except 'Reading' are related to motion.

***Ex* 02** Find the odd word.

(a) Knife (b) Scissors (c) Axe (d) Hammer

Solution (d) All except 'Hammer' are used for cutting.

***Ex* 03** Find the odd word.

(a) Car (b) Bus (c) Scooter (d) Jeep

Solution (c) All except 'Scooter' are four wheelers.

***Ex* 04** Pick the odd one out. « SSC GD Constable 2018

(a) Detect (b) Perceive (c) Ignorance (d) Observe

Solution (c) Except Ignorance, all others are verbs.

***Ex* 05** Find the odd word.

(a) Ghaziabad (b)Varanasi (c) Gorakhpur (d) Bhagalpur

Solution (d) All except 'Bhagalpur' are in the state of Uttar Pradesh.

***Ex* 06** Find the odd word.

(a) Commander (b) Major
(c) Brigadier (d) Captain

Solution (a) All except 'Commander' are ranks of army.

***Ex* 07** Find the odd one out. « WBCS Pre 2018

(a) Square (b) Circle
(c) Parallelogram (d) Rectangle

Solution (b) Except circle, all other are made up of straight lines.

***Ex* 08** Find the odd word.

(a) Bhagwad Geeta (b) Quran
(c) Ramayana (d) Mahabharata

Solution (b) All except 'Quran' are religious epics of Hindus.

***Ex* 09** Find the odd word.

(a) Silver (b) Iron (c) Gold (d) Hydrogen

Solution (d) All except 'Hydrogen' are metals.

***Ex* 10** Find the odd state out of the following. « CG Revenue Officer 2017

(a) Chhattisgarh (b) Uttaranchal
(c) Jharkhand (d) Telangana

Solution (d) Chhattisgarh, Uttaranchal and Jharkhand came into being in November, 2000 as new States. And, all belong to North India.
Hence, Telangana is the odd one.

***Ex* 11** Pick out the odd word from given options?

(a) Tongue (b) Lips (c) Brain (d) Nose

Solution (c) All except 'Brain' are sense organs of human.

***Ex* 12** Find the odd word.

(a) Slip (b) Diamond (c) Googli (d) Doosra

Solution (b) All except 'Diamond' are terms related to cricket.

***Ex* 13** Find the odd word.

(a) Orange (b) Apple (c) Guava (d) Grapes
(e) Pomegranate

Solution (d) Only Grapes grow in bunches and so it is odd one among others.

***Ex* 14** Find the odd word.

(a) Peso (b) Drachma (c) Shora (d) Baht

Solution (c) All others are currencies, while 'Shora' is the Parliament of Afganistan.

***Ex* 15** Find the odd word.

(a) Puppet (b) Documentary
(c) Animation (d) Commentary

Solution (d) 'Commentary' is the description of all other shows.

***Ex* 16** Four words are given in which three are alike in a certain way and one is different. Choose the the odd word. « SSC (10+2) 2020

(a) Chirp (b) Bleat (c) Jump (d) Neigh

Solution (c) Except jump, all others are sound made by different animals or birds.

***Ex* 17** Find the odd word. « SSC (Multitasking) 2010

(a) Square (b) Sphere (c) Rectangle (d) Circle

Solution (b) All except Sphere are two-dimensional figures.

***Ex* 18** Select the option which is different from the given alternatives.

England, New Zealand, Wales, Scotland. « UP Police SI 2017

(a) Wales (b) Scotland
(c) England (d) New Zealand

Solution (d) Except New Zealand, all other countries comes under the United Kingdom where as New Zealand comes under oceania.

***Ex* 19** Eight words have been given, out of which seven are alike in some manner and one is different. Select odd word. « SSC (CGL) 2020

Monitor, Headphone, Mouse, Keyboard, Windows, Printer, Scanner, Speaker

(a) Printer (b) Windows (c) Monitor (d) Mouse

Solution (b) Windows is a Software, whereas rest of the items i.e., Monitor, Headphone, Keyboard, Printer, Scanner and Speaker are Hardwares.

Practice/CORNER 3.1

DIRECTIONS ~ (Q. Nos. 1-121) *In the following questions, three or four alternatives are same in a certain way out of four or five and so form a group. Find the odd word that does not belong to the group.*

1. (a) Sitar (b) Guitar (c) Flute (d) Violin
« SSC (10+2) 2015

2. (a) Sweetness (b) Elegant (c) Bright (d) Beautiful

3. (a) Mile (b) Centimetre (c) Litre (d) Yard

4. (a) Green (b) Cricket (c) Bat (d) Ball
« SSC (Steno) 2016

5. (a) 14th November (b) 15th August (c) 26th January (d) 2nd October

6. (a) Bus (b) Scooter (c) Cycle (d) Boat

7. (a) Goat (b) Cat (c) Hen (d) Cow
« UPSSSC 2018

8. (a) Orange (b) Apple (c) Rose (d) Melon
« SSC (CPO) 2019

9. (a) Tomato (b) Potato (c) Carrot (d) Onion

10. (a) January (b) June (c) July (d) August

11. (a) Chop (b) Slit (c) Chirp (d) Slice

12. (a) Bear (b) Sparrow (c) Pigeon (d) Owl
« SSC (Steno Grade C&D) 2019

13. (a) Iron (b) Mercury (c) Silver (d) Gold

14. (a) Zinc (b) Bronze (c) Silver (d) Platinum

15. (a) Petrol (b) Coal (c) Air (d) Natural Gas
« SSC (Steno) 2017

16. (a) Temple (b) Worship (c) Mosque (d) Church « SSC (CGL) 2016

17. (a) Sea (b) River (c) Ocean (d) Swimming Pool
« SSC (CPO) 2019

18. (a) Cuckoo (b) Swan (c) Duck (d) Deer

19. (a) Bengaluru (b) Patna (c) Bhagalpur (d) Ranchi

20. (a) Carpenter (b) Goldsmith (c) Blacksmith (d) Driver
« SSC (10+2) 2017

21. (a) Islamabad (b) Kabul (c) Canberra (d) Sydney
« SSC (10+2) 2017

22. (a) Bat (b) Parrot (c) Crow (d) Pigeon

23. (a) Cube (b) Square (c) Cuboid (d) Sphere

24. (a) Daughter (b) Mother (c) Sister (d) Brother

25. (a) Father (b) Mother (c) Friend (d) Brother

26. (a) Red (b) Blue (c) Yellow (d) Black

27. (a) Kanpur (b) Lucknow (c) Lahore (d) Patna

28. (a) Ample (b) Copious (c) Plentiful (d) Abundance

29. (a) Lawyer (b) Doctor (c) Engineer (d) Education « SSC CPO 2018

30. (a) NILE (b) LIEN (c) LINE (d) LEAN
« SSC (Steno) 2016

31. (a) Parrot (b) Bat (c) Crow (d) Sparrow

32. (a) Diamond (b) Ruby (c) Marble (d) Sapphire

33. (a) Rifle (b) Cannon (c) Sword (d) Pistol

34. (a) Orange (b) Litchi (c) Apple (d) Guava

35. (a) Criminal (b) Killer (c) Dacoit (d) Thief
« SSC Steno Grade (C & D) 2019

36. (a) Papaya (b) Watermelon (c) Jackfruit (d) Guava

37. (a) Beijing (b) Melbourne (c) Paris (d) Athens

38. (a) Stag (b) Kitten (c) Colt (d) Fawn
« SSC (CGL) 2011

39. (a) Bitch (b) Horse (c) Cow (d) Vixen

40. (a) Ring (b) Tyre (c) Plate (d) Bangle (e) Rubber Tube

41. (a) Giraffe (b) Zebra (c) Lion (d) Horse

42. (a) Bake (b) Fry (c) Roast (d) Peel

43. (a) Tomato (b) Potato (c) Rice (d) Rose (e) Mango

44. (a) Crow (b) Vulture (c) Sparrow (d) Bat

45. (a) Graph (b) Chart (c) Model (d) Drawing (e) Figur

46. (a) Mattress (b) Pillow (c) Bed sheet (d) Curtain

47. (a) Needle (b) Pencil (c) Spade (d) Candle

48. (a) Basket (b) Barrel (c) Bag (d) Barrow

49. (a) Cricket (b) Baseball (c) Football (d) Billiards

50. (a) Genius (b) Geyser (c) Gesture (d) Revenge

51. (a) Zoology (b) Physiology (c) Botany (d) Philosophy « WBSC 2020

52. (a) Scorpio (b) Cancer (c) Capricorn (d) Equator

53. (a) Ladder (b) Staircase (c) Bridge (d) Escalator « SSC (10+2) 2015

54. (a) Hydrometer (b) Barometer (c) Diameter (d) Hygrometer

55. (a) Sneeze (b) Whistle (c) Snore (d) Cough

56. (a) King (b) Cow (c) Spider (d) Web « RRB Group D 2018

57. (a) Bhils (b) Todas (c) Sikhs (d) Nagas

58. (a) Cricket (b) Hockey (c) Shuttle Cock (d) Tennis

59. (a) Tired (b) Tardy (c) Slow (d) Late « SSC (Steno) 2016

60. (a) Jug (b) Pitcher (c) Tumbler (d) Bottle (e) Saucer

61. (a) Van (b) Truck (c) Cargo (d) Trolley (e) Tempo « Canara Bank (PO) 2008

62. (a) Camel (b) Horse (c) Ox (d) Cat (e) Ass

63. (a) Leaf (b) Flower (c) Fruit (d) Branch (e) Root

64. (a) Pen (b) Marker (c) Paper (d) Pencil

65. (a) Blackmail (b) Smuggling (c) Snobbery (d) Forgery

66. (a) Yen (b) Lira (c) Dollar (d) Ounce

67. (a) Spring (b) Autumn (c) Windy (d) Summer « UPSSSC (VDO) 2018

68. (a) Raft (b) Chariot (c) Sledge (d) Cart

69. (a) Book (b) Pages (c) Index (d) Chapters

70. (a) Huge (b) Tiny (c) Heavy (d) Small

71. (a) Spring (b) Heat (c) Winter (d) Autumn

72. (a) Igloo (b) House (c) Hut (d) Flat (e) Factor

73. (a) Cholera (b) AIDS (c) Cancer (d) Health (e) Jaundice

74. (a) Humorous (b) Comical (c) Hilarious (d) Gangster « SSC (CGL) 2018

75. (a) Sky (b) Star (c) Planet (d) Comet

76. (a) Rigveda (b) Yajurveda (c) Atharvaveda (d) Ayurveda

77. (a) Teeth (b) Tongue (c) Palate (d) Chin

78. (a) Torrent (b) Lake (c) River (d) Stream

79. (a) Barter (b) Purchase (c) Sale (d) Borrow

80. (a) Political Science (b) History (c) Philosophy (d) Physics « SSC (CPO) 2013

81. (a) Gandhi (b) Buddha (c) Mahavira (d) Christ

82. (a) Agitation (b) Confusion (c) Commotion (d) Annihilation « SSC (Steno) 2016

83. (a) Java (b) Tasmania (c) Sri Lanka (d) Malaysia

84. (a) Anger (b) Destroy (c) Irritation (d) Rage

85. (a) Mountain (b) Hill (c) Plateau (d) Plane

86. (a) Triangle (b) Tangent (c) Square (d) Rhombus

87. (a) Asia (b) Australia (c) America (d) England

88. (a) Konark (b) Madurai (c) Ellora (d) Khajuraho

89. (a) Trident (b) Triumph (c) Tripod (d) Triangle

90. (a) Peak (b) Mountain (c) Hillock (d) Valley

91. (a) Mumbai (b) Bhubaneshwar (c) Hyderabad (d) Jaipur (e) Allahabad

92. (a) Thorium (b) Uranium (c) Radium (d) Sodium « SSC (CGL) 2018

93. (a) Bus (b) Train (c) Truck (d) Wheel (e) Taxi

94. (a) Building (b) Toy (c) Vehicle (d) Mountain (e) Machine

95. (a) Friendship (b) Intimacy (c) Attachment (d) Enmity « UPSC Assistant Commandant 2019

96. (a) Volume (b) Size (c) Shape (d) Weight

97. (a) Guava (b) Orange (c) Apple (d) Litchi (e) Pear

98. (a) Aluminium (b) Copper (c) Mercury (d) Iron

99. (a) Swimming (b) Sailing (c) Diving (d) Driving

100. (a) Gallon (b) Ton (c) Quintal (d) Kilogram

101. (a) Stream (b) Spring (c) Dam (d) River

102. (a) Mare (b) Stag (c) Lioness (d) Bitch

103. (a) Green (b) Indigo (c) Pink (d) Violet

104. (a) Debit (b) Deposit (c) Deduction (d) Withdrawal

105. (a) Jupiter (b) Uranus (c) Mercury (d) Earth

106. (a) Rain (b) Shower (c) Sleet (d) Raisin

107. (a) Bhutan (b) Bangladesh (c) China (d) Pakistan

108. (a) John F Kennedy (b) Abraham Lincoln (c) George Washington (d) Gerald Ford

109. (a) Gun (b) Pistol (c) Dagger (d) Atom bomb

110. (a) Indira Gandhi (b) Lal Bahadur Shastri (c) Jawahar Lal Nehru (d) Dr Rajendra Prasad

111. (a) Head (b) Heed (c) Sledge (d) Heap

112. (a) Author (b) Novelist (c) Poet (d) Publisher

113. (a) Cheese (b) Wine (c) Milk (d) Curd

114. (a) Bronze (b) Silver (c) Cadmium (d) Platinum

115. (a) Herd (b) Flight (c) Hound (d) Swarm

116. (a) Frequency polygon (b) Rectangle (c) Bar (d) Pie

117. (a) Silicon (b) Platinum (c) Arsenic (d) Antimony

118. (a) Brass (b) Steel (c) Bronze (d) Tin
« SSC (CPO) 2015

119. (a) Wife (b) Bachelor (c) Widow (d) Spinster « SSC (CGL) 2014

120. (a) Dilution (b) Distribution (c) Dispersion (d) Diversion « SSC (CGL) 2014

121. (a) Quran (b) Gita (c) Panchsheel (d) Bible
« SSC (Multitasking) 2014

DIRECTIONS ~ (Q. Nos. 122-126) *Five words have been given, out of which four are alike in some manner and one is different. Select the odd one.*
« UPSSSC Junior Assistant 2020

122. Canoe, Dinghy, Igloo, Raft, Yacht
(a) Raft (b) Igloo (c) Canoe (d) Dinghy

123. Cliffs, Lapies, Stalactites, Sinkholes, Stalagmites
(a) Stalactites (b) Stalagmites (c) Lapies (d) Cliffs

124. Semicircle, Semicolon, Semifinal, Seminar, Semitone
(a) Semitone (b) Semicircle (c) Seminar (d) Semicolon

125. Five colours have been given, out of which four are alike in some manner and one is different. Select the odd one.
Green, Indigo, Pink, Orange, Yellow
(a) Orange (b) Pink (c) Green (d) Yellow

126. Five subjects have been given, out of which four are alike in some manner and one is different. Select the odd one.
Physics, Chemistry, Geography, Botany, Zoology
(a) Botany (b) Chemistry (c) Physics (d) Geography

Answers WITH EXPLANATIONS

1. (*c*) All are music instruments except Flute. All have strings to play the music but flute does not have strings.

2. (*a*) All except Sweetness are related with beauty but sweetness is related with taste.

3. (*c*) All others except Litre are units to measure distance.

4. (*a*) Green is a colour. All others are related to sport.

5. (*a*) All others except 14th November are national holidays.

6. (*d*) All others except Boat are road vehicles.

7. (*c*) Except Hen, all other animals have four legs.

8. (*c*) Except Rose, all others are fruits.

9. (*a*) All others except Tomatoes grow under soil.

10. (*b*) All others except June have 31 days.

11. (*c*) Except 'Chirp', all other are related to cutting.
Whereas chirp which means sound of birds.

12. (*a*) Except Bear, all other are birds.

13. (*b*) All others except Mercury are solid metals.

14. (*b*) 'Bronze' is an alloy, whereas rest are metals.

15. (*c*) All these are fossil fuels except Air.

16. (*b*) All others except worship are worship places.

17. (*d*) Except, Swimming pool all other are natural resources of water.

18. (*d*) Here, Duck, Swan and Cuckoo comes under the category of bird and Deer comes under the category of animal.
Hence, Deer is different from others.

19. (*c*) All others except Bhagalpur are capital cities of Indian states.

20. (*d*) Except 'Driver', all three can make articles in their specialisation and are related to production but only 'Driver' serves his work.

21. (*d*) Except Sydney, all other are the capitals of different countries while Sydney is one of the cities in Australia.

22. (*a*) Except 'Bat', all other are birds.

23. (*b*) All others except Square are three-dimensional bodies.

24. (*d*) All others except Brother are females.

25. (*c*) All others except Friends are family members.

26. (*d*) All others except Black are primary colours.

27. (*c*) All others except Lahore are Indian cities.

28. (*d*) Except 'Abundance', all mean sufficient amount but abundance is used for more than sufficient amount.

29. (*d*) Except Education, all other are professionals.

30. (*a*) Except (a) all other are meaningful words.

31. (*b*) All others are birds while bat is a mammal.

32. (*c*) All others except Marble are precious stones.

33. (*c*) All others except Sword are fire arms.

34. (*a*) 'Orange' is the only citrus fruit in the group.

35. (*a*) Killer, Dacoit and Thief are different types of criminals. Hence, Criminal is the odd one.

36. (*b*) All others grow on trees, while 'Watermelon' grows on creepers.

37. (*b*) All others are capitals of the countries, while 'Melbourne' is the city of Australia.

38. (*a*) All others are the young ones of animals, while 'Stag' is an adult animal.

39. (*b*) All others except Horse are female animals.

40. (*c*) Except, 'Plate', all other things have holes.

41. (*d*) All others except Horse are wild animals.

42. (*d*) All others except Peeling are different form of cooking.

43. (*d*) All others except Rose are food items.

44. (*d*) All others except Bat fly in the day time.

45. (*c*) Except 'Model', all are same because all are made on paper.

46. (*d*) All except 'Curtain' are parts of bed-spread.

47. (*d*) Except 'Candle', all other articles have one of its ends sharp or pointed.

48. (*d*) 'Barrow' is man-driven cart whereas others are usual containers.

49. (*d*) Except 'Billiards', all others are outdoor games.

50. (*b*) Only 'Geyser' is tangible whereas all others are intangible.

51. (*d*) Except Philosophy all others are related to Science.

52. (*d*) Except 'Equator', all others are zodiac signs.

53. (*c*) Bridge is different from the other three. Except Bridge, all others are used for vertical movement.

54. (*c*) Except Diameter, all others are apparatus to measure something.

55. (*b*) 'Whistling' is the voluntary act or process whereas others are spontaneous acts.

56. (*d*) Except Web, all others are living beings.

57. (*c*) All others except Sikhs are different tribes whereas Sikhism is a religion.

58. (*c*) 'Shuttle cock' is different from the other three because cricket, hockey and tennis are the name of different games.

59. (*d*) Late is the result of the other given options. A tired, tardy or slow attitude makes a work late.

60. (*e*) All others except Saucer can be filled up with something.

61. (*c*) Except Cargo, all others are vehicle.

62. (*d*) Except Cat, all others are herbivorous.

63. (*e*) Except Root, all others grow above the soil.

64. (*c*) We can write with pen, marker, pencil on paper. So, Paper is different from others.

65. (*c*) Except Snobbery, all other terms are related to the crimes.

66. (*d*) Except Ounce, all other terms represent the different currencies.

67. (*c*) Except (c), all are name of seasons.

68. (*a*) All except 'Raft' are drawn by animals.

69. (*a*) Except book, all other items are contained in a book.

70. (*c*) All other terms except Heavy are used to denote the size.

71. (*b*) All other terms except Heat represent the season.

72. (*e*) All others are dwelling places of human being, while 'Factory' is a working place.

73. (*d*) Except 'Health', all other are different kinds of diseases.

74. (*d*) Gangster is a criminal, whereas rest are not.

75. (*a*) All other items except Sky belong to the same class.

76. (*d*) 'Ayurveda' is the branch of medicine, whereas, all others are Vedas.

77. (*d*) Except 'Chin' all other parts are inside the mouth.

78. (*d*) 'Stream' is present in all forms given in other options.

79. (*d*) Except 'Borrow,' all the options are the terms of business.

80. (*d*) Political Science, History and Philosophy are the subjects related with humanity while Physics is a subject of Science.

81. (*a*) Except 'Gandhi' all other persons are founder of different religions.

82. (*b*) Except (b) all others are done in group. Confusion is a state which can be experienced by an individual.

83. (*d*) 'Malaysia' is peninsula whereas other countries are islands.

84. (*b*) Except 'Destroy', all others are different type of moods.

85. (*d*) Except 'Plane', all items have height.

86. (*b*) All other figure except Tangent enclose areas.

87. (*d*) Except 'England', all others are continents.

88. (*c*) 'Ellora' is famous for caves, all others are famous for temples.

89. (*b*) Except 'Triumph', Tri stands for three in all the other terms.

90. (*d*) Except 'Valley', are elevated feautures.

91. (*e*) All others except Allahabad are state capitals.

92. (*d*) All except sodium are radio isotopes, while sodium is a metal.

93. (*d*) All others except Wheels are vehicles.

94. (*d*) All others except Mountain are man made.

95. (*d*) Friendship, Intimacy, Attachment have similar meaning that's why they are synonyms. 'Enmity' means 'Apathy' which is opposite to others that's why it is an antonym.

96. (*a*) Except 'Volume' all other words have two vowels. Volume has three vowels.

97. (*b*) 'Orange' is the only citrus fruit.

98. (*c*) 'Mercury' is liquid at room temperature.

99. (*d*) Except 'Driving', all activities are related to water but driving is related to road.

100. (*a*) Only 'Gallon' is different because this is use for liquid measurement.

101. (*c*) 'Dam' is different among the given alternatives as dam is used to stop the water from flowing while in spring, stream and river, water flows.

102. (*b*) 'Stag' is male deer while mare, lioness and bitch are female. Thus, stag is different from others.

103. (*c*) The colours Green, Indigo and Violet are constituents of the pattern 'VIBGYOR'. Whereas Pink is not a part of VIBGYOR.

104. (*b*) In this question, the words Debit, Deduction and Withdrawal are very much similar in the meaning, whereas Deposit is antonym of these words.

105. (*c*) Each of Jupiter, Uranus and Earth has its satellite while Mercury doesn't have its satellite. Thus, Mercury is different.

106. (*d*) Here, all options are related to rain or water except Raisin. The meaning of 'Raisin' is a partially dried grapes which is different from all others.

107. (*c*) All except China are democratic countries.

108. (*d*) Among these four persons, Gerald Ford has never been the President of America.

109. (*c*) Among all these weapons, 'Dagger' is an ancient sword, whereas all the other weapons are modern.

110. (*d*) 'Dr Rajendra Prasad' was the President of India, whereas others were the Prime Ministers.

111. (*a*) 'Head' is different from all other.

112. (*d*) Except the 'Publisher' all other are related to 'literature'.

113. (*b*) Wine is obtained from grapes while other are obtained from milk.

114. (*a*) 'Bronze' is an alloy while silver, cadmium and platinum are the elements.

115. (*c*) Except 'Hound', all represent group.

116. (*b*) Frequency polygon, Bar and Pie are different type of graphs while 'rectangle' is a geometrical figure.

117. (*b*) Silicon, Arsenic and Antimony are metalloids while 'Platinum' is an element.

118. (*d*) Except Tin, all other are solid metals.

119. (*b*) Wife, Widow and Spinster can only be a woman. While either a man or a women can be 'Bachelor'.

120. (*a*) Except 'Dilution', all others signifies division. While Dilution is a process of reducing concentration.

121. (*c*) Except 'Panchsheel', all are holy books of different religion.

122. (*b*) Except, 'Igloo' all other are watercrafts

123. (*d*) A Cliff is a mass of rock that rises very high and is almost vertical, but Stalactites, Stalagmites and Lapies are types of short rock formation. So, 'Cliffs' is odd one here.

124. (*c*) Except 'seminar', all other indicates toward something which is half, whereas seminar a meeting for discussion.

125. (*b*) Except, Pink, all other are rainbow colours present in rainbow.

126. (*d*) Except 'Geography', all other are branches of Science.

TYPE 02

Choosing the Odd Pair or Group of Words

In this type of questions certain pairs or groups of words are given, out of which the words in all the pairs/groups except one bear a certain common relationship. The candidate is required to decipher this relationship and choose the pair/group in which the words are differently related, as the answer.

DIRECTIONS ~ (Example Nos.20-23) *Following are given four pairs/groups of words out of which three are similar and hence they form a group. Find the pair /group which is different from other groups.*

***Ex* 20**

(a) Horse : Neigh (b) Lion : Grunt
(c) Owl : Hoot (d) Sheep : Bleat

***Solution* (b)** All except 'Lion-Grunt' are correct match of animals and their sounds.

***Ex* 21** « SSC (CPO) 2010

(a) Student : Scholar (b) Paddy : Rice
(c) Soldier : Warrior (d) Politician : Leader

***Solution* (b)** In all pairs except (b), the first, when becomes an expert or become mature is known as second.

***Ex* 22** « SSC GD Constable 2018

(a) Grapes : Bunch (b) Flowers : Bouquet
(c) Bees : Swarm (d) Man : Class

***Solution* (d)** A group of grapes is called bunch, a group of flowers is called bouquet and a group of bees is called swarm. Hence, option (d) is odd one out.

***Ex* 23**

(a) Calculator, Heater, Pen
(b) Fan, Tube-light, Television
(c) Mobile, Tempo, Cutter
(d) Axe, Radio, LCD TV

***Solution* (b)** Because all things work through electricity.

Practice / CORNER 3.2

DIRECTIONS ~ (Q. Nos. 1-59) *In each of the following questions, certain pairs of words are given, out of which the words in all pairs except one, bear a certain common relationship. Choose the odd pair.*

1. (a) Clerk : File (b) Lawyer : Client
(c) Doctor : Patient (d) Shopkeeper : Customer

2. (a) Seldom : Often (b) Good : Nice
(c) Honest : Cheat (d) Extravagant : Thifty

3. (a) Pen : Stationery (b) Earth : Moon
(c) Sun : Star (d) Painter : Artist
« SSC (Steno) 2016

4. (a) Crime : Punishment (b) Judgement : Advocate
(c) Enterprise : Success (d) Exercise : Health

5. (a) Needle : Prick (b) Gun : Fire
(c) Auger : Bore (d) Chisel : Carve
« SSC (LDC) 2012

6. (a) Lion - Roar (b) Snake - Hiss
(c) Bees - Hum (d) Frog - Bleat
(e) Dog - Bark
« IBPS (Clerk) 2011

7. (a) Oil : Lamp (b) Water : Tap
(c) Oxygen : Life (d) Power : Machine
« SSC (CPO) 2018

8. (a) Flaw : Defect (b) Mend : Repair
(c) Vacant : Empty (d) Sink : Float

9. (a) Captain : Team (b) Boss : Gang
(c) Prime Minister : Cabinet (d) Artist : Troupe
« RRB (TC/CC) 2012

10. (a) Hard : Soft (b) Pointed : Blunt
(c) Sweet : Sour (d) Long : High
(e) Day : Night
« LIC (AAO) 2012

11. (a) Ice cube : Cold (b) Iron : Hard
(c) Marble : Smooth (d) Purse : Money

12. (a) Petrol : Car (b) Electricity : Television
(c) Ink : Pen (d) Dust : Vaccum cleaner
(e) Pen : Paper
« LIC (AAO) 2012

13. (a) Lion : Den (b) Bird : Nest
(c) Cat : Mew (d) Bee : Hive
« UPSSSC Junior Assistant 2016

14. (a) Water : Thirst (b) Talent : Education
(c) Food : Hunger (d) Air : Suffocation

15. (a) Tree : Stem (b) Face : Eye
(c) Chair : Sofa (d) Plant : Flower

16. (a) Profit : Gain (b) Debit : Credit
(c) Income : Expenditure (d) Assets : Liabilities
« UPSSSC Junior Assistant 2016

17. (a) Principal : School (b) Soldier : Barrack
(c) Artist : Troupe (d) Singer : Chorus

18. (a) Death : Disease (b) Milk : Butter
(c) Grape : Wine (d) Water : Oxygen

19. (a) Room : House (b) Page : Book
(c) Engine : Car (d) Food : Hunger
« SSC (Steno) 2017

20. (a) Aphid : Paper (b) Moth : Wool
(c) Termite : Wood (d) Locust : Plant
« SSC (10 + 2) 2013

21. (a) Broom : Sweep (b) Spoon : Feed
(c) Nut : Crack (d) Soap : Bathe

22. (a) Door : Bang (b) Piano : Play
(c) Rain : Patter (d) Drum : Beat

23. (a) Circle : Arc (b) Line : Dot
(c) Hexagon : Angle (d) Square : Line
« SSC (10+2) 2013

24. (a) Day : Night (b) Up : Down
(c) Across : Along (d) Small : Large
« SSC (10+2) 2013

25. (a) Flag : Flagship (b) Court : Courtship
(c) War : Worship (d) Friend : Friendship
« SSC (10+2) 2013

26. (a) Gold : Ornaments (b) Cloth : Garments
(c) Wood : Furniture (d) Leather : Footwear
(e) Earthen pots : Clay
« SBI (PO) 2009

27. (a) Ornithology : Birds (b) Mycology : Fungi
(c) Biology : Botany (d) Phycology : Algae
(e) Entomology : Insects

28. (a) Fish : Shoal (b) Cow : Herd
(c) Sheep : Flock (d) Man : Mob
(e) Bee : Swarm

29. (a) Shoe : Leather (b) Iron : Axe
(c) Table : Wood (d) Jewellery : Gold
(e) Shirt : Fabric
« RBI (Clerk) 2013

30. (a) Mason : Wall (b) Cobbler : Shoe
(c) Farmer : Crop (d) Chef : Cook
(e) Choreographer : Ballet

31. (a) Daring : Timid (b) Beautiful : Pretty
(c) Clear : Vague (d) Youth : Adult
(e) Native : Alien

32. (a) See : Eyes (b) Hear : Ears
(c) Smell : Nose (d) Touch : Skin
(e) Tongue : Taste
« IOB (PO) 2005

33. (a) Oxygen - Gas (b) Metal - Platinum
(c) Liquid - Water (d) Solid - Iron
« SSC (10+2) 2018

34. (a) Solder : Tin (b) Hae matite : Iron
(c) Bauxite : Aluminium (d) Malachite : Copper

35. (a) Whale : Mammal (b) Salamander : Insect
(c) Snake : Reptile (d) Frog : Amphibian

36. (a) Onomatology : Name (b) Nidology : Nests
(c) Psychology : Algae (d) Concology : Shells

37. (a) Hanger : Aeroplane (b) Yard : Train
(c) Depot : Bus (d) Scooter : Garage
« SSC (Steno) 2017

38. (a) Newspaper : Editor (b) Film : Director
(c) Stamps : Philatelist (d) Book : Author

39. (a) Periyar : Kerala (b) Corbett : Himanchal Pradesh
(c) Kaziranga : Assam (d) Gir : Gujrat

40. (a) Steel : Utensils (b) Bronze : Statue
(c) Duralumin : Aircraft (d) Iron : Rails

41. (a) Pistol : Gun (b) Knife : Dagger
(c) Engine : Train (d) Car : Bus

42. (a) Cat : Paw (b) Lizard : Pad
(c) Horse : Hoof (d) Man : Leg

43. (a) Avesta : Parsi (b) Torah : Jew
(c) Tripitaka : Buddhist (d) Temple : Hindu

44. (a) Stamp : Letter (b) Ticket : Train
(c) Ink : Pen (d) Car : Engine

45. (a) Tree : Branch (b) Hand : Finger
(c) Table : Chair (d) Room : Floor

46. (a) Taiwan : Taipei (b) China : Mongolia
(c) Iran : Teheran (d) Japan : Tokyo

47. (a) Bouquet : Flowers (b) Bunch : Grapes
(c) Furniture : Chair (d) Album : Photos

48. (a) Chaff : Wheat (b) Grit : Pulses
(c) Grain : Crop (d) Dregs : Wine

49. (a) Rice : Corn (b) Tomato : Potato
(c) Student : Class (d) Book : Library

50. (a) Ammeter : Current (b) Hygrometer : Pressure
(c) Odometer : Speed (d) Seismograph : Earthquakes

51. (a) Proteins : Marasmus (b) Sodium : Rickets
(c) Iodine : Goiter (d) Iron : Anaemia

52. (a) Church : Monument (b) Car : Bus
(c) Pond : Lake (d) Pistol : Gun
« SSC (CPO) 2005

53. (a) Ink - Inkpot (b) Pen - Nib
(c) Oil - Lamp (d) Water - Bucket
« MP Police Constable 2017

54. (a) Pelican : Reptile (b) Gnu : Antelope
(c) Elk : Deer (d) Shark : Fish

55. (a) Crop-Rice (b) Crop-Rubber
(c) Crop- Wheat (d) Crop-Bajra
« SSC (CHSL Tier-I) 2018

DIRECTIONS ~ (Q. Nos. 56-59) *In the following questions, choose the option in whcih all the words, bear common relationship with one an other.*

56. (a) Orange, Apple, Guava
(b) Brinjal, Pomegranate, Wheat
(c) Rice, Pulses, Cotton
(d) Cumin, Coriander, Millet

57. (a) Coffee, Barley, Millet
(b) Beans, Corn, Rice
(c) Cotton, Coffee, Jute
(d) Watermelon, Muskmelon, Banana

58. (a) Ostrich, Hen, Swan (b) Duck, Lion, Horse
(c) Zebra, Cabbage, Rose (d) India, World, Mobile

59. (a) Keyboard, Mouse, Category
(b) Leveret, Cub, Elephant
(c) Yen, Pound, Currency
(d) Hertz, Calorie, Watt

Answers / WITH EXPLANATIONS

1. (*a*) In all others, second is the person for whom the first works to earn money.

2. (*b*) All others are antonyms.

3. (*b*) Except (b) in all others first thing falls under the second. Earth is a planet not moon.

4. (*b*) In all others, second is the result of the first.

5. (*a*) Only this is not an instrument for action pair.

6. (*d*) Frogs don't bleat, they always croak.

7. (*b*) In all other pairs, second requires the first to function.

8. (*d*) Except (d) in all other pairs both the words are similar in meaning. But sink and float are opposite to each other.

9. (*d*) Artist is just a part of a troupe whereas in others the first is the head of the second.

10. (*d*) Except 'Long-High', all options having opposite words.

11. (*d*) In all other pairs, second denotes a characteristics of the first.

12. (*d*) Except 'Dust-Vaccum cleaner', all second things in the options come in use with help of first.

13. (*c*) In all other options except (c). Creatures and their living places are given while Mew is the voice of Cat.

14. (*b*) In all other pairs, lack of first causes the second.

15. (*c*) In all other pairs, second is a part of the first.

16. (*a*) Profit and Gain are synonyms to each other all others are antonyms to each other.

17. (*a*) In all other pairs, second is a collective group of the first.

18. (*a*) In all other pairs, second is a product obtained from the first.

19. (*d*) Except (d), in all others, first is a part of the second.

20. (*a*) In all the others, second is damaged/eaten by the first.

21. (*c*) In all other pairs, second is the purpose for which the first is used.

22. (*b*) In all other pairs, second is the noise made by the first.

23. (*c*) Hexagon is not made by angles, whereas in rest of the options the first is made by second.

24. (*c*) Day-Night, Up-Down and Small-Large word pairs denote the opposite relationship among them, but Across and Along are synonyms'.

25. (*c*) War and Worship are not related to each other, while all others are related to each other.

26. (*e*) In all pairs except (e), the first element is used as raw material to make the second.

27. (*c*) In all pairs except (c), first is the study of second.

28. (*d*) In all pairs except (d), second is the collective group of first.

29. (*b*) In all pairs except (b), second item is used for the manufacture of first item.

30. (*d*) In all pairs except (d), second is prepared by first.

31. (*b*) Except (b), all are antonym pairs.

32. (*e*) In all pairs except (e), first is the work of second.

33. (*a*) Except option (a), in all other options first represents the state of second.

34. (*a*) In all pairs except (a), first is the ore from which metal can be obtained and second is the name of that metal which is obtained. On the other hand, Solder is an alloy.

35. (*b*) In all pairs except (b), first is the animal and second is the class of that animal to which it belongs.

36. (*d*) In all pairs except (d), first is known as the study of second.

37. (*d*) Except (d) all other options represent the pair of vehicle and its parking place.

38. (*c*) In all pairs except (c), second is related to first.

39. (*b*) In all other pairs, first is the names of national park/sanctuary while the second denoted the state in which it is located.

40. (*d*) In all pairs except (d), first is an alloy and second is thing which is made by that alloy but Iron is a metal not an alloy.

41. (*c*) In all pairs except (c), both the words belong to same class.

42. (*d*) In all pairs except (d), second is the name of the foot of first.

43. (*d*) In all pairs except (d), first is the religious book that belongs to second.

44. (*d*) In all pairs except (d), first is required for second to use.

45. (*c*) In all pairs except (c), second is attached with first.

46. (*b*) In all pairs except (b), first is a name of country and second is the capital of that country.

47. (*c*) In all pairs except (c), first is known as the collection of second.

48. (*c*) In all pairs except (c), first is the wastage of second.

49. (*b*) In all pairs except (b), first is present in second.

50. (*b*) In all pairs except (b), first is the name of instrument which is used to measure the second.

51. (*b*) In all pairs except (b), deficiency of first causes the disease in second part.

52. (*a*) In all pairs except (a), both the words belongs to the same class.

53. (*b*) Except pen and nib, in all other option, first is kept in the second. Hence, pen and nib is odd.

54. (*a*) In all pairs except (a), first is a type of second.

55. (*b*) Except rubber, rice, wheat and Bajra are the examples of crop.

56. (*a*) Option (a) is correct because all are juicy fruits.

57. (*c*) Option (c) is correct because all are related to cash crops.

58. (*a*) Only option (a) is correct because all are birds in that group.

59. (*d*) Only option (d) is correct because all are the units, which are related to Science.

TYPE 03

Choosing the Odd Letter/Group

Under this classification, a single letter or group/pair of letters are given in each of four or five options. Three or four of them are similar to each other in some manner while one is different and this is to be chosen by the candidate as the answer.

But before moving on to the different types of letter classification, we must know the following

1. **Forward Order Letter Positions** (Left to Right)

A	B	C	D	E	F	G	H	I	J	K	L	M	N	O	P	Q	R	S	T	U	V	W	X	Y	Z
1	2	3	4	5	6	7	8	9	10	11	12	13	14	15	16	17	18	19	20	21	22	23	24	25	26

2. **Backward Order Letter Positions** (Right to Left)

A	B	C	D	E	F	G	H	I	J	K	L	M	N	O	P	Q	R	S	T	U	V	W	X	Y	Z
26	25	24	23	22	21	20	19	18	17	16	15	14	13	12	11	10	9	8	7	6	5	4	3	2	1

3. **Opposite Letters**

A	B	C	D	E	F	G	H	I	J	K	L	M
Z	Y	X	W	V	U	T	S	R	Q	P	O	N

Now, we can move on to actual types of letter classification.

A. Single Letter Classification

It is of following two types

Based on Vowels and Consonants

There are 5 vowels and 21 consonants in English alphabet

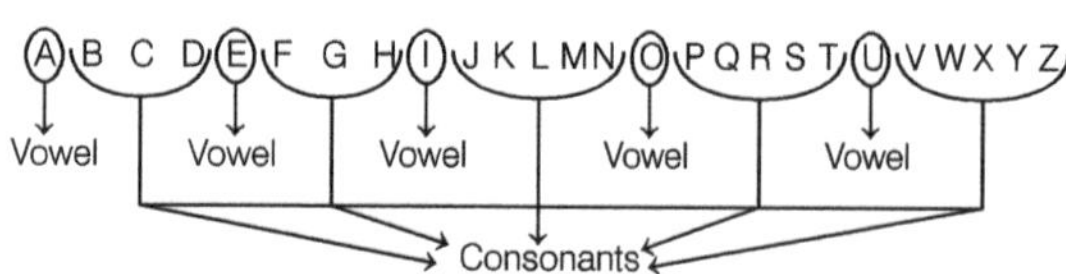

***Ex* 24** Find the odd letter.

(a) V (b) L (c) A (d) M

Solution (c) All except 'A' are consonants.

Based on Letters' Positional Value

In this type of classification, the odd letter is classified on the basis of its positional value in English alphabetical order.

***Ex* 25** Find the odd letter.

(a) B (b) L (c) Q (d) Z

Solution (c) Except Q, all others given letters are at even position, in English alphabet from left end.

2	12	17	26
B	L	Q	Z

B. Two Letters Classification

In this type of classification, the odd pair is classified based on the sum or difference of two letters in a pair.

***Ex* 26** Find out the odd pair.

(a) AZ (b) BY
(c) CX (d) DV

***Solution* (d)**

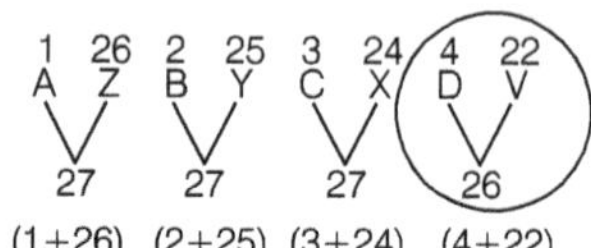

So, option (d) is the correct answer.

***Ex* 27** Select the odd word/letters/number/number pair from the given alternatives. « SSC (10+2) 2017

(a) EG (b) EB (c) BY (d) GD

***Solution* (a)**

It is clear from above that EG is different from others.

C. Three Letters Classification

It is of following types

Based on Similarity of Places of any two Letters

Here, odd group is classified based on the similarity of places of first and second letters or second and third letters or first and third letters.

***Ex* 28** Find the odd group of letters.

(a) HJA (b) NPE (c) OQU (d) XYZ

« SSC (CGL) 2009

***Solution* (d)** All except 'XYZ' have a difference of two positions between their first two letters.

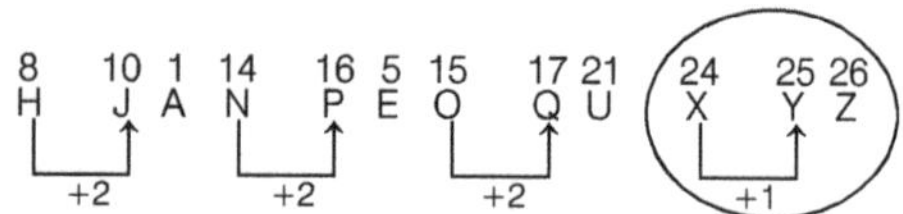

***Ex* 29** Which of the following letters group is an odd one?

(a) BJN (b) FPT (c) LQU (d) JTV

Solution (d) All except 'JTV' have a difference of four positions between last two letters.

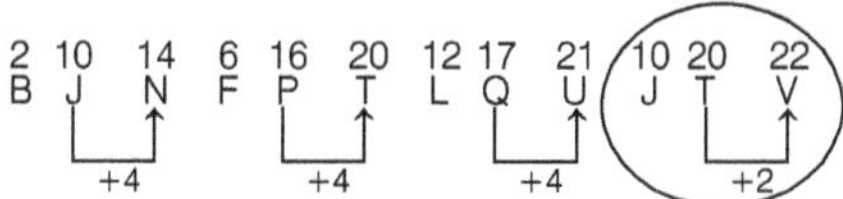

Ex 30 Find the odd group of letters.
(a) AOE (b) EUI
(c) OUT (d) IEM

Solution (c) All except 'OUT' have a difference of four positions.

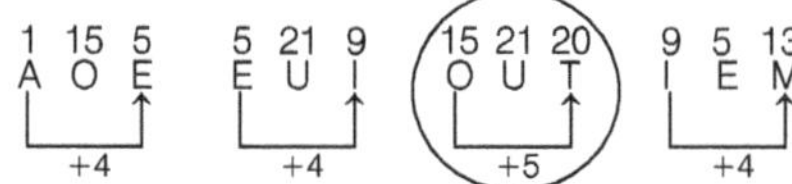

Based on Similarity of Places of All Three Letters

In this classification relative positions of all three letters are considered.

Ex 31 Which of the following is the odd letters group?
« SSC (CGL) 2019
(a) FHJ (b) DFH
(c) LNP (d) TVW

Solution (d) All except 'TVW' have a difference of two positions between first and second and second and third letters.

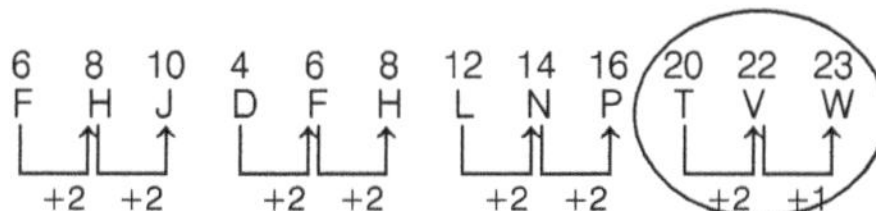

Ex 32 Which of the following is the odd letters group?
(a) LNJ (b) RTP (c) NPK (d) FHD
« RRB Group D 2018

Solution (c)

+2 +2 +2 +2
L N J R , T P N P K and F H D
−2 −2 −3 −2

∴ Letters group NPK follows different pattern from other. Hence, NPK does not belong to the group.

D. Four Letters Classification

It is of following types

Based on Similarity of Places of any Two Letters

In this classification, the relative position of first and second letters or first and third letters or second and third letters or third and fourth letters or first and fourth letters or second and fourth letters among the group provides the basis of classification.

Ex 33 Find the odd one out of the four options given below.
(a) ACDE (b) FHIJ
(c) KMNO (d) PQRS

Solution (d) All except 'PQRS' have a difference of two positions between first and second letter.

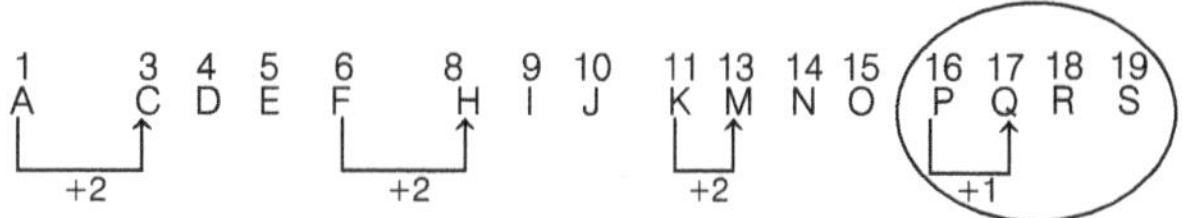

Ex 34 Pick the odd group of letters.
(a) ABDE (b) FGIJ (c) KLMN (d) OPRS

Solution (c) All except 'KLMN' have a difference of three positions between first and third letter.

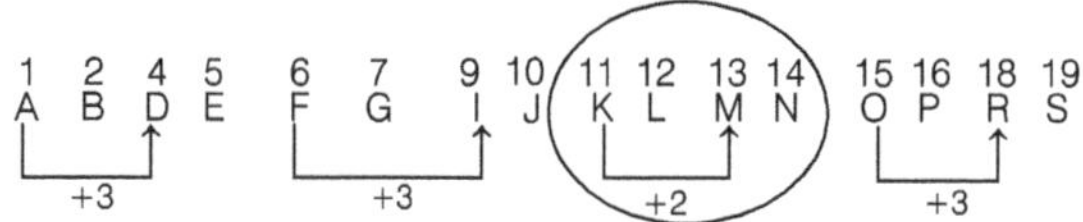

Ex 35 Find the odd group of letters.
(a) ABDE (b) FGIJ (c) KLOP (d) QRTU

Solution (c) All except 'KLOP' have a difference of two positions between second and third letter.

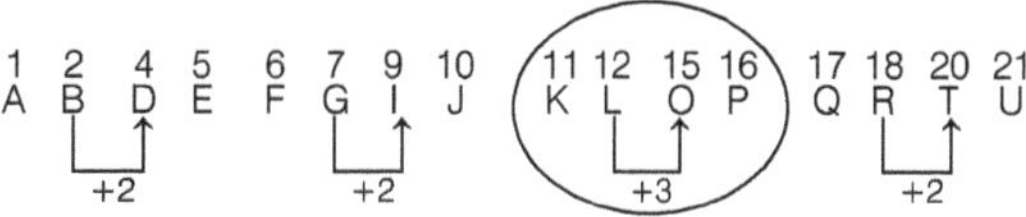

Ex 36 Find out the different group of letters out of the group options.
(a) DEFG (b) UVXZ (c) PQRT (d) JKMO

Solution (a) All except 'DEFG' have a difference of two positions between last two letters.

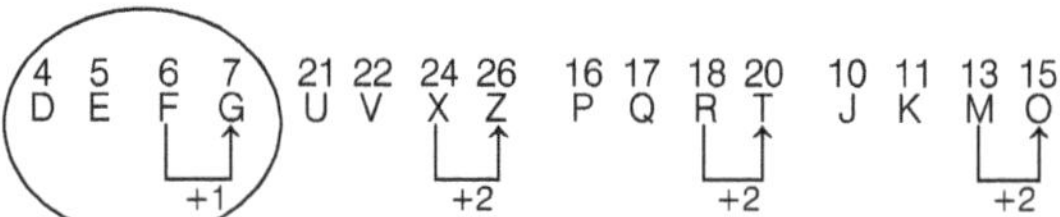

Ex 37 Which of the following groups is an odd one?
« SSC (CPO) 2012
(a) ABDF (b) GHJM (c) NOQS (d) TUWY

Solution (b) All except 'GHJM' have a difference of five positions between first and fourth letter.

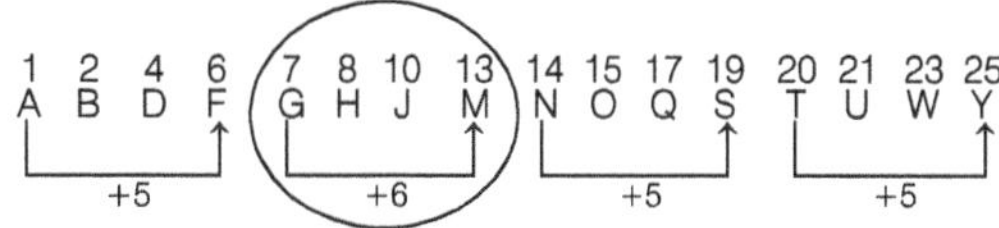

Ex 38 Find out the odd one.
(a) ABCF (b) GHIK
(c) LMNP (d) QRSU

Solution (a) All except 'ABCF' have a difference of three positions between second and fourth letter.

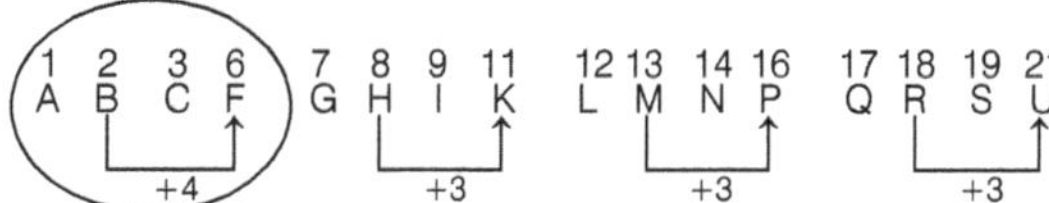

Based on Similarity of Place of All the Four Letters

Here, the relative position of all the letters is necessary for classification.

***Ex* 39** Find the odd one. « SSC (Constable) 2011

(a) NOPQ (b) JKLM (c) FGHI (d) ABCE

Solution (d) All except 'ABCE' are consecutive letters.

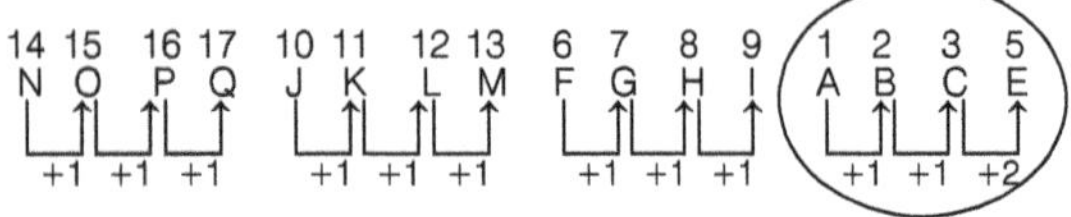

E. Classification Based on Letters Pair/Group

In this type the classification can based on consecutive letters, opposite letter pairs etc.

DIRECTIONS ~ (Example Nos. 40-43) *Choose the odd letter pair/group in each of the following questions.*

***Ex* 40**

(a) LO (b) EV (c) PT (d) NM

Solution (c) All except 'PT' are group of opposite letters.

***Ex* 41**

(a) M–O (b) P–R (c) A–C (d) E–F

M A P E
+2↓ +2↓ +2↓ +1↓
O C R F

Solution (d) In all other options, second letter is obtained from first letter after addition of 2 places.

***Ex* 42**

(a) MN–NM (b) BY–DW
(c) CX–DW (d) JQ–KP

Solution (b) Except option (b) all other pairs of letters have opposite consecutive letters.

MN – NM (+1), opposite opposite
BY – DW (+2), opposite opposite
CX – DW (+1), opposite opposite
JQ – KP (+1), opposite opposite

***Ex* 43**

(a) CDE–FGH (b) WXY–ZYX
(c) LMN–OPQ (d) TUV–WXY

« SSC (CGL) 2009

Solution (b) Except option (b), all having consecutive letters pair.

F. Miscellaneous

Based on Number of Letters

In this type of classification a group having different number of letters from others is classified as the odd group.

***Ex* 44** Which of the following option is odd one?

(a) PQRS (b) LMNOP
(c) BCDE (d) IJKL

Solution (b) All except 'LMNOP' have only four consecutive letters.

Based on Number of Small and Capital Letters

In this type of classification, odd group is that group which does not follow the sequence of small and capital letters.

***Ex* 45** Take out the odd one.

(a) TuvL (b) IJKL
(c) EfgH (d) PqrS

Solution (b) All except 'IJKL' have two small and two capital letters.

Based on Place of Small and Capital Letters

This classification is simply based on the places of capital and small letters.

***Ex* 46** Find out the odd one.

(a) TuvW (b) IjkL
(c) EfgH (d) PSqr

Solution (d) All except 'PSqr' have capital letters at first and fourth place.

Based on Presence or Absence of Vowels

In this type, absence or presence of vowels is used as a base for classification.

***Ex* 47** Find out the odd one. « SSC CGL 2015

(a) TPLI (b) YUQM
(c) RNJF (d) SOKJ

Solution (c) Option (c) is correct as except 'RNJF' all others have a vowel.

Based on Equality of Number of Vowels

Here, number of vowels present in a group serves as the basis of classifying the odd group out.

***Ex* 48** Which of the following is an odd letter group?

« SSC (10 + 2) 2010

(a) EBCDA (b) GFHIJ
(c) KOLNM (d) QRSTU

Solution (a) All except 'EBCDA' have only one vowel, whereas EBCDA has two vowels 'E' and 'A'.

Based on Meaningful and Non-meaningful Words

Here, odd group is classified on the basis that either they are meaningful words or not.

***Ex* 49** Find out the odd one.

(a) DEAR (b) NEAR
(c) BEAR (d) KEAR

Solution (d) All except 'KEAR' are meaningful words.

Note *Apart from all the given patterns of letter classification, students may be ready to face some surprising patterns.*

Practice CORNER 3.3

DIRECTIONS ~ (Q. Nos. 1-69) *In each of the following questions, some groups of letters are given, all of which except one, share a common similarity while one is different. Select the odd one.*

1. (a) I (b) J (c) K (d) L

2. (a) A (b) E (c) M (d) I

3. (a) O (b) I (c) E (d) B

4. (a) S (b) M (c) Q (d) U

« SSC (Steno) 2019

5. (a) KM (b) PO (c) HU (d) BA

« SSC Steno Grade (C&D) 2019

6. (a) DOG (b) DIN (c) OUT (d) FED (e) JOT

7. (a) MNOM (b) BDCB (c) XZYX (d) PRQP

« SSC (CGL) 2016

8. (A) NEXFL (B) ZGPKU (C) LANCP (D) FRGSP
(a) D (b) C (c) B (d) A

« RRB NTPC 2016

9. (a) FE (b) NM (c) DC (d) QR

« SSC MTS 2017

10. (a) BD (b) KM (c) HK (d) PR (e) TV

11. (a) CE (b) KI (c) FD (d) WU (e) MK

12. (a) HJ (b) PR (c) NP (d) BE (e) VX

« UCO Bank (PO) 2009

13. (a) EDC (b) MLK (c) NPR (d) XWV

« SSC (Steno) 2017

14. (a) BDH (b) CFL (c) EJU (d) DHP

15. (a) EHG (b) JML (c) PSR (d) UYX

16. (a) FGE (b) NOR (c) KLJ (d) YZX

« SSC (CGL) 2017

17. (a) LNP (b) DFH (c) FHJ (d) TVW

18. (a) CAE (b) KGM (c) NLP (d) YWA

19. (a) bbb fff jjj (b) mmm qqq ttt
(c) kkk ooo sss (d) ccc ggg kkk

« SSC (CPO) 2015

20. (a) VTR (b) HJL (c) UWY (d) PRT

RRB ALP 2018

21. (a) UST (b) QMO (c) LHJ (d) IEG

« UPSSSC 2018

22. (a) RUY (b) SQO (c) OMK (d) FDB (e) YWU

23. (a) ELS (b) HOV (c) CJQ (d) KRX

24. (a) BEA (b) PSO (c) WZV (d) RTQ

25. (a) GDF (b) VRT (c) KHJ (d) NKM

26. (a) MOR (b) GIL (c) SUX (d) VXZ

27. (a) HKI (b) UXV (c) CFD (d) MQN

28. (a) MrW (b) ChN (c) KpU (d) BgL

29. (a) JKL (b) GHI (c) OPQ (d) ILT (e) MNO

30. (a) CJQ (b) AGA (c) HOV (d) ELS (e) KRY

31. (a) JLN (b) GIK (c) NPR (d) TVY

« SSC (Steno) 2017

32. (a) DAH (b) IFM (c) ROV (d) QNT

33. (a) PQO (b) AZY (c) TWS (d) VBU

34. (a) GDA (b) OLI (c) VSP (d) WYZ

35. (a) HJL (b) VWX (c) PQR (d) EFG

« RRB (ALP) 2018

36. (a) GHI (b) XYZ (c) VUT (d) CDE

« SSC CGL 2017

37. (a) HJN (b) JLP (c) PRU (d) QSW (e) ACG

38. (a) BEG (b) KNP (c) WZB (d) JLN (e) DGI

39. (a) LNJ (b) RTP (c) NPK (d) FHD (e) WYU

40. (a) NKHE (b) MIDA (c) KHEB (d) WTQN

41. (a) YXVU (b) ORQP (c) KJHG (d) MLJI

42. (a) CDFE (b) JKLM (c) STVU (d) WXZY (e) HIKJ

43. (a) NKMJ (b) FCEB (c) URTQ (d) TQRP

44. (a) BEHK (b) ADGJ (c) FHKM (d) JMPS

« SSC (CGL) 2020

45. (a) dcba (b) zyxw (c) srpq (d) hgfe

« SSC (Multitasking) 2014

46. (a) TWXZ (b) ADEG (c) EHIK (d) LNOQ

« SSC (10+2) 2013

47. (a) GAEF (b) TSWX (c) WQUV (d) PJNO (e) RLPQ

« IDBI Executive 2018

48. (a) FUGT (b) KPLO (c) DWEV (d) CWDX

« RRB JE 2019

49. (a) GDFE (b) QMPO (c) TQSR (d) CZBA

50. (a) DEGJ (b) QRTW (c) JKNQ (d) YZBE

51. (a) ALMZ (b) BTUY (c) CPQX (d) DEFY

« CG Patwari 2017

52. (a) ZYAB (b) TSGH (c) ONLM (d) UTFH

53. (a) JKOP (b) MNRS (c) CABD (d) OPTU

« SSC (CPO) 2013

54. (a) BdEg (b) PrSu (c) KmNp (d) TwXz

55. (a) CdaB (b) VwtU (c) LmjK (d) RsqP

56. (a) JIHG (b) RQPO (c) WXUV (d) UTSR (e) NMLK

57. (a) LJHN (b) FDBH (c) SQOU (d) PNKR

58. (a) BJLQ (b) TPDC (c) BKDF (d) OLTF

« SSC (CGL) April 2014

59. (a) DFHB (b) KMOJ (c) PRTN (d) XZBV

60. (a) DGEF (b) HNLJ (c) TWUV (d) MSOQ

« SSC (CGL) 2018

61. (a) RKMQ (b) GDCF (c) LIHK (d) TQPS

62. (a) FIJL (b) RUVX (c) DGHJ (d) NPQS

63. (a) XTCG (b) NJMQ (c) EAUZ (d) SOHL

64. (a) GJHI (b) MPNO (c) RUST (d) UVXW

« SSC (Steno) 2017

65. (a) ABDG (b) CDFI (c) EFHK (d) GHJK (e) HIKN

« IBPS (Clerk) 2011

66. (a) u a i e o (b) c g k o s (c) e i m q u (d) h l p t x

« UPSSSC (VDO) 2018

67. (a) BDFHJ (b) NOQST (c) QSUWY (d) EGIKM

« SSC (CPO) 2019

68. (a) KKlmn (b) EEfgg (c) CCdee (d) TTuvv

69. (a) LNPRT (b) NPRTV (c) HJMOR (d) DFHJL

« SSC CPO 2018

DIRECTIONS ~ (Q. Nos 70 and 71) *Choose the odd letter pair/group in each of the following questions.*

70. (a) B–F (b) J–N (c) M–Q (d) T–U

71. (a) E–J–O–T (b) C–F–I–L (c) B–D–F–H (d) A–B–E–F

Answers WITH EXPLANATIONS

1. (*a*) Except I, all others are consonants.

2. (*c*) Except M, all others are vowels.

3. (*d*) Except B, all others are the vowels.

4. (*d*) Except U, all others are vowels.

5. (*a*) Except KM, all other pairs have one vowel.

6. (*c*) All others have only one vowel.

7. (*a*) Only in option (a) first 3 alphabets are in alphabetical order.

8. (*a*) Except FRGSP, all other options contain one vowel.

9. (*d*)

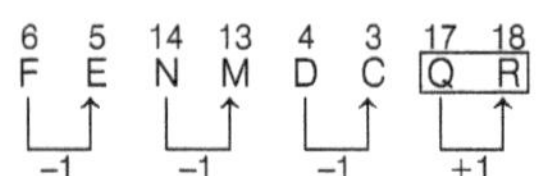

It is clear from above except QR, in all other have the difference of – 1.

10. (*c*)

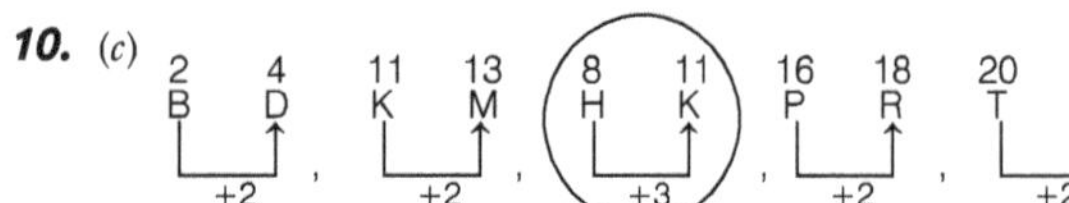

So, option (c) is different from others.

11. (*a*)

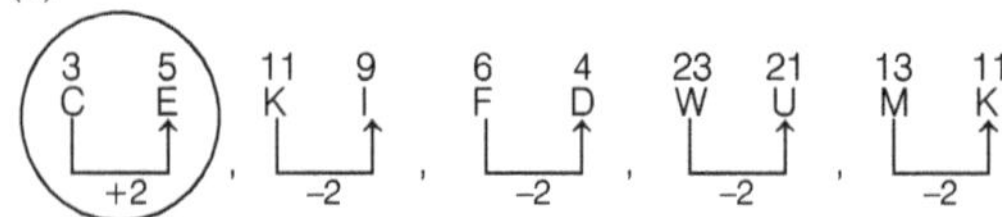

Now, it is clear that all options, except option (a), follow the same pattern.

12. (*d*)

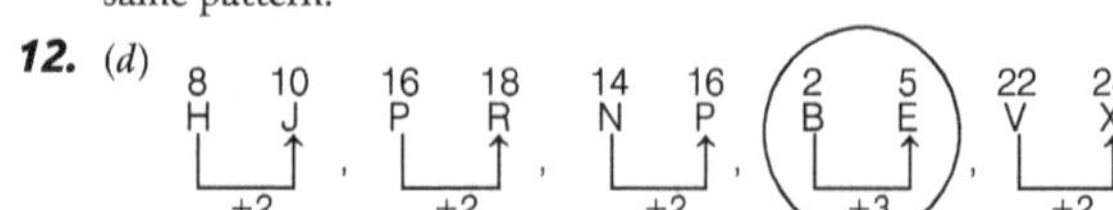

Therefore, BE is different from others.

13. (*c*)

Except (c), in all other option letters are written in same sequence.

14. (*c*)

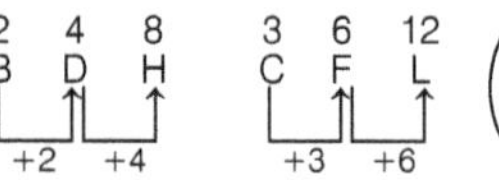

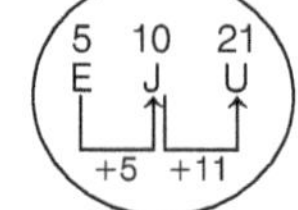

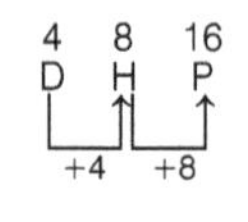

Clearly, 'EJU' is different from the other options because in all the others the second difference is twice the first difference.

15. (*d*)

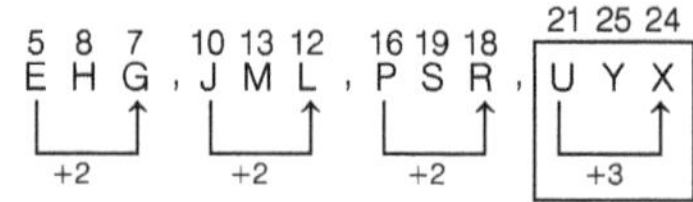

Except (d), in all other, there is a gap of one letter between first and third letter.

16. (*b*)

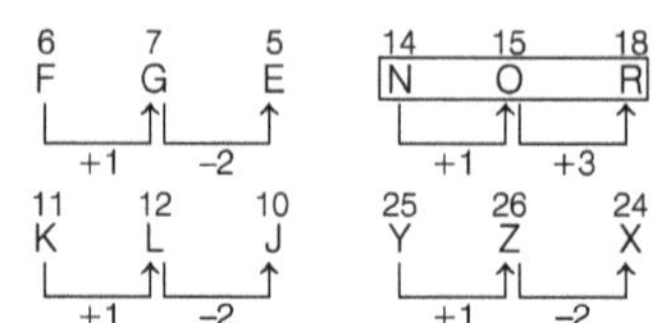

Clearly, NOR is different from others.

17. (*d*)

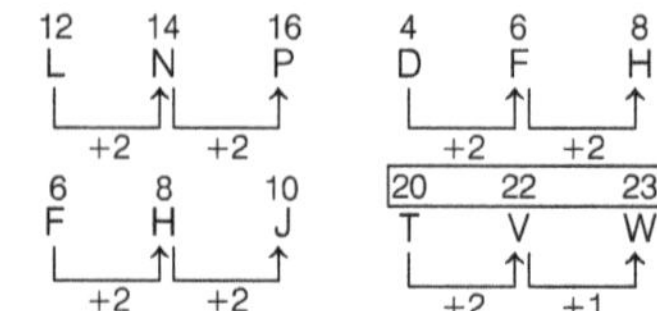

Clearly, 'TVW' follows different pattern from others.

18. (*b*)

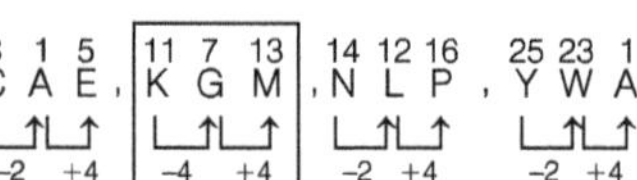

Clearly, 'KGM' is different from the others.

19. (*b*)

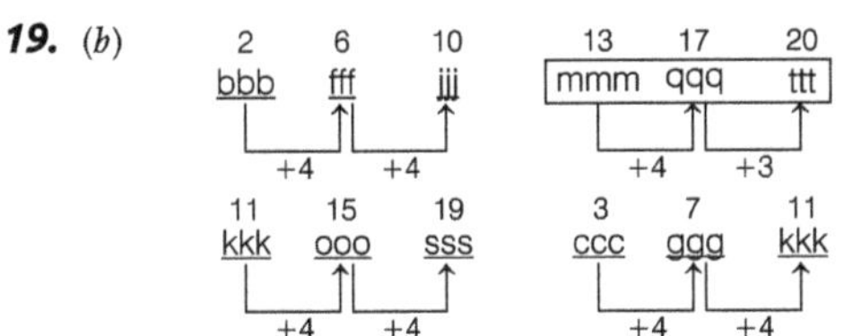

So, it is clear from above that option (b) is different.

20. (*a*)

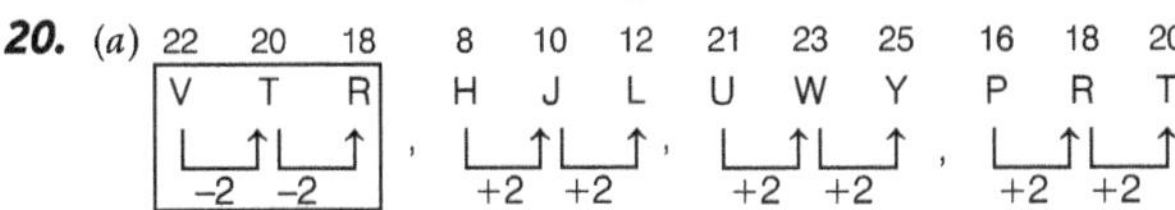

Clearly, VTR is different from the rest.

21. (*a*) 21 19 20 U S T (+2 +1), 17 13 15 Q M O (+4 +2), 12 8 10 L H J (+4 +2), 9 5 7 I E G (+4 +2)

Clearly, 'UST' is different from the rest.

22. (*a*) 18 21 25 R U Y (+3 +4), 19 17 15 S Q O (−2 −2), 15 13 11 O M K (−2 −2), 6 4 2 F D B (−2 −2), 25 23 21 Y W U (−2 −2)

∴ 'RUY' is the odd one out and does it belong to the group.

23. (*d*) 5 12 19 E L S (+7 +7), 8 15 22 H O V (+7 +7), 3 10 17 C J Q (+7 +7), 11 18 24 K R X (+7 +6)

Clearly, 'KRX' is different from the others.

24. (*d*) 2 5 1 B E A (+3 +4), 16 19 15 P S O (+3 +4), 23 26 22 W Z V (+3 +4), 18 20 17 R T Q (+2 +3)

Clearly, 'RTQ' is different from the others.

25. (*b*) 7 4 6 G D F (−3 +2), 22 18 20 V R T (−4 +2), 11 8 10 K H J (−3 +2), 14 11 13 N K M (−3 +2)

Clearly, 'VRT' is different from the others.

26. (*d*) 13 15 18 M O R (+2 +3), 7 9 12 G I L (+2 +3), 19 21 24 S U X (+2 +3), 22 24 26 V X Z (+2 +2)

Clearly, 'VXZ' is different from the others.

27. (*d*) 8 11 9 H K I (+3 −2), 21 24 22 U X V (+3 −2), 3 6 4 C F D (+3 −2), 13 17 14 M Q N (+3 −3)

Clearly, 'MQN' is different from the others.

28. (*b*) 13 18 23 M r W (+5 +5), 3 8 14 C h N (+5 +6), 11 16 21 K p U (+5 +5), 2 7 12 B g L (+5 +5)

Clearly, 'ChN' is different from the others.

29. (*d*)

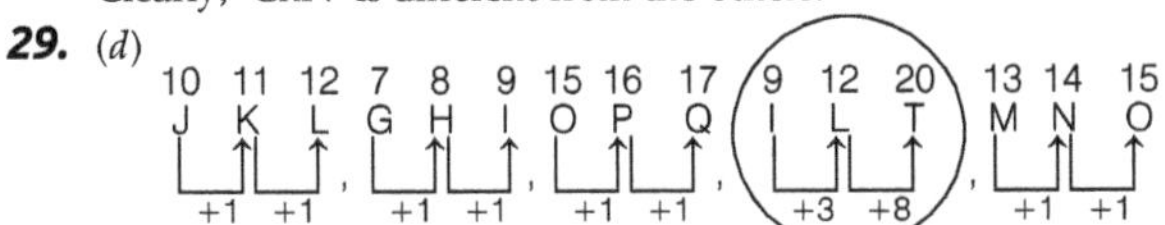

So, 'ILT' is different because other options have consecutive letters.

30. (*b*)

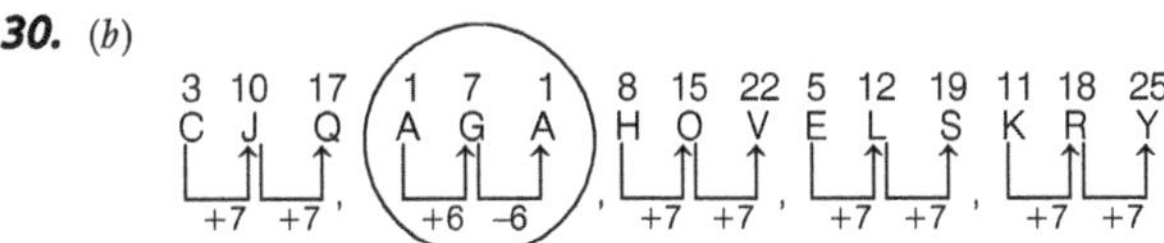

Clearly, AGA is different from other four.

31. (*d*)

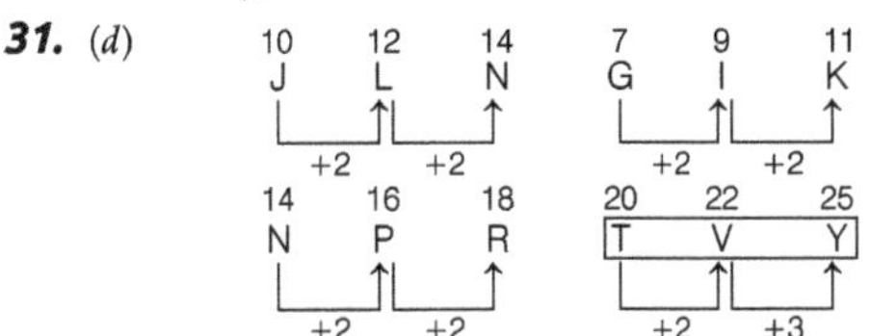

Clearly, TVY is different from others.

32. (*d*)

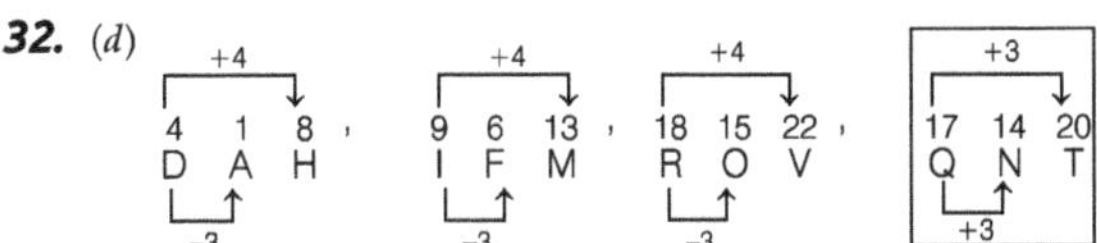

Clearly, 'QNT' is different from others.

33. (*b*) 16 17 15 P Q O (−1), 1 26 25 A Z Y (−2), 20 23 19 T W S (−1), 22 2 21 V B U (−1)

Clearly, 'AZY' is different from others.

34. (*d*) 7 4 1 G D A (−3 −3), 15 12 9 O L I (−3 −3), 22 19 16 V S P (−3 −3), 23 25 26 W Y Z (−2 −1)

Clearly, 'WYZ' is different from others.

35. (*a*) Here the pattern is

H (8) →(+2) J (10) →(+2) L (12), V (22) →(+1) W (23) →(+1) X (24)

P (16) →(+1) Q (17) →(+1) R (18), E (5) →(+1) F (6) →(+1) G (7)

Clearly, HJL follows a pattern, which is different from others. Hence, it is the odd one.

36. (*c*) 7 8 9 G H I (+1 +1), 24 25 26 X Y Z (+1 +1), 22 21 20 V U T (−1 −1), 3 4 5 C D E (+1 +1)

It is clear from above that VUT is different from others.

37. (*c*) 8 10 14 H J N (+2 +4), 10 12 16 J L P (+2 +4), 16 18 21 P R U (+2 +3), 17 19 23 Q S W (+2 +4), 1 3 7 A C G (+2 +4)

Clearly, 'PRU' is different from others.

38. (*d*)

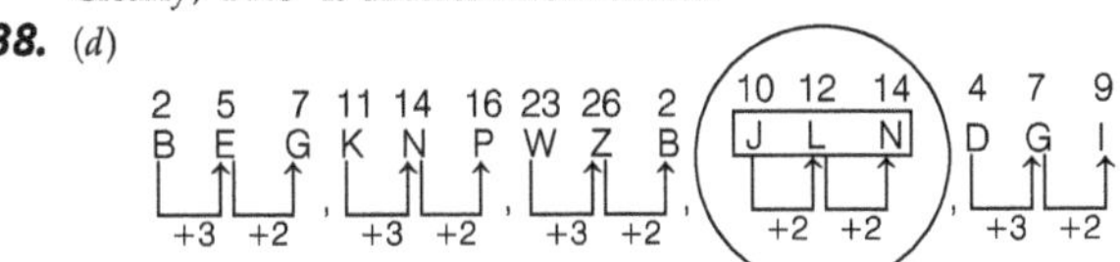

Clearly JLN is different from other.

39. (*c*)

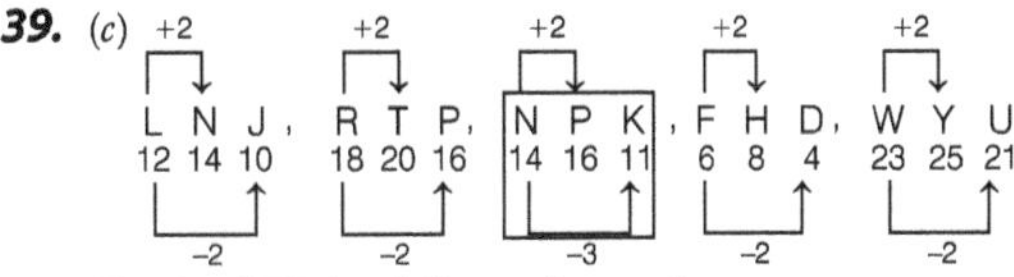

Clearly, 'NPK' is different from others.

40. (*b*) Except (b), all other follow the same pattern.

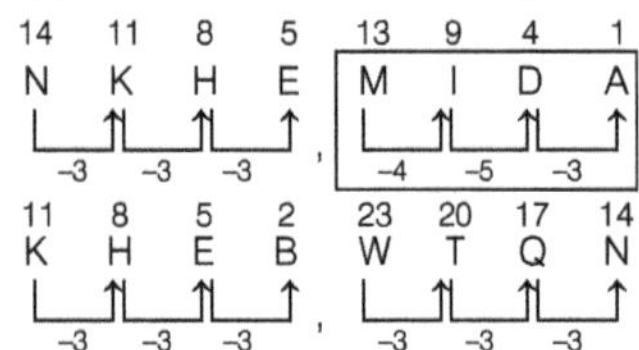

Clearly, MIDA is different from others.

41. (*b*) Except ORQP, all others have the same gap between the adjacent letters.

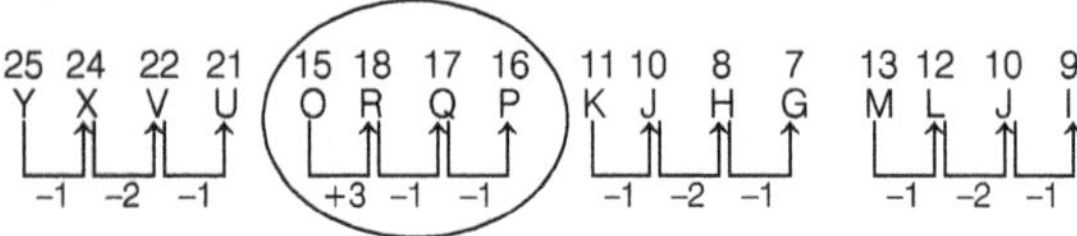

Clearly, ORQP is different from other options.

42. (*b*)

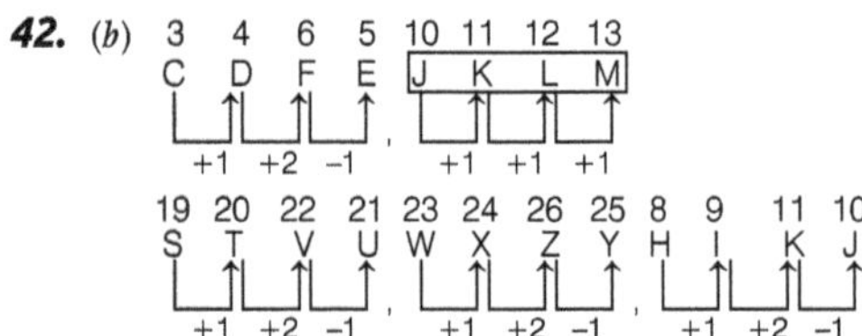

Clearly, 'JKLM' is different from the others.

43. (*d*)

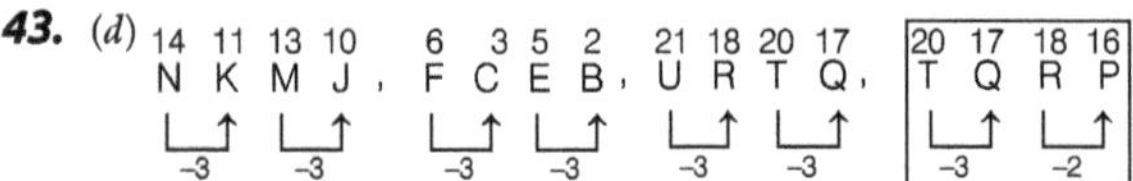

Clearly, 'TQRP' is different from the others.

44. (*c*)

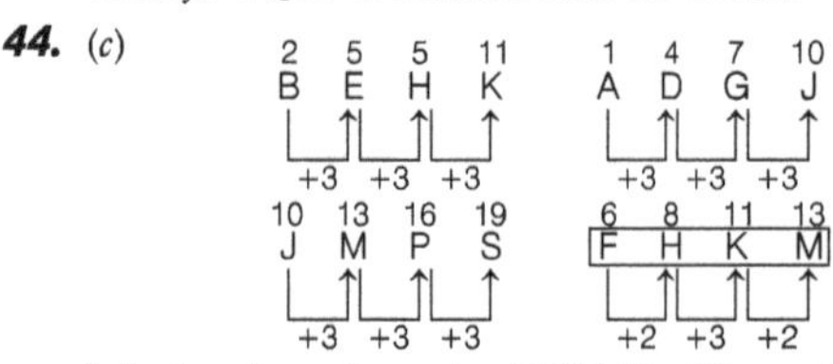

It is clear from above that FHKM is different from others.

45. (*c*)

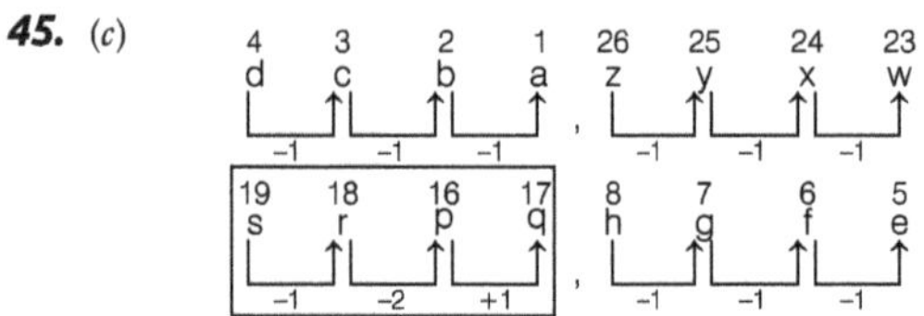

Clearly, 'srpq' is different from the others.

46. (*d*)

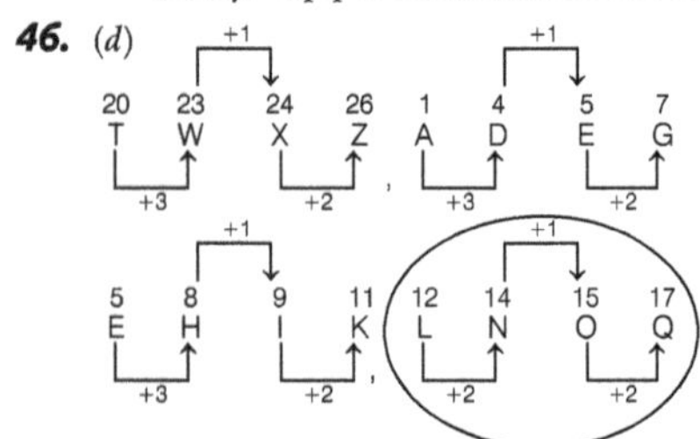

Clearly, LNOQ is different from other. Hence, option (d) is the answer.

47. (*b*)

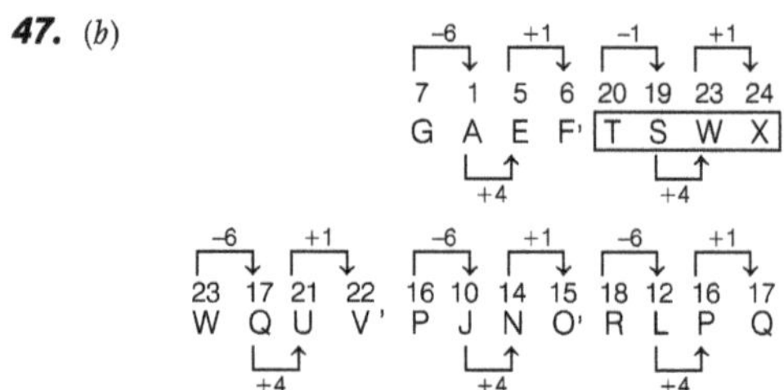

Clearly, 'TSWX' is different from others.

48. (*d*)

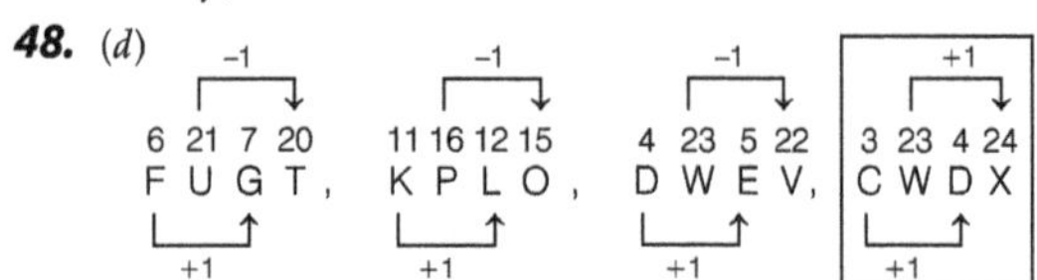

Clearly, CWDX is the odd one.

49. (*b*)

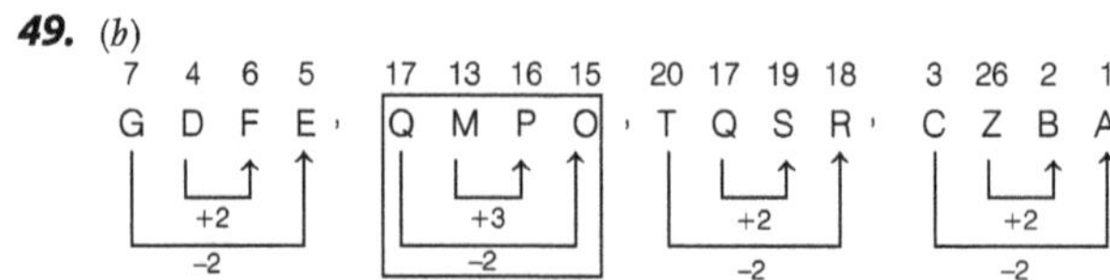

Clearly, 'QMPO' is different from the others.

50. (*c*)

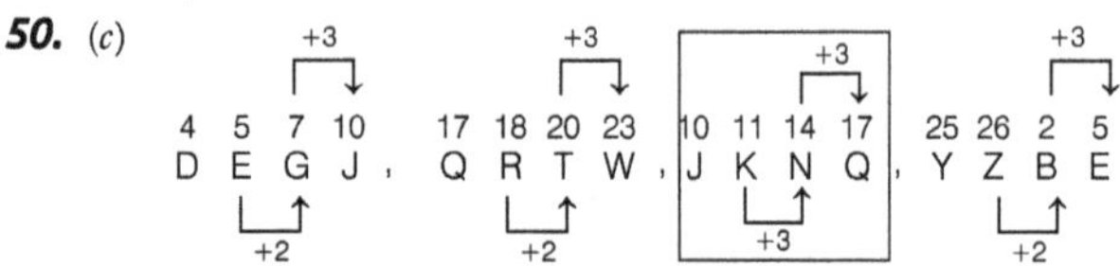

Clearly, 'JKNQ' is different from the others.

51. (*d*)

+1 +1
A L M Z, B T U Y
1 12 13 26 2 20 21 25

+1 +1
C P Q X, D E F Y
3 16 17 24 4 5 6 25

Except DEFY In all the other groups, the first and the last letter occupy same position in the alphabetical and reverse alphabetical series.

52. (*d*)

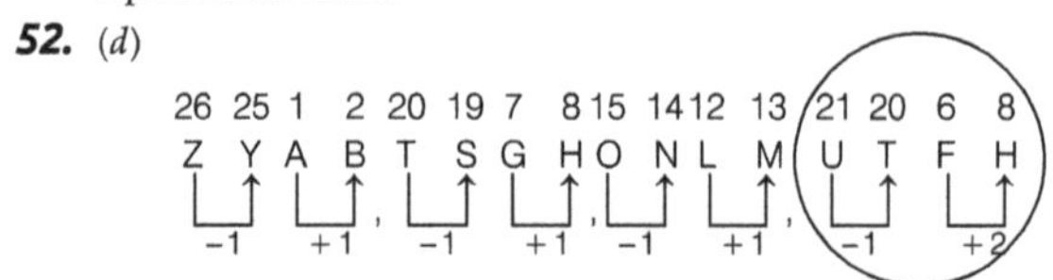

Clearly, option (d) is different from others.

53. (*c*)

J (10) —+1→ K (11) —+4→ O (15) —+1→ P (16)

M (13) —+1→ N (14) —+4→ R (18) —+1→ S (19)

C (3) —−2→ A (1) —+1→ B (2) —+2→ D (4)

O (15) —+1→ P (16) —+4→ T (20) —+1→ U (21)

Clearly, 'CABD' is different from others.

54. (*d*)

2 4 5 7 | 16 18 19 21 | 11 13 14 16 | 20 23 24 26
B d E g, | P r S u, | K m N p, | T w X z
+2 +2 | +2 +2 | +2 +2 | +3 +2

Clearly, 'TWXZ' is different from the others.

55. (*d*)

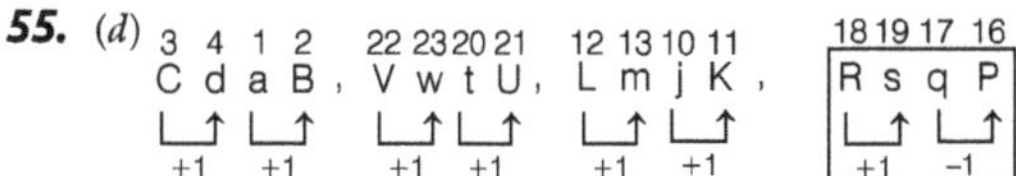

Clearly, 'RsqP' is different from the others.

56. (*c*)

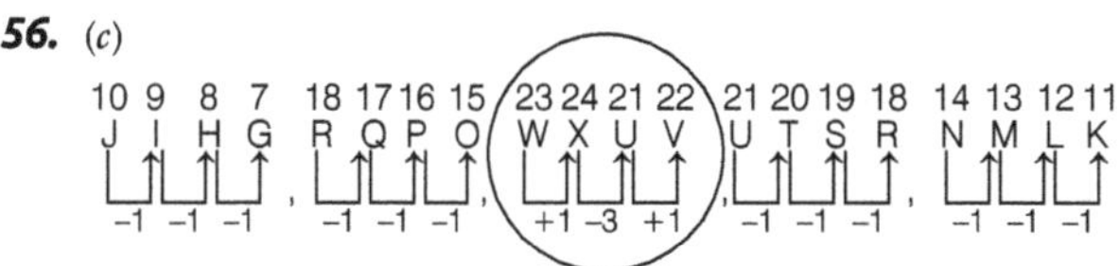

So, 'WXUV' is following different pattern from others.

57. (*d*)

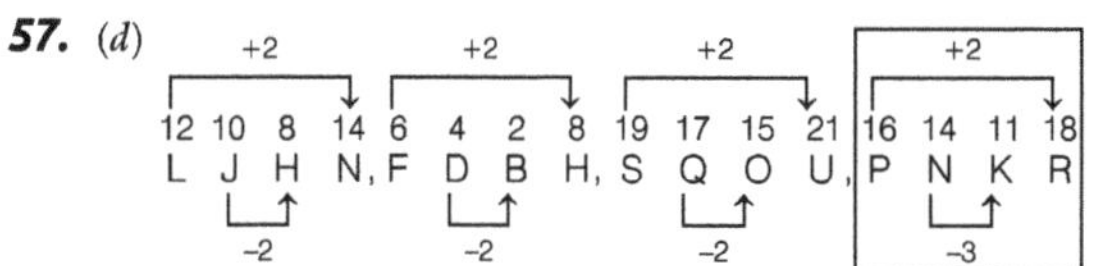

Clearly, 'PNKR' is different from the others.

58. (*d*) Except OLTF, none of the groups of letters has any vowel.

59. (*b*)

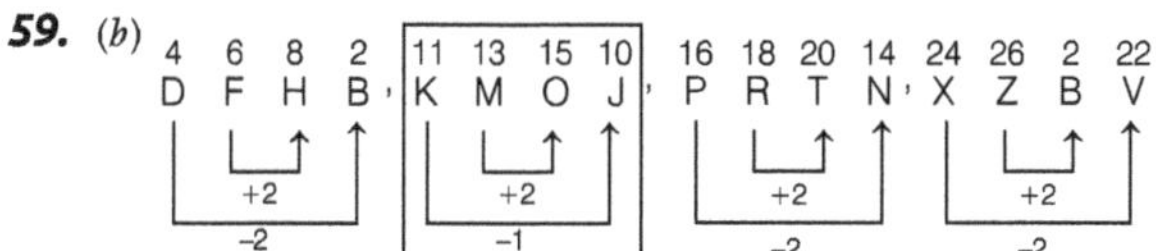

Clearly, 'KMOJ' is different from the others.

60. (*b*)

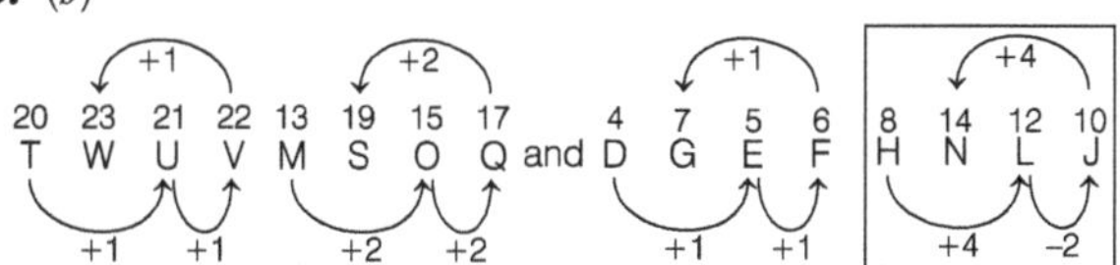

Except 'HNLJ', all others are showing same certain pattern.

61. (*a*)

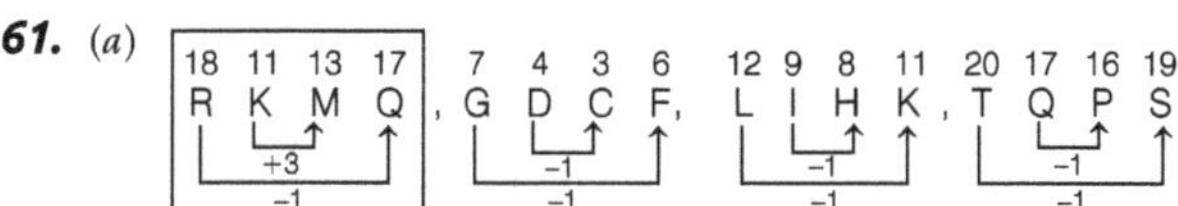

Clearly, 'RKMQ' is different from others.

62. (*d*) The pattern of the question is,

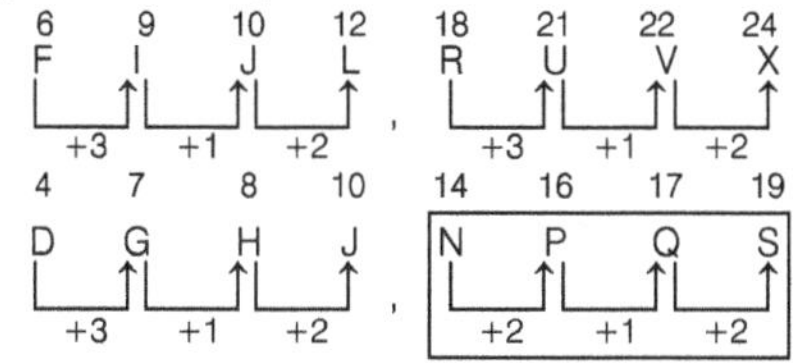

Clearly, option (d) is different from the others.

63. (*c*)

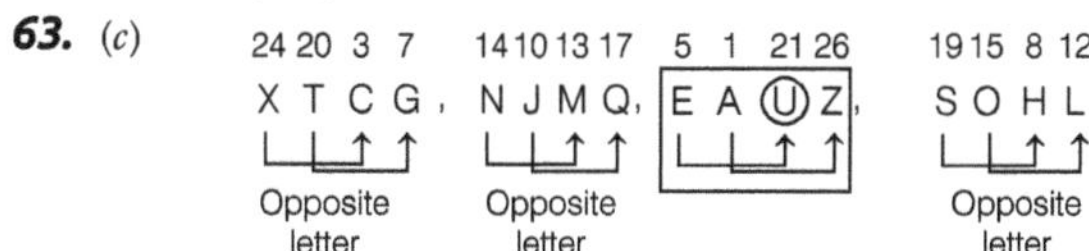

It is clear from above that EAUZ is different from others.

64. (*d*)

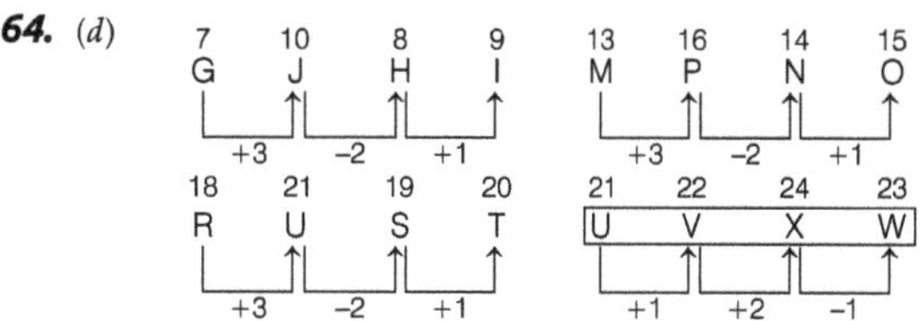

∴ Clearly, UVXW is different from others.

65. (*d*)

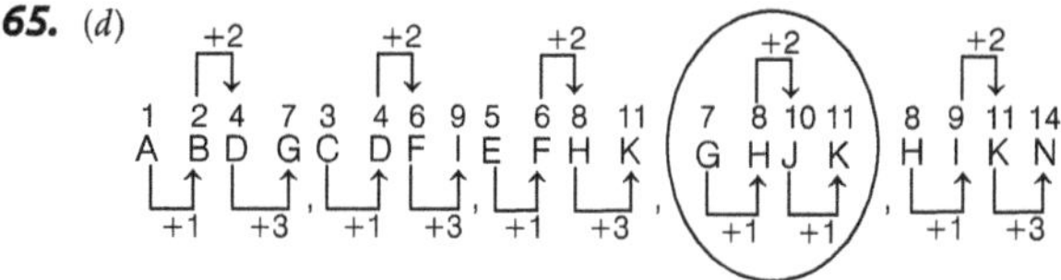

Therefore, GHJK is different from the other three.

66. (*a*) These are all vowels while other have consonents also.

67. (*b*)

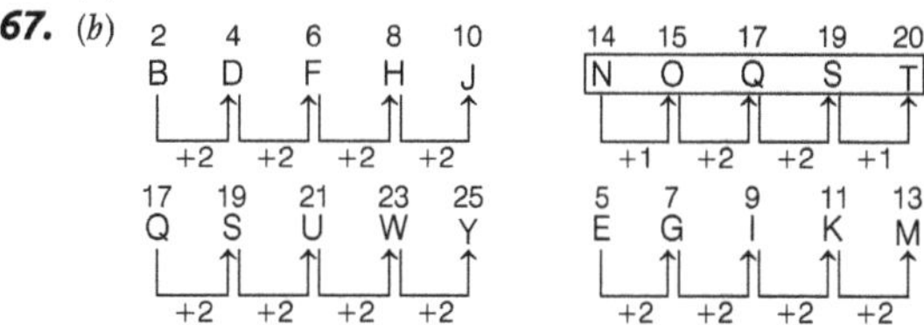

Clearly, 'NOQST' is different from others.

68. (*a*)

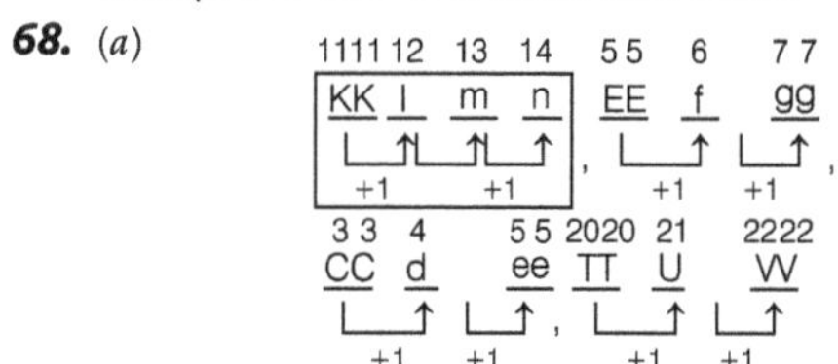

Hence, 'KKlmn' is different from others.

69. (*c*) 12 14 16 18 20 14 16 18 20 22
L N P R T, N P R T V
+2 +2 +2 +2, +2 +2 +2 +2
8 10 13 15 18 4 6 8 10 12
HJMOR, D F H J L
+2 +3 +2 +3, +2 +2 +2 +2

Hence, HJMOR is different from others.

70. (*d*)

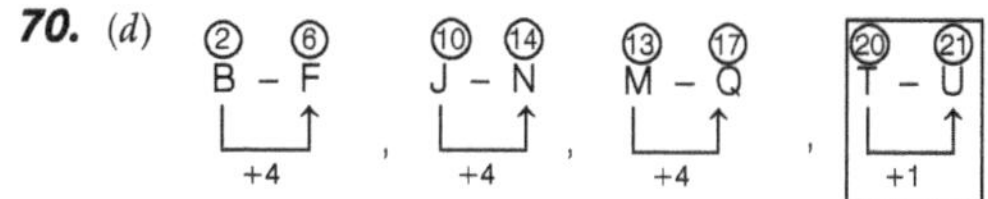

Clearly, T-U is different from others.

71. (*d*)

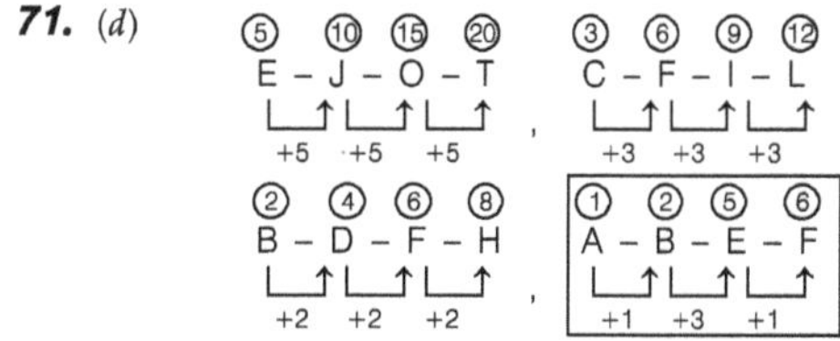

Clearly, A-B-E-F is different from others.

TYPE 04

Choosing the Odd Number/Number Pair/Group

In this type of questions, certain numbers/pairs/groups of numbers are given, out of which all except one may have the same property or may be related to each other according to the same rule or pattern. The candidate is required to choose the odd numbers/pair/group of numbers.

Let us see the types of number classifications

A. Classification Based on Single Digit/Number

In this type of questions a group of numbers or digits is given, in which you have to find out the digit/number which does not show similarity as other numbers i.e. different from others.

The numbers are classified on the following basis.

Classification Based on Even/Odd Numbers

The natural numbers exactly divisible by 2 (leaving no remainder) are called even numbers, *e.g.*, 2, 4, 6, 8, 10, 14 etc.

The natural numbers not exactly divisible by 2 are called odd numbers, e.g., 1, 3, 5, 7, 9, 11, 13, ...

***Ex* 50** Four numbers have been given, out of which three are alike in some manner and one is different. Select the number that is different from the rest. « SSC (10+2) 2020

(a) 255 (b) 212
(c) 268 (d) 124

Solution (a) Except '255' all other numbers are even.

***Ex* 51** Select the odd number from the given alternatives.

(a) 43 (b) 22
(c) 13 (d) 41

Solution (b) Except 22, all other numbers are odd.

Classification Based on Prime Or Non-Prime (Composite) Numbers

The natural numbers greater than one and divisible by 1 and only itself, are called prime numbers.

Non-prime (composite) numbers are exactly divisible by 1, itself and some other numbers also.

e.g., 4, 6, 8, 10, 12 , 14, 15, ...

***Ex* 52** Find out the odd one. « SSC (CPO) 2016

(a) 53 (b) 43
(c) 73 (d) 63

Solution (d) All except '63' are prime numbers.

***Ex* 53** Find the number different from others.

(a) 345 (b) 133
(c) 225 (d) 216

Solution (b) All except '133' are non-prime numbers.

Classification Based on Squares/Cube of Numbers

When a number is multiplied by itself, then the number obtained is called the square of that particular number.

e.g., Square of $2 = 2 \times 2 = 4$,
Square of $3 = 3 \times 3 = 9$,
Square of $4 = 4 \times 4 = 16$

When a number is multiplied two times with itself, then the number obtained is called the cube of that particular number.

e.g., Cube of $2 = 2 \times 2 \times 2 = 8$,
Cube of $3 = 3 \times 3 \times 3 = 27$,
Cube of $4 = 4 \times 4 \times 4 = 64$

***Ex* 54** Find the odd one out of the numbers given below.

(a) 225 (b) 255 (c) 289 (d) 196

Solution (b) All except '255' all others are squares of natural numbers.

***Ex* 55** Find the odd one.

(a) 216 (b) 33 (c) 8 (d) 64

Solution (b) All except '33' are cubes of natural numbers.

Classification Based on Divisibility/Multiplication

In this type of questions, all numbers are divisible/multiple of a particular number except only one number.

***Ex* 56** Find the odd one. « SSC (CPO) 2019

(a) 18 (b) 25 (c) 33 (d) 24

Solution (b) All except '25' are divisible by 3.

***Ex* 57** Find the odd man out of the given numbers.

(a) 108 (b) 320
(c) 498 (d) 32

Solution (c) Except 498, all are completely divisible by 4.

Classification Based on Increasing/ Decreasing Order of Digits

Here, the sequence of digits in options are given in increasing/decreasing order.

***Ex* 58** Take out the odd one.

(a) 456 (b) 234 (c) 123 (d) 465

Solution (d) All except '465' are in increasing order of digits.

***Ex* 59** Find the odd one. « SSC (CGL) 2009

(a) 345 (b) 321 (c) 876 (d) 654

Solution (a) All except '345' are in decreasing order of digits.

Classification Based on Repetation of Digits in Number

Here, in each number, except one or two or three digits are same.

Ex 60 Find the odd one.

(a) 311 (b) 232 (c) 344 (d) 567

Solution (d) Except 567, in all other numbers two digits are same.

Classification Based on Addition of Digits

Here, in each number, except one the sum of all the digits are equal.

Ex 61 Select the odd number from the given alternatives. « SSC (10+2) 2017

(a) 2378 (b) 7562 (c) 6662 (d) 1155

Solution (d)

$2378 \Rightarrow 2+3+7+8=20$
$7562 \Rightarrow 7+5+6+2=20$
$6662 \Rightarrow 6+6+6+2=20$
$1155 \Rightarrow 1+1+5+5=12$

It is clear from above that except 1155, sum of digit of all other numbers are 20 whereas sum of digit of 1155 is 12. Hence, 1155 is different from others.

B. Classification Based on Pair or Group of Digits/Numbers

The pair can consists of numbers with same difference, one is multiple of other etc.

DIRECTIONS ~ (Example Nos. 62-63) *In the following questions, four pairs of numbers are given, which all except one are similar in some manner and hence they form a group. You have to find the pair which is different and therefore discarded from the group of similar pair.*

Ex 62 « SSC (MTS) 2017

(a) 6-12 (b) 7-14
(c) 3-5 (d) 4-8

Solution (c) All except '3-5' have the second number which is twice the first number.

Ex 63 « SSC (10+2) 2018

(a) 27-32 (b) 31-36
(c) 33-38 (d) 23-27

Solution (d) Except option (d) in each pair, the second number is five more than the first number.

C. Classification Based on Group of Three Numbers

Three different numbers form a group possessing some common property.

Ex 64

(a) 25, 50, 56 (b) 20, 40, 46
(c) 18, 36, 40 (d) 12, 24, 30

Solution (c) All except '18, 36, 40' have second number double the first number and third number 6 more than the second number.

Practice / CORNER 3.4

DIRECTIONS ~ (Q. Nos. 1-44) *In each of the following questions, four/five options are given. Out of these, three/four are alike in a particular way but remaining one is different. Find the odd one from the given options which is different from others.*

1. (a) 25 (b) 9 (c) 16 (d) 18 « SSC (Multitasking) 2013

2. (a) 4867 (b) 5555 (c) 6243 (d) 6655

3. (a) 27 (b) 64 (c) 81 (d) 125 « WBCS 2020

4. (a) 61 (b) 51 (c) 97 (d) 89 « SSC (CPO) 2017

5. (a) 149 (b) 157 (c) 199 (d) 121 « SSC (10+2) 2017

6. (a) 13 (b) 43 (c) 63 (d) 23 (e) 53

7. (a) 78 (b) 91 (c) 85 (d) 26 « SSC (Steno) 2016

8. (a) 12 (b) 28 (c) 52 (d) 68 (e) 96

9. (a) 26 (b) 34 (c) 72 (d) 46 (e) 38 « SBI (PO) 2009

10. (a) 11 (b) 17 (c) 45 (d) 37

11. (a) 130 (b) 60 (c) 52 (d) 78 « SSC Sub-Inspector 2018

12. (a) 67 (b) 47 (c) 17 (d) 57 « SSC (Steno-Grade C&D) 2019

13. (a) 68 (b) 72 (c) 48 (d) 96 « SSC (GD) Constable 2018

14. (a) 729 (b) 123 (c) 423 (d) 621

15. (a) 48 (b) 96 (c) 59 (d) 12 « SSC (Steno) 2016

16. (a) 15 (b) 27 (c) 37 (d) 39

17. (a) 16 (b) 25 (c) 35 (d) 49

18. (a) 21 (b) 55 (c) 63 (d) 49

19. (a) 8110 (b) 9100 (c) 1189 (d) 1234 « SSC (CPO) 2015

20. (a) 162 (b) 405 (c) 567 (d) 644 « SSC (10+2) 2015

21. (a) 30 (b) 18 (c) 24 (d) 26
« RRB (ASM) 2011

22. (a) 43 (b) 53 (c) 63 (d) 73

23. (a) 26 (b) 124 (c) 728 (d) 64

24. (a) 49 (b) 140 (c) 112 (d) 21

25. (a) 121 (b) 169 (c) 225 (d) 289

26. (a) 119 (b) 154 (c) 85 (d) 51

27. (a) 12 (b) 14 (c) 56 (d) 30
« SSC (CGL) 2018

28. (a) 143 (b) 171 (c) 117 (d) 195

29. (a) 17 (b) 44 (c) 29 (d) 13
« SSS (Steno) 2013

30. (a) 63 (b) 126 (c) 124 (d) 342

31. (a) 272 (b) 210 (c) 240 (d) 304
« SSC (CGL) 2013

32. (a) 144 (b) 196 (c) 288 (d) 324

33. (a) 120 (b) 72 (c) 108 (d) 98

34. (a) 28 (b) 42 (c) 35 (d) 21 (e) 65

35. (a) 115 (b) 145 (c) 195 (d) 155 (e) 75

36. (a) 120 (b) 6 (c) 24 (d) 64
« SSC (CGL) April 2014

37. (a) 73 (b) 53 (c) 87 (d) 67

38. (a) 437 (b) 369 (c) 279 (d) 159 (e) 819

39. (a) 215 (b) 143 (c) 247 (d) 91 (e) 65

40. (a) 626 (b) 841 (c) 962 (d) 1090

41. (a) 488 (b) 929 (c) 776 (d) 667

42. (a) 3216 (b) 2338 (c) 3205 (d) 2015

43. (a) 572 (b) 671 (c) 264 (d) 427

44. (a) 144 (b) 324 (c) 196 (d) 210

DIRECTIONS ~ (Q. Nos. 45-76) *Choose the odd numbers pair/group in each of the following questions.*

45. (a) 72572 (b) 35453 (c) 78378 (d) 46246

46. (a) 46, 57 (b) 38, 49 (c) 41, 52 (d) 64, 73

47. (a) 18-22 (b) 11-13 (c) 12-14 (d) 17-19

48. (a) 20-36 (b) 30-36 (c) 50-56 (d) 60-66

49. (a) 117-39 (b) 164-41 (c) 198-66 (d) 213-71

50. (a) 54 : 17 (b) 36 : 13 (c) 90 : 29 (d) 72 : 23
« SSC (Steno Grade C&D) 2019

51. (a) 3 - 28 (b) 2 - 9 (c) 5 - 124 (d) 4 - 65
« SSC (Steno) 2017

52. (a) 25631 (b) 33442 (c) 34424 (d) 52163

53. (a) 23-29 (b) 19-25 (c) 13-17 (d) 3-5

54. (a) 18, 45 (b) 23,14 (c) 29, 82 (d) 36,27

55. (a) 65-101 (b) 26-50 (c) 17-37 (d) 49-82 « SSC (CGL) 2018

56. (a) 1 : 4 (b) 10 : 24 (c) 8 : 18 (d) 22 : 46

57. (a) 5 : 9 (b) 7 : 11 (c) 13 : 17 (d) 43 : 47

58. (a) 70-80 (b) 54-62 (c) 28-32 (d) 21-24
« CG (Patwari) 2017

59. (a) 147 : 741 (b) 253 : 352 (c) 518 : 816 (d) 303 : 303

60. (a) 93 : 117 (b) 63 : 81 (c) 133 : 171 (d) 119 : 153

61. (a) 22 : 44 (b) 45 : 1625 (c) 18 : 164 (d) 24 : 464

62. (a) 17-34 (b) 19-38 (c) 23-46 (d) 27-56
« SSC (CHSL) Tier I 2018

63. (a) 22 : 0 (b) 24 : 12 (c) 23 : 5 (d) 24 : 18

64. (a) 64-100 (b) 25-36 (c) 16-49 (d) 48-81
« SSC (CPO) 2019

65. (a) 16-25 (b) 64-81 (c) 36-49 (d) 100-110
« SSC (10+2) 2015

66. (a) 4 : 8 (b) 9 : 27 (c) 49 : 2401 (d) 25 : 125 « RRB (JE) 2018

67. (a) 286, 628 (b) 397, 739 (c) 475, 574 (d) 369, 936

68. (a) 919, 949 (b) 646, 686 (c) 828, 848 (d) 434, 464

69. (a) 39-72 (b) 57-38 (c) 42-12 (d) 28-60 « SSC (CGL) 2020

70. (a) 9-90 (b) 6-42 (c) 5-30 (d) 4-36 « SSC (Steno) 2019

71. (a) 7-46 (b) 9-80 (c) 6-35 (d) 4-15 « SSC (CGL) 2018

72. (a) 561, 615, 165 (b) 426, 642, 246 (c) 289, 829, 928 (d) 632, 325, 236
« SSC (CPO) 2019

73. (a) 14, 17, 23 (b) 19, 22, 28 (c) 17, 20, 26 (d) 21, 23, 30

74. (a) 2-4-8 (b) 4-16-32 (c) 3-9-27 (d) 5-25-125

75. (a) 11, 17, 23 (b) 12, 14, 16 (c) 8, 10, 12 (d) 18, 36, 72

76. (a) 12, 72, 144 (b) 26, 156, 312 (c) 17, 102, 204 (d) 14, 90, 180

Answers WITH EXPLANATIONS

1. (*d*) All except '18', are square of natural numbers.
$(5)^2 = 25, (3)^2 = 9, (4)^2 = 16$

2. (*d*) $4867 \rightarrow 4 + 8 + 6 + 7 = 25$, which is divisible by 5.
$5555 \rightarrow 5 + 5 + 5 + 5 = 20$, which is divisible by 5.
$6243 \rightarrow 6 + 2 + 4 + 3 = 15$, which is divisible by 5.
$6655 \rightarrow 6 + 6 + 5 + 5 = 22$, which is not divisible by 5.

3. (*c*) All the numbers are perfect cube except 81, which is a perfect square number, $9^2 = 81$.

4. (*b*) Except 51, all other are prime numbers.

5. (*d*) Except 121, all other are prime numbers while 121 is a square number of prime number 11.

6. (*c*) Except 63, all others are prime numbers.

7. (*c*) Except (c) all others are divisible by 13.

8. (*e*) Except 96, all others have only 3 factors.
$12 = 2 \times 2 \times 3,\ 28 = 2 \times 2 \times 7, 52 = 2 \times 2 \times 13$
$68 = 2 \times 2 \times 17, 96 = 2 \times 2 \times 2 \times 2 \times 2 \times 3$

9. (*c*) Except 72, all others have only 2 factors with prime numbers.
$26 = 2 \times 13, 34 = 2 \times 17,\ 72 = 2 \times 2 \times 2 \times 3 \times 3,$
$46 = 2 \times 23, 38 = 2 \times 19$

10. (*c*) Except 45, all others are prime numbers.

11. (*b*) Except 60, all other number are multiple of 13.
$13 \times 10 = 130$
$13 \times 4 = 52 \Rightarrow 13 \times 6 = 78$
Hence, 60 is different from others.

12. (*d*) Except 57, all other are prime numbers, while 57 is a composite number because it is divisible by 3.

13. (*a*) Except 68, all others are divisible by 8.
Hence, 68 is odd one out.

14. (*a*) Only '729' is a perfect cube $729 = 9^3$

15. (*c*) Except (c), all others are divisible by 12.

16. (*c*) 37 is the only prime number in the group.

17. (*c*) 35 is the only non-square number in the group.

18. (*d*) 49 is the only complete (perfect) square in the group.

19. (*c*) Except 1189, sum of digits of all other numbers is 10.

20. (*d*) $162 \Rightarrow 16 \div 2 = 8$
$405 \Rightarrow 40 \div 5 = 8$
$567 \Rightarrow 56 \div 7 = 8$
$644 \Rightarrow 64 \div 4 = 16$

21. (*d*) Except 26, all others are divisible by 6.

22. (*c*) Except 63, all others are prime numbers.

23. (*d*) Except 64, all other numbers are one less than the cube of natural numbers whereas, 64 is a cube of a natural number $4^3 = 64$.

24. (*a*) 49 is the only square in the group.

25. (*c*) Except 225, all others are squares of prime numbers.

26. (*b*) Except 154, all others are divisible by 17.

27. (*b*) $12 = 3 \times 4$ and $(4 - 3) = 1$
$14 = 2 \times 7$ and $(7 - 2) = 5$
$30 = 5 \times 6$ and $(6 - 5) = 1$
$56 = 7 \times 8$ and $(8 - 7) = 1$
$\therefore$ Except 14 in rest of the numbers the difference between their factors is 1.

28. (*b*) Except 171, all others are divisible by 13.

29. (*b*) Except '44', all are prime numbers.

30. (*b*) Except 126, all others are one less than the cube of a number.

31. (*c*) $\therefore\ 272 = 2 + 7 + 2 = 11$
$210 = 2 + 1 + 0 = 3$
$240 = 2 + 4 + 0 = 6$
$304 = 3 + 0 + 4 = 7$
The sum of digit of all numbers except 240 is a prime number, whereas sum of digits of the number 240 is a non-prime. Hence, it is different from all others.

32. (*c*) Except 288, all others are perfect square of natural number.

33. (*d*) Except 98, all others are divisible by 12.

34. (*e*) Except 65, all others are divisible by 7.

35. (*e*) Only 75 is divisible by 15.

36. (*d*) Except '64', none of the numbers is a square or a cube whereas, $64 = 4^3$.

37. (*c*) Except '87', all are prime numbers 87 is divisible by 3.

38. (*d*) In all other options, digit at the second place is the difference of first and third digits.

39. (*a*) Except 215, all others are divisible by 13.

40. (*b*) Except '841', all are even numbers.

41. (*d*) Except 667, in all other options, sum of the digits is 20.

42. (*d*) $3216 \Rightarrow 3 + 2 + 6 - 1 = 10;\ 2338 \Rightarrow 2 + 3 + 8 - 3 = 10;$
$3205 \Rightarrow 3 + 2 + 5 - 0 = 10;\ 2015 \Rightarrow 2 + 0 + 5 - 1 = 6$
Therefore, 2015 is different from the other three.

43. (*d*) Except 427, in all other options, digit in the middle is the sum of the other two digits.

44. (*d*) Except 210, all others are complete squares.

45. (*b*) Except 35453, in all others first and last two digits are same.

46. (*d*) Except '64, 73' all are having difference of 11.

47. (*a*) Except 18-22, in all others, 2nd number is 2 more than the first.

48. (*a*) Except 20-36, in all others, 2nd number = lst number + 6

49. (*b*) Except 164-41, in all other, 2nd number $= \frac{\text{1st number}}{3}$

50. (*b*) $54 : 17 \quad \Rightarrow 17 \times 3 + 3 = 54$
$90 : 29 \quad \Rightarrow 29 \times 3 + 3 = 90$
$72 : 23 \quad \Rightarrow 23 \times 3 + 3 = 72$
But $\boxed{36 : 13 \quad \Rightarrow 13 \times 3 + 3 \neq 36}$

51. (*c*) $3 - 28 \Rightarrow 3^3 + 1 = 28$
$2 - 9 \Rightarrow 2^3 + 1 = 9$
$5 - 124 \Rightarrow 5^3 + 1 \neq 124$
$4 - 65 \Rightarrow 4^3 + 1 = 65$
$5 \rightarrow 124$ is the odd one.

52. (*b*) Except 33442, in all other numbers the sum of the digits is 17.

53. (*b*) Except 19-25, all other pairs consists of prime number only.

54. (*c*) Except 29-82, in all other pairs, the difference between the two numbers is a multiple of 9.

55. (*d*)

65 – 101 , 26 – 50
↓ ↓ ↓ ↓
8^2+1 10^2+1 5^2+1 7^2+1

17 – 37 , 49 – 82
↓ ↓ ↓ ↓
4^2+1 6^2+1 7^2+1 9^2+1

Clearly, 49-82 is different from others.

56. (*b*) Except 10 : 24, in all others, 2nd number = (2 × 1st number) + 2

57. (*a*) Except 5 : 9, second number is the next prime number to the first number.

58. (*d*) In all the pairs both number 70 – 80, 54 – 62, 28 – 32 in each pairs is even numbers, whereas in 21 – 24 one number is odd and one is even.

59. (*c*) Except 518 : 816, second number is the reverse of the first number.

60. (*a*) $93 \to 31 \times 3, 117 \to 13 \times 9$

$63 \to 9 \times 7, 81 \to 9 \times 9$

$119 \to 17 \times 7, 153 \to 17 \times 9$

$133 \to 19 \times 7, 171 \to 19 \times 9$

Except 93 : 117 in all other pairs both the numbers have either 7 or 9 as one of the factor.

61. (*d*) Except 24 : 464, each digit of second number is the square of the respective digit of the first number.

62. (*d*) Given pairs are

$17 - 34 \Rightarrow 17 \times 2 = 34$

$19 - 38 \Rightarrow 19 \times 2 = 38$

$23 - 46 \Rightarrow 23 \times 2 = 46$

and $27 - 56 \Rightarrow 27 \times 2 = 54 \neq 56$

Hence, 27 – 56 is odd option.

63. (*d*) Except 24 : 18, second number is the difference of the square of the digits of the first number.

64. (*d*) In all other pairs have both numbers are square of a natural numbers.

65. (*d*) All the other numbers are perfect squares of consecutive numbers.

66. (*c*)

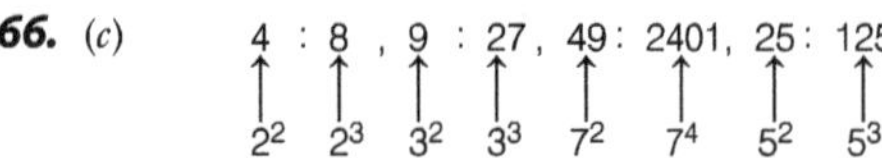

Clearly, 49 : 2401 is the odd one.

67. (*c*)

2 8 6⟶6 2 8 , 4 7 5⟶5 7 4

3 9 7⟶7 3 9 , 3 6 9⟶9 3 6

So, except option (c) all have the same rule or pattern for swapping.
Hence, '475, 574' is different from other three.

68. (*a*) In all the given numbers, the middle digit is twice in second group.

69. (*b*) Only option (b) has difference of prime number.

$39 \sim 72 = 33$

$57 \sim 38 = 19$ (prime number)

$42 \sim 12 = 30$

$28 \sim 60 = 32$

70. (*d*) $9 - 90 \Rightarrow 9 \times 10 = 90$

$6 - 42 \Rightarrow 6 \times 7 = 42$

$5 - 30 \Rightarrow 5 \times 6 = 30$

$4 - 36 \Rightarrow 4 \times 5 = 20 \neq 36$

∴ 4 – 36 is the odd one.

71. (*a*) As, $4 : 15 \Rightarrow 4^2 - 1 = 15$

$9 : 80 \Rightarrow 9^2 - 1 = 80$

$6 : 35 \Rightarrow 6^2 - 1 = 35$

But $7 : 46 \Rightarrow 7^2 - 1 = 48 \neq 46$

Hence, 7 : 46 is the odd one.

72. (*d*) In all other options, the three numbers have same digits.

73. (*d*) $14 + \boxed{3} = 17 \to 17 + \boxed{6} = 23,$

$19 + \boxed{3} = 22 \to 22 + \boxed{6} = 28$

$17 + \boxed{3} = 20 \to 20 + \boxed{6} = 26,$

$\boxed{21 + 2 = 23 \to 23 + 7 = 30}$

74. (*b*) In all the options except (b), second and third numbers are the square and cube of first number respectively.

75. (*a*) Except (a) in all the other options, numbers are even numbers but in option (a) all numbers are prime numbers.

76. (*d*) All others groups follow below pattern

I number $\xrightarrow{\times 6}$ II number $\xrightarrow{\times 2}$ III number

TYPE 05

Choosing the Odd Letter-Number Group

In this type of questions four/five letter group. Number or letter-number group is given, out of which one is odd or doesn't belong to the group. Candidates have to choose that odd letter number group or letter group-number as answer.

1. Based on the Position of Letters in English Alphabetical Series

Ex 65 Choose the odd letter number pair from the given options.

(a) B-4 (b) I-81 (c) J-64 (d) F-36

Solution (c) Except J-64, in rest of the groups the given number is square of the position of the given letters in the English alphabetical series.

$\overset{2}{B} \to 2^2 = 4$ $\overset{9}{I} \to 9^2 = 81$

$\overset{10}{J} \to (10)^2 = 100 \neq 64$ $\overset{6}{F} \to 6^2 = 36$

2. Based on the operations on position of letters in alphabetical series and given number in a letter-number groups.

Ex 66 Find the odd one out.

(a) PB - 14 (b) UK - 10
(c) MN - 11 (d) RB - 16

Solution (c) Except MN-11, in rest of the groups, the given numbers is equal to the difference of positional values of the letters given in the group.

$\overset{16}{P}\overset{2}{B} \to 16-2=14$; $\overset{21}{U}\overset{11}{K} \to 21-11=10$

$\overset{13}{M}\overset{14}{N} \to 13-14=-1 \neq 11$; $\overset{18}{R}\overset{2}{B} \to 18-2=16$

Ex 67 Find the odd-one out.

(a) TE-4 (b) UG-3 (c) YE-7 (d) PB-8

Solution (c) Except (c), In rest of the groups, the given number is obtained by dividing the positional value of first letter by the second

$\overset{20}{T}\overset{5}{E} \to 20 \div 5 = 4$; $\overset{21}{U}\overset{7}{G} \to 21 \div 7 = 3$

$\overset{25}{Y}\overset{15}{E} \to 25 \div 5 = 5 \neq 7$; $\overset{16}{P}\overset{2}{B} \to 16 \div 2 = 8$

3. Based on Independent letter and number.

Ex 68 Find the add-one out

(a) A 7 B 14 C 28
(b) P 5 Q 10 R 20
(c) K 3 L 5 M 12
(d) T 12 U 18 V 24

Solution (d)

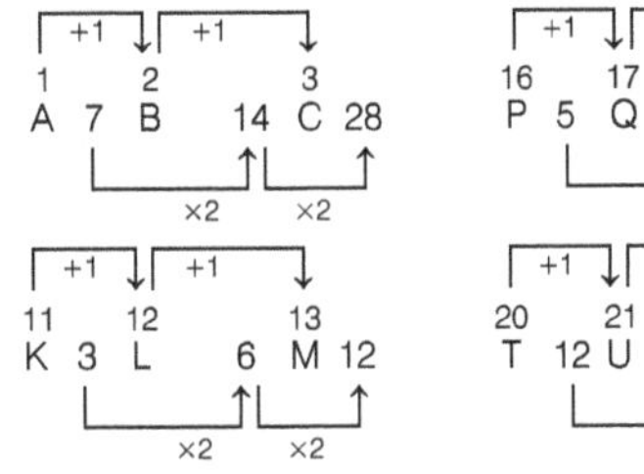

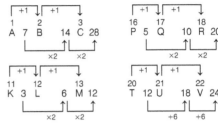

Hence, group 'T 12 U 18 V 24' is clearly the odd one.

Practice / CORNER 3.5

DIRECTIONS (Q.Nos. 1-25) *Choose the odd numbers pair/group in each of the following questions.*

1. (a) L-12 (b) Q-16 (c) X-24 (d) T-20

2. (a) 1 P 6 (b) 0 G 7 (c) 1 K 1 (d) 1 N 3

3. (a) K-1 (b) V-4 (c) W-6 (d) L-3

4. (a) I-18 (b) R-9 (c) D-23 (d) H-8

5. (a) U-36 (b) Z-1 (c) W-9 (d) V-25

6. (a) A-1 (b) B-8 (c) G-434 (d) D-64

7. (a) K-2 (b) R-9 (c) N-5 (d) M-3

8. (a) I-82 (b) J-111 (c) L-145 (d) G-50

9. (a) G-15 (b) I-19 (c) K-21 (d) N-29

10. (a) G-25 (b) C-1 (c) F-16 (d) J-49

11. (a) MT-33 (b) RS-37 (c) OP-32 (d) JK-21

12. (a) DE-18 (b) FG-26 (c) EO-40 (d) LT-56

13. (a) AB-5 (b) BC-13 (c) EB-29 (d) DG-121

14. (a) CM-39 (b) JD-40 (c) IC-27 (d) ON-29

15. (a) MD-9 (b) PB-14 (c) XL-12 (d) UB-23

16. (a) TT-40 (b) MJ-13 (c) BO-30 (d) OF-9

17. (a) BC-36 (b) AI-81 (c) AJ-81 (d) DE-400

18. (a) NB-7 (b) PH-2 (c) LD-3 (d) TJ-10

19. (a) ABC-6 (b) DEF-15 (c) MNO-42 (d) BCD-14

20. (a) HIC-24 (b) NBG-4 (c) DAG-28 (d) LHF-16

21. (a) R 2 T 3 V 5 (b) V 7 X 8 Z 10
(c) P 5 R 6 T 7 (d) M 4 O 5 Q 7

22. (a) P 1 O 2 Q 9 (b) D 9 C 16 B 25
(c) K 25 J 36 I 49 (d) V 100 U 121 T 144

23. (a) A 1 F 2 K 4 (b) E 8 J 16 N 33
(c) R 3 W 6 A 13 (d) M 4 R 8 V 17

24. (a) A C F 2 4 9 (b) P R U 3 6 13
(c) K M P 1 2 5 (d) S U X 4 8 15

25. (a) A Z B Y 1 2 4 (b) M N B C 0 1 3
(c) C X G T 3 4 8 (d) E V M N 2 3 6

Answers / WITH EXPLANATIONS

1. (*b*) 12 → L – 12 ; 17 → Q – 16 (boxed)

24 → X – 24 ; 20 → T – 20

2. (*d*) 16: 1 P 6 ; 07: 0 G 7

11: 1 K 1 ; 13: 1 N 3 (boxed)

3. (*d*) $\overset{11}{K} \rightarrow 1\times1 = 1 \Rightarrow K-1$;

$\overset{22}{V} \rightarrow 2\times2 = 4 \Rightarrow V-4$;

$\overset{23}{W} \rightarrow 2\times3 = 6 \Rightarrow W-6$;

$\overset{12}{L} \rightarrow 1+2 = 3 \Rightarrow L-3$ (boxed)

4. (*d*) Except H-8, rest of the options have pair of an alphabet and its position in reverse alphabatical series.

5. (*c*) 21 U – 36, $(27-21)^2$; 26 Z – 1, $(27-26)^2$

23 W – 9 (boxed), $(26-23)^2$; 22 V – 25, $(27-22)^2$

6. (*c*) 1 A – 1, $(1)^3$; 2 B – 8, $(2)^3$

7 G – 434 (boxed), $(7)^3+91$; 4 D – 64, $(4)^3$

7. (*d*) 11 K – 2, (1+1) ; 18 R – 9, (1+8)

14 N – 5, (1+4) ; 13 M – 3 (boxed), (1×3)

8. (*b*) 9 I – 82, $(9)^2+1$; 10 J – 111 (boxed), $(10)^2+11$

12 L – 145, $(12)^2+1$; 7 G – 50, $(7)^2+1$

9. (*c*) 7 G – 15, 7×2+1 ; 9 I – 19, 9×2+1

11 K – 21 (boxed), 11×2–1 ; 14 N – 29, 14×2+1

10. (*d*) 7 G – 25, $(7-2)^2$; 3 C – 1, $(3-2)^2$

6 F – 16, $(6-2)^2$; 10 J – 49 (boxed), $(10-3)^2$

11. (*c*)

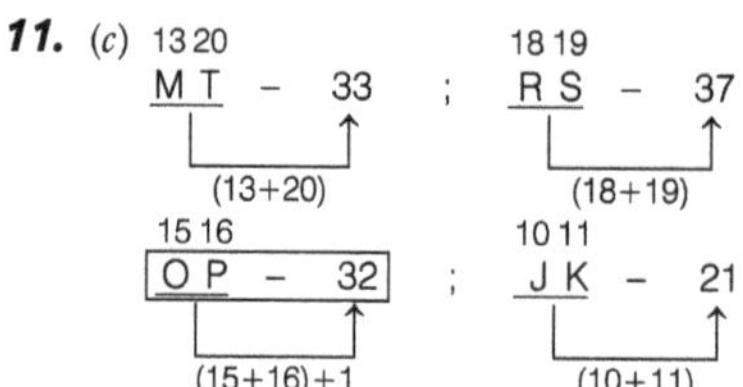

13 20 MT – 33, (13+20) ; 18 19 RS – 37, (18+19)

15 16 OP – 32 (boxed), (15+16)+1 ; 10 11 JK – 21, (10+11)

12. (*d*) 4 5 DE – 18, (4+5)×2 ; 6 7 FG – 26, (6+7)×2

5 15 EO – 40, (5+15)×2 ; 12 20 LT – 56 (boxed), (12+20)×2–8

13. (*d*) 1 2 AB – 5, $(1)^2+(2)^2$; 2 3 BC – 13, $(2)^2+(3)^2$

5 2 EB – 29, $(5)^2+(2)^2$; 4 7 DG – 121 (boxed), $(4+7)^2$

14. (*d*) 3 13 CM – 39, 3×13 ; 10 4 JD – 40, 10×4

9 3 IC – 27, 9×3 ; 15 14 ON – 29 (boxed), 15+14

15. (*d*) 13 4 MD – 9, 13–4 ; 16 2 PB – 14, 16–2 ;

24 12 XL – 12, 24–12 ; 21 2 UB – 23 (boxed), 21+2

16. (*c*) 20 20 TT – 40, (20×20)÷10 ; 13 10 MJ – 13, (13×10)÷10

2 15 BO – 30 (boxed), (2×15) ; 15 6 OF – 9, (15×6)÷10

17. (*c*) 2 3 BC – 36, $(2\times3)^2$; 1 9 AI – 81, $(1\times9)^2$

1 10 AJ – 81 (boxed), $(10-1)^2$; 4 5 DE – 400, $(4\times5)^2$

18. (*d*)

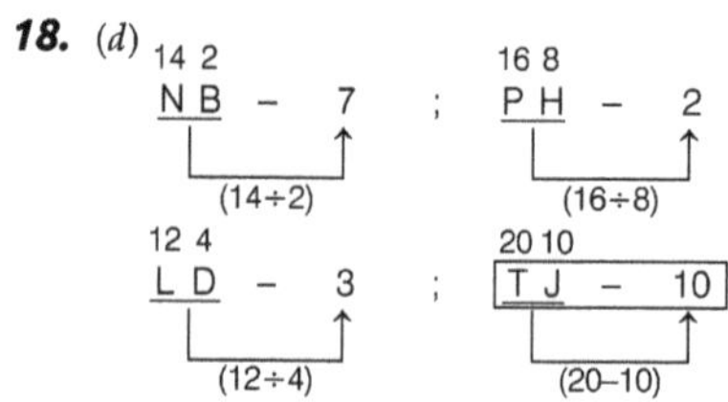

14 2 NB – 7, (14÷2) ; 16 8 PH – 2, (16÷8)

12 4 LD – 3, (12÷4) ; 20 10 TJ – 10 (boxed), (20–10)

19. (*d*)

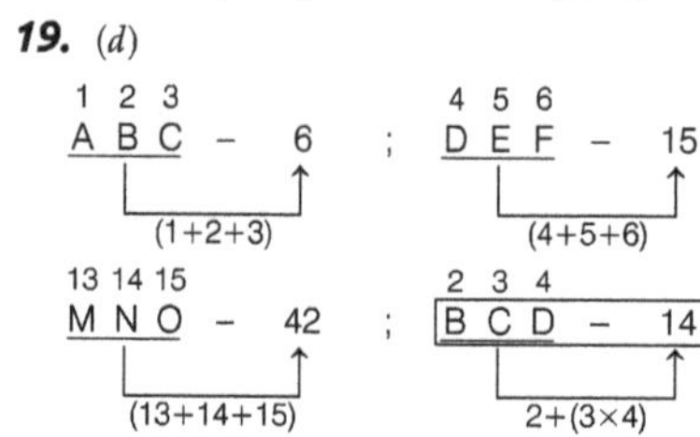

1 2 3 ABC – 6, (1+2+3) ; 4 5 6 DEF – 15, (4+5+6)

13 14 15 MNO – 42, (13+14+15) ; 2 3 4 BCD – 14 (boxed), 2+(3×4)

20. (*c*)

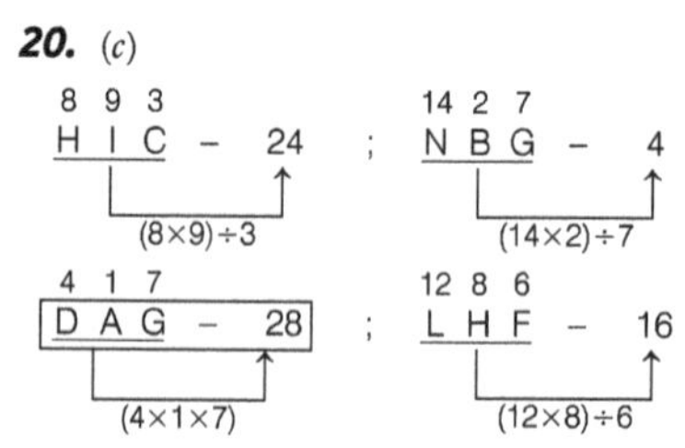

8 9 3 HIC – 24, (8×9)÷3 ; 14 2 7 NBG – 4, (14×2)÷7

4 1 7 DAG – 28 (boxed), (4×1×7) ; 12 8 6 LHF – 16, (12×8)÷6

21. (*c*)

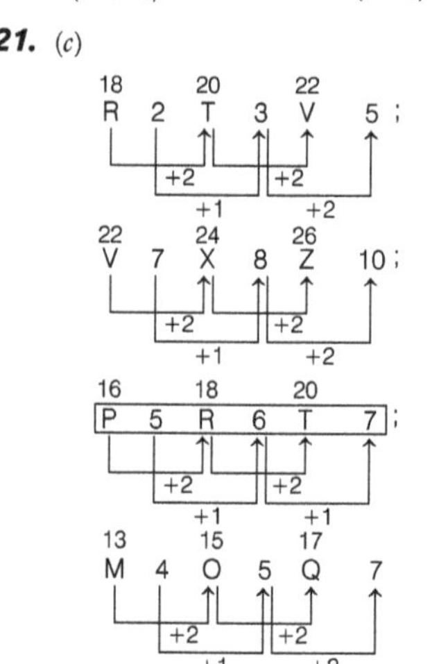

18 R 2 20 T 3 22 V 5 ; (+2, +2, +1, +2)

22 V 7 24 X 8 26 Z 10 ; (+2, +2, +1, +2)

16 P 5 18 R 6 20 T 7 (boxed) ; (+2, +2, +1, +1)

13 M 4 15 O 5 17 Q 7 (+2, +2, +1, +2)

22. (*a*)

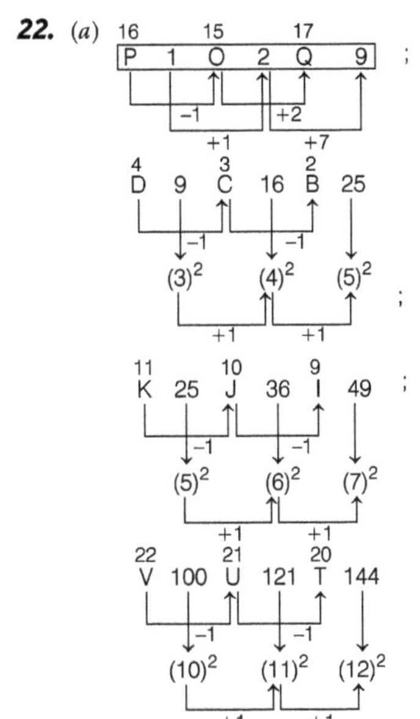

23. (*a*)

24. (*d*)

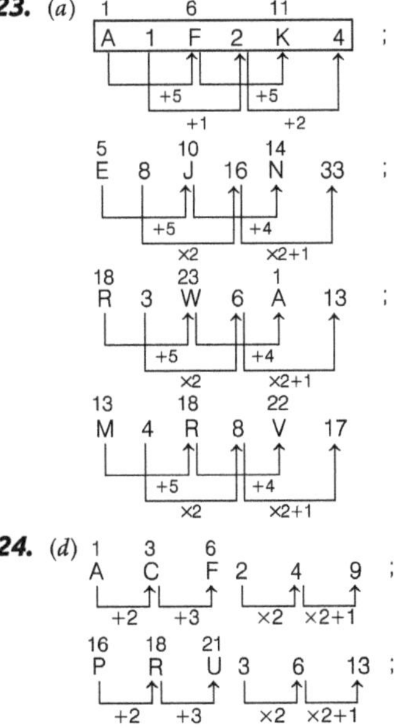

25. (*b*)

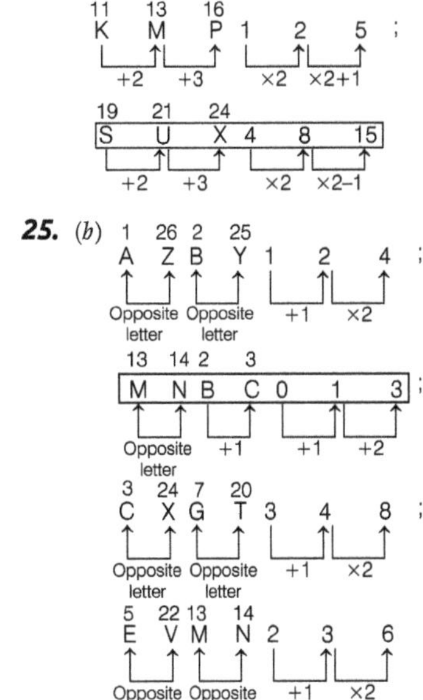

Master Exercise

DIRECTIONS ~ (Q. Nos. 1-9) *In each of the following questions, three out of the four alternatives contains letters/ numbers of the alphabet having a similar pattern. Find the one that does not belong to the group.*

1. (a) ZAN (b) ACF (c) UXA (d) BFC
« SSC (CPO) 2016

2. (a) C9F (b) H20L (c) N31Q (d) E29Y

3. (a) GK (b) MQ (c) PU (d) SW

4. (a) CEH (b) KMP (c) XZC (d) NPT

5. (a) DW (b) LO (c) JR (d) HS

6. (a) PUS (b) HLJ (c) UYW (d) BFD

7. (a) MLI (b) FEB (c) UTQ (d) SRN

8. (a) A8C (b) D22G (c) H42M (d) F34J

9. (a) ZS12 (b) PM4 (c) RJ16 (d) FD2

DIRECTIONS ~ (Q. Nos. 10-17) *In each of the following questions/three and five/four are alike in a certain way and so form a group. Which is the one that does not belong to the group?*

10. (a) Cotton (b) Nylon (c) Silk (d) Linen (e) Fibre

11. (a) Bus (b) Car (c) Truck (d) Aeroplane
« SSC (MTS) 2017

12. (a) Cumin (b) Groundnut (c) Clove (d) Pepper

13. (a) Leaf (b) Stem (c) Branches (d) Garden (e) Root

14. (a) Marigold (b) Tulip (c) Lotus (d) Rose
« SSC (CPO) 2015

15. (a) Eyes (b) Nose (c) Ears (d) Vestibular
« SSC (CGL) 2015

16. (a) Radium (b) Thorium (c) Sodium (d) Uranium (e) Radon

17. (a) Stationery (b) Pencil (c) Pen (d) Marker

DIRECTIONS ~ (Q. Nos. 18-25) *In the following questions, numbers are given in three out of the four alternatives having same relationship. You have to choose the one which does not belong to the group?*

18. (a) 3 : 8 (b) 6 : 35 (c) 7 : 50 (d) 1 : 0

19. (a) 1 : 2 (b) 3 : 28 (c) 4 : 65 (d) 2 : 7

20. (a) 21 : 24 (b) 28 : 32 (c) 14 : 16 (d) 54 : 62

21. (a) 95-15 (b) 305-50 (c) 160-25 (d) 185-30
« UP Police (SI) 2017

22. (a) 6361-16 (b) 5921-16 (c) 4361-14 (d) 2963-20
« SSC Delhi Police Constable 2017

23. (a) 8 : 20 (b) 10 : 25 (c) 18 : 81 (d) 12 : 36

24. (a) 10-100 (b) 12-144 (c) 13-171 (d) 15-225
« SSC Delhi Police Constable 2017

25. (a) 14, 6 (b) 7, 12 (c) 21, 4 (d) 41, 2
« SSC CPO 2018

DIRECTIONS ~ (Q. Nos. 26-70) *In each of the following questions, five/four words/number are given, out of which four/three are same in one way or the other and the fifth/forth one is different from these four/three. Select the odd one.*

26. (a) Sun (b) Moon (c) Venus (d) Mars

27. (a) Microphone (b) Microscope (c) Spectacles (d) Telescope

28. (a) Artery (b) Ventricle (c) Pharynx (d) Aorta

29. (a) Talking (b) Walking (c) Sleeping (d) Running
« SSC (10+2) 2015

30. (a) Red (b) White (c) Blue (d) Yellow

31. (a) ADZW (b) NOML (c) EGVT (d) TUGD
« SSC (10+2) 2020

32. (a) CAFD (b) TSWV (c) IGLJ (d) OMRP
« SSC (10+2) 2015

33. (a) Sand (b) Cement (c) Building (d) Wood (e) Brick

34. (a) Black (b) Yellow (c) Red (d) Green (e) Violet

35. (a) Nephew (b) Cousin (c) Mother (d) Brother (e) Sister

36. (a) Coriander (b) Onion (c) Beetroot (d) Ginger

37. (a) Cup (b) Jug (c) Tumbler (d) Plate (e) Pitcher

38. (a) Diamond (b) Ruby (c) Emerald (d) Turquoise

39. (a) Crimson (b) Scarlet (c) Vermilion (d) Cardinal

40. (a) Shorthand (b) Morse (c) Semaphore (d) Record

41. (a) River (b) Earth (c) Aeroplane (d) Breeze

42. (a) 12 (b) 28 (c) 52 (d) 68 (e) 96

43. (a) 97 (b) 143 (c) 241 (d) 157 (e) 181

44. (a) Plastic (b) Nylon (c) Polythene (d) Terylene (e) Silk

45. (a) TEETH (b) SLEEP (c) SHEEP (d) GREED « SSC (CPO) 2013

46. (a) LOJ (b) FID (c) RUP (d) ILN (e) CFA

47. (a) DHM (b) GKO (c) IMQ (d) LPT « SSC (10+2) 2018

48. (a) MOQS (b) ZADE (c) CEGI (d) SUWY « SSC (CPO) 2016

49. (a) JMSP (b) STZA (c) UVFX (d) NMPO

50. (a) ZUPK (b) TOJD (c) WRMH (d) VQLG « SSC (CPO) 2017

51. (a) JQK (b) BYC (c) LRM (d) CXD (e) OPX « IBPS (PO Pre) 2018

52. (a) FGH (b) AEI (c) IOU (d) OUA « SSC (Constable) 2018

53. (a) Long (b) Tall (c) High (d) Short (e) Dim

54. (a) 78 (b) 48 (c) 72 (d) 54

55. (a) Sweet (b) Cake (c) Pastry (d) Bread (e) Biscuit

56. (a) 31 (b) 39 (c) 47 (d) 41 (e) 43

57. (a) 25 (b) 81 (c) 189 (d) 225 (e) 121

58. (a) 169 (b) 225 (c) 289 (d) 441 (e) 255

59. (a) 27 (b) 64 (c) 125 (d) 384

60. (a) 84 (b) 120 (c) 72 (d) 108 (e) 98

61. (a) 143 (b) 257 (c) 195 (d) 15 (e) 63

62. (a) 26 (b) 34 (c) 72 (d) 46 (e) 38

63. (a) Cuckoo (b) Crow (c) Bat (d) Parrot (e) Sparrow

64. (a) Fruit (b) Flower (c) Leaf (d) Tree

65. (a) Garo (b) Khaasi (c) Kangra (d) Jaintia

66. (a) Radish (b) Carrot (c) Garlic (d) Gourd (e) Ginger

67. (a) 39 (b) 69 (c) 57 (d) 129 (e) 117

68. (a) Tree (b) Plant (c) Shrub (d) Farm

69. (a) Sharpener (b) Calculator (c) Eraser (d) Pencil (e) Stapler

70. (a) 17 (b) 19 (c) 23 (d) 27 (e) 29 « Corporation Bank (PO) 2008

DIRECTIONS ~ (Q. Nos. 71-80) *Find out the odd one from the given options which is different from others.*

71. (a) Flurry : Blizzard (b) Moisten : Drench (c) Prick : Stab (d) Scrub : Polish

72. (a) Thyroxine (b) Adrenaline (c) Iodine (d) Insulin « SSC (10+2) 2013

73. (a) Scurvy (b) Rickets (c) Night-blindness (d) Influenza « SSC (CGL) 2013

74. (a) Dim : Bright (b) Wrong : Right (c) Shallow : Deep (d) Genuine : Real

75. (a) Book : Page (b) Table : Drawer (c) Loom : Cloth (d) Car : Wheel

76. (a) Stale : Fresh (b) Truth : Lie (c) Slow : Sluggish (d) Teach : Learn (e) Kind : Cruel « Bank (PO) 2013

77. (a) Apple : Jam (b) Lemon : Citrus (c) Orange : Squash (d) Tomato : Pury

78. (a) Cow : Fodder (b) Crow : Carrion (c) Poultry : Farm (d) Vulture : Prey

79. (a) Chandragupta : Mauryan (b) Babar : Mughal (c) Kanishka : Kushan (d) Mahavira : Jainism

80. (a) Cockroach : Antennae (b) Lizard : Flagella (c) Hydra :Tentacles (d) Plasmodium : Cilia

DIRECTIONS ~ (Q. Nos. 81-91) *Choose the odd one out.*

81. (a) HJM (b) OQT (c) BDG (d) VXZ

82. (a) GMS (b) EKQ (c) JOU (d) LRX

83. (a) ROQP (b) KHJI (c) VSUT (d) JHIG

84. (a) KQ14 (b) AY13 (c) MR11 (d) GW15 « MAT 2014

85. (a) Intestines (b) Eyes (c) Hands (d) Ears « NMAT 2005

86. (a) Shovel : Mud (b) Screwdriver : Screw (c) Hammer : Nail (d) Pen : Pencil « Hotel Mgmt 2004

87. (a) BCGK (b) MNRV (c) RSVZ (d) EFJN

88. (a) DFIMR (b) CEHLQ (c) GILPU (d) HJMPT

89. (a) 12-28 (b) 14-82 (c) 23-64 (d) 36-72 « SNAP 2011

90. (a) DIRAMLOG (b) ERENIGEN (c) UIHCSSBI (d) AFOLDFID « SNAP 2013

91. (a) JN : QM (b) DH : WS (c) RV : IE (d) PR : IJ « SSC Steno Grade C&D 2019

DIRECTIONS ~ (Q. Nos. 92-96) *Rearrange the jumbled alphabets in the following four options and find the odd word among them.* « MAT 2014

92. (a) FLOW (b) WCO (c) ILNO (d) ERTIG « RRB ALP 2018

93. (a) LPAEP (b) AYAPAP
(c) AVGAU (d) SRAHDI

94. (a) LIWLOP (b) RSTESMTA
(c) TSROFE (d) UTQLI

95. (a) THIRS (b) SSCOK
(c) CEILNP (d) TANP

96. (a) OSCETOR (b) EPNAL
(c) ROTOM KEBI (d) ELCYC

97. Find the word that does not belong to the group
Biscuits, Cake, Bread, Chocolate
(a) Bread (b) Chocolate
(c) Biscuits (d) Cake

98. Choose the odd one out. « RRB NTPC 2016
A. incisors B. canines C. molars D. bones
(a) D (b) A
(c) C (d) B

99. Find the odd one out of the below geometrical shapes. Rhombus, Triangle, Square, Parallelogram, Rectangle, Trapezium « UPSSSC Combined Lower Subordinate 2019
(a) Rhombus (b) Triangle
(c) Parallelogram (d) Trapezium

100. Find the odd one out from the below group of names. Guava, Watermelon, Lettuce, Apple, Kiwi, Mango, Pear, Pomegranate
« UPSSSC Combined Lower Subordinate 2019
(a) Lettuce (b) Kiwi (c) Pear (d) Pomegranate

Answers / WITH EXPLANATIONS

1. (*d*) Except BFC, all other option contain one vowel.

2. (*d*) Alphabetical position,

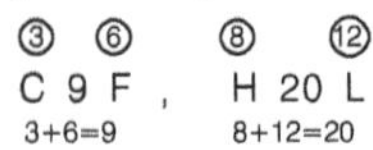

⑭ ⑰
N 31 Q ,
14+17=31

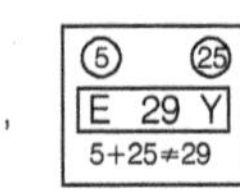

Clearly, 'E29Y' doesn't belong to the group.

3. (*c*)

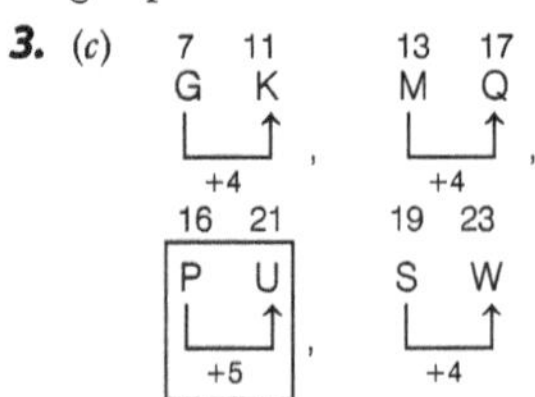

Clearly, 'PU' doesn't belong to the group.

4. (*d*)

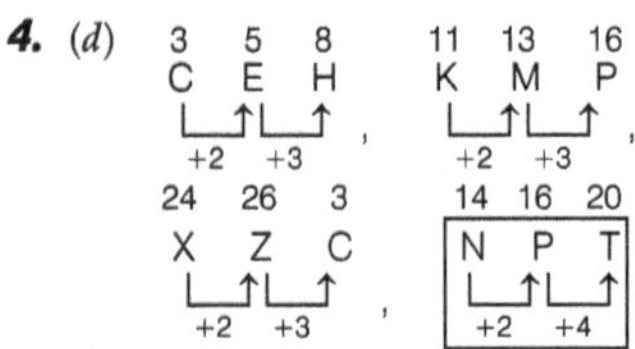

Clearly 'NPT' doesn't belong to the group.

5. (*c*) Alphabetical position,

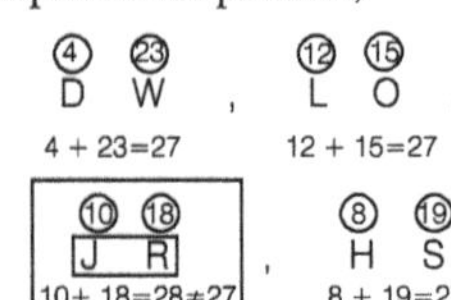

Clearly, 'J R' doesn't belong to the group.

Alternate method except option (c) letters given in opposite to each other.

6. (*a*)

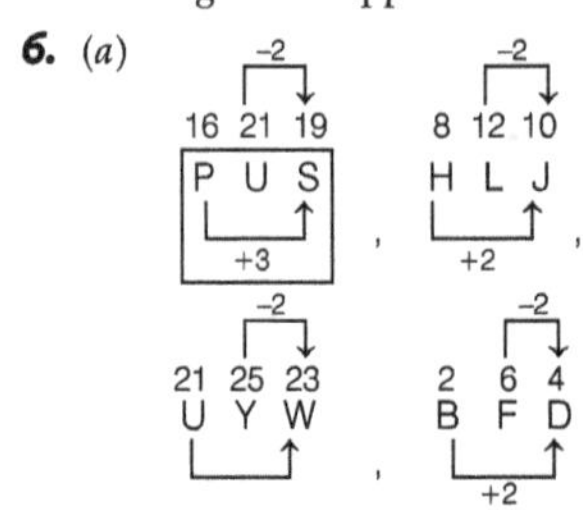

Clearly, 'PUS' doesn't belong to the group.

7. (*d*)

13 12 9 M L I (−1 −3), 6 5 2 F E B (−1 −3), 21 20 17 U T Q (−1 −3), 19 18 14 S R N (−1 −4)

Clearly, 'SRN' doesn't belong to the group.

8. (*d*) Alphabetical position,

① ③ A 8 C: 1 + 3 = 4, 4 × 2 = 8

④ ⑦ D 22 G: 4 + 7 = 11, 11 × 2 = 22

⑧ ⑬ H 42 M: 8 + 13 = 21, 21 × 2 = 42

⑥ ⑩ F 34 J: 6 + 10 = 16, 16 × 2 ≠ 34

Clearly, F34J does't belong to the group.

9. (*c*)

26 19 Z S 12 — No. of letter between Z and S=6 ∴ 6×2=12

16 13 P M 4 — No. of letter between P and M=2 ∴ 2×2=4

18 10 R J 16 — No. of letter between R and J=7 ∴ 7×2 ≠ 16

6 4 F D 2 — No. of letter between F and D=1 ∴ 1×2=2

Hence, 'RJ16' doesn't belong to the group.

10. (*b*) Only 'Nylon' is synthetic in nature.

11. (*d*) Except Aeroplane, all other vehicles run on the road whereas aeroplane fly in the sky.

12. (*b*) All the rest are spices while 'Groundnut' is a dry fruit.

13. (*d*) Except 'Garden' all the others are the parts of a tree.

14. (*b*) Except Tulip, all other are flowers whereas Tulip is a kind of a plant.

15. (*d*) Except 'Vestibular', the rest are external organs.

16. (*c*) Except 'Sodium', all other are radioactive.

17. (*a*) All other are 'Stationery' items.

18. (*c*) $3:8$, $6:35$,
$3^2-1=8$, $6^2-1=35$,
$7:50$, $1:0$
$7^2-1\neq 50$, $1^2-1=0$.
$\therefore$ 7 : 50 is the odd one and doesn't belong to the group.

19. (*d*) $1:2$, $3:28$,
$1^3+1=2$, $3^3+1=28$,
$4:65$, $2:7$
$4^3+1=65$, $2^3+1\neq 7$
Clearly, 2 : 7 doesn't belong to the group.

20. (*d*)

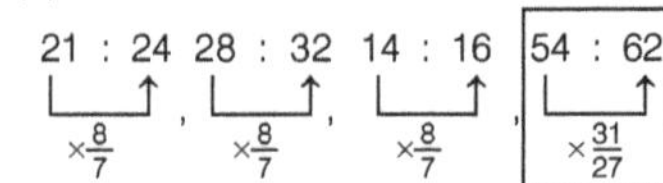

Clearly, 54 : 62 doesn't belong to the group.

21. (*c*) Except pair 160-25, all other pairs have the following rule.

Right side number × 6 + 5 = Left side number.

22. (*b*) Here, except 5921-16, in all other pairs, sum of digits of left side is given on right side whether it is not given option (b).
Here, $5 + 9 + 2 + 1 - 16 \Rightarrow 17 \neq 16$
Hence, 5921 –16 is different from others.

23. (*a*) $10 : 25 \rightarrow 10 \div 2 = 5$
$\Rightarrow \quad 5^2 = 25$
$18 : 81 \Rightarrow 18 \div 2 = 9 \Rightarrow 9^2 = 81$
$12 : 36 \Rightarrow 12 \div 2 = 6 \Rightarrow 6^2 = 36$
But, $\boxed{8 : 20} \Rightarrow 8 \div 2 = 4$
$\Rightarrow \quad 4^2 = 16 \neq 20$
Hence, 8 : 20 is different from others.

24. (*c*)

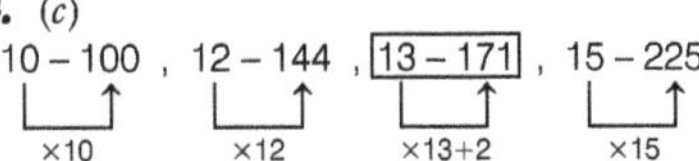

10 – 100 , 12 – 144 , 13 – 171 , 15 – 225
×10
×12
×13+2
×15

Hence, it is clear from above that 13-171 is different from others.

25. (*d*) $14 \times 6 = 84, 7 \times 12 = 84$
$21 \times 4 = 84, 41 \times 2 = 82 \neq 84$
Hence, 41, 2 is different from others.

26. (*b*) All the terms except 'Moon' are related to the solar system.

27. (*a*) All the terms except 'Microphone' are related to 'vision'.

28. (*c*) Except 'Pharynx' all other terms are related to heart.

29. (*c*) Sleeping is different from the other three. Except sleeping, all other activities involves some actions.

30. (*b*) Except 'white' all the other colours are present in the rainbow (VIBGYOR).

31. (*d*)

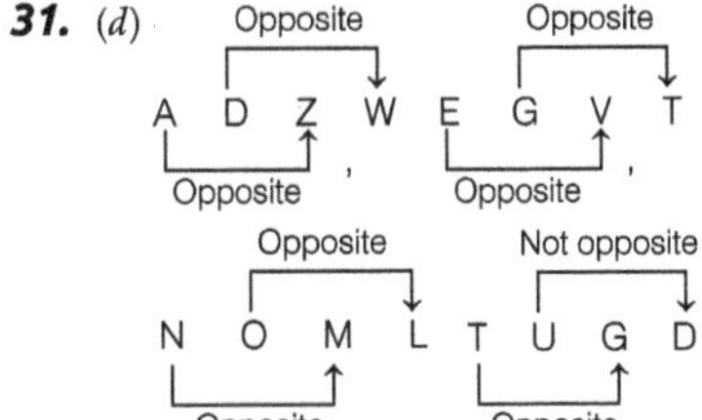

Clearly, TUGD is different from other.

32. (*b*)

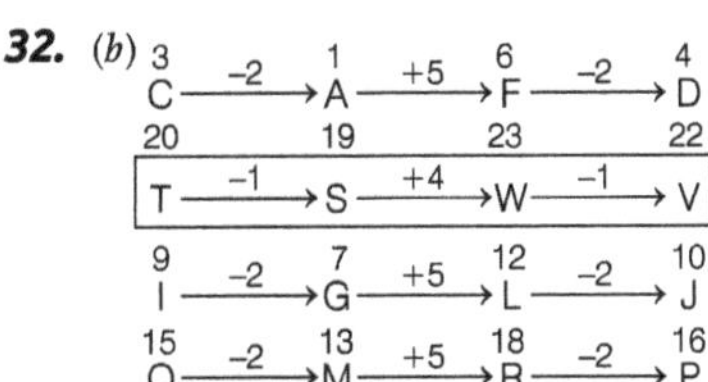

Clearly, 'TSWV' is different from others.

33. (*c*) Except 'building' all the others are materials used in a building.

34. (*a*) Except 'Black', all the others are primary colours.

35. (*b*) Except in 'cousin', the sex of the others can be determined

36. (*a*) Except (coriander), all others are modified stem.

37. (*d*) Except 'Plate', all the others are used to contain liquid.

38. (*a*) Except 'Diamond' all other are coloured stones.

39. (*d*) Except 'Cardinal' all the terms are related to red colour.

40. (*d*) Except 'Record' all the terms are related to secret system of sending messages.

41. (*d*) Except 'Breeze' all other things can be seen. Breeze can be felt.

42. (*e*) Except '96', all the others are obtained by multiplying 4 with a prime number.

43. (*b*) Except '143', all others are prime numbers.

44. (*e*) Except 'Silk', all the others are artificial fibres.

45. (*a*) In SLEEP, SHEEP and GREED, place of 'EE' is second from the right end while in TEETH, EE is second from the left end.

46. (*d*)

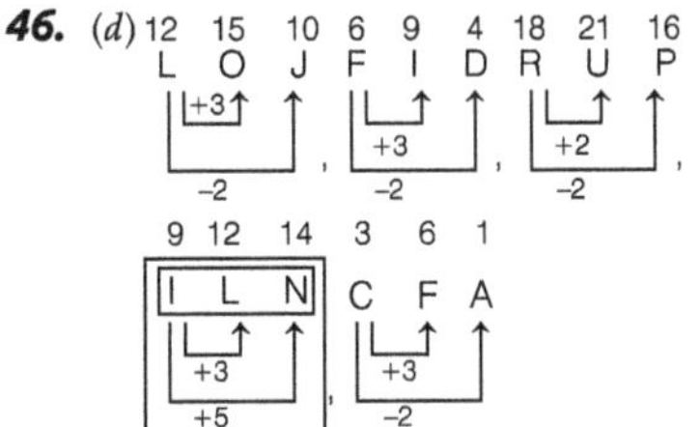

Clearly, 'ILN' doesn't belong to the group.

47. (*a*)
$\boxed{D \xrightarrow{+4} H \xrightarrow{+4} M}$ (4, 8, 13), $G \xrightarrow{+4} K \xrightarrow{+4} O$ (7, 11, 15),
$I \xrightarrow{+4} M \xrightarrow{+4} Q$ (9, 13, 17), $L \xrightarrow{+4} P \xrightarrow{+4} T$ (12, 16, 20)
Hence, DHM is odd.

48. (*b*)
13 15 17 19: M O Q S (+2 +2 +2)
26 1 4 5: $\boxed{Z\ A\ D\ E}$ (+1 +3 +1)
3 5 7 9: C E G I (+2 +2 +2)
19 21 23 25: S U W Y (+2 +2 +2)
So, ZADE is odd.

49. (*a*) Except JMSP, all other option contain one vowel.

50. (*b*)
26 21 16 11: Z U P K (–5 –5 –5), 20 15 10 4: $\boxed{T\ O\ J\ D}$ (–5 –5 –6)
23 18 13 8: W R M H (–5 –5 –5), 22 17 12 7: V Q L G (–5 –5 –5)
Hence, it is clear from above that TOJD is different from others.

51. (*e*) Except OPX, in all other alternatives the first and third letter are consecutive letters.

52. (*a*) Except 'FGH', all other contains vowel letters whereas in FGH, all letters consonants. Hence, FGH is odd one.

53. (*e*) Except Dim, all others are adjectives denoting size.

54. (*a*) Except '78', if you subtract 1, all the others give a prime number.

55. (*a*) Except 'Sweet', all the others are baked items.

56. (*b*) Except '39', all the others are prime numbers, while 39 is a composite number. As, $39 \rightarrow 13 \times 3$

57. (*c*) Except '189', all the others are square numbers.
$25 \rightarrow 5^2, 81 \rightarrow 9^2, 225 \rightarrow 15^2$ and $121 \rightarrow 11^2$.

58. (*e*) Except '255', all the others are perfect squares of natural numbers.

59. (*d*) Except '384', all the others are perfect cubes of natural numbers.

60. (*e*) Except '98',all the others are multiples of 6.
$84 \rightarrow 6 \times 14, 120 \rightarrow 6 \times 20,$
$72 \rightarrow 6 \times 12, 108 \rightarrow 6 \times 18$

61. (*b*) $143 \rightarrow 12^2 - 1$, $\boxed{257 \rightarrow 16^2 + 1,}$
$195 \rightarrow 14^2 - 1,$
$15 \rightarrow 4^2 - 1,$
$63 \rightarrow 8^2 - 1$
Hence, '257' is odd.

62. (*c*) Except '72', all the others give a prime number, when divided by 2.

63. (*c*) Except 'Bat', all the others are birds but bat is a mammal.

64. (*d*) Except 'Tree', all the others are its parts.

65. (*c*) 'Kangra' is the name of a valley and others are mountain ranges of North-East

66. (*d*) Except 'Gourd', all the others grow beneath the ground.

67. (*e*) Except '117', all the others give a prime number when divided by 3.

68. (*d*) Except 'Farm', all the others are form of plants.

69. (*b*) Except 'Calculator', all the others work mechanical device whereas calculator is an electronic device.

70. (*d*) Except '27', all the others are prime numbers.

71. (a) Except option (a), second word shows the higher intensity of first.

72. (*c*) Except (c), all are produced by various glands inside the human body.

73. (*d*) Except 'Influenza' all the other diseases are caused by lack of any vitamins.

74. (*d*) Except (d), in all other pairs, the two words are antonyms to each other.

75. (*c*) Except (c), in all others, second is the part of first.

76. (*c*) In all pairs except (c), both the words are antonyms of each other.

77. (*b*) In all pairs except (b), second is made by first.

78. (*c*) In all pairs except (c), second is the food for first.

79. (*d*) In all pairs except (d), first is the founder of second.

80. (*b*) In all others except (b), second is the organ used by first for its movement.

81. (*d*)
8 10 13 — H J M (+2 +3), 15 17 20 — O Q T (+2 +3),
2 4 7 — B D G (+2 +3), 22 24 26 — V X Z (+2 +2)

Clearly, 'VXZ' doesn't belong to the group.

82. (*c*)
7 13 19 — G M S (+6 +6), 5 11 17 — E K Q (+6 +6),
10 15 21 — J O U (+5 +6), 12 18 24 — L R X (+6 +6)

Clearly, 'JOU' doesn't belong to the group.

83. (*d*)

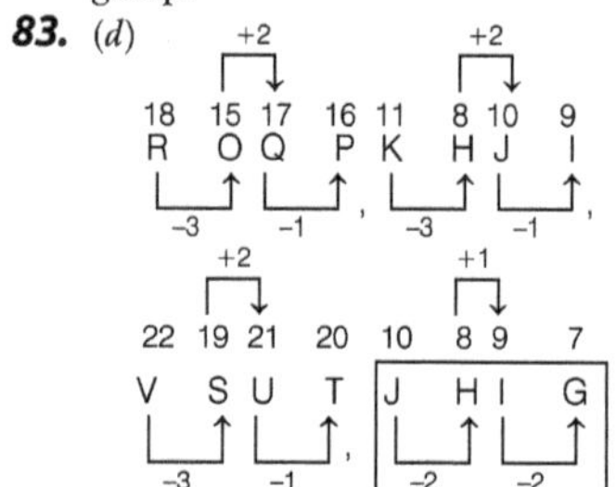

Clearly, 'JHIG' doesn't belong to the group.

84. (*c*)

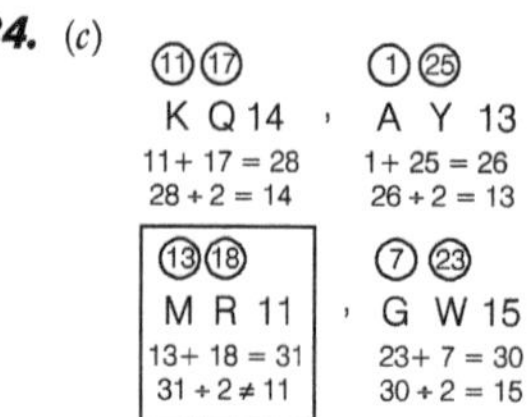

Clearly, MR11 doesn't belong to the group.

85. (*a*) Except intestines, all other are external organs of the human body.

86. (*d*) In all pairs except (d), first is a tool which works on second.

87. (*c*)

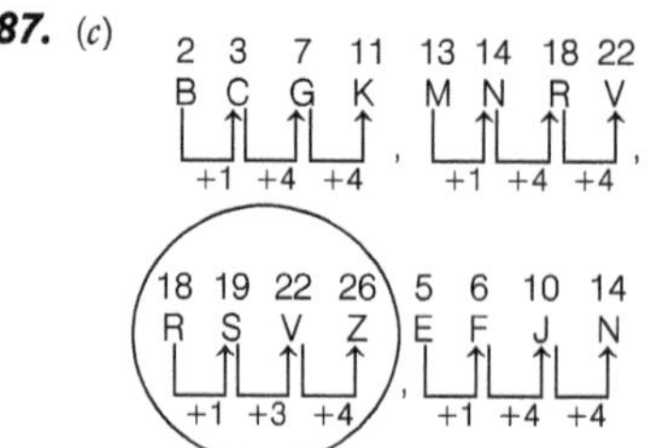

Therefore, 'RSVZ ' is different from other three.

88. (*d*)
4 6 9 13 18 — D F I M R (+2 +3 +4 +5), 3 5 8 12 17 — C E H L Q (+2 +3 +4 +5),
7 9 12 16 21 — G I L P U (+2 +3 +4 +5), 8 10 13 16 20 — H J M P T (+2 +3 +3 +4)

Clearly 'HJMPT' doesn't belong to the group.

89. (*d*) In all other options, second value is more than twice of the first value.

$12-28 \Rightarrow 28 > (12 \times 2)$

$14-82 \Rightarrow 82 > (14 \times 2)$

$23-64 \Rightarrow 64 > (23 \times 2)$

$36-72 \Rightarrow 72 = (36 \times 2)$

90. (*b*) According to the given information,

(a) DIRAMLOG - MARIGOLD
(b) ERENIGEN - ERENIGEN
(c) UIHCSSBI - HIBISCUS
(d) AFOLDFID - DAFFODIL

All except 'ERENIGEN' are related to the 'flowers'.

91. (*d*) Pattern of groups,

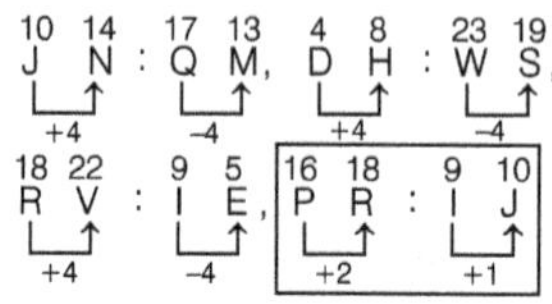

∴ PR : IJ is different from others.

92. (*b*)
FLOW ⇒ WOLF
WCO ⇒ COW
ILNO ⇒ LION
ERTIG ⇒ TIGER

Except COW, other animals are carnivorous.

93. (*d*) According to the given information,

(a) LPAEP - APPLE
(b) AYAPAP - PAPAYA
(c) AVGAU - GUAVA
(d) SRAHDI - RADISH

Except 'RADISH' all others are fruits whereas Radish is vegetable.

94. (*c*) According to the given information,

(a) LIWLOP - PILLOW
(b) RSTESMTA - MATTRESS
(c) TSROFE - FOREST
(d) UTQLI - QUILT

So, 'Forest' is different from others.

95. (*c*) Options (a), (b), (c) and (d) when rearranged become SHIRT, SOCKS, PENCIL and PANT respectively. So option (c) is odd one out here.

96. (*b*) Options (a), (b), (c) and (d) when rearranged become SCOOTER, PANEL, MOTOR BIKE and CYCLE respectively.

So, option (b) is the odd one out.

97. (*b*) Except Chocolate, all other are bakery items. So, Chocolate does not belong to the group.

98. (*a*) Except bones, all others are different types of teeth.

99. (*b*) Except triangle, all other geometrical shapes have four sides, whereas triangle has only three sides.

100. (*a*) Except 'Lettuce', all other are fruits, whereas lettuce is vegetable.

CHAPTER / 04

Coding-Decoding

Coding

When any letter/word/sentence is written or said in such **a language which hides the actual meaning** of that particular letter/word/sentence from others except the desired person that process is called coding.

Decoding

It means in **tracing out the actual meaning of a coded letter/word/sentence**. Generally, coding is done on the basis of the letters of English alphabet and their corresponding positions.

In these questions, a word is coded in a particular way and candidates are asked to code other word in the same way. As the matter of fact, there exists no uniform and particular type or category of these questions according to which we could classify questions of coding-decoding.

To solve the questions based on coding-decoding, first of all it is necessary to remember the positions of all alphabetical letters, both in forward and backward order. Several ways for remembering these positions easily are discussed here.

Positions of letter are of two types

Forward Order Position (Left to Right)

English Letter	A	B	C	D	E	F	G	H	I	J	K	L	M
Forward Position	1	2	3	4	5	6	7	8	9	10	11	12	13
English Letter	N	O	P	Q	R	S	T	U	V	W	X	Y	Z
Forward Position	14	15	16	17	18	19	20	21	22	23	24	25	26

Backward Order Position (Right to Left)

English Letter	Z	Y	X	W	V	U	T	S	R	Q	P	O	N
Backward Order	1	2	3	4	5	6	7	8	9	10	11	12	13
English Letter	M	L	K	J	I	H	G	F	E	D	C	B	A
Backward Order	14	15	16	17	18	19	20	21	22	23	24	25	26

Students find it difficult to remember backward order positions but, if they keep forward order positions of letters in their mind, they can easily calculate the backward order position of letters in the following way

Note *Backward order position of any letter = 27 – Forward order position of that letter*

∴ Backward order position of A = 27 – Forward order position of A

$= 27 - 1 = 26$

Backward order positions of letters can be remembered in the following ways.

(i) Here is a gap of four letters between each letters of the word group, 'VQLGB'.

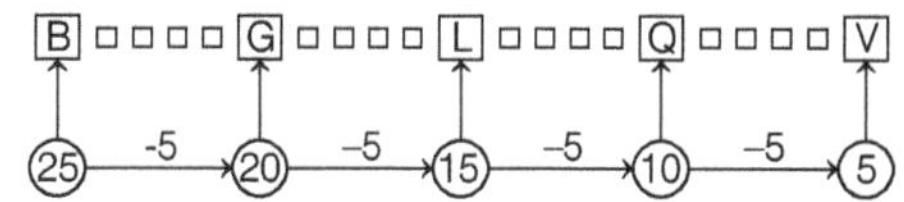

(ii) Backward order position of vowels can be remembered with following trick.

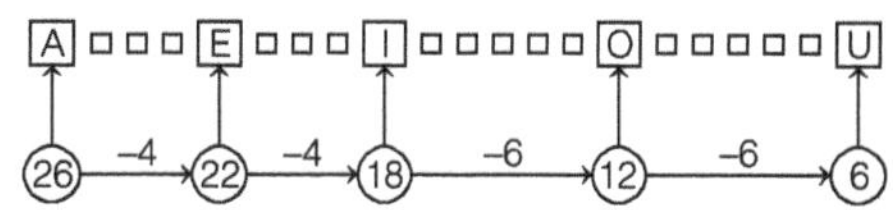

Trick to Learn Position/Rank of the Alphabets

Forward order positions of letters can be remembered in the following ways

A to D First four letters A to D's, rank is 1 to 4 (Easy to learn). No trick is required to learn them.

E For this you have to learn one word "EJOTY".

E	J	O	T	Y
5	10	15	20	25

Learning this word helps you to learn the position of 5 letters which are the multiple of 5.

F For this you have to learn another word "CFILORUX".

C	F	I	L	O	R	U	X
3	6	9	12	15	18	21	24

Learning this word helps you to learn the position of 8 letters which are the multiple of 3.

G Everybody know G-7 Nations.
The position of G is 7.

H If you join the 2 lines of H, it will become 8 or you can say H looks like 8. Thus the position of H is "8".

I "I know (9) you". Learn this sentence and you will get position of "I".

Or

Remember the term "CFILORUX"
The position of I is "9".

J Remember the term "EJOTY".
The position of J is "10".

K K for **Kelvin** and which is similar to "**eleven**" in Pronunciation.
The position of K is "11".

L Remember the term "CFILORUX". The position of L is "12".

M M looks like 3 (when we rotate M). The position of M is "13".

N N For November and November 14 is **children's day**. Thus, the position of N is "14".

O Again the term EJOTY. The position of O is "15".

P When we see water image of P, it look like six (6). The position of P is "16".

Q Write Q like Q7. Here we can see "7" on right end of Q. The position of Q is "17".

R Remember the term 'CFILORUX'. or When we stretch R like R, it looks like 8. The position of R is "18".

S We write Nineteen, UNISSS 19(S) in Hindi. The position of S is "19".

T T-20 Match

Or

Remember the term 'EJOTY'.
The position of T is "20".

U Again remember the term "CFILORUX." The position of U is "21".

V V for victory.
You require two fingers to represents victory. The position of "V" is "22".

W If you rotate anti-clockwise the letter "W", it looks like 3, its position is 23.

X Remember the term 'CFILORUX'.

Or

It is being divided into four parts.

The position of X is "23".

Y Remember the term "EJOTY".
The position of Y is 25.

Z Last letter is Z.
Its position is "26".

Opposite Letters

These are called opposite letters as the forward order corresponding position of an opposite letter is as same as the backward order corresponding position of its opposite letter.

	A	B	C	D	E	F	G	H	I	J	K	L	M
Alphabet Starting to End	1	2	3	4	5	6	7	8	9	10	11	12	13
	26	25	24	23	22	21	20	19	18	17	16	15	14
	↕	↕	↕	↕	↕	↕	↕	↕	↕	↕	↕	↕	↕
	Z	Y	X	W	V	U	T	S	R	Q	P	O	N
Alphabet Starting to End	26	25	24	23	22	21	20	19	18	17	16	15	14
	1	2	3	4	5	6	7	8	9	10	11	12	13

A and Z is a pair of opposite letters.

Now, it is clear from the above presentation that two letters are called opposite to each other, if sum of their corresponding positions is equal to 27.

Note *Opposite position of any letter = 27 – Corresponding position of that letter*

∴ *Opposite position of A = 27 – Corresponding position of A*

= 27 – 1 = 26 = Z

The pairs of opposite letters can easily be remembered in following ways

Trick to Remember Opposite Letters

AZ	Remember (ZA) of 'go' in Hindi/AZad
BY	Remember the word 'by'/BoY
CX	Remember CIX (like 'Six')/CraX
DW	Remember DW of the word DEW
EV	Remember EV (Evening) loVE
FU	Remember FU of 'Full'/For U
GT	Remember GT Road (Built by Shershah)
HS	Higher Secondary/High School
IR	Indian Railway
JQ	Jack and Queen (in the game of cards)
KP	Kevin Peterson (England cricket Player)/Kal-Prso
LO	Remember LO of the word LOVE
MN	Remember MN of the word MAN

TYPE 01

Letter Coding

In this type of questions, the letters of a certain word are arranged in different orders which can be a reverse order or a fragmented order in which first-half of the word follows some other rule and second part of the word follows some other rule for coding.

The candidates are therefore required to understand the different patterns of the letter coding and solve different types of problems based on these patterns which are discussed below.

1. Coding Based on Rearrangement of Letters

In this type of coding, the letters of the original word are rearranged in a particular manner to obtain the code.

Such coding can be of following types

(a) When all the letters of a word are written in reverse order.

Ex 01 In a certain code, if MAHESH is written as HSEHAM, then how will MANEGER written in that code?
« SSC Steno Grade C and D 2019

(a) REGENAM (b) REEGANM
(c) REGEANM (d) REGNEAM

Solution (a)

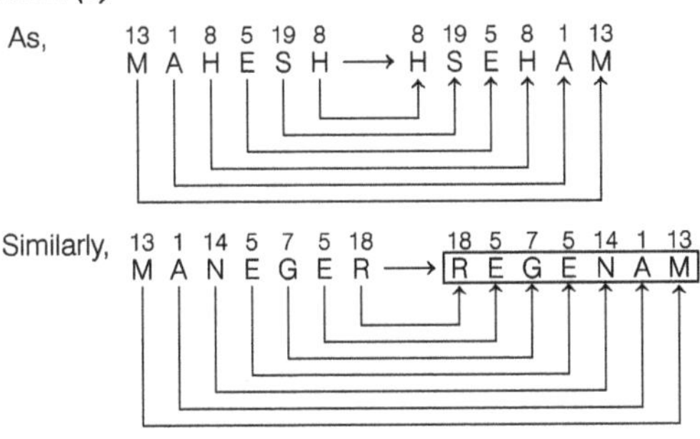

∴ MANEGER ⇒ REGENAM

Ex 02 If in a certain language, if 'EXECUTIVE' is coded as 'EVITUCEXE', then how is 'MAUSOLEUM' coded in that language? « SSC (MTS) 2019

(a) AUUCOSLMM (b) MUELOSUAM
(c) MUELOSUMA (d) ALUEOSUMM

Solution (b)

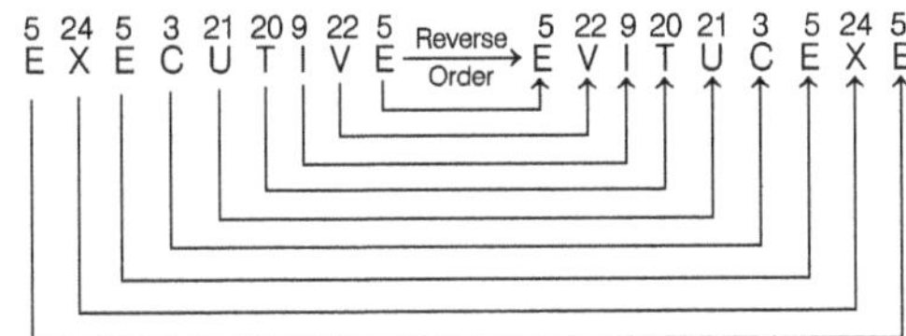

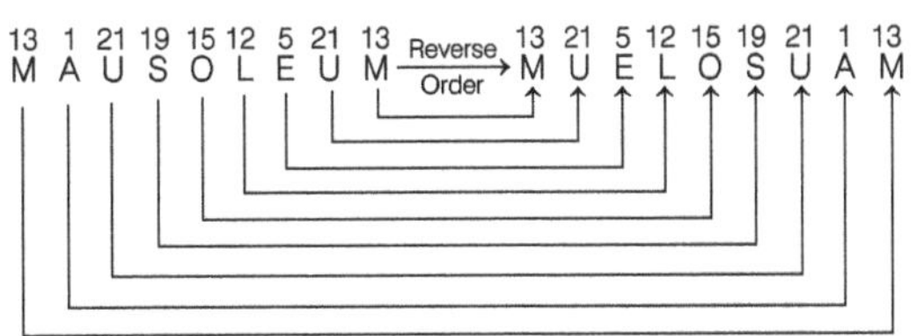

∴ MAUSOLEUM ⇒ MUELOSUAM

(b) When letters of the word are divided into two parts and then both the parts are written in reverse order or the first part is written in reverse order at the place of second part and second part is written in reverse order at place of first part.

Following situations can arise in such cases

(i) When the number of letters of the word is even

Coding of A B C D E F
1 2 3 4 5 6

can be done in certain ways as follows

A B C	F E D	1 2 3	6 5 4
C B A	D E F	3 2 1	4 5 6
C B A	F E D	3 2 1	6 5 4
D E F	A B C	4 5 6	1 2 3
D E F	C B A	4 5 6	3 2 1
F E D	A B C	6 5 4	1 2 3

Ex 03 If in a certain code language 'THREAT' is written as 'RHTTAE', then how will 'PEARLY' be written in that code?

(a) YLRAEP (b) YLRPAE
(c) AEPYLR (d) AEPRYL

Solution (c)

As, T H R E A T ⟶ R H T T A E
1 2 3 4 5 6 → 3 2 1 6 5 4

Similarly, P E A R L Y ⟶ A E P Y L R
1 2 3 4 5 6 → 3 2 1 6 5 4

∴ PEARLY ⇒ AEPYLR

(ii) When the number of letters of the word is odd

Coding of A B C D E
1 2 3 4 5

can be done in certain ways as follows

A B C	E D	1 2 3	5 4
B A C	E D	2 1 3	5 4
B A C	D E	2 1 3	4 5
D E C	A B	4 5 3	1 2
E D C	A B	5 4 3	1 2
D E C	B A	4 5 3	2 1

Ex 04 If in a certain code language 'GREAT' is written as 'GRETA', then how will 'FIGHT' be written in that code?

(a) FIGTH (b) FGITH
(c) FGIHT (d) FITGH

Solution (a) As,

	G R E A T	⟶	G R E T A
	1 2 3 4 5		1 2 3 5 4
Similarly,	F I G H T	⟶	F I G T H
	1 2 3 4 5		1 2 3 5 4

∴ FIGHT ⇒ FIGTH

(iii) When letters of the word are divided into two or more groups and then all or some particular groups are written in reverse order

Coding of A B C D E F
1 2 3 4 5 6

can be done in certain ways as follows

BA	CD	EF	21	34	56
BA	DC	EF	21	43	56
BA	DC	FE	21	43	65

Ex 05 If in a certain code language 'SECTOR' is written as 'ESCTOR', then how will 'MOTHER' be written in that code?

(a) MOHTER (b) OMHTER
(c) OMHTRE (d) OMTHER

Solution (d) As,

	S E C T O R	⟶	E S C T O R
	1 2 3 4 5 6		2 1 3 4 5 6
Similarly,	M O T H E R	⟶	O M T H E R
	1 2 3 4 5 6		2 1 3 4 5 6

∴ MOTHER ⇒ OMTHER

(iv) When first and last letter of the word remains at the same place but middle letters get reversed

Coding of A B C D E F
1 2 3 4 5 6

can be done in following way

A E D C B F | 1 5 4 3 2 6

Ex 06 If in a certain code language 'SECTOR' is written as 'SOTCER', then how will 'MOTHER' be written in that code?

(a) MTOHER (b) MEHTOR
(c) MEHOTR (d) METOHR

Solution (b)

	S E C T O R	⟶	S O T C E R
As,	1 2 3 4 5 6		1 5 4 3 2 6
Similarly,	M O T H E R	⟶	M E H T O R
	1 2 3 4 5 6		1 5 4 3 2 6

∴ MOTHER ⇒ MEHTOR

(v) When each letter of the word is written at a certain place

Coding of A B C D E
1 2 3 4 5

can be done in certain ways as follows

B	D	A	E	C	2	4	1	5	3
D	B	C	E	A	4	2	3	5	1
C	D	A	E	B	3	4	1	5	2
B	E	C	A	D	2	5	3	1	4

Ex 07 If in a certain code language 'MIGHT' is written as 'GHMTI', then how will 'EARTH' be written in that code?

(a) RTEHA (b) RTEAH (c) RTAEH (d) RETHA

Solution (a)

	M I G H T	⟶	G H M T I
As,	1 2 3 4 5		3 4 1 5 2
Similarly,	E A R T H	⟶	R T E H A
	1 2 3 4 5		3 4 1 5 2

∴ EARTH ⇒ RTEHA

2. Coding Based on Replacement of Letters

In this type of coding, the letters of the words are replaced by other letters following a certain pattern to obtain the code.

Such coding can be of following types

A. Forward Sequence Coding

Under this pattern of coding, every letter of a letter group/word is coded in increasing order of English alphabet.

Let us consider the coding of ABCD which can be done in following ways

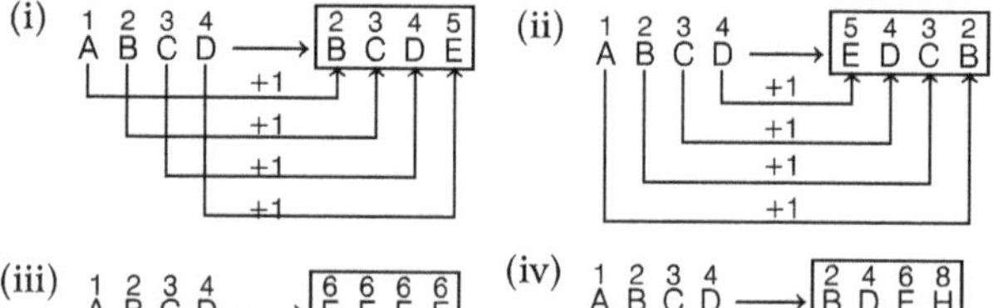

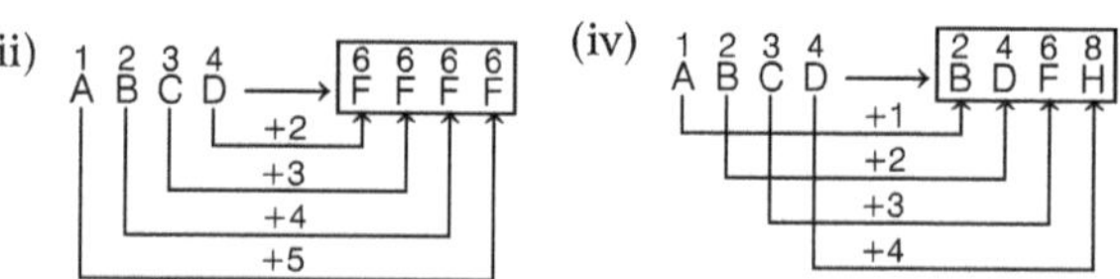

Ex 08 If 'PEACE' is coded as 'RGCEG', then how is 'MICKY' coded in that code? « SNAP 2013

(a) MOUSE (b) OKEMA (c) LHBJX (d) JDLJ

Solution (b)

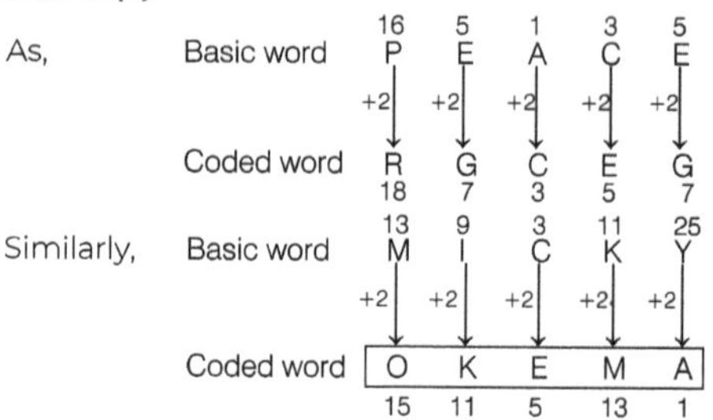

∴ MICKY = OKEMA

Ex 09 If RATIONAL is CLETZYLW, then EXPERIENCE is « RRB NTPC 2016

A. OIZOCTOYMO B. QJBDUQZOQ
C. OHZBSOXMO D. PIAPCTPYNP

(a) A (b) C (c) D (d) B

Solution (c)

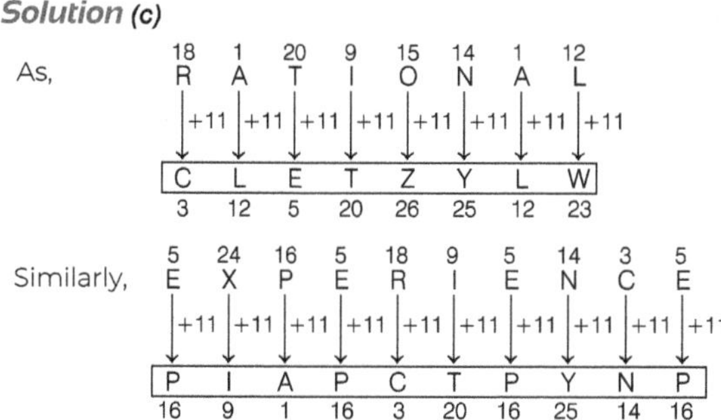

∴ EXPERIENCE ⇒ PIAPCTPYNP

B. Backward Sequence Coding

Under this pattern of coding, every letter of a letter group/word is coded in decreasing order of English alphabetical series.

Let us consider the coding of ABCD which can be done in following ways

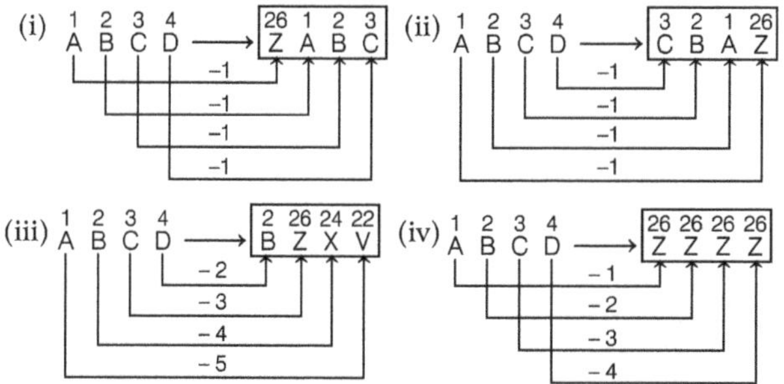

***Ex* 10** If in a certain code language 'FRESH' is written as 'EQDRG', then how will 'BLEND' be written in that code?

(a) AKDMC (b) AKDCM
(c) AKMDC (d) AKCMD

Solution (a)

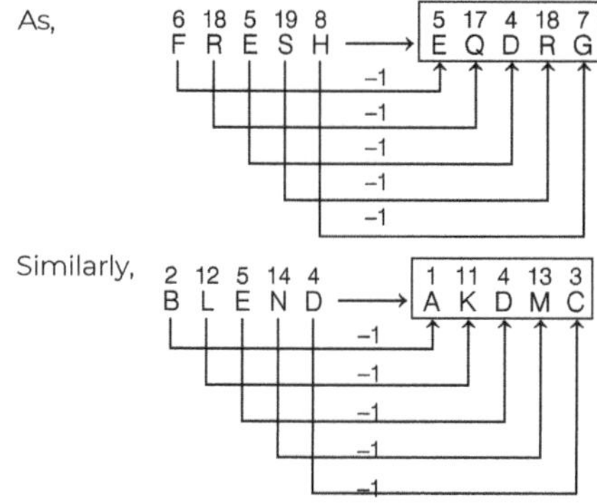

∴ BLEND = AKDMC

C. Mixed Sequence Coding (Forward and Backward)

Under this pattern, forward and backward sequence coding takes place simultaneously.

Let us consider the coding of ABCD which can be done in following ways

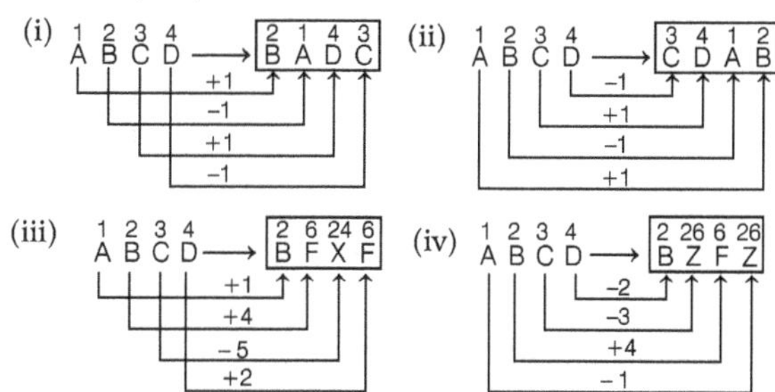

***Ex* 11** In a certain code language "NIGHT" is written as "ODDGM" and "DARK" is written as "GOYC". How is "GREEN" written in that code language?

« RRB JE 2019

(a) IABPF (b) MCBNB
(c) OGHVL (d) FPBAI

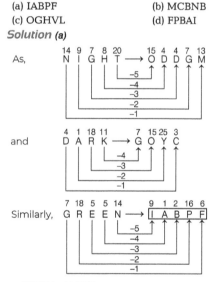

Solution (a)

As,
14 9 7 8 20
N I G H T → O D D G M
15 4 4 7 13
−5 −4 −3 −2 −1

and
4 1 18 11
D A R K → G O Y C
7 15 25 3
−4 −3 −2 −1

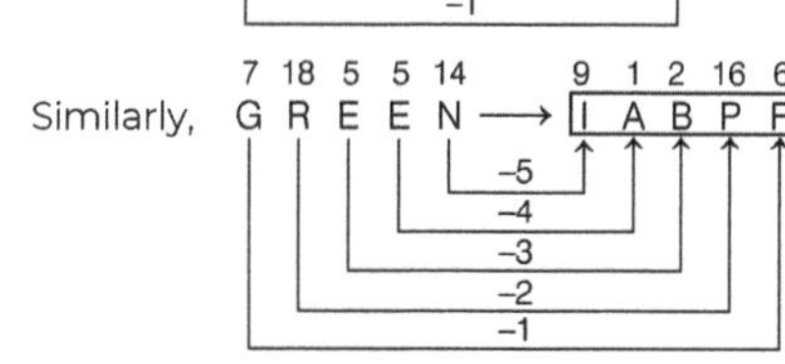

∴ GREEN = IABPF

D. Direct Letter Coding

In this type of coding, some letter group/words are assigned some codes which do not follow any particular rule but are direct codes for a particular letter of the letter group/ words. These direct codes are then used to form the codes of an another given word.

Example given below will give a better idea about such type of questions

Ex 12 In a certain code language, 'GRASP' is written as INOPQ and BROWN is written as RNSTU. How will SPARROW be written as in that code language?

« UPSSSC Junior Assistant 2020

(a) RSQGGSU (b) QQONMOT
(c) PPONNSU (d) PQONNST

Solution (d) As,

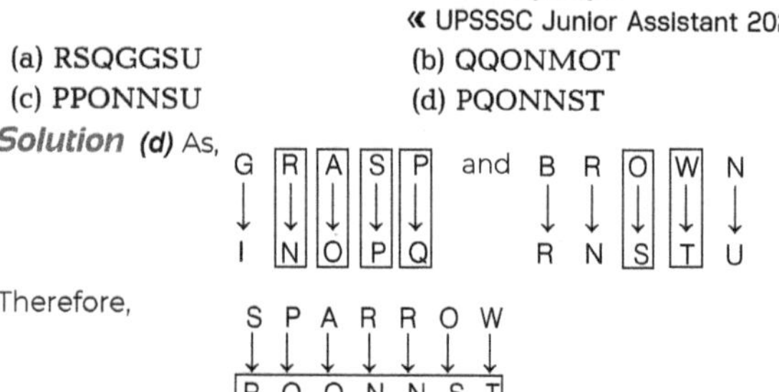

∴ SPARROW = PQONNST

3. Opposite Letters Coding

Under this pattern, each letter of a word is coded with its opposite letter.

Let us consider the coding of ABCD which can be done in following ways

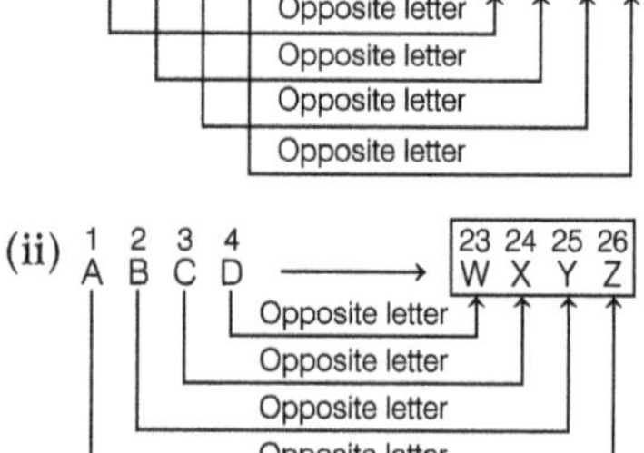

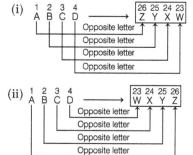

Ex 13 In a coded language, INDIA is written as RMWRZ. In the same language, how should CHINA be written?

« UKPSC Asst. Conservator of Forest 2019

(a) YRSNZ (b) XSRMZ (c) XRSMZ (d) YSRMZ

Solution (b) As,

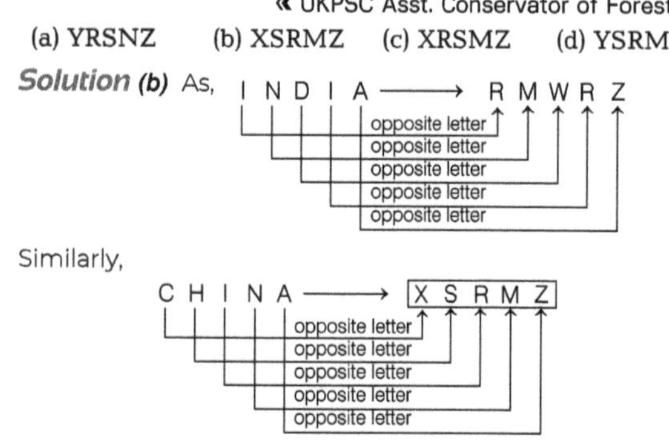

∴ CHINA = XSRMZ

4. Coding of Letters by Their Left and Right Letters of English Alphabet

Under this pattern each letter of a letter group/word is coded by its left and right letters of English alphabet.

Let us consider the coding of ABCD

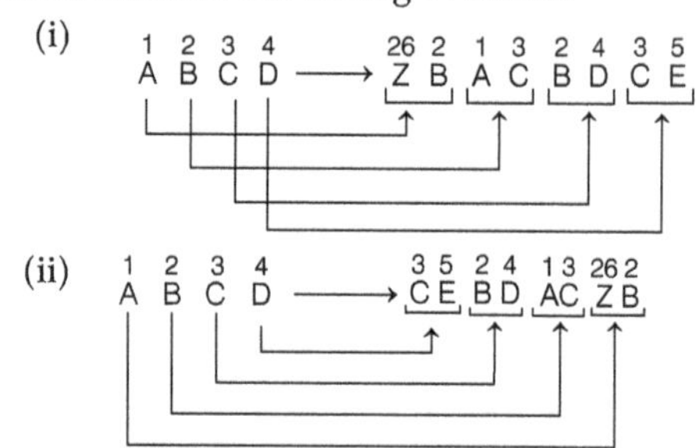

Ex 14 If in a certain code language 'BAT' is written as 'ACZBSU', then how will 'SIX' be written in that code?

(a) RTHJYW (b) RHTJYW
(c) RTHWJY (d) RTHJWY

Solution (d) Here, each letter is coded by its left and right letters.

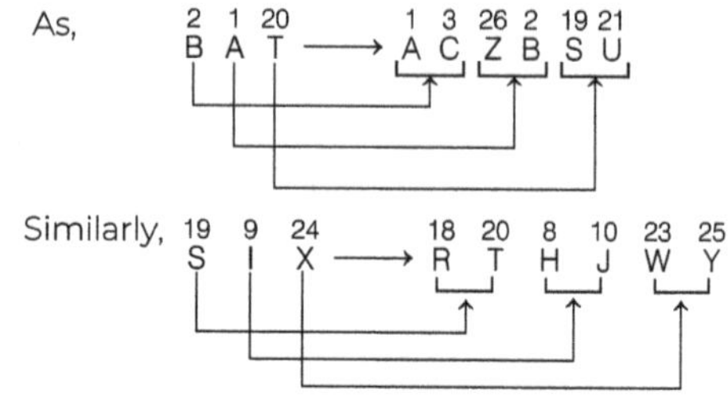

∴ SIX = RTHJWY

5. Decoding

(Finding the Original Word of a code)

In this type of questions the code of a word or letters group is given. The candidates are also given a coded word/letters group and they have to find out the original word/letters group of that code.

Ex 15 In a certain code language NOBEL is written as QIEQO, then in the same code language which word would be written as YLJKS?

(a) RIGHT (b) MIGHT
(c) BRIGHT (d) LIGHT

Solution (a) As,

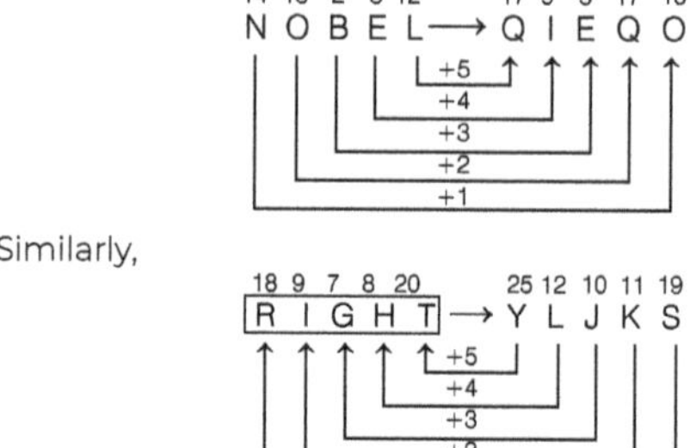

∴ RIGHT ⇒ YLJKS

Practice / CORNER 4.1

1. In a certain language, WOMEN is written as OWMNE. How will NOTES be written as in that code language?
« UPSSSC Junior Assistant 2020

(a) TONES (b) SETNO (c) ONTSE (d) ONETS

2. If NOVEMBER is coded REBMEVON and DECEMBER is coded REBMECED, then how is OCTOBER coded? « MP Police 2017

(a) RETBOCO (b) RTECBRO
(c) REBTOOC (d) REBOTCO

3. If in a certain code, 'GIGANTIC' is written as 'GIGTANCI'. How 'MIRACLES' be written in that language?

(a) MIRLCAES (b) MIRLACSE
(c) RIMCALSE (d) RIMLCAES

4. If in a certain code, 'EXPLAINING' is written as 'PXEALNIGNI'. How will 'PRODUCED' be written in that language?

(a) ORPBUDEC (b) ROPUDECD
(c) ORPUDDEC (d) DORPDECU

5. If in a certain code language 'SYSTEM' is written as 'SYSMET', 'NEARER' is written as 'AENRER', then how will 'FRACTION' be written in that language?

(a) CARFNOIT (b) CARFTION
(c) ARFCNOIT (d) FRACNOIT

6. If 'MEAT' is written as 'TEAM', then 'BALE' is written as

(a) ELAB (b) EABL (c) EBLA (d) EALB

7. In a certain coded language, if 'LITMUS' is written as 'SMIUTL' and 'INDIGO' is written as 'OINGDI', then how is the word 'JAGGER', would be written in that language? « UPSSSC Combined Lower Subordinate 2019

(a) RGAEGJ (b) RGJEGA
(c) RGAGEJ (d) RGJEAG

8. If 'SWAMINATHAN' is coded as 'NAHTANIMAWS' in a certain code language, then how would you code 'SIRNAME' in that language?

(a) EMAMSIR (b) EMARNIS
(c) EMNARIS (d) EMANRIS

9. In a certain code language 'BREAKDOWN' is written as 'NWODKAERB', then how will 'TRIANGLES' be written in that language?

(a) SELGNTRIA (b) AIRTNSELG
(c) SELGNAIRT (d) AIRTGNSEL
(e) None of these

10. In a certain coding system, PAPER is written as PERPA and SUBJECT is written as JECTSUB, what should be the code for COUNCIL? « SBI Clerk 2016

(a) NCILCOU (b) LICNOUC
(c) NCOUCIL (d) NLICUOC
(e) None of the above

11. If in a certain code, 'DAUGHTER' is written as 'TERDAUGH', how will 'APTITUDE' be written in that code?

(a) DEUAPTIT (b) UDEAPTIT
(c) DUEAPTIT (d) DAUEPTIT

12. If STOVE is coded as EVOTS and CANDLE is coded as ELDNAC, then REPORT is coded as?
« SSC GD Constable 2015

(a) QDONQS (b) SEQPSU
(c) PORTRE (d) TROPER

13. In a certain code, 'REFRIGERATOR' is coded as 'ROTAREGIRFER'. Which words from the following would be coded as 'NOITINUMMA'?

(a) ANMOMIUTMI (b) AMNTOMUIIN
(c) AMMUNITION (d) NMMUNITIOA

14. If 'VEHEMENT' is written as 'VEHETNEM', then how 'MOURNFUL' be written in that code language?

(a) MOURLUFN (b) MOUNULER
(c) OURMNFUL (d) URNFULMO

15. In a certain code language, 'COMPUTRONE' is written as 'PMOCTUENOR'. How is 'ADVANTAGES' written in that same code?

(a) ADVANSEGAS (b) ADVTANSEAG
(c) AVDANTAGES (d) AVDATNSEGA

16. In a certain language, 'EXECUTIVE' is coded as 'TCIEUXVEE', then how is 'MAUSOLEUM' coded in that same language?

(a) LSEUOAUMM (b) AUUCOSLMM
(c) AUEUOSEMM (d) SLUEOAUMM

17. A military code writes SYSTEM as SYSMET and NEARER as AENRER. Using the same code, FRACTION can be written as « UPSC Pre 2016

(a) CARFTION (b) FRACNOIT
(c) NOITCARF (d) CARFNOIT

18. If 'NEUROTIC' can be written as 'TICRONEU' then how can 'PSYCHOTIC' be written?

(a) TICOCHPSY (b) TICCHOPSY
(c) TICCOHPSY (d) TICHCOPSY

19. In a certain code language, 'BRAIN' is written as 'CSBJO', then how is 'MAKER' written in that code language? « UPSC Pre 2016

(a) BNLFS (b) NBLFS
(c) FSLBN (d) NBLFT

20. If in a certain code language 'NAME' is written as 'MZLD', then how will 'PEON' be coded in that language?

(a) ODNM (b) ODMN
(c) ONDM (d) OMND

21. In a certain code, 'PAISE' is coded as 'QBJTF' and 'CEASE' is coded as 'DFBTF'. How will 'TRANGLE' be coded in the same code? « FCI Assistant 2015

(a) USBOIMF (b) USBMHMF
(c) USOBIMF (d) USBOHMF

22. If in a certain code language 'MARS' is written as 'ZNEF', then how will 'ARMS' be written in that language?

(a) NEZF (b) FENZ (c) NFZE (d) MEZF

23. 'BEHK' is related to 'DGJM' in the same way as 'NQTW' is related to « UP Police Constable 2018

(a) PRTV (b) ORTV (c) PSVY (d) PRUX

24. If in a certain code language 'SISTER' is written as 'RHRSDQ', then how will 'UNCLE' be written in that language?

(a) TMBDK (b) TMBKD (c) TMDKB (d) TMKBD

25. In a code language, if BUTTER is coded as EXWWHU and MILK is coded as PLON, then in the same code language, how will EARTH be coded?

(a) HDWUK (b) HDUWK
(c) KHDUW (d) KHUWD

26. If in a code language DIAMONDS is written as EIBMPNES, how will PLATINUM be written as in the same language? « UPSSSC Combined Lower Subordinate 2016

(a) QLTBNJVM (b) PMAUIOUN
(c) PMAIVOUN (d) QLBTJNVM

27. In a certain code DREAMING is written as BFSEFMHL, how is SELECTED written in that code? « SBI PO 2015

(a) FMFTCDSB (b) FMFTEFUD
(c) EKDRCDSB (d) EKDREFUD
(e) None of these

28. In a certain code, 'FLOWERS' is written as 'EKNVDQR'. How will 'SUPREME' be written in that code?

(a) TQDROLD (b) RTODQLD
(c) TQDDROL (d) RTOQDLD

29. If in a certain code language 'TRIVENDRUM' is written as 'VTKXGPFTWO', then how will 'ERNAKULAM' be written in that language?

(a) GTPCMWNOC (b) GTPCMWNCO
(c) GTPCMNWCO (d) GTPMCWNCO

30. In a certain code language, SKEW is written as POCY. Which word will be written as JYQV as in that code language ? « UPSSSC Junior Assistant 2020

(a) JUST (b) MUST (c) LUST (d) HUSK

31. In a certain language, 'MADRAS' is coded as NBESBT, how is 'BOMBAY' coded in that language?

« UKPSC Lower Subordinate Service 2016

(a) DPNCBX (b) CPNCBZ
(c) CPNCBY (d) DPNCBZ

32. In a certain coded language, if 'TABLE' is written as 'VEDNI' and 'CHAIR' is written as 'EJEOT', then how is the word 'BENCH' would be written in that language? « UPSSSC Combined Lower Subordinate 2019

(a) DIPFJ (b) DGPEJ (c) DIPEJ (d) DGPFT

33. If in a certain code language 'VANDANA' is coded as 'TYLBYLY', 'TOP' is coded as 'RMN', then how will 'SUMPTUOUS' be coded in that language?

(a) QSKNRSMSQ (b) QSKNRSMQS
(c) QSKNRMSQS (d) QSKRNMSQS

34. In a certain code language, 'BROWSE' is written as 'GUYQTD'. How will 'AMALGAM' be written as in that language? « SSC (10+2) 2020

(a) CONCICO (b) OCINCOC
(c) DPMDGCP (d) PMDGCPD

35. If in a certain code language 'TEAM' is written as 'YJFR', then how will 'CREATE' be written in that language?

(a) HWJFJY (b) HWJFYJ (c) HWFJYZ (d) HWFJYJ
(e) None of these

36. If HANDLE is coded AHDNEL, then how is DISTANCE coded?

(a) IDTSNAEC (b) IDTSNACE
(c) IDTSANEC (d) DISTNACE

37. In a certain code language LESSON is coded as NGUQML. How will PUZZLE be coded in that code language?

(a) RWXBJP (b) RVBXJC
(c) RWBXJC (d) RUBJXC

38. In a certain code language 'SHORE' is written as 'QFMPC', then how will 'WNKGL' is written in that language?

(a) NIMPY (b) YPMIN (c) ULIEJ (d) ULIGE
(e) None of these

39. In a certain code, SOBER is written as RNADQ. How can LOTUS be written in that code?

(a) KNSTR (b) MPUWT (c) KMSTR (d) LMRST

40. In a certain code language, 'GROUND' is written as 'BMJPIY.' What will be the code for 'FREAK' in that code language? « SSC MTS 2019

(a) BOAYH (b) AMYVF (c) BNAWG (d) AMZVF

41. If MINARET is coded as JFKXOBQ, then how will BUY be coded? « UPSSSC Mandi Parishad 2018

(a) YRV (b) ZBD (c) EHK (d) LOR

42. If code for 'SET' is 'UGV', then what would be the code for 'BRICK'?

(a) CSJDL (b) DSJEM (c) DTKEM (d) DTKFM

43. In a certain code 'RAIN' is written as 'TCKP'. How is 'CLOUD' written in that code?

(a) ENQWF (b) EMQWF (c) FNQWE (d) ENRWF

44. If 'DAILY' is coded as 'XKHZC' in a code language, then how would you code 'FERTILE' in that code language?

(a) DKHSEDQS (b) DMHUQFE
(c) DKHSQDE (d) DJHRQCE

45. If in a certain code language 'ARIHANT' is written as 'BTLLFTA', then how will 'HONESTY' be written in that code?

(a) IQQIZFX (b) IQQXIZF
(c) IQQIXZF (d) IQQIXFZ

46. If GOODNESS is coded as HNPCODTR, how GREATNESS can be written in that code?
« Delhi Police CAPF 2015

(a) HQZSMFRT (b) HQFZUFRTM
(c) HQFZUODTR (d) HQFZUMFRT

47. If 'MUSICAL' is written as 'KWQKACJ', then how can 'SPRINKLE' be written? « SSC (CGL) 2013

(a) QRBKCNJG (b) QNPGLIJC
(c) QRPKLMJG (d) URTKPMNG

48. If LSJXVC is the code for MUMBAI, then code for DELHI is « UPPSC Pre 2018

(a) CCIDD (b) CDKGH
(c) CCJFG (d) CCIFE

49. If in a certain code language 'RUNNER' is written as 'SUMMER', then how will 'WINTER' be written in that language? « UPPCS 2006

(a) XIMSER (b) VINTER
(c) SINVER (d) XIOUER

50. In a certain coded language if 'JOKER' is coded as 'KNLDS' and 'CLOWN' is coded as 'DMNXO', then how is the word 'FUNNY' coded? « UPSSSC Cane Supervisor 2016

(a) GVOOZ (b) GTOMZ (c) GTOOZ (d) GTMOZ

51. In a certain code language, 'FRANK' is written as 'GQBML'. How is 'MARCO' written in that code language? « SSC 10+2 2018

(a) NYTPB (b) MZSCQ
(c) NZSBP (d) NQPBT

52. If in a certain code language 'KAMLESH' is written as 'GUJLMCO', then how will 'NATURAL' be written in that language?

(a) TCNUPCV (b) TCOUPVC
(c) TCUOPVC (d) TCOUVCP

53. If in a certain code language 'GREAT' is written as 'UBESH', then how will 'NIGHT' be written in that language?

(a) UIJOG (b) UIGOK (c) UIGOJ (d) UIGJO

54. If in a certain code language 'WHEN' is written as 'VGFO', then how will 'POLICE' be written in that language? « UBI (Clerk) 2011

(a) ONKHBD (b) ONKJDF
(c) OPKJBF (d) QPMHBD
(e) None of these

55. If in a certain code 'BOXER' is written as 'AQWGQ', then how will 'VISIT' be written in that language?

(a) UKRKU (b) UKRKS
(c) WKRKU (d) WKRKS

56. If in a certain code language 'PAINTER' is written as 'NCGPRGP', then how will 'REASON' be written in that language?

(a) PCYQMN (b) PGYQMN
(c) PGYUMP (d) PGYUPM

57. In a certain language, if BOXER is coded as CQAIW, which word will be coded as BEWSW?
« RRB Group D 2018

(a) AFTOR (b) ADTOR (c) ACTOR (d) ACSOR

58. If 'BEAUTY' is coded as 'DHEZZF', then how will 'FLOWER' be written in that language?

(a) HSOBYK (b) HBOSKY
(c) HOSBKY (d) SBKYOH

59. If in a certain code language the word POLITICAL is written as QNMHUHDZM, then in the same code language how will you write the word 'SOCIAL'?
« SSC GD Constable 2018

(a) DBKNTH (b) NTHDBK
(c) DHBKTN (d) TNDHBK

60. In a certain language, EMBEZZLE is coded as MEEBZZEL. How will MAXIMIZE be coded in the same language?

(a) AIMXMIEZ (b) AMIXIMEZ
(c) AMIMIXEZ (d) EMIXIMEM

61. If in a certain code language 'COMPUTE' is coded as 'FSVONND', then how will 'DISTURB' be coded in that language? « OBC (PO) 2009

(a) CSVSTHE (b) CQVSTHE
(c) CQVTSHE (d) CSVTSHE
(e) None of these

62. In a certain code language, 'RIGIDS' is written as 'TFIFFP'. What will be the code for 'CORNET' in that code language ? « SSC MTS 2019

(a) GNVMIS (b) FMULHR
(c) ELTKRQ (d) ELTKGQ

63. If in a certain code language 'FAME' is written as 'LGGY', then how will 'LION' be coded in that language?

(a) RHIO (b) ROIH (c) RHOI (d) RIOH

64. If in a certain code language 'RELATED' is written as 'EFUBKDQ', then how will 'RETAINS' be written in that language? « PNB (Clerk) 2010

(a) SDQBTOJ (b) JOTBQDS
(c) JOTBSDQ (d) TOJBSDQ
(e) None of these

65. In a certain coded language if 'MONSOON' is coded as 'PMQQPMO' and 'WINTERS' is coded as 'UPGRPGY', then how is 'SUMMERS' coded? « UPSSSC VDO 2018

(a) TVNNFST (b) TCQKWOS
(c) QWKOCTS (d) UPGKOSU

66. In a certain code language, 'HAMMER' is written as 'ICPQJX'. How will 'WRENCH' be written as in that language? « SSC (CGL) 2020

(a) XTIRHN (b) XTHRHN
(c) XTIRIN (d) XTHRIN

67. If in a certain language GAMBLE is coded as FBLCKF, how is FLOWER coded in that language ?
« UPSC Assistant Commandant 2019

(a) GMPVDS (b) GKPVFQ
(c) EMNXDS (d) EMNTDS

68. In a certain code, 'BISLERI' is written as 'CHTKFQJ' and 'AQUA' is written as 'BPVZ'. How is 'KINGFISHER' written in that same code?

(a) LHOFGHTGFQ (b) LHOGFTHGFQ
(c) LHOQFTHGFQ (d) LHOHGTFGFQ

69. In a certain code language, 'CURATIVE' is written as 'BSVDDUHS'. How 'STEAMING' is to be written in the same code language?

(a) BFUTFMHL (b) TUFBFMHL
(c) BFUTLHMF (d) BFUTHOJN

70. In a certain code, 'MOUSE' is written as 'PRUQC'. How is 'SHIFT' written in that same code? « Vijaya Bank (Clerk) 2010

(a) VKIRD (b) VKIDR (c) VJIDR (d) VIKRD
(e) None of these

71. If 'LOFTY' is coded as 'LPFUY', then 'DWARF' will be written as « RBI (Grade 'B') 2011

(a) DXASF (b) DXBSG (c) DXATF (d) DWBSG

72. In a certain code 'PRISM' is written as 'OSHTL' and 'RUBLE' is written as 'QVAMD'. How will 'WHORL' be written in that code? « Allahabad Bank (PO) 2011

(a) XIPSM (b) VINSK
(c) UINSK (d) XGPQM
(e) None of these

73. In a certain code language, U is written as C. K is written as H, L is written as U, N is written as E, S is written as L, E is written as K, and C is written as N, How will 'KNUCKLES' be written as in that language? « SSC CGL 2019

(a) KECNKUHL (b) CHUECKN
(c) HECNHULK (d) HECNHUKL

74. If in a certain code language 'TEMPERATURE' is written as 'BZQDYXVBNXZ', then how will 'RAMP' be written in that language?

(a) XQVD (b) XDVQ (c) XVDQ (d) XVQD

75. If in a certain code language, 'RAW' is written as 'TIN', 'NET' is written as 'SHG', how is 'WATER' written in that code ? « SSC MTS 2019

(a) GHTIN (b) TINGH
(c) NIGHT (d) NIGTH

76. In a language, FIFTY is written as CACTY. CAR as POL, TAR as TOL. How can TARIFF be written in that language? « Delhi Police CAPF 2015

(a) TOEFDD (b) TOEFEL
(c) TOLADD (d) TOLACC

77. If in a certain code language 'STAG' is written as 'HGZT', 'HORN' is written as 'SLIM', then how will 'NORTH' be written in that language? « SSC (MTS) 2010

(a) NLGMI (b) MLIGS
(c) MGLIS (d) NLGIS

78. If in a certain code language 'PEN' is written as 'NZO', 'BARK' is written as 'CTSL', then how will 'PRANK' be written in that language? « SSC (MTS) 2013

(a) NZTOL (b) CSTZN
(c) NSTOL (d) NTSLO

79. In a certain code language, APPROACH is coded as CHOAPRAP. How will RESTRICT be coded? « SSC CGL 2016

(a) CTRISTER (b) ERTSIRTC
(c) CTRISTRE (d) TCIRSTRE

80. If in a certain code language 'PARENT' is written as 'BDFGJK' and 'CHILDREN' is written as 'MOXQUFGJ', then how will 'REPRINT' be written in that language? « SSC (CPO) 2005

(a) FGBFXGD (b) BGBFXJK
(c) FGBUXJK (d) FGBFXJK

81. If the word 'TABLECLOTH' is coded as 'XEMRANRIXT', how can 'HOTEL' be coded? « RRB (ASM) 2011

(a) RIXAT (b) TIXAR
(c) TAXIR (d) RAXIT

82. If in a certain code 'OPERATION' is written as 'BWDATXPBJ' and 'PARENT' is written as 'WTADJX', how will 'ORIENT' be written in that code? « SSC CAPF 2018

(a) PSJFOU (b) BAPDJX
(c) BPADJX (d) BWPDJX

83. If the word 'EARTH' is written as 'QPMZS' in a coded form, how can 'HEART' be written in the same coding language?

(a) SQPZM (b) SQMPZ (c) SPQZM (d) SQPMZ

84. In a certain code language 'CANDLE' is written as 'D1OEM2' and 'MODERN' is written as N4E2SO. How will 'BEWARE' be written in the same code language? « SSC CAPF 2018

(a) D2OEM2 (b) C2X2S2
(c) CFY2S2 (d) C2X1S2

85. In a code language, 'APPLE' is written as 'PQQRS', 'RIS' is written as 'ABC' and 'MANGO' is written as 'TPXYZ'. How will 'ROSE' be written in that same code language?

(a) ABCS (b) ACBS (c) AZSC (d) AZCS

86. In a code language, 'PRINCE' is written as 'FLOWER' and 'PRINCESS' is written as 'FLOWERSS'. Which of the following word would be coded as 'SLOWERS'?

(a) SRINCES (b) SIRNCES
(c) SRNICES (d) None of these

87. In a code language, 'ORGANISATION' is written as 'CBDWLQJWYQCL' and 'OPERATION' is written as 'CXFBWYQCL'. How would 'SEPARATION' be coded?

(a) EJXEBYQCL (b) JFQYWBCXQL
(c) JFXWBWYQCL (d) QCLYWBFXJE

88. In a certain code, 'ZOOM' is written as 'POON' and 'ROAD' is written as 'QOBE'. How would 'NOMP' be coded in that code language?

(a) PONX (b) QOHB (c) XONY (d) MONZ

89. In a certain code, 'FIRE' is written as 'QHOE' and 'MOVE' is written as 'ZMWE'. Following the same rule of coding, what should be the code for the word 'OVER'?

(a) MWED (b) MWEO (c) MWOE (d) MWZO

90. In certain code, FARMER is written as MAFMRE, in that code which word will be written as GIWALE? « SSC CGL 2018

(a) VIALEGL (b) VAGIELL
(c) RIGAEL (d) VELAIGL

91. In a certain code, 'CERTAIN' is coded as 'XVIGZRM' and 'SEQUENCE' is coded as 'HVJFVMXV'. How would 'REQUIRED' be coded?

(a) FJIVWVIR (b) VJIFWTRV
(c) WVJRIFVI (d) IVJFRIVW

92. If 'WATER' is written as 'YCVGT', then what is written as 'HKTG'? « SSC (CGL) 2013

(a) IRFE (b) FIRE
(c) REFI (d) ERIF

93. If in a certain code language 'POPULAR' is written as 'QPQVMBS', then what word will be written for the code 'GBNPVT'?

(a) FASOUM (b) FAMOUS
(c) FAMOSU (d) FAMSUO

94. If in a certain code language 'ORIENTAL' is written as 'DHQNMBUO', then how will 'SCHOOLED' be written in that language?

(a) RBGNPMFE (b) NGBREFMP
(c) RBGNEFMP (d) NGBRPMFE
(e) None of these

95. If in a certain code language 'CROWNED' is written as 'PSDVEFO', then how will 'STREAMS' be written in that language?

(a) SUTDBNT (b) TUSDTNB
(c) SUTDTNB (d) QSRDTNB
(e) None of these

96. If in a certain language 'SOLDIER' is written as 'JFSCRNK', then how will 'GENIOUS' be written in that language?

(a) PVTHHFO (b) PNTHFDM (c) PVTHMDF
(d) TVPHFDM (e) None of these

97. CALANDER is coded in a code as CLANAEDR. Find the code for CIRCULAR under the same rule. « IB 2017

(a) CRIVACLR (b) CRIUCALR
(c) CRUICALR (d) CRIVCALR

98. In a certain code, 'TERMINAL' is written as 'NSFUMBOJ' and 'TOWERS' is written as 'XPUTSF'. How is 'MATE' written in that same code? « IBPS (Clerk) 2012

(a) FUBN (b) UFNB (c) BNFU (d) BNDS
(e) None of these

99. In a certain code language, COMBINE is written as XLNYRMV. How will TOWARDS be written in that code language? « SBI Clerk 2016

(a) FLDZIWJ (b) GLDZIWH
(c) GLEZJWH (d) FLEZIWH

100. If GRASP is coded as TIZHK, what will be coded as OVTZXB? « MPPSC 2018

(a) LEGATE (b) LEAGUE
(c) LEGACY (d) LEDGER

101. If in a certain code language 'ARIHANT' is coded as 'ZIRSZMG', 'BIRD' is written as 'YRIW', then how will 'PAINTER' be coded in that language?

(a) KZRMVGI (b) KZRMIGV
(c) KZRMGIV (d) KZRMGVI

102. If in a certain code language 'NATURAL' is coded as 'MZGFIZO', then how will 'CARE' be written in that language?

(a) XZIV (b) XZVI (c) XVZI (d) XIZV

103. If 'CAMERA' is coded as 'ZIVNZX' in a certain code language, then how would you code 'CHAPRA' in that code language?

(a) ZISKZX (b) ZIKSZX
(c) ZIKXSZ (d) ZIKZSX

104. If in a certain code language 'NEETA' is written as 'MVVGZ', then what word will be written for 'IZHSNR'?

(a) VANDAN (b) RASHMI
(c) ANJALI (d) POONAM

105. If in a certain code language 'TIGER' is written as 'GRTVI', then what word will be written for 'HMZPV'?

(a) GREAT (b) TRACK (c) PLATE (d) SNAKE

106. In a certain code, 'CLOCK' is written as 'XOLXP'. How will 'LOTUS' be written in that same code?

(a) OGLFH (b) OLGFH (c) LOGFH (d) OLGHF

107. In a certain code, 'LATE' is written as 'VGZO'. How will 'SHINE' be written in that same code?

(a) VRMSH (b) VMSHR
(c) VMRSH (d) MVRSH

108. If in a certain code language 'GO' is written as 'FHNP', then how will 'SUN' be written in that language?

(a) RTTOMV (b) RTTOVM
(c) RTTVOM (d) RTTVMO

109. If in a certain code language 'LAP' is coded as 'KMZBOQ', then how will 'NOTE' be written in that language? « Syndicate Bank (Clerk) 2011

(a) MONPSUFD (b) MONPUSDF
(c) MNOPSUDF (d) MONPSUDF
(e) None of these

110. If in a certain code language 'TOP' is written as 'OQNPSU', 'RAT' is written as 'SUZBQS', then how will 'GUN' be coded in that language?

(a) MTOHFV (b) MOTHFV
(c) MOTVHF (d) MOTVFH

111. If in a certain code language 'RAM' is written as 'QSZBLN', 'LOVE' is written as 'KMNPUWDF', then how will 'ACT' be written in that language?

(a) ZBBDSU (b) ZBBDUS
(c) ZBDBSU (d) ZDSUBB

112. If in a certain code language 'NAME' is written as 'MOZBLNDF', 'PUN' is written as 'OQTVMO', then how will 'TALK' be coded in that language?

(a) SUZBKMJL (b) SUZBKMLT
(c) SUZKBMLT (d) SUZKBIML

113. If in a certain code, HORSE is written as GINPQSRTDF, how will JOCKEY be written in that language ? « SSC CPO 2019

(a) IKNPBDJLDFXZ (b) IKNPDBJLFDZX
(c) KINPBDJLDFZX (d) KIPNBDJLDFXZ

114. If in a certain code language 'PICK' is coded as 'OQHJBDJL', then how will 'FLAT' be written in that language?

(a) EGKMZBSU (b) EGKMZBUS
(c) EGKMBZSU (d) EKGMZBSU

115. In a certain code language 'CHAT' is written as 'SUZBGIBD'. How will 'APT' be coded in that language?

(a) SUOBZQ (b) SUOZQB
(c) SUOQBZ (d) SUOQZB

116. In a certain code language 'PINKY' is coded as 'XZJLMOHJOQ'. How will 'VANDY' be coded in that language?

(a) XZCEMOZBUW (b) XZCEMOZBWU
(c) XZECMOBZUW (d) ZXCEMOZBWU

117. If in a certain code language 'TRUE' is coded as 'USSQVTFD', then what is the code for 'PRAY' in the same language?

(a) QSOQBZXZ (b) QOSQBZXZ
(c) QOSQBZZX (d) QOSBQZZX

Answers WITH EXPLANATIONS

1. (*c*) As

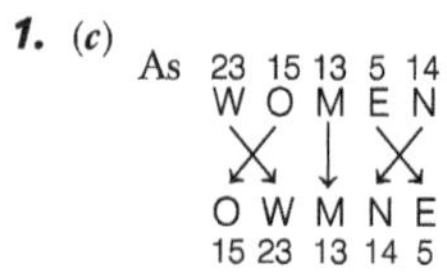

Similarly,

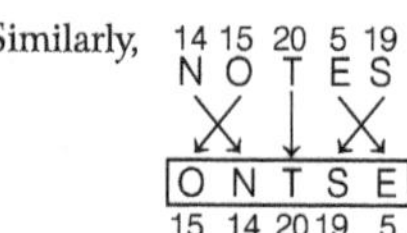

∴ NOTES ⇒ ONTSE

2. (*d*) As, NOVEMBER → REBMEVON
(1 2 3 4 5 6 7 8 → 8 7 6 5 4 3 2 1)

and DECEMBER → REBMECED
(1 2 3 4 5 6 7 8 → 8 7 6 5 4 3 2 1)

Similarly, OCTOBER → REBOTCO
(1 2 3 4 5 6 7 → 7 6 5 4 3 2 1)

3. (*b*) As,

1 2 3 4 5 6 7 8
G I G A N T I C

G I G T A N C I
1 2 3 6 4 5 8 7

Similarly,

1 2 3 4 5 6 7 8
M I R A C L E S

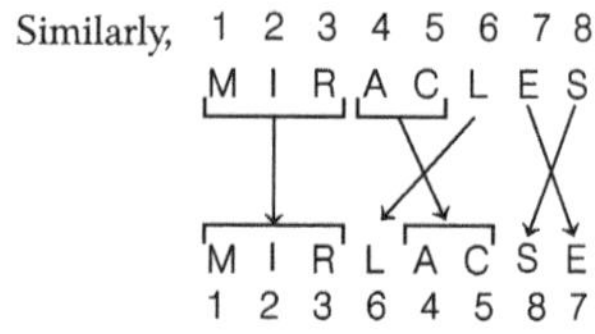

M I R L A C S E
1 2 3 6 4 5 8 7

∴ MIRACLES ⇒ MIRLACSE

4. (*c*) As, EXPLAINING → PXEALNIGNI
(1 2 3 4 5 6 7 8 9 10 → 3 2 1 5 4 7 6 10 9 8)

Similarly, PRODUCED → ORPUDDEC
(1 2 3 4 5 6 7 8 → 3 2 1 5 4 8 7 6)

∴ PRODUCED ⇒ ORPUDDEC

Here, the first three and the last letters are reversed as pairs and the rest of the letters are reversed in pair of two letters.

5. (*a*) As, SYSTEM → SYSMET
(1 2 3 4 5 6 → 3 2 1 6 5 4)

and NEARER → AENRER
(1 2 3 4 5 6 → 3 2 1 6 5 4)

Similarly, FRACTION → CARFNOIT
(1 2 3 4 5 6 7 8 → 4 3 2 1 8 7 6 5)

∴ FRACTION ⇒ CARFNOIT

Here, the first half and second half of letter are within the reverse order.

6. (*d*)

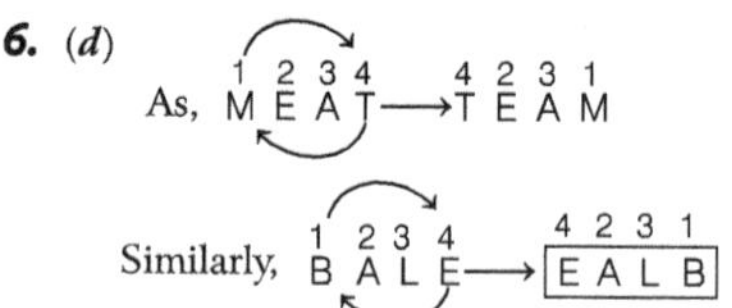

∴ BALE ⇒ EALB

7. (*a*) As,

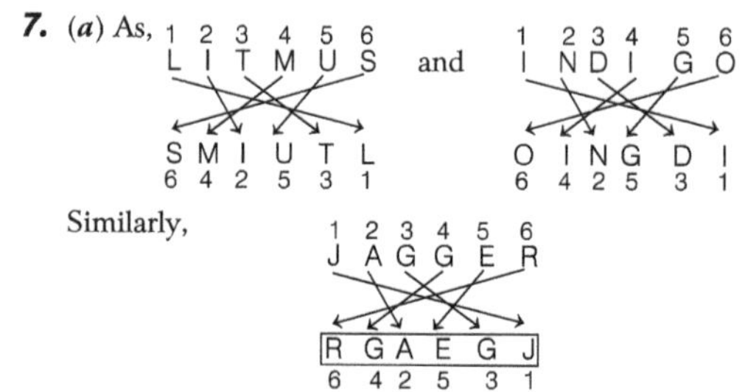

∴ JAGGER ⇒ RGAEGJ

8. (*d*) As,

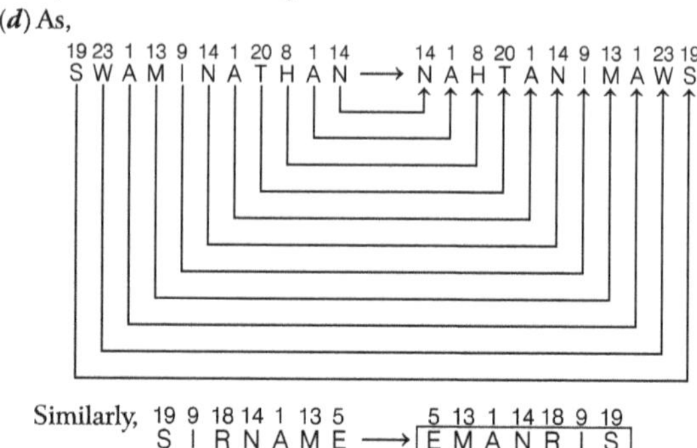

Similarly,

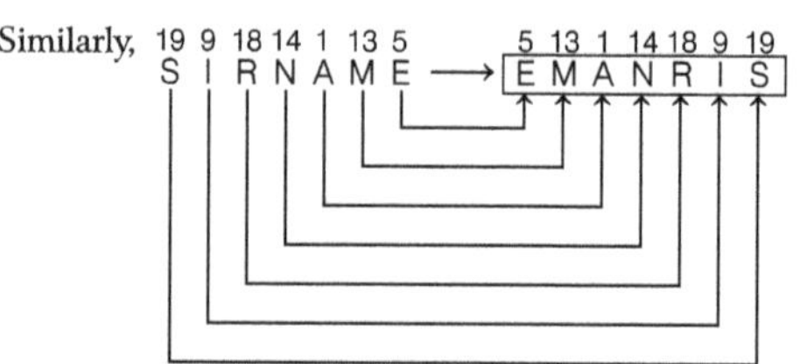

∴ SIRNAME ⇒ EMANRIS

9. (*c*) As, BREAKDOWN → NWODKAERB
(1 2 3 4 5 6 7 8 9 → 9 8 7 6 5 4 3 2 1)

Similarly, TRIANGLES → SELGNAIRT
(1 2 3 4 5 6 7 8 9 → 9 8 7 6 5 4 3 2 1)

∴ TRIANGLES ⇒ SELGNAIRT

10. (*a*) As,

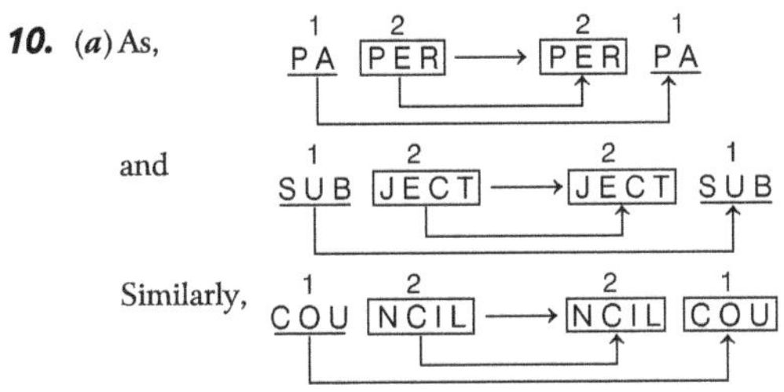

∴ COUNCIL ⇒ NCILCOU

11. (*b*) As, D A U G H T E R → T E R D A U G H
1 2 3 4 5 6 7 8 → 6 7 8 1 2 3 4 5

Similarly, A P T I T U D E → U D E A P T I T
1 2 3 4 5 6 7 8 → 6 7 8 1 2 3 4 5

∴ APTITUDE ⇒ UDEAPTIT

12. (*d*) As, STOVE (1 2 3 4 5) —Reverse order→ EVOTS (5 4 3 2 1)

and CANDLE (1 2 3 4 5 6) —Reverse order→ ELDNAC (6 5 4 3 2 1)

Similarly, REPORT (1 2 3 4 5 6) —Reverse order→ TROPER (6 5 4 3 2 1)

∴ REPORT ⇒ TROPER

13. (*c*) As, R E F R I G E R A T O R
1 2 3 4 5 6 7 8 9 10 11 12
→ R O T A R E G I R F E R
12 11 10 9 8 7 6 5 4 3 2 1

Similarly, A M M U N I T I O N
1 2 3 4 5 6 7 8 9 10 →
N O I T I N U M M A
10 9 8 7 6 5 4 3 2 1

∴ AMMUNITION ⇒ NOITINUMMA

Here, all letters are coded in reverse order.

14. (*a*)

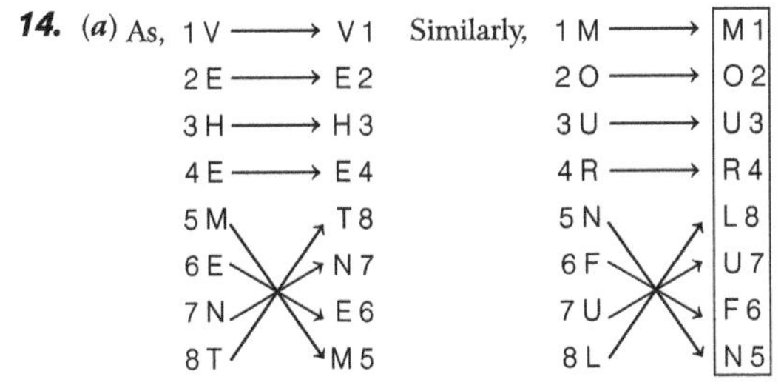

∴ MOURNFUL ⇒ MOURLUFN

15. (*d*)

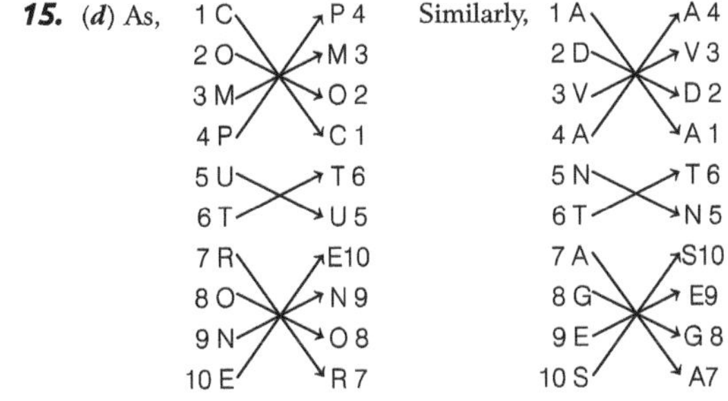

∴ ADVANTAGES ⇒ AVDATNSEGA

16. (*a*) As, E X E C U T I V E → T C I E U X V E E
1 2 3 4 5 6 7 8 9 → 6 4 7 3 5 2 8 1 9

Similarly, M A U S O L E U M → L S E U O A U M M
1 2 3 4 5 6 7 8 9 → 6 4 7 3 5 2 8 1 9

∴ MAUSOLEUM ⇒ LSEUOAUMM

17. (*d*) As,

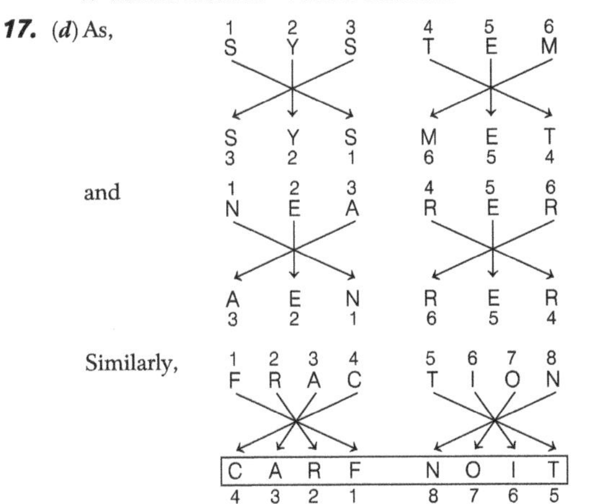

∴ FRACTION ⇒ CARFNOIT

18. (*b*) As,

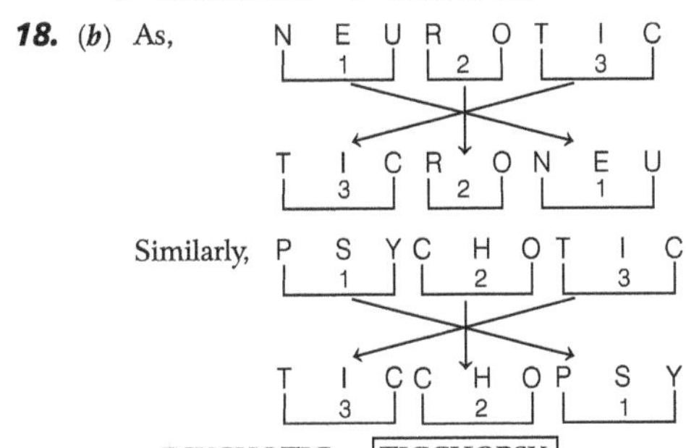

∴ PSYCHOTIC ⇒ TICCHOPSY

19. (*b*) As, B (2) R (18) A (1) I (9) N (14) —(+1 each)→ C (3) S (19) B (2) J (10) O (15)

Similarly, M (13) A (1) K (11) E (5) R (18) —(+1 each)→ N (14) B (2) L (12) F (6) S (19)

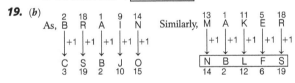

∴ MAKER ⇒ NBLFS

20. (*a*) As,

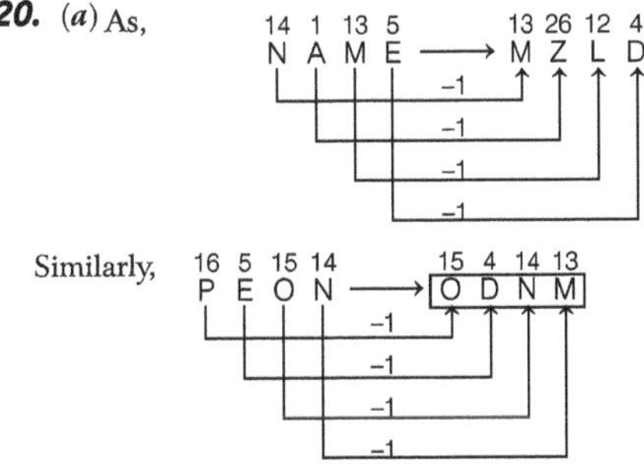

∴ PEON ⇒ ODNM

21. (*d*) In a certain code language, PAISE is coded as QBJTF

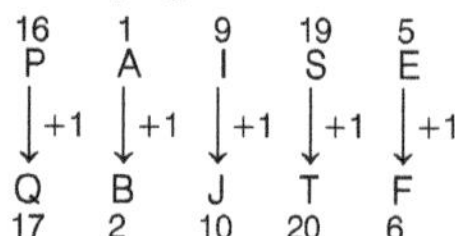

The above code follow a pattern of +1 in alphabetical position.

Also, CEASE is coded as DFBTF

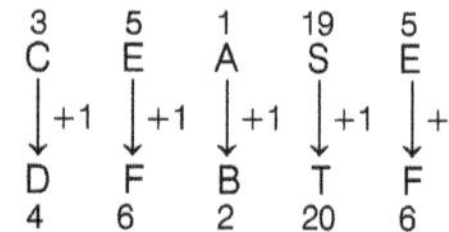

The above code also follow a pattern of +1 in alphabetical position.

Similarly, we can write the code for the word TRANGLE.

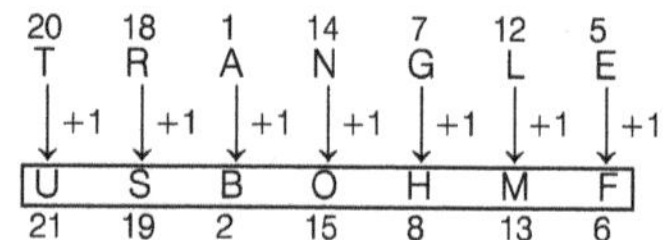

∴ TRANGLE ⇒ USBOHMF

22. (*a*) As,

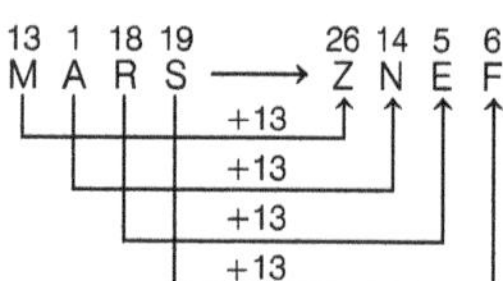

Similarly,

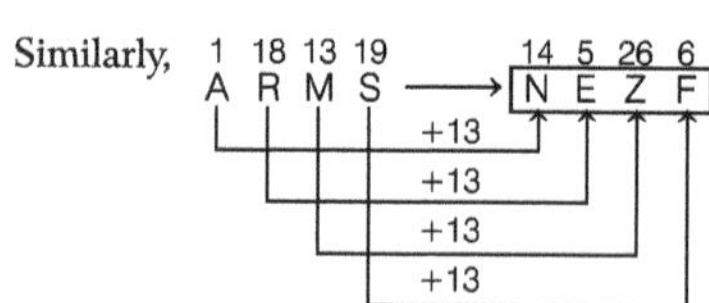

∴ ARMS ⇒ NEZF

23. (*c*) As,

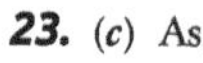

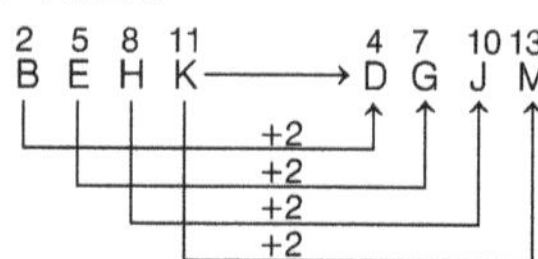

Similarly,

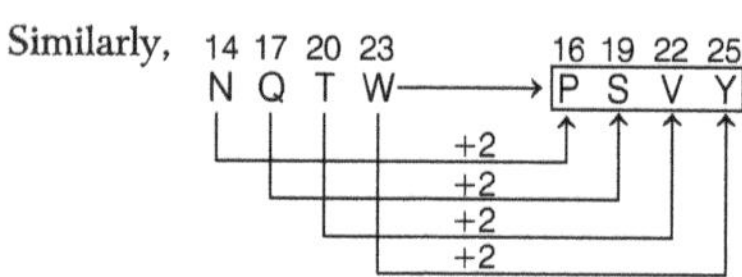

∴ NQTW ⇒ PSVY

24. (*b*) As,

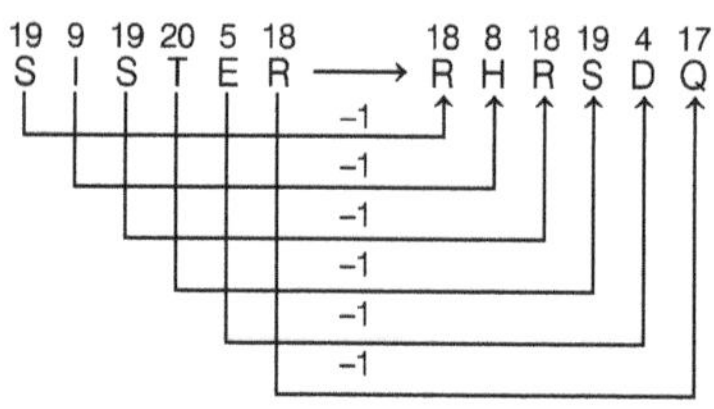

Similarly,

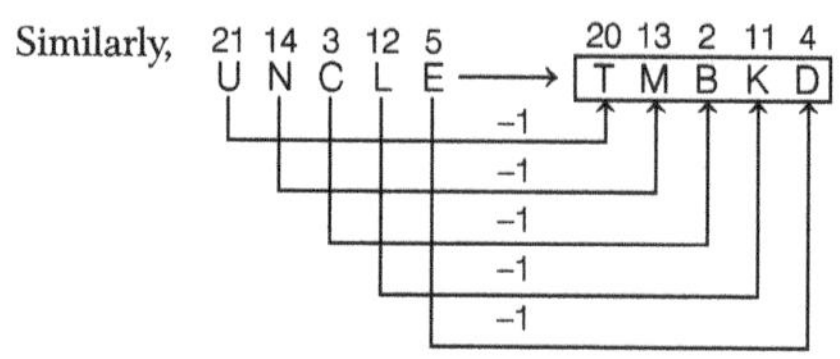

∴ UNCLE ⇒ TMBKD

25. (*b*) As,

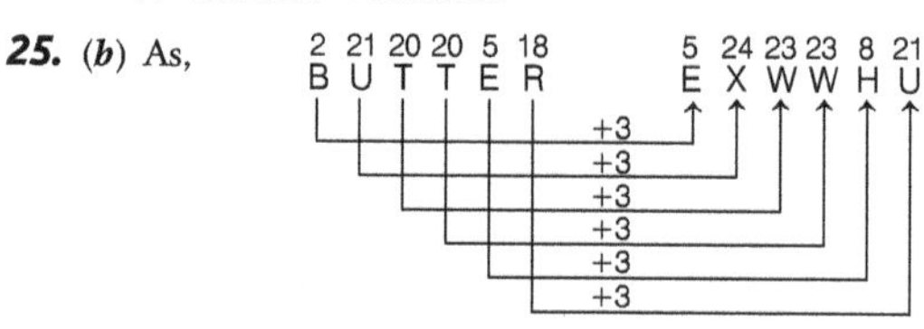

And

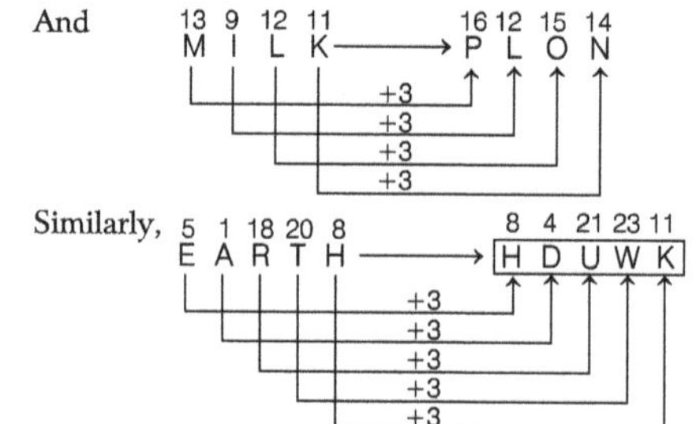

Similarly,

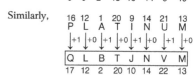

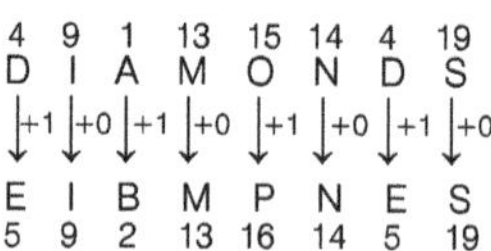

∴ EARTH ⇒ HDUWK

26. (*d*) As,

4 9 1 13 15 14 4 19
D I A M O N D S
+1 +0 +1 +0 +1 +0 +1 +0
E I B M P N E S
5 9 2 13 16 14 5 19

Similarly,

16 12 1 20 9 14 21 13
P L A T I N U M
+1 +0 +1 +0 +1 +0 +1 +0
Q L B T J N V M
17 12 2 20 10 14 22 13

∴ PLATINUM ⇒ QLBTJNVM

27. (*a*) As,

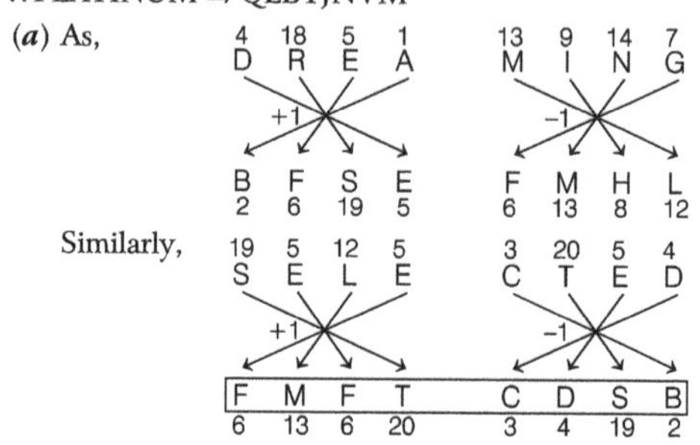

∴ SELECTED ⇒ FMFTCDSB

28. (*d*) As,

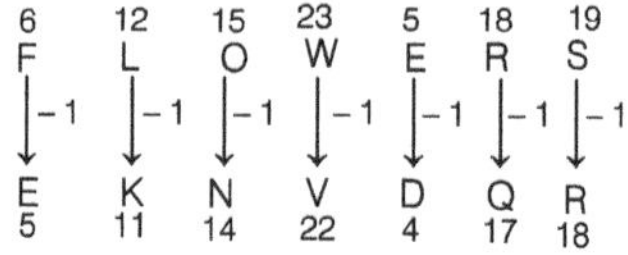

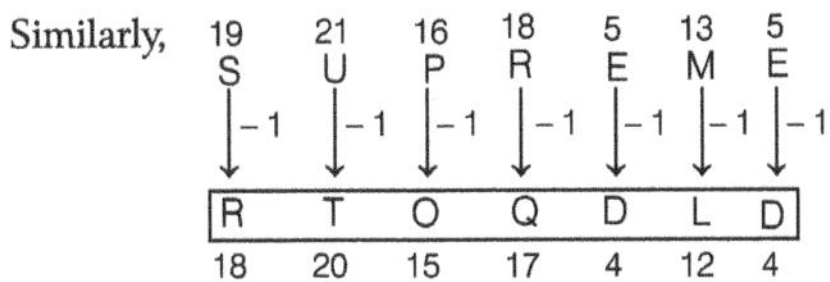

∴ SUPREME ⇒ RTOQDLD

29. (*b*) As,

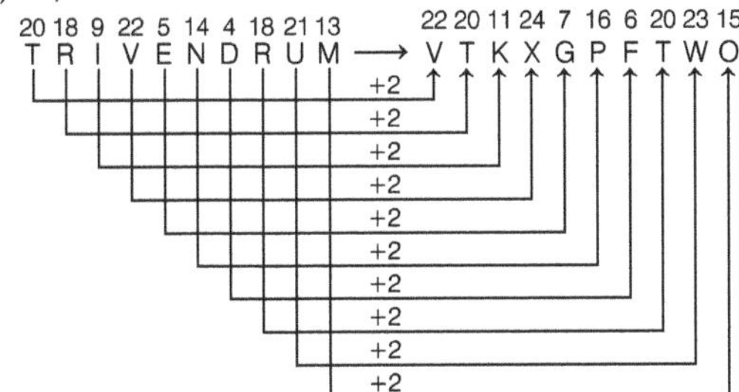

Similarly,

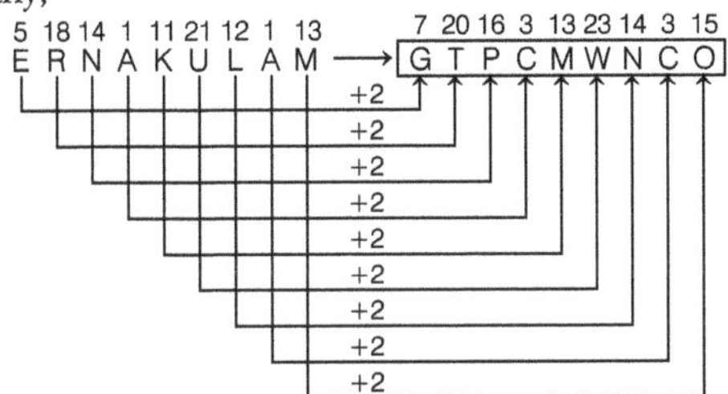

∴ ERNAKULAM ⇒ GTPCMWNCO

30. (*b*) As,

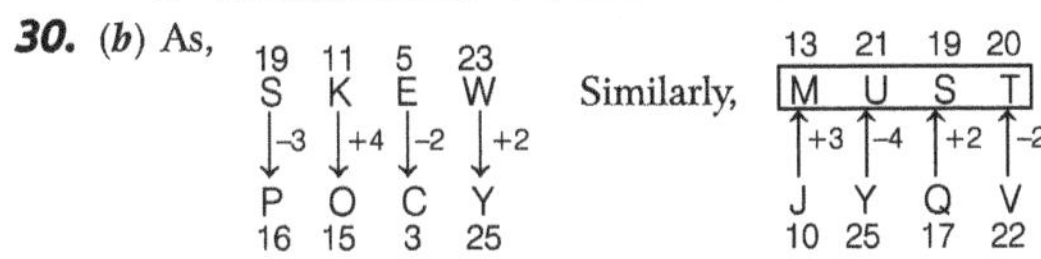

∴ MUST ⇒ JYQV

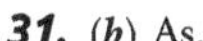

31. (*b*) As,

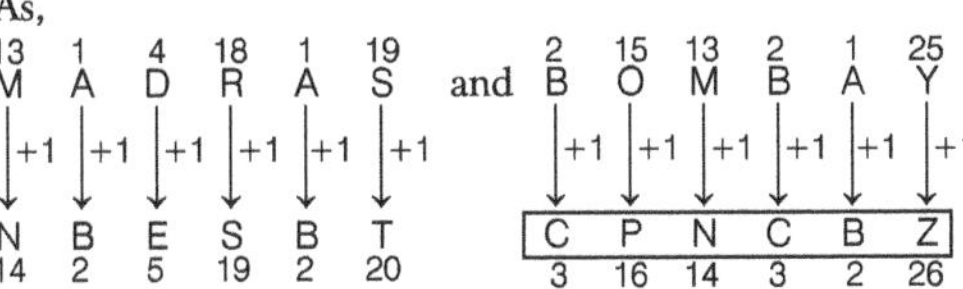

∴ BOMBAY ⇒ CPNCBZ

32. (*c*) As,

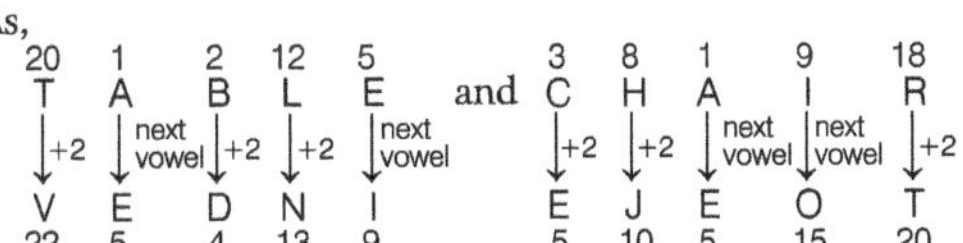

In this coding, the consonants are coded by the letters which are two places ahead of them and the vowels are coded with the next vowel according to the alphabetical series.

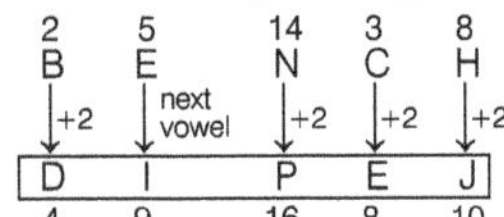

33. (*a*) As,

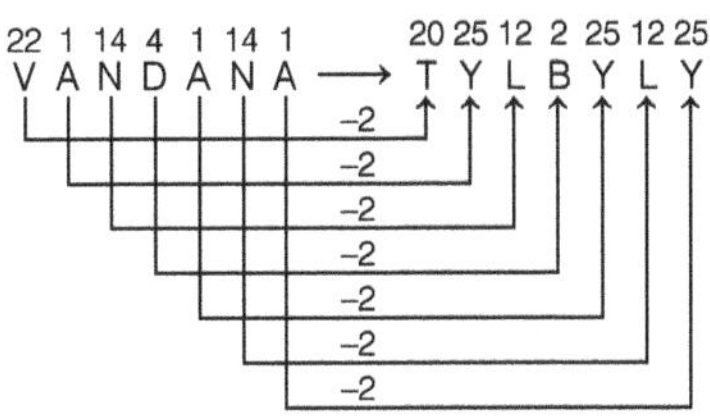

and

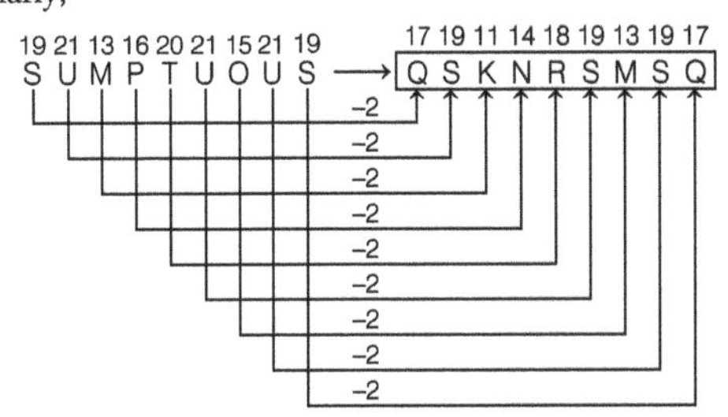

∴ LAVISH ⇒ JUKXCN

34. (*b*) As,

Similarly,

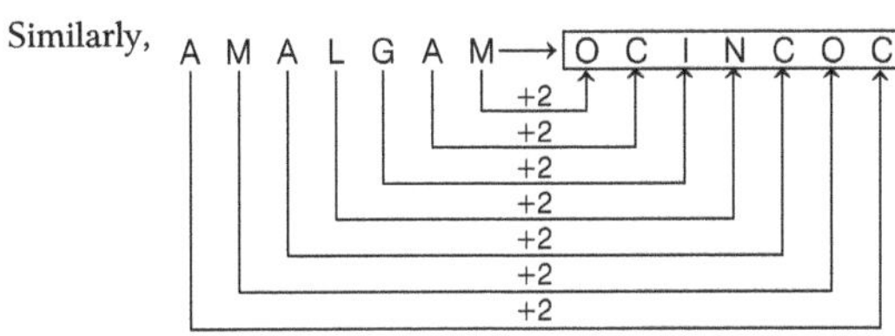

35. (*b*) As,

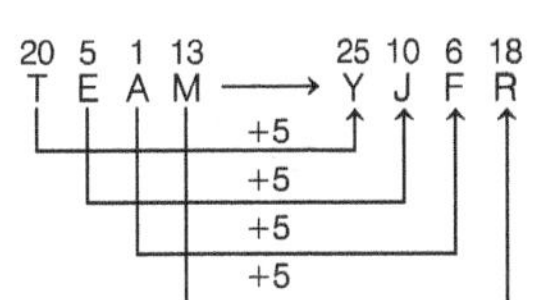

Similarly,

3 18 5 1 20 5
C R E A T E ⟶ H W J F Y J
8 23 10 6 25 10
+5 +5 +5 +5 +5 +5

∴ CREATE ⇒ HWJFYJ

36. (*a*) As,

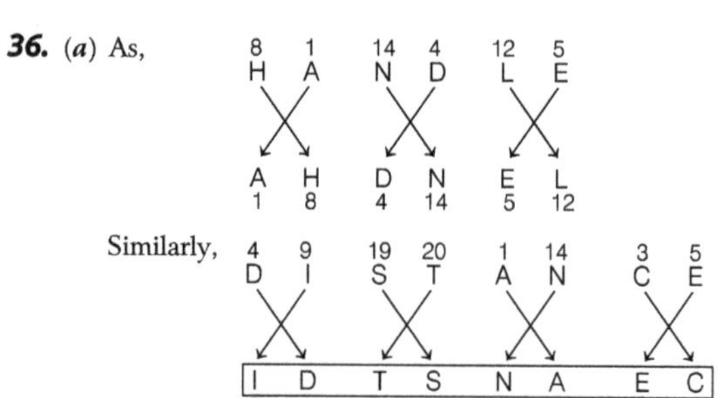

Similarly,

∴ DISTANCE ⇒ IDTSNAEC

37. (*c*) As,

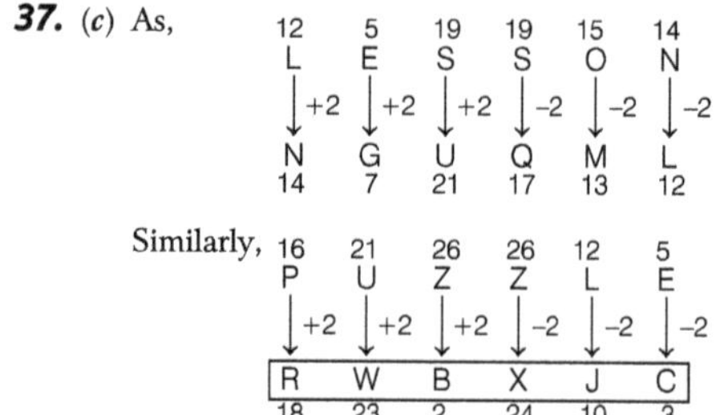

Similarly,

∴ PUZZLE ⇒ RWBXJC

38. (*c*) As,

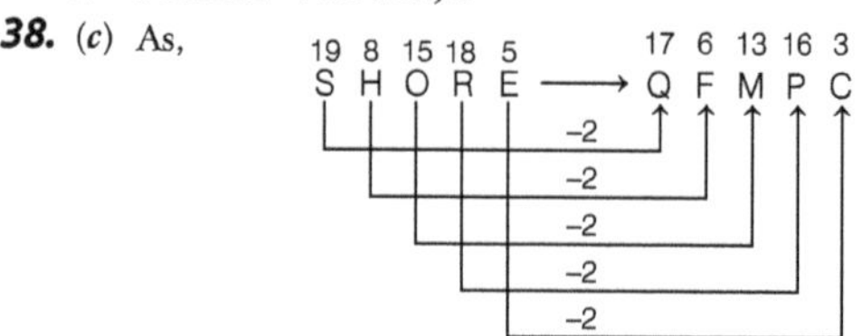

Similarly,

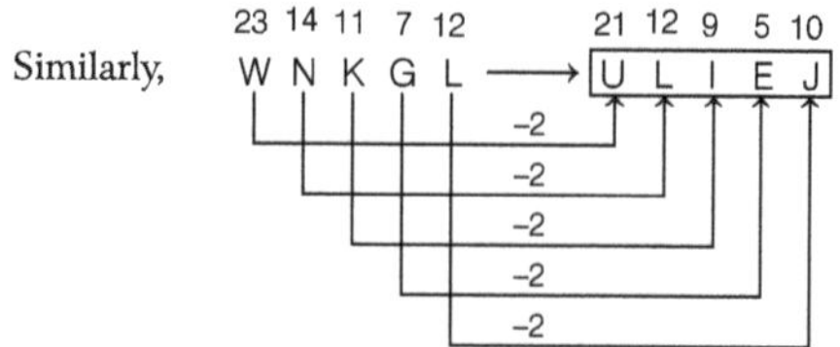

∴ WNKGL ⇒ ULIEJ

39. (*a*) As, Similarly,

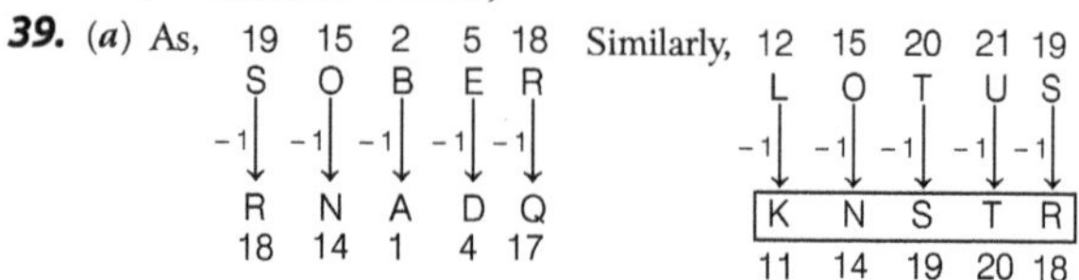

∴ LOTUS ⇒ KNSTR

40. (*d*) As,

Similarly,

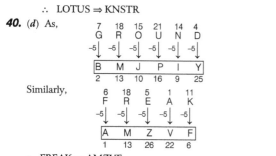

∴ FREAK ⇒ AMZVF

41. (*a*) As, Similarly,

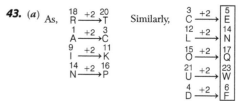

42. (*c*) As, Similarly,

∴ BRICK ⇒ DTKEM

43. (*a*) As, Similarly,

∴ CLOUD ⇒ ENQWF

44. (*c*) As,

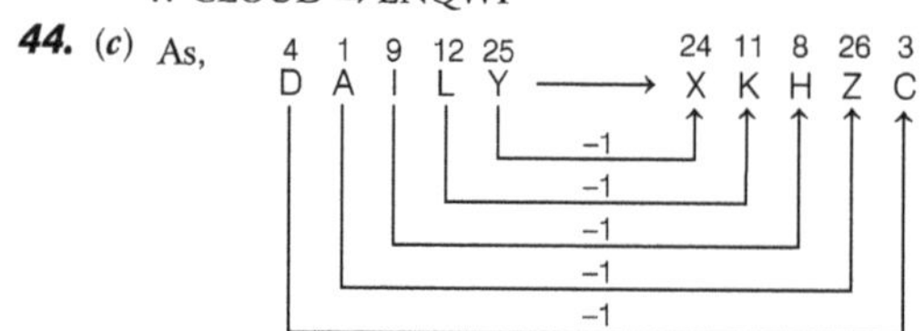

Similarly,

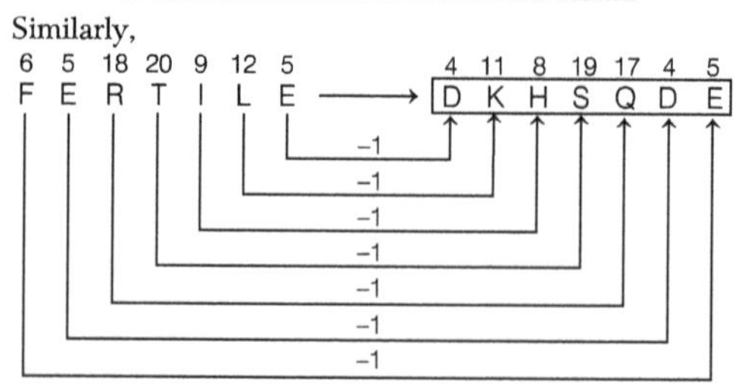

∴ FERTILE ⇒ DKHSQDE

45. (*c*) As,

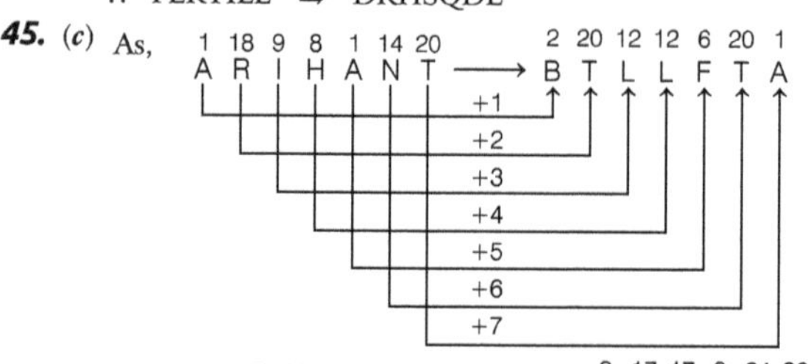

Similarly,

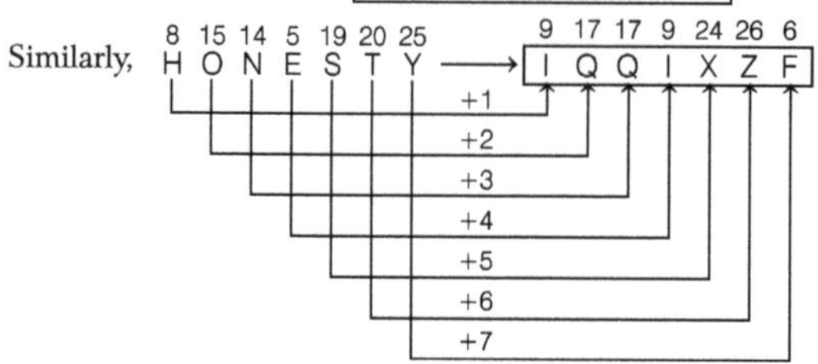

∴ HONESTY ⇒ IQQIXZF

46. (*d*) As,

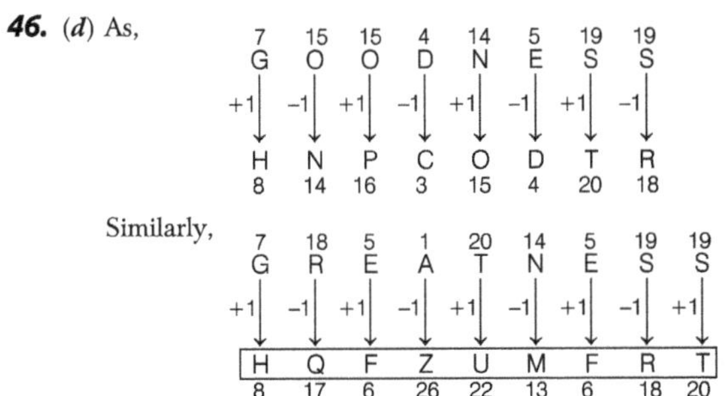

Similarly,

∴ GREATNESS ⇒ HQFZUMFRT

47. (*c*) As,

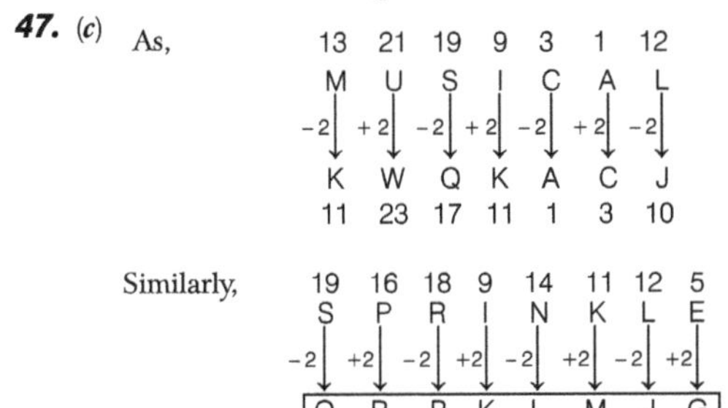

Similarly,

∴ SPRINKLE ⇒ QRPKLMJG

48. (*a*) As,

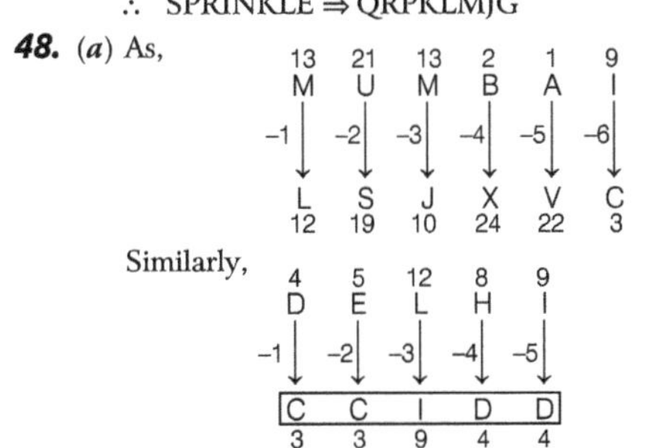

Similarly,

∴ DELHI ⇒ CCIDD

49. (*a*) As,

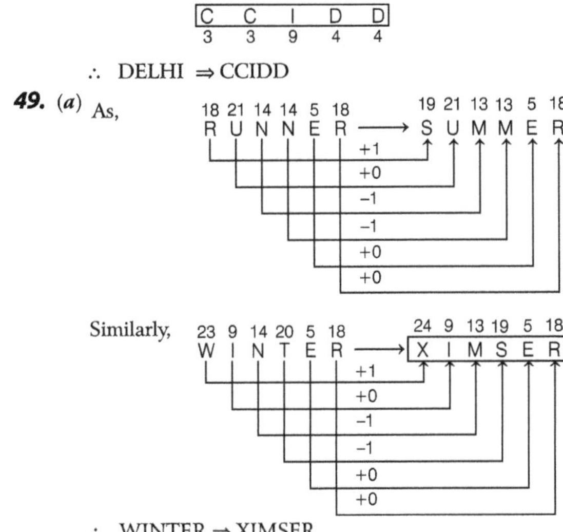

Similarly,

∴ WINTER ⇒ XIMSER

50. (*c*) As,

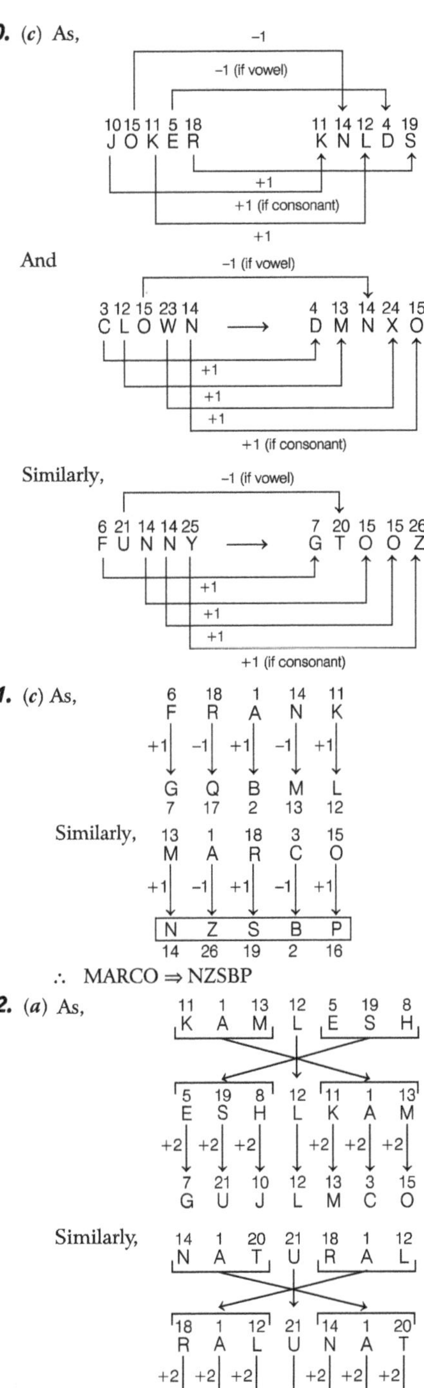

And

Similarly,

51. (*c*) As,

Similarly,

∴ MARCO ⇒ NZSBP

52. (*a*) As,

Similarly,

∴ NATURAL ⇒ TCNUPCV

53. (*d*) As,

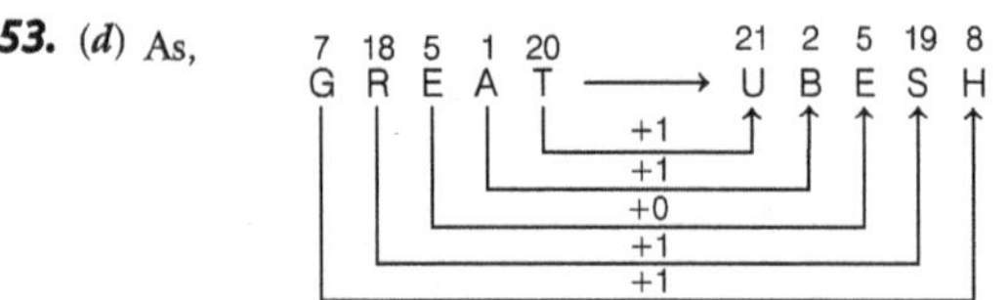

Similarly,

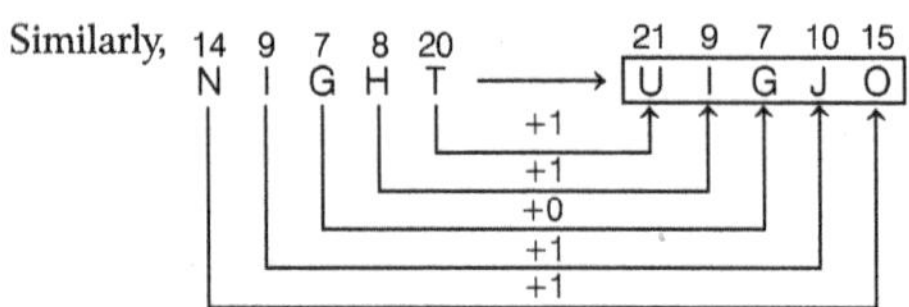

∴ NIGHT ⇒ UIGJO

54. (*b*) As,

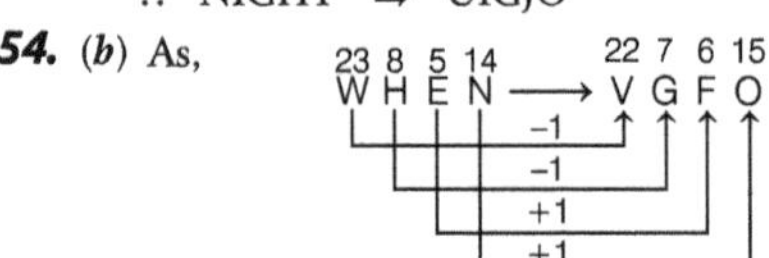

Similarly,

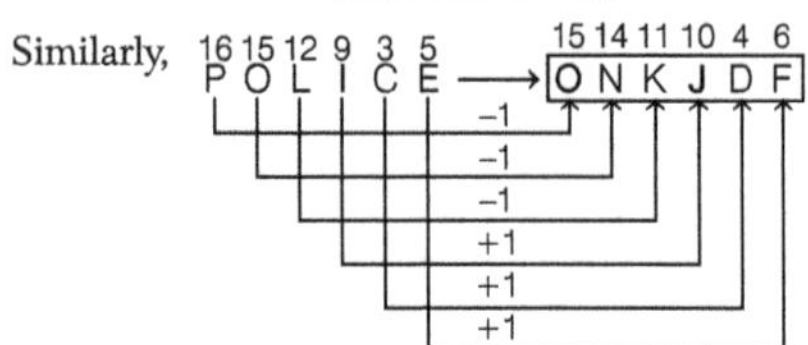

∴ POLICE ⇒ ONKJDF

55. (*b*) As,

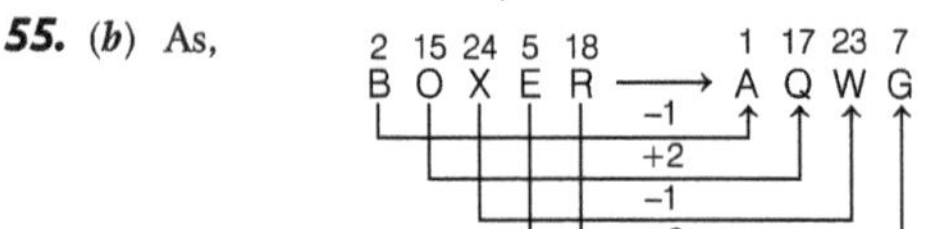

Similarly,

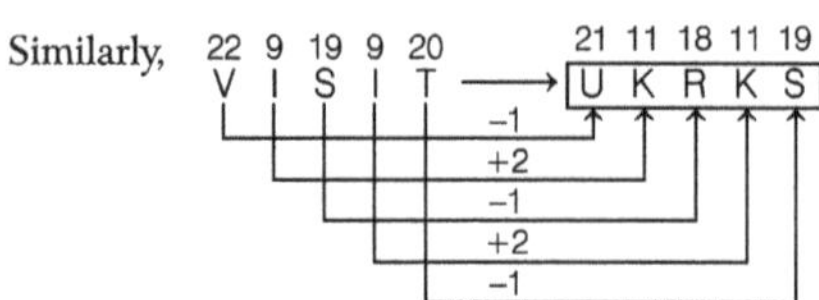

∴ VISIT ⇒ UKRKS

56. (*c*) As,

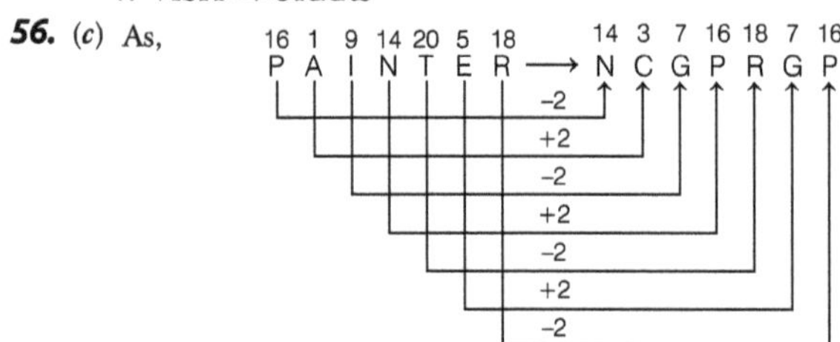

Similarly,

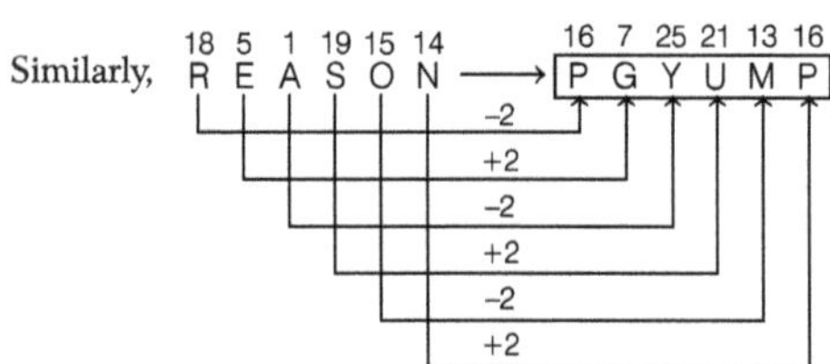

∴ REASON ⇒ PGYUMP

57. (*c*) As,

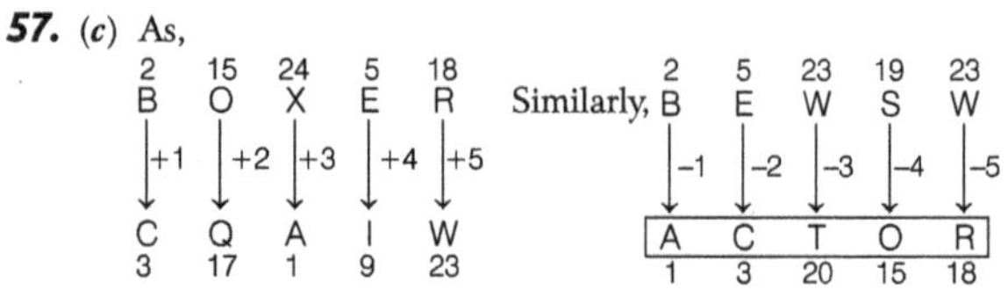

∴ BEWSW ⇒ ACTOR

58. (*c*) As,

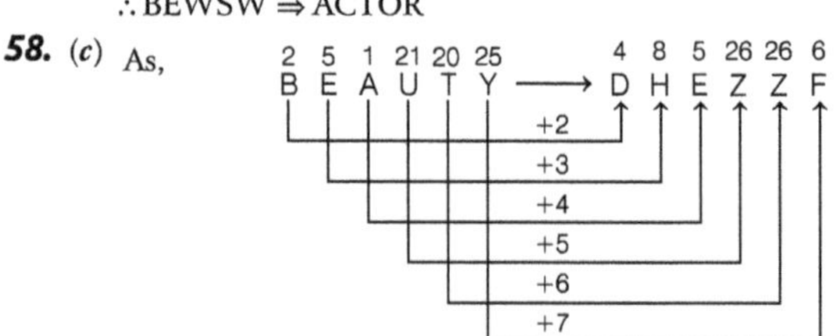

Similarly,

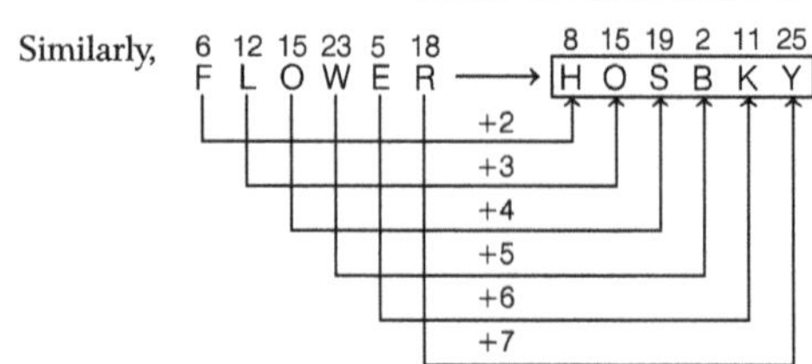

∴ FLOWER ⇒ HOSBKY

59. (*d*) As,

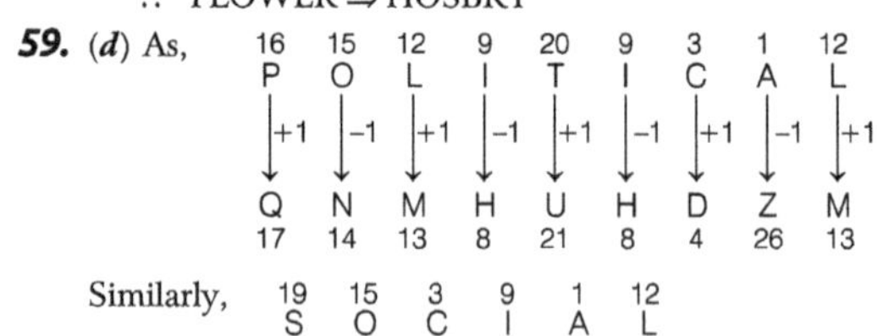

Similarly,

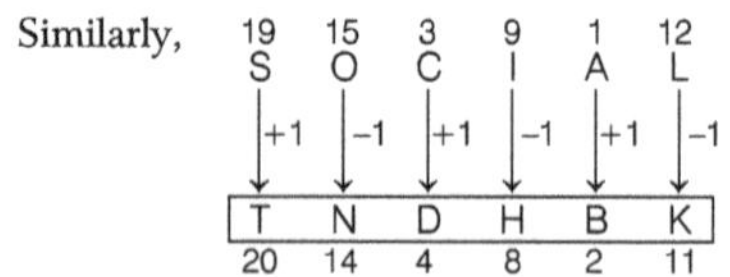

∴ SOCIAL ⇒ TNDHBK

60. (*b*) As,

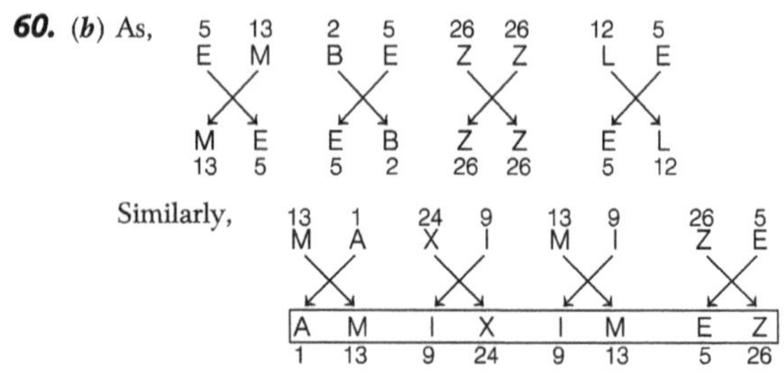

∴ MAXIMIZE ⇒ AMIXIMEZ

61. (*b*) As,

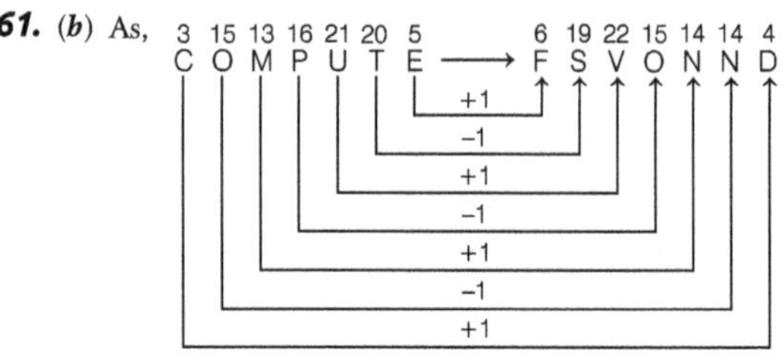

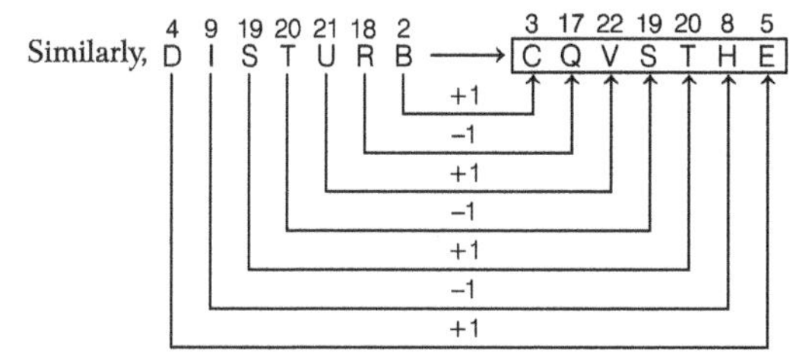

∴ DISTURB ⇒ CQVSTHE

62. (*d*) As,

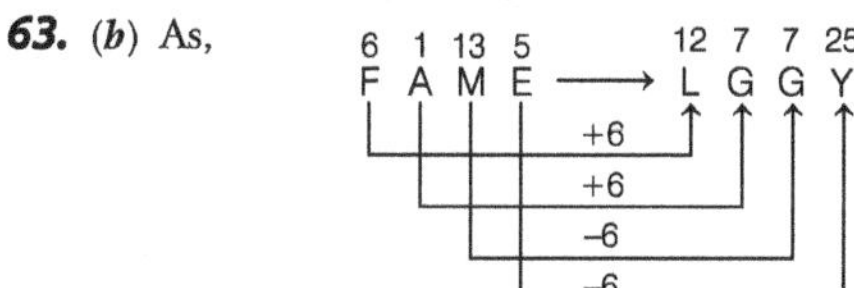

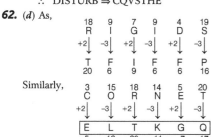

∴ CORNET ⇒ ELTKGQ

63. (*b*) As,

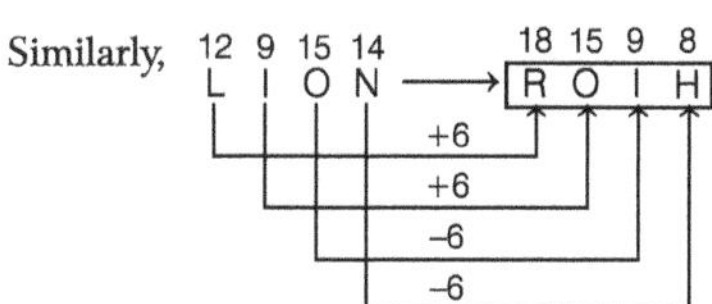

∴ LION ⇒ ROIH

64. (*d*) As,

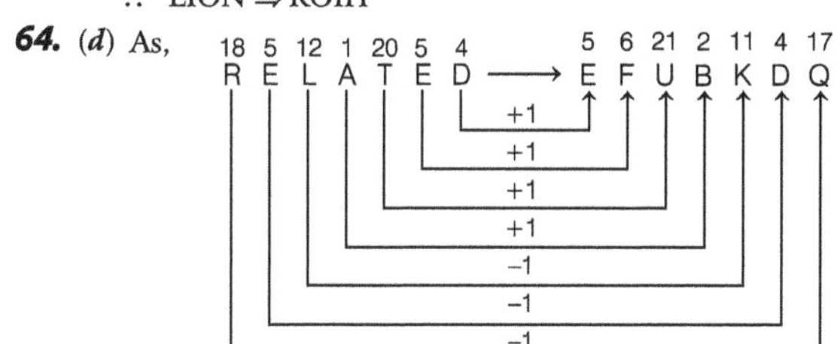

Similarly,

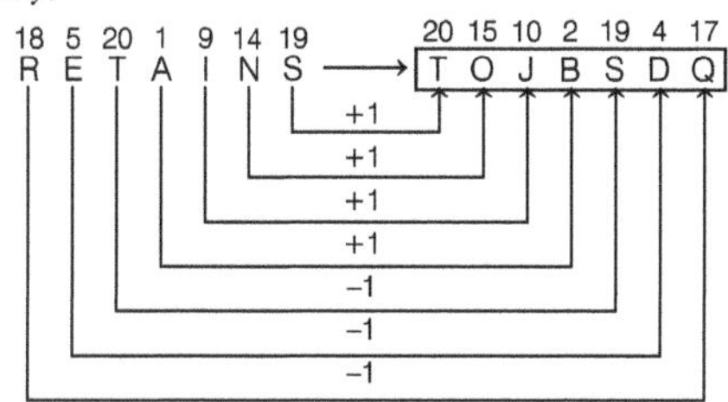

∴ RETAINS ⇒ TOJBSDQ

65. (*d*) As,

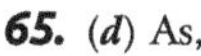

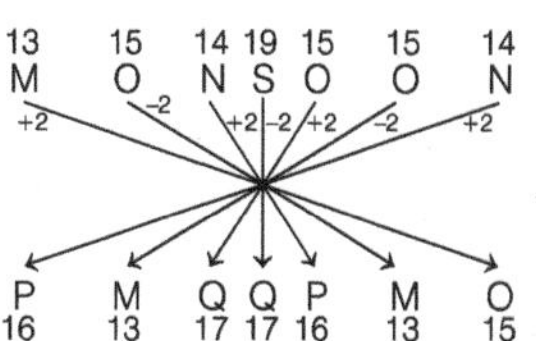

And

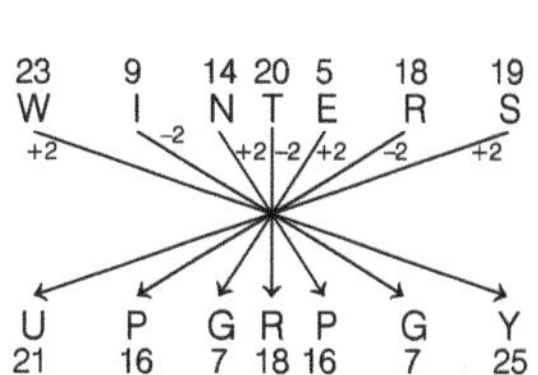

Similarly,

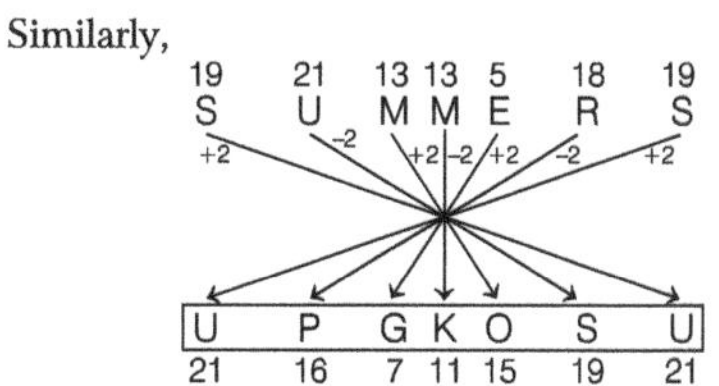

∴ SUMMER ⇒ UPGKOSU

66. (*b*) As, H A M M E R → I C P Q J X

Similarly, W R E N C H → X T H R H N

67. (*c*) As, FLOWER

∴ FLOWER ⇒ EMNXDS

68. (*a*)

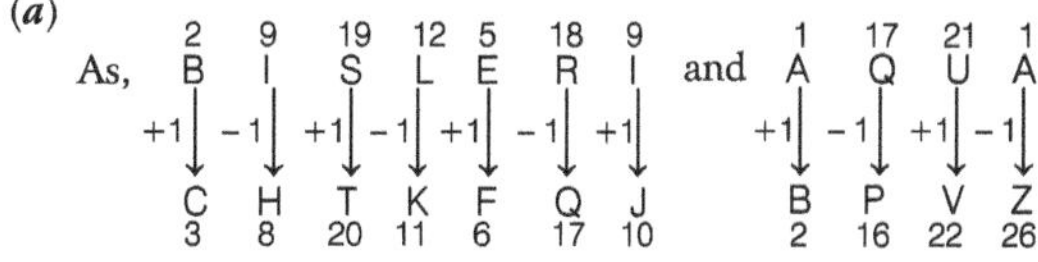

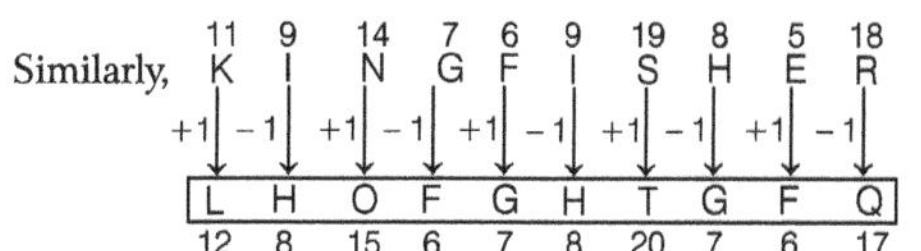

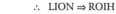

∴ KINGFISHER ⇒ LHOFGHTGFQ

69. (*a*) As,

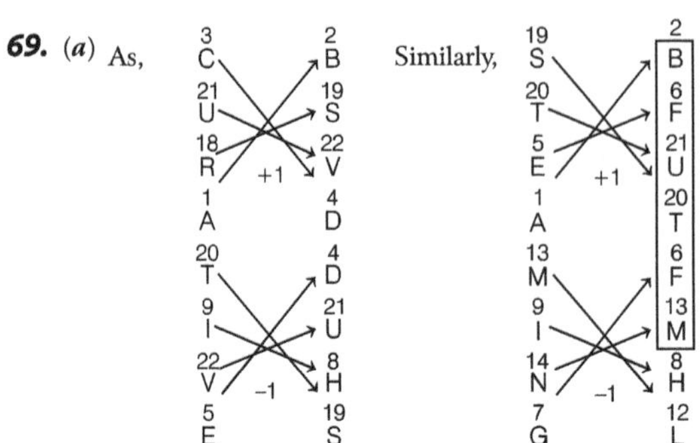

∴ STEAMING ⇒ BFUTFMHL

70. (*b*) As,

13 M $\xrightarrow{+3}$ 16 P
15 O $\xrightarrow{+3}$ 18 R
21 U ⟶ 21 U
19 S $\xrightarrow{-2}$ 17 Q
5 E $\xrightarrow{-2}$ 3 C

Similarly,

19 S $\xrightarrow{+3}$ 22 V
8 H $\xrightarrow{+3}$ 11 K
9 I ⟶ 9 I
6 F $\xrightarrow{-2}$ 4 D
20 T $\xrightarrow{-2}$ 18 R

∴ SHIFT ⇒ VKIDR

71. (*a*) As,

12 L	15 O	6 F	20 T	25 Y
↓ +0	↓ +1	↓ +0	↓ +1	↓ +0
L 12	P 16	F 6	U 21	Y 25

Similarly,

4 D	23 W	1 A	18 R	6 F
↓ +0	↓ +1	↓ +0	↓ +1	↓ +0
D 4	X 24	A 1	S 19	F 6

∴ DWARF ⇒ DXASF

72. (*b*) As,

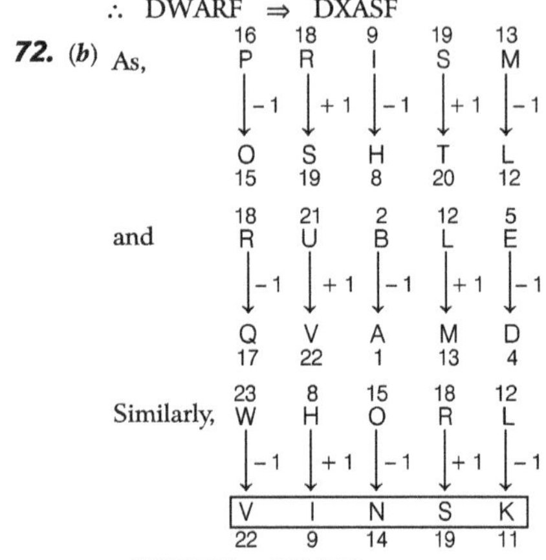

∴ WHORL ⇒ VINSK

73. (*d*) U → C, K → H, L → U, N → E, S → L, E → K, C → N

K	N	U	C	K	L	E	S
↓	↓	↓	↓	↓	↓	↓	↓
H	E	C	N	H	U	K	L

74. (*d*) As,

T	E	M	P	E	R	A	T	U	R	E
↓	↓	↓	↓	↓	↓	↓	↓	↓	↓	↓
B	Z	Q	D	Y	X	V	B	N	X	Z

Similarly,

R	A	M	P
↓	↓	↓	↓
X	V	Q	D

∴ RAMP ⇒ XVQD

75. (*c*)

R ⟶ T　　N ⟶ S
A ⟶ I　　E ⟶ H
W ⟶ N　　T ⟶ G

According to the above coded relation, we would write same code for 'WATER'

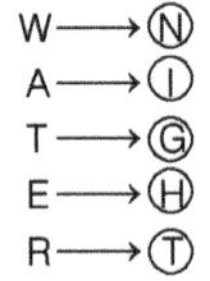

∴ WATER ⇒ NIGHT

76. (*d*) As,

F	I	F	T	Y
↓	↓	↓	↓	↓
C	A	C	T	Y

,

C	A	R
↓	↓	↓
P	O	L

and

T	A	R
↓	↓	↓
T	O	L

Similarly,

T	A	R	I	F	F
↓	↓	↓	↓	↓	↓
T	O	L	A	C	C

∴ TARIFF ⇒ TOLACC

77. (*b*) As,

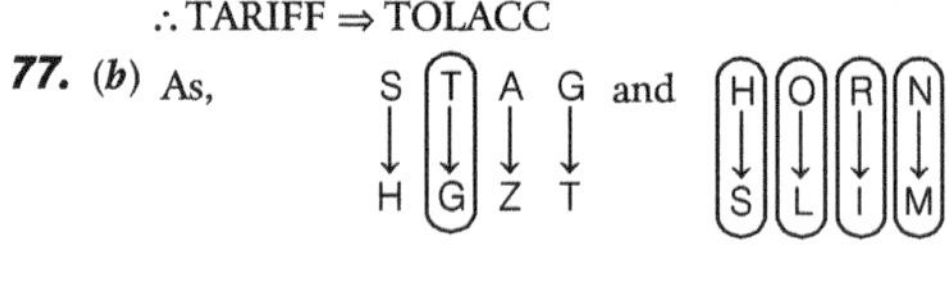

Similarly,

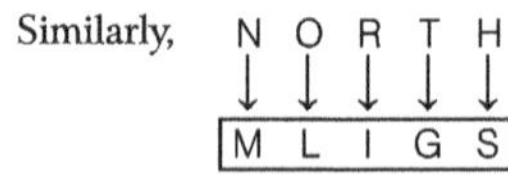

∴ NORTH ⇒ MLIGS

78. (*c*) As,

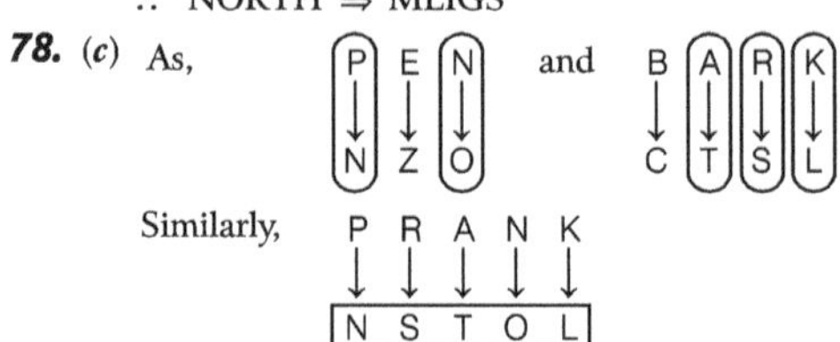

∴ PRANK ⇒ NSTOL

79. (*c*) As,

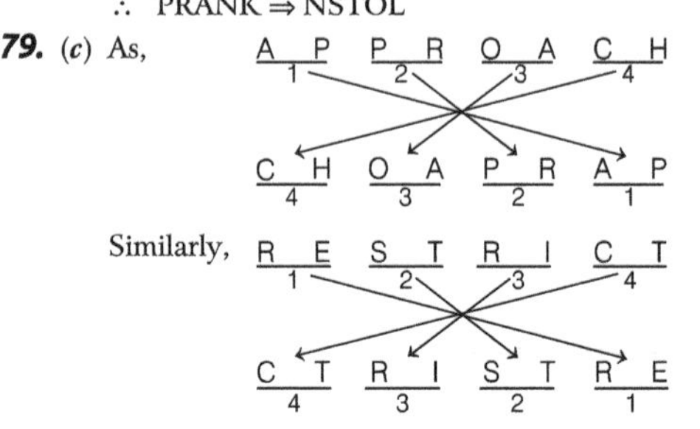

∴ RESTRICT ⇒ CTRISTRE

80. (*d*) As,

P → B, A → D, R → F, E → G, N → J, T → K

and

C → M, H → O, I → X, L → Q, D → U, R → F, E → G, N → J

Similarly,

R E P R I N T → F G B F X J K

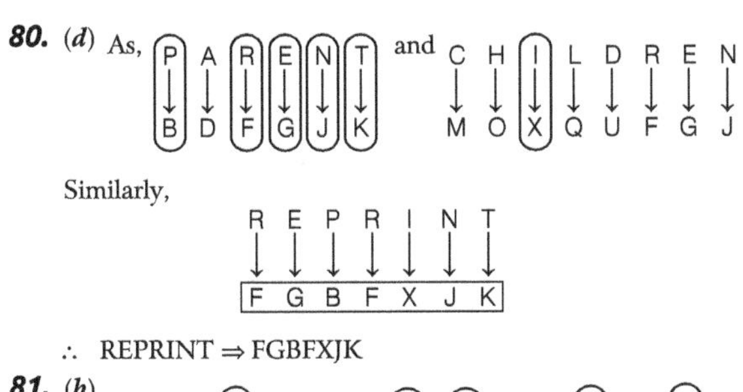

∴ REPRINT ⇒ FGBFXJK

81. (*b*) As,

T → X, A → E, B → M, L → R, E → A, C → N, L → R, O → I, T → X, H → T

Similarly, H O T E L → T I X A R

∴ HOTEL ⇒ TIXAR

82. (*b*) As,

O → B, P → W, E → D, R → A, A → T, T → X, I → P, O → B, N → J

and

P → W, A → T, R → A, E → D, N → J, T → X

Therefore, O R I E N T → B A P D J X

∴ ORIENT ⇒ BAPDJX

83. (*d*) As,

E → Q, A → P, R → M, T → Z, H → S

and

H → S, E → Q, A → P, R → M, T → Z

∴ HEART ⇒ SQPMZ

84. (*d*) As,

C (3) +1 → D (4), A → 1, N (14) +1 → O (15), D (4) +1 → E (5), L (12) +1 → M (13), E → 2

and

M (13) +1 → N (14), O → 4, D (4) +1 → E (5), E → 2, R (18) +1 → S (19), N (14) +1 → O (15)

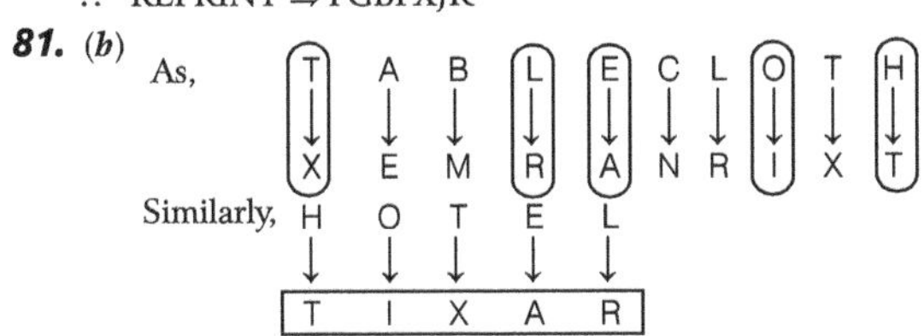

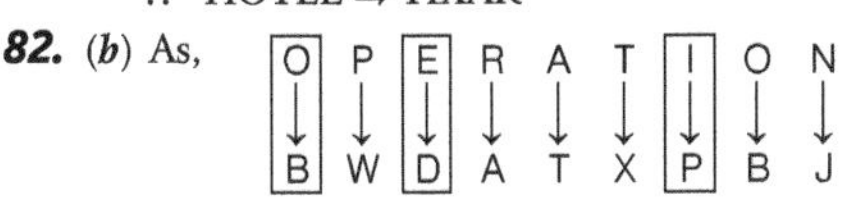

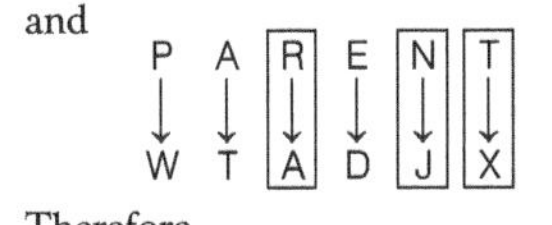

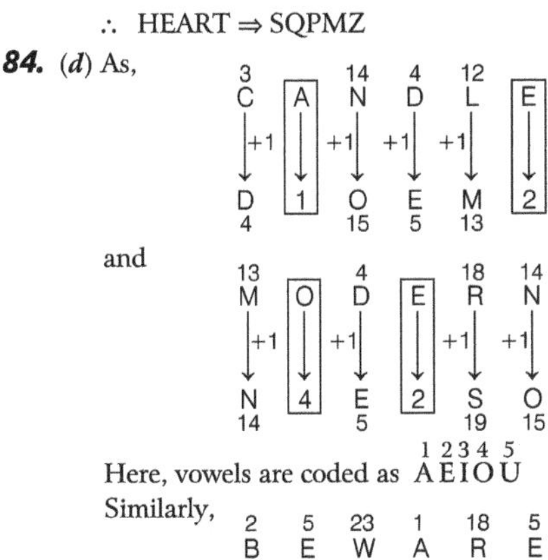

Here, vowels are coded as A E I O U (1 2 3 4 5)

Similarly,

B (2) +1 → C (3), E (5) → 2, W (23) +1 → X (24), A (1) → 1, R (18) +1 → S (19), E (5) → 2

∴ BEWARE ⇒ C2X1S2

85. (*d*) As,

A → P, P → Q, P → Q, L → R, E → S

R → A, I → B, S → C

and

M → T, A → P, N → X, G → Y, O → Z

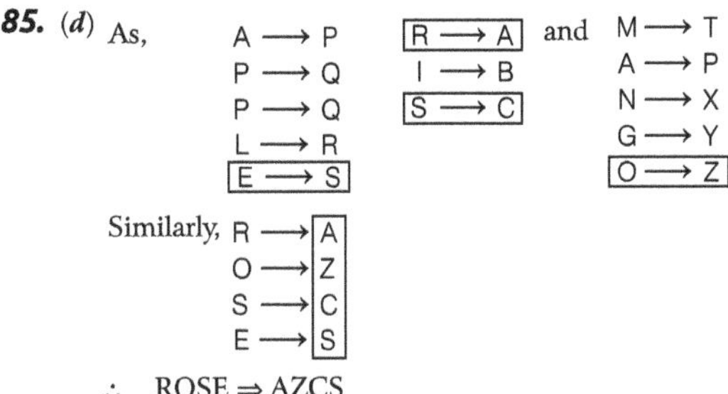

Similarly, R → A, O → Z, S → C, E → S

∴ ROSE ⇒ AZCS

86. (*a*) As,

P → F, R → L, I → O, N → W, C → E, E → R

and

P → F, R → L, I → O, N → W, C → E, E → R, S → S, S → S

Similarly, S ⟷ S, L ⟷ R, O ⟷ I, W ⟷ N, E ⟷ C, R ⟷ E, S ⟷ S

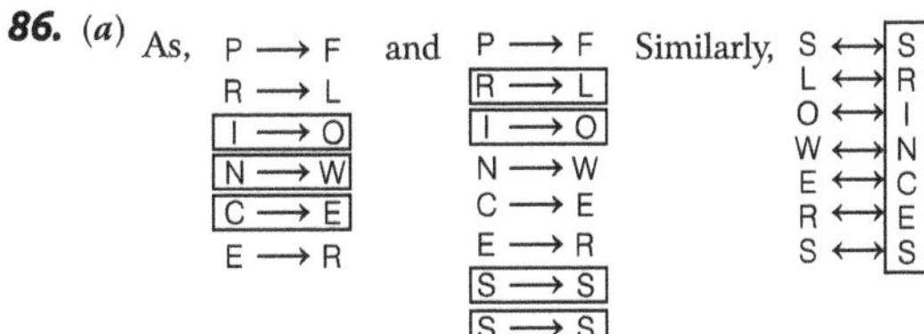

∴ SLOWERS ⇒ SRINCES

87. (*c*) As,

O → C, R → B, G → D, A → W, N → L, I → Q, S → J, A → W, T → Y, I → Q, O → C, N → L

and

O → C, P → X, E → F, R → B, A → W, T → Y, I → Q, O → C, N → L

Similarly, S → J, E → F, P → X, A → W, R → B, A → W, T → Y, I → Q, O → C, N → L

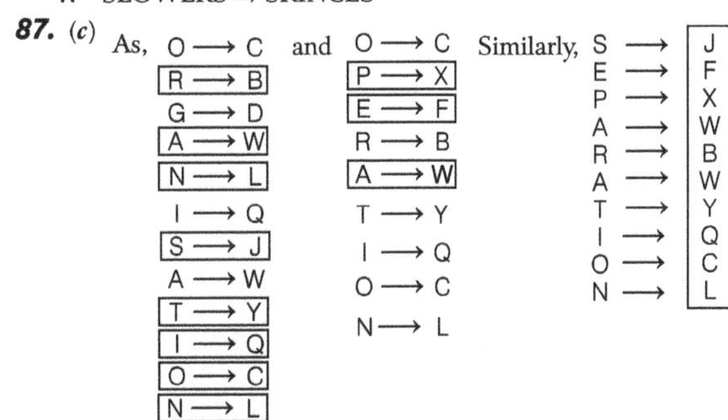

∴ SEPARATION ⇒ JFXWBWYQCL

88. (*d*) As,

Z → P, O → O, O → O, M → N

and

R → Q, O → O, A → B, D → E

Similarly, N → M, O → O, M → N, P → Z

∴ NOMP ⇒ MONZ

89. (*b*) As,

F → Q, I → H, R → O, E → E

and

M → Z, O → M, V → W, E → E

Similarly, O → M, V → W, E → E, R → O

∴ OVER ⇒ MWEO

90. (*c*) As.

F A R (12, 18) → M A F (R −5 → M, 13)

M E R → M R E

Similarly, G I W (23) A L E → R I G A E L (W −5 → R, 18)

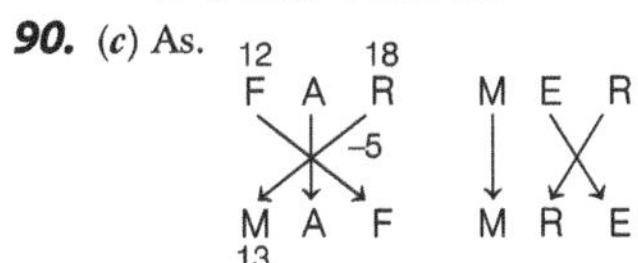

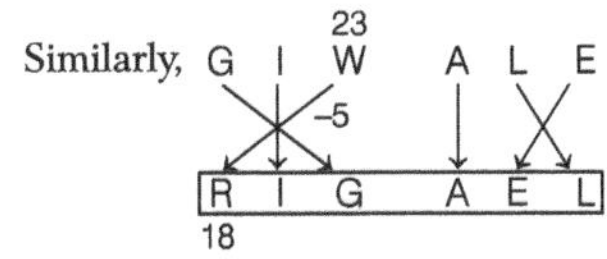

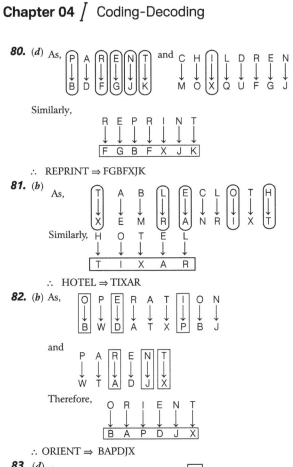

∴ GIWALE ⇒ RIGAEL

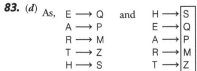

91. (*d*) As,

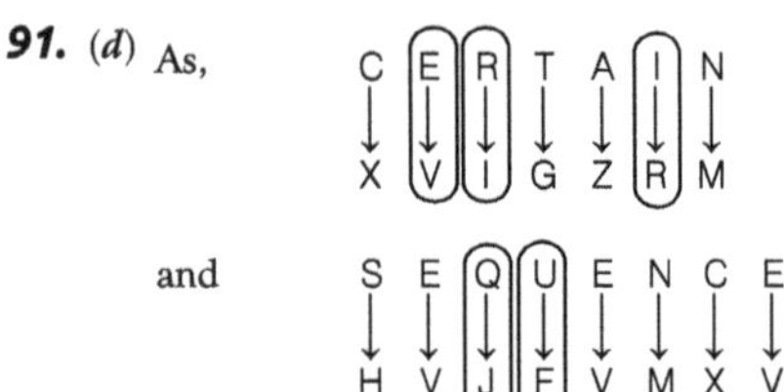

Code with opposite letters

Similarly,

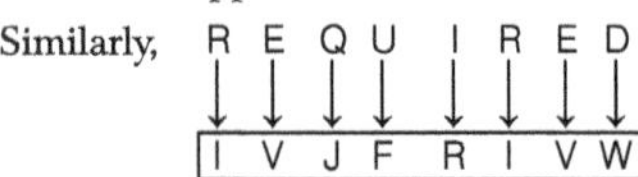

∴ REQUIRED ⇒ IVJFRIVW

92. (*b*) As,

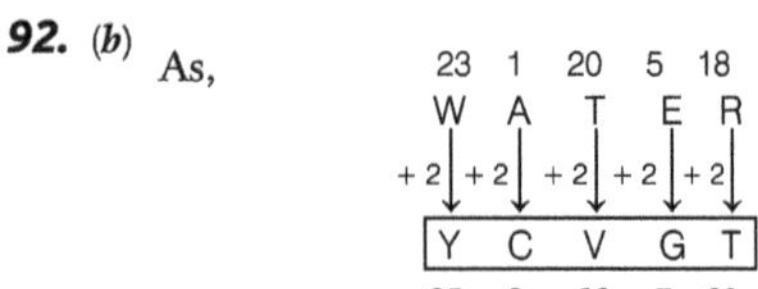

Similarly,

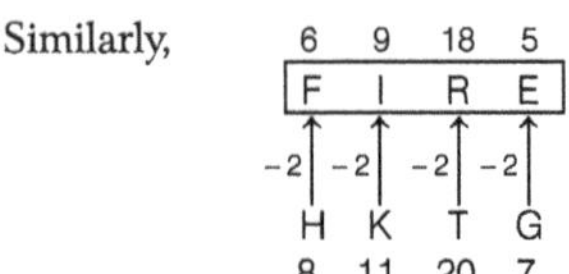

∴ FIRE ⇒ HKTG.

93. (*b*) As,

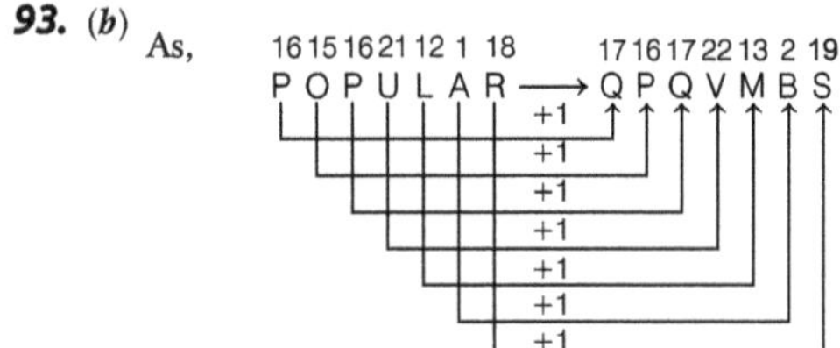

Similarly,

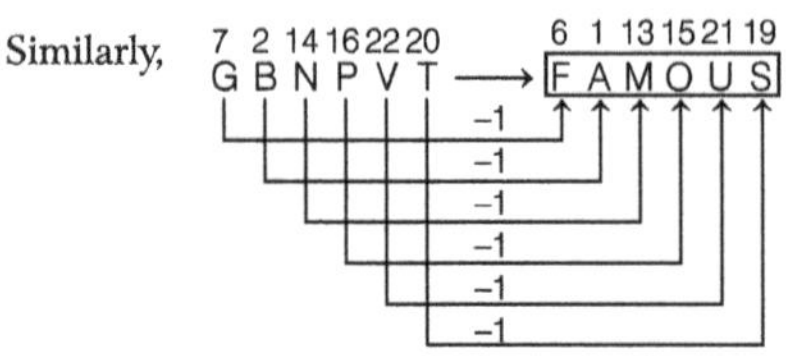

∴ GBNPVT ⇒ FAMOUS

94. (*b*) As,

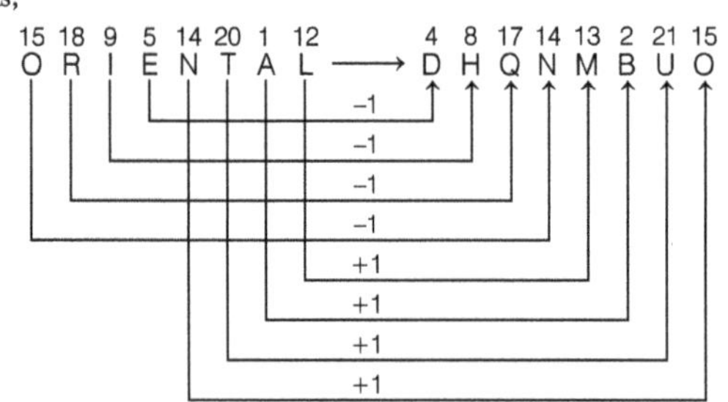

Similarly,

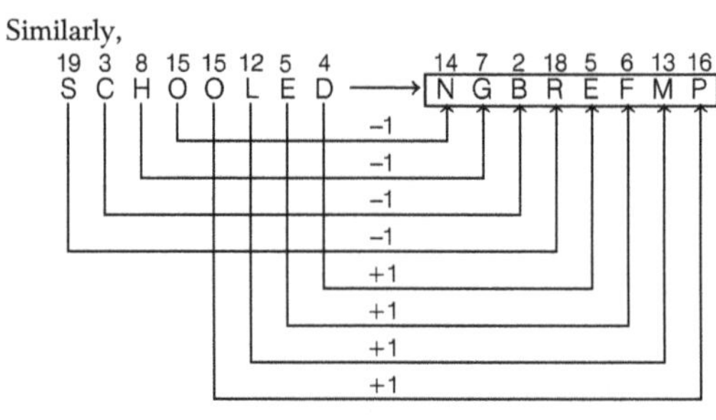

∴ SCHOOLED ⇒ NGBREFMP

95. (*c*) As,

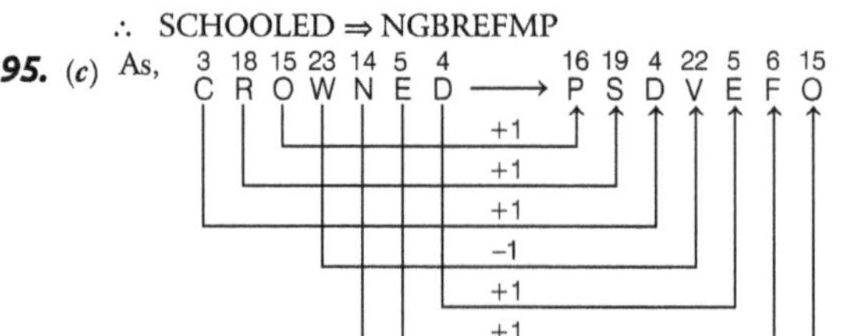

Similarly,

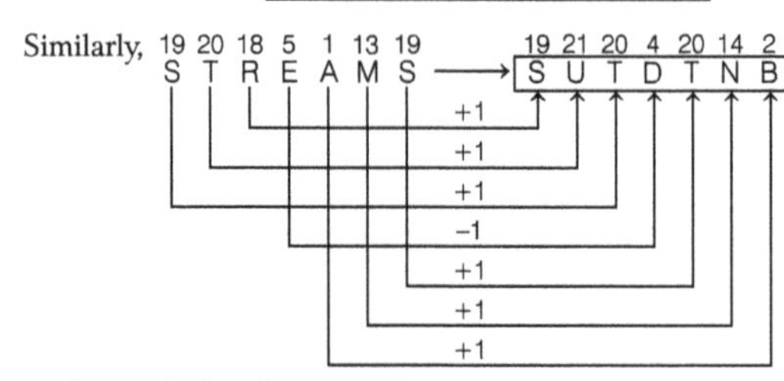

∴ STREAMS ⇒ SUTDTNB

96. (*e*) As,

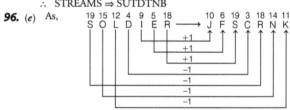

19 15 12 4 9 5 18
S O L D I E R ⟶ J F S C R N K
10 6 19 3 18 14 11
+1, +1, +1, −1, −1, −1, −1

Similarly,

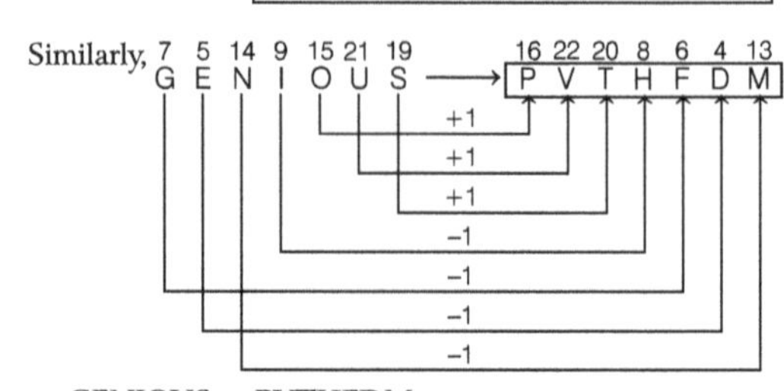

∴ GENIOUS ⇒ PVTHFDM

97. (*b*) As,

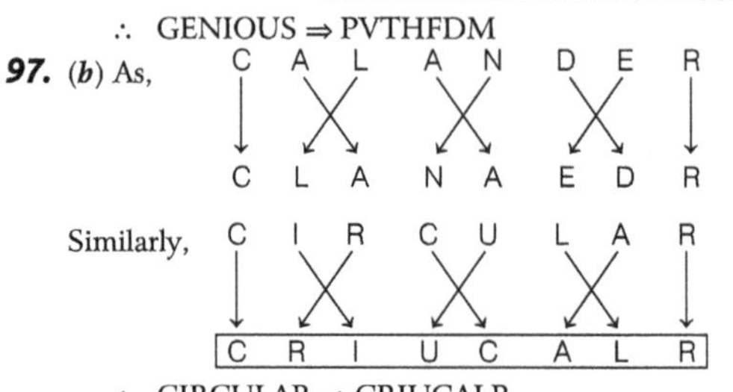

∴ CIRCULAR ⇒ CRIUCALR

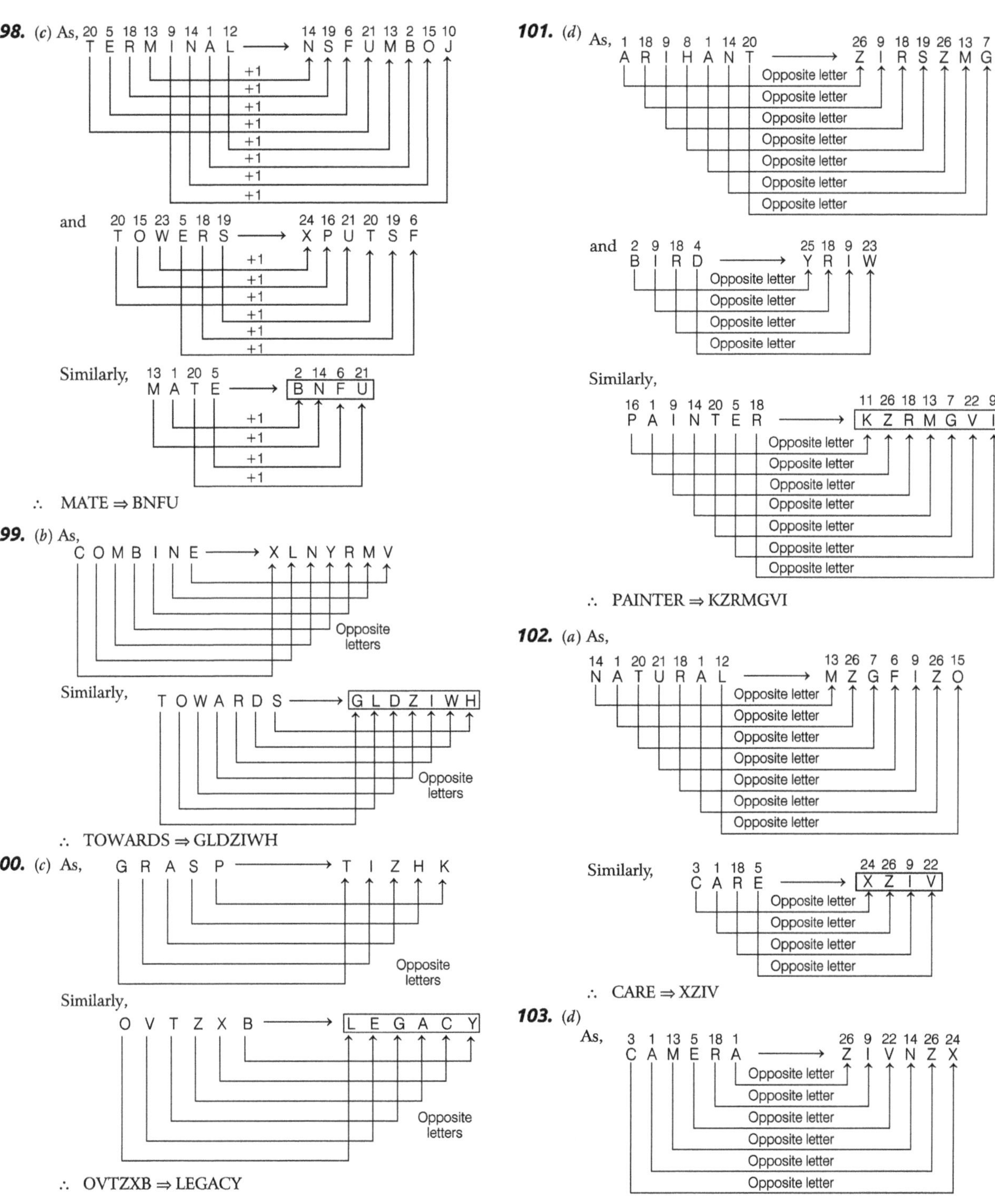
98. (c) As, 20 5 18 13 9 14 1 12
T E R M I N A L → N S F U M B O J
14 19 6 21 13 2 15 10
+1
and 20 15 23 5 18 19
T O W E R S → X P U T S F
24 16 21 20 19 6
+1
Similarly, 13 1 20 5
M A T E → B N F U
2 14 6 21
+1
∴ MATE ⇒ BNFU
99. (b) As,
C O M B I N E → X L N Y R M V
Opposite letters
Similarly,
T O W A R D S → G L D Z I W H
Opposite letters
∴ TOWARDS ⇒ GLDZIWH
100. (c) As, G R A S P → T I Z H K
Opposite letters
Similarly,
O V T Z X B → L E G A C Y
Opposite letters
∴ OVTZXB ⇒ LEGACY
101. (d) As, 1 18 9 8 1 14 20
A R I H A N T → Z I R S Z M G
26 9 18 19 26 13 7
Opposite letter
and 2 9 18 4
B I R D → Y R I W
25 18 9 23
Opposite letter
Similarly,
16 1 9 14 20 5 18
P A I N T E R → K Z R M G V I
11 26 18 13 7 22 9
Opposite letter
∴ PAINTER ⇒ KZRMGVI
102. (a) As,
14 1 20 21 18 1 12
N A T U R A L → M Z G F I Z O
13 26 7 6 9 26 15
Opposite letter
Similarly, 3 1 18 5
C A R E → X Z I V
24 26 9 22
Opposite letter
∴ CARE ⇒ XZIV
103. (d)
As, 3 1 13 5 18 1
C A M E R A → Z I V N Z X
26 9 22 14 26 24
Opposite letter

Similarly,

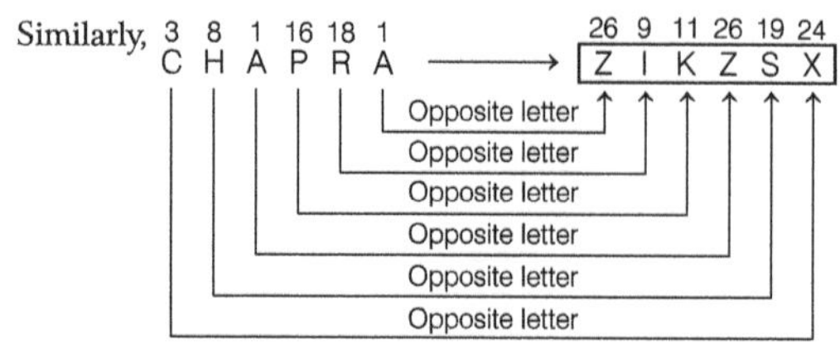

∴ CHAPRA ⇒ ZIKZSX

104. (*b*) As,

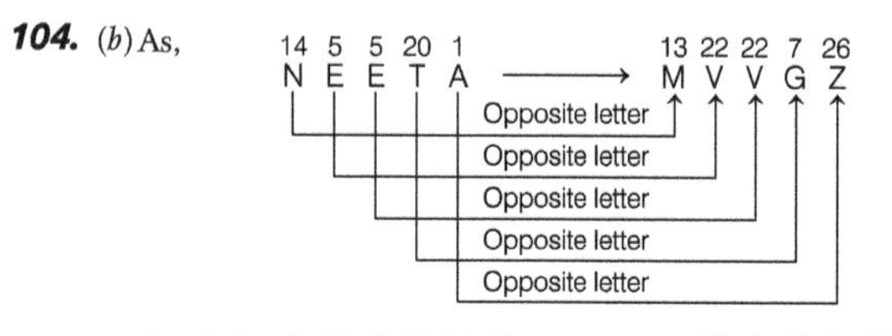

Similarly,

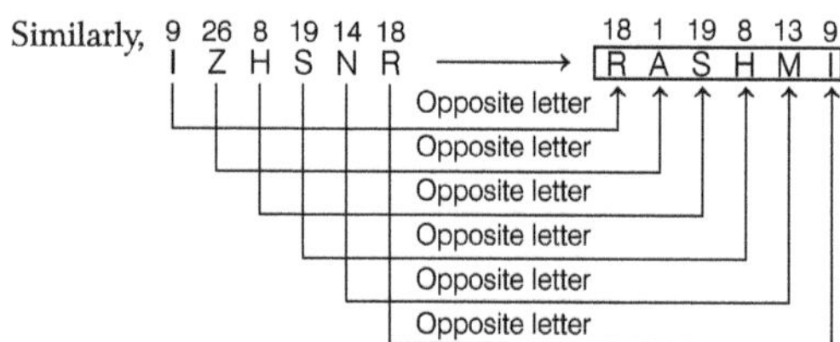

∴ IZHSNR ⇒ RASHMI

105. (*d*) As,

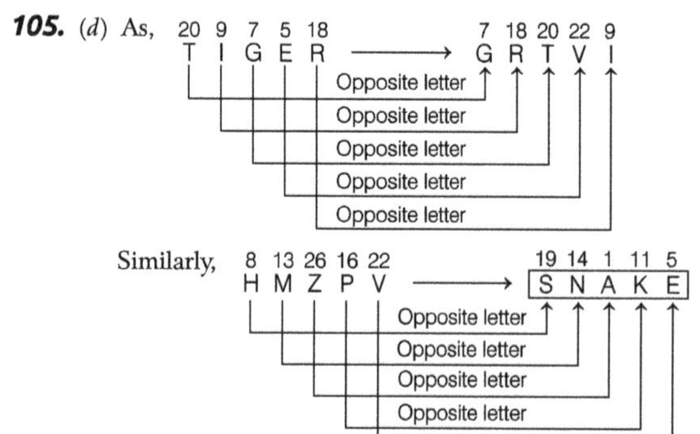

∴ HMZPV ⇒ SNAKE

106. (*b*) As,

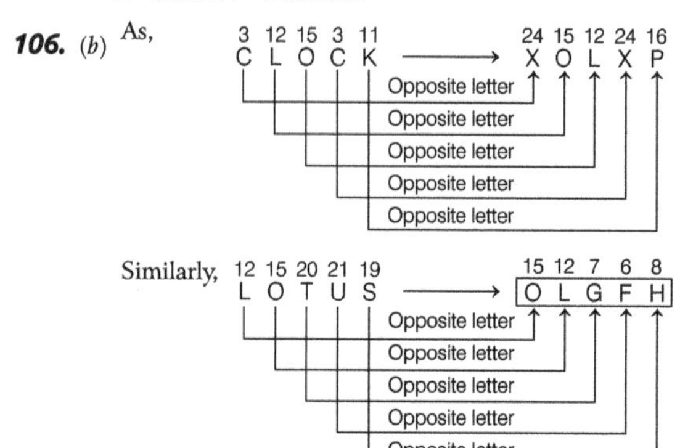

∴ LOTUS ⇒ OLGFH

107. (*c*) As,

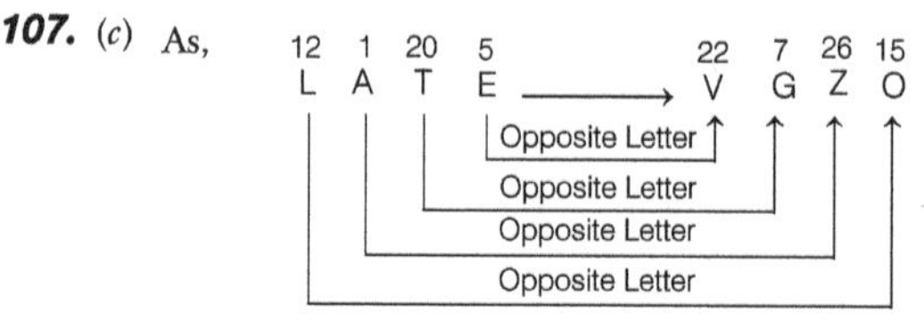

Similarly,

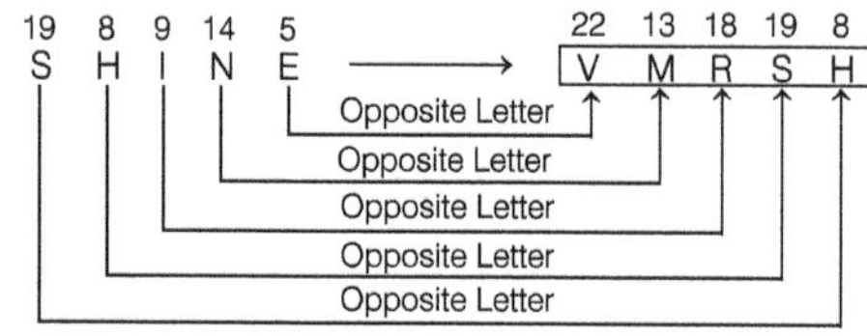

∴ SHINE ⇒ VMRSH

108. (*d*) Each letter is coded with its left and right letters in English alphabetical series.

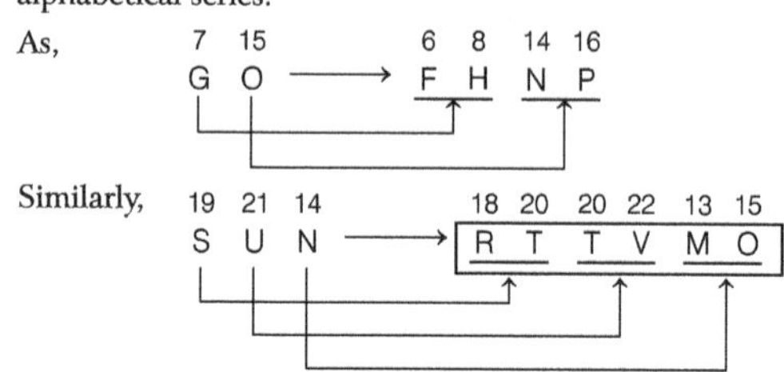

∴ SUN ⇒ RTTVMO

109. (*d*) Each letter is coded with its left and right letters in English alphabet.

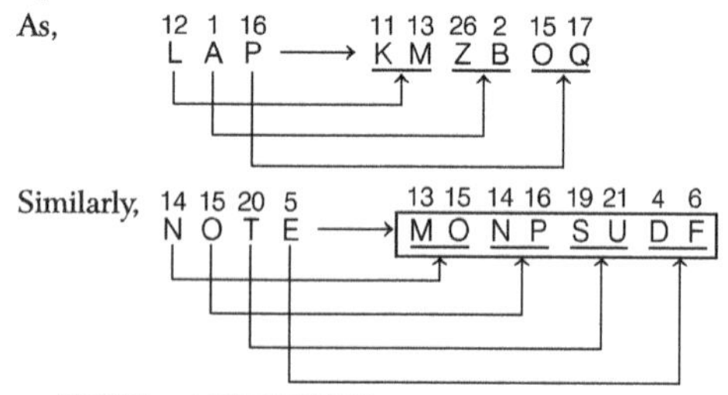

∴ NOTE ⇒ MONPSUDF

110. (*d*) Starting from right end, each letter is coded with its left and right letters in English alphabetical series.

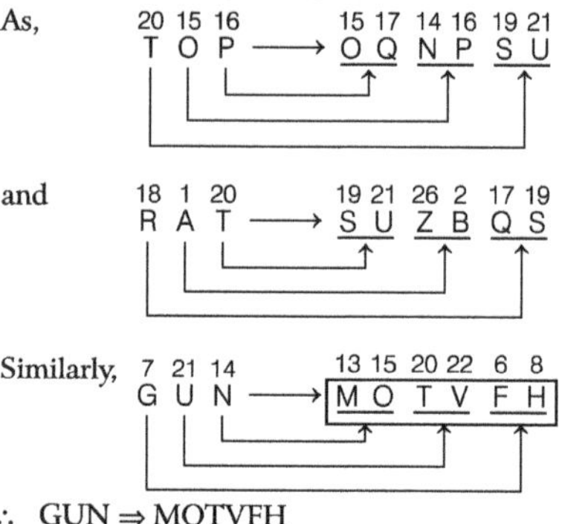

∴ GUN ⇒ MOTVFH

111. (*a*) Each letter is coded with its left and right letters in English alphabetical series.

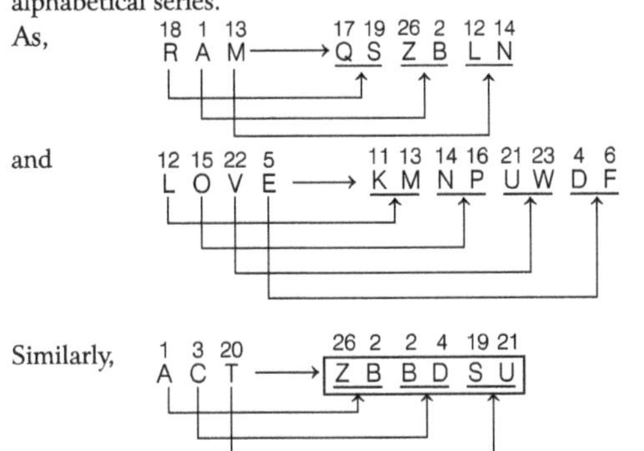

∴ ACT ⇒ ZBBDSU

112. (*a*) Each letter is coded with its left and right letters in English alphabetical series.

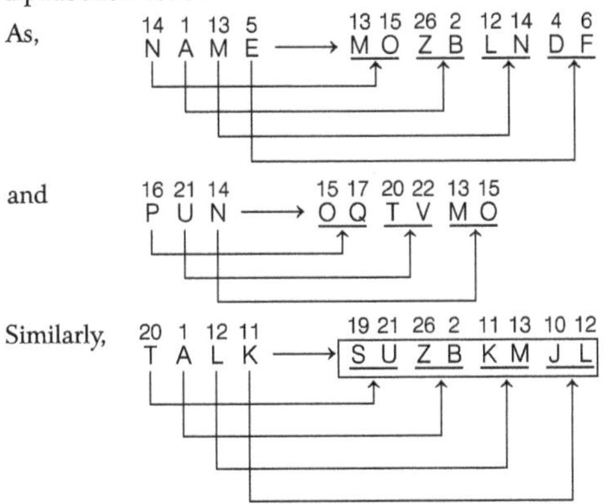

∴ TALK ⇒ SUZBKMJL

113. (*a*) Each letter is coded with its left and right letters in English alphabetical series.

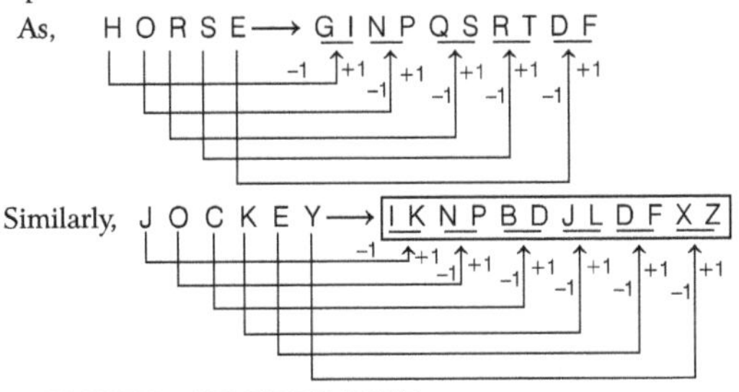

∴ JOCKEY ⇒ IKNPBDJLDFXZ

114. (*a*) Each letter is coded with its left and right letters in English alphabetical series.

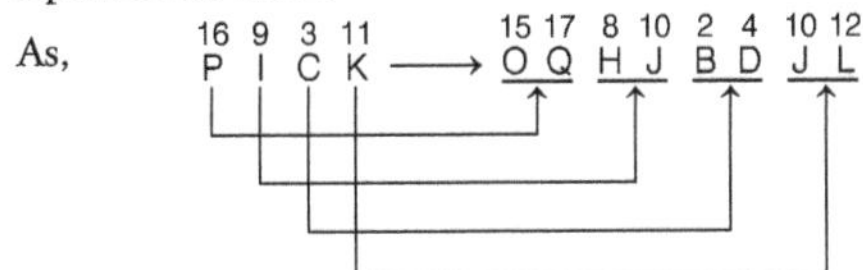

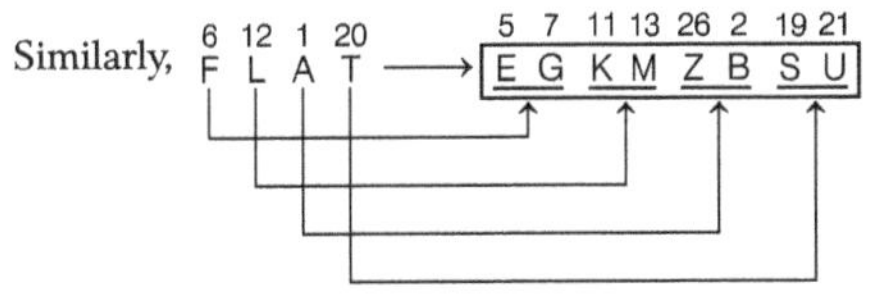

∴ FLAT ⇒ EGKMZBSU

115. (*d*) Starting from right end, each letter is coded with its left and right letters in English alphabetical series.

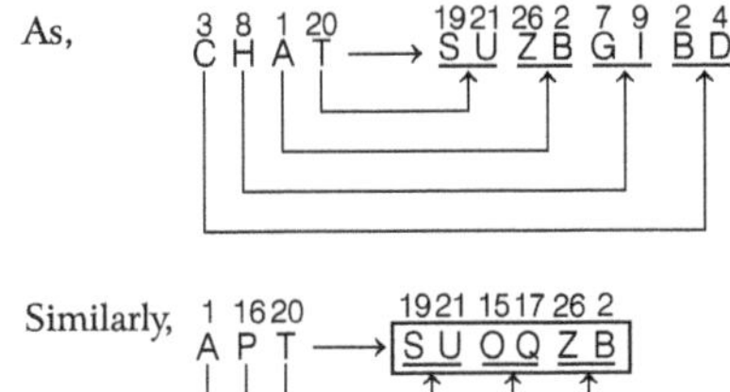

∴ APT ⇒ SUOQZB

116. (*a*) Starting from right end, each letter is coded with its left and right letters in English alphabetical series.

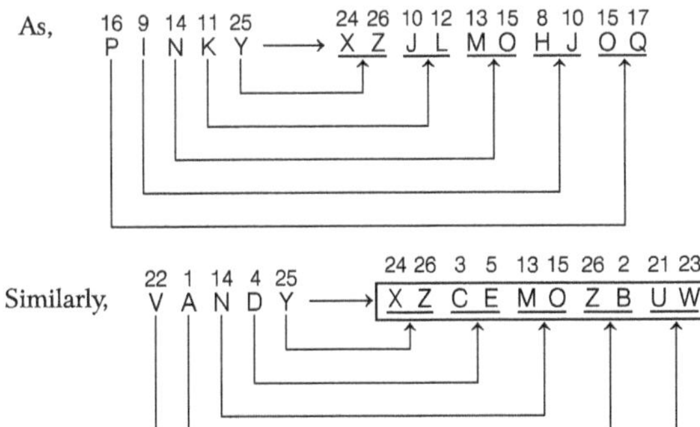

∴ VANDY ⇒ XZCEMOZBUW

117. (*c*) Each letter is coded with its right and left letters respectively in English alphabetical series.

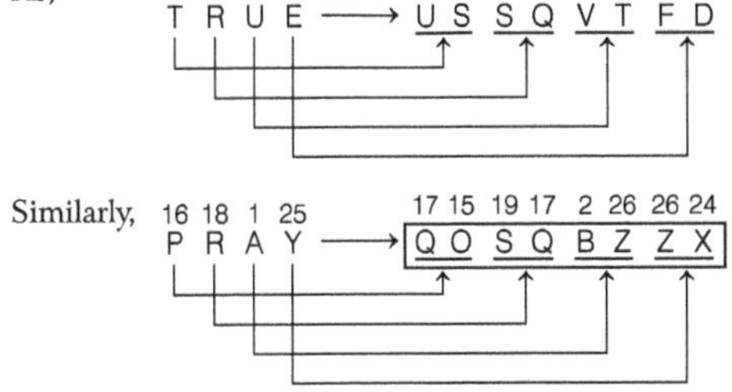

∴ PRAY ⇒ QOSQBZZX

TYPE 02

Number Coding

In number coding, numerical code is assigned to the word or alphabetical letters and candidates are required to analyse the codes as per the correlation between these numbers and letters. This correlation is based on certain pattern according to the position of letters in English alphabet as per a set of given rules.

Following example will give you a better idea about the type of question asked

***Ex* 16** If 'MYSTICAL' is coded as '1325192093112' in a code language, how would 'DUMBBELL' be coded in the same language ?

« UPSSSC Combined Lower Subordinate Services 2016

(a) 421132251112 (b) 421132241212
(c) 421132251212 (d) 421032251212

Solution (c) As,

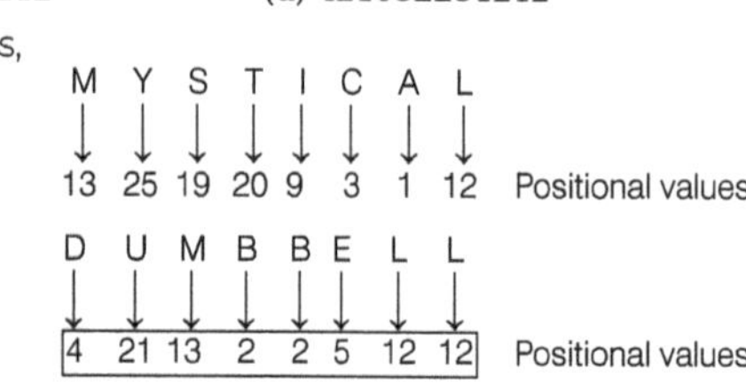

∴ DUMBBELL ⇒ 421132251212

***Ex* 17** In a certain code language, 'ROK' is written as '44' and 'MIG' is written as '29'. What will be the code for 'TAL' in that code language? « SSC MTS 2019

(a) 33 (b) 34 (c) 41 (d) 43

Solution (a) Here, the positional values of letters are added to obtain the code.

As, ROK (18 15 11) = 18 + 15 + 11 = 44

and MIG (13 9 7) = 13 + 9 + 7 = 29

Similarly, TAL (20 1 12) = 20 + 1 + 12 = 33

***Ex* 18** If PRIVATE is coded as 1234567 and RISK as 2398, how will be RIVETS coded?

« UKPSC Assit. Conservator of Forest 2019

(a) 232679 (b) 243769 (c) 234769 (d) 234976

Solution (c) As,

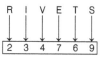

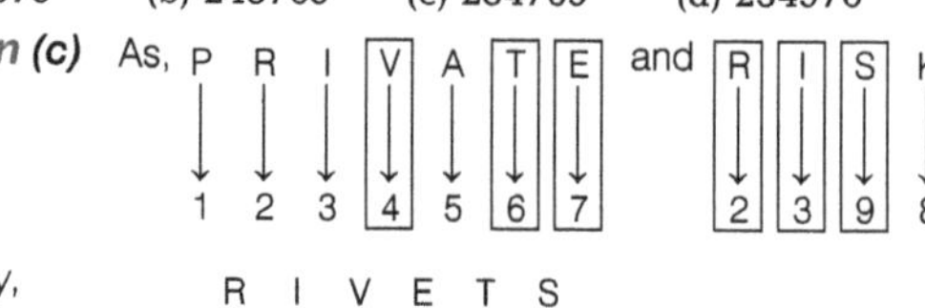

Similarly,

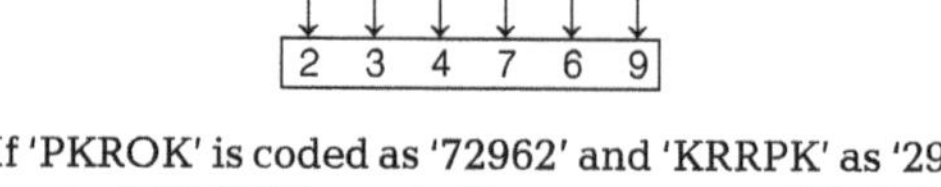

***Ex* 19** If 'PKROK' is coded as '72962' and 'KRRPK' as '29972', then how can 'NJMLZ' be coded? « SSC (CGL) 2014

(a) 45176 (b) 74314 (c) 91592 (d) 51430

Solution (d)

As, P(16) → 1+6 → 7, K(11) → 1+1 → 2, R(18) → 1+8 → 9, O(15) → 1+5 → 6, K(11) → 1+1 → 2
and K(11) → 1+1 → 2, R(18) → 1+8 → 9, R(18) → 1+8 → 9, P(16) → 1+6 → 7, K(11) → 1+1 → 2

P is coded as 7, K as 2, R as 9 and O as 6 that means code of NJMLZ does not have either 7, 2, 9 or 6. Hence, required code will be 51430, which is given in option (d).

***Ex* 20** If M = 14, TANK = 62, then STARDOM = ?

« RRB NTPC 2016

(a) 79 (b) 89 (c) 99 (d) 109

Solution (c) Given, M = 14 ⇒ M = 27 − 13 = 14

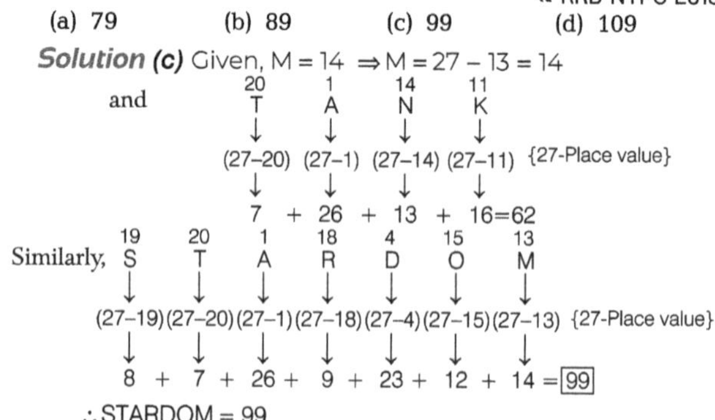

∴ STARDOM = 99

Practice CORNER 4.2

1. If 'NASCENT' is written as '2734526', how is 'SENTENCE' is written in that code? « MP Police 2017

(a) 35265245 (b) 35256245
(c) 35265235 (d) 35256275

2. If 'FACE' is coded as '6135' and 'DEAD' is coded as '4514', then 'HIGH' will be coded as

« UPSSSC Junior Assistant 2015

(a) 9556 (b) 6536 (c) 8978 (d) 9887

3. If in a certain code language 'BHAI' is written as '2819', then how will 'CDGH' be written in that language ?

« SSC MTS 2019

(a) 3478 (b) 8437 (c) 3487 (d) 7348

4. If 'INK' is coded as '91411' and 'RED' is coded as '1854', then 'PEN' will be coded as « CGPSC 2017

(a) 16514 (b) 14176 (c) 14562 (d) 151614
(e) None of these

5. In a certain code 'DIRTY' is coded as '24759' and 'FOAM' is coded as '1863'. Using the same code 'ARID' will be coded as « RRB ALP 2018

(a) 6742 (b) 1579 (c) 9165 (d) 2489

6. If in a certain code language 'RUN' is written as '182114' and 'PEN' is written as '16514', then how will 'RANSOM' be coded in that language?

(a) 1841491315 (b) 18114131915
(c) 18114191315 (d) 18114191513

7. If 'GERMANY' is written as '7, 5, 18, 13, 1, 14, 25', how can 'FRANCE' be written in that code?
(a) 6, 18, 1, 14, 3, 5 (b) 6, 3, 18, 14, 1, 5
(c) 8, 2, 14, 5, 13, 6 (d) 8, 16, 14, 3, 1, 5

8. In a certain code language if '41095' is 'READY' and '840327' is 'FRAILS', then '83145 419' is
A. FEARY RED B. FIERY RED
C. FAIRY RED D. FIREY RED
(a) D (b) B (c) C (d) A

9. If 7 is coded as 'CBRT343', then '9' is coded as
(a) CBRT27 (b) SQRT81
(c) CBRT729 (d) CBRT6561

10. If each letter of the English alphabet is assigned an odd numerical value in increasing order, such as A = 1, B = 3 and so on, then what will be the code of HONEY? « SSC CGL 2019
(a) 132725747 (b) 152927949
(c) 152927947 (d) 132725745

11. If 'HELLO' is coded as 15 | 12 | 12 | 5 | 8, then 'WHERE' is coded as
(a) 16|13|13|6|9 (b) 5|18|5|8|23
(c) 5|5|18|23|8 (d) 5|5|18|8|23

12. In a certain code language, 'PEN' is coded as '321028'. How will 'TUB' be coded as in that language? « SSC (CGL) 2020
(a) 44024 (b) 40422 (c) 42404 (d) 40424

13. If 'PAINT' is coded as '74128' and 'EXCEL' is coded as '93596', how is 'ACCEPT' coded?
(a) 455978 (b) 459578 (c) 457958 (d) 459758

14. In a certain code language, 'DANGER' is written as '145237' and 'RANCOR' is written as '745967'. How is 'RAGE' written in that code language? « UPSC 2016
(a) 7231 (b) 7234 (c) 7423 (d) 7441

15. If in a certain code language 'HONESTY' is written as '5132468' and 'POVERTY' is written as '7192068', then how will 'HORSE' be written in that language?
(a) 50124 (b) 51042 (c) 51024 (d) 52014

16. If in a certain code language 'REFORM' is written as '426349' and 'FORMULA' is written as '6349871', then how will 'MULE' be written in that language?
(a) 8792 (b) 7982 (c) 9872 (d) 2978

17. If 'DREAM' is coded as '78026' and 'CHILD' is coded as '53417', how can 'LEADER' be coded?
(a) 102078 (b) 102708
(c) 102087 (d) 102780

18. If in a certain code language 'BOAT' is written as '5937' and 'TIME' is written as '7826', then how will 'BEAM' be written in that language?
(a) 5362 (b) 7632 (c) 5632 (d) 5862
(e) None of these

19. If in a certain code language 'BOARD' is written as '53169', 'NEAR' is written as '2416', then how will 'NODE' be written in that language?
(a) 2394 (b) 2894 (c) 2934 (d) 2694
(e) None of these

20. If in a certain code language 'DEAF' is written as '3587' and 'FILE' is written as '7465', then how will 'IDEAL' be written in that language?
(a) 48536 (b) 43568
(c) 63548 (d) 43586
(e) None of these

21. If in a certain code language 'GOAL' is written as '5139' and 'LAME' is written as '9327', then how will 'MOLE' be written in that language?
(a) 2197 (b) 2917 (c) 3197 (d) 2157
(e) None of these

22. If in a certain code language 'BRACKET' is written as '9341285', 'DEAR' is written as '6843', then how will 'TRADE' be written in that language?
(a) 59468 (b) 34568 (c) 53468 (d) 53648
(e) None of these

23. If in a coded language, 'COIN' is coded as '8574' and 'UNTIL' is coded as '94371', then 'COCONUT' will be « UPSSSC VDO 2018
(a) 9393596 (b) 8585493 (c) 8585321 (d) 9393593

24. In a certain code language, FILE is written as 7465 and IDEAL is written as 43586. How will DEAF be written in that code language? « UP Police Constable 2018
(a) 3478 (b) 3588
(c) 3587 (d) 4578

25. If in a coded language, 'JOIN' is coded as '8574' and 'POKER' is coded as '95321', then 'JOKER' will be coded as « UPSSSC VDO 2018
(a) 93596 (b) 83593 (c) 85321 (d) 93593

26. If in a certain code language 'TERRACE' is written as 70, then in the same code language how will you write the word BALCONY? « SSC GD Constable 2018
(a) 74 (b) 73 (c) 72 (d) 71

27. If ABLE is written as 5324 and BINGO is written as 36178, then BANGLE can be written as « SSC Steno 2016
(a) 351724 (b) 356724
(c) 321846 (d) 362417

28. If in a certain code language 'BEAUTIFUL' is coded as '573041208' and 'BUTTER' is coded as '504479', then how will 'FUTURE' be coded in that language?
(a) 204097 (b) 201497
(c) 704092 (d) 204079

29. If 'RACKET' is written as '813524' in a certain code, how would 'TRACK' be written in that code? « MP Police 2017
(a) 81253 (b) 41835 (c) 48135 (d) 28153

30. If 'WOOD' is coded as 23|225|4, then MEET is coded as
(a) |3|5|5|20 (b) |13|10|20
(c) |13|25|20 (d) None of these

31. If 'RAMON' is written as '12345' and 'DINESH' as '675849', then 'HAMAM' will be written as « UPPSC 2018
(a) 92233 (b) 92323 (c) 93322 (d) 93232

32. In a certain code language 'MOBILITY' is coded as '46293927'. How will 'EXAMINATION' be coded as in that code language? « UPSSSC Junior Assitant 2020

(a) 27159415955 (b) 67038401834
(c) 56149512965 (d) 12250623034

33. In a certain code language, 'GOURD' is written as 21-4-5-10-24. How will 'BRINJAL' be written in the same code language ? « SSC CPO 2019

(a) 25-9-3-14-18-1-15 (b) 26-10-5-14-18-2-16
(c) 26-10-3-14-18-1-16 (d) 2-10-3-14-18-1-12

34. If 'RED' is coded as '360', then 'GREEN' can be coded as

(a) 44400 (b) 41400 (c) 44110 (d) 44100

35. In a certain code language, 'DOME' is written as '8943' and 'MEAL' is written as '4321'. What group of letters can be formed for the code '38249'?

(a) EOADM (b) MEDOA
(c) EMDAO (d) EDAMO
(e) None of these

36. If in a certain code language, 'EAT' is written as '318' and 'CHAIR' is written as '24156', then how 'TEACHER' be written in that code language?

(a) 8313426 (b) 8312436
(c) 8321436 (d) 8312346

37. In certain code 'NEPALI' is written as '6-15-0-15-10-13'. How will 'STEXQG' be written in that code? « UPPSC Lower Subordinate 2016

(a) 21-20-23-4-8-18 (b) 24-20-21-8-18-1
(c) 18-8-24-20-21-5 (d) 20-21-24-5-8-18

38. If in a certain code language 'TALK' is written as '2121312', then how will 'PATNA' be coded in that language?

(a) 17212152 (b) 17221251
(c) 17221125 (d) 17221152

39. If in a certain code language 'GRADUATE' is written as '2092623626722', then how will 'ARIHANT' be written in that language?

(a) 269181926137 (b) 269181926173
(c) 269811926137 (d) 269181962137

40. If in a certain code language 'PERFECT' is written as '116', then how will 'COMPACT' be written in that code?

(a) 85 (b) 111 (c) 98 (d) 118

41. In a certain code language, 'PING' is written as '4' and 'METAL' is written as '5'. What will be the code for 'STEADYS' in that code language ? « SSC MTS 2019

(a) 8 (b) 7 (c) 5 (d) 6

42. If in a certain code language 'SON' is written as '81213', 'LIFE' is written as '15182122', then how will 'NEVER' be written in that language?

(a) 13225229 (b) 22135229
(c) 13225292 (d) 13222529

43. If in a certain code language 'IPL' is written as '37' and 'POLISH' is written as '79', then how will 'GRAVITY' be coded in that language?

(a) 102 (b) 205 (c) 115 (d) 95

44. If 'TISSUE' is coded as '93' in a code language, how would ROCKET be coded in the same language ? « UPSSSC Combined Lower Subordinate Services 2016

(a) 68 (b) 70 (c) 71 (d) 72

45. If E = 5 and EVEN = 46, then ENTER = ?

(a) 62 (b) 52 (c) 72 (d) 42

46. If A = 1 and LOT = 47, then MAT = ?

(a) 40 (b) 66 (c) 34 (d) 51

47. If M = 13 and MAT = 34, then WAX = ?

(a) 47 (b) 25 (c) 48 (d) 23

48. If E = 5 and AMENDMENT = 89, then SECRETARY = ?

(a) 115 (b) 112 (c) 114 (d) 100

49. If A = 1 and VAN = 37, then FAT = ?

(a) 21 (b) 20 (c) 26 (d) 27

50. In a certain code language, N is coded as 30 and COT is coded as 78. How will PET be coded as in that language? « SSC (10+2) 2020

(a) 41 (b) 100 (c) 70 (d) 84

51. If ZIP = 30 and ZAP = 38, what will be VIP = ? « FCI Uttarakhand Watch Man 2018

(a) 174 (b) 43 (c) 34 (d) 113

52. If P = 16 and PUT = 6720, then PICK = ?

(a) 4137 (b) 4590
(c) 4032 (d) 4752

53. If P = 16 and TAP = 37, then CUP = ?

(a) 40 (b) 38 (c) 36 (d) 39

54. If N = 14 and NOT = 4200, then NAME = ?

(a) 937 (b) 822 (c) 915 (d) 910

55. If E = 5 and HEN = 27, then PET = ?

(a) 31 (b) 41 (c) 52 (d) 28

56. If T = 20 and TEAM = 39, then TREE = ?

(a) 39 (b) 54 (c) 48 (d) 36

57. If M = 13 and MAD = 52, then MOOD = ?

(a) 11700 (b) 10181
(c) 12500 (d) 95000

58. In a certain code, if 'GANESH' is written as '54', then how will 'PARVATI' written in that code? « SSC Steno Grade C & D 2019

(a) 87 (b) 85 (c) 81 (d) 83

59. If 'MACHINE' is coded as 19-7-9- 14-15-20-11, then how will you code 'DANGER' in the same code? « CGPSC Pre 2016

(a) 11-7-20-16-11-24 (b) 13-7-20-9-11-25
(c) 10-7-20-13-11-24 (d) 13-7-20-10-11-25
(e) None of the above

60. If 'FLARE' is coded as 21, 15, 26, 9, 22, then how would 'BREIF' be coded in the same language?

(a) 25, 9, 22, 21, 18 (b) 5, 37, 11, 19, 13
(c) 13, 19, 11, 37, 5 (d) 25, 9, 22, 18, 21

61. If in a certain code language 'NOTION' is written as '348', then how will 'TOTAL' be written in that language?
(a) 381 (b) 275
(c) 385 (d) 272

62. If in a certain language 'JNU' is written as '101714132106', then how will 'PUSA' be written in that language? « UP PCS 2008
(a) 1611210619080126 (b) 1611210619080162
(c) 1611210619086201 (d) 1161216019080126

63. If in a certain code language 'GAME' is written as '0720012613140522', then how will 'NOT' be coded in that language?
(a) 121413152007 (b) 131415122007
(c) 141315127002 (d) 141315122007

64. If in a certain code language 'IPL' is written as '81256144', then how will 'BUT' be written in that language?
(a) 4441400 (b) 4444100
(c) 4100444 (d) 4144400

65. If in a certain code language 'GOAT' is coded as '40014467649', then how will 'DO' be written in that language?
(a) 529144 (b) 222591 (c) 592225 (d) 529522

66. If in a certain code language 'RAMAN' is written as '23.5' and 'CAP' is written as '10', then how will 'CAPACITY ' be written in that code?
(a) 48 (b) 39 (c) 49 (d) 35

67. If in a certain code language 'LOT' is written as '111314161921', 'SIP' is written as '18208101517', then how will 'GO' be written in that language?
(a) 681416 (b) 864161
(c) 681476 (d) 681461

68. If in a certain code language 'KOMAL' is written as '31462', 'POT' is written as '267', then how will 'TIGER' be written in that language?
(a) 95927 (b) 95279
(c) 95729 (d) 95792

69. If in a certain code language 'HUT' is written as '9722202119', 'TO' is written as '21191614', then how will 'FOG' be written in that language?
(a) 75161486 (b) 75161468
(c) 75614168 (d) 57161486

70. If in a certain code language 'DEW' is written as '1625529', 'GET' is written as '4925400', then how will 'TWO' be written in that language?
(a) 400529522 (b) 400529225
(c) 400925225 (d) 400225925

71. In a certain code language 'PEN–TAN' is written as '0'. How is "DEN–COB" written in that code language?
(a) 8 (b) 3
(c) 9 (d) 7

72. If 'REASON' is coded as 5 and 'BELIEVED' as 7, what is the code number for 'GOVERNMENT'?
(a) 10 (b) 6 (c) 9 (d) 8

Answers WITH EXPLANATIONS

1. (a) As,

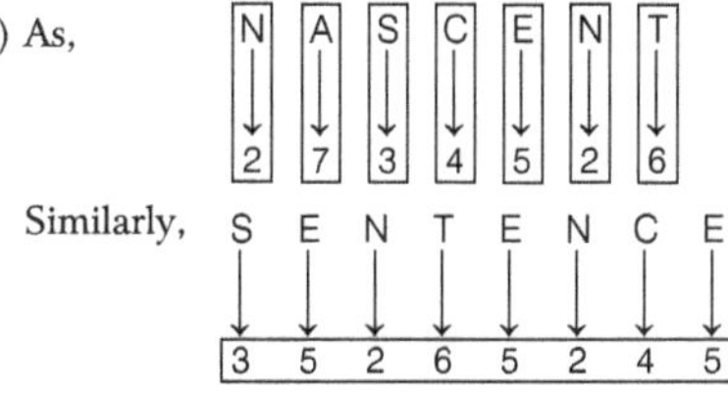

∴ SENTENCE ⇒ 35265245

2. (c) As, FACE ⟶ 6135
and DEAD ⟶ 4514
Similarly, HIGH ⟶ 8978
∴ HIGH ⇒ 35265245

3. (a) B ⟶ 2
H ⟶ 8
A ⟶ 1
I ⟶ 9

Alphabets are coded according to their alphabetical position

In the given series, alphabetical positions of alphabet are alphabets used to make the code,
Similarly,
C ⟶ ③
D ⟶ ④
G ⟶ ⑦
H ⟶ ⑧

∴ CDGH ⇒ 3478

4. (a) As,

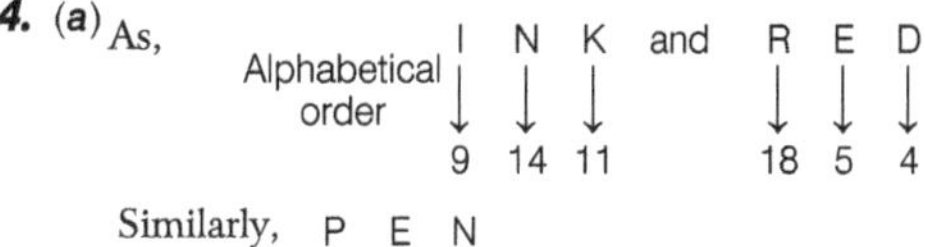

Similarly,

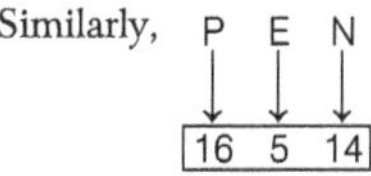

∴ PEN ⇒ 16514

5. (a) As,

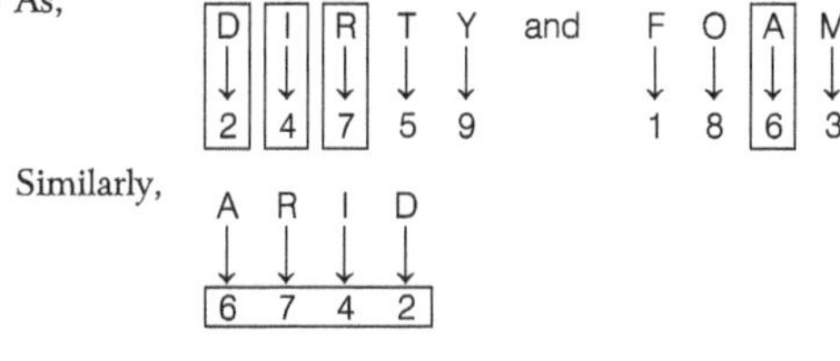

∴ ARID ⇒ 6742

6. (d) Letters are coded with their corresponding positions in alphabetical series.

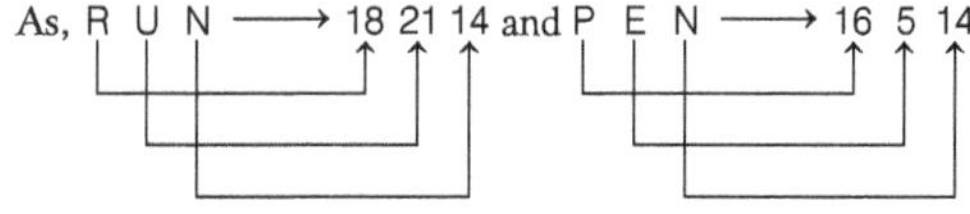

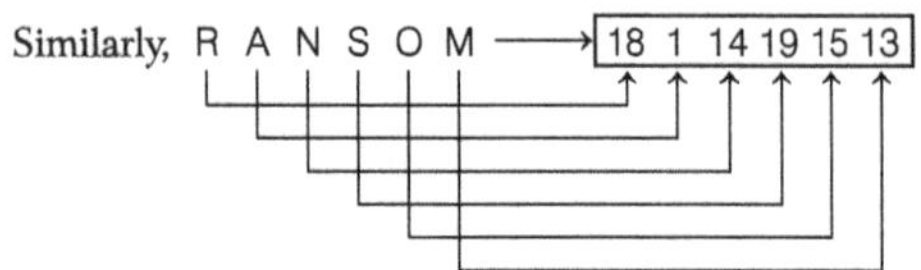

∴ RANSOM ⇒ 18114191513

7. (*a*) Letters are coded with their corresponding positions in alphabetical series.

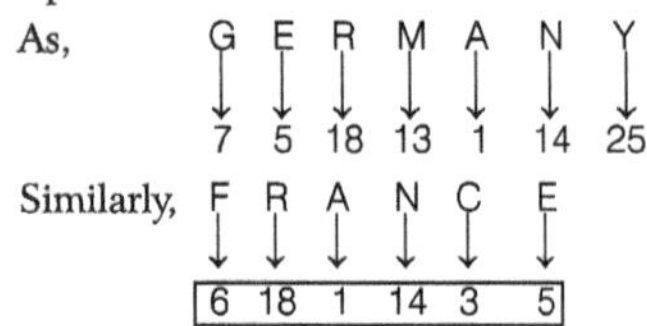

∴ FRANCE ⇒ 6, 18, 1, 14, 3, 5

8. (*b*)

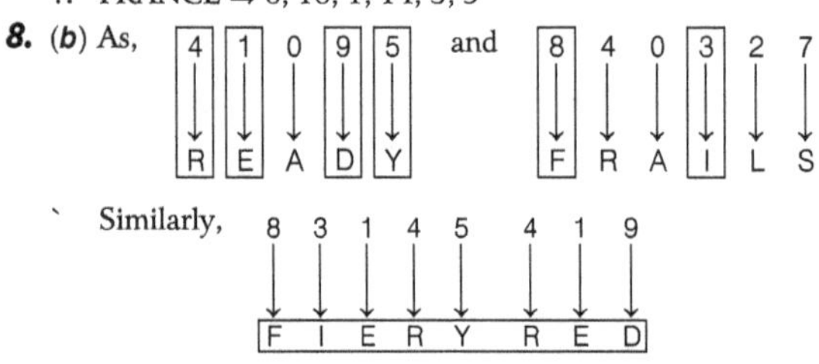

∴ 83145 419 ⇒ FIERY RED

9. (*c*) 7 is coded as CBRT 343.

343 is the cube of 7 *i.e.*, ($7^3 = 343$).

Similarly, 9 is coded as CBRT 729.

729 is the cube of 9 *i.e.*, ($9^3 = 729$).

10. (*b*) A = 1, B = 3, C = 5, D = 7, E = 9, F = 11, G = 13, H = 15, I = 17, J = 19, K = 21, L = 23, M = 25, N = 27, O = 29, P = 31, Q = 33, R = 35, S = 37, T = 39, U = 41, V = 43, W = 45, X = 47, Y = 49, Z = 51

∴ HONEY = 1 5 2 9 2 7 9 4 9

11. (*b*) Basic word H E L L O → 15 12 12 5 8

'H' has 8th position in the alphabetical order and 'O' has 15th position as in the alphabetical order. Both the positions of numeric form are interchanged as shown in the above figure. Similarly, 'L' has 12th position which is interchanged with 'E's position i.e., '5' and so on in the same way.

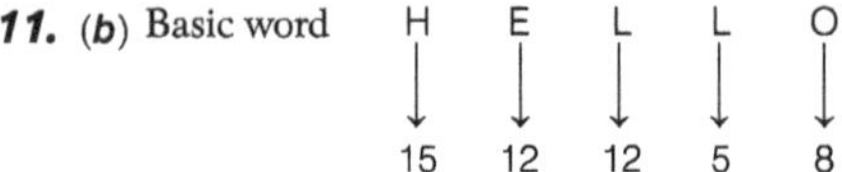

∴ WHERE ⇒ 5/18/5/8/23

12. (*d*)

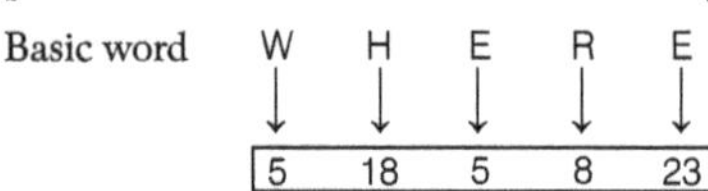

PEN ⇒ 321028

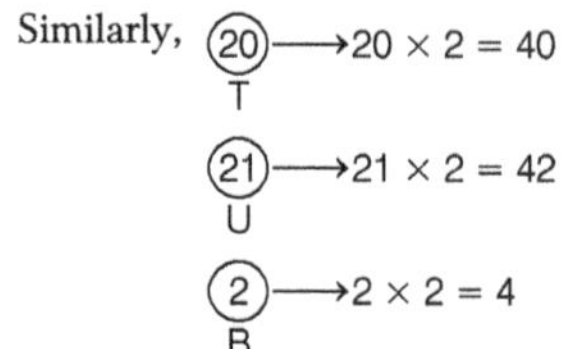

∴ TUB = 40424

13. (*a*)

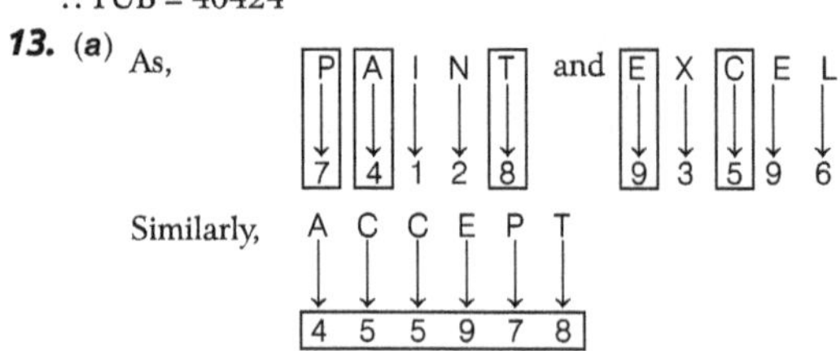

∴ ACCEPT ⇒ 455978

14. (*c*)

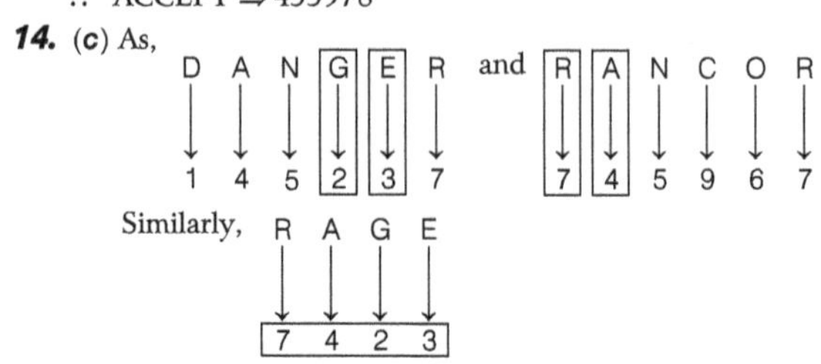

∴ RAGE ⇒ 7423

15. (*b*)

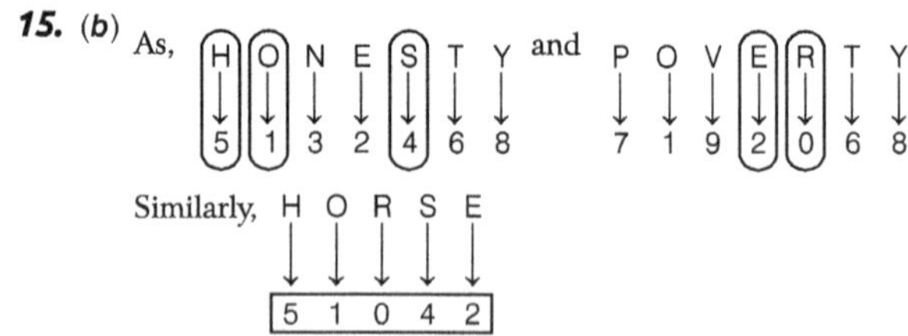

∴ HORSE ⇒ 51042

16. (*c*)

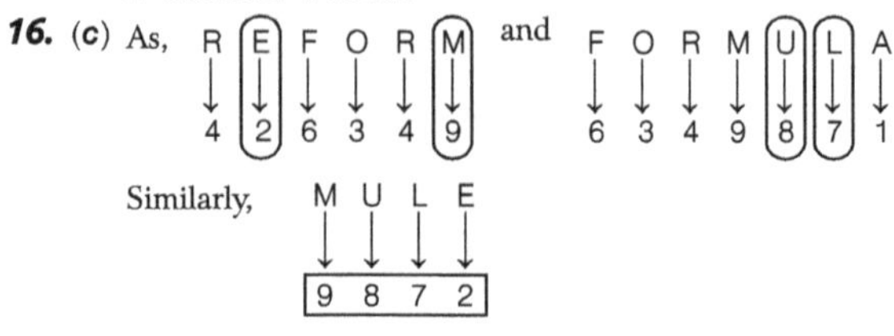

∴ MULE ⇒ 9872

17. (*b*)

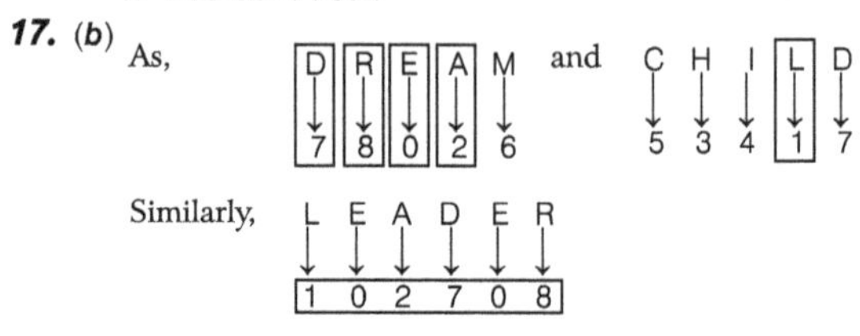

∴ LEADER ⇒ 102708

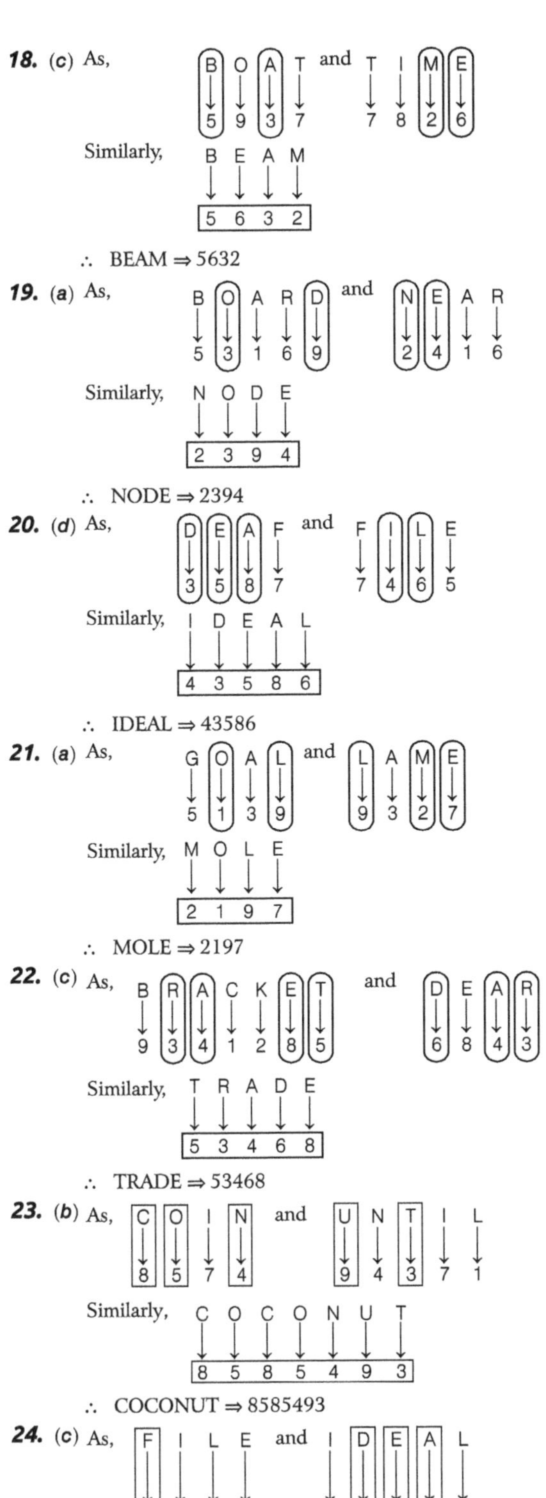

18. (*c*) As, BOAT → 5937 and TIME → 7826

Similarly, BEAM → 5632

∴ BEAM ⇒ 5632

19. (*a*) As, BOARD → 53169 and NEAR → 2416

Similarly, NODE → 2394

∴ NODE ⇒ 2394

20. (*d*) As, DEAF → 3587 and FILE → 7465

Similarly, IDEAL → 43586

∴ IDEAL ⇒ 43586

21. (*a*) As, GOAL → 5139 and LAME → 9327

Similarly, MOLE → 2197

∴ MOLE ⇒ 2197

22. (*c*) As, BRACKET → 9341285 and DEAR → 6843

Similarly, TRADE → 53468

∴ TRADE ⇒ 53468

23. (*b*) As, COIN → 8574 and UNTIL → 94371

Similarly, COCONUT → 8585493

∴ COCONUT ⇒ 8585493

24. (*c*) As, FILE → 7465 and IDEAL → 43586

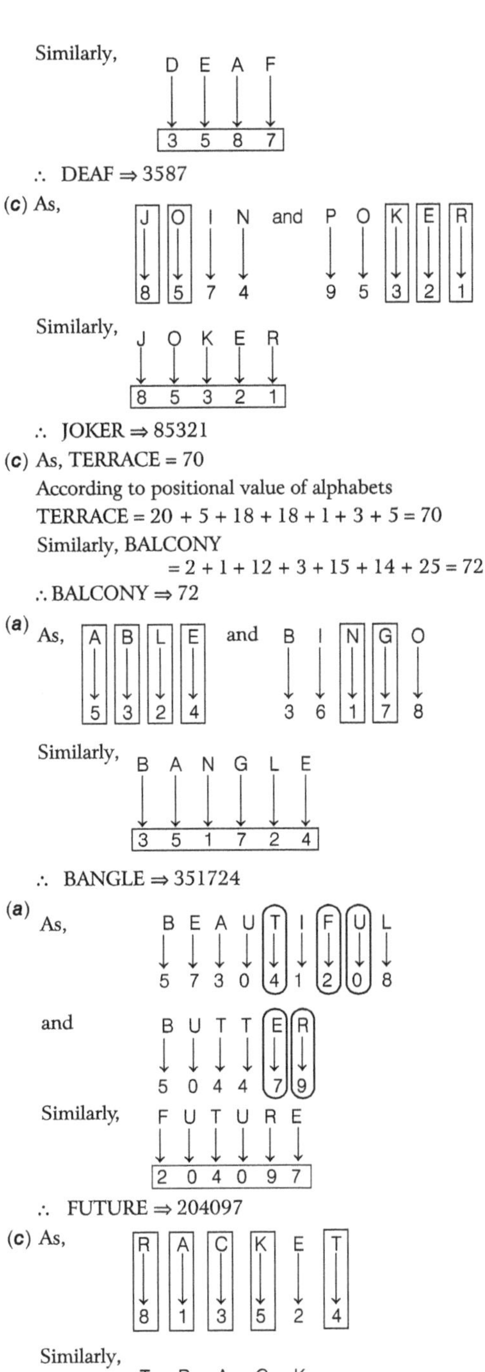

Similarly, DEAF → 3587

∴ DEAF ⇒ 3587

25. (*c*) As, JOIN → 8574 and POKER → 95321

Similarly, JOKER → 85321

∴ JOKER ⇒ 85321

26. (*c*) As, TERRACE = 70

According to positional value of alphabets

TERRACE = 20 + 5 + 18 + 18 + 1 + 3 + 5 = 70

Similarly, BALCONY

= 2 + 1 + 12 + 3 + 15 + 14 + 25 = 72

∴ BALCONY ⇒ 72

27. (*a*) As, ABLE → 5324 and BINGO → 36178

Similarly, BANGLE → 351724

∴ BANGLE ⇒ 351724

28. (*a*) As, BEAUTIFUL → 573041208

and BUTTER → 504479

Similarly, FUTURE → 204097

∴ FUTURE ⇒ 204097

29. (*c*) As, RACKET → 813524

Similarly, TRACK → 48135

∴ TRACK ⇒ 48135

30. (c)

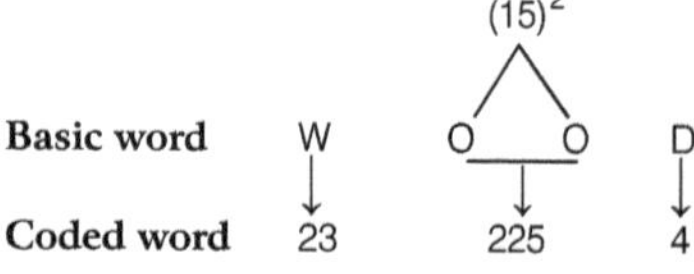

In this 'W' has 23rd position in the alphabetical order, 'D' has 4th position, 'O' has 15th position in the alphabetical order and 225 is the square of number 15.

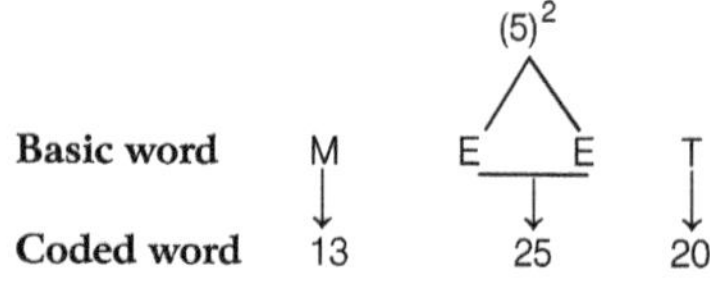

'M' has 13th position, 'T' has 20th position and 'E' has 5th position in alphabetical order and 25 is the square of number 5.

∴ MEET ⇒ /13/25/20

31. (b) As,

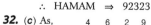

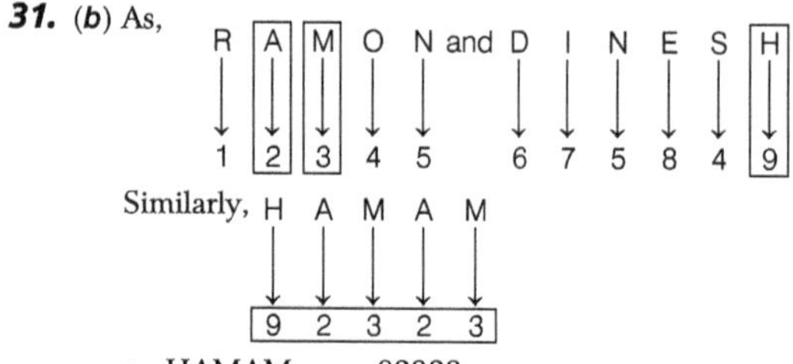

∴ HAMAM ⇒ 92323

32. (c) As,

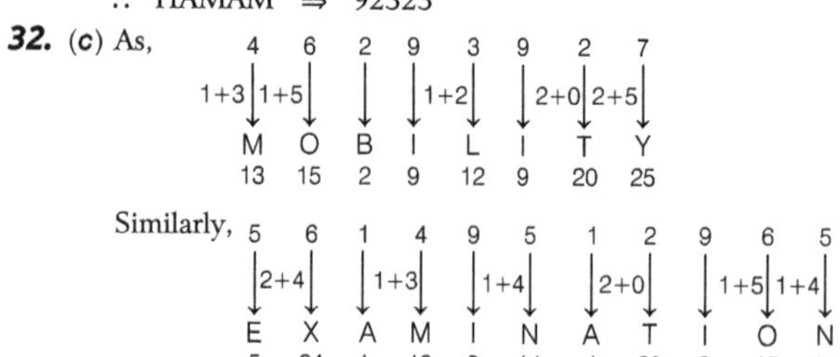

∴ EXAMINATION ⇒ 56149512965

33. (c) Here vowels are coded as A = 1, E = 2, I = 3, O = 4, U = 5 and consonant are coded as backward position in English alphabet +1

As,

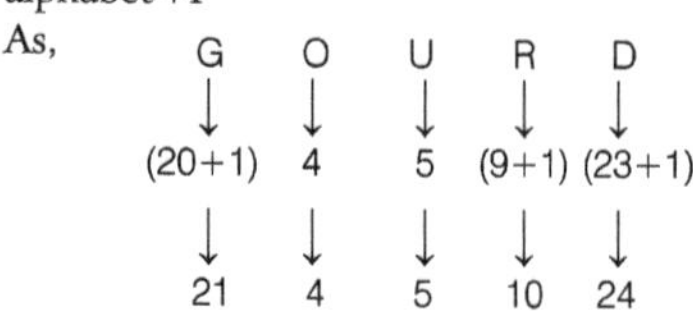

Similarly,

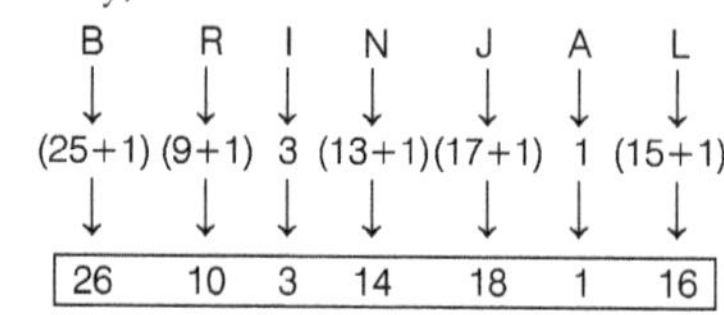

∴ BRINJAL ⇒ 26 – 10 – 3 – 14 – 18 – 1 – 16

34. (d) As, RED ⟶ 18 × 5 × 4 = 360

Similarly, GREEN ⟶ 7 × 18 × 5 × 5 × 14 = 44100

Hence, GREEN can be coded as 44100.

35. (d) As,

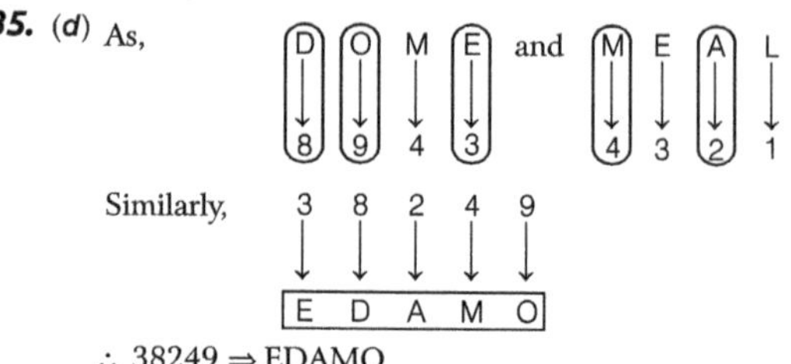

∴ 38249 ⇒ EDAMO

36. (b) As,

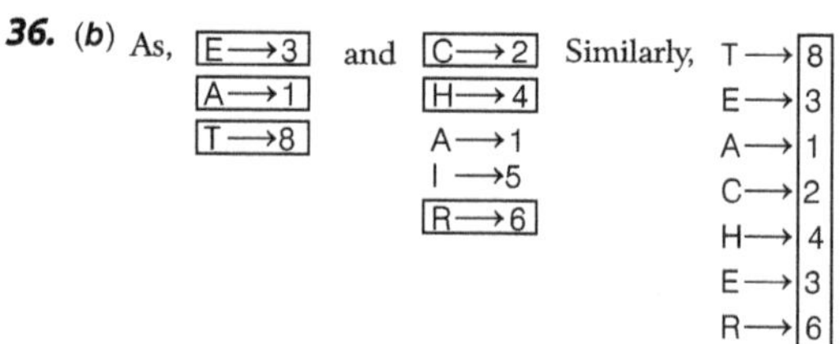

∴ TEACHER ⇒ 8312436

37. (a) As,

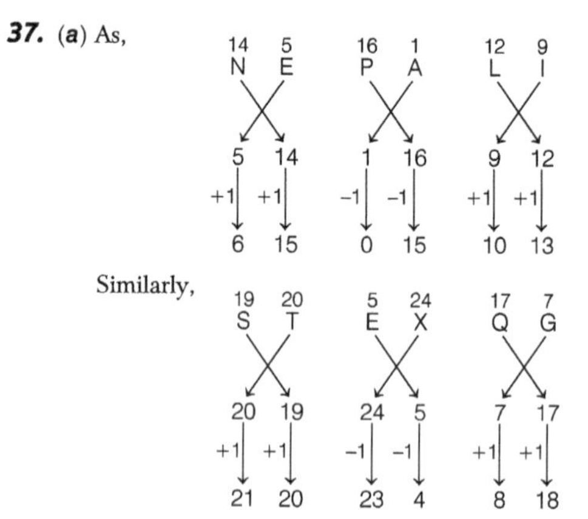

∴ STEXQG ⇒ 21-20-23-4-8-18

38. (d) As,

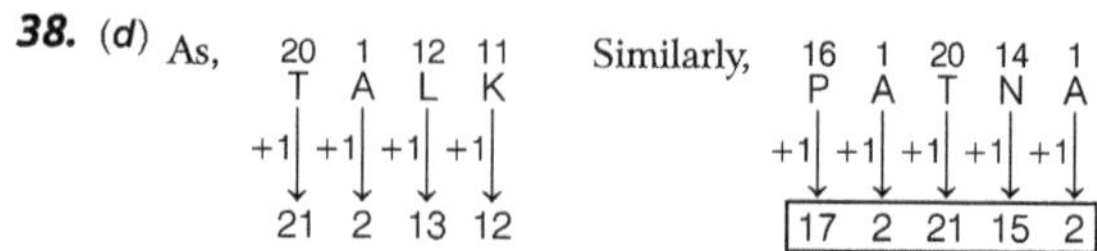

∴ PATNA ⇒ 17221152

39. (a) Each letter is coded with its backward order letter position.

As,

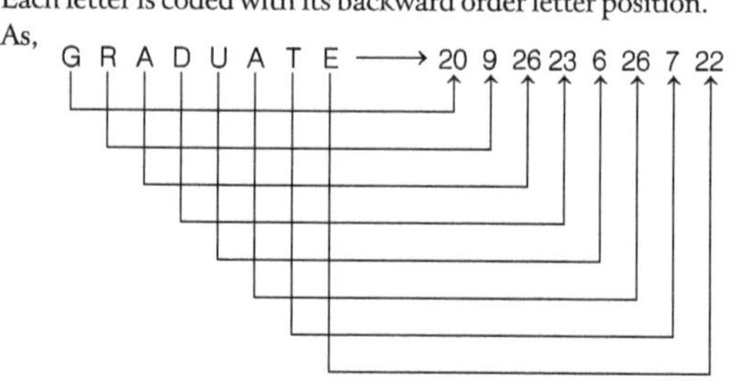

Similarly,

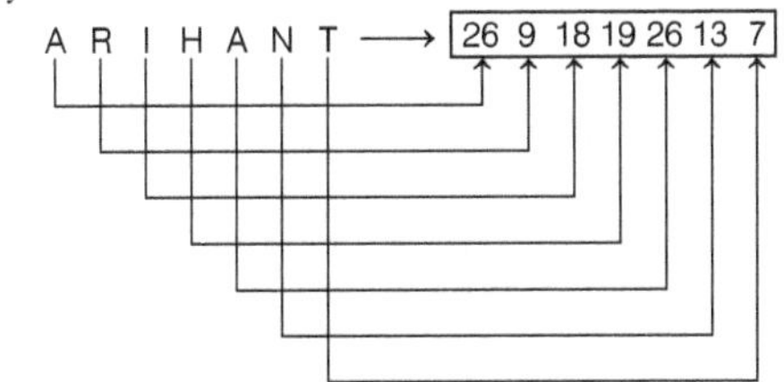

∴ ARIHANT ⇒ 269181926137

40. (*d*) Reverse alphabetical positions of letters are added.

As,

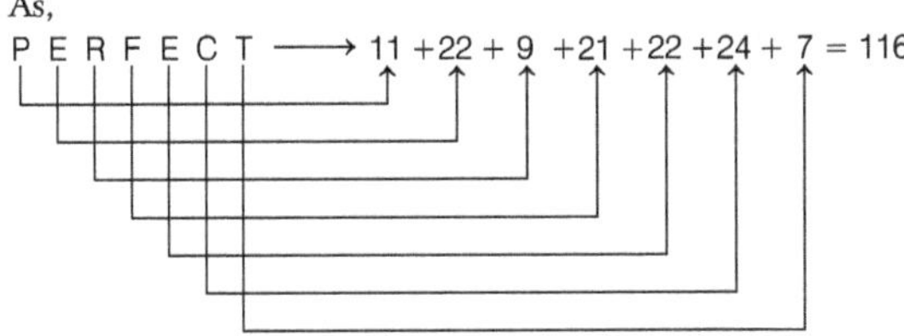

P E R F E C T → 11 + 22 + 9 + 21 + 22 + 24 + 7 = 116

Similarly,

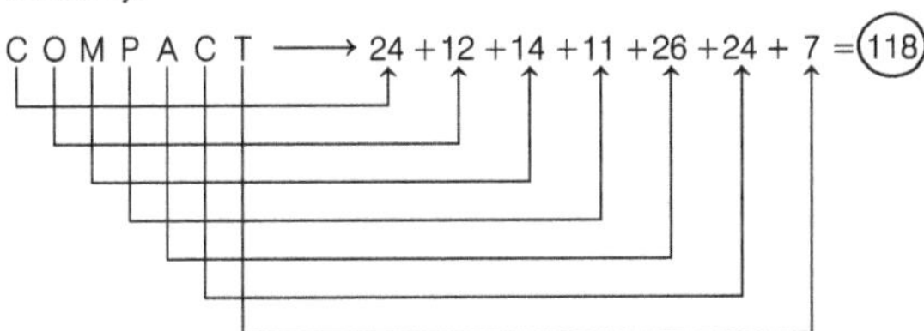

C O M P A C T → 24 + 12 + 14 + 11 + 26 + 24 + 7 = 118

∴ COMPACT ⇒ 118

41. (*b*) As, PING = 4 (∵ Number of letters = 4)

and METAL = 5 (∵ Number of letters = 5)

Similarly, STEADYS = 7 (∵ Number of letters = 7)

42. (*a*) Letters are coded with their reverse alphabetical position.

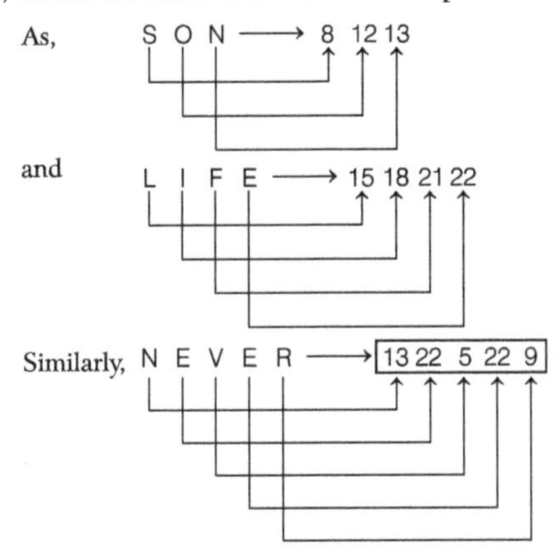

∴ NEVER ⇒ 13225229

43. (*a*) Required answer = Sum of their alphabetical position.

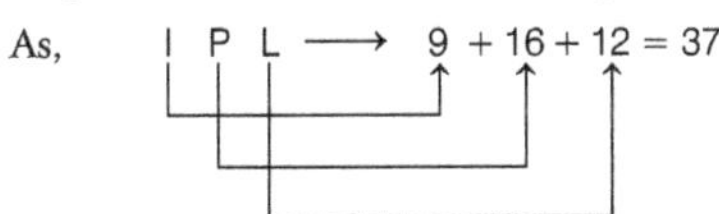

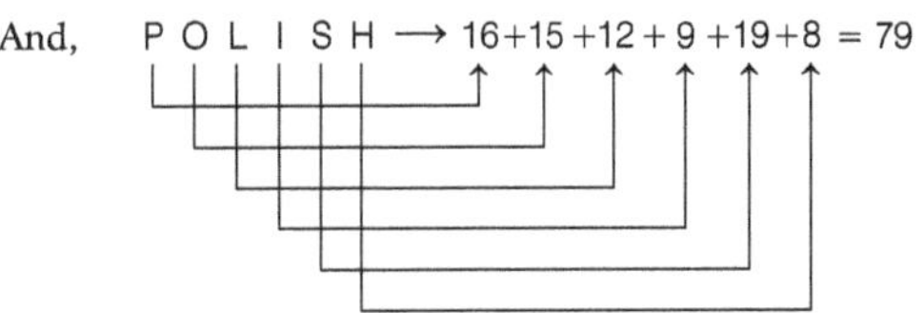

Similarly,

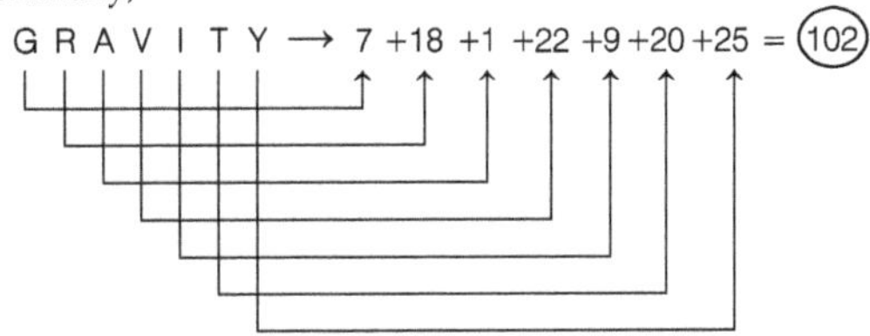

G R A V I T Y → 7 +18 +1 +22 +9 +20 +25 = 102

∴ GRAVITY = 102

44. (*d*) T(20) I(9) S(19) S(19) U(21) E(5)

⇒ 20 + 9 + 19 + 19 + 21 + 5 = 93

Similarly, R(18) O(15) C(3) K(11) E(5) T(20)

⇒ 18 + 15 + 3 + 11 + 5 + 20 = 72

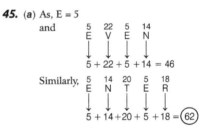

∴ ROCKET ⇒ 72

45. (*a*) As, E = 5

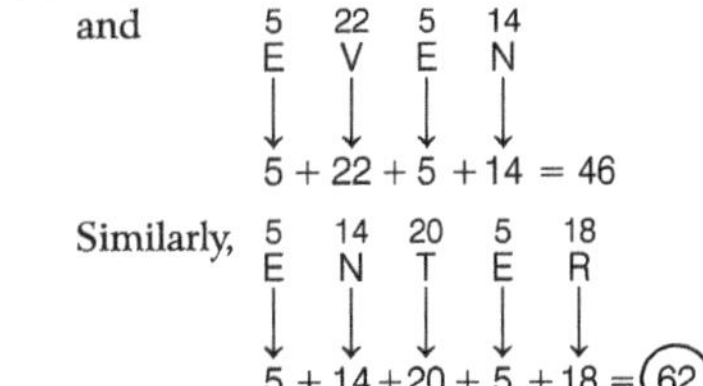

∴ ENTER = 62

46. (*c*) As, A = 1

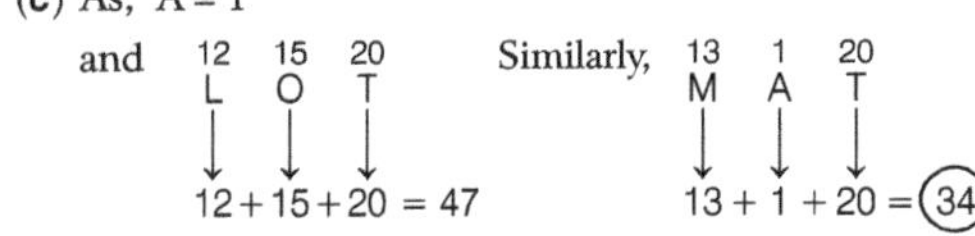

∴ MAT ⇒ 34

47. (*c*) As, M = 13

and M(13) A(1) T(20) → 13 + 1 + 20 = 34

Similarly, W(23) A(1) X(24) → 23 + 1 + 24 = 48

∴ WAX ⇒ 48

48. (*c*) As, E = 5

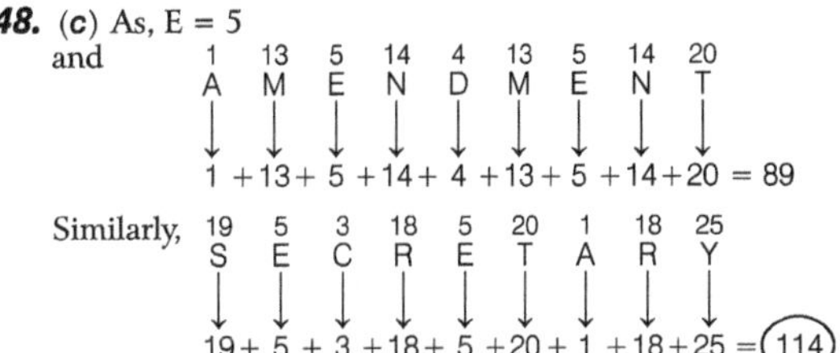

∴ SECRETARY ⇒ 114

49. (*d*) As, A = 1

and V(22) A(1) N(14) → 22 + 1 + 14 = 37

Similarly, F(6) A(1) T(20) → 6 + 1 + 20 = (27)

∴ FAT ⇒ 27

50. (*d*) As, N(14) ⇒ (14 × 2) + 2 = 30

and C(3) O(15) T(20) ⇒ (3 + 15 + 20) × 2 + 2

= 38 × 2 + 2

= 76 + 2 = 78

Similarly, P(16) E(5) T(20) ⇒ (16 + 5 + 20) × 2 + 2

= 41 × 2 + 2 = 82 + 2 = [84]

51. (*c*) As, ZIP —Opposite letter→ ARK → 1 + 18 + 11 = 30

and ZAP —Opposite letter→ AZK → 1 + 26 + 11 = 38

Similarly, VIP —Opposite letter→ ERK → 5 + 18 + 11 = [34]

∴ VIP = 34

52. (*d*) As, P = 16

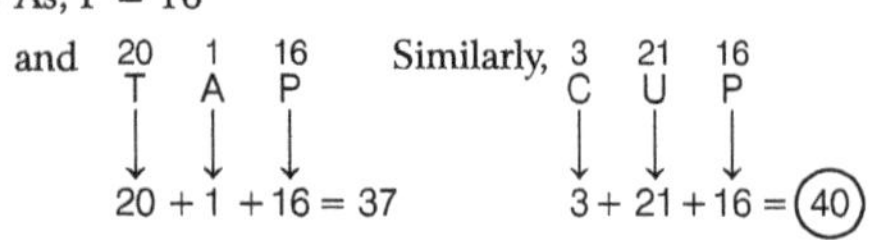

∴ PICK ⇒ 4752

53. (*a*) As, P = 16

and T(20) A(1) P(16) → 20 + 1 + 16 = 37

Similarly, C(3) U(21) P(16) → 3 + 21 + 16 = (40)

∴ CUP ⇒ 40

54. (*d*) As, N = 14

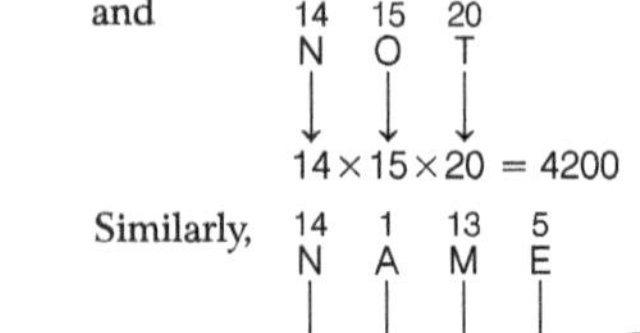

∴ NAME ⇒ 910

55. (*b*) As, E = 5

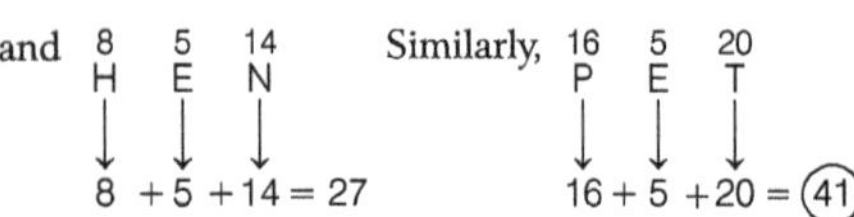

∴ PET ⇒ 41

56. (*c*) As, T = 20

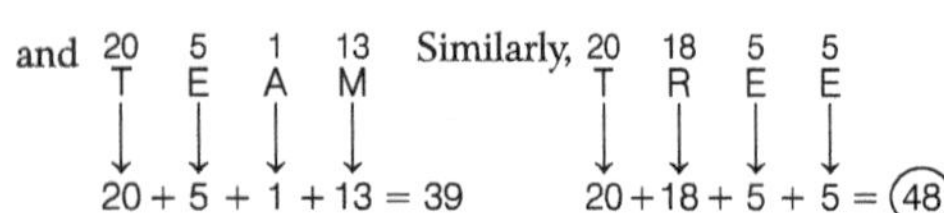

∴ TREE ⇒ 48

57. (*a*) As, M = 13

and M(13) A(1) D(4) → 13 × 1 × 4 = 52

Similarly, M(13) O(15) O(15) D(4) → 13 × 15 × 15 × 4 = (11700)

∴ MOOD ⇒ 11700

58. (*a*) As, G(7) A(1) N(14) E(5) S(19) H(8) → 7 + 1 + 14 + 5 + 19 + 8 = 54

Similarly, P(16) A(1) R(18) V(22) A(1) T(20) I(9) →

16 + 1 + 18 + 22 + 1 + 20 + 9 = [87]

∴ PARVATI ⇒ 87

59. (*c*) As,

M(13) —+6→ 19
A(1) —+6→ 7
C(3) —+6→ 9
H(8) —+6→ 14
I(9) —+6→ 15
N(14) —+6→ 20
E(5) —+6→ 11

Similarly,

D(4) —+6→ 10
A(1) —+6→ 7
N(14) —+6→ 20
G(7) —+6→ 13
E(5) —+6→ 11
R(18) —+6→ 24

∴ DANGER ⇒ 10-7-20-13-11-24

60. (*d*) Each letter is coded with its reverse order letter position.

∴ BRIEF ⇒ 25, 9, 22, 18, 21

61. (*d*) Coded with (Sum of the corresponding alphabetical series) × 4.

As,

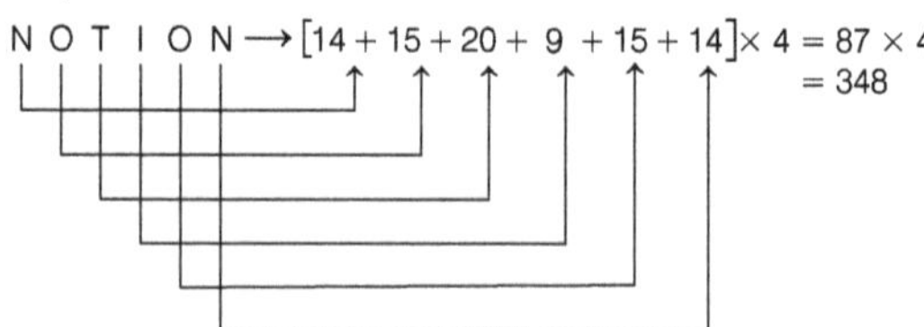

N O T I O N → [14 + 15 + 20 + 9 + 15 + 14] × 4 = 87 × 4
= 348

Similarly,

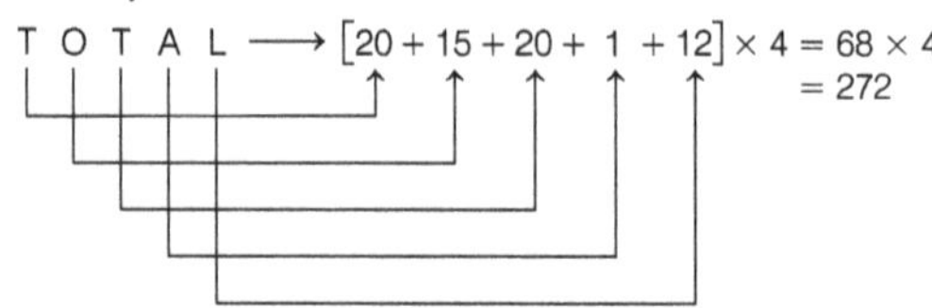

T O T A L → [20 + 15 + 20 + 1 + 12] × 4 = 68 × 4
= 272

∴ TOTAL ⇒ 272

62. (*a*) As,

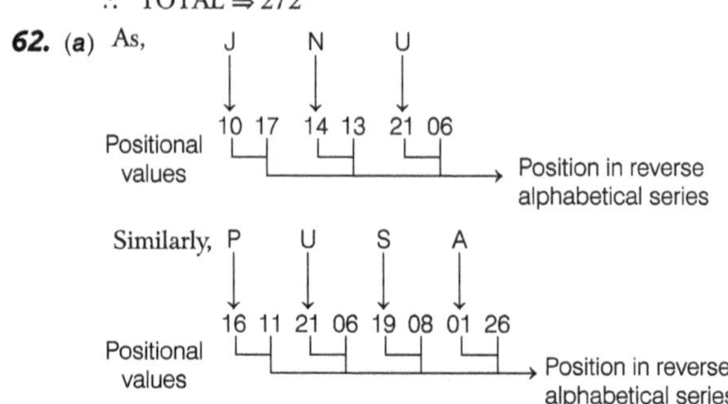

∴ PUSA ⇒ 1611210619080126

63. (*d*) As,

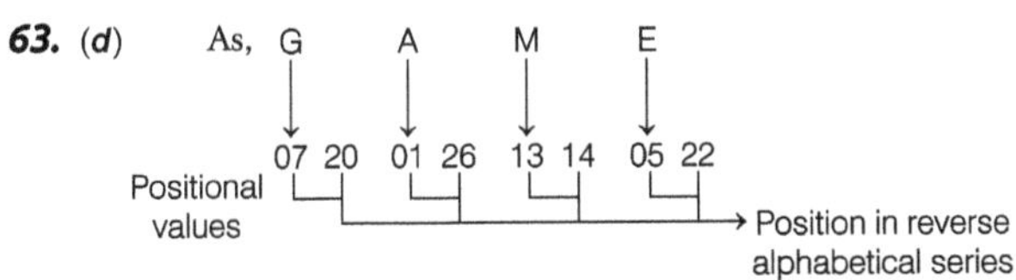

Similarly,

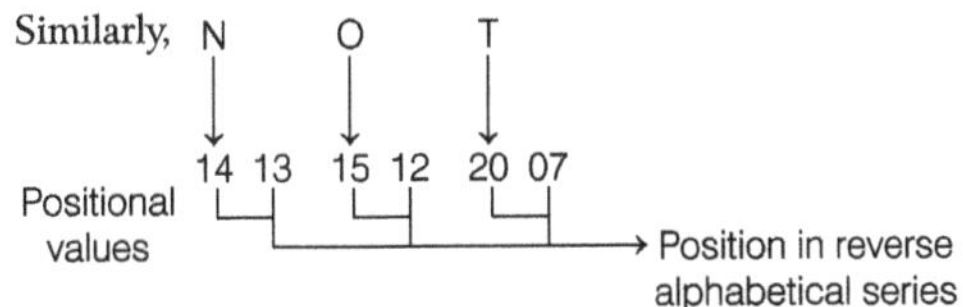

∴ NOT ⇒ 141315122007

64. (*a*) Square of the position of the alphabets in the alphabetical sertics.

As,

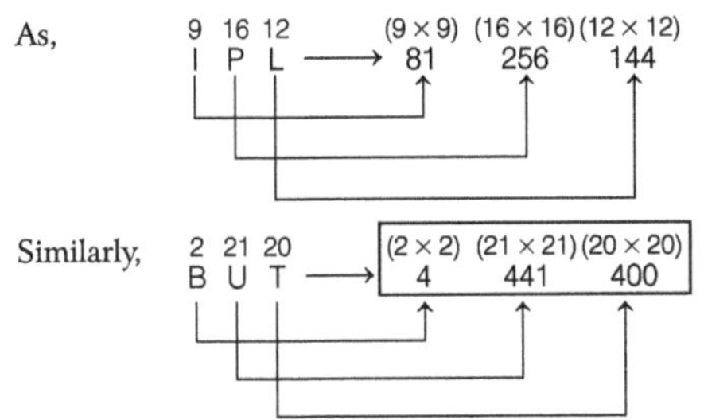

∴ BUT ⇒ 4441400

65. (*a*) Square of the reverse alphabetical position. Let us see

As,

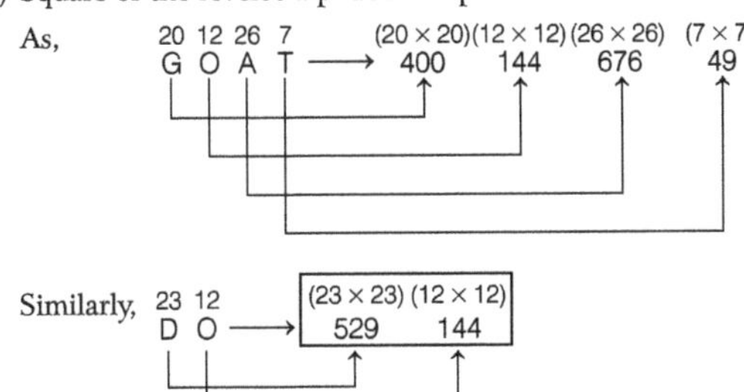

∴ DO ⇒ 529144

66. (*b*) Required answer

$$= \frac{\text{Sum of the corresponding alphabetical positions}}{2}$$

As,

R A M A N ⟶ [18 + 1 + 13 + 1 + 14] , 2 ÷ 47/2 = 23.5

Positional values

Also,

C A P ⟶ [3 + 1 + 16] , 2 ÷ 20/2 = 10

Positional values

Similarly,

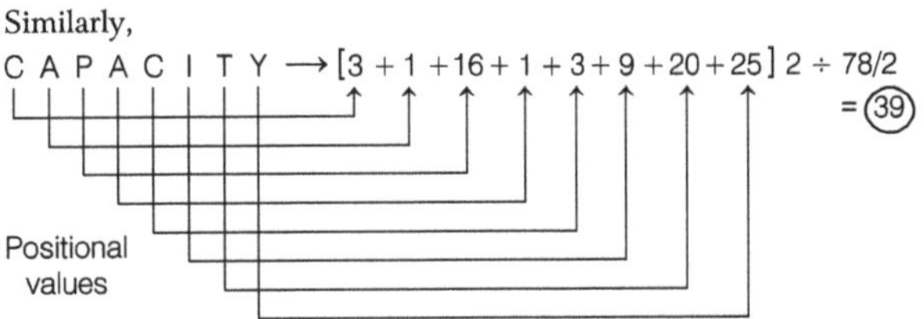

∴ CAPACITY ⇒ 39

67. (*a*) Each letter is coded with its left and right letter positions in alphabetical series.

As,

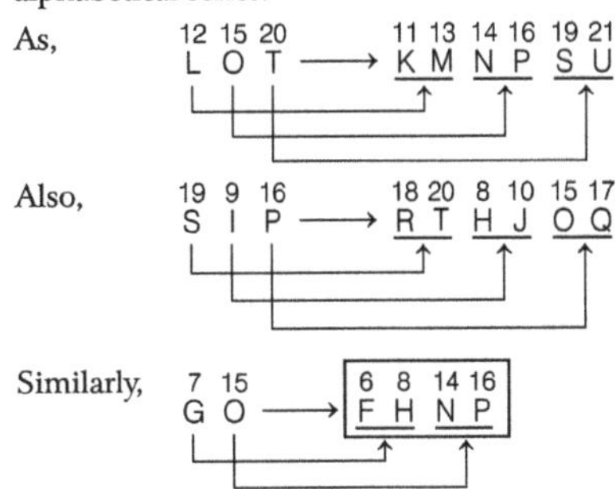

∴ GO ⇒ 681416

68. (*d*) Starting from right, each letter is coded with the digits sum of its corresponding position in alphabetical series.

As,

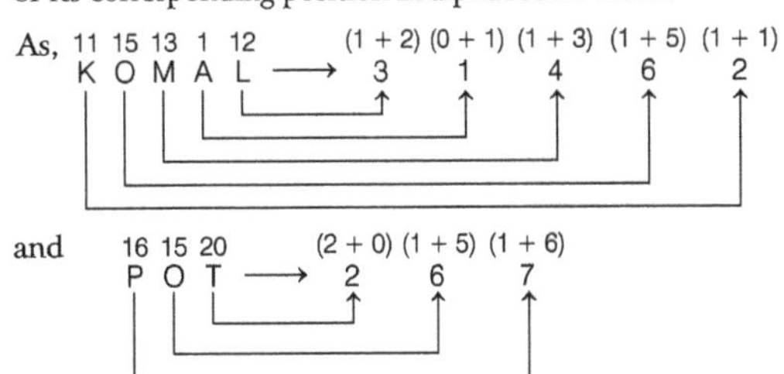

Similarly,

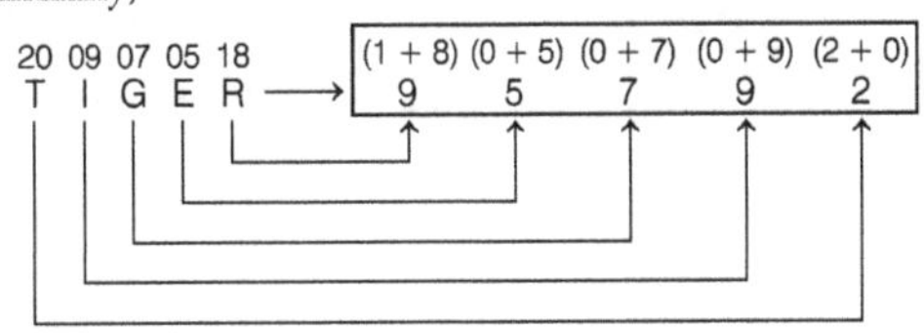

∴ TIGER ⇒ 95792

69. (*a*) Each letter is coded with its right and left letters positions, respectively.

As,

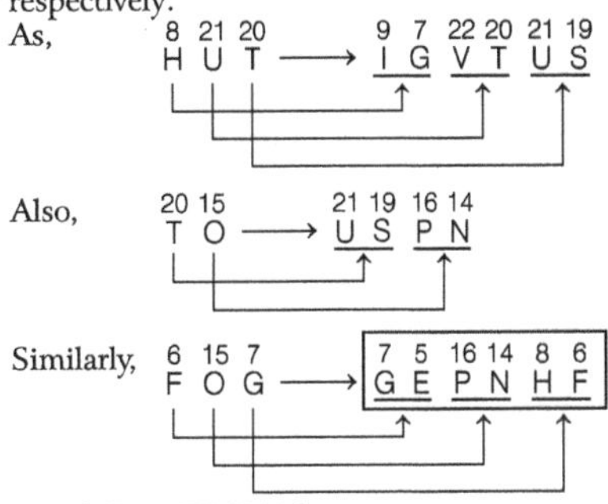

∴ FOG ⇒ 75161486

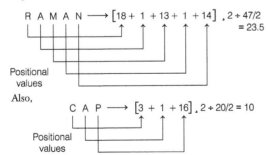

70. (*b*) Each letter is coded with the square of its letter positions in alphabetical series.

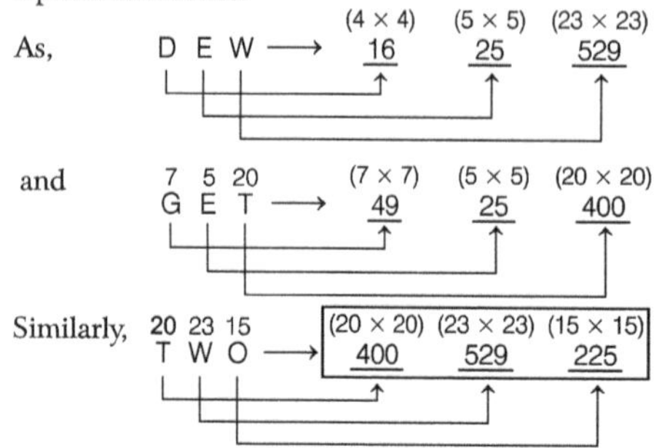

∴ TWO ⇒ 400529225

71. (*b*) Each letter is coded with the digits sum of its letters positions in English alphabetical series. Let us see

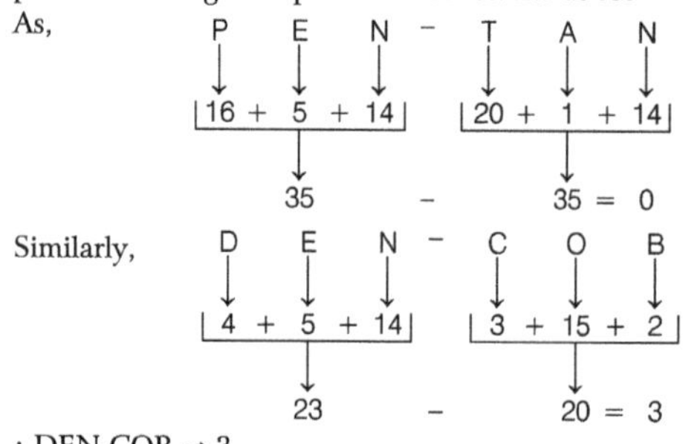

∴ DEN-COB ⇒ 3

72. (*c*) Given, REASON = 5 and BELIEVED = 7
Here, number of letters in the word −1= code
Similarly, GOVERNMENT =10 − 1
∴ GOVERNMENT = 9

TYPE 03

Symbol Coding Based on Similarity

In symbol coding, various symbols are assigned to the letters of a word and based upon their correlation or similarity, the candidates are required to determine the rules or pattern which is being followed.

Under this pattern each letter of a letter group/word is coded on the basis of the similarity of two or more given codes.

Following example will give you a better idea about the type of questions asked.

***Ex* 21** In a certain code language, SHOUT is written as *$59# and HATES is written as $4#6*. How will HOUSE be coded in the same code language? « RBI Assistant 2017

(a) $59#2
(b) 6$295
(c) #95$6
(d) Cannot be determined
(e) $59*6

Solution (*e*)

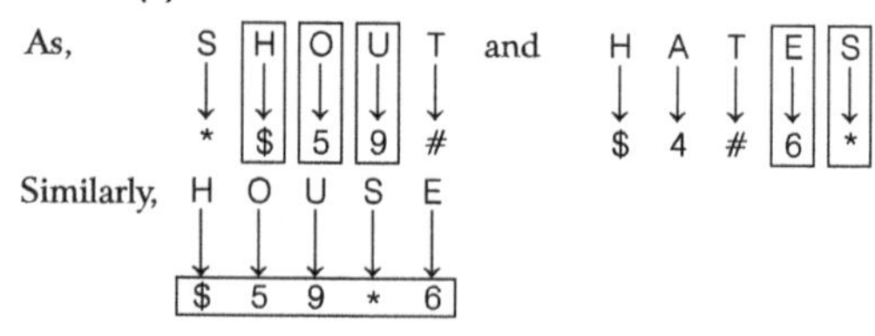

∴ HOUSE ⇒ $5 9*6

Practice CORNER 4.3

1. If in a certain code language 'STAR' is written as '5 $ ★ 2', 'TORE' is written as '$ 3 2 @', then how will 'OATS' be written in that language? « LIC (ADO) 2009

(a) 3 ★ 5 $ (b) 3 ★ $ 5
(c) 3 $ ★ 5 (d) 3 5 ★ $
(e) None of these

2. If in a certain code language 'GONE' is written as '5 @ © 9' and 'SEAL' is written as '6 9 % ★', then how will 'LOGS' be written in that language? « SBI (Clerk) 2010

(a) ★ © 5 6 (b) ★ 9 © 6
(c) ★ @ 6 5 (d) ★ @ 5 6
(e) None of these

3. If in a certain code language 'FIRE' is written as '# % @ $' and 'DEAL' is written as '© $ ★ ↑', then how will 'FAIL' be written in that language?

(a) # ★ % ↑ (b) # $ % ↑
(c) # ★ @ $ (d) # ★ © ↑

4. If in a certain code language 'ROPE' is written as '% 5 7 $', 'DOUBT' is written as '3 5 # 8 ★', and 'LIVE' is written as '@ 2 4 $', then how will 'TROUBLE' be written in that language?

(a) ★ % 5 $ 8 @ $ (b) ★ % # 58 @ $
(c) ★ % 5 # 8 @ 4 (d) ★ % # 58 $ 8
(e) None of these

5. In a certain code, 'BASKET' is written as '5$3%#1' and 'TRIED' is written as '14 ★ # 2'. How is 'SKIRT' written in that code?

(a) 3 % ★ 4 1 (b) 3 ★ % 4 1 (c) 3 % # 4 1 (d) 3 # 4 % 1
(e) None of these

6. If in a certain code language 'HEART' is written as '@8531', 'FEAST' is written as '#8541', then how will 'FARTHEST' be written in that language?

(a) @ 8 5 4 3 # 1 8 (b) # 5 3 1 4 @ 8 1
(c) # 5 3 1 @ 8 4 1 (d) 4 5 3 1 @ 8 4 5
(e) None of these

7. If in a certain code language 'RAT' is written as '★Δ%', 'CAT' is written as '#Δ%' and 'FAT' is written as '$Δ%', then how will 'CAR' be written in that language?
(a) $ % Δ (b) # % $ (c) # H Δ (d) # Δ H
(e) None of these

8. If in a certain code language 'RAIN' is written as '8 $ % 6', 'MORE' is written as '7 # 8 @', then how will 'REMAIN' be written in that language?
(a) 8 @ 7 $ % 6 (b) 7 @ # $ % 6
(c) # @ 7 $ % 6 (d) None of these

9. If RESEARCH is $#!#%$ & @, then SCARE is « RRB NTPC 2016
A. !&%$# B. !@%$#
C. !$%#& D. !@%#$
(a) D (b) A (c) B (d) C

10. In a certain code, P is #, A is %, C is ϕ and E is @. How is PEACE written in that code?
(a) # @ % @ # (b) # @ # ϕ @
(c) % # @ ϕ % (d) # @ % ϕ @
(e) None of these

11. In a certain code, 'DOWN' is written as '5@9#' and 'NAME' is written as '#6%3'. How would 'MODE' be written in that code?
(a) %653 (b) %@63 (c) %5@3 (d) %@53
(e) None of these

12. In a certain code language, 'SAFER' is written as '5@3#2' and 'RIDE' is written as '2© %#', how would 'FEDS' be written in that code? « RBI (Grade 'B') 2009
(a) 3 # © 5 (b) 3 @ % 5
(c) 3 # % 5 (d) 3 # % 2
(e) None of these

Answers / WITH EXPLANATIONS

1. (b) As,

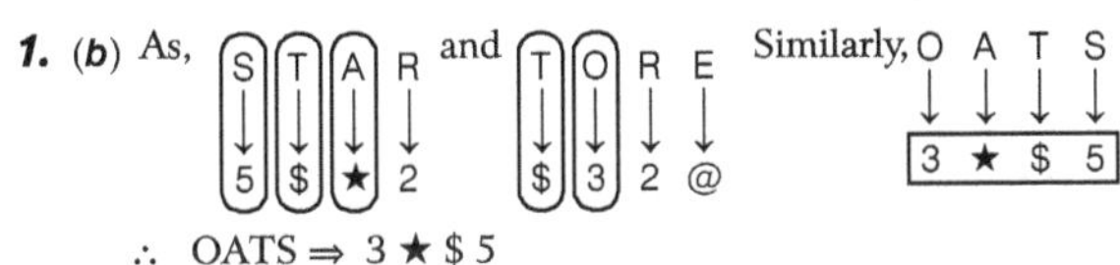

∴ OATS ⇒ 3 ★ $ 5

2. (d) As,

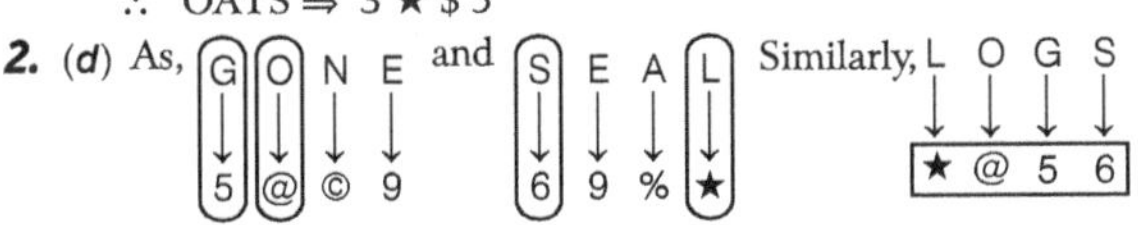

LOGS ⇒ ★ @ 5 6

3. (a) As,

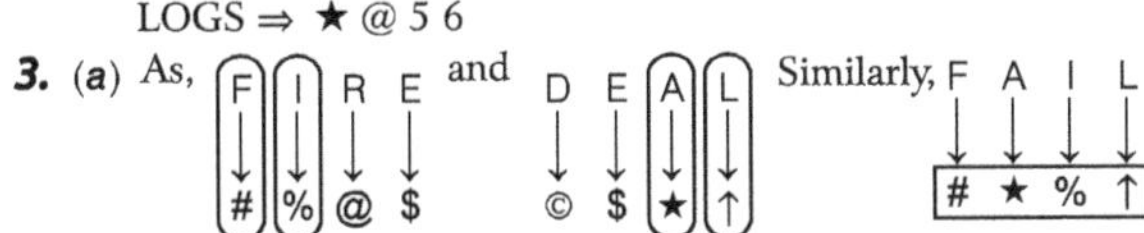

∴ FAIL ⇒ # ★ % ↑

4. (e) As,

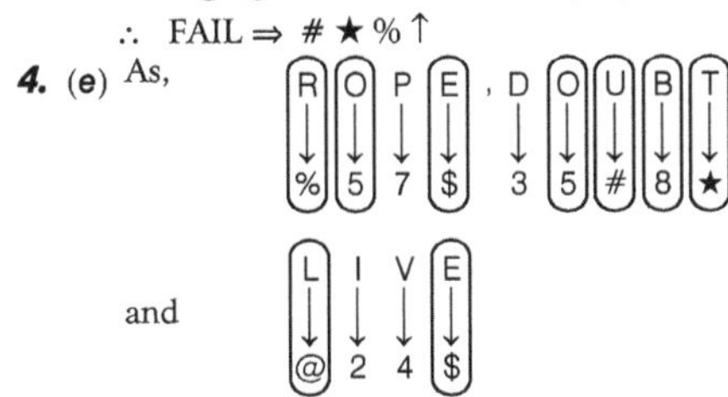

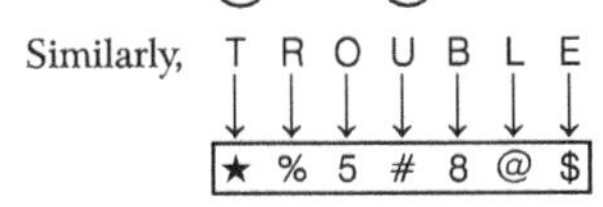

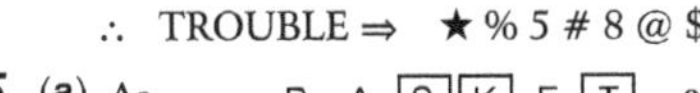

∴ TROUBLE ⇒ ★ % 5 # 8 @ $

5. (a) As,

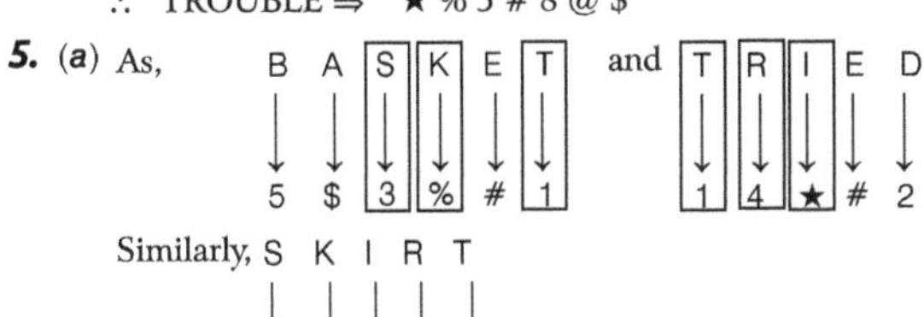

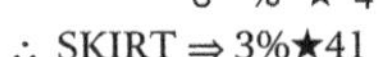

∴ SKIRT ⇒ 3%★41

6. (c) As,

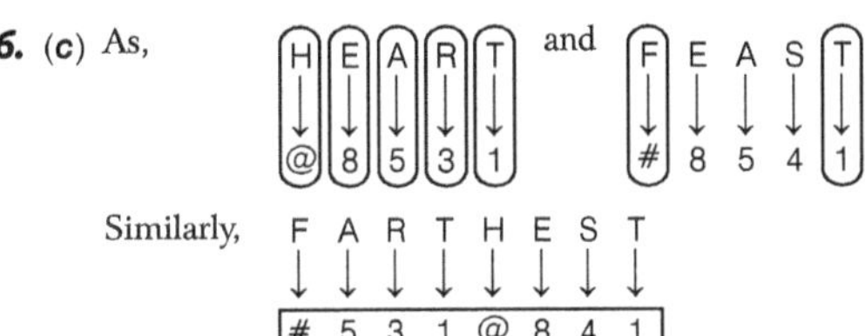

∴ FARTHEST ⇒ #531@841

7. (e) As,

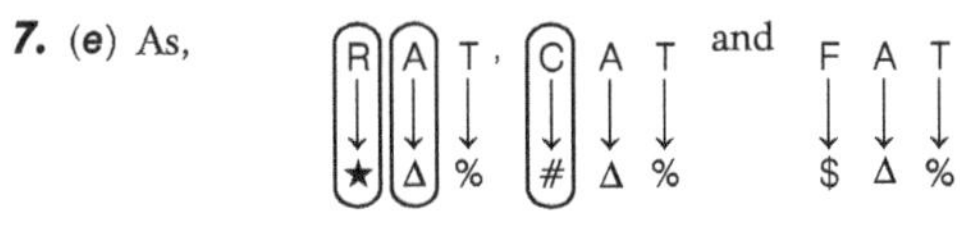

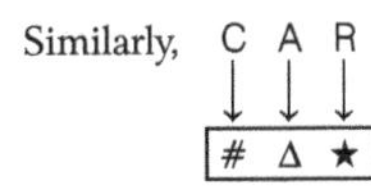

∴ CAR ⇒ # Δ ★

8. (a) As,

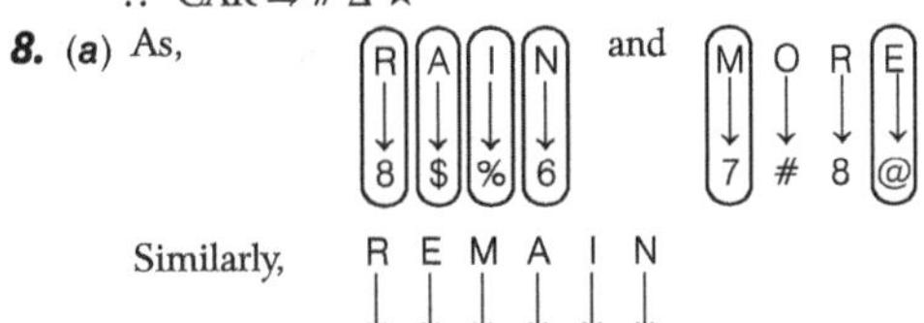

∴ REMAIN ⇒ 8 @ 7 $ % 6

9. (b) As,

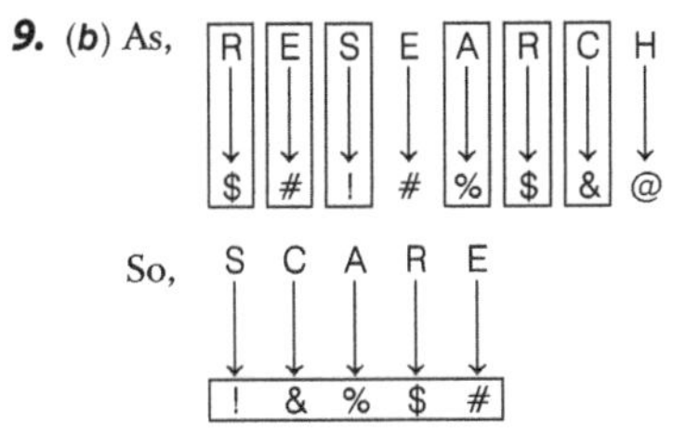

∴ SCARE ⇒ ! & % $ #

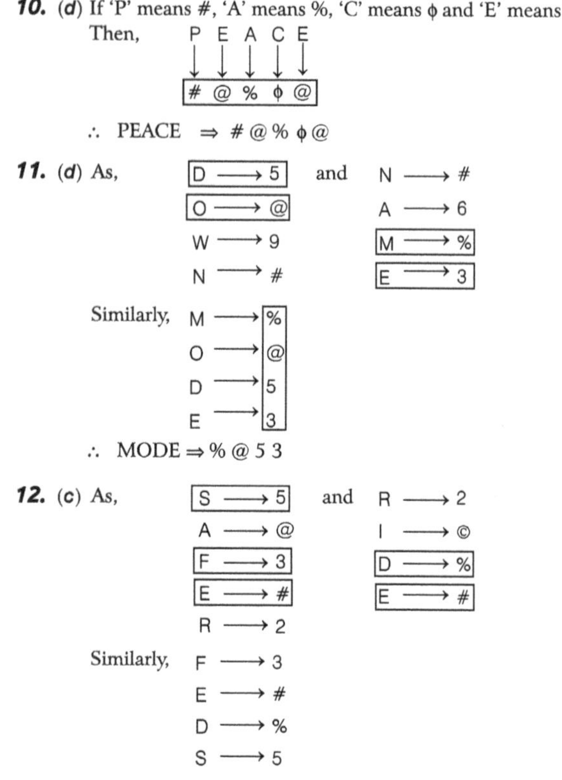

10. (*d*) If 'P' means #, 'A' means %, 'C' means ϕ and 'E' means @.
Then, P E A C E → # @ % ϕ @

∴ PEACE ⇒ # @ % ϕ @

11. (*d*) As, D → 5, O → @, W → 9, N → # and N → #, A → 6, M → %, E → 3

Similarly, M → %, O → @, D → 5, E → 3

∴ MODE ⇒ % @ 5 3

12. (*c*) As, S → 5, A → @, F → 3, E → #, R → 2 and R → 2, I → ©, D → %, E → #

Similarly, F → 3, E → #, D → %, S → 5

∴ FEDS → 3 # % 5

TYPE 04

Coding by Substitution/ Word Replacement

In substitution or word replacement, a confusing code is provided by giving a different name to the word. Under this pattern, a series of words is given and each word of this series is coded with another word. Candidates are required to find out the code for a word in the given series and then provide the right information regarding the word.

Following examples will give you a better idea about the type of questions asked

***Ex* 22** If 'green' is called 'red', 'red' is called 'blue', 'blue is called white', 'white' is called 'yellow', 'yellow' is called 'violet', then what is the colour of grass?

(a) Blue (b) Yellow (c) Violet (d) Red

***Solution* (*d*)** As, colour of grass is 'green' but here 'green' is called 'red' and hence according to the given information colour of grass must be 'red'.

***Ex* 23** If 'blue' means 'green', 'green' means 'white', 'white 'means' 'yellow', 'yellow' means 'black', 'black' means 'red' and 'red' means 'brown', then what is the colour of 'milk'?

« NIFT (UG) 2014

(a) Black (b) White (c) Yellow (d) Green

***Solution* (*c*)** Colour of 'milk' is 'white' but here 'white' means 'yellow'. Hence, colour of 'milk' is yellow.

Practice/CORNER 4.4

1. If 'RED' is called 'GREEN', 'GREEN' is called 'YELLOW', 'YELLOW' is called 'VIOLET', 'VIOLET' is called 'BLUE',' BLUE' is called 'ORANGE', then what is the colour of 'Lady Finger'?

(a) GREEN (b) BLUE
(c) VIOLET (d) YELLOW

2. If 'DOG' is called 'COW', 'COW' is called 'LION, 'LION' is called 'BUFFALO', 'BUFFALO' is called 'OX', 'OX' is called 'CAT', then which of the following animals is wild one?

(a) DOG (b) BUFFALO (c) LION (d) OX

3. If 'CAR' is called 'BIKE', 'BIKE' is called 'BICYCLE', 'BICYCLE' is called 'SCOOTER', 'SCOOTER' is called 'TRAIN', 'TRAIN' is called 'AEROPLANE', then which one of the following options is associated with railways?

(a) BIKE (b) TRAIN
(c) AEROPLANE (d) SCOOTER

4. If 'orange' is called 'butter', 'butter' is called 'soap', 'soap' is called 'ink', 'ink' is called' 'honey and 'honey' is called 'orange', which of the following is used for washing clothes? « FCI Uttarakhand Watchman 2018

(a) Soap (b) Honey
(c) Orange (d) Ink

5. If 'ROAD' is called 'CAR', 'CAR' is called 'TRAIN', 'TRAIN' is called 'SCHOOL', 'SCHOOL' is called 'HOUSE', 'HOUSE' is called 'OFFICE', then where do children go to study? « UCO Bank (Clerk) 2011

(a) HOUSE (b) TRAIN
(c) SCHOOL (d) OFFICE
(e) None of these

6. If 'bucket' is known as 'tub', 'tub' is known as 'glass', 'glass' is known as 'saucer', 'saucer' is known as 'spoon', then which utensil will be used for drinking water?

(a) Tub (b) Saucer
(c) Glass (d) Spoon

7. If 'HINDI' is called 'ENGLISH', 'ENGLISH' is called 'URDU', 'URDU' is called 'HISTORY', 'HISTORY' is called 'ECONOMICS', 'ECONOMICS' is called 'BIOLOGY', then in which subject we read the story of Mughal King Shahjahan?

(a) History (b) English
(c) Urdu (d) Economics

8. If 'blue' is called 'green', 'green' is called 'white', 'white' is called 'red', 'red' is called 'black', then what is the colour of clear sky?

(a) Blue (b) Green (c) White (d) Black

9. If 'green' is called 'black', 'black' is called 'blue', 'blue' is called 'red', 'red' is called 'white' and 'white' is called 'orange', then what is the colour of blood?

(a) Red (b) Black (c) Green (d) White
(e) None of these

10. If 'tiger' is called 'fox', 'fox' is called 'lion', 'lion' is called 'rat', 'rat' is called 'goat', 'goat' is called 'cow', then which of the following is the king of forest?

(a) Fox (b) Lion (c) Rat (d) Cow

11. In a certain code language, pink is called wood, wood is called pen, pen is called colour and colour is called brown. In this language, which of the following is used for writing ? « SSC CPO 2019

(a) Pen (b) Pink (c) Brown (d) Colour

12. If 'blue' is called 'green', 'green' is called 'orange', 'orange' is called 'yellow', 'yellow' is called 'black', 'black' is called 'red' and 'red' is called 'white', then what is the colour of turmeric?

(a) Orange (b) Green (c) White (d) Black
(e) None of these

13. If 'flower' is called 'tree', 'tree' is called 'red', 'red' is called 'gold' and 'gold' is called 'white', then with which of the following items, jewellery is made? « IBPS (PO) 2011

(a) Tree (b) Red (c) White (d) Flower
(e) None of these

14. If 'lion' is called 'fish', 'fish' is called 'parrot', 'parrot' is called 'rat', 'rat' is called 'cat' and 'cat' is called 'tiger', then which of the following is a bird?

(a) Fish (b) Parrot
(c) Rat (d) Tiger

15. If 'goat' is called 'cow', 'cow' is called 'lion', 'lion' is called 'ass', 'ass' is called 'rat', 'rat' is called 'cat', 'cat' is called 'dog'; then which of the following is a rodent?

(a) Lion (b) Ass (c) Rat (d) Cat

16. If 'football' is called 'hockey', 'hockey' is called 'badminton', 'badminton' is called 'cricket', 'cricket' is called 'tennis', 'tennis' is called 'squash' and 'squash' is called 'chess', then which game Sachin Tendulkar associated with?

(a) Squash (b) Cricket
(c) Badminton (d) Tennis

17. If 'lily' is called 'lotus', 'lotus' is called 'rose', 'rose' is called 'sunflower' and 'sunflower' is called 'marigold', then which will be the national flower of India?

(a) Lily (b) Lotus
(c) Rose (d) Marigold

18. On another planet, the local terminology for 'earth', 'water', 'light', 'air' and 'sky' are 'sky', 'light', 'air', 'water' and 'earth', respectively. If someone is thirsty there, what would he drink?

(a) Light (b) Air (c) Sky (d) Water

19. If the animals which can walk are called 'swimmers', animals who crawl are called 'flying', those living in water are called 'snakes' and those which fly in the sky are called 'hunters', then what will a lizard be called?

(a) Swimmers (b) Snakes
(c) Flying (d) Hunters

20. If rain is water, water is road, road is cloud, cloud is sky, sky is sea and sea is path, where do aeroplanes fly?
« UKPSC Asst. Conservator of forest 2019

(a) Road (b) Sea (c) Cloud (d) Water

Answers WITH EXPLANATIONS

1. (d) Colour of 'Lady Finger' is green but here green is called yellow. Hence, colour of 'Lady Finger' is yellow.

2. (b) 'Lion' is a wild animal but here 'lion' is called 'buffalo'. Hence, in this case 'buffalo' is a wild animal.

3. (c) 'Train' is associated with 'railways' but here train is called 'aeroplane'. Hence, in this case 'aeroplane' is associated with railways.

4. (d) Soap is used for washing clothes and soap is called ink. Therefore, ink is used for washing clothes.

5. (a) Children study in 'school' but here 'school' is called 'house'. Hence, in this case 'house' is the place where children go to study.

6. (b) 'Glass' is used for drinking water and here 'glass' is called as 'saucer'. Hence, in this case saucer is used for drinking 'water'.

7. (d) In 'History', we read the story of Shahjahan; but here History is called 'Economics'. Hence, in this case, we read about Shahjahan in Economics.

8. (b) The colour of clear sky is 'blue' but here 'blue' is called 'green'. Hence, in this case colour of clear sky is 'green'.

9. (d) Colour of blood is 'red' but here 'red' is called 'white'. Hence, in this case colour of blood is 'white'.

10. (c) The king of forest is 'lion' but here 'lion' is called 'rat'. Hence, in this case rat is the king of forest.

11. (d) Pen is used for writing but here, pen is called colour. So, colour is used for writing.

12. (d) The colour of turmeric is 'yellow' but here, 'yellow' is called 'black'. Hence, in this case colour of turmeric is 'black'.

13. (c) 'Jewellery' is made of 'gold' but here 'gold' is called 'white'. Hence, in this case jewellery is made of white.

14. (*c*) 'Parrot' is a bird but here 'parrot' is called 'rat'. Hence, in this case 'rat' is a bird.

15. (*d*) Rat is a rodent but here rat is called cat. Hence, in this case cat is a rodent.

16. (*d*) Sachin Tendulkar is a cricketer but here cricket is called tennis. Hence, in this case Sachin Tendulkar is associated with tennis.

17. (*c*) We know that, national flower of 'India' is 'lotus' and here 'lotus' is called 'rose'. Hence, in this case 'rose' is the national flower of India.

18. (*a*) 'Water' quenches thirst and here 'water' is called as 'light'. Hence, in this case 'light' quenches thirst.

19. (*c*) Lizard crawls and here 'crawl' is called 'flying'. Hence, in this case, lizard is 'flying'.

20. (*b*) Since aeroplanes fly in the sky and sky is called sea. Therefore, aeroplanes fly in the sea.

TYPE 05

Fictitious Language Coding

In this type of questions, some messages are provided in the code language and some codes are assigned to each word of the messages.

The candidates are required to decipher the code of each word by finding the common code for two words and this process is followed to decipher the code for each word thereafter and hence the entire message is decoded.

In some cases, there is no common word/number in the message given. In those cases, the words/numbers are coded separately. You have to identify the correct pattern of coding and find the code for the word or message given in the question.

Following examples will give you a better idea about the type of questions asked

***Ex* 24** In a certain code language 'he is great' is written as 'ka pa ra' and 'is Ram hungry' is written as 'na sa ka'. Find the code for 'is'.

(a) na (b) sa (c) ka (d) ra

Solution (c) he (is) great ⟶ (ka) pa ra

(is) Ram hungry ⟶ na sa (ka)

Clearly, code for 'is' = ka

In the above example, code for 'he' = pa or ra

code for 'great' = pa or ra

code for 'Ram' = na or sa

code for 'hungry' = na or sa

In place of fictious language, words can also be coded with digits (1, 2, 3, ...), letters (A, B, C, ...) or symbols (ϕ, %, +, ⇒, ...).

***Ex* 25** In a certain code language, 'po ki top ma' means 'Usha is playing cards', 'kop ja ki ma' means 'Asha is playing tennis', 'ki tap sop ho' means 'they are playing football' and 'po sur kop' means 'cards and tennis'. Which word in that language means 'Asha'? « RPSC 2013

(a) ja (b) ma (c) kop (d) top

Solution **(a)** According to the given information,

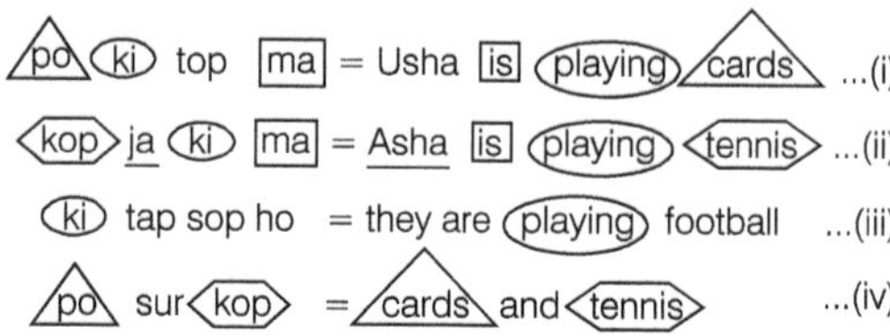

From Eqs. (i), (ii) and (iv), 'ja' means 'Asha'.

***Ex* 26** In a certain code language, '1 2 3' means 'hot filtered coffee', '3 5 6' means 'very hot day' and '5 8 9' means 'day and night'. How will 'very' be coded as in that code language? « UPSSSC Junior Assistant 2020

(a) 6 (b) 7 (c) 1 (d) 2

Solution **(a)** According to the given information,

1 2 (3) ⇒ (hot) filtered coffee ...(i)

(3) [5] {6} ⇒ {very} (hot) [day] ...(ii)

[5] 8 9 ⇒ [day] and night ...(iii)

From Eqs. (i), (ii) and (iii),

very ⇒ 6

DIRECTIONS ~ (Example Nos. 27-30) *Study the following information carefully and answer the given questions.* « IDBI Executive 2018

In a certain code language,
'here is tunnel she stop' is written as 'isa kin ha ti la',
'he goes through tunnel' is written as 'nit ti pi sit'
'she goes here often' is written as 'sit la tin isa' and
'tunnel is far through here' is written as 'ha nit la ti fa'

***Ex* 27.** Which of the following is the code for 'tunnel'?

(a) nit (b) ti (c) la (d) na
(e) None of these

***Ex* 28.** What does code 'sit' stand for?

(a) goes (b) through
(c) he (d) Cannot be determined
(e) None of these

***Ex* 29.** 'he is often' can be coded as ....

(a) sa pi la (b) fa tin ha (c) pi ha tin (d) kin tip sit
(e) None of these

***Ex* 30.** Which of the following is the code for 'stop'?

(a) la (b) tip (c) sit (d) kin
(e) None of these

Solution (Example Nos. 27-30) According to the given information,

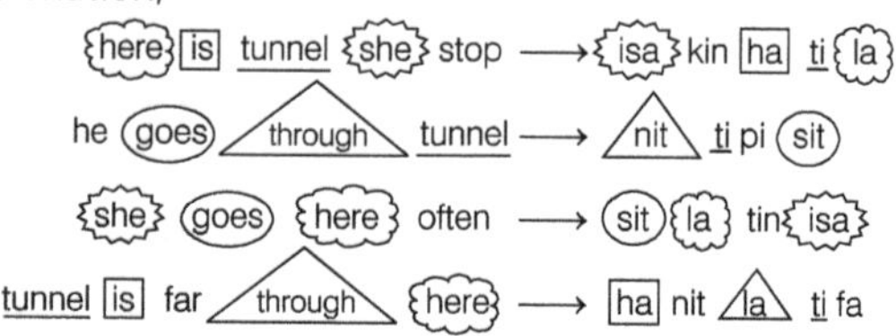

27. (b) The code for 'tunnel' is 'ti'.

28. (a) The code for 'sit' is 'goes'.

29. (c) The code for 'he is often' is 'pi ha tin'.

30. (d) The code for 'stop' is 'kin'.

DIRECTIONS ~ (Example Nos. 31-33) *Study the information below and answer the following questions.*

In a certain code language,

'Thin paper neatly folded' is written as @D6, %R5, !N4, ?Y6

'Four people from USA' is written as @M4, % E6, #A3, @K4

'Urban development programme launched' is written as %E9, *T11, #N5, &D8

'Dhaya likes forties hero' is written as @S7, &S5, *A5, $O4

***Ex* 31** The code for the word 'People' is

(a) @M4 (b) %E6
(c) #A3 (d) @R4
(e) None of these

***Ex* 32** The code '*A5' denotes which of the following word?

(a) Likes (b) Hero
(c) Forties (d) Dhaya
(e) None of these

***Ex* 33** The code word of 'Paper' is

(a) @R4 (b) %E6
(c) @M4 (d) #A3
(e) None of these

Solutions (Example Nos. 31-33) First code-symbol is as per the first letter of the word.

T	P	N	F	U	D	L	H
!	%	?	@	#	*	&	$

Second code-last letter of the word.
Third code–Number of letters in the word

31. (b) Code of 'People' is %E6.

32. (d) *A5 is the code for 'Dhaya'.

33. (e) Code for Paper is %R5.

DIRECTIONS ~ (Example Nos. 34-36) *Study the information and answer the following questions.*

In a certain code language,

'Kite fly in sit' is coded as 'X25G D5L S20T M14J'

'exam date are search' is coded as 'L13F D5B D5E G8T'

'solution is must for' is coded as 'M14T S20N R19J Q18G'

'very problem may wrong is coded as

'F7X X25N L13Q X25W'

***Ex* 34** What is the code for 'School' in the given code language ?

(a) K21R (b) R12K
(c) K12T (d) K34R
(e) R14K

***Ex* 35** What is the code for 'fight problem' in the given code language ?

(a) L13Q S19G (b) G20S L13Q
(c) S20G L13Q (d) L13Q S19T
(e) None of these

***Ex* 36** What may be the possible code for 'money quick sky' in the given code language ?

(a) X25N J11R T25X (b) J11R X25T N25X
(c) J11S X25U N25X (d) X25N X25T J11R
(e) X16N J12N X20S

Solutions (Example Nos. 34-36)

According to the given information,

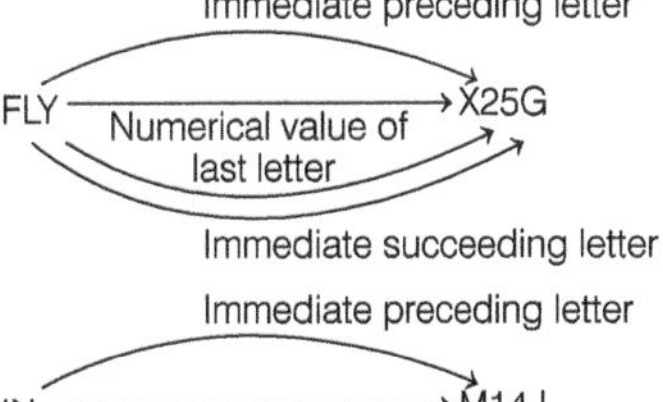

Immediate preceding letter
IN
M14J
Numerical value of last letter
Immediate succeeding letter

34. (c) School = K12T

35. (c) Fight problem = S20G L13Q

36. (d) Money quick sky = X25N X25T J11R

Practice / CORNER 4.5

1. In a certain code language 'lu ja ka hu' means 'will you meet us', 'lu ka hu pa' means 'will you sold us'. Then what is the code of 'meet' in this code language?
« SBI Clerk 2016

(a) ja (b) lu (c) ka (d) hu
(e) None of these

2. In a certain code « UKPSC Asst. Conservator of Forest 2019

157 = He is naughty
723 = She is cute
825 = Cute and naughty
What is the code for 'She'?

(a) 2 (b) 3 (c) 5 (d) 7

3. If in a certain code language 'pick and choose' is written as 'ko ho po' and 'pick up and come' is written as 'to no ko po', then how will 'pick' be written in that language?
« LIC (ADO) 2011

(a) ko (b) po
(c) ko or po (d) Cannot be determined
(e) None of these

4. In a certain code, 'ki pit lit' means 'some small houses', 'les ki tim' means 'some good buildings' and 'tim nis lit' means' many small buildings' . What is the code for 'houses'? « FCI Assistant 2015

(a) lit (b) ki (c) pit (d) tim

5. In a certain code language, 'Sue Re Nik' means 'She is brave', 'Pi Sor Re Nik' means 'She is always smiling' and 'Sor Re Zhi' means 'Is always cheerful'. What is the code used for the word' smiling' ? « SSC (CGL) 2014

(a) Sor (b) Nik
(c) Re (d) Pi

6. If in a certain code language 'nik ka pa' means 'who are you', 'ka na ta da' means 'you may come here' and 'ho ta sa' means 'come and go', then what does 'nik' mean in that language? « IBPS (Clerk) 2011

(a) who (b) are
(c) 'who' or 'are' (d) Data inadequate
(e) None of these

7. If in a certain code language 'how can you go' is written as 'ja da ka pa', 'you come here' is written as 'na ka sa' and 'come and go' is written as 'ra pa sa', then how will 'here' be written in that language? « IOB (PO) 2010

(a) ja (b) na
(c) pa (d) Data inadequate
(e) None of these

8. In a certain language 'la pil ta' means 'fruit is sweet', 'na sa pil' means 'flower and fruit'; 'na tee la', means 'flower is beautiful'. In that language what stands for 'sweet'? « CGPSC 2016

(a) la (b) ta
(c) sa (d) pil
(e) None of the above

9. In a certain code language, '786' means 'study very hard' '958' means 'hard work pays and '645' means 'study and work'. Which of the following is the code for 'very'? « MP Patwari 2017

(a) 9 (b) 8
(c) 6 (d) 7

10. If in a certain code language 'how old are you' is written as 'ko to po ha' and 'you are very beautiful' is written as 'na po da to', then how will 'how' be written in that language?

(a) ko (b) ha
(c) 'ko' or 'ha' (d) Data inadequate
(e) None of these

11. If in a certain code language 'no more food' is written as 'ta ka da' and 'more than that' is written as 'sa pa ka', then how will 'that' be written in that language?

(a) sa (b) ka
(c) sa or pa (d) Data inadequate
(e) None of the above

12. If in a certain code language 'nik ma de' is written as 'he has come', 'de lit pa' is written as 'come here fast' and 'ma la se' is written as 'she has gone' then how will 'he' be written in that language?

(a) nik (b) ma
(c) de (d) cannot be determined
(e) None of these

13. If in a certain code language 'monday is a holiday' is written as 'sa da pa na' and 'they enjoy a holiday' is written as 'da na ta ka', then how will 'monday' be written in that language? « IBPS (Clerk) 2011

(a) sa (b) pa
(c) 'sa' or 'pa' (d) Data inadequate
(e) None of these

DIRECTIONS ~ (Q. Nos. 14 and 15) *Study the following information carefully and answer the given questions.* « SBI Clerk 2018

In a certain code language,
'good key friends' in coded as 'xo pe cm'
'key law found' is coded as 'xo og bt'
'data key good' is coded as 'tu xo pe'

14. Which of the following is the code for 'good'?

(a) xo (b) pe (c) tu (d) cm
(e) None of these

15. Which of the following word is coded as 'og'?

(a) Law (b) Good
(c) Found (d) Either 'a' or 'c'
(e) None of the above

DIRECTIONS ~(Q. Nos. 16-20) *Study the given information carefully to answer the given questions.* « IBPS PO 2015

In a certain code language.
'few organise farming techniques' is written as 'li gs da ce'
'fertilizer products few available' is written as 'fo pz nb gs'
'organise waste into fertilizer' is written as 'nb ce pt mk'
'disposal of farming waste' is written as 'hu mk li yu'
(All codes are two-letter codes only)

16. What will be the code for 'few waste' in the given code language?

(a) mk gs (b) gs li (c) pt da (d) da mk
(e) Other than those given as options

17. What is the code for 'organise' in the given code language?

(a) is (b) ce (c) da (d) pt
(e) Other than those given as options

18. In the given code language, what does the code 'yu' stand for?

(a) farming (b) techniques
(c) Either 'of' or 'disposal' (d) waste
(e) Either 'into' or 'few'

19. If 'waste management techniques' is coded as 'ax da mk' in the given code language, then how will 'farming fertilizer management' be coded as?

(a) ax nb cr (b) li ax pt
(c) nb li ax (d) gs li nb
(e) Other than those given as option

20. What is the code for 'available' in the given code language?

(a) Either 'pz' or 'fo' (b) Either 'nb' or 'mk'
(c) li (d) hu
(e) Other than those given as options

DIRECTIONS ~ (Q. Nos. 21-25) *Study the following information carefully and answer the questions given below.* « IBPS RRB PO 2019

In a certain code language
'left right centre' is written as 'yo vo na',
'ahead below behind, is written as 'sa ra la',
'above centre right' is written as 'ha vo na', and
'behind below above' is written as 'ha ra la'

21. What is the code for 'left' ?
(a) sa (b) ha (c) yo (d) na
(e) None of these

22. 'behind' will be written as ?
(a) ra (b) ha
(c) la (d) either (a) or (c)
(e) None of these

23. What is the code for 'ahead' ?
(a) sa (b) yo
(c) la (d) ha
(e) Can not be determined

24. What does 'ha' stand for ?
(a) behind (b) below
(c) ahead (d) above
(e) None of these

25. What is the code for 'centre' ?
(a) la (b) yo (c) sa (d) ha
(e) Can not be determined

DIRECTIONS ~ (Q.Nos. 26-30) *Study the given information and answer the given questions.* « SBI Clerk 2015

In a certain code language
'dress code for meeting' is written as 'dk pd jn te'
'wear black formal dress' is written as 'pd ro ld le'
'formal meeting this weekend' is written as 'yi te le vr'
'black code this weekend' is written as 'jn vr ld yi'
(All the codes are two-letter codes).

26. In the given code language, what does 'le' stands for?
(a) this (b) formal (c) dress (d) black
(e) None of these

27. In the given code language, what is the code for 'dress'?
(a) jn (b) ro (c) ld (d) pd
(e) None of these

28. What does 'ld' stand for in the given code language?
(a) meeting
(b) weekend
(c) formal
(d) Other than those given as options
(e) None of the above

29. Which of the following possibly means 'security code' in the given code language?
(a) ux vr (b) vr tc (c) pd ux (d) jn ux
(e) None of these

30. What is the code for 'weekend' in the given code language?
(a) Either yi or vr (b) le
(c) te (d) jn
(e) ld

DIRECTIONS ~ (Q. Nos. 31-35) *Study the following information carefully to answer the given questions.* « SBI (PO) 2013

In a certain code language.
'economics is not money' is written as 'ka la ho ga'
'demand and supply economics' is written as 'mo ta pa ka'
'money makes only part' is written as 'zi la ne ki'
'demand makes supply economics' is written as 'zi mo ka ta'

31. What is the code for 'money' in the given code language?
(a) ga (b) mo (c) pa (d) ta
(e) la

32. What is the code for 'supply' in the given code language?
(a) Only ta (b) Only mo
(c) Either pa or mo (d) Only pa
(e) Either mo or ta

33. What may be the possible code for 'demand only more' in the given code language?
(a) xi ne mo (b) mo zi ne
(c) ki ne mo (d) mo zi ki
(e) xi ka ta

34. What may be the possible code for 'work and money' in the given code language?
(a) pa ga la (b) pa la lu
(c) mo la pa (d) tu la ga
(e) pa la ne

35. What is the code for 'makes' in the given code language?
(a) mo (b) pa
(c) ne (d) zi
(e) ho

DIRECTIONS ~ (Q.Nos. 36-39) *Study the following information carefully to answer the given questions.* « IBPS Clerk 2017

In a certain code language
'work for earning money' is coded as 'Go3 None 5Xor4 Farnin7'
'like six years passed' is coded as 'Ti3 Qasse6 Zear5 Mik4'
'hence good amount received' is coded as 'Seceive8 Ienc5 Hoo4 Bmoun6'.

36. What is the code for 'last earning was money'?
(a) Xa3 Mas4 None5 Farnin7
(b) None5 Xa3 Mas4 Darnin7
(c) None5 Mas4 Farnin7 Xa3
(d) Mas4 one5 Farnin7 Xa3
(e) None of the above

37. If 'money makes man perfect' is coded as 'Nake5 Qerfec7 Na3 None5, then what is the code for good people always perfect?
(a) Qeopl6 Hoo4 Blway6
(b) Hoo4 Qerfec7 Blway6 Qeopl6
(c) Qeopl6 Hoo4 Qerfec7 Blway6
(d) Qerfec7 Blway6 Qeopl5 Hoo5
(e) None of the above

38. What is the code for 'hence always wrong hance'?

(a) Blway6 Iance5 Xron5 Ienc5
(b) Ianc5 Xron5 Blway5 Ienc5
(c) Ianc5 Xron5 Blway5 Ienc5
(d) Blway6 Ienc5 Ianc5 Xron5
(e) Ianc6 Xron6 Blway5 Ienc5

39. 'Farming' is coded as

(a) Garmin7 (b) Gramin8
(c) Garing8 (d) Earnin7
(e) Earnin8

DIRECTIONS ~ (Q.Nos. 40 and 41) *Study the following information carefully and answer the questions given below.*

In a certain code language
'Given time simple plan is written as
'@E4 & N4 %N5 #E6'
'tired solution plant great' is written as
'#N8 @D5 %T5 & T5'
'sick point good turn' is written as '#K4 % D4@ N4 & @T5'
'garden sister phone team' is written as
'&E5#R6%N6@M4'

40. Which of the following is the code for 'translate' ?

(a) @E8 (b) @E9 (c) #E8 (d) #T8
(e) #T9

41. In the given code language, what does the code '%D4' represent ?

(a) Point (b) Turn
(c) Sick (d) Good
(e) None of these

DIRECTIONS ~ (Q.Nos. 42-44) *Study the following arrangement carefully and answer the questions given below.* « IBPS PO 2018

In a certain code language.
'alarm forest cuddle morning' is written as '%f6 !m7#a5@c6',
'sight fire making criticism' is written '#c9@f4 %s5!m6',
'raising centre recent alarm' is written as '@c6%r6#a5 !r7',
and strike arm ignoring sight is written as '!i8%s5@s6#a3'.

42. What is the code for 'raising'?

(a) !r7 (b) @c6
(c) #a5 (d) %r6
(e) Cannot be determined

43. What is the code for 'fire arm morning'?

(a) @c6 !m6 %s5 (b) #a3 ! i8@c6
(c) @f4 !m7 #a3 (d) !C7@a4#m3
(e) Cannot be determined.

44. What does '@s6 %s5 !m6' stand for?

(a) Ignoring cuddle forest (b) Sight morning arm
(c) Making strike sight (d) Strike raising fire
(e) Cannot be determined

DIRECTIONS ~ (Q.Nos. 45-47) *Study the following information carefully and answer the questions given below.*

In a certain code language
'year puzzle for solve' is written as '–1# ÷10@ + 20@ × 7#'
'with book the comet' is written as '×23#–24@–3# + 6@'
'sky chat across enjoy' is written as '÷ 25# × 21# –23# + 7#'
'tea lucky paint charge' is written as '× 10@ × 14@ + 6@ ÷ 23#'

45. Which of the following is the code for pickle' ?

(a) –16@ (b) ÷16@
(c) +10# (d) @14+
(e) ÷ 10@

46. Which of the following can be coded as '–14@' ?

(a) Look (b) Note
(c) Lie (d) Not
(e) Limca

47. Which of the following word is coded as '+3#'?

(a) Win (b) Wit
(c) Witty (d) Work
(e) Either a or b

DIRECTIONS ~(Q.Nos. 48-52) *Study the information and answer the following questions.*

In a certain code language.
"Seemed peer attend" is coded as "18BV 20BZ 19CW"
"Arrive Assessing file" is coded as "22BZ 19 DZ 12RV"
"Double systems possible" is coded as "19BY 21LY 25CV"

48. What is the code for 'asking' ?

(a) 19ZH (b) 20ZH
(c) 21XH (d) 19HX
(e) 19HZ

49. What is the code for 'Support'?

(a) 22DL (b) 21CL
(c) 21BL (d) 22BL
(e) None of these

50. What is the code for 'peer loom' ?

(a) 15CO 18BC
(b) 15BO 18BV
(c) 15BO 18CV
(d) 18CO 15BV
(e) None of the above

51. What is the code for 'Less' ?

(a) 20BZ (b) 19BV
(c) 21CV (d) 19BZ
(e) None of these

52. What is the code for 'Announced" ?

(a) 21CZ (b) 21ZC
(c) 23BZ (d) 22CZ
(e) None of these

Answers / WITH EXPLANATIONS

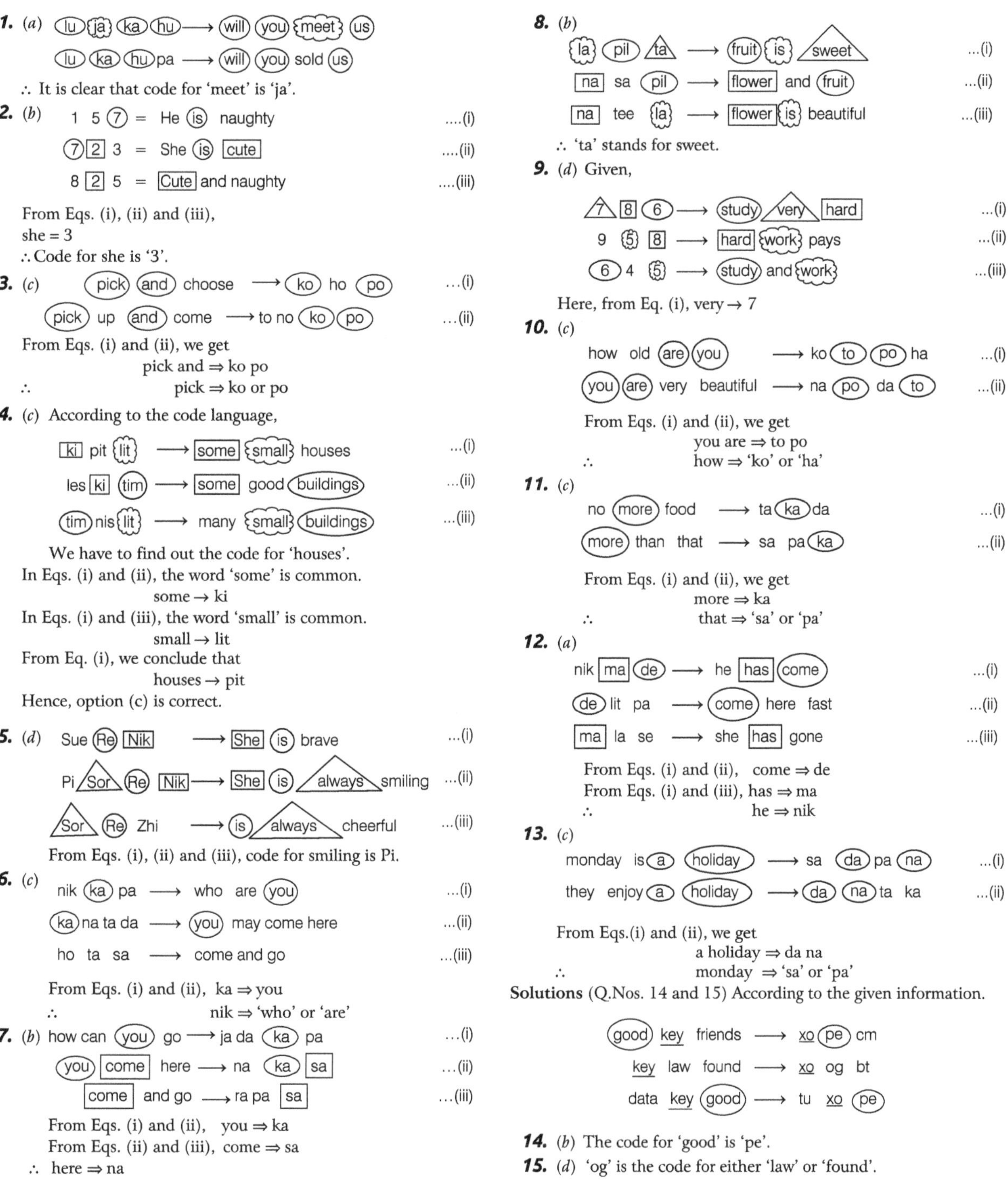

1. (*a*) lu ja ka hu ⟶ will you meet us

lu ka hu pa ⟶ will you sold us

∴ It is clear that code for 'meet' is 'ja'.

2. (*b*) 1 5 7 = He is naughty ....(i)

7 2 3 = She is cute ....(ii)

8 2 5 = Cute and naughty ....(iii)

From Eqs. (i), (ii) and (iii),

she = 3

∴ Code for she is '3'.

3. (*c*) pick and choose ⟶ ko ho po ...(i)

pick up and come ⟶ to no ko po ...(ii)

From Eqs. (i) and (ii), we get

pick and ⇒ ko po

∴ pick ⇒ ko or po

4. (*c*) According to the code language,

ki pit lit ⟶ some small houses ...(i)

les ki tim ⟶ some good buildings ...(ii)

tim nis lit ⟶ many small buildings ...(iii)

We have to find out the code for 'houses'.

In Eqs. (i) and (ii), the word 'some' is common.

some → ki

In Eqs. (i) and (iii), the word 'small' is common.

small → lit

From Eq. (i), we conclude that

houses → pit

Hence, option (c) is correct.

5. (*d*) Sue Re Nik ⟶ She is brave ...(i)

Pi Sor Re Nik ⟶ She is always smiling ...(ii)

Sor Re Zhi ⟶ is always cheerful ...(iii)

From Eqs. (i), (ii) and (iii), code for smiling is Pi.

6. (*c*) nik ka pa ⟶ who are you ...(i)

ka na ta da ⟶ you may come here ...(ii)

ho ta sa ⟶ come and go ...(iii)

From Eqs. (i) and (ii), ka ⇒ you

∴ nik ⇒ 'who' or 'are'

7. (*b*) how can you go ⟶ ja da ka pa ...(i)

you come here ⟶ na ka sa ...(ii)

come and go ⟶ ra pa sa ...(iii)

From Eqs. (i) and (ii), you ⇒ ka

From Eqs. (ii) and (iii), come ⇒ sa

∴ here ⇒ na

8. (*b*)

la pil ta ⟶ fruit is sweet ...(i)

na sa pil ⟶ flower and fruit ...(ii)

na tee la ⟶ flower is beautiful ...(iii)

∴ 'ta' stands for sweet.

9. (*d*) Given,

7 8 6 ⟶ study very hard ...(i)

9 5 8 ⟶ hard work pays ...(ii)

6 4 5 ⟶ study and work ...(iii)

Here, from Eq. (i), very → 7

10. (*c*)

how old are you ⟶ ko to po ha ...(i)

you are very beautiful ⟶ na po da to ...(ii)

From Eqs. (i) and (ii), we get

you are ⇒ to po

∴ how ⇒ 'ko' or 'ha'

11. (*c*)

no more food ⟶ ta ka da ...(i)

more than that ⟶ sa pa ka ...(ii)

From Eqs. (i) and (ii), we get

more ⇒ ka

∴ that ⇒ 'sa' or 'pa'

12. (*a*)

nik ma de ⟶ he has come ...(i)

de lit pa ⟶ come here fast ...(ii)

ma la se ⟶ she has gone ...(iii)

From Eqs. (i) and (ii), come ⇒ de

From Eqs. (i) and (iii), has ⇒ ma

∴ he ⇒ nik

13. (*c*)

monday is a holiday ⟶ sa da pa na ...(i)

they enjoy a holiday ⟶ da na ta ka ...(ii)

From Eqs.(i) and (ii), we get

a holiday ⇒ da na

∴ monday ⇒ 'sa' or 'pa'

Solutions (Q.Nos. 14 and 15) According to the given information.

good key friends ⟶ xo pe cm

key law found ⟶ xo og bt

data key good ⟶ tu xo pe

14. (*b*) The code for 'good' is 'pe'.

15. (*d*) 'og' is the code for either 'law' or 'found'.

Solutions (Q. Nos. 16-20) According to the given information, we have to find the possible code for a particular word

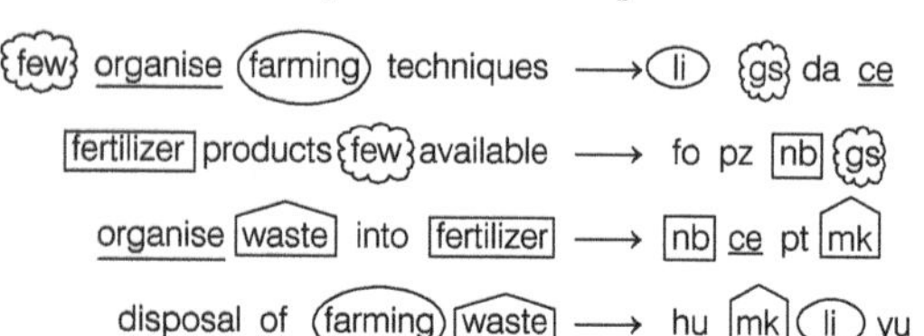

16. (*a*) The code for 'few waste' will be 'mk gs'.

17. (*b*) The code for 'organise' is 'ce'.

18. (*c*) 'yu' stands for either 'of' or 'disposal'.

19. (*c*) As, 'waste management techniques' is coded as 'ax da mk', then 'farming fertilizer management' will be coded as 'nb li ax'.

20. (*a*) The code for 'available' is either 'pz' or 'fo'.

Solutions (Q. Nos. 21-25) On the basis of given information,

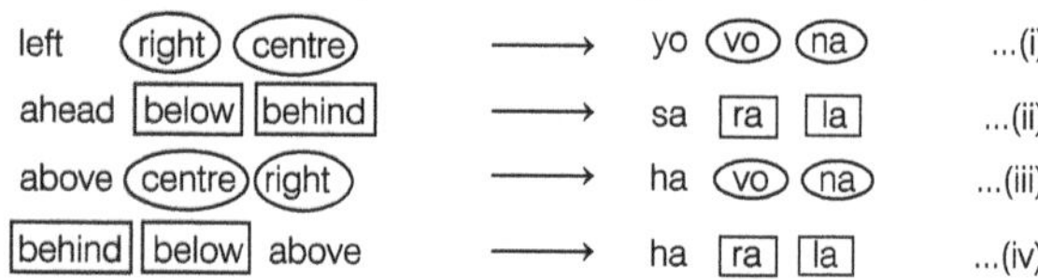

21. (*c*) left ⟶ yo

22. (*d*) behind ⟶ ra/la

23. (*a*) ahead ⟶ sa

24. (*d*) ha ⟶ above

25. (*e*) centre ⟶ vo/na

Solutions (Q.Nos. 26-30)

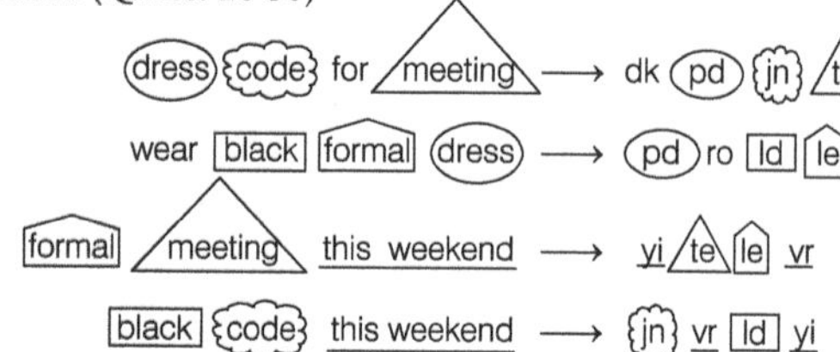

26. (*b*) 'le' stands for 'formal'.

27. (*d*) The code for 'dress' is 'pd'.

28. (*d*) 'ld' stand for 'black'.

29. (*d*) ∵ code ⟶ jn ∴ security code ⟶ jn ux

30. (*a*) The code for weekend is 'yi or vr'.

Solutions (Q. Nos. 31-35) On the basis of given information,

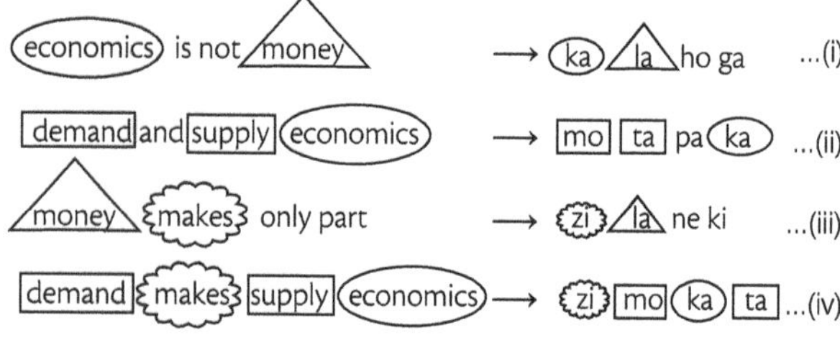

From Eqs. (i), (ii) and (iv), economics ⇒ ka

From Eqs. (i) and (iii), money ⇒ la

From Eqs. (iii) and (iv), makes ⇒ zi

From Eqs. (ii) and (iv), demand ⇒ mo/ta

supply ⇒ mo/ta

From Eq. (i), is ⇒ ho/ga

not ⇒ ho/ga

From Eq. (ii), and ⇒ pa

From Eq (iii), only ⇒ ne/ki

part ⇒ ne/ki

31. (*e*) It is clear that money ⇒ la

32. (*e*) According to the question,
code for supply ⇒ 'mo' or 'ta'

33. (*a*) According to the question,
demand ⇒ mo/ta, only ⇒ ne/ki
So, according to option (a) code for 'more' will be xi.
Hence, demand only more ⇒ xi ne mo

34. (*b*) According to the question,
and ⇒ pa
money ⇒ la
In option (a) third code is 'ga', which is either for 'is' or 'not'. So, it is incorrect.
In opiton (b) third code is 'lu', which is not for any other word in question.
So, 'lu' is for 'work'.
Hence, the possible code for 'work and money' will be 'pa la lu'.

35. (*d*) The code for makes is zi.

Solutions (Q.Nos. 36-39) According to the given information,

work for earning money ⟶ Go3 None5 Xor4 Farnin7 ...(i)

like six years passed ⟶ Ti3 Qasse6 Zear5 Mik4 ...(ii)

hence good amount received ⟶
Seceive8 Ienc5 Hoo4 Bmoun6 ...(iii)

36. (*c*) From Eq. (i) and option (c),
earning money ⟶ None5 Farnin7
∴ Last earning was money ⟶ None5 Mas4 Farnin7 Xa3

37. (*b*) Money makes man perfect ⟶ Nake6 Qerfec7 Na3 None5
Now, from Eq. (iii); good ⟶ Hoo4
∴ good people always perfect ⟶ Hoo4 Qerfec7 Blway6 Qeopl6

38. (*d*) From Eq. (iii)
hence ⟶ Ienc5
always ⟶ Blway6
∴ hence always wrong hance ⟶ Blway6 Ienc5 Ianc5 Xron5

39. (*a*) Farming ⟶ Garmin7

Solutions (Q. Nos. 40 and 41) Here, symbols are coded as per the first letter of the word.
As for 'g' symbol is %.
Similarly 'p' ⟶ &, 't' ⟶@ and 's' ⟶ #
The number in the code represents the number of letters in the word and the letter in the code represents the last letter of the word. e.g. In the word "Given" g = %, last letter = N and number of letters = 5
∴ Given = % N 5

40. (*b*) Code for translate ⟶ @E9

41. (*d*) % ⟶ g. So, from the options %D4 ⟶ Good

Solutions (Q. Nos. 42-44) # for last letter m, % for last letter t, @ for last letter e, and ! for last letter g. Number represents number of alphabets in word and alphabet represents the first letter of word.

42. (*a*) The code for 'raising' is '!r7'

43. (*c*) The code for 'fire arm morning' is '@f4 !m7 #a3'.

44. (*c*) '@s6 %s5 !m6' stands for 'making strike sight'.

Solutions (Q. Nos. 45-47) In this code language, we have to find the exact code used for the words.

Step 1 The initial symbol used are the four mathematical operators. The words have three, four, five and six alphabets. In Statement IV, 2 five letter words are used and '×' is used twice in the symbols. Therefore, five letter word is started with '×'. Using same logic on other statements, we get the symbols for words as below.

Number of letters in the word	Symbol
3	+
4	−
5	×
6	÷

Step 2 From the first step, tea would be +6@. Now, T is 7th letter from the end in the English dictionary and is coded as (7 − 1 = 6).

Step 3 In Statement III, the numeral symbols are 7, 23, 25 and 21 which are odd. All the symbols finish with #. Therefore, # is used for odd number while @ is used for even number numeral. For e.g. Tea = = +6@

45. (*e*) Pickle = ÷(11 − 1) = ÷10@

46. (*a*) −14@ = *a* four letter word starting from 'L'. Thus, Look is the correct option.

47. (*e*) According to the code '+3#' the words starts with W and is a three letter word. So, 'Win' or 'Wit' could be the word.

Solutions (Q. Nos. 48-52) **For the digit of the code** Number in the code will be the place value of the highest place value of letter present in the word.

e.g. peer = 18

For the first letter of the code

Case I If the given word has some repeated letters, then the code will be according to the given order.

Number of repeated letter in the word	Code
2	B
3	C
4	D

For e.g. peer in this word repeated letter is 'e' for two times. So the first letter of code for peer is 'B' ?

Case II If the given word has no repeated letter, then first letter of the code will be coded as opposite letter of the second letter of the word.

e.g. File = R (opposite)

For the last letter of the code The opposite letter of the smallest place value letter present in the word according to the English alphabet.

e.g. peer = V (opposite of Smaller)

48. (*e*) asking = 19HZ

49. (*c*) support = 21BL

50. (*b*) Peer Loom = 18BV15BO ⇒ 15BO 18BV

51. (*b*) Less = 19 BV

52. (*a*) Announced = 21 CZ

TYPE 06

Coding by Comparison

Under this pattern, some words are given in one column and their codes are given in another column. But the given codes are not in the same order of words given. Candidates are required to find out the codes of words on the basis of comparison of their properties, traits etc.

***Ex* 37** In the given table, some words are given in Column I and their codes are given in Column II. The code of the words given in Column II are not given in the order of given words. Find the corresponding codes of words and answer the following question.

Column I	Column II
BAT	dead
WIFE	dip
GREAT	sector
NATURE	training
TERMINAL	right

Find the code for the word 'GREAT'.

(a) dip
(b) dead
(c) right
(d) sector

***Solution* (c)** As in Column I 'GREAT' is the only word having five letters and in Column II 'right' is the only word having five letters. Therefore, code for 'GREAT' is 'right'.

Practice / CORNER 4.6

DIRECTIONS ~(Q. Nos. 1-5) *Read the following information to answer the questions that follow, In Column I, some words are given. In Column II, their codes are given and they are arranged in the same order in which they are in Column I but the letters in the code in Column II are not in the same order in which the letters of the words are given in Column I. Study the columns and give your answer on the basis of that.* « Delhi Police (Constable) 2010

Column I	Column II
(i) FLOUR	(A) xncap
(ii) TAP	(B) ksd
(iii) ROSE	(C) cmrn
(iv) LOTUS	(D) smcpx
(v) SAIL	(E) kptm

1. Find the code for F.
(a) p (b) c (c) a (d) x

2. Which letter is the code for P?
(a) k (b) s (c) c (d) d

3. Find the code for L.
(a) n (b) c (c) k (d) p

4. What is the code for E?
(a) c (b) m (c) r (d) n

5. Which of the following options is the code for O?
(a) x (b) c (c) m (d) r

DIRECTIONS ~(Q. Nos. 6-10) *Read the following information to answer the questions that follow. In the following questions, two Columns I and II have been given. In Column I, few words are given and in Column II, their codes have been given using a particular rule. The order of the smaller letter have been placed in jumbled up form. You have to decode the language and choose the alternative which is equal to the letter asked in the question.*

Column I	Column II
(i) DESIGN	(A) uklbjz
(ii) INFORM	(B) cbxkqy
(iii) MOTHER	(C) ygzwxc
(iv) RIGHTS	(D) bjucgw
(v) TAILOR	(E) wcpybv
(vi) GARDEN	(F) vzcjlk

6. What is the code for the letter N?
(a) u (b) k (c) c (d) g

7. What is the code for the letter F?
(a) i (b) b (c) q (d) g

8. What is the code for the letter O?
(a) y (b) k (c) v (d) c

9. What is the code for the letter S?
(a) z (b) w (c) u (d) x

10. What is the code for the letter G?
(a) i (b) p (c) b (d) j

DIRECTIONS ~(Q. Nos. 11-18) *Read the following information to answer the questions that follow. According to a code language, words in capital letters in Column I are written in small letters in Column II. The letters in Column II are jumbled up. Decode the language and choose the correct code for the word given in each question.*

Column I	Column II
(i) CROWDY	(A) blooppv
(ii) CRONY	(B) jkgotv
(iii) NET	(C) ijktv
(iv) CRUX	(D) ikmop
(v) ADDRESS	(E) cjmv
(vi) SOUND	(F) abi

11. Find the code for 'TRUE'.
(a) mvba (b) vbam (c) avmb (d) ambv

12. What is the code for 'NATURE'?
(a) ilamvb (b) ilambv (c) ilmabv (d) limabv

13. Find the code for 'SECTOR'.
(a) bpajkv (b) pbjakv (c) pbjavk (d) bpjakv

14. The code for 'TRUCE' is
(a) avmjb (b) avmbj
(c) avjmb (d) vajmb

15. Which one of the following options is the code for 'DOCTOR'?
(a) jkoavk (b) okjavk (c) kojatrv (d) okjakv

16. Find the code for 'WOOD'.
(a) kogk (b) gkko
(c) gokk (d) kgok

17. Which of the following options stands for 'TODAY'?
(a) altko (b) aoktl
(c) akotl (d) akolt

18. ... stands for 'ROSE'.
(a) vkpb (b) bpkv
(c) kpvb (d) vkbp

Answers / WITH EXPLANATIONS

Solutions (Q. Nos. 1-5)

Given that, FLOUR = xncap ...(i)

TAP = ksd ...(ii)

ROSE = cmrn ...(iii)

LOTUS = smcpx ...(iv)

SAIL = kptm ...(v)

From Eqs. (ii) and (v),

T (A) P = (k) s d
S (A) I L = (k) p t m

∴ A = k

From Eqs. (ii) and (iv),

(T) A P = k (s) d
L O (T) U S = (s) m c p x

∴ T = s ⇒ P = d

From Eqs. (iii) and (v),

R O (S) E = c (m) r n
(S) A I L = k p t (m)

∴ S = m

From Eqs. (iv) and (v),

(L) O T U S = s m c (p) x
S A I (L) = k (p) t m

∴ L = P ⇒ I = t

From Eqs. (iii) and (iv),

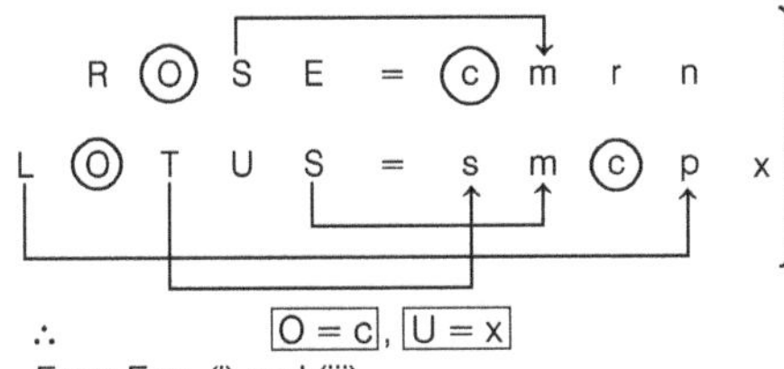

∴ O = c, U = x

From Eqs. (i) and (iii),

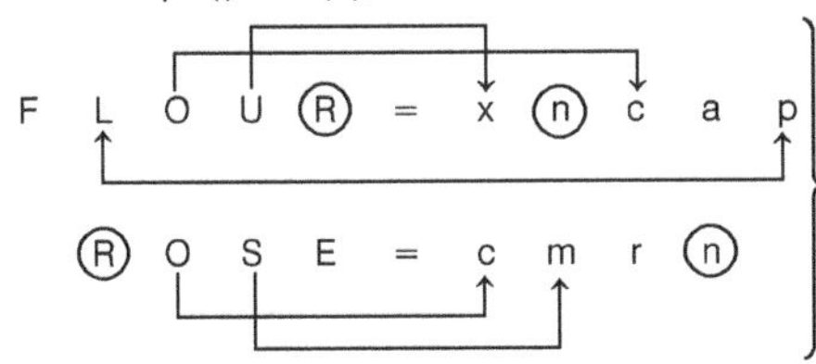

∴ R = n, E = r, F = a

Now, as per the given information, code of each letter is as below

1. (*c*) Clearly, the code for F is a.

2. (*d*) Clearly, the code for P is d.

3. (*d*) Clearly, the code for L is p.

4. (*c*) Clearly, the code for E is r.

5. (*b*) Clearly, the code for O is c.

6. (*b*) In Statements (i) and (ii), common letters are I and N and common codes are b and k.

Therefore, it is clear that IN stands for bk but not necessarily in the same order. From Statement (vi), it is clear that the word has letter N and code k is given for it. Hence, code for N is k.

7. (*c*) In the Statement (ii), it is clear that the word has letter F in it, which is not contained by any other word. Similarly, its code has letter q, which is not contained by any other code. Hence, F stands for q.

8. (*a*) From Statements (iii) and (v), it is clear that TOR = ywc. From Statement (ii), OR = yc. From Statement (vi), R = c. Hence, O = y.

9. (*c*) From Statements (i) and (iv), it is clear that SIG = ubj. From Statement (i), we have already found that I= b. Therefore, SG = uj. Now, from Statement (vi), G = j, therefore S = u.

10. (*d*) We have already found in sol.10 that G = j

Solutions (Q. Nos. 11-18)

The only 3 letter word = NET. So, its code = abi

The only 4 letter word = CRUX. So, its code = cjmv

The only 6 letter word = CROWDY. So, its code = jkgotv

The only 7 letter word = ADDRESS. So, its code = blooppv

The two five letter words are SOUND and CRONY and two codes for five letter words are ikmop and ijktv. CRONY has two common letters C and R with CRUX and the letters j and v in the code for CRUX are common with the code ijktv.

Hence, code for CRONY = ijktv

and code for SOUND = ikmop

After rearranging words and codes, we have

NET = abi ...(i)

CRUX = cjmv ...(ii)

CRONY = ijktv ...(iii)

SOUND = ikmop ...(iv)

CROWDY = jkgotv ...(v)

ADDRESS = blooppv ...(vi)

From Eqs. (i) and (iii),

(N) E T = a b (i)
C R O (N) Y = (i) j k t v

∴ N = i

From Eqs.(i) and (vi),

N (E) T = a (b) i
A D D R (E) S S = (b) l o o p p v

E = b, T = a

(∴N = i in NET)

From Eqs. (ii) and (vi),

C (R) U X = c j m (v)
A D D (R) E S S = b l o o p p (v)

∴ R = v

From Eqs. (ii) and (iii),

(C) R U X = c (j) m v
(C) R O N Y = i (j) k t v

∴ C = j

From Eqs. (ii) and (iv),

C R (U) X = c j (m) v
S O (U) N D = i k (m) o p

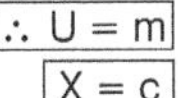

∴ U = m, X = c

From Eqs. (iii) and (iv),

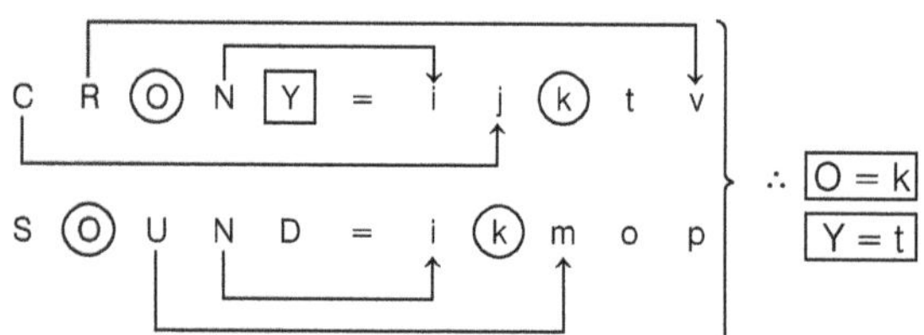

From Eqs. (iv) and (v),

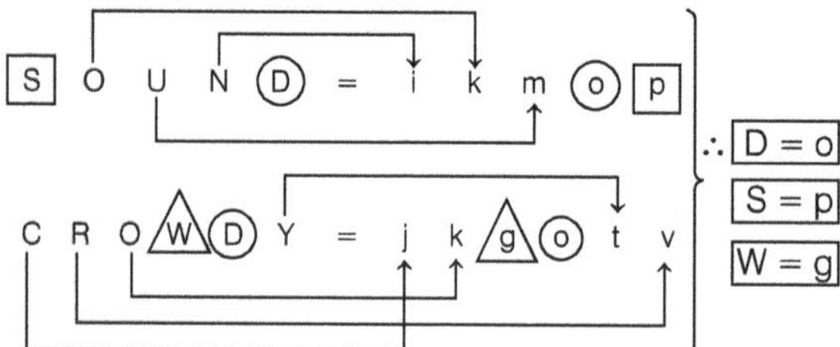

From Eq. (vi),

Now, as per the given information, code of each letter is as below

Letter	A	C	D	E	N	O	R	S	T	U	W	X	Y
Code	I	j	o	b	i	k	v	p	a	m	g	c	t

11. (*c*) We have,

∴ TRUE ⇒ avmb

12. (*a*) We have,

∴ NATURE ⇒ ilamvb

13. (*b*) We have,

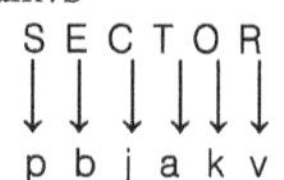

∴ SECTOR ⇒ pbjakv

14. (*a*) We have,

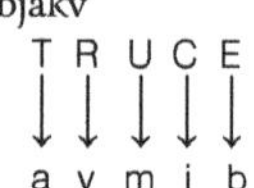

∴ TRUCE ⇒ avmjb

15. (*d*) We have,

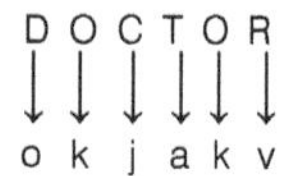

∴ DOCTOR ⇒ okjakv

16. (*b*) We have,

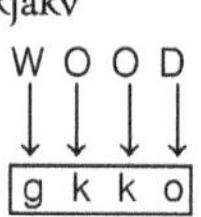

∴ WOOD ⇒ gkko

17. (*d*) We have,

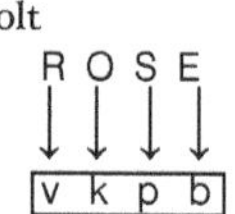

∴ TODAY ⇒ akolt

18. (*a*) We have,

R O S E
↓ ↓ ↓ ↓
v k p b

∴ ROSE ⇒ vkpb

TYPE 7

Conditional Coding

Under this pattern, letters/numbers are given and their codes are given right under them. Candidates are required to find out code for a particular letter group/word/number according to the given conditions.

***Ex* 38** In the question below, is given a group of letters followed by four combinations of digits/symbols. You have to find out which of the combinations correctly represents the group of letters based on the following coding system and the conditions that follow and mark your answer accordingly.

Letter	M	J	R	A	D	B	W	Z	P	E	I	H	G	U	K
Digits/Symbol code	8	4	@	9	c	1	2	$	3	#	5	6	%	7	★

Conditions

(i) If both first and last letters are vowels, their codes are to be interchanged.

(ii) If the first letter is a consonant and the last letter is a vowel, both are to be coded as the code for the vowel.

(iii) If the first letter is a vowel and the last letter is a consonant, both are to be coded as the code for the consonant.

Find the code for 'IBHJRE'.

(a) #614@5 (b) 5164@% (c) %164@# (d) #164@5

***Solution* (*d*)** When condition is not applied, the coding is done as follows.

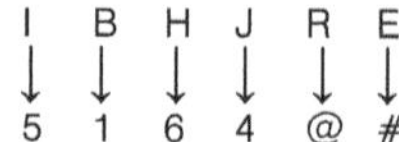

But here the 1st letter (I) and the last letter (E) are vowels and therefore condition (i) is applied here. As condition (i) is applied here, I and E will interchange their codes.

∴ Code for IBHJRE ⇒ #164@5

***Ex* 39** In the question below, is given a group of numbers followed by four combinations of letters/symbols. You have to find out which of the combinations correctly represents the group of numbers based on the following coding system and the conditions that follow and mark your answer accordingly.

Digit	3	8	0	7	4	6	9	2	5	1
Code	H	$	R	A	M	%	L	K	E	@

Conditions

(i) If a number begins and ends with a non-zero odd digit, then the first and the last digits are to be coded as Y and #, respectively.

(ii) If a number begins and ends with an even digit (including zero), then the first and the last digits are to be coded as B and X, respectively.

What will be the code for 764981?

(a) A % M L $ @
(b) Y % M L $ @
(c) Y % M L $ #
(d) A % M L $ #

Solution (c) When condition is not applied, the coding is done as follows

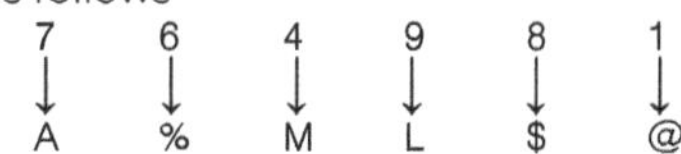

But here the number begins and ends with a non-zero odd digit and therefore, condition (i) is applied here. As condition (i) is applied here, 7 and 1 will be coded as Y and #, respectively.

∴ Code for 764981 ⇒ Y%ML$#

Practice / CORNER 4.7

DIRECTIONS ~ (Q. Nos. 1-6) *In each question below, is given a group of letters followed by four combinations of digits/symbols numbered (a), (b), (c) and (d). You have to find out which of the four combinations correctly represents the group of letters based on the following coding system and the conditions that follow and mark the number of that combination as your answer. If none of the combinations correctly represents the group of letters, mark (e), i.e., 'None of these', as your answer.*

« Indian Bank (PO) 2010

Letter	R	E	A	U	M	D	F	P	Q	I	O	H	N	W	Z	B
Digit/Symbol code	7	#	$	6	%	8	5	★	4	9	@	©	3	d	1	2

(i) If the first letter is a consonant and the third letter is a vowel, their codes are to be interchanged.

(ii) If the first letter is a vowel and the fourth letter is a consonant, both are to be coded as the code for the vowel.

(iii) If the second and the third letters are consonants, both are to be coded as the code for the third letter.

1. NABAQE
(a) 263$4# (b) 326$4# (c) 362$4# (d) 362$3#
(e) None of these

2. FWZERA
(a) 5d #7$ (b) 5dd #7$ (c) d17#$ (d) 511 #7$
(e) None of these

3. HUBDIN
(a) © 62893 (b) © 2689%
(c) © 6289© (d) © 62© 9%
(e) None of these

4. EMIRDP
(a) #%978★ (b) #%9#8★
(c) 7%9#8★ (d) #9%78★
(e) None of these

5. OREDHM
(a) @7#8© % (b) #7#8© %
(c) @78#© % (d) @7#@© %
(e) None of these

6. PQIMHZ
(a) ★49%©1 (b) %49★©1 (c) ★49★©1 (d) 949%©1
(e) None of these

DIRECTIONS ~ (Q. Nos. 7-11) *In each of the questions below, a group of numerals is given followed by four groups of symbol / letter combinations labelled (a), (b), (c) and (d). Numerals are to be coded as per the codes and conditions given below. You have to find out which of the combinations (a), (b), (c) and (d) is correct and indicate your answer accordingly. If none of the four combinations represents the correct code, mark (e) as your answer.*

Numerals	3	5	7	4	2	6	8	1	0	9
Letter/Symbol code	★	B	E	A	@	F	K	%	R	M

(i) If the first digit, as well as the last digit is odd, both are to be coded as 'X'.

(ii) If the first digit as well as the last digit is even, both are to be coded as $.

(iii) If the last digit is 0, it is to be coded as #.

7. 546839
(a) XAFK★M (b) BAFK★M
(c) XAFK★X (d) BAFK★X
(e) None of these

8. 713540
(a) E%★BA# (b) X%★BA#
(c) X%★BAR (d) E%★BAR
(e) None of these

9. 765082
(a) XFBRK@ (b) EFB#K@ (c) EFBR#K (d) EFBRK@
(e) None of these

10. 487692
(a) AKEFM@ (b) $KEFM@ (c) AKEFM$ (d) $KEFM$
(e) None of these

11. 364819
(a) XFAK@M (b) ★FAK%X (c) ★FAK%M (d) ★EAK%X
(e) None of these

DIRECTIONS ~ (Q. Nos. 12-16) *In each question below, is given a group of letters followed by four combinations of digits/symbols numbered (a), (b), (c) and (d). You have to find out which of the four combinations correctly represents the group of letters based on the following coding system and the conditions that follow and mark the number of that combination as your answer. If none of the combinations correctly represents the group of letters, mark (e), i.e., 'None of these', as your answer.* « Allahabad Bank (PO) 2010

Letter	W	P	J	Q	E	T	I	A	U	F	D	B	V	M	H
Digit/Symbol code	5	6	9	1	2	3	@	4	©	8	%	★	7	#	$

(i) If the first letter is a consonant and the fourth letter is a vowel, both are to be coded as the codes for the vowel.
(ii) If the second letter is a vowel and the last letter is a consonant, both are to be coded as 8.
(iii) If both the first and the last letter are consonants, both their codes are to be interchanged.

12. MBUVWE
(a) #★©#52 (b) 7★©#52 (c) #©★752 (d) #©★7528
(e) None of these

13. AJBMFU
(a) 49★48© (b) #9★#8© (c) 49★#8© (d) ©9©#84
(e) None of these

14. AEIMVH
(a) 42@#7$ (b) 42@47$ (c) #2@47$ (d) 48@#78
(e) None of these

15. THAFIQ
(a) 3$48@3 (b) 1$48@3 (c) 1$48@1 (d) 3$48@1
(e) None of these

16. WMEIJU
(a) @#2@9© (b) 5#2@9© (c) @#259© (d) 5#259©
(e) None of these

DIRECTIONS ~ (Q. Nos. 17-19) *In each of the questions below, a group of numerals is given followed by four groups of symbol / letter combinations labelled (a), (b), (c) and (d). Numerals are to be coded as per the codes and conditions given below. You have to find out which of the combinations (a), (b), (c) and (d) is correct and indicate your answer accordingly. If none of the four combinations represents the correct code, mark (e) as your answer.*

Digit	7	3	5	0	2	1	6	4	9	8
Code	N	H	L	T	F	D	R	Q	G	P

(i) If the first digit is even and the last digit is odd, they are to be coded as $ and @, respectively.
(ii) If the first digit is odd and the last digit is even, they are to be coded as # and £, respectively.
(iii) If 0 is preceded as well as followed by an odd digit, then 0 is to be coded as ↑.
(iv) If 0 is preceded as well as followed by an even digit, then 0 is to be coded as ↓.
(v) 0 is not considered as either even or odd.

17. What will be the code for 36250098?
(a) $RFLTTG£ (b) #RFLTTG@ (c) #RFLTTG£
(d) $RFLTTG@ (e) None of these

18. $QRL↑H@ could be the code for which of the following numbers?
(a) 8465032 (b) 8456037 (c) 8465034 (d) 6475031
(e) None of these

19. QLP↓RNT is the code for which of the following numbers?
(a) 6580470 (b) 4780650
(c) 6580470 (d) Data inadequate
(e) None of these

DIRECTIONS ~ (Q. Nos. 20-25) *In each question below, is given a group of letters followed by four combinations of digits/symbols numbered (a), (b), (c) and (d). You have to find out which of the four combinations correctly represents the group of letters based on the following coding system and the conditions that follow and mark the number of that combination as your answer. If none of the combinations correctly represents the group of letters, mark (e), i.e., 'None of these', as your answer.*
« Punjab & Sindh Bank (PO) 2010

Letter	B	A	D	E	F	H	J	K	M	I	U	O	W	F	P
Digit/Symbol code	6	$	7	8	#	1	2	★	%	3	©	4	9	@	5

(i) If the first letter is a vowel and the last letter is a consonant, their codes are to be interchanged.
(ii) If both the first and the last letters are consonants, both are to be coded as 'δ'.
(iii) If the first letter is a consonant and the last letter is a vowel, both are to be coded as the code for the vowel.

20. EKFUDH
(a) 8★#©78 (b) 1★#©78 (c) δ★#©78 (d) 1★#©71
(e) None of these

21. JMEIUD
(a) δ%83©δ (b) 2%83©2 (c) 7%83©7 (d) 2%83©7
(e) None of these

22. PEJDWU
(a) 58279© (b) δ8279δ (c) ©8279© (d) 582795
(e) None of these

23. DMEAKJ
(a) 7%8$★2 (b) 2%8$★7 (c) 7%8$★7 (d) δ%8$★δ
(e) None of these

24. IBHWPO
(a) 361954 (b) 461953 (c) 361953 (d) 461954
(e) None of these

25. UKPDMI
(a) ©5★7%3 (b) δ★57%δ (c) 3★57%© (d) ©★5%73
(e) None of these

DIRECTIONS ~ (Q. Nos. 26-30) *In each of the following questions below is given a group of letters followed by four combinations of digits/symbols numbered (a), (b), (c) and (d). You have to find out which of the combinations correctly represents the group of letters based on the following coding system and mark the number of that combination as the answer. If none of the four combinations correctly represents the group of letters, mark (e), i.e. 'None of these', as the answer.* « IBPS Clerk Main 2018

Note *More than one condition may apply.*

Letter	R	G	F	A	P	Q	U	M	E	I	B	J	S	O	L
Digit/Symbol	#	2	7	μ	%	3	&	9	1	@	5	©	6	8	$

Conditions

(i) If first letter is vowel and last letter is consonant, then both are coded with the code of the consonant.

(ii) If both the 2nd and the last letter is vowel, then their codes are to be interchanged.

(iii) If the second letter is a consonant and the 2nd last letter is a vowel, both are to be coded as the code for the vowel.

(iv) If both 1st and fifth letter is consonant, then both are coded as the code of third letter.

(v) If only one condition is applied among the above given, then the code of first letter is interchanged with code of second letter and third letter code interchanged with 4th letter and so on after that applied condition.

26. AMGFIS

(a) 6@27@4 (b) 6@27@6 (c) 6@27#6 (d) 6@2@76 (e) None of these

27. PUGRLE

(a) 2122#& (b) 221#2& (c) 212#&2 (d) 212#2& (e) None of these

28. UAIMUI

(a) @&9@μ& (b) @&@9μ& (c) @9&@μ& (d) @&99μ& (e) None of these

29. MJGLBF

(a) ©2$227 (b) ©$2272 (c) ©$2227 (d) ©$2$2 (e) None of these

30. GFPQMB

(a) %7%3%5 (b) 27%395 (c) 7%3%5% (d) %7%395 (e) None of these

Answers / WITH EXPLANATIONS

1. (e) Here, none of the conditions is applied, so the coding is done as follows.

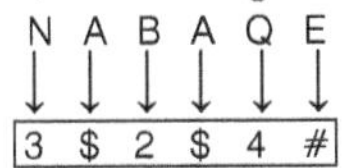

∴ Code for NABAQE ⇒ 3$2$4#

2. (d) When no conditions is applied, the coding is done as follows.

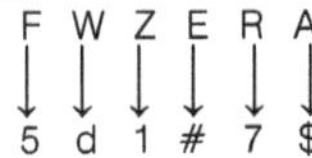

But here the second and third letters are consonants, therefore condition (iii) is applied here. As condition (iii) is applied here, both the second and third letters are to be coded as the code for the third letter.

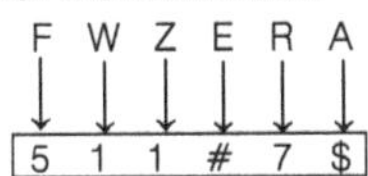

∴ Code for FWZERA ⇒ 511#7$

3. (a) Here, none of the conditions is applied, so the coding is done as follows.

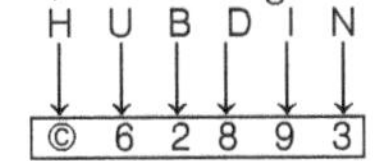

∴ Code for HUBDIN ⇒ ©62893

4. (b) When no conditions is applied, the coding is done as follows.

But here the first letter is a vowel and the fourth letter is a consonant, therefore condition (ii) is applied.

As condition (ii) is applied here, both the first and the fourth letters are to be coded as the code for the vowel.

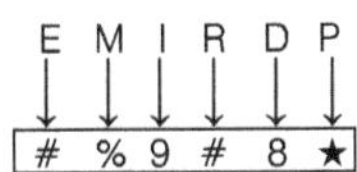

∴ Code for EMIRDP ⇒ #%9#8★

5. (d) When no condition is applied, the coding is done as follows.

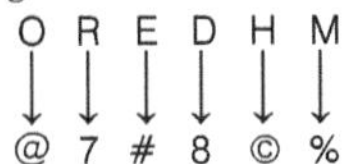

But here the first letter is a vowel and the fourth letter is a consonant, therefore condition (ii) is applied. As condition (ii) is applied here, both the first and fourth letters are to be coded as the code for the vowel.

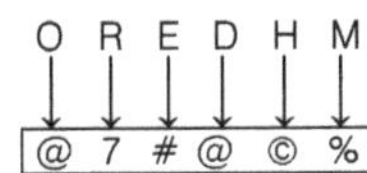

∴ Code for OREDHM ⇒ @7#@©%

6. (e) When no condition is applied, coding is done as follows.

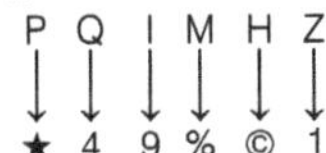

But here the first letter is a consonant and the third letter is a vowel, therefore condition (i) is applied. As condition (i) is applied here, the codes for first and third letters are to be interchanged.

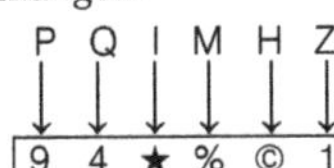

∴ Code for PQIMHZ ⇒ 94★%©1

7. (c) When condition is not applied, the coding is done as follows.

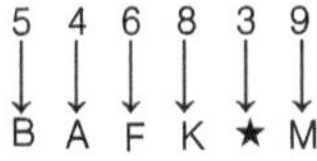

But here the first and the last digits are odd, therefore condition (i) is applied here. As condition (i) is applied here, 5 and 9 will be coded as X.

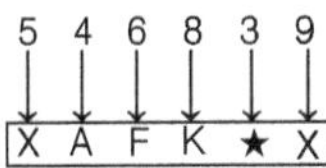

∴ Code for 546839 ⇒ XAFK★X

8. (a) When condition is not applied, the coding is done as follows.

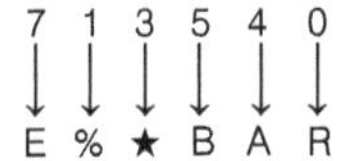

But here the last digit is 0, therefore condition (iii) is applied here. As condition (iii) is applied here, 0 will be coded as #

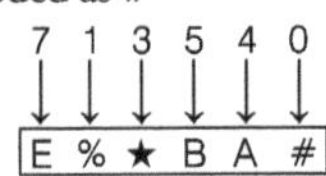

∴ Code for 713540 ⇒ E%★BA#

9. (d) Here, none of the conditions is applied, so the coding will be done as follows.

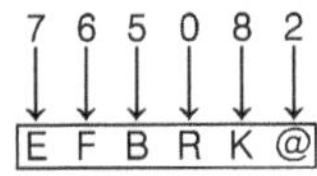

∴ Code for 765082 ⇒ EFBRK@

10. (d) When condition is not applied, the coding is done as follows.

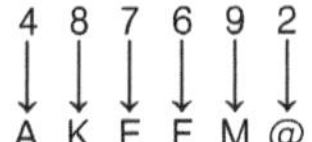

But here the first and the last digits are even, therefore condition (ii) is applied here. As condition (ii) is applied here, 4 and 2 will be coded as $.

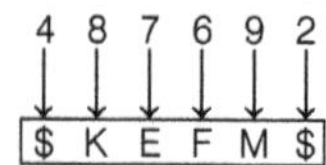

∴ Code for 487692 ⇒ $KEFM$

11. (*e*) When condition is not applied, the coding is done as follows.

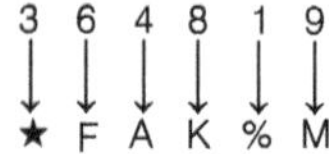

But here the first and the last digits are odd, therefore condition (i) is applied here. As condition (i) is applied here, 3 and 9 will be coded as X.

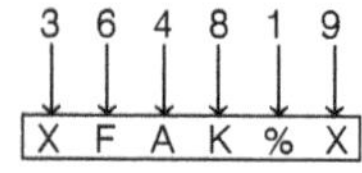

∴ Code for 364819 ⇒ XFAK%X

12. (*e*) Here, none of the conditions is applied, so the coding is done as follows.

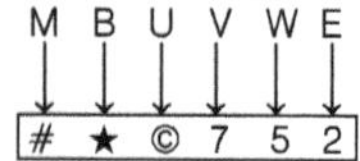

∴ Code for MBUVWE ⇒ #★©752

13. (*c*) Here, none of the conditions is applied, so the coding is done as follows.

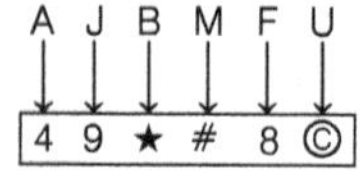

∴ Code for AJBMFU ⇒ 49★#8©

14. (*d*) When condition is not applied, the coding is done as follows.

But here the second letter is a vowel and the last letter is a consonant, therefore condition (ii) is applied here. As condition (ii) is applied here, both the second and the last letters are to be coded as 8.

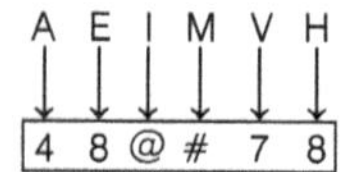

∴ Code for AEIMVH ⇒ 48@#78

15. (*b*) When condition is not applied, the coding is done as follows.

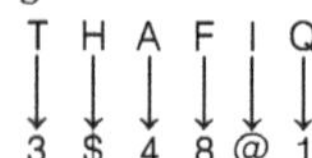

But here both the first and the last letters are consonants, therefore condition (iii) is applied here. As condition (iii) as applied here, the codes for the first and the last letters are interchanged.

∴ Code for THAFIQ ⇒ 1$48@3

16. (*a*) When condition is not applied, the coding is done as follows.

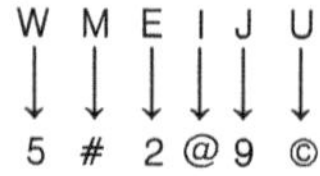

But here the first letter is a consonant and the fourth letter is a vowel, therefore condition (i) is applied here. As condition (i) is applied here, both the first and the fourth letters are to be coded as the codes for the vowel.

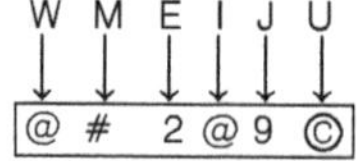

∴ Code for WMEIJU ⇒ @#2@9©

17. (*c*) When condition is not applied, the coding is done as follows.

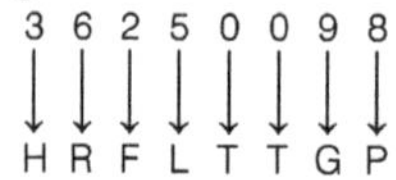

But here the first digit is odd and the last digit is even, therefore condition (ii) is applied here. As condition (ii) is applied here, 3 is coded as # and 8 is codest as £ ↑ is code for 0.

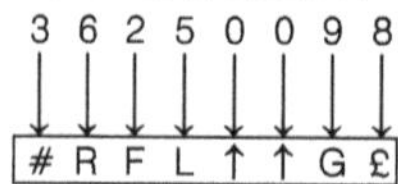

∴ Code for 36250098 ⇒ #RFL↑↑G£

18. (*e*) Q, R, L, H are the codes for 4, 6, 5, 3 respectively. ↑ is the code for 0.

So, $QRL↑H@ shall be the code of a number of the form ?46503?, in which the first digit must be even and the last digit must be odd. Clearly, there is no such number in the given alternatives.

19. (*e*) Q, L, P, ↓, R, N and T are the codes for 4, 5, 8, 0, 6, 7 and 0 respectively. So, the required number is 4580670.

20. (*b*) When condition is not applied, the coding is done as follows.

But here the first letter is a vowel and the last letter is a consonant, therefore, condition (i) is applied here. As condition (i) is applied here, the codes for the first and the last letters are interchanged.

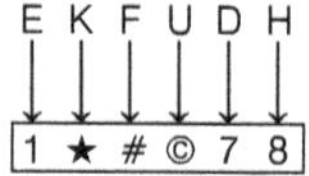

∴ Code for EKFUDH ⇒ 1★#©78

21. (*a*) When condition is not applied, the coding is done as follows.

But here both the first and the last letters are consonants, therefore condition (ii) is applied here. As condition (ii) is applied here, both the first and the last letters are to be coded as δ.

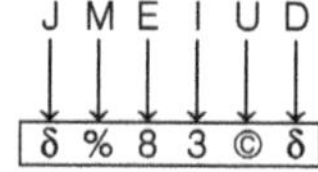

∴ Code for JMEIUD ⇒ δ%83©δ

22. (*c*) When condition is not applied, the coding is done as follows.

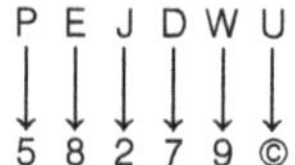

But here the first letter is a consonant and the last letter is a vowel, therefore condition (iii) is applied here. As condition (iii) is applied here, both the first and the last letters are to be coded as the code for the vowel.

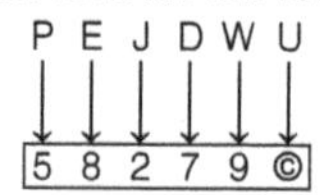

∴ Code for PEJDWU ⇒ ©8279©

23. (*d*) When condition is not applied, the coding is done as follows.

But here both the first and the last letters are consonants, therefore condition (ii) is applied here. As condition (ii) is applied here, both the first and the last letters are to be coded as δ.

∴ Code for DMEAKJ ⇒ δ%8$★δ

24. (*a*) Here, none of the conditions is applied, so the coding is done as follows.

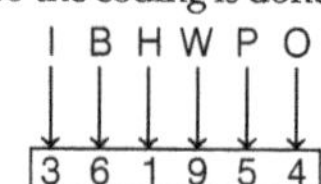

∴ Code for IBHWPO ⇒ 361954

25. (*e*) Here, none of the condition is applied, so the coding is done as follows.

U K P D M I

↓ ↓ ↓ ↓ ↓ ↓

© ★ 5 7 % 3

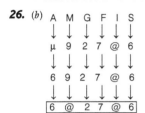

∴ Code for UKPDMI ⇒ ©★57%3

26. (*b*) A M G F I S

↓ ↓ ↓ ↓ ↓ ↓

μ 9 2 7 @ 6

↓ ↓ ↓ ↓ ↓ ↓

6 9 2 7 @ 6 [from condition (i)]

↓ ↓ ↓ ↓ ↓ ↓

6 @ 2 7 @ 6 [from condition (iii)]

27. (*d*) P U G R L E

↓ ↓ ↓ ↓ ↓ ↓

% & 2 # $ 1

↓ ↓ ↓ ↓ ↓ ↓

% 1 2 # $ & [from condition (ii)]

↓ ↓ ↓ ↓ ↓ ↓

2 1 2 # 2 & [from condition (iv)]

28. (*a*)

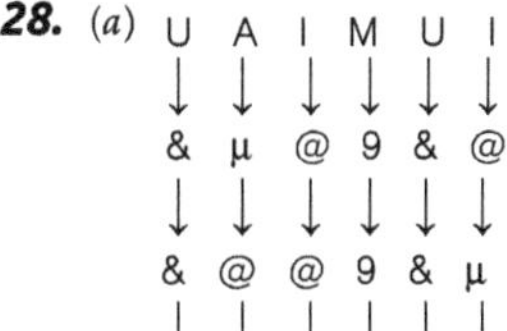

U A I M U I

↓ ↓ ↓ ↓ ↓ ↓

& μ @ 9 & @

↓ ↓ ↓ ↓ ↓ ↓

& @ @ 9 & μ [from condition (ii)]

↓ ↓ ↓ ↓ ↓ ↓

@ & 9 @ μ & [from condition (v)]

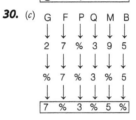

29. (*e*) M J G L B F

↓ ↓ ↓ ↓ ↓ ↓

9 © 2 $ 5 7

↓ ↓ ↓ ↓ ↓ ↓

2 © 2 $ 2 7 [from condition (iv)]

↓ ↓ ↓ ↓ ↓ ↓

© 2 $ 2 7 2 [from condition (v)]

30. (*c*) G F P Q M B

↓ ↓ ↓ ↓ ↓ ↓

2 7 % 3 9 5

↓ ↓ ↓ ↓ ↓ ↓

% 7 % 3 % 5 [from condition (iv)]

↓ ↓ ↓ ↓ ↓ ↓

7 % 3 % 5 % [from condition (v)]

Master Exercise

1. If 'PARK' is coded as '5394', 'SHIRT' is coded as '17698' and 'PANDIT' is coded as '532068', how would you code 'NISHAR' in that code language?

(a) 266734 (b) 231954
(c) 201739 (d) 261739

2. If in a certain code language, 'O' is written as 'E', 'A' as 'C', 'M' as 'I', 'S' as 'O', 'N' as 'P', 'E' as 'M', 'I' as 'A', 'P' as 'N' and 'C' as 'S', then how will 'COMPANIES' be written in that code language?

(a) SEIACPAMO (b) SMINCPAMO
(c) SEINCPAMO (d) SEINCPMIO
(e) None of these

3. In a certain code language 'TREAD' is written as '7%#94' and 'PREY' is written as '$%#8'. How is 'ARTERY' written in that code?

(a) 9#7%#8 (b) 9#%7#8
(c) 9%7#%8 (d) 9%#7%8

4. If '6' is coded as 'T', '8' is coded as 'I', '3' is coded as 'N', '9' is coded as 'Q', '2' is coded as 'Y', '5' is coded as 'D' and '7' is coded as 'R', then what is the uncoded form of 'DRINTQ'?

(a) 573869 (b) 578396
(c) 576839 (d) 578329
(e) None of these

5. If in a certain coded language, UNCLE is written as 94672, SISTER is written as 535821 and SON is written as 584, then what will be the code of NOISE in that coded language?

(a) 64825 (b) 84652 (c) 46356 (d) 48352

6. In a certain code language 'TRAIN' is written as '39★7%' and 'MEAL' is written as '4$★@'. How is 'REAM' written in that code language?

(a) 3$★9 (b) 74 $ 9
(c) 4★$ 9 (d) 9 $★4

7. In a certain code language 'BEAUTIFUL' is coded as '573041208', 'BUTTER' as '504479'. How is 'FUTURE' coded in that code language?

(a) 201497 (b) 204097
(c) 704092 (d) 204079

8. In a certain code MOAN is written as 5%3$ and NEWS is written as $1@8. How is SOME written in that code?

(a) 8 % 51 (b) 85 % 8
(c) 8 @ 51 (d) 8 % 31

9. In a certain code language 'BASKET' is written as '5$3%#1' and 'TRIED' is written as '14★#2'. How is 'SKIRT' written in that code language?

(a) 3%★41 (b) 3★%41
(c) 3% #41 (d) 3#4%1
(e) None of these

10. In a certain code language 'ROAM' is written as '5913' and 'DONE' is written as '4962'. How is 'MEAN' written in that code language?

(a) 5216 (b) 3126 (c) 3216 (d) 9126
(e) None of these

11. In a certain code language 'DINE' is writtten as '1537' and 'WORTH' is written as '$#96@'. How is 'WITHER' written in that code language?

(a) $5@679 (b) $567@9
(c) $56@79 (d) $56@97

12. In a certain code language 'ROPE' is written as '%57$', 'DOUBT' is written as '35#8★' and 'LIVE' is written as '@24$'. How is 'TROUBLE' written in that code language?

(a) ★%5#8@$ (b) ★%#58@$
(c) ★%5#8@4 (d) ★%#58$@
(e) None of these

13. If 'GERMAN' is coded as 126534, 'FOOD' is coded as 9770 and CORN is coded as 8764, then what will be the code for 'FRANCE'?

(a) 961063 (b) 963482
(c) 963428 (d) 964382

14. If 'LION' is called 'TIGER', 'TIGER is called 'DOG' 'DOG' is called 'ASS', 'ASS' is called 'BIRD', 'BIRD' is called 'CUP', 'CUP' is called 'PLATE', then which of the following does fly in the sky?

(a) ASS (b) LION (c) CUP (d) BIRD

15. If 'PARROT' is called 'SPARROW', 'SPARROW' is called 'CROW', 'CROW' is called 'DUCK', 'DUCK' is called 'COW ', 'COW' is called 'PIGEON' and 'PIGEON' is called 'CUCKOO', then which of the following has four legs?

(a) COW (b) PIGEON
(c) CUCKOO (d) DUCK

16. If 'DOG' is called 'CAT', 'CAT' is called 'FOX', 'FOX' is called 'SNAKE', 'SNAKE' is called 'MONKEY', 'MONKEY' is called 'OX' and 'OX' is called 'HORSE', then which of the following is a reptile?

(a) FOX (b) SNAKE (c) MONKEY (d) OX

17. If 'WATER' is called 'FOOD', 'FOOD' is called 'TREE', 'TREE' is called 'SKY', 'SKY' is called 'WALL', on which of the following does a 'FRUIT' grow?

(a) WATER (b) FOOD (c) TREE (d) SKY

18. If 'TELEVISION' is called 'CALCULATER', 'CALCULATER' is called 'PEN', 'PEN' is called 'BOOK', 'BOOK' is called 'PILLOW', 'PILLOW' is called 'BED', then what do we use to write?

(a) CALCULATER (b) PEN
(c) BOOK (d) PILLOW

DIRECTIONS ~ (Q. Nos. 19-23) *Read the given information and answer the following questions.*

In a certain code language

'For profit order now' is written as 'ho ja ye ga'

'right now for him' is written as 'ga ve ja se'

'place order for profit' is written as 'ga bl ho ye'

'only in right order' is written as 've du ye zo'

19. What is the code for 'him' in the given code language?

(a) Cannot be determined (b) ga
(c) ve (d) se
(e) aj

20. Which of the following may represent 'only for now' in the given code language?

(a) zo ga ja (b) zo ga ye (c) ja bl zo (d) du bl ja
(e) du zo ga

21. What is the code for 'profit' in the given code language?

(a) ye (b) ho (c) ga (d) ja (e) bl

22. 'fo ve du' could be a code for which of the following in the given code language?

(a) only in profit (b) order only him
(c) place in right (d) in right spirits
(e) order only now

23. What does 'bl' stand for in the given code language?

(a) profit (b) for (c) place (d) order
(e) now

24. If TRUTH is coded as SUQSTVSUGI, then how will LIES be coded? « UP Police Constable 2018

(a) KMJHDFTR (b) KMHJDFRT
(c) HJDFRTKM (d) KMJHFDTR

25. If 'CHAMBER' is coded as 'XSZNYVI', how will coded word 'WLFYOV' relate to the basic word through that coding language?

(a) DOVBLE (b) DOUCLF
(c) DLUBOE (d) DOUBLE

26. If in a coded language 'PEASANT' is written as 'RQYVYHN', how will 'RANCHER' be written in the same language ?
« UPSSSC Combined Lower Subordinate 2019

(a) PHFFPDL (b) PLDPHFF
(c) PHFFLDP (d) PFFHLDP

27. If in a certain code language 'MANUAL' is coded as '1311421112', 'TRIANGLE' is coded as '201891147125', then how will 'FIVE' be coded in that language?

(a) 65229 (b) 69225 (c) 62925 (d) 62295

28. If in a certain code language 'GOOD' is coded as '20121223', 'ONE' is coded as '121322', then how will 'FRUIT' be coded in that language?

(a) 2196187 (b) 2196178
(c) 2198167 (d) 2169187

29. In a certain code language '123' stands for 'I am servant', '279' stands for 'servant always miserable', and '684' stands for 'poverty is curse'. Then, 'miserable' stands for which numeric?

(a) 2 (b) 7
(c) 9 (d) Cannot be determined

30. In a certain code language, '493' means 'Friendship Big Challenge', '961' means 'Struggle Big Exam' and '178' means 'Exam Confidential Subject'. What does 'Confidential' stand for?

(a) 7 or 8 (b) 7 or 9
(c) 8 (d) 8 or 1

31. In a code language '157' means 'mother always lovable', '619' means 'always happy future' and '952' means 'mother very happy'. What does the word 'future' stand for in the same language?

(a) 9 (b) 6
(c) 1 (d) Cannot be determined

DIRECTIONS ~ (Q. Nos. 32-35) *Study the information and answer the following questions.* « IBPS PO Pre 2018

In a certain code language

'Get details for venue' is written as 'fe wi mo rs'

'Venue book required details' is written as 'rs gt rd wi'

'Details required book guest' is written as 'wi gt rd ra'

'Guest get more venue' is written as 'ra fe gk rs'

32. What is the code for 'details' in the given code language?

(a) fe (b) mo
(c) wi (d) ra
(e) None of these

33. What is the code for the word 'guest venue' in the given code language?

(a) gt gk (b) fe mo
(c) rs ra (d) gt ra
(e) None of these

34. What is the code for the word 'get' in the given code language?

(a) gt (b) fe (c) rs (d) rd
(e) None of these

35. If the code for the words 'for ...' is coded as 'mo gk' in the coded language, then what will be the missing word?

(a) book (b) required (c) guest (d) more
(e) Either (a) or (d)

DIRECTIONS ~ (Q. Nos. 36-39) *Study the information and answer the following questions.* « SBI PO Pre 2018

In a certain code language

"Entire Money Board Perfect" is written as "Q7 N5 F6 C5",

"Sleeve Washing World Stories" is written as "X7 T6 T7 X5",

"Moving Parly Falls Objects" is written as "N6 P7 G5 Q6",

36. What is the code for 'Radio' in the given code language?

(a) S5 (b) R5 (c) S4 (d) R6
(e) None of these

37. What is the code for the word 'Rising Normal' in the given code language?

(a) S5 O6 (b) O5 S6
(c) O6 S6 (d) O5 S5
(e) None of these

38. If the code for the words 'they forward ....' is coded as 'U4 G7 T5' in the coded language, then what will be the missing word?
(a) South (b) Mount (c) Stone (d) Climb
(e) Either (a) or (c)

39. What is the code for 'Elegant' in the given code language?
(a) G7 (b) D7 (c) F6 (d) F7
(e) None of these

40. In a certain code language, 'WEAVE' is written as 'FEZVX'. How WILL 'ELEVATE' be written in that code language? « UPSSSC Lower Subordinate 2016
(a) ELFUATF (b) FLEAUTF
(c) FLEUAFT (d) FLEUATF

41. If DEMOCRATIC is written as EDMORCATCI, how CONTINUOUS will be written in the same code? « CGPSC 2013
(a) OCTNNIOUSU (b) OTCNINUOUS
(c) OCNTNIUOSU (d) CONNITUOSU
(e) None of these

42. In a certain code language 'what else can you do for me Mr Ajay' is written' as 'you Mr what can Ajay else do me for'. How will 'anyone else who can do such favour to me' be written in that code language?
(a) Can to who anyone me else do favour such
(b) Can favour anyone who me else do to such
(c) Can to anyone who me else do such favour
(d) Can to anyone who me do else favour such
(e) None of the above

43. In a certain code language '975' means 'throw away garbage', '528' means 'give away smoking' and '213' means 'smoking is harmful'. Which digit in that code language means 'smoking'?
(a) 5 (b) 8 (c) 2 (d) 3

44. In a certain code, 'bi n pi' means 'some good books', 'n bat lik' means 'some real characters', 'pi lik tl' means 'many good characters'. Then what is the code of 'Many good books' « SSC Steno Grade C&D 2019
(a) tl pi bi (b) pi bat bi (c) n pi bi (d) n bat bi

45. In a certain code language, 'veny heny steny' means 'get out man'; 'steny shomy shelt' means 'out of danger'. Which is the word for 'steny' in that code language? « MP Police 2017
(a) man (b) of (c) out (d) danger

46. 165135 is to 'PEACE' as 1215225 is to
(a) LEAD (b) LOVE (c) LOOP (d) AURA

47. In a certain code language 'DESCRIBE' is written as 'FCJSDTFE'. How will 'CONSIDER' be written in that code language?
(a) SFEJTOPD (b) SEFJTOPD
(c) QFETJOPD (d) QEFJTOPD

48. If FRIEND is coded as HUMJTK, how is CANDLE written in that code? « FCI Uttarakhand watchman 2018
(a) EDRIRL (b) DCQHQK
(c) ESJFME (d) DEQJQM

49. If the word 'LEADER' is coded as 20-13-9-12-13-26, how would you write 'LIGHT'?
(a) 20-16-17-15-27 (b) 20-15-16-18-23
(c) 20-17-15-16-28 (d) 20-16-15-17-22

50. In a certain coded language if 'MOBILE' is coded '13-U-2-O-12-I' and 'GADGET' is coded as '7 E-4-7-I-20', then how is the word 'IPHONE' coded in that language ? « UPSSSC Cane Supervisor 2016
(a) 9-16-8-I-14-I (b) O-16-8-15-14-I
(c) O-16-8-U-14-I (d) J-16-8-P-14-F

51. If in a certain code, DIAGRAM is written as AFXDOXJ, then how can PICTURE be written in that code? « SSC Steno 2016
(a) NGARSPC (b) MGAQRPB
(c) NFYQROC (d) MFZQROB

52. If LACK is written as 396, then BACK is written as
(a) 56 (b) 72 (c) 66 (d) 86

53. In a certain language, C is 5 and CEAT is written as 37. Then, JAPAN is « UPSSSC VDO 2018
(a) 56 (b) 47 (c) 52 (d) 42

54. In a certain coding system, PAPER is written as PERPA and SUBJECT is written as JECTSUB, what should be the code for COUNCIL? « SBI Clerk 2016
(a) NCILCOU (b) LICNOUC
(c) NCOUCIL (d) NLICUOC
(e) None of these

55. If RED is coded as 6720, then how would GREEN be coded ? « UGC NET 2019
(a) 16717209 (b) 1677209
(c) 9207716 (d) 1677199

56. If 'SYNDICATE' is written as 'SYTENDCAI', then how can 'PSYCHOTIC' be written?
(a) PSYICTCOH (b) PSYCOHTCI
(c) PSICYOCTH (d) PSICYCOTH

57. If the code for 'KAMAL' = '1626142615', then find the code for 'NO'.
(a) 1312 (b) 13125 (c) 1213 (d) 192406

58. If 'NINE' is coded as 'OMJHOMFD', then 'LOT' is coded as
(a) MKPNUS (b) KMPNUS
(c) MKNPUS (d) MKPNSU

59. In a particular code, 'IUIJT' means 'GREEN'. What does XLSQKA mean in the same code?
(a) VIOLET (b) ORANGE
(c) INDIGO (d) PURPLE

60. In a certain code language, the word 'HEAD' is written as 'IFBE' and 'IRON' is written as 'JSPO'. How is the word 'JANE' be written in that code? « UP Police SI 2017
(a) KBOF (b) BFOB
(c) KOBF (d) KBFO

61. In a certain code, LIFE is written as KMHJEGDF. How is WORD written in that code? « UGC Net 2018
(a) XVPNSQCE (b) XVPNSQEC
(c) VXNPQSCE (d) VXNPQSEC

62. In a certain code language, '743' means 'mangoes are good', '657' means 'eat good food' and '934' means 'mangoes are ripe'. Which digit means 'ripe' in that language? « FCI Uttarakhand Watchman 2018

(a) 9 (b) 4 (c) 5 (d) 7

DIRECTIONS ~ (Q. Nos. 63-65) *Study the following information carefully and answer the given questions.*

In alphabetical series A–Z each letter except vowels is assigned a different number from 1-5 (For ex-B is coded as 1, C–2...., G-5) and again those numbers get repeated (For ex- H-1, J-2....so on).

Also each vowel (A, E, I, O, U) is assigned a different symbol viz. #, $, %, @, & respectively.

In coded language–

'Solar Power Energy" is coded as–

5&4@42&3#4/#1#455

"Need to Change" is coded as –1##31&21@15#

'Less Economic Revenue" is coded as–

4#55#2&1&5$24#2#1%#

Besides the above example, following operations are to be applied for coding, the words given in the questions below.

(i) If both first and last letters of a word is consonant, then the codes of both the consonants are interchanged.

(ii) If first letter of a word is vowel and last letter is consonants then both are to be coded as *.

(If the word does not satisfy the conditions given above, then the letters of that word are to be coded as per the directions given above.)

63. What can be the code of 'Nuclear Bomb' ?

(a) 4%24#@1 15&1 (b) 4%42#@11&51
(c) 4%24#@1 1&51 (d) 4%24@#11&51
(e) None of these

64. What can be the code of 'War and Peace'

(a) 3@41 *2 #@2#* (b) 4@3 *1* 2#@2#
(c) 4@3 @13 2#@2# (d) 4@3 *1* 2#2@#
(e) None of these

65. What can be the code of 'Own life' ?

(a) &3* 4$4# (b) *3* 44$# (c) &33 4$4# (d) *3* 4$4#
(e) None of these

DIRECTIONS ~(Q. Nos. 66-68) *Study the following information and answer the given questions.*

In alphabetical series consonant is assigned a different number from 1-7 (for ex-B is coded as 1, C – 2........J – 7) and again those numbers get repeated (Fir ex- K-1, L-2.....so on).

Besides the above information, following operations are to be applied for coding the words given in the questions below.

Each letter of the given questions will be coded as per the given conditions.

I. Vowels appearing before 'M' in the alphabetical series will be coded as '**'.

II. Vowels appearing after 'M' in the alphabetical series will be coded as '$$'.

III. Number immediately preceded by vowel will be coded as '#1'.

IV. Number immediately followed by vowel will be coded as '@#'.

66. What will possibly be the code of "ANNUAL' ?

(a) **@##1$$**@# (b) *1@##1$$**@#
(c) **##@1$$**@# (d) *2@##1$$**@#
(e) None of these

67. What will possible be the code for 'NORMAL' ?

(a)#1$$@##2**@# (b) #1$$@##1**@#
(c) #3$$@##1**@# (d) #1$#@##1**@#
(e) None of these

68. What will possible be the code of 'SMITTLE' ?

(a) 1#1**@#2#1** (b) 1#1**@#2#11*
(c) 1#1**@#2#1*1 (d) 2#1**@#2#1**
(e) None of these

DIRECTIONS ~(Q. Nos. 69-73) *In each of the questions below, a group of numerals is given followed by four groups of symbol/letter combinations lettered (a), (b), (c) and (d). Numerals are to be coded as per the codes and conditions given below. You have to find out which of the combinations (a), (b), (c) and (d) is correct and indicate your answer accordingly. If none of the four combinations represents the correct code, mark (e) as your answer.*
« Dena Bank (PO) 2008

Numerals	3	5	7	4	2	6	8	1	0	9
Letter/Symbol code	★	B	E	A	@	F	K	%	R	M

Following conditions apply

(i) if the first digit as well as the last digit is odd, both are to be coded as 'X'.

(ii) if the first digit as well as the last digit is even, both are to be coded as $.

(iii) if the last digit is 'zero', it is to be coded as #.

69. 487692

(a) $KEFM@ (b) AKEFM@ (c) AKEFM$ (d) $KEFM$
(e) None of these

70. 713540

(a) X%★BA# (b) E%★BA# (c) E%★BAR (d) X%★BAR
(e) None of these

71. 765082

(a) EFB#K@ (b) XFBRK@
(c) EFBRK@ (d) EFBR#K
(e) None of these

72. 364819

(a) ★FAK%X (b) XFAK&M
(c) ★FAK%M (d) ★EAK%X
(e) None of these

73. 546839

(a) XAFK★X (b) XAFK★M
(c) BAFK★X (d) BAFK★M
(e) None of these

DIRECTIONS ~ (Q. Nos. 74-79) *In each question below is given a group of letters followed by four combinations of digits/symbols numbered (a), (b), (c) and (d). You have to find out which of the four combinations correctly represents the group of letters based on the following coding system and the conditions that follow and mark the number of that combination as your answer. If none of the* *combinations correctly represents the group of letters, mark (e), i.e., 'None of these', as your answer.*

Letter	Digit/Symbol code	Letter	Digit/Symbol code
R	∝	Q	4
E	#	I	η
A	$	O	@
U	6	H	©
M	%	N	3
D	1	W	δ
F	9	Z	8
P	★	B	2

Conditions

(i) If the first letter is a consonant and the third letter is a vowel, their codes are to the interchanged.

(ii) If the first letter is a vowel and the fourth letter is a consonant, both are to be coded as the code for the vowel.

(iii) If the second and the third letters are consonants, both are to be coded as the code for the third letter.

74. NUBAQE

(a) 263$4# (b) 326$4# (c) 362$4# (d) 362$3#
(e) None of these

75. FWZORH

(a) 9 δ 8 @ ∝ © (b) 9 δ δ @ ∝ ©
(c) 9 δ 8 ∝ @ © (d) 988 @ ∝ ©
(e) None of these

76. MBIUHQ

(a) η 2 % 6 © 4 (b) % 2 η 6 © 4
(c) % 2 % 6 © 4 (d) η % 2 6 © 4
(e) None of these

77. OPAIHM

(a) @$ ★ η © (b) @★$ η © %
(c) η $ ★ @ © % (d) @ ★ η $ © %
(e) None of these

78. EAMWBN

(a) # $ % δ 2 3 (b) δ $ % # 2 3
(c) δ $ % # 2 3 (d) # $ % # 2 3
(e) None of these

79. AIWEZB

(a) $ η $ # 8 2 (b) δ η $ # 8 2 (c) δ η δ # 8 2 (d) $ η 8 # 8 2
(e) None of these

DIRECTIONS ~ (Q. Nos. 80-83) *Study the given information carefully and answer the given questions.*

Circle (○) represents (2), Right triangle (◺) represents (1) and triangle (△) represents (0), if it appears at unit place then its value is as it is, if it appears at tens place its is thrice and so on.

Such as:

◺ = 1

○ ◺ △ = 18 + 3 + 0 = 21

◺ △ ○ = 9 + 0 + 2 = 11

When circle is in unit place, its value is 2 and when it is in tens place its value is thrice of 2 which is 6; when it is in hundredth place, thrice of 6 which is 18.

80. What will be the resultant of the following code given below?

$$\frac{◺◺△△◺○◺}{△△○○○} = ?$$

(a) ○○◺◺ (b) ◺△○○
(c) ◺◺△○ (d) △○△○
(e) ◺◺△◺

81. How will you represent '1874' in this code language?

(a) ○△◺△○○◺

(b) ○○○△◺△○

(c) ○△◺△△◺△

(d) ◺○△◺△○○

(e) ○◺○△◺△○

82. How will you represent '383' in this code language?

(a) ◺△△◺△○

(b) ◺○△△◺○

(c) ◺◺○△◺○

(d) ◺△◺○◺◺

(e) ◺△△◺○◺

83. Which of the following is not divisible by 5 in this code language?

(a) △◺○◺○

(b) ◺◺◺◺

(c) ◺○△◺○

(d) △◺○△

(e) ◺◺◺◺○

Answers / WITH EXPLANATIONS

1. (*d*) As,

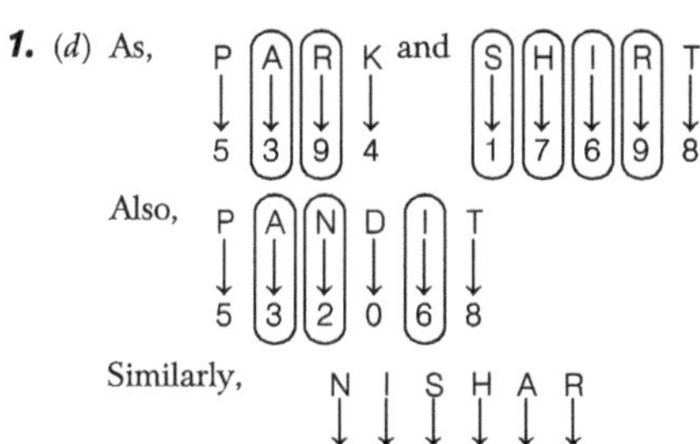

∴ NISHAR ⇒ 261739

2. (*c*)

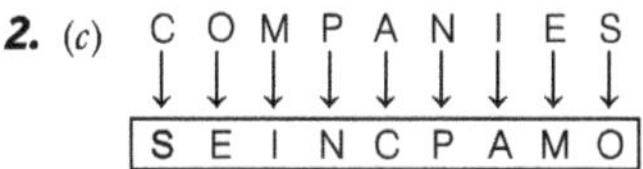

∴ COMPANIES ⇒ SEINCPAMO

3. (*c*) As,

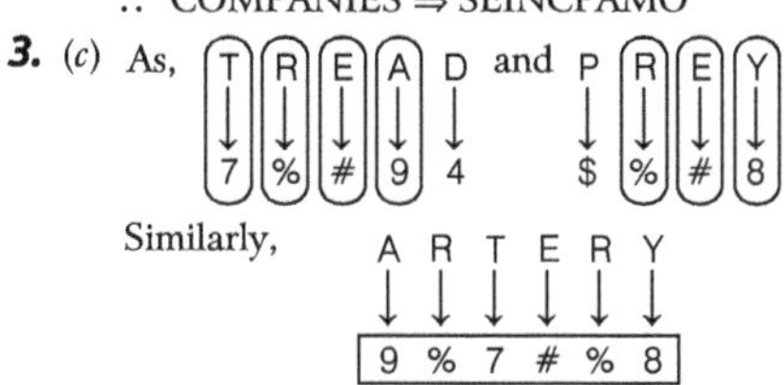

∴ ARTERY ⇒ 9%7#%8

4. (*e*)

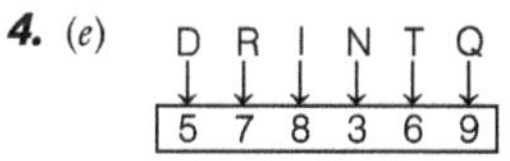

∴ DRINTQ ⇒ 578369

5. (*d*) From the given coded language, it is clear that
U – 9, N – 4, C – 6 L – 7, E – 2,
S – 5 I – 3, T – 8, R – 1 O – 8
∴ NOISE ⇒ 48352

6. (*d*) As,

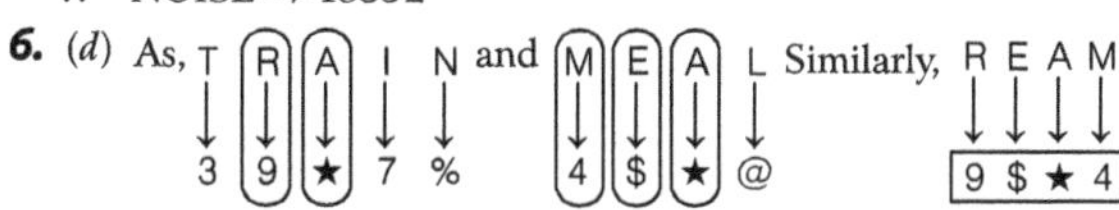

∴ REAM ⇒ 9$★4

7. (*b*) As,

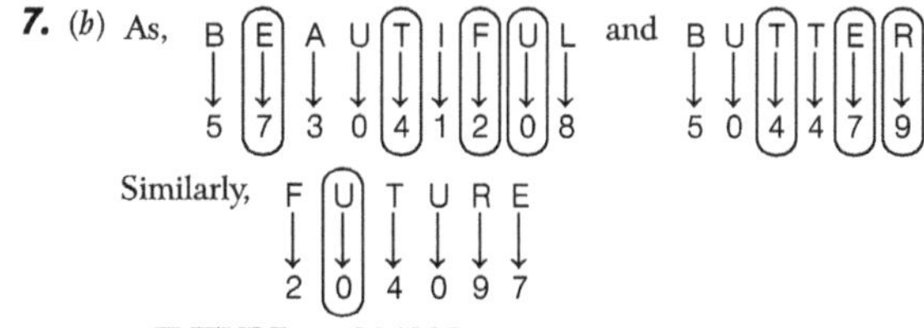

∴ FUTURE ⇒ 204097

8. (*a*) From the given coded language, it is clear that
M – 5, O – %, A – 3, N – $, E – 1, W – @, S – 8
∴ SOME ⇒ 8 % 51

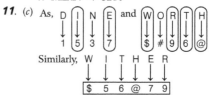

9. (*a*) As,

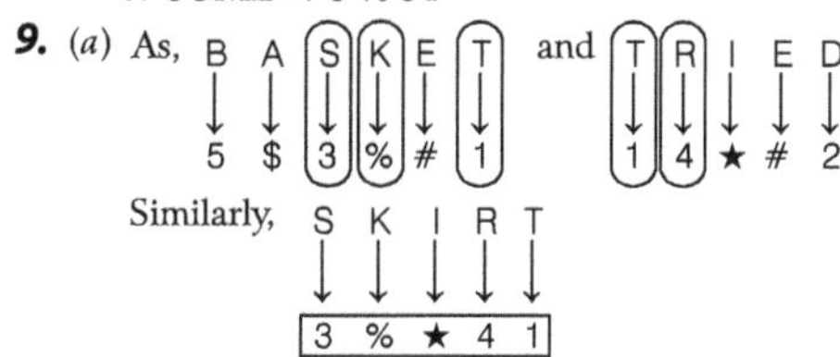

∴ SKIRT ⇒ 3% ★ 41

10. (*c*) As,

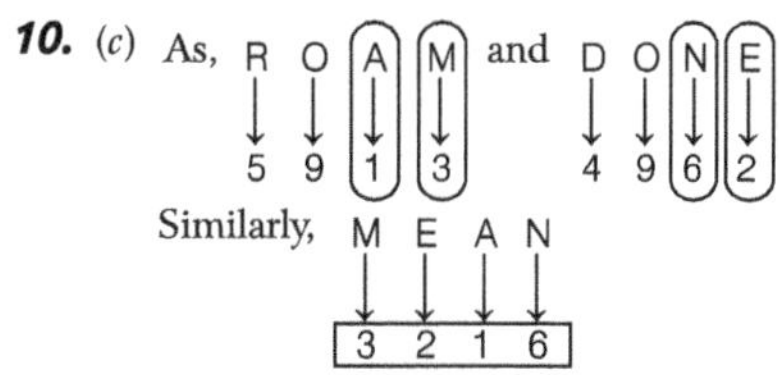

∴ MEAN ⇒ 3216

11. (*c*) As, D I N E and W O R T H
1 5 3 7 $ # 9 6 @
Similarly, W I T H E R → $ 5 6 @ 7 9

∴ WITHER ⇒ $56@79

12. (*a*) As,

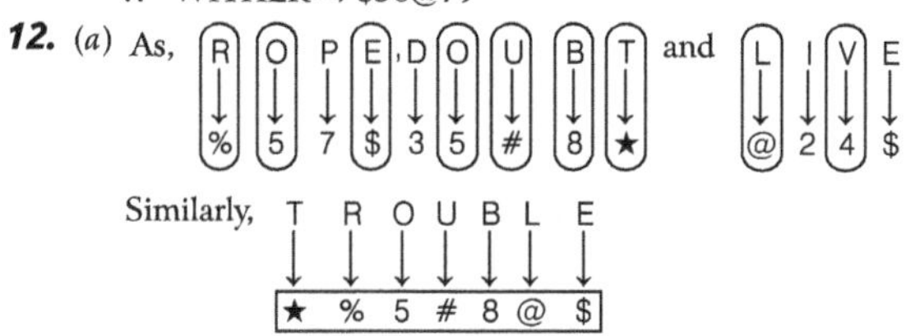

∴ TROUBLE ⇒ ★ % 5 # 8 @ $

13. (*b*) As,

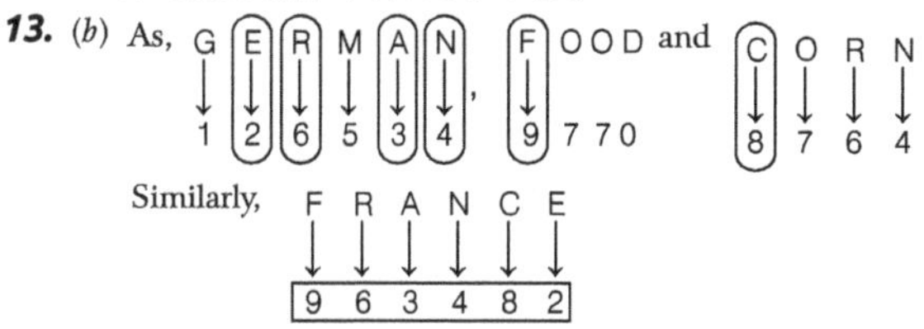

∴ FRANCE = 963482

14. (*c*) As we know that, a 'bird' flies in the sky but here 'bird' is called 'cup'. Hence, in this case 'cup' will fly in the sky.

15. (*b*) As we know that, 'COW' has four legs but here 'COW' is 'called' 'PIGEON'. Hence, in this case 'PIGEON' has four legs.

16. (*c*) As we know that, 'SNAKE' is a reptile but here 'SNAKE' is called 'MONKEY'. Hence, in this case 'MONKEY' is a reptile.

17. (*d*) 'Fruit' grows on 'TREE' and here 'TREE' is called 'SKY'.
∴ Fruit grows on 'SKY'.

18. (*c*) We use 'pen' to write but here, 'PEN' is called 'BOOK'. Hence, in this case we use 'BOOK' to write.

Solutions (Q.Nos. 19-23) According to the given information,

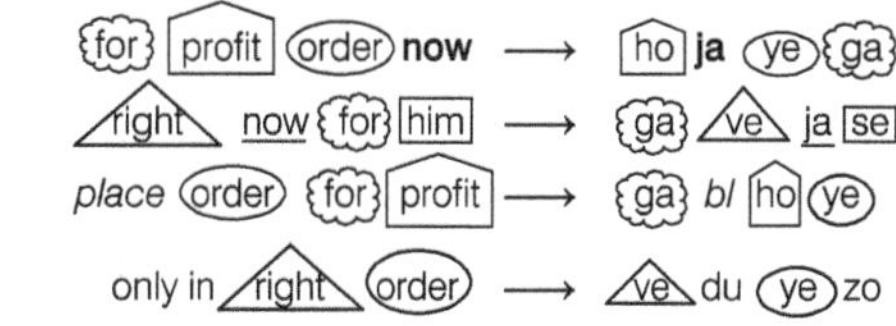

19. (*d*) The code for 'him' is 'se'.

20. (*a*) The code for 'only for now' is 'zo ga ja'

21. (*b*) The code for profit is 'ho'.

22. (*d*) 'in right spirits' could be the code for 'fo ve du'.

23. (*c*) 'bl' stands for 'place'.

24. (*b*) As,

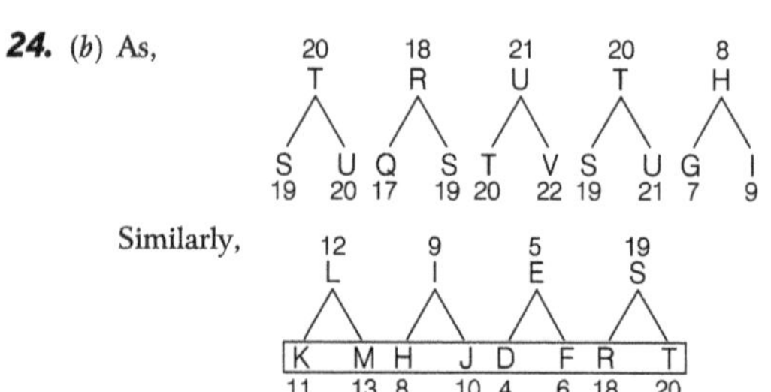

∴ LIES ⇒ KMHJDFRT

25. (*d*) As,

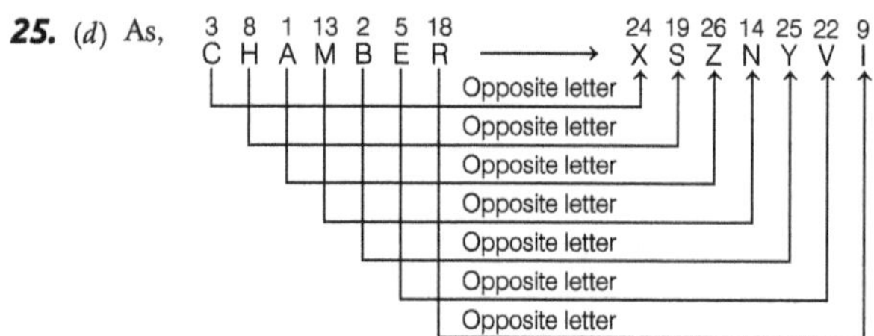

Similarly,

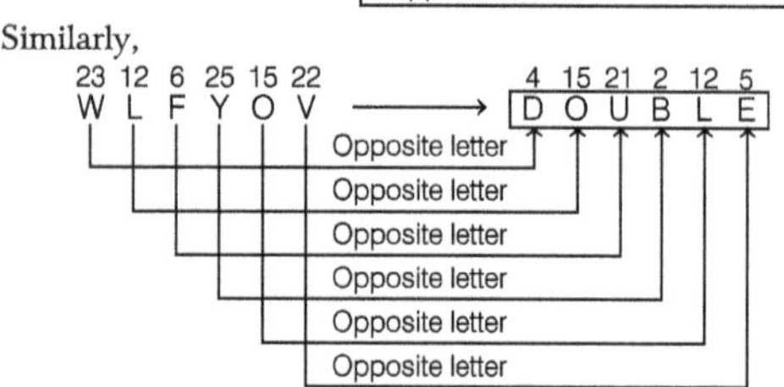

∴ WLFYOV ⇒ DOUBLE

26. (*c*) As,

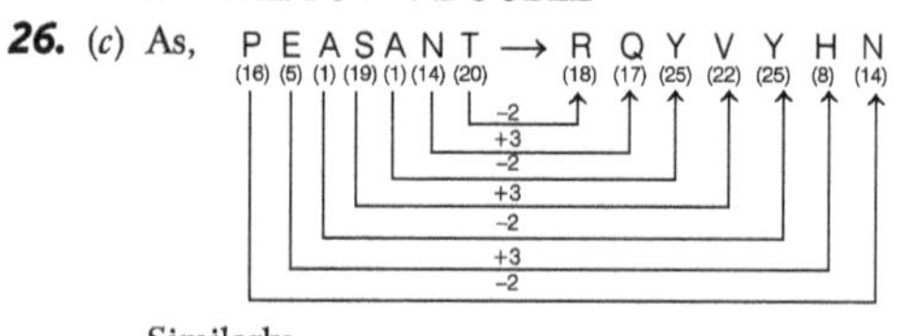

Similarly,

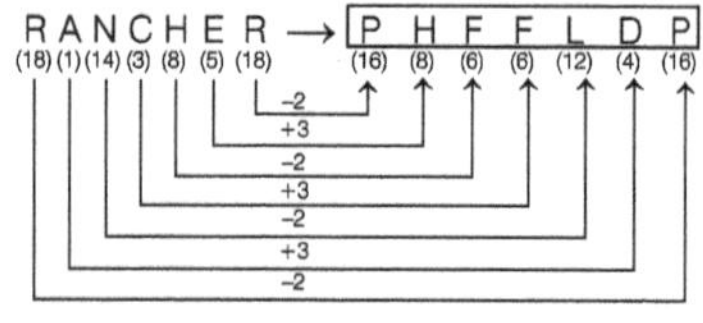

∴ RANCHER ⇒ PHFFLDP

27. (*b*) Each letter is coded with its corresponding letter position in the English alphabetical series.

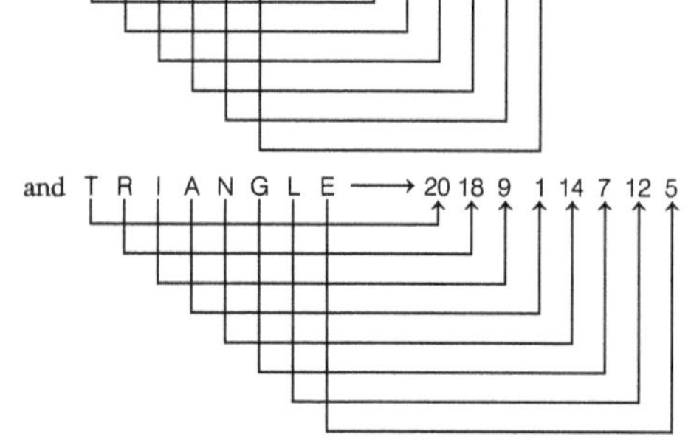

Similarly,

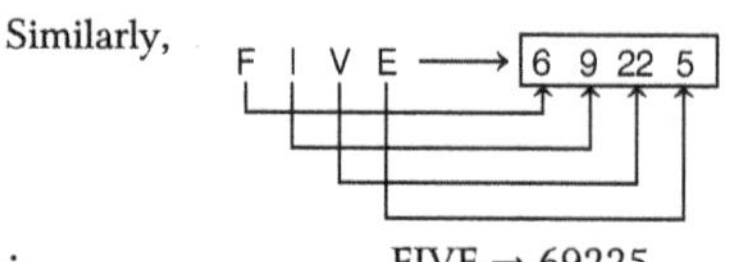

∴ FIVE ⇒ 69225

28. (*a*) Each letter is coded with its its position in reverse alphabetical series. Let us see

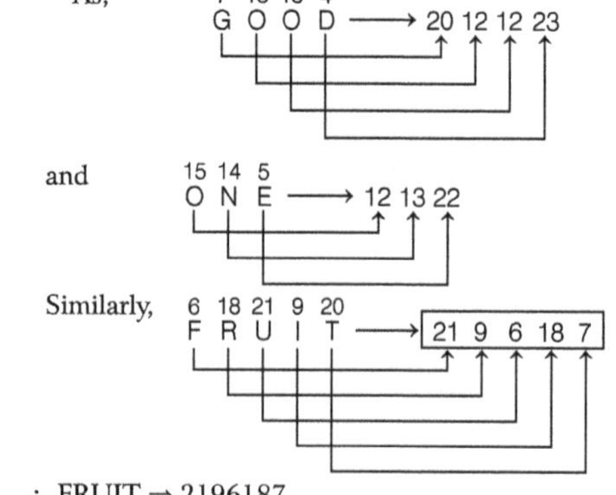

∴ FRUIT ⇒ 2196187

29. (*d*)

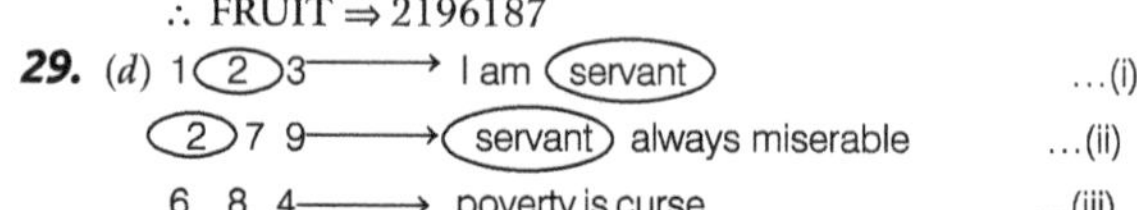

6 8 4 ⟶ poverty is curse ...(iii)

From Eqs. (i) and (ii), we get

2 ⇒ servant

∴ 1 ⇒ I/am

3 ⇒ I/am

7 ⇒ always/miserable

9 ⇒ always/miserable

∴ miserable ⇒ 7 or 9

Clearly, it cannot be definitely said how will 'miserable' be written.

30. (*a*) 4 9 3 ⟶ Friendship Big Challenge ...(i)

9 6 1 ⟶ Struggle Big Exam ...(ii)

1 7 8 ⟶ Exam Confidential Subject ...(iii)

From Eqs. (i) and (ii), 9 ⇒ Big

From Eqs. (ii) and (iii), 1 ⇒ Exam

∴ 7 ⇒ Confidential/Subject

8 ⇒ Confidential/Subject

∴ Confidential ⇒ 7 or 8

31. (*b*)

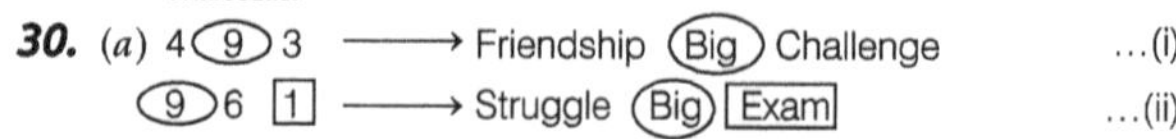

9 5 2 ⟶ mother very happy ...(iii)

From Eqs. (i) and (ii), 1 ⇒ always

From Eqs. (ii) and (iii), 9 ⇒ happy

∴ future ⇒ 6

Solutions (Q. Nos. 32-35) According to the given question,

Get details for venue ⟶ fe wi mo rs ...(i)

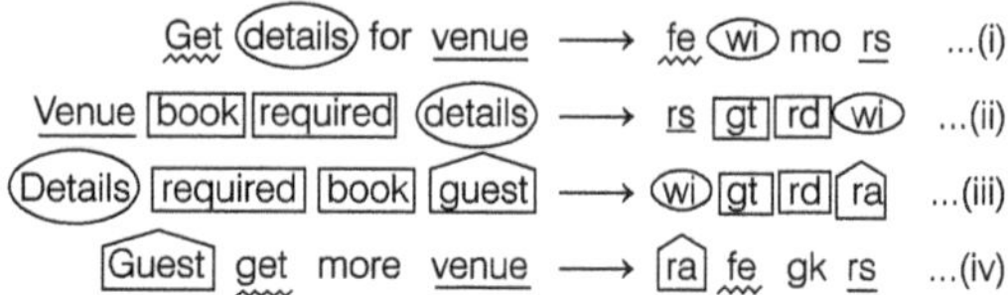

Guest get more venue ⟶ ra fe gk rs ...(iv)

	Word	Code
From (i), (ii) and (iv)	venue	rs
From (i), (ii) and (iii)	details	wi
From (iii) and (iv)	guest	ra
From (i) and (iv)	get	fe
From (ii) and (iii)	book	gt/rd
From (ii) and (iii)	required	gt/rd

32. (*c*) The code for 'details' is 'wi'.

33. (*c*) The code for 'guest venue' is 'rs ra'.

34. (*b*) The code for 'get' is 'fe'.

35. (*d*) The missing word is 'more'.

Solutions (Q.Nos. 36-39) Here, the alphabet in the code represents the next letter of the first alphabet of the word and the number represents the number of alphabets in the word.

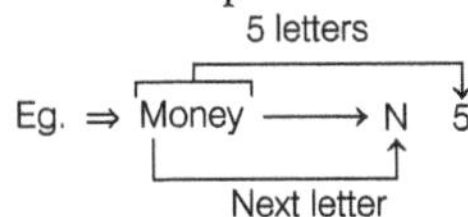

36. (*a*) The code for Radio is S5.

37. (*c*) The code for 'Rising Normal is 'O6 S6'.

38. (*e*) They forward → U4 G7 Now, 'T5' must be 'Stone' or 'South' as both contains 5 letters and starts with 'S'.

39. (*d*) Code for 'Elegant' is 'F7'.

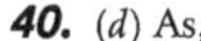

40. (*d*) As,

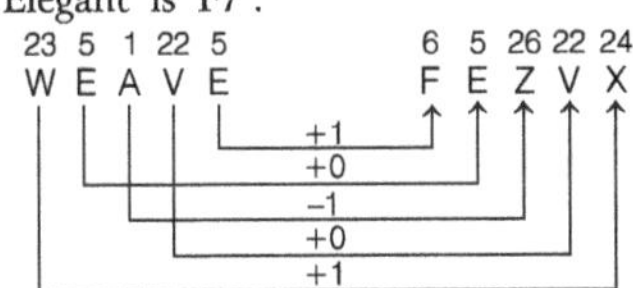

Similarly,

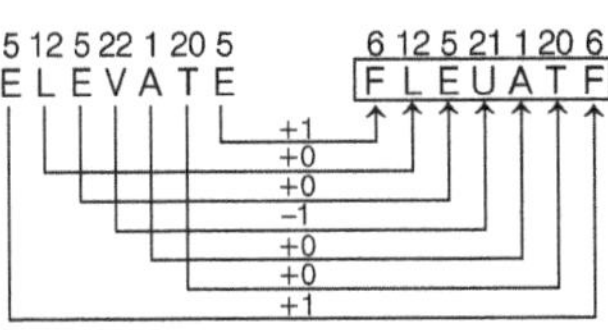

∴ ELEVATE ⇒ FLEUATF

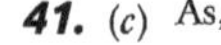

41. (*c*) As,

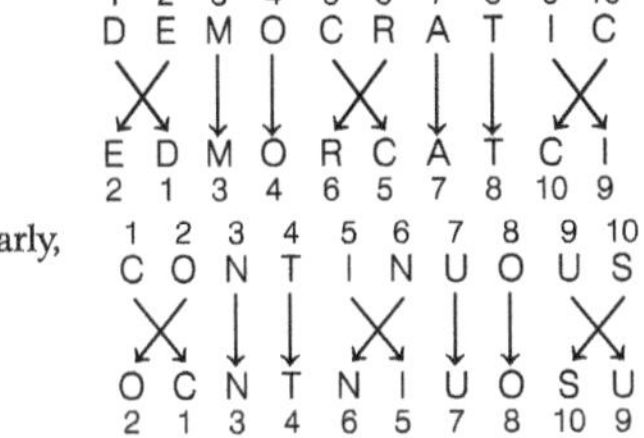

∴ CONTINUOUS ⇒ OCNTNIUOSU

42. (*e*) As,

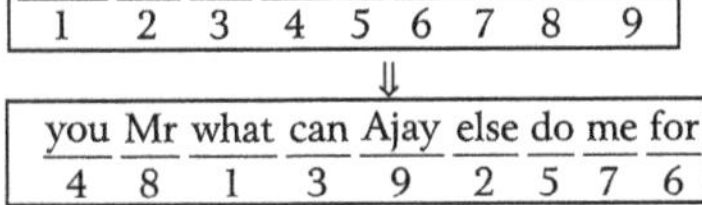

Similarly,

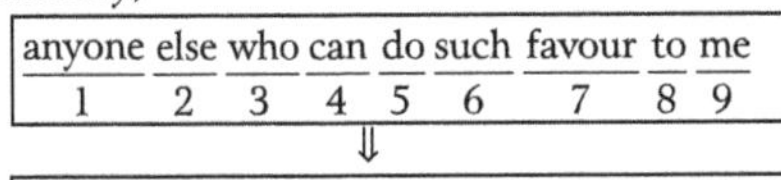

∴ Anyone else who can do such favour to me ⇒ can to anyone who me else do favour such.

43. (*c*)

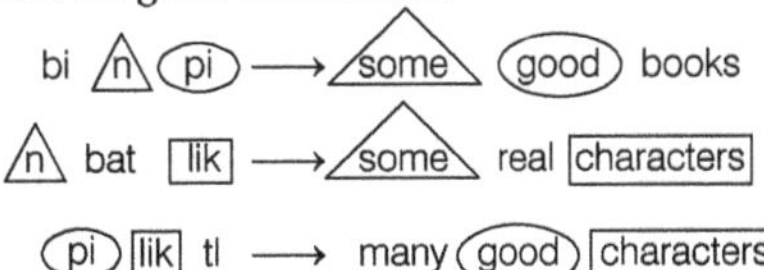

From Eqs. (ii) and (iii), 2 ⇒ smoking

44. (*a*) From the given information,

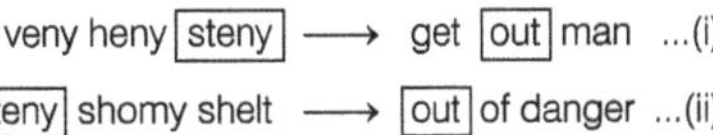

∴ Code for 'Many good books is "tl pi bi"

45. (*c*) From given information,

veny heny steny ⟶ get out man ...(i)

steny shomy shelt ⟶ out of danger ...(ii)

From Eqs. (i) and (ii), we get steny → out

46. (*b*) As,

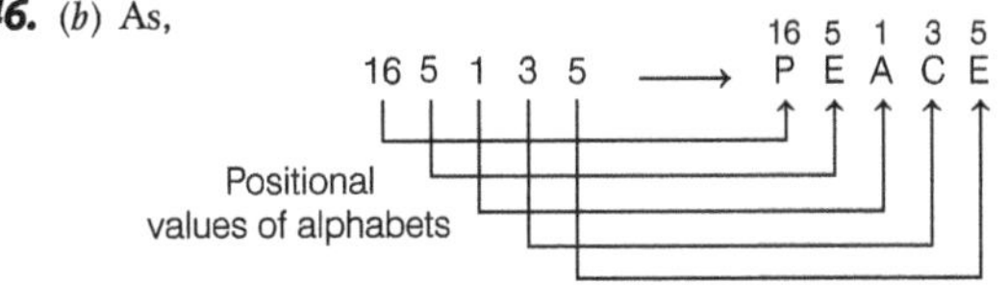

Similarly,

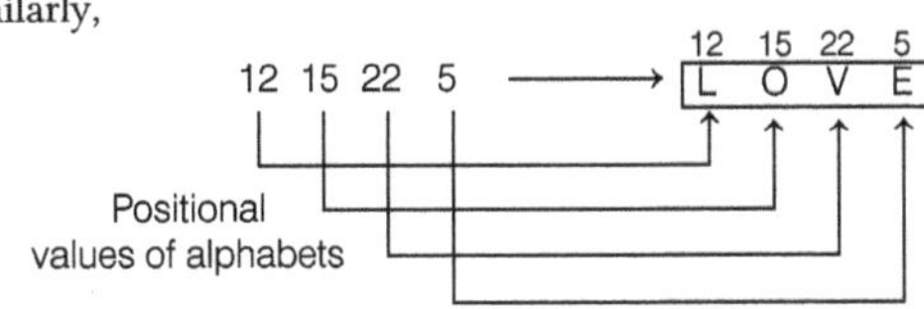

∴ LOVE ⇒ 1215225

47. (*a*) As,

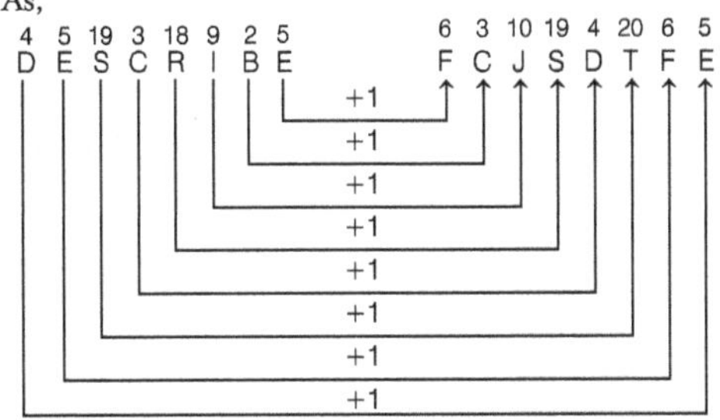

Similarly,

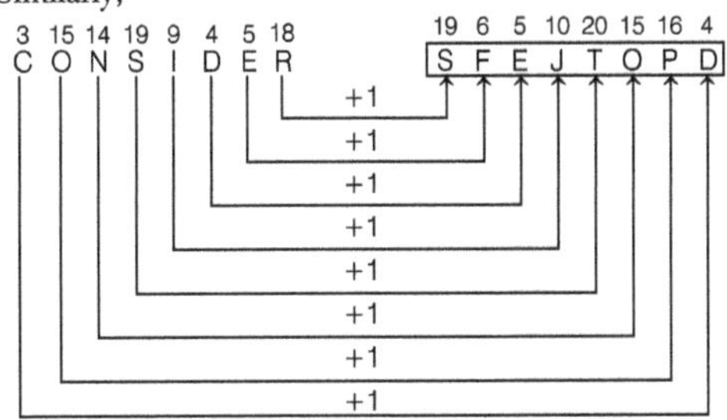

∴ CONSIDER ⇒ SFEJTOPD

48. (*a*) As,

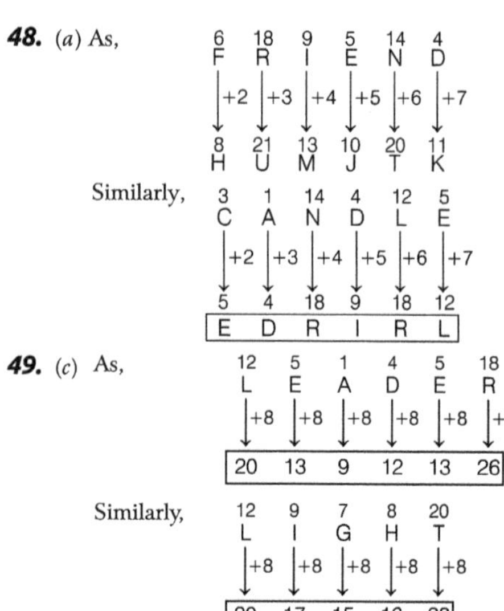

49. (*c*) As,

12 5 1 4 5 18
L E A D E R
+8 +8 +8 +8 +8 +8
20 13 9 12 13 26

Similarly,

12 9 7 8 20
L I G H T
+8 +8 +8 +8 +8
20 17 15 16 28

∴ LIGHT ⇒ 20-17-15-16-28

50. (*c*) As,

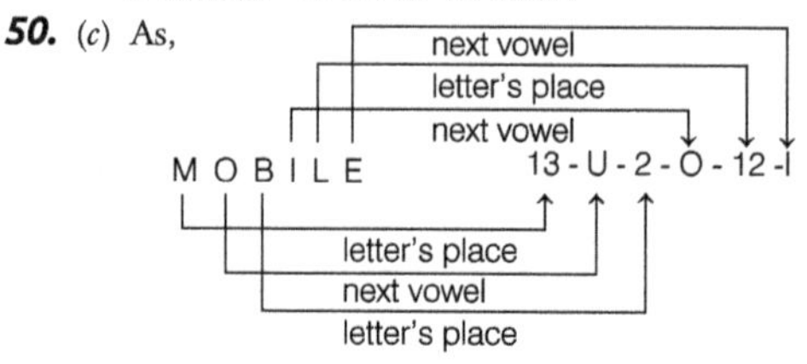

And

Place value
Next value
Place value
G A D G E T 7 – E – 4 – 7 – I – 20
Place value
Next value
Place value

Similarly,

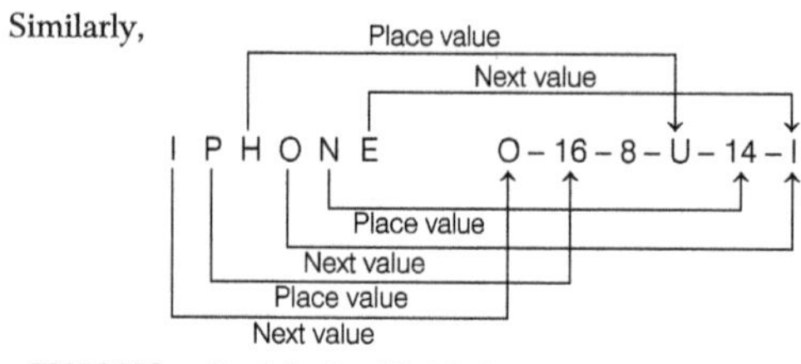

∴ IPHONE ⇒ O – 16 – 8 – U - 14 - I

51. (*d*) As,

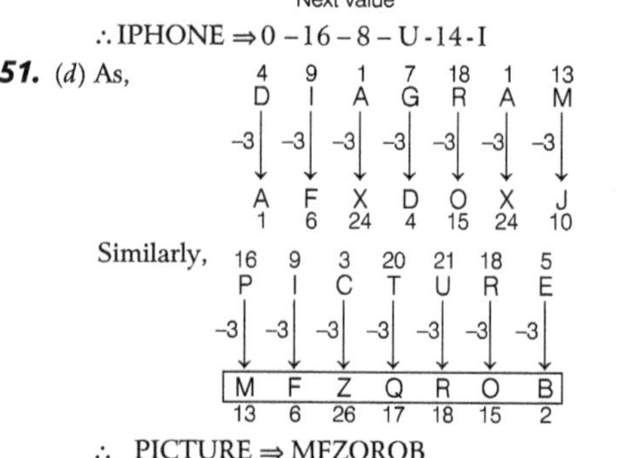

∴ PICTURE ⇒ MFZQROB

52. (*c*) The code number of LACK is 396

'L' comes at 12th place of alphabetical series.
'A' comes at 1st place of alphabetical series.
'C' comes at 3rd place of alphabetical series.
'K' comes at 11th place of alphabetical series.
Multiplying all the places, we get the code number of LACK as 396.
Then code number for BACK = $2 \times 1 \times 3 \times 11 = 66$
∴ BACK ⇒ 66

53. (*c*) As, C→ 5(3 + 2), C→ 5(3 + 2), E→ 7(5 + 2), A→ 3(1 + 2)

$T \rightarrow \frac{22\ (20 + 2)}{37}$

∴ CEAT ⇒ 37

Similarly,

10 J	1 A	16 P	1 A	14 N
(10+2)	(1+2)	(16+2)	(1+2)	(14+2)
12	3	18	3	16

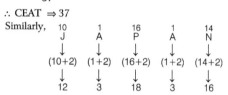

⇒ 12 + 3 + 18 + 3 + 16 ⇒ 52

∴ JAPAN ⇒ 52

54. (a)

As, PA[PER] ⟶ PERPA
and SUB[JECT] ⟶ JECTSUB
Similarly, COU[NCIL] ⟶ NCILCOU
∴ COUNCIL ⇒ NCILCOU

55. (*b*) As,

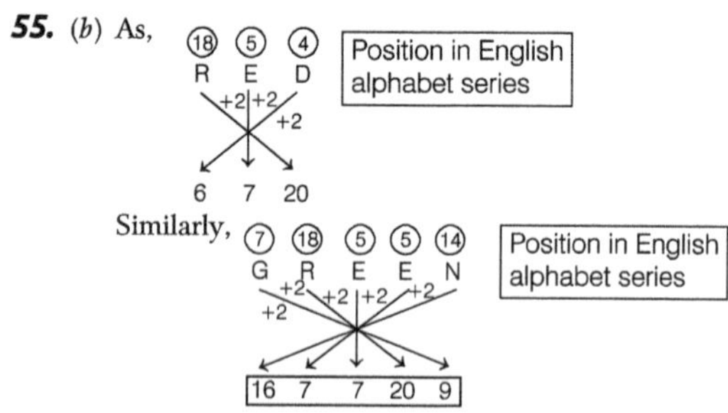

Hence, GREEN will be coded as 1677209.

56. (*d*) As,

S Y N D I C A T E ⟶ S Y T E N D C A I
1 2 3 4 5 6 7 8 9   1 2 8 9 3 4 6 7 5

Similarly, P S Y C H O T I C ⟶ P S I C Y C O T H
1 2 3 4 5 6 7 8 9   1 2 8 9 3 4 6 7 5

57. (*a*) Each letter is coded with the position of its opposite letter.

As,

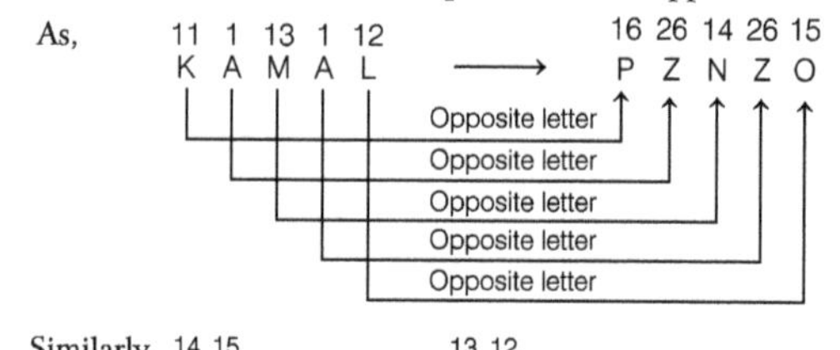

Similarly,

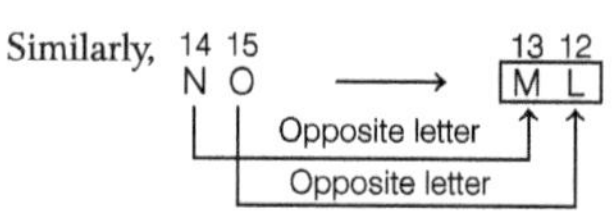

∴ N O ⇒ 13 12

58. (*a*) Each letter is coded with its right and left letters.

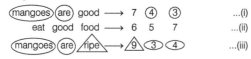

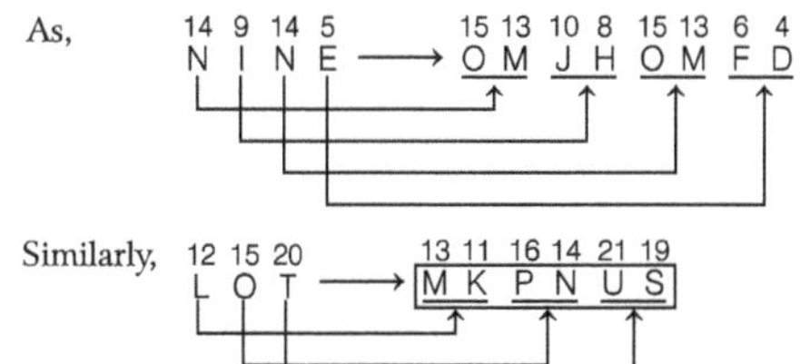

∴ LOT ⇒ MKPNUS

59. (*a*)

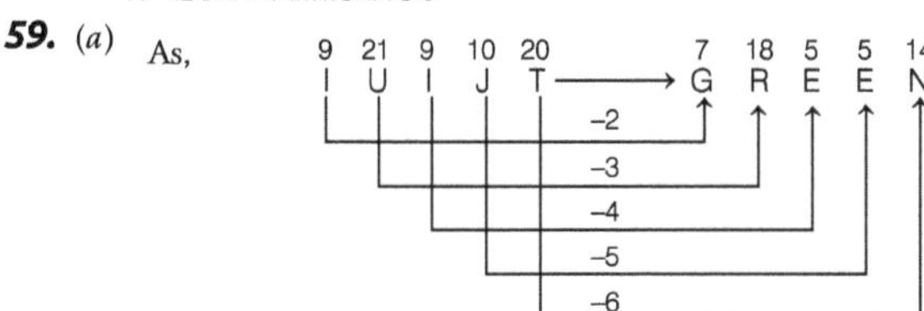

Similarly,

24	12	19	17	11	1
X	L	S	Q	K	A
–2 ↓	–3 ↓	–4 ↓	–5 ↓	–6 ↓	–7 ↓
V	I	O	L	E	T
22	9	15	12	5	20

∴ XLSQKA ⇒ VIOLET

60. (*a*)

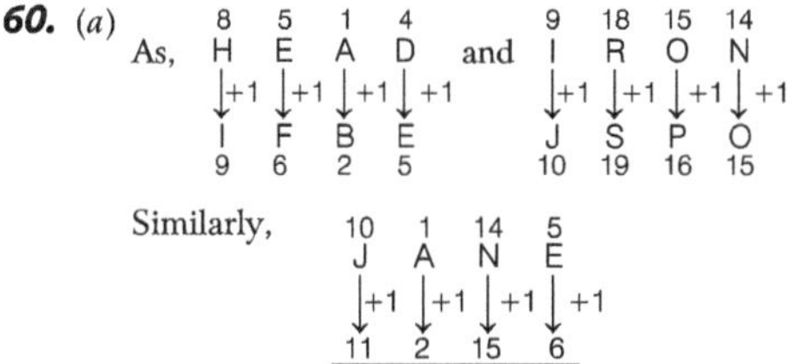

∴ JANE ⇒ KBOF

61. (*c*) As,

11 12 13 8 9 10 5 6 7 4 5 6
K [L] M , H [I] J , E [F] G , D [E] F
–1 +1 –1 +1 –1 +1 –1 +1

Similarly,

22 23 24 14 15 16 17 18 19 3 4 5
V [W] X , N [O] P , Q [R] S , C [D] E
–1 +1 –1 +1 –1 +1 –1 +1

∴ WORD ⇒ VXNPQSCE

62. (*a*) From given information,

(mangoes) (are) good ⟶ 7 ④ ③ ...(i)
eat good food ⟶ 6 5 7 ...(ii)
(mangoes) (are) △ripe ⟶ △9 ③ ④ ...(iii)

∴ Code for 'ripe' is '9'.

Solutions (Q. Nos. 63-65) Here each letter, except vowel, is assigned a number from 1-5 So, B-1, C-2, D-3, F-4, G-5, H-1, J-2, K-3, L-4, M-5, N-1, P-2, Q-3, R-4, S-5, T-1, V-2, W-3, X-4, Y-5, Z-1.

Each vowel is assigned a different symbol as– %, #, $, @, &

So, for vowels the symbols are –A-@, E-#, I-$, O-&, U-%

63. (c) Nuclear Bomb – Condition (i) applied–4%24#@1 1&51

64. (b) War–Condition
(i) applied–4@3 And–Condition (ii) applied– *1*
Peace–No condition applied–2#@2#
∴ War and peace ⇒ 4@3*1*2#@2 #

65. (d) Own condition (ii) applied– *3*
Life–No Condition applied –4$4#
∴ Own life ⇒ *3*4$4#

Solutions (Q. Nos. 66-68)

The different number codes for all the consonants as per the given conditions are
B-1, C-2, D-3, F-4, G-5, H-6, J-7
K-1, L-2, M-3, N-4, P-5, Q-6, R-7
S-1, T-2, V-3, W-4, X-5, Y-6, Z-7

According to Step 1,
A → * *
E → * *
I → * *

According to Step 2,
O–$ $
U–$ $

66. (a) A N N U A L
Step-1 : A 4 4 U A 2
Step-2 : * * @ # # 1 $ $ * * @ #
The code for 'ANNUAL' is "**@##1$$***a*#".

67. (b) N O R M A L
Step 1 : 4 O 7 3 A 2
Step 2 : # 1 $$ @ ## 1 ** @#
The code for "NORMAL" is "# 1 $$ @ # # 1 **@#".

68. (a) S M I T T L E
Step 1 : 1 3 I 2 2 2 E
Step 2 : 1 # 1 ** @ # 2 #1 **
The code for 'SMITTLE' is '1#1**@#2#1**'.
'1 # 1 * * @ # 2 # 1 * *'

Solutions (Q. Nos. 69-73)

Numerals	3	5	7	4	2	6	8	1	0	9
Letter/Symbol code	★	B	E	A	@	F	K	%	R	M

Conditions

(i) 1st digit odd, Last digit odd — Both are coded as X

(ii) 1st digit even, Last digit even — Both are coded as $

(iii) Last digit zero — code is #

69. (*d*)

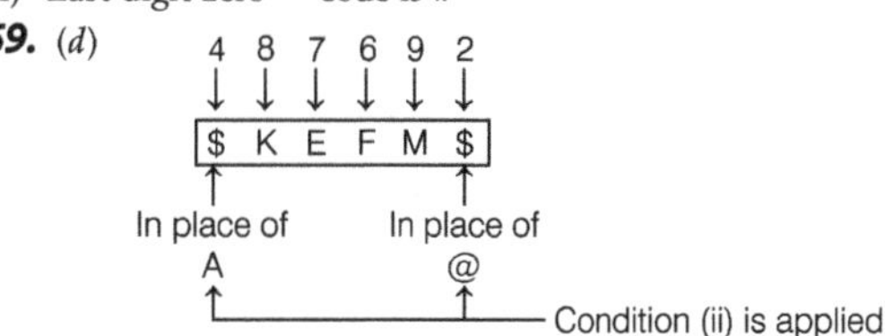

∴ 487692 ⇒ $ KEFM$

70. (*b*)

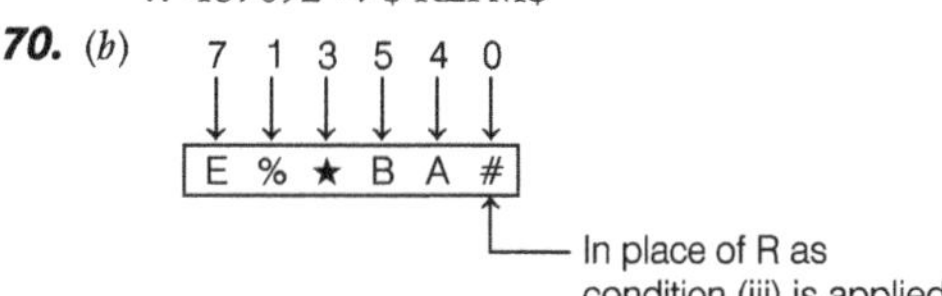

∴ 713540 ⇒ E%★BA#

71. (*c*)

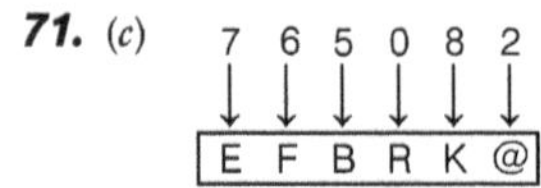

No condition applied.

∴ 765082 ⇒ EFBRK@

72. (*e*)

3 6 4 8 1 9

X F A K % X

In place of ★   In place of M

Condition (i) is applied.

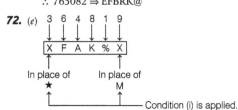

∴ 364819 ⇒ XFAK%X

73. (*a*)

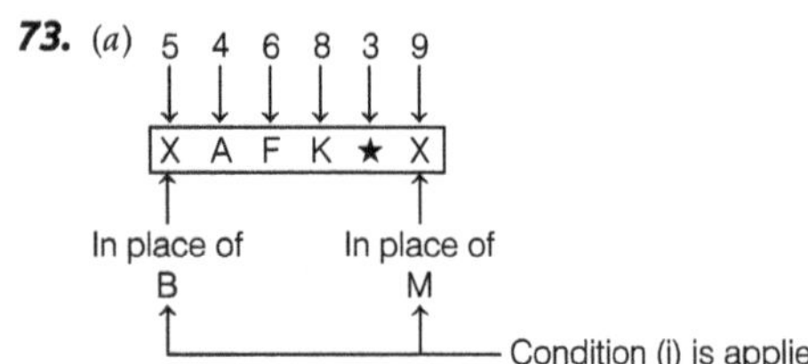

∴ 546839 ⇒ XAFK★X

74. (*c*) Here, none of the condition is applied, so the coding is done as follows

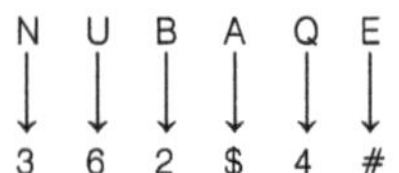

∴ Code for NUBAQE ⇒ 362$4#

75. (*d*) When no condition is applied, the coding is done as follows

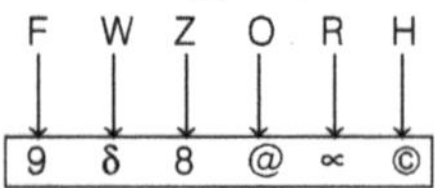

But here the second and third letters are consonants, therefore condition (iii) is applied here. As condition (iii) is applied here, both the second and third letters are to be coded as the code for the third letter.

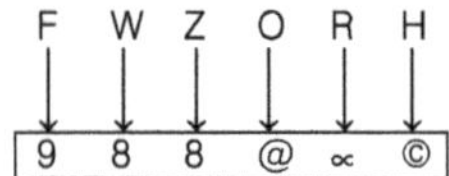

∴ Code for FWZORH ⇒ 988@∝©

76. (*a*) When no condition is applied, the coding is done as follows

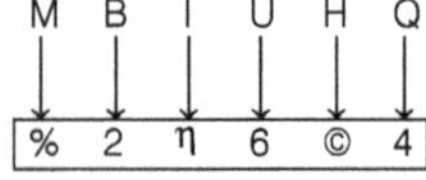

But here the first letter is a consonant and the third letter is a vowel, therefore condition (i) is applied here. As condition (i) is applied here, the codes for first and third letters are interchanged.

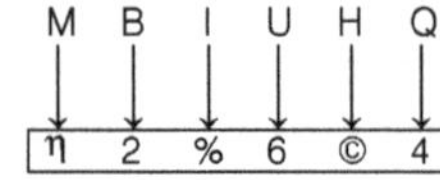

∴ Code for MBIUHQ ⇒ η 2%6©4

77. (*b*) Here, none of the condition is applied, so the coding is done as follows

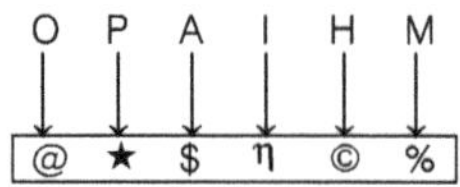

∴ Code for OPAIHM ⇒ @★ $ η © %

78. (*d*) When no condition is applied, the coding is done as follows.

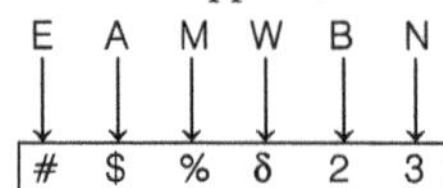

But here the first letter is a vowel and the fourth letter is a consonant, therefore condition (ii) is applied here.
As condition (ii) is applied, both the first and the fourth letters are to be coded as the code for the vowel.

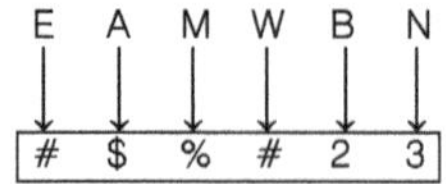

∴ Code for EAMWBN ⇒ #$%#23

79. (*e*) Here, none of the condition is applied, so the coding is done as follows.

∴ Code for AIWEZB ⇒ $ η δ # 8 2

Solutions (Q. Nos. 80-83)

	Triangle	Right Triangle	Circle
Place 1	0	1	2
Place 2	0	3	6
Place 3	0	9	18
Place 4	0	27	54
Place 5	0	81	162
Place 6	0	243	486
Place 7	0	729	1458

80. (*c*)

$$\frac{◺◺△△◺○◺}{△△○○○}$$

$$= \frac{729 + 243 + 0 + 0 + 9 + 6 + 1}{0 + 0 + 18 + 6 + 2} = \frac{988}{26} = 38$$

38 = ◺◺△○

81. (*e*) ○◺○△◺△○ = 1874

82. (*c*) ◺◺○△◺○ = 383

83. (*e*)

△◺○◺○ = 50

◺◺◺◺ = 40

◺○△◺○ = 140

△◺○△ = 15

◺◺◺◺○ = 122

CHAPTER / 05

Series

Series is a sequential order of letters, numbers or both arranged in such a way that each term in the series is obtained according to some specific rules. These rules can be based on mathematical operations, place of letters in alphabetical order etc.

In questions based on series, a specified sequence/order of letters, numbers or a combination of both is given where one of the terms (letter/number/letter and number) of the series is missing either at the end of the series or in between the series or one of its term is incorrect which does not fit into the series.

The candidate is required to identify the pattern involved in the formation of series and accordingly find the missing or wrong term of the series.

On the basis of various types of questions that are asked in competitive exams, we have classified series into several types as follows.

TYPE 01

Number Series

In such types of questions, a series of numbers is given with one number/term missing from its place.
The candidate is required to recognise the pattern involved in the formation of series and find the missing number accordingly.

Various different patterns are involved in the formation of series. Now, let us discuss some most common patterns involved in the formation of series.

1. Addition Series

In this type of series, each time the same digit/number or digit/number in increasing/decreasing order is added to previous element to obtain the next element.

Ex 01 What comes in place of question mark (?) in the series given below? « SSC 10+2 2018

17, 20, 23, 26, 29, ?

(a) 31 (b) 34
(c) 30 (d) 32

Solution (d) The pattern of the series is as follows

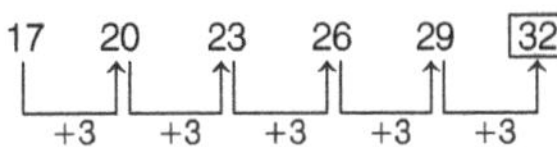

$\therefore$? = 32

Ex 02 9, 12, 16, 21, ?, 34. « RRB NTPC 2016

(a) 30 (b) 27 (c) 28 (d) 35

Solution (b) The pattern of the series is as follows

9 12 16 21 [27] 34
+3 +4 +5 +6 +7

$\therefore$? = 27

2. Subtraction Series

In this type of series, the difference between the two consecutive elements is same or in increasing or decreasing order.

Ex 03 Find the next number in the following series. « RRB Group D 2018

71, 63, 55, ?

(a) 48 (b) 47 (c) 46 (d) 45

Solution (b) The pattern of the series is as follows

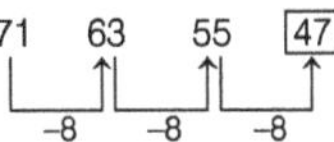

$\therefore$? = 47

Ex 04 What comes in place of question mark (?) in the following number series?

95, 94, 92, 89, 85, 80, ?

(a) 74 (b) 69 (c) 75 (d) 77

***Solution* (a)** The pattern of the series is as follows

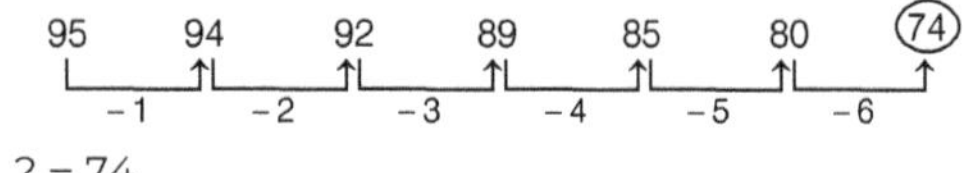

∴ ? = 74

3. Multiplication Series

In this type of series, the ratio between two consecutive elements is same or in increasing/decreasing order, i.e. in this case, every time the previous element is multiplied by the same digit/number or the digits in increasing/ decreasing order to obtain the next element.

***Ex* 05** What comes in place of question mark (?) in the following number series? « SSC CHSL 2017

3, 12, 48, ?

(a) 96 (b) 184
(c) 192 (d) 384

***Solution* (c)** The pattern of the series is as follows

3 12 48 192
×4 ×4 ×4

∴ ? = 192

***Ex* 06** What number should come next in the sequence 6, 18, 72 360, 2160, …… ? « WBCS 2020

(a) 12120 (b) 13120
(c) 14120 (d) 15120

***Solution* (d)** The pattern of the series is as follows

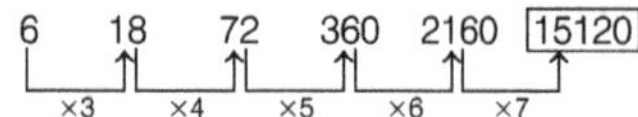

∴ ? = 15120

4. Division Series

In this type of series, each time the previous element is divided by the same digit/number or the digits in increasing/decreasing order to obtain the next element.

***Ex* 07** Find the missing number in the sequence. « CLAT 2018

9, 3, ___, 1/3, 1/9

(a) 2 (b) 6 (c) 1/2 (d) 1

***Solution* (d)** The pattern of the series is as follows

$9 \xrightarrow{\div 3} 3 \xrightarrow{\div 3} \boxed{1} \xrightarrow{\div 3} \frac{1}{3} \xrightarrow{\div 3} \frac{1}{9}$

∴ ? = 1

***Ex* 08** Find the missing number in the sequence « UPSSSC Junior Assistant 2020

600 120 ? 10 5 5

(a) 20 (b) 40 (c) 30 (d) 25

***Solution* (c)** The pattern of the series is as follows

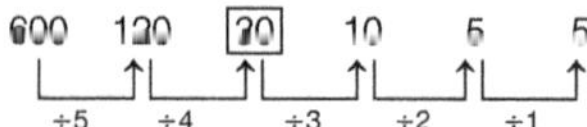

∴ ? = 30

5. Double Addition Series

In this type of series, each time the digit/number is added to the previous element in increasing order in such a way that numbers to be added make another series.

***Ex* 09** Replace the question mark(?) in the following number series.

1, 9, 22, 41, 67, ?

(a) 101 (b) 102
(c) 108 (d) 115

***Solution* (a)** The pattern of the series is as follows

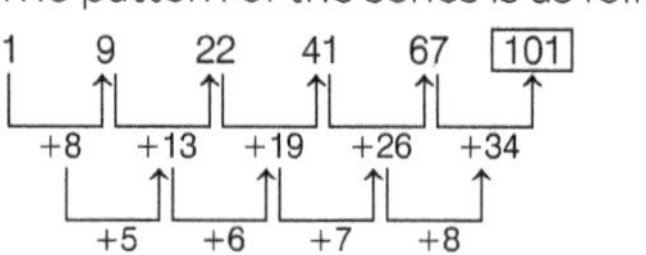

∴ ? = 101

6. Double Addition and Subtraction Series

In this type of series, next element is obtained by subtracting and adding some numbers from and to the previous number in alternate manner in increasing or decreasing order.

The numbers to be added and subtracted make a further series, the logic behind which is found by again subtracting and adding some numbers from and to the previous number in alternate manner in increasing or decreasing order.

***Ex* 10** What comes in place of question mark (?) in the following number series? « SBI PO 2018

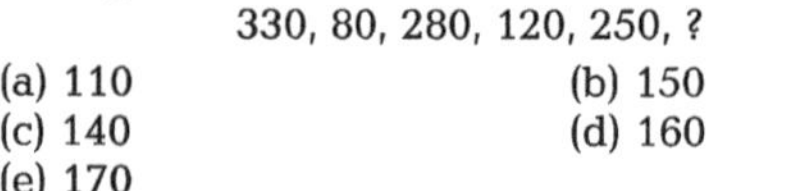

330, 80, 280, 120, 250, ?

(a) 110 (b) 150
(c) 140 (d) 160
(e) 170

***Solution* (c)** The pattern of the series is as follows

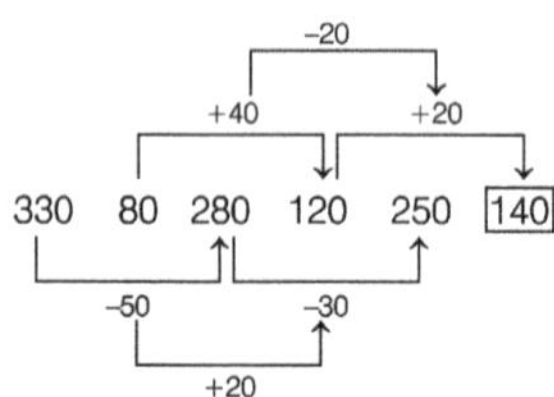

∴ ? = 140

7. Same Number Multiplication and Same Number Addition Series

In this type of series, the next element is obtained by multiplying the previous number by a certain number and by adding a certain number in this multiplication.

***Ex* 11** Replace the question mark (?) in the following number series with the suitable option.

5, 11, 23, 47, 95, ?

(a) 191 (b) 185
(c) 194 (d) 198

Solution **(a)** The pattern of the series is as follows

∴ ? = 191

8. Same Number Multiplication and Addition in Increasing Order Series

In this type of series, each previous element is multiplied by same number while numbers in increasing order are added respectively, in these multiplications to obtain the next element.

***Ex* 12** Select the correct option that will fill in the blank and complete the series. « SSC Steno 2019

6, 13, 28, 59, ?, 249

(a) 120 (b) 118 (c) 98 (d) 122

Solution **(d)** The pattern of the series is as follows

6 13 28 59 122 249
×2+1 ×2+2 ×2+3 ×2+4 ×2+5

∴ ? = 122

9. Increasing Order Multiplication and Same Number Addition Series

In this type of series, each previous element is multiplied respectively by numbers in increasing order and then a certain number is added in such multiplications to obtain the next element.

***Ex* 13** Replace the question mark (?) in the given series with suitable option.

3, 6, 15, 48, 195, ?

(a) 978 (b) 897 (c) 688 (d) 945

Solution **(a)** The pattern of the series is as follows

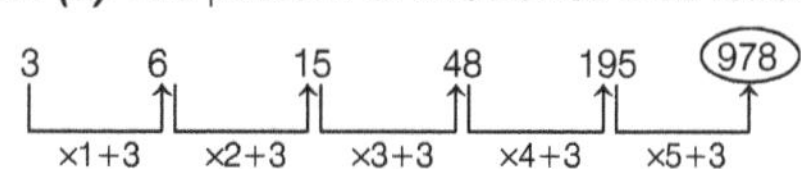

∴ ? = 978

10. Increasing Order Multiplication and Increasing Order Addition Series

In this type of series, the previous elements are multiplied respectively by numbers in increasing order and then numbers in increasing order are added respectively in such multiplications to obtain the next elements.

***Ex* 14** What comes in place of question mark (?) in the following number series?

4, 5, 12, 39, 160, ?

(a) 225 (b) 695 (c) 805 (d) 790

Solution **(c)** The pattern of the series is as follows

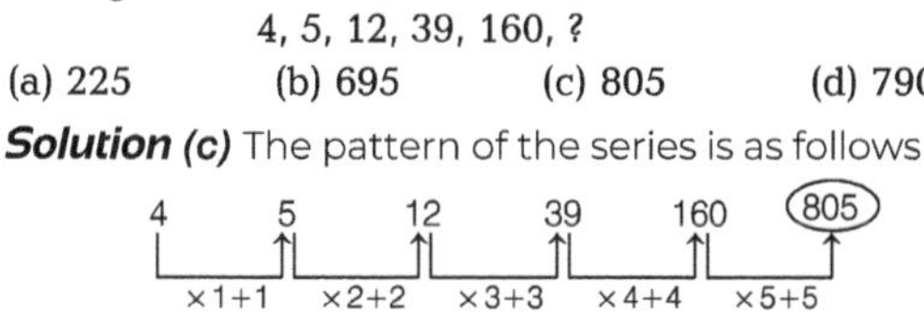

∴ ? = 805

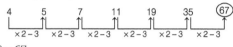

11. Same Number Multiplication and Same Number Subtraction Series

In this type of series, each previous element is multiplied by a certain number and then a certain number is subtracted from this multiplication to obtain each next element.

***Ex* 15** Replace the question mark (?) in the series given below with the correct option.

4, 5, 7, 11, 19, 35, ?

(a) 67 (b) 76 (c) 55 (d) 45

Solution **(a)** The pattern of the series is as follows

4 5 7 11 19 35 67
×2−3 ×2−3 ×2−3 ×2−3 ×2−3 ×2−3

∴ ? = 67

12. Same Number Multiplication and Subtraction in Increasing Order Series

In this type of series, each previous element is multiplied by a certain number and then from such multiplications, numbers in increasing order are subtracted, respectively to obtain each next element.

***Ex* 16** What comes in place of question mark (?) in the following number series?

4, 7, 12, 21, 38, ?

(a) 75 (b) 71 (c) 78 (d) 77

Solution **(b)** The pattern of the series is as follows

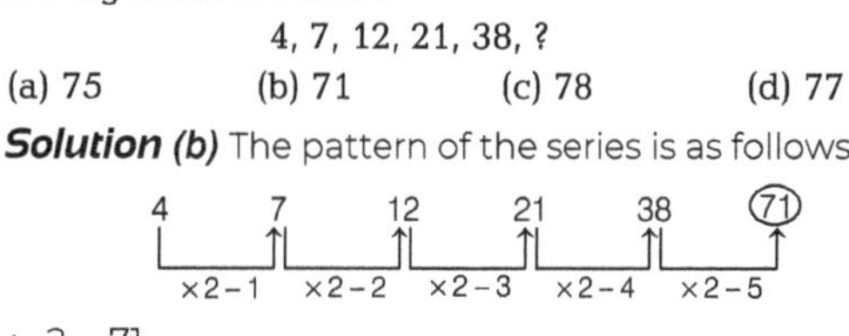

∴ ? = 71

13. Increasing Order Multiplication and Same Number Subtraction Series

In this type of series, each previous element is multiplied by numbers in increasing order respectively and then from such multiplications, a certain number is subtracted to obtain each next element.

***Ex* 17** What comes in place of question mark (?) in the following number series?

4, 6, 16, 62, 308, ?

(a) 990 (b) 1721 (c) 698 (d) 1846

Solution **(d)** The pattern of the series is as follows

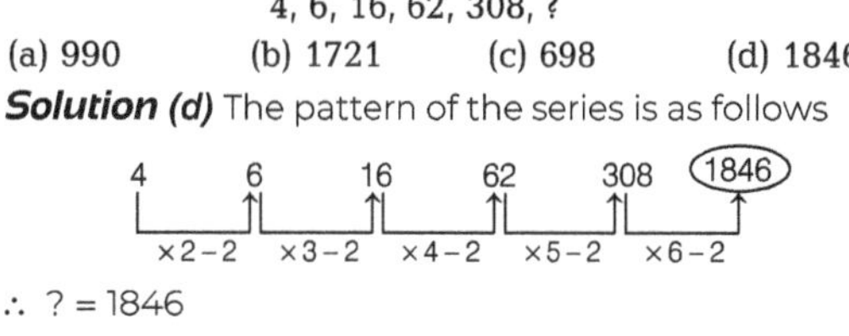

∴ ? = 1846

14. Increasing Order Multiplication and Increasing Order Subtraction Series

In this type of series, previous elements are multiplied respectively by numbers in increasing order and then numbers in increasing order are subtracted respectively from such multiplications to obtain each next element.

***Ex* 18** What comes in place of question mark (?) in the following number series?

3, 5, 13, 49, 241, ?

(a) 1541 (b) 4411
(c) 1600 (d) 1441

***Solution* (d)** The pattern of the series is as follows

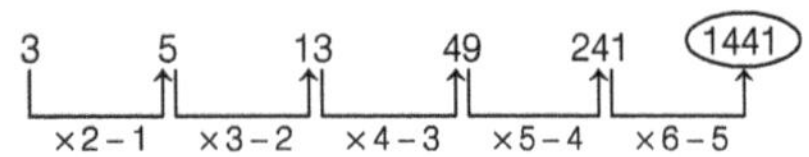

∴ ? = 1441

15. Multiplication and Division Series

In this type of series, each next element is obtained by the operation of multiplication and division alternately.

***Ex* 19** Replace the question mark (?) in the given series with the suitable option.

24, 72, 36, 108, 54, ?

(a) 145 (b) 162
(c) 158 (d) 165

***Solution* (b)** The pattern of the series is as follows

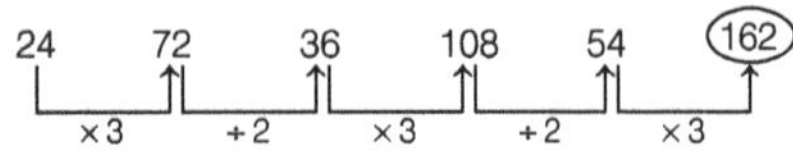

∴? = 162

***Ex* 20** Replace the question mark (?) in the given series with the suitable option.

6, 3, 9, 4.5, 13.5, ?

(a) 6.75 (b) 7 (c) 8.4 (d) 8

***Solution* (a)** The pattern of the series is as follows

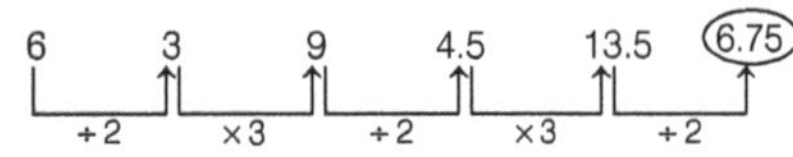

∴ ? = 6.75

16. Square Series

In this type of series, each element is the square of a number in a certain sequence.

***Ex* 21** Replace the question mark (?) in the series given below with the suitable option.

49, 64, ?, 100, 121 « SSC CGL 2017

(a) 74 (b) 80
(c) 75 (d) 81

***Solution* (d)** The pattern of the series is as follows

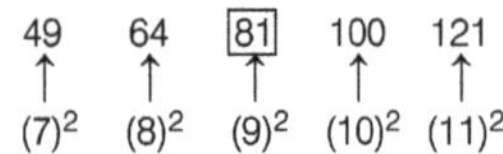

∴ ? = 81

17. Cube Series

In this type of series, each element is the cube of a number in a certain sequence.

***Ex* 22** Replace the question mark (?) in the series given below with the suitable option.

1, 8, 27, 64, 125, ?

(a) 155 (b) 216 (c) 210 (d) 177

***Solution* (b)** The pattern of the series is as follows

1	8	27	64	125	216
↑	↑	↑	↑	↑	↑
$(1)^3$	$(2)^3$	$(3)^3$	$(4)^3$	$(5)^3$	$(6)^3$

∴ ? = 216

18. Square Addition/Subtraction Series

In this type of series, square of numbers in a particular manner are added or subtracted respectively to each element to obtain the next element.

***Ex* 23** Which number will come next in the following series?

3, 7, 16, 32, 57, ... « SSC CPO 2018

(a) 85 (b) 80 (c) 98 (d) 93

***Solution* (d)** The pattern of the series is as follows

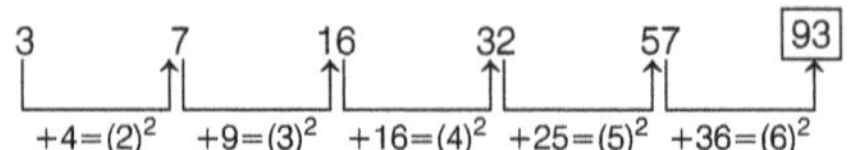

19. Cube Addition/Subtraction Series

In this type of series, cube of numbers in a particular manner are added or subtracted, respectively to each element to obtain the next element.

***Ex* 24** What comes in place of question mark (?) in the series given below?

1, 2, 10, 37, 101, ?

(a) 226 (b) 215 (c) 218 (d) 229

***Solution* (a)** The pattern of the series is as follows

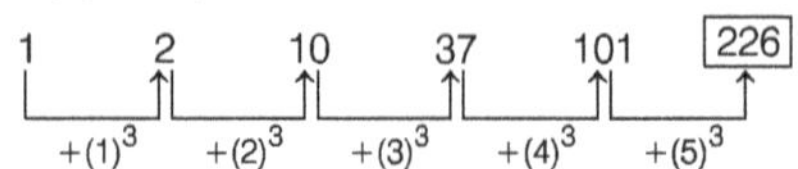

∴ ? = 226

20. Square and Cube Addition Series

In this type of series, square and cube of numbers are added alternately in increasing order respectively to obtain next element.

***Ex* 25** What comes in place of question mark (?) in the series given below?

2, 3, 7, 34, 50, ?

(a) 180 (b) 175 (c) 160 (d) 165

***Solution* (b)** The pattern of the series is as follows

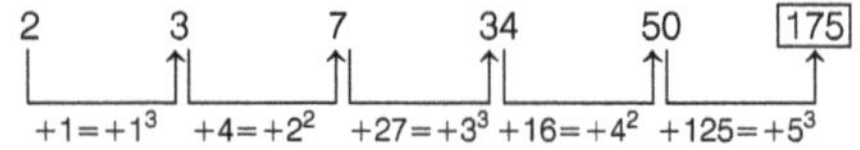

∴ ? = 175

21. Prime Number Series

In this type of series, each element is prime number in certain sequence.

Ex 26 What replaces the question mark (?) in the following number series?

2, 3, 5, 7, 11, ?

(a) 14 (b) 15
(c) 13 (d) 17

Solution (c) The pattern of the series is as follows

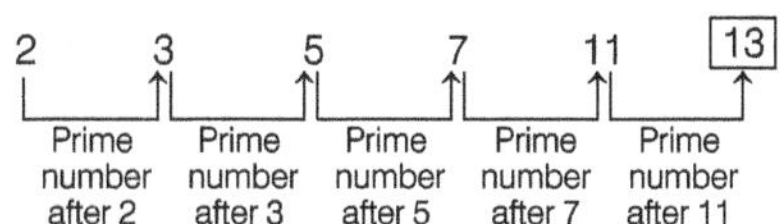

∴ ? = 13

22. Digital Operation of Number Series

In this type of series, the digits of each number are operated in a certain way to obtain the next elements of the series.

Ex 27 What replaces question mark (?) in the series given below?

88, 64, 24, ?

(a) 8 (b) 6
(c) 2 (d) 5

Solution (a) The pattern of the series is as follows

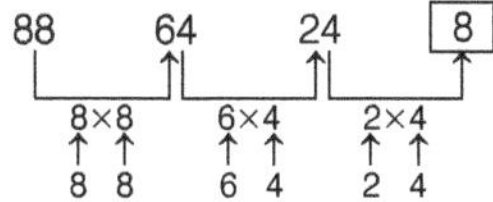

∴ ? = 8

Ex 28 What comes in place of question mark (?) in the given number series?

4, 24, 6, 48, 8, 80, ?

(a) 8 (b) 9
(c) 10 (d) 4

Solution (c) The pattern of the series is as follows

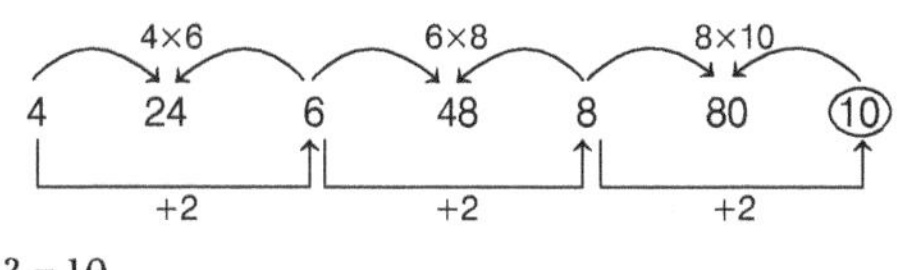

∴ ? = 10

23. Mixed/Combination Series

In this type of series, odd place elements make one series while the even place elements make another series.

Ex 29 Replace the question mark (?) in the following number series. « MAT 2015

0, 2, 3, 5, 8, 10, 15, 17, 24, 26, ?

(a) 28 (b) 30
(c) 32 (d) 35

Solution (d) The pattern of the series is as follows

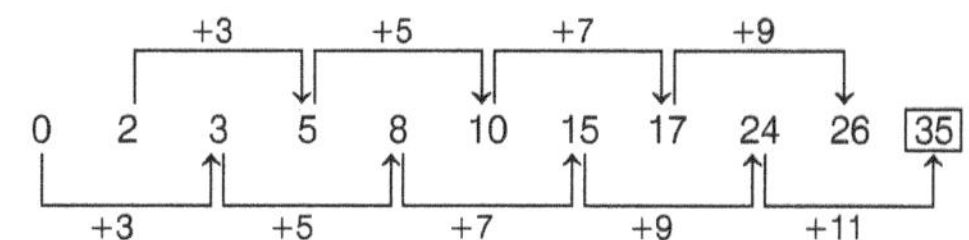

∴ ? = 35

Ex 30 Find the next three terms of the given series. « RRB Group D 2018

61, 61, 37, 67, 67, 52, 71, 71,__, __, __

(a) 65, 73, 73 (b) 65, 75, 75
(c) 67, 75, 75 (d) 67, 73, 73

Solution (d) The pattern of the series is as follows

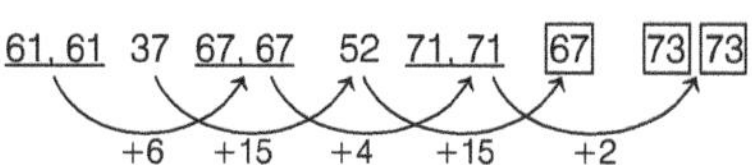

Ex 31 Replace the question mark (?) in the following number series. « SSC CGL 2016

1, 4, 2, 3, 2, ?

(a) 2 (b) 5
(c) 3 (d) 4

Solution (d) The pattern of the series is as follows

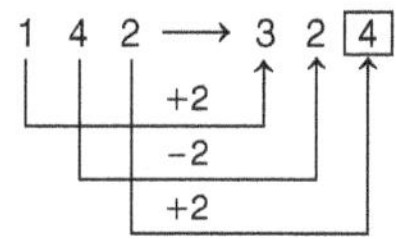

∴ ? = 4

24. New Series

In this type of series, a number series is given. Below this series another number series is there, in which first number is given but another numbers are named as (A), (B), (C), (D) and (E). In the first series, numbers are arranged from left to right based on some mathematical operations.

The candidate has to follow the same mathematical operations in second series and find out the values of (A), (B), (C), (D) and (E) according to the question.

Ex 32 2 7 12 17 22 27
3 (A) (B) (C) (D) (E)

which number comes in place of (D)?

(a) 18 (b) 19 (c) 20 (d) 23

Solution (d) The pattern of the series is as follows

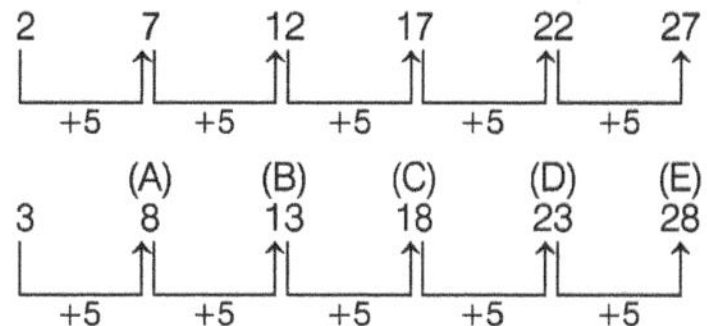

∴ D = 23

Practice CORNER 5.1

DIRECTIONS ~ (Q. Nos. 1-84) *In the following series, replace the question mark (?) with the suitable option.*

1. 6, 9, 12, 15, 18, ?
(a) 21 (b) 20 (c) 19 (d) 22

2. −1.3, −0.8, −0.3, ?, 0.7, 1.2 « RRB ALP 2018
(a) 0.2 (b) 0.4 (c) 0.1 (d) 0.3

3. 2, 3.5, 5, 6.5, 8, ?
(a) 9.0 (b) 9.5 (c) 10.5 (d) 11.0

4. 3.5, 7, 10.5, 14, ?
(a) 15.5 (b) 16.5 (c) 18.5 (d) 17.5

5. 15, 23, 31, 39, ? , 55, 63
(a) 45 (b) 47 (c) 46 (d) 44

6. 173, 188, 203, 218, ? « Delhi Police MTS 2018
(a) 232 (b) 233 (c) 235 (d) 231

7. 4, 5, 7, 10, 14, 19, ?
(a) 28 (b) 23 (c) 22 (d) 25

8. 2, 3, 5, 9, 17, ?
(a) 34 (b) 31 (c) 32 (d) 33

9. 0, 3, 8, 15,?
(a) 25 (b) 26
(c) 35 (d) None of these

10. 6, 9, 13, 18, 24, ? « SSC CHSL 2018
(a) 31 (b) 34 (c) 29 (d) 28

11. 100, 105, 111, 118, 126, 135, ?
« UPSSSC Tech Assist. Agri Service 2018
(a) 147 (b) 144 (c) 146 (d) 145

12. 2, 7, 14, 23, ?, 47 « UPSSSC Junior Assistant 2020
(a) 21 (b) 38
(c) 34 (d) 28

13. 55, 58, 64, ?, 85 « SSC CGL 2020
(a) 25 (b) 26 (c) 27 (d) 28

14. 6, 11, 21, 36, 56, ... ? « WBCS 2020
(a) 78 (b) 81 (c) 82 (d) 86

15. 40, 50, 61, 73, 86, ?, 115 « SSC CPO 2019
(a) 99 (b) 105 (c) 100 (d) 98

16. 8, 16, 28, 44, ?
(a) 62 (b) 64 (c) 66 (d) 60

17. 173, 151, 129, 107, ? « Delhi Police MTS 2018
(a) 84 (b) 83 (c) 87 (d) 85

18. 445, 444, 442, 439, 435, ?
(a) 427 (b) 418 (c) 430 (d) 425

19. 107, 97, 82, 62, ?
(a) 52 (b) 42 (c) 47 (d) 37

20. 18, 16, 13, 9, ? « MP Constable 2017
(a) 4 (b) 2 (c) 6 (d) 7

21. 36, 28, 24, 22, ? « SSC CPO 2010
(a) 18 (b) 19 (c) 21 (d) 22

22. 462, 420, 380, ?, 306
(a) 322 (b) 332 (c) 342 (d) 352

23. 71, 59, 48, 38, 29, ?
(a) 18 (b) 21 (c) 20 (d) 12

24. 36, 34, 30, 28, 24, ?
(a) 23 (b) 26 (c) 20 (d) 22

25. 15, 30, 60, 120, 240, ?
(a) 480 (b) 518 (c) 445 (d) 715

26. 3, 9, 27, 81, 243, 729, ?
« UPSSSC Tech Assist. Agri Service 2018
(a) 1458 (b) 1823 (c) 2187 (d) 2923

27. 3, 4.5, ?, 10.125, 15.1875
(a) 6 (b) 6.45 (c) 5.75 (d) 6.75

28. 980, 392, 156.8, ?, 25.088, 10.0352
(a) 65.04 (b) 60.28 (c) 62.72 (d) 63.85
(e) None of these

29. 12, 12, 24, 72, 288, ?
(a) 1440 (b) 1326 (c) 1456 (d) 1235

30. 3, 6, 18, 72, ?
(a) 144 (b) 216 (c) 288 (d) 360

31. 51975, 9450, 2100, 600, 240, 160, ?
(a) 80 (b) 120 (c) 320 (d) 240
(e) None of these

32. 360, 180, 90, 45, 22.5, ?
(a) 15 (b) 11.25 (c) 20 (d) 10.5

33. 1800, ?, 60, 15, 5, 2.5 « SBI Clerk 2019
(a) 300 (b) 600 (c) 120 (d) 240
(e) 360

34. ?, 100, 150, 375, 1312.5 « SBI Clerk 2019
(a) 50 (b) 100 (c) 75 (d) 25
(e) 200

35. 5, 11, 17, 25, 33, 43, ? « RRB JE CBT 2019
(a) 49 (b) 51 (c) 52 (d) 53

36. 24, 60, 120, 210, ?
(a) 300 (b) 336 (c) 420 (d) 525

37. 7, 17, 41, 85, ?, 257 « SSC CPO 2019
(a) 155 (b) 105 (c) 165 (d) 150

38. 11, ?, 16, 21, 29, 41 « SBI Clerk 2019
(a) 12 (b) 14 (c) 15 (d) 13 (e) 11

39. 0, 4, 18, 48, ?, 180
(a) 58 (b) 68 (c) 84 (d) 100

40. 27, 32, 30, 35, 33, ?
(a) 28 (b) 31 (c) 36 (d) 38

41. 17, 14, 15, 12, 13, ?, ?
(a) 10, 11 (b) 14, 11 (c) 11,13 (d) 12, 15

42. 97, 86, 99, 88, 101, ?, ?
(a) 88, 99 (b) 90, 103 (c) 121, 108 (d) 114, 103

43. 165, 195, 255, 285, 345, ? « CGPSC 2017
(a) 453 (b) 455 (c) 535 (d) 375
(e) None of these

44. 2, 20, 74, 110, ? « UPSSSC Junior Assistant 2020
(a) 152 (b) 182 (c) 190 (d) 210

45. What comes next in the sequence 1, 3, 7, 15, 31, 63, ...? « WBCS 2020
(a) 127 (b) 125 (c) 121 (d) 129

46. 4, 3, 4, 9, 32, ? « SBI Clerk 2019
(a) 75 (b) 155 (c) 125 (d) 175
(e) 165

47. 17, 36, 74, 150, ?, 606,
(a) 250 (b) 303 (c) 300 (d) 302

48. 7, 12, 22, 42, 82,?
(a) 143 (b) 173 (c) 162 (d) 183

49. 4, 9, 19, 39, 79, ?
(a) 159 (b) 119 (c) 139 (d) 169

50. 2, 5, 17, 71, ? « RRB JE 2019
(a) 131 (b) 247 (c) 359 (d) 419

51. 45, 46, 70, 141, ?, 1061.5
(a) 353 (b) 353.5 (c) 352.5 (d) 352
(e) None of these

52. 6, 13, 38, ?, 532, 2675
(a) 129 (b) 123 (c) 172 (d) 164
(e) None of these

53. 5, 16, 51, 158, ?
(a) 1452 (b) 483 (c) 481 (d) 1454

54. 77, 59, 55, 35, 25, ?
(a) 24 (b) 28 (c) 20 (d) 27

55. 99, 82, 18, 11, ?
(a) 5 (b) 10 (c) 2 (d) 9

56. 113, 225, 449, ?, 1793
(a) 897 (b) 789 (c) 987 (d) 978

57. 5, 9, 21, 37, 81, ?
(a) 163 (b) 153 (c) 181 (d) 203

58. 10, 9, 16, 45, 176, ?
(a) 815 (b) 222 (c) 555 (d) 875

59. 5, 16, 51, 158, ?
(a) 1452 (b) 483 (c) 481 (d) 1454

60. 104, 108, 54, 58, 29, ?
(a) 31 (b) 29 (c) 38 (d) 33

61. 1, 4, 9, 16, 25, ?
(a) 49 (b) 60 (c) 30 (d) 36

62. 16, 20, 29, 45, 70, ? « SSC MTS 2019
(a) 106 (b) 116 (c) 96 (d) 126

63. 4, ?, 144, 400, 900, 1764
(a) 25 (b) 36 (c) 49 (d) 100

64. 2, 10, 84, ? « SSC Constable 2018
(a) 1028 (b) 1229 (c) 1124 (d) 1032

65. 11, 29, 55, ?, 131
(a) 110 (b) 810 (c) 89 (d) 78

66. 198, 194, 185, 169, ?
(a) 92 (b) 136 (c) 144 (d) 112

67. 101, 100, ? , 87, 71, 46
(a) 92 (b) 88 (c) 89 (d) 96

68. 0, 3, 8, 15, 24, ?, 48
(a) 41 (b) 29 (c) 37 (d) 35

69. 0, 4, 18, 48, ?, 180
(a) 58 (b) 68 (c) 84 (d) 100

70. 0, 6, 24, 60, 120, 210, ?
(a) 290 (b) 240 (c) 336 (d) 504

71. 0, 6, 24, 60, ?, 210 « SBI Clerk 2019
(a) 130 (b) 170 (c) 90 (d) 120 (e) 150

72. 1, 8, 4, 27, 9, ? « IB ACIO 2017
(a) 8 (b) 9 (c) 64 (d) 16

73. 8, 3, 11, 14, 25, ?
(a) 50 (b) 39 (c) 29 (d) 11 (e) 48

74. 3, 15, 35, 63, ?, 143
(a) 120 (b) 110 (c) 99 (d) 91

75. 4, 10, 40, 190, 940, ?, 23440
(a) 4690 (b) 2930 (c) 5140 (d) 3680
(e) None of these

76. 1, 4, 4, 16, 64, ? « SSC CPO 2018
(a) 216 (b) 1024 (c) 128 (d) 1026

77. 5, 10, 8, 12, 11, 14, ?, 16
(a) 17 (b) 13 (c) 20 (d) 14

78. 40, 37, 43, 34, 46, ? « SSC CGL 2019
(a) 41 (b) 51 (c) 61 (d) 31

79. 3, 128, 6, 64, 9, ?, 12, 16, 15, 8
(a) 32 (b) 12 (c) 108 (d) 72

80. 100, 50, 52, 26, 28, ?, 16, 8
(a) 30 (b) 36 (c) 14 (c) 32

81. 6, 7, 20, ?, 34, 19 « UP Police SI 2017
(a) 17 (b) 23 (c) 13 (d) 27

82. 125, 13, 150, 39, 175, 117, 200, ? « RRB JE 2019
(a) 131 (b) 351 (c) 359 (d) 419

83. 22, 33, 66, 88, ? « UPSSSC Junior Assistant 2020
(a) 84 (b) 97 (c) 115 (d) 165

84. 7, 9, 13, 21, 37, ? « UPSSSC Junior Assistant 2020
(a) 58 (b) 63 (c) 69 (d) 72

85. The next term in the sequence « BPSC 2019
1, 3, 9, 15, 25, 35, 49 will be
(a) 80 (b) 64 (c) 81 (d) 63
(e) None of the above/More than one of the above

86. What is X in the sequence 4, 196, 16, 144, 36, 100, 64, X? « UPSC CSAT 2019
(a) 48 (b) 64
(c) 125 (d) 256

87. 132, 129, 124, 117, 106, 93, X? « UPSC CSAT 2019
(a) 74 (b) 75
(c) 76 (d) 77

88. 3947, 4379, 7493, 9734, ?
« UPSSSC Combined Subordinate 2019
(a) 9437 (b) 7934
(c) 4793 (d) 3947

89. The below two series are based on mathematical operations. Which number comes in place of (D) in second series?

8 16 18 36 38
7 (A) (B) (C) (D)

(a) 34 (b) 64 (c) 32 (d) 40

90. The below two series are based on mathematical operations. Which number comes in place of (C) in second series?

3 8 18 38 78
5 (A) (B) (C) (D)

(a) 54 (b) 56 (c) 58 (d) 60

Answers WITH EXPLANATIONS

1. (*a*) The pattern is as follows

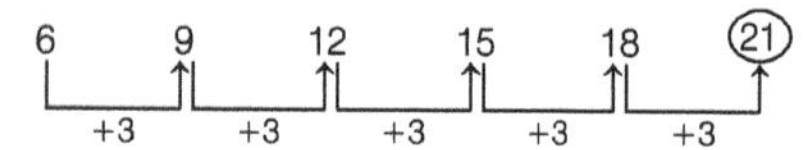

∴ ? = 21

2. (*a*) The pattern is as follows

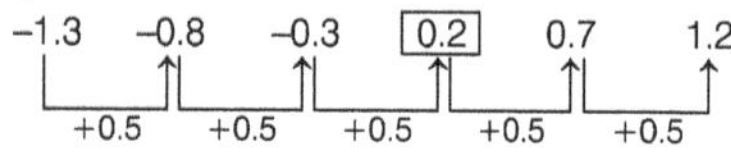

∴ ? = 0.2

3. (*b*) The pattern is as follows

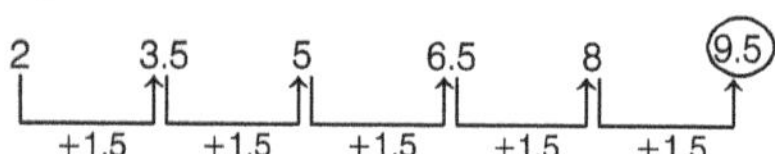

∴ ? = 9.5

4. (*d*) The pattern is as follows

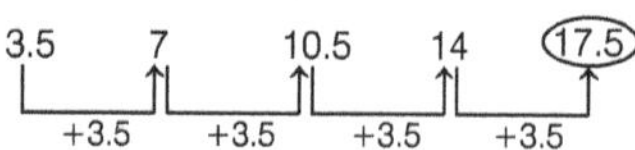

∴ ? = 17.5

5. (*b*) The pattern is as follows

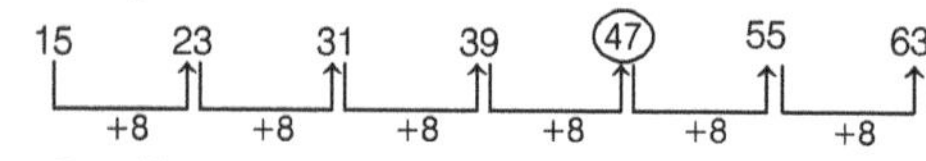

∴ ? = 47

6. (*b*) The pattern is as follows

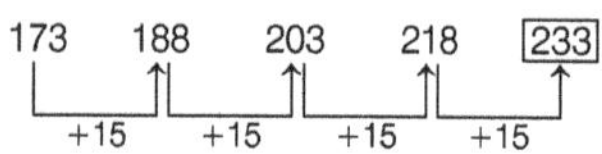

∴ ? = 233

7. (*d*) The pattern is as follows

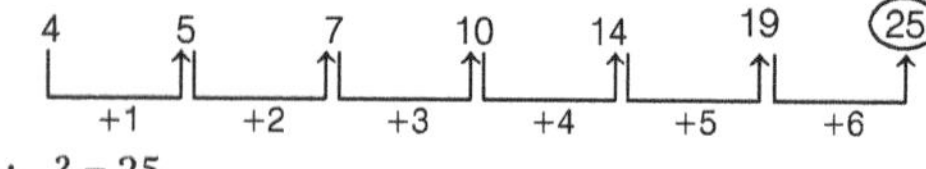

∴ ? = 25

8. (*d*) The pattern is as follows

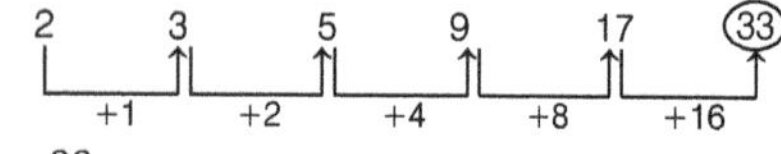

∴ ? = 33

9. (*b*) The pattern is as follows

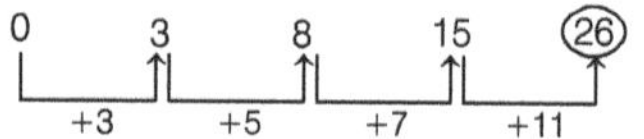

Addition of prime numbers.

∴ ? = 26

10. (*a*) The pattern is as follows

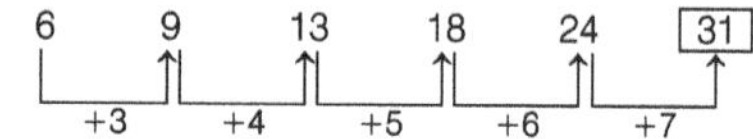

∴ ? = 31

11. (*d*) The pattern is as follows

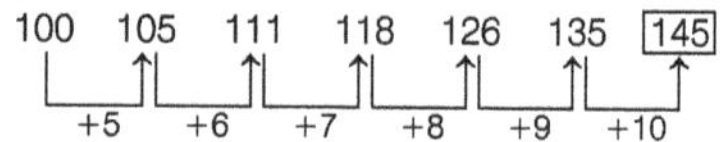

∴ ? = 145

12. (*c*) The pattern is as follows

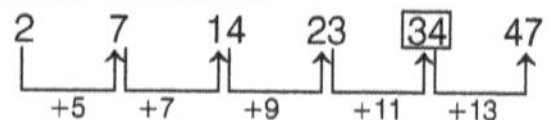

∴ ? = 34

13. (*d*) The pattern is as follows

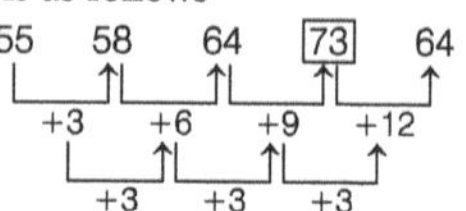

∴ ? = 73

14. (*b*) The pattern is as follows

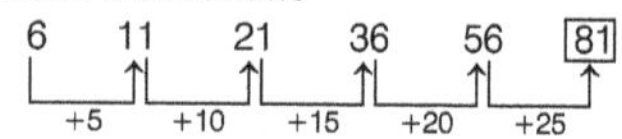

∴ ? = 81

15. (*c*) The pattern is as follows

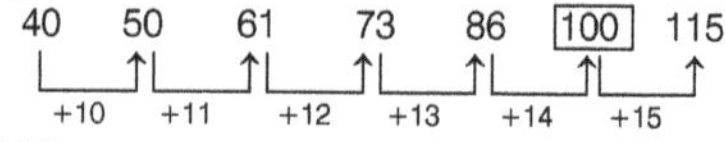

∴ ? = 100

16. (*b*) The pattern is as follows

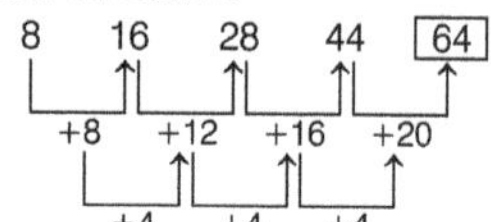

∴ ? = 64

17. (*d*) The pattern is as follows

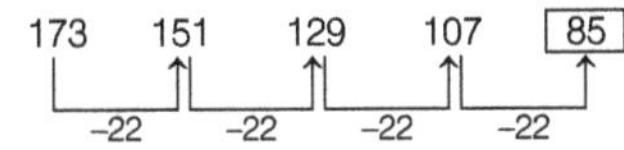

∴ ? = 85

18. (*c*) The pattern is as follows

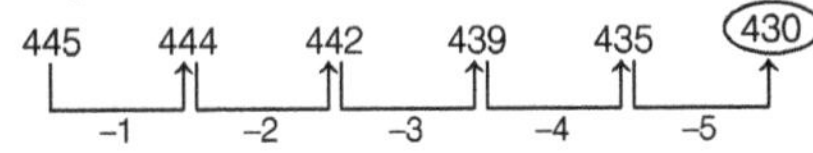

∴ ? = 430

19. (*d*) The pattern is as follows

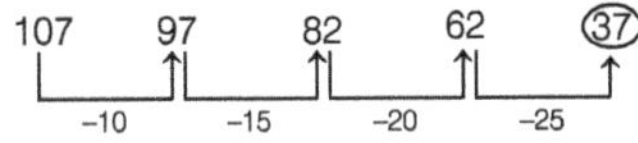

∴ ? = 37

20. (*a*) The pattern is as follows

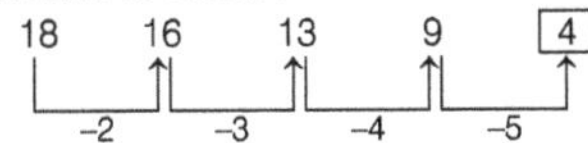

∴ ? = 4

21. (*c*) The pattern is as follows

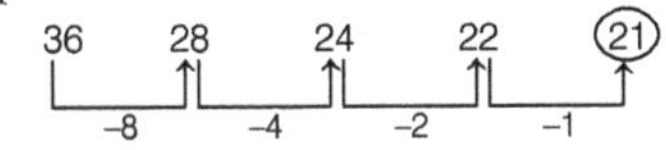

∴ ? = 21

22. (*c*) This pattern is as follows

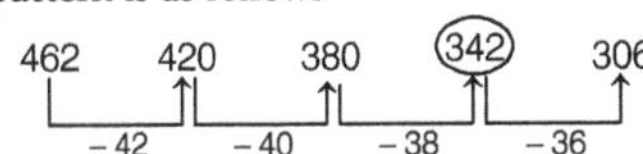

∴ ? = 342

23. (*b*) The pattern is as follows

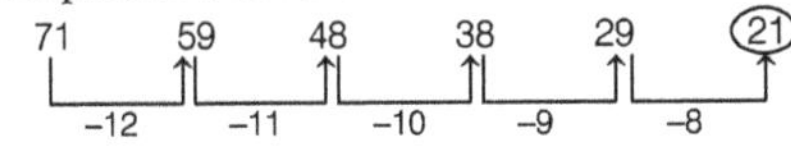

∴ ? = 21

24. (*d*) The pattern is as follows

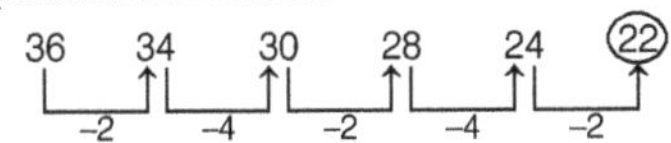

∴ ? = 22

25. (*a*) The pattern is as follows

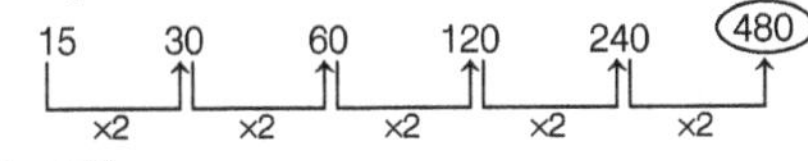

∴ ? = 480

26. (*c*) The pattern is as follows

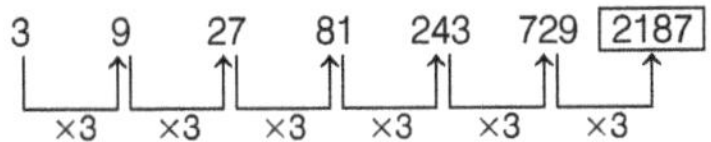

∴ ? = 2187

27. (*d*) The pattern is as follows

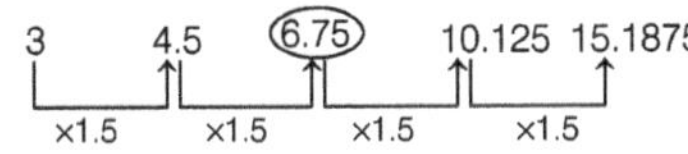

∴ ? = 6.75

28. (*c*) The pattern is as follows

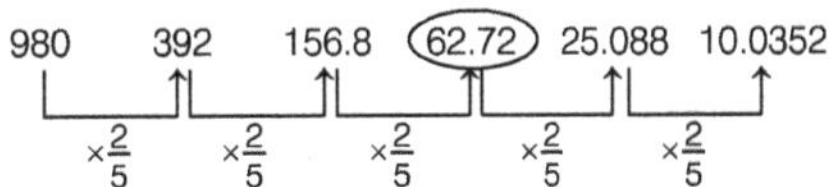

∴ ? = 62.72

29. (*a*) The pattern is as follows

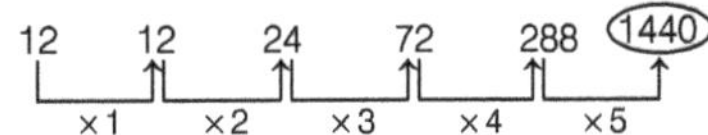

∴ ? = 1440

30. (*d*) The pattern is as follows

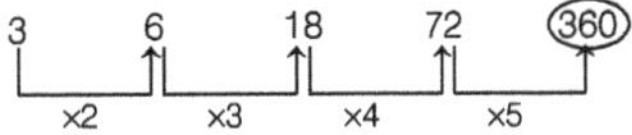

∴ ? = 360

31. (*c*) The pattern is as follows

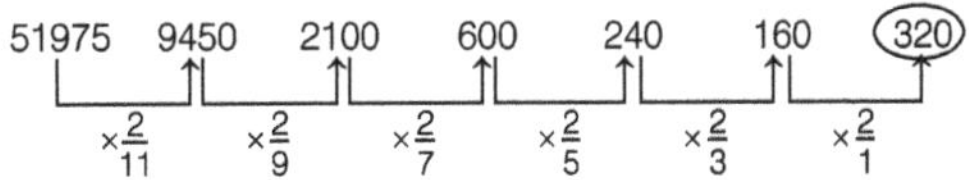

∴ ? = 320

32. (*b*) The pattern is as follows

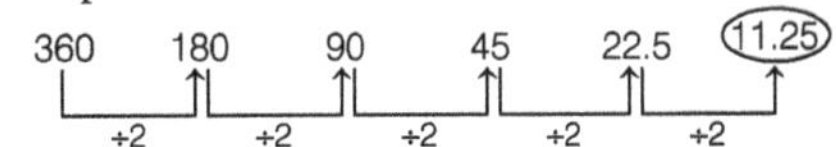

∴ ? = 11.25

33. (*a*) The pattern is as follows

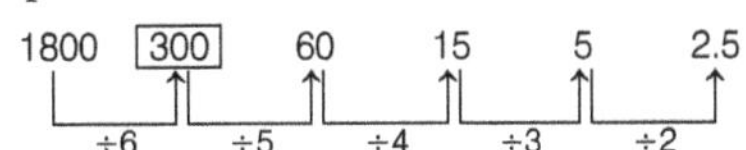

∴ ? = 300

34. (*e*) The pattern is as follows

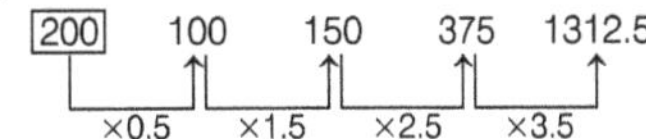

∴ ? = 200

35. (*d*) The pattern is as follows

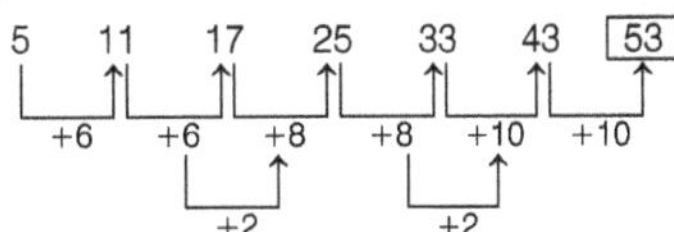

∴ ? = 53

36. (*b*) The pattern is as follows

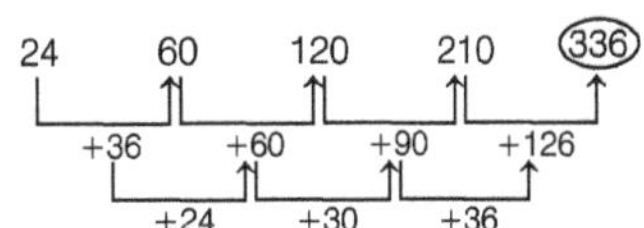

∴ ? = 336

37. (*a*) The pattern is as follows

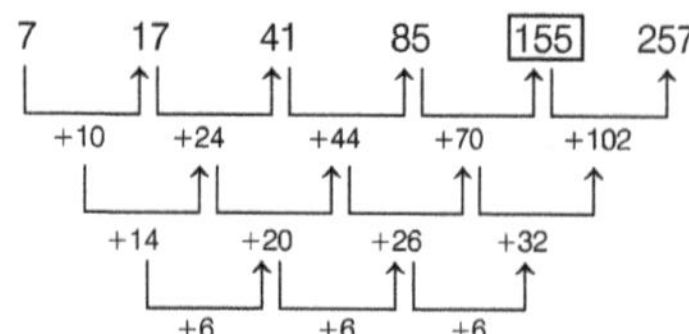

∴ ? = 155

38. (*d*) The pattern is as follows

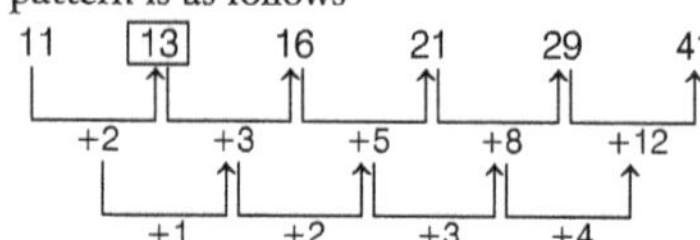

∴ ? = 13

39. (*d*) The pattern is as follows

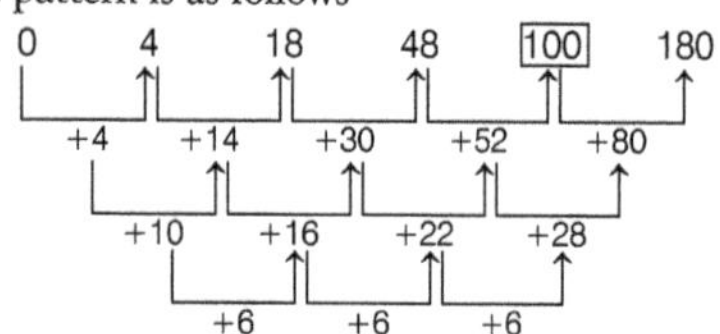

∴ ? = 100

40. (*d*) The pattern is as follows

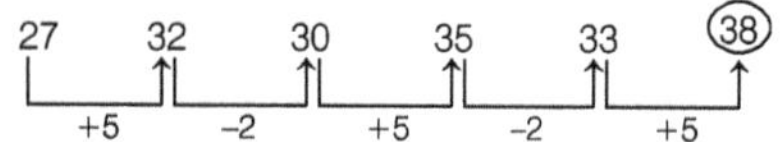

∴ ? = 38

41. (*a*) The pattern is as follows

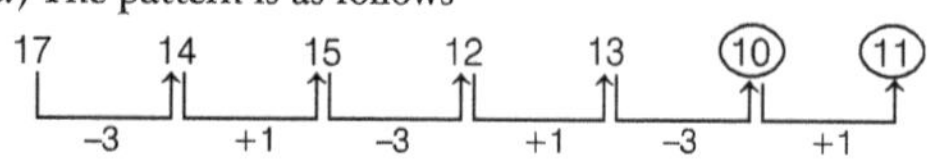

First (?) = 10 and second (?) = 11

∴ Required answer = 10, 11

42. (*b*) The pattern is as follows

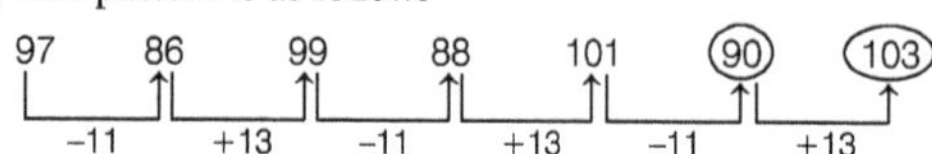

∴ First (?) = 90 and second (?) = 103

∴ Required answer = 90, 103

43. (*d*) The pattern is as follows

∴ ? = 375

44. (*b*) As, 2 = 2

20 ⇒ 2 + 0 = 2

74 ⇒ 7 + 4 = 11 = 1 + 1 = 2

110 ⇒ 1 + 1 + 0 = 2

Therefore, 182 ⇒ 1 + 8 + 2 = 11 ⇒ 1 + 1 = 2

In this pattern, ultimately we get 2 after addition.

45. (*a*) The pattern is as follows

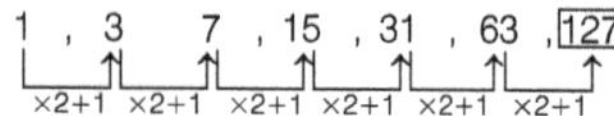

∴ ? = 127

46. (*b*) The pattern is as follows

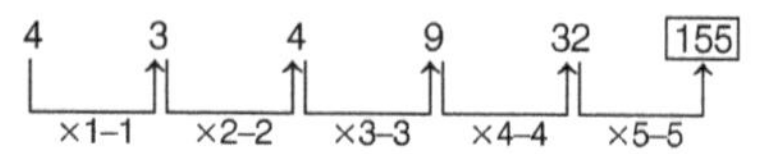

∴ ? = 155

47. (*d*) The pattern is as follows

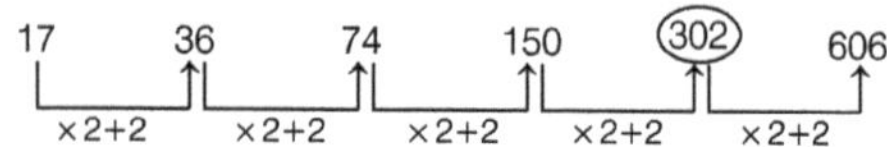

∴ ? = 302

48. (*c*) The pattern is as follows

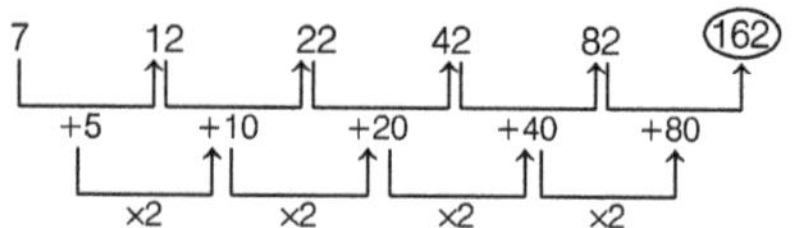

∴ ? = 162

49. (*a*) The pattern is as follows

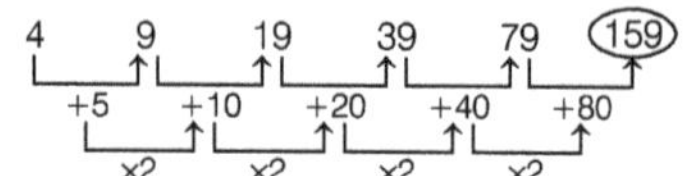

∴ ? = 159

50. (*c*) The pattern is as follows

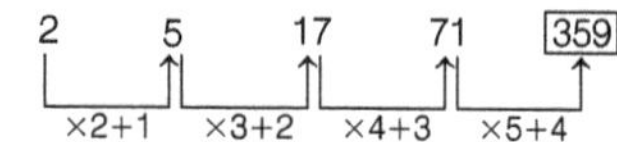

∴ ? = 359

51. (*b*) The pattern is as follows

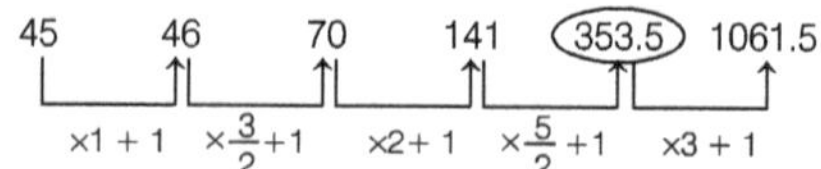

∴ ? = 353.5

52. (*a*) The pattern is as follows

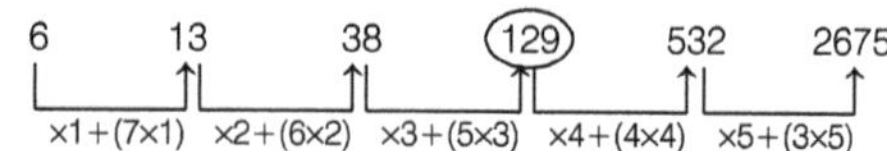

∴ ? = 129

53. (*c*) The pattern is as follows

$5 \times 3 + 1 = 16$

$16 \times 3 + 3 = 51$

$51 \times 3 + 5 = 158$

$158 \times 3 + 7 = 481$

∴ ? = 481

54. (*c*) Digits of each element are multiplied and then 10 is added to this multiplication to obtain the next element.

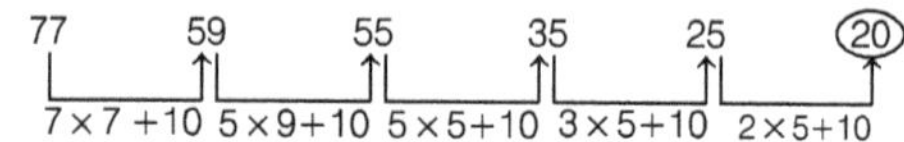

∴ ? = 20

55. (*a*) Digits of each term are multiplied and then 1, 2, 3 and 4 are added, respectively to obtain the next elements.

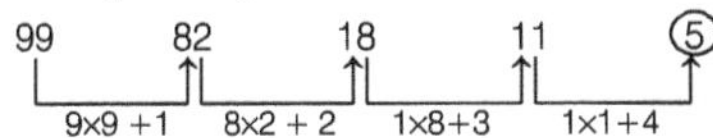

$\therefore \; ? = 1 \times 1 + 4 = 1 + 4 = 5$

56. (*a*) The pattern is as follows

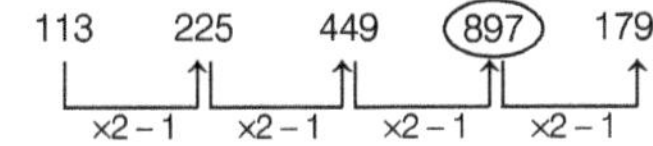

$\therefore \; ? = 897$

57. (*b*) The pattern is as follows

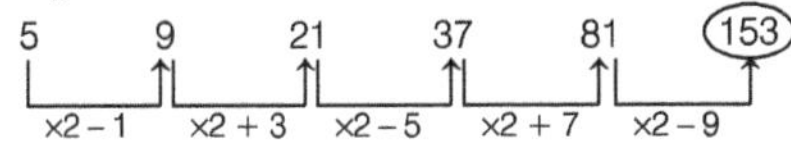

$\therefore \; ? = 153$

58. (*d*) The pattern is as follows

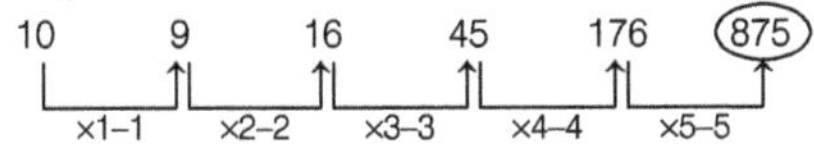

$\therefore \; ? = 176 \times 5 - 5 = 875$

59. (*c*) The pattern is as follows

$$5 \times 3 + 1 = 16$$
$$16 \times 3 + 3 = 51$$
$$51 \times 3 + 5 = 158$$
$$158 \times 3 + 7 = \boxed{481}$$

So, next term will be 481 in the series.

60. (*d*) The pattern is as follows

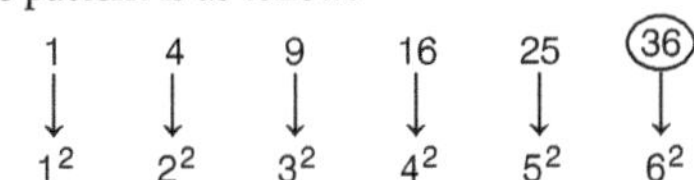

$\therefore \; ? = 33$

61. (*d*) The pattern is as follows

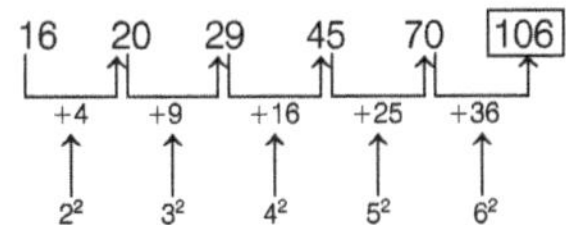

$\therefore \; ? = 36$

62. (*a*) The pattern is as follows

$\therefore \; ? = 106$

63. (*b*) The pattern is as follows

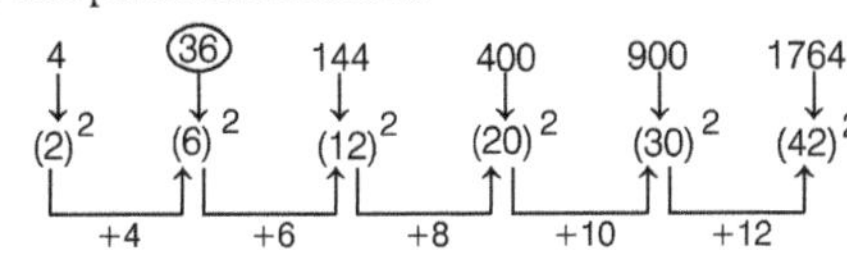

$\therefore \; ? = 36$

64. (*a*) The pattern is as follows

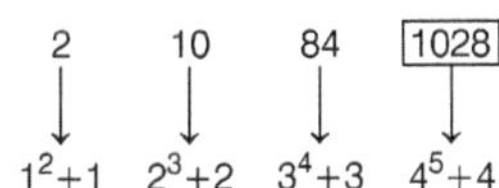

$\therefore \; ? = 1028$

65. (*c*) The pattern is as follows

$$3^2 + 2 = 11, \; 5^2 + 4 = 29,$$
$$7^2 + 6 = 55, \; 9^2 + 8 = \textcircled{89},$$
$$11^2 + 10 = 131$$

$\therefore \; ? = 89$

66. (*c*) The pattern is as follows

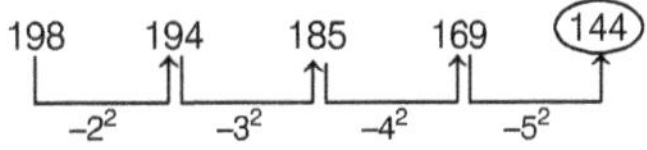

$\therefore \; ? = 144$

67. (*d*) The pattern is as follows

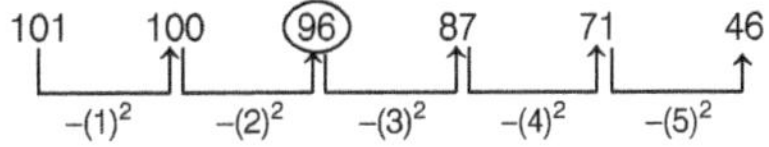

$\therefore$ Missing number $= 100 - (2)^2 = 100 - 4 = 96$

68. (*d*) The pattern is as follows

$$1^2 - 1 = 0, \; 2^2 - 1 = 3$$
$$3^2 - 1 = 8, \; 4^2 - 1 = 15$$
$$5^2 - 1 = 24, 6^2 - 1 = \textcircled{35},$$
$$7^2 - 1 = 48$$

$\therefore \; ? = 35$

69. (*d*) The pattern is as follows

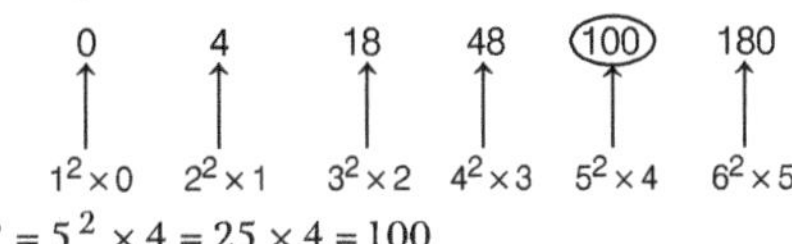

$\therefore \; ? = 5^2 \times 4 = 25 \times 4 = 100$

70. (*c*) The pattern is as follows

$$1^3 - 1 = 0, \quad 2^3 - 2 = 6,$$
$$3^3 - 3 = 24, \quad 4^3 - 4 = 60,$$
$$5^3 - 5 = 120, \; 6^3 - 6 = 210,$$
$$7^3 - 7 = \textcircled{336}$$

$\therefore \; ? = 336$

71. (*d*) The pattern is as follows

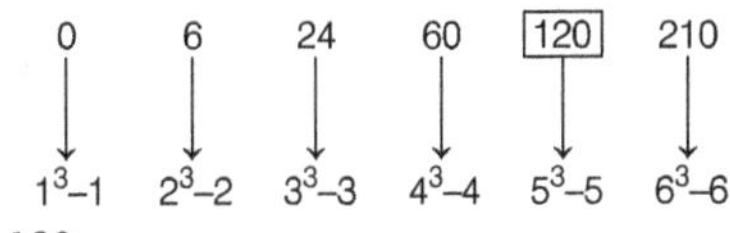

$\therefore \; ? = 120$

72. (*c*) The pattern is as follows

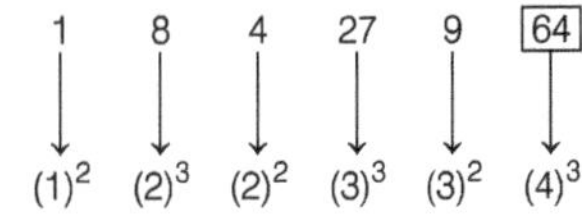

$\therefore \; ? = 64$

73. (*b*) Every third element is the sum of previous two elements.

$$8 + 3 = 11$$
$$3 + 11 = 14$$
$$11 + 14 = 25$$
$$14 + 25 = \textcircled{39}$$

$\therefore \; ? = 39$

74. (*c*) The pattern is as follows

$3 = 1 \times 3 \Rightarrow 15 = 3 \times 5$

$35 = 5 \times 7 \Rightarrow 63 = 7 \times 9$

$\boxed{99 = 9 \times 11} \Rightarrow 143 = 11 \times 13$

$\therefore \quad ? = 99$

75. (*a*) The pattern is as follows

$4 + 6 = 10$

$10 + (6 \times 5) = 40$

$40 + (30 \times 5) = 190$

$190 + (150 \times 5) = 940$

$940 + (750 \times 5) = 4690$

$4690 + (3750 \times 5) = 23440$

$\therefore \quad ? = 4690$

76. (*b*) The pattern is as follows

$1 \times 4 = 4$

$4 \times 4 = 16$

$4 \times 16 = 64$

$16 \times 64 = \boxed{1024}$

$\therefore \quad ? = 1024$

77. (*d*) There are two alternate series

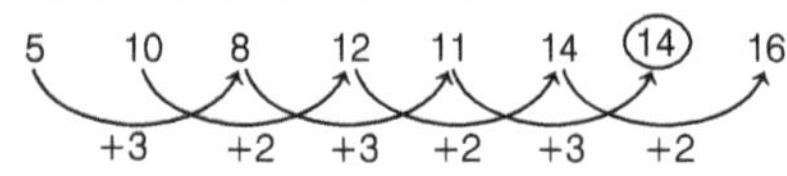

$\therefore \quad ? = 14$

78. (*d*) There are two interwoven series here

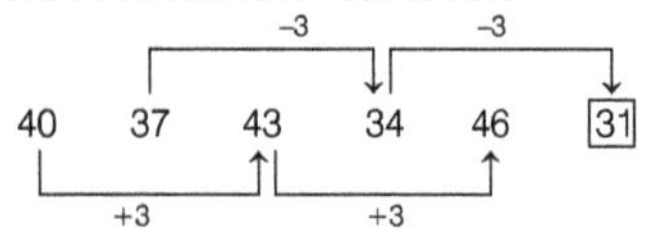

$\therefore \quad ? = 31$

79. (*a*) The pattern is as follows

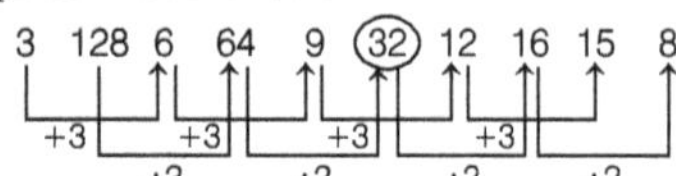

$\therefore \quad ? = 32$

80. (*c*) The pattern is as follows

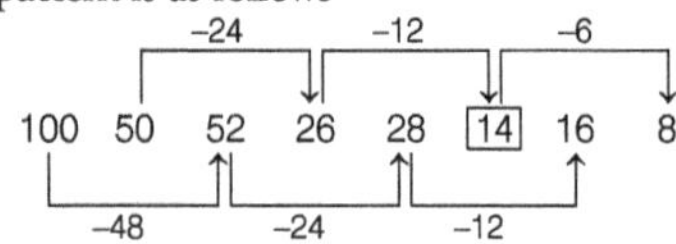

$\therefore \quad ? = 14$

81. (*c*) The pattern is as follows

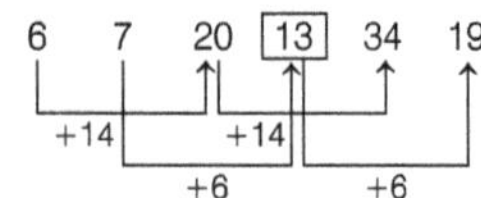

$\therefore ? = 13$

82. (*b*) The pattern is as follows

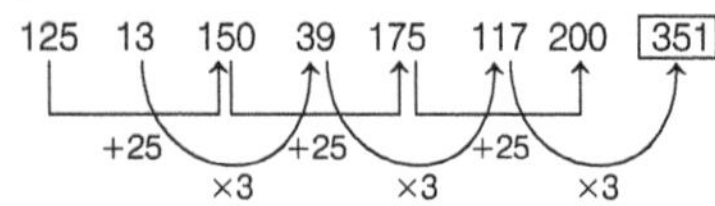

$\therefore ? = 351$

83. (*d*) The pattern is as follows

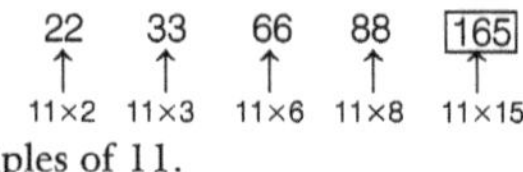

All are multiples of 11.

$\therefore \quad ? = 165$

84. (*c*) The pattern is as follows

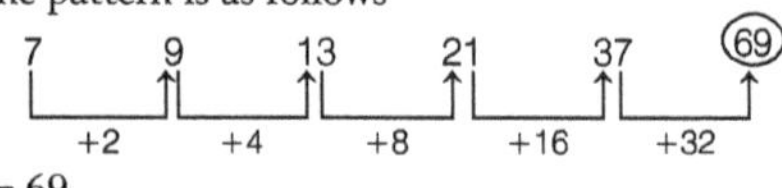

$\therefore \; ? = 69$

85. (*d*) The pattern is as follows

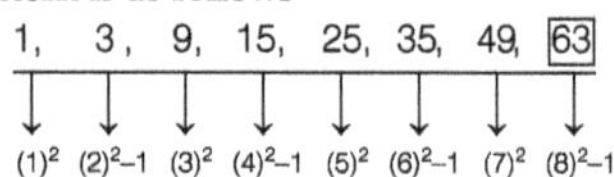

So, the correct option is (d).

86. (*b*) The pattern is as follows

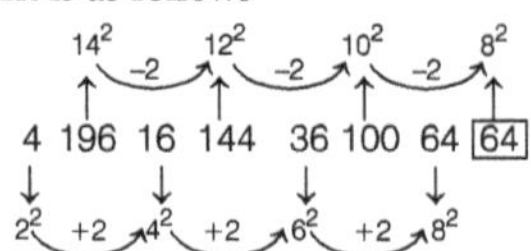

So, X = 64

87. (*c*) The pattern is as follows

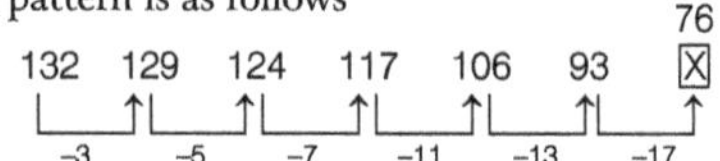

Here, consecutive prime numbers are subtracted.

$\therefore \quad X = 76$

88. (*d*) 3947, 4379, 7493, 9734

In the above series, in each successive number, the second last digit of the previous number comes at the first place, the first digit shifts to the second place and rest two digits shifts to the last after interchanging their positions.

e.g. Step I 3947 ⇒ 4397

Step II 4397 ⇒ 4379

Following this pattern, the last number will be

Step I 9734 ⇒ 3974

Step II 3974 ⇒ $\boxed{3947}$

89. (*a*) The pattern is as follows

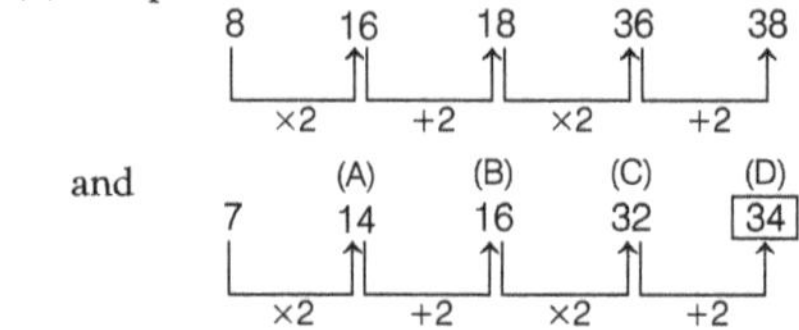

$\therefore$ Required number = 32 + 2 = 34

90. (*a*) The pattern is as follows

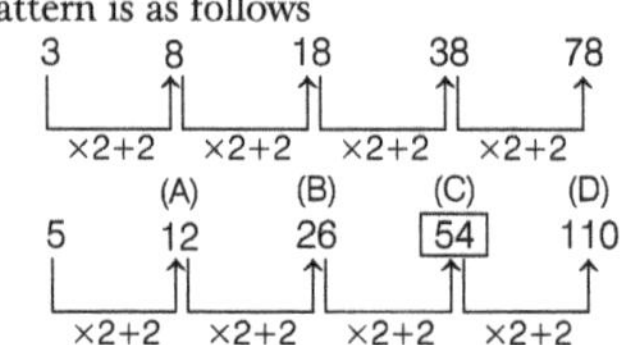

$\therefore$ Required number = $26 \times 2 + 2 = 52 + 2 = 54$

TYPE 02

Letter Series

Letter series is a sequence of letters or group of letters taken from English alphabet and such sequence follows a certain logical pattern. In letter series, certain logical pattern means that every next element of the series is obtained according to a certain change.

In this series, candidates are required to find out the next letter or group of letters in the series or the missing letter in the series.

To solve problems of this kind, candidates are required to find the rules followed in the series and determine the pattern of the series.

1. Addition Series

In such series, every next term is obtained by adding certain digit/number (either same or different) to the corresponding position of previous letter given in a particular series.

***Ex* 33** Find the letter in place of question mark (?) in the series given below. « RRB Group D 2018

A, D, G, J, M , ?

(a) R (b) B
(c) W (d) P

***Solution* (d)** The pattern of the series is as follows

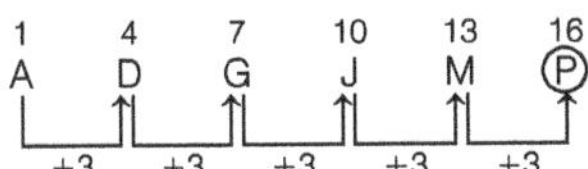

∴ Required letter = P

***Ex* 34** What comes in place of question mark (?) in the series given below?

B, C, E, H, L, ?

(a) M (b) N (c) P (d) Q

***Solution* (d)** The pattern of the series is as follows

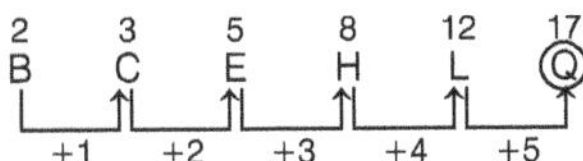

∴ Required letter = Q

***Ex* 35** What comes in place of question mark (?) in the series given below? « SSC CHSL 2018

FT, JX, NB, RF, ?

(a) TX (b) LJ
(c) VJ (d) YJ

***Solution* (c)** The pattern of the series is as follows

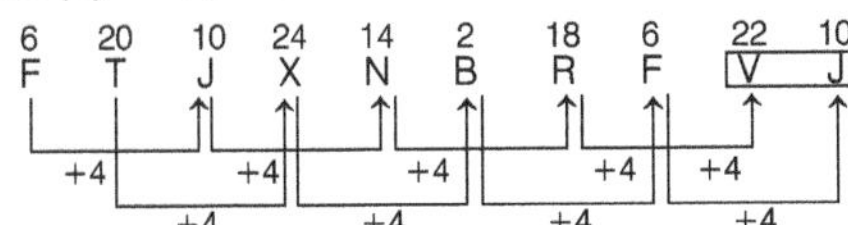

∴ Required letters = V, J

2. Subtraction Series

In such series, every next term is obtained by subtracting certain digit/number (either same or different) from its previous term (letter).

***Ex* 36** Which letter will replace the question mark in the following series. « SSC CPO 2018

Z, X, V, T, R, ?

(a) S (b) O (c) P (d) Q

***Solution* (c)** The pattern of the series is as follows

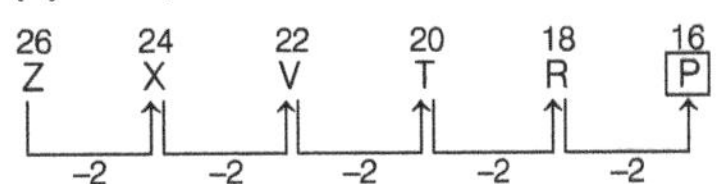

∴ Required letter = P

***Ex* 37** What comes in place of question mark (?) in the following series?

P, O, M, J, F, ?

(a) X (b) A
(c) Y (d) Cannot be determined

***Solution* (b)** The pattern of the series is as follows

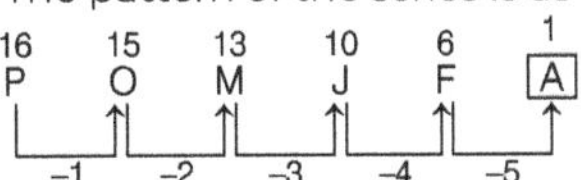

∴ Required letter = A

***Ex* 38** Which letter will replace the question mark in the following series? « SSC CHSL 2018

KHQ, HEN, EBK, ?, YVE

(a) ZWF (b) AXG
(c) CZI (d) BYH

***Solution* (d)** The patterns of the series is as follows

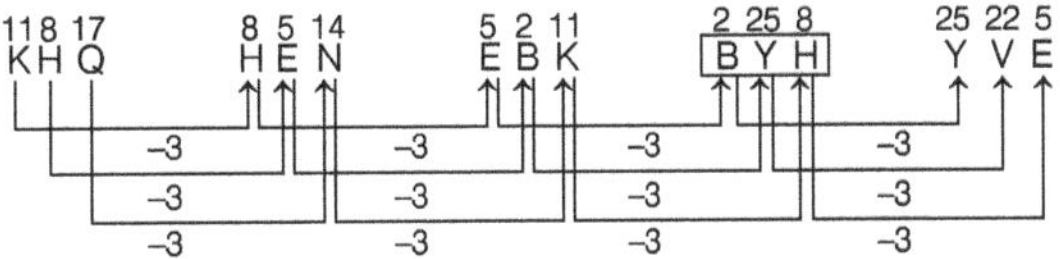

∴ Required letters = BYH

3. Addition-Subtraction Series

In such series, addition and subtraction (or subtraction-addition) take place alternatively to obtain the terms of the series.

***Ex* 39** What comes in place of question mark (?) in the following series?

A, E, C, G, E, I, ?

(a) H (b) E
(c) G (d) J

***Solution* (c)** The pattern of the series is as follows

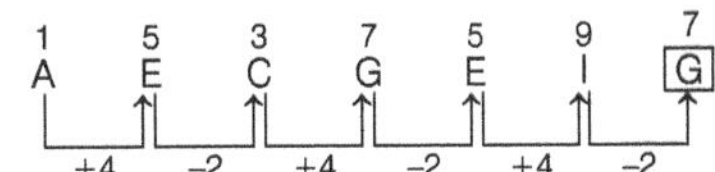

∴ Required letter = G

Ex 40 In the below series, identify what can come in place of '?' « UPSSSC VDO 2018

BX, DU, FR, HO, JL, LI, ?

(a) MF (b) NE
(c) NF (d) ME

***Solution* (c)** The pattern of the series is as follows

B(2) —+2→ D(4) —+2→ F(6) —+2→ H(8) —+2→ J(10) —+2→ L(12) —+2→ [N](14)
X(24) —−3→ U(21) —−3→ R(18) —−3→ O(15) —−3→ L(12) —−3→ I(9) —−3→ [F](6)

∴ Required letters = NF

4. Mixed/Combination Series

Such series have two or more interwoven series. In another words, we can say that a single series is formed with the combination of more than one series.

Ex 41 Replace the question mark (?) in the series given below.

B, B, A, D, Z, F, Y, H, X, ?

(a) J (b) N (c) M (d) O

***Solution* (a)** This series has two parts. In first part, every next term is obtained by subtracting 1 from the corresponding position of its previous letter. While in second part, every next term is obtained by adding 2 to the corresponding position of its previous term (letter).

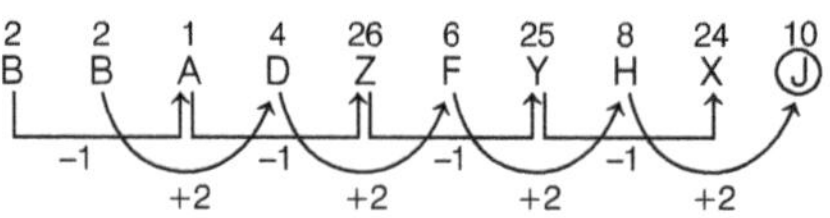

∴ Required letter = J

Ex 42 Replace the question mark (?) in the series given below.

NL, MM, LN, KO, ?

(a) JO (b) PJ (c) JP (d) KO

***Solution* (c)** The pattern of the series is as follows

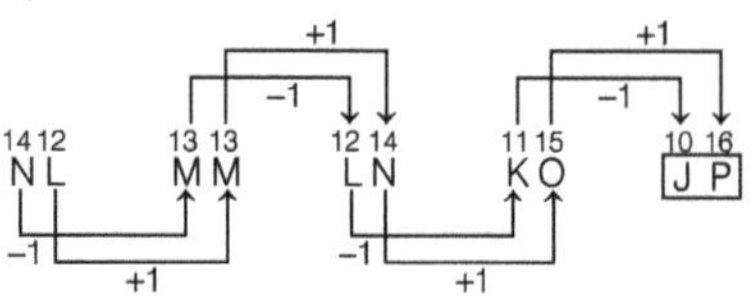

∴ Required letters = JP

5. Reverse Order Repetition Series

In such series, first part is written in reverse order in the second part of the series and this process may be repeated further.

Ex 43 What comes in place of question mark (?) in the series given below?

A, B, D, G, K, N, P, ?

(a) Q (b) R (c) S (d) T

***Solution* (a)** The pattern of the series is as follows

A(1) —+1→ B(2) —+2→ D(4) —+3→ G(7) —+4→ K(11) —+3→ N(14) —+2→ P(16) —+1→ [Q](17)

∴ Required letter = Q

6. Series Having Same Group of Letters as its Elements

In such series, each element consists of group of same letters instead of a single letter that follows certain pattern.

Ex 44 What comes in place of question mark (?) in the series given below?

LDP, DPL, PLD,?

(a) LPD (b) PDL (c) DLP (d) LDP

***Solution* (d)** In every next term, the last letter is the first letter of its previous term, middle letter is the last letter of its previous term and first letter is the middle letter of its previous term.

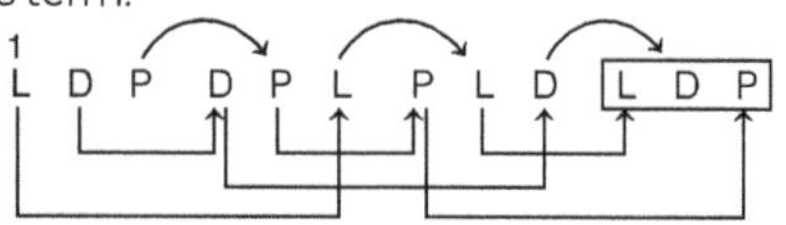

∴ Required letter= LDP

7. Frequency Series

In such series, frequency of occurrence of a letter increases/decreases in every next element.

Ex 45 Replace the question mark (?) in the following series.

ABCABABAB, ABABCABAB, ABABABCAB, ABABABABC, ACBABABAB, ? « SSC CHSL 2018

(a) ABABCABAB (b) ABCABABAB
(c) ABACBABAB (d) ABABACBAB

***Solution* (c)** The pattern of the series is as follows,
ABCABABAB, ABABCABAB, ABABABCAB,
ABABABABC, ACBABABAB, [ABACBABAB]

∴ Required term = ABACBABAB

Ex 46 What comes in place of question mark (?) in the series given below?

MNO, MMNO, MMNNO, MMNNOO, ?

(a) MMNNOOP (b) MMNNOODD
(c) MMMNNOO (d) MMMNNNOOO

***Solution* (c)** According to the following pattern
From 1st to 2nd element, one M is added → MMNO
From 2nd to 3rd element, one N is added → MMNNO
From 3rd to 4th element, one O is added → MMNNOO
From 4th to 5th element, one M is added → MMMNNOO
∴ Required element = MMMNNOO

8. Small-Capital letter Series

In such series, the sequence consists of small and capital letters in various patterns.

Ex 47 Replace the question mark (?) in the given series

mm, OO, qq, SS, ?

(a) Sq (b) Rs (c) St (d) uu

***Solution* (d)** The pattern of the series is as follows

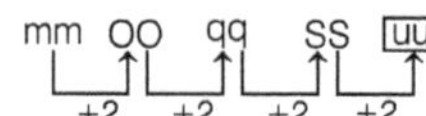

Here, the letters occur in pairs and are written small and capital in alternate manner and in every next term, the letters move two positions forward from the previous term.

***Ex* 48** Select the letter that can replace the question mark (?) in the following series « SSC CPO 2019

K, J, L, I, ?, H

(a) D (b) N
(c) L (d) M

Solution (d) The pattern of the series is as follows

11	10	12	9	13	8
K	J	L	I	[M]	H

Differences: −1, +2, −3, +4, −5

∴ ? = M

***Ex* 49** Select the letter-cluster that can replace the question mark in the following series « UPSSSC Junior Assistant 2020

K P A, L Q B, M R C, N S D, ?

(a) OTE (b) PER
(c) LTQ (d) MOL

Solution (a) The pattern of the series is as follows

$\overset{11}{K} \xrightarrow{+1} \overset{12}{L} \xrightarrow{+1} \overset{13}{M} \xrightarrow{+1} \overset{14}{N} \xrightarrow{+1} \overset{15}{O}$

$\overset{16}{P} \xrightarrow{+1} \overset{17}{Q} \xrightarrow{+1} \overset{18}{R} \xrightarrow{+1} \overset{19}{S} \xrightarrow{+1} \overset{20}{T}$

$\overset{1}{A} \xrightarrow{+1} \overset{2}{B} \xrightarrow{+1} \overset{3}{C} \xrightarrow{+1} \overset{4}{D} \xrightarrow{+1} \overset{5}{E}$

∴ ? = OTE

***Ex* 50** The next term of the series « UPSC Assistant Commandant 2019

BCYX, EFVU, HISR, KLPO, ... is

(a) NOML (b) NOLM
(c) ONML (d) ONLM

Solution (a) The pattern of the series is as follows

$\overset{2}{B} \xrightarrow{+3} \overset{5}{E} \xrightarrow{+3} \overset{8}{H} \xrightarrow{+3} \overset{11}{K} \xrightarrow{+3} \overset{14}{N}$

$\overset{3}{C} \xrightarrow{+3} \overset{6}{F} \xrightarrow{+3} \overset{9}{I} \xrightarrow{+3} \overset{12}{L} \xrightarrow{+3} \overset{15}{O}$

$\overset{25}{Y} \xrightarrow{-3} \overset{22}{V} \xrightarrow{-3} \overset{19}{S} \xrightarrow{-3} \overset{16}{P} \xrightarrow{-3} \overset{13}{M}$

$\overset{24}{X} \xrightarrow{-3} \overset{21}{U} \xrightarrow{-3} \overset{18}{R} \xrightarrow{-3} \overset{15}{O} \xrightarrow{-3} \overset{12}{L}$

9. Words Based Series

In this type of series, words series is given in which by moving from left to right letters of the words either increase or decrease in a particular order or a letter in each next word is shifted left or right.

The candidate has to find the pattern of the given series to complete the series.

***Ex* 51** Replace the question mark (?) in the following series

At, Bat , Flag, Mount, ?

(a) Lion (b) Seven (c) Linear (d) Elephant

Solution (c) In the given series by moving from left to right number of alphabets in each word is increased by one.

At	Bat	Flag	Mount	Linear
2 Letters	3 Letters	4 Letters	5 Letters	6 Letters

***Ex* 52** Replace the question mark (?) in the following series. « SSC CGL 2017

rupees, arena, pursue, spare, separate, ?

(a) rapid (b) pusher (c) person (d) super

Solution (b) In the given series, by moving from left to right, the position of r in each word is shifted by one.

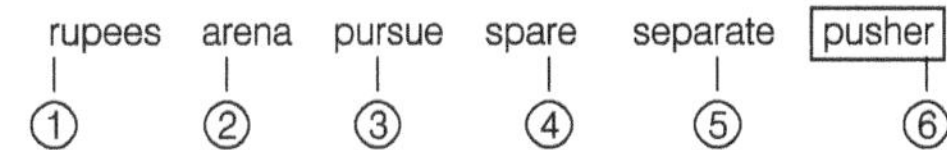

Practice / CORNER 5.2

DIRECTIONS ~ (Q. Nos. 1-51) *What comes in place of question mark(s) in the following letter series?*

1. A, C, E, G, I, ?
(a) K (b) J (c) M (d) L

2. J, M, P, ?, V, Y « SSC CGL 2020
(a) R (b) T (c) O (d) S

3. B, D, F, I, L, P, ?
(a) U (b) R (c) S (d) T
(e) None of these

4. C, E, I, K, O, Q, ?
(a) R (b) S (c) T (d) U
(e) None of these

5. AB, GH, MN, ST, ? « SSC Constable 2018
(a) YZ (b) VW (c) UV (d) XY

6. AR, CU, EX, GA, ? « SSC MTS 2019
(a) JE (b) ID (c) IF (d) KF

7. PBA, QDC, RFE, ?
(a) SHG (b) OAB (c) TJI (d) ULK

8. CIG, FLJ, IOM, ?
(a) LRP (b) JLG
(c) PSU (d) QUB

9. OTE, PUF, QVG, RWH, ?
(a) SYJ (b) TXI (c) SXJ (d) SXI

10. FTB, IQE, LNH, OKK, ? « SSC CPO 2019
(a) RHN (b) RGM (c) SHM (d) SHN

11. bdf, hjl, ?, tvx « SSC Steno 2019
(a) twy (b) suv (c) suw (d) npr

12. CBDA, GFHE, KJLI, ? « RRB NTPC 2016
(a) NOPM (b) MNOP (c) PMNO (d) ONPM

13. ACE, BDF, CEG, ?
(a) DFE (b) DEF (c) DFH (d) DEH

14. L, N, R, Z, ?
(a) E (b) J (c) P (d) O

15. P, N, L, J, ?, F, D
(a) K (b) H (c) L (d) C

16. X, V, T, R, P, ? « MP Constable 2017
(a) N (b) O (c) M (d) L

17. R, O, L, I, F, ?, Z
(a) A (b) C (c) E (d) I

18. Y, ?, ?, M, I, E
(a) Z, X (b) P, R (c) Q, T (d) U, Q

19. Y, X, V, S, O, ?
(a) J (b) M (c) E (d) F

20. Z, X, U, Q, L, ?
(a) F (b) E (c) G (d) H

21. Z, X, ?, N, F
(a) T (b) R (c) Q (d) O

22. W, U, S, P, M, I, ?
(a) E (b) A (c) H (d) F
(e) None of these

23. YW, US, ?, MK
(a) RP (b) BD (c) FH (d) QO

24. W, T, P, M, I, F, B, ?, ?
(a) Z, V (b) X, U (c) Y, U (d) Y, V

25. BRH, ZUD, ?, VAV, TDR, RGN
(a) XYZ (b) XZZ (c) XXZ (d) XZY

26. WYV, ?, IKH, BDA SSC Steno 2013
(a) OPR (b) ROP (c) PRO (d) OQN

27. aYd, fTi, kOn, pJs, ? « SSC CGL 2019
(a) uEw (b) VeX (c) uEx (d) uFw

28. BDZ, DGX, FJV, HMT, JPR, ? « SSC CPO 2018
(a) MSP (b) LSP (c) LTP (d) LSO

29. XWA, VTC, SPF, OKJ, ?
(a) JDN (b) JEO (c) LPN (d) JDP
(e) None of these

30. AZY, EXW, IVU, ?
(a) MTS (b) MQR (c) NRQ (d) LST

31. DKM, FJP, HIS, JHV, ?
(a) LGY (b) HGY (c) IGZ (d) IGY

32. FUGT, HSIR, JQKP, ?
(a) KNLO (b) LNNM
(c) LOMM (d) LOMN

33. XYZ, ABC, UVW, DEF, RST, GHI, ?
(a) UVW (b) JKL (c) OPQ (d) NOP

34. AYBZC, DWEXF, GUHVI, JSKTL, ?
(a) MQORN (b) QMONR (c) MQNRO (d) NQMOR

35. BEH, DGJ, ?, EJO, GLQ, INS « IB ACIO 2017
(a) FLR (b) FIS (c) FKO (d) FIL

36. A, P, C, Q, E, R, G, ?, ?
(a) S, I (b) H, I (c) I, S (d) T, J

37. A, Z, C, X, E, ?
(a) U (b) W (c) V (d) Y

38. POQ, SRT, VUW, ?
(a) XYZ (b) XZY (c) YZY (d) YXZ

39. H, V, G, T, F, R, E, P, ? « IB ACIO 2017
(a) K, L (b) D, N (c) C, D (d) L, K

40. ABC, PQR, DEF, STU, ?
(a) GKL (b) VWX (c) GHI (d) IJK

41. K, A, M, A, L, L, A, M, A, ?
(a) L (b) M (c) K (d) J

42. PMK, MPK, MKP, KMP, ?
(a) PMK (b) KMP (c) MPK (d) KPM

43. CD, HI, MN, ?
(a) QS (b) OP (c) PQ (d) RS

44. PRIMARILY, RIMARILY, RIMARIL, ?
(a) IMAR (b) RIMARI
(c) IMARIL (d) RIMA
(e) None of these

45. NATURAL, NATURA, ATURA, ?
(a) ATUR (b) TURA (c) RUTA (d) ARUT
(e) None of these

46. XYZ, XZY, YZX, ?, ZXY
(a) XZZ (b) YXZ (c) YZW (d) ZYX

47. bc, cde, de, efg, fg, ?
(a) hij (b) ljk (c) ghi (d) fgh

48. DD, jjj, PP, vvv, B ?
(a) BB (b) B (c) C (d) CC

49. Qx, Di, ?p
(a) M (b) m (c) l (d) L

50. S, n, ?, V, ?, H, ?, f, E, B, b, B
(a) Kay (b) KjY (c) KJY (d) KgY

51. ?, p, Lis, ?, lw, Q, o, ?, U
(a) fNb (b) BFn (c) fNc (d) Hbn

52. Select the letter cluster that will replace the question mark in the following series
ACEGI, BDFHJ, KMOQS, ?, UWYAC, VXZBD
(a) PQRTV (b) LPRTV (c) TUVWX (d) LNPRT

DIRECTIONS ~ (Q. Nos. 53-56) *A series is given. Choose the next missing term from the given alternatives.*

53. A B C D E F Z Y X W V U A B C D E Z Y X W V U A B C D E Z Y X W V
(a) U (b) A (c) B (d) Z
(e) None of these

54. BDFHJLN/ACEGIKM/BDFHJL/ ACEGIK/ BDFHJ « SBI Clerk 2009

(a) B (b) L (c) M (d) F
(e) None of these

55. A B C D E F G H A B C D E F G A B C D E F « BOI Clerk 2009

(a) H (b) G (c) A (d) E
(d) None of these

56. A A B A B C A B C D A B C D E A B C D E F A B C D E F G A B C D E F G « SBI Clerk 2011

(a) A (b) I (c) H (d) B
(e) None of these

DIRECTIONS ~ (Q. Nos. 57 and 58) *A series is given, with one term missing. Choose the correct alternatives from the given ones that will complete the series.*

57. YXWv, TSrQ, OnML, jIHG EDCb, ? « SSC CGL 2017

(a) YXwV (b) ZYxW (c) XwVU (d) YxWV

58. AB, DEF, HIJK, ?, STUVWX « NIFT UG 2015

(a) LMNC (b) LMNOP (c) MNOPQ (d) QRSTU

DIRECTIONS ~ (Q. Nos. 59 and 60) *A series is given, with one term missing. Choose the correct alternatives from the given ones that will complete the series.*

59. bat, thin, reply, length, ? « SSC CGL 2017

(a) terror (b) display (c) dome (d) scolding

60. win, note, grain, broker, ? « SSC CGL 2017

(a) refund (b) pony (c) banking (d) mutually

DIRECTIONS ~ (Q. Nos. 61 and 62) *A series is given, with one word missing. Choose the correct alternatives from the given ones that will complete the series.* « SSC CGL 2017

61. nature, ensure, tense, spent, spurn, ?

(a) pushup (b) thrash (c) upturn (d) asset

62. Money, Amity, Camera, Animal, Telomere, ?

(a) Talisman (b) Litmus (c) Matter (d) Shame

Answers / WITH EXPLANATIONS

1. (*a*) Every next term is obtained by adding 2 to the corresponding position of its previous term (letter).

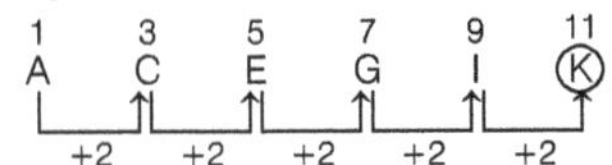

∴ ? = K

2. (*d*) The pattern is as follows

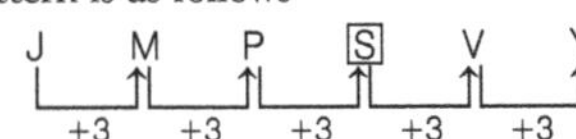

∴ ? = S

3. (*d*) The pattern is as follows

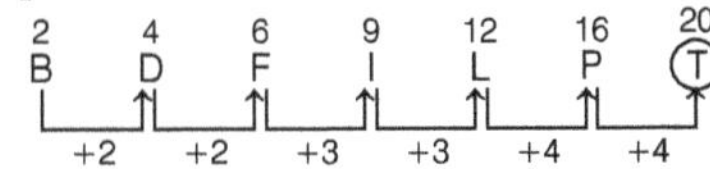

∴ ? = T

4. (*d*) The pattern is as follows

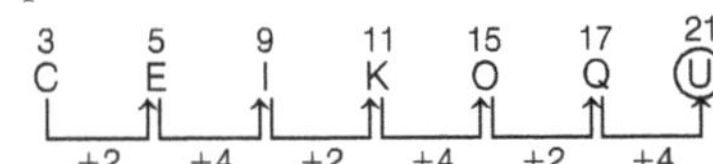

∴ ? = U

5. (*a*) The pattern is as follows

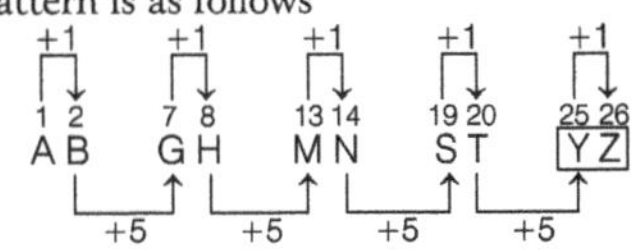

∴ ? = YZ

6. (*b*) The pattern is as follows

1 A —+2→ 3 C —+2→ 5 E —+2→ 7 G —+2→ 9 I
18 R —+3→ 21 U —+3→ 24 X —+3→ 1 A —+3→ 4 D

∴ ? = ID

7. (*a*) The pattern is as follows

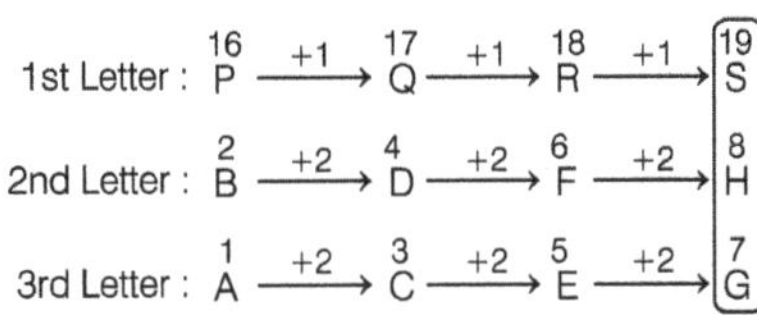

∴ ? = SHG

8. (*a*) The pattern is as follows

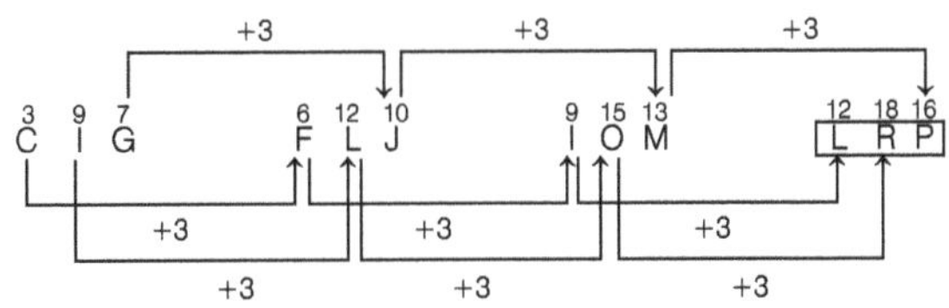

∴ ? = LRP

9. (*d*) The pattern is as follows

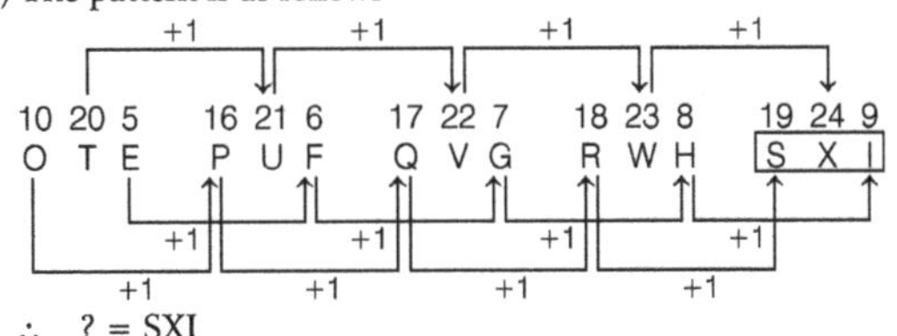

∴ ? = SXI

10. (*a*) The pattern is as follows

6 F —+3→ 9 I —+3→ 12 L —+3→ 15 O —+3→ 18 R
20 T —−3→ 17 Q —−3→ 14 N —−3→ 11 K —−3→ 8 H
2 B —+3→ 5 E —+3→ 8 H —+3→ 11 K —+3→ 14 N

∴ ? = RHN

11. (*d*) The pattern is as follows

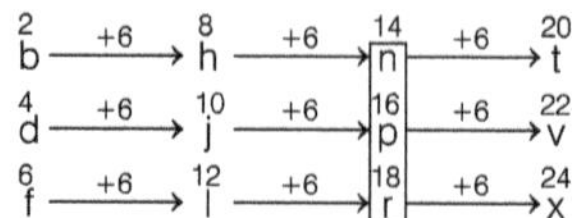

∴ ? = npr

12. (*d*) The pattern is as follows

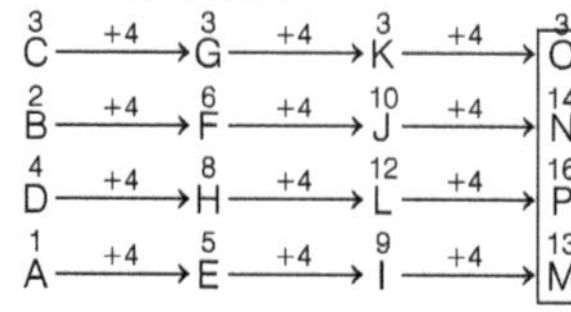

∴ ? = ONPM

13. (*c*) The pattern is as follows

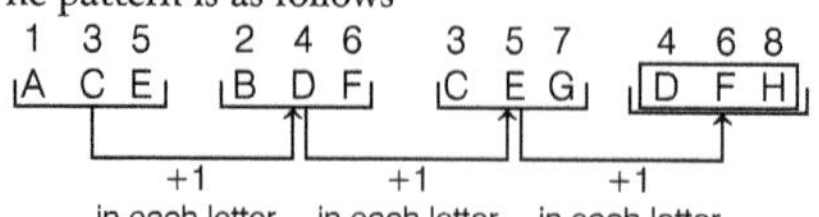

∴ ? = DFH

14. (*c*) The pattern is as follows

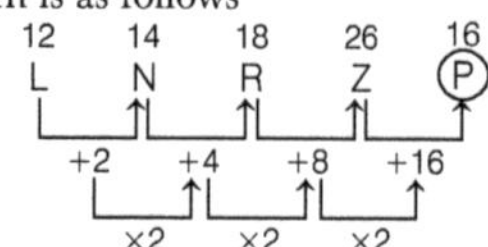

∴ ? = P

15. (*b*) Every next term is obtained by subtracting 2 from the corresponding position of its previous term (letter).

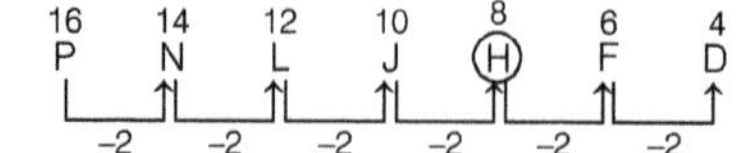

∴ ? = H

16. (*a*) The pattern is as follows

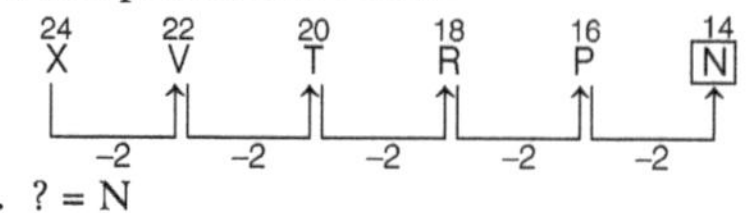

∴ ? = N

17. (*b*) The pattern is as follows

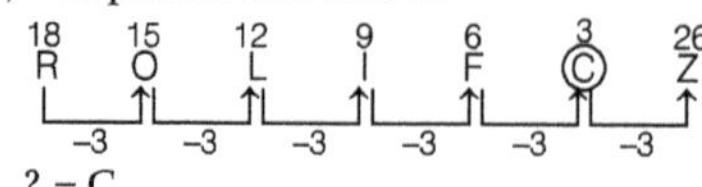

∴ ? = C

18. (*d*) The pattern is as follows

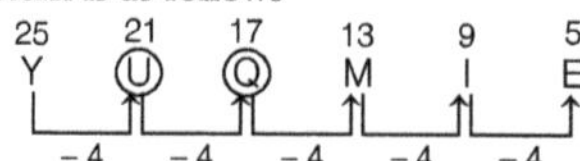

∴ First (?) = U and second (?) = Q

∴ Required answer = U, Q

19. (*a*) Every next term is obtained by subtracting 1, 2, 3, 4 and 5 respectively from its corresponding position.

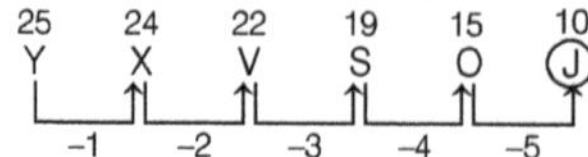

∴ ? = J

20. (*a*) The pattern is as follows

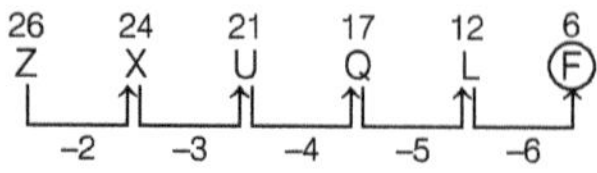

∴ ? = F

21. (*a*) The pattern is as follows

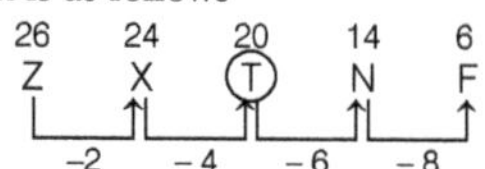

∴ ? = T

22. (*a*) The pattern is as follows

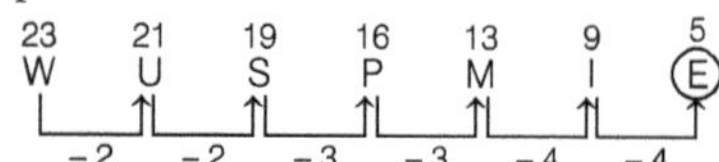

∴ ? = E

23. (*d*) The pattern is as follows

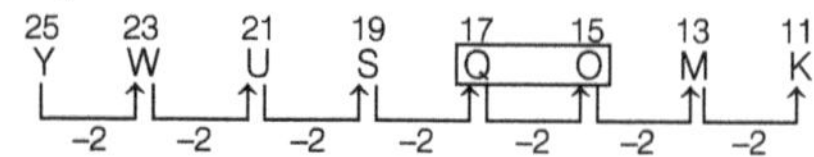

∴ ? = QO

24. (*c*) The pattern is as follows

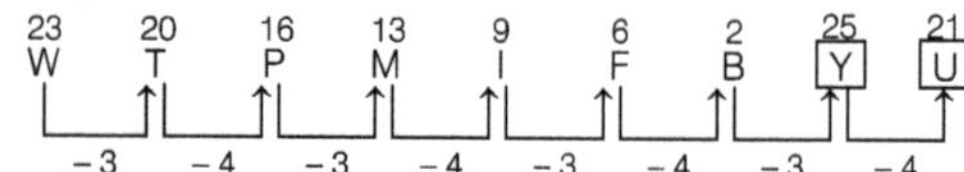

∴ Required answer = Y, U

25. (*d*) The pattern is as follows

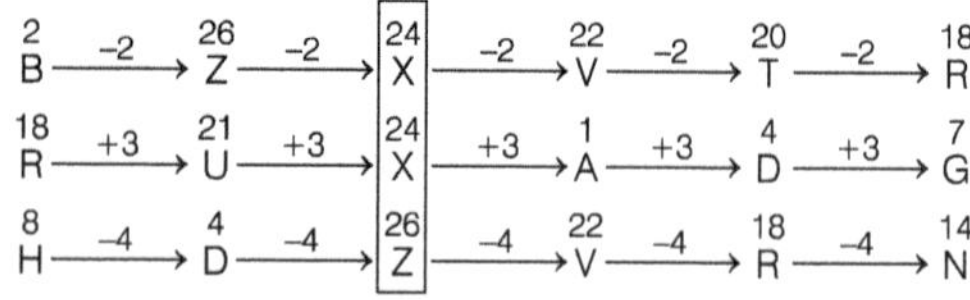

∴ ? = HFD

26. (*c*) The pattern is as follows

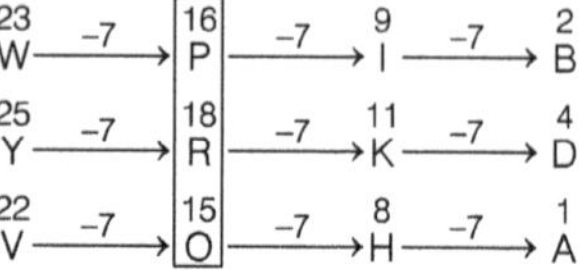

∴ ? = PRO

27. (*c*) The pattern is as follows

1 a +5 6 f +5 11 k +5 16 p +5 21 u
25 Y −5 20 T −5 15 O −5 10 J −5 5 E
4 d +5 9 i +5 14 n +5 19 s +5 24 x

∴ ? = uEx

28. (*b*) The pattern of the series is as follows

2 B +2 4 D +2 6 F +2 8 H +2 10 J +2 12 L
4 D +3 7 G +3 10 J +3 13 M +3 16 P +3 19 S
26 Z −2 224 X −2 22 V −2 20 T −2 18 R −2 16 P

∴ ? = LSP

29. (*b*) The pattern is as follows

1st Letter : X (24) —(−2)→ V (22) —(−3)→ S (19) —(−4)→ O (15) —(−5)→ [J (10)]

2nd Letter : W (23) —(−3)→ T (20) —(−4)→ P (16) —(−5)→ K (11) —(−6)→ [E (5)]

3rd Letter : A (1) —(+2)→ C (3) —(+3)→ F (6) —(+4)→ J (10) —(+5)→ [O (15)]

∴ ? = JEO

30. (*a*) The pattern is as follows

A (1) —(+4)→ E (5) —(+4)→ I (9) —(+4)→ [M (13)]

Z (26) —(−2)→ X (24) —(−2)→ V (22) —(−2)→ [T (20)]

Y (25) —(−2)→ W (23) —(−2)→ U (21) —(−2)→ [S (19)]

∴ ? = MTS

31. (*a*) The pattern is as follows

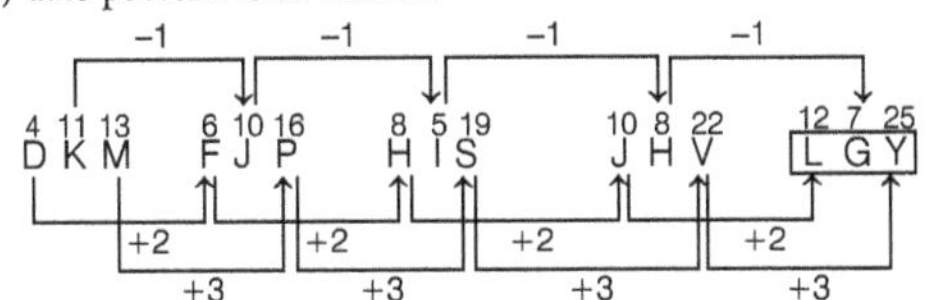

∴ ? = LGY

32. (*d*) The pattern is as follows

F (6) —(+2)→ H (8) —(+2)→ J (10) —(+2)→ [L (12)]

U (21) —(−2)→ S (19) —(−2)→ Q (17) —(−2)→ [O (15)]

G (7) —(+2)→ I (9) —(+2)→ K (11) —(+2)→ [M (13)]

T (20) —(−2)→ R (18) —(−2)→ P (16) —(−2)→ [N (14)]

∴ ? = LOMN

33. (*c*) Considering odd places elements first.

1st Letter : X (24) —(−3)→ U (21) —(−3)→ R (18) —(−3)→ [O (15)]

2nd Letter : Y (25) —(−3)→ V (22) —(−3)→ S (19) —(−3)→ [P (16)]

3rd Letter : Z (26) —(−3)→ W (23) —(−3)→ T (20) —(−3)→ [Q (17)]

Considering even place elements secondly.

1st Letter : A (1) —(+3)→ D (4) —(+3)→ G (7)

2nd Letter : B (2) —(+3)→ E (5) —(+3)→ H (8)

3rd Letter : C (3) —(+3)→ F (6) —(+3)→ I (9)

∴ ? = OPQ

34. (*c*) The pattern is as follows

1st Letter : A (1) —(+3)→ D (4) —(+3)→ G (7) —(+3)→ J (10) —(+3)→ [M (13)]

2nd Letter : Y (25) —(−2)→ W (23) —(−2)→ U (21) —(−2)→ S (19) —(−2)→ [Q (17)]

3rd Letter : B (2) —(+3)→ E (5) —(+3)→ H (8) —(+3)→ K (11) —(+3)→ [N (14)]

4th Letter : Z (26) —(−2)→ X (24) —(−2)→ V (22) —(−2)→ T (20) —(−2)→ [R (18)]

5th Letter : C (3) —(+3)→ F (6) —(+3)→ I (9) —(+3)→ L (12) —(+3)→ [O (15)]

∴ ? = MQNRO

35. (*d*) The pattern is as follows

B (2) —(+2)→ D (4) —(+2)→ [F (6)] —(−1)→ E (5) —(+2)→ G (7) —(+2)→ I (9)

E (5) —(+2)→ G (7) —(+2)→ [I (9)] —(+1)→ J (10) —(+2)→ L (12) —(+2)→ N (14)

H (8) —(+2)→ J (10) —(+2)→ [L (12)] —(+3)→ O (15) —(+2)→ Q (17) —(+2)→ S (19)

∴ ? = FIL

36. (*a*) There are two interwoven series.

The pattern is as follows

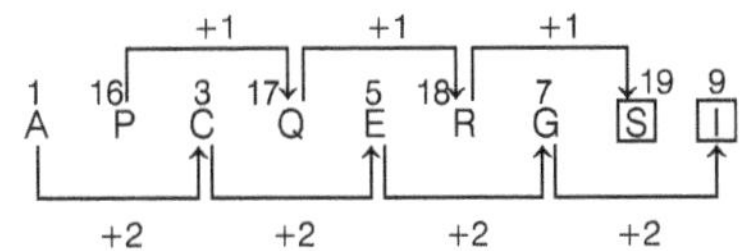

∴ Required answer = S, I

37. (*c*) There are two interwoven series.

The pattern is as follows

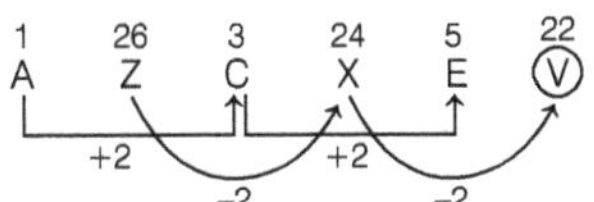

∴ ? = V

38. (*d*) The pattern is as follows

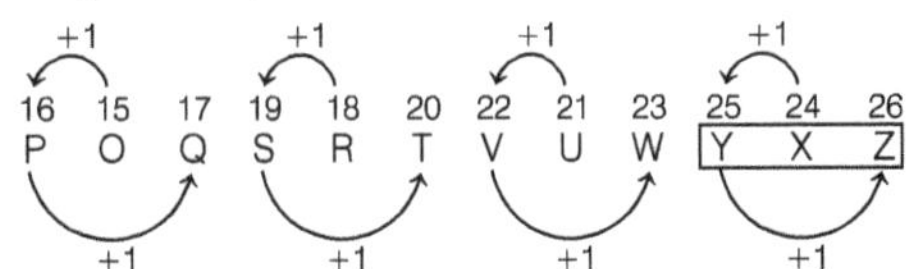

∴ ? = YXZ

39. (*b*) The pattern is as follows

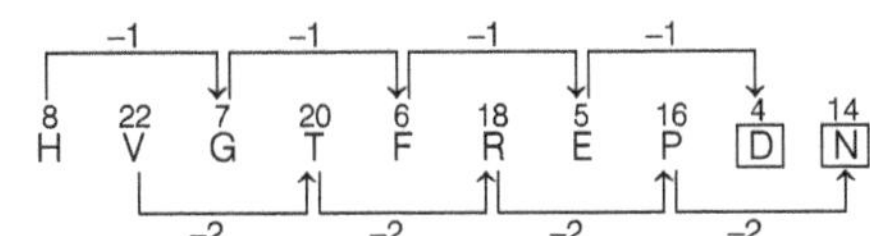

∴ ? = D,N

40. (*c*) The pattern is as follows

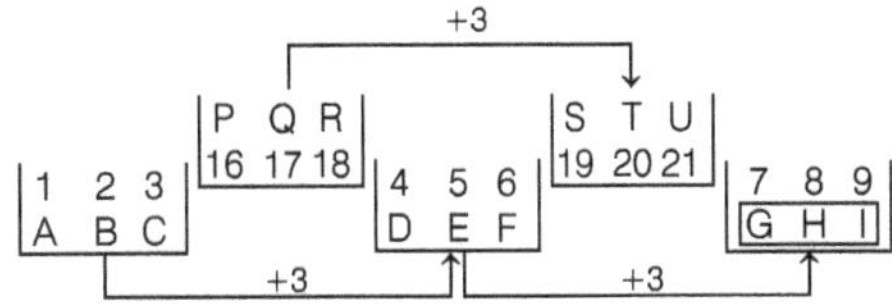

∴ ? = GHI

41. (*c*) Here, the reverse order repetition pattern is followed

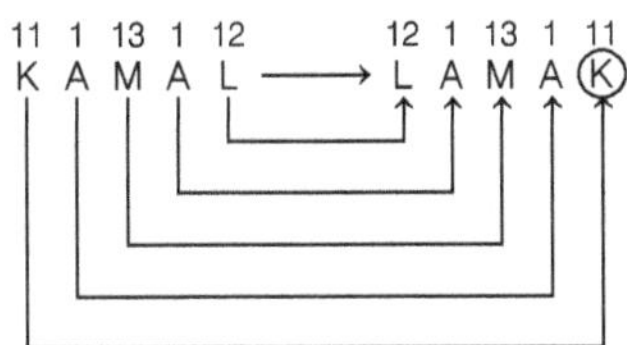

∴ ? = K

42. (*d*) First two letters and last two letters interchange their positions alternately.

∴ ? = KPM

43. (*d*) Here, three letters are skipped between each term of the series.

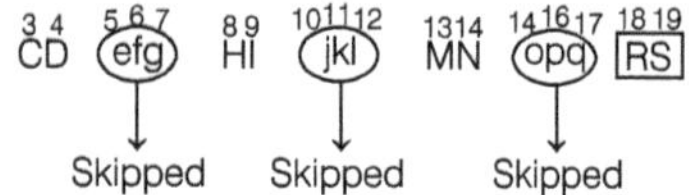

∴ ? = RS

44. (*c*) First and last letters disappear alternately.

∴ ? = IMARIL

45. (*a*) Last and first letters get disappear alternately.

∴ ? = ATUR

46. (*b*) The pattern is as follows

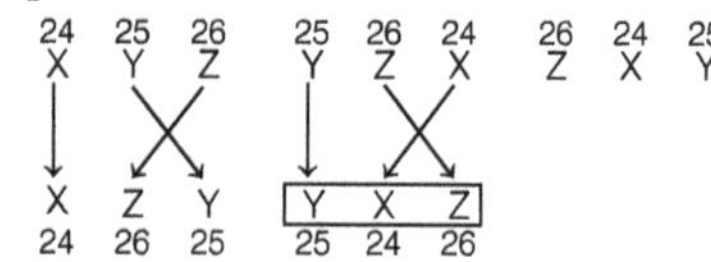

∴ ? = YXZ

47. (*c*) The pattern is as follows

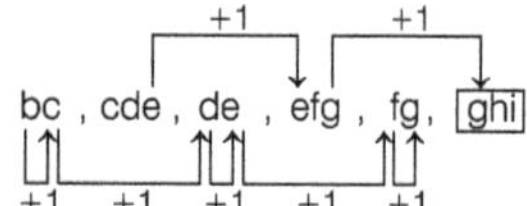

∴ ? = ghi

48. (*b*) The series progresses as D (efghi) j (klmno) P (qrstu) v (wxyza) B . The capital letters are repeated twice, while small letters are repeated thrice.

49. (*a*) The series is: Q(rstuvw) x (yzabc) D (efgh)i (jkl) M (no) p.

50. (*b*) The pattern is as follows

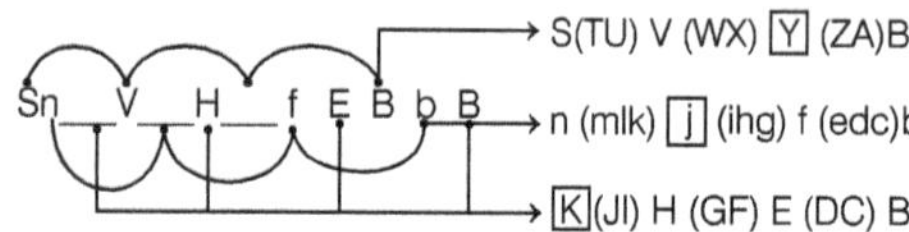

∴ Required answer = KjY

51. (*a*) The pattern is as follows

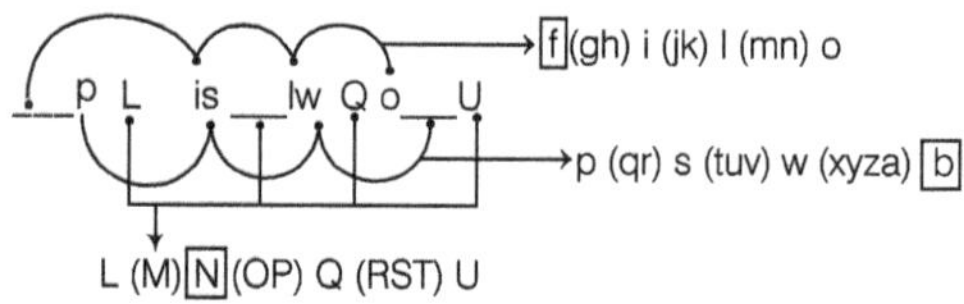

∴ Required answer = fNb

52. (*d*) The pattern is as follows

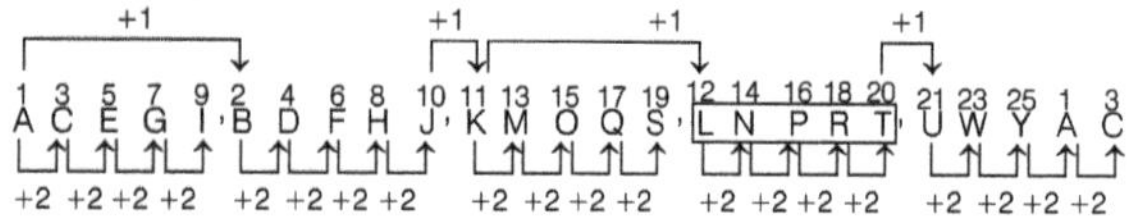

∴ Required answer = LNPRT

53. (*b*) The pattern is as follows

A B C D E F/Z Y X W V U
A B C D E/Z Y X W V U
A B C D E/Z Y X W V

Hence, next missing term would be A.

54. (*e*) The pattern is as follows

B D F H J L N/ A C E G I K M/ B D F H J L/ A C E G I K/ B D F H J/ A

Letters in the given series is increased by two and last letter of each term will disappear one by one.

Hence, next missing term would be A.

55. (*c*) The pattern is as follows

A B C D E F G H
A B C D E F G
A B C D E F
A

In the given series, one letter from right end is disappeared in each step.

Hence, next term would be A.

56. (*c*) The pattern is as follows

A/ A B / A B C / A B C D/ A B C D E / A B C D E F / A B C D E F G/ A B C D E F G H

Hence, next term would be H.

57. (*b*) The pattern is as follows

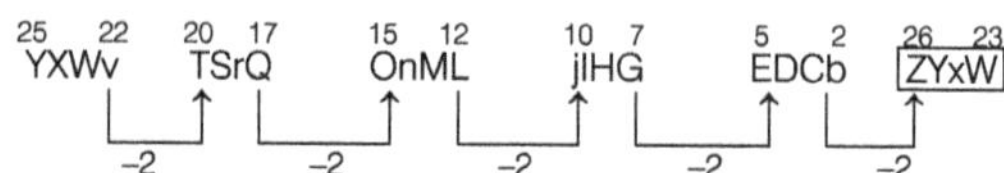

∴ ? = ZYxW

58. (*c*) The pattern is as follows

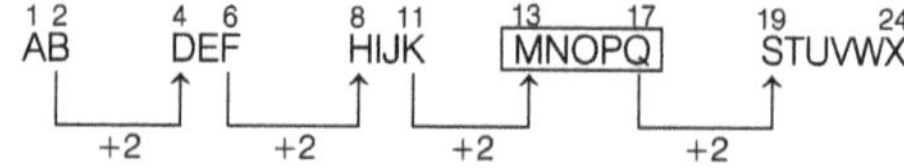

∴ ? = MNOPQ

59. (*b*) In the given series, by moving from left to right number of letters is increased by one.

bat	thin	reply	length	display
3	4	5	6	7

∴ ? = display

60. (*c*) In the given series, by moving from left to right number of letters is increased by one.

win	note	grain	broker	banking
3	4	5	6	7

∴ ? = banking

61. (*c*) In the given series, the position of 'n' is shifting by one.

Hence, nature (1), ensure (2), tense (3), spent (4), spurn (5), upturn (6)

∴ ? = upturn

62. (*a*) In the given series, the position of 'M' is shifting by one.

Hence, Money (1), Amity (2), Camera (3), Animal (4), Telomere (5), Talisman (6)

∴ ? = Talisman

TYPE 03

Alpha-Numeric Series

Alpha-numeric series comprises of both, the letters and numbers which are presented in jumbled format but each of them follow certain pattern based on either the alphabetical position of the letters or the numbers in different correlation etc.

The importance of this topic lies in expanding the skills of the candidates who are required to recognise the pattern in both manner and complete the series by inserting the missing number or detecting the wrong number in the series.

1. Separate Series of Letters/Numbers

In this type of series, letters and numbers both exist simultaneously but series of letters is associated only with letters and series of numbers is associated only with numbers.

***Ex* 53** In the below series, identify what can come in place of '?' « UPSSSC VDO 2018

C2, F5, I11, L17, ?, R31, U41, X47

(a) O25 (b) Q23 (c) Q21 (d) O23

Solution (d) The pattern is as follows

Prime Numbers

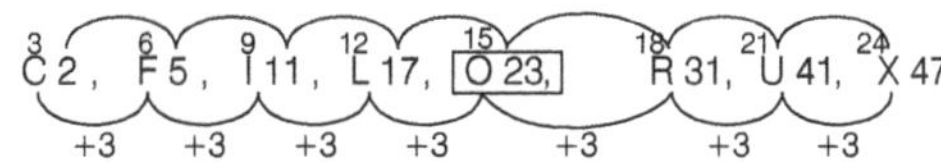

There is 1 missing prime between the alternative numbers.

***Ex* 54** Find the next term in the series. « RRB Group D 2018

3X24C, 5V22E, ?

(a) 9T21G (b) 8T21G
(c) 7T20G (d) 8T20G

Solution (c) The pattern is as follows

3 —(+2)→ 5 —(+2)→ 7
X —(−2)→ V —(−2)→ T
24 —(−2)→ 22 —(−2)→ 20
C —(+2)→ E —(+2)→ G

∴ ? = 7T20G

2. Combined Series of Letters and Numbers

In this type of series, letters and numbers both exist simultaneously and the series of letters is associated with the series of numbers in a particular manner.

***Ex* 55** Replace the question mark (?) in the following series with suitable option.

C5, F4, E7, H6, ?

(a) 8G (b) G9 (c) F9 (d) D7

Solution (b) The pattern of given alpha-numeric series is as follows

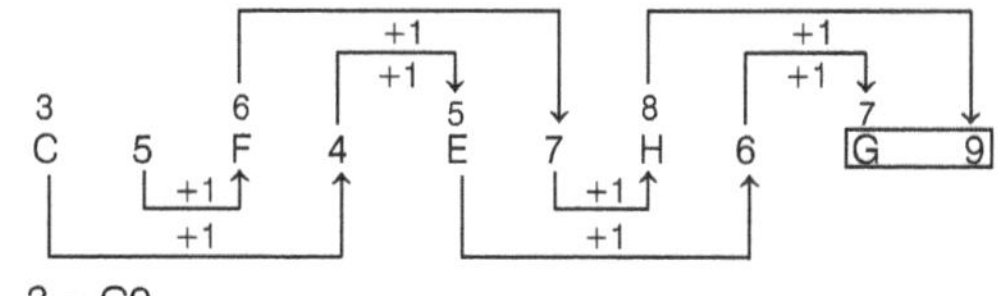

∴ ? = G9

Practice / CORNER 5.3

DIRECTIONS ~ (Q. Nos. 1-27) *What should come in the place of question mark (?) in the following alpha-numeric series?*

1. C-3, E-5, G-7, I-9, ?, ?
(a) X-24, M-21 (b) K-11, M-13
(c) O-15. X-24 (d) M-18, K-14

2. 3W, 7V, 11U, 15T, ? « RRB NTPC 2016
(a) 19Z (b) 20P (c) 22Q (d) 19S

3. 3F, 6G, 11I, 18L,?
(a) 27P (b) 25N (c) 27Q (d) 21'O'

4. P3C, R5F, T8I, V12L, ?
(a) X16O (b) Y17O (c) X17M (d) X 17O
(e) None of these

5. X7D, V11G, T13J, ?, P19P « CLAT 2018
(a) Q15M (b) R17M (c) Q17L (d) R15M

6. C4X, F9U, I16R, ?
(a) L25P (b) K25P (c) L27P (d) L25O

7. KM5, IP8, GS11, EV14,?
(a) BY17 (b) CZ17 (c) BX17 (d) CY17

8. A26H, C24F, G20B, ? « BPSC 2016
(a) M13D (b) O11C (c) M12B (d) M14E
(e) None of these

9. Q1F, S2E, U6D, W24C,?
(a) Y120B (b) Y44B (c) Z88B (d) Y66B

10. ST39, UV43, WX47, ?
(a) YZ47 (b) YZ52 (c) YZ51 (d) YX50

11. 2Z5, 7Y7, 14X9, 23W11, 34V13, ?
(a) 27U24 (b) 47U15 (c) 45U15 (d) 47V14

12. 4D3C, 7G6F, 10J9I, ? « RRB Group D 2018
(a) 13K12L (b) 12L13N (c) 13L12M (d) 13M12L

13. AB 11 CD, EF 13 GH, IJ 17 KL, ?
(a) MN18 OP (b) MN19 OP
(c) MN 21 OP (d) MN 23 OP

14. T49S64, R81Q100, P121O144, ?
(a) N169M196 (b) N160M190
(c) N164M194 (d) U36T46

15. B_2CD, ?, BCD_4, ?, BC_6D
(a) B C_3D, B_5CD (b) B C_2D, B C_3D
(c) B C_3D, C_3CD (d) B C_3D, BC_5D

16. P3, M8, ?, G24, D35
(a) K15 (b) J13 (c) I13 (d) J15

17. A1, C3, F6, J10, O15, ? « CLAT 2014

(a) U21 (b) V21 (c) T20 (d) U20

18. CO3KP, DO4KQ, EO5KR, FO6KS ?

(a) GO7KP (b) GO6KT (c) GO6KP (d) GO7KT

19. 27 CD 72, 26 FG 62, 25 IJ 52, ?, 23 OP 32 « MAT 2014

(a) 24 KI 42 (b) 24 LM 42
(c) 24 ML 42 (d) 24 MN 42

20. 86 XW 68, 85 UT 58, 84 RQ 48, ?, 82 LK 28 « MAT 2014

(a) 83 ON 38 (b) 83 PO 38
(c) 83 RP 38 (d) 83 NO 38

21. BA 2500 ZY, DC 1600 XW, FE 900 VU, ?, JI 100 RQ

(a) GH 600 ST (b) HG 400 TS
(c) HG 500 TS (d) HG 300 TS

22. 31 MN 97, 37 PQ 89, 41 ST 83, ?, 47 YZ 73 « MAT 2014

(a) 43 VW 79 (b) 45 VW 80
(c) 43 VW 81 (d) 44 YW 82

23. 71 XW 13, 67 UT 17, ?, 59 ON 23, 53 LK 29 « MAT 2014

(a) 65 RQ 18 (b) 63 RQ 19
(c) 61 RQ 19 (d) 60 RQ 126

24. AB11CD, EF13GH, IJ17KL, '?'

(a) MN18OP (b) MN19OP
(c) MN21OP (d) MN23OP

25. T144R121, P100N81, L64J49, ?

(a) H36F25 (b) H34F20
(c) H32F22 (d) H38F30

26. BD3FH, AC5EG, JL7NP, '?'

(a) IK9MO (b) IK11MO
(c) IK13MO (d) IK17MO

27. GAS27, IEU35, MIY47, OMA29, SOE39, USI49, ?
« UPSSSC Combined Lower Subordinate 2019

(a) WUM57 (b) WWO61
(c) YUM59 (d) YWN62

Answers WITH EXPLANATIONS

1. (*b*) In this series, every letter is given its alphabetical position number and one letter is skipped in between each term. Hence, the missing terms are K-11 and M-13.

2. (*d*) The pattern is as follows

3 →(+4) 7 →(+4) 11 →(+4) 15 →(+4) **19**
W(23) →(−1) V(22) →(−1) U(21) →(−1) T(20) →(−1) **S(19)**

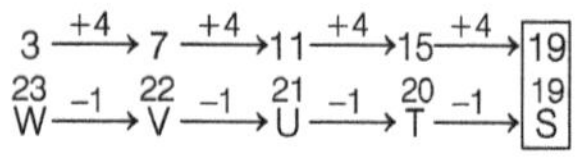

∴ ? = 19 S

3. (*a*) Pattern of given alpha-numeric series is as follows

Numbers: 3 →(+3) 6 →(+5) 11 →(+7) 18 →(+9) 27
Letters: F(6) →(+1) G(7) →(+2) I(9) →(+3) L(12) →(+4) P(16)

3 F 6 G 11 I 18 L **27 P**

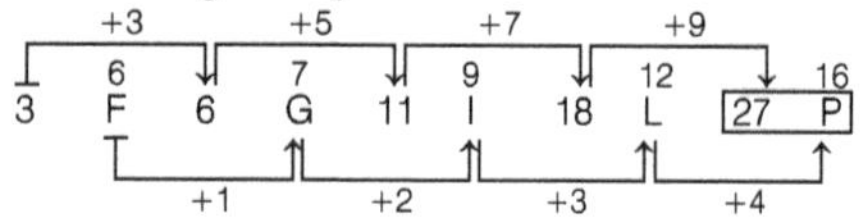

∴ ? = 27P

4. (*d*) Pattern of given alpha-numeric series is as follows

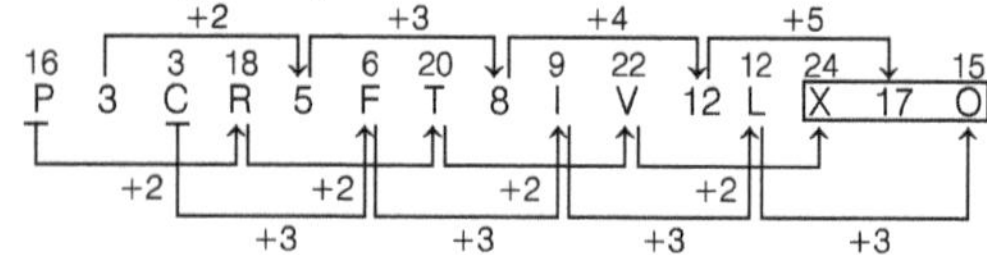

∴ ? = X17O

5. (*b*) The pattern is as follows

X(24) →(−2) V(22) →(−2) T(20) →(−2) **R(18)** →(−2) P(16)
7 →(+4) 11 →(+2) 13 →(+4) **17** →(+2) 19
D(4) →(+3) G(7) →(+3) J(10) →(+3) **M(13)** →(+3) P(16)

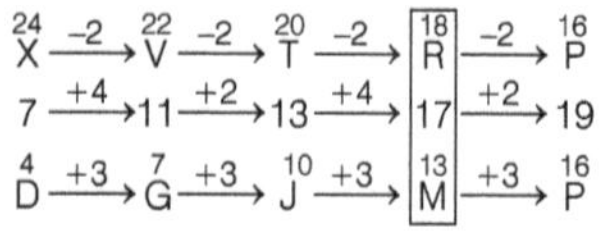

∴ ? = R17M

6. (*d*) Pattern of given alpha-numeric series is as follows

C(3) →(+3) F(6) →(+3) I(9) →(+3) **L(12)**
4 →(+5) 9 →(+7) 16 →(+9) **25**
X(24) →(−3) U(21) →(−3) R(18) →(−3) **O(15)**

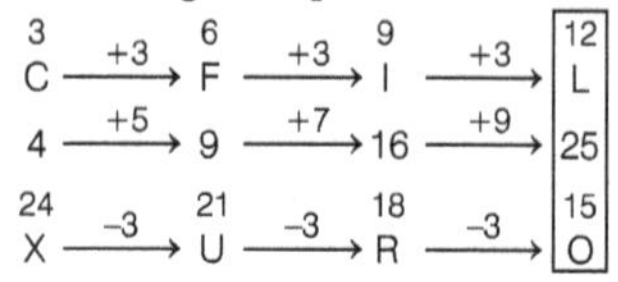

∴ ? = L 25 O

7. (*d*) Pattern of given alpha-numeric series is as follows

K(11) →(−2) I(9) →(−2) G(7) →(−2) E(5) →(−2) **C(3)**
M(13) →(+3) P(16) →(+3) S(19) →(+3) V(22) →(+3) **Y(25)**
5 →(+3) 8 →(+3) 11 →(+3) 14 →(+3) **17**

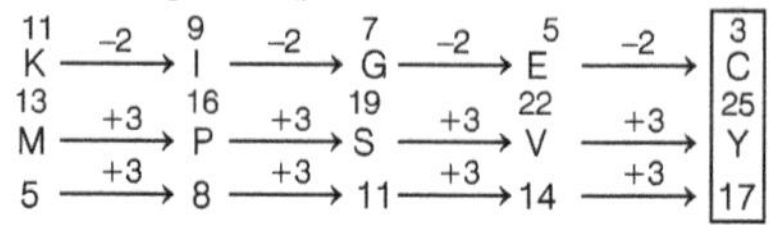

∴ ? = C Y 17

8. (*e*) The pattern is as follows

A →(+2) C →(+4) G →(+6) **M**
26 →(−2) 24 →(−4) 20 →(−6) **14**
H →(−2) F →(−4) B →(−6) **V**

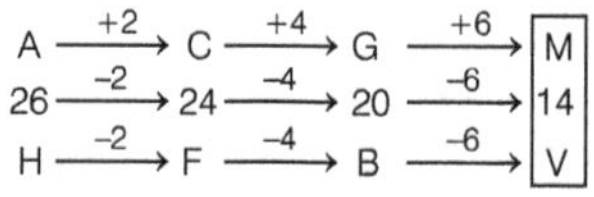

∴ ? = M 14 V

9. (*a*) Pattern of given alpha-numeric series is as follows

Q(17) →(+2) S(19) →(+2) U(21) →(+2) W(23) →(+2) **Y(25)**
1 →(×2) 2 →(×3) 6 →(×4) 24 →(×5) **120**
F(6) →(−1) E(5) →(−1) D(4) →(−1) C(3) →(−1) **B(2)**

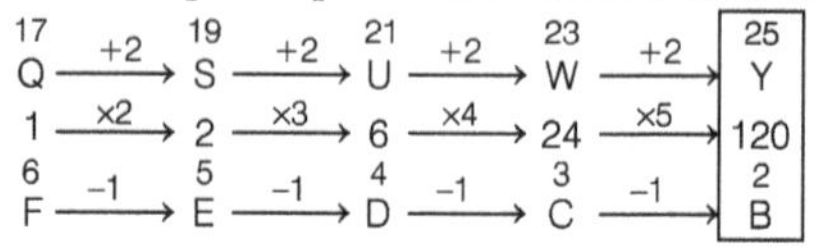

∴ ? = Y 120 B

10. (*c*) Pattern of given alpha-numeric series is as follows

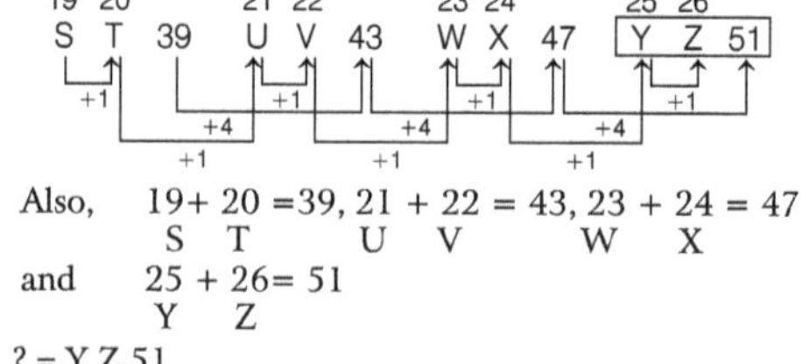

Also, 19 + 20 = 39, 21 + 22 = 43, 23 + 24 = 47
(S T, U V, W X)

and 25 + 26 = 51
(Y Z)

∴ ? = Y Z 51

11. (*b*) Pattern of given alpha-numeric series is as follows

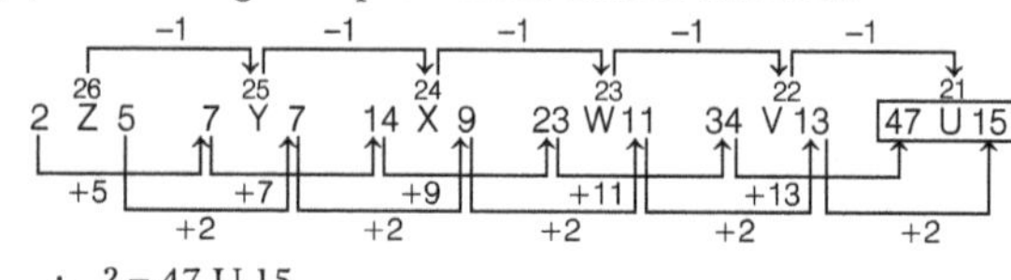

∴ ? = 47 U 15

12. (*d*) The pattern is as follows

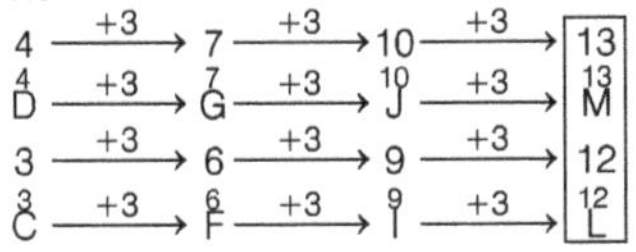

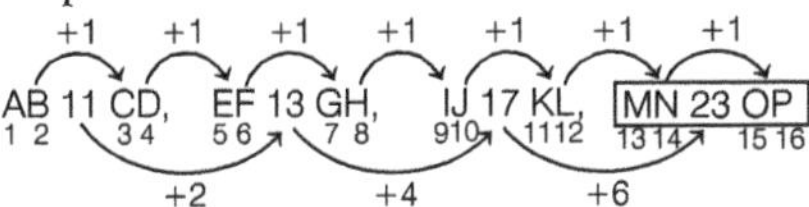

∴? = 13 M12L

13. (*d*) The pattern is as follows

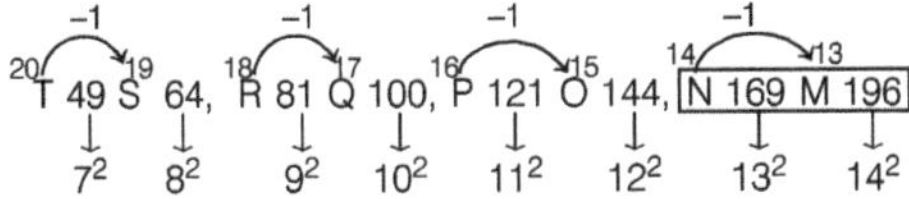

∴ ? = MN23OP

14. (*a*) The pattern is as follows

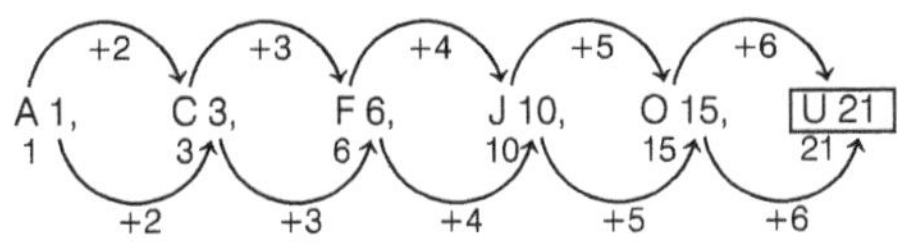

∴ ? = N169M196

15. (*a*) In this problem, we can see the number in the next term is increasing by 1 and it is also changing the position alphabetically. Hence, the series would be

B_2CD, $\underline{BC_3D}$, BCD_4, $\underline{B_5CD}$, BC_6D

∴ ?, ? = BC_3D, B_5CD

16. (*d*) $\overset{16}{P} \xrightarrow{-3} \overset{13}{M} \xrightarrow{-3} \overset{10}{J} \xrightarrow{-3} \overset{7}{G} \xrightarrow{-3} \overset{4}{D}$

$3 \xrightarrow{+5} 8 \xrightarrow{+7} 15 \xrightarrow{+9} 24 \xrightarrow{+11} 35$

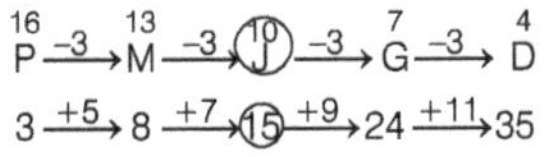

17. (*a*) Pattern of given alpha-numeric series is as follows

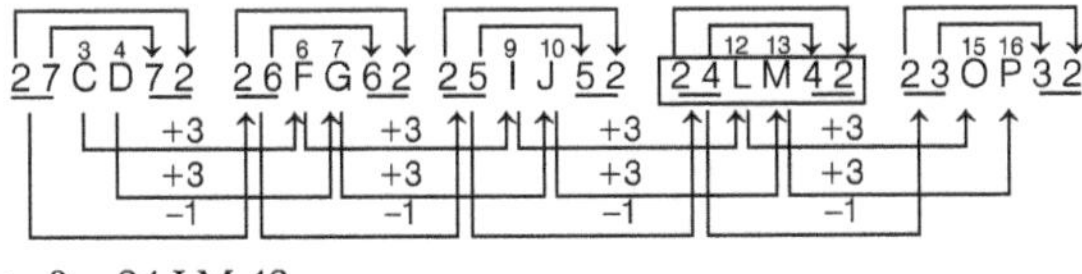

∴ ? = U21

18. (*d*) Pattern of given alpha-numeric series is as follows

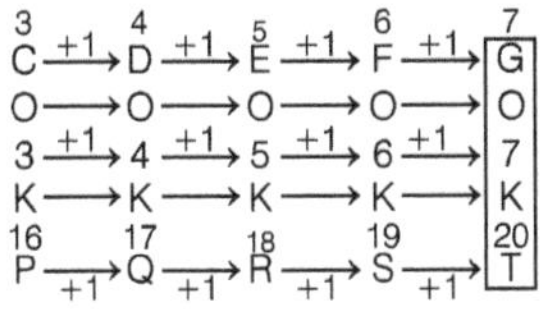

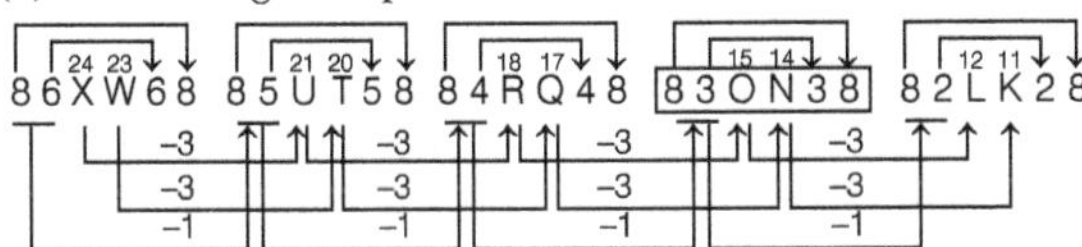

∴ ? = GO7KT

19. (*b*) Pattern of given alpha-numeric series is as follows

∴ ? = 24 LM 42

20. (*a*) Pattern of given alpha-numeric series is as follows

∴ ? = 83 ON 38

21. (*b*) Pattern of given alpha-numeric series is as follows

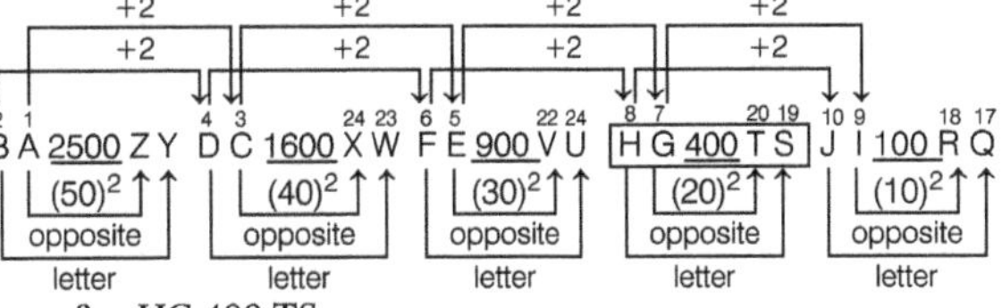

∴ ? = HG 400 TS

22. (*a*) Pattern of given alpha-numeric series is as follows

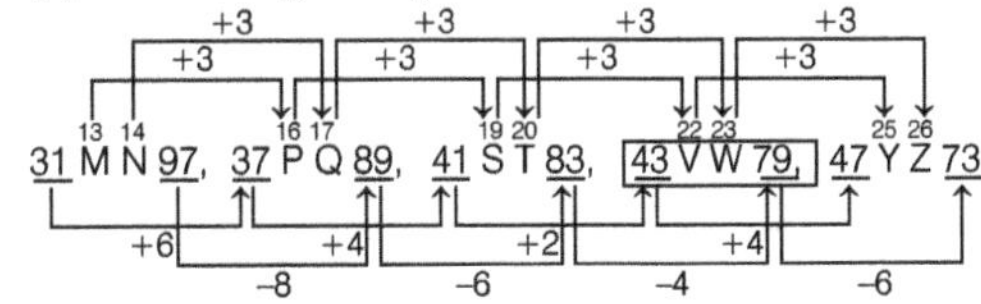

∴ ? = 43 V W 79

23. (*b*) Pattern of given alpha-numeric series is as follows

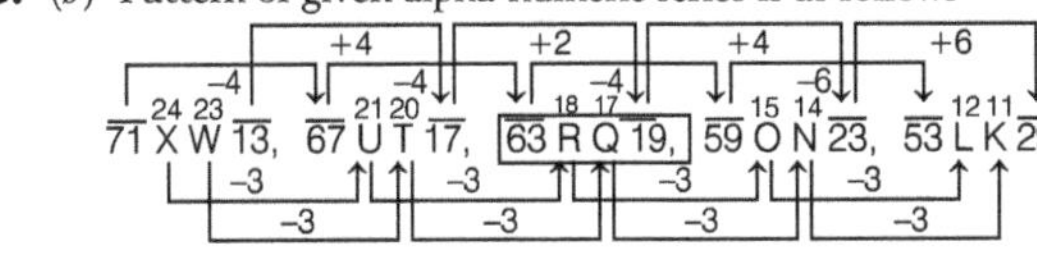

∴ ? = 63 RQ 19

24. (*d*) The pattern is as follows

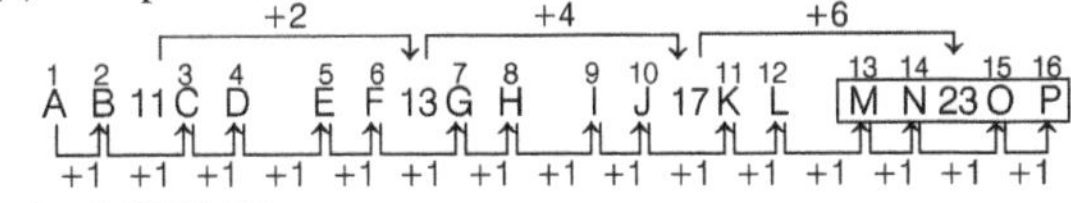

∴ ? = MN23OP

25. (*a*) The pattern is as follows

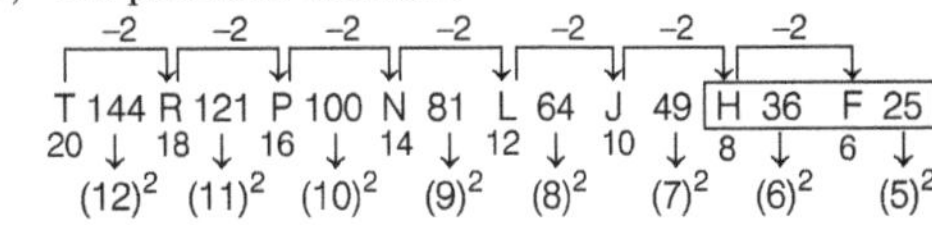

∴? = H36F25

26. (*a*) The pattern is as follows

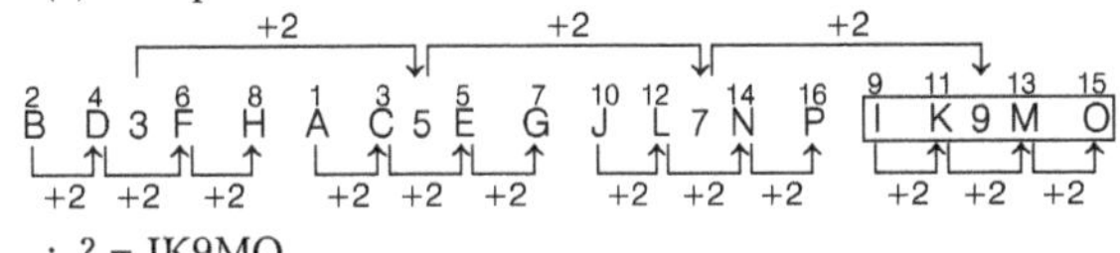

∴ ? = IK9MO

27. (*c*) The pattern is as follows

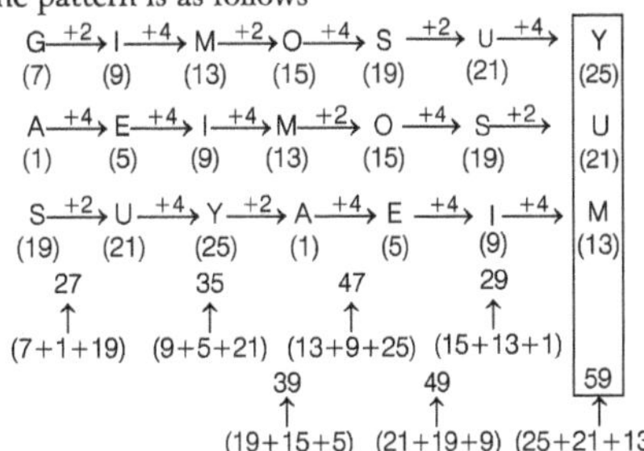

In the given series, the vowels are coded by the letter which are four places ahead of them and consonants are coded by the letters which are two places ahead of them in English alphabetical series. The number given in each term is the sum of the places of each alphabet in English alphabetical series.

TYPE 04

Find the Wrong Term (Number/Alphabet)

In this type of questions, a series of numbers/alphabets is given which follows a certain pattern and one of its terms is incorrect and does not fit into the series.

The candidate is required to identify the pattern involved in the formation of series and then find out that number/alphabet(s) which does not follow the specific pattern of the series.

***Ex* 56** Four numbers have been given, out of which three are alike in some manner and one is different. Select the number that is different from the rest.
UPSSSC Junior Assistant 2020

720, 120, 24, 8, 2, 1, 1

(a) 24 (b) 8 (c) 2 (d) 120

***Solution* (b)** Pattern of series is as follows

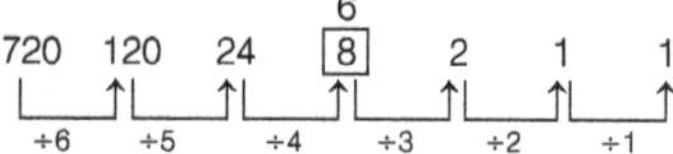

Hence, 8 is odd one here, 6 will replace it.

***Ex* 57** One term is wrong in the following series. What is that term? « CGPSC 2017

130, 126, 110, 78, 10

(a) 78 (b) 110 (c) 10 (d) 130
(e) None of these

***Solution* (a)** The pattern is as follows

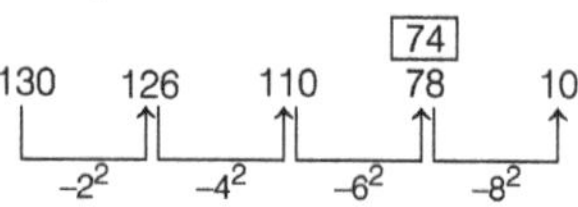

Hence, number 78 is wrong in the given series. It should be replaced by 74.

***Ex* 58** Find out the wrong term in the series
E G K M P S « UP Police SI 2017

(a) Q (b) K (c) E (d) P

***Solution* (d)** The pattern is as follows

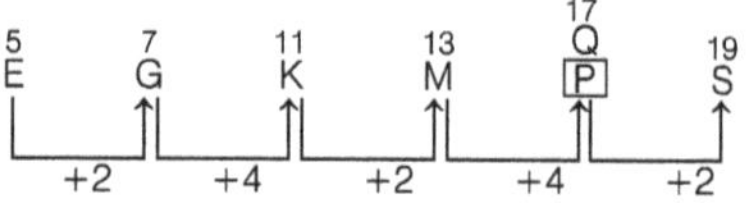

Hence, P is wrong term.

Practice / CORNER 5.4

DIRECTIONS ~ (Q. Nos. 1-55) *In each of the following questions, one number is wrong in the series. Find out the wrong number.*

1. 4, 5, 7, 10, 14, 18, 25, 32
(a) 7 (b) 14 (c) 18 (d) 32

2. 1, 2, 5, 14, 41, 124
(a) 2 (b) 5 (c) 14 (d) 124

3. 3, 5, 7, 12, 17, 19, 23
(a) 23 (b) 19 (c) 17 (d) 12

4. 4, 10, 22, 40, 84, 94, 130
(a) 22 (b) 40 (c) 94 (d) 84

5. 4, 19, 49, 93, 154, 229, 319
(a) 93 (b) 229 (c) 319 (d) 19

6. 189, 186, 181, 174, 165, 155, 141 « RBI Office Assistant 2020
(a) 189 (b) 181 (c) 165 (d) 155 (e) 141

7. 225, 289, 338, 374, 397, 415, 424
(a) 415 (b) 289 (c) 338 (d) 397

8. 7.5, 47.5, 87.5, 157.5, 247.5, 357.5, 487.5
(a) 357.5 (b) 87.5 (c) 157.5 (d) 7.5
(e) 47.5

9. 5, 9, 25, 59, 125, 225, 369 « RBI Office Assistant 2020
(a) 369 (b) 225 (c) 25 (d) 59 (e) 9

10. 9, 14, 19, 25, 32, 40
(a) 14 (b) 25 (c) 32 (d) 9

11. 17, 36, ,53, 68, 83, 92
(a) 92 (b) 53 (c) 68 (d) 83

12. 2, 6, 12, 48, 240, 1440, 10080 « RBI Office Assistant 2020
(a) 12 (b) 6 (c) 2 (d) 28 (e) 240

13. 2.5, 3.5, 15, 60, 300, 1800 « LIC AAO 2019
(a) 3.5 (b) 15 (c) 60 (d) 300 (e) 2.5

14. 2, 4, 8, 16, 48, 64, 128, 256
(a) 4 (b) 8 (c) 16 (d) 48

15. 385, 462, 572, 396, 427, 671, 264
(a) 385 (b) 427 (c) 671 (d) 264

16. 2, 10, 18, 54, 162, 486, 1458
(a) 18 (b) 54 (c) 162 (d) 10 (e) 486

17. 2, 6, 12, 72, 865, 62208
(a) 72 (b) 12 (c) 62208 (d) 865 (e) 6

18. 33, 321, 465, 537, 573, 590, 600
(a) 321 (b) 465 (c) 573 (d) 537 (e) 590

19. 56, 72, 90, 110, 132, 150
(a) 72 (b) 90 (c) 110 (d) 150
(e) None of these

20. 10, 14, 28, 32, 64, 68, 132
(a) 28 (b) 32 (c) 64 (d) 132

21. 100, 97, 90, 86, 76, 71, 62, 55
(a) 55 (b) 62 (c) 76 (d) 86

22. 8424, 4212, 2106, 1051, 526.5, 263.25, 131.625
(a) 131.625 (b) 1051 (c) 4212
(d) 8424 (e) 263.25

23. 4, 11, 30, 67, 128, 221, 346 « RBI Office Assistant 2020
(a) 11 (b) 4 (c) 221 (d) 67 (e) 346

24. 20, 40, 200, 400, 2000, 4000, 8000
(a) 200 (b) 2000 (c) 8000 (d) 4000
(e) None of these

25. 540, 550, 575, 585, 608, 620, 645
« RBI Office Assistant 2020
(a) 608 (b) 550 (c) 575 (d) 645 (e) 585

26. 212, 242, 278, 324, 392, 482, 602 « LIC AAO 2019
(a) 212 (b) 324 (c) 392 (d) 602 (e) 278

27. 35, 118, 280, 600, 1238, 2504, 5036
(a) 118 (b) 280 (c) 600 (d) 1238

28. 11, 30, 67, 120, 219, 346 « SSC CPO 2018
(a) 11 (b) 120 (c) 67 (d) 346

29. 1, 5, 9, 15, 25, 37, 49
(a) 25 (b) 37 (c) 9 (d) 15 (e) 590

30. 9, 16, 25, 36, 49, 61
(a) 16 (b) 9 (c) 49 (d) 61

31. 189, 701, 1044, 1263, 1385, 1449, 1476 « LIC AO 2019
(a) 1263 (b) 701 (c) 189 (d) 1449 (e) 1476

32. 8, 27, 125, 343, 1331
(a) 8 (b) 343 (c) 1331 (d) None of these

33. 2, 8, 3, 27, 4, 64, 5, 225
(a) 27 (b) 8 (c) 225 (d) 64

34. 2, 3, 9, 27, 112, 565, 3396
(a) 565 (b) 9 (c) 112 (d) 27

35. 1, 4, 8, 16, 31, 64, 127, 256
(a) 31 (b) 16 (c) 8 (d) 6

36. 12, 13, 28, 87, 351, 1765, 10596 « LIC AO 2019
(a) 87 (b) 1765 (c) 10596 (d) 12 (e) 351

37. 3, 5, 13, 43, 176, 891, 5353
(a) 5 (b) 13 (c) 43 (d) 176 (e) 891

38. 49, 56, 64, 71, 81, 90, 100, 110
(a) 56 (b) 64 (c) 71 (d) 81

39. 12, 18, 30, 48, 72, 126, 204 « LIC AAO 2019
(a) 18 (b) 72 (c) 126 (d) 48 (e) 204

40. 18, 119, 708, 3534, 14136, 42405
(a) 708 (b) 3534 (c) 14136 (d) 42405 (e) 119

41. 5, 14, 55, 274, 1641, 11500 « LIC AAO 2019
(a) 55 (b) 274 (c) 1641 (d) 11500 (e) 5

42. 513, 257, 129, 65, 31, 17, 9 « LIC AAO 2019
(a) 257 (b) 129 (c) 65 (d) 31 (e) 17

43. 1788, 892, 444, 220, 112, 52, 24
(a) 52 (b) 112 (c) 220 (d) 444
(e) None of these

44. 7, 12, 40, 222, 1742, 17390, 208608
(a) 7 (b) 12 (c) 40 (d) 1742
(e) 208608

45. 80, 42, 24, 13.5, 8.75, 6.375, 5.1875
(a) 8.75 (b) 13.5 (c) 24 (d) 6.375 (e) 42

46. 2, 9, 32, 105, 436, 2195, 13182
(a) 436 (b) 2195 (c) 9 (d) 32 (e) 105

47. 4, 2.5, 3.5, 6.5, 15.5, 41.25, 126.75
(a) 2.5 (b) 3.5 (c) 6.5 (d) 15.5 (e) 41.25

48. 3, 2, 8, 9, 13, 22, 18, 32, 23, 42 « NIFT PG 2014
(a) 22 (b) 13 (c) 9 (d) 8

49. 1236, 2346, 3456, 4566, 5686
(a) 1236 (b) 3456 (c) 4566 (d) 5686
(e) None of these

50. 1, 5, 5, 9, 7, 11, 11, 15, 12, 17
(a) 11 (b) 12 (c) 17 (d) 15
(e) None of these

51. 1, 3, 9, 31, 128, 651, 3913 « SBI PO 2018
(a) 9 (b) 1 (c) 128 (d) 31 (e) 3913

52. 291, 147, 75, 39, 22, 12, 7.5 « SBI PO 2018
(a) 22 (b) 291 (c) 147 (d) 75 (e) 7.5

53. 26, 27, 34, 58, 106, 186, 306 « SBI PO 2018
(a) 26 (b) 34 (c) 58 (d) 106 (e) 27

54. 5.9, 6, 6.1, 6.4, 7.9, 18.5, 112.9 « SBI PO 2018
(a) 6 (b) 5.9 (c) 6.1 (d) 18.5
(e) 112.9

55. 330, 80, 280, 120, 250, 130, 240 « SBI PO 2018
(a) 330 (b) 130 (c) 280 (d) 240 (e) 80

DIRECTIONS ~ (Q. Nos. 56-66) *In each of the following questions, one letter group of letters is wrong in the series. find out the wrong number.*

56. A C A E A G A J A K
(a) G (b) K (c) J (d) C

57. P, U, R, N, T, Q, V, O
(a) P (b) U (c) N (d) V

58. Z Y X W T S R Q N M L K G
(a) Q (b) G (c) R (d) N

59. E, O, I, S, M, W, Q, A, V
(a) S (b) V (c) W (d) M

60. ZX, YV, WS, PT, PJ
(a) PT (b) WS (c) ZX (d) YV

61. AD, GJ, MP, RS
(a) AD (b) RS (c) MP (d) GJ

62. AC, FH, KM, RP
(a) AC (b) KM (c) RP (d) FH

63. ABC, PQR, DEF, STU, HGI
(a) ABC (b) DEF (c) HGI (d) STU

64. AHI, BGJ, KFC, DEL
(a) KFC (b) DEL (c) BGJ (d) AHI

65. SHG, RIF, QJE, PKD, NMB
(a) RIF (b) PKD (c) QJE (d) NMB

66. CBCB, HEFG, LIJK, PMNO, TQRS
(a) LIJK (b) PMNO
(c) CBCB (d) TQRS

Answers WITH EXPLANATIONS

1. (*c*) The pattern is as follows

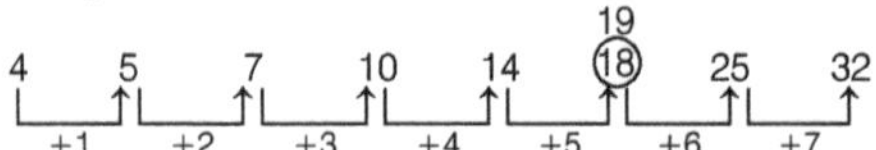

Hence, number 18 is wrong and should be replaced by 19.

2. (*d*) The pattern is as follows

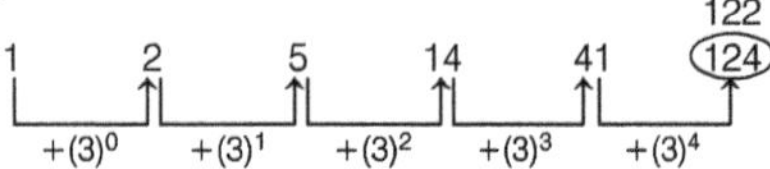

Hence,number 124 is wrong and should be replaced by 122.

3. (*a*) The pattern is as follows

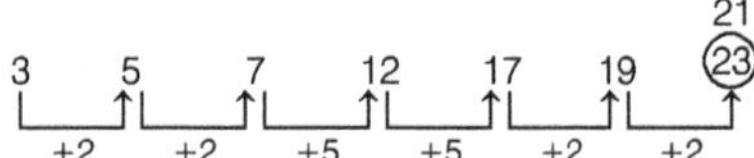

Hence, number 23 is wrong and should be replaced by 21.

4. (*d*) The pattern is as follows

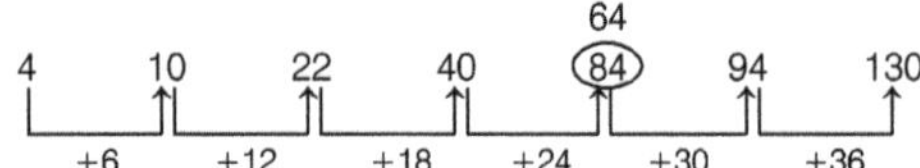

Hence, number 84 is wrong and should be replaced by 64.

5. (*a*) The pattern is as follows

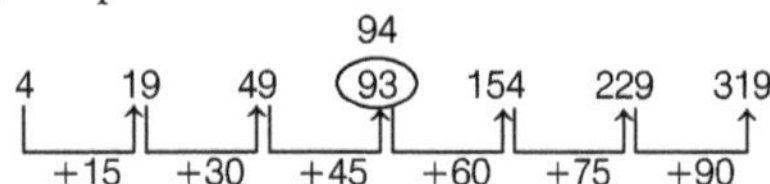

Hence, number 93 is wrong and should be replaced by 94.

6. (*d*) The pattern is as follows

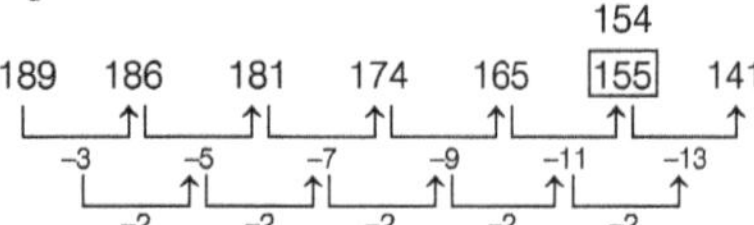

Hence, 155 is the wrong number and will be replaced by 154.

7. (*d*) The pattern is as follows

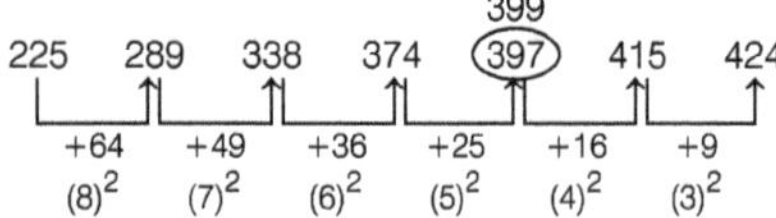

Hence, number 397 is wrong and should be replaced by 399.

8. (*e*) The pattern is as follows

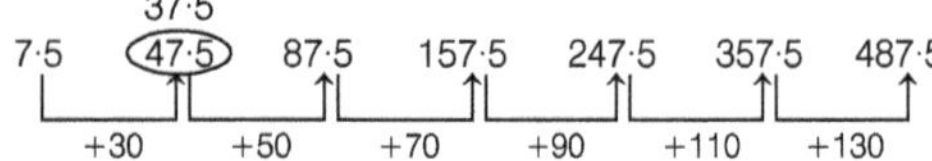

Hence, number 47.5 is wrong and should be replaced by 37.5.

9. (*d*) The pattern is as follows

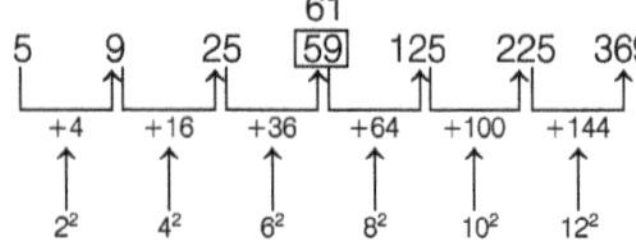

Hence, 59 is the wrong number and will be replaced by 61.

10. (*d*) The pattern is as follows

Hence, number 9 is wrong and should be replaced by 10.

11. (*d*) The pattern is as follows

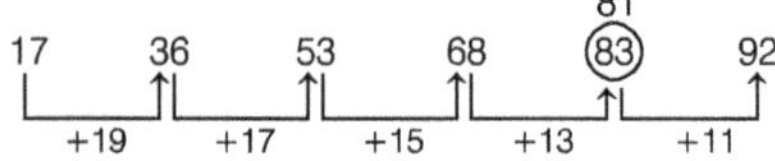

Hence, number 83 is wrong and should be replaced by 81.

12. (*b*) The pattern is as follows

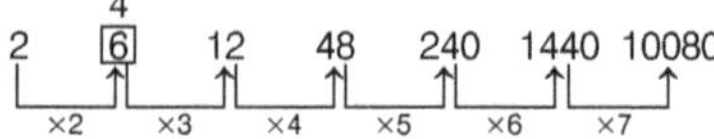

Hence, number 6 is the wrong and should be replaced by 4.

13. (*a*) The pattern is as follows

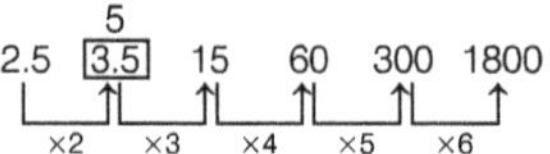

Hence, number 3.5 is Wrong and should be replaced by 5.

14. (*d*) The pattern is as follows

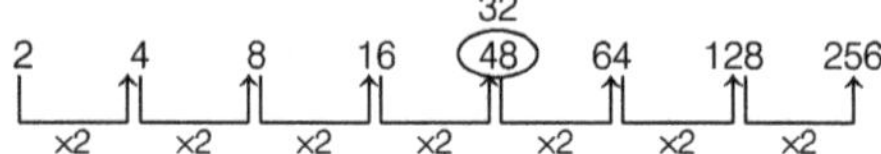

Hence, number 48 is wrong and should be replaced by 32.

15. (*b*) In this series, all the numbers are the multiples of 11, except the number 427 which is not a multiple of 11.

Hence, number 427 is wrong and should be replaced by the multiple of 11.

16. (*d*) The pattern is as follows

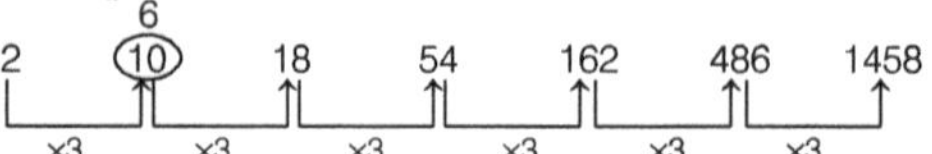

Hence, number 10 is wrong and should be replaced by 6.

17. (*d*) The pattern is as follows

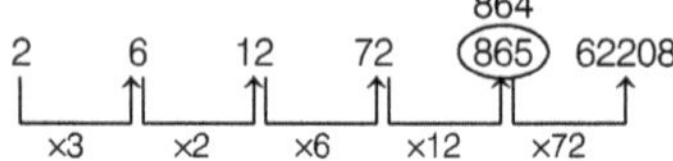

Here, $3 \times 2 = 6,\ 6 \times 2 = 12,\ 12 \times 6 = 72$

Hence, number 865 is wrong and should be replaced by 864.

18. (*e*) The pattern is as follows

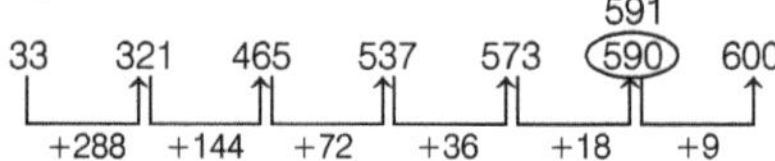

Hence, number 590 is wrong and should be replaced by 591.

19. (*d*) The numbers are

$$7 \times 8, 8 \times 9, 9 \times 10, 10 \times 11, 11 \times 12 \text{ and } 12 \times 13.$$

Hence, number 150 is wrong and must be replaced by (12×13) i.e., 156.

20. (*d*) The pattern is as follows

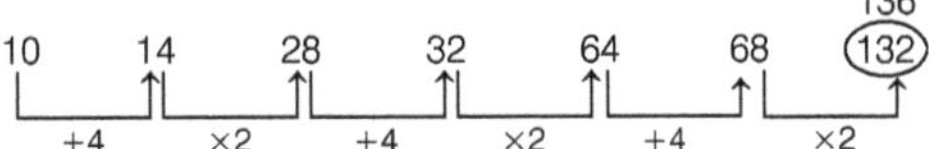

Hence, number 132 is wrong and should be replaced by 136.

21. (*a*) The pattern is as follows

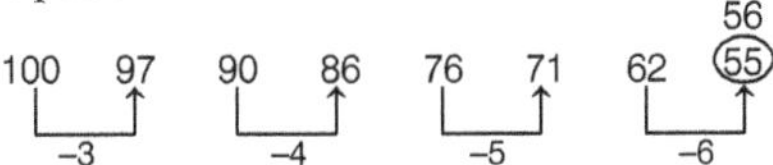

Hence, number 55 is wrong and should be replaced by 56.

22. (*b*) The pattern is as follows

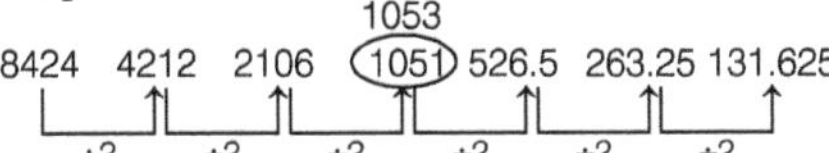

Hence, number 1051 is wrong and should be replaced by 1053.

23. (*c*) The pattern is as follows

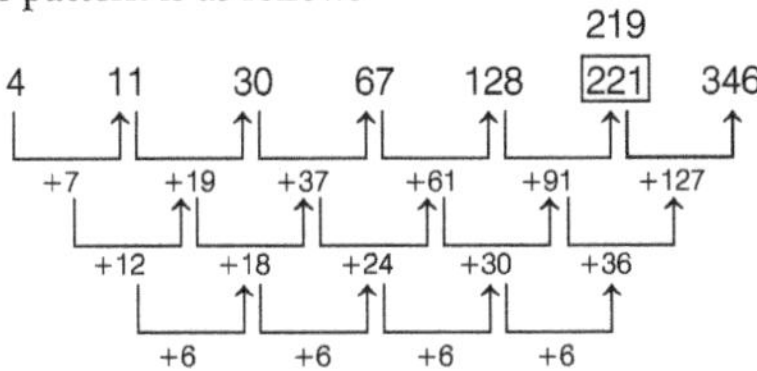

Hence, number 221 is wrong and should be replaced by 219.

24. (*c*) The pattern is as follows

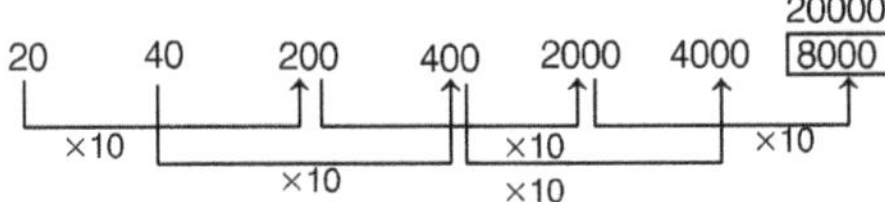

Hence, number 8000 is wrong and should be replaced by 20000.

25. (*a*) The pattern is as follows

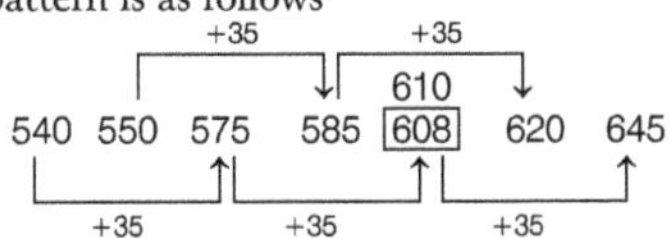

Hence, number 608 is wrong and should be replaced by 610.

26. (*b*) The pattern is as follows

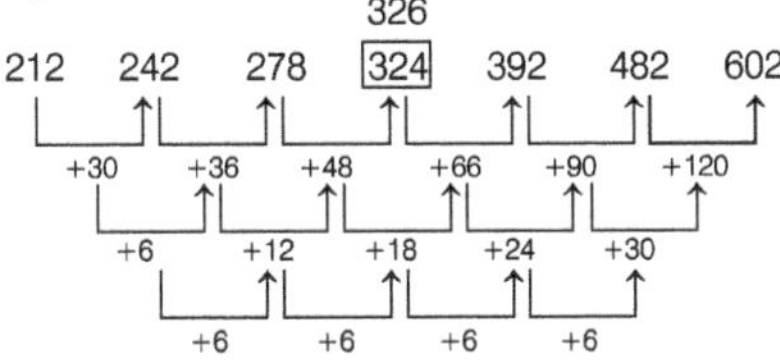

Hence, 324 is the wrong number and should be replaced by 326.

27. (*d*) The pattern is as follows

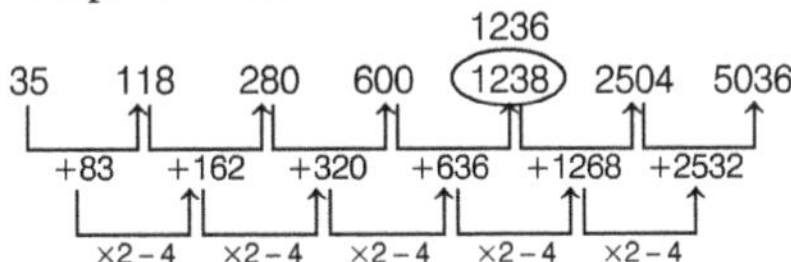

Hence, number 1238 is wrong and should be replaced by 1236.

28. (*b*) The pattern is as follows

$2^3 + 3 = 11, 3^3 + 3 = 30, 4^3 + 3 = 67,$

$5^3 + 3 = 128 \neq 120,\ 6^3 + 3 = 219, 7^3 + 3 = 346$

Hence, number 120 is wrong and should be replaced by 128.

29. (*d*) The pattern is as follows

17

1 5 9 (15) 25 37 49

↓ ↓ ↓ ↓ ↓ ↓ ↓

1^2 (2^2+1) 3^2 (4^2+1) 5^2 (6^2+1) 7^2

Hence, number 15 is wrong and should be replaced by 17.

30. (*d*) The pattern is as follows

64

9 16 25 36 49 (61)

↓ ↓ ↓ ↓ ↓ ↓

$(3)^2$ $(4)^2$ $(5)^2$ $(6)^2$ $(7)^2$ $(8)^2$

Hence, number 61 is wrong and should be replaced by 64.

31. (*a*) The pattern is as follows

1260

189 701 1044 [1263] 1385 1449 1476

+512 $(8)^3$, +343 $(7)^3$, +216 $(6)^3$, +125 $(5)^3$, +64 $(4)^3$, +27 $(3)^3$

Hence, 1263 is the wrong number and should be replaced by 1260.

32. (*d*) The numbers are cubes of prime numbers *i.e.*, $2^3, 3^3, 5^3, 7^3, 11^3$. Clearly, none is wrong.

33. (*c*) The pattern of the series is

$$2^3 = 8, 3^3 = 27, 4^3 = 64, 5^3 = 125$$

Hence, number 225 is wrong and should be replaced by 125.

34. (*b*) Series follows the pattern $2 \times 1 + 1 = 3, 3 \times 2 + 2 = 8,$ $8 \times 3 + 3 = 27, 27 \times 4 + 4 = 112$ and so on.
Hence, the number 9 is wrong and should be replaced by 8.

35. (*c*) The pattern is as follows

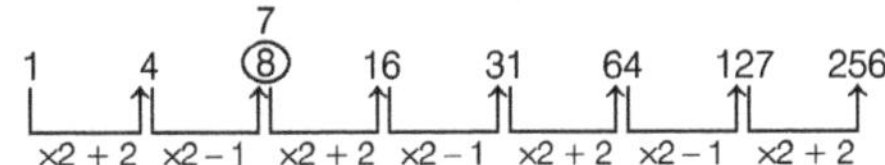

Hence, number 8 is wrong and should be replaced by 7.

36. (*e*) The pattern is as follows

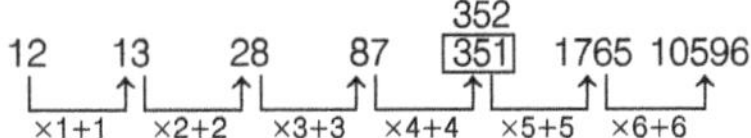

Hence, 351 is the wrong number and should be replaced by 352.

37. (*d*) The pattern is as follows

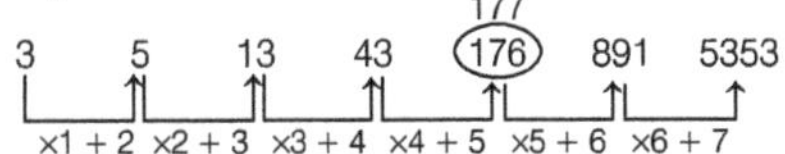

Hence, number 176 is wrong and should be replaced by 177.

38. (*c*) The pattern is as follows

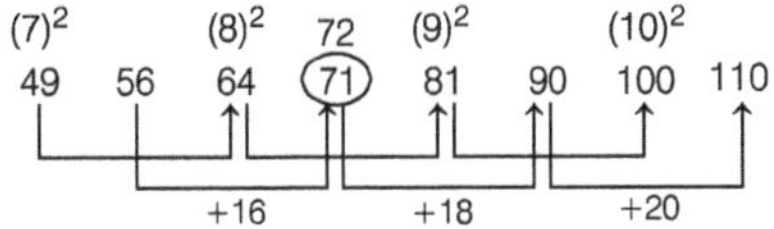

Terms at odd places are $7^2, 8^2, 9^2, 10^2$ and terms at even places are 56, 72, 90, 110 *i.e.*, with differences of 16, 18 and 20.
Hence, number 71 is wrong and should be replaced by 72.

39. (*b*) 12, 18, 30, 48, 72, 126, 204
Above series is following the sequence of

$$12 + 18 = 30$$
$$18 + 30 = 48$$
$$30 + 48 = 78 \neq \boxed{72}$$
$$48 + 78 = 126$$
$$78 + 126 = 204$$

Hence, 72 is the wrong number and should be replaced by 78.

40. (*b*) The pattern is as follows

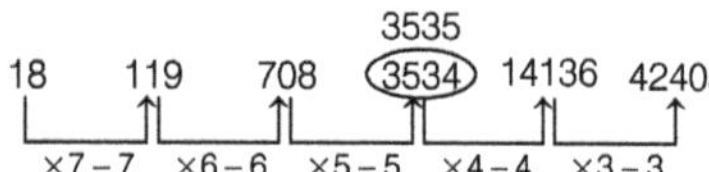

Hence, number 3534 is wrong and should be replaced by 3535.

41. (*c*) The pattern of the series is as follows

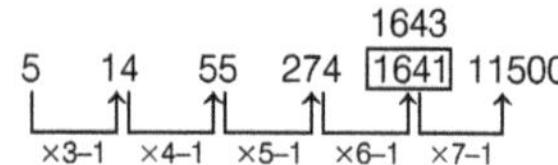

∴ Wrong number is 1641.

42. (*d*) The pattern of the series is as follows

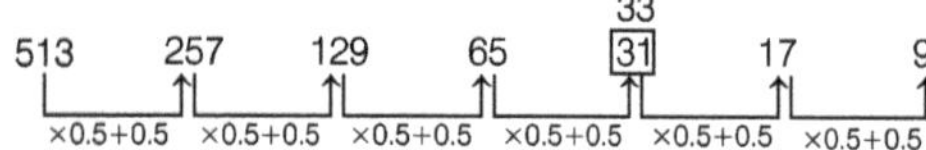

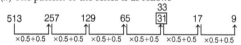

∴ Wrong number is 31.

43. (*b*) The pattern is as follows

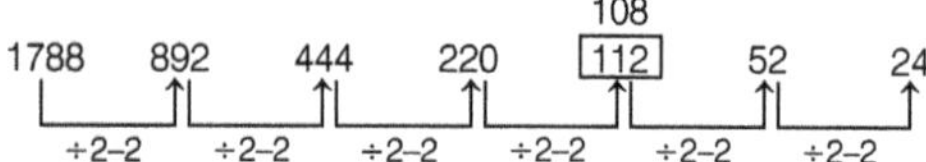

Hence, number 112 is wrong and should be replaced by 108.

44. (*d*) The pattern is as follows

$$7 \times 2 - 2 \times 1 = 12$$
$$12 \times 4 - (4 \times 2) = 40$$
$$40 \times 6 - (6 \times 3) = 222$$
$$222 \times 8 - (8 \times 4) \neq 1742 = 1744$$
$$1744 \times 10 - (10 \times 5) = 17390$$
$$17390 \times 12 - (12 \times 6) = 208608$$

Hence, number 1742 is wrong and should be replaced by 1744.

45. (*c*) The pattern is as follows

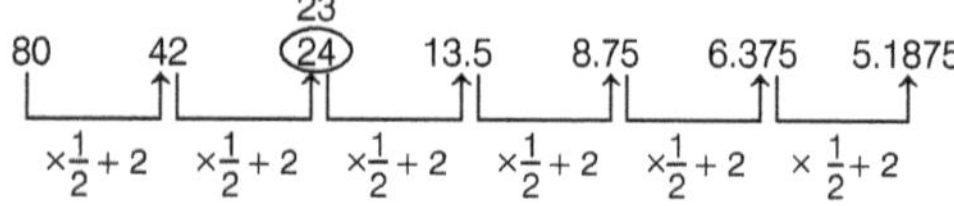

Hence, number 24 is wrong and should be replaced by 23.

46. (*d*) The pattern is as follows

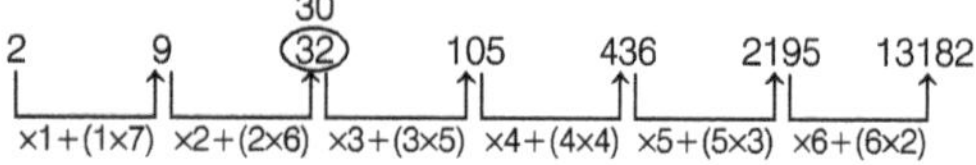

Hence, number 32 is wrong and should be replaced by 30.

47. (*c*) The pattern is as follows

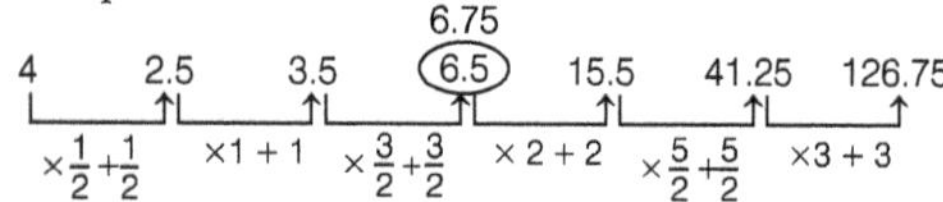

Hence, number 6.5 is wrong and should be replaced by 6.75.

48. (*c*) The given sequence is the combination of two series.

I. 3, 8, 13, 18, 23 II. 2, (9), 22, 32, 42
12

The pattern (I) is (+5) and the pattern in (II) is (+10). So, in (II), number 9 is wrong and should be replaced by (2+10), *i.e.*, 12.

49. (*d*) The first digits of the numbers form the series 1, 2, 3, 4, 5 the second digits form the series 2, 3, 4, 5, 6 and the third digits form the series 3, 4, 5, 6, 7 while the last digit in each of the numbers is 6. Hence, number 5686 is wrong and must be replaced by 5676.

50. (*b*) The given sequence is a combination of two series

+4 +2 +4 +2
I. 1, 5, 7, 11, 12, 13

+4 +2 +4 +2
II. 5, 9, 11, 15, 17

The pattern in both I and II is + 4, + 2, + 4, + 2.
Hence, number 12 is wrong and must be replaced by (11 + 2) *i.e.*, 13.

51. (*c*) The pattern is as follows

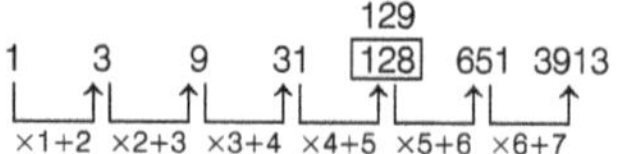

Hence, number 128 is wrong and should be replaced by 129.

52. (*a*) The pattern is as follows

21
291 147 75 39 22 12 7.5
÷2+1.5 ÷2+1.5 ÷2+1.5 ÷2+1.5 ÷2+1.5 ÷2+1.5

Hence, number 22 is the wrong and should be replaced by 21.

53. (*e*) The pattern is as follows

26
26 27 34 58 106 186 306
$+1^2-1$ $+3^2-1$ $+5^2-1$ $+7^2-1$ $+9^2-1$ $+11^2-1$

Hence, number 27 is wrong and should be replaced by 26.

54. (*d*) The pattern is as follows

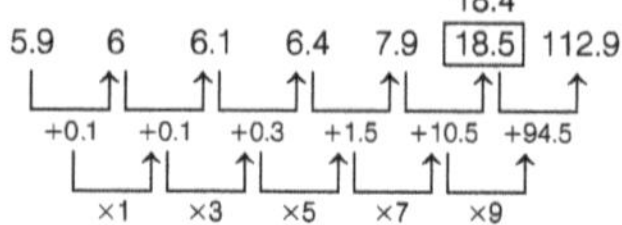

Hence, number 18.5 is wrong and should be replaced by 18.4.

55. (*b*) The pattern is as follows

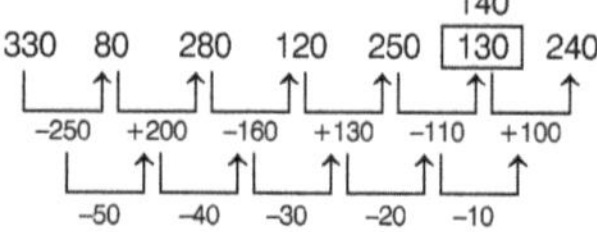

Hence, number 130 is wrong and should be replaced by 140.

56. (*c*) The pattern is as follows

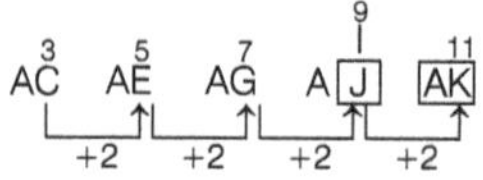

Hence, J should be replaced by I.

57. (*c*) The pattern is as follows

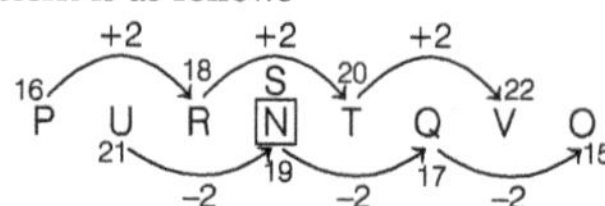

Hence, N should be replaced by S.

58. (*b*) The pattern is as follows

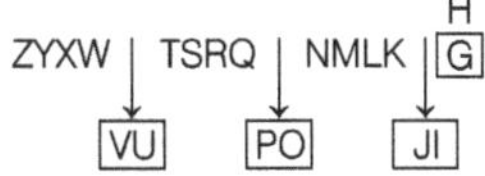

Hence, G should be replaced by H.

59. (*b*) The pattern is as follows

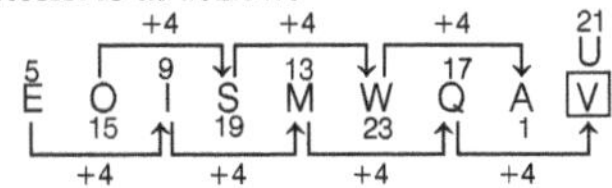

Hence, V should be replaced by U.

60. (*a*) The pattern is as follows

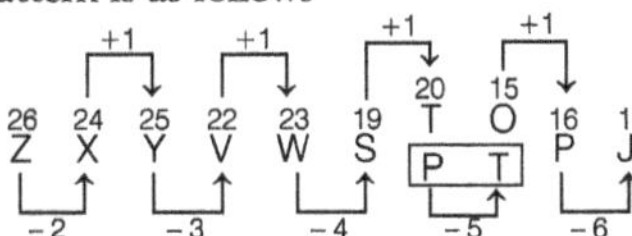

Hence, PT should be replaced by TO.

61. (*b*) The pattern is as follows

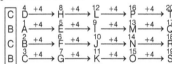

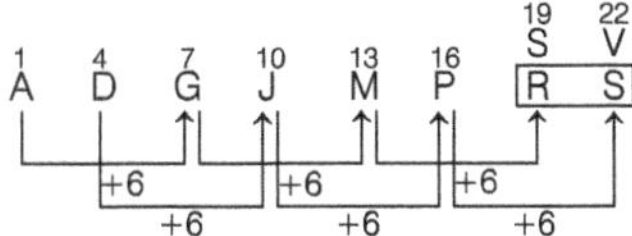

Hence, RS should be replaced by SV.

62. (*c*) The pattern is as follows

1 3 6 8 11 13 16 18

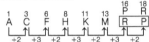

A C F H K M [R P] → P R

+2 +3 +2 +3 +2 +3 +2

Hence, RP should be replaced by PR.

63. (*c*) The pattern is as follows

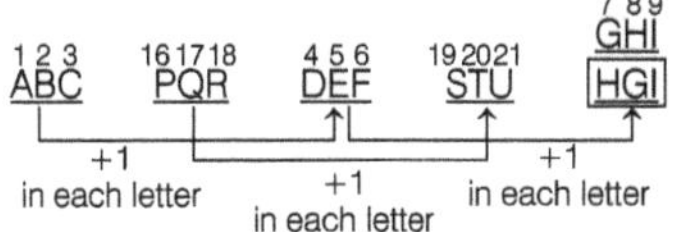

Hence, HGI should be replaced by GHI.

64. (*a*) The pattern is as follows

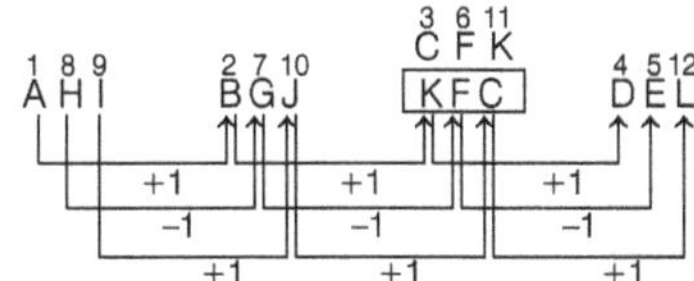

Hence, KFC should be replaced by CFK.

65. (*d*) The pattern is as follows

S(19) −1→ R(18) −1→ Q(17) −1→ P(16) −1→ N | O(15)

H(8) +1→ I(9) +1→ J(10) +1→ K(11) +1→ M | L(12)

G(7) −1→ F(6) −1→ E(5) −1→ D(4) −1→ B | C(3)

Hence, NMB should be replaced by OLC.

66. (*c*) The pattern is as follows

C | D(4) +4→ H(8) +4→ L(12) +4→ P(16) +4→ T(20)

B | A(1) +4→ E(5) +4→ I(9) +4→ M(13) +4→ Q(17)

C | B(2) +4→ F(6) +4→ J(10) +4→ N(14) +4→ R(18)

B | C(3) +4→ G(7) +4→ K(11) +4→ O(15) +4→ S(19)

Hence, CBCB should be replaced by DABC.

TYPE 05

Continuous Pattern Series

Continuous pattern series generally consists of letters of English alphabet or numbers or combination of letters and numbers, where the letters/numbers are arranged in a certain pattern. However, some letters/numbers are missing from the series.

The candidate is required to identify the pattern and accordingly find the proper sequence of these missing letters/numbers from the given alternatives.

Following examples will give you a better idea about the type of questions.

DIRECTIONS ~ (Example Nos. 58-60) *Find the missing term in the following series.*

Ex 58 _ aa_ba_bb_ab_aab

(a) aaabb (b) babab
(c) bbaab (d) None of these

Solution (c) The series is as follows

baab/baab/baab/baab

∴ Required answer = bbaab

Ex 59 P_R_S_QRR_ « SSC CHSL 2017

(a) QPRS (b) QRPS (c) QRPP (d) QPSR

Solution (b) The series is as follows

PQRRS/PQRRS

∴ Required answer = QRPS

Ex 60 12_41_34123_ _234 « SSC CGL 2015

(a) 3212 (b) 2134 (c) 3241 (d) 1432

Solution (c) The series is as follows

1234/1234/1234/1234

∴ Required answer = 3241

Ex 61 In the following question, which set of letters and numbers, when sequentially placed at the gaps in the given series, shall complete it? « RRB ALP 2018

1_2x_bb_yy_cc_6zzz

(a) a345c (b) 3a45c
(c) 3a45b (d) 3a4b5

Solution (a) The pattern is as follows

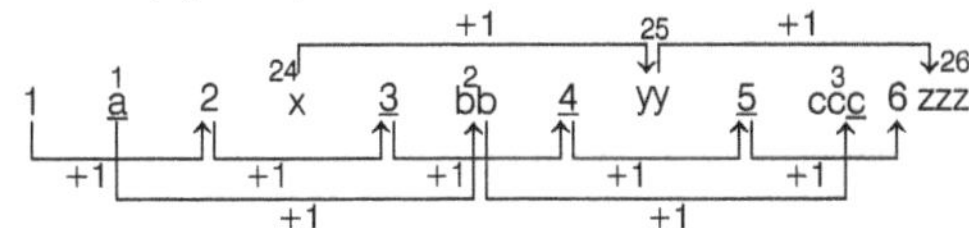

∴ Required answer = a345c

Practice / CORNER 5.5

DIRECTIONS ~ (Q. Nos. 1-31) *In each of the following letter series, some of the letters are missing which are given in that order as one of the alternatives below it. Select the correct alternative.*

1. ybb_byy_y_byb_yby « SSC Steno 2019
(a) ccyc (b) ybby (c) ybyb (d) yybb

2. _baa_abb_a_a_baa « IB ACIO 2017
(a) bbaabb (b) acbba (c) baabb (d) ababa

3. CDEF_EDC_DE_FED_ « SSC 10+2 2017
(a) FCFC (b) FCCD (c) DCCC (d) DEFC

4. gfe_ig_eii_fei_gf_ii « SSC CGL 2016
(a) ifgie (b) figie (c) eifgi (d) ifige

5. h_t_l_tt_lht_m_htt_l « SSC CGL 2016
(a) m m h t l t m
(b) h m m t t l m
(c) t m h m t l m
(d) l m t m h m t

6. llmn_oppq_rstt_vvw_xy « UPSSSC 2018
(a) n q v w (b) m p v w (c) n r u x (d) m r v x

7. ac_ga_eg_ce_
(a) dbag (b) ecag (c) deag (d) ebdg

8. ba_ b_aab_a_b
(a) abaa (b) abba (c) baab (d) babb

9. a_c_ ba_ca_cb
(a) abcc (b) acba (c) bcaa (d) bcba

10. b_ab_ b_aab_b
(a) abbb (b) abba (c) baaa (d) aaba

11. ac_cab_baca_aaa_aba
(a) aabc (b) aacb (c) babb (d) bcbb

12. a_ cacbc_ baca_ _ b « SSC CGL 2015
(a) baba (b) babc (c) abab (d) cacb

13. cccbb_aa_cc_bbbaa_c
(a) acbc (b) baca (c) baba (d) aaba

14. _opqn_pq no_qnop_
(a) onqp (b) noqp (c) nopq (d) pqno

15. a_ ba _ bb _ ab_ a
(a) baab (b) aaba (c) abab (d) baaa

16. f_hg_fh_gf_hg_fh_g « SSC CGL 2019
(a) gfgfhf (b) fghfgh (c) ghfghf (d) hfghfg

17. _b_baaabb_a_ _bb_a_
(a) abbaaba (b) ababbaa (c) babaaba (d) baabaab

18. _sr_tr_srs_r_srst_
(a) ttssrr (b) tsrtsr (c) strtrs (d) tstttr

19. a_b_ba_ _b_ ba
(a) bbaab (b) bbabb (c) aabab (d) aabba

20. aba_ccdab_b_ _dababc_ _ « SSC 10+2 2020
(a) bbaab (b) babba (c) baaba (d) aabba

21. _bb_c_bg _b_ g
(a) cbgbc (b) cgbcb (c) cgbcc (d) gbcbb

22. _A'B_ B'AA' _ BB' _ A
(a) A'BAB' (b) A'B'AB (c) ABAB (d) AB'A'B

23. a_ba_c_aad_aa_ea
(a) babbb (b) babbd (c) babbc (d) bacde

24. _zy_zxy_yxzx_zyx_xy
(a) yxzyz (b) zxyzy (c) yzxyx (d) xyzzy

25. aa_aabb_b_aa_aabb_bb
(a) bbbaa (b) bbbba (c) aabbb (d) babba

26. abab_b_bcb_ dcdcded _ d « CSAT 2020
(a) abcd (b) abde (c) acce (d) bcde

27. a_b_c_a _ bc _b _cb
(a) acbcab (b) ccbcca (c) ccaccb (d) cacabe

28. pqr_ _ rs _ rs _ _ s_ q_
(a) spqpprr
(b) pqrrppq
(c) sqppqpr
(d) sqprrqr

29. mnonopqopqrs _ _ _ _ _ _
(a) mnopqr (b) oqrstu (c) pqrstu (d) qrstup

30. abc_yabc_xw abcdev_
(a) zdu (b) d x u (c) c d u (d) z y w
(e) None of these

31. c_a c c a a_a a_b c_b « UPSC CSAT 2019
(a) abba (b) cbbb (c) bbbb (d) cccc

DIRECTIONS ~ (Q. Nos. 32-36) *In each of the following number series, some of the numbers are missing which are given in that order as one of the alternatives below it. Select the correct alternative.*

32. 87_5_7258_ _5872_
(a) 28725
(b) 28752
(c) 28275
(d) 28572

33. 75_ _7_12_5_2
(a) 12517 (b) 12175 (c) 12571 (d) 12715

34. 32_3_732_ _27
(a) 7237 (b) 2737 (c) 7223 (d) 7273

35. 87_8 8_78_ _78_778
(a) 87877
(b) 77788
(c) 88777
(d) 77878

36. 9_ _990_9_00_
(a) 9900
(b) 00099
(c) 90009
(d) 00990

37. In the following question letters and numbers are in accordance with a pattern. Discover the pattern and pick the correct answer from the answer choices.
Z 26_1_25 B 2 X _ _ 3 « SSC CGL 2014
(a) A Y 24 C
(b) B X 23 D
(c) Z X 21 D
(d) X Y Z 22

Answers WITH EXPLANATIONS

1. (*b*) Series pattern is as follows
ybby/byyb/ybby/byyb/y
∴ Required answer = ybby

2. (*d*) Series pattern is as follows
abaa/babb/aaba/a baa
∴ Required answer = ababa

3. (*a*) Series pattern is as follows
CDEF/FEDC/CDEF/FEDC
∴ Required answer = FCFC

4. (*a*) Series pattern is as follows
gfeii/gfeii/gfeii/gfeii
∴ Required answer = ifgie

5. (*c*) Series pattern is as follows
httml/httml/httml/httml
∴ Required answer = tmhmtlm

6. (*c*) Series pattern is as follows
llmnnoppqrrsttuvvwxxy
∴ Required answer = nrux

7. (*b*) Series pattern is as follows
aceg/aceg/aceg
∴ Required answer = ecag

8. (*b*) Series pattern is as follows
baab/baab/baab
∴ Required answer = abba

9. (*d*) Series pattern is as follows
abc/cba/bca/acb
∴ Required answer = bcba

10. (*d*) Series pattern is as follows
baabab/baabab
∴ Required answer = aaba

11. (*a*) aca/cab/aba/cab/aaa/cab/a
∴ Required answer = aabc

12. (*b*) Series pattern is as follows
abcac/bcaba/cab cb
∴ Required answer = babc

13. (*b*) Series pattern is as follows
cccbbbaaa/cccbbbaaa/c
∴ Required answer = baca

14. (*c*) Series pattern is as follows
nopq/nopq/nopq/nopq
∴ Required answer = nopq

15. (*a*) Series pattern is as follows
ab ba/ a bb a/abb a
∴ Required answer = baab

16. (*c*) Series pattern is as follows
fgh/ghf/hfg/fgh/ghf/hfg
∴ Required answer = ghfghf

17. (*a*) Series pattern is as follows
abb/baa/abb/baa/abb/baa
∴ Required answer = abbaaba

18. (*d*) Series pattern is as follows
tsr/str/tsr/str/tsr/str
∴ Required answer = tsttr

19. (*b*) Series pattern is as follows
abb/bba/a bb/bba
∴ Required answer = bbabb

20. (*c*) The pattern of the series is as follows
a b a b c c d/a b a b c c d/a b a b c c d
⇒ baccd

21. (*b*) Series pattern is as follows
cb bg /cb bg/c bb g
∴ Required answer = cgbcb

22. (*c*) Series pattern is as follows
AA′ B/BB′A/A′AB/B′ BA
∴ Required answer = ABAB

23. (*d*) Series pattern is as follows
abba/acca/adda/aeea
∴ Required answer = bacde

24. (*a*) Series pattern is as follows
yzy/xzx/yzy/xzx/yzy/xzx/y
∴ Required answer = yxzyz

25. (*d*) Series pattern is as follows
a a b aa/ bb a bb/ aa b aa / bb a bb
∴ Required answer=babba

26. (*c*) Given series is as follows
ab ab a/bcbcb/cdcdc/deded
∴ Missing letters = a, c, c, e

27. (*b*) Series pattern is as follows
a c b/c c b/a c b/c c b/ a c b
∴ Required answer = 'ccbcca'

28. (*c*) Series pattern is as follows
p q r s/ q r s p/ r s p q/s p q r
∴ Required answer = sqppqpr

29. (*c*) Series pattern is as follows
mno/nopq/opqrs/p q r s t u
∴ Required answer =pqrstu

30. (*a*) Series pattern is as follows
abczy / abcdxw / abcdevu
∴ Required answer = zdu

31. (*b*) Series pattern is as follows
ccacc/aabaa/bbcbb
∴ Required answer = cbbb

32. (*a*) Series pattern is as follows
= 8725/8725/87 25/8725
∴ Required answer = 28725

33. (*c*) Series pattern is as follows
= 751 2/7512/7512
∴ Required answer = 12571

34. (*d*) Series pattern is as follows
= 327/327/327/327
∴ Required answer = 7273

35. (*d*) Series pattern is as follows
= 8778/8778/8 778/8778
∴ Required answer = 77878

36. (*b*) Series pattern is as follows
= 90 09/9009/9009
∴ Required answer = 00099

37. (*a*) The number written after each letter is its position in the English alphabet.
Z → 26, A → 1, Y → 25,
B → 2, X → 24, C → 3
So, the complete pattern is
Z 26 A 1 Y 25 B 2 X 24 C 3
Required answer A Y 24 C

Master Exercise

DIRECTIONS ~ (Q. Nos. 1-59) *Find the missing number in the series given below.*

1. 1.5, 3, 4.5, 6, 7.5, 9, ?, 12, 13.5, 15 « UPSSSC Junior Assist. 2017
(a) 9.5 (b) 10
(c) 10.5 (d) 11.5

2. – 3.2, – 2.3, – 1.4, – 0.5, ?, 1.3 « UPSSSC Mandi Parishad 2019
(a) 0.4 (b) 0.5
(c) 0.6 (d) 0.3

3. 173, 195, 217, 239, ? « Delhi Police MTS 2018
(a) 261 (b) 259
(c) 263 (d) 260

4. 3, 11, 23, 39, ?
(a) 58 (b) 59
(c) 60 (d) 61

5. 1, 3, 7 13, 21, 31, 43, ?
(a) 55 (b) 57
(c) 59 (d) 61

6. 1, 9, 17, 33, 49, 73, ? « UPSC Assistant Commandant 2019
(a) 99 (b) 97
(c) 95 (d) 91

7. 16, 22, 34, 58, 106, ?, 394
(a) 178 (b) 175
(c) 288 (d) 202

8. 101, 123, 147, 173, ? « SSC Constable 2018
(a) 236 (b) 201
(c) 214 (d) 223

9. 7, 8, 11, 16, 23, ?
(a) 31 (b) 32
(c) 37 (d) 40

10. 17, 43, 81, 131, ?
(a) 375 (b) 468
(c) 300 (d) 193

11. 30, 68, 130, 222, ?, 520, 738
(a) 420 (b) 350
(c) 250 (d) 280

12. 15, 17, 20, 22, 27, 29, ?, ?
(a) 31, 38 (b) 36, 38
(c) 36, 43 (d) 38, 45

13. 5, 12, ?, 41, 87, 214 « IB ACIO 2017
(a) 19 (b) 35
(c) 22 (d) 26

14. –1, 5, 15, 29, ? « UGC NET 2018
(a) 59 (b) 63 (c) 36 (d) 47

15. 3, 4, 7, 11, 18, 29, ?
(a) 31 (b) 39
(c) 43 (d) 47

16. 0,1, 1, 2, 3, 5, 8, 13, 21, ?
(a) 34 (b) 35
(c) 33 (d) 36

17. 1, 3, 4, 8, 15, 27, ? « CGPSC 2017
(a) 37 (b) 44
(c) 48 (d) 55
(e) None of these

18. 1, 2, 3, 5, 8, 13, ? « MP Constable 2017
(a) 21 (b) 24 (c) 18 (d) 17

19. 37, 52, 77, 112, ? « SSC Steno 2019
(a) 157 (b) 156
(c) 167 (d) 155

20. 6, 13, 27, 48, ? « MP Constable 2017
(a) 76 (b) 94
(c) 136 (d) 121

21. 121, 112, ?, 97, 91, 86
(a) 102 (b) 108
(c) 99 (d) 104

22. 975, 864, 753, 642, ?
(a) 431 (b) 314
(c) 531 (d) 532

23. 285, 253, 221, 189,? « SSC Steno 2013
(a) 122 (b) 153
(c) 157 (d) 151

24. 758, 753, 748, 744, 740, 736, ?
(a) 732 (b) 733 (c) 734 (d) 735

25. 3, 9, 36, 180, ? « SSC Steno 2019
(a) 1080 (b) 900
(c) 1260 (d) 980

26. 6, 42, ?, 1260, 5040, 15120, 30240
(a) 546 (b) 424
(c) 252 (d) 328
(e) None of these

27. 14, 16, 35, 109, 441, ?
(a) 2651 (b) 2205
(c) 2315 (d) 2211

28. 3, 22, ?, 673, 2696, 8093
(a) 133 (b) 155
(c) 156 (d) 134

29. 5, 11, 23, 47, 95, ? « SSC CGL 2013
(a) 190 (b) 191
(c) 161 (d) 169

30. 1, 3, 7, 15, 31, ? « SSC 10+2 2013
(a) 37 (b) 36
(c) 73 (d) 63

31. 13 (168) 13, 14(181) 13, 15 (?) 13
(a) 190 (b) 196
(c) 195 (d) 194

32. 14, ?, 13, 17.5, 21.75
(a) 10 (b) 12
(c) 12.5 (d) 13.25

33. 2, 5, 9, 19, ? « RRB Group D 2018
(a) 37 (b) 43 (c) 41 (d) 36

34. 10, 33, 102, 309, ? « SSC Steno 2013
(a) 1030 (b) 1050
(c) 928 (d) 930

35. 2807, 1400, 697, ?, 171, 84 « SSC MTS 2019
(a) 697 (b) 84
(c) 371 (d) 346

36. 4, 9, 20, 43,?
(a) 90 (b) 84 (c) 96 (d) 95

37. 8, 24, 12, ?, 18, 54
(a) 28 (b) 36 (c) 46 (d) 38

38. 48, 24, 72, 36, 108, ?
(a) 115 (b) 216
(c) 121 (d) 54

39. 31, 13, 45, 54, ?, 63
(a) 36 (b) 54 (c) 61 (d) 58

40. 5, 7, 11, ?, 35
(a) 23 (b) 17 (c) 13 (d) 19

41. 3, 5, 7, ?, 13, 17, 19, 23
(a) 9 (b) 11 (c) 8 (d) 10
(e) None of these

42. 823543, 46656, 3125, 256, ?, 4, 1
(a) 28 (b) 27
(c) 36 (d) 49

43. 0, 2, 6, 12, 20, ? « Delhi Police MTS 2018
(a) 28 (b) 29 (c) 30 (d) 31

44. 8, 27, 64, ? « SSC Steno 2013
(a) 216 (b) 224
(c) 64 (d) 125

45. 90, 61, 52, 63, 94, ?, 18
(a) 72 (b) 46
(c) 54 (d) 81

46. 875, 874, 866, 839, 775, 650, 434, ?
(a) 322 (b) 281
(c) 91 (d) 18

47. 4, 18, ?, 100, 180, 294
« IB ACIO 2013
(a) 32 (b) 36
(c) 48 (d) 40

48. 7, 8, 24, 105, 361, ?
(a) 986 (b) 617
(c) 486 (d) 1657
(e) None of these

49. 2, 8, 18, 32, 50, ?
(a) 64 (b) 72
(c) 70 (d) 68

50. 2, 3, 4, 9, 3, 4, 5, 12, 4, 5, 6, 15, 5, ?, 7, 18
(a) 8 (b) 7 (c) 6 (d) 9

51. 2, 29, 38, 47, ?
(a) 59 (b) 56 (c) 52 (d) 58

52. 2, 9, 23, 3, 8, 25, 4, ?, 27
(a) 7 (b) 29
(c) 23 (d) 14

53. 1, 0, 4, 2, 9, 6, 16, 12, 25, ?
« SSC Steno 2019
(a) 36 (b) 21 (c) 27 (d) 20

54. 7, 10, 8, 11, 9, 12, ? « CLAT 2018
(a) 7 (b) 10
(c) 12 (d) 13

55. 11, 13, 17, 19, 23, ?, ? « CGPSC 2017
(a) 27 and 29 (b) 31 and 33
(c) 31 and 35 (d) 29 and 31
(e) None of these

56. 11, 7, 20, 12, 38, ?, 74, 42
« CGPSC 2017
(a) 32 (b) 28
(c) 26 (d) 24
(e) None of these

57. 4/12/95, 1/1/96, 29/1/96, 26/2/96, ?
« UPSC 2018
(a) 24/3/96 (b) 25/3/96
(c) 26/3/96 (d) 27/3/96

58. 3, 13, 1113, 3113, ?
« UPSSSC Technical Assist. Agri. service 2018
(a) 331113 (b) 132113
(c) 131313 (d) 313311

59. 82, 70, 76, 64, 70, 58, ?
« RRB NTPC 2016
(a) 52 (b) 76
(c) 64 (d) 48

DIRECTIONS ~ (Q. Nos. 60-85) *In each of these questions, a number series is given. In each series, only one number is wrong. Find out the wrong number.*

60. 6 7 9 13 26 37 69
(a) 7 (b) 26
(c) 69 (d) 37
(e) None of these

61. 22, 37, 52, 67, 84, 97
« SSC MTS 2013
(a) 52 (b) 84 (c) 97 (d) 67

62. 4, 7, 13, 25, 49, 97, 153
(a) 25 (b) 49
(c) 97 (d) 153

63. 7, 56, 447, 3584, 28672
(a) 3584 (b) 56
(c) 7 (d) 447

64. 32, 43, 45, 54, 65, 76
« MP Constable 2017
(a) 76 (b) 43
(c) 54 (d) 45

65. 10, 14, 28, 32, 64, 68, 132
(a) 28 (b) 32
(c) 132 (d) 64

66. 87, 54, 28, 13, 5, 2, 2
(a) 28 (b) 54
(c) 13 (d) 2

67. 11, 42, 39, 164, 525, 421, 749
(a) 164 (b) 421
(c) 525 (d) 749

68. 10, 41, 94, 1624, 2516, 3625, 4936
(a) 1624 (b) 2516
(c) 3625 (d) 4936

69. 1 3 10 36 152 760 4632
(a) 3 (b) 36
(c) 4632 (d) 760
(e) None of these

70. 258, 130, 66, 34, 18, 8, 6
(a) 130 (b) 66
(c) 34 (d) 8

71. 2, 6, 24, 96, 285, 568, 567
(a) 6 (b) 24
(c) 96 (d) 285

72. 4, 5, 14, 39, 103, 169, 290
(a) 5 (b) 14
(c) 39 (d) 103

73. 2, 3, 6, 15, 37.5, 157.5, 630
(a) 3 (b) 6
(c) 15 (d) 37.5

74. 2, 5, 11, 27, 58, 121, 248
(a) 5 (b) 11
(c) 27 (d) 58

75. 1, 2, 6, 21, 86, 445, 2676
(a) 2 (b) 6
(c) 21 (d) 86

76. 644, 328, 164, 84, 44, 24, 14
(a) 328 (b) 164
(c) 84 (d) 44

77. 157.5, 45, 15, 6, 3, 2, 1
(a) 1 (b) 2 (c) 6 (d) 157.5

78. 5531 5506 5425 5304 5135 4910 4621
(a) 5531 (b) 5425
(c) 4621 (d) 5136
(e) None of these

79. 864, 420, 200, 96, 40, 16, 6
(a) 420 (b) 200
(c) 96 (d) 40

80. 4, 12, 30, 68, 146, 302, 622
(a) 12 (b) 30
(c) 68 (d) 302

81. 3, 6, 9, 22.5, 67.5, 236.25, 945
(a) 6 (b) 9 (c) 22.5 (d) 67.5

82. 6072, 1008, 200, 48, 14, 5, 3
(a) 1008 (b) 200 (c) 48 (d) 14

83. 10, 13, 26, 37, 51, 85, 154
(a) 10 (b) 26 (c) 51 (d) 154

84. 895, 870, 821, 740, 619, 445, 225
(a) 870 (b) 821
(c) 740 (d) 445

85. 4 3 9 34 96 219 435
(a) 4 (b) 9 (c) 34 (d) 435
(e) None of these

DIRECTIONS ~ (Q. Nos. 86-128) *What comes in place of question mark (?) in the series given below?*

86. Q, T, W, Z, ?, F « RRB Group D 2018
(a) C (b) M (c) G (d) K

87. Z, U, Q, ?, L
(a) I (b) K (c) M (d) N

88. BA, ED, IH, NM, ? « RRB ASM 2016
(a) TS (b) ST (c) TU (d) SU

89. AN, DQ, GT, JW, ? « UPSSSC 2017
(a) MA (b) NZ (c) MZ (d) LY

90. ay, cw, eu, gs, iq, ko, ?
« UPSSSC Tech. Assist. Agri. Service 2018
(a) nm (b) mm (c) mn (d) nn

91. DK, FN, HQ, ? « RRB JE 2019
(a) KS (b) JT (c) KT (d) JS

92. AZ, BY, CX, ? « SSC Steno 2013
(a) EW (b) EU
(c) GH (d) DW

93. AC, FH, K? , PR, UW
(a) L (b) J (c) M (d) N

94. AC, FH, KM, PR,?
(a) UX (b) TV
(c) UW (D) VW

95. AI, BJ, CK, ?
(a) DC (b) DM
(c) DL (d) CM

96. B E H, K N Q, T W Z, ?
(a) C F I (b) D G H
(c) P R S (d) F I J

97. C, U, R, E, G, T, W, ?
(a) X (b) E (c) F (d) Z

98. KNQ, OPR, SRS, ? « SSC Steno 2019
(a) TVT (b) TWT
(c) WTT (d) TTW

99. AEI, DHL, IMQ, ? « SSC Steno 2019
(a) PTX (b) WPS (c) WSP (d) PWS

100. TU, ?, NO, XY
(a) IJ (b) FG (c) DF (d) DE

101. BDF, GIK, ?, QSU, VXZ
(a) LNP (b) XZU (c) KGI (d) PLN

102. ?, LMN, RST, WXY « SSC CHSL 2017
(a) FEG (b) DFE (c) DEF (d) EFG

103. CFI, DHL, ILO, LPT, ? « CLAT 2018
(a) ORU (b) RUW
(c) OQT (d) OSV

104. ABD, DGK, HMS, MTB, SBL, ? « UGC NET 2018
(a) ZKW (b) KZU
(c) ZKU (d) ZCA

105. BQT, VDT, VXG, IXA, CKA, CEN, ? « UPSSSC VDO 2018
(a) EGP (b) PEG
(c) FHQ (d) PEH

106. AEN, MQZ, CGP,?
(a) OSB (b) PUE
(c) MPX (d) OTC

107. DPJ, LJK, F?I « SSC Steno 2019
(a) K (b) N (c) L (d) M

108. AMN,BOP,CQR,?
(a) BAS (b) DST
(c) EQP (d) FRS

109. DKY, FJW, HIU, JHS, ?
(a) LFQ (b) LGQ
(c) KGR (d) KFR

110. OAC, PBD, QCE, RDF, ?
(a) SGH (b) SHI
(c) SEG (d) SIJ

111. BCD, BDC, CBD, ?, DCB
(a) CDB (b) CCD
(c) CDE (d) DCB

112. CEG, IKM, OQS, ?
(a) VXZ (b) TVX
(c) TUV (d) UWY

113. BDF, HJL, NPR, ?
(a) OQS (b) TUV
(c) TVX (d) UVW

114. XWA, VTC, SPF, OKJ, ?
(a) JDN (b) JEO
(c) LPN (d) JDP

115. BEAG, DGCI, FIEK,?
(a) HMIE (b) HKGM
(c) HGKJ (d) HKLJ

116. AGMSY, CIOUA, EKQWC, ? , IOUAG, KQWCI
(a) GMSYE (b) FMSYE
(c) GNSYD (d) FMYES

117. ABCD, BCDA, CDAB, ?, ABCD
(a) BADC (b) DABC
(c) DBAC (d) DACB

118. bc, cde, de, efg, fg, ?
(a) ghi (b) fgh (c) hij (d) ijk

119. PQRS, QPRS, RPQS, ?
(a) SQRP (b) RPQS
(c) QSPR (d) SQPR

120. TSMD, TSDM, TMDS, ?
(a) TSDM (b) SDTM
(c) TMDS (d) SDMT

121. STARE, ASSET, TASTE, SAUTE, STAVE, WASTE, TAXES, ?
(a) FAEST (b) FEAST
(c) YEAST (d) WESAT

122. ST, ND, RD, TH, ?, ?
(a) TH, TH (b) VW, SW
(c) RW, KH (d) ST, MN

123. URY, NUS, RTH, ARS, TER, URN, NUS, UNE, ?
(a) UTO (b) UFO
(c) NET (d) FSO

124. A, R, C, S, E, T, G, ?, ?
(a) X, Z (b) U, I
(c) W, Y (d) V, B

125. AIBJCK??
(a) EM (b) EL (c) DL (d) DM

126. KlMnO, qRsTu, WxYzA, cDeFg, ? « SSC CGL 2017
(a) iJkLm (b) HiJkL
(c) IjKlM (d) hijKl

127. AbC, dEfG, hIjKl, MnOpQr, ?
(a) StUvWxY (b) StUvWx
(c) StUvWxYZ (d) sTuVwXy

128. MIXTURE, IXTURE, IXTUR, ?, XTU « SSC Steno 2019
(a) XTRU (b) XTUR
(c) RTUX (d) TURE

DIRECTIONS ~(Q. Nos. 129-134) *A series is given, with one word missing. Choose the correct alternative from the given over that will complete the series.*

129. Shy, Food, Plate, Recess, ? « SSC CGL 2017
(a) Monsoon (b) Soon
(c) Eat (d) Lunch

130. tub, size, latin, formal, ?
(a) smooth (b) idle
(c) scramble (d) capital

131. Smart, Aspire, Castle, Abysma, Accost, ? « SSC CGL 2017
(a) Shop (b) Class
(c) Showman (d) Duties

132. upset, aurora, spurn, strut, status, ? « SSC CGL 2017
(a) treasure (b) perfect
(c) right (d) unique

133. XIIIII, IXIIII, IIXIII, IIIXII, IIIIXI, ? « SSC CGL 2017
(a) IIIIXII (b) IIIIXI
(c) IIIIIX (d) XIIIIX

134. Lieutenant, Captain, ?, Lieutenant colonel « SSC CHSL 2017
(a) Brigadier
(b) Major
(c) Sub-Lieutenant
(d) Major General

DIRECTIONS ~ (Q. Nos. 135-153) *In each of the following question, continuous pattern series is given. Some of the letters of the series are missing. These missing letters are given in that order as one of the four alternatives below the series. Find out the correct alternatives.*

135. _WOO_OO_OOW_ « SSC Steno 2019
(a) OOOW (b) OWWO
(c) OOWO (d) OWOO

136. BA_BA_BAC_ACB_CBAC
(a) AACB (b) BBCA
(c) CCBA (d) CBAC

137. a_yz_bz_xb_xy_c « UPSSSC Mandi Parishad 2019
(a) xacyz (b) xacyx
(c) xaycz (d) axcyx

138. _ml_nl_mlm_l_mlmn_ « SSC CPO 2017
(a) nnmmll (b) nmlnml
(c) mnlnlm (d) nmnnnl

139. a_a_abab_ba_
(a) abab (b) baab
(c) abba (d) bbab

140. c_bba_cab_ac_ab_ac
(a) acbcb (b) bcacb
(c) babcc (d) abcbc

141. ab_cabb_caa_bccab_cab_cc
(a) abbcc (b) baabc
(c) bcbbb (d) bcaac
(e) None of these

142. adb_ac_da_cddcb_dbc_cbda
(a) bccba (b) cbbaa
(c) ccbba (d) bbcad

143. c_bba_cab_ac_ab_ac
(a) b, c, b, a, c
(b) c, a, b, c, b
(c) a, c, c, b, c
(d) a, c, b, c, b

144. b_acbda_bd_cb_a_
(a) baadc (b) dcadc
(c) cbdca (d) cdacb

145. ab _ d _ bc _ a _ c _ ab _ d
(a) cadbdc (b) cabbcd
(c) abbcdd (d) caddbc

146. c_abbcc_bb_cab_c_abb
(a) abcca (b) babac
(c) cbbca (d) cacbc

147. bc_bca_cab_ab_a_ca
(a) abcab (b) cabac
(c) abccb (d) cabca

148. mc_m_a_ca_ca_c_mc
(a) acmmma (b) camcam
(c) aaacmm (d) acmmmc

149. a_a_abab_ba _
(a) abab (b) baab
(c) abba (d) bbab

150. aa_aaa_aaaa_aaaa_b
(a) baaa (b) bbaa
(c) bbbb (d) bbba

151. a_cdaab_cc_daa_bbb_ccddd
(a) bdbda (b) bddca
(c) abdcb (d) bbdac

152. ab_bcbca_ _ c _ bab
(a) aabc (b) baaa
(c) abcc (d) ccaa

153. _A _ A _ _ B A B _ B _ B A B A
(a) BBABAA
(b) BBBAAA
(c) ABABBA
(d) BBAABB

DIRECTIONS ~(Q. Nos. 154-156) *In each of the following question, continuous pattern series is given. Some of the numbers in the series are missing.*
These missing numbers are given in that order as one of the four alternatives below the series. Find out the correct alternatives.

154. 01_3_12_ _ 1 _ 30
(a) 12031 (b) 20302
(c) 20132 (d) 00121

155. 4 8_9_8_ _ 1 9 8_4 8 1_8_
(a) 1848898 (b) 4891914
(c) 8491941 (d) 9411198

156. 0_1 0 0 1_0 0 1 1 _ _ 110
(a) 1010 (b) 0111
(c) 1100 (d) 0110

157. The below two series are based on mathematical operations. Which number comes in place of (D) in second series?
5 10 20 25 50 55
15 (A) (B) (C) (D) (E)
(a) 90 (b) 95
(c) 80 (d) 85

158. The below two series are based on some mathematical operations. Which number comes in place of (C) in second series?
6 13 27 55 111
10 (A) (B) (C) (D)
(a) 87 (b) 85
(c) 83 (d) 81

DIRECTIONS ~(Q. Nos. 159-163) *In each of the following question, one letter/group of letters is wrong in the series. Find out the wrong number.*

159. CFI, FIL, JLQ, LOR, ORU
(a) JLQ (b) FIL
(c) LOR (d) ORU

160. AZA, BXF, CXK, DWP
(a) AZA (b) BXF
(c) CXK (d) DWP

161. EGP, GHQ, IIS, KJV, NKW
(a) GHQ (b) IIS
(c) KJV (d) NKW

162. ZVA, EWE, JXI, OYQ, TZU
(a) EWE (b) OYQ
(c) TZU (d) ZVA

163. PUB, QVD, RWG, SXQ, TYP
(a) PUB (b) QVD
(c) RWG (d) SXQ

DIRECTIONS ~ (Q. Nos. 164-179) *What value should come in place of the question mark (?) in the series given below?*

164. A2C, B4D, C8E, D16F, ?, F64H « UPSSSC Junior Assist. 2017
(a) E24G (b) E32F
(c) E32G (d) E36G

165. 3X24C, 5V22E, ? « RRB Group D 2018
(a) 9T21G (b) 8T21G
(c) 7T20G (d) 8T20G

166. 5E, 7G, 9I, 11K, ? « RRB Group D 2018
(a) 14M (b) 13M (c) 13N (d) 14N

167. Y4X9, W16V25, '?', S64R81
(a) U39T49 (b) U36T49
(c) U32T48 (d) U36T46

168. X24C3, V22E5, T20G7, '?'
(a) R16I7 (b) R17I9
(c) R18I9 (d) R19I10

169. D-23, E-22, F-21, G-20, H-19, ?
(a) I-18 (b) I-9 (c) I-20 (d) I-15

170. 2B, 4C, 8E, 14H, ?
(a) 16 K (b) 20I
(c) 20L (d) 22L

171. 2, A, 9, B, 6, C, 13, D, ?
(a) 9 (b) 10 (c) 12 (d) 19

172. 128, 61, Y, 64, 63, S, 32, 65, N, 16, 67, J, 8, 69, G, ?, ?, ?
(a) 2, 70, J (b) 3, 70, E
(c) 4, 70, E (d) 4, 71, E

173. N5V, K7T, ?, E14P, B19N
(a) H9R (b) H10Q
(c) H10R (d) I10R

174. DE-9, FC-9, LP-28, GT-?
(a) 35 (b) 8 (c) 27 (d) 6

175. CD-12, LB-24, BP-32, NE-?
(a) 70 (b) 75 (c) 45 (d) 95

176. Q1, P2, R6, N24, V120, ?
(a) W600 (b) X720
(c) F720 (d) F600

177. A1Z, E2V, I6R, M21N, Q88J, ?
(a) F 445 U (b) U 445 F
(c) G342 C (d) V 441 G
(e) T 267 N

178. W-144, ?, S-100, Q-81, O-64
(a) U-121 (b) U-122
(c) V-121 (d) V-128

179. BD3FH, AC5EG, JL7NP, ?
(a) IK9MO (b) NP7QS
(c) KM11MO (d) IK9NO

Answers / WITH EXPLANATIONS

1. (*c*) The pattern is as follows

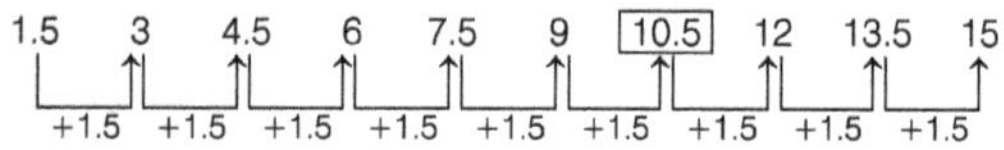

$\therefore$? = 10.5

2. (*a*) The pattern is as follows

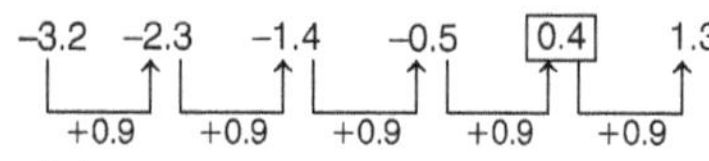

$\therefore$? = 0.4

3. (*a*) The pattern is as follows

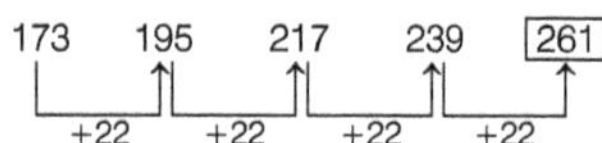

$\therefore$? = 261

4. (*b*) The pattern is as follows

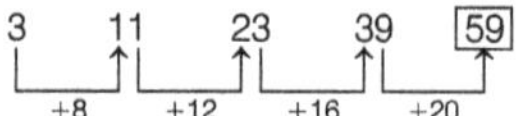

$\therefore$? = 59

5. (*b*) The pattern is as follows

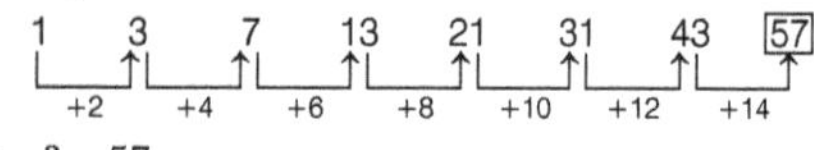

$\therefore$? = 57

6. (*b*) The pattern is as follows

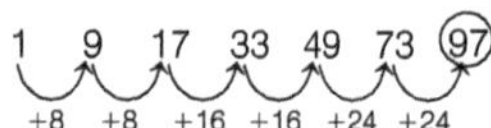

$\therefore$? = 97

7. (*d*) The pattern is as follows

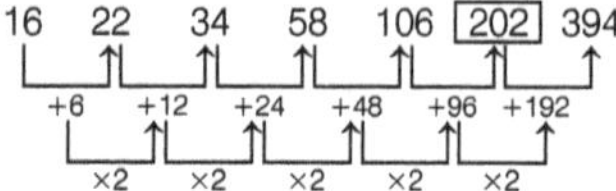

$\therefore$? = 202

8. (*b*) The pattern is as follows

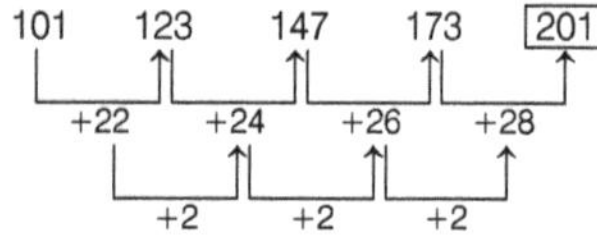

$\therefore$? = 201

9. (*b*) The pattern is as follows

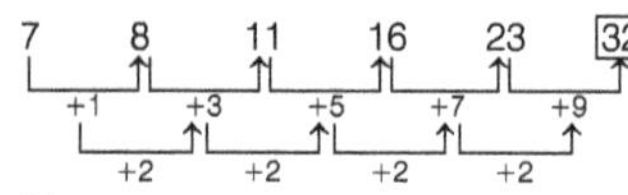

$\therefore$? = 32

10. (*d*) The pattern is as follows

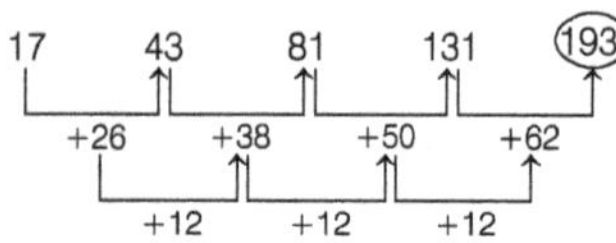

$\therefore$? = 193

11. (*b*) The pattern is as follows

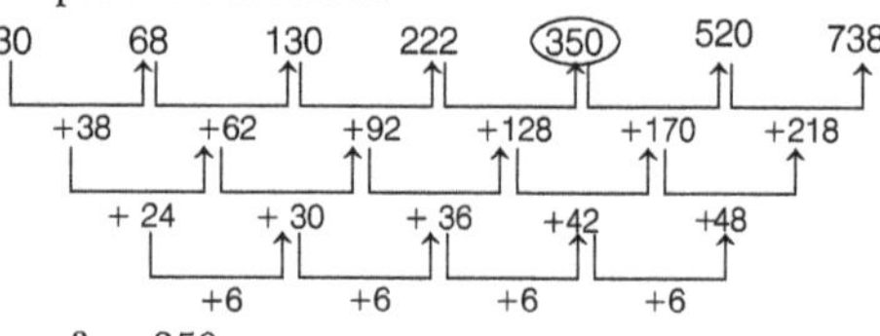

$\therefore$? = 350

12. (*b*) The pattern is as follows

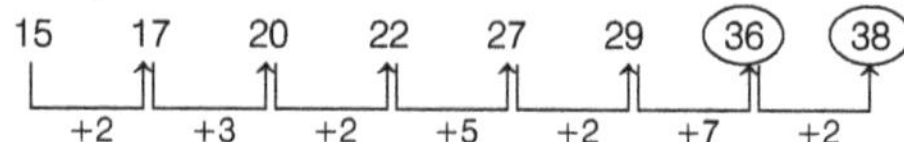

$\because$ First ? = 36 and second ? = 38

$\therefore$ Required answer = 36, 38

13. (*c*) The pattern is as follows

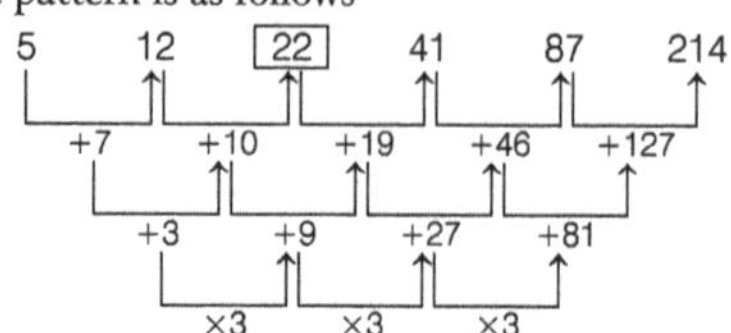

$\therefore$? = 22

14. (*d*) The pattern is as follows

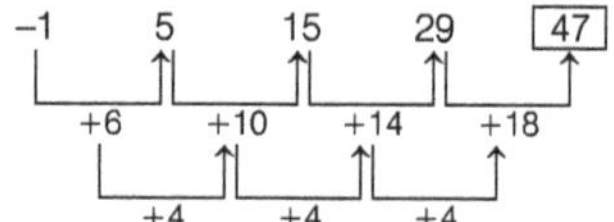

$\therefore$? = 47

15. (*d*) Every third element is the sum of its previous two elements.

3 + 4 = 7, 4 + 7 = 11

7 + 11 = 18, 11 + 18 = 29

18 + 29 = 47

$\therefore$? = 47

16. (*a*) Since, each term is obtained by adding two previous term,

$\therefore$? = 13 + 21 = 34

This type of sequence called fibonacci sequence, such that each number is the sum of the two preceding ones starting from 0 and 1.

17. (*e*) The pattern is as follows

1 + 3 = 4, 1 + 3 + 4 = 8,

3 + 4 + 8 = 15, 4 + 8 + 15 = 27,

8 + 15 + 27 = 50

$\therefore$? = 50

18. (*a*) The pattern is as follows

2 + 1 = 3, 3 + 2 = 5

5 + 3 = 8, 8 + 5 = 13

13 + 8 = 21

$\therefore$? = 21

19. (*a*) The pattern is as follows

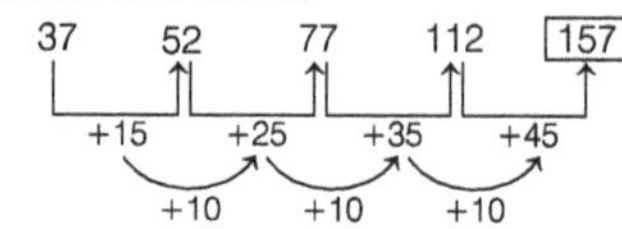

$\therefore$? = 157

20. (*a*) The pattern is as follows

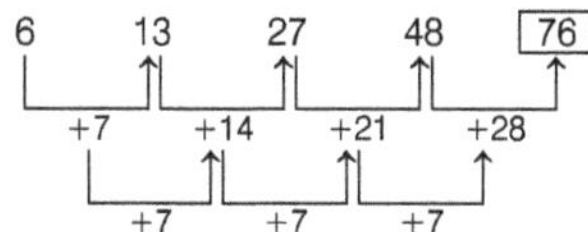

$\therefore$? = 76

21. (*d*) The pattern is as follows

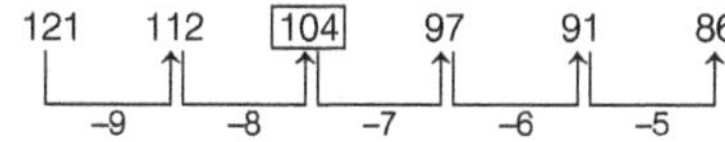

$\therefore$? = 104

22. (*c*) The pattern is as follows

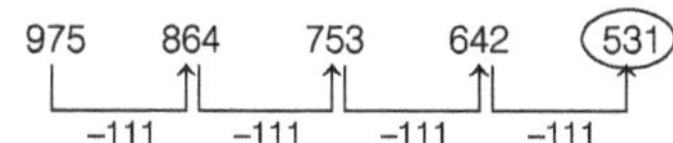

$\therefore$? = 531

23. (*c*) The pattern is as follows

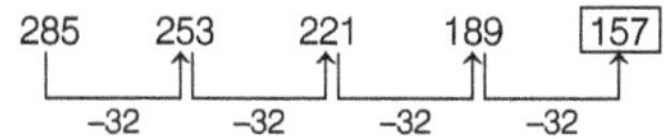

$\therefore$? = 157

24. (*b*) Deduct the middle digit each time to obtain the next number.

$758 - 5 = 753$, $753 - 5 = 748$

$748 - 4 = 744$, $744 - 4 = 740$

$740 - 4 = 736$, $736 - 3 = \boxed{733}$

$\therefore$? = 733

25. (*a*) The pattern is as follows

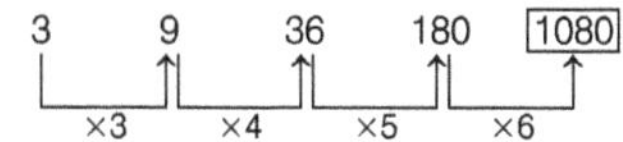

$\therefore$? = 1080

26. (*c*) The pattern is as follows

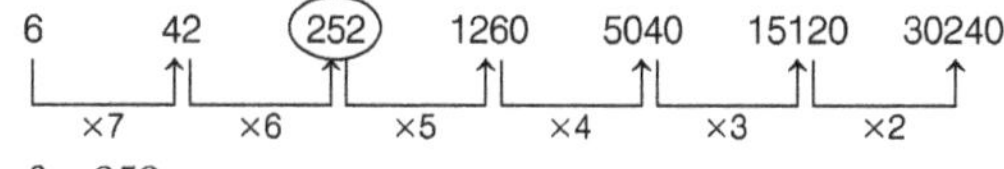

$\therefore$? = 252

27. (*d*) The pattern is as follows

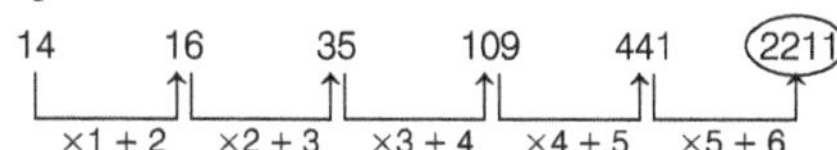

$\therefore$? = 2211

28. (*d*) The pattern is as follows

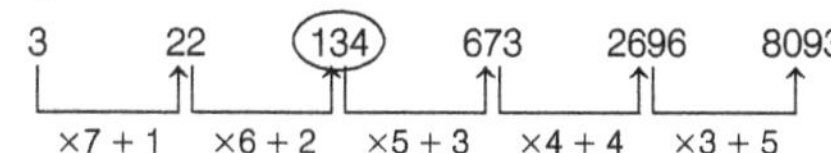

$\therefore$? = 134

29. (*b*) The pattern is as follows

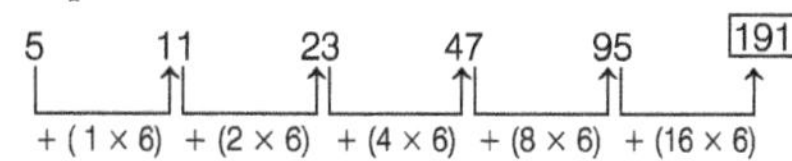

$\therefore$? = 191

30. (*d*) The pattern is as follows

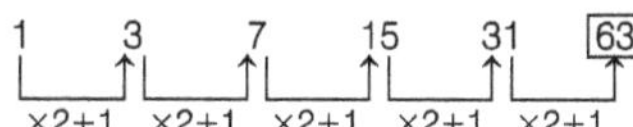

$\therefore$? = 63

31. (*d*) The pattern is as follows

$13 \times 13 = 169 \Rightarrow 169 - 1 = 168$

$14 \times 13 = 182 \Rightarrow 182 - 1 = 181$

$15 \times 13 = 195 \Rightarrow 195 - 1 = \boxed{194}$

$\therefore$? = 194

32. (*b*) The pattern is as follows

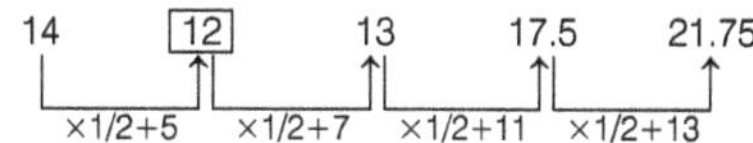

$\therefore$? = 12

33. (*a*) The pattern is as follows

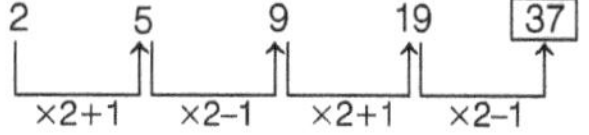

$\therefore$? = 37

34. (*d*) The pattern is as follows

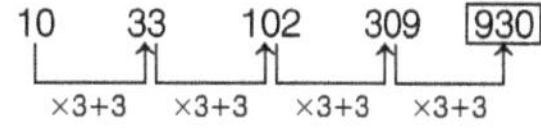

$\therefore$? = 930

35. (*d*) The pattern is as follows

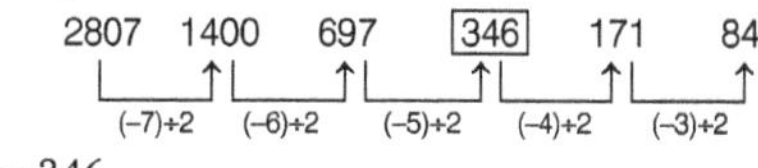

$\therefore$? = 346

36. (*a*) The pattern of series is as follows

$4 \times 2 + 1 = 9$, $9 \times 2 + 2 = 20$

$20 \times 2 + 3 = 43$, $43 \times 2 + 4 = \boxed{90}$

$\therefore$? = 90

37. (*b*) The pattern is as follows

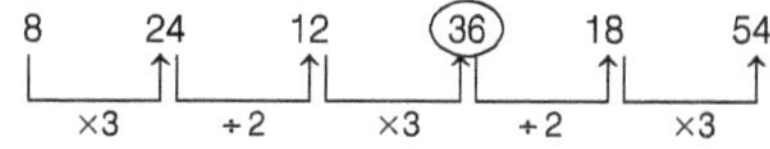

$\therefore$? = 36

38. (*d*) Here, the pattern is as follows

Divide by 2, multiple by 3 and the same process is repeated

$48 \div 2 = 24$, $24 \times 3 = 72$

$72 \div 2 = 36$, $36 \times 3 = 108$

$108 \div 2 = 54$

$\therefore$? = 54

39. (*a*) The pattern is as follows

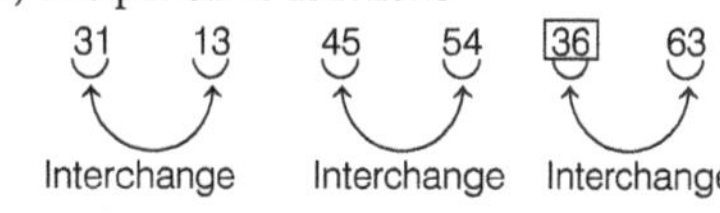

$\therefore$? = 36

40. (*d*) The pattern is as follows

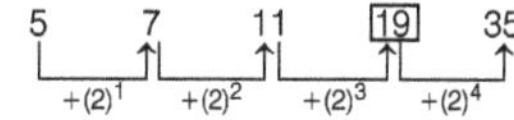

$\therefore$? = 19

41. (*b*) The given series is the series of prime numbers.

$3, 5, 7, \boxed{11}, 13, 17, 19, 23$

$\therefore$? = 11

42. (*b*) The sequence is $7^7, 6^6, 5^5, 4^4, 3^3, 2^2, 1^1$

$\therefore$? $= 3^3 = 27$

43. (*c*) The pattern is as follows

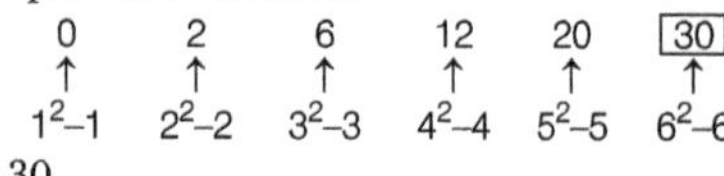

$\therefore$? = 30

44. (*d*) The pattern is as follows

8 27 64 125

↑ ↑ ↑ ↑

(2^3) (3^3) (4^3) (5^3)

$\therefore$? = 125

45. (*b*) When the digits of the numbers are reversed, these are the perfect squares 09, 16, 25, 36, 49, 64, 81 consecutively

$\therefore$? = Reverse of 64 = 46

46. (*c*) Keep subtracting the next larger perfect cube *i.e.,* 1, 8, 27, 64, 125, 216, 343.

$\therefore$? = 434 − 343 = 91

47. (*c*) The pattern of series is as follows

4 18 48 100 180 294

↓ ↓ ↓ ↓ ↓ ↓

$2^2\times1$ $3^2\times2$ $4^2\times3$ $5^2\times4$ $6^2\times5$ $7^2\times6$

$\therefore$? = 48

48. (*a*) The pattern is as follows

$$7 + 1^2 = 8,\quad 8 + 4^2 = 24$$
$$24 + 9^2 = 105,\ 105 + 16^2 = 361$$
$$361 + 25^2 = 986$$

$\therefore$? = 986

49. (*b*) The pattern is as follows

$$1^2 + 1^2 = 1 + 1 = 2,$$
$$2^2 + 2^2 = 4 + 4 = 8$$
$$3^2 + 3^2 = 9 + 9 = 18,$$
$$4^2 + 4^2 = 16 + 16 = 32$$
$$5^2 + 5^2 = 25 + 25 = 50,$$
$$6^2 + 6^2 = 36 + 36 = 72$$

$\therefore$? = 72

50. (*c*) The pattern is as follows

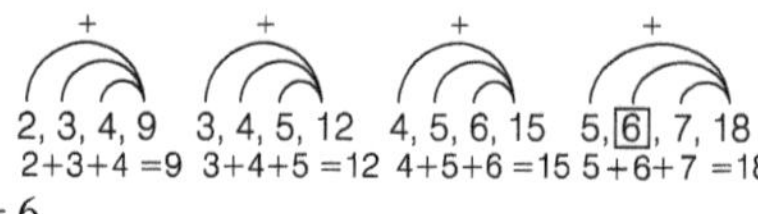

$\therefore$? = 6

51. (*b*) The pattern is as follows

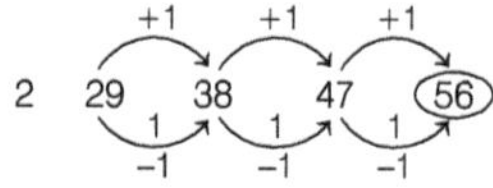

So, the correct alternative is 56.

52. (*a*) There are three alternative series 2, 3, 4, ... (consecutive numbers), 9, 8, 7 ... (consecutive number in descending order) and 23, 25, 27, ... Hence, 7 will come in place of the missing number.

53. (*d*) The pattern is as follows

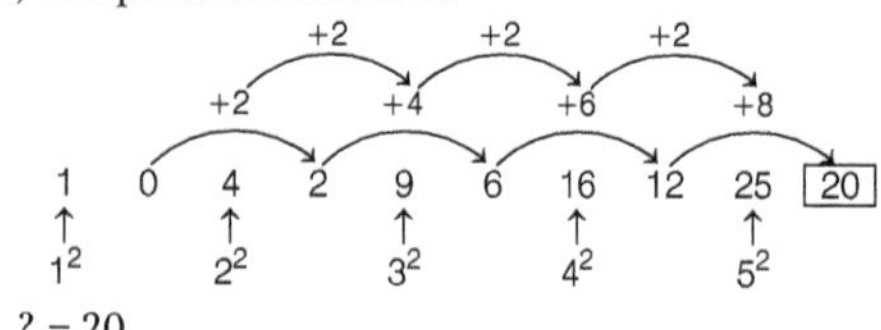

$\therefore$? = 20

54. (*b*) The pattern is as follows

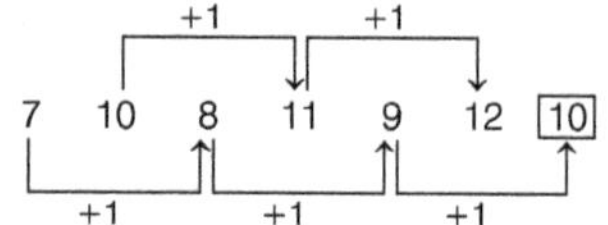

$\therefore$? = 10

55. (*e*) The pattern is as follows

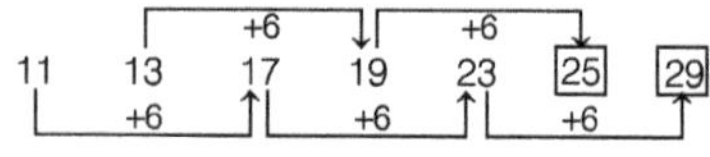

$\therefore$?, ? = 25, 29

56. (*e*) The pattern is as follows

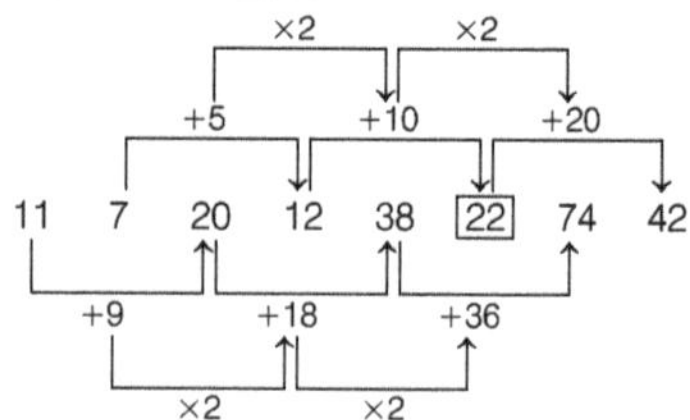

$\therefore$? = 22

57. (*b*) Given sequence

4/12/95, 1/1/96, 29/1/96, 26/2/96

if we observe they are calender dates with 28 days gap between them.

December 4, 1995, January 1, 1996,

January 29, 1996, February 26, 1996.

Hence, next date would be March 25, 1996.

Because 1996 is leap year it has February 29.

$\therefore$ Option (b) is correct answer.

58. (*b*) The pattern is as follows

3 → Number of three's is one i.e. one three → 13

13 → Number of one's is one and number of three's is one i.e. one one one three → 1113

1113 → Number of one's are three and number of three is one i.e. three one one three → 3113

3113 → Number of three is one and number of one's are two and number of three is one i.e. one three two one one three → 132113

$\therefore$? = 132113

59. (*c*) The pattern is as follows

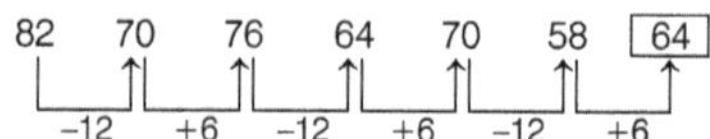

$\therefore$? = 64

60. (*b*) The pattern is as follows

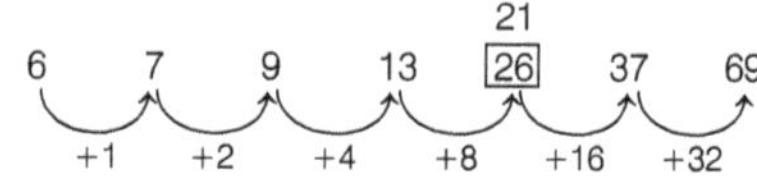

Hence, 21 should come in place of 26 in the series.

61. (*b*) The pattern is as follows

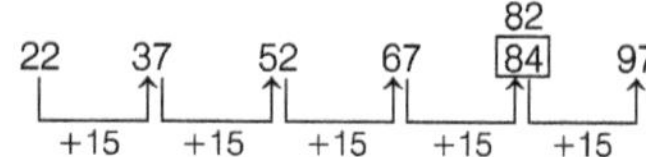

So, 84 is the incorrect term, it should be 82.

62. (*d*) The pattern is as follows

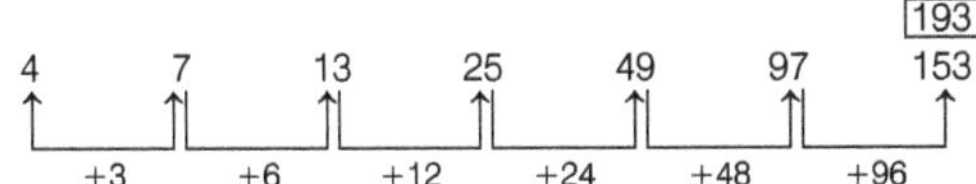

So, 153 is the incorrect term, it should be 193.

63. (*d*) The pattern is as follows

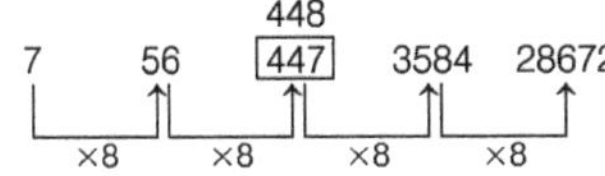

So, 447 is the incorrect term, it should be 448.

64. (*d*) The pattern is as follows

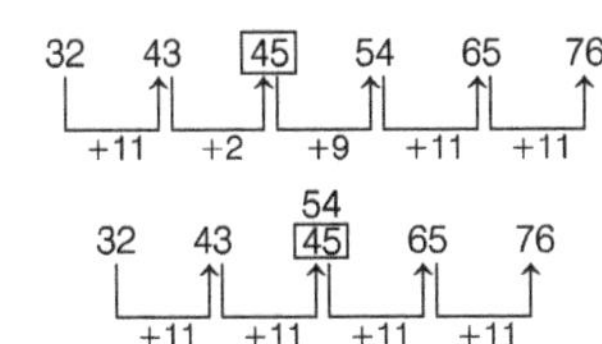

So, 45 is the wrong term in the series.

65. (*c*) The pattern is as follows

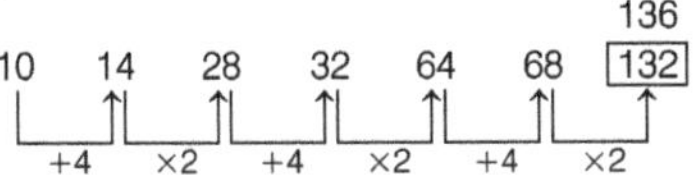

Hence, number 132 is wrong term, should be replaced by 136.

66. (*b*) The pattern is as follows

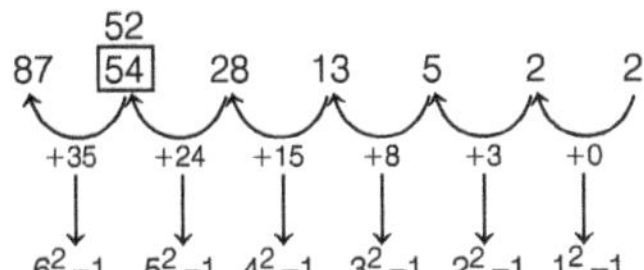

Hence, number 54 is wrong term, should be replaced by 52.

67. (*b*) The pattern is as follows

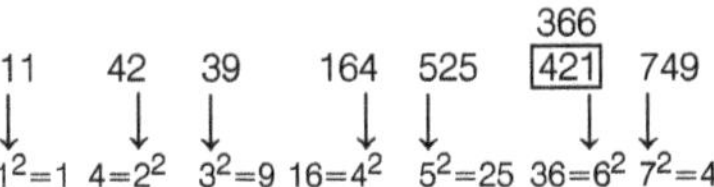

Hence, number 421 is wrong term, should be replaced by 366.

68. (*a*) The pattern is as follows

$10 \rightarrow (1)^2\ (0)^2, 41 \rightarrow (2)^2\ (1)^2, 94 \rightarrow (3)^2\ (2)^2,$

$2516 \rightarrow (5)^2\ (4)^2, 3625 \rightarrow (6)^2\ (5)^2, 4936 \rightarrow (7)^2\ (6)^2$

but in 1624 it is not so.

69. (*d*) The pattern is as follows

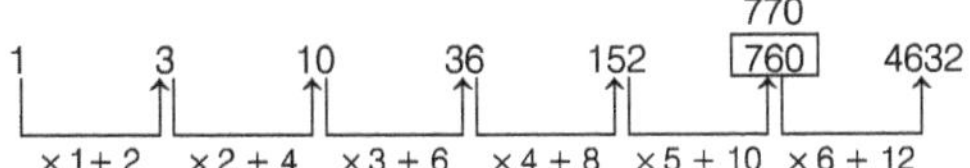

From above, we can say that 760 is wrong in the given series. 770 should come in place of 760.

70. (*d*) The pattern is as follows

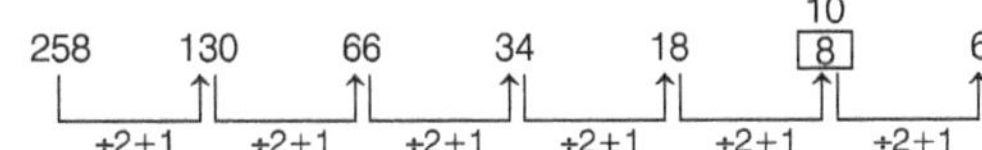

Hence, number 8 is wrong term, should be replaced by 10.

71. (*b*) The pattern is as follows

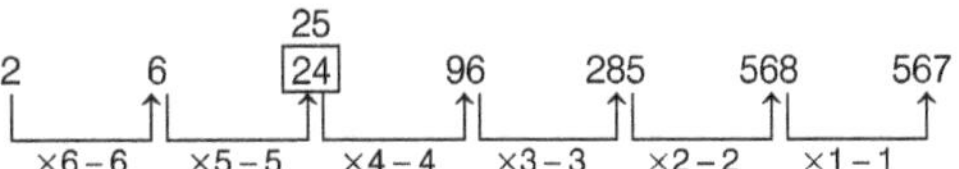

Hence, number 24 is wrong term, should be replaced by 25.

72. (*d*) The pattern is as follows

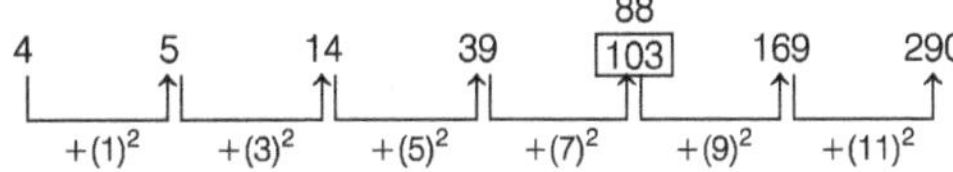

Hence, number 103 is wrong term, should be replaced by 88.

73. (*d*) The pattern is as follows

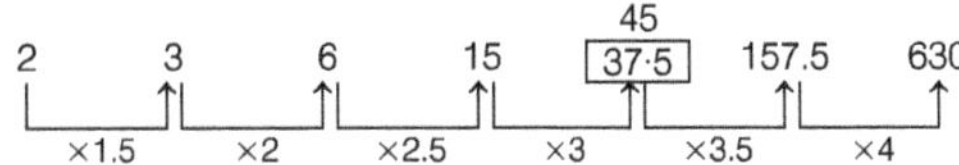

Hence, number 37.5 is wrong term, should be replaced by 45.

74. (*b*) The pattern is as follows

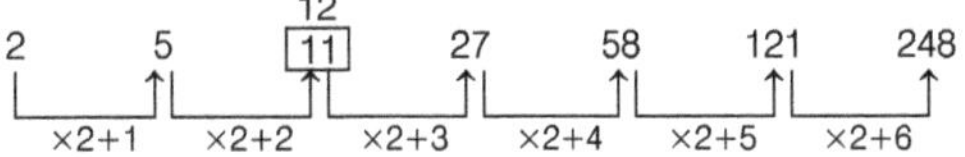

Hence, number 11 is wrong term, should be replaced by 12.

75. (*d*) The pattern is as follows

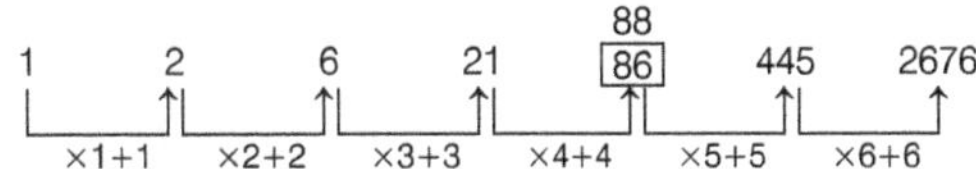

Hence, number 86 is wrong term, should be replaced by 88.

76. (*a*) The pattern is as follows

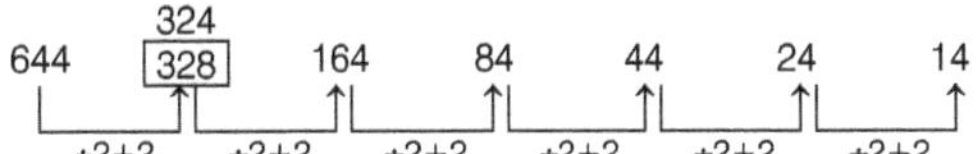

Hence, number 328 is wrong term, should be replaced by 324.

77. (*a*) The pattern is as follows

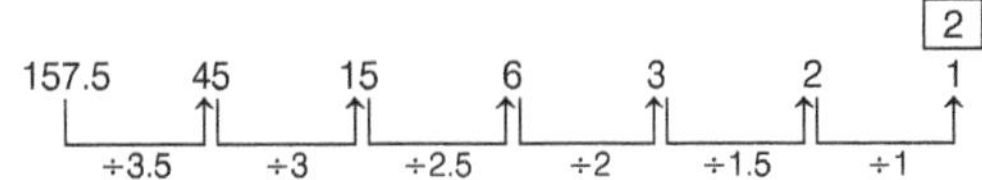

From above, 2 should come in place of 1 in given series.

78. (*a*) The pattern is as follows

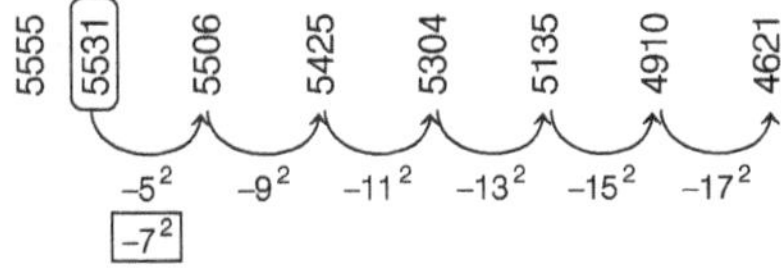

From above, we can say that 5531 is wrong in the series. 5555 should come in place of 5531.

79. (*c*) Pattern of the series from the right end follows the rule

$6 \times 2 + 4 = 16, 16 \times 2 + 8 = 40, 40 \times 2 + 12 = 92,$

$92 \times 2 + 16 = 200$ ... and so on.

Therefore, number 96 should be replaced by 92.

80. (*d*) The series is written using the pattern

$4 \times 2 + 4 = 12, 12 \times 2 + 6 = 30,$

$30 \times 2 + 8 = 68, 68 \times 2 + 10 = 146,$

$146 \times 2 + 12 = 304, 304 \times 2 + 14 = 622.$

Therefore, number 302 should be replaced by 304.

81. (*a*) Pattern of the series is

$$3 \times 1.5 = 4.5, 4.5 \times 2 = 9, 9 \times 2.5 = 22.5,$$
$$22.5 \times 3 = 67.5, 67.5 \times 3.5 = 236.25$$

Therefore, number 6 should be replaced by 4.5.

82. (*a*) The pattern is as follows

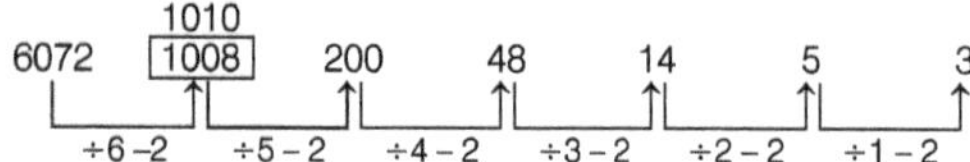

Hence, number 1008 is wrong term, should be replaced by 1010.

83. (*c*) The pattern is as follows

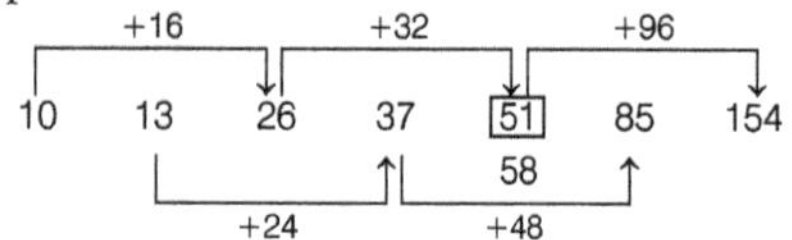

Hence, number 51 is wrong term, should be replaced by 58.

84. (*d*) The pattern is as follows

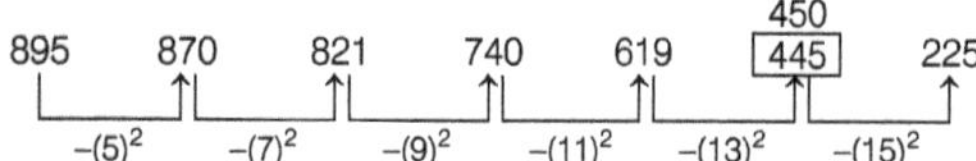

Hence, number 445 is wrong term, should be replaced by 450.

85. (*d*) The pattern is as follows

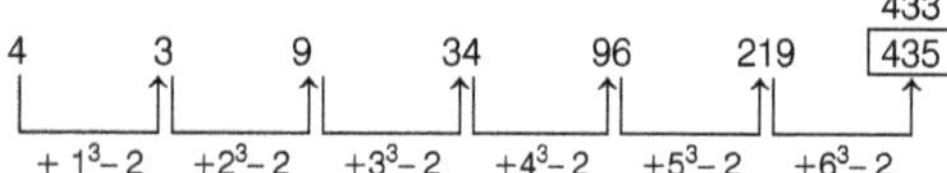

From above, we can say that 435 is wrong in the given series. 433 should come in place of 435.

86. (*a*) The pattern is as follows

17 Q, 20 T, 23 W, 26 Z, 14 C, 12 F (+3, +3, +3, +3, +3)

$\therefore$? = C

87. (*d*) The pattern is as follows

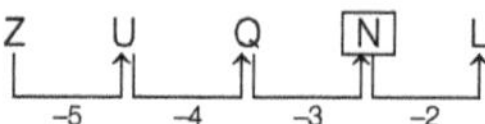

$\therefore$? = N

88. (*a*) The pattern is as follows

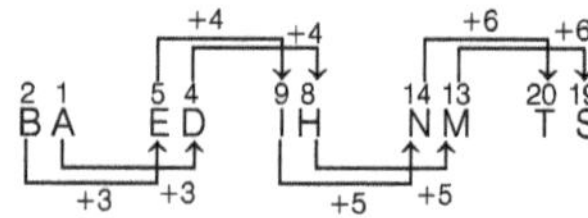

$\therefore$? = TS

89. (*c*) The pattern is as follows

1 A →(+3) 4 D →(+3) 7 G →(+3) 10 J →(+3) 13 M

14 N →(+3) 17 Q →(+3) 20 T →(+3) 23 W →(+3) 26 Z

$\therefore$? = MZ

90. (*b*) The pattern is as follows

1 a →(+2) 3 c →(+2) 5 e →(+2) 7 g →(+2) 9 i →(+2) 11 k →(+2) 13 m

25 y →(−2) 23 w →(−2) 21 u →(−2) 19 s →(−2) 17 q →(−2) 15 o →(−2) 13 m

$\therefore$? = mm

91. (*b*) The pattern is as follows

4 D →(+2) 6 F →(+2) 8 H →(+2) 10 J

11 K →(+3) 14 N →(+3) 17 Q →(+3) 20 T

$\therefore$? = JT

92. (*d*) The pattern is as follows

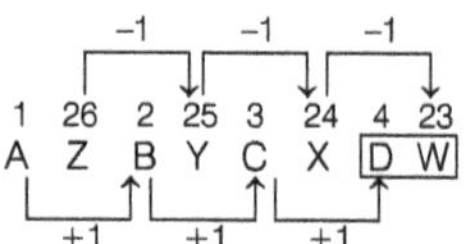

$\therefore$? = DW

93. (*c*) The pattern is as follows

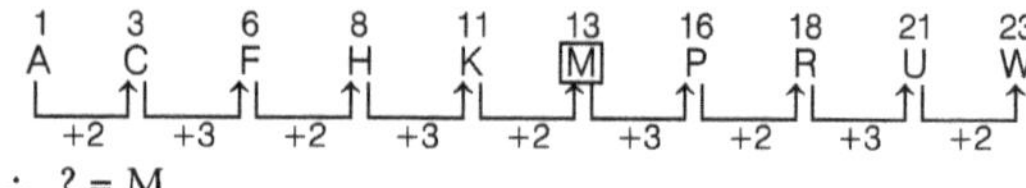

$\therefore$? = M

94. (*c*) The pattern is as follows

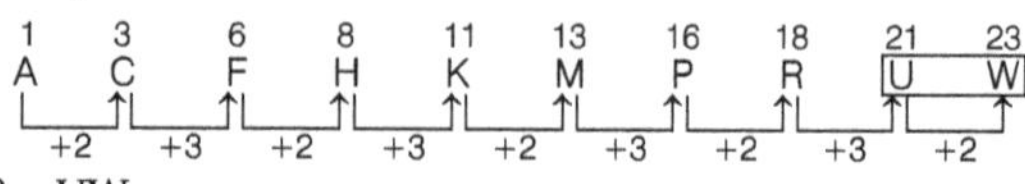

$\therefore$? = UW

95. (*c*) The pattern is as follows

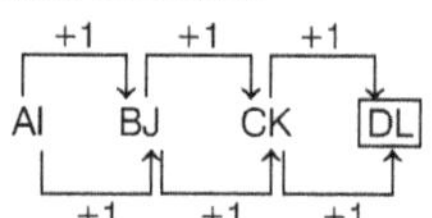

$\therefore$? = DL

96. (*a*) The pattern is as follows

2 5 8 11 14 17 20 23 26
B(cd) E(fg) H(ij), K(lm) N(op) Q(rs), T(uv) W(xy) Z(ab),
3 6 9
C(de) F(gh)I (+3 in each letter)

$\therefore$? = CFI

97. (*b*) The pattern is as follows

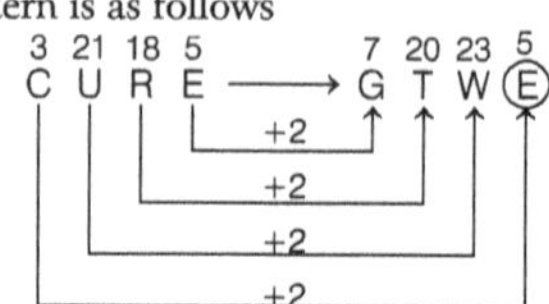

$\therefore$? = E

98. (*c*) The pattern is as follows

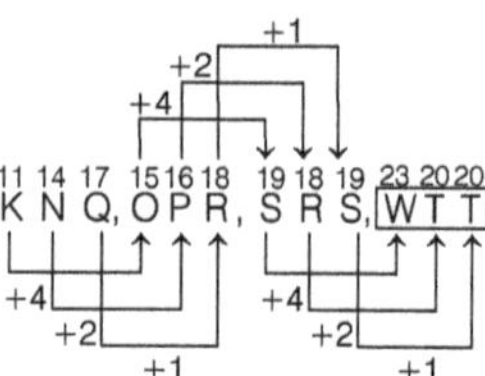

$\therefore$? = WTT

99. (*a*) The pattern is as follows

1 A →(+3) 4 D →(+5) 9 I →(+7) 16 P

5 E →(+3) 8 H →(+5) 13 M →(+7) 20 T

9 I →(+3) 12 L →(+5) 17 Q →(+7) 24 X

$\therefore$? = PTX

100. (*d*) The pattern is as follows

$\overset{20}{T}\overset{21}{U}$ $\boxed{\overset{4}{D}\overset{5}{E}}$ $\overset{14}{N}\overset{15}{O}$ $\overset{24}{X}\overset{25}{Y}$ (+10, +10, +10 above; +10, +10, +10 below)

∴ ? = DE

101. (*a*) The pattern is as follows

$\overset{2}{B} \xrightarrow{+5} \overset{7}{G} \xrightarrow{+5} \boxed{\overset{12}{L}} \xrightarrow{+5} \overset{17}{Q} \xrightarrow{+5} \overset{22}{V}$

$\overset{4}{D} \xrightarrow{+5} \overset{9}{I} \xrightarrow{+5} \boxed{\overset{14}{N}} \xrightarrow{+5} \overset{19}{S} \xrightarrow{+5} \overset{24}{X}$

$\overset{6}{F} \xrightarrow{+5} \overset{11}{K} \xrightarrow{+5} \boxed{\overset{16}{P}} \xrightarrow{+5} \overset{21}{U} \xrightarrow{+5} \overset{26}{Z}$

∴ ? = LNP

102. (*d*) The pattern is as follows

$\boxed{\overset{5}{E}} \xrightarrow{+7} \overset{12}{L} \xrightarrow{+6} \overset{18}{R} \xrightarrow{+5} \overset{23}{W}$

$\boxed{\overset{6}{F}} \xrightarrow{+7} \overset{13}{M} \xrightarrow{+6} \overset{19}{S} \xrightarrow{+5} \overset{24}{X}$

$\boxed{\overset{7}{G}} \xrightarrow{+7} \overset{14}{N} \xrightarrow{+6} \overset{20}{T} \xrightarrow{+5} \overset{25}{Y}$

∴ ? = EFG

103. (*a*) The pattern is as follows

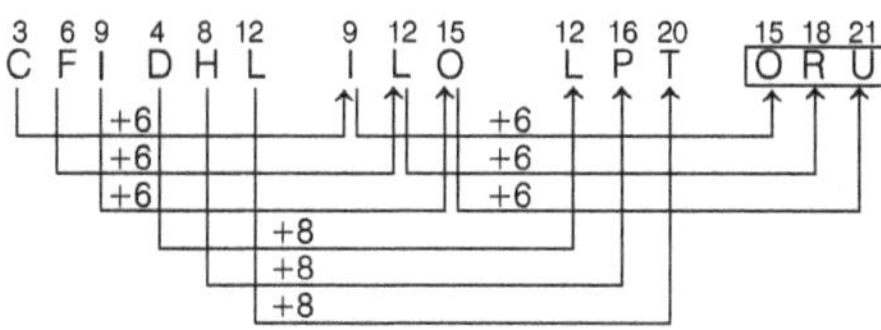

∴ ? = ORU

104. (*a*) The pattern is as follows

$\overset{1}{A} \xrightarrow{+3} \overset{4}{D} \xrightarrow{+4} \overset{8}{H} \xrightarrow{+5} \overset{13}{M} \xrightarrow{+6} \overset{19}{S} \xrightarrow{+7} \boxed{\overset{26}{Z}}$

$\overset{2}{B} \xrightarrow{+5} \overset{7}{G} \xrightarrow{+6} \overset{13}{M} \xrightarrow{+7} \overset{20}{T} \xrightarrow{+8} \overset{2}{B} \xrightarrow{+9} \boxed{\overset{11}{K}}$

$\overset{4}{D} \xrightarrow{+7} \overset{11}{K} \xrightarrow{+8} \overset{19}{S} \xrightarrow{+9} \overset{2}{B} \xrightarrow{+10} \overset{12}{L} \xrightarrow{+11} \boxed{\overset{23}{W}}$

∴ ? = ZKW

105. (*d*) The pattern is as follows

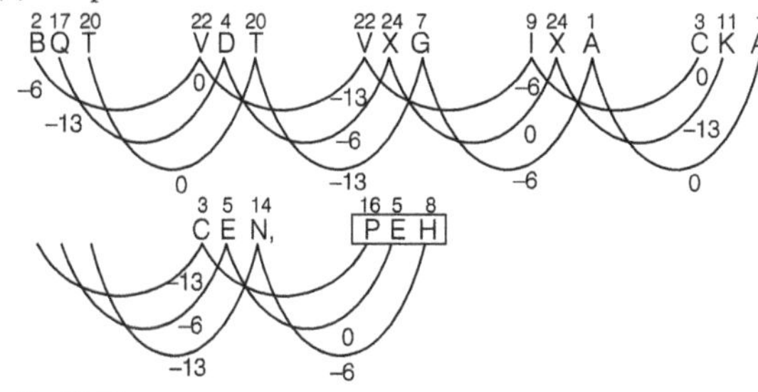

∴ ? = PEH

106. (*a*) The pattern is as follows

$\overset{1}{A} \xrightarrow{+12} \overset{13}{M} \xrightarrow{-10} \overset{3}{C} \xrightarrow{+12} \boxed{\overset{15}{O}}$

$\overset{5}{E} \xrightarrow{+12} \overset{17}{Q} \xrightarrow{-10} \overset{7}{G} \xrightarrow{+12} \boxed{\overset{19}{S}}$

$\overset{14}{N} \xrightarrow{+12} \overset{26}{Z} \xrightarrow{-10} \overset{16}{P} \xrightarrow{+12} \boxed{\overset{2}{B}}$

∴ ? = OSB

107. (*c*) Here, the position of alphabet at the corner is obtained by taking mean of the first two alphabets.

As, $\overset{4}{D} + \overset{16}{P} = \dfrac{4+16}{2} = 10 = J$ and $\overset{12}{L} + \overset{10}{J} = \dfrac{12+10}{2} = 11 = K$

Similarly, $\dfrac{F+?}{2} = I$

$\Rightarrow \quad \dfrac{6+?}{2} = 9 \Rightarrow 6 + ? = 9 \times 2$

$\therefore\ ? = 9 \times 2 - 6 = 12 = \boxed{L}$

108. (*b*) The pattern is as follows

$\overset{1}{A} \xrightarrow{+1} \overset{2}{B} \xrightarrow{+1} \overset{3}{C} \xrightarrow{+1} \boxed{\overset{4}{D}}$

$\overset{13}{M} \xrightarrow{+2} \overset{15}{O} \xrightarrow{+2} \overset{17}{Q} \xrightarrow{+2} \boxed{\overset{19}{S}}$

$\overset{14}{N} \xrightarrow{+2} \overset{16}{P} \xrightarrow{+2} \overset{18}{R} \xrightarrow{+2} \boxed{\overset{20}{T}}$

∴ ? = DST

109. (*b*) The pattern is as follows

$\overset{4}{D} \xrightarrow{+2} \overset{6}{F} \xrightarrow{+2} \overset{8}{H} \xrightarrow{+2} \overset{10}{J} \xrightarrow{+2} \boxed{\overset{12}{L}}$

$\overset{11}{K} \xrightarrow{-1} \overset{10}{J} \xrightarrow{-1} \overset{9}{I} \xrightarrow{-1} \overset{8}{H} \xrightarrow{-1} \boxed{\overset{7}{G}}$

$\overset{25}{Y} \xrightarrow{-2} \overset{23}{W} \xrightarrow{-2} \overset{21}{U} \xrightarrow{-2} \overset{19}{S} \xrightarrow{-2} \boxed{\overset{17}{Q}}$

∴ ? = LGQ

110. (*c*) The pattern is as follows

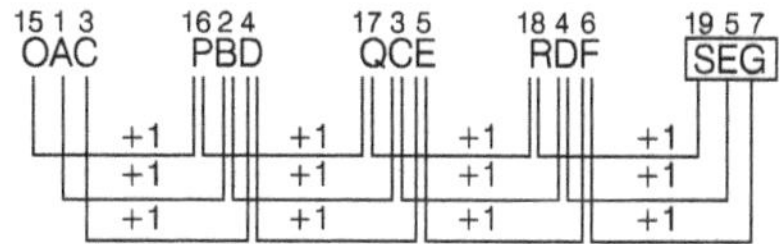

∴ ? = SEG

111. (*a*) The pattern is as follows

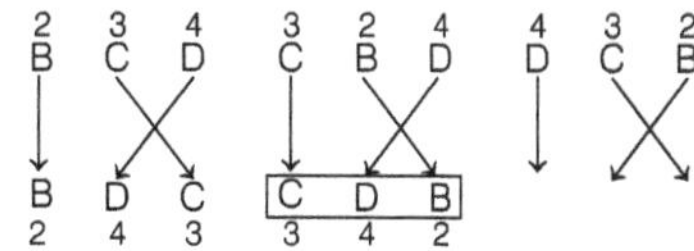

∴ ? = CDB

112. (*d*) The pattern is as follows

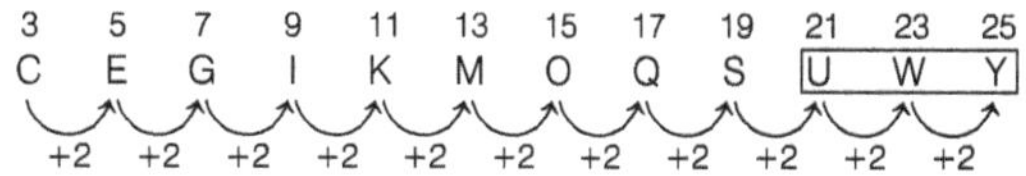

∴ ? = UWY

113. (*c*) The pattern is as follows

1st Letter : $\overset{2}{B} \xrightarrow{+6} \overset{8}{H} \xrightarrow{+6} \overset{14}{N} \xrightarrow{+6} \boxed{\overset{20}{T}}$

2nd Letter : $\overset{4}{D} \xrightarrow{+6} \overset{10}{J} \xrightarrow{+6} \overset{16}{P} \xrightarrow{+6} \boxed{\overset{22}{V}}$

3rd Letter : $\overset{6}{F} \xrightarrow{+6} \overset{12}{L} \xrightarrow{+6} \overset{18}{R} \xrightarrow{+6} \boxed{\overset{24}{X}}$

∴ ? = TVX

114. (*b*) The pattern is as follows

1st Letter : $\overset{24}{X} \xrightarrow{-2} \overset{22}{V} \xrightarrow{-3} \overset{19}{S} \xrightarrow{-4} \overset{15}{O} \xrightarrow{-5} \boxed{\overset{10}{J}}$

2nd Letter : $\overset{23}{W} \xrightarrow{-3} \overset{20}{T} \xrightarrow{-4} \overset{16}{P} \xrightarrow{-5} \overset{11}{K} \xrightarrow{-6} \boxed{\overset{5}{E}}$

3rd Letter : $\overset{1}{A} \xrightarrow{+2} \overset{3}{C} \xrightarrow{+3} \overset{6}{F} \xrightarrow{+4} \overset{10}{J} \xrightarrow{+5} \boxed{\overset{15}{O}}$

∴ ? = JEO

115. (*b*) The pattern is as follows

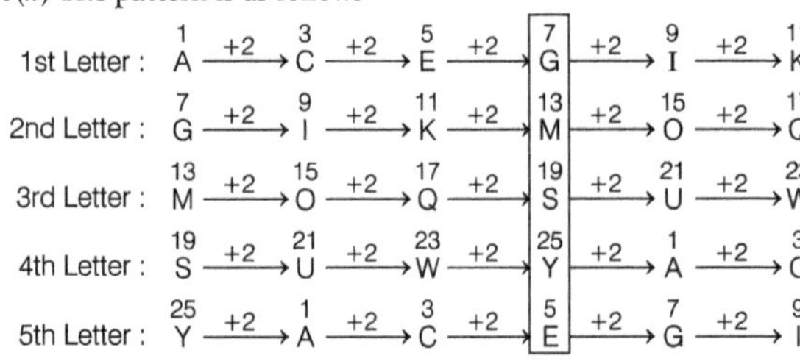

∴ ? = HKGM

116. (*a*) The pattern is as follows

1st Letter :	A (1)	+2	C (3)	+2	E (5)	+2	G (7)	+2	I (9)	+2	K (11)
2nd Letter :	G (7)	+2	I (9)	+2	K (11)	+2	M (13)	+2	O (15)	+2	Q (17)
3rd Letter :	M (13)	+2	O (15)	+2	Q (17)	+2	S (19)	+2	U (21)	+2	W (23)
4th Letter :	S (19)	+2	U (21)	+2	W (23)	+2	Y (25)	+2	A (1)	+2	C (3)
5th Letter :	Y (25)	+2	A (1)	+2	C (3)	+2	E (5)	+2	G (7)	+2	I (9)

∴ ? = GMSYE

117. (*b*) In the following series, the next term is obtained by shifting the first letter of the previous term to the last place.

∴ ? = DABC

118. (*a*) There are two interwoven series here.

bc, de, fg, (Each next term is formed by next two letters)
cde, efg, ghi (last letter of the previous term starts the new term and next two letters are included in the same term).

∴ ? = ghi

119. (*a*) From element first to second, first two letters get reversed, from second to third, first three letters get reversed and from third to last, all the four letters get reversed.

∴ Required answer = SQRP

120. (*d*) From element first to second, last two letters are written in reverse order, from element second to third, last three letters are written in reverse order and from element third to fourth, all the four letters are written in reverse order.

∴ Required answer = SDMT

121. (*c*) These are all anagrams of SEAT with one extra letter added. The letters added, in order are

R, S, T, U, V, W, X, Y.

Required answwer ⇒ YEAST

122. (*a*) This sequence consists of the last pair of letters in the words FIRST, SECOND, THIRD, FOURTH, FIFTH, SIXTH.

Required la

123. (*a*) These are the last three letters of the names of the planats in our solar system.

MERCURY, VENUS, EARTH, MARS, JUPITER, SATURN, URANUS, NEPTUNE, PLUTO

124. (*b*) The pattern is as follows

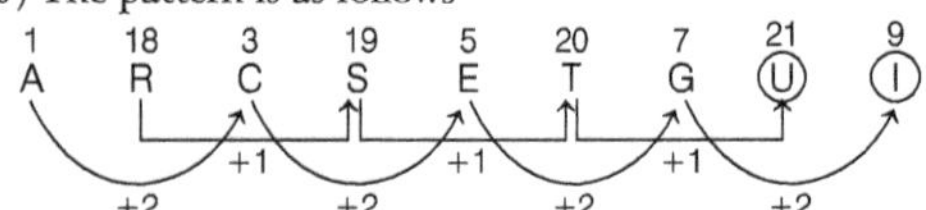

∴ First ? = U, Second ? = I

∴ Required answer = U, I

125. (*c*) The pattern is as follows

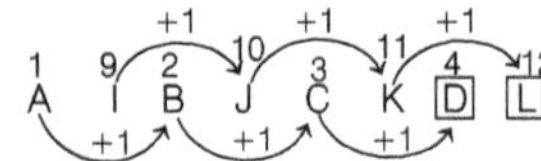

∴ First ? = D

Second ? = L

∴ Required answer = D,L

126. (*c*) The pattern is as follows

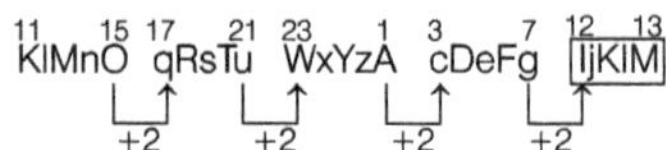

∴ ? = IjKIM

127. (*a*) The pattern is as follows

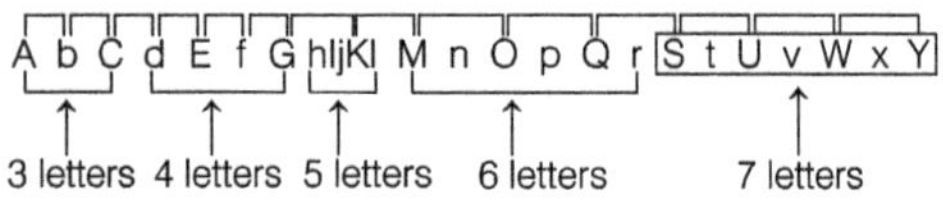

∴ ? = StUvWxY

128. (*b*) Here, the next term is obtained by removing first and last letter from the word alternately.

M I X T U R E, I X T U R E, I X T U R, X T U R, X T U.

Required answer → × TUR

129. (*a*) First word has 3 letters, 2nd word has 4 letters and so on. Thus, last word will have 7 letters i.e. Monsoon.

So, word Monsoon will come in place of question mark (?) in the given series.

130. (*d*) In the given series, by moving from left to right number of letters is increased by one.

tub (3), size (4), latin (5), formal (6), capital (7)

? = capital

131. (*d*) In the given series, the position of 's' is shifting by one.

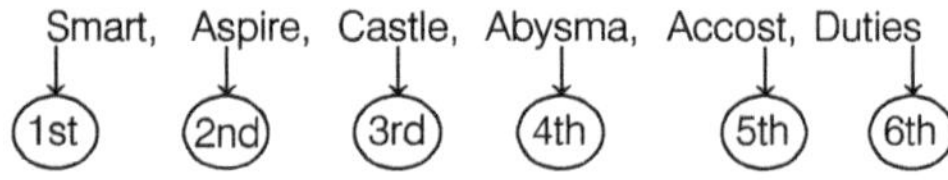

∴ ? = Duties

132. (*a*) In the given series, the position of 'u' is shifting by one.

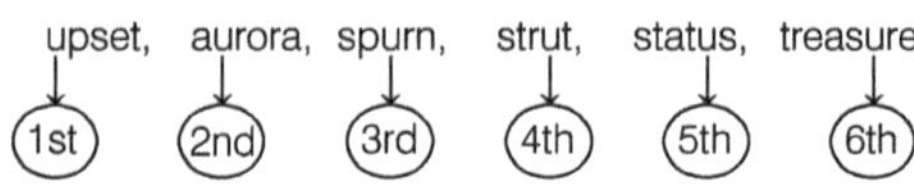

∴ ? = treasure

133. (*c*) In each successive step, one line is shifted from right to left.

Hence, IIIIIX will come in place of question mark.

134. (*b*) The given series is arranged according to the officers ranks in the Indian Army.

Lieutenant → Captain → Major → Lieutenant colonel

Required answer ⇒ Major

135. (*b*) The series pattern is as follows

O/WOO/WOO/WOO/WO

∴ Required answer = O W W O

136. (*c*) The series pattern is as follows

BAC/BAC/BAC/BAC/BAC/BAC

∴ Required answer = CCBA

137. (*c*) The series pattern is as follows

a/xyz/ab/zyx/bc/xyz/c

∴ Required answer = xaycz

138. (*d*) The series pattern is as follows

nml/mnl/nml/mnl/nml/mnl

∴ Required answer = nmnnnl

139. (*d*) The pattern is as follows

ab/ab/ab/ab/ab/ab

∴ Required answer = bbab

140. (*a*) The pattern is as follows

cab/bac/cab/bac/cab/bac

∴ Required answer = acbcb

141. (*c*) Series pattern : abbcabbcc / aabbcc/abbcabbcc

∴ Required answer = bcbbb

142. (*b*) In the given series, the letters are equidistant from the begining and the end.

adbcacbdabcddcbadbcacbda

Hence, the missing letters are cbbaa.

143. (*d*) Series pattern : cab/bac/cab/bac/cab/bac

∴ Required answer = acbcb

144. (*b*) Series pattern : bdac/bdac/bdac/bdac

∴ Required answer = dcadc

145. (*a*) Here, in the series letters 'abcd' are repeated

abcd/a bcd/abcd/abcd

So, the missing letters are cadbdc.

146. (*d*) Series pattern : ccabb/ccabb/ccabb/ccabb

∴ Required answer = cacbc

147. (*c*) Series pattern : bc/abc/abc/abc/abc/abc/a

∴ Required answer = abccb

148. (*a*) Series pattern : mca /mca/mca/mca/mca/mc

∴ Required answer = acmmma

149. (*d*) Here, in the series letters 'ab' are repeated.

ab/ab/ab/ab/ab/ab = bbab

∴ ? = bbab

150. (*d*) Series pattern : aab/aaab/aaaab/aaaaab

Clearly, the number of 'a' is increasing by one in the successive sequence.

∴ Required answer = bbba

151. (*d*) Series pattern a bcd/aab bcc dd/aa abbb cccddd

Clearly, each letter of first sequence is repeated two times in the second sequence and three times in the third sequence.

∴ Required answer = bbdac

152. (*d*) Series pattern : ab cbc/bca c a/c abab

Clearly, the series consists of three sequences, the first sequence begins with a, the second with b and the third with c. Each sequence consists of a letter followed by the pair of other two letters repeated twice.

∴ Required answer = ccaa

153. (*b*) Here in the series word 'BABA' is repeated,

B A B A B A B A B A B A B A B A B A

So, the missing letters are BBBAAA.

154. (*b*) Series pattern is as follows

0 1 2 3/0 1 2 3/0 1 2 3/0

∴ Required answer = 20302

155. (*a*) Series pattern is as follows

4 8 1 9 8 8/4 8 1 9 8 8/4 8 1 9 8 8

∴ Required answer = 1848898

156. (*c*) Series pattern is as follows

0 1 1 0/0 1 1 0/0 1 1 0/0 1 1 0

∴ Required answer = 1100

157. (*a*) The pattern is as follows

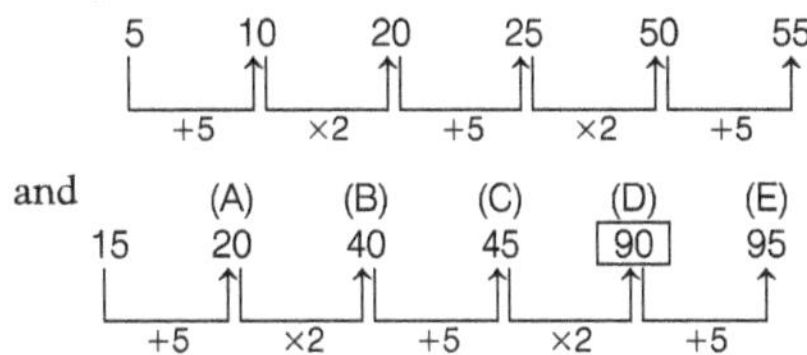

∴ Required number = 90

158. (*a*) The pattern is as follows

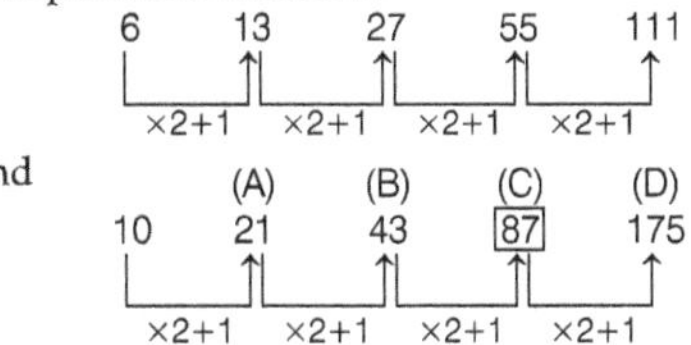

∴ Required number = 87

159. (*a*) The pattern is as follows

C(3) —+3→ F(6) —+3→ [J] I(9) —+3→ L(12) —+3→ O(15)

F(6) —+3→ I(9) —+3→ [L] L(12) —+3→ O(15) —+3→ R(18)

I(9) —+3→ L(12) —+3→ [Q] O(15) —+3→ R(18) —+3→ U(21)

∴ Wrong term = JLQ

160. (*b*) The pattern is as follows

A(1) —+1→ [B] B(2) —+1→ C(3) —+1→ D(4)

Z(26) —−1→ [X] Y(25) —−1→ X(24) —−1→ W(23)

A(1) —+5→ [F] F(6) —+5→ K(11) —+5→ P(16)

∴ Wrong term = BXF

161. (*d*) The pattern is as follows

E(5) —+2→ G(7) —+2→ I(9) —+2→ K(11) —+2→ [N] M(13)

G(7) —+1→ H(8) —+1→ I(9) —+1→ J(10) —+1→ [K] K(11)

P(16) —+1→ Q(17) —+2→ S(19) —+3→ V(22) —+4→ [W] Z(26)

∴ Wrong term = NKW

162. (*b*) The pattern is as follows

Z(26) —+5→ E(5) —+5→ J(10) —+5→ O(15) —+5→ T(20)

V(21) —+1→ W(23) —+1→ X(24) —+1→ Y(25) —+1→ Z(26)

A(1) —+4→ E(5) —+4→ I(9) —+6→ [Q] O(15) —+6→ U(21) (Vowels)

∴ Wrong term = OYQ

163. (*d*) The pattern is as follows

P(16) —+1→ Q(17) —+1→ R(18) —+1→ [S](19) —+1→ T(20)

U(21) —+1→ V(22) —+1→ W(23) —+1→ [X](24) —+1→ Y(25)

B(2) —+2→ D(4) —+3→ G(7) —+4→ [Q] K(11) —+5→ P(16)

∴ Wrong term = SXQ

164. (*c*) The pattern is as follows

$\overset{1}{A} \xrightarrow{+1} \overset{2}{B} \xrightarrow{+1} \overset{3}{C} \xrightarrow{+1} \overset{4}{D} \xrightarrow{+1} \boxed{\overset{5}{E}} \xrightarrow{+1} \overset{6}{F}$

$2 \xrightarrow{\times 2} 4 \xrightarrow{\times 2} 8 \xrightarrow{\times 2} 16 \xrightarrow{\times 2} \boxed{32} \xrightarrow{\times 2} 64$

$\overset{3}{C} \xrightarrow{+1} \overset{4}{D} \xrightarrow{+1} \overset{5}{E} \xrightarrow{+1} \overset{6}{F} \xrightarrow{+1} \boxed{\overset{7}{G}} \xrightarrow{+1} \overset{8}{H}$

∴ ? = E32G

165. (*c*) The pattern is as follows

$3 \xrightarrow{+2} 5 \xrightarrow{+2} \boxed{7}$

$\overset{24}{X} \xrightarrow{-2} \overset{22}{V} \xrightarrow{-2} \boxed{\overset{20}{T}}$

$24 \xrightarrow{-2} 22 \xrightarrow{-2} \boxed{20}$

$\overset{3}{C} \xrightarrow{+2} \overset{5}{E} \xrightarrow{+2} \boxed{\overset{7}{G}}$

∴ ? = 7T20G

166. (*b*) The pattern is as follows

$5 \xrightarrow{+2} 7 \xrightarrow{+2} 9 \xrightarrow{+2} 11 \xrightarrow{+2} \boxed{13}$

$\underset{5}{E} \xrightarrow{+2} \underset{7}{G} \xrightarrow{+2} \underset{9}{I} \xrightarrow{+2} \underset{11}{K} \xrightarrow{+2} \boxed{\underset{13}{M}}$

∴ ? = 13 M

167. (*b*) The pattern is as follows

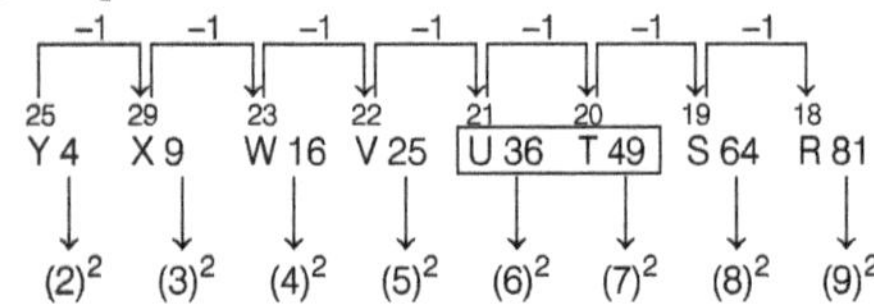

∴ ? = U36T49

168. (*c*) The pattern is as follows

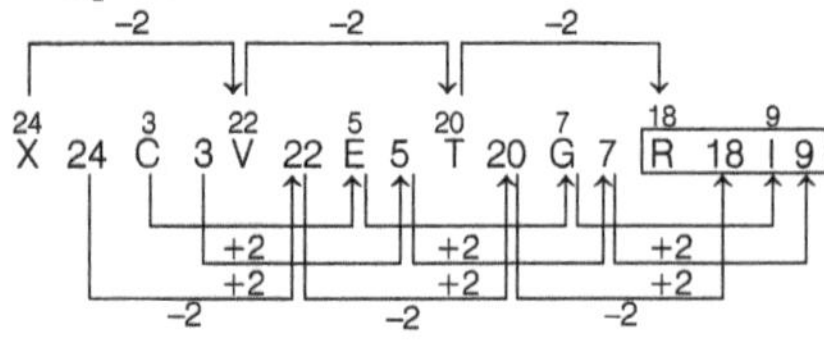

∴ ? = R18I9

169. (*a*) The letters in the given series are in continuous sequence of forward order English alphabet with each letter showing its backward order position in the alphabet.

∴ ? = I-18

170. (*d*) The pattern is as follows

Numbers $2 \xrightarrow{+2} 4 \xrightarrow{+4} 8 \xrightarrow{+6} 14 \xrightarrow{+8} (22)$

Letters $\overset{2}{B} \xrightarrow{+1} \overset{3}{C} \xrightarrow{+2} \overset{5}{E} \xrightarrow{+3} \overset{8}{H} \xrightarrow{+4} (\overset{12}{L})$

∴ ? = 22 L

171. (*b*) The given sequence has two parts.

Part I 2, 9, 6, 13

Part II A, B, C, D

Series pattern of part I is as follows

$2 \xrightarrow{+7} 9 \xrightarrow{-3} 6 \xrightarrow{+7} 13 \xrightarrow{-3} (10)$

∴ ? = 10

172. (*d*) There are three interwoven sequences here.

128, 64, 32, 16, 8, $\boxed{4}$ (dividing each time by 2)

61, 63, 65, 67, 69, $\boxed{71}$ (adding 2 each time)

Y, S, N, J, G, $\boxed{E}$

(move 6 letters backward then 5, then 4, 3, 2)

173. (*c*) The pattern is as follows

1st letter $\overset{14}{N} \xrightarrow{-3} \overset{11}{K} \xrightarrow{-3} (\overset{8}{H}) \xrightarrow{-3} \overset{5}{E} \xrightarrow{-3} \overset{2}{B}$

Middle number $5 \xrightarrow{+2} 7 \xrightarrow{+3} (10) \xrightarrow{+4} 14 \xrightarrow{+5} 19$

3rd letter $\overset{22}{V} \xrightarrow{-2} \overset{20}{T} \xrightarrow{-2} (\overset{18}{R}) \xrightarrow{-2} \overset{16}{P} \xrightarrow{-2} \overset{14}{N}$

∴ ? = H10R

174. (*c*) Letter positions are added.

4 + 5 = 9	6 + 3 = 9
D E	F C
12 + 16 = 28	7 + 20 = 27
L P	G T

∴ ? = 27

175. (*a*) Letter positions are multiplied.

3 × 4 = 12	12 × 2 = 24
C D	L B
2 × 16 = 32	14 × 5 = 70
B P	N E

∴ ? = 70

176. (*c*) The letters move back and forth by powers of 2 starting from 2^0, 2^1 and so on.

i.e., −1, +2, −4, +8, −16

The numbers multiply each time by a number one higher *i.e.*, × 2, × 3, × 4, × 5, × 6.

∴ ? = F720

177. (*b*) The pattern is as follows

$\overset{1}{A}\,1\,\overset{26}{Z}$, $\overset{5}{E}\,2\,\overset{22}{V}$, $\overset{9}{I}\,6\,\overset{18}{R}$, $\overset{13}{M}\,21\,\overset{14}{N}$, $\overset{17}{Q}\,88\,\overset{10}{J}$, $\overset{21}{U}\,445\,\overset{6}{F}$

+4 (1×1)+1 −4 | +4 (2×2)+2 −4 | +4 (6×3)+3 −4 | +4 (21×4)+4 −4 | +4 (88×5)+5 −4

∴ ? = U445F

178. (*a*) The pattern is as follows

Numbers $\overset{23}{W} \xrightarrow{-2} (\overset{21}{U}) \xrightarrow{-2} \overset{19}{S} \xrightarrow{-2} \overset{17}{Q} \xrightarrow{-2} \overset{15}{O}$

Letters $\overset{(12)^2}{144} \longrightarrow (\overset{(11)^2}{121}) \longrightarrow \overset{(10)^2}{100} \longrightarrow \overset{(9)^2}{81} \longrightarrow \overset{(8)^2}{64}$

∴ ? = U-121

179. (*a*) The pattern is as follows

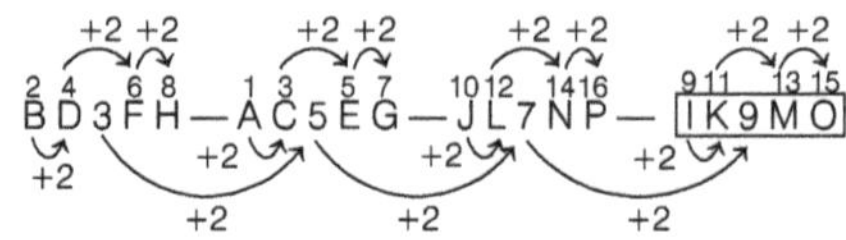

∴ ? = IK9MO

CHAPTER / 06

Logical Arrangement of Words

Logical Arrangement is the meaningful arrangement of words in accordance with the natural laws and universally accepted concepts.

In this type of problems, a sequence is to be formed with the given number of words in such a way that the particular arrangement of the words gives a logical step by step completion of some process or activity. In these questions, generally four/five/six words are given which are related to each other in some or other way.

The candidate is required to find out the proper logical arrangement of these words from the given alternatives.

Several types of problems based on logical arrangement of words asked in various competitive exams are categorised as follows

TYPE 01

Meaningful Arrangement of Words

In this type of questions, the given words are related to a particular event, class/group or represent the various stages of a certain process or arranged on the basis of increasing/ decreasing order of their size, age, need or intensity etc.

A candidate is required to choose that option from the given alternatives, which represents the correct logical sequence of the process.

***Ex* 01** Which one of the given responses would be a logical sequence of the following words? « CG APO 2017

1. Plant 2. Fruit 3. Seed
4. Flower 5. Tree

(a) 3, 1, 5, 4, 2 (b) 3, 1, 2, 4, 5
(c) 3, 1, 5, 2, 4 (d) 4, 3, 2, 5, 1

Solution* *(a) The logical sequence of given word is as follows

Seed (3) → Plant (1) → Tree (5) → Flower (4) → Fruit (2)

i.e. 3, 1, 5, 4, 2

***Ex* 02** Arrange the following words in a meaningful order.

1. Injury 2. Recovery 3. Accident 4. Showroom
5. Drive 6. Car « SSC CPO 2018

(a) 6, 4, 3, 5, 1, 2 (b) 5, 6, 3, 2, 1, 4
(c) 4, 6, 5, 3, 1, 2 (d) 4, 6, 5, 3, 2, 1

Solution* *(c) Logical sequence of the given word is as below

Showroom (4) → Car (6) → Drive (5) → Accident (3) → Injury (1) → Recovery (2)

i.e. 4, 6, 5, 3, 1, 2

***Ex* 03** Arrange the following words in a logical sequence.

1. Trillion 2. Thousand
3. Billion 4. Hundred
5. Million « SSC MTS 2009

(a) 1, 2, 4, 3, 5 (b) 1, 5, 3, 2, 4
(c) 4, 2, 3, 5, 1 (d) 4, 2, 5, 3, 1

Solution* *(d) All the words represent the counting numbers and their increasing order is given as below

Hundred (4)→Thousand (2)→Million (5)→Billion (3)→Trillion (1)

This order is given in option (d) i.e. 4, 2, 5, 3, 1.

***Ex* 04** Arrange the given words in a meaningful sequence and then choose the most appropriate sequence from amongst the options provided below. « SSC Steno 2016

1. Printer 2. Publisher 3. Writer
4. Editor 5. Seller

(a) 2, 3, 4, 1, 5 (b) 3, 4, 2, 1, 5
(c) 3, 4, 1, 2, 5 (d) 2, 4, 3, 5, 1

Solution* *(b) Meaningful sequence of the given words is as below

Writer (3) → Editor (4) → Publisher (2) → Printer (1) → Seller (5)

i.e. 3, 4, 2, 1, 5

***Ex* 05** Arrange the following words in a meaningful order.

1. Andhra Pradesh 2. Universe 3. Tirupati
4. World 5. India « SSC FCI 2012

(a) 3, 1, 4, 5, 2 (b) 1, 3, 5, 4, 2
(c) 3, 1, 5, 4, 2 (d) 3, 1, 2, 4, 5

Solution (c) Tirupati is a city situated in the Andhra Pradesh state of India. India is a part of the world and world is a part of the universe.

So, the correct sequence of part to whole is given as

Tirupati (3) → Andhra Pradesh (1) → India (5) → World (4) → Universe (2)

and the correct option showing this sequence is (c)

i.e. 3, 1, 5, 4, 2

Ex 06 Arrange the words given below in a meaningful sequence. « MP Police SI 2017

1. Wall 2. Clay 3. House 4. Room 5. Bricks

(a) 1, 2, 3, 4, 5 (b) 2, 5, 1, 4, 3
(c) 5, 2, 1, 4, 3 (d) 2, 5, 4, 1, 3

Solution (b) Meaningful sequence of given words is as below

Clay (2) → Bricks (5) → Wall (1) → Room (4) → House (3)
i.e. 2, 5, 1, 4, 3

Ex 07 Arrange the following in a logical sequence from small to big. « SSC CGL 2019

1. Crocodile 2. Lizard 3. Whale 4. Housefly 5. Monkey

(a) 4, 3, 2, 1, 5 (b) 4, 5, 2, 1, 3
(c) 4, 2, 5, 1, 3 (d) 3, 5, 4, 1, 2

Solution (c) The logical sequence of the given words is as below

Housefly (4) → Lizard (2) → Monkey (5) → Crocodile (1) → Whale (3)

i.e. 4, 2, 5, 1, 3

TYPE 02

Sequential Order of Words According to Dictionary

In such type of questions, the candidate is required to choose that option from the given alternatives, which is having the correct sequential order of words according to the English dictionary.

To check the order of words in English dictionary, first of all check the first letter of each word to find which among these comes first in English alphabet followed by second letter and so on. The word whose letter comes first in English alphabet comes first, the word whose letter comes second in English alphabet comes second and so on.

Moreover, let us take an overview of how the given words are arranged according to English dictionary with the help of an example in the following steps.

e.g. Arrangement of Pencil, Pen, Panel, Pick

***Step* I** Here, each word starts with the same letter P, so go through the second letter of the given words. Here, second letters are e, e, a, i. Alphabet 'a' comes first in the English alphabetical order, so first word will be Panel.

Panel, Pencil/Pen/Pick

***Step* II** Now go through the second letter of rest three words. Second letters are e, e and i. The letter 'e', comes first and 'i' comes later in the English alphabet so the words pencil and pen will set before the word pick in the final arrangement.

Panel, Pencil/Pen, Pick

***Step* III** Now, compare the words pen and pencil. In these two words first, second and third letters are same, so go through the fourth letter. We find that pen will be the second word of the arrangement because there is no letter after 'n' in this word as given in pencil and pick remains last word, so we have the final arrangement as

Panel, Pen, Pencil, Pick

Ex 08 Arrange the following words in alphabetical order and select the correct sequence from the given options. « SSC Steno 2019

1. Glamorous 2. Glucose 3. Galvanise
4. Gelatin 5. Ground

(a) 3, 4, 1, 2, 5 (b) 1, 2, 3, 5, 4
(c) 4, 3, 1, 2, 5 (d) 3, 4, 2, 1, 5

Solution (a) The sequence of the given words as per the dictionary is as below

Galvanise(3) → Gelatin (4) → Glamorous (1) → Glucose (2) → Ground (5)

i.e. 3, 4, 1, 2, 5

Ex 09 Arrange the given words in the sequence in which they occur in the dictionary. « SSC Delhi Police Constable 2017

1. Doom 2. Down 3. Drone
4. Drape 5. Ding

(a) 5, 1, 2, 4, 3 (b) 5, 1, 2, 3, 4
(c) 5, 2, 1, 4, 3 (d) 5, 2, 1, 3, 4

Solution (a) Sequence of given words as per the dictionary is as below

Ding (5) → Doom (1) → Down (2) → Drape (4) → Drone (3)
i.e. 5, 1, 2, 4, 3

Ex 10 Arrange the following words according to English dictionary. « SSC MTS 2013

1. Episode 2. Epistle 3. Episcope 4. Epigraph

(a) 1, 2, 3, 4 (b) 4, 2, 1, 3 (c) 3, 2, 1, 4 (d) 4, 3, 1, 2

Solution (d) As per the English dictionary, the correct sequential order of words is

Epigraph (4) → Episcope (3) → Episode (1) → Epistle (2)
i.e. 4, 3, 1, 2.

Ex 11 If the given words are arranged according to English dictionary, which word will be in third place? « SSC CGL 2016

1. KNOW 2. KNACK 3. KNIT 4. KNOB

(a) KNACK (b)KNIT (c) KNOW (d) KNOB

Solution (d) Sequence of given words according to dictionary is as follows

KNACK → KNIT → KNOB → KNOW

It is clear from above that KNOB is on third place.

Ex 12 Which of the following words will come fourth in English dictionary? « SSC Steno 2015

(a) Degrade (b) Density
(c) Deterioration (d) Determination

Solution (d) The sequence of given words as per the dictionary is as given below

Degrade → Density → Deterioration → Determination

So, the word 'Determination' will come fourth.

Practice / CORNER

DIRECTIONS ~ (Q. Nos. 1-49) *In each of the following questions, arrange the given words in meaningful sequence and choose the correct sequence from the given alternatives.*

1. 1. District 2. Village 3. State 4. Block
(a) 2, 1, 4, 3 (b) 2, 3, 4, 1 (c) 2, 4, 1, 3 (d) 3, 2, 1, 4

2. 1. Tired 2. Night 3. Day 4. Sleep 5. Work « SSC CPO 2010
(a) 1, 3, 5, 2, 4 (b) 3, 5, 1, 4, 2
(c) 3, 5, 1, 2, 4 (d) 3, 5, 2, 1, 4

3. 1. Poverty 2. Population 3. Death
4. Unemployment 5. Disease « UK PSC 2017
(a) 3, 4, 2, 5, 1 (b) 2, 4, 1, 5, 3
(c) 2, 3, 4, 5, 1 (d) 1, 2, 3, 4, 5

4. 1. Nation 2. Village 3. State 4. District 5. Town « CG (APO) 2017
(a) 1, 2, 5, 3, 4 (b) 2, 1, 3, 4, 5
(c) 2, 5, 4, 1, 3 (d) 2, 5, 4, 3, 1

5. 1. Flat 2. Street 3. Room 4. Apartment 5. City « SSC (10+2) 2020
(a) 3, 5, 1, 4, 2 (b) 5, 4, 3, 2, 1
(c) 3, 1, 4, 2, 5 (d) 3, 4, 1, 2, 5

6. 1. Vegetable 2. Market 3. Cutting 4. Cooking
5. Food
(a) 1, 2, 3, 4,5 (b) 2, 1, 3, 4, 5
(c) 3, 1, 2, 5, 4 (d) 5, 2, 1, 3, 4

7. 1. Punishment 2. Prison 3. Arrest 4. Crime
5. Judgement
(a) 5, 1, 2, 3, 4 (b) 4, 3, 2, 5, 1
(c) 4, 3, 5, 1, 2 (d) 2, 3, 1, 4, 5

8. 1. Elephant 2. Cat 3. Mosquito 4. Tiger
5. Whale « SSC CGL 2015
(a) 1, 3, 5, 4, 2 (b) 2, 5, 1, 4, 3
(c) 3, 2, 4, 1, 5 (d) 5, 3, 1, 2, 4

9. 1. Country 2. District 3. State 4. Village
5. Continent
(a) 5, 4, 3, 2, 1 (b) 1, 3, 2, 5, 4
(c) 4, 2, 3, 1, 5 (d) 2, 1, 3, 5, 4

10. 1. Frog 2. Eagle 3. Grasshopper
4. Snake 5. Grass « SSC CGL 2015
(a) 1, 3, 5, 2, 4 (b) 3, 4, 2, 5, 1
(c) 5, 3, 1, 4, 2 (d) 5, 3, 4, 2, 1

11. 1. Mother 2. Child 3. Milk 4. Cry 5. Smile
(a) 1, 5, 2, 4, 3 (b) 2, 4, 1, 3, 5
(c) 2, 4, 3, 1, 5 (d) 3, 2, 1, 5, 4

12. 1. Child 2. Job 3. Marriage 4. Infant
5. Education « SSC Constable 2015
(a) 1, 3, 5, 2, 4 (b) 4, 3, 5, 2, 1
(c) 4, 1, 5, 2, 3 (d) 2, 3, 1, 4, 5

13. 1. Plant 2. Fruit 3. Seed 4. Flower
(a) 3, 2, 4, 1 (b) 3, 1, 2, 4 (c) 3, 1, 4, 2 (d) 3, 2, 1, 4

14. 1. Protect 2. Pressure 3. Relief 4. Rain 5. Flood
(a) 2, 4, 3, 1, 5 (b) 2, 4, 5, 1, 3
(c) 2, 5, 4, 1, 3 (d) 3, 2, 4, 5, 1

15. 1. Hexagon 2. Nonagon 3. Pentagon
4. Heptagon 5. Octagon « SSC (CGL) 2020
(a) 1, 4, 5, 2, 3 (b) 4, 3, 1, 2, 5
(c) 3, 1, 4, 5, 2 (d) 1, 3, 4, 5, 2

16. 1. Consultation 2. Illness 3. Doctor 4. Treatment
5. Recovery « SSC CPO 2012, WBCS (Pre) 2018
(a) 2, 3, 1, 4, 5 (b) 2, 3, 4, 1, 5
(c) 4, 3, 1, 2, 5 (d) 5, 1, 4, 3, 2

17. 1. Rainbow 2. Rain 3. Sun 4. Happy 5. Child
(a) 2, 1, 4, 3, 5 (b) 2, 3, 1, 5, 4
(c) 4, 2, 3, 5, 1 (d) 4, 5, 1, 2, 3

18. 1. Study 2. Job 3. Examination
4. Earn 5. Apply
(a) 1, 2, 3, 4, 5 (b) 1, 3, 2, 5, 4
(c) 1, 3, 5, 4, 2 (d) 1, 3, 5, 2, 4

19. 1. Key 2. Door 3. Lock 4. Room
5. Switch on
(a) 5, 1, 2, 4, 3 (b) 4, 2, 1, 5, 3
(c) 1, 2, 3, 5, 4 (d) 1, 3, 2, 4, 5

20. 1. Farmer 2. Seed 3. Food 4. Cultivation
(a) 1, 2, 4, 3 (b) 2, 1, 3, 4 (c) 4, 2, 3, 1 (d) 3, 1, 4, 2

21. 1. Weaving 2. Cotton 3. Cloth 4. Thread
(a) 2, 4, 1, 3 (b) 2, 4, 3, 1 (c) 4, 2, 1, 3 (d) 3, 1, 4, 2

22. 1. Compose 2. Appreciation 3. Money
4. Think 5. Sing
(a) 1,4, 2, 5, 3 (b) 4, 1, 5, 2, 3
(c) 2, 4, 3, 5, 1 (d) 5, 4, 2, 1, 3
(e) 3, 2, 4, 1, 5

23. 1. Sending 2. Encoding 3. Receiving 4. Decoding « SSC 10+2 2013
(a) 2, 4, 3,1 (b) 4, 2, 1, 3 (c) 1, 2, 3, 4 (d) 2, 1, 3, 4

24. 1. Birth 2. Death 3. Funeral 4. Marriage
5. Education
(a) 4, 5, 3, 1, 2 (b) 2, 3, 4, 5, 1
(c) 1, 5, 4, 2, 3 (d) 1, 3, 4, 5, 2

25. 1. Honey 2. Flower 3. Bee 4. Wax
(a) 1, 3, 4, 2 (b) 2, 1, 4, 2,
(c) 2, 3, 1, 4 (d) 4, 3, 2, 1

26. 1. Lungs 2. Nostrils 3. Windpipe 4. Blood
(a) 1, 2, 3, 4 (b) 2, 3, 1, 4
(c) 1, 3, 4, 2 (d) 4, 3, 2, 1

27. 1. Pupa 2. Larva 3. Moth 4. Egg « SSC CGL 2013
(a) 4, 2, 1, 3 (b) 4, 1, 2, 3
(c) 4, 3, 2, 1 (d) 4, 3, 1, 2

28. 1. Atom 2. Matter 3. Molecule 4. Electron « SSC 10+2 2015
(a) 4, 1, 3, 2 (b) 1, 2, 3, 4
(c) 3, 4, 1, 2 (d) 3, 1, 4, 2

29. 1. Ornaments 2. Gold 3. Goldsmith
4. Jewellery shop 5. Bride « SSC CPO 2019
(a) 4, 2, 5, 3, 1 (b) 2, 5, 4, 3, 1
(c) 2, 4, 5, 1, 3 (d) 2, 3, 1, 4, 5

30. 1. Red fort 2. World 3. Delhi 4. India
5. Universe « UPSSSC Junior Assist. 2017
(a) 1, 3, 4, 5, 2 (b) 1, 3, 4, 2, 5
(c) 1, 4, 3, 2, 5 (d) 1, 3, 2, 4, 5

31. 1. Lake 2. Pond 3. Sea 4. Ocean 5. Puddle « KVS LDC 2017
(a) 5, 2, 4, 3, 1 (b) 5, 2, 1, 3, 4
(c) 1, 5, 3, 2, 4 (d) 5, 2, 3, 1, 4

32. 1. Protect 2. Rain 3. Pressure 4. Flood 5. Relief
(a) 2, 3, 4, 1, 5 (b) 3, 2, 4, 1, 5
(c) 2, 3, 5, 1, 4 (d) 3, 2, 4, 5, 1

33. 1. Animal 2. Feline
3. Leopard 4. Mammal
5. Vertebrate 6. Cat « WBCS Pre 2018
(a) 1, 2, 3, 4, 5, 6 (b) 1, 3, 5, 4, 2, 6
(c) 1, 4, 3, 2, 5, 6 (d) 1, 5, 4, 2, 3, 6

34. 1. Rivulet 2. Ocean 3. Tributary 4. River
5. Sea 6. Rain « SSC CGL 2015
(a) 5, 6, 1, 3, 2, 4 (b) 6, 5, 3, 1, 2, 4
(c) 6, 1, 3, 4, 5, 2 (d) 6, 4, 1, 3, 5, 2

35. 1. Index 2. Contents 3. Title 4. Chapters
5. Introduction « SSC CPO 2015
(a) 3, 2, 5, 1, 4 (b) 2, 3, 4, 5, 1
(c) 5, 1, 4, 2, 3 (d) 3, 2, 5, 4, 1

36. 1. Butterfly 2. Cocoon 3. Egg 4. Worm
(a) 1, 3, 4, 2 (b) 1, 4, 3, 2 (c) 2, 4, 1, 3 (d) 3, 4, 2, 1

37. 1. Chapter 2. Word 3. Letter
4. Phrase 5. Paragraph 6. Sentence « SSC CPO 2019
(a) 3, 2, 4, 6, 5, 1 (b) 2, 3, 4, 1, 6, 5
(c) 3, 2, 6, 4, 5, 1 (d) 3, 2, 4, 6, 1, 5

38. 1. Design 2. Need 3. Launching 4. Research
5. Testing 6. Identify « CLAT 2018
(a) 4, 1, 6, 2, 3, 5 (b) 2, 6, 4, 1, 5, 3
(c) 3, 5, 4, 1, 6, 2 (d) 2, 4, 1, 5, 6, 3

39. 1. Kilobyte 2. Byte
3. Megabyte 4. Terabyte
5. Gigabyte 6. Bit « UGC NET 2018
Give your answer from the following codes
(a) 6, 2, 1, 3, 5, 4 (b) 6, 2, 1, 4, 3, 5
(c) 6, 2, 1, 3, 4, 5 (d) 6, 2, 1, 4, 5, 3

40. 1. Windows 2. Walls 3. Floor
4. Foundation 5. Roof 6. Room
(a) 4, 5, 3, 2, 1, 6 (b) 4, 3, 5, 6, 2, 1
(c) 4, 2, 1, 5, 3, 6 (d) 4, 1, 5, 6, 2, 3

41. 1. Twilight 2. Dawn 3. Noon 4. Night
(a) 2, 1, 3, 4 (b) 2, 3, 1, 4
(c) 1, 2, 3, 4 (d) 1, 3, 2, 4

42. 1. Caste 2. Family
3. Newly married couple 4. Clan
5. Species « FCI Constable 2018
(a) 2, 3, 1, 4, 5 (b) 3, 2, 1, 4, 5
(c) 3, 4, 5, 1, 2 (d) 4, 5, 3, 2, 1

43. 1. Postbox 2. Letter 3. Envelope 4. Delivery
5. Clearance
(a) 3, 2, 4, 5, 1 (b) 3, 2, 1, 5, 4
(c) 3, 2, 1, 4, 5 (d) 2, 3, 1, 4, 5

44. 1. Probation 2. Interview
3. Selection 4. Appointment
5. Advertisement 6. Application
(a) 5, 6, 2, 3, 4, 1 (b) 5, 6, 3, 2, 4, 1
(c) 5, 6, 4, 2, 3, 1 (d) 6, 5, 4, 2, 3, 1

45. 1. Presentation 2. Recommendation
3. Arrival 4. Discussion
5. Introduction
(a) 3, 5, 1, 2, 4 (b) 3, 5, 4, 2, 1
(c) 5, 3, 1, 2, 4 (d) 5, 3, 4, 1, 2

46. 1. Atomic age 2. Metallic age
3. Stone age 4. Alloy age
(a) 1, 3, 4, 2 (b) 2, 3, 1, 4
(c) 3, 2, 4, 1 (d) 4, 3, 2, 1

47. 1. Station 2. Boarding 3. Train
4. Deboarding 5. Destination « SSC CGL 2015
(a) 1, 2, 3, 4, 5 (b) 1, 3, 2, 5, 4
(c) 3, 2, 1, 4, 5 (d) 5, 4, 3, 2, 1

48. 1. Euphoria 2. Happiness 3. Ambivalence
4. Ecstasy 5. Pleasure
(a) 1, 4, 2, 5, 3 (b) 2, 1, 3, 4, 5
(c) 3, 2, 5, 1, 4 (d) 4, 1, 3, 2, 5

49. 1. Implementation 2. Conceptual Modelling
3. Requirements Analysis 4. Logical Modelling
5. Physical Model 6. Scheme Refinement
(a) 3, 2, 4, 6, 5, 1 (b) 1, 3, 2, 6, 5, 4
(c) 3, 2, 5, 4, 6, 1 (d) 3, 2, 1, 4, 6, 5

50. Which one of the given responses would be a meaningful order of the following continents in descending order of area?
1. South America 2. Africa
3. Europe 4. Australia
5. North America
(a) 2, 1, 5, 3, 4 (b) 2, 5, 1, 3, 4
(c) 2, 5, 1, 4, 3 (d) 2, 1, 5, 4, 3

51. If the given words are arranged in descending order, then which of the following be last? « SSC CGL 2016

Sapling, Tree, Plant, Seed

(a) Sapling (b) Plant (c) Seed (d) Tree

DIRECTIONS ~ (Q. Nos. 52-61) *Which one of the given responses would be a meaningful order of the following words?*

52. 1. Reading 2. Composing 3. Writing 4. Printing

(a) 1, 3, 4, 2 (b) 2, 3, 4, 1
(c) 3, 1, 2, 4 (d) 3, 2, 4, 1

53. 1. Family 2. Community 3. Member 4. Locality 5. Country

(a) 3, 1, 2, 4, 5 (b) 3, 1, 2, 5, 4
(c) 3, 1, 4, 2, 5 (d) 3, 1, 4, 5, 2

54. 1. Income 2. Status 3. Education 4. Well-being 5. Job « RRB NTPC 2016

(a) 1, 3, 2, 5, 4 (b) 1, 2, 5, 3, 4
(c) 3, 1, 5, 2, 4 (d) 3, 5, 1, 2, 4

55. 1. Gold 2. Iron 3. Sand 3. Platinum 5. Diamond

(a) 2, 4, 3, 5, 1 (b) 3, 2, 1, 5, 4
(c) 4, 5, 1, 3, 2 (d) 5, 4, 3, 2, 1

56. 1. Foetus 2. Child 3. Baby 4. Adult 5. Youth

(a) 1, 2, 4, 3, 5 (b) 1, 3, 2, 4, 5
(c) 2, 3, 5, 4, 1 (d) 5, 4, 2, 3, 1

57. 1. Weekly 2. Daily 3. Monthly 4. Fortnightly 5. Bimonthly

(a) 1, 4, 3, 2, 5 (b) 2, 1, 4, 3, 5
(c) 4, 1, 2, 3, 5 (d) 5, 1, 2, 3, 4

58. 1. Shoulder 2. Wrist 3. Elbow 4. Palm 5. Finger

(a) 5, 4, 2, 3, 1 (b) 3, 4, 5, 2, 1
(c) 3, 1, 4, 2, 5 (d) 2, 4, 5, 3, 1

59. 1. Hecto 2. Centi 3. Deca 4. Kilo 5. Deci

(a) 2, 5, 3, 1, 4 (b) 1, 3, 4, 5, 2
(c) 1, 5, 3, 4, 2 (d) 5, 2, 1, 4, 3

60. 1. Collector 2. Governor 3. Chief Secretary 4. President 5. Clerk

(a) 1, 2, 3, 4, 5 (b) 5, 1, 3, 2, 4
(c) 5, 1, 3, 4, 2 (d) 5, 1, 4, 3, 2

61. 1. Star 2. Satellite 3. Galaxy 4. Planet 5. Universe « SSC CPO 2019

(a) 5, 3, 1, 4, 2 (b) 2, 1, 5, 3, 4
(c) 5, 1, 3, 2, 4 (d) 3, 1, 5, 2, 4

DIRECTIONS ~ (Q. Nos. 62-79) *Arrange the following words as per order in the dictionary.*

62. 1. Joke 2. Jockey 3. Jocular 4. Jocund « SSC CHSL 2017

(a) 4, 2, 1, 3 (b) 2, 3, 4, 1
(c) 2, 3, 1, 4 (d) 4, 2, 3, 1

63. 1. Tinned 2. Timber 3. Tinkle 4. Thunderstorm 5. Thursday « SSC CHSL 2018

(a) 5,3,2,1,4 (b) 2,1,3,4,5 (c) 4,5,2,3,1 (d) 1,2,4,3,5

64. 1. Theme 2. Thirst 3. Thing 4. Thames 5. Thurst « SSC MTS 2017

(a) 4,2,3,5,1 (b) 4,1,2,3,5 (c) 4,3,2,5,1 (d) 4,1,3,2,5

65. 1. Banquet 2. Bangle 3. Bandage 4. Bantam 5. Bangalore « Delhi Police Constable 2017

(a) 5, 1, 2, 4, 3 (b) 4, 5, 3, 1, 2
(c) 3, 5, 2, 1, 4 (d) 4, 1, 2, 5, 3

66. 1. Mobile 2. Mandate 3. Mandarin 4. Monkey 5. Master « SSC CPO 2017

(a) 3, 2, 5, 1, 4 (b) 3, 1, 2, 5, 4
(c) 3, 5, 2, 4, 1 (d) 3, 5, 2, 1, 4

67. 1. Drink 2. Drinking 3. Drive 4. Dictionary 5. Dracula « SSC CPO 2017

(a) 4, 5, 1, 2, 3 (b) 4, 1, 5, 3, 2
(c) 4, 2, 5, 1, 3 (d) 4, 5, 2, 1, 3

68. 1. Divide 2. Divisions 3. Devine 4. Divest 5. Direct

(a) 5, 4, 3, 1, 2 (b) 5, 4, 1, 3, 2 (c) 1, 2, 3, 4, 5 (d) 3, 5, 4, 1, 2

69. 1. Hair 2. Heena 3. Harmonium 4. Host

(a) 2, 3, 4, 1 (b) 1, 3, 4, 2
(c) 1, 3, 2, 4 (d) 3, 1, 2, 4

70. 1. Bound 2. Bonus 3. Bunch 4. Board

(a) 1, 4, 2, 3 (b) 2, 4, 3, 1 (c) 4, 2, 1, 3 (d) 4, 3, 2, 1

71. 1. Joker 2. Humanistic 3. Carpenter 4. Animated

(a) 4, 3, 2, 1 (b) 4, 1, 2, 3 (c) 3, 2, 4, 1 (d) 1, 3, 2, 4

72. 1. Billion 2. Bifurcate 3. Bilateral 4. Bilirubin

(a) 2,1,3,4 (b) 4,3,2,1 (c) 2,3,4,1 (d) 2,3,1,4

73. 1. Piquant 2. Pierce 3. Patent 4. Perjury 5. Pasture « SSC CPO 2019

(a) 5, 3, 4, 1, 2 (b) 3, 4, 5, 1, 2
(c) 5, 3, 4, 2, 1 (d) 3, 5, 4, 1, 2

74. 1. Ambitious 2. Ambiguous 3. Ambiguity 4. Animation 5. Animals

(a) 3, 2, 4, 1, 5 (b) 3, 2, 5, 4, 1
(c) 3, 2, 1, 5, 4 (d) 3, 2, 4, 5, 1

75. 1. Artistic 2. Anonymous 3. Antonymous 4. Arrogant

(a) 1, 2, 3, 4 (b) 2, 3, 4, 1 (c) 3, 2, 1, 4 (d) 3, 4, 1, 2

76. 1. Necrology 2. Necromancy 3. Necropolis 4. Necrophilia

(a) 2,1, 4, 3 (b) 1, 2, 3, 4 (c) 1, 2, 4, 3 (d) 2, 1, 3, 4

77. 1. Important 2. Impart 3. Improvise 4. Improve

(a) 1, 2, 3, 4 (b) 2, 1, 4, 3
(c) 3, 4, 1, 2 (d) 2, 1, 3, 4

78. 1. Aqueous 2. Aquarium 3. Aquiline 4. Aquatic

(a) 4, 3, 2, 1 (b) 1, 2, 3, 4 (c) 2, 4, 1, 3 (d) 3, 1, 4, 2

79. 1. Epitaxy 2. Episode 3. Epigene 4. Epitome 5. Epilogue « WBCS Pre 2018
(a) 1, 2, 3, 4, 5 (b) 3, 2, 1, 5, 4
(c) 3, 5, 2, 1, 4 (d) 1, 3, 2, 5, 4

80. From the given alternatives, according to dictionary, which word will come at second position?
1.Charity 2. Cardigan 3. Caravan 4. Carton 5. Challenge
(a) Charity (b) Challenge (c) Cardigan (d) Caravan

81. MABELA, MABLE, MABUSE, MABEPEARL,?
If the above given words are arranged in the dictionary then the last word is « RRB ALP 2018
(a) MABUSE (b) MABEPEARL
(c) MABELA (d) MABLE

82. Arrange the following words as per the English dictionary and find the last word.
Leaf, Lean, Leave, Less
(a) Lean (b) Leave (c) Less (d) Leaf

83. Which one of the following words will appear last in the English dictionary? « MP Patwari 2017
(a) Encradle (b) Encode (c) Encourage (d) Encounter

84. If the following words are arranged in alphabetical order, which word will come in the middle?
Electric, Elector, Elect, Election, Electrode « UKPSC Pre 2017
(a) Elector (b) Electric (c) Election (d) Electrode

85. Which of the following word will come fourth if arranged according to the English dictionary? « SSC Steno 2016
(a) Rain (b) Reef (c) Ready (d) Rainbow

DIRECTIONS ~(Q. Nos. 86-90) *In the following questions, which of the following words will come fifth if arranged according to the English dictionary.*

86. (a) June (b) July (c) Jury (d) Judo (e) Jump « SBI PO 2012

87. (a) Keg (b) Kea (c) Ked (d) Key (e) Ken « SBI Clerk 2011

88. (a) Kill (b) Kick (c) Kink (d) Kilt (e) Kind

89. (a) Leak (b) Leal (c) Lean (d) Lead (e) Leaf « IBPS Clerk 2011

90. 1. Onion 2. Owl 3. Omnious 4. Ostrich 5. Oxford « SSC Steno 2017
(a) Ostrich (b) Owl (c) Oxford (d) Onion

Answers WITH EXPLANATIONS

1. (*c*) The logical sequence of the given words is as below
Village (2) → Block (4) → District(1) → State(3)
i.e. 2, 4, 1, 3

2. (*c*) The logical sequence of the given words is as below
Day (3) → Work(5) → Tired (1) → Night(2) → Sleep(4)
i.e. 3, 5, 1, 2, 4

3. (*b*) The logical sequence of the given words is as below
Population (2) → Unemployment (4) → Poverty(1) → Disease(5) → Death(3)
i.e. 2, 4, 1, 5, 3

4. (*d*) The logical sequence of given words is as follows
Village (2) → Town(5) → District(4) → State(3) → Nation(1)
i.e. 2, 5, 4, 3, 1

5. (*c*) The logical and meaningful order of the given words is as follows.
Room(3) → Flat(1) → Apartment(4) → Street(2) → City (5)
i.e. 3, 1, 4, 2, 5

6. (*b*) The logical sequence of the given words is as below
Market(2) → Vegetable(1) → Cutting(3) → Cooking (4) → Food (5)
i.e. 2, 1, 3, 4, 5

7. (*c*) The logical sequence of the given words is as below
Crime(4) → Arrest(3) → Judgement(5) → Punishment (1) → Prison(2)
i.e. 4, 3, 5, 1, 2

8. (*c*) The logical sequence of the given words is as below
Mosquito(3) → Cat (2) → Tiger(4) → Elephant(1) → Whale(5)
i.e. 3, 2, 4, 1, 5

9. (*c*) The logical sequence of the given words is as below
Village (4) → District (2) → State(3) → Country(1) → Continent(5)
i.e. 4, 2, 3, 1, 5

10. (*c*) The logical sequence of the given words is as below
Grass(5) → Grasshopper(3) → Frog(1) → Snake(4) → Eagle(2)
i.e. 5, 3, 1, 4, 2

11. (*b*) The logical sequence of the given words is as below
Child(2) → Cry(4) → Mother(1) → Milk(3) → Smile(5)
i.e. 2, 4, 1, 3, 5

12. (*c*) The logical sequence of the given words is as below
Infant(4) → Child(1) → Education(5) → Job(2) → Marriage(3)
i.e. 4, 1, 5, 2, 3

13. (*c*) The logical sequence of the given words is as below
Seed (3) → Plant(1) → Flower(4) → Fruit(2)
i.e. 3, 1, 4, 2

14. (*b*) The logical sequence of the given words is as below
Pressure(2) → Rain(4) → Flood(5) → Protect(1) → Relief(3)
i.e. 2, 4, 5, 1, 3

15. (*c*) The logical sequence of the given words is as below
Pentagon (5 sides polygon) (3) → Hexagon (6 sides polygon) (1) → Heptagon (7 sides polygon) (4)
Octagon (8 sides polygon) (5) → Nonagon (9 sides polygon) (2)
i.e. 3, 1, 4, 5, 2

16. (*a*) The logical sequence of the given words is as below
Illness (2) → Doctor (3) → Consultation(1) → Treatment (4) → Recovery(5)
i.e. 2, 3, 1, 4, 5

17. (*b*) The logical sequence of the given words is as below
Rain(2) → Sun (3) → Rainbow(1) → Child(5) → Happy(4)
i.e. 2, 3, 1, 5, 4

18. (*d*) The logical sequence of the given words is as below
Study(1) → Examination(3) → Apply(5) → Job (2) → Earn(4)
i.e. 1, 3, 5, 2, 4

19. (*d*) The logical sequence of the given words is as below
Key (1) → Lock (3) → Door (2) → Room(4) → Switch on(5)
i.e. 1, 3, 2, 4, 5

20. (*a*) The logical sequence of the given words is as below
Farmer(1) → Seed(2) → Cultivation(4) → Food(3)
i.e. 1, 2, 4, 3

21. (*a*) The logical sequence of the given words is as below
Cotton(2) → Thread (4) → Weaving(1) → Cloth(3)
i.e. 2, 4, 1, 3

22. (*b*) The logical sequence of the given words is as below
Think(4) → Compose(1) → Sing(5) → Appreciation(2) → Money(3)
i.e. 4, 1, 5, 2, 3

23. (*d*) The logical sequence of the given words is as below
Encoding (2) → Sending(1) → Receiving (3) → Decoding(4)
i.e. 2, 1, 3, 4

24. (*c*) The logical sequence of the given words is as below
Birth (1) → Education(5) → Marriage(4) → Death (2) → Funeral(3)
i.e. 1, 5, 4, 2, 3

25. (*c*) The logical sequence of the given words is as below
Flower(2) → Bee (3) → Honey (1) → Wax(4)
i.e. 2, 3, 1, 4

26. (*b*) The logical sequence of the given words is as below
Nostrils (2) → Windpipe (3) → Lungs(1) → Blood (4)
i.e. 2, 3, 1, 4

27. (*a*) The logical sequence of the given words is as below
Egg(4) → Larva(2) → Pupa (1) → Moth(3)
i.e. 4, 2, 1, 3

28. (*a*) The logical arrangement of the given words is
Electron (4) → Atom (1) → Molecule(3) → Matter (2)
i.e. 4, 1, 3, 2

29. (*d*) The correct logical order of words is as follows
Gold(2) → Goldsmith(3) → Ornaments(1) → Jewellery shop (4) → Bride(5)
i.e. 2, 3, 1, 4, 5

30. (*b*) The logical sequence of given words is as follows
Red fort(1) → Delhi(3) → India(4) → World(2) → Universe(5)
i.e. 1, 3, 4, 2, 5

31. (*b*) The logical sequence of the words is as given below
Puddle (5) → Pond (2) → Lake (1) → Sea (3) → Ocean(4)
i.e. 5, 2, 1, 3, 4

32. (*b*) The logical sequence of the given words is as below
Pressure (3) → Rain (2) → Flood (4) → Protect (1) → Relief (5)
i.e. 3, 2, 4, 1, 5

33. (*d*) The logical sequence of the given words is as below
Animal (1) → Vertebrate (5) → Mammal (4) → Feline (2) → Leopard (3) → Cat (6)
i.e. 1, 5, 4, 2, 3, 6

34. (*c*) The logical arrangement of the given words is as below
Rain(6) → Rivulet (1) → Tributary (3) → River (4) → Sea (5) → Ocean(2)
i.e. 6, 1, 3, 4, 5, 2

35. (*d*) The logical sequence of the given words is as below
Title(3) → Contents(2) → Introduction(5) → Chapters(4) → Index(1)
i.e. 3, 2, 5, 4, 1

36. (*d*) The logical sequence of the given words is as below
Egg(3) → Worm(4) → Cocoon(2) → Butterfly(1)
i.e. 3, 4, 2, 1

37. (*a*) The logical sequence of the given words is as below
Letter(3) → Word (2) → Phrase(4) → Sentence(6) → Paragraph (5) → Chapter(1)
i.e. 3, 2, 4, 6, 5, 1

38. (*b*) The logical sequence of the given words is as below
Need(2) → Identify(6) → Research(4) → Design(1) → Testing (1) → Launching(3)
i.e. 2, 6, 4, 1, 5, 3

39. (*a*) These are Units of Computer Memory Measurements,
Hence the logical sequence of the given words is as below
Bit(6) → Byte (2) → Kilobyte (1) → Megabyte(3) → Gigabyte (5) → Terabyte(4)
i.e. 6, 2, 1, 3, 5, 4

40. (*c*) The logical sequence of the given words is as below
Foundation(4) → Walls(2) → Windows (1) → Roof (5) → Floor (3) → Room (6)
i.e. 4, 2, 1, 5, 3, 6

41. (*b*) The logical sequence of the given words is as below
Dawn(2) → Noon (3) → Twilight(1) → Night(4)
i.e. 2, 3, 1, 4

42. (*b*) The logical sequence of the given words is as below
Newly married couple (3) → Family(2) → Caste (1) → Clan (4) → Species(5)
i.e. 3, 2, 1, 4, 5

43. (*b*) The logical sequence of the given words is as below
Envelope(3) → Letter(2) → Postbox(1) → Clearance(5) → Delivery(4)
i.e. 3, 2, 1, 5, 4

44. (*a*) The logical sequence of the given words is as below
Advertisement (5) → Application (6) → Interview(2) → Selection (3) → Appointment (4) → Probation(1)
i.e. 5, 6, 2, 3, 4, 1

45. (*a*) The logical sequence of the given words is as below
Arrival (3) → Introduction (5) → Presentation (1) → Recommendation (2) → Discussion (4)
i.e. 3, 5, 1, 2, 4

46. (*c*) The logical sequence of the given words is as below
Stone age (3) → Metallic age(2) → Alloy age (4) → Atomic age (1)
i.e. 3, 2, 4, 1

47. (*b*) The logical arrangement of the given words is
Station (1) → Train (3) → Boarding (2) → Destination (5) → Deboarding (4)
i.e. 1, 3, 2, 5, 4

48. (*c*) The logical sequence of the given words is as below

Ambivalence(3)→ Happiness (2)
→ Pleasure(5) → Euphoria(1)
→ Ecstasy(4)
i.e. 3, 2, 5, 1, 4

49. (*c*) The logical sequence of the given words is as below
Requirements Analysis (3)
→ Conceptual Modelling(2)
→ Physical Model (5)
→ Logical Modelling(4)
→ Scheme Refinement(6)
→ Implementation(1)
i.e. 3, 2, 5, 4, 6, 1

50. (*b*) The logical sequence of the given words as per the descending order of area is as below
Africa(2)→ North America(5)
→ South America (1) → Europe(3)
→ Australia (4)
i.e. 2, 5, 1, 3, 4

51. (*c*) Descending order of the given words is as follows
Tree → Plant → Sapling → Seed
It is clear from above that seed come at the last.

52. (*d*) The given words represent the various stages in the process of publishing.
Firstly, the matter is written, followed by composition of that written matter.
Then, this composed matter is printed followed by reading. So, the correct order is 3 → 2 → 4 → 1.

53. (*a*) The arrangement takes place according to the following logic.
Member(3)→ Family(1)→Community(2)
→ Locality(4) → Country(5)
i.e. 3, 1, 2, 4, 5

54. (*d*) The logical sequence of the given words is as below
Education (3) → Job (5) → Income(1)
→ Status(2)→ Well-being(4)
i.e. 3, 5, 1, 2, 4

55. (*b*) All the given words represent substance which can be arranged in the increasing order of their cost.
The least costly is sand after which comes the cost of iron, followed by gold, diamond and the costliest among all is platinum.
So, they can be arranged in a logical order as
3 → 2 → 1 → 5 → 4.

56. (*b*) The logical sequence of the given words is as below
Foetus (1) → Baby (3) → Child (2)
→ Adult (4)→ Youth (5)
i.e. 1, 3, 2, 4, 5

57. (*b*) The logical sequence of the given words is as below
Daily(2)→ Weekly(1)→ Fortnightly(4)
→ Monthly(3) → Bimonthly(5)
i.e. 2, 1, 4, 3, 5

58. (*a*) The logical sequence of the given words is as below
Finger (5)→ Palm (4) → Wrist(2)
→ Elbow(3)→ Shoulder(1)
i.e. 5, 4, 2, 3, 1

59. (*a*) The logical sequence of the given words is as below
Centi (2) → Deci (5) → Deca (3)
→ Hecto (1) → Kilo(4)
i.e. 2, 5, 3, 1, 4

60. (*b*) The logical sequence of the given words is as below
Clerk(5)→ Collector(1)
→ Chief Secretary(3)
→ Governor(2)→ President(4)
i.e. 5, 1, 3, 2, 4

61. (*a*) The logical sequence of the given words is as below
Universe (5) → Galaxy (3) → Star (1)
→ Planet (4) → Satellite (2)
i.e. 5, 3, 1, 4, 2

62. (*b*) The sequence of the given words as per dictionary is as follows
Jockey (2) → Jocular (3) → Jocund (4)
→ Joke(1)
i.e. 2, 3, 4, 1

63. (*c*) The sequence of the given words as per dictionary is as follows
Thunderstorm (4) → Thursday (5)
→ Timber(2)→ Tinkle (3)
→ Tinned(1)
i.e. 4, 5, 2, 3, 1

64. (*d*) Sequence of given words as per dictionary is as follows
Thames (4) → Theme (1) → Thing (3)
→ Thirst(2)→ Thurst(5)
i.e. 4, 1, 3, 2, 5

65. (*c*) Sequence of given words as per dictionary is as follows
Bandage (3) → Bangalore(5)
→ Bangle(2)→ Banquet(1)
→ Bantam(4)
i.e. 3, 5, 2, 1, 4

66. (a) The sequence of given words as per dictionary order is as follows
Mandarin (3) → Mandate (2)
→ Master(5)→ Mobile(1)
→ Monkey(4)
i.e. 3, 2, 5, 1, 4

67. (*a*) The sequence of given words as per dictionary order is as follows
Dictionary(4)→Dracula(5)→ Drink(1)
→ Drinking (2) → Drive(3)
i.e. 4, 5, 1, 2, 3

68. (*d*) The sequence of the given words as per dictionary order is as follows
Devine(3)→ Direct(5)→ Divest (4)
→ Divide(1)→ Divisions(2)
i.e. 3, 5, 4, 1, 2

69. (*c*) The sequence of the given words as per dictionary order is as follows
Hair (1) → Harmonium(3)
→ Heena (2) → Host(4)
i.e. 1, 3, 2, 4

70. (*c*) The sequence of the given words as per dictionary order is as follows
Board (4) → Bonus (2) → Bound (1)
→ Bunch(3)
i.e. 4, 2, 1, 3

71. (*a*) The sequence of the given words as per dictionary is as follows
Animated (4) → Carpenter (3)
→ Humanistic(2)→ Joker(1)
i.e. 4, 3, 2, 1

72. (*c*) The sequence of the given words as per dictionary order is as follows
Bifurcate (2) → Bilateral (3)
→ Bilirubin(4)→ Billion(1)
i.e. 2, 3, 4, 1

73. (*c*) The sequence of the given words as per dictionary order is as follows.
Pasture (5) → Patent (3) → Perjury (4) → Pierce (2) → Piquant (1)
i.e., 5, 3, 4, 2, 1

74. (*c*) The sequence of the given words as per dictionary order is as follows
Ambiguity (3) → Ambiguous (2)
→ Ambitious(1)→ Animals (5)
→ Animation (4)
i.e. 3, 2, 1, 5, 4

75. (*b*) The sequence of the given words as per dictionary order is as follows
Anonymous(2)→ Antonymous (3)
→ Arrogant(4)→ Artistic(1)
i.e. 2, 3, 4, 1

76. (*c*) The sequence of the given words as per dictionary order is as follows
Necrology(1)→ Necromancy(2)
→ Necrophilia(4)→ Necropolis(3)
i.e. 1, 2, 4, 3

77. (*b*) The sequence of the given words as per dictionary order is as follows
Impart (2) → Important(1)
→ Improve(4)→ Improvise(3)
i.e. 2, 1, 4, 3

78. (*c*) The sequence of the given words as per dictionary order is as follows
Aquarium (2) → Aquatic (4)
→ Aqueous(1)→ Aquiline(3)
i.e. 2, 4, 1, 3

79. (*c*) The sequence of the given words as per dictionary order is as follows

Epigene (3) → Epilogue (5) → Episode(2) → Epitaxy (1) → Epitome(4)

i.e. 3, 5, 2, 1, 4

80. (*c*) Arrangement of words as per the English dictionary is as follows

Caravan → Cardigan → Carton → Challenge → Charity

i.e. 3, 2, 4, 5, 1

Hence, Cardigan will be come on second position.

81. (*a*) Arrangement of words as per the English dictionary is as follows

MABELA, MABEPEARL, MABLE, MABUSE

i.e. c, b, d, a

Hence, word MABUSE will come at the last.

82. (*c*) Arrangement of the given words as per English dictionary is as follows

Leaf → Lean → Leave → Less

i.e. d, a, b, c

It is clear from above that last word is Less.

83. (*a*) Arrangement of the given words as per English dictionary is as follows

Encode→ Encounter→ Encourage → Encradle

i.e. b, d, c, a

Hence, word Encradle will appear last in the English dictionary.

84. (*a*) Arrangement of the given words as per English dictionary is as follows

Elect → Election → Elector → Electric → Electrode

Hence, word Elector will come in the middle.

85. (*b*) The arrangement of words according to the dictionary

Rain→ Rainbow→ Ready→ Reef

Hence, Reef will come fourth.

86. (*c*) The sequence of the given words as per the dictionary order is as follows

Judo→ July→ Jump→ June→ Jury

i.e. d, b, e, a, c

Hence, word Jury will come on fifth position.

87. (*d*) The sequence of the given words as per the dictionary order is as follows

Kea→ Ked→ Keg→ Ken → Key

i.e. b, c, a, e, d

Hence, word Key will come on fifth position.

88. (*c*) The sequence of the given words as per the dictionary order is as follows

Kick→ Kill→ Kilt→ Kind → Kink

i.e. b, a, d, e, c

Hence, word Kink will come on fifth position.

89. (*c*) The sequence of the given words as per the dictionary order is as follows

Lead → Leaf → Leak → Leal → Lean

i.e. d, e, a, b, c

Hence, word Lean will come on fifth position.

90. (*c*) The sequence of the given words as per the dictionary order is as follows

Omnious → Onion → Ostrich → Owl → Oxford

i.e. 3, 1, 4, 2, 5

Hence, word Oxford will come on fifth position.

CHAPTER / 07

Direction and Distance

Direction is a measurement of position of one thing with respect to another thing or a reference point.

Distance is the amount of space between two points or the displacement between two points.

Concept of Directions

It is based on the position of the Sun. The Sun rises in the East and sets in the West.

(i) If we face the Sun when it rises, then our position is as follows

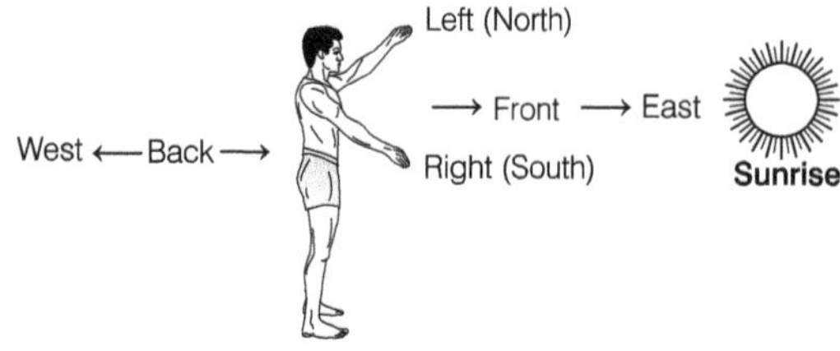

- Direction towards our front = **East**
- Direction towards our back = **West**
- Direction towards our left hand = **North**
- Direction towards our right hand = **South**

(ii) If we face Sunset, then our position is as follows

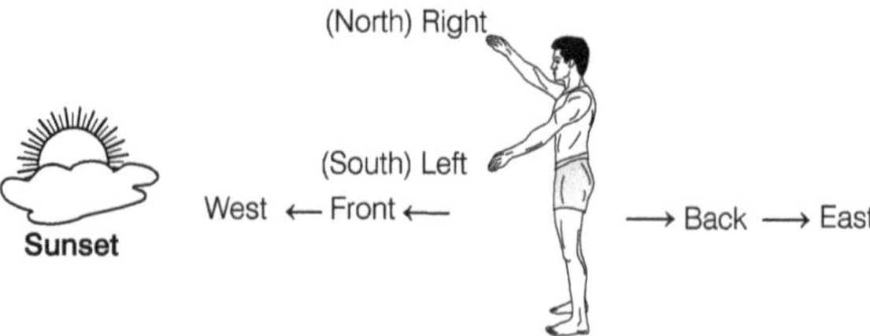

- Direction towards our back = **East**
- Direction towards our front = **West**
- Direction towards our right hand = **North**
- Direction towards our left hand = **South**

Prime Directions

There are four prime directions as shown below

1. North 2. South 3. East 4. West

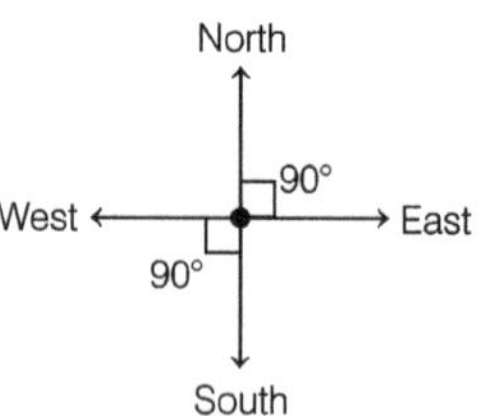

The angle between any two adjacent prime directions is 90°.

Subdirections/Cardinal Directions

A direction between two adjacent main or prime directions is known as a subdirection/cardinal direction.

There are four subdirections as given below

1. North-East (NE) 2. South-East (SE)
3. South-West (SW) 4. North-West (NW)

The various directions discussed above are represented on paper as shown below

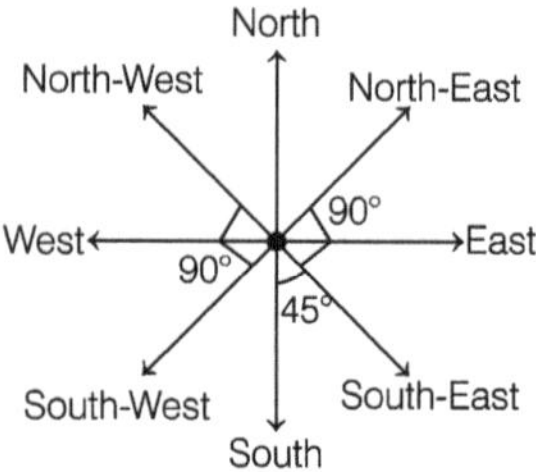

The angle between any two adjacent subdirections is 90°.

Chapter Tips

- Q is to the East of P.

  P ——→ Q

- Q is to the West of P.

  Q ←—— P

- Q is to the North of P.

- Q is to the South of P.

- Q is to the North East of P.

- Q is to the North West of P.

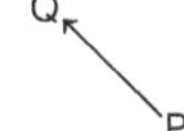

- Q is to the South East of P.

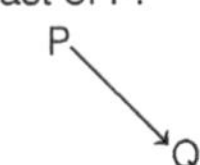

- Q is to the South West of P.

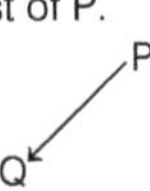

Concept of Turn

1. **Left Turn** (Anti-clockwise Turn)—When a person turns in a direction opposite to motion of a clock, then this turn is called left turn or anti-clockwise turn.

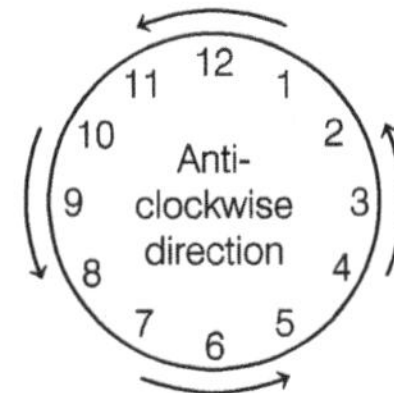

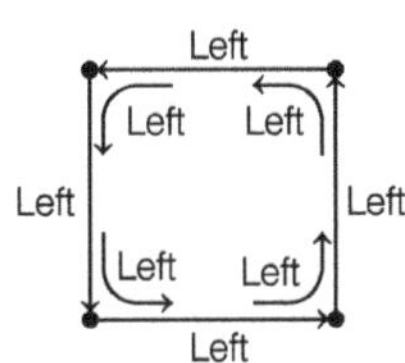

2. **Right Turn** (Clockwise Turn)—When a person takes a turn in the direction of motion of clock, then this turn is called right turn or clockwise turn.

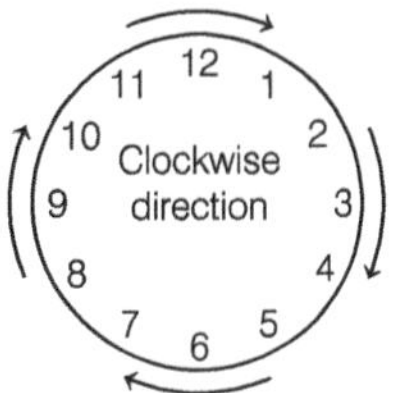

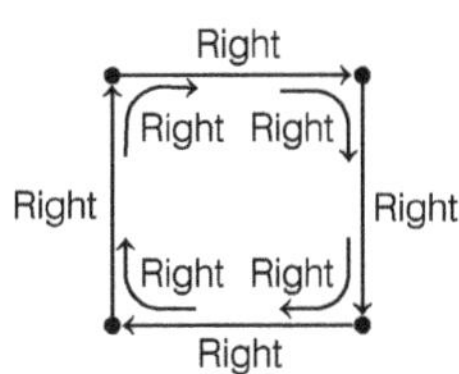

If the angle at which a turn takes place is not given, then the angle is assumed to be right angle, i.e. 90°. If it is said that a person turns left (anti-clockwise), then the turn will be leftward at 90° and if it is said that a person turns right (clockwise), then the turn will be rightward at 90°.

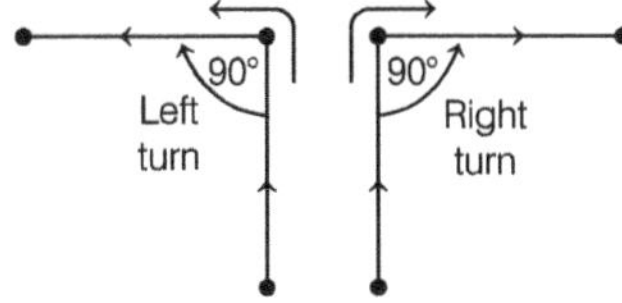

Concept of Degree

The position of the directions can be changed by angular movement in clockwise or anti-clockwise direction.

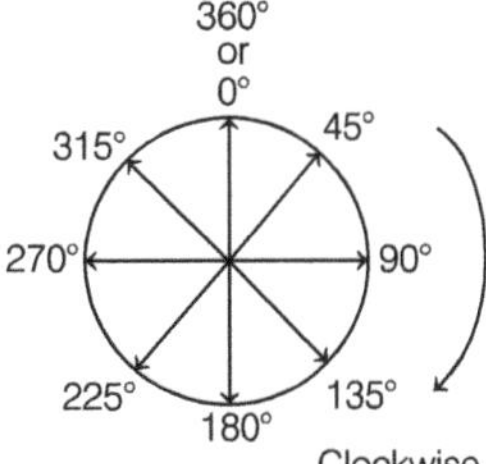

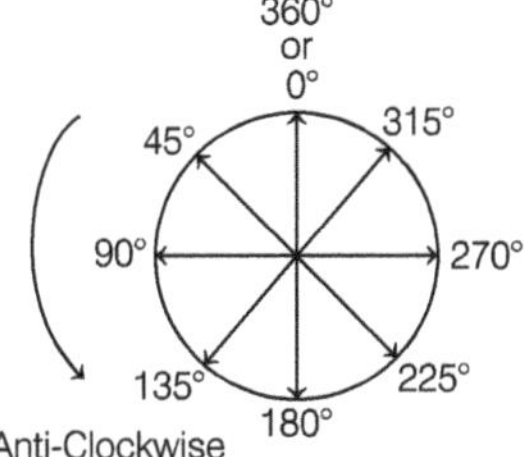

e.g. A girl is going towards West, then she turned left, then turned 90° in clockwise direction. In which direction is she going now?

Solution According to the question, the direction diagram will be as follows

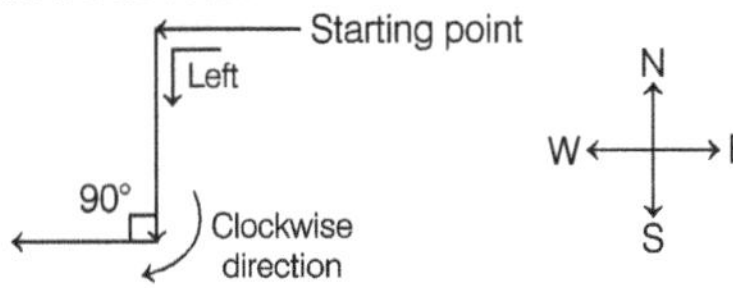

Clearly, the direction diagram shows that the girl is going in West direction.

Concept of Shadow

In the morning, when the Sun rises in the East, the shadow of any person or object is in the West direction. Similarly, in the evening, when the sun sets in the West, the shadow of a person or an object is towards the East.

Shadow at the time of sunrise

Shadow at the time of sunset

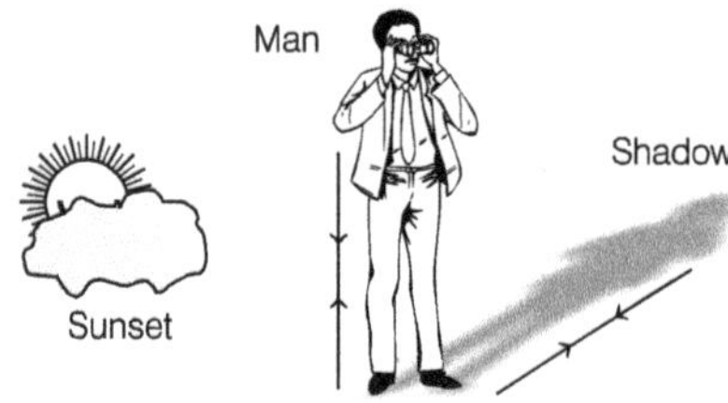

At 12:00 noon, there will be no shadow as the rays of the Sun are vertically downwards at that time.

Type of Questions

Based on the diversity of the type of questions that are asked in various competitive exams, we have classified the questions into the following types

TYPE 01

Finding the Direction Only

There are broadly seven types of questions asked in various competitive examinations based on finding the direction only

A. When Initial Direction is Given

In this type of questions, initial direction of a person's movement along with the various turns taken during the course of a journey is given. The objective is to determine the final direction in which the person is moving.

***Ex* 01** Julia started walking towards North direction from her house. After a while she turned left and later on turned right. She further turned right. Which direction is she facing now? « RRB NTPC 2016

(a) East (b) West (c) North (d) South

***Solution* (a)**

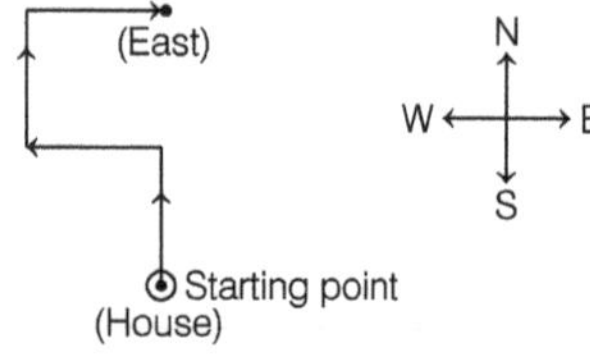

It is clear from the diagram that Julia is facing East direction.

***Ex* 02** Ashok went 8 km South and turned West and walked 3 km. Again he turned North and walked 5 km. He took a final turn to East and walked 3 km. In which direction was Ashok from the starting point? « RRB JE 2019

(a) East (b) North (c) West (d) South

***Solution* (d)**

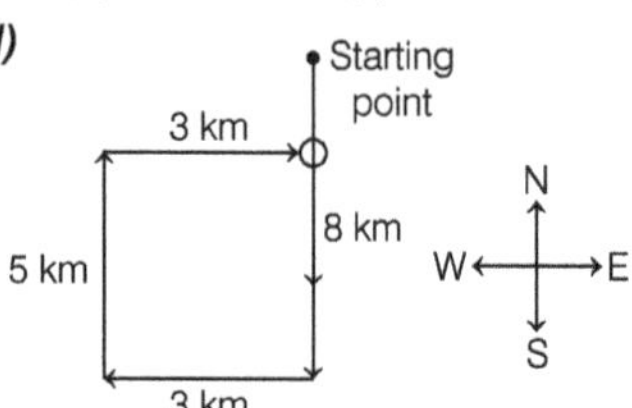

∴ Ashok was in South direction from starting point.

***Ex* 03** Lata starts from point A and walks for 2 km towards North, then turns to her right and walks for 2 km, then again turns to her right and walks for another 2 km. In which direction is she facing now? « UP Police SI 2017

(a) West (b) South (c) North (d) East

***Solution* (b)** Direction diagram of Lata is as given below

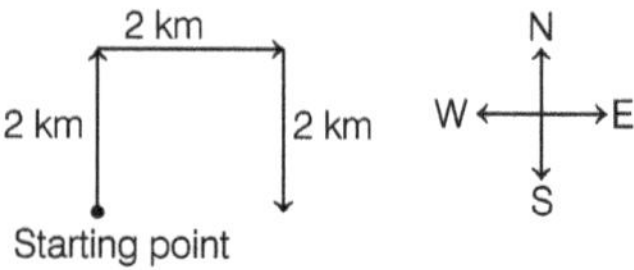

It is clear from diagram that Lata is facing in South direction now.

***Ex* 04** Going 50 m to the South of her house, Radhika turns left and goes another 20 m. Then turning to the North, she goes 30 m and then starts walking to her house. In which direction is the walking now? « WBCS 2020

(a) North (b) South-East
(c) North-West (d) West

***Solution* (c)** According to the question,

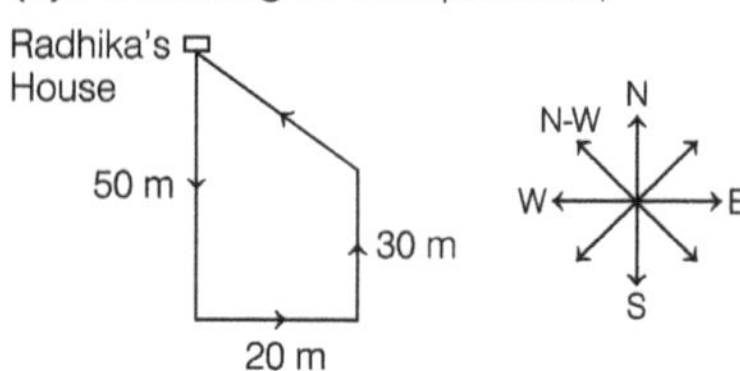

∴ The required direction is North-West direction.

B. When Final Direction is Given

In this type of questions, various turns taken during a journey are given along with the final direction.
The initial direction is required to be determined.

***Ex* 05** Shiv goes 4 km straight from his school. He turns to his right and walks 3 km. He again moves 2 km after turning right to reach his house. If his house is located in South-East from his school, then in which direction Shiv started moving initially from his school?

(a) North-East (b) West
(c) East (d) North

Solution ***(c)*** According to the information stated in the question, direction diagram can be drawn as follows

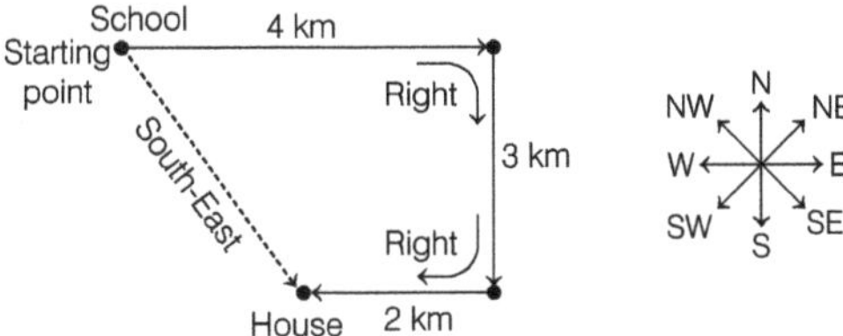

Clearly, he started moving towards East initially.

C. Directions After Replacement

In this type of questions, one direction gets designated by some other direction, thereby changing the designation of other directions accordingly.

It is required to determine the new designation of any one (or more) of the remaining directions.

Ex 06 If South-East becomes North, North-East becomes West and so on, what will South-West become? « SSC CPO 2018

(a) North (b) West
(c) East (d) South

Solution ***(c)*** According to the question,

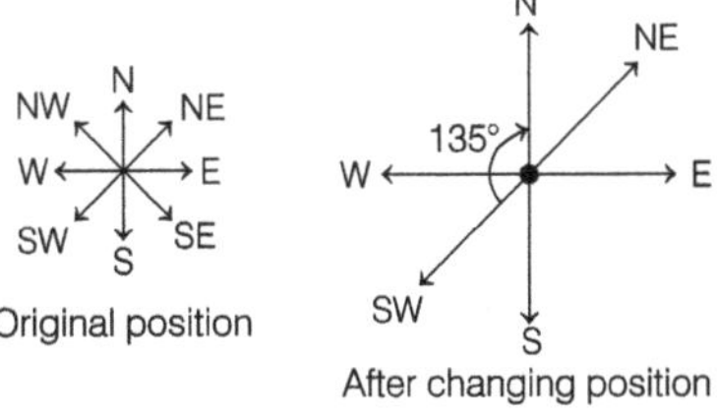

Here, directions are rotating 135° clockwise. Hence, South- West becomes East.

D. When Shadow is Given/or Two Person are Sitting in a Standard Position of Playing

In this type of questions, the direction of shadow during sunrise or sunset is given and based on this information the direction of a person is to be find out.

In other type of questions, two persons are sitting in a standard position of playing i.e. in front of each other. Between these two persons the direction of a person is given and the direction of other person is asked.

Ex 07 At sunrise, Amit and Deepak are having a conversation standing in front of each other. The shadow of Deepak is formed towards the right hand of Amit. What direction is Deepak facing? « SSC Steno 2016

(a) North-East (b) South
(c) East (d) North

Solution ***(d)*** According to the question, the direction diagram is drawn as

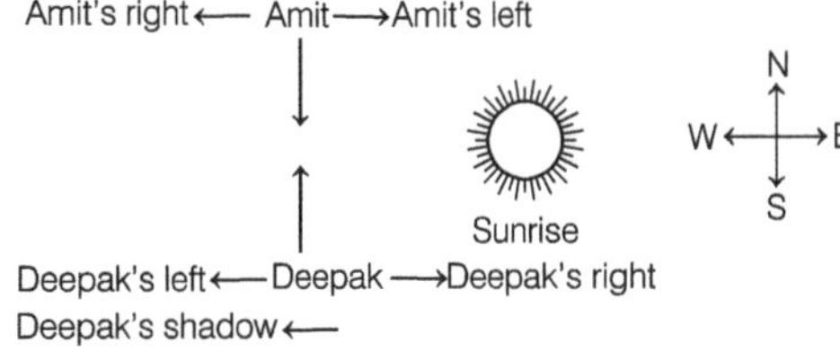

Clearly, Deepak is facing North.

Ex 08 Sunil and Manohar are playing carrom. If sunil faces towards North-East, then his opponent Manohar faces is which direction? « RRB Group D 2018

(a) South-West (b) North-East
(c) North-West (d) South-East

Solution ***(a)*** According to the question,

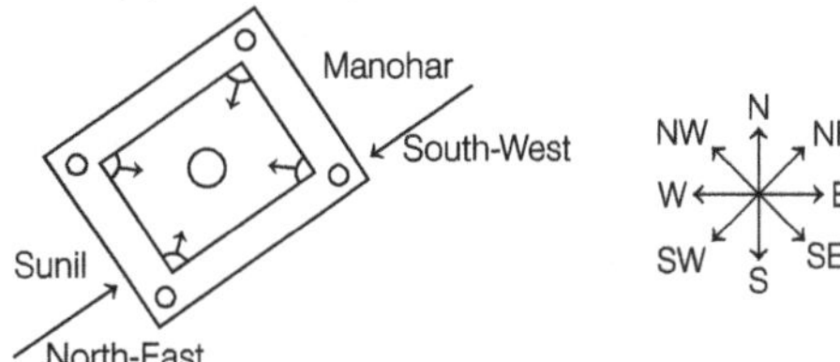

Hence, while playing carrom if Sunil faces North-East direction then Manohar will face his opposite direction i.e. South-West.

E. When Angular Rotation is Given

In this type of questions, the person stands in a particular direction. Now as per the question, that person rotates by some angle in clockwise or anti-clockwise direction.

The candidate is asked to find out the final direction in which that person is moving.

Ex 09 Facing East, X turns 150° clockwise and 105° anti-clockwise. Which direction is X facing now? « RRB ALP 2018

(a) South-East (b) South-West
(c) North-East (d) North-West

Solution ***(a)***

N
150° Clockwise
W E
105° anti-clockwise
S (S-E)

X is facing towards South-East direction.

F. Clock Based Directions

Sometimes direction based problems involve application of knowledge of clocks and the relative positioning of both hands of clocks at particular time.

In these type of questions, direction of minute or hour hand is to be found out as per the given time.

***Ex* 10** A watch shows 6 pm where the hour hand points East. In which direction is the minute hand facing when the time is 9:15 pm? « RRB ALP 2018

(a) West (b) East (c) South (d) North

Solution (d) At 6 pm, hour hand points East.

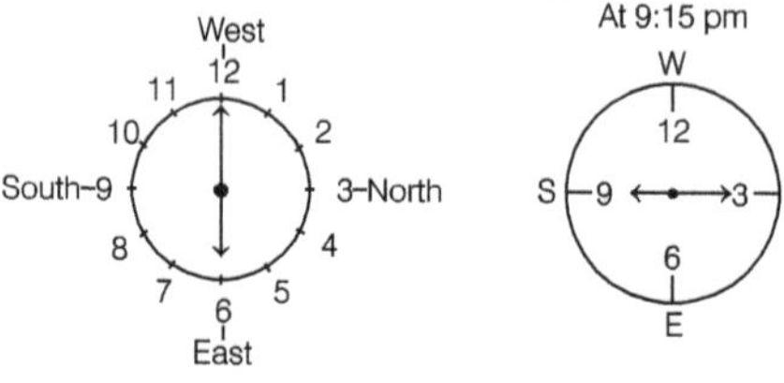

At 9 : 15 pm, minute hand is in North direction.

G. Finding Relative Directions

In these questions, relative positions of two or more objects/persons are given and based on this information, the candidate is required to find out the direction as asked in the question.

***Ex* 11** If M is in the South of B and B is in the West of N, then in which direction is N from M? « MP Police SI 2017

(a) South-East (b) North (c) North-East (d) East

Solution (c) From given information, direction diagram is as follows

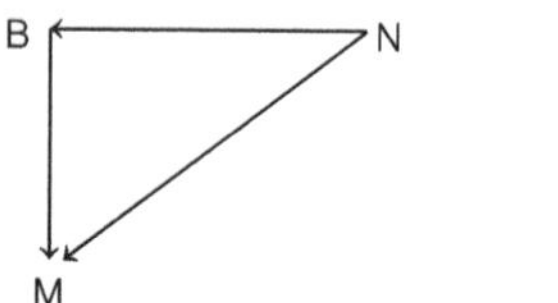

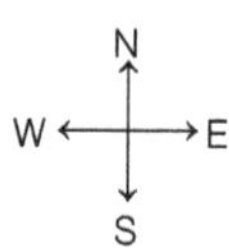

Hence, it is clear from diagram that N is in the North-East of M.

***Ex* 12** If Kamla is 50 m South-West of Neeta and Rita is 50 m South-East of Neeta, then Rita is in which direction with respect to Kamla? « RRB ALP 2018

(a) East (b) West
(c) North-West (d) North-East

Solution (a) According to the question,

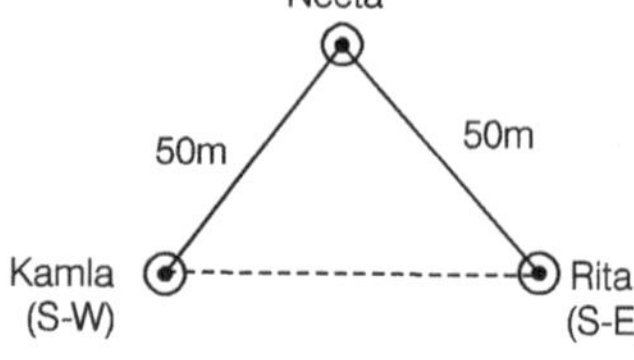

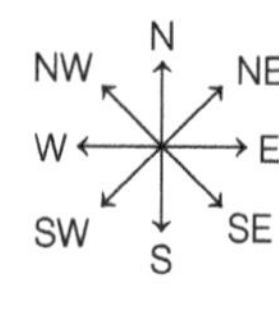

Rita is in East direction with respect to Kamla.

Practice /CORNER 7.1

1. John, in the morning, started walking towards North and then turn towards opposite side of the Sun. He then turn left again and stop. Which direction is he facing now? « SSC CGL 2016

(a) North (b) West (c) South (d) East

2. Sunita goes towards the South, turns left, then turns right and then goes to the left. Which direction is Sunita facing now? « UP Police Constable 2018

(a) East (b) West (c) North (d) South

3. A man goes 5 km East, then he turns right and goes 4 km, then he turns left and goes 5 km. Which direction is he facing now? « SSC CGL 2015

(a) North (b) South (c) East (d) West

4. A man starts for his office in the North direction. He turns to his left, and then to his right and again to his right. In which direction will he be facing? « SSC CPO 2016

(a) South (b) West (c) East (d) North

5. A man walks 5 km toward South and then turns to the right. After walking 3 km he turns to the left and walks 5 km. Now in which direction is he from the starting place? « Delhi Police MTS 2018

(a) West (b) South
(c) North-East (d) South-West

6. Manoj walks a distance of 5 m towards North, then he turns to East and walks a distance of 10 m. Then he turns to his right and covers a distance of 15 m. He then turns to his left and covers a distance of 15 m . Which direction is he facing now? « CLAT 2019

(a) North (b) East
(c) West (d) South

7. Neeraj wants to go to school from his house. First of all he goes to the crossing, from here he turns to right and reaches the bus stand. Bus stand is opposite to the library. In which direction is school locate?

(a) North (b) East
(c) Cannot be determined (d) West

8. A person starts towards South direction. Which of the following orders of directions will lead him to East direction?

(a) Right, Right, Right (b) Left, Left, Left
(c) Left, Right, Right (d) Right, Left, Right

9. A man starts from his house and walked straight for 10 m towards North and turned left and walked 25 m. He then turned right and walked 5 m and again turned right and walked 25 m. Which direction is he facing now? « SSC CGL 2012

(a) North (b) East
(c) South (d) West

10. Kunal travels 10 m from his shop and turns to his left. After that he turns to right from the crossing. After moving certain yards, he turns to left and again turns to left after moving some distance. Finally, he turns to right. If at final position he is facing North direction, then which direction he was facing while coming out of his shop?

(a) South (b) West (c) East (d) North

11. A policeman left his police post and proceeded South 4 km on hearing a loud sound from point A. On reaching the place, he heard another sound and proceeded 4 km to his left to the point B. From B he proceeded left to reach another place C, 4 km away. In which direction, he has to go to reach his police post?

(a) North (b) South (c) East (d) West

12. There are four roads. I have come from the South and want to go to the temple. The road to the right leads me away from the coffee house while straight road leads only to a college. In which direction is the temple?

(a) North (b) East (c) South (d) West

13. Sachin Tendulkar hits a ball towards North in a one day international cricket match between India and Pakistan. A Pakistani fielder, Shahid Afridi comes straight from East to field the ball. Which direction does Shahid Afridi come from to field the ball?

(a) South (b) North (c) West (d) East

14. A train runs 120 km in West direction, 30 km in South direction and then 80 km in East direction before reaching the station. In which direction is the station from the train's starting point?

(a) South-West (b) North-West
(c) South-East (d) South

15. Amutha's college bus is facing North when it reaches her college. After starting from Amutha's house, it turned right twice and then left before reaching the college. What direction was the bus facing when it left the bus stop in front of Amutha's house?

« UPSSSC Junior Assist. 2017

(a) East (b) West (c) South (d) North

16. A man walks down the backside of his house straight 25m, then turns to the right and walks 50m again, then he turns towards left and again walks 25m. If his house faces to the East, what is his direction from the starting point? « UPSC CSAT 2020

(a) South-East (b) South-West
(c) North-East (d) North-West

17. Raj is standing in the middle of a square field. He starts walking diagonally to North-East. Then, he turns right and reaches the far end of the field. Then, he turns right and starts walking. In the midway, he again turns right and starts walking. In halfway, he turns to his left and reaches a new far end. In what direction is Raj now?

(a) North (b) South
(c) North-West (d) South-West

18. Kate walks 4 km towards South. She, then turns towards her left and walks 8 km more. After that she turns left again and walks another 8 km. Here, she meets her friend coming from the opposite direction and they both stop here. Which direction would she be facing?

(a) North (b) South (c) East (d) West

19. A boy was misdirected from his way while returning to his home from his school. In order to reach his home, he first moved 3 km in South direction and then turned to his left and moved 2 km in straight direction on the road leading to the East. From there he moved to his left and walked 3 km. After this, he again turned to his left and moved 1 km. Finally he reached his home. The home of the boy was in which direction from his school?

(a) South (b) West (c) North (d) East

20. Rani and Sarita started from a place X. Rani went West and Sarita went North, both travelling with the same speed. After sometime, both turned their left and walked a few steps, if they again turned to their left, in which directions' the faces of Rani and Sarita will be with respect to X?

(a) North and East (b) North and West
(c) West and North (d) East and South

21. Mohan started from point A and proceeded 7 km straight towards East, then he turned left and proceeded straight for a distance of 10 km. He then turned left again and proceeded straight for a distance of 6 km and then turned left again and proceeded straight for another 10 km. In which direction is Mohan from his starting point? « MP Patwari 2017

(a) East (b) West
(c) North (d) South

22. A girls leaves from her home. She first walks 30 m in North-West direction and then 30 m in South-West direction. Next, she walks 30 m in South-East direction. Finally, she turns towards her home. In which direction is she moving? « CG PSC Pre 2018

(a) North-West (b) North-East
(c) South-East (d) South-West
(e) None of these

23. If East is replaced by South-East, then West will be replaced by which of the following directions?

(a) North-East (b) North
(c) East (d) North-West

24. If South-East becomes North and North-East becomes West and all the rest directions are changed in the same manner, what will be the direction for the West?

(a) North-East (b) South
(c) South-East (d) South-West

25. If North-West becomes West and South-East becomes East. North-East becomes North and all other directions are changed in a similar manner, then what will be the direction of South?

(a) South-West (b) South-East
(c) North-East (d) None of these

26. In a military secret service map, South-East is shown as North, North-East as West and so on. What will West become? « CLAT 2017

(a) South-West (b) North-West
(c) North-East (d) South-East

27. One evening before sunset, two friends Raman and Arjun were talking to each other face to face. If Raman's Shadow was exactly to his left side, which direction was Arjun facing?

(a) West (b) East
(c) North (d) South

28. In the morning X and Y walk towards each other in a park. When they meet, Y's shadow falls towards the right side of X. In which direction was X facing?

(a) South (b) East (c) West (d) North

29. Roshan, Vaibhav, Vinay and Sumit are playing cards. Roshan and Vaibhav are partners. Sumit faces towards North. If Roshan faces towards West, then who faces towards South?

(a) Vinay (b) Vaibhav
(c) Sumit (d) Data is inadequate

30. Sangitha was facing North-West direction. If she was playing carom with Sudha in the Standard seating pattern, in which direction was Sudha facing

« RRB Group D 2018

(a) North-West (b) North-East
(c) South-West (d) South-East

31. Kamal is facing South. He turns 135° in the anti-clockwise direction and then 180° in the clockwise direction. What direction is he facing now?

(a) North (b) South-West (c) East (d) North-West

32. Surbhi is facing East. She turns 100° in the clockwise direction and then 145° in the anti-clockwise direction. Which direction is she facing now?

(a) West (b) North-East
(c) North (d) South-West

33. A girl is facing North. She turns 180° in the anti-clockwise direction and then 225° in the clockwise direction. Which direction is she facing now?

(a) West (b) North-East
(c) South-West (d) East
(e) North-West

34. While facing East you turn to your left and walk 10 yard. Then, turn to your left and walk 10 yard and now turn 45° to your right and go straight to cover 50 yard. Now, in what direction are you with respect to the starting point?

(a) North-East (b) North
(c) South-East (d) North-West

35. A man is facing West. He turns 45° in the clockwise direction and then another 180° in the same direction and then 270° in the anti-clockwise direction. Which direction is he facing now?

(a) South (b) North-West
(c) West (d) South-West

36. Sumi ran a distance of 40m towards the South. She then turned to the right and ran for about 15m, turned right again and ran 50m. Turning to right, then ran for 15m. Finally she turned to the left an angle of 45° and ran. In which direction was she running finally?

(a) South-East (b) South-West
(c) North-East (d) North-West

37. Sandhya and Ramani were facing East direction. Sandhya turns 45° anti-clockwise and then 135° clockwise direction. How much turns Ramani would have to take to face opposite to Sandhya?

« RRB Group D 2018

(a) 180° anti-clockwise (b) 90° anti-clockwise
(c) 180° clockwise (d) 135° anti-clockwise

38. Manika moves around the boundary of her rectangular field with same speed. She started moving towards West and then turns 45° towards her right and then moves 500m. Which direction is she facing now?

« RRB Group D 2018

(a) North-West (b) North-East
(c) South-East (d) South-West

39. A watch reads 4:30. If the minute hand points East, in what direction will the hour hand point?

« UKPSC Asst. Conservator of Forest 2019

(a) South-East (b) North-East
(c) South-West (d) North-West

40. The time in a clock is quarter past twelve. If the hour hand points to the East, which is the direction opposite to the minute hand? « UP PSC 2013

(a) South-West (b) South (c) West (d) North

41. One morning at 7 O'clock, Naresh started walking with his back towards the Sun. Then, he turned towards left, walked straight and then turned towards right and walked straight. Then, he again turned towards left. Now, in which direction is he facing?

« SSC 10+2 2013

(a) North (b) East (c) West (d) South

42. Ramraj is wearing a watch. At 6:00 for instance, if the hour needle points towards West, then in which direction minutes hand was pointing out?

« RRB NTPC 2016

(a) South (b) West (c) North (d) East

43. City C is to the South of City B and City A is to the North of City C. In which direction City A is located with respect to City B? « Canara Bank PO 2010

(a) North (b) South (c) East
(d) Cannot be determined (e) West

44. City D is to the West of City M. City R is to the South of City D. If City K is to the East of City R, then in which direction is City K located with respect to City D?

(a) North (b) East
(c) North-East (d) South-East
(e) None of these

45. Y is in the East of X which is in the North of Z. If P is in the South of Z, then in which direction of Y, is P?

« Delhi Police MTS 2018

(a) North (b) South
(c) South-East (d) None of these

46. If Ram's house is located to the South of Krishna's house and Govinda's house is to the East of Krishna's house, in what direction is Ram's house situated with respect to Govinda's house?

(a) North-East (b) North-West
(c) South-East (d) South-West

47. Town D is towards East of Town F. Town B is towards North of Town D. Town H is towards South of Town B. Towards which direction is town H from Town F?

(a) East (b) South-East
(c) North-East (d) Data inadequate
(e) None of these

48. B is to the South-West of A, C is to the East of B and South-East of A and D is to the North of C in line with B and A. In which direction of A is D located? « IBPS Clerk 2015

(a) North (b) East
(c) South-East (d) North-East
(e) None of these

49. C is to the West of B and South-West of A.D is to the North-West of A and North to C and is in line with AB. In which direction from the point of A, B is located?

(a) North-East (b) South-East
(c) North-West (d) South-West

50. A direction pole was situated on the road crossing. Due to an accident, the pole turned in such a manner that the pointer which was showing East, started showing South. Sita, a traveller went to the wrong direction thinking it to be West. In what direction actually she was travelling?

(a) North (b) West
(c) East (d) South

DIRECTIONS ~ (Q. Nos. 51 and 52) *Study the following information carefully and answer the quetions given below.*

P is to the North of Q and S is to the East of P who is to the South of W. T is to the West of P. « SBI Clerical Cadre 2016

51. Who among the following is towards South of W and North of Q?

(a) P (b) T (c) S (d) Q
(e) None of these

52. W is in which direction with respect to T?

(a) North (b) North-East
(c) South-West (d) West
(e) None of these

DIRECTIONS ~ (Q. Nos. 53-55) *Study the following information carefully and answer the questions given below .* « RBI (Office Assistant 2020)

Ramesh goes to his office from point M. He walks 8 m in East and reaches at point N. Then, he turns his left and walk 4 m to reach at point O. Now, he turns to his right and walk 5 m to reach at point P. Again, he turns to his right and walk 8 m to reach at point Q. Again, he turns to his right and walk 5 m to reach at point R. Then, he turns to his left and walk 5 m to reach at point S. Finally, he turns to his right and walk 8 m to reach his office.

53. What is the direction of point P with respect to point S?

(a) South-East (b) North-East (c) North
(d) South (e) None of these

54. Which of the following points are in stright line?

(a) P, O, S (b) N, O, S (c) P, N, Q (d) M, N, S
(e) None of these

55. Ramesh's office is in which direction with respect to point M?

(a) North (b) North-West
(c) South-East (d) South
(e) None of these

Answers / WITH EXPLANATIONS

1. (c) Walking diagram of John is as follows

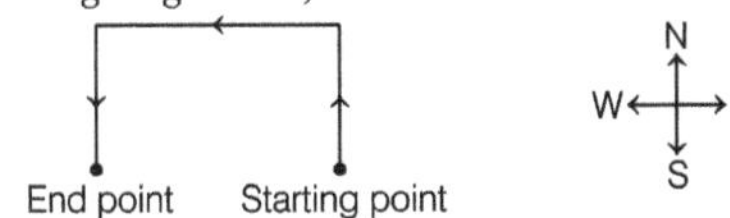

It is clear from diagram that John is in facing South direction now.

2. (a) According to the question,

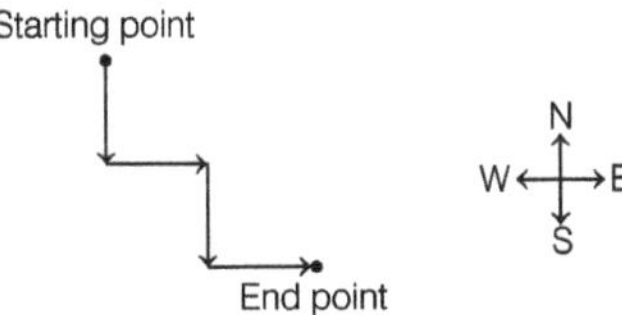

Clearly, now Sunita is facing towards East direction.

3. (c) According to the question, the direction diagram will be as follows

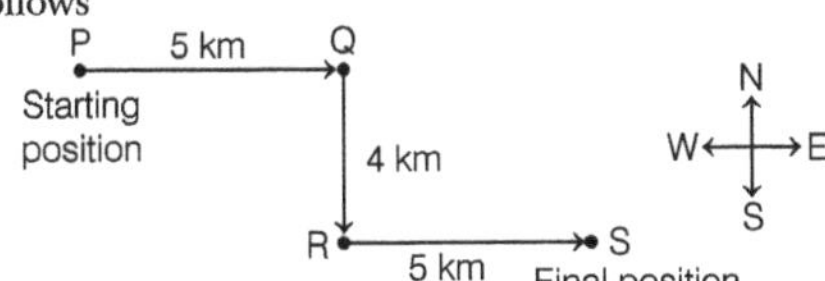

Clearly, man is facing East.

4. (c) According to the question, the direction diagram will be as follows

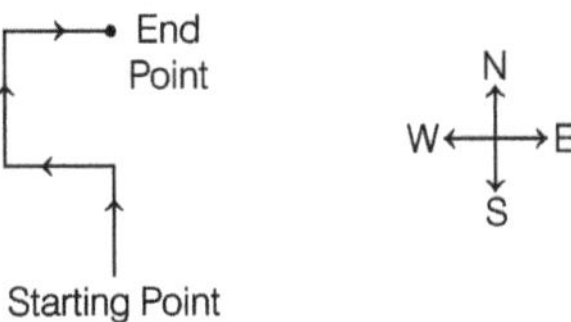

Clearly, the man will be facing East.

5. (d) From the given information,

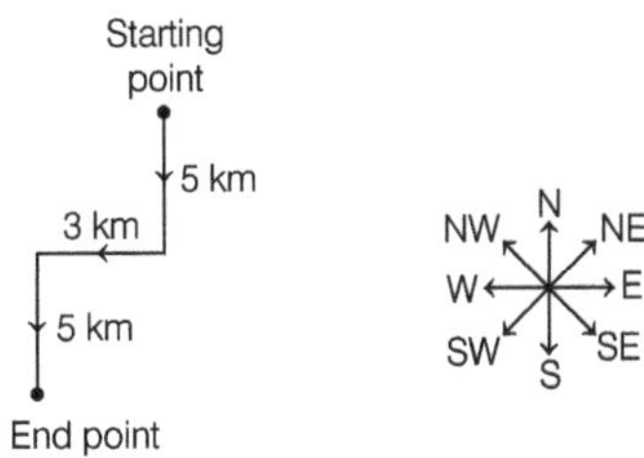

Clearly, he is in South-West direction from his starting point.

6. (*b*) According to the question,

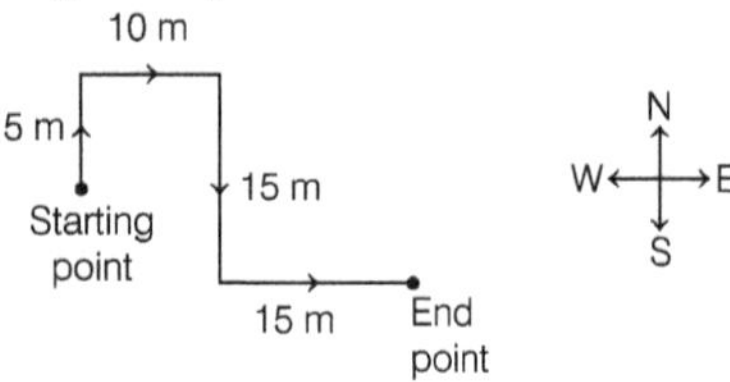

Hence, finally Manoj is facing East direction.

7. (*c*) Neither initial nor final direction is given. Hence, the direction cannot be determined.

8. (*a*) According to the question, the direction diagram will be as follows

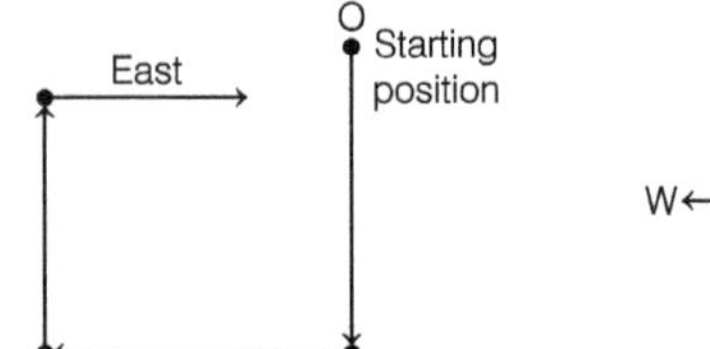

Clearly, right, right and right turns lead towards East.

9. (*b*) According to the question, the diagram will be as follows

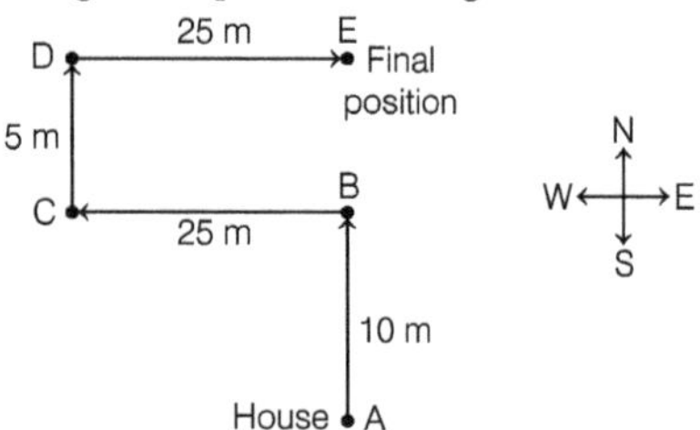

Clearly, he is facing East.

10. (*c*) According to the question, the direction diagram will be as follows

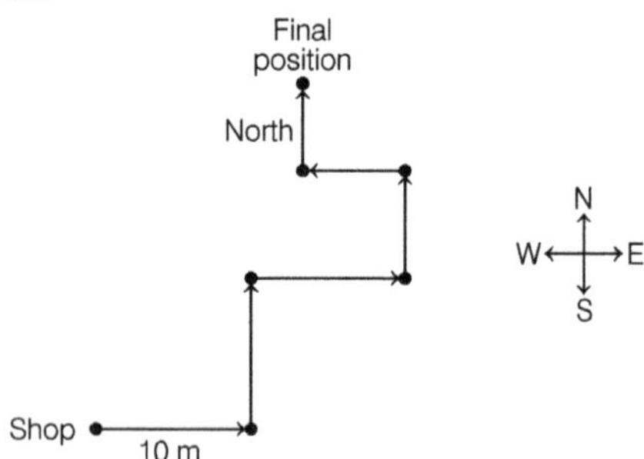

Clearly, Kunal is facing East while coming out of his shop.

11. (*d*) According to the question, the direction diagram will be as follows

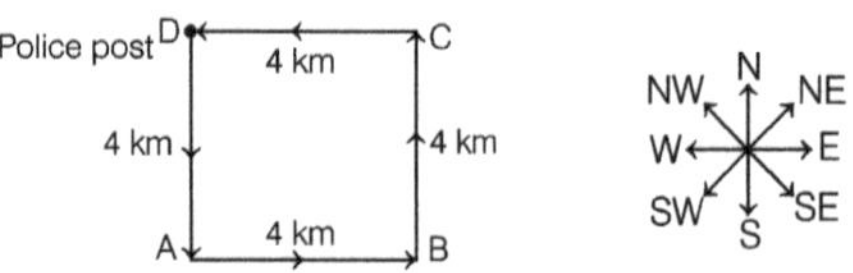

Clearly, from point C the policeman will have to go towards West to reach police post at point D.

12. (*b*) If I come from the South, then my left hand denotes West and right hand denotes East and straight is North.

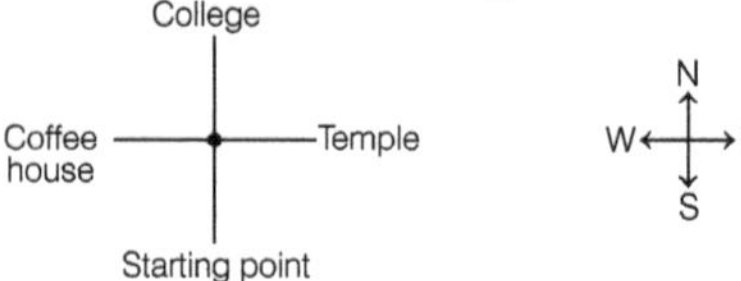

Hence, only the remaining direction on the road i.e. the East leads towards the temple.

13. (*d*) According to the question, the direction diagram will be as follows

So, from the above diagram, it is clear that Shahid Afridi came from East.

14. (*a*) According to the question, the direction diagram will be as follows

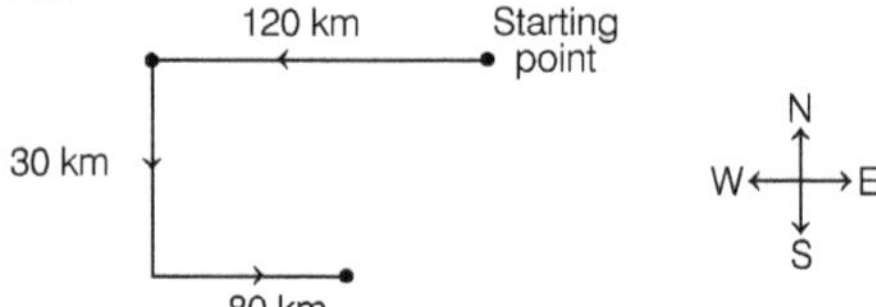

Clearly, station is in South-West direction from the train's starting point.

15. (*b*)

Amutha's College

N
W
E
S

Amutha's house

Clearly, bus is facing West when it left the bus stop.

16. (*d*) According to the question, the direction diagram will be as follows

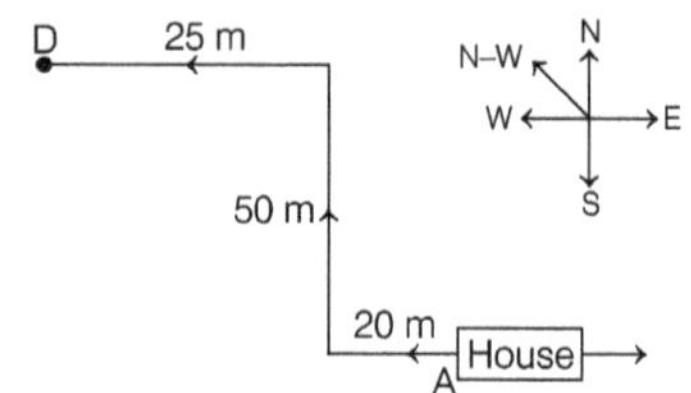

A = Starting point, D = End point

Hence, now the man is facing North-West direction.

17. (*d*) Path of Raj is as follows

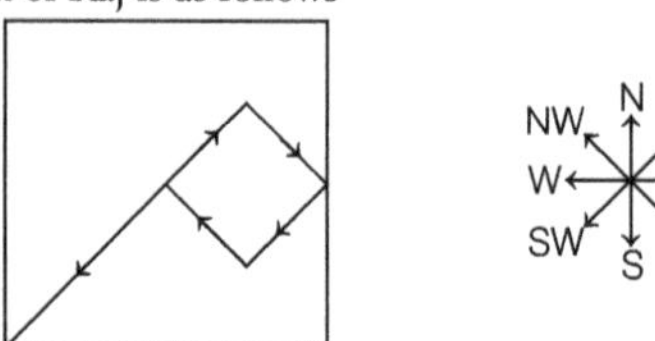

It is clear from the above figure that now Raj is in South-West direction.

18. (*a*) According to the question, we have the following direction diagram

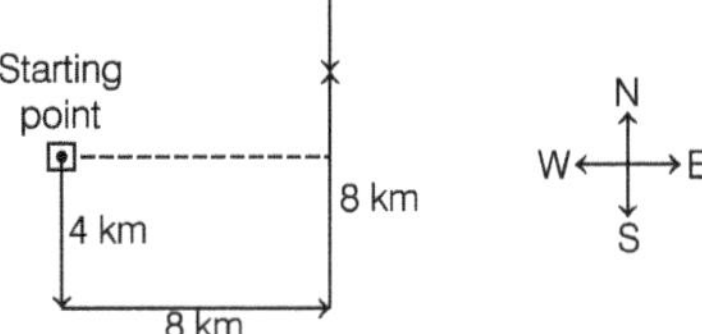

So, Kate is facing towards North.

19. (*d*) According to the question, the direction diagram is as follows

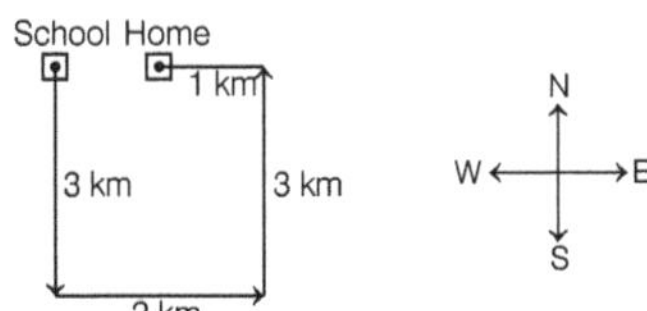

The home of boy was in East direction from his school.

20. (*d*) According to the question, the direction diagram is as follows

So, Rani is facing towards East and Sarita is facing towards South.

21. (*a*) From given information, walking diagram is as follows

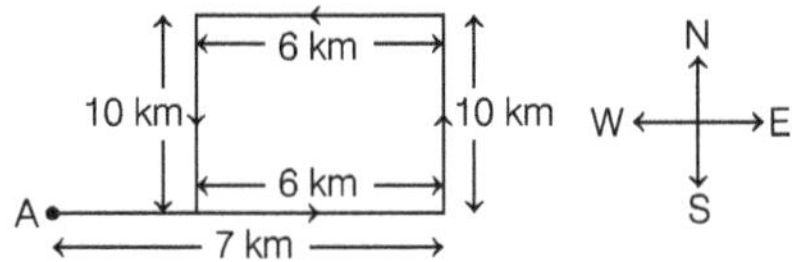

It is clear from diagram, he is in East with respect to starting point.

22. (*b*) From given information direction diagram of girl is as given below

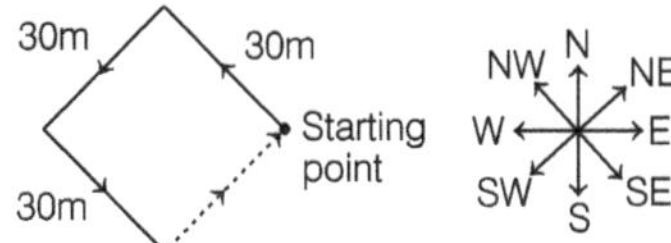

Hence, It is clear from diagram that the girl is moving in North-East direction.

23. (*d*) According to the question, the diagram will be as follows

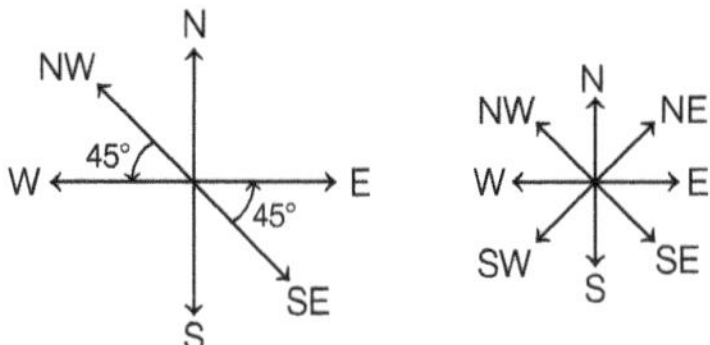

Clearly, West will be replaced by North-West.

24. (*c*) According to the question, the direction diagram will be as follows

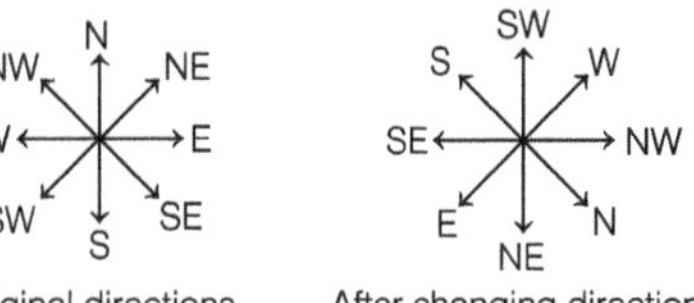

Now, from the above diagrams, it is clear that South-East will be the direction for West.

25. (*b*) According to the question, the direction diagram will be as follows

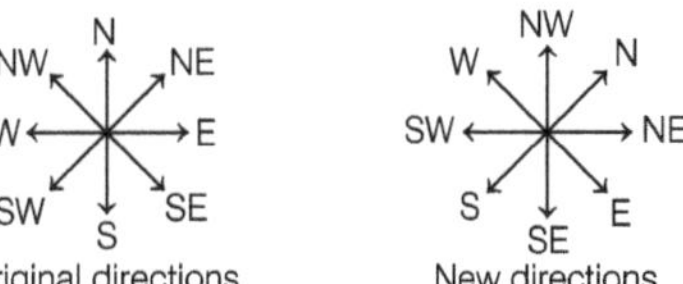

Now, from the above diagram, it is clear that the direction for South is South-East.

26. (*d*) According to the question,

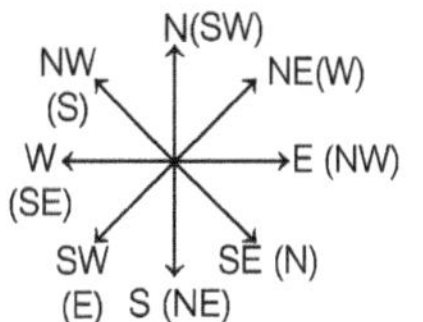

Hence, West will become South-East.

27. (*c*) According to the question,

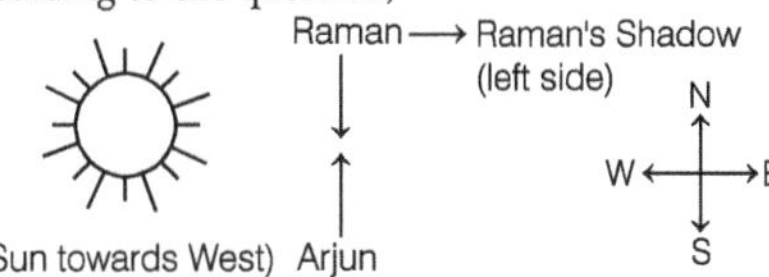

So, Arjun was facing North.

28. (*a*) In the morning Sun is in the East direction. According to the question, Y's shadow falls towards the right side of X i.e. West direction on the right side of X. Hence, X is facing towards South direction.

29. (*d*) According to the question, we have the following direction diagram

Vinay/Vaibhav
N
Vinay/Vaibhav W ⟵ ⟶ E Roshan
S
Sumit

Here, it is not clear that the partners Roshan and Vaibhav sit opposite to each other or next to each other.

30. (*d*) According to the question,

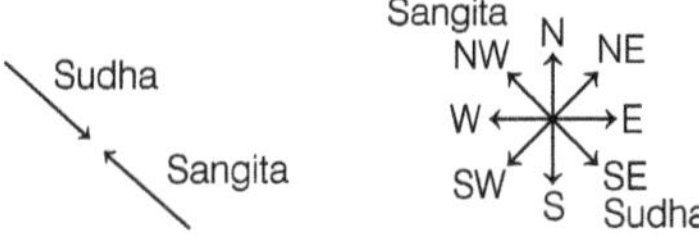

As per the standard seating pattern, they should face each other, So, Sudha will face South-East direction.

31. (*b*) According to the question, the direction diagram is as follows

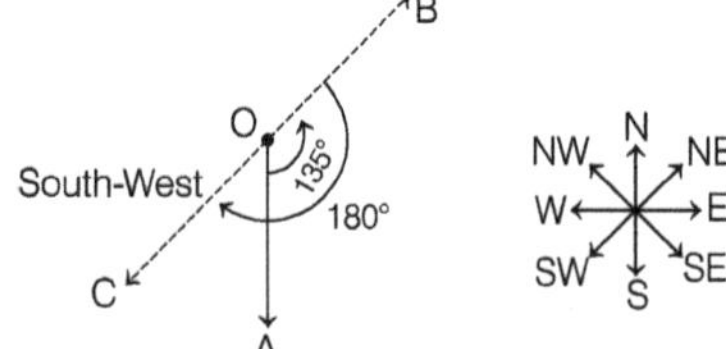

Clearly, Kamal is facing South-West.

32. (*b*) According to the question, the direction diagram will be as follows

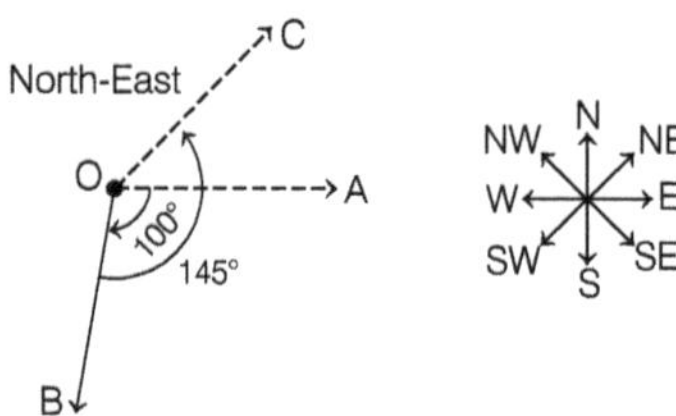

Clearly, Surbhi is facing North-East.

33. (*b*) According to the question, the direction diagram will be as follows

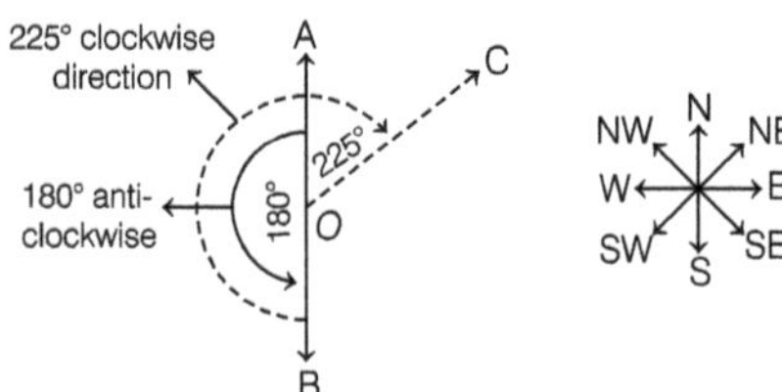

Clearly, the girl is facing North-East.

34. (*d*) Let *A* be the initial position of the man. He initially faced East and then turned his left in the direction of North and walked 10 yard.

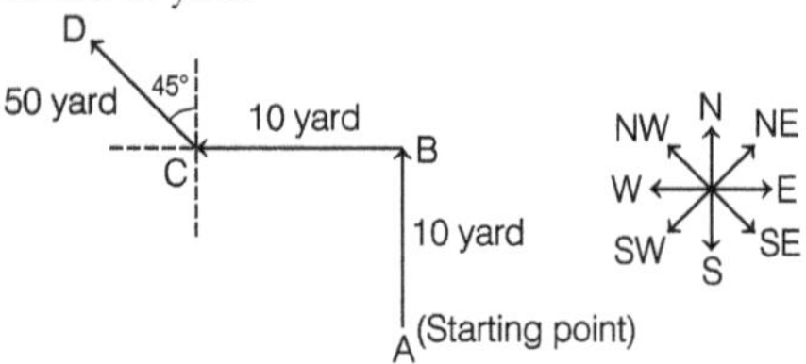

Then, turned his left in the direction of West and walked 10 yard. Now, he turned 45° to his right and walked 50 yard straight in the same direction.

Now, the direction of the man with respect to his starting point is North-West.

35. (*d*) According to the question, the direction diagram can be drawn as

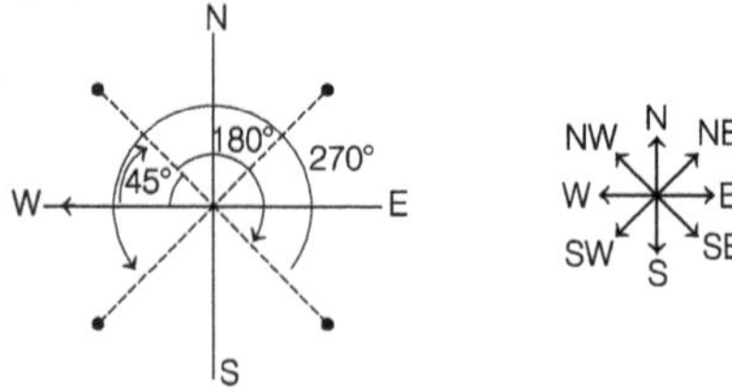

Finally, man is facing the South-West direction.

36. (*c*) According to the question,the direction diagram is as follows

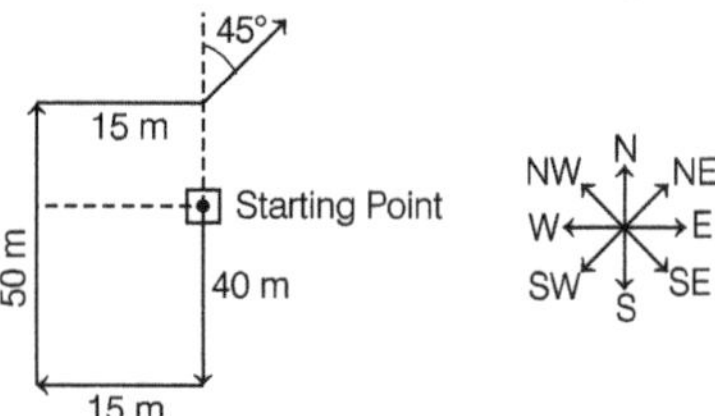

So, she is running in the North-East direction.

37. (*b*) According to the question,

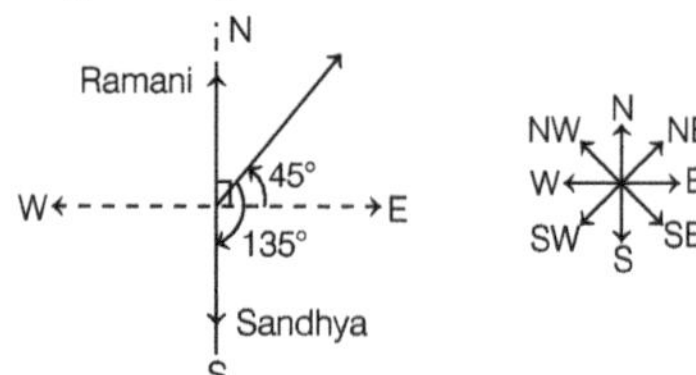

From the diagram Ramani have to turn 90° anti-clockwise to face opposite to Sandhya.

38. (*a*) According to the question,

Clearly, she is facing North-West direction.

39. (*b*) According to the question, the diagrams will be as follows

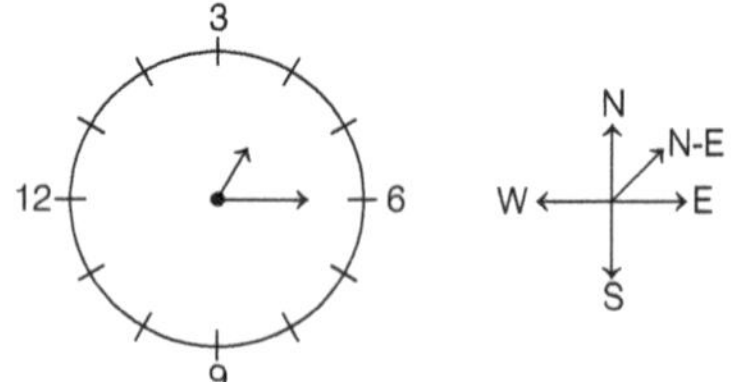

∴ The hour hand points towards North-East direction.

40. (*d*) Time quarter past twelve means that the time is 12:15.

Hence, when hour hand is pointing towards East, then the minute hand is pointing towards South.
So, the direction opposite to minute hand is North.

41. (*d*) According to the question, the direction diagram will be as follows

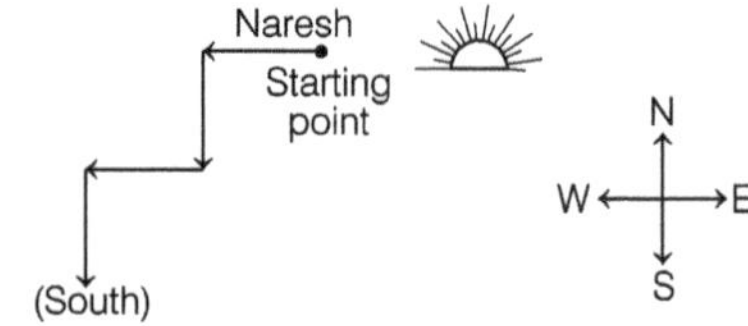

So, Naresh is facing towards South.

42. (*d*) According to the question,

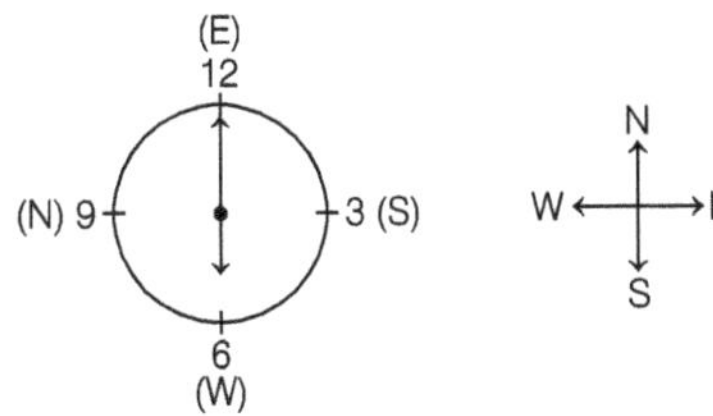

At 6:00 if the hour needle points towards West, then minute hand was pointing out towards East direction.

43. (*d*) According to the question, the diagram will be as follows

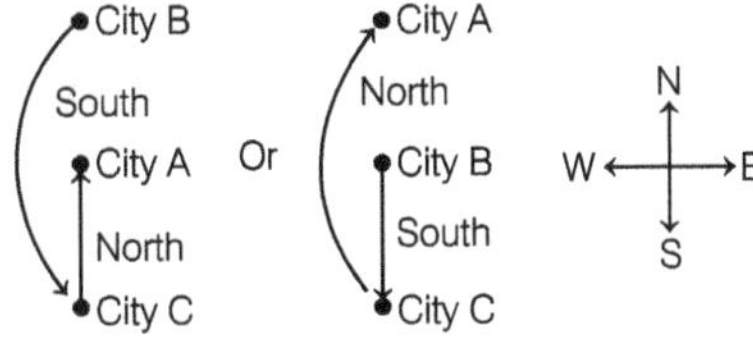

Therefore, the direction of City A with respect to City B cannot be determined.

44. (*d*) According to the question, the direction diagram is as follows

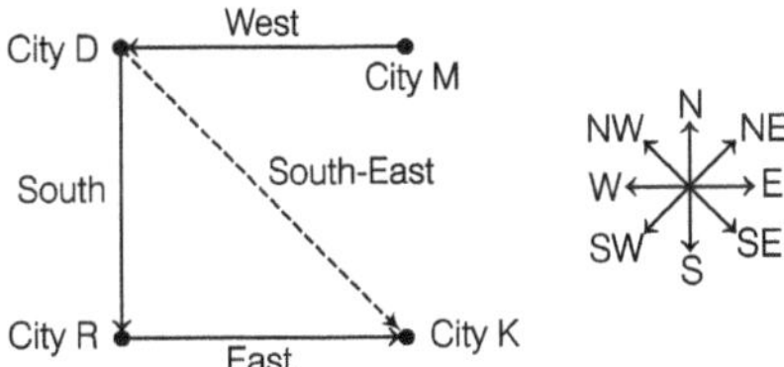

Hence, city K is located in the South- East direction.

45. (*d*) From the given information,

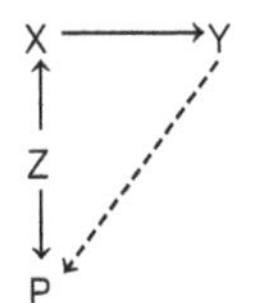

Clearly, P is in the South-West of Y.

46. (*d*) According to the question, the direction diagram will be as follows

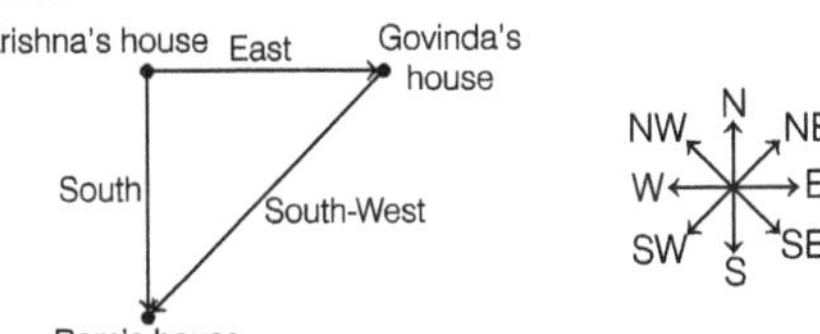

Clearly, Ram's house is to the South-West of Govinda's house.

47. (*d*) According to the question, the direction diagram is as follows

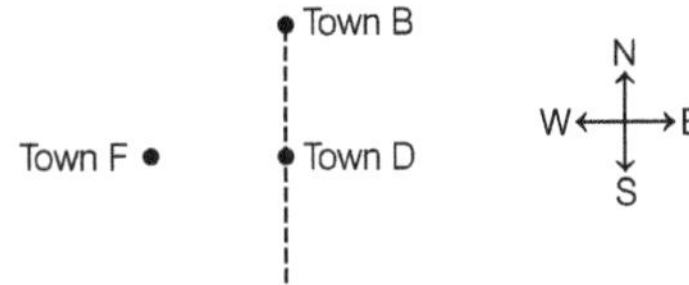

Now, H may lie anywhere on the dotted line. Hence, direction of H with respect to F cannot be determined definitely as data given is inadequate.

48. (*d*) According to the question, the direction diagram will be as follows

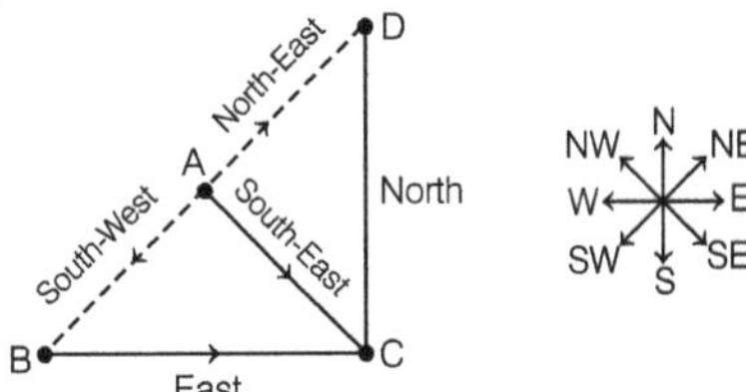

Clearly, D is to the North-East of A.

49. (*b*) According to the question, the direction diagram will be as follows

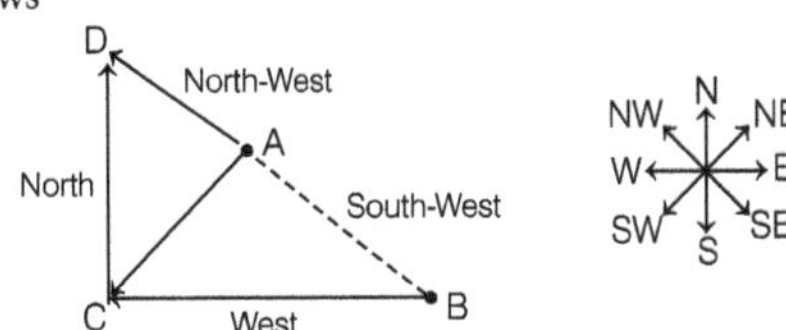

Clearly, the point B is located in the South-East direction from point A.

50. (*a*) According to the question,

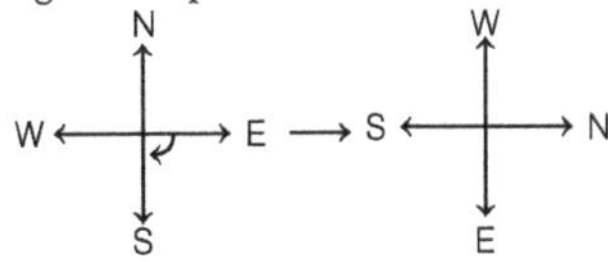

The, pointer which was showing West started showing South. Hence, the pointer turned 90° clockwise.
Now, Sita went to the direction thinking it as West. The original direction will be +90° clockwise i.e. North direction.

Solutions (Q. Nos. 51 and 52) *Direction diagram is as follows*

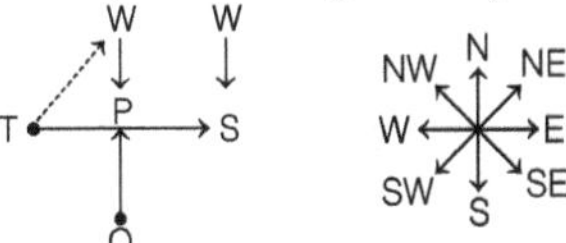

51. (*a*) It is clear from diagram that P is towards South of W and North of Q.

52. (*b*) W is an North-East direction with respect to T.

Solutions (Q. Nos. 53-55) According to the given information,

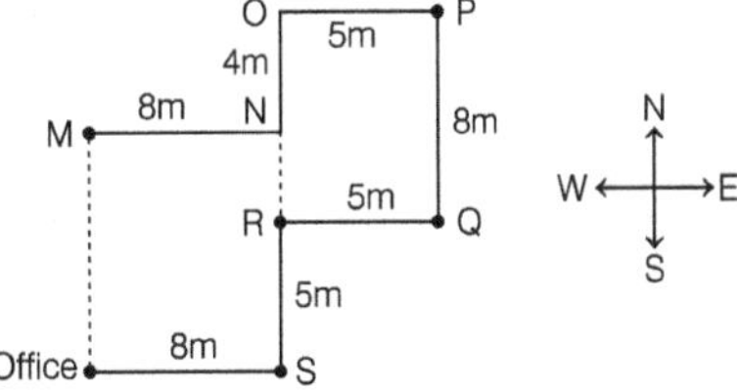

53. (b) Point P is in North-East direction with respect to Point S.

54. (b) Points N, O and S are in straight line.

55. (d) Ramesh's office is in South direction with respect to point M.

TYPE 02

Finding the Distance Only

In this type of questions, the candidate is asked to find out the distance between initial position and final position as per the information given in the question.

There are two types of questions based on finding the distance that are asked in various competitive examinations

A. Finding the Total Distance

In this type of questions, the candidate is asked to determine the total distance covered by a particular person or object.

***Ex* 13** Vipul goes Northward 10 m. He turns left and walks 30 m, then again turns left and walks 50 m. How much distance Vipul travelled?

(a) 60 m (b) 20 m
(c) 10 m (d) 90 m

***Solution* (d)** According to the question, the direction diagram is drawn as

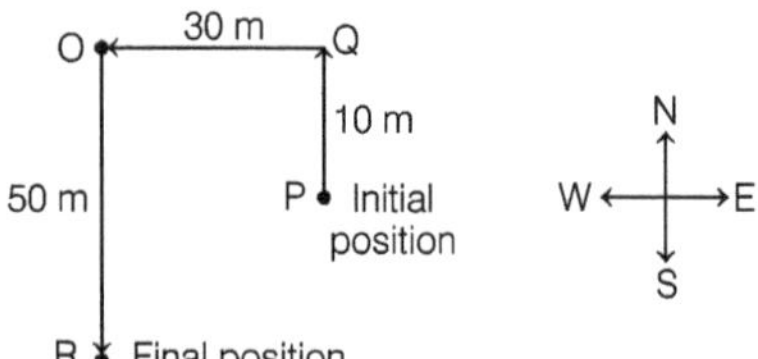

Total distance = PQ + QO + OR

= 10 + 30 + 50 = 90 m

B. Finding the Minimum (Shortest) Distance

The shortest distance between two points may be different from the total distance covered in going from one point to the other.

In this type of questions, minimum distance between initial and final points is to be determined.

To find the minimum distance between the starting and end point, there are two cases

***Case A* When right angled triangle is formed**

When a right angled triangle is formed, we use the Pythagoras theorem to find the minimum distance between the initial and final points.

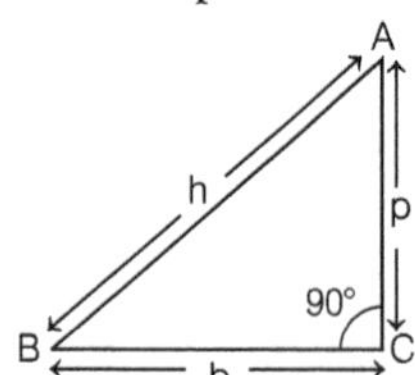

According to this theorem,

"In a right angled triangle, square of the hypotenuse (h) is equal to the sum of the squares of its base (b) and perpendicular (p).

$$h^2 = p^2 + b^2$$

where, h = AB = Hypotenuse, b = BC = Base,
p = AC = Perpendicular

AB or BA is the minimum or shortest distance to reach A from B or to reach B from A.

***Ex* 14** Kavi walks Northward upto 10 m. He turns left and walks 30 m. Finally, he turns left and walks 50 m. At what distance Kavi is now from his starting position?

(a) 50 m (b) 10 m (c) 20 m (d) 90 m

***Solution* (a)** According to the question, the direction diagram is drawn as shown in adjacent figure

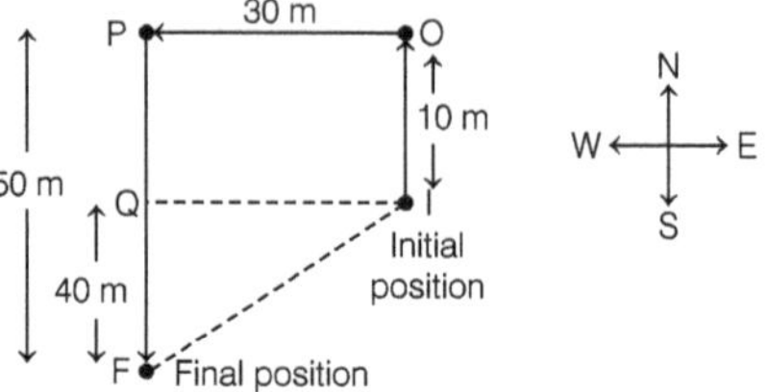

IO = 10 m, OP = 30 m, PF = 50 m,

QI = OP = 30 m, PQ = IO = 10 m

QF = PF − PQ = 50 − 10 = 40 m

F represents the final position.

$\therefore$ Required distance, $IF = \sqrt{(QI)^2 + (QF)^2}$

$= \sqrt{(30)^2 + (40)^2}$

$= \sqrt{900 + 1600}$

$= \sqrt{2500} = 50$ m

***Ex* 15** Prachi starting from place A towards East upto place B covered a distance of 10 ft, then she turned right and moved 3 ft, again she turned right and moved 14 ft. At how much distance from place A is she? « CGPSC Pre 2018

(a) 4 ft (b) 5 ft (c) 27 ft (d) 24 ft
(e) None of the above

***Solution* (b)** According to the question,

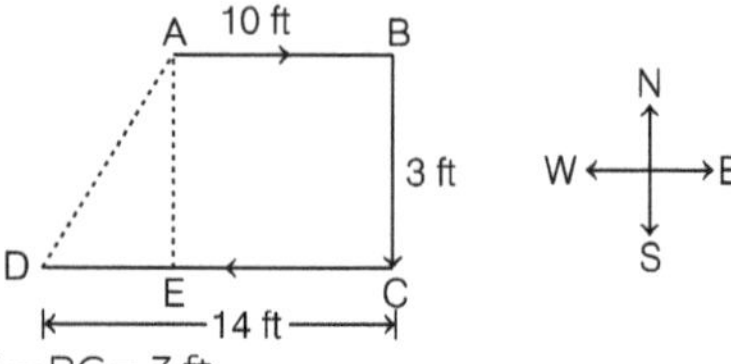

In ΔADE, AE = BC = 3 ft

DE = CD − CE = CD − AB = 14 − 10 = 4

$\therefore \quad AD^2 = AE^2 + DE^2 = 3^2 + 4^2 = 9 + 16 = 25$

$\therefore \quad AD = \sqrt{25} = 5$ ft

Hence, Prachi is 5 ft from place A.

Case B **When right angled triangle is not formed**

In this type of questions, we find the minimum distance by comparing the line opposite to the line that joins initial and final point.

***Ex* 16** Rema walked 10 km South and turned right and walked 5km. Then again, she turned right and walked 10 km. Then she turned left and walked 10 km. How many kilometer will Rema have to walk to reach the starting point? « RRB JE 2019

(a) 25 km (b) 20 km (c) 5 km (d) 15 km

Solution (d) According to the question,

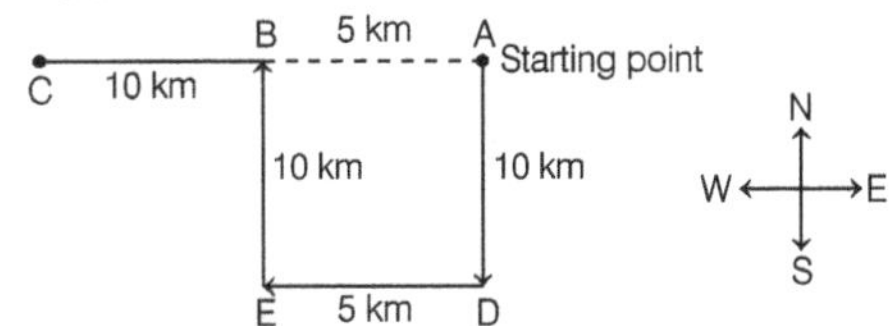

Rema walk to reach the starting point (CA)
= CB + BA = CB + ED
= 10 + 5 = 15 km

Practice / CORNER 7.2

1. Pihu walks 2 km towards North. Then she turns to East and walks 10 km. After this she turns to North and walks 3 km. Again she turns towards East and walks 2 km. Total distance covered by Pihu is
   (a) 10 km (b) 17 km (c) 12 km (d) 14 km

2. The length and breadth of a room are 8m and 6m respectively, A cat runs along all the four walls to catch a rat. How much total distance is covered by the cat?
   (a) 28 m (b) 20 m (c) 30 m (d) 25 m

3. I walk 12 km to the North, then 10 km East and then 12 km South. How far am I from the starting point? « SSC CPO 2016
   (a) 34 km (b) 22 km (c) 24 km (d) 10 km

4. From her house, Rani first walks 15m straight in front and then 15 m to the right. Then, every time turning to her left, she walks 10 m, 25 and 25 m respectively. How far is she now from her house? « UPSSSC Junior Assist. 2017
   (a) 25 m (b) 20 m
   (c) 15 m (d) 10 m

5. Anita started from a place A and walked 2m towards West. She then took a right turn and walked 3m before turning to left and walked 5m. Now, she took a left turn and walked again 3m to stop at place B. How far is the place A from B? « UKPSC Asst. Conservator of Forest 2019
   (a) 2 m (b) 6 m (c) 7 m (d) 8 m

6. Suman is fond of driving. One day, she left her home early and drove towards East for 8 km and then turned 90° anti-clockwise and drove for 15 km to reach a lake. What is the shortest distance of the lake from her home? « UPSSSC VDO 2018
   (a) 15 km (b) 16 km
   (c) 17 km (d) 18 km

7. A and B start walking from the same point A goes North and covers 3 km, then turns right and covers 4 km. B goes West and covers 5 km, then turns right and covers 3 km. How far apart are they from each other? « SSC CPO 2012
   (a) 10 km (b) 9 km
   (c) 8 km (d) 5 km

8. Molly travelled from point A to point B which is 5 ft. He, then travelled 6 ft to his right and then turned to left and went 4 ft. Finally, he again went 6 ft to his left. How far is he from the point B now? « SSC CGL 2012
   (a) 10 ft (b) 6 ft (c) 5 ft (d) 4 ft

9. W walked 40 m towards West, took a left turn and walked 30 m. He, then took a right turn and walked 20 m. He again took a right turn and walked 30 m. How far was he from the starting point?
   « Allahabad Bank PO 2010
   (a) 70 m (b) 60 m
   (c) 90 m (d) Cannot be determined
   (e) None of these

10. Sheela walks 2 km from A to B. She turns right at 90° and goes 3 km upto C. She, then again turns right at 90° and goes 8 km upto D. Again she takes right turn at 90° and goes 3 km upto K. From K she takes right turn at 90° again and reaches at F after covering 4 km. Find the distance between A and F. « MAT 2011
    (a) 2 km (b) 4 km
    (c) 6 km (d) 8 km

11. A man goes 5 km East from his office. He then takes left turn and walks 3 km. He again takes left turn and walks 5 km. How far is he from starting point? « RRB TC/CC 2010
    (a) 3 km (b) 4 km (c) 6 km (d) 7 km

12. Rohit drives a car from Bengaluru to Mysore. After 80 km he turns right and goes 50 km. After that he again turns to his right and moves on 70 km. Finally, he turns to his right and stops after moving a distance of 50 km. At what distance is Rohit now from Bengaluru? « MAT 2014
    (a) 10 km (b) 40 km
    (c) 20 km (d) 30 km

13. A man starts from his home and walks 10 km towards South. Then, he turns right and walks 6 km, again he turns right and goes 10 km. Finally, he turns right and walks 5 km. At what distance is he from his straight point? « UPPSC 2012
    (a) 3 km (b) 2 km
    (c) 1 km (d) 5 km

14. A house faces North. A man coming out of his house walked straight for 10 m, turned left and walked 25 m. He then turned right and walked 5 m and again turned right and walked 25 m. How far is he from his house?

(a)15 m (b) 55 m (c) 60 m (d) 65 m

15. John's house is 100 m North of his uncle's office. His uncle's house is located 200 m West of his uncle's office. Kabir is the friend of John and he stays 100 m East of John's house. The office of Kabir is located 100 m South of his house. Then, how far is his uncle's house from Kabir's office?

(a) 200 m (b) 300 m
(c) 400 m (d) 500 m

16. Rachel starts walking towards North. After walking 15 m, she turns towards South and walks 20 m. She then turns towards East and walks 10 m. Then, again she walks 5 m towards North. How far is she from her starting point and in which direction?

(a) 10 m, West (b) 5 m, East
(c) 5 m, North (d) 10 m, East

17. Rohan walks a distance of 3 km towards North, then turns to his left and walks for 2 km. He again turns left and walks for 3 km. At this point he turns to his left and walks for 3 km. How many kilometres is he from the starting point?

(a) 1 km (b) 2 km (c) 3 km (d) 4 km

18. Seema walks 30 m North. Then, she turns right and walks 30 m then she turns right and walks 55 m. Then, she turns left and walks 20 m. Then, she again turn left and walks 25 m. How many metres away is she from her original position?

(a) 45 m (b) 50 m (c) 66 m (d) 55 m

19. A man walks Southwards and covers 10 km distance. He, then turns to his right and walks 15 km, after which he turns to his right again and walks 10 km. What is the shortest distance from his start to end point?

(a) 35 km (b) $10\sqrt{2}$ km
(c) 10 km (d) 15 km

20. One day, Ravi left home and cycled 10 km Southwards, turned right and cycled 5 km and turned right and cycled 10 km and turned left and cycled 10 km. How many kilometres will he now have to cycle in straight line to reach his home?

(a) 10 km (b) 15 km (c) 20 km (d) 25 km

21. A man walks 7 km Eastwards, turns right and walks 3 km and further turns right and walks 11 km. How far is he from the starting point? « CGPSC Pre 2017

(a) 8 km (b) 3 km (c) 6 km (d) 5 km
(e) None of these

22. A man travels 4 km due North, then travels 6 km due East and further travels 4 km due North. How far he is from the starting point? « IBPS RRB Officer grade B 2015

(a) 6 km (b) 14 km
(c) 8 km (d) 10 km
(e) Other than those given as options

23. Mohan walked 30 m towards South, took a left turn and walked 15 m. He, then took a right turn and walked 20 m. He again took a right turn and walked 15 m. How far is he from the starting point?

(a) 95 m (b) 50 m (c) 70 m
(d) Cannot be determined (e) None of these

24. Ankit started walking towards North. After walking 30 m, he turned towards left and walked 40 m. He, then turned left and walked 30 m. He again turned left and walked 50 m. How far is he from his original position?

(a) 50 m (b) 40 m (c) 30 m (d) None of these

25. Laxman went 15 km to the West from house, then turned left and walked 20 km. He, then turned East and walked 25 km and finally turning left covered 20 km. How far is he now from his house?

(a) 15 km (b) 20 km (c) 25 km (d) 10 km

26. Madhuri travels 14 km Westwards and then turns left and travels 6 km and further turns left and travels 26 km. How far is Madhuri now from the starting point?

(a) $\sqrt{180}$ km (b) $\sqrt{80}$ km
(c) $\sqrt{100}$ km (d) None of these

27. Shyam walks 6 m towards East, then turns right and walks 9 m. Again, he turns to his left and walks 6 m. At what distance is he now from his original point?

(a) 15 m (b) 21 m (c) 18 m
(d) Cannot be determined (e) None of these

28. Ram and Shyam start walking towards North and cover 20 m. Ram turns to his left and Shyam to his right. After sometime, Ram walks to 10 m in the same direction in which he turned. On the other hand, Shyam walks only 7 m. Later, Ram turns towards his left and Shyam to his right. Both walk 25 m forward. How far is Ram from Shyam now? « SSC CGL 2015

(a) 10 m (b) 20 m (c) 17 m (d) 5 m

DIRECTIONS ~(Q. Nos. 29 and 30) *Read the following information carefully and answer the questions that follow.* « IBPS PO 2012, NIACL AO 2015

Point H is 6 m towards the East of Point G, Point R is 8 m North of Point G. Point Q is exactly midway between point R and Point G. Point K is 10 m to the South of point Q. Point L is 3 m towards the East of Point Q. Point S is exactly midway between Point G and Point H.

29. If a persons walks 4 m towards the South from point L, takes a right turn and walks for another 3 m, then which of the following points would he reach?

(a) Q (b) G (c) K (d) H
(e) None of these

30. If a person walks 8 m towards North from Point S, then which of the following points would he cross and how far will he be from point R?

(a) G, 4 m (b) H, 3 m (c) L, 6 m (d) L, 3 m
(e) G, 8 m

31. A person starts from his home for collecting money from various shops A, B, C, D and E. After collecting money from shop A, he reaches shop B which is 12 m to the West of shop A. Then he took a left turn to reach shop C, which is 5 m from shop B. Again he took two consecutive left turns, where he gets to go through the mid-point of shop A and shop B. Finally he reaches the shop E which is 3 m North from the mid-point of shop A and shop B. What is the distance between shop C and shop E? « UP Police SI 2017

(a) 8 m (b) 11 m (c) 10 m (d) 14 m

32. A man starts from a point and moves 9 km South and then turns to East and goes 3 km. He turns South and walks 3 km and then moves 8 km towards West. How far is he from the starting point? « SSC CPO 2016

(a) 13 km (b) 15 km
(c) 12 km (d) 11 km

33. In an open ground, Rakesh walks 20 m towards North, turns left and goes 40 m. He turns to his left again to walk 50 m. How far is he from starting point? « MP PCS 2015

(a) 110 m (b) 70 m
(c) 50 m (d) 40 m

34. Shahid and Rohit start from the same point in opposite directions. After each 1 km, Shahid always turns left and Rohit always turns right. Which of the following statements is correct? « CSAT 2015

(a) After both have travelled 2 km, the distance between them is 4 km
(b) They meet after each has travelled 3 km
(c) They meet for first time after each has travelled 4 km
(d) They go on without ever meeting again

35. A boy starts from home in early morning and walks straight for 8 km facing the Sun. Then, he takes a right turn and walks for 3 km. Then, he turns right again and walks for 2 km and then turns left and walks for 1 km. Again he turned right and walked 1 km. Then, he turns right and travels for 4 km straight. How far is he from the starting point? « SSC CGL 2013

(a) 5 km (b) 6 km
(c) 2 km (d) 4 km

36. A and B both are walking away from point 'X'. A walked 3 m and B walked 4 m from it, then A walked 4 m North of X and B walked 5 m South of A. What is the distance between them now? « SSC CGL 2013

(a) 9.5 m (b) 9 m (c) 16 m (d) 11. 40 m

Answers WITH EXPLANATIONS

1. (*b*) According to the given information,

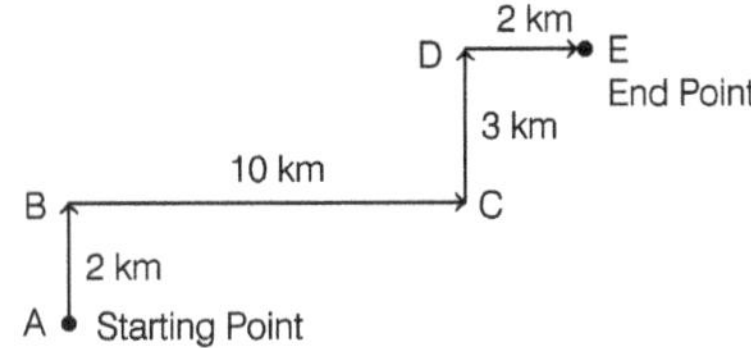

∴ Total distance covered by Pihu = AB + BC + CD + DE
= 2 + 10 + 3 + 2 = 17 km

2. (*a*) According to the given information,

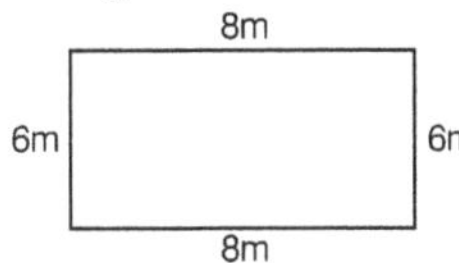

∴ Total distance covered by the Cat = 6 + 8 + 6 + 8 = 28 m

3. (*d*) According to the given information,

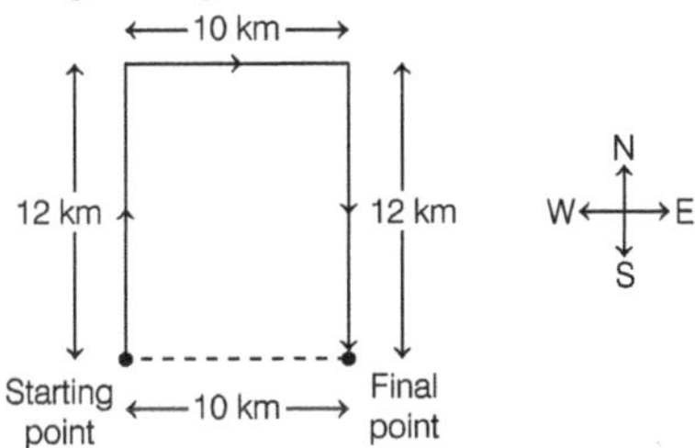

It is clear from the direction graph that the distance between starting and final point is 10 km.

4. (*d*) According to the given information,

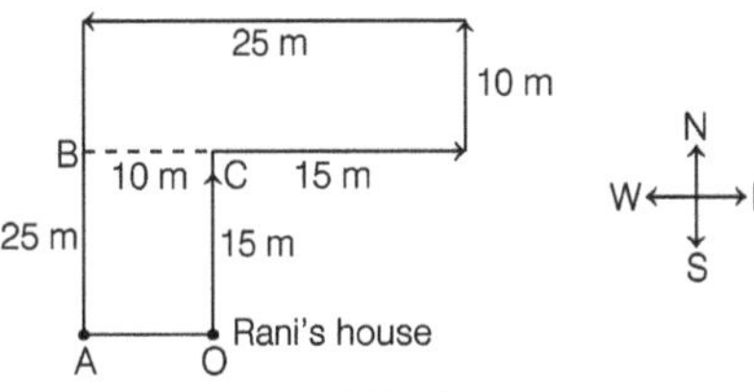

∴ Required distance = AO = BC = 10 m.

5. (*c*) According to the given information,

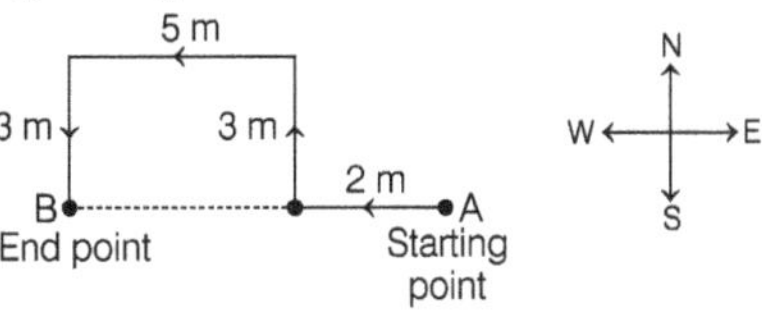

∴ Distance between A and B = 2 + 5 = 7m

6. (*c*) According to the question,

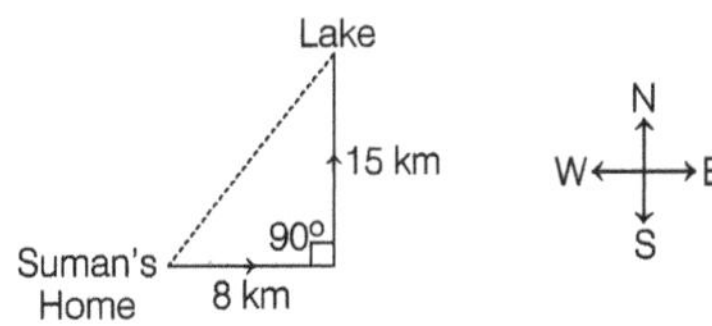

Shortest distance of lake from her home,

$= \sqrt{(15)^2 + (8)^2}$

$= \sqrt{(225 + 64)} = \sqrt{289} = 17$ km

7. (*b*) According to the question, the direction diagram is as follows

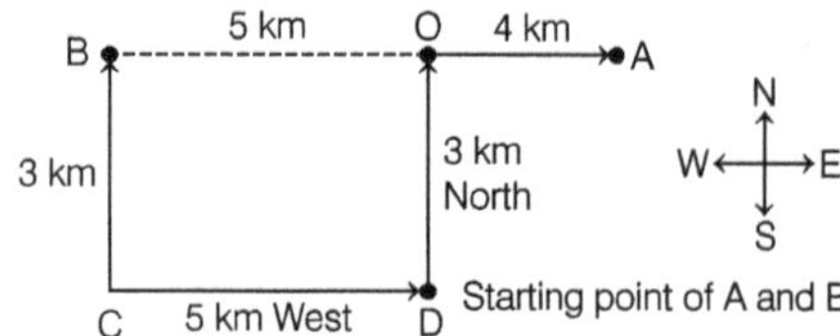

D = Starting point for A and B
CD = BO = 5 km
BC = OD = 3 km
∴ Required distance, AB = BO + OA
= 5 + 4 = 9 km

8. (*d*) According to the question, the direction diagram will be as follows

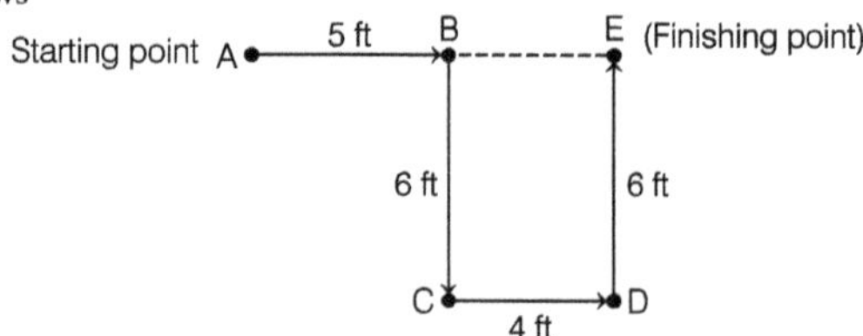

A = Initial point, E = Finishing point AB = 5 ft
BC = DE = 6 ft, BE = CD = 4 ft
∴ Required distance, BE = 4 ft

9. (*b*) According to the question, the direction diagram will be as follows

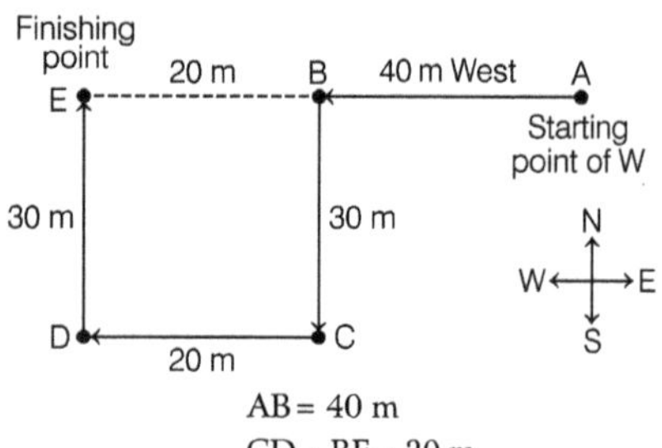

AB = 40 m
CD = BE = 20 m
∴ Required distance,
AE = AB + BE = 40 + 20 = 60 m

10. (*a*) According to the question, the direction diagram will be as follows

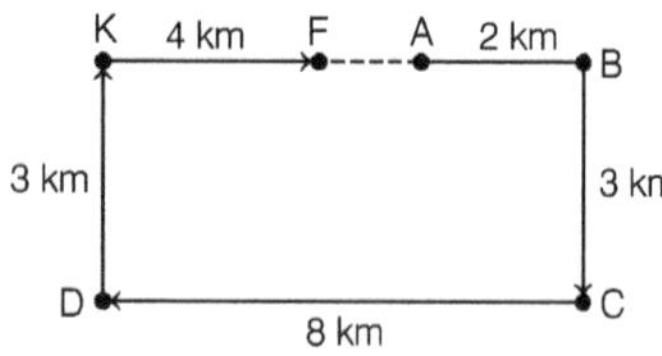

BC = KD = 3 km
CD = 8 km, AB = 2 km, KF = 4 km
∴ Required distance, AF = BK − (KF + AB)
= 8 − (4 + 2)
= 8 − 6 = 2 km

11. (*a*) According to the question, the direction diagram is as follows

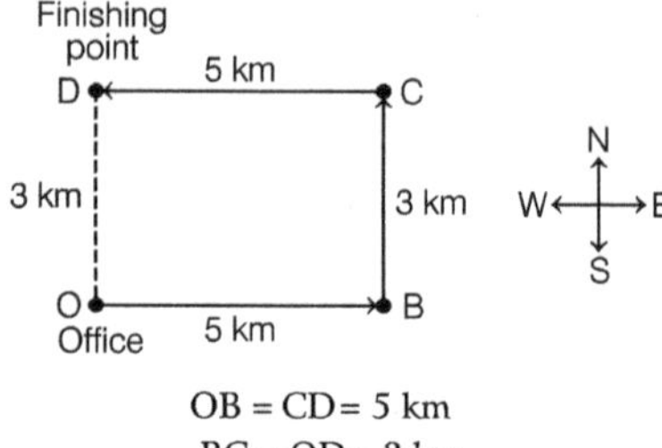

OB = CD = 5 km
BC = OD = 3 km
∴ Required distance, OD = 3 km

12. (*a*) According to the question, the direction diagram is as follows

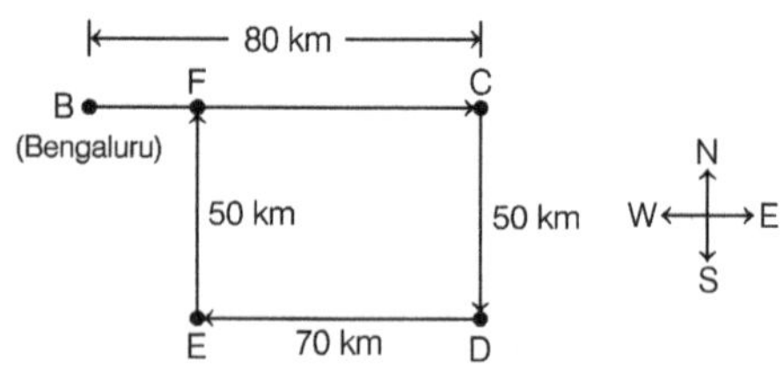

BC = 80 km, CD = FE = 50
DE = FC = 70 km
∴ Required distance, BF = BC − FC
= 80 − 70 = 10 km

13. (*c*) According to the question, the direction diagram will be as follows

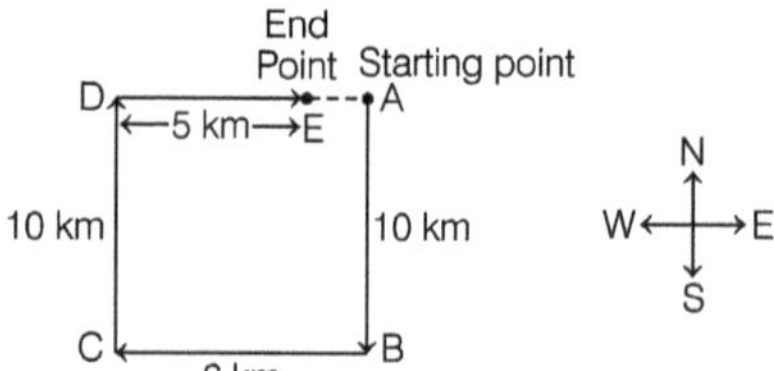

Now, CD = AB = 10 km,
BC = AD = 6 km,
ED = 5 km
∴ Required distance, AE = AD − ED
= 6 − 5 = 1 km

14. (*a*) According to the question, the direction diagram will be as follow

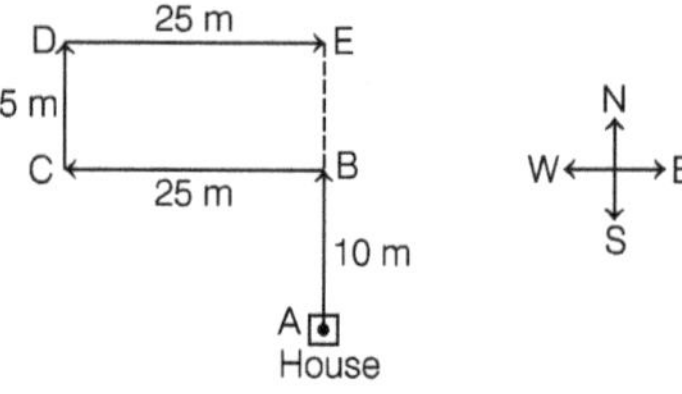

DC = EB = 5m
∴ Required distance, AE = AB + BE
= (10 + 5) m = 15 m

15. (*b*) According to the question, the direction diagram will be as follow

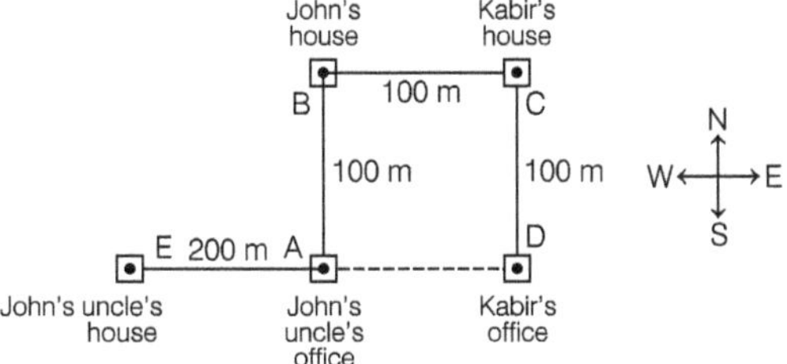

$$BC = AD$$

$\therefore$ Required distance, $DE = EA + AD$
$= 200\text{ m} + 100\text{ m}$
$= 300\text{ m}$

16. (*d*) Let the initial point of Rachel be 'A'. According to the question, the direction diagram will be as follow

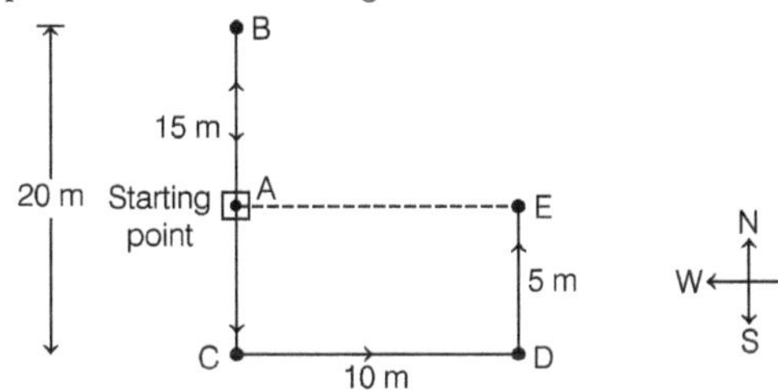

$\therefore$ Required distance, $AE = CD = 10\text{ m}$

So, Rachel is 10 m towards East from the starting point.

17. (*a*) According to the question, we have the following direction diagram

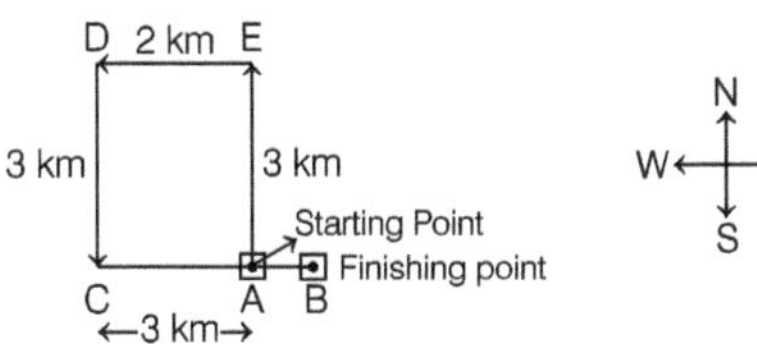

$$DE = AC = 2$$

$\therefore$ Required distance, $AB = BC - AC$
$= 3 - 2 \Rightarrow 1\text{ km}$

18. (*b*) According to the question, the direction diagram will be as follow

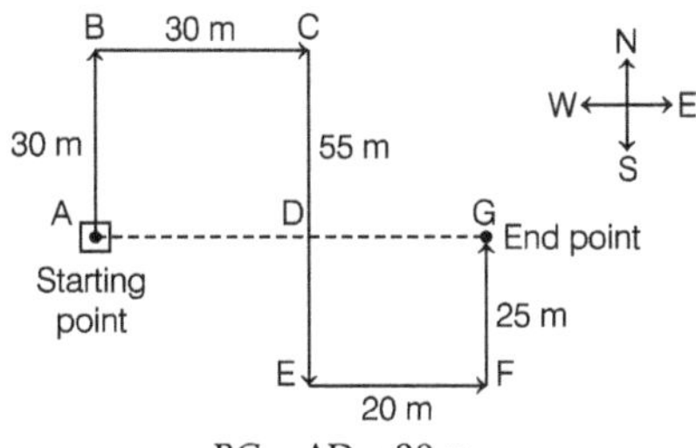

$BC = AD = 30\text{ m}$
$EF = DG = 20\text{ m}$

$\therefore$ Required distance, $AG = AD + DG$
$= 30\text{ m} + 20\text{ m}$
$= 50\text{m}$

19. (*d*) Let A be the starting point.

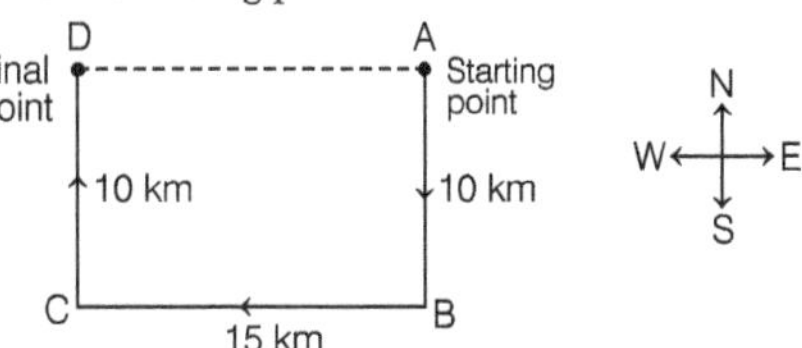

$\therefore$ Shortest distance between the points A and D,
$= AD = BC = 15\text{ km}.$

20. (*b*) According to the question, the direction diagram will be as follows

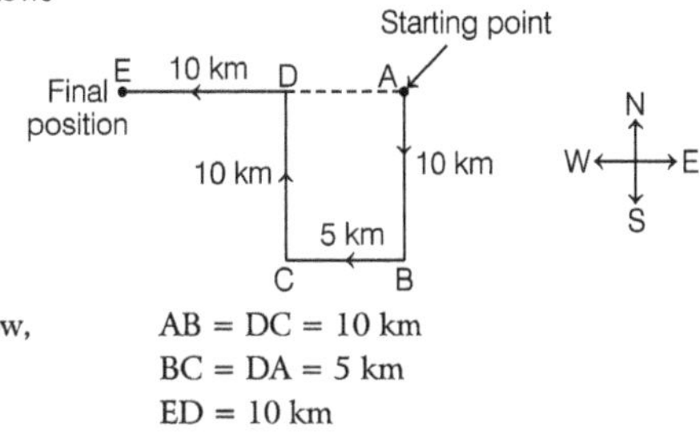

Now, $AB = DC = 10\text{ km}$
$BC = DA = 5\text{ km}$
$ED = 10\text{ km}$

$\therefore$ Required distance, $EA = ED + DA = 10 + 5 = 15\text{ km}$

21. (*d*) From given information, direction diagram of man is as follows.

Here, $AB = CE = 7\text{ km}$ and $BC = AE = 3\text{ km}$

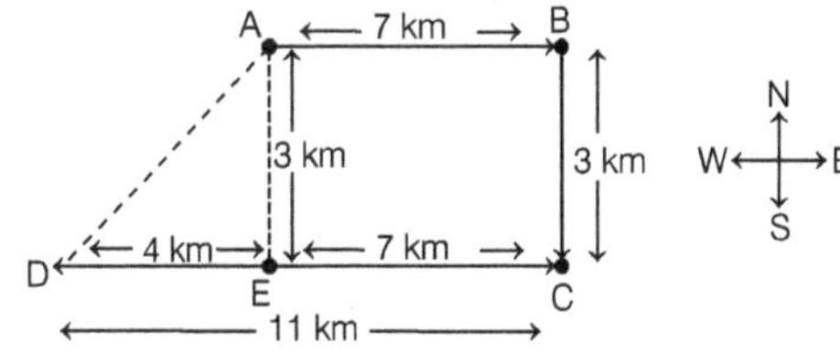

$\therefore$ $DE = 11 - 7 = 4\text{ km}$

$\therefore$ $AD = \sqrt{(DE)^2 + (AE)^2}$ [Pythagoras Theorem]

$AD = \sqrt{(4)^2 + (3)^2} = \sqrt{16 + 9} = \sqrt{25}$

$AD = 5\text{ km}$

Hence, man is 5 km far away from his starting point.

22. (*d*) According to the question,

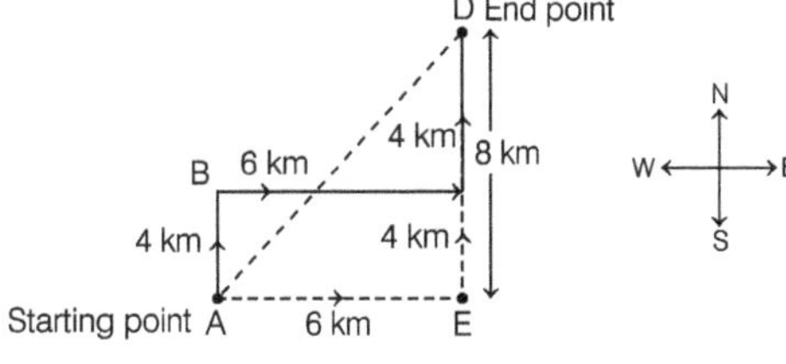

Distance between the starting point and end point is AD.

By Pythagoras theorem, in ΔADE

Now, $AD^2 = AE^2 + DE^2$

$AD^2 = (6)^2 + (8)^2$

$AD = \sqrt{36 + 64}$

$= \sqrt{100} = 10\text{ km}$

23. (*b*) According to the question, direction diagram will be as follows

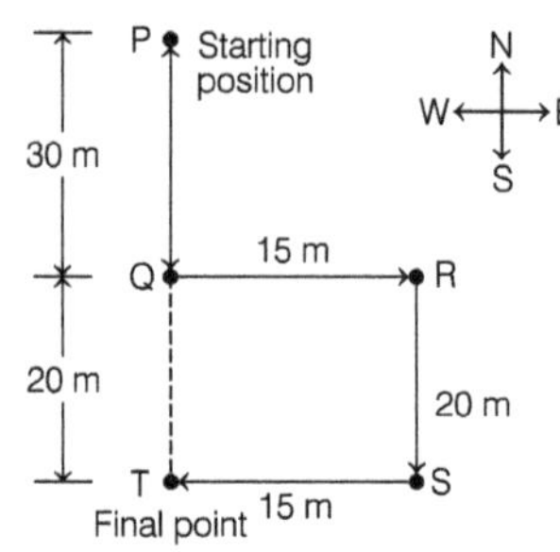

PQ = 30 m
QR = TS = 15 m
QT = RS = 20 m

∴ Required distance, PT = PQ + QT = 30 + 20 = 50 m

24. (*d*) According to the question, the direction diagram will be as follows

P = Starting point, T = Finishing point, PQ = RS = 30 m

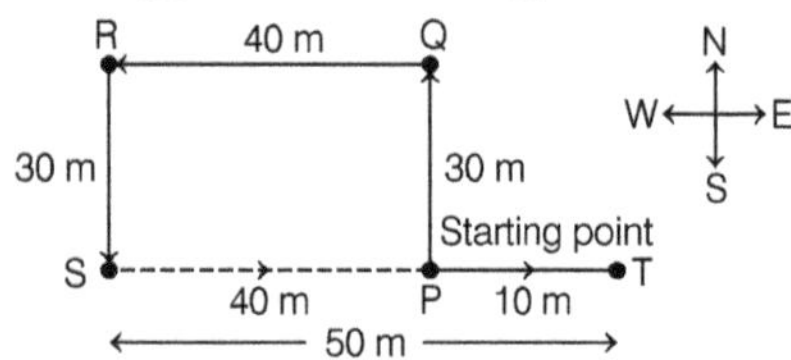

QR = SP = 40 m, ST = 50 m

∴ Required distance, PT = ST – SP = 50 – 40 = 10 m

25. (*d*) According to the question, the direction diagram will be as follows

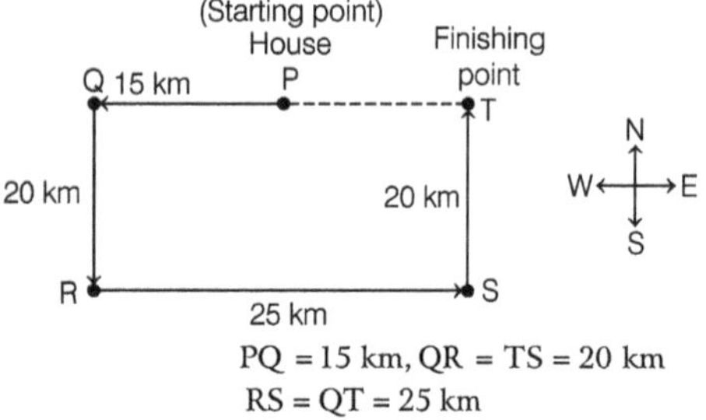

PQ = 15 km, QR = TS = 20 km
RS = QT = 25 km

∴ Required distance, PT = QT – QP = 25 – 15 = 10 km

26. (*a*) According to the question, the direction diagram will be as follows

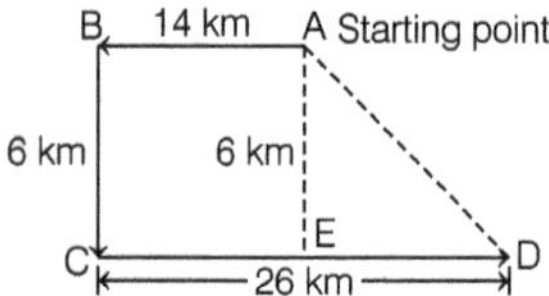

Now, AB = CE = 14 km, BC = AE = 6 km, CD = 26 km
ED = CD – CE = 26 – 14 = 12 km

∴ Required distance, $AD = \sqrt{(AE)^2 + (ED)^2}$ (by Pythagoras theorem)

$= \sqrt{6^2 + 12^2} = \sqrt{180}$ km

27. (*a*) According to the question, the direction diagram is as follows

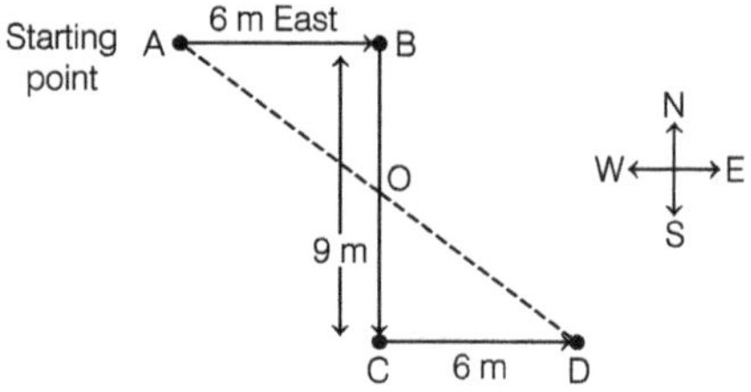

AB = 6 m, BC = 9 m, CD = 6 m

O is the mid-point of BC and AD.

$OB = OC = \frac{9}{2} = 4.5$ m

$OA = \sqrt{(AB)^2 + (OB)^2} = \sqrt{(6)^2 + (4.5)^2}$

$= \sqrt{36 + 20.25} = \sqrt{56.25} = 7.5$ m

OD = OA = 7.5 m

∴ Required distance, AD = AO + OD = 7.5 + 7.5 = 15 m

28. (*c*) According to the question, figure is drawn as

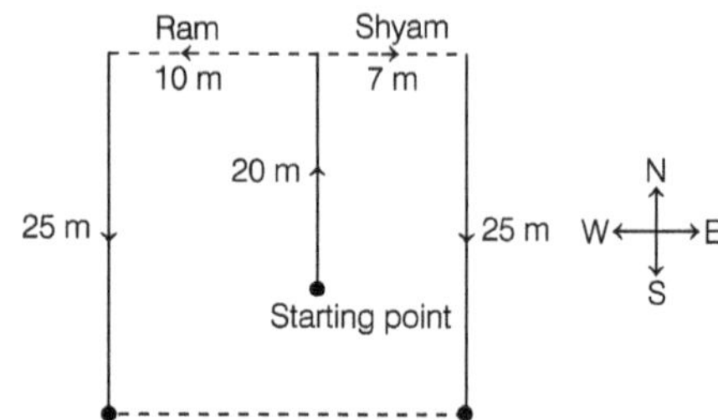

∴ The distance between Ram and Shyam at the end = 10 + 7 = 17 m

Solutions (Q. Nos. 29 and 30)

According to the question, the direction diagram will be as follows

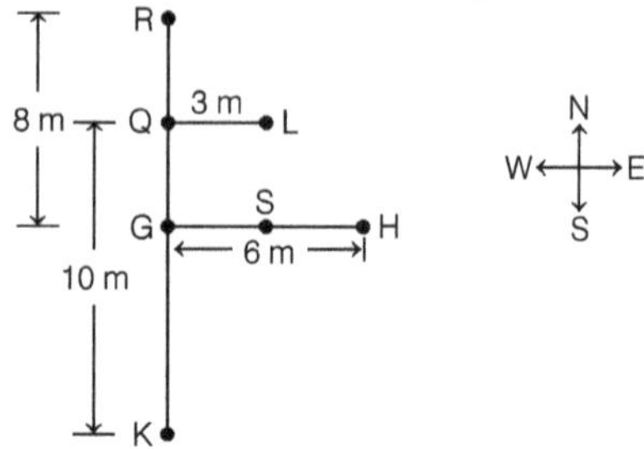

$RQ = QG = \frac{8}{2} = 4$ m as Q is the mid-point between R and G.

$GS = SH = \frac{6}{2} = 3$ m as S is the mid-point between G and H.

RG = 8 m, QK = 10 m, GH = 6 m, QL = 3 m.

29. (*b*)

L Starting point

4 m

G

3 m

Clearly, the person starts from Point L goes 4 m Southward and reaches Point S from where he takes right turn and walks 3 m to reach Point G.

30. (*d*)

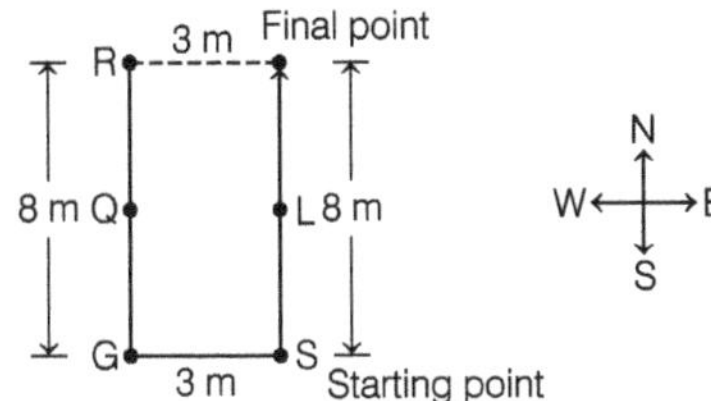

Clearly, man will cross point L and at the final point, he will be at a distance of 3 m from point R.

31. (*c*) Direction diagram is as given below

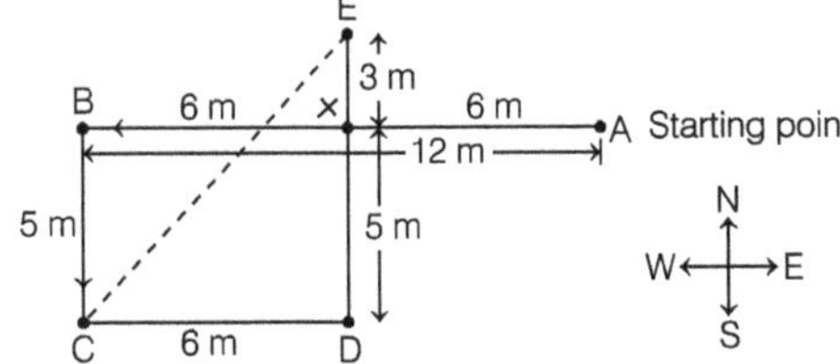

Here, CE = ? , CD = 6 m, DE = 5 + 3 = 8 m

Now, in Δ CDE, $(CE)^2 = (CD)^2 + (DE)^2$

$\Rightarrow \quad (CE)^2 = (6)^2 + (8)^2$

$\Rightarrow \quad (CE)^2 = 36 + 64 \Rightarrow CE = \sqrt{100} \Rightarrow CE = 10 \text{ m}$

Hence, distance between shop C and shop E is 10 m.

32. (*a*) According to the information given in question,

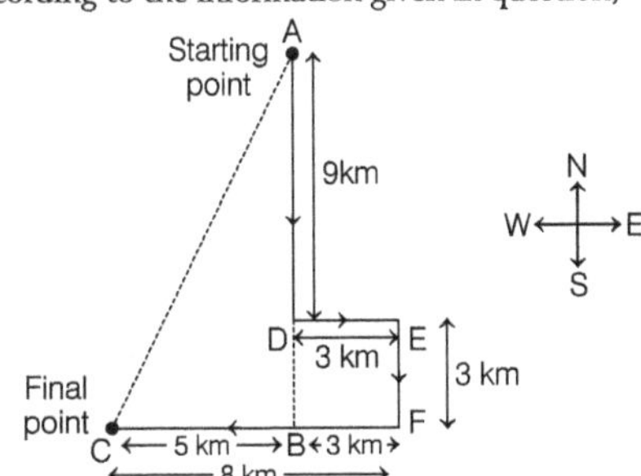

EF = DB = DE = BF = 3 km

AC = ?

Now, $AC^2 = AB^2 + BC^2 = 12^2 + 5^2 = 144 + 25$

$AC^2 = 169 \Rightarrow AC = 13$

So, distance between starting point A and final point C is 13 km.

33. (*c*) According to the question, the direction diagram is as follows

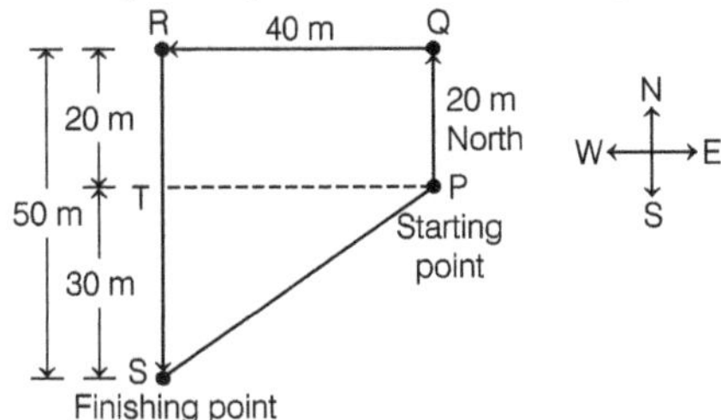

Here, PQ = RT = 20 m, QR = TP = 40 m

and RS = 50 m

Now, TS = RS − RT = 50 − 20 = 30 m

∴ Required distance, $PS = \sqrt{(TP)^2 + (TS)^2}$

$= \sqrt{(40)^2 + (30)^2}$

$= \sqrt{1600 + 900}$

$= \sqrt{2500}$

$= 50 \text{ m}$

34. (*b*) According to the information in the question, we can make a direction diagram. Given, after each 1 km, Shahid always turns left and Rohit always turns right

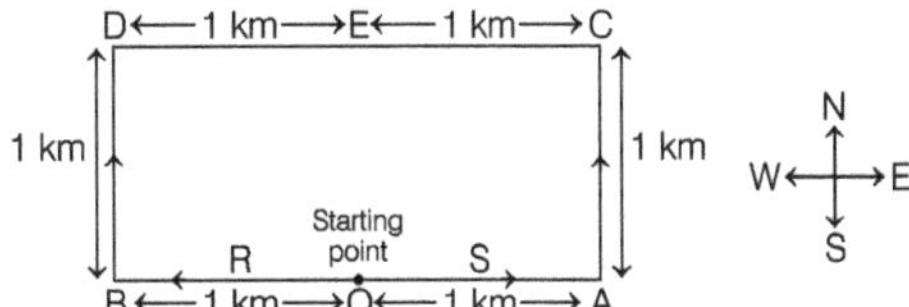

So, according to the diagram, they meet after each has travelled 3 km.

35. (*a*) According to the question, the direction diagram will be as follow

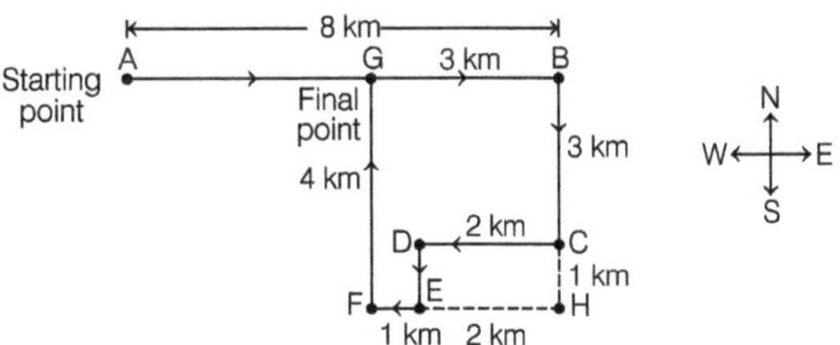

Let point A is the starting point and G is the final point of the boy.

Now, distance between starting point and final point

(AG) = AB − BG

= (8 − 3) km = 5 km

36. (*d*) According to the question, the direction diagram will be as follow

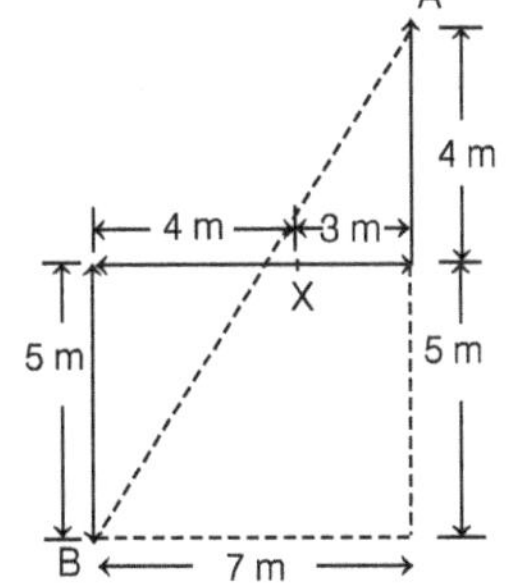

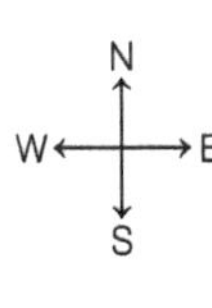

∴ Required distance, $AB = \sqrt{7^2 + 9^2}$

$= \sqrt{130} = 11.40 \text{ m}$

TYPE 03

Finding Both the Distance and Direction

In this type of questions, the information related to both distance and direction is given and based on this information, the candidate is asked to determine both distance and direction.

***Ex* 17** Mayank's house faces South. He leaves from the back gate of his house and walks 18 m. Then he turns right and walks 28 m. Then he turns right and walks 35 m. Then he turns left and walks 12 m. He then turns left and walks 17 m. In which direction and how many metres away is he from the original position? SSC CPO 2018

(a) 20 m, North (b) 17 m, South
(c) 30 m, West (d) 40 m, East

Solution (d) According to the question,

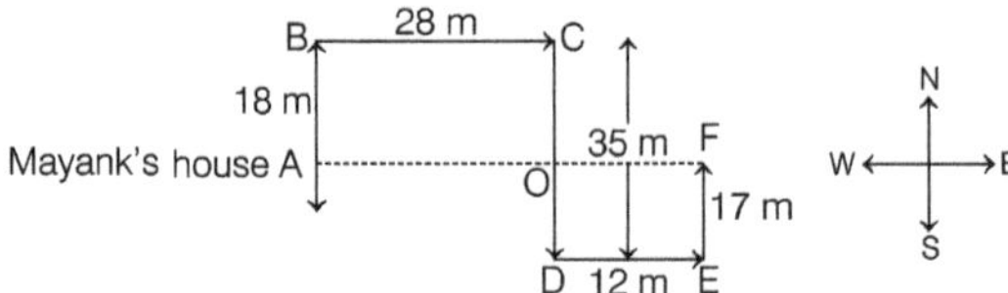

Required distance,

AF = AO + OF = 28 + 12 [∵ AO = BC, DE = OF]
= 40 m

Hence, Mayank is 40 m, East from his original position.

***Ex* 18** A postman starts from the post office and cycles 13 km South, then turns West and cycles 10 km, then turns North and cycles 8 km, then turns East and cycles 2 km and then turns to his left and cycles 5 km. Where is he now with reference to his starting position? RRB ALP 2019

(a) 8 km, East (b) 12 km, West
(c) 8 km, West (d) 12 km, East

Solution (c) According to the question,

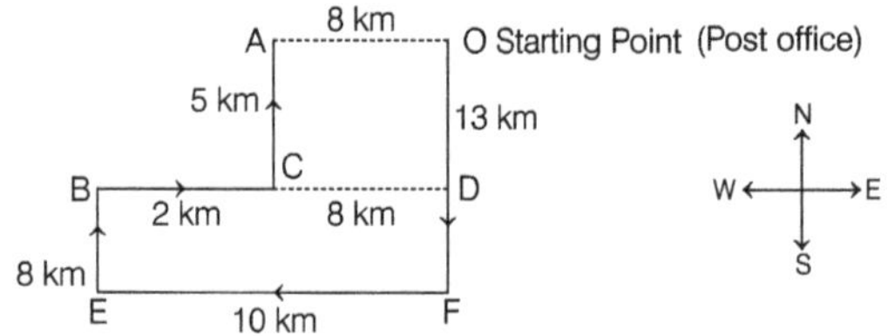

Required distance, OA = BD − BC = 10 − 2 = 8 km

Hence, postman is 8 km, West to his starting position.

***Ex* 19** From a place A, Rahul walked 18 m to South, then turned left and walked 25 m, again turned to left and walked 24 m and then turning to left reached at B after walking 17 m.
How far away he is from place A and in which direction?
UKPSC Asst. Conservator of Forest 2019

(a) 10 m, North-East (b) 10 m, East
(c) 10 m, South-East (d) 10 m, South-West

Solution (a) According to the question,

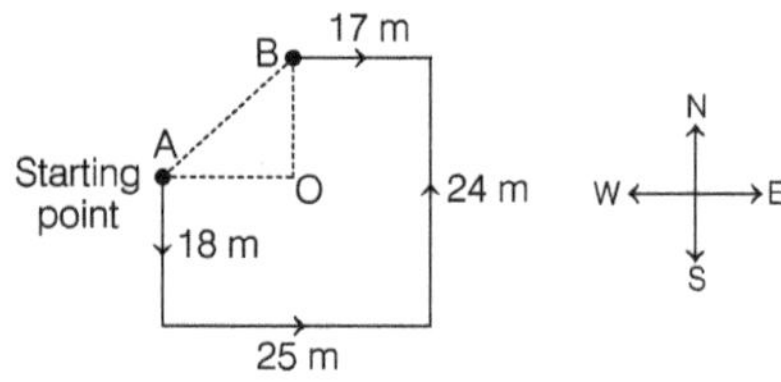

From the figure,

$$OA = 25 - 17 = 8 \text{ m}$$
$$OB = 24 - 18 = 6 \text{ m}$$
$$AB^2 = OA^2 + OB^2$$
$$AB = \sqrt{8^2 + 6^2}$$
$$= \sqrt{64 + 36} = \sqrt{100} = 10 \text{ m}$$

∴ B is 10 m North-East from A.

***Ex* 20** Point A is 30 m to the South of Point B. Point C is 20 m to the East of Point A. Point D is 15 m to the South of Point C. Point D is exactly midway between Points E and F in such a manner that Point E, D and F form a horizontal straight line of 40 m. Point E is to West of Point D. How far and in which direction is Point E from Point B? « SBI PO 2015

(a) 45 m towards South
(b) 25 m towards South
(c) 30 m towards West
(d) 35 m towards North
(e) 45 m towards North

Solution (a) According to the question,

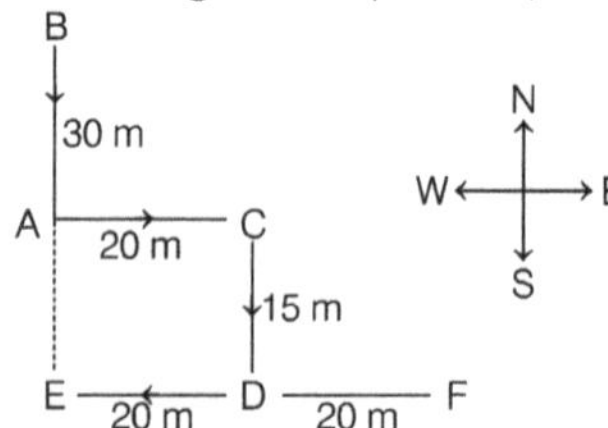

Thus, point E is (30 + 15)
∵ CD = AE = 15m i.e., 45 m away in the South of B.

DIRECTIONS ~ (Example Nos. 21-23) *Study the following information carefully and answer the questions given below* « SBI Clerk 2020

A is 14 m West of B.C is 17 m South of A. D is 16 m West of C. E is 30 m North of D. G is 23 m South of B. F is 30 m East of E.

***Ex* 21** If H is 16 m West of A, then what is the shortest distance between H and E?

(a) 11 m (b) 12 m
(c) 13 m (d) 14 m
(e) None of these

***Ex* 22** What is the shortest distance between F and G?

(a) 25 m (b) 27 m
(c) 36 m (d) 28 m
(e) None of these

***Ex* 23** Four of the following five are alike in certain way and hence form a group, find the one which does not belong to that group?

(a) A-F (b) B-E
(c) D-A (d) C-B
(e) None of these

Solutions (Example Nos. 21-23)

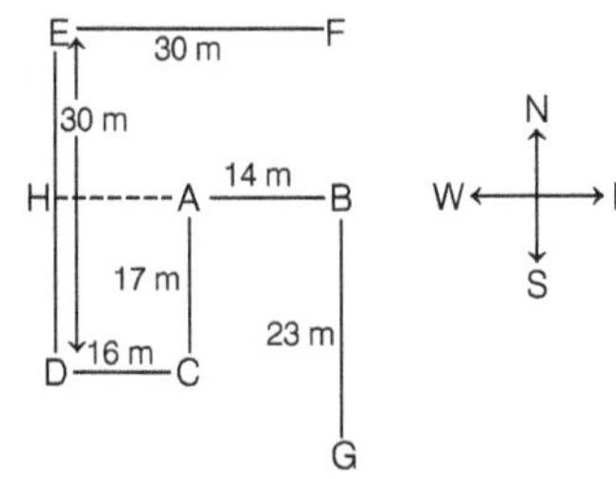

21. (c) Required distance, HE = 30 − 17 = 13 m

22. (c) Required distance, FG = (30 − 17) + 23
= 13 + 23 = 36 m

23. (b) Except B-E in all other pairs second point is in North-East direction of the first point.

DIRECTIONS (Example Nos. 24 and 25) *In the following questions, the symbols #, *, @ and $ are used with the following meanings as illustrated below. Study the following information and answer the given questions*

Note The directions which are given indicated exact directions.

P*Q Q or P is in the South direction of P or Q at distance of 6 m.

P@Q Q or P is in the North direction of P or Q at distance of 3 m

P#Q Q or P is in the East direction of P or Q at distance of 5 m.

P$Q Q or P is in the West direction of P or Q at distance of 4 m.

P*#Q Q or P is in the South-East direction of P or Q.

P*$Q Q or P is in the South-West direction of P or Q.

P@#Q Q or P is in the North-East direction of P or Q.

P@$Q Q or P is in the North-West direction of P or Q.

***Ex* 24** If B@#C#D*A is related to each other, point B is to the East of point A and the distance between them is 8 m and B is to the North-East of D, then find out the how far and in which direction is B with respect to C?

(a) $2\sqrt{5}$ m, South
(b) $3\sqrt{5}$ m, North-East
(c) $\sqrt{35}$ m, West
(d) 5 m, South-East
(e) None of the above

Solution *(b)*

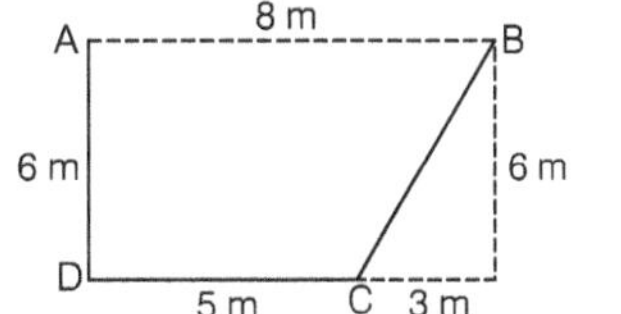

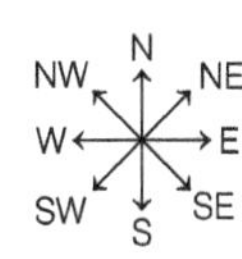

The distance between B and C $= \sqrt{BX^2 + CX^2}$
$= \sqrt{6^2 + 3^2}$
$= \sqrt{45}$ m $= 3\sqrt{5}$ m

Thus, point B is $3\sqrt{5}$m away in North-East of C.

***Ex* 25** If B@$C#D* A is related to each other, point A, D and B are inline and point B is the mid-point of AD and C is not in the North-West of A, then find out the probable distance between point B and C?

(a) $\sqrt{35}$ m (b) $\sqrt{39}$ m
(c) $5\sqrt{2}$ m (d) $\sqrt{34}$ m
(e) None of these

Solution *(d)*

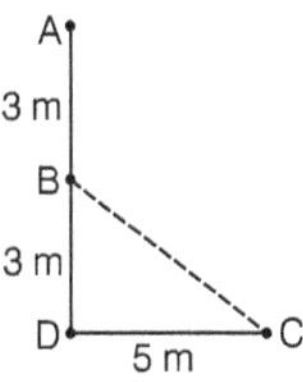

The distance between point B and C
$= \sqrt{BD^2 + DC^2}$
$= \sqrt{3^2 + 5^2} = \sqrt{34}$ m

Practice / CORNER 7.3

1. Sharada started to move in the direction of South. After moving 15 m, she turned to her left twice and moved 15 m each time. Now, how far is she and in which direction from her starting point? « SSC CGL 2014

(a) 20 m, West (b) 15 m, East
(c) 15 m, South (d) 30 m, East

2. Priya cycles 5 km North, then turns East and cycles 4 km, then turns South and cycles 5 km, then turns to her right and cycles 6 km. Where is she now with reference to her starting position? « SSC CGL 2017

(a) 2 km, East (b) 2 km, West
(c) 10 km, West (d) 10 km, East

3. Anil walks 4 m towards the East, takes a right turn and walks 3 m. He then takes a left turn and walks 5 m before taking a final left turn and walking 3 m. Towards which direction and how far should Anil walk to reach the point from where he initially started walking? « SBI Clerk 2016

(a) 8 m towards West (b) 8 m towards East
(c) 7 m towards West (d) 9 m towards West
(e) 9 m towards East

4. A man walks 15 m towards South from a fixed point. From there he goes 12 m towards North and then 4 m towards West. How far and in which direction is he from the fixed point? « UKPSC Pre 2017

(a) 3 m, South (b) 7 m, South-West
(c) 5 m, South-West (d) 5 m, South-East

5. A, E, L, B, I and T are 6 points marked on a map. A is 10 km to the East of P, which is 10 km to the North of E, which is 10 km to the East of T, which is 10 km to the North of L, which is 10 km to the North of B, which is 20 km to the West of I. Where is A with respect to I? « UPSSSC Mandi Parishad, 2019

(a) 30 km to the North of I (b) 20 km to the North of I
(c) 30 km to the South of I (d) 20 km to the South of I

6. Vinod starts from his house and travels 4 km in East direction, after that he turns towards left and moves 4 km. Finally, he turns towards left and moves 4 km. At what distance and in which direction he finally stands from his starting point?

(a) North, 4 km (b) North-East, 4 km
(c) South, 12 km (d) West, 4 km

7. A person moves 15 km in East direction, then turns towards North and moves 4 km. From here he turns towards West and travels 12 km. How far and in which direction is he from his starting point?

(a) 31 km, South-West (b) 5 km, North-East
(c) 19 km, North-East (d) 27 km, South-West

8. Sanjay's school is $10\sqrt{2}$ km in North-West direction from his house. The office of his father is 10 km in South direction from the school. The multiplex hall is 10 km towards East from the school. How far and in which direction is the multiplex hall from the office of his father?

(a) $10\sqrt{2}$ km, North-East (b) 20 km, North-East
(c) Cannot be determined (d) 10 km, South-East

9. Pankaj travels 10 m in North direction, he turns right and travels 20 m. Again he turns towards right and travels 25 m. Then, he turns towards left and travels 15 m. In which direction and how far is Pankaj from his original position?

(a) 35 m, East (b) 10 m, West
(c) 25 m, East (d) None of these

10. Starting from a point, Raju walked 12 m North, he turned right and walked 10 m, he again turned right and walked 12 m, then he turned left and walked 5 m. How far is he now and in which direction from the starting point?

(a) 27 m towards East (b) 5 m towards East
(c) 10 m towards West (d) 15 m towards East

11. Rachel starts walking towards North. After walking 15 m, she turns towards South and walks 20 m. She then turns towards East and walks 10 m. Then, again she walks 5 m towards North. How far is she from her starting point and in which direction?

(a) 10 m, West (b) 5 m, East
(c) 5 m, North (d) 10 m, East

12. A school bus driver starts from the school, drives 2 km towards North, takes a left turn and drives for 5 km. He, then takes a left turn and drives for 8 km before taking a left turn again and driving for further 5 km. The driver finally takes a left turn and drives 1 km before stopping. How far and towards which direction should the driver drive to reach the school again?

(a) 3 km towards North (b) 7 km towards East
(c) 6 km towards South (d) 6 km towards West
(e) 5 km towards North

13. Rajnikanth left his home for office in car. He drove 15 km straight towards North and then turned Eastwards and covered 8 km. He, then turned to left and covered 1 km. He again turned left and drove for 20 km and reached office. How far and in what direction is his office from the home?

(a) 21 km, West (b) 15 km, North-East
(c) 20 km, North-West (d) 26 km, North-West

14. In an exercise, Krishnan walked 25 m towards South and then he turned to his left and moved for 20 m. He again turned to his left and walked 25 m. Thereafter, he turned to his right and walked 15 m. What is the distance and direction of his present location with reference to the starting point?

(a) 74 m, North-East (b) 60 m, North
(c) 35 m, East (d) 40 m, South-East

15. Amit starts from a point A and walks 5 m towards North-East direction and reaches point B. From here, he travels 8 m in East direction and reaches point C. From C, he travels towards South-West direction and reaches point D after travelling a distance equal to AB. At last, he turns towards West direction and reaches point A. How much distance has been covered by Amit and which geometrical figure has been formed by the path travelled by him?

(a) 26 m, square (b) 26 m, parallelogram
(c) 26 m, trapezium (d) 16 m, parallelogram

DIRECTIONS ~ (Q. Nos. 16 and 17) *Study the given information carefully and answer the given questions.*
« IBPS RRB office Asst. 2020

- Point D is 10 m North of point P.
- Point Y is 14 m East of point D.
- Point Q is 8 m North of point Y.
- Point S is 20 m West of point Q.
- Point H is 8 m South of point S.

16. What is the shortest distance between point H and point D?

(a) 8 m (b) 6 m
(c) 4 m (d) 10 m
(e) None of these

17. In which direction is point P with respect to point Q?

(a) South-East (b) North-West
(c) South-West (d) North-East
(e) None of these

DIRECTIONS ~ (Q. Nos. 18 and 19) *Study the given information carefully to answer the given questions.*
« LIC AAO 2016

Meenal starts from point A, walks 15 m to the East and reaches point B. She then takes a left turn and walks 4 m. She finally takes a right turn and walks 5 m and steps at point D. Reena who is standing at point Z which is 7 m to the South of point B walks 9 m towards West, takes right turn and walks for 11 m and steps at point Y.

18. How far and in which direction is point Y with respect to point D?

(a) 14 m towards, West (b) 9 m towards, East
(c) 13 m towards, East (d) 9 m towards, West
(e) 14 m towards, East

19. If Meenal walks 11 m towards South from point D, in which direction will she have to walk in order to reach point Z?

(a) North (b) South-East
(c) West (d) North-West
(e) East

DIRECTIONS ~ (Q. Nos. 20 and 21) *Study the following information carefully to answer the given questions.*

Point P is 9 m towards the East of point Q. Point R is 5 m towards the South of point P. Point S is 3 m towards the West of point R. Point T is 5 m towards the North of point S. Point V is 7 m towards the South of point S.

20. If a person walks in a straight line for 8 m towards West from point R, which of the following points would he cross the first?

(a) V (b) Q
(c) T (d) S
(e) Cannot be determined

21. Which of the following points are in a straight line?

(a) P, R, V (b) S, T, Q
(c) P, T, V (d) V, T, R
(e) S, V, T

DIRECTIONS ~ (Q. Nos. 22 and 23) *Study the following information carefully to answer the given questions.*

Point B is 12 m South of point A. Point C is 24 m East of point B. Point D is 8 m South of point C. Point D is 12 m East of point E and point F is 8 m North of point E.

22. If a man has to travel to point E from point A (through these points by the shortest distance), which of the following points will he pass through first?

(a) Point C (b) Point D
(c) Point F (d) Point B
(e) None of these

23. If a man is standing facing North at point C, how far and in which direction is point F?

(a) 12 m, West (b) 24 m, East
(c) 12 m, East (d) 24 m, West
(e) None of these

DIRECTIONS ~ (Q. Nos. 24-26) *Study the following information and answer the questions given below.*

There are AB axis in such a way that A is in North and B is in South direction. There is XY axis in such a way that X is in West direction and Y is in East direction. AB axis and XY axis intersect at a point Q in such a way that AQ is 15 m, QB is 17 m, QX is 12 m, QY is 24 m.

Pratyaksha starts from Point X and walks 20 m in South direction and then she turns her left and walks 32 m. Pihu starts from Point A and walks 20 m in East direction. Astha starts from Point Y and walks 5 m in North direction and then she turns her left and walk 4 m and again she turns her left and walks 22 m.
« IBPS Clerk Mains 2017

24. Point Y is in which direction with respect to Pratyaksha's current position?

(a) North (b) East
(c) North-East (d) North-West
(e) South

25. Point B is in which direction with respect to Pihu's current position?

(a) South (b) South-East
(c) South-West (d) West
(e) North-West

26. What is distance between Astha's current position and Pratyaksha's current position?

(a) 3 m (b) 5 m (c) 13 m (d) 22 m
(e) 27 m

DIRECTIONS ~ (Q. Nos. 27-31) *In the following questions, the symbols #, &, @ and $ are used with the following meanings as illustrated below. Study the following information and answer the given questions.*

« IBPS PO Mains 2017

Note *The directions which are given indicates exact directions.*

P#Q Q is in the South direction of P.

P@Q Q is in the North direction of P.

P&Q Q is in the East direction of P at distance of either 12 m or 6 m.

P$Q Q is in the West direction of P at distance of either 15 m or 3 m.

P#&Q Q or P is in the South-East direction of P or Q.

P@&Q P or Q is in the North-East direction of Q or P.

27. K#&T$M#&S&K&Z are related to each other such that K is in North of M, then what is the probable direction of Z with respect to M?

(a) North-East (b) West
(c) South-West (d) East
(e) Can't be determined

28. K#&T$M#&S&K&Z are related to each other such that K is in North of M. M and K are inline vertically when MT > SK, then what is the sum of SK and MT?

(a) 27 m (b) 21 m
(c) 15 m (d) Either (a) or (b)
(e) Either (b) or (c)

29. K#&T$M#&S&K&Z are related to each other such that K is in North of M. M and K are inline vertically when MT > SK, then what is the distance between S and Z when KZ = 12 m?

(a) 24 m (b) 18 m
(c) 15 m (d) Either (a) or (b)
(e) None of these

30. If A&B#&C$D&E@F are related to each other such that F is placed exactly between A and B on line AB. Similarly D and A are vertically inline then what is the possible shortest distance between F and B when DE (length of segment DE) < DC/2 and EC < 10 m?

(a) 12 m (b) 5 m
(c) 4 m (d) 6 m
(e) None of these

31. If A&B#&C$D&E@F are related to each other such that D, A are inline, DE = 6 m and a perpendicular drawn from E on AB divides AB in two equal parts and D@&B, then what is the probable direction of A with respect to F?

(a) North-West (b) West
(c) South-West (d) East
(e) Can't be determined

DIRECTIONS ~ (Q. Nos. 32 and 33) *Read the following information carefully to answer the questions that follow. The questions are based on following coding formats*

P1Q means – P is in North of Q

P2Q – P is in South of Q

P3Q – P is in East of Q

P4Q – P is in West of Q

@ means – Either 2 or 7 m

– Either 5 or 10 m

& – Either 8 or 13 m

Conditions given are as

I. A @ 1 B II. A &3 D III. F #3 E
IV. G @4 F V. E #1 D

32. In which direction is point G with respect to D?

(a) South-West (b) North-West
(c) North (d) North-East
(e) Can't be determined

33. What could be the shortest distance between E and B considering the smallest among the given two-possible distances?

(a) $\sqrt{113}$ (b) $\sqrt{111}$
(c) $\sqrt{115}$ (d) $\sqrt{117}$
(e) None of these

DIRECTIONS ~ (Q. Nos. 34-36) *Study the following information carefully and answer the questions given below*

« IBPS Clerk 2018

A%B(7) A is 12 m in North of B.

A$B(12) A is 17 m in South of B.

A#B(32) A is 37 m in East of B.

A&B(14) A is 19 m in West of B.

Statement M%K(33), J#K(9), G%J(19), H&G(23), N$H(25)

34. K is in which direction with respect to G?

(a) North (b) West
(c) North-West (d) East
(e) South-West

35. If Z is the mid-point of the line formed between H and G, then what is the distance between H and Z?

(a) 12 m (b) 14 m
(c) 16 m (d) 17 m
(e) 30 m

36. If X is in West of J and lies on the line formed by H and N, then what is the distance between X and N?

(a) 10 m (b) 24 m
(c) 6 m (d) 16 m
(e) 14 m

Answers WITH EXPLANATIONS

1. (*b*) Let Sharada starts from point A and passing through B and C, she reaches D.

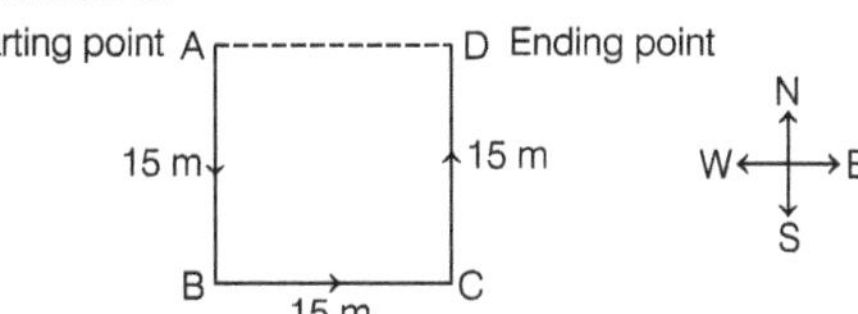

Clearly, she is in East and at a distance of 15 m from her original position.

2. (*b*) According to the question,

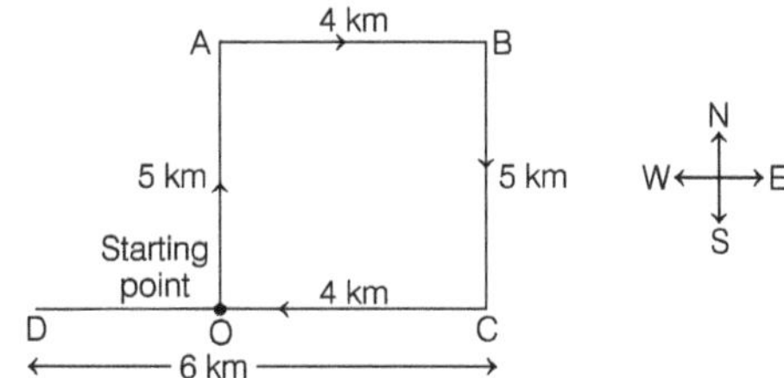

Required distance OD = DC − OC = 6 − 4 = 2 km

∴ Hence, Priya is 2 km, West with reference to her starting position.

3. (*d*) According to the question,

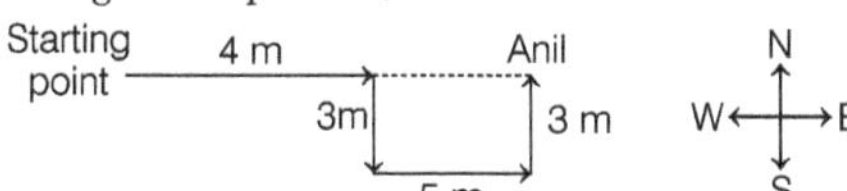

So, to reach at the initial point, Anil should go (4 + 5) = 9 m towards West.

4. (*c*) Walking diagram of a man is as follows

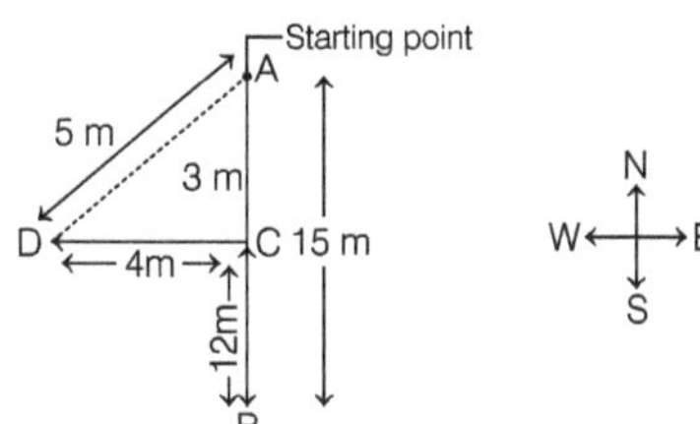

Let A is the fixed point and D is the last point where man has reached.

Now, AB = 15 m, BC = 12 m

∴ $AC = AB - BC$

$= 15 - 12 = 3$ m

∴ $AD = \sqrt{(CD)^2 + (AC)^2}$

$= \sqrt{(4)^2 + (3)^2}$

$= \sqrt{16 + 9}$

$= \sqrt{25} = 5$ m

Hence, man is 5 m far away from fixed point and from South-West direction.

5. (*a*) According to the given information,

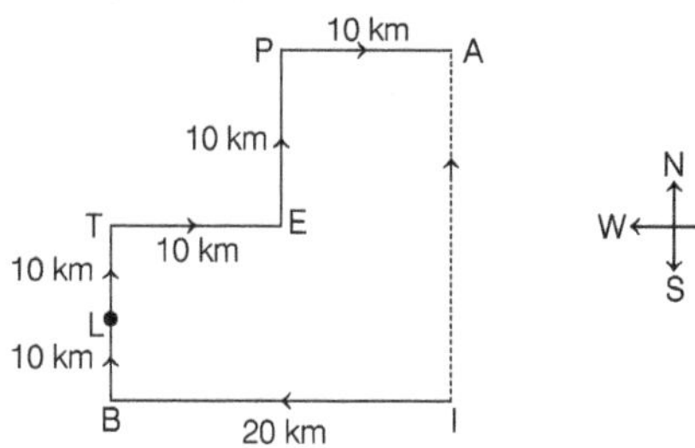

Distance, AI = PE + TL + LB

= 10 + 10 + 10

= 30 km

Hence, A is 30 km North to the I.

6. (*a*) According to the question, the direction diagram is as follows

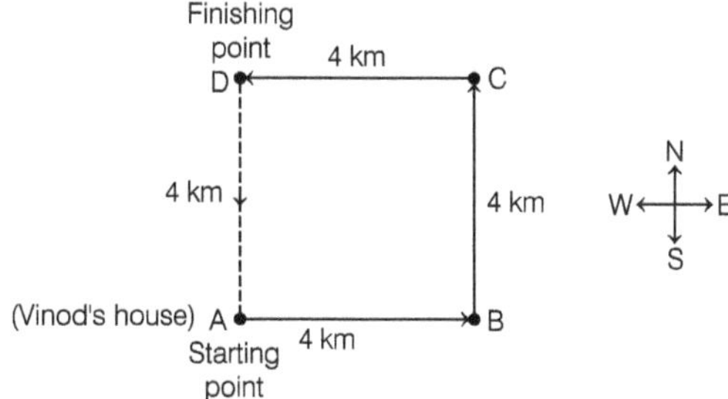

Clearly, at finishing point, he is 4 km, North from the starting point.

7. (*b*) According to the question, the direction diagram is as follows

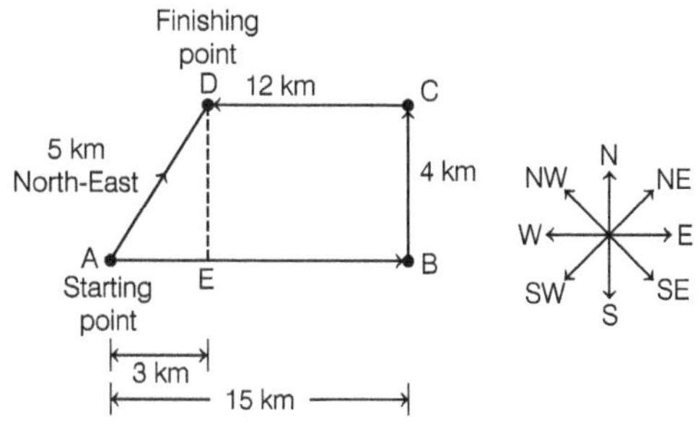

AB = 15 m

BC = DE = 4 km

CD = EB = 12 km

AE = AB − CD = 15 − 12 = 3 km

∴ Required distance, $AD = \sqrt{(DE)^2 + (AE)^2}$

$= \sqrt{4^2 + 3^2}$

$= \sqrt{16 + 9} = \sqrt{25} = 5$ km

Hence, D is 5 km North-East from the starting point A.

8. (*a*) According to the question, the direction diagram will be as follows

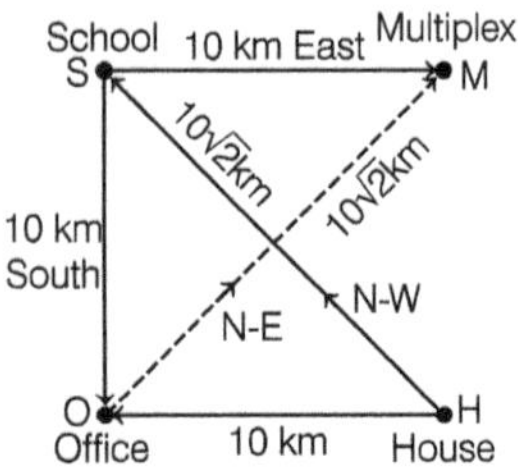

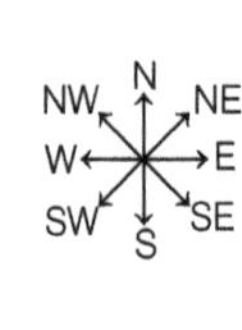

As in a square, diagonals are equal.

∴ $SH = OM = 10\sqrt{2}$ km

∴ Required distance, OM

= Distance between office and multiplex

$= 10\sqrt{2}$ km

Also, it is clear from diagram that multiplex (M) is to the North-East of O (office).

So, the multiplex is $10\sqrt{2}$ km North-East from office.

9. (*d*) According to the question, the direction diagram will be as follows

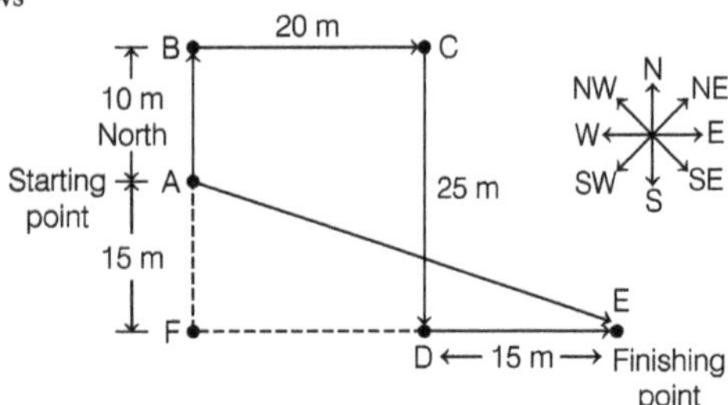

A = Starting point, E = Finishing point

DE = 15 m, BC = FD = 20 m

FE = FD + DE = 20 + 15 = 35 m

AF = BF − AB = 25 − 10 = 15 m

∴ Required distance, $AE = \sqrt{(AF)^2 + (FE)^2} = \sqrt{(15)^2 + (35)^2}$

$= \sqrt{225 + 1225} = \sqrt{1450} = 38.078$

$= 38.08$m

So, Pankaj is 38.08m towards South-East from starting point.

10. (*d*) According to the question, the direction diagram is as follows

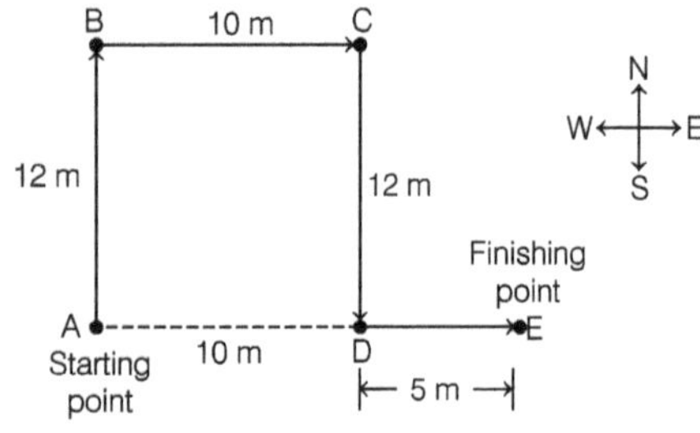

AB = CD = 12 m

BC = AD = 10 m, DE = 5 m

∴ Required distance, AE = AD + DE = 10 + 5 = 15 m

Hence, at finishing point E, Raju is 15 m East from starting point A.

11. (*d*) Let the initial point of Rachel be 'A'.

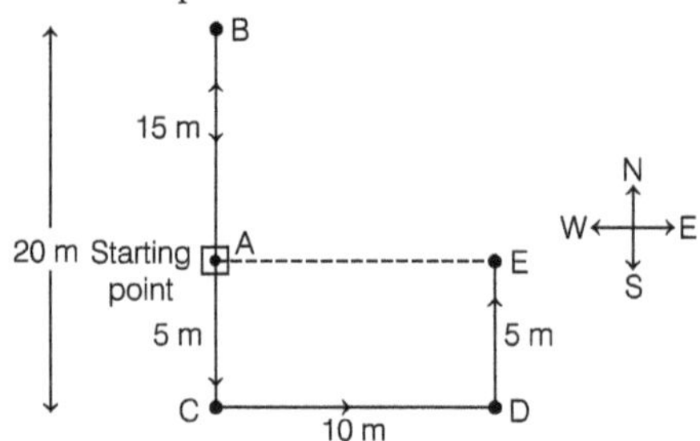

∴ Required distance, AE = 10 m

So, Rachel is 10 m towards East from the starting point.

12. (*e*) According to the question, the direction diagram will be as follows

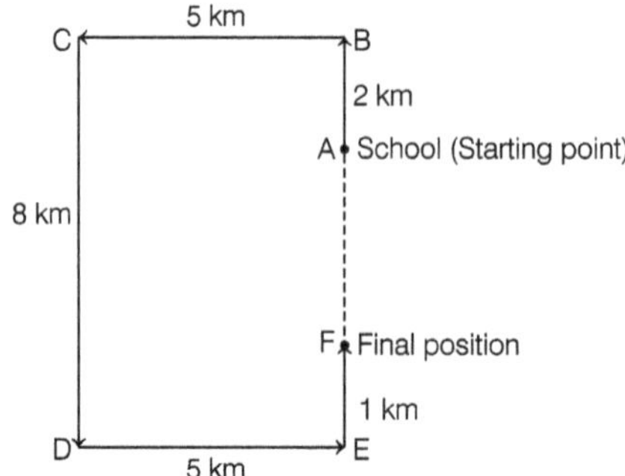

Now, BC = DE = 5 km, CD = BE = 8 km

AB = 2 km, EF = 1 km

∴ Required distance, AF = BE − (AB + EF)

= 8 − (2 + 1) = 8 − 3 = 5 km

From the direction diagram, it is clear that the bus is present finally in the South direction of school. So, the driver needs to drive 5 km towards North direction to reach the school.

13. (*c*) According to the question, the direction diagram will be as follows

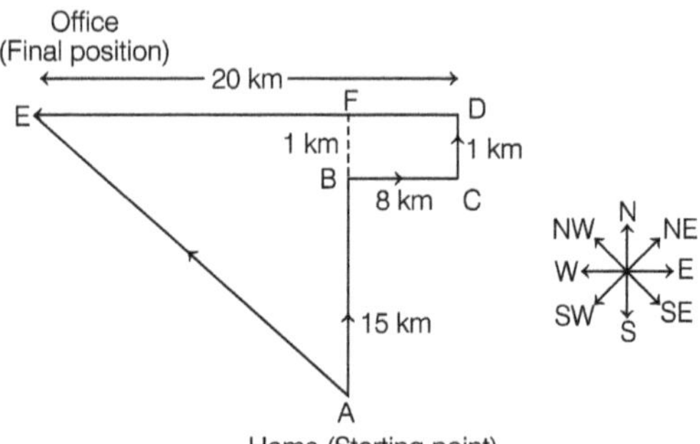

Now, AB = 15 km, CD = BF = 1 km

AF = AB + BF = 15 + 1 = 16 km

DE = 20 km, DF = BC = 8 km

EF = DE − DF = 20 − 8 = 12 km

∴ Required distance, $AE = \sqrt{(AF)^2 + (EF)^2}$

$= \sqrt{(16)^2 + (12)^2}$

$= \sqrt{256 + 144} = \sqrt{400} = 20$ km

So, his office is 20 km North-West From his home.

14. (*c*) According to the question, the direction diagram will be as follows

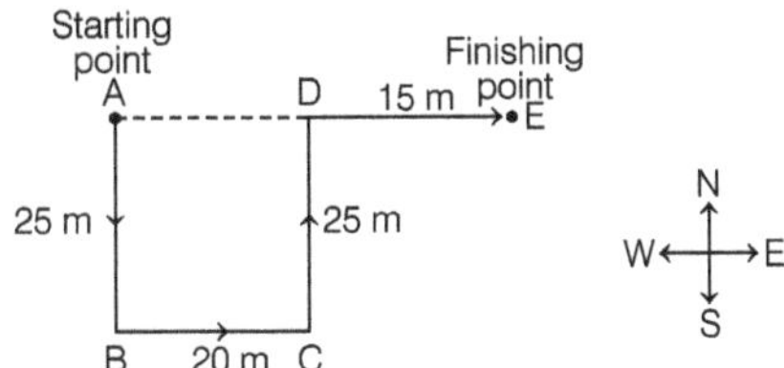

Now, AB = CD = 25 m, BC = AD = 20 m, DE = 15 m

∴ Required distance, AE = AD + DE,

AE = 20 + 15 = 35 m

Also, E is to the East of A.

15. (*b*) According to the question, the direction diagram is as follows

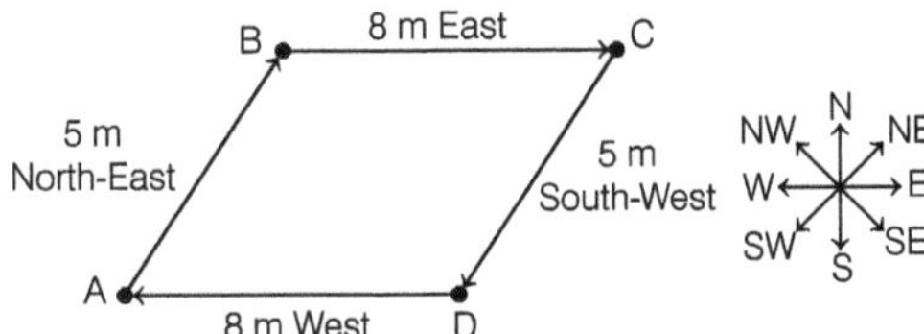

BC = AD = 8 m, AB = CD = 5 m

∴ Required distance = AB + BC + CD + DA

= 5 + 8 + 5 + 8 = 26 m

and the geometrical figure formed is parallelogram.

Solutions (Q. Nos. 16 and 17) According to the question,

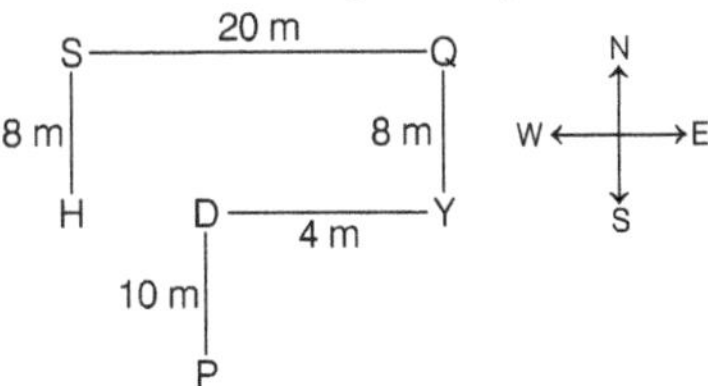

16. (*b*) The shortest distance between H and D

= SQ − DY = 20 − 14 = 6 m

17. (*c*) Point P is in South-West direction with respect to Q.

Solutions (Q. Nos. 18 and 19) According to the given information, the direction diagram is as follows

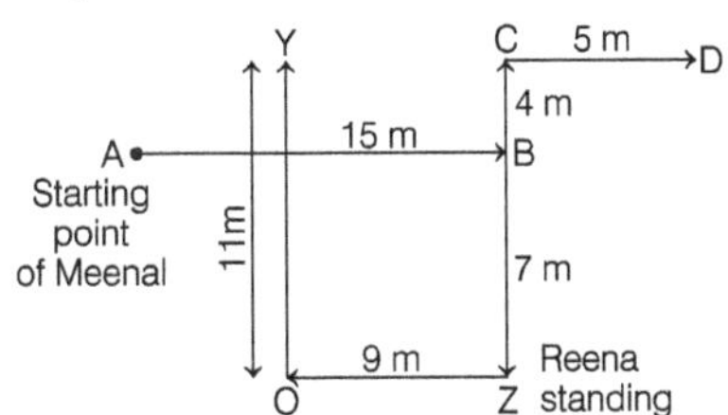

18. (*a*) In the above diagram, it is clearly shown that

OZ = YC = 9 m and CD = 5 cm

Therefore, YD = DC + YC,

YD = 5 + 9 = 14 m

and point Y is in West of D.

So, point Y is 14 m toward West of D.

19. (*c*) If Meenal walks 11 m towards South from point D, then

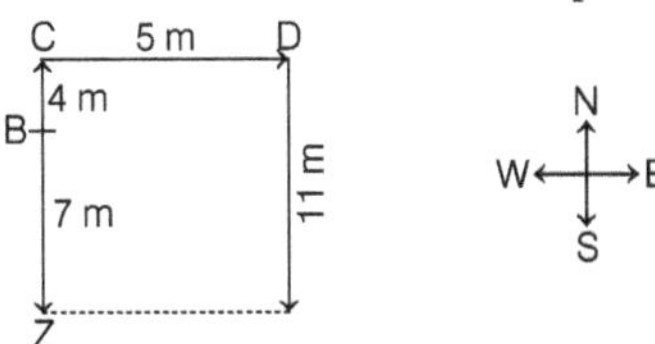

She will have to walk in West direction to reach point Z.

Solutions (Q. Nos. 20 and 21) According to the question,

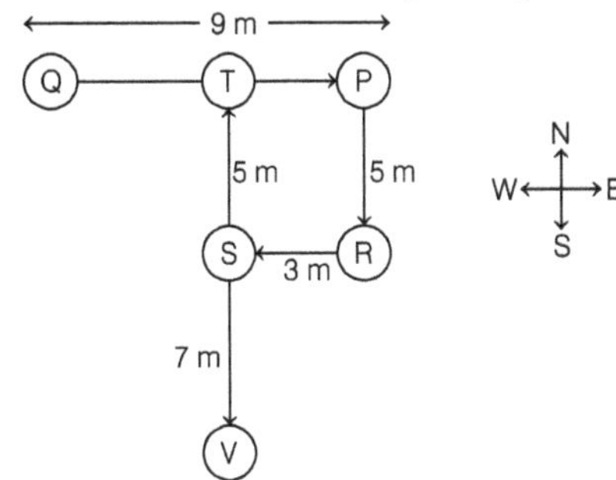

20. (*d*) If a person walks in a straight line for 8 m towards West from point R, then he would cross S.

21. (*e*) S, V, T are in straight line.

Solutions (Q. Nos. 22 and 23) According to the question,

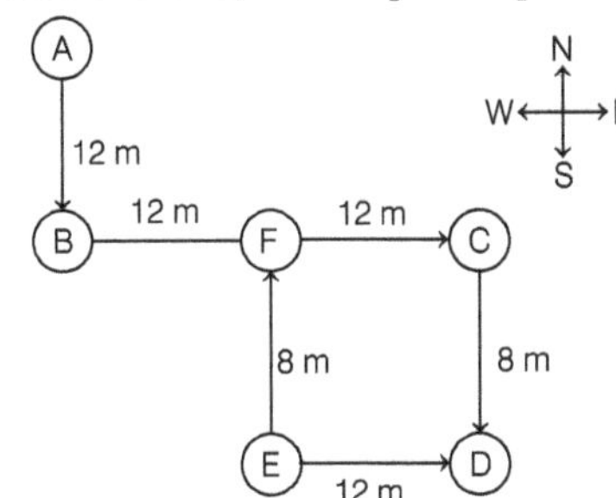

22. (*d*) To reach point E from point A he will cross point B first.

23. (*a*) The point F is 12 m, West of point C.

Solutions (Q. Nos. 24-26) According to the question,

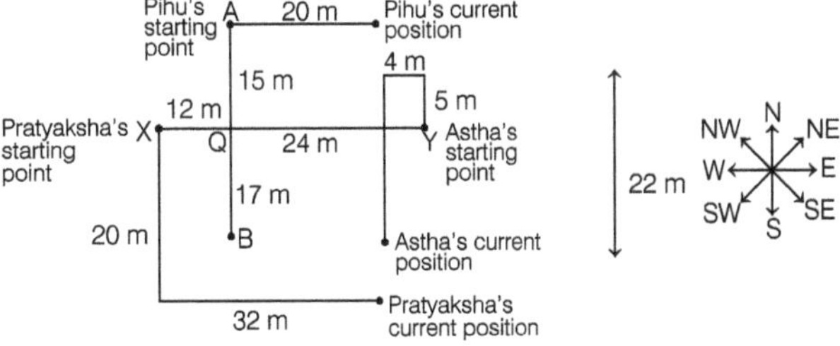

24. (*c*) Point Y is in North-East direction with respect to Pratyaksha's current position.

25. (*c*) Point B is in South-West direction with respect to Pihu's current position.

26. (*a*) Required distance = 20 − (22 − 5) = 20 − 17 = 3 m

27. (*a*)

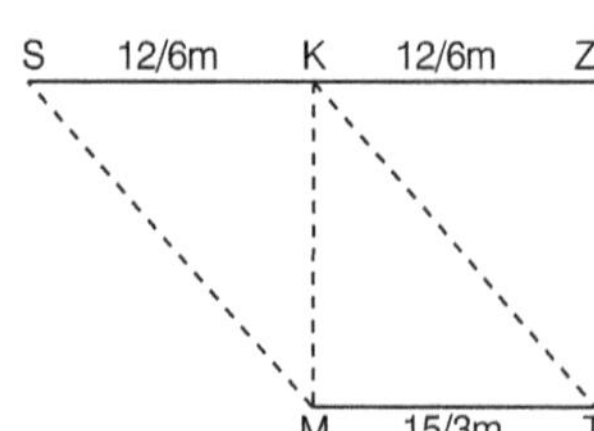

It is clear that Z is in North-East from M.

28. (*d*)

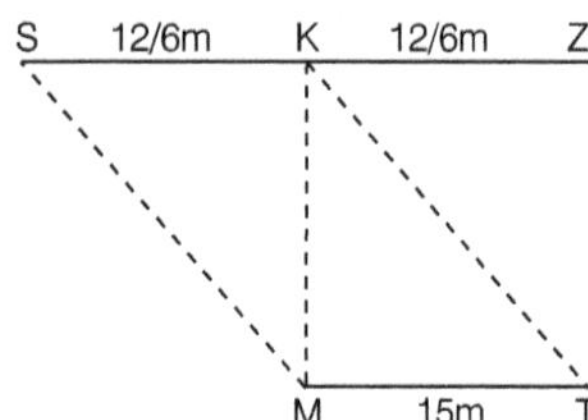

It is given that MT > SK, so MT = 15 m and SK = 12 m or 6 m
SK + MT = (12 + 15) or (15 + 6) = 27 m or 21 m

29. (*d*)

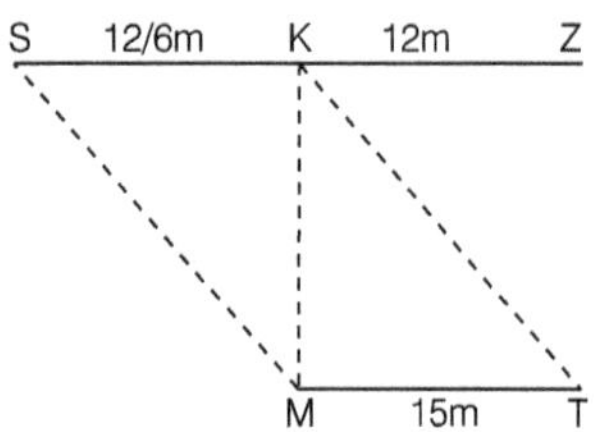

It is given that MT > SK, so MT = 15 m, KZ = 12 m and SK = 12 m or 6 m, so that value of SZ
= (12 + 12) or (12 + 6) = 24 m or 18 m

30. (*d*)

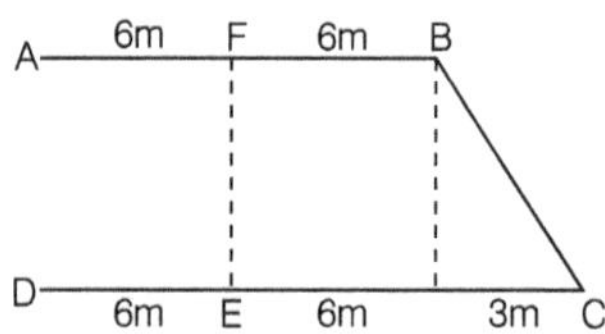

It is given that DE < DC/2, so that value of DC = 15 m and AB = 12 m or 6 m, D and A are inline, so DE = AF,
If DE = 6 m, EC = 15 − 6=9 m
If DE = 3 m, EC = 15 − 3 = 12 m
It is given that EC < 10, so DE = 6 m and AB = 12 m
Hence, FB = 6 m

31. (*e*)

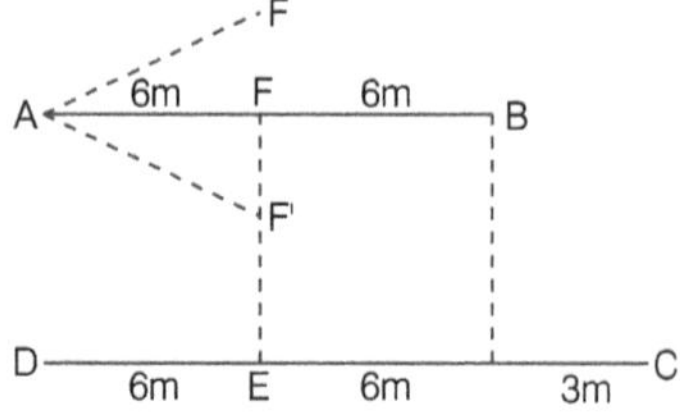

The direction of F with respect to E is given but the exact distance from E is not given, so we can't find out the exact position of F hence the direction of F with respect to A can't be determined.

Solutions (Q. Nos. 32 and 33) According to the question,

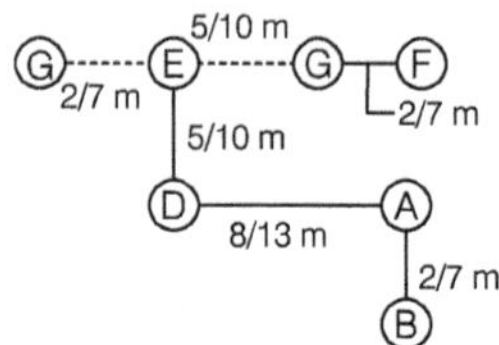

32. (*e*) Can not be determined.

33. (*a*)

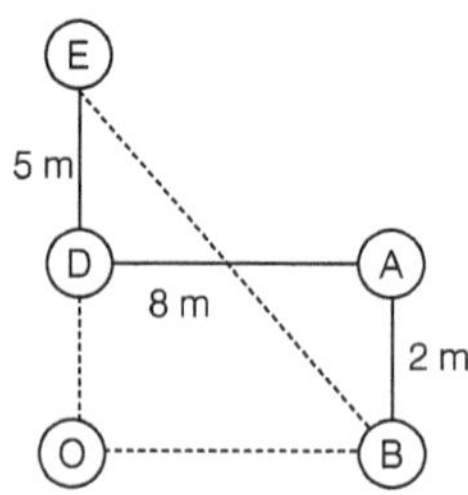

Required distance $EB = \sqrt{EO^2 + OB^2}$
$= \sqrt{7^2 + 8^2}$ [$\because$ EO = 5 + 2 = 7 m, OB = DA = 8 m]
$= \sqrt{49 + 64} = \sqrt{113}$

Solutions (Q. Nos. 34-36) According to the given information,
Given statements,
M%K (33) means - M is 30 m North of K. [$\because$ 33 + 5 = 38 m]
J#K (9) means - J is 14 m East of K. [$\because$ 9 + 5 = 14 m]
G%J (19) means - G is 24 m North of J.
H&G (23) means - H is 28 m West of B.
N$H (25) means - N is 30 m South of B.

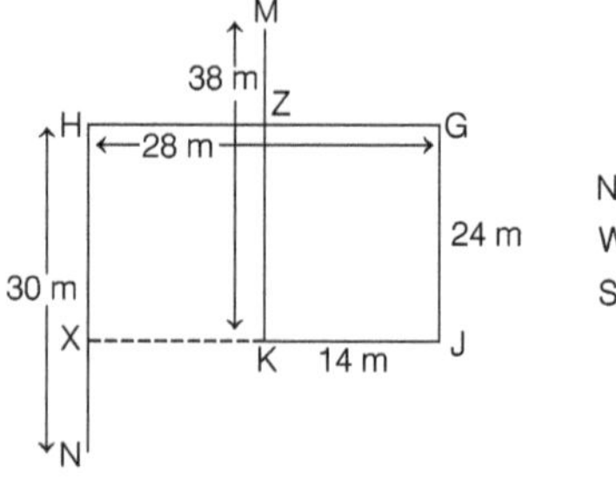

34. (*e*) K is South-West with respect to G.

35. (b) Distance between HG = 28 m
Mid-point = Z
Hence, distance between H and Z
$= \frac{28}{2} = 14$ m

36. (c) Distance between X and N
= HN − HX
= 30 − 24 = 6 m

Master Exercise

1. Rahul walks 2 km to West and then he turns to North and walks 5 km. Again he turns to West and walks 3 km. After this he turns to North and walks 7 km. In which direction is he from the starting point? « UPPSC Lower Subordinate 2016

(a) North-East (b) North
(c) North-West (d) East

2. Rani and Radha were walking in opposite directions. If Radha was walking in North-East direction, then in which direction was Rani walking? « RRB Group D 2018

(a) North-West (b) North-East
(c) South-East (d) South-West

3. During the time of sunset, at the railway platform, Sachin and Anjali are standing opposite to each other. If Anjali's shadow is to the left of Sachin. Then, which direction is Sachin facing? « RRB Group D 2018

(a) North (b) West (c) East (d) South

4. First of all Ahmad goes 20 m to the North from his place, then he walks 15 m to his right. Again he turns to the right and moves 20m.
Immediately turning to the left he walks 25 m. How far is Ahmad now from his starting point?
« UPSSSC Junior Assist. 2015

(a) 40 m (b) 35 m (c) 45 m (d) 50 m

5. A, B, C, D, E, F, G and H are sitting in a circular manner in the same order for lunch at equal distance. Their positions are clockwise. If C sits in the East, then what will be the position of H? « SSC Steno 2019

(a) South (b) North-West
(c) East (d) South-East

6. Mohan is going to the market in the North-West direction. To avoid heavy traffic, he turns 90° in the clockwise direction. He then finds himself in a traffic jam. He takes another route by running 135° in the anti-clockwise direction. In which direction is Mohan facing now? « CMAT 2015

(a) South (b) East (c) West (d) North

7. A motorcycle is going West wards. It makes a 45° turn to its left and goes for 3 km. It then turn 90° to its left and goes for 2 km. It then makes a 180° turn. In which direction is the motorcycle going now?
« UPSSSC Mandi Parishad 2019

(a) South-East (b) North-West
(c) South-West (d) North-East

8. Sudiksha was facing North-West direction. If she was playing chess with Sakshat in the standard seating pattern, in which direction was Sakshat facing?

(a) North-West (b) North-East
(c) South-West (d) South-East

9. Two friends park their vehicles outside a garden. The parking lot is 500 m away and towards 90° left from the entry point of the garden. If the entry point of the garden is towards East, then the parking lot is in which direction? « RRB Group D 2018

(a) East (b) West
(c) South (d) North

10. A watch shows the time of 4 : 30 h (4 h and 30 min). If the minute hand points East, in what direction will the hour hand point? « CGPSC 2015

(a) North-East (b) South-East
(c) North (d) North-West
(e) None of these

11. If you start running from a point towards North and after covering 4 km you turn to your left and run 5 km and then again turn to your left and run 5 km and then turn to left again and run another 6 km and before finishing you take another left turn and run 1 km, then answer the following question based on this information.
From the finishing point if you have to reach the point from where you started, in which direction will you have to run?

(a) East (b) West (c) North (d) South

12. Rakesh leaves from his house. He walks 10 m in North-West direction and then 20m in South-West direction. Next he moves 20 m in South-East direction. Finally he turns towards his house. In which direction is Rakesh going? « CGPSC 2015

(a) South-East (b) North-West
(c) South-West (d) North-East
(e) None of these

13. Praveen's house is 300 m away in the South-East direction of Rajiv's house. Joseph's house is 300 m away in the North-East direction of Rajiv's house. Gopal's house is 300 m away in the North-West direction of Joseph's house. Kavin's house is located 300m away is the South-West direction of Gopal's house.
What is the position of Kavin's in relation to that of Praveen? « UP Police SI 2017

(a) South-East (b) South-West
(c) North-West (d) North-East

14. Nikhil walked 30 m towards East took a left turn and walked 20 m. He again took a left turn and walked 30 m. How far and in which direction is he from his starting point?

(a) 20 m, North (b) 80 m, North
(c) 20 m, South (d) 80 m, South
(e) Data inadequate

15. Mohan walked 30 m towards South, took a left turn and walked 15 m. He, then took a right turn and walked 20 m. He again took a right turn and walked 15 m. How far is he from the starting point?

(a) 95 m (b) 50 m
(c) 70 m (d) Cannot be determined
(e) None of these

16. Two buses start from the opposite points of a main road, 150 km apart. The first bus runs for 25 km and takes a right turn and then runs for 15 km. It then turns left and runs for another 25 km and takes the direction back to reach the main road. In the mean time, due to the minor break down the other bus has run only 35 km along the main road. What would be the distance between the two buses at this point ?

(a) 65 km (b) 80 km (c) 75 km (d) 85 km

17. The houses of A and B face each other on a road going North-South, A's being on the western side, A comes out of his house, turns left, travels 5 km, turns right, travels 5 km to the front of D's house. B does exactly the same and reaches the front of C's house. In this context, which one of the following statements is correct? « IB ACIO 2017

(a) C and D live on the same street
(b) C's house faces South
(c) The houses of C and D are less than 20 km apart
(d) None of the above

18. Go through the below image and answer the question below

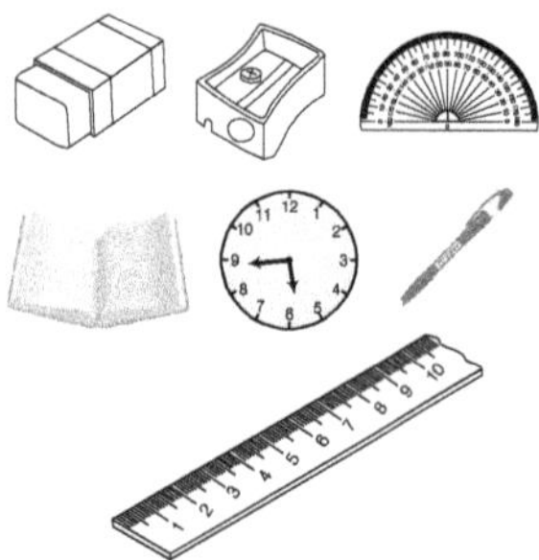

Imagine you are standing at the scale and facing the pen. Which is the correct image from the following to represent the spatial orientation pointing to the book?
« UPSSSC Tubewell Operator 2018

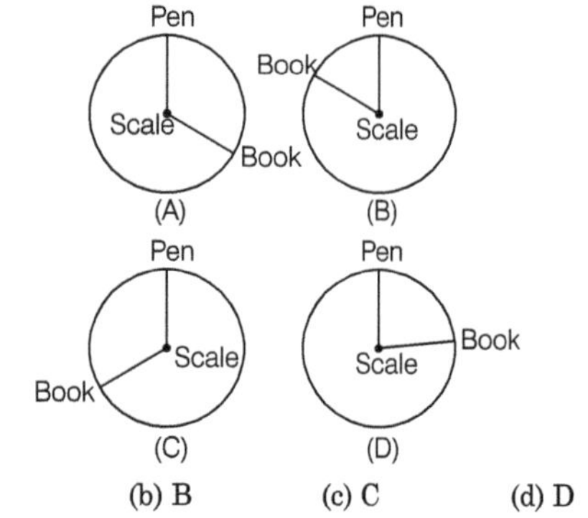

(a) A (b) B (c) C (d) D

19. Town D is to the West of Town M. Town R is to the South of Town D. Town K is to the East of Town R. Town K is towards which direction of Town D?

(a) South (b) East
(c) North-East (d) South-East
(e) None of these

20. A person walks 12 km due North, then 15 km due East, after that 19 km due West and then 15 km due South. How far is he from the starting point?
« Civil Services CSAT 2016

(a) 5 km (b) 9 km
(c) 37 km (d) 61 km

21. Mahu goes 40 km North, turns right and goes 80 km, turns right again and goes 30 km. In the end, he turns right again and goes 80 km. How far is he from his starting point if he goes straight ahead another 50 km and turns left to go his last 10 km?

(a) 30 km (b) 30 km
(c) 40 km (d) 50 km

22. A migrating bird flies 40 km North, then turns East and flies 50 km, then turns North and flies 110 km and turns to its left and flies 50 km. Where is it now with reference to its starting position? « SSC CGL 2017

(a) 150 km, South
(b) 150 km, North
(c) 70 km, North
(d) 70 km, South

23. If South-East becomes North, North-East becomes West and soon will West become? « CLAT 2017

(a) South-East (b) North
(c) East (d) North-West

24. Debu walks towards East, then towards North and turning 45° right walks for a while and lastly turns towards left. In which direction is he walking now?

(a) North (b) East
(c) South-East (d) North-West

25. A villager places a map of his farm in a gram panchayat meeting for resolving his dispute. He places the map in a way that South-East becomes North and North-East becomes West. The Sarpanch is confused. His assistant comes to help and turns the anti-clockwise by 90°. If the Sarpanch has to see the South side in the map, which side will he look? « SNAP 2017

(a) North (b) South-West
(c) South (d) West

26. Dr. Mruthula walks 24 m East from point A and reaches point B in Apollo hospital. From point B she takes left turn and walks 8 m and then she takes right turn and walks 12 m and again she takes right turn and walks 14 m and again takes right turn and reaches point M. If it is given that the starting point is in North from point where she ends her journey, then what is the distance between the points A and M?
« SSC Steno 2019

(a) 4 m (b) 5 m (c) 6 m (d) 3 m

27. From his fishpond, Niyaz went to the fish market. First, he went straight towards the North for 2 km and then turned right. Thereafter, he walked for a distance of 3 km straight and then turning left, he walked 2 km to reach the fish market. What is the shortest distance between Niyaz's fishpond and the fish market?

« UPSSSC Agri. Services Tech. Assist. 2018

(a) 5.5 m (b) 4.5 km
(c) 5 km (d) 3.5 km

28. Seeta and Ram both start from a point towards North. Seeta turns to left after walking 10 km. Ram turns to right after walking the same distance. Seeta waits for sometime and then walks another 5 km, whereas Ram walks only 3 km. They both then return to their respective South and walk 15 km forward. How far is Seeta from Ram?

(a) 12 km (b) 15 km
(c) 10 km (d) 8 km

29. Deepak left his office and walked towards East for 5 km and then turned left and walked for 12 km to reach his home. Madan, who works in the same office, left the office and walked towards West for 5 km and then turned left and walked for 12 km to reach his home.

What is the shortest distance between Deepak's and Madan's home? « UPSSSC VDO 2018

(a) 17 km (b) 24 km
(c) 26 km (d) 34km

30. Mr Raghav went in his car to meet his friend John. He drove 30 km towards North and then 40 km towards West. He then turned to South and covered 8 km. Further he turned to East and moved 26 km. Finally he turned right and drove 10 km and then turned left to travel 19 km. How far and in which direction is he from the starting point? « IIFT 2014

(a) East of starting point, 5 km
(b) East of starting point, 13 km
(c) North-East of starting point, 13 km
(d) North-East of starting point, 5 km

31. Ravi starts walking towards North. After walking 15 m he turns towards South. After walking 20 m, he turns towards East and walks 10 m. He, then turns towards North and walks 5 m. How far is he from his original position and in which direction? « CMAT 2015

(a) 10 m, North (b) 10 m, South
(c) 10 m, East (d) 10 m, West

32. Starting from point O facing West a man walks 4 km to reach point A. He turns right, walks 4 km and reaches point B. He then turns right, walks 4 km and reaches point C. Then, he turns right walks 3 km and reaches point D. He turns left, walks 4 km and reaches point E. Then, he turns right, walks 5 km and reaches point F. The shortest distance between point A and point E is

« RRB Group D 2018

(a) $5\sqrt{65}$ km (b) $2\sqrt{65}$ km
(c) $\sqrt{68}$ km (d) $\sqrt{65}$ km

33. A person climbs a hill in a straight path from point 'O' on the ground in the direction of North-East and reaches a point 'A' after travelling a distance of 5 km. Then, from the point 'A' he moves to point 'B' in the direction of North-West. Let the distance AB be 12 km. Now, how far is the person away from the starting point 'O'? « Civil Services CSAT, 2016

(a) 7 km (b) 13 km (c) 17 km (d) 11 km

34. X and Y start from the same point. X walks 40 m North, then turns West and walks 80 m, then turns to his right and walks 50 m. At the same time, Y walks 90 m North. Where is Y now with respect to the position of X?

(a) Y is 30 m to the East of X « SSC CGL 2017
(b) Y is 80 m to the West of X
(c) Y is 30 m to the West of X
(d) Y is 80 m to the East of X

35. Two bikers P and Q start from the same point P rides 8 km Northwards, then turns Westwards and rides 6 km, then turns to his right and rides 4 km. Q rides 4 km Westwards, then turns Northwards and rides 12 km, then turns to his right and rides 9 km. Where is Q now with respect to the current position of P?

« UPSSSC Mandi Parishad 2019

(a) 11 km, Westwards (b) 11 km, Eastwards
(c) 19 km, Eastwards (d) 19 km, Westwards

36. A person starts walking from his home towards his friend's place. He walks for 25 m towards West. He takes a 90° right turn and walks for 20 m. He again takes a 90° right turn and walks for 10 m. He then walks for another 10 m after taking a 90° left turn. Turning 90° towards his right, he walks for 15m to reach his friend's place. How far and in which direction is the friend's place from his home? « SBI PO 2015

(a) 30 m towards East (b) 30 m towards North
(c) 40 m towards South (d) 30 m towards South
(e) 40 m towards North

DIRECTIONS ~ (Q. Nos. 37-40) *Read the following information carefully and answer the questions given below.*

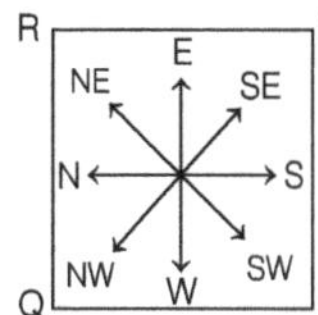

Four security guards P, Q, R and S have been posted at the four corners of a huge cashew plantations farm as show in the above figure.

37. Given the condition that none of the corners should be unmanned and both P and R start moving towards diagonally opposite corners, in which direction should S start moving, so that he occupies a corner by travelling the minimum possible distance?

(a) Clockwise
(b) Anti-clockwise
(c) Either clockwise or anti-clockwise
(d) None of the above

38. From the original position, P and Q move one arm length clockwise and then cross over to the corner diagonally opposite, R and S move one arm length anti-clockwise and cross over to the corner diagonally opposite. The original setting PSQR has now changed to

(a) RSPQ (b) SRPQ
(c) RQSP (d) None of these

39. From the original position, P and R move diagonally to opposite corners and then one side each in the clockwise direction. Which of the corners is unmanned at the moment?

(a) South-West (b) South-East
(c) North-East (d) North-West

40. After the movement in 25, who is at the North-West corner?

(a) Q Only (b) Q and R
(c) P and Q (d) S and R

DIRECTIONS ~ (Q. Nos. 41 and 42) *Read the following information carefully to answers the questions that follow.*

Two boys Anil and Shyam walk in opposite directions for 3 km. Anil is walking towards East. After 3 km each, both turn right and again walk 3 km each both turn to face each other.

41. In which direction is Shyam looking? « DMRC CRA 2012

(a) South (b) South-East
(c) East (d) North-West

42. In which direction is Anil looking? « DMRC (CRA) 2012

(a) North (b) North-West
(c) West (d) South-East

DIRECTIONS ~ (Q. Nos. 43-45) *Study the information and answer the following questions.* « IBPS PO 2018

D is 20m in South of A. C is 5 m East of D. E is 10m North of C. F is 10m East of E. G is 15 m South of F. X is 15 m West of G. B is 10 m to the East of A. Z is 10 m to the South of B. L is 10 m to East of C.

43. In which direction is point A with respect to point G?

(a) North-West (b) South-East(c) North
(d) South-West (e) North-East

44. Four of the following are alike in a certain way so form a group, which of the following does not belong to that group?

(a) EF (b) EC (c) LG (d) BZ
(e) CL

45. What is distance between point F and L?

(a) 10 m (b) 5 m (c) 15 m (d) 20 m
(e) 25 m

DIRECTIONS ~ (Q. Nos. 46-48) *Read the information carefully and answer the questions.*

Point U is 10 m North of Point Q. Point T is 10 m East of Point U. Point S is 15 m South of Point T.

Point P is 20 m South of Point Q. Point R is 25 m East of point P. Point L is 15 m East of Point S. Point M is the mid-point of Points U and P. « SBI Clerk 2018

46. What is the distance between Points L and R?

(a) 10 m (b) 15 m
(c) 5 m (d) 20 m
(e) 25 m

47. In which direction is point T with respect to P?

(a) North-West (b) South-West
(c) South-East (d) North-East
(e) None of these

48. Which of the following points are inline?

(a) P, R, S (b) Q, M, L
(c) U, S, T (d) M, S, L
(e) Q, S, L

DIRECTIONS ~ (Q. Nos. 49 and 50) *Study the following information carefully and answer the questions given below.*

Point C is 15 m in the East of Point F. Point A is 10 m West of Point B which is 15 m North of Point H. Point D is 15m West of Point E. Point B is 15 m South of Point C. Point E is 5 m East of Point H. Point G is 15 m North of Point A. « IBPS Clerk 2018

49. In which direction and at what distance is Point G from Point C?

(a) 10 m, East (b) 5 m, East
(c) 10 m, West (d) 5 m, West
(e) None of these

50. Point D is in which direction with respect to Point A?

(a) South (b) North
(c) North-East (d) West
(e) None of these

DIRECTIONS ~(Q.Nos. 51-53) *Study the following information carefully and answer the questions given below.*

Point S is 15m West of Point R. Point R is 30m South of Point Q. Point P is 20m West of Point Q. Point U is 15m South of Point P. Point T is 35 m North of Point S. « SBI Clerk 2019

51. If Point V is exactly between Point Q and R, then how far and in which direction is Point U with respect to V?

(a) 15 m, North-East
(b) 15 m, East
(c) 10 m, North-West
(d) 20 m, West
(e) 20 m, North-East

52. Four of the following are alike in a certain way, so form a group. Which of the following does not belong to that group?

(a) P, T (b) U, Q
(c) R, P (d) S, Q
(e) U, T

53. If Point W is in 5m East of Point U, then what is the distance between Point W and Point S?

(a) 5 m (b) 15 m
(c) 25 m (d) 10 m
(e) 20 m

DIRECTIONS ~ (Q. Nos. 54-56) *Study the following information carefully and answer the questions given below.* « LIC (AAO) 2019

Point A is 20 m East of B. Point D is 15m West of Point C. Point E is 45m South of Point D. Point C is 30 m North of Point B. Point F is 15m North of Point A. G is the mid-point of Point B and Point C.

54. If H is the 15m South of Point D, then what is the distance between Point E and Point H?
(a) 20 m (b) 25 m
(c) 30 m (d) 45 m
(e) None of these

55. Four of the following five belongs to a group find the one that does not belong to that group?
(a) F,C (b) A,G
(c) A,C (d) E,B
(e) B, D

56. In which direction and at what distance is point G, with respect to point F?
(a) 20 m, East (b) 310 m, West
(c) 30 m, East (d) 20 m, West
(e) None of these

DIRECTIONS ~ (Q. Nos. 57-59) *Study the following information carefully and answer the questions given below.* « SBI PO 2019

Point R is 5 m West of Point Q. Point P is 16 m North of Point Q. Point R is 25 m South of Point T. Point T is 10 m West of Point V. Point V is 9 m North of Point J.

57. Point J is at how much distance and in which direction with respect to point P?
(a) 10, South-East (b) 5m, South
(c) 5 m, East (d) 10, North-West
(e) 5m, West

58. If point W is West of point J and North of point R , then what is the distance between T and W?
(a) 15m (b) 9m
(c) 12m (d) 10m
(e) 5m

59. What is the direction of Point V with respect to point R?
(a) North (b) South-West
(c) North-East (d) South
(e) North-West

DIRECTIONS ~ (Q. Nos. 60-64) *In the following questions, the symbols #, &, @ and $ are used with the following meaning as illustrated below. Study the following information and answer the given questions.* « SBI PO 2018

Note The directions which are given indicates exact directions.

P#Q - P is in the South direction of Q.
P@Q - P is in the North direction of Q.
P&Q - P is in the East direction of Q.
P$Q - P is in the West direction of Q.
P£QS - P is the mid-point of QS vertically.

Note For South-East direction it used to be written as P#&Q and so on .... .

When it is given that the Car honks once then it will be considered as the car taken a left turn and if it is given as the car honks twice then it will be considered as the car takes a right turn.

Point S is & 15 m of Point B. Point J is @ 33 m of Point S. Point K is @ 25 m of Point B. Point L is $20 m of Point K. Point Q is #40 m of Point L. Point F is &40 m Point Q. Point E £ DF. Point D is @30 m of Point F.

60. What distance the car has to travel from Point D to reach the airplane which is parked at Point J?
(a) 22 m (b) 50 m (c) 43 m (d) 23 m
(e) 35 m

61. What could the possible shortest route to reach Point K from Point J?
(a) Started in East till 15 m, honks once, cover 8 m
(b) Started in West till 15 m, honks twice, cover 8 m
(c) Started in South till 25 m, honks once, cover 8 m
(d) Started in North till 5 m, honks once, cover 8 m
(e) Started in West till 15 m, honks once, cover 8 m

62. Point D is in which direction from point Q?
(a) # (b) @$ (c) #$ (d) @&
(e) #&

63. If Point U is #15 m of point B then which of the following is the position of U with respect to F?
(a) @, 24 m (b) $, 25 m
(c) #, 15 m (d) $, 20 m
(e) None of these

64. Point E is in which direction from point B?
(a) # (b) @ (c) $ (d) &
(e) #&

Answers WITH EXPLANATIONS

1. (*c*) From the given information,

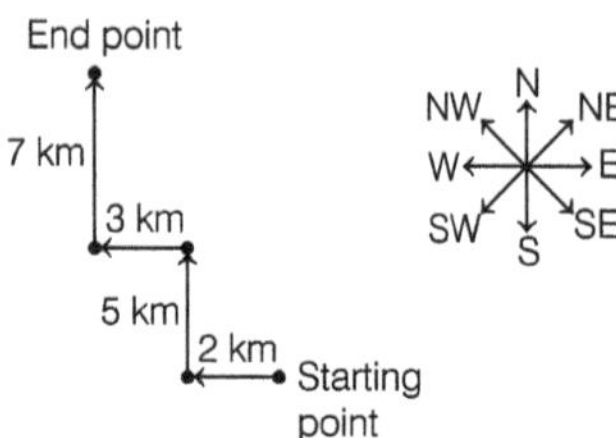

So, Rahul is in the North-West from his starting point.

2. (*d*) From the given information,

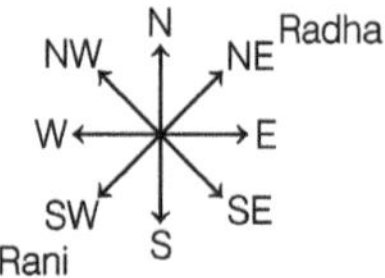

∴ Rani is walking in South-West direction.

3. (*d*) From the given information,

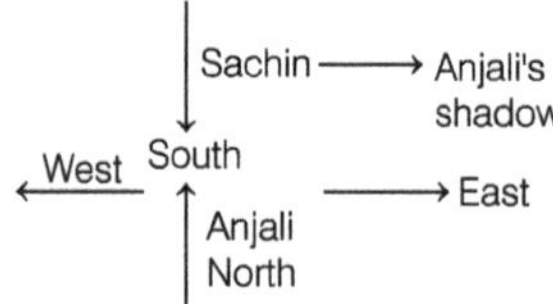

∴ Sachin is facing South.

4. (*a*) Walking diagram of Ahmad is as given below

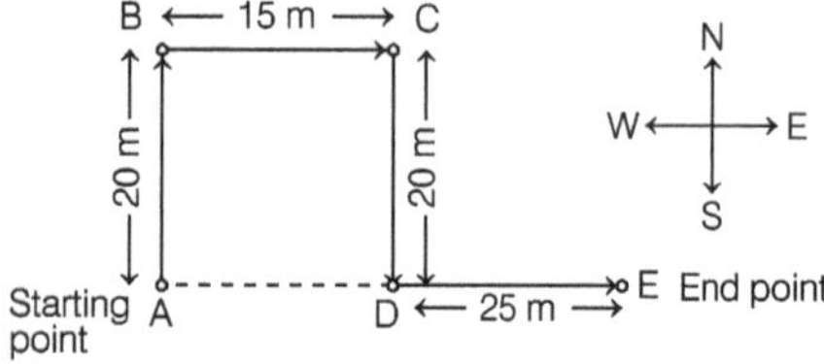

Let point A is the starting point and point E is the end point of walking of Ahmad.

∴ Distance of Ahmad from his starting point

$= AD + DE = BC + DE \quad (\because AD = BC)$

$= (15 + 25) = 40$ m

5. (*b*) From the given information,

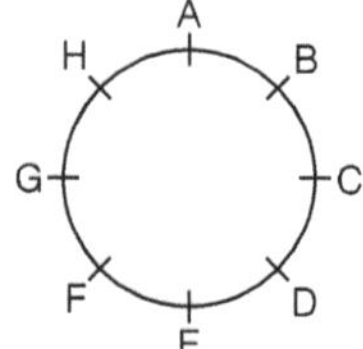

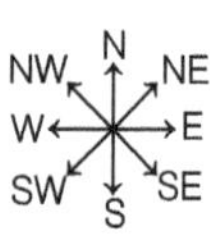

Clearly, H sits in North-West direction.

6. (*c*) From the given information,

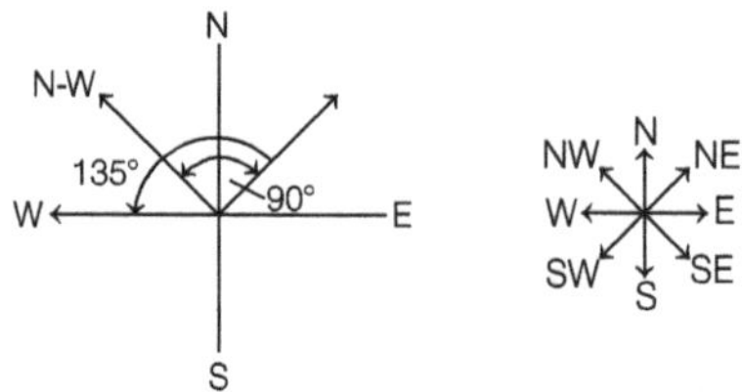

It is clear from the diagram, that Mohan is facing West.

7. (*b*) From the given information,

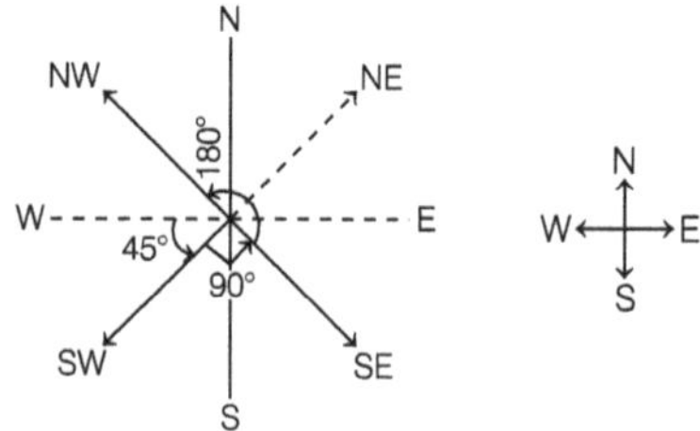

It is clear from the diagram that motorcycle is going in North-West direction.

8. (*d*) From the given information,

As Sudiksha was facing North-West direction and Sakshat was seating opposite to Sudiksha. Hence, Sakshat was facing South-East.

9. (*d*) From the given information,

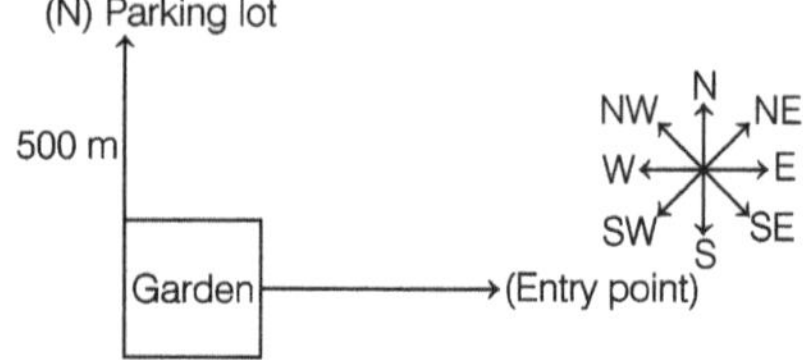

Parking lot is in North direction.

10. (*a*) From the given information,

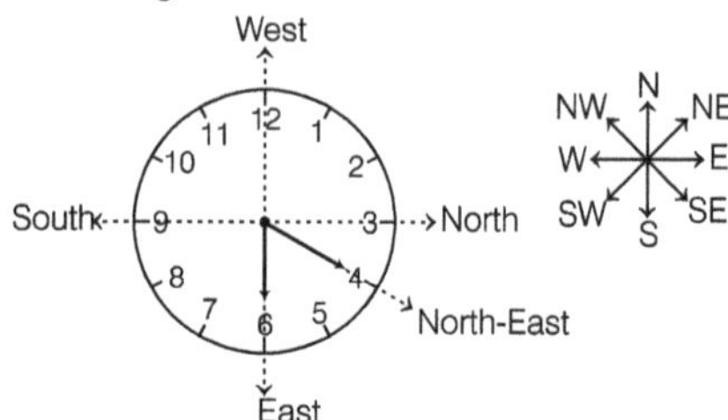

It is clear from diagram that if minute hand points East, then hour hand points North-East direction.

11. (*b*) The direction is as follows

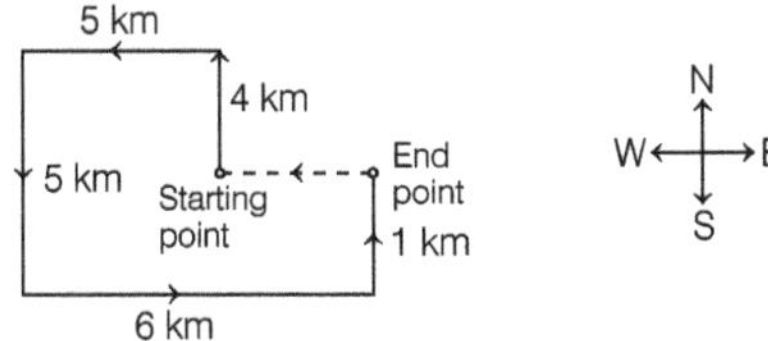

You will have to run in West.

12. (*d*) Walking diagram of Rakesh is as given below

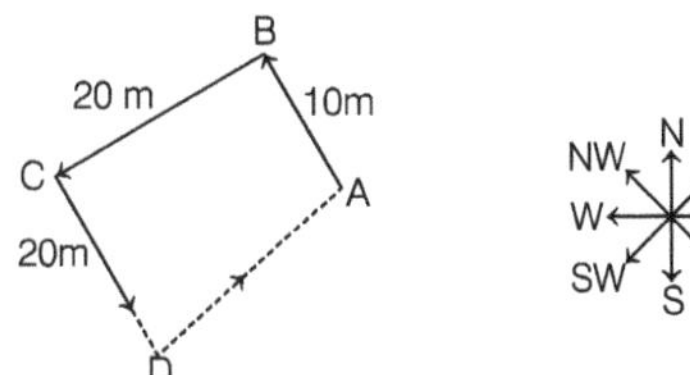

It is clear from diagram that Rakesh is going to the direction of North-East now.

13. (*c*) Direction diagram is as below

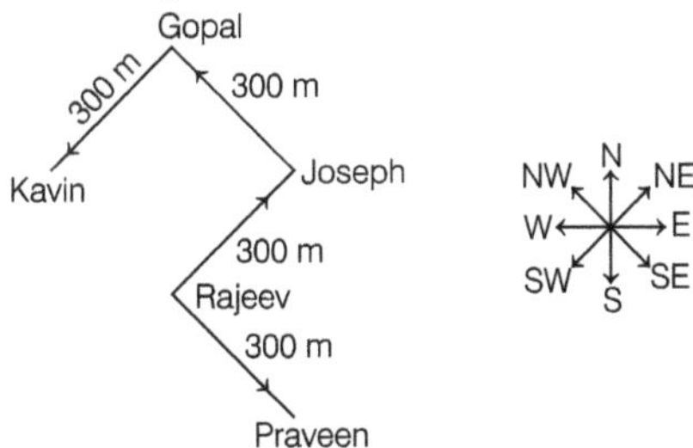

It is clear from diagram that position of Kavin's house to that of Praveen's house is in North-West.

14. (*a*) According to the question, the direction diagram is as follows

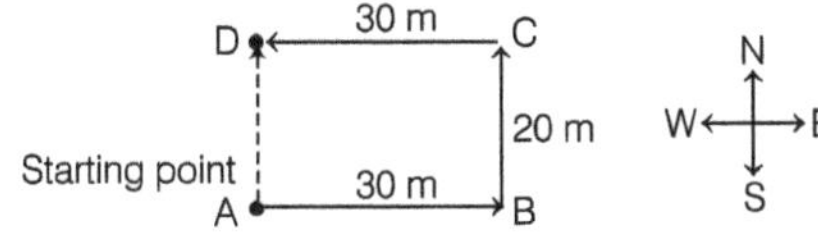

$\therefore$ Required distance = AD = BC = 20 m

So, Nikhil is 20 m, North from his starting point.

15. (*b*) From the given information,

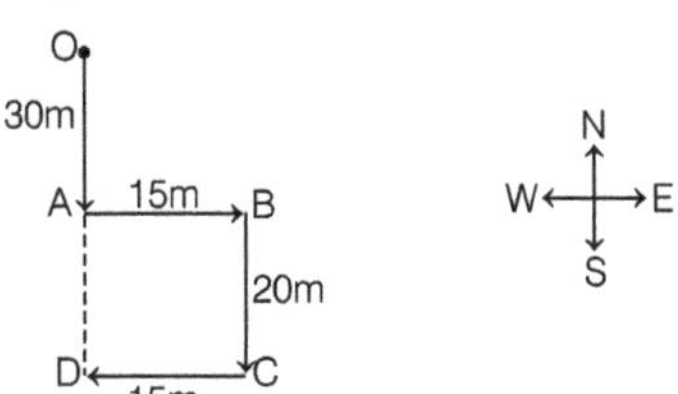

$\therefore$ Required distance = OD = OA + AD

= OA + BC $\quad (\because$ AD = BC)

= 30 + 20 = 50 m

So, Mohan is 50m away from his starting point.

16. (*a*) From the given information,

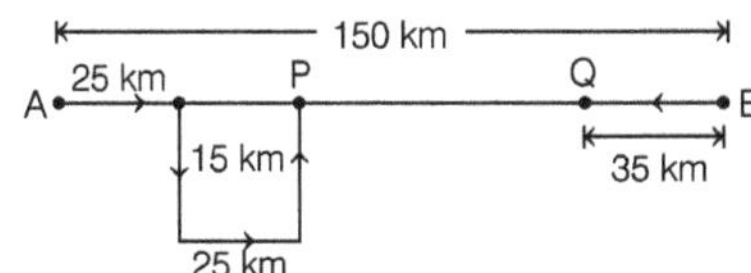

$\therefore$ Required distance = PQ = 150 − (25 + 25 + 35) = 65 km

So, the distance between the buses is 65 km.

17. (*c*) According to the question, the direction diagram will be as follows

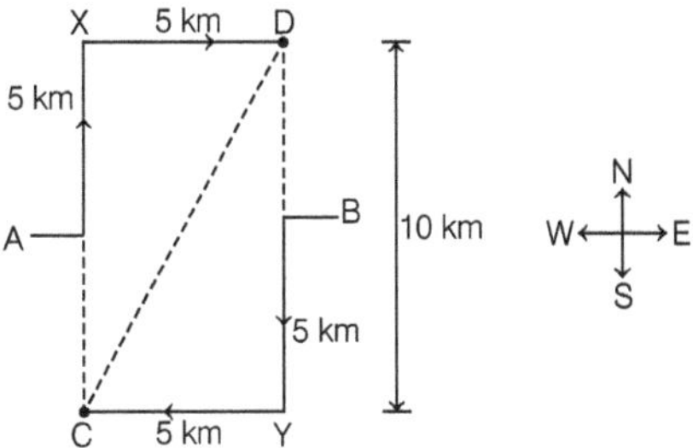

Now, AX = DB = BY = CA = 5 km, XD = CY = 5 km

XC = XA + AC = 5 + 5 = 10 km

$\therefore$ Distance between C and D,

$$CD = \sqrt{(XD)^2 + (XC)^2} \quad \text{[by Pythagoras theorem]}$$

$$= \sqrt{5^2 + 10^2} = \sqrt{25 + 100}$$

$$= \sqrt{125} = 5\sqrt{5} = 5 \times 2.23 = 11.15 \text{ km}$$

So, it is clear from the figure that the houses of C and D are less than 20 km apart.

18. (*b*) According to the given image,

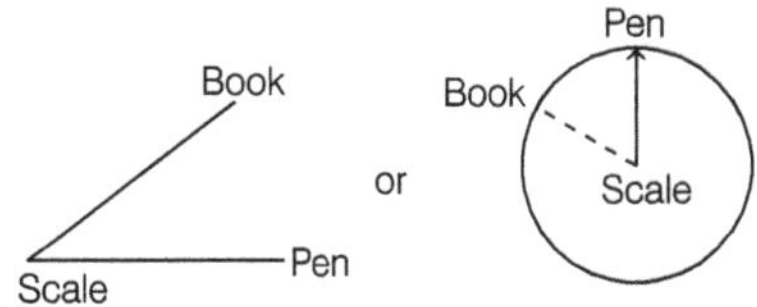

Hence, it is clear that option (b) is correct.

19. (*d*) According to the question, the direction diagram is as follows

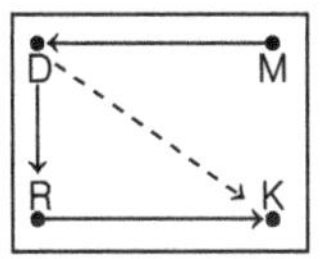

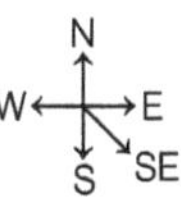

Hence, town K is towards South-East of town D.

20. (*a*) According to the given information,

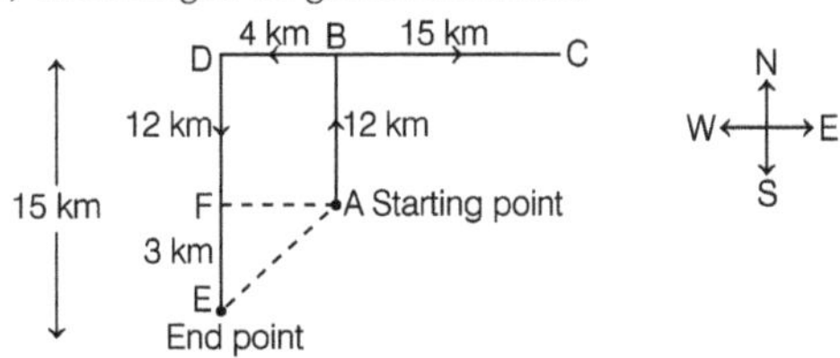

Here, AF = 4 km, FE = 3 km

$\therefore \quad AE = \sqrt{4^2 + 3^2} = \sqrt{16 + 9} = \sqrt{25} = 5 \text{ km}$

21. (*d*) According to the question, the direction diagram is as follows

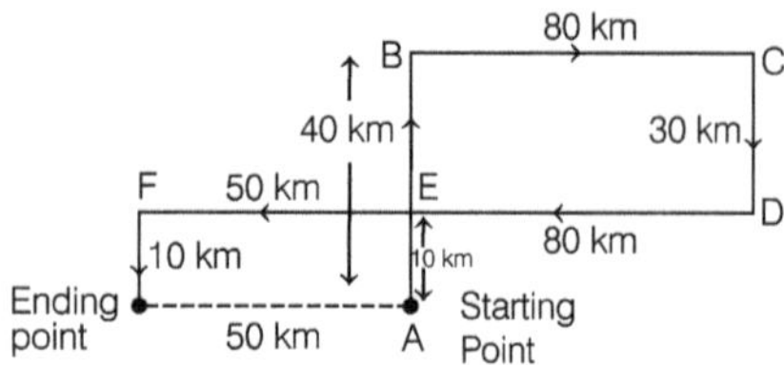

Clearly, he is 50 km far from his starting point.

22. (*b*)

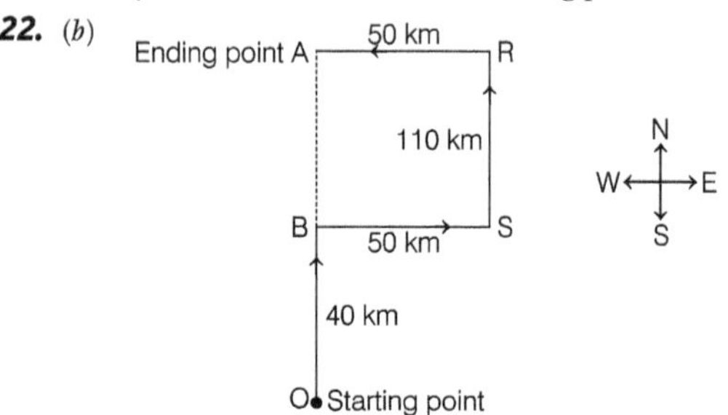

Required distance, OA = OB + BA (where, BA = RS)
= 40 + 110 = 150 km

∴ Hence, migrating bird is 150 km North of its starting position.

23. (a) According to the given information,

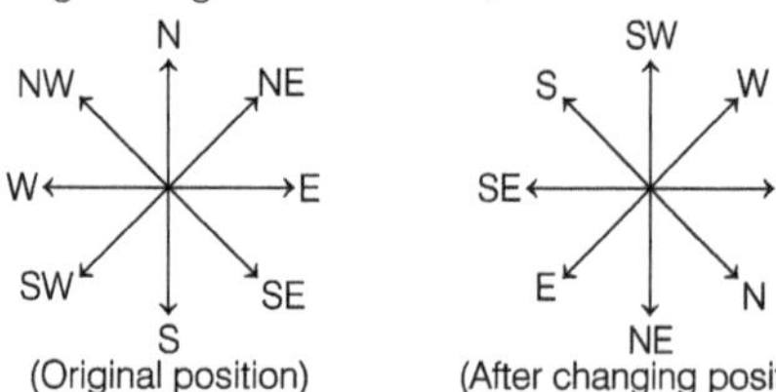

South-East becomes North.
Similarly, North-West becomes South,
North-East becomes West,
South-West becomes East,
Hence, West will become South-East.

24. (*d*) According to the given information,

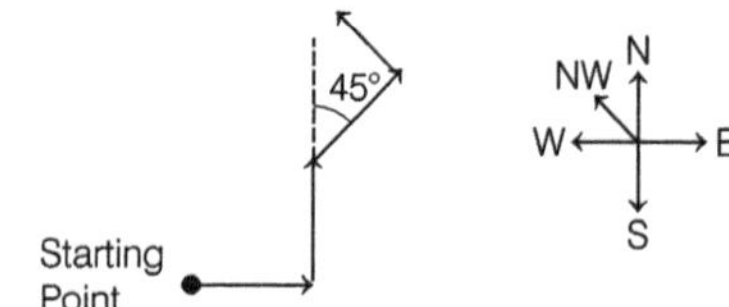

Clearly, debu is walking in North-West direction.

25. (*b*)

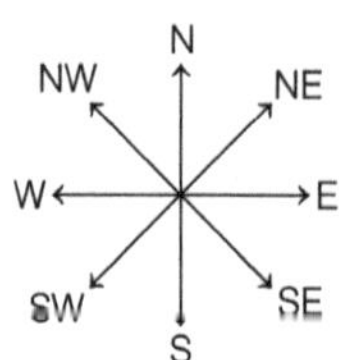

(i) Original position

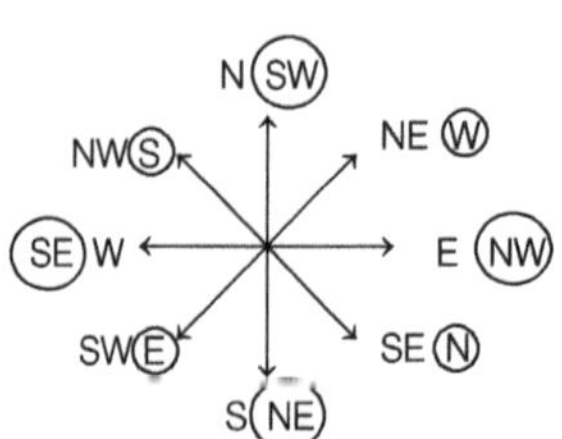

(ii) After Changing Position,

(iii) After turning 90° anti-clockwise

It is clear from diagram i, ii and iii, that to see the South side of the diagram, the Sarpanch has to see South-West side of the actual diagram i.e., diagram (i).

26. (*c*) From the given information,

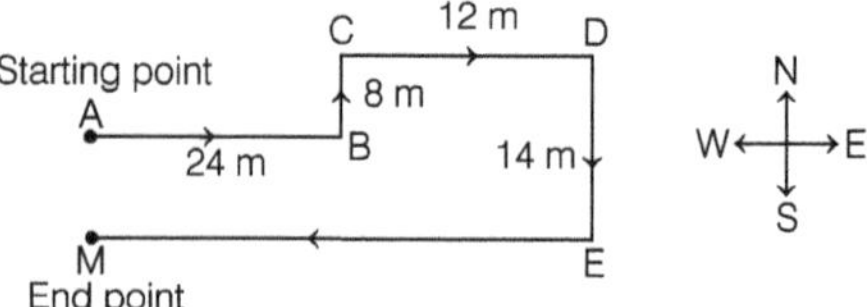

∴ Required distance = AM = DE − BC = 14 − 8 = 6 m
Thus, the distance between A and M is 6m.

27. (*c*) In ΔAOB, OB = DC = 3 km
AB = AC + BC = 2 + 2 = 4 km

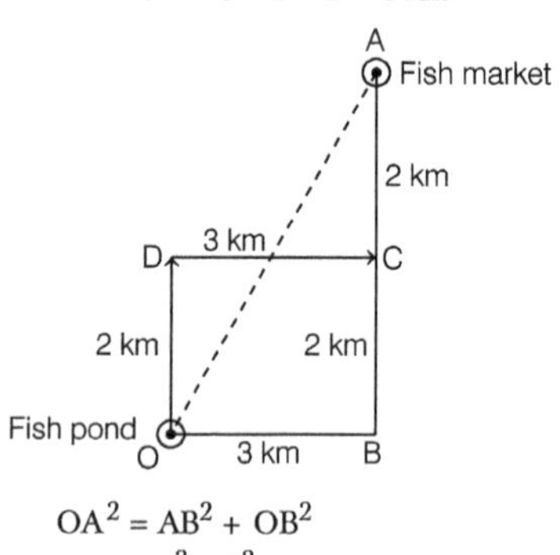

$$OA^2 = AB^2 + OB^2$$
$$= 4^2 + 3^2$$
$$= 16 + 9 = 25$$
$$OA = 5 \text{ km}$$

Hence, distance between fishpond and the fish market = 5 km

28. (*d*) According to the given information,

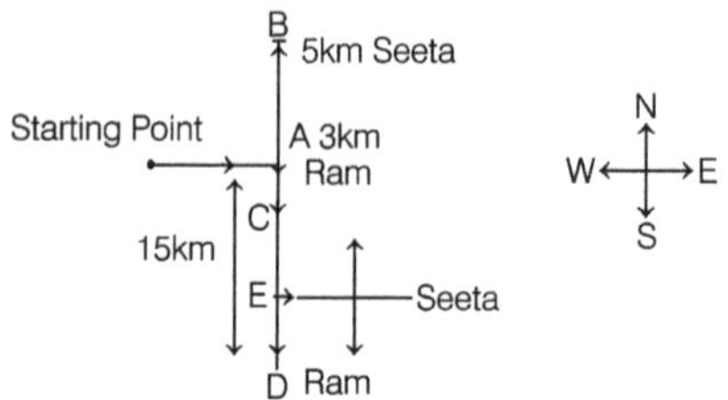

∴ Distance between Seeta and Ram,

$$CD = AD - AE$$
$$= (15 + 3) - 10$$
$$= 18 - 10 = 8 \text{ km}$$

29. (*c*) According to the given information,

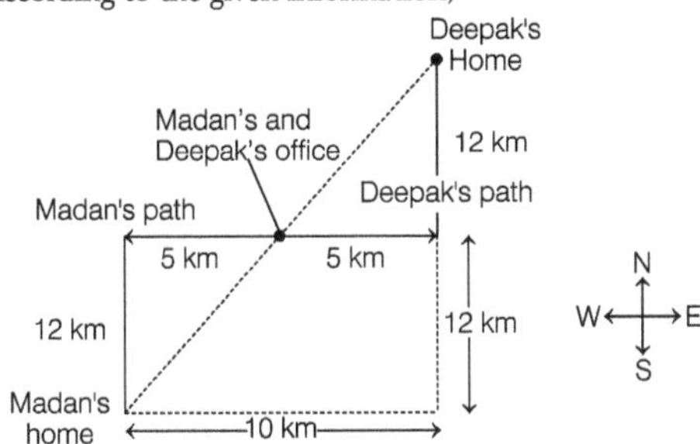

∴ Shortest distance between Deepak's and Madan's home

$$= \sqrt{24^2 + 10^2} = \sqrt{576 + 100}$$
$$= \sqrt{676} = 26 \text{ km}$$

30. (*c*) According to the question, direction diagram is as follows

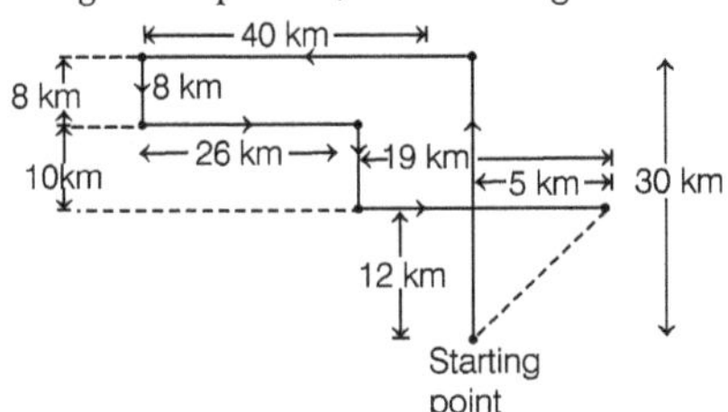

∴ Required distance $= \sqrt{(12)^2 + (5)^2}$
$= \sqrt{169} = 13$ km, North-East

31. (*c*) According to the question, direction diagram is as follows

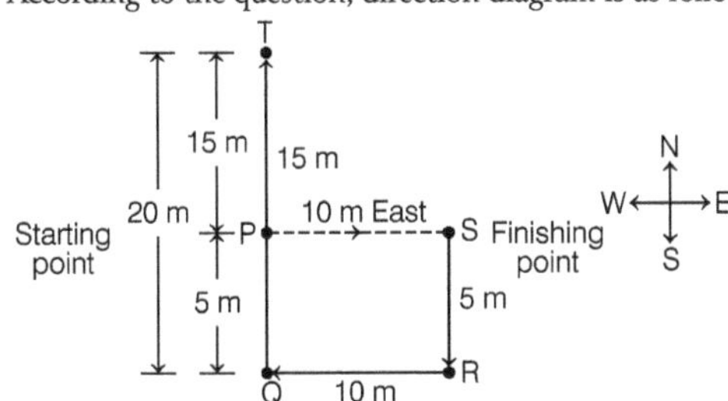

P = Starting point, S = Finishing point
PS = QR = 10 m, TQ = 20 m towards east
TP = 15 m, PQ = SR = 5 m

Now, it is clear from the diagram,
Required distance, PS = 10 m towards East
Clearly, at finishing point S, Ravi is 10 m East from starting Point P.

32. (*d*) Let O be the starting point.

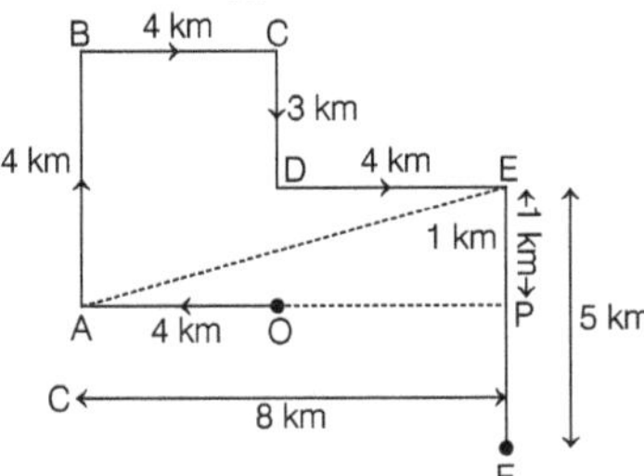

In ΔAEP, AP = AO + OP = 4 + 4 = 8 km

EP = EF − PF = 5 − 4 = 1 km

⇒ $AE^2 = AP^2 + PE^2 = 8^2 + 1^2 = 65$

∴ $AE = \sqrt{65}$ km

33. (*b*) According to the given information,

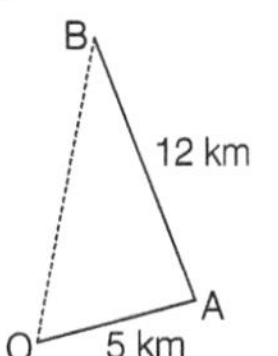

∴ Required distance, $OB = \sqrt{5^2 + 12^2} = \sqrt{25 + 144}$
$= \sqrt{169} = 13$ km

34. (*d*) From given information, diagram is as follows

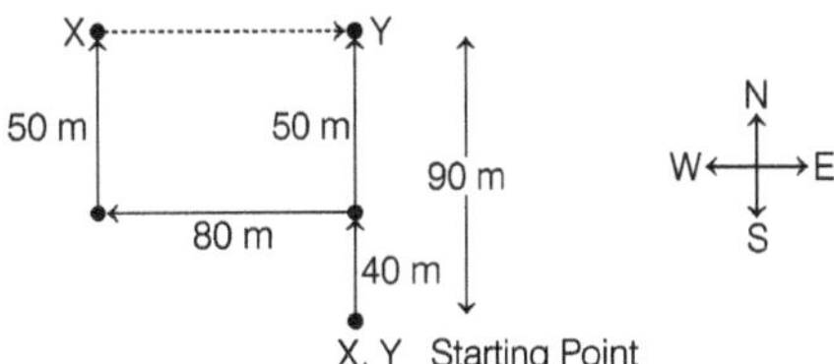

It is clear from the above diagram that Y is 80 m to the East of X.

35. (*b*) According to the given information,

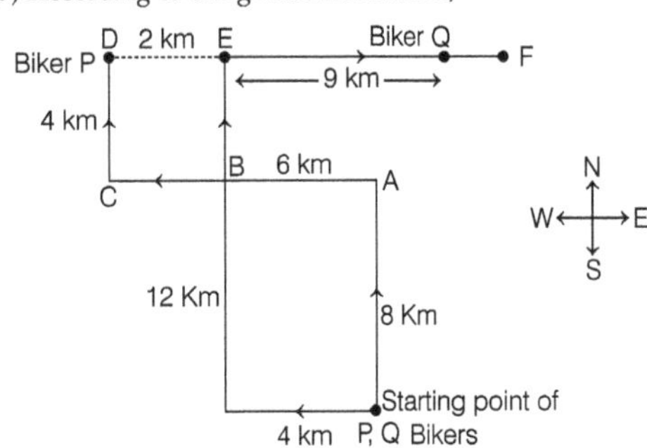

∴ Distance DF = DE + EF = 2 + 9 = 11 km
Hence, Q is 11 km Eastward with respect to P.

36. (*b*) A person starts walking from his home towards his friend's place.
The following figure shows its movement

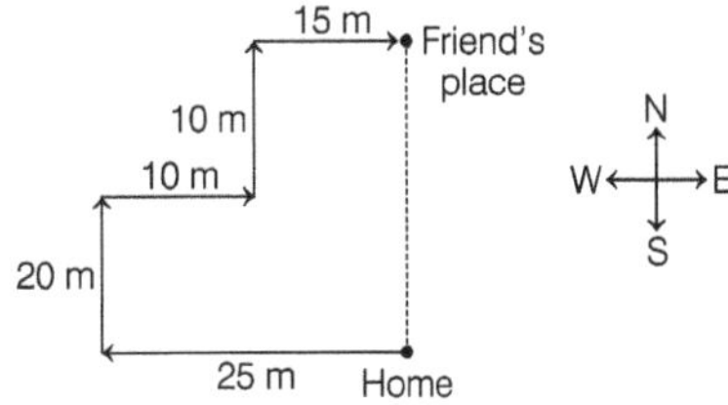

∴ The friend's place is (20 + 10 = 30 m) in the North direction from his home.

37. (*b*) When P and R move towards diagonally opposite coners the two top positions become vacant. Hence, in order S should travel minimum distance, he should move anti-clockwise to occupy P's position.

38. (*c*) Original setting of PSQR change to RQSP, as shown below

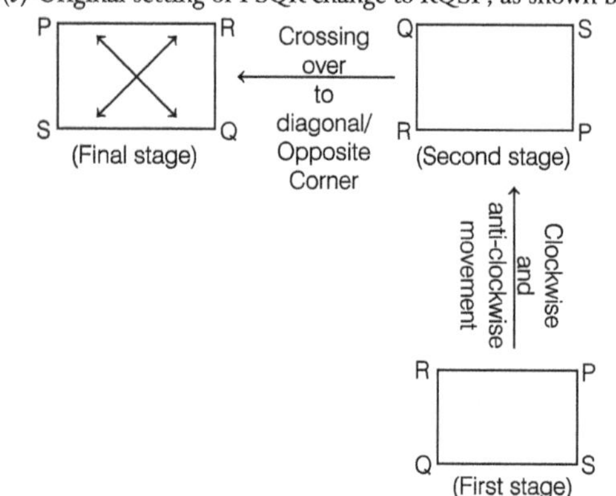

39. (*b*) Final positions of PSQR is shown below

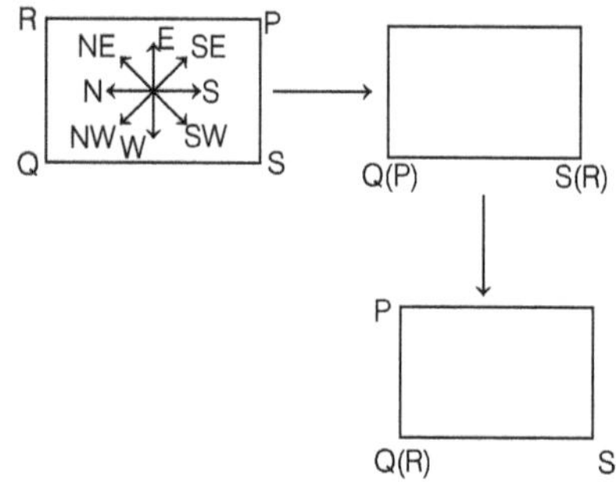

It is clear from the figure that the position in South-East (old position of P) remains unmanned.

40. (*c*) At the North-West position, Q and P are there.

Solutions (Q. Nos. 41 and 42) According to the given information,

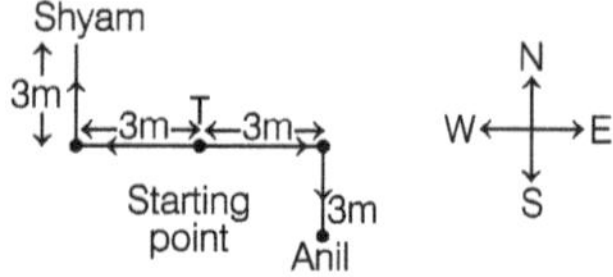

41. From the above diagram, it is clear that, Shyam is looking in South-East direction.

42. (*b*) From the above diagram Anil is looking in North-West direction.

Solutions (Q. Nos. 43-45) According to the given information,

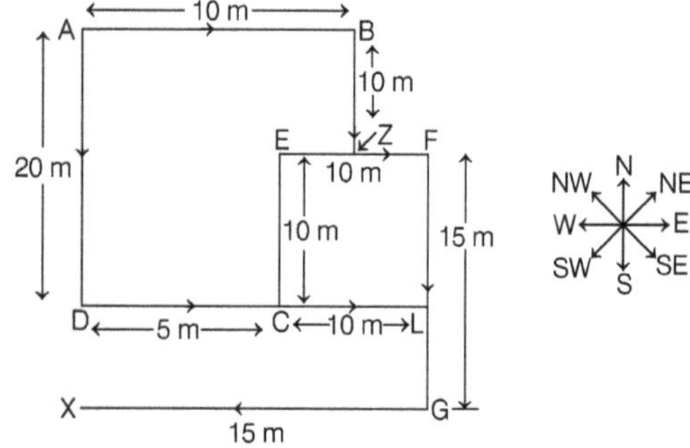

43. (*a*) Point A is in North-West of point G.

44. (*c*) Except LG, all pairs have distance 10 m.

45. (*a*) Distance between F and L = 10 m.

Solutions (Q. Nos. 46-48) According to the given information,

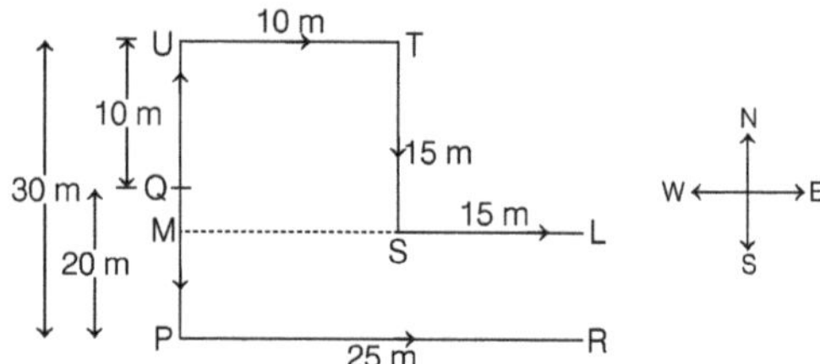

46. (*b*) Distance between L and R = MP = $\frac{UP}{2} = \frac{30}{2} = 15$ m.

47. (*d*) T is in North-East with respect to P.

48. (*d*) Points M, S and L are in line.

Solutions (Q. Nos. 49 and 50)

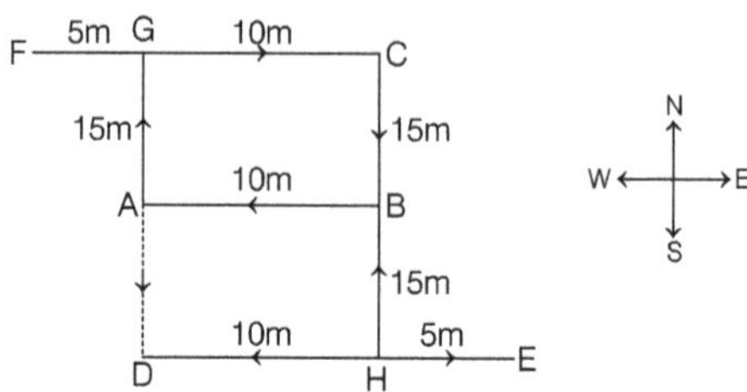

49. (*c*) Point G is 10m West of C.

50. (*a*) Point D is in South with respect to Point A.

51. (*d*)

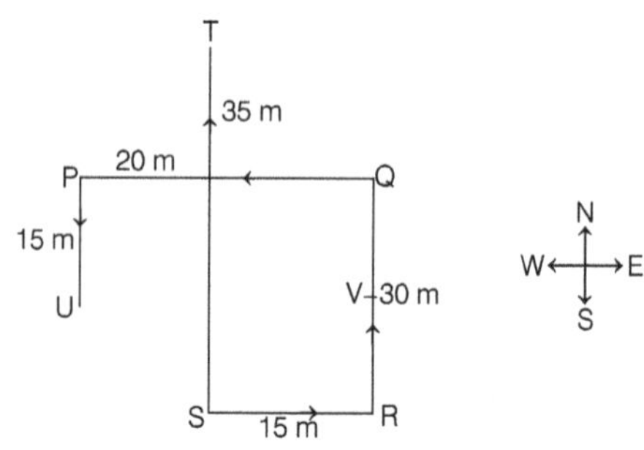

It is clear from the diagram that point U is 20m, West with respect to point V.

52. (*c*) In all of given options except (*c*) i.e. R, P, first point is in West-South direction with respect to second point but in option (*c*) R is in South-East direction with respect to Point P.

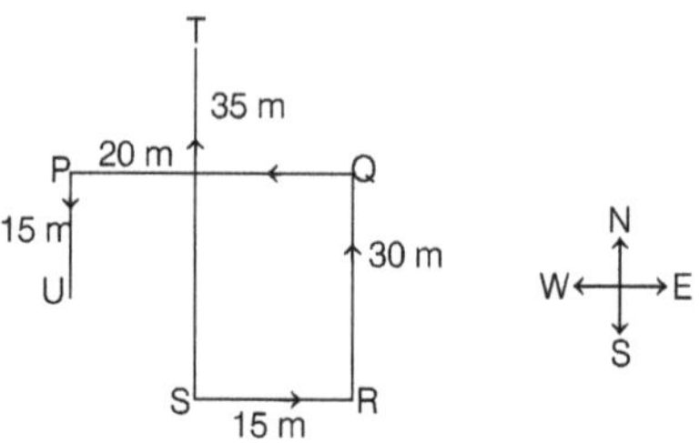

53. (*b*) According to the information,

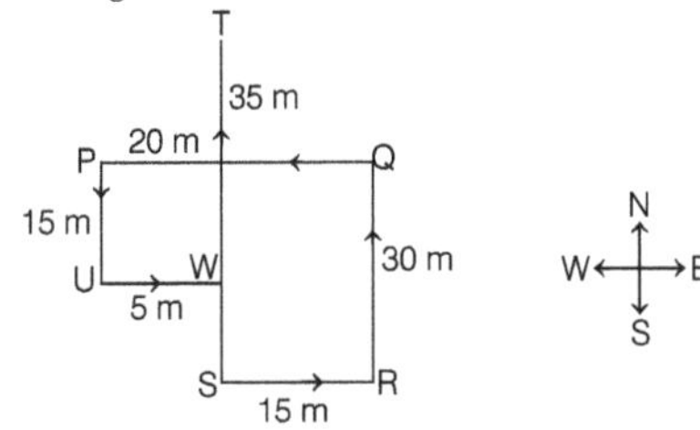

The distance between point W and point S

$= QR - PU = 30 - 15 = 15$ m

Solutions (Q. Nos. 54-56) According to the information,

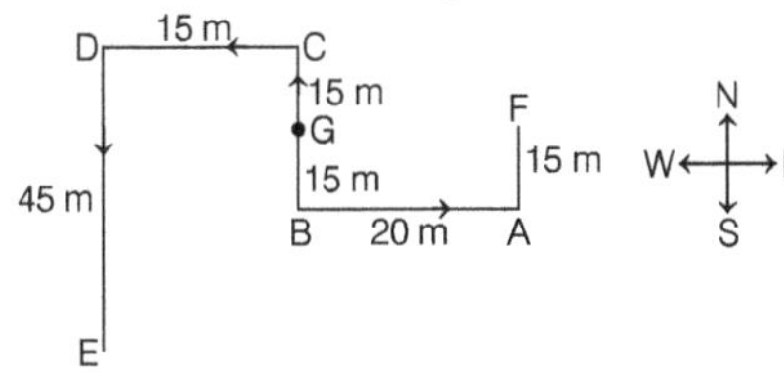

54. (*c*) If H is the 15m South of point D, then DE = DH + HE

$45 = 15 + EH$ [$\because$ HE = EH]

$EH = 45 - 15 = 30$m

55. (*d*) In all of the given options except (d), first point is in South-East direction with respect to second point and in option (d) E is in South-West direction with respect to point B.

56. (*d*) G is in West direction, with respect to point and distance between points G and F, GF = AB = 20m

Solutions (Q.Nos. 57-59) According to the information,

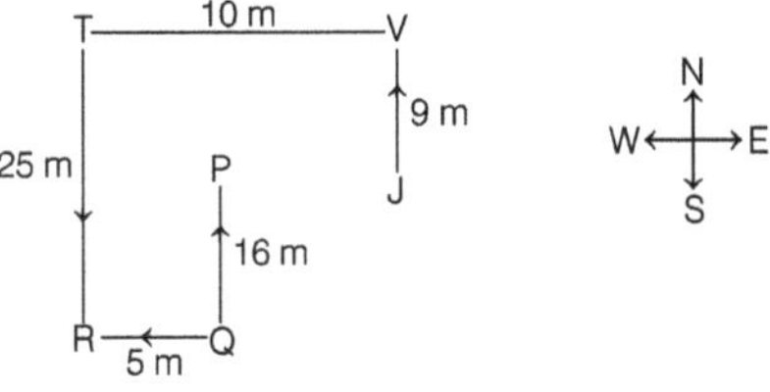

57. (*c*) It is clear from the diagram that point J is in East direction with respect to point P and distance between points J and P

$JP = TV - RQ = 10 - 5 = 5$m

58. (*b*) It is clear from the above diagram, distance between points T and W is $TW = TR - RW = TR - PQ$ [$\because RW = PQ$]

$= 25 - 16 = 9$m

59. (*c*) It is clear from the diagram that point V is in North-East direction with respect to point R.

Solutions (Q. Nos. 60-64) According to the given information,

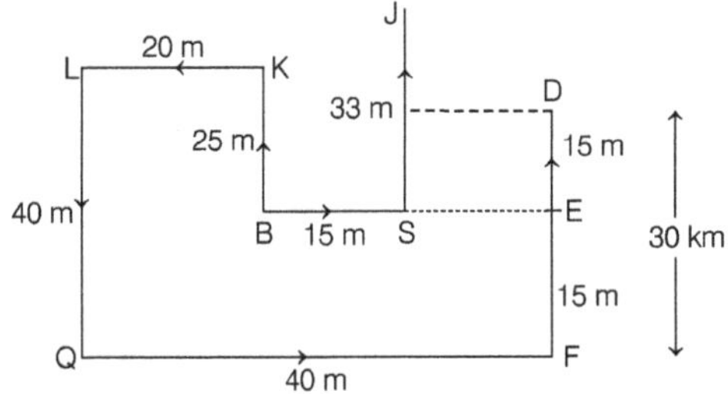

Point S is & 15 m of point B

⇒ Point S is 15m East of Q.

Point J is @ 33 m of point S

⇒ Point J is 33 m North of S.

Point K is @ 25 m of point B

⇒ Point K is 25 m North of B.

Point L is $ 20 m of point K

⇒ Point L is 20 m West of K.

Point Q is # 40 m of point L

⇒ Point Q is 40 m South of Q.

Point F is & 40 m point Q

⇒ Point F is 40 m East of Q.

point E £ DF

⇒ Point E is mid-point of DF vertically.

point D is @ 30 m of point F

⇒ Point D is 30 m North of F.

60. (*d*)

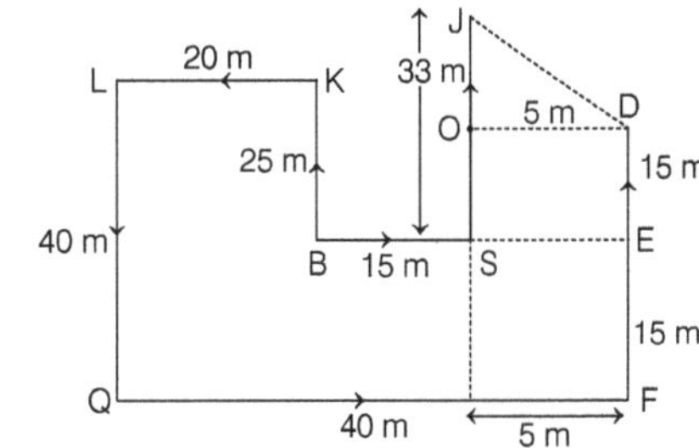

The distance covered by car from Point D to reach Point J = DO + OJ

$= 5 + 18 = 23$ m $\left[\begin{array}{l}\because OJ = SJ - DE \\ = 33 - 15 = 18\text{m}\end{array}\right]$

61. (*e*)

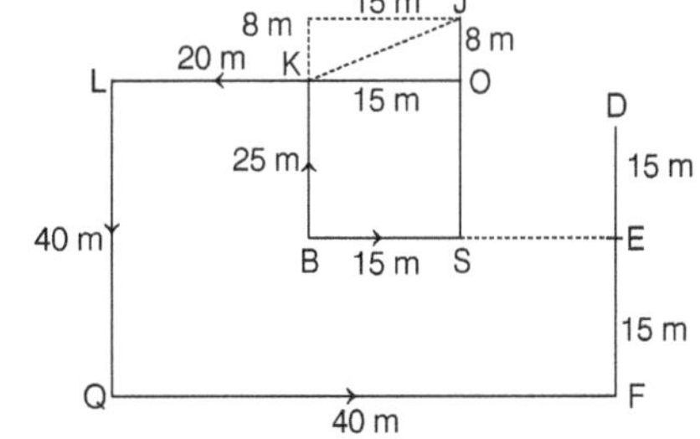

From option (e), started from J towards 15 m West and turn left and cover 8 m.

62. (*d*) Point D is in North-East of Point Q. According to the given information,

Code for North-East direction = @&.

63. (*d*) Point U is 20 m West of point F.

According to the given information,

Code for West direction = $

Hence, position of U with respect to F = $, 20 m.

64. (*d*) Point E is in East direction from Point B, but code for East direction is &.

Hence, position of Point E with respect to Point B is &.

CHAPTER / 08

Blood Relations

Blood relation between two individuals is defined as a relation between them by the virtue of their birth rather than by their marriage or any other reasons.

Blood relation questions involve analysis of information showing the relationship among members of the family. In this, a chain of relationships is given in the form of information and on the basis of this relation between any two members of the chain is asked from the candidate.

Candidates are supposed to be familiar with the knowledge of different relationships in the family. Generally, the questions based on blood relation deal with the hierarchical structure of the family

(i.e., seven generations of the family) which is generally three generation above and three generation below the current generation.

Different relationships between the family members of different generations

Generation	Male	Female
Three generations above ↑↑↑	(i) Great grandfather (ii) Maternal great grandfather (iii) Great grandfather-in-law	(i) Great grandmother (ii) Maternal great grandmother (iii) Great grandmother-in-law
Two generations above ↑↑	(i) Grandfather (ii) Maternal grandfather (iii) Grandfather- in- law	(i) Grandmother (ii) Maternal grandmother (iii) Grandmother-in-law
One generation above ↑	(i) Father (ii) Uncle, (iii) Maternal uncle (iv) Father-in-law	(i) Mother (ii) Aunt (iii) Maternal aunt (iv) Mother-in- law
Current generation (self) →	(i) Husband (ii) Brother (iii) Cousin (iv) Brother-in-law	(i) Wife (ii) Sister (iii) Cousin (iv) Sister-in-law
One generation below ↓	(i) Son (ii) Nephew (iii) Son-in-law	(i) Daughter (ii) Niece (iii) Daughter-in-law
Two generations below ↓↓	(i) Grandson (ii) Grandson-in-law	(i) Granddaughter (ii) Granddaughter-in-law
Three generations below ↓↓↓	(i) Great grandson (ii) Great grandson-in-law	(i) Great granddaughter (ii) Great granddaughter-in-law

Maternal and Paternal Relations

The relation on mother's side is called maternal, e.g., maternal uncle or aunt. The relation on father's side is called paternal e.g. Paternal uncle or aunt.

Important Blood Relations

Relation	Relation Name
+ Father of grandfather or grandmother	Great grandfather
+ Mother of grandfather or grandmother	Great grandmother
+ Father of father or mother	Grandfather
+ Mother of father or mother	Grandmother
+ Wife of grandfather	Grandmother
+ Husband of grandmother	Grandfather
+ Father-in-law of father/mother	Grandfather
+ Mother-in-law of father/mother	Grandmother
+ Father's father/mother only son	Father
+ Only daughter-in-law of father's father/father's mother	Mother
+ Husband of mother	Father
+ Wife of father	Mother
+ Second wife of father	Step mother
+ Brother of father or mother	Uncle
+ Sister of father or mother	Aunt
+ Husband of aunt	Uncle
+ Wife of uncle	Aunt
+ Son of grandfather/grandmother	Father/Uncle
+ Daughter of father-in-law/ mother-in-law of father	Mother/Aunt
+ Father of wife/husband	Father-in-law
+ Mother of wife/husband	Mother-in-law
+ Children of same parents	Siblings
+ Father's /mother's only son/daughter	Oneself/only brother/only sister
+ Son of father or mother	Brother
+ Daughter of father or mother	Sister
+ Son of second wife of father	Step brother
+ Daughter of second wife of father	Step sister
+ Son/daughter of uncle/aunt	Cousin
+ Brother of husband or wife	Brother-in-law
+ Sister of husband or wife	Sister-in-law
+ Husband of sister/sister-in-law	Brother-in-law
+ Son of father	Oneself/Brother
+ Mother of son/daughter	Oneself / Wife
+ Father of daughter/son	Oneself/Husband
+ Son of son of grandmother/grandfather	Cousin/Oneself/ Brother
+ Daughter of son of grandmother/ grandfather	Cousin/Oneself/ Sister
+ Son of brother or sister or brother-in-law or sister-in-law	Nephew
+ Daughter of brother or sister or brother-in-law or sister-in-law	Niece
+ Grandson of father/mother or mother-in-law or father-in-law	Son/Nephew
+ Granddaughter of father/mother or mother-in-law or father-in-law	Daughter/Niece
+ Husband of daughter	Son-in-law
+ Wife of brother/brother-in-law	Sister-in-law
+ Wife of son	Daughter-in-law
+ Son of Son/ Daughter/son-in-law/ daughter -in-law	Grandson
+ Daughter of Son/Daughter/son-in-law / daughter-in-law	Granddaughter
+ Son's/Daughter's grandson/sons-in-law/ daughter-in-law/	Great grandson
+ Son-in-law/daughter-in-law/Son's/ Daughter's granddaughter	Great granddaughter

Family Diagram

In the questions related to Blood Relations, the diagram formed by representing the various relations with the help of symbols, is called family tree.

S.No.	Symbols	Meaning
1.	$\oplus$	Male
2.	$\ominus$	Female
3.	$\oplus \leftrightarrow \ominus$	Husband-Wife (Married couple)
4.	$\oplus — \oplus$	Brother-Brother
5.	$\ominus — \ominus$	Sister-Sister
6.	$\oplus — \ominus$	Brother-Sister
7.	$\oplus$ (above) | $\oplus$ (below)	Father-Son
8.	$\oplus$ (above) | $\ominus$ (below)	Father-Daughter
9.	$\ominus$ (above) | $\oplus$ (below)	Mother-Son
10.	$\ominus$ (above) | $\ominus$ (below)	Mother-Daughter

With the help of following information one can easily understood, that how to make a family tree.

Suppose G, P, R, S and T are the members of a family in which

I. P and S are married couple.

II. S is not a male.

III. T is the son of P while P is the son of G.

IV. R is the sister of T.

On the basis of given information, now we can draw a family diagram

***Step* I** From Statement I, P and S are married couple and this can be represented as below

$$P \leftrightarrow S$$

***Step* II** From Statement II, S is not a male means S is definitely a female. Now, as S and P are married couple, P is definitely a male. This can be represented as follows

$$P^{\oplus} \leftrightarrow S^{\ominus}$$

This step makes it clear that P is the husband and S is the wife.

***Step* III** From Statement III, T is the son of P and P is the son of G. Now, the family diagram will be given as follows

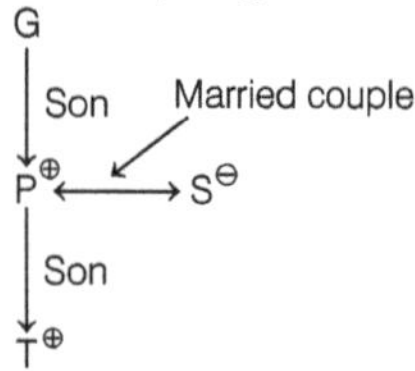

***Step* IV** From Statement IV, R is the sister of T.

T⊕ —Sister→ R⊖

Now, combining all the steps, following family diagram can be drawn

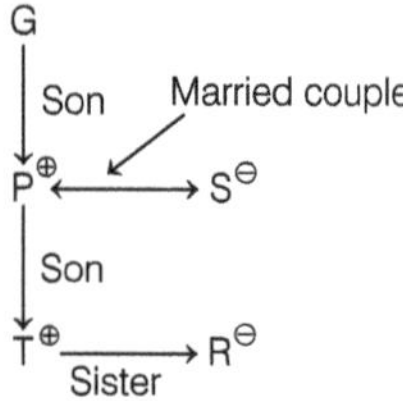

Note *Here, ⊕ sign symbolises a male and ⊖ sign symbolises a female.*

The following conclusions can be drawn from this final diagram

I. S is the daughter-in-law of G.
II. T is the grandson of G.
III. R is the granddaughter of G.
IV. P is the father of R and T.
V. R is the daughter of P and S.
VI. T is the son of P and S.
VII. S is the mother of T and R.
VIII. T is the brother of R.
IX. R is the sister of T.
X. G is grandmother/grandfather of T and R.
XI. G is father/mother of P and father-in-law/mother in law of S.

Points to be Kept in Mind While Solving the Questions

- Firstly try to find out the two persons among whom the relation is to be found. Then, based on the relations between the other members of the family given as intermediaries, try to establish the relation between the two required persons.
- Never predict the gender of a person on the basis of name, unless otherwise it is mentioned, as it may lead to a wrong answer.
- Correlating the relations given in question with your personal relations will help you to understand the question in a better way.
- Always use pictorial representation to solve the question because in this form you can systematically arrange the data and this will make easy for a student to understand the relations.
- When pointing to a picture it may be possible that a person is pointing towards himself in the picture but when a person points to another person, then it is not possible that the person is himself.

Different types of questions covered in this chapter are as follows

TYPE 01

Blood Relation Based on Conversation

In such questions, a person gives information to another person either about a particular person in a photograph or a person present in front of him.

Using this information, a candidate is required to establish a relationship between a given person and the person in the photograph/the person about whom the information is provided.

***Ex* 01** Amit said to Mohan, "That boy in red shirt is younger of the two brothers of the daughter of my father's wife". How is the boy in red shirt related to Amit. Who is a boy?

(a) Father (b) Uncle (c) Brother (d) Nephew

***Solution* (c)** Let us draw the family diagram,

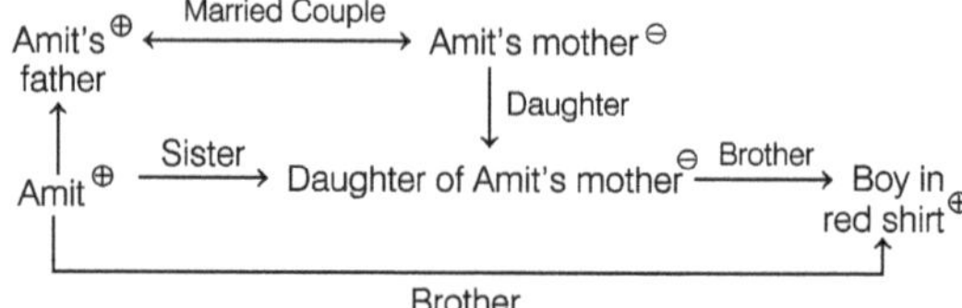

Now, it is clear that the boy in red shirt is the brother of Amit.

***Ex* 02** Gopal said, pointing to Govind, "His father is my father's only son". How is Gopal related to Govind?

« SSC (FCI) 2012

(a) Grandfather (b) Grandson
(c) Son (d) Father

***Solution* (d)** Let us draw the family diagram,

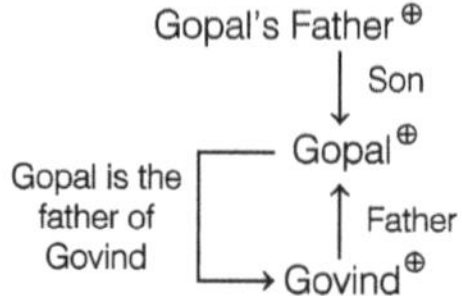

Clearly, the only son of Gopal's father is Gopal himself. This means Gopal is the father of Govind.

***Ex* 03** Introducing Kavi, Veena said, "She is sister of my husband's wife's son." How is Veena related to Kavi?

« SSC CGL 2019

(a) Aunty (b) Daughter (c) Sister (d) Mother

***Solution* (d)** Let us draw the family diagram,

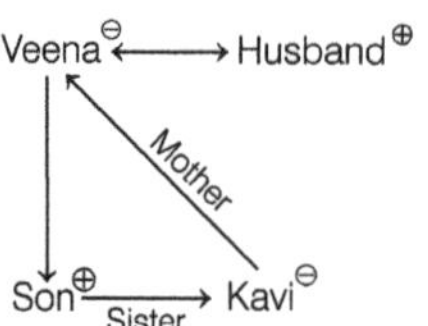

Now, it is clear that Veena is the mother of Kavi.

Ex 04 Pointing to a man in a photograph, a man said to a woman, "His mother is the only daughter of your father". How is the woman related to the man in the photograph? « SSC (CPO) 2009

(a) Sister (b) Mother
(c) Wife (d) Daughter

Solution (b) Let us draw the family diagram,

Father of the woman in conversation⊕
↓ Daughter
Mother of man in photograph⊖ (women in conversation)
↑ Mother
Man in Photograph⊕

Now, it is clear that the only daughter of the woman's father is the woman herself and hence, the man in the photograph is her son. Therefore, woman is the mother of the man in the photograph.

Ex 05 Pointing to a lady a man said, "The son of her only brother is the brother of my wife." How is the lady related to the man? « MAT 2008

(a) Mother's sister
(b) Grandmother
(c) Mother-in-law
(d) Sister of father-in-law

Solution (d) Let us draw the family diagram,

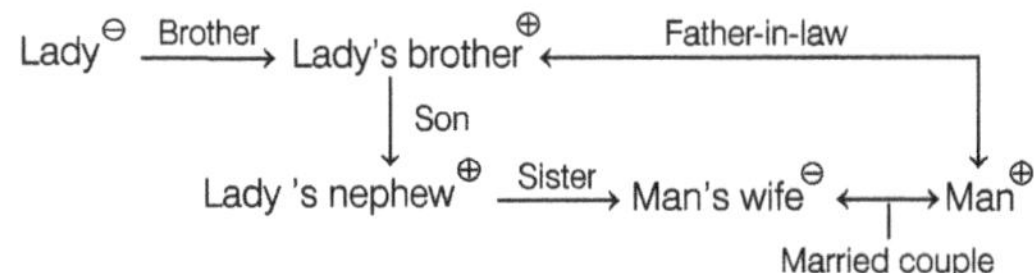

Now, it is clear that the lady is the sister of man's father-in-law.

Ex 06 Pointing to a photograph Yuvraj says, "He is the only brother of the only daughter of my sister's maternal grandmother". Pointing to another photograph Sourav says "he is the only brother of the only daughter of my sister's maternal grandmother". If among the two photographs, one was either of Sourav or Yuvraj and the photograph, towards which Yuvraj was pointing, was not of Sourav, then how is Yuvraj related to Sourav? « IIFT 2008

(a) Paternal uncle (b) Maternal uncle
(c) Grandfather (d) None of these

Solution (b) According to Yuvraj, the only daughter of my sister's maternal grandmother means Yuvraj's mother and man in photograph is the only brother of Yuvraj's mother. So, man in photograph is the maternal uncle of Yuvraj.

Similarly, another man in photograph is the maternal uncle of Sourav. Again, it is given that among the two photographs, one was either of Sourav or Yuvraj and the photograph towards which Yuvraj was pointing was not of Sourav, then that towards which Sourav was pointing is definitely of Yuvraj. Hence, Yuvraj is maternal uncle of Sourav.

Practice / CORNER 8.1

1. Pointing towards a photo, Rakesh said, "She is the daughter of the only son of my grandfather." How is the girl related to Rakesh? « RRB JE 2019

(a) Sister (b) Daughter
(c) Granddaughter (d) Cousin

2. Neelam, who is Rohit's daughter, says to Indu, Your mother Reeta is the younger sister of my father, who is third child of Sohanji". How is Sohanji related to Indu?

(a) Maternal uncle (b) Father
(c) Grandfather (d) Father-in-law

3. Pointing towards a woman, Suresh said, "She is the daughter of my father's sister". How is the woman related to Suresh?

(a) Brother (b) Cousin
(c) Uncle (d) Sister
(e) None of these

4. Looking at a photograph, a person said, "I have no brother or sister but that man's father is my father's son". At whose photograph was the person looking at?

(a) His son's (b) His nephew's
(c) His father's (d) His own

5. Looking at a woman sitting next to him, Amit said, "She is the sister of the husband of my wife". How is the woman related to Amit? « MPPCS 2018

(a) Niece (b) Daughter
(c) Sister (d) Wife

6. Introducing Asha to guests, Bhaskar said, "Her father is the only son of my father". How is Asha related to Bhaskar?

(a) Niece (b) Granddaughter
(c) Mother (d) Daughter

7. Fatima while introducing Mustafa to her husband said, "His brother's father is the only son of my grandfather". How is Fatima related to Mustafa?

(a) Aunt (b) Sister
(c) Niece (d) Mother

8. Pointing towards a man, a lady said, "He is the son of my husband's brother.' How is the lady's husband related to the man? « SSC Constable 2017

(a) Son (b) Uncle
(c) Brother (d) Husband

9. Pointing towards a photograph, Binod said, "she is the daughter of my wife's mother's only daughter". How is Binod related to the girl in the photograph?
(a) Cousin (b) Uncle
(c) Father (d) Cannot be determined
(e) None of these

10. Pointing towards a girl, Arun said, "she is the only daughter of my grandfather's son". How is that girl related to Arun? « Syndicate Bank (Clerk) 2011
(a) Daughter (b) Sister
(c) Cousin (d) Data inadequate
(e) None of these

11. Pointing towards a photograph, Ram said, "She is the mother of my brother's son's wife's sister". How is the lady in the photograph related to Ram's brother?
(a) Sister (b) Daughter-in-law
(c) Daughter (d) None of these

12. Pointing to a lady Simon said, " She is the daughter of the only sister of my father." How is lady related to Simon?
(a) Mother (b) Aunt
(c) Sister (d) Cousin sister

13. Pointing to a girl, Mihir said, "She is the only daughter of my grandfather's only child." How is the girl related to Mihir? « MP Patwari 2017
(a) Daughter (b) Niece
(c) Sister (d) None of these

14. Introducing Alka to guests, Brijesh said, "Her father is the only son of my father". How is Alka related to Brijesh?
(a) Daughter (b) Mother
(c) Sister (d) Niece

15. If Neena says, "Anita's father Raman is the only son of my father-in-law, Mahipal", then how is Bindu, who is the sister of Anita, related to Mahipal?
(a) Niece (b) Daughter
(c) Wife (d) Granddaughter

16. Pointing towards a girl, Mihir said, "She is the only daughter of only child of my grandfather". How is the girl related to Mihir?
(a) Daughter (b) Niece
(c) Sister (d) Data inadequate
(e) None of these

17. Pointing to a woman in the photograph, Rajesh said, "The only daughter of her grandfather is my wife". How Is Rajesh related to that woman?
(a) Uncle (b) Father
(c) Maternal Uncle (d) Brother

18. In a family of five persons, Dinesh is Jairam's son and Gopal's brother while Meeta is Gopal's mother and Jayanti's daughter. If there are no step brothers or half brothers in the family, which of the following statements is true?
(a) Jayanti is Dinesh's mother
(b) Meeta is Dinesh's mother
(c) Jayanti is Jairam's grandmother
(d) All of the above

19. Mathew told his friend Sham, pointing to a photograph, "Her father is the only son of my mother." The photograph is of whom?
(a) Mathew's niece (b) Mathew's mother
(c) Mathew's daughter (d) Mathew's sister

20. Introducing a man, a woman said, "His wife is the only daughter of my mother." How is the woman related with the man?
(a) Sister-in-Law (b) Wife
(c) Aunt (d) Mother-in-law

21. Pointing to a lady, Diwakar said, "Her mother's only grandson is my son." How is that lady related to Diwakar? « SSC (CGL) 2017
(a) Aunt (b) Sister
(c) Mother (d) Wife

22. Pointing towards a girl, Chetan said "She is the daughter of the only child of my grandmother". How is Chetan related to that girl? « SSC (CGL) 2017
(a) Father (b) Son
(c) Brother (d) Husband

23. Pointing at a picture on the wall, a boy said, "That man in the picture is the father-in-law of the wife of the son-in-law of the father of my mother who is the only child of her parents," How is the boy related to the man in the picture? « UPSSSC (Cane Supervisor) 2019
(a) Son (b) Grandson
(c) Nephew (d) Great grandson

24. A woman introduces a man as the son of the brother of her mother. How is the man related to the woman?
(a) Nephew (b) Son
(c) Cousin (d) Uncle

25. Introducing a boy, a girl says, he is the son of the only sister of my mother's brother'. How is the boy related to that girl? « SSC (10+2) 2017
(a) Father-in-law (b) Brother
(c) Cousin (d) Niece

26. Pointing towards a photo, Rakesh said, "She is the daughter of the only son of my grandfather." How is the girl related to Rakesh? « SSC (CGL) 2016
(a) Sister (b) Daughter
(c) Grand Daughter (d) Cousin

27. Pointing to a photograph a man said 'I have no brother or sister but that man's father is my father's son'. Whose photograph was it? « OPSC 2018
(a) His son's (b) His own
(c) His father's (d) His nephew's

28. Ravi was showing a photograph to his friend, Gopi. Pointing at a boy in the photograph, Ravi said 'The boy sitting at the left is the son of the wife of the only son of the grandmother of my younger brother'. What is the relation between the boy in the photograph and Ravi? « CLAT 2017
(a) Nephew and uncle (b) Ravi's brother-in-law
(c) First Cousins (d) Brothers

Answers / WITH EXPLANATIONS

1. (*a*) Let us draw the family diagram,

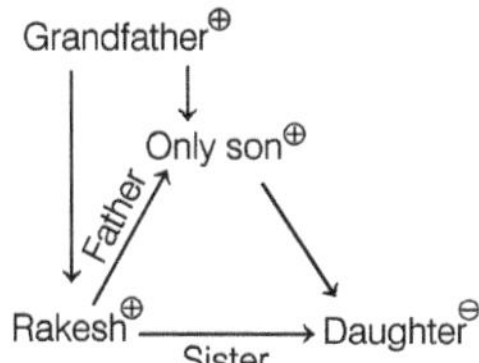

Now, it is clear that girl in photo is the sister of Rakesh.

2. (*c*) After seeing the options, we can consider Sohanji as a male member.

Now, let us draw the family diagram,

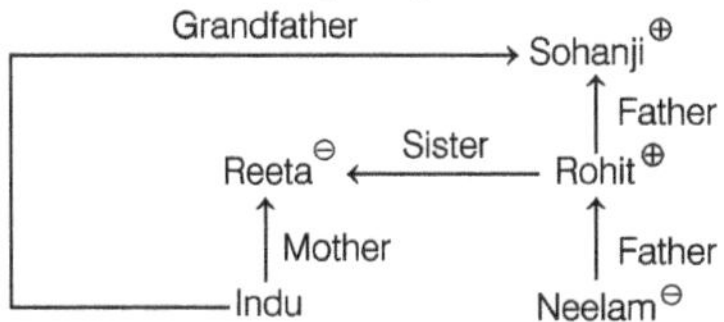

Now, it is clear that Sohanji is the grandfather of Indu.

3. (*b*) Let us draw the family diagram,

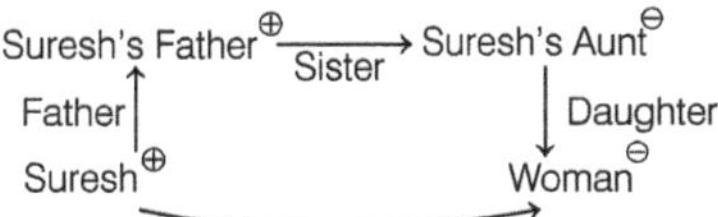

Clearly, woman is the cousin of Suresh.

4. (*a*) Let us draw the family diagram

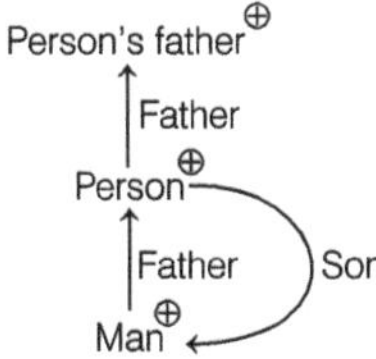

Clearly, the man in photograph is his son.

5. (*c*) Husband of Amit's wife = Amit

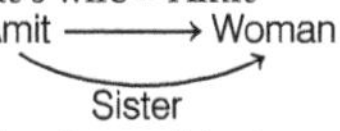

Clearly, woman is the sister of Amit.

6. (*d*)

Bhaskar's father

Father (Bhaskar)

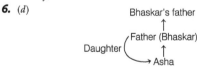

Daughter

Asha

Clearly, Asha is the daughter of Bhaskar.

7. (*b*) Let us draw the family diagram

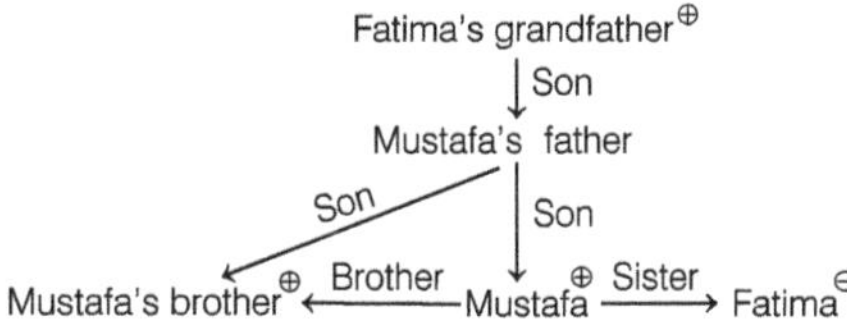

So, it is clear that Fatima is the sister of Mustafa.

8. (*b*) Let us draw the family diagram,

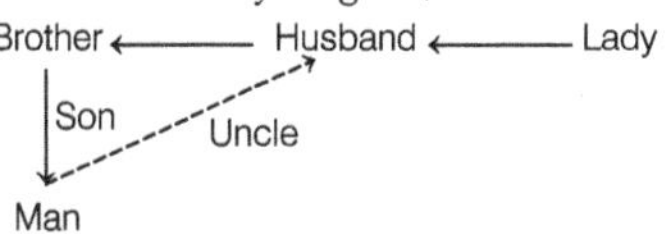

Clearly, Lady's husband is the uncle of the man.

9. (*c*) Let us draw the family diagram

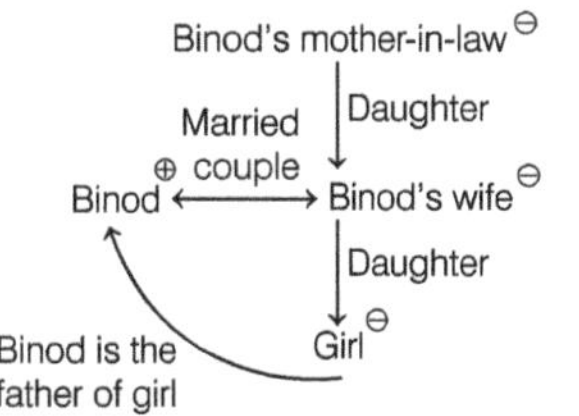

Clearly, Binod is the father of the girl in the photograph.

10. (*d*) Let us draw the family diagram,

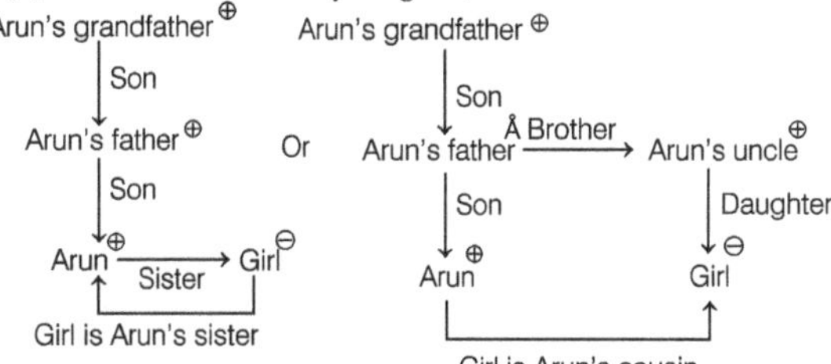

Clearly, the above diagrams make it clear that girl is either sister or cousin of Arun. Here, no definite relation can be established between Arun and girl on the basis of given information. Hence, the data is inadequate to answer the question.

11. (*d*) Let us draw the family diagram

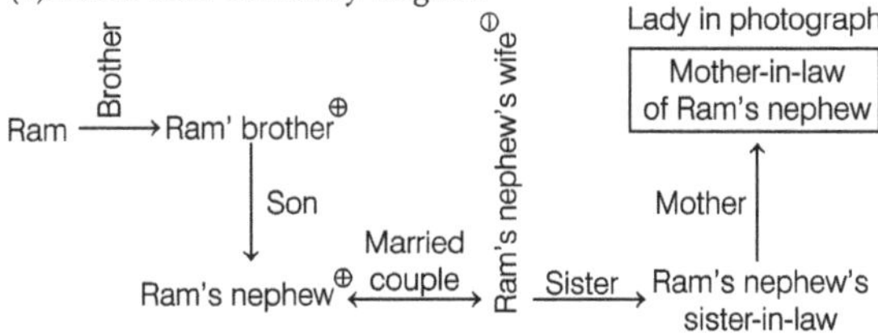

Hence, it is clear that the lady in the photograph is mother-in-law of Ram's nephew.

12. (*d*) Let us draw the family diagram,

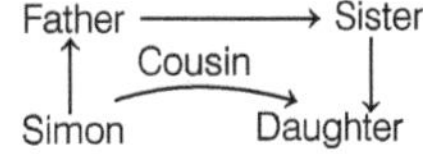

Thus, the lady is cousin sister of Simon.

13. (*c*) According to the question,

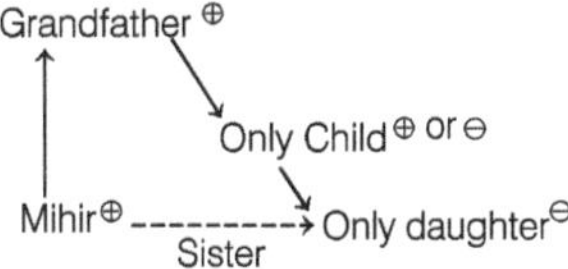

Clearly, the girl is the sister of Mihir.

14. (*a*) Let us draw the family diagram

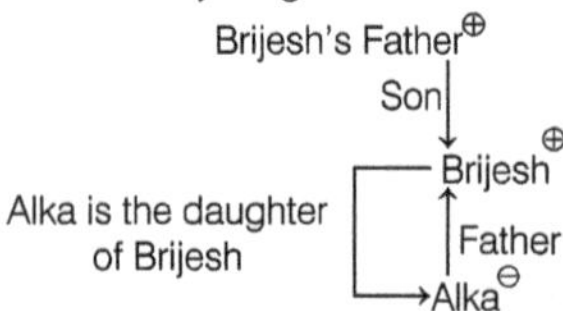

Clearly, the only son of Brijesh's father is Brijesh himself. This means Brijesh is the father of Alka. Hence, Alka is the daughter of Brijesh.

15. (*d*)

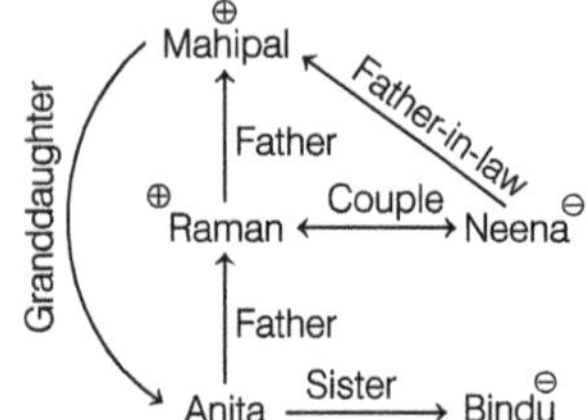

So, Bindu is granddaughter of Mahipal.

16. (*c*) Let us draw the family diagram

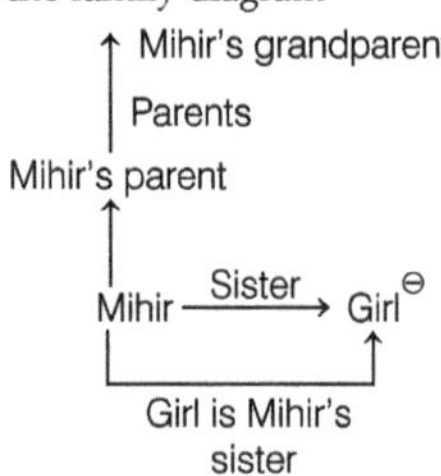

Clearly, only child of Mihir's grandfather is Mihir's father/mother and only daughter of Mihir's father/mother is Mihir's sister. Hence, the girl is Mihir's sister.

17. (*b*)

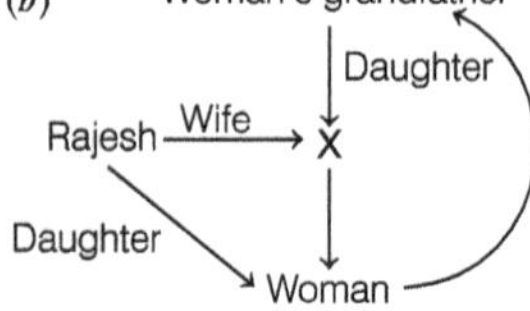

So, Rajesh is father of that woman.

18. (*b*) Let us draw the family diagram

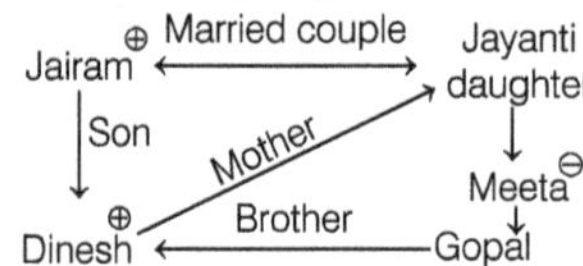

Now, it is clear that Meeta is Dinesh's mother.

19. (*c*) Let us draw the family diagram

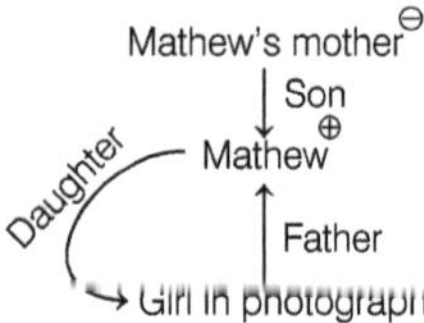

Clearly, her father is the only son means Mathew himself and the photograph is of Mathew's daughter.

20. (*b*) Let us draw the family diagram

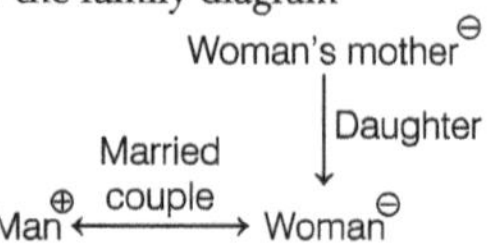

So, it is clear that woman is the wife of that man.

21. (*d*) Let us draw the family diagram,

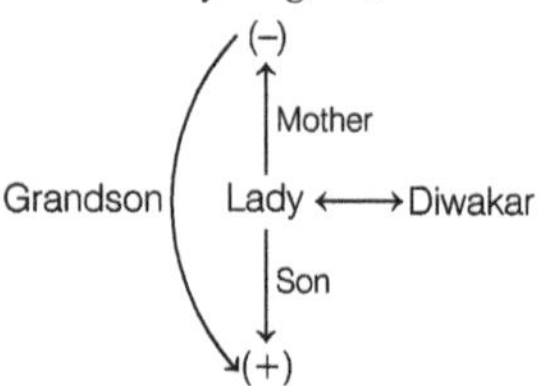

Clearly, the lady is the wife of Diwakar.

22. (*c*) Let us draw the family diagram,

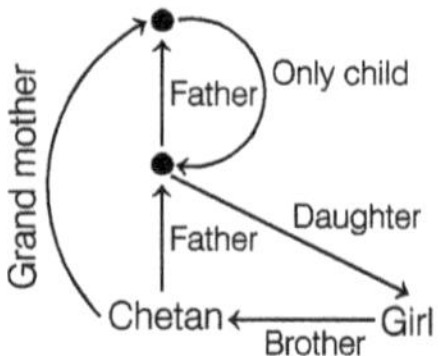

Clearly, Chetan is the brother of the girl.

23. (*b*) From the information given in the question, Blood-relation diagram is as follows;

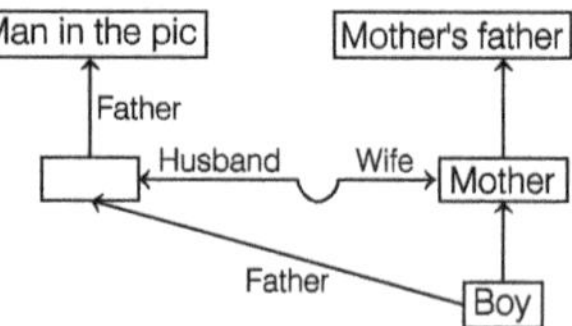

∴ Boy is the grandson of the pointed man.

24. (*c*) According to the question,

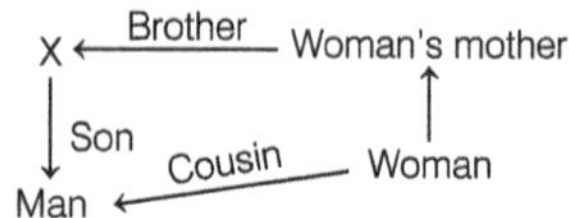

So, from above, the man is the cousin of woman.

25. (*b*) Girl's mother's brother's only sister is her mother and the son of her mother is her brother.

26. (*a*) It is clear from given information that only son of Rakesh's grandfather is Rakesh's father and his daughter is the sister of Rakesh. Hence, girl in photograph is the sister of Rakesh.

27. (*a*) That man's father's son means that man himself or we can say, that this man is the father of the person in the photograph. Hence, the man is pointing towards his son's photograph.

28. (*d*) The blood relation is as follows

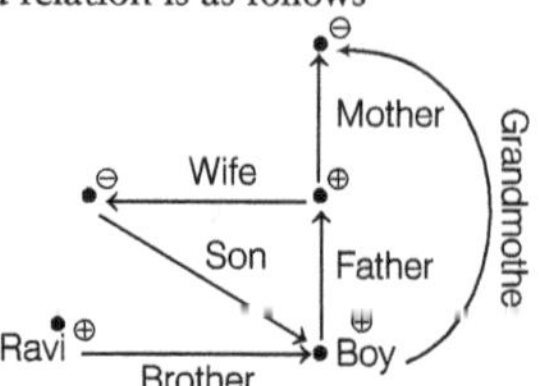

Hence, boy and Ravi are brothers.

TYPE 02

Blood Relation Based on Puzzle

In such questions, more than one information in the form of some puzzle is given and based on the informations, a candidate is required to deduce the relation between the two individuals.

Ex 07 If A is B's sister, C is B's mother, D is C's father and E is D's mother, then how is A related to D? « SSC (DEO) 2010

(a) Granddaughter (b) Daughter
(c) Aunt (d) Father

Solution **(a)** Let us draw the family diagram,

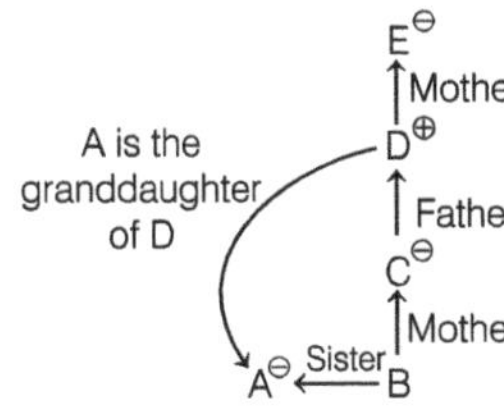

Now, it is clear that A is the granddaughter of D.

Ex 08 Rajesh is the brother of Ankit. Shano is the sister of Shubham. Ankit is the son of Shano. How is Rajesh related to Shano?

(a) Father (b) Brother (c) Son (d) Nephew

Solution **(c)** Let us draw the family diagram,

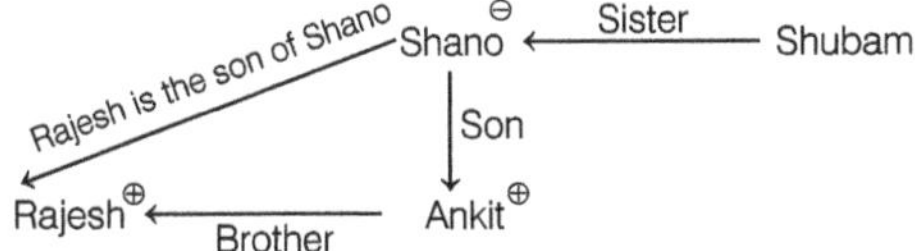

Now, it is clear that Rajesh is the son of Shano.

DIRECTIONS ~ (Example Nos. 9-12) *Read the following information carefully and answer the questions given below.*

There are six children playing football, namely P,Q,R, S, T and U. P and T are brothers, U is the sister of T. R is the only son of P's uncle, Q and S are the daughters of the only brother of R's father.

Ex 09 How is R related to U?

(a) Cousin (b) Brother
(c) Son (d) Uncle

Ex 10 How many male players are there?

(a) One (b) Three
(c) Four (d) Five

Ex 11 How many female players are there?

(a) One (b) Two
(c) Three (d) Four

Ex 12 How is S related to P?

(a) Uncle (b) Sister
(c) Niece (d) Cousin

Solutions (Example Nos. 9-12) *Let us draw the family diagram,*

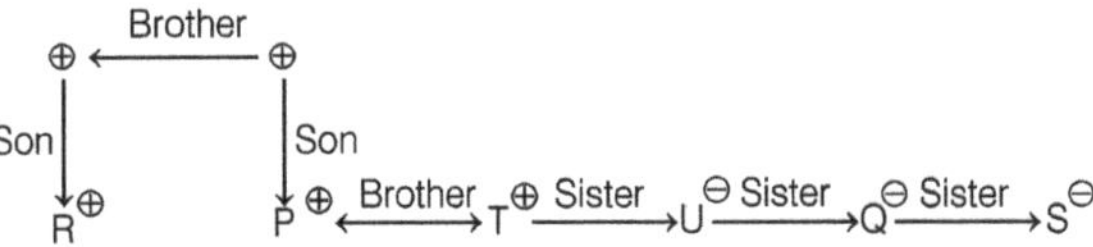

9. (a) R is the cousin of U.

10. (b) Clearly, there are three male players among them.

11. (c) Number of female players is 3.

12. (b) S is the sister of P.

Practice / CORNER 8.2

1. C is the mother of A and B. If D is the husband of B, then what is C to D? « SSC (10+2) 2013

(a) Mother (b) Aunt
(c) Mother-in-law (d) Sister

2. A is C's son. C and Q are sisters. Z is Q's mother. P is son of Z. How is P related to A? « WBCS 2020

(a) Brother (b) Maternal uncle
(c) Uncle (d) Grandfather

3. If M is brother of N, B is brother of N and M is brother of D, then which one of the following statements is definitely true? « UPSC Assistant Commandant 2019

(a) N is brother of B
(b) N is brother of M
(c) N is brother of D
(d) M is brother of B

4. P is the father of Q and R is the son of S. T is the brother of P. Q is the sister of R. How is S related to T? « SSC (CGL) 2019

(a) Brother-in-law (b) Daughter
(c) Sister-in-law (d) Brother

5. Bharat and Sapna are husband and wife. Rohit and Bharat are brothers. Suresh is the father of Rohit. Sapna's son is Krish. How is Krish related to Suresh? « SSC (CGL) 2019

(a) Son (b) Father (c) Uncle (d) Grandson

6. A is brother of B. C is sister of A. D is brother of E. E is daughter of B. Who is uncle of D? « UKPSC Asst. Conservator of forest 2019

(a) A (b) B
(c) C (d) D

7. P's mother is Q's daughter. P's maternal aunt is R and Q's sister is S. How is S related to R? « MP Police SI 2018

(a) None of these (b) Sister
(c) Sister-in-law (d) Niece

8. Raghu and Babu are twins. Babu's sister is Reema. Reema's husband is Rajan. Raghu's mother is Lakshmi. Lakshmi's husband is Rajesh. How is Rajesh related to Rajan?

(a) Uncle (b) Son-in-law
(c) Father-in-law (d) Cousin

9. B is the father of Q. B has only two children. Q is the brother of R. R is the daughter of P. A is the granddaughter of P and S is the father of A. How is S related to Q?

(a) Son (b) Son-in-law
(c) Brother (d) Brother-in-law
(e) None of these

10. Deepak has a brother named Aditya. Deepak is the son of Kuldeep. Bunty is Kuldeep's father. How is Aditya related to Bunty? « SSC (10 + 2) 2017

(a) Uncle (b) Brother
(c) Grandson (d) Grandfather

11. Vishwas's father's only son is the husband of Kritika. Anshula is married to Vivek's only brother. Vishwas is the son of Anshula. Vaibhavi is the daughter of Kritika. Raj and Vivek are brothers. How is Raj related to Vaibhavi? « UPSSSC Combined Lower Subordinate 2019

(a) Father (b) Grandson
(c) Paternal grandfather (d) Maternal grandfather

12. A joint family consists of seven members A, B, C, D, E, F and G with three females. G is a widow and sister-in-law of D's father F. B and D are siblings and A is daughter of B. C is cousin of B. Who is E ? « UPSC (CSAT) 2019

1. Wife of F 2. Grandmother of A 3. Aunt of C

Select the correct answer using the code given below

(a) 1 and 2 (b) 2 and 3
(c) 1 and 3 (d) All of these

13. V is married to W. R is the only sister of W. A is the mother of R. A has three children. G is the niece of R and P. V has no siblings. R is unmarried. Then, how is P related to V? « SBI PO 2018

(a) Mother-in-law (b) Sister
(c) Brother-in-law (d) Brother
(e) None of these

14. A is brother of B. B is sister of T. T is mother of P. If R is the maternal grandfather of P, how is T related to R? « UKPSC Asst. Conservator of Forest 2019

(a) Grand daughter (b) Sister
(c) Daughter (d) Wife

15. D is K's brother. M is K's sister. T is R's father who is M's brother, F is K's mother. Atleast how many sons do T and F have?

(a) 2 (b) 3
(c) 4 (d) Data inadequate
(e) None of these

16. F is the mother of T. T is the sister of W who is the only son of K. J is the brother of K. How is the mother of W related to K? « SSC Delhi Police Constable 2017

(a) Mother (b) Sister (c) Wife (d) Niece

17. A is the father of B, C is the brother of A, F is the sister of B. If M is the father of A, then establish relationship between F and C. « WBCS Pre 2018

(a) Daughter and father (b) Husband and wife
(c) Brother and sister (d) Niece and uncle

18. A, Q, Y and Z are different persons. Z is the father of Q. A is the daughter of Y and Y is the son of Z. If P is the son of Y and B is the brother of P, then

(a) B and Y are brothers (b) A is the sister of B
(c) Z is the uncle of B (d) Q and Y are brothers
(e) None of these

19. Sunil has a son Karna and a sister Sangeeta who is the mother of Jagdish and Vijay. Harnish is Jagdish's maternal uncle. How is Harnish related to Karna? « RRB NTPC 2016

(A) Brother (B) Father
(C) Nephew (D) Maternal uncle
(a) D (b) A (c) B (d) C

20. Given that

1. A is the brother of B. 2. C is the father of A.
3. D is the brother of E. 4. E is the daughter of B.

Then, the uncle of D is « UPSSSC Lower Sub Ordinate 2016

(a) A (b) B (c) C (d) E

DIRECTIONS ~(Q. Nos. 21 and 22) *Read the information given below and answer the questions.*

All the given members belong to the same the family. J is the brother of L. J is the only son of R. W is the father-in-law of L. D is the maternal grandfather of P, who is a male. Q is the only son of W. W is the grandfather of N and C is the daughter of N. « SBI Clerk 2018

21. How L is related to C?

(a) Mother (b) Son (c) Brother (d) Father
(e) None of these

22. How P is related to N?

(a) Mother (b) Son (c) Brother (d) Father
(e) None of these

DIRECTIONS ~ (Q. Nos. 23-25) *Study the following information and answer the given questions.*

B is married to S. G is the brother of B. A is the father of G. R is the only daughter of A. R is the mother of P. G is married to E. « RBI Office Assist. 2017

23. How is B related to P?

(a) Uncle (b) Aunt
(c) Cousin (d) Brother-in-law
(e) Cannot be determined

24. If Q is the mother-in-law of S, then how is Q related to R?

(a) Sister-in-law (b) Mother-in-law
(c) Grandmother (d) Aunt
(e) Mother

25. How is A related to E?

(a) Brother (b) Uncle
(c) Grandfather (d) Father-in-law
(e) Father

DIRECTIONS ~(Q. Nos. 26 and 27) *Study the following information carefully and answer the questions given below.*

Eight members are living in a family. Q is the only son of P. T is wife of U. T is sister of Q and R. V is daughter in law of W. S is son of T. W is the mother of Q. « IBPS RRB PO 2019

26. How is S related to R?

(a) Son (b) Daughter (c) Nephew (d) Niece
(e) Cannot be determined

27. How many male members are in the family?

(a) Four (b) Five (c) Three (d) Six
(e) None of these

DIRECTIONS ~(Q. Nos. 28-30) *Study the given information carefully to answer the given questions.*

L is the daughter of K. K is married to D. R is the mother of both D and M. M is the only son of Y. Y is the brother of G. « RBI Office Assistance 2016

28. If G is the mother of X, then how is X related to R?

(a) Sister-in-law (b) Granddaughter
(c) Brother-in-law (d) Cannot be determined
(e) Son

29. How is K related to Y?

(a) Father-in-law (b) Son-in-law
(c) Father (d) Nephew
(e) Son

30. How is L related to M?

(a) Niece (b) Aunt
(c) Granddaughter (d) Daughter
(e) Daughter-in-law

DIRECTIONS ~ (Q. Nos. 31-33) *Read the following information carefully to answer the questions that follow.*

I. There is a family of six members.
II. Members are A, B, C, D, E and F.
III. A and B are married couple, B being the female member.
IV. B is the daughter-in-law of F.
V. D is the only son of C.
VI. E and D are siblings.
VII. F's husband is not alive.
VIII. C is A's brother.

31. How is F related to C?

(a) Sister (b) Mother
(c) Aunt (d) Mother-in-law

32. How is E related to C?

(a) Mother (b) Aunt
(c) Cousin (d) Daughter

33. Who is C to B?

(a) Nephew (b) Brother
(c) Brother-in-law (d) Son-in-law

DIRECTIONS ~ (Q. Nos. 34-36) *Study the following information carefully and answer the questions given below.* « RBI Office Assistant 2020

There are eight members of three generations are living in a family. F is grandfather of G who is child of A. B and D are siblings of E who is only son of F. H is only grandson of F. C is spouse of B who have only one child. G is child of D.

34. How many male members are there in the family?

(a) Three (b) Four (c) Five (d) Six
(e) Can't be determined

35. How G is related to E?

(a) Daughter (b) Son (c) Nephew (d) Niece
(e) Can't be determined

36. If P is spouse of F, then how P is related to B?

(a) Father (b) Son (c) Mother (d) Aunt
(e) Can't be determined

Directions (Q.Nos 37-39) *Study the following information carefully and answer the questions given below.* « IBPS Clerk 2019

There are seven members in a family of three generation. A is mother of P. P is brother of G. K is married to G. S is aunt of M. K is child of L. S is sister of K.

37. If L is married to J, then how J is related to G?

(a) Grand daughter (b) Grand son
(c) Son-in-law (d) Daughter-in-law
(e) Can't be determined

38. If A is married to R, then how R is related to M?

(a) Grand father (b) Brother-in-law
(c) Uncle (d) None of these
(e) Can't be determined

39. How S is related to G?

(a) Sister (b) Sister-in-law
(c) Aunt (d) Mother-in-law
(e) None of these

DIRECTIONS ~ (Q. Nos. 40-42) *Study the following information carefully and answer the questions given below.*

Seven members are living in the family. Q is the daughter of P. B is the brother of R. G is the mother-in-law of A. B is married with A. B is the uncle of Q. D is the father of B. P is sister-in-law of B. « IBPS (PO) 2019

40. What is the relation of Q with respect to G?

(a) Brother (b) Sister-in-law
(c) Mother-in-law (d) Granddaughter
(e) Aunt

41. If C is the brother of B, then what is the relation of C with respect to Q?

(a) Aunt (b) Uncle (c) Father (d) Mother
(e) Sister

42. If M is the brother of Q, then what is the relation of M with respect to D?

(a) Grandson (b) Husband
(c) Father (d) Father-in-law
(e) Cousin

DIRECTIONS ~(Q. Nos. 43 and 44) *Study the information carefully and answer the questions given below.*

P is the husband of Q. R is the grandchild of P. P has only one child (son) who is married to T's child. T has only two children one son and one daughter. X is grandson of T. S is brother in law of son of T. U and V are children of T. W is married to the son of T. X is son of U's brother.

43. How is X related to V? « SBI PO Mains 2017
(a) Son (b) Daughter
(c) Son-in-law (d) Daughter-in-law
(e) Husband

44. If T is married to Y than how is T related to R?
(a) Grandfather (b) Grandmother
(c) Maternal Grandfather (d) Maternal Grandmother
(e) Either (c) or (d)

DIRECTIONS ~ (Q. Nos. 45 and 46) *Study the following information carefully and answer the questions given below.*

There are some members in the family. L is brother of M, who has only one son. A is the sister-in-law of R and is the mother of D. R is the child of M. A is daughter-in-law of K. G and T are siblings. G is the son of L. S is the sister-in-law of M and has only two sons. D is not the female member of the family. T and G are the cousins of J. S is not the sister of K, who is the grandmother of E. J has only one daughter. R is the daughter of K.

45. How is M related to 'T'?
(a) Father (b) Brother-in-law (c) Mother
(d) Grandfather (e) None of these

46. How is M related to J?
(a) Brother (b) Mother (c) Father (d) Sister
(e) None of these

Answers WITH EXPLANATIONS

1. (c) Let us draw the family diagram,

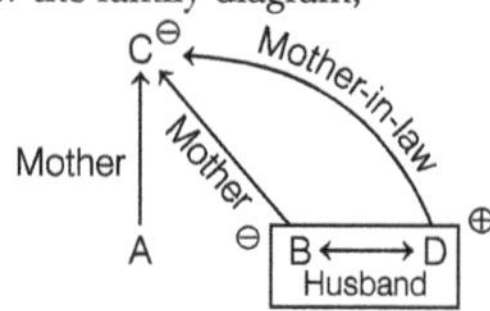

So, C is mother-in-law of D.

2. (c) From the information,

Z^- — mother → Q^-; C^- — sister → Q^- — sister → P^+; C^- — mother → A^+

Where,
– Denotes Female
+ Denotes Male

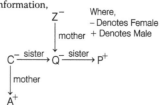

From the above blood-diagram, it is clear that P is the uncle of A.

3. (d) From the information, M ← Brother — N; B ← Brother — N; M ← Brother — D

M is Brother of B.

4. (c) Let us draw the family diagram,

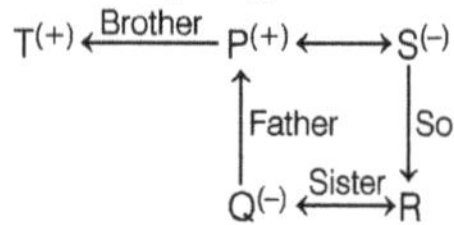

Clearly, S is the sister-in-law of T.

5. (d) Let us draw the family diagram,

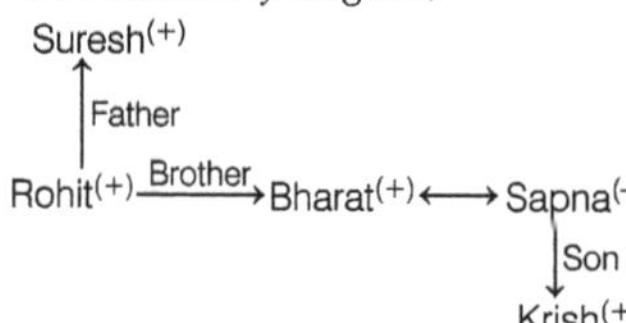

Clearly, Krish is the grandson of Suresh.

6. (a) According to the question,

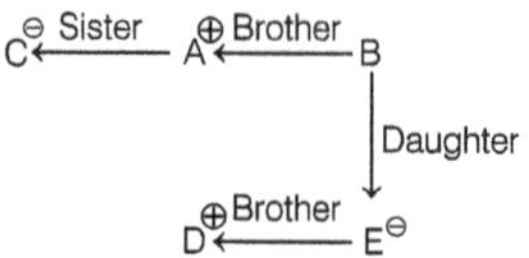

∴ A is the uncle of D.

7. (a) Let us draw the family diagram,

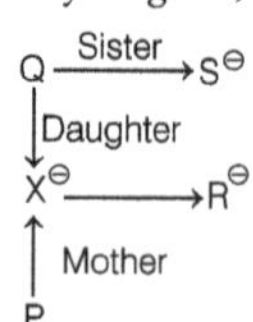

Clearly, S is the aunt of R.

8. (c) Let us draw the family diagram,

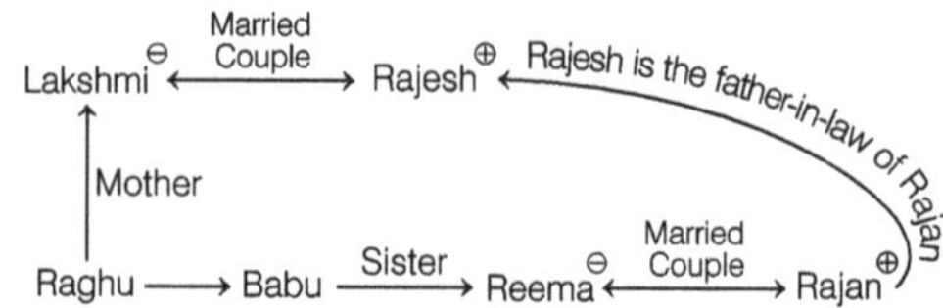

So, it is clear that Rajesh is the father-in-law of Rajan.

9. (d) Let us draw the family diagram,

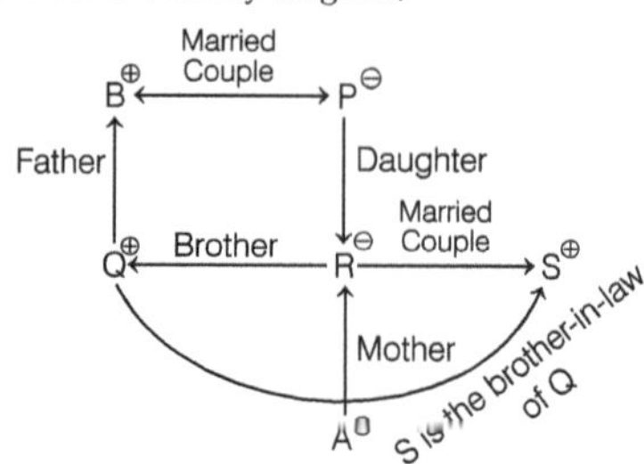

Hence, S is the brother-in-law of Q.

10. (*c*) Let us draw the family diagram,

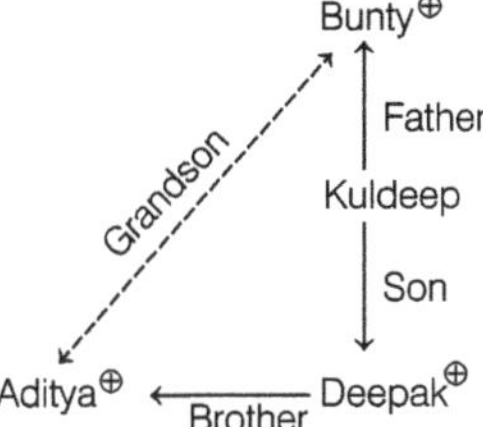

Clearly, Aditya is the grandson of Bunty.

11. (*c*) Let us draw the family diagram,

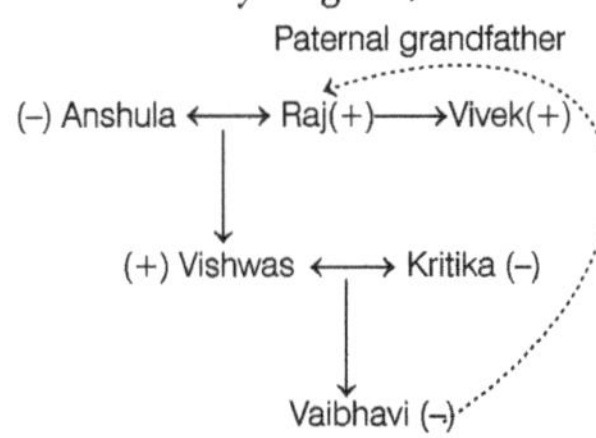

Clearly, Raj is paternal grandfather of Vaibhavi.

12. (*d*) Let us draw the family diagram,

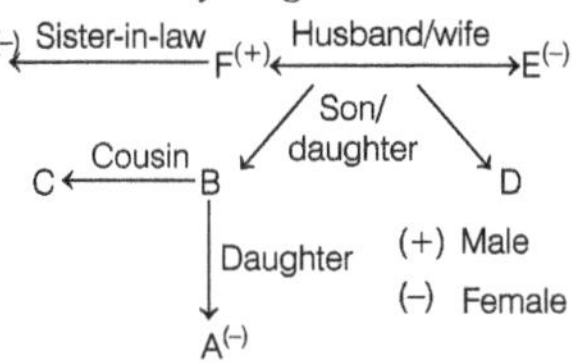

From the above diagram,

∴ E will be aunt of C, A will be grand-daughter of E and E is the wife of F.

∴ All the statements are correct.

13. (*c*) Let us draw the family diagram,

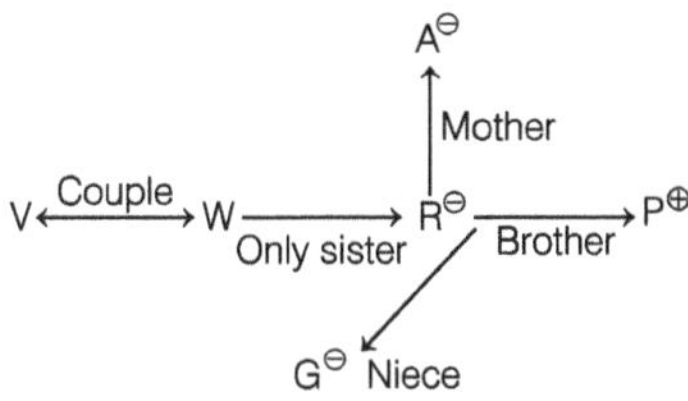

Clearly, P is the brother-in-law of V.

14. (*c*) According to the question,

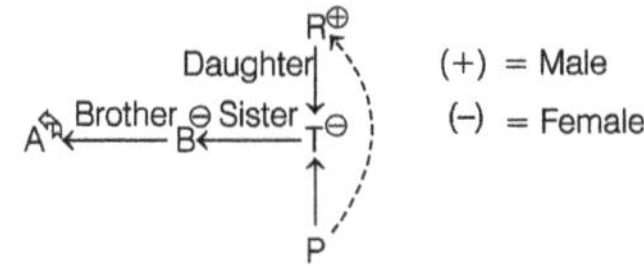

∴ T is the daughter of R.

15. (*a*) Let us draw the family diagram,

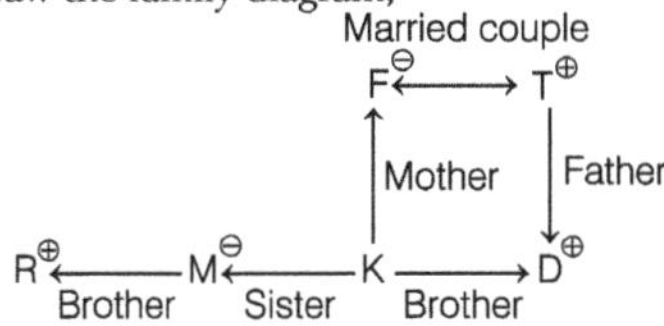

Clearly, F and T have atleast two son i.e. R and D.

16. (*c*) Let us draw the family diagram,

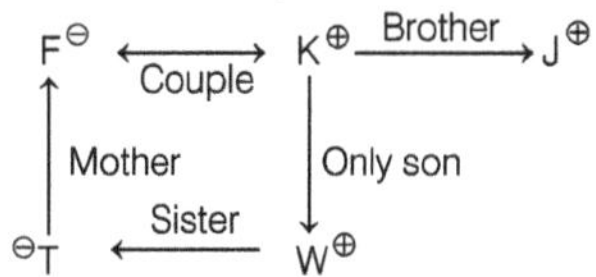

Clearly, F is the wife of K.

17. (*d*) Let us draw the following diagram,

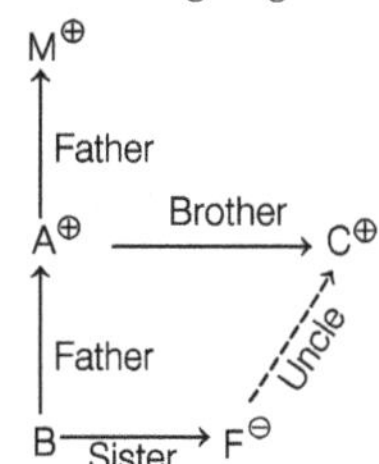

Clearly, F is niece and C is uncle.

18. (*b*) Let us draw the family diagram

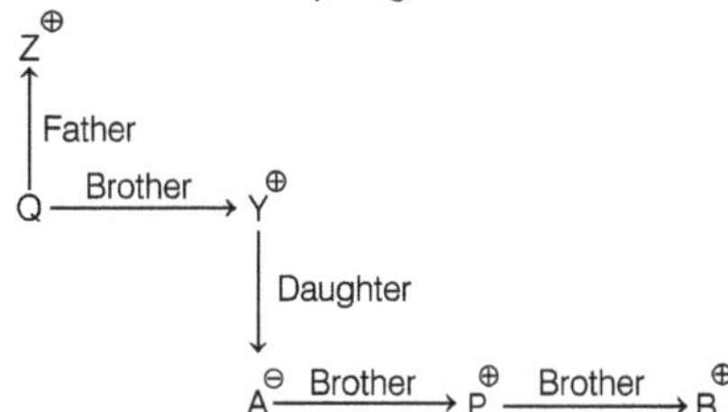

From the above diagram, it is clear that A is the sister of B.

19. (*a*) According to the question,

It is clear from diagram that Harnish is maternal uncle of Karna.

20. (*a*) According to the question,

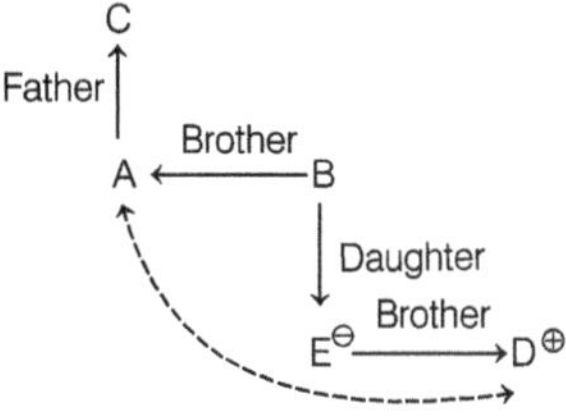

So, A is uncle of D.

Solutions (Q. Nos. 21 and 22) *Let us draw the family diagram,*

R⊖ Couple D⊕ W⊕
Only son Only son
J⊕ Brother L⊖ Couple Q⊕
Son
P⊕ ← N
C⊖

21. (*e*) Clearly, L is grandmother of C.

22. (*c*) Clearly, P is brother of N.

Solutions (Q. Nos. 23-25) *Let us draw the family diagram,*

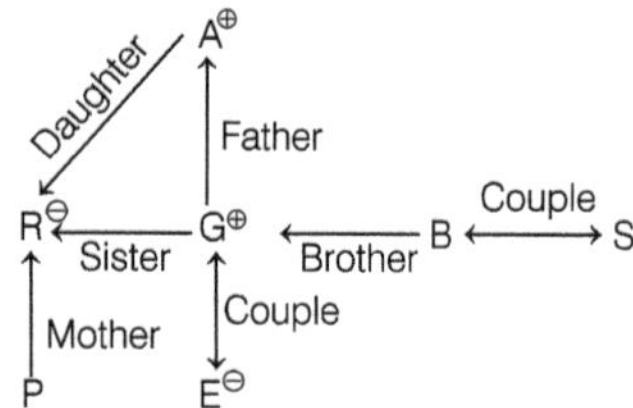

23. (*e*) Since, the gender of the B is not known.

24. (*e*) If Q is the mother-in-law of S, she is the wife of A. R is the daughter of A. So, Q is the mother of R.

25. (*d*) Clearly, A is the father-in-law of E.

Solutions (Q. Nos. 26 and 27) *Let us draw the family diagram,*

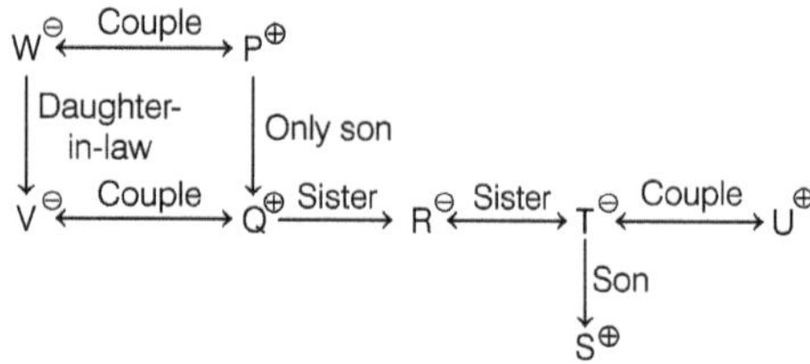

26. (*c*) S is nephew of R.

27. (*a*) Four male members are there in the family.

Solutions (Q. Nos. 28-30) *According to the question,*

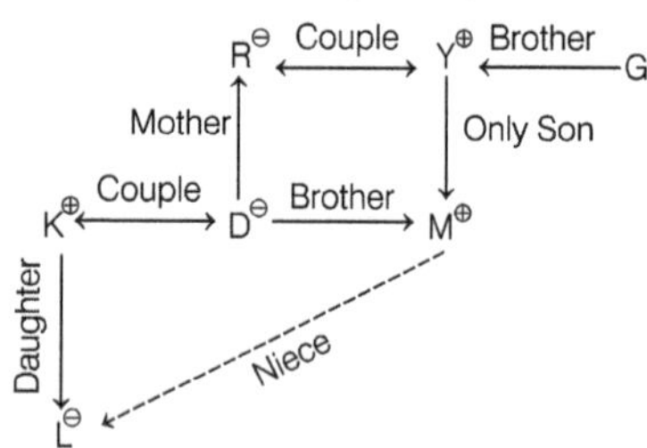

28. (*d*) Gender of X is not known, therefore relation of X related to R cannot be determined.

29. (*b*) K is the son-in-law of Y.

30. (*a*) L is the niece of M.

Solutions (Q. Nos. 31-33) *Let us draw the family diagram,*

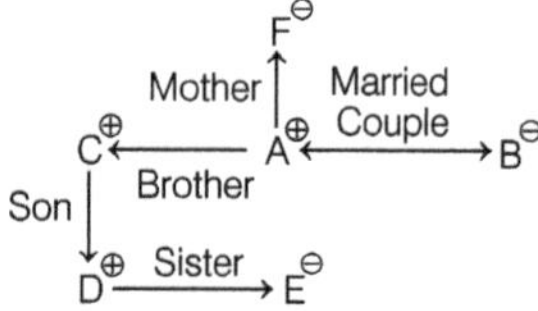

31. (*b*) F is C's mother.

32. (*d*) E is C's daughter.

33. (*c*) C is B's brother-in-law.

Solutions (Q.Nos. 34-36) *According to the given information,*

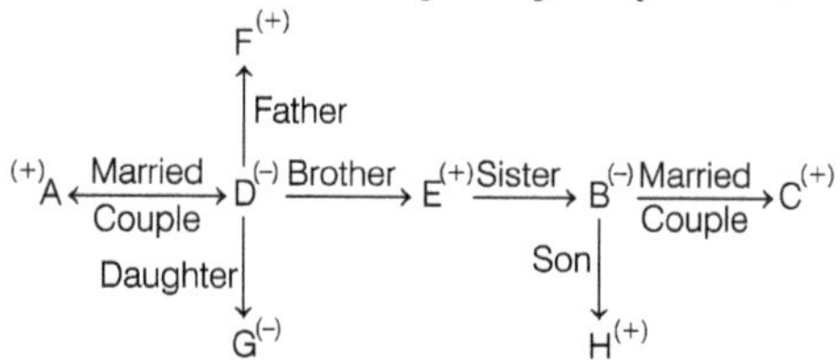

34. (*c*) Five male members (F, A, E, H and C) are there in the family.

35. (*d*) **36.** (*c*)

Solutions (Q. Nos. 37-39) *According to the given information.*

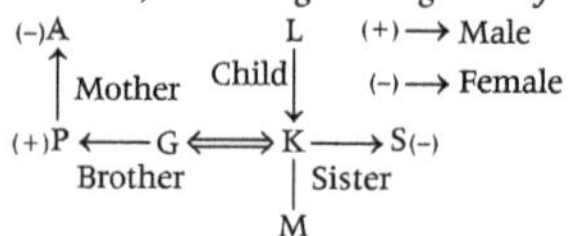

37. (*e*) The gender of both J and L is not clear. So, the relation of J with G can not be determined.

38. (*a*) If A is married to R then R will be the grandfather of M.

39. (*b*) S is the sister-in-law of G.

Solutions (Q. Nos. 40-42)

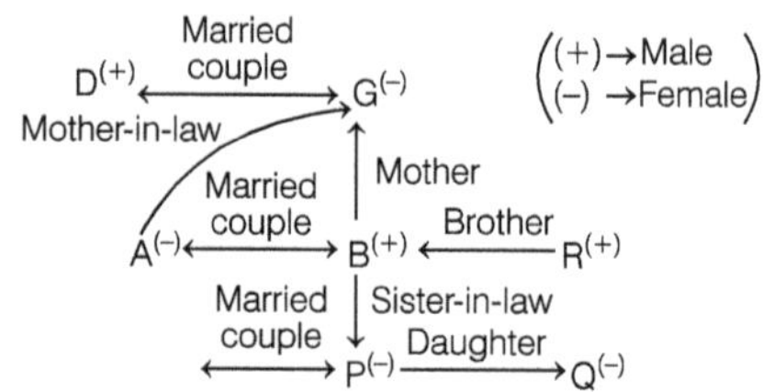

40. (*d*) Q is the granddaughter of G.

41. (*b*) If C is the brother of B, then he will be the uncle of Q.

42. (*a*) If M is the brother of Q, then he will be the grandson of D.

Solutions (Q.Nos. 43-44)

T P(+)⟺Q(−)
W(−)⟺V(+)— U(−)⟺S(+)
X(+) R

43. (*a*) X is the son of V.

44. (*e*) If T is married to Y than T will be either maternal grandfather or maternal grandmother of R.

Solutions (Q.Nos. 45-46)

K⟺M — L⟺S
(−) (+) (+) (−)
A⟺J — R G — T
(−) (+) (−) (+) (+)
E — D
(−) (+)

45. (*e*) M is the uncle of T.

46. (*c*) M is the father of J.

TYPE 03

Symbolically Coded Blood Relationship

In such questions certain symbols and codes such as +, –, ×, ÷, \$, *, Δ etc., are used to present information in coded form. The candidate is required to decode the information with the help of symbols to be used for making family diagram and then find out the relationship between the two required persons.

Points to be kept in mind while solving the questions

- If in a coded language 'A + B' means 'A is the father of B', then it is confirmed that A is male but nothing can be predicted about the gender of B (either B is son or daughter).
- If in a coded language 'A ÷ B' means 'A is the wife of B', then in this case, it is confirmed that A is female and the gender of B is also confirmed that he is male as B is the husband.

***Ex* 13** If A\$B means A is the husband of B. A#B means A is the brother of B and A*B means A is the mother of B, then what does P\$Q* R#S mean? « RRB ALP 2018

(a) P is the son of S (b) P is the brother-in-law of S
(c) P is the father of S (d) P is the brother of S

***Solution* (c)** By decoding the given information, with symbols of family diagram, we get

(A \$ B) = A⊕ ←Husband-Wife→ B⊖ | (A # B) = A⊕ ←Brother— B | (A* B) = A(–) ↑Mother B

Now, applying above decoding method, we draw the following family diagram,

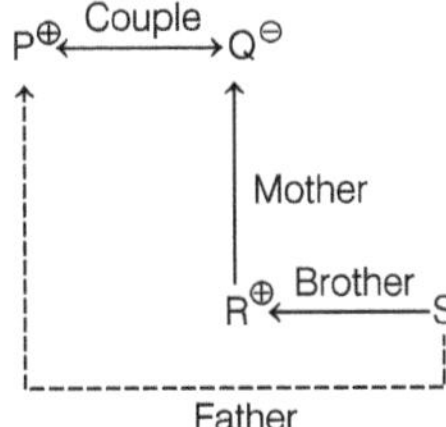

Clearly, P is the father of S.

DIRECTIONS ~ (Example Nos. 14 and 15) *Read the following information carefully and answer the questions given below.* « PNB (PO) 2010

I. 'P × Q' means 'P is sister of Q'.
II. 'P + Q' means 'P is mother of Q'.
III. 'P – Q' means 'P is father of Q'.
IV. 'P ÷ Q' means 'P is brother of Q'.

***Ex* 14** Which of the following represents 'M is the nephew of R'?

(a) M ÷ T – R (b) R ÷ T – M
(c) R × T + M × J (d) R ÷ T – M ÷ J
(e) None of the above

***Ex* 15** Which of the following represents 'W is grandfather of H'?

(a) W + T – H (b) W ÷ T – H (c) W × T + H (d) W ÷ T + H
(e) None of these

Solutions (Example Nos. 14 and 15) *By decoding given information with symbols of family diagram, we get*

(P × Q) = P⊖ ←Sister— Q | (P + Q) = P⊖ ↑Mother Q | (P – Q) = P⊕ ↑Father Q

(P ÷ Q) = P⊕ ←Brother— Q

14. (d) By applying above decoding method, we can check all the options for the required relationship.

(a) (M ÷ T– R) = Rejected

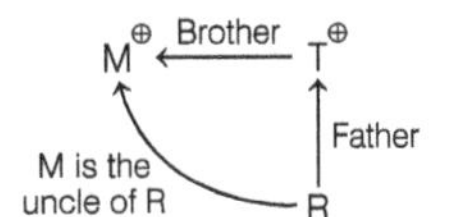

(b) (R ÷ T – M) = Rejected

R⊕ ←Brother— T⊕ ↑Father M

Here, gender of M is not known. So, M is either niece or nephew of R.

(c) (R × T + M × J) = Rejected

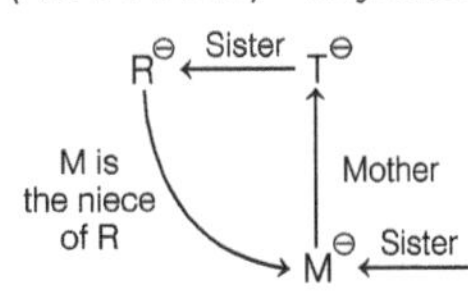

(d) (R ÷ T – M ÷ J) = Selected

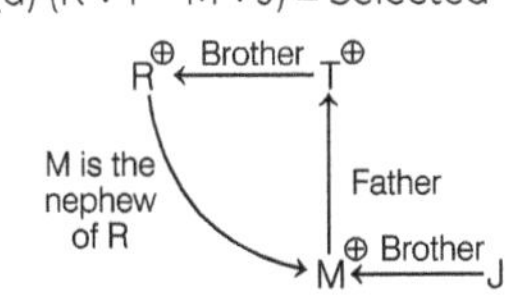

Hence, only option (d) satisfies the given relation between M and R.

15. (e) By applying above decoding method, we can check all the options for the required relationship.

(a) (W + T – H) = Rejected

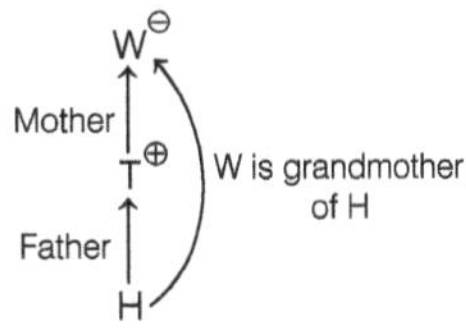

(b) (W ÷ T – H) = Rejected

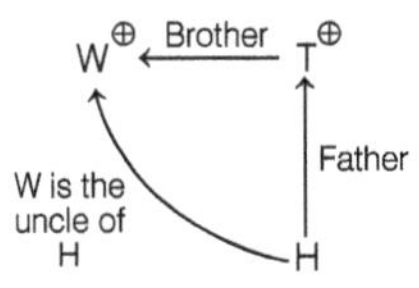

(c) (W × T + H) = Rejected

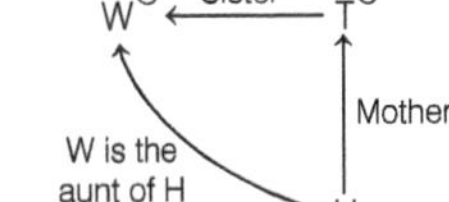

(d) (W ÷ T + H) = Rejected

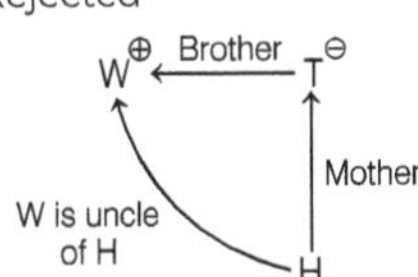

There is no option which satisfies the required relationship between W and H. So, option (e) is correct to answer.

Practice / CORNER 8.3

1. If A + B means 'A is the brother of B';
A × B means 'A is the son of B'; and A % B means 'B is the daughter of A' then which of the following means M is the maternal uncle of N? « FCI Uttarakhand 2018

(a) M + O × N (b) M % O × N + P
(c) M + O % N (d) None of these

2. If C$D means 'C is daughter of D', C&D means 'C is mother of D' and C % D means 'C is son of D', then what does W$X&Y%Z mean? « RRB ALP 2018

(a) Z is daughter of W.
(b) Z is wife of W.
(c) Z is father of W.
(d) Z is mother of W.

3. 'R + S' means 'R is mother of S', 'R – S' means 'R is wife of S', 'R × S' means 'R is son of S' and 'R ÷ S' means 'R is father of S'. « SSC (10 + 2) 2018

Which of the following represents K as the grandson of T?

(a) K + T × J × R (b) J + K × L × T
(c) R + T – S ÷ K (d) K + L × R ÷ T

4. If 'P – Q', means 'Q is son of P', 'P × Q' means 'P is brother of Q', 'P ÷ Q' means 'Q is sister of P' and 'P + Q' means 'P is mother of Q', then which of the following is definitely true about 'N × K – M ÷ L' ?

(a) K is father of L and M.
(b) L is daughter of K and niece of uncle N.
(c) K is father of L and M, his son and daughter respectively.
(d) M is uncle of K's brother N.

5. If P@Q means 'P is the husband of Q';J#L means 'L is the son of J' and N$M means 'N is the brother of M', then which of the below options definitely States that 'B is the mother of A'?
« UPSSSC Combined Lower Subordinate 2019

(a) A#B$C@D
(b) C$D@A#B
(c) B$C#A@D
(d) D@B#C$A

6. A + B means 'A is the daughter of B'.
A – B means 'A is the wife of B'.
A × B means 'A is the husband of B'.
A ÷ B means 'A is the father of B'.
If V + P × R + Q – S ÷ U × T, then which of the following statement is not correct?
« UPSSSC Combined Lower Subordinate 2019

(a) R is the mother of V.
(b) U is the brother of R.
(c) S is the paternal grandfather of V.
(d) Q is the mother of R.

7. A + B means 'B is the brother of A.
A – B means 'A is the mother of B'.
A × B means 'A is the son of B'.
A ÷ B means 'A is the son of B'.
If, P + R × T – Q ÷ S + U, then how is S related to R?
« SSC (CGL) 2020

(a) Son-in-law (b) Grandson
(c) Grandfather (d) Brother

8. 'A + B means 'A is the sister of B'.
'A – B means 'A is the brother of B'.
A × B means 'A is the mother of B'.
A ÷ B means 'A is the father of B'.
If V + S × Q – P ÷ T + R × U, then how is R related to S?
« SSC (CGL) 2019

(a) Grandson
(b) Daughter
(c) Grand-daughter
(d) Maternal Grandmother

9. A + B means 'A is the brother of B'.
A – B means 'A is the wife of B'.
A × B means 'A is the daughter of B'.
A ÷ B means 'A is the father of B'.
If P + S × Q × R – T ÷ V ÷ U, then how is T related to P?
« SSC (CGL) 2019

(a) Paternal grandmother
(b) Maternal grandmother
(c) Maternal grandfather
(d) Paternal grandfather

DIRECTIONS ~ (Q. Nos. 10 and 11) *Read the following information carefully to answer the questions that follow.*

I. 'A + B' means 'A is the son of B'.
II. 'A – B' means 'A is the wife of B'.
III. 'A × B' means 'A is the brother of B'.
IV. 'A ÷ B' means 'A is the mother of B'.
V. 'A = B' means 'A is the sister of B'.

10. What does 'P × R ÷ Q' mean?

(a) P is the nephew of Q. (b) P is the uncle of Q.
(c) P is the brother of Q. (d) P is the father of Q.

11. What does 'P = R ÷ Q' mean?

(a) P is the aunt of Q. (b) Q is the daughter of P.
(c) P is the sister of Q. (d) Q is the niece of P.

DIRECTIONS ~ (Q. Nos. 12-14) *Read the following information carefully and answer the questions given below.*

I. 'P × Q' means 'P is the father of Q'.
II. 'P – Q' means 'P is the sister of Q'.
III. 'P + Q' means 'P is the mother of Q'.
IV. 'P ÷ Q' means 'P is the brother of Q'.

12. In the expression B + D × M ÷ N, how is M related to B?
(a) Granddaughter
(b) Son
(c) Grandson
(d) Cannot be determined
(e) None of the above

13. Which of the following represent 'J is the son of F'?
(a) J ÷ R − T × F (b) J + R − T × F
(c) J ÷ M − N × F (d) Cannot be determined
(e) None of these

14. Which of the following represents 'R is the niece of M'?
(a) M ÷ K × T − R (b) M − J + R − N
(c) R − M × T ÷ W (d) Cannot be determined
(e) None of these

DIRECTIONS ~ (Q. Nos. 15-18) *Study the following information carefully to answer these questions.*
« SBI (PO) 2005

I. 'A $ B' means 'A is mother of B'.
II. 'A # B' means 'A is the father of B'.
III. 'A @ B' means 'A is the husband of B'.
IV. 'A % B' means 'A is daughter of B'.

15. P@Q$M#T indicates what relationship of P with T?
(a) Maternal grandfather (b) Paternal grandfather
(c) Maternal grandmother (d) Cannot be determined
(e) None of the above

16. Which of the following expressions indicates 'R is the sister of H'?
(a) R$D@F#H (b) H%D@F$R
(c) R%D@F$H (d) H$D@F#R
(e) None of these

17. If F@D%K#H, then how is F related to H?
(a) Brother-in-law (b) Sister
(c) Sister-in-law (d) Cannot be determined
(e) None of these

18. Which of the following expressions indicates 'H is the brother of N'?
(a) N%F@D$H (b) N%F@D%H
(c) N%F@D$H#R (d) H#R$D$N
(e) None of these

DIRECTIONS ~(Q. Nos. 19 and 20) *Read the following information carefully to answer the questions that follow.*

I. 'P + Q' means 'P is the father of Q'.
II. 'P − Q' means 'P is the mother of Q'.
III. 'P × Q' means 'P is brother of Q'.
IV. 'P ÷ Q' means 'P is the sister of Q.

19. Which of the following means 'H' is paternal grandfather of T?
(a) H + J + T (b) T × K + H
(c) H + J × T (d) H − J + T
(e) None of these

20. Which of the following means 'M is maternal uncle of T?
(a) M ÷ K − T (b) M × K − T
(c) M × K + T (d) M ÷ K + T
(e) None of these

DIRECTIONS ~ (Q. Nos. 21-26) *Read the following information carefully to answer the questions given below it.*

I. 'A + B' means that 'A is the father of B'.
II. 'A − B' means that 'A is the wife of B'.
III. 'A × B' means that 'A is the brother of B'.
IV. 'A ÷ B' means that 'A is the daughter of B'.

21. If it is given 'P ÷ R + S + Q', then which of the following is true?
(a) P is the daughter of Q (b) Q is the aunt of P
(c) P is the aunt of Q (d) P is the mother of Q

22. If it is given 'P − R + Q', then which of the following statements is true?
(a) P is the mother of Q (b) Q is the daughter of P
(c) P is the aunt of Q (d) P is the sister of Q

23. If it is given P × R ÷ Q, then which of the following is true?
(a) P is the uncle of Q (b) P is the father of Q
(c) P is the brother of Q (d) P is the son of Q

24. If it is given 'P × R − Q', then which of the following is true?
(a) P is the brother-in-law of Q
(b) P is the brother of Q
(c) P is the uncle of Q
(d) P is the father of Q

25. If 'P + R ÷ Q', then which of the following is true?
(a) P is the husband of Q
(b) P is the brother of Q
(c) P is the son of Q
(d) P is the father of Q

26. If 'P − R × Q', then which of the following is true?
(a) P is the sister of Q
(b) Q is the son of P
(c) Q is the husband of P
(d) P is the sister-in-law of Q

DIRECTIONS ~ (Q. Nos. 27-29) *Read the following information carefully to answer the question that follows.*

I. 'P * Q' means 'P is father of Q'.
II. 'P − Q' means 'P is sister of Q'.
III. 'P + Q' means 'P is mother of Q'.
IV. 'P ÷ Q' means 'P is brother of Q'. « NICL AO 2015

27. For B + D * M ÷ N, how M is related to B?
(a) Grand daughter (b) Son
(c) Grandson (d) Daughter
(e) None of these

28. Which of the following correctly represents J is son of F?
(a) J ÷ R − T * F (b) J + R − T * F
(c) J ÷ M − N * F (d) Cannot be determined
(e) None of these

29. Which of the following represents R is niece of M?
(a) M ÷ K * T − R (b) M − J + R − N
(c) R − M * T ÷ W (d) Cannot be determined
(e) None of these

DIRECTIONS ~ (Q. Nos. 30-31) *Read the following information carefully and answer the questions which follow.* « IBPS (PO) 2019

I. If, 'A × B' means 'A is father of B'
II. If, 'A + B' means 'A is wife of B'
III. If, 'A ÷ B' means 'A is daughter of B'
IV. If, 'A − B' means 'A is son of B'.

30. Which of the following relations are true based upon the relations given in the equations 'A − B × C + D − E'?
(a) C is mother of A. (b) E is wife of B.
(c) D is brother of A. (d) E is mother-in-law of C.
(e) None is true

31. What will come in the place of the question mark, to establish that Q is the nephew of T in the expression?
'Q? R ÷ S × T'
(a) + (b) × (c) − (d) ÷
(e) Either − or ÷

DIRECTIONS ~ (Q. Nos. 32-33) *In the following questions the symbols #, &, @, *, $, % and © are used with the following meanings as illustrated below. Study the following information and answer the given questions.*

P#Q — P is the son of Q.
P@Q — Q is the child of P.
P©Q — P is the parent of Q.
P$Q — P is elder than Q.
P*Q — P is the husband of Q.
P&Q — Q is the daughter-in-law of P.
P%Q — P is the wife of Q. « IBPS (PO Mains) 2017

32. If H*M©O$N#M, the age of N is 20 yr and age of H is 40 yr then what is the probable age of O?
(a) 17 yr (b) 15 yr (c) 23 yr (d) 45 yr
(e) 12 yr

33. If A@B*D&G%E$F#D then how F is related A?
(a) Grandfather (b) Grandson
(c) Daughter (d) Wife
(e) None of these

DIRECTIONS ~ (Q. Nos. 34-36) *In the following questions, the symbols #, &, @, *, $, % and © are used with the following meanings as illustrated below. Study the following information and answer the given questions.*

A@B — A is the child of B.
A©B — A is the parent of B.
A%B — A is elder to B.
A&B — A is younger to B.
A$B — A is brother of B.
A*B — A is wife of B.
A#B — A is sister-in-law of B.

34. If G©A@T#J*O$L@P©G then how is J related to A?
(a) Uncle (b) Brother-in-law
(c) Daughter-in-law (d) Aunt
(e) None of these

35. If G©A@T#J*O$L@P©G and P is the wife of U then how is P related to T?
(a) Mother
(b) Mother-in-law
(c) Sister-in-law
(d) Daughter-in-law
(e) None of these

36. If Y%H@J$U&K%Y, the age of H is 22 yr and age of K is 33 yr, so what can be the age of Y?
(a) 17 yr (b) 13 yr
(c) 29 yr (d) 40 yr
(e) 36 yr

Answers WITH EXPLANATIONS

1. (d) Given, A + B → A is the brother of B.
A × B → A is the son of B.
A % B → B is the daughter of A.
Hence, from none of the given option means M is the maternal uncle of N.

2. (c) Given, W$X&Y%Z
So, we get

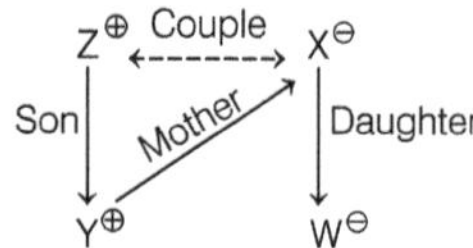

Clearly, Z is father of W.

3. (b) From the option (b),
J + K × L × T

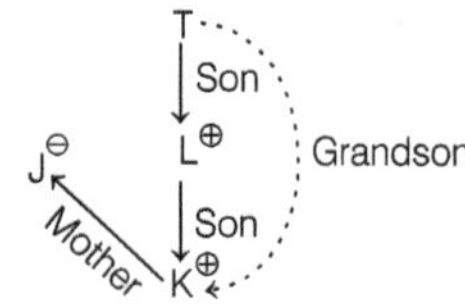

∴ K is grandson of T.

4. (b) According to the question,

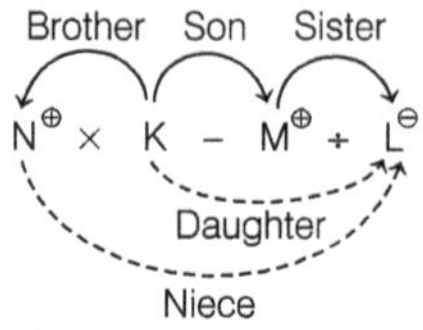

Clearly, L is daughter of K and niece of N.

5. (d) D @ B # C $ A

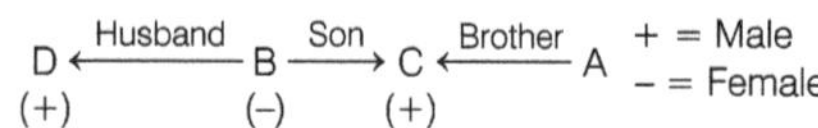

∴ It is clear that B is the mother of A.

6. (c)

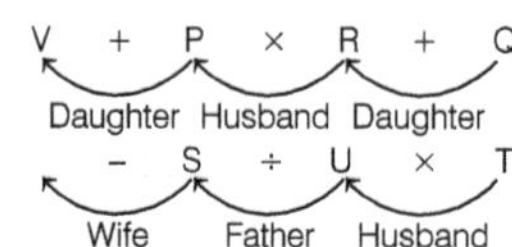

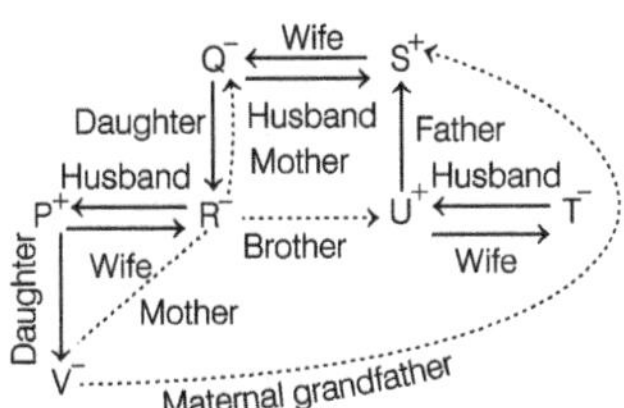

S is maternal grandfather of V.

7. (*a*) Blood relation figure is as follows:

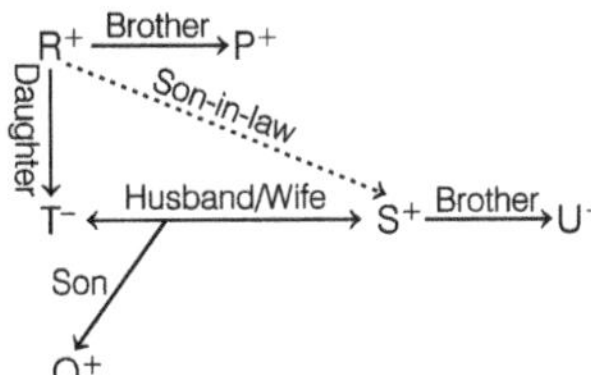

∴ S is son-in-law of R.

8. (*c*) $+ \rightarrow$ Sister, $- \rightarrow$ Brother, $\times \rightarrow$ Mother, $\div \rightarrow$ Father

$\Rightarrow V + S \times Q - P \div T + R \times U$

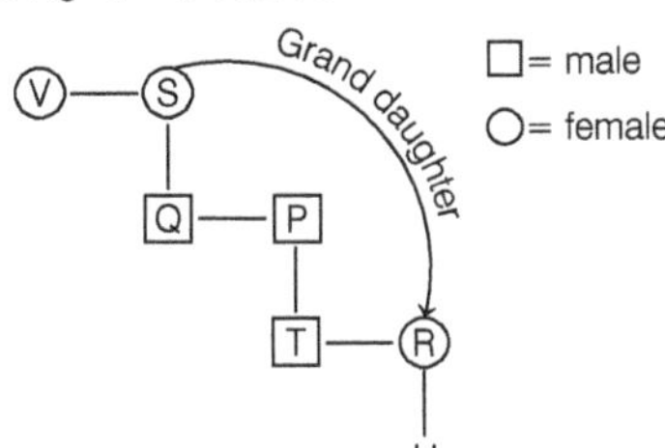

9. (*c*)

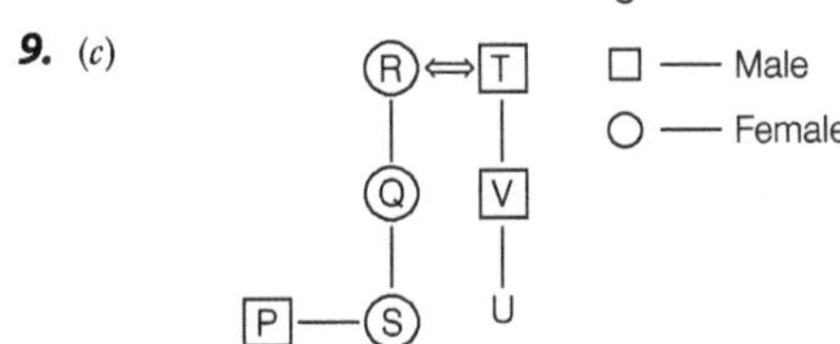

∴ T is maternal grandfather of P.

Solutions (Q. Nos. 10 and 11) *By decoding given information with symbols of family diagram, we get*

$(A + B) = B$, Son ↓ $A^{\oplus}$	$(A - B) = A^{\ominus} \longleftrightarrow B^{\oplus}$ (Married couple)	$(A \times B) = A^{\oplus} \xleftarrow{\text{Brother}} B$
$(A \div B) = A^{\ominus}$, Mother ↑ B	$(A = B) = A^{\ominus} \xleftarrow{\text{Sister}} B$	

10. (*b*) According to the question,

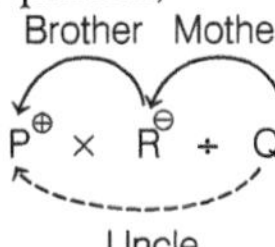

Clearly, P is the uncle of Q.

11. (*a*) According to the question,

Sister Mother

$P^{\ominus} = R^{\ominus} \div Q$

Aunt

Clearly, P is the aunt of Q.

Solutions (Q. Nos. 12-14) *By decoding given information with symbols of family diagram, we get*

$(P \times Q) = P^{\oplus}$, Father ↑ Q	$(P - Q) = P^{\ominus} \xleftarrow{\text{Sister}} Q$	$(P + Q) = P^{\ominus}$, Mother ↑ Q
$(P \div Q) = P^{\oplus} \xleftarrow{\text{Brother}} Q$		

12. (*c*) By applying above method for $(B + D \times M \div N)$, we draw the following family diagram

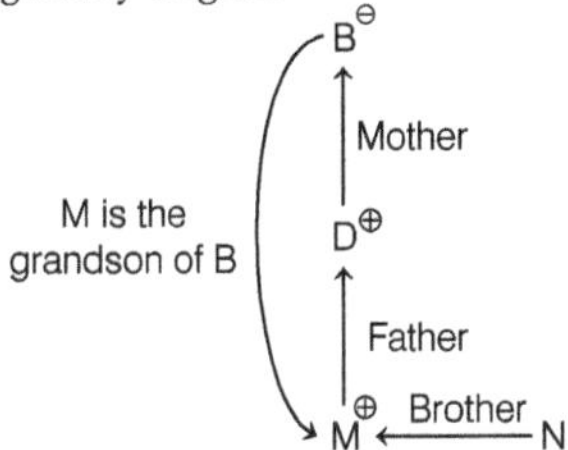

Hence, it is clear that M is the grandson of B.

13. (*e*) By applying above decoding method, we can check all the options for the required relationship.

(a) $(M \div T - R \times F) =$ Rejected

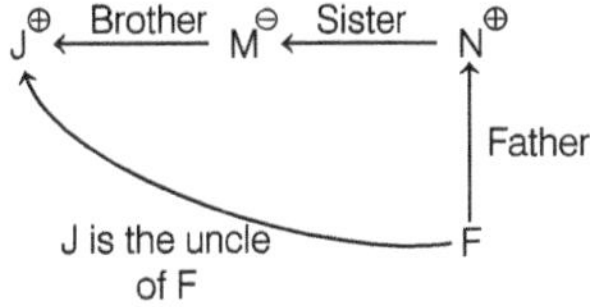

(b) $(J + R - T \times F) =$ Rejected

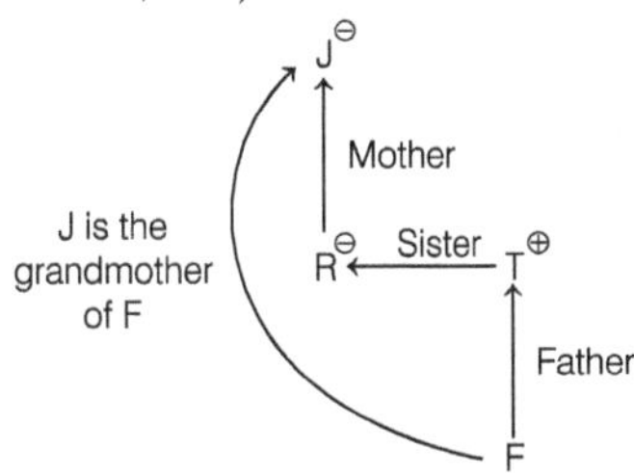

(c) $(J \div M - N \times F) =$ Rejected

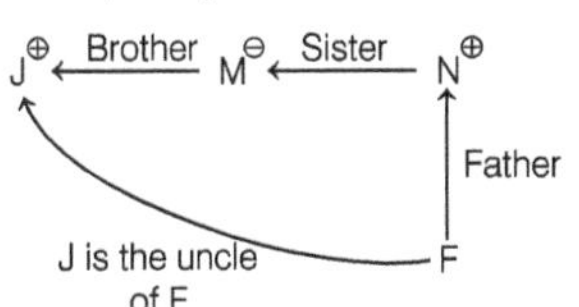

So, none of the options is correct to answer the question. So, option (e) will follow.

14. (*b*) By applying above decoding method, we can check all the options for the required relationship

(a) (M ÷ K × T – R) = Rejected

$M^{\oplus} \xleftarrow{\text{Brother}} K^{\oplus}$; K ↑ Father — $T^{\ominus}$; $T^{\ominus} \xleftarrow{\text{Sister}} R$

Here, gender of R is not known. So, R is either niece or nephew of M.

(b) (M – J + R – N) = Selected

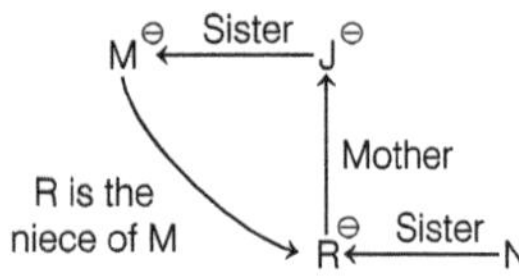

As, we have already obtained the answer, so there is no need to check other options.

Solutions (Q. Nos. 15-18) *By decoding given information with symbols of family diagram, we get*

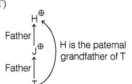

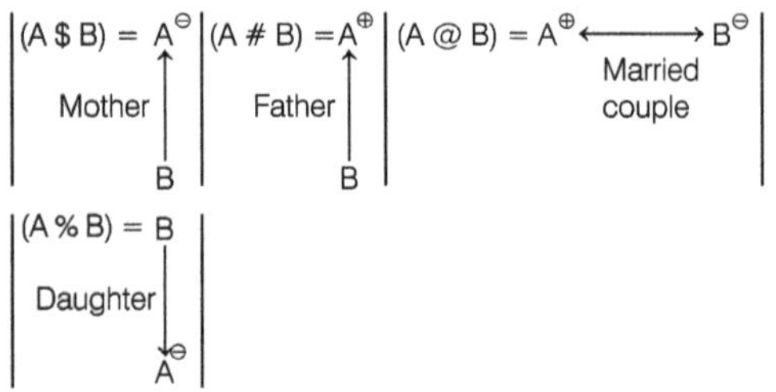

15. (*b*) According to the question,

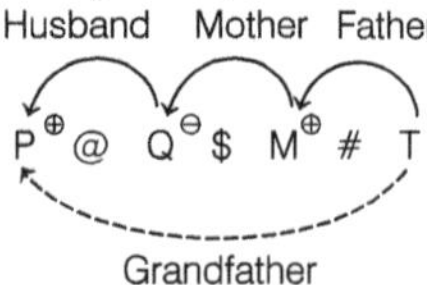

Clearly, P is paternal grandfather of T.

16. (*c*) According to the question, From option (c),

Clearly P 18.

17. (*a*) According to the question,

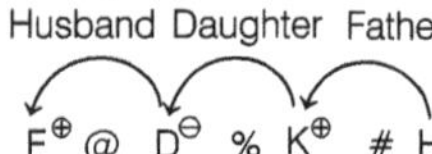

Clearly, F is the brother-in-law of H.

18. (*c*) According to the question, from option (c),

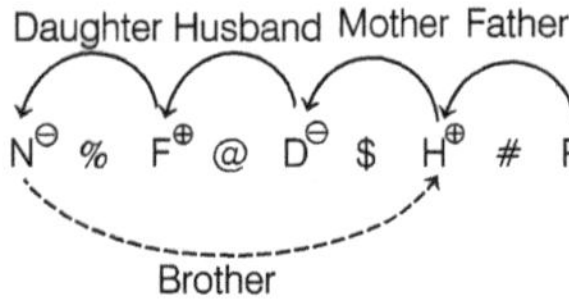

Clearly, H is the brother of N.

Solutions (Q. Nos. 19 and 20) *By decoding given information with symbols of family diagram, we get*

(P + Q) = $P^{\oplus}$	(P – Q) = $P^{\ominus}$	(P × Q) =	(P ÷ Q) =
Father ↑ Q	Mother ↑ Q	$P^{\oplus} \xleftarrow{\text{Brother}} Q$	$P^{\ominus} \xleftarrow{\text{Sister}} Q$

19. (*a*) By applying above decoding method, we can check all the options for the required relationship

(a) (H + J + T)

$H^{\oplus}$ ↑ Father — $J^{\oplus}$ ↑ Father — T

H is the paternal grandfather of T

Hence, there is no need to check other options, as we have already obtained the answer.

20. (*b*) By applying above decoding method, we can check all the options for the required relationship

(a) (M ÷ K – T) = Rejected

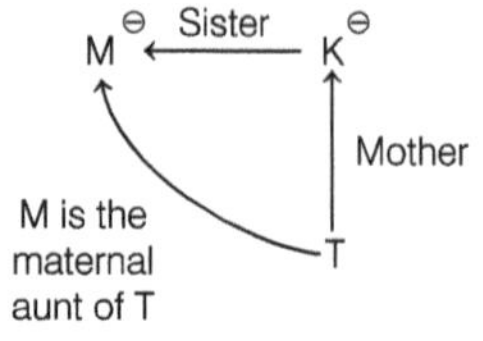

(b) (M × K – T) = Selected

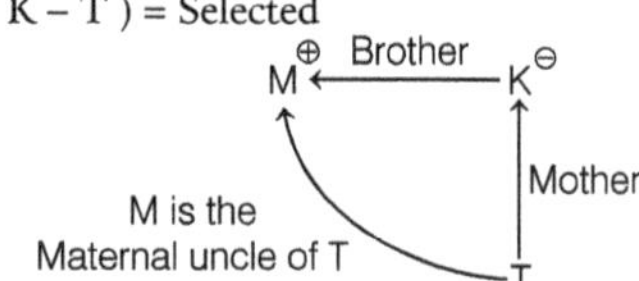

Hence, there is no need to check other options.

Solutions (Q. Nos. 21-26) *By decoding given information with symbols of family diagram, we get*

(A + B) = $A^{\oplus}$	(A – B) = $A^{\ominus}$ ⟷ $B^{\oplus}$	(A × B) = $A^{\oplus} \xleftarrow{\text{Brother}} B$
Father ↑ B	Married couple	

(A ÷ B) = B
Daughter ↓ $A^{\ominus}$

21. (*c*) According to the question,

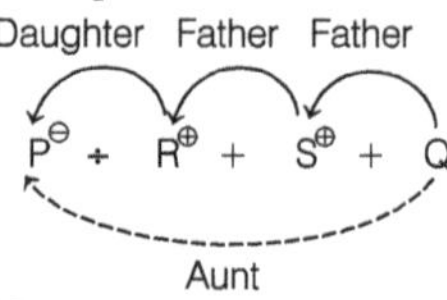

P is the aunt of Q is true.

22. (*a*) According to the question,

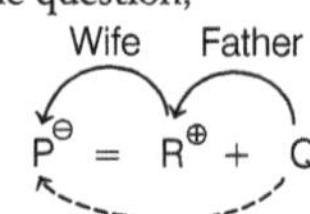

P is the mother of Q is true.

23. (*d*) According to the question,

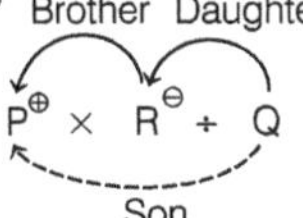

P is the son of Q.

24. (*a*) According to the question,

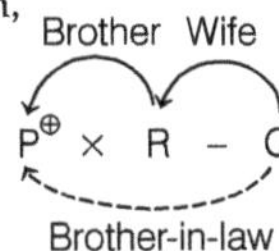

'P is the brother-in-law of Q' is true.

25. (*a*) According to the question,

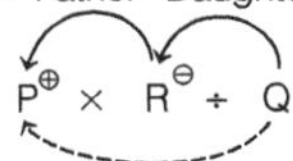

'P is the husband of Q' is true.

26. (*d*) According to the question,

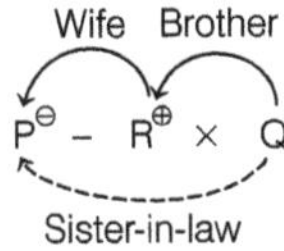

'P is sister-in-law of Q' is true.

Solutions (Q. Nos. 27-29) *By decoding given information with symbols of family diagram, we get*

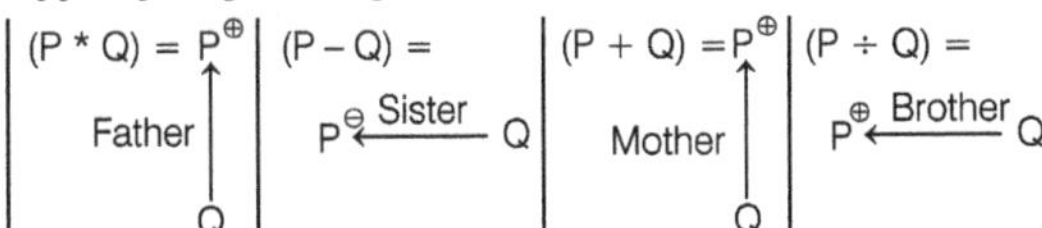

27. (*c*)

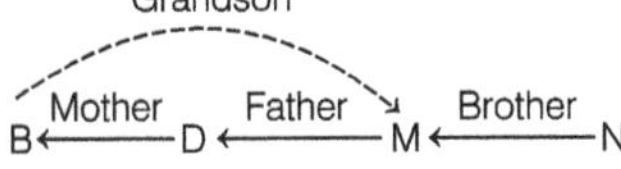

M is grandson of B.

28. (*a*) From option (a),

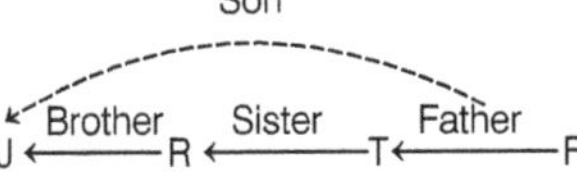

∴ Option (a) correctly shows J is son of F.

29. (*b*) From option (b),

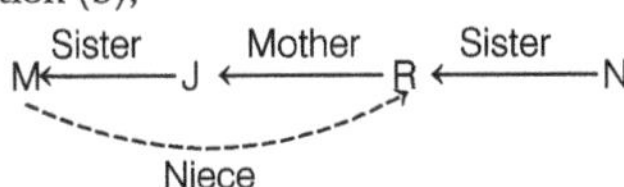

∴ Option (b) correctly shows that R is niece of M.

Solutions (Q. Nos. 30-31) *By decoding given information with symbols of family diagram, we get*

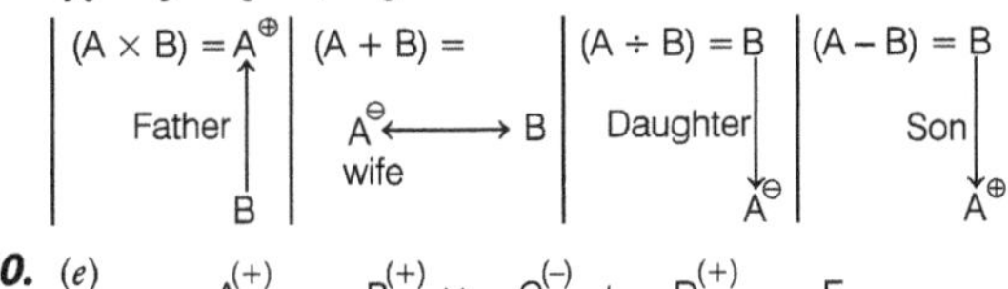

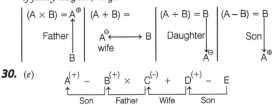

30. (*e*)

$A^{(+)} - B^{(+)} \times C^{(-)} + D^{(+)} - E$

Son Father Wife Son

Hence, none is true.

31. (*c*) From option (c), On putting sign (−) in place of question mark (?), we get

Nephew

$Q^{(+)} - R^{(-)} \div S^{(+)} \times T$

Son Daughter Father

From the above figure, it is clear that Q is the nephew of T.

Solutions (Q. Nos. 32-33) *By decoding given information with symbols of family diagram, we get*

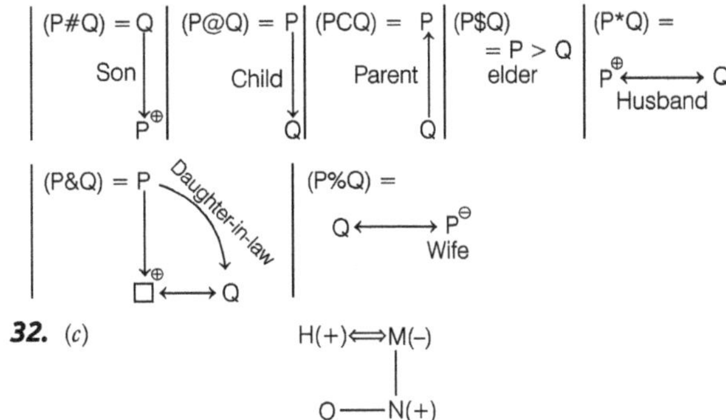

32. (*c*)

H(+)⟺M(−)
|
O—N(+)

Clearly, the possible age of O is 23 yr.

33. (*b*)

A
|
B(+)⟺D(−)
|
F(+)—E(+)⟺G(−)

Clearly, F is the grandson of A.

Solutions (Q. Nos. 34-36) *By decoding given information with symbols of family diagram, we get*

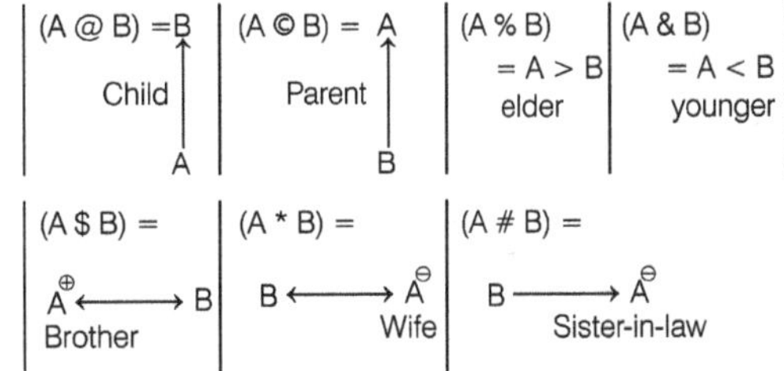

34. (*d*)

P
|
J(−)⟺O(+)—L—G(+)⟺T(−)
|
A

J is the aunt of A.

35. (*b*)

(−)P⟺U(+)
|
J(−)⟺O(+)—L—G(+)⟺T(−)
|
A

P is the mother-in-law of T.

36. (*c*)

J(+)— U<K
|
Y>H
& K>Y>H

Y's age is more than 22 yr and less than 33 yr. So, the age of Y can be 40 yr.

Master Exercise

1. K is the mother-in-law of P. P is married to S. K has only one daughter. L is the daughter of P. How is S related to K? « UP Police SI 2017
(a) Daughter (b) Son-in-law
(c) Son (d) Mother

2. Pointing towards a girl, Anurag says, "This girl is the daughter of the only child of my father". What is the relation of Anurag's wife with the girl?
(a) Sister (b) Aunt
(c) Daughter (d) Mother
(e) None of these

3. D is B's father, B is C's sister-in-law and A's daughter. How is A related to D?
(a) Wife (b) Mother
(c) Father (d) Husband

4. A's mother is sister of B and daughter of C. D is the daughter of B and sister of E. How is C related to E?
(a) Sister
(b) Mother
(c) Father
(d) Grandmother or grandfather

5. S is the only son of V. V is married to R. M is the daughter of R. R is the grandmother of A. How is S definitely related to A? « SBI PO 2018
(a) Uncle (b) Cannot be determined
(c) Father (d) Brother
(e) Sister

6. Pointing to a lady, a man said, "The son of her only brother is the brother of my wife." How is the lady related to the man?
(a) Daughter (b) Sister of father-in-law
(c) Grandmother (d) Mother's sister
(e) None of these

7. Sohan said to Mohan, "This girl is the wife of the grandson of my mother". How is Sohan related to this girl?
(a) Grandfather (b) Father
(c) Husband (d) Father-in-law

8. Kamal told Vimal, "Yesterday I defeated the only brother of the daughter of my grandmother." Whom did Kamal defeated?
(a) Father (b) Son
(c) Brother (d) Father-in-law

9. A and B are brothers, C and D are sisters. A's son is D's brother, then how is B related to C?
(a) Father (b) Brother
(c) Grandfather (d) Uncle

10. D is the son- in-law of B, who is the brother-in-law of A, who is the brother of C. How is A related to B?
(a) Father (b) Son
(c) Data inadequate (d) None of these

11. Pointing to a lady, Chouhan said, 'She is the only daughter of my father-in-law's wife. How is this lady related to Chouhan?
(a) Mother (b) Wife
(c) Cousin (d) Sister

12. Pointing towards a Boy Veena said "He is the son of only son of my grandfather". How is that boy related to Veena?
(a) Uncle (b) Brother
(c) Cousin (d) Data inadequate

13. P is the only son of Q who is the only daughter of S. D is the mother of B and daughter-in-law of Q. How is B related to Q?
(a) Grandson (b) Granddaughter
(c) Son (d) Cannot be determined

14. P's father is 'Q's son. M is the paternal uncle of P and N is the brother of Q. How is N related to M?
(a) Brother (b) Nephew
(c) Cousin (d) None of these

15. Anil is brother of Daya who is the son of Chandra. Bimal is Chandra's father. In terms of relationship, what is Anil of Bimal?
(a) Son (b) Grandson
(c) Brother (d) Grandfather

16. P's father is Q's son. M is the paternal uncle of P and N is the brother of Q. How is M related to N?
(a) Nephew (b) Cousin
(c) Data inadequate (d) None of these

17. Introducing Shyam, a lady said, 'The father of his father-in-law is my father-in-law'. How is Shyam related to the lady?
(a) Son (b) Husband
(c) Son-in-law (d) Father

18. There are six members in a family. A is the father of D, E is the grandfather of D. B is the daughter-in-law of C. F is the uncle of D. what is the relationship of C with F?
(a) Sister (b) Mother-in-law
(c) Mother (d) Data inadequate

19. Pointing to a man on the stage, Rita said, "He is the brother of the daughter of the wife of my husband". How is the man on the stage related to Rita?
(a) Son (b) Husband
(c) Cousin (d) Nephew

20. Deepak said to Nitin, "That boy playing with the football is the younger of the two brothers of the daughter of my father's wife". How is the boy playing football related to Deepak?

(a) Son (b) Brother
(c) Cousin (d) Brother-in-law

21. Anil introduced Rohit as the son of the only brother of his father's wife. How is Rohit related to Anil?

(a) Cousin (b) Son
(c) Uncle (d) Son-in-law

22. Introducing Amrita, Raj said, "Her mother is the only daughter of my mother-in law". How is Raj related to Amrita?

(a) Husband (b) Father
(c) Wife (d) Uncle

23. If A + B means 'A is the mother of B', A – B means 'A is the brother of B'; A % B means 'A is the father of B' and A × B means 'A is the sister of B', which of the following shows that 'P is the maternal uncle of Q'? « SSC MTS 2018

(a) Q – N + M × P (b) P + S × N – Q
(c) P – M + N × Q (d) Q – S % P

24. A man showed a boy next to him and said, "He is the son of my wife's sister-in-law but I am the only child of my parents." How is my son related to him?

(a) Cousin (b) Brother
(c) Uncle (d) Nephew

25. Sunil is the son of Kesav. Simran, Kesav's sister, has a son Maruti and daughter Sita. Prem is the maternal uncle of Maruti. How is Sunil related to Maruti?

(a) Cousin (b) Uncle
(c) Brother (d) Nephew

26. Based on the statements given below, find out who is the uncle of 'P'. « UKPSC 2016

I. K is the brother of J.
II. M is the sister of K.
III. P is the brother of N.
IV. N is the daughter of J.

(a) K (b) J
(c) N (d) Cannot be determined

27. Suppose A is the daughter of B, B is the daughter of C, C is the brother of D and D is the mother of E. If E is male, how is A related to E? « UPSSSC VDO 2018

(a) Nephew (b) Niece
(c) Brother (d) Sister

28. Looking at the photo of a man, Sunil said, "His mother is the wife of my Father's son. Brothers and sisters I have none." How the man in the photo is related to Sunil?

(a) Sunil's son (b) Sunil's uncle
(c) Sunil's nephew (d) Sunil's cousin
(e) None of these

29. Pinky, who is Victor's daughter, say to Lucy, "Your mother Rosy is the younger sister of my father, who is the third child of Joseph". How is Joseph related to Lucy?

(a) Father-in-law (b) Father
(c) Maternal uncle (d) Grandfather

30. Pointing to a lady, Rishi said, 'The son of her brother is the brother of my wife'. How is this lady related to Rishi?

(a) Mother-in-law (b) Mother's sister
(c) Sister of father-in-law (d) None of these

31. 'S × T' means that S is the mother of T, 'S +T means that S is the father of T, 'S –T' means that S is the sister of T. On the basis of this information, you have to select the option which shows that A is the grandfather of T?

(a) A + S + B – T (b) A × B + C – T
(c) A + B – C × T (d) A – C + B × T

32. Z is maternal uncle of Y, X is maternal grandfather of Z. S is grandson of X. How is S related to Y?

(a) Maternal grandfather
(b) Maternal uncle
(c) Cousin brother
(d) None of the above

33. Arti and Saurabh are the children of Mr and Mrs Shah. Ritu and Shaki are the children of Mr and Mrs Mehra. Saurabh and Ritu are married to each other and two daughter Mukti and Shruti are born to them. Shakti is married to Rina and two children Subhash and Reshma are born to them. How is Arti related to Shruti?

(a) Mother (b) Mother-in-Law
(c) Sister (d) Aunt

34. T, S and R are three brothers. T's son Q is married to K and they have one child Rahul blessed to them. M the son of S is married to H and this couple is blessed with a daughter Madhvi. R has a daughter N who is married to P. This couple has one daughter Karuna born to them. How is Madhvi related to S ? « MAT 2013

(a) Daughter (b) Niece
(c) Granddaughter (d) None of these

DIRECTIONS ~ (Q. Nos. 35-38) *Read the following information carefully to answer the questions that follow.*

There are six children taking part in an essay competition, namely A, B, C, D, E and F. A and E are brothers. F and D are the sisters of E. C is the only son of A's uncle. B and D are the daughters of the brother of C's father.

35. How is D related to A?

(a) Uncle (b) Sister
(c) Niece (d) Cousin

36. How many male competitors are there?

(a) 6 (b) 5 (c) 4 (d) 3

37. How many female competitors are there?
(a) 5 (b) 4
(c) 3 (d) 2

38. How is C related to F?
(a) Cousin (b) Brother
(c) Son (d) Uncle

DIRECTIONS ~ (Q. Nos. 39-41) *Read the following information carefully and answer the questions given below.*

T is sister of D. D is married to P. P is son of M. T is mother of J. Y is father of U. Y has only one son and one daughter. U is daughter of T. Q is son of D. « SBI PO 2015

39. How is P related to T?
(a) Brother (b) Cousin
(c) Brother-in-law (d) Cannot be determined
(e) None of these

40. How is J related to D?
(a) Son (b) Niece
(c) Son-in-law (d) Nephew
(e) Daughter

41. How is Q related to M?
(a) Son-in-law (b) Grandson
(c) Nephew (d) Son
(e) Cannot be determined

DIRECTIONS ~ (Q. Nos. 42-44) *Study the following information carefully to answer the given questions.*

S is the husband of Q. A is the brother of D. A is the only son of B. D is the sister of Q. R is married to D. M is the father of R. N is the daughter of Q. « IBPS RRB Officer 2016

42. If V is the grandfather of N, then how is B related to R?
(a) Uncle (b) Mother-in-law
(c) Grandmother (d) Aunt
(e) Father-in-law

43. How is S related to A?
(a) Father (b) Grandfather
(c) Brother-in-law (d) Uncle
(e) Nephew

44. How is D related to N?
(a) Mother (b) Sister-in-law
(c) Cousin (d) Mother-in-law
(e) Aunt

DIRECTIONS ~ (Q. Nos. 45-48) *Read the information carefully and answer the following questions.*

J is married to C. B and D are the children of C. D is married to daughter of K, who is married to M. K is mother of R, who is husband of N. H is the grandson of C and K. L is daughter of N. V is only sibling of H. D has only one daughter. « SBI PO 2019

45. How is D related to K?
(a) Son (b) Wife
(c) Son-in-law (d) Daughter
(e) None of these

46. If T is only daughter of K, then how is T related to D?
(a) Wife (b) Son-in-law
(c) Daughter (d) Husband
(e) None of these

47. How is L related to K?
(a) Wife (b) Granddaughter
(c) Daughter (d) Son
(e) Grandson

48. Who is father of R?
(a) M (b) D
(c) B (d) J
(e) C

DIRECTIONS ~ (Q. Nos. 49-51) *Study the following information carefully to answer the questions based on it.*

A is the mother of B. B is the sister of C. D is the son of C. E is the brother of D. F is the mother of E. G is the grand daughter of A. H has only two children B and C. « IBPS PO/MT 2017

49. How is F related to H?
(a) Son-in-law (b) Daughter-in-law
(c) Father-in-law (d) Granddaughter
(e) Niece

50. How is C related to E?
(a) Father (b) Son
(c) Mother (d) Cousin
(e) Grandfather

51. Who is mother of G, if sister of C is unmarried?
(a) C (b) B
(c) F (d) Either B or F
(e) Either C or F

DIRECTIONS ~(Q. Nos. 52-54) *Read the following information carefully to answer the questions that follow*

A family consists of six members P, Q, R, X, Y and Z. Q is the son of R but R is not the mother of Q. P and R are married couple. Y is the brother of R. X is the daughter of P and Z is the brother of P.

52. Who is the brother-in-law of R?
(a) P (b) Z (c) Y (d) X

53. How many female members are there in the family?
(a) One (b) Two
(c) Three (d) Four

54. Which of these is a pair of brothers?
(a) P and X (b) P and Z
(c) Q and X (d) R and Y

55. In a family, there are seven only child persons, comprising two married couples, T is the only child of M and the grandson of K. M is a widower. M and R are brothers and W is the daughter-in-law of J, who is the mother of R and the grandmother of 'D'. How is D related to M?
(a) Son (b) Son-in-law
(c) Nephew or niece (d) Brother

56. A family of two generations consisting of six members P, Q, R, S, T and U has three males and three females. There are two married couples and two unmarried siblings. U is P's daughter and Q is R's mother-in-law. T is an unmarried male and S is a male. Which one of the following is correct? « UPSC CSAT 2020

(a) R is U's husband (b) R is S's wife
(c) S is unmarried (d) None of these

57. M said to N, "You are my daughter-in-law's father-in-law's mother-in-law's son". How is N related to M? « UPSSSC Mandi Parishad 2018

(a) N is the brother-in-law of M
(b) N is the father of M
(c) N is the son of M
(d) N is the brother of M

58. Mohan is the Son of Arun's father's sister. Prakash is the son of Reva, who is the mother of Vikas and grandmother of Arun. Pranab is the father of Neela and the grandfather of Mohan. Reva is the wife of Pranab. How is the wife of Vikas related to Arun's Aunt? « NIFT (PG) 2013

(a) Sister (b) Sister-in-law
(c) Niece (d) None of these

DIRECTIONS ~ (Q. Nos. 59-62) *Study the given information carefully to answer the given questions.* « MHT MBA 2017

L's sibling is married to J's daughter. K is the wife of J. Q is the brother of J's only son-in-law. P is the only brother of Q. A is the mother of L. M is the only sibling of A's daughter-in-law. Both Q and M are unmarried. V is the nephew of M. A has only three children. L's spouse has no siblings.

59. If R is the sister-in-law of L, then how is R related to P?

(a) Aunt (b) Daughter (c) Wife (d) Cousin
(e) Sister-in-law

60. How is V related to A?

(a) Grandson (b) Husband
(c) Cannot be determined (d) Son-in-law
(e) Brother-in-law

61. If S is the son of L, then how is S related to Q?

(a) Father (b) Brother-in-law
(c) Uncle (d) Cousin
(e) Nephew

62. How is K related to M?

(a) Sister (b) Mother-in-law
(c) Daughter (d) Mother
(e) Aunt

63. If A@B means 'A is the daughter of B', A# B means 'A is the sister of B' and if A*B means 'A is the father of B', then what does W@X*Y#Z means if W has one brother and one sister? « UPSSSC Mandi Parishad 2018

(a) Z is the grandson of X.
(b) Z is the granddaughter of X.
(c) Z is the brother of X.
(d) Z is the son of X.

DIRECTIONS ~ (Q. Nos. 64-68) *Read the information carefully and answer the following questions.* « SBI (PO) 2013

If 'A+ B' means 'A is the father of B'.
If 'A× B' means 'A is the sister or B'.
If 'A $ B' means 'A is the wife of B'.
If 'A % B' means 'A is the mother of B'.
If 'A÷ B' means 'A is the son of B'.

64. What should come in place of the question mark, to establish that J is the brother of T in the expression?

J ÷ P % H ? T % L

(a) × (b) ÷
(c) $ (d) Either + or X
(e) None of these

65. Which among the given expressions indicate that M is the daughter of D?

(a) L % R $ D + T × M
(b) L + R $ D + M × T
(c) L % R % D + T ÷ M
(d) L $ D ÷ R % M ÷ T
(e) None of the above

66. Which among the following options is true, if the expression 'I + T % J × L ÷ K' is definitely true?

(a) L is the daughter of T.
(b) K is the son-in-law of I.
(c) I is the grandmother of L.
(d) J is the brother of L.
(e) None of the above

67. Which among the following expressions is true, if Y is the son of X is definitely false?

(a) W % L× T× Y÷ X
(b) W+ L× T× Y÷ X
(c) X+ L× T× Y÷ W
(d) W $ X + L + Y + T
(e) W % X× T× Y÷ L

68. What should come in place of the question mark, to establish that T is the sister-in-law of Q in the expression

R % T × P ? Q+ V

(a) + (b) %
(c) × (d) $
(e) Either $ or ×

69. Rajesh, his sister, his son and his daughter are fond of golf and often play together. The following statement are true for all the four.

I. The best player's twin and worst player are of the opposite sex.

II. The best player and the worst player are of the same age. Assuming that both twins are members of the group of four, who is the best player. « UGC NET 2018

(a) Daughter of Rajesh
(b) Son of Rajesh
(c) Rajesh
(d) Sister of Rajesh

Answers WITH EXPLANATIONS

1. (*a*) According to the question,

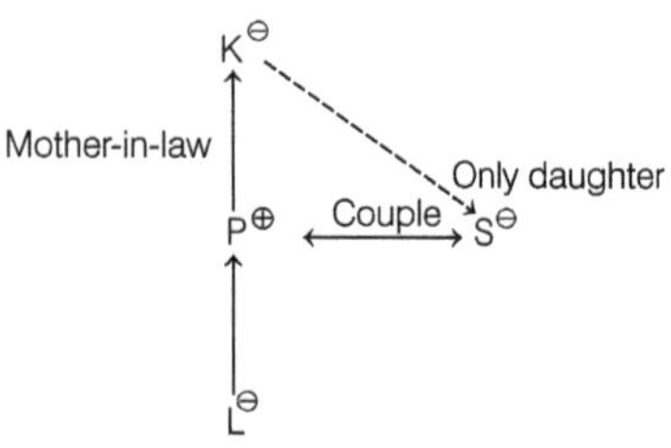

Clearly, S is the daughter of K.

2. (*d*) Let us draw the family tree

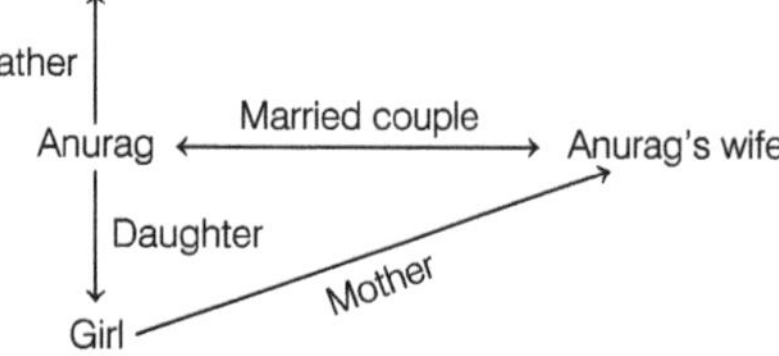

Clearly, Anurag's wife is the mother of the girl.

3. (*a*) Let us draw the family diagram,

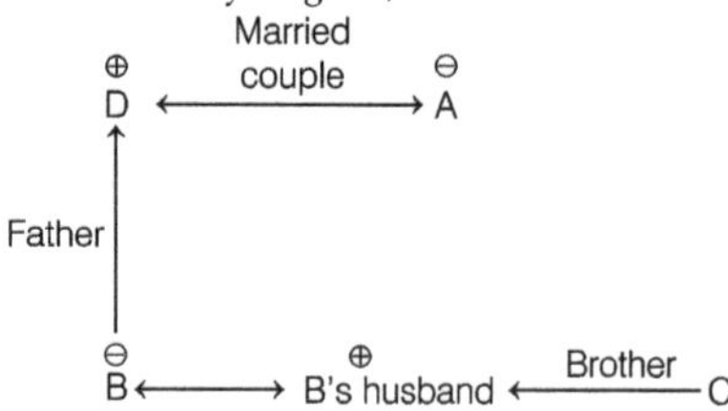

Clearly, A is D's wife.

4. (*d*) Let us draw the family diagram,

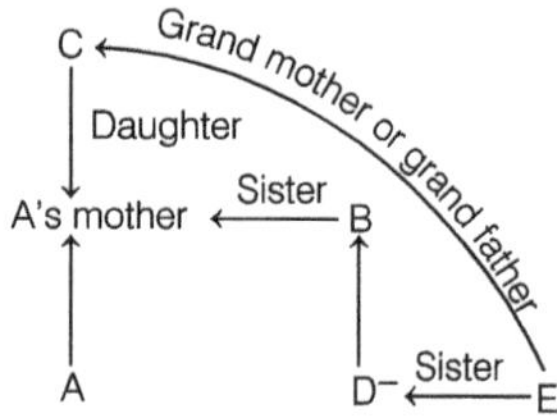

Now, it can be concluded that C is either grandmother or grandfather of E.

5. (*c*) The relation between S and A cannot be determined.

6. (*b*) According to the question,

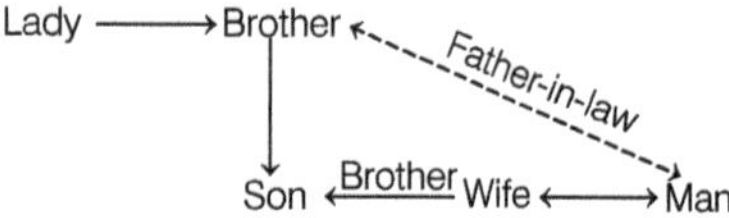

Clearly, the lady is sister of his father-in-law.

7. (*d*) Let us draw the family diagram,

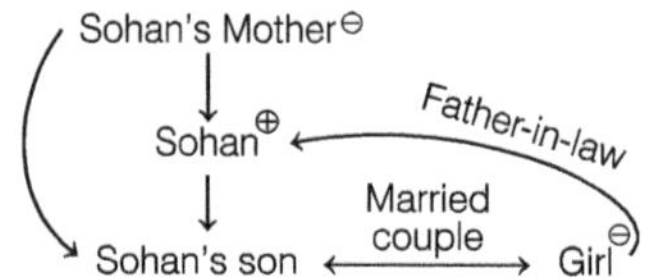

So, Sohan is father-in-law of that girl.

8. (*a*) Let us draw the family diagram,

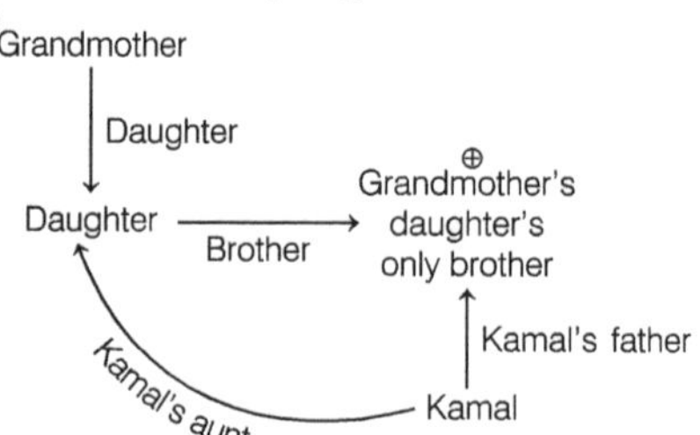

Hence, Kamal has defeated his father.

9. (*d*) A and B are brothers.
C and D are sisters.
A's son is D's brother

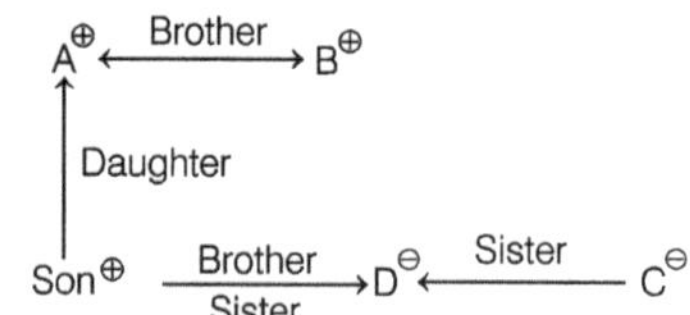

(since, '+' indicates male and – indicates female)
Hence, B is the uncle of C.

10. (*d*)

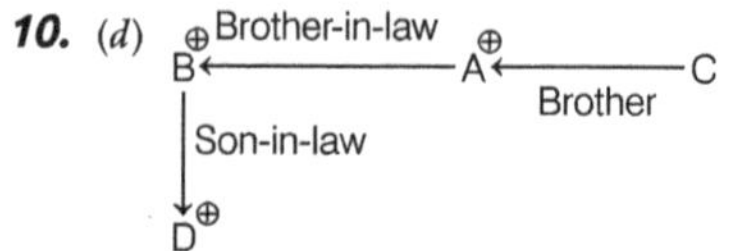

Brother of C ⇒ A
Brother-in-law of A ⇒ B (∵ A is male)
Clearly, A is also the brother-in-law of B.

11. (*b*) Let us draw the family diagram,

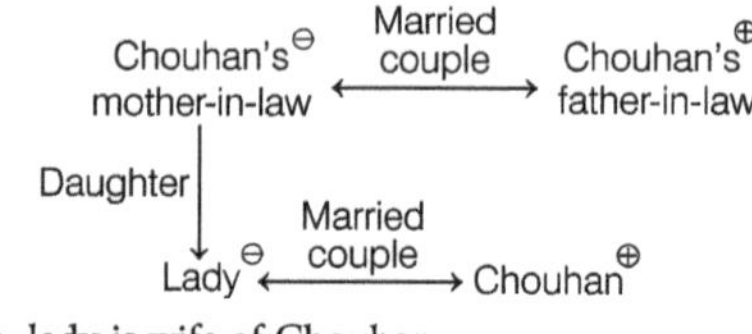

So, lady is wife of Chouhan.

12. (*b*) Let us draw the family diagram,

Veena's Grandfather ⊕
Son
Veena's father ⊕
father
Veena —Brother→ Boy ⊕

So, boy is the brother of Veena.

13. (*d*) Only son of Q ⇒ P
Only daughter of S ⇒ Q
D ⇒ B's mother
D ⇒ Q' daughter in-law
Q ⇒ B's grandmother
B ⇒ Q's grandson or granddaughter

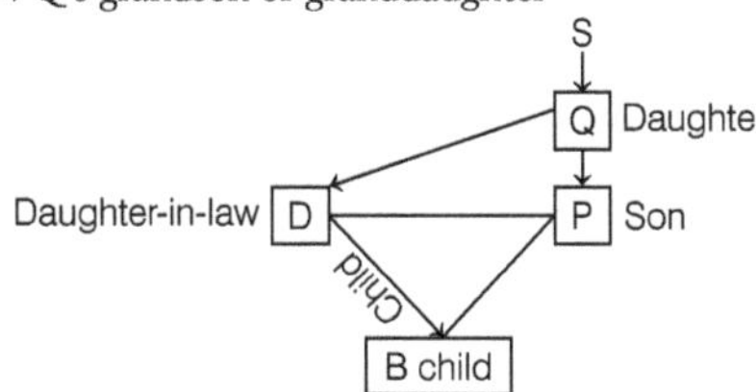

Clearly, the relationship cannot be determined because the gender of B is not clear.

14. (*d*) Let us draw the family diagram,

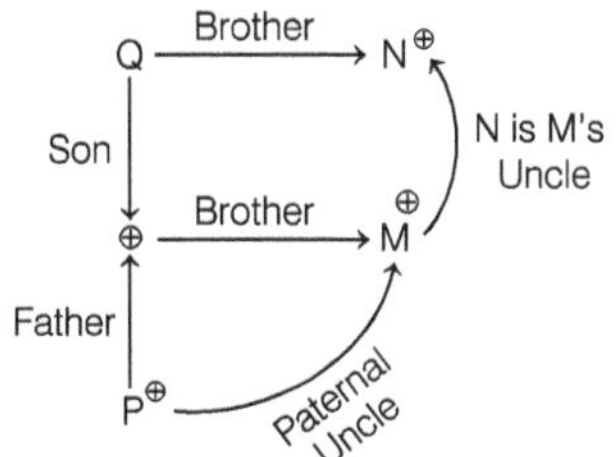

As, N is M's uncle, none of the options is correct.

15. (*b*) Let us draw the family diagram,

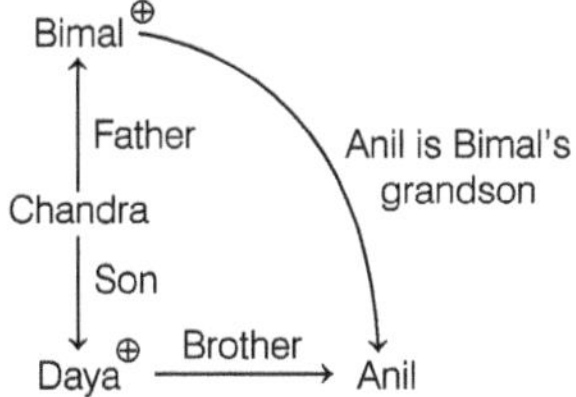

So, Anil is Bimal's grandson.

16. (*a*) M ⇒ Paternal uncle of P
N ⇒ Brother of Q
P's father ⇒ Q's son

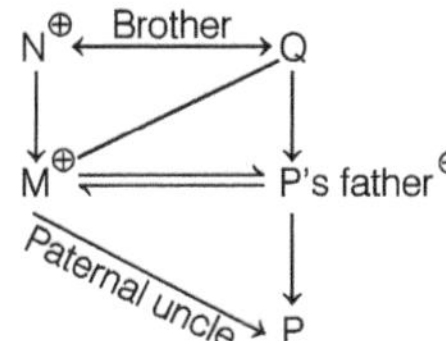

Clearly, N is brother of Q and M is brother of P's father who is Q's son.
So, M is nephew of N.

17. (*c*) Let us draw the family diagram,

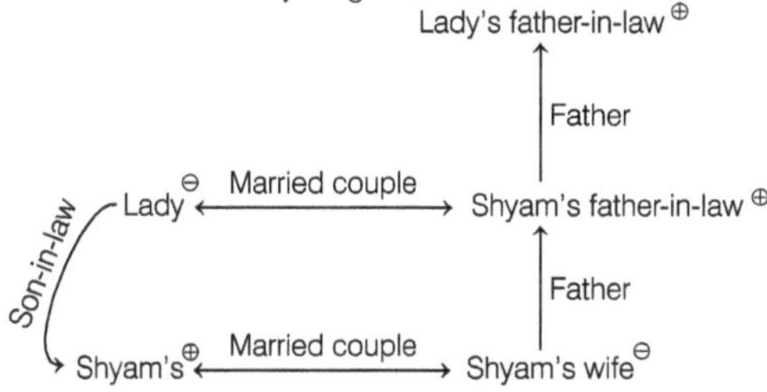

Clearly, Shyam is the son-in-law of that lady.

18. (*d*) Cannot be determined, since the relation of B and C is not given with other family members. Hence, data is inadequate.

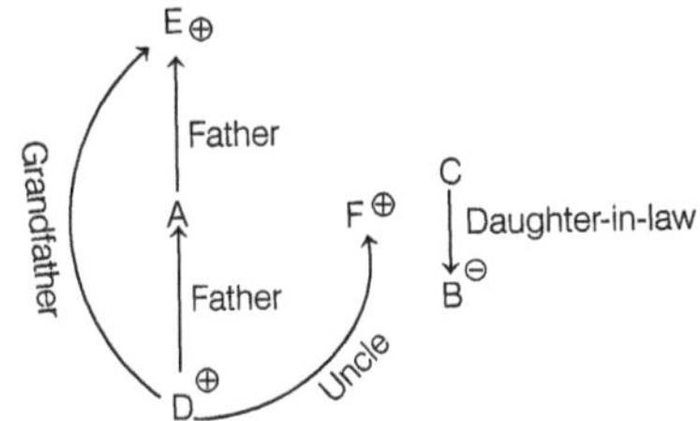

19. (*a*) Brother of daughter means son. Wife of my husband means herself. So, the man is son of Rita.

20. (*b*) Let us draw the family diagram,

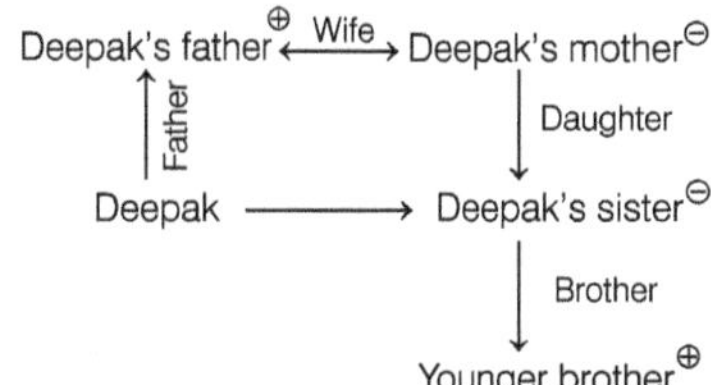

So, the boy is brother of Deepak.

21. (*a*) Let us draw the family diagram,

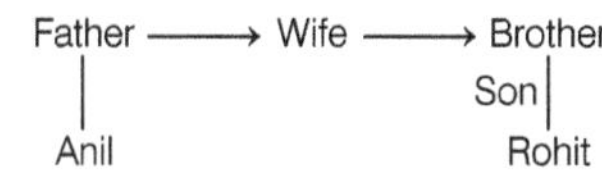

Clearly, Anil and Rohit are the cousins.

22. (*b*) Let us draw the family diagram,

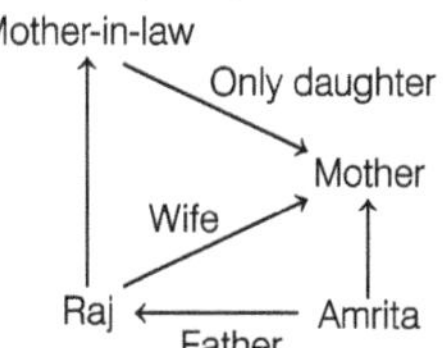

Clearly, Raj is the father of Amrita.

23. (*c*) According to the question,
From option (c),

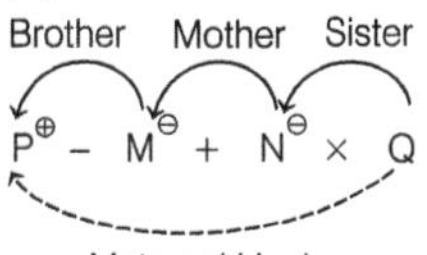

Clearly, P is the maternal uncle of Q.

24. (*a*) Let us draw the family diagram,

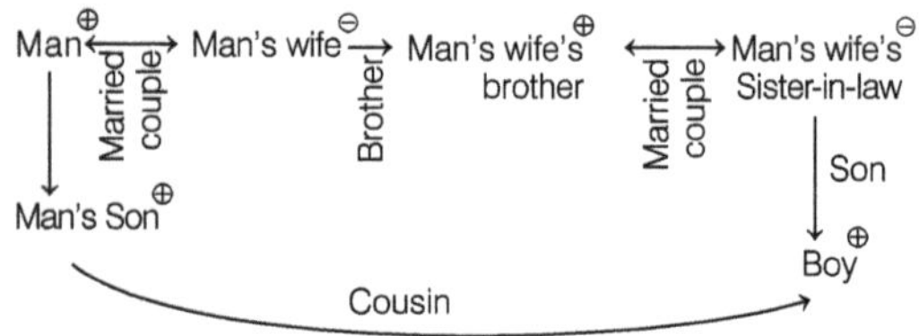

Hence, man's son is the cousin of that boy.

25. (*a*) Let us draw the family diagram,

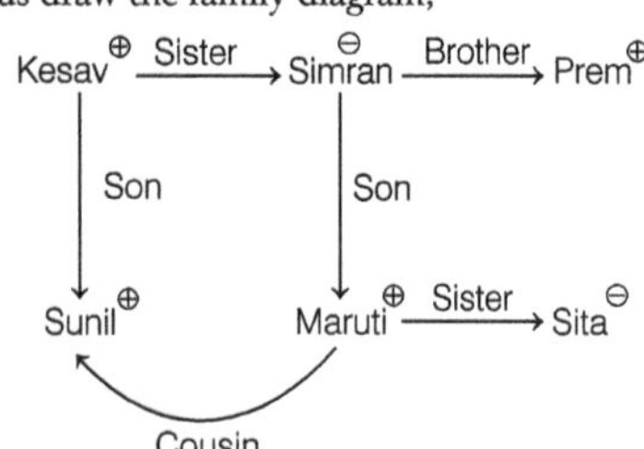

Clearly, Sunil is the cousin of Maruti.

26. (*a*) According to the question,

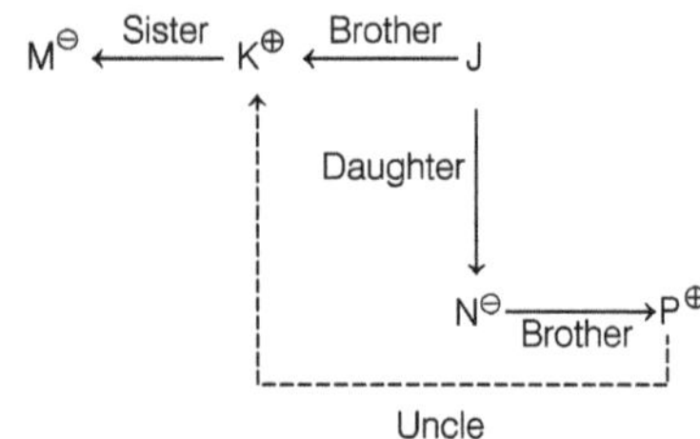

Clearly, K is the uncle of P.

27. (*b*) According to the question,

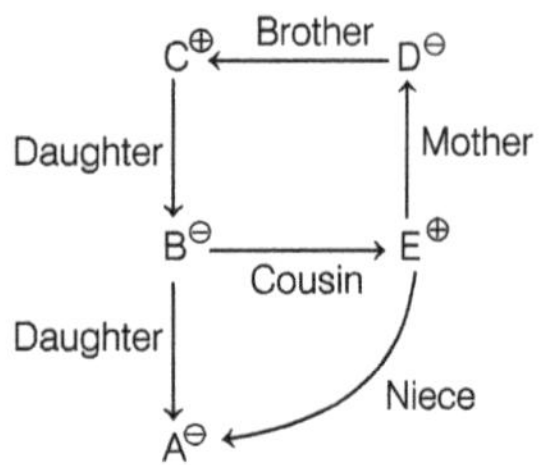

Clearly, A is the niece of E.

28. (*a*) Since, Sunil has no brother of sister. So, he is own his own son of his father and his wife will be mother of that person. Hence, the man in the photo is son of Sunil.

29. (*d*) Let us draw the family diagram,

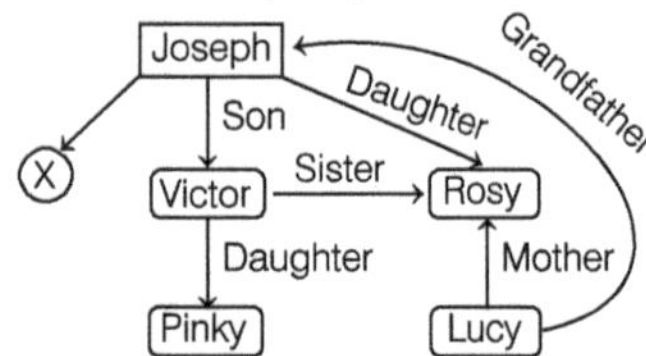

Joseph has three children, one is X, second is Victor and third is Rosy. Here, it is not clear 'X' is male or female.
Rosy is the mother of Lucy.
So, Joseph is the grandfather of Lucy.

30. (*c*) Let us draw the family diagram,

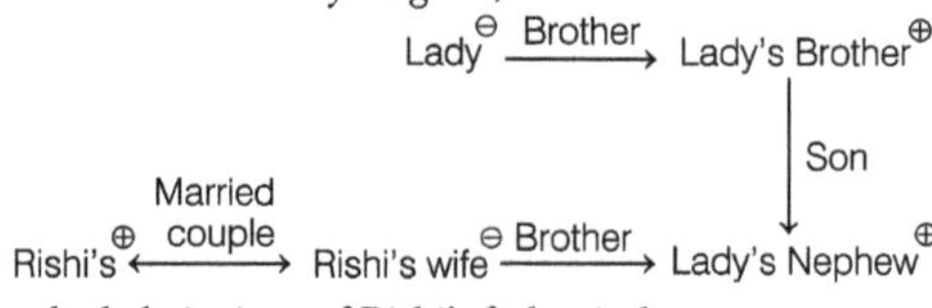

So, the lady is sister of Rishi's father-in-law.

31. (*a*) By using option (a) *i.e.*, A + S + B − T

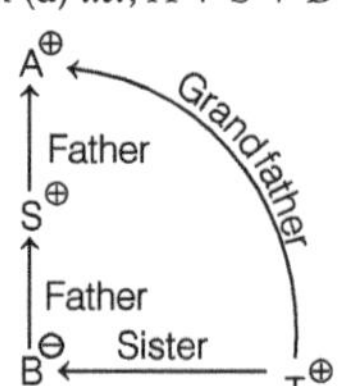

Now, from the diagram it is clear that A is grandfather of T

32. (*b*) Let us draw the family diagram,
X ⇒ Maternal grandfather of Z , S ⇒ Grandson of X

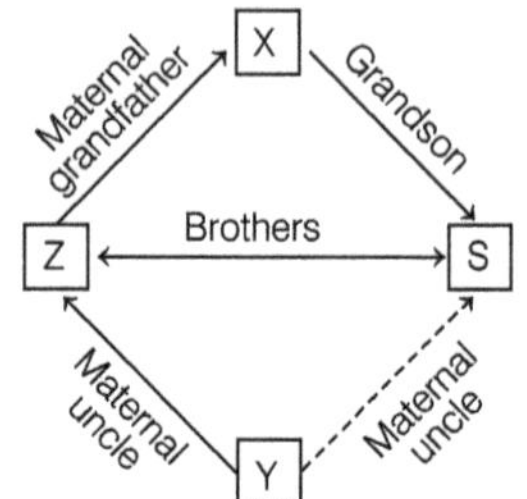

So, Z and S are brothers.
∵ Z ⇒ Maternal uncle of Y.
Clearly, S is also the maternal uncle of Y.

33. (*d*) Let us draw the family diagram,

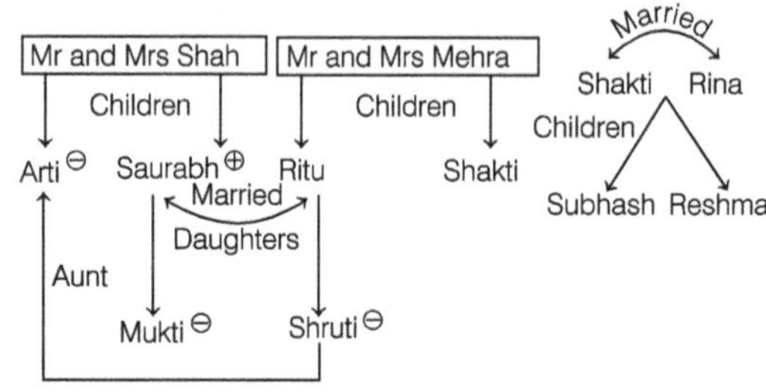

Clearly, Arti is aunt of Shruti.
Note We consider Arti as female on the basis of options.

34. (*c*) Let us draw the family diagram,

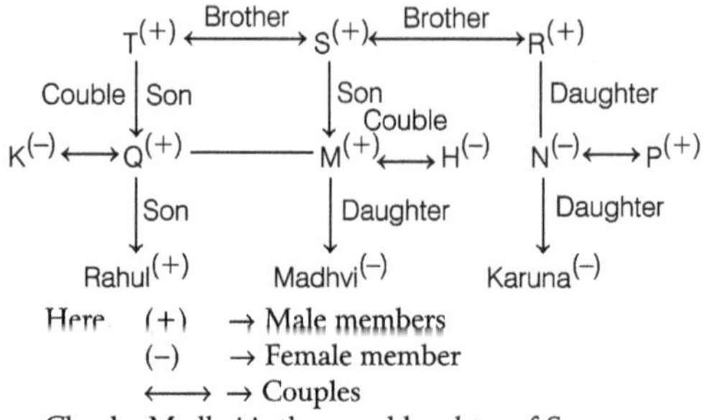

Here (+) → Male members
(−) → Female member
⟷ → Couples

Clearly, Madhvi is the granddaughter of S.

Solutions (Q. Nos. 35-38) *Let us draw the family diagram,*

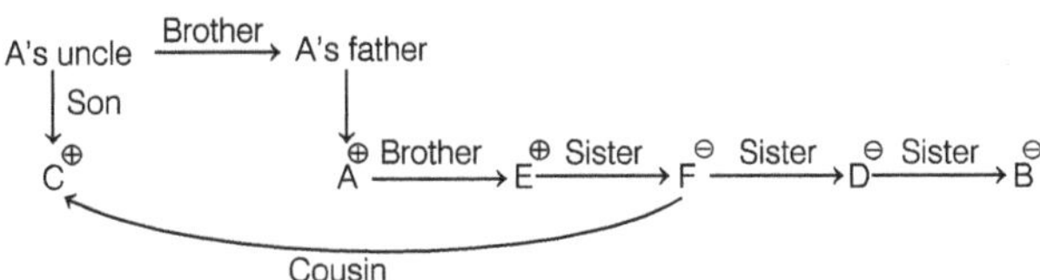

35. (*b*) D is A's sister.

36. (*d*) Males are A, E and C.

37. (*c*) Females are B, D and F.

38. (*a*) C is the cousin of F.

Solutions (Q. Nos. 39-41) *Let us draw the family diagram,*

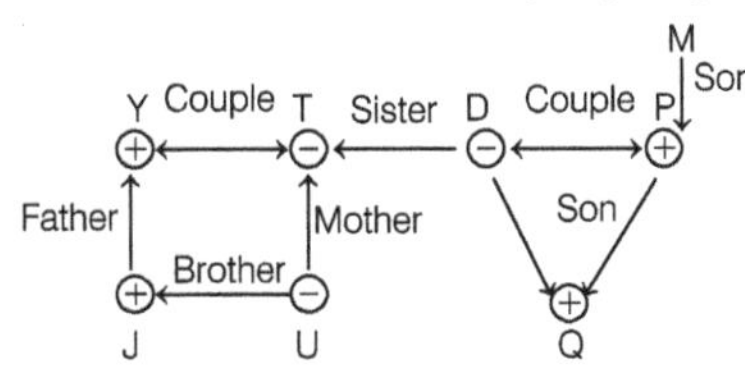

39. (*c*) P is brother-in-law of T.

40. (*d*) J is nephew of D.

41. (*b*) Q is grandson of M.

Solutions (Q. Nos. 42 - 44) *According to the question,*

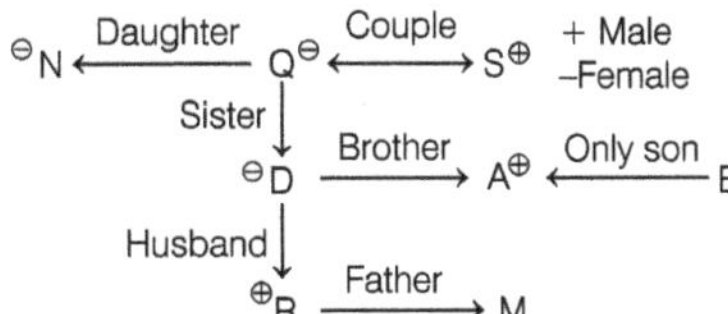

42. (*b*) B is the mother-in-law of R.

43. (*c*) S is the brother-in-law of A.

44. (*e*) D is the aunt of N.

Solutions (Q. Nos. 45-48) *Let us draw the family diagram,*

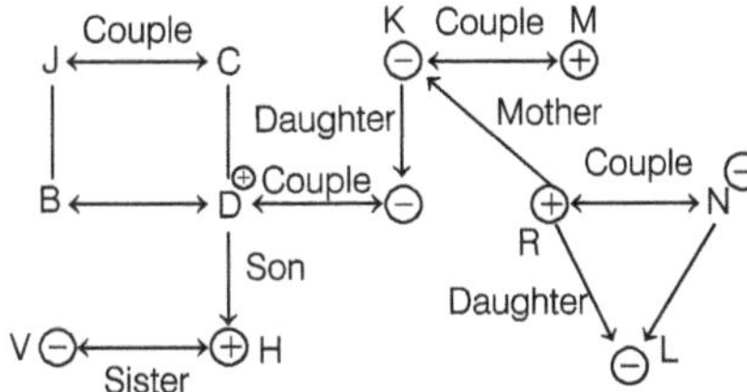

45. (*c*) D is son-in-law of K.

46. (*a*) It is clearly shown that if T is only daughter of K, then T will be the wife of D.

47. (*b*) L is the granddaughter of K.

48. (*a*) The father of R is M.

Solutions (Q. Nos. 49 -51) *According to the question,*

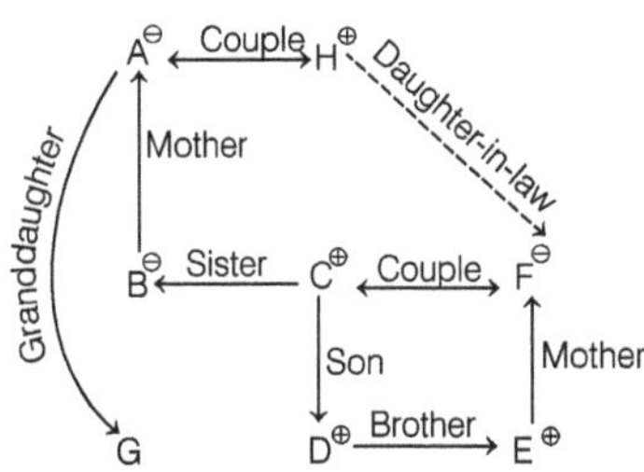

49. (*b*) F is the daughter-in-law of H.

50. (*a*) C is the father of E.

51. (*c*) F is the mother of G.

Solutions (Q. Nos. 52-54) *Let us draw the family diagram,*

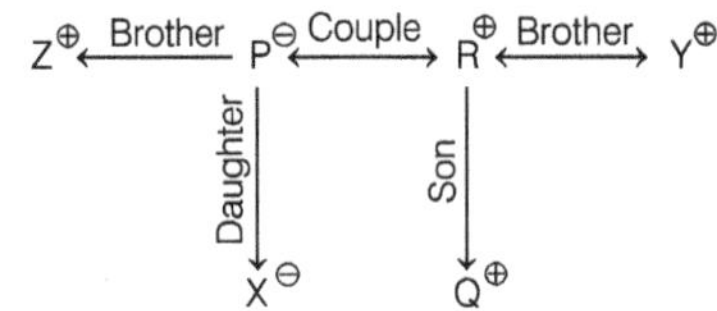

52. (*b*) Z is brother-in-law of R.

53. (*b*) X and P are females.

54. (*d*) R and Y is the pair of brothers.

55. (*c*) Let us draw the family diagram,

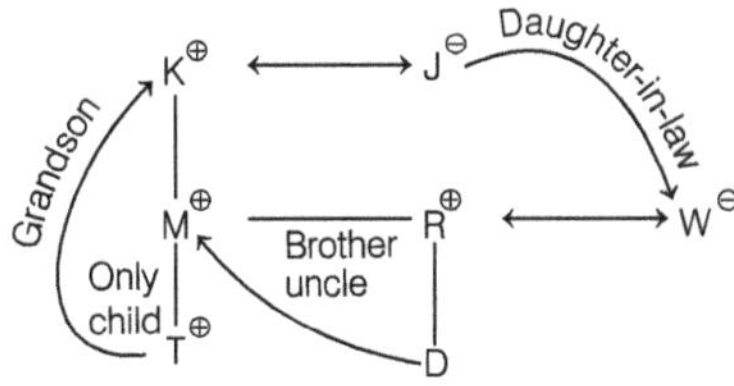

⊕ → Male member

⊖ → Female member

⟷ → Married couples

Clearly, M is uncle of D or D is nephew or niece of M because the gender of D is not clear.

56. (*b*) According to given information,

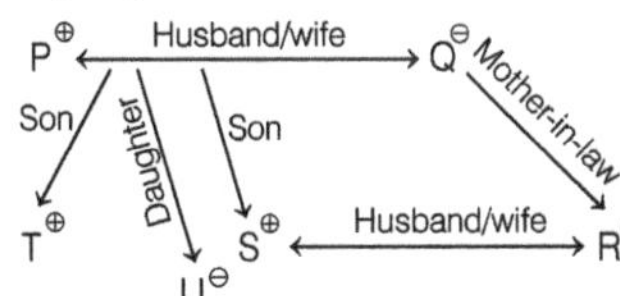

Hence, it is clear from the above diagram that R is the wife of S.

57. (*d*) According to the question,

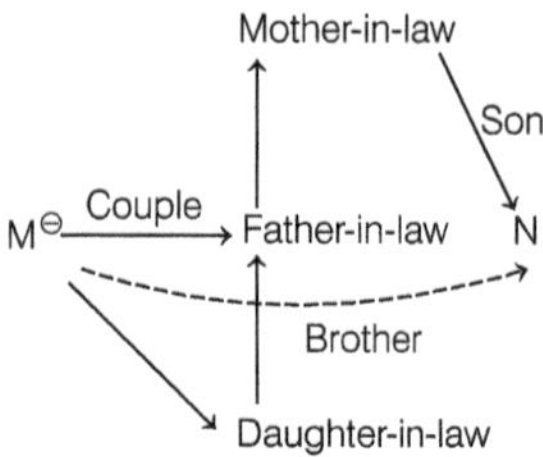

Clearly, N is the brother of M.

58. (*b*) Let us draw the family diagram,

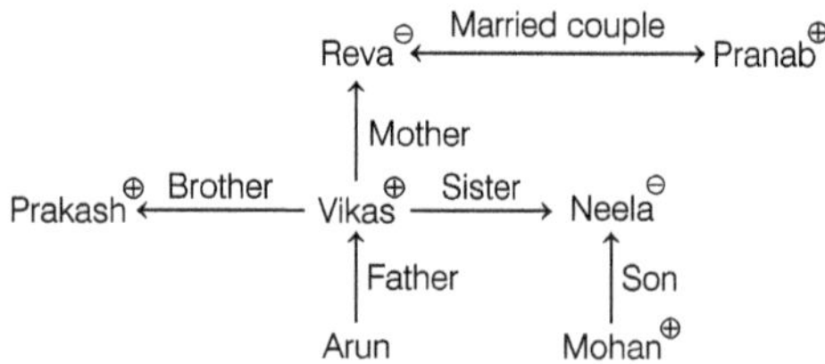

As, Vikas is Neela's brother, Vikas wife will be Neela's sister-in-law.

Solutions (Q. Nos. 59 - 62) *According to the question,*

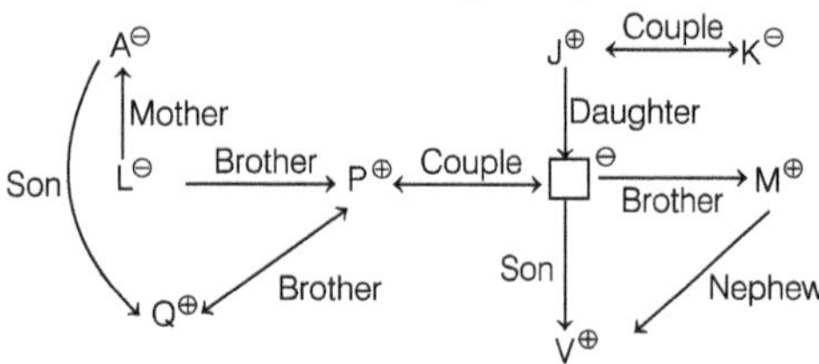

59. (*c*) Clearly, R will be the wife of P.

60. (*a*) Clearly, V is the grandson of A.

61. (*e*) Clearly, S will be the nephew of Q.

62. (*d*) Clearly, K is the mother of M.

63. (*d*) According to the question,

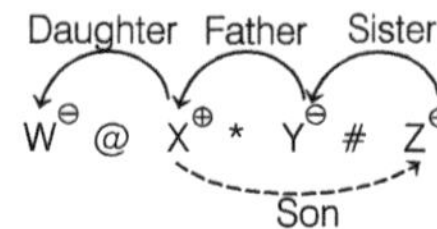

Clearly, Z is the son of X.

Solutions (Q. Nos. 64-68)

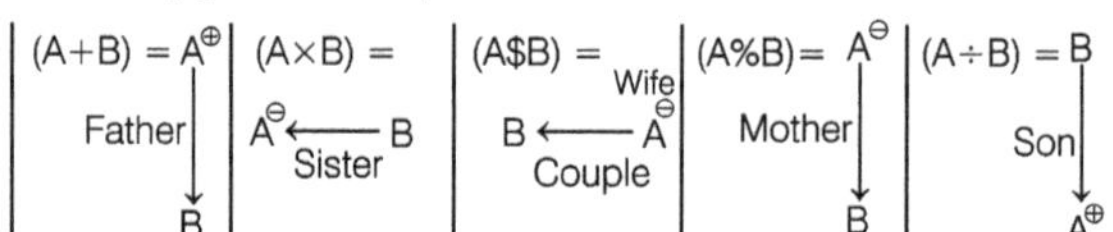

64. (*a*) According to the question,

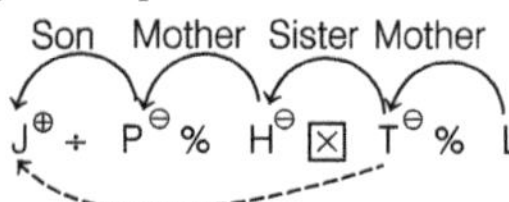

Clearly, from option (a), it is established that J is the brother of T.

65. (*b*) According to the question,

From option (b),

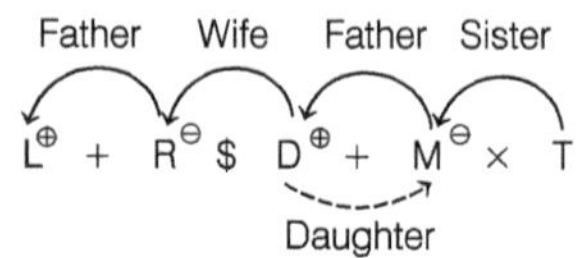

Clearly, M is the daughter of D.

66. (*b*) According to the question,

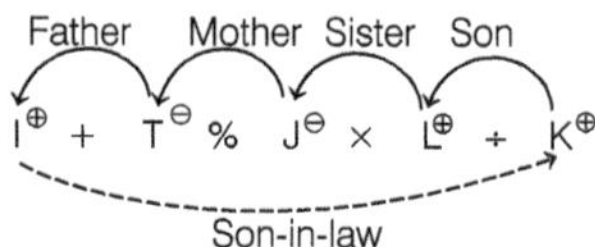

Clearly, K is the son-in-law of I is true.

67. (*d*) According to the question,

From option (a),

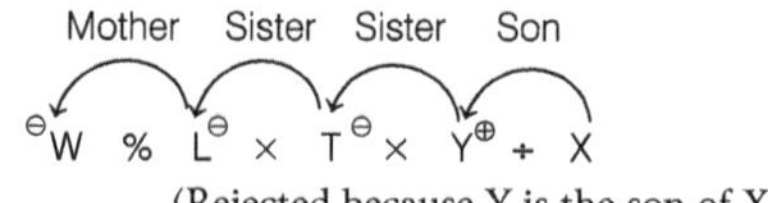

(Rejected because Y is the son of X)

From option (b),

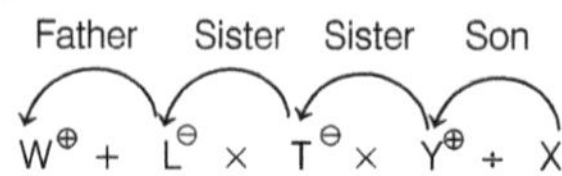

(Rejected because Y is the son of X)

From option (c),

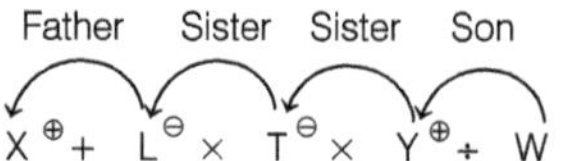

(Rejected because Y is the son of X)

From option (d),

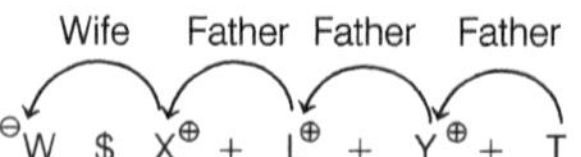

(Selected because Y is the grandson of X)

From option (e),

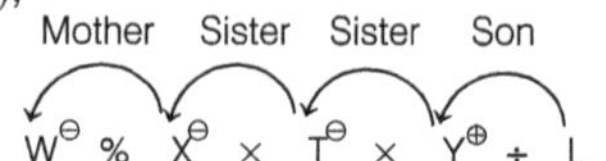

(Rejected because Y is the son of X)

68. (*d*) According to the question,

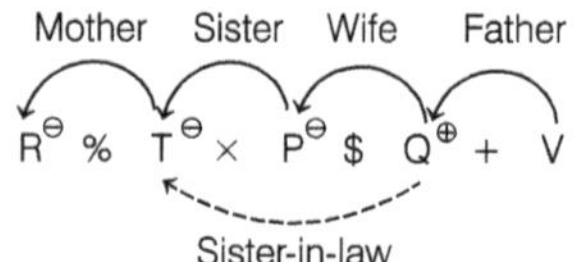

Clearly, option (d) will replace the question mark.

69. (*a*) Let us draw the family diagram,

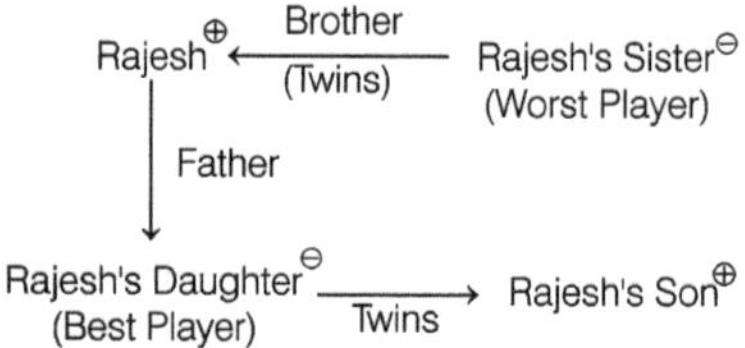

Clearly, best player is daughter of Rajesh.

CHAPTER / 09

Ranking and Time Sequence Test

This chapter broadly deals with the problems related to the arrangement of persons/objects in ascending/descending order (based on different parameters like height, weight, merit, position etc.), determining the position of a person/object in a row/queue and the problems related to the time sequence test wherein the candidate has to find out a particular day based on some given conditions.

Several types of problems based on this section that are asked in various competitive exams are classified as follows

TYPE 01

Sequential Order of Arrangement

This type of questions involves determining the sequential order of two or more persons/things on the basis of comparison based on different parameters such as age, height, marks, salary, weight, length, size etc.

These questions are generally given with a set of information in jumbled form, based on which the candidates are required to systematically arrange the given information and determine the sequential order of arrangement of the various persons/objects.

Generally, we compare the things, objects and persons using various notations such as greater than (>), smaller than (<), equal to (=), greater than or equal to (≥), less than or equal to (≤), etc.

The candidates are required to understand the given constraints and conditions to provide appropriate notation of comparison to reach the conclusion.

While solving problems under this section, use of the following symbols is required

1. Greater/Heavier/Taller/Higher/More (>)
   $A > B$ means
   A is greater/heavier/taller/higher/more than B.

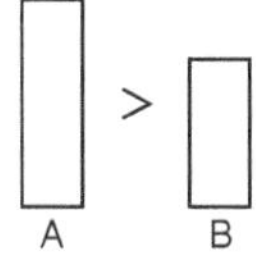

2. Smaller/Lighter/Shorter/Lower/Less (<)
   $A < B$ means
   A is smaller/lighter/shorter/lower/less than B.

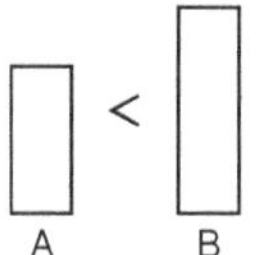

3. Equal (=)
   $A = B$ means
   A is equal to B.
   On the basis of above mentioned symbols, following two sequences are used while solving problems.

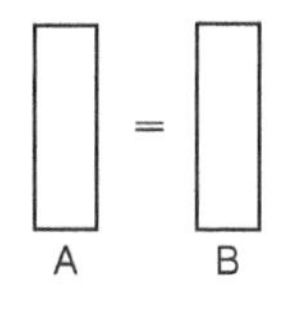

Ascending Order Sequence

In this sequence, the persons are arranged in ascending order of their heights/weight/ages or any other parameters.

Let us see $A < B < C < D$

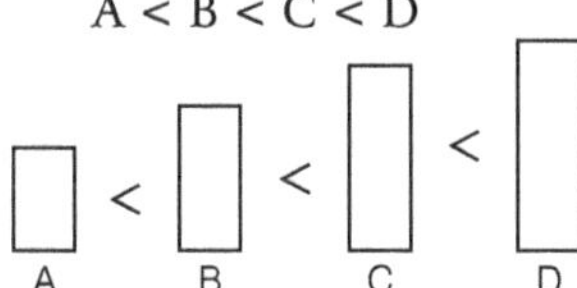

Descending Order Sequence

In this sequence, the persons are arranged in descending order of their heights/weight/ages or any other parameters.

Let us see A > B > C > D

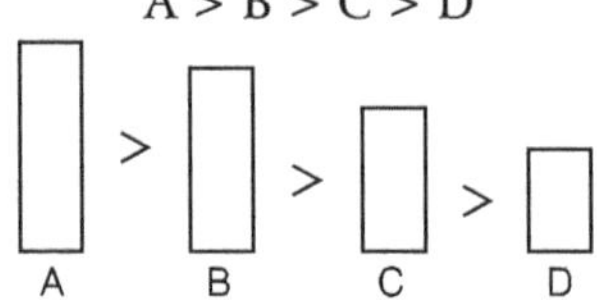

Parameters of Comparison

Various parameters of comparison of two or more persons or things are given as follows

Comparison Based on Length or Height

In this type of questions, comparison of lengths or heights of different persons/objects is given separately. We have to arrange the given information in the ascending/descending order and answer the related question(s).

The examples given below will help you to understand such type of questions

***Ex* 01** **Mohan is taller than Shyam but shorter than Ramesh. Ramesh is taller than Rajat but shorter than Gautam. If Shyam is taller than Rajat, then who is the shortest among all?** « MP PSC 2018

(a) Gautam (b) Rajat (c) Shyam (d) Ramesh

Solution (b) From given information,

Ramesh > Mohan > Shyam ...(i)

Gautam > Ramesh > Rajat ...(ii)

Shyam > Rajat ...(iii)

Combining Eqs. (i), (ii) and (iii), we have

Gautam > Ramesh > Mohan > Shyam > Rajat

Hence, Rajat is the shortest among all.

***Ex* 02** **D is taller than C and E. A is not as tall as E. C is taller than A. D is not as tall as B. Then, who is the 2nd tallest person?** « WBCS 2020

(a) B (b) C (c) D (d) E

Solution (c) From the information given in the question,

D > C and E; E > A ; C > A ; B > D

On arranging the above data, B > D > C and E > A

∴ D is the 2nd tallest person.

Comparison Based on Age

In this type of questions, the ages of different persons are given in comparison with one another and we have to arrange the given information in a logical order either ascending or descending and answer the question(s) related to the data.

***Ex* 03** **X is elder than Z, Y is younger than Z, Z is elder than W, W is younger than X, who is the eldest?** « SSC Steno 2015

(a) X (b) Y
(c) W (d) Z

Solution (a) According to the question,

X > Z > Y ...(i)

Z > W ...(ii)

and X > W ...(iii)

From Eqs. (i), (ii) and (iii), we get

X > Z > Y and W

So, it is clear that X is the eldest.

Comparison Based on Weight

In this type of questions, the weight of different persons are given in comparison with one another and we have to arrange the given information in the logical order either ascending or descending and answer the related question(s).

***Ex* 04** **Sunil is heavier than Abhinav but not as heavier as Rajiv. Abhinav is heavier than Jayesh. Kashi is heavier than Sunil but not as heavier as Rajiv. Who is the heaviest?**

(a) Sunil (b) Abhinav
(c) Rajiv (d) Kashi

Solution (c) According to the question,

Rajiv > Sunil > Abhinav

Abhinav > Jayesh

Rajiv > Kashi > Sunil

On arranging the above data, we get

(Rajiv) > Kashi > Sunil > Abhinav > Jayesh

Clearly, Rajiv is the heaviest.

Comparison Based on Merit

In this type of questions, persons are compared on the basis of their merit or competency or intelligence and we have to deduce the logical order of merit from the given information and answer the related question(s).

***Ex* 05** **Five students participated in the scholarship examination. Sudha scored higher than Puja. Kavita scored lower than Suma but higher than Sudha. Mamta scored between Puja and Sudha. Who scored lowest in the examination?** « MAT 2018

(a) Kavita (b) Puja
(c) Mamta (d) Sudha

Solution (b) According to the question,

Sudha > Puja

Suma > Kavita > Sudha

Puja > Mamta > Sudha or Sudha > Mamta > Puja

On arranging the above data, we get

Suma > Kavita > Sudha > Mamta > Puja

∴ Puja scored the lowest.

Practice / CORNER 9.1

1. John, Aries and Joseph are brothers with different ages. « WBCS 2020

Given that :

(i) Aries is the oldest. (ii) Joseph is not the oldest.

(iii) John is not the youngest.

Who is the youngest?

(a) Aries (b) John (c) Joseph
(d) Cannot be determined from the given information.

2. A is taller than B but not as tall as C. D is taller than E but not as tall as B.E is taller than F but not as tall as D. Who among them is the tallest?

(a) B (b) C (c) D (d) F

3. A pole is taller than a Giraffe which is taller than a tree. A signal is shorter than a pole but taller than a building which is taller than a Giraffe. Which is the shortest? « RRB NTPC 2016

(a) Signal (b) Giraffe
(c) Tree (d) Building

4. Among five boys, Vasant is taller than Manohar but not as tall as Raju. Jayant is taller than Dutta but shorter than Manohar. Who is the tallest in the group?

« FCI Watchman 2018

(a) Raju (b) Manohar
(c) Vasant (d) Jayant

5. Among 5 boys in a class, P is taller than M; M is taller than N; S is taller than M; R is taller than S. Which one of the following statements can definitely be concluded from the above information?

(a) S is taller than P
(b) R is the tallest among the given boys
(c) P is taller than R
(d) N is the shortest among the given boys

6. There are five friends–Sachin, Kunal, Mohit, Amit and Sohan. Sachin is shorter than Kunal, but taller than Sohan. Mohit is the tallest. Amit is little shorter than Kunal and little taller than Sachin. If they stand in the order of increasing heights, who will be the third?

« UPSC Assistant Commandant 2019

(a) Amit (b) Sohan
(c) Sachin (d) Kunal

7. N is more intelligent than M. M is not as intelligent as Y. X is more intelligent than Y but not as good as N. Who is the most intelligent of all?

(a) N (b) M (c) X (d) Y

8. Mohan is taller than Rohan but shorter than Farhan. Kannan is shorter than Mohan but taller than Rohan. Shanker is taller than Rohan and Farhan. Who is the tallest? « RRB NTPC 2016

A. Mohan B. Farhan
C. Shanker D. Kannan

(a) A (b) B (c) C (d) D

9. The height of banana tree and coconut tree is same. Mango tree is shorter than plum. Guava tree is smaller than mango but bigger than banana. Find out which is the tallest tree? « UPSSSC Amin 2016

(a) Mango (b) Banana
(c) Coconut (d) Plum

10. Shailendra is shorter than Keshav but taller than Rakesh, Madhav is the tallest. Aashish is a little shorter than Keshav and little taller than Shailendra. If they stand in the order of increasing heights, who will be the second?

(a) Aashish (b) Shailendra
(c) Rakesh (d) Madhav

11. The age of Amit is same as Sumit because they are twins, Richa is younger than Sumit, Richa is younger than Jyotsana but elder than Saurabh, Sumit is younger than Jyotsana. Who is the eldest among them?

(a) Amit (b) Jyotsana
(c) Richa (d) Saurabh

12. If Pen < Pencil, Pencil < Book and Book > Cap, then which one of the following is always true?

« UPSC Civil Services 2018

(a) Pen > Cap (b) Pen < Book
(c) Pencil = Cap (d) Pencil > Cap

13. Simi is older than Renu. Geeta is younger than Renu. Priya is older than Simi. Who is the eldest of them?

« MP Police SI 2017

(a) Simi (b) Priya (c) Geeta (d) Renu

14. Priti scored more than Rahul, Yamuna scored as much as Divya. Lokita scored less than Manju. Rahul scored more than Yamuna. Manju scored less than Divya. Who scored the lowest?

(a) Manju (b) Yamuna
(c) Lokita (d) Rahul

15. Sita is older than Kanika. Ila is older than Kanika but younger than Sita, Shempa is younger than both Manas and Kanika, Kanika is older than Manas. Who is the youngest?

(a) Shempa (b) Manas (c) Ila (d) Kanika

16. P, Q, R and S are four males. P is the eldest in the group but he is not the poorest, R is the richest but not the eldest, Q is elder than S but he is not elder than P or R, P is richer than Q but he is not richer than S. How the four persons can be arranged in decreasing order of their age and money?

(a) PQRS, RPSQ (b) PRQS, RSPQ
(c) PRQS, RSQP (d) PRSQ, RSPQ

17. Weight of P is twice that of Q. Weight of Q is half of R. Weight of R is 3 times of T. Weight of T is half of S. The weight of Q is greater than the weight of how many persons among P, R, S and T? « SSC Steno 2017

(a) 1 (b) 2 (c) 3 (d) 4

18. Lakshmi is elder than Meenu. Leela is elder than Meenu but younger than Lakshmi. Latha is younger than both Meenu and Hari but Hari is younger than Meenu. Who is the youngest? « SSC 10+2 2013

(a) Lakshmi (b) Meenu (c) Leela (d) Latha

19. Sashi is 2 yr elder than Sunita, Sunita is 3 yr elder than Bindu, Shekhar is 1 yr elder than Bindu. Who is the youngest in the group? « SSC 10+2 2010

(a) Sashi (b) Shekhar (c) Bindu (d) Sunita

20. Five men P, Q, R, S and T are reading a newspaper. The one who reads it first, gives it to T. The one who reads it last, had taken it from R. Q is not first or last one to read it. There were two readers between P and R. Who is the third one to read the newspaper? « SSC Constable GD 2019

(a) R (b) Q (c) S (d) P

21. At a public meeting there were 8 speakers A, B, C, D, E, F, G and H. Each spoke for some time according to the following scheme

I. 'A' spoke after 'F' and took more time than 'B'.
II. 'C' spoke before 'G' and after 'B' and took less time than E.
III. 'D' spoke after 'H' and before 'B' and took less time than 'H' but more time than 'E'.
IV. 'H' spoke after 'A' and took less time than 'B'.

Who spoke for the longest time? « FCI 2015

(a) A (b) B (c) C (d) D

DIRECTIONS ~ (Q. Nos. 22 and 23) *Read the following information given below to answer the questions that follow.*

Among A, B, C and D, B is heavier than A and C but C is taller than him. D is not as tall as C while A is the shortest. C is not as heavy as A. D is heavier than B but shorter than him.

22. Who is the heaviest?

(a) B (b) A (c) D (d) C

23. Who is the tallest?

(a) D (b) C
(c) Either A or D (d) Cannot be determined

DIRECTIONS ~ (Q. Nos. 24-28) *Read the following information carefully to answer the questions that follow.*

I. Anita, Mahima, Rajan, Lata and Deepti are five cousins.
II. Anita is twice as old as Mahima.
III. Rajan is half the age of Mahima.
IV. Anita is half the age of Deepti.
V. Rajan is twice the age of Lata.

24. Who is the youngest?

(a) Deepti (b) Rajan (c) Lata (d) Anita

25. Who is the eldest?

(a) Deepti (b) Lata (c) Anita (d) Rajan

26. Which of the following pairs of persons are of the same age?

(a) Mahima and Lata (b) Anita and Mahima
(c) Mahima and Rajan (d) There is no such pair

27. Anita is younger than whom?

(a) Rajan (b) Mahima (c) Deepti (d) Lata

28. If Mahima is 16 yr old, then what is the age of Lata?

(a) 4 yr (b) 5 yr (c) 7 yr (d) 14 yr

DIRECTIONS ~ (Q. Nos. 29-31) *Study the following information carefully and answer the questions given below.* « IBPS RRB Office Assistant 2020

Five persons A, B, C, D and E have different heights. Less than two persons are shorter than D. As many persons are taller than D as shorter than C. A is taller than B, but shorter than E. B is not the shortest person. The height of third tallest person is 86 cm.

29. If the height of shortest person is 68 cm, then what may be the height of B?

(a) 69 cm (b) 81 cm
(c) 78 cm (d) All the given heights
(e) None of these

30. How many persons are taller than C?

(a) None (b) One
(c) Two (d) Three
(e) None of these

31. Who among the following is just shorter than E?

(a) None (b) C (c) A
(d) D (e) None of these

DIRECTIONS ~(32-34) *Read the following information Carefully and answer the questions that follow.* « SBI PO 2015

(i) A, B, C, D, E and F are six students in a class.
(ii) B and C are shorter than F but heavier than A.
(iii) D is heavier than B and taller than C.
(iv) E is shorter than D but taller than F.
(v) F is heavier than D.
(vi) A is shorter than E but taller than F.

32. Who among them is the tallest?

(a) B (b) A (c) D (d) E
(e) None of these

33. Who is third from the top when they are arranged in descending order to their height?

(a) A (b) E (c) B (d) C
(e) None of these

34. Which of the following statements is true for F as regarding height and weight?

(a) He is heavier than B and C but shorter than D
(b) He is lighter than B and C but taller than D
(c) He is heavier than B and taller than E
(d) He is lighter than E and also shorter than E
(e) He is lighter than E and taller than E

DIRECTIONS ~ (Q. Nos. 35-37) *Study the given information carefully to answer the given questions.* « IBPS PO 2017

Six books A, B, C, D, E and F each of different thickness, are kept on a table. C is thicker than A, but thinner than E. A is thicker than both B and D. E is not the thickest. The third thinnest book is 9 cm thick and the thickest book is 16 cm thick.

Note *the thickness of all the books are in whole numbers.*

35. If E is 5 cm thicker than A, then how thick is E?
(a) 11 cm (b) 9 cm (c) 12 cm (d) 14 cm
(e) Cannot be determined

36. With respect to the thickness of the given books, if C + F = 27, then A + C = ?
(a) 20 (b) Other than those given as options
(c) 23 (d) 15
(e) 19

37. If B is 8 cm thick,then which of the following is true about B?
(a) B is the third thinnest book of all.
(b) F is 5 cm thicker than B.
(c) B is thicker than D.
(d) All the given statements are true.
(e) Other than those given as options

DIRECTIONS ~ (Q. Nos. 38-40) *Study the following information and answer the given questions.*

Each of the six stores P, Q, R, S, T and U sold different number of books in one day. Only three stores sold less books than U. P sold more books than R. T did not sell the highest number of books. S sold more books than R and P but less than U. The store which sold the second highest number of books sold 72 books. « SBI PO 2017

38. How many books did Q probably sell?
(a) 43 (b) 58 (c) 71 (d) 65 (e) 89

39. Which of the following stores sold the second lowest number of books?
(a) T (b) P (c) S (d) R (e) Q

40. If the total number of books sold by P and T is 125, then how many books did P sell?
(a) 51 (b) 76 (c) 68 (d) 45 (e) 53

DIRECTIONS ~ (Q. Nos. 41-46) *Read the following information carefully and answer the questions that follow.*

I. Seven students P, Q, R, S, T, U and V take a series of tests.
II. No two students get similar marks.
III. V always scores more than P.
IV. P always scores more than Q.
V. Each time either R scores the highest and T gets the least or alternatively S scores the highest and U or Q scores the least.

41. If V is ranked fifth, which of these must be true?
(a) S scores the highest (b) R is ranked second
(c) T is ranked third (d) Q is ranked fourth

42. If R gets the most, V should be ranked not lower than
(a) second (b) third (c) fourth (d) fifth

43. If S is ranked second, which of the following can be true?
(a) P gets more than R (b) V gets more than S
(c) P gets more than S (d) U gets more than V

44. If S is ranked sixth and Q is ranked fifth, which of the following can be true?
(a) V is ranked fifth or fourth
(b) R is ranked second or third
(c) P is ranked second or fourth
(d) U is ranked third or fourth

45. If R is ranked second and Q is ranked fifth, which of these must be true?
(a) S is ranked third (b) P is ranked third
(c) V is ranked fourth (d) T is ranked sixth

46. Information given in which of the statements is superfluous?
(a) Only II (b) Only I
(c) Only IV (d) All are needed

Answers WITH EXPLANATIONS

1. (*c*) From the information,
Aries ↑
John | increasing ages
Joseph |
∴ Joseph is the youngest.

2. (*b*) According to the given information, the descending order of height of A, B, C, D, E and F is
(C) > A > B > D > E > F
Hence, C is the tallest.

3. (*c*) From given information, the descending order of height
Pole > Giraffe> Tree ...(i)
and Pole > Signal > Building > Giraffe ...(ii)
Now, from Eqs. (i) and (ii), we have
Pole > Signal > Building > Giraffe > (Tree)
Hence, tree is the shortest.

4. (*a*) From given information,
Raju > Vasant > Manohar ...(i)
Manohar > Jayant > Dutta ...(ii)
Now, combined Eqs. (i) and (ii), we have
(Raju) >Vasant > Manohar > Jayant > Dutta
Hence, Raju is the tallest in the group.

5. (*d*) From the given information, we get
P > M > (N) ...(i)
and R > S > M ...(ii)
Certainly, N is shortest among the given boys.

6. (*a*) Sohan < Sachin < Kunal ...(i)
Mohit is tallest. ...(ii)
Sachin < Amit < Kunal ...(iii)
From Eqs. (i), (ii) and (iii)
Sohan < Sachin < (Amit) < Kunal < Mohit
Amit is third.

7. (*a*) According to the question,
N > M
Y > M
N > X > Y
On arranging the above data, we get
∵ (N) > X > Y > M
So, N is the most intelligent among them.

8. (*c*) From the given information,
(Shanker) > Farhan > Mohan > Kannan > Rohan
Clearly, Shanker is the tallest.

9. (*d*) According to the question,
(Plum) > Mango > Guava > Banana = Coconut
So, Plum tree is the tallest.

10. (*b*) According to the question,
K > S > R

Madhav is the tallest.

$K > A > S$

On arranging the above data, we get

$M > K > A > S > R$

K = Keshav
S = Shailendra
R = Rakesh
M = Madhav
A = Aashish

or $R < (S) < A < K < M$

R	S	A	K	M
↓	↓	↓	↓	↓
1	2	3	4	5

Hence, Shailendra will be the second.

11. (*b*) Amit = Sumit, Sumit > Richa
Jyotsana > Richa > Saurabh
Jyotsana > Sumit
On arranging the above data, we get
(Jyotsana) > Sumit = Amit > Richa > Saurabh
So, Jyotsana is the eldest among them.

12. (*b*) Given, Pen < Pencil, ...(i)
Pencil < Book, ...(ii)
Book > Cap ...(iii)
From Eqs. (i) and (ii), we can derive that
Pen < Book
Hence, option (b) is the correct answer.

13. (*b*) From given information,
Simi > Renu ...(i)
Renu > Geeta ...(ii)
and Priya > Simi ...(iii)
Now, combined all the three equations, we have
(Priya) > Simi > Renu > Geeta
It is clear that Priya is the eldest.

14. (*c*) According to the question,
Priti > Rahul ; Yamuna = Divya
Lokita < Manju ; Rahul > Yamuna
Manju < Divya
∴ Priti > Rahul > Yamuna = Divya > Manju > (Lokita)
So, it is clear from the above arrangement, Lokita scored lowest among them.

15. (*a*) According to the question,
Sita > Kanika
Sita > Ila > Kanika
Manas/ Kanika > Shempa
Kanika > Manas
∴ Sita > Ila > Kanika > Manas > (Shempa)
So, Shempa is the youngest among them.

16. (*b*) Decreasing order (agewise)
$P > R > Q > S$
Decreasing order (moneywise)
$R > S > P > Q$
Hence, option (b) is correct answer.

17. (*a*) Let weight of $Q = x$
Then, weight of $P = 2x$
weight of $R = 2x$, weight of $T = \frac{2x}{3}$
and weight of $S = \frac{4x}{3}$

$\frac{2x}{3} < x < \frac{4x}{3} < 2x \Rightarrow T < Q < S < R$
⇒ weight of Q is only greater than weight of T.
∴ Option (a) is the correct answer.

18. (*d*) According to the question,
Lakshmi > Meenu
Lakshmi > Leela > Meenu
Meenu > Hari > Latha
On arranging the above data, we get
Lakshmi > Leela > Meenu > Hari > (Latha)
Hence, Latha is the youngest.

19. (*c*) According to the question,
Sashi > Sunita (2 yr)
Sunita > Bindu (3 yr)
Shekhar > Bindu (1 yr)
∴ Sashi > Sunita > Shekhar > (Bindu)
So, youngest person in the group is Bindu.

20. (*b*) According to the given information,

Order of Reading Newspaper	Men
1st	P
2nd	[T]
3rd	Q
4th	R
5th (Last)	S

∴ Clearly Q is the third one to read the newspaper.

21. (*a*) There are 8 speakers A, B, C, D, E, F, G and H.
According to the question,
A spoke after F and H spoke after A.
F
A
H
D spoke after H and before B.
F
A
H
D
B
C spoke before G and after B.
So, the sequence becomes
F
A
H
D
B
C
G
Now, we arrange them according to the time.
A took more time than B i.e. A > B
H took less time than B i.e. B > H
C took less time than E i.e. E > C
D took less time than H but more time than E i.e H > D > E

Now, the sequence becomes
(A) > B > H > D > E > C
It is clear that A spoke for the longest time.

Solutions (Q. Nos. 22 and 23) *Here, H and T in the subscript denoting heavier and taller persons.*

$B_H > A_H$ and C_H $C_T > B_T$
$A_H > C_H$ $C_T > D_T$, $D_T > A_T$
$D_H > B_H$ $B_T > D_T$

22. (*c*) $(D_H) > B_H > A_H > C_H$
Here, D is the heaviest.

23. (*b*) $(C_T) > B_T > D_T > A_T$
Here, C is the tallest.

Solutions (Q. Nos. 24-28)
Let age of Mahima = x yr
Then, age of Anita = $2x$ yr
Age of Rajan = $\frac{x}{2}$ yr
Age of Deepti = $4x$ yr
Age of Lata = $\frac{x}{4}$ yr
Now, we have the following arrangement in descending order
Deepti > Anita > Mahima > Rajan > Lata

24. (*c*) Lata is the youngest.

25. (*a*) Deepti is the eldest.

26. (*d*) There are no two persons of the same age as per the given information.

27. (*c*) Anita is younger than Deepti.

28. (*a*) Mahima's age = 16 yr
∴ Lata's age = $\frac{16}{4} = 4$ yr

Solutions (Q. Nos. 29-31) *According to the given information, the arrangement of persons according to height is as follows*
$C > E > A > B > D$
↑
86 cm

29. (*d*) If the height of the shortest person D is 68 cm, then the height of *B* can be all 69 cm, 78 cm and 81 cm.

30. (*a*) None of the persons is taller than C.

31. (*c*) A is just shorter than E.

Solutions (Q. Nos. 32-34) Let H and T subscript denote heavier and taller persons. From the given information,
$F_H > B_H$ ...(i)
$F_H > C_H$ ...(ii)
$B_T > A_T$ ...(iii)
$C_T > A_T$ ...(iv)
$D_T > B_T$ ...(v)
$D_H > C_H$ ...(vi)
$D_H > E_H$ ...(vii)
$E_H > F_H$ ...(viii)
$F_T > D_T$ ...(ix)

$E_H > A_H$ ...(x)

$A_H > F_H$ ...(xi)

From Eqs. (i) to (xi),

$D_H > E_H > A_H > F_H > B_H > C_H$ ...(xii)

$F_T > D_T > B_T > A_T$ ...(xiii)

$C_T > A_T$ ...(xiv)

32. (*c*) From Eq. (xii), D is the tallest.

33. (*a*) From Eq. (xii), A is third from the top.

34. (*a*) From Eq. (xii) and (xiii), it is clear that F is heavier than B and C but shorter than D.

Solutions (Q. Nos. 35-37) *According to the given information, arrangement is as follows*

F>E>C>A>B/D >B/D

↓ ↓

16 cm 9cm

35. (*d*) Here, third thinnest book = A

Given, thickness of book A = 9 cm

∴ Thickness of book E = 9 + 5 = 14 cm

36. (*a*) Given, C + F = 27

$\therefore C = 27 - F = 27 - 16 = 11$ cm [∵ F = 16]

Now, A = 9 cm and C = 11 cm

∴ A + C = 9 + 11

= 20 cm

37. (*c*) If B is 8 cm thick, then B is thicker than D.

Solutions (Q. Nos. 38-40) *From the given information, arrangement is as follow*

Q > T > U > S > P > R

72

38. (*e*) It is given that the store which sold the second highest number of books sold 72 books. From above it is clear that store T sold the second highest number of books.
So, store Q sold the highest number of books. By option, we can say store Q sold 89 books because 72 is the second highest.

39. (*b*) From the given arrangement, it is clear that store P sold the second lowest number of books.

40. (*e*) Given, P + T = 125 and T = 72

∴ P + 72 = 125 ⇒ P = 125 − 72 = 53

Hence, store P sold 53 books.

Solutions (Q. Nos. 41-46)
According to the question,

V > P ; P > Q

∴ V > P > Q

If R scores highest and T gets the least, we have R > ... >T
If S scores the highest and U or Q, scores the least, we have

S > ... > Q or S > ... > U

41. (*a*) If V ranks fifth, then P and Q coming after V will occupy sixth and seventh places respectively *i.e.,* Q ranks the least.
So, S will score the highest.

42. (*c*) If R gets the most, T ranks lowest and occupies seventh place. Since V always ranks above P and Q, so at the maximum, P and Q will occupy fifth and sixth places.
Hence, V will not rank lower than fourth.

43. (*d*) If S ranks 2nd, R ranks 1st and T ranks lowest. The order V > P > Q will be followed. Out of all the given options, only the arrangement given as per option (d)
i.e., R > S > U > V > P > Q > T is possible.

Clearly, options (a), (b) and (c) cannot follow. So, option (d) is correct.

44. (*d*) If S is ranked 6th and Q is ranked 5th , we have

– > – > – > – > Q > S > –

In this case, R will rank the highest and thus T will rank the least.
We have, R > – > – > – Q > S > T

Also, the order V > P > Q will be maintained.

The possible arrangements are

R > U > V > P > Q > S > T

or R > V > U > P > Q > S > T

or R > V > P > U > Q > S > T

Thus, option (d), *i.e.,* U can be ranked third or fourth is true.

45. (*d*) If R is ranked 2nd, S will rank 1st and Q or U lowest but Q ranks 5th. So, U ranks lowest.

Also, the order V > P > Q will be followed.

∴ Arrangement

S > R > V > P > Q > T > U
1 2 3 4 5 6 7

Hence, 6th place will be occupied by T.

46. (*d*) All information is needed.

TYPE 02

Position Test

In this type of questions, the rank or position of person(s)/ objects from either of the two ends of a row/queue is given and it is asked to determine the total number of persons in the group or the number of persons to the left/right (or above/below) of a particular person/objects etc. Sometimes, such questions are given in the form of a puzzle involving interchanging of seats by two or more persons/objects.

Different types of position tests will give you a better idea about such type of questions.

Rank of a Person/Object from Top or Bottom/from Left or Right

In this type of questions, it is asked to determine the rank or position of a person/object in a group of persons/objects either from the left (or right) or from the top (or bottom) depending upon the arrangement.

The position or rank can be calculated with the help of following formulae

(i) Position (or rank) from the left end (or top)
= Total number of persons/students
– Rank from the right end (or bottom) + 1

(ii) Position (or rank) from the right end (or bottom)
= Total number of persons/students
– Rank from the left end (or top) + 1

Examples given below will help you to understand this type of questions

Ex 06 In a class of 45 students, rank of Ayush is 15 from top, then rank of Ayush from bottom is « SSC MTS 2009

(a) 30 (b) 32 (c) 31 (d) 35

***Solution* (c)**

Top
15th
45
Ayush
Bottom

Ayush's rank from the bottom = Total number of students – Rank of Ayush from top + 1 = 45 – 15 + 1 = 31

***Ex* 07** In a row of 40 girls, when Komal was shifted to her left by 4 places, her place from the left end of the row became 10. What is the position of Swati from the right end of the row, if Swati was three places to the right of Komal's original position? « Syndicate Bank Clerk 2010

(a) 22 (b) 23 (c) 25 (d) 24
(e) None of these

***Solution* (d)** On shifting 4 places to the left, Komal is 10th from the left end of the row. Thus, Komal's original position was 14th from the left end.

Swati is 3 places to the right of Komal's original position. Clearly, Swati is 17th from the left end.

This can be easily understood from the following figure

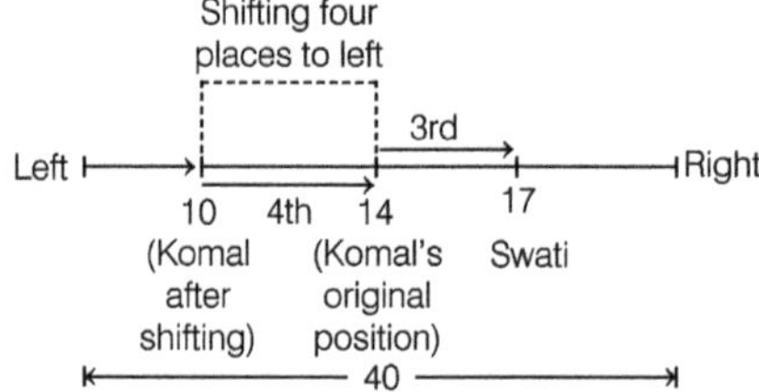

Now, Swati's position from right = (Total number of girls – Swati's position from left) + 1 = 40 – 17 + 1 = 23 + 1 = 24

So, Swati is 24th from the right end of the row.

Total Number of Objects/Persons in Queue

In this type of questions, it is asked to calculate the total number of persons when the rank of a person from both the ends is given. Following formula is helpful in the calculation of total number of objects/persons in a queue.

> Total number of objects/persons in a row or queue = Position (or rank) of object/person from the left end (or top or front) + Position (or rank) of object/person from the right end (or bottom or last) – 1

Examples discussed below will help you to understand this type of questions

***Ex* 08** In a class of students, Sandeep is 25th from top and 32nd from bottom in a class, then total number of students in the class is

(a) 56 (b) 50
(c) 57 (d) 58

***Solution* (a)** The information given in the question can be represented as shown figure

Top
25th
Sandeep
32nd
Bottom

Total students in a class
= (Rank of Sandeep from top + Rank of Sandeep from bottom) –1 = 25 + 32 – 1 = 57 – 1 = 56

***Ex* 09** In a class of thirty students, Mahesh is 14th from the left and Ramesh is 20th from the right end. How many students are there between Ramesh and Mahesh? « SSC CPO 2010

(a) 3 (b) 2
(c) 4 (d) Data inadequate

***Solution* (b)**

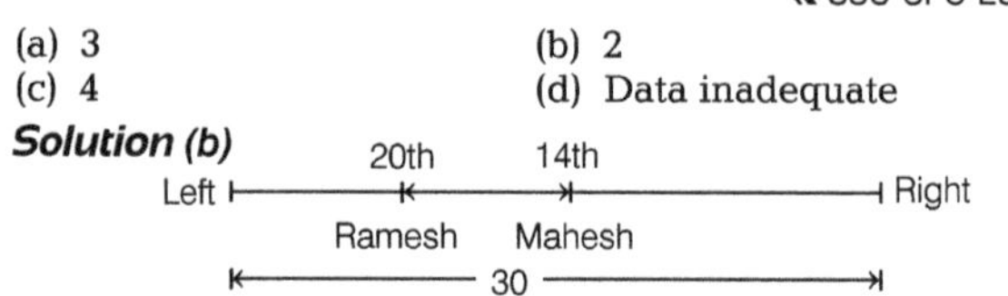

Ramesh's position from left = 30 – 20 + 1 = 10 + 1 = 11th

Mahesh's position from left = 14th

Clearly, there are 2 students in between Ramesh and Mahesh.

Hence, option (b) is the correct answer.

***Ex* 10** There are 17 girls in a row. The position of the girl at the middle is 9th from the beginning. What will be the position of the girl at the middle from the end? « MP Police SI 2017

(a) 9th (b) 10th (c) 7th (d) 8th

***Solution* (a)** Here, number of girls are odd. So, position of the girl at the middle will be same from the beginning and the end.

∴ Position of the girl at the middle from the end = Position of the girl at the middle from the beginning = 9 th.

***Ex* 11** In a row of students, Anil is 7th from the left while Jack is 18th from right. Both of them interchange their positions such that Anil becomes 21st from the left. How many people are there in the row? « SSC CGL 2011

(a) 38 (b) 39
(c) 40 (d) None of these

***Solution* (a)** Anil's original position from left = 7th

Jack's original position from right = 18th

Anil's position from left after interchange = 21st

Since, Anil exchanged his seat with Jack, it means Jack's original position is 21st from the left.

∴ Total number of people = (Initial position of Jack from the right + Initial position of Jack from the left) – 1
= 18 + 21 – 1 = 38

New Position of a Person (s) After Interchange of Positions between Two Persons

In this type of questions, the positions of two persons/objects are interchanged and it is asked to determine their new positions (from the left or right) which can be calculated with the help of following formulae

> (i) New position/place of first person/object after the interchange
> = [Difference of two positions / places of second person / object]
> + [Initial position/place of second person/object]
>
> (ii) New position /place of second person/object after the interchange
> = [Difference of two positions / places of second person / object]
> + [Initial position/place of second person/object]

Example discussed below will help you to understand this type of questions

***Ex* 12** In a queue of boys, Sandeep is 10th from left and Lalit is 5th from right. The places of Sandeep and Lalit are interchanged. If the new position of Sandeep is 15th from left, then the new position of Lalit from right is

(a) 10th (b) 11th
(c) 12th (d) 13th

Solution (a)

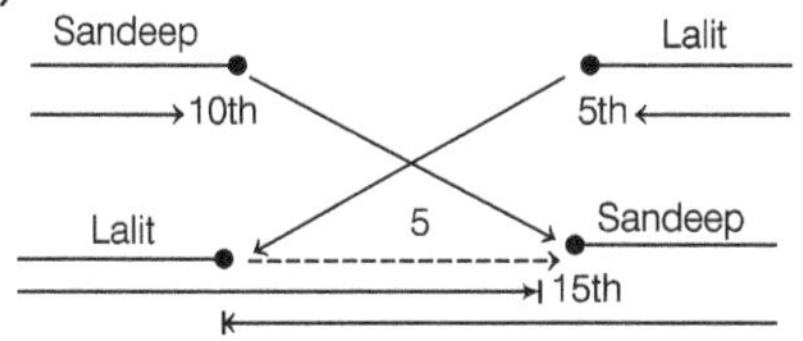

New position of Lalit from right end = [Difference of the two positions of Sandeep] +[Initial position of Lalit]
= (15 −10)+5 = 5+5
= 10th position

Number of Persons/Objects between the Original and Changed Position

In this type of questions, total number of persons/objects between the original and new position of a person/object is asked which can be calculated by the given formula.

> Total number of persons between two positions
> = New position − Old position −1

Example given below will help you to understand this type of questions

***Ex* 13** In a queue of girls, Akanksha is 9th from left and Mona is 17th from right. If the positions of Akanksha and Mona are interchanged, then new position of Akanksha is 15th from left. Find the number of girls between Mona and Akanksha.

(a) 4 (b) 5
(c) 6 (d) 7

Solution (b)

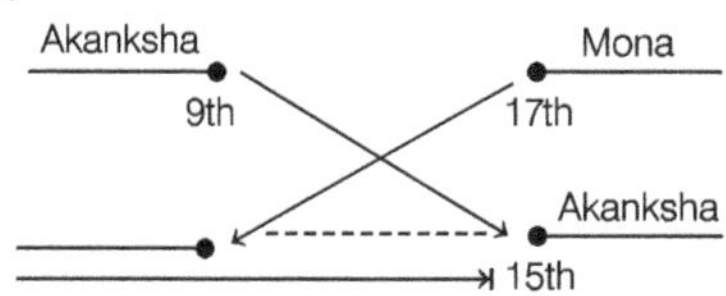

Total number of persons between Mona and Akanksha
= 15 − 9 − 1 = 5

Number of Persons in an Alternate Order

In these type of questions, number of persons standing in an alternate order under certain conditions is asked. The candidate is required to analyse the given information and answer the questions accordingly.

Example given below will help you to understand this type of questions

***Ex* 14** At a ticket counter there are 17 persons in a queue. If every second person in the queue is a female and also in the starting and at the end there is a female, then the total number of males in the queue is

(a) 7 (b) 10 (c) 8 (d) 9

Solution (c) Queue of the 17 persons can be shown as

F M F M F M F M F M F M F M F M F

∴ Total number of males = 8

Maximum and Minimum Number of Persons in a Row

If positions of two persons from the two opposite ends and the total number of places between these two positions is given, then

(i) Maximum number of persons that can be present in the row
= Sum of positions of both persons
+ Number of places in the middle

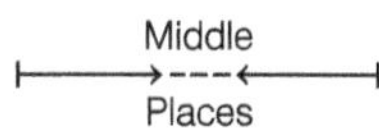

(ii) Minimum number of persons that can be present in the row
= Sum of positions of both persons
− Number of places in the middle − 2

Middle
Places

Example given below will help you to understand this type of questions

***Ex* 15** If in a row, Rohan is 10th from left and Mukesh is 13th from right and there are four persons in between Rohan and Mukesh, then find the maximum and minimum number of persons in the row.

(a) 27, 18 (b) 27, 17 (c) 30, 15 (d) 30, 19

Solution (b) For maximum number of persons, arrangement in the row will be as follows

Left — 10th Rohan — 4 — 13th Mukesh — Right

Total number of persons = Sum of positions of both persons
+ Number of places in middle
= 10 + 13 + 4 = 27

For minimum number of persons, arrangement in the row will be given as follows

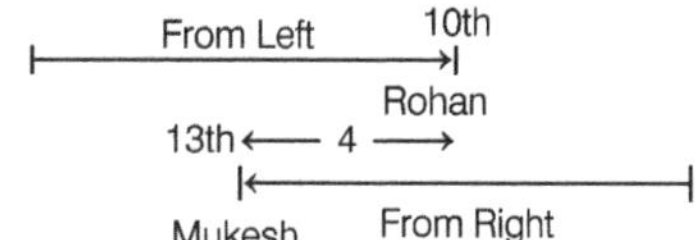

∴ Total number of persons = Sum of positions of both places
− Number of places in middle − 2
= (10 + 13) − 4 − 2 = 17

Hence, option (b) is the correct answer.

Practice CORNER 9.2

1. Rashmi is 14th from the right end in a row of 40 girls. What is her position from the left end?
(a) 25th (b) 27th
(c) 21st (d) None of these

2. Kavi ranked 9th from the top and 38th from the bottom in a class. How many students are there in the class?
(a) 45 (b) 42
(c) 46 (d) 44

3. A class of girls stands in a single line. One girl is 19th in order from both the ends. How many girls are there in the class?
(a) 27 (b) 37
(c) 38 (d) 39

4. Surbhi ranks 18th in a class of 49 students. What is her rank from the last?
(a) 31 (b) 28
(c) 35 (d) 32

5. Sohan ranks 7th from the top and 26th from the bottom in a class. How many students are there in the class?
(a) 31 (b) 32
(c) 33 (d) 34

6. In a row of letters, a letter is 5th from left end and 12th from the right end. How many letters are there in a row?
(a) 15 (b) 16 (c) 17 (d) 18

7. Sunita is the 11th from either end of a row of girls. How many girls are there in that row?
(a) 19 (b) 20
(c) 21 (d) 22

8. If Ramya's rank is 22nd out of 46 students. What is her rank from the last? « SSC 10+2 2015
(a) 25th (b) 29th
(c) 32nd (d) 24th

9. Ravi and Kishor got 13th and 14th rank, respectively from the top in the class. If there are total of 39 students in class, then what will be the position of both from bottom? « UPSSSC VDO 2015
(a) 26th and 25th (b) 27th and 26th
(c) 29th and 28th (d) 27th and 28th

10. In a row of boys, Jeevan is 7th from the start and 11th from the end. In another row of boys, Vikas is 10th from the start and 12th from the end. How many boys are there in both the rows together?
(a) 38 (b) 40
(c) 32 (d) Cannot be determined
(e) None of these

11. In a row of girls, Veena is 12th from the start and 19th from the end. In another row of girls, Sunita is 14th from the start and 20th from the end. How many girls are there in both the rows together?
(a) 72 (b) 65 (c) 63 (d) 61

12. In a line of boys Aman is 12th from top and Baman is 18th from bottom. If there are 6 boys between Aman and Baman, then how many maximum boys are there in the row? « SSC CPO 2017
(a) 34 (b) 36 (c) 35 (d) 37

13. Some books are arranged in a row. There are 5 books between 21st book from the right and 28th book from the left. The total number of books is more than 42. Find out the total number of books. « UPSSSC Amin 2016
(a) 44 (b) 49 (c) 52 (d) 54

14. 37 girls are standing in a row facing the school building. Ayesha is fifteenth from the left end. If she is shifted six places to the right what is her position from the right end? « SBI Clerk 2016
(a) 16th (b) 21st
(c) 20th (d) 18th
(e) None of these

15. In a row of 25 children, Nayan is 14th from the right end. Arun is 3rd to the left of Nayan in the row. What is Arun's position from the left end of the row?
(a) 8th (b) 9th (c) 7th (d) 10th
(e) None of these

16. There are 35 students in a class. Suman ranks third among the girls in the class. Amit ranks 5th among the boys in the class. Suman is one rank below Amit in the class. No, two students hold the same rank in the class. What is Amit's rank in the class?
(a) 7th (b) 5th
(c) 8th (d) Cannot be determined

17. In a row of thirty-seven boys facing South. 'R' is eighth to the right of 'T' who is fourteenth to the left of 'D'. How many boys are there between 'D' and 'R in the row? « UPSSSC Revenue Inspector 2016
(a) 4 (b) 5
(c) 8 (d) Data inadequate

18. In a row of children facing North, Ritesh is 12th from the left end. Sudhir, who is 22nd from the right end is 4th to the right of Ritesh. Total how many children are there in the row?
(a) 35 (b) 36 (c) 37 (d) 34
(e) None of these

19. In a class of 45 students, a boy is ranked 20th. When two boys joined, his rank was dropped by one. What is his new rank from the end?
(a) 25th (b) 26th
(c) 27th (d) 28th

20. There are 25 boys in a horizontal row. Rahul was shifted by three places towards his right side and he occupies the middle position in the row. What was his original position from the left end of the row?
(a) 15th (b) 16th
(c) 12th (d) 10th
(e) None of these

21. Aman is 16th from the left end in a row of boys and Vivek is 18th from the right end. Gagan is 11th place from Aman towards the right and 3rd from Vivek towards the right end. How many boys are there in the row?

(a) 40 (b) 42
(c) 48 (d) 41
(e) None of these

22. Kusum's position from left side of a line consisting of 16 girls, becomes 8th when she was displaced 2 positions towards left. Kusum's position, from right side of the line, before displacement, was « CGPSC Pre 2016

(a) 9th (b) 8th (c) 7th (d) 5th
(e) None of these

23. In a row, 'X' is at 14th position from the beginning and 'Y' is at 17th position from the end, while 'Z' is exactly in the middle way of 'X' and 'Y'. If there are total of 48 persons in the row, then how many persons are there between 'X' and 'Z'? « UPSSSC VDO 2016

(a) 6 (b) 7
(c) 8 (d) 9

24. In a row of girls, Kamya is fifth from the left and Preeti is sixth from the right. When they exchange their positions, then Kamya becomes thirteenth from the left. What will be Preeti's position from the right?

(a) 7th (b) 14th
(c) 11th (d) 18th

25. In a row at a bus stop, A is 7th from the left and B is 9th from the right. They both interchange their positions. Now, A becomes 11th from the left. How many people are there in the row? « MPPSC 2018

(a) 10 (b) 20 (c) 19 (d) 18

26. In a row 'A' is in the 11th position from the left and 'B' is in the 10th position from the right. If 'A' and 'B' interchange, then 'A' becomes 18th from the left. How many persons are there in the row other than 'A' and 'B'? « WBCS 2020

(a) 27 (b) 26 (c) 25 (d) 24

27. Consider a group comprising of 4 students : Reena, Beena, Meena and Neena, who stand in a row. Reena and Beena stand in 6th and 7th positions respectively from the left. Meena and Neena stand in the 4th and 5th positions respectively from the right. When Beena and Meena exchange their positions, then Beena will be 15th from the left. Reena's position from the right is

(a) 6 (b) 18 (c) 13 (d) 14

28. A hawker is in the middle compartment of an interconnected train with 17 bogies. He moves six compartments backward and gets down on the next station. Now he enters in the third compartment next to engine. How many compartments he is far away from his original position? « UPSSSC Junior Assist. 2015

(a) 3 (b) 6 (c) 5 (d) 8

29. In a row of boys, Sachin is eleventh from the left and Raj is seventh from the right. If they interchange their places, Sachin becomes sixteenth from the left. How many boys are there in the row? « UPSSSC Forest Guard 2018

(a) 21 (b) 22 (c) 23 (d) 24

30. Ram is standing in a line of students and his position is 10th from left and Shyam's position is 5th from right. Ram and Shyam interchanged their positions, then Ram is on 15th position from left. Find out the position of Shyam from right? « UPSSSC Excise Constable 2016

(a) 10th (b) 11th (c) 12th (d) 13th

Answers / WITH EXPLANATIONS

1. (*b*) Required position = (40 + 1 – 14) = 27th from left.

2. (*c*) Required number = (38 + 9 – 1) = 47 – 1 = 46

3. (*b*) Clearly, the girl at the 19th position is exactly in the middle of both the ends.
∴ Total number of girls = (18 + 1 + 18) = 37

4. (*d*) Surbhi's rank from last = (49 + 1 – 18) = 32

5. (*b*) Total students in the class = 7 + 26 – 1 = 33 – 1 = 32

6. (*b*) Number of letters in the row = 5 + 12 – 1 = 16

7. (*c*) Total number of girls = 11 + 11 – 1 = 22 – 1 = 21

8. (*a*) Ramya's rank from the last
= Total students – rank from start + 1 = 46 – 22 + 1 = 25th

9. (*b*) Ravi's position from bottom = Total number of students – Ravi's position from top +1
= 39 – 13 + 1 = 27th

Kishor's position from bottom
= Total number of students – Kishor's position from top +1
= 39 – 14 + 1 = 26 th

10. (*a*) Total number of boys
= (Number of boys in Jeevan's row) + (Number of boys in Vikas's row)
= (6 + 1 + 10) + (9 + 1 + 11) = (17 + 21) = 38

11. (*c*) In first row, Veena is 12th from start and 19th from end.
Then, total number of girls = (12 + 19 – 1) = 30
In second row, Sunita is 14th from start and 20th from the end.
Then, total number of girls = (14 + 20 – 1) = 33
∴ Total number of girls = 30 + 33 = 63

12. (*b*) Number of boys between Aman and Baman = Total number of boys in row – (Aman's rank from top + Baman's rank from bottom)
⇒ 6 = Total number of boys in row –(12 + 18)
∴ Total number of boys in row = 6 + 30 = 36

13. (*d*) Total number of books = 28 + 21 + 5 = 54

14. (*e*) Present position of Ayesha = 15 + 6 = 21st from left
∴ Position of Ayesha from right = 37 – 21 + 1 = 17th

15. (*b*) Nayan's position from left = (25 + 1 – 14) = 12th
∴ Arun's position = (12 – 3) = 9th from left

16. (*a*) Suman ranks 3rd in the class among the girls.
Amit ranks 5th among the boys.
Suman comes one rank after Amit in the class.
It means two girls and four boys rank higher than Amit in the class.
So, Amit ranks 7th in the class.

17. (*b*) According to the question,

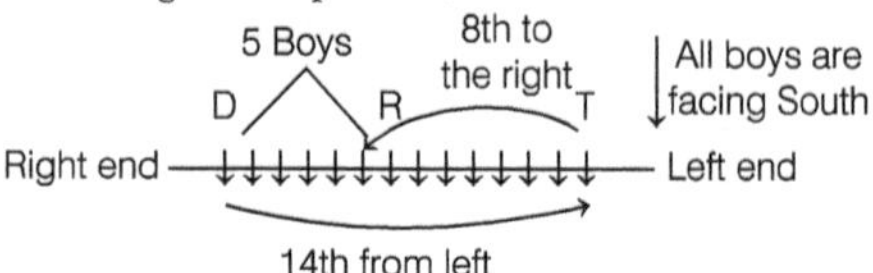

Hence, it is clear from the above diagram that 5 boys are there between D and R.

18. (*c*)

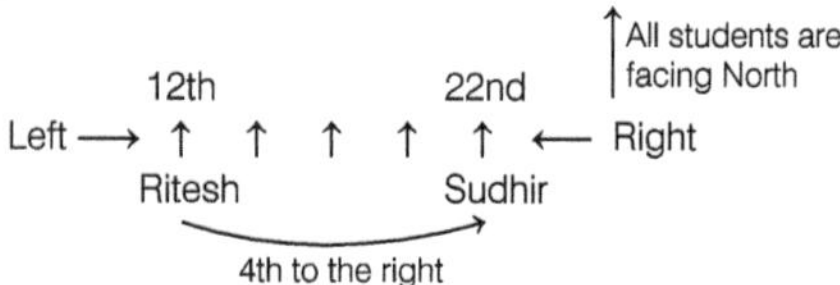

Sudhir's position from left = (12 + 4) = 16 th from left
Clearly, there are three students between Ritesh and Sudhir.

∴ Total number of children = (12 + 3 + 22) = 37

19. (*c*) Total number of boys after 2 new boys joined = 47
Since, the rank of the boy dropped by 1, it became 21st 20th.

∴ His new rank from the end = 47 − 21 + 1 = 27th

20. (*d*) When Rahul was shifted by three places towards his right side, then he occupies the middle position *i.e.*, 13th position.

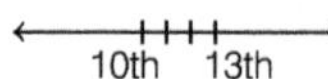

Thus, his original position from the left end of the row
= 13 − 3 = 10th

21. (*d*) Vivek is 18th from the right end and Gagan is third to the right of Vivek. So, Gagan is 15th from the right end. There are 15 boys to the left of Aman, 10 boys between Aman and Gagan and 14 boys to the right of Gagan.

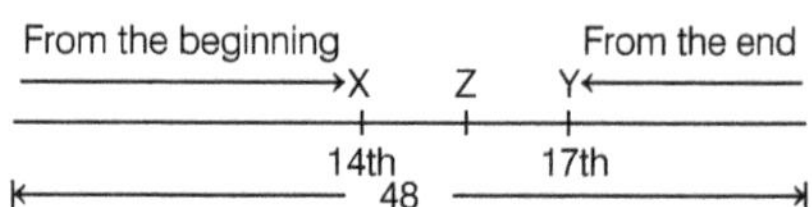

∴ Number of boys in the row = 15 + 1 + 10 + 1 + 14 = 41

22. (*c*) Kusum's position from left before displacement would have been 10th. There are 6 more girls to her right. Hence, her position from right, before displacement was 7th.

23. (*c*) According to the question,

∵ Total number of persons = 48
Then, the number of persons between X and Y
= 48 − (14 + 17) = 48 − 31 = 17

∴ Total number of persons between X and Z = $\frac{17-1}{2} = 8$

24. (*b*) Kamya's new position is 13th from left. But it is the same as Preeti's earlier position which is 6th from the right.

The row consists of (12 + 1 + 5) = 18 girls

Now, Preeti's new position is Kamya's earlier position which is 5th from the left.

∴ Preeti's new position from the right = 18 − 5 + 1 = 13 + 1 = 14th

25. (*c*)

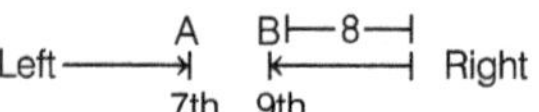

After interchanging the positions, A becomes 11th from left

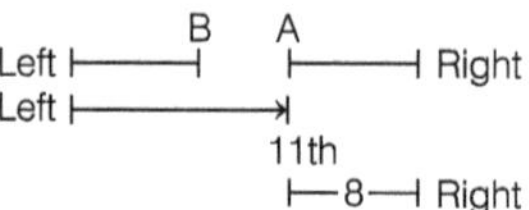

Total number of people in the row = 11 + 8 = 19

26. (*c*) According to the question,

If they interchange;

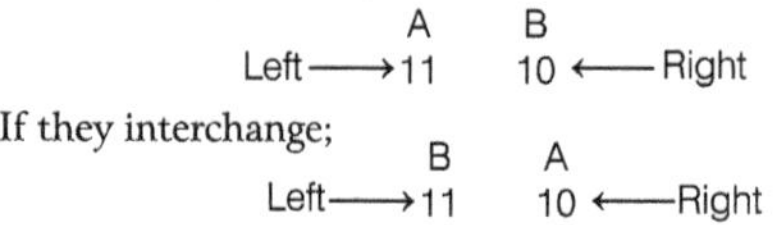

∴ Total number of persons = 18 + 10 − 1 = 27
Number of persons other than A and B = 27 − 2 = 25

27. (*c*) From given information,

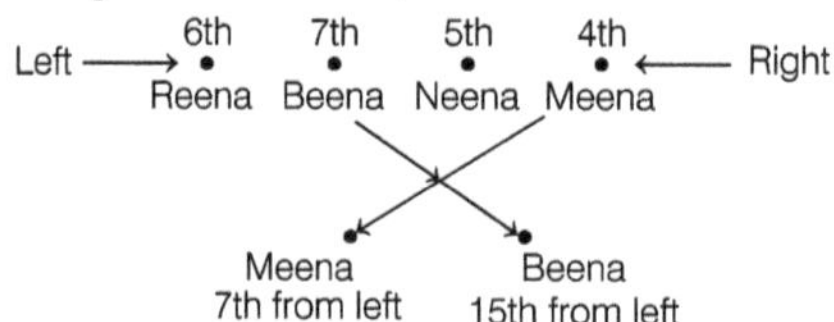

Total number of students = 15 + 4 − 1 = 18
Reena's position from left = 6th
Then, Reena's position from right = 18 − 5 = 13th

28. (*c*) According to the question,

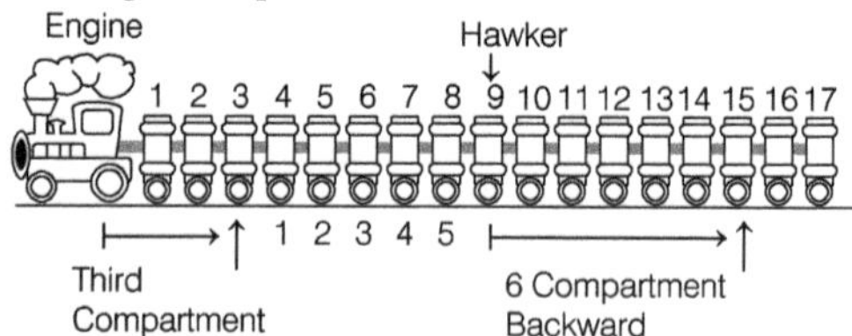

Starting position of hawker
= Middle compartment of 17 bogies train
$= \frac{17+1}{2} = \frac{18}{2} = 9$th compartment

On next station, he enters in the third compartment next to engine.

∴ New position of hawker = Third compartment from engine
Now, distance from his original position = (9 − 3) − 1
= 5th compartment

Hence, hawker is 5th compartment far away from his original position.

29. (*b*) According to the question,

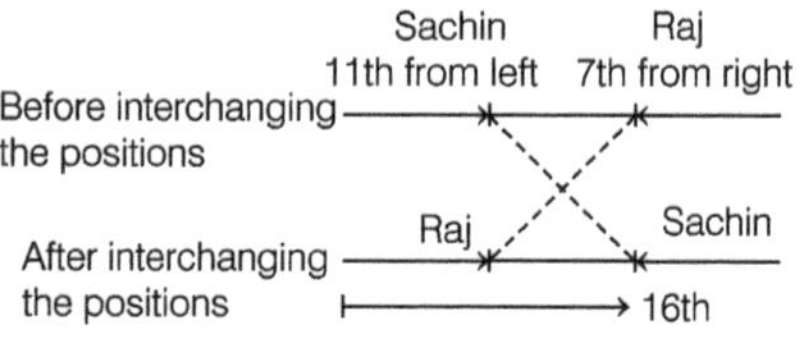

∴ Total number of boys in the row = (Raj's earlier position + Sachin's new position) − 1
= (7 + 16) − 1 = 22

30. (*a*) According to the question,

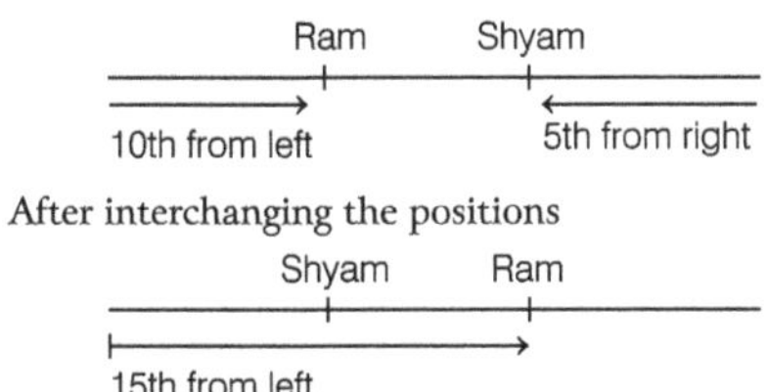

∴ Total number of students in the row $= 15 + 5 - 1 = 19$
After interchanging the position of Shyam from right
$= 19 + 1 - 10 = 10$ th

TYPE 03

Time Sequence Test

In these questions, the candidate is required to find out a particular day/date on the basis of several statements provided to them or given in the question. The questions asked from this section neither require a special methodology nor any special formulae. The questions are very basic in nature and require common sense and logical ability.

Examples given below will help you to understand these type of questions

Ex 16 Kamal remembers that his brother Dinu's birthday falls after 20th May but before 28th May, while Garima remembers that Dinu's birthday falls before 22nd May but after 12th May. On what date Dinu's birthday falls?

(a) 22nd May (b) 21st May
(c) Cannot be determined (d) None of these

Solution (*b*) According to Kamal, Dinu's birthday falls on one of the days —(21st/22nd/23rd/24th/25th/26th/27th) May.

According to Garima, Dinu's birthday falls on one of the days (13th/14th/15th/16th/17th/18th/19th/20th/21st) May.

The common date in both the group of dates = 21st May

Clearly, Dinu's birthday falls on 21st May.

Ex 17 Arun remembers that his mother's birthday is after April 17 but before April 21 whereas his sister Urmila remembered that their mother's birthday is after 19th but before April 24. Which of the following days in April is definitely their mother's birthday? « MP Patwari 2017

(a) 21st (b) 19th
(c) 20th (d) 22nd

Solution (c) According to Arun his mother's birthday falls on one of the day (18th/19th/20th) April.

According to Urmila her mother's birthday falls on (20th /21st/22nd/23rd) April.

Since 20th is common in both , therefore mother's birthday is definitely on 20th April.

Practice / CORNER 9.3

1. Ayush remembers that Sanjay's birthday is certainly after January 12 but not later than 16th January. If Mehar remembers that Sanjay's birthday is before 17th of Jan but not before 13th Jan. On which of the following days was Sanjay's birthday?

(a) 14th (b) 15th
(c) 16th (d) Either 14th or 15th

2. A remembers that B celebrated his birthday after 17 but before June, 22 while B remembers that the birthday was celebrated before 24 but after the June 20. On which date was the birthday celebrated? « CGPSC 2016

(a) June 23 (b) June 22
(c) June 21 (d) June 17
(e) None of these

3. Pratap correctly remembers that his mother's birthday is before 23rd April but after 19th April, whereas his sister correctly remembers that their mother's birthday is not on or after 22nd April. On which day in April is definitely their's mother's birthday? « Canara Bank PO 2010

(a) 20th (b) 21st
(c) 20th or 21st (d) 22nd
(e) None of these

4. Rajat correctly remembers that his mother's birthday is not after 18th of June. His sister correctly remembers that their mother's birthday is before 20th June but after 17th June.On which day in April was definitely their mother's birthday?

(a) 17th (b) 19th
(c) 18th (d) 17th or 18th

5. Meena correctly remembers that her father's birthday is after 18th May but before 22nd May. Her brother correctly remembers that their father's birthday is before 24th May but after 20th May. On which date in May was definitely their father's birthday? « Andhra Bank PO 2010

(a) 20th (b) 19th
(c) 18th (d) Cannot be determined
(e) None of these

6. Mohan correctly remembers that his father's birthday is before 20th January but after 16th January whereas his sister correctly remembers that their father's birthday is after 18th January but before 23rd January. On which date in January is definitely their father's birthday? « Syndicate Bank PO 2010

(a) 18th (b) 19th
(c) 20th (d) Data inadequate
(e) None of these

7. Satish read a book on Sunday. Sudha read that book one day prior to Anil but 4 days after Satish. On which day did Anil read the book?

(a) Friday (b) Thursday (c) Tuesday (d) Saturday

8. Nitin correctly remembers that Nidhi's birthday is before Friday but after Tuesday. Deepak correctly remembers that Nidhi's birthday is after Wednesday but before Saturday. On which of the following days does Nidhi's birthday definitely fall? « PNB Clerk 2009

(a) Monday (b) Tuesday (c) Wednesday (d) Thursday
(e) Cannot be determined

9. Samant remembers that his brother's birthday is after 16th but before 20th of January, while his sister remembers that her brothers' birthday is after 17th but before 19th of February. On which date of January, is Samant's brother's birthday?

(a) 16 th (b) 18 th (c) 19 th (d) 17 th

10. Vinay remembers that his brother Anupam's birthday is after 20th of August but before 28th of August, while Rita remembers that Anupam's birthday is before 22nd of August but after 12th of August. On which date does Anupam's birthday fall? « RRB PO 2010

(a) 20th August (b) 21th August
(c) 22nd August (d) Cannot be determined
(e) None of these

11. Sneha correctly remembers that her father's birthday is before 16th june but after 11th june whereas, her younger brother correctly remembers that their father's birthday is after 13th june but before 18th june and her elder brother correctly remembers that their father's birthday is on an even date. On what date in june, is definitely their father's birthday?
« Vijaya Bank Clerk 2010

(a) Sixteenth (b) Twelfth
(c) Fourteenth (d) Data inadequate
(e) None of these

12. Ranjana correctly remembers that Kiran's birthday was after Tuesday but before Friday. Rajan correctly remembers that Kiran's birthday was after Wednesday but before Sunday. On which day of the week does Kiran's birthday definitely fall ? « CBI Clerk 2009

(a) Monday (b) Thursday
(c) Saturday (d) Cannot be determined
(e) None of these

Answers / WITH EXPLANATIONS

1. (*d*) Days by Ayush, [13, [14, 15]] in January
Days by Mehar, [[14, 15], 16] in January
Clearly, 14th and 15th January are common in both the groups.
Hence, the correct answer is either 14th or 15th January.

2. (*c*) According to A,
B's birthday falls on (18th/19th/20th / (21st)) June
According to B, B's birthday falls on((21st)/ 22nd/23rd) June
The only common date is 21 June.

3. (*c*) Days by Pratap, [[20 /21]/ 22] in April
Days by his sister, not on or after 22 April
Clearly, the answer is [[20 / 21]] in April i.e. 20th / 21st April.

4. (*c*) Days by Rajat, June (18) or earlier.
Days by his sister, June (18) or June 19.
Clearly, June 18 is the required day.

5. (*e*) Days by Meena, [19th / 20th / (21st)] May.
Days by her brother, (21st) / 22nd / 23rd May.
Clearly, 21st May is common in both the groups and hence, it is the required day.

6. (*b*) Days by Mohan, [17th / 18th / (19th)] January.
Days by sister, [(19th), 20th, 21st or 22nd] January.
Required day is 19th January as it is common in both the groups.

7. (*a*) Sudha read the book 4 days after Sunday. It means Sudha read the book on Thursday. Hence, Anil will read the book on Friday.

8. (*d*)

According to	Nitin's Birthday
Nitin	Wednesday/[Thursday]
Deepak	[Thursday] / Friday

Here, Thursday is common to both. Hence, correct day is Thursday.

9. (*b*)

According to	Possibility of Date of January
Samant	17/ (18) / 19
Sister	(18)

Here, 18th is common to both. Hence, the correct date is 18th January.

10. (*b*)

According to	Possibility of Date of August
Vinay	(21)/ 22/ 23/24/25/26/27
Rita	13/14/15/16/17/18/19/20/(21)

Here, 21 is common to both. So, the correct date is 21st August.

11. (*c*)

According to	Possibility of Date of June
Sneha	12/13/(14) /15
Younger Brother	(14) /15/16/17
Elder Brother	...,(14) /16, ...

Here, 14 is common to all the groups. Hence, the correct date is 14th, June.

12. (*b*)

According to	Possiblity of Day
Ranjana	Wednesday/ [Thursday]
Rajan	[Thursday]/ Friday/Saturday

Clearly, Thursday is common to both. Hence, the correct day is Thursday.

Master Exercise

DIRECTIONS ~ (Q. Nos. 1-3) *Read the following information carefully and answer the questions that follow.*

I. There is a group of five girls.
II. Kamini is second in height but younger than Rupa.
III. Pooja is taller than Monika but younger in age.
IV. Rupa and Monika are of the same age but Rupa is tallest between them.
V. Neelam is taller than Pooja and elder to Rupa.

1. If they are arranged in the ascending order of height, who will be in the third position?
(a) Monika (b) Monika or Rupa
(c) Rupa (d) None of these

2. If they are arranged in descending order of their ages, who will be in the fourth position?
(a) Monika or Rupa (b) Monika
(c) Kamini (d) None of these

3. To answer the question, "Who is the youngest person in the group", which of the following statements is superfluous?
(a) Only I (b) Only V
(c) Only II (d) Either I or IV

4. There are four persons A, B, C and D. The total amount of money with A and B together is equal to the total amount of money with C and D together but the total amount of money with B and D together is more than the amount of money with A and C together. The amount of money with A is more than that with B. Who has the least amount of money?
(a) B (b) C
(c) D (d) Cannot be determined

5. Among five people J, K, L, M and N (each running at a different speed), who ran at the third fastest speed? M run faster than L but slower than K. J ran slower than only one person. L did not run at the slowest speed.
« NICL Assist. 2015
(a) Cannot be determined (b) M
(c) N (d) L
(e) K

DIRECTIONS ~(Q. Nos. 6-10) *Read the following information carefully and answer the following questions.*

A blacksmith has five iron articles A, B, C, D and E each having a different weight.

I. A weighs twice as much as B.
II. B weighs four and half times as much as C.
III. C weighs half as much as D.
IV. D weighs half as much as E.
V. E weighs less than A but more than C.

6. Which of the following is the lightest in weight?
(a) A (b) B (c) C (d) D

7. E is lighter in weight than which of the other two articles?
(a) A, B (b) D, C (c) A, C (d) D, B

8. E is heavier than which of the following two articles?
(a) D, B (b) D, C (c) A, C (d) A, B

9. Which of the following is the heaviest in weight?
(a) A (b) B (c) C (d) D

10. Which of the following represents the descending order of weights of the articles?
(a) A, B, E, D, C (b) B, D, E, A, C
(c) A, B, C, D, E (d) C, D, E, B, A

11. In a row at a bus stop, A is 7th from the left and B is 9th from the right. They both interchange their positions. Now, A becomes 11th from the left. How many people are there in the row?
(a) 10 (b) 20
(c) 19 (d) 18

DIRECTIONS ~ (Q. Nos. 12-14) *Read the given information carefully and answer the questions.*

Each of the six buildings P, Q, R, S, T and U houses different number of offices. S has more offices than only T and R. Q has more number of offices than P but less than U. R does not have the least number of offices. The building which has the least number of offices has 5 offices. The building which has second highest number of offices has 23 offices. S has 11 less number of offices than Q.
« IBPS PO 2015

12. Which of the following buildings has the second least number of offices?
(a) Q (b) U (c) R (d) P
(e) T

13. If the number of offices in P is an even number which is divisible by 2 as well as 3. How many does P have?
(a) 20 (b) 24 (c) 16 (d) 18
(e) 12

14. Which of the following is the number of offices in R?
(a) 25 (b) 12 (c) 13 (d) 14
(e) 11

15. A, B, C, D and E are five persons who obtained different marks in some test. B obtained more marks than C only. D and E obtained marks less than A only. Who obtained the minimum marks? « CGPSC Pre 2016
(a) D (b) E
(c) B (d) Insufficient data
(e) None of these

DIRECTIONS ~ (Q. Nos.16-19) *Read the following information and answer the questions that follow.*

In a study of five brands of pain relieving tablets P, Q, R, S and T, the brands were tested and ranked against each other as more or less effective per dose. The following results were obtained

I. P was more effective than Q.
II. The effectiveness of R was less than that of S.
III. T was the least effective brand tested.
IV. Q and R were equally effective.
V. The effectiveness of S was greater than that of Q.

16. If the above statements are true, which of the following must also be true?
(a) P and S were equally effective.
(b) P was the most effective.
(c) S was the most effective.
(d) R was less effective than P.

17. All the informations in the results given above can be derived from which of the following groups of statements?
(a) Statements I, II and III (b) Statements I, III and IV
(c) Statements I, III and V (d) Statements I, II, III and IV

18. If a sixth brand M is tested and found to be more effective than S, then which of the following must be true, if the findings of the study are correct?
(a) M is the most effective of all the six brands tested.
(b) Atleast four of the six brands tested are less effective than M.
(c) M is more effective than P.
(d) M is less effective than P.

19. If R is more expensive per dose than P and T is less expensive per dose than R, which of the following must be true, according to the study, for a consumer, who wishes to buy a pain reliever with the greatest effectiveness for the amount spent per dose?
(a) P should be purchased instead of R.
(b) P should be purchased instead of S.
(c) T should be purchased instead of R.
(d) Q should be purchased instead of R, if Q is of the same price as S.

DIRECTIONS ~ (Q. Nos. 20-25) *Read the following information carefully and answer the questions that follow.*

Six compounds are being tested for possible use in a new anti-poison, 'Sweet 'N' Deadly'.

I. U is sweeter than V and more deadly than Z.
II. V is sweeter than Y and less deadly than Z.
III. W is less sweet than X and less deadly than U.
IV. X is less sweet and more deadly than Y.
V. Y is less sweet and more deadly than U.
VI. Z is sweeter than U and less deadly than W.

20. Which is the sweetest?
(a) U (b) W (c) X (d) Z

21. Which of the following is/are both sweeter and more deadly than V?
(a) Only U (b) Only W (c) Only Z (d) U and Z

22. Which of the following statement adds no new information about sweetness to the statements that precede it?
(a) I (b) III
(c) IV (d) V

23. Which of the following is/are sweeter than Y and more deadly than W?
(a) Only U (b) Only V
(c) Only Z (d) U and V

24. Which is the least deadly?
(a) U (b) V (c) W (d) Y

25. Which is the most deadly?
(a) Z (b) W (c) Y (d) X

26. Six ropes viz A, B, C, D, E and F each of different length are kept on a table but not necessarily in the same order. B is shorter than A but longer than F. D is longer than A. C is shorter than A but longer than B. F is not the shortest. Which is the shortest rope? « MHT MBA 2017
(a) A (b) E (c) C (d) B (e) D

27. Roshan is taller than Hardik who is shorter than Sushil. Niza is taller than Harry but shorter than Hardik. Sushil is shorter than Roshan. Who is the tallest?
(a) Roshan (b) Sushil
(c) Hardik (d) Harry

28. A is taller than B. D is shorter than C but taller than E. Only D is between A and B in terms of height. Who is the tallest of all? « UPSSSC Junior Assist. 2015
(a) D (b) A (c) B (d) C

29. Gita is older than her cousin Mita. Mita's brother Bhanu is older than Gita. When Mita and Bhanu are visiting Gita, all three like to play a game of Monopoly. Mita wins more often than Gita does.

Which of the following can be concluded from the above?
(a) When he plays Monopoly with Mita and Gita, Bhanu often loses
(b) Of the three, Gita is the oldest
(c) Gita hates to lose at Monopoly
(d) Of the three, Mita is the youngest

30. Priya is taller than Tiya and shorter than Siya. Riya is shorter than Siya and taller than Priya. Riya is taller than Diya, who is shorter than Tiya. Arrange them in order of descending heights.
(a) Priya > Siya > Riya > Tiya > Diya
(b) Riya > Siya > Priya > Diya > Tiya
(c) Siya > Riya > Priya > Tiya > Diya
(d) Siya > Priya > Riya > Diya >Tiya

31. There is a group of seven friends Rani, Neha, Mira, Juhi, Hema, Isha and Kuku. Mira is taller than Hema and Kuku. Rani is not the tallest but taller than Mira. Neha is shorter than Hema. Juhi is taller than Hema but shorter than Kuku. If they are ranked in the ascending order of their heights, who will be ranked fifth? « MAT 2019
(a) Kuku (b) Mira (c) Isha (d) Juhi

32. There are five rivers A, B, C, D and E. A is shorter than B but longer than E. C is the longest one. If D is shorter than B but longer than A, then which is the shortest river? « UPSSSC Excise Constable 2016

(a) E (b) A (c) D (d) B

33. There are five books A, B, C, D and E. Book C lies above D, book E is below A, D is above A and B is below E. Which book is at the bottom?

(a) E (b) B (c) A (d) C

34. A is 16th from the left end in a row of boys and V is 18th from the right end. G is 11th from A towards the right and 3rd from V towards the right end. How many boys are there in the row? « UPSC CSAT 2020

(a) 40 (b) 41 (c) 42
(d) Cannot be determined due to insufficient data

35. Mohit correctly remembers that his father's birthday is not after 18th of April. His sister correctly remembers that their father's birthday is before 20th but after 17th of April. On which day in April was definitely their father's birthday? « Corporation Bank Clerk 2010

(a) 17th (b) 19th
(c) 18th (d) 17th or 18th
(e) None of these

36. In a row of girls, Kanta is 12th from the left and Kirti is 8th from the right. If they interchange their seats, Kanta becomes 15th from the left.

How many girls are there in the row?

« UKPSC Assist. Conservator of Forest 2019

(a) 20 (b) 21 (c) 22 (d) 24

37. Jaya's position from the left in a row of students is 12th and Rekha's position from the right is 20th. After interchanging their position, Jaya becomes 22nd from the left. How many students are there in the row?

(a) 30 (b) 31 (c) 41 (d) 34

38. Samant remembers that his brother's birthday is after 16th but before 19th of February while his sister remembers that her brother's birthday is after 14th but before 18th of February. On which date in February is Samant's brother's birthday?

(a) 16th (b) 18th (c) 19th (d) 17th

39. In a class among the passed students Neeta is 22nd from the top and Kalyan, who is 5 ranks below Neeta is 34th from the bottom. All the students from the class appeared for an examination. If the ratio of the students who passed in the examination to those who failed is 4 : 1 for the class, how many students were there in the class?

(a) 90 (b) 60
(c) 75 (d) Data inadequate
(e) None of these

40. Seema correctly remembers that she took leave after 21st October and before 27th October. Her colleague Rita took leave on 23rd October but Seema was present on that day. If 24th October was a public holiday and 26th October was Sunday, on which day in October did Seema take leave? « IDBI Bank PO 2010

(a) 22nd October (b) 25th October
(c) 22nd or 25th October (d) 23rd October
(e) None of these

41. In a running race, Rekha came ahead of Mala by a 10 s margin; Inika came ahead of Aarushi by 12 s and Vasantha came ahead of Gauri by 18 s. Mala came just a second after Vasantha and Inika came 2 s after Gauri. Who among the given friends came third in the race? « UPSSSC VDO 2018

(a) Inika (b) Rekha (c) Mala (d) Gauri

DIRECTIONS ~ (Q. Nos. 42 and 43) *Read the following information carefully and answer the questions that follow.* « SNAP 2013

Six students A, B, C, D, E and F participated in a dancing competition wherein they won prizes 12000, 10000, 8000, 6000, 4000, 2000 according to the position secured. The following information is known to us

I. A won less money than B.
II. The difference between the winning of C and F was ₹ 2000.
III. The difference between the winning of D and F was at least ₹ 4000.
IV. E won the ₹ 8000 prize.

42. Which of the following could be the ranking from first place to sixth place of students?

(a) A, D, E, B, F, C (b) B, A, E, C, F, D
(c) F, B, E, A, C, D (d) B, A, E, D, C, F

43. If A won ₹ 4000, how much in total did C and F win?

(a) ₹ 6000 (b) ₹ 10000 (c) ₹ 22000 (d) ₹ 18000

DIRECTIONS ~ (Q. Nos. 44-46) *Study the following information carefully and answer the questions given below.*

There are six persons who all are of different height. A is taller than C and D but shorter than E. The one who is third shortest is 102 cm in height B is taller than A, E is not the tallest. The one who is second tallest is 119 cm in height. Neither A nor C is the third shortest person among all. C is not the shortest among all. F is taller than D. « IBPS Clerk 2018

44. Who among the following is the second tallest?

(a) F (b) E (c) A (d) C
(e) None of these

45. What will be the possible height of A?

(a) 120 cm (b) 100 cm (c) 112 cm (d) 101 cm
(e) None of these

46. Who among the following is third shortest?

(a) A (b) C (c) B (d) F
(e) None of these

DIRECTIONS ~(Q. Nos. 47 and 48) *For the following 2 (Two) questions : Read the following statements* S1 *and* S2 *and answer the two questions that follow* « UPSC CSAT 2019

S1 : Twice the weight of Sohan is less than the weight of Mohan or that of Rohan.

S2 : Twice the weight of Rohan is greater than the weight of Mohan or that of Sohan.

47. Which one of the following statements is correct?

(a) Weight of Mohan is greatest
(b) Weight of Sohan is greatest
(c) Weight of Rohan is greatest
(d) 'Whose weight is greatest' cannot be determined.

48. Which one of the following statement is correct?

(a) Weight of Mohan is least
(b) Weight of Sohan is least
(c) Weight of Rohan is least
(d) 'Whose weight is least' cannot be determined

DIRECTIONS ~ (Q. Nos. 49-51) *For the following 3 (three) questions. Read the following information and answer the three questions that follow*

« UPSC CSAT 2019

Six students A, B, C, D, E and F appeared in several tests. Either C or F scores the highest. Whenever C scores the highest. then E scores the least. Whenever F scores the highest, B scores the least. In all the tests they got different marks : D scores higher than A, but they are close competitors; A scores higher than B; C scores higher than A.

49. If F stands second in the ranking, then the position of B is

(a) Third (b) Fourth (c) Fifth (d) Sixth

50. If B scores the least, then rank of C will be

(a) Second (b) Third
(c) Fourth (d) Second or third

51. If E is ranked third, then which one of the following is correct?

(a) E gets more marks than C (b) C gets more marks than E
(c) A is ranked fourth (d) D is ranked fifth

Answers / WITH EXPLANATIONS

Solutions (Q. Nos. 1-3) *Descending order of heights and ages is as given below*

Arrangement of persons according to Height
Rupa > Kamini > Neelam > Pooja > Monika

Arrangement of persons according to Age
Neelam > Rupa = Monika > Pooja > Kamini
or Neelam > Rupa = Monika > Kamini > Pooja

1. (*d*) Neelam will be in the third position when the persons are arranged in ascending order of height.

2. (*d*) Fourth position cannot be determined, if they are arranged in descending order of their ages.

3. (*a*) Only Statement I is superfluous.

4. (*b*) According to the question,

$A+B=C+D$; $B+D>A+C$; $A>B$

Now, $B+D>A+C$ and $A>B$

$\Rightarrow \quad B+D>A+C>B+C$

$\Rightarrow \quad B+D>B+C \Rightarrow D>C$

Now, $B+D>A+C$

$\Rightarrow \quad B+D=A+C+K \quad$ ...(i)

Also, $A+B=C+D$

$\Rightarrow \quad B-D=C-A \quad$ ...(ii)

$\Rightarrow \quad 2B=2C+K$

$\Rightarrow \quad B>C \Rightarrow A>B>C$

$D>C$

Clearly, each one of A, D and B has more amount than C.

Hence, C has the least amount.

5. (*b*) According to the information, the arrangement is as follows

K > J > (M) > L > N

Third from the left

So, 'M' ran at the third fastest speed.

Solutions (Q. Nos. 6-10)

$A = 2B$, $B = \frac{9}{2}C$, $D = 2C$, $E = 2D$,

A > E > C
or A > B > E > D > C

6. (*c*) C is the lightest.

7. (*a*) E is lighter than A and B.

8. (*b*) E is heavier than D and C.

9. (*a*) A is heaviest in weight.

10. (*a*) A, B, E, D, C represents the arragement in descending order of weight.

11. (*c*)

7th 9th
Left ⟶ [A] ||| [B] ⟵ Right

After interchanging the places,

⟶ [A] ||| [B] ⟵ Right
Left ⟶ 11th

Total number of people in the row
$= 11 + 9 - 1 = 19$

Solutions (Q. Nos. 12-14) According to the given information, the arrangement is as following

S > T / R ...(i)
U > Q > P ...(ii)

By combining both the Eqs. (i) and (ii), we get

U > Q > P > S > R > T – Building
23 12 5 – offices

The difference between Q and S is 11.

The second highest number of offices has 23 offices.

The building which has the least number of offices has 5 offices.

12. (*c*) The building R has the second least number of offices.

13. (*d*) If the number of offices in P is an even number which is divisible by 2 and 3 then P have 18 offices.

14. (*e*) The number of offices building R has should be more than 12 and less than 5.

∴ Out of the given options, option (c) satisfies the condition.

Therefore, Building R has 11 offices.

15. (*e*) A > D/E > D/E > B > C

'C' obtained the minimum marks.

Solutions (Q. Nos. 16-19)

According to the question,

P > Q, S > R

T is least effective.

Q = R, S > Q

∴ S/P > S/P > Q = R > T

16. (*d*) R was less effective than P.

17. (*d*) Statement V is not required.

18. (*b*) It is clear from the ranking order so obtained that brand S may be less effective than P or equal to P or more effective than P. It means that position of S is not fixed. Now as per question, sixth brand *i.e.,* M is more effective than S which implies that whatever be the position of S, there will be atleast four brands which will be less effective than M.

19. (*a*) Now, it is given that P is less expensive than R and from the order, P is more effective than R. It means that P should be purchased as it is more effective and less expensive than R.

Solutions (Q. Nos. 20-25) *The compounds can be arranged according to their taste and effectiveness as shown below*

Taste (sweet) Z > U > V > Y > X > W

Effectiveness (deadly)

X > Y > U > W > Z > V

20. (*d*) From the above taste (sweet) ranking, we find that Z is the sweetest.

21. (*d*) It is clear that both Z and U are sweeter and more deadly than V.

22. (*d*) Statement V does not add any new information about the sweetness of drugs.

23. (*a*) Compound U is sweeter than Y and more deadly than W.

24. (*b*) Compound V is the least deadly.

25. (*d*) Compound X is the most deadly.

26. (*b*) As per the given information, we have

D > A > C > B > F > (E)

∴ E is the shortest rope.

27. (*a*) Descending order of the heights is as

(Roshan) > Sushil > Hardik > Niza > Harry.

Therefore, the tallest person is Roshan.

28. (*b*) From given information, we have

A > B ...(i)

C > D > E ...(ii)

and A > D > B ...(iii)

On combining Eqs. (i), (ii) and (iii), we have

(A) > D > B > C > E

Hence, A is the tallest of all.

29. (*d*) Gita > Mita ; Bhanu > Gita

∴ Bhanu > Gita > (Mita)

30. (*c*) Given, Siya > Priya > Tiya ...(i)

Siya >Riya >Priya ...(ii)

and Riya > Tiya >Diya ...(iii)

On combining Eqs. (i), (ii) and (iii), we get

Siya > Riya > Priya> Tiya > Diya

31. (*b*) Arranging the persons in ascending order of their heights, we get

Neha < Hema < Juhi < Kuku < Mira < Rani < Isha

∴Mira ranked fifth in ascending order.

32. (*a*) According to information the arrangement is as

C > B > D > A > (E)

So, E is the shortest.

33. (*b*) All the books are arranged as follows

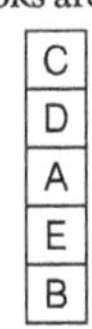

Hence, book B is at the bottom.

34. (*b*)

18th ← Right end

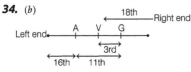

Left end — A V G

3rd

16th 11th

V's position from right hand = 18th

V's position from left hand

= (16 + 11 – 3) = 24th

Hence, total number of boys in row

= (18 + 24 – 1) = 41

35. (*c*)

According to	Birthday Date in April
Mohit	.../(18)
Mohit's Sister	(18) / 19

Here, 18 is common to both.
Hence, the correct date is 18th.

36. (*c*) According to the question,

12th from left Kanta Kirti 8th from right

After interchanging of seats Kirti Kanta 8th from right

15th from left

Number of girls in the row

= 15 + 8 – 1 = 22

37. (*c*) Position of Rekha is 20th from the right which is occupied by Jaya after interchanging takes place and Jaya becomes 22nd from the left.
Therefore, total number of students in the row = (20+ 22) – 1 = 41

38. (*d*)

According to	Birthday Date in February
Samant	(17) /18
Samant's sister	15/16/(17)

Here, 17 is common to both.
Hence, the correct date is 17th.

39. (*c*) From among those who passed Neeta is 22nd from the top and Kalyan is 22+ 5= 27th from the top and 34th from the bottom. Therefore, total number of students who passed the examination = 27+ 34– 1= 60.
Therefore, total number of students in the class = $\frac{60}{4} \times 5 = 75$

40. (*c*)

According to	Leave Date
Seema	22/23/24/25/26

But Seema was present on 23rd. Also, it was holiday on 24th and 26th October was Sunday.

Hence, possible date may be either 22nd or 25th October.

41. (*c*)

Mala —10 s→ Rekha

Aarushi —12 s→ Inika

Gauri —18 s→ Vasantha

Mala —1 s→ Vasantha

Inika —2 s→ Gauri

5th 4th 3rd 2nd 1st

Inika Gauri Mala Vasantha Rekha

So, clearly Mala came third in the race.

42. (*d*) Out of all the given options, only the ranking given in (d) satisfies the given conditions.

B – 12000 (A won less money than B)

A – 10000

E – 8000 (E won ₹ 8000 prize)

D – 6000

C – 4000 and the difference between winning of C and F was ₹ 2000.

F – 2000 and the difference between winning of D and F was atleast ₹ 4000.

43. (*c*) If A won ₹ 4000, then the only possible ranking is

C – 12000, F – 10000

E – 8000, B – 6000

A – 4000, D – 2000

The total of C and F

= 12000 + 10000 = ₹ 22000.

Solutions (Q. Nos. 44-46) *According to the given question, the arrangement according to height is as follows*

B > E > A > F > C > D

↓ 119 cm (B) ↓ 102 cm (D)

44. (*b*) E is the second tallest.

45. (*c*) The height of A should be less than 119 cm and more than 102 cm.

∴ Out of the given options only option (c) satisfies the condition.
Therefore, possible height of A must be 112 cm.

46. (*d*) F is the third shortest.

Solutions (Q.Nos. 47-49)

According to the given information,

2 Sohan < Mohan ⇒ Sohan < Mohan

2 Sohan < Rohan ⇒ Sohan < Rohan

2 Rohan > Mohan

2 Rohan > Sohan

47. (*d*) According to the above information, 'whose weight is greatest' cannot be determined.

48. (*b*) From above information, we get

Sohan < Mohan or Rohan

∴ Sohan's weight is the least.

Solutions (Q. Nos. 49-51) *According to the given information,*

	Case I	Case II
Highest Marks	C	Highest Marks → F
	F	C
	D	D
	A	A
	B	Least Marks → B
Least Marks	E	E (Possible positions of E)

49. (*c*) Now, if F stands on second in ranking,

Then according to case I, B is on fifth position.

50. (*d*) If B scores the least, then according to case II the rank of C would be either second or third.

51. (*b*) If E is ranked third, then according to case II, C gets more marks than E.

CHAPTER / 10

Sitting Arrangement

The process of arranging the persons/objects according to the given sitting conditions is called sitting arrangement.

Sitting arrangement questions are based on the sitting sequence pattern, direction, facing outside or inside etc. The candidate is required to understand all the conditions given in the question as the given information may be in jumbled form. The candidate has to segregate this information and make the arrangement as per the given conditions.

Based on the various patterns of sitting arrangement, they can be divided into the following four types.

TYPE 01

Linear Arrangement

In linear arrangement, persons/objects are required to be placed in proper order either in one straight line or in two straight lines.

In these questions, the candidate is required to identify the exact position of the objects and their positions with respect to one another based on the information given.

The linear arrangement can further be of two types, based on the number of rows

A. One Row Sequence

In such an arrangement, objects/ persons are placed in a single row as shown below.

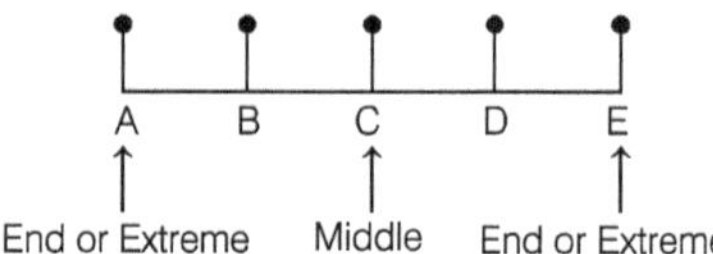

Case I In the above arrangement, if direction of face is not given, then we should take ourself as a base to determine left and right of the objects/persons.

In other words, we can say that in such cases our left and right are the left and right of the objects/persons.

Let us see

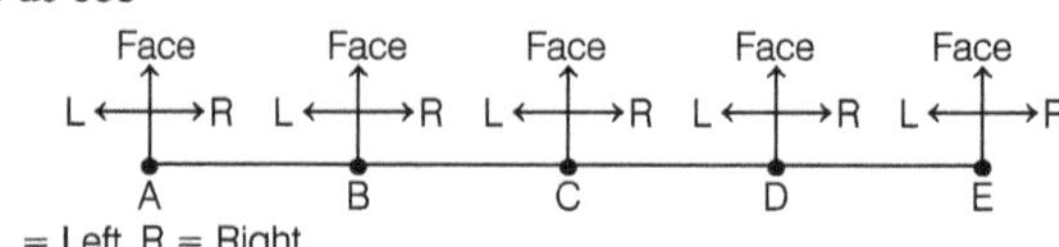

From the above diagram, it is clear that,

(i) B, C, D, E are to the right of A but only B is to the immediate right of A.

(ii) D, C, B, A are to the left of E but only D is to the immediate left of E.

(iii) C, D, E are to the right of B but only C is to the immediate right of B.

(iv) C, B, A are to the left of D but only C is to the immediate left of D.

(v) D and E are to the right of C but only D is to the immediate right of C.

(vi) B and A are to the left of C but only B is to the immediate left of C.

(vii) A is to the immediate left of B while E is to the immediate right of D.

Now, consider the following example to understand the steps to solve linear based seating arrangement questions.

Ex 01 6 persons are sitting in a row. They are A, B, C, D, E and F. D is sitting on the extreme right end. B is between F and D. E is between A and C. A is not sitting beside F and D. Who is immediate right of A?

(a) B (b) C (c) D (d) E

Solution (d) **Step I** D is sitting on extreme right.

Left • — • — • — • — • — • Right
D

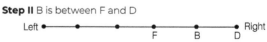

Step II B is between F and D

Left • — • — • — • — • — • Right
F B D

Step III E is between A and C but A is not sitting beside F. So, the final arrangement is.

Clearly, E is sitting to the immediate right of A.

***Ex* 02** There are five houses P, Q, R, S and T. P is right of Q and T is left of R and right of P. Q is right of S. Which house is in the middle? « IIFT 2013

(a) P (b) Q (c) T (d) R

***Solution* (a)** According to the question, the houses can be arranged as,

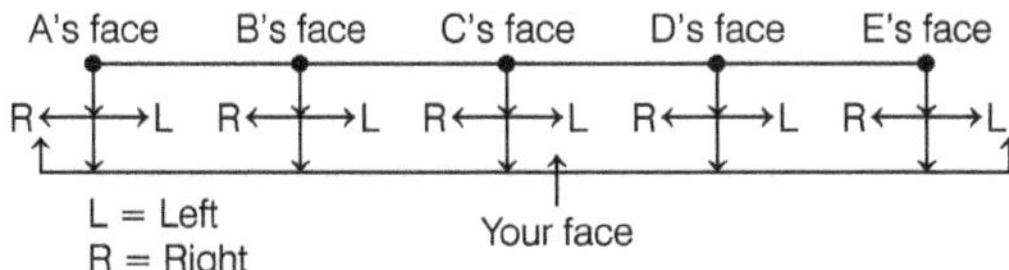

Clearly, the house P is in the middle of all the houses.

Case II If direction of face is given, then left and right is taken according to the given direction of face.

e.g., If 5 students are sitting in a row and their faces are towards you, then in this case, the direction of faces of students is opposite to the direction of your face.

Let us see

A's face B's face C's face D's face E's face

R←→L R←→L R←→L R←→L R←→L

L = Left
R = Right

Your face

From the above diagram, it is clear that

(i) Left of A = B, C, D and E
(ii) Right of E = D, C, B and A
(iii) B is immediate left of A, C is immediate left of B, D is immediate left of C and E is immediate left of D.
(iv) D is immediate right of E, C is immediate right of D, B is immediate right of C and A is immediate right of B.

***Ex* 03** 5 persons A, B, C, D and E are sitting in a row facing North such that D is on the left of C and B is on the right of E. A is on the right of C and B is on the left of D. If E occupies a corner position, then who is sitting in the centre?

(a) A (b) B (c) C (d) D

***Solution* (d)** Arrangement according to the question is as follows

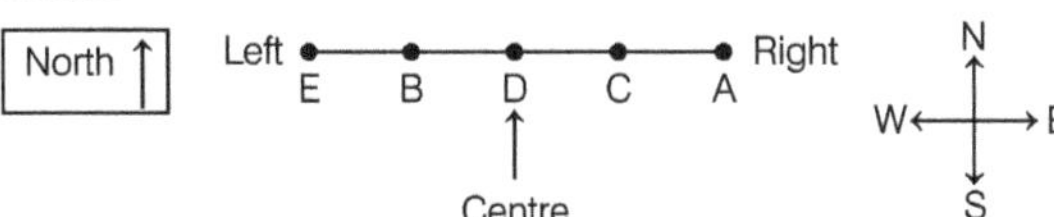

Clearly, D is sitting in the centre.

***Ex* 04** Five friends are sitting in a row facing the South direction. Among them Mohan is between Balu and Raju, and Raju is to the immediate right of Parveen. In the same way, Amit is to the right of Balu. Who is at the extreme right end? « SSC GD 2017

(a) Amit (b) Balu
(c) Parveen (d) Mohan

***Solution* (a)** According to the question, the sitting arrangement is as follows

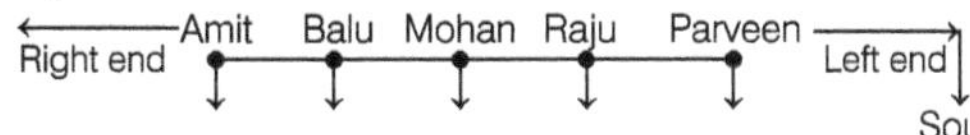

Clearly, Amit is at the extreme right end.

B. Two Row Sequence

In such arrangement, objects/persons are arranged in two different rows facing each other as follows

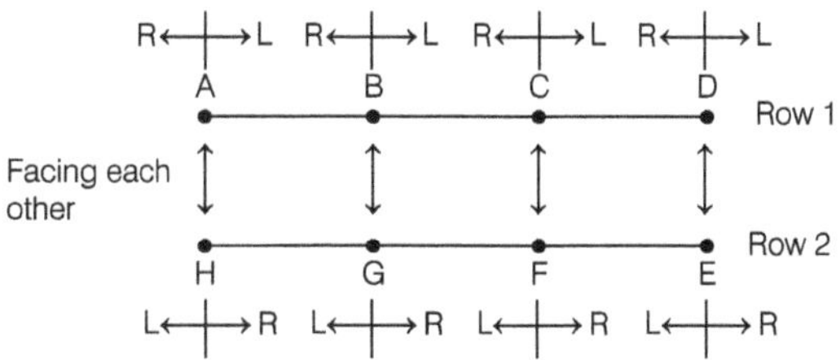

From the above diagram, it is clear that

(i) A is sitting opposite to H.
(ii) B is sitting opposite to G.
(iii) C is sitting opposite to F.
(iv) D is sitting opposite to E.
(v) A and E are sitting at diagonally opposite positions.
(vi) D and H are sitting at diagonally opposite positions.

***Ex* 05** 8 persons A, B, C, D, E, F, G and H are sitting in two rows opposite to each other. Each row has 4 persons. B and C are sitting in front of each other. C is between D and E. H is sitting to the immediate left of E. H and F are diagonally opposite. G and B are not near to each other. Who is in front of A?

(a) E (b) D (c) C (d) B

***Solution* (a)** Arrangement of persons, according to the question, is as follows

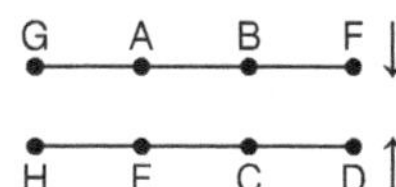

Clearly, E is in front of A.

DIRECTIONS ~(Example Nos. 6-10) *Study the following information carefully and answer the given questions.*

Twelve persons are sitting in two parallel rows at equal distance facing each other. Q, R, S, T, U and V are sitting in Row-1 facing South. B, C, D, E, F and G are sitting in Row-2 facing North (but not necessarily in the same order).

G sits third to the right of B and one of them sits at the end of the row. Q sits at the right end of the row. Three persons sit between Q and T. F sits to the immediate left of G. Two persons sit between F and C. C who faces R sits to the immediate right of E. S faces D. U sits to the immediate left of S. « IBPS Clerk Pre 2018

***Ex* 06** Which of the following pair sits at the extreme ends of the Row 2?

(a) B and E (b) G and E
(c) B and C (d) G and C
(e) None of these

***Ex* 07** Who sits second to the left of the person facing V?

(a) B (b) D (c) F (d) C
(e) G

Ex 08 What is the position of U with respect to R?

(a) Third to the left (b) Second to the left
(c) Second to the right (d) Third to the right
(e) None of these

Ex 09 Who is facing F?

(a) T (b) U (c) Q (d) S
(e) None of the above

Ex 10 If the positions of all persons sitting in Row 2 are arranged as per the English alphabetical order from left to right, then who among the following faces D?

(a) Q (b) R (c) S (d) T
(e) None of the above

Solution (Example Nos. 6-10) According to the given information,

```
Q S U V T R
↓ ↓ ↓ ↓ ↓ ↓  Row-1   (Facing South)

↑ ↑ ↑ ↑ ↑ ↑  Row-2   (Facing North)
B D F G E C
```

6. ***(c)*** B and C sits at the extreme ends of Row-2.
7. ***(b)*** G faces V and D sits second to the left of G.
8. ***(d)*** U is third to the right of R.
9. ***(b)*** U is facing F.
10. ***(e)*** If all the persons sitting in Row-2 are arranged as per the English alphabetical order from left to right then, U will face D.

Practice CORNER 10.1

1. Five friends are sitting on a bench. A is to the left of B but on the right of C. D is to the right of B but on the left of E. Who are at the extreme ends?

(a) A, B (b) A, D
(c) B, D (d) C, E

2. In a college party, 5 girls are sitting in a row. P is to the left of M and to the right of O. R is sitting to the right of N but to the left of O. Who is sitting in the middle?

(a) O (b) R (c) P (d) M

3. Five boys A, B, C, D and E are standing in a row. D is on the right of E. B is on the left of E but on the right of A. D is on the left of C, who is standing on the extreme right. Who is standing in the middle?

(a) B (b) C (c) D (d) E

4. Five boys A, B, C, D and E are sitting in a row facing south. A is to the right of B and E is to the left of B but to the right of C. A is to the left of D. Who is second from the left end?

(a) D (b) A (c) E (d) B

5. There are five different houses, A to E, in a row. A is to the right of B and E is to the left of C and right of A, B is to the right of D. Which of the houses is in the middle?

(a) A (b) B
(c) C (d) D

6. Five friends P, Q, R, S and T are sitting in a row facing North. Here, S is between T and Q and Q is to the immediate left of R. P is to the immediate left of T. Who is in the middle?

(a) S (b) T
(c) Q (d) R

7. Six children A, B, C, D, E and F are standing in a row. B is between F and D. E is between A and C. A does not stand next to either F or D. C does not stand next to D. F is between which of the following pairs of children?

(a) B and E (b) B and C
(c) B and D (d) B and A

8. Six persons L, M, N, O, P and Q sit in a linear row adjacent to each other facing North. Three persons sit between Q and P. N sits immediate left of Q. Two persons sit between N and M. How many persons sit to the left of M? « IBPS Clerk Mains 2018

(a) One (b) Two (c) Three (d) Four
(e) None

9. In a gathering, seven members are sitting in a row. 'C' is sitting left to 'B' but on the right of 'D'. 'A' is sitting right to 'B'. 'F' is sitting right to 'E' but left to 'D'. 'H' is sitting left to 'E'. Find the person sitting in the middle.

(a) C (b) D (c) E (d) F

10. Six people viz. A, B, C, D, E and F are standing in a straight line facing North but not necessarily in the same order. A stands second from one of the extreme ends of the line. Only two people stand between A and B. Only three people stand between B and D. F stands to the immediate right of B. More than one person stands between F and C. What is the position of E with respect to A? « MHT MBA 2017

(a) Second to the right (b) Second to the left
(c) Third to the right (d) Immediate left
(e) Immediate right

11. Six persons M, N, O, P, Q and R are sitting in two rows with three persons in each row. Both the rows are in front of each other. Q is not at the end of any row. P is second to the left of R. O is the neighbour of Q and diagonally opposite to P. N is the neighbour of R. Who is in front of N?

(a) R (b) Q (c) P (d) M

12. Six persons A, B, C, D, E and F are sitting in two rows, three in each row.

I. E is not at the end of any row.
II. D is second to the left of F.
III. C, the neighbour of E, is sitting diagonally opposite to D.
IV. B is the neighbour of F.

Which of the following are in one of the two rows?

(a) D, B and F (b) C, E and B (c) A, E and F (d) F, B and C

13. Five boys are standing in a row facing East. Pavan is to the left of Tavan, Vipin, Chavan. Tavan, Vipin and Chavan are to the left of Nakul. Chavan is between Tavan and Vipin. If Vipin is fourth from the left, then how far is Tavan from the right?

(a) First (b) Second (c) Third (d) Fourth

DIRECTIONS ~(Q. Nos. 14 and 15) *Read the following information carefully and then answer the questions that follow.*

A group of seven singers, facing the audience, are standing in a line on the stage as follow.

I. D is to the right of C. II. F is standing beside G.
III. B is to the left of F. IV. E is to the left of A.
V. C and B have one person between them.
VI. A and D have one person between them.

14. Who is on the extreme right?

(a) D (b) F (c) G (d) E

15. If we start counting from the left, on which number is C?

(a) 1st (b) 2nd (c) 3rd (d) 5th

DIRECTIONS ~(Q. Nos. 16-20) *Study the following information carefully to answer the given questions.*

A, B, C, D, E, F, G and H are seated in straight line facing North. C sits fourth to left of G. D sits second to right of G. Only two people sit between D and A. B and F are immediate neighbours of each other. B is not an immediate neighbour of A. H is not an immediate neighbour of D.

16. Who amongst the following sits exactly in the middle of the persons who sit fifth from the left and the person who sits sixth from the right?

(a) C (b) H (c) E (d) F

17. Who amongst the following sits third to the right of C?

(a) B (b) F (c) A (d) E

18. Which of the following represents persons seated at the two extreme ends of the line?

(a) C, D (b) A, B (c) B, G (d) D, H

19. What is the position of H with respect to F?

(a) Third to the left (b) Immediate right
(c) Second to right (d) Fourth to left

20. How many persons are seated between A and E?

(a) One (b) Two (c) Three (d) Four

DIRECTIONS ~(Q. Nos. 21-23) *Read the following information carefully and then answer the questions that follow.*

Eight persons P, M, R, T, Q, U, V and W are sitting in front of one another in two rows. Each row has 4 persons. P is between U and V and facing North. Q, who is to the immediate left of M is facing W. R is between T and M and W is to the immediate right of V.

21. Who is sitting in front of R?

(a) U (b) Q (c) V (d) P
(e) None of these

22. Who is to the immediate right of R?

(a) M (b) U
(c) M or T (d) Cannot be determined
(e) None of these

23. In which of the following pairs, persons are sitting in front of each other?

(a) MV (b) RV (c) TV (d) UR
(e) None of these

DIRECTIONS ~(Q. Nos. 24-28) *Read the following information carefully and answer the questions based on it.*

Ten students A, B, C, D, E, F, G, H, I and J are sitting in a row facing West.

I. B and F are not sitting on either of the edges.
II. G is sitting to the left of D and H is sitting to the right of J.
III. There are four persons between E and A.
IV. I is to the North of B and F is to the South of D.
V. J is in between A and D and G is in between E and F.
VI. There are two persons between H and C.

24. Who is sitting at the seventh place counting from left?

(a) H (b) C
(c) J (d) Either H or C

25. Who among the following is definitely sitting at one of the ends?

(a) C (b) H
(c) E (d) Cannot be determined

26. Who are immediate neighbours of I?

(a) BC (b) BH
(c) AH (d) Cannot be determined

27. Who is sitting second left of D?

(a) G (b) F (c) E (d) J

28. If G and A interchange their positions, then who become the immediate neighbours of E?

(a) G and F (b) Only F (c) Only A (d) J and H

DIRECTIONS ~ (Q. Nos. 29-33) *Study the following information carefully and answer the questions given below.*

Seven persons, A, B, C, D, E, F and G are sitting in a straight line facing North (but not necessarily in the same order). E sits third from the right end. B sits third to the right of G, who is not an immediate neighbour of either C or A, who sits third to the left of D, who is an immediate neighbour of G. E sits between D and B, who sits on the immediate left of C. Neither B nor F sits at any end of the line. There is only one person sit between C and E but that person is neither G nor F.

29. Who among the following is second to the left of D?

(a) B (b) C (c) F
(d) Other than those given as options
(e) A

30. Who among the following sit at the ends of the rows?

(a) G and D (b) C and B
(c) A and D (d) Cannot be determined
(e) Other than those given as options

31. Who among the following sits third to the left of B?
(a) C (b) G
(c) A (d) Cannot be determined
(e) Other than those given as options

32. What is the position of C with respect to G?
(a) Second to the left (b) Third to the left
(c) Fourth to the right (d) Fifth to the right
(e) Other than those given as options

33. Which of the following statements is true?
(a) C sits on the immediate left of A.
(b) The person who sits exactly between C and E is G.
(c) The person who sits exactly between G and A is F.
(d) Both (b) and (c) are true
(e) None of the true

DIRECTIONS ~ (Q. Nos. 34-38) *Study the following information carefully and answer the questions given below.* « LIC AAO 2019

Ten person i.e., A, B, C, D, E, P, Q, R, S and T are sitting in a single row and all are facing to the North direction, but not necessarily in same order.

A sits 4th from the extreme end. Three persons sit between A and B. C sits immediate right of B. Two persons sit between C and D. Three person sits between R and C. R sits immediate left of P. E sits to the right of R. Two persons sit between S and T. S sits to the left of T.

34. Who among the following person sits third to the left of P?
(a) C (b) T (c) Q (d) A
(e) None of these

35. How many persons sit between R and T?
(a) None (b) One (c) Two (d) Three
(e) More than three

36. Who among the following persons are sitting at extreme end?
(a) A and B (b) B and C (c) C and D (d) D and E
(e) None of these

37. Who among the following person sit second to the right of S?
(a) A (b) B (c) C (d) E
(e) None of these

38. The number of persons sitting left of B is same as the number of persons sitting right of which of the following person?
(a) P (b) R (c) Q (d) S
(e) None of these

DIRECTIONS ~ (Q. Nos. 39-43) *Study the following information carefully and answer the questions given below.* « RBI Office Assistant 2020

Ten persons are sitting in two rows, In row 1– A, B, C, D, E are sitting and they are facing North. In row 2– P, Q, R, S, T are sitting and they are facing South. Each person sitting in row 1 is facing another person sitting in row 2. All information is not necessarily in same order.

Two persons sit between P and R who faces A. D sits 2nd to the right of C who doesn't sit next to A. E faces T who sits immediate left of R. B faces the person who sits immediate left of Q.

39. Who among the following faces the person who sits immediate right of S?
(a) C (b) D (c) A (d) B
(e) None of these

40. How many persons/sit to the left of B?
(a) Two (b) Three (c) Four (d) One
(e) None

41. Which of the following is true ?
(a) D faces Q.
(b) Two persons sit between S and T.
(c) No person sits left to B.
(d) Both A and C sit at extreme end.
(e) None is true.

42. What is the position of B with respect to A?
(a) Immediate left (b) Immediate right
(c) 2nd to the right (d) 2nd to the left
(e) None of these

43. If A is related to T, E is related to Q then, in the same manner C is related to?
(a) P (b) R (c) S (d) B
(e) None of these

DIRECTIONS ~ (Q. Nos. 44-48) *Study the following information carefully and answer the questions given below.* « IBPS Clerk 2019

Twelve persons are sitting in the two parallel rows containing six persons in each row in such a way that there is an equal distance between adjacent persons. In the first row, A, B, C, D, E and F are seated and all of them are facing North.

In the second row, P, Q, R, S, T and U are seated and all of them are facing South. Therefore, in the given seating arrangement, each member seated in a row faces another member of the other row.

E sits 4th to the right of B. Q faces to E. The number of persons sit to the left of Q is same as sit to the right of S. F sits immediate left of D. A sits to the left of C and to the right of F. P faces the one who is an immediate neighbour of A. U is the only neighbour of Q. R sits to the right of T.

44. Four of the following five are alike in a certain way and hence they form a group. Which one of the following does not belong to that group?
(a) R (b) P (c) U (d) C (e) B

45. Who among the following faces to F?
(a) P (b) U (c) S (d) R
(e) Either (a) or (c)

46. What is the position of F with respect to B?
(a) Immediate to the left (b) 2nd to the left
(c) 3rd to the right (d) 4th to the left
(e) Immediate to the right

47. Which of the following is true as per the given information?
(a) S sits to the immediate right of P.
(b) U faces to A.
(c) F sits at the extreme end.
(d) Both (b) and (c) are true.
(e) All are true.

48. Who among the following sits 3rd to the right T?
(a) U (b) R (c) S (d) P
(e) None of these

DIRECTIONS ~ (Q. Nos. 49-52) *Read the following information carefully to answer the questions given below.* « SBI PO 2018

Fourteen persons i.e., A, B, C, D, E, F, G, M, N, O, P, Q, R and S are sitting in two parallel rows such that A, B, C, D, E, F and G sits in Row 1 faces towards South direction and M, N, O, P, Q, R and S sits in the Row 2 such that all are facing North direction. Person sitting in the Row 1 faces the person sitting in Row 2.

A sit third to the right of B. Either B or A sits at the end of the row. N sits third to the right of O. Neither N nor O faces A and B. The one who faces C sits third to the right of M. None of the immediate neighbour B Faces O. C sits third to the left of F. O does not face F. One of the immediate neighbour of F Faces Q, who does not sit at the end of the row. D is not the immediate neighbour of C. G sits on the left of E, but not on the immediate left. P does not face G and C. S does not face C. R and S are immediate neighbours. E does not sit at the end of the row. D does not face P.

49. Who among the following faces P?
(a) B (b) A (c) F (d) G
(e) None of these

50. Who among the following sits at the end of the row?
(a) P,C (b) P, D (c) O,G (d) A,S
(e) None of these

51. How many persons sits to the right of B?
(a) Two (b) More than Three (c) Three
(d) One (e) None of these

52. Who among the following faces N?
(a) D (b) B (c) F (d) G
(e) None of these

DIRECTIONS ~ (Q. Nos. 53-55) *Study the following information carefully and answer the questions given below.* « SBI Clerk 2019

A certain number of persons are sitting in the row. All of them are facing towards North. Q sits sixth from the right of S. T sits fourth to left of Q. Only two persons sit between Q and P. R sits fourth to the left of S. U sits between S and T. V sits second to the right of U. W is third from any of the end. S is eight from the left end of the row. Six persons sit between W and V.

53. How many numbers of persons could sit in the row?
(a) 14 (b) 18 (c) 23 (d) 15
(e) 20

54. What is the position of W with respect to Q?
(a) Fourth to the right (b) Fifth to the right
(c) Fourth to the left (d) Eighth to the right
(e) Sixth to the left

55. If X sits immediate right of V, then how many persons can sit between X and P?
(a) Five (b) Six (c) Four (d) Three
(e) None of these

DIRECTIONS ~ (Q. Nos. 56-60) *Study the following information carefully and answer the questions given below.* « IBPS PO 2018

Eight persons K, L, M, N, O, P, Q and R sitting in a row. Some of them are facing North while some are facing South. N sits fifth to the right of M, but none of them sits at an extreme end. Q sits third to N. L sits second to the right of Q. Only one person sit between L and P. R sits third to the left of P. K sits second to the left of O. Both the persons sitting at extreme ends faces opposite direction to each other. Both the immediate neighbours of M faces same direction. R sits to the left of L and both of them are facing opposite direction to each other. R does not face North direction.

56. Who among the following sits third to the right of R?
(a) Q (b) K (c) M (d) N
(e) None of these

57. Which among the following pair sit at the end of the row?
(a) Q, L (b) R, K (c) O, P (d) L, R
(e) None of these

58. How many persons sit to the right of K?
(a) Two (b) More than three
(c) Three (d) One
(e) None of these

59. Who among the following sits second to the right of Q?
(a) L (b) N (c) M (d) O
(e) None of these

60. Four of the following are alike in a certain way so form a group, which of the following does not belong to that group?
(a) K (b) N (c) R (d) O (e) P

DIRECTIONS ~ (Q. Nos. 61-65) *Study the following information carefully and answer the questions given below.*

Eight friends A, B, C, D, E, F, G and H are sitting in a straight line (but not necessarily in the same order). Some of them are facing South while some are facing North.

(Note: Facing the same direction means. If one is facing North then the other also faces North and *vice-versa.* Facing opposite directions means if one is facing North then the other faces South and *vice verse*).

B sits third to left of F. Two persons sit between B and H. F does not sit at any of the extreme end of the row. C does not sit adjacent to B and H. D sits second to right of G. C sits fourth to right of A. D does not sit adjacent to A. Immediate neighbour of G faces opposite direction (opposite direction means if one neighbour faces North then other will face South and *vice versa*). The one who sit at extreme end faces opposite direction. D faces North and sits immediate left of B. D and B faces same direction. Immediate neighbour of F faces same direction as F (If F faces north then both neighbour of F will face north and *vice versa*).

61. Who sits immediate right of E?
(a) A (b) C (c) No one (d) D
(e) B

62. Who among the following pair sits at extreme ends?
(a) H,E (b) D,H
(c) D,E (d) G, H
(e) None of these

63. How many persons sits between D and E?
(a) One (b) None
(c) Three (d) Two
(e) None of these

64. Who sits third to the left of D?
(a) B (b) A (c) G (d) C (e) E

65. Four of the following five are alike in a certain way based on the given seating arrangement and thus form a group. Which is the one that does not belong to that group?
(a) A (b) C (c) F (d) G
(e) H

Answers / WITH EXPLANATIONS

1. (*d*) Arrangement according to the question is as follows

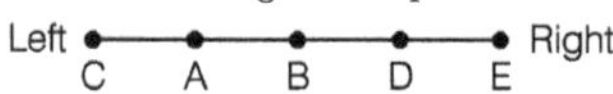

Clearly, C and E are at the extremes.

2. (*a*) Arrangement according to the question is as follows

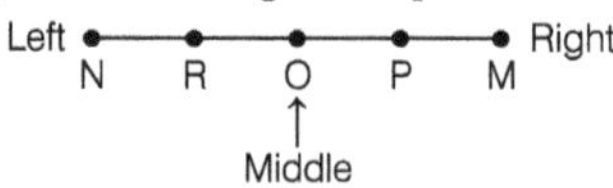

Clearly, O is sitting in the middle.

3. (*d*) The sequence of boys in the row is as follows

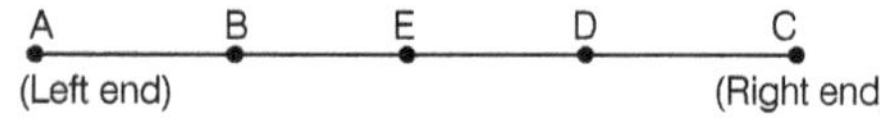

Clearly, E is standing in the middle.

4. (*c*) Arrangement according to the question is as follows

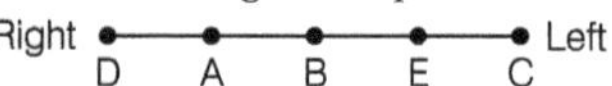

Clearly, E is second from the left end.

5. (*a*) According to the given information, houses in the row are arranged as follows

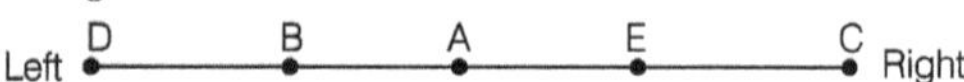

Clearly, the house in the middle is A.

6. (*a*) According to the question, sitting arrangement of all the five friends is as follow

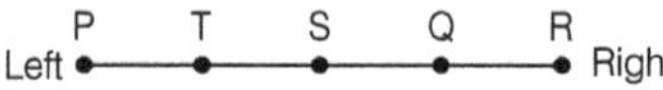

Hence, S is in the middle.

7. (*b*) According to the given information, the arrangement in which children are standing in the row is as follows

Clearly, F is standing between B and C.

8. (*c*) According to the given information the arrangement is as follows

Clearly, three persons sit to the left of M.

9. (*b*) According to the question,
Arranging the seven members in a row

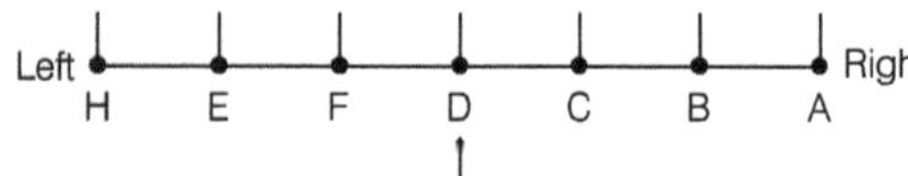

Hence, D is sitting in the middle.

10. (*a*) As per the given information, we have

So, E is second to the right of A

11. (*b*) Arrangement according to the question is as follows

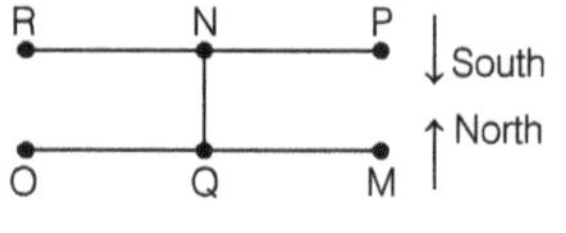

Or

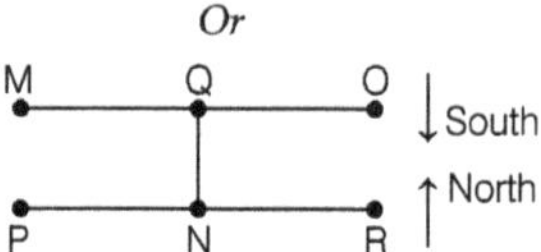

Clearly, Q is sitting opposite to N.

12. (*a*) First row

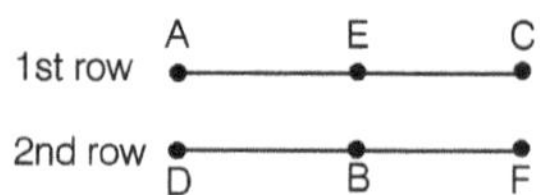

Clearly, D, B and F are in one of the two rows.

13. (*d*) Five boys standing in a row are Pavan, Tavan, Vipin, Chavan and Nakul

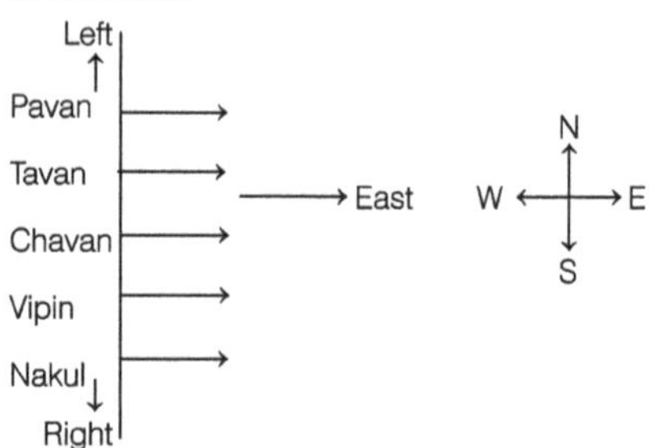

From the given information, the five boys are standing in the row as shown above. Clearly, Tavan is fourth from the right end.

Solutions (Q. Nos. 14 and 15) *On the basis of given information, the arrangement of the singers in a line is as follows*

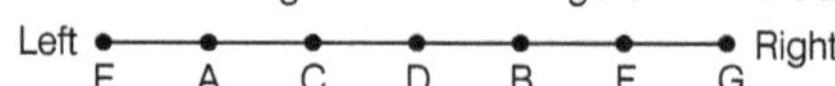

14. (*e*) Clearly, singer G is on the extreme right of the line

15. (*c*) C is third from the left.

Solutions (Q. Nos 16-20) *Arrangement according to the question is as follows*

16. (*d*) 5th from left = A
6th from the right = B
Clearly, the person between B and A is F.

17. (*c*)

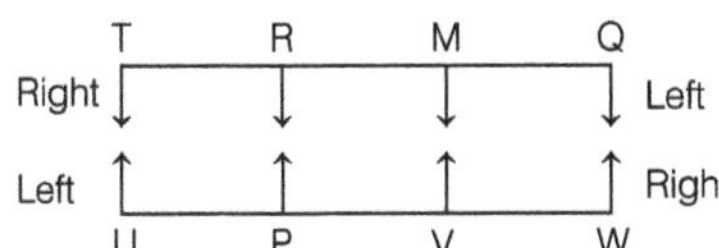

Clearly, A sits third to the right of C.

18. (*d*) Clearly, D and H are at the extreme ends.

19. (*a*) Clearly, H is third to the left of F.

20. (*a*) Only one person *i.e.*, G is sitting between A and E.

Solutions (Q. Nos. 21-23) *Arrangement according to the question is as follows*

T R M Q
Right Left
Left Right
U P V W

21. (*d*) Clearly, P is sitting in front of R.

22. (*e*) Clearly, T is to the immediate right of R.

23. (*a*) Clearly, M and V are sitting in front of each other.

Solutions (Q. Nos. 24-28) *On the basis of the given information exact positions of C and H cannot be determined. However, they will occupy the first and the fourth positions. Now, the arrangement is as follows*

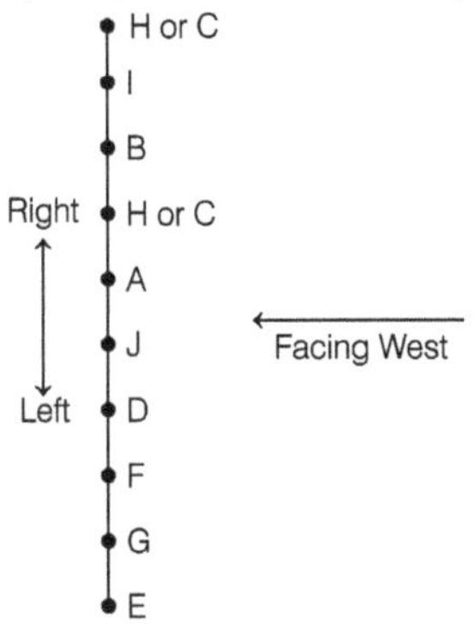

24. (*d*) Either H or C will occupy seventh position from the left.

25. (*c*) Clearly, E is definitely sitting at one of the ends.

26. (*d*) The immediate neighbours of I cannot be determined because the position of H and C are not fixed.

27. (*a*) G is sitting to the second left of D.

28. (c) 'A' will become the immediate neighbour of E after interchanging position.

Solutions (Q. Nos. 29-33) *From the given information we get*

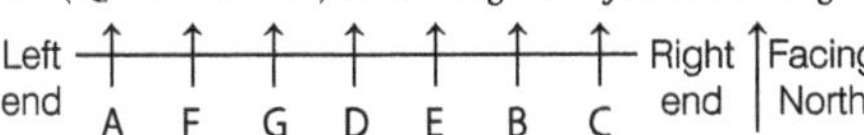

29. (*c*) F sits second to the left of D.

30. (*e*) A and C are those persons who sit on the extreme ends of the row.

31. (*b*) G is sitting third to the left of B.

32. (*c*) C is sitting fourth to the right of G.

33. (*c*) F is exactly sitting between A and G. So this is correct statement.

Solutions (Q. Nos. 34-38) *From the given information, we get*

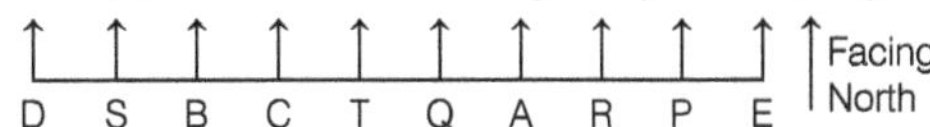

34. (*c*) Q sits third to the left of P.

35. (*c*) Q and A i.e., two persons are sitting between R and T.

36. (*d*) D and E are sitting at extreme ends where D is at extreme left and E is at extreme right.

37. (*c*) C sits second to the right of S.

38. (*b*) There are two persons sitting to the left of B and there are two persons sitting to the right of R.

Solutions (Q.Nos. 39-43) *According to the given information*

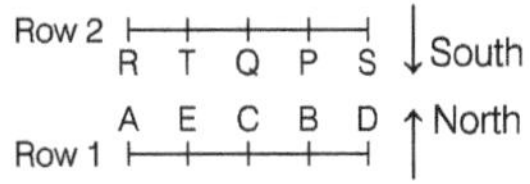

39. (*d*) B faces P, who sits immediate right of S.

40. (*b*) Three person (A, E and C) sit to the left of B.

41. (*b*) Two persons (Q and P) sits between S and T.

42. (*e*) B sits third to the right of A.

43. (*a*) According to the question,

Hence, C is related to P.

Solutions (Q. Nos. 44-48) According to the given information,

R S P T Q U South
B F D A E C North

44. (*b*) R, U, C and B are sitting at extreme ends. Therefore, P does not belong to that group.

45. (*c*) Clearly from the arrangement S faces F.

46. (*e*) F is immediate right to B.

47. (*a*) Clearly from the arrangements S sits to immediate right of P.

48. (*b*) Clearly R is sitting 3rd to the right of T.

Solutions (Q. Nos. 49-52) *From the given information we get*

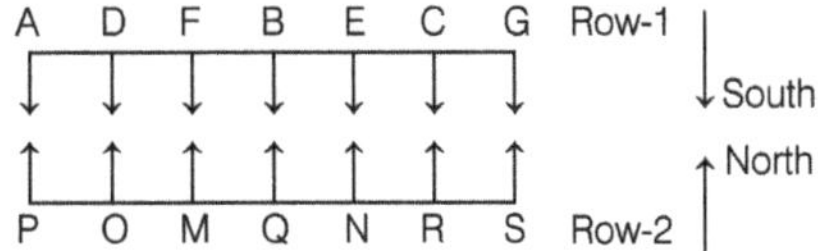

49. (*b*) A faces P.

50. (*d*) A and S sit to the end of the row.

51. (*c*) Three persons A, D and F sit to the right of B.

52. (*e*) E faces N.

Solutions (Q. Nos. 53-55) According to the question,

R S U T V Q P W North

53. (*e*) There are 20 seat in the row so 20 persons can sit.

54. (*a*) W is fourth to the right of Q.

55. (*c*) If X sits immediate right of V, then there will be 4 persons sitting between X and P.

Solutions (Q. Nos. 56-60) *From the given information we get*

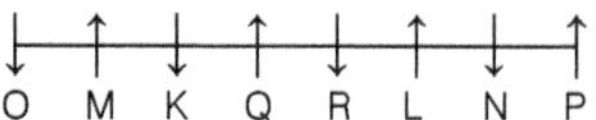

56. (*c*) M sits third to the right of R.
57. (*c*) O and P sit at the end of the row.
58. (*a*) Two persons M and O sit to the right of K.
59. (*a*) L sits second to the right of Q.
60. (*e*) P does not belong to the group.

Solutions (Q. Nos. 61-65) *According to the given information,*

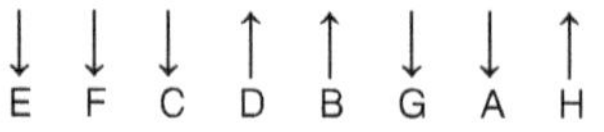

61. (c) No one is sitting right of E because E is sitting at extreme end of the line.
62. (a) H and E are the two persons who are sitting at extreme ends.
63. (d) Two persons i.e., F and C are sitting between D and E.
64. (e) E is sitting third to the left of D.
65. (e) Only H is the person in the given options who is facing North.

TYPE 02

Circular Arrangement

In this type of arrangement, objects/persons are placed around a circle either facing the centre or facing the direction opposite to centre. The left and right of each person/object in both the cases can be understood with the help of following diagrams.

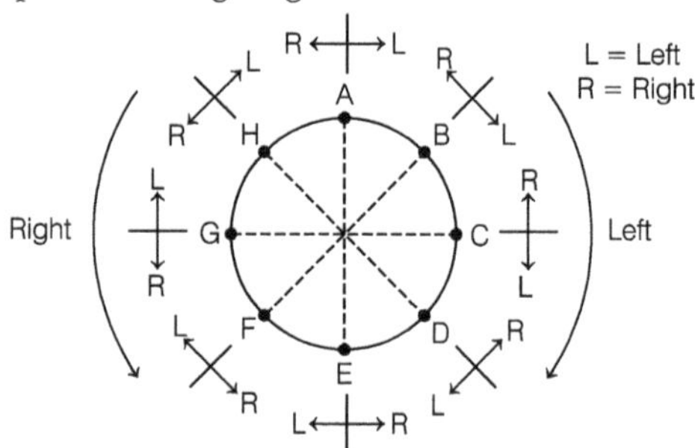

Facing the centre

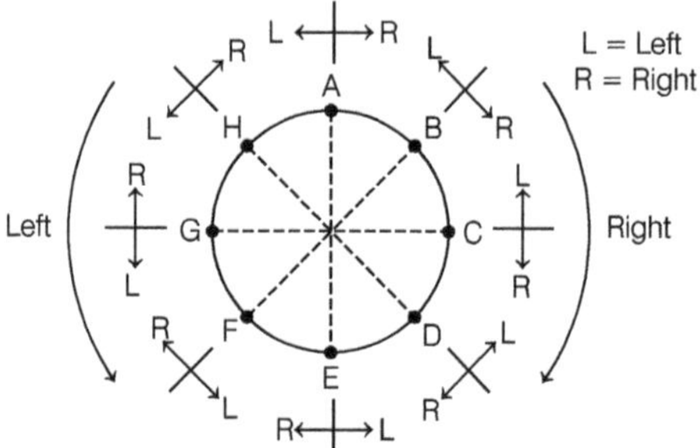

Facing the direction opposite to centre

	Left	Right
Center facing	**Clockwise**	**Anti-clockwise**
Outwards facing	Anti-clockwise	Clockwise

From the above diagram, it is clear that

(i) A and E are in front of each other.
(ii) B and F are in front of each other.
(iii) C and G are in front of each other.
(iv) D and H are in front of each other.

Now let's discuss the following example to understand how this type of questions are solved.

***Ex* 11** Five students are standing in a circle. Abhinav is between Alok and Ankur. Apurva is on the left of Abhishek. Alok is on the left of Apurva. Who is sitting next to Abhinav on his right?

(a) Apurva (b) Ankur
(c) Abhishek (d) Alok

Solution (d) Step I Abhinav is between Alok and Ankur. Here, we have two cases of arrangement as

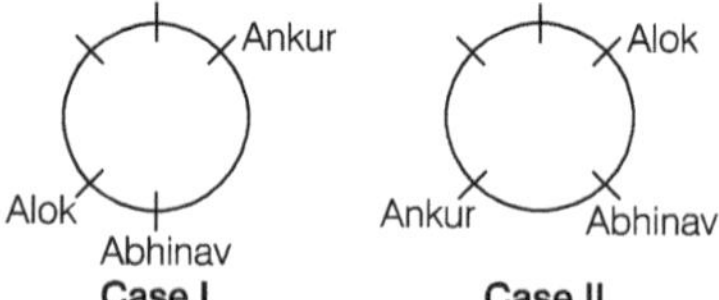

Step II Apurva is on the left of Abhishek.

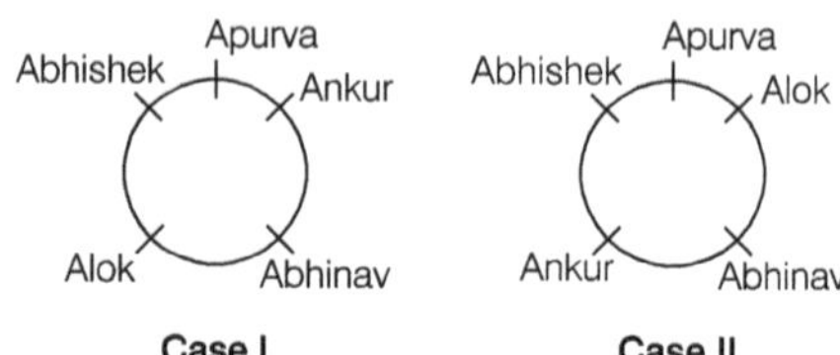

Step III Alok is on the left of Apurva. Here, Case I is eleminated. So, the final arrangement is

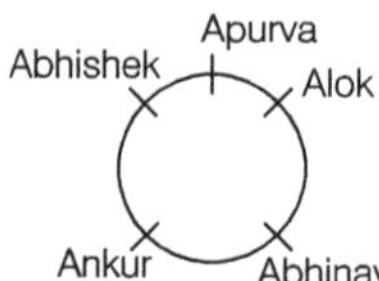

Clearly, Alok is sitting next to Abhinav on his right.

DIRECTIONS ~ (Example Nos. 12-16) *Study the following information carefully and answer the questions given below. Eight persons are sitting around a circular table facing to the centre but not necessarily in the same order.*
« SBI Clerk 2019

Two persons sit between Q and P (either from left or right). R sits immediate to the right of Q. One person sits between R and S, who faces to T. Q and T are not immediate neighbours of each other. W sits second to the left of V. Three persons sit between U and V.

Ex 12 Four of the following five are alike in a certain way and hence they form a group. Which one of the following does not belong to that group?

(a) Q-W (b) P-U (c) S-W (d) V-T
(e) Q-P

Ex 13 Who among the following sits immediate right of U?

(a) W (b) R (c) T (d) S
(e) V

Ex 14 The number of persons sit between Q and T, When counted to right of Q is same as the number of persons sit between W and ......, when counted to the left of ......

(a) P (b) S (c) T (d) U
(e) None of these

Ex 15 Who among the following faces R?

(a) U (b) V (c) P (d) W
(e) Q

Ex 16 Who among the following sits third to the right of S?

(a) P (b) U (c) Q (d) T
(e) None of these

Solutions (Example Nos. 12-16) *According to the given information,*

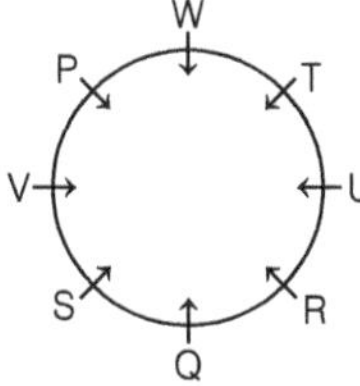

12. *(a)* Only Q-W is such a pair in which both the persons are sitting opposite to each other and three persons between them.

13. *(c)* T sits immediate right of U.

14. *(b)* For the given condition number of persons between Q and T = Number of persons between W and S.

15. *(c)* P faces R.

16. *(b)* U sits third to the right of S.

DIRECTIONS ~ (Example Nos. 17-19) *Study the information carefully and answer the given questions.*
« IDBI Executive 2018

L, M, N, O, P, Q, R and S are sitting around a circular area at equal distance between each other, but not necessarily in the same order. Some people face towards the centre while some face outside (i.e., in a direction opposite to the centre).

- O faces the centre. S sits third to the right of O. Only one person sits between S and L (either from left or right).
- P sits second to the left of L.
- R sits second to the right of N. N is not an immediate neighbour of S.
- Q sits to the immediate left of M. M and L face the same direction (i.e., M faces centre then L also faces the centre and *vice-versa*)
- Immediate neighbours of Q face opposite directions (i.e., If one neighbour faces the centre then the other faces outside and *vice-versa*)
- Immediate neighbours of O face opposite directions (i.e., If one neighbour faces the centre then the other faces outside and *vice-versa*)
- Immediate neighbours of S faces the same direction as S. (i.e., If S faces outside then both the immediate neighbours of S also faces outside and *vice-versa*)

Ex 17 What is M's position with respect to L?

(a) Second to the right (b) Third to the left
(c) Fourth to the right (d) Second to the left
(e) Third to the right

Ex 18 Who amongst the following are immediate neighbours of O?

(a) R,M (b) M,Q (c) P,M (d) L,Q
(e) L,N

Ex 19 Four of the following five are alike in a certain way, based on the given seating arrangement and so form a group. Which is the one that does not belong to that group?

(a) P (b) M (c) S (d) R
(e) Q

Solutions (Example Nos. 17-19) *According to the given information,*

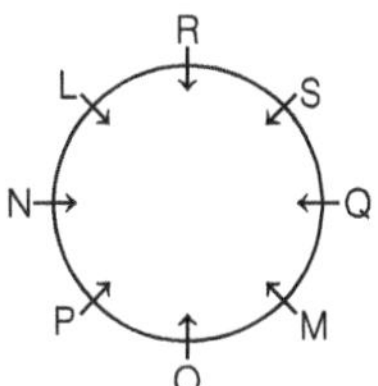

17. *(c)* M is fourth to the right of L.

18. *(c)* P and M are immediate neighbours of O.

19. *(b)* Except M, all other faces inside, whereas M faces outside.

Practice / CORNER 10.2

1. Four girls A, B, C and D are sitting around a circle facing the centre. B and C are in front of each other, which of the following is definitely true?

(a) A and D are in front of each other.
(b) A is not between B and C.
(c) D is to the left of C.
(d) A is to the left of C.

2. Eight persons A, B, C, D, E, F, G and H are sitting around the circle as given in the figure. They are facing the direction opposite to centre. If they move upto three places anti-clockwise, then

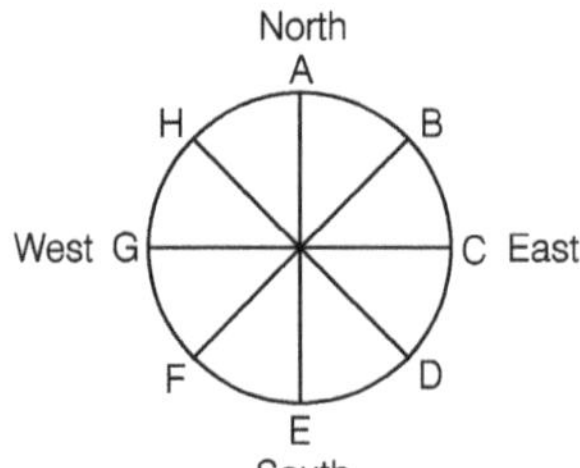

(a) B will face West. (b) E will face East.
(c) H will face North-West. (d) A will face South.

3. Five persons are sitting facing centre of a circle. Pramod is sitting to the right of Ranjan. Raju is sitting between Brejesh and Naveen. Raju is to the left of Brejesh and Ranjan is to right of Brejesh. Who is sitting to the left of Naveen?

(a) Pramod (b) Raju (c) Brejesh (d) Ranjan

4. Six persons are sitting in a circle facing the centre of the circle. Parikh is between Babita and Narendra. Asha is between Chitra and Pankaj. Chitra is to the immediate left of Babita. Who is to the immediate right of Babita?

(a) Parikh (b) Pankaj (c) Narendra (d) Chitra

5. Six persons are sitting around a circular table immediate facing centre. Ajay is facing Hemant who is sitting left of Arvind and immediate right of Sanjay. Suman is immediate right of Arvind. Manoj is facing Arvind. If Hemant and Manoj, Arvind and Sanjay mutually exchange their positions, who is now sitting to the right of Manoj?

(a) Arvind (b) Ajay
(c) Suman (d) None of these

6. Eight persons A, B, C, D, E, F, G and H are sitting around a round table each facing the centre. D is second to the left of F and third to the right of H. A is second to the right of F and an immediate neighbour of H. C is second to the right of B and F is third to the right of B. G is not an immediate neighbour of F. In the above information who is to the immediate left of A?

« WBSC Pre 2018

(a) H (b) E (c) G (d) B

7. Five people A, B, C, D and E are seated about a round table. Every chair is spaced equidistant from adjacent chairs.

1. C is seated next to A.
2. A is seated two seats from D.
3. B is not seated next to A.

Which of the following must be true?

I. D is seated next to B.
II. E is seated next to A.

Select the correct answer from the codes given below.

(a) Only I (b) Only II
(c) Both I and II (d) Neither I nor II

DIRECTIONS ~ (Q. Nos. 8 and 9) *Read the following information carefully and answer the questions that follow.*

Eight friends A, B, C, D, E, F, G and H are sitting in a circle facing the centre. B is sitting between G and D. H is third to the left of B and second to the right of A. C is sitting between A and G and B and E are not sitting opposite to each other.

8. Who is third to the left of D?

(a) F (b) E
(c) A (d) Cannot be determined

9. Which of the following statements is not correct?

(a) D and A are sitting opposite to each other
(b) C is third to the right of D
(c) E is sitting between F and D
(d) A is sitting between C and F

DIRECTIONS ~ (Q. Nos. 10-14) *Study the following information carefully and answer the questions given below.* « RBI Office Asst. 2020

Eight persons are sitting around a circular table facing towards the centre of the table. A sits second to the left of B. Only two persons sit between A and H. G sits third to the right of H. E sits immediate left of G. D sits second to the left of C. F sits third to the right of C.

10. Who among the following sits second to the left of H?

(a) C (b) D (c) B (d) F
(e) None of these

11. Who among the following faces D?

(a) A (b) H (c) E (d) G
(e) None of these

12. Four of the following five are alike in a certain way and hence form a group which of the following does not belong to the group?

(a) H-C (b) F-H (c) B-A (d) A-G (e) G-F

13. Which of the following is true regarding B?

(a) B sits third left of D
(b) B is an immediate neighbour of F
(c) B faces G
(d) Both (a) and (b)
(e) Both (a) and (c)

14. How many persons sit between H and E when counted from right of H?

(a) None (b) One
(c) Two (d) Three
(e) More than three

DIRECTIONS ~ (Q. Nos. 15-17) *Read the following information carefully to answer the questions that follow.*

Six girls are sitting in a circle facing centre. Sonia is sitting opposite to Radhika. Poonam is sitting right of Radhika but left of Deepti. Monika is sitting left of Radhika. Kamini is sitting right of Sonia and left of Monika. Now, Deepti and Kamini, Monika and Radhika mutually exchange their positions.

15. Who will be opposite to Sonia?

(a) Radhika (b) Monika
(c) Kamini (d) Sonia

16. Who will be sitting left of Kamini?

(a) Poonam (b) Deepti
(c) Radhika (d) Sonia

17. Who will be sitting left of Deepti?

(a) Sonia (b) Monika
(c) Radhika (d) Poonam

DIRECTIONS ~ (Q. Nos. 18-20) *Read the following information carefully to answer the questions given below* « RRB JE 2018

Five friends Ram, Shyam, Atul, Dev and Raj are sitting on a round table and all are facing outside. Atul is sitting third left to Ram and Shyam is sitting immediate left of Raj and immediate right of Atul.

18. Who is sitting immediate right to Dev?

(a) Atul (b) Raj (c) Ram (d) Shyam

19. Who is sitting between Ram and Shyam?

(a) Atul (b) Raj
(c) Dev (d) None of these

20. Who is second left of Raj?

(a) Atul (b) Dev
(c) Ram (d) Shyam

DIRECTIONS ~ (Q. Nos. 21-25) *Study the following information carefully and answer the questions given below.*

Nine persons i.e., A, B, C, D, E, F, G, H and J are sitting in a circular table but not necessarily in same order.

All are facing towards centre. A sits second to the right of B. F sits fourth to the left of A. Two persons sit between C and F. G is immediate neighbour of J. G sits second to the right of H. D sits second to the left of E. E is not an immediate neighbour of A. « LIC AAO 2019

21. Who among the following person sits third to the right of E?

(a) B (b) A (c) C (d) F
(e) None of these

22. How many persons sit between E and F?

(a) Two (b) One (c) Three (d) None
(e) More than three

23. Who among the following persons sits exactly between C and E?

(a) B (b) A (c) D (d) F
(e) None of these

24. Who among the following persons sits immediate right of A?

(a) B (b) C (c) D (d) G
(e) None of these

25. Four of the following five are alike in certain way based from a group, find the one which does not belong to that group?

(a) E-C (b) B-F (c) D-J (d) A-C
(e) C-H

DIRECTIONS ~ (Q. Nos. 26-30) *Study the following information carefully and answer the questions given below.* « IBPS RRB Clerk 2019

Seven people viz. P, Q, R, S, T, U and V are sitting around a circular table having equal distance between them. All of them are facing inside.

P sits immediate right of Q. Only one person sits between P and S (either from left or right). U sits third to the right of S. T is an immediate neighbour of U. R sits second to the left of V.

26. If all the persons are arranged according to the alphabetical order in anti-clockwise direction starting from P, then how many persons position will remain unchanged (except P)?

(a) Three (b) One (c) Two (d) None
(e) None of these

27. How many persons sits between Q and U. If counted from the left of Q?

(a) One (b) Two (c) Three (d) None
(e) None of these

28. Who sits second to the right of T?

(a) P (b) Q (c) R (d) S
(e) None of these

29. Four of the following five belongs to a group find the one that does not belongs to that group?

(a) VQ (b) PV (c) RT (d) SU (e) TQ

30. Who among the following sits second to the left of the one who sits fourth to the right of V?

(a) U (b) T (c) R (d) S
(e) None of these

DIRECTIONS ~ (Q. Nos. 31-35) *Study the following information carefully and answer the questions given below.* « SBI Clerk 2020

Eight persons are sitting around a circular table facing towards the centre of the table.

P sits second to the left of Q. Only two persons sit between P and U. T faces U. R sits third to the right of T. S sits third to the left of W. V is an immediate neighbour of W.

31. Who among the following person sits third to the left of S?

(a) R (b) T (c) P (d) Q (e) U

32. Four of the following five are alike in a certain way and hence form a group find the one which does not belong to that group?

(a) S-T (b) T-R (c) P-S (d) V-Q (e) W-T

33. Which of the following statement is true regarding W?

(a) W faces Q.
(b) W sits immediate left of V.
(c) V and U are immediate neighbours of W.
(d) W sits second to right of R.
(e) All are true.

34. How many persons sits between P and U when counted clockwise direction from P?

(a) One (b) Two (c) Three (d) None
(e) More than three

35. Who among the following person sits second to the right of the one who faces R?

(a) Q (b) T (c) P (d) S (e) U

DIRECTIONS ~ (Q. Nos. 36-40) *Study the following information carefully and answer the questions given below.* « RBI Office Assistant 2020

Eight persons are sitting around a circular table facing towards the centre of the table. A sits second to the left of B. Only two persons sit between A and H. G sits third to the right of H. E sits immediate left of G. D sits second to the left of C. F sits third to the right of C.

36. Who among the following sits second to the left of H?

(a) C (b) D (c) B (d) F
(e) None of these

37. Who among the following faces D?

(a) A (b) H (c) E (d) G
(e) None of these

38. Four of the following five are alike in a certain way and hence form a group which of the following does not belong to the group?

(a) H-C (b) F-H (c) B-A (d) A-G (e) G-F

39. Which of the following is true regarding B?

(a) B sits third left of D.
(b) B is an immediate neighbour of F.
(c) B faces G.
(d) Both (a) and (b)
(e) Both (a) and (c)

40. How many persons sit between H and E when counted from right of H?

(a) None (b) One (c) Two (d) Three
(e) More than three

DIRECTIONS ~ (Q. Nos. 41-43) *Study the following information carefully to answer the questions that follow.*

Six couples have been invited to a dinner party. They are Niti, Geeta, Lata, Rakhi, Sita, Champa and Farookh, Hari, Amit, Tilak, Ram, Ali. They are seated on a circular table, facing each other.

I. Geeta refuses to sit next to Ali.
II. Lata wants to be between Amit and Hari.
III. Champa refuses to sit next to Farookh.
IV. Niti is seated on Ali's right hand side.
V. Farookh and Tilak are seated exactly opposite to each other.
VI. Ram and Sita are seated to the left of Champa.
VII. Amit and Rakhi want to enjoy the company of Lata and Tilak respectively and are seated closest to them.
VIII. The seating arrangement is such that minimum one woman is always between two men.

41. Which of the following statements is correct?

(a) Lata is on Tilak's right.
(b) Ali is on Champa's right.
(c) Geeta is on Hari's right.
(d) Geeta is on Farookh's left.

42. If looked in an anti-clockwise manner, who are seated between Tilak and Farookh?

(a) Sita, Ram, Champa, Ali and Niti
(b) Sita, Ram, Rakhi, Amit and Lata
(c) Sita, Ram, Geeta, Hari and Lata
(d) Sita, Ram, Lata, Amit and Hari

43. Which of the following close neighbouring arrangements is correct?

(a) Ali, Champa and Ram (b) Tilak, Ram and Ali
(c) Niti, Farookh and Lata (d) Hari, Geeta and Amit

DIRECTIONS ~ (Q. Nos. 44-48) *Read the following information carefully to answer the given questions.*

V, U and T are sitting around a circle. A, B and C are sitting around the same circle but two of them are not facing centre (they are facing the direction opposite to centre). V is second to the left of C. U is second to the right of A. B is third to the left of T. C is second to the right of T. A and C are not sitting together.

44. Which of the following is not facing centre?

(a) BA (b) CA
(c) BC (d) Cannot be determined
(e) None of these

45. Which of the following is the position of T in respect of B?

(a) Third to the right (b) Second to the right
(c) Third to the left (d) Third to the left or right
(e) None of these

46. What is the position of V in respect of C?

(a) Second to the right (b) Third to the left
(c) Fourth to the right (d) Fourth to the left
(e) Cannot be determined

47. Which of the following statement is correct?

(a) A, B and C are sitting together
(b) V, U and T are sitting together
(c) Sitting arrangement of two persons cannot be determined
(d) Those who are not facing centre are sitting together
(e) Only two people are sitting between V and T

48. What is the position of A in respect of U?

(a) Second to the left (b) Second to the right
(c) Third to the right (d) Cannot be determined
(e) None of these

DIRECTIONS ~ (Q. Nos. 49-53) *Study the following information carefully and answer the questions given below.*

Eight friends M, N, O, P, Q, R, S and T are sitting around a circular table with equal distance between them but not necessarily in the same order. Some of them are facing the centre with some face outside (i.e., opposite to centre).

O sits second to the right of R, R faces the centre. Only two people sit between O and N (either from O's right or O's left). S sits second to the right of O. T sits to the immediate right of N. S and N face opposite direction. (i.e., if N faces the centre then S faces outside and *vice-versa*). Immediate neighbour of S face the same direction (i.e., If one neighbour faces the centre then the other also faces the centre and *vice-versa*). Only three people sit between P and Q. Neither P nor M is an immediate neighbour of R. Q sits second to the right of M. Both T and Q face a direction opposite to that of O (i.e., if O faces the centre then both T and Q faces outside and *vice-versa*).

49. Who sits exactly between M and P, when counted from left of M?
(a) N (b) S (c) R (d) Q
(e) None of these

50. How many people in the given arrangement face the centre?
(a) One (b) Three (c) Five (d) Four
(e) None of these

51. Who sits second to the right of T?
(a) O (b) Q (c) S (d) R
(e) Other than the given options

52. Four of the following five are alike in a certain way based on the given seating arrangement and so form a group. Which is the one that does that belong to that group?
(a) P (b) O (c) T (d) M (e) Q

53. What is P's position with respect to R?
(a) Second to the left (b) Third to the right
(c) Third to the left (d) Sixth to the right
(e) Second to the right

DIRECTIONS ~ (Q. Nos. 54-57) *Study the following information to answer the given questions.*

« IBPS Clerk Mains 2018

Twelve persons are sitting around two circular tables as one is inscribed in another one. All of them are facing towards the centre.

A, B, C, D, E, F six persons are sitting around the inner circular table.

P, Q, R, S, T, U six persons are sitting around the outer circular table.

Note The persons of outer circular table are sitting exactly behind the persons sitting around the inner circular table.

B is sitting second to the right of E. R is an immediate neighbour of the one who is sitting behind B. Only one person sits between A and F (either from the left or from the right). A is not an immediate neighbour of B. P is sitting behind F. Only two persons sit between R and T. U is an immediate neighbour of P. D is an immediate neighbour of A. T is not sitting behind D. Q is not an immediate neighbour of R.

54. How many persons are sitting between S and P?
(a) One (b) More than three
(c) Three (d) Two
(e) None

55. Four of the following five are alike in a certain way so form a group, which of the following does not belong to the group?
(a) A, P (b) C, R (c) E, T (d) B, U
(e) D, S

56. Who among the following person is sitting third to the left of A?
(a) F (b) E (c) D (d) B
(e) None of these

57. Who among the following person is sitting immediate right of S?
(a) P (b) T (c) U (d) R
(e) Q

DIRECTIONS (Q. Nos. 58-62) *Study the information carefully and answer the questions given below.*

« IBPS Clerk (mains) 2019

Certain number of persons are sitting around a circular table, which has a circumference of 546 cm. All the persons are facing towards the centre. They are sitting at distances to each other which are consecutive multiple of six. A is 3rd to the left of I. Two persons are sitting between K and I. M is immediate right to L. H sits to the left of G at a distance of 72 cm. The distance between A and D is 18 cm. The number of persons sitting between J and B is same as between B and F. The distance between E and F is LCM of 6 and 5. Neither M nor L is neighbour of K and H. The number of persons sitting between C and I is same as between I and E. The distance between K and I is not more than 162cm. Either C or E is neighbour of K.

58. Who among the following are immediate neighbour of J?
(a) K, L (b) G, A (c) H, M (d) F, D
(e) None of these

59. Which of the following represents the distance between B and F?
(a) 144 (b) 72 (c) 99 (d) 108
(e) None of these

60. Who among the following sits 4th to the right of the one who is 6th to the left of A?
(a) K (b) G (c) H (d) D
(e) None of these

61. Which of the following represents the distance between H and L?
(a) 144 (b) 180 (c) 345 (d) 108
(e) 280

62. Four of the following belongs to a group, find the one that does not belong to that group?
(a) B, C (b) M, J
(c) I, D (d) K, E
(e) L, M

Answers WITH EXPLANATIONS

1. (*a*) There are two possible arrangements of the four girls around the circle, as follows

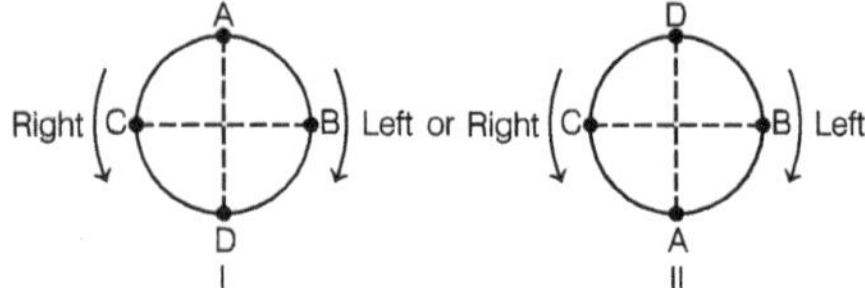

Clearly, A and D are in front of each other in both the arrangements.

2. (*a*) Following sitting arrangement is formed from the given information,

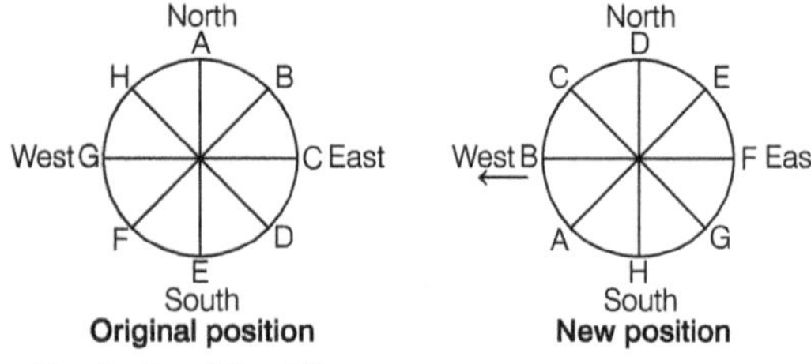

Clearly, B will face West

3. (*a*) Following sitting arrangement is formed from the given information,

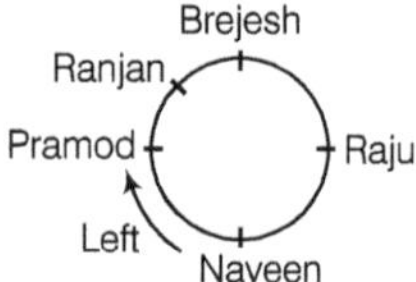

Clearly, Pramod is to the left of Naveen.

4. (*a*) Following sitting arrangement is formed from the given information,

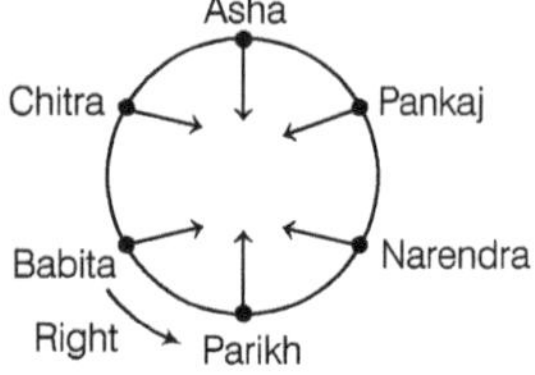

Clearly, Parikh is to the immediate right of Babita

5. (*d*) Following sitting arrangement is formed from the given information,

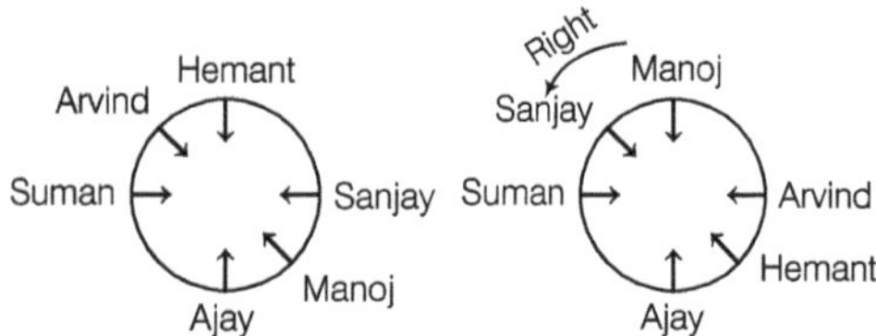

Clearly, Sanjay is sitting to the right of Manoj.

6. (*b*) Following sitting arrangement is formed from the given information,

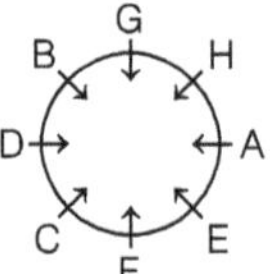

Hence, it is clear from diagram that E is the immediate left of A.

7. (*c*) According to the given information, there are four possible sitting arrangements as follows.

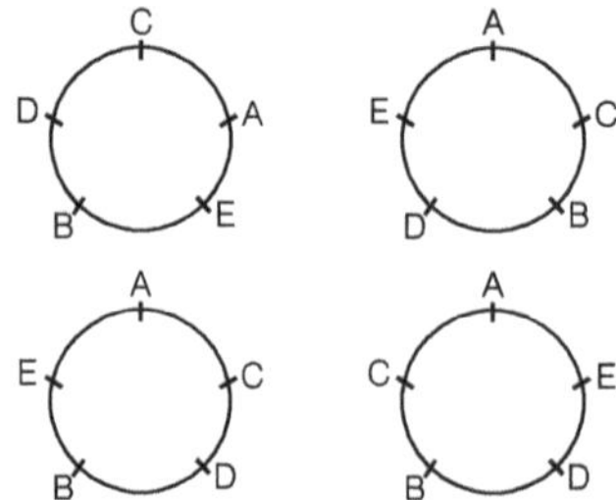

From the above arrangements, it is clear that D is seated next to B. Also, E is seated next to A. Clearly, both the Statements I and II are true.

Solutions (Q. Nos. 8 and 9) *On the basis of given information, the correct position of persons sitting around the circular table is as follows*

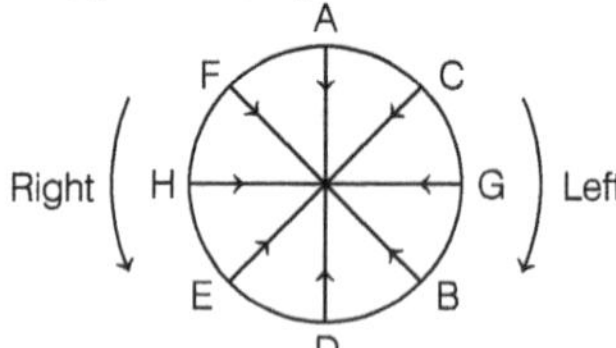

8. (*a*) Clearly, F is third to the left of D.

9. (*c*) E is sitting between H and D. Hence, statement (c) is not correct.

Solutions (Q. Nos. 10-14) *According to the given information,*

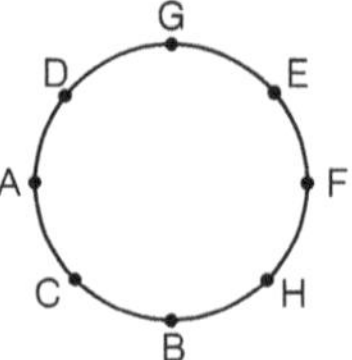

10. (*a*) C sits second to the left of H.

11. (*b*) H Faces D.

12. (*b*) Except 'F-H', in all other pairs one person sits between first person and second person.

13. (*c*) Only option (c) {B faces G} is true.

14. (*b*) One person (F) sit between H and E, when counted from right of H.

Solutions (Q. Nos. 15-17) *Arrangements according to the questions are as follows,*

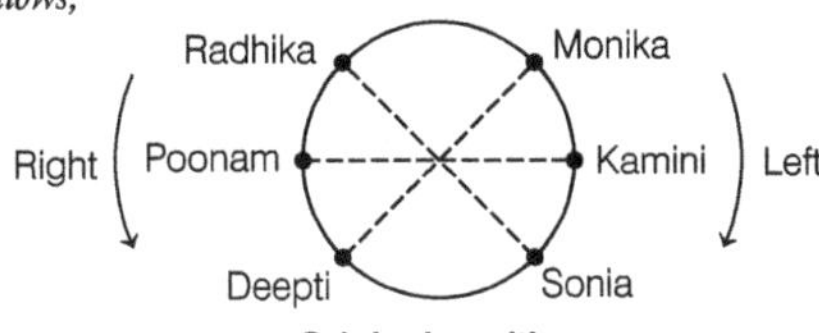

Original positions

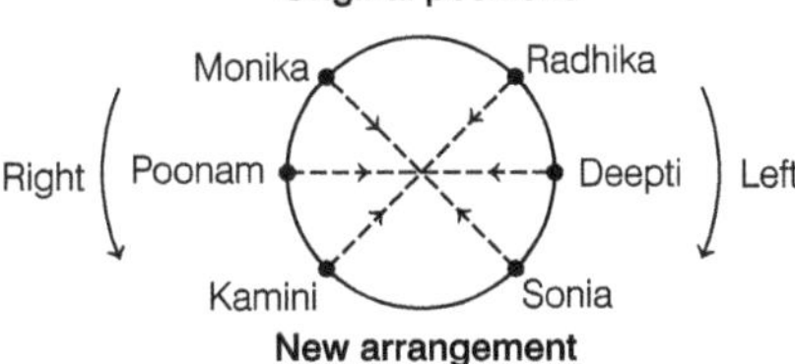

New arrangement

15. (*b*) Clearly, Monika will be opposite to Sonia.

16. (*a*) Clearly, Poonam will be sitting left of Kamini.

17. (*a*) Clearly, Sonia will be sitting left of Deepti.

Solutions (Q. Nos. 18-20) *Following sitting arrangement is formed from the given information,*

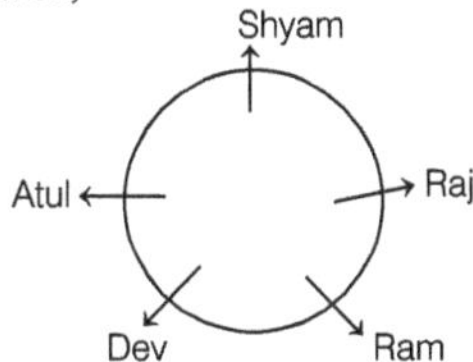

18. (*a*) Atul is sitting to the immediate right of Dev

19. (*b*) Raj is sitting between Ram and Shyam.

20. (*a*) Atul is second left of Raj.

Solutions (Q. Nos. 21-25) *Following sitting arrangement is formed from the given information*

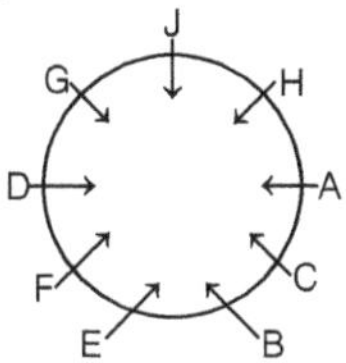

21. (*b*) A is sitting third to the right of E.

22. (*c*) E and F are immediate neighbour of each other so no one is sitting between them. (When counting from E's left)

23. (*a*) B is sitting exactly between C and E.

24. (*e*) H is sitting immediate right of A and H is not in the options.

25. (*d*) Except (d) each option contains pair of persons having one persons between them.

Solutions (Q. Nos. 26-30) *Following sitting arrangement is formed from the given information*

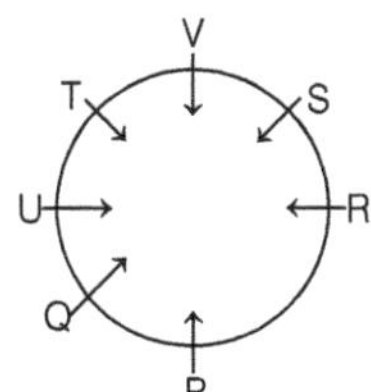

After rearranging, the arrangement is

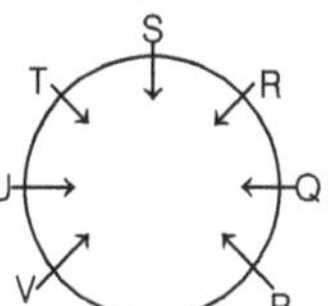

26. (*c*) So, T and U are the persons i.e., two persons whose positions remain unchanged.

27. (*d*) When counted from left of Q, there no one between Q and U because they are immediate neighbours of each other.

28. (*b*) Q is sitting second to the right of T.

29. (*e*) Except option (e), each option contains pair of persons having two persons between them when counted anti-clockwise from first person but option (e) has pair of persons having one person between them.

30. (*a*) P is sitting fourth to the right of V and U is second to the left of P.

Solutions (Q. Nos. 31-35)

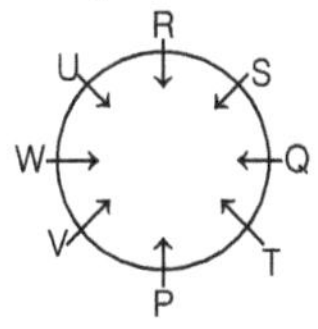

31. (*c*) P sits third to the left of S.

32. (*a*) Except S-T, in all other pairs second person is third to the right of first one.

33. (*e*) All the given statements are true.

34. (*b*) Two persons i.e., V and W sit between P and U when counted clockwise direction from P.

35. (*a*) P faces R and Q sits second to the right of P.

Solutions (Q. Nos. 36-40) *According to the given information,*

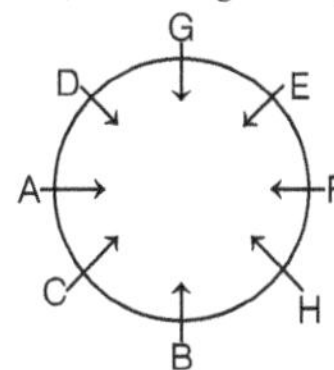

36. (*a*) C sits second to the left of H.

37. (*b*) H faces D.

38. (*b*) Except F-H, in all other pairs one persons sits between first person and second person.

39. (*c*) B faces G.

40. (*b*) One person (F) sit between H and E, when counted from right of H.

Solutions (Q. Nos. 41-43) *Following sitting arrangement is formed from the given information,*

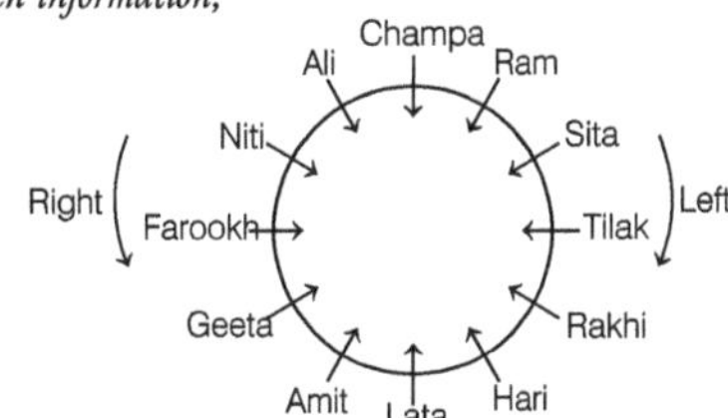

41. (*b*) Clearly, Ali is on Champa's right. So, statement (b) is correct.

42. (*a*) If looked in an anti-clockwise manner, Sita, Ram, Champa, Ali and Niti are seated between Tilak and Farookh.

43. (*a*) Clearly, Ali, Champa and Ram are close neighbours.

Solutions (Q. Nos. 44-48) *Arrangement according to the questions is as follows*

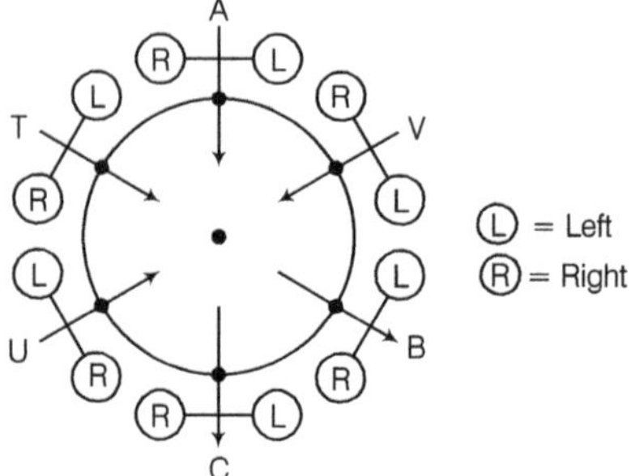

44. (*c*) B and C are not facing centre.

45. (*d*) T is sitting third to the left or right of B.

46. (*c*) V is fourth to the right of C.

47. (*d*) The persons who are not facing centre *i.e.,* B and C are sitting together.

48. (*a*) Clearly, A is second to the left of U.

Solutions (Q. Nos. 49-53) *Following sitting arrangement is formed from the given information,*

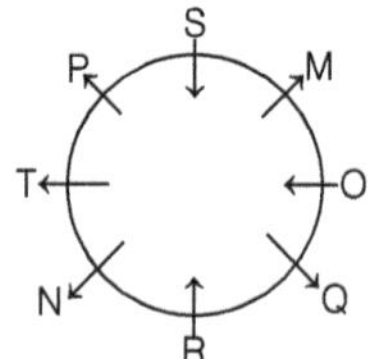

49. (*b*) S is sitting between M and P when counted from left of M.

50. (*b*) S, O and R, three people face the centre.

51. (*c*) S sits second to the right of T.

52. (*b*) P, T, M and Q are facing outside the centre whereas O is facing inside.

53. (*c*) P is sitting third to the left of R.

Solutions (Q. Nos. 54-57) *According to the given information the sitting arrangement is as follows.*

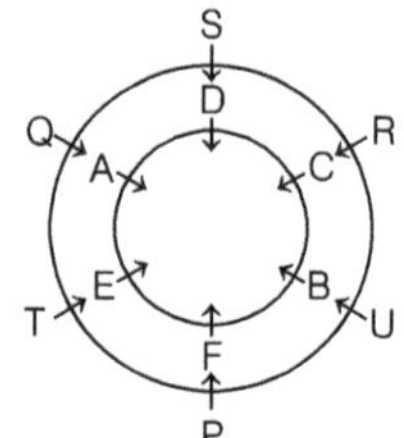

54. (*d*) Two persons (i.e., R and U or Q and T) are sitting between S and P in the outer circle.

55. (*a*) Except A, P in all other pairs second person is sitting behind the first person.

56. (*d*) B is sitting third to the left of A.

57. (*e*) Q is sitting immediate right of S.

Solutions (Q. Nos. 58-62)

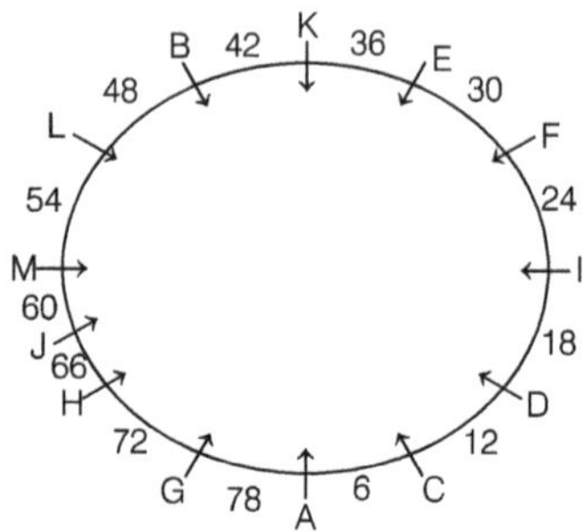

58. (*c*) M and H are immediate neighbours of J.

59. (*d*) Required distance BF = 42 + 36 + 30 = 108 cm

60. (*c*) B sits 6th to the left of A and H is 4th to the right of B.

61. (*b*) Required distance HL = 66 + 60 + 54 = 180 cm

62. (*a*) Except B, C in all other pairs both the persons are immediate neighbours of each other.

TYPE 03

Polygonal Arrangement

A polygon is a closed figure formed with three or more sides. So, in this type of questions, the arrangement of objects/persons may be done along triangular, quadrilateral, pentagonal shape etc.

The major arrangements are discussed as follows

A. Triangular Arrangement

In this type of arrangement, the objects/persons are placed around a triangular plane that may be a table or any triangular object. The left and right of each person/object in both the cases (i.e., facing the centre and facing the direction opposite to the centre) can be understood with the help of following diagrams.

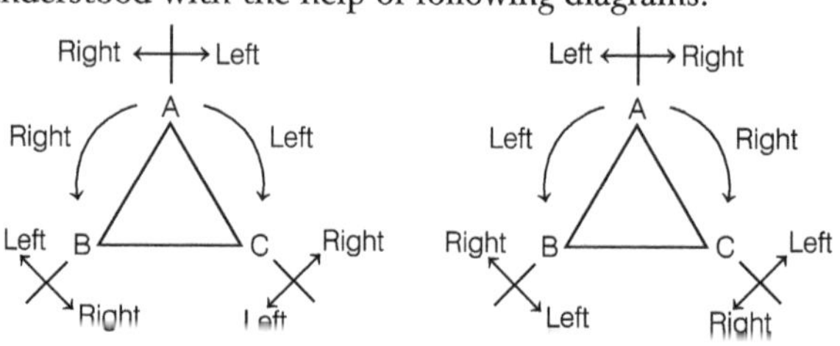

Ex 20 3 persons A, B and C are sitting along the corners of a triangular table facing centre. A is to right of B. Who is sitting to right of C?

(a) A (b) B
(c) C (d) None of these

Solution *(b)* Arrangement according to the question is as follows,

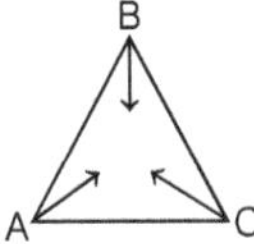

Clearly, B is sitting to the right of C.

B. Quadrilateral Arrangement

In this type of arrangement, four or more objects/persons are placed around a rectangular or a square shaped table or a park facing either the centre or the direction opposite to centre. The left and right of each person in both the cases can be understood with the help of following diagrams.

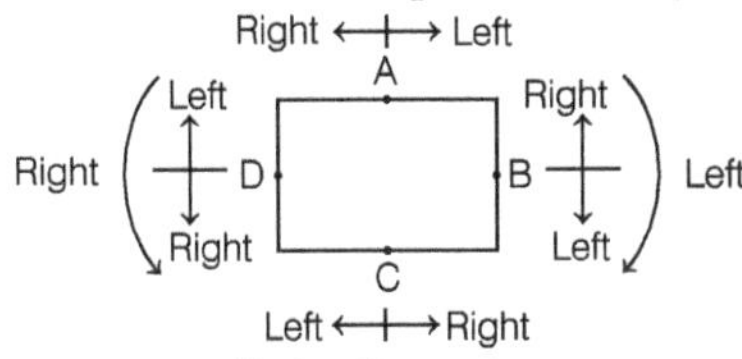

Facing the centre

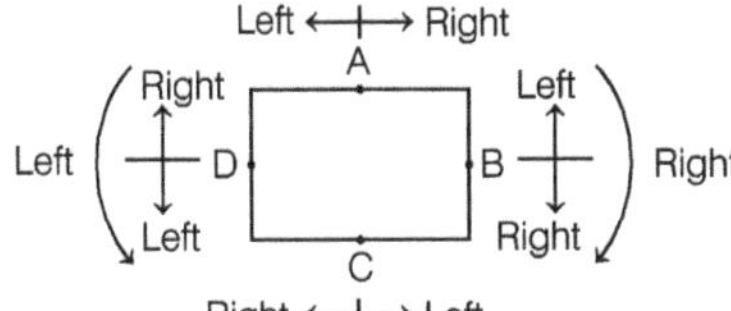

Facing the direction opposite to centre

Ex 21 A, B, C and D are playing cards. A, C and B, D are partners. D is to the right of C. The face of C is towards West. Find the direction that D is facing.

(a) West (b) East
(c) South (d) North

Solution *(c)* Arrangement according to the question is as follows,

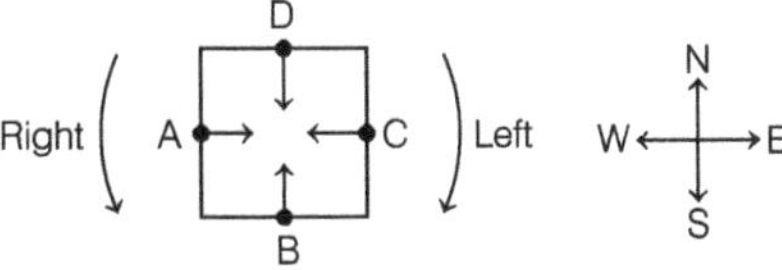

Clearly, D is facing South.

DIRECTIONS ~ (Ex. Nos. 22-26) *Study the following information carefully and answer the given questions.* « IBPS PO 2018

Eight friends A, B, C, D, W, X, Y and Z are sitting around a square table in such a way that four of them sit at four corners of the square while the other four sit in the middle of each sides. The ones who sit at the four corners face outside while those who sit in the middle of the sides face inside.

C is an immediate neighbour of A, who faces centre. W sits second to the left of C. Y sits fourth to the left of W. Two persons sit between Y and D (either from left or right). C is not an immediate neighbour of D. B sits second to the right of D. X sits second to the right of B.

Ex 22 How many persons sits between Z and C.

(a) None (b) One
(c) Two (d) Three
(e) More than three

Ex 23 What is the position of Y with respect to D?

(a) Third to the right (b) Second to the right
(c) Fourth to the left (d) Third to the left
(e) None of these

Ex 24 Four of the following five are alike in a certain way and so form a group. Who among the following does not belong to that group?

(a) Z (b) W
(c) D (d) C
(e) Y

Ex 25 Who sits second to the right of A?

(a) B (b) X
(c) Y (d) D
(e) None of these

Ex 26 Who among the following sits between B and C, when counted from the right of B?

(a) Y and Z (b) W and D
(c) X and Y (d) A and W
(e) A and D

Solutions (Example Nos. 22-26) *According to the given information,*

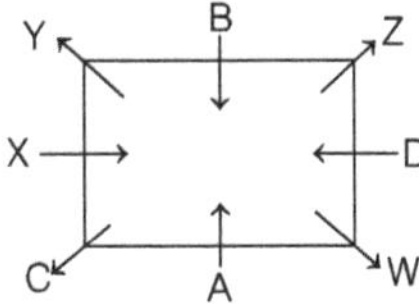

22. *(d)* Three person B, Y and X sits between Z and C, when counted from left of Z.

23. *(a)* Clearly, Y is third to the right of D.

24. *(c)* Except D, all other persons face outside.

25. *(d)* D sits second to the right of A.

26. *(c)* X and Y sits between B and C, when counted from the right of B.

C. Pentagonal Arrangement

In this arrangement, five persons/objects are placed around a pentagonal plane facing either the centre or the direction opposite to the centre. The left and right of each person in both the cases can be understood with the help of the following diagrams.

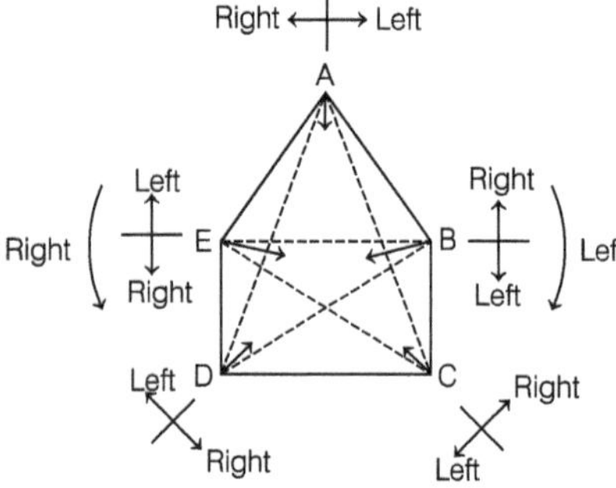

Facing the centre

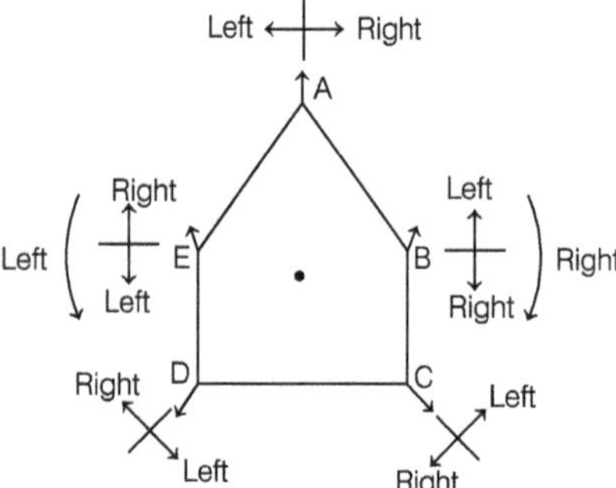

Facing the direction opposite to centre

***Ex* 27** 5 girls A, R, D, S and V are sitting around a pentagonal table facing centre. A is between R and D. S is to the left of V. R is to the left of S. Who is to the right of A?

(a) S (b) D
(c) R (d) V

Solution ***(c)*** Arrangement according to the question is as follows,

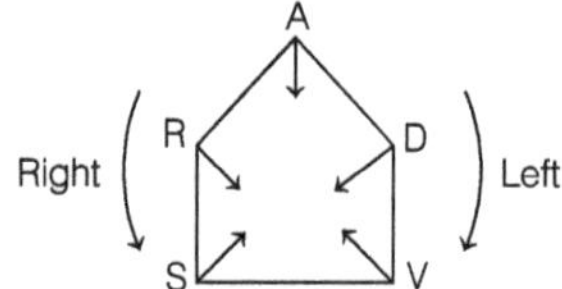

Clearly, R is to the right of A.

D. Hexagonal Arrangement

In this arrangement, six objects/persons are placed around a hexagonal plane facing either the centre or the direction opposite to centre.

The left and right of each person/object in both the cases can be understood with the help of following diagrams.

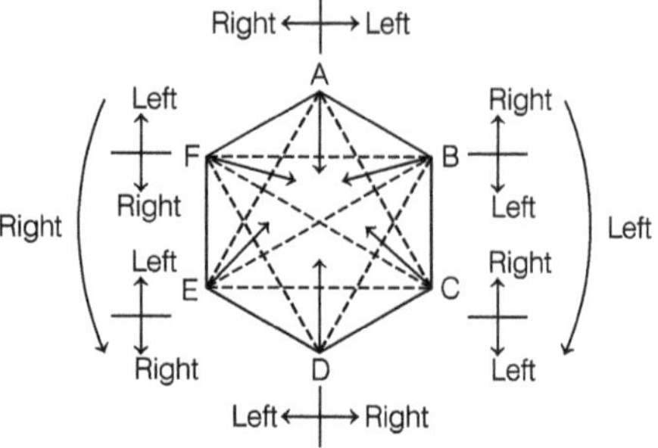

Facing the centre

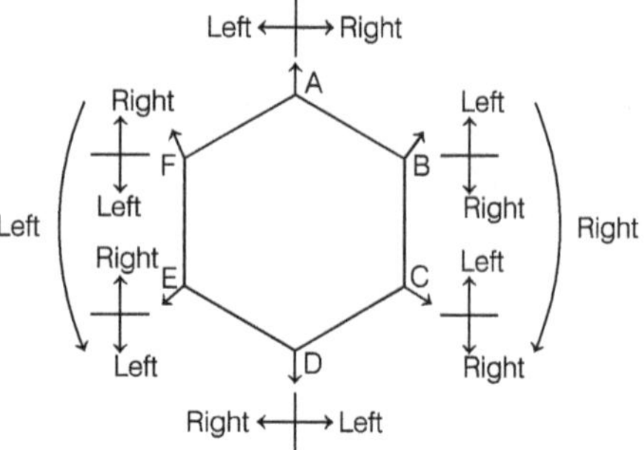

Facing the direction opposite to centre

***Ex* 28** 6 persons are sitting along a hexagonal dining table to have dinner. B is between F and C. A is between E and D and F is to the left of D. Who is between A and F?

(a) E (b) D (c) C (d) B

Solution ***(b)*** Arrangement according to the question is as follows,

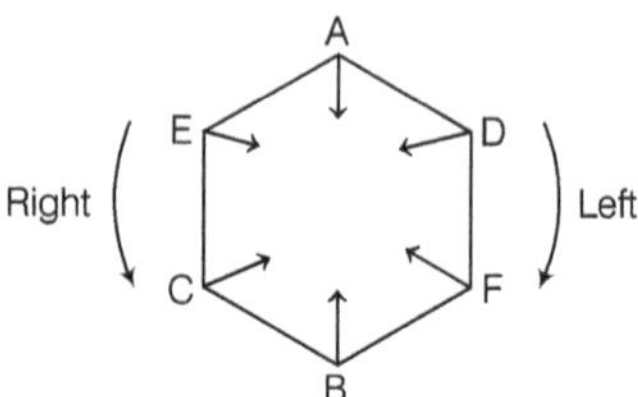

Clearly, D is between A and F.

***Ex* 29** Six persons are seated around a hexagonal table. Arup is seated opposite Belal, who is between chirag and Derek. Arup is between Ela and Farook. Ela is to the left of Derek. Which of the following pairs is facing each other?

« WBSC Pre 2020

(a) Ela and Farook (b) Derek and Ela
(c) Chirag and Ela (d) Chirag and Derek

***Solution* (c)** From given information, arrangement is as follows,

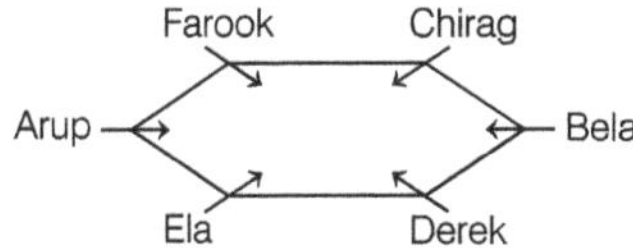

Hence, Chirag and Ela is facing each other.

E. Octagonal Arrangement

In this arrangement, eight objects/persons are placed around a octagonal plane facing either the centre or the direction opposite to centre. The left and right of each person/object in both the cases can be understood with the help of following diagrams.

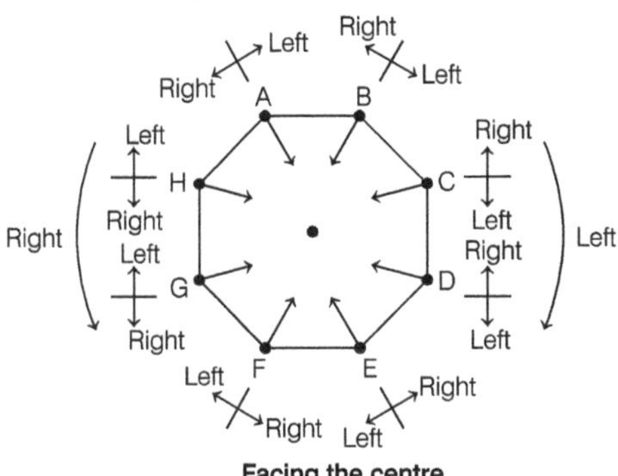

Facing the centre

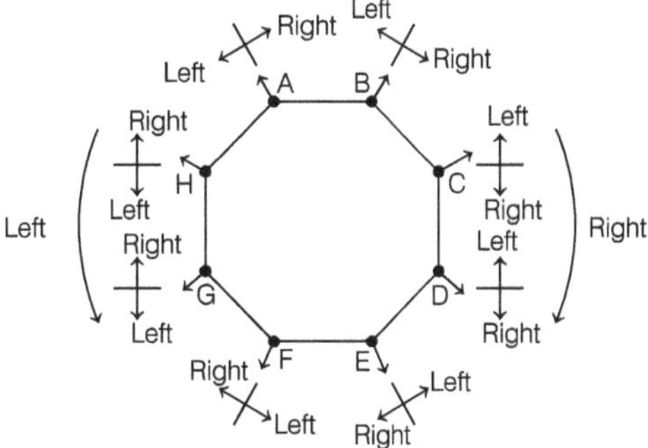

Facing the direction opposite to centre

***Ex* 30** 8 persons A, B, C, D, E, F, G and H are sitting around an octagonal dining table facing the centre. B is between G and D. H is third to the left of B and second to the right of A. C is between A and G. B and E are not in front of each other. Who is third to the left of D?

(a) H (b) G (c) F (d) E

***Solution* (c)** Arrangement according to the question is as follows

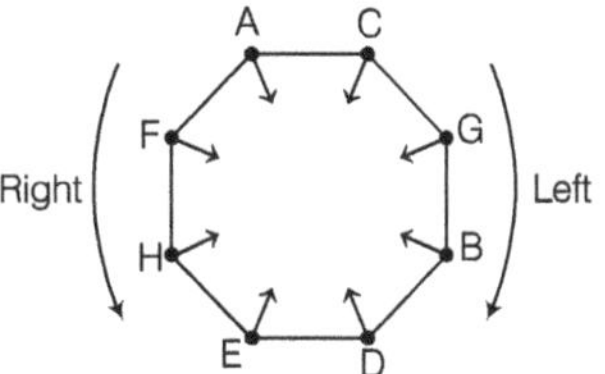

Clearly, F is third to the left of D.

Practice / CORNER 10.3

1. Three friends Ravi, Deepak and Mohit are sitting along the corners of a triangular field facing the centre. Ravi is to the left of Mohit. Who is sitting to right of Mohit?
   (a) Ravi (b) Deepak
   (c) Mohit (d) None of these

2. Radha, Sheela, Mahima and Seeta are sitting along a rectangular table facing centre. Radha is to the right of Sheela. Mahima is to the left of Seeta. Which of the persons given in the options are sitting opposite to each other?
   (a) Sheela-Seeta
   (b) Radha-Seeta
   (c) Radha-Sheela
   (d) Mahima-Radha

3. Five children A, B, C, D and E are sitting along the corners of a pentagonal table facing the centre. B is between E and C. D is to the right of E. Who is to the left of C?
   (a) B (b) A (c) D (d) C

4. Some friends are sitting at an octagonal place. Each person is sitting at one corner facing the centre. Mahima is sitting slantly in front of Ram. Ram is to the right of Sushma. Ravi is sitting beside Sushma and in front of Giridhar. Giridhar is to the left of Chandra. Savitri is not to the right of Mahima but is in front of Shalini. Who is sitting to the right of Shalini?
   (a) Ravi (b) Mahima
   (c) Giridhar (d) Ram

5. Four boys and four girls are sitting around a square facing the centre. One person is sitting at each corner and at the mid-point of each side of the square. Madhu is sitting diagonally opposite to Usha who is to the right of Geeta. Ram who is to the left of Geeta is diagonally opposite to Gopi who is to the left of Bose. Position of Suma is not to the right of Madhu but in front of Prema. Who is sitting opposite to Bose?
   (a) Geeta (b) Prema
   (c) Suma (d) Madhu

DIRECTIONS ~ (Q. Nos. 6-10) *Read the following information carefully to answer the given questions.*

Six people A, B, C, D, E and F are sitting on the ground in a hexagonal shape. All the sides of the hexagon, so formed are of same length. A is not adjacent to B or C. D is not adjacent to C or E. B and C are adjacent. F is in the middle of D and C.

6. Which of the following is not a correct neighbour pair?
(a) A and F (b) D and F
(c) B and E (d) C and F

7. Who is at the same distance from D as E is from D?
(a) B (b) C (c) D (d) F

8. Which of the following group has the correct order of arrangement?
(a) A, F, B (b) F, A, E (c) B, C, F (d) D, A, B

9. If one neighbour of A is D, who is the other one?
(a) B (b) C (c) E (d) F

10. Who is placed opposite to E?
(a) B (b) C (c) D (d) F

DIRECTIONS ~ (Q. Nos. 11-15) *Study the following information carefully and answer the given questions.* « RRB PO 2015

Eight persons G, H, I, J, K, L, M and N are sitting around a rectangular table, each of them facing the centre, but not necessarily in that order. Three persons sit along each of the longer sides of the table and one persons sits along each of the shorter sides.

- If H and J interchange their positions then M sits to the immediate left of J.
- If G and K interchange their positions then I sits opposite K.
- If H and L interchange their positions then N sits third to the right of L.
- G sits third to the left of H, who sits at the longer side of the table.
- If N and J interchange their positions then J sits third to the left of K.
- L and J sit opposite each other.

11. Who sits opposite to M?
(a) J (b) N
(c) K (d) Cannot be determined
(e) None of these

12. Who among the following sit along the longer side of the table?
(a) H, I, M (b) J, L, G
(c) H, I, N (d) Cannot be determined
(e) None of these

13. Who sits second to the left of J?
(a) H (b) K
(c) L (d) Cannot be determined
(e) None of these

14. Who among the following sits to the immediate right of G?
(a) L (b) N (c) K (d) J
(e) None of these

15. Who among the following sit along the shorter side of the table?
(a) J (b) K (c) G (d) M
(e) None of these

DIRECTIONS ~ (Q. Nos. 16-18) *Study the following information carefully and answer the following questions.* « SBI PO 2019

Six persons are sitting around a triangular table. Persons who are sitting at corner are facing towards the table and the persons who are sitting at middle of the table are facing outside the table. A sits at one of the corners of the table. M is an immediate neighbour of A. Two persons sit between M and B. C sits immediate right of B. N is to the immediate right of O. O does not sit at any of the corner of the table.

16. Who sits second to the right of B?
(a) M (b) A (c) N (d) O
(e) C

17. Who is sitting between A and N, when counted from the right of A?
(a) C (b) B (c) O (d) M
(e) None of these

18. Who sits immediate left of N?
(a) M (b) C (c) O (d) B
(e) None of these

DIRECTIONS ~ (Q. Nos. 19-23) *Study the following information carefully and answer the questions given below.*

Eight persons i.e. D, Q, G, H, K, S, E and W are sitting around a square table in such a way that four persons sit at the corner side of the table and other four persons sit in the middle side of the table. The persons who sit at the corner side are facing away from the centre and the persons who sit in the middle side are facing towards the centre. D sits at the corner side of the table. One person sits between D and G. Q sits third to the right of G. Three persons sit between Q and E. W sits second to the right of E. W is not an immediate neighbour of D. H sits second to the right of K.

19. Who among the following sits second to the right of S?
(a) Q (b) E (c) D (d) W
(e) None of these

20. How many persons sit between D and W when counted from the right of D?
(a) Three (b) Four
(c) One (d) Two
(e) None of these

21. Who among the following sits second to the left of G?
(a) D (b) K
(c) H (d) S
(e) None of these

22. Who among the following are the immediate neighbours to each other?
(a) K, E (b) Q, D
(c) G, H (d) W, S
(e) None of these

23. Four of the following five are alike in a certain way and hence form a group. Find the one who does not belong to that group?

(a) E (b) D (c) G (d) K
(e) H

DIRECTIONS (Q. Nos. 24-28) *Study the following information to answer the given questions.* « IBPS Clerk 2018

Eight students A, B, C, D, E, F, G and H are sitting around a square table in such a way four of them sit at four corners while four sit in the middle of each of the four sides. The one who sit at the corners face the centre and others facing outside.

A who faces the centre sits third to the left of F. E who faces the centre is not an immediate neighbour of F.

Only one person sits between F and G. D sits second to right of B. B faces the centre. C is not an immediate neighbour of A.

24. Which one does not belong to that group out of five?

(a) B (b) C (c) E (d) D
(e) A

25. Which will come in the place of?
BCE, EHA, AGD, ?

(a) DFB (b) DGA
(c) DCG (d) DCF
(e) None of these

26. What is the position of G with respect to C?

(a) Third to the right (b) Second to the left
(c) Second to the right (d) Fourth to the right
(e) None of these

27. Who sits third to the left of B?

(a) H (b) A (c) G (d) F
(e) None of these

28. Which is true from the given arrangement?

(a) G faces the centre. (b) B faces outside.
(c) H faces inside. (d) A faces the centre.
(e) None of these.

DIRECTIONS (Q. Nos. 29-33) *Study the following information carefully and answer the questons given below.* « IBPS RRB PO 2019

Eight persons are sitting around a square table. Four persons are sitting at middle of the sides of the square and all are facing towards inside. Remaining four are sitting at corners and they face outside.

Two persons are sitting between P and U. R who is an immediate neighbour of P, sits opposite to S. T sits third to the right of V. W sits immediate right of T. Q faces W.

29. Who among the following sits opposite to T?

(a) P (b) R
(c) S (d) W
(e) None of these

30. How many persons are sitting between P and V?

(a) Two (b) Three
(c) Four (d) Eight (a) or (c)
(e) None of these

31. What is the position of Q with respect to R?

(a) Immediate right.
(b) Immediate left.
(c) 2nd to the right.
(d) 2nd to the left.
(e) None of the above.

32. Who among the following person sit third to the right of Q?

(a) P (b) U (c) R (d) S
(e) None of these

33. Four of the following five are alike in certain way based from a group, find the one which does not belong to that group?

(a) Q (b) R (c) S (d) T
(e) U

DIRECTIONS (Q. Nos. 34-38) *Study the following information carefully and answer the questions given below.* « IBPS Clerk 2019

Eight persons i.e., F, J, K, M, N, P, S and V are sitting around a square table. Four of them are sitting at the corners and remaining are sitting at the middle side of the table. The persons sitting at the corners faces away from the centre and the persons sitting at the middle sides of the table faces towards the centre. All the information is not necessarily in the same order. F sits at the middle side of the table. N sits at the immediate left of V. Two persons sit between F and J. V sits at the immediate right of J. Three persons sit between S and N. M is an immediate neighbor of S. M is not an immediate neighbor of J. P faces inside.

34. How many persons are sitting between F and J when counting from the left of F?

(a) One (b) Two
(c) Three (d) Four
(e) More than four

35. Four of the following five are alike in a certain way and hence form a group, which of the following does not belong to the group?

(a) S (b) F
(c) J (d) K
(e) N

36. Which of the following statement is true?

(a) P sits second to the left of V.
(b) N is an immediate neighbor of S.
(c) Two persons sit between P and V.
(d) M sits opposite to N.
(e) J sits opposite to K.

37. Who among the following is sitting second to the left of M?

(a) P (b) V (c) J (d) F
(e) None of these

38. Who among the following is sitting opposite to P?

(a) V (b) J
(c) F (d) M
(e) None of these

Answers / WITH EXPLANATIONS

1. (*b*) Following sitting arrangement is formed from the given information,

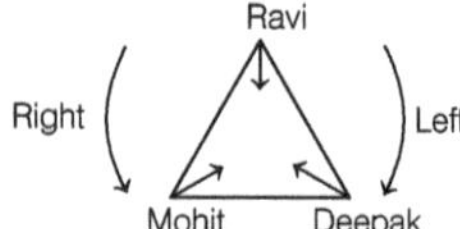

Clearly, Deepak is sitting to right of Mohit.

2. (*b*) Arrangement according to the questions is as follows

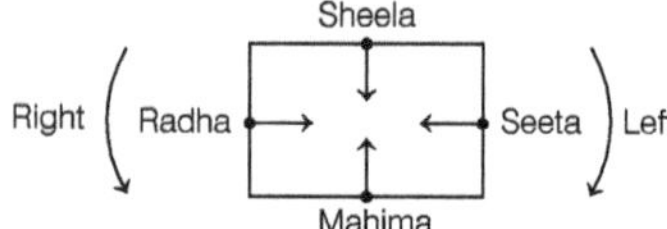

Clearly, Radha and Seeta are sitting opposite to each other.

3. (*b*) Following sitting arrangement is formed from the given information,

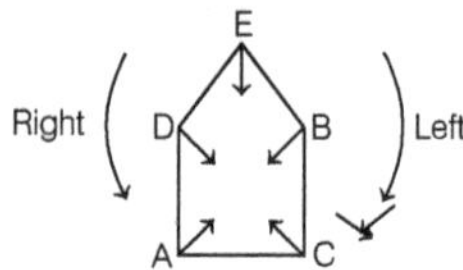

Clearly, A is to the left of C.

4. (*a*) Arrangement according to the question is as follows

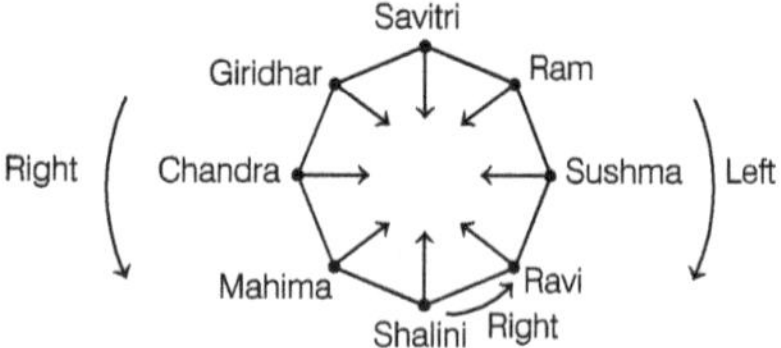

Clearly, Ravi is to the right of Shalini.

5. (*a*) Arrangement according to the questions is as follows

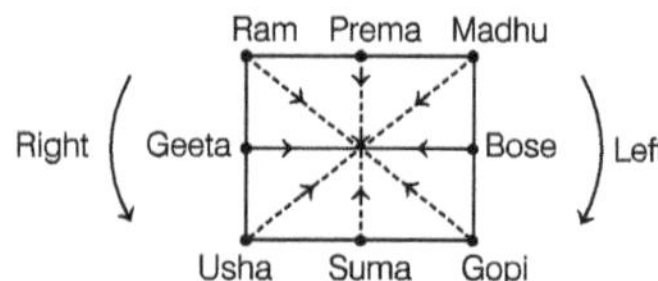

Clearly, Geeta is sitting opposite to Bose.

Solutions (Q. Nos. 6-10) *According to the given information, there are two possible arrangements as follows*

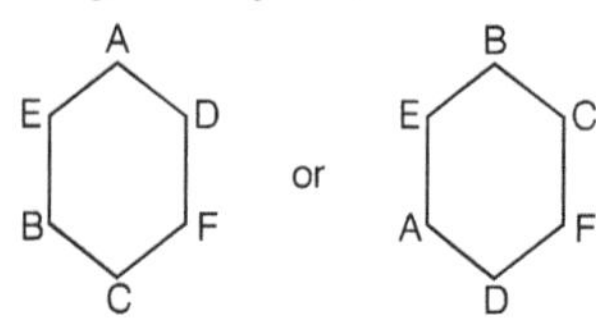

6. (*a*) A and F are not neighbours.

7. (*b*) Both E and C are two places apart from D.

8. (*c*) B, C and F are given in correct order.

9. (*c*) The other neighbour of A is E.

10. (*d*) F is placed opposite to E.

Solutions (Q. Nos. 11-15) *Following sitting arrangement is formed from the given information,*

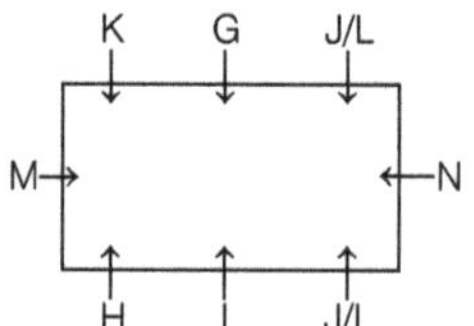

11. (*b*) N is sitting opposite of M.

12. (*b*) There are six persons sitting along the longer side i.e., K, G, J, L, I and H. Hence, option (b) J, L, G is correct.

13. (*d*) Since, the position of J is not confirmed so we can not conclude that who is sitting second to the left of J.

14. (*c*) K is sitting to the immediate right of G.

15. (*d*) M and N are the two persons who are sitting along the shorter side.

Solutions (Q. Nos. 16-18) *Following sitting arrangement is formed from the given information,*

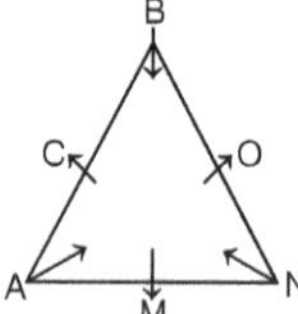

16. (*b*) A sits second to the right of B.

17. (*d*) When counted from right of A, then we see that M is sitting between A and N.

18. (*a*) M is sitting immediate left of N.

Solutions (Q. Nos. 19-23) *According to the given information the arrangement is as follows*

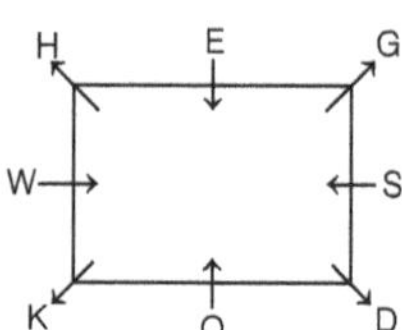

19. (*b*) E sits second to the right of S.

20. (*d*) Two persons (Q and K) sit between D and W, when counted from right of D.

21. (*c*) H sits second to the left of G.

22. (*b*) Q and D are immediate neighbours to each other.

23. (*a*) Except E, all other sits at the corner of the table.

Solutions (Q. Nos. 24-28) *According to the given information,*

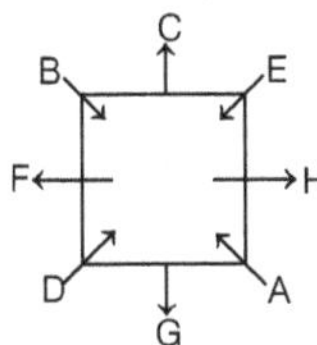

24. (*b*) Except C, all other faces the centre. Hence, C does not belong to that group.

25. (*a*) Following the same pattern, DFB will come in place of question mark.

26. (*d*) G is fourth to the right of C.

27. (*a*) H sits third to the left of B.

28. (*d*) A faces the centre is true.

Solutions (Q. Nos. 29-33) *Following sitting arrangement is formed from the given information,*

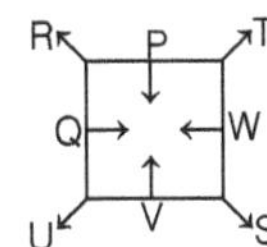

29. (*e*) U sits opposite to T.

30. (*b*) Three persons i.e., T, W and S are sitting between P and V when counted from left of P.

31. (*b*) Q sits immediate left of R.

32. (*d*) S sits third to the right of Q.

33. (*a*) Only Q is the person given in the option who faces inside while rest four persons i.e., R, S, T and U are facing outside.

Solution (Q. Nos. 34-38) *According to the given information,*

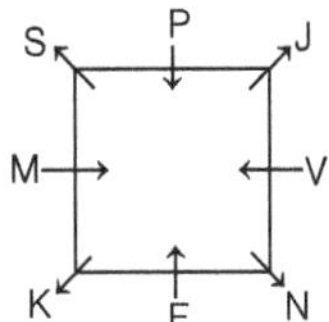

34. (*d*) K, M, S and P i.e., four persons are sitting between F and J.

35. (*b*) S, J, K and N are sitting at the corners but F is sitting at middle of side.

36. (*e*) Clearly from arrangement J is sitting opposite to K.

37. (*a*) P is sitting second to the left of M.

38. (*c*) From the arrangement F is sitting opposite to P.

TYPE 04

Floor Based Arrangement

This type of arrangement is based on different persons/objects residing on different floors of a building. In this type of questions a group of persons or objects are given, with certain set of conditions. Candidates have to analyse the conditions and decode the arrangement to answer the given questions.

Ex 31 Six persons, P, Q, R, S, T and U live on 6 different floors of a same building. Bottommost floor is first, the floor above it is second and so on till topmost floor which is sixth. P lives on odd numbered floor. R lives immediately below P. Two floors gap between floors of R and U. S lives immediately above U. Q lives above T, who lives below U. How many persons live below T? « IBPS Clerk 2018

(a) Four (b) One
(c) Two (d) Three
(e) None

Solutions (e) According to the given information the arrangement is as follows

Floors	Persons
6	S
5	U
4	Q
3	P
2	R
1	T

Clearly, no one lives below T.

Ex 32 Five persons Amit, Anil, Ajay, Atul and Anand live in a five storey building on different floors. Amit lives above Ajay, but below Anand. Atul lives above, but below Amit. Anil lives below Anand, but above Atul. In which floor does Anil live? « UGC NET 2018

(a) Third floor
(b) Second floor
(c) Either third floor or fourth floor
(d) Fourth floor

Solution (c) Following table can be drawn from given information,

Persons	Floor
Anand	5
Amit / Anil	4
Anil / Amit	3
Atul	2
Ajay	1

Therefore, Anil lives either on third floor or on fourth floor.

DIRECTIONS ~ (Example Nos. 33-36) *Study the following information and answer the given questions.* « NICL AO 2017

Maya, Pawan, Amit, Arvind, Raghu, Rajiv and Ashok are living on different floors of a building. The lower mostfloor is numbered 1. The floor immediately above the lowermost floor is numbered 2 and so on. The uppermost floor is numbered 7.

Arvind lives on an even numbered floor. Maya does not lives on any of floor above Arvind's floor. Pawan lives three floors above Rajiv's floor. Only one persons lives between Maya's floor and Rajiv's floor. Ashok lives on an odd numbered floor. Rajiv does not live on any of the floor below Arvind's floor. Amit lives on the floor immediately above the Ashok's floor.

***Ex* 33** Who lives on floor number 3?

(a) Maya (b) Raghu
(c) Rajiv (d) Amit
(e) Ashok

***Ex* 34** Who lives on the floor immediately above the Raghu's floor?

(a) Maya (b) Ashok
(c) Amit (d) Pawan
(e) Rajiv

***Ex* 35** Who lives on the upper most floor?

(a) Amit (b) Ashok
(c) Pawan (d) Raghu
(e) Maya

***Ex* 36** On which floor does Amit live?

(a) 7th floor (b) 6th floor
(c) 5th floor (d) 4th floor
(e) 3rd floor

Solutions (Example Nos. 33-36) According to the given information the arrangement is as follows.

Floor Number	Persons
7	Pawan
6	Amit
5	Ashok
4	Raghu
3	Rajiv
2	Arvind
1	Maya

33. (c) Rajiv lives on floor number 3.

34. (b) Ashok lives on the floor immediately above Raghu's floor.

35. (c) Pawan lives on the upper most floor.

36. (b) Amit lives on 6th floor.

DIRECTIONS ~ (Example Nos. 37-41) *Study the following information carefully and answer the questions given below.* « IBPS RRB Clerk 2019

Seven people viz. A, B, C, D, E, F and G live in a building on seven different floors such as ground floor is numbered 1, the floor just above is numbered 2 and so on till top floor numbered as seven but not necessarily in the same order. There are less than three floors above A. Only one persons lives between C and A. G lives immediately below D. D lives on an even number floor. B lives immediately above A. F lives above E. F does not lives on the 5th floor. F does not live on an even number floor.

***Ex* 37** Four of the following five belongs to a group find the one that does not belongs to that group?

(a) CD (b) EC (c) FB (d) AB
(e) GC

***Ex* 38** Who among the following lives on the top floor?

(a) E (b) B (c) F (d) D
(e) None of these

***Ex* 39** Number of persons lives above F is same as the number of persons below ...... ?

(a) B (b) D (c) C (d) G
(e) None of these

***Ex* 40** How many floors are there above the floor on which G lives?

(a) One (b) Two
(c) Three (d) More than Four
(e) Four

***Ex* 41** Who lives immediately below A?

(a) D (b) E
(c) F (d) C
(e) None of these

Solutions (Ex Nos. 37-41) According to the given information the arrangement is as follows.

Floor Number	Persons
7	F
6	B
5	A
4	E
3	C
2	D
1	G

37. (e) Only the pairs of persons given in option (e) i.e., GC has one persons between them while persons given in rest pairs are given in such a way that they are living on consecutive floors.

38. (c) F is living on top floor i.e., floor number 7.

39. (d) As there is no persons living above F in the same way, there is no persons living below G.

40. (d) Since, G lives on bottom floor so there are 6 persons live above G.

41. (b) E lives immediately below A.

Practice / CORNER 10.4

1. Five persons A, B, X, Y and Z lives on five floors of a building but not necessarily in this order. The ground floor is numbered 1 and the uppermost floor is numbered 5. There are three floors between A and B. X lives on anyone of the floors above Y. Who lives on the floor number 3. « SBI Clerk 2018

(a) B (b) A (c) X (d) Z
(e) Can not be determined

DIRECTIONS ~ (Q. Nos. 2-6) *Read the following information and answer the given questions.* « IBPS RRB 2017

Seven persons A, B, C, W, X, Y and Z lives on different floors of seven floored building but not necessarily in same order. The lower most floor is numbered 1.

The floor immediately above it is numbered 2 and so on. Only four persons lives between X and B. X lives on one of the floors above B. Only two persons live between B and W. A lives on the floor immediately above C. Only two persons live between B and W. A lives on the floor immediately above C. More than two persons live between Z and B. Y lives on one of the floors below Z.

2. Who lives below and above Z respectively?

(a) A, X (b) A, W (c) C, X (d) W, X
(e) W, C

3. On which floor does A live?

(a) Seventh (b) Fifth (c) Third (d) Fourth
(e) Sixth

4. If C interchanges his place with Z and B interchanges his place with A. Then, how many persons will be there between A and Z?

(a) Three (b) None (c) Two (d) One
(e) Four

5. According to the given arrangement. X is related to Z in a certain way and Z is related to W in the same way. According to this way, which of the following is related to A?

(a) Y (b) B (c) X (d) C
(e) None of these

6. According to the given arrangement, which of the following statements is true?

(a) No one lives between X and C.
(b) X lives on an even numbered floor.
(c) None of the given statements is true.
(d) No one lives on the floor below Y.
(e) Y lives on third floor.

DIRECTIONS ~ (Q. Nos. 7-11) *Read the following information and answer the given questions.* « SIDBI PO 2014

There are seven floor in a building. The ground floor is numbered 1. The floor immediately above ground floor is numbered 2 and so on. The top most floor is numbered 7. Seven persons L, M, N, O, P, Q and R live on these floors with each person occupying exactly one floor. O lives on fifth floor. Three persons live between N's and Q's floor respectively. N lives on one of the floors above O. P lives on the floor immediately above R's floor. Only one person lives between L's floor and P's floor.

7. Who lives on the floor immediately above M's floor?

(a) L (b) Q (c) O (d) N
(e) P

8. Who amongst the following lives on the floor exactly between O's and Q's floor?

(a) R (b) L (c) N (d) M
(e) P

9. Who amongst the following lives on topmost floor?

(a) N (b) M (c) L (d) Q
(e) O

10. Who amongst the following lives on fourth floor?

(a) M (b) Q (c) L (d) R
(e) P

11. Four amongst the following five are same and forms a group. Who does not belong to the group?

(a) N (b) O (c) Q (d) P
(e) R

DIRECTIONS ~ (Q. Nos. 12-16) *Study the following information carefully and answer the questions given below.*

There are eight persons namely A, B, C, D, E, F, G and H live on eight different floors from one to eight. Ground floor is number 1 and top floor is number eight but not necessarily in the same order. Only three persons live below the floor on which E lives. Two persons live between the floor on which E and H lives. More than one person live between the floor on which E and A lives. C lives immediately above G. C lives on odd numbered floor. Only one person lives between B and F. B lives one of the above floor on which F lives. D lives on even numbered floor but not on 2nd floor.

12. Who lives on third floor?

(a) C (b) F (c) E (d) D
(e) B

13. How many persons live between F and A?

(a) One (b) Three (c) Five (d) Two
(e) None of these

14. Who lives on floor number eight?

(a) B (b) C (c) A (d) D
(e) F

15. Four of the following five are alike in a certain way based on the given arrangement and thus form a group. Which is the one that does not belong to that group?

(a) F (b) D (c) G (d) E
(e) A

16. Who lives immediate below G?
(a) B (b) H (c) A (d) E
(e) F

DIRECTIONS ~ (Q. Nos. 17-20) *Study the following information and answer the questions that follows.* « IBPS PO 2019

Nine people live on separate floors of a 9- floor building. The ground floor is numbered 1, the first floor is numbered 2 and so on until the topmost floor is numbered 9. Less than four people live above M. Only four-person are living between M and X. P lives on a floor immediately above X. Only two person lives between P and S. S lives on one of the floor below P. As many people live below S as above T. O lives on an odd-numbered floor immediately above U. Only one person lives between O and R. Q lives on one of the floors below R.

17. Who among the following lives above U?
(a) O (b) M
(c) S (d) Both (a) and (b)
(e) None of these

18. How many persons are living between Q and O?
(a) 3 (b) 4
(c) 5 (d) More than 5
(e) None of these.

19. Find the odd one out of the rest.
(a) R (b) X (c) S (d) O (e) U

20. Who among the following lives on the eighth floor?
(a) M (b) O (c) T (d) U
(e) None of these

DIRECTIONS ~ (Q. Nos. 21-25) *Study the following information and answer the questions.* « IBPS RRB 2016

Nine friends A, B, C, D, E, F, G, H and I lives on nine different floors of a building, but not necessarily in the same order. The lower most floor of the building is numbered one, the one above that is numbered two and so on till the topmost floor is numbered nine.

I lives on floor numbered six. E lives on an odd numbered floor above I. Only three people live between E and G. A lives on an even numbered floor immediately below D, but not on the floor numbered eight. Only one person lives between A and F. C lives on one of the floors below F. The number of people living above C is equal to the number of people living below H.

21. Four of the following five are alike in a certain way as per the given arrangement and thus form a group.
Which of the following does not belong to that group?
(a) HB (b) FC (c) DE (d) EI (e) AG

22. How many persons live between A and the person living on the floor numbered seven?
(a) More than three (b) Two
(c) One (d) None
(e) Three

23. H lives on which of the following floor numbers?
(a) Eight (b) One (c) Five (d) Nine
(e) Other than those given as options

24. Which of the following is not true about B as per the given arrangement?
(a) B lives on an even numbered floor.
(b) All the given statements are true.
(c) Only one person lives between B and E.
(d) H lives immediately above B.
(e) Only one person lives above B.

25. In which of the following pairs of people, is even number of people living between them?
(a) G, C (b) H, E
(c) E, D (d) I, H
(e) B, I

DIRECTIONS ~ (Q. Nos. 26-30) *Read the following information carefully and answer the following questions.* « RRB PO 2015

Eight boxes A, B, C, D, E, F, G and H are placed one above the other in any particular order. Box number 1 is at the bottom and box number 8 is at the top.

Three boxes are placed between A and B. Box H is placed immediately below A. There are two boxes between H and G. There are as many boxes between C and D as between H and B. Box C is kept above D. Box E is kept immediately below box D. Three boxes are there between E and F.

26. How many boxes are there above box D?
(a) 4 (b) 3 (c) 6 (d) 2
(e) None of these

27. Which of the following boxes is kept at the top?
(a) B (b) A (c) D (d) E
(e) None of these

28. Choose the odd one out.
(a) B (b) G (c) A (d) D
(e) E

29. Which of the following boxes is kept between F and A?
(a) B (b) G (c) C (d) H
(e) None as box F is immediately above box A

30. How many boxes are there between C and A?
(a) Less than 2 (b) 4
(c) 5 (d) 6
(e) None of these

DIRECTIONS ~ (Q. Nos. 31-35) *Study the following information and answer the questions given below.* « RRB PO 2019

There are eleven boxes placed one above the other. Five boxes are placed between F and T. Not more than five boxes are kept above T. Two boxes are kept between T and M. Three boxes are kept between M and S and M is kept at one of the positions above S. There are only three boxes kept above the box J. One box is kept between R and S.

Two boxes are kept between R and H. Box D is kept at one of the positions below box K and at one of the positions above box C which is not above R. Box E is kept immediately above K.

31. How many boxes are placed between J and R?
(a) 5 (b) 6 (c) 3 (d) 4
(e) None of these

32. Which of the following statement is true regarding C?
(a) C is placed at one of the position above D.
(b) C is placed immediately below F.
(c) R is placed just above C.
(d) C is placed at the bottom most position.
(e) None of the above

33. Which of the following is not true regarding J?
(a) J is immediately below box T.
(b) One of the boxes below J is D.
(c) Number of boxes between J and S is four.
(d) One of the boxes above J is K.
(e) One box is kept between J and M.

34. Number of boxes above K is one less than the number of boxes below ....
(a) S (b) R (c) F (d) D
(e) None of these

35. How many boxes are there between M and H?
(a) One (b) Two
(c) Three (d) None
(e) More than three

DIRECTIONS ~ (Q. Nos. 36-40) *Study the following information carefully and answer the questions given below.* « RRB PO 2015

Seven persons P, Q, R, S, T, U and V live on eight different floors of a building, but not necessarily in the same order.

The lowermost floor of the building is numbered one; the one above it is number two and so on till the topmost floor is numbered eight and one floor is vacant.

V lives on fifth floor. P lives below U. Two persons lives between V and T. Neither R nor U lives on sixth number floor. Q does not live on third number floor. S lives immediate below T. R lives above U. Q does not live on an even numbered floor. More than one person lives between U and R.

36. Who among the following persons lives on floor number Eight?
(a) R (b) P (c) S (d) T
(e) Q

37. Who lives immediate below P?
(a) S (b) V (c) T (d) Q
(e) None of these

38. Who lives on floor number seven?
(a) S
(b) The floor is vacant
(c) The persons, who is immediate above vacant floor.
(d) T
(e) None of the above

39. How many persons live between Q and R?
(a) None (b) Three (c) Two (d) Four
(e) None of these

40. If U is related to T in a certain way and P is related to S in the same way, then which of the following is related to R?
(a) V (b) Q
(c) None of these (d) U
(e) Vacant floor

Answers / WITH EXPLANATIONS

1. (*e*) According to the given information,

Floor Number	Persons
5	A/B
4	Z/X
3	X/Y/Z
2	Y/Z
1	B/A

Clearly, X or Y or Z lives on third floor. Hence, the answer can not be determined.

Solutions (Q. Nos. 2-6) *According to the given information, the arrangement is as follows*

Floor Number	Persons
7	X
6	Z
5	W
4	A
3	C
2	B
1	Y

2. (*d*) W and X lives below and above Z respectively.

3. (*d*) A lives on fourth floor.

4. (*b*) According to the given information, the arrangement is as follows

Floor Number	Persons
7	X
6	C
5	W
4	B
3	Z
2	A
1	Y

Hence, no one lives between Z and A.

5. (*d*) As, Z lives below X and W lives below Z. Similarly, C lives below A.

6. (*d*) No one lives on the floor below Y. This statement is true.

Solutions (Q. Nos. 7-11) *According to the given information, the arrangement is as follows.*

Floor Number	Persons
7	N
6	M
5	O
4	L
3	Q
2	P
1	R

7. (*d*) N lives on the floor immediately above M's floor.

8. (*b*) L lives on the floor exactly between O's and Q's floor.

9. (*a*) N lives on the topmost floor.

10. (*c*) L lives on the fourth floor.

11. (*d*) Except 'P', all other live on the odd numbered floor.

Solutions (Q. Nos. 12-16) *According to the given information, the arrangement is as follows.*

Floor Number	Persons
8	A
7	B
6	D
5	F
4	E
3	C
2	G
1	H

12. (*a*) C lives on third floor.

13. (*d*) There are two persons i.e., B and D between F and A.

14. (*c*) A lives on floor numbered 8.

15. (*a*) Only F is the person who lives on odd numbered floor while rest three live on even numbered floor.

16. (*b*) H lives immediately below G.

Solutions (Q. Nos. 17-20)
According to the given information, the arrangement is as follows

Floor	Persons
9	T
8	M
7	O
6	U
5	R
4	P
3	X
2	Q
1	S

17. (*d*) O and M live above U.

18. (*b*) Four persons are living between Q and O.

19. (*e*) Except U all other persons are living on odd numbered floor.

20. (*a*) M lives on eight floor.

Solutions (Q. Nos 21-25) *According to the given information, the arrangement is as follows*

Floor Number	Persons
9	H
8	B
7	E
6	I
5	D
4	A
3	G
2	F
1	C

21. (*c*) $H \xrightarrow[\text{floor}]{-1} B$, $F \xrightarrow[\text{floor}]{-1} C$,
$D \xrightarrow[\text{floor}]{+2} E$, $E \xrightarrow[\text{floor}]{-1} I$, $A \xrightarrow[\text{floor}]{-1} G$
∴ DE does not belong to the group.

22. (*b*) Two people are living between A and the person living on the floor numbered 7.

23. (*d*) H lives on floor numbered 9.

24. (*c*) Only one persons lives between B and E is not true.

25. (*d*) Two people are living between I and H.

Solutions (Q. Nos. 26-30) *According to the given information, the arrangement is as follows.*

Number	Boxes
8	B
7	C
6	G
5	F
4	A
3	H
2	D
1	E

26. (*c*) Box D is placed at second position so there are six boxes above D.

27. (*a*) Box B at 8th position is kept at the top.

28. (*e*) Only box E is placed at odd position while rest three boxes are placed at even positions.

29. (*e*) Box F and A are placed at fifth and fourth positions respectively. So, there is no box between them.

30. (*e*) Two boxes G and F are there between boxes C and A.

Solutions (Q. Nos. 31-35) *According to the given information, the arrangement is as follows*

Number	Boxes
11	E
10	K
9	T
8	J
7	H
6	M
5	D
4	R
3	F
2	S
1	C

31. (*c*) There are 3 boxes i.e., H, M and D between J and R.

32. (*d*) C is placed at the bottom most position. This is the true statement.

33. (*c*) There are five boxes between J and S.

34. (*c*) There is only one box above K which one less than the number of box below F because there are two boxes below F.

35. (*d*) There is no one box between H and M.

Solutions (Q. Nos. 36-40) *According to the given information, the arrangement is as follows.*

Floor Number	Persons
8	R
7	Q
6	Vacant floor
5	V
4	U
3	P
2	T
1	S

36. (*a*) R lives on floor number 8.

37. (*c*) T on floor number 2 lives immediately below P.

38. (*c*) Q lives on floor number 7, who is immediate above vacant floor.

39. (*a*) Q lives on 7th floor and R on 8th floor so there is no one between R and Q.

40. (*e*) There is a one floor gap between first and second person and the second person lives below first person. In this way U is related T and P is related to S. In the similar manner R is related to vacant floor.

Master Exercise

1. A, B, C, D, E and F are six friends sitting in a long bench. E and F are at the centre while A and B are at the two extreme ends. C is sitting to the immediate left of A. Can you identify who is sitting to the immediate right of B? « SSC Constable 2018
(a) C (b) D (c) F (d) E

2. There are five books A, B, C, D and E. Book C lies above D. Book E is below A, D is above A and B is below E. Which book is at the bottom?
(a) E (b) B
(c) A (d) C

3. Six friends A, B, C, D, E and F are sitting in a row facing East. 'C' is between 'A' and 'E'. 'B' is just to the right of 'E' but left of 'D'. 'F' is not at the right end. How many persons are to the right of 'E'?
(a) 1 (b) 2
(c) 3 (d) 4

4. At a birthday party, 5 friends are sitting in a row. 'M' is to the left of 'O' and to the right of 'P'. 'S' is sitting to the right of 'T', but to the left of 'P'. Who is sitting in the middle?
(a) M (b) O
(c) P (d) S

5. A, B, C, D, E and F are sitting in a row. 'E' and 'F' are in the centre and 'A' and 'B' are at the ends. 'C' is sitting on the left of 'A'. Then who is sitting on the right of 'B'?
(a) A (b) D (c) E (d) F

6. Six friends A, B, C, D, E and F are sitting in a row facing towards North. C is sitting between A and E, D is not at the end, B is sitting at immediate right of E, F is not at the right end, but D is sitting at 3rd left of E. Which of the following is sitting to the left of D?
(a) A (b) F (c) E (d) C

7. Five girls are sitting in a row. Kalpita is to the left of Mridula. Megha is to the right of Arpana. Sangeeta is in the middle of Megha and Kalpita. Who among the following is to the right end of the row?
(a) Mridula (b) Arpana
(c) Kalpita (d) Cannot be determined

8. There are six houses in a row. Mr Lal has Mr Bhasin and Mr Sachdeva as neighbours. Mr Bhatia has Mr Gupta and Mr Sharma as neighbours. Mr Gupta's house is not next to Mr Bhasin or Mr Sachdava and Mr Sharma does not live next to Mr Sachdeva. Who are Mr Bhasin's next door neighbours?
(a) Mr Lal and Mr Bhasin
(b) Mr Lal and Mr Sachdeva
(c) Mr Sharma and Mr Lal
(d) Only Mr Lal

9. Seven children A, B, C, D, E, F and G are standing in a row. G is to the right of D and to the left of B. A is on the right of C, A and D have one child between them. E and B have two children between them. D and F have also two children between them. Who is exactly in the middle?
(a) A (b) C (c) D (d) G

10. Seven friends P, Q, R, S, T, U and V are watching hockey match sitting in a stadium. P and U are sitting at the extreme ends. S is sitting second right of P and between T and R. Q is sitting between U and V. R is sitting immediate left of V. Who is sitting at the middle of all? « SSC Steno 2019
(a) T (b) U (c) R (d) Q

11. Four people viz. P, Q, R and S are sitting around a square table such that each of them sits at the middle of each of the sides, but not necessarily in the same order. Two of them are facing the centre and two face outside (opposite to the centre). Only one person sits between P and Q. P faces outside. R sits to the immediate right of P. Both the immediate neighbours of R face the same direction (If one neighbour face the centre the other neighbour also faces the centre and *vice versa.*) What is the position of S with respect to Q? « MHT MBA 2017
(a) Immediate right (b) Immediate left
(c) Second to the right (d) Second to the left
(e) Cannot be determined

12. Study the following information carefully and answer the question given below.
P, A, D, Q, T, M, R and B are sitting around a circle facing at the centre. D is third to the left of T who is fifth to the right of P. A is third to the right of B who is second to the right of D. Q is second to the left of M.
Who is second to the right of D? « MP Police SI 2017
(a) Q (b) T (c) R (d) B

13. Six friends P, Q, R, S, T and U are sitting at a circular table facing the centre. S is sitting third to the left of T. R is not sitting between T and U. S is not the immediate neighbour of R. Q is seated second to the right of T. Who is sitting between U and Q? « SSC Constable 2018
(a) S (b) R (c) P (d) T

14. Six girls are sitting in a circle facing to the centre of the circle. They are P, Q, R, S, T and V. T is not between Q and S, but some other one. P is next to the left of V. R is fourth to the right of P. Which of the following statement is not true? « FCI Watchman 2018
(a) S is just next to the right to R.
(b) T is just next to the right of V.
(c) R is second to the left of T.
(d) P is second to the right of R.

15. Six persons are playing a card game. Suresh is facing Raghubir who is to the left of Ajay and to the right of Pramod. Ajay is to the left of Dhiraj. Yogendra is to the left of Pramod. If Dhiraj exchanges his seat with Yogendra and Pramod exchanges with Raghubir, who will be sitting to the left of Dhiraj?

(a) Yogendra (b) Raghubir
(c) Suresh (d) Ajay

DIRECTIONS ~ (Q. Nos. 16 and 17) *Read the following information carefully and then answer the questions given below.*

Seven boys A, B, C, D, E, F and G are standing in a line.

I. G is between A and E.
II. F and A have one boy between them.
III. E and C have two boys between them.
IV. D is to the immediate right of F.
V. C and B have three boys between them.

16. Who is second from left?

(a) C (b) G
(c) E (d) A

17. C is standing between.

(a) A and F (b) D and G
(c) A and D (d) F and G

DIRECTIONS ~ (Q. Nos. 18-20) *Study the following information carefully to answer the questions below.*

Five persons are standing in a queue. One of the two persons at the extreme ends is a professor and the other is a businessman. An advocate is standing to the right of a student. An author is to the left of the businessman. The student is between the professor and the advocate.

18. Counting from the left, the author is at which place?

(a) First (b) Second
(c) Third (d) Fourth

19. Which of the following is in the middle of the queue?

(a) Professor (b) Advocate
(c) Student (d) Businessman

20. If advocate and the businessman exchange their positions, and also the author and the student, then who will be standing to the left of student?

(a) Author (b) Businessman
(c) Professor (d) Advocate

DIRECTIONS ~ (Q. Nos. 21 and 22) *Read the following information carefully to answer these questions.*

I. P, Q, R, S, T, U and V are sitting along a circle facing the centre.
II. P is between V and S.
III. R, who is 2nd to the right of S, is between Q and U.
IV. Q is not the neighbour of T.

21. Which of the following is a correct statement?

(a) V is between P and S.
(b) S is 2nd to the left of V.
(c) R is third to the left of P.
(d) P is to the immediate left of S.

22. What is the position of T?

(a) Between R and V. (b) To the immediate left of V.
(c) 2nd to the left of R. (d) 2nd to the left of Q.

DIRECTIONS ~ (Q. Nos. 23 and 24) *Read the following information carefully and answer the questions that follow.*

I. Six flats on a floor in two rows facing North and South are allotted to P, Q, R, S, T and U.
II. Q gets a North facing flat and is not next to S.
III. S and U get diagonally opposite flats.
IV. R next to U, gets a South facing flat and T gets a North facing flat.

23. Whose flat is between Q and S?

(a) T (b) U (c) R (d) P

24. The flats of which of the pair, other than SU, are diagonally opposite to each other?

(a) PT (b) QP (c) QR (d) TS

DIRECTIONS ~(Q. Nos. 25-28) *Read the following information carefully and then answer the questions given below it.*

Five friends A, B, C, D and E are sitting on a bench.

I. A is sitting next to B.
II. C is sitting next to D.
III. D is not sitting with E.
IV. E is on the left end of the bench.
V. C is on second position from right end.
VI. A is on the right side of B and to the right side of E.
VII. A and C are sitting together.

25. At what position is A sitting?

(a) Between B and C (b) Between D and C
(c) Between E and D (d) Between C and E

26. Who is sitting at the centre?

(a) A (b) B (c) C (d) D

27. What is the position of B?

(a) Second from right (b) Centre
(c) Extreme left (d) Second from left

28. What is the position of D?

(a) Extreme left (b) Extreme right
(c) Third from left (d) Second from left

DIRECTIONS ~ (Q. Nos. 29 and 30) *Study the following information to answer the given questions.*

Five boxes are arranged from bottom to top (bottom is numbered as 1 and top is numbered as 5) in such a way that White box is just above Orange box. There are two boxes in between Blue and Pink box. Blue box is above Pink box. Black box is not immediately abvoe or below Blue box.

29. Which box is at bottom?

(a) White (b) Pink (c) Blue (d) Black
(e) Orange

30. Which box is at top?

(a) Black (b) Orange (c) Blue (d) White
(e) Pink

DIRECTIONS ~ (Q. Nos. 31-33) *Study the given information and answer the given questions.*

Six people—K, L, M, N, O and P lives on six different floors of a building not necessarily in the same order. The lower most floor of the building is numbered 1, the one above is numbered 2 and so on till the top most floor numbered 6. L lives on an even numbered floor. L lives immediately below K's floor and immediately above M's floor. P lives immediately above N's floor. P lives on an even numbered floor. O does not live on floor number 4.

31. Four of the following five are alike in a certain way based on the given arrangement and hence form a group. Which of the following does not belong to that group?

(a) MN (b) OL
(c) KM (d) LP
(e) PK

32. Who amongst the following lives on floor number 2?

(a) K (b) P (c) L (d) M
(e) O

33. On which floor does N live?

(a) 4 (b) 3 (c) 5 (d) 1
(e) 2

DIRECTIONS ~ (Q. Nos. 34-38) *Read the information given below to answer the questions.*

A, B, C, D, E, F, G and H want to have a dinner on a round table and they have worked out the following seating arrangements.

I. A will sit beside C.
II. H will sit beside A.
III. C will sit beside E.
IV. F will sit beside H.
V. E will sit beside G.
VI. D will sit beside F.
VII. G will sit beside B.
VIII. B will sit beside D.

34. Which of the following is wrong?

(a) A will be to the immediate right of C.
(b) D will be to the immediate left of B.
(c) E will be to the immediate right of A.
(d) F will be to the immediate left of D.

35. Which of the following is correct?

(a) B will be to the immediate left of D.
(b) H will be to the immediate right of A.
(c) C will be to the immediate right of F.
(d) B will be to the immediate left of H.

36. A and F will become neighbours, if.

(a) B agrees to change her sitting position.
(b) C agrees to change her sitting position.
(c) G agrees to change her sitting position.
(d) H agrees to change her sitting position.

37. During sitting,

(a) A will be directly facing C.
(b) B will be directly facing C.
(c) A will be directly facing B.
(d) B will be directly facing D.

38. H will be sitting between.

(a) C and B (b) A and F
(c) D and G (d) E and G

DIRECTIONS ~ (Q. Nos 39-43) *Read the following information carefully to answer the questions that follows.* « MAT 2018

(i) S, T, U, V, W, X and Y are sitting in a row all facing North.
(ii) V is sitting immediate left of U.
(iii) T is sitting at an extreme end and W is his neighbour.
(iv) V is third from one of the ends.
(v) Y is sitting between X and W.

39. Who is sitting on the right of Y?

(a) S (b) X
(c) V (d) U

40. Who is sitting exactly in the middle of the row?

(a) S (b) X
(c) W (d) U

41. Who is sitting immediately left to V?

(a) S (b) X
(c) W (d) U

42. Who is at the other end of the row?

(a) S (b) X
(c) V (d) U

43. Which of the following is correct regarding U?

(a) Sitting left of W.
(b) Sitting left of V.
(c) Sitting in the middle of the row.
(d) Sitting second from the other end.

DIRECTIONS ~ (Q. Nos. 44-48) *Read the following information carefully to answer the questions that follow.* « MAT 2018

Akansh, Binod, Chandana, Danesh, Isha and Farhad are seated in a semi circular table facing centre. Chandana is third to the right of Farhan and Binod is sitting second to the right of Chandana. Danesh is not sitting next to Chandana and Akansh is not sitting next to Binod.

44. Who is sitting between Chandana and Binod?

(a) Farhad (b) Isha
(c) Danesh (d) Akansh

45. If Farhad is sitting at the Northern most point of the table, then in which direction is Danesh sitting?

(a) West (b) North-West
(c) North-East (d) South-East

46. How many persons are seated between Akansh and Isha?

(a) 1 (b) 4 (c) 3 (d) 5

47. Who is sitting on the left of Farhad?

(a) Binod (b) Chandana
(c) Akansh (d) Danesh

48. Who is sitting diagonally opposite to Farhad ?

(a) Binod (b) Chandana
(c) Akansh (d) Danesh

DIRECTIONS ~ (Q. Nos. 49-53) *Study the following information carefully to answer the given questions.* « IBPS PO 2016

Seven boxes S, P, L, Q, R M and I are place one above the other in any particular order. Box number 1 is at the bottom and box number 7 is at the top.

Three boxes are placed between I and M. M is placed on the place above S, which did not place on an odd numbered place. P is neither placed on odd number place nor on topmost place. I did not place on bottom place. Two boxes are placed between R and S. Q is placed neither on the bottom nor on the fourth place. Box M is not placed on top place.

49. Which box is placed on just above M?
(a) L (b) P (c) Q (d) R
(e) None of these

50. How many boxes are there between L and P?
(a) None (b) One
(c) Two (d) Three
(e) Can not be determined

51. Which of the following pairs of boxes is placed on bottom most and the topmost place respectively?
(a) L, Q (b) Q, P
(c) I, Q (d) L, I
(e) Can not be determined

52. Which of the following box is placed on the topmost place?
(a) I (b) Q (c) P (d) L
(e) None of these

53. Which of the following combinations is true?
(a) 1-S (b) 4-R (c) 3-M (d) 6-I
(e) None of these

DIRECTIONS ~(Q. Nos. 54-58) *Study the following information carefully and answer the questions given below.* « SBI Clerk 2019

Ten persons are sitting in two parallel rows containing five persons in each row such a way that there is an equal distance between adjacent persons. In the first row, A, B, C, D and E are seated and all of them all of them are facing North. In the second row, P, Q, R, S and T are seated and all of them are facing South. Therefore, in the given seating arrangement, each member seated in a row faces another member of the other row.

E sits second from one of the extreme end of the row. P faces the one who sits second to the right of E. D sits second and all of them to the left of B, who does not sit at the extreme end. Two persons sit between S and Q. R sits immediate left of S. C sits next to B.

54. Who among the following faces Q?
(a) B (b) D (c) A (d) C
(e) None of these

55. Who among the following sits at the extreme end of the row?
(a) E (b) T (c) C (d) R
(e) P

56. Four of the following five are alike in a certain way and hence they form a group. Which one of the following does not belong to that group?
(a) Q (b) A (c) T (d) D
(e) P

57. Who among the following sits second to the right of P?
(a) S (b) R (c) Q (d) T
(e) None of these

58. What is the position of A with respect to E?
(a) third to the left (b) immediate to the left
(c) second to the left (d) third to the right
(e) second to the right

DIRECTIONS ~ (Q. Nos. 59-61) *Study the following information carefully and answer the questions given below.* « IBPS Clerk 2017

There are eight persons namely S, T, U, V, W, X, Y and Z lives on eight different floors from one to eight. Ground floor is number one and one above that is number two and so on till the topmost floor is number eight. X lives on odd number floor but does not live on third floor. Z lives immediate below X. More than two persons lives between Z and Y. There are six persons live between S and Y. V lives immediate above W, but live below T. U does not live above X. W does not live immediate above Y.

59. Who lives on floor number five?
(a) U (b) S
(c) Z (d) T
(e) None of these

60. How many persons live between W and X?
(a) One (b) Three
(c) Five (d) Two
(e) None of these

61. Who lives immediately above V?
(a) Z (b) T
(c) U (d) W
(e) None of these

DIRECTIONS ~ (Q. Nos. 62-66) *Read the following information carefully and answer the questions given below.* « RRB PO 2019

Twelve people are sitting in two parallel rows containing six people each in such a way that there is an equal distance between adjacent persons. In Row 1- P, Q, R, S, T and U are seated (but not necessarily in the same order) and all of them are facing South. In Row 2- A, B, C, D, E and F are seated (but not necessarily in the same order) and all of them are facing North. Therefore, in the given seating arrangement each member seated in a row faces another member of the other row.

P faces D. U does not face A, who sits left to E but not immediate left. R sit at one of the ends and diagonally opposite to B. Three persons sit between B and F, who does not face U. C sits immediate left to D but does not faces S. Two persons sit between Q and U, none of them sits at the end. The one who faces T sits second to the right of A.

62. Who among the following faces A?
(a) S (b) T
(c) Q (d) R
(e) None of these

63. How many persons sit to the right of R?
(a) None (b) One
(c) Two (d) Three
(e) Four

64. Four of the following five form a group, who among the following does not belongs to that group?
(a) U (b) T
(c) E (d) F
(e) A

65. If in a certain way R is related to C, T is related to E, then who among the following is related to D?
(a) U (b) T
(c) E (d) F
(e) Q

66. Who among the following sits third to the right of U?
(a) R (b) T
(c) P (d) S
(e) Q

DIRECTIONS ~ (Q. Nos. 67-71) *Study the following information carefully and answer the questions given below.* « IBPS Clerk 2019

A certain number of persons are sitting in a row facing in North direction. Four persons are sitting between P and Q. F sits second to the right of Q. One person sits between F and S. S sits at eighth position from one of the extreme ends. D sits third to the right of S. H sits fifth to the left of Q. Eight persons are sitting to the left of Q.

67. What is the maximum possible number of persons are sitting in a row?
(a) Twenty (b) Twenty-two
(c) Twenty-six (d) Twenty- five
(e) None of these

68. How many persons are sitting between P and S?
(a) Three (b) Five
(c) None (d) Two
(e) More than five

69. What is the position of D with respect to F?
(a) Fifth to the left (b) Sixth to the right
(c) Second to the left (d) Fifth to the right
(e) None of these

70. How many persons are sitting to the left of H?
(a) One (b) Three
(c) Two (d) Four
(e) None of these

71. If A is sitting exactly in between the P and D, then what is the position of A with respect to S?
(a) Third to the left (b) None of these
(c) Third to the right (d) Second to the left
(e) Second to the right

DIRECTIONS ~ (Q. Nos. 72-75) *Study the following information carefully and answer the below questions.* « IBPS PO 2019

Eight persons namely - A, B, C, D, E, F, G and H are sitting around a square table but not necessarily in the same order. One person sits at middle of the edge and one person sits at each corner. Person at the corner facing centre while person at the edges sits facing outward.

F is immediate neighbour of B, who doesn't facing to E. One person sits between G and H. Only two persons sits between B and D, who neither sits opposite to H nor F. C and G sit together. E is sitting third of F either from left or right. Immediate right person of A is not facing G. F sits at middle of the edge.

72. What is the position of H with respect to F?
(a) Second to right (b) Immediate left
(c) Second to left (d) Third to right
(e) None of these

73. Who sits opposite to A?
(a) D (b) C (c) F (d) E
(e) None

74. If E and A exchange their position with C and H respectively, then how many person are sitting between E and A after rearrangement when counting left of A?
(a) Two (b) Four
(c) One (d) Three
(e) None

75. Which of the following statement is not true?
(a) One person sits between A and C.
(b) D sits immediate left of G.
(c) The one who sits facing E sits second to right of B.
(d) Two person sits between F and the one who sits opposite to B.
(e) All the above statements are true.

DIRECTIONS ~ (Q. Nos. 76-80) *Study the following information carefully and answer the questions given below.* « SBI PO 2019

Nine persons are sitting in a row. Some of them are facing North and some are facing South. P sits second from one of the extreme ends. Two persons sit between P and R. S sits third to the left of R. U sits second to the right of S. Immediate neighbours of S faces opposite to S. T sits second to the right of U. W is an immediate neighbour of T. Persons sitting in an extreme end are facing opposite direction to each other. P sits second to the right of T. W and P does not face North. Q sits second to the left of V. X does not face South.

76. Who among the following persons sits third to the right of U?
(a) P (b) R (c) S (d) T
(e) None of these

77. How many persons are sitting between P and S?
(a) Two (b) Three (c) Five (d) Four
(e) One

78. Who among the following pair of persons are sitting at extreme end?

(a) S-V (b) V-X
(c) P-W (d) P-X
(e) None of these

79. How many persons are facing South?

(a) Two (b) Three
(c) Four (d) Five
(e) None of these

80. Four of the following five are alike in certain way based from a group, find the one which does not belong to that group?

(a) V (b) Q (c) W (d) X
(e) P

DIRECTIONS ~ (Q. Nos. 81-85) *Study the following information to answer the given questions.* « IBPS PO 2016

S, T, U, V, W, X, Y and Z are sitting in a straight line equidistant from each other (but not necessarily in the same order). Some of them are facing South while some are facing North. (Note: Facing the same direction means, if one is facing North then the other also faces North and *vice versa*. Facing the opposite directions means, if one is facing North then the other faces South and *vice versa*).

S faces North. Only two people sit to the right of S. T sits third to the left of S. Only one person sits between T and X. X sits to the immediate right of W. Only one person sits between W and Z. Both the immediate neighbours of T face the same direction. U sits third to the left of X. T faces the opposite direction as S. Y does not sit at any of the extremes ends of the line. V faces the same direction as W. Both Y and U face the opposite direction of Z.

81. How many persons in the given arrangement are facing North?

(a) More than four (b) Four
(c) One (d) Three
(e) Two

82. Four of the following five are alike in a certain way, and so form a group. Which of the following does not belong to the group?

(a) W, X (b) Z, Y
(c) T, S (d) T, Y
(e) V, U

83. What is the position of X with respect to Z?

(a) Second to the left (b) Third to the right
(c) Third to the left (d) Fifth to the right
(e) Second to the right

84. Who amongst the following sits exactly between Z and W?

(a) T (b) Y (c) X (d) V
(e) U

85. Who is sitting second to the right of T?

(a) Z (b) V (c) X (d) W
(e) None of these

DIRECTIONS ~ (Q. Nos. 86-90) *Study the information carefully and answer the questions given below.* « SBI PO 2019

There are ten persons J, P, Q, R, S, T, G, U, V and X living in a ten-floor building, such that ground floor is numbered as 1, just above the floor is numbered as 2 and so on the topmost floor is numbered as 10, but not necessary in the same order.

P lives on the 5th floor. Only three persons live between P and V. T lives immediate above J, who lives on an odd numbered floor. S lives on one of the floors below R. Number of persons lives between J and P is same as number of persons lives between T and R. There is only one floor in between U and X. W lives on an odd numbered floor. R does not live on top floor. S lives on an odd numbered floor above X but not on seventh floor. V lives below the floor on which P lives. U lives above the floor on which X lives. Q lives on an even numbered floor above P but not on top floor.

86. How many persons live between W and S?

(a) One (b) Four
(c) None (d) Three
(e) More than four

87. Who among the following lives on topmost floor?

(a) V (b) W (c) T (d) S
(e) U

88. Four of the following five are alike in certain way based form a group, find the one which does not belong to that group?

(a) Q (b) X
(c) U (d) W
(e) T

89. Who among the following lives immediate above Q?

(a) J (b) W
(c) P (d) S
(e) V

90. Which of the following statement is not true above U?

(a) U lives on 4th floor
(b) Two persons live between U and W
(c) V lives immediate below U
(d) P lives immediate above U
(e) All are true

DIRECTIONS ~ (Q. Nos. 91-95) *Study the information carefully and answer the questions.*

S, T, U, V, W, X, Y and Z are sitting around a circle area, with equal distance amongst each other but not necessarily in the same order.

Only two people face the centre and the rest face outside (i.e., in a direction opposite to the centre).

Y sits second to left of W. S sits second to left of Y. Only one person sits between S and Z. T sits to immediate right of S. T is not an immediate neighbour of Y. V is not an immediate neighbour of Y.

Both the immediate neighbours of X face the centre.

91. Who is sitting to immediate right of Z?
(a) Y (b) V (c) T (d) X
(e) W

92. Which of the following is true regarding U as per the given sitting arrangement?
(a) X sits second to left of U.
(b) Only three people sit between U and Y.
(c) Z is one of the immediate neighbours of U.
(d) U faces the centre.
(e) S sits to immediate left of U.

93. What is T's position with respect of Y?
(a) Second to the right (b) Second to the left
(c) Fifth to the left (d) Fourth to the right
(e) Third to the left

94. Which of the following groups represents the immediate neighbours of X?
(a) WY (b) VW
(c) TZ (d) VZ
(e) SU

95. Four of the following five are alike in a certain way based on the given seating arrangement and so form a group. Which is the one that does not belong to that group?
(a) Z (b) T (c) Y (d) V
(e) X

DIRECTIONS ~ (Q. Nos. 96-99) *Read the following information carefully and answer the questions that follow.* « UPSC Pre 2018

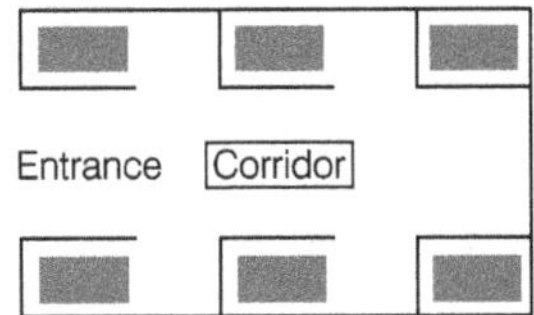

The above building plan shows an office block for six officers A, B, C, D, E and F. Both B and C occupy offices to the right of the corridor (as one enters the office block) and A occupies an office to the left of the corridor. E and F occupy offices on opposite sides of the corridor but their offices do not face each other. The offices of C and D face each other. E does not have a corner office. F's office is further down the corridor than A's but on the same side.

96. If E sits in his office and faces the corridor, whose office is to his left?
(a) A (b) B (c) C (d) D

97. Whose office faces A's office?
(a) B (b) C (c) D (d) E

98. Who is/are F's neighbour/(s)?
(a) Only A (b) A and D both
(c) Only C (d) B and C both

99. D was heard telling someone to go further down the corridor to the last office on the right. To whose room, was he trying to direct that person?
(a) A (b) B (c) C (d) F

DIRECTIONS ~ (Q. Nos. 100-104) *Study the information carefully and answer the questions given below.* « SBI PO 2018

There are fifteen people live on different floors in the given three building X, Y and Z such that each of the floors of the building is occupied by the given person. Building X is immediate West of building Y, which is immediate West to building Z. In the building ground floor is numbered as 1 above it is floor 2 and so on ... In the building floor 1 of building Y is immediate East of floor 1 of building X but immediate West of floor 1 of building Z and so on ....

Note *A is West to B does not mean A is immediate West to B. Above or below does not mean in the same building.*

N lives to the West of L on third floor. M is immediate West to I. K is immediate East to E. A lives on the top floor of the building such that none of the person lives above A in any of the building. The number of floors between J and H is same as between H and I. I lives below J. The one who is either immediate above or immediate below N is immediate left to B. Two persons live between B and M. M lives in the same building as B. B does not live in the same building as J. Building Z has more number of floor than building Y but less than building X. H is not in the same building as L. Two persons live between D and C. F live to the West of G. D lives above O, but in the same building. D does not live on the even number floor.

100. How many persons are living above B in the same building?
(a) Two (b) One (c) Three (d) Four (e) None

101. Who among the following lives to the immediate East of F ?
(a) L (b) J (c) H (d) B (e) A

102. Which of the following true regarding O?
(a) Lives in the same building as L
(b) Lives on second floor
(c) Lives to the West of G
(d) All are true
(e) None is true

103. On which of the following floor does C live?
(a) Third (b) First (c) Second (d) Fourth
(e) None of follows

104. Who among the following lives just above N in the same building?
(a) L (b) F (c) H (d) B (e) A

DIRECTIONS ~ (Q. Nos. 105-109) *Study the given information carefully and answer the given questions.*

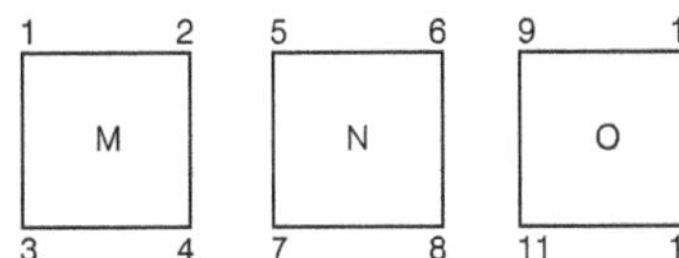

There are 3 square shape tables- M, N and O; placed as above and the corners of each table are numbered as 1, 2, 3......12. On each corner of each table a person viz. A, B, C, D, E, F, G, H, I, J, K and L, are sitting and facing the center. Each of the person likes different numbers viz. 25, 27, 29, 33, 49, 64, 65, 81, 100, 125, 153 and 196.

D is not an immediate neighbour of A. E and B are facing to each other. The one who likes the number which is square of 5 is not an immediate neighbour of that person who sits on that corner which is numbered as 10. G sits immediate right of D. B sits immediate right of J. F and C are facing to each other. The one who likes the number 25 is immediate neighbour of that person who sits on that corner which is numbered as 8. E is not the neighbour of A.

The one who likes square of 7, sits on that corner which is numbered as square of 3. I and G are facing to each other. J and K are facing to each other.

Note *Consider that all the positive integer are taken to square and cube.*

The numbers liked by them are as follows:

1. A likes the number 49.
2. B likes the number 100.
3. C likes the number 33.
4. D likes the number 27.
5. E likes the number 64.
6. F likes the number 125.
7. G likes the number 196.
8. H likes the number 25.
9. I likes the number 153.
10. J likes the number 65.
11. K likes the number 29.
12. L likes the number 81.

Conditions

1. If a person likes the number which is a cube, but not a square and not divisible by 3 then he sits on that corner which is numbered as 10.
2. If a person likes cube of 4 then he sits on that corner which is numbered as 3.
3. If a person likes square of 14 then he sits on that corner which is numbered as 5.

105. A is an immediate neighbour of ______ .

(a) F and C (b) D and I
(c) I and G (d) E and B
(e) Cannot be determined

106. J sits on table ______ .

(a) M (b) N
(c) O (d) Either (a) or (c)
(e) Either (b) or (c)

107. F sits immediate right of that person who likes ______ number.

(a) 49 (b) 64 (c) 81 (d) 33 (e) 29

108. D sits immediate left of ______ .

(a) A (b) I (c) H (d) E (e) G

109. Four of the following are alike in a certain way so form a group, which of the following does not belong to the group?

(a) L (b) A (c) B (d) H (e) J

DIRECTIONS ~ (Q. Nos. 110-114) *Study the given information carefully and answer the given questions.*

There are 7 cabins in an office. In each cabin an employee is working on a desktop. All cabins are lined together in a single row. The opening of only four cabins is in North and rest of them are in South. If the opening of the cabin is in North direction, the employee working in it is also facing north direction and same for the south. The name of the employees are A, B, C, D, E, F and G; and they all are having working experience of different years viz. 2, 4, 6, 8, 10, 12 and 14; but not necessarily in the same order.

The difference between the working experience of G and B is 1/3 of the combined working experience of A and D. The opening of that cabin in which D is working is in south direction. There is no gap between the cabin of the one who has working experience of 12 years and the one who has working experience of only 6 years. The cabin of A is at the end of the row. The opening of immediate cabins of that cabin in which B is working is in same direction. The cabin of C who is having 4 years of working experience is immediate right of G's cabin.

The cabin in which B is working is second to the right of the cabin in which C is working. The one who is having 10 years of working experience is A. There are more than three cabins between the cabin of the one who is having 2 years working experience and the one who is having 10 years working experience. The opening of G's cabin is in south direction. F has working experience of 14 years.

The opening of that cabin in which C is working is in opposite direction of that cabin's opening in which A is working. (i.e. if the opening of A's cabin is in north then the opening of C's cabin is in south direction and *vice-versa*). The working experience of G is more than 6 years but less than 12 years. The opening of that cabin in which B is working is in north direction.

The cabin in which A works is third to the left of F's cabin. The cabin in which B is working is second to the right of that cabin in which A is working. The working experience of E is more than D but less than B.

110. How many cabins are there between the cabin of the one who is having 8 years working experience and the cabin of the one who is having 6 years working experience?

(a) None (b) 1 (c) 2 (d) 3
(e) None of these

111. Four of the following five are alike in a certain way based on their cabin's positions and so form a group. Which of the following is different from the group?

(a) B (b) F (c) E (d) D
(e) C

112. The cabin of B is ______ of the cabin of D.

(a) 4th to the left (b) 3rd to the right
(c) immediate left (d) 4th to the right
(e) None of these

113. How many cabins are there between the cabin of the one who is having 12 years working experience and the cabin of the one who is having 14 years working experience?

(a) None (b) 1 (c) 2 (d) 3
(e) None of these

114. The cabin of A is ______ of the cabin of F.

(a) 3rd to the left (b) 4th to the right
(c) immediate right (d) 4th to the right
(e) None of these

Answers / WITH EXPLANATIONS

1. (*b*) According to the given information

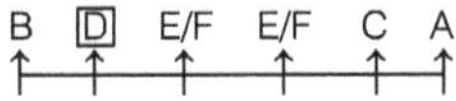

∴ Clearly, D is sitting to the immediate right of B.

2. (*b*) According to the given information, books are arranged as follows

Clearly, book at the bottom is B.

3. (*b*) According to the given information, following sitting arrangement is formed.

Clearly, 2 persons (*i.e.,* B and D) are to the right of E.

4. (*c*) Arrangement according to the question, is as follows

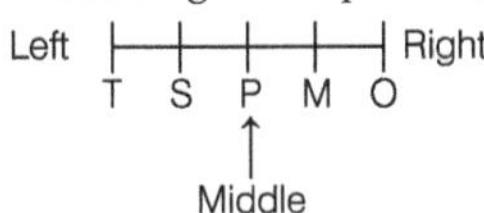

It is clearly show that 'P' is sitting in the middle.

5. (*b*) Arrangement according to the question is as follows

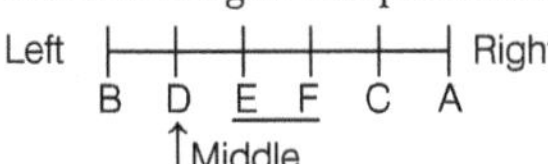

Clearly, 'D' is to the right of B. Hence, option (b) is the correct answer.

6. (*b*) According to the question, arrangement of A, B, C, D, E and F is as follows

Left F D A C E B Right

Clearly, F is sitting to the left of D.

7. (*a*) Arrangement according to the questions, is as follows

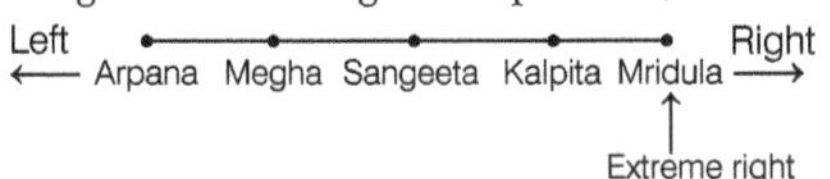

Clearly, Mridula is to the extreme right of the row.

8. (*c*) According to the question, the arrangement is as follow

Mr Sachdeva Mr Lal Mr Bhasin Mr Sharma Mr Bhatia Mr Gupta

Clearly, Mr Bhasin's next door neighbours are Mr Lal and Mr Sharma both.

9. (*c*) The sequence of children in the row is as follows,

Left C A E D G B F Right
Middle

Clearly, D is exactly in the middle.

10. (c) From the given information,

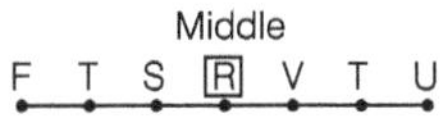

Clearly, R sits in the middle of all.

11. (*a*) As per given information, we have

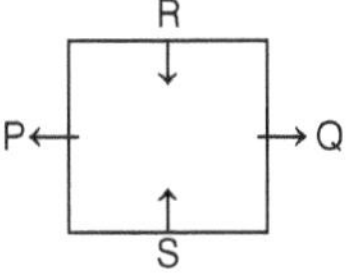

∴ S is to the immediate right of Q.

12. (*d*) From given information, arrangement is as follows

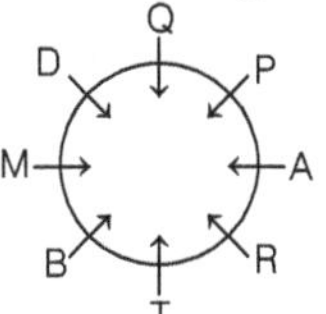

It is clear from above that B is second to the right of D.

13. (*a*) According to the given information,

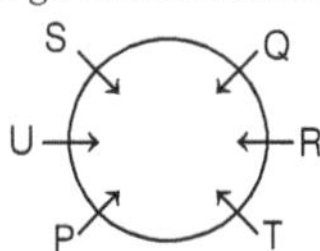

∴ Clearly, S is sitting between U and Q.

14. (*d*) From given information arrangement is as follows,

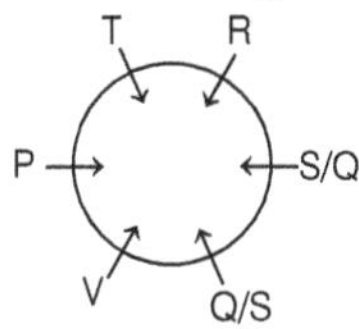

It is clear from diagram that P is second to the right of R.

15. (*c*) Arrangements according to the questions are as follows,

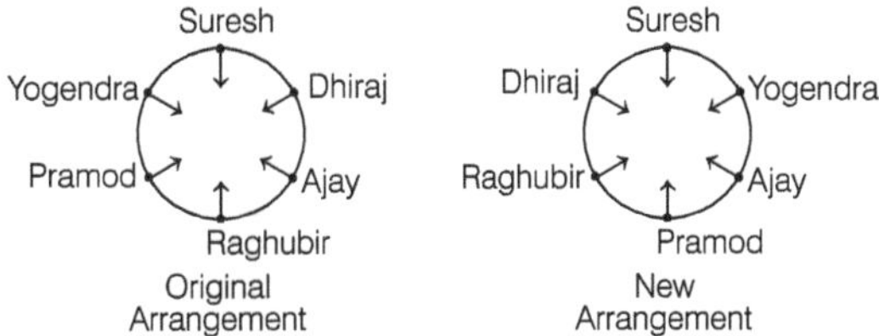

Clearly, Suresh is sitting to the left of Dhiraj.

Solutions (Q. Nos. 16 and 17) *Arrangement according to the questions is as follows*

16. (*c*) Clearly, E is second from left.

17. (*a*) Clearly, C is standing between A and F.

Solutions (Q. Nos. 18-20) *Arrangement according to the question, is as follows*

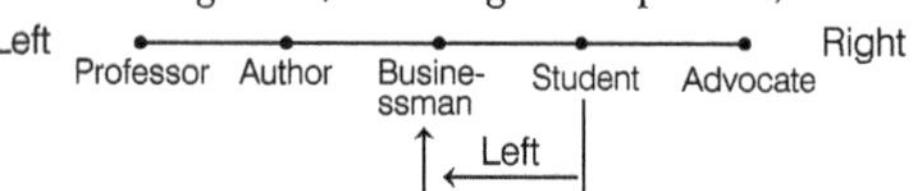

18. (*d*) Clearly, author is fourth from the left.
19. (*b*) Advocate is in the middle of the queue.
20. (*b*) New arrangement, according to the question, is as follows

Left Right
Professor Author Busine-ssman Student Advocate
Left

Clearly, businessman is standing to the left of student.

Solutions (Q. Nos. 21 and 22) *Following sitting arrangement is formed from the given information,*

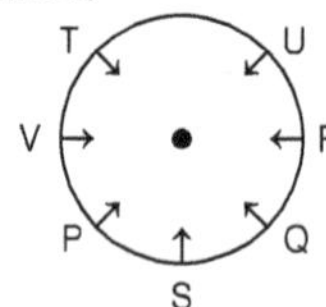

21. (*d*) Clearly, P is to the immediate left of S.
22. (*b*) Clearly, T is to the immediate left to V.

Solutions (Q. Nos. 23 and 24) *Arrangement according to the question, is as follows.*

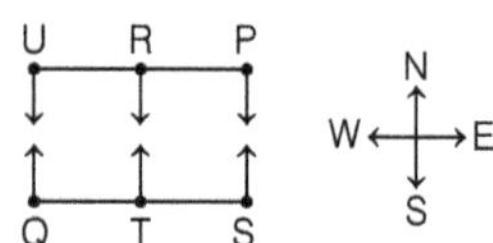

23. (*a*) Clearly, T's flat is between Q and S.
24. (*b*) Flats of Q and P both are diagonally opposite to each other.

Solutions (Q. Nos. 25-28) *Arrangement according to the question, is as follows*

Left E B A C D Right

25. (*a*) A is sitting between B and C.
26. (*a*) A is sitting at the centre.
27. (*d*) B is sitting second from left.
28. (*b*) D is at the extreme right.

Solutions (Q. Nos. 29 and 30) *According to the given information arrangement is as follows.*

Numbers	Boxes
5	Blue
4	White
3	Orange
2	Pink
1	Black

29. (*d*) Black box is placed at the bottom.
30. (*c*) Blue box is placed at the top.

Solutions (Q. Nos. 31-33) *Arrangement according to the question is as follows,*

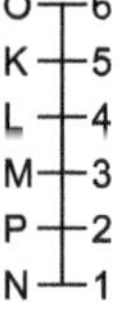

31. (*e*) Clearly, PK does not belongs to the group.
32. (*b*) Clearly, P lives on floor number 2.
33. (*d*) Clearly, N lives on floor number 1.

Solutions (Q. Nos. 34-38) *Following sitting arrangement is formed from the given information,*

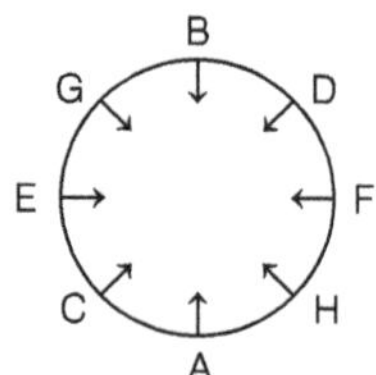

34. (*c*) Clearly, E is not to immediate right of A.
35. (*b*) Clearly, H will be to the immediate right of A.
36. (*d*) A and F will become neighbours, if H agrees to change her sitting position.
37. (*c*) Clearly, A will be directly facing B.
38. (*b*) Clearly, H is sitting between A and F.

Solutions (Q. Nos. 39-43) *From the given information the sitting arrangement is as follows*

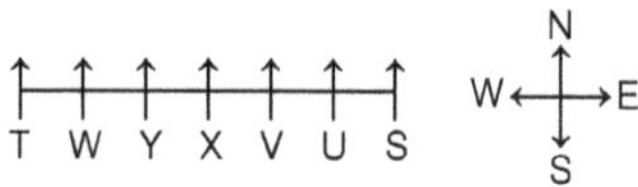

39. (*b*) X sits to the right of Y.
40. (*b*) X sits exactly in the middle of the row.
41. (*b*) X sits to the immediate left of V.
42. (*a*) S sits at the other end of the row.
43. (*d*) U's position is second from the other end is true.

Solutions (Q. Nos. 44-48) *The seating arrangement is as follows*

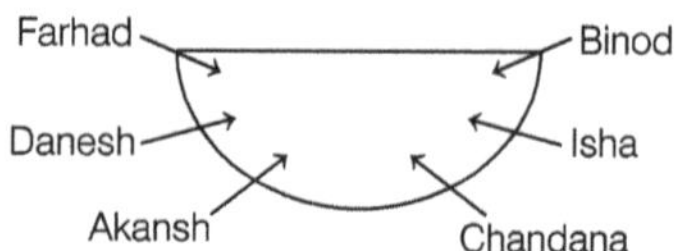

44. (*b*) Isha is sitting between Chandana and Binod.
45. (*b*) If Farhad is sitting at the Northern most point of the table, then Danesh is sitting is North-West direction.

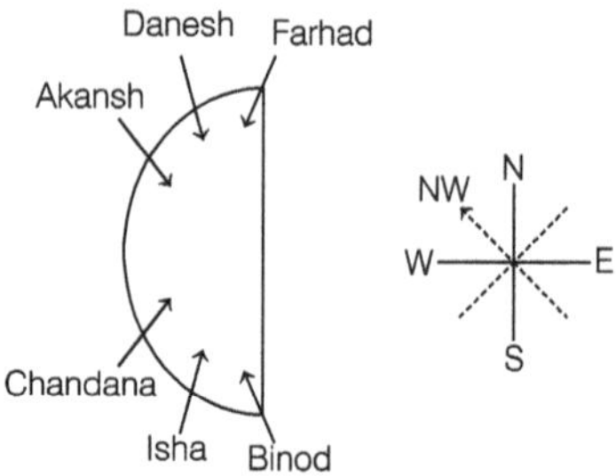

46. (*a*) Only one person is seated between Akansh and Isha.
47. (*a*) Binod is to the left of Farhad.
48. (*b*) Chandana is sitting diagonally opposite to Farhad.

Solutions (Q. Nos. 49-53) *According to the given information, arrangement is as follows.*

Numbers	Boxes
7	I
6	Q
5	R
4	P
3	M
2	S
1	L

49. (*b*) Box P is placed just above M.

50. (*c*) There are two boxes, M and S between L and P.

51. (*d*) L is placed at the bottom most place and I is placed at the top most place.

52. (*a*) Box I is placed at topmost place.

53. (*c*) Box M is placed at third place.

Solutions (Q. Nos. 54-58) *According to the given information, arrangement is as follows*

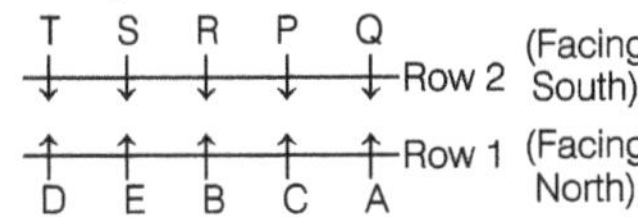

54. (*c*) Person A sitting in Row-1 faces the person Q.

55. (*b*) T sits at extreme right end of the Row-2.

56. (*e*) Except P, all persons given in the options sit at extreme ends.

57. (*a*) S sits second to the right of P.

58. (*d*) In Row-1, A sits third to the right of E.

Solutions (Q. Nos. 59-61) *According to the given information, arrangement is as follows.*

Floor Number	Persons
8	S
7	X
6	Z
5	T
4	V
3	W
2	U
1	Y

59. (*d*) T lives on floor number five.

60. (*b*) Three persons live between W and X.

61. (*b*) T lives immediately above V.

Solutions (Q. Nos. 62-66) *According to the given information, arrangement is as follows*

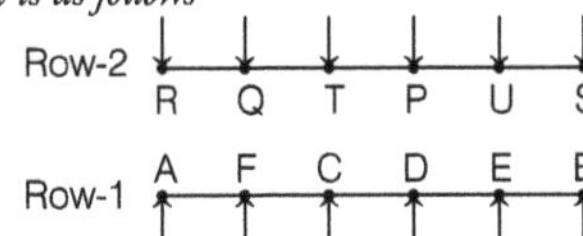

62. (*d*) R faces A.

63. (*a*) There is no any person sitting to the right of R.

64. (*e*) Only person, A given in option (e) is sitting at the extreme ends.

65. (*e*) As, R is related C and T is related E, in the same way Q is related to D or we can say that D is related to Q.

66. (*e*) Q sits third to the right of U.

Solutions (Q. Nos. 67-71) According to the given information,

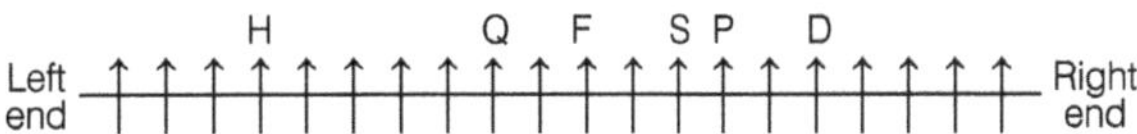

67. (*a*) Clearly from the arrangement maximum possible number of persons sitting are twenty.

68. (*c*) P and S are sitting together i.e., none of the person is sitting between them.

69. (*d*) D is sitting fifth to the right of F.

70. (*b*) Clearly three persons are sitting to the left of H.

71. (*e*) Position of A will be second to right of S.

Solutions (Q. Nos. 72-75)

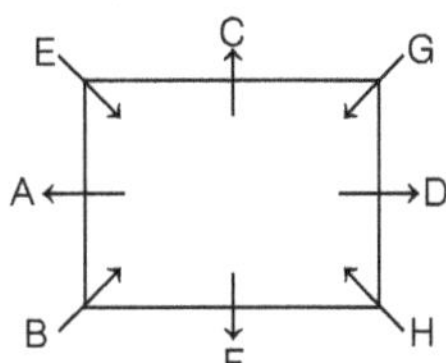

72. (*b*) H is immediate left of F.

73. (*a*) D Sits opposite to A.

74. (*b*)

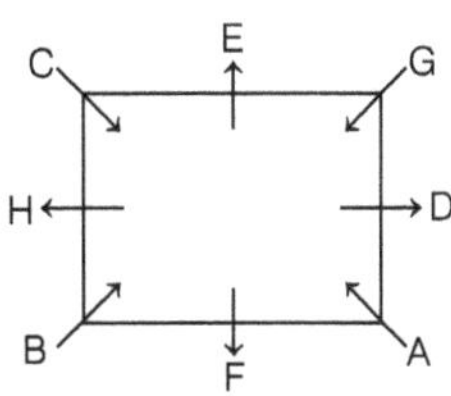

Now, four persons sit between E and A after rearrangement when counting left of A.

75. (*e*) All the given statements are true.

Solutions (Q. Nos. 76-80) *According to the given information, arrangement is as follows*

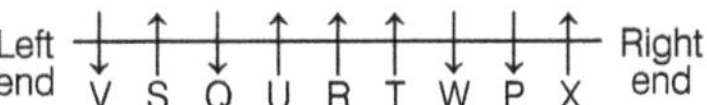

76. (*e*) W is the person who sits third to the right of U.

77. (*c*) Five persons sit between P and S.

78. (*b*) V and X are the person who sit at extreme ends.

79. (*c*) V, Q, W and P i.e., four persons are facing South.

80. (*d*) V, Q, W and P are facing South but X is facing North, so X does not belong to the group.

Solutions (Q. Nos. 81-85) *According to the given information, arrangement is as follows*

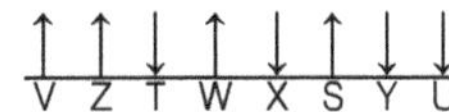

81. (*b*) Four persons V, Z, W and S are facing North.

82. (*d*) Except the pair of persons T and Y, in each pair, persons facing different directions are given.

83. (*b*) X is sitting third to the right of Z.

84. (*a*) T is sitting between Z and W.

85. (*b*) V is sitting second to the right of T.

Solutions (Q. Nos. 86-90) *According to the given information, arrangement is as follows.*

Floors	Persons
10	T
9	J
8	Q
7	W
6	R
5	P
4	U
3	S
2	X
1	V

86. (*d*) Three persons i.e., R, P and U live between W and S.

87. (*c*) T lives on topmost floor.

88. (*d*) Except W, all persons given in the option live on even number of floors.

89. (*a*) J on 9th floor lives immediately above Q.

90. (*c*) V does not live immediate below U, however there is two floor gap between U and V.

Solutions (Q. Nos. 91-95) *From the given information, sitting arrangement of all the persons is as follows.*

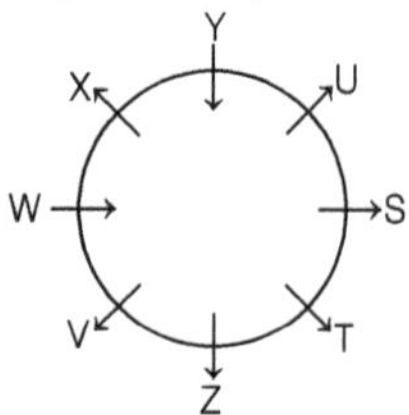

91. (*b*) V is sitting to the immediate right of Z.

92. (*a*) X sits second to the left of U.

93. (*e*) T is third to the left of Y.

94. (*a*) W and Y are immediate neighbours of X.

95. (*c*) Y is odd one as Y faces the centre and rest of the other faces outside.

Solutions (Q. Nos. 96-99) *After analysing the given information we can draw the following diagram.*

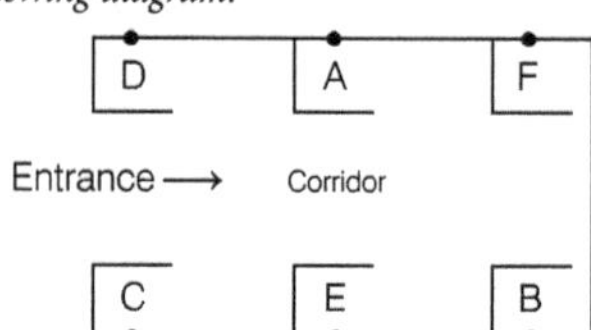

96. (*c*) C's office is to the left of E.

97. (*d*) E's office faces A's office.

98. (*a*) A is the only neighbour of F.

99. (*b*) B's office is the last office on the right side of corridor. So, D was trying to direct the person to B's office.

Solutions (Q. Nos. 100-104) *According to the given information, arrangement is as follows.*

Floors	Building X	Building Y	Building Z
6	A		
5	J		D
4	F	B	G
3	N	H	L
2	E	K	C
1	O	M	I

Persons

100. (*e*) No person live above B.

101. (*d*) B lives immediate East of F.

102. (*e*) None is true.

103. (*c*) C lives on second floor of building Z.

104. (*b*) F lives just above N Both are living in building X.

Solutions (Q. Nos. 105-109)

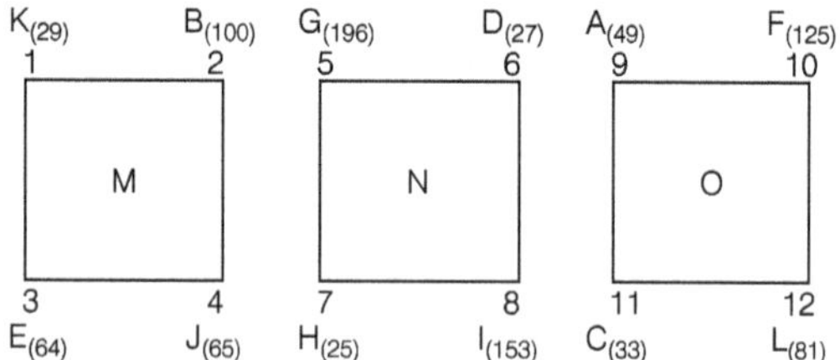

105. (*a*) A is an immediate neighbour of F and C.

106. (*a*) J sits on table M.

107. (*c*) L likes number 81.

108. (*e*) D sits immediate left of G.

109. (*e*) J likes the number 65, which is neither square nor cube.

Solutions (Q. Nos. 110-114)

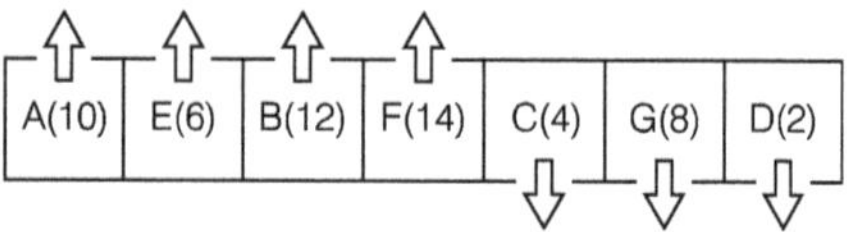

110. (*d*) There are 3 cabins in the given criteria.

111. (*c*) Except 'E', all other are consonants.

112. (*d*) Cabin of B is 4th, to the right of cabin of D.

113. (*a*) There is no cabin in the given criteria.

114. (*a*) Cabin of A is 3rd, to the left of cabin of F.

CHAPTER / 11

Puzzles

Puzzle is a collection of more than one statements/ informations in which the statements / informations are given in jumbled format.

These jumbled up informations/ statements express unclear meaning, although these statements/informations are true. But, when these jumbled up informations are arranged in a proper sequence or order, they express the clear meaning.

The informations/facts given in the puzzle, include more than one components or elements (like– names, professions, sports, favourite things etc.)

The candidates have to correlate the various given components/elements on the basis of the given information and arrange them in a proper sequence and on the basis of this arrangement, the answers to the questions are determined.

Best approach to attempt a puzzle

1. Note all the statements on the paper in simple form such that you do not have to look at the given puzzle again. e.g.
   Statement Bimal sits 2nd to the left of Suresh.
   Simple form "Bimal → 2L-Suresh."
   It will save your time.
2. In case of multiple possibilities, draw each possibility and rule out them one by one till you are left with just one final answer.
3. In the end, you will be left with only one case that will be in sync with all the positive as well as negative statements.
4. That will be your final answer.

Generally, the questions based on puzzles can be divided into following five types.

TYPE 01

Based on Classification

In this type of puzzles the persons and objects are classified separately on the basis of their characteristics, liking, disliking etc.

To solve these puzzles the candidates have to make a table. The rows and columns of the table are categorised into different categories and it is required to fill this table according to the given information.

After formation of the complete table, the answer to the questions can be easily found out from the table.

***Ex* 01** 1. Tom, Dick and Harry are intelligent.
2. Tom, Brown and Jack are hard working.
3. Brown, Harry and Jack are honest.
4. Tom, Dick and Jack are ambitious. « WBCS 2018

Which of the following person is neither hard working not ambitious?

(a) Tom (b) Dick (c) Harry (d) Jack

Solution (c) All the given information can be summarised in the tabular form as given below.

	Intelligent	Hardworking	Honest	Ambitious
Tom	✔	✔	✗	✔
Dick	✔	✗	✗	✔
Harry	✔	✗	✔	✗
Brown	✗	✔	✔	✗
Jack	✗	✔	✔	✔

Clearly, Harry is neither hard working nor ambitious.

DIRECTIONS (Ex. Nos. 2-6) *Study the following information carefully and answer the given questions.* « IBPS RRB Clerk 2016

A, B, C, D, E, F and G are seven friends. They play three types of games, viz Snooker, Ice hockey and Table tennis. Each game is played by at least two players. Each one of them has a favourite car, viz Honda, Fiat, Ferrari, Benz, Etios, Swift and Beleno, but not necessarily in the same order.

B likes Etios and does not play Table tennis. The one who likes Beleno plays the same game as E. C likes Fiat and plays the same game as G. D plays Ice hockey only with the one who likes Honda. G plays neither Ice hockey nor Table tennis. F does not like Beleno. G likes neither Benz nor Ferrari. D does not like Benz. E does not like Honda.

***Ex* 02** Which of the following groups play Snooker?

(a) B, G (b) A, B, C (c) B, C, G (d) D, G, B
(e) None of these

***Ex* 03** Who likes Ferrari Car?
(a) A (b) G (c) F (d) D
(e) None of these

***Ex* 04** Which of the following cars does A like?
(a) Ferrari (b) Beleno
(c) Honda (d) Either Beleno or Swift
(e) None of these

***Ex* 05** Which of the following combination is true?
(a) A-Beleno-Table tennis (b) G-Honda-Table tennis
(c) B-Etios-Ice hockey (d) D-Ferrari-Snooker
(e) None of true

***Ex* 06** Who likes Honda?
(a) G (b) A (c) E (d) C (e) F

Solutions (Ex. Nos. 5-9) Following table can be drawn from given information.

Cars	Person	Game
Beleno	A	Table tennis
Etios	B	Snooker
Fiat	C	Snooker
Ferrari	D	Ice hockey
Benz	E	Table tennis
Honda	F	Ice hockey
Swift	G	Snooker

2. (c) B, C, G play Snooker.
3. (*d*) D likes Ferrari car.
4. (*b*) A likes Beleno car.
5. (*a*) A-Beleno-Table tennis is true.
6. (*e*) F likes Honda.

DIRECTIONS (Ex. Nos. 7-9) *Read the following passage and answer the given questions.* « CGPSC (Pre) 2012

Seven friends Anu, Beena, Kanika, Mohini, Samina, Easther and Rani study different disciplines such as Arts, Commerce, Science, Engineering, Architecture, Management and Pharmacy, not necessarily in the same order. Each of them belongs to a different state viz. Andhra Pradesh, Uttar Pradesh, Maharashtra, Karnataka, Kerala, Chhattisgarh and Punjab but not necessarily in the same order.

Kanika studies Engineering and does not belong to either Uttar Pradesh or Punjab. The one who belongs to Chhattisgarh does not study Architecture or Pharmacy. Anu belongs to Maharashtra. Samina belongs to Kerala and studies Science. The one who belongs to Andhra Pradesh studies Commerce. Mohini studies Management and Rani studies Arts. Beena belongs to Karnataka and does not study Architecture. The one who studies Arts does not belong to Punjab.

***Ex* 07** Which of the following student and subject combination is correct?
(a) Anu-Architecture (b) Easther- Pharmacy
(c) Beena-Commerce (d) Mohini-Engineering
(e) None of the above

***Ex* 08** Which of the following state subject combination is/are correct?
I. Chhattisgarh-Engineering
II. Punjab-Pharmacy
III. Andhra Pradesh-Commerce
IV. Andhra Pradesh-Architecture

(a) I and II (b) II and III (c) I and IV (d) I and III
(e) None of these

***Ex* 09** Which of the following student state combination is/are correct?
I. Kanika-Chhattisgarh
II. Samina-Andhra Pradesh
III. Easther-Karnataka
IV. Mohini-Punjab
(a) I and II (b) I and III
(c) I and IV (d) II and III
(e) None of these

Solutions (Ex. Nos. 7-9) According to the given information, arrangement is following

	Disciplines							States						
Friends	Arts	Commerce	Science	Engineering	Architecture	Management	Pharmacy	AP	UP	Maharashtra	Karnataka	Kerala	Chhattisgarh	Punjab
Anu	✗	✗	✗	✗	✓	✗	✗	✗	✗	✓	✗	✗	✗	✗
Beena	✗	✗	✗	✗	✗	✗	✓	✗	✗	✗	✓	✗	✗	✗
Kanika	✗	✗	✗	✓	✗	✗	✗	✗	✗	✗	✗	✗	✓	✗
Mohini	✗	✗	✗	✗	✗	✓	✗	✗	✗	✗	✗	✗	✗	✓
Samina	✗	✗	✓	✗	✗	✗	✗	✗	✗	✗	✗	✓	✗	✗
Easther	✗	✓	✗	✗	✗	✗	✗	✓	✗	✗	✗	✗	✗	✗
Rani	✓	✗	✗	✗	✗	✗	✗	✗	✓	✗	✗	✗	✗	✗

7. (*a*) Anu-Architecture combination is correct.
8. (*d*) Chhattisgarh-Engineering and Andhra Pradesh-Commerce are correct.
9. (c) Kanika-Chhattisgarh and Mohini-Punjab are correct.

Practice CORNER 11.1

1. A ate grapes and pineapple; B ate grapes and oranges; C ate oranges, pineapple and apple; D ate grapes, apple and pineapple. After taking fruits, B and C fell sick.

   In the light of the above facts, it can be said that the cause of sickness was « UPSC (Pre) 2016

   (a) apple (b) pineapple
   (c) grapes (d) oranges

2. There are six books A, B, C, D, E and F. B, C and E have blue covers while the rest have red covers. D and F are new books while the rest are old books. A, C and D are law reports while the rest are of physics. Which is the red covered new law report book? « WBSC 2018

   (a) A (b) B
   (c) C (d) D

3. A, B, C, D and E belong to five different cities P, Q, R, S and T (not necessarily in that order). Each one of them comes from a different city. Further it is given that,

   I. B and C do not belong to Q.
   II. B and E do not belong to P and R.
   III. A and C do not belong to R, S and T.
   IV. D and E do not belong to Q and T.

   Which one of the following statements is not correct?

   (a) C belongs to P. (b) D belongs to R.
   (c) A belongs to Q. (d) B belongs to S.

4. Six students A, B, C, D, E and F are sitting on the ground. A and B belong to Ruby House, while the rest belong to Emerald House. D and F are tall, while others are short. C and D are wearing glasses, while others are not wearing. Which girl of Emerald House is tall and wearing glasses?

   (a) B (b) C (c) D (d) A

5. Six friends James, Deepak, Hari, Rahul, Vikram and Imran went for a picnic where they decided to play kabaddi. They divided themselves into two different teams with Deepak, Rahul and Vikram in Team 1 and rest in Team 2. Deepak and Imran were fat, but others were thin. Rahul and James were cheating, but other played the game fairly.

   Who was/were the friend/friends who played the game fairly from the Team 2? « CMAT 2015

   (a) Imran and James (b) Imran alone
   (c) Hari and Imran (d) Hari alone

DIRECTIONS ~(Q. Nos. 6-8) *Examine carefully the following statements and answer the three questions that follow.* « UPPSC (Pre) 2016

Out of four friends A, B, C and D; A and B play football and cricket. B and C play cricket and hockey. A and D play basketball and football. C and D play hockey and basketball.

6. Which game do B, C and D play?

   (a) Basketball (b) Hockey
   (c) Cricket (d) Football

7. Who play football, basketball and hockey?

   (a) D (b) C (c) B (d) A

8. Who does not play hockey?

   (a) D (b) C (c) B (d) A

DIRECTIONS ~ (Q. Nos. 9-13) *Study the following information carefully and answer the questions given below.* « IBPS Clerk 2018

There are seven persons i.e. A, B, C, D, E, F and G. They all belongs to the different cities i.e. Kolkata, Mumbai, Chennai, Pune, Lucknow, Ahmedabad and Delhi, but not necessarily in the same order.

D belongs to Pune. Neither A nor F belongs to Kolkata. B belongs to Ahmedabad. C does not belong to Kolkata and Lucknow. G belongs to Mumbai. A does not belongs to Lucknow and Chennai.

9. Who among the following belongs to Kolkata?

   (a) A (b) D (c) F (d) G
   (e) None of these

10. Which of the following statements is true?

    (a) A belongs to Chennai. (b) G belongs to Delhi.
    (c) E belongs to Kolkata. (d) F belongs to Pune.
    (e) None of these

11. F belongs to which of the following City?

    (a) Chennai (b) Mumbai
    (c) Delhi (d) Lucknow
    (e) None of these

12. Which of the following combination is true?

    (a) A-Delhi (b) D-Pune
    (c) E-Kolkata (d) All are correct
    (e) All are incorrect

13. A belongs to which of the following city?

    (a) Delhi (b) Mumbai (c) Kolkata (d) Chennai
    (e) None of these

DIRECTIONS ~ (Q. Nos. 14-18) *Study the following information carefully and answer the questions given below.* « SBI Clerk 2020

Eight persons have different designations i.e, Chairman (CHM), General Manager (GM), Assistant General Manager (AGM), Deputy General Manager (DGM), Manager, Assistant Manager, Probationary Officer, Clerk in a company. The order of seniority is the same as given above i.e, CHM is the senior-most designation and Clerk is the junior-most designation.

Only two persons are junior than J. Only one designation is there between J and O. Only two designation is there between O and M. M is senior than O. Number of persons who are senior than O is same as the number of persons who are junior than P. N is senior than P but junior than L. K is not in the junior-most post. Q is not the PO.

14. How many persons are junior than O?

    (a) Three (b) One (c) Two (d) None
    (e) Four

15. How many designations are there between N and M?
(a) One (b) Two (c) Three (d) Four
(e) Five

16. Number of persons who are junior than J is the same as the number of persons who are senior than .... ?
(a) M (b) L (c) K (d) N
(e) O

17. Which of the following designations is exactly between the designations of Q and O?
(a) Assistant Manager (b) Manager
(c) PO (d) CHM
(e) AGM

18. Who among the following is the Manager of the company?
(a) O (b) P (c) J (d) L
(e) N

DIRECTIONS ~ (Q. Nos. 19-21) *Consider the following information and answer the questions based on it.*
« RRB Non-Technical 2016

Y, R, M, J and B pursue five professions, namely, Designer, Teacher, Engineer, Technician and Accountant and have five gadgets, namely Mobile, Laptop, Calculator, Tablet and Computer, in random order. A person can pursue only one profession and have only one gadget.

(i) M has a calculator and is neither a teacher nor a technician.
(ii) The designer has a tablet.
(iii) The person who has a mobile is neither an accountant nor a teacher.
(iv) Y is an engineer who has neither computer nor mobile.
(v) J is a technician and B is not a teacher.

19. Which gadget does the accountant have?
A. Tablet B. Calculator
C. Mobile D. Laptop
(a) D (b) B (c) C (d) A

20. Which among the following is a right combination?
A. Teacher-Laptop B. Accountant-Tablet
C. Technician-Computer D. Engineer-Laptop
(a) D (b) B (c) A (d) C

21. Who has a computer?
A. B B. J
C. R D. Y
(a) A (b) D (c) B (d) C

DIRECTIONS ~ (Q. Nos. 22-26) *Study the following information carefully and answer the questions given below.*
« IBPS RRB PO 2015

At a recent International award function, five persons A, B, C, D and E participated. Every person observed some languages i.e. English, Portuguese, French, Spanish and Italian, but not necessarily in the same order. Each person belongs to some countries viz. Italy, Japan, France, London and Britain.

The following statements are

I. The only common language between C and E is Italian.
II. A does not belong to Italy or Britain.
III. Three persons can speak Portuguese.
IV. The most common language is Spanish.
V. D belongs to France. B and C speak English. Although when D joined them, they all changed to Spanish, the only common language among the three of them.
VI. C belongs to either London or Italy.
VII. The one who belongs to London cannot speak only French.
VIII. The only common language among A, B and E is French.
IX. The one who belongs to Britain could speak only Italian and French languages.
X. Each one of the five persons A, B, C, D and E knows either one, two, three, four and five languages (but not necessarily in the same order).

22. D does not speak which of the following languages?
I. French II. Italian
III. Portuguese
(a) Only I (b) I and II both
(c) I and III both (d) II and III both
(e) All I, II and III

23. A speaks which of the following languages?
I. French II. Italian
III. Portuguese
(a) Only I (b) I and II both
(c) I and III both (d) II and III both
(e) All I, II and III

24. Which of the following person belongs to Italy?
(a) D (b) E (c) B (d) C
(e) A

25. Four of the following five are alike in a certain way and hence they form a group. Which one of the following does not belong to that group?
(a) Japan (b) France (c) London (d) Italy
(e) Britain

26. In which of the following languages could not spoke by E?
I. Italian II. French
III. Spanish IV. English
V. Portuguese
(a) I, II and IV (b) II and V both
(c) III and V both (d) III, V and IV
(e) None of these

DIRECTIONS ~ (Q. Nos. 27-31) *Study the following information carefully and answer the questions given below.*
« IBPS Clerk Pre 2015

A, B, C, D, E, F and G are seven boys looking for three different types of shoes i.e. Canvas, Formal and Sports with at least two but not more than three for each type of shoe. Each of them has a liking for different shoe brands i.e. Nike, Adidas, Sparx, Reebok, Woodland, Bata & Puma but not necessarily in the same order.

C is looking for Sports shoes and his choice is Puma. F does not like Adidas and Bata and looking for same type of shoe only as of G among them. B is looking for same type of shoe as that of A but neither Sports nor Canvas. E is not looking for Sports shoes and he likes Reebok. The one who likes Nike is not looking for Canvas and Formal Shoes. A likes Sparx. The one who likes Bata is not looking for formal shoes.

27. Which is B's favourite brand?
(a) Nike (b) Puma (c) Bata (d) Adidas
(e) None of these

28. Which brand does D like?
(a) Bata (b) Sparx
(c) Nike (d) Data inadequate
(e) None of these

29. Which types of shoe does three of them have?
(a) Canvas (b) Formal
(c) Sports (d) Data inadequate
(e) None of these

30. Which is F's favourite brand?
(a) Adidas (b) Reebok (c) Bata (d) Nike
(e) None of these

31. What type of shoe does F like?
(a) Canvas (b) Formal
(c) Sports (d) Data inadequate
(e) None of these

DIRECTIONS ~ (Q. Nos. 32-36) *Study the following information carefully and answer the given questions.*
« SBI PO Pre 2015

I, J, K, L, M, N and O are seven shopkeepers of different shops, viz Grocery, Cosmetics, Clothes, Footwear, Gift items, Watches and Mobile phones, They go to supermarkets, viz. Big Bazaar, Max, Reliance Trends and Easy Day only on Sunday but not necessarily in the same order. At least one shopkeeper goes to one supermarket, but no super market is visited by more than two shopkeepers.

- N, who is a shopkeeper of Clothes, goes alone to Reliance Trends.
- The one who is a shopkeeper of Footwear does not go to Big Bazaar. Also, he never goes either with M or with O.
- L goes to Easy Day with the person who is the shopkeeper of Mobile phones.
- K goes to Max. O and J are not a shopkeeper of Mobile phones.
- The one who is the shopkeeper of Footwear goes to the market with the person who is the shopkeeper of Grocery.
- The one who is the shopkeeper of Gift items goes to Easy Day.
- I is a shopkeeper of neither Cosmetics nor Mobile phones.
- The one who is the shopkeeper of Watches goes to Big Bazaar neither with M nor with J.
- The person who is the shopkeeper of Cosmetics goes to the supermarket with I.

32. I goes in which of the following supermarkets?
(a) Easy Day (b) Max
(c) Big Bazaar (d) Reliance Trends
(e) None of these

33. Which of the following statement/statements is/are not true?
I. L is a shopkeeper of Mobile phones and goes to Easy Day.
II. K is a shopkeeper of Footwear and goes to Big Bazaar.
(a) Both I and II (b) Neither I nor II
(c) Either I or II (d) Only I
(e) Only II

34. Who among the following is shopkeeper of Gift items?
(a) J (b) L
(c) N (d) I
(e) None of these

35. Which of the following statements is definitely incorrect?
(a) K is a shopkeeper of Footwear.
(b) M is a shopkeeper of Mobile phones.
(c) O is shopkeeper of Grocery.
(d) All are incorrect.
(e) None of the above.

36. Big Bazaar is visited by which of the following persons?
(a) O and M both (b) Only L
(c) I and J both (d) Only N
(e) None of these

DIRECTIONS ~ (Q. Nos. 37-41) *Study the following information carefully to answer the given questions.*
« UBI PO 2016

Seven persons A, B, C, D, E, F and G are belongs to three different departments Production, Marketing and HR with at least 2 of them in any of these department. Each of them belongs to different cities i.e. Patna, Chandigarh, Kolkata, Delhi, Jaipur, Ranchi and Mumbai.

B works in Marketing department with E. E belongs to Mumbai. Those who work in Production department do not belong to Patna and Delhi. The one who belongs to Chandigarh works only with G in HR department. The one who belongs to Jaipur does not work in the same department with either E or G. A does not working in Marketing department. A belongs to Ranchi. D and F are working in the same department. F does not belong to Kolkata. The one who belongs to Delhi does not work in Marketing department.

37. In which department A, D and F work?
(a) Cannot be determined (b) Production
(c) Marketing (d) HR
(e) None of these

38. Who belongs to Patna?
(a) B (b) A
(c) C (d) D
(e) None of these

39. In which of the following city does E belong?
(a) Ranchi (b) Delhi
(c) Mumbai (d)Jaipur
(e) None of these

40. Which of the following combination is right?
(a) A - HR: Chandigarh
(b) G - Production: Jaipur
(c) F - HR: Delhi
(d) D - Production: Kolkata
(e) None of the above

41. C works in which department?
(a) Production
(b) Marketing
(c) HR
(d) Cannot be determined
(e) None of the above

DIRECTIONS ~ (Q. Nos. 42-46) *Study the following information carefully and answer the questions given below.* « IBPS PO MAINS-2016

Seven members P, Q, R, S, T, U and V are going different cities for attending a marriage function viz. Ahmedabad, Bangalore, Chennai, Hyderabad, Kolkata, Delhi and Mumbai but not necessarily in the same order. Also they are using different mode of transportation viz. Car, Train, Bike, Flight, Ship, Bus and Truck but not necessarily in the same order. Each one has a different mother tongue Tamil, Kannada, Telgu, Hindi, Marathi, Punjabi and Bangla but not necessarily in the same order.

R is going to Bangalore and his mother tongue is not Tamil or Marathi and he does not use Car or Ship for going to Bangalore. S's mother tongue is Punjabi and he is going to Ahmedabad by Flight. T and U are not going to Chennai and none of them has Marathi mother tongue and T uses neither Car nor Train as mode of transportation. Q is going to Hyderabad by Truck and his mother tongue is Telgu. The one who is going to Delhi has Bangla mother tongue and does not use Car. V is going to Mumbai and his mother tongue is Hindi and he does not use Train as transportation. T is not going to Kolkata and U is going by Ship. Bus and Bike are being used by T and P as a mode of transportation.

42. What is R's mother tongue?

(a) Telgu
(b) Hindi
(c) Bangla
(d) Kannada
(e) None of these

43. Who works in Chennai?

(a) P
(b) T
(c) U
(d) T or U
(e) None of these

44. Which of the following combination is correct?

(a) Marathi- Q -Hyderabad- Truck
(b) Tamil- U - Kolkata - Ship
(c) Marathi- Q - Chennai- Train
(d) Punjabi- S - Delhi - Bike
(e) None of these

45. Which of the following members is use Bus as a mode of transportation?

(a)P
(b) U
(c) T
(d) S
(e) Can't be determined

46. Which of the following members is use Bike as a mode of transportation?

(a) P
(b) U
(c) T
(d) S
(e) Can't be determined

DIRECTIONS ~ (Q. Nos. 47-51) *Study the following information carefully and answer the questions asked.*

(i) Seven teachers A, B, C, D, E, F and G teach in the science section of XII of a particular school. They teach one of the following subjects– Zoology, Botany, Chemistry, Physics and Maths.

(ii) Two teachers each teach Physics and Chemistry.

(iii) Both the Chemistry teachers and one from Zoology and Maths each has cleared UGC (NET).

(iv) Four teachers are females—B, C, F and G. Of them two are married. Two teachers are members of PTA executive council, out of which only one is male. However, none of the married teachers are its members.

(v) All the married teachers except one are class teachers of one class or the other. There are four married teachers A, B, D and F. There are three subject teachers.

(vi) None of the married women teacher have cleared UGC (NET). Two male teachers have cleared NET out of which one is married. He is Mr. A, a subject teacher. He is not from PCM stream. He teaches Botany or Zoology.

(vii) The PTA members are not from exclusive PCM or PCB stream. Both the teachers are subject teachers and not class teachers.

(viii) PTA members teach same subject.

(ix) Only Mrs. B teaches Botany. G is a class teacher.

47. What does G teach?

(a) Maths
(b) Physics
(c) Chemistry
(d) Can't be determined

48. Who is the male class teacher?

(a) F (b) D (c) A (d) Either D or E

49. Who among the following are the PTA members?

(a) A and B (b) B and C (c) C and D (d) C and E

50. Which of the following combinations is incorrect?

(a) E - Unmarried - Male - Chemistry
(b) C - Unmarried - Female - Chemistry
(c) A - Married - Male - Zoology
(d) G - Married - Female - Maths

51. Which of the following combinations is correct?

(a) A - NET cleared - Married - Botany
(b) B - NET not cleared - Married - Botany
(c) C - NET cleared - Married - Chemistry
(d) D - NET cleared - Married - Physics

DIRECTIONS ~ (Q. Nos. 52-56) *Study the following information carefully and answer the given questions.*

Eight persons K, L, M, D, E, F, G and H are travelling in three different cars namely P, Q and R but not necessarily in the same order. There are at least two persons in each Car and each Car has persons of both the sexes. Out of eight persons three are females. All of them like different colours Viz, Red, Green, Yellow, Blue, Black, White, Grey and Purple but not necessarily in the same order. Females do not like Grey or White colour.

D is travelling with G in the Car R. G likes Black colour.

The person who like Red and Purple colours, are travelling in the same Car. E does not like Purple colour and he is not travelling with H in the same car. K neither like purple nor Red colour. H is travelling in the car Q. L, M and H are females in the group. L likes Blue colour and travels with the person who likes Black Colour.

Red and Green Colours are liked by female members. The person who is travelling with H likes Grey colour. One of the persons travelling in Car R likes Yellow colour.

52. The female member who is travelling in the Car P likes which colour?

(a) Green (b) Blue (c) Yellow (d) Red
(e) None of these

53. Which of the following combinations of Person-Car-Colour is not correct?
(a) M - P - Red (b) F - P - Purple
(c) G - R-Black (d) D - R-Yellow
(e) E - Q-Grey

54. Who among the following are travelling with a female member M?
(a) E and G (b) K and D (c) E and F (d) D and E
(e) F and G

55. In which of the following Cars only two persons are travelling?
(a) Car P (b) Car Q
(c) Car R (d) Cannot be determined
(e) None of these

56. Who among the following likes Yellow colour?
(a) D (b) E
(c) K (d) F
(e) None of these

Answers / WITH EXPLANATIONS

1. (*d*) According to the given questions,

Person \ Fruit	Apple	Pineapple	Grapes	Orange
A		✓	✓	
B			✓	✓
C	✓	✓		✓
D	✓	✓	✓	

Since, B and C fell sick, so the cause of sickness is oranges which is eaten by both of them.

2. (*d*) Following table can be drawn from given information.

Books	Colour	Type	Subject
A	Red	Old	Law
B	Blue	Old	Physics
C	Blue	Old	Law
D	Red	New	Law
E	Blue	Old	Physics
F	Red	New	Physics

Therefore, D is Red covered new law report book.

3. (*d*) From the given information, following table can be drawn.

Persons \ Cities	P	Q	R	S	T
A	×	✓	×	×	×
B	×	×	×	×	✓
C	✓	×	×	×	×
D	×	×	✓	×	×
E	×	×	×	✓	×

Now, it is clear from the above table that B does not belong to S. So, Statement (d) is incorrect.

4. (*c*) We have total six students sitting on the ground :

[Ruby House → A, B
Emerald House → C, (D), E, F]

[Tall → (D), F
Short → A, B, C, E]

[Wearing glasses → C, (D)
Not Wearing glasses → C, B, E, F]

We have to find out the girl of Emerald House who is tall and wearing glasses. So, we have to find out the common students in the given condition. Therefore, D is the only student who is wearing glasses, tall and belongs to Emerald House.

5. (*d*) According to the question the arrangement is as follows

Friends	Team	Size	Playing Nature
James	Team-2	Thin	Cheating
Deepak	Team-1	Fat	Fairly
Hari	Team-2	Thin	Fairly
Rahul	Team-1	Thin	Cheating
Vikram	Team-1	Thin	Fairly
Imran	Team-2	Fat	Fairly

Hence, Hari played fairly from Team 2 and he is thin.

Solutions (Q. Nos. 6-8) *According to the given information,*

Friends \ Sports	Football	Cricket	Hockey	Basketball
A	✓	✓		✓
B	✓	✓	✓	
C		✓	✓	✓
D	✓		✓	✓

6. (*b*) B, C and D play hockey. Hence, the correct option is (b).

7. (*a*) D plays football, hockey and basketball. Hence, the correct option is (a).

8. (*d*) A does not play hockey. Hence, the correct option is (d).

Solutions (Q. Nos. 9-13) *According to the given information,*

Persons	Cities
A	Delhi
B	Ahmedabad
C	Chennai
D	Pune
E	Kolkata
F	Lucknow
G	Mumbai

9. (*e*) E belongs to Kolkata.

10. (*c*) E belongs to Kolkata, is true.

11. (*d*) F belongs to Lucknow.

12. (*d*) All of the given combinations are true.

13. (*a*) A belongs to Delhi.

Solutions (Q. Nos. 14-18) *According to given information,*

Designations	Persons
Chairman (CHM)	M
General Manager (GM)	L
Assistant General Manager (AGM)	N
Deputy General Manager (DGM)	O
Manager	P
Assistant Manager	J
Probationary Officer	K
Clerk	Q

14. (*e*) Four persons are junior than O.

15. (*a*) Only one designation i.e. General Manager (GM) is there between N and M.

16. (*d*) Two persons are junior than J and two persons are senior than N.

17. (*a*) Assistant Manager is exactly between the designation of Q and O.

18. (*b*) P is the Manager of company.

Solutions (Q. Nos. 19-21) *According to the given information,*

Person	Gadget	Profession
M	Calculator	Accountant
B	Tablet	Designer
R	Computer	Teacher
Y	Laptop	Engineer
J	Mobile	Technician

19. (*b*) The accountant has calculator.

20. (*a*) Engineer-Laptop is the right combination.

21. (*d*) R has a computer.

Solutions (Q. Nos. 22-26) *Following table can be drawn from given information.*

Languages→ Persons ↓	English	Italian	Spanish	French	Portuguese	Countries ↓
A	✗	✗	✓	✓	✓	Japan
B	✓	✓	✓	✓	✓	Italy
C	✓	✓	✓	✗	✓	London
D	✗	✗	✓	✗	✗	France
E	✗	✓	✗	✓	✗	Britain

22. (*e*) All of these.

23. (*c*) A speaks French and Portuguese.

24. (*c*) B belongs to Italy.

25. (*d*) Person belongs to Italy knows all five languages. Hence, he is different from others.

26. (*d*) E could not spoke Spanish, English and Portuguese.

Solutions (Q. Nos. 27-31) *Following table can be drawn from given information.*

Brand	Boys	Types of Shoes
Puma	C	Sports
Woodland	F	Canvas
Bata	G	Canvas
Adidas	B	Formal
Sparx	A	Formal
Reebok	E	Formal
Nike	D	Sports

27. (*d*) Adidas is B's favourite brand.

28. (*c*) D likes Nike.

29. (*b*) Three of them have Formal shoes.

30. (*e*) F's favorite brand is Woodland.

31. (*a*) F likes Canvas.

Solutions (Q. Nos. 32-36) *Following table can be drawn from given information.*

Shop	Shopkeeper	Super Market
Watch	I	Big Bazaar
Grocery/Footwear	J	Max
Footwear/Grocery	K	Max
Gift Items	L	Easy Day
Mobile Phones	M	Easy Day
Clothes	N	Reliance Trends
Cosmetics	O	Big Bazaar

32. (*c*) I goes in Big Bazaar.

33. (*a*) Both I and II are not true.

34. (*b*) L is shopkeeper of Gift Items.

35. (*c*) O is shopkeeper of Grocery is definitely incorrect.

36. (*e*) I and O goes to big bazar.

Solutions (Q. Nos. 37-41) *Following table can be drawn from given information.*

Person	City	Department
A	Ranchi	Production
B	Patna	Marketing
C	Chandigarh	HR
D	Kolkata	Production
E	Mumbai	Marketing
F	Jaipur	Production
G	Delhi	HR

37. (*b*) A, D and F works in production department.

38. (*a*) B belongs to Patna.

39. (*c*) E belongs to Mumbai.

40. (*d*) D-Production : Kolkata is the right combination.

41. (*c*) C works in HR department.

Solutions (Q. Nos. 42-46) *Following table can be drawn from given information.*

Member	Transportation	Language	City
R	Train	Kannada	Bangalore
S	Flight	Punjabi	Ahmedabad
U	Ship	Tamil	Kolkata
Q	Truck	Telgu	Hyderabad
T	Bus/Bike	Bangla	Delhi
V	Car	Hindi	Mumbai
P	Bus/Bike	Marathi	Chennai

42. (*d*) R's mother tongue is Kannada.
43. (*a*) P works in Chennai.
44. (*b*) Tamil-U-Kolkata-ship is correct.
45. (*e*) Either T or P.
46. (*e*) Either T or P.

Solutions (Q. Nos. 47-51) *According to the question the data can be arranged as*

Name	Sex	Marital Staus	UGC NET	Subject	Class /Subject	PTA
A	M	M	✓	Zoology	Sub. Tea.	×
B	F	M	×	Botany	Class. Tea.	×
C	F	UN	✓	Chemistry	Sub. Tea	✓
D	M	M	×	Physics	Class. Tea.	×
E	M	UN	✓	Chemistry	Sub. Tea	✓
F	F	M	×	Physics	Class. Tea.	×
G	F	UN	✓	Maths	Class. Tea.	×

47. (*a*) G teaches Maths.
48. (*b*) D is a Male class teacher.
49. (*d*) C and E are PTA members.
50. (*d*) Combination given in option (d) is incorrect.
51. (*b*) Combination given in option (b) is correct.

Solutions (Q. Nos. 52-56) *According to the given information,*

Car	Person	Gender	Colour
P	M	Female	Red
	E	Male	White
	F	Male	Purple
Q	K	Male	Grey
	H	Female	Green
R	D	Male	Yellow
	L	Female	Blue
	G	Male	Black

52. (*d*) M is the female member in the Car P and she likes Red colour.
53. (*e*) The combination E-Q-Grey is not correct. E travels in Car P and he likes White colour.
54. (*c*) E and F are travelling with Female member.
55. (*b*) Only two persons i.e., K and H are travelling in the Car Q.
56. (*a*) D likes Yellow colour.

TYPE 02

Based on Sitting and Order Arrangement

In this type of Puzzles, the information related to the sitting, placing and comparison of persons/objects on certain basis is given along with some additional information (like– favourite colour, age, profession, place, income etc.)

The candidates are required to arrange the given persons/objects in the order of their placing, sitting, rank etc. as given in information and answer the questions that are asked.

DIRECTIONS ~ (Ex. Nos. 10-14) *Study the given information and answer the given questions.*

« IBPS (Clerk) 2013

A, B, C, D, E, F and G are standing in a straight line facing North with equal distances between them, not necessarily in the same order.

Each one is pursuing a different profession— actor, reporter, doctor, engineer, lawyer, teacher and painter not necessarily in the same order.

G is fifth to the left of C. The reporter is third to the right of G. F is fifth to the right of A. E is second to the left of B. The engineer is second to the left of D. There are only three people between the engineer and the painter. The doctor is to the immediate left of the engineer. The lawyer is to the immediate right of the teacher.

***Ex* 10** What is A's profession?
(a) Painter (b) Doctor
(c) Teacher (d) Actor
(e) Engineer

***Ex* 11** Which of the following statements is true according to the given arrangement?
(a) F is the teacher.
(b) F is third to the left of E.
(c) The painter is to the immediate left of B.
(d) The lawyer is standing in the exact middle of the arrangement.
(e) None of the given statements is ture.

***Ex* 12** Who among the following is an actor?
(a) E (b) F (c) C (d) B
(e) A

***Ex* 13** What is D's position with respect to the painter?
(a) Third to the left (b) Second to the right
(c) Fourth to the right (d) Third to the right
(e) Second to the left

***Ex* 14** Four of the following five are alike in a certain way based on the given standing arrangement and so form a group. Which of the following does not belong to the group?
(a) AED (b) DFC
(c) GDB (d) EBF
(e) BFC

Solutions (Ex. Nos. 10-14) According to the given information, standing arrangement and profession of the persons are as follows.

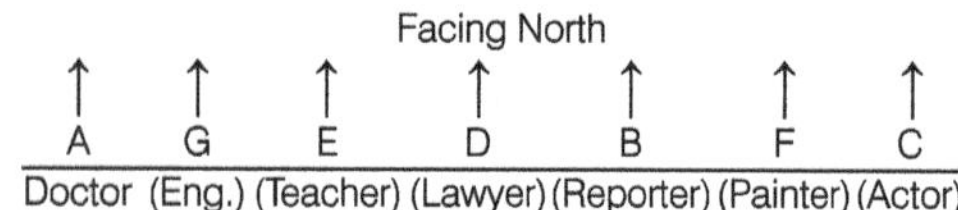

10. (b) A is a Doctor.

11. (d) The lawyer is standing in the exact middle of the arrangement.

12. (c) C is an Actor.

13. (e) D is second to the left of painter.

14. (e) BFC does not belong to the group.

DIRECTIONS ~ (Ex. Nos. 15-17) *Study the following information carefully to answer the questions based on it.* « IBPS (PO) Pre 2016

A, B, C, D, W, X, Y and Z are sitting in a circle (But not necessarily in the same order). Their faces are in the centre.

W is sitting third to the left of Y. The person, who is from Dwarka is to the immediate right of W and W is not from Okhla. B is sitting fourth to the right of Z. Z is not the neighbour of Y. Neither B nor Z is an immediate neighbour of W.

X is from Chanakyapuri and is sitting third to the right of the person from Dwarka. The person from Mehrauli is sitting second to the left of person from Chanakyapuri. The person from Rohini is sitting second to the left of W. A, who is from Lajpat Nagar, is sitting exactly between X and Z. The person from Saket is sitting second to the right of the person from Lajpat Nagar. C is sitting third to the left of X. Y is not from Karol Bagh.

***Ex* 15** Who amongst the following persons belongs to Okhla?

(a) Y (b) D (c) C (d) B (e) Z

***Ex* 16** What is A's position with respect to B?

(a) Third to the right
(b) Second to the right
(c) Third to the left
(d) Second to the left
(e) Fourth to the right

***Ex* 17** How many people are sitting between Z and C when counted in an anti-clockwise direction from C?

(a) One (b) Two (c) Three (d) Four
(e) None of these

Solutions (Ex. Nos. 15-17) According to the given information, arrangement is as follows

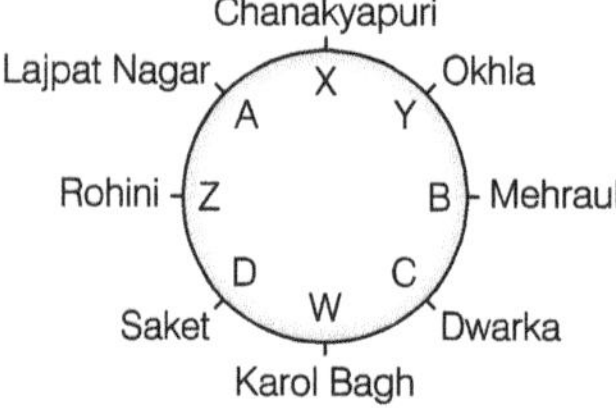

15. (a) Y belongs to Okhla.

16. (*a*) Position of A with respect to B, is third to the right.

17. (*d*) When counted in an anti-clockwise direction from C, then four people are sitting between Z and C.

DIRECTIONS (Ex. Nos. 18-22) *Read the given information to answer the given questions.* « SBI PO 2017

Eight people *viz.* X, G, T, C, P, J, A and M live on different floors of a building. The ground floor of the building is numbered one, the one above that is numbered two and so on till the topmost floor is numbered eight. All of them can perform a different form of dance *viz.* Kathak, Garba, Dandiya, Bhangra, Lavani, Odissi, Mohiniyattam and Sattriya.

Note *None of the given information is necessarily in the same order.*

T lives on an even numbered floor below floor number five. Only three people live between T and the one who performs Garba. As many people live between T and C as above the one who performs Lavani and sattriya. Number of people living between the one who performs Garba and Odissi is equal to the number of people living between C and P. C lives on an even numbered floor below P. Neither C nor P performs Garba or Lavani. The one who performs Kathak lives on an odd numbered floor below floor number four. P does not perform Kathak. The number of people between T and the one who performs Kathak is same as the number of people living between C and the one who performs Lavani. X lives on one of the floors below the one who performs Lavani. Number of people living between C and X is equal to the number of people living between C and M. The one who performs Odissi lives on an odd numbered floor immediately above the one who performs Bhangra. Only one people live between G and J. G lives on one of the floors above J. The one who performs Bhangra lives immediately above the one who performs Kathak.

***Ex* 18** Which of the following statements is true as per the given arrangement?

(a) C performs Odissi.
(b) The one who performs Garba lives on floor number six.
(c) T lives immediately above J.
(d) None of the given statements is true.
(e) Only two people live between M and J.

***Ex* 19** Four of the following five are alike in a certain way based on the given arrangement and thus form a group. Which one of the following does not belong to the group?

(a) T-Bhangra
(b) C-Dandiya
(c) Floor number three-Odissi
(d) G-Floor number eight
(e) J-Floor number six

***Ex* 20** How many people live between the one who performs Lavani and Bhangra?

(a) More than three
(b) Three
(c) None
(d) One
(e) Two

***Ex* 21** Who performs Sattriya?

(a) G
(b) A
(c) P
(d) T
(e) C

***Ex* 22** Which dance M performs?

(a) Bhangra
(b) Lavani
(c) Odissi
(d) Mohiniyattam
(e) Kathak

Solutions (Ex. Nos. 18-22) Following table can be drawn from given information.

Floor Number	People	Performance
8	G	Dandiya
7	P	Sattriya
6	J	Garba
5	M	Lavani
4	C	Mohiniyattam
3	X	Odissi
2	T	Bhangra
1	A	Kathak

18. (*b*) The one who performs Garba lives on floor number six is true.

19. (*b*) C-Dandiya is wrong combination.

20. (e) Two people live between the one who performs Lavani and Bhangra.

21. (*c*) P performs Sattriya.

22. (*b*) M performs Lavani.

Practice / CORNER 11.2

DIRECTIONS ~ (Q. Nos. 1-2) *Study the following information carefully and answer the questions given below.*
« FCI Asst. Grade II 2015

There were six persons U, V, W, X, Y and Z playing a game of cards. U's father, mother and uncle were in the group. There were two ladies in the group. 'V' the mother of 'U' got more points than her husband. 'X' got more points than 'Y' but less than 'Z'. Niece of 'Y' got lowest points. Father of 'U' got more points than 'Z' but could not win the game.

1. Who won the game and who got the lowest points respectively?
(a) V and U (b) W and U (c) W and Y (d) X and V

2. Who is the husband of V and what was his position in the game on the basis of points ?
(a) Z, II (b) Y, III (c) X, II (d) W, II

DIRECTIONS ~ (Q. Nos. 3-7) *Study the following information carefully and answer the questions given below.*
« SBI PO (Pre) 2016

Seven boxes J, K, L, M, N, O and P are kept one above the other, but not necessarily in the same order. Each box contains different elements–Cookies, Pencils, Spoons, Diaries, Colours, Jewellery and Watches, but not necessarily in the same order.

Only two boxes are kept between M and N. The pencil box is kept immediately below M. Only two boxes are kept between the pencil box and the Watch box. N is kept above the Watch box. The Diary box is kept immediately below the Watch box. Only three boxes are kept between the Diary box and J. The Jewellery box is kept immediately above the J. O is kept immediately above K. O is not a pencil box. P is kept immediately below the Cookies box. Only one box is kept between P and the Spoon box.

3. Which of the following boxes is kept immediately above M?
(a) P (b) O (c) L (d) Diary box
(e) Jewellery box

4. What is the position of O in the given stack of boxes?
(a) First from top (b) Second from top
(c) Third from bottom (d) Fifth from bottom
(e) Fourth from top

5. Which of the following boxes contains Spoons?
(a) Other than those given as options
(b) K
(c) M
(d) N
(e) L

6. Four of the following five are alike in a certain way and hence form a group. Which of the following does not belong to the group ?
(a) N-Diaries (b) P-Spoons
(c) O-Colours (d) K-Pencils
(e) M-Jewellery

7. How many boxes are kept between K and the Watch box?
(a) More than three (b) None
(c) Three (d) One
(e) Two

DIRECTIONS ~ (Q. Nos. 8-12) *Study the following information carefully and answer the questions given below.*
« IBPS RRB Office Assistant 2013

Seven persons A, B, C, D, E, F and G are sitting in a straight line facing North. Each of them plays atleast one game like-Chess, Polo, Football, Cricket, Badminton, Table Tennis and Tennis (but not necessarily in the same order.)

There are only two persons between F and E. E is on the extreme right end of the line. Chess player is second to the left of polo player. C is not the neighbour of E. There are four persons between C and the badminton player. B is third to the right of cricket player. Football player is fourth to the left of table tennis player. There is only one person between C and cricket player. Tennis player is second to the right of A. D is not the neighbour of polo player.

8. Four of the following five are alike in a certain way so form a group. Which is the one that does not belong to that group ?
(a) CG (b) GA
(c) AE (d) BF
(e) DF

9. Which of the following statements is true with respect to the given information?

(a) G, who is second to the left of A, plays chess.
(b) F, who is fourth to the right of C, plays tennis.
(c) G, who plays cricket is in middle of D and polo player.
(d) B, who is immediate neighbour of A, plays table tennis.
(e) None of the above.

10. Which game does F play?

(a) Cricket (b) Polo
(c) Table Tennis (d) Chess
(e) Tennis

11. Which of the following is true about A?

(a) Second to the right of E.
(b) Second to the left of G.
(c) Immediate right of B.
(d) Immediate left of F.
(e) Between F and badminton player.

12. Which of the following games do the neighbours of D play?

(a) Cricket (b) Table Tennis
(c) Polo (d) Football
(e) Both (a) and (d)

DIRECTIONS ~ (Q. Nos. 13-16) *Study the following information carefully and answer the below questions.* « IBPS PO 2019

Eight persons namely - A, B, C, D, E, F, G and H are sitting in a row facing north. Age (Year) of each persons are different *viz.*- 13, 16, 17, 18, 19, 21, 23 and 26 Yr. All the information are not necessary in same order.

G sits fourth to left of A, whose age is not prime number. Age of neither B nor D is 19 yr. Two persons sits between H and the one whose age is 19 yr. Three persons sits between the one whose age is 18 yr and the one whose age is 23 yr. H, whose age is not even, sits at one of the end of the row. Neither G nor A sits adjacent to H. Two persons sits between F and E, who sits immediate right of A. Age of the person two places away from H is twice the age of D. Two persons sits between D and the one whose age is 17 yr. Age of B is not 18 yr.

13. What is the position of the one whose age is 16 yr with respect to F?

(a) Second to right (b) Immediate left
(c) Second to left (d) Third to right
(e) None of these

14. What is the age of the one who sits third to right of B?

(a) 26 (b) 17 (c) 21 (d) 13
(e) None of these

15. What is the age of E?

(a) 21 (b) 17 (c) 26 (d) 18
(e) None of these

16. Which of the following statement is not true?

(a) The one whose age is 13 yr sits immediate left of G.
(b) Immediate right person of F is of 19 yr.
(c) Two persons sit between the one whose age is 26 yr and H.
(d) B sits second to left of C.
(e) All the above statements are true.

DIRECTIONS ~ (Q. Nos. 17-21) *Study the following information carefully and answer the questions given below.* « IBPS RRB Officers Grade B (Pre) 2015

Eight people E, F, G, H, W, X, Y and Z are sitting in two parallel rows containing four people each. E, F, G and H are sitting in row-1 facing North and W, X, Y and Z are sitting in row-2 facing South. (But not necessarily in the same order). Thus, each person sitting in row-1 faces another person sitting in row-2. Each of the two rows consists of one Professor, one Leader, one Technician and one Doctor (but not necessarily in the same order). The Doctor of row-1 sits second to the right of H. E is an immediate neighbour of H. E faces the Leader of row-2.

X sits to the immediate right of the Leader. X faces one of the immediate neighbours of the Professor of row-1. The Professor of row-1 does not sit at any of the extreme ends of the line.

W sits second to the left of Y. Z does not face G. F faces the Professor of row-2. In both the rows, only one person sits between the Professor and the Technician. W is not a Doctor.

17. Which of the following represent both the immediate neighbours of W?

(a) X and Leader of row-2
(b) Y and Technician of row-2
(c) Y and Doctor of row-2
(d) X and Professor of row-2
(e) Z and Doctor of row-2

18. Who amongst the following sits to the immediate left of the Leader of row-1?

(a) Professor of row-1 (b) F
(c) H (d) G
(e) Doctor of row-1

19. Which of the given statements is true with respect to the given arrangement?

(a) None of the given statements is true.
(b) Y sits to the immediate right of Z.
(c) H is a Teacher.
(d) Technician of one row faces the Doctor of another row.
(e) Y and H face each other.

20. If E and X interchange their places and so do G and Z, then who amongst the following will face W?

(a) Z (b) Other than those given as options.
(c) A (d) X (e) H

21. Which of the following represent the people sitting at extreme ends of both the lines ?

(a) F, H and Z, W (b) F, H and X, Y
(c) E, H and Y, Z (d) G, F and Z, Y
(e) G, F and W, Y

DIRECTIONS ~ (Q. Nos. 22-27) *Study the following information carefully and answer the questions given below.* « SBI Clerk (Mains) 2016

Eight friends P, Q, R, S, T, V, W and Z, out of whom one is a Pilot, Professor, Businessman, Doctor, Lawyer, Banker, Cricketer or an Architect (but not necessarily in the same order), are sitting around a circular table, facing the centre.

S, who is a banker sits third to the right of Z. The professor and the architect are immediate neighbours of each other. Neither the professor nor the architect is an immediate neighbour of either Z or S. The one, who is a professor sits second to the right of T, who is a lawyer. V, who is a cricketer, is not an immediate neighbour of the banker. Cricketer and the pilot are immediate neighbours of each other. Neither Z nor W is a pilot. Only R sits between the professor and the doctor. P sits third to the right of the pilot.

22. Who amongst the following sits exactly between T and Q?

(a) Doctor (b) Banker (c) Professor (d) Cricketer
(e) Architect

23. Who sits third to the right of the professor?

(a) Q (b) The Lawyer
(c) The Banker (d) S
(e) The Cricketer

24. Which of the following is true regarding R?

(a) He is an immediate neighbour of the professor.
(b) He is a doctor.
(c) None is true.
(d) He is an immediate neighbour of the pilot.
(e) R sits exactly between Q and T when counted from the right of Q.

25. What is the position of the businessman with respect to the pilot?

(a) Third to the left (b) Second to the left
(c) Immediately to the right (d) Fourth to the right
(e) Second to the right

26. What is the profession of Z?

(a) Doctor
(b) Other than those given as options
(c) Businessman
(d) Professor
(e) Architect

27. How many people sit between the 'banker' and 'W' when counted in anti-clockwise direction from banker?

(a) Three (b) Four
(c) One (d) None
(e) Two

DIRECTIONS ~ (Q. Nos. 28-32) *Study the following information carefully and answer the given questions.* « NABARD (Assistant Manager) 2016

Eight friends P, Q, R, S, T, U, V and W are sitting around a circular table facing the centre but not necessarily in the same order. Each one of them works in a different company *viz.* Microsoft, Sony, Dell, P & G, HTC, ONGC, Google and Amazon, but not necessarily in the same order.

The one who works in Microsoft sits third to the right of V. Only one person sits between the one who works in Microsoft and U. Only three people sit between T and U. R sits second to the left of U.

Both R and T are immediate neighbours of the one who works in P & G. Only three people sit between the one who works in P & G and S. S is one of the immediate neighbours of the one who works in Dell.

The one who works in ONGC sits second to the left of the one who works in Dell. W sits third to the left of the one who works in ONGC. P is one of the immediate neighbours of W.

The one who works in Google sits to the immediate left of the one who works in HTC.

Only three people sit between the one who works in Google and the one who works in Sony.

28. V is related to Google in a certain way based on the given arrangement. Following the same pattern, Q is related to Amazon. To which of the following companies is R related to following the same pattern?

(a) Microsoft (b) HTC (c) ONGC (d) Dell
(e) Sony

29. Q works in which of the following companies?

(a) HTC (b) P & G (c) Google (d) Sony
(e) Dell

30. What is the position of P with respect to Q?

(a) Third to the left (b) Fourth to the left
(c) Second to the left (d) Second to the right
(e) Third to the right

31. Which of the following is true with respect to the given arrangement?

(a) T sits second to right of U.
(b) Q is an immediate neighbour of the one who works in Google.
(c) P and the one who works in Dell are immediate neighbours of each other.
(d) S works in ONGC.
(e) R sits second to the right of the one who works in HTC.

32. Who amongst the following works in Amazon?

(a) R (b) Other than those given as options
(c) T (d) U
(e) P

DIRECTIONS ~(Q. Nos. 33-38) *Study the given information* carefully *to answer the given questions.* « IBPS PO 2017

Seven athletes M, N, O, P, Q, R and S live on seven different floors of a building but not necessarily in the same order. The lowermost floor of the building is numbered 1, the one above that is numbered 2 and so on till the topmost floor is numbered 7. Each one of them runs for a different distance in marathon – 850 m, 1300 m, 2200 m, 2800 m, 3300 m, 4000 m, and 4700 m, but not necessarily in the same order.

The one who runs for 2200 m lives on floor numbered 3. Only one person lives between O and the one who runs for 2200 m. The one who runs for 4000 m lives immediately above O. Only one person lives between the one who runs for 4000 m and the one who runs for 1300 m. The number of people living between O and the one who runs for 1300 m is same as that between the one who runs for 4000 m and R. N lives on an odd numbered floor. N ran for 2000 m more than the one who lives on floor number 4. Only two people live between Q and the one who runs for 3300 m. The one who runs for 2800 m lives on one of the floors below Q but not on the floor number 2, only two people live between M and S. The one who runs for 850 m lives immediately below M.

33. How many people live between S and N?
(a) Three (b) One
(c) Five (d) Four
(e) Two

34. Who amongst the following live(s) between P and the one who runs for 1300 m?
(a) Both Q and R
(b) Only S
(c) Both R and the one who runs for 850 m.
(d) Only the one who runs for 4000 m.
(e) Both R and the one who runs for 2200 m.

35. As per the given arrangement, four of the following five are alike in a certain way and so form a group. Which one of the following does not belong to the group?
(a) Q-3300 m (b) O-1300 m
(c) Floor number 4-S (d) Floor number 2-R
(e) Floor number 7-1300 m

36. Which of the following statements is true with respect to the given arrangement?
(a) Only two people live between P and O.
(b) Q runs for 4000 m.
(c) N lives on floor number 7.
(d) The one who runs for 850 m lives immediately above P.
(e) None of the above

37. If the total distance covered by B and M is 5300 m, then how much did B run alone?
(a) 2000 m (b) 4000 m (c) 3100 m (d) 1300 m
(e) 600 m

38. Who amongst the following runs for 2200 m?
(a) P (b) N (c) Q (d) R
(e) S

DIRECTIONS ~ (Q. Nos. 39-43) *Study the following information carefully to answer the given question.*
« RRB PO MAINS 2016

Seven different boxes namely P, Q, R, S, T, U, V having different number of articles in it placed one above the other. Number of articles is 2,6,9,11,15,16,20 but not necessarily in the same order. The following information is given below.

There are two boxes between S and the box in which there is 11 articles. Two boxes are placed between P and the box in which there is 9 articles. There are only three boxes between T and the box which have 9 articles.

S is placed below P. U is immediately below the box which has 15 articles. P doesn't have 15 articles. Only one box is there between Q and V.

There are two boxes between the boxes having 15 and 6 articles. S lies above the box having 11 articles. The difference between number of articles in boxes S and the box which is just above S is greater than 10. The number of articles in the box which is just above V is less than the number of articles in V. Q does not have 6 number of articles. U does not have 9 articles.

39. How many boxes is/are there between S and U?
(a) One (b) Two
(c) Three (d) Four
(e) None

40. How many articles are there in box 'S'?
(a) 11 (b) 15 (c) 20 (d) 16
(e) Can't be determined

41. Find the pair of articles and boxes which is not correct?
(a) Q-16 (b) U-11 (c) P-2 (d) V-6
(e) None of these

42. Which of the following condition is correct regarding the position of the box which contains 2 articles with respect to T?
(a) There is only one box between the box T and the box which contains 20 articles.
(b) Box T is immediately above the box which contains 2 articles.
(c) Box which contains 2 articles is immediately above box T.
(d) All of the above is true.
(e) None of the above is true.

43. Box P contains how many articles?
(a) 15 (b) 16 (c) 6 (d) 11
(e) None of these

DIRECTIONS ~ (Q. Nos. 44-49) *Study the following information carefully and answer the questions asked.*
« IBPS PO 2013

Seven friends A, B, C, D, E, F and G are sitting around a circular table facing either the centre or outside. Each one of them belongs to a different department viz. Finance, Marketing, Sales, HR, Corporate Finance, Investment Banking and Operations but not necessarily in the same order.

C sits third to the right of G. G faces the centre. Only one person sits between C and the person working in the HR department. Immediate neighbours of C face outside. Only one person sits between F and D. Both F and D face the centre. D does not work in the HR department. A works in Investment Banking Department. A faces the centre. Two people sit between the person who work in Investment Banking and Marketing Departments.

The person who works in Corporate Finance sits to the immediate left of E. C faces same direction as E. The person who works in Sales department sits to the immediate left of the person who works for Operations department.

44. For which of the following departments does B works ?
(a) Finance (b) Marketing
(c) HR (d) Corporate Finance
(e) Operations

45. What is the position of B with respect to the person who works for Sales department?
(a) Immediate right (b) Third to the left
(c) Second to the right (d) Second to the left
(e) Fourth to the right

46. Who sits to the immediate right of E?
(a) The person who works for marketing department.
(b) C
(c) B
(d) The person who works for HR department.
(e) A

47. Who amongst the following sits exactly between C and the person who works for HR department?

(a) B
(b) The person who works for Marketing department.
(c) The person who works Operations department.
(d) D
(e) G

48. Who amongst the following sit between the persons who work for Marketing and Investment Banking departments when counted for the left hand side of the person working for Marketing department?

(a) F and G (b) E and C (c) C and B (d) F and D
(e) B and D

49. How many people sit between the person who works for Operations department and A, when counted from the right hand side of A?

(a) One (b) Two (c) Three (d) Four
(e) More than four

DIRECTIONS ~ (Q. Nos. 50-52) *Study the following information carefully and answer the questions given below.* « SBI PO (Mains) 2017

Eight members A, B, C, D, E, F, G and H sitting in a row facing North but not necessary in the same order. No two successive members are sitting together according to alphabetical order.

For example A does not sit with B, similarly B does not sit with C and so on.

They also have a hobby like Playing game, Watching TV, Singing, Dancing, Online surfing, Chatting, Acting and Cooking, but not necessary in the same order.

Either A or H sits at the extreme end of the row. A is sitting third to the left of the person whose hobby is online surfing. B sits second to the right of the person who likes acting. C sits second to the right of F. G who likes watching TV is sitting second from the right end of the row. The person whose hobby is dancing is immediate neighbour of F who likes playing games. The person whose hobby is acting is not sitting adjacent to the person whose hobby is online surfing, C's hobby is neither acting nor online surfing. D and E do not sit at any extreme end of the row. One of the immediate neighbours of H likes cooking and the one whose hobby is singing sits left end of the row. Neither H nor D likes acting.

50. Which of the following member is sitting second to the left of the second from the right end of the row?

(a) E
(b) The one whose hobby is acting
(c) A
(d) The one whose hobby is cooking
(e) None of the above

51. A is related to B and F is related to E in the same way, how is the member whose hobby is dancing related to which of the following?

(a) The one whose hobby is acting
(b) G
(c) The one whose hobby is cooking
(d) C
(e) B

52. Which of the following combination is not true?

(a) A—singing (b) E—Acting
(c) G —Watching TV (d) B—Playing games
(e) D—Dancing

DIRECTIONS ~ (Q. Nos. 53-57) *Study the following information carefully and answer the questions which follow.* « RRB PO Mains 2016

Eight persons S, T, U, V, W, X, Y and Z live on 8 different floors in a building. The ground floor is numbered 1 then first floor is numbered 2 till then numbered 8. They like different colours i.e., Red, Pink, Orange, Blue, Grey, Green, Yellow and Purple but not necessarily in the same order..

There are four floors between W's floor and S's floor. W lives on an odd numbered floor. S likes Yellow colour. There are two floors between T's and W's floor. The one who likes Grey colour lives on immediate above the floor on which S lives. U lives immediate above Y. The one who likes Red colour lives on floor numbered one. There is no floor between T's floor and Z's floor. V does not live immediate above or below to W's floor. Only one person lives between the persons who like Yellow and Purple colours. The one who likes Pink colour lives immediate above the floor on which the person who likes Grey colour. Z likes Blue colour but does not live below to T. X likes Green colour.

53. On which floor Z lives?

(a) Third (b) Fourth (c) Fifth (d) Sixth
(e) Seventh

54. How many floors are below the floor on which Y lives?

(a) Three (b) Four (c) Five (d) Six
(e) Seven

55. Who among the following lives on the second floor?

(a) X (b) V (c) Y (d) U (e) S

56. Which colour is liked by V?

(a) Orange (b) Pink (c) Grey (d) Red
(e) Purple

57. Which of the following is true with respect to T?

(a) T likes Orange colour and lives on 4th floor.
(b) T likes Pink colour and lives on 8th floor.
(c) T likes Purple colour and lives on 4th floor.
(d) T likes Grey colour and lives on 7th floor.
(e) T likes Red colour and lives on 8th floor.

DIRECTIONS ~ (Q. Nos. 58-62) *Study the following information carefully and answer the questions asked.*

Eight persons A, B, C, D, E, F, G and H sit on the line and all of them face North direction but not necessarily in same order. All of them stay in different floors *viz.* 3rd, 6th, 13th, 19th, 27th, 31st, 43rd and 47th of a multi-storey building but not necessarily in same order.

The one who stays on 13th floor sits second to right of one who stays on 6th floor. C stays on 27th floor. A sits fourth to left of person who stays on 47th floor. D does not sit adjacent to H. Neither A nor the person who stays on 47th floor sit on the extreme end of the line. B sits third to left of F. There is only one person sitting between G, who lives on 3rd floor and the person who stays on 47th floor.

There are two persons sitting between G and the one who stays on 43rd floor. H sits immediate left of one who stays on 43rd floor. There are two persons between H and F who stays on 31st floor.

58. Who lives on 43rd floor?
(a) A (b) D (c) B (d) E (e) H

59. How many persons sit between A and B?
(a) Two (b) One (c) Three (d) Four
(e) None of these

60. D lives on which of the following floors?
(a) 6th (b) 13th (c) 19th (d) 47th
(e) 43rd

61. Who among the following sits immediate left of the person who lives on 3rd floor?
(a) A (b) F (c) D (d)B
(e) None of these

62. Who sits 3rd to the left of C?
(a) A (b) D (c) F (d) E
(e) None of these

DIRECTIONS (Q. Nos. 63-67) *Study the following information and answer the given questions.*
« IBPS PO (Pre) 2015

J, K, L, M, O, Q, R and S are sitting around a circular table facing the centre with equal distances between each other (but not necessarily in the same order). Each one of them is also related to M in some way or the other.

Only two people sit between Q and L. M sits second to the left of Q. Only three people sit between L and M's sister. M's son sits second to the right of M's sister. Only one person sits between M's son and S. J sits to the immediate right of R. R is neither the son nor the mother of M. S is an immediate neighbour of M's mother. Only three people sit between M's mother and M's brother. M's daughter sits second to the left of M's brother. M's father is not an immediate neighbour of M. M's wife sits third to the right of K.

63. Who sits second to the right of R ?
(a) M's brother (b) M (c) R (d) M's son
(e) M's daughter

64. How many people sit between K and L, when counted from the left of L?
(a) Six (b) One (c) None (d) Two
(e) Four

65. Which of the following statements is true with respect to the given information?
(a) R sits second to the right of M's wife.
(b) K is an immediate neighbour of R.
(c) M sits second to the left of L.
(d) All the given options are true.
(e) S is the daughter of L

66. How is K related to R?
(a) Son-in-law (b) Uncle (c) Niece (d) Brother
(e) Daughter

67. Who amongst the following is the wife of M?
(a) N (b) L (c) O (d) Q
(e) J

DIRECTIONS (Q. Nos. 68-74) *Study the following information carefully and answer the given questions.*
« MHT CET MBA 2016

Ten people are sitting in two parallel rows containing five people each, in such a way that there is equal distance between each adjacent persons. In row-1 J, K, L, M and N are seated and all of them are facing North. In row-2 P, Q, R, S and T are seated and all of them are facing South. Each of them likes a different fruit namely, Banana, Orange, Guava, Pineapple, Kiwi, Cherry, Mango, Apple, Strawberry and Litchi but not necessarily in the same order.

Therefore, in the given seating arrangement, each member seated in a row faces another member of the other row and each of them likes a different fruit. (Please Note : All the given information is not necessarily in the order) R sits second to the left of S. R does not sit at any of the extreme ends of the row. The one who faces R sits to the immediate left of the one who likes Cherry. Only two people sit between the one who likes Cherry and the one who likes Mango.

The one who faces the one who likes Mango sits third to the right of the one who likes Apple. Only one person sits between the one who likes apple and the one likes Litchi. The one who faces the one who likes Litchi sits third to the left of N. Only two people sit between N and M. L faces Q. The one who likes Orange sits to the immediate right of Q. The one who likes Strawberry sits second to the left of the one who likes Orange. P sits to the immediate left of the one who likes Guava. The one who likes Kiwi sits to the immediate right of the one who likes Banana. J does not like Mango.

68. Four of the given five are alike in a certain way based on the given arrangement and hence form a group. Which one of them does not belong to that group?
(a) J (b) S
(c) T (d) K
(e) N

69. Who amongst the following is facing K?
(a) The one who likes Pineapple
(b) The one who likes Guava
(c) R
(d) P
(e) The one who likes Kiwi

70. Who amongst the following is facing T?
(a) N
(b) The one who likes Kiwi
(c) The one who likes Mango
(d) The one who likes Orange
(e) J

71. Which of the following statements is true regarding J?
(a) Only two people sit between J and the one who likes Pineapple.
(b) J sits to the immediate right of the one who likes Cherry.
(c) None of the given statements is true.
(d) One of J's immediate neighbours faces the one who likes Litchi.
(e) J faces one of the immediate neighbour of the one who likes Strawberry.

72. What is the position of M with respect to T?
(a) M faces the one who sits to the immediate right of T.
(b) M faces the one who sits second to the left of T.
(c) M faces the one who sits second to the right of T.
(d) M faces the one who sits third to right of T.
(e) M faces the one who sits to the immediate left of T.

73. What is the position of S with respect to Q?
(a) Second to the left (b) Third to the right
(c) Third to the left (d) To the immediate right
(e) To the immediate left

74. Four of the given five are alike in a certain way based on the given arrangement and hence form a group. Which of them does not belong to that group?
(a) Orange—Kiwi (b) Strawberry—Banana
(c) Apple—Mango (d) Litchi—Pineapple
(e) Guava—Cherry

DIRECTIONS ~ (Q. Nos. 75-79) *Study the following information carefully and answer the given questions.*

There are ten candidates i.e. P, Q, R, S, T, A, B, C, D and E. All of them are seated in two parallel rows, each row consist of six chairs. P, Q, R, S and T sit in Row 1, which is facing South direction and A, B, C, D and E in Row 2, with faces north direction. One seat is vacant in each row. They all have birthday in different month i.e. January, March, April, May, June, July, August, September, November and December but not necessarily in the same order.

The one whose birthday is in June sits opposite to A. The one whose birthday is in January sits third to left of E. R does not sit at extreme end. The one whose birthday is in March sits second from right end of the Row 2. P faces vacant seat and S faces B. There are three seats between D and B. B does not face the one whose birhtday is in April. E sits opposite to the one whose birthday is in July who sits at extreme end. T sits just right of one vacant seat. C faces the vacant seat that is second to right of P. The one whose birthday is in April faces the one who sits fourth to left of the one whose birthday is in March. There is only one seat between the one who whose birthday is in June and the one who whose birthday is in April. The one whose birthday is in November sits immediate right of the one whose birthday is in September. The one whose birthday is in September sits near to Q. The one whose birthday is in August faces the one who sits adjacent to vacant seat. The one whose birthday is in May sits adjecent to the one who faces the one whose birthday is in June. One seat is vacant between A and B.

75. Who among the following has birthday in July?
(a) R (b) T (c) C (d) D (e) Q

76. Who among the following faces the one whose birthday is in June?
(a) P (b) A (c) B (d) E
(e) None of these

77. Who among the following sits third to right of D?
(a) A (b) B (c) E (d) C
(e) No one

78. Who among the following sits 2nd left of the one whose birthday is in November?
(a) P (b) R (c) C (d) D (e) Q

79. Which of the following sentence is correct?
(a) P faces the one who whose birthday is in August.
(b) T sits adjacent to vacant seat.
(c) E s birthday is in March month.
(d) C is not immediate neighbor of A.
(e) All are correct.

DIRECTIONS ~ (Q. Nos. 80-84) *Study the following information carefully and answer the given questions.*
« Indian Bank PO 2016

Seven people P, Q, R, S, T, U and V live on seven different floors of a building but not necessarily in the same order. The lower most floor of the building is numbered one, the one above that is numbered two and so on till the top most floor is numbered seven. Each one of them likes a different watch—Casio, Citizen, Fossil, Seiko, Tissot, Omega and Fastrack, but not necessarily in the same order.

U lives on floor number 4. Only two people live between U and the one who likes Citizen. Only three people live between the one who likes Citizen and the one who likes Fastrack. S lives on one of the even numbered floors above the one who likes Fastrack. Only one person lives between S and the one who likes Seiko. V lives one of the odd numbered floors below the one who likes Seiko. Only one person lives between V and the one who likes Fossil. P lives either immediately above or immediately below the one who likes fossil. T lives immediately above P. Only one person lives between Q and the one who likes Casio. The one who likes Tissot lives on one of the floors above the one who likes Omega.

80. Who lives immediately below S?
(a) T (b) Q
(c) U (d) The one who likes Omega
(e) The one who likes Tissot

81. How many people live above the one who likes Seiko?
(a) More than three (b) Two
(c) None (d) Three
(e) One

82. Which of the following watches does T like?
(a) Omega (b) Fastrack (c) Fossil (d) Tissot
(e) Casio

83. On which of the following floor numbers does Q live?
(a) 7 (b) 5 (c) 3 (d) 2 (e) 6

84. How many people live between the one who likes Fastrack and the one who likes Casio?
(a) None (b) One
(c) More than three (d) Two
(e) Three

DIRECTIONS ~ (Q. Nos. 85-89) *Study the following information carefully and answer the given questions.*
« IBPS RRB PO (Mains) 2017

Eight persons namely P, Q, R, S, W, X, Y and Z are sitting around a square table facing towards center. 4 of the persons are sitting in 4 corners while 4 of the persons are sitting in the middle of the sides. They have different ages. Those who sit in the corners having the ages multiple of 3.Those who sit at the middle of the sides having the ages multiple of 2.

P sits 2nd to the right of the one who has the age of 44. P is an immediate neighbour of the one who is 39 yr old.

Two persons sit between Q and the person having the age of 39. Q has not the age of 44, W sits 2nd to the left of Q. S is immediate right of the person having age of 15. Three persons sit between Z and the one having age of 15. The difference between the ages of Z and the one who is 2nd to the left of Z is 6. S is older than Z. Immediate neighbours of S are younger than S. Person having age of 22 sits 2nd to the right of the person having age of 10. Age of P is not 10. Y sits immediate left of the person having age of 22. Age of Y is 51. Age of R is greater than 20. Age of R is 24 yr more than X. Age of X is 3 yr more than age of P.

85. Who among the following is of 9 yr old?
(a) P (b) S (c) W (d) X
(e) No one

86. Who sits 2nd right of the one who sits immediate left of the one whose age is 51 yr old?
(a) R (b) S (c) Y (d) Q (e) W

87. How many persons sit between the one who is of 15 yr old and the one who is of 12 yr old, when counted anti-clockwise from the one who is of 15 yr old?
(a) One (b) Two
(c) Three (d) More than three
(e) None of these

88. Who among the following sits diagonally opposite to Z?
(a) X (b) T (c) S (d) P (e) W

89. Who among the following sits immediate right of S?
(a) P (b) W (c) Y (d) R (e) Z

DIRECTIONS ~ (Q. Nos. 90-93) *Study the following information carefully and answer the questions given below.* « IBPS Clerk (Mains) 2018

Six boxes A, B, C, D, E and F are placed in a stack one above other. Each contains different number of chocolates *viz.* 250, 190, 119, 175, 280 and 210.

Box A is placed immediately above box C. Three boxes are placed between C and the box which contains 250 chocolates. Box which has 175 chocolates is just above the box which has 250 chocolates. One box is placed between box E and the box which has 175 chocolates. F contains 210 chocolates. The box which contains 119 chocolates are placed below box F. Three boxes are placed between box D and the box which have 119 chocolates. One box is placed between box B and the box which have 190 chocolates.

90. Which box contains 210 chocolates?
(a) F (b) B (c) C (d) D (e) A

91. Box C and E together contain how many chocolates?
(a) 399 (b) 369 (c) 294 (d) 309 (e) 400

92. Which box is placed at topmost position?
(a) F (b) B (c) C (d) D
(e) A

93. How many boxes are placed between box B and the box which has 119 chocolates?
(a) one (b) two (c) three (d) four
(e) none

DIRECTIONS ~ (Q. Nos. 94-98) *Study the following information carefully and answer the questions given below.* « SBI PO 2017

There are 6 cars P, Q, R, S, T and U which are parked in a straight line. But adjacent cars cannot be alphabetically placed, like car P cannot be parked adjacent to car Q, car Q cannot be parked adjacent to car P and R and so on. Distance between each car is successive multiple of 4. Distance between cars P and Q is 60 m. Car P is to the left of car Q. There is one car between car P and car Q. Distance between cars Q and T is 84 m. Distance between cars R and U is a multiple of 3. Car U is parked somewhere right of car R.

From a point, car V moves 16 m East, takes a right turn, moves 12 m and stops at point Z. Point Z is 15 m North of car P.

If car U goes 7 m in South direction, takes a left turn and moves 16 m, then it turns right and moves 5 m, next takes a left turn again and moves 22 m, then it reaches to point X.

94. How many cars are parked between cars P and S?
(a) One (b) None (c) Three (d) Two
(e) Four

95. What is the distance between car Q and point X?
(a) 13 m (b) $2\sqrt{5}$ m (c) $6\sqrt{2}$ m (d) 14 m
(e) $6\sqrt{5}$ m

96. Car R will have to move how much distance and in which DIRECTION to reach to car V?
(a) 15 m North, 38 m East (b) 24 m East, 17 m North
(c) 44 m East, 15 m North (d) 17 m North, 38 m East
(e) 17 m North, 44 m East

97. Car S will have to move how much distance and in which DIRECTION to reach to point X?
(a) 10 m West, 30 m South (b) 12 m South, 30 m West
(c) 12 m South, 30 m East (d) 32 m West, 10 m West
(e) 36 m West, 10 m South

98. If car V moves 28 m East from point Z, takes a right turn and stops at point Y after moving 17 m, then car Q is in which direction with respect to point Y?
(a) North-West (b) South-East
(c) Cannot be determined (d) North-East
(e) South-West

DIRECTIONS ~ (Q. Nos. 99-103) *Read the following information carefully and answer the given questions.* « IBPS Clerk (Mains) 2015

There are six boxes M, N, O, P, Q, and S in a room and placed one above another, each having different number of toffees i.e. 10, 15, 18, 21, 24 and 32, also they are of different colours i.e, Red, Yellow, Pink, Green, White and Blue (but not necessarily in the same order).

Only three boxes are placed between box M and P, which has odd number of toffees. There is only one box is placed between P and N, which is of Yellow colour. Box Q is of Red colour and doesn't place just above and below box N, but placed one of the boxes above box N. The box which is placed just above P is of White colour. The box which is placed at top has 11 toffees more than box P. Box S's colour is not White. Green coloured box has 18 toffees. At least two boxes are placed below M, which has odd number of toffees. Box P is not of Blue colour and box O doesn't have 24 toffees.

99. What is the colour of the Box which has 10 toffees?
(a) White (b) Yellow
(c) Green (d) Blue
(e) None of these

100. Which of the following box is placed at top and how many toffees are there in it?
(a) N, 32 (b) Q, 24
(c) O, 18 (d) Q, 32
(e) None of these

101. How many boxes are placed between Q and the box which is of Pink colour?
(a) One (b) Three
(c) Two (d) More than three
(e) None of these

102. Which box is placed just above box N?
(a) S (b) P
(c) M (d) Q
(e) None of these

103. Which of the following box has maximum number of toffees?
(a) The box which is placed just above M
(b) N (c) Both (a) and (d)
(d) Red coloured box (e) None of these

DIRECTIONS ~ (Q. Nos. 104-108) *Study the following information carefully and answer the given questions.*
« SBI PO MAINS-2015

Seven different containers B, D, F, K, L, G and O contain seven different chocolates namely, viz. Dairy milk, Kit-kat, Perk, Galaxy, Bournville, Temptation and Snickers are arranged one above the other. The container at the bottom of arrangement is numbered 1, the above container is numbered 2 and so on.

The container which contains Galaxy chocolate is immediately below B. Only one container is between the Dairy milk container and G. O is immediately above the Temptation container. There are only three containers above the container that contains Dairy milk. Only two containers are between the Kitkat container and the container that contains Snickers. Only two containers are between the container which contains. The Galaxy chocolate and the container which contains Dairy milk. D is immediately above L. The container filled with Perk is neither at the top nor at the bottom of the arrangement. container D does not contain Dairy milk. Only one container is between D and the container which one is filled with Kitkat. D is placed above the Kitkat Container. F is placed immediately above G. Neither F nor O contains Galaxy.

104. Which of the following combination represents the position of F and the chocolate which it contains?
(a) 5 - Bournville (b) 4 - Temptation
(c) 1 - Galaxy (d) 4 - Dairy milk
(e) 7 - Bournville

105. Which amongst the following container is arranged exactly in between G and L?
(a) B (b) K (c) D (d) O
(e) Other than those given as options

106. Which of the following chocolate is filled in container "B"?
(a) Bournville (b) Snickers
(c) Temptation (d) Dairy milk
(e) None of the above

107. As per the given arrangement, K is related to Bournville and G is related to Temptation in a certain way. Then O is related to which of the following in the same way?
(a) Bournville (b) Snickers
(c) Perk (d) Dairy milk
(e) None of the above

108. Which of the following pairs of people occupies the top, middle and bottom positions of the arrangement?
(a) F,B,L (b) F,L,G (c) B,L,O (d) D,G,K
(e) F,L,K

DIRECTIONS ~ (Q. Nos. 109-113) *Study the information carefully and answer the questions given below.*
« MHT MNA 2017

7 friends P, Q, R, S, T, U and V stay on 9 floor building ground floor is numbered one and above the number one is floor number 2 and so on. But not necessary in the same order. Each one of them likes different colour viz. Black, Brown, Green, Yellow, Pink, Red and Grey but not necessary in the same order.

There are two floors which are vacant. U stay on an odd numbered floor but not above the floor number 6 and likes Black colour. There is a gap of one floor between U and both of the vacant floors. Neither P nor Q is an immediate neighbour of both vacant floors and they does not like Yellow and Pink colour. The person who likes Grey colour stay on the 2nd floor. Q stays on an odd numbered floor which is above P. There is one floor between P and R who likes Green colour. There are three floors between P and S who does not likes Yellow colour. The person who likes Brown colour stay on just above V.

109. Who among the following stay between vacant floor and U?
(a) S (b) T
(c) R (d) Either (a) or (b)
(e) Both (a) and (b)

110. How many persons stay between P and Q?
(a) None (b) One (c) Two (d) Three
(e) None of these

111. Which of the following floor belongs to V?
(a) 8th (b) 9th (c) 7th
(d) Can't be determined (e) None of these

112. Who among the following person stay on 5th floor?
(a) S (b) U (c) No one (d) T
(e) R

113. How many persons stay between S and R?
(a) No one (b) One (c) Two (d) Three
(e) Four

DIRECTIONS ~ (Q. Nos. 114-118) *Study the following information carefully and answer the questions given below.* « IBPS PO Mains 2017

Seven persons P, Q, R, S, T, U and V live on seven different floors of a building, but not necessarily in the same order. The lowermost floor of the building is numbered as one; the one above it is number two and so on till the topmost floor is number seven. Each of them also likes a different drink and fast-food i.e. drinks are- Pepsi, Miranda, Coca-Cola, Sprite, Thumps up, Frooti, Limca and fast-food are- Dosa, Idali, Burger, Bada-pao, Bread chaat, Chicken Baguette and Sandwich but not necessarily in the same order.

Only one person lives between the one who likes Thumps up and the one who likes Frooti. S does not like Thumps up. V does not like Pepsi. The one who likes Chicken Baguette lives immediate above the one who likes Thumps up. T lives on one of the floors below Q, but does not live on the lowermost floor. The one who lives on 7th floor is immediate above the one, who lives immediate below the one who likes Sandwich. There are three persons between Q and T. The one who likes Sprite lives on one of the odd-numbered floors below U. P lives immediately above U and does not like Coca-Cola. U does not like Bada-pao and Idali. The one who likes Burger lives immediate above the one who likes Bread chaat. The one who likes Frooti is also likes Idali. Only one person lives between Q and the one who likes Coca-Cola. The one who likes Bread chaat lives below the one who likes Dosa. Only two persons live between V and the one who likes Coca-Cola. The one who likes Miranda lives on one of the even-numbered floors above the one who likes Coca-Cola. The one who likes Limca lives immediately above V. S lives on one of the floors above R.T does not live on 2nd floor.

114. Who among the following persons like Bada-pao?

(a) R
(b) The one who likes Miranda
(c) The one who likes Coca-Cola .
(d) The one who likes Pepsi
(e) Q

115. Who lives immediate above the one who likes Idali?

(a) The one who likes Coca-Cola
(b) Both (a) and (e)
(c) S
(d) Q
(e) The one who likes Dosa

116. Which of the following persons like Limca?

(a) Q (b) P (c) V (d)T
(e) None of these

117. How many persons live between the one who likes Sprite and the one who likes Idali?

(a) None (b) Three
(c) Two (d) Can't be determined
(e) None of these

118. Four of the following five are alike in a certain way and hence they form a group. Which one of the following does not belong to that group?

(a) The one who likes Sprite
(b) The one who likes Chicken Baguette
(c) The one who lives on 5th floor
(d) The one who likes Bada-Pao.
(e) The one who likes Pepsi

DIRECTIONS ~ (Q. Nos. 119-123) *Study the following information carefully and answer the questions given below.* « IBPS PO (Mains) 2019

Seven square boxes of different areas are placed on seven shelves of different widths from bottom to top (such as bottom shelf is numbered as 1 and top is numbered as 7). Seven boxes of different areas contain different chocolates viz. 5-Star, Dairy milk, Kitkat, Perk, Bournville, Silk and Munch. Each box is of different colour viz. Blue, Black, Green, Orange, Purple, Pink and White. The width of each shelf is different viz. 5, 9, 11, 15, 17, 21, 35, but not necessarily in the same order.

The area of the box placed immediately below the top shelf is equal to the square of the width (which is a prime number) of the corresponding shelf. The area of the box of Kitkat is equal to the addition of the areas of the box of Silk and the one which is placed on the bottom shelf. The shelf which contain green box has highest width. There are only two boxes between the box of Orange colour and box of Perk, which is placed at even numbered shelf but below 5th shelf. Box of Bournville and Dairy milk are not of Blue colour and Pink colour. The box of dairy milk has its side, equal to the width of the corresponding shelf minus 1 and has equal number of shelf above and below it.

The sides of the boxes of Silk is 12 and Munch is 5. The ratio of the widths of shelf on which Pink and White box is equal to the ratio of the widths of shelf on which Green and Black box is kept. No box is placed above Pink box and it is neither Silk nor Munch. The area of the box of 5-star is equal to the square of the width of the shelf on which White colour box is kept. The box of Bournville is placed immediately above the box of Kitkat. The width of the shelf on which Pink box is kept is multiple of seven and width of the shelf on which White box is kept is a perfect square. The width of the shelf on which box of Kitkat is placed is least. Green box is placed at the bottom and it does not contain Silk. There are three boxes in between Purple and Blue box, which is not placed above the box of Silk. No two boxes have equal areas. The width of the shelf on which Blue box is kept is less than the width of the shelf on which Black box is kept. The box which has its area equal to the square of seven is placed immediately below Black box.

119. What is the colour of the box, which is placed immediately above the box, whose side is equal to the width of the corresponding shelf minus 1?

(a) White (b) Orange
(c) Blue (d) Pink
(e) None of these

120. What will be the area of the box of Bournville?

(a) 25 (b) 144 (c) 81 (d) 64
(e) 289

121. Which of the following combination is true regarding Silk in pattern of 'Shelves- Colour- Area- Width'?

(a) 2-Blue-144-11 (b) 3-Blue-144-11
(c) 3-Black-144-15 (d) 6-White-169-17
(e) None of the above

122. How many boxes are placed between the boxes of Kitkat and Munch?

(a) Three (b) Five
(c) Four (d) Two
(e) None of these

123. What will be difference between the widths of the shelfs of Purple and Black box?

(a) 2 (b) 14 (c) 20 (d) 8
(e) None of these

DIRECTIONS ~ (Q. Nos. 124-128) *Read the following information carefully and answer the questions that follow.* « IBPS PO Mains 2019

Eight cricketers P, Q, R, S, T, U, V and W are sitting around a circular table facing the centre. Each cricketer is wearing shoes of different brand viz. B, D, X, E, A, C, H and F, but not necessarily in the same order. Neither P nor U is wearing shoes of D brand. Age of the cricketer who sits opposite to the one who is wearing shoes of brand H is two third the age of the cricketer who sits opposite to R whose age is equal to the average of ages of T and S.

The cricketer wearing the shoes of D brand sits third to the right of V. R is an immediate neighbour of V. Q sits third to the right of W. W is wearing shoes of neither D nor E brand. The cricketer who sits between Q and the one who is wearing shoes of brand D is twenty five years old. Only one cricketer sits between R and the Cricketer who is wearing shoes of X brand. P and U are immediate neighbours of each other. The cricketer who sits opposite to R is two years older than the cricketer who sits immediate left of T.

The cricketer wearing shoes of brand B is not an immediate neighbour of the cricketer wearing shoes of brand D. Age of W is equal to the sum of the ages of the cricketers who are wearing shoes of brand X and E. The cricketer wearing shoes of brand C sits second to the left of P. The cricketer wearing shoes of F brand sits second to the right of P. Two cricketers sit between S and the cricketer wearing shoes of brand A. V is twice as old as one of his immediate neighbour. U is five years older than R. S is not wearing shoes of D brand. P is ten years younger than the cricketer who is wearing shoes of brand D. The cricketer who is wearing shoes of brand E sits second to the right of R.

124. Who is the oldest of them all?

(a) P (b) W
(c) R (d) U
(e) S

125. What is the sum of the ages of T, V and Q?

(a) 50 yr (b) 54 yr (c) 48 yr (d) 39 yr
(e) None of these

126. What is the position of U with respect to the cricketer who is wearing shoes of brand D?

(a) Second to the left (b) Second to the right
(c) Immediate right (d) Immediate left
(e) None of these

127. R is wearing shoes of which brand?

(a) W (b) E (c) C (d) D
(e) A

128. What is the sum of the ages of the immediate neighbours of the person who is sitting opposite to T?

(a) 58 yr (b) 55 yr
(c) 65 yr (d) Less than 50 yr
(e) None of these

DIRECTIONS ~ (Q. Nos. 129-133) *Study the following information carefully and answer the questions given below.* « SBI PO (Mains) 2017

There are 10 shelves numbered 1,2 ......, 10. They are arranged in two rows one above the other. The shelves 1, 2 ,......, 5 are in row 1 and rest in row 2 which is above row 1. The shelves are arranged in increasing order of number given to them. Like the shelf number 1 is placed on extreme left of row 1, then shelf number 2 and so on. Similarly the shelf number 6 is placed on extreme left of row 2, and so on. Each shelf contains a certain number of glass slabs and photo frames. There is atleast one glass slab in each shelf. The length of each glass slab is 15 cm and that of each photo frame is 6 cm.

The shelf 3 has length 33 cm. There is one shelf between shelf 3 and Yellow shelf. The Yellow shelf contains 1 glass slab and 6 photo frames more than that in shelf 3. The Silver shelf is just above the Yellow shelf. The Silver shelf contains same number of glass slabs as Yellow shelf and 1 photo frame. There are 2 shelves between Silver and Green slabs. The length of Green shelf is 3 cm greater than the Silver shelf. The Blue shelf is immediate next in number to Green shelf. The Blue shelf contains 1 glass slab more than that in Silver shelf and 1 photo frame less than that in Green shelf. There is one shelf between Blue and Orange shelves. The White shelf is just below the Orange shelf. There is one shelf between White and Red shelf. Black shelf is in row 2.

The Pink shelf is just below the Black shelf. The Black shelf has same number of photo frames and glass slabs. The Orange shelf has 1 glass slab more than Black shelf. The length of Orange shelf is 24 cm more than the length of Pink shelf. The length of Violet shelf is half the length of Yellow shelf. The Red shelf has greater than or equal to four glass slabs. The length of Pink shelf is 6 cm less than the shelf immediate next in number. The length of row 1 is 267 cm and that of row 2 is 249 cm.

129. How many more photo frames can the row 2 adjust?

(a) 1 (b) 2 (c) 3 (d) None
(e) 4

130. The colour of shelf 2 is

(a) Cannot be determined (b) Violet
(c) Red (d) White (e) Pink

131. How many total glass slabs do the Silver, Black and Red shelves contain?

(a) 7
(b) 9
(c) 10
(d) Other than those given in options
(e) 12

132. What is the total length of the Pink, Orange and Blue shelves?

(a) 146 cm (b) 134 cm (c) 141 cm (d) 133 cm
(e) None of these

133. If all the photo frames of Silver and White shelves are removed and added in Black shelf, then what will be the length of Black shelf?

(a) 67 cm (b) 66 cm (c) 61 cm (d) 69 cm
(e) 62 cm

Answers / WITH EXPLANATIONS

Solutions (Q. Nos. 1-2) *By information given, we can conclude that*

$$V > W > Z > X > Y > U$$

(Husband of V) (Niece of Y)

1. *(a)* V won the game and U got the lowest point.

2. *(d)* W is the husband of V and his position in the game on the basis of points is II.

Solutions (Q.Nos. 3-7) *From given information, arrangement is as follows*

Box	Item
N	Colours
O	Watches
K	Diaries
M	Cookies
P	Pencils
L	Jewellery
J	Spoons

3. *(d)* Diary box is kept immediately above M.

4. *(b)* O is second from top in the given stack of boxes.

5. *(a)* Box J contains Spoons.

6. *(c)*

N ⟶ (Colour – 2) ⟶ Diaries
P ⟶ (Pencils – 2) ⟶ Spoons
K ⟶ (Diaries – 2) ⟶ Pencils
M ⟶ (Cookies – 2) ⟶ Jewellery
O ⟶ (Watches + 1) ⟶ Colours

Cleary 'O-colours' follows different pattern, so it does not belong to the group.

7. *(b)* None

Solutions (Q. Nos. 8-12) *According to the information, the order of sitting is as follows*

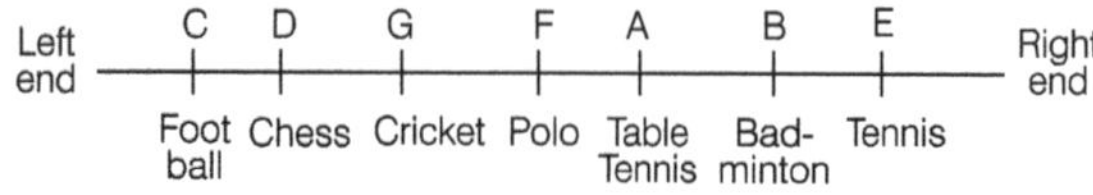

8. *(d)* Except 'BF' in all other groups first person is second to the left of second person, while in group 'BF' first person is second to the right of second person.

9. *(c)* G plays cricket and is in middle of D who plays chess and F who plays polo.

10. *(b)* F plays polo.

11. *(e)* A is in middle of F who plays polo and B who plays badminton.

12. *(e)* Clearly, C and G are the neighbours of D. C plays football, while G plays cricket.

Solutions (Q. Nos. 13-16) *From given information, the arrangement is as follows*

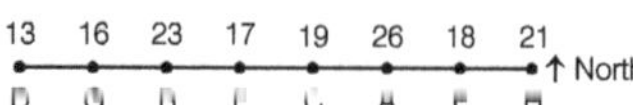

13. *(c)* The age of G is 16 yr. G sits second to the left of F.

14. *(a)* A sits third to the right of B and his age is 26 yr.

15. *(d)* The age of E is 18 yr.

16. *(c)* Two persons sit between the one whose age is 26 yr and H, is not true.

Solutions (Q. Nos. 17-21) *According to the given information, we get*

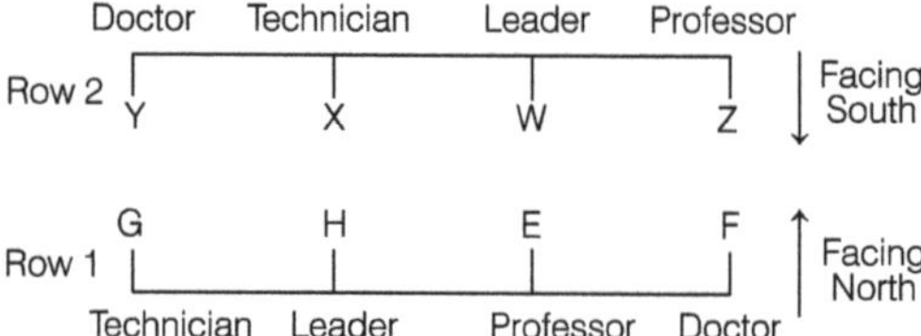

17. *(d)* X and the professor of row 2 are immediate neighbours of W.

18. *(d)* Technician G sits to the immediate left of the leader of row1.

19. *(d)* The technician of row 1 faces the Doctor of row 2.

20. *(d)* After rearrangement we get,

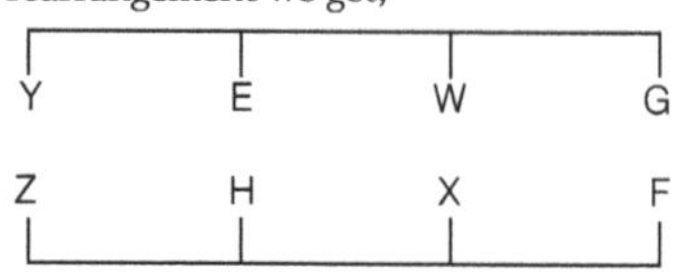

X will face W.

21. *(d)* G, F and Z, Y are sitting at extreme ends of both the lines.

Solutions (Q. Nos. 22-27) *From the given information, the arrangement*

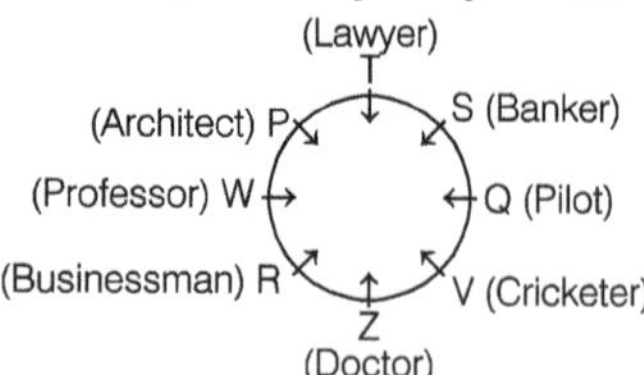

22. *(b)* S, the banker sits exactly between T and Q.

23. *(e)* V, the cricketer sits third to the right of the professor.

24. *(a)* R is an immediate neighbour of the professor, is true.

25. *(a)* Businessman is sitting third to the left of pilot.

26. *(a)* Z is a doctor.

27. *(e)* Only two people - T and P are sitting between the banker and W when counted in anti-clockwise direction from banker.

Solutions (Q. Nos. 28-32) *From given information, the arrangement is as follows*

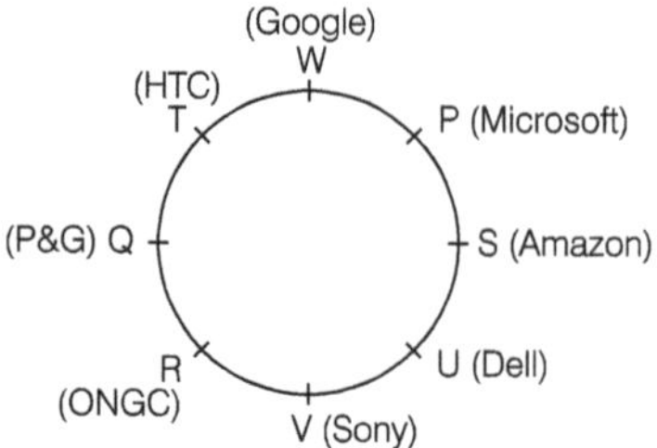

28. *(a)* As, V $\xrightarrow{\text{opposite}}$ W (Google)

and, Q $\xrightarrow{\text{opposite}}$ S (Amazon)

Similarly, R $\xrightarrow{\text{opposite}}$ P (Microsoft)

29. (*b*) Q works in P & G.

30. (*a*) P is sitting third to the left of Q.

31. (*e*) R sits second to the right of the one who works in HTC.

32. (*b*) S works in Amazon.

Solutions (Q. Nos. 33-38) *According to the given information, arrangement is as follows*

Person	Floor number	Distance
N	7	3300 m
M	6	4700 m
R	5	850 m
Q	4	1300 m
S	3	2200 m
P	2	4000 m
O	1	2800 m

33. (*a*) Three people live between S and N.

34. (*b*) Only S lives between P and the one who runs for 1300 m.

35. (*c*) Except pair, floor number 4-S, all other pairs have three places difference between the elements.

36. (*c*) N lives on floor number 7 is true.

37. (*e*) Here, M covered the distance = 4700 m

Given, distance covered by B and M = 5300 m

$\therefore$ B ran alone = 5300 − 4700 = 600 m

38. (*e*) S runs for 2200 m.

Solutions (Q. Nos. 39-43) *Following table can be drawn from given information.*

Boxes	Articles
T	16
P	2
V	6
S	20
Q	9
R	15
U	11

39. (*b*) There are two boxes between S and U.

40. (*c*) There are 20 articles in box S.

41. (*a*) Q-16 is not correct.

42. (*b*) Box T is immediately above the box which contains 2 articles is correct.

43. (*e*) Box P contains 2 articles.

Solutions (Q. Nos. 44-49) *According to the given information, sitting arrangement of all the seven friends is given below*

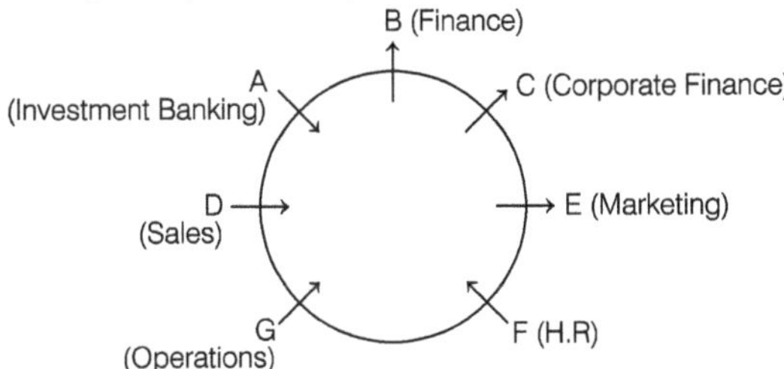

44. (*a*) B works in Finance Department.

45. (*d*) The person working in Sales Department is D and B is second to the left of D.

46. (*d*) The person who sits to the immediate right of E is F who works in HR Department.

47. (*b*) Clearly, E i.e. the person who works in Marketing Department sits between C and the person who works for HR Department i.e. F.

48. (*c*) The persons who work in Marketing and Investment Banking Departments are E and A, respectively and the person who sit between them are C and B when counted from the left of E.

49. (*a*) The person who works for operations department is G. Therefore, number of persons who sit between G and A, when counted from right hand side of A is one i.e. D.

Solutions (Q. Nos. 50-52)

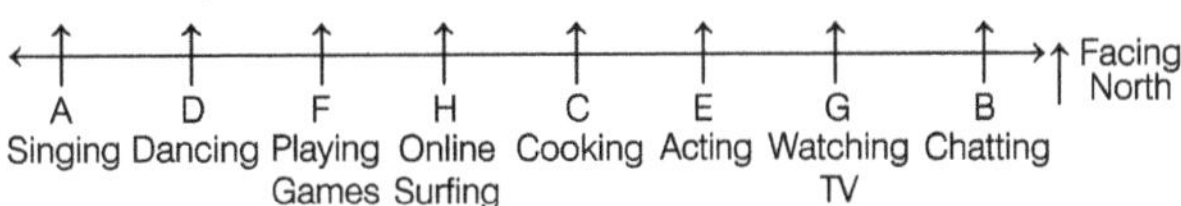

50. (*d*) Second from the right end is G. And, second to the left of G is C whose hobby is cooking.

51. (*b*) The member whose hobby is dancing is D and D is related to G whose hobby is watching TV.

52. (*d*) B-Playing games is not the correct combination.

Solutions (Q. Nos. 53-57) *Following table can be drawn from given information.*

Person	Colour	Floor
U	Pink	8
Y	Grey	7
S	Yellow	6
Z	Blue	5
T	Purple	4
V	Orange	3
X	Green	2
W	Red	1

53. (*c*) Z lives on fifth floor.

54. (*d*) Six floors are below the floor on which Y lives.

55. (*a*) X lives on second floor.

56. (*a*) V likes Orange colour.

57. (*c*) T likes Purple colour and lives on fourth floor is true.

Solutions (Q. Nos. 58-62)

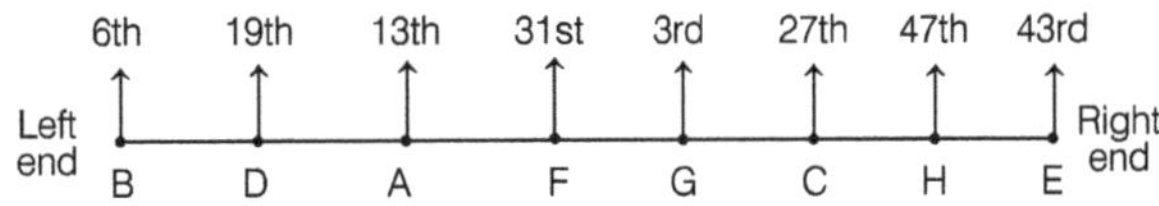

58. (*d*) E lives on 43rd floor.

59. (*b*) Only one person i.e. only D sits between A and B.

60. (*c*) D lives on 19th floor.

61. (*b*) G lives on 3rd floor and F sits to the immediate left of G.

62. (*a*) A sits 3rd to the left of C.

Solutions (Q. Nos. 63-67) *According to the information, the seating arrangement is as following,*

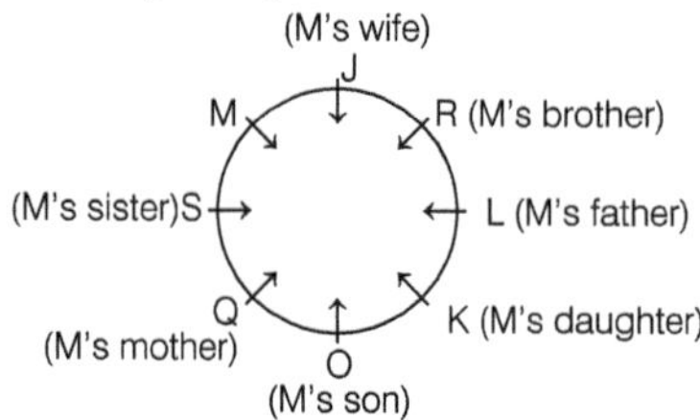

63. *(b)* M sits second to the right of R.

64. *(c)* 'None' sits between K and L, when counted from the left of L.

65. *(e)* Since S is M's sister and L is M's father, so clearly S is the daughter of L.

66. *(c)* R is the brother of M and K is the daughter of M, so K is niece of R.

67. *(e)* J is the wife of M.

Solutions (Q. Nos. 68-74) *According to the given information, the sitting arrangement of ten people in two parallel rows is as follows*

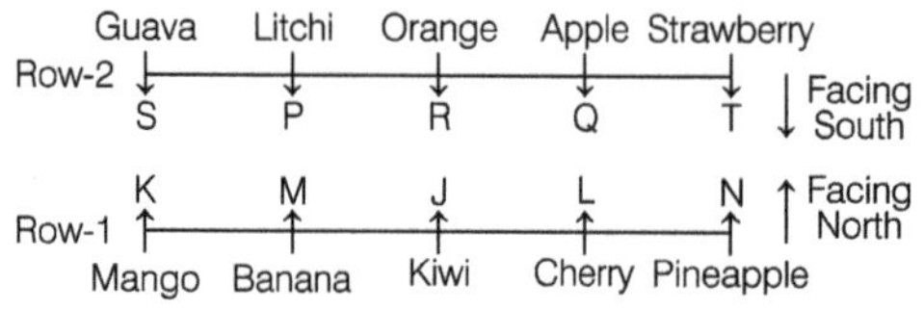

68. *(a)* Except J, all others are sitting at extreme ends of line.

69. *(b)* The one who likes Guava is facing K.

70. *(a)* N is facing T.

71. *(d)* One of J's immediate neighbours faces the one who likes Litchi, is true regarding J.

72. *(d)* M faces the one who sits third to right of T.

73. *(b)* S is third to right of Q.

74. *(a)* Except Orange—Kiwi, all others are having gap of two fruits between them.

Solutions (Q. Nos. 75-79) *According to the given information,*

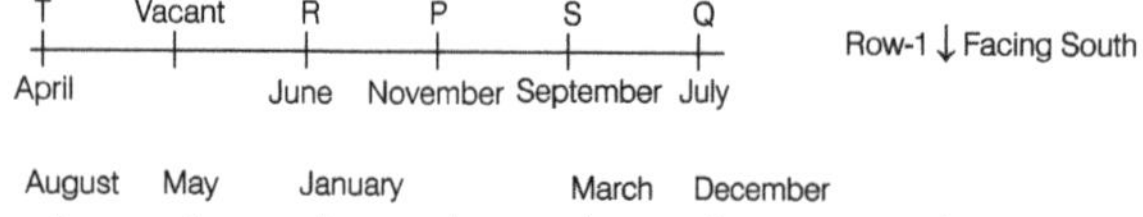

75. *(e)* Q's birthday is in July.

76. *(b)* A faces R, whose birthday is in June.

77. *(e)* Third seat to the right of D is vacant.

78. *(e)* Q sits second to the left of P, whose birthday is in November.

79. *(b)* T sits adjacent to vacant seat, is true.

Solutions (Q. Nos. 80-84) *According to the question the arrangement is as follows*

Persons	Floor	Watch
R	7	Casio
S	6	Tissot
Q	5	Fastrack
U	4	Seiko
T	3	Fossil
P	2	Omega
V	1	Citizen

80. *(b)* Q lives immediately below S.

81. *(d)* Three people — Q, S and R live above the one who likes Seiko.

82. *(c)* T likes Fossil.

83. *(b)* Q live on 5th floor.

84. *(b)* Only one person—S, lives between the one who likes Fastrack and the one who likes Casio.

Solutions (Q. Nos. 85-89)

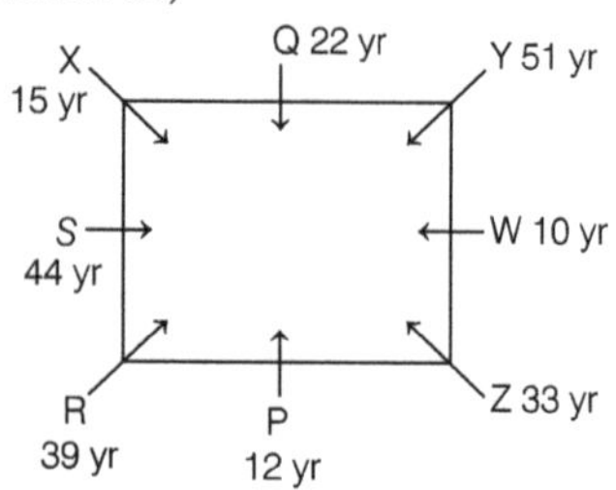

85. *(e)* No one is 9 yr old.

86. *(d)* W sits immediate left of the one who is 51 yr old and Q sits second to the right of W.

87. *(b)* Two people sit between the one who is of 15 yr old and the one who is 12 yr old.

88. *(a)* X sits diagonally opposite to Z.

89. *(d)* R sits immediate right of S.

Solutions (Q. Nos. 90-93) *According to the given information the arrangement is as follows*

Box	Number of Chocolates
B	175
D	250
E	190
F	210
A	280
C	119

90. *(a)* Box F contains 210 chocolates.

91. *(d)* Required number of chocolates = 119 + 190 = 309

92. *(b)* Box B is placed at topmost position.

93. *(d)* Four boxes are placed between box B and the box which has 119 chocolates.

Solutions (Q. Nos. 94-98)

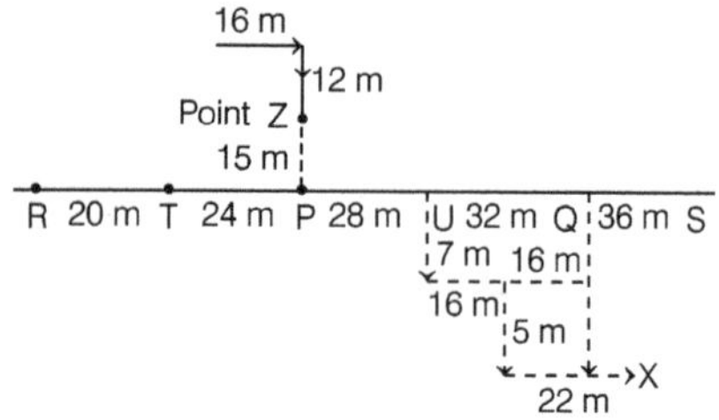

94. (*d*) Two cars U and Q are parked between cars P and S.

95. (*e*) Required distance = $\sqrt{(12^2 + 6^2)} = 6\sqrt{5}$ m

96. (*c*) 44 m East and 15 m North.

97. (*b*) 12 m South and 30 m West.

98. (*d*) According to the question,

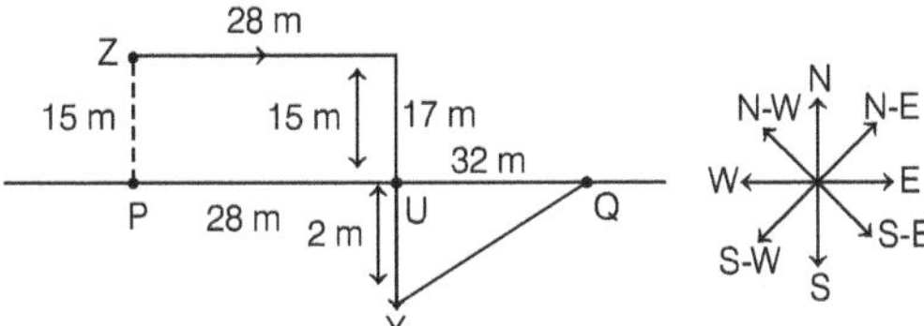

Hence, the car Q is in North-East direction of car Y.

Solutions (Q. Nos. 99-103) *Following table can be drawn from given information.*

Colour	Box	Number of Toffees
Red	Q	32
Blue	M	15
Green	S	18
Yellow	N	24
White	O	10
Pink	P	21

99. (*a*) Colour of the Box which has 10 toffees is White.

100. (*d*) Box Q is placed at top and 32 toffees are there in it.

101. (*d*) Four boxes are placed between Q and the box which is of Pink colour.

102. (*a*) Box S is placed just above box N.

103. (*a*) The box which is placed just above M has maximum number of toffees.

Solutions (Q. Nos. 104-108) *Following table can be drawn from given information.*

Chocolate	Position	Container
Bournville	7	F
Snickers	6	G
Perk	5	D
Dairy Milk	4	L
Kit Kat	3	O
Temptation	2	B
Galaxy	1	K

104. (*e*) 7-Bournville

105. (*c*) D is exactly between G and L.

106. (*c*) Temptation is in container B.

107. (*c*) As, Bournville - F First from top
Galaxy - K First from bottom
and Snickers - G Second from top
Temptation - B Second from bottom
Similarly, Perk - D Third from top
Kit Kat - O Third from bottom

108. (*e*) F $\rightarrow$ Top, L $\rightarrow$ Middle, K $\rightarrow$ Bottom

Solutions (Q. Nos. 109-113) *Following table can be drawn from given information.*

Friends	Colour	Floor
Q	Red	9
P	Brown	8
V	Yellow	7
R	Green	6
Vacant	–	5
S	Pink	4
U	Black	3
T	Grey	2
Vacant	–	1

109. (*e*) Both S and T stay between vacant floor and U.

110. (*a*) None

111. (*c*) 7th Floor belongs to V.

112. (*c*) No one stay on 5th floor, because the floor is vacant.

113. (*a*) No one stay between S and R, because the fllor is vacant.

Solutions (Q. Nos. 114-118) *Following table can be drawn from given information.*

Person	Floor	Fast Food	Drink
Q	7	Sandwich	Pepsi
P	6	Bada-Pao	Miranda
U	5	Dosa	Coca-Cola
S	4	Idali	Frooti
T	3	Chicken Baguette	Limca
V	2	Burger	Thumps Up
R	1	Bread Chaat	Sprite

114. (*b*) The one who likes Miranda likes Bada-pao.

115. (*e*) The one who likes Coca-cola likes Dosa.

116. (*d*) T likes Limca.

117. (*c*) Two persons live between the one who likes Sprite and the one who likes Idali.

118. (*d*) The one who likes Bada-Pao is different from others because all other lives on odd numbered floor.

Solutions (Q. Nos. 119-123) *Following table can be drawn from given information.*

Shelves	Boxes	Area of the box	Colour	Width of the shelf
7	5-Star	81	Pink	21
6	Bournville	289	Purple	17
5	Kitkat	169	Orange	5
4	Dairy milk	64	White	9
3	Silk	144	Black	15
2	Perk	49	Blue	11
1	Munch	25	Green	35

119. (*b*) The colour of required box is Orange.

120. (*e*) The area of the box of Bourniville is 289.

121. (*c*) Silk - 3 - Black - 144 - 15 is the correct combination.

122. *(a)* Three boxes are placed between the boxes of kitkat and munch.

123. *(a)* Required difference = 17 − 15 = 2

Solutions (Q. Nos. 124-128) *From the given information,*

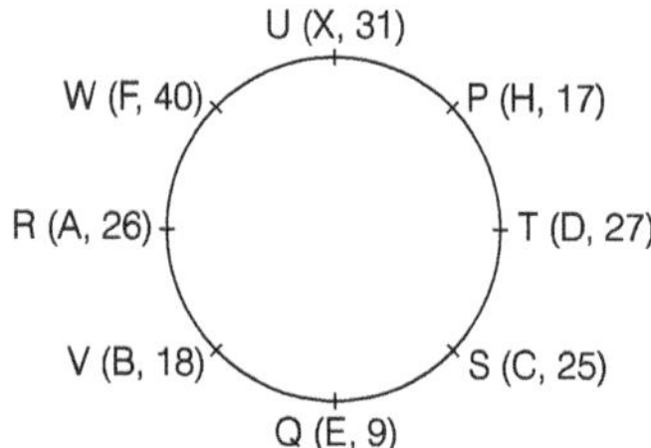

124. *(b)* W is the oldest.

125. *(b)* Required sum = 27 + 18 + 9 = 54 yr.

126. *(b)* T is wearing the shoes of brand D and U is second to the right of T.

127. *(e)* R is wearing the shoes of brand A.

128. *(a)* R is sitting opposite to T, and W and V are immediate neighbours of R. So, the sum of ages of W and V = 40 + 18 = 58 yr.

Solutions (Q. Nos. 129-133) *From the given information,*

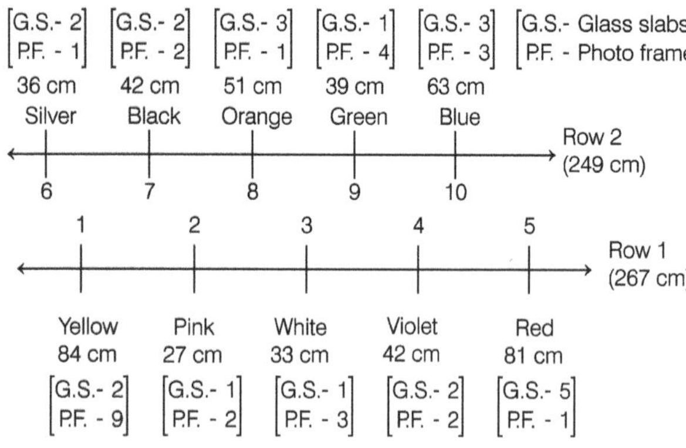

129. *(c)* In Row 2, total length given = 249 cm
Total length of glass slabs and photo frames given = 231
Therefore, spare length = $(249-231)\text{cm} = 18\,\text{cm}$
Hence, three more photo frames can be adjust in row-2.

130. *(e)* Colour of shelf-2 is Pink.

131. *(b)* Total number glass slabs of Silver, Black and Red shelves
$= (2+2+5) = 9$

132. *(c)* Total length of Pink, Orange and Blue shelves
$= (27+51+63)$
$= 141\,\text{cm}$

133. *(b)* Silver shelf contains 1 photo frame.
White shelf contains 3 photo frames.
Therefore, total number of photo frames in Black shelf
$= 2+1+3$
$= 6$
Total length of Black shelf = $(2\times15+6\times6)\text{cm}$
$= (30+36)\text{cm}$
$= 66\text{ cm}$

TYPE 03

Based on Sequential Order of Event

In this type of puzzles some clues are given regarding the occurrence of certain events. The candidate is required to analyse the given information, frame the right sequence and then answer the questions accordingly.

DIRECTIONS ~ (Ex. Nos. 23-27) *Study the following information carefully and answer the given questions.*
« IBPS RRBs Officer 2016

Sagar sells mobiles of seven different companise viz. Samsung, HTC, Lenovo, Intex, Micromax, Nokia and Oppo starting from Monday and ending on Sunday, but not necessarily in the same order.

Sagar sold HTC on Monday. He sold only three mobiles between HTC and Samsung. He does not sell any mobile between the day he sold Samsung and Lenovo. He sold only two mobiles between Lenovo and Oppo. He sold Micromax mobiles the day immediately before the day he sold Oppo mobiles. He sold Intex on one of the days after Oppo, but not on Sunday.

***Ex* 23** On which day Sagar sold Micromax?
(a) Thursday (b) Tuesday
(c) Friday (d) Saturday
(e) Wednesday

***Ex* 24** How many mobiles did Sagar sell between HTC and Lenovo?
(a) Four (b) Two
(c) One (d) None
(e) Three

***Ex* 25** Which of the following is not true as per the given arrangement?
(a) Sagar sells mobiles of anyone company between Samsung and Nokia.
(b) Sagar sells Intex on Thursday.
(c) Sagar did not sell mobiles of any other company between Oppo and Intex.
(d) All the given statements are true.
(e) Sagar sells Lenovo on Friday.

***Ex* 26** Four of the following five are alike in a certain way based on the given arrangement and thus form a group. Which is the one that does not belong to that group?
(a) Nokia-Friday
(b) Samsung-Thursday
(c) Micromax-Monday
(d) Intex-Wednesday
(e) Oppo-Tuesday

***Ex* 27** Which mobiles did Sagar sell on Sunday?
(a) Nokia (b) Lenovo
(c) Micromax (d) None of these
(e) Oppo

Solution (Ex. Nos. 23-27) Following table can be drawn from given information.

Day	Mobile
Monday	HTC
Tuesday	Micromax
Wednesday	Oppo
Thursday	Intex
Friday	Samsung
Saturday	Lenovo
Sunday	Nokia

23. (*b*) Sagar sold Micromax on Tuesday.

24. (*a*) Sagar sell four mobile between HTC and Lenovo.

25. (*e*) Sagar sells Lenovo on Friday is not true.

26. (*a*) Samsung → Thursday + 1 day = Friday (Actual day)

Micromax → Monday + 1 day = Tuesday (Actual day)

Intex → Wednesday + 1 day = Thursday (Actual day)

Oppo → Tuesday + 1 day = Wednesday (Actual day)

Nokia → Friday + 1 day = Saturday (But actual day is Sunday)

27. (*a*) Sagar sells Nokia on Sunday.

DIRECTIONS ~ (Ex. Nos. 28-33) *Study the following information carefully and answer the given questions.* « SBI PO (Pre) 2016

Seven people, namely K, L, M, N, O, P and Q have to attend a concert, but not necessarily in the same order, on seven different months (of the same year) namely January, February, April, May, June, September and November. Each of them also likes a different movie namely X-Men, Transformers, Frozen, Minions, Shrek, Tangled and Rio, but not necessarily in the same order.

M will attend a concert in a month, which has 31 days.

Only two people will attend a concert between M and the one who likes Frozen. The one who likes Frozen will attend a concert on one of the months after M. Only two people will attend a concert between the one who likes Frozen and the one who likes Transformers. The one who likes Transfromers will attend a concert in a month which has 31 days. K will attend a concert immediately after M. Only three people will attend concert between K and the one who likes Tangled. Only one person will attend a concert between the one who likes Tangled and L. Only two people will attend a concert between L and the one who like Rio. The one who likes X-Men will attend a concert immediately before the one who likes Shrek. Only one person will attend a concert between the one who likes Shrek and P. Only three people will attend a concert between Q and O. Q will not attend a concert in a month which has 30 days.

Ex 28 Who amongst the following likes X-Men?
(a) M (b) K
(c) O (d) L
(e) Q

Ex 29 How many people will attend a concert after M?
(a) More than three (b) One
(c) None (d) Two
(e) Three

Ex 30 Which of the following represents the people who will attend a concert immediately before and immediately after O?
(a) M, N (b) K, N (c) L, N (d) P, N
(e) N, M

Ex 31 As per the given arrangement, January is related to Q and May is related to K following a certain pattern, which of the following is April related to following the same pattern?
(a) P (b) O (c) M (d) L
(e) N

Ex 32 Which of the following represents the month in which K will attend a concert?
(a) September (b) June
(c) November (d) April
(e) Cannot be determined

Ex 33 Who amongst the following likes Minions?
(a) M
(b) L
(c) P
(d) Other than those given as options
(e) K

Solutions (Ex. Nos. 28-33) From the given information, arrangement is as follows

People	Months	Movies
P	January	Tangled
Q	February	X-Men
L	April	Shrek
M	May	Transformers
K	June	Minions
O	September	Rio
N	November	Frozen

28. (*e*) Q likes X-Men.

29. (*e*) Three people will attend a concert after M.

30. (*b*) K and N attend a concert immediately before and immediately after O.

31. (*c*) January → (P+1) Q; May → (M+1) K and April → (L+1) M

32. (*b*) K will attend a concert in June.

33. (*e*) K likes Minions.

DIRECTIONS ~ (Ex. Nos. 34-38) *Study the following information carefully and answer the questions given below:* « SBI Clerk 2020

Eight persons were born in four different months i.e. January, March, June and September and on two different dates i.e. 8 the and 15th of the same year. S was born on 8th in one of the months having 30 days. Only three persons were born between S and P. R and T were born in the same month. R was born after P. U was born immediately before P. Number of persons were born before R is same as number of persons were born after V. Q was born before W.

Ex 34 Who among the following was born on 8th of January?
(a) Q (b) R (c) P (d) T
(e) None of these

Ex 35 Who among the following was born between T and V?
(a) R (b) Q (c) P (d) S
(e) None of these

Ex 36 Who among the following was born in the same month as U?
(a) W (b) Q (c) P (d) V
(e) None of these

Ex 37 Four of the following five are alike in a certain way and hence form a group which of the following does not belong to the group?
(a) T-V (b) P-T (c) W-T (d) S-R
(e) V-U

Ex 38 How many persons were born before V?
(a) One (b) Two
(c) Three (d) Four
(e) More than four

Solutions (Ex. Nos. 34-38)

Months	Date	Person
January (31)	8	Q
	15	U
March (31)	8	P
	15	V
June (30)	8	R
	15	T
September (30)	8	S
	15	W

34. (*a*) Q was born on 8th January.
35. (*a*) R was born between T and V.
36. (*b*) Q was born in the same month as U i.e. January.
37. (*b*) Except P-T, in all other pairs both the persons were born on same date.
38. (*c*) Three persons were born before V.

Practice CORNER 11.3

DIRECTIONS ~ (Q. Nos. 1-5) *Study the given information carefully and answer the given questions.* « IBPS Clerk 2018

Seven persons A, B, C, D, E, F and G are watching movies on different days of the week (starting on Monday and ending on Sunday) not necessarily in the same order.

B is going to watch movie on Tuesday. F is going to watch movie on adjacent day of B. There are three days gap between the days on which F and A are going to watch movie. G is going to watch movie just after D. There are as many persons are watching movie between A and G, same as between D and C. C is watching movie before D, but not just before.

1. Who among the following is going to watch movie on Wednesday?
(a) B (b) C
(c) F (d) E
(e) None of these

2. Who among the following person is going to watch movie just after A?
(a) C (b) D
(c) F (d) G
(e) None of these

3. If F and G interchange their days of watching movie, then on which day G is watching movie?
(a) Monday (b) Wednesday
(c) Friday (d) Saturday
(e) None of these

4. C is watching movie on which day?
(a) Friday (b) Saturday
(c) Wednesday (d) Thursday
(e) Tuesday

5. How many persons are watching movie between B and A?
(a) Two (b) Three (c) One (d) Four
(e) None of these

DIRECTIONS ~ (Q. Nos. 6-10) *Study the following information carefully and answer the questions given below.* « RBI Office Assistant 2020

Eight persons i.e. P, Q, R, S, T, U, V, W attend meeting in different months i.e. January, March, April, May, July, August, September, October in same year, but not necessarily in same order.

Three persons attend meeting between T and P who attend meeting in the month of 30 days. W attend meeting before V and after R. There are as many persons attend meeting before P as after Q. U attend meeting before S and after Q. S attend meeting before V and W who doesn't attend meeting in May.

6. Who among the following attend meeting in July?
(a) P (b) Q (c) R (d) W
(e) None of these

7. There are as many persons who attend meeting before W as after ____?
(a) P (b) Q (c) V (d) R
(e) None of these

8. How many persons attend meeting before U?
(a) Two (b) Three (c) Four (d) One
(e) None of these

9. In which of the following month V attend meeting?
(a) January (b) July
(c) August (d) October
(e) None of these

10. Four of the following five are alike in certain way and hence form a group, find the one which does not belong to that group?

(a) R (b) Q
(c) T (d) U
(e) W

DIRECTIONS ~ (Q. Nos. 11-15) *Study the following information carefully and answer the questions given below.* « IBPS RRB PO 2019

Nine persons i.e. P, Q, R, S, T, U, V, W, X were born on different months i.e. January, March, April, May, July, August, September, October, November but not necessarily in same order.

Four persons were born between P and T. P was born before T. Q was born in the month of 30 days after July. T was born after Q and before R. There were as many persons born before X as after R. One person was born between U and V. S was born before U and after W.

11. How many persons were born between X and V?

(a) Two (b) Three
(c) One (d) Four
(e) More than four

12. In which of the following month S was born?

(a) March (b) April
(c) June (d) October
(e) None of these

13. Who among the following was born in August?

(a) R (b) S
(c) T (d) P
(e) None of these

14. Four of the following five are alike in certain way based form a group, find the one which does not belong to that group?

(a) R (b) S
(c) T (d) U
(e) V

15. If W is related to April, V is related to July then, P is related to which of the following?

(a) March (b) May
(c) June (d) August
(e) October

DIRECTIONS ~ (Q. Nos. 16-20) *Study the following information carefully and answer the questions given below.* « IBPS SO 2016

Seven friends, namely P, Q, R, S, T, U and V visit seven different countries namely Japan, Germany, China, India, Nepal, Australia and Malaysia, not necessarily in the same order, starting from Monday to Sunday (of the same week).

R visits on Thursday. Only two people visit between R and the one who visits Germany. Only four people visit between the one who visits Germany and V. The one who visits Malaysia visits immediately before V. Only two people visit between the one who visits Malaysia and P. S visits on one of the days after the one who visits Malaysia. U visits immediately after the one who visit Japan. U does not visit Malaysia. Only three people visit between the one who visits Japan and the one who visits Nepal. The one who visits Australia visits immediately before the one who visits China. Q does not visit on Monday.

16. On which of the following days does U visits a country?

(a) Friday (b) Saturday
(c) Sunday (d) Wednesday
(e) Tuesday

17. Which of the following is true about T?

(a) All the given options are true.
(b) T visits on Friday.
(c) T visits China.
(d) Only three people visit between T and R.
(e) T visits immediately before P.

18. Who amongst the following visits India?

(a) S (b) T
(c) P (d) G
(e) R

19. As per the given arrangement, P is related to the one who visits Japan in a certain way and V is related to the one who visits Nepal in the same way. To which of the following is R related to in the same way?

(a) The one who visits Australia.
(b) The one who visits China.
(c) The one who visits India.
(d) The one who visits Malaysia.
(e) The one who visits Germany.

20. Four of the following five are alike in a certain way and thus form a group as per the given arrangement. Which of the following does not belong to that group?

(a) U-Friday (b) Q-Thursday
(c) S-Saturday (d) V-Sunday
(e) T-Tuesday

DIRECTIONS ~ (Q. Nos. 21-25) *Study the following information carefully and answer the questions given below.* « IBPS PO (Pre) 2017

L, M, N, O, P, Q and R are seven employees who are working in the same company. They attend meeting in different departments *viz.* administrative, Security, Finance and HR department on different days from Monday to Sunday but not necessarily in the same order. One employee attends only one meeting and only one meeting is held on each day. There are two employees who attend meeting in Administrative, Security, HR department and only one employee attends meeting in Finance department.

L attends meeting on Thursday. There are two persons who attend meeting between L and the person who attends meeting in HR department. There are three persons who attend meeting between the persons who attend meeting in Administrative department and the one who attends meeting in Finance department. The one who attends meeting in Administrative department attends before the one who attends in Finance department. The one who attends meeting in Finance department does not attend on Saturday. The number of persons who attend meeting between L and the one who attend meeting in Finance department is same as the number of persons who attend meeting between O and the one who attends meeting in security department. The one who attends meeting in Security department attend before O. O does not attend meeting in HR department. Q attends meeting on the day immediately before the day on which L attends meeting. O does not attend meeting on the day just after the day on which L attends meeting.The number of persons who attend meeting between L and P is same as the number of persons who attend meeting between L and R. P attends meeting in one of the day before the day on which R attends meeting. N attends meeting in Administrative department. R does not attend meeting in Security department.

21. Who among the following person attend meeting on Friday?

(a) O (b) M (c) P (d) N
(e) R

22. Which of the following combinations of 'Person-Day' is true with respect to the given arrangement?

(a) R-Friday (b) M-Saturday
(c) Q-Thursday (d) P-Friday
(e) P-Tuesday

23. L attends meeting in which of the following department?

(a) Security (b) HR
(c) Administrative (d) Finance
(e) Either (a) or (b)

24. In this arrangement, Q is related to Monday, L is related to Security, then N is related to?

(a) Thursday
(b) Wednesday
(c) None of the given options is true
(d) HR
(e) Sunday

25. How many persons attend meeting between P and O?

(a) 3 (b) 4 (c) 2 (d) 1
(e) None of these

DIRECTIONS ~ (Q. Nos. 26-30) *Study the given information carefully to answer the given questions.* « UBI PO 2016

Seven people P, Q, R, S, T, U and V launched products in seven different months (of the same year), namely January, February, May, June, September, November and December but not necessarily in the same order. Each of them also likes a different state, namely Gujarat, Punjab, Odisha, Haryana, Assam, Sikkim and Telangana but not necessarily in the same order.

R launched the product in a month which has 31 days. Only three people launched the products between R and the one who likes Haryana. T launched the product immediately before the one who likes Haryana. T did not launch the product in a month which has less than 30 days. P launched the product immediately before the one who likes Odisha. P launched the product in a month which has 31 days. Only two people launched products between the one who likes Odisha and V. The one who likes Gujarat launched the products in a month which has more than 30 days but not in January. V likes neither Gujarat nor Sikkim. Q launched the product in a month immediately before the one who likes Sikkim. The one who likes Punjab launched the product after the one who likes Sikkim. U launched the product in a month which has lees than 30 days. The one who likes Assam launched the product in one of the months before U.

26. How many people launched the products between the months in which U and T launched the products?

(a) Two (b) More than three
(c) Three (d) One
(e) None

27. If V launched the product in May, then who amongst the following launched the product immediately before V?

(a) The one who likes Sikkim
(b) The one who likes Assam
(c) R
(d) T
(e) U

28. Four of the following five are alike in a certain way based on the given arrangement and hence form a group. Which of the following does not belong to that group?

(a) VT (b) RT (c) PS (d) PU (e) QU

29. Which of the following represents the people who launched the products in May and November respectively?

(a) P, S (b) M, R (c) R, T (d) T, Q
(e) S, U

30. Which of the following states does S like?

(a) Telangana (b) Haryana
(c) Odisha (d) Sikkim
(e) Other than those given as options

DIRECTIONS ~ (Q. Nos. 31-35) *Study the given information carefully to answer the given questions.* « SBI PO 2017

C, D, E, F, W, X, Y and Z have to attend a wedding in January, April, September and December months of the same year. In each month the wedding is on either the 11th or the 24th of the month. Not more than two of the given people have to attend a wedding in the same month. W has to attend a wedding on the 11th of the month which has only 30 days. Only three people have to attend a wedding between W and Y. C and Y have to attend a wedding neither on the same date nor in the same month. C does not have to attend a wedding in April. Only two people have to attend a wedding between C and F. X and F have to attend a wedding on the same date. D has to attend a wedding on one of the days before X. Only one person has to attend a wedding between D and E. Less than four people have to attend a wedding between E and Z.

31. How many people have to attend a wedding between F and Z?

(a) Two (b) Three
(c) None (d) More than three
(e) One

32. When does X have to attend a wedding?

(a) April 24 (b) Cannot be determined
(c) January 11 (d) September 24
(e) December 11

33. If all the people are made to attend the wedding in alphabetical order starting from January 11 and ending on December 24, the schedule of how many people will remain unchanged?

(a) One (b) Two
(c) Five (d) None
(e) Three

34. Who among the following has to attend a wedding before Y?

(a) C and X (b) Only W
(c) None (d) F and W
(e) Only F

35. As per the given arrangement, four of the following five are alike in a certain way and so form a group. Which of the following does not belong to the group?

(a) W (b) F (c) Z (d) Y
(e) X

DIRECTIONS ~ (Q. Nos. 36-39) *Study the following information carefully and answer the below questions.*

« IBPS PO 2019

Ten person namely - P, Q, R, S, T, U, V, W, Y and Z attends a seminar in five different month *viz.*- April, June, August, September and October. Seminar on each month scheduled at two different dates 12th and 13th. One person attends seminar only on one day of any of the month not necessary in same order.

V attends seminar on any day before R but after Q's seminar. At least two person attends seminar before S. Z attends seminar on any of the month having 30 days. S and Z attends seminar on different dates of different month. Number of person attending seminar between V and T is one more than number of person attending seminar between Q and U.

Two person attends seminar between P and Z. P and Y attends seminar in August. There is only one seminar after R's seminar. S neither attends seminar with R nor with Q. Number of person attending seminar between S and Z is same as number of person attending seminar between W and Y. W neither attends seminar with Z nor attends at last. At least two person attends seminar between U and R. Z doesn't attends seminar on 12th.

36. How many person attends seminar between R and Y?

(a) Two (b) Three
(c) Four (d) One
(e) None

37. Who among the following person attends seminar with S?

(a) W (b) V
(c) U (d) T
(e) None of these

38. Find odd among all five pairs.

(a) RZ (b) SQ (c) UP (d) RT
(e) ZP

39. Who attends seminar just after W?

(a) Q (b) V (c) T (d) S
(e) None of these

DIRECTIONS ~ (Q. Nos. 40-44) *Study the following information carefully and answer the below questions.*

« RBI Officers Grade B 2016

Seven flights are bound to fly to different cities *viz.* Dubai, Sydney, London, Paris, Zurich, Madrid and Rome from Monday to Sunday of the same week. Each flight departs at a different time *viz.* 4 pm, 5 pm, 6 pm, 7 pm, 8 pm, 9 pm and 10 pm, in the night on their respective days. None of the information given is necessarily in the same order.

- The flight to Dubai departs on Wednesday but neither at 5 pm nor at 8 pm.
- There is only one day between the flight to Dubai and the flight which departs at 10 pm.
- There are only three days between the flights which departs at 5 pm and the flight to Rome.
- The flight which departs at 5 pm departs before the Rome bound flight.
- The flight which departs on Monday neither departs at 5 pm nor does it fly to Sydney.
- The flight which departs on Saturday leaves at a time before the flight which departs on Tuesday (i.e. if the Tuesday flight departs at 7 pm, then the flight on Saturday departs at 6 pm, 5 or 4 pm.)
- The flight to London departs on the day immediately before the day on which the 8 pm flight departs.
- The flights to Paris departs at 7 pm.
- There is a difference of 2 h between the Zurich bound flight and the London bound flight (i.e. if a London bound flight departs at 4 pm, then the Zurich bound flight departs at either 2 pm or 6 pm on its respective day).

40. Which flight departs on the day immediately after the day on which the London bound flight departs?

(a) The flight which departs at 7 pm.
(b) The flight which departs on Thursday.
(c) None as the Paris bound flight departs on Saturday.
(d) The flight which departs at 5 pm.
(e) The Zurich bound flight.

41. At what time does the Sydney bound flight depart?

(a) 9 pm (b) 10 pm
(c) 6 pm (d) 5 pm
(e) 4 pm

42. Which flight departs exactly 1 h after the Sydney bound flight on its scheduled day?

(a) The flight which departs on Friday
(b) The flight which departs on Tuesday
(c) The flight which departs at 10 pm
(d) The London bound flight
(e) The Rome bound flight

43. The Dubai bound flight reaches Dubai in 4 h after its start. If the flight stops over at New Delhi at exactly half the total time, at what time would the fight arrive in New Delhi?

(a) 8 pm (b) 11 pm
(c) 7 pm (d) 6 pm
(e) 12 mid-night

44. Which of the following flights departs at 10 pm?
(a) The flight which departs on Friday.
(b) The Zurich bound flight.
(c) The flight which departs on Friday.
(d) The Paris bound flight.
(e) The flight departing on the day immediately before the Sydney bound flight.

DIRECTIONS ~ (Q. Nos. 45-48) *Study the following information carefully and answer the questions given below.* « IBPS Clerk (Mains) 2018

Twelve persons are born on three different dates 5, 12, 21 of four different months *viz.* March, May, September and November.

Only one person is born on one date of a month. J was born on 5 of month having 30 days. Only three persons were born between J and H. H does not born on an even date of a month. As many as persons born after H as born before A. Five persons born between A and D. Only two persons born between F and E. C born on an even date but immediately after K. Six persons born between C and B. E born immediately before B. M born on an even date after L but before G.

45. How many persons born between C and F?
(a) Two (b) More than three
(c) Three (d) One
(e) Now

46. Who among the following is born immediately before G?
(a) M (b) L (c) J (d) C
(e) D

47. H born on which of the following day?
(a) 21 May (b) 21 March
(c) 5 September (d) 5 March
(e) 5 May

48. Which of the following statements is true?
(a) J and G both were born in same month.
(b) F was born on odd date.
(c) G was born on 5th.
(d) B was born on 21st.
(e) All are true.

DIRECTIONS ~ (Q. Nos. 49-51) *Study the following information carefully and answer the questions given below.* « IBPS Clerk (Mains) 2017

There are five doctors of different types of viz., Cardiologist, Nephrologist, Psychiatrist, General Physician and Dental Surgeon in a hospital but not necessarily in same order. They attend their patients at different timing in a single day. The duration of their meeting with the patient is different.

The total duration of the meeting with the patients by all doctors is of 11 hour. There is no gap between the meeting time of all doctors. The duration of meeting either full hour or half an hour but not in one third or one fourth.

The one who is Nephrologist attends their patients from 12:30 to 3pm. The dental surgeon attends their patients immediate before or immediate after the Nephrologist. The meeting hour of dental surgeon with the patients is three hours. The duration of meeting with patients of General physician is more than duration of meeting of Psychiatrist with patients by 1 hour. General Physician attends meeting just after the meeting of Psychiatrist. The general Physician does not attend patients at the last. The Cardiologist attend their patients before the Nephrologist but not immediate before. The duration of meeting of Cardiologist is of 1.5 hours. The timing of Psychiatrist meeting is after 6:00 am.

49. Who among the following attends patients just after the Cardiologist?
(a) General physician
(b) Psychiatrist
(c) Nephrologist
(d) Dental Surgeon
(e) None of these

50. Who among the following attends patients from 3:00-6:00 pm?
(a) Cardiologist (b) Psychiatrist
(c) General physician (d) Dental Surgeon
(e) Nephrologist

51. What is the duration (in hours) of the Psychiatrist's meeting with the patients?
(a) 2.5 h (b) 3 h
(c) 3.5 h (d) 1.5 h
(e) 2 h

DIRECTIONS ~ (Q. Nos. 52-56) *Study the following information carefully and answer the given questions.*

There are seven students – A, B, C, D, E, F and G – who like different subjects *viz.* Hindi, English, Maths, History, Physics, Chemistry and Biology but not necessarily in the same order. They read on different days of the week starting from Monday. They also like different sports, *viz.* Hockey, Cricket, Football, Tennis, Badminton, Baseball and Kho-Kho but not necessarily in the same order.

B, who likes Baseball, reads on the fourth day of the week but neither Hindi nor Biology. Two students read between the days on which B and F read and neither of them read on the 1st day of the week. There is only one student who reads between A and C. But C does not read either on 1st or 3rd day of the week. C likes Cricket sport and reads Hindi. The one who reads Maths on the last day of the week likes Football sport. D does not read on the day either immediately before or immediately after the day on which A read, who doesn't like either Badminton or Hockey or Tennis sport. D does not read History. G reads immediately after C and he likes Hockey sport. E does not like Badminton sport and reads Chemistry. A does not read either Physics or History. The one who reads English takes class immediately after the day when Hindi has been read.

52. Which of the following combinations is definitely false?
(a) C – Cricket – Hindi
(b) A – Kho-Kho –Biology
(c) E – Tennis –Chemistry
(d) F – Cricket – Hindi
(e) None of these

53. Who among the following reads on the 6th day of the week?

(a) The student who likes Kho-Kho sport.
(b) The student who reads Maths.
(c) The student who reads English.
(d) The student who likes Tennis sport .
(e) None of the above

54. Who reads History?

(a) The student who likes Baseball sport.
(b) The student who likes Kho-Kho sport .
(c) The student who likes Badminton sport.
(d) The student who likes Football sport.
(e) None of the above

55. If 'B' is related to 'Cricket' and 'G' is related to 'Football', then which of the following is 'A' related to?

(a) Badminton
(b) Baseball
(c) Tennis
(d) Kho-Kho
(e) None of these

56. Who reads Physics?

(a) The student who reads on fourth day of the week .
(b) The student who reads just before E.
(c) The student who reads just after E.
(d) Cannot be determined
(e) None of the above

DIRECTIONS ~ (Q. Nos. 57-61) *Study the following information carefully and answer the questions given below:* « SBI (PO) 2018

Eight persons B, C, D, E, M, N, O, J were born in different months i.e. January, April, June, October on two different dates 16th or 24th. Only one person was born on one date. They all like different flowers i.e. lily, jasmine, hibiscus, marigold, rose, sunflower, lotus, daffodil but not necessarily in the same order.

B was born in April. Only one person was born between B and the one who like lotus, who was not born in January. One person was born between the ones who like lotus and sunflower. Five persons were born between C and N, who was born after C. N was not the youngest. E was born before O and both of them were born in the same month. No one was born before the one who likes hibiscus. The number of persons born before M is same as the number of persons born after the one who likes lotus. No one is born between B and the one who likes jasmine. D does not like jasmine. D was born before J but not immediately before. Four persons were born between the J, who likes rose and the one who likes marigold. J was born after the one who likes marigold. One of the person born in June likes Lily.

57. Who among the following likes marigold?

(a) D (b) J
(c) N (d) B
(e) None of these

58. Who was born exactly between the one who likes Rose and M?

(a) D (b) J (c) B (d) O
(e) None of these

59. Which of the following flower is liked by D?

(a) Lily (b) Rose
(c) Daffodil (d) Marigold
(e) None of these

60. Which among the following combination is not true?

(a) D- April (b) J- rose
(c) N- sunflower (d) O- June
(e) None of these

61. How many persons were born before O?

(a) Two (b) Six
(c) Five (d) Seven
(e) None of these

DIRECTIONS ~ (Q. Nos. 62-65) *Study the following information carefully and answer the questions given below.* « IBPS Clerk (Mains) 2018

Six persons P, Q, R, S, T and U are born in six different years 1946, 1958, 1963, 1971, 1994, 2006. All of them like different colours Red, Black, Orange, Pink, White, Yellow.

The sum of the ages of S and the one who likes Black colour is 86. The one who likes Pink colour was born in an even numbered year. S does not like Red colour. The one who likes Pink colour is older than the one who likes Black colour. S does not like Pink colour. Q is older than the one who like Pink colour. T likes Orange and was born in an odd numbered year. The sum of the ages of P and the one who likes Yellow colour is 81. U is younger than the one who likes Orange colour. R does not like Yellow colour.

Note *All the calculations of the ages are to be done on the basis of year 2019.*

62. Who among the following likes Red colour?

(a) P (b) U (c) S (d) R
(e) T

63. How many persons born after U?

(a) Two (b) Four
(c) Three (d) One
(e) None

64. Which of the following statement is not correct regarding Q?

(a) Q is younger than S.
(b) Q likes Yellow.
(c) Q is elder to P.
(d) The one who likes White is younger than Q.
(e) All are correct.

65. In which of the following years P was born?

(a) 1946 (b) 1958
(c) 1971 (d) 2006
(e) 1994

Answers / WITH EXPLANATIONS

Solutions (Q. Nos. 1-5) *According to the given information.*

Days	Persons
Monday	F
Tuesday	B
Wednesday	E
Thursday	C
Friday	A
Saturday	D
Sunday	G

1. *(d)* E is going to watch movie on Wednesday.

2. *(b)* D is going to watch movie just after A.

3. *(a)* F is going to watch movie on Monday. So, if F and G interchange their days of watching movie, the G is watching movie on Monday.

4. *(d)* C is watching movie on Thursday.

5. *(a)* Two persons *viz.* E and C are watching movie between B and A.

Solutions (Q.Nos. 6-10) *According to the given information.*

Persons	Months
R	January
Q	March
T	April
U	May
W	July
S	August
P	September
V	October

6. *(d)* W will attend the meeting in July.

7. *(e)* There are as many persons who attend meeting before W as after U.

8. *(b)* Three persons (R, Q and T) attend meeting before U.

9. *(d)* V will attend the meeting in October.

10. *(c)* Except T, all other persons attend the meeting in the month having 31 days.

Solutions (Q. Nos. 11-15) *According to the given information,*

Months	Persons
January	X
March	W
April	P
May	V
July	S
August	U
September	Q
October	T
November	R

11. *(a)* Two persons born between X and V.

12. *(e)* S born in July.

13. *(e)* U born in August.

14. *(a)* Except R, all other persons born in the month of 31 days.

15. *(b)* P is related to May.

Solutions (Q. Nos. 16-20) *On the basis of given information, the combination of friend-day-country is as below.*

Friends	Days	Countries
T	Monday	Germany
P	Tuesday	Japan
U	Wednesday	Australia
R	Thursday	China
Q	Friday	Malaysia
V	Saturday	Nepal
S	Sunday	India

16. *(d)* U visits a country on Wednesday.

17. *(e)* T visits immediately before P, is true.

18. *(a)* S visits India.

19. *(b)* As, P visits Japan itself and V visits Nepal itself. In the same way, R visits China itself.

20. *(a)* Except U—Friday, in all other groups there is a gap of one day between actual day and given day but in U-Friday, there is a gap of two days between actual day and given day.

Solutions (Q. Nos. 21-25) *According to the given information,*

Days	Departments	Employees
Monday	HR	M
Tuesday	Security	P
Wednesday	Administrative	Q
Thursday	Security	L
Friday	Administrative	N
Saturday	HR	R
Sunday	Finance	O

21. *(d)* N attends meeting on Friday.

22. *(e)* "P-Tuesday" is true with respect to given arrangement.

23. *(a)* L attends meeting in Security Departments.

24. *(b)* N is related to Wednesday.

25. *(b)* Four persons attend the meeting between P and O.

Solutions (Q. Nos. 26-30) *According to the given information,*

Months	Persons	States
January (31 days)	R	Assam
February (28/29 days)	U	Telangana
May (31 days)	P	Gujarat
June (30 days)	T	Odisha
September (30 days)	Q	Haryana
November (30 days)	S	Sikkim
December (31 days)	V	Punjab

26. (*d*) Only one person i.e. P launched the products between the months in which U and T launched the products.

27. (*e*) If V launched the product in May, then U launched product immediately before V.

28. (*d*) Except PU, in all other options two persons launched their products between first and second person.

29. (*a*) P and S represents the people who launched the products in May and November respectively.

30. (*d*) S likes Sikkim.

Solutions (Q. Nos. 31-35) *Following table can be drawn from given information.*

Peoples	Dates	Month
Y	11	January
D	24	January
F	11	April
E	24	April
W	11	September
C	24	September
X	11	December
Z	24	December

31. (*d*) 4 people have to attend a wedding between F and Z.

32. (*e*) X attend a wedding on 11 December.

33. (*a*) After arranging in alphabetical order.
C-11-January
D-24-January
E-11-April
F-24-April
W-11-September
X-24-September
Y-11-December
Z-24-December
i.e. Only one W remain unchanged.

34. (*c*) None

35. (*c*) Except Z, all other attend wedding on 11 of the month.

Solutions (Q. Nos. 36-39) *According to the given information,*

Months	Dates	Persons
April (30)	12	W
	13	Q
June (30)	12	S
	13	U
August (31)	12	P
	13	Y
September (30)	12	V
	13	Z
October (31)	12	R
	13	T

36. (*a*) Only two persons attend seminar between R and Y.

37. (*c*) U attends seminar with S.

38. (*e*) Except ZP persons in all other pairs have no seminar between them.

39. (*a*) Q attends seminar just after W.

Solutions (Q. Nos. 40-44) *The given information can be arranged as below*

Days	Cities	Time
Monday	Madrid	10 pm
Tuesday	Sydney	5 pm
Wednesday	Dubai	9 pm
Thursday	London	6 pm
Friday	Zurich	8 pm
Saturday	Rome	4 pm
Sunday	Paris	7 pm

40. (*e*) The Zurich bound flight departs on the day immediately after the day on which the London bound flight departs.

41. (*d*) The Sydney bound flight departs at 5 pm.

42. (*d*) The London bound flight departs exactly 1 h after the Sydney bound flight on its scheduled day.

43. (*b*) Total taken time = 4 h
Time to reach New Delhi = 2 h
The Dubai bound flight departs at 9 pm.
So, the flight arrived in New Delhi at 11 pm.

44. (*e*) The flight departing on the day immediately before the Sydney bound flight.

Solutions (Q. Nos. 45-48) *According to the given information the arrangement is as follows*

Months	Dates	Persons
	5	K
March (31)	12	C
	21	H
	5	D
May (31)	12	F
	21	L
	5	J
Sep (30)	12	E
	21	B
	5	A
Nov (30)	12	M
	21	G

45. (*a*) Two persons were born between C and F.

46. (*a*) M was born immediately before G.

47. (*b*) H was born on 21st March.

48. (*d*) B was born on 21st.

Solutions (Q. Nos. 49-51) *According to the given information,*

Doctors	Meeting hour	Duration
Cardiologist	7:00-8:30 am	1.5 h
Psychiatrist	8:30-10:00 am	1.5 h
General Physician	10:00-12:30 pm	2.5 h
Nephrologist	12:30-3:00 pm	2.5 h
Dental Surgeon	3:00-6:00 pm	3 h

49. (*b*) Psychiatrist attends patients just after Cardiologist.

50. (*d*) Dental surgeon attends patients from 3:00 to 6:00 pm.

51. (*d*) The duration of Psychiatrist's meeting with the patients is 1.5 h.

Solutions (Q. Nos. 52-56)

Days	Students	Sports	Subjects
Monday	D	Badminton	Physics
Tuesday	E	Tennis	Chemistry
Wednesday	A	Kho-Kho	Biology
Thursday	B	Baseball	History
Friday	C	Cricket	Hindi
Saturday	G	Hockey	English
Sunday	F	Football	Maths

52. (*d*) Combination F-Cricket- Hindi is definitely false.

53. (*c*) G, who reads English reads on the 6th day of the week.

54. (*a*) B, who likes Baseball reads History.

55. (*b*) According to the given pattern, A is related to Baseball.

56. (*b*) D, who reads just before E reads Physics.

Solutions (Q. Nos. 57-61) *Following table can be drawn from given information.*

Months	Dates	Person-Flower
January	16	C - Hibiscus
	24	D - Daffodil
April	16	B - Marigold
	24	M - Jasmine
June	16	E - Lotus
	24	O - Lily
October	16	N - Sunflower
	24	J - Roses

57. (*d*) B likes marigold.

58. (*d*) O born exactly between the one who like Rose and M.

59. (*c*) D likes Daffodil.

60. (*a*) D-April is not true.

61. (*c*) Five persons are born before O.

Solutions (Q. Nos. 62-65) *According to the given information the arrangement is as follows*

Years	Ages	Persons	Colours
1946	73	S	White
1958	61	R	Red
1963	56	Q	Yellow
1971	48	T	Orange
1994	25	P	Pink
2006	13	U	Black

62. (*d*) R likes Red Colour.

63. (*e*) No one was born after U.

64. (*d*) S likes White colour and he is older than Q. So, the Statement (d) is not correct.

65. (*e*) P was born in the year 1994.

TYPE 04

Complex Family Puzzles

In this type of puzzles, a chain of relationship among the members of a family is given alongwith some additional information (like their profession, vehicle, favourites colour etc) in puzzle form.

The candidates are required to establish the relationship of the members of a family with other members of the same family and also arrange the additional given information and relate them to the related members.

After arranging the given information the answers to the questions can be easily determined.

DIRECTIONS (Ex. Nos. 39-41) *Study the following information carefully and answer the given questions.* « UPSC CSAT 2011

A, B, C, D and E are members of the same family. There are two fathers, two sons, two wives, three males and two females. The teacher is the wife of a lawyer who is the son of a doctor. E is neither a male, nor a wife of a professional. C is the youngest person in the family and D is the eldest. B is a male.

Ex 39 How is D related to E?
(a) Husband
(b) Son
(c) Father
(d) Wife

Ex 40 Who are the females in the group?
(a) C and E
(b) C and D
(c) E and A
(d) D and E

Ex 41 Whose wife is a teacher?
(a) C (b) D
(c) A (d) B

Solutions (Ex. 39-41) According to the information,

$D^{(+)} \longleftrightarrow E^{(-)}$ Doctor
↓
Lawyer $B^{(+)} \longleftrightarrow A^{(-)}$ Teacher
↓
$C^{(+)}$

[(−) ⟶ Female; (+) ⟶ Male; ⟷ Husband/wife]

39. (*a*) D is the husband of E.

40. (*c*) A and E are females.

41. (*d*) B's wife, A is a teacher.

Practice / CORNER 11.4

1. P, Q, R, S, T and U are 6 members of family in which there are two married couples. T, a teacher, is married to a doctor who is mother of R and U. Q, the lawyer, is married to P. P has one son and one grandson. Of the two married ladies one is a housewife. There is also one student and one male engineer in the family.

Which of the following is true about the granddaughter of the family? « SSC (CGL) 2015

(a) She is a lawyer. (b) She is an engineer.
(c) She is a student. (d) She is a doctor.

DIRECTION ~ (Q. No. 2) *Study the following information carefully and answer the questions given below.* « MAT Feb 2010

A, B, C, D, E, F and G are members of a family consisting of 4 adults and 3 children, two of whom, F and G are girls, A and D are brothers and A is a doctor. E is an engineer married to one of the brothers and has two children. B is married to D and G is their child.

2. Who is C?

(a) G's father (b) F's father
(c) E's daughter (d) A's son

DIRECTIONS ~ (Q. Nos. 3-5) *Study the following information carefully and answer the questions given below.* « UPSC CSAT 2014

A, B, C, D, E and F are six members of a family. They are Engineer, Stenographer, Doctor, Draughtsman, Lawyer and Judge (not in order).

A , the Engineer is married to the lady Stenographer. The Judge is married to the Lawyer. F, the Draughtsman is the son of B and brother of E. C, the Lawyer is the daughter-in-law of D. E is the unmarried Doctor. D is the grandmother of F. There are two married couples in the family.

3. What is the profession of B?

(a) Judge (b) Lawyer
(c) Draughtsman (d) Cannot be determined

4. Which of the following is/are a couple/couples?

(a) Only AD (b) Only BC
(c) AD and BC (d) AC and BD

5. What is the profession of D?

(a) Judge (b) Stenographer
(c) Doctor (d) Cannot be determined

DIRECTIONS ~ (Q. Nos. 6-8) *Study the following information carefully and answer the questions given below.* « MAT 2013

There is family of six members A, B, C, D, E and F. They are lawyer, doctor, teacher, salesman, engineer and accountant not necessarily in that order. There are two married couples in the family.

D, the salesman, is married to the lady teacher. The doctor is married to the lawyer. F, the accountant, is the son of B and brother of E. C, the lawyer, is the daughter-in-law of A. E is the unmarried engineer. A is the grandmother of F.

6. How is E related to F?

(a) Brother (b) Sister
(c) Cousin (d) None of these

7. What is the profession of B?

(a) Teacher (b) Doctor
(c) Lawyer (d) Cannot be determined

8. Which of the following is one of the couples?

(a) F and D (b) D and B
(c) E and A (d) None of these

DIRECTIONS ~ (Q. Nos. 9-13) *Study the following information carefully and answer the questions given below.* « UPSSSC Lower Subordinate (Pre) 2016

The members of a bank are Mr. A, Mr. B, Mrs. C, Mrs. D, Mr. E and Mrs. F. The positions they occupy are Manager, Asstt. Manager, Cashier, Stenographer, Teller and a Clerk, though not necessarily in the same order.

The Asstt. Manager is Manager's Grandson. Cashier is Stenographer's son-in-law. Mr. A is bachelor. Mrs. D is Teller's step-sister and Mr. E is Manager's husband. Mr. B cannot have grandson or son-in-law as he is only 20 yr old. D and F are not Manager.

9. Who is the Manager?

(a) A (b) C
(c) E (d) None of these

10. Who is Asstt. Manager?

(a) A (b) F (c) C (d) B

11. Who is Teller?

(a) F (b) C
(c) A (d) D

12. Who is Clerk?

(a) B (b) D
(c) F (d) None of these

13. Who is the Cashier?

(a) Either A or D (b) F
(c) B (d) C

DIRECTIONS ~ (Q. Nos. 14-16) *Study the information below and answer the given questions.* « MPPSC 2018

Seven members, viz. A,B,C,D, E, F and G, are family members. Three of them are female members. There are two couples in the family. Each of them has a different profession, viz. Architect, Teacher, Lawyer, Doctor, Engineer, Manager and Music Director, but not necessarily in the same order.

B is a Lawyer and his wife is F, who is a Manager. A is brother of G, who is an Architect. C, who is a Doctor is a female and is unmarried. D is a Teacher and sister of G. E is not an Engineer and is father of C.

14. Which of the following combinations according to the given information is true?
(a) C- Female-Manager (b) B- Female-Lawyer
(c) F-Male-Manager (d) G-Male-Architect

15. Which of the following is true about A?
(a) A is husband of C (b) A is a Music Director
(c) A is brother of G and D (d) A is sister of E

16. If B is father of A, then what is the relation between F and G?
(a) G is mother of F (b) F is mother of G
(c) F is sister of G (d) Cannot be determined

DIRECTIONS ~(Q. Nos. 17-21) *Study the information below and answer the given questions.* « CLAT 2014

I. In a family of six persons, there are people from three generations. Each person has separate profession and also each one likes different colours. There are two couples in the family.
II. Charan is a CA and his wife is neither a doctor nor likes Green colour.
III. Engineer likes Red colour and his wife is a teacher.
IV. Vanita is mother-in-law of Namita and she likes Orange colour.
V. Mohan is grandfather of Raman and Raman, who is a principal, likes Black colour.
VI. Sarita is granddaughter of Vanita and she likes Blue colour. Sarita's mother likes White colour.

17. Who is an engineer?
(a) Sarita (b) Vanita
(c) Namita (d) Mohan

18. What is the profession of Namita?
(a) Doctor (b) Engineer
(c) Teacher (d) Cannot be determined

19. Which of the following is the correct pair of two couples?
(a) Mohan — Vanita and Charan — Sarita
(b) Vanita — Mohan and Charan — Namita
(c) Charan — Namita and Raman — Sarita
(d) Cannot be determined

20. How many ladies are there in the family?
(a) Two (b) Three (c) Four (d) None of these

21. Which colour is liked by CA?
(a) White (b) Blue
(c) Black (d) Cannot be determined

DIRECTIONS (Q. Nos. 22-26) *Study the information below and answer the given questions.* « RBI Grade B 2017

Seven people P, Q, R, S, T, U and V are related to each other in a certain way. Each person has different age, but not necessarily in this order.

(**Note** It is assumed that the husband's age is more than that of wife).

T's age is more than V but less than U. P is the mother of Q. R is the sister-in-law of P. R is unmarried. T is the daughter-in-law of S. S is the oldest person in the family. U is the father of only R and V. U doesn't have any brother or sister. V doesn't have any son. R is older than V. The third oldest person of family is 54 yr old. The youngest person of family is 4 yr old.

22. If in the given arrangement, Q + V =31, then the possible age of V is
(a) 27 yr (b) 56 yr (c) 23 yr (d) 30 yr
(e) 59 yr

23. If P is 24 yr old, then the sum of P's and T's ages is,
(a) 28 yr (b) 78 yr (c) 64 yr (d) 49 yr
(e) 75 yr

24. How is T related to Q?
(a) Grandmother (b) Granddaughter
(c) Aunt (d) Mother-in-law
(e) Mother

25. If M is married to S, then how is S related to R?
(a) Grandmother (b) Granddaughter
(c) Grandfather (d) Uncle
(e) Cannot be determined

26. Which of the following is younger than V?
(a) Both P and Q (b) Only Q
(c) Only P (d) Both P and U
(e) Cannot be determined

Answers WITH EXPLANATIONS

1. (c) According to the given information, arrangement is as follows

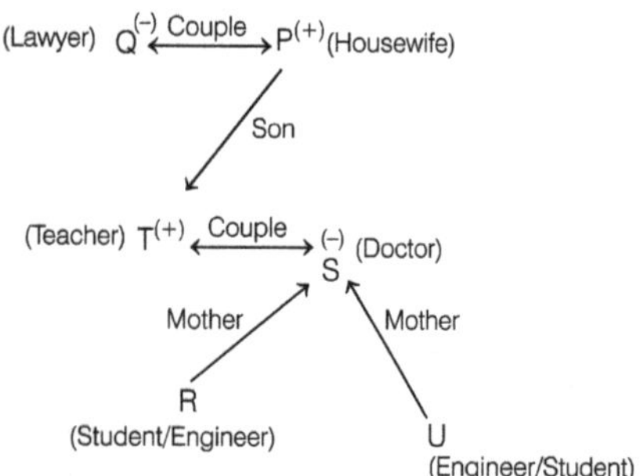

So, the granddaughter of the family is a student and either R or U is a student.

2. (d) Family diagram is as follows

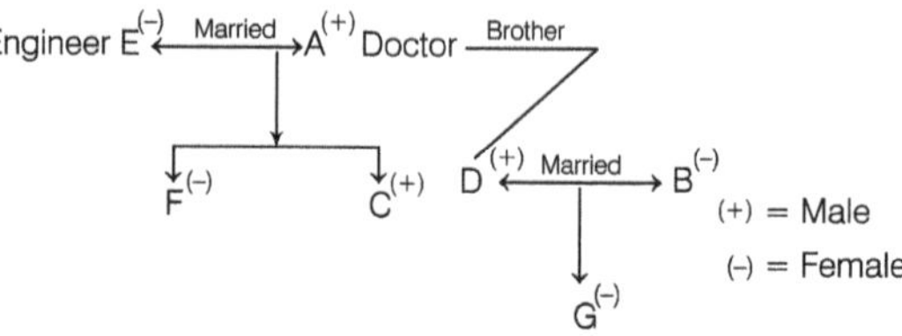

So, C is A's son.

Solutions (Q. Nos. 3-5) *From the given information, the relation chart can be drawn as*

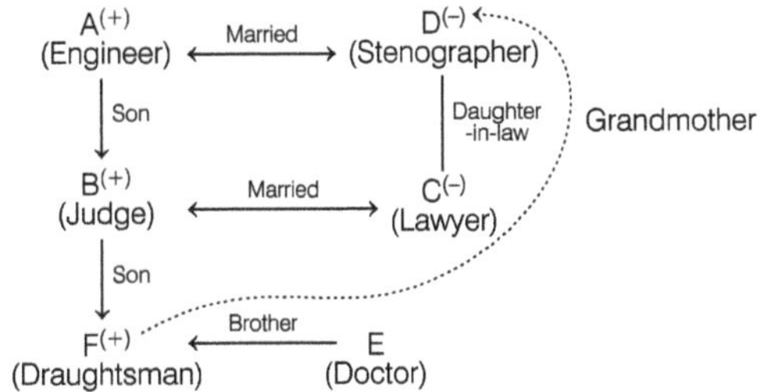

[Notation used (+) = Male, (–) = Female]

3. *(a)* From the above relation diagram, B is a Judge.

4. *(c)* Married couples are AD and BC.

5. *(b)* D is a Stenographer.

Solutions (Q. Nos. 6-8) *Let us draw the family diagram*

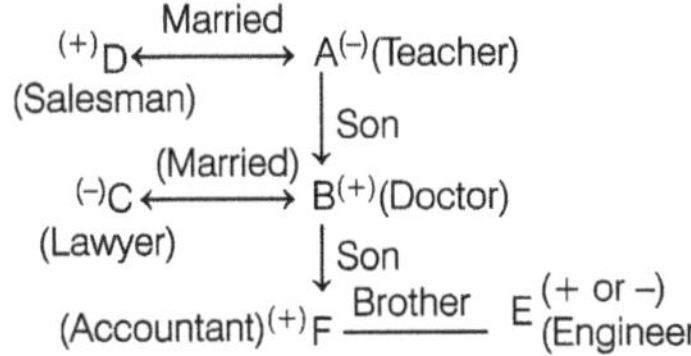

6. *(d)* As, it is not clear that E is male or female, so we cannot conclude that E is brother or sister of F.

7. *(b)* B is a doctor.

8. *(d)* D, A and C, B are married couples.

Solutions (Q.Nos. 9-13) *According to the given information,*

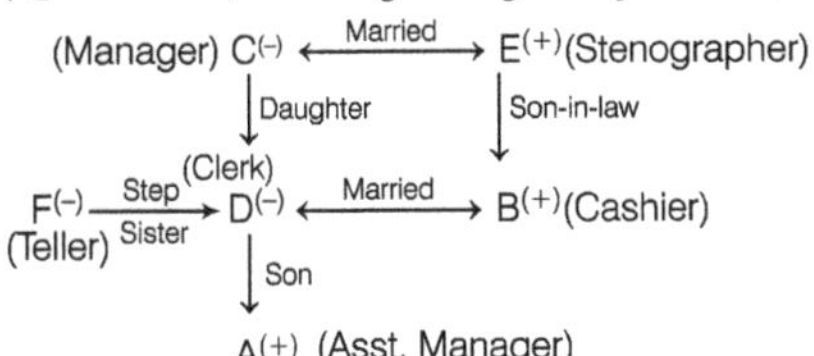

9. *(b)* Mrs. C is the Manager.

10. *(a)* Mr. A is Asst. Manager.

11. *(a)* Mrs. F is Teller.

12. *(b)* Mrs. D is Clerk.

13. *(c)* Mr. B is the Cashier.

Solutions (Q.Nos. 14-16) *As per the information, the arrangement is as follows*

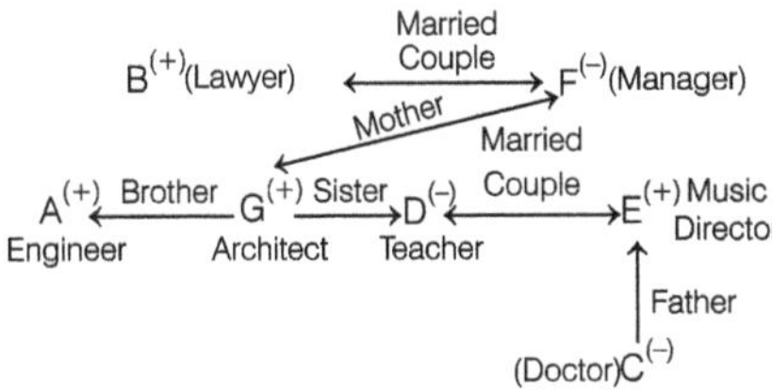

14. *(d)* G-Male-Architect is a true combination.

15. *(c)* A is brother of G and D.

16. *(b)* F is mother of G.

Solutions (Q. Nos. 17-21) *According to the given conditions, we can make a table as follows*

Grand-parents	Mohan (+) (Engineer) (Red)	Vanita (–) (Teacher) (Orange)
Parents	Charan (CA) (+)	Namita (White) (–)
Children	Raman (+) (Principal) (Black)	Sarita (Blue) (–)

17. *(d)* Mohan is an engineer.

18. *(d)* Namita's profession is not given.

19. *(b)* Pair of two couples are
Vanita – Mohan
Charan – Namita

20. *(b)* There are three ladies in the family.

21. *(d)* Charan is a CA and colour liked by him is not given.

Solutions (Q. Nos. 22-26) *According to the given information, the relation diagram is as follows*

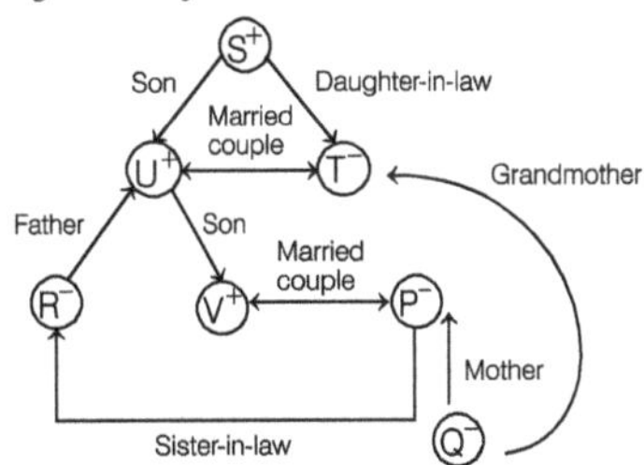

$S > U > T > R > V > P > Q$ (People in decreasing order of their age)

54   4

22. *(a)* Given, $Q + V = 31$

$\Rightarrow \quad 4 + V = 31$

$\Rightarrow \quad V = 31 - 4 = 27$

$\therefore \quad V = 27$

23. *(b)* Given, T = 54 yr, P = 24 yr

$\therefore \quad P + T = 24 + 54 = 78$ yr

24. *(a)* T is the grandmother of Q.

25. *(c)* If M is married to S, then M is the wife of S because it is given that S is the oldest person in the family and the age of husband is more than the age of his wife. Hence, S is the grandfather of R.

26. *(a)* Both P and Q are younger than V.

TYPE 05

Based on Condition, Grouping and Team Formation

In this type of puzzles, a large group of people or objects is given along with some conditions regarding selection or non-selection of persons or objects with respect to one another. The candidate is required to form one or more than one small groups according to the given conditions and on the basis of the same he/she has to answer the questions that are asked.

DIRECTIONS ~ (Ex. Nos. 42-44) *Read the following information carefully to answer the questions that follow.*

A combination of three colours is being chosen to decorate a room. The colour must be chosen from a group of seven colours A, B, C, D, E, F and G according to the following conditions.

I. If A or B is chosen, then other must also be chosen.
II. C and D cannot be chosen together.
III. Either C or A or both must be chosen.

***Ex* 42** Which of the following combinations of colours confirms to the conditions?

(a) A, C, D
(b) A, E, F
(c) B, C, G
(d) C, E, G

***Ex* 43** If D is chosen, which of the following pair of colours must also be chosen?

(a) A and B
(b) A and G
(c) B and C
(d) C and E

***Ex* 44** If E is chosen, which of the following pair of colours could also be chosen?

(a) A and C
(b) A and F
(c) B and C
(d) C and F

Solutions (Ex. Nos. 42-44) This puzzle is totally different from the puzzles discussed in earlier types and therefore, methods for solution discussed so far will not provide much help for its solution. The main difference in this puzzle is that, according to set of conditions given in the puzzles, there may be more than one valid combinations which may confirm to the given condition. Hence, our answer will vary according to the question asked.

42. *(d)* By condition I, if A or B is chosen, the other must also be chosen. In options (a) and (b), A is chosen but B is not. Hence, these options are not correct. While in option (c), B is chosen but A is not. Hence, this option is not correct. Only option (d) follows all conditions.

43. *(a)* According to the question, D is chosen. So, D works as a condition. Since, D is chosen, C cannot be chosen. So, option (c) and (d) are rejected. If A is chosen, B has to be chosen, so option (b) is rejected, option (a) complies with all the conditions.

44. *(d)* According to the question, E is chosen. So, E works as a condition. By condition I, if A or B is chosen, the other must also be chosen. Hence, options (a), (b) and (c) do not follow condition I, so these options are rejected. Only option (d) complies with all the conditions.

Practice / CORNER 11.5

1. Eight students A, B, C, D, E, F, G and H are going to college in two cars and following are conditions.

There are four students in each car.
A is in the same car in which D is sitting but H is not in the same car.
B and C are not in the car in which D is sitting.
F is sitting with A and E. « NTSE 2014

Four students sitting in the same car are

(a) A, B, G, H
(b) B, D, F, G
(c) B, C, G, H
(d) A, C, D, E

2. Four political parties W, X, Y and Z decided to set up a joint candidate for the coming parliamentary elections.

The formula agreed by them was the acceptance of a candidate by most of the parties. Four aspiring candidates A, B, C and D approached the parties for their tickets.

A was acceptable to W but not Z.
B was acceptable to Y but not X.
C was acceptable to W and Y.
D was acceptable to W and X.

When candidate B was preferred by W and Z, candidate C was preferred by X and Z and candidate A was acceptable to X but not to Y, who got the ticket?
« UPSC CSAT 2012

(a) A
(b) B
(c) C
(d) D

3. A society consists of only two types of people–fighters and cowards. Two cowards are always friends. A fighter and a coward are always enemies. Fighters are indifferent to one another. If A and B are enemies, C and D are friends, E and F are indifferent to each other, A and E are not enemies, while B and F are enemies.
« UPSC CSAT 2015

Which of the following statements is correct?

(a) B, C and F are cowards.
(b) A, E and F are fighters.
(c) B and E are in the same category.
(d) A and F are in different categories.

4. A five member business delegation to Pakistan has to be chosen from five politicians Khansaab, Lalaji, Mohanlal, Nathumal and Omprakash and four prominent businessmen Popatlal, Quareshi, Ramprasad and Sorabseth. But there are some conditions. Khansaab and Sorabseth have to be together. Mohanlal and Omprakash too cannot be separated. Nathumal and Quareshi cannot go together. Ramprasad has disputes with Popatlal and Lalaji, he will not go with any of these two. If Popatlal and atleast two other businessmen are selected.

Then members of the delegation besides Popatlal are « CMAT 2015

(a) Quareshi, Sorabseth, Khansaab, Lalaji
(b) Quareshi, Sorabseth, Lalaji, Nathumal
(c) Ramprasad, Sorabseth, Khansaab, Popatlal.
(d) Quareshi, Sorabseth, Mohanlal, Nathumal

5. A team of six members is to be selected from a bunch of boys B_1, B_2, B_3, B_4, B_5 and B_6 and four girls G_1, G_2, G_3 and G_4. Some of the criteria are as follow

B_2 and B_4 have to go together
B_3 cannot go with G_2.
B_6 cannot go with the B_1 and B_4.
G_1 and G_3 have to be together.
G_1 cannot go with G_4.
B_1 and B_5 have to be together.

If four of the members including B_5 have to be boys and one of the girls has to be G_3, then the team members are « CMAT 2015

(a) B_1, B_4, B_5, B_6, G_1, G_3 (b) B_2, B_4, B_5, B_6, G_1, G_3
(c) B_1, B_2, B_4, B_5, G_3, G_4 (d) B_1, B_2, B_4, B_5, G_1, G_3

DIRECTIONS ~ (Q. Nos. 6 and 7) *Study the following information carefully and answer the questions asked.* « SNAP 2010

Seven people A, B, C, D, E, F and G are planning to enjoy boating. There are only two boats and the following conditions are to be kept in mind.

I. A will go in the same boat in which E is to go.
II. F cannot go in the boat in which C unless D is also accompanying.
III. Neither B nor C can be given the boat in which G is.
IV. The maximum number of persons in one boat can be four only.

6. If F and B are in one boat, which of the following statements is true?

(a) G is in the other boat.
(b) D is in the other boat.
(c) C is in the other boat.
(d) E is with F and B in one boat.

7. If E gets boat with F, which of the following is the complete and accurate list of the people who must be sitting in other boat?

(a) F and E (b) G and A
(c) D and A (d) C, D and B

DIRECTIONS ~ (Q. Nos. 8-10) *Study the following information carefully and answer the questions asked.* « MAT May 2015

Hansraj College, Delhi is selecting a four person debate team. There are seven candidates of equal ability. X, Y and Z who attended the Science block courses and L, M, N and P who attended the Commerce block courses. The team must have two members from each block. Also, the members must be able to work well with all the other members of the team. Note that debaters Y and L, Z and N and L and M are incompatible pairs.

8. If debater Y is rejected and M is selected, the team will consist of

(a) L, M , X and Z (b) M, N, X and Z
(c) M, N, P and X (d) M, P, X and Z

9. If debater L is in the team, what other debaters must be in the team as well?

(a) M, X and Z (b) P, X and Z
(c) N, X and Z (d) P, N and Z

10. If both Y and Z are selected, which of the other debaters are there by assured of a place in the team?

(a) Both L and M (b) Both M and P
(c) Only N (d) Both N and P

11. At an electronic data processing unit, five out of the eight program sets P, Q, R, S, T, U, V and W are to be operated daily. On anyone day, except for the first day of a month, only three of the program sets must be the ones that were operated on the previous day. The program operating must also satisfy the following conditions.

I. If program P is to be operated on a day, V can't be operated on that day.
II. If Q is to be operated on a day, T must be one of the programs to be operated after Q.
III. If R is to be operated on a day, V must be one of the programs to be operated after R.
IV. The last program to be operated on any day must be either S or U.

Which of the following could be set of programs to be operated on the first day of a month? « MP Police Constable 2016

(a) V, Q, R, T, S (b) U, Q, S, T, W
(c) T, U, R, V, S (d) Q, S, R, V, U

DIRECTIONS ~ (Q. Nos. 12-14) *Study the following information carefully and answer the questions asked.* « IIFT 2015

There are three countries, USA, UAE and UK. An exporter can select one country or two countries or all the three countries subject to the conditions below.

Condition 1. Both USA and UAE have to be selected.

Condition 2. Either USA or UK, but not both have to be selected.

Condition 3. UAE can be selected only if UK has been selected.

Condition 4. USA can be selected only if UK is selected.

12. In how many ways countries can be selected, if no condition is imposed?

(a) 6 (b) 4 (c) 7 (d) 8

13. In how many ways countries can be selected to meet only condition 1?

(a) 0 (b) 2 (c) 1 (d) 3

14. In how many ways countries can be selected to meet only conditions 2 and 3?

(a) 0 (b) 2 or 1
(c) 0 or 1 (d) None of these

DIRECTIONS ~ (Q. Nos. 15-19) *Study the following information carefully and answer the questions asked.*

« CLAT 2011

From amongst six boys A, B, C, D, E and F and five girls P, Q, R, S and T, a team of six is to be selected under the following conditions;

I. A and D have be together.
II. C cannot go with S.
III. S and T have to be together.
IV. B cannot be teamed with E.
V. D cannot go with P.
VI. B and R have to be together.
VII. C and Q have to be together.

15. If there be five boys in the team, the only girl member is

(a) P (b) Q (c) R (d) S

16. If, including P, the team has three girls, the members other than P are

(a) BCFQR (b) ADEST (c) ADBST (d) BFRST

17. If the team including C consists of four boys, the other members of the team are

(a) ADEPQ (b) ABDQR (c) DEFAQ (d) BEFRQ

18. If four members including E have to be boys, the members other than E are

(a) ABCQR (b) ADFST
(c) BCFQR (d) ACDFQ

19. If four members have to be girls, the members of the team are

(a) BCPQRS (b) BFPRST
(c) BCQRST (d) BCPQRT

DIRECTIONS ~ (Q. Nos. 20 and 21) *Study the following information carefully and answer the questions asked.*

« IIFT 2014

Federation of Indian Chamber of Commerce and Industries organised a business conclave on India's emerging electronic goods sector. CEOs and Managing Directors of four leading companies, namely, Klentech Industries, Andromeda Infotech, Zoomerang Technologies and Spearhead Unlimited were invited to deliver lectures on this occasion. The CEOs of the four companies were Mr. Sethi, Mr. D'Souza, Mr. Puri and Mr. Bisht respectively, while the Managing Directors were Mr. Tandon, Mr. Arora, Mr. Karare and Mr. Reddy in that order. The speeches were delivered subject to the condition that each of the Managing Directors delivered their speeches immediately after that of the CEOs of their company.

20. The first CEO to speak was Mr. D'Souza and the next CEO to deliver his address was Mr. Puri. If Mr. Tandon is the third Managing Director to deliver his address, which of the following statements must be true?

(a) Mr. Bisht delivered his address sometime before Mr. Sethi.
(b) Mr. Reddy delivered his address sometime before Mr. Tandon.
(c) Mr. Puri delivered his address sometime before Mr. Reddy.
(d) Mr. Karare delivered his address sometime before Mr. Arora.

21. If Mr. Bisht was the second CEO to speak after Mr. D'Souza and two more Managing Directors speak after the address of the Managing Director of Spearhead Unlimited, then who is the last CEO to speak?

(a) Mr. Sethi (b) Mr. Puri
(c) Mr. Tandon (d) Cannot be determined

DIRECTIONS ~ (Q. Nos. 22-25) *Study the following information carefully and answer the questions asked.*

« SNAP 2015

A chef is trying a recipe for a tasty ice-cream using four ingredients. He can choose from three liquids for taste which are labelled A, B and C which are stable in nature and the choice for flavour can be from four liquids which are labelled W, X, Y and Z. For the new ice-cream recipe to be tasty, there must be two liquids from the taste giving liquids. Also certain liquids cannot be mixed because of their reactions which makes it unhealthy for human consumption and the same is given below

B cannot be mixed with W.

C cannot be mixed with Y.

Y cannot be mixed with Z.

22. If the chef calculated that Y is the most important flavour and must be used in the recipe, which other ingredients must be part of the recipe?

(a) A, B and W (b) A, B and X
(c) A, B and Z (d) B, C and X

23. If the chef rejected B because of its possible side effects but decided to use Z, which is a possible combination of the four ingredients in the recipe?

(a) A, C, W and Z (b) A, X, Y and Z
(c) A, W, X and Z (d) A, C, Y and Z

24. Which of the following combinations of liquids is impossible?

I. Using Y and W together.
II. Using B and C together.
III. Using W, X and Z together.

(a) Only I (b) Only II
(c) Both III and I (d) Both II and I

25. Which of the following must always be true?

I. If C is used W must be added.
II. If Y is used B must be added.
III. If C is not used W cannot be added.

(a) Both I and II (b) Both II and III
(c) I, II and III (d) Only II

DIRECTIONS ~ (Q. Nos. 26 and 27) *Study the following information carefully and answer the questions asked.*
« UPSC CSAT 2013

I. A guesthouse has six rooms A, B, C, D, E and F. Among these, A and C can accommodate two persons each, the rest can accommodate only one each.
II. Eight guests P, Q, R, S, T, U, W and X are to be kept in these rooms. Q, T and X are females while the other are males. The two sexes cannot be put together in the same room. No man is willing to stay in room C or F.
III. P wants to be alone but does not want to stay in room B or D. S needs a partner but is not ready to stay with U or W. X does not want to share her room.

26. Who among the following will stay in room E?
(a) U (b) W (c) P (d) Q

27. X will stay in which of the room?
(a) C (b) E (c) B (d) F

DIRECTIONS ~ (Q. Nos. 28-32) *Read the following information carefully and answer the questions given below.*
« RRB Clerk Mains 2016

Ten students G, H, I, J, K, L, M, N, O and P have come for audition for a Rock Band in the college. The college wants to select a Rock Band for its new event at the Fest. Among them, two are drummers, three are guitarists, three are pianists and the remaining are bassists. The band should contain at least one instrumentalist from the above four each.

- If H is selected, then P is not selected. One between O and M must be selected.
- H and L are experts in the same instrument, but are not pianists.
- Either K or I is selected in the Band. Neither of them is a guitarist. They play different instruments.
- If M, a bassist, is selected, then no other bassist is selected. N is either a drummer or a pianist.
- J has better expertise than O in playing the same instrument, but neither of them is a guitarist or a drummer. If the company wants to select only one person from their field then it can be neither J nor O.
- G, O and H are experts in different instruments.

28. If K is a drummer and the college want to select a band of four persons then which of the following is a possible band?
(a) N, K, G, L (b) O, P, M, N
(c) M, H, K, I (d) K, J, P, O
(e) None of these

29. If N is a pianist and all the three pianists are selected for the band, then who all are the co-pianists.
(a) O, M (b) K, I
(c) N, I (d) J, O
(e) None of these

30. If K and N are not selected for the band and two drummers are selected for the band, then who are they?
(a) I, K (b) J, I
(c) G, I (d) H, J
(e) None of these

31. If K is a bassist and all the bassists are selected for the band, then who is another co-bassist?
(a) G (b) M (c) I (d) P
(e) J

32. If the pianists J, O, N are selected for the band, then who among the following can be the guitarists?
(a) G, H, P (b) L, H, G (c) L, H, P (d) P, H, M
(e) None of these

DIRECTIONS ~ (Q. Nos. 33-35) *Study the following information carefully and answer the questions asked.*
« XAT 2011

Mrs Sharma has a house which she wants to convert to a hostel and rent it out to students of a nearby women's college. The house is a two storey building and each floor has eight rooms. When one looks from the outside, three rooms are found facing North, three found facing East, three found facing West and three found facing South. Expecting a certain number of students, Mrs Sharma wanted to follow certain rules while giving the 16 rooms on rent.

I. All sixteen rooms must be occupied.
II. No room can be occupied by more than three students.
III. Six rooms facing North is called North wing. Similarly, six rooms facing East, West and South are called as East wing, West wing and South wing. Each corner room would be in more than one wing. Each of the wings must have exactly 11 students. The first floor must have twice as many students as the ground floor.
IV. However, Mrs Sharma found that three fewer students have come to rent the rooms. Still, Mrs Sharma could manage to allocate the rooms according to the rules.

33. How many students turned up for renting the rooms?
(a) 24 (b) 27 (c) 30 (d) 33
(e) None of these

34. If Mrs Sharma allocates the North-West corner room on the ground floor to 2 students, then the number of students in the corresponding room on the first floor and the number of students in the middle room in the first floor of the East wing are
(a) 2 and 1 respectively.
(b) 3 and 1 respectively.
(c) 3 and 2 respectively.
(d) Both should have 3 students Such an arrangement is not possible.
(e) Such an arrangement is not possible.

35. If all the students that Mrs Sharma expected initially had come to rent the rooms and if Mrs Sharma had allocated the North-West corner room in the ground floor to 1 student, then the number of students in the corresponding room on the first floor and the number of students in the middle room in the first floor of the East wing would have been
(a) 1 and 2 respectively.
(b) 2 and 3 respectively.
(c) 3 and 1 respectively.
(d) More than one arrangement is possible.
(e) Such an arrangement is not possible.

Answers / WITH EXPLANATIONS

1. (c) By given conditions, there are two groups of students which are A, D, E, F and B, C, G, H.

2. (c) According to the given conditions, A was accepted by W and X. B was accepted by Y, W and Z. C was accepted by W, Y, X and Z. D was accepted by W and X.
So, C was accepted by all the four parties. Hence, option (c) is correct.

3. (*b*) From the given information,

Fighter	Coward
E	C
F	D
A	B

Given that,
A fighter and a coward are always → Enemies.
Two cowards are always → Friends
Thus, A, E and F are fighters.

4. (a) Option (b) is eliminated on the ground that Quareshi and Nathumal can't go together. Option (c) can be eliminated as Ramprasad has disputes with Popatlal, so they can't go together.
Option (d) is also eliminated, the reason is same as for the option (b).
So, right option is (a).

5. (d) From given conditions, B_2 and B_4 have to go together. So, option (a) is rejected. B_6 and B_4 cannot be go together, so option (b) is rejected. G_1 and G_3 have to be together. So, option (c) is also rejected.
Only option (d) satisfies the given conditions, hence it will be right choice.

Solutions (Q. Nos. 6 and 7)

6. (*a*) According to the question and given conditions, the possible cases are as follows

Case I $\frac{\text{Boat 1}}{\text{B, C, D, F}} + \frac{\text{Boat 2}}{\text{A, E, G}}$

Case II $\frac{\text{Boat 1}}{\text{A, E, G}} + \frac{\text{Boat 2}}{\text{B, C, D, F}}$

Clearly, G is in other boat. If B, C, D and F are in boat 1, then G is in boat 2 and if B, C, D and F are in boat 2, then G is in boat 1.

7. (*d*) According to the question and given conditions, the possible cases are as follows

Case I $\frac{\text{Boat 1}}{\text{E, F, A, G}} + \frac{\text{Boat 2}}{\text{C, D, B}}$

Case II $\frac{\text{Boat 1}}{\text{C, D, B}} + \frac{\text{Boat 2}}{\text{E, F, A, G}}$

Clearly, in either case C, D and B are sitting in other boat.

Solutions (Q. Nos. 8-10) Candidates from Science block courses-X, Y, Z. Candidates from Commerce block courses-L, M, N, P. Incompatible pairs-Y and L, Z and N, L and M.

8. (*d*) In option (a), L and M cannot be together. In option (b), N and Z cannot be together. In option (c), three persons from Commerce block, i.e. M, N and P are given, so it is also not possible.
Only the team given in option (d) can be possible.

9. (*b*) Option (a) is eliminated because M cannot be with L. Options (c) and (d) are also eliminated because Z and N cannot be in same team. Only the team given in option (b) can be formed.

10. (*b*) Option (a) is eliminated because L and M cannot be in same team. Options (c) and (d) are eliminated because N cannot be a member of Z's team. From the given alternatives, only M and P are assured to be the members of the team with Y and Z.

11. (*c*) From statement III, If R is operated then, V must be operated after R. So, option (a) is rejected. From statement IV the last program must be either S or U. So, option (b) is rejected. From statement II. If Q is operated, then T must be operated after Q. So, option (d) is rejected. The set of programs that could be operated on the first day is T, U, R, V, S.

Solutions (Q. Nos. 12-14)

12. (*c*) If no condition is applied, then selection
= USA + UAE + UK
+ {(USA, UAE) + (UAE, UK) + (USA, UK)}
+ (USA, UAE, UK)
= 3 + 3 + 1 = 7

13. (*b*) If condition 1 is applied, then selection
= (USA, UAE) + (USA, UAE, UK)
= 1 + 1 = 2

14. (*b*) USA + UK or (UK/UAE)
= 1 + 1 or 1 = 2 or 1

Solutions (Q. Nos. 15-19)

15. (*b*) Since, B cannot go with E, so we have two combinations of men *viz.* ABCDF or ACDEF. But if C is in the team, so Q must be in team. Also, B and R have to be together, but it is not possible to choose both Q and R. So, the team will be ACDEFQ.

16. (*a*) P can not go with D, so options (b) and (c) are not possible. If we consider option (d), then including P, we have four girls. So, option (d) is also not possible. Hence, the correct option is (a).

17. (*b*) By statement V, D cannot go with P. So, option (a) is not possible. Option (c) consists of four boys, if we include C, then we have five boys, so option (c) is also not possible. By statement IV, B cannot be teamed with E. So, option (d) is also not possible.
Hence, only option (b) is possible.

18. (*b*) There are four male members in option (d), including E we have five male members, So, option (d) is not correct. Options (a) and (c) do not follow conditions I and IV respectively. Hence, the correct option is (b).

19. (*b*) Options (a) and (c) do not follow condition II.
Option (d) does not follow condition III. Hence, the correct option is (b).

Solutions (Q. Nos. 20 and 21)

List of Companies' CEOs and Managing Directors

Companies	CEOs	Managing Directors
Klentech Industries	Mr. Sethi	Mr. Tandon
Andromeda Infotech	Mr. D'Souza	Mr. Arora
Zoomerang Technologies	Mr. Puri	Mr. Karare
Spearhead Unlimited	Mr. Bisht	Mr. Reddy

20. *(c)* According to the above table, Mr. Puri delivered his address sometime before Mr. Reddy.

21. *(d)* We cannot determine who is the last CEO to speak, as we don't know the CEO of which company will speak after Mr. Bisht.

Solutions (Q. Nos. 22-25)

22. *(b)* According to the question, Y cannot be mixed with Z and C. Here, Y is the most important flavour and must be used in the recipe. So, Z and C cannot be mixed. Out of three liquids there must be two liquids from taste, according to the question. So, two liquids are A and B and B cannot be mixed with W. So, remaining flavour will be X.

Hence, other ingredients are A, B and X.

23. *(a)* As, B is rejected, so W can be used in recipe. A and C are used as liquids because two liquids from the taste giving liquids are must to use in recipe. So, Y cannot be used in recipe. Hence, possible combinations of the four ingredients in the recipe are A, C, W and Z and A, C, X and Z.

But, from the given options A, C, W and Z is the required combination.

24. *(c)*

I. If we use Y and W together, we can not use B and C in recipe and according to the question out of three liquids i.e. A, B and C two are must to use in recipe.
So, combination of Y and W together is impossible.

II. B and C can be used together.

III. W, X and Z are three liquids for flavour and according to the question two liquids from the taste giving liquids are must to use in recipe.
Hence, combination of W, X and Z together is impossible.

25. *(b)* If B is used with C, then W cannot be used. So, statement I is not true.

Now, if Y is used then C cannot be used, So, A and B must be used. Also, if C is not used then A and B must be used. And W cannot be used with B.

Hence, statements II and III must always be true.

Solutions (Q. Nos. 26-27) Following table can be drawn from the given statements.

Rooms	Number of persons	Persons	M/F
A	2	S, R	M, M
B	1	U/W	
C	2	Q, T	F,F
D	1	U/W	
E	1	P	M
F	1	X	F

26. *(c)* From the table, it is clear that P will stay in room E.

27. *(d)* It is clear from the table that, X will stay in room F.

Solutions (Q. Nos. 28-32) Following table can be drawn from given information.

Case	Painists	Guitarists	Drummers	Bassists
1	J, O, K	L, H, P	I, N	M, G
2	J, O, I	L, H, P	K, N	M, G
3	J, O, K	L, H, P	G, N	M, I
4	J, O, N	L, H, P	G, I	M, K
5	J, O, I	L, H, P	G, N	M, K
6	J, O, N	L, H, P	K, G	M, I

28. (e) None of these

29. (d) J, O are the co-pianists

30. (c) Drummers are G, I.

31. (b) M is co-bassist.

32. (c) H, P are guitarists.

Solutions (Q. Nos. 33-35)

33. *(b)* The number of students who turned up for renting the rooms = 27. Let us see the diagram given below.

∴ Total students (ground floor + first floor)
$= 9 + 18 = 27$

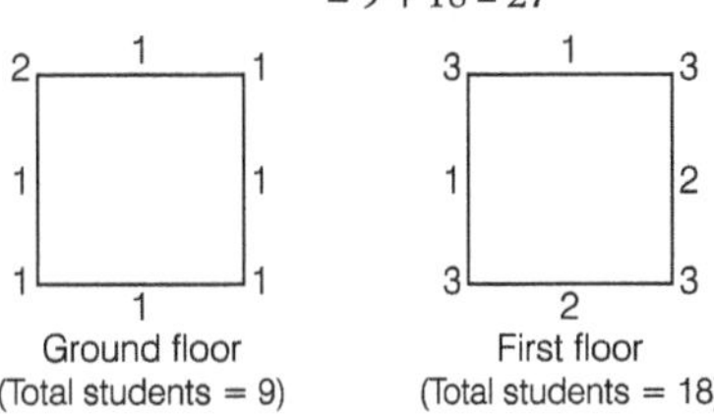

34. *(b)* If the North-West corner room is allotted to 2 students as in the diagram (Sol. No. 1), then the number of students in the corresponding room on the first floor and the number of students in, the middle room in the first floor of the East wing (as East wing consists of room facing East, it would be at West) would be 3 and 1, respectively.

35. *(d)* If all the 30 students had come, the arrangement according to the given conditions, would have more than one possibility.

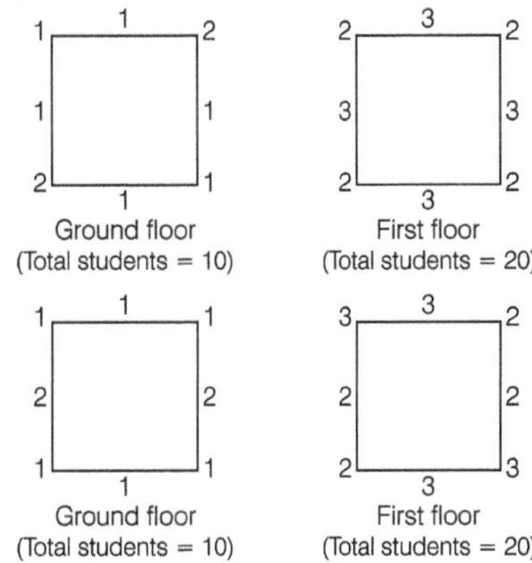

Master Exercise

DIRECTIONS ~ (Q. Nos. 1-5) *Study the following information carefully and answer the given questions.* « IBPS (PO) 2016

Seven persons E, F, G, H, S, T and U buys seven different items viz. Tie, Coat, Ring, Nail paint, Shirt, Diary and Goggles on different days. One person buys one item in a day.

Four persons buy items between E and the one who buys Tie. The one who buys coat buys immediately after the one who buys Tie. Two persons buy items between H and the one who buys Tie. T buys between the one who buys coat and the one who buys Shirt. S buys, Goggles was bought immediately after E. Two persons buy items between the one who buys Ring and the one who buys Diary. U buys his item before G.

1. Who among the following buys Nail paint?
(a) U (b) G (c) H (d) T
(e) None of these

2. Which item was bought immediately after Shirt?
(a) Diary (b) Goggles (c) Tie (d) Coat
(e) None of these

3. How many persons buys items between S and F?
(a) One (b) Two (c) Three (d) Four
(e) None of these

4. Which of the following combination is true?
(a) G-Tie (b) H-Diary (c) T-Goggles (d) E-Diary
(e) None is true

5. Who among the following buys item immediately before Ring?
(a) U (b) G (c) H (d) T
(e) None of these

DIRECTIONS ~ (Q. Nos. 6-10) *Study the following information carefully and answer the questions given below.*

Eight persons A, B, C, D, E, F,G and H are going to watch movie in different months i.e. January, April, May, June, July, August, October and December, but not necessarily in the same order.

F was going to watch movie in the month which has 30 days. There are three persons watching movie between F and C. H watches the movie just before A, who is watching the movie before 2 persons B watches the movie just before C. H is watching the movie in the month which has maximum number of days, but not in January. D is watching the movie in the month which has 30 days. G is watching the movie after D.

6. If E is related to F and H is related to C, then in the same way D is related to which of the following?
(a) H (b) F (c) C (d) B
(e) A

7. Which of the following statement is true as per the given information?
(a) D is going to watch movie after F.
(b) Two persons are watching movie between G and (B).
(c) B is watching the movie in January.
(d) A is watching the movie in August.
(e) None is true

8. The number of persons watching the movie between D and F is same as between B and .... ?
(a) E (b) F (c) H (d) A
(e) None of these

9. Four of the following five are alike in a certain way and hence they form a group. Which one of the following does not belong to that group?
(a) H (b) D (c) C (d) B
(e) G

10. How many persons are watching the movie between B and D?
(a) Five (b) Three (c) Four (d) Two
(e) None

DIRECTIONS ~ (Q. Nos. 11-15) *Study the following information carefully and answer the questions given below.* « SBI PO (Mains) 2015

Seven people A, B, C, D, E, F and G are having different hobbies, *viz.* Travelling, Reading, Dancing, Painting, Sculpting, Singing and Pottery-making, but not necessarily in the same order.

Each or them belong to different State, *viz.* Punjab, Odisha, Kerala, Rajasthan, Maharashtra, Gujarat and Karnataka, but not necessarily in the same order. A belongs to Maharashtra. D likes Pottery-making. The person who likes Sculpting is from Odisha. The person who likes Dancing is from Gujarat. F does not belong to Gujarat, Odisha, Punjab or Rajasthan.

F does not like Singing, Reading or Painting. B does not belong to Kerala, Odisha, Punjab or Rajasthan. B does not like Painting, Travelling, Reading or Singing. C does not like Sculpting and he is not from Rajasthan or Punjab. Neither D nor G belongs to Punjab A does not like Reading. The person from Kerala likes Singing.

11. Who among the following likes Singing?
(a) A (b) C (c) E (d) G
(e) Cannot be determined

12. According to the given information, which one of the following combinations is true?
(a) A—Travelling—Maharashtra
(b) C—Dancing—Gujarat
(c) E—Reading—Karnataka
(d) D—Pottery-making—Rajasthan
(e) All are true

13. Who among the following belongs to Karnataka?
(a) B (b) D (c) F (d) E
(e) Cannot be determined

14. Which of the following combinations is true about G?
(a) Sculpting—Odisha
(b) Pottery-making—Karnataka
(c) Dancing—Gujarat
(d) Singing—Kerala
(e) Travelling—Karnataka

15. The person who belongs to Punjab, likes
(a) Travelling (b) Sculpting
(c) Painting (d) Pottery-making
(e) Reading

DIRECTIONS ~ (Q. Nos. 16-20) *Study the following information carefully and answer the questions given below.* « IBPS PO Pre 2015

P, Q, R, S, T, U, V and W are eight employees working in three departments Marketing, Finance and Production. In each department, at least two and not more than three persons are working. Each of them has a different choice of TV channel i.e. Star, Zee, ESPN, DD, Sony, NDTV, Aaj Tak and BBC not necessarily in the same order.

S likes ESPN and he works in production department with only V. Q and U do not work in the same department. W likes DD and does not work in finance departments. U and R does not work in marketing department. T works with R in the same department and likes Star. Q likes Aaj Tak and none of his colleagues in the department like either Sony or NDTV. V likes Zee, U does not like Sony.

16. Which channel does P like?
(a) DD (b) NDTV
(c) BBC (d) Data inadequate
(e) None of these

17. In which department does U work?
(a) Marketing (b) Production
(c) Finance (d) Marketing or finance
(e) None of these

18. Which channel does U like?
(a) Zee (b) NDTV
(c) BBC (d) Data inadequate
(e) None of these

19. Which of the following groups work in marketing department?
(a) Q, P, V (b) Q, V, T (c) W, Q, T (d) Q, P, T
(e) None of these

20. In which department does Q work?
(a) Marketing (b) Production
(c) Finance (d) Data inadequate
(e) None of these

21. The music director of a film wants to select four persons to work on different aspects of the composition of a piece of music. Seven persons are available for this work, they are Rohit, Tanya, Shobha, Kaushal, Kunal, Mukesh and Jaswant. Rohit and Tanya will not work together. Kunal and Shobha will not work together. Mukesh and Kunal want to work together.

Which of the following is the most acceptable group of people that can be selected by the music director? « UPSC CSAT 2013

(a) Rohit, Shobha, Kunal and Kaushal
(b) Tanya, Kaushal, Shobha and Rohit
(c) Tanya, Mukesh, Kunal and Jaswant
(d) Shobha, Tanya, Rohit and Mukesh

22. Mr. Biswas is planning for 2 weeks holiday with his family to UK, Germany, France, Switzerland, Belgium, Italy, Norway and Austria. However, his family has imposed certain conditions for travel.

(i) Will travel to Austria and Switzerland in different weeks.
(ii) Germany must be visited after Belgium in the same week.
(iii) Switzerland must be visited after France in the same week.
(iv) Will travel to Germany and Norway in different weeks.
(v) Will travel to UK and France in different weeks.
(vi) Will travel to Austria and Belgium in the same week.
(vii) Italy must be visited in the 2nd week.
(viii) Equal number of places must be visited in week 1 and 2.

Which places are visited in week 2, if all places are visited only once? « CMAT 2015

(a) Italy, UK, Switzerland, Norway
(b) Italy, France, Germany, Norway
(c) Italy, UK, Austria, Switzerland
(d) Italy, France, Switzerland, Norway

DIRECTIONS ~ (Q. Nos. 23-28) *Study the given information carefully to answer the given questions.* « MHT MBA 2017

L, M, N, O, P, Q and R have to attend a meeting in January, June, October and November months of the same year. In each month, except in January, the meeting will be conducted on only 15th and 24th of the month. In January, the meeting will be conducted only on the 24th. Not more than two of the given people have a meeting in the same month. Each one of them also likes a different colour - Red, Violet, Pink, Green, Black, Silver and Yellow, but not necessarily in the same order.

N has meeting on the 24th of a month which has 30 days. Only one person has meeting between N and the one who likes Pink. The one who likes Pink has meeting before N. Only two people have a meeting between the one who likes Pink and the one who likes Silver. Both L and the one who likes Silver have meeting in the same month but not on the same date. M has a meeting after L but not in October. M and L have meetings on different dates. The number of people having a meeting between M and the one who likes Pink is same as that between R and the one who likes Silver.

Only one person has a meeting between R and the one who likes Violet. No one has a meeting after the one who likes Red. O and the one who likes Red have a meeting on the same date. P has a meeting on one of the days after Q. Neither P nor R likes the one who likes Green does not have a meeting in October.

23. How many people have a meeting after O?
(a) One (b) Five (c) Four (d) None
(e) Two

24. As per the given schedule, four of the following five are alike in a certain way and so form a group. Which of the following does not belong to group?
(a) Q-June (b) L-Silver (c) Yellow-November
(d) M-Violet (e) O-P

25. How many people have a meeting between P and the one who likes Yellow?
(a) Two (b) One (c) Three
(d) More than three (e) None

26. Which colour does P like?
(a) Red (b) Black (c) Pink (d) Silver
(e) Green

27. Which of the following statements is true as per the given schedule?
(a) M has a meeting on November 24.
(b) R likes Pink.
(c) None of the given statements is true.
(d) P has a meeting after M.
(e) The one who likes Pink has a meeting in October.

28. When does R have a meeting?
(a) October 11 (b) June 15
(c) October 24 (d) November 15
(e) January 24

DIRECTIONS ~ (Q. Nos. 29-33) *Study the following information carefully to answer the given questions.*
« SBI Clerk 2009

A group of people has six family members and an advocate. These are L, M, N, O, P, Q and R and having different professions. Each one of them is a journalist, businessman, architect, doctor and pilot but not necessarily in this order. There are three males and three females in the family out which there are two married couples. M is a businessman and is the father of P. Q is a doctor and grandfather of P who is a male. N is a housewife and is daughter-in-law of O. L is neither a pilot nor a journalist. R is an advocate. N is not the mother of P and O is not married to M. No lady is a journalist.

29. Which of the following groups represent the three ladies in the group?
(a) N, P, L (b) P, L, N (c) L, N, O (d) O, P, L
(e) None of these

30. Who is married to Q?
(a) N (b) O (c) L
(d) Cannot be determined (e) None of these

31. Who among the following family members is an architect?
(a) L (b) O (c) P
(d) Cannot be determined (e) None of these

32. Which of the following is the profession of P?
(a) Architect (b) Pilot (c) Architect or Pilot
(d) Journalist (e) None of these

33. How is Q related to O?
(a) Father (b) Mother
(c) Mother-in-law (d) Son-in-law
(e) None of these

DIRECTIONS ~ (Q. Nos. 34-38) *Study the following information carefully to answer the given questions.*
« IDBI PO 2017

Eight persons P, Q, R, S, T, U, V and W are sitting around a circular table with equal distance between each other, facing the centre, but not necessarily in the same order. Each one of them speaks a different language viz. Hindi, Urdu, Punjabi, Tamil, Marathi, Sanskrit, Gujarati and Bengali, but not necessarily in the same order.

S sits second to the left of the one who speaks Marathi. Only two people sit between S and U. The one who speaks Bengali is an immediate neighbour of U. Q sits third to the right of the one who speaks Bengali. Only three people sit between Q and the one who speaks Punjabi. Only two people sit between the one who speaks Punjabi and R. P sits second to the left of the one who speaks Urdu. P does not speak Bengali. T sits third to the left of W. Only three people sit between W and the one who speaks Gujarati. The one who speaks Tamil sits fourth to right of the one who speaks Hindi. The one who speaks Hindi is not an immediate neighbour of the one who speaks Marathi.

34. Which of the following statements is true about V ?
(a) V is an immediate neighbour of the one who speaks Bengali
(b) V speaks punjabi
(c) None of the given statements is true
(d) V sits to the immediate left of U
(e) Only two persons sit between V and R

35. Four of the following five are alike in a certain way based on their positions in the arrangement and hence form a group. Which one does not belong to that group?
(a) S-Marathi (b) Q-Gujarati
(c) W-Hindi (d) V-Punjabi
(e) P-Sanskrit

36. Who amongst the following is equidistant from T and the one who speaks Hindi, when counted from the left of the one who speaks Hindi?
(a) The one who speaks Marathi
(b) Q
(c) The one who speaks Gujarati
(d) R
(e) U

37. Who amongst the following speaks Sanskrit?
(a) R (b) P (c) T (d) U
(e) S

38. Who amongst the following sits third to the right of W?
(a) V (b) U
(c) The one who speaks Urdu (d) R
(e) The one who speaks Tamil

DIRECTIONS ~ (Q. Nos. 39-43) *Study the following information carefully and answer the questions given below.*
« SBI PO 2018

Seven boxes A , B, C, D, E, F, G are kept one above the other containing different number of chocolates ranging from 10-90. Not more than four boxes are kept above A. Two boxes are kept between A and the box containing 41 chocolates, which is kept below Box A. D contains thrice number of chocolates than box B. Box C contains 50 number of chocolates and is not kept at the top. The number of chocolates in box G is a cube of a number. Only one box is kept between box containing 41 chocolates and 39 chocolates. Box D has less number of chocolates than box A. One of the boxes contain 78 chocolates.

Five boxes are kept between box containing 64 chocolates and Box C. Box G is immediately above box E. Box D is not kept immediately above or below box B. Three boxes are kept between box D and box F. Box D is above box F.

39. Which among the following box/boxes is kept exactly between box D and box B?

(a) G, E (b) B, C (c) B, A (d) F, C
(e) None of these

40. How many chocolates are kept in box E?

(a) 50 (b) 13 (c) 78 (d) 41
(e) None of these

41. Which among the following boxes contains the maximum and minimum number of chocolates respectively?

(a) G, E (b) B, D (c) C, A (d) F, B
(e) None of these

42. Which of the following combination is not true?

(a) 50-D (b) 13-B (c) 41-E (d) 64-A
(e) None of these

43. Which among the following boxes is kept immediately below box B?

(a) G (b) C (c) A (d) F
(e) None of these

DIRECTIONS ~ (Q. Nos. 44-46) *Study the following information carefully to answer the given questions.* « IBPS Clerk (Main) 2017

There are some boxes which are arranged one above another such that one box is placed at the bottom and another box is placed just above that box and all are arranged in the same order.

Only two boxes are there in between Yellow box and box T and Yellow box is above box T. There is only one box in between box P and box Q. Box Q is Blue colour and is placed above box R. There are three boxes in between Yellow box and Brown box. Brown box is placed below T, which is not of Purple colour. Only one box is placed in between box R and Yellow box. More than four boxes are placed in between box P and Yellow box.

There are as same boxes placed between box Q and the box which is of Yellow colour as same as between the box which is of Yellow colour and the box which is of Brown colour. The box which is of Brown colour is placed at the bottom. Not more than two boxes are placed in between box S and box Q. Box R is placed just above the box of purple colour. Box S is not an immediate neighbour of Box Q. Box S is placed below box Q.

44. How many boxes are there in the arrangement?

(a) Ten (b) Eleven
(c) Fourteen (d) Twelve
(e) None of these

45. How many boxes are there between box R and box T?

(a) Five (b) One
(c) Four (d) Two
(e) None of these

46. Which box is immediately above Yellow box?

(a) Q (b) R (c) Blue box (d) S
(e) Brown box

DIRECTIONS ~ (Q. Nos. 47-49) *Study the following information carefully and answer the questions given below.*

Six persons i.e. A, B, C, E, F and G who all are sitting around a circular table facing outside. They all are of different age. F is third youngest person. Only two persons sit between E and F. G sits second to the left of C, who is 20 yr of age. The one who is second oldest person is of 24 yr of age. G is elder than A and C but not the eldest. C sits on the immediate right of E. B is elder than A and G. A and G are not immediate neighbours. The one who is the youngest is less than 20 yr of age. A is not younger than F.

47. What will be the possible age of A?

(a) 25 yr (b) 20 yr (c) 27 yr (d) 19 yr
(e) 22 yr

48. Who among the following is the youngest among all?

(a) A (b) E (c) C (d) F
(e) None of these

49. What is the position of G with respect to A?

(a) Third to the left (b) Third to the right
(c) Second to the left (d) Both (a) and (b)
(e) Second to the right

DIRECTIONS ~ (Q. Nos. 50-54) *Study the following information carefully and answer the questions that follow.* « IBPS Clerk (Mains) 2017

Seven people having their name as consecutive alphabets, are sitting in an alphabetical order from, West to East direction in a straight line. Four of them are facing South and remaining of them are facing North. All of them are of different age. The person whose age is square of four sits second to the left of K. Two persons sit between the one whose age is square of four and the one whose age is six years. Both the immediate neighbours of the one, whose age is six years face opposite direction to each other (i.e. if one faces to North, then the other faces to South *vice versa*). L's age is twice of the age of the one who sits second left of K.

The one whose age is four years more than the half of L's age sits second to the right to L. Only one person sits between M and the one, whose age is 5/4 of L's age. The person whose age is six year and the one whose age is 0.5 times of 18 are immediate neighbours. The one, whose age is square of five sits third to the right of the person whose age is four years more than the half of L's age. L and M face opposite direction to each other (i.e. If one faces North, then the other faces South *vice versa*). The one whose age is six years faces South. The person whose age is 5/4 of L's age faces North.

50. If 25 is related to K and 16 is related to M, then 32 is related to whom?

(a) L (b) J (c) Q (d) G
(e) None of these

51. Who among the following is sitting extreme left of the row?

(a) J (b) O (e) M (d) I
(e) L

52. What will be the age of the one who sits third to the right of L?

(a) 20 (b) 6 (c) 40 (d) 25
(e) 9

53. Who among the following person faces North direction?

(a) K (b) J (c) M (d) N
(e) O

54. Which of the following is the age of M?

(a) 16 (b) 40 (c) 9 (d) 25
(e) None of these

DIRECTIONS ~ (Q. Nos. 55-59) *Study the following information carefully and answer the questions that follow.*

Eight students A, B, C, D, E, F, G and H are seated around a two square table, in which one square table is smaller than 2nd square table. Four students have seated at the middle side of a larger square table , facing towards a centre and four students have seated at the middle side of smaller square table facing outside and facing that person who has seated on larger square table. They all are studying in different engineering stream i.e. ECE, ETC, ME, CE, Biotech, IT, CSE and EEE.

The one who is in ECE faces outside of the square table.There is one student between A and G. D sits to the immediate left of F who sits opposite of H who does not belong to ECE. The seat 2nd to the left of the one who is in ECE, belongs to CE. The one who belongs to ETC faces that student who sits immediate left of B. F does not faces E who sits 2nd right of C. H does not sits on larger square table. B faces the one who sits immediate left of G.

The one who belongs to ECE does not faces E who belongs to Biotech. The one who belongs to CE faces the one who belongs to EEE. The one who faces E belongs to ME. C does not belong to CSE. The one who belongs to Biotech, sits immediate right of the one who sits opposite of H.

55. Who belongs to EEE stream?

(a) A (b) B (c) C (d) D
(e) F

56. Who faces F?

(a) E (b) G (c) C (d) A
(e) B

57. Who faces the one who sits 3rd left of the one who belongs to ME?

(a) A (b) F (c) E (d) C
(e) F

58. Who belongs to ETC?

(a) G (b) B (c) A (d) F
(e) E

59. Who sits 2nd to the left of the one who belongs to IT?

(a) The one who belongs to ETC
(b) A
(c) E
(d) The one who belongs to IT
(e) None of the above

DIRECTIONS ~ (Q. Nos. 60-64) *Study the following information carefully and answer the questions that follow.*

There are ten girls who sit on two parallel rows of bench containing five people each, in such a way that there is an equal distance between adjacent girls, for doing some college work and they like different mobile phones *viz.* LG, Redmi Note 4, Redmi , Moto X, Lenovo, Samsung, Nokia, MI5, I Phone 6 and Vivo. In row 1- A, B, E, F and G are seated and some of them are facing South and some of them are facing North.

In row 2 – R, S, O, P and Q are seated and some of them are facing South and some of them are facing North. Therefore, in the given seating arrangement, each member seated in a row either faces another member of the other row or seated behind each other.

The girl who likes Moto X sits to the immediate right of S, who is seated exactly in the middle of the row. One of the immediate neighbours of the girl, who likes Lenovo, sits behind the girl facing towards South who likes Redmi. P does not like Redmi. F likes neither Lenovo nor Samsung. R sits immediate right of the girl who likes I Phone 6. E sits third to the right of the girl who likes Redmi note 4. R does not face. A and faces South direction.

The girl who likes LG sits exactly between the girls who like Vivo and Lenovo. A likes Lenovo and sits in the middle of the row 1. Q faces North direction and sits immediate left of S. Only one girl sits between the girls who like Redmi and Moto X. R faces one of the immediate neighbours of the girl who likes Redmi Note 4. F faces one of the immediate neighbours of the girl who likes Redmi. Only one girl sits between the girl who likes I Phone 6 and S who likes Nokia. E sits to the immediate right of the girl who faces P. Only two people sit between E and G. P likes neither LG nor MI5.

The girl who likes Lenovo sits second to the right of the one who faces North direction. O sits one of the extreme ends of the line and likes I Phone 6. A faces the opposite direction to the girl who likes Nokia. F faces North direction and the one who faces F, faces South direction. B faces North direction.

60. Who amongst the following faces the girl B?

(a) The girl who likes LG (b) F
(c) The girl who likes Lenovo (d) The girl who likes Moto X
(e) O

61. E likes which of the following Mobile phones?

(a) LG (b) Nokia (c) I Phone 6 (d) Samsung
(e) Redmi

62. Which of the following is true regarding Q?

(a) Q faces South direction.
(b) Q is E's immediate neighbour
(c) Q likes Redmi.
(d) The girl who likes MI5 faces Q.
(e) None of the given options is true.

63. Which one is the immediate neighbour of A?
(a) O (b) P
(c) The one who likes Redmi. (d) The one who likes LG.
(e) The one who likes Samsung.

64. Who amongst the following sits at middle of the row 1?
(a) G (b) B (c) E
(d) The girl who likes Lenovo
(e) None of these

DIRECTIONS ~ (Q. Nos. 65-69) *Study the following information carefully and answer the questions asked.*
« RBI Officers Grade B 2015

Eight family members S, T, U, V, W, X, Y and Z are sitting around a circular table but not necessarily in the same order. Some of them are females and some are males. All of them are related to each other in the same way or the other. Some of them are facing the centre while some are facing outside (i.e. opposite to the centre). Only two people sit between T and W. T faces the centre. X sits second to the right of T. W is the wife of S. No female is an immediate neighbour of W.

U is not an immediate neighbour of T. U is the daughter of W. Both the immediate neighbours of U face the centre.

Only three people sit between S and U's brother. X is not the brother of U. Neither S nor U's brother is an immediate neighbour of X.

Z, the wife of T, sits to the immediate left of V. Both Y and S face a direction opposite to that of U (i.e. if U faces the centre, then both Y and S face outside and vice-versa). U's husband sits second to the left of Y. T's father sits to the immediate right of W. T sits second to the right of S's father. Both the immediate neighbours of X are females.

65. How many people sit between T and S's father when counted from the right of T?
(a) Four (b) Three
(c) None (d) One
(e) Two

66. Who amongst the following sits exactly between Y and W when counted from the left of Y?
(a) T (b) X (c) S (d) Z
(e) U

67. Which of the following statements regarding T is definitely true?
(a) X and Z are immediate neighbours of T.
(b) T sits second to the left of X.
(c) T is the son of S.
(d) None of the given options is correct.
(e) V is the father of T.

68. Who amongst the following faces outside (i.e. opposite to the centre)?
(a) W (b) V (c) U (d) Z
(e) T

69. If it is given that Y is married to X, then what is the position of T with respect to Y's daughter-in-law?
(a) Third to the right (b) Second to the right
(c) Immediate right (d) Second to the left
(e) Third to the left

DIRECTIONS ~ (Q. Nos. 70-75) *Read the given information carefully and answer the given questions.*
« MHA CET MBA 2012

A, B, C, D, E, F, G and H are sitting around a square table in such a way that four of them sit at four corners of the square while four sit in the middle of each of the four sides. The ones who sit at the four corners face the centre of the table while those who sit in the middle of the sides face outside.

B, the wife of E is sitting second to left of G. G is sitting at one of the corners of the table. No female is an immediate neighbour of G.

D's daughter is sitting third to the right of F. F is the mother of H.

H and A are immediate neighbours of each other. Both A and H are daughters of C. H is not an immediate neighbour of F.

D is the brother of C. D is not an immediate neighbour of G. D sits to the immediate left of his father, E.

70. Who sits to the immediate right of F?
(a) A's grandmother (b) A
(c) F's brother-in-law (d) E
(e) C

71. What is the position of E with respect to his daughter-in-law?
(a) Immediate left (b) Third to the right
(c) Third to the left (d) Second to the right
(e) Fourth to the left

72. Four of the following are alike in a certain way based on the given information and so form a group. Which is the one that does not belong to that group?
(a) F (b) A (c) G (d) B
(e) C

73. Who amongst the following is D's daughter?
(a) H (b) G (c) A (d) B
(e) None of these

74. Which of the following is true with respect to the given seating arrangement ?
(a) B sits to the immediate left of her granddaughter.
(b) H sits at one of the corners of the table.
(c) No female is an immediate neighbour of D.
(d) D and H are immediate neighbour of each other.
(e) None of the above.

75. How many people sit between H and her cousin when counted from the left hand side of H?
(a) One (b) Two (c) Three (d) Four
(e) More than four

DIRECTIONS ~ (Q. Nos. 76-80) *Read the given information carefully and answer the given questions.*
« IBPS Clerk (Mains) 2016

There are five units i.e. 1, 2, 3, 4 and 5. Each unit has a different height. Also each unit contains books and boxes. unit 2 is above unit 1 and unit 3 is above unit 2 and so on. Every unit belongs to different country i.e. Beijing, Paris, London, Sydney and Zurich. The total height of all five units is equal to 252"ft.

- Total Height of Unit is equal to the total height of books plus total height of boxes in each unit.
- Height of books is not equal to the height of boxes. Unless specified so.

The unit belongs to London is an even unit. The total height of unit 1 is 75" ft. Sydney does not belong to unit 1. The total height of unit, which belongs to Sydney is 55" ft, There is only one unit between the units which belongs to London and Paris. The height of books and height of boxes in unit 3 are equal. The height of books in unit 2 is not less than 30" ft. The height of books in unit 4 is 4"ft more than height of books which is in unit 3.

The total height of unit which belongs to London is not 37" ft. Unit which has 37" ft will not be immediate above to unit which has 20" ft more height than unit which belongs to Sydney. The height of boxes in unit 2 is 23" ft. Unit belongs to Zurich does not equal height of books and boxes. The total height of unit 2 is an odd number and more than 50" ft and less than 55" ft. Height of boxes in unit 1 is 23" ft more than unit 4. Height of books in unit 5 is 7" ft less than unit 1.

76. What is the total height in unit 3?
(a) 37" ft (b) None of these (c) 32" ft
(d) 53" ft (e) 75" ft

77. Unit 3 belongs to which country?
(a) Paris (b) Zurich (c) Sydney (d) Beijing
(e) London

78. If 'Sydney' is related to 37" ft in the same way as 'Beijing' is related to 53" ft. Which of the following is 'Paris' related to, following the same pattern?
(a) 53" ft (b) 37" ft (c) 75" ft
(d) None of these (e) 32" ft

79. Four of the following five are alike in a certain way and hence they form a group. Which one of the following does not belong to that group?
(a) Sydney (b) 32" ft (c) 75" ft (d) Paris
(e) Beijing

80. What is the height of box in unit 4?
(a) 23" ft (b) 17" ft (c) 27" ft (d) 40"ft
(e) 20" ft

DIRECTIONS ~ (Q. Nos. 81-86) *Study the given information carefully to answer the given questions.*

« MHT MBA 2017

Eight boxes namely, A, B, C, D, E, F, G and H are placed from top to bottom not in the same order. They contain different chocolates, such as silk, temptation, fruit and nut, dairy milk, bubbly, milky bar, kit-kat and 5 star-boxes are packed with different colour paper, such as Yellow, Pink, Blue and Green. Exactly two boxes are packed with same colour paper. Consider the top position as Ist position.

1. There is one box between box B and box D and box D is packed with pink paper and both are in the top 4 positions when boxes are arranged from top to bottom.
2. The box containing dairy milk is kept immediately below blue paper packed box and is packed with same colour paper as E.
3. Box C is kept somewhere between G and H and H being below C.
4. The two green paper packed boxed are kept vertically adjacent to each other and one of the green paper packed box is immediately under the pink paper packed box.
5. Fruit and nut chocolate is kept exactly between F and the box containing milky bar.
6. H doesn't contain silk chocolate.
7. There is one box between box E and box G and box G is kept immediately below the box containing dairy milk.
8. The box containing 5-star chocolate is placed at even numbered place but is not placed at the bottom.
9. The yellow paper packed box which is kept at top either contains silk or kit-kat.
10. Box E is not packed with green paper.
11. F which contains Bubbly is packed with blue paper and among top five.
12. The box containing temptation is packed with blue paper.
13. C doesn't contain any of silk or 5-star chocolate.

81. Which of the following boxes is kept immediately above the box containing dairy milk?
(a) Box containing bubbly
(b) Box containing milky bar
(c) Box containing silk
(d) Box containing temptation
(e) None of the above

82. Four of the following five are alike in a certain way based on the given arrangement and hence form a group. Which of the following does not belong to the group?
(a) A-Dairy milk (b) G-Bubbly
(c) H-Kit-kat (d) B-Temptation
(e) D-5-Star

83. Which of the following boxes contains fruit and nut?
(a) E (b) A (c) D (d) H (e) G

84. What is the position of B in the given stack of boxes?
(a) First from the top (b) Third from the bottom
(c) Fifth from the top (d) Second from the bottom
(e) Second from the top

85. Which of the following represents the contents of box G?
(a) Temptation (b) 5-Star (c) Kit-Kat (d) Silk
(e) Bubbly

86. Which two boxes are packed with pink paper?
(a) D and F (b) C and H
(c) B and G (d) D and E
(e) G and C

DIRECTIONS ~ (Q. Nos. 87-91) *Read the given information carefully and answer the given questions.*

P, Q, R, S, E, F, G and H are eight friends sitting around a circular table. Four of them are facing away from the center and four of them are facing towards the center. Each of them has a different car- Ford, Toyota, Audi, Nissan, Fiat, Datsun, Ferrari and Bentley but not necessarily in the same order. All the given cars are of different colour viz. White, Blue, Orange, Pink, Green, Purple, Yellow and Red, but not necessarily in the same order.

E faces towards the centre and has a White colour car. Both the immediate neighbours of E face away from the center and have either Orange or Pink colour car. S faces away from the center and he has a Ford car. Both the immediate neighbours of S do not face away from the center. E sits third to the right of F, who has a green colour car. F faces away from the center. R sits third to the left of F. The one who has an Orange colour car sits opposite to F.

The one who has Blue colour car is not the immediate neighbour of F and faces away from the center. P sits second to the left of R and he has neither Yellow nor Red colour car. The one who has a Yellow colour car sits between H and F. Q faces away from the center and has Toyota car which is not of Blue colour. E has Ferrari car. The person who has Nissan car sits opposite to S. Audi car is of Purple colour. The person who has Bentley car is not near to G or E. R faces the person who has Datsun car.

87. Who among following has Orange colour car?

(a) E (b) F (c) Q (d) S (e) P

88. Who among following has Red colour car?

(a) Q (b) R (c) F (d) S
(e) None of these

89. G has which of the following car?

(a) Fiat (b) Ferrari (c) Dastun (d) Nissan
(e) Toyota

90. Who among the following has Pink colour car?

(a) Q (b) H (c) F (d) S
(e) None of these

91. Which of the following is S's position with respect to E?

(a) Fourth to the left (b) Third to the right
(c) Third to the left (d) Second to the right
(e) None of these

DIRECTIONS ~ (Q. Nos. 92-96) *Study the following information carefully and answer the questions below.* « IBPS Clerk Mains 2019

Seven persons A, B, C, D, E, F, G are going to participate in seven different races all of which are of different milestones *viz.* 200, 350, 500, 800, 1000, 1200 and 1500. Each of them got different ranks in their respective races as 1st, 2nd, 3rd ...and so on till 7th. Also each of them participated in the race in different years *viz.* 1995, 1998, 2000, 2002, 2007, 2010, 2011. The one who got 1st rank participated in 1200m race. C participated 2 yr after A. D got 4th rank. The milestone of F's race was 4 times of the milestone of the who participated in race in 2011. The one who participated first got 3rd rank. There is a difference of one year between B and G's participation year. F got the lowest rank. Only two person got lower rank than G. A's milestone of race is twice of the one whose rank is just lower than him.

The one who got 6th rank participated in odd numbered year. The one whose rank is just higher than G participated in an odd numbered year. The one whose rank is last participated after the one whose rank is first. The one who participated in 2007 does not have milestone which is a multiple of the one whose rank is 3rd. B does not get higher rank than A.

92. What will be the difference between the milestones of the one who got 3rd rank and the one who got 6th rank?

(a) 300m (b) 700m (c) 1000m (d) 200m
(e) None of these

93. Who got second rank in the race?

(a) B (b) G (c) A (d) D
(e) E

94. What is the milestone of C?

(a) 350m (b) 1500m
(c) 1000m (d) 1200m
(e) 500m

95. Who among the following participated in 1995?

(a) B (b) G (c) A (d) D
(e) E

96. Who among the following got 6th rank?

(a) B (b) G (c) A (d) D
(e) E

DIRECTIONS ~ (Q. Nos. 97-101) *Study the given information carefully and answer the questions that follow.* « IBPS RRB Officer Scale I (Mains) 2017

Eight friends A, B, C, D, E, F, G and H born on 7th, 9th, 16th and 19th in March and July. Each one of them likes either a colour or a fruit. The persons who likes colours were born on that day which is a perfect square and the colour they likes are Yellow, Green, Red and Blue. The persons who were born on the day which denotes a prime numbers like fruits Apple, Cherry, Mango and Banana.

The one who likes Yellow colour was born on a day which is a perfect square in the month of March. No person was born between D and the one who likes Yellow. D doesn't like colours.

Three persons were born between D and the one who likes Mango. There is no person born between the one who likes Mango and Blue colour. The number of people born after the one who likes Blue colour is one less than the number of persons born before A. The one who likes Apple was born immediately before B. B do not like Mango. The number of people born before B is same as the number of persons born after G.

Three persons were born between the one who likes Green and H. H and the one who likes Cherry was born in the same month but not in March. C was born after the one who likes Blue colour. E doesn't like any colour. F doesn't like Apple.

97. Who among the following likes Green colour?

(a) B (b) A (c) G (d) H (e) C

98. Who was born on 16th March?

(a) D (b) A (c) G (d) F (e) E

99. Who among the following likes Cherry?

(a) F (b) G (c) H (d) A (e) B

100. Who was born on 19th July?

(a) C (b) A (c) D (d) B (e) E

101. Who among the following likes Red colour?

(a) A (b) B (c) H (d) C (e) D

DIRECTIONS ~ (Q.Nos. 102-106) *Study the information given below and answer the questions based on it.*

« IBPS PO (Mains) 2019

There are 10 houses A, B, C, M, N, O, X, Y, Z and S in two sides of a street. The houses were built as shown in the figure below and the distances between each house in both the sides are successive integral multiple of 7. Each houses were painted in different colours viz. Green, Yellow, Orange, Blue, Brown, Pink, Red, Grey, Violet and Black but not necessarily in same order.

Note *The distance between two houses is same in both the sides such that each houses exactly faces other house on the other side.*

Facing South

100m

Facing North

The House Y is painted in Green colour. The house which is painted in Violet colour is opposite to the one which is 133 m to the right of Z . Neither B nor X is painted in Blue colour. The house O is opposite to the one which is 147 m to the left of the house that is painted in Red colour.

There is only one house between Z and Y. The house which is painted in Grey and Brown colour were facing opposite to one other. House N is opposite to S. The House which is painted in Pink colour faces the house which is painted in Orange colour. A is not facing North, but it is 210 m to the left of M, which is of Pink colour.

House O is at the end of the street which is painted in Grey. The house which is painted in Orange is on the immediate right of House X, which is at one end of the street. The House which is painted in Red and Violet are not facing North. House S is painted in Black colour. The person from House X walks 20 m South, now he takes a left turn and walks for 100 m to reach point L. The person from House B walks towards South for 56 m and takes an immediate right turn, walks for 89 m to reach point T.

102. How many houses are there between B and C?

(a) Two (b) Three (c) One (d) None
(e) Four

103. What is the minimum distance between L and T and in which direction is T with respect to Y?

(a) 64 m - North - East (b) 32 m - South - West
(c) 48 m - North - West (d) 64 m - North - West
(e) 32 m - South - East

104. What is the distance between House C and B?

(a) 119 m (b) 133 m (c) 210 m (d) 189 m
(e) 266 m

105. What is the distance between Yellow coloured house and Black coloured house?

(a) 189 m (b) 133 m (c) 119 m (d) 147 m
(e) 210 m

106. What is the colour of House B?

(a) Yellow (b) Violet (c) Orange (d) Brown
(e) Red

DIRECTIONS ~ (Q. Nos. 107-110) *Study the following information carefully and answer the questions asked.*

« Indian Bank PO 2017

Nine people namely P, Q, R, S, T, U, V, W and X like nine different movies namely, Twilight, Gladiator, Frozen, Inception, Cindrella, titanic, Watchmen, Vertigo and Dread. Each of them works in either of the three states Viz. Kerala, Haryana and Punjab. There are two posts in the states viz IFS and IPS except Kerala which has only the IFS post. Not more than two people in a state work at the same post.

R works as an IFS but not in Kerala. The one who likes Frozen works with R within the same post. The one who likes watchmen works as an IPS with the one who likes Twilight within the same post. The one who likes watchmen does not work in the state in which R works. T works in the same state in which the one who likes twilight works but not in the same post. Both X and P work as an IFS in the same state.

The one who likes Titanic works in the same post in the same state in which U works. Neither T nor the IPS likes Titanic. S likes Gladiator. S does not work in Haryana,. The one who likes Inception works with S. T does not like inception. V neither likes Watchmen nor works with S. The one who likes Vertigo works with V. Q does not work with the one who likes Vertigo. X does not like Dread.

107. Which of the following combination represents the posts for which P works and the movie he likes?

(a) IFS-Dread (b) IFS-Watchmen
(c) IPS-Vertigo (d) IPS-Dread
(e) None of these

108. Which of the following statements is not true as per the given arrangement?

(a) Q works in Punjab with the one who likes Cindrella.
(b) All the given statements are true.
(c) R works at the same post at which X works.
(d) Both T and V work in the same state.
(e) R likes Titanic.

109. Who amongst the following likes Cindrella?

(a) Q (b) V
(c) S (d) X
(e) T

110. Which of the following combination is true with respect to the given arrangement?

(a) U-IFS- Punjab - Inception
(b) P-IFS- Kerala - Cindrella
(c) T-Haryana-IPS-Vertigo
(d) V-IPS-Haryana- Twilight
(e) S-IFS- Kerala - Gladiator

DIRECTIONS ~ (Q. Nos. 111-115) *Read the following information carefully and answer the questions following it.*

« IBPS PO 2019

Twelve persons X, Y, Z, D, E, F, P, Q, R, K, L and M are staying on six different floors of Apex tower. The floors are 97th, 90th, 55th, 42nd, 23rd and 2nd. Total number of rooms on each of the given floors is different. The total number of rooms on these six floors could be one of the following nineteen, thirty-three, thirty-eight, twenty-four, seventeen and fourty but no two floors can have the same number of rooms. Two of the given persons are living on each floor. X, Y, Q, R, L and M are males while rest of them are females. Females stay on an odd numbered floor where as males are staying on an even numbered floor. X with only Y are staying on the some floor. Z is not staying on the same floor as D. E is not staying on second floor which has thirty-eight rooms. Neither floor 23rd nor floor 42nd has nineteen rooms. The floor which has seventeen rooms is an odd numbered floor but not 55th floor. L stays on the floor which has nineteen rooms. Neither floor 23rd nor floor 42nd has twenty-four rooms. F stay on floor 23rd with only D. P does not stay on the same floor as K. The floor which has nineteen rooms is even-numbered. R stays the floor which has thirty-three rooms whereas D stays on the floor which has fourty rooms. K does not stay on 55th floor.

111. Which of the following floor has the highest number of rooms?

(a) 2nd (b) 97th (c) 23rd (d) 55th
(e) 42nd

112. Which of the following floor has thirty-eight rooms?

(a) 55th (b) 90th (c) 97th (d) 2nd
(e) 23rd

113. Who among the following stays on floor 55th?

(a) P and Z (b) P and E
(c) Z and E (d) Data inadequate
(e) None of these

114. Who among the following are staying on the floor which has seventeen rooms?

(a) E and K (b) Z and K (c) P and Z
(d) Data inadequate (e) None of these

115. On which floor are X and Y staying?

(a) 90th (b) 42nd
(c) 2nd (d) Data inadequate
(e) None of these

DIRECTIONS ~ (Q. Nos. 116-120) *Study the given information carefully to answer the given questions.*

Twelve students namely *viz.* A, B, C, D, E, F, G, H, I, J, K and L of twelve different colleges have conference in six different months namely *viz.* January, February, June, July, September and October on twelve different days i.e. (all persons have different dates) from 9th to 20th of any month but not necessarily in the same order. Two students must have conference in the same month. Each student stays in a hostel in different floor.

The ground floor of the building is numbered 1, the one above that is numbered 2 and so on till the topmost floor is numbered 12.

There are five floors between the persons who have conference in June. The persons who have conference in June does not occupy the floor above the floor numbered 10 and also not occupy the floor below the floor numbered 4. G stayed on the second floor and has a conference on 19th. The one who stayed on the first floor has a conference in September. E has a conference on the date immediately after the date on which K has conference. There are two persons who live between G and H. The floor number and the conference date is same for the person B. The person who has conference on 15th lives immediately below E.

K has conference on one of the dates after 12 and before 16. There are four persons live between K and E.

K has conference in the month of June. B and I have conference in the same month which has 31 days. D who lived on floor numbered 11, has the conference in the month which has less than 30 days. Only one person lives between two persons who have conference in the month of October. The persons who have conference in the month of October lives on two of the floors above the floor numbered 6. There are five floors between B and I.

There are six floors between the person J and the person who has conference in the month of September. The person F stays in a middle between the person E and C. L does not have conference in the month of June. H does not have conference on 20th. L does not have conference on 16th. There is only one person living between the persons who have conference in the month of July.

There are four floors between the persons who have conference on 19th and 10th. The person who has conference on 17th lives immediately above the person who has conference on 20th. H does not have conference on 20th. A does not have conference on 11th. The person who has conference on 18th lives immediately above the person who has conference on 11.

116. F stays on which of the following floors?

(a) 12 (b) 8 (c) 7 (d) 4
(e) None of these

117. Who among the following has conference in September?

(a) A, B (b) J, F (c) B, E (d) D, G
(e) E, G

118. Four among the following five form a group in a certain way. Which of the following does not belong to group?

(a) C-October (b) J-September
(c) F-September (d) B-January
(e) E-October

119. Which of the following is correctly matched?

(a) 12-B-June-17 (b) 12-F-June-17
(c) 2-G-February-19 (d) 2-G-September-19
(e) 5-E-July-18

120. Who among the following has conference on 20th?

(a) A (b) C (c) B (d) D
(e) J

DIRECTIONS ~ (Q. Nos. 121-125) *Study the given information carefully to answer the given questions.*
« SBI PO Mains 2015

Ten people G, H, I, J, K, L, W, X, Y and Z live in a building with four floors. Each floor has 3 flats-flat 1, flat 2, and flat 3 in the same order from left to right. Ground floor is numbered floor 1 and top most floor is floor 4. Each flat is built in such a way that Flat 1 of floor 2 is just above Flat 1 of floor 1 and so on. The two flats in which no one lives are on even numbered floor and in even numbered flat respectively. G does not live on even numbered floor and even numbered flat. W lives in the flat which is just above H's flat.

The only flat which is between K and X is vacant and K lives in one of the flat above X. L lives in an odd numbered flat which is in the left of X on the same floor. Z and Y lives on the same floor and no one else is living with them on that floor. G lives on a floor and flat just above W's floor and flat. I live on one of the floor on which one flat is vacant. Z and I both live in the flat which is numbered 1.

121. Who is living just above X?

(a) K (b) G (c) J (d) Z
(e) None of these

122. Which of the following statement is true about G?

(a) G lives on an even numbered flat.
(b) K is the immediate neighbour of G.
(c) G lives on a floor on which one flat is vacant.
(d) None is true
(e) G and W lives on the same floor.

123. Which of the following lives on the ground floor?

(a) G (b) I (c) L (d) W
(e) Both (a) & (c)

124. Which of the following does not belong to a certain group?

(a) G (b) L (c) W (d) H (e) Y

125. Who is living in flat 1 on floor 4?

(a) Z (b) Y (c) No one (d) G
(e) W

DIRECTIONS ~ (Q. Nos. 126-130) *Study the given information carefully to answer the given questions.*

« SBI PO Mains 2016

The seven brothers M, N, O, P, Q, R and S of Gupta's family buy a building of seven floors in Mumbai and they live on different floors but not necessarily in the same order. The lower most floor of the building is numbered 1, the one above that numbered 2 and so on till the topmost floor are numbered 7. Each brother of Gupta's family consumes beers of different brands-Kings, Corona, Grolosch, Heineken, Carlsberg, Budweiser, Haywards but not necessary in the same order. They all are fond of expensive bikes. Each one has bike of different brands viz. Yamaha, BMW, Harley Davidson, Suzuki, Hero, Bajaj and Ducati (But not necessarily in the same order.)

M lives on an odd numbered floor but not on the floor numbered 3. M consumes beer of Grolosch brand. The one who has Hero bike lives immediately above M. Only two people live between P and the one who has Hero bike. No one consumes beer of Carlsberg brand who lives on floor number 2 or 4. The one who has BMW bike lives on one of the odd numbered floors above P. Only three people live between O and the one who has BMW bike. The one who has Suzuki bike consumes beer of Kings brand. The one who has Harley Davidson lives immediately above O.

The one who has Yamaha bike lives immediately above the one who has Ducati bike. The one who has Ducati bike does consume beer of Carlsberg brand. S lives on an odd numbered floor. N consumes beer of Corona brand. Only one person lives between N and Q. The person who consumes beer of Haywards brand have Bajaj bike. N lives on one of the floors above Q. Neither O nor M have Suzuki bike. Q does not consume beer of Budweiser brand. Q does not have Harley Davidson.

126. Which of the following bike does M have?

(a) Bajaj (b) Ducati (c) Harley Davidson
(d) BMW (e) Yamaha

127. Which of the following combinations is true with respect to the given arrangement?

(a) Bajaj-O- Haywards (b) BMW-R-Corona
(c) Ducati-S- Carlsberg (d) Hero-P-Carlsberg
(e) Suzuki-N-Kings

128. If all the people are made to sit in alphabetical order from top to bottom, the positions of how many people will remain unchanged?

(a) Four (b) None (c) Two (d) One (e) Three

129. Which of the following statements is true with respect to the given arrangement?

(a) The one who has Ducati bike lives immediately below M
(b) R have BMW bike
(c) None of the given options is true
(d) Only four people live between P and S
(e) S lives immediately below Q

130. Who amongst the following lives on the floor numbered 2?

(a) N (b) The one who likes corona
(c) The one who likes kings (d) P
(e) R

DIRECTIONS ~ (Q. Nos. 131-135) *Study the following information carefully and answer the questions given below.*

Seven persons are living in a 9-floor building whereas groundf loor is number 1 and just above the ground floor is number 2 and so on and topmost floor is number 9. There are two floors which are vacant floors. Persons are P, Q R, S, T, U and V but not necessary in the same order. They have different ages viz. 27, 25, 24, 31, 55, 81 and 9 but not necessary in the same order. Q sits one of the odd numbered floors above the floor number 5 and his age is 31yr. There are 2 floors between Q and the person whose age is 55yr. Both vacant floors are in even numbered floor. Floor number 8 is not the vacant floor. The age of U is square of the age of R, who does not live an even numbered floor. The number of floors between Q and T is same as between Q and P. P's age is perfect square. Difference between the age of the person, who lives in top floor and ground floor, is 15yr. There is only one person lives between Q and S, whose age is an odd number. Neither R nor V lives on topmost floor.

131. On which of the following floor does U live?

(a) 8th floor (b) 3rd floor
(c) 2nd floor (d) Can't be determined
(e) None of these

132. How many persons live between U and V?

(a) 3 (b) 4
(c) 5 (d) Can't be determined
(e) None of these

133. Who among the following persons live on ground floor and top floor respectively?

(a) TP (b) TS (c) RT (d) TR
(e) None of these

134. If all the persons live in an alphabetical order from top to bottom, then how many persons position will be changed (Vacant will be remain the vacant)?

(a) None (b) Two
(c) Three (d) Four
(e) None of these

135. What is the total age of U, R and V?

(a) 118 (b) 116 (c) 117 (d) 81
(e) None of these

DIRECTIONS ~ (Q. Nos. 136-139) *Study the given information carefully and answer the given questions.*

There is a figure of road network given below which connects various routes from one point to another. There are certain points viz. A, B, C, ... K.

There is a value between two points which denotes the distance between both point in kms.

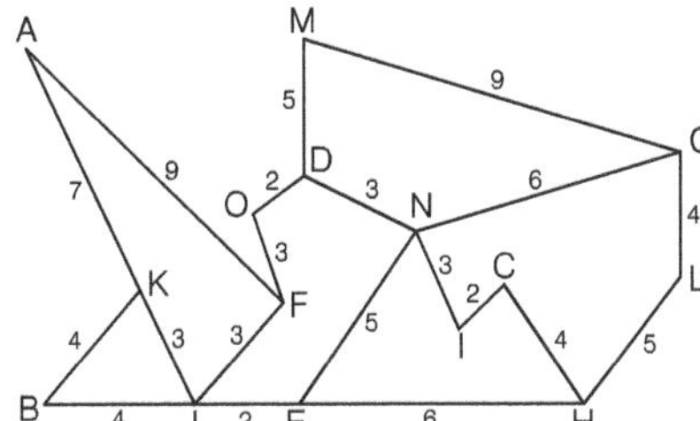

Conditions:

1. If a person is passing by a four wheeler through this road network, he has to pay ₹ 10 as toll tax, ₹ 7 as road tax and ₹ 5 as vehicle tax in addition to a charge of ₹ 2 per km.
2. If a person is passing by a two wheeler through this road network, he has to pay ₹ 8 as toll tax, ₹ 5 as road tax and ₹ 3 as vehicle tax in addition to a charge of ₹ 2 per km.
3. If a person is passing through this road network on foot, he has to pay road tax only which is equal to the distance between both the points.
(If a person walks 10 kms, he has to pay ₹ 10)

136. If Ram is going from point J to point G by a four wheeler, then what is the minimum expenditure he has to bear?

(a) ₹ 58 (b) ₹ 56 (c) ₹ 48 (d) ₹ 36 (e) ₹ 42

137. Four of the following five are alike in a certain way based on their seating positions and so form a group. Which of the following is different from the group?

(a) F (b) J (c) E (d) H (e) G

138. If Ramesh is going from point F to point N, what is the maximum expenditure bear by him, when he was going on foot. (When he'll not cross a point more than one time.)

(a) ₹ 88 (b) ₹ 58
(c) ₹ 37 (d) ₹ 25
(e) None of these

139. Which of the following is true according to a certain logic?

(a) H - N - 9 (b) D - G - 11
(c) F- N - 10 (d) E - G - 15
(e) None of these

DIRECTIONS ~ (Q. Nos. 140-144) *Study the given information carefully and answer the given questions.*

Four persons Prakhar, Deepak, Vishal and Rajeev participated in Annual grading of Arihant Publication India Limited. They have taken the objective test. Now, they are waiting for their turn for one to one in head office. They have different serial numbers for one to one round 1, 2, 3 and 4 but not necessarily in the same order.

They sat on different chairs-Chair 1, Chair 2, Chair 3 and Chair 4 (from left to right). These four persons are from different cities (branches)- Kanpur, Sitapur, Lucknow and Agra. These persons have different years of work experience in Arihant Publication viz. 9 years, 4 years, 6 years and 11 years (from left to right). Ages of these four persons are 42, 40, 36 and 38 but not necessarily in the same order.

Vishal sits to the left of the person who is from Agra (but not exact next) who gives his interview before Vishal who is 2 years younger than Vishal. Deepak is 4 years younger than the person who is from Sitapur and who is next to left of Deepak. The man who sits on Chair 1 is not Prakhar and gives interview next after the 42 years old. 40 years old person sits next to the right of the person who is from Kanpur and there are only one person gives interview between them.

The person who is from Lucknow gives interview next after the person who sits on Chair 4 (who doesn't give interview first); he is older than both the latter and Rajeev. The person who gives the interview on 2nd number, sits next to the one who gives interview on 4th number, who is more than two years older than the one who gives interview on 2nd number.

140. How many person/persons give/gives interview between Prakhar and the one who is from Agra branch?

(a) None (b) 1
(c) 2 (d) Either 1 or None
(e) Cannot be determined

141. Who is from Kanpur branch?

(a) Rajeev (b) Prakhar
(c) Deepak (d) Vishal
(e) Cannot be determined

142. What is the age difference between the one who is from Agra and who gives interview on 4 number (in days approx)?

(a) 1,460 days (b) 2,190 days
(c) 1,095 days (d) 730 days
(e) 1,825 days

143. What is the age and the branch of the person who sits on chair-1?

(a) 38-Lucknow (b) 42-Lucknow
(c) 36-Kanpur (d) 38-Kanpur
(e) 42-Agra

144. Which of the following is true?

(a) Rajeev-40 years-Agra
(b) Prakhar-42 years-Sitapur
(c) Deepak-36 years-Lucknow
(d) Vishal-40 years-Kanpur
(e) Deepak-42 years-Agra

Answers / WITH EXPLANATIONS

Solutions (Q. Nos. 1-5) *Following table can be drawn from given information.*

Persons	Item	Persons	Item
U	Tie	H	Nail Paint
G	Coat	T	Shirt
S	Ring	E	Diary
		F	Goggles

1. (*c*) H buys nail paint.

2. (*a*) Diary bought immediately after shirt.

3. (*c*) Three persons buys items between S and F.

4. (*d*) E-Diary is true.

5. (*b*) G buys item immediately before 'Ring'.

Solutions (Q.Nos. 6-10) *According to the given information,*

Month	Person	Month	Person
January	E	July	H
April	D	August	A
May	G	October	B
June	F	December	C

6. *(a)* F and C are third to E and H respectively. Similarly, D is related to H.

7. *(d)* From the table, A is watching the movie in August.

8. *(c)* Only one person is watching movie between D and F, therefore H will be the answer.

9. *(b)* H, C, B, and G are watching movie in a month having 31 days. But D is watching movie in a month having 30 days is April.

10. *(c)* From the table clearly four persons are watching movie between B and D.

Solutions (Q. Nos. 11-15) *Following table can be drawn from given information.*

Peoples	Hobby	States
A	Reading	Maharashtra
B	Dancing	Gujarat
C	Singing	Kerala
D	Pottery-making	Rajasthan
E	Reading	Punjab
F	Travelling	Karnataka
G	Sculpting	Odisha

11. (*b*) C likes Singing.

12. (*d*) D-pottery-making-Rajasthan is true.

13. (*c*) F belongs to Karnataka.

14. (*a*) Sculpting-Odisha is true.

15. (*e*) Person belongs to Punjab likes Reading.

Solutions (Q. Nos. 16-20) *Following table can be drawn from given information*

Name of Employee	Channel	Department
W	DD	Marketing
P	BBC	Marketing
Q	Aaj Tak	Marketing
R	Sony	Finance
U	NDTV	Finance
T	Star	Finance
S	ESPN	Production
V	Zee	Production

16. (*c*) P likes BBC.

17. (*c*) U works in Finance.

18. (*b*) U likes NDTV.

19. (*e*) None of the given group work in marketing department.

20. (*a*) Q works in Marketing.

21. (*c*) Rohit and Tanya cannot work together means that options (b) and (d) are out. Kunal and Shobha will not work together, so option (a) is out. Hence, the right answer is (c), where no one has problem working with another person of the group and Mukesh and Kunal will also work together.

22. (*d*)

1st Week Visiting	2nd Week Visiting
UK	France
Austria	Switzerland
Belgium	Italy
Germany	Norway

France and Switzerland must be visited in same week. So, option (a) is eliminated, option (b) is also eliminated on the same ground. Option (c) is also eliminated for the reason that Austria and Switzerland visited in different weeks. So, right option is (d).

Solutions (Q. Nos. 23-28) *Following table can be drawn from given information.*

Month	Date	People (Colour)
January	24th	R (Green)
June	15th	Q (Silver)
June	24th	L (Violet)
October	15th	P (Black)
October	24th	O (Pink)
November	15th	M (Yellow)
November	24th	N (Red)

23. (*e*) Two people have meeting after O.

24. (*d*) M and the one who likes Violet have meeting in different months while all others have meeting in the same months.

25. (*b*) One people have a meeting between P and the one who likes Yellow.

26. (*b*) P likes Black colour.
27. (*e*) The one who likes Pink has a meeting in October is true.
28. (*e*) R have a meeting on the 24 of January.

Solutions (Q. Nos. 29-33)

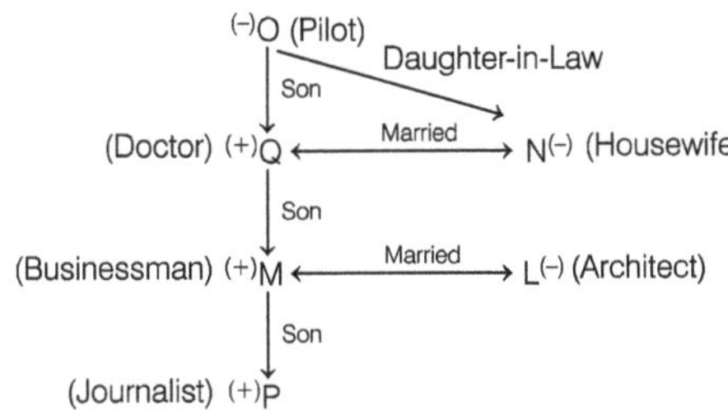

29. (*c*) L, N and O are the three ladies in the group.
30. (*a*) N is married to Q.
31. (*a*) L is an architect.
32. (*d*) P's profession is journalist.
33. (*e*) Q is the son of O.

Solutions (Q. Nos. 34-38) *Sitting arrangement of eight people is as follows*

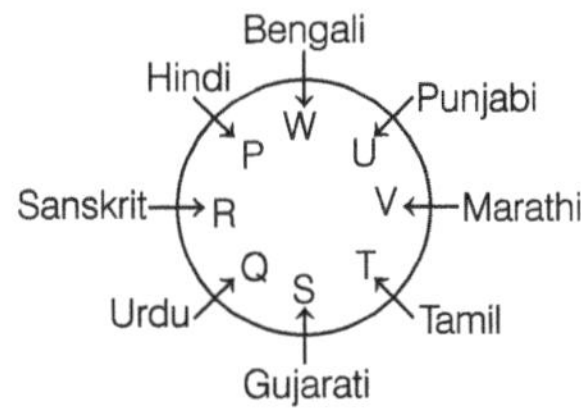

34. (*d*) V sits to the immediate left of U, is true.
35. (*a*) Except S-Marathi, in all others the given person is to the immediate left of the person who speaks the given language.
36. (*e*) U is equidistant from T and the one who speaks Hindi, when counted from the left of the person who speaks Hindi.
37. (*a*) R speaks Sanskrit.
38. (*c*) Q, who speaks Urdu sits third to the right of W.

Solutions (Q. Nos. 39-43) *Following table can be drawn from given information.*

S.No.	Box	Number of Chocolates
7	A	64
6	D	39
5	G	27
4	E	41
3	B	13
2	F	78
1	C	50

39. (*a*) Boxes G, E are kept exactly between box D and box B.
40. (*d*) 41 chocolates are kept in box E.
41. (*d*) Box F contains maximum number of chocolates i.e. 78. Box B contains minimum number of chocolate i.e. 13.
42. (*a*) 50-D, is not true.
43. (*d*) Box F is immediately below box B.

Solutions (Q. Nos. 44-46)

S. No.	Boxes	Colours
1.	P	......
2.	......	......
3.	Q	Blue
4.	......	......
5.	R	......
6.	S	Purple
7.	......	Yellow
8.	......	......
9.	......	......
10.	T	......
11.	......	Brown

44. (*b*) Eleven boxes are there in the arrangement.
45. (*c*) Four boxes are there between box R and box T.
46. (*d*) Box S is immediately above Yellow box.

Solutions (Q. Nos. 47-49) *According to the given information, the arrangement is as follows*

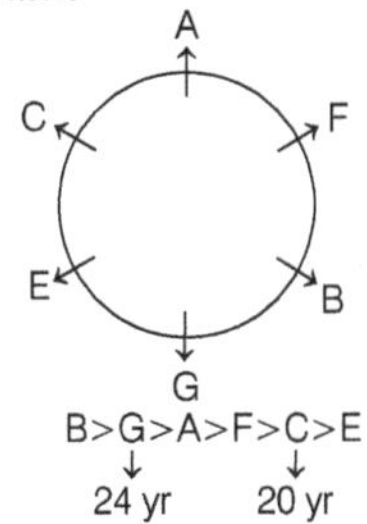

B>G>A>F>C>E

24 yr (G), 20 yr (C)

47. (*e*) A's age lies between 24 yr and 20 yr. So, the possible age of A = 22 yr
48. (*b*) E is the youngest among all.
49. (*d*) G is third to the left of A and also third to the right of A.

Solutions (Q. Nos. 50-54)

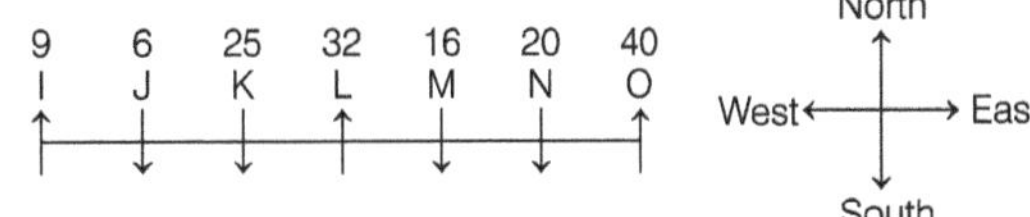

50. (*a*) As, the age of K is 25, the age of M is 16. Similarly, the age of L is 32.
51. (*d*) I is sitting extreme left of the row.
52. (*c*) O sits third to the right of L and his age is 40.
53. (*e*) O faces North direction.
54. (*a*) The age of M is 16 yr.

Solutions (Q. Nos. 55-59) *According to the given information,*

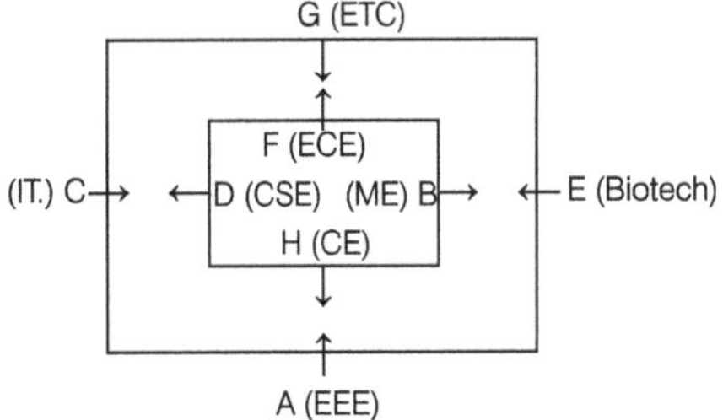

55. (a) A belongs to EEE.

56. (b) G faces F.

57. (a) A faces the one who sits 3rd to the left of the one who belongs to ME.

58. (a) G belongs to ETC.

59. (c) E sits second to the left of the one who belongs to IT.

Solutions (Q. Nos. 60-64)

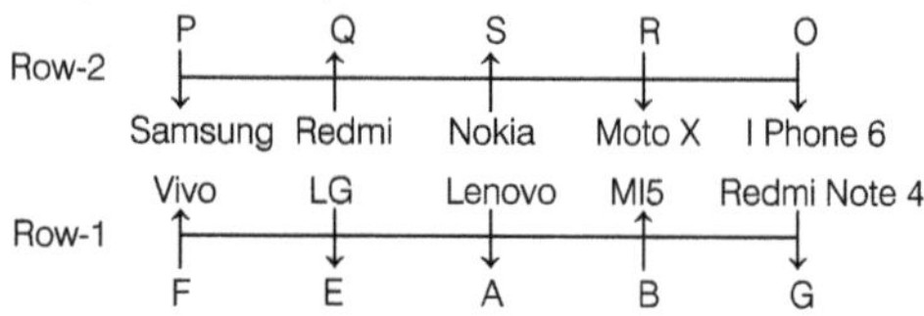

60. (d) The girl who likes Moto-X, faces B.

61. (a) E likes LG.

62. (c) Q likes Redmi.

63. (d) The one who likes LG is immediate neighbour of A.

64. (d) The girl who likes Lenovo i.e. A sits in the middle of row 1.

Solutions (Q. Nos. 65-69) *On the basis of given information the sitting arrangement is as following*

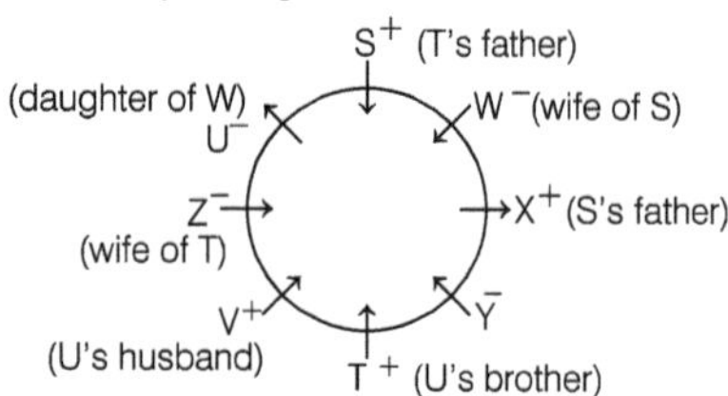

65. (d) There is only one person i.e. Y who sits between T and S's father when counted from the right of T.

66. (d) 'Z' sits exactly between Y and W when counted from the left of Y.

67. (c) T is the son of S is definitely true.

68. (c) Amongst the given alternatives, U faces outside.

69. (e) T is third to the left of W, who is Y's daughter-in-law.

Solutions (Q. Nos. 70-75) *According to the given information, sitting arrangement and relationship among the persons are given below.*

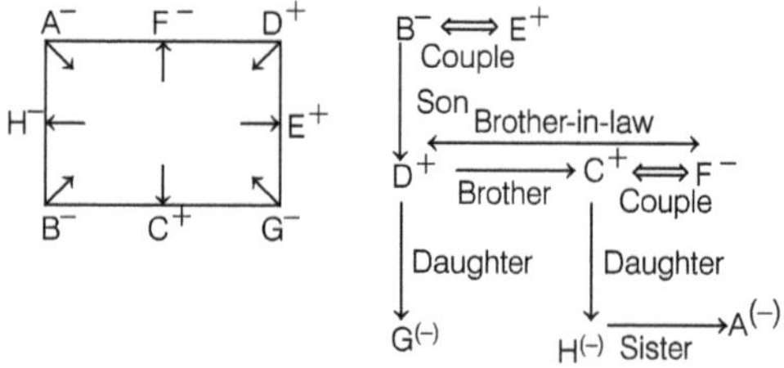

70. (c) The person who sits immediate right of F, is D who is F's brother-in-law.

71. (d) Daughter-in-law of E is F and E is sitting second to the right of F.

72. (e) Among F, A, G, B and C, only C is male while others are females.

73. (b) D's daughter is G.

74. (a) Statement (a) is true i.e. B sits to the immediate left of her granddaughter H.

75. (b) Cousin of H is G and number of persons between H and G is two when counted from the left hand side of H.

Solutions (Q.Nos. 76-80) *Following table can be drawn from the given information.*

Unit	Country	Height of (Books + Box) = Total height of Unit
5	Sydney	28" ft + 27" ft = 55" ft
4	Paris	20" ft + 17" ft = 37" ft
3	Beijing	16" ft + 16" ft = 32" ft
2	London	30" ft + 23" ft = 53" ft
1	Zurich	35" ft + 40" ft = 75" ft

76. (c) Height of unit 3 is 32" ft.

77. (d) Unit 3 belongs to Beijing.

78. (e) As, Sydney 55" ft + 1
Paris 37" ft,
and Beijing 32" ft + 1
London 53" ft
Similarly, Paris 37" ft + 1
Beijng 32" ft

79. (d) Except Paris, all other have odd numbered unit.

80. (b) Height of box in unit 4 is 17" ft.

Solutions (Q. Nos. 81-86) Following table can be drawn from given information.

S. No.	Box	Chocolate	Colour of Packing Paper
1	B	Silk	Yellow
2	A	Temptation	Blue
3	D	Dairy Milk	Pink
4	G	5-Star	Yellow
5	F	Bubbly	Blue
6	E	Fruit and nut	Pink
7	C	Milky bar	Green
8	H	Kit-Kat	Green

81. (d) Box containing temptation is kept immediately above the box containing dairy milk.

82. (c) A-Temptation, G-5-Star
D-Dairy Milk, F-Bubbey
H-Kit-Kat, B-Silk
A-Temptation
and D-Dairy Milk
G-5-Star
H-Kit-Kat is different from others.

83. (a) Box E contains Fruit and Nut.

84. (a) B is first from top.

85. (b) Box G contains 5-Star.

86. (d) D and E boxes are packed with Pink paper.

Solutions (Q. Nos. 87-91)

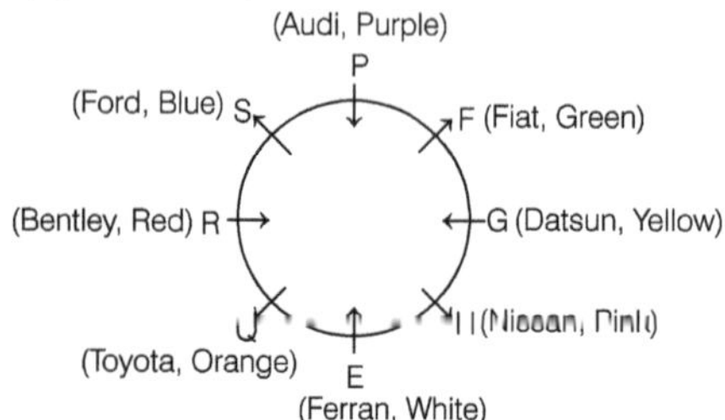

87. (c) Q has Orange colour car.

88. (b) R has Red colour car.
89. (c) G has Datsun car.
90. (b) H has Pink colour car.
91. (c) S is third to the left of E.

Solutions (Q. Nos. 92-96)

Persons	Rank	Milestone	Participation Year
A	2	1000	1998
B	6	200	2011
C	1	1200	2000
D	4	350	2007
E	3	500	1995
F	7	800	2002
G	5	1500	2010

Rank based comparison,
$C > A > E > D > G > B > F$

92. (a) E got 3rd rank and his milestone is 500 m and B got 6th rank and his milestone is 200 m.
∴ Required difference = 500 − 200 = 300 m
93. (c) A got second rank in the race.
94. (d) C's milestone is 1200 m.
95. (e) E participated in 1995.
96. (a) B got 6th rank.

Solutions (Q. Nos. 97-101) *According to the given information, we get the following results.*

Month	Date	Persons	Colour/Fruit
March	7	E	Apple
March	9	B	Green
March	16	A	Yellow
March	19	D	Banana
July	7	F	Cherry
July	9	H	Red
July	16	G	Blue
July	19	C	Mango

97. (a) B likes Green colour.
98. (b) A was born on 16th March.
99. (a) F likes Cherry.
100. (a) C was born on 19th July.
101. (c) H likes Red colour.

Solutions (Q. Nos. 102-106)

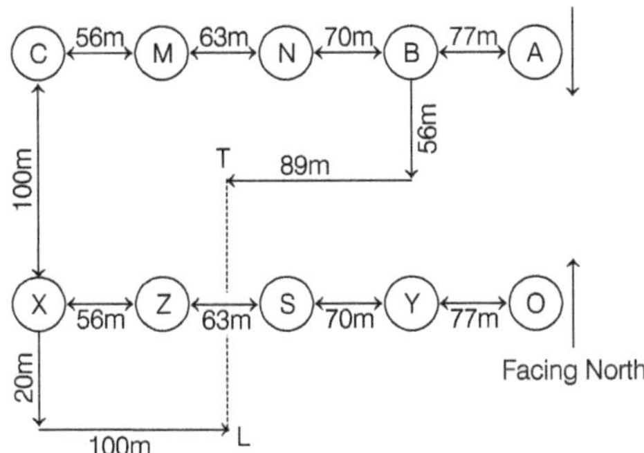

House	Paint Colour
A	Brown
B	Violet
C	Blue
M	Pink
N	Red
O	Grey
X	Yellow
Y	Green
Z	Orange
S	Black

102. (a) These are two houses between B and C.
103. (d) Minimum distance between L and T
$= (100 - 56) + 20$
$= 44 + 20 = 64$ m
Clearly, T is in North-West direction with respect to Y.
104. (d) The distance between C and B = 56 + 63 + 70 = 189 m
105. (c) X and S are Yellow and Black coloured house, respectively.
The distance between X and S = 56 + 63 = 119 m
106. (b) The colour of house B is violet.

Solutions (Q. Nos. 107-110)

Person	Movie	State	Post
P	Dread	Kerala	IFS
Q	Inception	Punjab	IPS
R	Titanic	Punjab	IFS
S	Gladiator	Punjab	IPS
T	Vertigo	Haryana	IFS
U	Frozen	Punjab	IFS
V	Twilight	Haryana	IPS
W	Watchmen	Haryana	IPS
X	Cindrella	Kerala	IFS

107. (a) P works as an IFS officer and he likes Dread movie.
108. (a) Statement (a) is not true as per the given arrangement.
109. (d) X likes Cindrella.
110. (d) V-IPS-Haryana-Twilight is the correct combination.

Solutions (Q. Nos. 111-115)

Floors	Person	Number of rooms
97th	E/Z and K	Seventeen
90th	M/Q and L	Nineteen
55th	Z/E and P	Twenty-four
42nd	Q/M and R	Thirty -three
23rd	F and D	Fourty
2nd	X and Y	Thirty-eight

Males = X, Y, Q, R, L and M
Females = Z, D, E, F, P and K

111. (c) Floor 23rd has highest number of rooms i.e. 40.
112. (d) 2nd floor has 38 rooms.

113. (*d*) Either Z or E and P stay on 55th floor. So, the correct answer is data inadequate.

114. (*d*) 97th floor has 17 rooms and either E or Z and K are staying on this floor. So, the correct answer is data inadequate.

115. (*c*) X and Y are staying on 2nd floor.

Solutions (Q. Nos. 116-120) *Given information can be arranged as below*

Floor	Person	Month	Date
12	B	January	12
11	D	February	17
10	A	June	20
9	E	October	14
8	F	September	15
7	C	October	10
6	I	January	18
5	H	July	11
4	K	June	13
3	L	July	9
2	G	February	19
1	J	September	16

116. (*b*) F stays on 8th floor.

117. (*b*) J and F have conference in September.

118. (*c*) Except F, all persons have conference on even dates. Hence F, September does not belong to group.

119. (*c*) 2-G-February-19 is correctly matched.

120. (*a*) A has conference on 20th.

Solutions (Q. Nos. 121-125) *Following table can be drawn from given information.*

Flat→ Floor↓	Flat 1	Flat 2	Flat 3
Floor 4	Z	Vacant	Y
Floor 3	J	K	G
Floor 2	I	Vacant	W
Floor 1	L	X	H

121. (*e*) None of these.

122. (*b*) K is the immediate neighbour of G.

123. (*c*) L lives on the ground floor.

124. (*b*) Except L, all are in flat 3.

125. (*a*) Z lives in flat 1 on floor 4.

Solutions (Q. Nos. 126-130) *Following table can be drawn from given information.*

Brother	Beer	Bike	Floor
S	Kings	Suzuki	7
N	Corona	Hero	6
M	Grolosch	BMW	5
Q	Heineken	Yamaha	4
P	Carlsberg	Ducati	3
R	Budeweiser	Harley Davidson	2
O	Haywards	Bajaj	1

126. (*d*) M have BMW.

127. (*a*) Bajaj-O-Haywards.

128. (*c*) Positions two people will remain unchanged.

129. (*c*) None of the given options is true.

130. (*e*) R lives on floor numbered 2.

Solutions (Q. Nos. 131-135) *Following table can be drawn from given information.*

Person	Age	Floor
T	24	9
V/U	27/81	8
Q	31	7
Vacant	-	6
P	25	5
S	55	4
U/V	81/27	3
Vacant	-	2
R	9	1

131. (*d*) We can't determine the floor on which U lives..

132. (*a*) 3 persons live between U and V.

133. (*c*) R lives on ground floor and T lives on top floor.

134. (*a*) None of the person will remain on same position..

135. (*c*) Total age of U, R and V is 117.

136. (*c*) Minimum expenditure $= (2 + 5 + 6) \times 2 + 10 + 7 + 5$
$= 26 + 10 + 7 + 5 =$ ₹ 48

137. (*b*) J is directly connected with 4 points, while all others are directly connected with 3 points.

138. (*b*) Route : F - A - K - B - J - E - H - L - G - M - D - N
$(9 + 7 + 4 + 4 + 2 + 6 + 5 + 4 + 9 + 5 + 3) =$ ₹ 58

139. (*a*) H - N - 9 is true. (9 is the minimum distance between H and N).

Solutions (Q. Nos. 140-144)

Person	Chair number	Experience (in years)	Sequence number for interview	Branch	Age
Rajeev	1	9	2	Kanpur	36
Vishal	2	4	4	Lucknow	40
Prakhar	3	6	1	Sitapur	42
Deepak	4	11	3	Agra	38

140. (*b*) Only one person gives the interview between given criteria.

141. (*a*) Rajeev is from Kanpur branch.

142. (*d*) From above table,
Age of person who is from Agra = 38 yr (Deepak)
Age of person who gives interview on 4th number = 40 yr (Vishal)

Required difference $= 40 - 38 = 2$ yr
$= 2 \times 365$ days $= 730$ days

143. (*c*) Rajeev is 36 yr old. His branch is Kanpur.

144. (*b*) Prakhar-42 yr-Sitapur is the correct answer.

CHAPTER / 12

Clock

A Clock is an instrument used for indicating the time. It is an electronic device that presents the duration of hour, minute and second.

The **face** or **dial** of a clock is divided along the circumference into **12 equal spaces** called **hour spaces** and **60 equal** spaces called **minute spaces**. The clock has mainly two hands. The **larger** one is called **minute hand** which gives minute and the **smaller** one is called **hour hand** which gives hour.

In some clocks, third **hand known** as **second hand** is also given.

The basic structure of a clock with three hands which is as follows

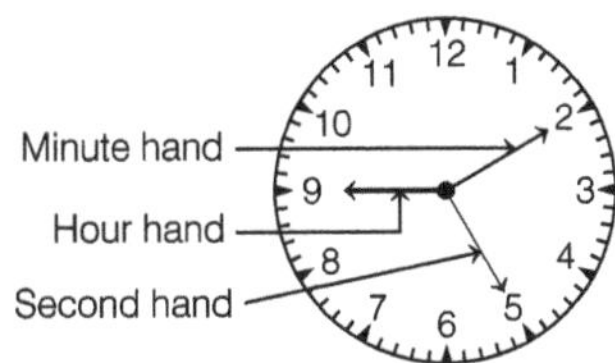

The clock represents two things *i.e.,* minute and hour.

The **minute** is a unit of time equal to $\frac{1}{60}$th of an hour or 60 Second *i.e.,* 1 min = 60 Second (s).

An **hour** is a unit of measurement for the time duration of 60 min or 3600 second.

i.e., 1 h = 60 min= 3600 s

Relative Movement of Hands of Clock

Clocks follow the principle of relative speed. Both hands move in the same direction *i.e.,* (clockwise direction). The minute hand moves around the whole circumference of the clock once in 1h.

The hour hand moves around the whole circumference of the clock once in 12h. Thus, the minute hand is twelve times faster than the hour hand.

The distance between two consecutive number in the clock is equal to 5 min.

In an hour, the hour hand crosses 5 min spaces while the minute hand crosses 60 min spaces.

∴ In 60 min, the minute hand gains (60 – 5) = 55 min over hour hand

∴ 1 min is gained by minute hand over hour hand in

$$\frac{60}{55} = \frac{12}{11} \text{ min}$$

Several types of questions based on clock are asked in various competitive exams.

TYPE 01

Angle Between the Hands of Clock

In this type of questions, a particular time is given and the candidate is asked to find out the angle between the hour hand and the minute hand at that particular time.

For solving these type of questions, a candidate is required to have a basic knowledge about the angles traced by hands of a clock at different time.

The circumference of the dial of a clock is equal to 360°. In other words, we can say that when minute hand, moving clockwise, starts from 12 and again reaches at 12, then it completes one round which is equal to 360°.

The angle between two consecutive digits/numbers of a clock is 30°. When minute hand completes one round, then it crosses 60 min spaces of dial.

It means 60 min spaces = 360°

$$\therefore \quad 1 \text{ min space} = \frac{360°}{60} = 6°$$

Clearly, minute hand traces an angle of 6° in 1 min.

When hour hand completes a round, then it crosses 12 h spaces of dial.

$$12 \text{ h} = 360° \Rightarrow 1 \text{ h} = \frac{360°}{12} = 30°$$

Hour hand traces an angle of 30° in 1 h

$$1 \text{ h} = 30° \Rightarrow 60 \text{ min} = 30°$$

$$\Rightarrow \quad 1 \text{ min} = \frac{30°}{60°} = \left(\frac{1}{2}\right)^{\circ}$$

Clearly, hour hand traces an angle of $\left(\frac{1}{2}\right)^{\circ}$ in 1 min.

Thus, angle traced per minute by

(i) Second hand = 360° (ii) Minute hand = 6°

(iii) Hour hand = $\left(\frac{1}{2}\right)^{\circ}$

Formulae to Find Angle between Hands of Clock

- When the minute hand is behind the hour hand and in clock, the time is x min past n, then the angle between these hands $=\left[30\left(n-\frac{x}{5}\right)+\frac{x}{2}\right]^{\circ}$
- When the hour hand is behind the minute hand and in clock, the time is x min past n, then the angle between these hands $=\left[30\left(\frac{x}{5}-n\right)-\frac{x}{2}\right]^{\circ}$

***Ex* 01** When the minute hand covers a distance of 1h 20 min, then what is the angular distance covered by it?

(a) 310° (b) 192° (c) 480° (d) 420°

***Solution* (c)** Total minute spaces = 1h + 20 min = 60 min + 20 min = 80 min

$\because$ 1 min space = 6°

$\therefore$ 80 min spaces = 80 × 6° = 480°

The relative speed of the minute hand with respect to hour hand is $5\frac{1}{2}^{\circ}$ per minute and at any time, they make an angle between 0° and 180° with each other. Whenever you get answer in decimals, then remember that the base is 60.

***Ex* 02** What is the angle traced by hour hand in15 min?

(a) 7.5° (b) 8° (c) 6.5° (d) 5°

***Solution* (a)** $\because$ Angle traced by hour hand in 1 min = $\left(\frac{1}{2}\right)^{\circ}$

$\therefore$ Angle traced by hour hand in 15 min = $15 \times \frac{1^{\circ}}{2} = 7.5^{\circ}$

***Ex* 03** What will be angle between the two hands of a clock when the time is 8 : 50?

(a) 65° (b) 30° (c) 55° (d) 35°

***Solution* (d)**

Method I $\because$ Angle traced by the hour hand in 12 h = 360°

So, angle traced by the hour hand in 8 h 50 min

i.e., $\frac{53}{6}$ h $=\left(\frac{360}{12}\times\frac{53}{6}\right)^{\circ}=265^{\circ}$

$\therefore$ Angle traced by the minute hand in 60 min = 360°

$\therefore$ Angle traced by minute hand in 50 min = $\frac{360^{\circ}}{60}\times 50 = 300^{\circ}$

$\therefore$ Required angle = (300° − 265°) = 35°

Method II In the given question, hour hand is behind the minute hand. Also, given, $n = 8$, $x = 50$

Then, according to the formula,

$\therefore$ Required angle $=\left\{30\left(\frac{x}{5}-n\right)-\frac{x}{2}\right\}^{\circ} \Rightarrow \left\{30\left(\frac{50}{5}-8\right)-\frac{50}{2}\right\}^{\circ}$

$\Rightarrow (30\times 2-25)^{\circ} = 35^{\circ}$

TYPE 02

Position of Hands of Clock

In this type of questions, some conditions are provided and the candidate is asked to find out the time regarding the hands of a clock.

To solve these questions, following facts related to hour hand and minute hand must be kept in mind.

(i) In every hour, both the hands are at right angles two times. In this case,

(a) Angle between the two hands = 90°

(b) The two hands are 15 min spaces apart.

(ii) In every hour, the two hands are in the same straight line two times.

(a) When both hands are coincident

- Angle between the two hands = 0°
- Minute spaces between the two hands = 0
- Both hands are in the same direction.

(b) When both hands are opposite to each other.

- Angle between the two hands = 180°
- The two hands are 30 min spaces apart.

(iii) In every 12 h, both hands coincide 11 times.

(between 11 and 1 O'clock there is a common position at 12 O'clock).

$\therefore$ In 24 h, both hands coincides $\frac{11\times 24}{12} = 22$ times

(iv) In every 12 h, both hands are in opposite direction 11 times.

(between 5 O'clock and 7 O'clock there is a common position at 6 O'clock).

$\therefore$ In 24 h, both hands are in opposite directions $\frac{11\times 24}{12}$ times = 22 times

(v) In every 12 h, the two hands are in the same straight line 22 times

$\therefore$ In 24 h, the two hands are in the same straight line $\frac{22\times 24}{12}$ times = 44 times

(vi) In every 12 h, the two hands are at right angles 22 times.

(between 2 O'clock and 4 O'clock there is a common position at 3 O'clock and also between 8 O'clock and 10 O'clock there is a common position at 9 O'clock).

$\therefore$ In 24 h, both the hands are at right angles $\frac{22\times 24}{12}$ times = 44 times

(vii) If both hands of a clock start moving together from the same position, then both hands will coincide after every $65\frac{5}{11}$ min.

The questions based on this type can be solved with the help of the facts discussed above. But we have some formulae to solve these questions quickly. These formulae are discussed below.

1. Between x and $(x+1)$ O'clock, Both Hands are t Minute Apart

Between x and $(x+1)$ O'clock, both hands of the clock are t minute apart, then the time in that clock is $\frac{(5x \pm t)\times 12}{11}$ min past x.

> **Note** *Use '+' sign when minute hand is ahead and '–' sign when hour hand is ahead.*

***Ex* 04** At what time between 3 O'clock and 4 O' clock, will the hands of a clock be 4 min apart?

(a) $20\frac{8}{11}$ min past 3 and 12 min past 3

(b) $20\frac{8}{11}$ min past 3 and 13 min past 3

(c) $20\frac{8}{7}$ min past 3 and 12 min past 3

(d) $20\frac{8}{9}$ min past 3 and 14 min past 3

***Solution* (a)**

Method I At 3 O'clock, minute hand is 15 min spaces behind the hour hand.

3 O'clock

***Case* I** When the minute hand is 4 min spaces behind the hour hand.

In this case, minute hand has to gain $(15-4)=11$ min spaces over hour hand

$\because$ 55 minute are gained in 60 min,

$\therefore$ 11 min are gained in $\frac{60\times 11}{55}$ min $=12$ min

Hence, the hands will be 4 min apart at 12 min past 3.

***Case* II** When the minute hand is 4 min spaces ahead of the hour hand.

In this case, minute hand has to gain $(15+4)=19$ min spaces over hour hand

$\because$ 55 min are gained in 60 min

$\therefore$ 19 min are gained in $\left(\frac{60}{55}\times 19\right)$ min $=\left(\frac{12\times 19}{11}\right)$ min $=20\frac{8}{11}$ min

Hence, the hands will be 4 min apart at $20\frac{8}{11}$ min past 3.

Method II Given that, $x=3$, $(x+1)=4$ and $t=4$

Then, according to the formula,

$$(5x \pm t)\frac{12}{11}=(5\times 3\pm 4)\times\frac{12}{11}\text{ min}=(15\pm 4)\times\frac{12}{11}\text{ min}$$

Separating '+' and '–' signs, we have

$$(15+4)\times\frac{12}{11}\text{ min past 3 and }(15-4)\times\frac{12}{11}\text{ min past 3}$$

$$=\frac{19\times 12}{11}\text{ min past 3 and }11\times\frac{12}{11}\text{ min past 3}$$

$$=20\frac{8}{11}\text{ min past 3 and 12 min past 3}$$

2. Between x and $(x+1)$ O'clock, Both Hands Coincide

Between x and $(x+1)$ O'clock, both hands of the clock coincide *i.e.* $t=0$, then the time in that clock is $\frac{60x}{11}$ min past x.

***Ex* 05** At what time between 1 O'clock and 2 O'clock will the hands of the clock be together? « CGPSC 2019

(a) $4\frac{5}{11}$ min past 1

(b) $5\frac{5}{11}$ min past 1

(c) $3\frac{4}{11}$ min past 1

(d) $6\frac{5}{11}$ min past 1

(e) None of these

***Solution* (b)**

Method I At 1 O'clock, hour hand is at 1 while minute hand is at 12.

It means, the two hands are 5 min spaces apart.

1 O'clock

To be together, minute hand will have to gain 5 min over the hour hand.

Since, 55 min are gained in 60 min

$\therefore$ 5 min will be gained in

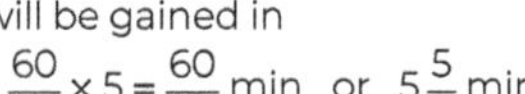

$$\frac{60}{55}\times 5=\frac{60}{11}\text{ min or }5\frac{5}{11}\text{ min}$$

Hence, the two hands will coincide at $5\frac{5}{11}$ min past 1.

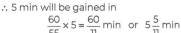

Method II In the given question, $x=1$, $(x+1)=2$

$\therefore$ Required answer $=\frac{60x}{11}$ min past 1 $=\frac{60\times 1}{11}$ min past 1 $=5\frac{5}{11}$ min past 1

3. Between x and $(x+1)$ O'clock, Both Hands are at Right Angle

Between x and $(x+1)$ O'clock, both hands of the clock are at right angle *i.e.* $t=15$ min, then the time in that clock is $\frac{(5x \pm 15)}{11}\times 12$ min past x.

> **Note** *Use '+' sign when minute hand is ahead and '–' sign when hour hand is ahead.*

***Ex* 06** At what time between 2 O'clock and 3 O'clock, will the hands of a clock make right angle?

(a) $10\frac{10}{11}$ min past 2

(b) $27\frac{3}{11}$ min past 2

(c) $10\frac{10}{15}$ min past 3

(d) Both 'b' and 'c'

***Solution* (b)**

Method I At 2 O'clock, both hands of the clock are 10 min apart. Both hands make right angle only when they are 15 min apart.

7 O'clock

$\therefore$ Minute hand must cover more than $10+15=25$ min

As we know 55 min spaces are gained in 60 min

∴ 25 min spaces will be gained in

$$\frac{60}{55} \times 25 \text{ min} = \frac{300}{11} = 27\frac{3}{11} \text{ min}$$

Hence, at $27\frac{3}{11}$ min past 2, both hands of the clock will make right angle.

Method II In the given question, $x = 2$ and $x + 1 = 3$

According to the formula,

Required time $= \left(\frac{5x + 15}{11}\right) \times 12$ min past x

'+' sign because minute hand is ahead

∴ Required time $= \left(\frac{5 \times 2 + 15}{11}\right) \times 12$ min past 2

$= \frac{25 \times 12}{11}$ min past 2 $= \frac{300}{11}$ min past 2 $= 27\frac{3}{11}$ min past 2

4. Between x and $(x + 1)$ O'clock, Both Hands are in Opposite Directions

Between x and $(x + 1)$ O'clock, both hands of the clock are in opposite directions, then the time in that clock is $(5x \pm 30) \times \frac{12}{11}$ min past x.

Note *Use '+' sign when $x < 6$ and '–' sign when $x > 6$.*

***Ex* 07** At what time between 7 O'clock and 8 O'clock, will the hands of a clock be in the same straight line but not together?

(a) $5\frac{5}{11}$ min past 7　(b) $5\frac{4}{11}$ min past 7

(c) $6\frac{5}{11}$ min past 7　(d) $3\frac{4}{11}$ min past 7

***Solution* (a)**

Method I At 7 O'clock, minute hand is at 12 while hour hand is at 7 and both the hands are 25 min spaces apart.

7 O'clock

To be in the same straight line (but not together) both hands will have to 30 min spaces apart.

∴ Minute hand will have to gain $(30 - 25) = 5$ min spaces over hour hand.

As we know, 55 min spaces are gained in 60 min.

∴ 5 min spaces will be gained in $\left(\frac{60}{55} \times 5\right)$ min

$$= \frac{60}{11} \text{ min} = 5\frac{5}{11} \text{ min}$$

Hence, the hands will be in the same straight line but not together at $5\frac{5}{11}$ min past 7.

Method II In the given question, $x = 7, (x + 1) = 8, x > 6$

According to the formula,

Hands will be in the same straight line at

$(5x - 30) \times \frac{12}{11}$ min past $x = (5 \times 7 - 30) \times \frac{12}{11}$ min past 7

$= (35 - 30) \times \frac{12}{11}$ min past 7 $= 5 \times \frac{12}{11}$ min past 7 $= 5\frac{5}{11}$ min past 7

Practice CORNER 12.1

1. If in a clock, the hour hand rotates 18°, then how much angle, the second hand will rotate in the same clock? « RRB ALP 2018

(a) 168°　(b) 276°　(c) 196°　(d) 216°

2. How much angular distance will be covered by the minute hand of a correct clock in a period of 2 h 20 min?

(a) 140°　(b) 840°　(c) 320°　(d) 520°

3. Find the angle traced by hour hand of a correct clock between 8 O'clock and 2 O'clock. « FCI Watchman 2018

(a) 180°　(b) 168°
(c) 150°　(d) 144°

4. What is the angle between the hour hand and the minute hand at half past two? « RRB ALP 2018

(a) 105°　(b) 120°
(c) 75°　(d) 90°

5. The angle between the minute hand and the hour hand of a clock, when the time is 4 : 20 is « [illegible] Pre 2017

(a) 0°　(b) 10°
(c) 5°　(d) 20°
(e) None of these

6. At half past 5 in the evening, the smaller angle between the hour and minute hands of a clock is « IB ACIO 2017

(a) 10°　(b) 12°　(c) 15°　(d) 18°

7. What degree of angle is made by the hands of clock at 10 : 35? « RRB (ALP) 2008

(a) $72\frac{1°}{2}$　(b) $97\frac{1°}{2}$　(c) $107\frac{1°}{2}$　(d) $117\frac{1°}{2}$

8. What will be the angle between the hands of clock at 7 : 10? « UP B. Ed. 2012

(a) 185°　(b) 155°　(c) 170°　(d) 165°

9. What will be the angle between the hands of clock at 9 : 30? « UP B. Ed. 2010

(a) 75°　(b) 90°　(c) 105°　(d) 120°

10. Find the angle between the two hands of clock at 4 : 10.

(a) 61°　(b) 68°　(c) 55°　(d) 65°

11. What will be the measurement of the angle made by the hands of a clock when the time is 8 : 35?

(a) 32.4°　(b) 37.5°　(c) 45°　(d) 47.5°

12. What angle will be traced by the hands of a clock at 12 : 55?
(a) $87\frac{1^\circ}{2}$ (b) $67\frac{1^\circ}{2}$ (c) $57\frac{1^\circ}{2}$ (d) $27\frac{1^\circ}{2}$

13. What angle will be traced by the hands of a clock at 7 : 35? « MAT 2010
(a) $7\frac{1^\circ}{2}$ (b) $17\frac{1^\circ}{2}$ (c) $27\frac{1^\circ}{2}$ (d) $37\frac{1^\circ}{2}$

14. In a clock at 7:30, what will be the angle between minute hand and hour hand? « UPSSSC VDO 2016
(a) 120° (b) 95° (c) 75° (d) 45°

15. What angle will be formed between the hands of clock at 3:30? « UPPSC Pre 2014
(a) 95° (b) 65° (c) 85° (d) 75°

16. What will be angle between the hands of clock at 8 : 30? « SSC (CPO) 2015
(a) 15° (b) 30° (c) 45° (d) 75°

17. Find the angle between the hands of clock at 8 : 20. « Hotel Mgmt 2012
(a) 130° (b) 115° (c) 125° (d) 140°

18. What will be the angle between the two hands of the clock at 4 : 37 pm? « RRB ALP 2018
(a) 83.5° (b) 18° (c) 18.5° (d) 6.5°

19. How many times do the hands of a clock coincide in a day?
(a) 24 (b) 22 (c) 21 (d) 20

20. In a week, how many times the minute hand and hour hand make right angle with each other? « RRB ALP 2018
(a) 44 (b) 24 (c) 54 (d) 308

21. How many times the hand of a clock are at right angle in a day?
(a) 24 (b) 48 (c) 22 (d) 44

22. How many times in 24 h the hands of a clock are in straight line but opposite in directions?
(a) 20 (b) 22
(c) 24 (d) 48

23. How many times in 24 h the hands of a clock are straight?
(a) 48 (b) 44
(c) 24 (d) 22

24. From 1 O'clock afternoon upto 10 O'clock in the night, the hands of a clock will be at right angle .... times. « IAS 2009
(a) 9 (b) 10
(c) 16 (d) 20

25. At what time between 4 O'clock and 5 O'clock will hands of a clock be together?
(a) $24\frac{9}{11}$ min past 4 (b) $23\frac{9}{11}$ min past 4
(c) $21\frac{9}{11}$ min past 4 (d) $21\frac{7}{11}$ min past 4

26. At what time between 4 O'clock and 5 O'clock will the hands of a watch point in opposite directions?
(a) 45 min past 4 (b) 40 min past 4
(c) $50\frac{4}{11}$ min past 4 (d) $54\frac{6}{11}$ min past 4

27. At what time between 6 O'clock and 7 O'clock will the hands of a clock be at right angle?
(a) $49\frac{1}{11}$ min past 6 and $16\frac{4}{11}$ min past 6
(b) $50\frac{1}{11}$ min past 6 and $16\frac{4}{11}$ min past 6
(c) $47\frac{1}{11}$ min past 6 and $42\frac{1}{11}$ min past 6
(d) $47\frac{1}{11}$ min past 6 and $16\frac{4}{11}$ min past 6

Answers WITH EXPLANATIONS

1. (*d*) In 1 min hour hand rotates $\left(\frac{1}{2}\right)^\circ$

Then, to rotate 18°, it will take
$$\frac{1}{\left(\frac{1}{2}\right)} \times 18 \text{ min} = 36 \text{ min}$$

We know that, minute hand rotates 6° in 1 min
Then, in 36 min, the minute hand will rotate $= 36 \times 6 = 216^\circ$

2. (*b*) Angle traced by minute hand per minute = 6°
∴ Angle traced by minute hand in 2 h 20 min
$= [(2 \times 60) + 20] \times 6^\circ$
$= (120 + 20) \times 6^\circ$
$= 140 \times 6^\circ = 840^\circ$

3. (*a*) ∵ Angle traced by hour hand per minute $= \left(\frac{1}{2}\right)^\circ$

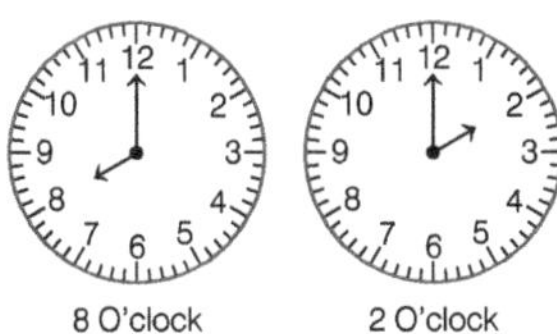

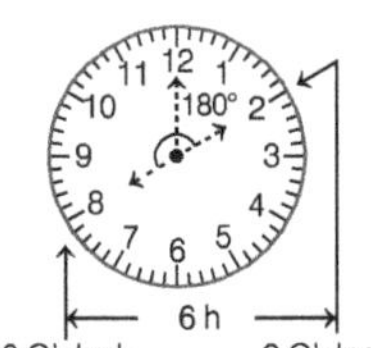

∴ Angle traced by hour hand in 1 h
$= \frac{1^\circ}{2} \times 60 = 30^\circ$

Time period between 8 O'clock to 2 O' clock = 6 h
∴ Angle traced by hour hand in 6h
$= 30^\circ \times 6 = 180^\circ$

4. (*a*) ∵ Angle traced by hour hand per minute $= \left(\frac{1}{2}\right)^\circ$

∴ Angle traced by hour hand in 2 h 30 min (half past two)
$= (2 \times 60 + 30) \times \frac{1^\circ}{2} = 150 \times \frac{1^\circ}{2} = 75^\circ$

∴ Angle traced by minute hand per minute = 6°
Angle traced by minute hand in 30 min = $30 \times 6^\circ = 180^\circ$
∴ Required angle $= 180^\circ - 75^\circ = 105^\circ$

5. (*b*) Given time = 4 : 20 *i.e.,* minute hand is behind the hour hand.
Then, angle between both the hands

$$= \left[30\left(n - \frac{x}{5}\right) + \frac{x}{2}\right]^\circ$$

Here, $n = 4$ and $x = 20$

∴ Angle between both the hands

$$= \left[30\left(4 - \frac{20}{5}\right) + \frac{20}{2}\right]^\circ$$
$$= [30(4-4)+10]^\circ$$
$$= (30 \times 0 + 10)^\circ = (0+10)^\circ = 10^\circ$$

6. (*c*) At 5 : 30 pm, hour hand is behind minute hand

∴ Angle between both the hands

$$= \left[30\left(\frac{x}{5} - n\right) - \frac{x}{2}\right]^\circ$$

Here, $n = 5$ and $x = 30$

∴ Required angle

$$= \left[30\left(\frac{30}{5} - 5\right) - \frac{30}{2}\right]^\circ$$
$$= [30(6-5)-15]^\circ$$
$$= (30 \times 1 - 15)^\circ$$
$$= (30-15)^\circ = 15^\circ$$

7. (*c*) **Method I** ∵ Angle traced by hour hand per minute $= \left(\frac{1}{2}\right)^\circ$

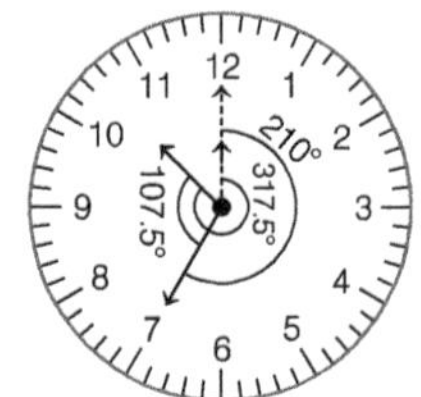

Time = 10 : 35

∴ Angle traced by hour hand in 10 h 35 min

$$= [(10 \times 60) + 35] \times \frac{1^\circ}{2}$$
$$= \left(\frac{635}{2}\right)^\circ = 317.5^\circ$$

∵ Angle traced by minute hand per minute = 6°

∴ Angle traced by minute hand in 35 min = 35 × 6° = 210°

∴ Required angle = (317.5° − 210°)

$$= 107.5^\circ = 107\frac{1}{2}^\circ$$

Method II Since at 10:35, the minute hand is behind the hour hand so the angle between the hands

$$= \left[30\left(n - \frac{x}{5}\right) + \frac{x}{2}\right]^\circ$$

Here, $n = 10$ and $x = 35$

∴ Required angle

$$= \left[30\left(10 - \frac{35}{5}\right) + \frac{35}{2}\right]^\circ$$
$$= \left[30 \times 3 + \frac{35}{2}\right]^\circ$$
$$= \left[90 + \frac{35}{2}\right]^\circ$$
$$= \frac{215^\circ}{2} = 107\frac{1^\circ}{2}$$

8. (*b*) ∵ Angle traced by hour hand per minute $= \left(\frac{1}{2}\right)^\circ$

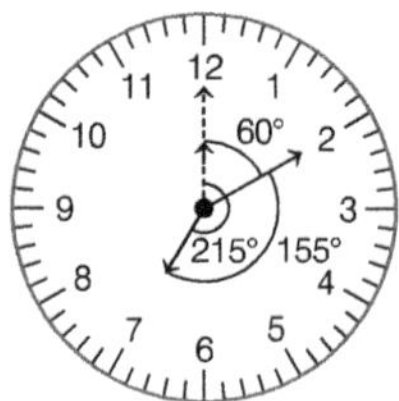

Time = 7 : 10

∴ Angle traced by hour hand in 7 h 10 min

$$= (7 \times 60 + 10) \times \frac{1^\circ}{2}$$
$$= 430 \times \frac{1^\circ}{2}$$
$$= 215^\circ$$

∵ Angle traced by minute hand per minute = 6°

∴ Angle traced by minute hand in 10 min

$$= 10 \times 6^\circ = 60^\circ$$

∴ Required angle = (215° − 60°)

$$= 155^\circ$$

9. (*c*) ∵ Angle traced by hour hand per minute $= \left(\frac{1}{2}\right)^\circ$

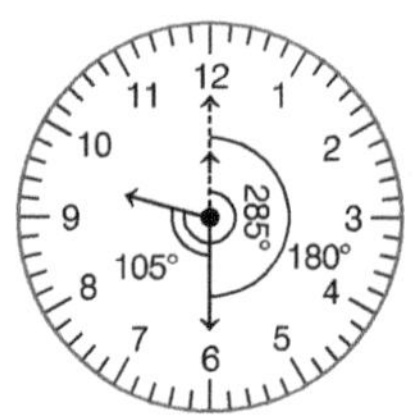

Time = 9 : 30

∴ Angle traced by hour hand in 9 h 30 min

$$= [(9 \times 60) + 30] \times \frac{1^\circ}{2}$$
$$= 570 \times \frac{1^\circ}{2}$$
$$= 285^\circ$$

∵ Angle traced by minute hand per minute = 6°

∴ Angle traced by minute hand in 30 min = 30 × 6° = 180°

∴ Required angle = (285° − 180°)

$$= 105^\circ$$

10. (*d*) ∵ Angle traced by hour hand per minute $= \left(\frac{1}{2}\right)^\circ$

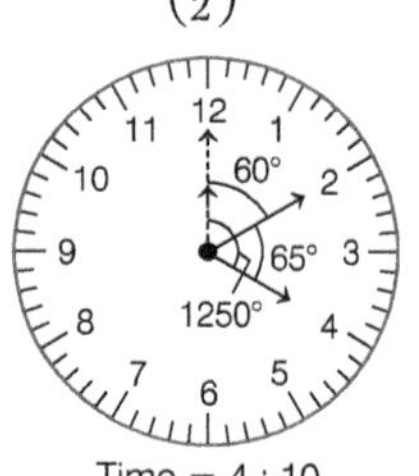

Time = 4 : 10

∴ Angle traced by hour hand in 4 h 10 min $= [(4 \times 60) + 10] \times \frac{1^\circ}{2}$

$$= 250 \times \frac{1^\circ}{2} = 125^\circ$$

∵ Angle traced by minute hand per minute = 6°

∴ Angle traced by minute hand in 10 min = 10 × 6° = 60°

∴ Required angle = 125° − 60°

$$= 65^\circ$$

11. (*d*) Angle traced by hour hand in 35 min after 8 $= 35 \times \frac{1^\circ}{2} = 17.5^\circ$

At 8 : 35, min hand is at 7, and angle between 8 and 7 = 30°

∴ Required angle between two hands at 8 : 35 = 30° + 17.5°

$$= 47.5^\circ$$

12. (*c*) ∵ Angle traced by hour hand per minute $= \left(\frac{1}{2}\right)^\circ$

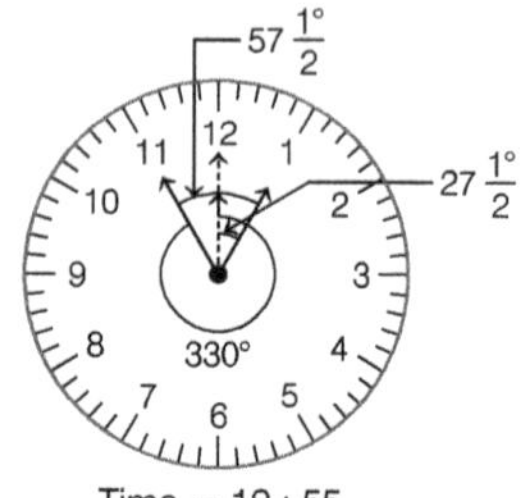

Time = 12 : 55

∴ Angle traced by hour hand in 12 h 55 min (*i.e.,* at 0 : 55)

$$= 55 \times \frac{1^\circ}{2} = 27\frac{1^\circ}{2}$$

∵ Angle traced by minute hand per minute = 6°

∴ Angle traced by minute hand in 55 min = 55 × 6° = 330°

∴ Required angle

$$= 360^\circ - \left(330^\circ - 27\frac{1^\circ}{2}\right)$$
$$= 360^\circ + 27\frac{1^\circ}{2} - 330^\circ$$
$$= 387\frac{1^\circ}{2} - 330^\circ = 57\frac{1^\circ}{2}$$

13. (*b*) ∵ Angle traced by hour hand per minute = $\left(\frac{1}{2}\right)^\circ$

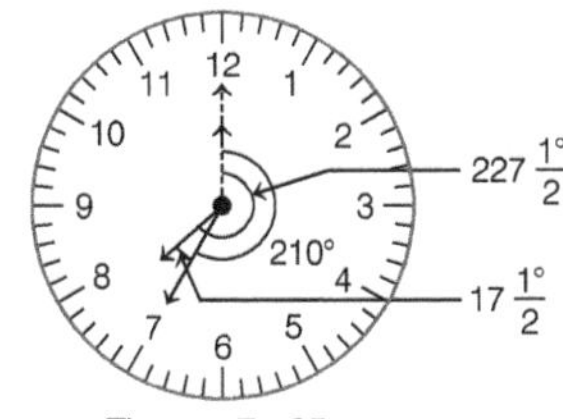

Time = 7 : 35

∴ Angle traced by hour hand in 7 h 35 min = $[(7 \times 60) + 35] \times \frac{1°}{2}$

$= (420 + 35) \times \frac{1°}{2}$

$= 455 \times \frac{1°}{2} = 227\frac{1°}{2}$

∴ Angle traced by minute hand per minute = 6°

Angle traced by minute hand in 35 min = 35 × 6° = 210°

∴ Required angle = $227\frac{1°}{2} - 210°$

$= 17\frac{1°}{2}$

14. (*d*) In $7\frac{1}{2}$ h, the angle covered by hour hand = $7\frac{1}{2} \times 30 = \frac{15}{2} \times 30 = 225°$

and in $\frac{1}{2}$ h or 30 min, the angle covered by minute hand = 30 × 6 = 180°

∴ Required angle = 225 − 180 = 45°

15. (*d*) **Method I** ∵ Angle traced by hour hand per minute = $\left(\frac{1}{2}\right)^\circ$

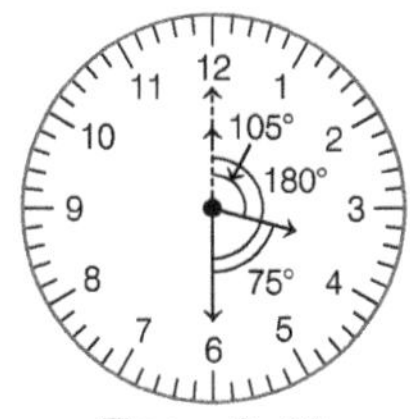

Time = 3 : 30

∴ Angle traced by hour hand in 3 h 30 min

$= [(3 \times 60) + 30] \times \frac{1°}{2}$

$= (180 + 30) \times \frac{1°}{2}$

$= 210 \times \frac{1°}{2} = 105°$

∵ Angle traced by minute hand per minute = 6°

∴ Angle traced by minute hand in 30 min = 30 × 6° = 180°

∴ Required angle = 180° − 105° = 75°

Method II Since at 3:30, the hour hand is behind the minute hand. So, the angle between the hands

$= \left[30\left(\frac{x}{5} - n\right) - \frac{x}{2}\right]^\circ$

Here, $n = 3$ and $x = 30$

∴ Required angle

$= \left[30\left(\frac{30}{5} - 3\right) - \frac{30}{2}\right]^\circ$

$= [30 \times 3 - 15]^\circ$

$= [90 - 15]^\circ = 75°$

16. (*d*) ∵ Angle traced by hour hand per minute = $\left(\frac{1}{2}\right)^\circ$

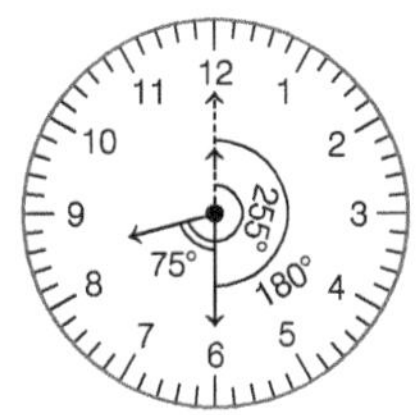

Time = 8 : 30

∴ Angle traced by hour hand in 8 h 30 min

$= \left[\{(8 \times 60) + 30\} \times \frac{1}{2}\right]^\circ$

$= \left[\{480 + 30\} \times \frac{1}{2}\right]^\circ$

$= 510 \times \left(\frac{1}{2}\right)^\circ = 255°$

∵ Angle traced by minute hand per minute = 6°

∴ Angle traced by minute hand in 30 min = 30 × 6° = 180°

∴ Required angle = (255° − 180°) = 75°

17. (*a*) ∵ Angle traced by hour hand per minute = $\left(\frac{1}{2}\right)^\circ$

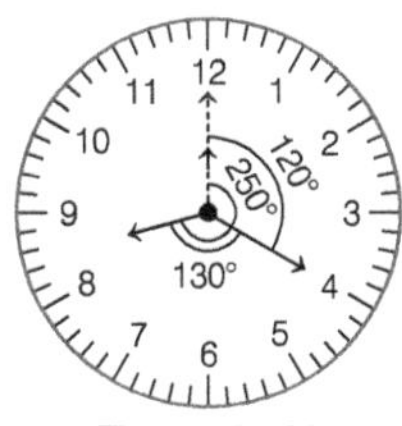

Time = 8 : 20

∴ Angle traced by hour hand in 8h 20 min

$= (8 \times 60 + 20) \times \frac{1°}{2} = 250°$

Again, angle traced by minute hand per minute = 6°

∴ Angle traced by minute hand in 20 min = 20 × 6° = 120°

∴ Required angle = (250° − 120°) = 130°

18. (*a*) **Method I**

∵ Angle traced by hour hand per minute = $\left(\frac{1}{2}\right)^\circ$

∴ Angle traced by hour hand in 4h 37 min = $(4 \times 60 + 37) \times \frac{1°}{2}$

$= \frac{277°}{2}$

∵ Angle traced by minute hand per minute = 6°

∴ Angle traced by minute hand in 37 min = 37 × 6° = 222°

∴ Required angle = $222° - \frac{277°}{2}$

$= 222° - 138.5°$

$= 83.5°$

Method II Since, the hour hand behind the minute hand

∵ Required angle = $\left\{30\left(\frac{x}{5} - n\right) - \frac{x}{2}\right\}^\circ$

Here, $x = 37$ and $n = 4$

∴ Required angle

$= \left\{30\left(\frac{37}{5} - 4\right) - \frac{37}{2}\right\}^\circ$

$= [6 \times 17 - 18.5]^\circ$

$= [102 - 18.5]^\circ$

$= 83.5°$

19. (*b*) We know that, hands of a clock coincide once in every hour but between 11 O'clock and 1 O'clock they coincide only once. Therefore, the hands of a clock coincide 11 times in every 12 h.

Hence, they will coincide (11 × 2) *i.e.*, 22 times in 24 h.

20. (*d*) As we know that, in every hour the minute and hour hands make right angle two times but in every 12 h, the two hands are at right angle 22 times. So, in 24 h (or 1 day), the minute hand and hour hand will be at right angle 22 × 2 = 44 times

Hence, in a week or 7 days, the minute and hour hands will make right angle = 44 × 7 = 308 times

21. (*d*) We know that, the hands of a clock are at right angle twice in every hour but between 2 O'clock and 4 O'clock there is a common position at 3 O'clock and also between 8 O'clock and 10 O'clock there is common position at 9 O'clock.

So, they are at right angle 22 times in 12 h and therefore, in 24 h or in a day they are at right angle 44 times.

22. (*b*) Once in every hour the hands of a clock are in the same straight line (but opposite in direction) 11 times in every 12 h, because between 5 O'clock and 7 O'clock, they point in opposite direction once at 6 O'clock only. Therefore, in a day (24 h) the hands points in the opposite direction $(2 \times 11) = 22$ times.

23. (*b*) The hands are in opposite direction (at angular distance of 180°) or coincide (at 0° angular distance) 22 times in every 12h. Hence, in 24 h, hands are straight (coincide or in opposite direction) $= 22 \times 2 = 44$ times.

24. (*c*) Time period from 1 O'clock afternoon to 10 O'clock night

$$= (10 - 1)\,h = 9\,h$$

As we know, hands are at right angle 2 times in an hour. But between 2 O'clock and 4 O'clock there is a common position at 3 O'clock and also between 8 O'clock and 10 O'clock there is a common position at 9 O'clock.

Hence, in 9 h they will be at right angle $3 + 3 + 2 + 8 = 16$ times

25. (*c*) **Method I** At 4 O' clock, hour hand is at 4 and minute hand is at 12. Hour hand is 20 min space ahead minute T and

Time = 4 O'clock

To be together with hour hand minute hand will have to gain 20 min.

As 55 min are gained by minute hand in 60 min.

∴ 20 min will be gained in

$$\left(\frac{60}{55} \times 20\right) \text{min} = \left(\frac{60 \times 4}{11}\right) \text{min}$$

$$= \frac{240}{11} \text{ min}$$

$$= 21\frac{9}{11} \text{ min}$$

Hence, the hands will be together at $21\frac{9}{11}$ min past 4.

Method II

Required time $= \frac{60x}{11}$ min past x

Here, $x = 4$ O'clock

∴ Required time $= \frac{60 \times 4}{11}$ min past 4

$$= \frac{240}{11} \text{ min past } 4 = 21\frac{9}{11} \text{ min past } 4$$

The hands will be at right angle between, 1 O'clock and 2 O'clock = 2 times 2 O'clock and 4 O'clock = 3 times 4 O'clock and 8 O'clock = 8 times 8 O'clock and 10 O'clock = 3 times

26. (*d*) **Method I** At 4 O' clock, both the hands are 20 min apart and for the hands to be in the opposite direction, they have to be 30 min apart.

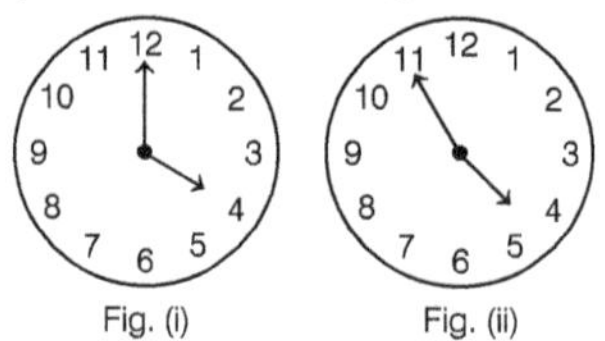

Fig. (i) Fig. (ii)

From Fig. (i) and Fig. (ii) it is clear , that minute hand has to travel $(20 + 30)$ min space in order to be in opposite direction to each other.

Now, 55 min space is gained by minute hand in 60 min.

Therefore, 50 min space will be gained in $\left(\frac{60}{55} \times 50\right)$ min $= 54\frac{6}{11}$ min

Hence, the hands of the clock will be in opposite direction at

$54\frac{6}{11}$ min past 4.

Method II

Required time

$$= \frac{(5x + 30)}{11} \times 12 \text{ min past } x$$

used '+' sign because $x = 4$ O'clock < 6

∴ Required time

$$= \frac{(5 \times 4 + 30)}{11} \times 12 \text{ min past } 4$$

$$= \frac{600}{11} \text{ min past } 4$$

$$= 54\frac{6}{11} \text{ min past } 4$$

27. (*a*) **Method I** At 6 O' clock, minute hand is 30 min spaces behind the hour hand. Now, for being at right angle the two hands will have to be 15 min spaces apart.

So, they are at right angles in the following cases

6 O'clock

***Case* I** When minute hand is 15 min spaces behind the hour hand.

In this case, minute hand will have to gain $(30 - 15) = 15$ min over the hour hand

Since, minute hand gains 55 min over hour hand in 60 min.

∴ Minute hand will gain 15 min in $\left(\frac{60}{55} \times 15\right)$ min

$$= \frac{60 \times 3}{11} \text{ min} = \frac{180}{11} \text{ min}$$

$$= 16\frac{4}{11} \text{ min}$$

Hence, they are at right angle at $16\frac{4}{11}$ min past 6.

***Case* II** When minute hand is 15 min spaces ahead of hour hand.

In this case, minute hand will have to gain $(30 + 15) = 45$ min over the hour hand.

Since, minute hand gains 55 min in 60 min

∴ Minute hand will gain 45 min in

$$\left(\frac{60}{55} \times 45\right) \text{min} = \left(\frac{60}{11} \times 9\right) \text{min}$$

$$= \frac{540}{11} \text{ min}$$

$$= 49\frac{1}{11} \text{ min}$$

Hence, hands will be at right angle at $49\frac{1}{11}$ min past 6.

Method II Required time

$$= (5x \pm 15) \times \frac{12}{11} \text{ min past } x$$

Here, $x = 6$ O'clock

∴ Required time

$$= (5 \times 6 \pm 15) \times \frac{12}{11} \text{ min past } 6$$

$$= (30 \pm 15) \times \frac{12}{11} \text{ min past } 6$$

Now, separating '+' and '–' sign, we have

∴ Required time

$$= (30 + 15) \times \frac{12}{11} \text{ min past } 6$$

and $(30 - 15) \times \frac{12}{11}$ min past 6

$$= \frac{540}{11} \text{ min past } 6$$

and $\frac{180}{11}$ min past 6

$$= 49\frac{1}{11} \text{ min past } 6$$

and $16\frac{4}{11}$ min past 6.

TYPE 03

Faulty Clocks

A clock which **gains or loses time** is called a faulty clock. If a clock indicates more than the actual time, then the clock is said to be fast. If a clock indicates 5 : 10 when the correct time is 5, it is said to be 10 min too fast.

If a clock indicates less than the actual time, then the clock is said to be slow. If a clock indicates 4 : 50, when the correct time is 5, it is said to be 10 min too slow.

Whenever a clock is too fast or too slow, then both the hands of the clock will not coincide at the intervals of $65\frac{5}{11}$ min.

In this type of questions, some conditions of faulty clocks are given and on that basis, the candidate is required either to find out the correct time or the time at which the clock will show the correct time.

Sometime the questions are asked about finding the comparative time of two faulty clocks.

Ex 08 Two clocks are set correctly at 9 am on Monday. Both the clocks gain 3 min and 5 min respectively in an hour. What time will the second clock register, if the first clock which gains 3 min in an hour shows the time as 27 min past 6 pm on the same day?

(a) 6 : 27 pm (b) 6 : 45 pm (c) 6 : 25 pm (d) 6 : 50 pm
(e) None of these

Solution (b) According to the question,

First clock gains = 3 min/h and second clock gains = 5 min/h

So, the difference in minutes between these two clocks in one hour = (5 – 3) min = 2 min

Total time from 9 pm to 6 pm on Monday = 9 h.

So, first clock gains in 9 h = (9 × 3) min = 27 min and shows the time as 6 : 27 pm.

Then, the second clock gains in 9 h = (9 × 5) min = 45 min and shows the time as 6 : 45 pm.

Ex 09 In the noon, a man observes that, his watch is 5 min too slow and showing 11:55 am instead of the correct time i.e. 12:00 pm. In the evening, he observes that, his watch is 9 min too fast and showing 7:09 pm instead of the correct time i.e. 7:00 pm. Find the time, when the watch would be showing the correct time.

(a) 12 : 30 pm (b) 1 : 30 pm
(c) 2 : 30 pm (d) 3 : 30 pm

Solution (c) According to the question, at 12 O'clock, the watch was 5 min too slow and at 7 O'clock, it is 9 min too fast. So, in this time duration, the watch becomes 9 + 5 = 14 min ahead.

From 12 O'clock to 7 O'clock there is 7 h.

So per hour, the clock becomes fast $= \frac{14}{7} = 2$ min

Because at the initial time, it was 5 min too slow, so it will show the correct time when it becomes 5 min fast.

∵ It becomes 2 min fast in 1 h

∴ It will becomes 5 min fast in $\frac{1}{2} \times 5$ h $= 2\frac{1}{2}$ h

So, the time = 12 O'clock + $2\frac{1}{2}$ h = 2 : 30 pm,

at which the clock would be showing the correct time.

TYPE 04

Time Gained or Lost by Clock

In this type of questions, the time interval of the correct time in which the minute hand of a clock overtakes the hour hand is given and the candidate is required to find out the time gained or lost by the clock.

If the minute hand of a clock overtakes the hour hand at intervals of x min of the correct time, then the clock loses or gains $\left(\frac{720}{11} - x\right)\left(\frac{60 \times 24}{x}\right)$ min in a day.

> **Note** *If the result is (+ ve), then clock gains and if the result is (– ve), then clock loses.*

Ex 10 The minute hand of a clock overtakes the hour hand at intervals of 63 min of the correct time. How much does a clock gain or lose in a day?

(a) $54\frac{8}{77}$ min (gain) (b) $56\frac{8}{77}$ min (gain)
(c) $53\frac{8}{77}$ min (loss) (d) $53\frac{8}{77}$ min (gain)

Solution (b)

Method I As we know, that in a correct clock, the minute hand gains 55 min spaces over the hour hand in 60 min.

To be together again, the minute hand must gain 60 min over the hour hand.

60 min are gained in $\left(\frac{60}{55} \times 60\right)$ min $= 65\frac{5}{11}$ min

But they are together after 63 min.

∴ Gain in 63 min $= \left(65\frac{5}{11} - 63\right) = 2\frac{5}{11}$ min $= \frac{27}{11}$ min

$$\text{Gain in 24 h} = \left(\frac{27}{11} \times \frac{60 \times 24}{63}\right) \text{min}$$
$$= \frac{4320}{77} \text{ min} = 56\frac{8}{77} \text{ min}$$

As result is positive, therefore clock gains $56\frac{8}{77}$ min.

Method II In the given question, $x = 63$ min

According to the formula,

$$\text{Required result} = \left(\frac{720}{11} - x\right)\left(\frac{60 \times 24}{x}\right) \text{min}$$
$$= \left(\frac{720}{11} - 63\right)\left(\frac{60 \times 24}{63}\right) \text{min}$$
$$= \frac{27}{11} \times \frac{60 \times 8}{21} = 56\frac{8}{77} \text{ min}$$

(gain as sign is positive)

TYPE 05

Exact Time/Duration

In this type of question, the candidate is required to find out the exact/real time or duration of some meeting/interview etc. based on some conditions.

Ex 11 The bus for Delhi leaves every 35 min from a bus stand. An enquiry clerk told a passenger that the bus has already left 10 min ago and the next bus will leave at 9:35. At what time did the enquiry clerk give this information to passenger? « UPSSSC VDO 2016

(a) 9 : 10 (b) 8 : 55 (c) 9 : 08 (d) 9 : 15

Solution (a) As next bus leaves at 9:35

∴ Previous bus left at (9 : 35 − 0 : 35) = 9 : 00

The time when enquiry clerk gave this information

= 9 : 00 + 0 : 10 = 9 : 10

Ex 12 The first period of a class start at 10:30 am and fourth ends at 13 : 45 pm. If periods are of equal duratioin and after each period a break of 5 min is given to the students, the exact duration of each period is « MPPSC Pre 2018

(a) 35 min
(b) 42 min
(c) 45 min
(d) 40 min

Solution (c) Time interval between the first period and fourth period = 1 : 45 pm − 10 : 30 am

= 3 h 15 min

∴ Total break = 3 × 5 = 15 min

∴ Time period of classes = (3 × 60) + 15 − 15

= 180 min

∴ Exact duration of each period

$= \frac{180}{4} = 45$ min

Practice / CORNER 12.2

1. A wall clock moves 10 min fast in every 24 h. The clock was set right to show the correct time at 8:00 am on Monday. When the clock shows the time 6:00 pm on Wednesday, what is the correct time? « UPSC CSAT 2019
   (a) 5 : 36 pm (b) 5 : 30 pm
   (c) 5 : 24 pm (d) 5 : 18 pm
2. A clock becomes 12 s fast in every 3 h. If it is made correct at 3 O'clock in the afternoon of Sunday, then what time will it show at 10 O'clock Tuesday morning?
   (a) 2 min 52 s past 10 (b) 2 min 54 s past 10
   (c) 2 min 50 s past 10 (d) 2 min 48 s past 20
3. At present a wall clock is showing 07 : 40 : 06. If it loses 4 s in each hour, then after $6\frac{1}{2}$ h, what time it will be showing? « UPSSSC Amin 2016
   (a) 14 : 09 : 40 (b) 14 : 09 : 38
   (c) 14 : 10 : 06 (d) 14 : 10 : 42
4. A clock becomes 15 min fast every day. If it is made correct at 12 O'clock in the afternoon, then what time will it show at 4 O'clock in the morning?
   (a) 4 : 10 (b) 4 : 15 (c) 4 : 20 (d) 4 : 30
5. A clock is set right at 5 am. The clock loses 16 min in 24 h. What will be the right time when the clock indicates 10 pm on the 3rd day?
   (a) 11 : 15 pm (b) 11 pm
   (c) 12 pm (d) 12 : 30 pm
6. A watch, which gains uniformly is 2 min slow at noon on Monday and is 4 min, 48s fast at 2 pm on the following Monday. At what time it was correct?
   (a) 2 pm on Tuesday (b) 2 pm on Wednesday
   (c) 3 pm on Thursday (d) 1 pm on Friday
   (e) None of these
7. A clock, which loses uniformly, is 15 min fast at 9 am on 3rd of the December and is 25 min less than the correct time at 3 pm on 6th of the same month. At what time it was correct?
   (a) 2 : 15 am on 3rd (b) 2 : 15 pm on 4th
   (c) 2 : 15 pm on 3rd (d) 2 : 15 am on 4th
8. Two clocks are set correctly at 10 am on Sunday. One clock loses 3 min in an hour while the other gains 2 min in an hour. By how many minutes do the two clocks differ at 4 pm on the same day?
   (a) 25 min (b) 20 min
   (c) 35 min (d) 30 min
9. The minute hand of a clock overtakes the hour hand at intervals of 65 min of the correct time. How much does a clock gain or lose in a day?
   (a) $10\frac{10}{143}$ min (gain) (b) $10\frac{10}{143}$ min (loss)
   (c) $9\frac{10}{143}$ min (gain) (d) $9\frac{10}{143}$ min (loss)
10. The minute hand of a clock overtakes the hour hand at intervals of 58 min of the correct time. How much does a clock gain or lose in a day?
    (a) $185\frac{25}{319}$ min (loss) (b) $185\frac{25}{319}$ min (gain)
    (c) $184\frac{25}{319}$ min (loss) (d) $184\frac{25}{319}$ min (gain)
11. The minute hand of a clock overtakes the hour hand at intervals of 62 min of the correct time. How much does a clock gain or lose in a day?
    (a) $81\frac{80}{341}$ min (loss) (b) $81\frac{80}{341}$ min (gain)
    (c) $80\frac{80}{341}$ min (loss) (d) $80\frac{80}{341}$ min (gain)

12. The minute hand of a clock overtakes the hour hand at intervals of 76 min of the correct time. How much does a clock gain or lose in a day?

(a) $198\frac{169}{209}$ min (loss) (b) $198\frac{169}{209}$ min (gain)
(c) $199\frac{169}{209}$ min (loss) (d) $199\frac{169}{209}$ min (gain)

13. In a college, a class is scheduled from 1:00 pm to 3:52 pm. If in this time duration, 4 lectures are held and before each lecture, there is gap of 4 min to go from one classroom to another, then find the time duration of each lecture. « UPSSSC Excise Constable 2018

(a) 39 min (b) 40 min
(c) 41 min (d) 42 min

14. The priest told the devotees, 'the bell is rung at regular intervals of 45 min. The last bell was rung 5 min ago. The next bell is due to be rung at 7 : 45 am. At what time did the priest give the information to be devotees?

(a) 6 : 55 am (b) 7 : 00 am (c) 7 : 05 am (d) 7 : 40 am

15. A bus for Delhi leaves every 30 min from a bus stand. An enquiry clerk, Rambabu told Shyamlal, a passenger that the bus has already left 10 min ago and the next bus will leave at 9:35 am. At what time did the enquiry clerk give this information to Shyamlal?

(a) 9 : 15 am (b) 9 : 10 am
(c) 9 : 20 am (d) 9 : 05 am

16. Aseem leaves his house at 20 min to 7 in the morning, reaching Kaushal's house in 25 min, they finish their breakfast in another 5 min and leave for their office which takes another 35 min. At what time do they leave Kaushal's house to reach their office?

(a) 7 : 55 am (b) 8 : 15 am
(c) 7 : 45 am (d) 7 : 20 am

17. Reaching the place of meeting 20 min before 8 : 50 h, Sujay found himself 30 min earlier than the person who came 40 min late. What was the scheduled time of meeting?

(a) 8 : 09h (b) 8 : 05h (c) 8 : 20h (d) 8 : 10h

Answers / WITH EXPLANATIONS

1. (*a*) Clock to move fast in 24 h = 10 min
Time from 8:00 am on Monday to till 6:00 pm on next Wednesday = 58 h
∴ Clock to move fast in 58 h
$= \frac{10}{24} \times 58$ min
$= 24.1 \approx 24$ min
∴ Correct time = 6:00 pm – 24 pm
= 5:36 pm

2. (*a*) Total time from 3 O' clock Sunday afternoon to 10 O' clock Tuesday morning = 43 h
Total increased time $= \frac{12}{3} \times 43$
= 172 s
= 2 min 52s
∴ Time at 10 O' clock Tuesday morning = 2 min 52 s past 10

3. (*a*) In each, the wall clock is losing 4s.
Then, in $6\frac{1}{2}$ h it will be losing
$= 4 \times 6\frac{1}{2} = 2 \times 13 = 26$ s
Hence, time after $6\frac{1}{2}$ h
= 07:40:06 + (6:30:00 – 00:00:26)
= 07:40:06 + 6:29:34 = 14:09:40

4. (*a*) Total time from 12 O' clock afternoon to 4 O' clock morning
= 12 O' clock after noon to 12 O' clock night + 12 O' clock night to 4 O'clock morning
= 12 + 4 = 16 h
Since, in 24 h (1 day), the clock becomes 15 min fast.
∴ In 16 h clock will be
$\frac{15 \times 16}{24} = 10$ min fast
∴ Required time
= 4 : 00 + 0 : 10 = 4 : 10

5. (*b*) Time from 5 am of a particular day to 10 pm on the 3rd day is 89 h. Now, the clock loses 16 min in 24 h or in other words, we can say that 23 h 44 min of this clock is equal to 24 h of the correct clock.
$\left(23 + \frac{44}{60}\right) = \frac{356}{15}$ h of this clock = 24h of the correct clock
∴ 89 h of this clock $= \left(\frac{24 \times 15}{356} \times 89\right)$ h the correct clock
= 90 h of the correct clock
or 89 h of this clock = 90 h of the correct clock. Therefore, it is clear that in 90 h this clock loses 1 h and hence, the correct time is 11 pm when this clock shows 10 pm.

6. (*b*) Time from Monday noon (12 O'clock) to 2 pm the following Monday
= 7 days 2 h = 170 h
Now, the watch gains $\left(2 + 4\frac{4}{5}\right)$ min from Monday (12 pm) to 2 pm, the following Monday.
In other words, the watch gains $\frac{34}{5}$ min in 170 h.
Therefore, it will gain 2 min in
$\left(\frac{170 \times 5}{34} \times 2\right) = 50$ h
= 2 days 2 h
Therefore, the watch is correct after 2 days 2 h from Monday noon or at 2 pm on Wednesday.

7. (*b*) According to the question,
Total time from 9 am on 3rd of the December to 3 pm on 6th of the December = 3 days 6 h = 78 h
Also, the clock loses in 78 h
= (15 + 25) = 40 min
So, the clock loses 15 min in
$= \frac{15}{40} \times 78 = 29$ h 15 min
Therefore, the clock is correct after 29 h 15 min from 9 am on 3rd December *i.e.*, at 2:15 pm on 4th December.

8. (*d*) According to the question,
One clock loses = 3 min/h
Other clock gains = 2 min/h
So, the difference in minutes between these two clocks in one hour
= 2 – (–3) = 5 min loss
(Loss in minutes = Negative sign)
Total time from 10 am to 4 pm on Sunday = 6 h
Therefore, the difference in minutes between these two clocks from 10 am to 4 pm on Sunday = (5 × 6) = 30 min

9. (*a*) Required result
$= \left(\frac{720}{11} - x\right)\left(\frac{60 \times 24}{x}\right)$ min
Here, $x = 65$
∴ Required result
$= \left(\frac{720}{11} - 65\right)\left(\frac{60 \times 24}{65}\right)$ min
$= \frac{5}{11} \times \frac{288}{13}$ min $\Rightarrow \frac{1440}{143}$ min
$= 10\frac{10}{143}$ min gain
(gain as sign is positive)

10. (*b*) Required result

$$= \left(\frac{720}{11} - x\right)\left(\frac{60 \times 24}{x}\right) \text{min}$$

Here, $x = 58$

∴ Required result

$$= \left(\frac{720}{11} - 58\right)\left(\frac{60 \times 24}{58}\right) \text{min}$$

$$= \frac{82}{11} \times \frac{720}{29} \text{ min}$$

$$= 185\frac{25}{319} \text{ min gain}$$

(gain as sign is positive)

11. (*d*) Required result

$$= \left(\frac{720}{11} - x\right)\left(\frac{60 \times 24}{x}\right) \text{min}$$

Here, $x = 62$

∴ Required result

$$= \left(\frac{720}{11} - 62\right)\left(\frac{60 \times 24}{62}\right) \text{min}$$

$$= \frac{38}{11} \times \frac{720}{31} \text{ min}$$

$$= 80\frac{80}{341} \text{ min gain}$$

(gain as sign is positive)

12. (*c*) Required result

$$= \left(\frac{720}{11} - x\right)\left(\frac{60 \times 24}{x}\right) \text{min}$$

Here, $x = 76$

∴ Required result

$$= \left(\frac{720}{11} - 76\right)\left(\frac{60 \times 24}{76}\right) \text{min}$$

$$= \frac{-116}{11} \times \frac{360}{19} \text{ min}$$

$$= -199\frac{169}{209} \text{ min}$$

(loss as sign is negative)

13. (*b*) Let the time duration of each lecture is t min. Then, according to the question,

$$t \times 4 + 4(4-1) = 3{:}52 - 1{:}00$$

$$\Rightarrow \quad 4t + 12 = 2 \text{ h } 52 \text{ min}$$

$$\Rightarrow \quad 4t = 172 - 12$$

$$\Rightarrow \quad t = \frac{160}{4} = 40 \text{ min}$$

∴ Each lecture of the class is of 40 min duration.

14. (*c*) Time of ringing last bell
= (7 : 45 – 0 : 45) = 7 : 00 am
But it happened 5 min before the priest gave the information to the devotees.
∴ Time of giving information
= 7 : 00 + 0 :05 = 7 : 05 am

15. (*a*) As next bus leaves at 9 : 35 am.
∴ Previous bus left at,
(9 : 35 – 0 : 30) = 9 : 05 am
The time when enquiry clerk gave this information
= 9 : 05 + 0 : 10 = 9 : 15 am

16. (*c*) Aseem leaves his house at 20 min to 7, *i.e.*, at 6 : 40 am.
He reaches Kaushal's house at
6 : 40 + 0 : 25 = 7 : 05 am
They finish their breakfast at
= 7 : 05 + 0 : 05 = 7 : 10 am
Then, both leave for office at
=7 : 10 + 0 : 35 = 7 : 45 am
Hence, option (c) is the correct answer.

17. (*c*) Time of Sujay's reaching the place
= (8 : 50 – 0 : 20)h
= 8 : 30 h
It is clear that, the person who was 40 min late would reach the place at 9 : 00 h.
∴ Scheduled time of meeting
= (9 : 00 – 0 : 40) h
= 8 : 20 h

Master Exercise

1. There are 20 people working in an office. The first group of five works between 8 am and 2 pm. The second group of ten works between 10 am and 4 pm and the third group of five works between 12 noon and 6 pm. There are three computers in the office which all the employees frequently use.
During which of the following hours, the computers are likely to be used the most?
(a) 2 : 00 pm - 4 : 00 pm (b) 12 noon - 2 : 00 pm
(c) 1 : 00 pm - 3 : 00 pm (d) 10 am - 12 noon

2. A man puts the switch ON of the bulb at 2 : 39 : 40 and puts the switch OFF at 12 : 30 : 34. Find the time duration when the bulb was switched ON. « RRB ALP 2018
(a) 9 h 50 min 54s (b) 10 h 9 min 6s
(c) 6 h 9 min 9s (d) 12 h 40 min 6s

3. A clock rings up one time at 1 O'clock, two times at 2 O'clock ... 12 times at 12 O'clock. In two days, how many times, the same clock will ring up? « WBCS 2018
(a) 78 (b) 264 (c) 312 (d) 444

4. The train for Chandigarh leaves every two and a half hour from New Delhi Railway Station. An announcement was made at the station that the train for Chandigarh had left 40 min ago and the next train will leave at 18 h. At what time was the announcement made?
(a) 17 : 05 h (b) 17 : 20 h
(c) 16 : 10 h (d) 15 : 30 h

5. There is a bus after every 40 min from a bus stand to Chennai. A clerk sitting at the enquiry counter told Q passenger that the bus has already left 10 min ago and the next bus will leave at 10:45. At what time did the enquiry clerk give this information to the passenger? « FCI 2015
(a) 10 : 25h (b) 9 : 55h (c) 10 : 15h (d) 10 : 35h

6. Raveena left house for the bus stop 15 min earlier than usual. It takes 10 min to reach the stop. She reached the stop at 8 : 40 am. What time does he usually leave home for the bus stop?
(a) 8 : 55 am (b) 8 : 45 am
(c) 8 : 30 am (d) 8 : 05 am

7. A tortoise walks 1 km in 4h. He takes rest of 20 min after every kilometer. So, you have to find out, how much time would be taken by tortoise to complete 3.5 km journey? « SSC (CGL) 2011
(a) 14 h (b) 13 h (c) 15 h (d) 12 h

8. How many times do the hands of a clock coincide in a day?

(a) 24 (b) 20 (c) 12 (d) 22

9. The minute hand of a clock overtakes the hour hand at intervals of 50 min of the correct time. How much does a clock gain or lose in a day?

(a) $443\frac{28}{55}$ min (gain) (b) $43\frac{28}{55}$ min (loss)
(c) $445\frac{5}{55}$ min (gain) (d) $444\frac{28}{55}$ min (loss)

10. The minute hand of a clock overtakes the hour hand at intervals of 88 min of the correct time. How much does a clock gain or lose in a day?

(a) $368\frac{112}{121}$ min (loss) (b) $368\frac{112}{121}$ min (gain)
(c) $369\frac{112}{121}$ min (loss) (d) $369\frac{112}{121}$ min (gain)

11. At what time, in between 6 O'clock and 7 O'clock, will the minute hand of a clock be ahead of hour hand by 3 min? « UPSC CSAT 2015

(a) 06 : 15h (b) 06 : 18h
(c) 06 : 36h (d) 06 : 48h

12. Find at what time between 8 O'clock and 9 O'clock will the hands of a clock be in the same straight line but not together?

(a) $10\frac{10}{11}$ min past 8 (b) $50\frac{10}{11}$ min past 8
(c) $10\frac{12}{11}$ min past 8 (d) 10 min past 8

13. At what time between 3 O'clock and 4 O'clock will the hands of a clock coincide?

(a) 45 min past 3 (b) $15\frac{10}{11}$ min past 3
(c) $10\frac{12}{11}$ min past 3 (d) $16\frac{4}{11}$ min past 3

14. At what time between 4 O'clock and 5 O'clock will the hands of a clock be at right angle?

(a) 30 min past 4 (b) $16\frac{3}{4}$ min past 4
(c) $38\frac{2}{11}$ min past 4 (d) 33 min past 4

15. At what time between 5 O'clock and 6 O'clock are the hands of a clock coincident?

(a) 22 min past 5 (b) 30 min past 5
(c) $22\frac{8}{11}$ min past 5 (d) $27\frac{3}{11}$ min past 5

16. At what time between 9 O'clock and 10 O'clock will the hands of a watch be together?

(a) 45 min past 9 (b) 50 min past 9
(c) $49\frac{1}{11}$ min past 9 (d) $48\frac{2}{11}$ min past 9

17. At what angle the hands of a clock are inclined at 15 min past 5?

(a) $72\frac{1}{2}^\circ$ (b) $67\frac{1}{2}^\circ$ (c) $58\frac{1}{2}^\circ$ (d) 64°

18. What angle will be formed by the hands of a clock at 11 : 20?

(a) 120° (b) 130°
(c) 140° (d) 150°

19. A clock is set right at 8 am. The clock gains 10 min in 24 h. What will be the right time when the clock indicates 1 pm on the following day?

(a) 12 : 40 pm (b) 12 : 48 pm
(c) 12 pm (d) 10 pm

20. A watch is one minute slow at 1 : 00 pm on Tuesday and 2 min fast at 1 : 00 pm on Thursday. When did it show the correct time? « UP PSC 2012

(a) 1: 00 am on Wednesday (b) 5: 00 am on Wednesday
(c) 1: 00 pm on Wednesday (d) 5: 00 pm on Wednesday

21. A clock is set right at 8 am, the clock uniformly loses 24 min in a day. What will be the right time when the clock indicates 4 pm on the next day?

(a) 4 : 50 pm (b) 4 : 30 pm
(c) 4 : 50 am (d) 4 : 32 am

22. A watch, which gains uniformly, is 3 min slow at 12 noon on Sunday and is 5 min 36 s fast at 4 pm on the next Sunday. At what time it was correct?

(a) 12 am on same day (b) 12 pm on Monday
(c) 12 am on Tuesday (d) 12 am on Wednesday

23. A class starts at 10 : 00 am lasts till 1 : 27 pm. Four periods are held during this interval. After every period, 5 min rest are given to the students. The exact duration of each period is « RPSC 2013

(a) 40 min (b) 48 min
(c) 51 min (d) 53 min

24. If the time in a clock is 20 min past 2, then find the angle between the hands of the clock. « IIFT 2013

(a) 45° (b) 50°
(c) 60° (d) 120°

25. If each of the twelve digits on a watch is replaced by English vowels a, e, i, o, u in sequence (1 by a, 2 by e, and so on), the hour hand will be between which pair of vowels at 9 : 30 am? « CMAT 2013

(a) ae (b) ei
(c) io (d) ou

26. A series of letters, digits and symbol is given below

L•4 P β ϕ N 7@9θ6 P• D ∗ EHT↓ M > 3 #

If the digits/numbers of the dial of clock are replaced in such a way that ϕ takes the place of 6, N takes the place of 7 and this arrangement goes on in the same way, then what comes in place of 11?

(a) 7 (b) θ
(c) ∗ (d) 9

27. The digits/numbers from 1 to 24 to be represented by the dial of a clock are replaced by the letters of English alphabet. The replacement is started with the letter C. Find the letter which represent 16 O'clock. « SSC (FCI) 2010

(a) W (b) P (c) S (d) R

Answers / WITH EXPLANATIONS

1. (*b*) It is obvious that computers would be used most when all the three groups are working simultaneously and this happens during the period 12 noon to 2 pm.

2. (*a*) Required time duration
$= 12:30:34 - 2:39:40$
$= 09:50:54 = 9$ h 50 min 54 s

3. (*c*) In 12 h, clock will ring up
$$= \frac{12 \times (12+1)}{2} = \frac{12 \times 13}{2} = 78 \text{ times}$$
Hence, in 24 h (or 1 day), clock will ring up $= 78 \times 2$ times and in 2 days, it will ring up $= 78 \times 2 \times 2 = 312$ times

4. (*c*) Time of the last train leaving the station
$= (18:00 - 2:30)\text{ h} = 15:30$ h
But this happens 40 min before the announcement is made.
$\therefore$ Time of making announcement
$= (15:30 + 0:40) = 16:10$ h

5. (*c*) The time of departure of the previous bus $= 10{:}45 - 0{:}40 = 10{:}05$
According to the question, this bus has left 10 min ago. So the time, at which the enquiry clerk gave the information $= 10{:}05 + 0{:}10 = 10{:}15$

6. (*b*) Clearly, Raveena left home 10 min before 8 : 40 am *i.e.*, at 8 : 30 am but it was 15 min earlier than usual, so she usually leaves for the stop at $(8:30 + 0:15) = 8:45$ am.

7. (*c*) Total time taken by tortoise
$= (4 + 4 + 4 + 2)$ h
and $(20 + 20 + 20)$ min
$= 14 \text{ h} + 60 \text{ min} = 15$ h

8. (*d*) The hands of a clock coincide 11 times in every 12 h (because between 11 O'clock and 1 O' clock, there is a common position at 12 O'clock).
Therefore, in a day the hands coincide 22 times.

9. (*c*) Required result
$$= \left(\frac{720}{11} - x\right)\left(\frac{60 \times 24}{x}\right) \text{min}$$
Here, $x = 50$
$\therefore$ Required result
$$= \left(\frac{720}{11} - 50\right)\left(\frac{60 \times 24}{50}\right) \text{min}$$
$$= \left(\frac{170}{11} \times \frac{144}{5}\right) \text{min}$$
$$= 445\frac{5}{55} \text{ min (gain)}$$
(gain as sign is positive)

10. (*a*) Required result
$$= \left(\frac{720}{11} - x\right)\left(\frac{60 \times 24}{x}\right) \text{min}$$
Here, $x = 88$
$\therefore$ Required result
$$= \left(\frac{720}{11} - 88\right)\left(\frac{60 \times 24}{88}\right) \text{min}$$
$$= \frac{-248}{11} \times \frac{180}{11} = -368\frac{112}{121} \text{ min}$$
(loss as sign is negative)

11. (*c*) In between 6 O'clock and 7 O'clock, 06:33 will be the time at which the minute hand will be ahead of hour hand.
As we know that, the minute hand covers a space of 1 min in $\frac{12}{11}$ min.
$\therefore$ In 3 min, it will covers a space of
$3 \times \frac{12}{11} = \frac{36}{11} = 3\frac{3}{11} \text{ min} \approx 3$ min
Hence, the required time
$= 06{:}33 + 00{:}03 = 06{:}36$h

12. (*a*) **Method I** Fig. (i) shows the positions of the hands of the clock at 8 O'clock and it is clear that they are 20 min apart. To be in the straight line, they have to be 30 min apart.

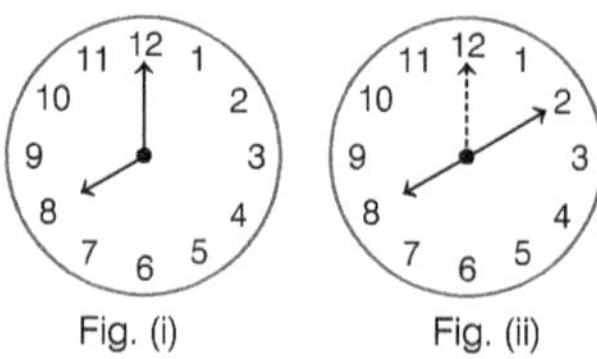

Fig. (i) Fig. (ii)

So, the minute hand will have to gain 10 min space in order to be 30 min apart from hour hand.
Since, 55 min are gained in 60 min
$\therefore$ 10 min will be gained in
$$\frac{60}{55} \times 10 = \frac{12}{11} \times 10 \text{ min}$$
Therefore, the hands will be in straight line but not together at
$10\frac{10}{11}$ min past 8.

Method II Required time
$$= \left(\frac{5x - 30}{11}\right) \times 12 \text{ min past } x$$
'–' sign is used because x (8 O'clock) > 6
$\therefore$ Required time
$$= \left(\frac{5 \times 8 - 30}{11}\right) \times 12 \text{ min past 8}$$
$$= \frac{120}{11} \text{ min past 8}$$
$$= 10\frac{10}{11} \text{ min past 8}$$

13. (*d*) **Method I** At 3 O'clock both the hands of the clock are 15 min apart. Hence, in order to be together, minute hand will have to gain 15 min spaces in order to coincide with the hour hand.
Now, 55 min are gained by minute hand in 60 min.
$\therefore$ 15 min will be gained in
$$\left(\frac{60}{55} \times 15\right) \text{min} = \left(\frac{12}{11} \times 15\right) \text{min}$$
$$= \frac{180}{11} \text{ or } 16\frac{4}{11} \text{ min}$$
Therefore, the hands will coincide at $16\frac{4}{11}$ min past 3.

Method II Required time
$$= \frac{60x}{11} \text{ min past } x$$
Here, $x = 3$ O'clock
$$\therefore \text{ Required time} = \frac{60 \times 3}{11} \text{ min past 3}$$
$$= 16\frac{4}{11} \text{ min past 3}$$

14. (*c*) **Method I** Between 4 O'clock and 5 O'clock the hands of the clock will be at right angle twice, first situation will occur when minute hand is 15 min spaces behind the hour hand and the second when minute hand is 15 min spaces ahead of the hour hand.

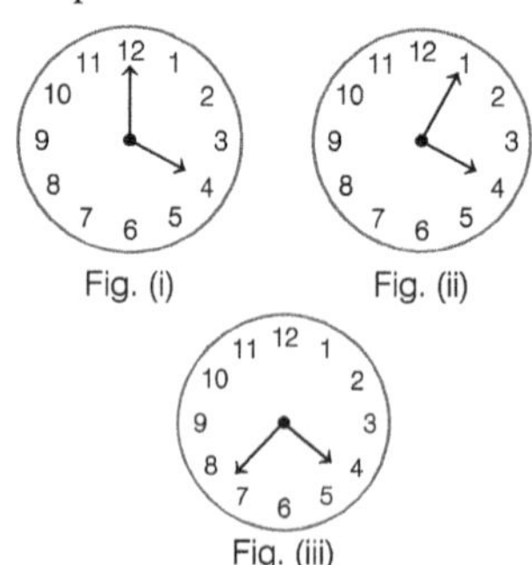

Fig. (i) Fig. (ii)
Fig. (iii)

Fig. (ii) shows the position when minute hand is 15 min spaces behind the hour hand. To come at this position, minute hand has to gain 5 min spaces from the position at 4 O'clock .
Now, 55 min are gained by minute hand in 60 min.
$\therefore$ 5 will be gained in
$$\frac{60}{55} \times 5 = \frac{60}{11} \text{ min}$$
It means that hands of the clock will be at right angle at $5\frac{5}{11}$ min past 5.
Fig. (iii) shows the position when minute hand is 15 min spaces ahead the hour hand.
To come at this position, minute hand has to gain 35 min spaces from the position at 4 O'clock.
Now, 55 min are gained in 60 min.
$\therefore$ 35 min spaces will be gained in

$60 \text{ min} = \frac{60}{55} \times 35 \text{ min} = \frac{420}{11} \text{ min}$

It means that second position will come at $38\frac{2}{11}$ min past 4.

Now, in options $38\frac{2}{11}$ min past 4 is available as option (c).

Method II Required time

$$= \left(\frac{5x+15}{11}\right) \times 12 \text{ min past } x$$

'+' sign is used because minute hand is ahead.

Here, $x = 4$ O'clock

∴ Required time

$$= \left(\frac{5 \times 4 + 15}{11}\right) \times 12 \text{ min past 4}$$

$$= \frac{420}{11} \text{ min past 4} = 38\frac{2}{11} \text{ min past 4}$$

15. (*d*) **Method I** From the figure, we find that min hand is 25 min spaces behind the hour hand. In order to coincide, it has to again 25 min spaces.

Now, 55 min are gained by minute hand in 60 min.

∴ 25 min will be gained in

$$\frac{60}{55} \times 25 = 27\frac{3}{11} \text{ min}$$

So, the hands will coincide at

$$27\frac{3}{11} \text{ min past 5.}$$

Method II Required time

$$= \frac{60x}{11} \text{ min past } x$$

Here, $x = 5$ O'clock

∴ Required time $= \frac{60 \times 5}{11}$ min past 5

$$= 27\frac{3}{11} \text{ min past 5}$$

16. (*c*) **Method I** Both the hands are 15 min spaces apart at 9 O'clock. To be together between 9 and 10, min O' clock hand has to gain 45 min.

Now, minute hand gains 55 min in 60 min.

∴ It will gain 45 min in

$$\frac{60}{55} \times 45 = 49\frac{1}{11} \text{ min}$$

Therefore, the hands will be together at $49\frac{1}{11}$ min past 9.

Method II Required time

$$= \frac{60x}{11} \text{ min past } x$$

Here, $x = 9$ O'clock

∴ Required time $= \frac{60 \times 9}{11}$ min past 9

$$= 49\frac{1}{11} \text{ min past 9}$$

17. (*b*) ∵ Angle traced by hour hand per minute $= \left(\frac{1}{2}\right)^\circ$

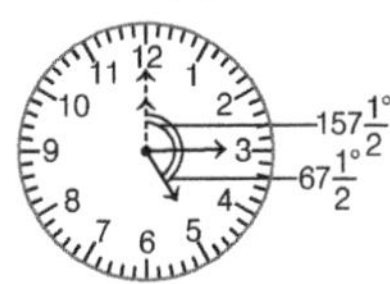

∴ Angle traced by hour hand in 5 h 15 min

$$= (5 \times 60 + 15) \times \frac{1}{2}^\circ$$

$$= 315 \times \frac{1}{2}^\circ = 157\frac{1}{2}^\circ$$

∵ Angle traced by minute hand per minute $= 6°$

∴ Angle traced by minute hand in 15 min

$$= 15 \times 6° = 90°$$

∴ Required angle

$$= 157\frac{1}{2}^\circ - 90° = 67\frac{1}{2}^\circ$$

18. (*c*) ∵ Angle traced by hour hand in 1 min $= \left(\frac{1}{2}\right)^\circ$

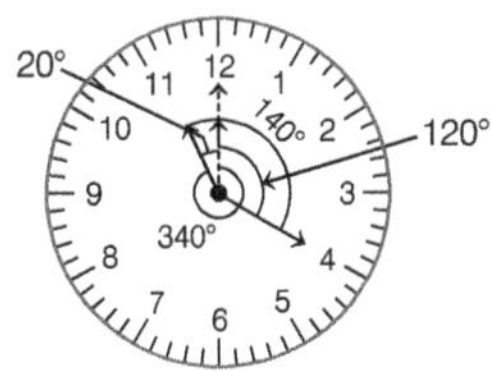

∴ Angle traced by hour hand in 11 h 20 min

$$= 360° - [(11 \times 60) + 20] \times \left(\frac{1}{2}\right)^\circ$$

$$= 360° - 680 \times \frac{1°}{2}$$

$$= 360° - 340° = 20°$$

∵ Angle traced by minute hand in 1 min = 6°

∴ Angle traced by minute hand in 20 min = 20 × 6° = 120°

∴ Required angle = 120° + 20°
= 140°

19. (*b*) Time from 8 am of a particular day to 1 pm on the following day = 29 h

Now, the clock gains 10 min in 24 h which means that 24 h 10 min of this clock is equal to 24 h of the correct clock.

i.e., $\frac{145}{6}$ h of this clock = 24 h of the correct clock

∴ 29 h of this clock $= \frac{24}{145} \times 6 \times 29$

= 28 h 48 min of correct clock

29 h of this clock = 28 h 48 min of the correct clock. It means that, the clock in question is 12 min faster than the correct clock.

Therefore, when clock indicates 1 pm, the correct time will be 48 min past 12 *i.e.*, 12 : 48 pm.

20. (*b*) As it is given that, on Tuesday at 1 : 00 pm the watch is one minute slow and on Thursday at 1 : 00 pm, it is 2 min fast, it means that the clock has gained 3 min in 48 h from Tuesday to Thursday.

Now, to show the correct time, the clock needs to gain only 1 min starting from 1 : 00 pm on Tuesday.

As, 3 min are gained in 48 h, 1 min is gained in $\frac{48}{3}$ h = 16 h

So,the clock showed the correct time at 5 : 00 am on Wednesday *i.e.*, 16 h later to 1:00 pm on Tuesday.

21. (*b*) According to the question,

Total time from 8 am of a particular day to 4 pm on the next day = 32 h

The clock loses 24 min in 24 h.

So, 23 h 36 min of this clock = 24 h of the correct clock

$$\Rightarrow \quad 23\frac{36}{60}$$

i.e., $\left(23 + \frac{3}{5}\right)$ h of this clock

= 24 h of the correct clock

$\Rightarrow \frac{118}{5}$ h of this clock

= 24 h of the correct clock

So, 32 h of this clock

$$= \left(\frac{32 \times 5 \times 24}{118}\right) \text{h of the correct clock}$$

= 32 h 30 min (approx)

Therefore, the right time is 32 h 30 min (approx) after 8 am

= 4 h 30 min = 4 : 30 pm

22. (*d*) According to the question, total time from Sunday noon (12 pm) to 4 pm the next Sunday = 7 days 4 h = 172 h

Also, the watch gains in 172 h

= 3 min + 5 min 36s

$$= 3 + 5\frac{36}{60}$$

$$= \left(3 + 5\frac{3}{5}\right) \text{min} = \frac{43}{5} \text{min}$$

$\therefore$ Watch gains 3 min in

$$= \left(\frac{3}{\frac{43}{5}}\right) \times 172 \text{ h}$$

$$= \left(\frac{3 \times 5 \times 172}{43}\right) \text{h}$$

$$= 60 \text{ h}$$

$$= 2 \text{ days } 12 \text{ h}$$

Therefore, the watch is correct after 2 days 12 h from Sunday, 12 noon *i.e.*, at 12 am on Wednesday.

23. (*b*) $\because$ Total time of class

$$= 3 \text{ h } 27 \text{ min}$$

and total time of rest

$$= 5 \times 3 = 15 \text{ min}$$

$\therefore$ Total time of all periods

$$= 3 \text{ h } 27 \text{ min} - 15 \text{ min}$$

$$= 3 \text{ h } 12 \text{ min}$$

$$= 192 \text{ min}$$

$\therefore$ Exact duration of each period

$$= \frac{192}{4} = 48 \text{ min}$$

24. (*b*) 20 min past 2

$$= 2 + \frac{20}{60} = 2 + \frac{1}{3}$$

$$= \frac{7}{3} \text{ h}$$

Angle traced by hour hand in $\frac{7}{3}$ h

$$= \frac{360°}{12} \times \frac{7}{3} = 70°$$

Angle traced by minute hand in

$$20 \text{ min} = \frac{360°}{60} \times 20 = 120°$$

$\therefore$ Required angle $= 120° - 70° = 50°$

25. (*d*) The clock is as shown in given figure. Clearly at 9 : 30 am, the hour hand will be between o and u.

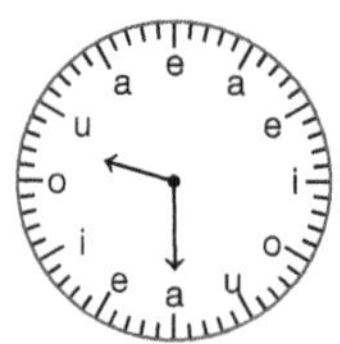

26. (*b*) According to the question, replacement is as follows,

Series	Number
L	1
•	2
4	3
P	4
β	5
ϕ	6
N	7
7	8
@	9
9	10
θ	11
6	12

Clearly, θ comes in place of 11.

27. (*d*) According to the question, replacement is as follows

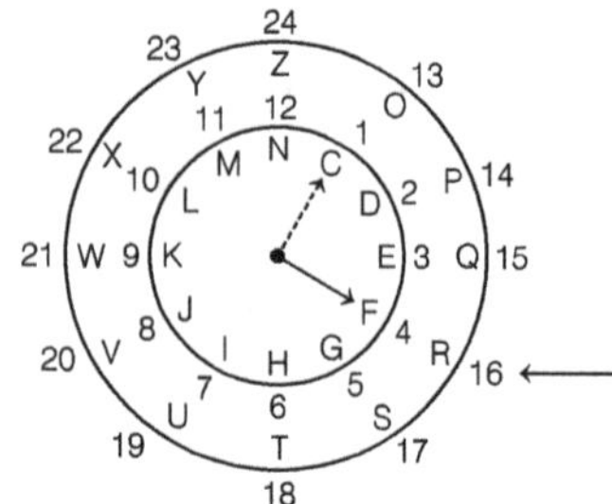

$\therefore$ R represents 16 O'clock.

CHAPTER / 13

Calendar

A calendar is a systematic arrangement of days, weeks and months in a defined pattern with which we can easily recognise the required date, month or week of a particular day.

Gregarian calendar is the world's most popular calendar. It also happens to be the Indian National Calendar and was adopted by India on 22nd March, 1957.

The Indian National Calendar contains the following

1. Day 2. Week 3. Month 4. Year 5. Date

The basics related to the calendars are given as follows

Day

A day is the 7th part of a week. It has 24 h. It is the smallest unit of a calendar.

Week

A week is the 52nd part of a year. It is a group of 7 days, which are given below

(i) Sunday (ii) Monday (iii) Tuesday
(iv) Wednesday (v) Thursday (vi) Friday
(vii) Saturday

Month

A month is the 12th part of a year. It has 28/29/30/31 days.

January	31 days
February	28 days (Ordinary year or Lunar year) 29 days (Leap year)
March	31 days
April	30 days
May	31 days
June	30 days
July	31 days
August	31 days
September	30 days
October	31 days
November	30 days
December	31 days

Year

A year is the 100th part of a century or a period of 12 months. It is the time taken by Earth to make one revolution around the Sun.

Date

Date is the

- 28th/29th/30th/31st part of a month
- 365th/366th part of a year (Lunar/Leap year)

In general, we can say that a date is a number given to each day.

Century

A block of 100 yrs is called a century e.g., Each one of the year 1100, 1800, 2000, 2100 and 2900 are century years.

Ordinary Year

- An ordinary year is a year which has 365 days (52 weeks + 1 odd day). Such years are not divisible by 4
  e.g., 2006, 2007, 2009, 2010, 2011, 2013, 2014, 2015, 2017 and 2018 etc.
- Ordinary years in the form of century are not exactly divisible by 400.
  e.g., 200, 500, 600, 700 and 900 etc.
- In an ordinary year, the first and last days of the year are same.
  e.g., In an ordinary year, if 1st January falls on Monday, then 31st December will also be on Monday.
- In any two consecutive ordinary years, date of the next year will be one day ahead of the same date of the previous year.
  e.g., If 2nd March, 2010 is Tuesday, then 2nd March, 2011 will be Wednesday.

Leap Year

- A leap year is a year which has 366 days (52 weeks + 2 days) and such years are exactly divisible by 4.
  e.g., 2004, 2008, 2012, 2016, 2020 etc.
- Leap years in the form of a century are exactly divisible by 400. e.g., 400, 800, 1200, 1600, 2000, 2400, etc.
- Last day of a leap year is one day ahead of the first day. e.g., In a leap year, if 1st January, 2004 falls on Monday, then 31st December, 2004 will be on Tuesday.

If a leap year comes immediately after an ordinary year, then the day on a certain date of the leap year will be

- 1 day ahead of the same date of the ordinary year upto February.
- 2 days ahead of the same date of the ordinary year from March to December.

If an ordinary year comes immediately after a leap year, then the day on a certain date of the ordinary year will be

- 2 days ahead of the same date of the leap year upto February.
- 1 day ahead of the same date of the leap year from March to December.

Odd Days

Extra days, apart from complete weeks in a given period are called odd days.

e.g. A period of 7 days = 7 + 0 extra day = 0 odd day

A period of 8 days = 7 + 1 extra day = 1 odd day

A period of 9 days = 7 + 2 extra days = 2 odd days

A period of 10 days = 7 + 3 extra days = 3 odd days

A period of 11 days = 7 + 4 extra days = 4 odd days

A period of 12 days = 7 + 5 extra days = 5 odd days

A period of 13 days = 7 + 6 extra days = 6 odd days

But a period of 14 days = 7 + 7 = 2 complete weeks = 0 odd days.

Counting of odd days

To calculate odd number of days in a given period, follow the rule given below.

Divide the period by 7 $\left(\textit{i.e.}, \dfrac{\text{Period}}{7} \right)$

- If $\dfrac{\text{Period}}{7}$ leaves no remainder, then there is zero odd days.
- If $\dfrac{\text{Period}}{7}$ leaves any remainder, then that remainder will be the number of odd days.

Let us understand the above rule with the following two cases

***Case* I** Finding number of odd days for 28 days period

7) 28 (4
28
0

No remainder found, so no odd day

A period of 28 Days = (4 × 7 + 0) days = 4 complete weeks + 0 odd day

As, 28 is exactly divisible by 7, hence, it leaves no remainder.

∴ Number of odd days = 0

***Case* II** Finding number of odd days for 30 days period

7) 30 (4
28
2 odd days

Here, 30 days = (4 × 7 + 2) days
= 4 complete weeks + 2 odd days

As, 30 is not exactly divisible by 7, it leaves 2 as remainder.

∴ Number of odd days = Remainder = 2

Similarly, the month with 31 days contains (4 × 7 + 3) days = 3 odd days and the month with 29 days contains (4 × 7 + 1) days = 1 odd days.

By following the same rule, number of odd days in each month of the year can be summarised as follows

Months	Number of odd days
January	3
February (ordinary year), February (leap year)	0, 1
March	3
April	2
May	3
June	2
July	3
August	3
September	2
October	3
November	2
December	3

1. Similarly, number of days in an ordinary year = 365 days

   ∴ 7) 365 (52
   35
   15
   14
   1 odd day or 365 = 52 × 7 + 1 = 1 odd day

   So, an ordinary year has 1 odd day.

2. Number of days in a leap year = 366 days

   ∴ 7) 366 (52
   35
   16
   14
   1 odd day or 366 = 52 × 7 + 2 = 2 odd day

   So, a leap year has 2 odd days.

3. 100 yrs = 76 ordinary years + 24 leap years

   ∴ Number of odd days in 100 yrs = 76 odd days of 76 ordinary years + (24 × 2) odd days of 24 leap years = 76 odd days + 48 odd days = 124 odd days

   7) 124 (17
   7
   54
   49
   5 odd days

   124 = 17 × 7 + 5 = 5 odd days

From above calculations we can conclude that

- Odd days in 1 ordinary year = 1 odd day
  = (52 weeks + 1 day)
- Odd days in 1 leap year = 52 weeks + 2 days = 2 odd days.
- Odd days in 100 yrs = 5 odd days
- Odd days in 200 yrs = (Odd days in 100 yrs) × 2
  = 5 × 2 = 10 days = 1 week + 3 days = 3 odd days
- Odd days in 300 yrs = (Odd days in 100 yrs) × 3
  = 5 × 3 = 15 days = 2 weeks + 1 day = 1 odd day
- Odd days for 400 yrs = (Odd days in 100 yrs) × 4 + 1 day
  = (5 × 4 + 1) days = 21 days = 3 weeks = 0 odd day

(i) As 400 yrs is a leap year, therefore 1 more day has been taken.

(ii) Similarly, each one of 800, 1200, 1600, 2000 and 2400 etc., has no odd days.

***Ex* 01** If the first day of the year (other than the leap year) was Sunday, then which was the last day of that year?
« UPSC Assistant Commandant 2019

(a) Monday (b) Sunday
(c) Saturday (d) None of these

***Solution* (b)** We know, in a year there are 365 day which is equal to 52 week 1 day.

In an ordinary year 1 odd day,

So, it 1st day of year is Sunday then last day of same year is also Sunday.

***Ex* 02** Which year will have the same calendar as that of 2016?

(a) 2020 (b) 2040
(c) 2025 (d) 2044

***Solution* (d)** Since, 2016 is a leap year.

∴ 2016 + 28 = 2044

(as we know that, a leap year repeats itself after 28 yr)

So, year 2044 will have the same calendar as that of 2016.

***Ex* 03** Which year has the same calendar as that of 2009?
« UPSC CSAT 2019

(a) 2018 (b) 2017
(c) 2016 (d) 2015

***Solution* (d)** To have the same calendar as that of year 2009, we must have 0 odd day between 2009 and the required year.

Years	2009	2010	2011	2012	2013	2014
Odd days	1	1	1	2	1	1

Total odd days = 1 + 1 + 1 + 2 + 1 + 1 = 7
= 1 complete week or 0 odd day.

Therefore, calendar for 2015 will be same as that of year 2009.

There are mainly three types of questions which are generally asked from this chapter in various competitive exams.

TYPE 01

Finding the Day on a Particular Date when reference Day/Date is Given

In this type of questions, a particular day and its date is given. On the basis of that the candidate has to find out the day on a given date.

There are following steps to solve these type of questions

***Step* I** Find the net number of odd days between the reference date and the date for which the day is to be determined (exclude the reference day but count the given day for counting the number of net odd days).

***Step* II** The day of the week on the particular date is equal to the number of net odd days ahead of the reference day, if the reference day was before this date. But if the reference day was ahead of this date, then the day of the week on the particular date is equal to number of odd days before the reference day.

***Ex* 04** If January 1 is a Friday, then what is the first day of the month of March in a leap year? « SSC (10 + 2) 2013

(a) Tuesday (b) Wednesday
(c) Thursday (d) Friday

***Solution* (a)** Total number of days from January 1 to March 1 = 30 + 29 + 1 = 60 days (February in a leap years = 29 days)

60 ÷ 7 = 8 weeks and 4 odd days

So, the fourth day from Friday = Tuesday

***Ex* 05** If 15th August, 2011 was Monday, what day of the week was on 17th September, 2011?

(a) Saturday (b) Sunday
(c) Friday (d) Thursday

Solution (*a*) Here, remaining days in August, 2011
= 31 − 15 = 16

and total days in September, 2011 (1st to 17th) = 17

Total days = 16 + 17 = 33

∴ 33 ÷ 7 ⇒ 7) 33 (4
28
5

33 days = (4 × 7 + 5) days = 4 weeks + 5 odd days

∴ Number of odd days = 5

Required day = Monday + 5 = Saturday

***Ex* 06** If 5th January, 1991 was Saturday, then what day of the week was it on 4th March 1992? « MAT 2009

(a) Monday (b) Wednesday
(c) Friday (d) Sunday

***Solution* (b)** **Method I** According to the question,

Remaining number of days in 1991 (365 − 5) = 360

Number of days in January 1992 = 31

Number of days in February 1992 = 29 (Leap year)

Number of days from 1st to 4th March 1992 = 4

Total days = 360 + 31 + 29 + 4 = 424

∴ 424 ÷ 7 ⇒ 7)424(60
42
4

424 days = (60 × 7 + 4) days = 60 weeks + 4 days

Number of odd days = 4

∴ Day on 4th March, 1992 = Saturday + 4 = Wednesday

Note *29 days have been taken in February as 1992 is exactly divisible by 4 and hence it is a leap year.*

Method II (By finding odd days for every segment)

Number of odd days in 1991 for (365 − 5 = 360) = 3
(360 = 51 × 7 + 3)

Number of odd days in January 1992 = 3

Number of odd days in February 1992 = 1 (Leap year)

Number of odd days from 1st to 4th March, 1992 = 4

∴ Total odd days = 3 + 3 + 1 + 4 = 11 = 1 week + 4 days
= 4 odd days

∴ Required day = Saturday + 4 = Wednesday

Ex 07 If 5th March 2012 was a Wednesday, what was the day on 5th November 2014? « UP Police SI 2017

(a) Saturday (b) Thursday
(c) Wednesday (d) Friday

Solution (d) 2012 is a leap year it has 2 odd days. But if we take dates from 5th March 2012 to 4th March 2013, it has only 1 odd day and number of odd days from 5th March 2013 to 4th March 2014 (an ordinary year) = 1 days and number of odd days from 5th March 2014 to 5th November 2014

= (31 − 5) + 30 + 31 + 30 + 31 + 31 + 30 + 31 + 5
= 245 days = (35 × 7) days
= 0 odd days

∵ Total number of odd days = 1 + 1 + 0 = 2 days

∴ Day on 5th November 2014 = Wednesday + 2 = Friday

Ex 08 Adam's birthday is on Friday 18th June. On what day of the week will be Eve's birthday in the same year if Eve's was born on 20th September?

(a) Wednesday (b) Monday
(c) Friday (d) Thursday

Solution (b) Total days from 18th June to 20th September in the same year

= (30 − 18) in June + 31 (July) + 31 (August) + 20 September

= 12 + 31 + 31 + 20 = 94 days

∵ Number of odd days

⇒ 7)94(13
7
24
21
3 odd days

∴ Required day i.e., Eve's birthday = Friday + 3 = Monday

Practice CORNER 13.1

1. If the 11th day of month is Saturday, then the date 27 of the same month will be on. « UPSSSC Amin 2016
(a) Monday (b) Saturday (c) Friday (d) Sunday

2. If 1st day of a year which is not a leap year is Friday, then find the last day of that year. « UP B.ed. 2012
(a) Sunday (b) Friday
(c) Monday (d) Wednesday

3. If there was Monday on 17 April in a year, then what was on 17 May in the same year?
(a) Sunday (b) Monday
(c) Friday (d) Wednesday

4. If 1st January, 2007 was Monday, then what day of the week lies on 1st January, 2008?
(a) Monday (b) Tuesday
(c) Wednesday (d) Sunday

5. If 1st January, 2008 is Tuesday, then what day of the week lies on 1st January, 2009?
(a) Monday (b) Wednesday
(c) Thursday (d) Sunday

6. Find the number of days from 26th January, 2011 to 23rd September, 2011 (both days are included). « SSC (CGL)2011
(a) 214 (b) 241
(c) 249 (d) 251

7. If 4th Saturday of a month was 22nd day, then what was the 13th day of that month?
(a) Tuesday (b) Wednesday
(c) Thursday (d) Friday

8. If 15th June falls on 3 days after tomorrow which is Friday, then what day of week will fall on last date of month?
(a) Monday (b) Tuesday
(c) Wednesday (d) Thursday

9. If the national day of a country was celebrated on the 4th Saturday of a month, then find the date of celebration, when the first day of that month is Tuesday. « SSC (CPO) 2011
(a) 24th (b) 25th
(c) 26th (d) 27th

10. If 26 January, 2011 was Wednesday, then what day of the week was it on 26th January,2012?
(a) Monday (b) Tuesday
(c) Wednesday (d) Thursday

11. If 15th August, 2011 was Tuesday, then what day of the week was it on 17th September, 2011?
(a) Thursday (b) Friday
(c) Saturday (d) Sunday

12. If Republic day was celebrated in 1996 on Friday, on which day in 2000 Independence day was celebrated? « SSC (CGL) 2012
(a) Monday (b) Tuesday
(c) Wednesday (d) Saturday

13. If the third day of a month is Monday, then which of the following will be the fifth day from 21st of that month? « MAT 2014
(a) Tuesday (b) Monday
(c) Wednesday (d) Thursday

14. If it was Saturday on 17th December, 1899, then what will be the day on 22nd December, 1901? « RPSC 2013
(a) Friday (b) Saturday
(c) Sunday (d) Monday

15. If 27 March, 1995 was a Monday, then what day of the week was 1 November, 1994? « MAT 2013
(a) Sunday (b) Monday
(c) Tuesday (d) Wednesday

16. Aayush's birthday is on Monday 22nd May. On what day of the week will be Neerav's birthday in the same year in Neerav was born on 30th October? « SSC CGL 2017
(a) Monday (b) Wednesday
(c) Friday (d) Thursday

17. Nasir's birthday is on Thursday May 18. On what day of the week will be Rehan's Birthday in the same year if Rehan was born on August 19? « SSC CGL 2017
(a) Wednesday (b) Saturday
(c) Friday (d) Thursday

18. Priya's birthday is on Tuesday 11th April. On what day of the week will be Rani's birthday in the same year if Rani was born on 31st August? « SSC CGL 2017
(a) Monday (b) Wednesday
(c) Tuesday (d) Thursday

19. Advik's birthday is on Monday 19th June. On what day of the week will be Nishith's birthday in the same year if Nishith was born on 17th November? « SSC CGL 2017
(a) Saturday (b) Wednesday
(c) Friday (d) Sunday

20. In a particular month of some year, there are three Mondays which have even dates. On which day of the week does the 15th of that month fall? « WBCS 2020
(a) Monday (b) Wednesday
(c) Friday (d) Sunday

Answers / WITH EXPLANATIONS

1. (*a*) Required day = Saturday
+ (7 + 7 + 2) days
= Saturday + 2 days = Monday

2. (*b*) As we know that, first and last day of an ordinary year is same.
∵ 1st day = Friday
⇒ Last day = Friday

3. (*d*) Number of days from 17th April to 17th May
= (30 − 17) + 17 = 30 days
= 4 weeks and 2 odd days
∴ Day on 17th May = Monday + 2 days
= Wednesday

4. (*b*) 2007 is an ordinary year and in an ordinary year
1st January = 31 st December
As, 1st January = Monday
∴ 31st December = Monday
∴ 1st January, 2008 = Monday + 1 odd day = Tuesday

5. (*c*) Since, 2008 is leap year.
In a leap year, last day = 1 st day + 1 odd day
= Tuesday + 1 odd day
= Wednesday
= 31 st December
∴ 1st January, 2009
= Wednesday + 1 odd day
= Thursday

6. (*b*) According to the question,
26th January to 31st January = 6 days
February = 28 days
March = 31 days
April = 30 days
May = 31 days
June = 30 days
July = 31 days
August = 31 days
1st September to 23rd September = 23 days
Total days = 241
∴ Required days = 241

7. (*c*) 4th Saturday = 22nd day
3rd Saturday = 22 − 7 = 15th day
∴ 13th day = Saturday − 2
= Thursday

8. (*b*) Tomorrow = Friday
3 days after tomorrow = 15th June
= Friday + 3 odd days
= Monday
Days from 15th to 30th June = 15
15 ÷ 7 ⇒ 7)15(2
14
1 odd day
30th June = Monday + 1 odd day
= Tuesday

9. (*c*) According to the question,
National day = 4th Saturday
∵ 1st day = Tuesday
∴ 1st Saturday = Tuesday + 4
= 1 + 4 = 5 th day
2nd Saturday = 5 + 7 = 12 th day
3rd Saturday = 12 + 7 = 19 th day
4th Saturday = 19 + 7 = 26 th day
So, National day was celebrated on 26th of that month.

10. (*d*) 26th January, 2011 to 26th January, 2012 will be considered as an ordinary year because 26th January in 2012 (a leap year) comes before 29th February. Hence, the period of this one year will have only 1 odd day.
∵ 26th January 2011 = Wednesday
∴ 26th January 2012
= Wednesday + 1 odd day
= Thursday

11. (*d*) ∵ Total days from 15th August, 2011 to 17 September, 2011 = 33
33 ÷ 7 ⇒ 7)33(4
28
5 odd days
∴ Required day
= Tuesday + 5 odd days = Sunday

12. (*b*) Number of days in 1996 (366-26) = 340
Number of days in 1997 = 365
Number of days in 1998 =365
Number of days in 1999 =365
Number of days from January 2000 to July 2000
= 31 + 29 + 31 + 30 + 31 + 30 + 31 =213
Number of days from 1st to 15th August, 2000 =15
∴ Total days
=340 + 365 + 365 + 365 + 213 + 15 =1663
1663 ÷ 7 ⇒
7) 1663 (237
14
26
21
53
49
4
∵1663 days = (237 × 7 + 4) days
= 237 weeks + 4 odd days
∴ Number of odd days =4
∴ Day on 15th August, 2000
= Friday +4 odd days = Tuesday

13. (*c*) Fifteen day from 21st will be 26th and Monday lies on 3rd, 10th, 17th, 24th. So, the day on 26th will be Wednesday.

14. (*b*) ∵ December 17, 1899 — Saturday
December 17, 1900 — Sunday
[∵ 1900 is not a leap year i.e. only one odd day]
December 18, 1901 — Tuesday
∴ December 22, 1901 — Saturday

15. (*c*) Here, 27th March, 1995 was Monday.
Now, for calculating total number of odd days. First, we calculate total number of days till 1st November, 1994.
∴ Number of days in March, 1995 = 27
Number of days in February, 1995 = 28
Number of days in January, 1995 = 31
Number of days in December, 1994 = 31
Number of days in November 1994 = 29 = 146
∴ Number of odd days = $\frac{146}{7}$
= $20\frac{6}{7}$
So, 6 odd days.
∴ On November 1, 1994
= Monday − 6 = Tuesday

16. (*a*) ∵Total days from 22nd May to 30th October in the same year
= (31 − 22) in May + 30 + 31 + 31 + 30 + 30 = 161 days
∵ Number of odd days ⇒161 ÷ 7
⇒ 7)161(23
14
21
21
0 odd day
∴ Required day i.e., Neerav's birthday
= Monday + 0
= Monday

17. (*b*) Total number of days from 18 May to 19 August = (31 − 18) May + 30 (June) + 31 (July) + 19 (August)
= 13 + 30 + 31 + 19
= 93days
Number of odd days
⇒ 7)93(13
7
23
21
2 odd days
∴ Rehan's birthday
= Nasir's birthday + 2
= Thursday + 2
= Saturday

18. (*d*) ∵ Total days from 11th April to 31st August in the same year

= (30 − 11) in April + 31 (May) + 30 (June) + 31 (July) + 31 (August)

= 142 days

Number of odd days

⇒ 142 ÷ 7

⇒ 7)142(20
140
2 odd days

Required day = Tuesday + 2 = Thursday

∴ Rani's birthday = Thursday

19. (*c*) ∵ Total days from Advik's birthday (19th June) to 17th November in the same year

= (30 − 19) + 31 + 31 + 30 + 31 + 17

= 151 days

⇒ 7)151(21
14
11
7
4 odd days

∴ Nishith's birthday = Monday + 4

= Friday (17th November)

20. (*d*) Three Monday on even dates in a month are only possible when 1st Monday is on 2nd day of the month.

So, Date 2 ⇒ Monday

Date 23 ⇒ Monday

Date 9 ⇒ Monday

Date 30 ⇒ Monday

Date 16 ⇒ Monday

∴ 16th date of the month falls on Monday. 15 th is on Sunday.

TYPE 02

Finding the Day on a Particular Date when Reference Day is not Given

To find the day on a particular date when reference day is not given we have to follow the following steps.

***Step* I** Find the net number of odd days upto the date for which the day is to be determined.

***Step* II** Write the name of the day according to the number of odd days as given below

If odd day = 0, then required day = Sunday

If odd day = 1, then required day = Monday

If odd days = 2, then required day = Tuesday

If odd days = 3, then required day = Wednesday

If odd days = 4, then required day = Thursday

If odd days = 5, then required day = Friday

If odd days = 6, then required day = Saturday

***Ex* 09** Find the day of the week on 26th January 2020.

(a) Friday (b) Sunday
(c) Monday (d) Saturday

***Solution* (b)** Number of odd days in 2000 yr = 0

Number of odd days in 19 yr = (4 × 2 + 15 × 1) = 23

(Since, there are 4 leap years and 15 ordinary years in the period of 19 yr)

Number of odd days in 26 days of January 2020 = 5

∴ Total odd days = 0 + 23 + 5 = 28 days

28 ÷ 7 ⇒ 7)28(4
28
0

i.e., 28 days = (4 × 7 + 0) days = 4 weeks

Number of odd days = 0

∴ Required day = Sunday

***Ex* 10** On which dates of March 2017 was Tuesday?

(a) 3, 10, 17 and 24 (b) 6, 13, 20 and 27
(c) 7, 14, 21 and 28 (d) 5, 12, 19 and 26

***Solution* (c)** Let us find out the day on 1st March 2017.

1st March 2017 = Odd days in 2000 yr + Odd days in 16 yr + Odd days in 2 months and 1 day.

Number of odd days in 16 yr = 0 + 4 × 2 + 12 × 1

= 20 days = 2 weeks and 6 odd days

[∵ In 16 yr = 4 leap year and 12 ordinary years]

2 months and 1 day = January (31) + February (28) + March (1)

= 31 + 28 + 1 = 60 days

Number of odd days in 60 days

⇒ 7)60(8
56
4 odd days

∴ Total number of odd days = 6 + 4 = 10 days

Number of odd days in 10 days

⇒ 7)10(1
7
3 odd days

= 3 odd days

Since, there are 3 odd days, so the day was Wednesday on 1st March 2017

∴ 7, 14, 21 and 28 were the Tuesday in March 2017.

Practice / CORNER 13.2

1. What day of the week was on 26th January, 1989? « RRB ALP 2018
   (a) Wednesday (b) Tuesday
   (c) Thursday (d) Sunday
2. On which day of the week does 4 July, 1776 fall?
   (a) Thursday (b) Monday
   (c) Tuesday (d) Saturday
3. What was the day of the week on 15th August, 1947?
   (a) Friday (b) Monday
   (c) Saturday (d) Sunday
4. What was the day of the week on 28th May, 2006?
   (a) Thursday (b) Friday (c) Saturday (d) Sunday
5. What was the day of the week on 30th June, 1980?
   (a) Friday (b) Wednesday
   (c) Monday (d) Saturday
6. On which day of the week does 28th August, 2009 fall?
   (a) Sunday (b) Monday
   (c) Tuesday (d) Friday
7. What day of the week was on 15th August, 1949?
   (a) Monday (b) Tuesday
   (c) Thursday (d) Saturday
8. On which day of the week does 18th September, 1991 fall?
   (a) Wednesday (b) Tuesday (c) Friday (d) Saturday
9. Ashu was born on August 19,1992 what day of the week was the born?
   (a) Sunday (b) Monday
   (c) Tuesday (d) Wednesday
10. What was the day on 1st January, 1901?
    (a) Monday (b) Wednesday
    (c) Sunday (d) Tuesday
11. What was the day of the week on 4th June, 2017?
    (a) Tuesday (b) Monday
    (c) Friday (d) Saturday
12. What was the day on 26th January 1950, when first Republic Day of India was celebrated?
    (a) Monday (b) Tuesday (c) Thursday (d) Friday
13. On which dates of April, 2012 will a Sunday come?
    (a) 5, 12, 19, 26 (b) 1, 8, 15, 22, 29
    (c) 3, 10, 17, 24 (d) 7, 14, 21, 28
14. On which dates of June 2015 was a Wednesday?
    (a) 1, 8, 15, 22 and 29 (b) 4, 11, 18 and 25
    (c) 6, 13, 20 and 27 (d) 5, 12, 19 and 26
15. On what dates in April, 2001, did Wednesday fall? « CGPSC Pre 2017
    (a) 1st, 8th, 15th, 22nd, 29th
    (b) 2nd, 9th, 16th, 23rd, 30th
    (c) 4th, 11th, 18th, 25th
    (d) 3rd, 10th, 17th, 24th

Answers / WITH EXPLANATIONS

1. (*c*) Number of odd days till 26 January 1989
= Odd days in 1600 yr + Odd days in 300 yr + Odd days in 88 yr + Odd days in 26 days
$= 0 + 1 + 22 \times 2 + 66 \times 1 + 5$
= 116 days
= 16 weeks and 4 odd days
∴ On 26th January 1989, there was Thursday.

2. (*a*) 1776 yr = 1600 yr + 100 yr + 75 yr
Number of odd days in 1600 yr = 0
Number of odd days in 100 yr = 5
Number of odd days in 75 yr
$= 18 \times 2 + 57 \times 1 = 93$ days
[∵ In 76 yr, there are 18 leap years and 57 ordinary years]
= 13 weeks and 2 odd days = 2 odd days
And odd days from 1 January 1776 to 4 July 1776
= odd days in
$(31 + 29 + 31 + 30 + 31 + 30 + 4)$ days
= odd days in 186 days
∵ 186 days = 26 weeks and 4 odd days
∴ Odd days = 4 days
Total number of odd days
$= 0 + 5 + 2 + 4 = 4$ odd days
There are 4 odd days, so the required day = Thursday

3. (*a*) Odd days in 1600 yr = 0
Odd days in 300 yr = 1
46 yr = (11 leap year + 35 ordinary year) $= (11 \times 2 + 35 \times 1) = 1$ odd day
∴ Odd days in 1946 yr $= (0 + 1 + 1) = 2$

Month	Odd days
January	3
February	0 (ordinary year)
March	3
April	2
May	3
June	2
July	3
August	1 (15 ÷ 7)
Total	17

17 ÷ 7 ⇒ 7)17(2
14
3 odd days
Total odd days = 2 + 3 = 5
∴ Required day = Friday

4. (*d*) Odd days in 1600 yr = 0
Odd days in 400 yr = 0
5 yr = (4 ordinary year + 1 leap year)
$= (4 \times 1 + 1 \times 2)$
= 6 odd days

Month	Odd days
January	3
February	0
March	3
April	2
May	0(28 ÷ 7)
Total	8

Total odd days = 8 + 6 = 14 = 0 odd day
∴ Required day = Sunday

5. (*c*) 30th June,1980 means 1979 complete years+ 6 months of 1980
Number of odd days in 1600 yr = 0
Number of odd days in 300 yr = 1
Number of odd days in 79 yr
= (19 leap years + 60 ordinary years)
$=19 \times 2 + 60 \times 1 = 38 + 60$
$=98 \Rightarrow 0$ odd days

January	3
February	1
March	3
April	2
May	3
June	2

Number of odd days in 1980
$= 3 + 1 + 3 + 2 + 3 + 2$
$= 14 \Rightarrow 0$ odd day
Total number of odd days till 30th June, 1980
$= 0 + 1 + 0 + 0 = 1$
So, the required day was Monday.

6. (*d*) 28th August, 2009 means 2008 complete years + First 7 months of year 2009 + 28 days of August
Number of odd days in 2000 yr = 0
Number of odd days from 2001 yr to 2008 yr

Year	Number of odd days
2001	1
2002	1
2003	1
2004	2
2005	1
2006	1
2007	1
2008	2

$= 1 + 1 + 1 + 2 + 1 + 1 + 1 + 2$
$= 10 = 7 \times 1 + 3 = 3$ odd days
Number of odd days in 2009,

January	3
February	0
March	3
April	2
May	3
June	2
July	3
August	0

$= 3 + 0 + 3 + 2 + 3 + 2 + 3 + 0$
$= 16 = 7 \times 2 + 2 = 2$ odd days
Total number of odd days till 28th August, 2009
$= 0 + 3 + 2 = 5$
So, the required day is Friday.

7. (*a*) 15th August, 1949 means, 1948 complete year + First 7 months of the years 1949 + 15 days of August
Number of odd days in 1600 yr = 0
Number of odd days in 300 yr = 1
Number of odd days in 48 yr
(36 non-leap years + 12 leap years)
$= 36 \times 1 + 12 \times 2 = 60$
$= 7 \times 8 + 4 = 4$ odd days
From 1st January, 1949 to 15th August, 1949
Number of odd days in 1949,

January	3
February	0
March	3
April	2
May	3
June	2
July	3
August	$(18 \div 7) = 4$

Total number of odd days in 1949
$= 3 + 0 + 3 + 2 + 3 + 2 + 3 + 1 = 17$
$= 7 \times 2 + 3 = 3$ odd days
Total odd days $= 1 + 4 + 3 = 8 = 1$ odd day
Since, 1 is the code for Monday. Therefore, the required day was Monday.

8. (*a*)18th September, 1991 means 1990 complete years + 8 months of 1991 + 18 days of September
Number of odd days in 1600 yr = 0
Number of odd days in 300 yr = 1
Number of odd days in 90 yr
(22 leap years + 68 ordinary years)
$= 22 \times 2 + 68 \times 1$
$= 44 + 68 = 112 \Rightarrow 0$ odd day
Number of odd days in 1991,

January	3
February	0
March	3
April	2
May	3
June	2
July	3
August	3
September	$18 \div 7 = 4$

$= 3 + 0 + 3 + 2 + 3 + 2 + 3 + 3 + 4$
$= 23 = 7 \times 3 + 2$
$\Rightarrow$ 2 odd days
Total number of odd days till 18th September, 1991
$= 0 + 1 + 0 + 2 = 3$
So, the required day was Wednesday.

9. (*d*) 19th August, 1992 means 1991 complete years + First 7 months of 1992 + 19 days of August
Number of odd days in 1600 yr = 0
Number of odd days in 300 yr = 1
Number of odd days in 91 yr
(22 leap years + 69 non-leap years)
$= 22 \times 2 + 69 \times 1 = 44 + 69$
$= 113 = 7 \times 16 + 1 = 1$ odd day
From 1st January, 1992 to 19th August, 1992 number of odd days in 1992,

January	3
February	1 (Since, 1992 is a leap year
March	3
April	2
May	3
June	2
July	3
August	$19 \div 7 = 5$

$= 3 + 1 + 3 + 2 + 3 + 2 + 3 + 5$
$= 22 = 7 \times 3 + 1 = 1$ odd day
$\therefore$ Number of odd days till 19th August, 1992
$= 0 + 1 + 1 + 1 = 3$
So, the required day was Wednesday.

10. (*d*) 1st January, 1901 means = (1900 yr and 1 day)
Now, 1600 yr have 0 odd day, 300 yr have 1 odd day
and 1 day has 1 odd day.
Total number of odd days
$= 0 + 1 + 1 = 2$ days
Therefore, the day on 1st January, 1901 was Tuesday.

11. (*b*) Odd days of 2000 yr = 0
Odd days in 16yr = 0
Odd days for period of 1st January, 2017 to 4th June, 2017 =
Jan Feb March April May June
3 +0 +3 +2 +3 +4 = 15
$\therefore$ Total odd days $= 0 + 15 = 15 = 2$ weeks + 1 day = 1 odd day
So, the required day is Monday.

12. (*c*) Number of odd days in 1600 yr = 0
Number of odd days in 300 yr = 1
$\therefore$ Number of odd days in 1900 yr
$= 0 + 1 = 1$
Now, in 49 yr, there are 12 leap year and 37 ordinary years.
$\therefore$ Number of odd days in 49 yr
$= 2(12) + 37$
[$\because$ a leap year has 2 odd days and an ordinary year has 1 odd day]
$= 24 + 37 = 61$
= 8 weeks + 5 odd days.
Number of odd days in 1949 yr
$= 1 + 5 = 6$
Now, for 26 January
$\Rightarrow$ Number of odd days = 5

∴ Total number of odd days
$= 6 + 5 = 11$
$= 1$ week + 4 odd days
Day related to 4 odd days = Thursday
Hence, the day on 26th January 1950 was Thursday.

13. (*b*) First of all, we have to find the day on 1st April, 2012. 1st April 2012 means (2011 yr 3 months and 1 day)
Now, 2000 yr have 0 odd days
11 yr have
(2 leap years and 9 ordinary years)
$= (2 \times 2 + 9 \times 1)$ odd days
$= (4 + 9)$ odd days
$= 13 = 6$ odd days
3 months and 1 day

January	31
February	29
March	31
April	1

= 92 days = 1 odd day
Total number of odd days
$= (6 + 1) = 7 \Rightarrow 0$ odd day
Hence, it was Sunday on 1st April 2012. (1st Sunday).
Subsequently, Sunday of the month were on 1st, 8th, 15th, 22nd and 29th.

14. (*b*) Let us find out the day on 1st June 2015
1st June 2015 = 2000 yr + 14 yr + 5 months +1 day
Now, calculate the number of odd days
Number of odd days in 2000 yr = 0
Number of odd days in 14 yrs
$= 3 \times 2 + 11 \times 1 = \frac{17}{7} = 3$ odd days
[∵ In 14 yr, 3 leap years and 11 ordinary years]
5 months and 1 day = January (31) + February (28) + March (31) + April (30) + May (31) + 1
$= 31 + 28 + 31 + 30 + 31 + 1$
= 152 days
Number of odd days in 152 days
⇒ 7)152(21
14
12
7
5 odd days

∴ Total number of odd days
$= 3 + 5$
$= 8 = 1$ odd day
Hence, on 1st June 2015, there was Sunday and on 4th June there was Wednesday.
∴ Total number of Wednesday = 4, 11, 18 and 25.

15. (*c*) First of all, we have to find the day on 1st April, 2001.
Now, 2000 yr have 0 odd day.
Number of odd days in 3 months and 1 day
$= \frac{31 + 28 + 31 + 1}{7}$
$= \frac{91}{7} = 0$ odd day
∵ Total number of odd days = (0 + 0)
= 0 odd day
Hence, it was Sunday on 1st April, 2001 and it was Wednesday on 4th April, 2001.
Subsequently, Wednesday of the month were on 4th, 11th, 18th and 25th.

TYPE 03

Finding a Week Day on the Basis of Another Week Day

In such questions, a week day is to be found out on the basis of some reference day of the week.

Important Concepts Regarding Days

(i) Yesterday = Today – 1 day
(ii) Tomorrow = Today + 1 day
(iii) Day after yesterday = Today
(iv) Day before yesterday = Today – 2 days
(v) Day after tomorrow = Today + 2 days
(vi) Day before tomorrow = Today
(vii) Day after the day before yesterday = (Yesterday – 1 day) + 1 day = Yesterday = Today – 1 day
(viii) Day before the day after tomorrow = (Tomorrow + 1 day – 1 day = Tomorrow = Today + 1 day
(ix) Day before the day after yesterday = (Yesterday + 1 day) – 1 day = Yesterday = Today – 1 day
(x) Day after the day before tomorrow = (Tomorrow – 1 day) + 1 day = Tomorrow = Today + 1 day

Ex 11 If today is Sunday, then what day of the week will be 3 days after tomorrow?
(a) Thursday (b) Wednesday
(c) Saturday (d) Friday

Solution **(a)** Today = Sunday
Tomorrow = Sunday + 1 = Monday
3 days after tomorrow = Monday + 3 odd days = Thursday

Ex 12 If the day before yesterday was Wednesday, when will Sunday be? « MPPSC Pre 2018
(a) Today
(b) Tomorrow
(c) Day after tomorrow
(d) Two days after tomorrow

Solution **(c)** If the day before yesterday was Wednesday, then yesterday ⇒ Wednesday + 1 = Thursday and today will be Friday and the day after tomorrow will be Sunday.
i.e.

Wednesday	Thursday	Friday	Saturday	Sunday
↓	↓	↓	↓	↓
Day before yesterday	yesterday	Today	Tomorrow	The day after tomorrow

Thus, the day after tomorrow will be Sunday.

Practice / CORNER 13.3

1. 2 days before yesterday was Friday, then what day of the week will be day after tomorrow?
(a) Monday (b) Sunday (c) Saturday (d) Wednesday

2. If a day before yesterday was Thursday, then when will Sunday fall? « SSC (10+2) 2010
(a) Today (b) 2nd day after today
(c) Tomorrow (d) A day after tomorrow

3. If day after tomorrow is Tuesday, then what day of the week will it be on 2 days after the day after tomorrow?
(a) Monday (b) Wednesday
(c) Saturday (d) Thursday

4. If day before yesterday was Thursday, then when will be the Monday? « UP B.Ed. 2011
(a) Day after tomorrow (b) Today
(c) Tomorrow (d) Two days after days

5. If a day before yesterday was Wednesday, then when will Sunday fall? « SSC (10+2) 2010
(a) 3rd days after today (b) Tomorrow
(c) Today (d) A day after tomorrow

6. If Tuesday falls 3 days after today, then what day of the week was it on 4 days before yesterday?
(a) Monday (b) Tuesday
(c) Wednesday (d) Sunday

7. If Thursday falls 2 days after tomorrow, then what day of the week was it on three days before yesterday?
(a) Monday (b) Tuesday
(c) Wednesday (d) Thursday

8. If day after tomorrow is Sunday, then what day of the week was it on day before yesterday?
(a) Wednesday (b) Friday
(c) Saturday (d) Monday

9. If a day before yesterday was Tuesday, then what day of the week will it be on a day after tomorrow?
(a) Monday (b) Wednesday
(c) Friday (d) Saturday

10. If day before yesterday was Saturday, then what day of the week will it be after tomorrow?
« UPSSSC Forest Guard 2015
(a) Friday (b) Thursday
(c) Wednesday (d) Tuesday

11. If the day before yesterday was Wednesday, when will Sunday be? « SSC (10+2) 2013
(a) Today
(b) Tomorrow
(c) Day after tomorrow
(d) Two days after tomorrow

12. The day before the day before yesterday is three days after Saturday. What day is it today?
« IB (ACIO) 2013, BSSC (CGL) 2015
(a) Tuesday (b) Wednesday
(c) Thursday (d) Friday

13. Sudha went to watch movie 9 days ago. She goes to watch movies only on Thursday, What is the day of the week today? « UPSSSC Excise Inspector 2016
(a) Thursday (b) Saturday
(c) Sunday (d) Monday

14. Anil reaches at a certain place on Friday and found he reaches the place 3 days before. If he had reached the place on coming Sunday, then how many days before or after he would have reached the place?
(a) One day before (b) One day after
(c) 2 days after (d) 2 days before

Answers / WITH EXPLANATIONS

1. (*d*) 2 days before yesterday = Friday
Yesterday = Friday + 2 = Sunday
Today = Sunday + 1 = Monday
∴ Day after tomorrow
= Monday + 2 = Wednesday
∴ Required day = Wednesday

2. (*c*) A day before yesterday = Thursday
Yesterday = Thursday + 1 = Friday
Today = Friday + 1 = Saturday
∴ Sunday = Saturday + 1
= Tomorrow
∴ Required day = Tomorrow

3. (*d*) A day after tomorrow = Tuesday
∴ Two days after the day after tomorrow
= Tuesday + 2 = Thursday
∴ Required day = Thursday

4. (*a*) Day before yesterday = Thursday
∴ Today = Thursday + 2 = Saturday
∴ Monday = Saturday + 2 = Day after tomorrow
∴ Required day = Day after tomorrow

5. (*d*) A day before yesterday
= Wednesday
Yesterday = Wednesday + 1 = Thursday
Today = Thursday + 1 = Friday
∴ Sunday = Friday + 2
= Day after tomorrow.
∴ Required day = Day after tomorrow

6. (*a*) Three days after today = Tuesday
Today = Tuesday − 3 = Saturday
Yesterday = Saturday − 1 = Friday
∴ 4 days before yesterday
= Friday − 4 = Monday
∴ Required day = Monday

7. (*d*) Two days after tomorrow = Thursday
Tomorrow = Thursday − 2 = Tuesday
Today = Tuesday − 1 = Monday
Yesterday = Monday − 1 = Sunday
∴ 3 days before yesterday
= Sunday − 3 = Thursday
∴ Required day = Thursday

8. (*a*) Day after tomorrow = Sunday
Tomorrow = Sunday − 1 = Saturday
Today = Saturday − 1 = Friday
Yesterday = Friday − 1 = Thursday
∴ Day before yesterday
= Thursday − 1 = Wednesday
∴ Required day = Wednesday

9. (*d*) A day before yesterday = Tuesday
Yesterday = Tuesday + 1
= Wednesday
Today = Wednesday + 1
= Thursday
Tomorrow = Thursday + 1 = Friday
∴ Day after tomorrow
= Friday + 1 = Saturday
∴ Required day = Saturday

10. (*c*) Day before yesterday = Saturday
Today = Saturday + 2 = Monday
∴ Tomorrow = Monday + 1
= Tuesday
∴ Day after Tomorrow
= Tuesday + 1
= Wednesday
∴ Required day = Wednesday

11. (*c*) If the day before yesterday was Wednesday, then today will be Friday and 'the day after tomorrow' will be 'Sunday'.

12. (*d*) Three days after Saturday is Tuesday and Tuesday is a day before a day before yesterday
So, yesterday is Thursday and today is Friday.

13. (*b*) Day 9 days ago = Thursday
∴ Today = Thursday + 9 = Thursday + 7 + 2
= Thursday + 2
= Saturday
∴ Required day = Saturday

14. (*a*) The correct day on which Anil has to reach the place = Friday + 3 = Monday. Therefore, if Anil reaches on Sunday, then he reaches there on the day which is (Monday – 1) or 1 day before the correct day.

Master Exercise

1. Which of the following is a leap year? « CG PSC 2013
(a) 2800 (b) 1800 (c) 2600 (d) 3000
(e) All of these

2. If day before yesterday was Saturday, then what day of the week will it be on day after tomorrow?
(a) Friday (b) Thursday
(c) Wednesday (d) Tuesday

3. If Monday falls on the first of October which day will fall three days after the 20th in that month? « UP PSC 2013
(a) Monday (b) Tuesday
(c) Wednesday (d) Sunday

4. The last day of a century cannot be either. « MAT 2013
(a) Monday (b) Wednesday
(c) Tuesday (d) Friday

5. Today is Monday, it will be ...... after 61 days.
(a) Wednesday (b) Saturday
(c) Tuesday (d) Thursday

6. If the date 7 of a month is on three days before Friday, then the date 19 of the same month will be on « UPSSSC VDO 2016
(a) Sunday (b) Monday
(c) Wednesday (d) Friday

7. If there was Thursday on 25th September in a year, then what day was on 25th October in the same year? « Haryana Police Constable 2016
(a) Sunday (b) Monday (c) Friday (d) Saturday

8. How many Monday's are there in a particular month of a particular year, if the month ends on Wednesday? « SNAP 2012
(a) 4 (b) 5
(c) 3 (d) Cannot be specified

9. The year next to 1990 which have the same calendar as that of the year 1990 is
(a) 1995 (b) 1997 (c) 1996 (d) 1992

10. A girl was born on September 6, 1970 which happened to be a Sunday. Her birthday would have fallen again on Sunday in « UP PSC 2012
(a) 1975 (b) 1977 (c) 1981 (d) 1982

11. In a month of 31 days, third Thursday falls on 16th, then what will be the last day of the month? « CG PSC 2013
(a) 5th Friday (b) 4th Saturday
(c) 5th Wednesday (d) 5th Thursday
(e) None of these

12. If there was Thursday on 11 January 2018, then what will be the day on 11 June 2019? « RRB ALP 2018
(a) Sunday (b) Wednesday
(c) Tuesday (d) Monday

13. If there was Monday on 5 January 2012, then what will be the day on 31st March 2013? « CGPSC 2019
(a) Sunday (b) Monday
(c) Tuesday (d) None of these

14. What was the day on 1st January, 1901?
(a) Monday (b) Wednesday
(c) Sunday (d) Tuesday

15. What was the day on 31st October, 1984?
(a) Friday (b) Sunday
(c) Wednesday (d) Monday

16. What was the day on 14th March, 1993?
(a) Friday (b) Thursday
(c) Sunday (d) Saturday

17. What was the day of the week on 2nd July, 1984?
(a) Wednesday (b) Tuesday
(c) Monday (d) Thursday

18. On what dates of August, 1980 did Monday fall?
(a) 4th, 11th, 18th and 25th
(b) 3th, 10th, 17th and 24th
(c) 6th, 13th, 20th, and 27th
(d) 9th, 16th, 23rd and 30th

19. On what dates of December,1984 did Sunday fall?
(a) 6th , 13th, 20th and 27th
(b) 7th , 14th, 21st and 28th
(c) 2nd , 9th, 16th, 23rd and 30th
(d) 1st , 8th, 15th and 22nd

20. If the Republic day of India in 1980, falls on Saturday, X was born on March 3,1980 and Y is older to X by four days, then Y's birthday fell on « IB (ACIO) 2013
(a) Thursday (b) Friday
(c) Wednesday (d) None of these

21. The day on 18.09.1977 was Sunday. A couple was married on this date.How many marriage anniversaries would fall on Sunday in the next 15 yr? « UP PSC 2013
(a) 1 (b) 2
(c) 5 (d) 9

Answers / WITH EXPLANATIONS

1. (*a*) The century year which is completely divisible by 400, is a leap year. Thus, the year 2800 is a leap year.

2. (*c*) Day before yesterday = Saturday
Yesterday = Saturday + 1 = Sunday
Today = Sunday + 1 = Monday
Tomorrow= Monday +1= Tuesday
Day after Tomorrow = Tuesday + 1 = Wednesday
∴ Required day = Wednesday

3. (*b*) Here, 1st October is Monday.
Three days after 20th of that month is 23rd October.
Number of days between 1st October and 23rd October = 22
Number of odd days = $\frac{22}{7}$ = 1 odd day
∴ Required day = Monday +1 odd day = Tuesday

4. (*c*) The last day of century cannot be Tuesday or Thursday or Saturday.

5. (*b*) Today = Monday
Number of odd days ⇒ 61 ÷ 7
⇒ 7) 61 (8
56
5 odd days
∴ Required day = Monday + 5 = Saturday

6. (*a*) The day falls on date 7 of the month = Friday – 3 = Tuesday
∴ Tuesday on that month will fall on = 7, 14, 21 and 28
The date 19 will fall on Tuesday – 2 days = Sunday
∴ Required day = Sunday

7. (*d*) Number of days from 25th September to 25th October
= (30 – 25) + 25 = 30 days
= 4 weeks and 2 odd days
∴ On 25 October, the day will be
= Thursday + 2 days = Saturday
∴ Required day = Saturday

8. (*d*) There are months of 30, 31 and 28 days and last day of month is Wednesday.
So, using 28 and 30 days, there are 4 Monday.
Using 31 days, there are 5 Monday.
So, it cannot be specified.

9. (*c*) The year 1990 has 365 days *i.e.*, 1 odd day, year 1991 has 365 days i.e., 1 odd day,year 1992 has 366 days i.e., 2 odd days. Likewise year 1993, 1994, 1995 have 1 odd day each. The sum of odd days, so calculated from years 1990 to 1995
(1 + 1 + 2 + 1 + 1 + 1)
= 7 odd days = 0 odd day
Hence, the year 1996 will have the same calendar as that of the year 1990.

10. (*c*) 1970 is an ordinary year. We know that the calendar of an ordinary year repeats after 6 yr or 11 yr.
6 yr after 1970 is 1976 and 11 yr after 1970 is 1981. In the given options, we have only year 1981.
So, we can easily eliminate rest of the options. Now, it is clear that her birthday would fall again on Sunday in 1981.

11. (*a*) Number of days left in the month after 16th = 31 – 16 = 15
Number of odd days
= $\frac{15}{7}$ = 2 weeks + 1 odd day
∴ Required day
= Thursday + 1 odd day = Friday
As, 16th of the month is third Thursday,the day which is two weeks after this day is fifth Thursday. So, one day after 5th Thursday is 5th Friday.

12. (*c*) Number of days from 11 January 2018 to 11 June 2019
= 365 + 20 + 28 + 31 + 30 + 31 + 11
= 516 days
Odd number of days = 516 ÷ 7 = 5 odd days
∴ Required days
= Thursday + 5 days = Tuesday

13. (*d*) Number of odd days from 5 January 2012 to 31 March 2013 = From 5 January 2012 to 5 January 2013 + From 5 January 2013 to 31 March 2013
= 2 + 26 + 28 + 31 = 87 odd days
= 3 odd days
∴ On 31 March, 2013, the day will be
= Monday + 3 days = Thursday

14. (*d*) 1st January, 1901 means (1900 yr and 1 day)
Now, 1600 yr have 0 odd day
300 yr have 1 odd day
1 day has 1 odd day
Total number of odd days = 0 + 1 + 1 = 2 days
Hence, the day on 1st January, 1901 was Tuesday.

15. (*c*) 31st October, 1984 means (1983 yr and 10 months)
Now, 1600 yr have 0 odd day
300 yr have 1 odd day
83 yr have 20 leap years and 63 ordinary years
=(20 × 2 + 63 × 1) odd days
= (40 + 63) odd days
= (103 odd days) i.e., 5 odd days
10 months of the year 1984 have 305 days.
(February is of 29 days, being the month of leap year).
305 days have 43 weeks and 4 odd days.
Total number of odd days
= (0 + 1 + 5 + 4)
= 10 odd days or 3 odd days
Hence, it was Wednesday on 31st October, 1984.

16. (*c*) 14th March, 1993 means (1992 yr, 2 months and 14 days)
Now, 1900 yr have 1 odd day,
92 yr have 23 leap years and 69 ordinary years
= (23 × 2 + 69 × 1) odd days
= odd days (46 + 69) =115 days
= 3 odd days
2 months + 14 days
= 31 + 28 + 14 = 73 = 3 odd days
Total number of odd days
= (1 + 3 + 3) = 7 i.e., 0 odd day
Hence, it was Sunday on 14th March, 1993.

17. (*c*) 2nd July, 1984 means
(1983 yr, 6 months and 2 days)
1900 yr have 1 odd day.
(∵ 1900 is not a leap year)

83 yr have 20 leap years and 63 ordinary years
= (40 + 63) odd days
= 103 = 5 odd days

Months	Number of days
January	31
February	29
March	31
April	30
May	31
June	30
July	2 (required)

= 184 days = 2 odd days
Total number of odd days
= (1 + 5 + 2) = 8 odd days
= 1 odd day
Hence, it was Monday on 2nd July, 1984.

18. (*a*) First of all, we have to find the day on 1st August, 1980.
1st August, 1980 means (1979 yr, 7 months and 1 day)
Now, 1900 yr have 1 odd day
79 yr have 19 leap years and 60 ordinary years,
which have $(19 \times 2 + 60 \times 1) = 98$ odd days = 0 odd day
7 months and 1 day

Months	Number of days
January	31
February	29
March	31
April	30
May	31
June	30
July	31
August	1 (required)

= 214 days = 4 odd days
Total number of odd days
= (1 + 4) = 5
So, it was Friday on 1 st August, 1980 and 1st Monday of the month was on 4th and subsequent Monday of the month were on 4th, 11th, 18th and 25th.

19. (*c*) First of all, we have to find the day on 1st December, 1984.
1st December, 1984 means (1983 yr, 11 months and 1 day)
Now, 1900 yr have 1 odd day.
83 yr have (20 leap years and 63 ordinary years)
= (40 + 63) odd days
= 103 odd days
= 5 odd days

11 months and 1 day

Jan	Feb	March	April	May	June	July	August
31	29	31	30	31	30	31	31

Sep	Oct	Nov	Dec
30	31	30	1 required

= 336 days
⇒ 0 odd day
Total number of odd days = (1 + 5 + 0) = 6
Hence, it was Saturday on 1st December, 1984 and 1st Sunday was on 2nd December, 1984. Subsequently, Sunday of the month were on 2nd, 9th, 16th, 23rd and 30th.

20. (*b*) Republic day in 1980 *i.e.,* January 26, 1980 = Saturday
Number of odd days till March 3, 1980

January February March
↓ ↓ ↓
5 29 3 → 37 odd days

or $\frac{37}{7} = 2$ odd days

So, March 3 is Monday and Y is 4 day older to X. So, his birthday must be four days ahead of X *i.e.,* on Friday.

21. (*b*) 1977 is an ordinary year. We know that the calendar of an ordinary year repeats after 6 yr or 11 yr. Let us check for the number of odd days in 6th and 11th yr.

Years	Number of odd days
1978	1
1979	1
1980	2
1981	1
1982	1
1983	1
1984	2

Years	1985	1986	1987	1988
Number of odd days	1	1	1	2

From the above table,
Number of odd days from 18.09.1977 to 18.09.1983 = 7, i.e., 0 odd day
It means that in 1983, 18th September would fall on Sunday.
From the above table, number of odd days from 18.09.1977 to 18.09.1988 = 14, i.e., 0 odd day.
Now, it is clear that 2 marriage anniversaries would fall on Sunday in the next 15 yr.

CHAPTER / 14

Mathematical Operations

Mathematical operation can be defined as the simplification of an expression containing numbers and different mathematical signs.

Under this segment of reasoning, the four mathematical operations *viz.* Addition, Subtraction, Multiplication and Division as well as signs such as 'less than', 'greater than', 'equal to', 'not equal to' are represented by unusual and different symbols. You may say such symbols as artificial ones.

The candidate is required to substitute the real signs in place of artificial symbols as given in the question to solve the questions.

First of all, a candidate is required to become familiar with all type of signs that are used for mathematical operations.

A list of these signs is given as follows

(i)	Addition	+
(ii)	Subtraction	–
(iii)	Multiplication	×
(iv)	Division	÷
(v)	Of	Of
(vi)	Circular bracket	( )
(vii)	Curly bracket	{ }
(viii)	Square bracket	[ ]
(ix)	Bar bracket/Vinculum	–
(x)	Greater than	>
(xi)	Less than	<
(xii)	Equal to	=

How to Solve the Questions

To solve this type of questions, substitute the real signs in the given expression and then solve the expression according to the VBODMAS rule. This rule gives us the correct order, in which various operations in simplification are performed.

Order of Operations-VBODMAS

Order of various operations is as same the order of letters in the 'VBODMAS' from left to right.

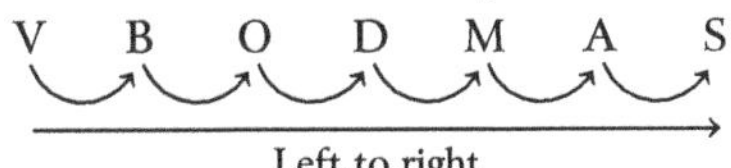

Clearly, the order will be as follows

Step **I** **V** (—) 'Vinculum' bracket is solved.

Step **II** **B** Brackets are to be solved in the order as given below.

( ) or small/circular bracket
{ } or middle/curly bracket
[ ] or large/square bracket

Step **III** **O** (Of) Operation of 'Of' is done.

Step **IV** **D** (÷) Operation of 'Division' (÷) is done.

Step **V** **M** (×) Operation of 'Multiplication' (×) is done.

Step **VI** **A** (+) Operation of 'Addition' (+) is done.

Step **VII** **S** (–) Operation of 'Subtraction' (–) is done.

Based on their diverse nature, we have classified mathematical operations into several types as given below

TYPE 01

Symbol Substitution

In this type of questions, a candidate is provided with substitutes for various mathematical symbols, followed by a question involving calculation of an expression or choosing the correct/incorrect equation.

The candidate is required to put in the real signs in the given equation and then solve the questions as required.

***Ex* 01** If '×' means '–', '÷' means '+', + means '×', then 18 × 5 ÷ 5 + 6 is equal to?

(a) 58 (b) 49 (c) 43 (d) 37

***Solution* (c)** According to the question,

$$? = 18 \times 5 \div 5 + 6$$
$$\downarrow \quad \downarrow \quad \downarrow$$
$$- \quad + \quad \times$$
$$= 18 - 5 + 5 \times 6$$
$$= 18 - 5 + 30 \quad \text{(using VBODMAS rule)}$$
$$= (18 + 30) - 5 = 43$$

***Ex* 02** In a certain code language '+' represents '×', '–' represents '+', '×' represents '÷' and '÷' represents '–'. What is the answer to the following question? « SSC CGL 2017

$$825 \times 25 - 27 \div 10 = ?$$

(a) 100 (b) 50 (c) 25 (d) 20

***Solution* (b)** According to the question,

$$825 \times 25 - 27 \div 10 = ?$$
$$\downarrow \quad \downarrow \quad \downarrow$$
$$\div \quad + \quad -$$
$$825 \div 25 + 27 - 10 = ?$$
$$33 + 27 - 10 = ? \quad \text{(using VBODMAS rule)}$$
$$50 = ?$$

***Ex* 03** If A means +, D means ÷, P means ×, and S means –, then 68A48D2S8P10 = ? « CGPSC 2019

(a) 46 (b) 64
(c) 12 (d) 500
(e) None of these

***Solution* (c)** Given expression,

$$68\,A\,48\,D\,2\,S\,8\,P\,10 = ?$$

On substituting the signs,

$$? = 68 + 48 \div 2 - 8 \times 10$$
$$\Rightarrow \quad ? = 68 + 24 - 8 \times 10$$
$$\Rightarrow \quad ? = 68 + 24 - 80$$
$$? = 92 - 80 \Rightarrow ? = 12$$

***Ex* 04** If '÷' denotes "multiplied by", "+" denotes "subtracted from", "–" denotes "added to"and "×" denotes "divided by", then which of the following equation is true? « RRB JE 2019

(a) $16 + 19 \times 21 - 5 = 201$ (b) $5 \times 6 + 4 \div 3 = \frac{37}{6}$

(c) $6 \times 3 + 12 \div 3 = 21$ (d) $18 \times 6 \div 8 - 12 = 36$

***Solution* (d)** Let us check all the options one by one

From option (a)

$$16 + 19 \times 21 - 5 = 201$$
$$\downarrow \quad \downarrow \quad \downarrow$$
$$- \quad \div \quad +$$
$$16 - 19 \div 21 + 5 = 201$$
$$\Rightarrow \quad 16 - \frac{19}{21} + 5 = 201 \quad \text{(using VBODMAS rule)}$$
$$\Rightarrow \quad \frac{336 - 19 + 105}{21} = 201$$
$$\Rightarrow \quad \frac{422}{21} = 201$$
$$\text{LHS} \neq \text{RHS}$$

From option (b)

$$5 \times 6 + 4 \div 3 = \frac{37}{6}$$
$$\downarrow \quad \downarrow \quad \downarrow$$
$$\div \quad - \quad \times$$
$$5 \div 6 - 4 \times 3 = \frac{5}{6} - 12 \quad \text{(using VBODMAS rule)}$$
$$= \frac{5}{6} - 12 = \frac{37}{6}$$
$$\text{LHS} \neq \text{RHS}$$

From option (c)

$$6 \times 3 + 12 \div 3 = 21$$
$$\downarrow \quad \downarrow \quad \downarrow$$
$$\div \quad - \quad \times$$
$$6 \div 3 - 12 \times 3 = 21$$
$$\Rightarrow \quad 2 - 36 = 21 \quad \text{(using VBODMAS rule)}$$
$$\Rightarrow \quad -34 = 21$$
$$\text{LHS} \neq \text{RHS}$$

From option (d)

$$18 \times 6 \div 8 - 12 = 36$$
$$\downarrow \quad \downarrow \quad \downarrow$$
$$\div \quad \times \quad +$$
$$18 \div 6 \times 8 + 12 = 36$$
$$\Rightarrow \quad 3 \times 8 + 12 = 36$$
$$\Rightarrow \quad 24 + 12 = 36 \quad \text{(using VBODMAS rule)}$$
$$\Rightarrow \quad 36 = 36$$
$$\text{LHS} = \text{RHS}$$

Practice CORNER 14.1

1. If + means '÷', – means '+', × means '–' and ÷ means '×', then what will be the value of the following expression?
$18 \div 6 - 27 + 3 \times 12 = ?$ « SSC CAPFs 2018

(a) 92 (b) 105
(c) 95 (d) 107

2. If '+' stands for multiplication; '–' stands for division, '×' stands for addition, '÷' stands for subtraction, then which one of the following equations is correct? « Delhi Police CAPFs 2016

(a) $12 \times 5 + 4 - 5 \div 4 = 20$ (b) $12 \div 5 + 4 - 5 \times 4 = 18$
(c) $12 \div 5 - 4 \times 5 + 4 = 22$ (d) $12 + 5 - 4 \times 5 \div 4 = 16$

3. If sign '×' is interchanged with '÷' and number '3' is interchanged with '2', then which of the following equations would be correct? « SSC CAPFs 2018

(a) $3 \div 2 \times 2 + 2 - 3 = 1$
(b) $3 \times 2 \div 2 + 2 - 3 = 3$
(c) $2 \times 3 \div 2 + 2 - 3 = 0$
(d) $2 \times 3 - 2 + 2 \div 3 = 0$

4. If P denotes '÷', Q denotes '×', R denotes '+' and S denotes '–', then the value of 18 Q 12 P 4 R 5 S 6 is « Chhattisgarh Patwari 2017

(a) 28 (b) 53 (c) 55 (d) 80

5. If '+' means 'minus', '–' means 'multiply', '÷' means 'plus' and '×' means 'divide', then

$10 \times 5 \div 3 - 2 + 3 = ?$

(a) 5 (b) $\frac{53}{3}$ (c) 21 (d) 36

6. If 'A' is replaced by '+', if 'B' is replaced by '–', C' is replaced by '÷' and 'D' is replaced by '×'. Find the value of the following equation.

27B29A45C9D4 « SSC Steno 2019

(a) 7 (b) 65
(c) 18 (d) 55

7. If '+' stands for division, '÷' stands for multiplication, '×' stands for subtraction and '–' stands for addition, which one of the following is correct? « Delhi Police CAPFs 2016

(a) $18 + 6 \div 7 \times 5 - 2 = 18$ (b) $18 \times 6 + 7 \div 5 - 2 = 16$
(c) $18 \div 6 \times 7 + 5 - 2 = 22$ (d) $18 \div 6 - 7 + 5 \times 2 = 20$

8. If '÷' means addition and '×' means subtraction, then $(15 \times 9) \div (12 \times 4) \times (4 \div 4)$ is equal to

(a) 96 (b) 6
(c) 3/128 (d) 143/8

9. If $ means 'divided by,' @ means 'multiplied by,' # means 'subtracted by,' then the value of 10#5@1$5 is « UPSC CSAT 2019

(a) 0 (b) 1 (c) 2 (d) 9

10. If ÷ stands for ×, × stands for –, – stands for + and + stands for ÷, then $48 + 6 - 12 \div 2 + 10 = ?$

(Do chronologically and not according to VBODMAS rule)

(a) 14 (b) 16 (c) 9 (d) 4

11. If '+' means '×', '–' means '÷', '×' means '–' and '÷' means '+', then find the value of the following equation.

$6 + 64 - 8 \div 45 \times 8$ « SSC CGL 2016

(a) 85 (b) 76 (c) 87 (d) 75

12. If A = '+', B = '–', C = '×' and D = '÷', then 5 C 5 D 5 A 5 B 5 = ?

(a) 0 (b) 5 (c) 10 (d) 15

13. If '+' stands for ÷, '×' stands +, '–' stands for ×, '÷' stands for '–', then which of the following equations is correct? « SSC Steno 2016

(a) $33 - 4 \div 5 \times 6 + 2 = 130$
(b) $33 \times 4 - 5 + 6 \div 2 = 26$
(c) $33 \div 4 \times 5 + 6 - 2 = 30$
(d) $33 - 4 + 5 \div 6 \times 2 = 24$

14. If > denotes +, < denotes –, + denotes ÷, ^ denotes ×, – denotes =, × denotes > and = denotes <, choose the correct statement among the following « SSC CGL 2014

(a) 28 + 4 ^ 2 = 6 ^ 4 + 2 (b) 13> 7 < 6 + 2 = 3 ^ 4
(c) 9 > 5 > 4 – 18 + 9 > 16 (d) 9 < 3 < 2 > 1 × 8 ^2

15. If Q means 'add to', J means 'multiply by', T means 'subtract from' and K means 'divide by', then 30K2Q3J6T5 = ? « CGPSC 2016

(a) 31 (b) 15 (c) 14
(d) 28 (e) None of these

16. If '–' stands for 'addition', '÷' for 'multiplication', '×' for 'subtraction' and '+' for 'division', then which of the following is correct? « SSC CGL 2013

(a) $25 \times 12 - 14 \div 4 + 6 = 16$
(b) $25 - 12 + 14 \div 2 \times 4 = 15$
(c) $25 - 15 + 5 \div 4 \times 16 = 21$
(d) $25 + 11 - 4 \div 10 \times 6 = 20$

DIRECTIONS ~ (Q. Nos. 17-19) *Study the following information carefully and answer the given questions.*

If '+' is coded as 'π', '×' is coded as '≠', '÷' is coded as '$' and '–' is coded as 'Δ', then what is the value of the following?

17. $2 \neq 7 \Delta 4$

(a) 9 (b) 3 (c) 13 (d) 10

18. $72 \pi 27 \Delta 99$

(a) 65 (b) 52 (c) 47 (d) 0

19. 17 ≠ 12 $ 3

(a) 98 (b) 87 (c) 75 (d) 68

20. If A stands for '–', B stands for '+' and C stands for '×', then what is the value of (5C4)A(2B3)B6? « UPSSSC Junior Assist. 2015

(a) 31 (b) 21 (c) 19 (d) 9

21. If P stands for '+', Q stands for '–', R stands for '×', then the value of (10R4)P(4R4)Q6 = « RRB NTPC 2016

A. 65 B. 56 C. 50 D. 60
(a) C (b) B (c) A (d) D

22. If S means '–', Q means '×', R means '÷' and P means '+', then 1 P 45 R 2 Q 2 S 4 = ?

(a) 40 (b) 42 (c) 36 (d) 46
(e) 38

23. If '#' means '+', '@' means '×', '&' means '/' and '$' means '–' then 200 & 5 @ 3 $ 20 # 5 = ? « SSC MTS 2019

(a) 105 (b) 100 (c) 85 (d) 120

24. If '–' stands for division, '+' stands for subtraction, '÷' stands for multiplication and '×' stands for addition, then which one of the following equations is correct?

(a) $70 - 2 + 4 \div 5 \times 6 = 44$ (b) $70 - 2 + 4 \div 5 \times 6 = 21$
(c) $70 - 2 + 4 \div 5 \times 6 = 341$ (d) $70 - 2 + 4 \div 5 \times 6 = 36$

25. If '–' stands for division, '+' for multiplication, '÷' for subtraction and '×' for addition, then which one of the following equations is correct?

(a) $19 + 5 - 4 \times 2 \div 4 = 11$ (b) $19 \times 5 - 4 \div 2 + 4 = 16$
(c) $19 \div 5 + 4 - 2 \times 4 = 13$ (d) $19 \div 5 + 4 - 2 \div 4 = 20$

26. If '–' stands for '÷', '+' stands for '×', '÷' stands for, '–' and '×' stands for '+', which one of the following equations in correct?

(a) $30 - 6 + 5 \times 4 \div 2 = 27$ (b) $30 + 6 - 5 \div 4 \times 2 = 30$
(c) $30 \times 6 \div 5 - 4 + 2 = 32$ (d) $30 \div 6 \times 5 + 4 - 2 = 40$

27. If '+' means '–', '–' means '×', '÷' means '+' and '×' means '÷', then $10 \times 5 \div 3 - 2 + 3 = ?$

(a) 5 (b) 21
(c) 53/3 (d) 18

28. If '+' stands for division, '–' stands for multiplication, '×' stands for subtraction and '÷' for addition, then find the value of (120 + 6 × 10) – 10 ÷ 5 « UPSSSC Amin 2016

(a) 125 (b) 135
(c) 75 (d) 105

29. If '×' stands for division, '÷' stands for addition, '–' stands for multiplication and '+' stands for subtraction, then (14 – 6 ÷ 18) × 6 is equal to « UPSSSC Amin 2016

(a) 107 (b) 17 (c) 104 (d) 15

30. If < means –, > means +, = means ×, $ means ÷, then find the value of 67>27$9<4 « SSC Steno 2019

(a) 66 (b) 62
(c) 68 (d) 64

31. In a certain code language, '–' represents '×', '÷' represents '+', '+' represents '÷' and '×' represents '–'. Find out the answer to the following question.

18 ÷ 12 – 5 + 30 × 6 = ? « SSC (10 + 2) 2018

(a) 19 (b) 15
(c) 41 (d) 14

32. If '<' denotes '–', '+' denotes '÷', '>' denotes '+', '–' denotes '=', '=' denotes '<' and '×' denotes '>', then which of the following statement is true?

A. 3 > 2 < 4 × 8 + 4 < 2 B. 3 + 2 > 4 = 9 + 3 < 2
C. 3 + 2 < 4 × 9 + 3 < 3 D. 3 > 2 > 4 = 18 + 3 < 1

(a) C (b) A (c) B (d) D

33. If + denotes 'multiplied by', '–' denotes 'added to', × denotes 'divided by' and ÷ denotes 'subtracted from', then which of the following option is true?

(a) 30 ÷ 8 × 4 – 6 + 1 = 32 (b) 8 + 5 – 20 × 4 ÷ 6 = 41
(c) 12 – 12 ÷ 6 × 6 + 3 = 21 (d) 6 + 7 × 3 – 4 ÷ 6 = 26

34. If '×' stands for 'addition', '÷' stands for 'subtraction', '+' stands for 'multiplication' and – stands for 'division', then 20 × 16 – 2 + 2 ÷ 8 = ? « UPSSSC VDO 2018

(a) 28 (b) 30 (c) 36 (d) 25

35. If '×' stands for 'addition', '÷' stands for 'subtraction', '+' stands for 'multiplication' and '–' stands for 'division', then 20 × 16 – 4 + 2 ÷ 8 = ? « UPSSSC VDO 2018

(a) 24 (b) 20 (c) 36 (d) 25

Answers / WITH EXPLANATIONS

1. *(b)* According to the question,

18 ÷ 6 – 27 + 3 × 12
↓ ↓ ↓ ↓
⇒ ? = 18 × 6 + 27 ÷ 3 – 12
⇒ ? = 18 × 6 + 9 – 12
⇒ ? = 108 + 9 – 12
⇒ ? = 117 – 12
⇒ ? = 105

2. *(d)* From option (d),
12 + 5 – 4 × 5 ÷ 4 = 16
Given that '+' → ×
'–' → ÷
'×' → +
'÷' → –
On substituting the signs,
12 × 5 ÷ 4 + 5 – 4
= 60 ÷ 4 + 5 – 4 = 15 + 5 – 4
= 20 – 4 = 16
So, option (d) is correct.

3. *(b)* From option (b),
3 × 2 ÷ 2 + 2 – 3 = 3
Now, according to the question, on interchanging the signs and numbers
2 ÷ 3 × 3 + 3 – 2 = 3
⇒ $\frac{2}{3} \times 3 + 3 - 2 = 3$
⇒ 2 + 3 – 2 = 3
⇒ 3 = 3

4. *(b)* P → ÷, Q → ×
R → +, S → –
18 Q 12 P 4 R 5 S 6
18 × 12 ÷ 4 + 5 – 6
18 × 3 + 5 – 6 (using VBODMAS rule)
= 54 – 1 = 53

5. *(a)* ? = 10 × 5 ÷ 3 – 2 + 3
= 10 ÷ 5 + 3 × 2 – 3
= 2 + 3 × 2 – 3
(using VBODMAS rule)
= 2 + 6 – 3 = 8 – 3 = 5

6. *(c)* Given,
A → +, B → –, C → ÷, D → ×
∴ 27 B 29 A 45 C 9 D 4
27 – 29 + 45 ÷ 9 × 4
= –2 + 5 × 4 = –2 + 20 = 18

7. *(a)* From option (a),
18 + 6 ÷ 7 × 5 – 2 = 18
According to the question,
18 + 6 ÷ 7 × 5 – 2
↓ ↓ ↓ ↓
÷ × – +
Now, 18 ÷ 6 × 7 – 5 + 2
= 3 × 7 – 5 + 2
= 21 – 3 = 18
So, option (a) is correct.

8. *(b)* According to the question,
Required answer
= (15 × 9) ÷ (12 × 4) × (4 ÷ 4)
↓ ↓ ↓ ↓ ↓
– + – – +
= (15 – 9) + (12 – 4) – (4 + 4)
= 6 + 8 – 8 (using VBODMAS rule)
= 6

9. *(d)* According to the question,
$ ⇒ ÷; @ ⇒ ×; # ⇒ –
∴ 10#5@1$5 ⇒ 10 – 5 × 1 ÷ 5
Now, 10 – 5 × 1 ÷ 5 = 10 – 5 × $\frac{1}{5}$
= 10 – 1 = 9

10. *(d)* Given expression,
48 + 6 – 12 ÷ 2 + 10 = ?
After changing the signs
48 ÷ 6 + 12 × 2 ÷ 10 = ?
⇒ 8 + 12 × 2 ÷ 10 = ?
⇒ $20 \times \frac{2}{10} = ?$
⇒ 4 = ?

11. *(a)* Given expression,
6 + 64 – 8 ÷ 45 × 8
After changing the signs
6 × 64 ÷ 8 + 45 – 8
= 6 × 8 + 45 – 8
= 48 + 45 – 8
= 93 – 8 = 85

12. *(b)* According to the question,
? = 5 C 5 D 5 A 5 B 5
↓ ↓ ↓ ↓
× ÷ + –
= 5 × 5 ÷ 5 + 5 – 5
= 5 × 1 + 5 – 5
(using VBODMAS rule)
= 10 – 5 = 5

13. *(a)* From option (a),
33 – 4 ÷ 5 × 6 + 2 = 130
After changing the signs,
33 × 4 – 5 + 6 ÷ 2 = 130
⇒ 132 – 5 + 3 = 130
⇒ 132 – 2 = 130
∴ 130 = 130

14. *(c)* From option (c),
9 > 5 > 4 – 18 + 9 > 16
After changing the signs,
9 + 5 + 4 = 18 ÷ 9 + 16
⇒ 18 = 18
So, option (c) is correct.

15. (*d*) According to the question,

30 K 2 Q 3 J 6 T 5

$\downarrow$ $\downarrow$ $\downarrow$ $\downarrow$

$\div$ + $\times$ −

Now, $30 \div 2 + 3 \times 6 - 5$

$= 15 + 18 - 5 = 28$

16. (*c*) From option (c),

$25 - 15 + 5 \div 4 \times 16 = 21$

$\downarrow$ $\downarrow$ $\downarrow$ $\downarrow$

+ $\div$ $\times$ −

$25 + 15 \div 5 \times 4 - 16 = 21$

$\Rightarrow \quad 25 + 3 \times 4 - 16 = 21$

(using VBODMAS rule)

$\Rightarrow \quad 25 + 12 - 16 = 21$

$\Rightarrow \quad 37 - 16 = 21 \Rightarrow 21 = 21$

$\Rightarrow$ LHS = RHS

So, option (c) is correct.

17. (*d*) Given expression,

$2 \neq 7 \Delta 4$

After changing the signs,

$2 \times 7 - 4 = 14 - 4 = 10$

18. (*d*) Given expression,

$72 \pi 27 \Delta 99$

After changing the signs,

$72 + 27 - 99 = 99 - 99 = 0$

19. (*d*) Given expression, $17 \neq 12 \$ 3$

After changing the signs,

$17 \times 12 \div 3 = 17 \times 4 = 68$

20. (*b*) Given, (5C4)A(2B3)B6

Now, place the mathematical sign of A, B and C

$= (5 \times 4) - (2 + 3) + 6$

$= 20 - 5 + 6$

$= 26 - 5 = 21$

21. (*a*) According to the question,

P $\longrightarrow$ '+'

Q $\longrightarrow$ '−'

R $\longrightarrow$ '×'

Given expression, (10R4)P(4R4)Q6

$= (10 \times 4) + (4 \times 4) - 6$

$= 40 + 16 - 6$

$= 50$

22. (*b*) Given expression

1 P 45 R 2 Q 2 S 4

After changing the signs.

$1 + 45 \div 2 \times 2 - 4 = ?$

$1 + 22.5 \times 2 - 4 = ?$

$1 + 45 - 4 = ?$

$46 - 4 = ?$

$42 = ?$

23. (*a*)

$\# \longrightarrow \oplus$

$@ \longrightarrow \otimes$

$\& \longrightarrow \oplus$

$\$ \longrightarrow \ominus$

Given, 200 & 5 @ 3 \$ 20 # 5 = ?

After replacing sign

$\Rightarrow \quad 200 \div 5 \times 3 - 20 + 5$

$\Rightarrow \quad 40 \times 3 - 20 + 5$

$\Rightarrow \quad 120 - 20 + 5$

$\Rightarrow \quad 105$

24. (*b*) According to the question,

− ⇒ ÷	+ ⇒ −
÷ ⇒ ×	× ⇒ +

From option (b),

$70 - 2 + 4 \div 5 \times 6 = 21$

$\Rightarrow \quad 70 \div 2 - 4 \times 5 + 6 = 21$

$\Rightarrow \quad 35 - 20 + 6 = 21$

$\Rightarrow \quad 41 - 20 = 21$

$\therefore \quad 21 = 21$

25. (*c*) According to the question,

− ⇒ ÷	+ ⇒ ×
÷ ⇒ −	× ⇒ +

From option (c),

$19 \div 5 + 4 - 2 \times 4 = 13$

$\Rightarrow \quad 19 - 5 \times 4 \div 2 + 4 = 13$

$\Rightarrow \quad 19 - 5 \times 2 + 4 = 13$

$\Rightarrow \quad 19 - 10 + 4 = 13$

$\therefore \quad 13 = 13$

26. (*a*) According to the question,

− ⇒ ÷	+ ⇒ ×
÷ ⇒ −	× ⇒ +

From option (a),

$30 - 6 + 5 \times 4 \div 2 = 27$

$\Rightarrow \quad 30 \div 6 \times 5 + 4 - 2 = 27$

$\Rightarrow \quad 5 \times 5 + 4 - 2 = 27$

$\Rightarrow \quad 25 + 4 - 2 = 27$

$\therefore \quad 27 = 27$

27. (*a*)

$+ \longrightarrow -$

$- \longrightarrow \times$

$\div \longrightarrow +$

$\times \longrightarrow \div$

Given, $10 \times 5 \div 3 - 2 \div 3 = ?$

After changing the signs,

$10 \div 5 + 3 \times 2 - 3$

$\Rightarrow \quad 2 + 6 - 3$

$\Rightarrow \quad 5$

28. (*d*) Given expression,

$(120 + 6 \times 10) - 10 \div 5$

After changing the signs,

$(120 \div 6 - 10) \times 10 + 5$

$= (20 - 10) \times 10 + 5$

$= 105$

29. (*b*) Given expression,

$(14 - 6 \div 18) \times 6$

After changing the signs,

$(14 \times 6 + 18) \div 6 = (84 + 18) \div 6$

$= 102 \div 6$

$= 17$

30. (*a*) Given expression,

$67 > 27 \$ 9 < 4$

After changing the signs,

$67 + 27 \div 9 - 4 = 67 + 3 - 4$

$= 70 - 4$

$= 66$

31. (*d*) Given expression,

$18 \div 12 - 5 + 30 \times 6 = ?$

After changing the signs,

$18 + 12 \times 5 \div 30 - 6$

$= 18 + 12 \times \frac{5}{30} - 6$

$= 18 + 2 - 6$

$= 14$

32. (*b*) Given,

$< \longrightarrow -$

$+ \longrightarrow +$

$> \longrightarrow +$

$- \longrightarrow =$

$= \longrightarrow <$

$\times \longrightarrow >$

From option (a),

$3 > 2 < 4 \times 8 + 4 < 2$

$3 + 2 - 4 > 8 \div 4 - 2$

$5 - 4 > 2 - 2$

$1 > 0$

33. (*c*) From option (c), given equation

$12 - 12 \div 6 \times 6 + 3 = 21$

After changing the signs,

$12 + 12 - 6 \div 6 \times 3 = 21$

$\Rightarrow \quad 12 + 12 - \frac{6}{6} \times 3 = 21$

$\Rightarrow \quad 12 + 12 - 1 \times 3 = 21$

$\Rightarrow \quad 12 + 12 - 3 = 21$

$\Rightarrow \quad 24 - 3 = 21$

$\therefore \quad 21 = 21$

34. (*a*) $20 \times 16 - 2 + 2 \div 8 = ?$

After changing the signs,

$20 + 16 \div 2 \times 2 - 8 = ?$

$\Rightarrow \quad 20 + 16 - 8 = ?$

$\Rightarrow \quad 36 - 8 = 28$

35. (*b*) $20 \times 16 - 4 + 2 \div 8 = ?$

After changing the signs,

$20 + 16 \div 4 \times 2 - 8$

$\Rightarrow \quad 20 + 4 \times 2 - 8$

$\Rightarrow \quad 20 + 8 - 8$

$\Rightarrow \quad 20$

TYPE 02

Balancing the Equation

In this type of questions, it is required to fill up the blank spaces with the signs given in one of the alternatives to balance the given equation.

***Ex* 05** If the following equations has to be balance, then the signs of which of the following options will be used?

24 ? 6 ? 12 ? 16

(a) –, + and + (b) ÷, + and ÷
(c) –, – and – (d) ÷, + and –

Solution ***(d)*** Let us check all the options one-by-one.

From option (a),

$$24 - 6 + 12 + 16 = 0$$
$$\Rightarrow (24 + 12 + 16) - 6 = 0$$
$$\Rightarrow 52 - 6 = 0$$
$$\Rightarrow 46 = 0$$
$$\Rightarrow \text{LHS} \neq \text{RHS}$$

Hence, option (a) is incorrect.

From option (b),

$$24 \div 6 + 12 \div 16 = 0$$
$$\Rightarrow 4 + 0.75 = 0$$
$$\Rightarrow 4.75 = 0$$
$$\Rightarrow \text{LHS} \neq \text{RHS}$$

Hence, option (b) is incorrect.

From option (c),

$$24 - 6 - 12 - 16 = 0$$
$$\Rightarrow 18 - 12 - 16 = 0$$
$$\Rightarrow 6 - 16 = 0$$
$$\Rightarrow -10 = 0$$
$$\Rightarrow \text{LHS} \neq \text{RHS}$$

Hence, option (c) is incorrect.

From option (d),

$$24 \div 6 + 12 - 16 = 0$$
$$\Rightarrow \frac{24}{6} + 12 - 16 = 0$$
$$\Rightarrow 4 + 12 - 16 = 0$$
$$\Rightarrow 16 - 16 = 0$$
$$\Rightarrow 0 = 0$$
$$\Rightarrow \text{LHS} = \text{RHS}$$

Hence, option (d) is correct.

***Ex* 06** In the following question, by using which mathematical operators will the expression become correct? « SSC CPO 2017

35 ? 5 ? 10 ? 15 ? 4

(a) ÷, +, = and × (b) ×, ÷, > and ×
(c) ÷, ×, > and × (d) ÷, ×, < and +

Solution ***(c)*** From option (c) in given equation,

$$35 \div 5 \times 10 > 15 \times 4$$
$$\Rightarrow \frac{35}{5} \times 10 > 15 \times 4$$
$$\Rightarrow 7 \times 10 > 15 \times 4 \Rightarrow 70 > 60 \quad \text{(True)}$$

Hence, using sign of option (c), equation will be correct.

TYPE 03

Interchange of Signs and Numbers

In this type of questions, the given equation becomes correct and fully balanced when either two signs of the equation or both the numbers and the signs of the equation are interchanged. The candidate is required to find the correct pair of signs and numbers from the given alternatives.

***Ex* 07** Which two signs should be interchanged to make the given equation correct?

$14 + 4 \div 5 - 18 \times 2 = 25$ « SSC CAPFs 2018

(a) ÷ and + (b) × and + (c) × and – (d) ÷ and ×

Solution ***(d)*** Given expression,

$$14 + 4 \div 5 - 18 \times 2 = 25$$

From option (d),

$$14 + 4 \times 5 - 18 \div 2 = 25 \Rightarrow 14 + 4 \times 5 - 9 = 25$$
$$\Rightarrow 14 + 20 - 9 = 25 \Rightarrow 34 - 9 = 25 \Rightarrow 25 = 25$$

***Ex* 08** Which one of the given interchanges in signs and numbers would make the given equation correct?

$16 - 8 \times 16 - 2 \div 4 + 3 = 15$ « SSC MTS 2011

(a) + and ÷, 3 and 4 (b) × and –, 16 and 4
(c) – and ÷, 8 and 2 (d) × and –, 16 and 2

Solution ***(c)*** Let us check all the options one by one.

From option (a),

$$16 - 8 \times 16 - 2 \div 4 + 3 = 15$$
(↓ ↓ ↓ ↓ : + 3 ÷ 4)
$$\Rightarrow 16 - 8 \times 16 - 2 + 3 \div 4 = 15$$
$$\Rightarrow 16 - 8 \times 16 - 2 + 0.75 = 15$$
$$\Rightarrow 16 - 128 - 2 + 0.75 = 15$$
$$\Rightarrow 16 + 0.75 - 130 = 15$$
$$\Rightarrow 16.75 - 130 = 15$$
$$\therefore 16.75 \neq 145$$

Hence, option (a) is incorrect.

From option (b),

$$16 - 8 \times 16 - 2 \div 4 + 3 = 15$$
(↓ ↓ ↓ ↓ ↓ ↓ : 4 × – 4 × 16)
$$\Rightarrow 4 \times 8 - 4 \times 2 \div 16 + 3 = 15$$
$$\Rightarrow 4 \times 8 - 4 \times 0.125 + 3 = 15$$
$$\Rightarrow 32 - 0.5 + 3 = 15 \Rightarrow 35 - 0.5 = 15$$
$$\therefore 34.5 \neq 15$$

Hence, option (b) is incorrect.

From option (c),

$$16 - 8 \times 16 - 2 \div 4 + 3 = 15$$
(↓ ↓ ↓ ↓ ↓ : ÷ 2 ÷ 8 –)
$$\Rightarrow 16 \div 2 \times 16 \div 8 - 4 + 3 = 15$$
$$\Rightarrow 8 \times 2 - 4 + 3 = 15$$
$$\Rightarrow 16 - 4 + 3 = 15 \Rightarrow 19 - 4 = 15$$
$$\therefore 15 = 15$$

Hence, option (c) is correct.

As, option (c) gives us the correct answer. Hence, there is no need to check option (d).

TYPE 04

Trick Based Mathematical Operations

In this type of questions, the values of equations or digits or numbers are given in the form of another digit or number. These questions can be based on several different patterns. The candidates are required to identify the pattern and find the value of the asked equation or digit or number following the same pattern.

You will get a better idea about the type of questions from the examples as given below

Ex 09 Some equations are solved on the basis of certain pattern. Find out the correct answer for the unsolved equation on that basis. « SI (Delhi Police & CAPFs) ASI (CISF) 2015

$7\times6\times4=674$, $8\times5\times3=583$, $9\times1\times2=?$

(a) 219 (b) 192

(c) 129 (d) 921

Solution (b) As,

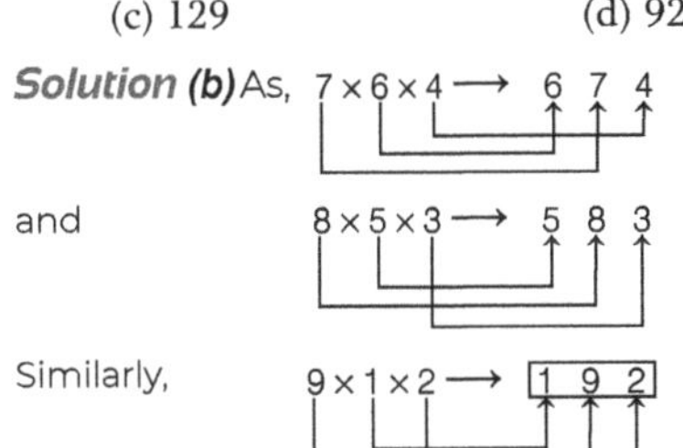

Ex 10 If $5\bigstar3=16$, $9\bigstar8=73$ and $6\bigstar7=43$, then $7\bigstar8$ is equal to

(a) 72 (b) 58

(c) 85 (d) 57

Solution (d) As, $5\bigstar3=5\times3+1=16$, $9\bigstar8=9\times8+1=73$, $6\bigstar7=6\times7+1=43$

Similarly, $7\bigstar8=7\times8+1=57$

Ex 11 If $\uparrow=12$, $\Delta=15$, $\text{O}=3$ and $\square=6$, then $\Delta-\uparrow+\text{O}=?$

(a) O (b) ↑ (c) Δ (d) □

Solution (d) $\Delta-\uparrow+\text{O}=15-12+3=15+3-12$

$=18-12=6\Rightarrow\square$

$\therefore$ $?=\square$

Ex 12 If 2 [3] 4 = 14 and 3 [4] 6 = 60, then 4 [5] 7 =? « UPSC Assistant commandant 2019

(a) 72 (b) 84

(c) 96 (d) 108

Solution (c) As, 2[3]4 = 14

$2\times[3+4]\times[4-3]=14$

$2\times7\times1=14$ and $3[4]6=60$

$3\times[4+6]\times[6-4]=60$

$3\times10\times2=60$

Similarly, $4[5]7=?$

$4\times[5+7]\times[7-5]=?$

$4\times12\times2=?\Rightarrow96=?$

Ex 13 If 3 = 7, 8 = 12, 9 = 13, then 7 = ? « UPSSSC Junior Assist. 2015

(a) 13 (b) 10

(c) 11 (d) 12

Solution (c) As, $3\xrightarrow{+4}7$,

$8\xrightarrow{+4}12$

and $9\xrightarrow{+4}13$

Similarly, $7\xrightarrow{+4}\boxed{11}$

Practice / CORNER 14.2

1. Which of the following sets of operation with the usual notations replacing the stars in the order given makes the statements valid?

$\sqrt{100}*\sqrt{16}*\sqrt{225}*\sqrt{1}$ « SSC Steno 2013

(a) ×, =, + (b) +, =, −

(c) +, =, × (d) −, ×, =

2. Select the correct combination of mathematical signs to replace * signs and to balance the following equation.

8 * 8 * 1 * 7 = 8 « SSC MTS 2014

(a) ×, ÷, + (b) +, ÷, × (c) ÷, ×, + (d) +, ×, ÷

3. Select the correct combination of mathematical signs to replace 'A' sequentially from left to right and balance the following equation.

26 A 2 A 3 A 3 A 13 « SSC (10+2) 2020

(a) ÷, ×, =, × (b) ×, ÷, +, =

(c) ÷, ×, =, − (d) ×, =, −, ÷

4. Select the correct combination of mathematical signs to replace the * signs and to balance the given equation

40 * 2 * 4 * 3 * 8 « SSC CPO 2013

(a) +,−,÷,= (b) ÷, +, =, ×

(c) +,÷,×,= (d) +, ×,−,=

5. Place appropriate mathematical operations in the shaded boxes to get the answer. All calculations are to be performed from left to right. « SSC Steno 2013

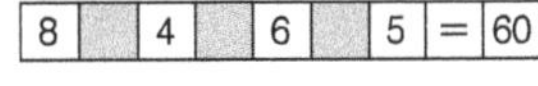

(a) −, ÷, + (b) ×, ÷, × (c) ×, ÷, − (d) ÷, ×, ×

6. Which sequence of mathematical symbols can replace * in the given equation to balance the equation?

(9 * 8 * 7) * 13 * 5 « SSC CPO 2019

(a) ×, −, ÷, = (b) −, ÷, ×, =

(c) ÷, −, =, × (d) ×, =, ÷, −

7. In the following question, * stands for any of the mathematical signs at different places, which are given as choices under each question. Select the choice with the correct sequence of signs which when substituted makes the question as a correct equation.

$24 * 4 * 5 * 4$

(a) ×, +, = (b) =, ×, + (c) +, ×, = (d) =, +, ×

8. Select the correct combination of mathematical signs to replace* signs and to balance the given equation.

$16 * 6 * 4 * 24$

(a) ÷, =, × (b) ×, =, ÷
(c) =, ÷, ÷ (d) ×, ÷, =

9. Select the correct combination of mathematical signs to replace* signs and to balance the given equation.

$9 * 3 * 3 * 3 * 6$

(a) ÷, ×, −, = (b) +, −, ×, =
(c) −, +, +, = (d) ×, +, −, =

10. Select the correct combination of mathematical signs to replace* signs and to balance the given equation.

$8 * 6 * 96 * 2 = 0$

(a) ×, ÷, − (b) ×, −, ÷
(c) −, ×, ÷ (d) ÷, −, ×

DIRECTIONS ~ (Q. Nos. 11-13) *What should be the correct signs to balance the following equations?*

11. $17 - 3 \times 6 = 45$

(a) ×, = and − (b) −, × and =
(c) =, × and − (d) ×, − and =

12. $3 + 2 \times 1 = 7$

(a) ×, +, and = (b) +, × and =
(c) =, × and + (d) × , = and +

13. 6 5 4 = 34

(a) − and + (b) × and +
(c) ÷ and × (d) × and −

14. Which two signs should be interchanged to make the given equation correct?

$36 \div 2 \times 12 + 3 - 6 = 24$ « SSC CGL 2020

(a) − and ÷ (b) × and −
(c) + and × (d) ÷ and ×

15. Which of the following interchange of numbers would make the given equation correct?

$8 \times 20 \div 3 + 9 - 5 = 38$

(a) 3, 9 (b) 3, 8
(c) 8, 9 (d) 3, 5

16. Which of the following interchange of signs or numbers would make the given equation correct?

$(18 \div 9) + 3 \times 5 = 45$

(a) × and ÷ (b) + and ÷
(c) 18 and 5 (d) 3 and 9

17. In the following question, correct the equation by interchanging two signs. « RRB JE 2019

$4 \times 3 - 6 \div 2 + 7 = 8$

(a) − and + (b) × and −
(c) ÷ and × (d) × and +

18. Which two signs should be interchanged in the following equation to make it correct? « SSC CGL 2019

$18 + 6 - 6 \div 3 \times 3 = 6$

(a) + and − (b) + and ÷
(c) − and ÷ (d) + and ×

19. Find out the two signs to be interchanged for making following equation correct. « SSC Steno 2019

$27 + 13 \times 12 - 6 \div 3 = 50$

(a) + and × (b) + and ÷
(c) − and ÷ (d) + and −

20. The following equation is incorrect. Which two signs should be interchanged to correct the equation?

$20 + 14 \div 35 - 10 \times 12 = 10$ « SSC (10 + 2) 2018

(a) + and × (b) + and ÷
(c) − and + (d) ÷ and ×

21. By interchanging which two signs the equation will be correct?

$16 + 31 - 3 \times 93 \div 11 = 966$

(a) + and − (b) − and ÷ (c) ÷ and × (d) × and +

22. Which one of the following interchange of signs would make the given equation correct?

$5 + 3 \times 8 - 12 \div 4 = 3$

(a) + and − (b) − and ÷
(c) + and × (d) + and ÷

23. Which one of the four interchange in signs and numbers would make the given equation correct?

$6 \times 4 + 2 = 16$

(a) + and ×, and 4 (b) + and ×, 2 and 4
(c) + and ×, 4 and 6 (d) None of these

24. If the two signs, '+ and ÷' are interchanged, which of the following equations will be correct?

« SSC MTS 2019

(a) $16 \div 9 + 4 \times 8 = 34$ (b) $16 \div 21 + 13 \times 26 = 56$
(c) $11 + 13 \times 4 \div 2 = 37$ (d) $13 \times 9 + 16 \div 2 = 125$

DIRECTIONS ~ (Q. Nos. 25-35) *In each of the following questions, all the equations except one have been solved according to a certain rule. You are required to solve the unsolved equation following the same rule and to choose the correct answer out of the given options.*

25. If 2463 = 36 and 5552 = 30, then 6732 = ?

(a) 32 (b) 36 (c) 34 (d) 39

26. $2 + 6 + 9 = 926, 1 + 8 + 2 = 218, 4 + 3 + 1 = ?$

(a) 314 (b) 341
(c) 143 (d) 431

27. $7 - 4 - 1 = 714, 9 - 2 - 3 = 932, 8 - 0 - 4 = ?$

(a) 804 (b) 840 (c) 408 (d) 480

28. If $4 + 5 = 41$ and $10 + 12 = 244$, then $6 + 8 = ?$

« SSC MTS 2019

(a) 200 (b) 88 (c) 96 (d) 100

29. $4 \times 6 \times 2 = 351, 3 \times 9 \times 8 = 287, 9 \times 5 \times 6 = ?$

(a) 270 (b) 845
(c) 596 (d) 659

30. If $5472 = 9$, $6342 = 6$ and $7584 = 6$, then what is 9236? « UPSC Assistant Commandant 2019

(a) 2 (b) 3
(c) 4 (d) 5

31. $4 \times 6 \times 9 = 694, 5 \times 3 \times 2 = 325, 7 \times 8 \times 2 = ?$

(a) 729 (b) 872
(c) 827 (d) 279

32. $9 * 7 = 32, 13 * 7 = 120, 17 * 9 = 208, 19 * 11 = ?$

(a) 64 (b) 160
(c) 240 (d) 210

33. If $5 * 6 * 7 = 789, 4 * 2 * 5 = 647, 5 * 1 * 7 = 739$, then $3 * 6 * 2 = ?$

(a) 584 (b) 484
(c) 251 (d) 473

34. 16 (27) 43, 29 (?) 56, 36 (12) 48

(a) 23 (b) 33
(c) 27 (d) 37

35. 10 (150) 15, 14 (224) 16, 13 (?) 15

(a) 205 (b) 195
(c) 178 (d) 197

36. If $3\%2 = 50, 2\% 4 = 60$, then what is the value of $5\% 4 = ?$ « SSC CGL 2017

(a) 16 (b) 9 (c) 90 (d) 20

37. If $16 \# 2 = 16$, $12 \# 6 = 36$ and $6 \# 1 = 3$, then find the value of $4 \# 4 = ?$ « SSC (10 + 2) 2018

(a) 2 (b) 4
(c) 10 (d) 8

38. Some equations are solved on the basis of a certain system. On the same basis, find out the correct answer for the unsolved equation.

$4-5-1=514, 3-5-6=563, 0-6-8=?$

(a) 860 (b) 680
(c) 806 (d) 068

39. If $34 \times 15 = 495$ and $43 \times 12 = 504$, then $98 \times 17 = ?$ « SSC CPO 2017

(a) 1649 (b) 1683 (c) 1763 (d) 1751

40. If 26(52) 8 and 48 (192) 16, then what is the value of 'A' in A(175)14?

(a) 50 (b) 25 (c) 35 (d) 40

41. If $64 + 7 = 460$ and $25 + 8 = 212$, then $43 + 8 = ?$ « SSC CPO 2017

(a) 360 (b) 376 (c) 332 (d) 356

42. If 13 L 4 A 7 = 41 and 14 A 3 L 12 = 54, then 12 L 3 A 9 = ? « SSC Steno 2017

(a) 84 (b) 39 (c) 42 (d) 56

43. If $73 + 82 = 14, 91 + 21 = 11$, then $86 + 24 = ?$

(a) 9 (b) 62 (c) 8 (d) 6

44. If $264 * 2 = 6$, $870 * 3 = 11$, then what should $735 * 5$ be?

(a) 05 (b) 12 (c) 16 (d) 03

45. Given, B = 8, L = 7, O = 5, C = 9 and K = 4. Using the given total, find out the missing symbol in the block.

L	?	K	K	K	=	24

(a) L (b) O (c) B (d) K

Answers / WITH EXPLANATIONS

1. (*b*) From option (b),
$$\sqrt{100} + \sqrt{16} = \sqrt{225} - \sqrt{1}$$
$$10 + 4 = 15 - 1$$
$$\Rightarrow 14 = 14$$

2. (*c*) From option (c),
$$8 * 8 * 1 * 7 = 8$$
$$\Rightarrow 8 \div 8 \times 1 + 7 = 8$$
$$\Rightarrow 1 \times 1 + 7 \Rightarrow 8 = 8$$

3. (*a*) Given, 26 A 2 A 3 A 3 A 13
From option (a), $26 \div 2 \times 3 = 3 \times 13$
$$\Rightarrow 13 \times 3 = 3 \times 13$$
$$\Rightarrow 39 = 39$$

4. (*b*) Given, 40* 2* 4 * 3 * 8
From option (b),
$$40 \div 2 + 4 = 3 \times 8$$
$$\Rightarrow 20 + 4 = 24 \Rightarrow 24 = 24$$
LHS = RHS
Hence, option (b) is correct.

5. (*d*) From option (d),
$$8 \div 4 \times 6 \times 5 = \frac{8}{4} \times 6 \times 5$$
$$= 2 \times 6 \times 5 = 60$$

6. (*a*) From option (a),
$$(9 \times 8 - 7) \div 13 = 5$$
$$(72 - 7) \div 13 = 5$$
$$65 \div 13 = 5$$
$$5 = 5$$

7. (*b*) From option (b),
$$24 = 4 \times 5 + 4$$
$$\Rightarrow 24 = 20 + 4$$
$$\Rightarrow 24 = 24$$

8. (*d*) From option (d),
$$16 \times 6 \div 4 = 24$$
$$\Rightarrow \frac{96}{4} = 24$$
$$\Rightarrow 24 = 24$$

9. (*a*) From option (a),
$$9 \div 3 \times 3 - 3 = 6$$
$$\Rightarrow 3 \times 3 - 3 = 6$$
$$\Rightarrow 9 - 3 = 6$$
$$\Rightarrow 6 = 6$$

10. (*b*) From option (b),
$$8 * 6 * 96 * 2 = 0$$
$$\Rightarrow 8 \times 6 - 96 \div 2 = 0$$
$$\Rightarrow 48 - 48 = 0$$

11. (*d*) From option (d),
$$17 - 3 \times 6 = 45$$
↓ ↓ ↓
× − =
$$\Rightarrow 17 \times 3 - 6 = 45$$
$$\Rightarrow 51 - 6 = 45$$
(using VBODMAS rule)
$$\Rightarrow 45 = 45$$
$\therefore$ LHS = RHS
So, option (d) is correct.

12. (*a*) Let us check all the options one by one.
From option (a),
$$3 + 2 \times 1 = 7$$
↓ ↓ ↓
× + =
$$\Rightarrow 3 \times 2 + 1 = 7$$
$$\Rightarrow 6 + 1 = 7$$
(using VBODMAS rule)
$$\Rightarrow 7 = 7$$
$\therefore$ LHS = RHS

13. (*b*) From option (b),
$6 \times 5 + 4 = 34$
$\Rightarrow 30 + 4 = 34$
(using VBODMAS rule)
$\Rightarrow 34 = 34$
$\Rightarrow$ LHS = RHS

14. (*b*) Given expression,
$36 \div 2 \times 12 + 3 - 6 = 24$
From option (b),
$36 \div 2 - 12 + 3 \times 6 = 24$
$\Rightarrow 18 - 12 + 18 = 24$
$\Rightarrow 36 - 12 = 24$
$\Rightarrow 24 = 24$

15. (*d*) Given expression,
$8 \times 20 \div 3 + 9 - 5 = 38$
After interchanging 3 and 5,
$8 \times 20 \div 5 + 9 - 3 = 38$
$\Rightarrow 8 \times 4 + 9 - 3 = 38$
$\Rightarrow 32 + 9 - 3 = 38$
$\Rightarrow 41 - 3 = 38$
$\Rightarrow 38 = 38$

16. (*b*) Given expression,
$(18 \div 9) + 3 \times 5 = 45$
After interchanging + and ÷,
$\Rightarrow (18 + 9) \div 3 \times 5 = 45$
$\Rightarrow 27 \div 3 \times 5 = 45$
$\Rightarrow 9 \times 5 = 45 \Rightarrow 45 = 45$

17. (*a*) Given expression,
$4 \times 3 - 6 \div 2 + 7 = 8$
From option (a), after interchanging signs, we get
$4 \times 3 + 6 \div 2 - 7 = 8$
$\Rightarrow 4 \times 3 + 3 - 7 = 8$
$\Rightarrow 12 + 3 - 7 = 8$
$\Rightarrow 15 - 7 = 8 \Rightarrow 8 = 8$

18. (*b*) Given expression,
$18 + 6 - 6 \div 3 \times 3 = 6$
Now on interchanging + and ÷, we get
$18 \div 6 - 6 + 3 \times 3 = 6$
$\Rightarrow 3 - 6 + 9 = 6$
$\Rightarrow 12 - 6 = 6 \Rightarrow 6 = 6$

19. (*c*) Given expression,
$27 + 13 \times 12 - 6 \div 3 = 50$
From option (c),
$27 + 13 \times 12 \div 6 - 3 = 50$
$\Rightarrow 27 + 13 \times 2 - 3 = 50$
$\Rightarrow 27 + 26 - 3 = 50$
$\Rightarrow 53 - 3 = 50$
$\Rightarrow 50 = 50$

20. (*a*) Given expression,
$20 + 14 \div 35 - 10 \times 12 = 10$
From option (a),
$20 \times 14 \div 35 - 10 + 12 = 10$
$\Rightarrow 20 \times 14 \times \frac{1}{35} - 10 + 12 = 10$
$\Rightarrow 8 + 2 = 10 \Rightarrow 10 = 10$

21. (*b*) Given expression,
$16 + 31 - 3 \times 93 \div 11 = 966$
From option (b),
$16 + 31 \div 3 \times 93 - 11 = 966$
$\text{LHS} = 16 + 31 \div 3 \times 93 - 11$
$= 16 + \frac{31}{3} \times 93 - 11$
$= 16 + 961 - 11 = 966 = \text{RHS}$

22. (*b*) Given expression,
$5 + 3 \times 8 - 12 \div 4 = 3$
After interchanging − and ÷,
$5 + 3 \times 8 \div 12 - 4 = 3$
$\Rightarrow 5 + 24 \div 12 - 4 = 3$
$\Rightarrow 5 + 2 - 4 = 3 \Rightarrow 3 = 3$

23. (*c*) Given expression, $6 \times 4 + 2 = 16$
From option (c), $4 + 6 \times 2 = 16$
$\Rightarrow 4 + 12 = 16$
$\Rightarrow 16 = 16$

24. (*a*) From option (a)
$16 \div 9 + 4 \times 8 = 34$
$\Rightarrow 16 + 9 \div 4 \times 8 = 34$
$\Rightarrow 16 + \frac{9}{4} \times 8 = 34$
$\Rightarrow 16 + 9 \times 2 = 34$
$\Rightarrow 16 + 18 = 34$
$\Rightarrow 34 = 34$

25. (*a*) As,
$2463 \rightarrow (2 + 4 + 6) \times 3 = 12 \times 3 = 36$
and
$5552 \rightarrow (5 + 5 + 5) \times 2 = 15 \times 2 = 30$
Similarly,
$6732 \rightarrow (6 + 7 + 3) \times 2 = 16 \times 2 = 32$

26. (*c*)
As, 2 + 6 + 9 → 926 (1 2 3 → 3 1 2)
1 + 8 + 2 → 218 (1 2 3 → 3 1 2)
Similarly, 4 + 3 + 1 → 143 (1 2 3 → 3 1 2)
∴ ? = 143

27. (*b*)
As, 7 − 4 − 1 → 714 (1 2 3 → 1 3 2)
9 − 2 − 3 → 932 (1 2 3 → 1 3 2)
Similarly, 8 − 0 − 4 → 840 (1 2 3 → 1 3 2)
? = 840

28. (*d*) $4 + 5 = 4^2 + 5^2 = 16 + 25 = 41$
$10 + 12 = 10^2 + 12^2$
$= 100 + 144 = 244$
Similarly, $6 + 8 = 6^2 + 8^2$
$= 36 + 64 = 100$
? = 100

29. (*b*) As, 4 × 6 × 2 → (−1 each) 3 5 1
and 3 × 9 × 8 → (−1 each) 2 8 7
Similarly, 9 × 5 × 6 → (−1 each) 8 4 5
? = 845

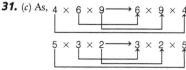

30. (*a*) $5 + 4 + 7 + 2 = 18 = 1 + 8 = 9$
$6 + 3 + 4 + 2 = 15 = 1 + 5 = 6$
$7 + 5 + 8 + 4 = 24 = 2 + 4 = 6$
Similarly,
$9 + 2 + 3 + 6 = 20 = 2 + 0 = 2$

31. (*c*) As, 4 × 6 × 9 → 6 × 9 × 4
5 × 3 × 2 → 3 × 2 × 5
Similarly,
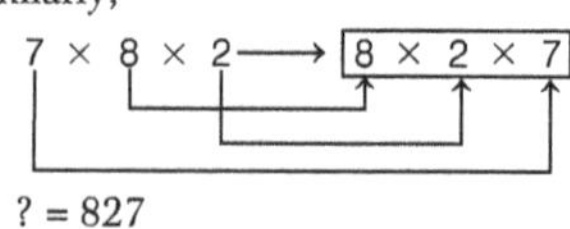
7 × 8 × 2 → 8 × 2 × 7
? = 827

32. (*c*) As, 9 * 7
$\Rightarrow (9 + 7)(9 - 7) = 16 \times 2 = 32;$
$13 * 7 \Rightarrow (13 + 7)(13 - 7)$
$= 20 \times 6 = 120;$
$17 * 9 \Rightarrow (17 + 9)(17 - 9)$
$= 26 \times 8 = 208;$
Similarly, 19 * 11
$\Rightarrow (19 + 11)(19 - 11)$
$= 30 \times 8 = 240$
∴ ? = 240

33. (*a*) As, 5 * 6 * 7, 4 * 2 * 5 → (+2 each) 7 8 9, 6 4 7
and 5 * 1 * 7 → (+2 each) 7 3 9
Similarly, 3 * 6 * 2 → (+2 each) 5 8 4
∴ ? = 584

34. (*c*) Here, right number − left number = middle number
As, 43 − 16 = 27, 48 − 36 = 12
Similarly, 56 − 29 = 27
∴ ? = 27

35. (*b*) Here, product of left and right numbers = middle number
As, $10 \times 15 = 150$,
$14 \times 16 = 224$
Similarly, $13 \times 15 = 195$
∴ ? = 195

36. (*c*) As, 3% 2 = 50
3 + 2 = 50
5 = 50 = 50

and 2% 4 = 60, 2 + 4 = 60

6 = 60 = 60

Similarly, 5% 4 = ?

5 + 4 = ?

9 = ?

$\boxed{90 = ?}$

37. (*d*) $16 \times 2 \div 2 = 16 \times 1 = 16$

$12 \times 6 \div 2 = 12 \times 3 = 36$

$6 \times 1 \div 2 = 6 \times 0.5 = 3$

$4 \times 4 \div 2 = 4 \times 2 = 8$

? = 8

38. (*b*) As, 4 – 5 – 1 ⟶ 5 1 4

and 3 – 5 – 6 ⟶ 5 6 3

Similarly, 0 – 6 – 8 ⟶ 6 8 0

? = 680

39. (*a*) As, $34 \times 15 = 495 \rightarrow 34 \times 15$

$= 510 - 15 = 495$

and $43 \times 12 = 504 \rightarrow 43 \times 12$

$= 516 - 12 = 504$

Same as, $98 \times 17 = ?$

$\Rightarrow \quad 98 \times 17 = 1666 - 17 = \boxed{1649}$

$\therefore \quad ? = 1649$

40. (*a*) As, $26(52)\,8 \rightarrow \dfrac{26 \times 8}{4} = 52$

and $48\,(192)\,16 \rightarrow \dfrac{48 \times 16}{4} = 192$

Similarly, $A\,(175)14 \rightarrow \dfrac{A \times 14}{4} = 175$

$\Rightarrow A = \dfrac{175 \times 4}{14} = \dfrac{175 \times 2}{7}$

$\Rightarrow A = 25 \times 2 \Rightarrow A = 50$

41. (*d*) As, 64 + 7 = 460

$\Rightarrow 64 \times 7 + 12 = 460$

and 25 + 8 = 212

$\Rightarrow 25 \times 8 + 12 = 212$

Same as, 43 + 8 = ?

$\Rightarrow \quad 43 \times 8 + 12 = \boxed{356}$

? = 356

42. (*b*) As, 13 L 4 A 7 = 41

$13 + 4 \times 7 = 41$

and 14 A 3 L 12 = 54

$14 \times 3 + 12 = 54$

Similarly, 12 L 3 A 9 = $12 + 3 \times 9 = 39$

43. (*c*) As, 73 + 82 = 14

$\Rightarrow (7 - 3) + (8 + 2) = 14$

$\Rightarrow \quad 4 + 10 = 14$

$\Rightarrow \quad 14 = 14$

and 91 + 21 = 11

$\Rightarrow (9 - 1) + (2 + 1) = 11$

$\Rightarrow \quad 8 + 3 = 11 \Rightarrow 11 = 11$

Similarly, 86 + 24 = (8 – 6) + (2 + 4)

= 2 + 6 = 8

44. (*b*) As, $\dfrac{264}{2} = 132$

$\Rightarrow \quad 1 + 3 + 2 = 6;$

$\dfrac{870}{3} = 290$

$\Rightarrow \quad 2 + 9 + 0 = 11$

Similarly, $\dfrac{735}{5} = 147$

$\Rightarrow \quad 1 + 4 + 7 = 12$

45. (*b*)

L	?	K	K	K	=	24

According to the question,

7 + ? + 4 + 4 + 4 = 24

$\Rightarrow \quad ? = 24 - 19$

= 5 = O

Hence, O is the missing symbol in the block.

TYPE 05

Find the Resultant Number in a Row

In this type of questions, two rows of numbers are given along with certain rules. On the basis of these rules, one is required to find out the resultant number in each row separately and question below the row is to be answered. The operation of numbers progresses from left to right. Firstly, operation for the first two numbers is done and the number obtained from this operation (operation of the first two numbers) and the third number is used to get the required answer.

DIRECTIONS ~ (Q. Nos. 14-18) *In each of the following questions two rows of numbers are given. The resultant number of each row is to be worked out separately based on the following rules and the question below the rows is to be answered. The operations of numbers progress from left to right.* « SBI PO Main 2016

Rules

(i) If an even number is followed by an another even number, they are to be added.

(ii) If an even number is followed by a prime number, they are to be multiplied.

(iii) If an odd number is followed by an even number, the even number is to be subtracted from the odd number.

(iv) If an odd number is followed by an another odd number, the first number is to be added to the square of the second number.

(v) If an even number is followed by a composite odd number, the even number is to be divided by the odd number.

***Ex* 14** **1st Row** 84 21 13

2nd Row 15 11 44

What is the half of the sum of the resultants of the two rows?

(a) 116 (b) 132 (c) 232 (d) 236

(e) None of these

***Ex* 15** **1st Row** 45 18 12

2nd Row 22 14 9

What is the product of the resultants of the two rows?

(a) 75 (b) 48 (c) 45 (d) 65

(e) None of these

***Ex* 16** **1st Row** 12 7 16

2nd Row 79 28 15

What is the difference between the resultants of the first row and second row?

(a) 276 (b) 176 (c) 100 (d) 156

(e) None of these

***Ex* 17** **1st Row** 36 13 39

2nd Row 77 30 7

What will be the outcome, if the resultant of the second row is divided by the resultant of the first row?

(a) 12 (b) 16 (c) 8 (d) 6

(e) None of these

***Ex* 18** **1st Row** 65 11 12

2nd Row 15 3 11

What is the sum of the resultants of the two rows?

(a) 366 (b) 66 (c) 264 (d) 462

(e) None of these

Solutions (Example Nos. 14-18)

Rules

(i) Even number + Even number

(ii) Even number × Prime number

(iii) Odd number − Even number

(iv) Odd number + $(\text{Odd number})^2$

(v) Even number ÷ Composite odd number

14. (a) **1st Row** 84 21 13

⇒ 84 ÷ 21 = 4 [rule (v)]

⇒ 4 × 13 = 52 [rule (ii)]

2nd Row 15 11 44

⇒ $15 + 11^2 = 136$ [rule (iv)]

⇒ 136 + 44 = 180 [rule (i)]

∴ Required answer $= \frac{180 + 52}{2} = \frac{232}{2} = 116$

15. (d) **1st Row** 45 18 12

⇒ 45 − 18 = 27 [rule (iii)]

⇒ 27 − 12 = 15 [rule (iii)]

2nd Row 22 14 9

⇒ 22 + 14 = 36 [rule (i)]

⇒ 36 ÷ 9 = 4 [rule (v)]

∴ Required answer = 15 × 4 = 60

16. (b) **1st Row** 12 7 16

⇒ 12 × 7 = 84 [rule (ii)]

⇒ 84 + 16 = 100 [rule (i)]

2nd Row 79 28 15

⇒ 79 − 28 = 51 [rule (iii)]

⇒ $51 + (15)^2 = 276$ [rule (iv)]

∴ Required answer = 276 − 100 = 176

17. (c) **1st Row** 36 13 39

⇒ 36 × 13 = 468 [rule (ii)]

⇒ 468 ÷ 39 = 12 [rule (v)]

2nd Row 77 30 7

⇒ 77 − 30 = 47 [rule (iii)]

⇒ $47 + 7^2 = 96$ [rule (iv)]

∴ Required answer $= \frac{96}{12} = 8$

18. (d) **1st Row** 65 11 12

⇒ $65 + 11^2 = 186$ [rule (iv)]

⇒ 186 + 12 = 198 [rule (i)]

2nd Row 15 3 11

⇒ $15 + 3^2 = 24$ [rule (iv)]

⇒ 24 × 11 = 264 [rule (ii)]

∴ Required answer = 198 + 264 = 462

Practice / CORNER 14.3

DIRECTIONS ~ (Q. Nos. 1-5) *In each of the following questions two rows of numbers are given. The resultant number in each row is to be worked out separately based on the following rules and the questions below the rows of numbers are to be answered. The operations of numbers progress from left to right.* « PNB PO 2007

Rules

(i) If a two-digit odd number is followed by a two-digit odd number, they are to be added.

(ii) If a two-digit even number is followed by a two digit odd number which is a perfect square, then even number is to be subtracted from the odd number.

(iii) If a three-digit number is followed by a two-digit number, the first number is to be divided by then second number.

(iv) If a prime number is followed by an even number, the two are to be added.

(v) If an even number is followed by an another even number, the two are to be multiplied.

1. 23 15 12
X 24 49
If 'X' is the resultant of the first row, what is the resultant of the second row?
(a) 24 (b) 25 (c) 28 (d) 22
(e) None of these

2. 37 12 21
38 81 14
What is the difference between the resultants of the two rows?
(a) 23 (b) 32 (c) 13 (d) 18
(e) None of these

3. 16 8 32
132 11 X^2
If X is the resultant of the first row, what is the resultant of the second row?
(a) 192 (b) 128
(c) 132 (d) 144
(e) None of these

4. 345 23 X
45 17 81
If 'X' is the resultant of the second row, what is the resultant of the first row?
(a) 285 (b) 33 (c) 135 (d) 34
(e) None of these

5. 12 28 84
37 22 18
What is the sum of the resultants of the two rows?
(a) 77 (b) 87
(c) 84 (d) 72
(e) None of the above

DIRECTIONS ~ (Q. Nos. 6-11) *In each of the following questions, two rows of numbers are given. The resultant number in each row is to be worked out separately based on the following rules and the questions below the rows of numbers are to be answered. The operations of numbers progress from left to the right.* « SBI PO 2008

Rules

(i) If an odd number is followed by an another composite odd number, they are to be added.
(ii) If an even number is followed by an odd number, they are to be added.
(iii) If an even number is followed by a number which is the perfect square, the even number is to be subtracted from the perfect square.
(iv) If an odd number is followed by a prime odd number, the first number is to be divided by the second number.
(v) If an odd number is followed by an even number, the second one is to be subtracted from the first number.

6. 15 8 21
p 3 27
If 'p' is the resultant of the first row, what will be the resultant of the second row?
(a) 58 (b) 76 (c) 27 (d) 82
(e) None of these

7. 12 64 17
20 m 16
If 'm' is the resultant of the first row, what will be the resultant of the second row?
(a) 69 (b) 85 (c) 101 (d) 121
(e) None of these

8. 85 17 35
16 19 r
If 'r' is the resultant of the first row, what will be the resultant of the second row?
(a) 175 (b) – 5 (c) 75 (d) 210
(e) None of these

9. 24 15 3
d 6 15
If 'd' is the resultant of the first row, what will be the resultant of the second row?
(a) 37 (b) 8 (c) 22 (d) 29
(e) None of these

10. 28 49 15
h 3 12
If 'h' is the resultant of the first row, what will be the resultant of the second row?
(a) 13 (b) 15 (c) 19 (d) 27
(e) None of these

11. 36 15 3
12 3 n
If 'n' is the resultant of the first row, what will be the resultant of the second row?
(a) $\frac{15}{17}$ (b) 32 (c) $\frac{12}{17}$ (d) 36
(e) None of these

DIRECTIONS ~ (Q. Nos. 12-16) *In each of the following questions two rows of numbers are given. The resultant number in each row is to be worked out separately based on the following rules and the questions below the rows of numbers are to be answered. The operations of numbers progress from left to right.* « PNB PO 2010

Rules

(i) If an odd number is followed by another composite odd number, they are to be multiplied.
(ii) If an even number is followed by an odd number, they are to be added.
(iii) If an even number is followed by a number which is a perfect square, the even number is to be subtracted from the perfect square.
(iv) If an odd number is followed by a prime odd number, the first number is to be divided by the second number.
(v) If an odd number is followed by an even number, the second one is to be subtracted from the first one.

12. 58 17 5
85 5 n
If 'n' is the resultant of the first row, what is the resultant of the second row?
(a) 255 (b) 32
(c) 49 (d) 34
(e) None of these

13. 24 64 15
m 11 15
If 'm' is the resultant of the first row, what is the resultant of the second row?
(a) 165 (b) 75
(c) 20 (d) 3
(e) None of these

14. 7 21 3
d 7 33
If 'd' is the resultant of the first row, what will be the resultant of the second row?
(a) 40 (b) 138
(c) 231 (d) 80
(e) None of the above

15. 73 34 13
32 p 15
If 'p' is the resultant of the first row, what is the resultant of the second row?
(a) 713 (b) 50
(c) 20 (d) 525
(e) None of these

16. 14 5 9
24 w 88
If 'w' is the resultant of the first row, what is the resultant of the second row?
(a) 171 (b) 283
(c) 195 (d) 107
(e) None of these

DIRECTIONS ~ (Q. Nos. 17-21) *In each of the following questions two rows of numbers are given. The resultant number in each row is to be worked out separately based on the following rules and the questions below the rows of numbers are to be answered. The operations of numbers progress from left to right.* « UCO Bank PO 2008

Rules

(i) If a two-digit even number is followed by an another even number, the first one is to be divided by the second one.

(ii) If an even number is followed by a prime number, the two are to be multiplied.

(iii) If an odd number is followed by an another odd number, the two are to be added.

(iv) If a three-digit number is followed by a two-digit number which is a perfect square, the second number is to be subtracted from the first number.

(v) If a three-digit number is followed by a two-digit number which is not a perfect square, the first number is to be divided by the second one.

17. 16 7 25
m 23 22
If 'm' is the resultant of the first row, what is the resultant of the second row?
(a) 132 (b) 88 (c) 122 (d) 78
(e) None of these

18. 97 45 71
48 8 11
What is the sum of the resultants of the two rows?
(a) 68 (b) 19 (c) 147 (d) 64
(e) None of these

19. 125 64 33
282 x 39
If 'x' is resultant of the first row, what is the resultant of the second row?
(a) 45 (b) 42 (c) 39 (d) 36
(e) None of these

20. 84 14 13
360 24 17
What is the difference between the resultants of the first row and the second row?
(a) 100 (b) 46
(c) 56 (d) 90
(e) None of these

21. 24 7 81
x 27 19
If 'x' is the resultant of the first row, what is the resultant of the second row?
(a) 87 (b) 114
(c) 4 (d) 6
(e) None of these

Answers WITH EXPLANATIONS

Solutions (Q. Nos. 1-5)

Rules

(i) (2-digit odd number) + (2-digit odd number)

(ii) 2-digit even number → 2-digit perfect square odd number then, (odd number) − (even number)

(iii) (3-digit number) ÷ (2-digit number)

(iv) (Prime number) + (Even number)

(v) (Even number) × (Even number)

1. (*e*) **1st Row** 23 15 12
⇒ $23 + 15 = 38$ [rule (i)]
$38 \times 12 = 456$ [rule (v)]
2nd Row X 24 49
⇒ 456 24 49
⇒ $456 \div 24 = 19$ [rule (iii)]
⇒ $19 + 49 = 68$ [rule (i)]
∴ Resultant of second row = 68

2. (*c*) **1st Row**
37 12 21
⇒ $37 + 12 = 49$ [rule (iv)]
⇒ $49 + 21 = 70$ [rule (i)]
2nd Row 38 81 14
⇒ $81 - 38 = 43$ [rule (ii)]
⇒ $43 + 14 = 57$ [rule (iv)]
∴ Required difference = 70 − 57
= 13

3. (*a*) **1st Row** 16 8 32
⇒ $16 \times 8 = 128$ [rule (v)]
⇒ $128 \div 32 = 4$ [rule (iii)]
X = 4
2nd Row 132 11 X^2
⇒ 132 11 16
⇒ $132 \div 11 = 12$ [rule (iii)]
⇒ $12 \times 16 = 192$ [rule (v)]
∴ Resultant of second row = 192

4. (*d*) **2nd Row** 45 17 81
⇒ $45 + 17 = 62$ [rule (i)]
⇒ $81 - 62 = 19$ [rule (ii)]
X = 19
1st Row 345 23 X
⇒ 345 23 19
⇒ $345 \div 23 = 15$ [rule (iii)]
⇒ $15 + 19 = 34$ [rule (i)]
∴ Resultant of first row = 34

5. (*e*) **1st Row** 12 28 84
⇒ $12 \times 28 = 336$ [rule (v)]
⇒ $336 \div 84 = 4$ [rule (iii)]
2nd Row 37 22 18
⇒ $37 + 22 = 59$ [rule (iv)]
⇒ $59 + 18 = 77$ [rule (iv)]
∴ Required sum = 4 + 77
= 81

Solutions (Q. Nos. 6-11)

Rules

(i) (Odd number) + (Composite odd number)

(ii) (Even number) + (Odd number)

(iii) (Even number) → (Perfect square number), then (Perfect square number) − (Even number)

(iv) (Odd number) ÷ (Prime odd number)

(v) (Odd number) − (Even number)

6. (*a*) **1st Row** 15 8 21
⇒ $15 - 8 = 7$ [rule (v)]
⇒ $7 + 21 = 28$ [rule (i)]
p = 28
2nd Row p 3 27
⇒ 28 3 27
⇒ $28 + 3 = 31$ [rule (ii)]
⇒ $31 + 27 = 58$ [rule (i)]
∴ Resultant of second row = 58

7. (*e*) **1st Row** 12 64 17
⇒ $64 - 12 = 52$ [rule (iii)]
⇒ $52 + 17 = 69$ [rule (ii)]
m = 69
2nd Row 20 m 16
⇒ 20 69 16
⇒ $20 + 69 = 89$ [rule (ii)]
⇒ $89 - 16 = 73$ [rule (v)]
∴ Resultant of second row = 73

8. (*b*) **1st Row** 85 17 35

$\Rightarrow$ $85 \div 17 = 5$ [rule (iv)]

$\Rightarrow$ $5 + 35 = 40$ [rule (i)]

$r = 40$

2nd Row 16 19 r

$\Rightarrow$ 16 19 40

$\Rightarrow$ $16 + 19 = 35$ [rule (ii)]

$\Rightarrow$ $35 - 40 = -5$ [rule (v)]

$\therefore$ Resultant of second row $= -5$

9. (*c*) **1st Row** 24 15 3

$\Rightarrow$ $24 + 15 = 39$ [rule (ii)]

$\Rightarrow$ $39 \div 3 = 13$ [rule (iv)]

$d = 13$

2nd Row d 6 15

$\Rightarrow$ 13 6 15

$\Rightarrow$ $13 - 6 = 7$ [rule (v)]

$\Rightarrow$ $7 + 15 = 22$ [rule (i)]

$\therefore$ Resultant of second row $= 22$

10. (*d*) **1st Row** 28 49 15

$\Rightarrow$ $49 - 28 = 21$ [rule (iii)]

$\Rightarrow$ $21 + 15 = 36$ [rule (i)]

$h = 36$

2nd Row h 3 12

$\Rightarrow$ 36 3 12

$\Rightarrow$ $36 + 3 = 39$ [rule (ii)]

$\Rightarrow$ $39 - 12 = 27$ [rule (v)]

$\therefore$ Resultant of second row $= 27$

11. (*a*) **1st Row** 36 15 3

$\Rightarrow$ $36 + 15 = 51$ [rule (ii)]

$\Rightarrow$ $51 \div 3 = 17$ [rule (iv)]

$n = 17$

2nd Row 12 3 n

$\Rightarrow$ 12 3 17

$\Rightarrow$ $12 + 3 = 15$ [rule (ii)]

$\Rightarrow$ $15 \div 17 = \frac{15}{17}$ [rule (iv)]

$\therefore$ Resultant of second row $= \frac{15}{17}$

Solutions (Q. Nos. 12-16)

Rules

(i) (Odd number) $\times$ (Composite odd number)

(ii) (Even number) + (Odd number)

(iii) (Even number) $\rightarrow$ (Perfect square number), then (Perfect square number) − (Even number)

(iv) (Odd number) $\div$ (Prime odd number)

(v) (Odd number) − (Even number)

12. (*a*) **1st Row** 58 17 5

$\Rightarrow$ $58 + 17 = 75$ [rule (ii)]

$\Rightarrow$ $75 \div 5 = 15$ [rule (iv)]

$n = 15$

2nd Row 85 5 n

$\Rightarrow$ 85 5 15

$\Rightarrow$ $85 \div 5 = 17$ [rule (iv)]

$\Rightarrow$ $17 \times 15 = 255$ [rule (i)]

$\therefore$ Resultant of second row $= 255$

13. (*b*) **1st Row** 24 64 15

$\Rightarrow$ $64 - 24 = 40$ [rule (iii)]

$\Rightarrow$ $40 + 15 = 55$ [rule (ii)]

$m = 55$

2nd Row m 11 15

$\Rightarrow$ 55 11 15

$\Rightarrow$ $55 \div 11 = 5$ [rule (iv)]

$\Rightarrow$ $5 \times 15 = 75$ [rule (i)]

$\therefore$ Resultant of second row $= 75$

14. (*c*) **1st Row** 7 21 3

$\Rightarrow$ $7 \times 21 = 147$ [rule (i)]

$\Rightarrow$ $147 \div 3 = 49$

$= d$ [rule (iv)]

2nd Row d 7 33

$\Rightarrow$ 49 7 33

$\Rightarrow$ $49 \div 7 = 7$ [rule (iv)]

$\Rightarrow$ $7 \times 33 = 231$ [rule (i)]

$\therefore$ Resultant of second row $= 231$

15. (*d*) **1st Row** 73 34 13

$\Rightarrow$ $73 - 34 = 39$ [rule (v)]

$\Rightarrow$ $39 \div 13 = 3 = p$ [rule (iv)]

2nd Row 32 p 15

$\Rightarrow$ 32 3 15

$\Rightarrow$ $32 + 3 = 35$ [rule (ii)]

$\Rightarrow$ $35 \times 15 = 525$ [rule (i)]

$\therefore$ Resultant of second row $= 525$

16. (*d*) **1st Row** 14 5 9

$\Rightarrow$ $14 + 5 = 19$ [rule (ii)]

$19 \times 9 = 171$ [rule (i)]

$w = 171$

2nd Row 24 w 88

$\Rightarrow$ 24 171 88

$\Rightarrow$ $24 + 171 = 195$ [rule (ii)]

$\Rightarrow$ $195 - 88 = 107$ [rule (v)]

$\therefore$ Resultant of second row $= 107$

Solutions (Q. Nos. 17-21)

Rules

(i) (2-digit even number) $\div$ (Even number)

(ii) (Even number) $\times$ (Prime number)

(iii) (Odd number) + (Odd number)

(iv) (3-digit number) − (2-digit perfect square number)

(v) (3-digit number) $\div$ (2-digit non-perfect square number)

17. (*e*) **1st Row** 16 7 25

$\Rightarrow$ $16 \times 7 = 112$ [rule (ii)]

$\Rightarrow$ $112 - 25 = 87 = m$ [rule (iv)]

2nd Row m 23 22

$\Rightarrow$ 87 23 22

$\Rightarrow$ $87 + 23 = 110$ [rule (iii)]

$\Rightarrow$ $110 \div 22 = 5$ [rule (v)]

$\therefore$ Resultant of second row $= 5$

18. (*a*) **1st Row** 97 45 71

$\Rightarrow$ $97 + 45 = 142$ [rule (iii)]

$\Rightarrow$ $142 \div 71 = 2$ [rule (v)]

2nd Row 48 8 11

$\Rightarrow$ $48 \div 8 = 6$ [rule (i)]

$\Rightarrow$ $6 \times 11 = 66$ [rule (ii)]

$\therefore$ Required sum $= 2 + 66 = 68$

19. (*b*) **1st Row** 125 64 33

$\Rightarrow$ $125 - 64 = 61$ [rule (iv)]

$\Rightarrow$ $61 + 33 = 94$ [rule (iii)]

$x = 94$

2nd Row 282 x 39

$\Rightarrow$ 282 94 39

$\Rightarrow$ $282 \div 94 = 3$ [rule (v)]

$\Rightarrow$ $3 + 39 = 42$ [rule (iii)]

$\therefore$ Resultant of second row $= 42$

20. (*b*) **1st Row** 84 14 13

$\Rightarrow$ $84 \div 14 = 6$ [rule (i)]

$\Rightarrow$ $6 \times 13 = 78$ [rule (ii)]

2nd Row 360 24 17

$\Rightarrow$ $360 \div 24 = 15$ [rule (v)]

$\Rightarrow$ $15 + 17 = 32$ [rule (iii)]

$\therefore$ Required difference $= 78 - 32$
$= 46$

21. (*d*) **1st Row** 24 7 81

$\Rightarrow$ $24 \times 7 = 168$ [rule (ii)]

$\Rightarrow$ $168 - 81 = 87$ [rule (iv)]

$= x$

2nd Row x 27 19

$\Rightarrow$ 87 27 19

$\Rightarrow$ $87 + 27 = 114$ [rule (iii)]

$\Rightarrow$ $114 \div 19 = 6$ [rule (v)]

$\therefore$ Resultant of second row $= 6$

Master Exercise

1. If '+' means '×', '×' means '÷', '÷' means '–' and '–' means '+', what is the value of (17 + 15 – 135 × 9 ÷ 70), ...?...
« UKPSC Asstt. Conservator of forest 2019
(a) 270 (b) 240 (c) 200 (d) 170

2. If J = 1, K = 2, L = 5 , M = 7, N = 11 , O = 13, P = 17, then what will come in the place of question mark in given expression? « SSC (10 + 2) 2017
(N × ? + M) ÷ K = 31
(a) L (b) P (c) J (d) O

3. If + means divide, × means subtract, ÷ means multiply and – means plus, then find the value of 9 + 3 ÷ 4 – 8 × 2.
« IB ACIO 2017
(a) 15 (b) 17 (c) 18 (d) 20

4. Find the correct group of signs to solve the equation.
24 * 16 * 8 * 32
(a) ÷, –, = (b) –, +, = (c) ×, ÷, = (d) +, –, =

5. Insert arithmetical signs in the equation for it to be correct 8 ? 4 ? 2 = 16 « IB ACIO 2017
(a) +, × (b) –, +
(c) ÷, + (d) +, ÷

6. If 84 × 13 = 8, 37 × 13 = 6, 26 × 11 = 6, then 56 × 22 = ?
(a) 3 (b) 5 (c) 7 (d) 9

7. Which of the following interchanges of numbers would make the given equation correct?
8 × 20 ÷ 3 + 9 – 5 = 38
(a) 3, 8 (b) 8, 9 (c) 3, 5 (d) 3, 9

8. Find the group of mathematical signs in the place of * in the given equation 7*7*2*1 = 12.
(a) ×, –, ÷ (b) +, –, ×
(c) ×, –, + (d) +, ×, –

9. The following equation is incorrect. Which two signs should be interchanged to correct the equation?
13 × 8 + 25 – 6 ÷ 10 = 20 « SSC (10 + 2) 2018
(a) ÷ and – (b) × and –
(c) + and ÷ (d) – and +

10. In a certain code language, '×' represents '+', '÷' represents '×', '–' represents '÷' and '+' represents '–'. Find out the answer to the following question.
20 + 16 × 6 ÷ 10 – 4 = ? « SSC (10 + 2) 2018
(a) 13 (b) 12 (c) 30 (d) 19

11. Some equations have been solved on the basis of a certain system. Find the correct answer for the unsolved equation on that basis « SSC Steno 2016
If 29 × 13 = 14,76 × 26 = 34, then 64 × 14 = ?
(a) 54 (b) 19 (c) 32 (d) 26

12. Select the most appropriate option to solve the equation. « UP Police Constable 2018
60 ÷ 5 × (16 – 8 ÷ 2) ÷ 3 = ?
(a) 48 (b) 16 (c) 1 (d) 32

13. If 64 + 7 = 460, and 25 + 8 = 212, then 43 + 8 = ?
« SSC CGL 2016
(a) 360 (b) 376 (c) 332 (d) 356

14. If 5 @ 6 = 61 and 8 @ 10 = 164, then 7 @ 9 = ?
« UKPSC 2016
(a) 125 (b) 63 (c) 130 (d) 32

15. What will be the value of the following equation if '÷' means 'addition', '+' means subtraction, '–' means multiplication and '×' means division? « SSC GD 2018
49 × 7 – 3 ÷ 9 + 4 = ?
(a) 31 (b) 26 (c) 25 (d) 39

16. Which of the following interchange of signs would make the given equation correct?
(20 – 4) × 4 + 16 = 36
(a) + and – (b) – and × (c) × and + (d) ÷ and –

17. Which two signs need to be interchanged to make the following equation correct?
73 – 13 × 42 ÷ 14 + 56 = 56 « SSC MTS 2019
(a) + and × (b) × and ÷
(c) – and + (d) – and ×

18. Put the correct mathematical signs in the following equation from the given alternatives.
33 ? 11 ? 3 ? 6 = 115
(a) +, –, × (b) ×, ÷, –
(c) ÷, ×, × (d) –, ×, +

DIRECTIONS ~ (Q. Nos. 19 and 20) *If the given interchanges are made in signs and numbers, then which one of the four equations would be correct?*

19. Given interchanges signs '–' and '÷' and numbers '4' and '8'.
(a) 16 ÷ 8 – 4 = 6 (b) 4 – 8 ÷ 6 = 2
(c) 6 – 8 ÷ 4 = –1 (d) 4 ÷ 8 – 2 = 6

20. Given interchanges signs '+' and '–', numbers '4' and '8'. « UKPSC Asst. Conservator of Forest 2019
(a) 4 ÷ 8 – 12 = 16 (b) 4 – 8 + 12 = 0
(c) 8 ÷ 4 – 12 = 24 (d) 8 – 4 ÷ 12 = 8

21. Select the correct combination of mathematical signs to replace * signs and to balance the given equation.
15 * 24 * 3 * 6 * 17
(a) +, ÷, –, = (b) ÷, ×, –, ÷
(c) –, ×, =, + (d) –, ÷, +, =

22. If 'K' means 'minus', 'L' means 'divided by', 'M' means 'plus' and 'D' means 'multiplied by', then « SSC (10 + 2) 2017

117 L 3 K 5 M 12 D 8 = ?

(a) 150 (b) 125 (c) 130 (d) 145

23. In a certain code language '+' represents '×', '–' represents '+', '×' represents '÷' and '÷' represents '–'. What is the answer to the following question? « SSC CGL 2017

$24 \times 6 - 8 + 2 = ?$

(a) 25 (b) 50 (c) 40 (d) 20

24. If 10$25 = 8, 12$25 = 10, then what is the value of 14$53 =? « SSC CGL 2017

(a) 13 (b) 15 (c) 11 (d) 9

25. If 8#12 = 10; 5#9 = 7; 6#10 = 8, then find the value of 14#4. « RRB ALP 2018

(a) 3 (b) 10 (c) 5 (d) 9

26. If $9 \times 3 = 3$, $15 \times 3 = 5$, $60 \times 5 = 12$, then what is the value of $27 \times 3 = ?$ « SSC CGL 2017

(a) 30 (b) 9 (c) 3 (d) 6

DIRECTIONS ~ (Q. Nos. 27 and 28) *In the following questions, some equations are solved on the basis of a certain system. On the same basis, find out the correct answer for the unsolved equation.* « SSC (10 + 2) 2013

27. If $5 \times 6 \times 4 = 456$ and $3 \times 6 \times 5 = 536$, then $4 \times 8 \times 7 = ?$

(a) 748 (b) 478 (c) 847 (d) 784

28. If 782 = 20 and 671 = 17, then 884 = ?

(a) 32 (b) 19 (c) 26 (d) 23

29. The two given expressions on both the side of the '=' sign will have the same value if two numbers from either side or both side are interchanged. Select the correct numbers to be interchanged from the given option.

$3 + 5 \times 4 - 24 \div 3 = 7 \times 4 - 3 + 36 \div 6$ « SSC CGL 2019

(a) 4, 7 (b) 24, 36 (c) 5, 7 (d) 6, 3

30. Find the correct group of signs to solve the equation

24 * 16 * 8 * 32

(a) +, –, = (b) ÷, –, =
(c) –, +, = (d) ×, ÷, =

31. Select the correct combination of mathematical signs to replace '*' signs and to balance the given equation.

9*7*2*3*10

(a) ÷, ×, +, = (b) –, +, ÷, =
(c) +,–,×,= (d) –, ÷, ×, =

DIRECTIONS ~ (Q. Nos. 32-34) *In each of the following questions, all the equations except one have been solved according to a certain rule. You are required to solve the unsolved equation following the same rule and to choose the correct answer out of the given options.*

32. If $8 \times 6 \times 1 = 168$ and $5 \times 2 \times 1 = 125$, then $4 \times 5 \times 7 = ?$

(a) 754 (b) 457
(c) 547 (d) 475

33. If 3 * 8 * 6 = 497 and 8 * 4 * 2 = 953, then 6 * 5 * 1 = ?

(a) 386 (b) 726
(c) 863 (d) 762

34. If 16 (55) 3 and 30 (157) 5, then 9 (?) 25

(a) 335 (b) 125
(c) 232 (d) 342

35. If 9#3 = 6; 15#3 = 9; 60#4 = 32, then what is the value of 27#3 = ? « SSC CGL 2017

(a) 24 (b) 15
(c) 13 (d) 33

36. If '+' denotes ÷, '–' denotes ×, '×' denotes – and '÷' denotes +, then $35 + 7 - 5 \div 5 \times 6 = ?$

(a) 36 (b) 24 (c) 20 (d) 14

37. If '+' means '–', '–' means '×', '×' means '÷' and '÷' means '+' then $2 \div 6 \times 6 \div 2 = ?$ « RRB JE 2019

(a) 1 (b) 0 (c) 10 (d) 5

38. If 'A' is replaced by '+', if 'B' is replaced by '–', 'C' is replaced by '÷' and 'D' replaced by '×', find the value of the following equation. « SSC Steno 2019

15A25B35C5D7

(a) 9 (b) –9 (c) 13 (d) 11

39. Select the correct combination of mathematical signs to replace * signs and to balance the given equation.

5 * 5 * 5 * 3 * 10

(a) ×, +, =, × (b) +, –, ×, = (c) +, ÷, =, × (d) +, ÷, ×, =

40. Some equations are solved by special method, on the basis of it, find the right answer of equation from the given options which is not solved?

$6 \times 4 \times 3 = 436$, $8 \times 4 \times ? = 468$, $6 \times 9 \times 8 = 986$

(a) 3 (b) 4 (c) 5 (d) 6

41. If 'P' means '+', 'Q' means '×', 'R' means '÷' and 'S' means '–', then 44 Q 9 R 12 S 6 Q 4 P 16 = ?

(a) 36 (b) 124
(c) 25 (d) 112

42. Which of the following interchange of signs would make the given equation correct?

$5 + 3 \times 8 - 12 \div 4 = 3$

(a) + and ÷ (b) + and –
(c) – and ÷ (d) + and ×

43. If '+' means '÷', '×' means '+', '–' means '×' and '÷' means '–', then which of the following equation is correct?

(a) $36 + 6 - 3 \times 2 = 20$ (b) $36 \times 6 + 3 - 2 < 20$
(c) $36 \times 6 + 3 \times 2 > 20$ (d) $36 + 6 \times 3 + 2 = 20$

44. If P + Q implies P – Q

P – Q implies P × Q

P × Q implies P ÷ Q

P ÷ Q implies P + Q

Which of the following is TRUE?

« UPSSSC Combined Lower Subordinate Service 2019

(a) $1 + 2 - 6 \times 3 \div 8 = 8$ (b) $6 + 2 - 3 \times 1 \div 4 = 12$
(c) $25 + 6 - 45 \times 9 \div 23 = 18$ (d) $10 + 4 - 3 \times 1 \div 2 = 5$

45. Select the correct combination of mathematical signs to replace * signs and to balance the given equation.

2 * 4 * 3 * 4 * 9

(a) +,−,=,÷ (b) +, ×, =, −
(c) ×, ÷,−,= (d) ×, −,+,=

46. If the symbols '+' and '−' are interchanged, '×' and '÷' are interchanged and also the digits '3' and '7' are interchanged, then what will be the value of the below equation? $87 \times 7 - 79 + 63 \div 7$

« UPSSSC Combined Lower Subordinate Service 2019

(a) −133 (b) −350
(c) 244 (d) 511

47. Select the correct combination of mathematical signs to replace * signs and to balance the following equation 6* 4* 12 *12

(a) ÷, −, = (b) +, −, ÷
(c) =,−,÷ (d) ×, −, =

DIRECTIONS ~ (Q. Nos. 48 and 49) *In following questions, some equations are solved on the basis of a certain system. On that basis find out the correct answer for unsolved equation.* « SSC 10+2 2013

48. If $3 \times 9 \times 7 = 379$ and $5 \times 4 \times 8 = 584$, then $1 \times 2 \times 3 = ?$

(a) 123 (b) 231 (c) 213 (d) 132

49. If 526 = 9 and 834 = 9, then 716 = ?

(a) 20 (b) 15
(c) 9 (d) 12

DIRECTIONS ~ (Q. Nos. 50 and 51) *In the following questions some equations are solved on the basis of a certain system. On the same basis, find out the correct answer for the unsolved equation.*

50. If 85 + 25 = 50 and 97 + 65 = 93, then 72 + 94 = ?

(a) 92 (b) 50
(c) 67 (d) 60

51. If 4267 = 10 and 3374 = 9, then 4255 = ?

(a) 12 (b) 10
(c) 20 (d) 8

52. If '+' means 'greater than'; '−' means 'smaller than' and '=' means 'not greater than', 'then, a + b and c − b' implies that « UPSSSC Junior Assist. 2015

(a) $ab + c$ (b) $a + c$
(c) $ac + b^2$ (d) $a = c$

Answers WITH EXPLANATIONS

1. (*c*) Given expression,

$17 + 15 - 135 \times 9 \div 70$

On substituting the signs

$17 \times 15 + 135 \div 9 - 70$
$= 17 \times 15 + 15 - 70$
$= 255 + 15 - 70$
$= 270 - 70 = 200$

2. (*a*) Given,

J = 1, K = 2, L = 5, M = 7, N = 11, O = 13 and P = 17

Let question mark (?) would be replace by x.

Then, putting the values in given expression

$\frac{(11 \times x + 7)}{2} = 31$

$\Rightarrow 11x + 7 = 62 \Rightarrow 11x = 55$
$\Rightarrow x = 5 \therefore x = 5 = L$

Hence, L will be come in place of question mark.

3. (*c*) Given, $9 + 3 \div 4 - 8 \times 2$

Now, changing the sign as per the question,

$9 \div 3 \times 4 + 8 - 2 \Rightarrow \frac{9}{3} \times 4 + 8 - 2$
$\Rightarrow 3 \times 4 + 8 - 2 \Rightarrow 12 + 8 - 2$
$\Rightarrow 20 - 2 \Rightarrow 18$

So, the required value is 18.

4. (*d*) From option (d),

$24 + 16 - 8 = 32$
$\Rightarrow 40 - 8 = 32 \Rightarrow 32 = 32$
$\Rightarrow$ LHS = RHS

So, option (d) is correct.

5. (*a*) Here, 8 ? 4 ? 2 = 16

Now, place the sign of option (a)

$8 + 4 \times 2 = 16$
$\Rightarrow 8 + 8 = 16$
$\Rightarrow 16 = 16$

Hence, option (a) is correct.

6. (*c*) As, $84 \times 13 = 8$

$\Rightarrow (8 + 4) - (1 + 3) = 8$
$\Rightarrow 12 - 4 = 8$
and $37 \times 13 = 6$
$\Rightarrow (3 + 7) - (1 + 3) = 6$
$\Rightarrow 10 - 4 = 6$
and $26 \times 11 = 6$
$\Rightarrow (2 + 6) - (1 + 1) = 6$
$\Rightarrow 8 - 2 = 6$
Same as, $56 \times 22 = ?$
$\Rightarrow (5 + 6) - (2 + 2) = ?$
$\Rightarrow 11 - 4 = ?$
$\therefore ? = 7$

So, option (c) is correct.

7. (*c*) From option (c),

$8 \times 20 \div 3 + 9 - 5 = 38$ (with 3 → 5 and 5 → 3)

$\Rightarrow 8 \times 20 \div 5 + 9 - 3 = 38$
$\Rightarrow 8 \times 4 + 9 - 3 = 38$
$\Rightarrow 32 + 9 - 3 = 38$
$\Rightarrow 41 - 3 = 38$
$\Rightarrow 38 = 38$
$\therefore$ LHS = RHS

So, option (c) is correct.

8. (*b*) From option (b),

$7 + 7 - 2 \times 1 = 12$
$\Rightarrow 7 + 7 - 2 = 12$
$\Rightarrow 14 - 2 = 12$
$\Rightarrow 12 = 12$
$\therefore$ LHS = RHS

So, option (b), is correct.

9. (*b*) LHS $= 13 \times 8 + 25 - 6 \div 10$

After interchanging the sign × and −, then

$13 - 8 + 25 \times 6 \div 10$
$= 13 - 8 + 15 = 28 - 8 = 20 =$ RHS

Hence, × and − are required answer.

10. (*d*) Given, × → +, ÷ → ×, − → ÷, + → −

Then, $20 + 16 \times 6 \div 10 - 4 = ?$

After changing sign, we have

$? = 20 - 16 + 6 \times 10 \div 4$
$? = 20 - 16 + \frac{6 \times 10}{4}$
$= 20 - 16 + 15 = 19$

So, the correct option is (d).

11. (*b*) Here, $29 \times 13 = 14$

$(2 \times 9) - (1 + 3) = 18 - 4 = 14$
and $76 \times 26 = 34$
$(7 \times 6) - (2 + 6) = 42 - 8 = 34$
Similarly, $64 \times 14 = ?$
$(6 \times 4) - (1 + 4) = 24 - 5 = \boxed{19}$

So, the correct option is (b).

12. (*a*) $60 \div 5 \times (16 - 8 \div 2) \div 3$

$= 12 \times (16 - 4) \div 3$
$= 12 \times 12 \div 3 = 12 \times 4 = 48$

So, the correct option is (a).

13. (*d*) As, $64 + 7 = 460$
$\Rightarrow 64 \times 7 + 12 = 460$
and $25 + 8 = 212$
$\Rightarrow 25 \times 8 + 12 = 212$
Same as, $43 + 8 = ?$
$\Rightarrow 43 \times 8 + 12 = \boxed{356}$
$\therefore ? = 356$
Hence, option (d) is correct.

14. (*c*) $5 @ 6 = 61$
$\Rightarrow 5^2 + 6^2 = 25 + 36 = 61$
$8 @ 10 = 164$
$\Rightarrow 8^2 + 10^2 = 64 + 100 = 164$
$7 @ 9 = ?$
$\Rightarrow 7^2 + 9^2 = 49 + 81 = 130$
Hence, option (c) is correct.

15. (*b*) According to the question,
$\div \Rightarrow +$
$+ \Rightarrow -$
$- \Rightarrow \times$
$\times \Rightarrow \div$
$\Rightarrow 49 \times 7 - 3 \div 9 + 4$
By changing signs,
$49 \div 7 \times 3 + 9 - 4$
$= 7 \times 3 + 5$
$= 21 + 5 = 26$
$\therefore ? = 26$
Hence, option (b) is correct.

16. (*d*) $(20 - 4) \times 4 + 16 = 36$
$\Rightarrow (20 \div 4) \times 4 + 16 = 36$
$\Rightarrow 5 \times 4 + 16 = 36$
$\Rightarrow 20 + 16 = 36$
$\Rightarrow 36 = 36$
Hence, option (d) is correct.

17. (*c*) Given, $73 - 13 \times 42 \div 14 + 56 = 56$
From option (c),
$73 + 13 \times 42 \div 14 - 56 = 56$
$\Rightarrow 73 + 13 \times 3 - 56 = 56$
$\Rightarrow 73 + 39 - 56 = 56$
$\Rightarrow 112 - 56 = 56$
$\Rightarrow 56 = 56$
Hence, option (c) is correct.

18. (*b*) From option (b),
$33 \times 11 \div 3 - 6 = 115$
$\Rightarrow 33 \times \frac{11}{3} - 6 = 115$
$\Rightarrow 121 - 6 = 115$
$\Rightarrow 115 = 115$
$\therefore$ LHS = RHS
So, option (b) is correct.

19. (*d*) From option (d),
$4 \div 8 - 2 = 6$
↓ ↓ ↓ ↓
$8 - 4 \div$
$\Rightarrow 8 - 4 \div 2 = 6$
$\Rightarrow 8 - 2 = 6$
$\Rightarrow 6 = 6$
$\Rightarrow$ LHS = RHS
Clearly, option (d) is correct.

20. (*b*) From option (b),
$4 - 8 + 12 = 0$
↓ ↓ ↓ ↓
$8 + 4 -$
$\Rightarrow 8 + 4 - 12 = 0$
$\Rightarrow 12 - 12 = 0$
$\Rightarrow 0 = 0$
$\Rightarrow$ LHS = RHS
So, option (b) is correct.

21. (*a*) From option (a),
$15 + 24 \div 3 - 6 = 17$
$\Rightarrow 15 + 8 - 6 = 17$
$\Rightarrow 23 - 6 = 17$
$\Rightarrow 17 = 17$
$\therefore$ LHS = RHS
So, option (a) is correct.

22. (*c*) Given, 117 L 3 K 5 M 12 D 8 = ?
Now, change the alphabet into the signs,
$? = 117 \div 3 - 5 + 12 \times 8$
$\Rightarrow ? = \frac{117}{3} - 5 + 12 \times 8$
$\Rightarrow ? = 39 - 5 + 96$
$\Rightarrow ? = 135 - 5 \Rightarrow ? = 130$
So, option (c) is correct.

23. (*d*) Given equation,
$? = 24 \times 6 - 8 + 2$
Now, changing the sign as per the question,
$? = 24 \div 6 + 8 \times 2$
$\Rightarrow ? = \frac{24}{6} + 8 \times 2$
$\Rightarrow ? = 4 + 16 \Rightarrow ? = 20$
So, option (d) is correct.

24. (*a*) As, $10\$25 \Rightarrow 1 + 0 + 2 + 5 = 8$
and $12\$25 \Rightarrow 1 + 2 + 2 + 5 = 10$
Similarly, $14\$53$
$\Rightarrow 1 + 4 + 5 + 3 = \boxed{13}$
So, option (a) is correct.

25. (*d*) As, $8\#12 = 10$
$\Rightarrow \frac{8+12}{2} = 10$
$\Rightarrow \frac{20}{2} = 10,$
$5\#9 = 7$
$\Rightarrow \frac{5+9}{2} = 7 \Rightarrow \frac{14}{2} = 7$
and $6\#10 = 8$
$\Rightarrow \frac{6+10}{2} = 8$
$\Rightarrow \frac{16}{2} = 8$
Similarly,
$14 \# 4 = ?$
$\Rightarrow \frac{14+4}{2} = ?$
$\Rightarrow \frac{18}{2} = ?$
$\Rightarrow ? = 9$
So, option (d) is correct.

26. (*b*) As, $9 \times 3 = 3$
$9 \div 3 = 3$
$15 \times 3 = 5$
$15 \div 3 = 5$
and $60 \times 5 = 12$
$60 \div 5 = 12$
Similarly, $27 \times 3 = ?$
$27 \div 3 = ?$
$? = 9$
So, option (b) is correct.

27. (*a*) As, $5 \times 6 \times 4 = 4\ 5\ 6$
and $3 \times 6 \times 5 = 5\ 3\ 6$
Similarly,

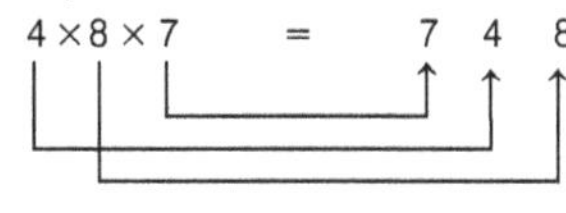

$\therefore ? = 748$
So, option (a) is correct.

28. (*d*) As, $782 = (7 + 8 + 2) + 3 = 20$
and $671 = (6 + 7 + 1) + 3 = 17$
Similarly, $884 = (8 + 8 + 4) + 3 = 23$
So, option (d) is correct.

29. (*c*) Given,
$3 + 5 \times 4 - 24 \div 3 = 7 \times 4 - 3 + 36 \div 6$
From option (c),
$\Rightarrow 3 + 7 \times 4 - 24 \div 3 = 5 \times 4 - 3 + 36 \div 6$
$\Rightarrow 3 + 28 - 8 = 20 - 3 + 6$
$\Rightarrow 31 - 8 = 26 - 3$
$\Rightarrow 23 = 23$
So, option (c) is correct.

30. (*a*) Given expression, $24 * 16 * 8 * 32$
From option (a),
$24 + 16 - 8 = 32$
$\Rightarrow 40 - 8 = 32$
So, option (a) is correct.

31. (*c*) From option (c),
$9 + 7 - 2 \times 3 = 10$
$\Rightarrow 9 + 7 - 6 = 10$
$\Rightarrow 10 = 10$
$\therefore$ LHS = RHS
So, option (c) is correct.

32. (*a*) As, $8 \times 6 \times 1 \longrightarrow 168$
and $5 \times 2 \times 1 \longrightarrow 125$
Similarly, $4 \times 5 \times 7 \longrightarrow \boxed{754}$
$\therefore ? = 754$
So, option (a) is correct.

33. (*d*) As,

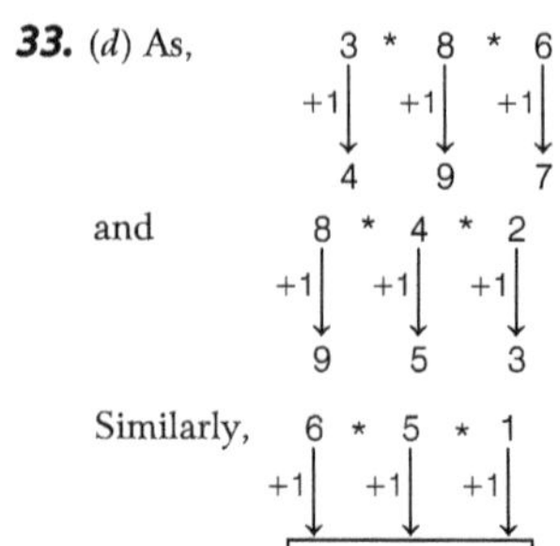

$\therefore$? = 762

So, option (d) is correct.

34. (*c*) As, $(16 \times 3) + 7 = 55$

and $(30 \times 5) + 7 = 157$

Similarly, $(9 \times 25) + 7 = 232$

$\therefore$? = 232

So, option (c) is correct.

35. (*b*) As, 9#3 = 6

$\Rightarrow \frac{9+3}{2} = 6 \Rightarrow \frac{12}{2} = 6,$

15#3 = 9

$\Rightarrow \frac{15+3}{2} = 9 \Rightarrow \frac{18}{2} = 9$

and 60#4 = 32

$\Rightarrow \frac{60+4}{2} = 32$

$\Rightarrow \frac{64}{2} = 32$

Similarly, 27#3=?

$\Rightarrow \frac{27+3}{2} = ? \Rightarrow \frac{30}{2} = ?$

$\Rightarrow ? = \boxed{15}$

So, option (b) is correct.

36. (*b*) According to the question,

? = 35 + 7 − 5 ÷ 5 × 6
↓ ↓ ↓ ↓
÷ × + −

$= 35 \div 7 \times 5 + 5 - 6$

$= 5 \times 5 + 5 - 6 = 25 + 5 - 6$

$= 30 - 6 = 24$

$\therefore$? = 24

So, option (b) is correct.

37. (*d*) Given,

2 ÷ 6 × 6 ÷ 2 = ?
↓ ↓ ↓
+ ÷ +

$2 + 6 \div 6 + 2 = ?$

$\Rightarrow 2 + 1 + 2 = ?$

$\Rightarrow 5 = ?$

So, option (d) is correct.

38. (*b*) Given,

15 A 25 B 35 C 5 D 7
↓ ↓ ↓ ↓
15 + 25 − 35 ÷ 5 × 7

$= 15 + 25 - 7 \times 7 = 40 - 49 = -9$

So, option (b) is correct.

39. (*a*) 5 * 5 * 5 * 3 * 10

$\Rightarrow 5 \times 5 + 5 = 3 \times 10$

$\Rightarrow 30 = 30$

So, option (a) is correct.

40. (*d*) As,

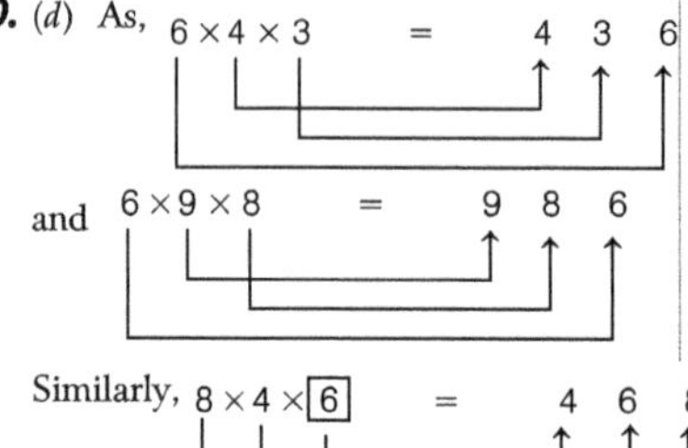

Similarly, 8 × 4 × $\boxed{6}$ = 4 6 8

$\therefore$? = 6

So, option (d) is correct.

41. (*c*) According to the question,

? = 44 Q 9 R 12 S 6 Q 4 P 16
↓ ↓ ↓ ↓ ↓
× ÷ − × +

$= 44 \times 9 \div 12 - 6 \times 4 + 16$

$= 44 \times \frac{9}{12} - 6 \times 4 + 16$

$= 33 - 24 + 16 = 49 - 24 = 25$

$\therefore$? = 25

So, option (c) is correct.

42. (*c*) From option (c),

5 + 3 × 8 − 12 ÷ 4 = 3
↓ ↓
÷ −

$\Rightarrow 5 + 3 \times 8 \div 12 - 4 = 3$

$\Rightarrow 5 + 3 \times \frac{8}{12} - 4 = 3$

$\Rightarrow 5 + 2 - 4 = 3$

$\Rightarrow 7 - 4 = 3$

$\Rightarrow 3 = 3$

$\Rightarrow$ LHS = RHS

So, option (c) is correct.

43. (*a*) From option (a),

36 + 6 − 3 × 2 = 20
↓ ↓ ↓
÷ × +

$\Rightarrow 36 \div 6 \times 3 + 2 = 20$

$\Rightarrow 6 \times 3 + 2 = 20$

$\Rightarrow 18 + 2 = 20$

$\Rightarrow 20 = 20$

$\Rightarrow$ LHS = RHS

So, option (a) is correct.

44. (*c*) $25 + 6 - 45 \times 9 \div 23 = 18$

On interchanging the signs.

LHS $25 - 6 \times 45 \div 9 + 23$

$\Rightarrow 25 - 6 \times \frac{45}{9} + 23$

$\Rightarrow 25 - 6 \times 5 + 23$

$\Rightarrow 25 - 30 + 23 \Rightarrow 25 - 7$

$\Rightarrow 18 = 18$ (RHS)

$\therefore$ Option (d) is correct.

45. (*d*) From option (d),

2 * 4 * 3 * 4 * 9

$2 \times 4 - 3 + 4 = 9$

$\Rightarrow 8 - 3 + 4 = 9$

$\Rightarrow 9 = 9$

$\therefore$ Option (d) is correct.

46. (*a*) $83 \times 7 - 79 + 63 \div 7$

On interchanging '+' with '−', '×' with '÷' and 3 with 7; we get

$87 \div 3 + 39 - 67 \times 3$

$\Rightarrow \frac{87}{3} + 39 - 67 \times 3$

$\Rightarrow 29 + 39 - 201$

$\Rightarrow 68 - 201 \Rightarrow -133$

$\therefore$ Option (a) is correct.

47. (*d*) 6 * 4 * 12 * 12

From option (d),

$6 \times 4 - 12 = 12$

$\Rightarrow 12 = 12$

$\therefore$ Option (d) is correct.

48. (*d*) As,

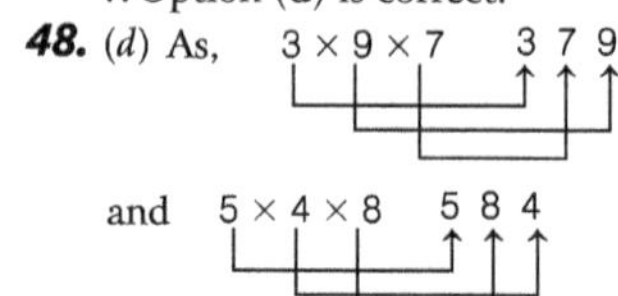

Similarly,

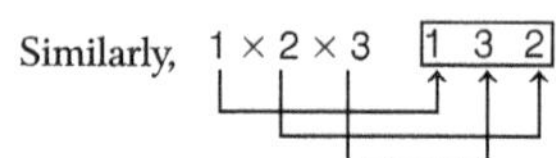

$1 \times 2 \times 3 = 132$

So, option (d) is correct.

49. (*d*) As, $5 + 6 - 2 = 9$

and $8 + 4 - 3 = 9$

Similarly, $7 + 6 - 1 = 12$

So, option (d) is correct.

50. (*b*) As, $85 + 25 \rightarrow 8 \times 5 + 2 \times 5$

$= 40 + 10 = 50$

and $97 + 65 \rightarrow 9 \times 7 + 6 \times 5$

$= 63 + 30 = 93$

Similarly,

$72 + 94 \rightarrow 7 \times 2 + 9 \times 4$

$= 14 + 36 = 50$

So, option (b) is correct.

51. (*b*) As,

$4267 \longrightarrow 4 \times 6 - 2 \times 7$

$= 24 - 14 = 10$ and

$3374 \longrightarrow 3 \times 7 - 3 \times 4$

$= 21 - 12 = 9$

Similarly,

$4255 \longrightarrow 4 \times 5 - 2 \times 5$

$= 20 - 10 = 10$

So, option (b) is correct.

52. (*b*) $a + b \longrightarrow a > b$ ...(i)

and $c - b \longrightarrow c < b$ ...(ii)

From Eqs. (i) and (ii), we have

$a > b > c \Rightarrow a > c \Rightarrow a + c$

So, option (b) is correct.

CHAPTER / 15

Mathematical Reasoning

Mathematical reasoning involves the ability to solve various problems through mathematical ability along with logical and mental ability.

Mathematical reasoning test is designed to test the ability of a candidate to solve the various Mathematical problems which are encountered in day to day life. To solve the problems on Mathematical reasoning, a candidate should have a knowledge of concepts of Arithmetic or basic Mathematics.

Examples given below, will give you a better idea about the types of questions asked in various examinations.

***Ex.* 01** A man climbing up a wall of 24 m high. He climbs 16 m in a day but slipped back by 3 m 40 cm in the evening. How far had the man reached on that day? « SSC (CPO) 2015

(a) 11.4 m (b) 12.6 m
(c) 12 m 40 cm (d) 19 m 40 cm

***Solution* (b)** Distance covered by man in a day

$= (16 - 3.4)$ m

$= 12.6$ m

***Ex.* 02** The weights of 4 boxes are 90, 40, 80 and 50 kilograms. Which of the following cannot be the total weight, in kilograms, of any combination of these boxes and in a combination a box can be used only once?

(a) 200 (b) 260
(c) 180 (d) 170

***Solution* (a)** For option (b), $90 + 40 + 80 + 50 = 260$

For option (c), $90 + 40 + 50 = 180$

For option (d), $90 + 80 = 170$

But in option (a), the sum of any numbers given in question is not 200.

***Ex.* 03** A shepherd had 17 sheeps. All but nine died. How many was he left with? « UPSSSC Lower Subordinate 2017

(a) 17 (b) 9 (c) Nil (d) 8

***Solution* (b)** According to the question, 'All but nine died'.

This statement means that 'All except nine died' i.e. nine sheeps remained alive and others died.

So, shepherd was left with 9 sheeps.

***Ex.* 04** John used to buy petrol at the rate of ₹ 80 per litre till last month. Now he buys it at the rate of ₹ 85 per litre. By what percentage did the petrol price increase as compared to last month? « SSC (10+2) 2020

(a) 6.25% (b) 8.35% (c) 5.5% (d) 10%

***Solution* (a)** Price increased = 85 − 80 = ₹ 5

$\therefore$ Percentage increased $= \frac{5}{80} \times 100 = 6.25\%$

***Ex.* 05** In an exam of 80 questions, a correct answer is given 1 mark, a wrong answer is given −1 mark and if a question is not attempted there are zero marks. If a student attempted only 80% of the questions and got 32 marks, then how many questions did he answer correctly? « SSC CGL 2020

(a) 48 (b) 16 (c) 56 (d) 32

***Solution* (a)** Question attempted = 80% of 80

$= \frac{80 \times 80}{100} = 64$

Now, let the number of questions answered correctly $= x$

$\therefore$ Number of questions answered wrongly $= 64 - x$

According to the question,

$$x \times 1 + (64 - x)x - 1 = 32$$

$$x - 64 + x = 32$$

$$\Rightarrow \quad 2x = 64 + 32 \Rightarrow 2x = 96$$

$$\therefore \quad x = 48$$

$\therefore$ Number of questions answered correctly = 48

***Ex.* 06** How many odd numbered pages are there in a book of 1089 pages?

(a) 542 (b) 545 (c) 544 (d) 546

***Solution* (b)** Odd pages in the book are 1, 3, 5, 7, 9, ... 1089.

Here, every alternate page is odd starting from 1. So, if the total number of pages was an even numbered, then the half number of pages will be odd numbered and half will be even. But, here the total number of pages is odd.

So, required number of pages

$$= \frac{\text{Total number of pages} + 1}{2}$$

$$= \frac{1089 + 1}{2} = \frac{1090}{2} = 545$$

Ex. 07 At the end of a business conference all the ten people present, shake hands with each other only once. How many handshakes were there altogether? « UKPSC Asst. conservator of Forest 2019

(a) 20 (b) 45 (c) 55 (d) 90

Solution (b) Clearly, the total number of hand shakes

$= 9 + 8 + 7 + 6 + 5 + 4 + 3 + 2 + 1 = 45$

It can also be calculated with the help of formula.

Total number of handshakes $= \frac{n(n-1)}{2}$

where, n = number of people

Total number of handshakes $= \frac{10\,(10-1)}{2}$

$= \frac{10 \times 9}{2} = \frac{90}{2} = 45$

Ex. 08 There are deer and peacocks in a zoo. By counting heads they are 80. The number of their legs is 200. How many peacocks are there? « SSC (CGL) 2015

(a) 60 (b) 50 (c) 20 (d) 30

Solution (a) Assuming deer = d and peacock = p

Head $\rightarrow d + p = 80 \xrightarrow{\times 4} 4d + 4p = 320$ ...(i)

Legs $\rightarrow 4d + 2p = 200 \rightarrow 4d + 2p = 200$ ...(ii)

(As, a deer has 4 legs and a peacock has 2 legs)

From subtracting Eq. (ii) from Eq. (i), we get

$2p = 120 \Rightarrow p = \frac{120}{2} = 60$

Ex. 09 In a music class, 12 students can play flute, 11 can play guitar and 10 can play violin. 6 students can play flute as well as guitar and 3 out of these can also play violin. 3 students can play only guitar and 4 students can play only violin. How many students can play only flute? « UPSSSC (Gram Panchayat Adhikari) 2018

(a) 4 (b) 5 (c) 6 (d) 7

Solution (b) According to the given information,

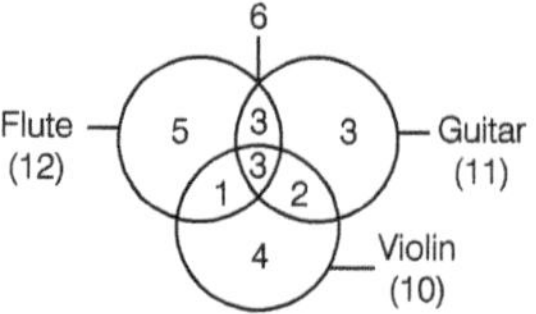

Students who can play only Guitar and Violin

$= 11 - (3 + 3 + 3) = 11 - 9 = 2$

Students who can play only Flute and Guitar

$= 10 - (3 + 2 + 4) = 10 - 9 = 1$

$\therefore$ Students who can play only Flute $= 12 - (3 + 3 + 1)$

$= 12 - 7 = 5$

Ex. 10 A survey of 100 candidates with respect to their choice of icecream flavour-vanilla, chocolate and strawberry produced the following information. 50 candidates like vanilla, 43 like chocolate, 28 like strawberry, 13 like vanilla and chocolate, 11 like chocolate and strawberry, 12 like strawberry and vanilla and 5 like all the three flavours. How many candidates like chocolate and strawberry, but not vanilla? « UPSSSC Junior Assistant 2020

(a) 24 (b) 10 (c) 32 (d) 6

Solution (d) According to the given information,

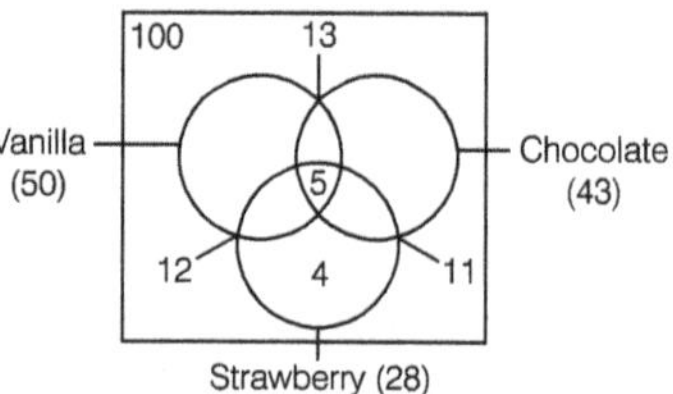

Since, number of candidates who like chocolate and strawberry = 11

And, number of candidates who like all the three flavours (chocolate, vanilla, strawberry) = 5

$\therefore$ Number of candidates who like chocolate and strawberry, but not vanilla = 11 − 5 = 6

Practice / CORNER

1. The sum of all the 3-digit numbers which are formed by the digits 1, 2 and 3 without repetition of digits, is « CGPSC 2014

(a) 1233 (b) 1321 (c) 1323 (d) 1332
(e) None of these

2. A florist had 133 roses. She sold 5/7 of them. How many roses had she left? « SSC Constable (GD) 2015

(a) 58 (b) 38 (c) 57 (d) 19

3. '4 is even and 8 is odd'. What is the truth value of this? « UPSSSC Lower Subordinate 2015

(a) Given statement is true
(b) Given statements is false
(c) 32
(d) Cannot be determined

4. At a party, the number of girls is half the number of boys. After an hours, five boys leave the party and three girls join the party. How many people were present at the party an hour before? « SSC CGL 2018

(a) 16 (b) 8 (c) 24 (d) 22

5. There are some balls of Red, Green and Yellow colour lying on a table. There are as many Red balls as there are Yellow balls. There are twice as many Yellow balls as there are Green ones. The number of Red balls is « UPSSSC Lower Subordinate, 2016

(a) is equal to the sum of Yellow and Green balls
(b) Is double the number of Green balls
(c) is equal to Yellow balls minus Green balls
(d) Cannot be ascertained

6. Two horses A and B run at a speed of 3 : 2 ratio in the first lap; during the second lap the ratio differs by 4 : 7; during the third lap the ratio differs by 8:9. What is the difference in ratio of speed altogether between the two horses? « SSC (CPO) 2015

(a) 4 (b) 1 (c) 3 (d) 2

7. The number of students in an art class is increasing month after month as follows. Find the number of students in June from the following information.

Month	Number of students
January	1
February	2
March	4
April	7
May	11
June	?

« SSC Constable (GD) 2015

(a) 16 (b) 13 (c) 15 (d) 14

8. The heights of three towers are in the ratio 5 : 6 : 7. If a spider takes 15 min to climb the smallest tower, how much time will it take to climb the highest one? « SSC CGL 2015

(a) 15 min (b) 18 min
(c) 21 min (d) 54 min

9. The weights of 4 boxes are 80, 60, 90 and 70 kg. Which of the following cannot be the total weight, in kilograms, of any combination of these boxes and in a combination a box can be used only once.

(a) 300 (b) 230 (c) 220 (d) 290

10. The price of onions is shown below for every fiftheen days. Find the price in the 3rd week of February.

Period	Dec. 1st week	Dec. 3rd week	Jan. 1st week	Jan. 3rd week	Feb. 1st week	Feb. 3rd week
Price	20	60	40	120	100	?

« UPSSSC Lower Subordinate 2017

(a) 140 (b) 300 (c) 180 (d) 320

11. 8 people are present in a meeting. In the end of meeting all people shake hand to each other. Find the number of handshakes at the end of a meeting?

(a) 56 (b) 28 (c) 48 (d) 64

12. A person is given 1 rupee for shooting at the target and if he misses, then he has to give 1 rupee. If he gets 30 rupees for 100 chances then how many chances did he miss?

(a) 25 (b) 35 (c) 40 (d) 45

13. There were a total of 10 bicycles and tricycles. If the total number of wheels was 24, how many tricycles were there?

(a) 2 (b) 6 (c) 18 (d) 4

14. P is greater than Q by 60% and greater than R by 30%. The ratio of Q and R is « WBPSC 2018

(a) 1 : 2 (b) 2 : 1 (c) 13 : 16 (d) 16 : 13

15. In a group of cows and hens, the number of legs are 14 more than twice the number of heads. Find the number of cows?

(a) 5 (b) 7 (c) 10 (d) 12

16. If it takes two workers, working separately but at the same speed, 2 h and 40 min to complete a particular task about how long will it take one worker, working at the same speed, to complete the same task alone?

(a) 1 h 20 min (b) 4 h 40 min
(c) 5 h (d) 5 h 20 min

17. Sonu and his friend Rahul went for shopping. Sonu had ₹ 500 with him while Rahul had ₹ 240. Sonu spent twice as much as Rahul on shopping. Now, Sonu has three times as much money as is left with Rahul. How much money did Sonu spend?

(a) ₹ 220 (b) ₹ 60 (c) ₹ 440 (d) ₹ 120

18. A man has ₹ 480 in the denominations of one-rupee notes, five-rupee notes and ten-rupees notes. The number of notes of each denomination is equal. What is the total number of notes that he has?

(a) 45 (b) 60 (c) 75 (d) 90

19. In a company, 60% workers are males. If the number of female workers in the company is 800, what is the number of male workers in the company? « CLAT-2017

(a) 1600 (b) 1400
(c) 1900 (d) 1200

20. The flowers kept in a basket doubles in every one minute. If the basket gets completely filled by flowers in 30 min, then in how many minutes $\frac{1}{4}$ th of the basket was filled with flowers?

(a) 15 min (b) 28 min (c) $\frac{15}{2}$ min (d) $\frac{45}{2}$ min

21. Some birds are sitting on two branches A and B. If one bird of the branch A fly away and sit on branch B, then the number of birds on both the branches will become equal. But if a bird from branch B flies and sits on the branch A then the number of birds on branch A is double of branch B. What number of birds were sitting on branch A at the beginning?

(a) 3 (b) 4 (c) 5 (d) 7

22. A factory produced 1858509 cassettes in the month of January, 7623 more cassettes in the month of February and owing to short supply of electricity produced 25838 less cassettes in March than in February. Find the total production in all? « RRB NTPC (Phase-1) 2016

(a) 5557312 (b) 5983245
(c) 5564935 (d) 5608988

23. Which number will be in the middle if the following numbers are arranged in descending order? 4456, 4465, 4655, 4665, 4565 « RRB NTPC (Phase-1) 2016

(a) 4456 (b) 4465 (c) 4565 (d) 4655

24. Two persons A and B get the same salary. Their basic pay are different. The allowances of A and B are 65% and 80% of the basic pay respectively. What is the ratio of the basic pay?

(a) 17 : 15 (b) 7 : 5
(c) 11 : 10 (d) 12 : 11

25. A train is running 3 min late and further being late 3 s/min. Find how long this train will be delayed one hour?

(a) 1140 min (b) 1150 min
(c) 1160 min (d) 1200 min

26. A machine cuts the wooden log into 10 m pieces and take 6 s to cut a 10 m piece. Find the time to cut the 3 km long wooden log into pieces?

(a) 174 s (b) 180 s
(c) 1794 s (d) 1800 s

27. A tailor has to cut 10 shirt pieces of equal length from a roll of fabric. He cuts at the rate of 45 shirt pieces in a minute. How many rolls would be cut in 24 min?

(a) 120 (b) 108
(c) 84 (d) 72

28. In a zoo, there are rabbits and pigeons. If heads are counted, there are 200 heads and if legs are counted there are 580 legs. How many pigeons are there?

(a) 90 (b) 100
(c) 110 (d) 120

29. In a plane, line X is perpendicular to line Y and parallel to line Z, line U is perpendicular to both lines V and W, line X is perpendicular to line V. Which one of the following statement is correct?

(a) Z, U and W are parallel.
(b) X, V and Y are parallel.
(c) Z, V and U are all perpendicular to W.
(d) Y, V and W are parallel.

30. Marry said, "a number which I am thinking is divisible by 2 or 3." This statement is false, if the number which I am thinking.

(a) 6 (b) 8 (c) 11 (d) 15

31. A father invites some boys and girls on his son's birthday. The number of boys is less than 2 the number of girls. Father gives ₹ 10 to boys and ₹ 20 to girls as a gift. If total amount spent is ₹ 280, find the number of boys.

(a) 8 (b) 10 (c) 12 (d) 14

32. 5 students A, B, C, D and E are present in an examination. If C got 5 marks less than B, D got 10 marks more than B and 20 marks less than A and E got 22 marks more than B and B got 40 marks. Then, how many marks did A get?

(a) 52 (b) 60 (c) 64 (d) 70

33. A group has some cows, bulls and 45 hens. Every 15 animals are herded by a herdsman. The number of bulls are twice the number of cows. If total numbers of heads is 186 less than total number of legs (with herdsman). Find the number of herdsmen?

(a) 6 (b) 8 (c) 10 (d) 12

34. Consider the following venn-diagram.

Math
50
12
12
5
English
30
10
75
Hindi

500 candidates appeared in an examination comprising of tests in English, Hindi and Mathematics. The diagram gives the number of candidates who failed in different tests. What is the percentage of the candidates who failed in atleast two subject?

(a) 0.078 (b) 1.0
(c) 6.8 (d) 7.8

35. According to a survey report, 62% people watch news on doordarshan, 44% people read newspaper and 24% people read newspaper and watch doordarshan both. How many percentage of people neither read newspaper nor watch doordarshan.

(a) 8% (b) 18%
(c) 10% (d) 0%

DIRECTIONS ~ (Q. Nos. 36-38) *Consider the following information and answer the questions based on it.*

« RRB NTPC (Phase-1) 2016

In a group of 75 students, 12 like only cabbage, 15 like only cauliflower, 21 like only carrot, 12 like both carrot and cabbage, 13 like only capsicum and 2 like both capsicum and cauliflower.

36. The difference between the people who like carrot and cauliflower is

(a) 6 (b) 18 (c) 16 (d) 4

37. What is the percentage of students that do not like cabbage?

(a) 16 (b) 32
(c) 24 (d) 68

38. How many students like only one vegetable?

(a) 60 (b) 61 (c) 65 (d) 71

DIRECTIONS ~ (Q. Nos. 39-41) *Read the following information and answer the following questions.*

« RRB NTPC (Phase-1) 2016

In a class of 40 students, 28 can speak Tamil and 30 can speak Telugu. All students can speak at least one of the two languages.

39. Find the number of students who can speak only Tamil.

(a) 8 (b)10
(c) 12 (d) 14

40. Find the minimum number of students who can speak both Tamil and Telugu.

(a) 12 (b) 15
(c) 18 (d) 22

41. Find the number of persons who can speak only Telugu?

(a) 8 (b) 10
(c) 12 (d) 14

42. A travel agent surveyed 100 people to find out how many of them had visited the cities of Mumbai and Bengaluru. 31 people had visited Mumbai, 26 people had visited Bengaluru and 12 people had visited both cities. Find the number of people who had visited neither Mumbai nor Bengaluru.
« UPSSSC Junior Assistant 2020

(a) 12 (b) 55 (c) 19 (d) 45

43. A survey of 500 TV viewers produced the following information. 285 viewers watch football games, 195 viewers watch hockey games, 115 viewers watch basketball game, 45 viewers watch football and basketball games, 70 viewers watch football and hockey games, 50 viewers watch hockey and basketball games and 50 viewers do not watch any of three games. How many viewers watch exactly one of the three games? « UPSSSC Junior Assistant 2020

(a) 440 (b) 365
(c) 205 (d) 325

44. In an airline, hot drinks and iced tea were served to 120 passengers. 75 passengers enjoyed hot drinks and 62 enjoyed iced tea. If 40 enjoyed both, then how many passengers enjoyed none of the beverages?
« UPSSSC Junior Assistant 2020

(a) 15 (b) 12
(c) 23 (d) 25

Answers / WITH EXPLANATIONS

1. (*d*) The 3-digit numbers which are formed by digits 1, 2 and 3 without repetition of digits are given below
$312 + 321 + 123 + 231 + 132 + 213 = 1332$

2. (*b*) Florist sold $= 133 \times \frac{5}{7} = 95$ roses
$\therefore$ Remaining roses $= 133 - 95 = 38$

3. (*b*) 4 is even but 8 is not odd.
So, the statement is false.

4. (*c*) Let the number of boys $= 2x$
$\therefore$ Number of girls $= x$
$\therefore$ Total number of persons $= 2x + x = 3x$
So, the total number of persons must be divided by 3.
$\therefore$ From the given alternatives, only 24 is divided by 3.
Hence, 24 people were present at the party an hour before.

5. (*b*) Let the number of Green balls $= x$
$\therefore$ Number of Yellow balls $= 2x$
$\therefore$ Number of Red balls $= 2x$
It is clear from above that the number of Red balls is twice the number of Green balls.

6. (*c*) Difference between ratio of speed of both horses
$= (2 + 7 + 9) - (3 + 4 + 8)$
$= 18 - 15 = 3$
$\Rightarrow$ Required difference = 3

7. (*a*) January $\Rightarrow 1$
February $\Rightarrow 1 + 1 = 2$
March $\Rightarrow 2 + 2 = 4$
April $\Rightarrow 4 + 3 = 7$
May $\Rightarrow 7 + 4 = 11$
$\therefore$ June $\Rightarrow 11 + 5 = 16$

8. (*c*) Spider climbs $5x$ units 15 min
$\therefore$ Spider will climb $7x$ units in
$\frac{15}{5} \times 7 = 21$ min

9. (*d*) For option (a)
$= 80 + 60 + 90 + 70$
$= 300$
For option (b) $= 80 + 60 + 90 = 230$
For option (c) $= 60 + 90 + 70 = 220$
And in option (d) the sum of any numbers given in option is 290.
So, option (d) cannot be the total weight, in kg, of any combination of these boxes.

10. (*b*) In each month the price of onions in 3rd week in 3 times to the price of onions in 1st week.
So, the price of onions in 3rd week of Feb $= 100 \times 3 = 300$

11. (*b*) Number of handshakes $= \frac{n(n-1)}{2}$
Here, $n = 8$
$\therefore$ Required number of handshakes
$= \frac{8(8-1)}{2}$
$= \frac{8 \times 7}{2} = 28$

12. (*b*) Assuming the number of chances missed by the person be x.
Number of chances to shoot the target $= 100 - x$
According to the question,
$(100 - x) - x = 30$
$\Rightarrow 100 - 2x = 30$
$\Rightarrow 2x = 100 - 30 = 70$
$x = \frac{70}{2} = 35$

13. (*d*) Let the required number of tricycles $= x$
Then, the number of bicycles $= 10 - x$
According to the question,
$3x + 2(10 - x) = 24$
[$\because$ Tricycles = 3 wheels; Bicycle = 2 wheels]
$\Rightarrow x + 20 = 24$
$\Rightarrow x = 4$
Therefore, the required number of tricycles $= x = 4$

14. (*c*) Given, P = 160% of Q = 130% of R
$\Rightarrow$ 160% of Q = 130% of R
$\Rightarrow Q \times \frac{160}{100} = R \times \frac{130}{100}$
$\Rightarrow Q \times 16 = R \times 13$
$\Rightarrow \frac{Q}{R} = \frac{13}{16}$
$\Rightarrow Q : R = 13 : 16$

15. (*b*) Let the number of hens be x and cows be y.
Number of legs in the group $= 2x + 4y$
Number of heads in the group $= x + y$
According to the question,
legs = 2 (heads) + 14
$2x + 4y = 2(x + y) + 14$
$\Rightarrow 2x + 4y = 2x + 2y + 14$
$\Rightarrow 2x - 2x + 4y - 2y = 14$
$\Rightarrow 2y = 14$
$y = 7$
(therefore number of cows = 7)

16. (*d*) Given that the two workers, working separately but at the same speed takes 2 h and 40 min to complete a particular task.
Then, one worker, working at the same speed, to complete the same task will take double time i.e. 5 h 20 min.

17. (*c*) Let expenditure of Rahul = ₹x
and expenditure of Sonu = ₹ $2x$
Now, $500 - 2x = 3(240 - x)$

$\Rightarrow \quad 500 - 2x = 720 - 3x$

$\Rightarrow \quad x = ₹\,220$

$\therefore$ Expenditure of Sonu $= 2x = ₹440$

18. (*d*) Let the number of notes of each denomination $= x$

Total amount = 480

$x + 5x + 10x = 480$

$\Rightarrow \quad 16x = 480$

$\Rightarrow \quad x = 30$

So, required total number of notes

$= x + x + x$

[number of notes of each denomination is equal]

$\Rightarrow 3x \Rightarrow 3 \times 30 \Rightarrow 90$

19. (*d*) Let the total number of workers $= x$

Given, number of female workers = 800

Then, according to the question,

$\frac{60}{100}$ of $x + 800 = x$

$\therefore \quad x - \frac{60x}{100} = 800$

$\Rightarrow \quad x = \frac{800}{0.4} = \frac{8000}{4} = 2000$

Number of male workers

$= \frac{60}{100} \times 2000 = 1200$

20. (*b*) $\because$ 30 min$\rightarrow$1 [Full]

$\therefore$ $(30-1)\text{min} \Rightarrow 29\text{ min} \rightarrow \frac{1}{2}$

$\therefore$ $(29-1)\text{min} \Rightarrow 28\text{ min} \rightarrow \frac{1}{4}$

Therefore, the expected time is 28 min.

21. (*d*) Assuming the number of birds on $A = x$ and $B = y$

In Ist stage, $x - 1 = y + 1$ ...(i)

In IInd stage, $x + 1 = 2(y - 1)$ ...(ii)

From Eqs. (i) and (ii), we get

$(x+1) = 2(x - 2 - 1)$

$\Rightarrow \quad x + 1 = 2(x - 3)$

$\Rightarrow \quad x + 1 = 2x - 6$

$\Rightarrow \quad 2x - x = 7$

$\Rightarrow \quad x = 7$

Therefore, total number of birds on branch '*A*' = 7.

22. (*c*) Production in January = 1858509

Production in February

$= 1858509 + 7623$

$= 1866132$

Production in March

$= 1866132 - 25838$

$= 1840294$

$\therefore$ Total production

$= 1858509 + 1866132 + 1840294$

$= 5564935$

23. (*c*) According to the question, arrangement of numbers in descending order

4665, 4655, 4565, 4465, 4456

$\therefore$ Number in middle = 4565

24. (*d*) Suppose basic pay of A = ₹ x

Basic pay of B = ₹ y

Ratio between basic pays

$\Rightarrow \quad \frac{x \times 165}{100} = \frac{y \times 180}{100}$

$\Rightarrow \quad \frac{x}{y} = \frac{180}{165}$

$= \frac{12}{11} = 12:11$

25. (*a*) Given, the train is running 3 min late. Therefore, to be delayed by one hour it has to be delayed $= 60 - 3$

$= 57$ min.

$\because$ The train is being late 3 sec or $\frac{3}{60}$ min in one minute.

$\therefore$ The train will be late by 57 min in

$= \frac{57 \times 1}{\frac{3}{60}} = \frac{57 \times 60}{3}$

$= 1140$ min

26. (*c*) The length of the wooden log = 3 km

$= 3 \times 1000 = 3000$ m

The length of the piece cut by machine = 10 m

$\therefore$ Total number of pieces cut by the machine $= \frac{3000}{10} = 300$

To cut 300 pieces the machine has to cut 299 pieces because in the last step when machine cut 299th piece then only one piece i.e. 300th piece will remain.

$\because$ Time required to cut a piece = 6 sec

$\therefore$ Time required to cut 299 pieces

$= 299 \times 6$

$= 1794$ sec

27. (*b*) Shirt pieces cut by the tailor in 24 min

$24 \times 45 = 1080$

$\because$ Number of shirt pieces in a roll = 10

$\therefore$ Required number of rolls $= \frac{1080}{10}$

$= 108$

28. (*c*) Let the number of rabbits is x and the number of pigeons is y.

According to the question,

$x + y = 200$ ...(i)

and $\quad 4x + 2y = 580$ ...(ii)

($\because$ A rabbit has 4 legs and a piegon has 2 legs)

or $\quad 2x + y = 290$ ...(iii)

From Eqs. (i) and (iii),

$x = 90$

and $\quad y = 110$

Hence, number of piegons = 110

29. (*d*) According to the question,

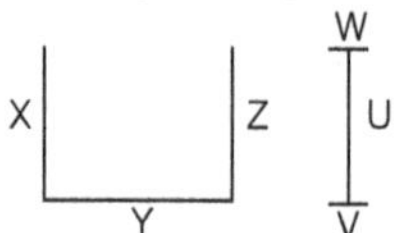

Clearly, Y, V and W are parallel.

30. (*c*) From the given options, number 6, 8 and 15 are divisible by either 2 or 3. Only number 11, is not divisible by 2 or 3.

Hence, the required number is 11.

31. (*a*) Let the number of girls $= x$

$\therefore$ Number of boys $= (x - 2)$

According to the question,

$(x-2) \times 10 + x \times 20 = 280$

$\Rightarrow \quad 10x - 20 + 20x = 280$

$\Rightarrow \quad 30x = 280 + 20$

$\Rightarrow \quad 30x = 300$

$\Rightarrow \quad x = 10$

$\therefore$ Number of boys $= 10 - 2 = 8$

32. (*d*) Given, B got = 40 marks

Then, C got = 40 − 5 = 35 marks

D got = 40 + 10 = 50 marks

A got = 50 + 20 = 70 marks

E got = 40 + 22 = 62 marks

Hence, it is clear from above that A got 70 marks in the examination.

33. (*a*) Let the number of cows be x, number of bulls be y and the number of herds man be z.

Then, according to the question,

$\frac{x + y + 45 + z}{16} = z$

$\Rightarrow \quad x + y + 45 = 16z - z$

$\Rightarrow \quad x + 2x + 45 = 15z \quad (\because y = 2x)$

$\Rightarrow \quad 3x + 45 = 15z$ ...(i)

and $(3x + z + 45)$

$= (4 \times 3x + 2 \times z + 2 \times 45) - 186$

$\Rightarrow \quad 15z + z = 12x + 2z + 90 - 186$

$\Rightarrow \quad 16z - 2z - 12x = -96$

$\Rightarrow \quad 14z - 12 \times \frac{(15z - 45)}{3} = -96$

$\Rightarrow \quad 14z - 4 \times (15z - 45) = -96$

$\Rightarrow \quad 14z - 60z + 180 = -96$

$\Rightarrow \quad -46z = -276$

$\therefore \quad z = 6$

Hence, it is clear from above that there are 6 herds man.

34. (*d*) According to the question,

Total number of candidates = 500

Candidates failed in Math and Hindi = 12

Candidates failed in Math and English = 12

Candidate failed in Hindi and English = 10

Candidates failed in three subjects = 5

So, number of candidates who failed in atleast two subjects

$= 12 + 12 + 10 + 5 = 39$

$\therefore$ Percent candidates failed in atleast two subjects $= \frac{39}{500} \times 100$

$= \frac{39}{5} = 7.8$

35. (*b*)

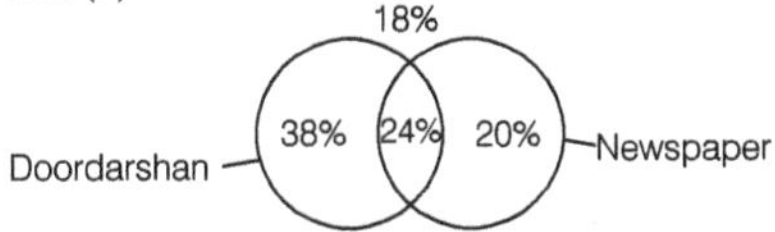

Total number of people who watch doordarshan and who read newspaper $(A \cup B)$

$= A + B - (A \cap B)$

$= 62 + 44 - 24 = 82\%$

Hence, percentage of people who neither read newspaper nor watch doordarshan = 100 − 82 = 18%

Solution (Q. Nos. 36-38)

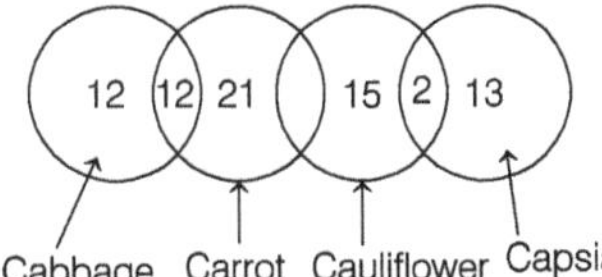

36. (*c*) Required difference

$= (12 + 21) - (15 + 2)$

$= 33 - 17 = 16$

37. (*d*) Students who do not like cabbage

$= 75 - (12 + 12) = 51$

$\therefore$ Required percent $= \frac{51}{75} \times 100$

$= 68\%$

38. (*b*) Number of students who like only one vegetable

$= 12 + 21 + 15 + 13 = 61$

Solutions (Q. Nos. 39-41) *According to the question,*

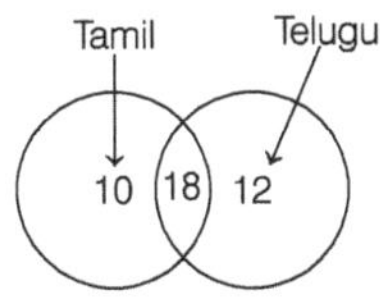

Let x students can speak both Tamil and Telugu.

So, only Tamil = $28 - x$

Only Telugu = $30 - x$

According to the question,

$\Rightarrow (28 - x) + (30 - x) + x = 40$

$\Rightarrow \quad 58 - x = 40$

$x = 18$

39. (*b*) Number of students who can speak only Tamil $= 28 - x = 28 - 18 = 10$

40. (*c*) Students who can speak both Tamil and Telugu $x \Rightarrow 18$.

41. (*c*) Number of students who can speak only Telugu $30 - 18 \Rightarrow 12$.

42. (*b*) Number of people who visited Mumbai = 31

Number of people who visited Bengaluru = 26

Number of people who visited both cities = 12

And, total number of people = 100

$\therefore$ Number of people who visited neither Mumbai nor Bengaluru

$= 100 - \{(31 + 26) - 12\}$

$= 100 - 57 + 12$

$= 112 - 57 = 55$

43. (*d*) Total number of people,

$n(P) = 500$

People who watch Basketball, $n(B) = 115$

People who watch Football, $n(F) = 285$

People who watch Hockey, $n(H) = 195$

People who watch Basketball and Hockey, $n(B \cap H) = 50$.

People who watch Football and Hockey, $n(H \cap F) = 70$

People who watch Basketball and Football, $n(B \cap F) = 45$

People who do not watch any games, $n(H \cup B \cup F) = 50$

Now,

$n(H \cup B \cup F) = n(P) - n(H \cup B \cup F)'$

$\Rightarrow n(H \cup B \cup F) = n(P) - [n(H) + n(B) + n(F) - n(H \cap B) - n(H \cap F) - n(B \cap F) + n(H \cap B \cap F)]$

$\Rightarrow 50 = 500 - [285 + 195 + 115 - 70 - 50 - 45 + n(H \cap B \cap F)]$

$\Rightarrow 50 = 500 - 430 - n(H \cap B \cap F)$

$\Rightarrow n(H \cap B \cap F) = 70 - 50 = 20$

$\therefore$ 20 people watch all three games.

Number of people who only watch Football $= 285 - (50 + 20 + 25) = 190$.

Number of people who only watch Hockey

$= 195 - (50 + 20 + 30)$

$= 195 - 100 = 95$

Number of people who only watch Basketball

$= 115 - (25 + 20 + 30)$

$= 115 - 75 = 40$

$\therefore$ Number of people who watch exactly one of the three games

$= 190 + 95 + 40 = 325$

44. (*c*) Total passenger $n(P) = 120$

Number of passenger enjoyed hot drinks $n(H) = 75$

Number of passenger enjoyed iced tea $n(I) = 62$

Number of passenger who enjoyed both $n(I \cap H) = 40$

Number of passenger who enjoyed at least one beverage

$n(H \cup I) = n(H) + n(I) - n(H \cap I)$

$= 75 + 62 - 40$

$= 97$

$\therefore$ Number of passenger enjoyed none of the beverages

$= n(P) - n(H \cap I)$

$= 120 - 97 = 23$

CHAPTER / 16

Problems Based on Ages

Age is defined as a period of time that a person has lived or a thing has existed. Age is measured in months, years, decades and so on.

Problems based on ages generally consist of information of ages of two or more persons and a relation between their ages in present/future/past. Using the information, it is asked to calculate the ages of one or more persons in present/future/past.

Important Formulas

Given below are a few formulas related to problems based on ages which may help to answer the questions quicker and also get a better idea of the concept.

1. Let the current age to be x, then the age after n yr will be $(x+n)$ yr.
2. Let the current age to be x, then the age before n yr will be $(x-n)$ yr.
3. If the age is given in the form of ratio, for example P : Q. Then, the age shall be considered as Px and Qx.
4. Let the current age to be x, then n times the current age will be $(x \times n)$ yr.
5. Let the current age to be x, then $\frac{1}{n}$ of the age will be $\frac{x}{n}$ yr.

Ex 01 The current age of Savan is four times the age of Akshan. 10 yr later from now, Savan's age will be twice the age of Akshan. What is Savan's current age? « SSC CGL 2018

(a) 30 yr (b) 20 yr
(c) 10 yr (d) 5 yr

Solution (b) Let the present age of Akshan = x yr

$\therefore$ Present age of Savan = $4x$ yr

According to the question, 10 yr later,

$$4x + 10 = 2(x + 10)$$
$$\Rightarrow 4x + 10 = 2x + 20$$
$$\Rightarrow 2x = 10 \Rightarrow x = 5$$

$\therefore$ Present age of Savan = $4 \times 5 = 20$ yr

Ex 02 The difference of the ages of Rohit and Axar is 12 yr. The ratio of their ages is 3 : 5. The age of Axar is « WBCS 2018

(a) 32 yr (b) 24 yr
(c) 28 yr (d) 30 yr

Solution (d) Let present ages of Rohit and Axar be $3x$ and $5x$, respectively.

According to the question, $5x - 3x = 12$

$$\Rightarrow 2x = 12 \Rightarrow x = 6$$

$\therefore$ The age of Axar = $5x = 5 \times 6 = 30$ yr

Ex 03 Ram is 4 times his son's age today. Five years later, hence Ram will be thrice his son's age. Find their current ages? « RRB NTPC 2016

(A) 60, 15 (B) 40, 10 (C) 20, 5 (D) 32, 8
(a) B (b) D (c) A (d) C

Solution (a) Let present age of Ram be '$4a$' yr.

$\therefore$ Present age of his son = $\frac{4a}{4} = a$ yr

According to the question,

$$4a + 5 = 3(a + 5)$$
$$\Rightarrow 4a + 5 = 3a + 15 \text{ or } a = 10$$

Hence, the present age of Ram and his son are 40 yr and 10 yr, respectively.

Ex 04 Maithri is aged three times more than her son Vishajith. After 8 yr she would be $2\frac{1}{2}$ times Vishajith's age. After further 8 yr, how many times would she be of Vishajith's age? « RRB Group D 2018

(a) 3 (b) $\frac{4}{5}$ (c) $\frac{11}{5}$ (d) 2

Solution (d) Let present age of Vishajith be 'a' yr.

$\therefore$ Present age of Maithri = $a + 3a = 4a$ yr

According to the question,

$$4a + 8 = \frac{5}{2}(a + 8) \Rightarrow 8a + 16 = 5a + 40$$
$$\Rightarrow a = \frac{24}{3} = 8$$

$\therefore$ Present age of Vishajith = 8 yr

and present age of Maithri = 32 yr

$\therefore$ Required number = $\frac{32 + 16}{8 + 16} = \frac{48}{24} = 2$ times

Ex 05 Abhay's age after 6 yr will be three-seventh of his father's age. Ten years ago, the ratio of their ages was 1 : 5. What is Abhay's father's age at present? « RRB Group D 2018

(a) 50 yr (b) 53 yr (c) 51 yr (d) 55 yr

Solution (a) Let the ages of Abhay and his father 10 yr ago be x and $5x$ yr respectively. Then,

Abhay's age after 6 yr $= (x + 10) + 6 = (x + 16)$ yr

Father's age after 6 yr $= (5x + 10) + 6 = (5x + 16)$ yr

$$\therefore \quad (x + 16) = \frac{3}{7}(5x + 16)$$

$$\Rightarrow \quad 7(x + 16) = 3(5x + 16)$$

$$\Rightarrow \quad 7x + 112 = 15x + 48$$

$$\Rightarrow \quad 8x = 64$$

$$\Rightarrow \quad x = 8$$

$\therefore$ Father's present age $= 5x + 10 = 50$ yr

Ex 06 In 2002, Meenu's age was one-third of the age of Meera, whereas in 2010, Meenu's age was half the age of Meera. What is Meenu's year of birth? « UPSC CSAT 2019

(a) 1992 (b) 1994
(c) 1996 (d) 1998

Solution (b) Let in 2002, Meenu's age be x and Meera's age be y.

$$\therefore \quad x = \frac{1}{3}y \quad \text{...(i)}$$

In 2010, i.e. after 8 yr

$$(x + 8) = \frac{1}{2}(y + 8)$$

$$\Rightarrow \quad x + 8 = \frac{1}{2}y + 4$$

$$\Rightarrow \quad x - \frac{1}{2}y = -4$$

Now, put $y = 3x$ from Eq. (i),

$$x - \frac{3x}{2} = -4 \Rightarrow -\frac{x}{2} = -4$$

$$\Rightarrow \quad x = 8$$

$\therefore$ In 2002, Meenu's age was 8 yr.

$\therefore$ Meenu's year of birth is $(2002 - 8) = 1994$

Ex 07 10 yr ago, a father's age was $3\frac{1}{2}$ times that of his son and 10 yr from now, the father's age will be $2\frac{1}{4}$ times that of the son. What will be the sum of the ages of the father and the son at present? « SSC CGL 2018

(a) 100 yr (b) 110 yr (c) 115 yr (d) 120 yr

Solution (b) Let the present ages of father and son be x yr and y yr respectively.

Now, according to question 10 yr ago

$$x - 10 = 3\frac{1}{2}(y - 10)$$

$$\Rightarrow \quad x - 10 = \frac{7}{2}(y - 10)$$

$$\Rightarrow \quad 2x - 20 = 7y - 70$$

$$2x - 7y = -50 \quad \text{...(i)}$$

Now, according to question, after 10 yr

$$x + 10 = 2\frac{1}{4}(y + 10)$$

$$\Rightarrow \quad x + 10 = \frac{9}{4}(y + 10)$$

$$\Rightarrow \quad 4x + 40 = 9y + 90$$

$$\Rightarrow \quad 4x - 9y = 50 \quad \text{...(ii)}$$

Multiplying Eq. (i) by 2 – Eq. (ii)

We get, $-5y = -150$

$\Rightarrow$ $y = 30$ yr

Now put $y = 30$ in Eq. (i),

$$2x - 210 = -50$$

$$2x = 160$$

$$\Rightarrow \quad x = 80 \text{ yr}$$

$\therefore$ The sum of present ages of son and father

$= x + y = 80 + 30 = 110$ yr

Practice / CORNER 16.1

1. 12 yr old Sami is three times as old as his brother Vinay. How old will Sami be when he is twice as old as Vinay? « Delhi Police (SI and ASI) 2016

(a) 14 yr (b) 16 yr
(c) 20 yr (d) 18 yr

2. The sum of the ages of 4 children born at the intervals of 4 yr is 48. Find the age of the youngest child. « RRB NTPC (Phase-1) 2016

(a) 4 yr (b) 5 yr
(c) 6 yr (d) 7 yr

3. The sum of ages of mother, daughter and son is 87 yr. What will be the sum of their ages after 8 yr? « SSC CHSL DEO & LDC 2015

(a) 101 (b) 110
(c) 111 (d) 105

4. The present ages of Vikas and Sujit are in the ratio of 5 : 4 respectively. Three years hence, the ratio of their ages will become 11 : 9 respectively. What is Sujit's present age in years? « UPSSSC Lower Subordinate II 2017

(a) 6 (b) 24 (c) 18 (d) 27

5. A person is 4 yr elder than his wife and his age is four times the age of his son. 4 yr hence his son's age will be 16 yr, then what is the present age of his mother?

(a) 48 yr (b) 45 yr
(c) 44 yr (d) 42 yr

6. At the time of my birth, my mother's age was 23 yr. After 6 yr, my sister was born, at that time my father's age is 34 yr. What is the difference between the ages of my father and mother? « UPSSSC Forest Guard 2015

(a) 5 yr (b) 6 yr (c) 8 yr (d) 11 yr

7. The average of age of three boys is 35 yr and the ratio of their ages is 3 : 5 : 7. What is the age of youngest boy?
« UPSSSC Combined Medical Service 2015
(a) 15 yr (b) 18 yr
(c) 21 yr (d) 12 yr

8. Jai and his father has an age difference of 35 yr now. After 5 yr the sum of their age is 135. What will be the age of Jai and his father after 12 yr from now?
(a) 51 and 85 (b) 52 and 87
(c) 40 and 75 (d) 45 and 70

9. Adam who is 20 yr old is 4 times as old as Mary. What will be Mary's age when Adam is twice as old as her?
« SSC CHSL DEO & LDC PA/SA 2015
(a) 35 yr (b) 15 yr
(c) 30 yr (d) 17 yr

10. A was twice as old as B, two yr ago. If the difference in their ages be 2 yr, find A's age.
« SSC CHSL DEO & LDC & PA/SA 2015
(a) 6 (b) 8 (c) 10 (d) 4

11. Mani is double the age of Prabhu. Ramona is half the age of Prabhu. If Mani is sixty year old, find out the age of Ramona. « SSC (10+2) Nov. 2014
(a) 20 (b) 15
(c) 10 (d) 24

12. Praveen is twice as old as Roopa and 6 yr older than Deepak. If Deepak is 12 yr, how old is Roopa?
« SSC Stenographer Sep. 2014
(a) 9 (b) 8 (c) 11 (d) 6

13. Govind is 48 yr old. He is twice as old as his son Prem is now. How old was Prem seven years before?
« SSC CPO 2014
(a) 16 (b) 17
(c) 13 (d) 18

14. Mr. Mani's age is 47 yr and John's age is 13 yr. In how many years will Mr. Mani's age be double of John's age?
(a) 20 yr (b) 21 yr
(c) 10 yr (d) 15 yr

15. The ratio of the present ages of Sunita and Vinita is 4 : 5. Six years, hence the ratio of their ages will be 14 : 17. What will be the ratio of their ages 12 yr hence?
(a) 15 : 19 (b) 13 : 45
(c) 13 : 15 (d) 16 : 19

16. Mahesh is 60 yr old. Ram is 5 yr junior to Mahesh and 4 yr senior to Raju. The youngest brother of Raju is Babu and he is 6 yr junior to him. What is the age difference between Mahesh and Babu?
(a) 18 (b) 15
(c) 13 (d) 06

17. Nikhil is 8 yr younger than his brother Rohan. How old will Rohan be when he is twice as old as Nikhil?
(a) 1 (b) 6
(c) 8 (d) 16

18. Rahim and his uncle difference in their ages by 30 yr. After 7 yr, if the sum of their ages is 66, what will be the age of his uncle? « SSC (10 + 2) 2013
(a) 51 (b) 49 (c) 39 (d) 41

19. Sita got married 6 yr ago. Sita's present age is $1\frac{1}{4}$ times her age at the time of marriage. Sita's son's age is 1/6 times her present age. Her son's age (in yr) is
(a) 5 (b) 2 (c) 3 (d) 4

20. Amit was born 5 yr before Rakesh. Rakesh is 3 yr younger to Anil. If Amit is now 17 yr old, how old is Anil?
(a) 8 yr (b) 12 yr
(c) 15 yr (d) 19 yr

21. 20 yr ago, Antony's age was 1/2 of what his age now is. What is the age now?
(a) 20 yr (b) 40 yr
(c) 35 yr (d) 30 yr

22. Neela is now three times as old as her daughter Leela. 10 yr back, Neela was five times as old as Leela. The age of Leela is « SSC (10+2) 2012
(a) 15 (b) 25 (c) 30 (d) 20

23. The average age of husband, wife and their child 3 yr ago was 27 yr and that of wife and the child 5 yr ago was 20 yr. The present age of husband is « SSC (10+2) 2012
(a) 40 yr (b) 50 yr
(c) 45 yr (d) 35 yr

24. A said to B, "When I was of your age, my age was twice as old as your age at that time. If the sum of their ages is 63 yr, then what is the present age of A?
« UPSSSC Junior Assistant 2015
(a) 45 yr (b) 18 yr
(c) 28 yr (d) 36 yr

25. A father's age is now three times that of his elder daughter. 5 yr back his age was eight times that of his younger daughter. If the difference of age of the two daughters is 5 yr, what is the age of the father now?
(a) 55 (b) 50 (c) 60 (d) 45

26. A person's present age is two-fifth of the age of his mother. After 8 yr, he will be one-half of the age of his mother. How old is the mother at present?
« SSC (10+2) 2012
(a) 40 yr (b) 48 yr (c) 32 yr (d) 36 yr

27. Mother was three times the age of her daughter 5yr ago. After 5yr, mother will be twice as old as her daughter. How old is the daughter today?
(a) 5 yr (b) 10 yr
(c) 15 yr (d) 20 yr

28. A father tells his son, "I was three times of your present age when you were born." If the father's present age is 48 yr, how old was the boy 4 yr ago?
(a) 24 yr (b) 8 yr
(c) 12 yr (d) 16 yr

29. The average age of 19 boys in a class is 21 yr. If the teacher's age is included, the average increases to 22 yr. What is the teacher's age?

(a) 39 yr (b) 41 yr (c) 40 yr (d) 44 yr

30. In a family, mother's age is twice that of daughter's age. Father is 10 yr older than mother. Brother is 20 yr younger than his mother and 5 yr older than his sister. What is the age of the father?

(a) 62 yr (b) 60 yr
(c) 58 yr (d) 55 yr

31. 2 yr ago, a mother was 4 times as old as her son. 6 yr from now her age will become more than double her son's age by 10 yr. What is the present ratio of their ages?

(a) 2 : 1 (b) 38 : 11
(c) 19 : 7 (d) 3 : 1

32. The sum of the ages of a father and a son presently is 70 yr. After 10 yr, the son's age is exactly half that of the father's. What are their ages now?

(a) 45 yr, 25 yr (b) 50 yr, 20 yr
(c) 47 yr, 23 yr (d) 50 yr, 25 yr

33. 'X' and her grandfather differ in their ages by 50 yr. After 6 yr, if the sum of their ages is 152, their present age are

(a) 24, 74 (b) 26, 76
(c) 45, 95 (d) 25, 75

34. The age of a father is twice that of his son's present age. After 5 yr, the sum of their ages will be 85. How old are they now?

(a) 40, 20 (b) 46, 23
(c) 60, 30 (d) 50, 25

35. A father's age is one more than 5 times of his son's age. After 3 yr, the father's age would be 2 less than four times the son's age. Find the present age of the father.

(a) 30 yr (b) 40 yr
(c) 31 yr (d) 29 yr

36. A man is 3 yr older than his wife and four times as old as his son. If the son beomces 15 yr old after 3 yr, what is the present age of the wife?

(a) 60 yr (b) 51 yr
(c) 48 yr (d) 45 yr

37. Hema was twice as old as Geetha 10 yr ago. How old is Geetha today, if Hema will be 40 yr old 10 yr, hence?

(a) 25 yr (b) 20 yr
(c) 15 yr (d) 35 yr

38. Ashok's mother was 3 times as old as Ashok 5 yr ago. After 5 yr she will be twice as old as Ashok. How old is Ashok today?

(a) 10 yr (b) 15 yr
(c) 20 yr (d) 25 yr

39. The average age of 30 students is 15 yr. If the teacher's age is also included, then the average age increases by 1 yr. The age of the teacher is « SSC CGL 2007

(a) 56 yr (b) 46 yr (c) 35 yr (d) 45 yr

40. A, B, C, D are four friends. Average age of A and C is 35 yr and that of B, and D is 40 yr. Average age of B, C and D is 40 yr. The sum of the ages of A and D is equal to that of B and C. Find out the age (in yr) of A, B, C and D.

(a) 20, 30, 40, 50
(b) 20, 25, 30, 35
(c) 30, 35, 40, 45
(d) 30, 40, 50, 60

41. A is 16 yr older than B. But half the age of B is equal to one-third of A's age. Find present age of A and B?

(a) A = 40, B = 32 (b) A = 48, B = 32
(c) A = 46, B = 30 (d) A = 32, B = 16

42. Ram's age was square of a number last year and it will be cube of a number next year. How long must he wait before his age is again the cube of a number?

(a) 39 yr (b) 10 yr
(c) 38 yr (d) 64 yr

43. 10 yr ago, average age of A and B is 20 yr. Average age of A, B and C is 30 yr today. How old C will be after 5 yr?

(a) 20 yr (b) 30 yr
(c) 35yr (d) 55 yr

44. In a family, a couple has a son and a daughter. The age of the father is three times that of his daughter and the age of the son is half of his mother. The wife is 9 yr younger to her husband and the son is seven years older than daughter. What is the age of the mother?

« UPSSSC Excise Constable 2017

(a) 40 yr (b) 45 yr
(c) 50 yr (d) 60 yr

45. In a particular situation 'A' is 4 yr elder to 'B'. 16 yr later 'A' will be thrice of his present age and 'B' will be five times of his present age. Find the ages of 'A' and 'B' two years before the given situation. « UPSSSC VDO 2016

(a) 6 yr and 2 yr (b) 10 yr and 6 yr
(c) 8 yr and 4 yr (d) 12 yr and 8 yr

46. The difference between the ages of two brothers is same as the difference between the ages of their parents. The age of elder brother is 15 yr. At the time of the birth of younger brother their mother's age is 37 yr. If father's age is 5 yr more than mother's age, then what was the age of father at the time of elder brother's birth? « UPSSSC Junior Assistant 2016

(a) 32 yr (b) 57 yr
(c) 25 yr (d) None of these

47. The difference between the ages of two brothers is same as the difference between ages of their father and mother. The age of the elder brother is 25 yr. At the time of the birth of younger brother his mother's age was 32 yr. If father's age is 5 yr more than mother's age, then what was the age of father at the time of elder brother's birth? « UPSSSC Amin 2016

(a) 55 yr (b) 32 yr
(c) 31 yr (d) 57 yr

Answers / WITH EXPLANATIONS

1. (*b*) If Sami is 12, one-third of his age is 4, which is his brother's age

Then, $12 + x = 2(4 + x)$

$\Rightarrow 12 + x = 8 + 2x$

$\Rightarrow 4 = x$

In 4 more years, Sami will be twice his brother's age.

So, Sami's age $= 12 + 4 = 16$ yr

2. (*c*) Let the ages of 4 children respectively are x, $x + 4$, $x + 8$ and $x + 12$.

$\therefore$ According to the question,

$x + (x + 4) + (x + 8) + (x + 12) = 48$

$\Rightarrow 4x + 24 = 48$

$\Rightarrow 4x = 24$

$\Rightarrow x = 6$

$\therefore$ The age of the youngest child = 6 yr

3. (*c*) Sum of ages of mother, daughter and son is 87 yr.

Sum of their age after 8 yr

$= 87 + (8 \times 3)$

$= 87 + 24$

$= 111$ yr

4. (*b*) Let the present age of Vikas and Sujit be $5x$ and $4x$ yr, respectively.

According to the question, after 3 yr

$$\frac{5x + 3}{4x + 3} = \frac{11}{9}$$

$\Rightarrow 45x + 27 = 44x + 33$

$\therefore x = 6$

$\therefore$ Present age of Sujit $= 4 \times 6 = 24$ yr

5. (*c*) According to the question,

The present age of son $= 16 - 4 = 12$ yr

The present age of father

$= 12 \times 4 = 48$ yr

$\therefore$ The present age of mother

$= 48 - 4 = 44$ yr

6. (*a*) At the time of my birth, my mother's age = 23 yr

$\therefore$ After 6 yr mother's age

$= 23 + 6 = 29$ yr

Father's age = 34 yrs

$\therefore$ Difference between the ages of father and mother $= 34 - 29 = 5$ yr

7. (*c*) Let the age of three boys are $3x$, $5x$, $7x$ respectively.

According to the question, average age of three boys = 35 yr

$$\therefore \frac{3x + 5x + 7x}{3} = 35$$

$\Rightarrow 15x = 35 \times 3$

$$\Rightarrow x = \frac{105}{15} = 7$$

$\therefore$ The age of youngest boy

$= 3 \times 7 = 21$ yr

8. (*b*) Let the age of Jai = x yr

Therefore, his father's age $= (x + 35)$ yr

According to the question,

$(x + 5) + (x + 35 + 5) = 135$

$\Rightarrow 2x + 45 = 135$

$\Rightarrow 2x = 135 - 45$

$$\therefore x = \frac{90}{2} = 45$$

Age of Jai after 12 yr $= x + 12$

$= 40 + 12$

$= 52$ yr

$\therefore$ Age of Jai's father after 12 yr

$= 40 + 35 + 12$

$= 87$ yr

9. (*b*) Age of Adam = 20 yr

Age of Mary $= \frac{20}{4} = 5$ yr

After 10 yr,

Age of Adam $= 20 + 10 = 30$ yr

Age of Mary $= 5 + 10 = 15$ yr

10. (*a*) Let the present age of A

$= (x + 2)$ yr

According to the question,

$2(x - 2) = x + 2 - 2$

$\Rightarrow 2x - 4 = x$

$\Rightarrow 2x - x = 4$

$\therefore x = 4$

Age of B = 4 yr

Age of A $= x + 2 = 4 + 2 = 6$ yr

11. (*b*) According to the question,

Age of Mani = 2 × Age of Prabhu

and age of Ramona $= \frac{1}{2} \times$ Age of Prabhu

Now, age of Mani = 60 yrs

$\Rightarrow 60 = 2 \times$ Age of Prabhu

$\Rightarrow$ Age of Prabhu = 30 yrs

$\therefore$ Age of Ramona $= \frac{1}{2} \times 30 = 15$ yr

12. (*a*) Let age of Praveen = P yr

Age of Roopa = R yr

and age of Deepak = D yr

Now, according to the question,

$P = 2R$ ...(i)

$P = D + 6$ ...(ii)

Given, $D = 12$

Then, from Eq. (ii), we get

$P = 12 + 6 = 18$

$\Rightarrow P = 18$

Now, from Eq. (i),

$18 = 2R$

$$\Rightarrow R = \frac{18}{2} = 9$$

$\Rightarrow R = 9$

Hence, age of Roopa is 9 yr.

13. (*b*) Govind's present age = 48 yr

$\therefore$ Prem's present age $= \frac{48}{2} = 24$ yr

Prem's age seven years ago

$= 24 - 7 = 17$ yr

14. (*b*) Given, Mr. Mani's present age

= 47 yr

and John's present age = 13 yr

Let in x years, Mr. Mani's age be double of John's age.

According to the question,

$47 + x = 2(13 + x)$

$\Rightarrow 47 + x = 26 + 2x$

$\Rightarrow 2x - x = 47 - 26$

$\Rightarrow x = 21$ yr

15. (*d*) Let the present ages of Sunita and Vinita be $4x$ yr and $5x$ yr, respectively.

Six years hence, their respective ages would be $(4x + 6)$ yr and $(5x + 6)$ yr.

According to the question,

$$\frac{4x + 6}{5x + 6} = \frac{14}{17}$$

$\Rightarrow 68x + 102 = 70x + 84$

$\Rightarrow 2x = 18$

$x = 9$

$\therefore$ There present ages are 36 yr and 45 yr respectively.

Ratio of their ages 12 yr.

Hence, $\frac{36 + 12}{45 + 12} = \frac{48}{57} = \frac{16}{19} = 16 : 19$

16. (*b*) According to the question,

Mahesh's age = 60 yr

Ram's Age = Mahesh − 5

$= 60 - 5 = 55$ yr

Again, Ram = Raju + 4

$\Rightarrow 55 = \text{Raju} + 4$

$\Rightarrow$ Raju's age $= 55 - 4 = 51$ yr

Now, Babu = Raju − 6

$= 51 - 6$

$= 45$ yr

Age difference between Mahesh and Babu $= 60 - 45 = 15$ yr

Hence, option (b) is correct.

17. (*d*) Let age of Nikhil = x yr

Then, age of Rohan $= (x + 8)$ yr

According to the question,

$x + 8 = 2x$

$\therefore x = 8$

Now, age of Rohan is $8 + 8 = 16$ yr

18. (*d*) Let the age of Rahim be x yr.
So, age of uncle will be $(x + 30)$ yr.
According to the question,

$$(x + 7) + (x + 30 + 7) = 66$$
$$\Rightarrow \quad 2x + 14 + 30 = 66$$
$$\Rightarrow \quad 2x + 44 = 66$$
$$\Rightarrow \quad 2x = 66 - 44$$
$$\therefore \quad x = \frac{22}{2} = 11$$

So, age of Rahim's uncle will be
$11 + 30 = 41$ yr

19. (*a*) Let the present age of Sita be x yr.
Then, according to the question,

$$x = 1\frac{1}{4}(x - 6)$$
$$\Rightarrow \quad x = \frac{5}{4}(x - 6)$$
$$\Rightarrow \quad 4x = 5x - 30$$
$$\therefore \quad x = 30$$

Thus, age of Sita's son $= \frac{30}{6} = 5$ yr
Hence, option (a) is correct.

20. (*c*) According to the question, the current age of Amit is 17 yr.
Current age of Rakesh $= 17 - 5 = 12$ yr
Now, current age of Anil $= 12 + 3$
$= 15$ yr

21. (*b*) Let the present age of Antony be x yr.
According to the question,
The age of Antony before 20 yr was $\frac{x}{2}$ yr.
Thus, we can write the given condition as

$$x - 20 = \frac{x}{2}$$
$$\Rightarrow \quad 2x - 40 = x$$
$$\Rightarrow \quad 2x - x = 40$$
$$\therefore \quad x = 40 \text{ yr}$$

Hence, option (b) is correct.

22. (*d*) Let the present age of Leela be x yr.
So, the present age of Neela $= 3x$ yr
According to the question,
10 yr ago, the age of Neela and Leela was related as

$$5(x - 10) = (3x - 10)$$
$$\Rightarrow \quad 5x - 50 = 3x - 10$$
$$\Rightarrow \quad 5x - 3x = 50 - 10$$
$$\Rightarrow \quad 2x = 40$$
$$\therefore \quad x = \frac{40}{2} = 20 \text{ yr}$$

$\because$ Present age of Leela = 20 yr

23. (*a*) According to the question,
3 yr ago, the total age of husband, wife and child was $= 27 \times 3 = 81$ yr
Also, total age of wife and child 5 yr ago was $20 \times 2 = 40$ yr.
$\therefore$ Total age of wife and child 3 yr ago was $= 40 + 4 = 44$ yr
$\therefore$ Now, age of husband 3 yr ago was
$= 81 - 44 = 37$ yr
Thus, the present age of husband
$= 37 + 3 = 40$ yr

Alternate Method
Let the present age of husband, wife and child be x, y and z yr, respectively.
Then, according to the question,

***Case* I**

$$\frac{(x - 3) + (y - 3) + (z - 3)}{3} = 27$$
$$\Rightarrow \quad x + y + z - 9 = 81$$
$$\Rightarrow \quad x + y + z = 90 \quad \ldots\text{(i)}$$

***Case* II**

$$\frac{(y - 5) + (z - 5)}{2} = 20$$
$$\Rightarrow \quad y + z - 10 = 40$$
$$\Rightarrow \quad y + z = 50 \quad \ldots\text{(ii)}$$

From Eqs. (i) and (ii), we get

$$x + 50 = 90$$
$$\Rightarrow \quad x = 40$$

$\therefore$ Present age of husband = 40 yr

24. (*d*) Let the present age of A be x yr and the present age of B be y yr.
Then, according to the question,

$$(x - t) = y \quad \ldots\text{(i)}$$
$$\text{and} \quad x = (y - t) \times 2 \quad \text{(Let } t \text{ yr ago)}$$
$$\Rightarrow \quad y + t = 2y - 2t$$
$$\Rightarrow \quad 3t = y \quad \ldots\text{(ii)}$$

From Eq. (i),

$$\Rightarrow \quad x - \frac{y}{3} = y$$
$$\Rightarrow \quad x = x + \frac{y}{3}$$
$$\Rightarrow \quad 3 \times x = 3y + y$$
$$\Rightarrow \quad 3x = 4y$$
$$\Rightarrow \quad 3x + 4x = 4y + 4x$$
$$\Rightarrow \quad 7x = 4 \times 63 \quad (\because x + y = 63)$$
$$\therefore \quad x = 4 \times 9 = 36 \text{ yr}$$

25. (*d*) Let the present age of younger daughter be x yr.
Then, present age of the elder daughter is $(x + 5)$ yr.
Present age of the father $= 3(x + 5)$ yr
According to the question,

$$8(x - 5) = 3x + 15 - 5$$
$$\Rightarrow \quad 8x - 40 = 3x + 10$$
$$\Rightarrow \quad 8x - 3x = 10 + 40$$
$$\therefore \quad x = \frac{50}{5} = 10 \text{ yr}$$

Thus, present age of the father
$= 3 \times 10 + 15$
$= 45$ yr

Alternate Method
Let the age of the elder daughter be x yr.
$\therefore$ Father's age $= 3x$ yr
5 yr back, age of elder daughter $= x - 5$
$\therefore$ 5 yr back, age of younger daughter
$= (x - 5) - 5 = x - 10$
According to the question,

$$(3x - 5) = 8(x - 10)$$
$$\Rightarrow \quad 3x - 5 = 8x - 80$$
$$\Rightarrow \quad 3x - 8x = -80 + 5$$
$$\Rightarrow \quad -5x = -75$$
$$\Rightarrow \quad x = \frac{75}{5}$$
$$\therefore \quad x = 15$$

$\therefore$ Present age of father $= 3 \times 15$
$= 45$ yr

26. (*a*) Let the present age of the mother
$= x$ yr
So, present age of the person $= \frac{2}{5}x$ yr
According to the question, the age of mother and person after 8 yr is related as

$$\left(\frac{2}{5}x + 8\right) = \frac{(x + 8)}{2}$$
$$\Rightarrow \quad 2\frac{(2x + 40)}{5} = x + 8$$
$$\Rightarrow \quad 4x + 80 = 5x + 40$$
$$\Rightarrow \quad 5x - 4x = 80 - 40$$
$$\therefore \quad x = 40 \text{ yr}$$

Present age of mother = 40 yr

27. (*c*) Let the present age of daughter
$= x$ yr
and the present age of mother $= y$ yr
According to the question,

$$3(x - 5) = (y - 5)$$
$$\Rightarrow \quad 3x - 15 = y - 5$$
$$\Rightarrow \quad 3x - y = 10 \quad \ldots\text{(i)}$$
$$\text{Again,} \quad 2(x + 5) = y + 5$$
$$\Rightarrow \quad 2x + 10 = y + 5$$
$$\Rightarrow \quad 2x - y = -5 \quad \ldots\text{(ii)}$$

After solving Eqs. (i) and (ii), we get
$x = 15$ yr

28. (*b*) Let the son's present age be x yr.
Father's present age = 48 yr
According to the question,

$$48 - x = 3x$$
$$\Rightarrow \quad x = 12$$

$\therefore$ Son's present age = 12 yr
and his age 4 yr ago $= 12 - 4 = 8$ yr

29. (*b*) According to the question,
The average age of 19 boys is 21 yr.
Then, total age of boys
$= 19 \times 21$
$= 399$ yr.

The average age of 19 boys and teacher is 22 yr.

Total age of 19 boys and teacher

$= 20 \times 22$

$= 440$ yr

Now, teacher's age $= 440 - 399$

$= 41$ yr.

Alternate Method

Let the age of the teacher be x yr.

Total age of 19 boys in class $= 19 \times 21$

$= 399$ yr

According to the question,

$399 + x = 20 \times 22$

$\Rightarrow \quad x = 440 - 399$

$\therefore \quad x = 41$ yr

Hence, option (b) is correct.

30. (*b*) Let the age of daughter be x yr.

Then, age of brother will be $(x + 5)$ yr and age of mother is $2x$ yr.

Now, according to the question,

We can write the given condition in following way

$2x - 20 = x + 5$

$\Rightarrow \quad 2x - x = 5 + 20$

$\Rightarrow \quad x = 25$ yr

$\therefore$ Age of mother $= 2x = 2 \times 25 = 50$ yr

Clearly, age of father $= 50 + 10$

$= 60$ yr

31. (*b*) Let the present age of son be x yr and the present age of mother be y yr

According to the question,

$4(x - 2) = y - 2$

$\Rightarrow \quad 4x - 8 = y - 2$

$\Rightarrow \quad 4x - y = 6 \quad \ldots(i)$

Again, $2(x + 6) + 10 = y + 6$

$\Rightarrow \quad 2x + 12 + 10 = y + 6$

$\Rightarrow \quad 2x - y = -16 \quad \ldots(ii)$

After solving Eqs. (i) and (ii), we get

$x = 11$

$\therefore \quad y = 4 \times 11 - 6 = 38$

Required ratio $= 38 : 11$

Alternate Method

Let the present age of mother $= x$ yr

$\therefore$ 2 yr ago her age $= x - 2$

$\therefore$ 2 yr ago her son's age $= \dfrac{(x-2)}{4}$

Mother's age after 6 yr from now

$= x + 6$

Son's age after 6 yr $= \dfrac{(x-2)}{4} + 2 + 6$

$= \dfrac{x-2}{4} + 8$

$= \dfrac{x - 2 + 32}{4}$

$= \dfrac{x + 30}{4}$

According to the question,

$$x + 6 = 2\left(\frac{x+30}{4}\right) + 10$$

$\Rightarrow \quad x + 6 = \dfrac{x}{2} + 15 + 10$

$\Rightarrow \quad \dfrac{x}{2} = 19$

$\Rightarrow \quad x = 38$

Son's age $= \dfrac{x-2}{4} + 2$

$= \dfrac{38-2}{4} + 2$

$= 9 + 2 = 11$

$\therefore$ Ratio of their ages $= 38 : 11$

32. (*b*) Let the present age of son $= x$ yr

The present age of father $= y$ yr

$\therefore \quad x + y = 70 \quad \ldots(i)$

According to the question,

We can write the given condition in following way,

$2(x + 10) = y + 10$

$\Rightarrow \quad 2x + 20 = y + 10$

$\Rightarrow \quad 2x - y = -10 \quad \ldots(ii)$

After solving Eqs. (i) and (ii), we get

$(x + y) + (2x - y) = 70 - 10$

$\Rightarrow \quad 3x = 60$

$\Rightarrow \quad x = 20$

Now, $y = 70 - 20 = 50$

$x = 20$ and $y = 50$

33. (*c*) Let the present age of X be x yr.

Her grandfather's present age

$= x + 50$ yr

According to the question,

We can write the given condition in following way

$x + 6 + x + 50 + 6 = 152$

$\Rightarrow \quad 2x + 62 = 152$

$\Rightarrow \quad 2x = 152 - 62 = 90$

$\therefore \quad x = \dfrac{90}{2} = 45$ yr

$\therefore \quad x + 50 = 45 + 50$

$= 95$ yr

Grandfather's present age $= 95$ yr

34. (*d*) Let the present age of son be x yr.

Then, age of father $= 2x$ yr

According to the question,

We can write the given condition in following way.

$x + 5 + 2x + 5 = 85$

$\Rightarrow \quad 3x + 10 = 85$

$\Rightarrow \quad 3x = 85 - 10 = 75$

$\Rightarrow \quad x = \dfrac{75}{3} = 25$ yr

$\therefore \quad 2x = 50$ yr

$\therefore$ Father's and son's respective ages are 50 yr and 25 yr

35. (*c*) Let the age of son be x yr.

Thus, the age of father will be $5x + 1$

According to the question,

$4(x + 3) - 2 = 5x + 1 + 3$

$\Rightarrow \quad 4x + 12 - 2 = 5x + 4$

$\Rightarrow \quad 10 - 4 = 5x - 4x$

$\therefore \quad x = 6$

Age of father $= 5x + 1$

$= 5 \times 6 + 1$

$= 31$ yr

36. (*d*) Let the present age of son is x yr.

Therefore, present age of the father

$= 4x$ yr

According to the question,

We can write the condition as

$x + 3 = 15$

Now, $\quad x = 15 - 3 = 12$ yr

The present age of father

$= 4x = 4 \times 12 = 48$ yr

$\therefore$ The present age of man's wife

$= 48 - 3 = 45$ yr

37. (*b*) Let the present age of Geetha is x yr

Present age of Hema $= 40 - 10 = 30$ yr

According to the question,

We can write the given condition in following way

$2(x - 10) = 30 - 10$

$\Rightarrow \quad 2x - 20 = 20$

$\Rightarrow \quad 2x = 20 + 20 = 40$

So, $\quad x = \dfrac{40}{2} = 20$ yr

38. (*b*) Let the present age of Ashok is x yr and that of his mother is y yr.

According to the question,

5 yr ago,

$3(x - 5) = (y - 5)$

$\Rightarrow \quad 3x - 15 = y - 5$

$\Rightarrow \quad 3x - y = 10 \quad \ldots(i)$

After 5 yr,

$2(x + 5) = (y + 5)$

$\Rightarrow \quad 2x + 10 = y + 5$

$\Rightarrow \quad 2x - y = -5 \quad \ldots(ii)$

After solving Eqs. (i) and (ii), we get

$x = 15$ yr

39. (*b*) The average age of 30 students is 15 yr.

Then, total age of 30 students

$= 30 \times 15 = 450$ yr.

Average age of 30 students and teacher is 16 yr.

Total age of 30 students and teacher

$= 16 \times 31 = 496$ yr

Now, age of teacher $= (496 - 450)$

$= 46$yr

Alternate Method

Let the teacher's age be x yr.

Total age of 30 students $= 30 \times 15$
$= 450$

According to the question,

$$\frac{450 + x}{31} = (15 + 1) = 16$$

$\Rightarrow \quad 450 + x = 496$

$\therefore \quad x = 46$

$\therefore$ Teacher's age = 46 yr

40. (*c*) As the average age of A and C is 35 yr and average age of B and D is 40 yr.

Then, $A + C = 70$ yr ...(i)

$B + D = 80$ yr ...(ii)

Also, average age of B, C and D is 40 yr

$B + C + D = 120$ yr ...(iii)

After solving Eqs. (i), (ii) and (iii), we get

$\boxed{C = 40 \text{ yr}}$

and $\boxed{A = 30 \text{ yr}}$

$A + D = B + C$

$\Rightarrow \quad 30 + D = B + 40$

$\Rightarrow \quad D - B = 10$ ...(iv)

From Eqs. (ii) and (iv),we get

$(B + D) + (D - B) = 90$

$\Rightarrow \quad D = 45$

$\therefore \quad \boxed{B = 35 \text{ yr}}$

and $\boxed{D = 45 \text{ yr}}$

41. (*b*) Suppose the age of A is x yr and that of B is y yr.

Then, $x - y = 16$ ...(i)

Again, $\frac{x}{3} = \frac{y}{2}$

$\Rightarrow \quad 2x = 3y$

$\Rightarrow \quad 2x - 3y = 0$ ...(ii)

From Eqs. (i) and (ii), we get

$x = 48$ yr

$\therefore \quad y = 48 - 16$
$= 32$ yr

Thus, A = 48 yr,
B = 32 yr

42. (*c*) Let the present age of Ram is 26 yr.

Last year his age $= 26 - 1 = 25 = (5)^2$

Next year his age $= 26 + 1 = 27 = (3)^3$

After 27yr, the next cube number is $64 = (4)^3$

So, he must wait for $= 64 - 26 = 38$ yr

43. (*c*) Let the present age of A, B and C be x yr, y yr and z yr, respectively.

According to the given condition, we have

$$\frac{(x - 10) + (y - 10)}{2} = 20$$

$\Rightarrow \quad x - 10 + y - 10 = 40$

$\Rightarrow \quad x + y = 60$ ...(i)

Again, $\frac{x + y + z}{3} = 30$

or $\quad x + y + z = 30 \times 3$
$= 90$ ...(ii)

After solving Eqs. (i) and (ii), we get

$z = 30$ yr

So, the age of C after 5 yr = 30 + 5
= 35 yr

44. (*d*) Let the daughter's age be x yr.

$\therefore$ Father's age $= 3x$ yr

Wife's age $= (3x - 9)$ yr

Son's age $= (x + 7)$ yr

According to the question,

$$(x + 7) = \frac{(3x - 9)}{2}$$

$\Rightarrow \quad 2(x + 7) = (3x - 9)$

$\Rightarrow \quad 2x + 14 = 3x - 9$

$\Rightarrow \quad x = 23$

$\therefore$ Mother's age $= 3 \times 23 - 9$
$= 69 - 9 = 60$ yr

45. (*a*) Let the age of B be x yr.

$\therefore$ A's age $= x + 4$ yr

According to the question,

$(x + 4)3 = (x + 4) + 16$

$\Rightarrow \quad 3x + 12 = x + 20$

$\Rightarrow \quad 3x - x = 20 - 12 \Rightarrow 2x = 8$

$\therefore \quad x = 4$

$\therefore$ A's age $= 4 + 4 = 8$ yr

$\therefore$ Two years before the ages of A and B are $= (8 - 2)$ yr and $(4 - 2)$ yr $= 6$ and 2 yr, respectively.

46. (*d*) Given, the age of elder brother
= 15 yr

$\because$ Difference between the ages of father-mother is 5 yr, therefore the difference between the age of two brothers is 5 yr.

$\therefore$ The age of younger brothre
$= 15 - 5 = 10$ yr

$\because$ The age of mother at the time of birth of younger brother = 37 yr

$\therefore$ The age of mother at the time of birth of elder brother $= 37 - 5 = 32$ yr

$\therefore$ The age of father at the time of birth of elder brother $= 32 + 5 = 37$ yr

47. (*b*) Difference between the ages of two brothers = Difference between the ages of mother and father.

$\because$ Father's age is 5 yr more than mother's age i.e. difference between the ages of father and mother is 5 yr.

Now, difference between the ages of two brothers is 5 yr, then the elder brother is 5 yr elder to his younger brother.

Given at the time of birth of younger brother, the age of mother = 32 yr.

$\therefore$ Father's age at the time of birth of younger brother $= 32 + 5 = 37$ yr

Mother's age at the time of birth of elder brother $= 32 - 5 = 27$ yr

$\therefore$ Father's age at the time of birth of elder brother $= 37 - 5 = 32$ yr

CHAPTER / 17

Inserting the Missing Character

Inserting the Missing Character is filling-up of the empty (missing) spaces in letter and number puzzles given in pictorial forms.

Under this segment of reasoning, numbers or letters or both are represented through one or more figures (geometrical or any other figure).

Such numbers or letters are arranged inside the figure according to a certain pattern (*i.e.,* based on particular logic and/or mathematical calculations) and one character is missing which is denoted by question mark (?).

The candidate is required to find out the character that can replace the question mark (?) satisfying the logic and calculations. Various puzzles based on inserting the missing character that are asked in various competitive exams are classified into following types.

- Number Puzzles
- Letter Puzzles
- Alpha-Numeric Puzzles

TYPE 01

Number Puzzles

In such type of problems, some numbers are arranged in a certain pattern, which follows a certain rules like the rule of addition, subtraction, multiplication, division, squaring or cubing of consecutive numbers etc.

Based on these different operations, we have to find the missing number in the given problems.

Following examples will give you better idea about such types of problems.

DIRECTIONS ~ (Example Nos. 1-11) *Find the missing number from the given alternatives.*

***Ex* 01**

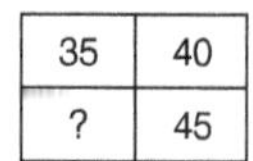

35	40
?	45

(a) 55 (b) 48 (c) 52 (d) 50

Solution (d) Moving clockwise, the pattern is as follows

$35 + 5 = 40$ and $40 + 5 = 45$

So, missing number $= 45 + 5 = \boxed{50}$

***Ex* 02**

45	11	1
12	0	1
57	11	?

« SSC CGL 2017

(a) 0 (b) 68 (c) 2 (d) 10

Solution (c) As, $45 + 12 = 57$ and $11 + 0 = 11$

Similarly, $1 + 1 = ?$

$\therefore$ $? = 2$

***Ex* 03**

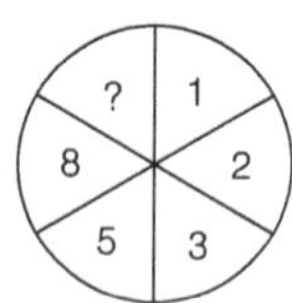

« LIC ADO 2010

(a) 10 (b) 15 (c) 13 (d) 12
(e) None of these

Solution (c) The pattern in clockwise direction is

$1 + 2 = 3$, $2 + 3 = 5$

$3 + 5 = 8$ and $5 + 8 = 13$

$\therefore$ $? = \boxed{13}$

***Ex* 04**

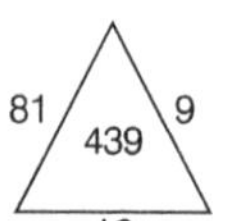

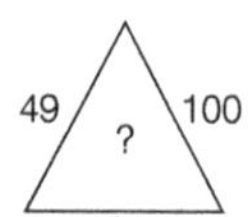

(a) 8710 (b) 1078 (c) 8107 (d) 789

Solution (c) Numbers placed along the sides of the triangle are the squares of the digits at the centre of the triangle, as shown below

$(4)^2 = 16, (3)^2 = 9, (9)^2 = 81$

Similarly, $\sqrt{64} = 8, \sqrt{100} = 10, \sqrt{49} = 7$

So, the missing number $= \boxed{8107}$

Ex 05

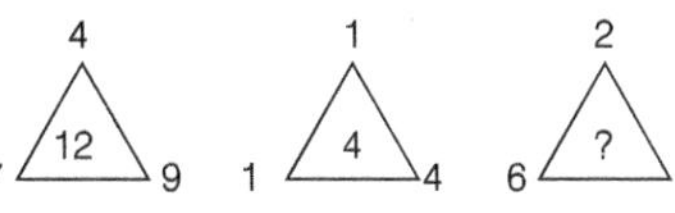

« FCI Uttarakhand 2018

(a) 5 (b) 8 (c) 9 (d) 11

Solution (c) As, $7 + 9 - 4 = 12$ and $1 + 4 - 1 = 4$

Similarly $6 + 5 - 2 = 9$

$\therefore$ $? = 9$

Ex 06

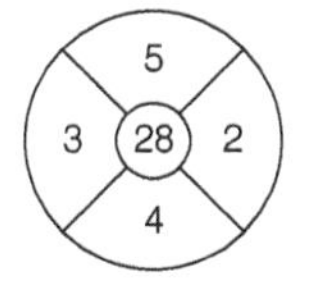

8
8 12 ?
4

(a) 3 (b) 9
(c) 1 (d) 2

Solution (d) As,

$$\{(5)^2 + (4)^2\} - \{(3)^2 + (2)^2\} = (25 + 16) - (9 + 4)$$
$$= 41 - 13 = 28$$

Similarly, $\{(8)^2 + (4)^2\} - \{(8)^2 + (?)^2\} = 12$

$\Rightarrow$ $(64 + 16) - \{64 + (?)^2\} = 12$

$\Rightarrow$ $16 - (?)^2 = 12$

$\Rightarrow$ $?^2 = 4$

$? = 2$

So, the missing number = $\boxed{2}$

Ex 07

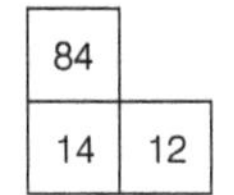

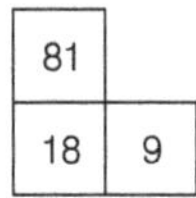

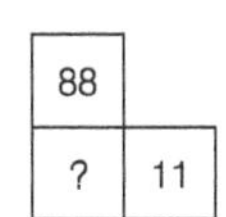

« SSC (CGL) 2013

(a) 7 (b) 16
(c) 21 (d) 28

Solution (b) As, $84 \div 12 = 7$; $7 \times 2 = 14$

and $81 \div 9 = 9$; $9 \times 2 = 18$

Similarly, $88 \div 11 = 8$ and $8 \times 2 = 16$

Ex 08

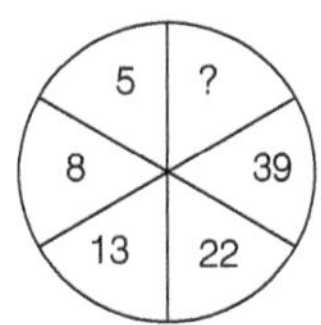

« SSC CPO 2013

(a) 66 (b) 72
(c) 71 (d) 78

Solution (b) The pattern is as follows

$$(5 \times 2) - 2 = 8$$
$$(8 \times 2) - 3 = 13$$
$$(13 \times 2) - 4 = 22$$
$$(22 \times 2) - 5 = 39$$
$$(39 \times 2) - 6 = 72$$

$\therefore$ $? = \boxed{72}$

Ex 09

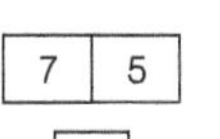

5	21

21	7

6 13 ?

« UPSC CSAT 2013

(a) 4 (b) 8
(c) 20 (d) 14

Solution (d) As, $\frac{7 + 5}{2} = 6$ and $\frac{5 + 21}{2} = 13$

Similarly, missing number $= \frac{21 + 7}{2} = \boxed{14}$

Ex 10

9	6	8
5	8	4
7	4	?
11	2	7

« SSC (10 + 2) 2017

(a) 4 (b) 7 (c) 3 (d) 6

Solution (c) As, in first column, $9 + 7 - 5 = 11$

In second column, $6 + 4 - 8 = 2$

In third column, $8 + ? - 4 = 7$

$\Rightarrow$ $? + 4 = 7$

$\Rightarrow$ $? = 7 - 4 = 3$

So, missing number = $\boxed{3}$

Ex 11

4	5	6
2	3	7
1	8	3
21	98	?

(a) 85 (b) 94
(c) 104 (d) 49

Solution (b) As, $(4)^2 + (2)^2 + (1)^2 = 21$

$(5)^2 + (3)^2 + (8)^2 = 98$

Similarly, missing number $= (6)^2 + (7)^2 + (3)^2 = \boxed{94}$

Practice / CORNER 17.1

DIRECTIONS ~ (Q. Nos. 1-56) *In each of the following questions, a set of figures carrying certain characters is given. Assuming that the characters in each set follow a similar pattern, find the missing character in each case.*

1. 

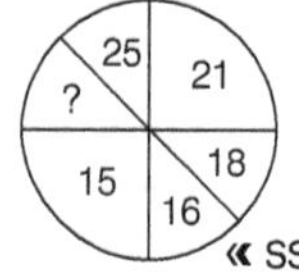

« SSC Steno 2017

(a) 28 (b) 30 (c) 35 (d) 27

2.

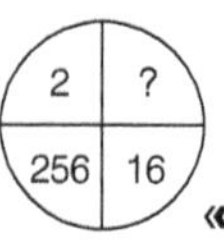

« UP B.Ed. 2007

(a) 8 (b) 4 (c) 32 (d) 16

3.

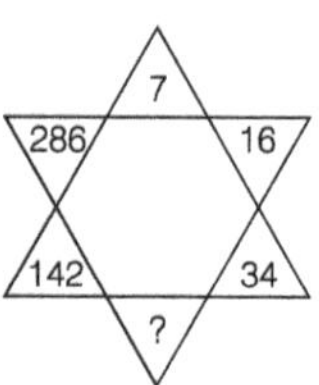

« UPSC Assit. Conservator of Forest 2019

(a) 72 (b) 70 (c) 68 (d) 66

4.

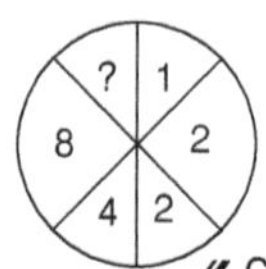

« CGPSC Pre 2017

(a) 10 (b) 15 (c) 32 (d) 12
(e) None of these

5.

7	22	5
5	9	11
9	11	15
38	77	?

(a) 160 (b) 120 (c) 83 (d) 55

6.

23	?	12
6	13	7
138	117	84

« SSC CGL 2017

(a) 9 (b) 13 (c) 17 (d) 15

7.

2	3	4	25
5	7	2	71
1	5	6	?

« SSC Delhi Police Constable 2017

(a) 31 (b) 33
(c) 37 (d) 43

8.

5	3	125
10	4	10000
2	5	?

« SSC CGL 2017

(a) 80 (b) 7 (c) 10 (d) 32

9.

11	3	49
5	19	?
7	13	100

« Chattisgarh Patwari 2016-17

(a) 49 (b) 121 (c) 169 (d) 144

10.

6	2	3
5	7	4
9	8	1
?	1	6

« UPPSC 2018

(a) 8 (b) 6 (c) 3 (d) 2

11.

5	4	41
15	6	?
9	11	202

« SSC CGL (Pre) 2020

(a) 209 (b) 212 (c) 122 (d) 261

12.

1	2	3
11	7	5
120	45	?

« SSC CGL 2016

(a) 19 (b) 16 (c) 15 (d) 17

13.

92	70	48
64	53	42
52	45	?

« SSC (MTS) 2014

(a) 36 (b) 40
(c) 38 (d) 42

14.

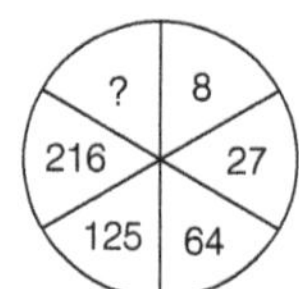

« SSC (CPO) 2010

(a) 729 (b) 343 (c) 305 (d) 4

15.

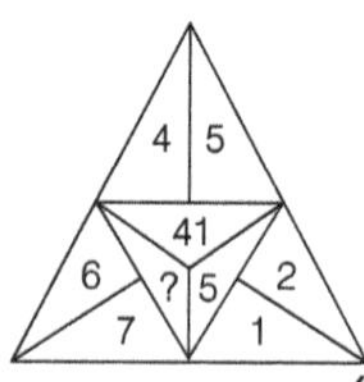

« CMAT 2013

(a) 16 (b) 9 (c) 85 (d) 112

16.

3	8	10	2	?	1
6	56	90	2	20	0

« UPSC CSAT 2015

(a) 5 (b) 0 (c) 7 (d) 3

17.

1	216	343
8	125	512
27	64	?

« SSC CGL 2015

(a) 575 (b) 340 (c) 615 (d) 729

18.

5	2	4
4	4	7
2	5	3
18	30	?

« CGPSC Pre 2017

(a) 42 (b) 43 (c) 32 (d) 33
(e) None of these

19.

24	20	37
31	25	?
26	36	19

« MPPSC Pre 2018

(a) 23 (b) 26 (c) 30 (d) 25

20.

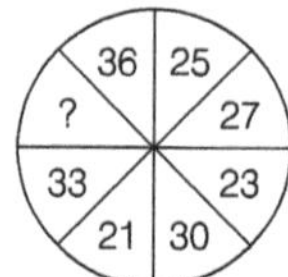

« SSC (CPO) 2005

(a) 19 (b) 22
(c) 32 (d) 35

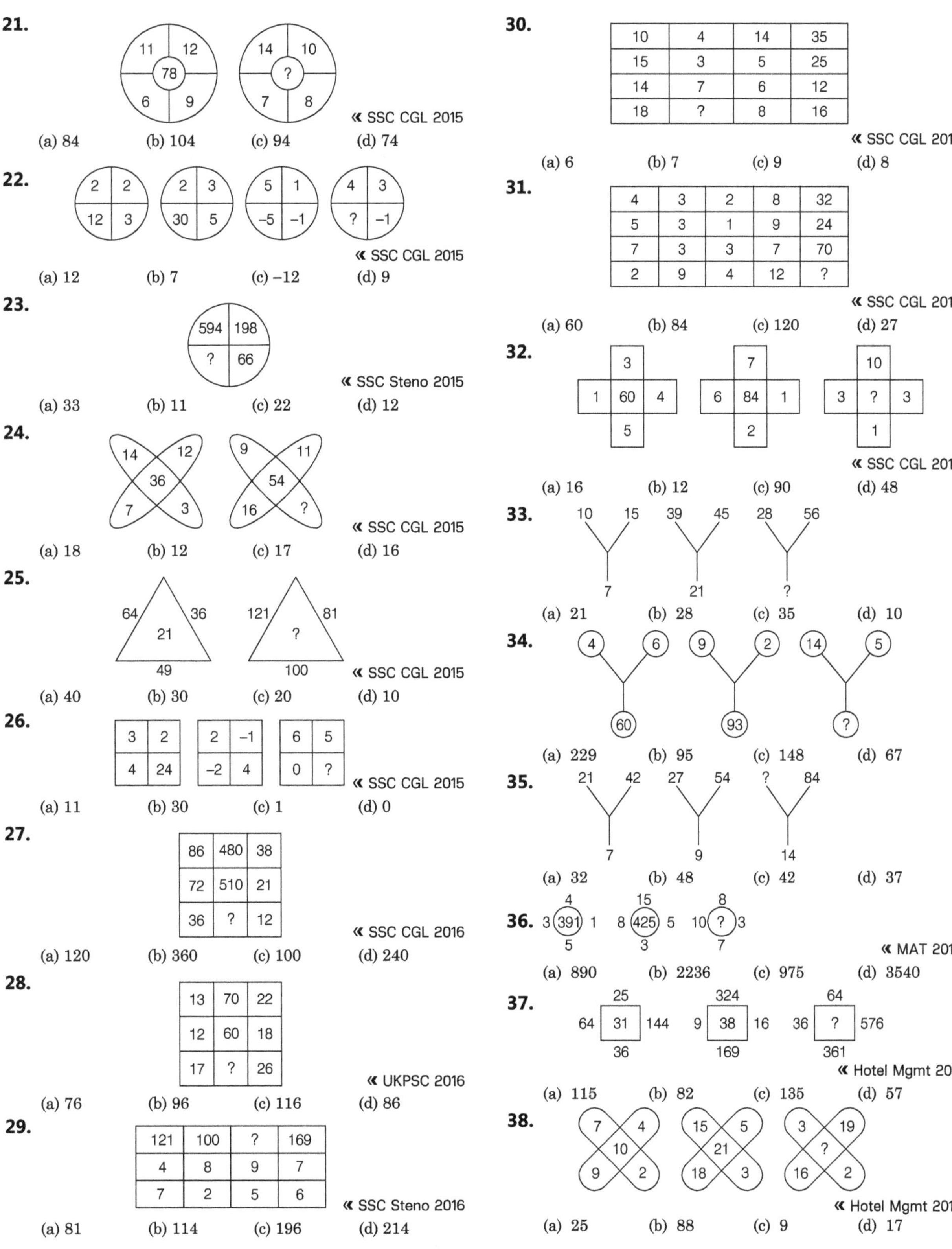

21.

« SSC CGL 2015

(a) 84 (b) 104 (c) 94 (d) 74

22.

« SSC CGL 2015

(a) 12 (b) 7 (c) –12 (d) 9

23.

« SSC Steno 2015

(a) 33 (b) 11 (c) 22 (d) 12

24.

« SSC CGL 2015

(a) 18 (b) 12 (c) 17 (d) 16

25.

« SSC CGL 2015

(a) 40 (b) 30 (c) 20 (d) 10

26.

« SSC CGL 2015

(a) 11 (b) 30 (c) 1 (d) 0

27.

86	480	38
72	510	21
36	?	12

« SSC CGL 2016

(a) 120 (b) 360 (c) 100 (d) 240

28.

13	70	22
12	60	18
17	?	26

« UKPSC 2016

(a) 76 (b) 96 (c) 116 (d) 86

29.

121	100	?	169
4	8	9	7
7	2	5	6

« SSC Steno 2016

(a) 81 (b) 114 (c) 196 (d) 214

30.

10	4	14	35
15	3	5	25
14	7	6	12
18	?	8	16

« SSC CGL 2015

(a) 6 (b) 7 (c) 9 (d) 8

31.

4	3	2	8	32
5	3	1	9	24
7	3	3	7	70
2	9	4	12	?

« SSC CGL 2015

(a) 60 (b) 84 (c) 120 (d) 27

32.

« SSC CGL 2015

(a) 16 (b) 12 (c) 90 (d) 48

33.

(a) 21 (b) 28 (c) 35 (d) 10

34.

(a) 229 (b) 95 (c) 148 (d) 67

35.

(a) 32 (b) 48 (c) 42 (d) 37

36.

« MAT 2012

(a) 890 (b) 2236 (c) 975 (d) 3540

37.

« Hotel Mgmt 2011

(a) 115 (b) 82 (c) 135 (d) 57

38.

« Hotel Mgmt 2012

(a) 25 (b) 88 (c) 9 (d) 17

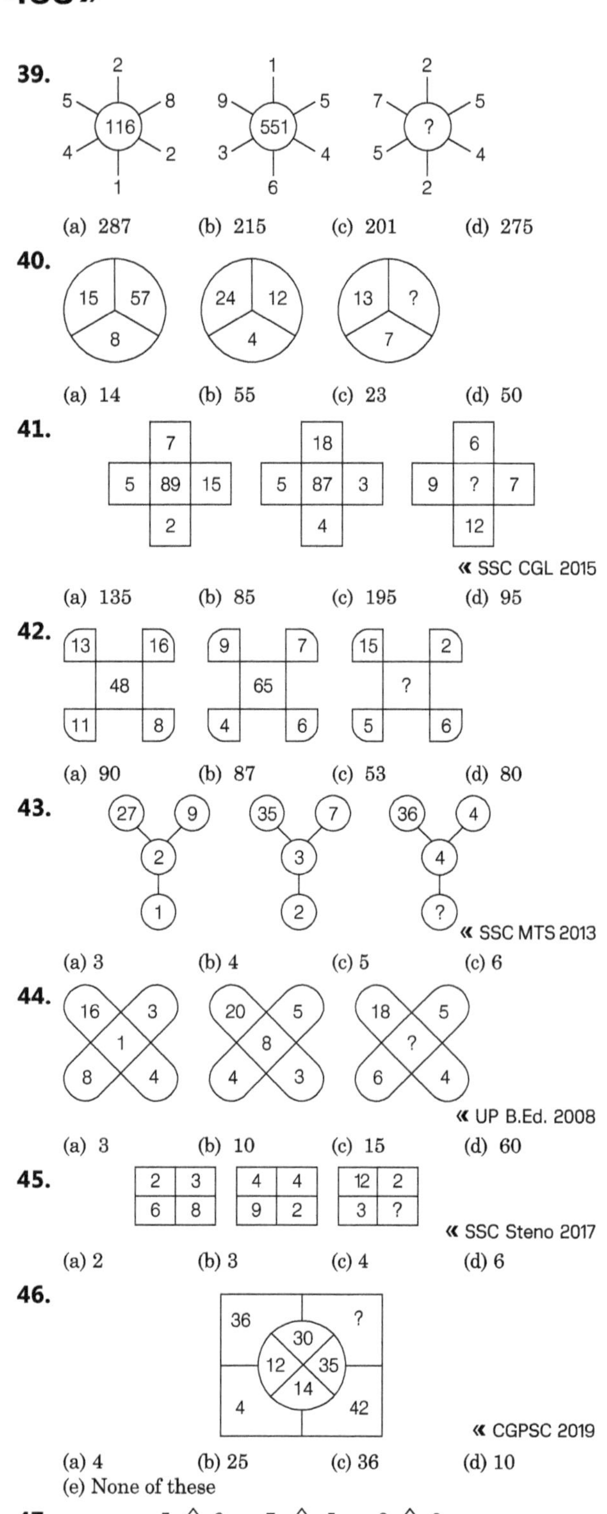

39. (a) 287 (b) 215 (c) 201 (d) 275

40. (a) 14 (b) 55 (c) 23 (d) 50

41. « SSC CGL 2015

(a) 135 (b) 85 (c) 195 (d) 95

42. (a) 90 (b) 87 (c) 53 (d) 80

43. « SSC MTS 2013

(a) 3 (b) 4 (c) 5 (c) 6

44. « UP B.Ed. 2008

(a) 3 (b) 10 (c) 15 (d) 60

45. « SSC Steno 2017

(a) 2 (b) 3 (c) 4 (d) 6

46. « CGPSC 2019

(a) 4 (b) 25 (c) 36 (d) 10

(e) None of these

47. « UPSSSC 2018

(a) 27 (b) 15 (c) 169 (d) 108

48.

2	5	4	51
4	7	9	65
3	3	8	47
1	8	4	?

« CG Revenue Inspector 2017

(a) 48 (b) 44 (c) 42 (d) None of these

49.

33	72	45	63
27	22	?	13
54	18	44	91
36	31	19	55

« CG Patwari 2019

(a) 81 (b) 28 (c) 18 (d) None of these

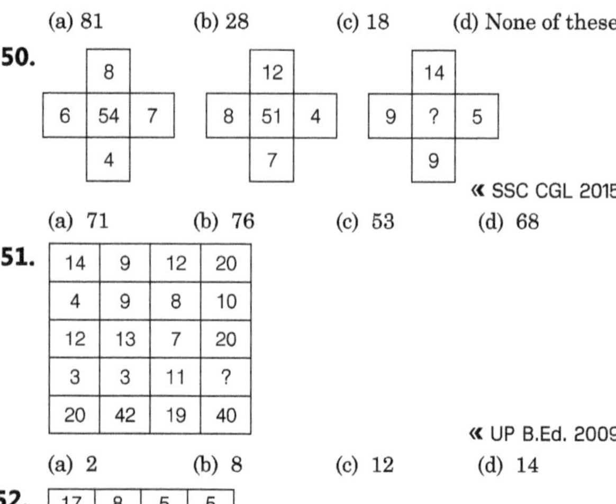

50. « SSC CGL 2015

(a) 71 (b) 76 (c) 53 (d) 68

51.

14	9	12	20
4	9	8	10
12	13	7	20
3	3	11	?
20	42	19	40

« UP B.Ed. 2009

(a) 2 (b) 8 (c) 12 (d) 14

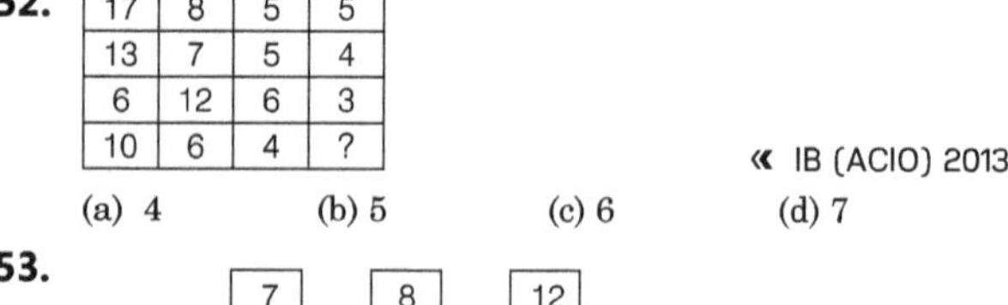

52.

17	8	5	5
13	7	5	4
6	12	6	3
10	6	4	?

« IB (ACIO) 2013

(a) 4 (b) 5 (c) 6 (d) 7

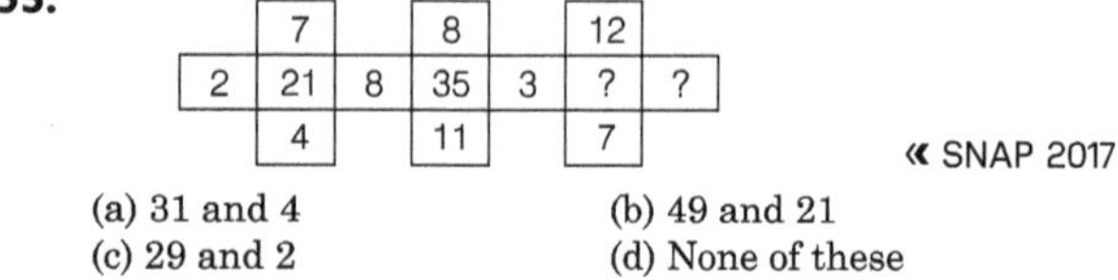

53. « SNAP 2017

(a) 31 and 4 (b) 49 and 21

(c) 29 and 2 (d) None of these

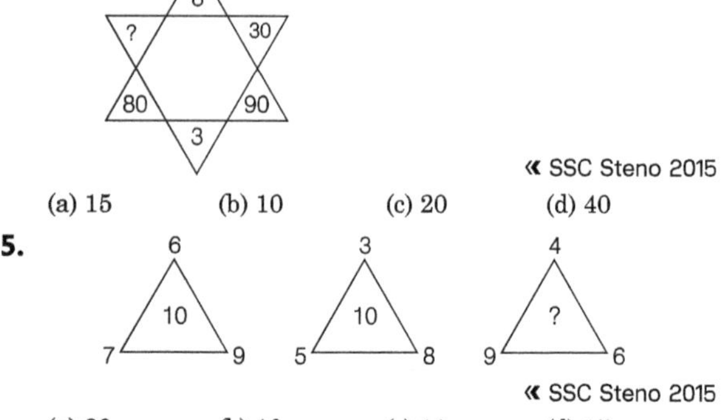

54. « SSC Steno 2015

(a) 15 (b) 10 (c) 20 (d) 40

55. « SSC Steno 2015

(a) 20 (b) 10 (c) 11 (d) 15

Answers / WITH EXPLANATIONS

1. (*b*) Moving anti-clockwise, the pattern is as follows

$15 + 1 = 16$

$16 + 2 = 18$

$18 + 3 = 21$

and $21 + 4 = 25$

So, missing number $25 + 5 = \boxed{30}$

2. (*b*) The pattern in clockwise direction

$2 \xrightarrow{\times 2} \boxed{4} \xrightarrow{\times 4} 16 \xrightarrow{\times 16} 256$

$\therefore\ ? = \boxed{4}$

3. (*b*) As, $7 \times 2 + 2 = 16$

$16 \times 2 + 2 = 34$

$34 \times 2 + 2 = \boxed{70}$

$\boxed{70} \times 2 + 2 = 142$

$142 \times 2 + 2 = 286$

$\therefore\ ? = 70$

4. (*c*) Moving in clockwise direction

As, $1 \times 2 = 2$

$2 \times 2 = 4$

$2 \times 4 = 8$

Similarly, $4 \times 8 = 32$

$\therefore\ ? = \boxed{32}$

5. (*a*) In I column, $(9 \times 5) - 7 \Rightarrow 38$

In II column, $(11 \times 9) - 22 \Rightarrow 77$

In III column, $(11 \times 15) - 5 \Rightarrow 160$

So, missing number is 160.

6. (*a*) As, $\frac{138}{6} = 23$ and $\frac{84}{7} = 12$

Similarly, $\frac{117}{13} = ?$

$\therefore\ ? = \boxed{9}$

7. (*a*) As, $2 \times 3 \times 4 = 24$

$\Rightarrow\ 24 + 1 = 25$

and $5 \times 7 \times 2 = 70$

$\Rightarrow\ 70 + 1 = 71$

Similarly, $1 \times 5 \times 6 = 30$

$\Rightarrow\ 30 + 1 = 31$

$(?) = \boxed{31}$

8. (*d*) As, $5^3 = 125$

$10^4 = 10000$

Similarly, $2^5 = ?$

$\Rightarrow\ 32 = ?$

$\therefore\ ? = \boxed{32}$

9. (*d*) As, $\frac{11 + 3}{2} = 7$

$7^2 = 49$ and $\frac{7 + 13}{2} = 10$

$10^2 = 100$

Similarly, $\frac{5 + 19}{2} = 12$

$\therefore\ 12^2 = ?$

$\Rightarrow\ ? = \boxed{144}$

10. (*d*) As, $3 + 4 - 1 = 6$

and $2 + 7 - 8 = 1$

Similarly, $6 + 5 - 9 = ?$

$\therefore\ ? = \boxed{2}$

11. (*d*) As,

In first row, $5^2 + 4^2 = 25 + 16 = 41$

In third row, $9^2 + 11^2 = 81 + 121 = 202$

Similarly, in

Second row,

$15^2 + 6^2 = 225 + 36 = 261$

$\therefore\ ? = 261$

12. (*b*) As, $11^2 - 1^2 = 121 - 1 = 120$

and $7^2 - 2^2 = 49 - 4 = 45$

Similarly, $5^2 - 3^2 = 25 - 9 = \boxed{16}$

13. (*c*) As, $92 + 64 + 52 = 208$ ⎤ -40

and $70 + 53 + 45 = 168$ ⎤ -40

Similarly, $48 + 42 + \boxed{38} = 128$

Hence, number $\boxed{38}$ will come in place of question mark (?).

14. (*b*) The pattern in clockwise direction is as $2^3, 3^3, 4^3, 5^3, 6^3$ and 7^3.

$\therefore\ ? = 7^3 = \boxed{343}$

15. (*c*) The pattern in the question is

$4^2 + 5^2 = 16 + 25 = 41,$

$2^2 + 1^2 = 4 + 1 = 5,$

$7^2 + 6^2 = 49 + 36 = \boxed{85}$

Hence, the missing number will be 85.

16. (*a*) The pattern of the number is

$3^2 - 3 = 6$

$8^2 - 8 = 56$

$10^2 - 10 = 90$

$2^2 - 2 = 2$

$5^2 - 5 = 20$

$1^2 - 1 = 0$

Hence, the missing number will be $\boxed{5}$.

17. (*d*) Here in the first, second and third columns cube of numbers from 1 to 9 is given.

$\therefore\ ? = (9)^3 = 729$

18. (*d*) As, $(5 + 4) \times 2$

$\Rightarrow\ 9 \times 2 = 18$ and $(2 + 4) \times 5$

$\Rightarrow\ 6 \times 5 = 30$

Same as, $(4 + 7) \times 3$

$\Rightarrow\ 11 \times 3 = \boxed{33}$

Hence, number in place of ? is 33.

19. (*d*) As, $24 + 20 + 37 = 81$

and $26 + 36 + 19 = 81$

Similarly, $31 + 25 + ? = 81$

$\Rightarrow\ 56 + ? = 81$

$\Rightarrow\ ? = 81 - 56 \Rightarrow ? = \boxed{25}$

20. (*a*) Starting from 27 and moving clockwise, the number in alternate segments form the series, 27, 30, 33, 36. The numbers in the remaining segments moving anti-clockwise, form the series as shown below.

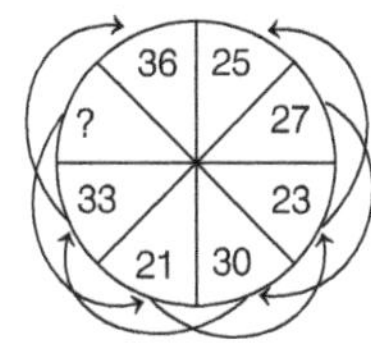

?, 21, 23, 25 or 21, 23, 25, ?

$\therefore\ ? = \boxed{19}$ or 27

21. (*a*) As,

$(11 \times 12) - (6 \times 9) = 132 - 54 = 78$

Similarly,

$(14 \times 10) - (7 \times 8) = 140 - 56 = \boxed{84}$

22. (*c*) As, $2 \times 2 \times 3 = 12$

$\Rightarrow\ 2 \times 3 \times 5 = 30$

and $5 \times 1 \times (-1) = -5$

Similarly, $4 \times 3 \times (-1) = \boxed{-12}$

23. (*c*) The pattern is given as

$\boxed{22} \xrightarrow{\times 3} 66 \xrightarrow{\times 3} 198 \xrightarrow{\times 3} 594$

$\therefore\ ? = \boxed{22}$

24. (*a*) As, $14 + 12 + 3 + 7 = 36$

Similarly, $9 + 11 + ? + 16 = 54$

$\Rightarrow\ ? = 54 - 36$

$\therefore\ ? = \boxed{18}$

25. (*b*) As,

$64 \uparrow (8)^2,\ 36 \uparrow (6)^2,\ 49 \uparrow (7)^2$

$8 + 6 + 7 = 21$

Similarly,

$121 \uparrow (11)^2,\ 81 \uparrow (9)^2,\ 100 \uparrow (10)^2$

$11 + 9 + 10 = \boxed{30}$

26. (*d*) As, $3 \times 2 \times 4 = 24$

and $2 \times (-1) \times (-2) = 4$

Similarly, $6 \times 5 \times 0 = 0$

$\therefore\ ? = \boxed{0}$

27. (*d*) As, $(86 - 38) \times 10 = 480$

and $(72 - 21) \times 10 = 510$

Similarly, $(36 - 12) \times 10 = 240$

$\therefore\ ? = \boxed{240}$

28. (*d*) As, $(13 + 22) \times 2 = 70$

and $(12 + 18) \times 2 = 60$

In the same way,

$(17 + 26) \times 2 = \boxed{86}$

29. (*c*) As, $(7+4)^2 = 121$,
$(2+8)^2 = 100$
and $(6+7)^2 = 169$
Similarly, $(5+9)^2 = 196$
$? = \boxed{196}$

30. (*c*) In first row, $(10 \div 4) \times 14 = 2.5 \times 14$
$= 35$
In second row,
$(15 \div 3) \times 5 = 5 \times 5 = 25$
In third row,
$(14 \div 7) \times 6 = 2 \times 6 = 12$
Similarly, in forth row, $(18 \div ?) \times 8 = 16$
$\Rightarrow \frac{18}{?} = \frac{16}{8}$
$\Rightarrow ? = \frac{18 \times 8}{16}$
$\Rightarrow ? = \boxed{9}$

31. (*b*) In each row of matrix,
As, $(4 \times 3 \times 2) + 8 = 32$,
$(5 \times 3 \times 1) + 9 = 24$
and $(7 \times 3 \times 3) + 7 = 70$
Similarly,
$(2 \times 9 \times 4) + 12 = 84$
$? = \boxed{84}$

32. (*c*) As, $1 \times 3 \times 4 \times 5 = 60$
and $6 \times 7 \times 1 \times 2 = 84$
Similarly, $3 \times 10 \times 3 \times 1 = 90$
$? = \boxed{90}$

33. (*a*) As, $(1+0+1+5) = 7$
and $(3+9+4+5) = 21$
Similarly, $(2+8+5+6) = 21$
$? = \boxed{21}$
Hence, option (a) is the correct answer.

34. (*a*) As, $(4^2 + 6^2) + 8 = 60$
and $(9^2 + 2^2) + 8 = 93$
Similarly, $(14^2 + 5^2) + 8 = 229$
$? = \boxed{229}$
Hence, number 229 will come in place of question mark (?).

35. (*c*) As, $7 \times 3 = 21$; $21 \times 2 = 42$
and $9 \times 3 = 27$; $27 \times 2 = 54$
Similarly, $14 \times 3 = 42$
$? = \boxed{42}$
and $42 \times 2 = 84$
So, the missing number $= \boxed{42}$
Hence, option (c) is the correct answer.

36. (*b*) As, $(4 \times 5)^2 - (3 \times 1)^2 = 391$
and $(15 \times 3)^2 - (8 \times 5)^2 = 425$
Similarly,
$(8 \times 7)^2 - (10 \times 3)^2 = \boxed{2236}$
Hence, 2236 will come in place of question mark (?).

37. (*d*) As, $(\sqrt{25} + \sqrt{64} + \sqrt{36} + \sqrt{144})$
$= 5 + 8 + 6 + 12 = 31$
and $(\sqrt{324} + \sqrt{9} + \sqrt{169} + \sqrt{16})$
$= 18 + 3 + 13 + 4 = 38$
Similarly,
$(\sqrt{64} + \sqrt{36} + \sqrt{361} + \sqrt{576})$
$= 8 + 6 + 19 + 24 = \boxed{57}$
Hence, option (d) is the correct answer.

38. (*a*) As, $(7 \times 4) - (9 \times 2) = 10$
and $(15 \times 5) - (18 \times 3) = 21$
Similarly, $(19 \times 3) - (16 \times 2) = 25$
$? = \boxed{25}$
Hence, option (a) is the correct answer.

39. (*c*) As, $528 - 412 = 116$
and $915 - 364 = 551$
Similarly, $725 - 524 = 201$
$? = \boxed{201}$

40. (*d*) As, $\frac{15 + 57}{9} = 8$ and $\frac{24 + 12}{9} = 4$
Similarly, $\frac{13 + ?}{9} = 7$
$\therefore\ ? = (7 \times 9) - 13 = 63 - 13 = \boxed{50}$

41. (*a*) As,
$(7 \times 2) + (5 \times 15) = 14 + 75 = 89$
and $(18 \times 4) + (5 \times 3) = 72 + 15 = 87$
Similarly,
$(6 \times 12) + (9 \times 7) = 72 + 63 = 135$
$? = \boxed{135}$

42. (*d*) As, $(13 - 11) \times (16 + 8) = 48$
and $(9 - 4) \times (7 + 6) = 65$
Similarly, $(15 - 5) \times (2 + 6) = 80$
$\therefore\ ? = \boxed{80}$

43. (*c*) As, $27 \div 9 - 2 = 3 - 2 = 1$
and $35 \div 7 - 3 = 5 - 3 = 2$
Similarly, $36 \div 4 - 4 = 9 - 4 = 5$
$\therefore\ ? = \boxed{5}$

44. (*a*) As, $16 - (3 + 4 + 8) = 1$
and $20 - (5 + 3 + 4) = 8$
Similarly, $18 - (5 + 4 + 6) = 3$
$\therefore\ ? = \boxed{3}$

45. (*a*) As, $2 + 3 + 6 + 8 = 19$
and $4 + 4 + 9 + 2 = 19$
Similarly, $12 + 2 + 3 + ? = 19$
$\therefore\ ? = 19 - 17 = 2 \Rightarrow ? = \boxed{2}$

46. (*d*) As, $35 - 14 \Rightarrow 21 \times 2 = 42$
$14 - 12 = 2 \Rightarrow 2 \times 2 = 4$
$30 - 12 = 18$
$\Rightarrow 18 \times 2 = 36$
Similarly, $35 - 30 = 5 \Rightarrow 5 \times 2 = 10$
$\therefore\ ? = \boxed{10}$

47. (*d*) As, $5^2 + 3^2 = 25 + 9 = 34 - (4)^2$
$= 34 - 16 = 18$
and $7^2 + 5^2 = 49 + 25 = 74 - (3)^2$
$= 74 - 9 = 65$
Similarly, $9^2 + 6^2 = 81 + 36$
$= 117 - (3)^2$
$= 117 - 9 = 108$
$\therefore\ ? = \boxed{108}$

48. (*c*) As, $2 \times 2 + 5 \times 3 + 8 \times 4 = 51$
$4 \times 2 + 7 \times 3 + 9 \times 4 = 65$
and $3 \times 2 + 3 \times 3 + 8 \times 4 = 47$
Similarly, $1 \times 2 + 8 \times 3 + 4 \times 4 = 42$
$? = \boxed{42}$

49. (*a*) In the given matrix, the digits of the numbers given in each row are interchanged and arranged accordingly in column.
As, in first row, 33, 72, 45, 63
∴ In first column, 33, 27, 54, 36
In fourth row, 36, 31, 19, 55
∴ In fourth column, 63, 13, 91, 55
Similarly, In second, row, 27, 22, ? , 13
In second column, 72, 22, 18, 31
In third row 54, 18, 44, 91
In third column, 45, $\boxed{?}$, 44, 19
$\therefore\ \boxed{?} = 81$

50. (*d*) As, $(6 \times 7) + (8 + 4) = 42 + 12 = 54$
and $(8 \times 4) + (12 + 7) = 31 + 19 = 51$
Similarly,
$(9 \times 5) + (14 + 9) = 45 + 23 = 68$
$? = \boxed{68}$

51. (*b*) As, $(14 \times 4 - 20) \div 12 = 3$
$(9 \times 9 - 42) \div 13 = 3$
and $(12 \times 8 - 19) \div 7 = 11$
Similarly, $(20 \times 10 - 40) \div 20 = 8$
$\therefore\ ? = \boxed{8}$

52. (*a*) Here, As In row 1 : $\frac{17 + 8}{5} = 5$
In row 2 : $\frac{13 + 7}{5} = \frac{20}{5} = 4$
In row 3 : $\frac{6 + 12}{6} = \frac{18}{6} = 3$
In row 4 : $\frac{10 + 6}{4} = \frac{16}{4} = 4 \Rightarrow ? = \boxed{4}$

53. (*b*) As, $4 - 2 = 2$; $8 - 7 = 1$
∴ Middle number = 21
and $11 - 8 = 3$; $8 - 3 = 5$
∴ Middle number = 35
Similarly, $7 - 3 = 4$; $21 - 12 = 9$
∴ Middle number = 49
Hence, required numbers are 49 and 21 respectively.

54. (*d*) As, $8 \times 10 = 80$
$\Rightarrow 80 + 10 = 90$
Similarly, $3 \times 10 = 30$
$\Rightarrow 30 + 10 = 40 \Rightarrow ? = \boxed{40}$

55. (*c*) In first figure,
$7 + 9 - 6 = 16 - 6 = 10$
In second figure,
$5 + 8 - 3 = 13 - 3 = 10$
In third figure,
$9 + 6 - 4 = 15 - 4 = 11 \Rightarrow ? = \boxed{11}$

TYPE 02

Letter Puzzles

In this type of problems, the arrangement of the letters of the English alphabet is done according to a certain pattern that may involve addition/subtraction of the positional values of letters, operations on the positional values of the letters in the English alphabetical series or reverse alphabetical series. The candidate is required to find out the pattern and then the missing character from the arrangement based on that pattern.

Following examples will give you better idea about such types of problems.

DIRECTIONS ~ (Example Nos. 12-16) *In each of the following questions, which character when placed at the sign of interrogation (?) shall complete the given pattern.*

Ex 12

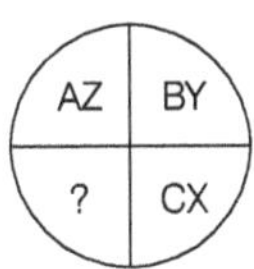

(a) DK (b) DW (c) DL (d) DE

Solution (b) Moving clockwise, starting with AZ, each quadrant is having a pair of opposite letters in succession.

A + Z = 1 + 26 = 27
B + Y = 2 + 25 = 27
C + X = 3 + 24 = 27

Similarly, [D + W] = 4 + 23 = 27

So, the missing character is DW.

Ex 13

A	D	G
D	I	N
I	P	?

(a) V (b) W (c) X (d) Y

Solution (b) According to English alphabet,

A (1) —+3→ D (4) —+3→ G (7)
D (4) —+5→ I (9) —+5→ N (14)
I (9) —+7→ P (16) —+7→ [W] (23)

So, the missing character is W.

Ex 14

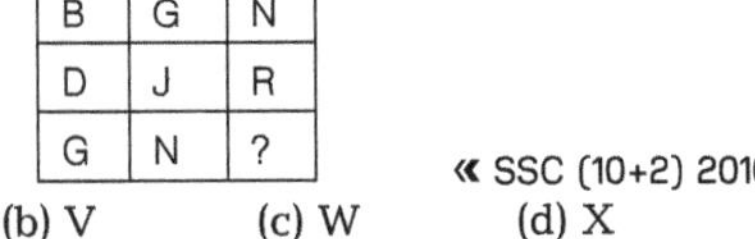

B	G	N
D	J	R
G	N	?

« SSC (10+2) 2010

(a) U (b) V (c) W (d) X

Solution (c) According to English alphabet,

B (2) —+5→ G (7) —+7→ N (14)
D (4) —+6→ J (10) —+8→ R (18)
G (7) —+7→ N (14) —+9→ [W] (23)

So, the missing character is W.

Ex 15

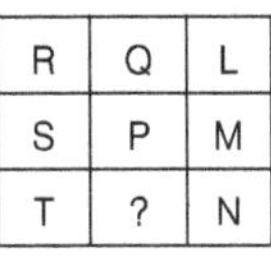

R	Q	L
S	P	M
T	?	N

« SSC (10+2) 2010

(a) O (b) R (c) W (d) V

Solution (a) According to English alphabet,
Moving columnwise

R (18) —+1→ S (19) —+1→ T (20)
Q (17) —−1→ P (16) —−1→ [O] (15)
L (12) —+1→ M (13) —+1→ N (14)

So, the missing character is O.

Ex 16

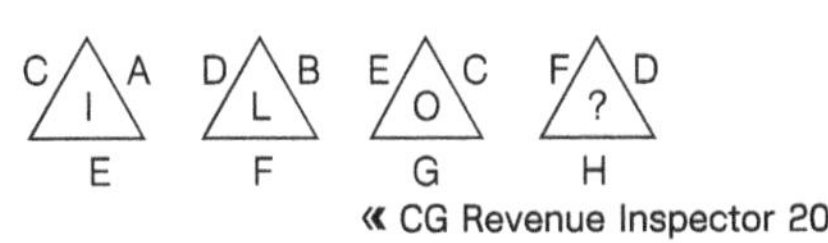

« CG Revenue Inspector 2017

(a) S (b) R (c) Q (d) N

Solution (b) The pattern of the letters at the center of the triangle is as follows

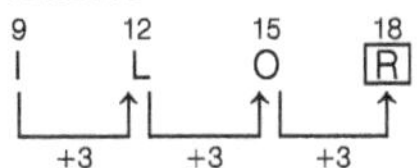

So, the missing character is R.

TYPE 03

Alpha-Numeric Puzzles

In this type of problems, a combination of numbers and alphabets/letters, arranged according to a pattern, is given in the form of a puzzle. The candidate is required to identify the underlying pattern and then find the missing term(s).

Following examples will give you better idea about such types of problems

DIRECTIONS ~ (Example Nos. 17-20) *In each of the following questions, which character will complete the given pattern when placed at the sign of interrogation(?)?*

Ex 17

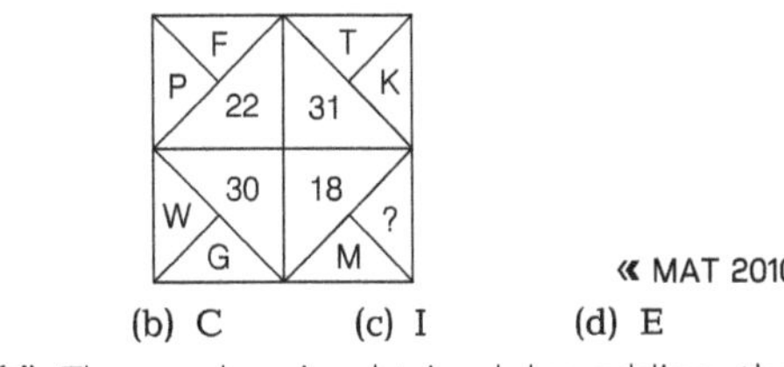

« MAT 2010

(a) F (b) C (c) I (d) E

Solution (d) The number is obtained by adding the positional values of alphabet in english alphabetical series

As, 16 + 6 = 22 (P F), 20 + 11 = 31 (T K) and 23 + 7 = 30 (W G)

Similarly, missing letter is E such that 13 + 5 = 18 (M E)

Hence, the answer is option (d).

Ex 18

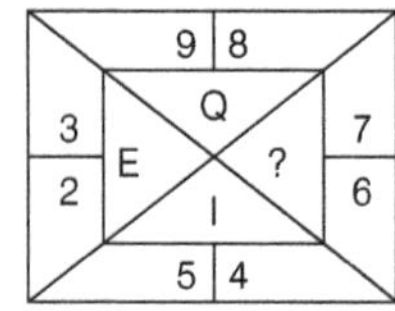

« UPSSSC Lower Subordinate III 2016

(a) R (b) N
(c) M (d) L

Solution (c) As, $3 + 2 = 5 \Rightarrow E$
$9 + 8 = 17 \Rightarrow Q$
and $5 + 4 = 9 \Rightarrow I$
Similarly, $7 + 6 = 13 \Rightarrow M$
$\therefore$? = M

Hence, the answer is option (c).

Ex 19

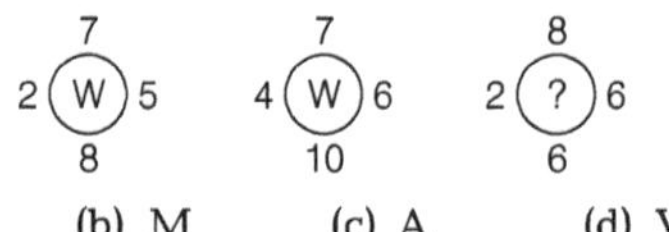

(a) R (b) M (c) A (d) V

Solution (a) As, $(7 \times 8) - (2 \times 5) = 56 - 10 = 46$
and $46 \div 2 = 23 = W$
and $(7 \times 10) - (4 \times 6) = 70 - 24 = 46$
and $46 \div 2 = 23 = W$
Similarly, $(8 \times 6) - (2 \times 6) = 48 - 12 = 36$
and $36 \div 2 = 18 = R$

Hence, the answer is option (a).

Ex 20

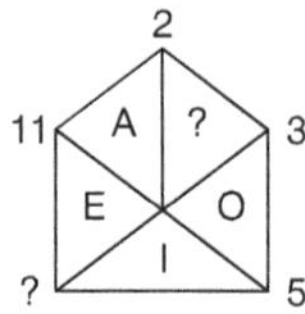

« SSC (CPO) 2009

(a) 8 and U (b) 8 and V
(c) 7 and U (d) 9 and V

Solution (c) According to the given sequence of groups of letters and numbers,
Prime numbers are increasing in clockwise direction.
Starting with A in anti-clockwise direction all letters are the group of vowels *i.e.*, A, E, I, O and U.
So, the missing number will be 7 and the last vowel will be U.
Hence, the answer is option (c).

Practice / CORNER 17.2

DIRECTIONS ~ (Q. Nos. 1-37) *In each of the following questions, which character will complete the given pattern, when placed at the sign of interrogation?*

1.

A	D
?	G

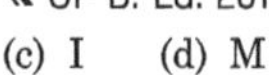

« UP B. Ed. 2010

(a) H (b) J (c) I (d) M

2.

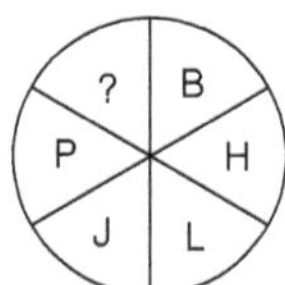

(a) U (b) V (c) T (d) X

3.

L	C	H	G	F
O	X	?	T	U

(a) S (b) K (c) T (d) Y

4.

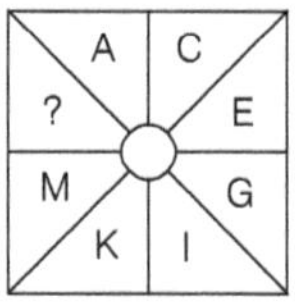

A C
? E
M G
K I

« SSC (CPO) 2011

(a) B (b) W (c) O (d) V

5.

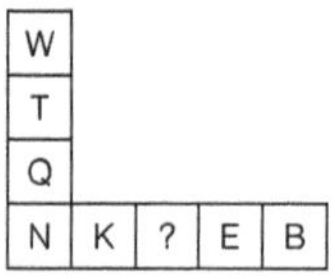

W
T
Q
N K ? E B

(a) H (b) L (c) G (d) F

6.

D	M	V
F	P	Z
H	S	?

« CG PSC 2013

(a) D (b) C (c) I (d) G
(e) K

7.

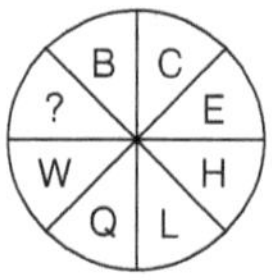

B C
? E
W H
Q L

(a) Z (b) X (c) I (d) D

8.

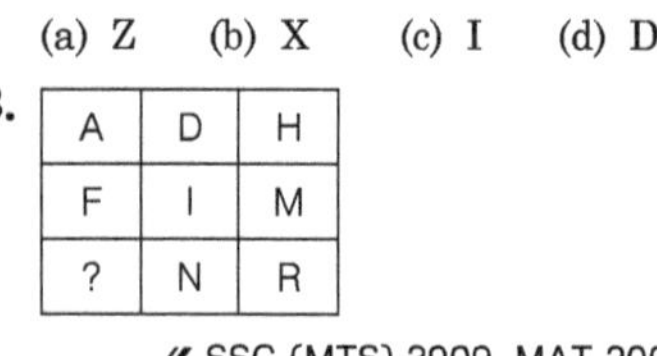

A	D	H
F	I	M
?	N	R

« SSC (MTS) 2009, MAT 2005

(a) K (b) N (c) O (d) P

9.

H	C	?
B	F	E
P	R	T

« IIFT 2012

(a) Y (b) O (c) D (d) G

10.

F	I	O
A	J	K
E	M	?

« Hotel Mgmt 2009

(a) P (b) R (c) S (d) V

11.

A	D	G
D	I	N
I	P	?

« UPSSSC Excise Constable 2016

(a) V (b) W (c) X (d) Y

12.

A	C	E
N	K	H
R	?	Z

« UPSSSC Lower Subordinate 2015

(a) S (b) T (c) V (d) W

13. 

P	M	Q
F	C	F
J	J	?

« SSC (10 + 2) 2017

(a) R (b) K (c) L (d) O

14.

AZ	BY	CX
DW	EV	FU
GT	?	IR

« SSC (CPO) 2011

(a) HR (b) HS (c) HV (d) HU

15.

A	M	B	N
R	C	S	D
E	U	F	?

(a) G (b) R (c) T (d) V

16. 

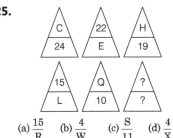

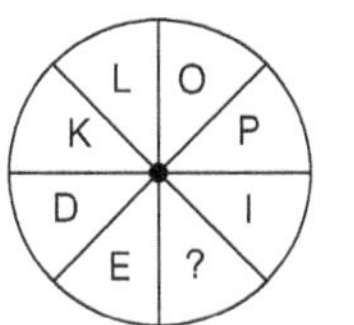

(a) G (b) U (c) V (d) H

17.

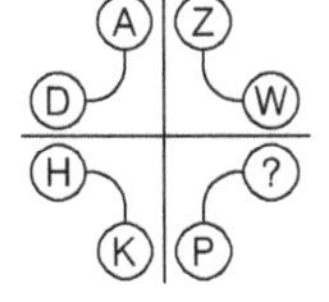

(a) Y (b) Q (c) S (d) R

18.

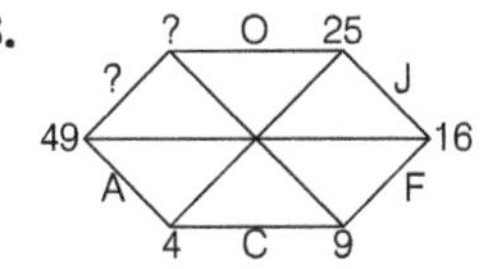

(a) Y and 40 (b) U and 36
(c) W and 64 (d) X and 81

19.

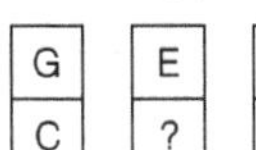

A	G	E	K	I
E	C	?	G	M

(a) H (b) D (c) I (d) F

20.

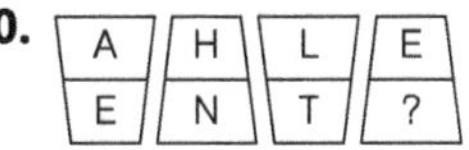

A	H	L	E
E	N	T	?

(a) U (b) V (c) W (d) O

21.

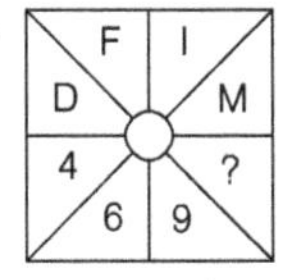

(a) 10 (b) 13 (c) 12 (d) 14

22.

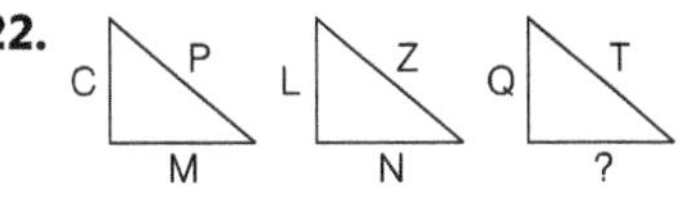

(a) O (b) C (c) S (d) J

23.

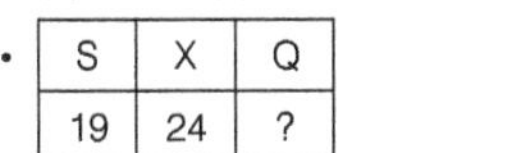

S	X	Q
19	24	?

(a) 25 (b) 17 (c) 30 (d) 26

24.

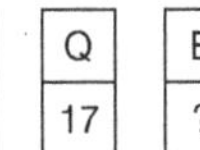

B	J	Q	E	?
2	10	17	?	8

(a) H and 5 (b) F and 6
(c) H and 6 (d) 5 and H

25.

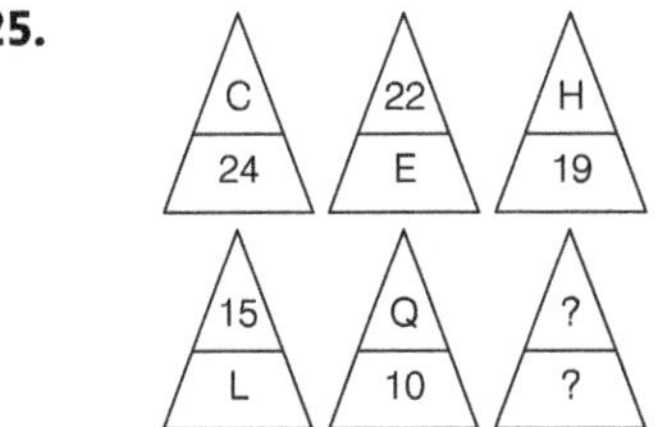

(a) $\frac{15}{R}$ (b) $\frac{4}{W}$ (c) $\frac{S}{11}$ (d) $\frac{4}{X}$

26.

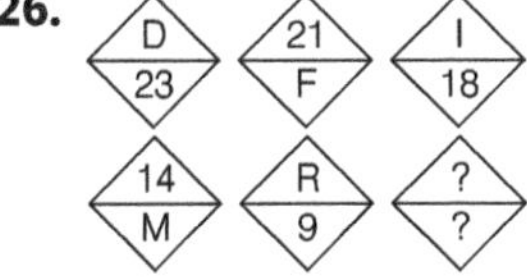

(a) $\frac{S}{10}$ (b) $\frac{3}{X}$ (c) $\frac{U}{4}$ (d) $\frac{6}{U}$

27.

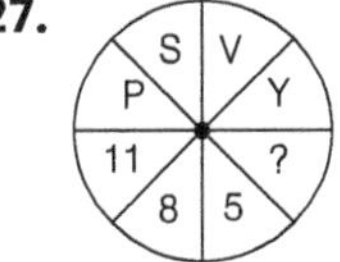

(a) 3 (b) 7 (c) 2 (d) 3

28.

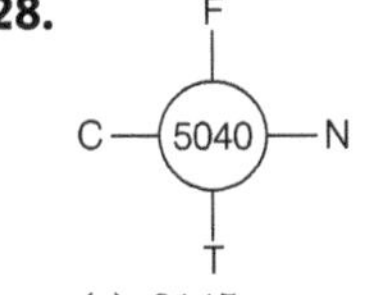

(a) 8145 (b) 3437
(c) 9256 (d) 4928

29.

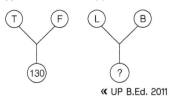

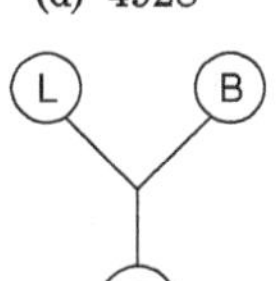

« UP B.Ed. 2011

(a) 118 (b) 75
(c) 205 (d) 70

30.

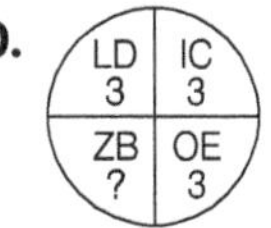

(a) 3 (b) 16 (c) 5 (d) 13

31.

CN 21	TV 220
FK 33	LI ?

« SSC (CGL) 2009

(a) 54 (b) 58 (c) 65 (d) 85

32.

4C	2B	3A
28A	?	45B
7C	8A	15B

« SSC (CPO) 2007

(a) 16 C (b) 12 C (c) 13 C (d) 7 C

33.

BC 5	TR 38
LG 19	XN ?

(a) 15 (b) 42 (c) 38 (d) 5

34.

A 2	C 4	E 6
G 3	I 5	?
M 5	O 9	Q14

« SSC (CGL) 2006

(a) J 15 (b) K 8 (c) K 15 (d) L 10

35.

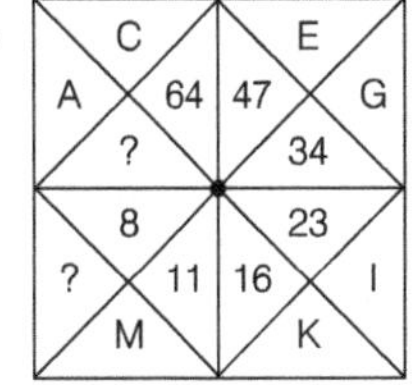

(a) J and 80 (b) O and 83
(c) N and 7 (d) P and 85

36.

JL4	KM5	LN20
MO7	NP3	OQ21
PR6	QS8	?

« UPSSSC Conductor Exam 2015

(a) RT14 (b) TR48
(c) RT48 (d) SR48

37.

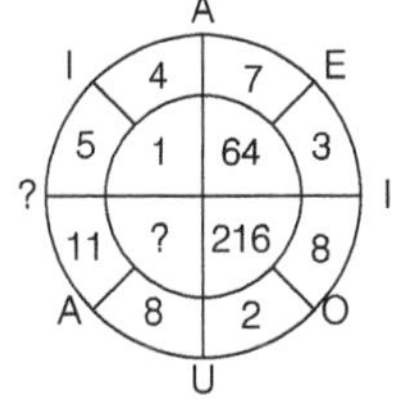

(a) U and 28 (b) I and 26
(c) E and 27 (d) A and 25

Answers WITH EXPLANATIONS

1. (*b*) Moving clockwise, each next letter is 3 letters forward in position of the previous letter.

$\overset{1}{A} \xrightarrow{+3} \overset{4}{D}$, $\overset{4}{D} \xrightarrow{+3} \overset{7}{G}$, $\overset{7}{G} \xrightarrow{+3} \boxed{\overset{10}{J}}$

So, missing character is J.

2. (*c*) As, $\overset{2}{B} \xrightarrow{+8} \overset{10}{J}$ and $\overset{8}{H} \xrightarrow{+8} \overset{16}{P}$

Similarly, $\overset{12}{L} \xrightarrow{+8} \overset{20}{T}$

So, missing character is T.

3. (*a*) LO, CX, GT and FU are pair of opposite letters. Similarly, the letter opposite to H is S.

Hence, option (a) is the correct answer.

4. (*c*) Starting from A in clockwise direction, add 2 in the position of each letter to obtain the next letter.

As, $\overset{1}{A} + 2 = \overset{3}{C}$

$\overset{3}{C} + 2 = \overset{5}{E}$

$\overset{5}{E} + 2 = \overset{7}{G}$

$\overset{7}{G} + 2 = \overset{9}{I}$

$\overset{9}{I} + 2 = \overset{11}{K}$

$\overset{11}{K} + 2 = \overset{13}{M}$

Similarly, $\overset{13}{M} + 2 = \boxed{\overset{15}{O}}$

Hence, option (c) is the correct answer.

5. (*a*) The pattern is as follows

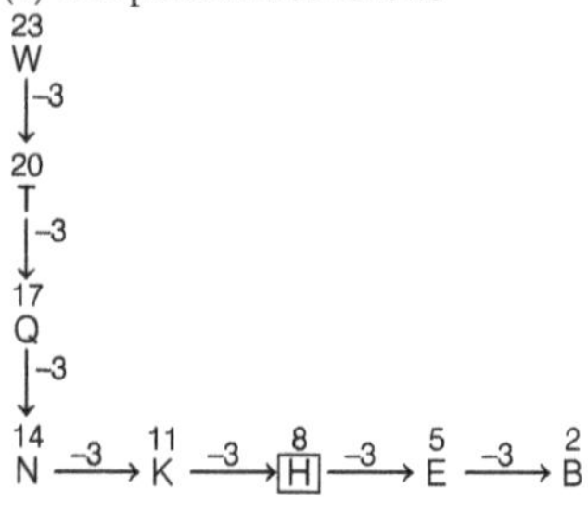

Hence, option (a) is the correct answer

6. (*a*) As, $\overset{4}{D} \xrightarrow{+2} \overset{6}{F} \xrightarrow{+2} \overset{8}{H}$

and $\overset{13}{M} \xrightarrow{+3} \overset{16}{P} \xrightarrow{+3} \overset{19}{S}$

Similarly, $\overset{22}{V} \xrightarrow{+4} \overset{26}{Z} \xrightarrow{+4} \boxed{\overset{4}{D}}$

So, missing character is D.

7. (*d*) Moving clockwise, the pattern is as follows

$\overset{2}{B} \xrightarrow{+1} \overset{3}{C} \xrightarrow{+2} \overset{5}{E} \xrightarrow{+3} \overset{8}{H} \xrightarrow{+4}$

$\overset{12}{L} \xrightarrow{+5} \overset{17}{Q} \xrightarrow{+6} \overset{23}{W} \xrightarrow{+7} \boxed{\overset{4}{D}}$

∴ So, missing character is D.

8. (*a*) As, $\overset{1}{A} \xrightarrow{+3} \overset{4}{D} \xrightarrow{+4} \overset{8}{H}$

and $\overset{6}{F} \xrightarrow{+3} \overset{9}{I} \xrightarrow{+4} \overset{13}{M}$

Similarly, $\boxed{\overset{11}{K}} \xrightarrow{+3} \overset{14}{N} \xrightarrow{+4} \overset{18}{R}$

Hence, option (a) is the correct answer.

9. (*c*) Here, H = 8, B = 2

and 8 × 2 = 16 = P

Similarly, C = 3, F = 6

and 3 × 6 = 18 = R

Now, in column III,

E = 5 and T = 20

∴ ? = D such that

4 × 5 = 20

↓

D

∴ ? = $\boxed{D}$

10. (*b*) As, 6 9 15

F + I = O

and 1 10 11

A + J = K

Similarly, $\overset{5}{E} + \overset{13}{M} = \boxed{\overset{18}{R}}$

Hence, option (b) is the correct answer.

11. (*b*) As, $\overset{1}{A} \xrightarrow{+3} \overset{4}{D} \xrightarrow{+3} \overset{7}{G}$ (In first row)

and $\overset{4}{D} \xrightarrow{+5} \overset{9}{I} \xrightarrow{+5} \overset{14}{N}$ (In second row)

Similarly, $\overset{9}{I} \xrightarrow{+7} \overset{16}{P} \xrightarrow{+7} \boxed{\overset{23}{W}}$ (In third row)

∴ ? = $\boxed{W}$

12. (*c*) As, $\overset{1}{A} \xrightarrow{+2} \overset{3}{C} \xrightarrow{+2} \overset{5}{E}$ (in first row)

and $\overset{14}{N} \xrightarrow{-3} \overset{11}{K} \xrightarrow{-3} \overset{8}{H}$ (in second row)

Similarly, $\overset{18}{R} \xrightarrow{+4} \boxed{\overset{22}{V}} \xrightarrow{+4} \overset{26}{Z}$ (in third row)

∴ ? = $\boxed{V}$

13. (*b*) Replacing the letters with their positional value in alphabetical series, we get,

16	13	17
6	3	6
10	10	?

As, 16 − 6 = 10 and 13 − 3 = 10

Similarly, 17 − 6 = 11

∴ 11 is the positional value of K in English alphabetical series.

∴ ? = K

14. (*b*) In each cell, pair of opposite letters in the alphabetical series is given.

∴ G $\xrightarrow{+1}$ H and opposite letter of H is S.

∴ HS will come in place of question mark.

15. (*d*) Consecutive letters occupy alternate positions in each row.

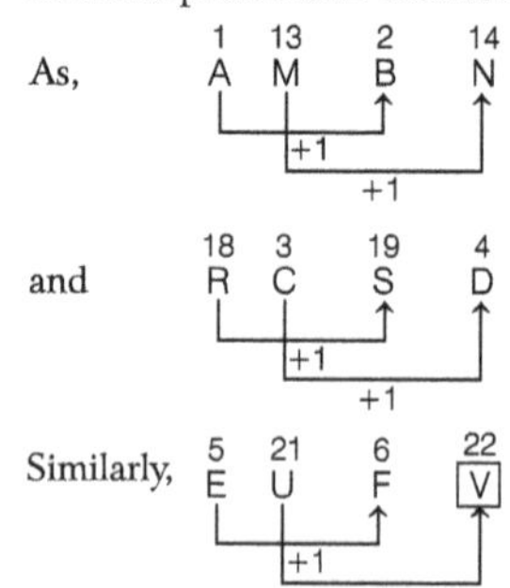

Hence, V will come in place of question mark.

16. (*d*) The pattern in the question is

Top part = KL (MN) OP

Bottom part = DE (FG) $\boxed{H}$ I

∴ H will come in place of question mark.

17. (*c*) There are four opposite letter pairs in the question and sum of their positional value is equal to 27.

Pairs are as follows

A Z, DW, H ? and KP

∵ Letter opposite to H is $\boxed{S}$

Hence, S will come in place of question mark.

18. (*b*) Starting from letter A in anti-clockwise direction,

$\overset{1}{A} \xrightarrow{+2} \overset{3}{C} \xrightarrow{+3} \overset{6}{F} \xrightarrow{+4} \overset{10}{J}$

$\xrightarrow{+5} \overset{15}{O} \xrightarrow{+6} \boxed{\overset{21}{U}}$

Starting from number 4 in anti-clockwise direction

$2^2 = 4$,

$3^2 = 9, 4^2 = 16, 5^2 = 25, 6^2 = \boxed{36}$

∴ ? = $\boxed{\text{U and 36}}$

Hence, option (b) is the correct answer.

19. (*c*) In the given question, the letters are zigzag from top to bottom and bottom to top with a gap of one letter each time.

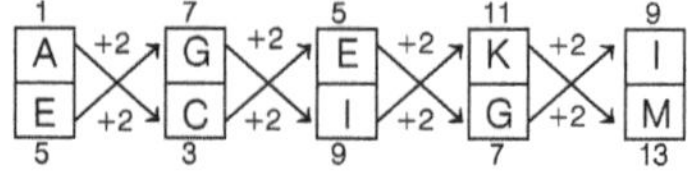

Hence, $\boxed{I}$ will come in place of question mark.

20. (*d*) So,

1	8	12	5
A	H	L	E
E	N	T	?
5	14	20	

The gaps between the top and bottom letters in each domino form the series 4, 6, 8, 10. The final gap will therefore be 10.

$\because$? = E + 10

? = 5 + 10 = 15 = 15 ⇒ O

21. (*b*) The letters in the upper half of square have their corresponding position numbers in the second half (bottom) of square.

$\therefore$? = 13 = M

22. (*b*) As, | 16 − 3 = 13 | and | 26 − 12 = 14 |
P C M ; Z L N

Similarly, | 20 − 17 = 3 |
T Q C

$\therefore$? = C (letter at 3rd position according to the English alphabetical series).

23. (*b*) Each letter has been denoted by its position according to the English alphabetical series.

As, position of S according to the English alphabetical series = 19 and position of X according to the English alphabetical = 24

Similarly, position of Q according to the English alphabetical = 17

$\therefore$? = 17

24. (*d*) In each box, letters of English alphabet and their corresponding positions are given.

As, position of B in English alphabetical series is 2,

Position of J in English alphabetical series is 10,

Position of Q in English alphabetical series is 17,

Similarly, position of E in English alphabetical series is 5 and letter H is present at 8th position in alphabetical series.

$\therefore$ Number = 5 (second row)

Letter = H (first row)

$\therefore$ Option (d) is the correct answer.

25. (*b*) The letters move from numerator to denominator and have gaps of 1, 2, 3, 4 and 5 letters (according to English alphabetical series). The numbers are their respective position numbers in backward order.

$\therefore$ $\frac{?}{?} = \frac{4}{W}$

26. (*b*) The letters are zigzag from top to bottom and have gaps of 1, 2, 3, 4 and 5. The numbers are their respective position numbers in backward order.

$\because$ R S, T, U, V, W X (5 letters)

And position of X in backward order is 3.

$\therefore$ $\frac{?}{?} = \frac{3}{X}$

27. (*c*) The letters in the upper half of the circle follow the sequence

16 19 22 25
P →(+3) S →(+3) V →(+3) Y

and the numbers represent their respective position in backward order

Hence, position of Y in backward order is 2.

28. (*d*) As, $3 \times 6 \times 14 \times 20 = 5040$
C F N T

Similarly, $7 \times 11 \times 4 \times 16$ = 4928
G K D P

Hence, 4928 will come in place of question mark.

29. (*d*) Sum of the letter positions is multiplied by 5.

As, | (20 + 6) × 5 = 130 |
T F

Similarly, | (12 + 2) × 5 = 70 |
L B

$\therefore$? = 70

30. (*d*) As, | 12 ÷ 4 = 3 |, | 9 ÷ 3 = 3 |
L D ; I C

and | 15 ÷ 5 = 3 |
O E

Similarly, | 26 ÷ 2 = 13 |
Z B

$\therefore$? = 13

31. (*a*) Number = $\frac{\text{Product of letter positions}}{2}$.

As, | (3 × 14) ÷ 2 = 21 |,
C N

| (20 × 22) ÷ 2 = 220 |
T V

and | (6 × 11) ÷ 2 = 33 |
F K

Similarly, | (12 × 9) ÷ 2 = 54 |
L I

$\therefore$? = 54

32. (*a*) In each row, each of the letters A, B, C must appear once. In each column, the product of the first and third number is equal to the second number.

$\therefore$ Missing number = (8 × 2) = 16

and missing letter = C

$\therefore$? = 16 C

Hence, option (a) is the correct answer.

33. (*c*) As, 2 + 3 = 5,
B C

20 + 18 = 38
T R

and 12 + 7 = 19
L G

Similarly, 24 + 14 = 38
X N

Hence, option (c) is the correct answer.

34. (*b*) The positional values of the letters in each row are increased by 2 to get the next letter.

Hence, missing letter = I (9) →(+2) K (11)

In each row, 1st number + 2nd number = 3rd number

$\therefore$ Missing number = 3 + 5 = 8

$\therefore$? = K8

Hence, option (b) is the correct answer.

35. (*b*) Starting from letter A in clockwise direction,

A(1) →(+2) C(3) →(+2) E(5) →(+2) G(7) →(+2) I(9) →(+2) K(11) →(+2) M(13) →(+2) O(15)

Starting from number 8 in anti-clockwise direction (prime number addition sequence)

8 →(+3) 11 →(+5) 16 →(+7) 23 →(+11) 34 →(+13) 47 →(+17) 64 →(+19) 83

$\therefore$? = O and 83

Hence, option (b) is the correct answer.

36. (c) As, J(10) L(12) 4 ; K(11) M(13) 5 ; L(12) N(14) 20 — letters +1 each; 4 × 5 = 20

(In first row)

and M(13) O(15) 7 ; N(14) P(16) 3 ; O(15) Q(17) 21 — letters +1 each; 7 × 3 = 21

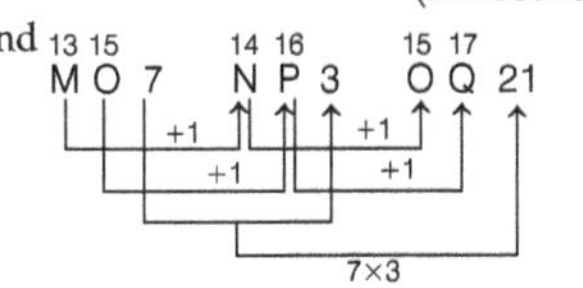

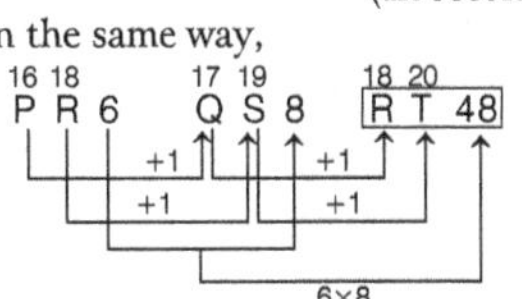

(In second row)

In the same way,

P(16) R(18) 6 ; Q(17) S(19) 8 ; R(18) T(20) 48 — letters +1 each; 6 × 8 = 48

(In third row)

$\therefore$? = RT48

37. (*c*) The letters form a repetitive sequence of vowels.

A, E, I, O, U, A, E (outer side)

On the inner side, (right half part)

$(7-3)^3 = 64$ and $(8-2)^3 = 216$

On inner side (left half part)

$(5-4)^3 = 1$

and $(11-8)^3$ = 27

$\therefore$? = E and 27

Hence, option (c) is the correct answer.

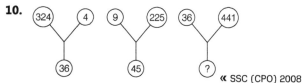

Master Exercise

DIRECTIONS ~ (Q. Nos. 1-66) *In each of the following questions, which number/character will complete the given pattern, when placed at the sign of interrogation (?).*

1.

25	17	41
32	83	11
26	?	31

(a) 26 (b) 25 (c) 34 (d) 38

2.

5	9	14	20
9	17	27	?

« WBSC 2020

(a) 35 (b) 37 (c) 39 (d) 41

3.

4	18	23
19	330	?
3	6	1

« SSC CPO 2019

(a) 350 (b) 529 (c) 550 (d) 530

4.

3	4	5	?
5	2	9	19
7	3	3	24
11	1	4	15

« Chattisgarh Revenue Inspector 2016-17

(a) 17 (b) 18 (c) 19 (d) 20

5.

16	17	28
21	23	27
?	391	756

« SSC CGL 2017

(a) 377 (b) 351 (c) 336 (d) 306

6.

91	299	493
?	23	29
7	13	17

« SSC CGL 2017

(a) 13 (b) 17 (c) 84 (d) 98

7.

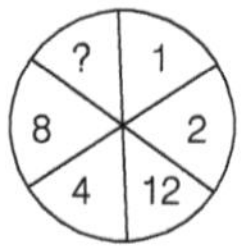

« UPSC Assistant Commandant 2019

(a) 12 (b) 16
(c) 32 (d) 48

8.

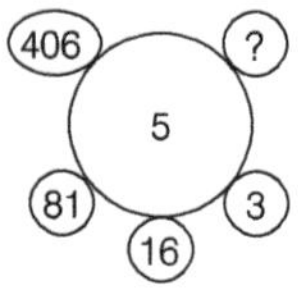

« CGPSC Pre 2017

(a) 2031 (b) 731
(c) 1625 (d) 1
(e) None of these

9.

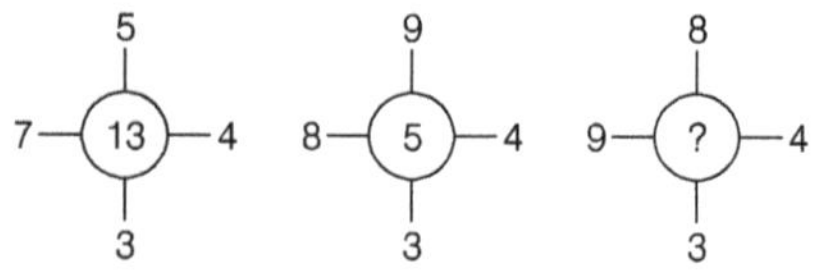

(a) 12 (b) 15 (c) 18 (d) 14

10.

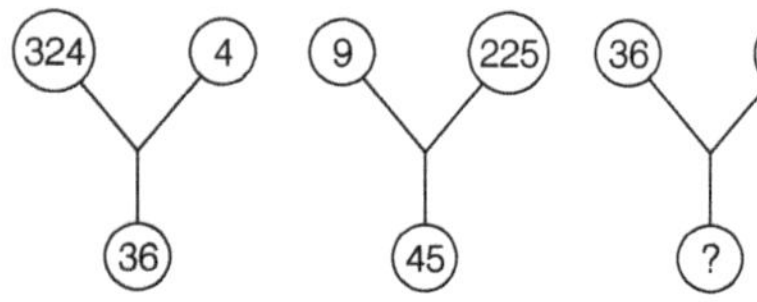

« SSC (CPO) 2008

(a) 180 (b) 59 (c) 126 (d) 88

11.

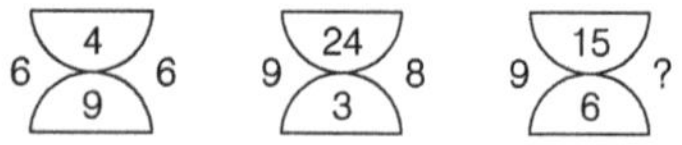

« SSC (10 + 2) 2004

(a) 8 (b) 7 (c) 10 (d) 12

12.

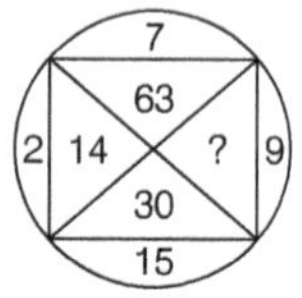

(a) 33 (b) 145 (c) 135 (d) 18

13.

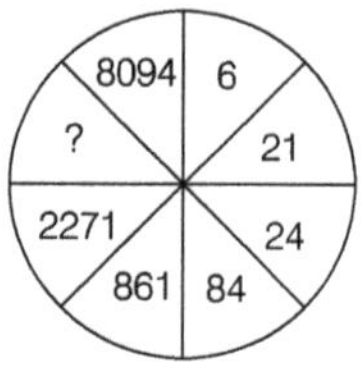

« UP Police SI 2017

(a) 2245 (b) 2454 (c) 2154 (d) 2254

14.

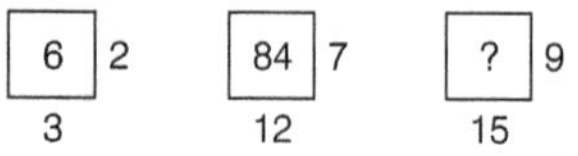

(a) 135 (b) 167
(c) 221 (d) 141

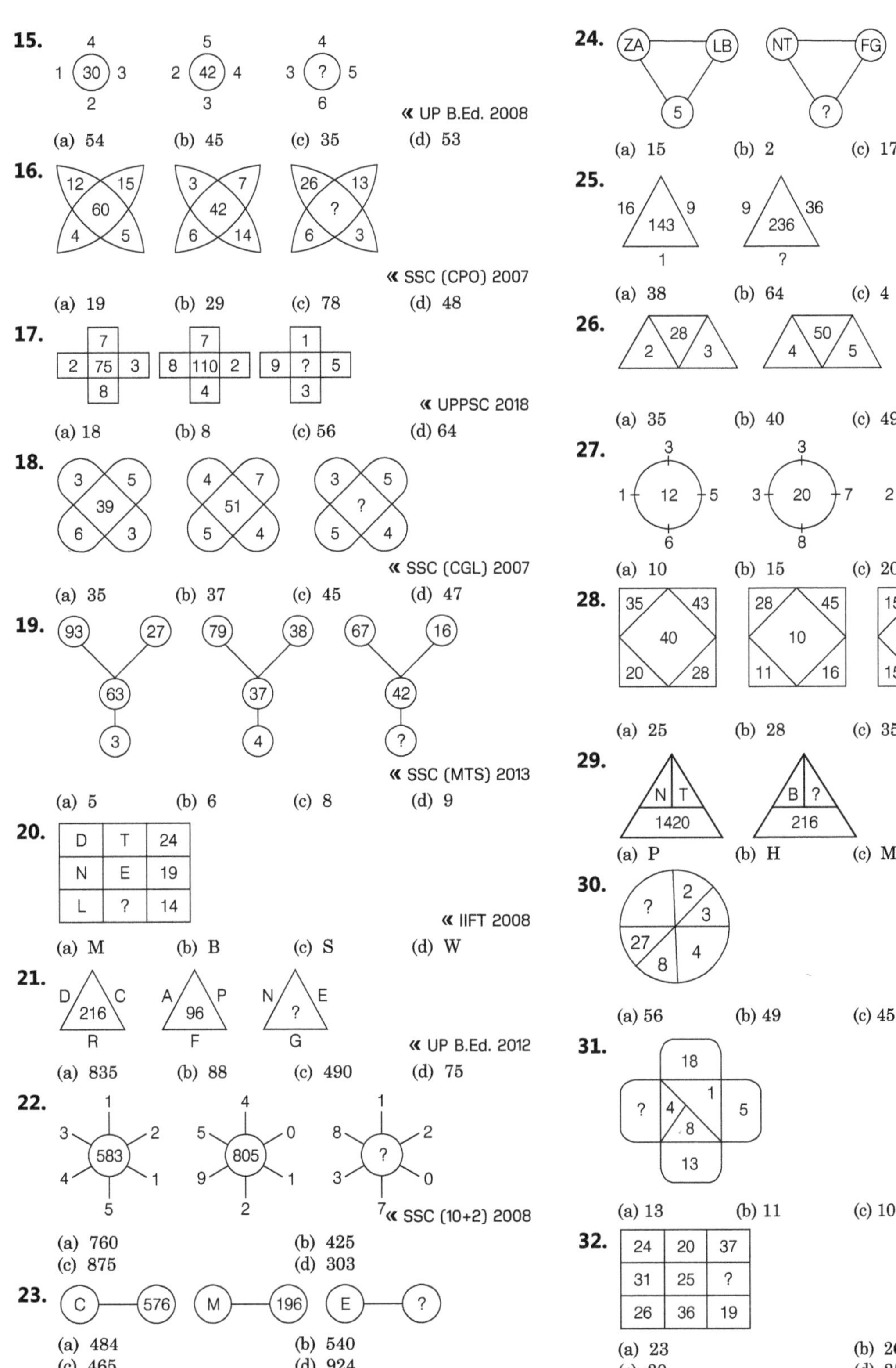

15. « UP B.Ed. 2008

(a) 54 (b) 45 (c) 35 (d) 53

16. « SSC (CPO) 2007

(a) 19 (b) 29 (c) 78 (d) 48

17. « UPPSC 2018

(a) 18 (b) 8 (c) 56 (d) 64

18. « SSC (CGL) 2007

(a) 35 (b) 37 (c) 45 (d) 47

19. « SSC (MTS) 2013

(a) 5 (b) 6 (c) 8 (d) 9

20.

D	T	24
N	E	19
L	?	14

« IIFT 2008

(a) M (b) B (c) S (d) W

21. « UP B.Ed. 2012

(a) 835 (b) 88 (c) 490 (d) 75

22. « SSC (10+2) 2008

(a) 760 (b) 425
(c) 875 (d) 303

23.

(a) 484 (b) 540
(c) 465 (d) 924

24.

(a) 15 (b) 2 (c) 17 (d) 8

25. « SSC CGL 2015

(a) 38 (b) 64 (c) 4 (d) 16

26. « SSC (CGL) 2004

(a) 35 (b) 40 (c) 49 (d) 53

27.

(a) 10 (b) 15 (c) 20 (d) 25

28. « SSC (DEO) 2007

(a) 25 (b) 28 (c) 35 (d) 38

29.

(a) P (b) H (c) M (d) L

30. « SSC (CGL) 2013

(a) 56 (b) 49 (c) 45 (d) 64

31. « MPSI 2017

(a) 13 (b) 11 (c) 10 (d) 17

32.

24	20	37
31	25	?
26	36	19

« SSC (CGL) 2014

(a) 23 (b) 26
(c) 30 (d) 25

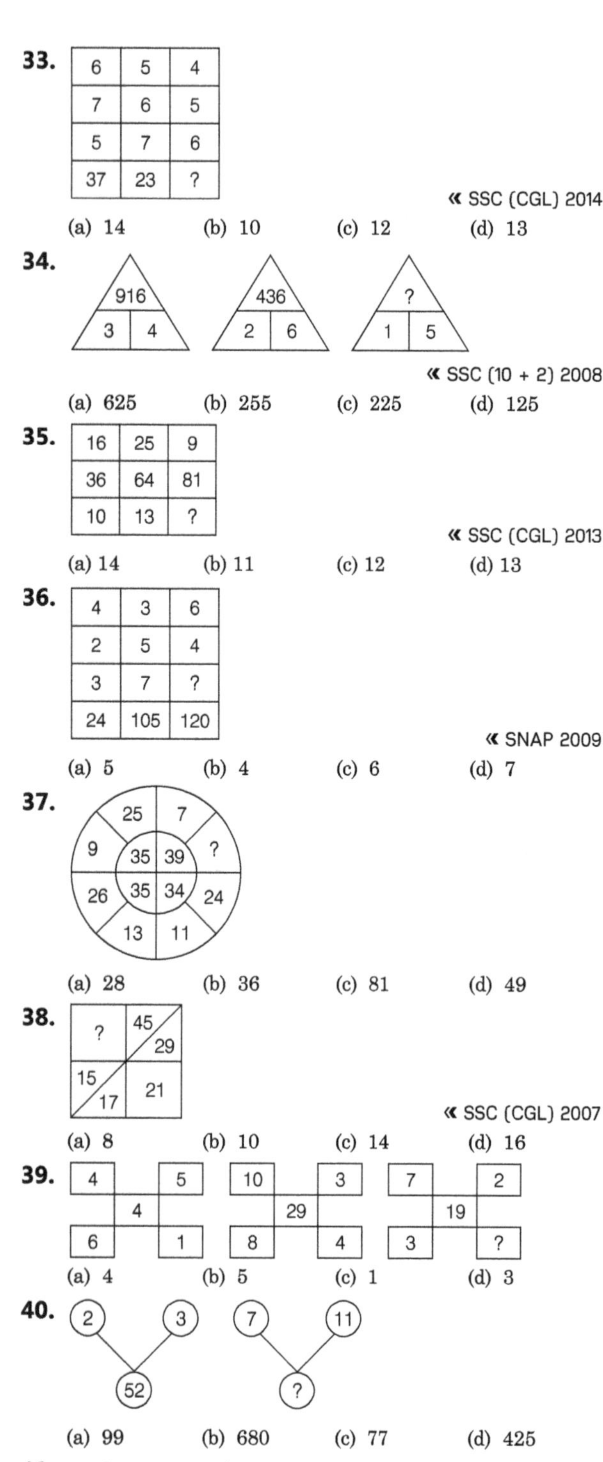

33.

6	5	4
7	6	5
5	7	6
37	23	?

« SSC (CGL) 2014

(a) 14 (b) 10 (c) 12 (d) 13

34.

916
3 4
436
2 6
?
1 5

« SSC (10 + 2) 2008

(a) 625 (b) 255 (c) 225 (d) 125

35.

16	25	9
36	64	81
10	13	?

« SSC (CGL) 2013

(a) 14 (b) 11 (c) 12 (d) 13

36.

4	3	6
2	5	4
3	7	?
24	105	120

« SNAP 2009

(a) 5 (b) 4 (c) 6 (d) 7

37.

25 7
9 ?
35 39
35 34
26 24
13 11

(a) 28 (b) 36 (c) 81 (d) 49

38.

? 45/29
15/17 21

« SSC (CGL) 2007

(a) 8 (b) 10 (c) 14 (d) 16

39.

4 5 / 4 / 6 1
10 3 / 29 / 8 4
7 2 / 19 / 3 ?

(a) 4 (b) 5 (c) 1 (d) 3

40.

2 3 → 52
7 11 → ?

(a) 99 (b) 680 (c) 77 (d) 425

41.

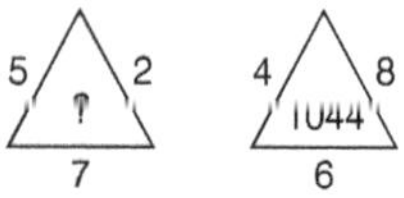

5 2 ? 7
4 8 1044 6

(a) 1678 (b) 415 (c) 8210 (d) 702

42.

?	13	49
9	17	69
13	11	59

« SSC (Constable) 2005

(a) 9 (b) 5 (c) 10 (d) 21

43.

1	2	3
11	7	5
120	45	?

« SSC (10 + 2) 2006

(a) 15 (b) 16 (c) 17 (d) 18

44.

11	6	8
17	12	?
25	34	19
19	28	11

(a) 13 (b) 15 (c) 16 (d) 9

45.

1	3	7
5	12	14
25	?	28
125	192	56

« SSC (DEO) 2011

(a) 40 (b) 48 (c) 56 (d) 64

46.

14	28	42
2	4	6
36	112	246
18	56	?

« SSC (10 + 2) 2007

(a) 120 (b) 201 (c) 123 (d) 303

47.

4	5	3	2	0
7	3	4	4	21
6	4	4	5	22
9	6	5	5	?

(a) 34 (b) 42 (c) 44 (d) 45

48.

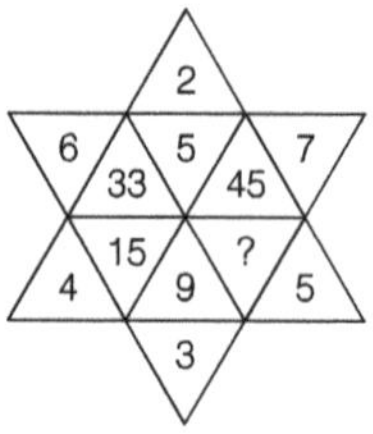

2
6 5 7
33 45
15 ?
4 9 5
3

« SSC (CGL) 2008

(a) 20 (b) 23 (c) 25 (d) 28

49.

K7	L4	M10
L8	M5	K12
M9	L6	?

« SSC (CPO) 2005

(a) K24 (b) L14 (c) K14 (d) M14

50.

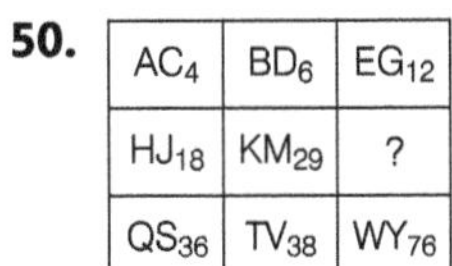

AC_4	BD_6	EG_{12}
HJ_{18}	KM_{29}	?
QS_{36}	TV_{38}	WY_{76}

(a) NP_{24} (b) OQ_{40} (c) NP_{49} (d) PQ_{68}

51.

DL	10	14	FR
RX	23	18	SM
KM	?	?	PV

« MAT 2011

(a) 18, 34 (b) 14, 21 (c) 56, 84 (d) 12, 18

52.

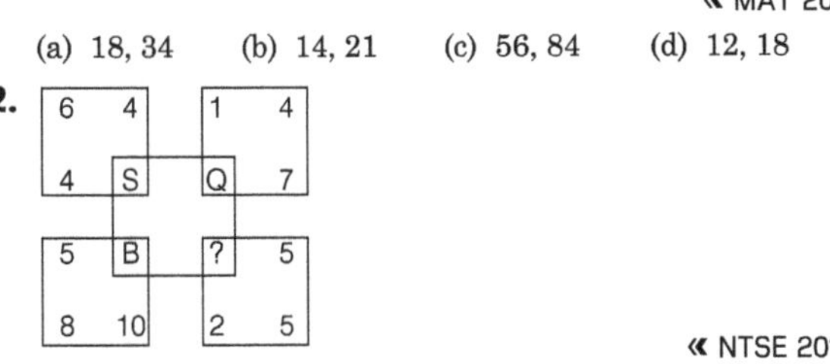

« NTSE 2015

(a) L (b) N (c) P (d) Q

53.

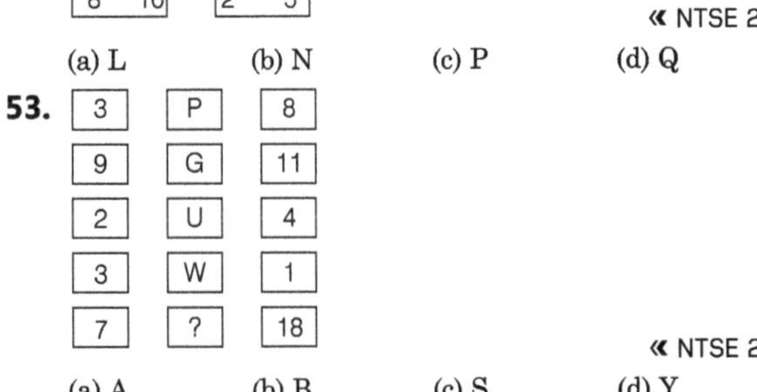

3	P	8
9	G	11
2	U	4
3	W	1
7	?	18

« NTSE 2015

(a) A (b) B (c) S (d) Y

54.

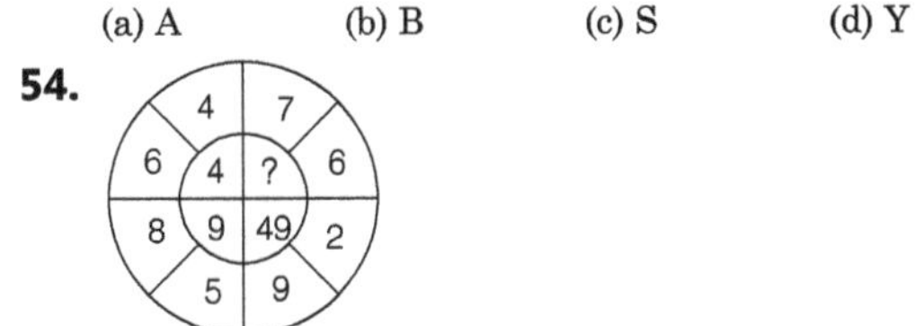

(a) 1 (b) 3 (c) 64 (d) 121

55.

4 3 2
5 3 5 1 1
6 1 2 8 3 3 1
7 2 8 4 3
9 ? 3

« IIFT 2011

(a) 1 (b) 4 (c) 12 (d) 6

56.

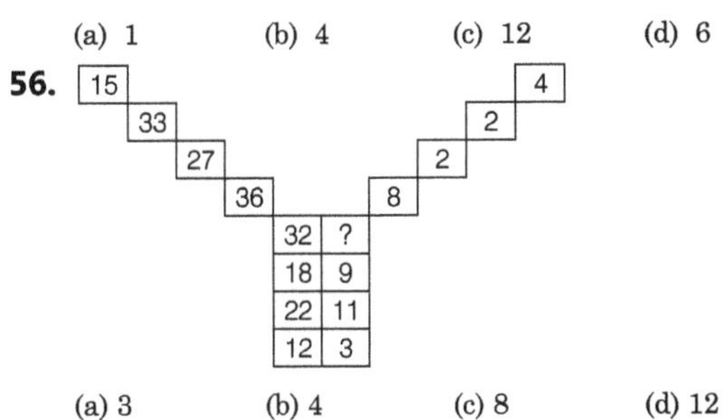

(a) 3 (b) 4 (c) 8 (d) 12

57.

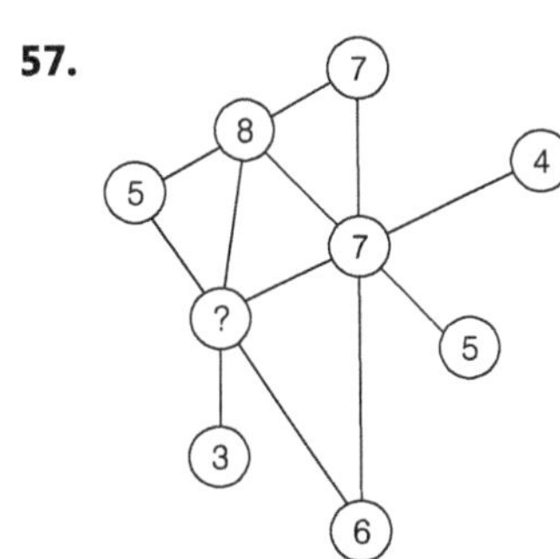

(a) 8 (b) 9 (c) 7 (d) 5

58.

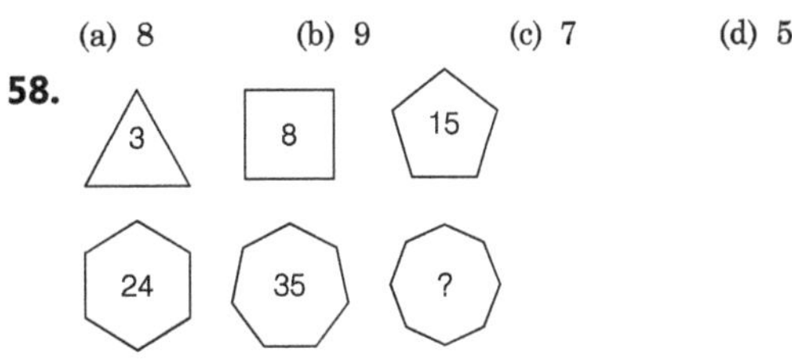

(a) 40 (b) 42 (c) 46 (d) 48

59.

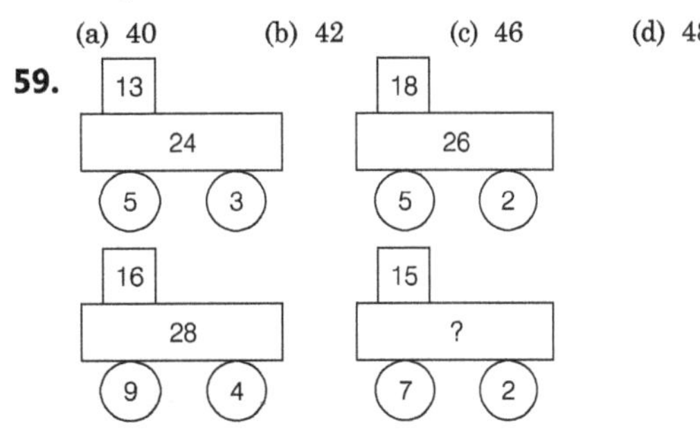

(a) 18 (b) 22 (c) 16 (d) 27

60.

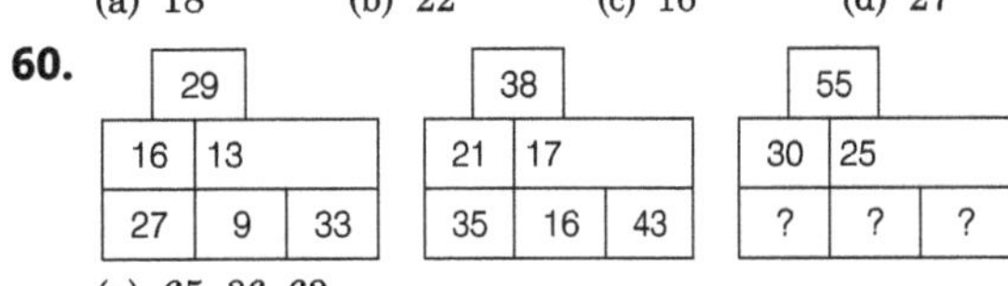

(a) 65, 36, 63
(b) 53, 24, 63
(c) 49, 32, 53
(d) 51, 25, 61

61.

F I
D 21 18 K
23 16
6 13
U 8 ? N
S ?

(a) 9/R (b) 11/P (c) 13/Q (d) 10/V

62.

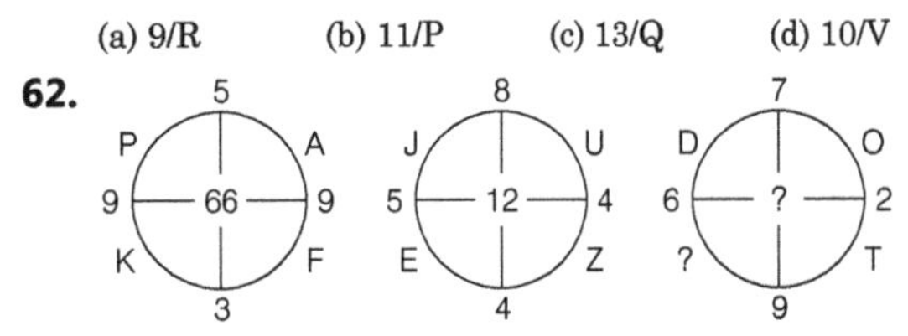

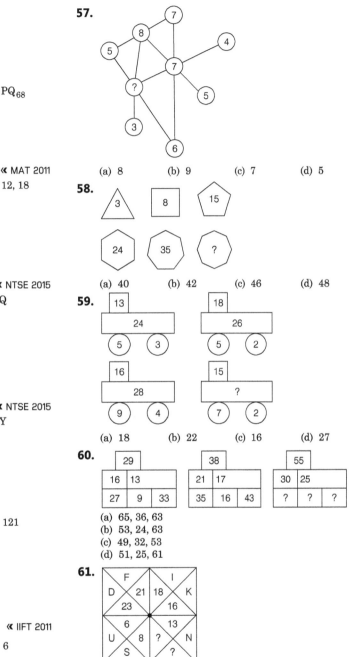

(a) 53 and Z (b) 51 and Y (c) 50 and Y (d) 52 and U

63.

2	9	11	7
8	5	13	– 3
7	?	10	– 4
6	4	10	?

« SSC (CGL) 2013

(a) 3 and (– 2)
(b) (– 3) and (– 2)
(c) 3 and 2
(d) (– 3) and 2

64.

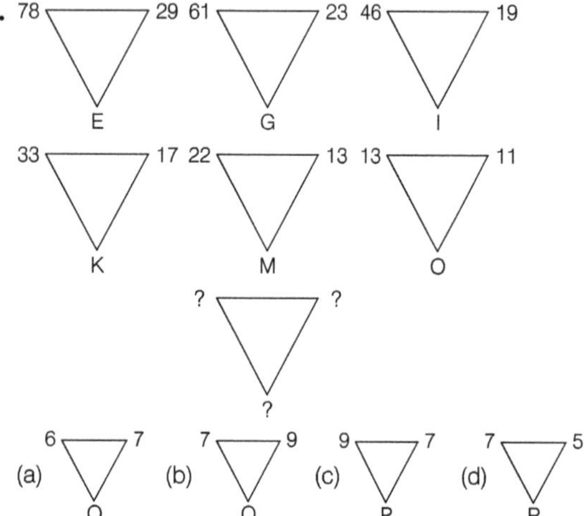

65.

1	4	–3	–1	?
–3	?	?	–5	?
5	?	1	?	?
?	?	–5	–3	16
14	17	?	?	?

(a) 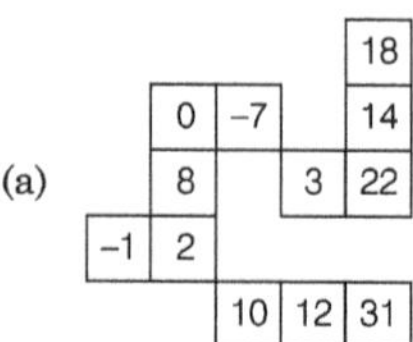

(b) 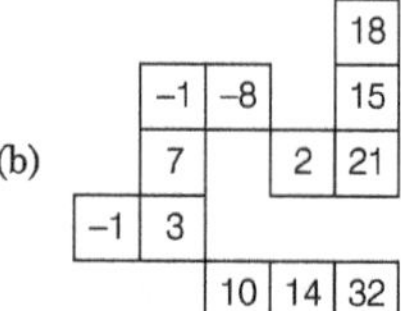

(c) 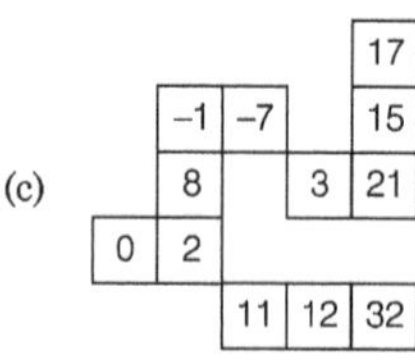

(d) 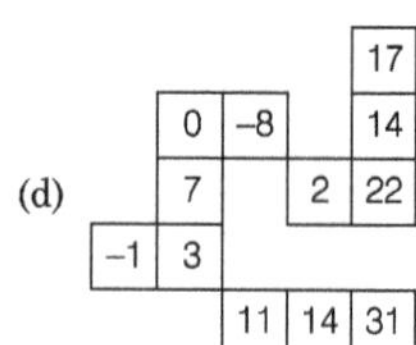

66.

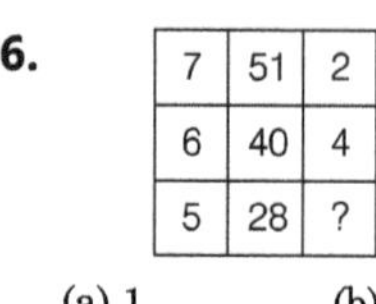

7	51	2
6	40	4
5	28	?

« UPPSC 2014

(a) 1 (b) 3 (c) 2 (d) 0

Answers WITH EXPLANATIONS

1. (*a*) In row,
$25+17+41=83, 32+83+11=126,$
$26+?+31=83,\ ?=83-57=\boxed{26}$
Similarly, in column,
$25+32+26=83$
$17+83+?=126 \Rightarrow ?=26$
$41+11+31=83$
∴ Option (a) is the correct answer.

2. (*c*) According to the question,
5 9 14 20
×2-1 ×2-1 ×2-1 ×2-1
9 17 27 $\boxed{39}$
∴ 39 is the required answer.

3. (*d*) In first column,
$4^2+3=16+3=19$
In second column,
$18^2+6=324+6=330$
Similarly, in third column,
$23^2+1=529+1=530$
∴ $?=\boxed{530}$

4. (*a*) As, II row → $5\times2+9=19$,
III row → $7\times3+3=24$
IV row → $11\times1+4=15$ and
Similarly, I row → $3\times4+5=17$
∴ $?=\boxed{17}$

5. (*c*) As, $28\times27=756$
$17\times23=391$
Similarly, $16\times21=336$
∴ $?=\boxed{336}$

6. (*a*) As, $29\times17=493$
$13\times23=299$
Similarly, $7\times?=91 \Rightarrow ?=\frac{91}{7}$
∴ $?=\boxed{13}$

7. (*d*) As, $1\times4=4, 2\times4=8$
Similarly, $12\times4=48$
∴ $?=\boxed{48}$

8. (*a*) Here,

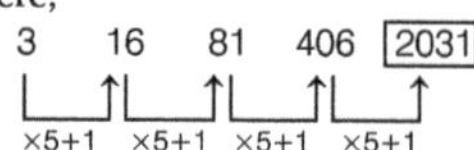

Hence, in the given figure, number 2031 will come in place of question mark (?).

9. (*a*) As, $(7\times4)-(5\times3)=13$
and $(8\times4)-(9\times3)=5$
Similarly, $(9\times4)-(8\times3)=12$
∴ $?=\boxed{12}$

10. (*c*) As, $\sqrt{324}\times\sqrt{4}=18\times2=36$
$\sqrt{9}\times\sqrt{225}=3\times15=45$
Similarly, $\sqrt{36}\times\sqrt{441}=6\times21=126$
∴ $?=\boxed{126}$

11. (*c*) As, $(4\times9)\div6=6,$
$(24\times3)\div9=8$
and $(15\times6)\div9=10$
∴ $?=\boxed{10}$

12. (*c*) As, $15\times2=30, 2\times7=14, 7\times9=63$
and $9\times15=\boxed{135}$
Hence, the missing number is 135.

13. (*b*) As, $6\times2=12 \Rightarrow 21$
(On reversing digits)
$21\times2=42 \Rightarrow 24$
$24\times2=48 \Rightarrow 84$
$84\times2=168 \Rightarrow 861$
$861\times2=1722 \Rightarrow 2271$
$2271\times2=4542 \Rightarrow 2454$
$2454\times2=4908 \Rightarrow 8094$
∴ $?=\boxed{2454}$

14. (*a*) As, $3\times2=6$ and $12\times7=84$
Similarly, $15\times9=135$
∴ $?=\boxed{135}$

15. (*a*) As, $(1+4+3+2)\times3=30$
and $(2+5+4+3)\times3=42$
Similarly, $(3+6+5+4)\times3=54$
∴ $?=\boxed{54}$

16. (*c*) As, $12\times5=15\times4=60$
and $3\times14=7\times6=42$

Similarly, $26 \times 3 = 13 \times 6 = 78$

$\therefore$? = $\boxed{78}$

17. (*c*) As, $(7 + 8) \times (2 + 3) = 15 \times 5 = 75$

and $(7 + 4) \times (8 + 2) = 11 \times 10 = 110$

Similarly, $(1 + 3) \times (9 + 5) = ?$

$\Rightarrow$ $4 \times 14 = ?$

$\Rightarrow$? = $\boxed{56}$

18. (*b*) As, $(3 \times 3) + (6 \times 5) = 39$

and $(4 \times 4) + (5 \times 7) = 51$

Similarly, $(4 \times 3) + (5 \times 5) = 37$

$\therefore$? = $\boxed{37}$

19. (*d*) As, $93 - (27 + 63) = 3$,

$79 - (38 + 37) = 4$

Similarly, $67 - (16 + 42) = \boxed{9}$

Hence, number 9 will come in place of question mark(?).

20. (*b*) Letters' positions in each row are added to get the numbers in the corresponding rows.

As, $\begin{vmatrix} 4 + 20 = 24 \\ D \quad T \end{vmatrix}$

and $\begin{vmatrix} 14 + 5 = 19 \\ N \quad E \end{vmatrix}$

Similarly, $\begin{vmatrix} 12 + ? = 14 \\ L \quad ? \end{vmatrix}$

$12 + ? = 14 \Rightarrow ? = 14 - 12 = 2$

$\therefore$? = $\boxed{B}$

21. (*c*) Numbers inside the triangles are products of alphabetical positions of the letters existing along the sides of triangles.

As, $\begin{vmatrix} 4 \times 3 \times 18 = 216 \\ D \quad C \quad R \end{vmatrix}$

and $\begin{vmatrix} 1 \times 16 \times 6 = 96 \\ A \quad P \quad F \end{vmatrix}$

Similarly, $\begin{vmatrix} 14 \times 5 \times 7 = 490 \\ N \quad E \quad G \end{vmatrix}$

$\therefore$? = $\boxed{490}$

22. (*a*) As, $\left.\begin{array}{l} 1 \times 5 = 5 \\ 2 \times 4 = 8 \\ 1 \times 3 = 3 \end{array}\right\} = 583$

and $\left.\begin{array}{l} 4 \times 2 = 8 \\ 0 \times 9 = 0 \\ 1 \times 5 = 5 \end{array}\right\} = 805$

Similarly, $\left.\begin{array}{l} 1 \times 7 = 7 \\ 2 \times 3 = 6 \\ 0 \times 8 = 0 \end{array}\right\} = 760$

$\therefore$? = $\boxed{760}$

23. (*a*) Here, each letter is represented by the square of the position of its opposite letter.

As, C $\rightarrow \underset{\text{(opposite of C)}}{\overset{(24)^2}{X}} = 576$

and M $\rightarrow \underset{\text{(opposite of M)}}{\overset{(14)^2}{N}} = 196$

Similarly, E $\rightarrow \underset{\text{(opposite of E)}}{\overset{(22)^2}{V}} = 484$

$\therefore$? = 484

24. (*b*) Letter positions are added till the sum gets converted into single digit.

As, $\begin{vmatrix} 26 + 1 + 12 + 2 = 41 ; 4 + 1 = 5 \\ Z \quad A \quad L \quad B \end{vmatrix}$

Similarly, $\begin{vmatrix} 14 + 20 + 6 + 7 = 47; \\ N \quad T \quad F \quad G \end{vmatrix}$

$4 + 7 = 11$ and $1 + 1 = 2$

$\therefore$? = $\boxed{2}$

25. (*c*) Clearly, the numbers along the sides of triangle are the squares of digits of the number at the centre.

As, $(1)^2 = 1, (4)^2 = 16, (3)^2 = 9$

Similarly,

$(2)^2 = \boxed{4}, (3)^2 = 9, (6)^2 = 36$

Hence, the missing number is 4.

26. (*b*) As, $2, 3 \rightarrow 23 + 5 = 28$

and $4, 5 \rightarrow 45 + 5 = 50$

Similarly, $3, 5 \rightarrow 35 + 5 = 40$

$\therefore$? = $\boxed{40}$

27. (*b*) As, $(5 - 1) \times (6 - 3) = 12$

$(7 - 3) \times (8 - 3) = 20$

Similarly, $? = (7 - 2) \times (6 - 3) = \boxed{15}$

Hence, option (b) is the correct answer.

28. (*d*) As, $(35 + 20 + 28) - 43 = 40$

and $(28 + 11 + 16) - 45 = 10$

Similarly, $(15 + 15 + 40) - 32 = 38$

$\therefore$? = $\boxed{38}$

29. (*a*) As, N T → 14 20 Alphabetical position

Similarly, 2 16 → B $\boxed{P}$

Hence, P is the missing character.

30. (*d*) As $2, (2)^3 = 8$, $3, (3)^3 = 27$,

$4, (4)^3 = \boxed{64}$

So, the missing number is 64.

31. (*d*) As, $5 + 8 = 13$ and $13 + 4 = \boxed{17}$

Same as, $17 + 1 = 18$

Note Here, number of outer box is added to the number of inner box respectively.

32. (*d*) As, $24 + 20 + 37 = 81$

and $26 + 36 + 19 = 81$

Similarly, $31 + 25 + ? = 81$

$\Rightarrow$ $? = 81 - 56$

$\Rightarrow$? = $\boxed{25}$

33. (*a*) As $6 \times 7 - 5 = 42 - 5 = 37$

and $5 \times 6 - 7 = 30 - 7 = 23$

Similarly, $4 \times 5 - 6 = 20 - 6 = \boxed{14}$

Hence, 14 is the missing number.

34. (*d*) As, $(3)^2, (4)^2 \rightarrow 916$

and $(2)^2, (6)^2 \rightarrow 436$

Similarly, $(1)^2, (5)^2 \rightarrow 125$

Hence, option (d) is the correct answer.

35. (*c*) $\sqrt{16} + \sqrt{36} = 4 + 6 = 10$;

$\sqrt{25} + \sqrt{64} = 5 + 8 = 13$

Similarly, $\sqrt{9} + \sqrt{81} = ?$

$\Rightarrow$ $3 + 9 = \boxed{?}$

$\therefore$? = $\boxed{12}$

36. (*a*) As, $24 \div (4 \times 2) = 3$

and $105 \div (3 \times 5) = 7$

Similarly, $120 \div (6 \times 4) = 5$

$\therefore$? = $\boxed{5}$

37. (*a*) As, $26 + 13 = 39, 11 + 24 = 35$

and $25 + 9 = 34$,

Similarly, $7 + ? = 35$

$\therefore$? = $\boxed{28}$

38. (*c*) As, $45 - 16 = 29, 29 - 8 = 21$,

$21 - 4 = 17, 17 - 2 = 15$

Similarly, $15 - 1 = 14$

$\therefore$? = $\boxed{14}$

39. (*b*) As,

$\{(4)^2 + (5)^2\} - \{(6)^2 + (1)^2\} = 4$

$\{(10)^2 + (3)^2\} - \{(8)^2 + (4)^2\} = 29$

$\{(7)^2 + (2)^2\} - \{(3)^2 + \boxed{5}^2\} = 19$

So, the missing number is 5.

40. (*b*) As, $(2^2 + 3^2) \times 4 = 52$

Similarly, $(7^2 + 11^2) \times 4 = 680$

$\therefore$? = $\boxed{680}$

41. (*d*) As, $(4^2 + 8^2 + 6^2) \times 9 = 1044$

Similarly, $(5^2 + 2^2 + 7^2) \times 9 = 702$

$\therefore$? = $\boxed{702}$

42. (*b*) Number in 3rd column = 2 × 1st block number + 3 × 2nd block number.

As, $(2 \times 13) + (3 \times 11) = 59$

and $(2 \times 9) + (3 \times 17) = 69$

Similarly, $(2 \times \boxed{?}) + (3 \times 13) = 49$

$2? + 39 = 49$

$2? = 49 - 39$

$? = \frac{10}{2} = 5$

Hence, the missing number is 5.

43. (*b*) Across each column, Number in 3rd cell

= (Number in 2nd cell)^2

− (Number in 1st cell)^2

$(11)^2 - (1)^2 = 120$

$(7)^2 - (2)^2 = 45$

Similarly, $(5)^2 - (3)^2 = \boxed{16}$

Hence, the missing number is 16.

44. (*c*) As, $(11 + 25) - 17 = 36 - 17 = 19$

and $(6 + 34) - 12 = 40 - 12 = 28$

Similarly, $(8 + 19) - ? = 11$

$? = 27 - 11$

$\Rightarrow$? = $\boxed{16}$

45. (*b*) In the first column, each number is multiplied by 5 to get the next number

i.e., $1 \times 5 = 5,\ 5 \times 5 = 25$

$25 \times 5 = 125$

Similarly, in 2nd column each number is multiplied by 4 to get the next number

i.e., $3 \times 4 = 12,\ 12 \times 4 = \boxed{48}$

and $48 \times 4 = 192$

Hence, the missing number is 48.

46. (*c*) Here, Number in 1st row = 7 × Number in 2nd row.

Number in the 3rd row = 2 × Number in the 4th row.

Hence, the missing number is $\boxed{123}$.

47. (*a*) As, $4 \times 2 - (5 + 3) = 0$

$7 \times 4 - (3 + 4) = 21$

$6 \times 5 - (4 + 4) = 22$

Similarly, $9 \times 5 - (6 + 5) = \boxed{34}$

Hence, the missing number is 34.

48. (*b*) $7 \times (7 - 1) = 42 \rightarrow 42 + 3 = 45$

$2 \times (2 - 1) = 2 \rightarrow 2 + 3 = 5$

$6 \times (6 - 1) = 30 \rightarrow 30 + 3 = 33$

$4 \times (4 - 1) = 12 \rightarrow 12 + 3 = 15$

$3 \times (3 - 1) = 6 \rightarrow 6 + 3 = 9$

$\therefore\ 5 \times (5 - 1) = 20 \rightarrow 20 + 3 = \boxed{23}$

Hence, option (b) is the correct answer.

49. (*c*) Each row consists of letters K, L and M. The difference in numeric portion of 3rd column is 2, i.e. 12 + 2 = 14.

Hence, the missing term is $\boxed{K\ 14}$.

50. (*c*) Each block comprises of two letters and a number. Letters occur in pairs with a gap of one letter in between. The 1st letter of 3rd block in each row is the letter next to the 2nd alphabet of 2nd block. Number in 3rd block of each row is 2 more than the sum of 1st and 2nd block numbers.

Hence, $\boxed{NP_{49}}$ is the correct answer.

51. (*b*) As, D L

↓ ↓

$4 + 12 = 16;\ \frac{16}{2} = 8$

and $8 + 2 = 10$

It means, positional value of letters are added and divided by 2, and the result thus obtained, is incremented by 2.

Similarly,

K M

↓ ↓

$11 + 13 = 24;\ \frac{24}{2} = 12$ and $12 + 2 = 14$

P V

↓ ↓

$16 + 22 = 38;\ \frac{38}{2} = 19$ and $19 + 2 = 21$

Hence, missing numbers are $\boxed{14 \text{ and } 21}$.

52. (*d*) As, $(6 + 4 + 4) + 5 = 19$

⇒ Positional value of S

$(1 + 4 + 7) + 5 = 17$

⇒ Positional value of Q

and $(5 + 8 + 10) + 5 = 28 = 26 + 2$

⇒ Positional value of B

Similarly, $(5 + 5 + 2) + 5 = 17$

⇒ Positional value of Q

$\therefore\ ? = \boxed{Q}$

53. (*b*) As, $27 - (3 + 8) = 27 - 11 = 16$

⇒ Positional value of P

$27 - (9 + 11) = 27 - 20 = 7$

⇒ Positional value of G

$27 - (2 + 4) = 27 - 6 = 21$

⇒ Positional value of U

$27 - (3 + 1) = 27 - 4 = 23$

⇒ Positional value of W

Similarly, $27 - (7 + 18) = 27 - 25 = 2$

⇒ Positional value of B

$\therefore\ ? = \boxed{B}$

54. (*a*) As, $(6 - 4)^2 = 2^2 = 4$

$(8 - 5)^2 = 3^2 = 9$

$(9 - 2)^2 = 7^2 = 49$

Similarly, $(7 - 6)^2 \Rightarrow 1^2 \Rightarrow ? = \boxed{1}$

Hence, option (a) is the correct answer.

55. (*d*) Starting with the top most row, the number at the center of each row is the sum of the other numbers divided by 2

1st row → $(4 + 2) \div 2 = 3$

2nd row → $(5 + 3 + 1 + 1) \div 2 = 5$

3rd row → $(6 + 1 + 2 + 3 + 3 + 1) \div 2 = 8$

4th row → $(7 + 2 + 4 + 3) \div 2 = 8$

5th row → $(9 + 3) \div 2 = 6$

$\therefore\ ? = \boxed{6}$

56. (*b*) The top left hand number is obtained by adding the bottom two numbers. The top right hand number is the result obtained after the division of bottom two numbers.

Thus, $12 + 3 = 15,\ 12 \div 3 = 4,$

$22 + 11 = 33,\ 22 \div 11 = 2,$

$18 + 9 = 27,\ 18 \div 9 = 2,$

So, $32 + ? = 36$ and $32 \div ? = 8$

or $? = \boxed{4}$

57. (*b*) Each connected straight line of three numbers makes sum equal to 20.

$\therefore\ 4 + 7 + ? = 20 \Rightarrow ? = 20 - 11$

$? = \boxed{9}$

58. (*d*) Each number is the product of the number of sides in the shape enclosing it and its position in the sequence. Since the octagon has 8 sides and is 6th in the sequence, the number inside it should be $8 \times 6 = \boxed{48}$.

$\therefore\ ? = 48$

59. (*c*) Here, the pattern is as follows (Smokestack – Left wheel) x Right wheel = Body

As, $(13 - 5) \times 3 = 8 \times 3 = 24$

$(18 - 5) \times ? = 13 \times ? = 26$

and $(16 - 9) \times 4 = 7 \times 4 = 28$

Similarly, $(15 - 7) \times 2 = 8 \times 2 = \boxed{16}$

$\therefore\ ? = 16$

60. (*d*) Here, the pattern is

	a	
b	c	
(2×c)+1	(b–c)^2	(2×b)+1

∴ First number = $(25 \times 2) + 1 = 51$

Second number = $(30 - 25)^2 = 25$

and third number = $(30 \times 2) + 1 = \boxed{61}$

Hence, 51, 25, 61 are the three missing terms.

61. (*b*) The letters progress in clockwise direction starting from D and the next letter is obtained by following the below skipping pattern

D (E) F (GH) I (J) K (LM) N (O) $\boxed{P}$ (QR) S (T) U. The numbers are their respective positions in reverse order.

$\therefore\ \frac{?}{?} = \frac{\boxed{11}}{\boxed{P}}$

62. (*b*) The pattern is

$9 \times 9 - 5 \times 3 = 66$

$8 \times 4 - 5 \times 4 = 12$

$9 \times 7 - 6 \times 2 = \boxed{51}$

A $\xrightarrow{+5}$ F $\xrightarrow{+5}$ K $\xrightarrow{+5}$ P

U $\xrightarrow{+5}$ Z $\xrightarrow{+5}$ E $\xrightarrow{+5}$ J

O $\xrightarrow{+5}$ T $\xrightarrow{+5}$ $\boxed{Y}$ $\xrightarrow{+5}$ D

Hence, $\boxed{51 \text{ and } Y}$ is the correct answer.

63. (*a*) $2 + 9 = 11$

$9 - 2 = 7$

Also, $8 + 5 = 13$

$5 - 8 = -3$

Now, $7 + ? = 10$

$? = 10 - 7 = \boxed{3}$

Also, $4 - 6 = ?$

$? = \boxed{-2}$

So, the correct options are 3 and (– 2).

64. (*a*) The numbers at the top left corners decrease by 17, then 15, then 13, etc. The numbers at the top right corners are consecutive primes in descending order. The letters move two letters forward each time.

i.e.,

$\overset{5}{E} \xrightarrow{+2} \overset{7}{G} \xrightarrow{+2} \overset{9}{I} \xrightarrow{+2}$

$\overset{11}{K} \xrightarrow{+2} \overset{13}{M} \xrightarrow{+2} \overset{15}{O} \xrightarrow{+2} \overset{17}{\boxed{Q}}$

So, the correct answer is

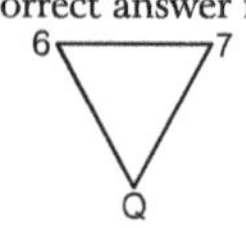

65. (*a*) In rows, the pattern is

+3, – 7, + 2, + 19

In columns, the pattern is

–4, + 8, – 6, + 15

So, the correct answer is as given in option (a).

66. (*b*) As, $7^2 + 2 = 49 + 2 = 51$

$6^2 + 4 = 36 + 4 = 40$

Similarly, $5^2 + ? = 28$

$\therefore\ ? = \boxed{3}$

CHAPTER / 18

Inequality

Inequality means state of being unequal. When a group of elements are given with a certain coded relationship denoted by 'less than' (<), 'greater than'(>), 'equal to' (=), 'not equal to' (≠) 'greater than or equal to' (≥), 'Smaller than or equal to' (≤).

In order to derive a definite conclusion by establishing relation between different sets of elements, first of all a candidate is required to become familiar with all types of signs that are used for establishing inequalities.

A table of these signs along with their meaning and explanation is given as follows–

Important Signs

Signs	Meaning	Example	Explanation
=	Equal to	A = B	(i) A is equal to B. (ii) A is neither greater nor smaller than B.
>	Greater than	A > B	(i) A is greater than B. (ii) A is neither smaller than nor equal to B.
<	Less than	A < B	(i) A is less than B. (ii) A is neither greater than nor equal to B.
≥	Greater than or equal to	A ≥ B	(i) A is greater than or equal to B. (ii) A is not less than B.
≤	Less than or equal to	A ≤ B	(i) A is less than or equal to B. (ii) A is not greater than B.
≠	Not equal to	A ≠ B	(i) A is not equal to B. (ii) A is either greater than or less than B.

e.g., $(4 \times 3) = 12$ Equal — Case of equality
$(4 \times 3) \neq 9$ Not equal — Case of inequality

As, $(4 \times 3) \neq 9$, we can write it as following

⇒ $(4 \times 3) > 9$ or (4×3) is greater than 9.

⇒ $12 > 9$ or 12 is greater than 9.

Similarly, $(4 \times 3) \neq 14$, we can write it as following
$(4 \times 3) < 14$ or (4×3) is less than 14

⇒ $12 < 14$ or 12 is less than 14.

Now, the table given below represents the relationships between certain statements and their conclusions.
Once you learn and understand these concepts, questions on inequality will become much easier to solve.

Statement	Conclusion	
A>B>C A>B≥C A≥B>C A=B>C A>B=C	A>C	
A<B<C A<B≤C A≤B<C A=B<C A<B=C	A<C	
A≥B≥C A=B≥C A≥B=C	A≥C (Either A>C or A=C)	
A≤B≤C A=B≤C A≤B=C	A≤C (Either A<C or A=C)	
A<B>C	No conclusion can be established or, Either (i) or (ii) follows, if any of the following cases (a, b, c and d) is given as they form a complementary pair.	
A≤B>C	(a) (i) A > C	(ii) A≤C
A<B≥C	(b) (i) A≥C	(ii) A<C
A > B<C	(c) (i) A<C	(ii) A≥C
A > B≤C	(d) (i) A≤C	(ii) A>C
A ≥ B <C		

Note *To derive a definite conclusion from the given statements, there must be a common term.*

e.g., ***Statements*** $x > y, y > z$

⇒ ∴ $x > y > z$

Conclusion $x > z$ (∵ *y is a common term or middle term)*

Two types of problems based on inequalities are asked in various competitive exams. In one type, real symbols are used to establish the relations between different sets of elements while in other type, substituted symbol (*i.e.*, coded symbols) in place of real symbols are used to establish the relations between different sets of elements.

In both the cases the candidate is required to find out the alternative that follows the given inequalities.

These two types of inequalities are explained below to have a deeper understanding about the type of questions asked

TYPE 01

Simple Inequalities

In this type of questions, certain relations between different sets of elements are given in terms of 'less than' (<), 'greater than' (>), 'equal to' (=) etc, using the real symbols. The candidate is required to analyse the given statements and then decide which of the relations given as alternatives, follows from those given in the statements.

Steps to Solve Simple Inequality Based Questions

e.g., **Statements** $H < J$, $F < H$, $I \le K = J$

Conclusions I. $H > I$ II. $I \ge F$

***Step* I** Write down all the statements as below

$H < J$ (i)

$F < H$ (ii)

$I \le K = J$ (iii)

***Step* II** Combine all the statements as below

Firstly, combine statements (i) and (ii) as H is common between both the statements.

$F < H < J$ (iv)

Secondly, combine statements (iii) and (iv), we get

$F < H < J = K \ge I$ (v)

***Step* III** Check the validity of the given conclusions with the help of statement (v)

I. $H > I$ (False)

II. $I \ge F$ (False)

Hence, neither conclusion I nor II is true.

DIRECTIONS ~ (Example Nos. 1-5) *In these questions, relationship between different elements is shown in the statements. The statements are followed by conclusions. Study the conclusions based on the given statements and select the appropriate answer.* « NICL (Assist.) 2015

Give Answer

(a) If only Conclusion I is true.
(b) If neither Conclusion I nor II is true.
(c) If both conclusions are true.
(d) If only Conclusion II is true.
(e) If either Conclusion I or II is true.

***Ex* 01** **Statement** $B > R \ge A = N < D \le S$

Conclusions I. $B > N$ II. $S \ge A$

***Solution* (a) Statement** $B > R \ge A = N < D \le S$

Conclusions I. $B > N$ (True) II. $S \ge A$ (False)

Only Conclusion I is true.

***Ex* 02** **Statement** $T \ge I < G \le E = R < S$

Conclusions I. $R > T$ II. $S > I$

***Solution* (d) Statement** $T \ge I < G \le E = R < S$

Conclusions I. $R > T$ (False) II. $S > I$ (True)

Only Conclusion II is true.

***Ex* 03** **Statements** $U > B \ge M \le G; L < Y \le M$

Conclusions I. $U > L$ II. $G \le L$

***Solution* (a)** Statements $U > B \ge M \le G; L < Y \le M$

$\therefore$ $U > B \ge M \ge Y > L$; $G \ge M \ge Y > L$

Conclusions I. $U > L$ (True) II. $G \le L$ (False)

Only Conclusion I is true.

***Ex* 04** **Statement** $P < R \le A \le I > S \ge E$

Conclusions I. $P < I$ II. $E \le A$

***Solution* (a) Statement** $P < R \le A \le I > S > E$

Conclusions I. $P < I$ (True)

II. $E \le A$ (False)

Only Conclusion I is true.

***Ex* 05** **Statement** $S \le T = E \le P = N \le G$

Conclusions I. $G > S$ II. $G = S$

***Solution* (b) Statement** $S \le T = E \le P = N \le G$

Conclusions I. $G > S$ (False)

II. $G = S$ (False)

Hence, neither Conclusion I nor II is true.

DIRECTIONS ~ (Example Nos. 6-8) *In each of the questions given below are given some statements followed by two conclusions. You have to take the given statements to be true even if they seem to be at variance with commonly known facts. Read all the conclusions and then decide which of the given conclusions logically follows from the given statements disregarding commonly known facts.* « RBI Office Assistant 2020

(a) If only Conclusion I follows.
(b) If only Conclusion II follows.
(c) If either Conclusion I or II follows.
(d) If neither Conclusion I nor II follows.
(e) If both Conclusions I and II follow.

***Ex* 06** **Statements**

$V > B \ge G = H > F < D \le T$, $Q < W = E \le F$

Conclusions I. $B > W$ II. $E \ge B$

***Solution* (a) Statements** $V > B \ge G = H > F < D \le T$

Or $V > B \ge G = H > F \ge E = W > Q$

Conclusions I. $B > W$ (True)

II. $E \ge B$ (False)

Hence, only Conclusion I is definitely true.

***Ex* 07** **Statement** $M < N = B \le V > C$, $L > K \ge J = H \ge B$

Conclusions I. $N \le H$ II. $B > J$

***Solution* (a) Statements** $M < N = B \le V > C$

Or $M < N = B \le H = J \le K$

Conclusions I. $N \le H$ (True)

II. $B > J$ (False)

Hence, only Conclusion I is definitely true.

Ex 08 Statement $P = L > O \geq K > U > M$, $N < H \leq M = B < K$

Conclusions I. $L > B$ II. $N < U$

Solution (e) **Statement** $P = L > O \geq K > U > M$

Or $P = L > O \geq K > U > M \geq H > N$

Or $L > O \geq K > U > M = B < K$

Conclusions I. $L > B$ (True)

II. $N < U$ (True)

Hence, both the conclusions are definitely true.

DIRECTIONS ~ (Example Nos. 9-13) *In these questions, a relationship between different elements is shown in the statements. The statements are followed by two conclusions. Give answer.* « SBI PO 2018

Ex 09 Statements $L \leq T \leq I \geq M < X$, $W < P \leq L \geq B \geq K$

Conclusions I. $K < X$ II. $W > M$

(a) If only Conclusion II is true.
(b) If only Conclusion I is true.
(c) If neither Conclusion I nor II is true.
(d) If either Conclusion I or II is true.
(e) If both Conclusions I and II are true.

Solution (c) **Statements** $L \leq T \leq I \geq M < X$, $W < P \leq L \geq B \geq K$

$\therefore$ $X > M \leq I \geq T \geq L \geq B \geq K$

and $W < P \leq L \leq I \geq M$

Conclusions I. $K < X$ (False)

II. $W > M$ (False)

$\therefore$ Neither Conclusion I nor II follows.

Ex 10 Statements $Z < U \leq D \leq A \leq M < S$, $Q > A \leq Y < G$

Conclusions I. $Z < Y$ II. $S > Q$

(a) If both Conclusions I and II are true.
(b) If only Conclusion I is true.
(c) If neither Conclusion I nor II is true.
(d) If either Conclusion I or II is true.
(e) If only Conclusion II is true.

Solution (b) **Statements** $Z < U \leq D \leq A \leq M < S$,

$Q > A \leq Y < G$

$\therefore$ $Y \geq A \geq D \geq U > Z$

and $S > M \geq A < Q$

Conclusions I. $Z < Y$ (True)

II. $S > Q$ (False)

$\therefore$ Only Conclusion I follows.

Ex 11 Statements $L \leq T \leq I \geq M < X$, $W < P \leq L \geq B \geq K$

Conclusions I. $K \geq M$ II. $P > M$

(a) If only Conclusion II is true.
(b) If either Conclusion I or II is true.
(c) If neither Conclusion I nor II is true.
(d) If only Conclusion I is true.
(e) If both Conclusions I and II are true.

Solution (c) **Statements**

$L \leq T \leq I \geq M < X$, $W < P \leq L \geq B \geq K$

$\therefore$ $K \leq B \leq L \leq T \leq I \geq M$ and $P \leq L \leq T \leq I \geq M$

Conclusions I. $K \geq M$ (False)

II. $P > M$ (False)

$\therefore$ Neither Conclusion I nor II follows.

Ex 12 Statements $Z < U \leq D \leq A \leq M < S$, $Q > A \leq Y < G$

Conclusions I. $M \geq U$ II. $G > Z$

(a) If only Conclusion II is true.
(b) If only Conclusion I is true.
(c) If neither Conclusion I nor II is true.
(d) If either Conclusion I or II is true.
(e) If both Conclusions I and II are true.

Solution (e) **Statements** $Z < U \leq D \leq A \leq M < S, Q > A \leq Y < G$

$\therefore$ $U \leq D \leq A \leq M$ and $G > Y \geq A \geq D \geq U > Z$

Conclusions I. $M \geq U$ (True)

II. $G > Z$ (True)

$\therefore$ Both Conclusions I and II are true.

Ex 13 Statement $J > K \geq H = U \geq B \leq T < F \leq R$

Conclusions I. $J > B$

II. $H < R$

(a) If only Conclusion II is true.
(b) If either Conclusion I or II is true.
(c) If neither Conclusion I nor II is true.
(d) If only Conclusion I is true.
(e) If both Conclusions I and II are true.

Solution (d) **Statement** $J > K \geq H = U \geq B \leq T < F \leq R$

Conclusions I. $J > B$ (True)

II. $H < R$ (False)

$\therefore$ Only Conclusion I is true.

Ex 14 If $M > N \leq O < P$ and $T < O > C \geq Z$ are true, then which of the following options is definitely true? « NICL (AO) 2017

(a) $M > O$ (b) $C = T$ (c) $O = Z$ (d) $T < P$
(e) $N \geq Z$

Solution (d) Given, $M > N \leq O < P, T < O > C \geq Z$

$\therefore$ $P > O > T$ and $N \leq O > C \geq Z$

(a) $M > O$ (false)

(b) $C = T$ (false)

(c) $O = Z$ (false)

(d) $T < P$ (true)

(e) $N \geq Z$ (false)

$\therefore$ Only option (d) is true.

Ex 15 Which of the following should be placed in the blank spaces respectively (in the same order from left to right in order to complete the given expression in such a manner that both $S > P$ as well as $A \leq E$ definitely hold true? « MHT MBA 2017

S _ H _ A _ P _ E

(a) $\geq, >, =, \leq$ (b) $>, \geq, <, <$
(c) $>, \geq, <, \leq$ (d) $>, >, \geq, =$
(e) $\geq, \geq, \leq, \leq$

Solution (a) Taking option (a), we have

$S \geq H > A = P \leq E$

$\therefore$ $S > P$ (true)

and $A \leq E$ (true)

***Ex* 16** Which of the following expressions will be true, if the given expression $K \geq G > H \leq F$ is definitely true?

« NABARD (PO) 2010

(a) $F \geq K$ (b) $H < K$ (c) $F < G$ (d) $K \geq H$
(e) None of these

***Solution* (b)** Given, $K \geq G > H \leq F$

Now, we can check all the options one by one

(a) $F \geq K$ (False) (b) $H < K$ (True)
(c) $F < G$ (False) (d) $K \geq H$ (False)

So, it is clear that option (b) is true.

***Ex* 17** In which of the following expressions the expression '$M > R$' does not hold true?

(a) $M = P > Q > R$ (b) $M > P \geq Q = R$
(c) $R = P < Q < M$ (d) $R < Q \leq P = M$
(e) $M = P < Q = R$

***Solution* (e)** We can check all the options one by one.

From option (a), $M = P > Q > R \Rightarrow M > R$

So, expression $M > R$ holds true for option (a).

From option (b),

$$M > P \geq Q = R \Rightarrow M < R$$

So, expression $M > R$ holds true for option (b).

From option (c),

$$R = P < Q < M \Rightarrow M > R$$

So, expression $M > R$ holds true for option (c).

From option (d),

$$R < Q \leq P = M \Rightarrow M > R$$

So, expression $M > R$ holds true for option (d).

From option (e),

$$M = P < Q = R \Rightarrow M < R$$

So, expression $M > R$ does not hold true for option (e).

Practice CORNER 18.1

DIRECTIONS ~ (Q. Nos. 1-5) *In each of the question, relationship between some elements are shown in the statements. These statements are followed by conclusions I and II. Read the statements.*

Give Answer « IBPS RRB Officers 2019

(a) If only Conclusion I follows.
(b) If only Conclusion II follows.
(c) If either Conclusion I or II follows.
(d) If neither Conclusion I nor II follows.
(e) If both Conclusions I and II follow.

1. Statement $C \leq L = E \leq R \leq K = P \geq O$
Conclusions I. $P = C$ II. $C < P$

2. Statement $W > A = S \geq H < I \leq N \leq G$
Conclusions I. $H < W$ II. $G > H$

3. Statement $C < O \leq D = S > A \geq P \geq Q$
Conclusions I. $Q < D$ II. $C < A$

4. Statement $F \leq B = I \leq C = A \geq S > E$
Conclusions I. $S \geq B$ II. $F > E$

5. Statement $I \geq N = T \geq E > L \geq G > M$
Conclusions I. $G < N$ II. $I \geq L$

DIRECTIONS ~ (Q. Nos. 6-8) *In each of the question relationship between some elements are shown in the statements. These statements are followed by conclusions I and II. Read the statements.*

Give Answer « SBI Clerk 2019

(a) If only Conclusion I follows.
(b) If only Conclusion II follows.
(c) If either Conclusion I or II follows.
(d) If neither Conclusion I nor II follow.
(e) If both Conclusions I and II follow.

6. Statement $A \geq B \geq C = D > E \leq F < G$
Conclusions I. $E < B$ II. $G > E$

7. Statements $P \leq R < T = U$, $Q \geq T \leq S \geq V$
Conclusions I. $Q > P$ II. $V < R$

8. Statements $L > M = O \geq P$, $N \leq M \geq S \geq T$
Conclusions I. $T \leq P$ II. $N < L$

DIRECTIONS ~ (Q. Nos. 9-11) *In these questions, a relationship between different elements is shown in the statements. The statements are followed by two conclusions.* « RRB Office Assistant 2017

Give Answer

(a) If only Conclusion I is true.
(b) If only Conclusion II is true.
(c) If either Conclusion I or II is true.
(d) If both Conclusions are true.
(e) If neither Conclusion I nor II is true.

9. Statement $G \leq I = A \leq N < T$
Conclusions I. $G < T$ II. $G = T$

10. Statement $B \leq C = X \geq Y < Z$
Conclusions I. $B > Z$ II. $B = Z$

11. Statement $G \leq H \leq R \geq S = T > U$
Conclusions I. $R \geq G$ II. $H > U$

DIRECTIONS ~ (Q. Nos. 12-16) *In these questions, a relationship between different elements is shown in the statements. The statements are followed by two conclusions.* « SBI Clerk 2016

Give Answer

(a) If only Conclusion I is true.
(b) If only Conclusion II is true.
(c) If either Conclusion I or II is true.
(d) If neither Conclusion I nor II is true.
(e) If both Conclusions are true.

12. Statements $A > B > C < D$, $C = E > G$
Conclusions I. $D > E$ II. $B > E$

13. Statements $P > Q > M > N$, $Q = S$
Conclusions I. $S > P$ II. $N < S$

14. Statement $S > M = Z > T < Q > V$
Conclusions I. $V = S$ II. $Q > M$

15. Statement $T < U = V < S > P > Q$

Conclusions I. $S > T$ II. $V < Q$

16. Statements $M < N > R > W$, $E = J > L > W$

Conclusions I. $E > W$ II. $M > L$

DIRECTIONS ~ (Q. Nos. 17-19) *In the following questions, relationship between different elements is shown in the statements. These statements are followed by two conclusions. Read them carefully and mark the appropriate answer.* « SBI Clerk 2016

Give Answer

(a) If either Conclusion I or II follows.
(b) If neither Conclusion I nor II follows.
(c) If only Conclusion II follows.
(d) If both conclusions follow.
(e) If only Conclusion I follows.

17. Statement $Y < J = P \geq R > I$

Conclusions I. $J > I$ II. $Y < R$

18. Statements $V \geq K > M = N$, $M > 5$, $T < K$

Conclusions I. $T < N$ II. $V = 5$

19. Statements $G \geq H = I < J$, $J > K$, $G < L$

Conclusions I. $K < H$ II. $L > I$

DIRECTIONS ~ (Q. Nos. 20-22) *In each of the questions below are given some statements followed by two conclusions. You have to take the given statements to be true even if they seem to be at variance with commonly known facts. Read all the conclusions and then decide which of the given conclusions logically follows from the given statements disregarding commonly known facts.* « RBI Office Assistant 2020

Give Answer

(a) If only Conclusion I follows.
(b) If only Conclusion II follows.
(c) If either Conclusion I or II follows.
(d) If neither Conclusion I nor II follows.
(e) If both Conclusions I and II follows.

20. Statements $V > B \geq G = H > F < D \leq T$,
$Q < W = E \leq F$

Conclusions. I. $B > W$ II. $E \geq B$

21. Statements $M < N = B \leq V > C$, $L > K \geq J = H \geq B$

Conclusions I. $N \leq H$ II. $B > J$

22. Statements $P = L > O \geq K > U > M$, $N < H \leq M = B < K$

Conclusions I. $L > B$ II. $N < U$

DIRECTIONS ~ (Q. Nos. 23-27) *In these questions, a relationship between different elements is shown in the statements. The statements are followed by two conclusions.* « IBPS PO/MT 2018

23. Statements $L \leq T \leq I \geq M < X$, $W < P \leq L \geq B \geq K$

Conclusions I. $K < X$ II. $W > M$

(a) If only Conclusion II is true
(b) If only Conclusion I is true
(c) If neither Conclusion I nor II is true
(d) If either Conclusion I or II is true
(e) If both Conclusions I and II are true

24. Statements $Z < U \leq D \leq A \leq M < S$,
$Q > A \leq Y < G$

Conclusions I. $Z < Y$
II. $S > Q$

(a) If both Conclusions I and II are true.
(b) If only Conclusion I is true.
(c) If neither Conclusion I nor II is true.
(d) If either Conclusion I or II is true.
(e) If only Conclusion II is true.

25. Statements $L \leq T \leq I \geq M < X$, $W < P \leq L \geq B \geq K$

Conclusions I. $K \geq M$
II. $P > M$

(a) If only Conclusion II is true.
(b) If either Conclusion I or II is true.
(c) If neither Conclusion I nor II is true.
(d) If only Conclusion I is true.
(e) If both Conclusions I and II are true.

26. Statements $Z < U \leq D \leq A \leq M < S$, $Q > A \leq Y < G$

Conclusions I. $M \geq U$ II. $G > Z$

(a) If only Conclusion II is true.
(b) If only Conclusion I is true.
(c) If neither Conclusion I nor II is true.
(d) If either Conclusion I or II is true.
(e) If both Conclusions I and II are true.

27. Statements $J > K \geq H = U \geq B \leq T < F \leq R$

Conclusions I. $J > B$ II. $H < R$

(a) If only Conclusion II is true.
(b) If either Conclusion I or II is true.
(c) If neither Conclusion I nor II is true.
(d) If only Conclusion I is true.
(e) If both Conclusions I and II are true.

DIRECTIONS ~ (Q. Nos. 28-32) *In these questions, relationship between different elements is shown in the statements. These statements are followed by two conclusions.* « SBI PO 2018

Give Answer

(a) If only Conclusion I follows.
(b) If only Conclusion II follows.
(c) If either Conclusion I or II follows.
(d) If neither Conclusion I nor II follows.
(e) If both Conclusions I and II follow.

28. Statements $X \geq G = H$, $G > J \geq L$, $J \geq K < Y$

Conclusions I. $X > L$ II. $K < G$

29. Statements $A > B = R \geq S \geq T$, $X < J \leq K < T$

Conclusions I. $A > X$ II. $R \geq T$

30. Statements $M > L \geq K \leq J$, $N \geq R \geq S = M$

Conclusions I. $R > J$ II. $J \geq R$

31. Statements $C \geq D = E$, $A = B \leq S \geq C$

Conclusions I. $C < A$ II. $D \leq B$

32. Statements $X \geq G > H \geq I$, $M > H \geq L$

Conclusions I. $X > M$ II. $X > L$

DIRECTIONS ~ (Q. Nos. 33-37) *In these questions, relationship between different elements is shown in the statements. These statements are followed by two conclusions.* « NABARD Grade-A, Grade-B, 2016

Give Answer

(a) If only Conclusion I follows.
(b) If only Conclusion II follows.
(c) If both conclusions follow.
(d) If none follows.
(e) If either conclusion I or II follows.

33. Statements $Q \geq U > I < C = K > L, G < L, C < H$
Conclusions I. $I < L$ II. $C > G$

34. Statements $M < O = N \leq K < E \geq Y = S, D < K \geq B$
Conclusions I. $M < K$ II. $O > B$

35. Statements $R < A = I \geq N, S \geq A$
Conclusions I. $S > N$ II. $N = S$

36. Statements $M < O = N \leq K < E \geq Y = S, D < K \geq B$
Conclusions I. $E > O$ II. $D < S$

37. Statements $Q \geq U > I < C = K > L, G < L, C < H$
Conclusions I. $Q > K$ II. $H > U$

DIRECTIONS ~ (Q. Nos. 38-42) *In these questions, relationship between different elements is shown in the statements. The statements are followed by conclusions. Study the conclusions based on the given statements and select the appropriate answer.* « SBI PO 2015

Give Answer

(a) If only Conclusion I is true.
(b) If neither Conclusion I nor II is true.
(c) If only Conclusion II is true.
(d) If both conclusions are true.
(e) If either Conclusion I or II is true.

38. Statements $M > A \geq B = Q \leq P < J \leq Y, Z \geq A > X$
Conclusions I. $B < Y$ II. $X \geq J$

39. Statements $M > A \geq B = Q \leq P < J \leq Y, Z \geq A > X$
Conclusions I. $Z = Q$ II. $Z > Q$

40. Statements $G < R = A \leq S, T < R$
Conclusions I. $G < S$ II. $S > T$

41. Statements $P = U < M < K \leq I > N, D \geq P, I \geq C$
Conclusions I. $M < C$ II. $N > U$

42. Statements $P = U < M < K \leq I > N, D \geq P, I \geq C$
Conclusions I. $D \geq K$ II. $I > P$

DIRECTIONS ~ (Q. Nos. 43-47) *In these questions, relationship between different elements is shown in the statements. The statements are followed by conclusions. Study the conclusions based on the given statements and select the appropriate answer.* « IBPS PO/MT 2015

Give Answer

(a) If only Conclusion II is true.
(b) If only Conclusion I is true.
(c) If both Conclusions I and II are true.
(d) If either Conclusion I or II is true.
(e) If neither Conclusion I nor II is true.

43. Statements $S \leq L \leq I = P \geq E > R, L > Q$
Conclusions I. $P \geq S$ II. $I > R$

44. Statements $G > R \geq E = A \leq T \leq S, D \leq A \leq J$
Conclusions I. $T \geq D$ II. $R > S$

45. Statement $A \geq B > C \leq D \leq E < F$
Conclusions I. $A \geq E$ II. $C < F$

46. Statements $G > R \geq E = A \leq T \leq S, D \leq A \leq J$
Conclusions I. $J > G$ II. $J = G$

47. Statements $S \leq L \leq I = P \geq E > R, L > Q$
Conclusions I. $L < R$ II. $E \geq Q$

48. Which of the given statements will be definitely true if the expression '$V < E > B = H \geq N \geq P$' is definitely true? « IBPS RRB 2015

(a) $P < B$ (b) $H < V$
(c) $N \geq V$ (d) $E \geq N$
(e) $E \geq P$

49. If the expression $S > T \geq U = V \leq W, Y \geq T < X$ are true, then which of the following conclusions is definitely true? « MHT MBA 2017

(a) $T \geq W$ (b) $W > Y$
(c) $X < V$ (d) $S > X$
(e) $V \leq Y$

50. In which of the following expressions will the expression $J \leq Y$ be definitely true? « MHT MBA 2017

(a) $J = P \leq S = N \leq V, N > Y$
(b) $Y \geq H \geq E = G \geq B \geq J$
(c) $N \leq Y \geq Q \geq T < S \leq J$
(d) $S \leq V = P \leq F \leq Y, J \geq S$
(e) $C < T \geq W \geq M \geq V = J, T \geq Y$

51. Which of the following symbols should be placed in blank spaces respectively (in the same order from left to right) in order to complete the given expression in such a manner that both $W > R$ as well as $E > S$ definitely hold true? « IBPS RRB officers 2015

W _ E _ A _ R _ S

(a) >, =, ≥, ≥ (b) >, ≥ =, >
(c) ≤, ≥, =, ≥ (d) ≤, =, >, ≥
(e) ≥, <, ≥, =

52. Which of the following symbols should replace the sign (@) and (%) respectively in the given expression in order to make the expression $L \geq U$ and $R > J$ definitely true?

$L \geq K \geq P = N = J \;@\; U \leq A \;\%\; R$ « IBPS Clerk 2018

(a) ≤, = (b) ≤, ≤
(c) >, ≤ (d) =, <
(e) ≥, <

53. Which of the following will be definitely true if the given expression $T \geq U \geq M = N < J = P < Q \leq R$ is definitely true? « IBPS Clerk 2018

(a) $T < J$ (b) $U > M$
(c) $R > N$ (d) $R \geq M$
(e) $T < P$

Answers WITH EXPLANATIONS

1. (*c*) **Statement** C ≤ L = E ≤ R ≤ K = P ≥ O
Conclusions I. P = C (May be true)
II. C < P (May be true)

2. (*e*) **Statement** W > A = S ≥ H < I ≤ N ≤ G
Conclusions I. H < W (True)
II. G > H (True)

3. (*a*) **Statement** C < O ≤ D = S > A ≥ P ≥ Q
Conclusions I. Q < D (True)
II. C < A (False)

4. (*d*) **Statement** F ≤ B = I ≤ C = A ≥ S > E
Conclusions I. S ≥ B (False)
II. F > E (False)

5. (*a*) **Statement** I ≥ N = T ≥ E > L ≥ G > M
Conclusions I. G < N (True)
II. I ≥ L (False)

6. (*e*) **Statement** A ≥ B ≥ C = D > E ≤ F < G
Conclusions I. E < B (True)
II. G > E (True)

7. (*a*) **Statements** P ≤ R < T = U, Q ≥ T ≤ S ≥ V
∴ Q ≥ T > R ≥ P and R < T ≤ S ≥ V
Conclusions I. Q > P (True)
II. V < R (False)

8. (*b*) **Statements** L > M = O ≥ P, N ≤ M ≥ S ≥ T
∴ T ≤ S ≤ M = O ≥ P and N ≤ M < L
Conclusions I. T ≤ P (False)
II. N < L (True)

9. (*a*) **Statement** G ≤ I = A ≤ N < T
Conclusions I. G < T (True)
II. G = T (False)
So, only Conclusion I follows.

10. (*e*) **Statement** B ≤ C = X ≥ Y < Z
Conclusions I. B > Z (False) II. B = Z (False)
So, neither Conclusion I nor II follows.

11. (*a*) **Statement** G ≤ H ≤ R ≥ S = T > U
Conclusions I. R ≥ G (True) II. H > U (False)
So, only Conclusion I follows.

12. (*e*) A > B > C < D, C = E > G
∴ A > B > C, C = E, C < D
∴ A > B > E = C < D
∴ B > E (True)
D > E (True)
Hence, both Conclusions are true.

13. (*b*) P > Q > M > N, Q = S
∴ P > S > M > N
∴ S > N (True)
Hence, only Conclusion II is true.

14. (*d*) S > M = Z > T < Q > V
∴ M < S > T < Q > V
Hence, neither Conclusion I nor II is true.

15. (*a*) T < U = V < S > P > Q
∴ T < U = V < S
∴ T < S ⇒ S > T (True) and V < Q (False)
Hence, only Conclusion I follows.

16. (*a*) M < N > R > W and E = J > L > W
∴ E > W
Hence, only Conclusion I is true.

17. (*e*) **Statement** Y < J = P ≥ R > I
Conclusions I. J > I (True)
II. Y < R (False)
So, only Conclusion I follows.

18. (*b*) On combining statements,
V ≥ K > M = N > 5, T < K
Conclusions I. T < N (False)
II. V = 5 (False)
So, neither Conclusion I nor II follows.

19. (*c*) On combining statements,
L > G ≥ H = I < J > K
Conclusions I. K < H (False)
II. L > I (True)
So, only Conclusion II follows.

20. (*a*) **Statements** V > B ≥ G = H > F < D ≤ T
Or V > B ≥ G = H > F ≥ E = W > Q
Conclusions I. B > W (True)
II. E ≥ B (False)
Hence, only Conclusions I is definitely true.

21. (*a*) **Statements** M < N = B ≤ V > C
Or M < N = B ≤ H = J ≤ K
Conclusions I. N ≤ H (True)
II. B > J (False)
Hence, only Conclusion I is definitely true.

22. (*e*) **Statements** P = L > O ≥ K > U > M
Or P = L > O ≥ K > U > M ≥ H > N
Or L > O ≥ K > U > M = B < K
Conclusions I. L > B (True)
II. N < U (True)
Hence, both Conclusions are definitely true.

23. (*c*) **Statements** L ≤ T ≤ I ≥ M < X, W < P ≤ L ≥ B ≥ K
∴ X > M ≤ I ≥ T ≥ L ≥ B ≥ K and W < P ≤ L ≤ I ≥ M
Conclusions I. K < X (False)
II. W > M (False)
∴ Neither Conclusion I nor II is true.

24. (*b*) **Statements** Z < U ≤ D ≤ A ≤ M < S, Q > A ≤ Y < G
∴ Y ≥ A ≥ D ≥ U > Z and S > M ≥ A < Q
Conclusions I. Z < Y (True)
II. S > Q (False)
∴ Only Conclusion I is true.

25. (*c*) **Statements** L ≤ T ≥ I ≥ M < X, W < P ≤ L ≥ B ≥ K
∴ K ≤ B ≤ L ≤ T ≤ I ≥ M and P ≤ L ≤ T ≤ I ≥ M
Conclusions I. K ≥ M (False)
II. P > M (False)

26. (*e*) **Statements** $Z < U \le D \le A \le M < S, Q > A \le Y < G$
$\therefore$ $U \le D \le A \le M$ and $G > Y \ge A \ge D \ge U > Z$
Conclusions I. $M \ge U$ (True)
II. $G > Z$ (True)

27. (*d*) **Statement** $J > K \ge H = U \ge B \le T < F \le R$
Conclusions I. $J > B$ (True)
II. $H < R$ (False)

28. (*e*) **Statements** $X \ge G = H, G > J \ge L, J \ge K < Y$
$\therefore$ $X \ge G = H > J \ge L$ and $G = H > J \ge K < Y$
Conclusions I. $X > L$ (True)
II. $K < G$ (True)
Hence, both I and II are true.

29. (*e*) **Statements** $A > B = R \ge S \ge T,\ X < J \le K < T$
$\therefore$ $A > B = R \ge S \ge T > K \ge J > X$
Conclusions I. $A > X$ (True)
II. $R \ge T$ (True)
Hence, both I and II are true.

30. (*d*) **Statements** $M > L \ge K \le J, N \ge R \ge S = M$
$\therefore$ $N \ge R \ge S = M > L \ge K \le J$
Conclusions I. $R > J$ (False)
II. $J \ge R$ (False)
Hence, Neither Conclusion I Nor II is true.

31. (*d*) **Statements** $C \ge D = E,\ A = B \le S \ge C$
$\therefore$ $A = B \le S \ge C \ge D = E$
Conclusions I. $C < A$ (may be true)
II. $D \le B$ (may be true)
Hence, neither Conclusion I nor II is true.

32. (*b*) **Statements** $X \ge G > H \ge I, M > H \ge L$
$\therefore$ $X \ge G > H < M$ and $X \ge G > H > L$
Conclusions I. $X > M$ (False)
II. $X > L$ (True)
Hence only conclusion II is true.

33. (*b*) **Statements** $Q \ge U > I < C = K > L > G,\ C < H$
Conclusions I. $I < L$ (False)
II. $C > G$ (True)

34. (*a*) **Statements** $M < O = N \le K < E \ge Y = S, D < K \ge B$
Conclusions I. $M < K$ (True)
II. $O > B$ (False)

35. (*e*) **Statements** $R < A = I \ge N, S \ge A$
Conclusions I. $S > N$ II. $N = S$
Either Conclusion I or Conclusion II follows.

36. (*a*) **Statements** $M < O = N \le K < E \ge Y = S, D < K \ge B$
Conclusions I. $E > O$ (True)
II. $D < S$ (False)

37. (*d*) **Statements** $Q \ge U > I < C = K > L, G < L, C < H$
Conclusions I. $Q > K$ (False)
II. $H > U$ (False)

38. (*a*) $Y \ge J > P \ge Q = B \le A > X$
Conclusions I. $Y > B$ (True)
II. $X \ge J$ (False)
So, only Conclusion I is true.

39. (*e*) $Z \ge A \ge B = Q$
Conclusions I. $Z = Q$ (True)
or
II. $Z > Q$ (True)
So, either Conclusion I or II is true.

40. (*d*) $S \ge A = R > G$
Conclusions I. $S > G$ (True)
and $S \ge A = R > T$
II. $S > T$ (True)
So, both conclusions are ture.

41. (*b*) $M < K \le I \ge C$
Conclusions I. $M < C$ (False)
$U < M < K \le I > N$
II. $N > U$ (False)
So, neither Conclusion I nor II is true.

42. (*c*) $D \ge P = U < M < K \le I > N, I \ge C$
Conclusions I. $D \ge K$ (False)
II. $I > P$ (True)
So, only Conclusion II is true.

43. (*c*) **Statements** $S \le L \le I = P \ge E > R, L > Q$
Conclusions I. $P \ge S$ (True)
II. $I > R$ (True)
So, both the Conclusions I and II are true.

44. (*b*) **Statements** $G > R \ge E = A \le T \le S$,
$D \le A \le J \Rightarrow D \le A \le T$
Conclusion I. $T \ge D$ (True)
II. $R > S$ (False)
So, only Conclusion I is true.

45. (*a*) **Statement** $A \ge B > C \le D \le E < F$
Conclusions I. $A \ge E$ (False)
II. $C < F$ (True)
So, only Conclusion II is true.

46. (*e*) **Statements** $G > R \ge E = A \le T \le S, D \le A \le J$
$\Rightarrow$ $G > R \ge E = A \le J$
Conclusions I. $J > G$ (False)
II. $J = G$ (False)
So, neither Conclusion I nor II is true.

47. (*e*) **Statements** $S \le L \le I = P \ge E > R, L > Q$
$\Rightarrow$ $Q < L \le I = P \ge E > R$
Conclusions I. $L < R$ (False)
II. $E \ge Q$ (False)
So, neither Conclusion I nor II is true.

48. (*a*) As, $V < E > B = H \ge N \ge P$
$P < B$, will be definitely true from the given expression.

49. (*e*) Given, $S > T \ge U = V \le W, Y \ge T < X$
$\therefore$ $V \le T \le Y$
Hence, $V \le Y$ is definitely true.

50. (*b*) In option (b), $J \le B \le G = E \le H \le Y$
$\therefore$ $J \le Y$ is definitely true.

51. (*b*) $W > E \ge A = R > S$ definitely holds true, $W > R$ as well as $E > S$ are true according to the expression.

52. (*d*) From option (d), $L \ge K \ge P = N = J = U \le A < R$
Here, $L \ge U$ and $R > J$ are definitely true.

53. (*c*) Given expression $T \ge U \ge M = N < J = P < Q \le R$
Option (a) - $T < J$ (False)
Option (b) - $U > M$ (False)
Option (c) - $R > N$ (True)
Option (d) - $R \ge M$ (False)
Option (e) - $T < P$ (False)

TYPE 02

Coded Inequalities

Unlike the simple inequalities, coded inequalities have all the signs (>, <, =, ≥, ≤) in coded form. i.e., substituted symbols are used in place of real symbols e.g., the sign of greater than (>) can be coded as ϕ / @/ * /$ etc.

The candidates are required to replace the codes with real signs and then solve the questions in the same way as the questions of simple inequalities are solved and answer the given question.

Steps to Solve Coded Inequality Based Questions

***Step* I Representation of Statements with Mathematical Operators**

First of all, represent the symbols used in statements with mathematical operators according to the given directions.

e.g. 1. A $ B means, A is not less than B.

2. A # B means, A is not greater than B.
3. A @ B means, A is neither less than nor equal to B.
4. A © B means, A is neither less than nor greater than B.
5. A % B means, A is neither greater than nor equal to B.

Now, replacing the symbols with mathematical operators, the statements become,

			Therefore,
1. A $ B	⇒	A ≥ B	$ ⇒ ≥
2. A # B	⇒	A ≤ B	# ⇒ ≤
3. A @ B	⇒	A > B	@ ⇒ >
4. A © B	⇒	A = B	© ⇒ =
5. A % B	⇒	A < B	% ⇒ <

Now, if any statement is given as follows

Statement M @ J, J $ T, T © N

Then, according to the given directions the statements can be represented with mathematical operators as follows

M @ J ⇒ M > J, J $ T ⇒ J ≥ T, T © N ⇒ T = N

***Step II* Combining the Statements According to Mathematical Rules**

e.g. M @ J ⇒ M > J, J $ T ⇒ J ≥ T, T © N ⇒ T = N

Combination M > J ≥ T = N

Chapter tip!

While combining the statements following points should kept in mind

- Don't assume anything from your side, only follow the given directions/instructions.
- Arrange/combine the given statements always in ascending or descending order.
- Arrange/combine maximum parts given in question, in one line.

***Step* III Representation of Conclusions with Mathematical Operators**

Conclusions

I. N # J II. T % N III. M @ N

Now, represent the conclusions with mathematical signs as follows

I. N # J ⇒ N ≤ J II. T % N ⇒ T < N

III. M @ N ⇒ M > N

***Step* IV Determining** (whether the conclusions are true or false) Now, the truth of the conclusions has to be determined.

Conclusions

I. N ≤ J (True) II. T < N (False)

III. M > N (True)

So, it is clear that Conclusions I and III are true.

DIRECTIONS ~ (Example Nos. 18-21) *In the questions that follow, the symbols are used as follows.*

A © B means, A is greater than B.

A $\underline{©}$ B means, A is either greater than or equal to B.

A = B means, A is equal to B.

A @ B means, A is smaller than B.

A $\underline{@}$ B means, A is either smaller than or equal to B.

Now, in each of the following questions, assuming the three statements to be true, state which of the two Conclusions I and II given below is definitely true.

Give Answer

(a) If only Conclusion I is true.
(b) If only Conclusion II is true.
(c) If either Conclusion I or II is true.
(d) If neither Conclusion I nor II is true.
(e) If both Conclusions I and II are true.

***Ex* 18** **Statements** Q @ R, R @ M, M © D
Conclusions I. D © R II. D © Q

***Ex* 19** **Statements** M @ K, K © R, R © P © D
Conclusions I. P @ K II. P @ M

***Ex* 20** **Statements** T © M, M = P, P © R
Conclusions I. R @ T II. T © R

***Ex* 21** **Statements** P @ Q, Q © K, K@ M
Conclusions I. M = Q II. M $\underline{©}$ Q

Solutions (Example Nos. 18-21)

Given that, A © B ⇒ A > B *i.e.*, © represents >

A $\underline{©}$ B ⇒ A ≥ B *i.e.*, $\underline{©}$ represents ≥

A = B ⇒ A = B *i.e.*, = represents =

A @ B ⇒ A < B *i.e.*, @ represents <

A $\underline{@}$ B ⇒ A ≤ B *i.e.*, $\underline{@}$ represents ≤

18. (d) According to the question,

Q @ R ⇒ Q < R ...(i)
R @ M ⇒ R < M ...(ii)
M © D ⇒ M > D ...(iii)

On combining the statements (i), (ii) and (iii), we get

Q < R < M > D

Conclusions I. D © R ⇒ D > R (False)
II. D © Q ⇒ D > Q (False)

So, it is clear that neither Conclusion I nor II is true.

19. ***(a)*** According to the question,

M @ K ⇒ M < K ...(i)
K © R ⇒ K > R ...(ii)
R © P © D ⇒ R > P > D ...(iii)

On combining the statements (i), (ii) and (iii), we get

M < K > R > P

Conclusions I. P @ K ⇒ P < K (True)
II. P @ M ⇒ P < M (False)

So, it is clear that only Conclusion I is true.

20. ***(e)*** According to the question,

T © M ⇒ T > M ...(i)
M = P ⇒ M = P ...(ii)
P © R ⇒ P > R ...(iii)

On combining the statements (i), (ii) and (iii), we get

T > M = P > R

Conclusions I. R @ T ⇒ R < T (True)
II. T © R ⇒ T > R (True)

So, it is clear that both Conclusions I and II are true.

21. ***(d)*** According to the question,

P @ Q ⇒ P < Q ...(i)
Q © K ⇒ Q > K ...(ii)
K @ M ⇒ K < M ...(iii)

On combining the statements (i), (ii) and (iii), we get

P < Q > K < M

Conclusions I. M = Q ⇒ M = Q (False)
II. M © Q ⇒ M ≥ Q (False)

So, it is clear that neither Conclusion I nor II is true.

DIRECTIONS ~ (Example Nos. 22-26) *In the following questions, the symbols @, ©, $, % and are used with the meaning as illustrated below.*

'A $ B' means 'A is not smaller than B'.
'A©B' means 'A is neither smaller than nor greater than B'.
'A @ B' means 'A is neither smaller than nor equal to B'.
'A # B' means 'A is not greater than B'.
'A % B' means 'A is neither greater than nor equal to B'.
In each of the following questions, assuming the given statements to be true, find which of the three Conclusions I, II and III given below is/are definitely true? « CGPSC 2017

Ex 22 **Statements** K © P, P @ Q, Q $ R

Conclusions I. K @ R II. R % P III. Q % R

(a) I and II are true. (b) II and III are true.
(c) Only III is true. (d) All are true.
(e) None of these.

Ex 23 **Statements** D © K, K # F, F @ P

Conclusions I. P @ D II. K # P III. F $ D

(a) Only I is true. (b) Only II is true.
(c) Only III is true. (d) II and III are true.
(e) None of these.

Ex 24 **Statements** M @ D, D © V, V $ W

Conclusions I. W @ M II. M % V III. D $ W

(a) II and III are true. (b) Only II is true.
(c) Only III is true. (d) Only I is true.
(e) None of these.

Ex 25 **Statements** M @ J, J $ T, T © N

Conclusions I. N # J II. T % M III. M @ N

(a) Only I is true. (b) I and II are true.
(c) All are true. (d) II and III are true.
(e) None of these.

Ex 26 **Statements** H % J, J © N, N @ R

Conclusions I. R % J II. H @ J III. N @ H

(a) I and II are true (b) I and III are true
(c) II and III are true (d) All are true
(e) None of these

Solutions (Example Nos. 22-26) *According to the given information,*

A $ B → A ≥ B, A © B → A = B, A @ B → A > B,
A # B → A ≤ B, A % B → A < B

22. (*d*) **Statements** K © P, P @ Q, Q $ R
⇒ K = P; P > Q; Q ≥ R ⇒ K = P > Q ≥ R

Conclusions

I. K @ R → K > R (True)
II. R % P → R < P (True)
III. Q % K → Q < K (True)

Hence, all conclusions are true.

23. (*c*) **Statements**

D © K, K # F, F @ P
⇒ D = K; K ≤ F; F > P ⇒ D = K ≤ F > P

Conclusions

I. P @ D → P > D (False)
II. K # P → K ≤ P (False)
III. F $ D → F ≥ D (True)

Hence, only Conclusion III is true.

24. (*c*) **Statements**

M @ D, D © V, V $ W
⇒ M > D, D = V, V ≥ W ⇒ M > D = V ≥ W

Conclusions

I. W @ M → W > M (False)
II. M % V → M < V (False)
III. D $ W → D ≥ W (True)

Hence, only Conclusion III is true.

25. (*c*) **Statements**

M @ J, J $ T, T © N
⇒ M > J, J ≥ T, T = N ⇒ M > J ≥ T = N

Conclusions

I. N # J → N ≤ J (True)
II. T % M → T < M (True)
III. M @ N → M > N (True)

Hence, all conclusions are true.

26. (*b*) **Statements** H % J, J © N, N @ R
⇒ H < J, J = N, N > R ⇒ H < J = N > R

Conclusions

I. R % J → R < J (True)
II. H @ J → H > J (False)
III. N @ H → N > H (True)

Hence, only Conclusions I and III are true.

Practice / CORNER 18.2

DIRECTIONS ~ (Q. Nos. 1-5) *In the following questions, the symbol ©, ©̳, @, @̳ and = are used as follows.*

A © B means A > B
A ©̳ B means A ≥ B
A = B means A = B
A @ B means A < B
A @̳ B means A ≤ B

Now, in each of the following questions, assuming the given statements to be true, find which of the two Conclusions I and II given below is/are definitely true.

Give Answer

(a) If only Conclusion I is true.
(b) If only Conclusion II is true.
(c) If either Conclusion I or II is true.
(d) If neither Conclusion I nor II is true.
(e) If both Conclusions I and II are true.

1. Statements B @ K, K @ M, M @ Z
Conclusions I. B @ Z II. B = Z

2. Statements R © B, B ©̳ M
Conclusions I. R © M II. R @ M

3. Statements M @̳ R, Q ©̳ P, P = R
Conclusions I. M @ P II. M = P

4. Statements M @ N, N @̳ R
Conclusions I. R ©̳ M II. R © M

5. Statements P @̳ Q, Q ©̳ M, M @̳ T
Conclusions I. P @̳ T II. P ©̳ T

DIRECTIONS ~ (Q. Nos. 6-8) *In the following questions, the symbol @, @̳, =, © and ©̳ are used with following meanings.*

P @ Q ⇒ P is greater than Q.
P @̳ Q ⇒ P is either greater than or equal to Q.
P © Q ⇒ P is smaller than Q.
P ©̳ Q ⇒ P is either smaller than or equal to Q.
P = Q ⇒ P is equal to Q.

Give Answer

(a) If only Conclusion I is true.
(b) If only Conclusion II is true.
(c) If either Conclusion I or II is true.
(d) If neither Conclusion I nor II is true.
(e) If both Conclusions I and II are true.

6. Statements B @ V, K © C, C ©̳ B
Conclusions I. V @ C II. B @ K

7. Statements K @ T, S = K, T © R
Conclusions I. S @ T II. T = R

8. Statements U = M, P @̳ U, M @̳ B
Conclusions I. P = B II. P @ B

DIRECTIONS ~ (Q. Nos. 9-14) *In the following questions, the symbols, ©, %, $ and @ are used with the following meaning as illustrated below.*

P © Q means, 'P is either smaller than or equal to Q'.
P * Q means, 'P is either greater than or equal to Q'.
P % Q means, 'P is smaller than Q'.
P $ Q means, 'P is greater than Q'.
P @ Q means, 'P is equal to Q'.

Now, in each of the following questions, assuming the given statements to be true, find which of the two Conclusions I and II given below then is/are definitely true.

Give Answer

(a) If only Conclusion I is true.
(b) If only Conclusion II is true.
(c) If either Conclusion I or II is true.
(d) If neither Conclusion I nor II is true.
(e) If both Conclusions I and II are true.

9. Statements M % T, T $ K, K © D
Conclusions I. T $ D II. D $ M

10. Statements F @ B, B % N, N $ H
Conclusions I. N $ F II. H $ F

11. Statements R * M, M @ K, K © J
Conclusions I. J $ M II. J @ M

12. Statements B $ N, N * R, R @ K
Conclusions I. K © N II. B $ K

13. Statements J © K, K $ N, N * D
Conclusions I. J % N II. D % K

14. Statements R @ D, D © M, M $ T
Conclusions I. T % D II. M * R

DIRECTIONS ~ (Q. Nos. 15-19) *Read the following information carefully and answer the questions that follows.* « SBI PO 2016

'P @ Q' means, 'P is neither greater than nor equal to Q'.
'P % Q' means, 'P is neither smaller than nor equal to Q'.
'P # Q' means, 'P is not greater than Q'.
'P $ Q' means, 'P is not smaller than Q'.
'P * Q' means, 'P is neither smaller than nor greater than Q'.

15. Statements A @ B, B % C, C * D, D $ E
Conclusions I. B % E II. A % E

(a) Only Conclusion I follows.
(b) Only Conclusion II follows.
(c) Either Conclusion I or II follows.
(d) Neither Conclusion I nor II follows.
(e) Both Conclusions I and II follow.

16. Statements A % B, B * C, C # D, D * E
Conclusions I. A % C II. E $ B

(a) Only Conclusion I follows.
(b) Only Conclusion II follows.
(c) Either Conclusion I or II follows.
(d) Neither Conclusion I nor II follows.
(e) Both Conclusions I and II follow.

17. Statements A * B, B $ C, C # D, D @ E
Conclusions I. E $ A II. C % A
(a) Only Conclusion I follows.
(b) Only Conclusion II follows.
(c) Either Conclusion I or II follows.
(d) Neither Conclusion I nor II follows.
(e) Both Conclusions I and II follow.

18. Statements A $ B, B $ C, C * D, D @ E
Conclusions I. A $ E II. E % C
(a) Only Conclusion I follows.
(b) Only Conclusion II follows.
(c) Either Conclusion I or II follows.
(d) Neither Conclusion I nor II follows.
(e) Both Conclusions I and II follow.

19. Statements A % E, E @ C, C % B, B * D
Conclusions I. C % D II. B @ A
(a) Only Conclusion I follows.
(b) Only Conclusion II follows.
(c) Either Conclusion I or II follows.
(d) Neither Conclusion I nor II follows.
(e) Both Conclusions I and II follow.

DIRECTIONS ~ (Q. Nos. 20-24) *In the following questions, the symbols @, ©, $, % and # are used with the following meaning as illustrated below.*

'A $ B' means, 'A is not smaller than B'.
'A # B' means, 'A is not greater than B'.
'A @ B' means, 'A is neither smaller than nor equal to B'.
'A © B' means, 'A is neither smaller than nor greater than B.'
'A % B' means 'A is neither greater than nor equal to B'.
Now, in each of the following questions, assuming the given statements to be true, find which of the three Conclusions I, II and III given below them is/are definitely true and give your answer accordingly.

20. Statements H % J, J© N, N @ R
Conclusions I. R % J II. H @ J III. N @ H
(a) Only II is true. (b) I and III are true.
(c) Only I is true. (d) Only III is true.

21. Statements M @ J, J $ T, T© N
Conclusions I. N # J II. T % M III. M @ N
(a) I and II are true. (b) II and III are true.
(c) I and III are true. (d) All are true.

22. Statements D © K, K # F, F @ P
Conclusions I. P @ D II. K # P III. F $ D
(a) Only II is true. (b) I and II are true.
(c) Only III is true. (d) II and III are true.

23. Statements R # D, D $ M, M© N
Conclusions I. R # M II. N # D III. N $ R
(a) Only I is true. (b) Only II is true.
(c) Only III is true. (d) None is true.

24. Statements K© P, P @ Q, Q $ R
Conclusions I. K @ R II. R % P III. Q % K
(a) I and II are true. (b) II and III are true.
(c) Only III is true. (d) All are true.

DIRECTIONS ~ (Q. Nos. 25-29) *In the following questions, the symbols $, %, @, © and * are used with the following meaning as illustrated below.* « SBI PO Mains 2015

A$B means A is not smaller than B.
A%B means A is not greater than B.
A@B means A is neither smaller than nor equal to B.
A©B means A is neither greater than nor equal to B.
A*B means A is neither greater than nor smaller than B.
Now, in each of the following questions, assuming the given statements to be true, find which of the three Conclusions I, II and III given below them is/are definitely true and give your answer accordingly.

25. Statements A © B, B % C, C @ D
Conclusions I. D © B II. C @ A III. C $ A
(a) Only I is true. (b) Only II is true.
(c) Either I or II true. (d) Only III is true.
(e) All I, II and III are true.

26. Statements P * Q, Q $ R, R @ S
Conclusions I. S © Q II. R % P III. S © P
(a) Only I is true. (b) Only II is true.
(c) Only III is true. (d) Neither I nor II true.
(e) All I, II and III are true.

27. Statements A $ B, B @ C, C % D
Conclusions I. D @ C II. C % A III. D @ A
(a) Only I is true. (b) Only II is true.
(c) Only III is true. (d) None follow.
(e) All I, II and III are true.

28. Statements M % N, N @ O, O $ P
Conclusions I. P © N II. P % N III. P © M
(a) Only I is true. (b) Only II is true.
(c) Only III is true. (d) Neither I nor II true.
(e) All I, II and III are true.

29. Statements W © X, X * Y, Y % Z
Conclusions I. Y @ W II. Z $ X III. Z @ W
(a) Only I is true. (b) Only II is true.
(c) Only III is true. (d) Neither I nor II true.
(e) All I, II and III are true.

DIRECTIONS ~ (Q. Nos. 30-35) *In the following questions, the symbols @, ©, $, % and # are used with the following meaning as illustrated below*

'P $ Q' means, 'P is not greater than Q.'
'P @ Q' means ,'P is neither smaller than nor equal to Q'.
'P # Q' means, 'P is not smaller than Q.'
'P © Q' means, 'P is neither greater than nor equal to Q.'
'P % Q' means, 'P is neither smaller than nor greater than Q'.
Now, in each of the following questions, assuming the given statements to be true, find which of the three Conclusions I, II and III given below is/are definitely true and give your answer accordingly.

30. Statements D # K, K @ T, T $ M, M % J
Conclusions I. J @ T II. J % T III. D @ T
(a) Only I is true. (b) Only II is true.
(c) Either I or II is true. (d) Either I or II and III are true.

31. Statements R @ N, N © D, D $ J, J # B
Conclusions I. R @ J II. J @ N III. B @ D
(a) None is true. (b) Only I is true.
(c) Only II is true. (d) Only III is true.

32. Statements W © B, B % V, V $ R, R @ K
Conclusions I. K© B II. R # B III. V @ W
(a) I and II are true. (b) I and III are true.
(c) II and III are true. (d) All I, II, III are true.

33. Statements H $ M, M # T, T @ D, D © R
Conclusions I. D © M II. R @ M III. H $ T
(a) None is true. (b) Only I is true.
(c) Only II is true. (d) Only III is true.

34. Statements B % J, J @ K, K© T, T $ F
Conclusions I. F @ K II. B @ K III. B @ F
(a) I and II are true. (b) I and III are true.
(c) II and III are true. (d) All are true.

35. Statements F # B, B $ M, M @ K, K© N
Conclusions I. N @ M II. F $ M III. K© B
(a) Only I is true. (b) Only II is true.
(c) Only III is true. (d) None is true.

DIRECTIONS ~ (Q. Nos. 36-40) *In the following questions, the symbols @, $, #, © and % are used with the following meaning as illustrated below.* « IBPS (PO) 2012

'P $ Q' means 'P is not smaller than Q'.
'P © Q' means 'P is neither greater than nor equal to Q'.
'P # Q' means 'P is neither smaller than nor equal to Q'.
'P % Q' means 'P is not greater than Q.'
'P @ Q' means 'P is neither greater than nor smaller than Q'.
Now, in each of the following question, assuming the given statements to be true, find which of the four Conclusions I, II, III and IV given below them is/are definitely true and give your answer accordingly.

36. Statements R # J, J $ D, D @ K, K % T
Conclusions I. T # D II. T @ D
III. R # K IV. J $ T
(a) Either I or II is true. (b) Only III is true.
(c) III and IV are true.
(d) Either I or II and III are true.
(e) None of these

37. Statements T % R, R $ M, M @ D, D © H
Conclusions I. D % R II. H # R
III. T© M IV. T % D
(a) Only I is true. (b) I and IV are true.
(c) I and II are true. (d) II and IV are true.
(e) None of these

38. Statements M @ B, B # N, N $ R, R© K
Conclusions I. K # B II. R© B
III. M $ R IV. N© M
(a) I and III are true. (b) I and II are true.
(c) II and IV are true. (d) II, III and IV are true.
(e) None of these

39. Statements F # H, H @ M, M© E, E $ J
Conclusions I. J © M II. E # H
III. M© F IV. F # E
(a) I and II are true. (b) II and III are true.
(c) I, II and III are true. (d) II, III and IV are true.
(e) None of these

40. Statements D % A, A @ B, B© K, K % M
Conclusions I. B $ D II. K # A
III. M # B IV. A© M
(a) I, II and IV are true. (b) I, II and III are true.
(c) II, III and IV are true. (d) I, III and IV are true.
(e) All are true.

DIRECTIONS ~ (Q. Nos. 41-45) *In the following questions, the symbols @, $, *, # and δ are used with the following meaning as illustrated below.* « SBI (PO) 2010

'P $ Q' means, 'P is not smaller than Q'.
'P @ Q' means, 'P is neither smaller than nor equal to Q'.
'P # Q' means, 'P is neither greater than nor equal to Q'.
'P δ Q' means, 'P is neither greater than nor smaller than Q.'
'P * Q' means, 'P is not greater than Q'.
Now, in each of the following questions assuming the given statements to be true, find which of the four Conclusions I, II, III and IV given below them is/are definitely true and give your answer accordingly.

41. Statements H @ T, T # F, Fδ E, E * V
Conclusions I. V $ F II. E @ T
III. H @ V IV. T # V
(a) I, II and III are true. (b) I, II and IV are true.
(c) II, III and IV are true. (d) I, III and IV are true.
(e) All are true.

42. Statements D # R, R * K, K @ F, F $ J
Conclusions I. J # R II. J # K
III. R # F IV. K @ D
(a) I, II and III are true (b) II, III and IV are true
(c) I, III and IV are true (d) All are true
(e) None of these

43. Statements Nδ B, B $ W, W # H, H * M
Conclusions I. M @ W II. H @ N
III. Wδ N IV. W # N
(a) Only I is true. (b) Only III is true.
(c) Only IV is true. (d) Either III or IV is true.
(e) Either III or IV and I are true.

44. Statements R * D, D $ J, J # M, M @ K
Conclusions I. K # J II. D @ M
III. R # M IV. D @ K
(a) None is true. (b) Only I is true.
(c) Only II is true. (d) Only III is true.
(e) Only IV is true.

45. Statements M $ K, K @ N, N * R, R # W
Conclusions I. W @ K II. M $ R
III. K @ W IV. M @ N
(a) I and II are true. (b) I, II and III are true.
(c) III and IV are true. (d) II, III and IV are true.
(e) None of these.

DIRECTIONS ~ (Q. Nos. 46-50) *In the questions given below, some relationship have been expressed through symbols as shown below. Study the meaning of these symbols and pickup the correct answer from the answer choices for each of the questions below.* « CMAT 2013

ϕ means ' less than' Δ means 'not greater than'
– means ' equal to' + means 'not equal to'
× mens 'not less than' = means 'greater than'

46. X ϕ Y + Z implies
(a) X – Y = Z (b) X × Y – Z (c) X Δ Y ϕ Z (d) X + Y = Z

47. X ϕ Y − Z implies
(a) X × Y − Z (b) X − Y × Z (c) X + Y × Z (d) X × Y = Z

48. X − Y + Z implies
(a) X + Y + Z
(b) X ϕ Y − Z
(c) X − Y ϕ Z
(d) None of these

49. X − Y = Z implies
(a) X + Y + Z (b) X Δ Y × Z (c) X + Y ϕ Z (d) X + Y × Z

50. X = Y = Z does not implies
(a) Y ϕ X = Z
(b) Z ϕ Y ϕ X
(c) Z ϕ X = Y
(d) None of these

DIRECTIONS ~ (Q. Nos. 51 and 52) *Based on the given data answer the following questions.* « IBPS PO Mains 2019

'P $ Q' means, 'P is not smaller than Q'.
'P @ Q' means, 'P is neither smaller than nor equal to Q'.
'P # Q' means, 'P is neither greater than nor equal to Q'.
'P & Q' means, 'P is neither smaller than nor greater than Q'.
'P * Q' means, 'P is not greater than Q'.

51. What symbol will come in between K and N such that all the given expressions R@K, K$N, K*R, M$N are definitely false?

M$K?N*R

(a) # (b) $ (c) * (d) @ (e) &

52. Which of the given symbols can be placed in blank spaces respectively (in the same order from left to right) such that all the three expressions V$F. T#V and E@T definitely holds true?

H ? T ? F ? E ? V

(a) $, #, &, *
(b) #, #, *, *
(c) $, #, *, &
(d) Either a or b or c
(e) None of these

DIRECTIONS ~ (Q. Nos. 53 and 54) *In each of the following question, find the relationship that can definitely be deduced on the basis of the relations given. The symbols used to define the relationship are as follows*

@ means, 'greater than'
# means, 'less than'
$ means, 'not equal to'
% means, 'equal to'

53. If it is given that, 3 M % 2 N and N % 30, then,
(a) @ M
(b) M #
(c) 20 % M
(d) None of these

54. If it is given that, N @ P, P # O, O @ M and N % M, then,
(a) O @ N
(b) O # N
(c) O $ N
(d) None of these

Answers / WITH EXPLANATIONS

Solutions (Q. Nos. 1-5)

Given that,
A © B ⇒ A > B *i.e.*, © represents >
A $\underline{\underline{©}}$ B ⇒ A ≥ B *i.e.*, $\underline{\underline{©}}$ represents ≥
A = B ⇒ A = B *i.e.*, = represents =
A @ B ⇒ A < B *i.e.*, @ represents <
A $\underline{\underline{@}}$ B ⇒ A ≤ B *i.e.*, $\underline{\underline{@}}$ represents ≤

1. (*a*) According to the question,
B @ K ⇒ B < K ...(i)
K @ M ⇒ K < M ...(ii)
M @ Z ⇒ M < Z ...(iii)
On combining the statements (i), (ii) and (iii), we get
B < K < M < Z
Conclusions
I. B @ Z ⇒ B < Z (True)
II. B = Z ⇒ B = Z (False)
So, it is clear that only Conclusion I is true.

2. (*a*) According to the question,
R © B ⇒ R > B ...(i)
B $\underline{\underline{©}}$ M ⇒ B ≥ M ...(ii)
On combining the statements (i) and (ii), we get
R > B ≥ M
Conclusions
I. R © M ⇒ R > M (True)
II. R @ M ⇒ R < M (False)
So, it is clear that only Conclusion I is true.

3. (*c*) According to the question,
M $\underline{\underline{@}}$ R ⇒ M ≤ R ...(i)
Q $\underline{\underline{©}}$ P ⇒ Q ≥ P ...(ii)
P = R ⇒ P = R ...(iii)
On combining statements (i), (ii) and (iii), we get
M ≤ R = P ≤ Q
Conclusions
I. M @ P ⇒ M < P (May be true)
or
II. M = P ⇒ M = P (May be true)
So, it is clear that either Conclusion I or Conclusion II is true.

4. (*b*) According to the question,
M @ N ⇒ M < N ...(i)
N $\underline{\underline{@}}$ R ⇒ N ≤ R ...(ii)
On combining the statements (i) and (ii), we get
M < N ≤ R
Conclusions
I. R $\underline{\underline{©}}$ M ⇒ R ≥ M (False)
II. R © M ⇒ R > M (True)
So, it is clear that only Conclusion II is true.

5. (*d*) According to the question,
P $\underline{\underline{@}}$ Q ⇒ P ≤ Q ...(i)
Q $\underline{\underline{©}}$ M ⇒ Q ≥ M ...(ii)
M $\underline{\underline{@}}$ T ⇒ M ≤ T ...(iii)
On combining the statements (i), (ii) and (iii), we get P ≤ Q ≥ M ≤ T
Conclusions I. P $\underline{\underline{@}}$ T ⇒ P ≤ T (False)
II. P $\underline{\underline{©}}$ T ⇒ P ≥ T (False)
So, it is clear that neither Conclusion I nor Conclusion II is true.

Solutions (Q. Nos. 6-8)

Given that,
P @ Q ⇒ P > Q *i.e.*, @ represents >
P $\underline{\underline{@}}$ Q ⇒ P ≥ Q *i.e.*, $\underline{\underline{@}}$ represents ≥
P © Q ⇒ P < Q *i.e.*, © represents <
P $\underline{\underline{©}}$ Q ⇒ P ≤ Q *i.e.*, $\underline{\underline{©}}$ represents ≤
P = Q ⇒ P = Q *i.e.*, = represents =

6. (*b*) According to the question,
B @ V ⇒ B > V ...(i)
K © C ⇒ K < C ...(ii)
C $\underline{\underline{©}}$ B ⇒ C ≤ B ...(iii)
On combining the statements (i), (ii) and (iii), we get
K < C ≤ B > V
Conclusions
I. V @ C ⇒ V > C (False)
II. B @ K ⇒ B > K (True)
So, it is clear that only Conclusion II is true.

7. (*a*) According to the question,
K @ T ⇒ K > T ...(i)
S = K ⇒ S = K ...(ii)
T © R ⇒ T < R ...(iii)
On combining the statements (i), (ii) and (iii), we get S = K > T < R
Conclusions
I. S @ T ⇒ S > T (True)
II. T = R ⇒ T = R (False)
So, it is clear that only Conclusion I is true.

8. (*c*) According to the question,
U = M ⇒ U = M ...(i)
P $\underline{\underline{@}}$ U ⇒ P ≥ U ...(ii)

$M @ B \Rightarrow M \geq B$ ...(iii)

On combining the statements (i), (ii) and (iii), we get

$P \geq U = M \geq B$

Conclusions

I. $P = B \Rightarrow P = B$ (May be true)
or
II. $P @ B \Rightarrow P > B$ (May be true)

So, it is clear that either Conclusion I or Conclusions II is ture.

Solutions (Q. Nos. 9-14)

Given that,

$P © Q \Rightarrow P \leq Q$ *i.e.,* © represents ≤
$P * Q \Rightarrow P \geq Q$ *i.e.,* * represents ≥
$P \% Q \Rightarrow P < Q$ *i.e.,* % represents <
$P \$ Q \Rightarrow P > Q$ *i.e.,* $ represents >
$P @ Q \Rightarrow P = Q$ *i.e., @ represents* =

9. (*d*) According to the question,

$M \% T \Rightarrow M < T$ ...(i)
$T \$ K \Rightarrow T > K$ ...(ii)
$K © D \Rightarrow K \leq D$ ...(iii)

On combining the statements (i), (ii) and (iii), we get $M < T > K \leq D$

Conclusions

I. $T \$ D \Rightarrow T > D$ (False)
II. $D \$ M \Rightarrow D > M$ (False)

So, it is clear that neither Conclusion I nor II is true.

10. (*a*) According to the question,

$F @ B \Rightarrow F = B$ ...(i)
$B \% N \Rightarrow B < N$ ...(ii)
$N \$ H \Rightarrow N > H$ ...(iii)

On combining the statements (i), (ii) and (iii), we get

$F = B < N > H$

Conclusions

I. $N \$ F \Rightarrow N > F$ (True)
II. $H \$ F \Rightarrow H > F$ (False)

So, it is clear that only Conclusion I is true.

11. (*c*) According to the question,

$R * M \Rightarrow R \geq M$ ...(i)
$M @ K \Rightarrow M = K$ ...(ii)
$K © J \Rightarrow K \leq J$ ...(iii)

On combining the statements (i), (ii) and (iii), we get $R \geq M = K \leq J$

Conclusions

I. $J \$ M \Rightarrow J > M$ (May be true)
or
II. $J @ M \Rightarrow J = M$ (May be true)

So, it is clear that either Conclusion I or Conclusion II is true.

12. (*e*) According to the question,

$B \$ N \Rightarrow B > N$ ...(i)
$N * R \Rightarrow N \geq R$ ...(ii)
$R @ K \Rightarrow R = K$ ...(iii)

On combining the statements (i), (ii) and (iii), we get $B > N \geq R = K$

Conclusions

I. $K © N \Rightarrow K \leq N$ (True)
II. $B \$ K \Rightarrow B > K$ (True)

So, it is clear that both the Conclusions I and Conclusion II is true.

13. (*b*) According to the question,

$J © K \Rightarrow J \leq K$ ...(i)
$K \$ N \Rightarrow K > N$ ...(ii)
$N * D \Rightarrow N \geq D$ ...(iii)

On combining the statements (i), (ii) and (iii), we get $J \leq K > N \geq D$

Conclusions

I. $J \% N \Rightarrow J < N$ (False)
II. $D \% K \Rightarrow D < K$ (True)

So, it is clear that only Conclusion II is true.

14. (*b*) According to the question,

$R @ D \Rightarrow R = D$ ...(i)
$D © M \Rightarrow D \leq M$ ...(ii)
$M \$ T \Rightarrow M > T$ ...(iii)

On combining the statements (i), (ii) and (iii), we get

$R = D \leq M > T$

Conclusions

I. $T \% D \Rightarrow T < R$ (False)
II. $M * R \Rightarrow M \geq R$ (True)

So, it is clear that only Conclusion II is true.

Solutions (Q. Nos. 15-19)

$@ \rightarrow <$ $\% \rightarrow >$
$\# \rightarrow \leq$ $\$ \rightarrow \geq$
$* \rightarrow =$

15. (*a*) $A < B, B > C, C = D, D \geq E$

$A < B > C = D \geq E$

Conclusions

I. $B > E$ (True)
II. $A > E$ (False)

Hence, only Conclusion I follows.

16. (*e*) $A > B, B = C, C \leq D, D = E$, $A > B = C \leq D = E$

Conclusions I. $A > C$ (True)
II. $E \geq B$ (True)

Hence, both Conclusions I and Conclusion II follow.

17. (*d*) $A = B, B \geq C, C \leq D, D < E$

$A = B \geq C \leq D < E$

Conclusions I. $E \geq A$ (False)
II. $C > A$ (False)

Hence, neither Conclusion I nor Conclusion II follow.

18. (*b*) $A \geq B, B \geq C, C = D, D < E$

$A \geq B \geq C = D < E$

Conclusions I. $A \geq E$ (False)
II. $E > C$ (True)

Hence, only Conclusion II follows.

19. (*a*) $A > E, E < C, C > B, B = D$

$A > E < C > B = D$

Conclusions I. $C > D$ (True)
II. $B < A$ (False)

Hence, only Conclusion I follows.

Solutions (Q. Nos. 20-24)

Given that,

$A \$ B \Rightarrow A \geq B$ *i.e.,* $ represents ≥
$A \# B \Rightarrow A \leq B$ *i.e.,* # represents ≤
$A @ B \Rightarrow A > B$ *i.e.,* @ represents >
$A © B \Rightarrow A = B$ *i.e.,* © represents =
$A \% B \Rightarrow A < B$ *i.e.,* % represents <

20. (*b*) According to the question,

$H \% J \Rightarrow H < J$ ...(i)
$J © N \Rightarrow J = N$ ...(ii)
$N @ R \Rightarrow N > R$ ...(iii)

On combining the statements (i), (ii) and (iii), we get

$H < J = N > R$

Conclusions

I. $R \% J \Rightarrow R < J$ (True)
II. $H @ J \Rightarrow H > J$ (False)
III. $N @ H \Rightarrow N > H$ (True)

So, it is clear that both Conclusions I and Conclusion III are true.

21. (*d*) According to the question,

$M @ J \Rightarrow M > J$ ...(i)
$J \$ T \Rightarrow J \geq T$ ...(ii)
$T © N \Rightarrow T = N$ ...(iii)

On combining the statements (i), (ii) and (iii), we get $M > J \geq T = N$

Conclusions

I. $N \# J \Rightarrow N \leq J$ (True)
II. $T \% M \Rightarrow T < M$ (True)
III. $M @ N \Rightarrow M > N$ (True)

So, it is clear that all the Conclusions I, II and III are true.

22. (*c*) According to the question,

$D © K \Rightarrow D = K$ ...(i)
$K \# F \Rightarrow K \leq F$ ...(ii)
$F @ P \Rightarrow F > P$ ...(iii)

On combining the statements (i), (ii) and (iii), we get $D = K \leq F > P$

Conclusions

I. $P @ D \Rightarrow P > D$ (False)
II. $K \# P \Rightarrow K \leq P$ (False)
III. $F \$ D \Rightarrow F \geq D$ (True)

So, it is clear that only Conclusion III is true.

23. (*b*) According to the question,

$R \# D \Rightarrow R \leq D$ ...(i)
$D \$ M \Rightarrow D \geq M$ ...(ii)
$M © N \Rightarrow M = N$ ...(iii)

On combining the statements (i), (ii) and (iii), we get

$R \leq D \geq M = N$

Conclusions

I. $R \# M \Rightarrow R \leq M$ (False)
II. $N \# D \Rightarrow N \leq D$ (True)
III. $N \$ R \Rightarrow N \geq R$ (False)

So, it is clear that only Conclusion II is true.

24. (*d*) According to the question,

$K © P \Rightarrow K = P$ ...(i)
$P @ Q \Rightarrow P > Q$ ...(ii)
$Q \$ R \Rightarrow Q \geq R$ ...(iii)

On combining the statements (i), (ii) and (iii), we get

$K = P > Q \geq R$

Conclusions

I. $K @ R \Rightarrow K > R$ (True)
II. $R \% P \Rightarrow R < P$ (True)

III. Q % K ⇒ Q < K (True)
So, it is clear that all the Conclusions I, II and III are true.

Solutions (Q. Nos. 25-29)
Given that,
$ → ≥
% → ≤
@ → >
© → <
* → =

25. (*b*) **Statements** A < B ≤ C > D
Conclusions I. D < B (False)
II. C > A (True)
III. C ≥ A (False)
Only Conclusion II is true.

26. (*e*) **Statements** P = Q ≥ R > S
Conclusions I. S < Q (True)
II. R ≤ P (True)
III. S < P (True)
All the Conclusions I, II and III are true.

27. (*d*) **Statements** A ≥ B > C ≤ D
Conclusions I. D > C (False)
II. C ≤ A (False)
III. D > A (False)
None of the conclusions follow.

28. (*a*) **Statements** M ≤ N > O ≥ P
Conclusions I. P < N (True)
II. P ≤ N (False)
III. P < M (False)
Only Conclusion I is true.

29. (*e*) **Statements** W < X = Y ≤ Z
Conclusions I. Y > W (True)
II. Z ≥ X (True)
III. Z > W (True)
All the Conclusions I, II and III are true.

Solutions (Q. Nos. 30-35)
Given that,
P $ Q ⇒ P ≤ Q *i.e.,* $ represents ≤
P @ Q ⇒ P > Q *i.e.,* @ represents >
P # Q ⇒ P ≥ Q *i.e.,* # represents ≥
P © Q ⇒ P > Q *i.e.,* © represents <
P % Q ⇒ P = Q *i.e.,* % represents =

30. (*d*) According to the question,
D # K ⇒ D ≥ K ...(i)
K @ T ⇒ K > T ...(ii)
T $ M ⇒ T ≤ M ...(iii)
M % J ⇒ M = J ...(iv)
On combining the statements (i), (ii), (iii) and (iv), we get
D ≥ K > T ≤ M = J
Conclusions
I. J @ T ⇒ J > T (Either I or II is True)
II. J % T ⇒ J = T
III. D @ T ⇒ D > T (True)
So, it is clear that either Conclusions I or Conclusion II and Conclusion III are true.

31. (*c*) According to the question,
R @ N ⇒ R > N ...(i)
N © D ⇒ N < D ...(ii)
D $ J ⇒ D ≤ J ...(iii)
J # B ⇒ J ≥ B ...(iv)
On combining the statements (i),(ii), (iii) and (iv), we get
R > N < D ≤ J ≥ B
Conclusions
I. K @ J ⇒ R > J (False)
II. J @ N ⇒ J > N (True)
III. B @ D ⇒ B > D (False)
So, it is clear that only Conclusion II is true.

32. (*c*) According to the question,
W © B ⇒ W < B ...(i)
B % V ⇒ B = V ...(ii)
V $ R ⇒ V ≤ R ...(iii)
R @ K ⇒ R > K ...(iv)
On combining the statements (i),(ii),(iii) and (iv), we get
W < b = V ≤ R > K
Conclusions
I. K © b ⇒ K < B (False)
II. R # B ⇒ R ≥ B (True)
III. V @ W ⇒ V > W (True)
So, it is clear that both Conclusions II and Conclusion III are true.

33. (*b*) According to the question,
H $ M ⇒ H ≤ M ...(i)
M # T ⇒ M ≥ T ...(ii)
T @ D ⇒ T > D ...(iii)
D © R ⇒ D < R ...(iv)
On combining the statements (i), (ii), (iii) and (iv), we get
H ≤ M ≥ T > D < R
Conclusions
I. D © M ⇒ D < M (True)
II. R @ M ⇒ R > M (False)
III. H $ T ⇒ H ≤ T (False)
So, it is clear that only Conclusion I is true.

34. (*a*) According to the question,
B % J ⇒ B = J ...(i)
J @ K ⇒ J > K ...(ii)
K © T ⇒ K < T ...(iii)
T $ F ⇒ T ≤ F ...(iv)
On combining the statements (i), (ii), (iii) and (iv), we get B = J > K < T ≤ F
Conclusions
I. F @ K ⇒ F > K (True)
II. B @ K ⇒ B > K (True)
III. B @ F ⇒ B > F (False)
So, it is clear that both Conclusions I and II are true.

35. (*d*) According to the question,
F # B ⇒ F ≥ B ...(i)
B $ M ⇒ B ≤ M ...(ii)
M @ K ⇒ M > K ...(iii)
K © N ⇒ K < N ...(iv)
On combining the statements (i), (ii), (iii) and (iv), we get
F ≥ B ≤ M > K < N
Conclusions
I. N @ M ⇒ N > M (False)
II. F $ M ⇒ F ≤ M (False)
III. K © B ⇒ K < B (False)
So, it is clear that none of the conclusions is true.

Solutions (Q. Nos. 36-40)
Given that,
P $ Q ⇒ P ≥ Q *i.e.,* $ represents ≥
P © Q ⇒ P < Q *i.e.,* © represents <
P # Q ⇒ P > Q *i.e.,* # represents >
P % Q ⇒ P ≤ Q *i.e.,* % represents ≤
P @ Q ⇒ P = Q *i.e.,* @ represents =

36. (*d*) According to the question,
R # J ⇒ R > J ...(i)
J $ D ⇒ J ≥ D ...(ii)
D @ L ⇒ D = K ...(iii)
K % T ⇒ K ≤ T ...(iv)
On combining the statements (i),(ii),(iii) and (iv), we get
R > J ≥ D = K ≤ T
Conclusions I. T # D ⇒ T > D
(Either I or II is true)
II. T @ D ⇒ T = D
III. R # K ⇒ R > K (True)
IV. J $ T ⇒ J ≥ T (False)
So, it is clear that either Conclusions I or II and Conclusion III are true.

37. (*a*) According to the question,
T % R ⇒ T ≤ R ...(i)
R $ M ⇒ R ≥ M ...(ii)
M @ D ⇒ M = D ...(iii)
D © H ⇒ D < H ...(iv)
On combining the statements (i), (ii), (iii) and (iv), we get T ≤ R ≥ M = D < H
Conclusions
I. D % R ⇒ D ≤ R (True)
II. H # R ⇒ H > R (False)
III. T © M ⇒ T < M (False)
IV. T % D ⇒ T ≤ D (False)
So, it is clear that only Conclusion I is true.

38. (*c*) According to the question,
M @ B ⇒ M = B ...(i)
B # N ⇒ B > N ...(ii)
N $ R ⇒ N ≥ R ...(iii)
R © K ⇒ R < K ...(iv)
On combining the statements (i), (ii), (iii) and (iv), we get M = B > N ≥ R < K
Conclusions
I. K # B ⇒ K > B (False)
II. R © B ⇒ R < B (True)
III. M $ R ⇒ M ≥ R (False)
IV. N © M ⇒ N < M (True)
So, it is clear that both Conclusions II and IV are true.

39. (*b*) According to the question,
F # H ⇒ F > H ...(i)
H @ M ⇒ H = M ...(ii)

M © E ⇒ M < E ...(iii)
E $ J ⇒ E ≥ J ...(iv)

On combining the statements (i), (ii), (iii) and (iv), we get F> H= M< E≥ J

Conclusions

I. J © M ⇒ J < M (False)
II. E # H ⇒ E > H (True)
III. M © F ⇒ M < F (True)
IV. F # E ⇒ F > E (False)

So, it is clear that both Conclusions II and Conclusion III are true.

40. (*e*) According to the question,

D % A ⇒ D ≤ A ...(i)
A @ B ⇒ A = B ...(ii)
B © K ⇒ B < K ...(iii)
K % M ⇒ K ≤ M ...(iv)

On combining the statements (i), (ii), (iii) and (iv), we get D≤ A= B< K≤ M

Conclusions

I. B $ D ⇒ B ≥ D (True)
II. K # A ⇒ K > A (True)
III. M # B ⇒ M > B (True)
IV. A © M ⇒ A < M (True)

So, it is clear that all the Conclusions I, II, III and IV are true.

Solutions (Q. Nos. 41-45)

Given that,

P $Q ⇒ P ≥Q *i.e.,* $ represents≥
P @Q ⇒ P >Q *i.e.,* @ represents>
P #Q ⇒ P < Q *i.e.,* # represents<
P δQ ⇒ P =Q *i.e.,* d represents=
P *Q ⇒ P ≤Q *i.e.,* * represents≤

41. (*b*) According to the question,

H @ T⇒H> T ...(i)
T # F ⇒T< F ...(ii)
F δE ⇒F = E ...(iii)
E * V ⇒E≤ V ...(iv)

On combining the statements (i), (ii), (iii) and (iv), we get H> T< F= E≤ V

Conclusions

I. V $ F ⇒ V≥ F (True)
II. E @ T ⇒ E> T (True)
III. H @ V ⇒H> V (False)
IV. T # V ⇒ T< V (True)

So, it is clear that Conclusions I, II and IV are true.

42. (*e*) According to the question,

D # R ⇒ D < R ...(i)
R * K ⇒ R ≤ K ...(ii)
K @ F ⇒ K > F ...(iii)
F $ J ⇒ F ≥ J ...(iv)

On combining the statements (i), (ii), (iii) and (iv), we get D< R≤ K> F≥ J

Conclusions

I. J # R ⇒ J < R (False)
II. J # K ⇒ J < K (True)
III. R # F ⇒ R < F (False)
IV. K @ D ⇒ K> D (True)

So, it is clear that Conclusions II and IV are true.

43. (*e*) According to the question,

N δ B ⇒ N = B ...(i)
B $ W ⇒ B ≥ W ...(ii)
W # H ⇒ W< H ...(iii)
H * M ⇒ H ≤ M ...(iv)

On combining the statements (i), (ii), (iii) and (iv), we get

N = B ≥ W < H ≤ M

Conclusions

I. M @ W ⇒ M > W (True)
II. H @ N ⇒ H > N (False)
III. W δ N ⇒ W = N
(Either III or IV is True)
IV. W # N ⇒ W< N

So, it is clear that either Conclusions III or IV and I are true.

44. (*a*) According to the question,

R * D ⇒ R ≤ D ...(i)
D $ J ⇒ D ≥ J ...(ii)
J # M ⇒ J < M ...(iii)
M @ K ⇒ M > K ...(iv)

On combining the statements (i), (ii), (iii) and (iv), we get R≤ D≥ J< M> K

Conclusions

I. K # J ⇒ K< J (False)
II. D @ M ⇒ D > M (False)
III. R # M ⇒ R < M (False)
IV. D @ K ⇒ D > K (False)

So, it is clear that none of the conclusion is true.

45. (*e*) According to the question,

M $ K ⇒ M ≥ K ...(i)
K @ N ⇒ K > N ...(ii)
N * R ⇒ N ≤ R ...(iii)
R # W ⇒ R < W ...(iv)

On combining the statements (i), (ii), (iii) and (iv), we get

M ≥ K > N ≤ R < W

Conclusions

I. W @ K ⇒ W > K (False)
II. M $ R ⇒ M ≥ R (False)
III. K @ W ⇒ K > W (False)
IV. M @ N ⇒ M > N (True)

So, it is clear that only Conclusion IV is true.

Solutions (Q. Nos. 46-50)

Given that,

φ → < + → ≠
Δ → ≯ × → ≮
− → = = → >

46. (*c*) Clearly, the meaning of the given symbols

X φ Y + Z
⇒ X < Y ≠ Z

Using the proper notations/symbols in option (c), we get

X Δ Y φ Z
⇒ X ≯ Y < Z
⇒ X < Y ≠ Z

Therefore, X φ Y + Z ⇒ X Δ Y φ Z

47. (*c*) Clearly, the meaning of the given symbols, X φ Y − Z ⇒ X < Y = Z

Using the proper symbols in option (c), we get

X + Y × Z
⇒ X ≠ Y ≮ Z ⇒ X < Y = Z

Therefore, X φ Y − Z ⇒ X + Y × Z

48. (*c*) Clearly, the meaning of the given symbols,

X − Y + Z ⇒ X = Y ≠ Z

Using the proper symbols in option (c), we get

X − Y φ Z ⇒ X = Y < Z
⇒ X = Y ≠ Z

Therefore, X − Y + Z ⇒ X − Y φ Z

49. (*b*) Clearly, the meaning of the given symbols,

X − Y = Z ⇒ X = Y > Z

Using the proper symbols in option (b), we get

X Δ Y × Z ⇒ X ≯ Y ≮ Z
⇒ X = Y > Z

Therefore, X − Y = Z ⇒ X Δ Y × Z

50. (*b*) Clearly, the meaning of the given symbols,

X = Y = Z ⇒ X > Y > Z *i.e..,* X > Y

Using the proper symbols in option (b), we get

Z φ Y φ X ⇒ Z < Y < X ⇒ X > Y > Z

Therefore, X = Y = Z ⇒ Z φ Y φ X

Solutions (Q.Nos. 51 and 52)

P $ Q ⇒ P ≥ Q, P @ Q
⇒ P > Q, P # Q ⇒ P < Q,
P & Q ⇒ P = Q, P * Q
⇒ P ≤ Q

51. (*d*) 1. R @ K ⇒ R > K 2. K $ N
⇒ K ≥ N
3. K * R ⇒ K ≤ R 4. M $ N ⇒ M ≥ N

From option (d), M $ K @ N * R

M ≥ K > N ≤ R

Here, all the above expression 1, 2, 3 and 4 are false.

52. (*d*) From (a), H ≥ T < F = E ≤ V

From (b), H < T < F ≤ E ≤ V

From (c), H ≥ T < F ≤ E = V

Here, V $ F ⇒ V ≥ F (True)
T # V ⇒ T < V (True)
E @ T ⇒ E > T (True)

Solutions (Q. Nos. 53 and 54)

@ means '>', # means '<', $ means '≠', % means '='

53. (*c*) Given, 3M % 2N and N % 30

⇒ 3M = 2N and N = 30
⇒ 3M = 2 × 30
⇒ 20 = M ⇒ 20 % M

54. (*a*) N @ P, P # O, O @ M and N % M

⇒ N > P, P < O, O > P and N = M
⇒ M = N > P < O ⇒ O > M = N
⇒ O > N ⇒ O @ N

Master Exercise

DIRECTIONS ~(Q. Nos. 1-3) *In these questions, relationship between different elements is shown in the statements. These statements are followed by two conclusions. Study the conclusion based on the given statements and select the appropriate answer.* « IBPS Clerk 2017

Give Answer

(a) If only Conclusion I follows.
(b) If only Conclusion II follows.
(c) If both conclusions follow.
(d) If either Conclusion I or II follows.
(e) If neither Conclusion I nor II follows.

1. Statement $Z > W > V = K < L < I$
Conclusions I. $W > K$ II. $I > K$

2. Statements $Q > B, K < E < B, J \geq E, R < Q$
Conclusions I. $Q > K$ II. $Q = E$

3. Statements $E = F < G < H, G \geq I$
Conclusions I. $H > I$ II. $E > I$

DIRECTIONS ~ (Q. Nos. 4 and 5) *In each of the following questions assuming the given statements to be true, find which of the two Conclusions I and II given below them is/are definitely true and give your answer accordingly.*

Give Answer « SBI Clerk 2020

(a) If only Conclusion I is true.
(b) If only Conclusion II is true.
(c) If either Conclusion I or II is true.
(d) If neither Conclusion I nor II is true.
(e) If both Conclusions I and II are true.

4. Statements $Q \geq P > R = T, T < U \geq V$
Conclusions I. $V > P$ II. $Q > T$

5. Statements $A > B < C \geq D > E, E > G = I > L$
Conclusions I. $D > I$ II. $B \geq L$

DIRECTIONS ~ (Q. Nos. 6-10) *In these questions, relationship between different elements is shown in the statements. The statements are followed by Conclusions I and II. Study the conclusions based on the given statements and select the appropriate option.*

Give Answer « IBPS RRBs Officer 2016

(a) If only Conclusion I is true.
(b) If only Conclusion II is true.
(c) If both conclusions are true.
(d) If none of the conclusions is true.
(e) If either Conclusion I or II is true.

6. Statements $P < E < T \leq R, T \geq K$
Conclusions I. $K > P$ II. $R \geq K$

7. Statements $X < W, A > C \geq H = W$
Conclusions I. $C > X$ II. $A > W$

8. Statements $B \leq N < D, K = R < D \leq W$
Conclusions I. $N = R$ II. $B < W$

9. Statement $J \leq L < B \leq S > Y < M$
Conclusions I. $J < M$ II. $L \geq Y$

10. Statements $B \leq N < D, K = R < D \leq W$
Conclusions I. $W > K$ II. $N \geq W$

DIRECTIONS ~(Q. Nos 11-15) *In these questions, relationship between different elements is shown in the statements. These statements are followed by two conclusions.* « LIC AAO 2019

Give Answer

(a) if only Conclusion I follows.
(b) if only Conclusion II follows.
(c) if either Conclusion I or II follows.
(d) if neither Conclusion I nor II follows.
(e) if both conclusions I and II follows.

11. Statements $A \geq M \geq H \geq K \geq L < N \leq B$
Conclusions I. $A > L$ II. $B \geq K$

12. Statements $A \geq M \geq H \geq K \geq L > N \geq B$
Conclusions I. $A \geq B$ II. $B < K$

13. Statements $P < A \leq R = K, S \leq R \leq N$
Conclusions I. $N > P$ II. $K \leq N$

14. Statements $M \leq E \leq L \leq T > S, L > V$
Conclusions I. $V \geq S$ II. $S > V$

15. Statements $P < A \leq R = K, S \leq R \leq N$
Conclusions I. $K > A$ II. $A \leq K$

DIRECTIONS ~ (Q. Nos. 16-22) *In these questions, relationship between different elements is shown in the statements. The statements are followed by conclusions.*

Give Answer « MHA CET 2012

(a) If only Conclusion I is true.
(b) If only Conclusion II is true.
(c) If either Conclusion I or II is true.
(d) If neither Conclusion I nor II is true.
(e) If both the Conclusions I and II are true.

16. Statements $P \geq Q < T, R < Q \geq S, V \geq T$
Conclusions I. $R \geq P$ II. $S > V$

17. Statements $P \geq Q < T, R < Q \geq S, V \geq T$
Conclusions I. $S \leq P$ II. $V > R$

18. Statements $H < I \leq J, R \geq I > A$
Conclusions I. $H < R$ II. $A > H$

19. Statements $R \geq I \leq J, A < I$
Conclusions I. $J > R$ II. $J > A$

20. Statements $J = K \geq L \leq M, K < S, J > T$
Conclusions I. $L < S$ II. $M > T$

21. **Statements** P < R ≥ I = C, L > E ≥ R
Conclusions I. E > C II. C = E

22. **Statements** B ≤ C = D > E, F > C
Conclusions I. F ≥ B II. C ≥ E

DIRECTIONS ~ (Q. Nos. 23 and 24) *Solve the following questions and mark the best possible option.*
« MHT MBA CET 2018

23. **Statements** P > A > S < R < K, G > O < S > L > Z
Conclusions I. P < Z II. G = K
(a) If only Conclusion I is true.
(b) If only Conclusion II is true.
(c) If either Conclusion I or II is true.
(d) If neither Conclusion I nor II is true.
(e) If both Conclusions I and II are true.

24. **Statements** P > A > S < R < K, G > O < S > L > Z
Conclusions I. O < R II. L > A
(a) If only Conclusion I is true.
(b) If only Conclusion II is true.
(c) If either Conclusion I or II is true.
(d) If neither Conclusion I nor II is true.
(e) If both Conclusions I and II are true.

DIRECTIONS ~ (Q. Nos. 25 and 26) *Solve the following questions and mark the best possible option.*
« MHT MBA CET 2018

25. **Statements** B ≥ D ≥ S ≥ U ≤ M, J ≤ P < U > F > V
Conclusions I. J ≤ M II. D > P
(a) If only Conclusion I is true.
(b) If only Conclusion II is true.
(c) If either Conclusion I or II is true.
(d) If neither Conclusion I nor II is true.
(e) If both Conclusions I and II are true.

26. **Statements** B ≥ D ≥ S ≥ U ≤ M, J ≤ P < U > F > V
Conclusions I. F < B II. D > V
(a) If only Conclusion I is true.
(b) If only Conclusion II is true.
(c) If either Conclusion I or II is true.
(d) If neither Conclusion I nor II is true.
(e) If both Conclusions I and II are true.

27. In which of the following expressions will the expression P > S be defintely false? « MHT MBA CET 2018
(a) P > Q ≥ R = S (b) S ≤ R ≤ Q < P
(c) R = P > Q ≥ S (d) S > Q ≥ R < P
(e) S < Q ≤ R < P

28. What should come in place of £ and # respectively in the expression B£A £ T # K, so that the expression K < B definitely holds true? « MHT MBA CET 2018
(a) > , < (b) =, < (c) ≥, > (d) ≤, <
(e) <, ≤

DIRECTIONS ~(Q. Nos. 29-33) *Read each statement carefully and answer the following questions.*
« SBI (PO) 2013

29. Which of the following expressions will be true, if the expression R > O = A > S < T is definitely true?
(a) O > T (b) S < R (c) T > A (d) S = O
(e) T < R

30. Which of the following symbols should replace the question mark (?) in the given expression in order to make the expressions 'P > A' as well as 'T < L' definitely true?

P > L ? A ≥ N = T

(a) ≤ (b) > (c) < (d) ≥
(e) Either ≤ or <

31. Which of the following symbols should be placed in the blank spaces, respectively (in the same order from left to right) in order to complete the given expression in such a manner that makes the expressions 'B > N' as well as 'D ≤ L' definitely true?

B _ L _ O _ N _ D

(a) = , =, ≥ , ≥ (b) >, ≥ , =, > (c) >, <, =, ≤ (d) >, =, =, ≥
(e) >, =, ≥, >

32. Which of the following symbols should be placed in the blank spaces, respectively (in the same order from left to right) in order to complete the given expression in such a manner that makes the expression 'A < P' definitely false? _ ≤ _ < _ > _
(a) L, N, P, A (b) L, A, P, N (c) A, L, P, N (d) N, A, P, L
(e) P, N, A, L

33. Which of the following symbols should be placed in the blank spaces, respectively (in the same order from left to right) in order to complete the given expression in such a manner that makes the expressions 'F > N' and 'U > D' definitely false?

F _ O _ U _ N _ D

(a) < , <, >, = (b) <, =, =, > (c) <, =, =, < (d) ≥ , =, =, ≥
(e) >, >, =, <

DIRECTIONS ~(Q. Nos. 34-38) *In the following questions, the symbols* $\beta, \gamma, \psi, \alpha$ *and* δ *are used with the following meanings.*
'$P \beta Q$' means 'P is not smaller than Q'.
'$P \gamma Q$' means 'P is neither greater than nor smaller than Q'.
'$P \psi Q$' means 'P is not greater than Q'.
'$P \alpha Q$' means 'P is neither smaller than nor equal to Q'.
'$P \delta Q$' means 'P is neither greater than nor equal to Q'.
Now in each of the following questions, assuming the given statements to be true, find which of the two Conclusions I and II given below is/are definitely true.
Give Answer « IBPS RRB Officer 2014
(a) If only Conclusion I is true.
(b) If only Conclusion II is true.
(c) If either Conclusion I or II is true.
(d) If neither Conclusion I nor II is true.
(e) If both Conclusions I and II are true.

34. **Statements** $M \beta N$, $H \psi Q$, $Q \beta M$
Conclusions I. $H \gamma M$ II. $Q \gamma N$

35. **Statements** $C \alpha B$, $L \delta S$, $S \psi C$
Conclusions I. $B \alpha S$ II. $C \alpha L$

36. **Statements** $I \beta H$, $E \alpha F$, $I \gamma F$
Conclusions I. $E \alpha I$ II. $H \delta E$

37. **Statements** $V \gamma O$, $R \gamma V$, $O \beta B$
Conclusions I. $R \gamma B$ II. $R \alpha B$

38. **Statements** $L \alpha U$, $T \gamma L$, $W \beta B$
Conclusions I. $T \alpha W$ II. $U \gamma W$

DIRECTIONS ~(Q. Nos 39-43) *In the following questions, the symbols Δ, Σ, @, © and # are used with the following meaning as illustrated below.* « IBPS RRB Officer 2013

'X Δ Y' means, 'X is neither greater than nor equal to Y.'
'X Σ Y' means, 'X is not smaller than Y.'
'X @ Y' means, 'X is not greater than Y.'
'X © Y' means, 'X is neither greater than nor smaller than Y.'
'X # Y' means, 'X is neither smaller than nor equal to Y'.
Now in each of the following questions assuming the given statements to be true, find which of the two Conclusions I and II given below is / are definitely true?

Give Answer

(a) If only Conclusion I is true.
(b) If only Conclusion II is true.
(c) If either Conclusion I or II is true.
(d) Is neither Conclusion I nor II is true.
(e) If both Conclusions I and II are true.

39. Statements R @ J, F Σ J, C Σ F
Conclusions I. R © C II. C # R

40. Statements W @ P, W # E, E Δ V
Conclusions I. P # E II. V © W

41. Statements J © R, P Σ R, Z # P
Conclusions I. R Δ Z II. J @ P

42. Statements G @ O, N © O, H # G
Conclusions I. O Δ H II. G © N

43. Statements Q Δ B, M © B, K Σ M
Conclusions I. K © B II. Q Δ K

DIRECTIONS ~ (Q. Nos 44-48) *In these questions the symbols #, $, % and ★ are used with different meanings as follow.*

'A @ B' means, 'A is not smaller than B'.
'A # B' means, 'A is neither smaller than nor equal to B'.
'A $ B' means, 'A is neither greater than nor smaller than B'.
'A % B' means, 'A is not greater than B'.
'A ★ B' means, 'A is neither greater than nor equal to B'.
In each question, four statements showing relationships have been given, which are followed by three Conclusions, II and III. Assuming that the given statements are true, find out which conclusion (s) is / are definitely true.

44. Statements V $ Y, Y @ Z, Z % X, X # T
Conclusions I. T # Z II. X # Y III. Z ★ Y
(a) None follows.
(b) Only I follows.
(c) II and III follow.
(d) I and III follow.
(e) Only III follows.

45. Statements R @ J, J % F, F ★ E, E % M
Conclusions I. M # J II. F % M III. M ★ R
(a) Only I follows.
(b) Only II follows.
(c) Only III follows.
(d) I and II follow.
(e) All follow.

46. Statements H # R, R @ L, L ★ W, W % F
Conclusions I. H # L II. F # L III. H $ F
(a) Only I follows. (b) I and II follow.
(c) II and III follow. (d) Either I or II follows.
(e) All follow

47. Statements M # K, M $ F, F % Q, Q ★ H
Conclusions I. H # K II. Q # K III. Q @ M
(a) I and II follow. (b) Either I or II follows.
(c) All follow. (d) II and III follow.
(e) None of these

48. Statements D ★ Q, Q $ L, L # T, T % H
Conclusions I. D ★ L II. L @ H III. H # L
(a) Only I follows. (b) I and II follow.
(c) Either II or III follows. (d) All follow.
(e) None follows

DIRECTIONS ~ (Q. Nos. 49-53) *Based on the information below answer the questions that follow*

'P $ Q' means, 'P is not smaller than Q'
'P @ Q' means, 'P is neither smaller than nor equal to Q'.
'P # Q' means, 'P is neither greater than nor equal to Q'.
'P & Q' means, 'P is neither greater than nor smaller than Q'.
'P * Q' means, 'P is not greater than Q'

49. Statements H @ T, T # F, F & E, E * V
Conclusions I. V $ F II. E @ T III. H @ V IV. T # V
(a) I, II and III are true. (b) I, II and IV are true.
(c) II, III and IV are true. (d) I, III and IV are true.
(e) I, II, III and IV are true.

50. Statements D # R, R * K, K @ F, F $ J
Conclusions I. J # R II. J # K III. R # F IV. K @ D
(a) I, II and III are true. (b) II, III and IV are true.
(c) I, III and IV are true. (d) All I, II, III and IV are true.
(e) None of these.

51. Statements N & B, B $ W, W # H, H * M
Conclusions I. M @ W II. H @ N III. W & N IV. W # N
(a) Only I is true. (b) Only III is true.
(c) Only IV is true. (d) Either III or IV is true.
(e) Either III or IV and I are true.

52. Statements R * D, D $ J, J # M, M @ K
Conclusions I. K # J II. D @ M III. R # M IV. D @ K
(a) None is true. (b) Only I is true.
(c) Only II is true. (d) Only III is true.
(e) Only IV is true.

53. Statements M $ K, K @ N, N ★ R, R # W
Conclusions I. M @ K II. M $ R III. K @ W IV. M @ N
(a) I and II are true. (b) III and IV are true.
(c) III or IV is true. (d) II, III and IV are true.
(e) None of these

Answers WITH EXPLANATIONS

1. (*c*) **Statement** Z > W > V = K < L < I
Conclusions
I. W > K (True) II. I > K (True)
Both Conclusions I and II are true.

2. (*a*) **Statements** Q > B > E > K, Q > B > E ≤ J, Q > R
Conclusions
I. Q > K (True) II. Q = E (False)
Only Conclusion I is true.

3. (*a*) **Statements** E = F < G < H, E = F < G ≥ I, I ≤ G < H
Conclusions
I. H > I (True)
II. E > I (False)
Only Conclusion I is true.

4. (*b*) **Statements**
Q ≥ P > R = T, T < U ≥ V
∴ P > R = T < U ≥ V
Conclusions
I. V > P (False)
II. Q > T (True)
∴ Only Conclusion II is true.

5. (*a*) **Statements** A > B < C ≥ D > E,
E > G = I > L
∴ D > E > G = I,
B < C ≥ D > E > G = I > L
Conclusions
I. D > I (True)
II. B ≥ L (False)
∴ Only Conclusion I is true.

6. (*b*) **Statements** P < E < T ≤ R, T ≥ K
On combining the statements, we get
P < E < T ≥ K
Conclusions
I. K > P (False)
II. R ≥ K (True)
So, Conclusion II follows.

7. (*c*) **Statements** X < W,
A > C ≥ H = W
On combining the statements, we get
A > C ≥ H = W > X
Conclusions
I. C > X (True)
II. A > W (True)
So, both conclusions follow.

8. (*b*) **Statements** B ≤ N < D;
K = R < D ≤ W
On combining the statements, we get
K = R < D > N ≥ B
Conclusions
I. N = R (False)
II. B < W (True)
So, Conclusion II follows.

9. (*d*) **Statements** J ≤ L < B ≤ S > Y < M
Conclusions
I. J < M (False)
II. L ≥ Y (False)
So, neither Conclusion I nor II follows.

10. (a) **Statements** B ≤ N < D;
K = R < D ≤ W
On combining the statements, we get
K = R < D > N ≥ B
Conclusions
I. W > K (True)
II. N ≥ W (False)
So, only Conclusion I follow.

11. (*d*) According to the given statements
A ≥ M ≥ H ≥ K ≥ L < N ≥ B
Conclusions
I. A > L (False)
II. B ≥ K (False)
Hence, neither Conclusion I nor II follows.

12. (*b*) According to the given statements,
A ≥ M ≥ H ≥ K ≥ L > N ≥ B
Conclusions
I. A ≥ B (False)
II. B < K (True)
Hence, only Conclusion II follows.

13. (*e*) According to the given statements
P < A ≤ R = K, S ≤ R ≤ N.
∴ P < A ≤ R ≤ N and K = R ≤ N
Conclusions
I. N > P (True)
II. K ≤ N (True)
Hence, both Conclusions I and II follow.

14. (*c*) According to the given statements
M ≤ E ≤ L ≤ T > S, L > V
∴ V < L ≤ T > S
Conclusions
I. V ≥ S (May be True)
II. S > V (May be True)
Hence, either Conclusion I or II follows.

15. (*b*) According to the given statements,
P < A ≤ R = K, S ≤ R ≤ N
Conclusions
I. K > A (False)
II. A ≤ K (True)
Hence, only Conclusion II follows.

16. (*b*) I. From given statement,
R > Q ≤ P ⇒ R ≤ P
So, Conclusion I is not true.
II. From given statements,
S ≤ Q < T ≤ V ⇒ S < V
So, Conclusion II is true.

17. (*e*) I. From given statements,
P ≥ Q ≥ S ⇒ S ≤ P
So, Conclusion I is true.
II. From given statements,
V ≥ T > Q > R ⇒ V > R
So, Conclusion II is true.

18. (*a*) I. From given statements,
H < I ≤ R ⇒ H < R
So, Conclusion I is true.
II. From given statement,
H < I > A
So, no relation can be found between H and A.

19. (*b*) I. From given statements.
R ≥ I ≤ J
So, no relation can be established between J and R.
II. From given statements,
A < I ≤ J ⇒ J > A
So, Conclusion II is true.

20. (*a*) I. Given statements are
J = K ≥ L ≤ M, K < S, J > T
From given statements,
L ≤ K < S ⇒ L < S (True)
So, Conclusion I is true.
II. From given statements,
T < J = K ≥ L ≤ M
So, no relation can be established between M and T.

21. (*c*) Given statements are
P < R ≥ I = C; L > E ≥ R
From given statements,
E ≥ R ≥ I = C ⇒ E ≥ C
⇒ E > C or E = C
So, either Conclusion I or II is true.

22. (*d*) Given statements are
B ≤ C = D > E, F > C
From given statements,
B ≤ C < F or B ≤ F (False)
and B ≤ C = D > E, C ≥ E (False)
So, neither Conclusion I nor II is true.

23. (*d*) On combining the statements, we get
P > A > S > L > Z,
G > O < S < R < K
I. P < Z (False)
II. G = K (False)
Hence, neither Conclusion I nor II is true.

24. (*a*) On combining the statements, we get
O < S < R, A > S > L
I. O < R (True)
II. L > A (False)
Hence, only Conclusion I is true.

25. (*b*) On combining the statements, we get

$J \le P < U \le M, \; D \ge S \ge U > P$

I. $J \le M$ (False)

II. $D > P$ (True)

Hence, only Conclusion II is true.

26. (*e*) On combining the statements, we get

$B \ge D \ge S \ge U > F$

$D \ge S \ge U > F > V$

I. $F < B$ (True)

II. $D > V$ (True)

Hence, both Conclusions I and II are true.

27. (*d*) In $S > Q \ge R < P$, no definite relation can be established between P and S.

Hence, $P > S$ is definitely false.

28. (*c*) From option (c), placing £ = ≥ and # = >.

$B \ge A \ge T > K$

$\therefore \; K < B$

29. (*b*) $S < R$ will be definitely true.

30. (*b*) From option (b) after replacing the symbol,

$P > L > A > N = T$

Hence, $P > A$ and $T < L$ is definitely true.

31. (*d*) From option (d) after placing the symbols,

$B > L = O = N \ge D$

Hence, $B > N$ and $D \le L$ is definitely true.

32. (*e*) From option (e) after placing the letters,

$P \le N < A > L$

Hence, $A < P$ is false.

33. (*c*) From option (c), after placing the symbols,

$F < O = U = N < D$

Hence, $F > N$ and $U > D$ is definitely false.

Solutions (Q. Nos. 34-38)

$\beta \rightarrow P \ge Q$

$\gamma \rightarrow P = Q$

$\psi \rightarrow P \le Q$

$\alpha \rightarrow P > Q$

$\delta \rightarrow P < Q$

34. (*d*) **Statements**

$M \beta N \Rightarrow M \ge N$

$H \psi Q \Rightarrow H \le Q$

$Q \beta M \Rightarrow Q \ge M$

$\therefore \; H \le Q \ge M \ge N$

Conclusions

I. $H \gamma M \Rightarrow H = M$ (False)

II. $Q \gamma N \Rightarrow Q = N$ (False)

Hence, neither Conclusion I nor II follows.

35. (*b*) **Statements**

$C \alpha B \Rightarrow C > B$

$L \delta S \Rightarrow L < S$

$S \psi C \Rightarrow S \le C$

$\Rightarrow \; L < S \le C > B$

Conclusions

I. $B \alpha S \Rightarrow B > S$ (False)

II. $C \alpha L \Rightarrow C > L$ (True)

Hence, only Conclusion II follows.

36. (*e*) **Statements**

$I \beta H \Rightarrow I \ge H$

$E \alpha F \Rightarrow E > F$

$I \gamma F \Rightarrow I = F$

$\therefore \; E > I = F \ge H$

Conclusions

I. $E \alpha I \Rightarrow E > I$ (True)

II. $H \delta E \Rightarrow H < E$ (True)

Hence, both Conclusions I and II follow.

37. (*c*) **Statements**

$V \gamma O \Rightarrow V = O$

$R \gamma V \Rightarrow R = V$

$O \beta B \Rightarrow O \ge B$

$\therefore \; R = V = O \ge B$ (May be True)

Conclusions

I. $R \gamma B \Rightarrow R = B$ (May be True)

II. $R \alpha B \Rightarrow R > B$ (May be True)

Hence, either Conclusion I or II follows.

38. (*d*) **Statements**

$L \alpha U \Rightarrow L > U$

$T \gamma L \Rightarrow T = L$

$W \beta U \Rightarrow W \ge U$

$\therefore \; T = L > U \le W$

Conclusions

I. $T \alpha W \Rightarrow T > W$ (False)

II. $U \gamma W \Rightarrow U = W$ (False)

Hence, neither Conclusion I nor II follows.

Solutions (Q. Nos. 39-43)

$\Delta \rightarrow X < Y$

$\Sigma \rightarrow X \ge Y$

$@ \rightarrow X \le Y$

$© \rightarrow X = Y$

$\# \rightarrow X > Y$

39. (*c*) **Statements**

$R @ J \Rightarrow R \le J$

$F \Sigma J \Rightarrow F \ge J$

$C \Sigma F \Rightarrow C \ge F$

$C \ge F \ge J \ge R$ (May be True)

Conclusions

I. $R © C \Rightarrow R = C$ (May be True)

II. $C \# R \Rightarrow C > R$ (May be True)

It is a complementary pair, hence either Conclusion I or II follows.

40. (*a*) **Statements**

$W @ P \Rightarrow W \le P$

$W \# E \Rightarrow W > E$

$E \Delta V \Rightarrow E < V$

$\therefore \; P \ge W > E < V$

Conclusions

I. $P \# E \Rightarrow P > E$ (True)

II. $V © W \Rightarrow V = W$ (False)

Hence, only Conclusion I follows.

41. (*e*) **Statements**

$J © R \Rightarrow J = R$

$P \Sigma R \Rightarrow P \ge R$

$Z \# P \Rightarrow Z > P$

$\therefore \; Z > P \ge R = J$

Conclusions

I. $R \Delta Z \Rightarrow R < Z$ (True)

II. $J @ P \Rightarrow J \le P$ (True)

Hence, both Conclusions I and II follow.

42. (*d*) **Statements**

$G @ O \Rightarrow G \le O$

$N © O \Rightarrow N = O$

$H \# G \Rightarrow H > G$

$\therefore \; H > G \le O = N$

Conclusions

I. $O \Delta H \Rightarrow O < H$ (False)

II. $G © N \Rightarrow G = N$ (False)

Hence, neither Conclusion I nor II follows.

43. (*b*) **Statements**

$Q \Delta B \Rightarrow Q < B$

$M © B \Rightarrow M = B$

$K \Sigma M \Rightarrow K \ge M$

$\therefore \; Q < B = M \le K$

Conclusions

I. $K © B \Rightarrow K = B$ (False)

II. $Q \Delta K \Rightarrow Q < K$ (True)

Hence, only Conclusion II follows.

Solutions (Q. Nos. 44-48) According to question,

★ ⇒ <

⇒ >

@ ⇒ ≥

% ⇒ ≤

$ ⇒ =

44. (*a*) **Statement** $V = Y \ge Z \le X > T$

Conclusions

I. $T \# Z \Rightarrow T > Z$ (False)

II. $X \# Y \Rightarrow X > Y$ (False)

III. Z ★ $Y \Rightarrow Z > Y$ (False)

So, none follows.

45. (*a*) **Statement** $R \ge J \le F < E \le M$

Conclusions

I. $M \# J \Rightarrow M > J$ (True)

II. $F \% M \Rightarrow F \le M$ (False)

III. M ★ $R \Rightarrow M < R$ (False)

So, only I follows.

46. (*b*) **Statement** H > R ≥ L < W ≤ F
Conclusions
I. H # L ⇒ H > L (True)
II. F # L ⇒ F > L (True)
III. H $ F ⇒ H = F (False)
So, I and II follow.

47. (*c*) **Statement** K < M = F ≤ Q < H
Conclusions
I. H # K ⇒ H > K (True)
II. Q # K ⇒ Q > K (True)
III. Q @ M ⇒ Q ≥ M (True)
So, all follow.

48. (*a*) **Statement** D < Q = L > T ≤ H
Conclusions
I. D ★ L ⇒ D < L (True)
II. L @ H ⇒ L ≥ H (False)
III. H # L ⇒ H > L (False)
So, only I follows.

Solutions (Q. Nos. 49-53) According to question,
$ → ≥, @ → >, # → <
& → =, * → ≤

49. (*b*) **Statements** H > T, T < F, F = E, E ≤ V
On combining the given statements,
H > T < F = E ≤ V
Conclusions
I. V ≥ F (True)
II. E > T (True)
III. H > V (False)
IV. T < V (True)
Hence, Conclusions I, II and IV are true.

50. (*e*) **Statements** D < R, R ≤ K, K > F, F ≥ J
On combining the given statements,
D < R ≤ K > F ≥ J
Conclusions
I. J < R (False)
II. J < K (True)
III. R < F (False)
IV. K > D (True)
Hence, Conclusions II and IV are true.

51. (*e*) **Statements** N = B, B ≥ W, W < H, H ≤ M
On combining the given statements,
N = B ≥ W < H ≤ M
Conclusions
I. M > W (True)
II. H > N (False)
III. W = N (May be True)
IV. W < M (May be True)
Conclusions III and IV are complementary pair.
∴ Conclusion I and either III or IV are true.

52. (*a*) **Statements** R ≤ D, D ≥ J, J < M, M > K
On combining the given statements,
R ≤ D ≥ J < M > K
Conclusions
I. K < J (False)
II. D > M (False)
III. R < M (False)
IV. D > K (False)
None of the conclusion is true.

53. (*e*) **Statements** M ≥ K, K > N, N ≤ R, R < W
On combining the given statements,
M ≥ K > N ≤ R < W
Conclusions
I. M > K (False)
II. M ≥ R (False)
III. K > W (False)
IV. M > N (True)
∴ Only IV is true.

CHAPTER / 19

Venn Diagram

A Venn Diagram is a representation method for all possible relations that can exist among the given elements of a group in a single figure.

Logical Venn diagram depicts the process of representing the things/objects/persons/departments/ organisations/ events etc., through diagrammatic medium by the use of figures such as square, circle, rectangle, parallelogram, trapezium, triangle etc.

The representation of various similarities and dissimilarities of the objects through the diagram provides a better insight to the candidate, regarding the role and area of representation of various objects.

Based on the variety of questions that are asked in various competitive exams, we have classified these logical Venn diagrams into two types as follows

TYPE 01

Identification of Relation Based Venn Diagram

The most common type of questions that we encounter in logical Venn diagram are based on circular Venn diagrams. The questions asked from this type contain, a group of some elements (things) and also some diagrams.

Here, a candidate is required to find out the diagram which classify the elements given in the group correctly or illustrates the relation between/among them.

The main motive of asking these type of questions is to analyse the candidate's ability to relate a certain given group of items and illustrate it diagrammatically.

Relation between Two Objects/Things/Places/Persons

Three types of relationships can be established between two objects/things/places/persons/organisations etc., which are given as follows

1. The given Venn diagram shows that one class completely belongs to the other class.

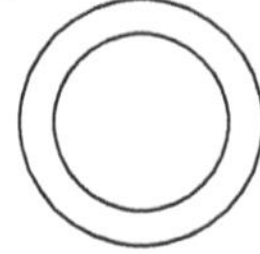

Ex 01 Which one of the following diagrams best depicts the relationship between Meerut and Uttar Pradesh?

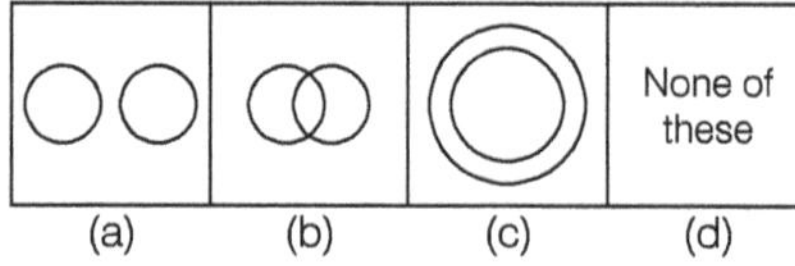

***Solution* (c)** Meerut is a city of Uttar Pradesh. It means Meerut exists completely in Uttar Pradesh. This relation can be expressed as given in option (c).

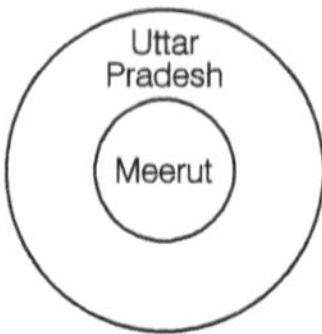

2. The given Venn diagram shows that no one class completely belongs to the other class but they are partly related to each other or have some common characteristics.

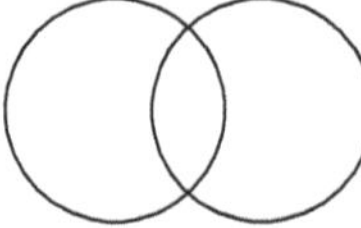

Ex 02 Which one of the following diagrams best depicts the relationship between Female and Teacher?

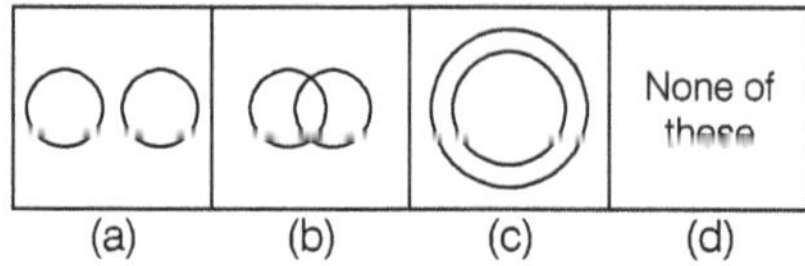

Solution (b) By profession, some females can be teachers, but there can also be some females who are not teachers. Also there can be some male teachers. So, this relation can be best expressed as given in option (b).

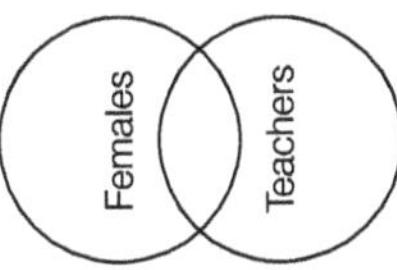

3. The given Venn diagram shows that there is no relation between two classes and no elements are common.

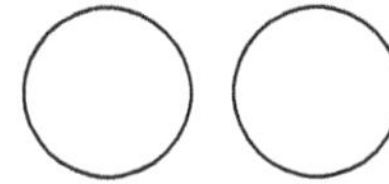

***Ex* 03** Which one of the following diagrams best depicts the relationship between Males and Females?

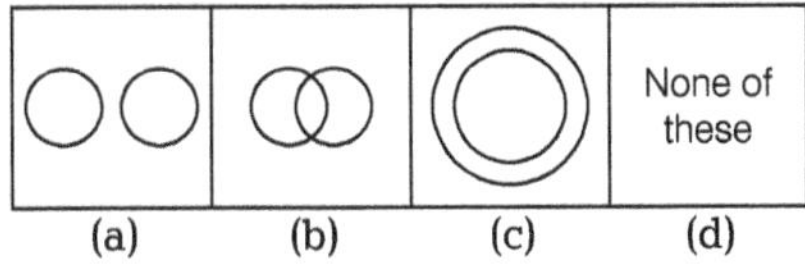

Solution (a) Males and females represents two different genders which are not related to each other in any manner. This can be expressed as given in option (a).

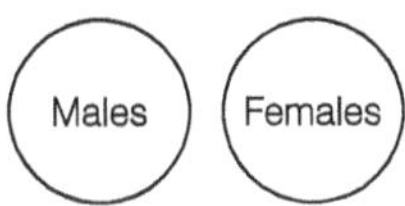

Relations between Three Objects/ Things/Places/Persons

Several types of relationships can be established between three objects/things/places/persons/ organisations etc., which are given as follows

1. The given Venn diagram shows that one class completely belongs to the second class and the second class completely belongs to the third class.

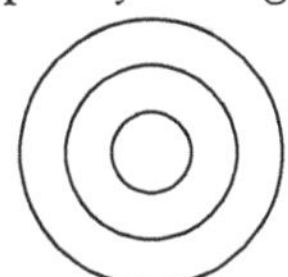

***Ex* 04** Which one of the following diagrams best depicts the relationship between Seconds, Minutes and Hours?

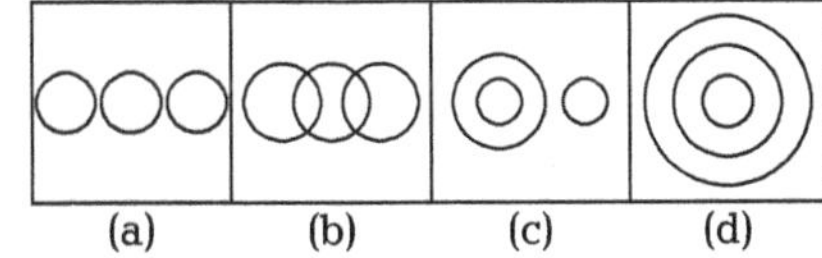

Solution (d) Seconds are the part of minute and minutes are the part of hour. This relation can be expressed by option (d).

Hours
Minutes
Seconds

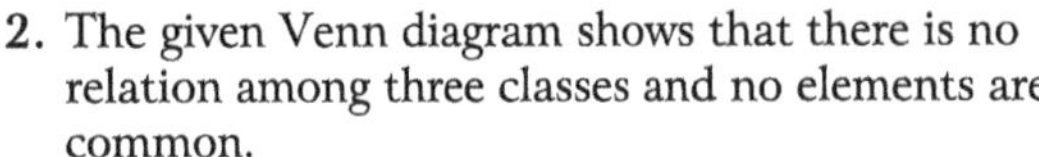

2. The given Venn diagram shows that there is no relation among three classes and no elements are common.

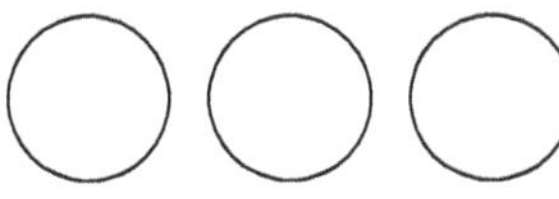

***Ex* 05** Which one of the following diagrams best depicts the relationship among Kanpur, Varanasi and Meerut?

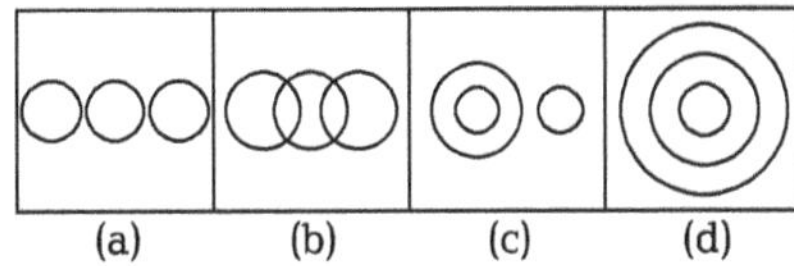

Solution (a) Kanpur, Varanasi and Meerut all are cities of Uttar Pradesh but they are entirely different from one another. This can be expressed by option (a).

3. The given Venn diagram shows that two classes partly belongs to the third and are themselves independent of each other.

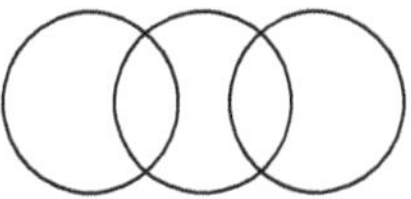

***Ex* 06** Which of the following diagrams best depicts the relationship between Dogs, Pets and Cats?

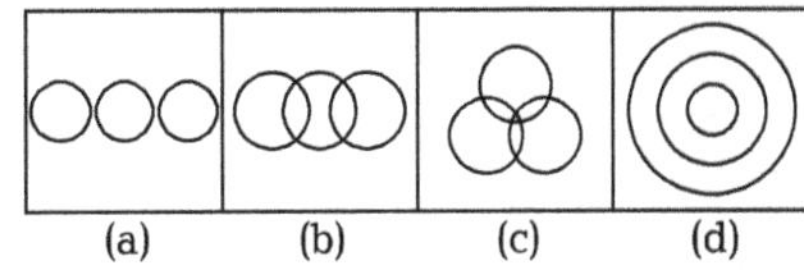

Solution (b) Some dogs are pets and some cats are pets. But all pets are not dogs or cats. Also, dogs and cats are completely different groups and are not related to each other. This can be expressed as given in option (b).

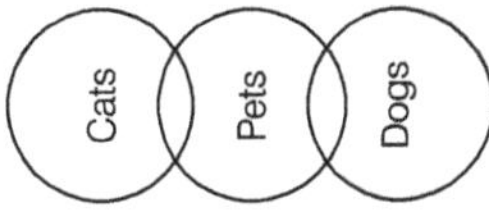

4. The given Venn diagram shows that three separate classes are partly related to one another and the shaded portion is common to all the three classes.

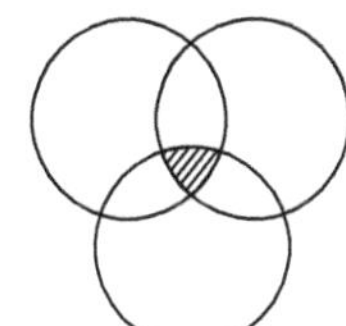

***Ex* 07** Which of the following diagrams best depicts the relationship between Married, Government employees and Teachers? « SSC Steno 2019

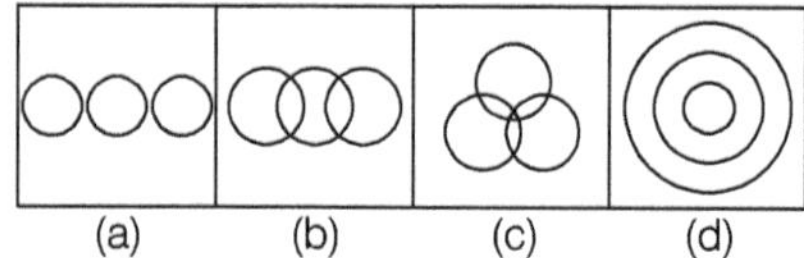

Solution (c) Some government employees are teachers. Some government employees are married. Some teachers are married. Some married government employees are teachers. This can be expressed as given in option (c).

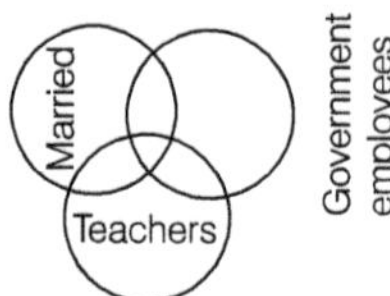

5. If one class belongs to the second class while the third class is entirely different from the two, then the diagram will be as follows

***Ex* 08** Which of the following diagrams best depicts the relationship between Doctors, Human beings and Cats?

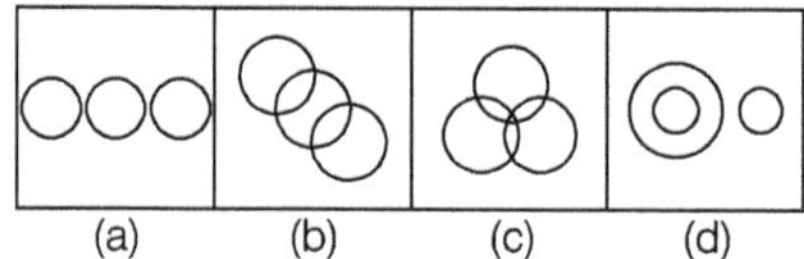

Solution (d) All doctors come under the group of human beings but all human beings do not come under the group of doctors and cats are entirely different from doctors and human beings. The relation can be expressed by the diagram as given in option (d).

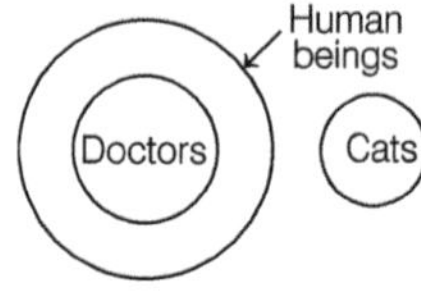

6. The given Venn diagram shows that two separate classes belong to the class of third.

***Ex* 09** Select the Venn diagram that best represents the relationship among the given set of classes:

Metals, Silver, Gold « SSC Constable 2019

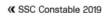

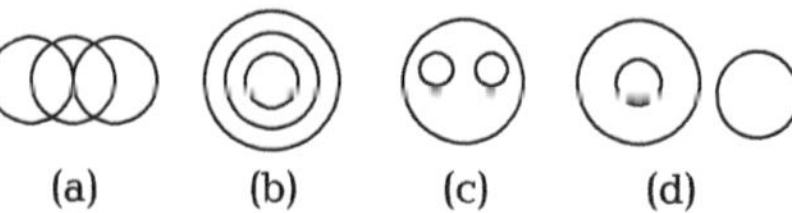

Solution (c) Gold and Silver are two different elements but both come under the group of metals. This can be expressed as given in option (c).

7. When two classes or groups belong to the class of third such that some items of each of these two groups are common, then the diagram will be as follows

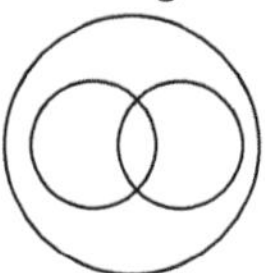

***Ex* 10** Which of the following diagram best depicts the relationship between Females, Mothers and Sisters?

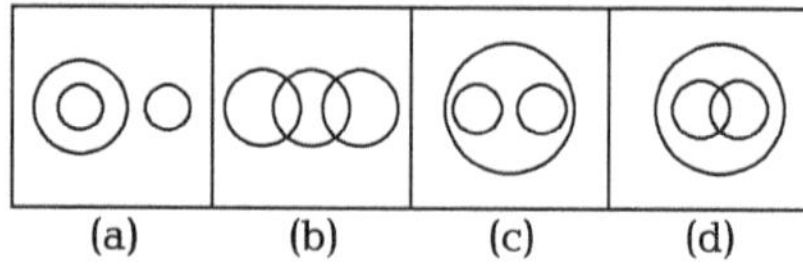

Solution (d) Some mothers are sisters and some sisters are mothers. Also, both mothers and sisters are females. This relationship can be expressed as given in option (d).

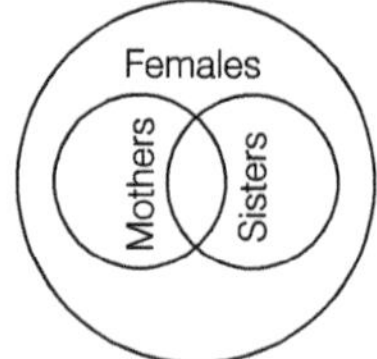

8. When one class belongs to the class of second and the third class is partly related to these two, then the diagram will be as follows

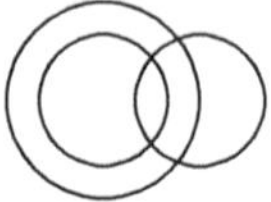

***Ex* 11** Which of the following diagrams best depicts the relationship between Males, Husbands and Doctors? « RRB ALP 2018

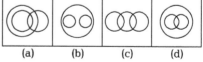

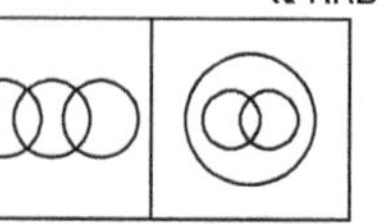

Solution (a) All husbands are males. Also, some husbands and some males can be doctors. This relationship can be expressed as given in option (a).

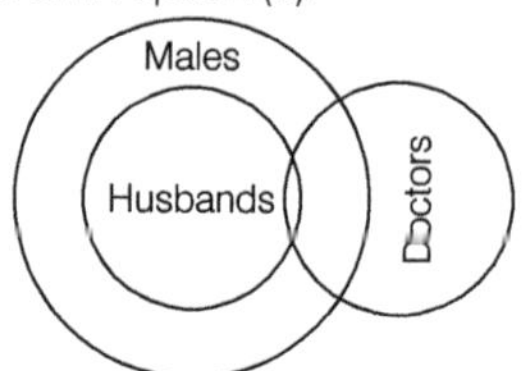

9. When one class belongs to the class of second and the third class is partly related to the second class, then the diagram will be as follows

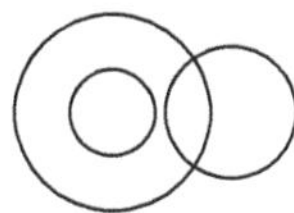

Ex 12 Which of the following diagram best depicts the relationship between Females, Mothers and Infants?

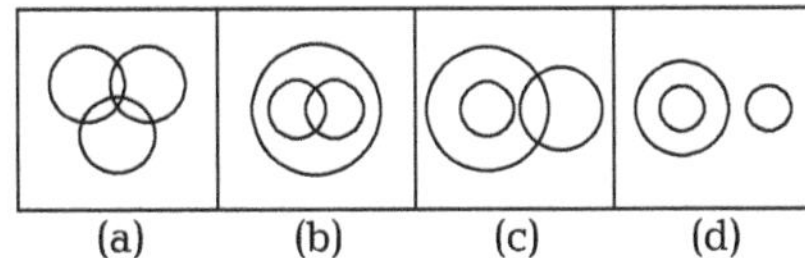

Solution (c) All mothers are females. Also, some infants are females but infants cannot be mothers. This can be expressed as given in option (c).

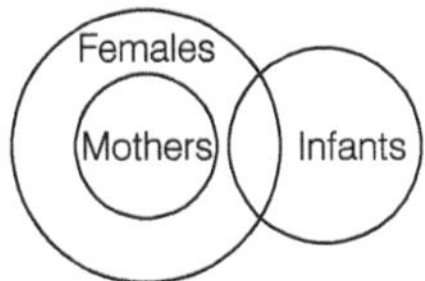

10. When two classes are partly related to each other and the third class is entirely different from these two, then the diagram will be as follows

Ex 13 Which of the following diagrams best depicts the relationship between Professor, Author and Infants?

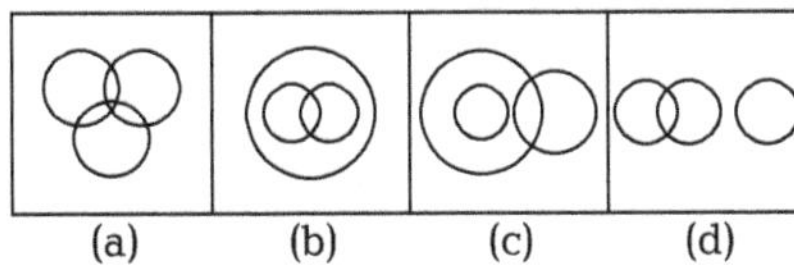

Solution (d) Some professors can be authors and some authors can be professors but the class of infants is entirely different from these two. This relationship can be expressed as given in option (d).

Association or Independency of Groups/Classes

Two or more groups/classes are associated to one another when they have some common items/part as shown below

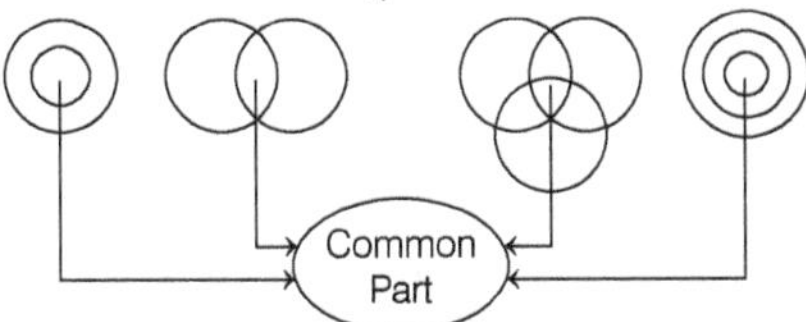

Two or more groups/classes are independent of one another when they have no common part/items at all. In this case, all the figures are separate from one another as shown below.

Ex 14 If L and M are two independent groups, then which of the following does not represent them?

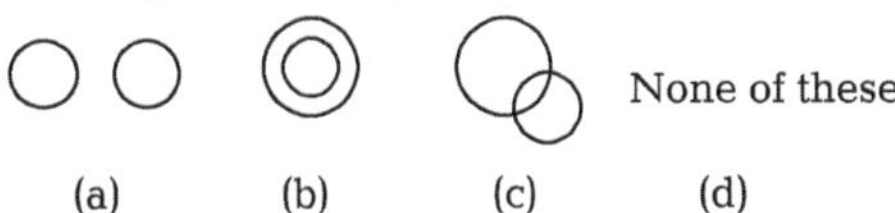

Solution (c) Option (c) has some part common to both the circles. It means both the groups represented by the two circles have certain relationship between them and hence cannot be independent from each other.

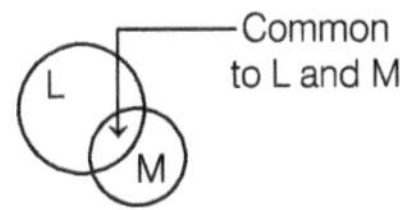

The following examples will give you a better idea about the type of questions asked in various competitive exams

Ex 15 Which of the following represents a correct relationship between India and Uttar Pradesh?

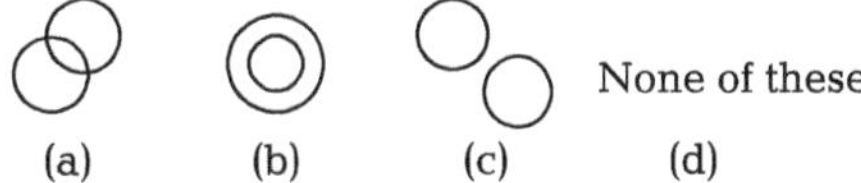

Solution (b) Uttar Pradesh is a state of India. It means Uttar Pradesh exists completely inside India.

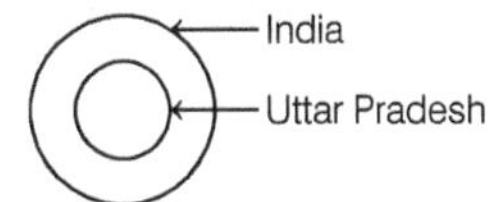

Ex 16 Which of the following diagrams represents a relationship between Animal and Cow?

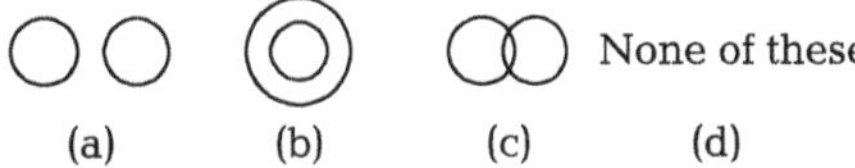

Solution (b) Cow is an animal . This relationship can be represented by option (b).

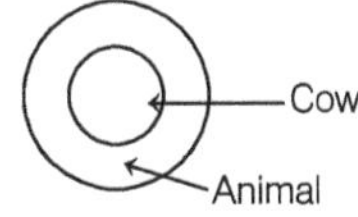

Ex 17 Which of the following Venn diagrams best represents the relationship among Europe, Paris and France?
« UPSSSC Mandi Parishad 2018

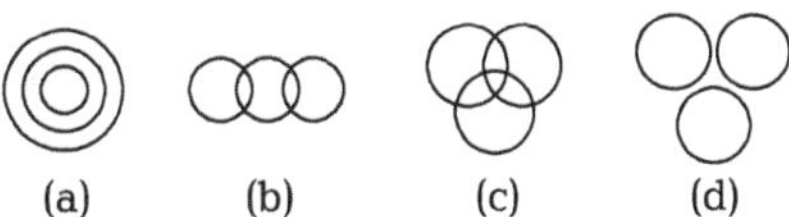

Solution (a) Paris is the capital of France and France is a country in Europe. Therefore, figure (a) depicts the relationship among given elements.

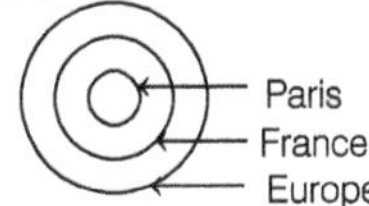

Ex 18 Which of the following diagrams represents the relationship among Apple, Banana and Mango?

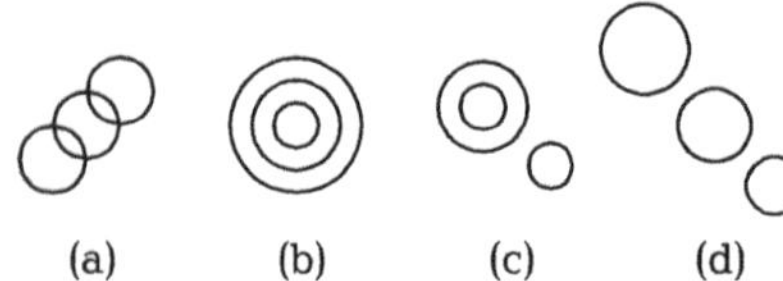

(a) (b) (c) (d)

Solution (d) Apple, banana and mango all are fruits but they are entirely different from one another.

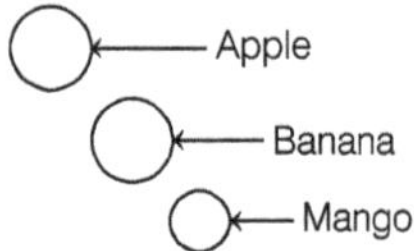

Ex 19 Which of the following diagrams represents the relationship among Bihar, Gaya and Darbhanga?

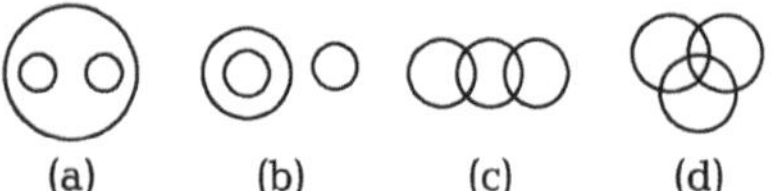

(a) (b) (c) (d)

Solution (a) Gaya and Darbhanga are two different towns of Bihar and hence option (a) depicts the relationship among the three.

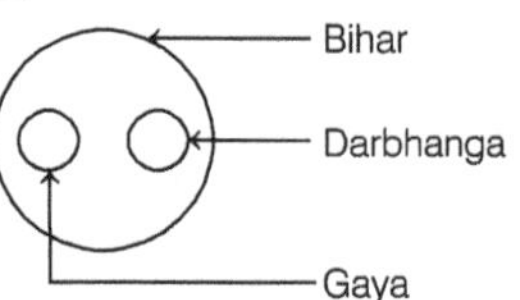

Ex 20 Which of the following is correct about the given diagram?

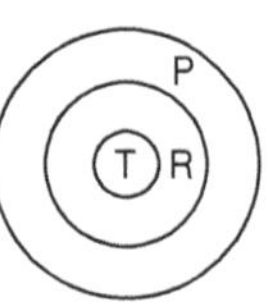

(a) All R are T
(b) All P are T
(c) All T are P
(d) All P are R

Solution (c) T is present completely inside R and R is present completely inside P. Hence, T is present completely inside P (i.e., all T are P).

Practice / CORNER 19.1

1. In a village, there are landlords of which some are literate. Which of the following best expresses the relationship between them? « SSC CGL 2016

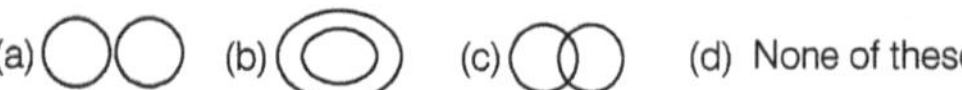

(a) (b) (c) (d) None of these

2. Which of the following diagrams represents a relationship between players and footballers? « UP B.Ed.2012

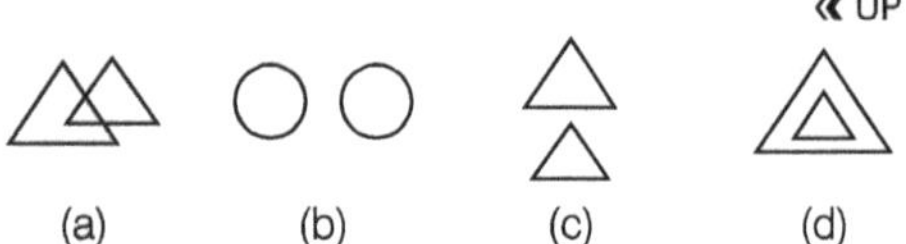

(a) (b) (c) (d)

3. Choose the Venn diagram from the given options that best represents the relationship amongst the following classes: « SSC CAPF 2018

Vienna, Europe, New Zealand

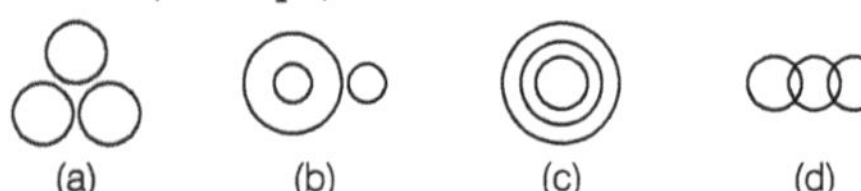

(a) (b) (c) (d)

4. Identify the diagram that best represents the relationship among the classes given below « SSC CGL 2015

Soda water, Mineral water, Liquid

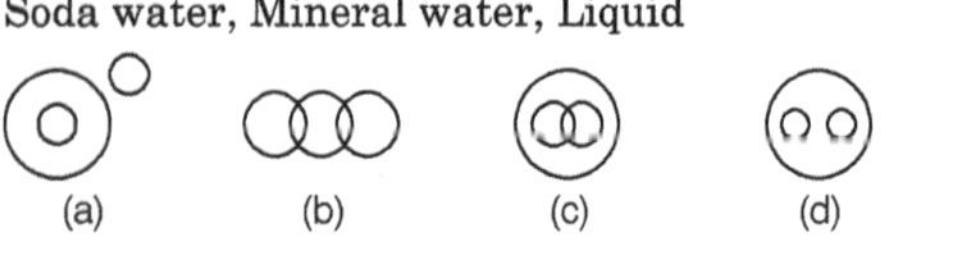

(a) (b) (c) (d)

5. Which figure represents the exact relationship with the variables given in questions? « MP SI 2017

Father, Female, Human

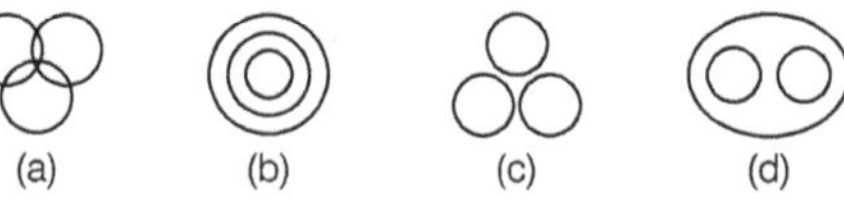

(a) (b) (c) (d)

6. Which of the following Venn diagram best represents the relationship among Indians, Doctors and Women? « RRB ALP 2018

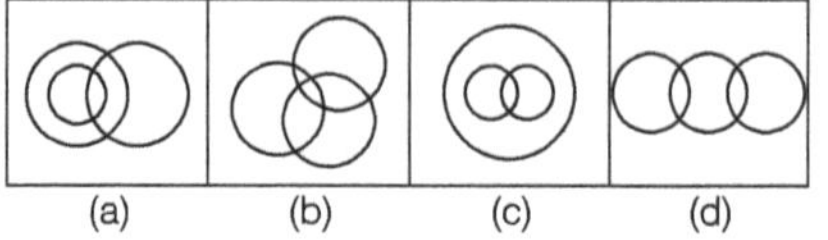

(a) (b) (c) (d)

7. Which of the following figures best depicts the relationship among Criminals (C), Thieves (T) and Judges (J)? « IB 2017

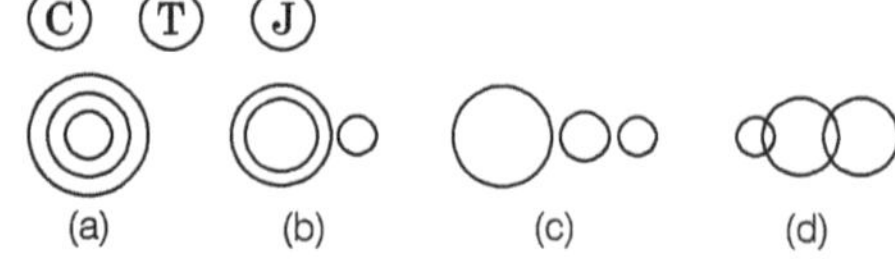

(a) (b) (c) (d)

DIRECTIONS ~ (Q. Nos. 8-10) *Which of the following diagrams best represents the relationship among given words.*

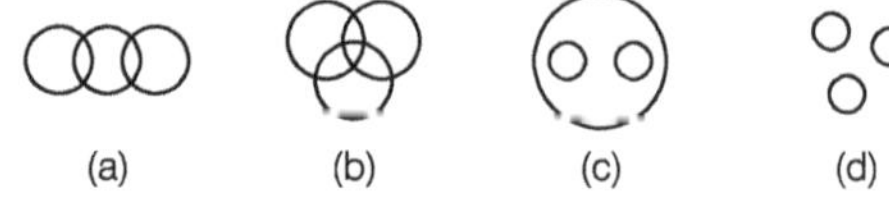

(a) (b) (c) (d)

8. Woman, Teacher, Student « RRB Group D 2009

9. Elephant, Wolf, Animal « UP B.Ed. 2008

10. Red, Green, Colour « UP B.Ed. 2012

DIRECTIONS ~(Q. Nos. 11-20) *Each of the questions given below contains three items. These items may or may not have some relation with one another. Each group of the items may fit into one of the diagrams* (a), (b), (c), (d) *and* (e). *You have to indicate that the group of items in each of these questions correctly fits into which of the diagram.* « SBI PO 2012

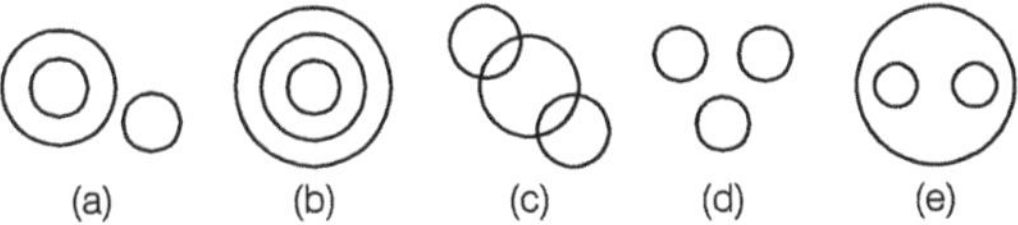

11. Universe, Earth, Europe

12. Picture, TV, Radio

13. Living beings, Animals, Men

14. Radio, TV, Cinema hall

15. Residence, Resident, Road

16. Notebook, Stationery, Car

17. Coal mines, Factory, Field

18. Clothes, Sari, Dhoti

19. Chapter, Book, Topic

20. Boys, Class, Girls

21. Identify the Venn diagram that best represents the relationship between the given classes « SSC MTS 2019

Painter, Lawyer, Singer

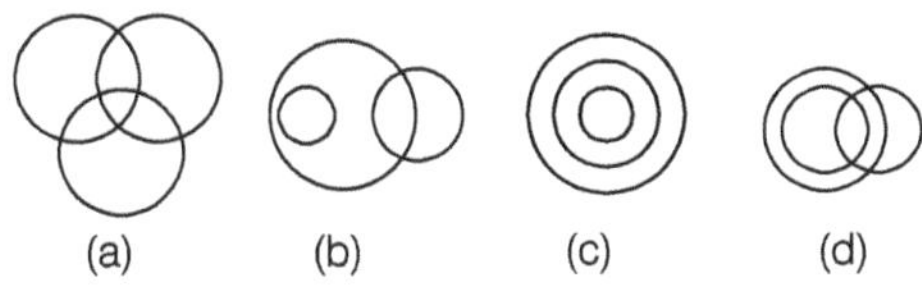

22. Choose from the 4 diagrams given below, the one that illustrates the relationship among Languages, Japanese, German. « Delhi Police CAPF 2016

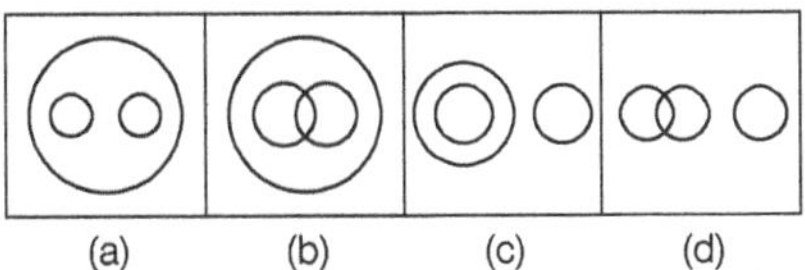

23. Which of the following diagrams best represents the relationship among Uttar Pradesh, Kanpur, Jaipur? « UP B.Ed. 2011

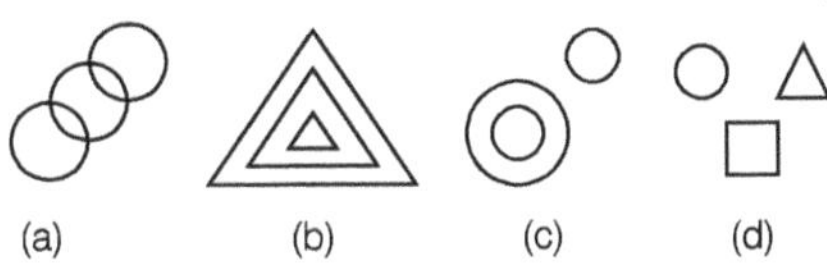

24. Identify the diagram that best represents the relationship among classes given below « SSC MTS 2014

Sportsmen, Cricketers, Batsman

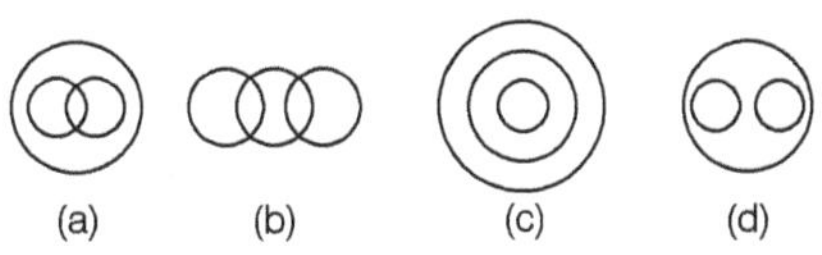

25. Which of the answer figures indicates the best relationship among Milk, Goat, Cow, Hen? « SSC Constable 2015

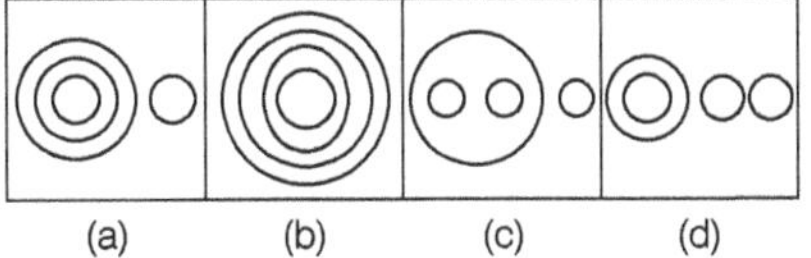

26. Which of the Venn diagrams correctly represents the given classes? « SSC Steno 2018

Dermatologist, Anthropologist, Cardiologist

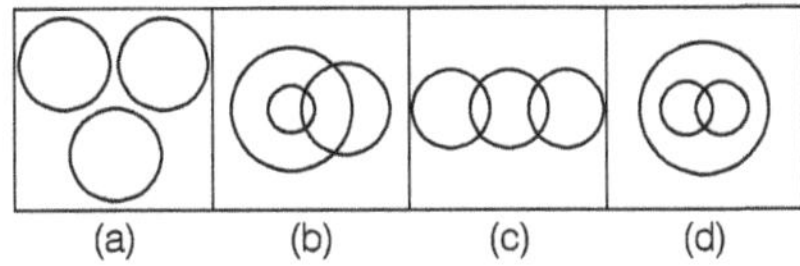

27. Choose the Venn diagram that best depicts the relation among State, District, City. « RRB Group D 2018

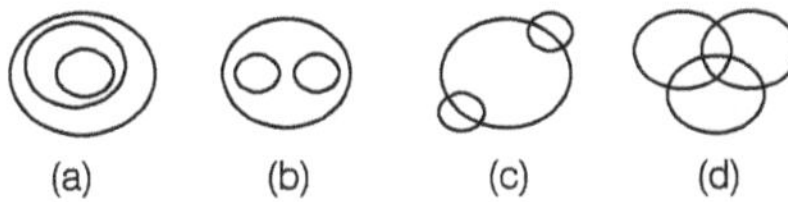

28. Identify the diagram that best represents the relationship among the given classes.

Circle, Square, Triangle « Delhi Police Constable 2017

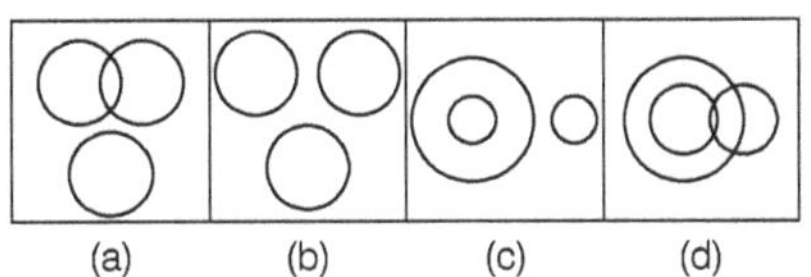

29. Choose the Venn diagram from the given options that best represents the relationship amongst the following classes. « SSC CAPF 2019

Mothers, Doctors, Homo sapiens

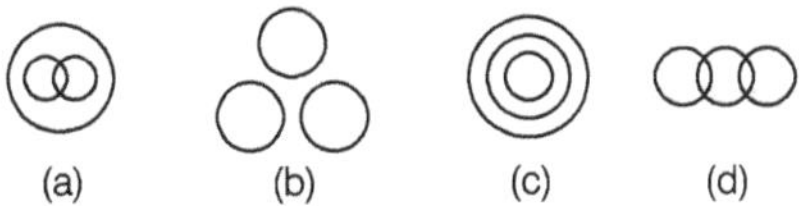

30. Choose the Venn diagram from the given options that best represents the relationship amongst the following classes.

Inert Gases, Chlorine, Helium « SSC CAPF 2019

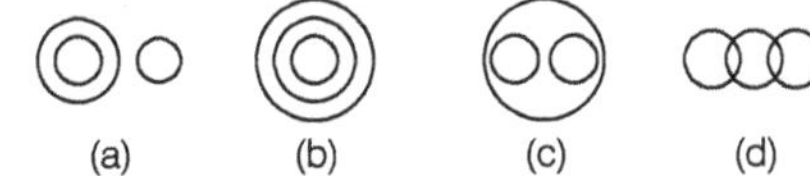

31. Which of the following diagrams represents the relationship among Nucleus, Protons, Neutrons? « UP Police SI 2018

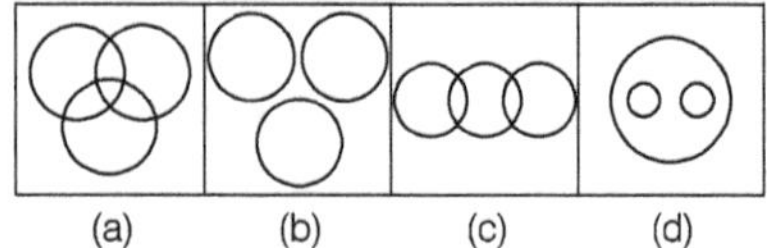

32. Identify the diagram that best represents the relationship among the given classes. « SSC 10+2 2017

Males, Doctors, Brothers

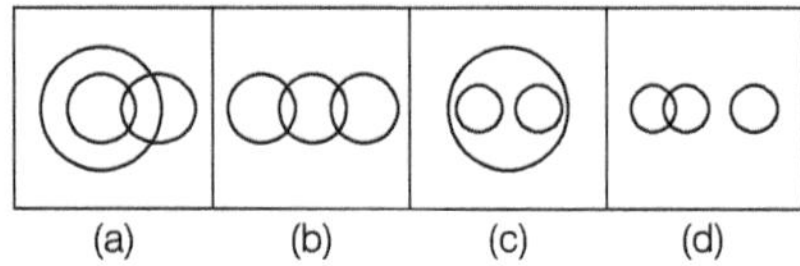

33. Which figure best represents the relationship among Religion, Mosque, Temple? « Delhi Police CAPF 2016

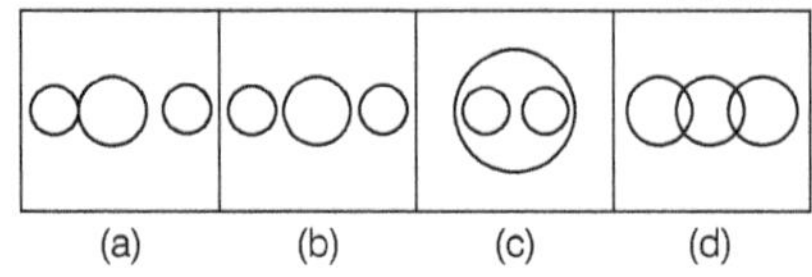

34. Choose the Venn diagram from the given options which best represents the relationship amongst the following classes : « SSC MTS 2019

Fishes, Sharks, Dolphins

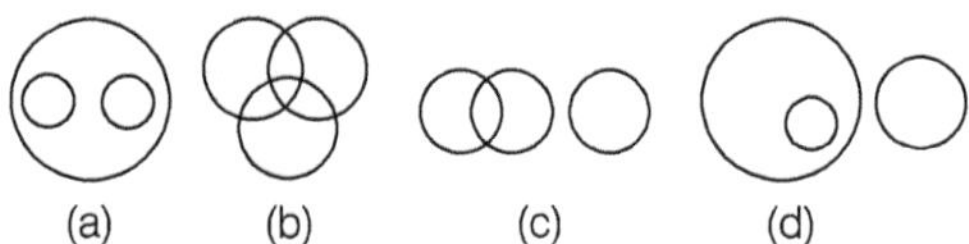

35. Choose the Venn diagram from the given options which best represents the relationship amongst the following classes : « SSC CPO 2019

Stars, Sun, Polaris

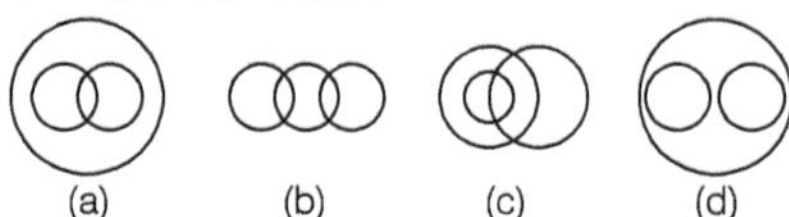

36. Which of the following diagrams represents the correct relationship among Herbivorous, Tigers and Animals? « SSC CGL 2013

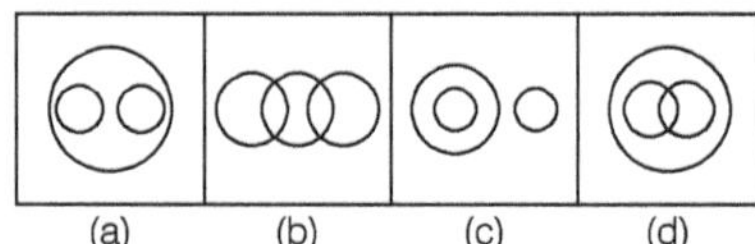

37. Select the Venn diagram that best represents the relationship between the following classes. « SSC 10+2 2020

Reptile, Mammal, Lizard

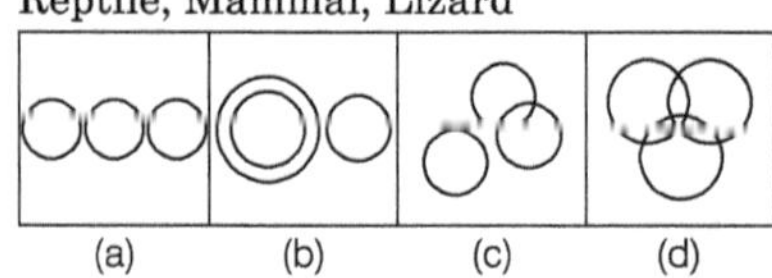

38. Which one of the following diagrams best depicts the relationship among Earth, Sea and Sun? « SSC CGL 2013

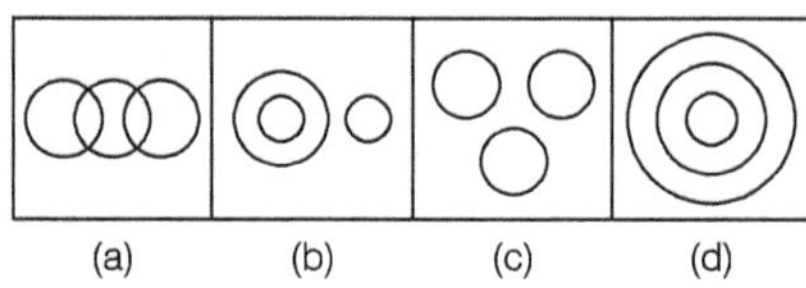

39. Which one of the following diagrams represents the correct relationship among Teachers, Educated, Employed? « SSC Steno 2013

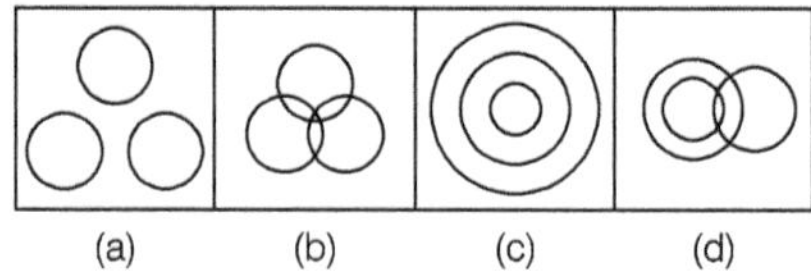

40. Identify the diagram that best represents the relationship among the classes given below

Police, Thief, Criminal « SSC MTS 2014, SSC Steno 2013

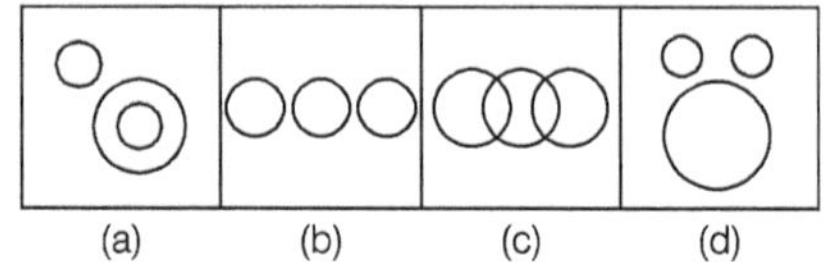

41. Which of the following diagrams correctly represents Brinjal, Food, Vegetable? « UPSSSC Junior Assist. Clerk 2019

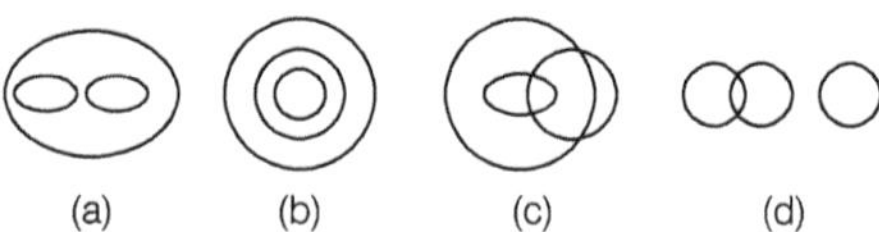

42. Which one of the following diagrams best depicts the relationship among Elephants, Wolves and Animals? « SSC Steno 2012

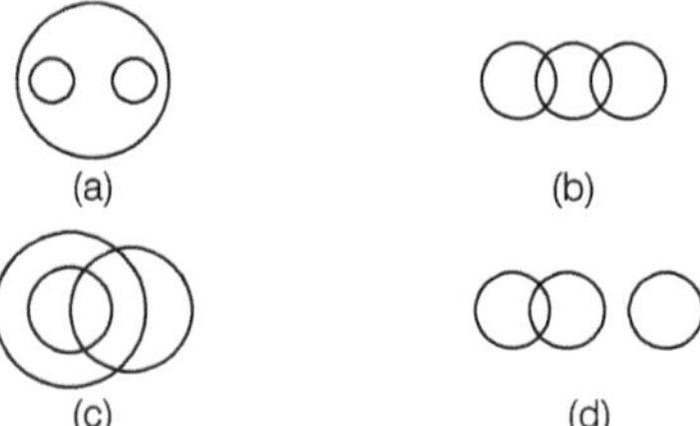

43. Which diagram correctly represents the relationship among Politicians, Poets and Women? « SSC CGL 2011

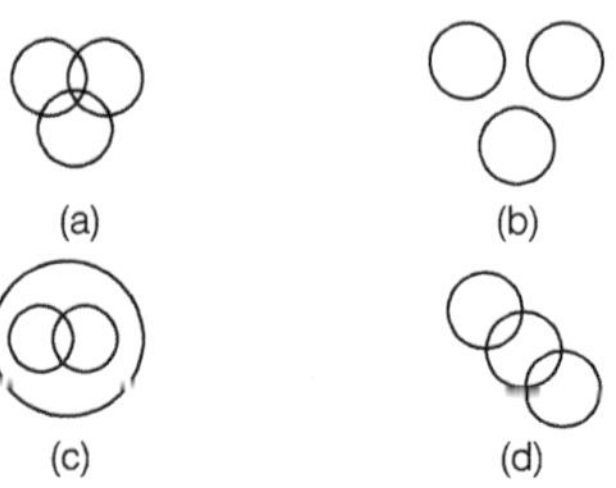

Answers WITH EXPLANATIONS

1. (*c*) Some landlords can be literate. Here this can be best depicted by option (c)

2. (*d*) All footballers are players. It means the class of footballers exists completely inside the class of players. This can be expressed as given in option (d).

3. (*b*) Vienna is a Europian country, but New Zealand is not a Europian country.
The figure given in option (b) best depicts this relationship.

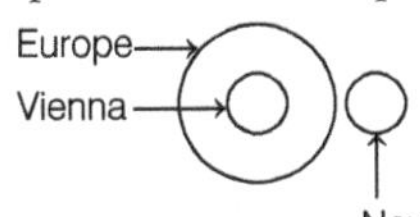

4. (*d*) Soda water and Mineral water both are different types of liquid. Hence, option (d) depicts the best relationship.

5. (*d*) Father and female both comes under the category of human. Hence, figure of option (d) represents the exact relationship with the elements given in question.

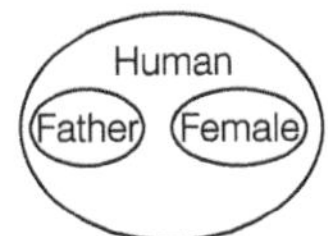

6. (*b*) Some Indian are women. Some Indian are doctor. Some women are doctor. Some Indian women are doctor. This can be expressed as given in option (b).

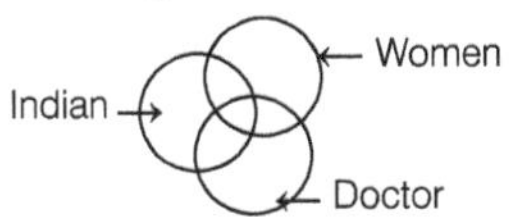

7. (*b*) Thieves are criminal, but judges are different this can be expressed as given in option (b)

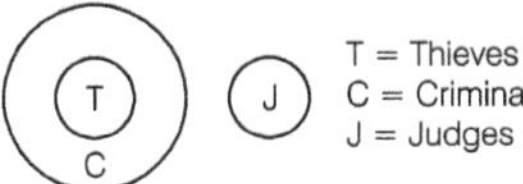

8. (*b*) Some women are teachers. Some women are students. Some teachers are students. Some women teachers are students. This can be expressed as given in option (b).

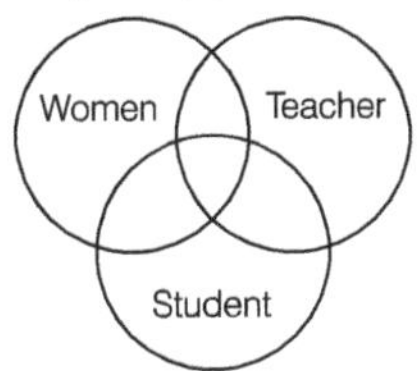

9. (*c*) Elephant and wolf both belong to the group of animals but they both are entirely different. This can be expressed as given in option (c).

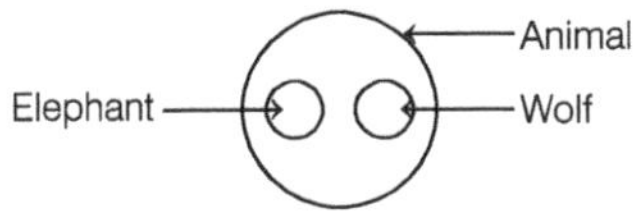

10. (*c*) Red and green both belong to the group of colours but they both are entirely different. This can be expressed as given in option (c).

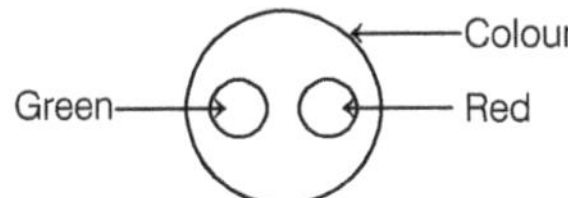

11. (*b*) Europe is a continent on earth and earth is a planet in universe. This relation can be expressed as given in option (b).

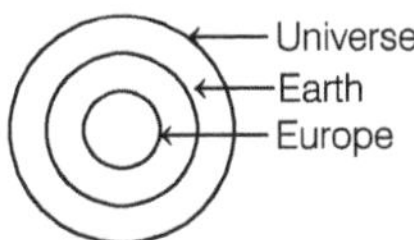

12. (*a*) Picture is there in TV while radio is not related to both of them. This can be expressed as given in option (a).

13. (*e*) Men and animals are entirely different but they both are living beings. This can be expressed as given in option (e).

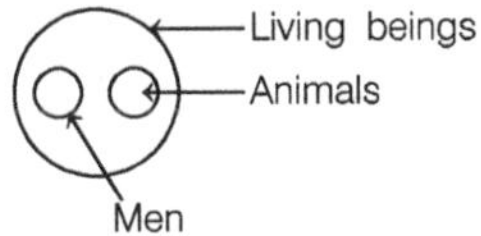

14. (*d*) Radio, TV and cinema hall are entirely different from one another. This can be expressed as given in option (d).

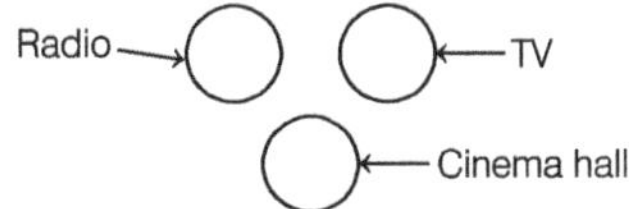

15. (*a*) Resident lives in the residence while road is entirely different from resident and residence. This can be expressed as given in option (a).

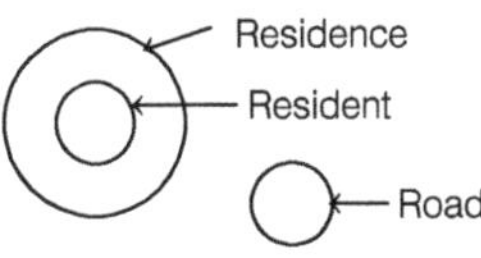

16. (*a*) Notebook is a stationery item while car is entirely different. This can be expressed as given in option (a).

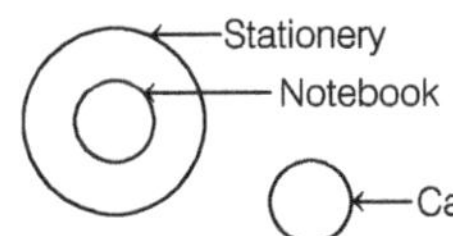

17. (*e*) Both coal mines and factory are located in the field. This can be expressed as given in option (e).

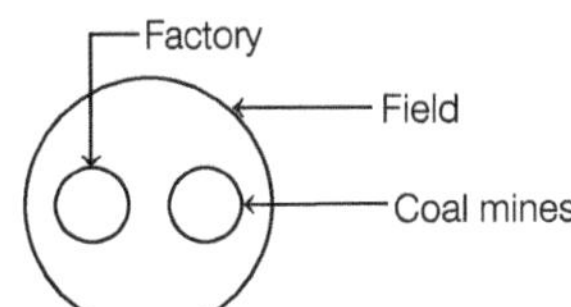

18. (*e*) Dhoti and Sari are entirely different but both belong to the group of clothes. This can be expressed as given in option (e).

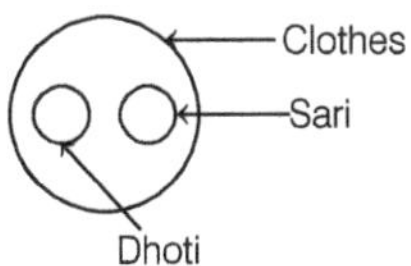

19. (*b*) A book consists of chapters and chapter consists of topics. This can be expressed as given in option (b).

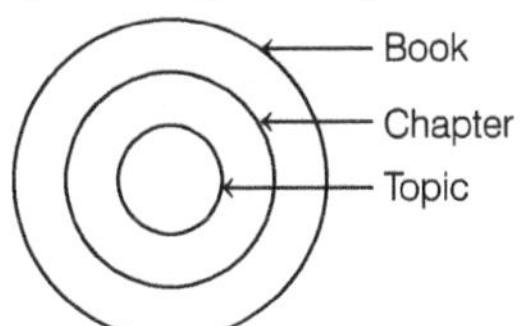

20. (*e*) A class has both boys and girls but boys and girls are entirely different from each other. This can be expressed as given in option (e).

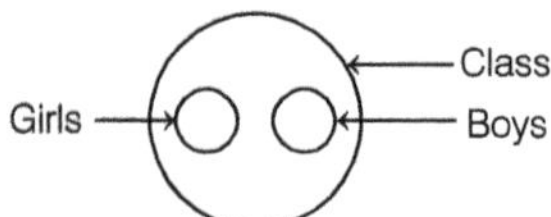

21. (*a*) Some painters are lawyers, some lawyers are singers, some singers are painters and some painters are lawyers as well as singers.

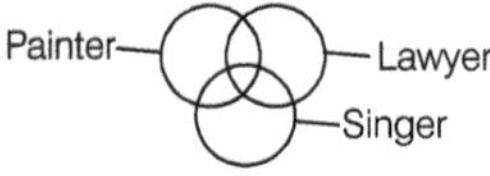

22. (*a*) Japanese and German are two different languages.

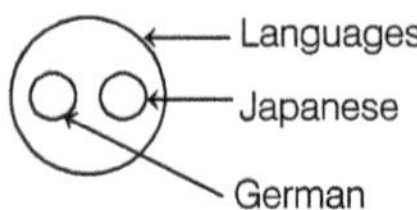

23. (*c*) Kanpur is a city in the state of Uttar Pradesh while Jaipur is entirely different as it is a city in Rajasthan. This can be expressed as given in option (c).

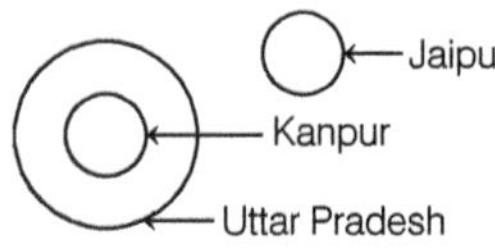

24. (*c*) A batsman is a cricketer and cricketers are sportsmen.

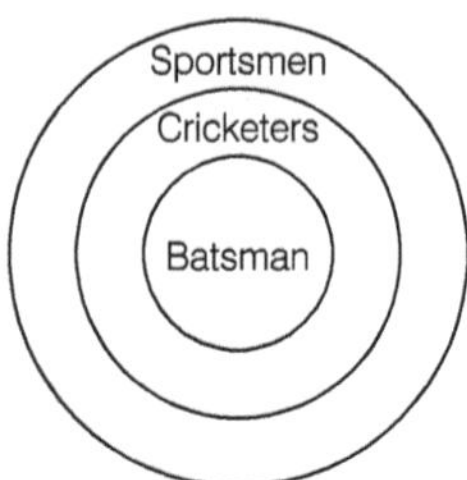

25. (*c*) Goat and cow gives milk, whereas hen does not give milk. This relationship can be best depicted by figure given in option (c).

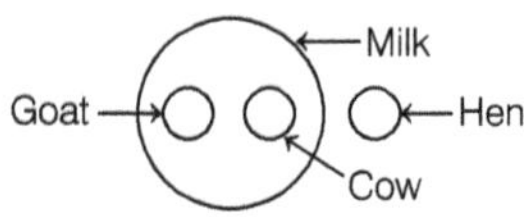

26. (*a*) Dermatologist, Anthropologist and Cardiologist are entirely different.

This relationship can be best depicted by figure given in option (a).

27. (*a*) City comes under district and district comes under state. This relationship can be best depicted by figure given in option (a).

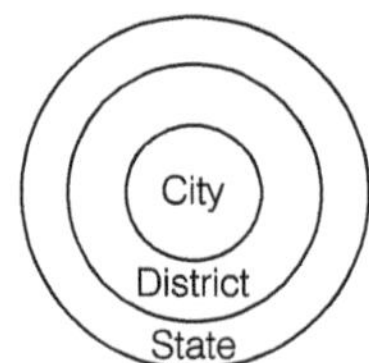

28. (*b*) Circle, square and triangle are different geometrical figures.

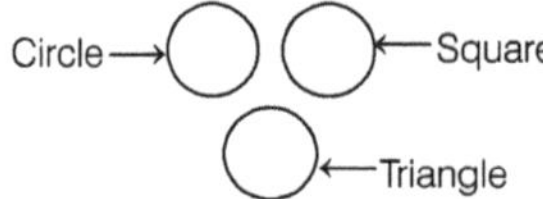

29. (*a*) Some mothers can be doctors and vice-versa. All mothers and doctors are homo sapiens. This relationship can be expressed by figure given in option (a).

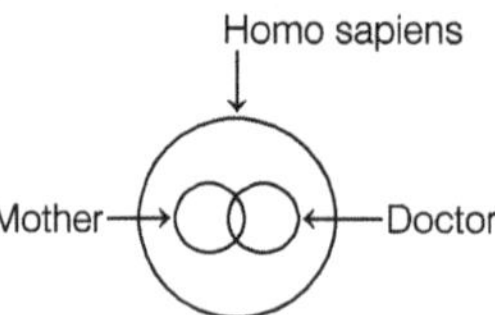

30. (*a*) Helium is an inert gas, but chlorine is not an inert gas. This relationship can be best depicted by figure given in option (a).

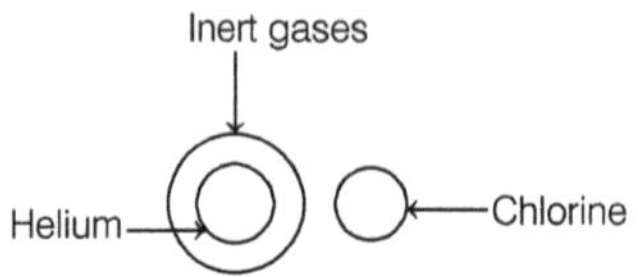

31. (*d*) We know that protons and neutrons live in nucleus. So, figure of option (d) represent the relationship between each of them.

32. (*a*) All brothers are males. Some males are doctors. Some doctors are males. Some brothers are doctors. Some doctors are brothers. Hence, figure given in option (a) best depicts the relationship.

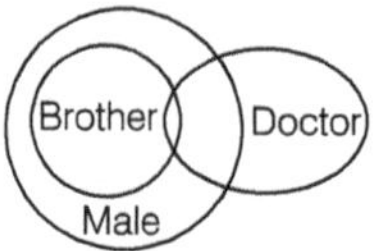

33. (*c*) Temples and Mosque, both are the places of religious congregation and activities. Hence, figure given in option (c) best depicts the given relationship.

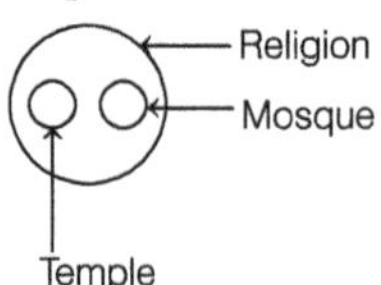

34. (*d*) Dolphins are warm blooded mammals and sharks are cold blooded fishes.

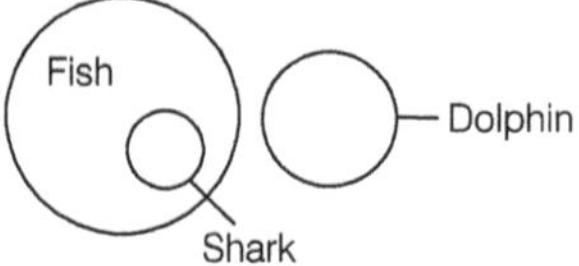

35. (*d*) Sun and Polaris are different Stars.

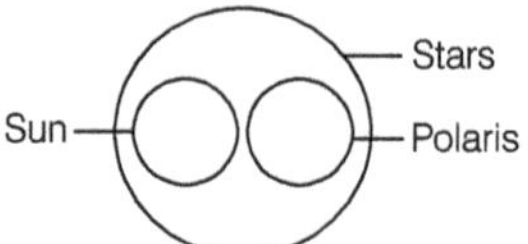

36. (*a*) Tigers are animals but not herbivorous. This can be expressed as given in option (a).

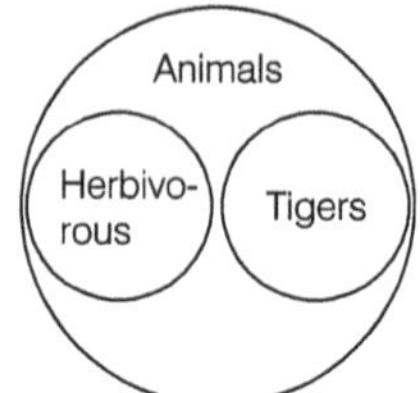

37. (*b*) Lizard is a reptile, not a mammal.

38. (*b*) Sea is a part of the Earth but Sun is present outside the Earth. This relation can be expressed as given in option (b).

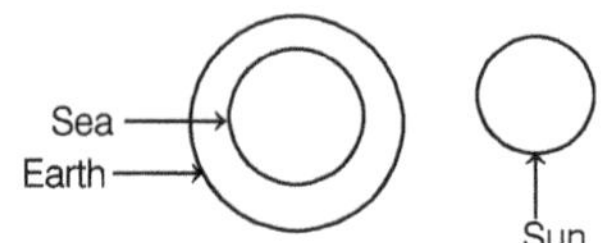

39. (*d*) All the teachers are educated but some are employed. This can be expressed as given in option (d).

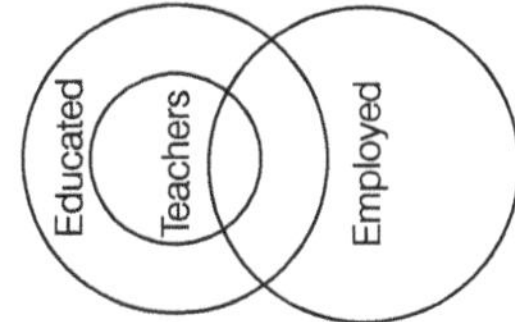

40. (*a*) Thief is a criminal but police is different. This can be expressed as given in option (a).

41. (*b*) Brinjal is a vegetable and vegetable is the part of the food.

So, the Venn-diagram of the three relates as follows

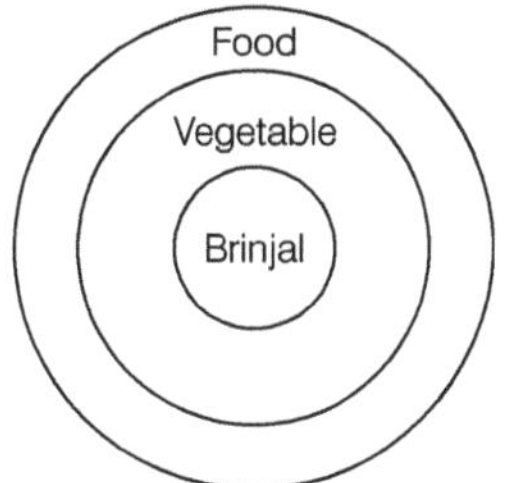

42. (*a*) Wolves and elephants both are animals but are different from each other. This can be expressed as given in option (a).

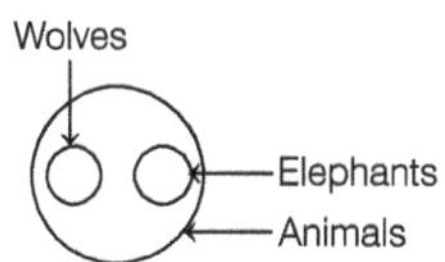

43. (*a*) Some women are poets. Some women are politicians. Some women politicians are poets.

This can be expressed as given in option (a).

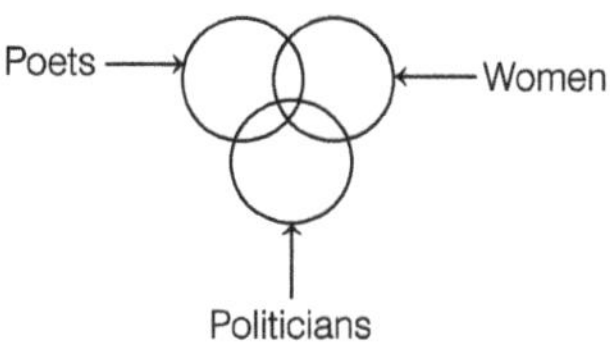

TYPE 02

Analysis Based Venn Diagram

In this type of questions, generally a Venn diagram comprising of different geometrical figures is given. Each geometrical figure in the diagram represents a certain class. The candidate is required to study and analyse the figure carefully and then answer the given questions based on it. Let's take an example

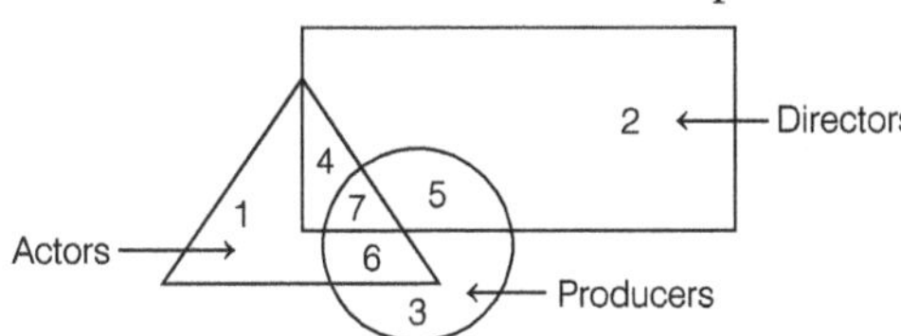

This diagram consists of three groups—Actors, Directors and Producers, represented by a triangle, a rectangle and a circle, respectively.

There are seven regions represented by numbers from 1 to 7 where each region represents the following

Region 1 Represents only Actors.

Region 2 Represents only Directors.

Region 3 Represents only Producers.

Region 4 Represents those Actors who are also Directors but not Producers.

Region 5 Represents those Directors who are also Producers but not Actors.

Region 6 Represents those Producers who are also Actors but not Directors.

Region 7 Represents those Actors who are Directors as well as Producers.

In some other questions, the candidate is required to find out the correct shaded Venn diagram which correctly depicts the situation given in the question.

Some solved examples given below will give you a better idea about both the types of questions asked

Ex 21 In the given diagram, square represents doctors, triangle represents lady and circle represents surgeon. Which of the following letters represents those ladies who are doctors and surgeon both?

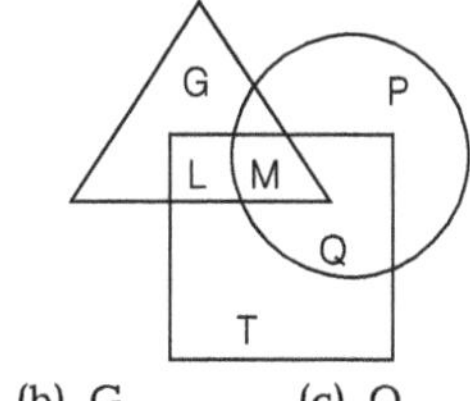

(a) M (b) G (c) Q (d) P

Solution (a) It is clear from the diagram that M is common in all the three figures i. e., square, triangle and circle. It means that required letter is M.

Ex 22 In the following figure, rectangle represents Authors, circle represents Art critics, triangle represents Tattooists and square represents Joggers. Which set of letters represents Joggers who are either Art critics or Authors?
« SSC 10+2 2018

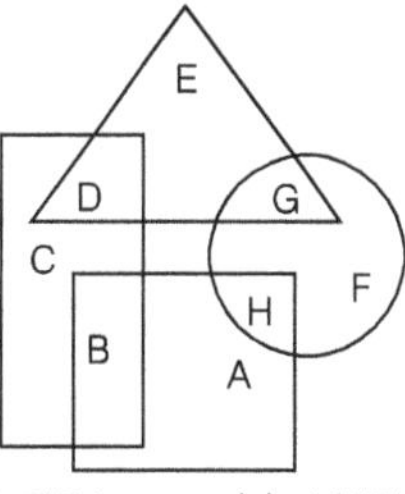

(a) BAH (b) CBA (c) AHF (d) BH

Solution (d) B and H, letters represent joggers who are either art critics or authors.

***Ex* 23** In the following figure 'B' represents businessmen, R represents rich men, and H represents honest men. Which number will represent rich businessmen? « UKPSC 2016

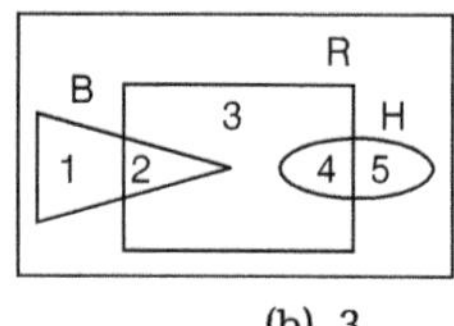

(a) 5 (b) 3
(c) 2 (d) 4

Solution (c) 2 is common between rich men and businessmen.

Hence, 2 is a rich businessmen.

***Ex* 24** A result of a survey of 1000 persons with respect to their knowledge of Hindi (H), English (E) and Sanskrit (S) is given below

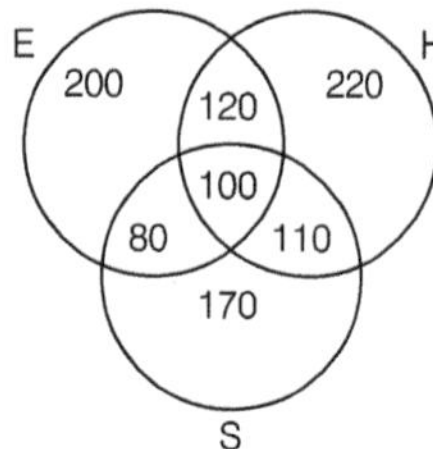

What is the ratio of those who know all the three languages to those who do not know Sanskrit?

(a) $\frac{5}{27}$ (b) $\frac{10}{17}$
(c) $\frac{1}{10}$ (d) $\frac{1}{9}$

Solution (a) The persons knowing all the three languages are represented by the region which is common to all the three circles. Hence, number of such persons = 100.

The persons who do not know Sanskrit are represented by the region outside circle S.

So, number of such persons = (200 + 120 + 220) = 540

$\therefore$ Required ratio $= \frac{100}{540} = \frac{5}{27}$

DIRECTIONS ~ (Example Nos. 25-28) *Read the following information carefully and answer the questions based on them.*

In the Venn diagram given below, the square represents women, the triangle represents persons who are in government services, the circle represents educated persons and the rectangle represents persons working in private sector.

Each section of the diagram is numbered. Your task is to study the diagram and answer the questions that follow.

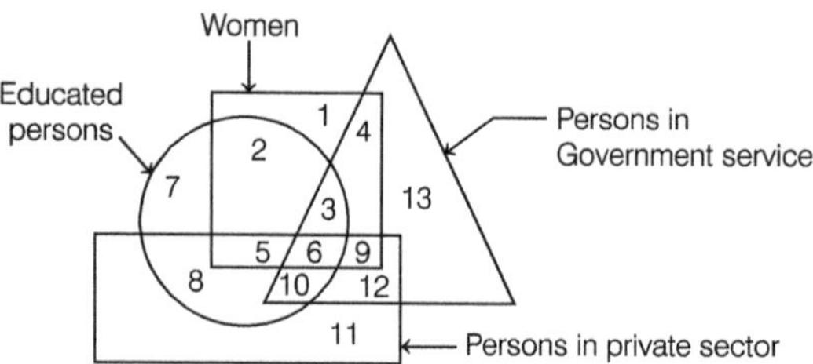

***Ex* 25** Which number represents educated women, who are in government jobs?

(a) 2 (b) 3
(c) 6 (d) 4

Solution (b) Educated women in government jobs are represented by number 3 as it occupies the area common to circle, square and triangle.

***Ex* 26** Which number represents the uneducated women, who have government jobs as well as jobs in private sectors?

(a) 6 (b) 4
(c) 12 (d) 9

Solution (d) Number 9 represents uneducated women who have government jobs as well as jobs in private sectors because it lies in the area which is common to square, triangle and rectangle.

***Ex* 27** Number 10 represents

(a) educated women in private jobs.
(b) uneducated men in government jobs.
(c) educated men working in private sectors.
(d) educated men having private as well as Government jobs.

Solution (d) Number 10 represents educated men having private jobs as well as government jobs because it lies in the area which is common to circle, triangle and rectangle .

***Ex* 28** Number 2 represents

(a) educated women who neither have government jobs nor have a private job.
(b) uneducated women with no jobs.
(c) educated men with government jobs.
(d) uneducated men with government jobs.

Solution (a) Number 2 represents educated women who neither have government job nor have private job because it lies in the area which is common to square and circle.

Practice CORNER 19.2

DIRECTIONS ~ (Q. Nos. 1-3) *Study the following diagram to answer these questions.*

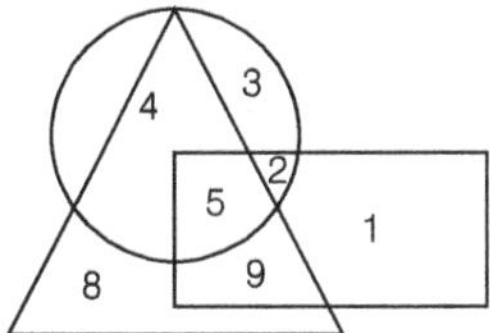

1. Find out the number that lies only inside the triangle.
(a) 4 (b) 3 (c) 8 (d) 1

2. What are the numbers that lie inside any two figures?
(a) 5, 1 (b) 4, 3, 1 (c) 8, 3 (d) 4, 9, 2

3. Find out the number that lies inside all the figures.
(a) 5 (b) 8 (c) 9 (d) 2

4. See the following diagram carefully to answer the question that follows

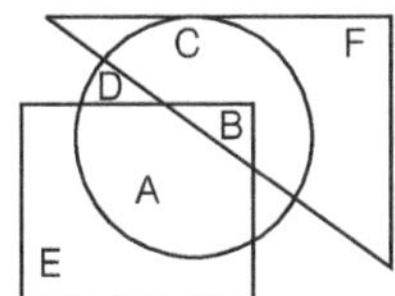

Which of the following statements is correct according to the diagram given above? « SSC LDC 2008

(a) A and B lie in all the three figures.
(b) E, A, B and C lie in all the three figures.
(c) F, C, D, B and A lie in all the three figures.
(d) Only B lies in all the three figures.

5. In the given Venn diagram, the 'circle' represents 'ladies,' the 'triangle' represents 'teachers' and the 'rectangle' represents 'unmarried persons.' The numbers given in the diagram represent the number of persons in that particular category. « SSC CGL 2020

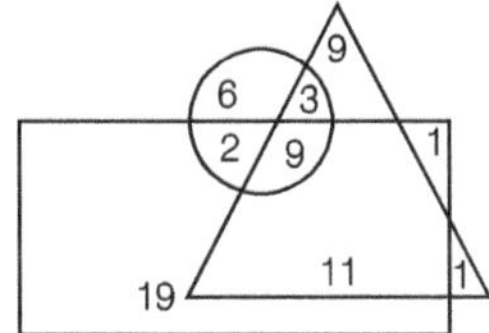

How many married ladies are teachers?
(a) 6 (b) 3 (c) 9 (d) 11

6. Identify the region that represents students who study Biology and Computer but not Mathematics.
« SSC CGL 2014

Mathematics students 1 4 2 Biology students
5
6 7
3 Computer students

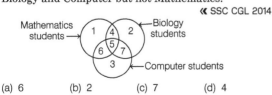

(a) 6 (b) 2 (c) 7 (d) 4

DIRECTIONS ~ (Q. Nos. 7-11) *Each of the following questions is based on the diagram given below. Study the diagram carefully and answer the questions.*
« LIC ADO 2010

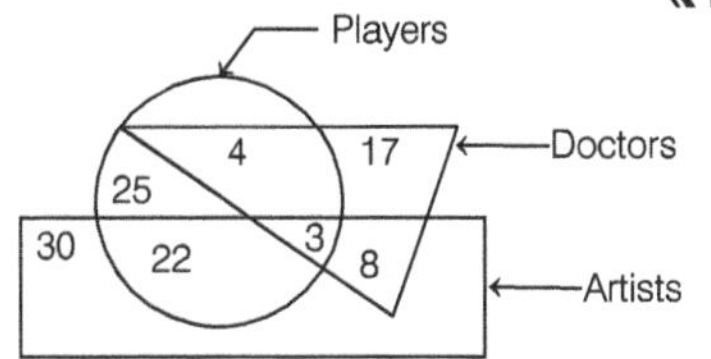

In the above diagram, rectangle represents 'artists', circle represents 'players' and triangle represents 'doctors'.

7. How many players are neither artists nor doctors?
(a) 25 (b) 22 (c) 4 (d) 29
(e) None of these

8. How many artists are players?
(a) 22 (b) 3 (c) 25 (d) 8
(e) None of these

9. How many artists are neither doctors nor players?
(a) 22 (b) 8 (c) 25 (d) 30
(e) None of these

10. How many doctors are neither players nor artists?
(a) 4 (b) 25 (c) 8 (d) 17
(e) None of these

11. How many doctors are players and artists both?
(a) 4 (b) 7 (c) 3 (d) 8
(e) None of these

12. Given below are three figures which represent Graduates, Post-graduates, Officers. Which part represents all the officers who are graduates and post-graduates? « SSC MTS 2013

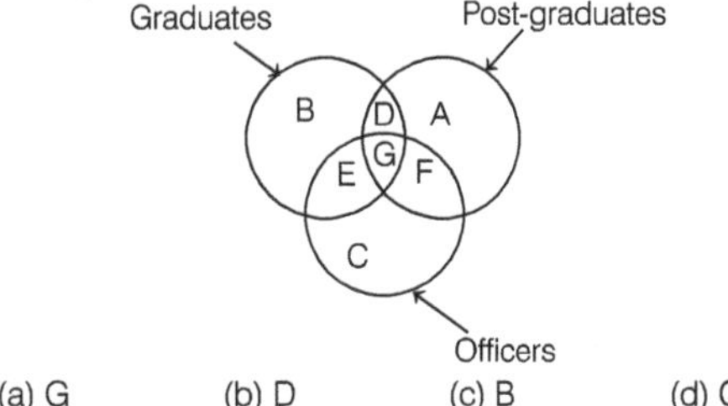

(a) G (b) D (c) B (d) C

13.

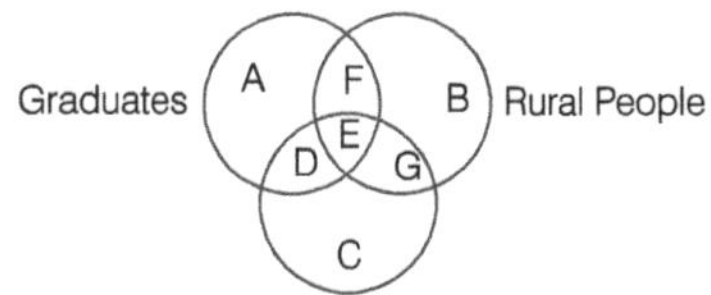

« CG Revenue Inspector 2017

The politicians, who are not graduate and not from rural area, will be represented by
(a) F (b) E (c) G (d) C

14. In the following diagram, identify the region that represents appointed educated persons whose job is not permanent.

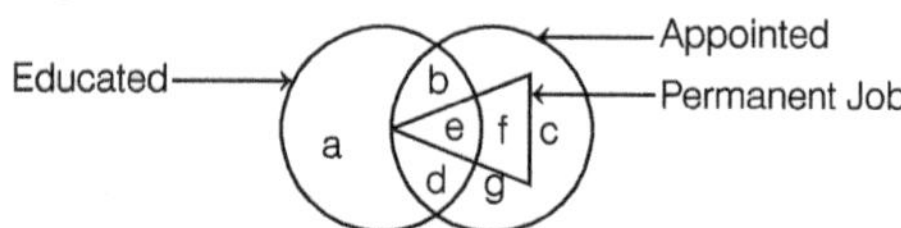

(a) b and g (b) a and d (c) a and c (d) b and d

15. Study the following figure and give the answer of the question : If rectangle represents artists, the circle represents players and the triangle represents doctors.

« CG Patwari 2017

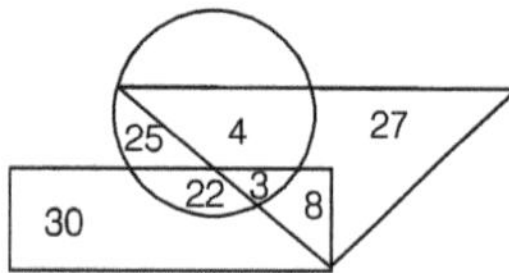

How many players are neither artists nor doctors?

(a) 3 (b) 4 (c) 22 (d) 25

16. In the following figure, square represents lawyers, triangle represents cyclists, circle represents men and rectangle represents post-graduates. Which set of letters represents men who are not cyclists?
« SSC CGL 2017

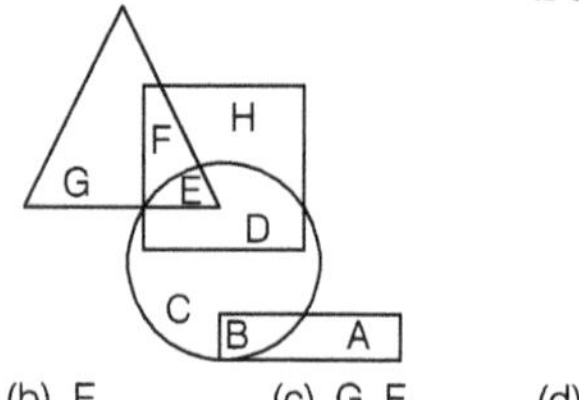

(a) B, C, D (b) E (c) G, F (d) G, F, H, A

DIRECTIONS ~ (Q. Nos. 17-19) *Read the following information and then answer the questions that follow. In the figure the rectangle stands for philosophers, circle for historians and triangle for magicians.*

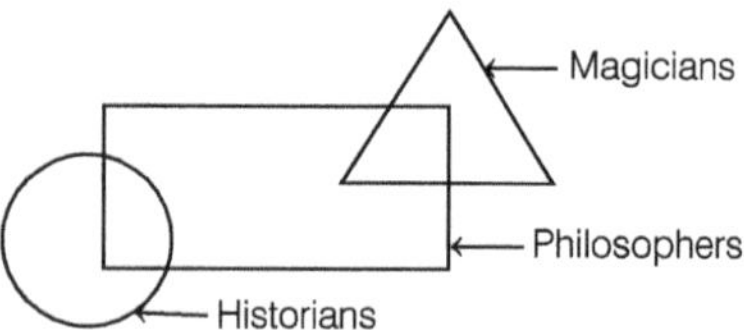

17. According to the given diagram, which one of the following statements is true?

(a) All philosophers are magicians but no magician is a historian.
(b) All magicians are either historians or philosophers.
(c) Some philosophers are historians and some magicians are philosophers.
(d) Some historians, who are philosophers, are magicians too.

18. According to the given diagram, which one of the following statements is true?

(a) All historians are magicians.
(b) Some magicians are philosophers as well as historians.
(c) All historians are either philosophers or magicians.
(d) Some historians are philosophers.

19. According to the given diagram, which one of the following statements is not true?

(a) Some magicians are philosophers.
(b) No magician is historian.
(c) Magicians, who are philosophers are historians also.
(d) Some philosophers are magicians.

20. In the following diagram, the triangle represents doctors, the circle represents players and the rectangle represents singers. Which region represents doctors who are singers but not players?

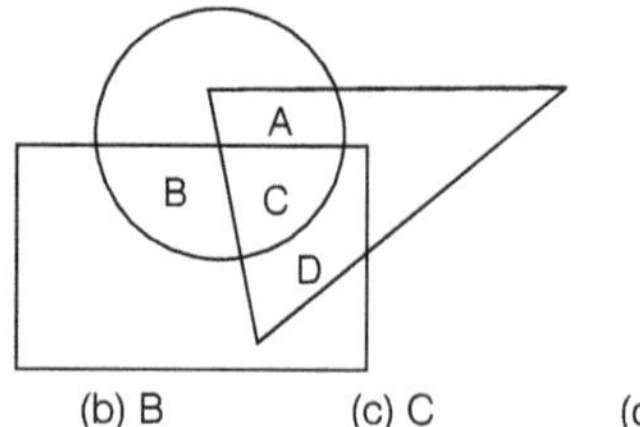

(a) A (b) B (c) C (d) D

21. The diagram below represents the students who study Physics, Chemistry and Mathematics.

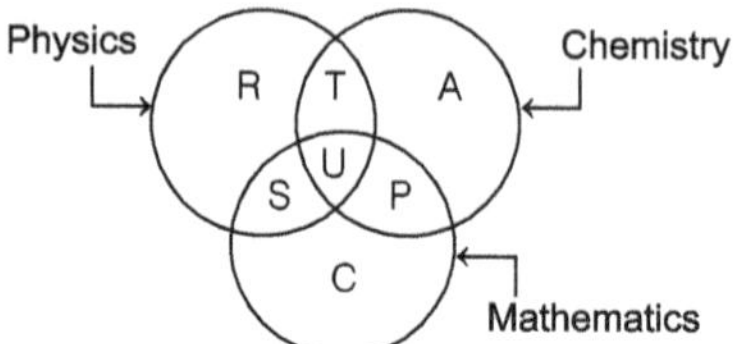

Study the diagram and identify the region which represents students who study both Physics and Chemistry but not Mathematics.

(a) T + S + U + P (b) C
(c) R + T + A + U + P + S (d) T

22. In the following figure, square represents Chinese, triangle represents dancers, circle represents male and rectangle represents architects. Which set of letters represents dancers who are male? « RRB ALP 2019

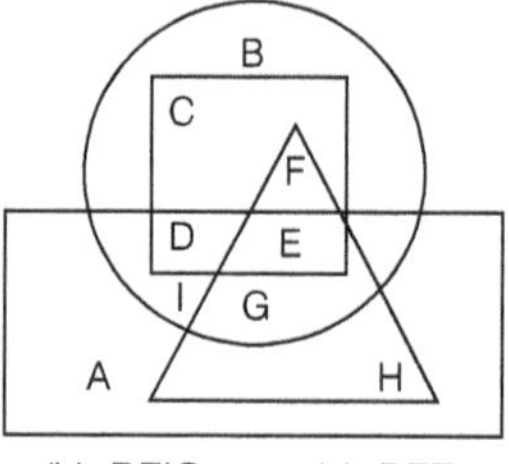

(a) IGH (b) DEIG (c) DEF (d) GEF

23. Which one of the areas marked I-VII represents the urban educated who are not hardworking?

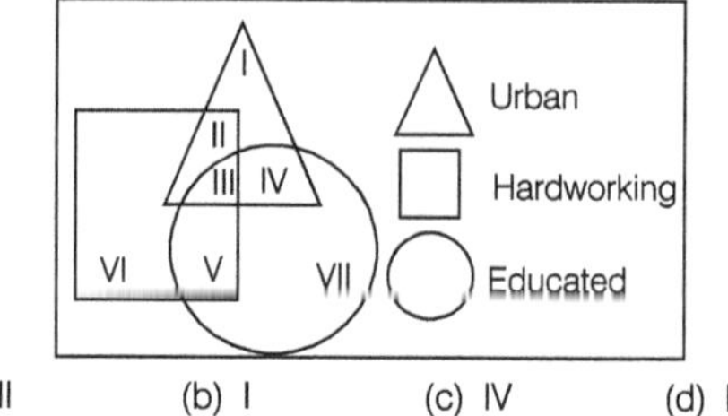

(a) II (b) I (c) IV (d) III

24. In the following figure, the triangle represents actors, the square represents professors, the circle represents Indians and the rectangle represents fathers. Which set of letters represents Indians who are either professors or fathers? « RRB ALP 2018

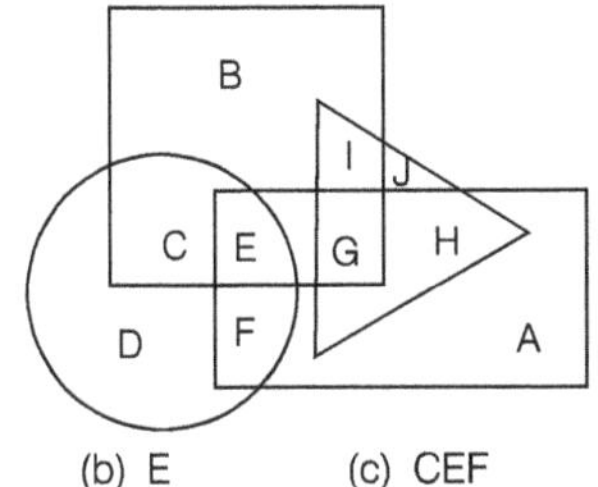

(a) IGH (b) E (c) CEF (d) G

DIRECTIONS ~ (Q. Nos. 25 and 26) *Consider the following figure and answer the questions.* « CMAT 2016

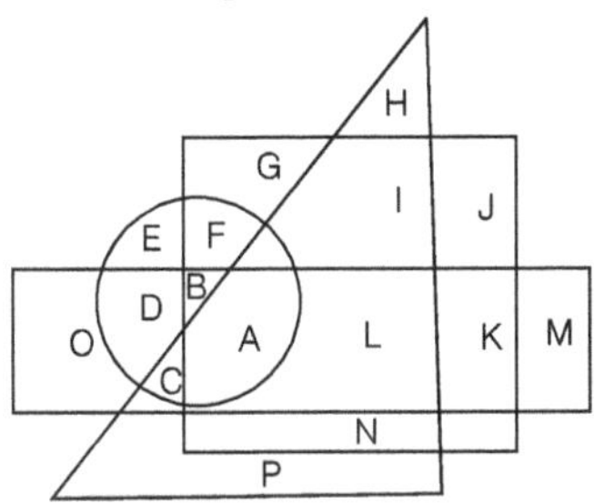

Rectangle indicates faculty members, square indicates research scholars, circle indicates Indians and triangle indicates Americans.

25. In the given figure show the area which indicates faculty members who are research scholars but are neither Indians nor Americans?

(a) L (b) N (c) K (d) G

26. In the given figure show the area which indicates Indian Americans who are faculty members but not research scholars?

(a) A (b) B (c) C (d) F

DIRECTIONS ~ (Q. Nos. 27 and 28) *Consider the following Venn diagram and answer the questions that follow.* « NIFT UG 2012

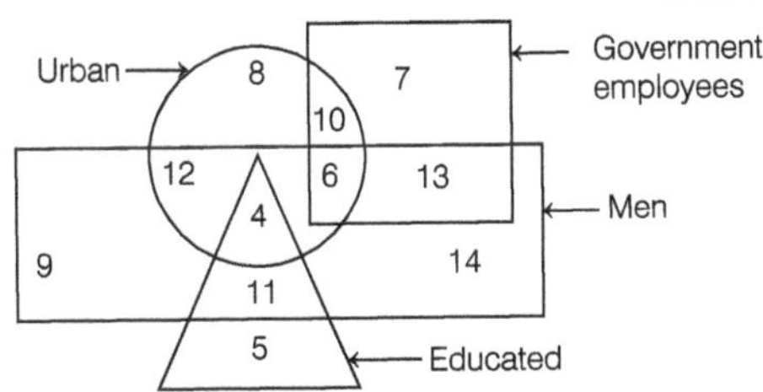

27. In the following diagram, which of the following represents the educated men but not urban?

(a) 9 (b) 5 (c) 4 (d) 11

28. In the following diagram, which of the following represents a man who is urban as well as a government employee?

(a) 7 (b) 13 (c) 10 (d) 6

DIRECTIONS ~ (Q. Nos. 29-31) *These are based on the diagram given below. Answer these questions.* « CGPSC 2017

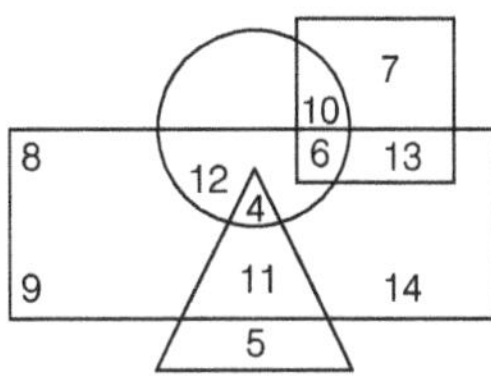

- Rectangle represents males;
- Triangle represents educated;
- Circle represents urban;
- Square represents civil servants.

29. How many among the following is an educated male who are not the urban resident?

(a) 11 (b) 9 (c) 5 (d) 4
(e) None of these

30. How many among the following is a female, urban resident and also a civil servant?

(a) 6 (b) 7 (c) 10 (d) 13
(e) None of these

31. How many among the following is uneducated and also an urban male?

(a) 18 (b) 11 (c) 3 (d) 2
(e) 12

32. In the given diagram, Set U is the universal set and Set L, M and N represent students studying History, Geography and Language, respectively. What is the total number of students studying History and Geography but not Language? « RRB ALP 2018

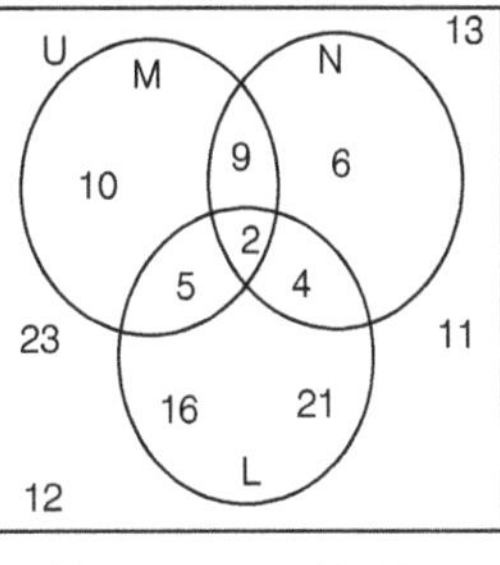

(a) 5 (b) 2 (c) 12 (d) 7

33. In the following diagram, triangle, square and circle shown represent urban, hardworking and educated people respectively. Which of these areas represents people who are urban and educated, but not hardworking? « FCI Uttarakhand Watchman 2018

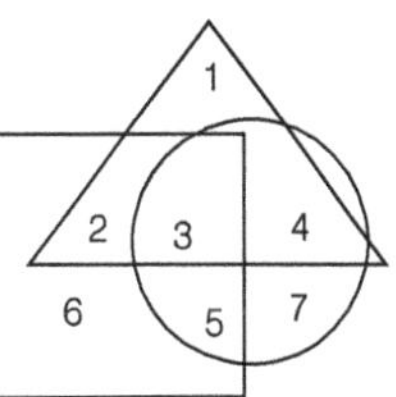

(a) 4 (b) 7 (c) 5 (d) 7

34. Study the following figure and give the answer of the question : If rectangle represents artists, the circle represents players and the triangle represents doctors.
« CG Patwari 2017

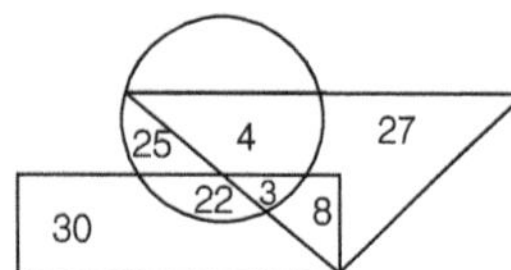

How many doctors are neither players nor artists?
(a) 30 (b) 22 (c) 27 (d) 8

DIRECTIONS ~ (Q. Nos. 35-38) *In the following figure, the smaller triangle represents the teachers, the big triangle represents the politicians, the circle represents the graduates and the square represents the members of parliament. Different regions are being represented by letters of English alphabet.*

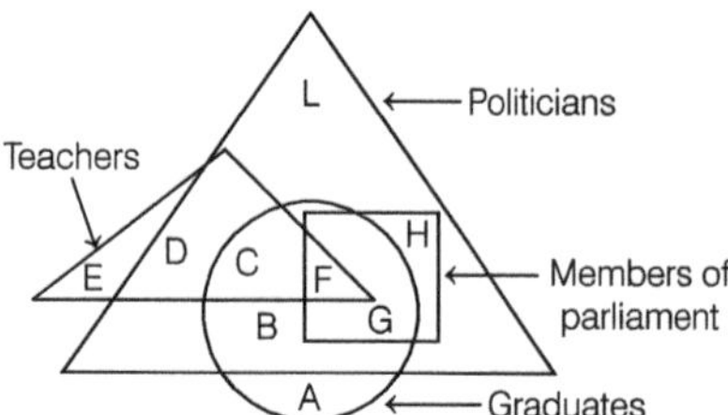

35. Who among the following are either graduates or teachers but not politicians?
(a) B, G (b) G, H (c) A, E (d) E, F

36. Who among the following politicians are graduates but not the members of parliament?
(a) B, C (b) L, B (c) D, L (d) A, H, L

37. Who among the following politicians are neither teachers nor graduates?
(a) E, F (b) D, E (c) C, D (d) L, H

38. Who among the following members of parliament is a graduate as well as a teacher?
(a) G (b) F (c) C (d) H

DIRECTIONS ~ (Q. Nos. 39-41) *Following questions are based on the given diagram. Study the diagram carefully to answer the questions. In the diagram, rectangle represents males, triangles represents educated, square represents public servants and circle represents urban.*

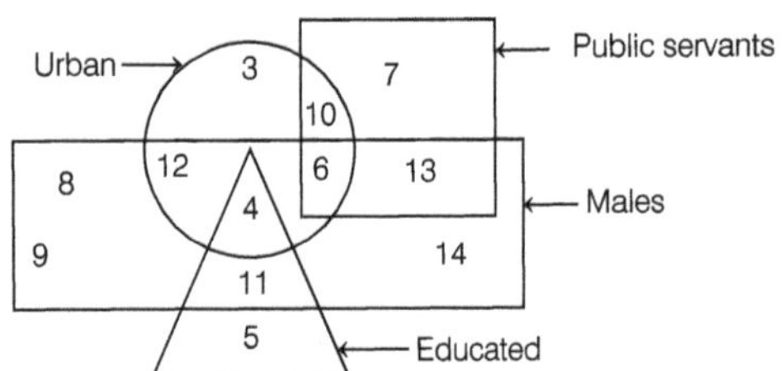

39. Out of the following options, how many educated males are not urban?
(a) 10 (b) 4
(c) 11 (d) 9

40. Out of the following options, how many persons are urban who are neither public servants nor educated or males?
(a) 3 (b) 5
(c) 6 (d) 10

41. Out of the following options, how many persons are related to educated males and urban region?
(a) 4 (b) 2
(c) 5 (d) 11

DIRECTIONS ~ (Q. Nos. 42-46) *Each of the questions below is based on the information given below. Four different sections have been projected with the help of four different figures.*

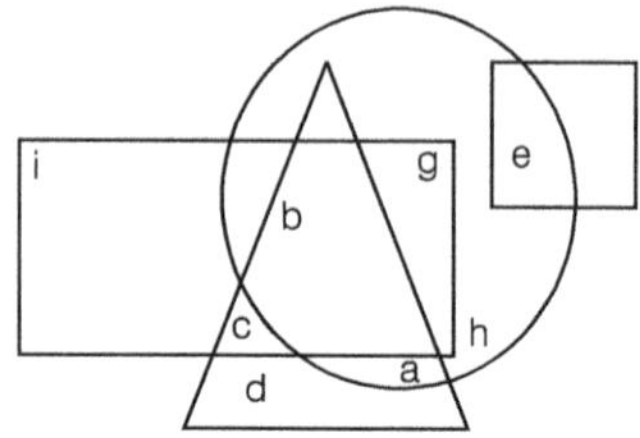

Rectangle represents female members, circle represents employees, triangle represents businessman and square represents post graduates. Based on this information, answer the questions given below.

42. Which of the following group of employees represents those employees, who are not businessmen?
(a) e, g, h (b) a, g, h
(c) b, g, e (d) a, e, g, h

43. Which of the following group represents the section, comprising persons who are either employees or businessmen but not female members?
(a) a, b, d (b) a, e, h
(c) a, g, h (d) a, d, e, h

44. Who among the following are female members as well as businessmen?
(a) a, h (b) b, g
(c) b, c (d) b, h

45. Who among the following are businessmen but are neither post graduates nor employees?
(a) b, d, g (b) a, d, h
(c) c, d (d) b, e

46. Who among the following are the female members but neither businessmen nor employees?
(a) i, g (b) b, c, i, g
(c) b, i, e (d) i

47. Question are based on the following figure. Various letters represent various types of persons. « MP SI 2017

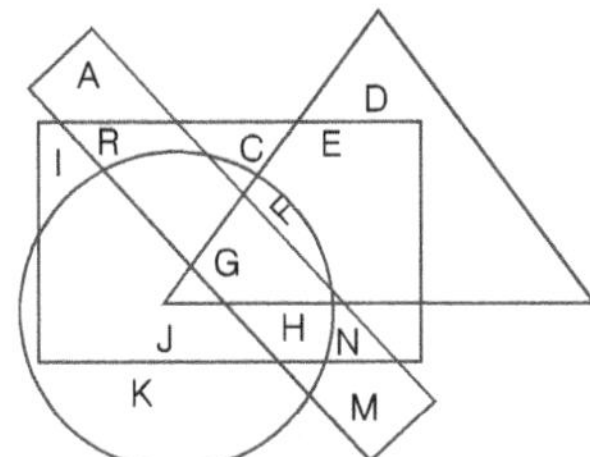

Square	-	Clerk	Triangle	-	Bachelor
Rectangle	-	Player	Circle	-	Male

The bachelor clerk who is a male player is represented by the letter

(a) G only (b) G and F (c) H only (d) I only

48. In the given figure, circle represents persons having car, triangle represents persons having motorcycle, square represents persons having autorickshaw, rectangle represents persons having cycle.

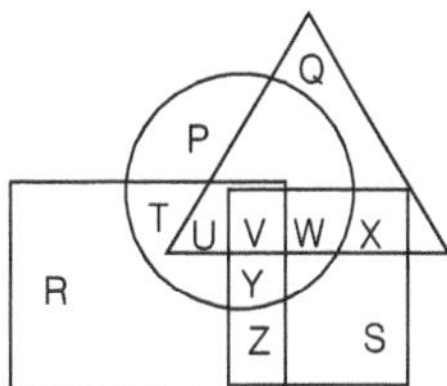

Find the region, which represents persons having car, motorcycle, cycle but no autorickshaw. « SSC CGL 2013

(a) X (b) U
(c) V (d) W

Answers / WITH EXPLANATIONS

1. (*c*) According to the diagram, number 8 lies only inside the triangle.

2. (*d*) Number common to circle and triangle = 4
Number common to rectangle and triangle = 9
Number common to circle and rectangle = 2

3. (*a*) According to the diagram, Common number that lies inside all figures = 5

4. (*d*) Statement given in option (d) is correct because only B is common in all three figures.

5. (*b*) Since, number 3 is common between circle and triangle, hence 3 married ladies are teachers.

6. (*c*) The region which represents students who study Biology and Computer but not Mathematics is '7'.

7. (*a*) There are 25 players who are neither artists nor doctors because this is the only region of the circle which is not common with either rectangle or triangle.

8. (*c*) Required number = 22 + 3 = 25

9. (*d*) There are 30 artists who are neither doctors nor players because this is the only region of the rectangle which is not common with either circle or triangle.

10. (*d*) There are 17 doctors who are neither players nor artists because this is the only region of the triangle which is not common with either circle or rectangle.

11. (*c*) The region 3 is common to triangle, circle and rectangle and hence, represents doctors who are players as well as artists.

12. (*a*) The part of figure representing officers, who are graduates and post-graduates is common to all three circles *i.e.*, G.

13. (*d*) Portion C represents the politicians who are not graduate and not from rural area.

14. (*d*) According to the diagram, regions b and d represent appointed educated persons whose job is not permanent.

15. (*d*) Players are represented by circle, artists are represented by rectangle, doctors are represented by triangle. So, players which are neither artists nor doctors are 25 in numbers, because 25 is not common to either rectangle or triangle.

16. (*a*) Set of letters B, C and D represents men who are not cyclists.

17. (*c*) Statement (c) is true because some portion of rectangle is common to both the triangle and the circle.

18. (*d*) The circle and the rectangle have some area in common which indicates that some historians are philosophers.

19. (*c*) Because no portion of the figure shows the common space among the three figures.

20. (*d*) Letter D represents those people who are doctors and singers but not players as it is common to triangle and rectangle but not circle.

21. (*d*) Region 'T' represents the students who study both Physics and Chemistry but not Mathematics.

22. (*d*) GEF represents dancers who are male.

23. (*c*) Area IV represents the urban educated who are not hardworking.

24. (*c*) CEF represents Indians who are either professors or fathers.

25. (*c*) In the given figure, the area K indicates faculty members who are research scholars but are neither Indians nor Americans.

26. (*c*) In the given figure, the area C indicates Indian-American who are faculty members but not research scholars.

27. (*d*) Educated men who are not urban are represented by the region which is common to both the triangle and the rectangle but not to the square and circle. So, the required region is 11.

28. (*d*) A man who is urban as well as a governments employee is common to the circle , square and rectangle but not to the triangle. So, the required region is 6.

29. (*a*) 11 educated males are at present not the urban resident.

30. (*c*) 10 females are urban resident and also a civil servant.

31. (*a*) 18 persons are uneducated and also an urban male.

32. (*a*) Number of students who study only History and Geography but not language, is represented by region which is common to L and M only, i.e. 5.

33. (*a*) In the given diagram, number 4 represents the person who are urban and educated but not hardworking.

34. (*c*) Triangle represents doctors, circle represents player, rectangle represents artists.

So, 27 is the number of doctors which are not common to either circle or triangle.

So, 27 is the number of doctors who are neither players nor artists.

35. (*c*) A and E are either graduates or teachers but not politicians because A and E do not fall under the big triangular space.

36. (*a*) B and C are graduate politicians but not the members of parliament because B and C do not fall under the square.

37. (*d*) L and H are the politicians who are neither teachers nor graduates because L and H do not fall under small triangular space and circular space.

38. (*b*) F is the member of parliament who is a graduate as well as a teacher because F is common to circle, square and the small triangle.

39. (*c*) Only 11 persons are educated males but not urban.

40. (*a*) Only 3 persons are urban, who are neither public servents nor educated or males.

41. (*a*) Only 4 educated males are there who belong to urban region.

42. (*a*) The group of employees e, g and h represents those employees who are not businessmen.

43. (*d*) The group of employees a, d, e and h represents persons who are either employees or businessmen but not female members.

44. (*c*) Letters b and c represents female members as well as businessmen.

45. (*c*) Letters c and d are businessmen but are neither post graduates nor employees.

46. (*d*) Only i represents the female members who are neither businessman nor employees.

47. (*a*) The bachelor clerk who is a male player is represented by letter G only.

48. (*b*) Letter U represents persons having car, motorcycle, cycle but no autorickshaw.

Master Exercise

1. Which of the following figures give the proper relation to Fruit, Red and Shirt? « SSC steno 2016

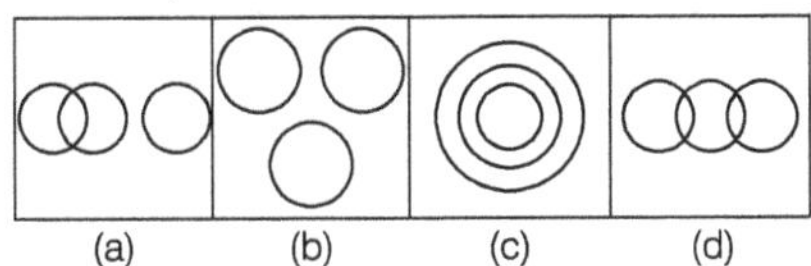

2. Which of the following diagrams represents India, Lucknow, USA? « NIFT UG 2013

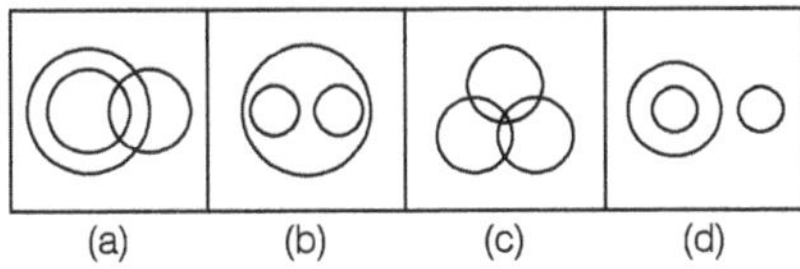

DIRECTIONS ~ (Q. Nos. 3-5) *Choose the Venn diagram that best illustrates the relationship among the three classes given below* « UP Police Constable 2018

3. Birds, Fish, Chicken.

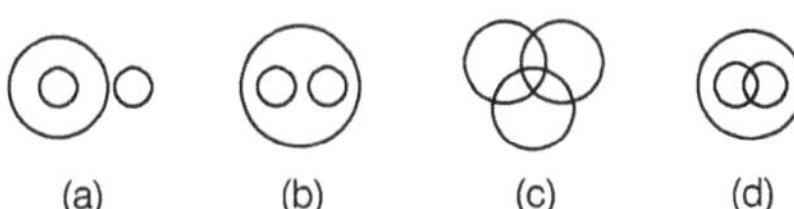

4. Sports, Football, Lizard.

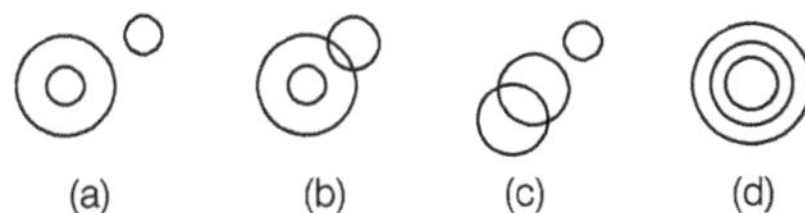

5. Pen, Pencil, Paper.

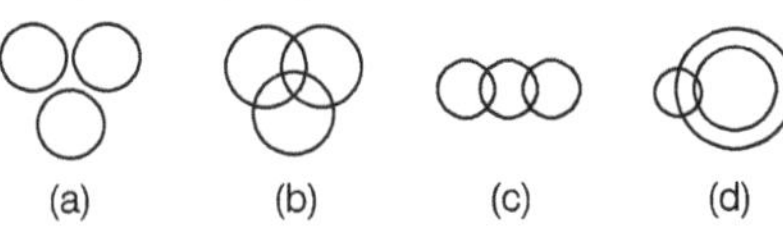

6. Which of the following diagrams represents the relationship among Library, Book, Pages? « UP Police SI 2018

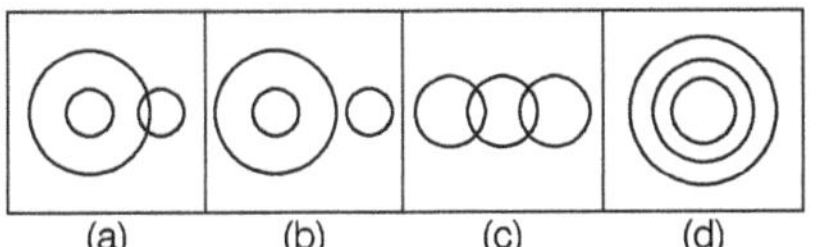

7. Which of the following diagrams correctly represents the relationship amongst Tiger, Elephant, Animal? « SSC CPO 2013

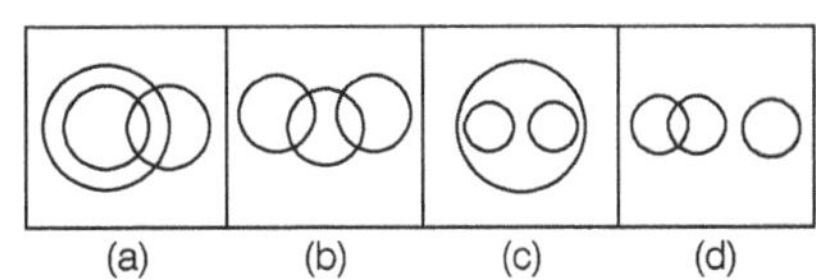

8. Select the Venn diagram that best illustrates the relationship between the following classes.
Parents, Rich persons, Farmers « SSC CGL 2019

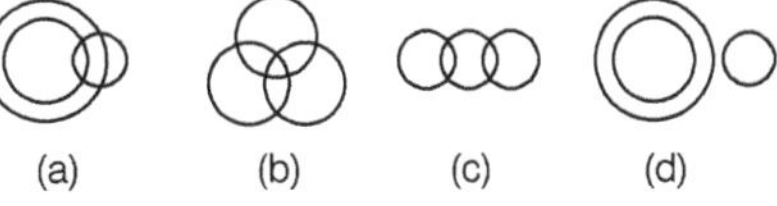

DIRECTIONS ~ (Q. Nos. 9-13) *Each of the questions given below has three items having certain relationship among them. The same relationship is expressed by sets of circles, each circle representing one item irrespective of its size. Match the items with right set of circles.*

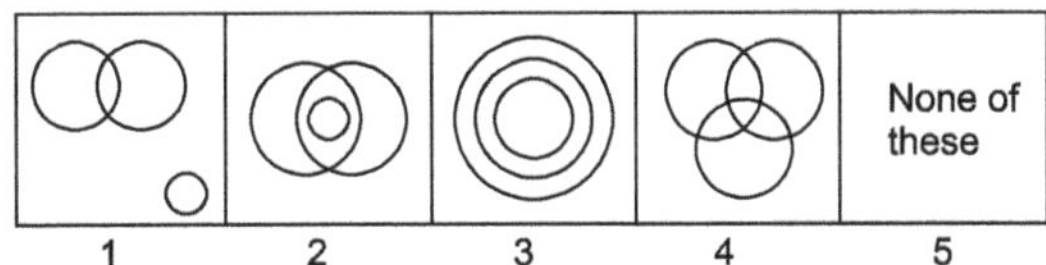

9. Rivers, Canals, Perennial source of water
(a) 1 (b) 2 (c) 3 (d) 5

10. Rings, Ornaments, Diamond rings
(a) 3 (b) 2 (c) 1 (d) 4

11. Women, Married persons, Wives who work
(a) 1 (b) 3 (c) 4 (d) 2

12. Computer skilled, Graduates, Employed
(a) 1 (b) 4 (c) 2 (d) 5

13. Students, First divisioners, Third divisioners
(a) 2 (b) 3 (c) 4 (d) 5

14. Which of the following diagrams represents Granite, Tree and Water? « CG PSC 2013

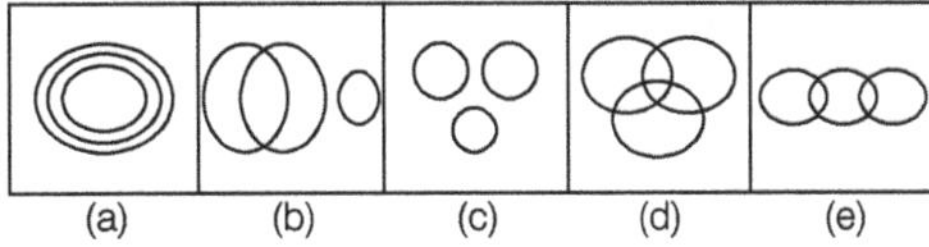

15. Choose the diagram in which the following groups of elements fit correctly
House, Brick and Bridge « CG Patwari 2017

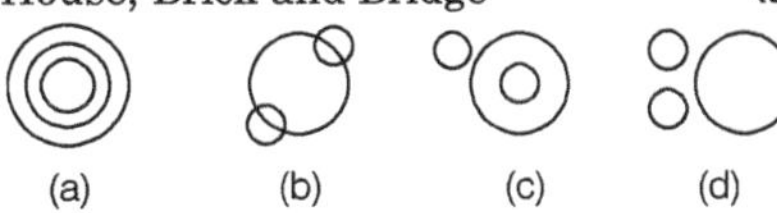

16. Which of the following combinations of circles best represents Athletes, Sprinters and Marathon runners? « NIFT (PG) 2013

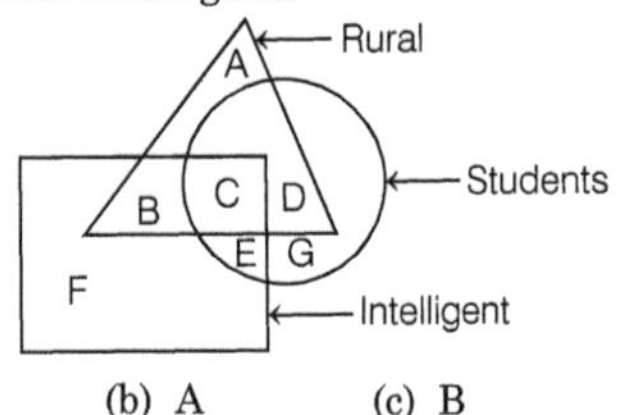

17. Find the region that represents those rural students who are not intelligent. « UP B.Ed. 2010

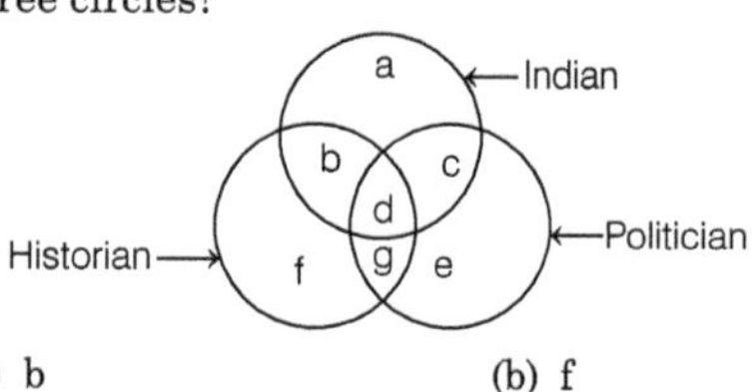

(a) D (b) A (c) B (d) G

18. Point out the letter which represents Indians and Historians, but not politicians on the basis of these three circles? WBSC 2018

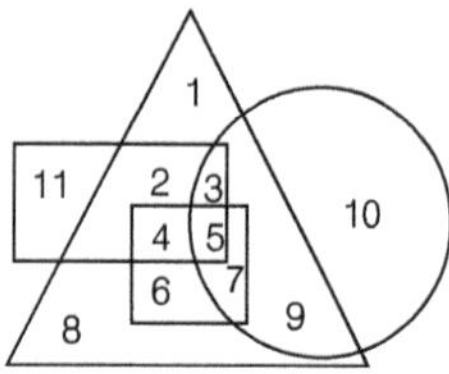

(a) b (b) f
(c) b and f (d) b and g

19. In the given diagram, circle represents professionals, square represents dancers, triangle represents musicians and rectangle represents Europeans. Different regions in the diagram are numbered 1 to 11.

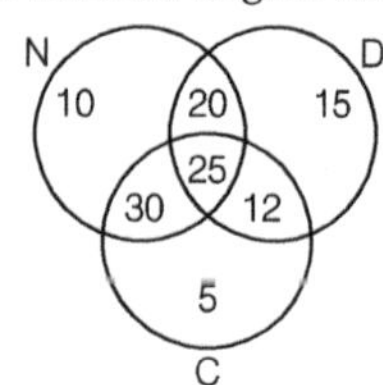

Who among the following is neither a dancer nor a musician but is professional and not a European? SSC CGL 2013

(a) 8 (b) 11 (c) 1 (d) 10

20. In the diagram given below, N represents non-degree holders, D represents degree holders and C represents the computer programmers. Among these, which number indicates the programmers, who are neither degree holders nor non-degree holders?

(a) 30 (b) 5 (c) 25 (d) 12

21. How many educated people are employed? « SSC (10+2) 2012

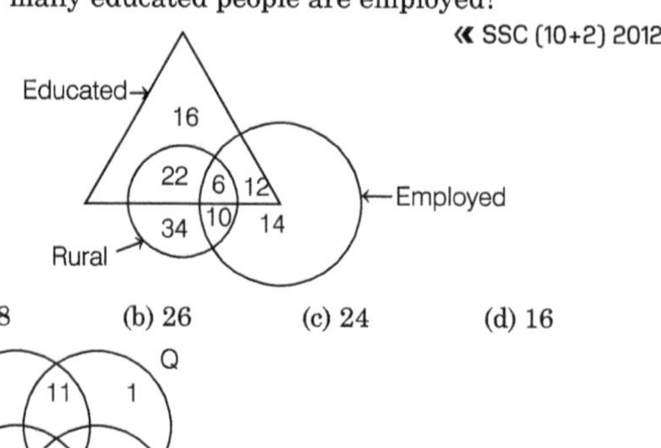

(a) 18 (b) 26 (c) 24 (d) 16

22.

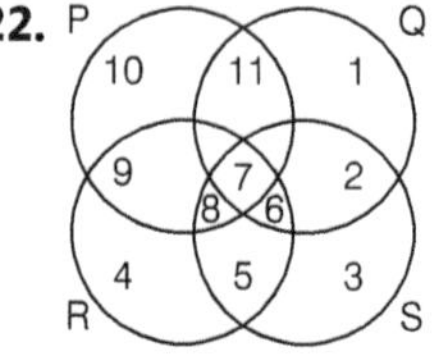

In the above diagram, circle P represents hardworking people, circle Q represents intelligent people, circle R represents truthful people and circle S represents honest people. Which region represents the people who are intelligent, honest and truthful but not hardworking? « UPSC CSAT 2012

(a) 6 (b) 7 (c) 8 (d) 11

23. Identify the diagram that best represents the relationship among classes given below « SSC (10+2) 2013

Mammal, Dog, Bat

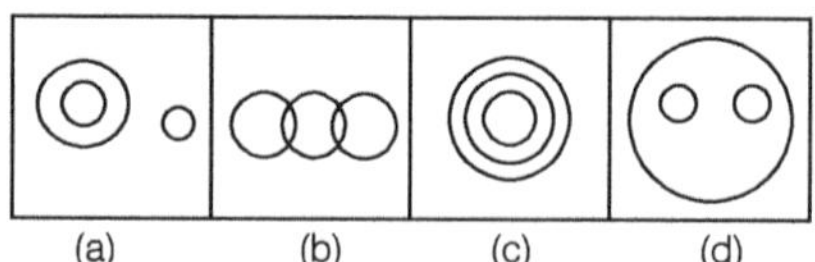

24. The given Venn diagram shows the number of students who have passed in the three exams, viz. English, Science and Maths. How many students passed in all the three exams? « RRB ALP 2018

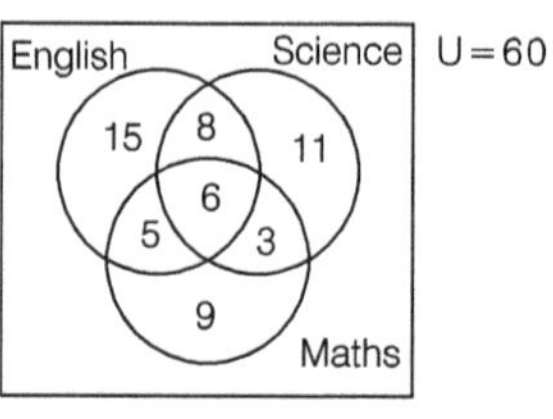

(a) 6 (b) 12 (c) 9 (d) 3

25. Read the following diagram and find the region representing persons who are educated and employed but not confirmed. « SSC CGL 2013

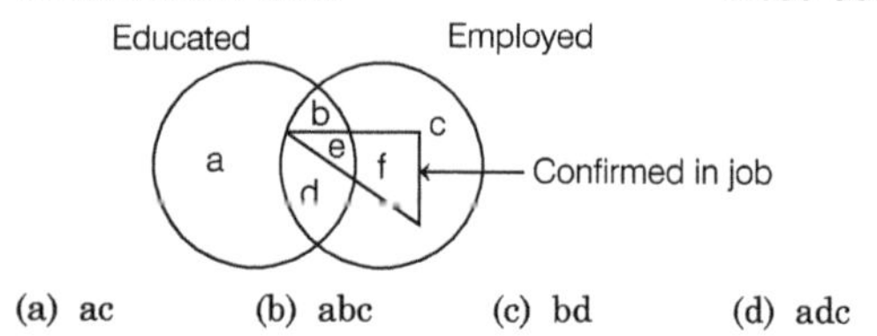

(a) ac (b) abc (c) bd (d) adc

26. In a class of 46 students, 18 played football, 17 played cricket including 6 who played football. 16 students played hockey including 4 who played cricket but not football. Five students played carrom but no out door games. Which of the following diagrams represents these facts?

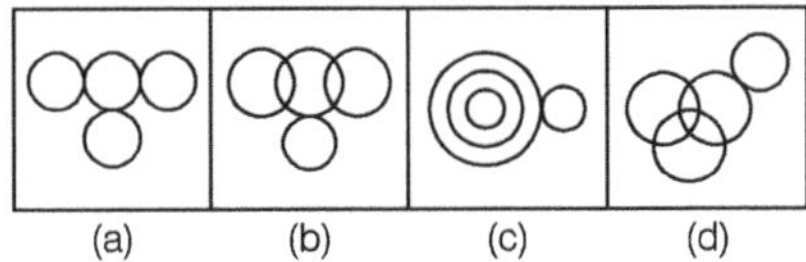

27. In the following diagram, square represents the area where jackfruit trees are grown, circle represents mango trees and triangle represents coconut trees.

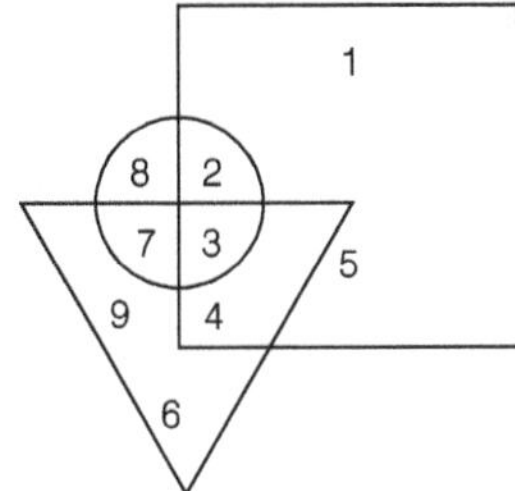

Which numbers represent the area where all types of trees are grown? « SSC CPO 2012

(a) 4 (b) 3 (c) 5 (d) 8

28. In the following figure, square represents Priests, triangle represents Singers, circle represents Therapists and rectangle represents Indians.

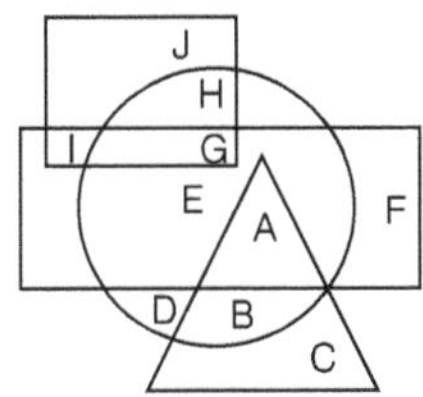

Which set of letters represents Indians who are not priests? « SSC CGL 2017

(a) E, F (b) I, G
(c) E, A, F (d) G, E, A

29. Study the following diagram and answer the question given below « SSC CPO 2013

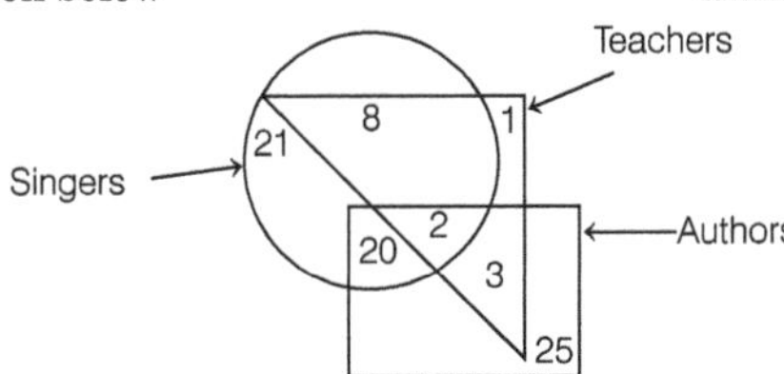

How many teachers are neither authors nor singers?

(a) 1 (b) 8 (c) 2 (d) 3

30. Study the below diagram and identify the option that is not correct. « UPSSSC Combined Lower Subordinate 2019

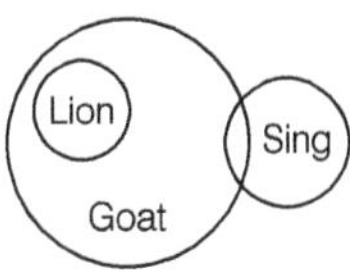

(a) Some lions are not goats. (b) Some goats are lions.
(c) Lions are not singers. (d) Some goats can sing.

DIRECTIONS ~ (Q. Nos. 31-35) *Study the diagram given below and answer the questions that follow.*

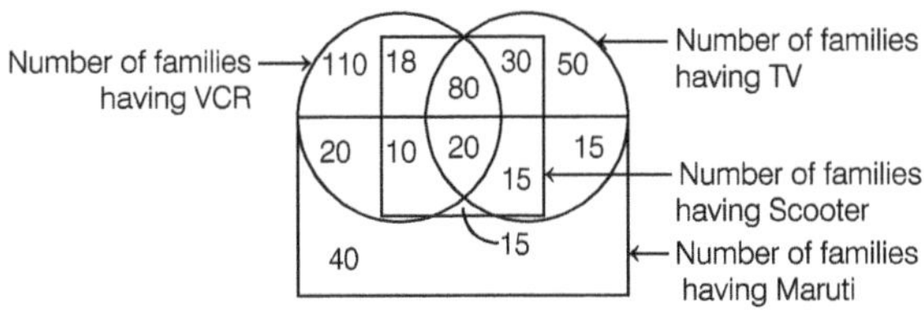

31. Find out the number of families which have all the four things mentioned in the diagram above.

(a) 40 (b) 30 (c) 35 (d) 20

32. Find out the number of families which have scooters.

(a) 145 (b) 100
(c) 188 (d) 240

33. Find out the number of families which have VCR and TV both.

(a) 84 (b) 24
(c) 104 (d) None of these

34. Find out the number of families which have only one thing, *i.e.*, either VCR or TV or scooter or maruti.

(a) 160 (b) 184
(c) 200 (d) 254

35. Find out the number of families which have TV and scooter both but have neither VCR nor maruti.

(a) 15 (b) 30 (c) 4 (d) 50

36. In the following diagram, Police Officer represents circle, Corrupt represents triangle, Poet represents square and Married represents rectangle. « SSC MTS 2013

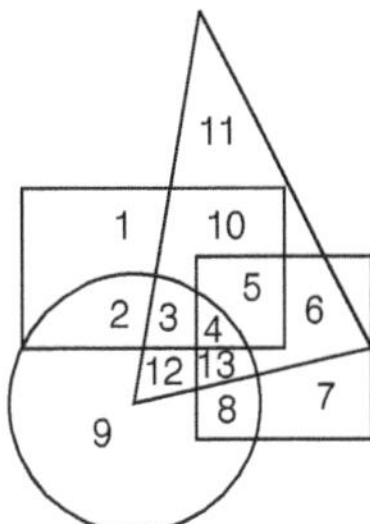

The area representing unmarried Police Officers who are not Corrupt but are Poets is

(a) 8 (b) 9 (c) 2 (d) 4

DIRECTIONS ~ (Q. Nos. 37-41) *In the following questions, answers are based on the diagram given below, where the triangle represents doctors, the circle represents players and the rectangle represents the artists.*

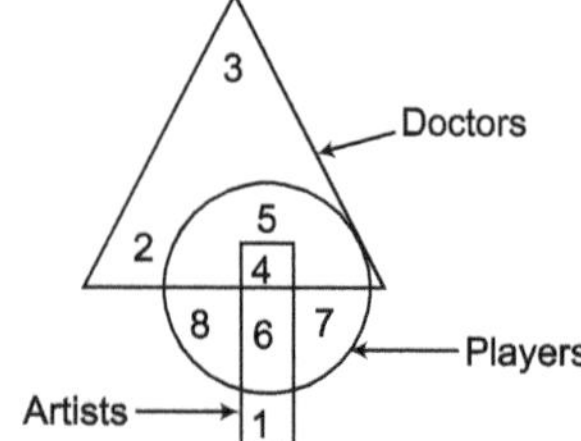

37. Which numbered space in the diagram represents doctors, who are also players and artists?

(a) 2 (b) 3
(c) 4 (d) 5

38. Which numbered space in diagram represents artists, who are players but not doctors?

(a) 6 (b) 7
(c) 8 (d) 4

39. Which numbered space in the diagram represents artists, who are neither players nor doctors?

(a) 1 (b) 2
(c) 3 (d) 4

40. Which numbered space in the diagram represents players, who are neither artists nor doctors?

(a) 1, 2 (b) 3, 4
(c) 6, 7 (d) 7, 8

41. Which numbered space in the diagram represents doctors, who are players but not artists?

(a) 2 (b) 3
(c) 4 (d) 5

DIRECTIONS ~ (Q. Nos. 42 and 43) *Study the following diagram carefully and answer the questions based on it.*

« SSC CGL 2013

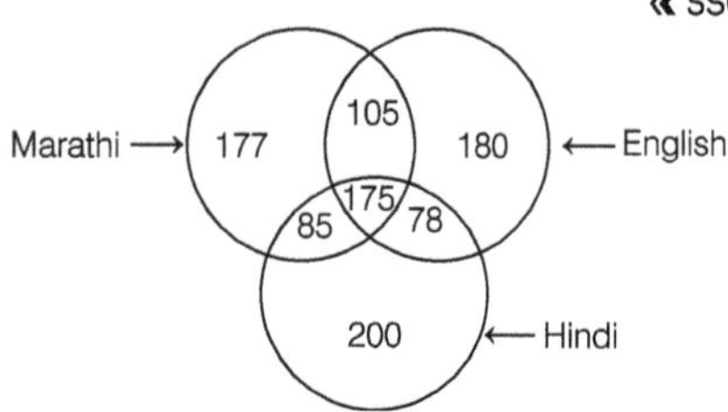

42. The diagram shows the survey on a sample of 1000 persons with reference to their knowledge of English, Hindi and Marathi. How many persons know all the languages?

(a) 78 (b) 175
(c) 105 (d) 85

43. The diagram shows the survey on a sample of 1000 persons with reference to their knowledge of English, Hindi and Marathi. 105 people know ... languages.

(a) Marathi, Hindi (b) English, Hindi
(c) Marathi, English (d) Hindi, Marathi, English

DIRECTIONS ~ (Q. Nos. 44-47) *In the following questions, answers are based on the diagram given below*

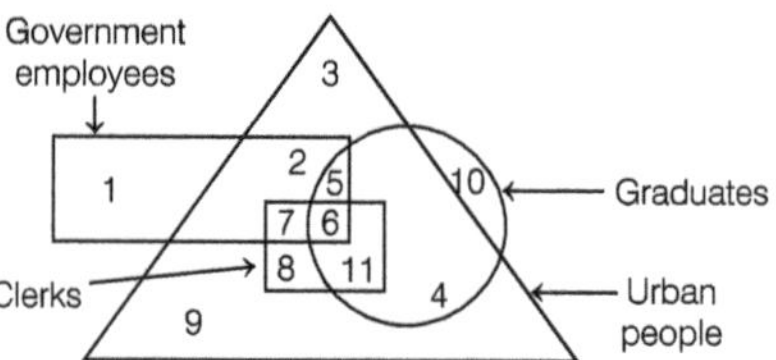

I. The rectangle represents government employees.
II. The triangle represents urban people.
III. The circle represents graduates.
IV. The square represents clerks.

44. Which of the following statements is true?

(a) All government employees are clerks.
(b) Some government employees are graduates as well as clerks.
(c) All government employees are graduates.
(d) All clerks are governments employees but not graduates.

45. Choose the correct statement

(a) Some clerks are government employees.
(b) No clerk is from urban areas.
(c) All graduates are from urban areas.
(d) All graduates are government employees.

46. Which of the following numbers represents urban government employees, who are graduate but not clerk?

(a) 9 (b) 4 (c) 10 (d) 5

47. Which number represents clerks, who are government employees but are neither graduates nor live in urban areas?

(a) 4 (b) 2 (c) 9 (d) None of these

DIRECTIONS ~ (Q. Nos. 48 and 49) *In the following diagram represents a group of persons. The triangle represents educated persons, the rectangle represents the administrative persons, the square represents the businessman and the circle represents income tax payers.*

« CG PSC 2013

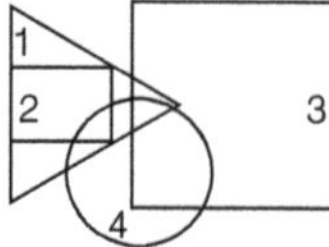

48. From the above figure, it can be concluded that

(a) All businessmen pay income tax.
(b) Some administrative persons are income tax payers.
(c) All income tax payers are educated.
(d) Educated persons which are not in administrative service do not pay income tax.
(e) All businessmen are educated.

49. According to the given figure, it can be inferred that

(a) None of the income tax payer is educated.
(b) All the administrative persons are income tax payers.
(c) None of the income tax payer is administrative person.
(d) Some of the persons who are neither businessman nor income tax payers are educated persons.
(e) None of the above.

50. In the given Venn diagram, the triangle represents students playing table tennis, the rectangle represents students playing badminton, the circle represents female students and the pentagon represents students playing football. The numbers given in the diagram represent the number of persons in that particular category. « SSC CGL 2019

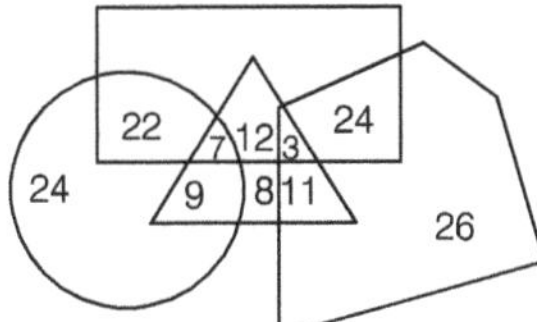

How many female students play both table tennis and badminton?

(a) 7 (b) 18 (c) 9 (d) 22

DIRECTIONS ~ (Q. Nos. 51-55) *In the following diagram, the circle stands for insurance agents, the square stands for hard working, the triangle stands for rural people and the rectangle stands for graduates. Study the diagram carefully and answer the questions that follow.* « LIC ADO 2008

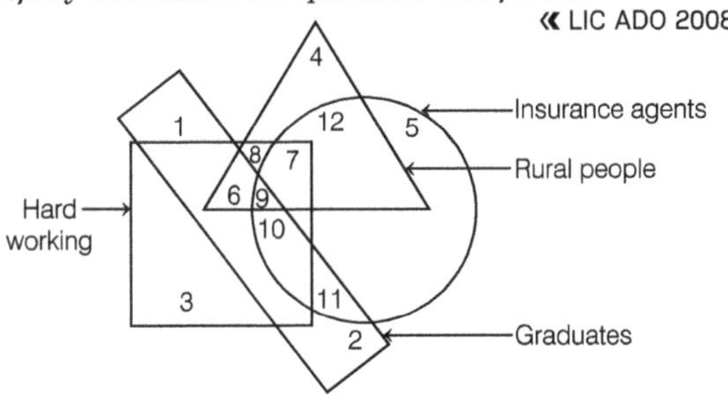

51. Non-rural and hard working insurance agents who are graduates are indicated by the region?

(a) 5 (b) 7 (c) 9 (d) 10
(e) None of these

52. Insurance agents who are neither graduates nor hard working but rural are represented by the region?

(a) 8 (b) 10 (c) 11 (d) 12
(e) None of these

53. Hard working, non-graduates, rural agents are represented by the region?

(a) 6 (b) 7
(c) 9 (d) 12
(e) None of these

54. Non-graduates insurance agents who are not hard working and who do not belong to rural areas are represented by the region?

(a) 5 (b) 6
(c) 8 (d) 11
(e) None of these

55. Insurance agents who are graduates, hard working and rural are represented by the region?

(a) 6 (b) 8
(c) 9 (d) 10
(e) None of these

DIRECTIONS ~ (Q. Nos. 56-58) *Read the diagram given below. Choose the answer from the given options of the following questions.*

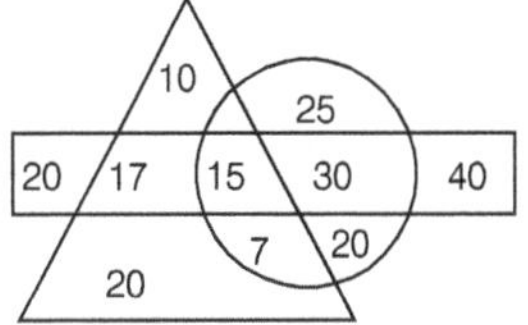

△ = Number of persons who drink tea
○ = Number of persons who drink coffee
▭ = Number of persons who drink wine

56. Number of those persons who drink only coffee?

(a) 25 (b) 45
(c) 20 (d) 90

57. Number of those persons who drink tea and coffee both?

(a) 7 (b) 17
(c) 20 (d) 25

58. Number of those persons who drink all, tea, coffee and wine?

(a) 15 (b) 32
(c) 22 (d) 24

Answers / WITH EXPLANATIONS

1. (*d*) Some fruits and some shirts can be of red colour. Hence, figure given in option (d) best depict the relationship.

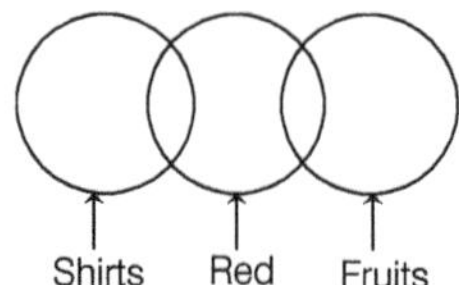

2. (*d*) Lucknow is a city in India while USA is entirely a different country. This can be expressed as given in option (d).

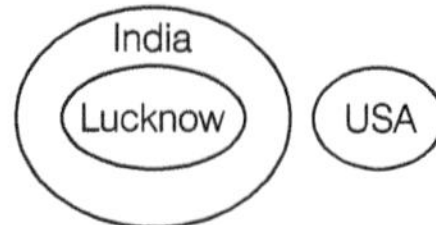

3. (*a*) Chicken are birds, whereas fish is different. Hence, figure given in option (a) best depict the given relationship.

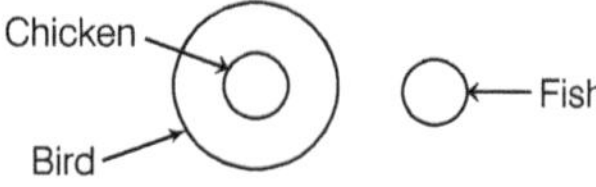

4. (*a*) Football is a type of sport, whereas lizard is a reptile. Hence, figure given in option (a) best depicts the given relationship.

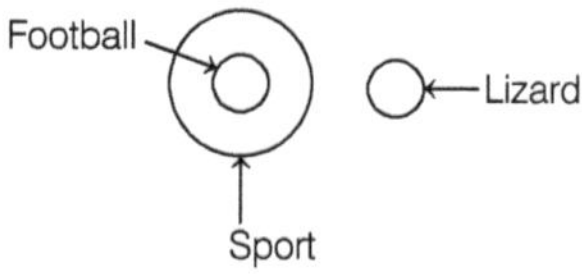

5. (*a*) Pen, pencil and paper all three are different types of stationary items. Hence, figure given in option (a) best depicts the relationship.

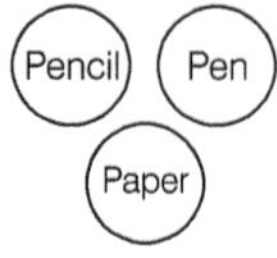

6. (*d*) Book is a collection of pages and library is a collection of books. Hence, figure given in option (d) best depicts the relationship.

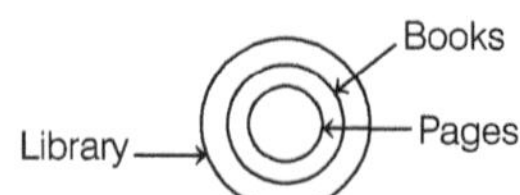

7. (*c*) We know that both tiger and elephant are animals. This relationship can be expressed as given as in option (c).

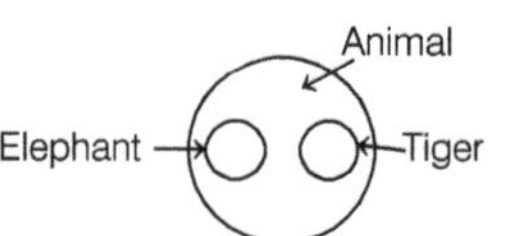

8. (*b*) Some parents are rich persons, some rich persons are farmers, some farmers are parents. Some parents are farmers and also a rich person.

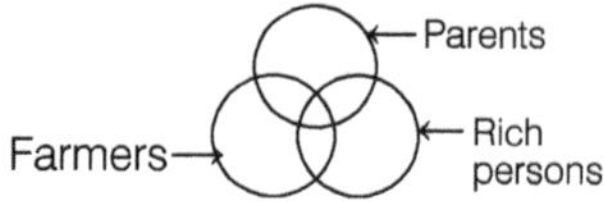

9. (*d*) Rivers and canals both are perennial sources of water and hence, both are included in it. This can be expressed by the following diagram.

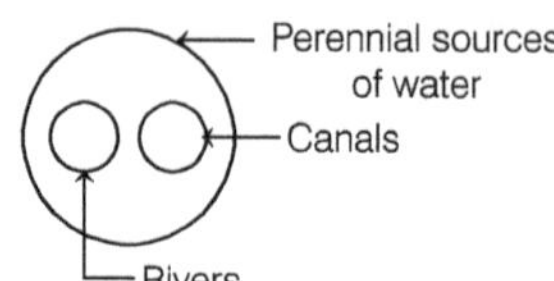

10. (*a*) Ring is a type of ornament and diamond ring is a variety of ring. This can be expressed as given in option (a).

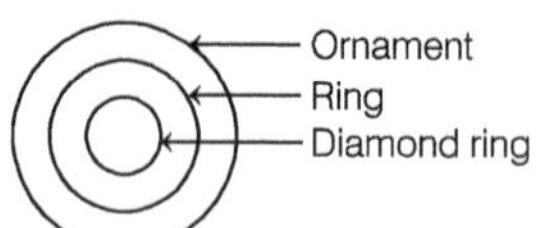

11. (*d*) This can be expressed as given in option (d)

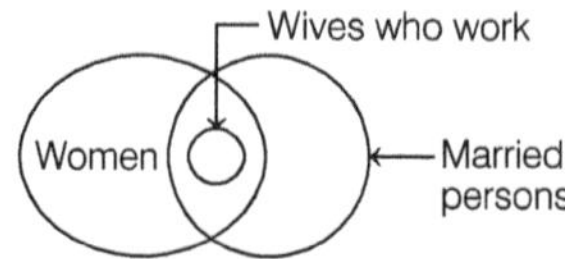

Here, small circle represents wives who work because wives who work are a part of married persons as well as women.

12. (*b*) Some graduates may be computer skilled, some graduates may be employed. Some computer skilled may be employed. Some computer skilled graduates may be employed.

This can be expressed as given in option (b).

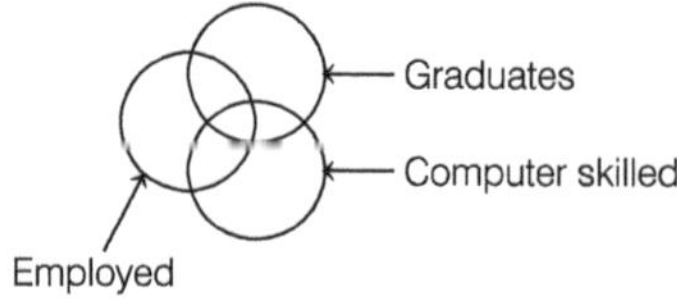

13. (*d*) First divisioners and third divisioners both are students and hence are completely included in the class of students. This can be expressed as given below.

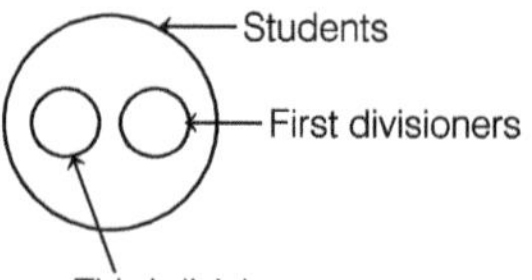

14. (*c*) Granite, Tree and Water are three different things and are not related to one another in any manner. This can be expressed as given in option (c).

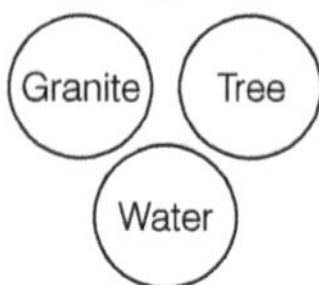

15. (*b*) Brick is used as a building material in both house and bridge. Hence, figure given in option (b) depicts the best relationship.

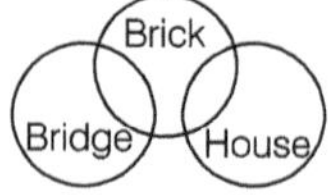

16. (*a*) All sprinters and marathon runners are athletes and also some sprinter can be marathon runners. So, this relation can be expressed as given in option (a).

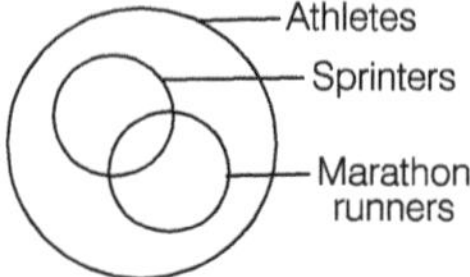

17. (*a*) Region D represents rural students who are not intelligent.

18. (*a*) b represents Indians and Historians but not politicians.

19. (*d*) The person who is neither a dancer nor a musician but is professional and not a European is represented by that region of circle which is not common with any other figure. It means that the required number is '10'.

20. (*b*) Only number 5 represents the programmers, who are neither degree holders nor non-degree holders.

21. (*a*) Number of educated and employed people = 12 + 6 = 18

22. (*a*) We want a region which represents the people who are intelligent, honest and truthful but not hardworking. So, region 6 represents such people.

23. (*a*)

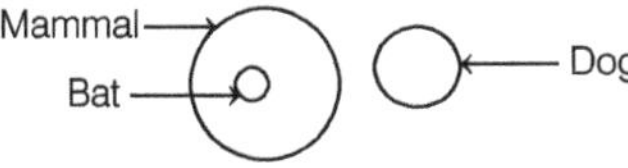

Bats are mammal but dog is different.

24. (*a*) The number common in all the three circles is 6. Therefore, 6 students passed in all the three exams.

25. (*c*) In the given figure, the persons who are educated and employed but not confirmed are represented by the region common to both the circles but outside the triangle.

So, the required region is 'bd'.

26. (*b*) Only figure given in option (b) represents the given facts. This can be illustrated by the help of following diagram

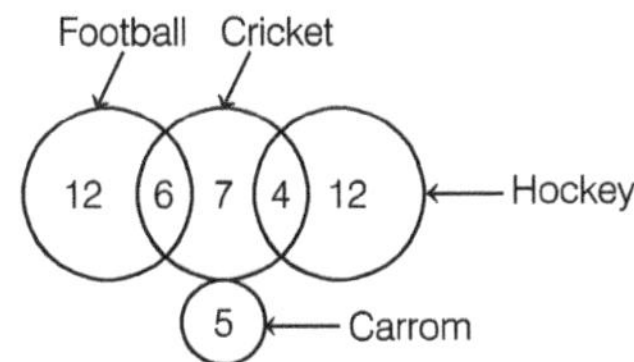

27. (*b*) All types of trees are grown in the area which is represented by the number 3.

28. (*a*) E and F represents Indians who are not priests.

29. (*a*) The teachers who are neither authors nor singers are represented by that region of triangle which is not common with any other figure. So, the required region is '1'.

30. (*a*) From the figure, it is clear that all lions are goat.
Hence, option (a) 'some lions are not goat' is not correct.

31. (*d*) Number 20 is common to all the four figures and hence, it can be concluded that 20 families have all the four things.

32. (*c*) Number of families having scooters are represented by the square and total of all the numbers present in square is given by
18+80+30+10+20+15+15 = 188

33. (*d*) 100 families have both VCR and TV as it is the sum of the numbers present on the portion common to both the circles *i.e.*, 80 and 20.

34. (*c*) Sum of 110, 50 and 40 will represent such families as all these numbers lie on the portion not common to other figures.

Hence, the required number of families = 110+50+40 = 200.

35. (*b*) Number 30 lies on the portion common to the figures representing families having TV and scooter both but neither VCR nor maruti.

36. (*a*) Unmarried police officers who are not corrupt but are poets are represented by the region common to circle and square but not the other figures. So, the required area is 8.

37. (*c*) The region 4 is common to triangle, circle and rectangle and hence, represents doctors who are players as well as artists.

38. (*a*) The region 6 is common to circle and rectangle only and hence represents the artists who are players.

39. (*a*) The region 1 of rectangle is not common to any other figure and hence is the required answer.

40. (*d*) The region 7 and 8 of circle is not common to any other figure and hence is the required answer.

41. (*d*) The region 5 is common to circle and triangle only and hence represents the required portion.

42. (*b*) Person knowing all the languages are represented by the region common to all the three circles *i.e.*, 175.

43. (*c*) 105 people know Marathi and English both.

44. (*b*) Statement (b) is correct as number 6 represent employees who are graduates as well as clerks.

45. (*a*) Statement (a) is correct as numbers 7 and 6 represent clerks, who are Government employees.

46. (*d*) Number 5 is common to rectangle, circle and triangle but not to square and hence, it represents urban Government employees who are graduates but not clerks.

47. (*d*) None of the number occupies the required space, which is common to rectangle and square only.

48. (*b*) From the figure, it is clear that some administrative persons are income tax payers as shown in the diagram.

49. (*d*) Some of the persons who are neither businessman nor income tax payers are educated persons as shown in the diagram.

50. (*a*)

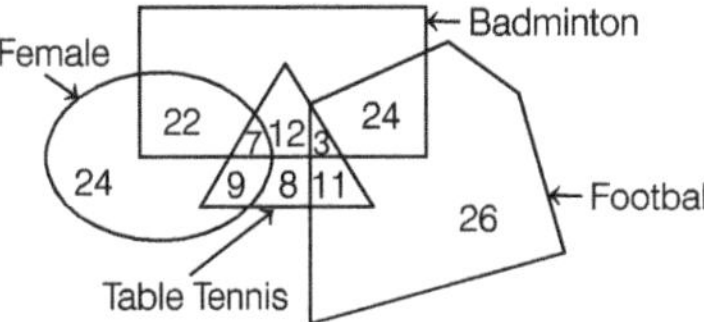

Clearly, 7 female students play both table tennis and badminton.

51. (*d*) Region 10 is common to the circle, rectangle and square and hence, represents the required region.

52. (*d*) Insurance agents who are neither graduates nor hard working but rural are represented by region 12 as it is common to circle and triangle.

53. (*b*) 7 is common region for hard working, non-graduates and rural agents.

54. (*a*) Region 5 represents non-graduates insurance agents who are not hard working and who do not belong to rural areas.

55. (*c*) Region 9 is common for all four figures and hence, represents the required region.

56. (*b*) The number of persons who drink coffee are = 25 + 20 = 45

57. (*a*) The number of persons who drink both tea and coffee are = 7

58. (*a*) The number of persons who drink tea, coffee and wine are = 15

CHAPTER / 20

Matrix Coding

Matrix is a set of elements presented in tabular form (in rows and columns).

Matrix coding is a method to represent the letters of English alphabet by two digits. One digit is represented by the corresponding row and the other digit is represented by the corresponding column.

The questions based on matrix coding consist of one or two matrices. Generally, each matrix has five columns and five rows.

In **one matrix** based questions, five columns and five rows are generally marked from 0 to 4.

In **two matrices** based questions, five columns and five rows are generally marked from 0 to 4, in Matrix I and in Matrix II, the five columns and five rows are generally marked from 5 to 9.

In these matrices five letters appear in each column and row but different in order. The candidates are required to find the assigned number to the letters of given word from the given matrices and select the group of numbers which accompanies the letter in the right format.

Let us discuss some examples to understand matrix coding.

***Ex* 01** A word is represented by only one set of numbers as given in any one of the alternatives. The sets of numbers given in the alternatives are represented by two classes of alphabets as in two matrices given below. The columns and rows of Matrix I are numbered from 0 to 4. A letter from the matrix can be represented first by its row and next by its column, e.g., 'N' can be represented by 00, 12 etc and 'K' can be represented by 01, 13 etc. Similarly, you have to identify the set for the word 'PINK'.

	0	1	2	3	4
0	N	K	P	L	I
1	P	I	N	K	L
2	K	N	L	P	I
3	N	L	I	K	P
4	K	P	L	N	I

(a) 10, 13, 43, 44 (b) 10, 32, 43, 01
(c) 43, 01, 32, 10 (d) 34, 10, 23, 13

***Solution* (b)**

	0	1	2	3	4
0	N	K	P		I
1	P	I	N	K	
2	K	N		P	I
3	N		I	K	P
4	K	P		N	I

Here, taking the row and column number of each letter, we have

P = 02, 10, 23, 34, 41 I = 04, 11, 24, 32, 44
N = 00, 12, 21, 30, 43 K = 01, 13, 20, 33, 40

Now, taking each option and comparing them with above values, we get

Option	P	I	N	K
(a)	10	13 ☒	43	44 ☒
(b)	10	32	43	01
(c)	43 ☒	01 ☒	32 ☒	10 ☒
(d)	34	10 ☒	23 ☒	12 ☒

Hence, only option (b) contains all the correct values.

***Ex* 02** A word is represented by only one set of numbers as given in anyone of the alternatives. The sets of numbers given in the alternatives are represented by two classes of alphabets as in the two matrices given below. The columns and rows of Matrix I are numbered from 0 to 4 and that of Matrix II are numbered from 5 to 9. A letter from these Matrices can be represented first by its row and next by its column, e.g. 'O' can be represented by 01, 33, etc and 'Q' can be represented by 55, 78 etc. Similarly, you have to identify the set for the word METAL. « SSC (Steno) 2016

Matrix I

	0	1	2	3	4
0	M	O	R	A	L
1	O	R	A	L	M
2	R	A	L	M	O
3	A	L	M	O	R
4	L	M	O	R	A

Matrix II

	5	6	7	8	9
5	Q	U	I	E	T
6	U	I	E	T	Q
7	I	E	T	Q	U
8	E	T	Q	U	I
9	T	Q	U	I	E

(a) 23, 67, 96, 40, 44 (b) 23, 76, 95, 40, 44
(c) 32, 76, 95, 44, 04 (d) 32, 76, 44, 95, 04

***Solution* (c)**

Matrix I

	0	1	2	3	4
0	M			A	L
1			A	L	M
2		A	L	M	
3	A	L	M		
4	L	M			A

Matrix II

	5	6	7	8	9
5				E	T
6			E	T	
7		E	T		
8	E	T			
9	T				E

Here, taking the row and column number of each letter, we have

M → 00, 14, 23, 32, 41
E → 58, 67, 76, 85, 99
T → 59, 68, 77, 86, 95
A → 03, 12, 21, 30, 44
L → 04, 13, 22, 31, 40

Now, taking each option and comparing them with above values, we get

Option	M	E	T	A	L
(a)	23	67	96 ✗	40 ✗	44 ✗
(b)	23	76	95	40 ✗	44 ✗
(c)	32	76	95	44	04
(d)	32	76	44 ✗	95 ✗	04

Hence, only option (c) contains all the correct values.

DIRECTIONS ~(Ex. Nos. 3-4) *Read the following information carefully and answer the questions that follow.*

In the following questions, a word is represented by only one set of numbers as given in any one of the alternatives. The sets of numbers given in the alternatives are represented by two classes of alphabets as in two Matrices given below.

The columns and rows of matrix I are numbered from 0 to 4 and that of Matrix II are numbered from 5 to 9. A letter from these matrices can be represented first by its row and next by its column.

e.g. 'M' can be represented by 01, (Row, Column) 20, (Row, Column) etc., in the same way 'T' can be represented by 57, 85 etc. Similarly, you have to identify the set for the word given in each question.

« SSC (CPO) 2015

***Ex* 03** LANE

Matrix I

	0	1	2	3	4
0	Z	M	S	R	C
1	J	L	D	B	G
2	M	B	C	M	H
3	R	L	N	S	I
4	B	D	M	R	J

Matrix II

	5	6	7	8	9
5	X	K	T	E	S
6	Q	A	U	Y	P
7	U	V	O	W	E
8	T	Y	A	E	U
9	X	O	E	V	A

(a) 11, 66, 33, 96
(b) 11, 67, 32,97
(c) 31, 66, 33, 97
(d) 31, 87, 32, 97

***Solution* (d)**

Matrix I

	0	1	2	3	4
0					
1		L			
2					
3		L	N		
4					

Matrix II

	5	6	7	8	9
5				E	
6		A			
7					E
8			A	E	
9			E		A

Here, taking the row and column number of each letter, we have

L = 11, 31　　A = 66, 87, 99
N = 32　　E = 58, 79, 88, 97

Now, taking each option and comparing them with above values, we get

Option	L	A	N	E
(a)	11	66	33 ✗	96 ✗
(b)	11	67 ✗	32	97
(c)	31	66	33 ✗	97
(d)	31	87	32	97

Hence, only option (d) contains all the correct values.

***Ex* 04** AIRS

Matrix I

	0	1	2	3	4
0	A	E	M	N	P
1	N	P	A	E	M
2	E	M	N	P	A
3	P	A	E	M	N
4	M	N	P	A	E

Matrix II

	5	6	7	8	9
5	I	L	R	S	T
6	R	S	T	I	L
7	T	I	L	R	S
8	L	R	S	T	I
9	S	T	I	L	R

(a) 43, 55, 86, 95　　(b) 12, 76, 99, 78
(c) 00, 68, 78, 88　　(d) 24, 69, 56, 78

***Solution* (a)**

Matrix I

	0	1	2	3	4
0	A				
1			A		
2					A
3		A			
4				A	

Matrix II

	5	6	7	8	9
5	I		R	S	
6	R	S		I	
7		I		R	S
8		R	S		I
9	S		I		R

Here, taking the row and column number of each letter, we have

A = 00, 12, 24, 31, 43　　I = 55, 68, 76, 89, 97
R = 57, 65, 78, 86, 99　　S = 58, 66, 79, 87, 95

Now, taking each option and comparing them with above values, we get

Option	A	I	R	S
(a)	43	55	86	95
(b)	12	76	99	78 ✗
(c)	00	68	78	88 ✗
(d)	24	69 ✗	56 ✗	78 ✗

Hence, only option (a), contains all the correct values.

Practice / CORNER 20

1. A word is represented by only one set of numbers as given in any one of the alternatives. The sets of numbers given in the alternatives are represented by two classes of alphabets as in the matrix given below. The columns and rows of matrix are numbered from 0 to 6. A letter from the matrix can be represented first by its row and next by its column, e.g., 'A' can be represented by 42, 62, etc. and 'P' can be represented by 15, 43, etc. Similarly, you have to identify the set for the word 'CALM'.

0	1	2	3	4	5	6
1	H	R	E	I	P	S
2	S	G	N	D	Z	I
3	B	U	F	T	K	L
4	V	A	P	C	Y	A
5	M	W	C	O	X	N
6	B	A	E	J	L	O

« SSC CGL 2013

(a) 53, 42, 65, 36 (b) 53, 54, 51, 31
(c) 44, 54, 65, 24 (d) 44, 62, 65, 51

2. A word is represented by only one set of numbers as given in any one of the alternatives. The sets of numbers given in the alternatives are represented by two classes of alphabets as in the matrix given below. The columns and rows of matrix are numbered from 1 to 6. A letter from the matrix can be represented first by its row and next by its column e.g., 'A' can be represented by 42, 46, 62 etc and 'P' can be represented by 15, 43, etc. Similarly, you have to identify the set for the word 'SNOW'.

	1	2	3	4	5	6
1	H	R	E	I	P	S
2	S	G	N	D	Z	J
3	B	U	F	T	K	L
4	V	A	P	C	Y	A
5	M	W	C	O	X	N
6	B	A	E	I	L	O

« SSC CGL 2013

(a) 21, 14, 22, 56 (b) 21, 56, 62, 44
(c) 16, 56, 46, 35 (d) 21, 23, 54, 52

3. A word is represented by only one set of numbers as given in any one of the alternatives. The sets of numbers given in the alternatives are represented by two classes of alphabets as shown in the given two matrices. The columns and rows of Matrix-I are numbered from 0 to 4 and that of Matrix-II are numbered from 5 to 9. A letter from these matrices can be represented first by its row and next by its column, for example 'D' can be represented by 24, 41 etc. and 'Y' can be represented by 57, 98 etc. Similarly, you have to identify for the word 'BREW'. « SSC (10+2) 2018

Matrix I

	0	1	2	3	4
0	C	J	H	G	A
1	G	I	H	D	C
2	F	C	H	E	D
3	M	B	A	L	E
4	E	D	K	B	G

Matrix II

	5	6	7	8	9
5	U	W	Y	X	W
6	Z	U	N	T	S
7	V	O	U	R	P
8	R	O	W	X	O
9	V	Q	S	Y	U

(a) 36, 68, 44, 95 (b) 43, 78, 23, 59
(c) 30, 66, 42, 96 (d) 23, 68, 22, 66

4. A word is represented by only one set of numbers as given in any one of the alternatives. The sets of numbers given in the alternatives are represented by two classes of alphabets as shown in the given two matrices. The columns and rows of Matrix-I are numbered from 0 to 4 and that of Martix-II are numbered from 5 to 9. A letter from these matrices can be represented first by its row and next by its column, for example, 'Y' can be represented by 00, 22, etc. and 'U' can be represented by 42, 59, etc. Similarly, you have to identify the set for the word "PARK".

Matrix-I

	0	1	2	3	4
0	Y	I	K	W	X
1	G	J	N	H	V
2	E	O	Y	K	T
3	M	G	W	L	R
4	A	E	U	N	K

Matrix-II

	5	6	7	8	9
5	N	I	X	P	U
6	K	V	O	T	S
7	L	P	R	A	D
8	O	H	J	L	N
9	P	J	Q	V	X

« SSC Steno 2017

(a) 58, 40, 86, 34 (b) 76, 55, 89, 23
(c) 23, 78, 34, 02 (d) 95, 40, 77, 65

5. A word is represented by only one set of numbers as given in any one of the alternatives. The sets of numbers given in the alternatives are represented by two classes of alphabets as in two matrices given below. The columns and rows of Matrix I are numbered from 0 to 3 and that of Matrix II are numbered from 4 to 7. A letter from these matrices can be represented first by its row and next by its column, e.g., D can be represented by 01 and R can be represented by 44. Similarly, you have to identify the set for the word TALE. « SSC Steno 2015

Matrix-I

	0	1	2	3
0	A	D	G	H
1	P	S	V	Z
2	C	F	I	M
3	T	L	E	Q

Matrix-II

	4	5	6	7
4	R	U	B	O
5	N	W	J	X
6	T	K	S	G
7	I	H	A	F

(a) 00, 31, 64, 32 (b) 64, 00, 31, 32
(c) 30, 76, 23, 32 (d) 46, 13, 00, 23

6. A word is represented by only one set of numbers as given in any one of the alternatives. The sets of numbers given in the alternatives are represented by two classes of alphabets as in two matrices given below. The columns and rows of Matrix I are numbered from 0 to 4 and that of Matrix II are numbered from 5 to 9. A letter from these matrices can be represented first by its row and next by its column, e.g. M can be represented by 01, 10 etc., and A can be represented by 56, 65 etc. Similarly, you have to identify the set for the word 'ROD'. « SSC (10+2) 2015

Matrix-I

	0	1	2	3	4
0	I	M	W	S	Q
1	M	W	S	Q	I
2	W	S	Q	I	M
3	S	Q	I	M	W
4	Q	I	M	W	S

Matrix-II

	5	6	7	8	9
5	O	A	D	R	N
6	A	D	R	N	O
7	D	R	N	O	A
8	R	N	O	A	D
9	N	O	A	D	R

(a) 58, 66, 78 (b) 56, 66, 86 (c) 67, 96, 57 (d) 58, 69, 65

7. A word is represented by only one set of numbers as given in any one of the alternatives. The sets of numbers given in the alternatives are represented by two classes of alphabets as shown in the given two matrices. The columns and rows of Matrix-I are numbered from 0 to 4 and that of Matrix-II are numbered from 5 to 9. A letter from these matrices can be represented first by its row and next by its column, for example, 'D' can be represented by 02, 79, etc., and 'Z' can be represented by 00, 77, etc. Similarly, you have to identify the set for the word MAKE. « SSC MTS 2017

Matrix-I

	0	1	2	3	4
0	Z	C	D	G	M
1	G	A	N	H	V
2	U	O	Y	K	T
3	D	G	M	L	R
4	A	E	U	C	K

Matrix-II

	5	6	7	8	9
5	F	R	O	T	W
6	K	M	J	C	S
7	L	P	Z	Y	D
8	F	E	J	A	N
9	U	W	Q	V	X

(a) 04, 11, 23, 86
(b) 11, 40, 45, 23
(c) 43, 88, 12, 41
(d) 66, 55, 67, 34

8. A word is represented by only one set of numbers as given in any one of the alternatives. The sets of numbers given in the alternatives are represented by two classes of alphabets as shown in the given two matrices. The columns and rows of Matrix-I are numbered from 0 to 4 and that of Matrix-II are numbered from 5 to 9. A letter from these matrices can be represented first by its row and next by its column, for example, 'V' can be represented by 31, 44, etc., and 'D' can be represented by 67, 86 etc. Similarly, you have to identify the set for the word 'GLOW'. « SSC CPO 2017

Matrix-I

	0	1	2	3	4
0	O	N	V	S	W
1	V	S	W	O	N
2	W	O	N	V	S
3	N	V	S	W	O
4	S	W	O	N	V

Matrix-II

	5	6	7	8	9
5	A	G	L	I	D
6	L	A	D	G	I
7	D	I	A	L	G
8	I	D	G	A	L
9	G	L	I	D	A

(a) 56, 89, 01, 04
(b) 68, 78, 21, 42
(c) 87, 65, 22, 41
(d) 95, 57, 13, 33

9. In this question, the sets of numbers given in the alternatives are represented. The columns and rows of Matrix I are numbered from 0 to 4 and that of Matrix II are numbered from 5 to 9. A letter from these matrices can be represented first by its row and next by its column, e.g., O can be represented by 03, 14 etc and 'K' can be represented by 56, 65, etc. Similarly you have to identify the set for the word 'EASE'. « SSC CGL 2017

Matrix-I

	0	1	2	3	4
0	E	S	U	O	H
1	S	U	H	E	O
2	O	H	E	S	U
3	U	E	O	H	S
4	H	O	U	S	E

Matrix-II

	5	6	7	8	9
5	E	K	A	N	S
6	K	A	S	E	N
7	N	S	E	K	A
8	A	E	N	S	K
9	S	N	K	A	E

(a) 55, 85, 44, 42
(b) 77, 85, 88, 44
(c) 77, 66, 31, 44
(d) 00, 98, 23, 98

10. A word is represented by only one set of numbers as given in any one of the alternatives. The sets of numbers given in the alternatives are represented by two classes of alphabets as shown in the given two matrices. The columns and rows of Matrix-I are numbered from 0 to 4 and that of Matrix-II are numbered from 5 to 9. A letter from these matrices can be represented first by its row and next by its column, for example, 'E' can be represented by 10, 22, etc., and 'O' can be represented by 56, 78 etc. Similarly, you have to identify the set for the word 'HALT'. « SSC CPO 2017

Matrix-I

	0	1	2	3	4
0	T	E	R	A	H
1	E	R	H	T	A
2	A	H	E	R	T
3	R	T	A	H	E
4	H	A	T	E	R

Matrix-II

	5	6	7	8	9
5	L	O	P	U	E
6	O	P	E	L	U
7	U	E	L	O	P
8	P	L	U	E	O
9	E	U	O	P	L

(a) 40, 03, 76, 24
(b) 21, 41, 68, 13
(c) 12, 14, 69, 00
(d) 34, 41, 87, 31

11. In the question, a word is represented by only one set of numbers as given in any one of the alternatives. The sets of numbers given in the alternatives are represented by two classes of alphabets as in two matrices given below. The columns and rows of Matrix I are numbered from 0 to 4 and that of Matrix II are numbered from 5 to 9. A letter from these matrices can be represented first by its row and next by its column, e.g., K can be represented by 00, 24, etc. and A can be represented by 55 etc. You have to identify the set for the word 'SHIP'. « SSC CGL 2016

Matrix-I

	0	1	2	3	4
0	K	G	E	A	S
1	P	V	H	R	Y
2	N	V	N	R	K
3	W	S	B	O	J
4	T	U	A	I	P

Matrix-II

	5	6	7	8	9
5	A	H	U	W	N
6	Y	R	B	T	V
7	O	I	H	B	Q
8	V	O	E	I	S
9	E	T	K	W	P

(a) 31, 56, 43, 10
(b) 89, 12, 40, 99
(c) 04, 21, 76, 44
(d) 89, 56, 34, 11

12. In the following question, a word is represented by only one set of numbers as given in anyone of the alternatives. The set of numbers given in the alternatives are represented by two classes of alphabets as in two matrices given below. The columns and rows of Matrix I are numbered 0 to 4 and that of Matrix II are numbered 5 to 9. A letter from these matrices can be represented first by its row and then by its column, example, P can be represented by 55,69 etc. and L can be represented by 59, 68 etc. Similarly, you have to identify the set for the word given in the question.

MASTER « SSC CPO 2016

Matrix-I

	0	1	2	3	4
0	S	M	A	R	T
1	M	A	R	T	S
2	A	R	T	S	M
3	R	T	S	M	A
4	T	S	M	A	R

Matrix-II

	5	6	7	8	9
5	P	E	R	I	L
6	E	R	I	L	P
7	R	I	L	P	E
8	I	L	P	E	R
9	L	P	E	R	I

(a) 01, 11, 23, 00, 88, 44
(b) 10, 34, 14, 31, 40, 12
(c) 01, 43, 41, 04, 65, 44
(d) 33, 02, 23, 30, 31, 97

13. In the following question, a word is represented by only one set of numbers as given in anyone of the alternatives. The set of numbers given in the alternatives are represented by two classes of alphabets as in two matrices given below. The columns and rows of Matrix I are numbered 0 to 4 and that of Matrix II are numbered 5 to 9. A letter from these matrices can be represented first by its row and then by its column, example, C can be represented by 55,69 etc. and D can be represented by 59, 68 etc. Similarly, you have to identify the set for the word given in the question.

ROUND « SSC CPO 2016

Matrix-I

	0	1	2	3	4
0	B	N	R	T	H
1	N	R	T	H	B
2	R	T	H	B	N
3	T	H	B	N	R
4	H	B	N	R	T

Matrix-II

	5	6	7	8	9
5	C	L	O	U	D
6	L	O	U	D	C
7	O	U	D	C	L
8	U	D	C	L	O
9	D	C	L	O	U

(a) 20, 66, 79, 67, 77
(b) 34, 66, 58, 33, 95
(c) 11, 75, 85, 42, 99
(d) 43, 67, 10, 68, 59

14. A word is represented by only one set of numbers as given in any one of the alternatives. The sets of numbers given in the alternatives are represented by two classes of alphabets as in two matrices given below. The columns and row of Matrix I are numbered from 0 to 4 and that on Matrix II are numbered from 5 to 9. A letter from these matrices can be represented first by its rows and next by its column, e.g., 'A' can be represented by 01, 14 etc., and E can be represented by 55, 66 etc. Similarly, you have to identify the set for the word 'ORGAN'. « SSC CGL 2015

Matrix-I

	0	1	2	3	4
0	P	A	G	R	Z
1	G	R	Z	P	A
2	Z	P	A	G	R
3	A	G	R	Z	P
4	R	Z	P	A	G

Matrix-II

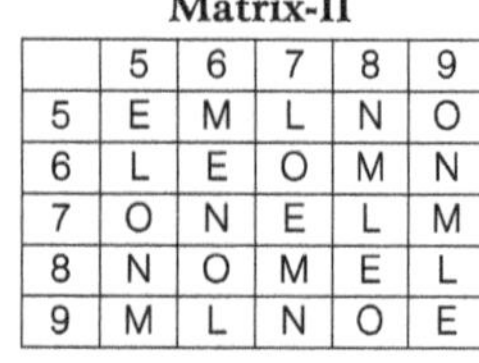

	5	6	7	8	9
5	E	M	L	N	O
6	L	E	O	M	N
7	O	N	E	L	M
8	N	O	M	E	L
9	M	L	N	O	E

(a) 75, 03, 11, 22, 76
(b) 67, 22, 31, 58, 22
(c) 86, 40, 23, 14, 96
(d) 98, 03, 44, 22, 58

15. A word is represented by only one set of numbers as given in any of the alternatives. The set of numbers given in the alternatives are represented by two classes of alphabets as in two matrices given below. The columns and rows of Matrix I are numbered from 0 to 4 and that of Matrix II are numbered from 5 to 9. A letter from these matrices can be represented first by its row and next by its column, e.g., 'A' can be represented by 55, 67, 86 etc., and R can be represented by 04, 23, 30 etc. Identify the set for the word 'DOOR'. « SSC (10+2) 2011

Matrix I

	0	1	2	3	4
0	F	O	M	S	R
1	S	R	F	O	M
2	O	M	S	R	F
3	R	F	O	M	S
4	M	S	R	F	O

Matrix II

	5	6	7	8	9
5	A	T	D	I	P
6	I	P	A	T	D
7	T	D	I	P	A
8	P	A	T	D	I
9	D	I	P	A	T

(a) 69, 44, 20, 43
(b) 76, 01, 44, 24
(c) 95, 20, 44, 12
(d) 57, 13, 32, 23

16. A word is represented by only one set of numbers as given in any of the alternatives. The sets of numbers given in the alternatives are represented by two classes of alphabets as in two matrices given below. The columns and rows of Matrix I are numbered from 0 to 4 and that of Matrix II are numbered from 5 to 9. A letter from these matrices can be represented first by its row and next by its column, e.g., 'A' can be represented by 01, 12, 33 etc., and 'K' can be represented by 57, 68, 85 etc. Identify the set for the word 'EAST'. « SSC (FCI) 2012

Matrix I

	0	1	2	3	4
0	E	A	R	W	P
1	W	P	A	E	R
2	A	W	P	R	E
3	P	R	E	A	W
4	R	E	W	P	A

Matrix II

	5	6	7	8	9
5	S	B	K	T	C
6	B	C	T	K	S
7	T	S	C	B	K
8	K	T	S	C	B
9	C	K	B	S	T

(a) 00, 12, 76, 58
(b) 32, 34, 76, 68
(c) 41, 20, 77, 59
(d) 24, 02, 55, 76

17. A word is represented by only one set of numbers as given in any of the alternatives. The set of numbers given in the alternatives are represented by two classes of alphabets as in two matrices, given below. The columns and rows of Matrix I are numbered from 0 to 3 and that of Matrix II are numbered from 4 to 7. A letter from these matrices can be represented first by its row and next by its column.

e.g., 'A' can be represented by 00, 76 and 'S' can be represented by 11, 66. Identify the set for the word 'PUSH'. « SSC (10+2) 2011

Matrix I

	0	1	2	3
0	A	D	G	H
1	P	S	V	Z
2	C	F	I	M
3	T	L	E	Q

Matrix II

	4	5	6	7
4	R	U	B	O
5	N	W	J	X
6	T	K	S	G
7	I	H	A	F

(a) 10, 66, 45, 03 (b) 30, 11, 54, 10
(c) 10, 45, 66, 75 (d) 01, 54, 66, 57

18. A word is represented by only one set of numbers as given in any of the alternatives. The set of numbers given in the alternatives are represented by two classes of alphabets as in two matrices given below. The columns and rows of Matrix I are numbered from 0 to 4 and that of Matrix II are numbered from 5 to 9. A letter from these matrices can be represented first by its row and next by its column. e.g., 'A' can be represented by 02, 14, 33, etc., and K can be represented by 57, 69, 88 etc. Identify the set for the word 'SOAP'. « SSC (Steno) 2012

Matrix I

	0	1	2	3	4
0	R	S	A	C	N
1	C	N	R	S	A
2	S	A	C	N	R
3	N	R	S	A	C
4	A	C	N	R	S

Matrix II

	5	6	7	8	9
5	O	B	K	E	P
6	E	P	O	B	K
7	B	K	E	P	O
8	P	O	B	K	E
9	K	E	P	O	B

(a) 13, 55, 21, 66 (b) 01, 56, 21, 67
(c) 32, 56, 20, 66 (d) 20, 56, 21, 66

19. A word is represented by only one set of numbers as given in any of the alternatives. The set of numbers given in the alternatives are represented by two classes of alphabets as in two matrices given below. The columns and rows of Matrix I are numbered from 0 to 4 and that of Matrix II are numbered from 5 to 9. A letter from these matrices can be represented first by its row and next by its column, e.g., 'T' can be represented by 00, 13, 30 and R can be represented by 56, 79, 87 etc. Identify the set for the word 'DEAL'. « SSC (10+2) 2010

Matrix I

	0	1	2	3	4
0	T	C	K	K	G
1	F	B	R	T	O
2	M	D	I	O	Q
3	T	A	U	A	N
4	Y	K	P	R	Y

Matrix II

	5	6	7	8	9
5	C	R	I	G	E
6	P	M	S	L	T
7	E	Y	N	B	R
8	A	U	R	O	A

(a) 11, 23, 76, 68 (b) 21, 75, 97, 68
(c) 21, 32, 86, 89 (d) 43, 75, 89, 69

20. A word is represented by only one set of numbers as given in any of the alternatives. The sets of numbers given in the alternatives are represented by two classes of alphabets as in two matrices given below. The columns and rows of Matrix I are numbered from 0 to 4 and that of Matrix II are numbered from 5 to 9. A letter from these matrices can be represented first by its row and next by its column. e.g., 'I' can be represented by 03, 22 etc., and 'R' can be represented by 57, 68 etc. Similarly, you have to identify the set for the word 'BALD'. « SSC (Multitasking) 2013

Matrix I

	0	1	2	3	4
0	B	T	D	I	F
1	I	D	B	F	T
2	F	B	I	T	D
3	T	I	F	D	B
4	D	F	T	B	I

Matrix II

	5	6	7	8	9
5	A	L	R	E	K
6	K	A	L	R	E
7	E	K	A	L	R
8	R	E	K	A	L
9	L	R	E	K	A

(a) 12, 99, 65, 24 (b) 21, 88, 95, 24
(c) 43, 55, 67, 04 (d) 34, 77, 76, 42

21. A word is represented by only one set of numbers as given in any of the alternatives. The sets of numbers given in the alternatives are represented by two classes of alphabets as in two matrices given below. The columns and rows or matrix I are numbered from 0 to 4 and that of matrix II are numbered from 5 to 9. A letter from these matrices can be represented first by its row and next by its column, e.g., D can be represented by 00, 12 etc., and 'P' can be represented by 56, 68 etc. Similarly, you have to identify the set for the word 'FIRE'. « SSC GD Constable 2015

Matrix I

	0	1	2	3	4
0	D	E	F	I	N
1	I	N	D	E	F
2	E	F	I	N	D
3	N	D	E	F	I
4	F	I	N	D	E

Matrix II

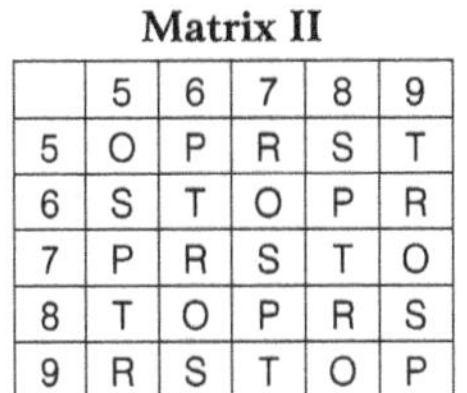

	5	6	7	8	9
5	O	P	R	S	T
6	S	T	O	P	R
7	P	R	S	T	O
8	T	O	P	R	S
9	R	S	T	O	P

(a) 02, 03, 57, 01 (b) 33, 34, 76, 22
(c) 14, 10, 69, 14 (d) 21, 22, 88, 33

22. A word is represented by only one set of numbers as given in any of the alternatives. The sets of numbers given in the alternatives are represented by two classes of alphabets as in two matrices given below. The columns and rows of matrix I are numbered from 0 to 4 and that of Matrix II are numbered from 5 to 9. A letter from these matrices can be represented first by its row and next by its column, e.g., 'A' can be represented by 01, 13, etc., and 'E' can be represented by 56, 67, etc. Similarly, you have to identify the set for the word 'BOTH'. « SSC (Steno) 2013

Matrix I

	0	1	2	3	4
0	F	A	N	O	I
1	I	O	F	A	N
2	A	N	O	I	F
3	O	F	I	N	A
4	N	I	A	F	O

Matrix II

	5	6	7	8	9
5	S	E	H	B	T
6	H	S	E	T	B
7	B	T	S	E	H
8	E	H	T	B	S
9	T	S	E	H	B

(a) 88, 30, 85, 86 (b) 58, 02, 68, 65
(c) 69, 67, 68, 59 (d) 75, 22, 76, 79

23. A word is represented by only one set of numbers given in any of the alternatives. The sets of numbers given in the alternatives are represented by two classes of alphabets as in two matrices given below. The columns and rows of Matrix I are numbered from 0 to 4 and that of Matrix II are numbered from 5 to 9. A letter from these matrices can be represented first by its row and next by its column, e.g., 'M' can be represented by 42, 31, etc. Similarly, you have to identify the set for the word given 'ROST'.

« SSC (CGL) 2014

Matrix I

	0	1	2	3	4
4	K	L	M	N	O
3	L	M	K	O	N
2	N	O	L	M	K
1	M	N	O	K	L
0	O	K	N	L	M

Matrix II

	5	6	7	8	9
9	P	Q	R	S	T
8	T	S	Q	P	R
7	R	T	S	Q	P
6	S	P	T	R	Q
5	Q	R	P	T	S

(a) 68, 33, 65, 58
(b) 56, 44, 67, 40
(c) 97, 21, 66, 29
(d) 75, 00, 10, 92

24. A word is represented by only one set of numbers as given in any of the alternatives. The sets of numbers given in the alternatives are represented by two classes of alphabets as in the two matrices given below. The columns and rows of matrix I are numbered from 0 to 4 and that of Matrix II are numbered from 5 to 9. A letter from these matrices can be represented first by its row and next by its column, e.g., 'E' can be represented by 00, 13, 32, etc., and 'S' can represented by 55, 76, 87, etc. Similarly, you have to identify the set for the word given CART.

« SSC (Multitasking) 2014

Matrix I

	0	1	2	3	4
0	E	A	R	W	P
1	W	P	A	E	R
2	A	W	P	R	E
3	P	R	E	A	W
4	R	E	W	P	A

Matrix II

	5	6	7	8	9
5	S	B	K	T	C
6	B	C	T	K	S
7	T	S	C	B	K
8	K	T	S	C	B
9	C	K	B	S	T

(a) 65, 33, 40, 86
(b) 66, 12, 40, 58
(c) 88, 44, 31, 89
(d) 59, 20, 32, 89

25. A word is represented by only one set of numbers as given in any of the alternatives. The sets of numbers given in the alternatives are represented by two classes of alphabets as in two matrices given below. The columns and rows of Matrix I are numbered from 0 to 4 and that of Matrix II are numbered from 5 to 9. A letter from these matrices can be represented first by its row and next by its column, e.g., 'H' can be represented by 02, 20, 43 etc., and 'V' can be represented by 58, 79, 95 etc. Similarly, you have to identify the set for the word given SOFT.

« SSC (Multitasking) 2014

Matrix I

	0	1	2	3	4
0	F	G	H	O	M
1	O	M	F	G	H
2	H	O	M	F	G
3	G	H	O	M	F
4	M	F	G	H	O

Matrix II

	5	6	7	8	9
5	S	T	U	V	W
6	U	V	W	S	T
7	W	S	T	U	V
8	T	U	V	W	S
9	V	W	S	T	U

(a) 55, 03, 22, 77
(b) 89, 32, 12, 97
(c) 68, 11, 12, 97
(d) 89, 03, 12, 98

26. A word is represented by only one set of numbers as given in anyone of the alternatives. The sets of numbers given in the alternatives are represented by two classes of alphabets as shown in the given two matrices. The columns and rows of Matrix I are numbered from 0 to 4 and that of Matrix II are numbered from 5 to 9. A letter from these matrices can be represented first by its row and next by its column, for example 'K' can be represented by 43, 04 etc., and 'Z' can be represented by 75, 66 etc. Similarly, you have to identify the set for the word 'MALE'.

Matrix I

	0	1	2	3	4
0	H	B	I	M	K
1	E	L	A	L	I
2	C	G	D	M	G
3	I	H	E	L	J
4	E	I	H	K	B

Matrix II

	5	6	7	8	9
5	S	W	Q	N	W
6	Y	Z	Y	P	X
7	Z	S	U	X	X
8	W	R	P	P	V
9	Q	R	O	T	P

(a) 11, 78, 32, 65
(b) 43, 01, 23, 67
(c) 03, 12, 11, 32
(d) 11, 02, 43, 76

27. A word is represented by only one set of numbers as given in any of the alternatives. The sets of numbers given in the alternatives are represented by two classes of alphabets as shown in the given two matrices. The columns and rows of Matrix I are numbered from 0 to 4 and that of Matrix II are numbered from 5 to 9. A letter from these matrices can be represented first by its row and next by its column, for example, 'K' can be represented by 42, 33 etc. and 'Z' can be represented by 56, 67 etc. Similarly, you have to identify the set for the word 'NOTE'.

Matrix I

	0	1	2	3	4
0	C	K	K	M	H
1	A	I	B	M	G
2	D	J	E	D	L
3	L	H	M	K	I
4	F	C	K	L	J

Matrix II

	5	6	7	8	9
5	V	Z	Q	U	W
6	Y	S	Z	S	W
7	T	X	X	O	R
8	W	X	Q	T	X
9	Y	S	S	T	N

(a) 04, 30, 85, 66
(b) 20, 40, 75, 69
(c) 40, 21, 69, 55
(d) 99, 78, 75, 22

28. In this question, the sets of numbers given in the alternatives are represented by two classes of alphabets as in two matrices given below. The columns and rows of Matrix I are numbered from 0 to 4 and that of Matrix II are numbered from 5 to 9. A letter from these matrices can be represented first by its row and next by its column, e.g., 'D' can be represented by 01, 13 etc., and 'N' can be represented by 59,66, etc. You have to identify the set for the word 'HEEL'.

Matrix I

	0	1	2	3	4
0	C	D	E	F	G
1	F	G	C	D	E
2	D	E	F	G	C
3	E	F	G	C	D
4	G	C	D	E	F

Matrix II

	5	6	7	8	9
5	H	K	L	I	N
6	I	N	H	K	L
7	K	L	I	N	H
8	L	I	N	H	K
9	N	H	K	L	I

(a) 67, 21, 14, 98
(b) 75, 88, 65, 01
(c) 68, 65, 60, 10
(d) 68, 65, 50, 01

29. A word is represented by only one set of numbers as given in any of the alternatives. The set of numbers given in the alternatives are represented by two classes of alphabets as in the two matrices given below. The columns and rows of Matrix I are numbered from 0 to 4 and that of Matrix II from 5 to 9. A letter can be represented first by its row and next by its column number. e.g., 'N' can be represented by 02, 21, etc. 'O' can be represented by 65, 96 etc. Similarly, you have to identify the correct set for the word given WEAR.

Matrix I

	0	1	2	3	4
0	P	W	N	I	S
1	I	S	P	W	N
2	W	N	I	S	P
3	S	P	W	N	I
4	N	I	S	P	W

Matrix II

	5	6	7	8	9
5	A	E	R	O	H
6	O	H	A	E	R
7	E	R	O	H	A
8	H	A	E	R	O
9	R	O	H	A	E

(a) 44, 68, 67, 87
(b) 44, 87, 98, 69
(c) 20, 86, 67, 87
(d) 32, 87, 78, 95

DIRECTIONS ~ (Q. Nos. 30 and 31) *Read the following information carefully and answer the questions given below.*

A word is represented by only one set of numbers as given in any of the alternatives. The set of numbers given in the alternatives are represented by two classes of alphabets as in the 2 matrices given below. The columns and rows of Matrix I are from 0 to 4 and that of Matrix II from 5 to 9. A letter can be represented first by its row and next by its column number. e.g., 'C' can be represented by 02, 21, etc. 'T' can be represented by 65, 96 etc. Similarly, you have to identify the correct set for the word given in each question.

Matrix I

	0	1	2	3	4
0	D	V	C	P	M
1	P	M	D	V	C
2	V	C	P	M	D
3	M	D	V	C	P
4	C	P	M	D	V

Matrix II

	5	6	7	8	9
5	S	A	U	T	J
6	T	J	S	A	U
7	A	U	T	J	S
8	J	S	A	U	T
9	U	T	J	S	A

30. DUST
(a) 00, 76, 86, 59
(b) 13, 76, 98, 89
(c) 21, 69, 55, 65
(d) 12, 57, 67, 58

31. CAMP
(a) 02, 57, 04, 34
(b) 14, 68, 42, 34
(c) 21, 75, 11, 41
(d) 40, 99, 42, 12

DIRECTIONS ~ (Q. Nos. 32 and 33) *Read the following information carefully and answer the questions given below.*

A word is represented by only one set of numbers as given in any of the alternatives. The sets of numbers given in the alternatives are represented by two classes of alphabets as in two matrices given below. The columns and rows of Matrix I are numbered from 0 to 4 and that of Matrix II are numbered from 5 to 9. A letter from these matrices can be represented first by its row and next by its column, e.g. 'A' can be represented by 01, 20 etc., and 'B' can be represented by 56, 65 etc. Similarly, you have to identify the set for the word given in each question.

32. CARS

Matrix I

	0	1	2	3	4
0	E	A	R	W	P
1	W	P	A	E	R
2	A	W	P	R	E
3	P	R	E	A	W
4	R	E	W	P	A

Matrix II

	5	6	7	8	9
5	S	B	K	T	C
6	B	C	T	K	S
7	T	S	C	B	K
8	K	T	S	C	B
9	C	K	B	S	T

(a) 96, 00, 23, 99
(b) 95, 01, 13, 77
(c) 66, 20, 31, 88
(d) 77, 33, 40, 69

33. SILK

Matrix I

	0	1	2	3	4
0	M	L	F	H	B
1	H	B	M	L	F
2	L	F	H	B	M
3	B	M	L	F	H
4	F	H	B	M	L

Matrix II

	5	6	7	8	9
5	L	K	S	U	N
6	U	N	I	K	S
7	K	S	U	N	I
8	N	I	K	S	U
9	S	U	N	I	K

(a) 76, 67, 32, 68
(b) 76, 67, 32, 65
(c) 76, 67, 33, 68
(d) 76, 66, 33, 68

DIRECTIONS ~ (Q. Nos. 34-36) *Read the following information carefully and answer the questions given below.*

In the given matrices, a letter can be represented first by its row number and followed by its column number. 'A' is represented by 12, 24 and 'R' by 57, 76 etc. In each of the questions following matrices, identify one set of number pairs out of (a, b, c, d) which represents the given word.

Matrix I

	0	1	2	3	4
0	A	E	S	T	H
1	T	H	A	E	S
2	E	S	T	H	A
3	H	A	E	S	T
4	S	T	H	A	E

Matrix II

	5	6	7	8	9
5	P	O	R	K	L
6	K	L	P	O	R
7	O	R	K	L	P
8	L	P	O	R	K
9	R	K	L	P	O

34. EAST
(a) 32, 31, 02, 04
(b) 20, 43, 33, 11
(c) 13, 12, 14, 10
(d) 44, 32, 21, 03

35. LAKE
(a) 85, 31, 77, 44
(b) 97, 00, 77, 12
(c) 66, 12, 58, 40
(d) 77, 43, 76, 31

36. ROSE
(a) 86, 67, 33, 44
(b) 88, 76, 31, 32
(c) 95, 75, 02, 32
(d) 57, 87, 32, 33

DIRECTIONS ~ (Q. Nos. 37-39) *Read the following information carefully and answer the questions given below.*

A word is represented by only one set of numbers as given in any of the alternatives. The set of numbers given in the alternatives are represented by two classes of alphabets as in two matrices given below. The columns and rows of Matrix I are numbered from 0 to 4 and that of Matrix II are numbered from 5 to 9. A letter from these matrices can be represented first by its row and next by its column. e.g., 'A' can be represented by 00, 12, 23 etc. and 'P' can be represented by 58, 69, 75 etc. Similarly, you have to identify the set for the word given in each question.

Matrix I

	0	1	2	3	4
0	A	R	S	N	C
1	N	C	A	R	S
2	S	N	C	A	R
3	R	S	N	C	A
4	C	A	R	S	N

Matrix II

	5	6	7	8	9
5	O	E	L	P	T
6	T	O	E	L	P
7	P	T	O	E	L
8	L	P	T	O	E
9	E	L	P	T	O

37. PAST

(a) 75, 21, 14, 65 (b) 86, 12, 31, 76
(c) 58, 41, 12, 67 (d) 88, 77, 41, 67

38. RATE

(a) 13, 12, 98, 67 (b) 42, 23, 56, 76
(c) 30, 14, 95, 89 (d) 24, 43, 89, 95

39. POET

(a) 69, 88, 67, 65 (b) 75, 56, 65, 67
(c) 77, 88, 98, 78 (d) 75, 66, 76, 78

DIRECTION ~ (Q.No. 40) *Given below are two matrices of 25 cells each containing two classes of number. The columns and rows of Matrix I are numbered from A to E and those of Matrix II from F to J. A number from these matrices can be represented first by its row number and next by its column number. e.g., '2' can be represented as AB, BD etc. Similarly, 1 can be represented by FJ, GF, etc. In each of the following examples identify one set of letters pair out of a, b, c and d which represents the given word.*

Matrix I

	A	B	C	D	E
A	0	2	3	4	5
B	5	3	0	2	4
C	2	5	4	3	0
D	3	0	5	4	2
E	2	0	5	3	4

Matrix II

	F	G	H	I	J
F	6	8	7	9	1
G	1	7	6	8	9
H	9	8	7	6	1
I	1	9	8	7	6
J	9	6	8	7	1

40. Determine the letter group in the given alternatives which correctly denotes 7 4 2 8 3 5?

(a) JI, BE, CA , HG, DA, AE (b) GG, CC, EE, FG, BB, CE
(c) II, DD, AA, EE, BB, CC (d) FH, AD, AC, AE, FG, AB

Answers WITH EXPLANATIONS

1. (*d*) From the given matrix,

C = 44, 53
A = 46, 42, 62
L = 36, 65
M = 51

∴ CALM = 44, 62, 65, 51

2. (*d*) From the given matrix,

S = 16, 21
N = 23, 56
O = 54, 66
W = 52

∴ SNOW = 21, 23, 54, 52

3. (*b*) B = 31, 43

R = 78 , 85
E = 23, 34, 40
W = 56, 59, 87

Hence, BREW = 43, 78, 23, 59

4. (*d*) According to the question,

P = 58, 76, 95
A = 40, 78
R = 34, 77
K = 02, 23, 44, 65

Hence, PARK→ 95, 40, 77, 65

5. (*b*) Representations of alphabets are

T→ 30, 64
A→ 00, 76
L→ 31
E→ 32

∴ TALE→ 64, 00, 31, 32

6. (*c*) From the given matrices,

R = 58, 67, 76, 85, 99
O = 55, 69, 78, 87, 96
D = 57, 66, 75, 89, 98

∴ ROD = 67, 96, 57

7. (*a*) According to the question,

M→04, 32, 66
A →11, 40, 88
K→23, 44, 653
E→ 41, 86

Hence, MAKE = 04, 11, 23, 86

8. (*d*) According to the question,

G = 56, 68, 79, 87, 95
L = 65, 57, 78, 89, 96
O = 00, 13, 21, 34, 42
W = 04, 12, 20, 33, 41

∴ GLOW = 95, 57, 13, 33

9. (*b*) According to the question,

E = 00, 13, 22, 31, 44 , 55, 68, 77, 86, 99
A = 57, 66, 79, 85, 98
S = 01, 10, 23, 34, 43, 59, 67, 76, 88, 91
E = 00, 13, 22, 31, 44, 55, 68, 77, 86, 99

∴ EASE = 77, 85, 88, 44

10. (*b*) According to the question,

H = 04, 12, 21, 33, 40
A = 03, 14, 20, 32, 41
L = 55, 68, 77, 86, 99
T = 00, 13, 24, 31, 42

∴ HALT – 21, 41, 68, 13

11. (*a*) S→ 04, 31, 89; H→ 12, 56, 77;
I→43, 76, 88; P→10, 44, 99

∴ SHIP = 31, 56, 43, 10

12. (*c*) M→01, 10, 24, 33, 42;

A→ 02, 11, 20, 34, 43
S→ 00, 14, 23, 32, 41
T→04, 13, 22, 31, 40
E→ 56, 65, 79, 88, 97
R→ 03, 12, 21, 30, 44

MASTER = 01, 43, 41, 04, 65, 44

13. (*b*) R→ 02, 11, 20, 34, 43

O→ 57, 66, 75, 89, 98
U→58, 67, 79, 85, 99
N→ 01, 10, 24, 33, 42
D→ 59, 68, 77, 86, 95

ROUND→ 34, 66, 58, 33, 95

14. (*d*) From the given matrix,

O = 59, 67, 75, 86, 98
R = 03, 11, 24, 32, 40
G = 02, 10, 23, 31, 44
A = 01, 14, 22, 30, 43
N = 58, 69, 76, 85, 97

∴ ORGAN = 98, 03, 44, 22, 58

15. (*d*) According to the matrices,

D— 57 , 69, 76, 88, 95
O— 01, 13 , 20, 32 , 44
O— 01, 13 , 20, 32, 44
R— 04, 11, 23 , 30, 42

DOOR ⇒ 57, 13, 32, 23

16. (*a*) According to the matrices,
E — 00, 13, 24, 32, 41
A — 01, 12, 20, 33, 44
S — 55, 69, 76, 87, 98
T — 58, 67, 75, 86, 99
∴ EAST ⇒ 00, 12, 76, 58.

17. (*c*) According to the matrices,
P — 10
U — 45
S — 11, 66
H — 03, 75
∴ PUSH ⇒ 10, 45, 66, 75.

18. (*a*) According to the matrices,
S — 01, 13, 20, 32, 44
O — 55, 67, 79, 86, 98
A — 02, 14, 21, 33, 40
P — 59, 66, 78, 85, 97
∴ SOAP ⇒ 13, 55 21, 66.

19. (*b*) According to the matrices,
D — 21
E — 59, 75
A — 31, 33, 85, 89, 97
L — 68
∴ DEAL ⇒ 21, 75, 97, 68

20. (*b*) According to the matrices,
B — 00, 12, 21, 34, 43
A — 55, 66, 77, 88, 99
L — 56, 67, 78, 89, 95
D — 02, 11, 24, 33, 40
∴ BALD ⇒ 21, 88, 95, 24

21. (*a*) F — 02, 14, 21, 33, 40
I — 03, 10, 22, 34, 41
R — 57, 69, 76, 88, 95
E — 01, 13, 20, 32, 44
∴ FIRE = 02, 03, 57, 01

22. (*d*) According to the matrices,
B — 58, 69, 75, 88, 99
O — 03, 11, 22, 30, 44
T — 59, 68, 76, 87, 95
H — 57, 65, 79, 86, 98
∴ BOTH ⇒ 75, 22, 76, 79

23. (*a*) According to the matrices,
R — 97, 89, 75, 68, 56
O — 44, 33, 21, 12, 00
S — 98, 86, 77, 65, 59
T — 99, 85, 76, 67, 58
∴ ROST ⇒ 68, 33, 65, 58

24. (*b*) According to the matrices,
C — 59, 66, 77, 88, 95
A — 01, 12, 20, 33, 44
R — 02, 14, 23, 31, 40
T — 58, 67, 75, 86, 89
∴ CART ⇒ 66, 12, 40, 58

25. (*d*) According to the matrices,
S — 55, 68, 76, 89, 97
O — 03, 10, 21, 32, 44
F — 00, 12, 23, 34, 41
T — 56, 69, 77, 85, 98
∴ SOFT ⇒ 89, 03, 12, 98

26. (*c*) According to the matrices,
M — 03, 23
A — 12
L — 11, 13, 33
E — 32, 10, 40
∴ MALE ⇒ 03, 12, 11, 32

27. (*d*) N — 99
O — 78
T — 75, 88, 98
E — 22
∴ NOTE ⇒ 99, 78,75, 22.

28. (*a*) H — 55, 67, 79, 88, 96
E — 02, 14, 21, 30, 43
E — 02, 14, 21, 30, 43
L — 57, 69, 76, 86, 98
∴ 'HEEL' ⇒ 67, 21, 14, 98.

29. (*b*) According to the matrices,
W — 01, 13, 20, 32, 44
E — 56, 68, 75, 87, 99
A — 55, 67, 79, 86, 98
R — 57, 69, 76, 88, 95
∴ WEAR ⇒ 44, 87, 98, 69

30. (*d*) According to the matrices,
D — 00, 12, 24, 31, 43
U — 57, 69, 76, 88, 95
S — 55, 67, 79, 86, 98
T — 58, 65, 77, 89, 96
∴ DUST ⇒ 12, 57, 67, 58

31. (*b*) According to the matrices,
C — 02, 14, 21, 33, 40
A — 56, 68, 75, 87, 99
M — 04, 11, 23, 30, 42
P — 03, 10, 22, 34, 41
∴ CAMP ⇒ 14, 68, 42, 34

32. (*d*) C — 95, 66, 59, 77, 88
A — 01, 20, 12, 33, 44
R — 40, 31, 02, 23, 14
S — 55, 76, 87, 98, 69
∴ CARS ⇒ 77, 33, 40, 69

33. (*a*) S — 57, 69, 76, 88, 95
I — 67, 79, 86, 98
L — 01, 13, 20, 32, 44
K — 56, 68, 75, 87, 99
∴ SILK ⇒ 76, 67, 32, 68

34. (*c*) According to the matrices,
E — 01, 13, 20, 32, 44
A — 00, 12, 24, 31, 43
S — 02, 14, 21, 33, 40
T — 03, 10, 22, 34, 41
∴ EAST ⇒ 13, 12, 14, 10

35. (*a*) According to the matrices,
L — 59, 66, 78, 85, 97
A — 00, 12, 24, 31, 43
K — 58, 65, 77, 89, 96
E — 01, 13, 20, 32, 44
∴ LAKE ⇒ 85, 31, 77, 44

36. (*c*) According to the matrices,
R — 57, 69, 76, 88, 95
O — 56, 68, 75, 87, 99
S — 02, 14, 21, 33, 40
E — 01, 13, 20, 32, 44
∴ ROSE ⇒ 95, 75, 02, 32

37. (*b*) According to the matrices,
P — 58, 69, 75, 86, 97
A — 00, 12, 23, 34, 41
S — 02, 14, 20, 31, 43
T — 59, 65, 76, 87, 98
∴ PAST ⇒ 86, 12, 31, 76

38. (*a*) According to the matrices,
R — 01, 13, 24, 30, 42
A — 00, 12, 23, 34, 41
T — 59, 65, 76, 87, 98
E — 56, 67, 78, 89, 95
∴ RATE ⇒ 13, 12, 98, 67

39. (*a*) According to the matrices,
P — 58, 69, 75, 86, 97
O — 55, 66, 77, 88, 99
E — 56, 67, 78, 89, 95
T — 59, 65, 76, 87, 98
∴ POET ⇒ 69, 88, 67, 65

40. (*a*) 7 — FH, GG, HH, II, JI
4 — AD, BE, CC, DD, EE
2 — AB, BD, CA, DE, EA
8 — FG, GI, HG, IH, JH
3 — AC, BB, CD, DA, ED
5 — AE, BA, CB, DC, EC
Clearly, the letter group JI, BE, CA, HG, DA, AE correctly represents the number 742835.

CHAPTER / 21

Data Sufficiency

Data Sufficiency is to check and test the given set of information, whether it is enough to answer a question or not. This test is designed to test candidate's ability to relate given information to reach to a conclusion.

In data sufficiency problems, a question on any of the topics of sequences, ranking, puzzle test, coding-decoding, blood relations, ordering or mathematical calculations etc., is given followed by two, three or any number of statements. These statements may contain information to arrive at the answer to the question. You have to decide which of the statement(s) is/are sufficient to answer the given questions.

Steps to Solve the Questions

***Step* 1** The first step in solving a data sufficiency problem is to look at the question asked without the statements. You will not be able to answer the question because you will need more data.

***Step* 2** Now, examine Statement I alone. See whether you have enough data to answer the question or not.

***Step* 3** Now, look at Statement II alone and see whether it provides enough data to enable you to answer the question.

***Step* 4** If neither Statement I alone nor Statement II alone is sufficient to answer the question, then check for both the statements together to answer the question.

Similar steps are also followed when more than two statements are given, to obtain the answer.

The questions based on data sufficiency are divided into following two types

TYPE 01

Problems Based on Two Statements

In this type of problems, a question is followed by two statements which contain some information. The candidates are required to analyse and solve the question with the help of these statements and accordingly choose the correct option.

***Ex* 01** Read the given question and decide which of the following statements is/are sufficient to answer the question.

Question

Which word represents 'blue' in the code language ?

Statements « RRB Group D 2018

I. 'Here is a pen' is written as 'Hya eys e pena'.

II. 'Here is a blue pen' is written as 'Hya eys e Nel pena'.

(a) Statements I and II together are sufficient.
(b) Statement I alone is sufficient.
(c) Statements I and II together are insufficient.
(d) Statement II alone is sufficient.

***Solution* (a)** From Statement I,

Here is a pen ⇒ Hya eys e pena.

From Statement II,

Here is a [blue] pen ⇒ Hya eys e [Nel] pena.

From Statements I and II together,

Code for blue is Nel.

∴ Statements I and II together are sufficient.

***Ex* 02** Read the given question and decide which of the following statements is/are sufficient to answer the question.

Question

What is the age of Sriram? « RRB Group D 2018

Statements

I. Sriram is 32 yr elder to Shyam.

II. Shyam is 2 yr old now.

(a) Only II is sufficient. (b) Either I or II is sufficient.
(c) Only I is sufficient. (d) Both I and II are sufficient.

***Solution* (d)** From both the statements,

Shyam's present age = 2 yr and Sriram = 32 + 2 = 34 yr

∴ Both the statements are sufficient to answer the question.

DIRECTIONS ~ (Example Nos. 3-8) *Each of the questions below consists of a question and two statements numbered* I *and* II *given below it. You have to decide whether the data provided in the statements are sufficient to answer the question.*

Give answer

(a) If the data in Statement I alone are sufficient to answer the question, while the data in Statement II alone are not sufficient to answer the question.

(b) If the data in Statement II alone are sufficient to answer the question, while the data in Statement I alone are not sufficient to answer the question

(c) If the data either in Statement I alone or in Statement II alone are sufficient to answer the question
(d) If the data in both Statements I and II together are not sufficient to answer the question.
(e) If the data in both Statements I and II together are necessary to answer the question.

Ex 03 Sharvan's birthday is in which of the following month in a year? « IDBI Executive 2018

I. Sharvan's mother correctly remembers that Sharvan's birthday will come after September, but not in the month which has 30 days.
II. Sharvan's father correctly remember that Sharvan's birthday will not come in first and last month of the year.

Solution (e) From Statement I,

Months according to Sharvan's mother = October, December
From Statement II,
Months according to Sharvan's father
= February to November
∴ From Statements I and II,
Sharvan's birthday = October

Hence, the data in both the statements are necessary to answer the question.

Ex 04 How many sisters does Madhu have? « SBI Clerk 2016

I. Madhu's parents have four children.
II. Madhu has three brothers.

Solution (e) From Statement I, Madhu has three siblings,

From Statement II, Madhu has three brothers.

So, from both statements we can say that Madhu has no sister.

Ex 05 H is in which direction in respect of L?

I. L is to the East of M which is to the North of H.
II. L is to the North of J which is to the East of H.

Solution (c) From Statement I,

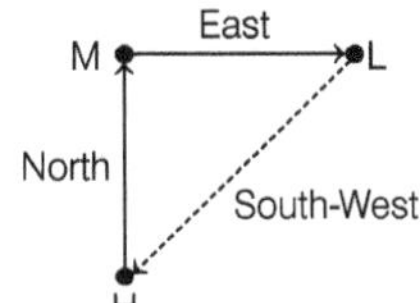

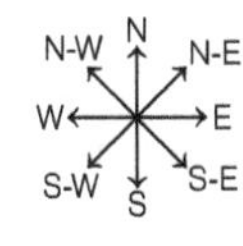

Clearly, H is to the South-West of L.

From Statement II,

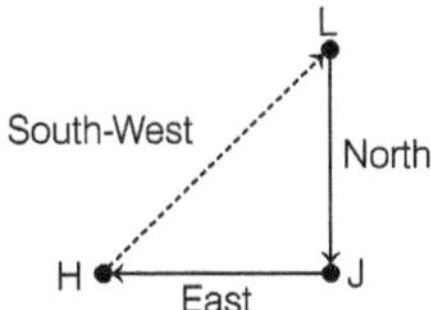

Clearly, H is to the South-West of L.

So, either Statement I or II alone is sufficient to answer the question.

Ex 06 Among A, B, C, D and E, seated in a straight line, but not necessarily in the same order, facing North, who sits exactly in the middle of the line? « SBI (Clerk) 2016

I. A sits third to left of D. B sits to the immediate right of C.
II. B sits second to right of A. E is not an immediate neighbour of D.

Solution (e) From Statement I, A C B D

From Statement II, A _ B

From Statements I and II, E A C B D

So, C is in the middle of the line.

So, two Statements I and II together are necessary to answer the question.

Ex 07 How many people are standing in straight line (Note : All are facing North)? « IBPS (SO) 2015

I. Q stands third from the right end of the line. Only one person stands between Q and S. S stands at the extreme left end of the line.
II. Q stands exactly in the centre of the line. P and M are immediate neighbours of Q. Only one person stands to the left of P.

Solution (e) From both statements,

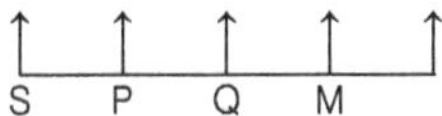

So, there are five people standing in straight line.

Hence, data in both statements together are necessary to answer the question.

Ex 08 How far is Point M from Point S? « IBPS (SO) 2015

I. Point S is 7 m to the South of Point M. Point T is 4 m to the East of Point S. Point R is 4 m to the North of Point T. Point Q is to the West of Point P. Point R is 4 m to the North of Point Q.
II. Point R is 4 m to the West of Point Q. Point P is 4 m to the North of Point Q. Point X is 4 m to the North of Point R. Point M is 6 m to the East of Point X.

Solution (a) From Statement I,

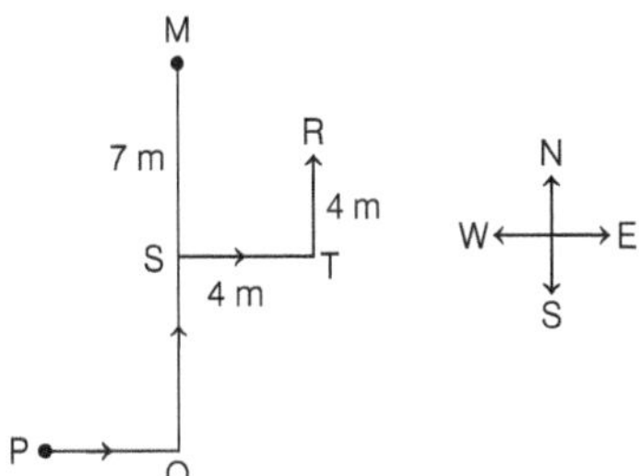

It is clear from diagram that Point M is 7 m far from Point S.

Hence, data in Statement I alone are sufficient to answer the question.

Practice / CORNER 21.1

1. You are given a question and two statements. Identify which of the statement(s) is/are necessary/sufficient to answer the question.

   Question

   Towards which direction is X from Y?

   Statements « RRB Group D 2018

   I. X is exactly to the East of W.

   II. W is exactly to the South of Y.

   (a) Statement II alone is sufficient, while Statement I alone is not sufficient.
   (b) Either Statement I or II alone is sufficient.
   (c) Statement I alone is sufficient, while Statement II alone is not sufficient.
   (d) Both Statement I and Statement II together are sufficient.

2. Consider the following question and decide which of the statement is sufficient to answer the question.

   Question

   How is Bhavna related to Satish ? « RRB Group D 2018

   Statements

   I. Bhavna's mother is Rajyam.

   II. Rajyam's son is Satish.

   (a) Only Statement I is sufficient, while Statement II is not
   (b) Neither Statement I nor II is sufficient
   (c) Only Statement II is sufficient, while Statement I is not
   (d) Both Statements I and II are sufficient

3. Three statements S_1, S_2 and S_3 are given below followed by a question:

   S_1 : C is younger than D , but older than A and B.

   S_2 : D is the oldest.

   S_3 : A is older than B.

   Question

   Who among A, B, C and D is the youngest?

   Which one of the following is correct in respect of the above statements and the question? « CSAT 2020

   (a) S_1 alone is sufficient to answer the question
   (b) S_1 and S_2 together are sufficient to answer the question
   (c) S_2 and S_3 together are sufficient to answer the question
   (d) S_1 and S_3 together are sufficient to answer the question

DIRECTIONS ~ (Q. Nos. 4-48) *Each of the following questions below consists of a question and two statements numbered* I *and* II *given below it. You have to decide whether the data provided in the statements are sufficient to answer the question.*

Give answer

(a) If the data in Statement I alone are sufficient to answer the question, while the data in.
Statement II alone are not sufficient to answer the question.
(b) If the data in Statement II alone are sufficient to answer the question, while the data in Statement I alone are not sufficient to answer the question.
(c) If the data either in Statement I alone or Statement II alone are sufficient to answer the question.
(d) If the data in both the Statements I and II together are not sufficient to answer the question.
(e) If the data in both the Statements I and II are together necessary to answer the question.

4. What does '$' mean in a certain code language?

   I. '5 $ # 3' means 'flowers are really good'.

   II. '7 # 3 5' means 'good flowers are available'.

5. Which of the following means 'very' in a certain code language?

   I. 'pit jo ha' means 'very good boy' in that code language.

   II. 'jo na pa' means 'she is good' in that code language.

6. What is the code of 'fat' in a certain code language?

   I. In that code language, 'she is fat' is written as 'he ra ca'.

   II. In that code language, 'fat boy' is written as 'ra ka'.

7. How is 'call' written in a code language?

   I. 'call me back' is written as '531' in that code language.

   II. 'you can call me any time' is written as '94163' in that code language.

8. How will 'must' be written in a certain code?

   I. In that code language, 'you must see' is written as 'la pa ni' and 'did you see' is written as 'jo ni pa'.

   II. In that code language 'you did that' is written as 'pa si jo'. « SBI (PO) 2009

9. What is the code of 'right' in a certain code language?

   I. The code of 'every right to reject' is '%47 *32 $53 *95'.

   II. The code of 'never reject right turn' is '%62 %47 $51 *32'. « SBI Clerk 2018

10. How is 'also' written in a code language?

    I. 'he also show data' is written as 'sx fa mn ca' and 'now many person also' is written as 'zb ct sx ya' in that code language.

    II. 'she visit the also' is written as 'sx lm nc ty' and 'she visit the always' is written as 'lm kc ty nc' in that code language. « IDBI Executive 2018

11. In a code language, 'al ed hop' means 'we play chess'. What is the code of word 'chess'?

    I. 'id nim hop' means 'we are honest'.

    II. 'gob ots al' means 'they play cricket'.

12. In a certain code language, '146' means 'adopt good habits'. What is the code of 'habit' in that language?

    I. '473' means ' like good pictures'.

    II. '826' means 'passion becomes habits'.

13. If 'over and above' is written as 'ja na ta' in a code language, how is 'and' written in that code language?

    I. 'come and go' is written as 'ha la ja' in that code language.

    II. 'he and you' is written as 'da ja ma' in that code language.

14. How is 'cost' written in the given code language?
I. In the code language 'tell me the cost' is coded as '@ 0 # 9' and 'cost was very high' is coded as '& 6 # 1'.
II. In the code language 'some cost was discount' is coded as '187#' and 'some people like discount' is coded as '875%'.

15. On which day in June did the school reopen?
I. Manoj correctly remembers that the school reopened after 12th June but before 16th June.
II. Manoj's classmate Ashok correctly remembers that the school reopened after 14th June but before 18th June.

16. On which day of the same week is Ramesh's exam scheduled (Monday being the first day of the week)?
I. Ramesh correctly remembers that his exam is scheduled on a day after Tuesday but before Thursday of the same week.
II. Ramesh's friend correctly remembers that Ramesh's exam is scheduled on the third day of the week

17. Is R the grand-daughter of C? « SBI Clerk 2016
I. The only sister of A is the mother of R's brother, B.
II. C, the mother of A has only one grandson, B.

18. How many sisters does P have?
I. T and V are only sisters of D.
II. D is brother of P.

19. How is Nalini related to Sameer?
I. Brother of Nalini is the only grandson of Sameer's father.
II. Sameer is the only son of his father.

20. How is D related to M?
I. D has two brothers and one sister.
II. Brother of M is married to D's sister.

21. How many sisters does P have?
I. M and T are sisters of K.
II. D is husband of B who is mother of K and P.

22. Among P, K, D and R, who is the son of M?
I. P and K are sisters of R.
II. D is the mother of K and wife of M.

23. Point X is in which direction in respect of Point Y?
I. Point Z is at equal distance from Point X and Point Y.
II. Point X is at a distance of 5 km from Point Y.

24. Kumud is facing towards which direction?
I. Nikhil is facing towards North and if he turns to his left he faces opposite direction as that of Kumud.
II. Saroj who is not towards facing East is to the right of Kumud.

25. Point Q is in which direction with respect to Point P?
I. Point P is in East of Point L. Point L is in North of Point M. Point M is in West of Point N. Point N is in South of Point O. Point O is in West of Point Q.
II. Point L is in West of Point P and North of Point M. Point M is in East of Point N which is South of Point O. Point Q is in East of Point O and North of Point L. « IDBI Executive 2018

26. Among five friends M, N, O, P and Q (each earning a different amount), who earns the least? « SBI Clerk 2016
I. M earns more than O, P and N.
II. P earns more than only O.

27. Who amongst P, Q, R, S and T is the tallest?
I. P is taller than Q. T is not the tallest.
II. R is taller than P. S is not the tallest.

28. Among Sanjay, Suresh, Navin, Prakash and Karan, who has secured maximum marks in Mathematics?
I. Karan has secured more marks in Mathematics than Suresh and Navin.
II. Sanjay and Prakash have secured less marks in Mathematics than Navin.

29. What is the difference in the ages of P and K?
I. P is 20 yr older than M.
II. M is 2 yr younger than Z.

30. The sum of ages of M, N and O is 50 yr. What is N's age?
I. N is 10 yr older than M.
II. O is 30 yr old.

31. Find the number of boys and number of girls in the row? « SBI Clerk 2018
I. R sits 18th from left end of the row and Y sits 11th from the right end of the row. R and Y interchange their positions, after interchanging the position R's position is 20th from left end.
II. Total 43 students are in the row and all are facing is same direction.

32. Among five friends— J, K, L, M and N each of a different height, who is the second tallest?
I. N is taller than M and K. K is shorter than M.
II. L is taller than N. J is not the tallest.

33. How many students are there in the class?
I. There are more than 20 but less than 27 students in the class.
II. There are more than 24 but less than 31 students in the class. The number of students in the class can be divided into groups such that each group contains 5 students.

34. Six boys J, K, L, M, N, O are there in a classroom each of them is of different heights. Who among the following is the tallest?
I. M is taller than N and K. J is taller than M but not as tall as O. L is taller than K.
II. M is taller than only three boys. J is taller than K.

35. How many children are there in the row of children facing North?
I. Vasudha who is fifth from the left end is eight to the left of Anish who is twelfth from the right end.
II. Rahul is fifth to the left of Neeta who is seventh from the right end and eighteenth from the left end.

36. Among five friends S, T, U, V and W, who owns the maximum number of houses ?
« United India Insurance Company (AO) 2016

(Each owning a different number of houses)

I. T owns more houses than V. V owns more houses than S but less than W. U does not own the least number of houses.

II. Only one person owns more number of houses than W. S and V own less number of houses than U. T owns more houses than S.

37. Four friends A, B, C and D are seated in circle facing the centre but not necessarily in the same order. Is anyone seated exactly between C and D, when counted from the left of C? « SBI Clerk 2016

I. B is seated to the immediate right of C.

II. B is seated to the immediate left of A. D is not an immediate neighbour of B.

38. Among five people — A, B, C, D and E sitting around a circular table facing the centre, who is sitting second to the left of D?

I. C is second to the left of A. B and D are immediate neighbours of each other.

II. D is to the immediate left of B. E is not an immediate neighbour of D and B.

39. Seven people A, B, C, D, E, F and G are standing in a straight line facing North, not necessarily in the same order. What is the position of D with respect to G?
« United India Insurance Company (AO) 2016

I. F stands fifth to the right of B. Only one person stands between F and G. D is neither an immediate neighbour of B nor F.

II. C stands at one of the extreme ends of the line. Only two people stand between C and G. D stands second to the right of B.

40. Six persons viz A, B, C, D, E and F are sitting on a circular table for lunch, who among them sits immediate left of F (If all the persons are facing towards the centre)? « IDBI Executive 2018

I. A sits third to right of F. One person sits between A and C. E sits third to left of C.

II. Only one person sits between E and D. F sits second to right of D. A sits third to left of F.

41. Seventeen people are standing in a straight line facing South. What is Bhavna's position from the left end of the line?

I. Sandeep is standing second to the left of Sheetal. Only five people stand between Sheetal and the one who is standing at the extreme right end of the line. Four people stand between Sandeep and Bhavna.

II. Anita is standing fourth to the left of Sheetal. Less than three people are standing between Bhavna and Anita. « SBI (PO) 2013

42. Six persons A, B, C, D, E and F are sitting in row. All of them are facing North direction. Who among the following sits second from the right end?

I. B sits at end extreme end of the row. A sits second to the right of B. Only one person sits between A and C. E sits immediate right of C.

II. E sits third to the right of D. Only one person sits between E and A. F sits to the right to E. C is an immediate neighbour of E.

43. Who sits immediate to the left of Ravi, who is sitting in row. All the persons who are sitting in a row facing North direction ? « SBI Clerk 2018

I. There are only two persons sit between Sahil and Geeta. More than three persons sit to the left of Geeta.

II. Not more than 8 persons can sit in a row. Ravi sits second to the left of Sahil. Diya sits 6 places away from Geeta.

44. A certain number of boxes have been stacked one above the other. How many boxes are there in the stack?
« United India Insurance Company (AO) 2016

I. Only three boxes are kept between U and B. M is kept immediately below B but not at the bottom of the stack. Only five boxes are kept between M and D.

II. R is kept exactly in the middle of the stack. Only two boxes are kept between R and U. S is kept immediately above U.

45. A certain number of boxes have been stacked one above the other. How many boxes are there in the stack ?
« United India Insurance Company (AO) 2016

I. G is kept fifth from the bottom of the stack. Only two boxes are kept between G and Y. Only three boxes are kept above Y.

II. F is kept third from the top of the stack. Y is kept immediately below F. Only two boxes are kept between Y and B.

46. Seven people P, Q, R, S, T, U and V are standing in a straight line facing North, not necessarily in the same order. What is the position of R with respect to T ?
« United India Insurance Company (AO) 2016

I. S stands second to the right of R. P stands third to the left of R. Only one person stands between P and T.

II. Q stands second from the left end of the line. T is an immediate neighbour of Q. R stands to the immediate left of U.

47. Six persons R, S, T, U, V and W live on a six storey building such as ground floor is numbered as 1 and above it 2 floor and so on ... upto top floor numbered as 6. How many persons live between R and T?

I. T lives on an even numbered floor, but not on top floor. Only two persons live between W and T. R lives below W.

II. Four persons live between S and U. No one lives between S and T. V lives immediately above R.

48. What is the value of 144$16★7#9?

I. '$' means '÷', '★' means '×' and '#' means '+'.

II. 1 6 $ 4 ★ 2 # 2 = 10

Answers WITH EXPLANATIONS

1. (*d*) From Statements I and II,

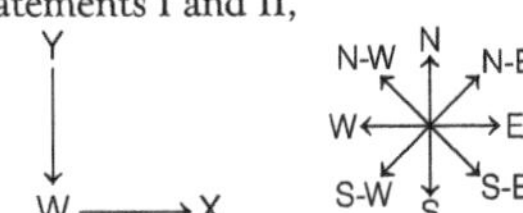

Clearly, X is in South-East direction from Y.
Hence, both the statements together are sufficient.

2. (*b*) From Statements I and II, we get

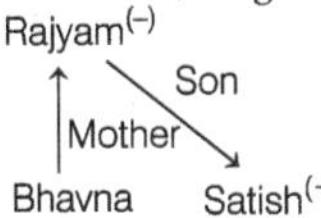

As, gender of Bhavna is not clear. So, both the statements together are not sufficient to answer the question.

3. (*d*) From S_1 : $C < D$
$C > A$
$C > B$
From S_3 : $A > B$
∴ Combining both S_1 and S_3, we get
$D > C > A > B$
Hence, youngest is B.
Therefore, S_1 and S_3 together are sufficient to answer the question.

4. (*e*) From Statements I and II,

(5) $ (#) (3) = (flowers) (are) really (good.)
(7) (#) (3)(5) = (good)(flowers) (are) available

∴ $ = really
So, both statements are required to answer the question.

5. (*d*) From Statements I and II,

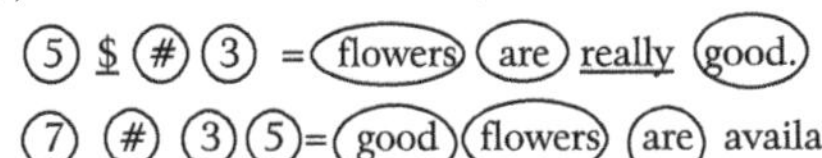

(jo) na pa = she is (good)

∴ very = pit/ha
So, both the statements are not sufficient to answer the question.

6. (*e*) From Statement I, she is fat = he ra ca
From, Statement II, fat boy = ra ka
Clearly, fat = ra
So, both statements are required to answer the question.

7. (*d*) From Statements I and II,
call me back = 5 3 1
you can call me any time = 9 4 1 6 3
∴ call = 3/1
So, both the statements are not sufficient to answer the question.

8. (*a*) From Statement I, (you) must (see) = la (pa) (ni)
did (you)(see) = jo (ni)(pa)
Clearly, must = la
From Statement II, you did that = pa si so
So, Statement I alone is sufficient to answer the question.

9. (*d*) From Statements I and II together,
every right to reject
⇒ %47 *32 $53 *95
never reject right turn
⇒ %62 %47 $51 *32
∴ Code for right is either %47 or *32
Hence, both the statements together are not sufficient to answer the question.

10. (*c*) From Statement I,
he (also) show data ⟶ (sx) fa mm ca
now many person (also) ⟶ zb ct (sx) ya
∴ also = sx,
From Statement II,
[she][visit][the] also ⟶ sx [lm][nc][ty]
[she][visit][the] always ⟶ [lm] kc [ty][nc]
∴ also = sx
Hence, the data in either Statement I or in Statement II alone are sufficient to answer the question.

11. (*e*) Given that,
(al) ed [hop] = [we] (play) chess ...(A)
From Statement I, id nim [hop] = [we] are honest
From Statement II, gob ots (al) = they (play) cricket
From Statement I and (A), we = hop
From Statement II and (A), play = al
Clearly, chess = ed
So, both statements are required to answer the question.

12. (*b*) Given that, 1 4 6 = adopt good habits ...(A)
From Statement I, 4 7 3 = like good pictures
From Statement II, 8 2 6 = passion becomes habits
From Statement II and (A), 6 = habits
So, Statement II alone is required to answer the question.

13. (*c*) Given that, over and above = ja na ta ...(A)
From Statement I, come and go = ha la ja
From Statement II, he and you = da ja ma
Clearly, either from (A) and Statement I or from (A) and Statement II, and = ja
So, either Statement I or Statement II alone is sufficient to answer the question.

14. (*a*) From Statement I,
tell me the cost → @ 0 # 9
cost was very high → & 6 # 1
cost → #
From Statement II,
some cost was discount → 1 8 7 #
some people like discount → 8 7 5 %
⇒ some discount → 8 7
and cost → either 1 or #
Thus, we can get the code of 'cost' from Statement I only.
Hence, data in Statement I alone are sufficient to answer the question.

15. (*e*) According to the Manoj,
Required day = 13th June/14th June/15th June
According to the Ashok,
Required day = 15th June/16th June/17th June
∴ Required day = 15th June
So, both statements are required to answer question.

16. (*c*) From Statement I,

Between Tuesday and Thursday

Required day = Tuesday, Wednesday, Thursday

From Statement II,

Required day = Monday, Tuesday, Wednesday

3rd day of the week

So, either Statement I or II alone is sufficient to answer the question.

17. (*e*) From Statements I and II,

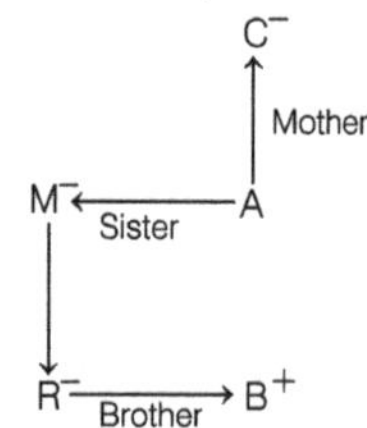

So, from Statements I and II, R is the grand-daughter of C.

18. (*e*) From Statements I and II,

Hence, it is clear P has two sisters T and V.
So, both statements are required to answer the question.

19. (*e*) From Statement I, and II,

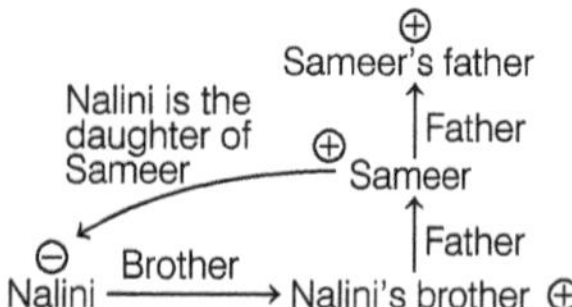

Clearly, Nalini is the daughter of Sameer.
So, both Statements are required to answer the question.

20. (*d*) From Statement II,

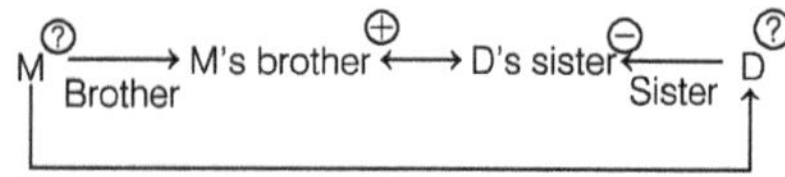

Hence, Statement II is not insufficient.
Further, no relation is possible from Statements I and II also.
So, both statements are insufficient to answer the question.

21. (*d*) Statement I alone is not sufficient as P is not available in it. Statement II alone is insufficient as gender of K is unknown.
From Statements I and II,

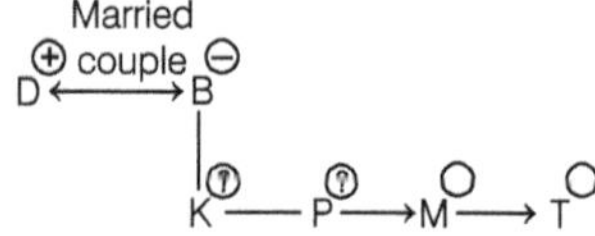

Hence, Statements I and II both are insufficient as gender of K is not known.

22. (*d*) It is clear that neither of the given statements is sufficient alone.
From Statements I and II,

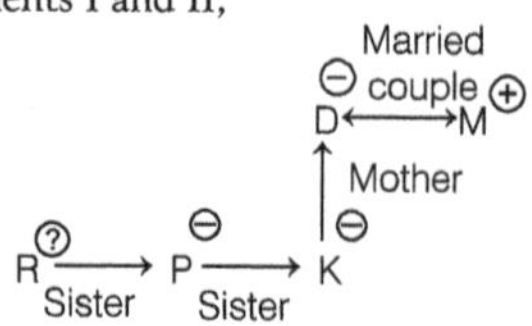

Gender of R is unknown, hence Statements I and II together are not sufficient to answer the question.

23. (*d*) Both statements are not sufficient to answer the question as directions is not given in any of the statements or we can say that data is inadequate.

24. (*a*) From Statement I,

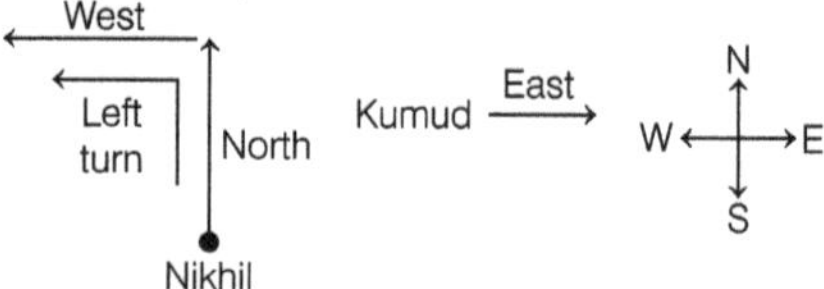

Clearly, after left turn Nikhil will face West. Hence, Kumud will face the direction opposite to what Nikhil will face after the left turn. Hence, Kumud will face East which is opposite to West what Nikhil is facing.
Hence, Statement I alone is sufficient to answer the question.
From Statement II, it is not clear that Kumud is facing which direction. Hence, only Statement I alone is sufficient to answer the question.

25. (*b*) From Statement II,

Clearly, Q is in North-West direction with respect to P.
Hence, data in Statement II alone are sufficient.

26. (*d*) From Statement I,

$$M > O, P, N$$

Nothing is given about Q.
From Statement II, ... $P > O$
So, none of the statement is sufficient to answer the question.

27. (*e*) It is clear that neither of the statements alone is sufficient.
From Statements I and II, $R > P > Q$ and T and S are not the tallest.
Hence, R is the tallest. So, both Statements I and II are required to answer the question.

28. (*e*) From Statement I, Karan > Suresh/Navin
Clearly, Statement I alone is insufficient.
From Statement II, Navin > Sanjay/Prakash
Clearly, Statement II alone is insufficient.
But from both Statements I and II, it is clear that Karan has secured maximum marks. So, both statements are required to answer the question.

29. (*d*) Relation between P and K cannot be established with the help of both Statements I and II. So, both the statements are not sufficient to answer the question.

30. (*e*) As given in the question, $M + N + O = 50$ yr
On combining Statements I and II, we get

$$N = 15 \text{ yr}$$

So, both statements are required to answer the question.

31. (*d*) No information regarding boys or girls is given in any of the statement.
Hence, both the statements together are not sufficient to answer the question.

32. (*d*) From Statement I, N > M > K
From Statement II, L > N
From both the Statements, L > N > M > K
But height of J is not clear.
Thus, second tallest friend cannot be determined.
Hence, data neither in Statement I nor in Statement II are sufficient to answer the question.

33. (*e*) From Statement I,
Number of students in class = 21 or 22 or 23 or 24 or 25 or 26
From Statement II,
Number of students in class = 25 or 26 or 27 or 28 or 29 or 30
Since, number of students can be divided into groups of 5 students, therefore number of students must be a multiple of 5.
∴ Number of students in the class = 25 or 30
On combining Statements I and II,
Number of students in the class = 25
Hence, the data in both the Statements I and II together are necessary to answer the question.

34. (*e*) From Statement I,
O > J > M > N and K
also, L > K
From Statement II,
J > K
and M is taller than three boys.
From Statements I and II together,
O > J > M > __ > __ > __
Clearly, O is tallest.
Hence, both the statements are required to answer the question.

35. (*c*) From Statement I,
Total number of students = 12 + 8 + 5 − 1 = 24
From Statement II,
Total number of students = 18 + 7 − 1 = 24
Therefore, both the statements are individually sufficient to answer the question.

36. (*d*) From Statement I,
T > V, W > V>S
∴ T > W> V> S, U
From Statement II,
U > S/V,T >S, Only one > W
Hence, both Statements I and II together are not sufficient to answer the question.

37. (*b*) From Statement I,

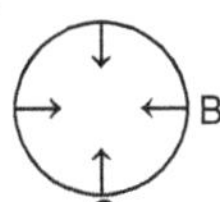

From Statement II,

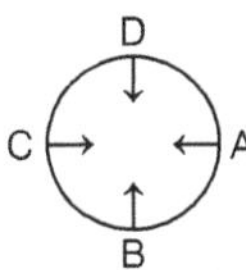

So, from Statement II, we can say that there is no person between C and D.

38. (*b*) From Statement II,

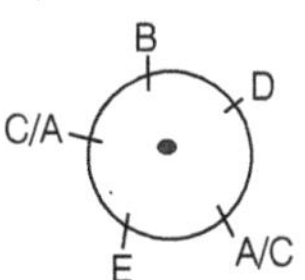

So, E is sitting second to the left of D.
Hence, data in Statement II alone are sufficient to answer the question.

39. (*c*) From Statement I,

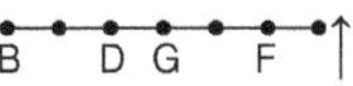

From Statement II,

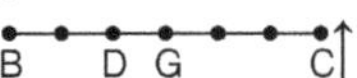

So, position of D is one of the immediate neighbour of G.
Hence, data either in Statement I or II alone are sufficient to answer the question.

40. (*e*) From Statement I,

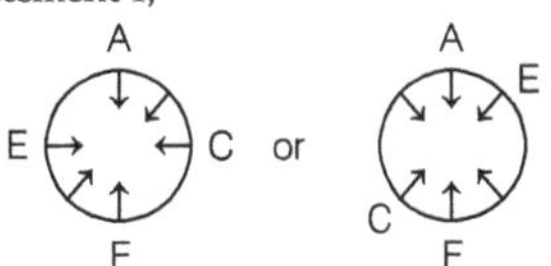

From Statement II,

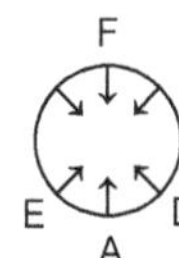

Now, from Statements I and II,

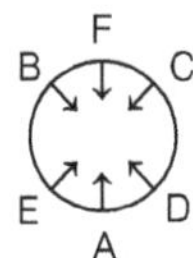

Clearly, C sits to the immediate left of F. Hence, data in both the statements are required to answer the question.

41. (*e*) From Statements I and II,

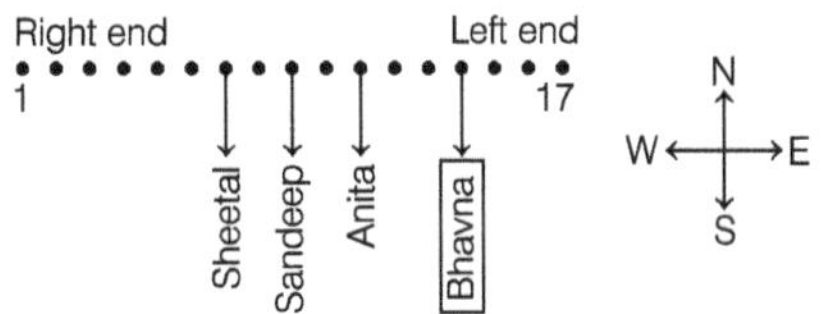

Thus, position of Bhavna can be found out by using both of the statements.

42. (*a*) From Statement I,

Clearly, C sits at second position from right end.
From Statement II, more than one arrangement is possible.
So, we cannot determine who sits at second position from right end.
Hence, only Statement I is sufficient.

43. (*e*) From Statement I,
Sahil/Geeta ___ ___ Geeta/Sahil and more than three people sit to the left of Geeta.
From Statement II,
Not more than 8 people can sit in a row.
Ravi ___ Sahil
and Diya sits 6 place away from Geeta.
From Statements I and II together.
Diya Ravi ___ Sahil ___ ___ Geeta ___
Clearly, Diya sits to the immediate left of Ravi.
Hence, data in both Statements I and II together are necessary to answer the question.

44. (*e*) From both statements.

–	B	M	–	R	–	S	U	D

From above arrangement it is clear that there are nine boxes in the stack.
Hence, data in both Statements I and II together are necessary to answer the question.

45. (*e*) From both statements,

B	–	F	Y	–	–	G	–	–	–	–

From above arrangement it is clear that there are eleven boxes in the stack.
Hence, data in both Statements I and II together are necessary to answer the question.

46. (*a*) From Statement I,

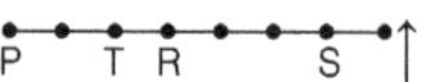

From Statement II,

From Statement II, we are unable to find the exact position of R. But from Statement I position of R is clear position of R is immediate right of T.
Hence, data in Statement I alone are sufficient to answer the question, while the data in Statement II alone are not sufficient to answer the question.

47. (*e*) From both the statements,

Floor	Person	Floor	Person
6	U	3	R
5	W	2	T
4	V	1	S

Clearly, no one lives between R and T. Hence, both the statements are necessary to answer the question.

48. (*a*) From Statement I, 144 $ 16 ★ 7 # 9

$\Rightarrow \quad 144 \div 16 \times 7 + 9 \Rightarrow \frac{144}{16} \times 7 + 9 \quad \Rightarrow \quad 63 + 9 \Rightarrow 72$

Hence, Statement I alone is sufficient to answer the question.

TYPE 02

Problems Based on Three Statements

In this type of questions, three statements are provided, which contain certain information. The candidates are required to analyse the statements to solve the given question and accordingly choose the correct option.

The given alternatives include whether any one of the statement, combination of two or combination of the three statements are required to solve the problem or either of the statement or neither of the statements are sufficient to answer these problem.

***Ex* 09** You are given a question and three statements. Identify which of the statements is/are necessary/ sufficient to answer the question. « RRB Group D 2018

Question Find the age of M after 10 yr from now.

Statements

I. L is 2 yr old now.
II. M is L's older sister.
III. M's age is half to five times the age of L.

(a) Statement II alone is sufficient
(b) Statements I and III together are sufficient
(c) Statements I, II and III together are insufficient
(d) Statement I alone is sufficient

***Solution* (b)** From Statement 1, L's age = 2 yr

From Statement III,

$$\text{M's age} = \frac{5 \times 2}{2} = 5 \text{ yr}$$

$\therefore$ M's age 10 yr, hence = 5 + 10 = 15 yr

Therefore, Statements I and III together are sufficient.

DIRECTIONS ~ (Example Nos. 10-12) *Each of the question below consists of a question and three statements numbered I, II and III. You have to decide whether the data provided in the statements are sufficient to answer the questions.*

Give answer « IBPS Clerk 2017

(a) If the Statements II and III are sufficient to answer the question but Statement I alone is not sufficient to answer the question.
(b) If all the statements taken together are not sufficient to answer the question.
(c) If the Statements I and II are sufficient to answer the question but Statement III is not sufficient to answer the question.
(d) If all the statements together are sufficient to answer the question.
(e) If Statements I and III are sufficient to answer the question but Statement II alone is not sufficient to answer the question.

***Ex* 10** Which of the following represents 'come' in a code language?

I. 'pit na ja od' means 'you may come here' in that language.
II. 'ja ta ter' means 'come and go' in that code language.
III. 'od na pit ter' means 'you may go home' in that code language.

***Solution* (c)** From Statements I, II and III

you may (come) here	⟶	pit na (ja) od	...(i)
(come) and [go]	⟶	(ja) ta [ter]	...(ii)
you may [go] home	⟶	od na pit [ter]	...(iii)

From Eqs. (i) and (ii), come ⟶ ja
Hence, it is clear that Statements I and II are sufficient to answer the question.

Ex 11 How many son/sons does D has?

I. B and F are brothers of A.
II. C is the sister of A and F.
III. C and E are daughters of D.

Solution ***(d)*** From Statement I,

Here, it is clear that B and F are brother of A. So, B and F are sons of D, whereas the gender of A is not clear.
From Statements II and III, it is clear that gender of A is male. Hence, A is also son of D. So, D have three sons, A, B and F.
Hence, all the three statements are sufficient to answer the question.

Ex 12 Who amongst P, Q, R, S and T is in the middle while standing in a line?

I. Q is to the right of T.
II. S is between P and T.
III. Q is between T and R.

Solution ***(d)*** From Statements I, II and III,

P S T Q R

It is clear from above that T is in the middle while standing in the line.
Hence, all the three statements are sufficient to answer the question.

Practice / CORNER 21.2

DIRECTIONS ~ (Q. Nos. 1-20) *In each question below, three Statements* I, II *and* III *are given. You are required to find out which of the given statement (s) is/are sufficient to answer the question. Mark your answer accordingly.*

1. On Which day Suresh went to Chennai, if week starts on Monday?

I. Suresh took leave on Wednesday.
II. Suresh went to Chennai the next day of the day his mother came to his house.
III. Suresh's mother came to his house neither on Monday nor Friday.

(a) II and III (b) I and II
(c) I and III (d) All are needed
(e) Even I, II and III together are not sufficient

2. In which year was Tarun born?

I. Tarun is 6 yr older than Rabin.
II. Rabin's brother was born in 1982.
III. Tarun's brother is 2 yr younger than Rabin's brother who was 8 yr younger than him.

(a) I and III (b) II and III
(c) All I, II and III (d) I and II

3. Who among Girish, Prashant, Kamlesh and Jayesh is the youngest?

I. Kamlesh is younger than Jayesh but older than Girish and Prashant.
II. Jayesh is the oldest.
III. Girish is older than Prashant.

(a) I and II (b) I and III
(c) II and III (d) Only I

4. Who among P, Q, R, S and T is in the middle while standing in a line?

I. Q is to the right of T.
II. S is between P and T.
III. Q is between T and R.

(a) I and II (b) II and III
(c) I and III (d) All I, II, III

5. Point D is in which direction with respect to Point B? « IBPS (PO) 2012

I. Point A is to the West of point B, Point C is to the North of Point B, Point D is to the South of Point C.
II. Point G is to South of Point D. Point G is 4 m from Point B. Point D is 9 m from Point B.
III. Point A is to the West of Point B. Point B is exactly midway between Point A and E. Point F is to the South of Point E. Point D is to the West of Point F.

(a) I and III (b) II and III
(c) All required (d) I and II
(e) None of these

6. How old was Deepak on 30th July, 1996?

I. Deepak is 6 yr older than his brother Prabir.
II. Prabir is 29 yr younger than his mother.
III. Deepak's mother celebrated her 50th birthday on 15th June, 1996.

(a) I and II (b) All I, II and III
(c) II and III (d) None of these

7. On which day of the last week did Mohan definitely meet Pramod in his office?

I. Pramod went to Mohan's office on Tuesday and Thursday.
II. Mohan was absent for three days in the week excluding Sunday.
III. Mohan was not absent on any two consecutive days of the week.

(a) I and II
(b) I and III
(c) II and III
(d) Even I, II and III, together are not sufficient.

8. Which of the following represents 'touch' in a code language?

I. '4231' means 'It may touch here' in that language.
II. '526' means 'touch and go' in that code language.
III. '7345' means 'It may go home' in that code language.

(a) I and II or I and III (b) I and II
(c) All I, II and III (d) II and III

9. Who among P, Q, R, S and T is the lightest?

I. Q is lighter than P and S and heavier than T.
II. P is heavier than Q and lighter than S.
III. R is heavier than Q.

(a) I and II (b) I and III
(c) I, II and III (d) II and III

10. How is Q related to T?

I. M and R are brothers.

II. S has two sons and one daughter, R being one of the sons.

III. S is the mother of T and married to Q.

(a) I and III (b) Only III

(c) I and II (d) II and III

11. Who amongst Suraj, Neeraj, Tara, Meena and Anil is the first to take the lecture ?

I. Suraj takes lecture before Meena and Neeraj but not before Anil.

II. Tara is not the first to take the lecture.

III. Meena is not the last to take the lecture.

(a) Only I

(b) Only I and II

(c) Only I and either II or III

(d) All I, II and III are necessary

(e) Question cannot be answered even with the information in all three statements

12. Who among A, B, C, D, E and F each having a different height, is the tallest ?

I. B is taller than A but shorter than E.

II. Only two of them are shorter than C.

III. D is taller than only F.

(a) Only I and II

(b) Only II and III

(c) Only I and III

(d) All I, II and III are required to answer the question.

(e) All I, II and III are not sufficient to answer the question.

13. Who among A, B, C, D and E is the lightest?

I. B is lighter than A & D and heavier than E.

II. A is heavier than B and lighter than D.

III. C is heavier than B.

(a) I and II only (b) I and III

(c) I, II and III (d) II and III only

(e) None of these

14. How many daughters does L have ?

I. C and D are sisters of M.

II. M's father T is husband of L.

III. Out of the three children which T has only one is a boy.

(a) Only I and III

(b) All, I, II and III are required to answer the question

(c) Only II and III

(d) Question cannot be answered even with all I, II and III

(e) Only I and II

15. There are six members P, Q, R, S, T and U in a family, how is T related to S?

I. S is son of R, P and U are child of Q . T is grandfather of P.

II. R is mother - in law of Q, who is a female member.

III. S has no brother.

(a) I and III only

(b) III only

(c) I and II only

(d) II and III only

(e) All I, II and III are required

16. How is Aditya related to Mayank?

I. Pinki is the mother-in-law of Rashmi, the wife of Aditya.

II. Pinki's brother is Aditya's maternal uncle.

III. Pinki's husband is the only son of Mayank.

(a) Only I and II

(b) Only I and III

(c) Only I and either II or III

(d) Any two of the three

(e) Question cannot be answered even with the information in all three statements

17. How is 'DATE' written in the code language ?

I. DEAR is written as $#@? in that code language.

II. TREAT is written as %?#@% in that code language.

III. TEAR is written as %#@? in that code language.

(a) Only I and II

(b) Only II and III

(c) All I, II and III

(d) Only I and either II or III

(e) None of the above

18. Towards which direction is village J from village W ?

I. Village R is to the West of village W and to the North of village T.

II. Village Z is to the East of village J and to the South of village T.

III. Village M is to the North-East of village J and North of village Z.

(a) Only III

(b) Only II and III

(c) All I, II and III are required to answer the question

(d) Question cannot be answered even with all I, II and III

(e) None of the above

19. What is Sudha's rank from top in the class of 45 students?

I. Sudha is five ranks below Samir who is 15th from the bottom.

II. Radha is 30th from the top and Neeta is 5th from the bottom.

III. Sudha is exactly in the middle of Radha and Neeta.

(a) Only I

(b) Only II and III

(c) Either Only I or only II and III

(d) Only I and either II or III

(e) None of the above

20. There are six letters W, A, R, S, N and E. Is 'ANSWER' the word formed after performing the following operations using these six letters only? « IBPS Clerk 2011

I. E is placed fourth to the right of A. S is not placed immediately next to either A or E.

II R is placed immediately next (either left or right) to E. W is placed immediately next (either left or right) to S.

III. Both N and W are placed immediately next to S. The word does not begin with R. A is not placed immediately next to W.

(a) Only I (b) Only I and III

(c) Only I and either II or III (d) Only II and III

(e) None of the above

Answers / WITH EXPLANATIONS

1. (*e*) Statements I, II and III together are not sufficient as the required day can be anyone of Wednesday, Thursday, Friday and Sunday.

2. (*c*) From Statements II and III, it is clear that Rabin's brother was born in 1982, Tarun's brother was born in 1984 and Rabin was born in 1974.
From Statement I, it is given that Tarun is six year older than Rabin, hence we know that Tarun was born in 1968.
So, all Statements I, II and III are required to answer the question.

3. (*b*) From Statement I, Jayesh > Kamlesh > Girish/Prashant
Clearly, Statement I alone is insufficient.
From Statement III, Girish > Prashant
Clearly, Statement III alone is insufficient.
From both Statements I and III,

Jayesh > Kamlesh > Girish > Prashant

Clearly, Prashant is the youngest.
So, Statements I and III are required to answer the question.

4. (*d*) From all the Statements I, II and III, the order of ranking of P, Q, R, S and T in a line is as

Hence, T is in between the line.
So, all the Statements I, II and III are required to answer the question.

5. (*a*) From Statements I and II,

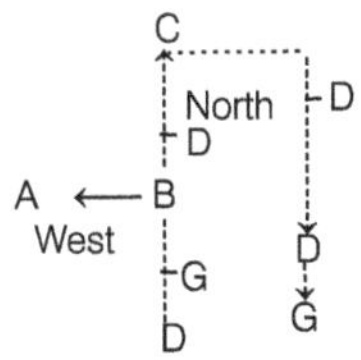

Clearly, Points D and G can be anywhere on the dotted line.
Hence, exact direction of D cannot be determined.
From Statements II and III,

A B E
-------------------F

Point D can be anywhere on the dotted line. Hence, positions of G and D and their directions in respect of B cannot be determined.
From Statements I and III,

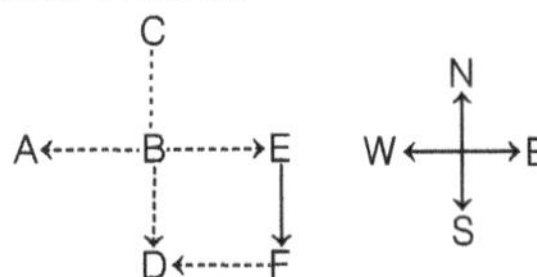

Clearly, D is to the South of B.
So, Statements I and III are required to answer the question.

6. (*b*) From Statement III,
Deepak's mother's age as on 15th June, 1996 = 50 yr
From Statements II and III,
Prabir's age as on 15th June, 1996 = 50 − 29 = 21 yr
From Statements I, II and III,
Deepak's age as on 15th June, 1996 = Prabir's age + 6
= 21+6 =27 yr

∴ Deepak's age as on 30th July, 1996
= 27 yr and 1.5 months

So, all Statements I, II and III are required to answer the question.

7. (*d*) All the statements taken together are insufficient to answer the question.

8. (*b*) From Statements I and II,

4 [2] 3 1 ⟶ It may [touch] here
5 [2] 6 ⟶ [touch] any go

Statements I and II are required to find the answer.

9. (*b*) From Statements I and II,

S > P > Q > T

But no information is given about R.
Hence, I and II are not sufficient.
From Statements II and III,

S > P > Q
Also, R > Q

But no comparison is given between P, S and R and information about T is missing.
From Statements I and III,

S / P / R > Q > T

Clearly, T is the lightest.
So, Statements I and III are sufficient to answer the question.

10. (*b*) From Statements I and II, it is not possible as no information is given about Q and T.
From Statement III, it is obvious that Q is the father of T (from Statements I and III) or (Statements II and III) is not possible as Statement III alone is sufficient.
As Statement III alone is sufficient, (I + II + III) is also not possible.
So, only Statement III is sufficient to answer the question.

11. (*b*) From Statement I,

Anil > Suraj > Meena, Neeraj

From Statement II,
Tara is not first means Tara is somewhere after Anil.
From Statement III,
Meena is not last but from Statement I, she cannot be first.
Therefore, Anil is the first to take the lecture.
Hence, Statements I and II are sufficient to give answer.

12. (*d*) From Statement I,

E > B > A

From Statement II,

– > –>–>C>–>–

From Statement III,

– > –>–>–>D>F

On combining I, II and III

E >B > A > C > D > F

Therefore, E is the tallest.
Hence, Statements I, II and III all are sufficient to give answer.

13. (*b*) From Statement I,

A, D>B>E

From Statement II,

D > A > B

From Statement III,

C > B

on combining I and III

D, A > C > B > E

Therefore, E is the lightest.

Hence, Statements I and III are sufficient to find the question.

14. (*c*) From Statements I and II,

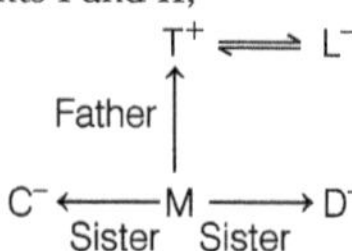

Gender of M is not known.

From Statements II and III,

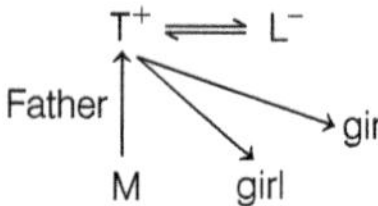

Therefore, from Statement III it is clear that T has three children out of which two are girls. Hence, Statements II and III are sufficient to give answer.

15. (*e*) From Statements I, II and III,

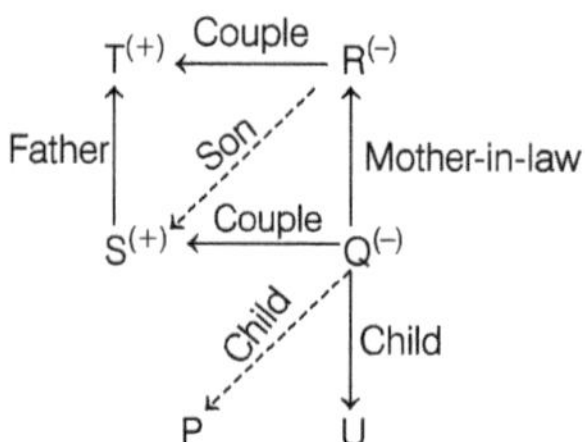

∴ T is father of S.

Hence, Statements I, II and III all are sufficient to give the answer.

16. (*b*) From Statements I and II,

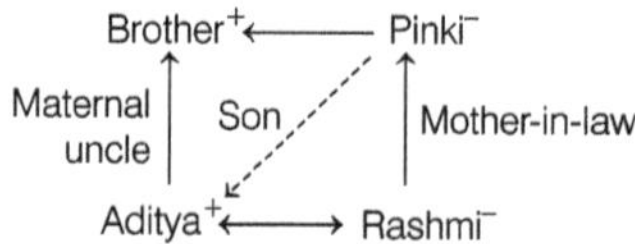

From Statements I and III,

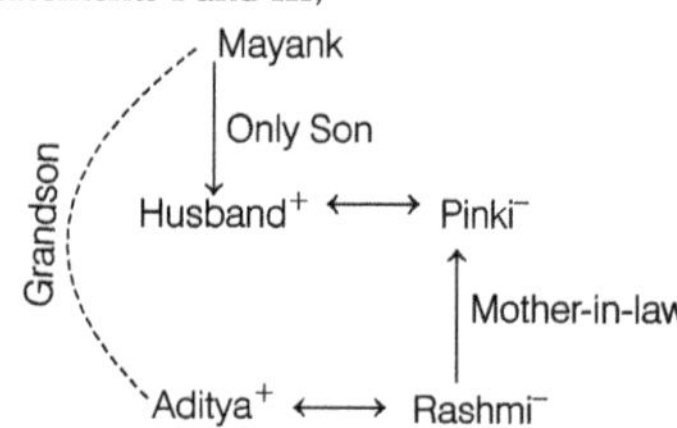

Therefore, Aditya is grand son of Mayank.

Hence, Statements I and III are sufficient.

17. (*d*) From Statements I and II,

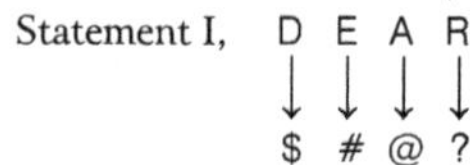

Statement II, T R E A T
↓ ↓ ↓ ↓ ↓
% ? # @ %

So, code for DATE → $@%#

From Statements I and III,

Statement I, D E A R
↓ ↓ ↓ ↓
$ # @ ?

Statement III, T E A R
↓ ↓ ↓ ↓
% # @ ?

So, code for DATE → $@%#

Hence, only I and either II or III.

18. (*e*) From Statements I and II,

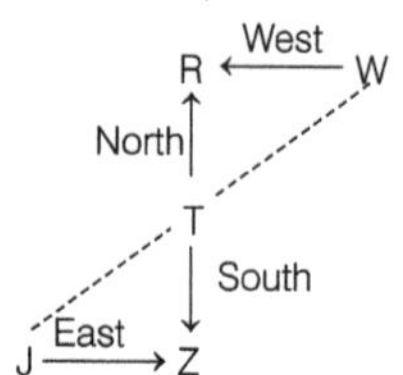

Therefore, village J is in the South-West of village W.

Hence, Statements I and II are sufficient to give answer.

19. (*a*) From Statement I,

Rank of Samir from the top

= 45 – 15 + 1 = 31

Rank of Sudha = Rank of Samir + 5

= 31 + 5

= 36

From Statements II and III,

29 Students → R | | | | | | | | | | N ← 4 Students
30th From top — 5th From bottom

There are 10 students between Radha and Neeta. So, there would not be exact middle position.

Hence, only Statement I is sufficient to give answer.

20. (*b*) From Statement I,

A S E or A S U

From Statement II,

E R or R E and S W or W S

From Statement III, N S W or W S N

A is not placed next to W and the word does not begin with R.

From Statements I and III together,

A N S W E R

Hence, data only in Statements I and III are sufficient to answer the question, while the data in Statement II is not required to answer the question.

Master Exercise

1. Read the question given below.

   Question What is the relation between A and C?

   Read the statement below.

   Statement A is the son of B and C is the daughter of D.

   Which of the below information is additionally required to answer the above question definitely ? « UPSSSC VDO 2018

   (a) A is elder to C
   (b) C is taller than A
   (c) B is male and D is female
   (d) D is the wife of B

2. A set of statements is given.

   A. Ginny is facing in North direction.

   B. Hemant and Ginny are facing in perpendicular directions.

   Which of the given set of statements should be used to decide the solution to the problem. Is Hemant facing South-East? « UPSSSC Tubewell Operator 2018

   (a) Only A
   (b) Only B
   (c) Both A and B together
   (d) Not possible to decide even with both A and B

3. Read the question given below.

   Question How many students are seated between Deepak and Satish? « UPSSSC VDO 2018

   Read the statement given below.

   Statement A group of 20 students are seated in a row watching a movie. Rajesh is at the 5th position from the left. Satish has 5 students on his right.

   Deepak is seated somewhere between Rajesh and Satish ?

   Which of the below information is additionally required to answer the above question ?

   (a) Deepak has more number of students on his right hand than Satish.
   (b) Rajesh and Satish has 9 students between them.
   (c) Deepak has 8 students on his left side.
   (d) Satish has 14 students on his left including Deepak.

4. Read the question below.

   Who is seated to the immediate right hand of B among eight friends? « UPSSSC VDO 2018

   Read the statements given below

   Eight friends A, B, C, D, E, F, G and H are seated around a round table and having dinner. Facing the centre A is seated exactly opposite to B and E is seated exactly opposite to F. C is exactly between E and A. D is on the immediate right hand of A.

   Which of the below information is additionally required to answer the above question ?

   (a) A is between C and D.
   (b) C is seated exactly opposite G.
   (c) B is seated between G and H.
   (d) D is seated between A and F.

5. A is the brother of B, who is the sister of C. A, B and C are the children of E and F. How is F related to B?

   Which of the below information is additionally required to answer the above question? « UPSSSC VDO 2018

   (a) C is the son of F.
   (b) E is the father of A.
   (c) E and F have 1 son and 2 daughters.
   (d) E and F have 2 sons and 1 daughters.

6. In a certain class, the roll number of Dinesh is 10 while that of Uma is 16. What is the roll number of Damyanti? Which of the below information is additionally required to answer the above question ? « UPSSSC VDO 2018

   (a) There are 20 students in the class.
   (b) The roll number of Damyanti is 6 places away from roll number of Dinesh.
   (c) The roll number of Damyanti is after Uma.
   (d) The number of students having roll number between Damyanti and Dinesh is the same as the students having roll number between Damyanti and Uma.

DIRECTIONS ~ (Q. Nos. 7-55) *Each of the questions below consists of a question and two statements numbered* I *and* II *given below. You have to decide whether the data provided in the statements are sufficient to answer the question. Read both the statements.*

Give answer

(a) If the data in Statement I alone are sufficient to answer the question, while the data in Statement II alone are not sufficient to answer the question.
(b) If the data in Statement II alone are sufficient to answer the question, while the data in Statement I alone are not sufficient to answer the question.
(c) If the data either in Statement I alone or in Statement II alone are sufficient to answer the question.
(d) If the data given in both the Statements I. and II together are not sufficient to answer the question
(e) If the data in both the Statements I and II together are necessary to answer the question.

7. What is Sudhir's rank from top in the class of 40 students?

   I. Sudhir's rank is 10 rank below Nandini who is 35th from the bottom.

   II. Sudhir's rank is 10 rank above Samir who is 24th from the top.

8. How is 'over' written in a code language?
I. 'Over and again' is written as 'ka ja ha' in that code language.
II. 'Came and go' is written as 'ja pa na' in that code language.

9. In a row of boys facing South who is immediate left to Ramakant?
I. Suresh is immediate right to Chandrakant, who is Fourth to the right of Ramakant.
II. Suresh is third to the right of Ramakant and Naresh is second to the right of Suresh. « SBI PO 2015

10. Who among M, T, K, J and R is the shortest but one?
I. T is taller than J and R.
II K is shorter than R and M.

11. Who amongst L, M, N, O and P is the shortest.
I. O is shorter than P but taller than N.
II. M is not as tall as L. « NIACL 2014

12. Point A is towards which direction from Point B?
I. If a person walks 4 m towards the North from Point A and takes two consecutive right turns, each after walking 4 m, he would reach Point C, which is 8 m away from Point B.
II. Point D is 2 m towards the East of Point A and 4 m towards the West of Point B. « NIACL 2014

13. Which code word stands for 'well' in the coded sentence 'sin lo bye' which means 'He is well'?
Statements
I. In the same code language, 'lo mot det' means 'They are well'.
II. In the same code language, 'sin mic bye' means 'He is strong'. « UPSSSC VDO 2018

14. Who is the heaviest among Amol, Prabhu, Narayan and Navin?
I. Amol and Prabhu are of the same weight.
II. Prabhu's weight is more than Narayan but less than Navin.

15. How many daughters does 'L' have?
I. R's father has three daughters.
II. T is R's sister and the daughter of L.

16. Rajiv's rank is 17th in his class. What is his rank from the last?
I. There are 70 students in his class.
II. Abhijeet, who ranks 20th in Rajiv's class is 51st from the last.

17. How is 'also' written in a code language?
I. 'he also show data' is written as 'sx fa mn ca' and 'now many person also' is written as 'zb ct sx ya' in that code language.
II. 'she visit the also' is written as 'sx lm nc ty' and 'she visit the always' is written as 'lm kc ty nc' in that code language.

18. D is the sister of C. How is D related to A?
I. A is sister of B. II. B is the brother of C.

19. In a six storey building (consisting of floors numbered 1 to 6, wherein the topmost floor is numbered 6 and the ground floor is numbered 1), each of the six friends namely A, B, C, D, E and F lives on a different floor. On which floor number does E live? « NABARD Grade A & Grade B 2016
I. A lives on floor numbered 3. Only one person lives between A and F. E lives on an odd numbered floor below F.
II. B lives on floor numbered 4. A lives on one of the floors below B but not on floor numbered 1. D lives on even numbered floor above A. C lives immediately above E.

20. How is 'buyer' definitely coded in the given language ? « NABARD Grade A & Grade B 2016
I. 'help find a buyer' is coded as 'ni ka po sn' and 'a small help given' is coded as 'tk sn ru ni'.
II. 'must find small buyer' is coded as 'ka hp tk po' and find a help soon is coded as 'mj ni sn ka'.

21. Five boxes *viz.* A, B, C, D and E are kept one above the other in a stack. How many boxes are kept between box E and box B? « Canara Bank (PO) 2018
Statements
I. Only two boxes are kept between Box C and Box D. Only one box is kept between Box C and Box B. Only two boxes are kept between Box E and Box A. Box E is kept at one of the positions above Box A and below Box C.
II. No box is kept between Box D and Box B. Only two boxes are kept between Box C and Box D. Box E is kept at one of the positions above box A but below Box C.

22. How many rooms does your house have?
I. The number of rooms is the same as the number of family members in our house.
II. The number is sufficient to accommodate our family members.

23. Who is the best salesman in the company?
I. Rohit sold maximum number of air conditioners this summer.
II. The company made the highest profit this year.

24. What is the colour of the curtains on the stage?
I. The curtains have the same colour as the walls of the hall.
II. The colour of the curtains is quite appealing.

25. Who is a better artist–Abid or Hussain?
I. Abid had more art exhibitions.
II. The number of paintings sold by Hussain is more.

26. Six persons viz. A, B, C, D, E and F are sitting on a circular table for lunch, who among them sits immediate left of F (If all the persons are facing towards the centre)?
I. A sits third of right of F. One person sits between A and C. E sits third to left of C.
II. Only one person sits between E and D. F sits second to right of D. A sits third to left of F.

27. Kamal's birthday is in which of the following month in a year?
I. Kamal's mother correctly remembers that Kamal's birthday will come after January but not in the month which has 31days.
II. Kamal's father correctly remember that Kamal's birthday will not come after March.

28. In which month (of the same year) did Ravi join office?
I. Ravi's mother correctly remembers that Ravi joined office after June but before October and that month had less than 31days.
II. Ravi's father correctly remembers that Ravi joined office after August but before December and the month had only 30 days. « SBI PO 2015

29. Five letter A, E, G, N and R are arranged left to right according to certain conditions. Which letter is placed third? « SBI (PO) 2013
I. G is placed second to the right of A. E is to the immediate right of G. There are only two letter between R and G.
II. N is exactly between A and G. Neither A nor G is at the extreme end of the arrangement.

30. What is position of P?
I. T and V are immediate neighbours of P. Only Q stands between V and U. Only R stands between S and T.
II. U and S stand at the extreme ends of the row. Only three people stand between U and T. R stands exactly between S and T. Q stands to the immediate left of U. « SBI PO 2015

31. Is M the mother of L?
I. T is the mother of M. M is married to J. K is the son of J. F is the sister of K. L is the sister of F.
II. K is the grandson of T. K is the brother of F. F is the sister of L. L is the daughter of J. J is the son-in-law of T. « SBI PO 2015

32. Who among A, B, C, D and E teaches history ?
I. Each one of them teaches only one subject. B teaches Mathematics, while E teaches Science. A or C does not teach Geography. A or D does not teach English.
II. C and E are teachers of English and Science respectively and A is the teacher of Mathematics. « SBI PO 2015

33. Who is to the immediate right of Mohan when Mohan, Salil, Bhusan, Suresh and Jayesh are sitting around a circle facing at the centre?
I. Salil is 3rd to the left of Mohan.
II. Bhusan is between Salil and Jayesh.

34. How is N related to K?
I. N's brother is married to D.
II. D's sister is married to K.

35. B is the brother of D, D is the sister of K, K is the brother of M. How is M related to B?
I. P is mother of B.
II. H is husband of P.

36. A six story building with floors numbered 1, 2, 3, 4, 5 and 6, houses different people *viz.* A, B, C, D and E. Floor number 3 is vacant. On which of the floor does A live? « MHA-CET 2011
I. C lives on an even numbered floor. A lives on a floor immediately above C's floor.
II. B lives on an even numbered floor. B's floor is not immediately above or immediately below the vacant floor. Only one person lives between B and C's floors. D lives immediately below E's floor.

37. In which year was Ranjith born?
Statements
I. At present, Ranjith is 24 years younger to his mother.
II. Ranjith's brother, who was born in 2001, is 31 years younger to his mother. « UPSSSC VDO 2018

38. What will be the total cost of 28 bags if each of them costs the same?
Statements
I. One-fifth of the cost of each bag is ₹ 50.
II. The total cost of three bags is ₹ 250 more than the total cost of two bags. « UPSSSC VDO 2018

39. How is 'Marbles' coded in the code language ?
Statements
I. 'Na Mg AI Si' means 'Some stones are Marbles' and 'Si P CI' means 'Marbles don't break'.
II. 'Na Mg AI Si' means 'Some stones are Marbles' and 'Si Al Ar' means 'Marbles are strong'. « UPSSSC VDO 2018

40. How is 'gone' written in a code language? « IBPS (PO) 2012
I. 'you will be gone' is written as 'ka pa ni sa' in that code language.
II. 'he will be there' is written as 'ja da ka ni' in that code language.

41. Towards which direction is P with respect to the starting point? « IBPS (PO) 2012
I. P walked 20 m, took a right turn and walked 30 m again took right turn and walked 20 m towards West.
II. P walked 30 m, took a left turn and walked 20 m again took left turn and walked 30 m towards East.

42. Lal is taller than Nand, Jim is taller than Harry. Who among them is the tallest?
I. Jim is taller than Nand. II. Lal is taller than Harry.

43. How many brothers does Bharat have?
I. Shiela, the mother of Bharat, has only three children.
II. Meena, the grandmother of Bharat, has only one grand-daughter. « NIACL 2014

44. Are all the five friends viz. Leena, Amit, Arun, Ali and Ken who are seated around a circular table facing the centre?
I. Leena sits second to the left of Amit. Amit faces the centre. Arun sits second to the right of Leena.
II. Ali sits third to the left of Ken. Ken faces the centre. Amit sits to the immediate left of Ali but Ken is not an immediate neighbour of Amit. « NIACL 2014

45. A, B, C, D, E and F are sitting in a circle, some of them facing towards the centre while some are facing away from the center of the circle. How many persons are facing inside?
I. F is on the immediate left of E. Only D is between B and E. C is immediate right of F. C is second to the left of B. A does not face same direction as E. D and C face opposite direction of A.
II. A is facing D. Only C is between A and B. Only F is between E and A. E sits second to the right of B. Both F and C face same direction but opposite to B. F does not sits to the immediate left E.

46. Six peoples S, T, U, V, W and X are sitting around a circular table facing the centre. What is T 's position with respect to X? « SBI (PO) 2013

I. Only two people sit between U and W, X is second to the left of W, V and T are immediate neighbours of each other.

II. T is to the immediate right of V. There are only two people between T and S. X is an immediate neighbour of S but not of V.

47. How many people are sitting in a circle, where all the people are facing the centre?

I. K sits third to the right of L. M is an immediate neighbour of K. Only three people sit between L and M.

II. N sits third to the left of M. Only one person sits between N and K. K is an immediate neighbour of M. « NABARD Grade A & Grade B 2016

48. How far and in which direction is Point B with respect to Point A? « Canara Bank (PO) 2018

Statements

I. Point G is 6 m to the East of Point A. Point C is 9 m to the North of Point G. Point F is 3 m to the West of Point C. Point B is 6 m away from Point F.

II. Point M is 8 m to the West of Point B. Point R is 8 m to the South of Point M. Point A is 11 m to the East of Point R. Point C is to the North-East of Point A.

49. How far is Point M from Point K?

I. Point D is 5m to the South of Point P. Point M is 8 m to the West of Point D. Point S is 2.5m to the North of Point M. Point O is 10 m to the East of Point S. Point K is 2.5 m to the South of Point O.

II. Point K is 10 m to the East of Point M. Point U is 8m to the West of Point M. Point D is to the East of Point M. Point M is the midpoint of the lines formed by joining Points U and D. « IBPS (SO) 2017

50. Amongst the people viz. A, B, C, D, E and F sitting around a circular table facing the centre, who sits second to the right of A? « Canara Bank (PO) 2018

Statements

I. A sits second to the right of F. Only two people sit between A and D. B is neither an immediate neighbour of D nor F.

II. Only one person sits between A and F (either from left or right). Only two people sit between F and B. C sits to the immediate neighbour of B.

51. Amongst P, Q, R, S and T all of them are of different price. Also they are placed one above another. Which book is placed at the top?

I. Price of the book R is more than the price of book P. Only two books are placed between book R and P. Price of the Book S is second costliest among all and is placed above T.

II. Price of the book Q is more than only P and T and costliest book is not placed at top. The third costliest book is exactly in the middle.

52. Six people *viz.* I, J, K, L, M and N live in a building on different floors from top to bottom (such as ground floor numbered as 1 and top is numbered as 6). Each of them likes different colours Black, White, Blue, Pink, Purple, Grey. Which colour is liked by the one who lives on 4th floor?

I. Only one person lives between L and M. J lives above I who likes Black color. There is a gap of three floors between J and L and both of them lives on odd number of floor. The one who lives on top floor likes Purple color.

II. K likes White color. The one who likes Grey colour lives above I. J does not like Grey colour.

53. How many minutes does the clock lose a day?

I. The clock reads 6:00 when it is really 5:48.

II. The clock is 40 s fast each hour.

54. Ram and Esha are in a line to purchase tickets. How many people are in the line? « NIFT (PG) 2013

I. There are 20 people behind Ram and 20 people in front of Esha.

II. There are 5 people between Ram and Esha.

55. Among six people viz. C, D, E, F, G and H sitting in a straight line with equal distance, between each other and facing North, who sits second to the left of G? « Canara Bank (PO) 2018

Statements

I. C sits third from the left end of the line. Only one person sits between C and H. Only two people sit between E and G. G sits at one of the position to the right of E.

II. E sits third to the left of G. G does not sit at any extreme end of the line. More than three people sit between H and F. F sits at one of the positions to the right of H.

DIRECTIONS ~(Q. Nos. 56-60) *Each of the question below consists of a question and three statements numbered I, II and III given below it . You have to decide whether the data provided in the statement are sufficient to answer the question.* « IBPS (PO) 2011

56. Point D is in which direction with respect to Point B?

I. Point A is to the West of Point B.
Point C is to the North of Point B.
Point D is to the South of Point C.

II. Point G is to the South of Point D.
Point G is 4 m from point B. Point D is 9 m from Point B.

III. Point A is to the West of Point B. Point B is exactly midway between Points A and E. Point F is to the South of Point E. Point D is to the West of Point F.

(a) II and III are sufficient to answer the question.
(b) I and III are sufficient to answer the question.
(c) I and II are sufficient to answer the question.
(d) All I, II, and III are required to answer the question.
(e) None of the above.

57. How many daughters does of W have?

I. B and D are the sister of M.

II. M's father T is the husband of W.

III. Out of the three childrens which T has, only one is a boy.

(a) I and III are sufficient to answer the question.
(b) All I, II and III are required to answer the question.
(c) II and III are sufficient to answer the question.
(d) Question cannot be answered even with all I, II and III.
(e) I and II are sufficient to answer the question.

58. Who among A, B, C, D, E and F, each having a different height is the tallest?
I. B is taller than A but shorter than E.
II. Only two of them are shorter than C.
III. D is taller than only F.
(a) I and II are sufficient to answer the question.
(b) I and III are sufficient to answer the question.
(c) II and III are sufficient to answer the question.
(d) All I, II and III are required to answer the question.
(e) All I, II and III even together are not sufficient to answer the question.

59. Towards which direction is Village J from Village W?
I. Village R is to the West of Village W and to the North of Village T.
II. Village Z is to the East of Village J and to the South of Village T.
III. Village M is to the North-East of Village J and to the North of Village Z.
(a) Only III is sufficient to answer the question.
(b) II and III sufficient to answer the question.
(c) All I, II and III are required to answer the question.
(d) Question cannot be answered even with all I, II and III.
(e) None of the above

60. How is 'go' written in a code language?
I. 'now or never again' is written as 'torn ka na sa' in that code language.
II. 'you come again now' is written as 'ja ka ta sa' in that code language..
III. 'again go now or never' is written as 'na ha ka sa torn' in that code language.
(a) I and III are sufficient to answer the question.
(b) II and III are sufficient to answer the question.
(c) I and II are sufficient to answer the question.
(d) All I, II and III are required to answer the question.
(e) None of the above.

Answers WITH EXPLANATIONS

1. (*d*) According to the question,

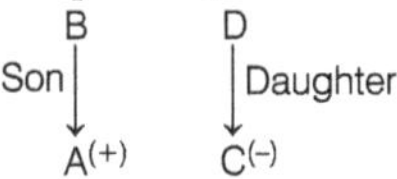

From option (d),

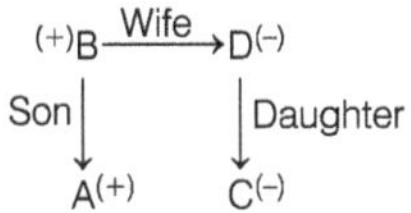

Hence, A and C are brother and sister, respectively.

2. (*c*) From Statements A and B,

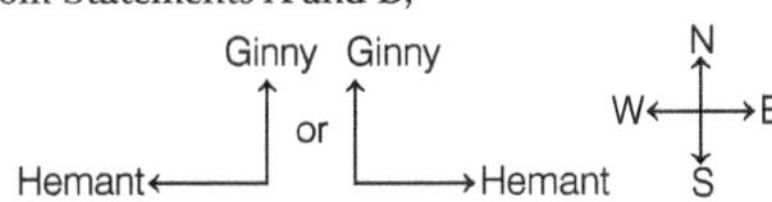

Hence, Hemant is not facing South-East. He is facing either East or West.

3. (*c*) According to the question,

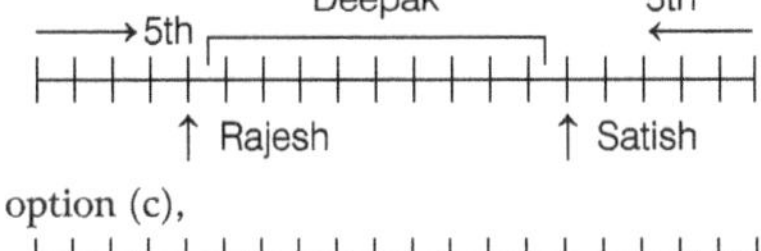

From option (c),

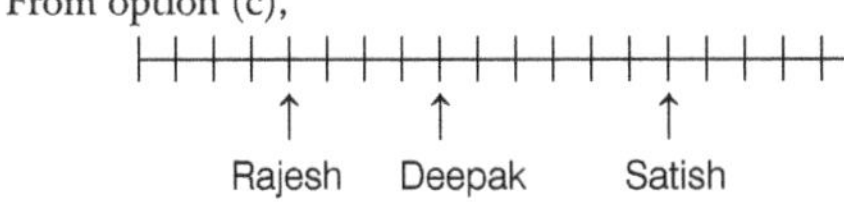

Hence, 5 students are seated between Deepak and Satish.

4. (*b*) According to the question,

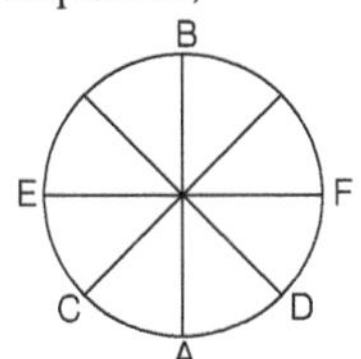

From option (b),

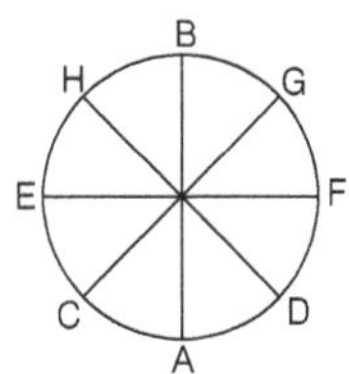

Hence, H is seated to the immediate right of B.

5. (*b*) According to the question,

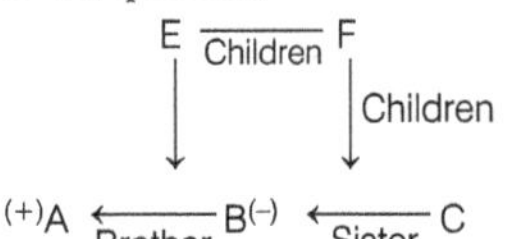

From option (b),

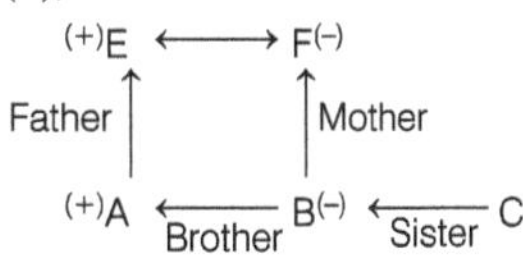

Hence, F is the mother of A, B and C.

6. (*d*) According to the question,

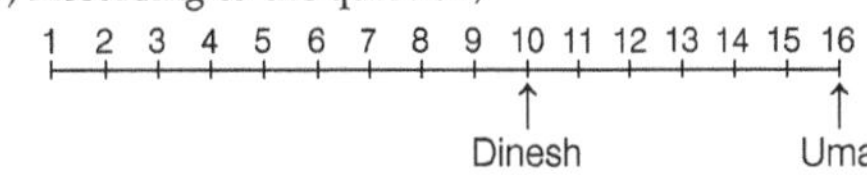

From option (d),

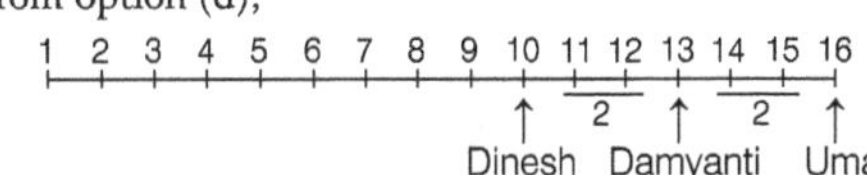

Hence, it is clear that the roll number of Dinesh is 13.

7. (*c*) From Statement I,
Required rank = $[40 - (35 - 10) + 1] = 16$th
From Statement II, Required rank = $(24 - 10) = 14$th
So, either Statement I or II alone are sufficient to answer the question.

8. (*d*) From Statements I and II,

over [and] again → ka [ja] ha

came [and] go → [ja] pa na

∴ Over = ka / ha

Hence, both the statements are not sufficient to answer the question.

9. (*d*) From Statement I,

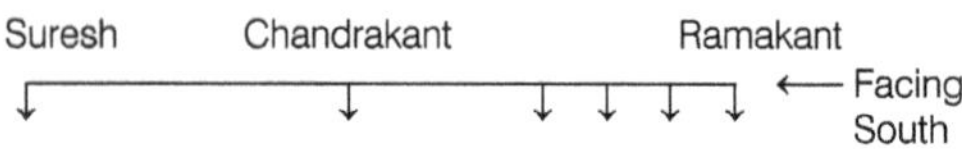

From Statement II,

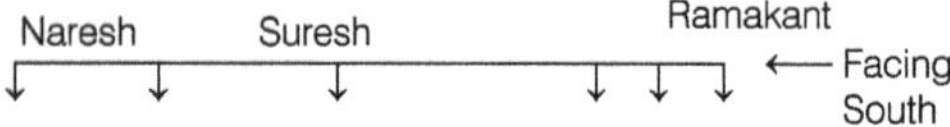

Hence, both the Statements I and II together are not sufficient to give answer.

10. (*d*) From both the statements,

T > J, R and R, M > K

So, both Statements I and II are insufficient to answer the question.

11. (*d*) From Statement I,

P > O > N

From Statement II,

L > M

Hence, data in both the Statements I and II together are not necessary to give answer.

12. (*b*) From Statement I,

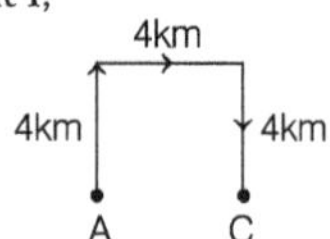

From Statement II,

A —2m— D —4m— B (N, S, E, W)

Therefore, Point A is towards the West of Point B.

Hence, data in Statement II alone are sufficient to give answer.

13. (*c*) From Statement I

(lo) mot det ⇒ They are (well)

sin (lo) bye ⇒ He is (well)

From Statement II,

sin lo bye ⇒ He is well

sin mic bye ⇒ He is strong

Hence, well can coded by lo.

So, Either Statement I or II is sufficient.

14. (*e*) It is very obvious that both the statements alone are insufficient.

From Statements I and II, Navin > Amol = Prabhu > Narayan

Therefore, Navin is the heaviest.

Hence, Statements I and II both are sufficient to answer the question.

15. (*e*) From Statement II, it is clear that T is R's sister and it is given in Statement I that R's father has three daughters it means that L is the father of R and T both

Hence, L has three daughters.

So, both statements are required to answer the question.

16. (*c*) Statements I and II are sufficient to answer the question.

From Statement I,

Rajiv's rank from the last = 70 − 17 + 1 = 54th

From Statement II, we can calculate the total number of students in the class = 20 + 51 − 1 = 70.

Now, we can calculate Rajiv's rank from the last.

So, either Statement I or II alone are sufficient to answer the question.

17. (*c*) From Statement I,

he (also) show data → (sx) fa mn ca

now many person (also) → zb ct (sx) ya

∴ also = sx

From Statement II,

[she] [visit] [the] also ⟶ sx [lm] [nc] [ty]

[she] [visit] [the] always ⟶ [lm] kc [ty] [nc]

∴ also = sx

Hence, the data in either Statement I or II in Statement II alone is sufficient to answer the question.

18. (*e*) Statement I is insufficient as relation link between B, C and D is missing. Statement II is insufficient as A is not available in it.

From Statements I and II,

D⊖ ←Sister— C —Brother→ B⊕ —Sister→ A⊖

D is sister of A

So, both Statements I and II are needed to answer the question.

19. (*c*) From Statement I

Floor	Person
6	
5	F
4	
3	A
2	
1	E

From Statement II

Floor	Person
6	D
5	F
4	B
3	A
2	C
1	E

It is clear from above that E lives on floor number 1.

Hence, data either in Statement I or II alone are sufficient to answer the question.

20. (*e*) From Statement I,

[help] find [a] buyer ⟶ [ni] ka po [sn]

[a] small [help] given ⟶ tk [sn] ru [ni]

From Statement II,

must [find] small buyer ⟶ (ka) hp tk po

[find] a help soon ⟶ mj ni sn (ka)

On combining Statements I and II,

[help] {find} (a) [buyer] ⟶ (ni) {ka} [po] [sn] ...(i)

(a) small [help] given ⟶ tk [sn] ru (ni) ...(ii)

must {find} small [buyer] ⟶ {ka} hp tk [po] ...(iii)

{find} (a) [help] soon ⟶ mj (ni) [sn] ka ...(iv)

Now, from Eqs. (i) and (iii), we get buyer → po

Hence, both statements are required to answer the given question.

21. (*a*) From Statement I,

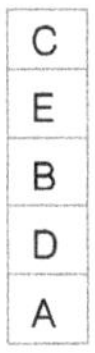

C
E
B
D
A

So, no box is kept between Box E and Box B.
Hence, Statement I alone is sufficient to answer the question.

22. (*d*) Data inadequate both Statements I and II are not sufficient to answer the question.

23. (*a*) Since, Rohit has sold the maximum number of items, hence he is the best salesman. So, Statement I alone is sufficient to answer the question.

24. (*d*) Data inadequate both Statements I and II are not sufficient to answer the question.

25. (*b*) As given in Statement II, the number of paintings sold by Hussain is more, hence he is the better artist.
So, Statement II alone is sufficient to answer the question.

26. (*e*) From Statement I,

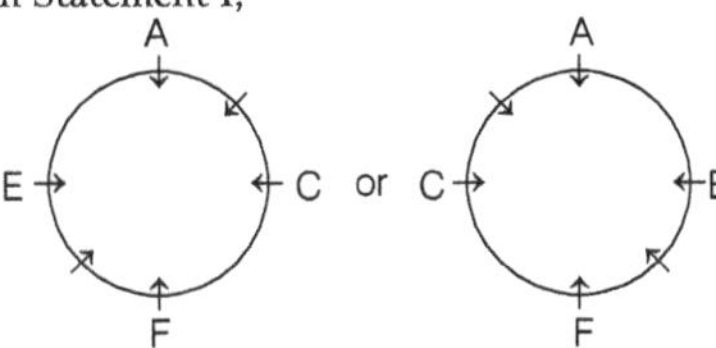

From Statement II,

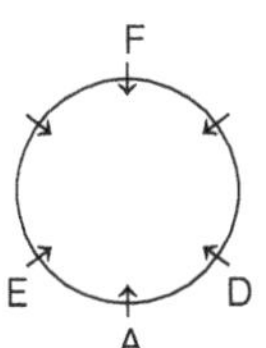

Now, from Statements I and II,

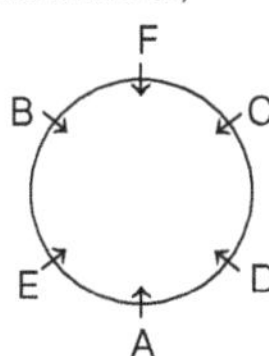

Clearly, C sits to the immediate left of F.
Hence, data in both the statements are required to answer the question.

27. (*e*) From Statement I,
Months according to Kamal's mother = February, April, June, September, November
From Statement II,
Months according to Kamal's father = January, February November
From Statements I and II,
Kamal's birthday = February.
Hence, the data in both the statements are necessary to answer the question.

28. (*e*) From Statement I,
According to Ravi's mother → September (only month which has 30 days.)
From Statement II,
According to Ravi's Father → September, October, November
On combining I and II, September is common.
Hence, both the Statements I and II together are necessary to answer the question.

29. (*c*) From Statement I, R A _G E
Clearly, left place which is third, is replaced by N.
From Statement II, _A N G_ or _G N A_
Clearly, N is at third place.
Hence, the data in Statement I alone or in Statement II alone is sufficient to answer the question.

30. (*e*) From Statement I,

U Q V P T R S

From Statement II,

S R T _ _ Q U

On Combining I and II,

S R T P V Q U

Therefore, P is at the middle in the row seven persons.
Hence, both the Statements I and II together are necessary to answer the question.

31. (*e*) From Statement I,

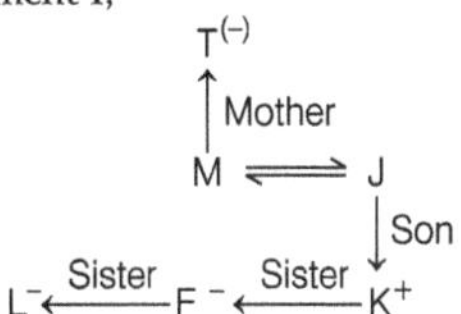

From Statement II,

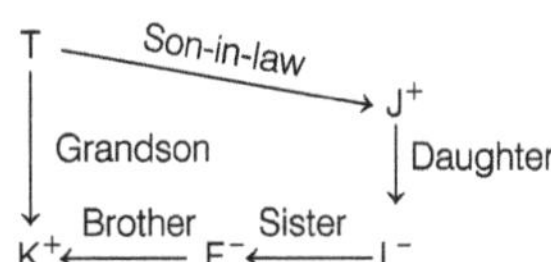

On combining Statements I and II,

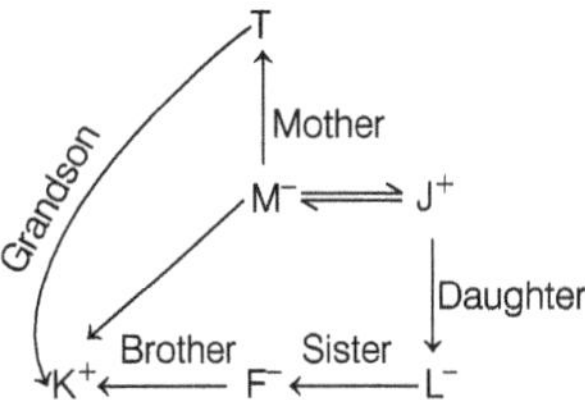

Hence, both the Statements I and II together necessary to answer the question.

32. (*a*)

From Statement I,

Name	Subject
A	History
B	Mathematics
C	English
D	Geography
E	Science

From Statement II,

Name	Subject
A	Mathematics
B	__
C	English
D	__
E	Science

Therefore, from Statement I it is clear that A teaches History.
Hence, only Statement I is sufficient to give answer.

33. (*e*) Both the statements are required to answer the question.

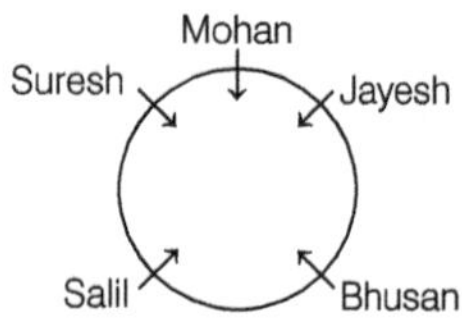

Hence, it is clear that Suresh is to the immediate right of Mohan.
So, Statements I and II are required to answer the question.

34. (*e*) From Statement I, D is sister-in-law of N.
From Statement II, K is husband of D's sister.

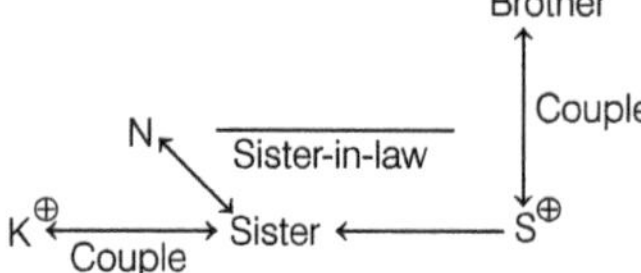

So, both the Statements I and II are required to answer the question.

35. (*d*) From Statement I,

P⊖
Mother
B⊕ ← Brother — D⊖ ← Sister — K⊕ ← Brother — M?

M is brother or sister of B but gender of M is not known, so exact relation of M with respect to B cannot be determined.
Hence, Statement I alone is insufficient and Statement II is also clearly insufficient.
From Statements I and II,

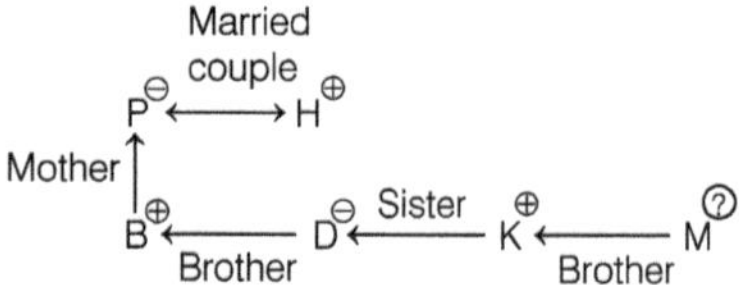

Again, gender of M is not given.
Hence, relation of M with respect to B cannot be determined.
So, Statements I and II together are not sufficient.

36. (*c*) From Statement I, C lives on an even numbered floor and A lives on floor immediately above C's floor. Also, floor 3 is vacant. So, it is obvious that C lives on 4th floor and A lives on 5th floor.
Hence, Statement I alone is sufficient to answer the question.
From Statement II,

People	B	A	C	—	E	E
Floor	6	5	4	3	2	1

Clearly, A lives on 5th floor.
Hence, Statement II alone is sufficient to answer the question.
So, either Statement I or II alone are sufficient to answer the question.

37. (*e*) Ranjith's brother was born in 2001. Ranjith's brother is 31 years younger to his mother and Ranjith is 24 years younger to his mother.
The above statement clearly shown that Ranjith is elder to this brother and he is 7 years elder than his brother.
So, birth year of Ranjith = 7 years before 2001,
i.e. The year of birth of Ranjith = 1994
Hence, both statements are required to get the age of Ranjith.

38. (*c*) From Statement I,
$\frac{1}{5}$th cost of each bag = ₹ 50
Complete cost of bag = 50 × 5 = ₹ 250
From Statement II,
Total cost of 3 bags – Total cost of 2 bags = ₹ 250
Total cost of 1 bag = ₹ 250
Hence, either Statement I or II is sufficient to get the cost of bag.

39. (*c*) From Statement I,
Na Mg Al Si ⇒ some stones are Marbles
Si P Cl ⇒ Marbles don't break
From Statement II,
Na Mg Al Si ⇒ Some stones are Marbles
Si Al Ar ⇒ Marbles are strong
Marbles is coded as Si.
Hence, either Statement I or II is sufficient.

40. (*d*) From Statements I and II,
you will be gone = ka pa ni sa
he will be there = ja da ka ni
Clearly, 'will be' = ka ni
∴ you gone = pa sa
∴ gone = pa/sa
So, both statements are insufficient to answer the question.

41. (*c*) From Statement I,

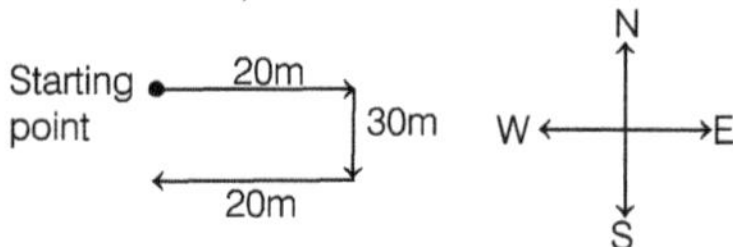

Clearly, P is in South direction with respect to starting point from Statement II,

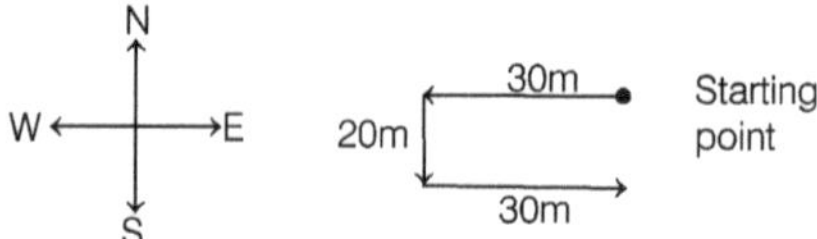

Clearly, P is in South direction with respect to starting point .
Hence, either Statement I or II alone are sufficient to answer the question.

42. (*d*) Given that, Lal > Nand
Jim > Harry
From Statement I,
Jim > Harry/Nand
Also, Lal > Nand
But no comparison is given between Lal and Jim.
Hence, Statement I alone is insufficient.
From Statement II, Lal > Harry/Nand
Also, Jim > Harry
But again no comparison is given between Lal and Jim. Hence, II alone is also insufficient.
Even it is very obvious from Statements I and II that they are together insufficient to answer the question.

43. (*e*) From Statement I,

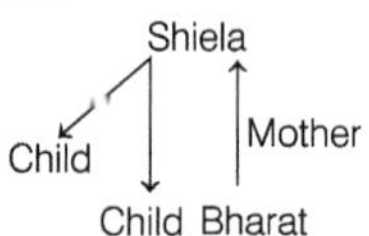

From Statement II,

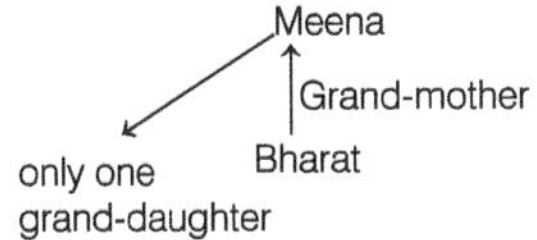

On combining both statements I and II,

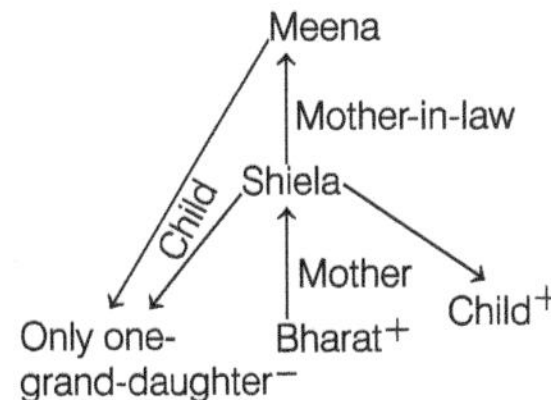

Therefore, Bharat have only one brother.
Hence, data in both the Statements I and II together are necessary to give answer.

44. (*e*) From Statement I,

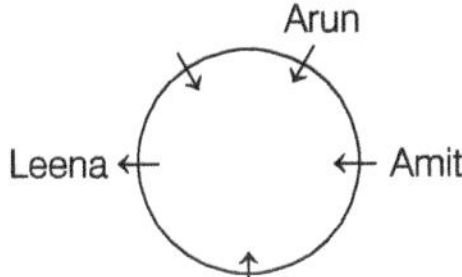

From Statement II,

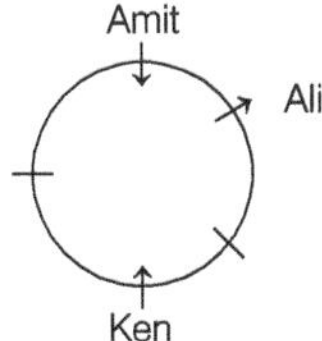

On combining I and II,

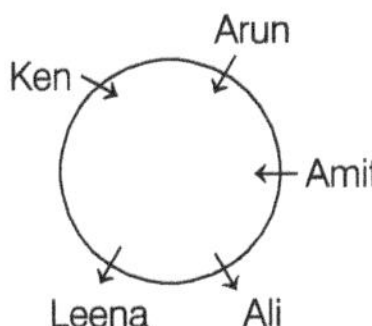

It is clear from diagram that all five friends have not facing the centre of circular table.
Hence, data in both the Statements I and II together are necessary to give answer.

45. (*c*) From Statement I,

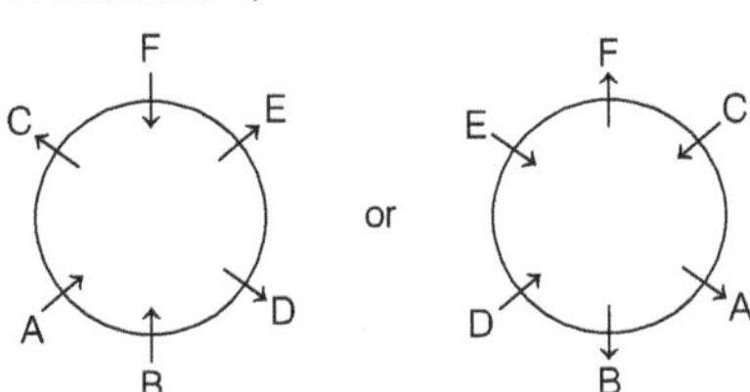

From both of the above cases we get that three persons are facing inside.

From Statement II,

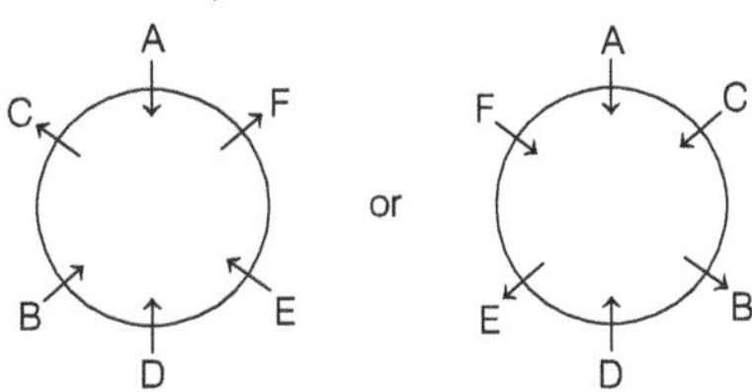

From both of the above cases we get that four persons are facing inside.
So, either Statement I or II is sufficient to answer the question.

46. (*b*) From Statement I,

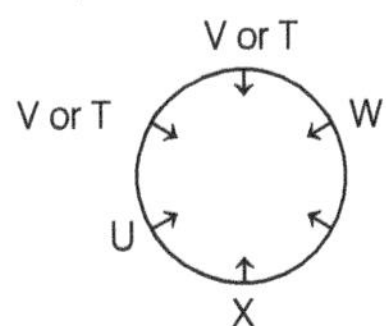

Hence, position to T with respect to X cannot be found out using the data provided in Statement I alone.
From Statement II,

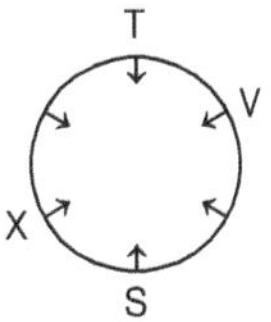

Here it is clear that T is second to the left of X.
Hence, the data is Statement II alone are sufficient to answer the question.

47. (*e*) From Statement I,

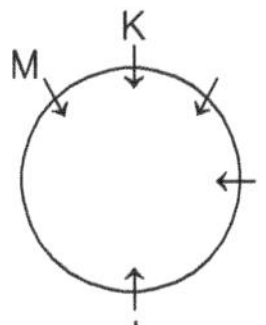

From Statement II,

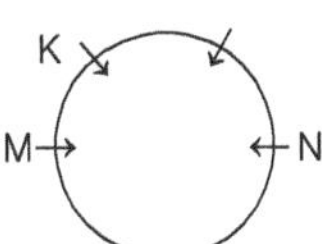

On combining I and II,

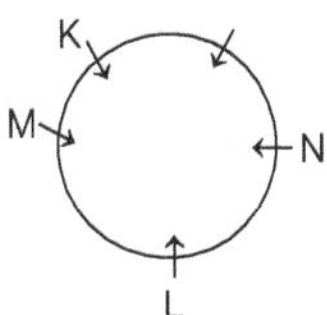

Therefore, it is clear that there are five persons sitting in a circle.
Hence, data in both Statements I and II together are necessary to answer the question.

48. (*b*) From Statement I,

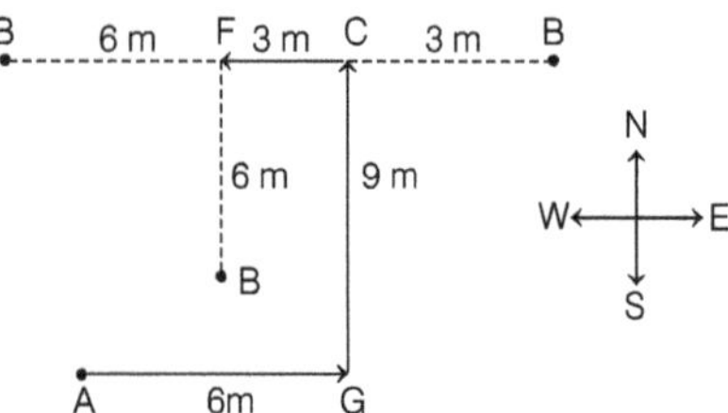

We can not determine the position of B.
From Statement II,

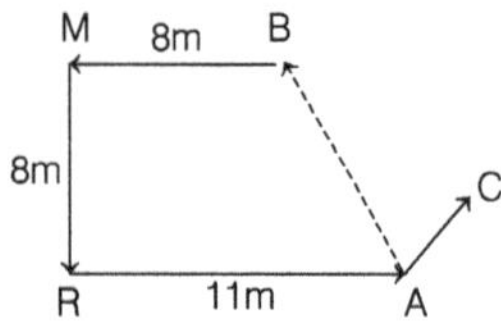

So, Point B is in the North-West direction with respect to Point A.
Thus, Statement II alone is sufficient to answer the question.

49. (*c*) From Statement I,

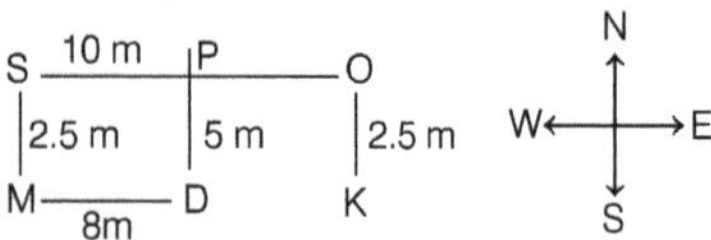

Clearly, Point M is 10m away from point K.
From Statement II, Point K is 10m to the East of Point M.
Hence, data in either of the two statements is sufficient to answer the question.

50. (*b*) From Statement I,

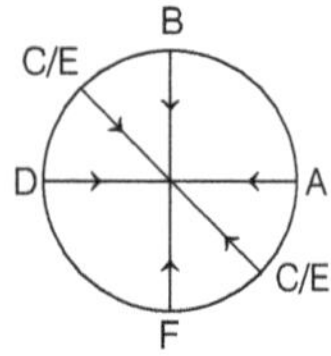

Either C or E is second to right of A.
From Statement II,

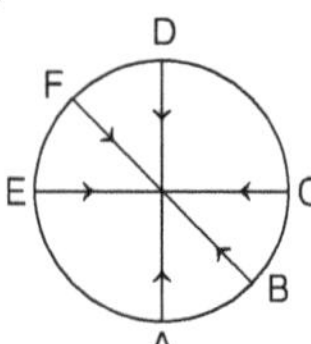

C is sitting second to the right of A.
Hence, Statement II alone is sufficient to answer the question.

51. (*d*) From Statement I,

R > P and - > S > - > - >

Books
R/P
R/P

From Statement II, Q > P, T

Books
Q

From Statements I and II,

R > S > Q > P/T> P/T

Books
S
R/P
Q
T
R/P

OR

Books
P
S
Q
R
T

As, even by combining both we can say either books S or P is placed at top.
So, data in both the Statements I and II together are not sufficient to answer the question.

52. (*a*) From Statement I,

Floors	Persons	Colours
6		Purple
5	J	
4	I/	Black/
3	M	
2	I/	Black/
1	L	

From Statement II, K likes white colour. The one who likes Grey colour lives above I.
From Statements I and II,

Floors	Persons	Colours
6		Purple
5	J	
4	K	White
3	M	Grey
2	I	Black
1	L	

So, from both Statements I and II we get that K lives on 4th floor and likes white colour.

53. (*e*) Statement I says clock is 12 min fast at 6:00.
Statement II says clock become fast by 40 s after each hour.
Thus, by combining these two equations we can find that how many minutes will the clock lose in 24 h.
So, both the Statements I and II together are sufficient to answer the question but neither statement alone is sufficient.

54. (*d*) From Statements I and II together, there are two possibilities

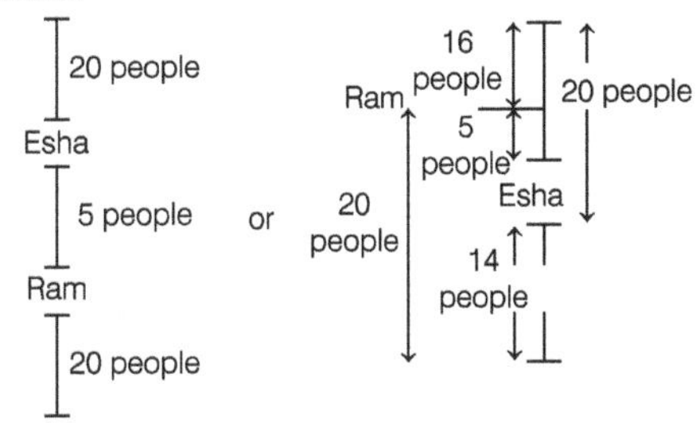

∴ Total people in line = 14 + 1 + 5 + 1 + 14 = 35
∴ Total people in line = 20 + 1 + 5 + 1 + 20 = 47
So, both statements taken together are not sufficient to answer the question.

55. (*e*) From Statement I,

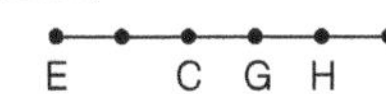

From Statement II,

On combining Statements I and II,

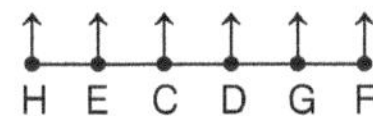

Hence, C sits second the left of G. The data in both Statements I and II are together necessary to answer the question.

56. (*b*) From Statement I,

C C
↑ ↓
A ← B , D

From Statement III,

A ←— B —→ E

D ←——— F

By combining Statements I and III, we get

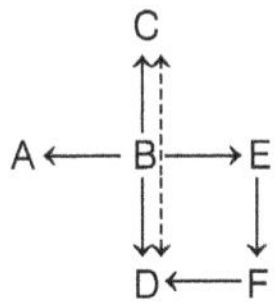

So, the data in Statements I and III are sufficient to answer the question, while the data in Statement II is not required to answer the question.

57. (*c*) From Statement II, T is the husband of W i.e., T and W are a married couple.
From Statement III, Out of 3 childrens of T, one is a boy i.e., he has two daughters and one son.
By combining Statements II and III, W has two daughters.
So, Statements II and III are sufficient to answer the question.

58. (*a*) By combining Statements I and II,

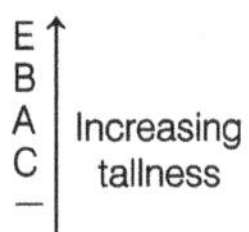

Hence, E is the tallest.
So, only Statements I and II are sufficient to answer the question.

59. (*e*) From Statement I,

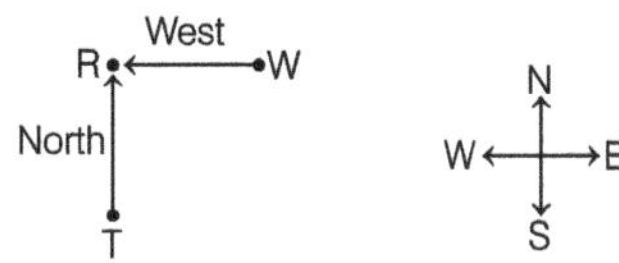

From Statement II,

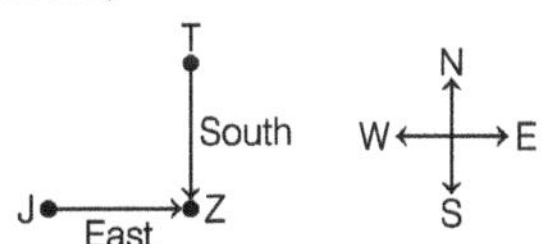

By combining Statements I and II,

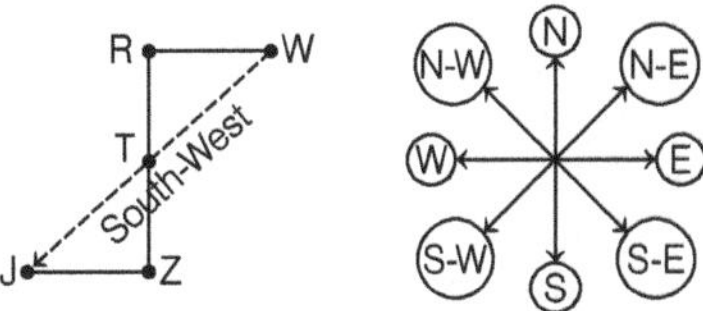

Clearly, J is in South-West direction from village W.
So, Statements I and II are required to answer the question.

60. (*a*) From Statements I and III,

now or never again ⟶ torn ka na sa

again go now or never ⟶ na ha ka sa torn

∴ go = ha

So, Statements I and III are sufficient to answer the question.

CHAPTER / 22

Input-Output

Input-Output is a process of rearrangement of data or sequence consisting of words or numbers or both based on some rule.

In such type of questions, the candidate is given a word and number arrangement. With each subsequent operation, the arrangement of words and numbers changes following a particular pattern. These operations are performed untill a final arrangement is reached or is performed in a loop. The candidate is required to identify the hidden pattern in the rearrangement and apply it to the questions.

Input → Machine → Output

Points to be remembered while solving input-output questions

- First of all, observe the given input line of words or numbers and the last step of rearrangement, so that candidate may get an idea about the changes in various steps of rearrangement.
- In order to know what changes have been made in each step, observe two consecutive steps carefully.
- Now, correlate the input, the last step and any one of the middle steps. This will enable you to identify the rule of arrangement.
- Observe the pattern to know that how many elements are arranged in each step *i.e.*, one or more then one.
- The arrangement can be done in any direction, i.e. from left to right or right to left.
- The words can also be arranged according to vowels and consonants.

The questions based on Input-Output are divided in following four types.

TYPE 01

Problems Based on Shifting

Shifting problem consists of sequence in which the elements are shifted from one position to other according to a certain set of rules/patterns.

DIRECTIONS ~ (Example Nos. 1-5) *Study the following information carefully and answer the questions given below it.*

The admission ticket for an exhibition bears a password which is changed after every clock hour based on set of words chosen for each day. The following is an illustration of the code and steps of rearrangement for subsequent clock hours. The time is 9 am to 3 pm.

Batch I (9 am to 10 am)	is not ready cloth simple harmony burning
Batch II (10 am to 11 am)	ready not is cloth burning harmony simple
Batch III (11 am to 12 noon)	cloth is not ready simple harmony burning
Batch IV (12 noon to 1 pm)	not is cloth ready burning harmony simple
Batch V (1 pm to 2 pm) and so on	ready cloth is not simple harmony burning.

Ex 01 If the password for batch I was ...... 'rate go long top we let have', then which batch will have the password .... 'go rate top long have let we'?

(a) II (b) III (c) IV (d) V
(e) None of these

Ex 02 Day's first password ..... 'camel road no toy say me not'. What will be the password for fourth batch, *i.e.*, 12 noon to 1 pm?

(a) road camel toy no not me say
(b) no road camel toy not me say
(c) toy no road camel not me say
(d) toy camel road no say me not
(e) None of the above

Ex 03 If batch II has the password ...... 'came along net or else key lot', then what could be the password for batch IV *i.e.*, 12 noon to 1 pm?

(a) net or cams along else key lot
(b) came or net along lot key else
(c) or net along came lot key else
(d) along net or came else key lot
(e) None of the above

***Ex* 04** If the password for 11 am to 12 noon was ..... 'soap shy miss pen yet the she', then what was the password for Batch I?

(a) pen miss shy soap she the yet
(b) shy miss pen soap yet the she
(c) soap pen miss shy she the yet
(d) miss shy soap pen she the yet
(e) None of the above

***Ex* 05** If the password for batch VI, *i.e.*, 2 pm to 3 pm is .... 'are trap cut he but say lap', then what will be the password for batch II, *i.e.*, 10 to 11 am?

(a) trap are he cut lap say but
(b) he cut trap are lap say but
(c) cut he are trap but say lap
(d) are he cut trap lap say but
(e) None of the above

Solutions (Example Nos. 1-5)

Different steps followed in change of password for different batches is understood as follows

Mark each word with a suitable number for reference to track the method of shifting used in various steps.

is → 1, not → 2, ready → 3, cloth → 4, simple → 5, harmony → 6, burning → 7

Now,

First step *i.e.*, Batch I

is	not	ready	cloth	simple	harmony	burning
1	2	3	4	5	6	7

Second step *i.e.*, Batch II

3	2	1	4	7	6	5

Third step *i.e.*, Batch III

4	1	2	3	5	6	7

∴ **Batch II** First three and last three words of the previous batch are written in reverse order.

Batch III First four and last three words of the previous batch are written in reverse order.

These two patterns are repeated alternately for generating pass codes for the subsequent batches.

∴ The complete sets of pass code with number representation can be written as follows

Batch I (9 am to 10 am)

1 2 3 4 5 6 7

Batch II (10 am to 11 am)

3 2 1 4 7 6 5

Batch III (11 am to 12 noon)

4 1 2 3 5 6 7

Batch IV (12 noon to 1 pm)

2 1 4 3 7 6 5

Batch V (1 pm to 2 pm)

3 4 1 2 5 6 7

Batch VI (2 pm to 3 pm)

1 4 3 2 7 6 5

1. (*c*) Batch I

rate	go	long	top	we	let	have
1	2	3	4	5	6	7

Now, given password is

go	rate	top	long	have	let	we
2	1	4	3	7	6	5

Therefore, required password is for batch IV.

2. (*a*) Batch I (9 am to 10 am)

camel	road	no	toy	say	me	not
1	2	3	4	5	6	7

So, Batch IV (12 noon to 1 pm)

road	camel	toy	no	not	me	say
2	1	4	3	7	6	5

3. (*d*) Batch II (10 am to 11 am)

came	along	net	or	else	key	lot
3	2	1	4	7	6	5

So, Batch IV (12 noon to 1 pm)

along	net	or	came	else	key	lot
2	1	4	3	7	6	5

4. (*b*) Batch III (11 am to 12 noon)

soap	shy	miss	pen	yet	the	she
4	1	2	3	5	6	7

So, Batch I password is obtained as

shy	miss	pen	soap	yet	the	she
1	2	3	4	5	6	7

5. (*c*) Batch VI (2 pm to 3 pm)

are	trap	cut	he	but	say	lap
1	4	3	2	7	6	5

So, password for batch II (10 am to 11 am) will be

cut	he	are	trap	but	say	lap
3	2	1	4	7	6	5

Practice CORNER 22.1

DIRECTIONS ~(Q. Nos. 1-5) *Read the information carefully and answer the questions given below. A word rearrangement machine when given an input line of words, rearranges them following a particular rule in every step. The following is an illustration of input and the steps of rearrangement.* « Central Bank of India PO 2010

Input Sachin's shots are really hot in cricket
***Step* I** Sachin's in are really hot shots cricket
***Step* II** Really are in Sachin's cricket shots hot
***Step* III** in are really hot shots cricket Sachin's
***Step* IV** in cricket really hot shots are Sachin's
***Step* V** hot really cricket in Sachin's are shots.

The further steps go on in the same manner.
As per the pattern followed in the above steps. Find the appropriate step for the given input or vice-versa in questions given below

1. **Input** 'team sudden now to act police staff'. Which of the following steps would be 'police staff to act sudden now team'?
(a) Step I (b) Step II (c) Step III (d) Step IV
(e) None of these

2. If Step IV of an input is 'none of the politicians have toured India', find the Step VI.
(a) have politicians none the toured India of
(b) India politicians have toured the none of
(c) have the none politicians toured India of
(d) India have politicians none of the toured
(e) None of the above

3. **Input** 'Most of the politicians were given ultimatum'. Which of the following will be the Step IV for the given input?
(a) ultimatum were given the most politicians of
(b) the politicians of most were given ultimatum
(c) ultimatum given were the politicians most of
(d) given ultimatum politicians were of the most
(e) None of the above

4. If Step V of an input is 'no of the has happy at all', then which of the following will definitely be the input?
(a) happy all at of no has the (b) all at happy no of has the
(c) the has no of at all happy (d) cannot be determined
(e) None of these

5. If Step I of an input is 'in the four of three be serious', find out the VII step of that input.
(a) serious in three be four of the
(b) in the three be four of serious
(c) serious in three be the of four
(d) cannot be determined
(e) None of the above

DIRECTIONS ~ (Q.Nos. 6-10) *Read the information carefully and answer the questions given below. A word and number arrangement machine when given a particular input, rearranges it following a particular rule. The following is the illustration of input and the steps of arrangement.*

Input 15 give not hot 45 33 for
***Step* I** for give not hot 45 33 15
***Step* II** for not give hot 33 45 15
***Step* III** 15 not give hot 33 45 for
***Step* IV** 15 give not hot 45 33 for
***Step* V** for give not hot 45 33 15

6. If '19 36 43 50 31 22 25' is the input, then find out the Step IV.
(a) 43 19 36 50 31 22 25 (b) 25 22 31 50 43 36 19
(c) 50 31 22 25 43 36 19 (d) 19 36 43 50 31 22 25
(e) None of these

7. If 'rat cat fat chat that hat mat' is the Step II, then what would be the input?
(a) mat fat cat chat hat that rat
(b) chat mat fat cat rat that hat
(c) fat mat chat cat rat hat that
(d) that hat rat cat chat mat fat
(e) None of the above

8. If input is '16 nine 32 ten two five six', then find Step V.
(a) 32 ten two five 16 nine six
(b) 32 six ten two five 16 nine
(c) six nine 32 ten two five 16
(d) 16 five two ten 32 nine six
(e) None of the above

9. We have Step V as '24 99 100 121 fine wine dine', then what would be the Step II?
(a) 24 100 99 121 wine fine dine
(b) dine fine wine 24 100 99 121
(c) wine fine dine 24 100 99 121
(d) 121 99 100 24 dine fine wine
(e) None of the above

10. Step III '39 40 41 59 35 tap map'. Find the input.
(a) map 41 40 59 tap 35 39 (b) 39 35 tap 59 40 41 map
(c) tap 41 40 59 map 35 39 (d) tap map 39 35 59 40 41
(e) None of these

DIRECTIONS ~(Q. Nos. 11-15) *Read the information carefully and answer the questions given below. A word arrangement machine, when given an input line of words, rearranges them following a particular rule in each step. The following is the illustration of the input and the steps of arrangement.* « BOI PO 2009

Input Dhoni cannot but feel sorry for him
***Step* I** but cannot Dhoni sorry feel him for
***Step* II** cannot but feel sorry Dhoni for him
***Step* III** but cannot sorry feel him for Dhoni
***Step* IV** sorry cannot but him feel Dhoni for

and so on for subsequent steps. You have to find out the logic and answer the questions given below.

11. If Step V read "weeks of tepid slothful and weak ideas", then what would Step IV read?
(a) ideas weeks and tepid of weak slothful
(b) of weeks and slothful tepid ideas weak
(c) of tepid slothful ideas weak and weeks
(d) ideas and tepid weeks of weak slothful
(e) None of the above

12. If Step I read "it was the name bestowed upon him", then what would be the arrangement for Step VII?
(a) bestowed it was the name upon him
(b) him it name bestowed the was upon
(c) it was him the name bestowed upon
(d) upon the him was it bestowed name
(e) None of the above

13. If Step VI reads "workers must take a stand against working", then what will be the last word of step III?
(a) workers (b) must (c) take (d) a
(e) None of these

14. If Step III reads "the best way of promoting our sports", then what will be the arrangement of the input?
(a) best the sports way of our promoting
(b) our promoting the best sports way of
(c) sports best the of way our promoting
(d) of our best the way sports promoting
(e) None of the above

15. If the given input is "it is good approach with care", then what will be Step IV?
(a) with approach it is a good care
(b) approach is a care good it with
(c) a good approach it is with care
(d) care with a good approach is it
(e) None of the above

Answers WITH EXPLANATIONS

Solutions (Q. Nos. 1-5)

Let reference chart be

Sachin's = 1 shots = 2 are = 3 really = 4
hot = 5 in = 6 cricket = 7

Replacing words with digits, we get

Input	1	2	3	4	5	6	7
Step **I**	1	6	3	4	5	2	7
Step **II**	4	3	6	1	7	2	5
Step **III**	6	3	4	5	2	7	1
Step **IV**	6	7	4	5	2	3	1
Step **V**	5	4	7	6	1	3	2
Step **VI**	7	4	5	2	3	1	6
Step **VII**	7	1	5	2	3	4	6

1. (*d*) Given, **Input**

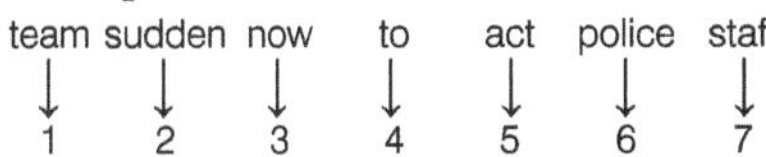

Then, the given step

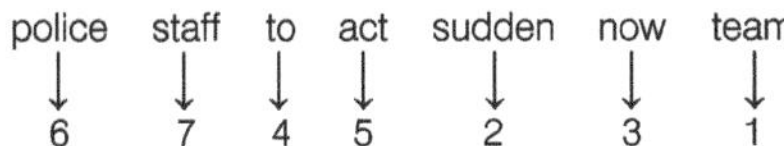

From reference chart,
Step IV 6, 7, 4, 5, 2, 3, 1

2. (*b*) Here Step IV follows, the same process of shifting as Step I follows from the input So Step IV can be considered as first step and then process of shifting can be done.

Step IV → Step I

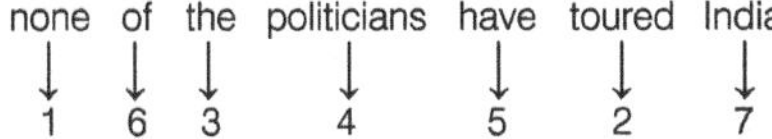

Now, from reference chart (taking digits for Step VI and putting words for them)

Step VI

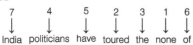

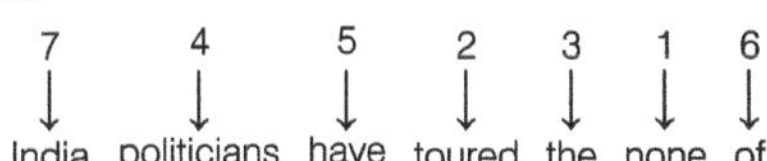

3. (*d*) Given, **Input**

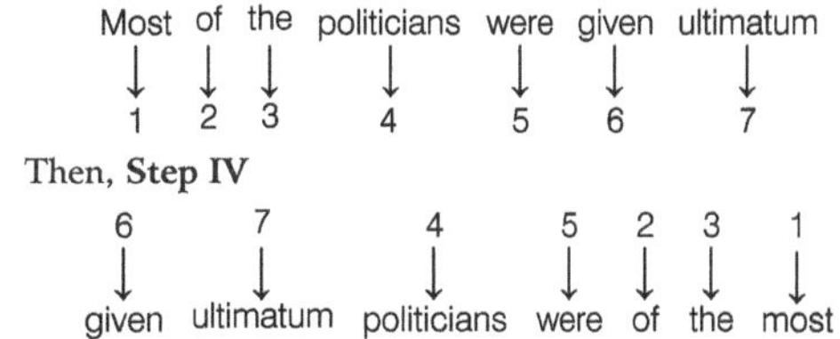

4. (*a*) Given, **Step V**

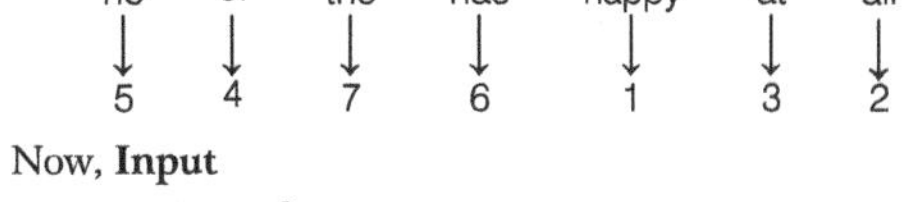

Now, **Input**

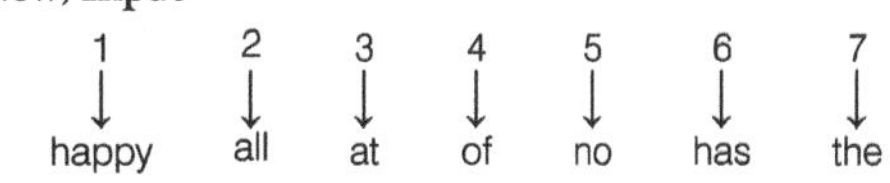

5. (*a*) Given, **Step I**

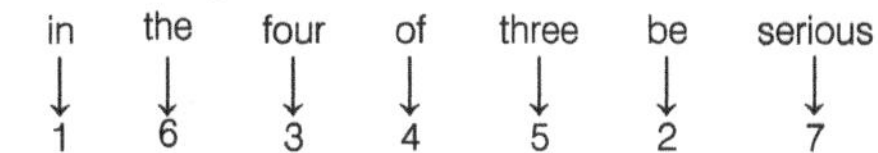

Now, from reference chart (taking digits for step VII for replacing them with appropriate words)

Step VII

Solutions (Q. Nos. 6-10) Let reference chart be

15 = 1 give = 2 not = 3 hot = 4
45 = 5 33 = 6 for = 7

Input	1	2	3	4	5	6	7
Step **I**	7	2	3	4	5	6	1
Step **II**	7	3	2	4	6	5	1
Step **III**	1	3	2	4	6	5	7
Step **IV**	1	2	3	4	5	6	7
Step **V**	7	2	3	4	5	6	1

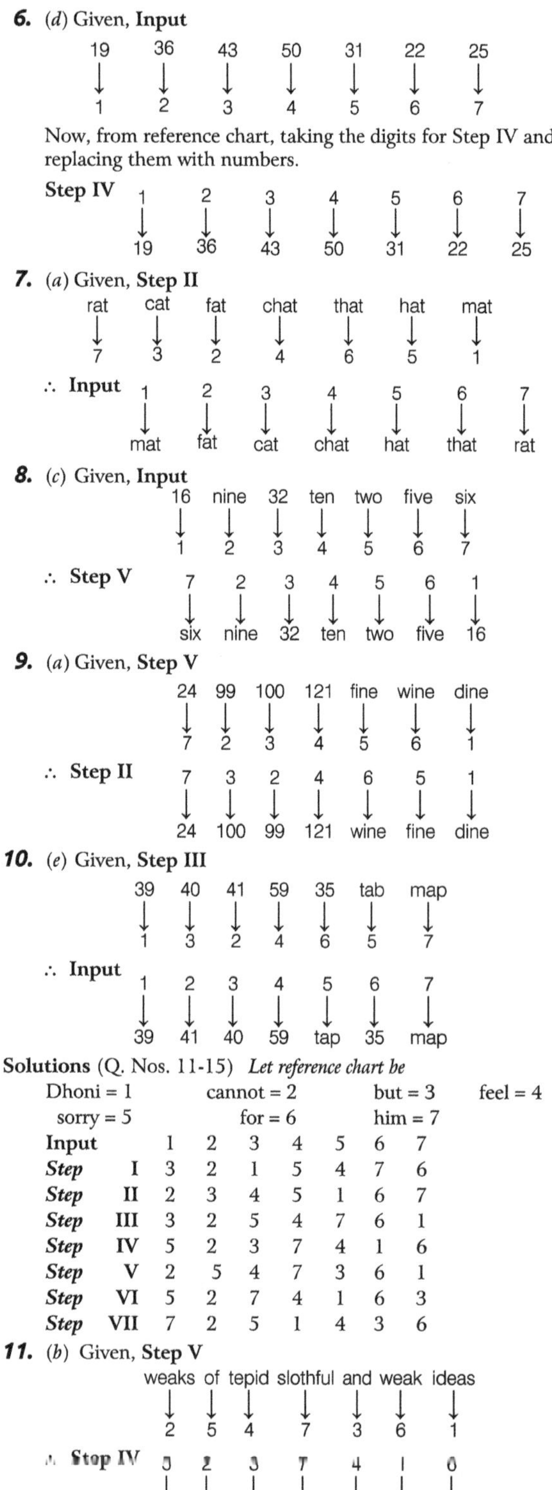

6. (*d*) Given, **Input**

19 36 43 50 31 22 25
↓ ↓ ↓ ↓ ↓ ↓ ↓
1 2 3 4 5 6 7

Now, from reference chart, taking the digits for Step IV and replacing them with numbers.

Step IV 1 2 3 4 5 6 7
↓ ↓ ↓ ↓ ↓ ↓ ↓
19 36 43 50 31 22 25

7. (*a*) Given, **Step II**

rat cat fat chat that hat mat
↓ ↓ ↓ ↓ ↓ ↓ ↓
7 3 2 4 6 5 1

∴ **Input** 1 2 3 4 5 6 7
↓ ↓ ↓ ↓ ↓ ↓ ↓
mat fat cat chat hat that rat

8. (*c*) Given, **Input**

16 nine 32 ten two five six
↓ ↓ ↓ ↓ ↓ ↓ ↓
1 2 3 4 5 6 7

∴ **Step V** 7 2 3 4 5 6 1
↓ ↓ ↓ ↓ ↓ ↓ ↓
six nine 32 ten two five 16

9. (*a*) Given, **Step V**

24 99 100 121 fine wine dine
↓ ↓ ↓ ↓ ↓ ↓ ↓
7 2 3 4 5 6 1

∴ **Step II** 7 3 2 4 6 5 1
↓ ↓ ↓ ↓ ↓ ↓ ↓
24 100 99 121 wine fine dine

10. (*e*) Given, **Step III**

39 40 41 59 35 tab map
↓ ↓ ↓ ↓ ↓ ↓ ↓
1 3 2 4 6 5 7

∴ **Input** 1 2 3 4 5 6 7
↓ ↓ ↓ ↓ ↓ ↓ ↓
39 41 40 59 tap 35 map

Solutions (Q. Nos. 11-15) *Let reference chart be*

Dhoni = 1 cannot = 2 but = 3 feel = 4
sorry = 5 for = 6 him = 7

Input	1	2	3	4	5	6	7
Step **I**	3	2	1	5	4	7	6
Step **II**	2	3	4	5	1	6	7
Step **III**	3	2	5	4	7	6	1
Step **IV**	5	2	3	7	4	1	6
Step **V**	2	5	4	7	3	6	1
Step **VI**	5	2	7	4	1	6	3
Step **VII**	7	2	5	1	4	3	6

11. (*b*) Given, **Step V**

weaks of tepid slothful and weak ideas
↓ ↓ ↓ ↓ ↓ ↓ ↓
2 5 4 7 3 6 1

∴ **Step IV** 5 2 3 7 4 1 6
↓ ↓ ↓ ↓ ↓ ↓ ↓
of weaks and slothful tepid ideas weak

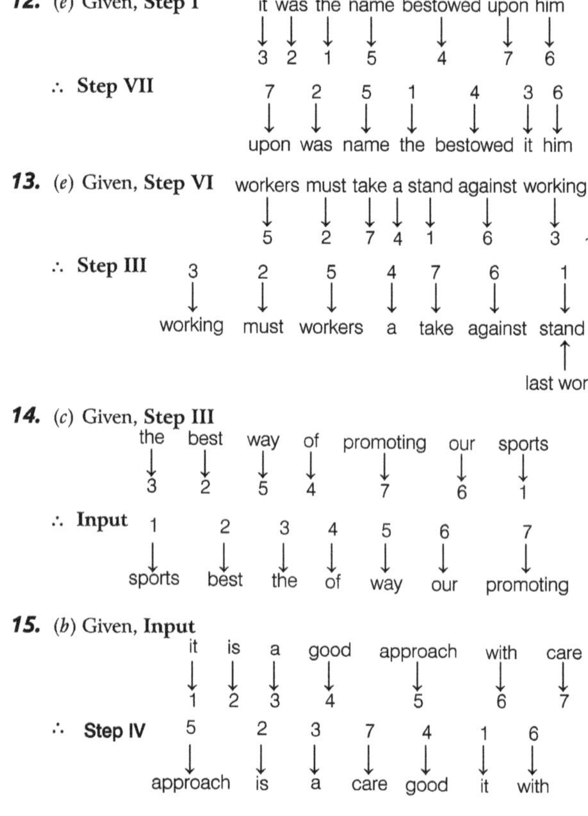

12. (*e*) Given, **Step I**

it was the name bestowed upon him
↓ ↓ ↓ ↓ ↓ ↓ ↓
3 2 1 5 4 7 6

∴ **Step VII** 7 2 5 1 4 3 6
↓ ↓ ↓ ↓ ↓ ↓ ↓
upon was name the bestowed it him

13. (*e*) Given, **Step VI**

workers must take a stand against working
↓ ↓ ↓ ↓ ↓ ↓ ↓
5 2 7 4 1 6 3

∴ **Step III** 3 2 5 4 7 6 1
↓ ↓ ↓ ↓ ↓ ↓ ↓
working must workers a take against stand
↑
last word

14. (*c*) Given, **Step III**

the best way of promoting our sports
↓ ↓ ↓ ↓ ↓ ↓ ↓
3 2 5 4 7 6 1

∴ **Input** 1 2 3 4 5 6 7
↓ ↓ ↓ ↓ ↓ ↓ ↓
sports best the of way our promoting

15. (*b*) Given, **Input**

it is a good approach with care
↓ ↓ ↓ ↓ ↓ ↓ ↓
1 2 3 4 5 6 7

∴ **Step IV** 5 2 3 7 4 1 6
↓ ↓ ↓ ↓ ↓ ↓ ↓
approach is a care good it with

TYPE 02

Problems Based on Arrangement

In such problems, words or numbers or both are arranged. Words are arranged alphabetically while numbers are arranged in their increasing or decreasing order.

DIRECTIONS ~ (Example Nos. 6 -10) *A word arrangement machine when given an input line of words, rearranges them following a particular rule in each step. The following is the illustration of the input and the steps of arrangement.*

Input	vani is the most beautiful girl on earth
Step **I**	beautiful vani is the most girl on earth
Step **II**	beautiful earth vani is the most girl on
Step **III**	beautiful earth girl vani is the most on
Step **IV**	beautiful earth girl is vani the most on
Step **V**	beautiful earth girl is most vani the on
Step **VI**	beautiful earth girl is most on vani the
Step **VII**	beautiful earth girl is most on the vani

Since the words are already arranged, the machine stops after this step. Otherwise the machine may carry on its logic until the words get fully arranged.

Study the logic and answer the questions that follow

Ex 06 **Input** 'is you are again famous on this'. Find the Step III.

(a) again are famous is you on this
(b) on this you is famous are again
(c) this on you is famous are again
(d) famous this on you is are again
(e) None of the above

Ex 07 If given, Step IV 'option pen rose Seema tape yolk', what will be the input?

(a) pen option rose tape Seema yolk
(b) yolk Seema tape rose option pen
(c) tape Seema yolk rose option pen
(d) Cannot be determined
(e) None of the above

Ex 08 **Input** 'no gum to sum fame game'. Find the Step I.

(a) game no gum to sum fame
(b) gum no to sum fame game
(c) game gum no to sum fame
(d) Cannot be determined
(e) None of the above

Ex 09 **Input** 'He is a great Indian cricketer'. Find out the last step for this input.

(a) VII (b) VI (c) IV
(d) Cannot be determined
(e) None of these

Ex 10 **Input** 'when men ten gain rain'. What would be the second step for this input?

(a) gain when men ten rain
(b) gain men when ten rain
(c) rain ten men when gain
(d) Cannot be determined
(e) None of the above

Solutions (Example Nos. 6-10) *In this problem we notice,*

(i) It is a forward order alphabetical arrangement.
(ii) Arrangement takes place from left side only.

6. (*a*) **Input** 'is you are again famous on this'

Step I again is you are famous on this

Step II again are is you famous on this

Step III again are famous is you on this

Hence, option (a) is the correct answer.

Quicker Method We pick first three words in forward alphabetical order (again, are, famous) and place them before the remaining words that gives.

Step III again are famous is you on this

7. (*d*) Option (d) is the correct answer as in the arrangement problem previous steps cannot be determined. (see Rule B)

8. (e) Input no gum to sum fame game

Step I fame no gum to sum game

Hence, option (e) is the correct answer.

9. (c) **Input** He is a great Indian cricketer

Step I a He is great Indian cricketer

Step II a cricketer he is great Indian

Step III a cricketer great he is Indian

Step IV a cricketer great he Indian is

Hence, option (c) is correct.

Quicker Method The complete arrangement will take atmost 6 – 1 = 5 steps

So, it is very much clear that total steps will be either 5 or less. Thus, this rule automatically rejects option (a) and (b) and option (d) will also be rejected.

10. (*b*) Input when men ten gain rain

Step I gain when men ten rain

Step II gain men when ten rain

Hence, option (b) is correct.

DIRECTIONS ~ (Example Nos. 11-16) *Study the following information carefully and answer the given questions.*
« IBPS PO 2016

A word and number arrangement machine given an input line of words and numbers rearranges them following a particular rule in each step. The following is an illustration of input and rearrangement.

Input	day case 20 13 now for 49 56
Step I	13 day case 20 now for 49 56
Step II	13 now day case 20 for 49 56
Step III	13 now 20 day case for 49 56
Step IV	13 now 20 for day case 49 56
Step V	13 now 20 for 49 day case 56
Step VI	13 now 20 for 49 day 56 case

and Step VI is the last step.

As per the rules followed in the above steps. Find out in each of the following questions the appropriate step for the given input.

Ex 11 **Input** yes 21 far 32 17 12 wide goal

Which of the following will be Step V of the above input?

(a) 12 yes 21 wide 32 far 17 goal
(b) 12 yes 21 wide far 32 17 goal
(c) 12 yes 21 far 32 17 wide goal
(d) There will be no such step
(e) None of the above

Ex 12 Step IV of an input is, 17 hotel 29 father 83 76 door eye

Which of the following will be Step VII?

(a) 17 hotel 29 father 76 door 83 age
(b) 17 hotel 29 father 76 age 83 door
(c) 17 hotel 29 father 76 83 door age
(d) There will be no such step
(e) None of the above

Ex 13 Step III of an input is, 25 win 32 85 73 tax break home

How many more steps will be required to complete the rearrangement?

(a) Five (b) Four (c) Six (d) Seven
(e) None of these

Ex 14 Step III of an input is, 37 yellow 42 61 53 violet green red. How many more steps will be required to complete the rearrangement?

(a) 3 (b) 4 (c) 5 (d) 6
(e) None of these

***Ex* 15** Input can you go there 22 36 13 46

How many steps will be required to complete, rearrangement?

(a) 7 (b) 8
(c) 6 (d) 5
(e) None of these

***Ex* 16** Input 42 36 go and come back 20 15

Which of the following steps will be the last but one?

(a) IV (b) V
(c) VII (d) VIII
(e) None of these

Solutions (Example Nos. 11-16) After careful analysis of input and various steps of rearrangement it is evident that in each step one number or word is rearranged. The numbers are arranged in ascending order and words are arranged in reverse alphabetical order.

11. (e) **Input** yes 21 far 32 17 12 wide goal
Step I 12 yes 21 far 32 17 wide goal
Step II 12 yes 17 21 far 32 wide goal
Step III 12 yes 17 wide 21 far 32 goal
Step IV 12 yes 17 wide 21 goal far 32
Step V 12 yes 17 wide 21 goal 32 far

12. (*d*) **Step IV** 17 hotel 29 father 83 76 door eye
Step V 17 hotel 29 father 76 83 door eye
Step VI 17 hotel 29 father 76 eye 83 door
So, there will be no such step.

13. (e) **Step III** 25 win 32 85 73 tax break home
Step IV 25 win 32 tax 85 73 break home
Step V 25 win 32 tax 73 85 break home
Step VI 25 win 32 tax 73 home 85 break
So, three more steps are required to complete the rearrangement.

14. (*a*) **Step III** 37 yellow 42 61 53 violet green red
Step IV 37 yellow 42 violet 61 53 green red
Step V 37 yellow 42 violet 53 61 green red
Step VI 37 yellow 42 violet 53 red 61 green
So, three more steps are required to complete rearrangement.

15. (a) **Input** can you go there 22 36 13 46
Step I 13 can you go there 22 36 46
Step II 13 you can go there 22 36 46
Step III 13 you 22 can go there 36 46
Step IV 13 you 22 there can go 36 46
Step V 13 you 22 there 36 can go 46
Step VI 13 you 22 there 36 go can 46
Step VII 13 you 22 there 36 go 46 can
So, seven steps are required to complete rearrangement.

16. (b) **Input** 42 36 go and come back 20 15
Step I 15 42 36 go and come back 20
Step II 15 go 42 36 and come back 20
Step III 15 go 20 42 36 and come back
Step IV 15 go 20 come 42 36 and back
Step V 15 go 20 come 36 42 and back
Step VI 15 go 20 come 36 back 42 and
So, the step from last but one is V.

DIRECTIONS ~(Example Nos. 17-20) *A word and number arrangement machine when given an input line of words and numbers rearranges them following a particular rule in each step. The following is an illustration of input and rearrangement (all the numbers are two digit numbers).* « IBPS PO 2015

Input talk 47 12 rise at 99 75 32 wise joke high 28 56 be
***Step* I** 12 talk 47 rise 99 75 32 wise joke high 28 56 be at
***Step* II** 28 12 talk 47 rise 99 75 32 wise joke high 56 at be
***Step* III** 32 28 12 talk 47 rise 99 75 wise joke 56 at be high
***Step* IV** 47 32 28 12 talk rise 99 75 wise 56 at be high joke
***Step* V** 56 47 32 28 12 talk 99 75 wise at be high joke rise
***Step* VI** 75 56 47 32 28 12 99 wise at be high joke rise talk
***Step* VII** 99 75 56 47 32 28 12 at be high joke rise talk wise

Step VII is the last step of the above rearrangement as the desired arrangement is obtained.

Input 83 why sat 14 32 no be ink feet 50 27 vain 67 92

***Ex* 17** Which step number is the following output?
32 27 14 83 why sat no 50 vain 67 92 be feet ink

(a) Step V (b) Step VI (c) Step IV (d) Step I
(e) Other than those given as options

***Ex* 18** Which word/number would be at fifth position from the right in Step V?

(a) 14 (b) 92 (c) feet (d) be
(e) sat

***Ex* 19** How many elements (words or numbers) are there between 'feet' and '32' as they appear in the last step of the output?

(a) One (b) Three (c) Four (d) Five
(e) Two

***Ex* 20** Which of the following represents the position of 'why' in the fourth step?

(a) Eighth from the left (b) Fifth from the right
(c) Sixth from the left (d) Fifth from the left
(e) Other than those given as options

Solutions (Example Nos. 17-20) By careful analysis of input and various steps of output we find that in each step a number and also a word is rearranged. Numbers are rearranged as the left end in ascending order and words are rearranged at right end in alphabetical order. Also, when a new number is rearranged, the previously arranged numbers are shifted towards right and when a new word is rearranged, the previously arranged words to are shifted towards left.

Input 83 why sat 14 32 no be ink feet 50 27 vain 67 92
Step I 14 83 why sat 32 no ink feet 50 27 vain 67 92 be
Step II 27 14 83 why sat 32 no ink 50 vain 67 92 be feet
Step III 32 27 14 83 why sat no 50 vain 67 92 be feet ink
Step IV 50 32 27 14 83 why sat vain 67 92 be feet ink no
Step V 67 50 32 27 14 83 why vain 92 be feet ink no sat
Step VI 83 67 50 32 27 14 why 92 be feet ink no sat vain
Step VII 92 83 67 50 32 27 14 be feet ink no sat vain why

17. (e) The given output matches with Step III.

18. (*d*) 'be' would be at fifth position from the right in Step V.

19. (*b*) Three elements are there between 'feet' and '32' as they appear in the last step of the output.

20. (c) 'why' is sixth from the left in the fourth step.

Practice / CORNER 22.2

DIRECTIONS ~ (Q. Nos. 1-5) *Read the information carefully and answer the questions given below.*

« IDBI (Office Executive) 2018

A word and number arrangement machine when given a particular input, rearranges it following a particular rule. The following is the illustration of input and the steps of arrangement.

Input cup for hot 34 69 72 tea 27
***Step* I** 27 cup for hot 34 69 72 tea
***Step* II** 27 tea cup for hot 34 69 72
***Step* III** 27 tea 34 cup for hot 69 72
***Step* IV** 27 tea 34 hot cup for 69 72
***Step* V** 27 tea 34 hot 69 cup for 72
***Step* VI** 27 tea 34 hot 69 for cup 72
***Step* VII** 27 tea 34 hot 69 for 72 cup

And Step VII is the last step of the above arrangement

As per the rules followed in the above steps, find out in each of the following question, the appropriate step for the given input.

1. Input kind 12 96 heart water 59 42 yes
How many steps will be required to complete the rearrangement?
(a) Three (b) Four
(c) Five (d) Six
(e) None of these

2. Input Jungle 43 mode 25 basket 39 target 19
Which of the following steps will be the last but one?
(a) VII (b) VIII (c) IX (d) VI
(e) None of these

3. Step III of an input is : 12 world 31 ask cart ball 87 75
Which of the following will definitely be the input?
(a) 31 ask cart ball 87 75 world 12
(b) 31 ask cart ball 87 75 12 world
(c) 31 ask 12 world cart ball 87 75
(d) Cannot be determined
(e) None of the above

4. Step II of an input is– 24 year 56 43 last part 64 over
How many more steps will be required to complete the rearrangement?
(a) Five (b) Six (c) Seven (d) Four
(e) None of these

5. Step III of an input: 32 station 46 81 73 march go for
Which of the following will be Step VI?
(a) 32 station 46 march 73 go for 81
(b) 32 station 46 march 73 81 go for
(c) 32 station 46 march 73 go 81 for
(d) There will be no such step
(e) None of the above

DIRECTIONS ~ (Q.Nos 6-9) *Study the following information carefully and answer the given questions. A word and number arrangement machine when given an input line of words and numbers rearranges them following a particular rule in each step. The following is an illustration of input and rearrangement.*

« UCO Bank (PO) 2010

Input 'sale data 18 23 for 95 then 38'
***Step* I** data sale 18 23 for 95 then 38
***Step* II** data 95 sale 18 23 for then 38
***Step* III** data 95 for sale 18 23 then 38
***Step* IV** data 95 for 38 sale 18 23 then
***Step* V** data 95 for 38 sale 23 18 then
***Step* VI** data 95 for 38 sale 23 then 18

and step VI is the last step of the rearrangement of the above input.

As per the rules followed in the above steps, find out in each of the following questions the appropriate step for the given input.

6. Input 'year 39 stake 47 house full 94 55'
How many steps will be required to complete the rearrangement?
(a) Five (b) Six (c) Four (d) Seven
(e) None of these

7. Step II of an input is car 83 lost ever 32 46 74 now
How many more steps will be required to complete the rearrangement?
(a) Three (b) Four
(c) Five (d) Six
(e) None of these

8. Step III of an input is and 79 code 27 18 new goal 34
Which of the following will definitely be the input?
(a) code and 79 27 18 new goal 34
(b) code 27 18 new goal 34 and 79
(c) code 27 and 18 79 new goal 34
(d) Cannot be determined
(e) None of the above

9. Input 'water full never 35 78 16 height 28'
Which of the following steps will be the last?
(a) VI (b) VII (c) VIII (d) IX
(e) None of these

DIRECTIONS ~ (Q.Nos. 10-13) *Study the following information to answer the given questions. A word arrangement machine, when given an input line of words, rearranges them following a particular rule in each step. The following is an illustration of input and the steps of rearrangement.*

Input 'As if it on as zoo figure Of in at'
***Step* I** as As if it on zoo figure Of in at
***Step* II** as As at if it on zoo figure Of in
***Step* III** as As at figure if it on zoo Of in
***Step* IV** as As at figure if in it on zoo Of.
***Step* V** as As at figure if in it Of on zoo

and Step V is the last step for this input.

As per the rules followed in the above steps, find out in the questions below, the appropriate steps for the given input.

10. **Input** 'you are at fault on this'—Which of the following steps would be 'are at fault on you this'?

(a) I (b) II (c) III (d) IV (e) V

11. **Input** 'am ace all if Is'—Which of the following will be the IInd step?

(a) all am ace if Is (b) ace all am Is if
(c) ace all am if Is (d) Is if am ace all
(e) None of the above

12. If IVth step an input is 'an apple at cot was red on one side' —Which of the following will definitely be the input?

(a) apple at an cot was red on one side
(b) cot an at apple was red on one side
(c) was cot red an on at one apple side
(d) Cannot be determined
(e) None of the above

13. **Input** 'Him and His either of her', which step will be the last step for this input?

(a) I (b) II (c) III (d) V (e) VII

DIRECTIONS ~ (Q. Nos. 14-18) *Study the following information carefully and answer the given questions.*

A word and number arrangement machine when given an input line of words and numbers rearrange them following a particular rule in each step. The following is an illustration of input and rearrangement. (all the numbers are two-digit numbers). « SBI PO 2015

Input gate 20 86 just not 71 for 67 38 bake sun 55
***Step* I** bake gate 20 just not 71 for 67 38 sun 55 86
***Step* II** for bake gate 20 just not 67 38 sun 55 86 71
***Step* III** gate for bake 20 just not 38 sun 55 86 71 67
***Step* IV** just gate for bake 20 not 38 sun 55 86 71 67
***Step* V** not just gate for bake 20 sun 86 71 67 55 38
***Step* VI** sun not just gate for bake 86 71 67 55 38 20

Step VI is the last step of the arrangement the above input. As per the rule followed in the above steps, find out in each of the following questions the appropriate step for the given input.

Input 31 rise gem 15 92 47 aim big 25 does 56 not 85 63 with moon

14. How many steps will be required to complete the rearrangement?

(a) Eight (b) Six (c) Seven (d) Five
(e) None of these

15. Which word number would be at 7th position from the left end in Step IV ?

(a) rise (b) aim (c) big (d) 15
(e) 47

16. Which step number is the following output?
Rise not moon gem does big aim 15 with 92 85 63 56 47 31 25

(a) Step V (b) Step VII (c) Step IV (d) Step VIII
(e) There is no such step

17. Which of the following represents the position of '92' in Step VI?

(a) Ninth from the left end (b) Fifth from the right end
(c) Sixth from the right end (d) Ninth from the right end
(e) Seventh from the left end

18. Which word/number would be at 5th position from the right end in the last step?

(a) gem (b) 63 (c) 56 (d) 85 (e) does

DIRECTIONS ~ (Q. Nos. 19-23) *Study the following information carefully and answer the given questions.*

When a word and number arrangement machine is given an input line of words and numbers, it arranges them following a particular rule. The following is an illustration of Input and rearrangement. « SBI PO 2016

Input expect 30 more funny 41 52 sea 61 ring 36 89 joy
***Step* I** expect funny 30 more 41 52 sea 61 ring 36 89 joy
***Step* II** expect funny 89 61 30 more 41 52 sea ring 36 joy
***Step* III** expect funny 89 61 joy more 30 41 52 sea ring 36
***Step* IV** expect funny 89 61 joy more 52 41 30 sea ring 36.
***Step* V** expect funny 89 61 joy more 52 41 ring sea 30 36
***Step* VI** expect funny 89 61 joy more 52 41 ring sea 36 30

And step VI is the last step of the above input. As per the rules followed in the above step, find out the appropriate step for the given output.

Input best 11 all 25 my 47 81 equal 49 strength 16 and explanation.

19. Which of the following term exactly comes between 49 and equal in Step III?

(a) my (b) 11 (c) Strength (d) best
(e) None of these

20. How many elements are there between 25 and 16 in Step V?

(a) One (b) Three (c) Two (d) Five
(e) None of these

21. In Step VI, if 'equal' and 'my'. '11' and '49' interchanged then how many elements are there between 49 and equal?

(a) Two (b) Three (c) Four (d) Six
(e) None of these

22. What is the position of 25 in Step IV from the right end?

(a) Third (b) Fourth (c) Sixth (d) Fifth
(e) None of these

23. Which of the following will be the final step of the given input?

(a) all and 16 11 best equal 25 47 my strength 49 81
(b) my and 49 81 equal best 47 25 all strength 16 11
(c) all and 81 49 best equal 25 47 my strength 11 16
(d) all best 81 49 and equal 47 25 my strength 16 11
(e) None of the above

DIRECTIONS ~(Q. Nos. 24-28) *Study the given information and answer the questions.*

When a word and number arrangement machine is given an input line of words and numbers. It arranges them following a particular rule. The following is an illustration of input and rearrangement. « LIC AAO 2015

(All the numbers are two-digit numbers)

Input 24 method 87 67 of data 34 collection 45 12 specified now
***Step* I** 12 method 87 67 of data 34 collection 45 specified now 24

Step II 34 12 method 87 67 of data collection specified now 24 45

Step III 67 34 12 method of data collection specified now 24 45 87

Step IV collection 67 34 12 method of specified now 24 45 87 data

Step V method collection 67 34 12 of specified 24 45 87 data now

Step VI of method collection 67 34 12 24 45 87 data now specified

Step VI is the last step of the above arrangement as the intended arrangement is obtained.

As per the rules followed in the given steps, find out the appropriate steps for the given input.

Input chemical 68 11 reaction 87 is 21 hard to 53 92 detect

24. In which step are the elements 'to 92 detect 21' found in the same order?

(a) Sixth (b) Third
(c) The given order of elements is not found in any step.
(d) Second (e) Fifth

25. What is the position of '21' from the right end in the last step?

(a) Tenth (b) Eighth (c) Fifth (d) Fourth
(e) Sixth

26. In which step are the elements '87 53 11 reaction' found in the same order?

(a) Sixth (b) Fifth
(c) Fourth (d) Fourth and Fifth
(e) None of these

27. Which element is fifth to the left of the element which is ninth from the left end of the fourth step?

(a) 11 (b) 87 (c) 53 (d) reaction
(e) chemical

28. Which element is exactly between 'chemical' and '87' in the second step of the given arrangement?

(a) 53 (b) hard (c) reaction (d) is (e) 68

DIRECTIONS ~(Q. Nos. 29-33) *Study the following information carefully and answer the questions given below.* « Bank of Maharashtra PO 2016

When a word and number arrangement machine is given an input line of words and numbers. It arranges them following a particular rule. The following is an illustration of input and arrangement. (All the numbers are two digit numbers).

Input wait 47 19 rose door 23 aim less 85 year 99 68

Step I year 19 wait 47 rose door 23 aim less 85 99 68

Step II year 19 47 rose door aim less 85 99 68 23 wait

Step III rose 47 year 19 door aim less 85 99 68 23 wait

Step IV rose 47 year 19 door aim 85 99 23 wait 68 less

Step V door 85 rose 47 year 19 aim 99 23 wait 68 less

Step VI door 85 rose 47 year 19 23 wait 68 less 99 aim

Step VI is the last step of the above arrangement as the intended output of the arrangement is obtained. As per the rules followed in the given steps, find the appropriate steps for the given input.

Input band 85 zen 54 den fit 25 37 home 41 sun 73

29. How many elements are there between 'band' and '73' in Step IV?

(a) Five (b) One (c) Two (d) None
(e) Four

30. Which is the third element to the left of the ninth element from the left in the third step?

(a) zen (b) ban (c) 54 (d) 85 (e) fit

31. In which of the following steps 41, 73, 37' found consecutively in the same order?

(a) Step II (b) Step IV (c) Step I (d) Step III
(e) Step V

32. In Step V, 'home' is related to '25' following a certain pattern. Following the same pattern, '37' is related to 'fit' in Step VI. In Step I, with which of the following is 'band' related to following the same pattern?

(a) fit (b) den (c) 81 (d) sun
(e) home

33. Which of the following combinations represents the first two and the last two elements in the Step V of the given input?

(a) den, 41; 54, fit (b) home, 73; 85, band
(c) den, 25; 37, sun (d) den, 85; 54 home
(e) den, 73; 54, fit

DIRECTIONS ~ (Q. Nos. 34-38) *When a number arrangement machine is given an input line of numbers, it arranges them following a particular rule.* « IBPS PO(Pre) 2017

The following is an illustration of input and rearrangement (All the numbers are two digit numbers)

Input 81 63 79 42 15 24 86 37 96 19

Step I 15 19 81 63 79 42 24 86 37 96

Step II 96 86 15 19 81 63 79 42 24 37

Step III 24 37 96 86 15 19 81 63 79 42

Step IV 81 79 24 37 96 86 15 19 63 42

Step V 42 63 81 79 24 37 96 86 15 19

Step V is the last step of the above arrangement as the intended output of arrangement is obtained.

As per the rules followed in the given steps, find the appropriate steps for the given input.

Input 26 69 13 82 55 21 71 34 93 47

34. Which is the fourth element to the left of the seventh element from the left end in Step III of the given arrangement?

(a) 93 (b) 82 (c) 13 (d) 26
(e) 55

35. What will be the resultant if the fifth element from right end in Step V is subtracted from the second element from left end in Step II as per the given arrangement?

(a) 59 (b) 79 (c) 56 (d) 48 (e) 67

36. In which of the following steps '26 69 55' found consecutively in the same order as per the given arrangement?

(a) Only II (b) I and II
(c) II and III (d) There is no such step
(e) Only III

37. As per the given arrangement, in Step I '21' is related to '69' in a certain pattern. Following the same pattern, '26' is related to '93' in Step IV. In which of the following is '47' related to following the same pattern in Step V?

(a) 71 (b) 21 (c) 34 (d) 69 (e) 55

38. How many elements appear to the right of '26' in Step IV of the given arrangement?

(a) Six (b) None (c) Two (d) Five
(e) Seven

DIRECTIONS ~(Q. Nos. 39-43) *Study the given information carefully and answer the given questions.* « UBI PO 2016

When a word and number arrangement machine is given an input line of words and numbers, it arranges them following a particular rule. The following is an illustration of input and rearrangement.(All the numbers are two-digit numbers.)

Input 30 overcome ado 67 18 lie so 85 74 come
***Step* I** admit 30 overcome 67 18 lie so 74 come 84
***Step* II** commit admit 30 overcome 67 18 lie so 84 73
***Step* III** limit commit admit 30 overcome 18 so 84 73 66
***Step* IV** overcommit limit commit admit 18 so 84 73 66 29
***Step* V** smit overcommit limit commit admit 84 73 66 29 17

And Step V is the last step of the above arrangement as the intended output of the above arrangement is obtained. As per the rules followed in the given steps, find the appropriate steps for the given input.

Input 61 ox herb 33 86 intern sums 28 49 perk.

39. In Step III, how many elements are there between '85' and the third element from the left end?

(a) None (b) One (c) Three
(d) More than three (e) Two

40. Which of the following is the sixth element from the left end in Step II?

(a) sums (b) hermit (c) intern (d) perk (e) 28

41. 'intermit' is related to '85' in the same way as 'omit' is related to '60' in Step V. Following the same pattern which element is 'permit' related to in Step IV?

(a) intermit (b) omit (c) 28 (d) 32
(e) 48

42. What is the difference between the fourth element from the right end in Step IV and the fourth element from the right end in Step V?

(a) 27 (b) 12 (c) 18 (d) 5
(e) Other than those given as options

43. In Step V, which of the following elements does not appear between 'permit' and the fourth element from the right end?

(a) intermit (b) hermit (c) omit (d) 32 (e) 85

DIRECTIONS ~ (Q. Nos. 44-48) *Study the following information carefully to answer the given questions.* « IBPS RRB (PO) 2017

A word and number arrangement machine when given an input line of words and numbers rearranges them following a particular rule. The following is an illustration of input and rearrangement.

Input 97 nosy 21 snow cold 32 asian 46 65 viral 83 high
***Step* I** 211 97 nosy snow cold asian 46 65 viral 83 high 322
***Step* II** asian 211 97 nosy snow 46 65 viral 83 high 322 cold
***Step* III** 463 asian 211 97 nosy snow viral 83 high 322 cold 654
***Step* IV** high 463 asian 211 97 snow viral 83 322 cold 654 nosy
***Step* V** 835 high 463 asian 211 snow viral 322 cold 654 nosy 976
***Step* VI** snow 835 high 463 asian 211 322 cold 654 nosy 976 viral

Step VI is the last step of the rearrangement. As per the rules followed in the above steps, find out in each of the following questions the appropriate steps for the given input.

Input peak 18 utility 76 emerge 27 beautiful 37 51 visible 86 know

44. Which of the following would be the difference of the numbers which is 2nd from left end in step IV and 2nd from right end in Step II?

(a) 290 (b) 83 (c) 193 (d) 101
(e) None of these

45. How many steps would be needed to complete the arrangement?

(a) X (b) VIII (c) V (d) VII
(e) None of these

46. Which of the following element will be 6th to the left of 3rd from the right end in Step V?

(a) 181 (b) beautiful (c) 373 (d) know
(e) None of these

47. What will the addition of the numbers which is fifth from the left end in Step II and 5th from the right end in Step IV?

(a) 312 (b) 210 (c) 162 (d) 165
(e) None of these

48. In Step IV, which of the following word/number would be on 4th position from the left end?

(a) visible (b) 181 (c) 97 (d) utility
(e) None of these

DIRECTIONS ~ (Q. Nos. 49-53) *Study the following information carefully and to answer the questions given below.* « Indian Bank PO 2017

When a word and number arrangement machine is given an input line of words and numbers, it arranges them following a particular rule. The following is an illustration of input and rearrangement.

(All the numbers are two digit numbers)

Input turn 12 84 mist hike 45 vast 26 site gate 72 56
Step I gate turn 12 mist hike 45 vast 26 site 72 56 84
Step II 72 gate turn 12 mist 45 vast 26 site 56 84 hike
Step III mist 72 gate turn 12 45 vast 26 site 84 hike 56
Step IV 45 mist 72 gate turn 12 vast 26 84 hike 56 site
Step V turn 45 mist 72 gate 12 vast 84 hike 56 site 26
Step VI 12 turn 45 mist 72 gate 84 hike 56 site 26 vast

Step VI is the last step of the above arrangement as the intended arrangement is obtained.

As per the rules followed in the given steps, find the appropriate steps for the given input.

Input 15 role air 96 63 born with 77 like 39 some 52

49. How many elements are there between 'with' and 'born' in Step IV?
(a) None (b) One (c) Two (d) Three
(e) Five

50. In which of the following steps is ' 15 some 52' found consecutively in the same order?
(a) Step IV (b) Step VI (c) Step II (d) Step I
(e) Step III

51. Which of the following is second element to the left of the ninth element from the left in the second step?
(a) like (b) 39 (c) with (d) role (e) air

52. In Step I, 'some' is related to '77' following a certain pattern. Following the same pattern, in Step V, 'role' is related to '96' In Step IV, to which of the following is 'born' related to?
(a) With (b) 63 (c) like (d) role (e) 39

53. In Step II, which element(s) appear(s) exactly between '77' and '15'?
(a) Only 'role' (b) Both 'born' and '52'
(c) Only 'air' (d) Only 'some'
(e) Both 'like' and '39'

DIRECTIONS ~ (Q. Nos. 54-58) *Study the following information to answer the given questions:*

A word and number arrangement machine when given an input of words, rearranges them following a particular rule. The following is an illustration of input and rearrangement.

Input code word right you thing like
Step I youv code word right thing like 211
Step II worde youv code right thing like 211 44
Step III thingh worde youv code right like 211 44 77
Step IV rightu thingh worde youv code like 211 44 77 200
Step V likef rightu thingh worde youv code 211 44 77 200 55
Step VI codef likef rightu thingh worde youv 211 44 77 200 55 55

Step VI is the last step of the rearrangement.

As per the rules followed in the above steps, find out in each of the following questions the appropriate steps for the given input.

Input quite similar dull go test vice

54. What will the difference of the numbers which is third from the right end in Step III and Ist from the right end in Step IV?
(a) 12 (b) 0 (c) 18 (d) 11
(e) None of these

55. Which of the following element will be 6th to the left of 3rd from the right end in Step V?
(a) quitef (b) dull (c) similars (d) 200
(e) None of these

56. How many steps would be needed to complete the arrangement?
(a) Ten (b) Eight (c) Nine (d) Six
(e) None of these

57. Which of the following would be the cube root of the sum of the numbers which is 2nd from right end in Step IV and 2nd from right end in Step VI?
(a) 9 (b) 8 (c) 13 (d) 7
(e) None of these

58. In Step IV, which of the following word/number would be on 4th position (from the left end)?
(a) vicef (b) 188 (c) 55 (d) quite
(e) None of these

DIRECTIONS ~(Q. Nos. 59-63) *Study the following information carefully and answer the given questions.*

When a word and number arrangement machine is given an input line of words and numbers, it arranges them following a particular rule. The following is an illustration of input and rearrangement.

Input camps 59 to 91 concentration 48 including 85 Auschwitz 35.
Step I Auschwitz 35 camps 59 to 91 concentration 48 including 85.
Step II Auschwitz 35 camps 91 59 to concentration 48 including 85.
Step III Auschwitz 35 camps 91 to 48 59 concentration including 85.
Step IV Auschwitz 35 camps 91 to 48 concentration 85 59 including.
Step V Auschwitz 35 camps 91 to 48 concentration 85 including 59.

And Step V is the last step of the above input. As per the rules followed in the above step, find out the appropriate step for the given output.

Input 84 warsaw has 72 14 already 49 come 83 under sharp 37 from 21.

59. In Step VI, what is the sum of 4th element from the left end and 7th element from the right end?
(a) 56 (b) 51 (c) 48 (d) 54
(e) None of these

60. What is the position of '**Under**' in the Step IV?
(a) Fourth from the right end
(b) Sixth from the left end
(c) None of given options
(d) Fourth from the left end
(e) Eighth from the right end

61. In which of the following step numbers, '37 84 49' found in the same order?
(a) Step II (b) Step VII
(c) Step IV (d) Step VI
(e) None of these

62. Which step number would be the following output?
"already 21 Warsaw 14 has 72 under 37 sharp 83 from 84 come 49"
(a) Step VII (b) Step IV (c) Step V (d) Step VI
(e) Step III

63. Which element is exactly between the elements which are fourth from left end and third from right end in Step V?
(a) Sharp (b) 72 (c) Under (d) 37
(e) None of these

Answers / WITH EXPLANATIONS

Solutions. (Q. Nos. 1-5)

1. (*c*) **Input** kind 12 96 heart water 59 42 yes
Step I 12 kind 96 heart water 59 42 yes
Step II 12 yes kind 96 heart water 59 42
Step III 12 yes 42 kind 96 heart water 59
Step IV 12 yes 42 water kind 96 heart 59
Step V 12 yes 42 water 59 kind 96 heart

2. (*e*) **Input** jungle 43 mode 25 basket 39 target 19
Step I 19 jungle 43 mode 25 basket 39 target
Step II 19 target jungle 43 mode 25 basket 39
Step III 19 target 25 jungle 43 mode basket 39
Step IV 19 target 25 mode jungle 43 basket 39
Step V 19 target 25 mode 39 jungle 43 basket
Hence, Step IV is the last but one.
i.e. second from last. None of the given options matches the final output.

3. (*d*) **Input** cannot be determined

4. (*d*) *Step* II 24 year 56 43 last part 64 over
Step III 24 year 43 56 last part 64 over
Step IV 24 year 43 part 56 last 64 over
Step V 24 year 43 part 56 over last 64
Step VI 24 year 43 part 56 over 64 last
Hence, four more steps are required to complete the rearrangement.

5. (*c*) *Step* III 32 station 46 81 73 March go for
Step IV 32 station 46 March 81 73 go for
Step V 32 station 46 March 73 81 go for
Step VI 32 station 46 March 73 go 81 for

Solutions (Q. Nos. 6-9) In the Step I, the word coming first alphabetically comes at the 1st place from left pushing the remaining line right word; in Step II, largest number comes at the 2nd position from left pushing the remaining line rightward; in Step III, the word coming second alphabetically comes at the 3rd place from left pushing the remaining line rightward; in Step IV, the 2nd largest number comes at the 4th position from left pushing the remaining line rightward. Thus, word and number get arranged alternately till the words are in forward alphabetical order and the numbers in decreasing order.

6. (*b*) **Input** year 39 stake 47 house full 94 55
Step I Full year 39 stake 47 house 94 55
Step II Full 94 year 39 stake 47 house 55
Step III Full 94 house year 39 stake 47 55
Step IV Full 94 house 55 year 39 stake 47
Step V Full 94 house 55 stake year 39 47
Step VI Full 94 house 55 stake 47 year 39
∴ Required steps = Six

7. (*b*)
Step II Car 83 lost ever 32 46 74 now
Step III Car 83 ever lost 32 46 74 now
Step IV Car 83 ever 74 lost 46 now 32
Step V Car 83 ever 74 lost 46 32 now
Step VI Car 83 ever 74 lost 32 46 now
∴ Required more steps = Four

8. (*d*) In arrangement problem, previous steps cannot be determined.

9. (*a*) **Input** Water full never 35 78 16 height 28
Step I Full water never 35 78 16 height 28
Step II Full 78 water never 35 16 height 28
Step III Full 78 height water never 35 16 28
Step IV Full 78 height 35 water never 16 28
Step V Full 78 height 35 never water 16 28
Step VI Full 78 height 35 never 28 water 16
∴ Last step = Step VI

Solutions (Q. Nos. 10-13) Here, each word of the input has been arranged in the alphabetical order giving preference to the word starting with the small letter.

10. (*d*) **Input** you are at fault on this
Step I are you at fault on this
Step II are at you fault on this
Step III are at fault you on this
Step IV are at fault on you this

11. (*c*) **Input** am ace all if Is
Step I ace am all if Is
Step II ace all am if Is

12. (*d*) We cannot determine the input for the given step, as the position of each word cannot definitely be known in the input.

13. (*c*) **Input** Him and His either or her
Step I and Him His either or her
Step II and either Him His or her
Step III and either her Him His or

Solutions (Q. Nos. 14-18) By analysis carefully, of input and various steps we find that in each step a word and also a number is rearranged. Words are rearranged at left end in alphabetical order and numbers are rearranged at right end in descending order. Also, when a new word is rearranged, the previously arranged words are shifted towards right and when a new number is rearranged, the previously arranged numbers are shifted towards left.

Input 31 rise gem 15 92 47 aim big 25 does 56 not 85 63 with moon
Step I aim 31 rise gem 15 47 big 25 does 56 not 85 63 with moon 92
Step II big aim 31 rise gem 15 47 25 does 56 not 63 with moon 92 85
Step III does big aim 31 rise gem 15 47 25 56 not with moon 92 85 63
Step IV gem does big aim 31 rise 15 47 25 not with moon 92 85 63 56
Step V moon gem does big aim 31 rise 15 25 not with 92 85 63 56 47
Step VI not moon gem does big aim rise 15 25 with 92 85 63 56 47 31
Step VII rise not moon gem does big aim 15 with 92 85 63 56 47 31 25
Step VIII with rise not moon gem does big aim 92 85 63 56 47 31 25 15

14. (*a*) VIII steps will be required to complete the rearrangement.

15. (*d*) **Step IV** gem does big aim 31 rise 15 47 25 not with moon 92 85 63 56
15 is at 7th position from the left end.

16. (*b*) rise not moon gem does big aim 15 with 92 85 63 56 47 31 25 is step number VII.

17. (*c*) **Step VI** not moon gem does big aim rise 15 25 with 92 85 63 56 47 31
Here, 92 is at 6th position from the right end.

18. (*c*) **Last step** with rise not moon gem does big aim 92 85 63 56 47 31 25 15

'56' is at 5th position from the right end.

Solutions (Q. Nos. 19-23) By analysis carefully of given input and various steps of output we find that

In Step 1, two words are arranged in alphabetical order and placed at the left corner. In Step 2, two numbers are arranged in descending order and placed next to words and so on.

Input best 11 all 25 my 47 81 equal 49 strength 16 and
Step **I** all and best 11 25 my 47 81 equal 49 strength 16
Step **II** all and 81 49 best 11 25 my 47 equal strength 16
Step **III** all and 81 49 best equal 11 25 my 47 strength 16
Step **IV** all and 81 49 best equal 47 25 11 my strength 16
Step **V** all and 81 49 best equal 47 25 my strength 11 16
Step **VI** all and 81 49 best equal 47 25 my strength 16 11.

19. (*d*) 'best' comes between 49 and equal in Step III.

20. (*b*) 3 elements are there between 25 and 16 in Step V.

21. (*a*) After interchanging there will be two elements between 49 and equal in Step VI.

22. (*d*) 25 is fifth from right end in Step IV.

23. (*e*) None of the given options matches the final output.

Solutions (Q. Nos. 24-28)

Input chemical 68 11 reaction 87 is 21 hard to 53 92 detect.
Step **I** 11 chemical 68 reaction 87 is hard to 53 92 detect 21.
Step **II** 53 11 chemical reaction 87 is hard to 92 detect 21 68.
Step **III** 87 53 11 chemical reaction is hard to detect 21 68 92.
Step **IV** chemical 87 53 11 reaction is hard to 21 68 92 detect.
Step **V** hard chemical 87 53 11 reaction to 21 68 92 detect is
Step **VI** reaction hard chemical 87 53 11 21 68 92 detect is to.

24. (*d*) In Step II elements 'to 92 detect 21' found in the same order.

25. (*e*) Step VI reaction hard chemical

87 53 11 (21) 68 92 detect is to

Clearly, 21 is as 6th position from the right end in the last step.

26. (*c*) In Step IV,

'87 53 11 reaction' found in the same order.

27. (*a*) Required element = 11

28. (*c*) 'reaction' is exactly between 'chemical' and '87' in the second step.

Solutions (Q. Nos. 29-33) After careful analysis of the given input and various steps of rearrangement we find that, in each step a word and also a number is rearranged. In first step, the word which comes last in the dictionary is moved to the extreme left end and the lowest number is moved to the second position from the left. In second step, the word which comes second last in the dictionary is moved to the extreme right end and the second lowest number is moved to the second position from the right. This process is continued upto last step.

Input band 85 zen 54 den fit 25 37 home 41 sun 73
Step **I** zen 25 band 85 54 den fit 37 home 41 sun 73
Step **II** zen 25 band 85 54 den fit home 41 73 37 sun
Step **III** home 41 zen 25 band 85 54 den fit 73 37 sun
Step **IV** home 41 zen 25 band 85 den 73 37 sun 54 fit
Step **V** den 73 home 41 zen 25 band 85 37 sun 54 fit
Step **VI** den 73 home 41 zen 25 37 sun 54 fit 85 band

29. (*c*) Only two elements are there between 'band' and '73' in Step IV.

30. (*d*) 85 is the third element to left of the ninth element from the left in the Step III.

31. (*a*) In Step II, '41, 73, 37' found consecutively.

32. (*b*) Step V Home $\xrightarrow{+2}$25

Step VI 37 $\xrightarrow{+2}$ fit

Then, same pattern in Step I–band $\xrightarrow{+2}$ den

33. (*e*) den 73; 54 fit

Solutions (Q. Nos. 34-38) From given information, arrangement is as follows

Input 26 69 13 82 55 21 71 34 93 47
Step **I** 13 21 26 69 82 55 71 34 93 47
Step **II** 93 82 13 21 26 69 55 71 34 47
Step **III** 26 34 93 82 13 21 69 55 71 47
Step **IV** 71 69 26 34 93 82 13 21 55 47
Step **V** 47 55 71 69 26 34 93 82 13 21

34. (*a*) Fourth element to left of the seventh element from the left end in Step III is '93'.

35. (*d*) Fifth element from the eight end in Step V = 34 and second element from left end in Step II = 82 then

Resultant = 82 − 34 = 48

36. (*a*) In Step II only '26, 69, 55' found consecutively.

Step II 93 82 13 21 <u>26 69 55</u> 71 34 47

37. (*a*) **Step I**

13 (21) 26 69 82 55 71 34 93 43

Step IV

71 69 (26) 34 93 82 13 21 55 47

In same way

Step V

(47) 55 71 69 26 34 93 82 13 21

'47' is related to '71'

38. (*e*) There are seven elements to the right of 26 in Step IV.

Solutions (Q. Nos. 39-43) By analysis carefully of input and various steps of rearrangement we find that, in each step a word and also a number is rearranged. Words are rearranged at the left end in an alphabetical order by replacing the last letter with 'mit' and numbers are rearranged at the right end in descending order with subtraction of 'one' to each number. The process continous upto the last step.

Input 61 ox herb 33 86 intern sums 28 49 perk
Step **I** hermit 61 ox 33 intern sums 28 49 perk 85
Step **II** intermit hermit ox 33 sums 28 49 perk 85 60
Step **III** omit intermit hermit 33 sums 28 perk 85 60 48
Step **IV** permit omit intermit hermit sums 28 85 60 48 32
Step **V** summit permit omit intermit hermit 85 60 48 32 27

39. (*d*) Four elements are there between hermit and 85 in Step III.

40. (*e*) Sixth element from left end in Step II is 28.

41. (*e*) Following the same relation permit is related to 48.

42. (*e*) Fourth element from right end in Step IV → 85

Fourth element from right end in Step V → 60

∴ Required difference = 85 − 60 = 25

43. (*d*) 32 does not appear between permit and fourth element from right end in Step V, *i.e.,* 60.

Solutions (Q. Nos. 44-48) There are six numbers and six words in the input. In the first step the numbers are arranged in ascending order from both the ends with a natural number starting from 1 at unit place in left end number and with a natural number 2 at unit place in right end number. After that in second step the words are arranged in alphabetical order from both the ends. And then again numbers are arranged in third step and words are arranged in forth step and so on.

Input peak 18 utility 76 emerge 27 beautiful 37 51 visible 86 know
Step I 181 peak utility 76 emerge beautiful 37 51 visible 86 know 272
Step II beautiful 181 peak utility 76 37 51 visible 86 know 272 emerge
Step III 373 beautiful 181 peak utility 76 visible 86 know 272 emerge 514
Step IV know 373 beautiful 181 utility 76 visible 86 272 emerge 514 peak
Step V 765 know 373 beautiful 181 utility visible 272 emerge 514 peak 866
Step VI utility 765 know 373 beautiful 181 272 emerge 514 peak 866 visible

44. (*d*) Required difference = 373 − 272 = 101

45. (*e*) Six steps are required to complete the arrangement.

46. (*b*) 'beautiful' is 6th to the left of 3rd from the right end in Step V.

47. (*c*) Required addition = 76 + 86 = 162

48. (*b*) '181' is at 4th position from the left end is Step IV.

Solutions (Q. Nos. 49-53) By carefully analysis of input and various steps of output we find that, in each step a word and a number is rearranged. The words are rearranged in alphabetical order and the numbers are arranged in descending order. In first step, word is rearranged at the left end and number is rearranged at the right end. In second step, number is rearranged at the left end and word is rearranged at the right end. The process continues upto last step.

Input 15 role air 96 63 born with 77 like 39 some 52
Step I air 15 role 63 born with 77 like 39 some 52 96
Step II 77 air 15 role 63 with like 39 some 52 96 born
Step III like 77 air 15 role with 39 some 52 96 born 63
Step IV 52 like 77 air 15 with 39 some 96 born 63 role
Step V Some 52 like 77 air 15 with 96 born 63 role 39
Step VI 15 some 52 like 77 air 96 born 63 role 39 with

49. (*d*) Three elements are there between 'with' and 'born' in step IV.

50. (*b*) '15 some 52' found consecutively in Step VI

51. (*a*) In 2nd Step, 9th Element from left → some
2nd Element from left of 'some' → like

52. (*e*) In Step I, '77' is third to the left of 'some'.
In Step V, '96' is third to the left of 'role'.
Similarly, in Step IV '39 ' is third to the left of 'born'

53. (*c*) Only 'air' appears exactly between '77' and '15'.

Solutions (Q. Nos. 54-58) In each step the words are arranged in reverse alphabetical order such that next letter of the last letter of that word is also placed with it. Also, in each step a number is placed at the right end which is the positional value of the last letter of the word which is arranged, with the last digit of that number (positional value) is repeated once in it. For example, you (positional value of u = 21) so 211 is placed at the rightmost end.

Input quite similar dull go test vice
Step I vicef quite similar dull go test 55
Step II testu vicef quite similar dull go 55 200
Step III similars testu vicef quite dull go 55 200 188
Step IV quitef similars testu vicef dull go 55 200 188 55
Step V gop quitef similars testu vicef dull 55 200 188 55 155
Step VI dullm gop quitef similars testu vicef 55 200 188 55 155 122

54. (*b*) Required difference = 55 − 55 = 0

55. (*c*) Step V gop quitef

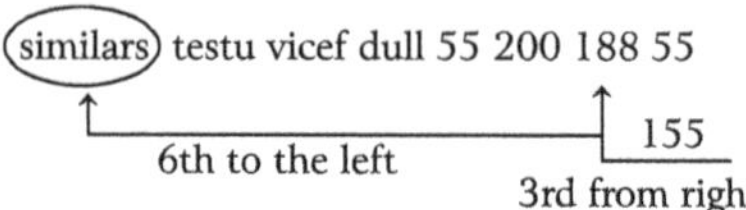

56. (*d*) Six steps are required to complete the arrangement.

57. (*d*) Required sum = 188 + 155 = 343
∴ Cube root of 343 = $\sqrt[3]{343} = 7$

58. (*a*) Step IV

quitef similars testu (vicef) dull go 55 200 188 15
4th from left

Solutions (Q. Nos. 59-63) One word and one number is arranged in each step simultaneously, words and numbers both are arranged from left end.

For words Words are arranged in decreasing alphabetical order according to the last letter of the word and same will be followed in further steps.

For numbers Numbers are arranged in increasing order, according to addition of their digits. (For example 35 = 3 + 5 = 8)

Input 84 Warsaw has 72 14 already 49 come 83 under sharp 37 from 21.
Step I already 21 84 Warsaw has 72 14 49 come 83 under sharp 37 from.
Step II already 21 Warsaw 14 84 has 72 49 come 83 under sharp 37 from.
Step III already 21 Warsaw 14 has 72 84 49 come 83 under sharp 37 from.
Step IV already 21 Warsaw 14 has 72 under 37 84 49 come 83 sharp from.
Step V already 21 Warsaw 14 has 72 under 37 sharp 83 84 49 come from.
Step VI already 21 Warsaw 14 has 72 under 37 sharp 83 from 84 49 come.
Step VII already 21 Warsaw 14 has 72 under 37 sharp 83 from 84 come 49.

59. (*b*) Required sum = 14 + 37 = 51

60. (*e*) **Step IV** already 21 Warsaw 14 has

72 (under) 37 84 49 come 83 sharp from.
8th from right end

61. (*c*) **Step IV** already 21 Warsaw 14 has 72 under 37 84 49 come 83 sharp from

62. (*a*) **Step VII** already 21 Warsaw 14 has 72 under 37 sharp 83 from 84 come 49.

63. (*d*) **Step V**

already 21 Warsaw 14 has 72 under (37) sharp 83 84 49 come from
4th from left
3rd from right

TYPE 03

Problems Based on Mathematical Operations

In this type of questions, the input has some numbers. Different steps are obtained by taking the numbers of the input and different arithmetic operations are performed after that.

Such type of problems can be better understood with the following format of the questions

DIRECTIONS ~ (Example Nos. 21-25) *Study the following information to answer the following questions. A number arrangement machine, when given a particular input, rearranges it following a particular rule. The following is the illustration of the input and the steps of the arrangement.*

Input	44	35	18	67	22	28	36
Step **I**	36	27	10	59	14	20	28
Step **II**	16	15	8	42	4	16	18
Step **III**	132	105	54	201	66	84	108
Step **IV**	50	41	24	73	28	34	42
Step **V**	8	8	9	4	4	1	9
Step **VI**	64	64	81	169	16	100	81
Step **VI**	20	19	12	46	8	20	22

***Ex* 21** What will be the 4th step of the following input?
Input '24, 88, 22, 34, 81, 90, 38'

(a) 30, 94, 28, 40, 87, 92, 40
(b) 30, 94, 28, 40, 87, 96, 44
(c) 44, 96, 87, 40, 28, 94, 30
(d) Cannot be determined
(e) None of the above

***Ex* 22** The second step of a given input is 45, 27, 35, 28, 42, 15. What will be Step VII for the input?

(a) 49, 31, 39, 32, 46, 19 (b) 50, 31, 40, 22, 37, 19
(c) 19, 46, 32, 39, 31, 49 (d) Cannot be determined
(e) None of these

***Ex* 23** In how many steps would the following arrangement be yielded by the given input?

Input '91, 45, 67, 51, 32, 17'

Arrangement 100, 81, 169, 36, 25, 64

(a) VI (b) III
(c) V (d) VII
(e) None of these

***Ex* 24** What will be the Step V of the following input?
Input '37, 48, 91, 22, 49'

(a) 10, 12, 10, 4, 13 (b) 4, 4, 1, 3, 1
(c) 1, 3, 1, 4, 4 (d) Cannot be determined
(e) None of these

***Ex* 25** Find the Step III of the following input.
Input '17, 50, 37, 23, 35'

(a) 51, 150, 111, 69, 105
(b) 8, 5, 10, 6, 8
(c) 150, 51, 111, 69, 105
(d) Cannot be determined
(e) None of the above

Solutions (Q. Nos. 21-25)

Logic

***Step* I** (Each number of the input) – 8
***Step* II** Product of the digits of each number of the input
***Step* III** (Each number of the input) × 3
***Step* IV** (Each number of the input)+ 6
***Step* V** Keep adding the digits of each number of the input till they are converted into single digit
***Step* VI** (Digit sum of each number of input)^2
***Step* VII** (Each number of Step II) + 4

21. (*b*) Step IV = (Each number of the input) + 6

Hence, 30, 94, 28, 40, 87, 96, 44 is the 4th step.

22. (*a*) Step VII = (Each number of Step II) + 4

Hence, 49, 31, 39, 32, 46, 19 is the 7th step.

23. (*a*) As given arrangement
= (Digit sum of each number of input)^2
Which is the logic of Step VI.

24. (*a*) As in Step V, digits of each number of given input are added till each number get converted into single digit. Let us see

$37 \Rightarrow 3+7=10 \Rightarrow 1+0=1$
$48 \Rightarrow 4+8=12 \Rightarrow 1+2=3$
$91 \Rightarrow 9+1=10 \Rightarrow 1+0=1$
$22 \Rightarrow 2+2=4$
$49 \Rightarrow 4+9=13 \Rightarrow 1+3=4$

25. (*a*) Step III = (Each number of the input) × 3

Hence, 51, 150, 111, 69, 105 is the 3rd step.

DIRECTIONS ~ (Example Nos. 26-28) *Read the following information carefully and answer the questions.*
« SBI (PO) 2017

A number arrangement machine arranges two digit numbers into a typical manner. Each step gives output taking input from the previous step. The following is an illustration of input and rearrangement. Using the illustration answer the questions given below.

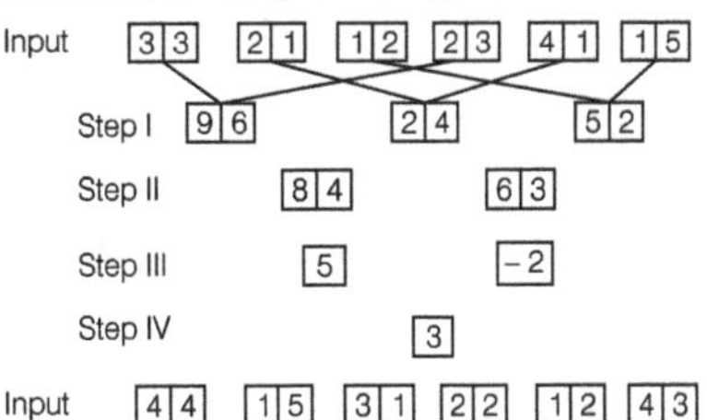

***Ex* 26** If the value "2" is multiply with the final output, then what will be the resultant value?

(a) 18 (b) 16 (c) 06 (d) 12
(e) – 12

***Ex* 27** If in the first step the second digit of every number is added and subtracted by 5, then which will be the resultant value?

(a) 14 (b) 12 (c) 10 (d) 08
(e) 16

***Ex* 28** Which of the following combinations represent the second digit of the third value and the first digit of the second value in Step I of the given input respectively?

(a) 3, 2 (b) 2, 4 (c) 4, 2 (d) 2, 2
(e) 2, 8

Solutions (Example Nos. 26-28)

Step I Multiply the first digit of the first number with the second digit of the fourth number. Multiply the second digit of the first number with the first digit of the fourth number.

Step II Add the first digit of all numbers in Step I and the second digit of all number in Step I and then multiply by 3 and write down in the reverse order.

[e.g. 8 + 2 +9 = 19; 19 × 3 = 57 and now output will be 75]

Step III Subtract the second digit of second from the first digit of the first. Subtract the first digit of second from the second digit of the first value. [e.g. 7−5=2; 5−1=4]

Step IV Add both numbers

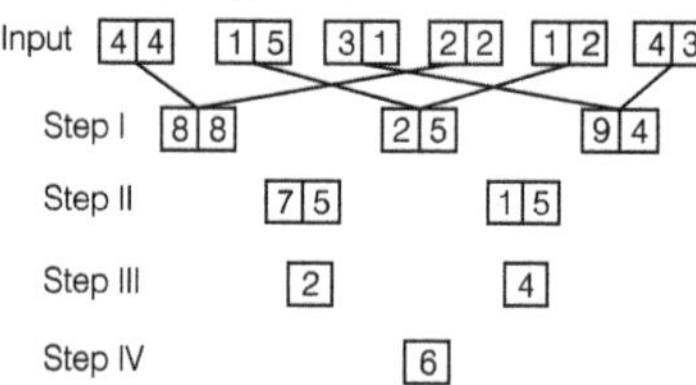

26. (*d*) Resultant value will be 12.

27. (*b*) Resultant value will be 12.

28. (*c*) Second digit of the third value = 4
First digit of the second value = 2

TYPE 04

Miscellaneous Problems

There is no fixed pattern of questions coming under this category. Infact, questions under this category come before you as a real surprise.

DIRECTIONS ~(Example Nos. 29-33) *Study the following information to answer the following questions. A number arrangement machine when given an input line of numbers, rearranges them following a particular rule in each step. The following is an illustration of input and steps of arrangement.*

Input	'35	261	15	812	12	127'
Step I	53	126	51	281	21	712
Step II	305	2061	105	8012	102	1027
Step III	53	612	51	128	21	271
Step IV	3	26	1	81	1	12
Step V	350	2610	150	8120	120	1270

***Ex* 29** **Step V** 160 850 900 750 590. Find out the input.
(a) 150 850 900 750 590 (b) 85 16 90 75 59
(c) 16 85 90 75 59 (d) Cannot be determined
(e) None of these

***Ex* 30** **Input** 72 25 85 97 43 91. What would be the Step IV?
(a) 7 2 8 9 4 9 (b) 2 5 5 7 3 1
(c) 9 4 9 8 2 7 (d) Cannot be determined
(e) None of these

***Ex* 31** **Step II** 204 5018 800 902 401 6017. What would be the input?
(a) 20 51 80 90 40 60 (b) 24 518 80 92 41 617
(c) 617 41 92 80 518 24 (d) Cannot be determined
(e) None of these

***Ex* 32** **Step IV** 2 29 1 92 35 48. Find out the input.
(a) 29 292 15 925 352 483
(b) 28 296 18 928 356 482
(c) 22 293 17 923 355 486
(d) Cannot be determined
(e) None of the above

***Ex* 33** **Step I** 39 44 68 58 18 182. Find out the input.
(a) 93 44 86 85 81 812 (b) 93 39 44 68 58 182
(c) 93 44 85 86 81 812 (d) 93 44 85 81 86 812
(e) None of these

DIRECTIONS ~ (Example Nos. 34 and 35) *Study the following diagram and convert it into other diagrams by implementing the instructions which is given in each step to get next step.* « SBI PO 2017

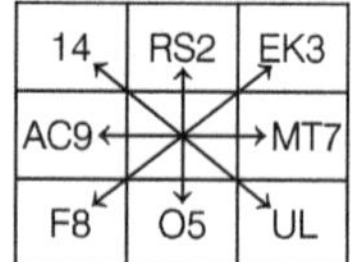

Interchange the Alphabets to get Step I as arrows mention in the above figure.

UL4	02	F3
MT9		AC7
EK8	RS5	1

Step I for Step II

(i) If the alphabets contain one consonant and one vowel and the number with them is greater than 3, then subtract 3 from the given number.

(ii) If the alphabets are two consonant and the number with them is greater than 5, then change the letters with the previous letter in alphabetical series.

UL1	02	F3
LS9		AC4
EK5	RS5	1

Step II For Step-III : Step III is coded in some special pattern.

.EK5	R2	1
UL1		F3
LS9	WX5	AC4

Step III As per the rules followed in the above step, find out the appropriate steps for the given input.
And answer the following questions.

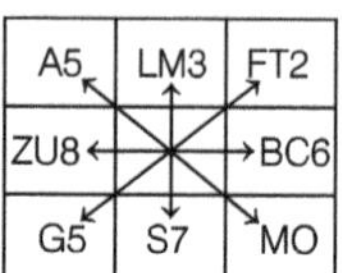

***Ex* 34** Which element comes in Step-II in the second column of third row?
(a) LM7 (b) KL7
(c) ZU3 (d) AB8
(e) None of these

***Ex* 35** Which element replaces AB8 in step III?

(a) PQ7
(d) ZU3
(c) FT5
(d) MO2
(e) None of the above

Solutions (Example Nos. 29-33)

Logic

Step I Last digit becomes first.
Step II 0 comes after the 1st digit.
Step III 1st digit becomes last in two-digit numbers while middle digit becomes the 1st digit in three-digit numbers.
Step IV Last digit get removed.
Step V 0 comes at the end.

29. (*c*) 0 is removed from the end of every number.
30. (*a*) Last digit from every number is removed.
31. (*b*) 0 after the 1st digit is removed.
32. (*d*) It is not possible to find out last digits and hence input cannot be determined.
33. (*a*) 1st digit becomes last in two-digit numbers and middle digit becomes 1st in three-digit numbers.

Solutions (Q. Nos. 34 and 35)

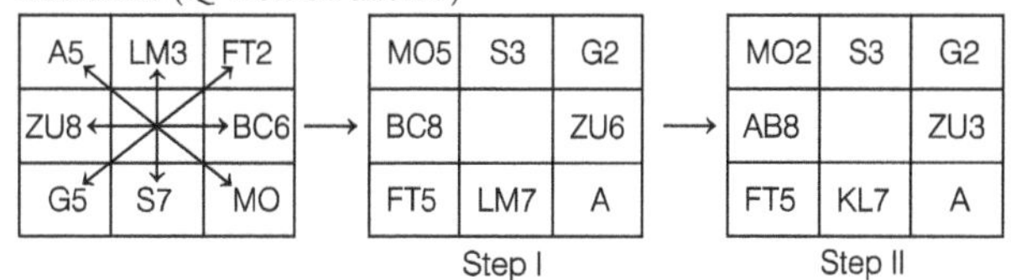

In step III, the elements are changed according to the following pattern.

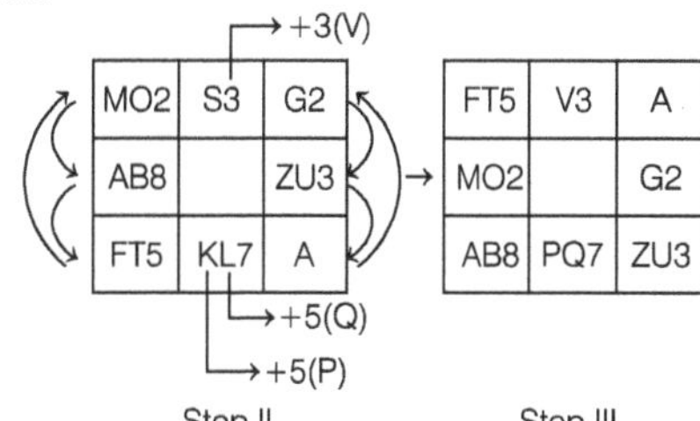

34. (*b*) Element KL7 comes in Step-II in the second column of third row.
35. (*d*) MO2 element replaces AB8 in Step III.

Practice / CORNER 22.3

DIRECTIONS ~ (Q.Nos. 1-5) *Study the following information to answer the following questions. A number arrangement machine, when given an input line of numbers, rearranges them following a particular rule in each step. The following is the illustration of the input and the steps of arrangement.*

Input	'13	25	9	17	15	32	7	20'
***Step* I**	8	20	4	12	10	27	2	15
***Step* II**	22	34	18	26	24	41	16	29
***Step* III**	121	529	49	225	69	900	25	324
***Step* IV**	169	625	81	289	225	1024	49	400
***Step* V**	144	576	64	256	196	961	36	361
***Step* VI**	676	2500	324	1156	900	4096	196	1600

1. What will be the fourth step of the following input?
Input '8 18 28 38 48 58 68 27'

(a) 46, 289, 784, 1444, 2304, 3364, 4624, 729
(b) 64, 324, 784, 1444, 2304, 3364, 4624, 729
(c) 64, 324, 648, 1444, 2304, 3364, 4624, 729
(d) 64, 324, 748, 1444, 2304, 3364, 4624, 729
(e) None of the above

2. The sixth step for a given input is
1156, 5776, 2304, 324, 1296, 2916, 7056, 576
What will be the input?

(a) 15, 36, 22, 7, 16, 25, 40, 10
(b) 17, 38, 24, 9, 18, 27, 42, 12
(c) 19, 40, 26, 11, 20, 29, 44, 14
(d) 21, 42, 28, 13, 22, 31, 46, 16
(e) None of the above

3. In how many steps, the arrangement given below the following input would be arrived at?
Input '11, 17, 22, 34, 8, 25, 38, 43'
Arrangement 100, 256, 441, 1089, 49, 576, 1369, 1764

(a) 3 steps (b) 5 steps (c) 4 steps (d) 6 steps
(e) None of these

4. The second step of a given input is
57, 41, 37, 53, 44, 26, 17, 32
What will be the input?

(a) 109, 1404, 38, 58, 1928, 32, 829, 925
(b) 2304, 1024, 784, 1936, 1225, 289, 64, 529
(c) 4023, 1042, 874, 1936, 1225, 289, 64, 529
(d) 2304, 1024, 874, 1936, 1225, 289, 64, 529
(e) None of the above

5. What would be Step VI for the following input?
8, 12, 16, 24, 6, 15, 2, 13

(a) 17, 21, 25, 33, 15, 24, 11, 21
(b) 3, 7, 11, 19, 1, 10, −3, −8
(c) 256, 576, 1024, 2304, 144, 900, 16, 676
(d) 64, 144, 256, 576, 36, 225, 4, 169
(e) None of the above

DIRECTIONS ~(Q.Nos. 6-10) *Study the given information carefully and answer the questions based on it.*

An input-output is given in different steps. Some mathematical operations are done in each step. No mathematical operation is repeated in next step but it can be repeated with some other mathematical operation (as multiplication can be used with subtraction in Step I and same can be used with addition in Step II).

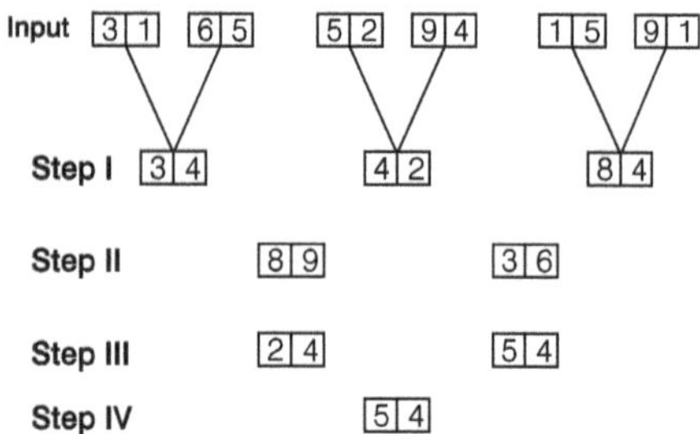

As per the rules followed in the steps given above, find out in each of the following questions the appropriate step for the given input.

Input 41 16 25 38 25 78

6. Find the multiplication of two numbers obtained in Step II.
(a) 1409 (b) 1505 (c) 1615 (d) 1705
(e) None of these

7. Find the addition of the three numbers obtained in Step I.
(a) 101 (b) 100 (c) 102 (d) 103
(e) None of these

8. Find the difference between the two numbers obtained in Step III.
(a) 3 (b) 4 (c) 5 (d) 6
(e) None of these

9. Find the cube of number which is obtained in Step IV.
(a) 4096 (b) 3375 (c) 6859 (d) 5832
(e) None of these

10. If digit is exchanged within the each block, then find the multiplication of two new numbers obtained in Step II.
(a) 1500 (b) 1812 (c) 1902 (d) 1802
(e) None of these

DIRECTIONS ~(Q.Nos.11-13) *Study the given information carefully and answer the given questions.*

An input-output is given in different steps. Some mathematical operations are done in each step. No mathematical operation is repeated in next step « SBI PO 2017

53 12 24 21 43 24
Step I 56 38 88
Step II 16 22
Step III 3.5 2
Step IV 1.5

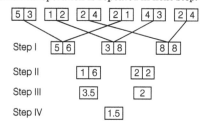

As per the rules followed in the steps given above, find out in each of the following questions the appropriate step for the given input.

42 51 29 32 71 14

11. Find the addition of the two numbers obtained in Step III?
(a) 1.5 (b) 3 (c) 7 (d) 3.5
(e) None of these

12. Find the difference between sum of numbers which obtained in 1st step and sum of numbers obtained in all other steps?
(a) 232 (b) 185 (c) 188 (d) 183.5
(e) None of these

13. Find the multiplication of the numbers obtained in Step II?
(a) 426 (b) 462 (c) 188 (d) 98
(e) None of these

DIRECTIONS ~ (Q. Nos. 14-16) *Study the following information carefully to answer the given questions.*
« IBPS Clerk (Mains) 2018

A word and number arrangement machine when given an input line of words and numbers rearranges them following a particular rule. The following is an illustration of input and rearrangement.

Input	2538	5628	8516	7524	6325	2645
Step I	2358	2568	1568	2457	2356	2456
Step II	1568	2356	2358	2456	2457	2568
Step III	56	35	35	45	45	56
Step IV	11	8	8	9	9	11

Step IV is the last step of the rearrangement. As per the rules followed in the above steps, find out in each of the following questions the appropriate steps for the given input.

Input 3846 9213 8273 7341 5218 3285 6925 4758

14. What will be the addition of the numbers which is second, fourth, sixth and eighth from the left end in Step IV?
(a) 23 (b) 83 (c) 39 (d) 38
(e) 32

15. Which of the following would be the difference of the numbers which is second from left end in Step I and fourth from right end in Step II?
(a) 1138 (b) 1287 (c) 1040 (d) 2125
(e) 1139

16. Which of the following element will be third to the left of seventh from the left end in Step III?
(a) 35 (b) 37 (c) 25 (d) 34
(e) None of these

DIRECTIONS ~(Q.Nos. 17-21) *Study the following informations to answer the given questions. A number arrangement machine when given an input line of numbers, rearranges them following a particular rule in each step. The following is an illustration of input and steps of arrangement.*

Input	23	132	38	27	430	287
Step I	2	13	3	2	43	28
Step II	3	32	8	7	30	87
Step III	32	231	83	72	034	782
Step IV	3	2	4	3	5	3
Step V	34	233	49	38	531	388

17. What will be Step V for the following input?
Input '135, 88, 24, 215, 16'
(a) 236, 99, 35, 316, 27 (b) 136, 99, 25, 216, 17
(c) 17, 216, 25, 99, 136 (d) Cannot be determined
(e) None of these

18. If **Step II** is '16, 9, 22, 416, 25, 67', then find the input.
(a) 18, 11, 24, 418, 27, 69
(b) 11, 18, 24, 418, 27, 69
(c) 69, 27, 418, 24, 11, 18
(d) Cannot be determined
(e) None of these

19. What will be the Step III for the following input?
Input '777, 29, 435, 115, 61, 37'
(a) 777, 92, 436, 116, 62, 37
(b) 777, 92, 534, 16, 511, 73
(c) 777, 92, 534, 511, 16, 73
(d) Cannot be determined
(e) None of these

20. If **Step I** of an input is '4, 16, 121, 8, 17', then find the input.
(a) 45, 163, 1217, 87, 178 (b) 46, 163, 1213, 85, 172
(c) 41, 161, 1216, 82, 176, (d) Cannot be determined
(e) None of these

21. What will be Step IV for the following input?
220, 197, 15, 37, 89, 75
(a) 3, 2, 2, 4, 9, 8 (b) 1, 8, 6, 8, 10, 6
(c) 6, 10, 8, 6, 8, 1 (d) 8, 9, 4, 2, 2, 3
(e) None of these

DIRECTIONS ~ (Q.Nos. 22-25) *Study the following information to answer the given questions. A word arrangement machine when given as input line of words, rearranges them following a particular rule in each step. The following is an illustration of input and steps of arrangement.*

Input	every	now	and	then	same
***Step* I**	every	ow	nd	hen	ame
***Step* II**	ever	no	an	the	sam
***Step* III**	vry	nw	nd	thn	sm
***Step* IV**	ee	o	a	e	ae
***Step* V**	ery	w	d	en	me

22. What will be the Step V for the following input?
Input you are the one great person
(a) u e e e eat rson (b) e e u e eat rson
(c) yo ar th on gr pe (d) Cannot be determined
(e) None of these

23. If Step IV of an input is 'e i a oo ou', then find the input.
(a) get will an spoon you
(b) left wit at noon you
(c) net wit at noon you
(d) Cannot be determined
(e) None of these

24. Find Step II for the following input.
Input 'you must be agree'.
(a) ou ust e gree (b) yu mst b ee
(c) yo mus b agre (d) Cannot be determined
(e) None of these

25. What will be Step IV for the input given below?
Input items are very good
(a) ie ae e oo (b) ie ar ve go
(c) ms ar ry od (d) Cannot be determined
(e) None of these

DIRECTIONS ~ (Q. Nos. 26 and 27) *Study the following diagram and convert it into other diagram by implementing the instructions which is given in each step to get next step.* « SBI (PO) 2017

Input
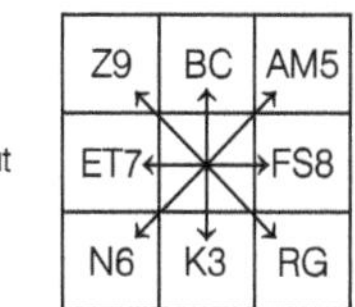

Interchange the alphabets to get Step I as arrows mention in the above figure.

Step I
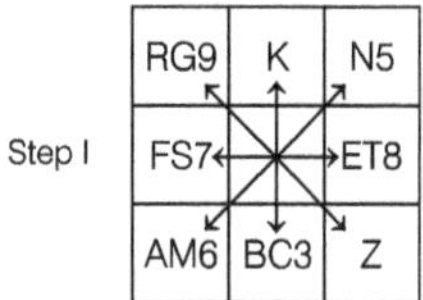

(i) If the alphabets contain two consonants and the number with them is greater than 6, then subtract 2 from the given number.
(ii) If the alphabets has single consonant and no number, then change the letters with the next letter in the alphabetical series.
(iii) If the alphabets contain one consonant and one vowel and the number with them is greater than 4, then subtract 3 from the given number.

Step II

RG 7	L	N5
FS 5		ET5
AM 3	BC3	A

Step III

SH 8	BC 3	O 6
ET 5		FS 5
BN 4	L	B

As per the rules followed in the above steps, find out the appropriate steps for the given input and answer the following questions.

T 8	OP	QL 7
GM 5		TF 9
C 1	K 4	RE

26. Which element comes in the third row of third column in Step II?
(a) TF 5 (b) U (c) QL 1 (d) GM 7
(e) RE 5

27. Which element comes in the second row of first column in Step II?
(a) LU (b) RE 5 (c) TF 5 (d) C 7
(e) V

Answers / WITH EXPLANATIONS

Solutions (Q. Nos. 1-5)

Logic

Step I (Each number of input) – 5
Step II (Each number of input) + 9
Step III (Each number of input – 2)^2
Step IV (Each number of input)^2
Step V (Each number of input – 1)^2
Step VI (Each number of input × 2)^2

1. (*b*) Step IV = (Each number of input)^2

2. (*b*) As Step VI = (Each number of input × 2)^2

$\Rightarrow$ Each number of input = $\frac{\sqrt{\text{Step VI}}}{2}$

3. (*b*) As Step V = (Each number of input – 1)^2

4. (*e*) As Step II = (Each number of input) + 9

$\Rightarrow$ Each number of input = (Step II) – 9

Hence, it is clear that out of the given options (a), (b), (c) and (d), no one can be correct.

5. (*c*) As Step VI = (Each number of input × 2)^2

Solutions (Q.Nos. 6-10) In the given arrangement, the patterns followed in each step are as follow

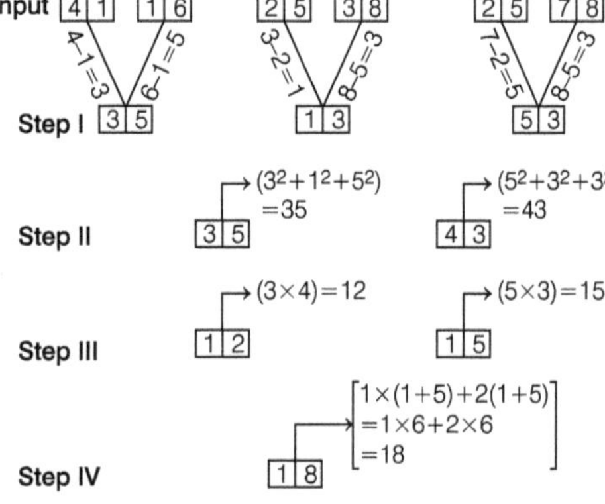

6. (*b*) Required answer = 35 × 43 = 1505

7. (*a*) Required answer = 35 + 13 + 53 = 101

8. (*a*) Required answer = 15 – 12 = 3

9. (*d*) Required answer = $(18)^3$ = 5832

10. (*d*) Numbers obtained after interchanging the digits 53 and 34.

∴ Required answer = 53 × 34 = 1802

Solutions (Q. Nos. 11-13) As per the rules, the appropriate steps for the given input are as follows.

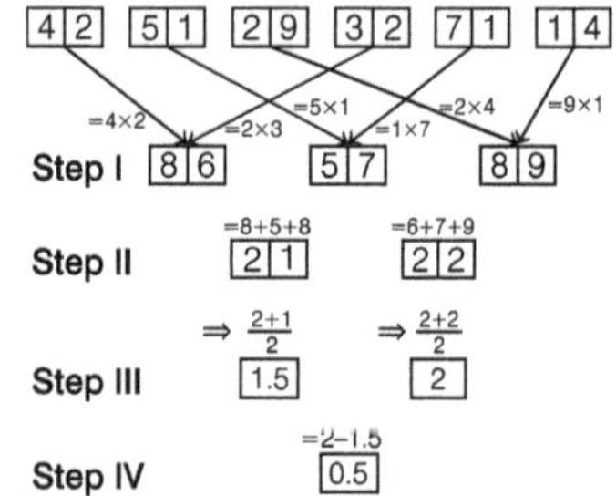

11. (*d*) Required addition = 1.5 + 2 = 3.5

12. (*b*) Required difference

= (86 + 57 + 89) – (21 + 22 + 1.5 + 2 + 0.5)
= 232 – 47 = 185

13. (*b*) Required multiplication = 21 × 22

= 462

Solutions (Q Nos. 14-16) In the given arrangement step-by-step logic followed is given as below.

Step I In each of the given numbers, all the digits are arranged in ascending order within the numbers.

Step II All the numbers obtained in Step I are arranged in ascending order from left end to right end.

Step III First and last digits of the numbers obtained in Step II are removed.

Step IV The digits of the numbers obtained in Step III are added.

Now, the arrangement of the given input is as follows.

Input	3846	9213	8273	7341	5218	3285	6925	4758
Step I	3468	1239	2378	1347	1258	2358	2569	4578
Step II	1239	1258	1347	2358	2378	2569	3468	4578
Step III	23	25	34	35	37	56	46	57
Step IV	5	7	7	8	10	11	10	12

14. (*d*) Required addition = 7 + 8 + 11 + 12 = 38

15. (*e*) Required difference = 1239 ~ 2378 = 1139

16. (*a*) Step III 23 25 34 (35) 37 56 46 57

3rd to the left

7th from the left

∴ Required element = 35

Solutions (Q. Nos. 17-21)

Logic

Step I Rightmost digit of each number of input gets disappeared

Step II Leftmost digit of each number of input is disappeared

Step III Leftmost and rightmost digits of each number of input are interchanged

Step IV Leftmost digit of each number of input + 1

Step V Leftmost and rightmost digits of each number of input increase by 1

17. (*a*) In Step V, leftmost and rightmost digits of each number of input increase by 1.

Hence, 236, 99, 35, 316, 27 will be Step V for the given input.

18. (*d*) In Step II, right most digit of each number of input gets disappeared but it is impossible to get the input from Step II.

19. (*c*) In Step III, leftmost and rightmost digits of each number of input are interchanged.

20. (*d*) In Step I, rightmost digit of each number of input gets disappeared but practically it is impossible to find out the rightmost digit of input from Step I.

21. (*a*) ∵ Step IV = Leftmost digit of each number of input + 1

Hence, 3, 2, 2, 4, 9, 8 will be Step IV for the given input

Solutions (Q. Nos. 22-25)

Logic

***Step* I** First letters disappear of input
***Step* II** Last letters disappear of input
***Step* III** Vowels disappear of input
***Step* IV** Consonants disappear of input
***Step* V** First two letters disappear of input

22. (*a*) As in Step V, first two letters in each word of input get disappeared.

23. (*d*) It is very obvious, that previous step/input cannot be determined.

24. (*c*) As in Step II, last letter in each word of input gets disappeared.

25. (*a*) As in Step IV, consonants in each word of input get disappeared.

Solutions (Q. Nos. 26 and 27)

Step 1

RE 8	K	C 7
TF 5		GM 9
QL 1	OP 4	T

Step 2

RE 5	L	C 7
TF 5		GM 7
QL 1	OP 4	U

Step 3

SF 6	OP 4	D 8
GM 7		TF 5
RM 2	L	V

26. (*b*) U comes in the third row of third column in Step II.

27. (*c*) TF 5 comes in the second row of first column in Step II.

Master Exercise

DIRECTIONS ~ (Q. Nos. 1-6) *Read the following information carefully and answer the questions given below. A famous museum issues entry passes to all its visitors for security reasons. Visitors are allowed in batches after every one hour. In a day there are six batches. A code is printed on entry pass which keeps on changing for every batch. Following is an illustration of passcodes issued for each batch.* « Vijaya Bank PO 2007

Batch I houses neat and clean liked are all by
Batch II by houses neat all are and clean liked
Batch III liked by houses clean and neat all are and so on

1. If passcode for the third batch is 'you succeed day and hard work to for', then what will be the passcode for the sixth batch?
(a) work hard to for succeed you and day
(b) hard work for and succeed you to day
(c) work hard for to succeed you and day
(d) hard work for to succeed you and day
(e) None of the above

2. If 'visit in 15 should the we time 40' is the passcode for the fifth batch, '15 we the should visit 40 time in' will be the passcode for which of the following batches?
(a) II (b) IV
(c) I (d) III
(e) VI

3. Naman visited the museum in the fourth batch and was issued a passcode 'to one rush avoid not do very run'. What would have been the passcode for him had he visited the museum in the second batch?
(a) rush do not avoid to run very one
(b) rush not do avoid to run very one
(c) avoid rush not do to run very one
(d) Data inadequate
(e) None of the above

4. Kamal went to visit the museum in the second batch. He was issued a passcode 'length the day equal of an night are'. However, he could not visit the museum in the second batch as he was a little late. Then, he preferred to visit in the fourth batch. What will be the new passcode issued to him?
(a) and of are night the length equal day
(b) and are of night the length equal day
(c) and of are night the equal day length
(d) and of are the night length day equal
(e) None of the above

5. If passcode for the second batch is 'to come hard you did work and success', then what will be the passcode for the fourth batch?
(a) did success to you hard come and work
(b) did success you to hard come and work
(c) did success to you hard come work and
(d) did to success you hard come and work
(e) None of the above

6. If the passcode issued for the last (sixth) batch is the pencil by all boys used are pen', then what will be the passcode for the first batch?
(a) pencil the pen are used by all boys
(b) pen the pencil used are by all boys
(c) pen the pencil are used by all boys
(d) pencil the pen are used all by boys
(e) None of the above

DIRECTIONS ~ (Q.Nos. 7-13) *Study the following information carefully and then answer the questions given below it. A word arrangement machine when given on input line of words rearranges them following a particular rule in each step. The following is an illustration of the input and rearrangement.* « Central Bank (PO) 2006

Input	Zeal for and yellow bench state goal on
***Step* I**	and zeal for yellow bench state goal on
***Step* II**	and bench zeal for, yellow state goal on
***Step* III**	and bench for zeal yellow state goal on
***Step* IV**	and bench for goal zeal yellow state on
***Step* V**	and bench for goal on zeal yellow state
***Step* VI**	and bench for goal on state zeal yellow
***Step* VII**	and bench for goal on state yellow zeal

And Step VII is the last step.

As per the rules followed in the above steps, find out in each of the following questions, the appropriate steps for the given input.

7. **Input** 'ginger year town sour cat bring ink pot'. Which of the following steps will be the last but one?
(a) VI (b) V (c) VII (d) VIII
(e) None of these

8. **Input** 'your job is not very important to him'. Which of the following steps will be the last?
(a) VIII (b) VII (c) VI (d) IX
(e) None of these

9. **Step II** of an input is car down table pen jug water fall sign.
How many more steps will be required to complete the rearrangement?
(a) Four (b) Five (c) Three (d) Six
(e) None of these

10. **Step III** of an input is ball elephant goat trade over horse never there.
Which of the following is definitely the input?
(a) goat ball trade elephant over horse never there
(b) trade horse ball goat elephant over never there
(c) horse trade ball goat elephant over never there
(d) Cannot be determined
(e) None of the above

11. **Step II** of an input is crown divine victory sky force take lane honey. Which of the following will be Step V?
(a) crown divine force honey lane take victory sky
(b) crown divine force honey lane victory sky take
(c) crown divine force honey victory sky take lane
(d) crown divine force victory sky take lane honey
(e) None of the above

12. **Input** 'carry over there until you are held down'. Which of the following will be Step IV?
(a) are carry down over there until you held
(b) are carry down held over there until you
(c) are carry over there until you held down
(d) there will be no such step
(e) None of the above

13. **Input** 'he was getting ready to start for office'. How many steps will be required to complete the arrangement?
(a) 4 (b) 5 (c) 6 (d) 3
(e) None of these

DIRECTIONS ~(Q.Nos. 14-20) *Study the following information carefully and then answer the questions given below it. A word and number arrangement machine when given on input line of words and numbers rearranges them following a particular rule in each step. The following is an illustration of input and rearrangement.* « Corporation Bank PO 2006

Input	'Past back 32 47 19 own fear 25'
***Step* I**	19 past back 32 47 own fear 25
***Step* II**	19 past 25 back 32 47 own fear
***Step* III**	19 past 25 own back 32 47 fear
***Step* IV**	19 past 25 own 32 back 47 fear
***Step* V**	19 past 25 own 32 fear back 47
***Step* VI**	19 past 25 own 32 fear 47 back

And Step VI is the last step.

As per rules followed in the above steps, find out in each of the following questions, the appropriate step for the given input.

14. Which of the following will be Step VI?
(a) 21 win 39 tyre 46 file case 51
(b) 21 win 39 tyre 46 file 51 case
(c) 21 win 39 tyre file 46 51 case
(d) 21 win 39 tyre 46 case file 51
(e) There will be no such step

15. **Input** 83 42 bench lower 13 upper floor 37. Which of the following will be Step III?
(a) 13 upper 37 83 42 bench lower floor
(b) 13 upper 37 lower 83 42 bench floor
(c) 13 83 42 bench lower upper floor 37
(d) 13 upper 83 42 bench lower floor 37
(e) None of the above

16. **Step II** of an input is 27 ultra open case 45 35 now 12. Which of the following is definitely the input?
(a) ultra open 27 case 45 35 now 12
(b) open case ultra 27 45 35 now 12
(c) open case 27 45 35 now 12 ultra
(d) Cannot be determined
(e) None of the above

17. **Input** Case over 12 36 49 long ago 42. Which of the following steps will be the last but one?
(a) V (b) VI (c) VII (d) VIII
(e) None of these

18. **Input** Judge retire home 62 53 41 34 task. How many steps will be required to complete the arrangement?
(a) 6 (b) 5 (c) 4 (d) 7
(e) None of these

19. **Step IV** of an input is 24 step 27 pick 94 85 76 bring down. How many more steps will be required to complete the rearrangement?
(a) 2 (b) 3 (c) 4 (d) 5
(e) None of these

20. **Step III** of an input is 17 vice 22 85 and car oil 42. How many more steps will be required to complete the rearrangement?
(a) 3 (b) 4 (c) 5 (d) 6
(e) None of these

DIRECTIONS ~ (Q.Nos. 21-24) *Study the following information carefully and answer the given questions. A word and number arrangement machine when given an input line of words and numbers rearranges them following a particular rule in each step. The following is an illustration of input and rearrangement. (All the numbers are two-digit numbers)* « IBPS (PO) 2012

Input 'tall 48 13 rise alt 99 76 32 wise jar high 28 56 barn'
***Step* I** 13 tall 48 rise 99 76 32 wise jar high 28 56 barn alt
***Step* II** 28 13 tall 48 rise 99 76 32 wise jar high 56 alt barn
***Step* III** 32 28 13 tall 48 rise 99 76 wise jar 56 alt barn high
***Step* IV** 48 32 28 13 tall rise 99 76 wise 56 alt barn high jar
***Step* V** 56 48 32 28 13 tall 99 76 wise alt barn high jar rise
***Step* VI** 76 56 48 32 28 13 99 wise alt barn high jar rise tall
***Step* VII** 99 76 56 48 32 28 13 alt barn high jar rise tall wise

And Step VII is the last step of the above input, as the desired arrangement is obtained.
As per the rules followed in the above steps, find out in each of the following questions the appropriate step for the given input.

Input 84 why sit 14 32 not best ink feet 51 27 vain 68 92
(All the numbers are two-digit numbers)

21. Which step number is the following output?
32 27 14 84 why sit not 51 vain 92 68 feet best ink
(a) Step V (b) Step VI
(c) Step IV (d) Step III
(e) There is no such step

22. Which word/number would be at 5th position from the right in Step V?
(a) 14 (b) 92 (c) feet (d) best
(e) why

23. How many elements (words or numbers) are there between 'feet' and '32' as they appear in the last step of the output?
(a) One (b) Three
(c) Four (d) Five
(e) Seven

24. Which of the following represents the position of 'why' in the fourth step?
(a) Eighth from the left
(b) Fifth from the right
(c) Sixth from the left
(d) Fifth from the left
(e) Seventh from the left

DIRECTIONS ~ (Q.Nos. 25-30) *Study the following information to answer the questions given below it. A number sorting machine, when given an input of numbers, rearranges the numbers in a particular manner step by step as indicated below—till all the numbers are arranged in a particular order.*

Input	29	2	15	5	20	11	50	105	28	19	30	140
***Step* I**	2	29	15	5	20	11	50	105	28	19	30	140
***Step* II**	2	140	15	5	20	11	50	105	28	19	30	29
***Step* III**	2	140	5	15	20	11	50	105	28	19	30	29
***Step* IV**	2	140	5	105	20	11	50	15	28	19	30	29
***Step* V**	2	140	5	105	11	20	50	15	28	19	30	29
***Step* VI**	2	140	5	105	11	50	20	15	28	19	30	29
***Step* VII**	2	140	5	105	11	50	15	20	28	19	30	29
***Step* VIII**	2	140	5	105	11	50	15	30	28	19	20	29
***Step* IX**	2	140	5	105	11	50	15	30	19	28	20	29
***Step* X**	2	140	5	105	11	50	15	30	19	29	20	28

25. Which of the following is the input of the following final output?
Final output '16 159 19 160 40 161 80 162'
(a) 19 16 159 40 162 80 160 161
(b) 162 16 40 19 161 159 80 160
(c) 80 159 19 16 40 160 162 161
(d) Cannot be determined
(e) None of the above

26. Which of the following will be the Step II for the following input?
Input '16 13 400 26 150 200 19.'
(a) 13 16 400 26 150 200 19
(b) 13 400 19 26 150 200 16
(c) 13 400 16 26 150 200 19
(d) Cannot be determined
(e) None of the above

27. Which of the following will be the first step for the following input?
Input '100, 500, 2, 400, 20, 3, 800, 1, 999, 666'
(a) 1, 500, 2, 400, 20, 3, 800, 100, 999, 666
(b) 2, 500, 100, 400, 20, 3, 800, 1, 999, 666
(c) 999, 500, 2, 400, 20, 3, 800, 1, 100, 666
(d) Cannot be determined
(e) None of the above

28. How many steps would be required in getting the final output for the following input?
Input '10, 4, 1, 9, 8 12'.
(a) One (b) Two (c) Three (d) Four
(e) None of these

29. Which of the following will be the Vth step for the following input?
Input '15, 19, 90, 3, 50, 16, 4, 99, 91'
(a) 3, 99, 4, 91, 50, 16, 90, 19, 15
(b) 3, 99, 4, 91, 15, 16, 90, 19, 50
(c) 3, 99, 4, 91, 15, 90, 16, 19, 50
(d) Cannot be determined
(e) None of the above

30. Which of the following will be the IIIrd step for the following input?
Input '20, 10, 50, 55, 40, 19, 12'
(a) 10 55 50 20 40 19 12 (b) 10 20 50 55 40 19 12
(c) 10 55 12 40 20 19 50 (d) Cannot be determined
(e) None of these

DIRECTIONS ~ (Q.Nos. 31-35) *Study the following information carefully to answer the given questions.*
Number arrangement machine when given an input line of numbers rearranges them following a particular rule in each step. The following is an illustration of input and rearrangement. « SBI PO 2018

Input 91 53 72 14 39 24 85 76 61 67
***Step* I** 15 91 53 72 39 85 76 61 67 25
***Step* II** 40 15 91 72 85 76 61 67 25 54
***Step* III** 62 40 15 91 72 85 76 25 54 68
***Step* IV** 73 62 40 15 91 85 25 54 68 77
***Step* V** 86 73 62 40 15 25 54 68 77 92

Step V, is the last step.

Input 58 40 99 28 63 84 16 34 71 87

31. How many numbers are there between 59 and the one which 3rd to left of 85 in Step V?
(a) One (b) More than three (c) Three
(d) None (e) Two

32. How many numbers are there between the one which is 2nd from the left end and 99 in Step II?
(a) One (b) More than three (c) Three
(d) None (e) Two

33. What is the position of 35 from the left end in second last step?
(a) First (b) Fifth (c) Second (d) Third
(e) Sixth

34. Which of the following number is 6th to the left of 29 in the Step III?
(a) 35 (b) 59 (c) 17 (d) 99
(e) None of these

35. Which of the following number is 5th from the right end in Step V?
(a) 35 (b) 59 (c) 17 (d) 29
(e) None of these

DIRECTIONS ~(Q.Nos. 36-40) *Study the following information carefully to answer the given questions.*

Number arrangement machine when given an input line of numbers rearranges them following a particular rule in each step. The following is an illustration of input and rearrangement. « SBI PO Pre 2018

Input 91 53 72 14 39 24 85 76 61 67
***Step* I** 15 91 53 72 39 85 76 61 67 25
***Step* II** 40 15 91 72 85 76 61 67 25 54
***Step* III** 62 40 15 91 72 85 76 25 54 68
***Step* IV** 73 62 40 15 91 85 25 54 68 77
***Step* V** 86 73 62 40 15 25 54 68 77 92

Step V is the last step.

Input 58 40 99 28 63 84 16 34 71 87

36. How many numbers are there between 59 and the one which 3rd to left of 85 in Step V?
(a) One (b) More than three (c) Three
(d) None (e) Two

37. How many numbers are there between the one which is 2nd from the left end and 99 in Step II?
(a) One (b) More than three (c) Three
(d) None (e) Two

38. What is the position of 35 from the left end in second last step?
(a) First (b) Fifth (c) Second (d) Third
(e) Sixth

39. Which of the following number is 6th to the left of 29 in the Step III?
(a) 35 (b) 59 (c) 17 (d) 99
(e) None of these

40. Which of the following number is 5th from the right ond in Stop V?
(a) 35 (b) 59 (c) 17 (d) 29
(e) None of these

DIRECTIONS ~ (Q. Nos. 41-45) *Study the given information carefully and answer the given questions.*

An input-output is given in different steps. Some mathematical operations are done in each step. No mathematical operation is repeated in next step but it can be repeated with some other mathematical operation (as multiplication can be used with subtraction in Step I and same can be used with addition in Step II)

Input 68 35 49 13 12 27
Step I 22 23 12
Step II 17 43
Step III 16 63
Step IV 25

As per the rules followed in the steps given above, find out in each of the following questions the appropriate steps for the given input.

Input 63 56 63 41 26 35

41. Find the addition of the three numbers obtained in Step I.
(a) 57 (b) 56 (c) 55 (d) 58
(e) None of these

42. Find the difference of two numbers obtained in Step II.
(a) 41 (b) 61 (c) 91 (d) 56
(e) None of these

43. Find the multiplication of the two numbers obtained in Step III.
(a) 2007 (b) 1747 (c) 3087 (d) 1841
(e) None of these

44. Find the multiplication of unit and tens digit of number which is obtained in Step IV.
(a) 72 (b) 60 (c) 50 (d) 36
(e) 40

45. Which of the following number is obtained in Step IV?
(a) 34 (b) 98 (c) 48 (d) 66
(e) None of these

DIRECTIONS ~ (Q. Nos. 46-50) *Study the following information carefully and answer the questions given below.*

When a word and number arrangement machine is given an input line of words and numbers, it arranges them following a particular rule. The following is an illustration of input and arrangement.
(All the numbers are two digit numbers)

Input 48 height marker 13 92 kneel school 29 65 barrier
***Step* I** barriers 48 height marker 92 kneel school 29 65 12
***Step* II** 28 barriers 48 marker 92 kneel school 65 12 heights
***Step* III** kneels 28 barriers marker 92 school 65 12 heights 47
***Step* IV** 64 kneels 28 barriers 92 school 12 heights 47 markers
***Step* V** schools 64 kneels 28 barriers 12 heights 47 markers 91

Step V is the last step of the above arrangement as the intended output of arrangement is obtained. As per the rules followed in the given steps, find the appropriate steps for the given input. « Bank of Baroda (PO) 2016

Input 84 layer 97 packet 51 damage narrow 75 32 table

46. Which of the following represents the sum of the fourth element from the left end in Step V and the second element from the right end in Step II?

(a) 105 (b) 125 (c) 114 (d) 147 (e) 81

47. 'damages' is related to '97' in Step III in the same way as 'narrow' is related to 'table' in Step I. Following the same pattern to which element is '31' related to in Step IV?

(a) 50 (b) 74 (c) packets (d) damages (e) 97

48. Which of the following represents the element that is fifth to the left of 'layers' in the last step?

(a) narrows (b) 50 (c) packets (d) 83 (e) table

49. In Step IV, how many elements are there between '50' and the fourth element from the right end?

(a) More than three (b) None (c) Three (d) Two (e) One

50. Which of the following is the third to the left of the ninth element from the left end of Step II?

(a) narrow (b) 97 (c) packet (d) damages (e) 75

DIRECTIONS ~ (Q. Nos. 51-55) *A word and number arrangement machine when given an input line of words and numbers rearranges them following a particular rule in each step. The following is an illustration of input and rearrangement.*

Input	juhs elok 65 17 32 15 pnir veox
***Step* I**	ednc 6511 juhs elok 17 32 15 pnir
***Step* II**	kmhi 325 ednc 6511 juhs elok 17 15
***Step* III**	qtsh 178 kmhi 325 ednc 6511 elok 15
***Step* IV**	donp 156 qtsh 178 kmhi 325 ednc 6511

Answer the following questions based on the following input.

Input wder 76 yqok 33 54 isxv 13 zcjf

51. What will be the Step II of the given input?

(a) Step II-bjnp 549 axqu 76 wder 33 isxv 13
(b) Step II-bjnp 549 axqu 7613 wder isxv 13
(c) Step II-549 bjnp axqu 7613 wder 33 isxv 13
(d) Step II-bjnp 546 axqu 7613 wder 33 isxv 13
(e) None of the above

52. What will be the difference of the number which is second from the left end of Step II and which is second from the left end of Step III?

(a) 252 (b) 218 (c) 213 (d) 191 (e) None of these

53. What will be the difference of second number from the right end of Step IV and second number from left end of Step IV?

(a) 384 (b) 424 (c) 828 (d) 415 (e) None of these

54. In which of the following step '7613 isxv 13' found in the same order?

(a) Step II (b) Step I (c) Step IV (d) Step III (e) None of these

55. Which of the following word/number will be third to the left of sixth from the left end in Step III?

(a) 134 (b) bjnp (c) 336 (d) dwdi (e) None of these

DIRECTIONS ~ (Q. Nos. 56-60) *Study the following information carefully and answer the given questions.*

When a word and number arrangement machine is given an input line of words and numbers, it arranges them following a particular rule. The following is an illustration of input and rearrangement.

Input	18 quora 26 diagnose 89 maths 27 eat
***Step* I**	fkcipqug quora 26 89 maths 27 eat 18
***Step* II**	gcv fkcipqug quora 26 89 maths 18 27
***Step* III**	ocvju gcv fkcipqug quora 89 18 27 26
***Step* IV**	swqtc ocvju fkcipqug 18 27 26 89

And Step IV is the last step of the above input. As per the rules followed in the above step, find out the appropriate step for the given output.

Input Queen 79 apple 38 vowel 19 jungle 26

56. What is the position 'vowel' in the Step II?

(a) Seventh from the right end (b) Sixth from the left end
(c) Fourth from the right end (d) Fourth from the left end
(e) None of these

57. Which element is exactly between the elements which are fourth from left end and third from right end in Step IV?

(a) 79 (b) 26 (c) 38 (d) 19 (e) None of these

58. In Step II, what is the sum of 7th element and 6th element from left end?

(a) 56 (b) 54 (c) 48 (d) 45 (e) None of these

59. Which of the following would be at the third position from the left end in Step IV?

(a) swggp (b) lwping (c) crrng (d) 19 (e) None of these

60. Which step number would be the following output? "swggp lwping crrng 79 vowel 19 38 26"

(a) Step III (b) Step IV (c) Step I (d) Step II (e) None of these

DIRECTIONS ~ (Q. Nos. 61-65) *Study the following information carefully and answer the given questions. A number arrangement machine, when given as input line of number rearranges them following a particular rule in each step. The following is the illustration of the input and the steps of arrangement.*

Input	25	22	15	36	29	99
***Step* I**	7	4	6	9	11	18
***Step* II**	10	4	5	18	18	81
***Step* III**	625	484	225	1296	841	9801
***Step* IV**	15625	10648	3375	46656	24389	970299
***Step* V**	5	4.4	3	7.2	9.76	19.8

Step VI	7	4	6	9	2	9
Step VII	27	24	17	38	31	101
Step VIII	20	17	10	31	24	94
Step IX	75	66	45	108	87	297
Step X	14	8	12	18	22	36
Step XI	3	0	4	3	7	0
Step XII	–3	0	– 4	–3	–7	0
Step XIII	49	16	36	81	121	324

61. If Input is 11, 15, 19, 12, 14, then find the Step XIII for this input.

(a) 36, 4, 100, 9, 25 (b) 4, 36, 100, 9, 25
(c) 2, 6, 10, 3, 5 (d) Cannot be determined
(e) None of these

62. If Step I of a given input is as follows '7, 9, 6, 15, 16, 18', then find the input.

(a) 25, 63, 42, 96, 88, 99 (b) 52, 36, 24, 69, 88, 99
(c) 25, 36, 24, 96, 88, 99 (d) Cannot be determined
(e) None of the above

63. If Step V is '6, 9, 12, 75, 8', then find the input.

(a) 30, 45, 60, 375, 40 (b) 24, 54, 26, 78, 56
(c) 40, 375, 60, 45, 30 (d) 10, 13, 16, 79, 12
(e) None of these

64. If input is '35, 95, 43, 45, 98, 81', then find Step XII.

(a) – 2, 4, – 1, 1, – 1, 7 (b) – 2, 4, 1, – 1, 1, 7
(c) 2, 6, 5, 4, 3,2 (d) Cannot be determined
(e) None of these

65. If input is '78, 12, 27, 16, 87, 45', then find the Step II.

(a) 56, 2, 14, 6, 56, 20 (b) 15, 3, 9, 7, 15, 9
(c) 76, 9, 25, 14, 85, 43 (d) Cannot be determined
(e) None of these

DIRECTIONS ~ (Q.Nos. 66-69) *Study the following information carefully and answer the given questions.*

« IBPS PO Mains 2019

The following is an illustration of input and rearrangement. Using the illustration answer the questions given below.

Step-I Interchange the Alphabets/Numbers (follow the same pattern as shown in figure.)

Step-II

(a) If both letters are vowel and number is less than 6, then vowels change to next letter in English alphabetical series and add 2 to the number.

(b) If both letters are consonant and number is greater than or equal to 6, then consonants change to the previous letter in English alphabetical series and subtract 3 from the number.

(c) If both letters are vowel and number is greater than or equal to 6, then vowels change to the previous letter in English alphabetical series and subtract 3 from the number.

(d) If both letters are consonant and number is less than 6, then consonants change to next letter in English alphabetical series and add 3 to the number.

(e) If there are one vowel and one consonant, then vowel change to next letter and consonant change to the previous letter and add 2 to the number.

(f) If there is single consonant, then consonant change to the previous letter and subtract 3 from the number.

(g) If there is a single vowel, then vowel change to next letter and add 3 to the number.

Step- III Follow both Steps I and II

Example

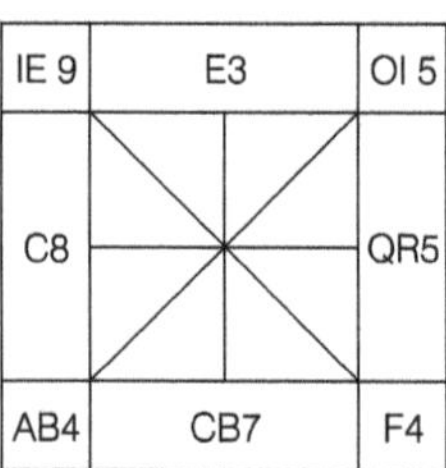

Step I

F4	CB3	AB4
QR8		C5
OI5	E7	IE9

Step II

E1	DC6	BA6
PQ5		B2
PJ7	F10	HD6

Step III

GC3	E3	OI4
A2		QR5
AB8	ED7	F4

Input

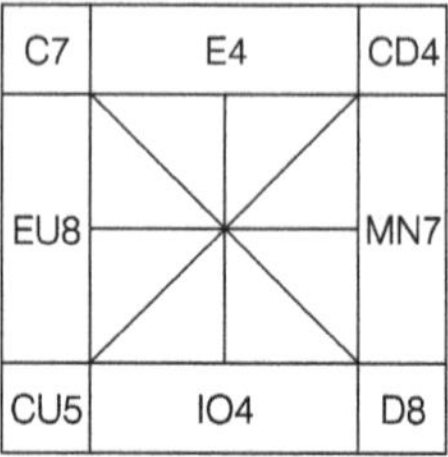

66. In Step II, what is the product of the sum of numbers in the first column and the sum of numbers in the third column?

(a) 245 (b) 285 (c) 275 (d) 255 (e) 235

67. In Step III, what is the difference between the sum of numbers in the first row and the sum of numbers in the third row?

(a) 5 (b) 6 (c) 3 (d) 4
(e) None of these

68. In Step II, if the sum of the numbers in the third row is divided by the sum of numbers in the second row, then what will be the resultant?

(a) 8 (b) 7 (c) 6 (d) 4 (e) 2

69. In Step III, what is the sum of numbers in the first row?
(a) 15 (b) 11 (c) 12 (d) 13
(e) None of these

DIRECTIONS ~ (Q. Nos. 70-74) *A word and number arrangement machine when given an input line of words and numbers rearranges them following a particular rule in each step. The following is an illustration of input and rearrangement.*

Input utys hltk 37 21 19 48 gmrd fexn
***Step* I** gdwo 100 utys hltk 37 21 48 gmrd
***Step* II** hlqe 100 gdwo 100 utys hltk 21 48
***Step* III** iksl 9 hlqe 100 gdwo 100 utys 48
***Step* IV** vsxt 144 iksl 9 hlqe 100 gdwo 100

Answer the following questions based on the following input

Input qewb 23 plsf 17 15 cjrx 36 ytvd

70. Which of the following word/number will be third to the left of sixth from the left end in Step II?
(a) 25 (b) rdvc
(c) 64 (d) diqy
(e) None of these

71. What will be the difference of the number which is second from the left end of Step I and which is third from the right end of Step III?
(a) 52 (b) 28 (c) 0 (d) 91
(e) None of these

72. What will be the third step of the given input?
(a) **Step III**-rdvc 36 qkrg 25 diqy 64 32 ytvd
(b) **Step III**-qkrg 36 25 rdvc diqy 64 36 ytvd
(c) **Step III**-rdvc 36 qkrg 25 diqy 64 36 ytvd
(d) **Step III**-qkrg 36 rdvc 25 diqy 64 ytvd 36
(e) None of the above

73. In Step IV, what is the sum of 2nd element from the left end and 5th element from the right end?
(a) 107 (b) 89
(c) 117 (d) 106
(e) None of these

74. What will be the twice of the difference of sixth number from the left end of Step I and fifth number from right end of step IV?
(a) 34 (b) 42 (c) 28 (d) 44
(e) None of these

DIRECTIONS ~ (Q. Nos. 75-79) *Study the following information carefully and answer the given questions.*

A word and number arrangement machine when given an input line of words and numbers rearranges them following a particular rule in each step. The following is an illustration of input and rearrangement.

Input Draft 95 alliance 67 ideological 58 complex 62
***Step* I** revlmlhrdzm draft 95 alliance 58 complex 62 67
***Step* II** revlmlhrdzm eszgu alliance 58 complex 62 67 95
***Step* III** revlmlhrdzm eszgu dlnqmvy alliance 62 67 95 58
***Step* IV** revlmlhrdzm eszgu dlnqmvy zmmrzodv 67 95 58 62

Input tactics 89 constrained 73 macro 56 hardline 42

75. Which of the following word/number will be at fifth position from right end in Step III?
(a) 73 (b) nzdsl
(c) 56 (d) constrained
(e) None of these

76. How many steps are required to rearrange the given input?
(a) 3 (b) 6 (c) 5 (d) 4
(e) None of these

77. What is the addition of 2nd and 5th element from the right end in Step II?
(a) 130 (b) 129 (c) 128 (d) 121
(e) None of these

78. Which step gives following output?
"uzdurdt nzdsl izsemrov constrained 56 73 89 42"
(a) Step-I (b) Step-II
(c) Step-III (d) Step-IV
(e) None of these

79. What will be the second step of the given input?
(a) uzdurdt nzdsl constrained 56 hardline 73 42 89
(b) uzdurdt nzdsl constrained 42 hardline 56 73 89
(c) uzdurdt nzdsl constrained 56 hardline 42 73 89
(d) uzdurdt nzdsl constrained 73 56 hardline 42 89
(e) None of the above

DIRECTIONS ~ (Q. Nos. 80-82) *Study the following information carefully to answer the given questions*
« IBPS PO Mains 2019

A number arrangement machine when given an input line of numbers rearranges them following a particular rule. The following is an illustration of input and rearrangement.

Input Study tips strategies article week vocabulary
***Step* I** article strategies study tips vocabulary week
***Step* II** IO14 GV30 GW10 RK12 LI30 VV12
***Step* III** 5 3 1 3 3 3
***Step* IV** 15 9 3

Step IV is the last step of the rearrangement. As per the rules followed in the above steps, find out in each of the following questions the appropriate steps for the given input.

Input english current affairs based hindu thoughts

80. What will the addition of the numbers which is third from the right end in step III and 1st from the left end in step IV?
(a) 24 (b) 30 (c) 61 (d) 12
(e) None of these

81. Which of the following element is 3rd from the right end in step II?
(a) UR18 (b) ZV10
(c) FM14 (d) MH14
(e) None of these

82. Which of the following is the product of the numbers which are 2nd from right in Step IV and 3rd from left end in Step III?
(a) 5 (b) 8 (c) 2 (d) 11
(e) None of these

Answers / WITH EXPLANATIONS

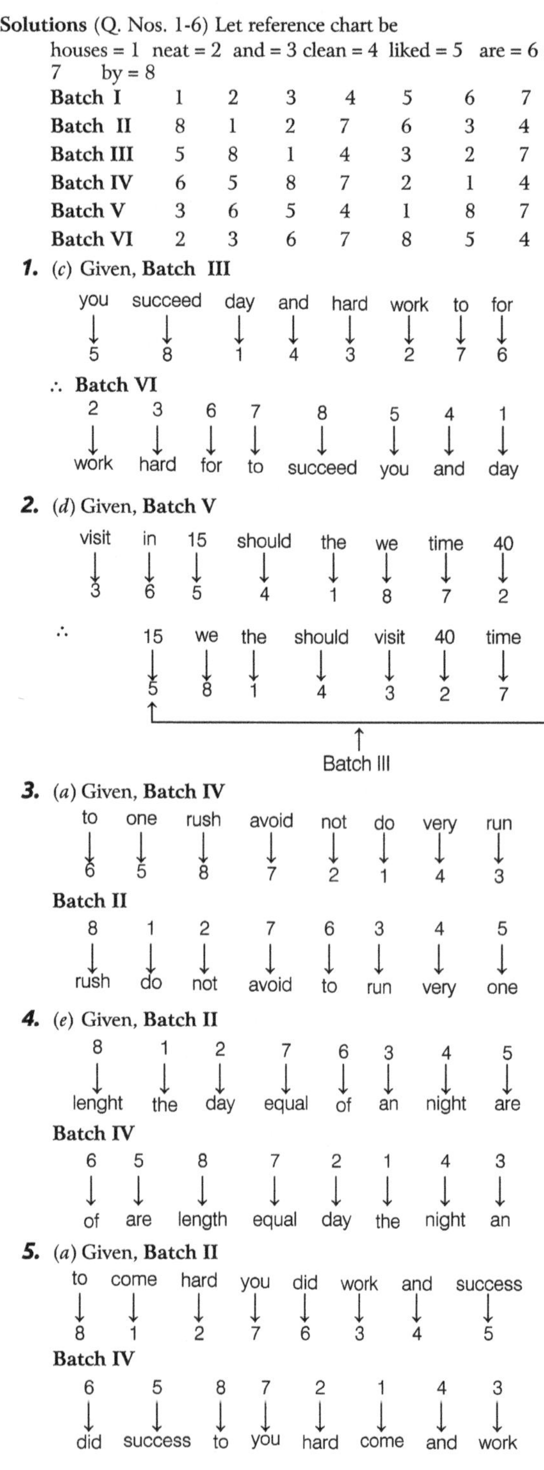

Solutions (Q. Nos. 1-6) Let reference chart be

houses = 1 neat = 2 and = 3 clean = 4 liked = 5 are = 6 all = 7 by = 8

Batch I	1	2	3	4	5	6	7	8
Batch II	8	1	2	7	6	3	4	5
Batch III	5	8	1	4	3	2	7	6
Batch IV	6	5	8	7	2	1	4	3
Batch V	3	6	5	4	1	8	7	2
Batch VI	2	3	6	7	8	5	4	1

1. (*c*) Given, **Batch III**

you ↓ 5, succeed ↓ 8, day ↓ 1, and ↓ 4, hard ↓ 3, work ↓ 2, to ↓ 7, for ↓ 6

∴ **Batch VI**

2 ↓ work, 3 ↓ hard, 6 ↓ for, 7 ↓ to, 8 ↓ succeed, 5 ↓ you, 4 ↓ and, 1 ↓ day

2. (*d*) Given, **Batch V**

visit ↓ 3, in ↓ 6, 15 ↓ 5, should ↓ 4, the ↓ 1, we ↓ 8, time ↓ 7, 40 ↓ 2

∴ 15 ↓ 5, we ↓ 8, the ↓ 1, should ↓ 4, visit ↓ 3, 40 ↓ 2, time ↓ 7, in ↓ 6

↑ Batch III

3. (*a*) Given, **Batch IV**

to ↓ 6, one ↓ 5, rush ↓ 8, avoid ↓ 7, not ↓ 2, do ↓ 1, very ↓ 4, run ↓ 3

Batch II

8 ↓ rush, 1 ↓ do, 2 ↓ not, 7 ↓ avoid, 6 ↓ to, 3 ↓ run, 4 ↓ very, 5 ↓ one

4. (*e*) Given, **Batch II**

8 ↓ lenght, 1 ↓ the, 2 ↓ day, 7 ↓ equal, 6 ↓ of, 3 ↓ an, 4 ↓ night, 5 ↓ are

Batch IV

6 ↓ of, 5 ↓ are, 8 ↓ length, 7 ↓ equal, 2 ↓ day, 1 ↓ the, 4 ↓ night, 3 ↓ an

5. (*a*) Given, **Batch II**

to ↓ 8, come ↓ 1, hard ↓ 2, you ↓ 7, did ↓ 6, work ↓ 3, and ↓ 4, success ↓ 5

Batch IV

6 ↓ did, 5 ↓ success, 8 ↓ to, 7 ↓ you, 2 ↓ hard, 1 ↓ come, 4 ↓ and, 3 ↓ work

6. (*c*) Given, **Batch VI**

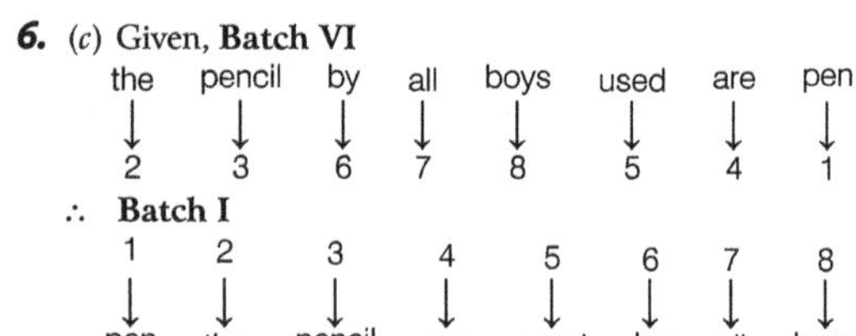

the ↓ 2, pencil ↓ 3, by ↓ 6, all ↓ 7, boys ↓ 8, used ↓ 5, are ↓ 4, pen ↓ 1

∴ **Batch I**

1 ↓ pen, 2 ↓ the, 3 ↓ pencil, 4 ↓ are, 5 ↓ used, 6 ↓ by, 7 ↓ all, 8 ↓ boys

Solutions (Q. Nos. 7-13) The given problem is based on arrangement in which words of the input get arranged in alphabetical order from left to right. In Step I, the word coming first alphabetically comes at the first position from left pushing the remaining line towards right; in step II, the word coming second alphabetically comes at the second position from left pushing the remaining line rightward; in Step III, word coming 3rd alphabetically comes at the 3rd position from left pushing the rest of the line rightward and further steps are obtained in the same manner till all the words of the input get arranged.

7. (*b*) **Input** ginger year town sour cat bring ink pot.

Step I bring ginger year town sour cat ink pot
Step II bring cat ginger year town sour ink pot
Step III bring cat ginger ink year town sour pot
Step IV bring cat ginger ink pot year town sour
Step V bring cat ginger ink pot sour year town
Step VI bring cat ginger ink pot sour town year

Step VI is the last step, hence Step V will be last but one.

8. (*b*) **Input** your job is not very important to him

Step I him your job is not very important to
Step II him important your job is not very to
Step III him important is your job not very to
Step IV him important is job your not very to
Step V him important is job not your very to
Step VI him important is job not to your very
Step VII him important is job not to very your

∴ Last step = Step VII

9. (*a*)

Step II car down table pen jug water fall sign
Step III car down fall table pen jug water sign
Step IV car down fall jug table pen water sign
Step V car down fall jug pen table water sign
Step VI car down fall jug pen sign table water (final step)

Four more steps are required to reach the final step.

10. (*d*) In the arrangement problem input/previous steps can never be determined.

11. (*b*)

Step II crown divine victory sky force take lane honey
Step III crown divine force victory sky take lane honey
Step IV crown divine force honey victory sky take lane
Step V crown divine force honey lane victory sky take

Shortcut Just take five words alphabetically and put them before the rest of the words. (See 'Rule D' under the section arrangement)

12. (*d*) **Input** carry over there until you are held down

Step I are carry over there until you held down
Step II are carry down over there until you held
Step III are carry down held over there until you

As Step III is the last step of the given input, hence Step IV is not possible.

13. (*c*) **Input** he was getting ready to start for office
Step I for he was getting ready to start office
Step II for getting he was ready to start office
Step III for getting he office was ready to start
Step IV for getting he office ready was to start
Step V for getting he office ready start was to
Step VI for getting he office ready start to was
∴ Step VI is the last step.
Hence, required number of steps = 6.

Solutions (Q.Nos. 14-20) The given problem is based on arrangement in which numbers and words get arranged alternately. Numbers get arranged in ascending order while words get arranged in reverse alphabetical order.

14. (*e*) *Step* II 21 win tyre 46 39 case file 51
Step III 21 win 39 tyre 46 case file 51
Step IV 21 win 39 tyre 46 file case 51
Step V 21 win 39 tyre 46 file 51 case.
This is the last step. Hence, there will be no VI step.

15. (*a*) **Input** 83 42 bench lower 13 upper floor 37
Step I 13 83 42 bench lower upper floor 37
Step II 13 upper 83 42 bench lower floor 37
Step III 13 upper 37 83 42 bench lower floor

16. (*d*) Input cannot be determined.

17. (*e*) **Input** case over 12 36 49 long ago 42
Step I 2 case over 36 49 long ago 42
Step II 12 over case 36 49 long ago 42
Step III 12 over 36 case 49 long ago 42
Step IV 12 over 36 long case 49 ago 42
Step V 12 over 36 long 42 case 49 ago
Thus, Vth step is the last step.
∴ Last but one step is IV.

18. (*a*) **Input** Judge retire home 62 53 41 34 task
Step I 34 Judge retire home 62 53 41 task
Step II 34 task judge retire home 62 53 41
Step III 34 task 41 judge retire home 62 53
Step IV 34 task 41 retire judge home 62 53
Step V 34 task 41 retire 53 judge home 62
Step VI 34 task 41 retire 53 judge 62 home
Hence, VI steps are required.

19. (*c*) *Step* IV 24 stop 27 pick 94 85 76 bring down
Step V 24 stop 27 pick 76 94 85 bring down
Step VI 24 stop 27 pick 76 down 94 85 bring
Step VII 24 stop 27 pick 76 down 85 94 bring
Step VIII 24 stop 27 pick 76 down 85 bring 94
This is the last step. Hence, four more steps will be required to complete the rearrangement.

20. (*a*) **Step** III 17 vice 22 85 and car oil 42
Step IV 17 vice 22 oil 85 and car 42
Step V 17 vice 22 oil 42 85 and car
Step VI 17 vice 22 oil 42 car 85 and
This is the last step. Hence, three more steps will be required to complete the rearrangement.

Solutions (Q.Nos. 21-24) The machine rearranges words and numbers in such a way that numbers are arranged form left side with the smallest number coming first and move subsequently, so that in the last step numbers are arranged in descending order while the words are arranged from right side as they appear in English alphabetical order.

Input 84 why sit 14 32 not best ink feet 51 27 vain 68 92
Step I 14 84 why sit 32 not ink feet 51 27 vain 68 92 best
Step II 27 14 84 why sit 32 not ink 51 vain 68 92 best feet
Step III 32 27 14 84 why sit not 51 vain 68 92 best feet ink
Step IV 51 32 27 14 84 why sit vain 68 92 best feet ink not
Step V 68 51 32 27 14 84 why vain 92 best fet ink not sit
Step VI 84 51 32 27 14 why 92 best feet ink not sit vain
Step VII 92 84 51 32 27 14 best feet ink not sit vain why

21. (*e*) There is no such step.

22. (*d*) Required word = best.

23. (*b*) 27, 14 and best are the three elements between 'feet' and '32' in the last step which is Step VII.

24. (*c*) Sixth from left.

Solutions (Q.Nos. 25-30) Final arrangement of the input shows that there are two series — one in ascending order and other in descending order. In the first step, the smallest number is exchanged with the first number of the input. In the second step, largest number is exchanged with the second number of the Step I. In the third step, second smallest number is exchanged with the third number of Step II. Likewise, series continues to get arranged.

25. (*d*) We cannot determine the input for the given step as original position of numbers in input cannot be determined.

26. (*c*) **Input** 16 13 400 26 150 200 19
Step I 13 16 400 26 150 200 19
Step II 13 400 16 26 150 200 19
Hence, 13, 400, 16, 26, 150, 200, 19 will be the Step II for the input.

27. (*a*) **Input** 100 500 2 400 20 3 800 1 999 666
Step I 1 500 2 400 20 3 800 100 999 666
Hence, 1, 500, 2, 400, 20, 3, 800, 100, 999, 666, will be the Step I for the input.

28. (*d*) **Input** 10 4 1 9 8 12
Step I 1 4 10 9 8 12
Step II 1 12 10 9 8 4
Step III 1 12 4 9 8 10
Step IV 1 12 4 10 8 9
Hence, option (d) is correct.

29. (*b*) **Input** 15 19 90 3 50 16 4 99 91
Step I 31 9 90 15 50 16 4 99 91
Step II 3 99 90 15 50 16 4 19 91
Step III 3 99 4 15 50 16 90 19 91
Step IV 3 99 4 91 50 16 90 19 15
Step V 3 99 4 91 15 16 90 19 50
Hence, 3, 99, 4, 91, 15, 16, 90, 19, 50, will be the Step V for the given input.

30. (*e*) **Input** 20 10 50 55 40 19 12
Step I 10 20 50 55 40 19 12
Step II 10 55 50 20 40 19 12
Step III 10 55 12 20 40 19 50
Hence, 10, 55, 12, 20, 40, 19, 50 will be the 3rd Step for the input.

Solutions (Q. Nos. 31-35) In the following number arrangement the lowest number is placed at first with the addition of +1 and second lowest number is placed at last with the same pattern. This pattern is followed in every step.

For e.g., In input series the lowest number is 16, so in Step I it is written at starting as 17(16 + 1 = 17) and the second lowest number is 28 and it is written as 29(28 + 1) at last position.

Input 58 40 99 28 63 84 16 34 71 87
***Step* I** 17 58 40 99 63 84 34 71 87 29
***Step* II** 35 17 58 99 63 84 71 87 29 41
***Step* III** 59 35 17 99 84 71 87 29 41 64
***Step* IV** 72 59 35 17 99 87 29 41 64 85
***Step* V** 88 72 59 35 17 29 41 64 85 100

31. (*e*) Two elements *i.e.,* 35 and 17 are there between 59 and the element, which is third to the left of 85.

32. (*a*) One number *i.e.,* 58 is between 99 and 17 which is second from left end in Step II.

33. (*d*) 35 is third from left end in Step IV.

34. (*a*) 35 is 6th to the left of 29 in Step III.

35. (*d*) 29 is 5th from right end in Step V.

Solutions (Q. Nos. 36-40) The machine first rearranges the lowest number at left end and the second lowest number at the right end. Also, 1 is added to all the numbers which are getting arranged. Thus, the numbers are arranged in descending order from both the ends.

Input	58	40	99	28	63	84	16	34	71	87
***Step* I**	17	58	40	99	63	84	34	71	87	29
***Step* II**	35	17	58	99	63	84	71	87	29	41
***Step* III**	59	35	17	99	84	71	87	29	41	64
***Step* IV**	72	59	35	17	99	87	29	41	64	85
***Step* V**	88	72	59	35	17	29	41	64	85	100

36. (*e*) Two numbers are there between 59 and 29, which is third to the left of 85.

37. (*a*) One number is there between 17 and 99 in Step II.

38. (*d*) 35 is third from left end in Step IV.

39. (*a*) 35 is 6th to the left of 29 in Step III.

40. (*d*) 29 is 5th from right end in Step V.

Solutions (Q.Nos. 41-45) From the given information arrangement is as follows,

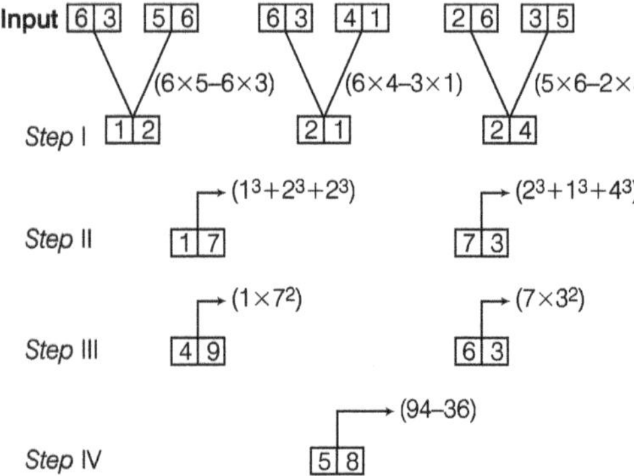

41. (*a*) Required answer = 12 + 21 + 24 = 57

42. (*d*) Required difference = 73 − 17 = 56

43. (*c*) Required answer = 3087

44. (*e*) Required answer = 8 × 5 = 40

45. (*e*) '58' is obtained in Step IV.

Solutions (Q. Nos. 46-50) By careful analysis of input and various steps we find that, in first step the smallest letter according to dictionary is arranged with addition of 's' at extreme left end and the smallest number is arranged at extreme right end by subtracting 'I'. In next step second smallest number among all is arranged at extreme left end by subtracting 'I' and second smallest letter according to dictionary is arranged at extreme right end with addition of 's'. This process is continued upto last step.

Input 84 layer 97 packet 51 damage narrow 75 32 table
***Step* I** damages 84 layer 97 packet 51 narrow 75 table 31
***Step* II** 50 damages 84 97 packet narrow 75 table 31 layers
***Step* III** narrows 50 damages 84 97 packet table 31 layers 74
***Step* IV** 83 narrows 50 damages 97 table 31 layers 74 packets
***Step* V** tables 83 narrows 50 damages 31 layers 74 packets 96

46. (*e*) Fourth element from the left end in Step V = 50
Second element from the right end Step II = 31
∴ Required sum = 50 + 31 = 81

47. (*b*) Second element is second to the right of first element.
∴ In Step IV, '31' is related to 74.

48. (*d*) '83' is fifth to the left of 'layer' in the Step V.

49. (*c*) There are three elements (damages 97 table) between '50' and the fourth element from the right end, *i.e.,* '31'.

50. (*a*) In Step II, 9th element from left end → '31'
Hence, 3rd element to the left of '31' is 'narrow'.

Solutions (Q. Nos. 51-55) The word which is last according to the alphabetical series is arranged first from the left end in Step I, then the word which is second last according to the alphabetical order is arranged from the left end in Step II and so on ... .

Also each of the consonant in the word is replaced by its opposite letter and each vowel is replaced by its previous letter while arrangement.

For numbers-only one number is arranged along with one word in each step. The numbers are arranged in decreasing order as the highest number is arranged in Step I with the word, then second highest number is arranged in Step II with the next word and so on... .

Each number is arranged along with one word in such a way that the sum of the digits of that number is placed next to it.

Input wder 76 yqok 33 54 isxv 13 zcjf
***Step* I** axqu 7613 wder yqok 33 54 isxv 13
***Step* II** bjnp 549 axqu 7613 wder 33 isxv 13
***Step* III** dwdi 336 bjnp 549 axqu 7613 isxv 13
***Step* IV** hhce 134 dwdi 336 bjnp 549 axqu 7613

51. (*b*) **Step II** bjnp 549 axqu 7613 wder 33 isxv 13

52. (*c*) Required difference = 549 − 336 = 213

53. (*d*) Required difference = 549 − 134 = 415

54. (*d*) **Step III** dwdi 336 bjnp 549 axqu 7613 isxv 13

55. (*b*) **Step III**

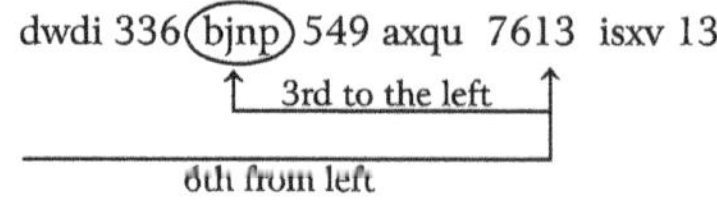

Solutions (Q. Nos. 56-60) The machine rearranges one word and one number in each step simultaneously, words are arranged from left end and numbers are arranged from right end.

Words are arranged in increasing alphabetical order with each letter of word is replaced by its 2nd succeeding letter according to alphabetical series and same will be followed in further steps.

Numbers are arranged in decreasing order, according to difference of their digits. (For example 79 = 9 − 7 = 2)

Input Queen 79 apple 38 vowel 19 jungle 26
***Step* I** crrng queen 79 38 vowel jungle 26 19
***Step* II** lwping crrng queen 79 vowel 26 19 38
***Step* III** swggp lwping crrng 79 vowel 19 38 26
***Step* IV** xqygn swggp lwping crrng 19 38 26 79

56. (*c*) **Step II**

57. (*d*) **Step IV**

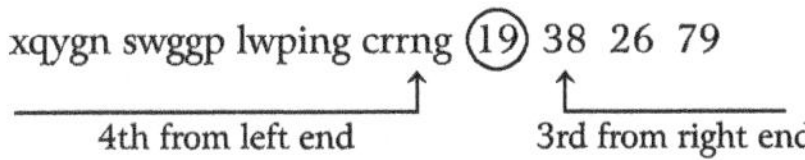

58. (*d*) Required sum = 26 + 19 = 45

59. (*b*) **Step IV**

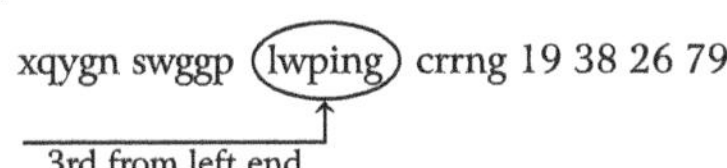

60. (*a*) **Step III** swggp lwping crrng 79 vowel 19 38 26

Solution (Q. Nos. 61-65)

Logic
***Step* I** Digit-sum of input.
***Step* II** Product of the digits of input
***Step* III** Square of the each number of the input
***Step* IV** Cube of the each number of the input
***Step* V** Each number of the input is divided by 5
***Step* VI** Keep adding digits till they are converted into single digit
***Step* VII** Each number of the input + 2
***Step* VIII** Each number of the input − 5
***Step* IX** Each number of the input × 3
***Step* X** Digit sum of each number of input × 2
***Step* XI** Difference between digits of each number of input
***Step* XII** (1st digit − 2nd digit) of each number of input
***Step* XIII** (Digit sum of each number of input)^2 of each number of input

61. (*b*) (Digits sum of each number of input)^2 of each number of input

62. (*d*) As it is very obvious.

63. (*a*) $\because$ Step V = $\dfrac{\text{Each number of the input}}{5}$

$\therefore$ Each number of the input = (Step V) × 5

64. (*b*) (1st digit − 2nd digit) of each number of the input.

65. (*a*) Product of digits of each number of the input.

Solutions (Q. Nos. 66-69)

Input

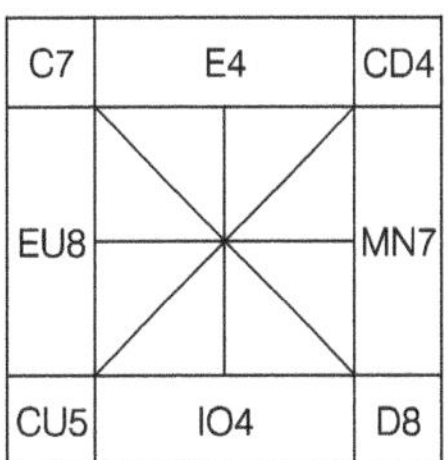

Step I

D8	IO4	CU5
MN8		EU7
CD4	E4	C7

Step II

C5	JP6	BV7
LM5		DT4
DE7	F7	B4

Step III

A1	E3	CF9
EU8		MN7
AU4	IO4	B2

66. (*d*) Required product
$= (5 + 5 + 7) \times (7 + 4 + 4) = 17 \times 15 = 255$

67. (*c*) Required difference
$= (1 + 3 + 9) - (4 + 4 + 2)$
$= 13 - 10 = 3$

68. (*e*) Required result $= (7 + 7 + 4) \div (5 + 4) = 18 \div 9 = 2$

69. (*d*) Required sum $= 1 + 3 + 9 = 13$

Solutions (Q. Nos. 70-74) Here, one word and one number is being arranged simultaneously in each step.

For Words The word which comes first according to alphabetical series will be arranged from left end in first step, such that its first and last letter will be replaced with its next letter and rest of the letters are replaced with their preceding letter. Then, the next word according to alphabetical order will be arranged in second step from the left end and so on ....

For numbers All the numbers are arranged with the one word simultaneously in each step, such that first the prime numbers are arranged in ascending order and then non-prime numbers will be arranged.

Each of the number will be arranged as number will be replaced with the square of the addition of the digits of that number after arrangement.

Input qewb 23 plsf 17 15 cjrx 36 ytvd

***Step* I** diqy 64 qewb 23 plsf 15 36 ytvd

***Step* II** qkrg 25 diqy 64 qewb 15 36 ytvd

***Step* III** rdvc 36 qkrg 25 diqy 64 36 ytvd

***Step* IV** zsue 81 rdvc 36 qkrg 25 diqy 64

70. (*d*) **Step II**

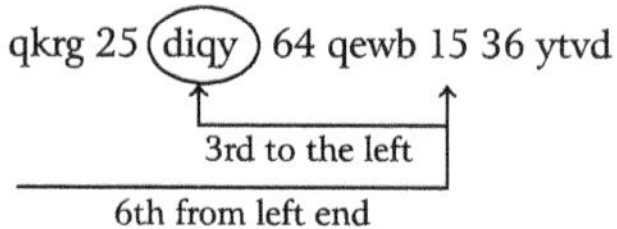

71. (*c*) Required difference = 64 − 64 = 0

72. (*c*) **Step III** rdvc 36 qkrg 25 diqy 64 36 ytvd

73. (*c*) Required sum = 81 + 36 = 117

74. (*b*) Required difference = 36 − 15 = 21

And, twice of 21 is 42.

Solutions (Q. Nos. 75-79) In this arrangement one word and one number is arranged in each step. The words are arranged from the left end such that in 1st step word is arranged in extreme left end than 2nd word is arranged in 2nd left end and so on... while the numbers are arranged from the right end.

For words Words are arranged according to reverse alphabetical order from left end with each vowel of word is replaced by its opposite letter according to alphabetical series while each consonant of word is replaced by its succeeding letter according to alphabetical series and same will be followed in further steps.

For numbers Numbers are arranged in ascending order from right end in such a way that first all odd numbers are arranged after that all even numbers are arranged.

Input tactics 89 constrained 73 macro 56 hardline 42

***Step* I** uzdurdt 89 constrained macro 56 hardline 42 73

***Step* II** uzdurdt nzdsl constrained 56 hardline 42 73 89

***Step* III** uzdurdt nzdsl izsemrov constrained 56 73 89 42

***Step* IV** uzdurdt nzdsl izsemrov dlotuszrove 73 89 42 56

75. (*d*) **Step III**

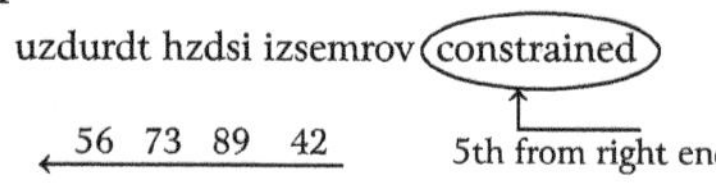

76. (*d*) Four step are required to rearranges the given input.

77. (*b*) Required addition = 73 + 56 = 129

78. (*c*) **Step III** uzdurdt nzdsl izsemrov constrained 56 73 89 42

79. (*c*) **Step II** uzdurdt nzdsl constrained 56 hardline 42 73 89

Solutions (Q. Nos. 80-82) **For step I** Words are arranged according to alphabetical order.

Step II For letter-Reverse of the 2nd letter and the 2nd last letter.

For Number-If the total number of letters is even, then it is multiplied with 3 and if it is odd, then it is multiplied with 2.

Step III The digits of the numbers in the previous step are added.

Step IV The first number is multiplied with last number, similarly 2nd number from left is multiplied with 2nd number from right.and 3rd number from left is multiplied with 3rd number from right

Input english current affairs based hindu thoughts

***Step* I** affairs based current english hindu thoughts

***Step* II** UI14 ZV10 FM14 MH14 RW10 SG24

***Step* III** 5 1 5 5 1 6

***Step* IV** 30 1 25

80. (*e*) Required sum 5 + 30 = 35

81. (*d*) Step II U I14 ZV10 FM14 MH14 RW10 SG24

↑3rd from right

82. (*a*) Required Product = 1 × 5 = 5

CHAPTER / 23

Decision Making

Decision making is a process in which a final decision is taken by analysing the given information. In decision making questions, some conditions are given. Candidates need to analyse the given conditions and then decide the suitable decision from the given options.

Different types of questions covered in this chapter are as follows

TYPE 01

Situation Reaction Test (SRT)

In Situation Reaction Test (SRT), you are given a situation and it is asked to choose a suitable reaction.

For solving these questions, first of all try to analyse the demand of the situation. Depending upon the need, try to analyse the pros and cons of each alternative and then choose that alternative which solves the problem and the purpose without any negative effect.

While attempting SRT problems following points should be kept in mind

- Grasp the essentials of the situation before you react i.e., understand the situation.
- Don't be vague in your reaction.
- The candidate should use his presence of mind.
- The reaction to the given situation should be ideal.
- The reaction to the situation should be the best way to solve the problem.
- The reaction to the situation should be morally correct.
- The reaction to the situation should be an immediate action to the problem.
- The reaction to the situation should be positive.
- The decision/reaction should be a responsible one.

***Ex* 01** If on a tough day you are the only person available to handle the customers, you should

(a) ask for additional help from the boss.
(b) take leave and go back home.
(c) just do your part of the work.
(d) try and work to the maximum of your ability to satisfy customers.

***Solution* (d)** Clearly, an ideal professional is expected not to shirk his duties but to work hard and strive to satisfy his customers.

***Ex* 02** Your friends like smoking and influence you to do the same. You will

(a) smoke only because your friends are smoking.
(b) refuse to smoke.
(c) smoke but only in their presence.
(d) refuse and lie to them that you have asthma.

***Solution* (b)** Clearly, one should have a strong will-power, so as not to yield to easy temptations and indulge in any activity that shall later prove to be harmful.

***Ex* 03** While travelling in a train, you notice that a man fall off the train from the coach behind your coach. You would « Hotel Mgmt 2010

(a) pull the alarm chain, so that the train may stop and the man may be helped.
(b) shout at the falling man asking him to get up quickly and catch the train.
(c) jump off the train to assist the falling man.
(d) wait till the train stops at the next station and inform the railway authorities there.

***Solution* (a)** Clearly, the situation demands taking quick action to provide help to the victim which in turn requires that the train be stopped immediately.

***Ex* 04** You are a team manager. You find that your employee's performance is inappropriate that induces/creates stress for you. You should « CG PSC 2013

(a) explore the reason of inappropriate performance and report to the higher authorities.
(b) start an incentive mechanism for better performance.
(c) create an organisational culture in which the employee feels to be concerned.
(d) implement special human resource training for the employees.

***Solution* (c)** Reporting the reasons to the higher authorities as mentioned in option (a) shows your inability to tackle the problem while options (b) and (d) do not serve the purpose effectively.

For improving employee's performance, Team manager should create an organisational culture in which the employee feels to be concerned as mentioned in option (c).

So, option (c) is the best possible solution to this problem.

***Ex* 05** If you are a manager and one of your employees is not working properly, as a manager you would
(a) fire him.
(b) give the man two weeks to improve.
(c) try to develop the man's abilities and interest in another job.
(d) talk to him and try to find out his problem.

Solution (d) Clearly, the work of manager is to manage and see to his employee's problem if any such situation arises and leads to improper work by him/her. So, as a manager He should talk to him and try to find out his problem.

***Ex* 06** While attending your friend's party, you see your friend's muffler catching fire from the candle on the table behind him. You would
(a) ask your friend to see behind him.
(b) rush to call friend's mother.
(c) rush and take out the muffler from his neck, drop it and pour water on it.
(d) take out the muffler and throw it away.

Solution (c) Clearly, the situation demands to rescue the friend from fire, so correct reaction is given in option (c) *i.e.,* to rush and take out the muffler from his neck, drop it and pour water on it.

***Ex* 07** You have come to know that one of your cousins has not completed the compulsory vaccination of his one-year old child. What will be your most logical response in this situation? « UPSSSC Combined Lower Subordinate 2019
(a) You will ask the cousin to complete the vaccination later.
(b) You will ask him to meet the doctor for completing the vaccination on priority.
(c) You will insult both the parents of the newborn for their mistake.
(d) You will tell them it's not a matter of concern.

Solution (b) In this senario, we should ask him to meet the doctor for completing the vaccination on priority.

***Ex* 08** After having committed to your family that you would be taking them out on a vacation, you suddenly find yourself wanted in a board meeting which unfortunately clashes with the vacation. What would you do? « Hotel Mgmt 2004
(a) Assuming it to be urgent, start making necessary arrangement to ensure that the reason for the meeting is fulfilled, thus cancelling the vacation.
(b) Find out what the urgent meeting is all about and make necessary arrangements and postpone your vacation.
(c) Proceed with your vacation plans without making any arrangement.
(d) Try and get out of that situation by asking your colleague to cover up for you.

Solution (b) As a responsible working professional, you need to fulfill the demand of the situation. In this situation, you have to postpone your vacation, find out the cause of the meeting and need to make necessary arrangements.

Practice / CORNER 23.1

1. When you get angry, you usually
(a) throw things.
(b) withdraw yourself and start crying.
(c) leave the situation and engage yourself in a different activity.
(d) None of the above.

2. Your maid has invited you to her daughter's wedding. You would « Hotel Mgmt 2008
(a) completely ignore her.
(b) attend the wedding.
(c) buy a gift for her daughter and help in wedding.
(d) congratulate her and make up some excuse for not being able to attend.

3. When you see a blind man trying to cross the road, you
(a) wait till he crosses the road.
(b) ask someone to help him.
(c) go and help him.
(d) ignore and move on.

4. You are walking down the street and suddenly you see two hundred rupee notes on the pavement. What action will you take?
(a) Deposit it in the nearest police station.
(b) Pocket it yourself.
(c) Leave it where it is.
(d) Give the money to a beggar.

5. Your bathroom tap is leaking and is a constant source of irritating noise. You would
(a) sleep with pillows upon your ears.
(b) put a bucket underneath.
(c) call a plumber to repair the tap.
(d) try to put up a cork upon the mouth of the tap.

6. You are having tea in your office, some of the tea spills on your clothes. You will « CG PSC 2013
(a) call the peon to wipe off the tea from your clothes.
(b) yourself wipe off the tea from your clothes.
(c) hide the stain marks.
(d) ask the peon to fetch clothes from your house.

7. If in an examination hall, you find the question paper is too tough to be answered satisfactorily by you, the best thing to do for you is to « NIFT UG 2005
(a) tell the examiner that the questions are out of course.
(b) provoke the candidates to walk out of the examination hall.
(c) try to know something from your neighbour.
(d) try to solve the questions as much as you know with a cool head.

8. You are a member of the sports team of your college. One day due to misunderstanding, other members stop talking to you. You
(a) ask someone to mediate.
(b) wait till they come and start talking again.
(c) keep to yourself and let things take their time for improving.
(d) go forward and start talking.

9. You are a guest at a dinner. The host asks you to take one more chapatti after your stomach is full. You would
(a) make a bad face at him.
(b) take the chapatti.
(c) politely say that the food was too good and you have already eaten much.
(d) make a blunt refusal.

10. You are head of your office. Some media people come to your office and request you to brief them about the pension plan of your office. You will « CGPSC 2013
(a) aks the media people to come some another day.
(b) immediately accept the offer and brief them.
(c) get them turned out of your office.
(d) ask them to wait and to consult the officials concerned.

11. Your classmate, who got you in a fix recently with a teacher, has met with an ancient. You
(a) feel that God taught him/her a lesson.
(b) carry on with life unaffected.
(c) tell others that this is the way one suffers for making others suffer.
(d) decides to visit him/her in the hospital.

12. After a purchase, the shopkeeper returns ₹ 100 extra to you. You will « NIFT UG 2005
(a) treat your friends to a lunch.
(b) offer ₹ 20 at a temple and pray for more such instance.
(c) hope he will give another ₹ 100 extra.
(d) return the extra money to the shopkeeper.

13. Your family is going to your aunt's house, whom you do not particularly like. What would you do?
(a) Stay at home and enjoy yourself.
(b) Go to your aunt's house but stay outside.
(c) Go to your aunt's place and maintain a comfort level.
(d) Try and convince your brother and sister to stay back with you as you cannot stay back at home.

14. Your colleague is not performing his duties upto the mark. You will
(a) just do your part of the duties and enjoy your work.
(b) take advantage of it to promote yourself.
(c) report to the seniors.
(d) try and handle his customers to maintain the company's status.

15. When someone demands something undesirable, you
(a) always try to avoid the man.
(b) neglect the person and leave the place.
(c) always try to explain your inability to meet the demand.
(d) try to teach him a lesson, so that he does not repeat the same behaviour.

16. Your classmate who is usually very energetic and happy all the time looks very down and upset. You
(a) carry on with your work.
(b) tell one of your friends to go and talk to her.
(c) go up to her and ask the reason.
(d) wait for her to come up and tell you the reason.

17. You are in a bus. The bus reaches your stop but still you have not purchased the ticket because of heavy rush. What will you do?
(a) Jump out quickly to avoid embarrassment.
(b) Call the conductor give him the money and get the ticket.
(c) Hand the money to someone sitting nearby to give it to the conductor.
(d) Give the money to the driver.

18. You are getting late for your college and no bus is available. In such a situation
(a) you start walking.
(b) you drop the idea of going to college that day and return home.
(c) you think about other possible conveyance.
(d) you wait patiently for the bus though you are late for the class.

19. Suppose one of your friends drops your camera while handling it carelessly. You would
(a) ask him to buy a new camera and replace it.
(b) never keep any connection with him.
(c) be very much annoyed.
(d) tell him to be careful while handling such delicate things.

20. You are alone in the house and your sister-in-law is suddenly experiencing labour pains. You
(a) would definitely get upset and do not know what is the right step.
(b) go out of the house to call your family doctor.
(c) walk her to the nearest hospital.
(d) call an ambulance for emergency.

21. You are a sincere and dedicated manager in a reputed five star hotel. You have been appointed as the Chief Manager of the Guwahati branch which needs to be developed. Your salary has been hiked.
(a) You give it a shot for two months and see how it goes.
(b) You accept the challenge and go ahead with the project.
(c) You accept another offer and leave the job.
(d) You crib for limited resources and try to convince the superior to send somebody else instead of you.

22. You are competing with your batchmate for a prestigious award to be decided based on an oral presentation. Ten minutes are allowed for each presentation. You have been asked by the committee to finish on time. Your friend, however is allowed more than the stipulated time period. You would « UPSC CSAT 2012
(a) lodge a complaint to the chairperson against the discrimination.
(b) not listen to any justification from the committee.
(c) ask for withdrawal of your name.
(d) protest and leave the place.

23. While travelling in a train, you observe some college students pulling the alarm chain simply to get down at their desired point. You would.
   (a) with the help of some passengers, stop them from doing so.
   (b) let them pull the chain but check them from deboprding
   (c) inform the guard of the train as soon as it stops.
   (d) keep quiet and do nothing.

24. You have been transferred to a new department. You find that most of the staff members criticise one another. You should « CG PSC 2013
   (a) try to know the weakness of staff members.
   (b) hold a meeting and try to create an organisation culture.
   (c) overlook the matter.
   (d) complain to the higher authorities.

25. You are the manager of the department. You get to know that one of the subordinates is having a problem with his family, since his father is supposed to undergo bypass surgery but at the same time the subordinate is very important for the current project which you have undertaken. The subordinate wants two weeks' leave. What would you do?
   (a) Give him your support by assuring him that his duty towards his father is more important.
   (b) Not empathise with the employee's situation and ask him to stay.
   (c) Get an extension for the project to be submitted as the employee is very efficient and you cannot trust anyone else.
   (d) Transfer the work to some other employee of similar caliber.

26. You have to accomplish a very important task for your headquarters within the next two days. Suddenly you meet with an accident. Your officer insists that you complete the task. You would « UPSC CSAT 2011
   (a) ask for an extension of deadline.
   (b) inform headquarters of your inability to finish on time.
   (c) suggest alternate person to Headquarters who may do the needful.
   (d) stay away till you recover.

27. You are passing by a river and you know swimming. Suddenly you hear the cry of a drowning child. You would
   (a) wait to see, if some other person is there to help.
   (b) dive into the river to save him.
   (c) look for professional divers.
   (d) console the childs parents.

28. You have been asked to give an explanation for not attending an important official meeting. Your immediate boss who has not informed you about the meeting is now putting pressure on you not to place an allegation against him/her. You would « UPSC CSAT 2013
   (a) send a written reply explaining the fact.
   (b) seek an appointment with the top boss to explain the situation.
   (c) admit your fault to save the situation.
   (d) put the responsibility on the coordinator of the meeting for not informing.

29. You are a team leader and you are supposed to hold a convention on HR issues but your team members are unable to get adequate sponsorship.
   (a) You put in your money and hold the event as scheduled.
   (b) You try and motivate them that they can do it.
   (c) You postpone the event and give them some more time.
   (d) You tell them things can work out like this and cancel the event.

30. You are a manager of a company and an employee does not turn up for work because his son was ill. You will « Hotel Mgmt 2004
   (a) tell him to come on time now onwards no matter what.
   (b) ask him how his son is and give him a day off.
   (c) give him a strict warning.
   (d) ask how his son is and tell him to call the office, if even in future he decides not to come.

31. Your friend has lost his/her purse with your important documents in it. You would
   (a) feel angry but do not react as anyone can make mistakes.
   (b) feel angry and ask him/her to replace/duplicate the documents.
   (c) understand the situation and tell him/her that it's ok and not to worry about it.
   (d) blame him/her for being careless and stop talking to him/her.

32. After your graduation, you are offered a well paid Government job. However, your friend says that you have to pay bribe to get the appointment order. You « Hotel Mgmt 2004
   (a) go to some influential politician who can help.
   (b) accept the job by paying the bribe, consoling yourself that this is the present social setup.
   (c) accept the job by paying the bribe but firmly resolve that this is the last time you will pay bribe.
   (d) flatly refuse the offer.

33. You are alone in the house and there is quite a danger of thieves around. Just then, you hear a knock at the door. You would
   (a) open the door to see who is there.
   (b) first peep out from the window to confirm whether you know the person.
   (c) not open the door.
   (d) ask the servant to see who is there.

34. While travelling in your car, certain persons stop you on the way asking you to take an injured child to the hospital. You would
   (a) ask them to leave your way and then drive away.
   (b) ask them to first call the police.
   (c) immediately take the child to hospital.
   (d) get out of the car and ask some other person to help them.

35. You are handling a time bound project. During the project review meeting, you find that the project is likely to get delayed due to lack of cooperation of the team members. You would « UPSC CSAT 2012
   (a) warn the team members for their non-cooperation.
   (b) look into reasons for non-cooperation.
   (c) ask for the replacement of team members.
   (d) ask for extension of time citing reasons.

36. You are in the middle of an important dinner party when the waiter spills steaming hot soup all over the boss'lap. How would you cope?

(a) You panic and start shouting on the waiter.
(b) Arrange for the first aid and make arrangements to rush him or her off to the hospital.
(c) You dab frantically at the ruined outfit with a napkin while screaming at the waiter.
(d) You pour the entire contents of a jug of water over his lap, explaining that your prompt action will prevent burns and then lay out a change of clothes in the guest bedroom and return to the party while the boss changes.

37. While addressing people in an open ground, it begins to rain. Your address is important and you cannot afford to postpone it. What will you do? you would « CGPSC 2013

(a) ask someone to arrange an umbrella.
(b) stop your address for a while.
(c) continue the address without bothering the rain.
(d) postpone it for a day.

38. You are playing football in a park. When you kick the ball, it strikes and breaks the window pane of a nearby house. You would

(a) demand your ball back from the house owner.
(b) say that it was no fault of yours.
(c) stealthily get your ball back.
(d) apologise to the house owner and contribute to replace the glass.

39. You are moving across the road on a scooter when you observe that two boys on a bike snatch a lady's gold chain and side away. You would

(a) console the women.
(b) chase the boys to catch hold of them.
(c) inform the police about the matter.
(d) stand and see what happens.

40. On reaching the railway station, you find that the train you wanted to catch is just to start and there is hardly any time for purchasing the ticket. The best thing for you is to

(a) rush to the train rather than miss it and inform the T.T.I. at the next stoppage about your inability to purchase the ticket.
(b) rush to the train and perform your journey quietly.
(c) first purchase the ticket and then catch the train, if it is there.
(d) miss the train than take the risk of boarding the moving train.

41. A train is coming and you are standing at the station. Suddenly you notice that the railway track is broken. You will

(a) inform the authority to take necessary action.
(b) leave the station.
(c) use some means to stop train immediately.
(d) None of the above.

42. You are driving your car on the road when you hit against a fruit vendor's cart. You would

(a) escape from the site by driving away.
(b) abuse the fruit vendor for putting his cart on the way.
(c) pay the fruit vendor for the damage done to him.
(d) insist that it was not your fault.

43. You are an officer incharge for providing basic medical facilities to the survivors of an earthquake affected area. Despite your best possible effort, people put allegations against you for making money out of the funds given for relief. You would « UPSC CSAT 2011

(a) let an enquiry be set up to look into the matter.
(b) ask your senior to appoint some other person in your place.
(c) not pay attention to allegations.
(d) stop undertaking any initiative till the matter is resolved.

44. You are suffering from diabetes. When you see a whole lot of chocolates, you are tempted to eat them but you also realise that they are not good for you in the long run. What do you do? « Hotal Mgmt 2005

(a) You would not eat them because you know the harmful effects.
(b) You decide not to eat them but keep thinking about them.
(c) You would eat them but feel guilty about what you have done.
(d) You would give in to the temptation and eat the chocolates without being bothered about the consequences.

45. You want to get married to a person of your choice, but your family members give their own reasons why you should not marry that person, which you do not find very convincing. What would you do?

(a) Go by what your family says.
(b) Become thoroughly confused and still remain undecided.
(c) Marry the person of your choice.
(d) Try to convince your family about your choice.

46. You just got to know that your friend has met with an accident and hearing this you immediately leave for the accident spot along with one more friend. In a hurry, you forgot to take your licence and helmet. You were flagged down to stop at the traffic intersection by the traffic constable. You will « CGPSC 2013

(a) dodge the policeman.
(b) stop and pay fine.
(c) stop and reason it out with about the policeman.
(d) stop and use references.

47. You are handling a priority project and have been meeting all the deadlines and are therefore planning your leave during the project. Your immediate boss does not grant your leave citing the urgency of the project. You would « UPSC CSAT 2012

(a) proceed on leave without waiting for the sanction.
(b) pretend to be sick and take leave.
(c) approach higher authority to reconsider the leave application.
(d) tell the boss that it is not justified.

48. If you find yourself in a situation where you are required to make a power point presentation and you are already bogged down by too much work, as the manager what would you do?

(a) Take an alternative mode of presentation.
(b) Cancel the seminar and reschedule according to your convenience.
(c) Pass the buck to your subordinate, you are the boss, on one can question you.
(d) Prioritise your work and try to squeeze out time for it.

49. You have worked hard on an idea which you believe would be a breakthrough but the presentation does not go as you had hoped it would. You « Hotel Mgmt 2004

(a) ignore all the suggestions and believe that you were correct.
(b) break down and get all the emotional.
(c) take this as a learning experience and convince yourself that you would do better the next time.
(d) feel like a loser.

50. You have taken up a project to create night shelters for homeless people during the winter season. Within a week of establishing the shelters, you have received complaints from the residents of the area about the increase in theft cases with a demand to remove the shelters. You would « UPSC CSAT 2011

(a) ask them to lodge a written complaint in the police station.
(b) assure residents of an enquiry into the matter.
(c) ask residents to consider the humanitarian effort made.
(d) continue with the project and ignore their complaint.

51. You have a pharmaceutical company. You have received information that someone who is not an employee has tampered with a certain type of tablets in a specific area, which has caused some deaths in that area. In this type of crisis, what will you do?
« Hotel Mgmt 2006

(a) This incident can have a negative effect on your company's reputation and earnings and can lead to loss. In order to avoid this you don't launch a campaign to alert the people.
(b) Launch a campaign to alert the public and recall tablets from the specific area.
(c) Recall tablets from only the specific area and not the whole country.
(d) Recall those tablets from the entire country despite the fact that the tampering of tablets occurred in a certain area.

52. While sitting in a park, you observe that a smart young man comes to the place on a scooter, leaves it there and goes away with someone else on a motorbike. You would

(a) call back the person.
(b) remain engaged in your enjoyment.
(c) chase the person.
(d) inform the police at the nearby booth.

53. A person lives in a far off village which is almost two hours by bus. The villager's neighbour is a very powerful landlord who is trying to occupy the poor villager's land by force.

You are the District Magistrate and busy in a meeting called by a local minister. The villager has come all the way, by bus and on foot, to see you and give an application seeking protection from the powerful landlord.

The villager keeps on waiting outside the meeting hall for an hour. You come out of the meeting and are rushing to another meeting. The villager follows you to submit his application. What would you do?
« UPSC CSAT 2013

(a) Tell him to wait for another two hours till you come back from your next meeting.
(b) Tell him that the matter is actually to be dealt by a junior officer and that he should give the application to him.
(c) Call one of your senior subordinate officers and ask him to solve the villager's problem.
(d) Quickly take the application from him, ask him a few relevant questions regarding his problem and then proceed to the meeting.

Answers / WITH EXPLANATIONS

1. (*c*) The best mode to overcome anger is not to vent it on things or people around you but to divert your mind to a different indulgence. Hence, the answer is option (c).

2. (*c*) Clearly, the situation demands helping the maid by contributing towards the wedding as much as one can. Hence, the best answer is option (c).

3. (*c*) Here, you must have to show your humanity by helping the blind man in crossing the road.

4. (*a*) As the money lying on the street is not yours, so keeping it with yourself or giving it to a beggar is not ethical. The correct action in this situation is to deposit that money in the nearest police station so that the genuine owner of the money will receive that money.

5. (*c*) As the tap is leaking, sleeping, putting a bucket underneath or putting a cork upon the mouth of the tap will not solve the problem, so you must call a plumber to repair the tap.

6. (*b*) Here, option (a) is not valid on moral grounds while option (c) shows that you are more concerned about your clothes and grooming rather than your work. In this case, option (b) will be the best reaction to perform.

7. (*d*) Clearly, an ideal student shall never be exposed to create a row over such an issue or try to copy the answers. Also, a situation can best be tackled by not creating panic rather trying to solve it with a cool head.
Hence, the best answer is option (d).

8. (*d*) As you are a member of the team, so to maintain the healthy relationship with other team members you must try to clear the misunderstandings by talking to the other members.

9. (*c*) In the given situation, you must be polite enough to the host of the dinner while refusing to take more chapatti. So, the action given in option (c) is appropriate.

10. (*d*) Here, options (a) and (c) are not appropriate as these are not valid on ethical grounds while option (b) is also not valid as you are the head of the office and you have certain important tasks to accomplish.
In this case, option (d) would be the best course of action as there are certain officials for each work in every office, so one has to consult them.

11. (*d*) In the given situation, you must have to show humanity but not revenge on moral ground. So, here the best action is to visit him/ her in the hospital.

12. (*d*) As the extra money which the shopkeeper has given to you doesnot belong to you. Therefore, you must return it to the shopkeeper.

13. (*c*) As your whole family is going to your aunt's house, you also have to go with your family. In that situation, you need to maintain a comfort level at your aunts's house.

14. (*d*) In the given situation as a committed employee, you have to try and handle your colleague customers to maintain the company's status.

15. (*c*) When someone demands something undesirable, avoiding or neglecting the person does not solve the problem. You must try to explain the person about your inability to meet the demand.

16. (*c*) As you know that, your classmate usually remains happy and energetic, you have to go to her and ask about the reason for her being upset.

17. (*b*) As you have travelled in the bus but was unable to purchase the ticket during the journey due to heavy rush, you must give the money to the conductor and get the ticket before leaving the bus.

18. (*c*) As you are getting late for the college and no bus is available. In that situation you must have to go for other possible conveyance, so as to reach the college at time other options are not the solution to this problem.

19. (*d*) In this situation, you have to be polite with your friend but also you make him understand that these delicate things must be handled carefully.

20. (*d*) Clearly, the situation demands taking the lady to the hospital without much delay. Leaving her alone at home to go out in search of help or to make her do excess strain in the act of reaching hospital shall surely not be appropriate.

21. (*b*) As you are a sincere and dedicated manager, you must be committed to the work which is assigned to you. So, you must have to accept the challenge and go ahead with the project.

22. (*a*) Withdrawal of your name is an escapist attitude. Protesting is correct but lodging a complaint to the concerned authority will give the result. So, option (a) is the best course of action.

23. (*a*) Pulling the alarm chain of the train without any emergency is a crime. You must have to take help of other passengers to stop the students from doing this wrong act.

24. (*b*) Here option (a) does not serve the purpose. Option (c) shows your negligence that you are not interested in maintaining healthy working environment in your department while option (d) shows your inability to tackle the problem. So, in this case option (b) is the best possible solution.

25. (*d*) As both completion of your project and your subordinate attending to his father are important. So, you must transfer your subordinate work to some other employee of similar caliber.

26. (*b*) Informing headquarters of your inability to finish the work on time, explaining the reason is the best action. So, answer is option (b).

27. (*b*) The situation demands immediate action to save the child. As you know swimming, you must have to dive into the river for saving the child without any delay for waiting someone else to come for help.

28. (*a*) As you have been asked to give an explanation, so it is the best way to give a written reply explaining the fact. Hence, answer is option(a).

29. (*b*) As you have the responsibility to hold the convention, so canceling or postponing the event does not hold good for you. In this situation, you have to try to motivate your team members, so as to achieve an adequate sponsorship.

30. (*d*) As the son of your employee was ill, asking about his son's health is humane. Also, you have to make him understand that informing about the leave is necessary, so that the work can be managed accordingly.

31. (*a*) In the given situation, you must understand your friends's situation as anyone can make mistakes. So, you need not react to the situation.

32. (*d*) Offering bribe is an unethical action. So, you must not indulge in these type of activities and flatly refuse the offer.

33. (*b*) As you are alone in the house and there is a danger of thieves, you must check who is at the door before opening the door so that you must be sure that the person coming to you is not unknown.

34. (*c*) Here, the injured child needs immediate treatment. So, calling the police or leaving the child for someone else help shall surely not be appropriate as it will lead to much delay in the treatment process clearly, the situation demands taking the child immediately to the hospital.

35. (*b*) Looking into reasons for non-cooperation and then rectifying it is the correct step. Options (c) and (d) show lack of leadership qualities. Option (a) will not solve the problem permanently. So, option (b) is correct.

36. (*d*) In the given situation, pouring water over your boss lap is required as it will prevent burns. Also, the dinner party is equally important, you can arrange changing of clothes for your boss and return to the party.

37. (*c*) Asking someone to arrange an umbrella as mentioned in option (a) will not be moral while options (b) and (d) do not serve the purpose as it is mentioned that it is important and you cannot afford to postpone it.
Here, in this case continuing the address without bothering the rain as mentioned in option (c) will be the best course of action.

38. (*d*) As the glass was broken because of your fault, you must apologise to the house owner and contribute to replace the glass.

39. (*b*) In this situation, you should chase the boys to catch hold of them the best answer is (b).

40. (*a*) In the given situation, rush to the train rather than miss it and inform the T.T.I at the next stoppage about your inability to purchase the ticket. In this case the option (a) is the best action to perform.

41. (*c*) Obviously, you cannot let thousands of innocent people die, just like that. You have to act immediately, as a fraction of second might prove to be all the difference.

42. (*c*) In the given situation, you must have to show humanity. You should pay the fruit vendor for the damage done to him. So, the best is option (c).

43. (*c*) As you are doing your work honestly and with complete dedication, so that best action is not to pay attention to the allegations. Hence, answer is option (c).

44. (*a*) As you are diabetic, you would not eat then because it will lead to harmful effects in the long run.

45. (*d*) The best way to settle a conflict is always to arrive at a consensus through peaceful talks and mutual discussions rather than stick to any one side and ignore the other.

In the given situation, since the person concerned doesn't find the views of the family members convincing, he should try to convince them and mound their views to match his own.

Just following his own choice shall hurt the family's sentiments and obeying the family members blindly shall surely be disloyalty towards the person you love.

46. (*b*) The policeman is doing his duty, so he won't understand your reason. Also, that would be a wastage of time, so option (c) is eliminated. Dodging the policeman is making a crime, hence it is also not ethical.

Using references is again not an ethical behaviour.

Hence, the most appropriate option is (b) as you have done a mistake, so you have to pay fine for it.

47. (*c*) Option (a) shows your adamant attitude. Option (b) is ethically not permitted. Arguing with the immediate boss is not correct as it will not bring any result. Option (c) is the best course of action.

48. (*d*) A manager is one who has the expertise to manage tasks properly. So, it becomes his prime responsibility to rearrange his work schedule properly and work out the required time for the project rather than postpone it or hand it over to someone else.

Hence, the best answer is option (d).

49. (*c*) To be a successful person, you must learn from your mistakes and convince yourself that you would do better the next time.

50. (*b*) As a responsible project manager, it is your responsibility to pacify the residents, who have complained to you. The best action in such situation is to assure residents of an inquiry into the matter.

51. (*b*) In this crisis situation, you must take an authoritative step to launch a campaign to alert the public and also you have to recall the tablets that specific area.

52. (*d*) The given situation demands a prompt action as there may be some bomb or some other illegal things in the scooter which he has left there chasing the person on your own may be risky. So, the correct action in this situation is to inform the police at the nearby booth.

53. (*d*) Here, we have two objectives to achieve at the same time. Firstly, we have to help the villager who has come from far off. Secondly, we have to reach the second meeting on time. Option (d) allows us to achieve both.

Option (c) also achieves the same objectives though it means that the villager will have to wait for a little more time.

Options (a) and (b) are wrong as, they will increase the troubles of the villager who might not be able to wait longer.

TYPE 02

Eligibility Test

In these type of questions, a set of necessary conditions and qualifications required to be fulfilled by the candidate for a certain vacancy in job/ promotion / admission in a college, along with the biodata of certain candidates who have applied for the same is given.

You are required to evaluate and assess a candidate's eligibility and thereby decide upon the appropriate course of action to be taken from among the given alternatives.

Let us consider following examples to understand the format of questions asked and the basic step involved in solving these questions

***Ex* 09** A junior college inducts students based on the following criteria. « RRB NTPC 2016

1. Students who scored above 75% in Physics, 85% in Mathematics and 70% in Chemistry.
2. Students who scored at least 60% in English.
3. Students who are good in a sport or play a musical instrument or know a dance form.

Which student among the following will the college definitely take?

(A) Shakti with 80% in Physics, 65% in Chemistry, 85% in Mathematics, 61% in English and plays Veena.

(B) Megha secured 80% in Physics, 87% in Mathematics, 70% in English, 75% in Chemistry and is a singer.

(C) Sheela secured 78% in Physics, 70% in Chemistry 85% in Mathematics, 75% in English knows Manipuri folk dance.

(D) Mallika secured 70% in Chemistry, 70% in Mathematics, 85% in Physics, 65% in English and plays basketball.

(a) C (b) B (c) D (d) A

***Solution* (a)** In this question, three basic conditions are given which must be fulfilled by the candidate.
Now, we will check the biodata of each candidate and then we will decide that which candidate will be taken by the college.

(A) Shakti secured 65% marks in Chemistry but according to the condition 1 the candidate must secured 70% marks in Chemistry. So, Shakti is rejected.

(B) Megha fulfills all the conditions except condition 3. She is a singer but according to the condition 3, student must be good in a sport or play a musical instrument or know a dance form. So, Megha is rejected.

(C) Sheela fulfills all the three conditions. So college will definitely take Sheela.

(D) Mallika secured 70% in Mathematics but according to the condition 1, the student must secured 85% in Mathematics. So, Mallika is rejected.

DIRECTIONS ~ (Example Nos. 10-12) *Read the following information carefully and answer the questions given below it.*

Following are the conditions for short listing candidates for the post of Customer Relations Officers (CRO) for XYZ Limited. The candidate to be called for interview must

A. be a graduate in Science *i.e.*, B.Sc. with minimum 55% marks.
B. have atleast 3 yr experience in selling/ marketing.
C. have participated in debating or drama or sports at the inter college level onwards.
D. have secured minimum 60% marks in the written examination.
E. be ready to deposit ₹ 10000 as security deposit.

However, in case of a candidate who fulfils all these criteria except

(i) (D) above but has secured minimum 60% in B. Sc. may be referred to the Chief Manager, Customer Relations (CR).
(ii) (A) above but has passed M.Sc. *i.e.*, post-graduation in Science, with minimum 50% marks, may be referred to DGM (CR).

Based on these criteria and information provided decide the courses of action in each case. You are not to assume anything. If the data provided is not adequate to decide the given course of action, your answer will be 'data inadequate'. All the candidates given below fulfil the criteria for age.

Give answer

(a) Selected for interview
(b) Not to be selected
(c) Data inadequate
(d) Refer to the Chief Manager (CR)
(e) Refer to the DGM (CR)

***Ex* 10** Rohan is the son of a marketing executive, Rohan has obtained money as prizes in inter college/university debates and drama events. He has worked as marketing executive for 5 yr after completing his B.Sc. and MBA with 62% and 70% marks, respectively. He is ready to give security deposit of ₹ 10000. He has obtained 65% marks in written exam.

***Ex* 11** Kanchan has 6 yr of experience in marketing consumer products. She has completed her B.Sc., M.Sc. and MBA with 65%, 56% and 62% marks, respectively. She is ready to pay the security deposit. She participated at debating competitions and has won many prizes in inter college/university events. She is interested in social work.

***Ex* 12** Jadunath is a Science graduate having done post-graduate diploma in Journalism. He is having 4 yr experience of marketing consumer products. He is ready to deposit ₹ 10000 as security deposit. He had been participating in dramas at inter college level and above and has won many prizes. He has secured 55% and 65% marks at written exam and B.Sc., respectively.

Solutions (Example Nos. 10-12) *First of all, let us understand the contents of the questions*

- **Basic conditions** A, B, C, D and E
- **Additional conditions** (i) and (ii)
- **Bio data** Personal details given in each example.

To solve these questions, we have to follow a step by step approach. Steps involved in the process are as follows

***Step* I** Read carefully the basic conditions A, B, C, D and E.

***Step* II** Read carefully the additional conditions (i) and (ii) and find out with which basic conditions (A, B, C, D or E), these additional conditions (i) and (ii) are attached.

- We find that additional condition (i) is attached with basic condition D.
- Additional condition (ii) is attached with basic condition A.

There is no any other additional condition. It means apart from A and D, other basic conditions (B, C and E) are independent.

***Step* III** Make table for the questions as given below

Ex. Nos.	Candidate	A (ii)	B	C	D (i)	E	Answers
10.	Rohan						
11.	Kanchan						
12.	Jadunath						

Here, Additional condition (ii) is attached with basic condition A.
Additional condition (i) is attached with basic condition D.

***Step* IV** Read information about each candidate and then put following symbols in the table made in step III.

✓ For basic condition fulfilled.
✗ For unfulfilled basic condition.
(✓) For basic condition unfulfilled but additional condition attached to the basic condition is fulfilled.
(✗) For the violation of both basic and additional condition.
–/? For data inadequate. (x) can also be written as x.

Now, let us fill the table

Q. Nos.	Candidates	A (ii)	B	C	D (i)	E	Answers
10.	Rohan	✓	✓	✓	✓	✓	a
11.	Kanchan	✓	✓	✓	?	✓	c
12.	Jadunath	✓	✓	✓	(✓)	✓	d

Condition A This condition is fulfilled by all candidates, hence '✓' is put for them.

Condition B This condition is also fulfilled by all candidates, hence '✓' is put for them.

Condition C This condition is also fulfilled by all the candidates, hence '✓' is put for them.

Condition D (i) Rohan, fulfils basic condition D. Hence, '✓' is put for them.

Jadunath violates basic condition D but fulfil additional condition (i) attached to D. Hence, (✓) is put for them.

Biodata of **Kanchan** does not give any information about **her percentage of marks in written examination**. As we lack definite information in case of Kanchan, we put '?' for her.

Condition E All candidates fulfil basic condition E. Hence, '✓' is put for them.

Now, we have our table ready to answer the given questions. Let us answer the questions as follows.

10. (a) **Rohan** All basic conditions are fulfilled. Hence, he will be selected.

11. (*c*) **Kanchan** Except condition D, all basic conditions are fulfilled. But there is no information about his percentage of marks in the written exam. It means data is inadequate.

12. (*d*) **Jadunath** Basic conditions A, B, C and E are fulfilled. Further, basic condition D is not fulfilled. But additional condition (i) attached with D is fulfilled. Therefore, case will be referred to Chief Manager (CR).

After solving the above examples we deduce some important rules that must be kept in mind while solving the problems

***Rule* 1** For selection all basic conditions must be fulfilled.

***Rule* 2** For rejection atleast one independent basic condition must be violated/basic '+' additional condition must be violated.

***Rule* 3** If a basic condition is violated but an additional condition attached with it is fulfilled and all other remaining basic conditions are fulfilled, then the case will be referred to the person given in the question.

***Rule* 4** Once the symbol ✗ / (✗) is put in the table, there is no need to check further conditions as person is declared rejected at this stage only.

***Rule* 5** If for one basic condition, the data is not given while all other basic conditions are fulfilled, it means data is inadequate.

***Rule* 6** If any information is not given and answer choices don't have data inadequate option, then condition related to that particular information is supposed to be violated.

DIRECTIONS ~ (Example Nos. 13-19) *A chemical Company X decided to recruit management trainees for its ammonia plant. The company laid down the following criteria for selecting the candidates.*

A. should be a chemical engineering graduate with minimum 65% marks.

B. should have done atleast a diploma in business management.

C. should not be less than 21 yr of age and more than 28 yr of age as on 1st July, 2005.

D. should have secured a minimum of 75% marks in the Common Entrance Test (CET).

However, if the candidate fulfils all the criteria except

(i) A above but has secured marks above 60% and below 65% and also has a working experience of one year, his case may be referred to the Managing Director (MD).

(ii) B above and has secured more than 80% marks in CET, his case may be referred to the General Manager (GM) of the plant.

(iii) D above but has passed the CET examination with atleast 65% marks and has secured more than 70% marks in chemical engineering degree examination, his case may be referred to the Vice-President.

Based on the above criteria and information given in each of the following questions, you have to take a decision regarding to each case. You cannot assume anything. These cases are given to you as on 1st July, 2005.

Give answer

(a) If the candidate is to be selected.

(b) If the candidate is to be referred to the Managing Director.

(c) If the candidate is to be referred to General Manger of the plant.

(d) If the candidate is to be referred to the Vice-President.

(e) If the candidate is not to be selected.

***Ex* 13** Subhash Chandra, who is working in a chemical factory as junior engineer (chemicals), since 30th June, 2004, is a chemical engineering graduate with 72% marks. He has passed CET with 85% marks. His date of birth is 23rd December, 1983.

***Ex* 14** Arundhati a 27 yr old lady, is chemical engineer with 61% marks and has also done as diploma course in the information technology. She has been working in a private company as manager, software science for past 3 yr. She has obtained a post-graduate degree in business management. She has secured 75% marks in CET.

***Ex* 15** Shirish Gupta has completed his graduation in chemical engineering with 75% marks and diploma in business management with 60% marks. He has passed the CET with 69% marks. He celebrated his 27th birthday on 17th March, 2005.

***Ex* 16** Dilip Khare is an engineering graduate passed out in 2002, with 70% marks. He has secured 68% marks in CET. His date of birth is 25th October, 1982. He has completed his post-graduate diploma in business management from a reputed institute.

***Ex* 17** Rajiv Mhatre is a 25 yr old chemical engineering graduate with 62% marks in graduation. He is working in a private chemical company as an assistant manager for last 2 yr. He has passed CET with 52% marks and has done diploma in business management in 2001.

***Ex* 18** Mamta is an electrical engineer with 74% marks. She has done diploma in business management as well as in chemical technology securing 66% and 62% marks, respectively. Her date of birth is 16th December, 1979. She has passed CET with 80% marks.

***Ex* 19** Subodh Roy is studying for post-graduate degree in chemical engineering at present. He has secured 73% marks in BE chemical engineering. His date of birth is 25th June, 1984. He has also completed the diploma in business management and has passed CET with 82% marks. He has no working experience.

Solutions (Example Nos. 13-19) *The given information can be tabulated as follows.*

Exp. Nos.	Candidates	A (i)	B (ii)	C	D (iii)	Answers
13.	Subhash	✓	(✓)	✓	✓	c
14.	Arundhati	(✓)	✓	✓	✓	b
15.	Shirish	✗	✓	✓	(✓)	d
16.	Dilip	✗	—	—	—	e
17.	Rajiv	(✓)	✓	✓	✗	e
18.	Mamta	✗	—	—	—	e
19.	Subodh	✓	✓	✓	✓	a

For Dilip, It is given that Dilip is an engineering graduate with 70% marks. On the basis of this information we cannot be sure that he is a chemical engineering graduate or not. It means, we should put the symbol of data inadequate '?' for condition A. But point to be noted that in the answer option, data inadequate has not been given. Further additional condition (i) attached with A is also not fulfilled, if we suppose A is violated. Hence, we put (✗) for A(i).

For Subhash, There is no information about the basic condition B. Hence, according to general rule we should put the symbol of data inadequate '?' for condition B but point to be noted that in the answer option data inadequate has not been given. In this situation we suppose, for Subhash basic condition B is violated. When we suppose B is violated, then we go on to check additional condition ii attached with B. Here, we find that additional condition ii attached with B is fulfilled. Hence, we put (✓) for B(ii).

For Dilip and Mamta, Rule IV is applied

For Subhash, Arundhati and Shirish, Rule III is applied.

For Rajiv, Rule II is applied.

For Subodh, Rule I is applied

Practice / CORNER 23.2

1. A college council is auditioning students for a cultural festival. they must satisfy the following criteria.

1. Student must know atleast one dance form.
2. Student must know to play atleast one musical instrument.
3. Student must have good acting skills.

Which one of the following will the council definitely select? « RRB NTPC 2016

(a) Z is a Bharat Natyam dancer, a violinist but does not have any acting skills.
(b) P plays football, guitar, has acted in road shows and is a classical dancer.
(c) J is a contemporary dancer, a great actor and is planning to learn flute.
(d) A plays sitar, is a hip-hop dancer and does not have any acting skills.

DIRECTIONS ~(Q. Nos. 2-6) *Read the following informations carefully and answer the question given below it.*

Following are the criteria for selection of interpreter in different embassies in India.

A. The candidate should be a graduate from a recognised university.
B. He or she should be 23 to 26 yr of age as on 7th March, 2006.
C. The candidate should have the ability to read, write and speak English and Hindi besides the foreign language to which he/she has applied.
D. The candidate should have his/her own accommodation, either rental or own, in Delhi.

However, if a candidate fulfils all criteria except.

(i) At D but he/she has accommodation either rental or own, in NCT Delhi, his/her case is to be referred to foreign secretary.
(ii) At B but he/she has a PG degree in any discipline, his/her case is to be referred to personal assistant, foreign secretary.

Now, based on the given criteria and the information given below, you have to take decision in regard to each case. You are not to assume any information which is not available.

Give answer

(a) If to be referred to foreign secretary.
(b) If to be referred to PA foreign secretary.
(c) If data is inadequate.
(d) If to be selected.
(e) If not to be selected.

2. Sweta Singh is a Hindi Hons. graduate from Hindu College, Delhi. Recently, she has celebrated her 23rd birthday on 9th January, 2006. She possesses her own house in Vikaspuri, Delhi. She can speak, write and read English, Hindi and French equally well.

3. Miss Anu knows how to speak, write and read Hindi, English and Portuguese. She also knows how to handle computers. She has done GNIIT after doing her graduation from a recognised university. She can arrange a house in Delhi for her accommodation.

4. Pinki has done her graduation from Oxford University. Her date of birth is 9th November, 1979. She knows how to speak, write and read Hindi, English and Spanish. Her grandfather owns a house in Ghaziabad, in NCT, Delhi. She can live with her grandfather during her job in Delhi.

5. Kiran, wife of Ajay and a graduate from a recognised university, lives with her husband at Kamla Nagar in North. Delhi in their rental house. She has passed her post-graduation in History in February, 2003 at the age of 23 yr. She can speak, read and write Maithili,

Hindi, English and Nepali. There languages Nepali, Maithili and Bhojpuri are being spoken in Nepal.

6. Reena has done her graduation from Jabalpur University, Madhya Pradesh. She can arrange her accommodation with her brother-in-law in Delhi. Her date of birth is 12th January, 1983. She can speak more than two languages including a foreign language.

DIRECTIONS ~(Q. Nos. 7-15) *Study the following information carefully to answer these questions.*

Following are the conditions stipulated by XYZ Company for recruitment of trainees engineers.

The candidate must

A. be an engineering graduate with atleast 60% marks.
B. be not less than 21 yr and to more than 25 yr of age as on 1st May, 2006.
C. have passes the selection test with atleast 55% marks.
D. be willing to pay a deposit of ₹ 50000 to be refunded on completion of training.

However, if a candidate fulfils all the above mentioned criteria except

(i) at (A) above but has appeared to the last semester examination and has obtained an aggregate of minimum 65% marks in first seven semesters, his/her case may be referred to VP of the company.
(ii) at (D) above but in willing to pay an amount atleast ₹ 25000 and has obtained atleast 70% marks at engineering degree; the case may be referred to the general manager of the company.

In each of the following questions, details of one candidate are given as regards his/her candidature. You have to read the information provided and decide his/her status bases on the conditions given above and the information provided. You are not to assume anything other than the informations provided in each of the following questions. All these cases are given to you as on 1st May, 2006.

Give answer

(a) If the candidate is to be selected.
(b) If the case is to be referred to the general manager.
(c) If the case is to be referred to the VP.
(d) If the data provided is not adequate to take a decision.
(e) If the candidate is not to be selected.

7. Sachin, who has just completed 23 yr of age passed out degree in civil engineering with 70% marks. He has cleared the selection test with 61% marks. He is willing to pay the amount of ₹ 25000 only and will not be able to pay ₹ 50000.

8. Anjali is an IT engineer passed out in 2003 with 52% marks. After getting the engineering degree she has done MBA with specialisation in finance. She has cleared the selection test with 60% mark. She can pay the deposit of ₹ 50000. Her date of birth is 15th September, 1982.

9. Mohan Rao is an electronics engineer (BE electronics) and passed out in 2004 with 66% marks. He has passed the selection test with 59% marks and is willing to pay the required amount of deposit.

10. K Shiv Kumar is a student of B.Tech. in mechanical engineering and has appeared for the last semester examination. Results of the last semester examinations are expected in June 2006. He is expecting to score 65% marks in the last semester as his aggregate percentage of the first seven semester is 67%. He has passed the selection test with 60% marks and has no problem in paying the amount of ₹ 50000 as deposit. He is 22 yr old at present.

11. Rajeev Andhare has appeared for the last semester of engineering degree examination and is hoping to score atleast 70% marks. His aggregate score upto seventh semester is 72%. He has just completed 21 yr of age. He has scored 63% marks in the selection test and is ready to pay an amount of ₹ 50000 as deposit.

12. Nachiket is an engineering graduate with 75% marks at degree level. His date of birth is 16th April, 1982. He has obtained 66% marks in the selection test and is ready to pay 50% of the required amount of deposit at the time of selection and the remaining amount subsequently.

13. Nikita has passes out chemical engineering degree in June 2005 with 74% marks. She appeared for the selection test which she cleared with 72% marks. Her date of birth is 26th August, 1983. She is not in a position to pay ₹ 50000 but will arrange to pay ₹ 30000 as deposit.

14. Vinod has passed computer engineering degree examination with 68% marks in 2005 at the age of 22 yr and is working with a private engineering firm since last six months. He has cleared the selection test with 63% marks. He will manage to pay ₹ 50000 as deposit.

15. Aniket has appeared for the last semester examination of diploma in mechanical engineering and the results are awaited. He secured first class in each of the first 3 semesters. He has recently completed 22 yr of age. He has no problem in paying the required amount of ₹ 50000 as deposit. He has passes the selection test with 58% marks.

DIRECTIONS ~ (Q. Nos. 16-20) *Study the following information carefully and answer the questions given below.* « IBPS PO 2013

An organisation wants to recruit system analysts. The following conditions apply.

The candidate must

(i) be an engineering graduate in computer/IT with atleast 60% marks.
(ii) have working experience in the field of computer atleast for 2 yrs after acquiring the requisite qualification.
(iii) have completed minimum 25 yr and maximum 30 yr of age as on 01.12. 2013.
(iv) be willing to sign a bond for ₹ 50000.
(v) have secured minimum 55% marks in selection test.

However, if the candidate fulfils all other conditions.

Except

(a) at (i) above, but is an Electronics engineer with 65% or more marks the case is to be referred to the general manager (GM)-IT.

(b) at (iv) above, but has an experience of atleast 5 is as a Software Manager, the case is to be referred to the VP.

In each question below, detailed information of candidate is given. You have to carefully study the information provided in each case and take one of the following courses of actions based on the information and the conditions given above.

You are not to assume anything other than the information provided in each question. All these case are given to you as on 01.12.2013.

You have to indicate your decision by marking answers to each question as follows

Give Answer

(a) If the case is to be referred to VP.
(b) If the case is to be referred to GM.
(c) If the data provided is not sufficient to take a decision.
(d) If the candidate is to be selected.
(e) If the candidate is not to be selected.

16. Ms. Suneeta is an IT Engineer with 60% marks at graduation as well as in selection test. She is working as a Software Engineer for last 3 yr after completing engineering degree and has completed 27 yr of age. She is willing to sign the bond of ₹ 50000.

17. Rakesh Rao is a Computer Engineer graduate and thereafter is working as a Software Manager for last 6 yr. He has secured 72% marks at graduation and 67% marks in selection test. His date of birth is 5th December, 1984. He is not willing to sign the bond for ₹ 50000.

18. Ramkumar is an engineering graduate in computers with 78% marks passed out in 2007 at the age of 23 yr. Since, then he is working as a Software Manager in an engineering firm. He does not want to sign the bond for ₹ 50000. He has leared the selection test with 72% marks.

19. Nishant is an electronics engineer passed out in June, 2010 at the age of 22yr. Since, then he is working as a programmer in a software company. He has passed the selection test with 66% marks and is willing to sign the bond.

20. Kalyani is an engineer with 72% marks in telecommunicator. She has just completed 27 yr of age. She has cleared the selection test with 59% marks. She is willing to sign the bond.

DIRECTIONS ~(Q. Nos. 21-25) *Study the following information carefully and answer the questions given below.* « IBPS PO 2012

Following are the conditions for selecting Manager-HR in an organisation

(i) be atleast 30 yr and not more than 35 yr as on 1st March, 2012.
(ii) have secured atleast 60% marks in graduation in any discipline.
(iii) have secured atleast 65% marks in the post-graduate degree/diploma in personnel management/ HR.
(iv) have post qualification work experience of atleast five years in the personnel/ HR department of an organisation.
(v) have secured atleast 50 % marks in the selection process.

However, in the case of a candidate who satisfies all the above conditions except

(a) (ii) above but has secured atleast 55% marks in graduation in any discipline and atleast 70% marks in post-graduate, degree/diploma in personnel management/HR, the case is to be referred to GM-HR.

(b) (iv) above but has post qualification work experience of atleast four years out of which atleast two years as deputy manager-HR, the case is to be referred to President-HR.

In each question below are given details of one candidate. You have to take one of the following courses of actions based on the information provided and the conditions and subconditions given above and mark the number of that course of action as your answer. You are not to assume anything other than the information provided in each question. All these cases are given to you as on 1st March, 2012.

Give answer

(a) If the candidate is not to be selected.
(b) If the data provided are not adequate to take a decision.
(c) If the case is to be referred to President-HR.
(d) If the case is to be referred to GM-HR.
(e) If the candidate is to be selected.

21. Rita Bhatt was born on 25th July, 1978. She has secured 62% marks in graduation and 65% marks in post-graduate diploma in management. She has been working for the past 6 yr in the personnel department of an organisation after completing her post-graduation. She has secured 55% marks in the selection process.

22. Ashok Pradhan was born on 8th August, 1980. He has been working in the personnel department of an organisation for the past 4 yr after completing his post-graduate degree in personnel management with 67%. Out of his entire experience, he has been working for the past 2 yr as deputy Manager-HR. He has secured 62% marks in graduation and 58% marks in the selection process.

23. Alok Verma was born on 4th March, 1976. He has been working in the personnel department of an organisation for the past 6 yr after completing his post-graduate diploma in personnel management with 66% marks. He has secured 57% marks in the selection process and 63% marks in graduation.

24. Swapan Ghosh has been working in the personnel department of an organisation for the past 5 yr after completing his post-graduate degree in HR with 72% marks. He has secured 56% marks in graduation. He was born on 12th May, 1977. He has secured 58% marks in the selection process.

25. Seema Behl has been working in the personnel department of an organisation for the past 7 yr after completing her post-graduate diploma in personnel management with 70% marks. She was born on 5th July, 1979. She has secured 65% marks in graduation and 50 % marks in the selection process.

DIRECTIONS ~(Q. Nos. 26-30) *Study the following information carefully and answer the questions given below.*

Following are the conditions for selecting Senior Manager Credit in a bank. The candidate must

(i) be a graduate in any discipline with atleast 60% marks.
(ii) have post qualification work experience of atleast 10 yr in the Advances Section of a bank.
(iii) be atleast 30 yr and not more than 40 yr on 1.4.2010.
(iv) have secured atleast 40% marks in the group discussion.
(v) have secured atleast 50% marks in interview.

In the case of a candidate who satisfies all the condition except.

(a) At (i) above but has secured atleast 50% marks in graduation and atleast 60% marks in post-graduation in any discipline the case is to be referred to the General Manager Advances.
(b) At (ii) above but has total post qualification work experience of atleast seven years out of which atleast three years as Manager Credit in a bank, the case is to be referred to Executive Director.

In each question below details of one candidate is given. You have to take one of the following courses of action based on the information provided and the conditions and sub-conditions given above and mark the number of that course of action as your answer.

You are not to assume anything other than the information provided in each question. All these cases are given to you as on 01.04.2010.

Give answer

(a) If the case is to be referred to Executive Director
(b) If the case is to be referred to General Manager Advances
(c) If the data are inadequate to take a decision
(d) If the candidate is not to be selected
(e) If the candidate is to be selected

26. Amrit Saini was born on 4th August, 1977. He has secured 65% marks in post graduation and 58% marks in graduation. He has been working for the past ten years in the Advances Department of a bank after completing his post graduation. He has secured 45% marks in the group discussion and 50% marks in the interview.

27. Raman Sharma was born on 28th May, 1974. He has been in the Advances Department of a bank for the past eleven years after completing his B. Sc. degree with 65% marks. He has secured 55% marks in the group discussion and 50% marks in the interview.

28. Ritesh Mehta has secured 50% marks in interview and 40% marks in the group discussion, he has been working for the past eight years out of which four years as Manager Credit in a bank after completing his B.A. degree with 60% marks. He was born on 12th September, 1978.

29. Ruchit Gupta was born on 8th March, 1974. He has been working in a bank for the past twelve years after completing his B. Com. degree with 70% marks. He has secured 50% marks in both the group discussion and the interview.

30. Kanika Saxena has been working in the Advances Department of a bank for the past twelve years after completing her B. Com. degree with 60% marks. She has secured 50% marks in the group discussion and 40% marks in the interview. She was born on 15th February, 1972.

DIRECTIONS ~ (Q. Nos. 31-37) *Study the following information carefully and answer the questions given below.* « UCO Bank PO 2010

Following are the condition for selecting marketing manager in an organisation.

The candidate must

(i) be a graduate in any discipline with atleast 55% marks.
(ii) have a post-graduate degree/diploma in marketing management with atleast 60% marks.
(iii) have post qualification work experience of atleast five years in the marketing division of an organisation.
(iv) have secured atleast 45% marks in the selection examination.
(v) have secured atleast 40% marks in the selection interview. In the case of a candidate, who satisfies all the conditions except
(a) at (iii) above but has post qualification work experience of atleast three years as deputy marketing manager, the case is to be referred to GM-Marketing.
(b) at (v) above, but has secured atleast 60% marks in the selection examination, the case is to be referred to VP-Marketing.

In each question below, details of one candidate are given. You have to take one of the following courses of action based on the information provided and the conditions and subconditions given above and mark the number of that courses of action as your answer. You are not to assume anything other than the information provided in each question. All these cases are given to you as on 01st May, 2010.

Give answer

(a) If the candidate is to be selected.
(b) If the candidate is not to be selected.
(c) If the case is to be referred to GM-Marketing.
(d) If the case is to be referred to VP-Marketing.
(e) If the data provided are not adequate to take a decisions.

31. Nidhi Agarwal has secured 60% marks in the selection interview and 40% marks in selection examination. She has been working in the marketing division of an organisation for the past 8 yr after completing her post-graduate degree in the marketing management with 65% marks. She has secured 59% marks is B.Sc.

32. Navin Desai has secured 56% marks in BA. He has been working in the marketing division of an organisation for the past 7 yr after completing his post-graduate degree in marketing with 62% marks. He has secured 62% marks in the selection examination and 38% marks in the selection interview.

33. Sabina Handa has been working for the past 4 yr as deputy marketing manager in an organisation after completing her post-graduate diploma in marketing management with 65% marks. She has secured 45% marks in both selection examination and selection interview. She has also secured 58% marks in B.Com.

34. Manoj Malhotra has secured 65% marks in B.Sc. and 60% marks in post-graduate degree in marketing management. He has also secured 50% marks in both selection examination and selection interview. He has been working in the marketing division of an organisation for the past 6 yr after completing his post-graduation in marketing.

35. Varsha Akolkar has secured 59% marks in BA. She has secured 42% marks in the selection interview and 48% marks in the selection examination. She has been working in the marketing division of an organisation for the past 7 yr after completing her post-graduation in marketing management with 57% marks.

36. Utpal Goswami has been working in the marketing division of an organisation for the past 5 yr after completing his post-graduate diploma in marketing management with 65% marks. he is a first class Science graduate with 60% marks. He has secured 45% marks in the selection examination and 40% marks in the selection interview.

37. Anindita Ghosh has been working for the past 8 yr in an organisation after completing her post-graduate degree in marketing management with 70% marks. She has secured 56% marks in BA. She has also secured 50% marks in the selection examination and 45% marks in the selection interview.

DIRECTIONS ~ (Q. Nos. 38-42) *Study the following information carefully and answer the questions given below. A company decided to appoint Content Manager (CM) to give a new impetus to its business. Following are the criteria laid down by the company.*

« IDBI Executive 2018

The candidate must have

(i) a graduate degree from a recognised university with at least 65% marks.
(ii) qualified in atleast 5 written examinations of Bank PO.
(iii) obtained atleast 60% marks in the written test (total marks = 200) conducting by the company.
(iv) obtained atleast 40% marks out of 75 marks in the interview for the above post conducted by the company.
(v) a working knowledge of computers.
(vi) completed 30 yr of age as on January 14, 2012.

However, in case of a candidate who fulfils all these criteria except.

1. (i) above, but is a graduate, is to be referred to the Director of the company.
2. (iii) above, is to be referred to the Assistant Vice-President of the company.

Based on the above criteria and the information given in each of the following cases, you have to take decision. You are not assume anything. In case you find that the given data is insufficient to make a decision, given 'data inadequate' as your answer. The cases are being given to you as on January 14, 2012.

Give answer

(a) If the candidates is to be selected as CM.
(b) If the candidate is not to be selected as CM.
(c) If the case is to be referred to the Director of the company.
(d) If the case is to be referred to the Assistant. Vice-President of the company.
(e) If the data are inadequate to take any decision

38. Surbhi Gaurav, was born on January 12, 1981, has done her graduation with 67% marks. It was the fifth interview for him when she appeared before the interview board constituted for Union Bank of India. She has a working knowledge of computers. She got 121 marks and 38 marks in the written examination and interview respectively, conducted by the company.

39. Vineet Pehal has a working knowledge of computers. He got 125 marks and 32 marks in the written examination and interview respectively, conducted by the company. When he appeared before the interview board for PO for Bank of India, it was his sixth interview for Bank PO. He performed a good dance on January 10, 2012, on the eve of the birthday of his sister, who is 8 yr younger than him.

40. Malik Aanand a talented working computer engineer, is 31 yr of age. He has already qualified six exams for Bank POs. He is a graduate with 65% marks. He got 60% marks in the interview and 40% marks in the written test conducted by the company for CM.

41. Shobha Vijay has a working knowledge of computers. She is a graduate with 65% marks. She has qualified five written examinations of Bank PO. She has obtained 40% marks and
60% marks in interview and written examinations respectively, conducted by the company for CM. For the last three years her age has been more than 18.

42. Alankrita Mangal is graduate with 65% marks. She has obtained 30 marks in the interview and 123 marks in the written examination conducted by the company, for CM. She is 32 yr old and possesses working knowledge of computers. She has given more than five interview of Bank Po.

DIRECTIONS ~(Q. Nos. 43-47) *Study the following information carefully and answer the questions given below.*

Following are the conditions for selection Senior. Manager-General Banking in bank.

The candidate must

(i) have secured atleast 60% marks in Std XII.
(ii) have secured atleast 55% marks in graduation in any discipline.
(iii) have secured atleast 60% marks in post-graduate degree/diploma in Management/ Economics/ Statistics.
(iv) be atleast 25 yr and not more than 35 yr as on 1st March, 2010.
(v) have post qualification work experience of atleast 2 yr as general banking officer in a bank.
(vi) have secured atleast 50% marks in the written examination.
(vii) have secured atleast 40% marks in the personal interview.

In the case of candidate, who satisfies all the above conditions except

(a) at (iii) above but has secured atleast 60% marks in CA or ICWA, the case is to be referred to VP-Recruitment.
(b) at (vii) above but has secured atleast 60% marks in the written examination and atleast 35% marks in the personal interview, the case is to be referred to President-Recruitment.

In each question below are given details of one candidate. You have to take one of the following courses of action based on the information provided and the conditions and subconditions given above and mark the number of that courses of action as your answer. You are not to assume anything other than the information provided in each question. All these cases are given to you as on 1st March, 2010.

Give answer

(a) If the data provided are inadequate to take a decision.
(b) If the case is to be referred to VP-Recruitment.
(c) If the case is to be referred to President-Recruitment.
(d) If the candidate is to be selected.
(e) If the candidate is not to be selected.

43. Kesav Vora was born on 8th November, 1978. He has secured 65% marks in Std XII and 60% marks in graduation. He has secured 58% marks in MA Economics and 60% marks in ICWA. He has been working in a bank as a generalist officer for the past 2 yr after completing his education. He has also secured 50% marks in the written examination and 45% marks in the personal interview.

44. Arindam Ghosh has been working in a bank as a generalist officer for the past 4yr after completing his post-graduate diploma in management with 60% marks. He has secured 50% marks in the written examination and 40% marks in the personal interview. He has also secured 70% marks in Std XII. He was born on 25th February, 1975.

45. Sohan Majhi has secured 65% marks in B.Sc. and 70% marks in M.Sc. Statistics. He has been working in bank as a generalist officer for the past 3 yr after completing his post-graduation. He has secured 55% marks in the written examination and 50% marks in the personal interview. He was born on 8th July, 1982.

46. Neha Salve has been working in bank as a generalist officer for the past 4 yr after completing her post-graduate degree in Economics with 60% marks. She has secured 60% marks in both graduation and Std XII. She was born on 24th August, 1979. She has secured 70% marks in the written examination and 38% marks in the personal interview.

47. Neeta Jaiswal was born on 2nd June, 1980. She has been working in bank as a generalist officer for the past 3 yr after completing her post-graduate degree in Economics with 60% marks. She has secured 68% marks in HSC and 58% marks in B.Com. She has also secured 50% marks in both the written examination and personal interview.

Directions (Q. Nos. 48-57) *Read the following information carefully and then answer the questions given below it.*

Following are the conditions for selecting a 'research officer' for a reputed research institution.

The candidate must

A. be a post-graduate with minimum 60% marks.
B. have Ph.D. degree.
C. have research experience of atleast 3 yr.
D. have fluency in Hindi and English.
E. have published atleat 5 research papers.
F. not be less than 25 yr and more than 35 yr as on 1st July, 1993.
G. have diploma in Statistical Applications.

In the case of a candidate who

(i) satisfies all other criteria except A above but has post-graduate degree with more than 55% marks, his case will be referred to the director of the institute.
(ii) satisfies all other criteria except C above will be referred to the join director.

Now, read the information provided in the case of the candidates in each of the questions given below and decide on the basis of the information provided and above conditions, which of the following courses of action is to be taken.

Give answer

(a) If candidate is to be referred to the director.
(b) If the data provided are inadequate to decide the courses of action.
(c) If the candidate is to be selected.
(d) If the candidate is to be referred to the joint director.
(e) If the candidate is not to be selected.

48. 28 yr old Sudhir has obtained his Ph.D. degree and is a post-graduate with 70% marks. He has diploma in Statistical Applications and research experience of 2 yr. He has got published 5 research papers and is fluent in English and Hindi.

49. 27 yr old Rajesh is a post-graduate with 61% marks and has obtained Ph.D. degree. He is fluent in Hindi and English. He has got 5 research papers published and has research experience of 4 yr. He has completed diploma in Statistical Applications.

50. 32yr old Vishal has obtained Ph.D. degree and diploma in Statistical Applications. He obtained 53% marks in post-graduation. He has research experience of 4 yr and has got published 6 research papers. He is fluent in English and Hindi.

51. Rahul is a post-graduate with 65% marks and has obtained Ph.D. degree. He is fluent in Hindi and English. He was born on 1st June, 1968. He has research experience of 4 yr and has published 6 research papers.

52. Anubhav is post-graduate with 62% marks. He has obtained Ph.D. degree and has published 5 research papers. He has research experience of $3\frac{1}{2}$ yr and fluent in Hindi and English. He has completed diploma in Statistical Applications. His date of birth is 1st September, 1968.

53. Sunder has obtained Ph.D. degree and diploma in Statistical Applications. He has 65% marks in post-graduation. He has research experience of 4 yr and has 6 research papers published. He is fluent in Hindi and English. His date of birth is 29th September, 1958.

54. Vasudha is post-graduate with 63% marks and has obtained Ph.D. degree and diploma in Statistical Applications. She is fluent in Hindi and English. She has research experience of $2\frac{1}{2}$ yr and has got 7 research papers published.

55. Radhey Raman is a post-graduate with 67% marks. He has obtained Ph.D. degree and diploma in Statistical Applications. He has research experience of 4 yr and has got 7 research papers published.

56. Chandrashekhar is post-graduate with 56% marks and has obtained Ph.D. degree. He is fluent in Hindi and English. He got 5 research papers published and has research experience of 4 yr. His date of birth is 1st September, 1958. He has obtained diploma in Statistical Applications.

57. 34 yr old Kumar is a post-graduate with 64% marks. He has obtained Ph.D. degree and diploma in Statistical Applications. He has research experience of 5 yr and has got 7 research papers published.

DIRECTIONS ~ (Q. Nos. 58-67) *Study the following information carefully and answer the questions given below.* « IDBI Bank PO 2014

Following are the conditions for selecting Manager Accounts in an organisation.

The candidate must

(i) be atleast 25 yr and not more than 35 yr as on 01.01.2010.

(ii) be a graduate in Commerce with atleast 55% marks.

(iii) be a post graduate in Commerce with atleast 60% marks.

(iv) have post qualification work experience of atleast 6 yr in the Accounts Department of an organisation.

(v) have secured atleast 45% marks in the personal interview.

In the case of a candidate who satisfies all the conditions except

(A) at (iii) above, but is an MBA-Finance with atleast 65% marks, the case is to be referred to GM-Accounts.

(B) at (iv) above, but is a CA/ICWA and has work experience of atleast 1 yr in an organisation, the case is to be referred to Executive Director.

In each question below, details of one candidate are provided. You have to take one of the following courses of actions based on the information provided and the conditions and subconditions and mark the number of that course of action as your answer. You are not required to assume anything other than the information provided in each question. All these cases are given to you as on 01.01.2010.

Give Answer

(a) If the case is to be referred to Executive Director.
(b) If the case is to be referred to GM-Accounts.
(c) If the data provided are not adequate to take a decision.
(d) If the candidate is to be selected.
(e) If the candidate is not to be selected.

58. Prashant Mishra has secured 60% in B. Com. and 65% marks in M.Com. He has been working in the Accounts department of an organisation for the past 7 yr after completing his M.Com. He has secured 50% marks in personal interview. His date of birth is 15.09.1984.

59. Samir Malhotra was born on 25th July 1982. He has been working in the Accounts department of an organisation for the past 6 yr after obtaining his M.Com. degree with 58% marks. He has secured 70% marks in B.Com. and 60% marks in personal interview.

60. Sudha Agarwal was born on 5th January, 1978. She has been working in the Accounts department of an organisation for the past 7 yr after obtaining her MBA in Finance with 70% marks. She has secured 68% marks in B.Com. and 52% marks in personal interview.

61. Arun Ramnathan has secured 62% marks in M.Com. and 58% marks in B.Com. He has been working in an organisation for the past 6 yr after completing his M.Com. He has secured 46% marks in the personal interview. His date of birth is 20th May, 1981.

62. Mohan Das was born on 8th February, 1980. He has been working for the past 2 yr in an organisation after completing his CA. He has secured 60% marks in both B.Com. and M.Com. He has secured 50% marks in personal interview.

63. Atul Ghosh has secured 65% marks in B.Com. and 65% marks in M.Com. He has been working for the past 8 yr in the Accounts department of an organisation after completing his M.Com. He was born on 12th march, 1981.

64. Seema Jaiswal was born on 19th January, 1978. She has secured 62% marks in both B.Com. and M.Com. She has been working in the Accounts department of an organisation for the past 6 yr after completing her M.Com. She has secured 48% marks in personal interview.

65. Navin Gosh has secured 68% marks in B.Com. and 57% marks in M.Com. He has been working in the Accounts department of an organisation for the past 7 yr after completing his M.Com. He has secured 47% marks in the personal interview.

66. Kapil Sonawane was born on 4th November, 1976. He has been working for the past 1 yr in an organisation after completing his ICWA. He has secured 65% marks in both B.Com. and M.Com. He has secured 60% marks in personal interview.

67. Sonam Khanna was born on 28th December, 1979. She has secured 62% marks in M.Com. She has been working for the past 8 yr in the Accounts department of an organisation after completing her MBA- Finance with 75% marks. She has secured 54% marks in B.Com. She has secured 60% marks in personal interview.

68. Study the following information carefully and answer the question given below. Following are the conditions for selecting Marketing manager in an organisation.

The candidate must

(i) be a Graduate in any discipline with atleast 55% marks.
(ii) have secured atleast 40% marks in the selection interview.
(iii) have post qualification work experience of atleast five years in the marketing division of an organisation.
(iv) have secured atleast 45% marks in the selection examination.
(v) have a post Graduate degree/diploma in Marketing-Managment with at least 60% marks.

Study the following information carefully and find which of the following condition show candidate is not selected?

(a) Candidate is daughter of a renowned freedom fighter from another state.
(b) Candidate has a post Graduate degree in Finance with 60% marks.
(c) Candidate has completed his graduation with 80% marks.
(d) Candidate does not own a house in Noida
(e) Candidate has secured 56% marks in cap Gemini's interview.

DIRECTION ~ (Q. Nos. 69-71) *Following are the conditions for the selection of Head Coach for Indian Cricket Team. The conditions are* « UP SI 2017

(i) Candidate should have successfully coached a cricket team of any of the member countries of the International Cricket Council (ICC), at the first class or at the international level.
(ii) Candidate should be qualified through a certification/ assessment program conducted by any of the full member countries and should currently possess such a valid certification.
(iii) Communication skills benefitting the coach of an international team are mandatory along with the ability to effectively convey the light massage and must demonstrate proficiency in English.
(iv) Candidate should have an impeccable personal record, devoid of any past or current disputes, with any of the member boards of the ICC or its affiliates.

A person is selected as Head Coach of Indian Cricket team, if he fulfils the above criteria except,

A. If the candidate does not fulfil anyone of the criteria and his name is asked to be included by all of the 3 cricket Advisory committee members then he can be selected as Head Coach.
B. Candidate doesn't have any coaching experience, but he was a caption of International Cricket Council (ICC) world cup wining team then he may be referred to the Board of Control for Cricket in India (BCCI) secretary.
C. Candidate doesn't have proficiency in English but he is able to communicate in Hindi and other regional Indian Languages then he may be referred to the Cricket Advisory committee members.

69. What is the decision to be taken in his case?

Jaffer has coached the Indian Railways team in the first class cricket and has the certification of the ICC and is well versed in English communication and he has no records of disputes.

(a) Data inadequate.
(b) The candidate is not be selected.
(c) The candidate is to be selected.
(d) Referred to the cricket Advisory committee members/BCCI secretary.

70. What is the decision to be taken in his case?

Pandey is a player in Indian team and has no experience in coaching any of the team. But his name is included by all of the 3 cricket advisory committee members.

(a) Referred to the cricket Advisory committee members/BCCI secretary.
(b) The candidate is not to be selected.
(c) Data inadequate.
(d) The candidate is to be selected.

71. What is the decision to be taken in his case?

Surya Rahul has coached Mumbai team in the domestic cricket and has the certification of the ICC and he doesn't have proficiency in English but he is able to communicate in Hindi and regional languages.

(a) The candidate is not to be selected.
(b) The candidate is to be selected.
(c) Data inadequate.
(d) Referred to the cricket Advisory committee members/BCCI secretary.

Answers / WITH EXPLANATIONS

1. (b) P fulfils all the criteria, so he will be definitely selected.

Solutions (Q. Nos. 2-6)

Q. Nos.	Candidates	A	B (ii)	C	D (i)	Answers
2.	Sweta	✓	✓	✓	✓	d
3.	Miss Anu	✓	?	✓	✓	c
4.	Pinki	✓	✗	—	—	e
5.	Kiran	✓	(✓)	✓	✓	b
6.	Reena	✓	✓	?	✓	c

2. (*d*) ***3.*** (*c*) ***4.*** (*e*)
5. (*b*) ***6.*** (*c*)

Solutions (Q. Nos. 7-15)

Q. Nos.	Candidates	A (i)	B	C	D (ii)	Answers
7.	Sachin	✓	✓	✓	(✓)	b
8.	Anjali	✗	—	—	—	e
9.	Mohan	✓	?	✓	✓	d
10.	K Shiv Kumar	✓	(✓)	✓	✓	c
11.	Rajeev	✓	(✓)	✓	✓	c
12.	Nachiket	✓	✓	✓	(✓)	b
13.	Nikita	✓	✓	✓	(✓)	b
14.	Vinod	✓	✓	✓	(✓)	a
15.	Aniket	✗	✓	✓	(✓)	e

7. (*b*) ***8.*** (*e*) ***9.*** (*d*)
10. (*c*) ***11.*** (*c*) ***12.*** (*b*)
13. (*b*) ***14.*** (*a*) ***15.*** (*e*)

Solutions (Q. Nos. 16-20)

Q. Nos.	Candidates	(i)	(ii)	(iii)	(iv)	(v)	a	b	Answers
16.	Suneeta	✓	✓	✓	✓	✓			d
17.	Rakesh	✓	✓	✓	–	✓		✓	a
18.	Ramkumar	✓	✓	✓	–	✓		✓	a
19.	Nishant	–	✓	✓	✓	✓			c
20.	Kalyani	✗	?	✓	✓	✓			e

16. (d) ***17.*** (a) ***18.*** (a)
19. (c) ***20.*** (e)

Solutions (Q. Nos. 21-25)

Q. Nos.	Candidates	(i)	(ii) (a)	(iii)	(iv) (b)	(v)	Answers
21.	Rita	✓	✓	?	✓	✓	b
22.	Ashok	✓	✓	✓	(✓)	✓	c
23.	Alok	✗	—	—	—	—	a
24.	Swapan	✓	✓	✓	✓	✓	d
25.	Seema	✓	✓	✓	✓	✓	e

21. (*b*) ***22.*** (*c*) ***23.*** (*a*)
24. (*d*) ***25.*** (*e*)

Solutions (Q. Nos. 26-30)

Q. Nos.	Candidates	(i) (a)	(ii) (b)	(iii)	(iv)	(v)	Answer
26	Amrit Saini	(✓)	✓	✓	✓	✓	b
27	Raman Sharma	✓	✓	✓	✓	✓	e
28	Ritesh Mehta	✓	(✓)	✓	✓	✓	a
29	Ruchit Gupta	✓	–	✓	✓	✓	c
30	Kanika Sexena	✓	✓	✓	✓	✗	d

26. (b) ***27.*** (e) ***28.*** (a)
29. (c) ***30.*** (d)

Solutions (Q. Nos. 31-37)

Q. Nos.	Candidates	(i)	(ii)	(iii) (a)	(iv)	(v) (b)	Answers
31.	Nidhi	✓	✓	✓	✗		b
32.	Navin	✓	✓	✓	✓	(✓)	d
33.	Sabina	✓	✓	(✓)	✓	✓	c
34.	Manoj	✓	✓	✓	✓	✓	a
35.	Varsha	✓	✗	—	—	—	b
36.	Utpal	✓	✓	✓	✓	✓	a
37.	Anindita	✓	✓	?	✓	✓	e

31. (*b*) ***32.*** (*d*) ***33.*** (*c*)
34. (*a*) ***35.*** (*b*) ***36.*** (*a*)
37. (*e*)

Solutions (Q. Nos. 38-42) *According to the given information*

Q. Nos.	Candidates	(i) or	(1)	(ii)	(iii) or	(2)	(iv)	(v)	(vi)	Answers
38.	Surbhi Gaurav	✓	—	—	✓	—	✓	✓	✓	e
39.	Vineet Pehal	—	—	✓	✓	—	✓	✓	—	e
40.	Malik Aanand	✓	—	✓	✗	✓	✓	✓	✓	d
41.	Shobha Vijay	✓	—	✓	✓	—	✓	✓	—	e
42.	Alankrita Mangal	✓	—	✓	✓	—	✓	✓	✓	a

38. (e) ***39.*** (e)
40. (d) ***41.*** (e)
42. (a)

Solutions (Q. Nos. 43-47)

Q. Nos.	Candidates	i	ii	iii (a)	iv	v	vi	vii (b)	Answers
43.	Kesav	✓	✓	(✓)	✓	✓	✓	✓	b
44.	Arindam	✓	?	✓	✗	✓	✓	✓	e
45.	Sohan	?	✓	✓	✓	✓	✓	✓	a
46.	Neha	✓	✓	✓	✓	✓	✓	(✓)	c
47.	Neeta	✓	✓	✓	✓	✓	✓	✓	d

43. (*b*) **44.** (*e*) **45.** (*a*) **46.** (*c*) **47.** (*d*)

Solutions (Q. Nos. 48-57)

Q. Nos.	Candidates	A (i)	B	C (ii)	D	E	F	G	Answers
48.	Sudhir	✓	✓	(✓)	✓	✓	✓	✓	d
49.	Rajesh	✓	✓	✓	✓	✓	✓	✓	c
50.	Vishal	(✗)	-	-	-	-	-	-	e
51.	Rahul	✓	✓	✓	✓	✓	✓	?	b
52.	Anubhav	✓	✓	✓	✓	✓	✗	-	e
53.	Sunder	✓	✓	✓	✓	✓	✓	✓	c
54.	Vasudha	✓	✓	?	✓	✓	?	✓	b
55.	Radhey	✓	✓	✓	?	✓	?	✓	b
56.	Chandrashekhar	(✓)	✓	✓	✓	✓	✓	✓	a
57.	Kumar	✓	✓	✓	?	✓	✓	✓	b

48. (*d*) **49.** (*c*) **50.** (*e*) **51.** (*b*) **52.** (*e*) **53.** (*c*)
54. (*b*) **55.** (*b*) **56.** (*a*) **57.** (*b*)

Solutions (Q. Nos. 58-67) *All the information can be summarised as in the given table.*

Q. Nos.	Name	Conditions fulfilled							Answers
		(i) Age 25-35 yr on 1-1-10	(ii) Gradu. in Comm ≥55%	(iii) PG Comm ≥60%	(iii)/(A) MBA-F ≥65%	(iv) Work Exp ≥6 yr	(iv)/(B) CA/ICWA+1 yr Exp.	(v) Interview 45%	
58.	Prashant Mishra	✓	✓	✓	—	✓	—	✓	d
59.	Samir Malhotra	✓	✓	✗	—	✓	—	✓	e
60.	Sudha Agarwal	✓	✓	—	✓	✓	—	✓	b
61.	Arun Ramnathan	✓	✓	✓	—	—	—	✓	c
62	Mohan Das	✓	✓	✓	—	✗	✓	✓	a
63.	Atul Ghosh	✓	✓	✓	—	✓	—	—	c
64.	Seema Jaiswal	✓	✓	✓	—	✓	—	✓	d
65.	Navin Ghosh	—	✓	✗	—	✓	—	✓	e
66.	Kapil Sonawane	✓	✓	✓	—	✗	✓	✓	a
67.	Sonam Khanna	✓	✗	✓	✓	✓	—	✓	e

58. (*d*) **59.** (*e*) **60.** (*b*) **61.** (*c*) **62.** (*a*) **63.** (*c*) **64.** (*d*)
65.(*e*) **66.** (*a*) **67.** (*e*) **68.** (*b*)

Solutions (Q. Nos. 69-71) *All the infor*

Q. Nos.	Candidate	(i)	(ii)	(iii)	(iv)	A	B	C	Answers
69.	Jaffer	✓	✓	✓	✓				c
70.	Pandey	✗	?	?	?	✓			c
71.	Surya Rahul	✓	✓	✗	?			✓	c

69. (c) **70.** (c) **71.** (c)

CHAPTER / 24

Verification of Truth of the Statement

Examining the reality of a statement based on practical knowledge is called "Verification of Truth of the Statement".

In the questions asked from this chapter, an event/sentence is given in the form of a statement.

The candidates are required to carefully read the given statement and determine on the basis of their practical knowledge, what is the reality of the statement or what is most necessary for the sentence given in the statement.

In other words, candidates are required to stress only on truth of facts that always hold.

Generally two types of questions are asked from this chapter.

TYPE 01

Questions Based on the Reality of the Event

In this type of questions, an incident is given in the form of a statement. On the basis of this event, it is asked whether the given event is always or often or sometimes happens or never happens.

***Ex* 01** A boy is sitting at the back seat of a car. When the driver suddenly starts moving the car (in forward direction), the boy experiences a backward force.

(a) Always
(b) Never
(c) Often
(d) Sometimes

***Solution* (a)** When a car suddenly starts, then anyone will always experience backward force because the lower part of the body will be in the motion while the uppero part of the body will be at rest.

***Ex* 02** If we are going early in the morning towards the South, the Sun will be visible at our left.

(a) Always (b) Never (c) Often (d) Sometimes

***Solution* (a)** Early in the morning the Sun rises in the East. Now, if we are going towards South, then our face will be in South direction and our left hand will be in East direction. Hence, the Sun will be visible at our left.

TYPE 02

Questions Based on Best Choice

In this type of questions, a sentence is given in the form of a statement. The candidates have to determine that what is required for an object in this statement? In these questions while choosing the correct option the candidate should use his practical knowledge.

***Ex* 03** A school always has « RRB ALP 2018

(a) Teacher (b) Principal
(c) Building (d) Library

***Solution* (a)** A school may not have a principal, building or library but it is compulsory to have a teacher.

***Ex* 04** A pen always has

(a) Tube (b) Cap
(c) Holder (d) Nib

***Solution* (d)** A nib is a necessary part of a pen.

***Ex* 05** Which one of the following is always associated with 'tree'?

(a) Flowers (b) Leaves
(c) Fruits (d) Roots

***Solution* (d)** A tree may not have flowers, leaves or fruits but a tree must have roots.

Practice / CORNER

DIRECTIONS ~ (Q. Nos. 1-16) *In each of the following questions an event is given. Read the questions carefully and choose the correct option.*

1. Gold is more valuable than silver. « RRB ALP 2018
(a) Sometimes (b) Often (c) Always (d) Never

2. There are four elephants in the game of chess. « RRB ALP 2018
(a) Always (b) Sometimes
(c) Often (d) Never

3. Sun rises in the West early in the morning.
(a) Always (b) Sometimes
(c) Often (d) Never

4. A boy going to Luna bending forward when hitting a break.
(a) Sometimes (b) Never
(c) Often (d) Always

5. Yesterday, i saw an ice cube which had already melted due to heat of a nearby furnace.
(a) Always (b) Never
(c) Often (d) Sometimes

6. The main function of Rajya Sabha is to implement the law.
(a) Never (b) Sometimes
(c) Often (d) Always

7. A piece of ice floats on water.
(a) Often (b) Sometimes
(c) Never (d) Always

8. My ten years old niece is taller than my twelve years old son.
(a) Always (b) Never
(c) Often (d) Sometimes

9. In barter, exchange of goods takes place.
(a) Often (b) Sometimes
(c) Always (d) Never

10. In India, a widow can marry her brother-in-law although a man cannot marry the sister of his dead wife.
(a) Always (b) Never
(c) Often (d) Sometimes

11. A library has computer.
(a) Never (b) Always
(c) Often (d) None of these

12. A mobile has cover.
(a) Always (b) Never
(c) Often (d) None of these

13. A computer has CPU.
(a) Always (b) Sometimes
(c) Never (d) None of these

14. A knife has an edge.
(a) Always (b) Sometimes
(c) Never (d) None of these

15. A hospital has doctor.
(a) Always (b) Never
(c) Often (d) Sometimes

16. An elephant has a trunk.
(a) Always (b) Sometimes
(c) Never (d) None of these

DIRECTIONS ~ (Q. Nos. 17-35) *In each of the following questions a statement is given. Read the question carefully and choose the correct option.*

17. A mirror always
(a) Reflects (b) Retracts
(c) Distorts (d) Refracts

18. A book always has
(a) Chapters (b) Pages
(c) Words (d) Pictures

19. A factory always has
(a) Electricity (b) Chimney
(c) Workers (d) Files

20. Atmosphere always has
(a) Oxygen (b) Air
(c) Germs (d) Moisture

21. A hill always exists « FCI 2018
(a) Height (b) Way (c) Tree (d) Water

22. A shirt always has « RRB ALP 2018
(a) Button (b) Cloth
(c) Collar (d) Pocket

23. A bank always has
(a) Manager (b) Locker
(c) Account holder (d) ATM

24. The office always has « RRB ALP 2018
(a) Kitchen (b) Roof
(c) Officers (d) Car

25. A train always has
(a) Engine (b) Driver
(c) Guard (d) Passengers

26. A fan always has
(a) Switch (b) Blades
(c) Current (d) Wiro

27. All animals have
(a) Eyes (b) Four legs
(c) Horns (d) Instincts

28. A disease always has
(a) Cure (b) Medicine
(c) Cause (d) Germs

29. A diamond has
(a) Hardness (b) Brilliance
(c) Use (d) Conductivity

30. A jail always has
(a) Bars (b) Jailor
(c) Lawyer (d) Locks

31. A camera always has
(a) Lens (b) Reels
(c) Flash (d) Photograph

32. Which of the following is always with bargain?
(a) Sumptuousness (b) Exchange
(c) Triviality (d) Eloquence

33. A newspaper always has
(a) Advertisement (b) News
(c) Editor (d) Paper

34. Cricket always has
(a) Stumps (b) Pitch
(c) Glove (d) Bat

35. The dead have no
(a) Sensation (b) Heartbeats
(c) Movement (d) Breathing

Answers / WITH EXPLANATIONS

1. (*c*) Gold is always more valuable than silver.

2. (*a*) The game of chess always consists of four elephants i.e. two White and two Black.

3. (*d*) We know that the Sun always rises in the East. Therefore, Sun never rises in the West.

4. (*d*) If we hit a break in a moving object, then the person sitting in it will bend forward.

5. (*b*) Since, the ice cube has already melted, so after this ice can not remain as ice cube.

6. (*a*) To implement the law is not the function of Rajya Sabha.

7. (*d*) We know that the density of ice is less than the density of water, thats why the piece of ice floats on water.

8. (*d*) The height of a person depends on various factors along with age. Hence, sometimes it can be possible that the height of any person will be more than the height of any person who elder to him/her.

9. (*c*) Barter means exchange of goods. Hence, option (c) is correct.

10. (*d*) As there is no tradition. Hence, this will happen sometimes.

11. (*c*) A computer is necessary for library. But it doesn't mean that every library must have computer. Hence, sometimes a library has a computer.

12. (*c*) Often a mobile has a cover.

13. (*a*) We know that the CPU is an integral part of computer. Hence, a computer always has CPU.

14. (*a*) A knife always has edge.

15. (*a*) A hospital always has doctor.

16. (*a*) An elephant is recognised by his trunk. So, an elephant always has a trunk.

17. (*a*) A mirror always reflects.

18. (*b*) A book can be without words i.e. it may have only picture. Similarly, it may have only words. Also, it can be possible to have a book without chapters. But it cannot be possible to have a book without pages.

19. (*c*) A factory may not have electricity, chimney or files. But it is not possible to have a factory without workers.

20. (*b*) The air is most vital part of atmosphere. Without air there can be no atmosphere.

21. (*a*) It can be possible that there is no tree, water or way on a hill but a hill always has height.

22. (*b*) A shirt always has cloth. A shirt may not have button, collar or pocket.

23. (*c*) A bank may not have manager, locker or ATM. But a bank always has account holders.

24. (*c*) An office can not be an office without its officers.

25. (*d*) A train may not have driver, guard or passenger but to run a train must have an engine.

26. (*b*) Fan cannot be a fan without its blades.

27. (*d*) All animals have instincts.

28. (*c*) There is always a cause behind any disease.

29. (*a*) A diamond always has hardness.

30. (*d*) A jail cannot be a jail without locks.

31. (*a*) A camera may not have reels, flash or photograph. But it always contains lens.

32. (*b*) Exchange is always with bargain.

33. (*b*) A newspaper may not have advertisement, editor or paper. But it always contains news.

34. (*d*) Bat is necessary to play cricket.

35. (*c*) Any dead object can not have any movement.

A New Approach to

REASONING

NON-VERBAL REASONING

CHAPTER / 01

Series

A series is described as a sequential arrangement of figures following a certain pattern of transition from one element to other.

Each next figure in the series is obtained from the previous figure by clockwise or anti-clockwise rotation, movement of symbols inside the figure, addition or deletion of designs, replacement or rearrangement of designs etc.

In order to solve these questions candidates must have a clear vision of the concepts like rotation, angles, steps of movement, etc., as these concepts are utilised for identifying the correct answer figure that will complete the given series of figures.

Concept of Rotation

The movement of a block (figure) around a fixed point is known as rotation. The simplest example of rotation is the movement of hour and minute hands of the clock. Such movements are of two types.

1. **Clockwise Rotation** When a figure rotates in the direction of the hands of a clock, then this rotation/ movement is called clockwise rotation. This can be better understood with the help of direction of arrows.

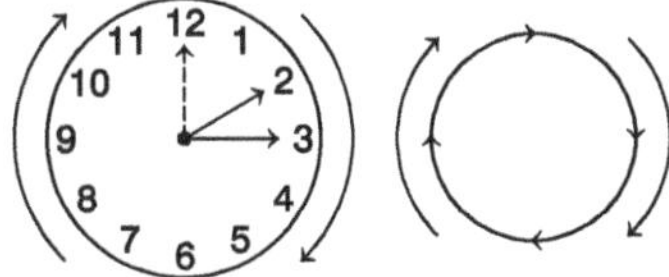

Clockwise rotation

2. **Anti-clockwise Rotation** When a figure rotates in the opposite direction of the hands of a clock, then this rotation movement is known as anti-clockwise rotation. This can be understood with the help of direction of arrows.

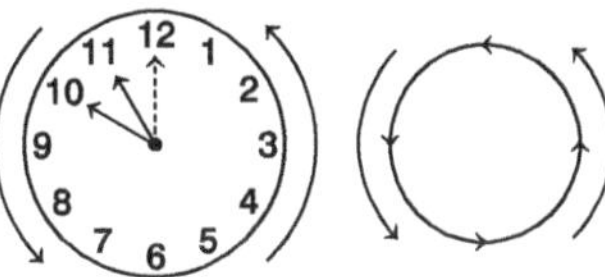

Anti-clockwise rotation

Concept of Angles

The figures are rotated either clockwise or anti-clockwise by a certain angle. The concept of angles can be better understood with the help of following figures where the dotted line shows the original/initial position, dark line shows the final position and the direction of arrow shows the direction of rotation.

Angle	Clockwise Rotation	Anti-Clockwise Rotation
45°	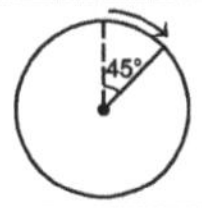 45°	 45°
90°	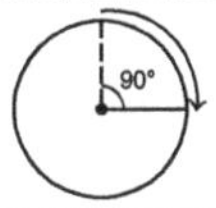 90°	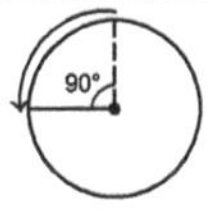 90°
135°	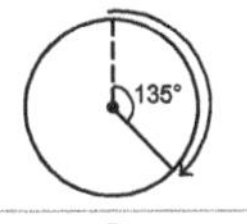 135°	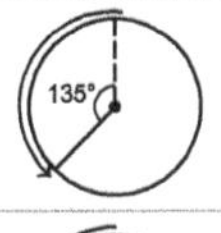 135°
180°	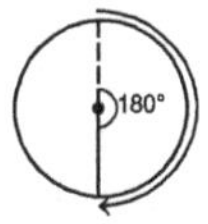 180°	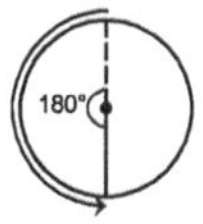 180°
225°	 225°	 225°

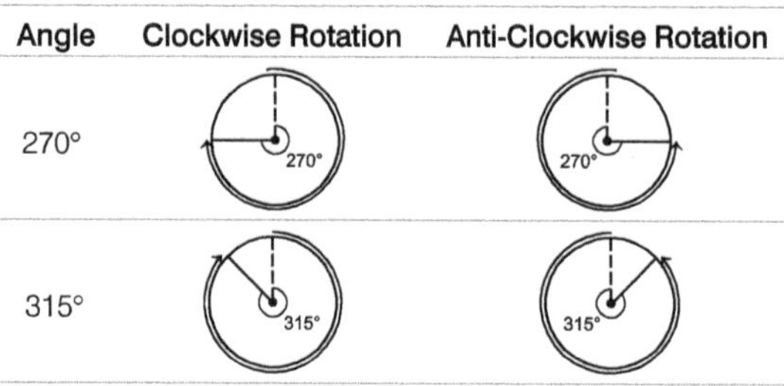

Concept of Steps

In some type of questions based on series, the whole figure is not rotated to obtain the another figure but one or more than one elements/symbols inside the figure moves some steps in an orderly manner to obtain the subsequent figures. So, it is required to have a clear understanding, about the concept of steps.

As we have already understood the concept of angles, we can extend the concept of angles to explain the concept of steps.

Let us consider the following two figures

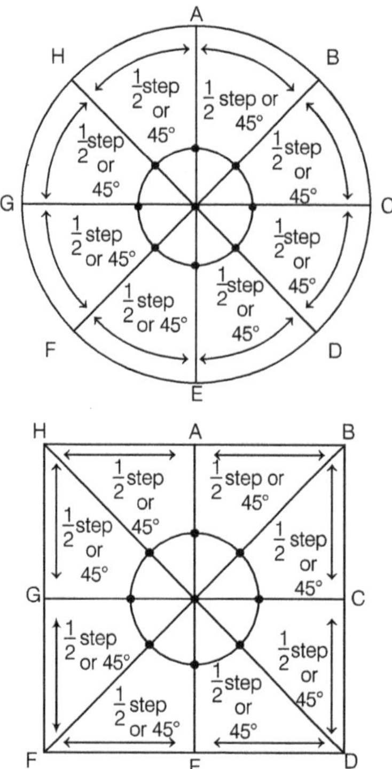

From the above figures, it is clear that the length of arc or side corresponding to 45° is taken as half step.

So, $\frac{1}{2}$ step = 45°

Now, we can calculate some more steps as given below

$\left(\frac{1}{2}+\frac{1}{2}\right)$ steps $= 45° + 45°$ $\Rightarrow$ 1 step $= 90°$

$\left(1+\frac{1}{2}\right)$ steps $= 90° + 45°$ $\Rightarrow$ $1\frac{1}{2}$ steps $= 135°$

$\left(1\frac{1}{2}+\frac{1}{2}\right)$ steps $= 135° + 45°$ $\Rightarrow$ 2 steps $= 180°$

$\left(2+\frac{1}{2}\right)$ steps $= 180° + 45°$ $\Rightarrow$ $2\frac{1}{2}$ steps $= 225°$

$\left(2\frac{1}{2}+\frac{1}{2}\right)$ steps $= 225° + 45°$ $\Rightarrow$ 3 steps $= 270°$

$\left(3+\frac{1}{2}\right)$ steps $= 270° + 45°$ $\Rightarrow$ $3\frac{1}{2}$ steps $= 315°$

$\left(3\frac{1}{2}+\frac{1}{2}\right)$ steps $= 315° + 45°$ $\Rightarrow$ 4 steps $= 360°$

Let us consider the following series of figures

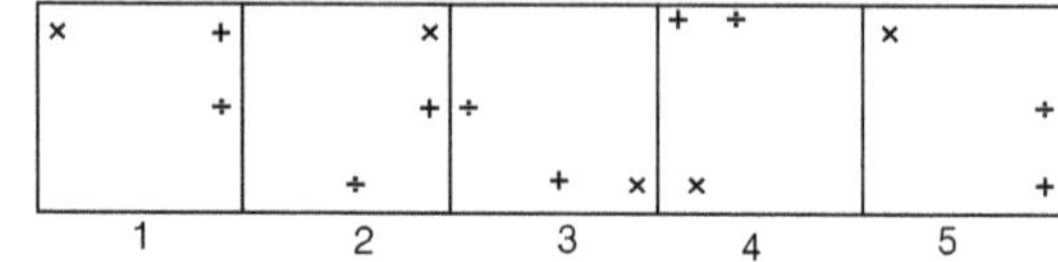

In the above series, the symbols/elements '×' and '+' move one step clockwise in the each subsequent figure while the symbol '+' moves $\frac{1}{2}$, 1, $1\frac{1}{2}$ and 2 steps clockwise in each subsequent figure.

Patterns Involved in Series Formation

The most commonly applied patterns for the formation of a series are as follows

A. Clockwise or Anti-clockwise Rotation of Designs

In this type of questions, each preceding figure in the series is rotated at a certain angle either in clockwise or anti-clockwise direction to obtain the subsequent figure. This rotation of figures can be done either by same angle or by some different angles in an orderly manner.

This concept can be better understood with the help of following examples

DIRECTIONS ~ (Example Nos. 1 and 2) *In the sequence given below, which answer figure will come next?*

***Ex* 01** **Problem Figures**

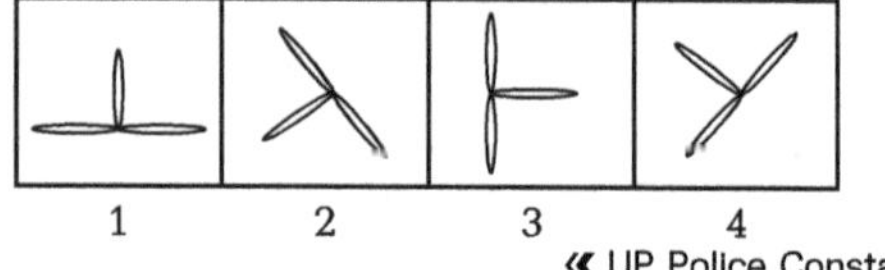

« UP Police Constable 2014

Answer Figures

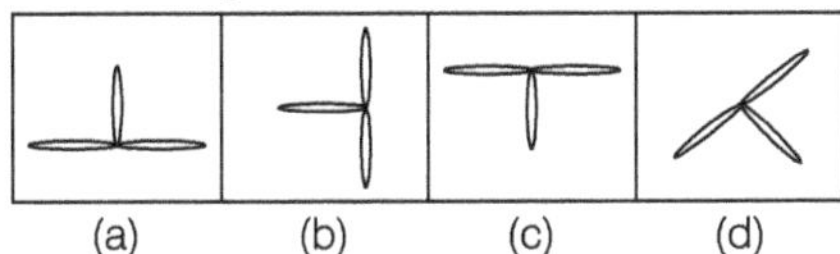

(a) (b) (c) (d)

Solution (c) It is clear from the sequence given in problem figures, the whole figure is rotating 135° anti-clockwise in each successive step. Hence, the answer figure (c) will be the next in the given series.

***Ex* 02 Problem Figures**

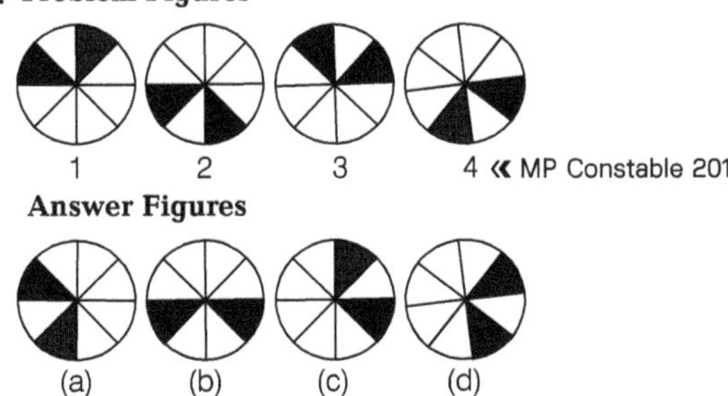

« MP Constable 2017

Solution (a) After careful analysis of the problem figures, we find that in each subsequent figure, the shaded portions are moving 3, 4, 5 and 6 steps respectively in anti-clockwise direction.

DIRECTIONS ~ (Example Nos. 3 and 4) *In each of the following questions, a group of five figures following a certain sequence is given as problem figures. Problem figures are followed by another group of four/five figures known as answer figures marked as* (a), (b), (c), (d) *and* (e). *Find out the figure from the answer figures which when placed next to the problem figures will continue the sequence of problem figures.*

***Ex* 03 Problem Figures**

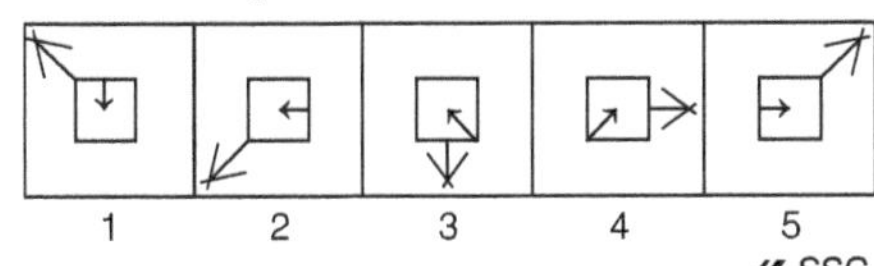

1 2 3 4 5

« SSC Steno 2019

Answer Figures

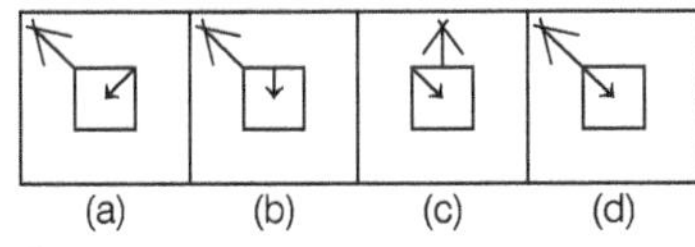

(a) (b) (c) (d)

Solution (b) It is clear from the problem figures that the outer arrow rotates through an angle of 90° and 45° anti-clockwise alternatively and inner arrow rotates through an angle of 90° and 45° clockwise in alternate blocks.

***Ex* 04**

Problem Figures

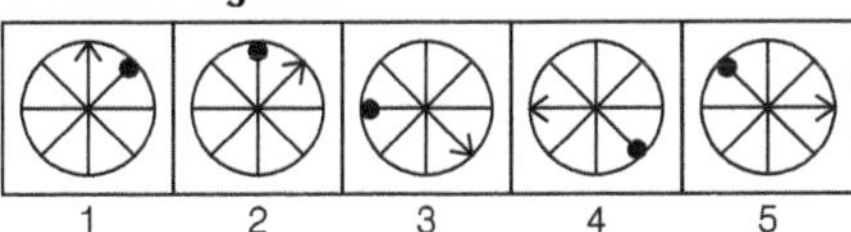

1 2 3 4 5

Answer Figures

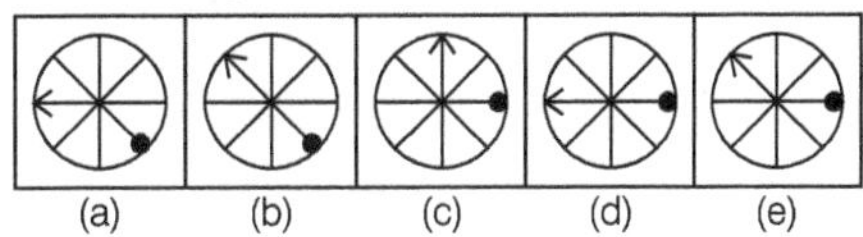

(a) (b) (c) (d) (e)

Solution (e) It is clear from the problem figure that the arrow rotates clockwise making an angle of 45°, 90°, 135° and 180° in each subsequent block and the dot rotates in the same way but in anti-clockwise direction. Thus, in answer figure, the arrow and dot will rotate by an angle of 225° in clockwise and anti-clockwise direction with respect to figure (1).

Hence, answer figure (e) will continue the given sequence.

B. Addition and Deletion of Designs/Lines

In this type of questions, each subsequent figure of the series is obtained by addition and /or deletion of designs/lines in the preceding figure. Sometimes this addition and/ or deletion of designs/lines can also take place along with the rotation of figures.

Following examples will give a better understanding of this concept

***Ex* 05** Which option will replace the question mark and complete the given figure series? « SSC Constable 2018

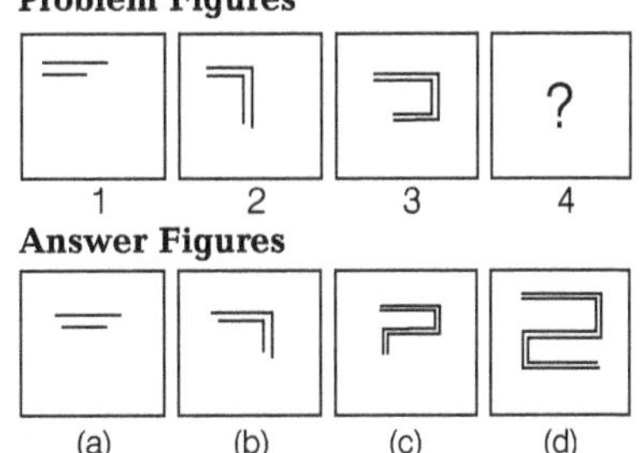

Solution (c) In each successive figure, the number of straight lines is increasing by 2 in a set pattern. Therefore, the last figure in problem figures will have 8 straight lines.

DIRECTIONS ~ (Example Nos. 6-8) *In each of the following questions, a group of five figures following a certain sequence is given as problem figures. Problem figures are followed by another group of five figures known as answer figures marked as* (a), (b), (c), (d) *and* (e). *Find out the figure from the answer figures which when placed next to the problem figures will continue the sequence of problem figures.*

***Ex* 06 Problem Figures**

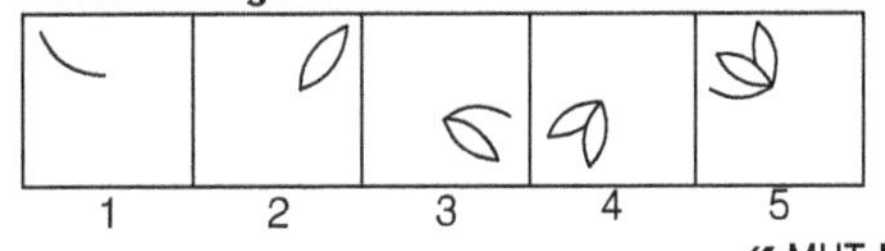

1 2 3 4 5

« MHT MBA 2017

Answer Figures

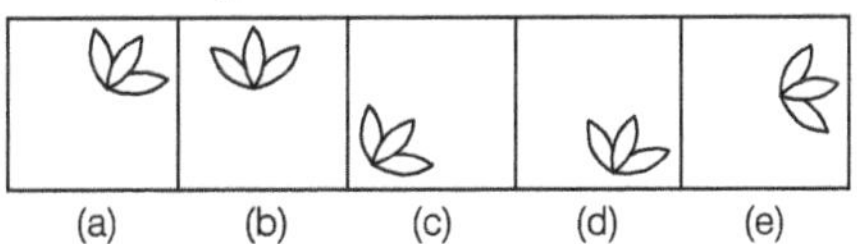

(a) (b) (c) (d) (e)

***Solution* (a)** In each successive block, the figure rotates 90° in clockwise direction and also a new arc is added in each step.

***Ex* 07**

Problem Figures

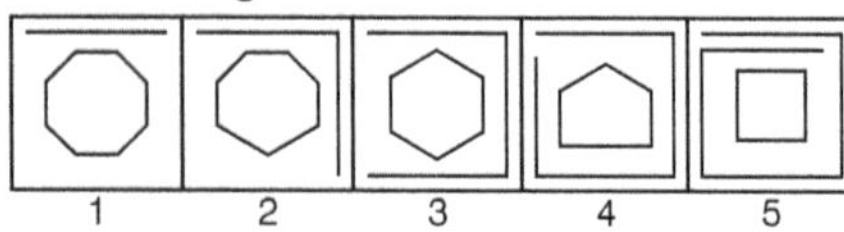

Answer Figures

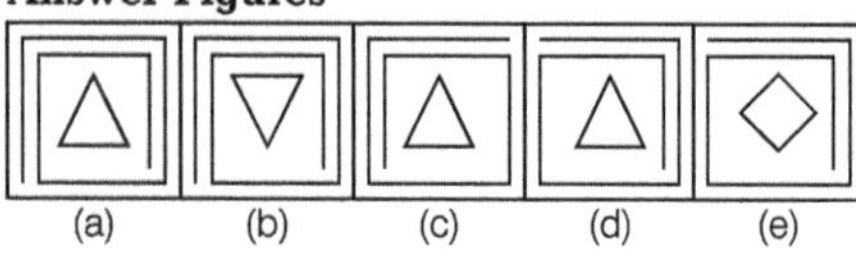

***Solution* (d)** The number of sides in the outer figure is increased by one in clockwise directions and number of sides in the inner figure is decreased by one in each subsequent block.

***Ex* 08**

Problem Figures

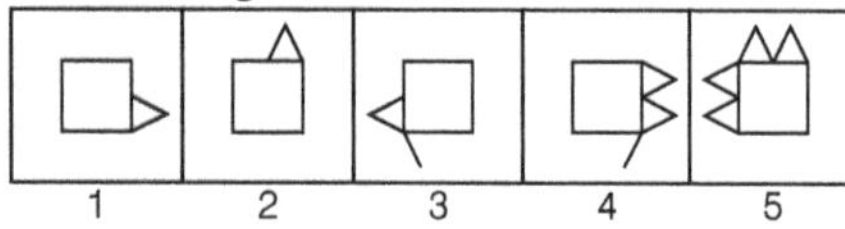

Answer Figures

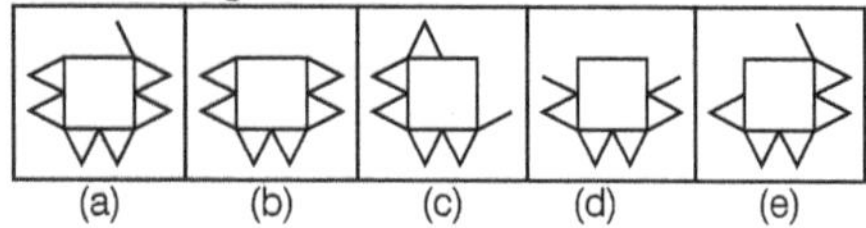

***Solution* (b)** In each subsequent figure, 0, 1, 2, 3,...lines are added in anti-clockwise and clockwise directions alternatively.

C. Replacement and Rearrangement of Designs

In this type of questions, each subsequent figure of the series is obtained when the designs inside the preceding figure are replaced by new designs or the position of the designs are rearranged with some modifications or alterations. Sometimes this replacement and rearrangement of designs can also take place along with the rotation and addition/deletion of the design.

Following examples will give a better understanding of this concept

***Ex* 09** Which of the following answer figures will continue the series made by problem figures?

Problem Figures

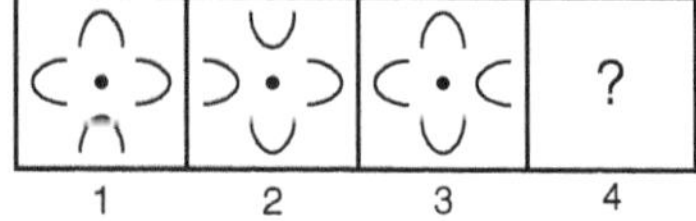

Answer Figures

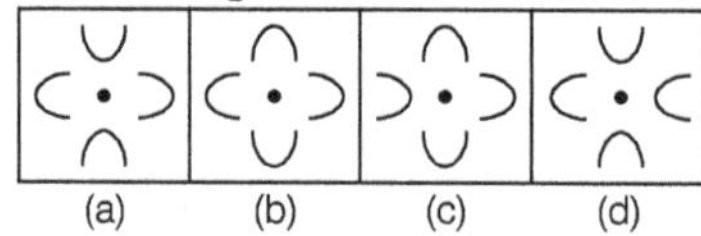

***Solution* (a)** In each subsequent figure of problem figures, three designs are inverted respectively in anti-clockwise direction. So, following the same pattern answer figure (a) will be the correct, figure for the next block.

DIRECTIONS ~ (Example Nos. 10 and 11) *In each of the following questions, a group of five figures following a certain sequence is given as problem figures. Problem figures are followed by another group of five figures known as answers figures marked as* (a), (b), (c), (d) *and* (e). *Find out the figure from the answer figures which when placed next to the problem figures will continue the sequence of problem figures.*

***Ex* 10**

Problem Figures

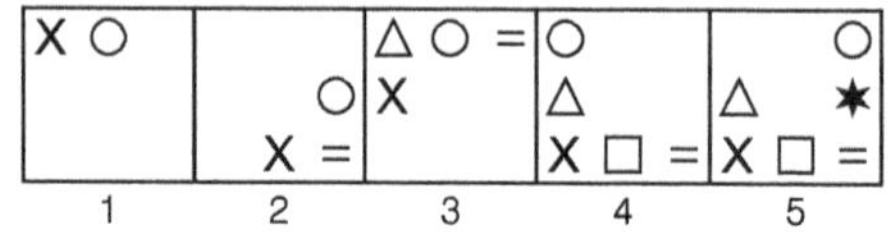

Answer Figures

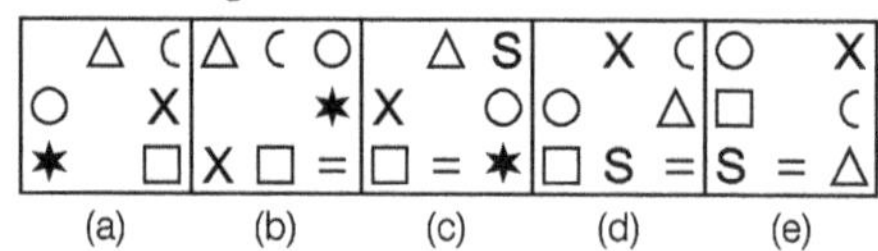

***Solution* (c)** Symbols of each block of problem figures are moving clockwise in such a way that first symbol moves one side and is immediately preceded by new symbol in subsequent block and the second symbol moves $2\frac{1}{2}$, 3, $3\frac{1}{2}$, 4 and $4\frac{1}{2}$ sides in subsequent blocks. Hence, first symbol (Δ) of problem figure (5) will move one side and will be preceded by new symbol and second symbol (X) will move $4\frac{1}{2}$ side.

***Ex* 11**

Problem Figures

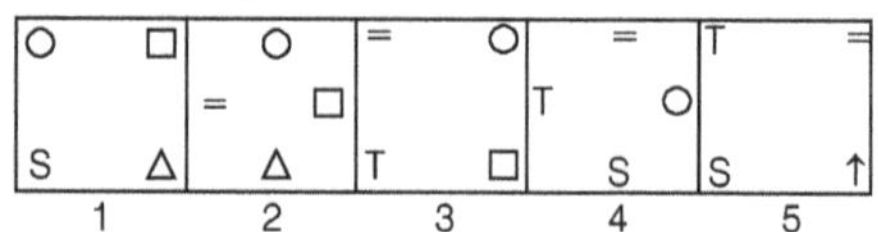

« MHT MBA 2017

Answer Figures

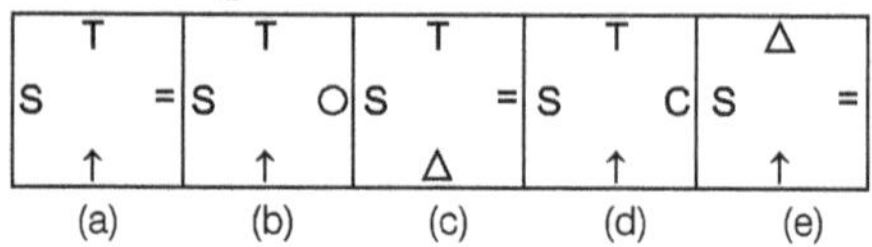

***Solution* (d)** All the symbols move 45° clockwise and a symbol is replaced by a new symbol in each subsequent block.

Different types of questions covered in this chapter are as follows

TYPE 01

Choosing the Next Term in the Series

In this type of questions, a series of figures is given which follows a certain pattern/rule of transition or change between the successive figures. The series of figures is termed as problem figures and is followed by another set of figures known as answer figures.

Candidates are required to select one figure from the answer figures which will continue the series following the same pattern/rule as used in the problem figure series. When placed next to the last problem figure.

This type of questions are explained in the following examples.

***Ex* 12** Find the next figure in the following series.
« SSC CGL 2019

Problem Figures

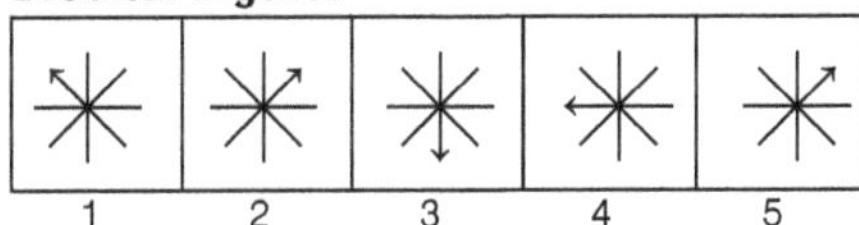

Answer Figures

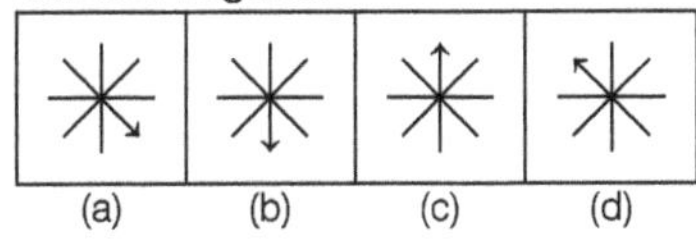

***Solution* (a)** In each successive figure, the arrow is rotating 90° and 135° alternatively in clockwise direction. Following the same pattern, answer figure (a) will be the next figure.

DIRECTIONS ~ (Example Nos. 13 and 14) *Each of the following questions consists of four/five problem figures marked* 1, 2, 3, 4 *and* 5 *and four/five answer figures marked* (a), (b), (c), (d) *and* (e). *Select a figure from the answer figures which will continue the series established by the four/five problem figures.*

***Ex* 13**

Problem Figures

Answer Figures

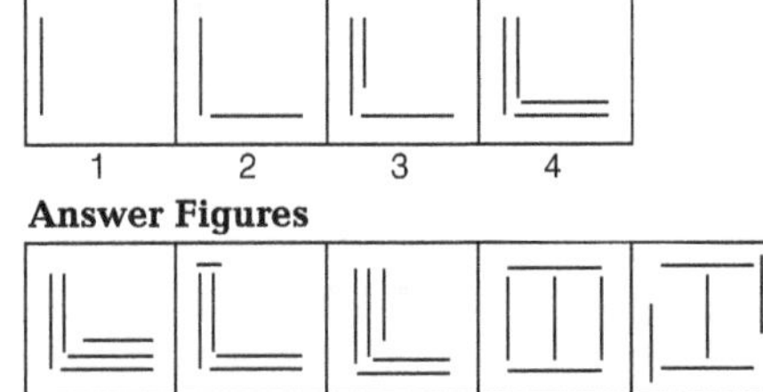

***Solution* (c)** By careful analysis of the problem figures, we find that, horizontal and vertical line segments are added to the figure alternately. So, in the next figure a vertical line segment will be added.

***Ex* 14**

Problem Figures

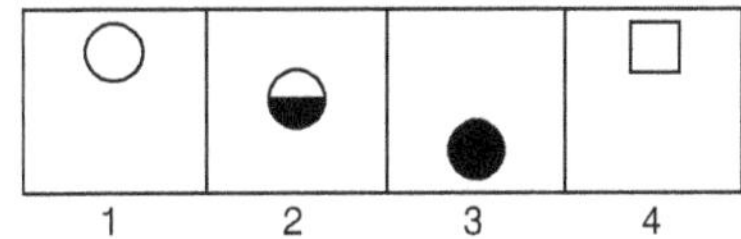

Answer Figures

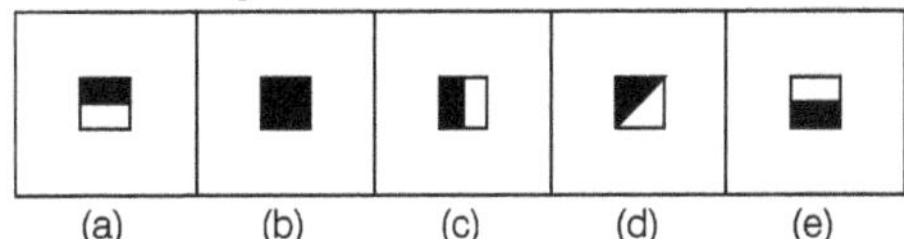

***Solution* (e)** In the first step, the lower half of the figure gets shaded; in the second step, the complete figure gets shaded and in the third step, the figure gets replaced by a new figure. The three steps will be repeated for the new figure also. So, in the next figure, a lower half shaded square placed in the centre, will appear.

DIRECTIONS ~ (Example Nos. 15-17) *Each of the following questions consists of five problem figures marked* 1, 2, 3, 4 *and* 5 *followed by five answer figures* (a), (b), (c), (d) *and* (e). *Find out the figure from the answer figures which will continue the given series.*

***Ex* 15**

Problem Figures

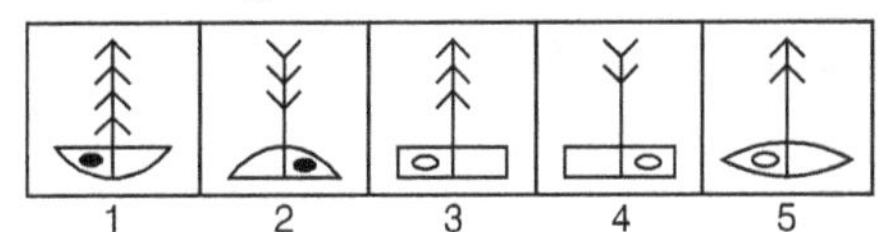

Answer Figures

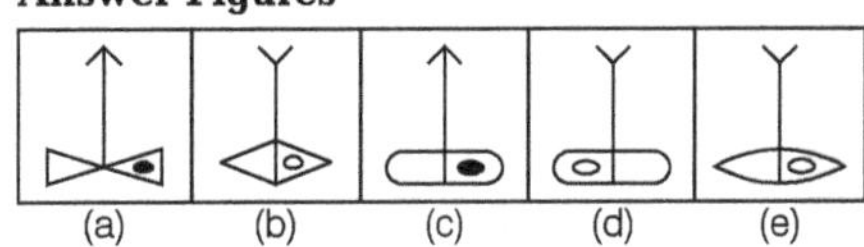

***Solution* (e)** Here, deletion of a design in the figure takes place with some changes. An arrow is deleted in each alternate block with the re-reversal in design. Similarly, base is also reversed with shifting of shaded or unshaded portion on either side.

***Ex* 16**

Problem Figures

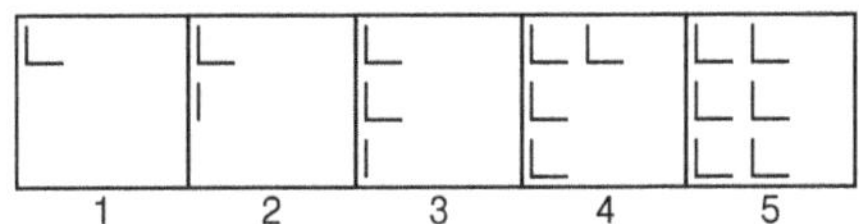

Answer Figures

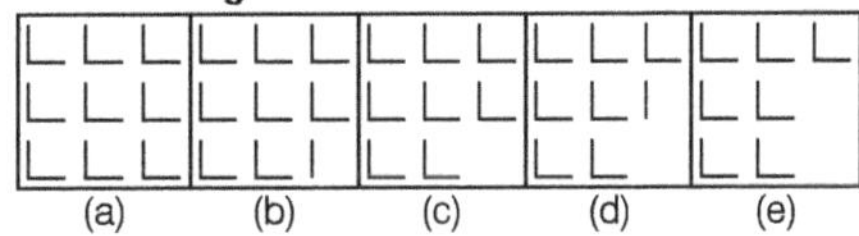

***Solution* (b)** In every successive figure, there is an addition of 1, 2, 3, 4, 5,... lines, respectively.

***Ex* 17 Problem Figures**

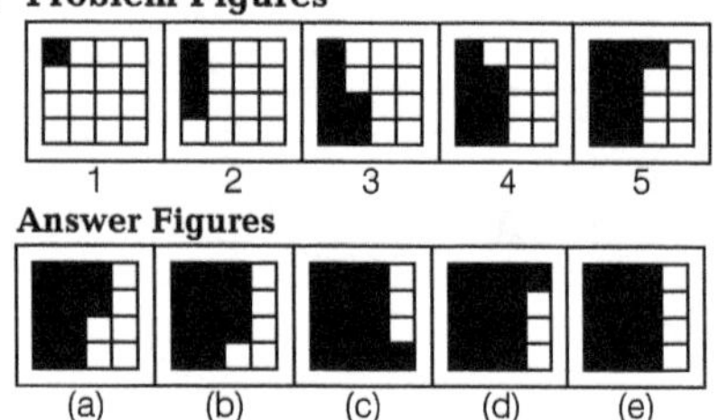

Answer Figures

***Solution* (e)** In subsequent figures, 2, 3, 1, 2, 3, 1, ... boxes respectively are shaded in a set order.

***Ex* 18 Problem Figures**

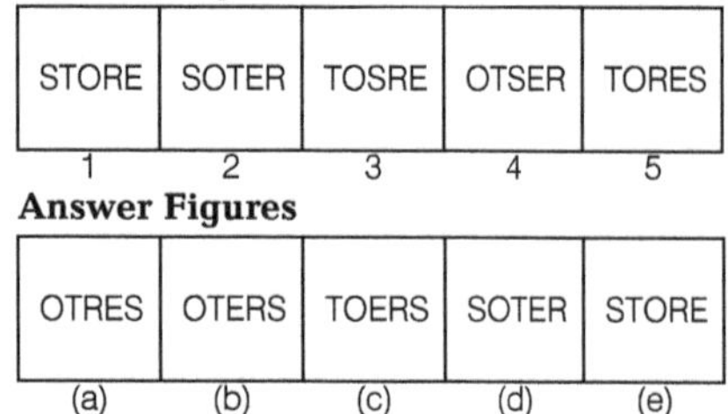

STORE	SOTER	TOSRE	OTSER	TORES
1	2	3	4	5

Answer Figures

OTRES	OTERS	TOERS	SOTER	STORE
(a)	(b)	(c)	(d)	(e)

***Solution* (b)** From problem figures (1) to (3) and (3) to (5), 'S' moves two positions ahead (from left to right).

Similarly, from problem figures (2) to (4) and (4) to answer figure (b), 'S' moves two positions ahead (from left to right).

***Ex* 19**

Problem Figures

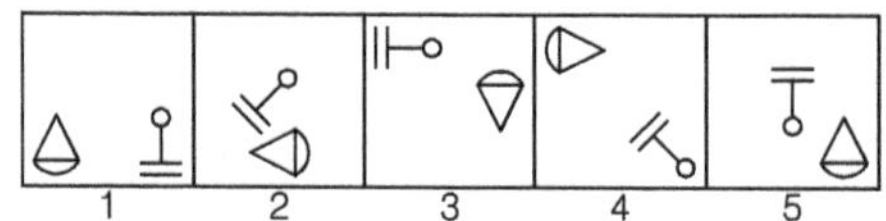

Answer Figures

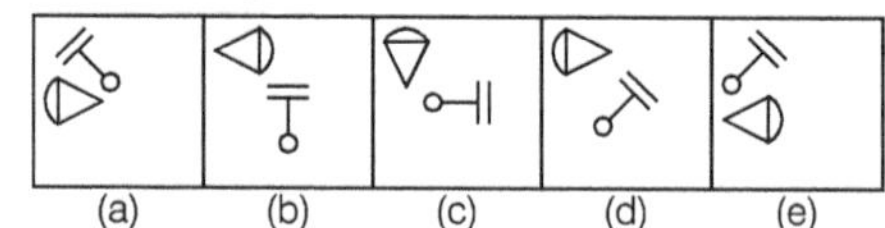

***Solution* (e)** Figure △ moves $\frac{1}{2}$, 1, $1\frac{1}{2}$ and 2 sides in anti-clockwise direction making an angle of 90° anti-clockwise. The another figure ⫯ makes an angle of 45° in clockwise direction and also shifts to the middle, top and bottom positions diagonally.

Practice CORNER 1.1

DIRECTIONS ~ (Q. Nos. 1-62) *Each of the questions consists of four/five figures marked* 1, 2, 3, 4 *and* 5 *named as the problem figures and is followed by four/five answer figures marked* (a), (b), (c), (d) *and* (e). *Select a figure from the answer figures which will continue the series established by the four/five problem figures.*

1. Problem Figures

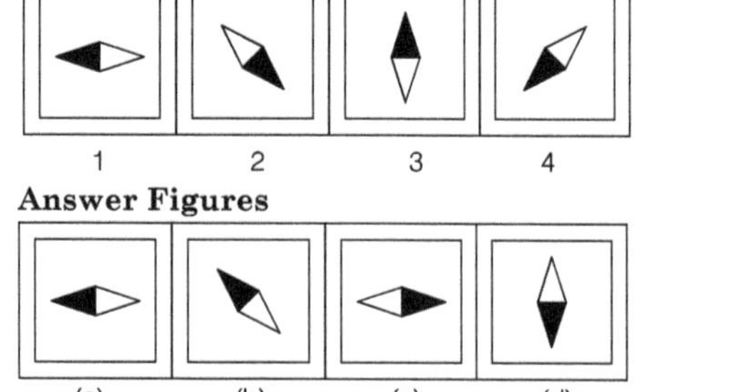

Answer Figures

« UPSSSC 2018

2. Problem Figures

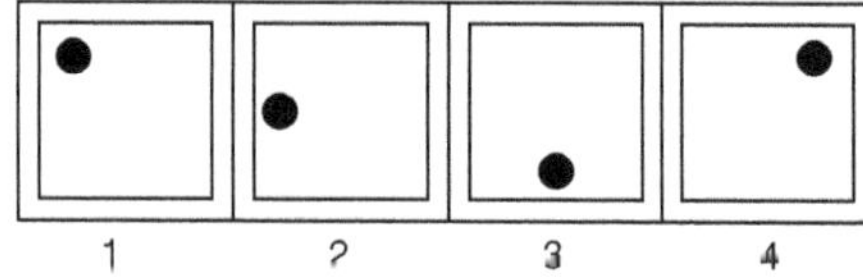

Answer Figures

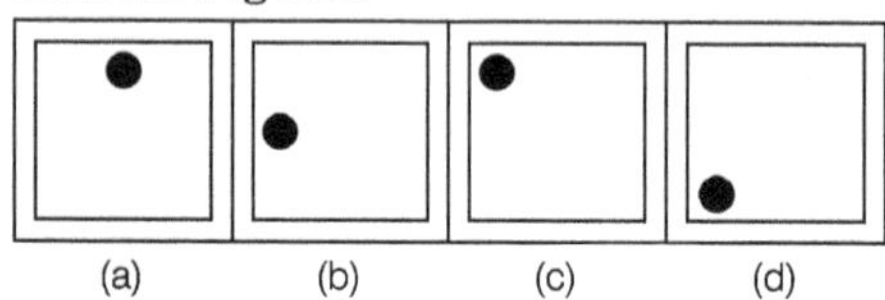

3. Problem Figures

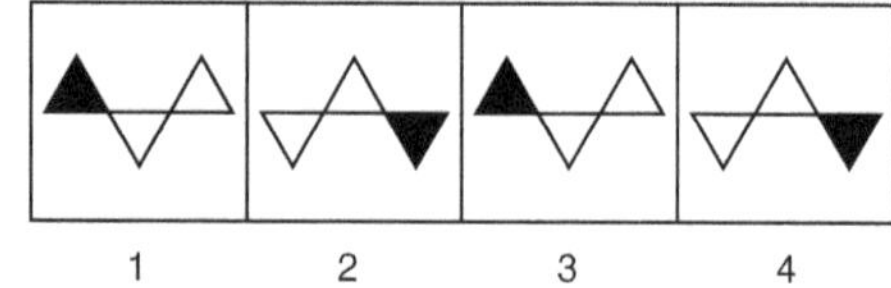

Answer Figures

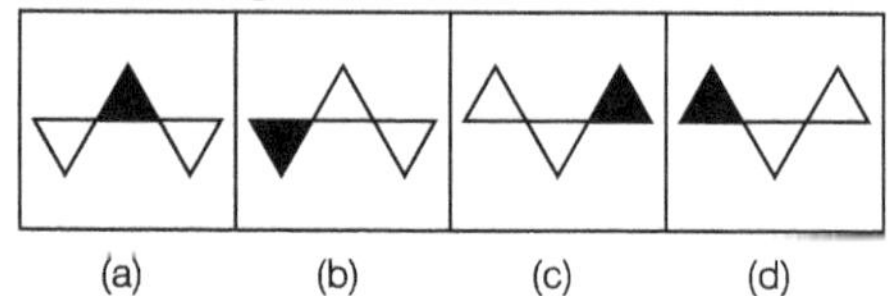

4. Problem Figures

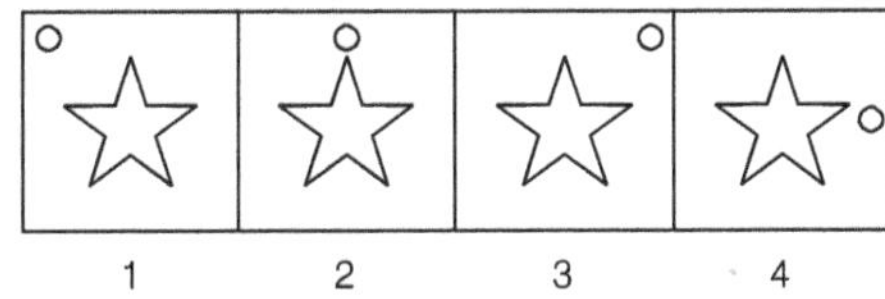

Answers Figures

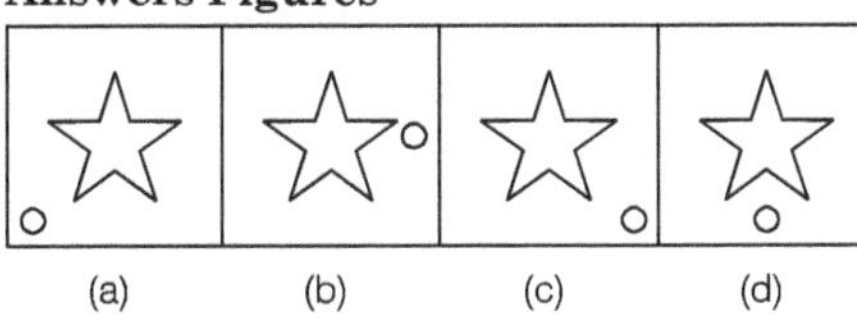

5. Problem Figures

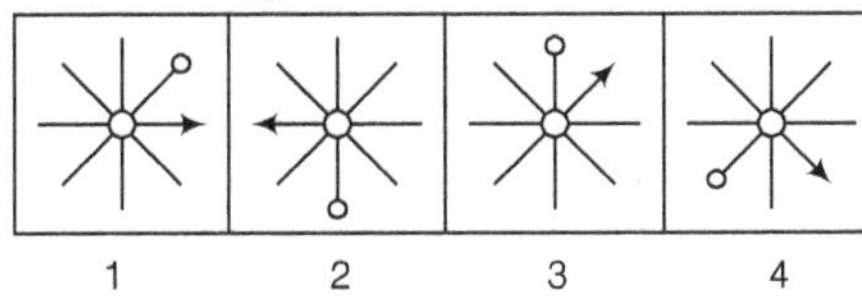

Answers Figures

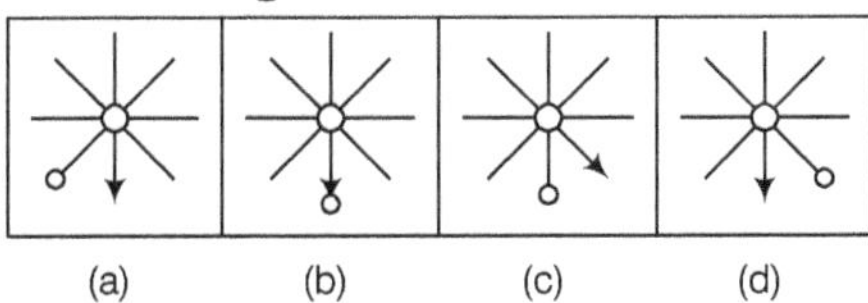

6. Problem Figures

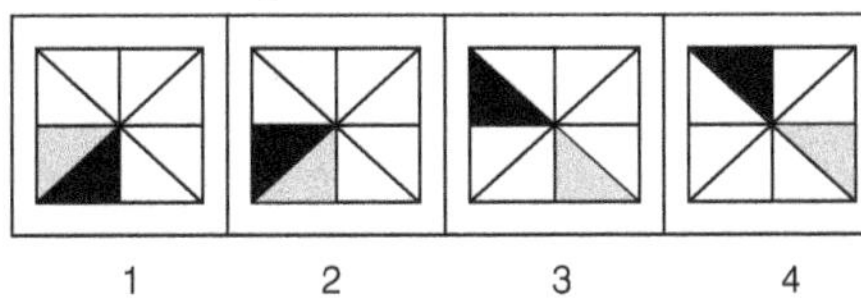

Answers Figures

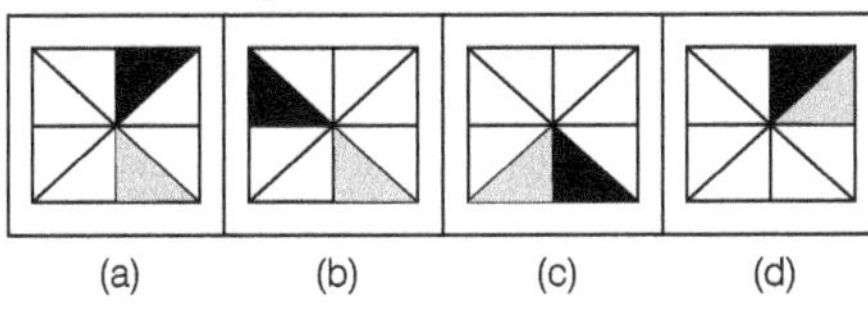

« Rajasthan Police Constable 2018

7. Problem Figures

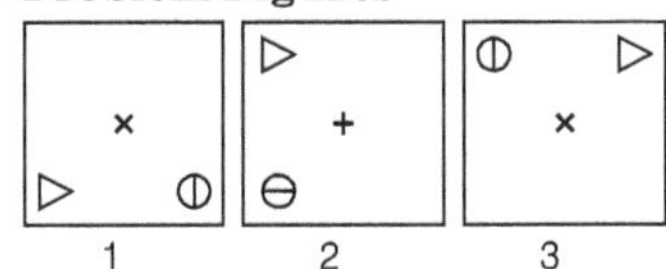

Answers Figures

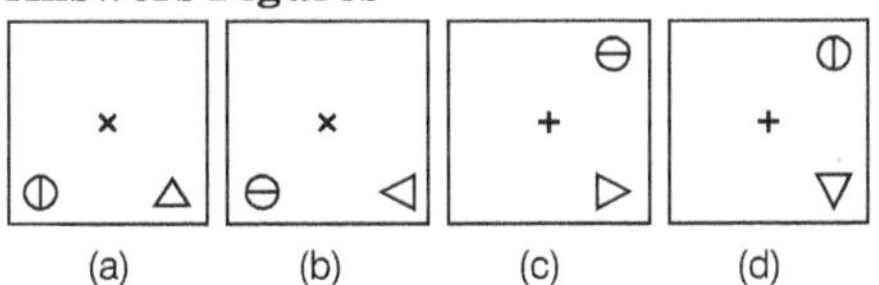

« UPSSSC 2018

8. Problem Figures

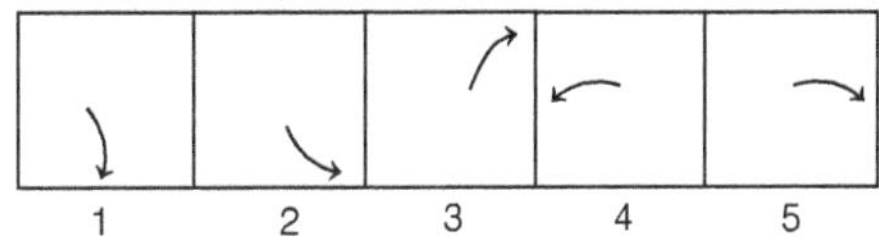

Answers Figures

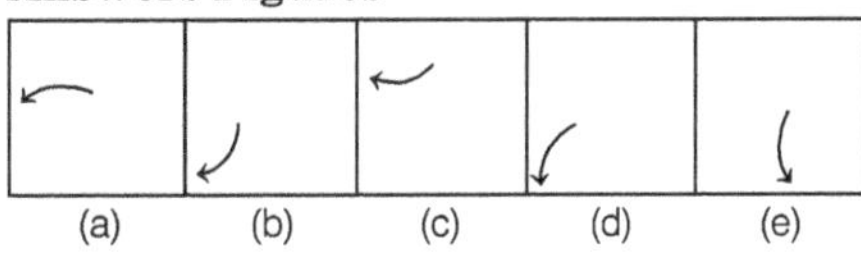

« MHT MBA 2017

9. Problem Figures

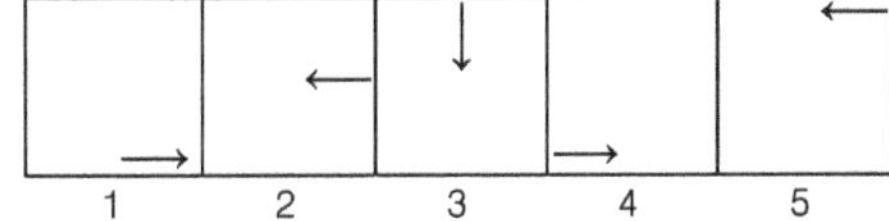

Answers Figures

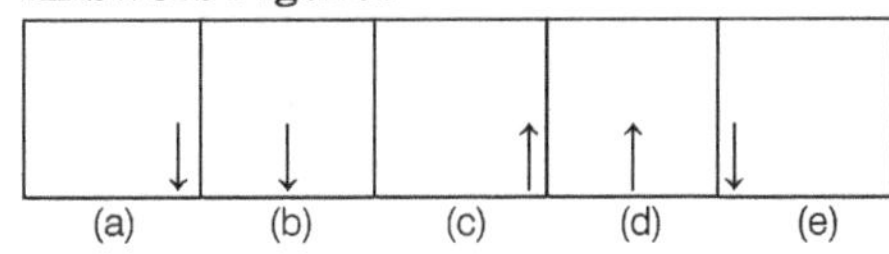

« MHT MBA 2017

10. Problem Figures

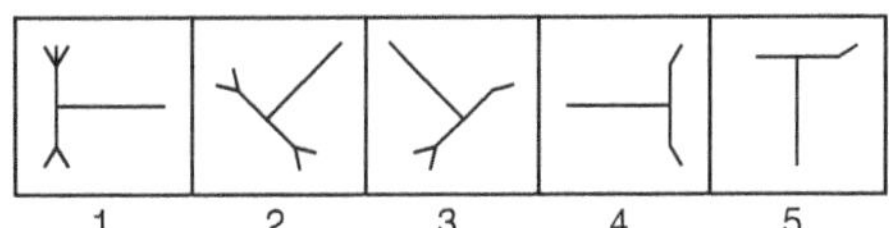

Answers Figures

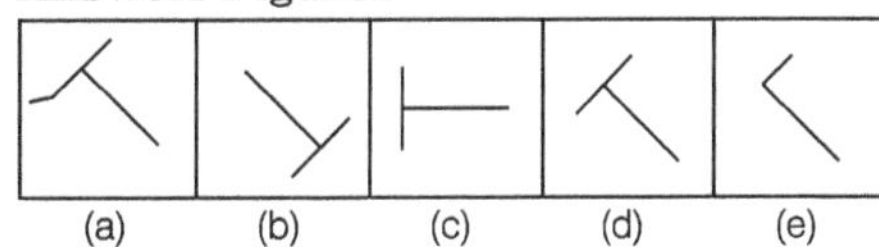

11. Problem Figures

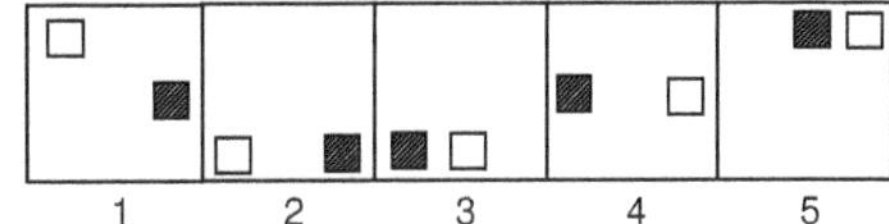

Answers Figures

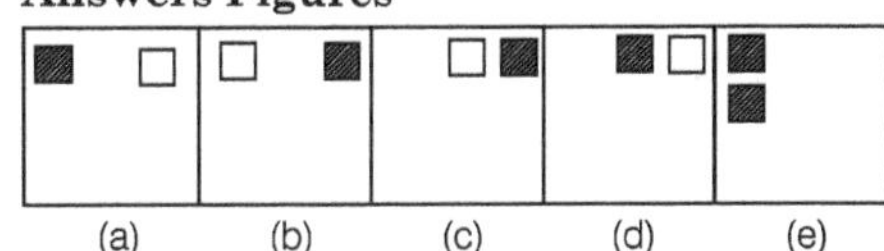

« NIFT UG 2013

12. Problem Figures

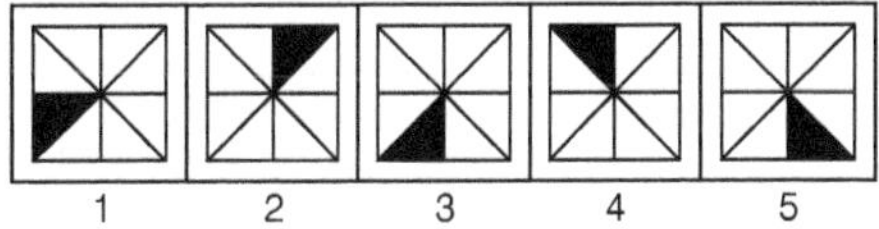

Answers Figures

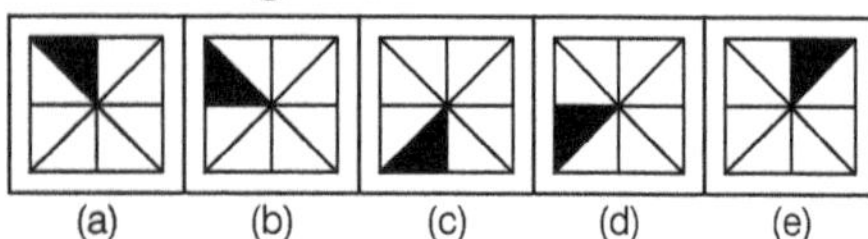

13. Problem Figures

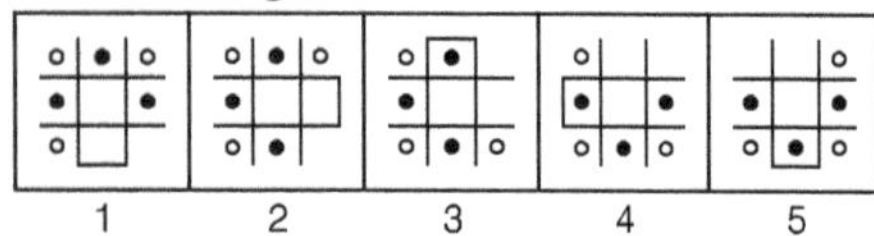

Answers Figures

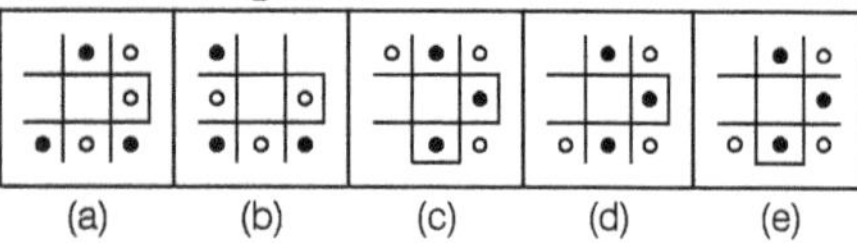

14. Problem Figures

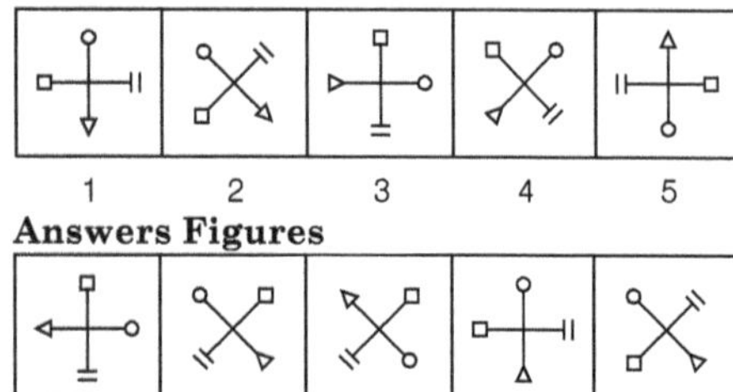

« SBI Clerk 2011

15. Problem Figures

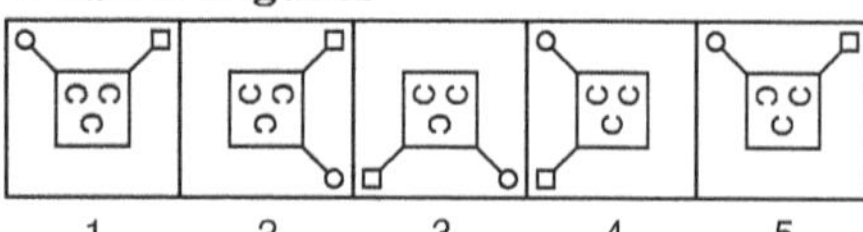

Answers Figures

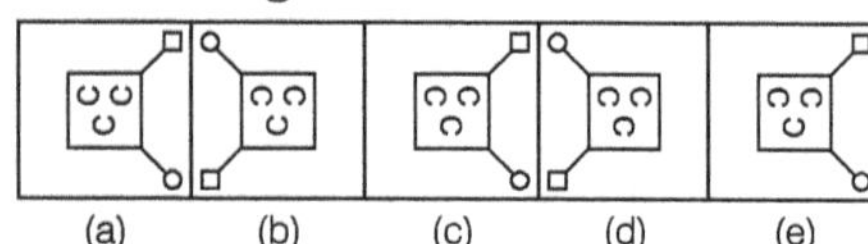

16. Problem Figures

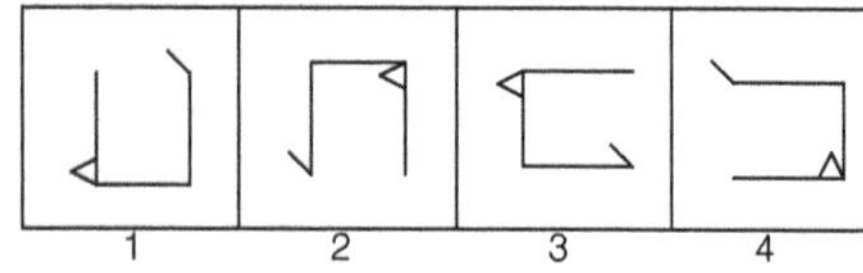

Answers Figures

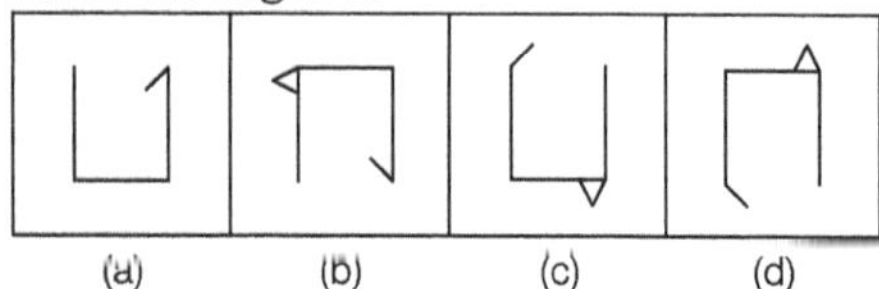

« SSC 10+2 2010

17. Problem Figures

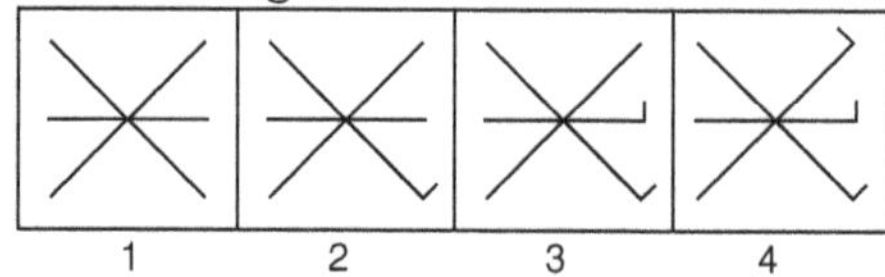

Answers Figures

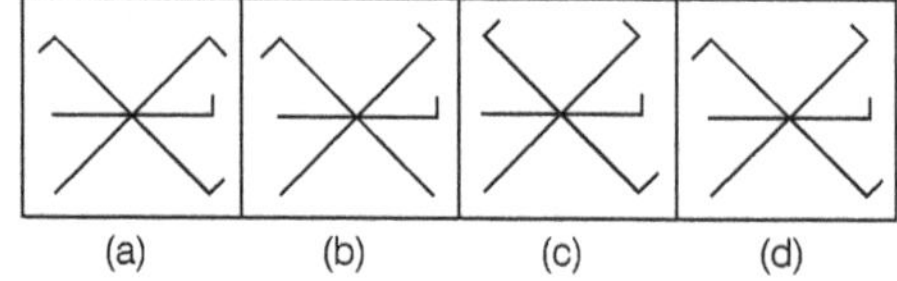

18. Problem Figures

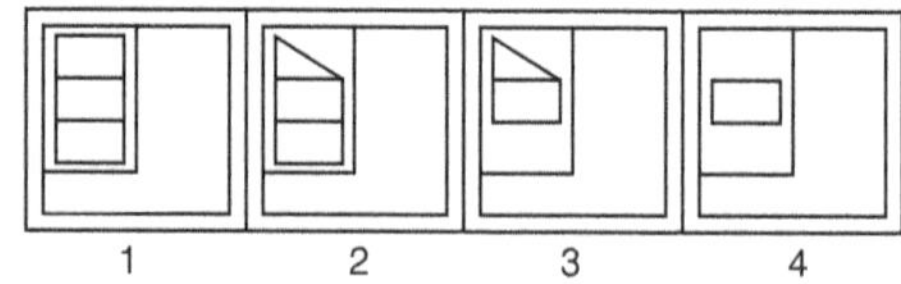

Answers Figures

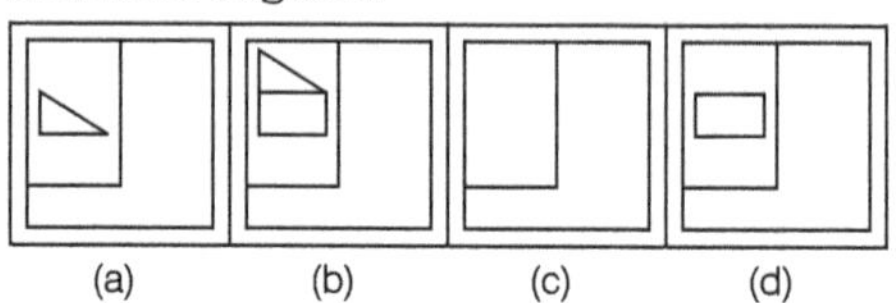

19. Problem Figures

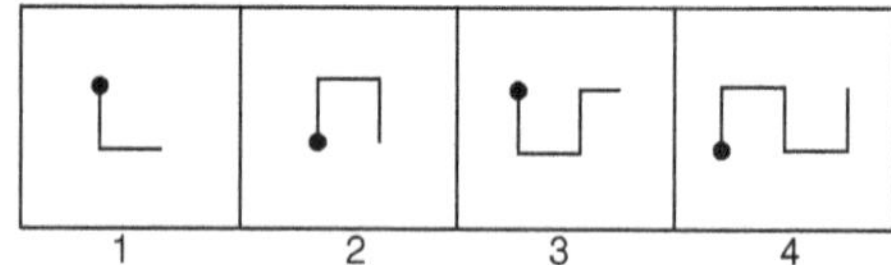

Answers Figures

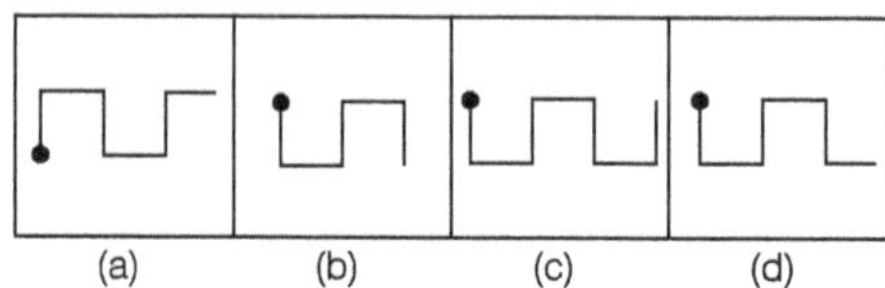

20. Problem Figures

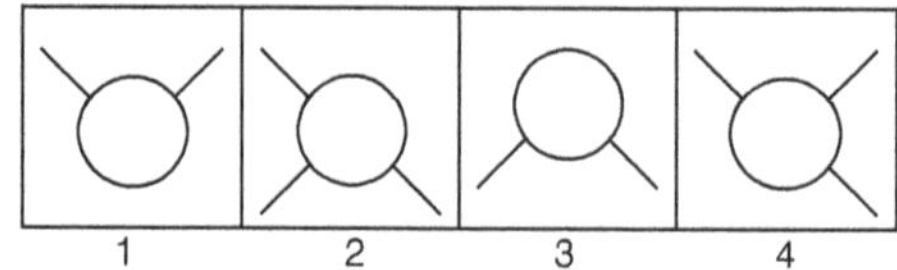

Answers Figures

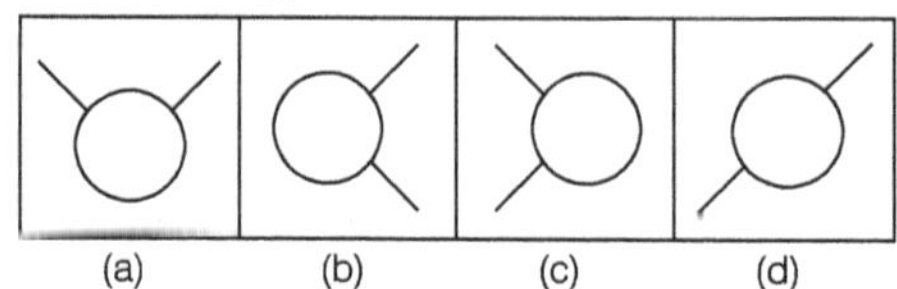

21. Problem Figures

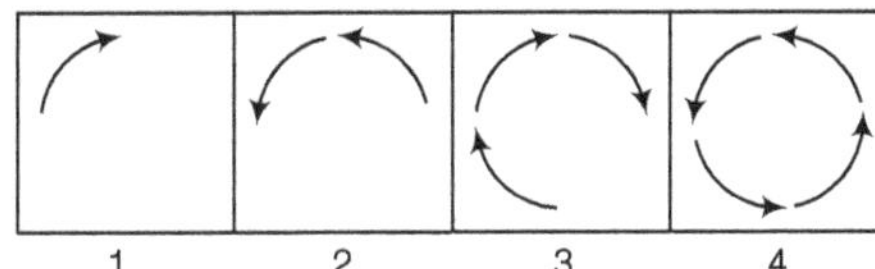

1 2 3 4

Answers Figures

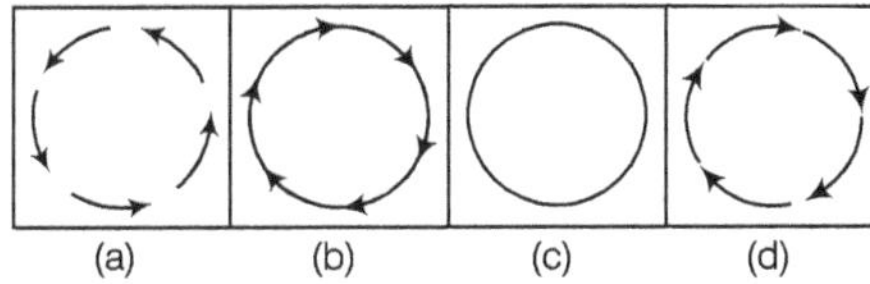

(a) (b) (c) (d)

22. Problem Figures

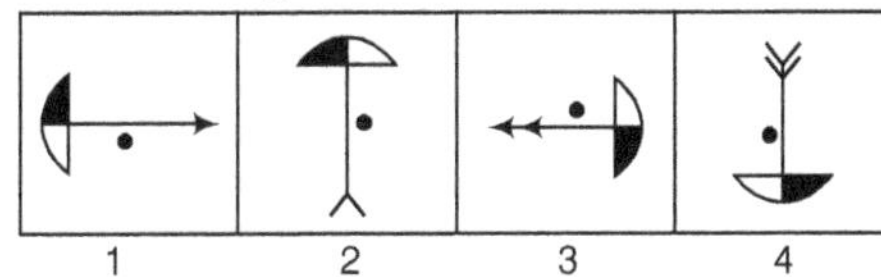

1 2 3 4

Answers Figures

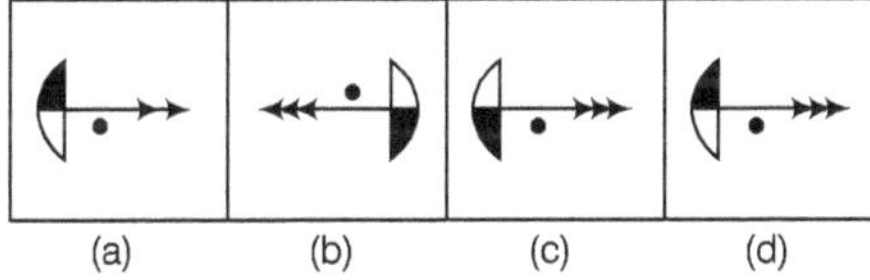

(a) (b) (c) (d)

23. Problem Figures

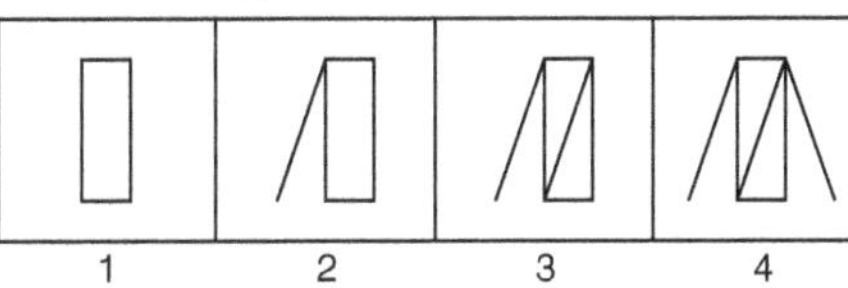

1 2 3 4

Answers Figures

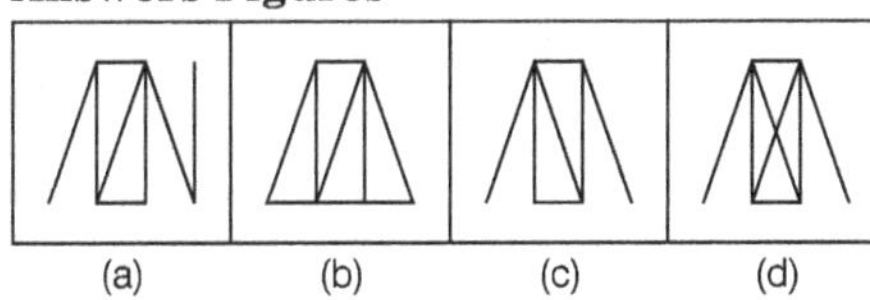

(a) (b) (c) (d)

« SSC 10+2 2014

24. Problem Figures

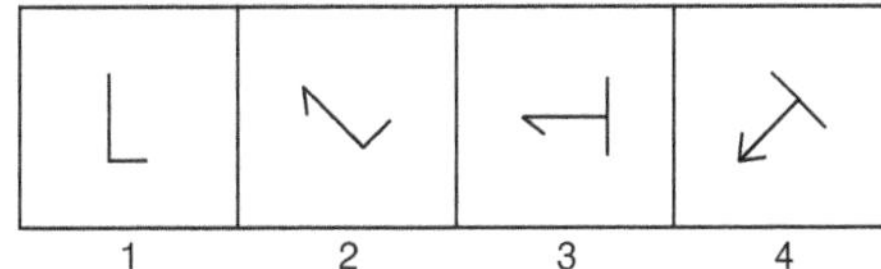

1 2 3 4

Answers Figures

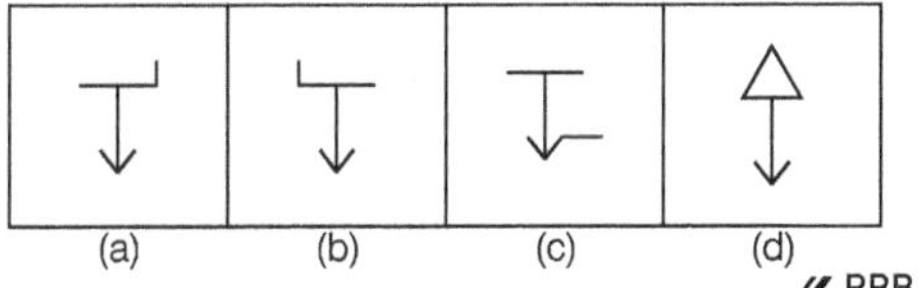

(a) (b) (c) (d)

« RRB ALP 2010

25. Problem Figures

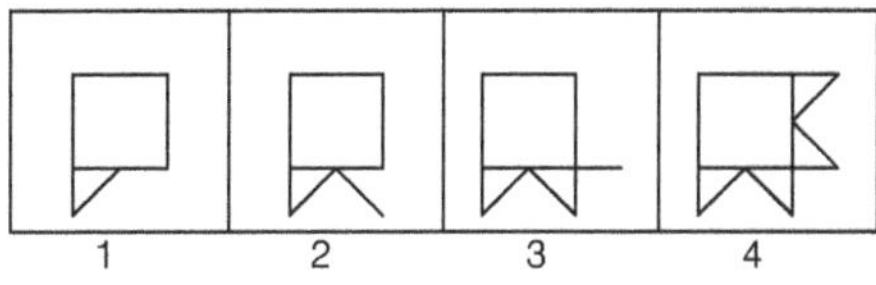

1 2 3 4

Answers Figures

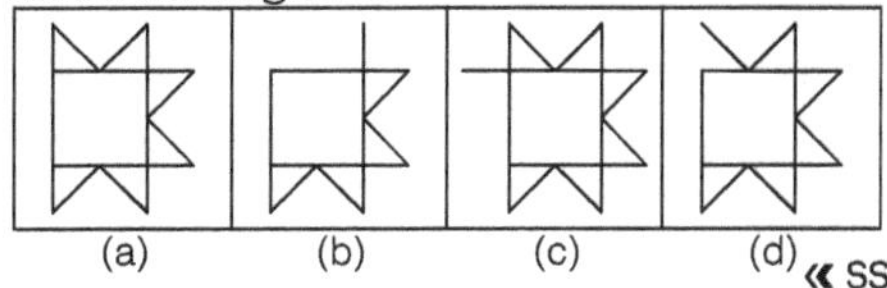

(a) (b) (c) (d)

« SSC MTS 2011

26. Problem Figures

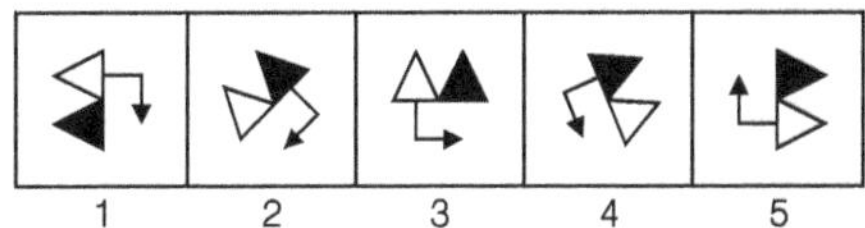

1 2 3 4 5

Answers Figures

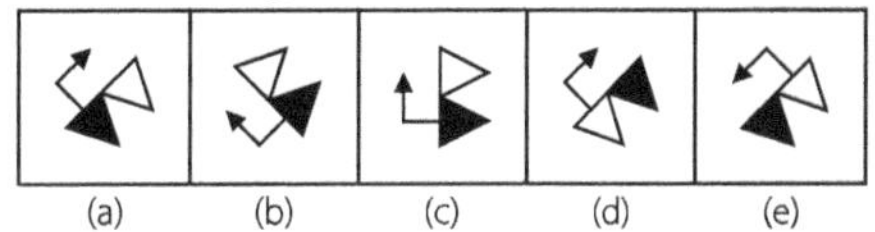

(a) (b) (c) (d) (e)

27. Problem Figures

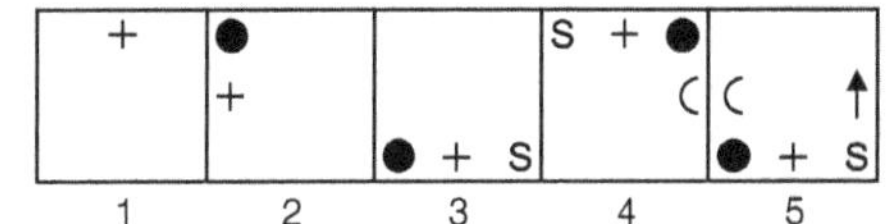

1 2 3 4 5

Answers Figures

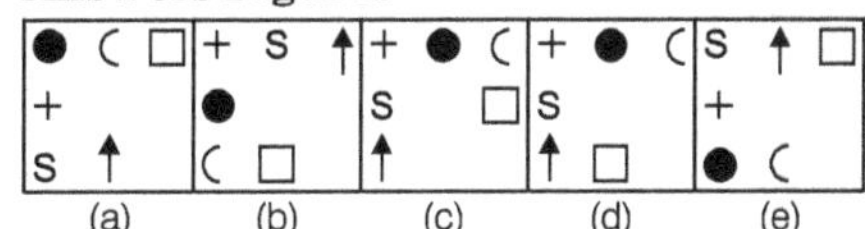

(a) (b) (c) (d) (e)

« Union Bank PO 2010

28. Problem Figures

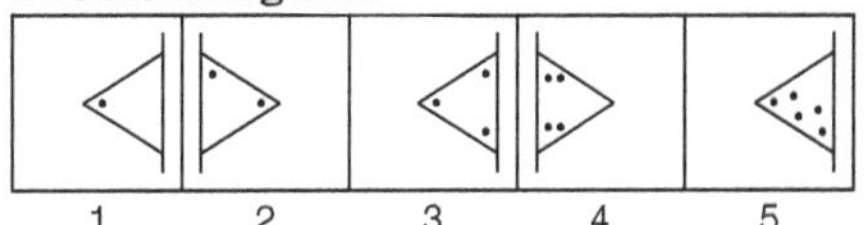

1 2 3 4 5

Answers Figures

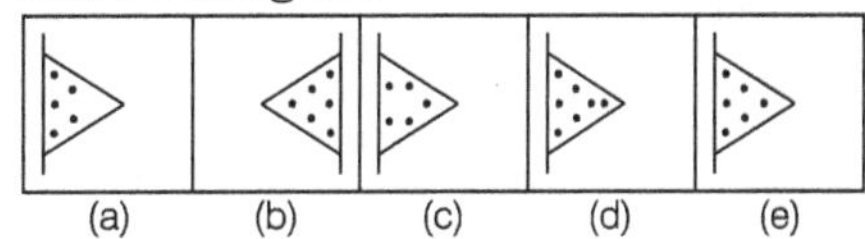

(a) (b) (c) (d) (e)

« Corporation Bank PO 2011

29. Problem Figures

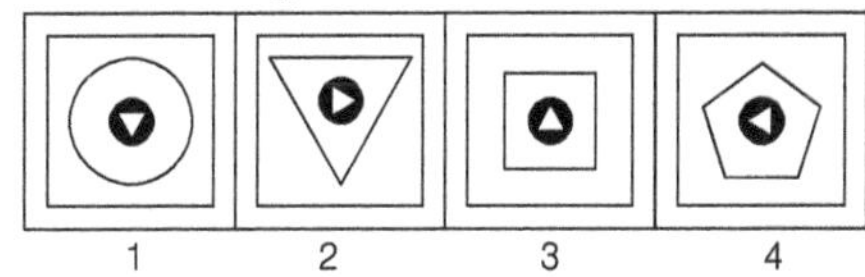

1 2 3 4

Answers Figures

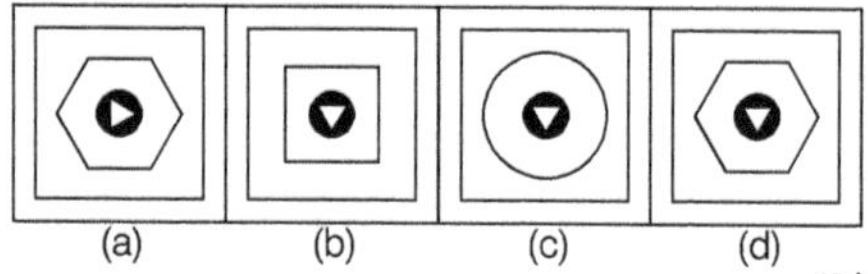

« UPSSSC 2018

30. Problem Figures

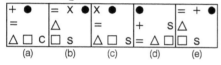

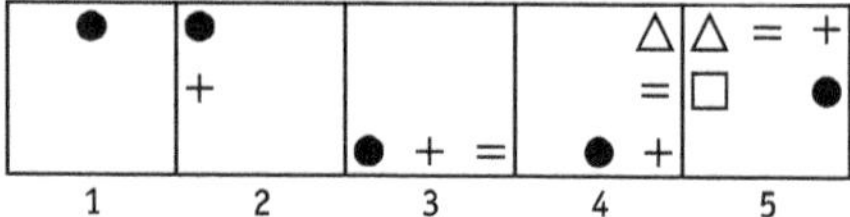

Answers Figures

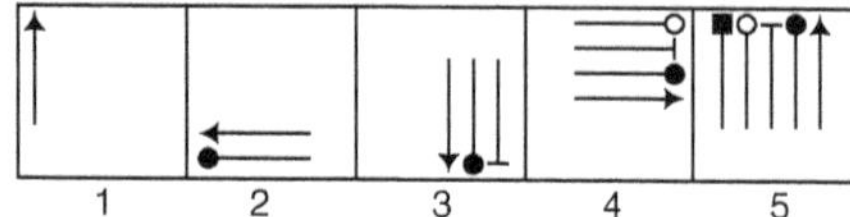

31. Problem Figures

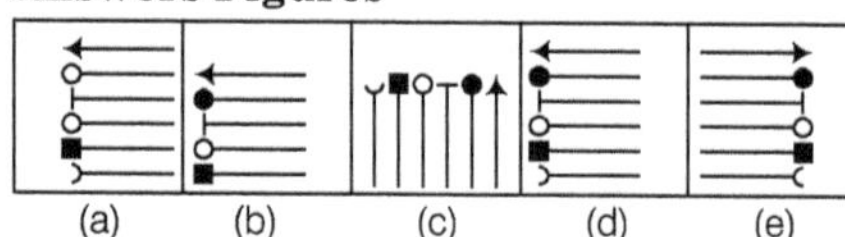

Answers Figures

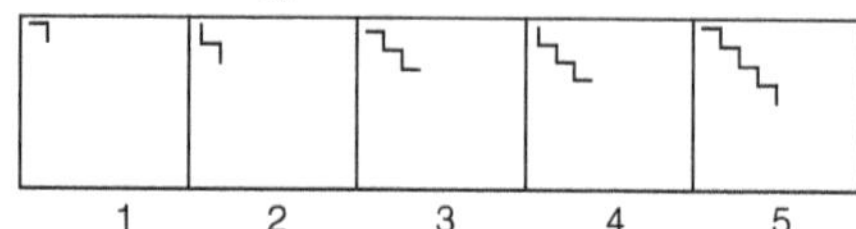

« Rajasthan Grameen Bank PO 2011

32. Problem Figures

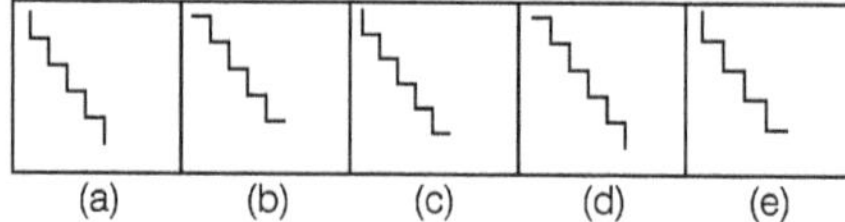

Answers Figures

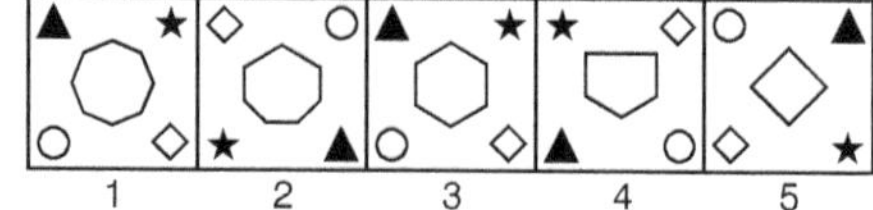

« MHT MBA 2017

33. Problem Figures

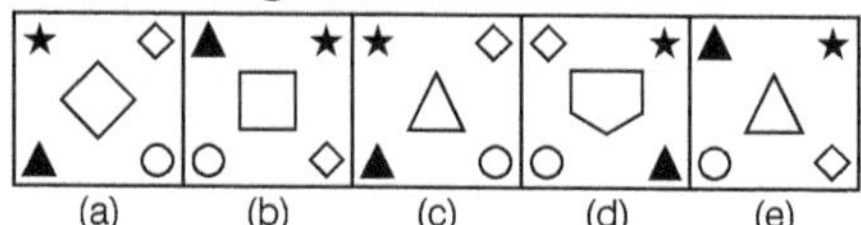

Answers Figures

34. Problem Figures

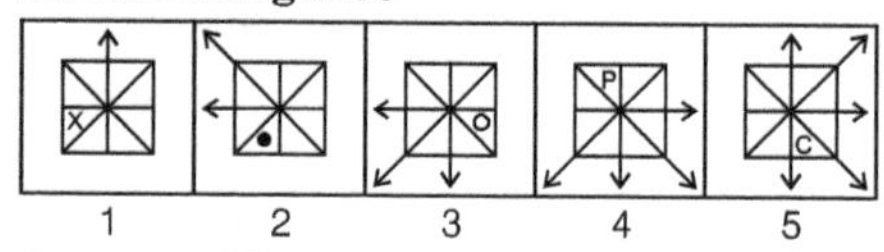

Answers Figures

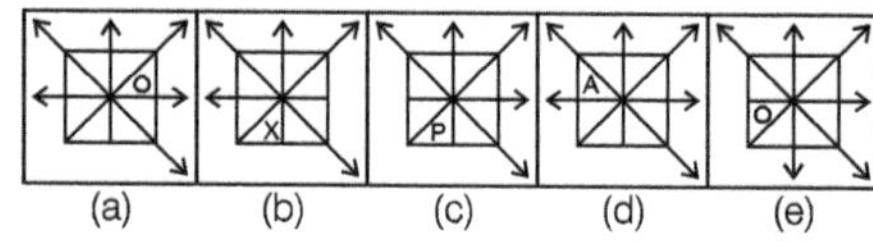

35. Problem Figures

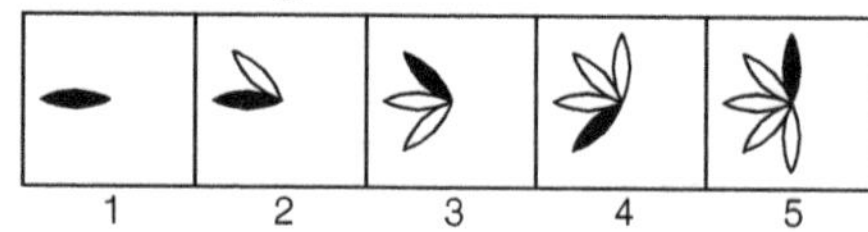

Answers Figures

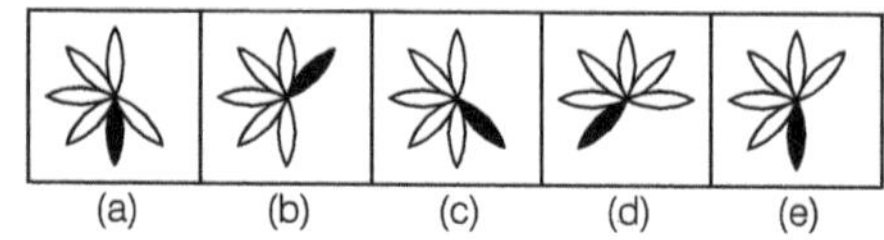

36. Problem Figures

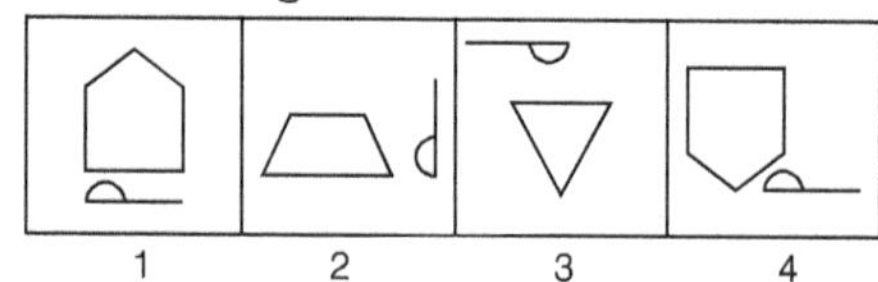

Answers Figures

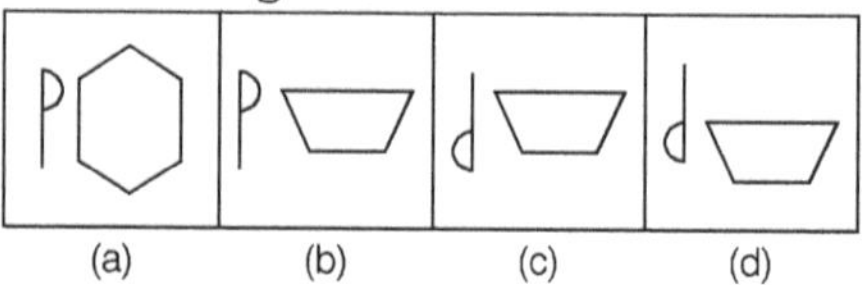

« SSC 10+2 2015

37. Problem Figures

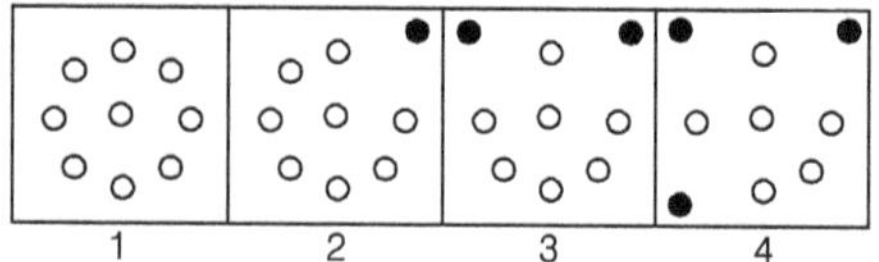

Answers Figures

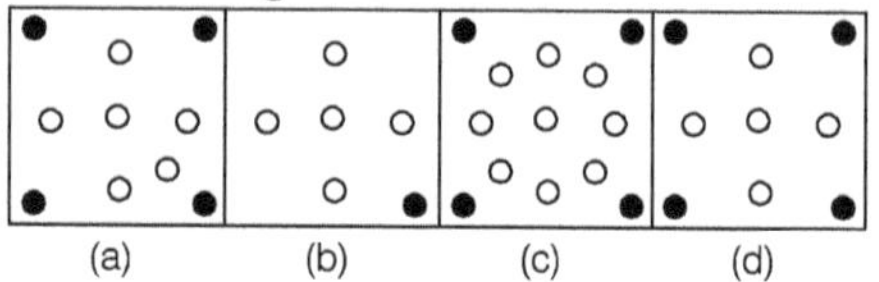

38. Problem Figures

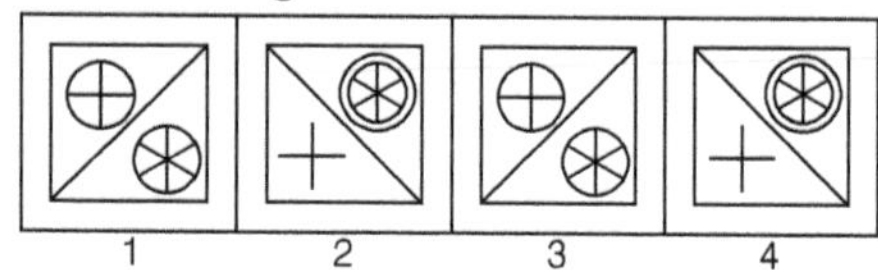

Answers Figures

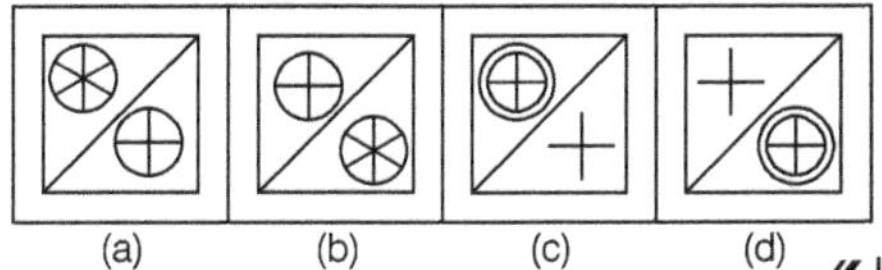

« UP B.Ed 2011

39. Problem Figures

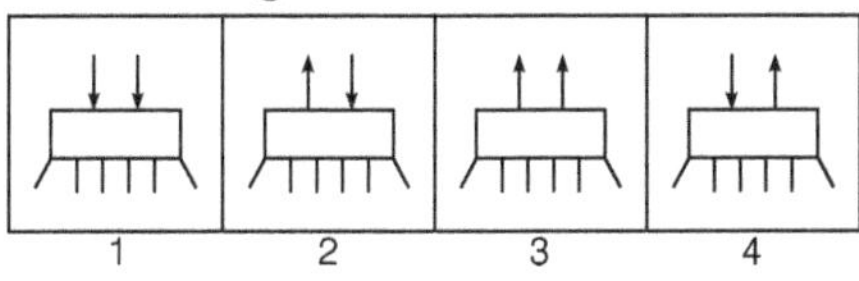

Answers Figures

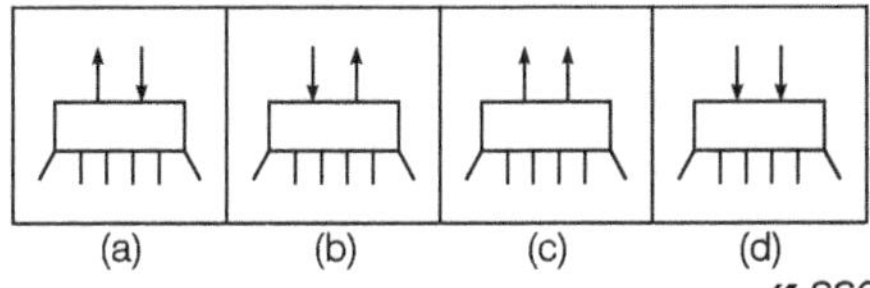

« SSC Steno 2008

40. Problem Figures

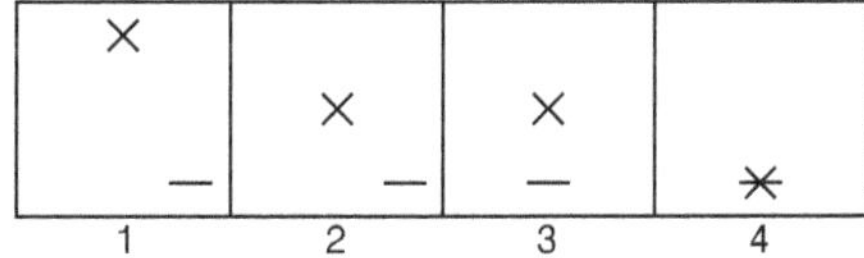

Answers Figures

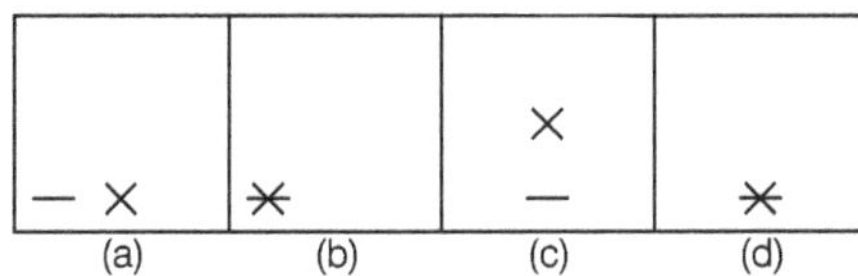

« RRB ALP 2009

41. Problem Figures

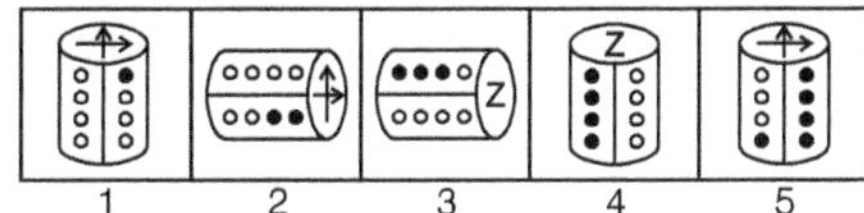

Answers Figures

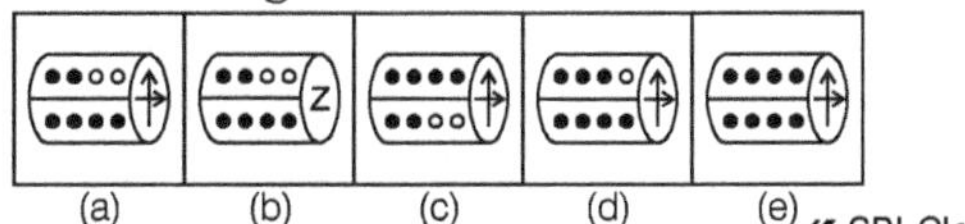

« SBI Clerk 2012

42. Problem Figures

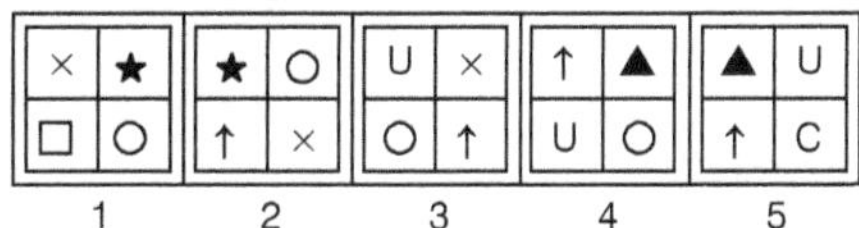

Answers Figures

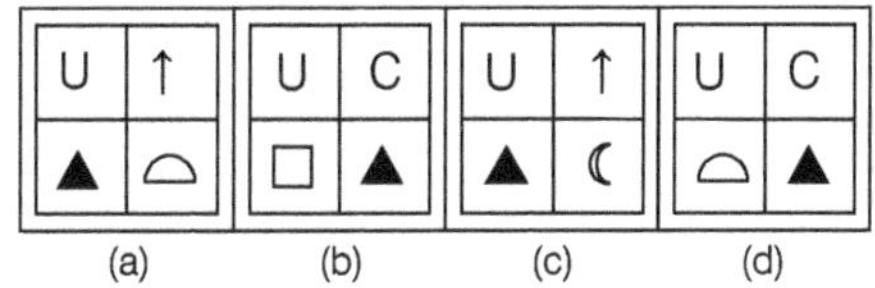

« SSC Stenographer C & D 2019

43. Problem Figures

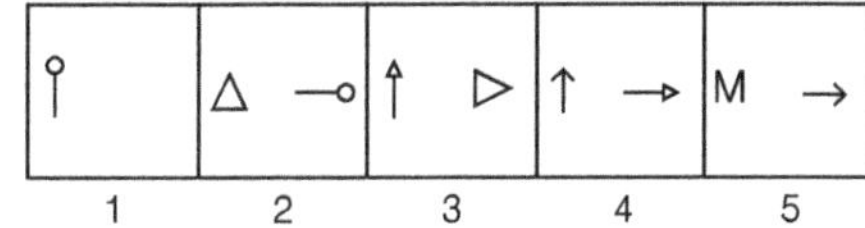

Answers Figures

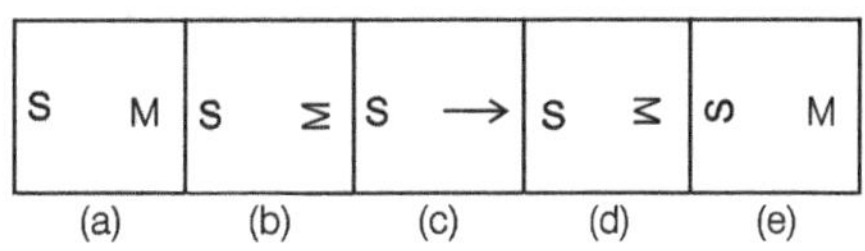

« NIFT PG 2013

44. Problem Figures

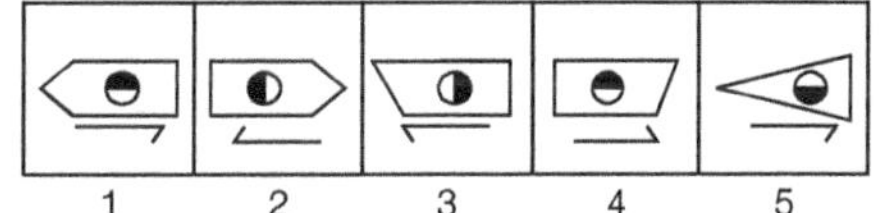

Answers Figures

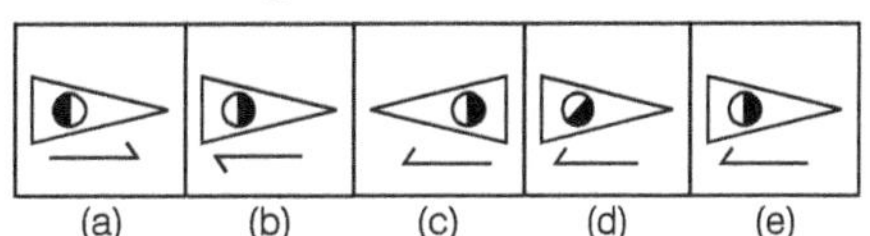

« OBC Clerk 2009

45. Problem Figures

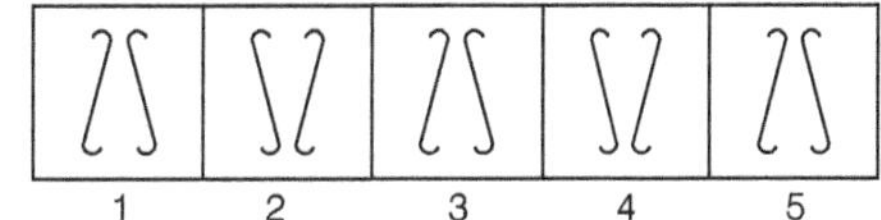

Answers Figures

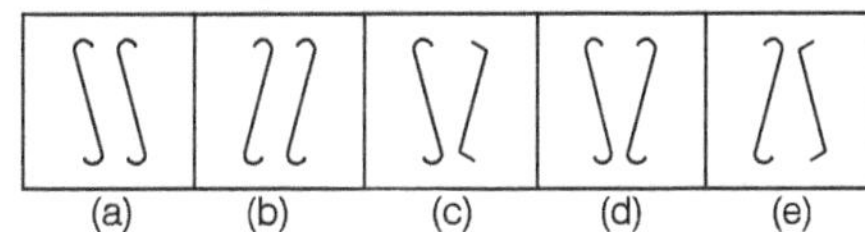

« Corporation Bank PO 2011

46. Problem Figures

● □ / △ S	□ S / ● ★	S ● / □ Z	● Z / S ⋛	Z S / ● ⬭
1	2	3	4	5

Answers Figures

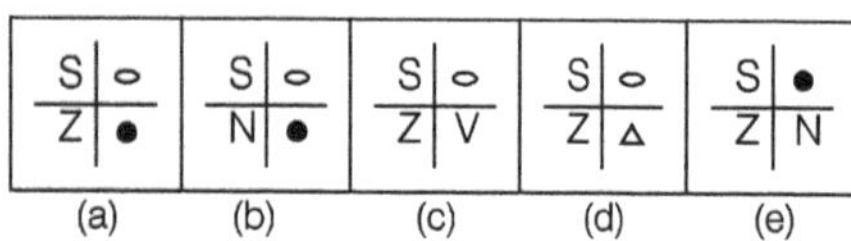

« Corporation Bank PO 2011

47. Problem Figures

Answers Figures

« SBI Clerk 2012

48. Problem Figures

Answers Figures

« Allahabad Bank PO 2011

49. Problem Figures

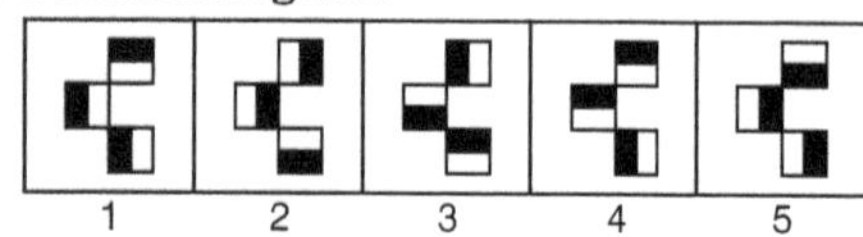

Answers Figures

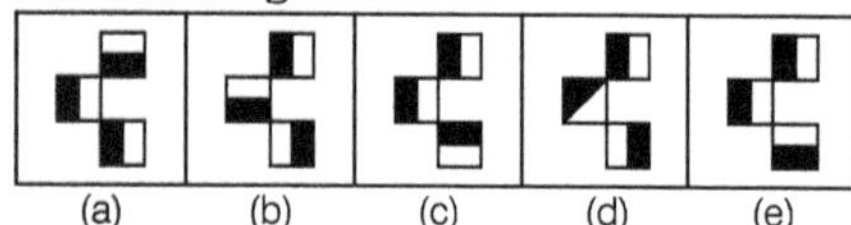

50. Problem Figures

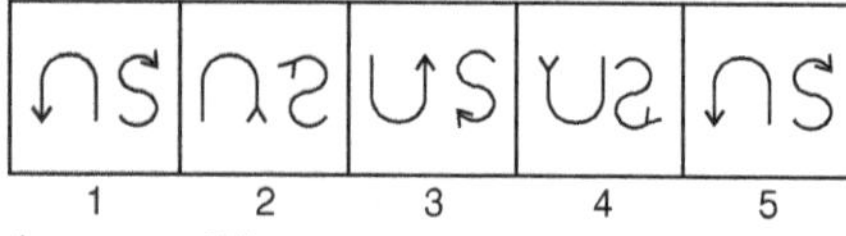

Answers Figures

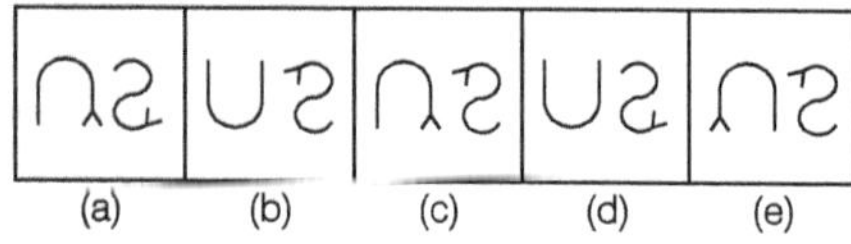

« PNB PO 2010

51. Problem Figures

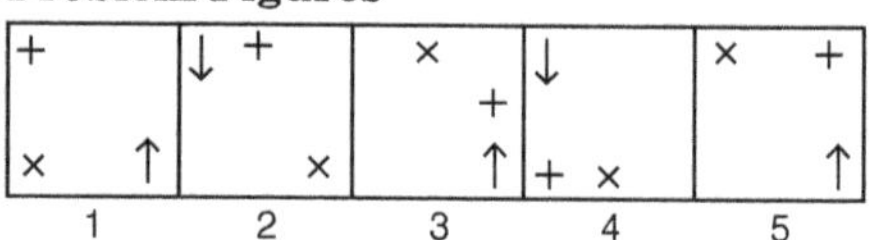

Answers Figures

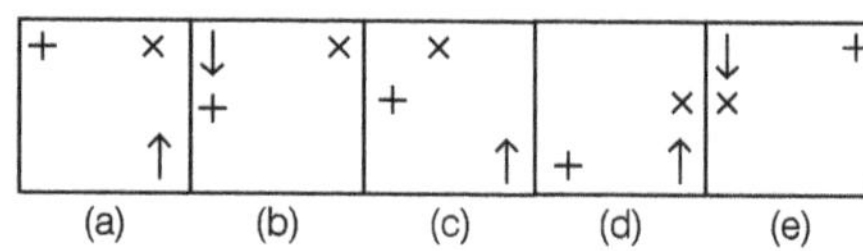

« NIFT PG 2013

52. Problem Figures

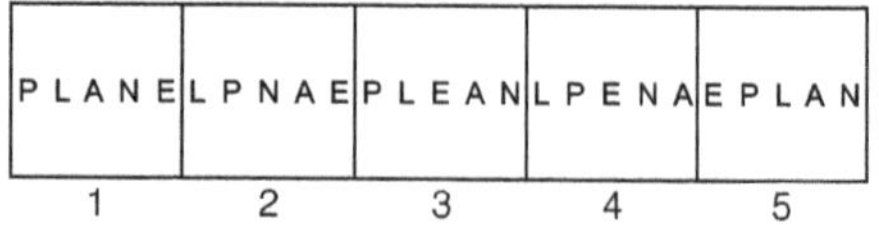

Answers Figures

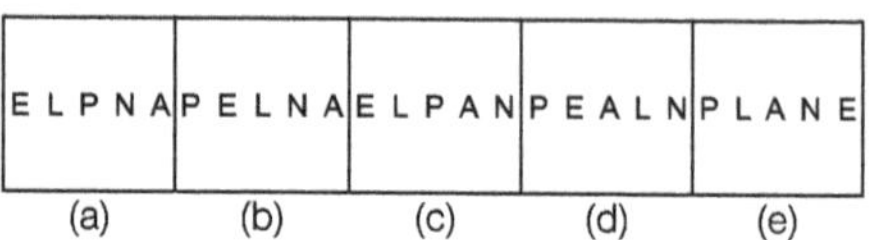

« Rajasthan Grameen Bank PO 2011

53. Problem Figures

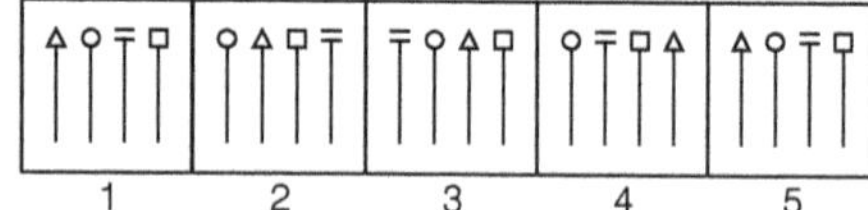

Answers Figures

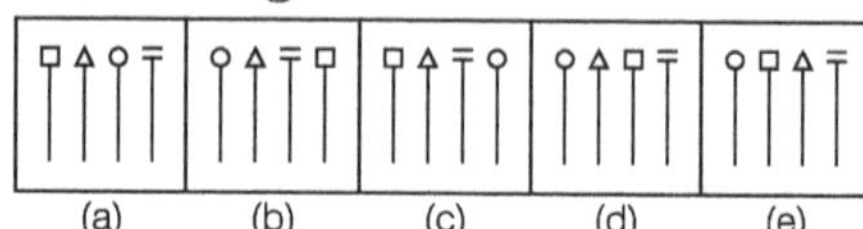

« PNB Clerk 2011

54. Problem Figures

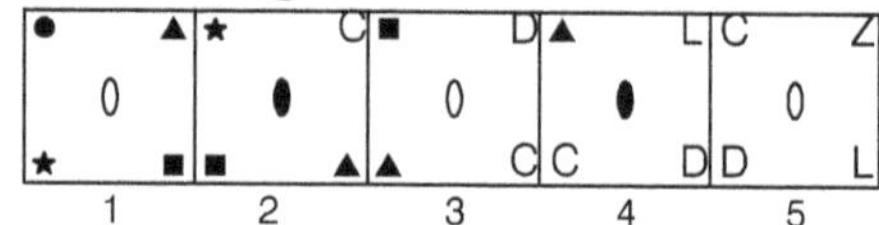

Answers Figures

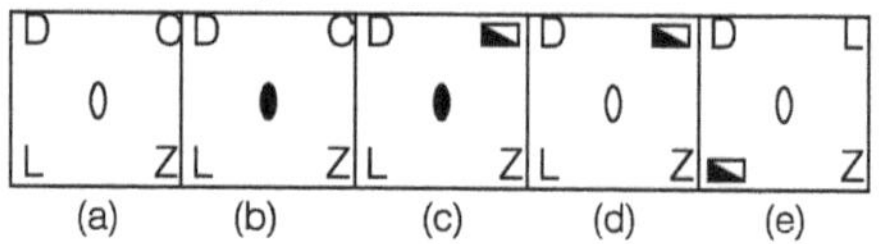

« Corporation Bank PO 2011

55. Problem Figures

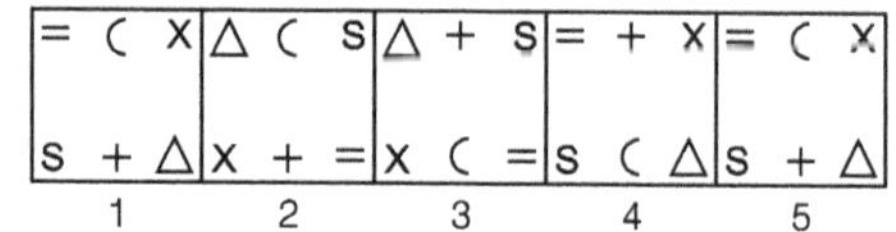

Answers Figures

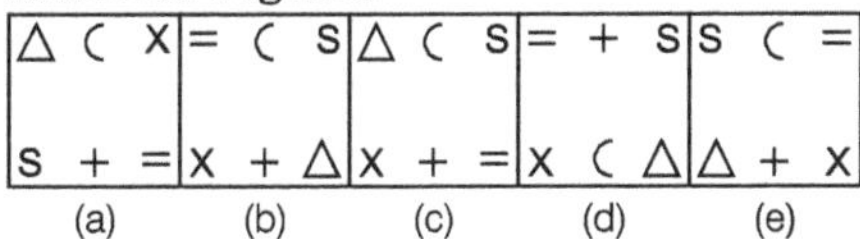

56. Problem Figures

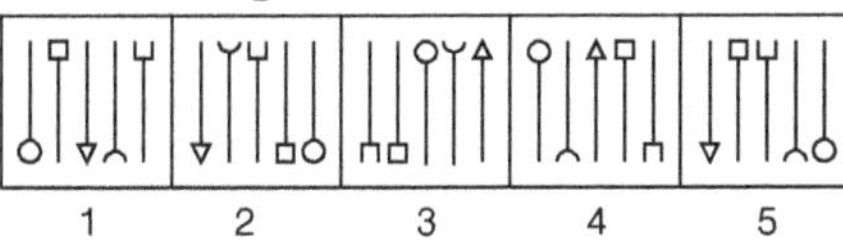

Answers Figures

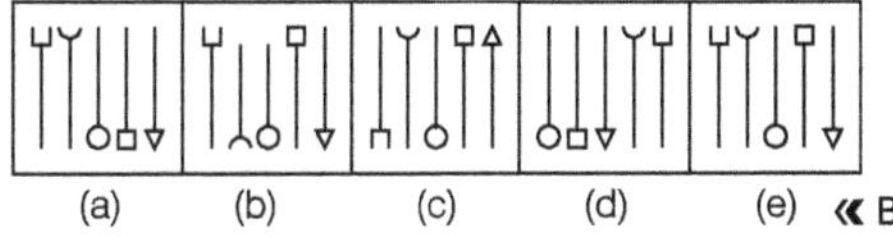

« BOB PO 2011

57. Problem Figures

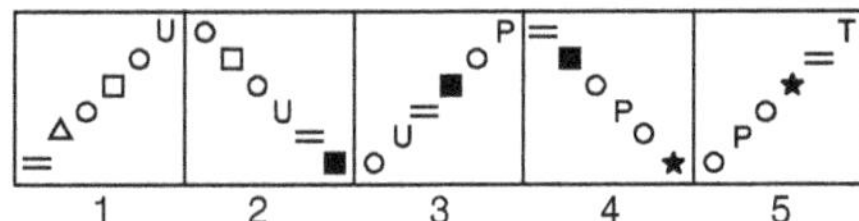

Answers Figures

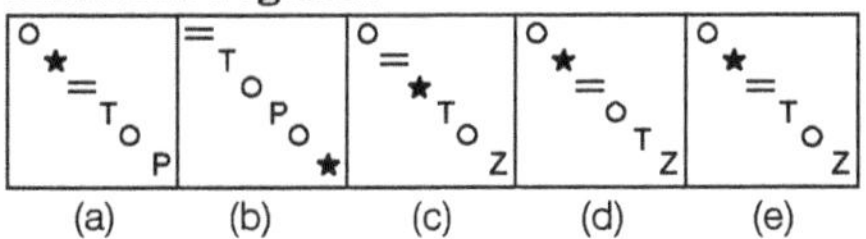

« BOB PO 2011

58. Problem Figures

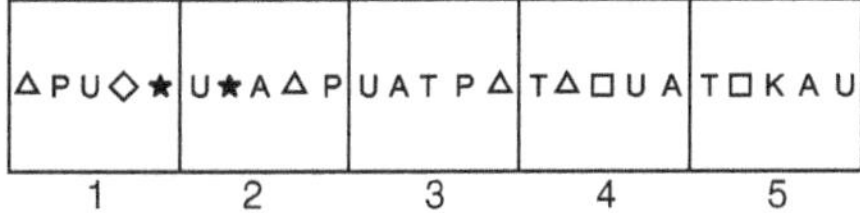

Answers Figures

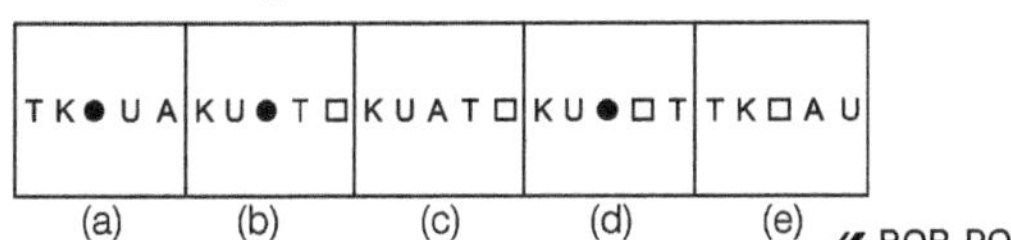

« BOB PO 2011

59. Problem Figures

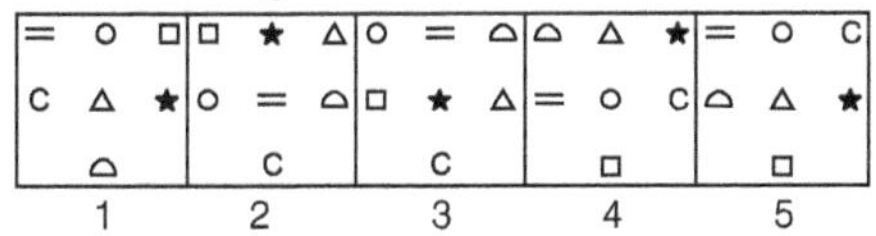

Answers Figures

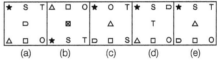

(a)	(b)	(c)	(d)	(e)
C ★ △ / ○ = □ / ⌓	C ⌓ △ / □ = ○ / ★	△ ★ = / ○ C □ / ⌓	C □ △ / ★ = ⌓ / ○	⌓ △ ★ / = ○ C / □

« Rajasthan Grameen Bank PO 2011

60. Problem Figures

1	2	3	4	5
★ = T / ○ / □ ⊃ △	□ T = / ★ / ⊃ △ ○	△ ○ ⊃ / = / ★ □ T	⊃ △ ○ / S / □ T ★	□ ○ △ / ⊃ / T ★ S

Answers Figures

(a)	(b)	(c)	(d)	(e)
★ S T / ⊃ / △ □ ○	△ □ ○ / ⊠ / ★ S T	★ ○ T / △ / ⊃ □ S	★ S ⊃ / T / △ □ ○	★ S T / △ / ⊃ □ ○

« Corporation Bank PO 2011

61. Problem Figures

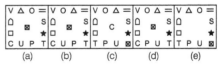

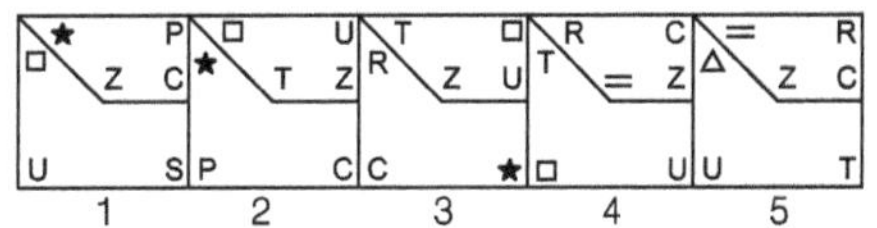

Answers Figures

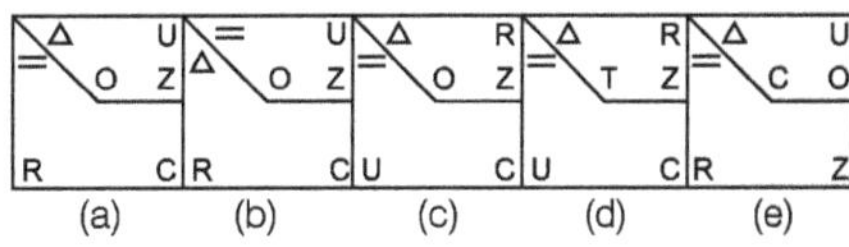

« Indian Bank PO 2011

62. Problem Figures

1	2	3	4	5
L O △ C / V = / Z / ⌂ S / □ P U ★	V U P = / ⌂ S / L / □ ★ / C △ O Z	Z △ U C / ★ □ / ⊠ / S ⌂ / = O P V	★ P O □ / S ⌂ / Z / = V / C U △ ⊠	⊠ U P C / V = / T / ⌂ S / □ △ O ★

Answers Figures

(a)	(b)	(c)	(d)	(e)
V △ O = / ⌂ S / ⊠ / □ ★ / C U P T	V O △ = / ⌂ S / ⊠ / □ ★ / C U P T	V O △ = / ⌂ S / C / □ ★ / T P U ⊠	V O △ = / ⌂ S / ⊠ / □ ★ / C P U T	V △ O = / ⌂ S / □ ★ / T P U ⊠

« Indian Bank PO 2011

Answers / WITH EXPLANATIONS

1. (*c*) The given shape is rotating 135° in anti-clockwise direction in each step.

2. (*d*) The shaded circle moves sequentially $\frac{1}{2}, 1, 1\frac{1}{2}, 2$ in anti-clockwise direction.

3. (*d*) The shaded portion moves either side of the figure and there is a reversal of the whole figure in each successive block.

OR Similar figure repeats in every second step.

4. (*c*) The circle moves half step in clockwise direction in each successive figure.

5. (*d*) The arrow moves sequentially by spaces clockwise and the pin moves $2\frac{1}{2}, \frac{2}{0}, 1\frac{1}{2}, 1$ ... spaces in direction anti-clockwise.

6. (*d*) In each problem figure, the gray colour shade is moving half step in anti-clockwise direction whereas the black colour shade is moving half step in clockwise direction.

7. (*c*) The triangle is moving one step in clockwise direction. The circle is moving one step in clockwise direction and also it is rotating 90° in each step. The middle symbol is rotating 90° in each step.

8. (*d*) In each step, the arrow moves $\frac{1}{2}, 1, 1\frac{1}{2}, 2$ and $2\frac{1}{2}$ steps respectively in anti-clockwise direction and gets laterally inverted.

9. (*b*) The arrow moves $\frac{1}{2}, 1, 1\frac{1}{2}, 2$ and $2\frac{1}{2}$ steps in each subsequent figure. Also, the arrow rotates 180° and 90° anti-clockwise in second and third figures, respectively. After the third figure, this process is repeated from the fourth figure.

10. (*d*) The figure rotates in anti-clockwise direction through an angle of 45°, 90°, 45°, 90°,... and so on and every time one line is deleted from the figure.

11. (*b*) Blank box is moving one step and half step alternatively and filled or lined box is moving clockwise half step and one step alternatively. So, the answer figure (b) will be the next figure.

12. (*b*) The shaded portion moves $1\frac{1}{2}$ and 2 steps alternatively in clockwise direction in the successive figures.

13. (*d*) From figure (1) to (2) black dots and main figure move one step in anti-clockwise direction.

From figure (2) to (3) white circles and main figure move one step in anti-clockwise and this process goes on in alternate steps.

14. (*c*) There is an alternate rotation of 45° anti-clockwise and 225° clockwise and also the square and triangle attached with the line are rotating alternatively according to a certain pattern.

15. (*e*) In the first step the line containing circle comes to the opposite corner but the line containing square remains stationary and in the next step, the line containing square comes to the opposite corner but the line containing circle remains stationary and so on. The '∩' figure inside the big square changes orientation one-by-one in each step.

16. (*d*) In each successive figure, the main design is rotated 180°, 90°, 180°, 90°, ... respectively in anti-clockwise direction. The small triangle moves from left to right, right to left and the line segment attached with the main design changes its position from inside to outside and outside to inside at the opposite corner of triangle.

17. (*d*) A new small line segment is added to one of the lines in the figure sequentially in anti-clockwise direction.

18. (*c*) Half portion of the upper most rectangle is removed in one step and one complete rectangle of the lower most is removed in the next step.

19. (*d*) In each step, the figure gets vertically inverted and a line segment is added to the RHS end.

20. (*a*) Similar figure repeats in every second step and each time a particular figure reappears, it gets rotated through 180°.

21. (*d*) The figure gets laterally inverted and also the number of arrows increases by one in each step.

22. (*d*) Similar figure repeats in every second step. Each time a particular figure reappears, it gets rotated through 180° and the number of arrowheads increases by one.

23. (*d*) In each successive figure, a line segment is added to the main figure in a fixed pattern.

24. (*b*) The main figure rotates 45° anti-clockwise in every successive step and at both the ends of the line a small line segment is added, respectively in every alternate figure, first at the right side and then at the left side.

25. (*a*) In each successive figure, one, two, three and four lines are added to the main figure in anti-clockwise direction.

26. (a) The figure rotates 45° clockwise in each successive figure. The shaded triangle shifts to the other side from problem figure (1) to (2) and arrow is shifted to the other side from problem figure (2) to (3) and then this process is repeated alternatively.

27. (*a*) The sign '+' moves 1, 1, 2, 2, 3,... steps anti-clockwise, in each of the successive figures and one new symbol is added before and after it.

28. (*e*) The triangle is reversed and the dot is increased by one in each step.

29. (*d*) In the problem figures, triangles given in dark shades is moving 90° anti-clockwise in each step and the number of lines surrounding the triangles is increased by one in each step.

30. (*e*) Circle moves $\frac{1}{2}$ and 1 steps anti-clockwise alternatively in each subsequent block and a new figure is added before it.

Also each time the new figure is preceded by another new figure in the subsequent block.

31. (*d*) In each problem figure one new design is added and after rotating 90° in anti-clockwise direction, the design shifts one place in anti-clockwise direction.

32. (*a*) In each step, the figure gets laterally inverted and one and two lines are added alternately.

33. (*c*) The number of sides in the central figure is reducing by 1, so the triangle will come in the centre of the answer figure.

Other elements shift 2 steps in clockwise or anti-clockwise directions.

34. (*d*) From problem figures (1) to (2), arrow rotates 45° anti-clockwise and one more arrow is added ahead of it in anti-clockwise direction and the same pattern is repeated in the subsequent figures.

The figure in the middle moves in anti-clockwise manner with 1, 2, 3, 4,... spaces and is replaced by a new figure in each of the subsequent figures respectively.

35. (*e*) The black leaf rotates 0°, 45°, 90°,... anti-clockwise and clockwise alternatively and a white leaf is added in each step at the end other than that where the black leaf is present.

36. (*b*) In the problem figures, the geometrical shape given in fourth figure is the inverse of first figure and the shape P is moving $1, 1\frac{1}{2}, 2...$ steps in anti-clockwise direction.

37. (*d*) In each step, one of the circles turns black and moves to a corner of the square boundary.

38. (*b*) Every alternate figure is same. So, following the same pattern answer figure (b), will be obtained as the correct answer figure.

39. (*d*) In the first step, the left arrow at the top of the main figure is inverted. In second step, the right arrow as the top of the main figure is inverted. This process continues from third to fourth and from fourth to the answer figure.

40. (*a*) In the first step '×' sign moves one position downward and in next step '–' sign moves one step towards left. These steps are repeated alternatively.

41. (*a*) The elements at the face of the cylinder remain same for two consecutive figures.

Among the two consecutive figures, one is vertical while the other is horizontal. As problem figure (5) is vertical, the answer figure must be horizontal.

Also, the number of shaded dots are increased by one in each subsequent figure.

42. (*d*) From first to second figure

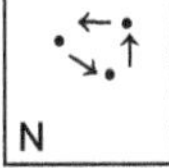

From second to the third figure

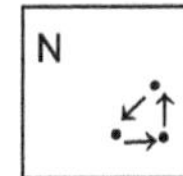

From third to the fourth figure

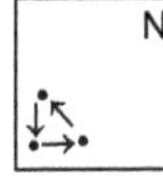

From fourth to the fifth figure

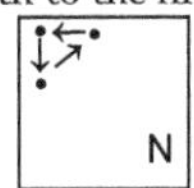

where, N is a new figure.

Similarly, from fifth to the answer figure

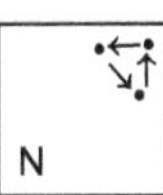

Figure (d) is the figure which will be formed by following the same pattern.

43. (*d*) From problem figure (1) to (2), the symbol on the left side rotates 90° clockwise and gets shifted to the right side and a new symbol is added on the left side. The same pattern follows from problem figure (3) to (4) and (5) to the answer figure.

44. (*e*) Line at the bottom in figure (1) is same as the line at the bottom in figure (5). Therefore, the line in answer figure must be same as in figure (2). Main figure is same for two consecutive figures but with the mirror image. Also, the shaded portion of the circle in figure (5) is opposite of figure (1). Hence, it will be opposite of figure (2)in the answer figure.

45. (*d*) Figures 1, 3 and 5 are same. Similarly figures 2, 4 and the answer figure (d) will be same.

46. (*e*) Dark circle moves anti-clockwise in a triangular pattern, rest of the symbols move anti-clockwise and a new symbol is also added.

47. (*d*) The series of letters present horizontally is moving one position downwards in each subsequent figures along with addition of a new element in the vertical series in place of an old element. Also, from problem figures (1) to (2), the two letters present on the left side of the vertical line interchange their position. Same is the case for right side letters. From problem figures (2) to (3), the pair of letters present on left side interchanges its position with the pair of letters present on the right side. Now, the same process repeats.

48. (*b*) In the 1st step two lower elements interchange their places while the other three shift anti-clockwise in cyclic order. In the next step the upper two elements interchange their places while the remaining three shift one step anti-clockwise in a cyclic order. In the next step, all the elements which are present in the horizontal line move one position downwards while elements present at corners move 90° anti-clokwise. Now, the whole process repeats except that the shifting of three elements is now clockwise.

49. (*c*) Problem figure (5) is same as figure (1) with shifting of shaded portion in opposite direction. Therefore, answer figure will be same as figure (2) with shifting of the shaded portion.

50. (*c*) The third figure is obtained by rotating the symbols of first figure 180° anti-clockwise, fourth figure is obtained by rotating the symbols of second figure 180° clockwise. Similarly, answer figure will be obtained by rotating the symbols of fourth figure 180° clockwise.

51. (*b*) It is clear that '+' (plus sign) is moving $\frac{1}{2}, 1, 1\frac{1}{2}, 2,...$steps in clockwise direction, '×' (multiplication sign) is moving $1, 1\frac{1}{2}, 2, 2\frac{1}{2}$ ... steps in anti-clockwise direction and '↑' (arrow sign) is changing its place from bottom right to top left position alternately and getting inverted.

52. (*a*) From problem figure (1) to (3) and (3) to (5) letter E comes two place left and other letters have been written in same order. Similar pattern follows from problem figure (2) to (4) and (4) to the answer figure.

53. (*d*) Change in the position of elements from problem figure (1) to (2) is similar to the changing position of the elements from problem figure (3) to (4). Similarly, the pattern from problem figure (2) to (3) is same as the pattern from problem figure (4) to (5). So, the pattern from problem figure (5) to the answer figure must be similar to the pattern from problem figure (3) to (4).

54. (*c*) Central circle becomes dark and white alternately. All four elements are moving clockwise and a new element replaces the old one at the upper corner of right hand side of the figure.

55. (*c*) Problem figure (1) is same as the figure (5), hence answer figure will be same as the figure (2).

56. (*a*) From problem figure (1) to (2), (3) to (4) and (5) to the answer figure, the following sequence takes place.

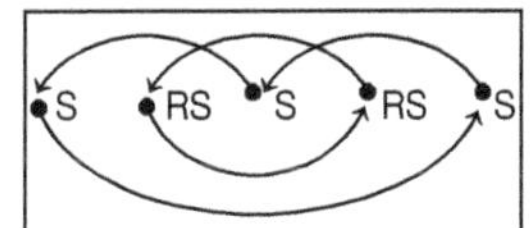

S = Same design
RS = Reverse the same design

57. (*e*) From problem figure (1) to (2), (3) to (4) and (5) to the answer figure, the following sequence (whole figure rotates 45° in clockwise direction) takes place.

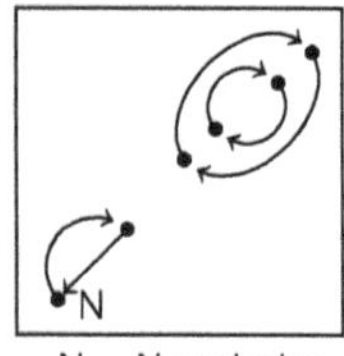

N = New design

58. (*b*) From problem figure (1) to (2), (3) to (4) and (5) to the answer figure, the following sequence takes place.

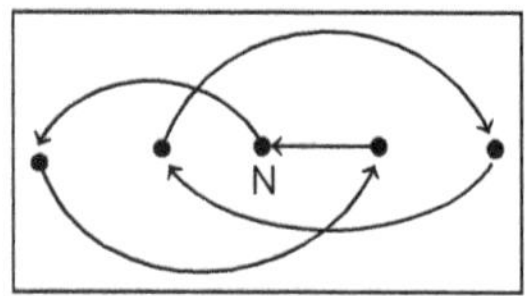

N = New design

59. (*a*) The sequence of the problem figures is

Problem figure (1) to (2)

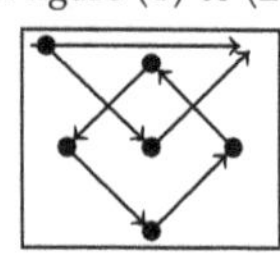

Problem figure (3) to (4)

Problem figure (5) to the answer figure

60. (*e*)

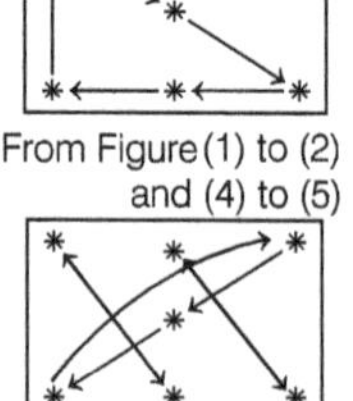

From Figure (1) to (2) and (4) to (5)

From Figure (2) to (3) and (5) to the answer figure

61. (*a*) Diagrams are moving as follows

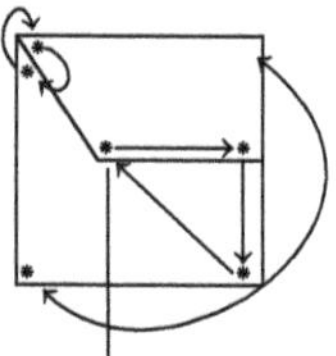

a new diagram takes place

Problem figure (1) to (2), Problem figure (3) to (4), Problem figure (5) to the answer figure.

62. (*d*) Diagrams are moving as follows

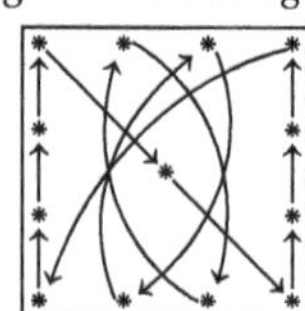

Problem figure (1) to (2)
Problem figure (3) to (4)
Problem figure (5) to the answer figure.

TYPE 02

Choosing the Missing Figure in the Series

In this type of questions, one figure from the set of problem figures is missing and is represented by the sign '?'. Based on certain pattern or rule followed by the problem figures, candidates are asked to choose one figure from the set of answer figures which replaces the sign '?'. This type of questions are explained in the following examples

DIRECTIONS ~ (Example Nos. 20-30) *Each of the following questions consists of three/four/five problem figures marked as 1, 2, 3, 4 and 5 followed by four/five answer figures marked as (a), (b), (c), (d) and (e). If one of these answer figures is placed in the place of '?' in the problem figures, a series is established and the figure which should replace the '?' is your answer.*

***Ex* 20** **Problem Figures**

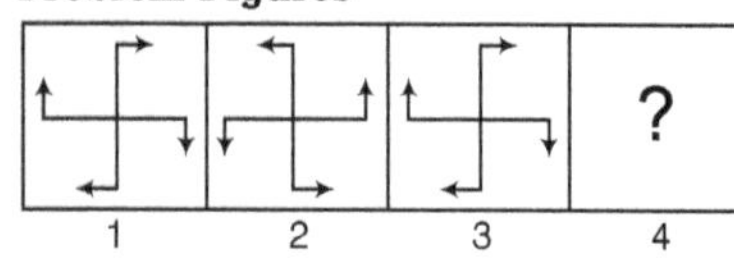

1 2 3 4

Answer Figures

(a) (b) (c) (d) (e)

***Solution* (d)** The figure gets laterally inverted in each step. Clearly, figure (d) is obtained by the lateral inversion of figure (3).

***Ex* 21** **Problem Figures**

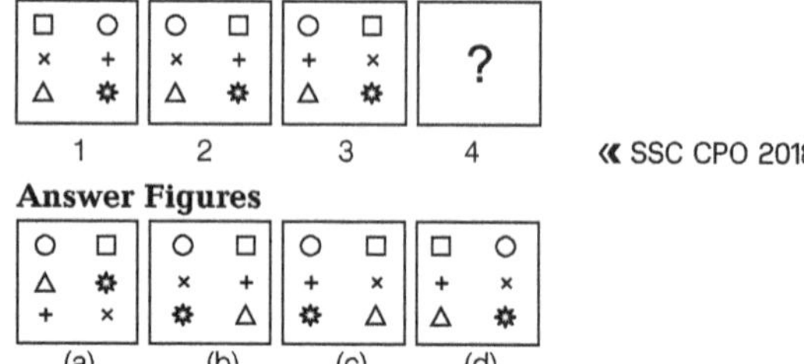

« SSC CPO 2018

***Solution* (c)** From first to second figure, top two elements interchange their positions. From second to third figure, middle two elements interchange their positions. From third to fourth figure, bottom two elements will interchange their positions. Hence, answer figure (c) will come next in the given series.

***Ex* 22** **Problem Figures**

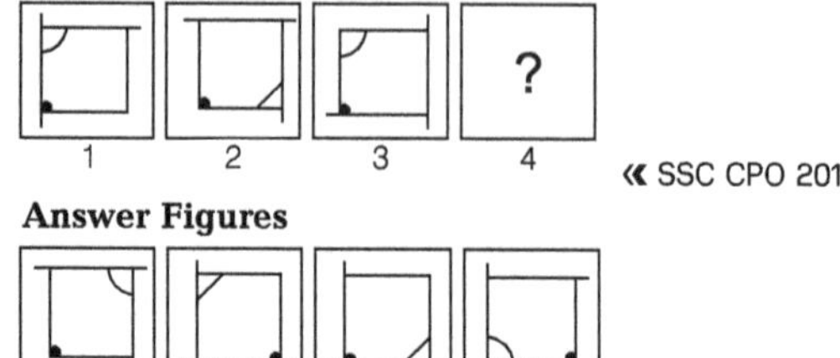

« SSC CPO 2018

Solution (c) In each successive step, the main figure is rotating through 90° in clockwise direction. The curve given in first figure gets converted into a straight line and shifts at the opposite corner in second figure and then the straight line in the curve in third figure also shifted at the opposite corner. This process continues.

Hence, option figure (c) will replace'?'.

Ex 23 **Problem Figures**

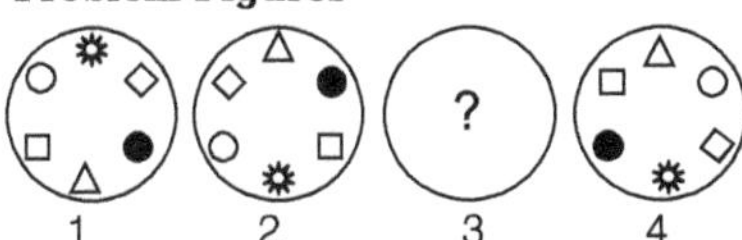

Answer Figures

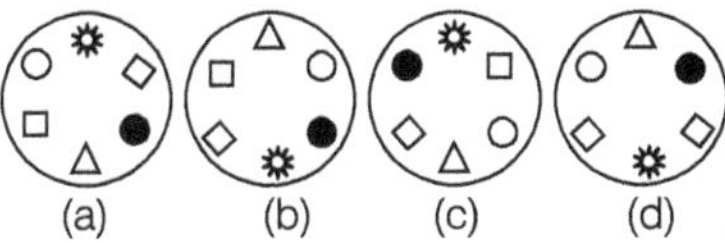

« RRB NTPC 2016

Solution (c) In each successive figure symbols 'Δ' and ✲ are interchanging their positions and rest of the symbols are moving in anti-clockwise direction in a cyclic order.

Ex 24 **Problem Figures**

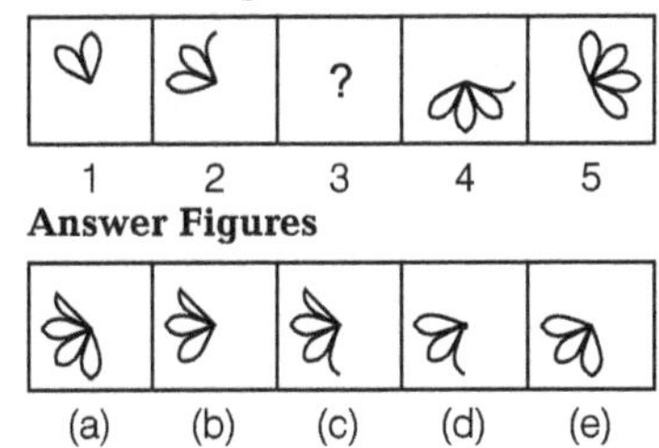

Solution (e) The figure rotates 45° and 90° alternatively in anti-clockwise direction and half leaf is added everytime to the figure respectively.

Ex 25 **Problem Figures**

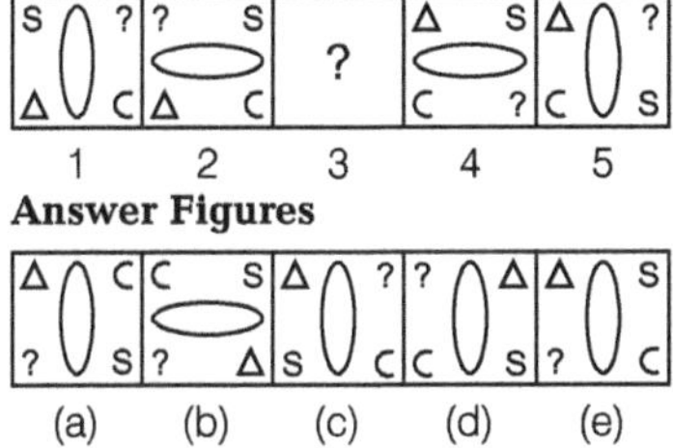

Solution (e) The '?' rotates 90° anticlockwise while the other symbols at the corner sides rotates 90° clockwise. The middle 'oval' shaped figure rotates 180° in each successive figure.

Ex 26 **Problem Figures**

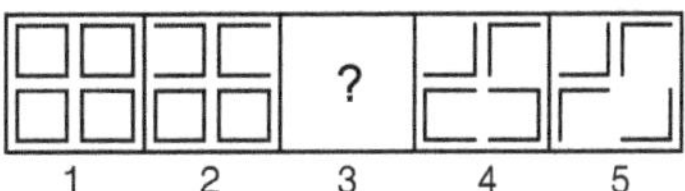

Answer Figures

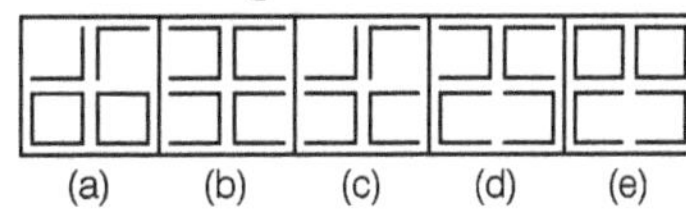

Solution (d) Two lines from the upper pair of squares and two lines from the lower pair of squares disappear in alternate manner.

Ex 27 **Problem Figures**

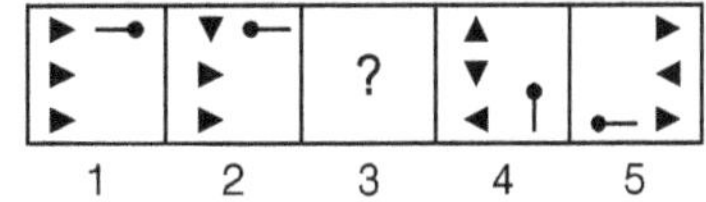

Answer Figures

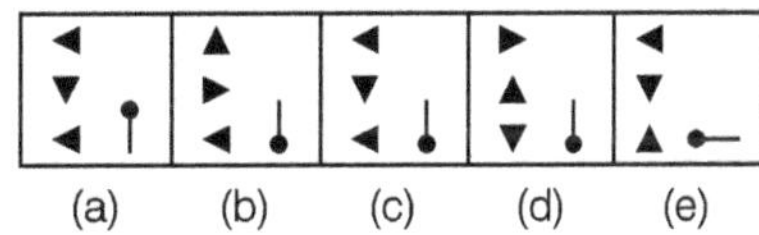

Solution (c) The uppermost triangle rotates through an angle of 90° clockwise in each successive figure, the middle triangle rotates through an angle of 90° clockwise in every second figure and the lowermost triangle rotates through an angle of 180° in every second figure.

The line with the black head is inverted at the same position from problem figure (1) to (2) and so it will from figure (3) to (4).

Ex 28 **Problem Figures**

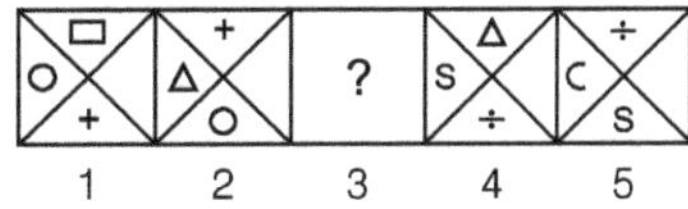

Answer Figures

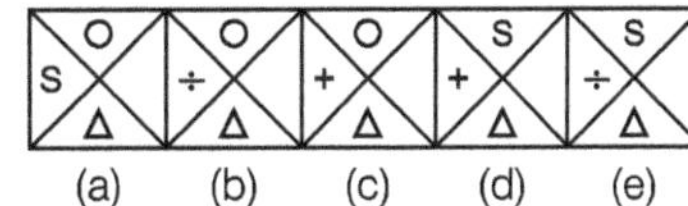

Solution (b) All the symbols move anti-clockwise in a triangular order and the symbol on left hand side is replaced by a new symbol in the subsequent figure.

***Ex* 29** **Problem Figures**

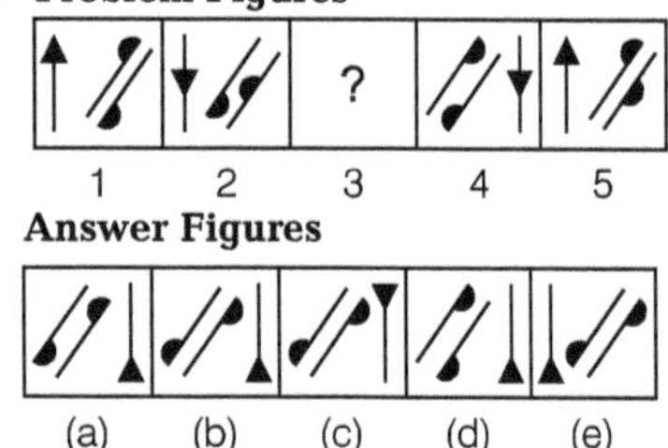

1 2 3 4 5

Answer Figures

(a) (b) (c) (d) (e)

Solution (b) The head of arrow travels half step every time and is reversed in each successive figure. The head of the upper line moves to other side of the line and the line is reversed from figure (1) to (2) but it does not move from figure (4) to (5) but only gets reversed at the same position. It implies that from figure (2) to (3), the head will not move but it will be reversed at the same position. The head of the lower line moves half step and gets reversed at the same position.

***Ex* 30**

Problem Figures

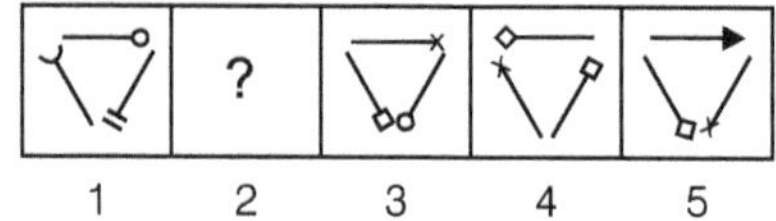

1 2 3 4 5

Answer Figures

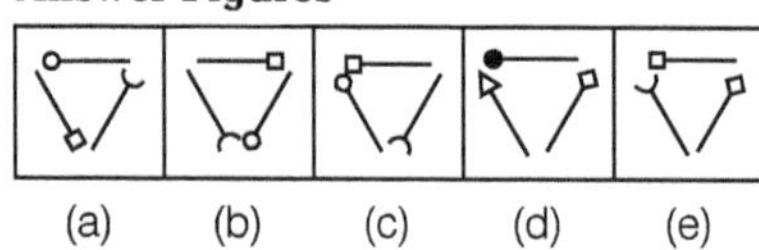

(a) (b) (c) (d) (e)

Solution (c) Each symbol of the figure rotates in anti-clockwise direction and a new symbol replaces the symbol at the top which is inverted alternatively in each of the successive figures.

Practice / CORNER 1.2

DIRECTIONS ~ (Q. Nos. 1-61) *In each of the following questions, there are two sets of figures i.e. problem figures and answer figures. Problem figures contain four/five/six figures marked by numbers 1, 2, 3, 4, 5 and 6 and answer figures contain four/five figures marked by letters (a), (b), (c), (d) and (e). A series will be established, if one of the four/five answer figures is placed in place of the sign '?' in the problem figures and that figure is your answer.*

1. Problem Figures

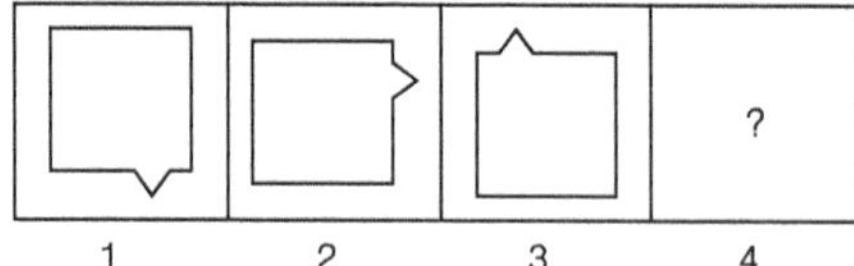

1 2 3 4

Answer Figures

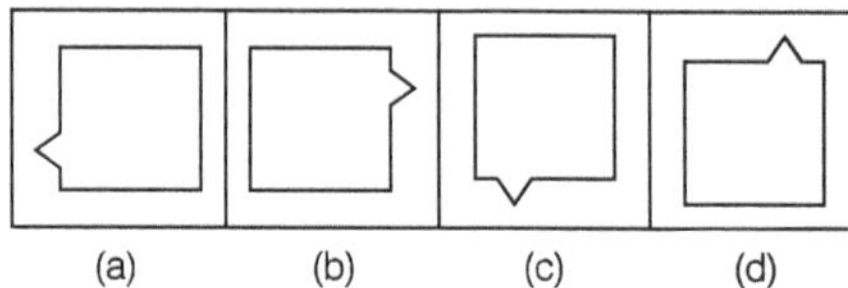

(a) (b) (c) (d)

« SSC 10+2 2009

2. Problem Figures

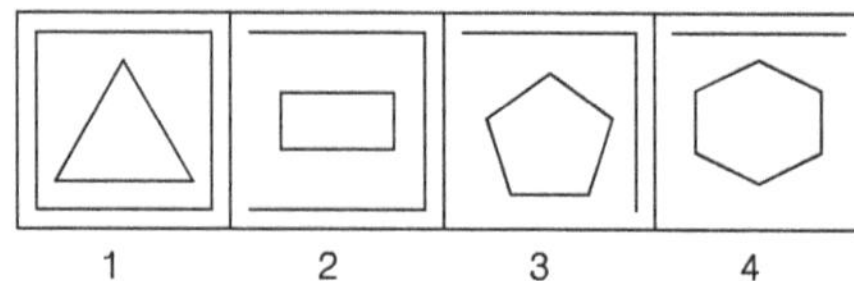

1 2 3 4

Answer Figures

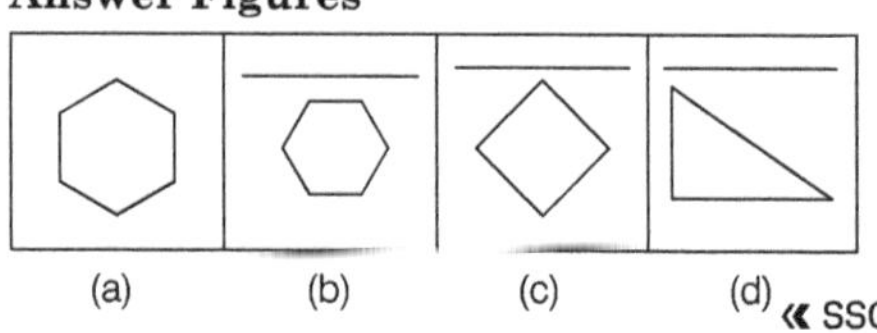

(a) (b) (c) (d) « SSC 10+2 2020

3. Problem Figures

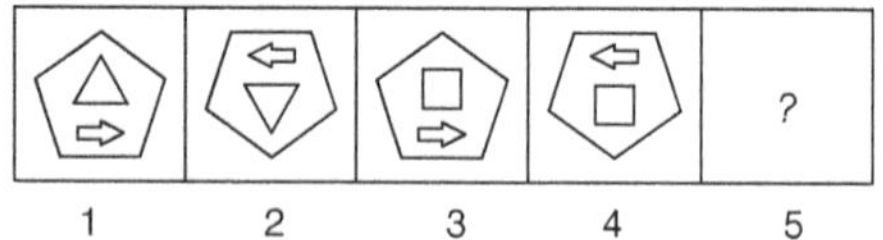

1 2 3 4 5

Answer Figures

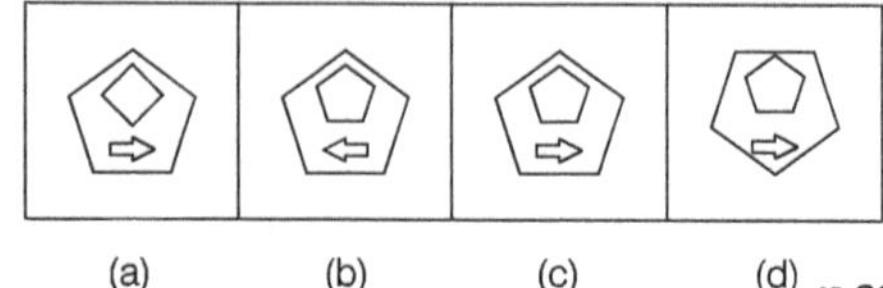

(a) (b) (c) (d) « SSC CGL 2020

4. Problem Figures

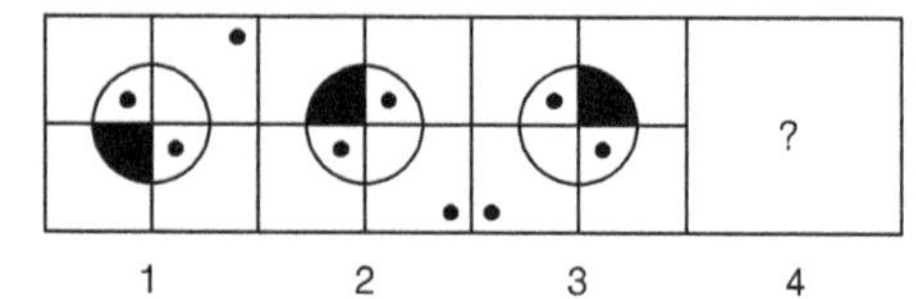

1 2 3 4

Answer Figures

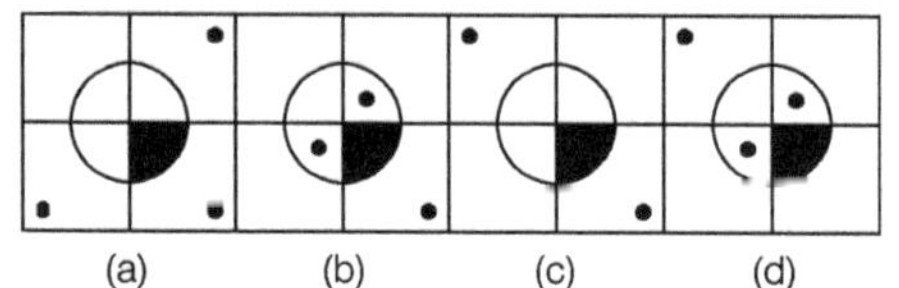

(a) (b) (c) (d)

5. Problem Figures

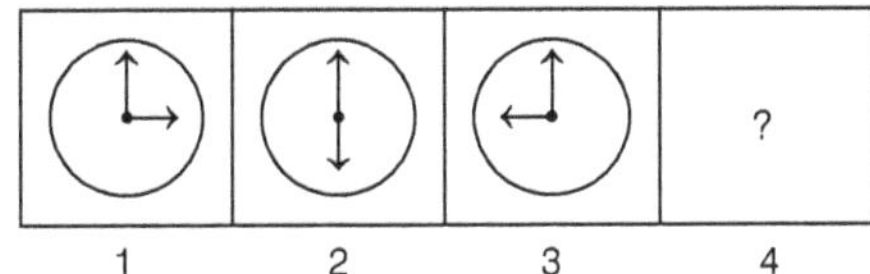

Answer Figures

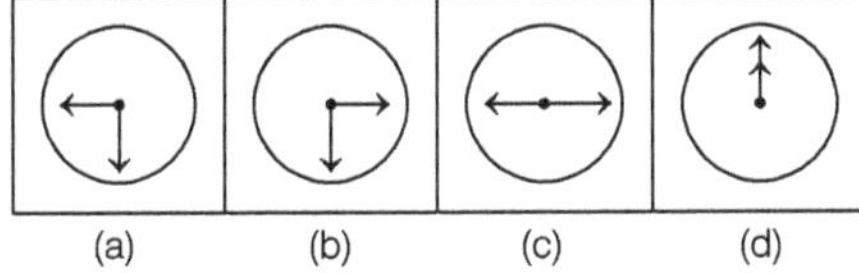

6. Problem Figures

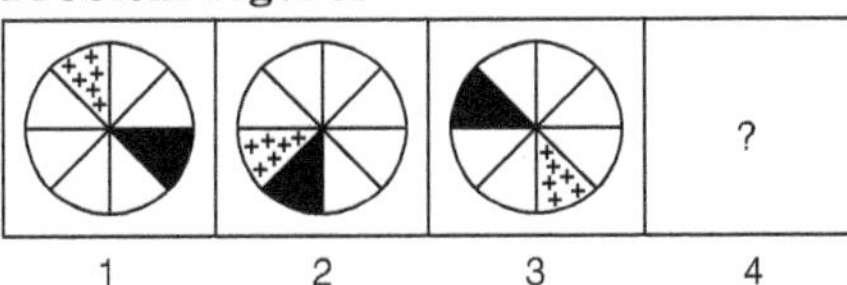

Answer Figures

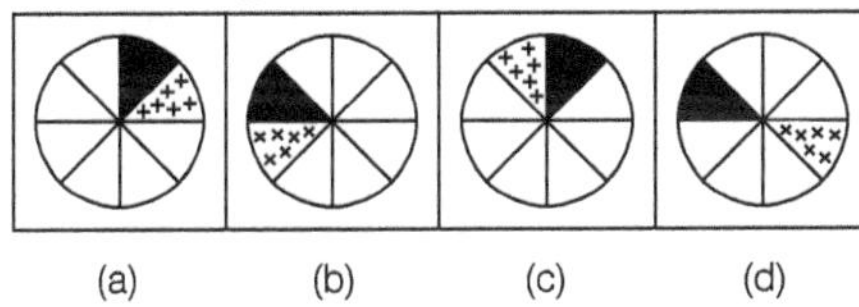

« SSC 10+2 2012

7. Problem Figures

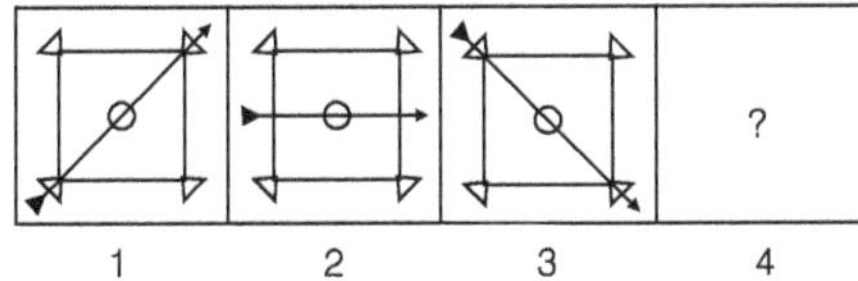

Answer Figures

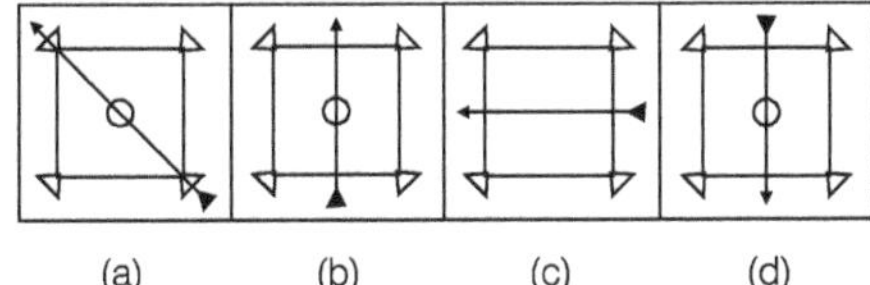

8. Problem Figures

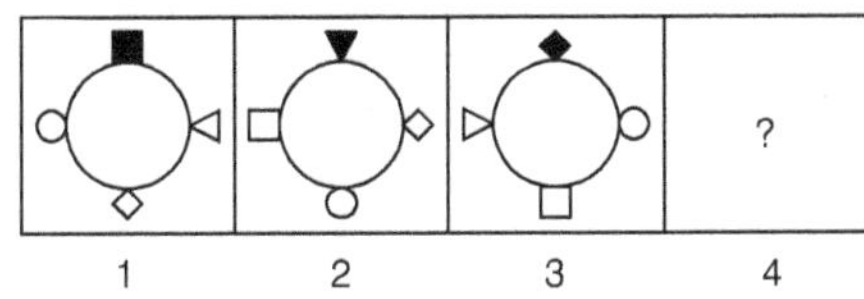

Answer Figures

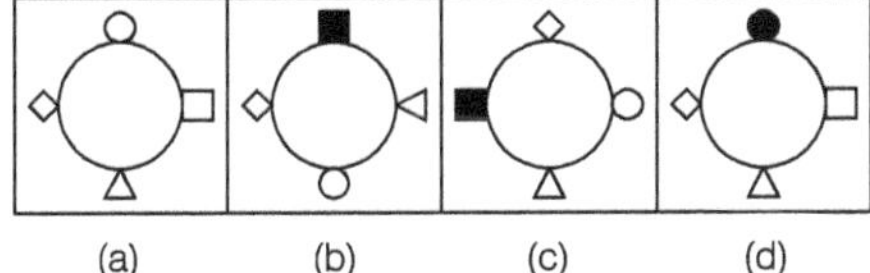

9. Problem Figures

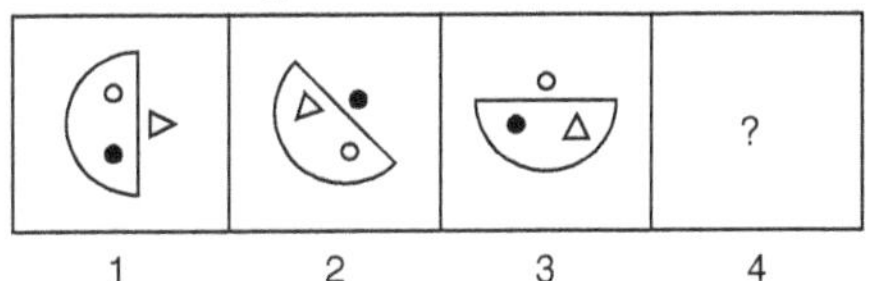

Answer Figures

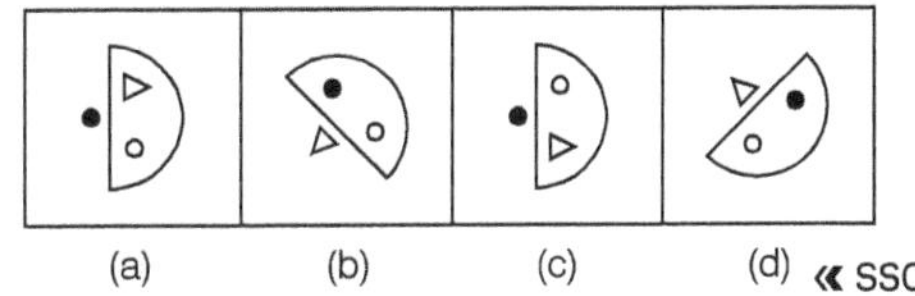

« SSC 10+2 2011

10. Problem Figures

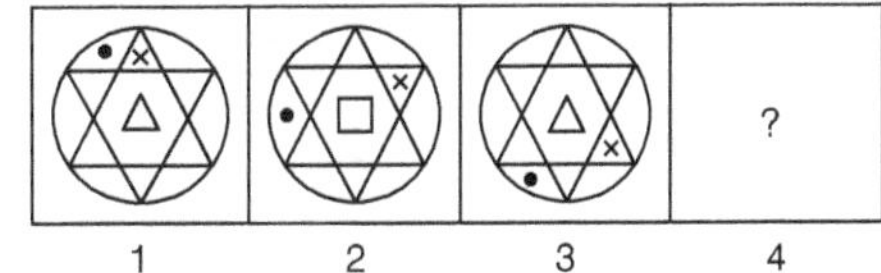

Answer Figures

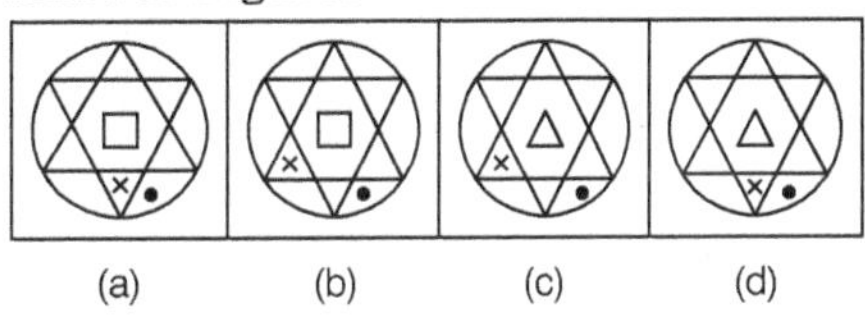

11. Problem Figures

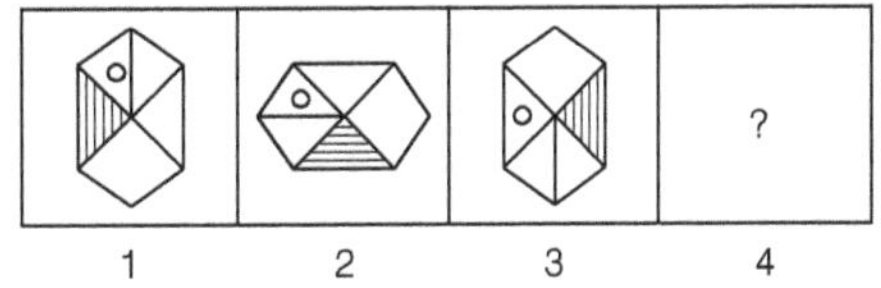

Answer Figures

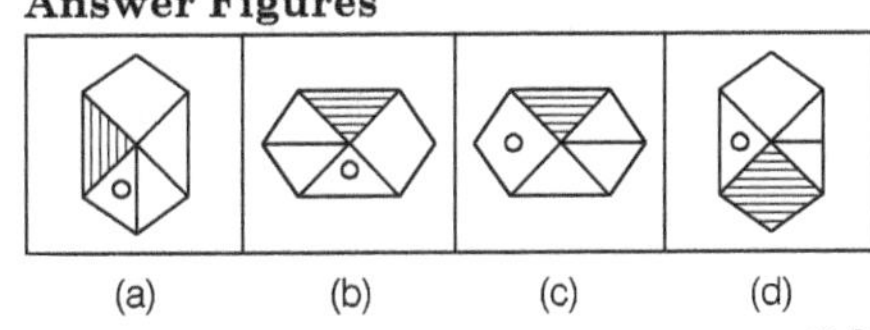

« SSC 10+2 2013

12. Problem Figures

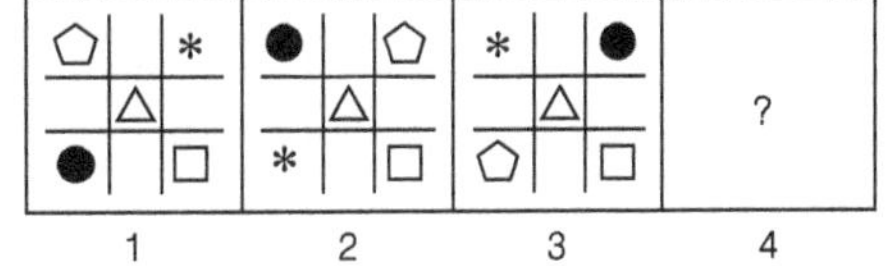

Answer Figures

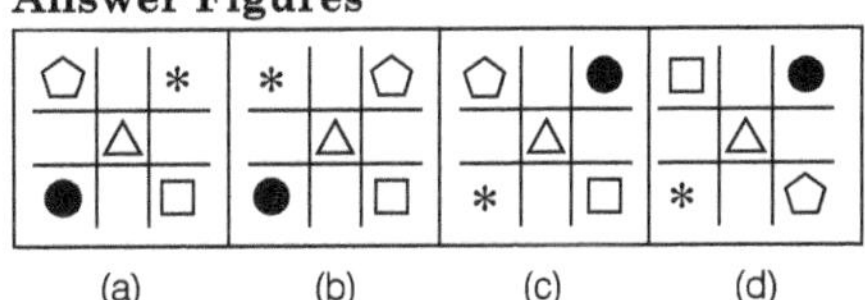

13. Problem Figures

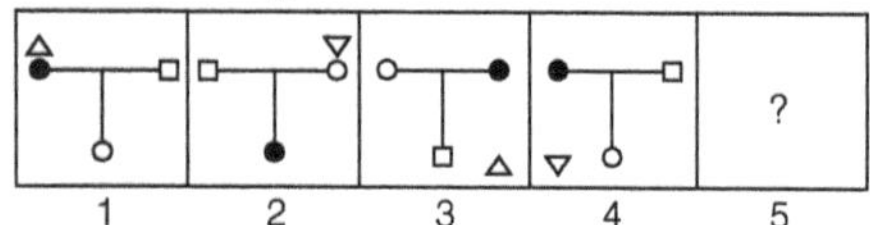

Answer Figures

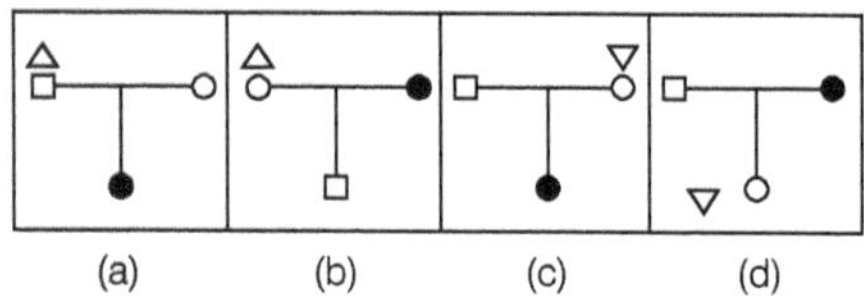

« UPSC CSAT 2015

14. Problem Figures

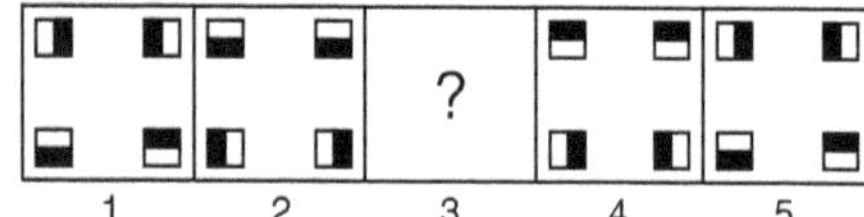

Answer Figures

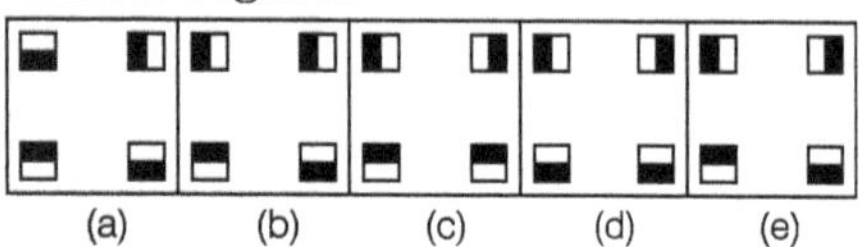

15. Problem Figures

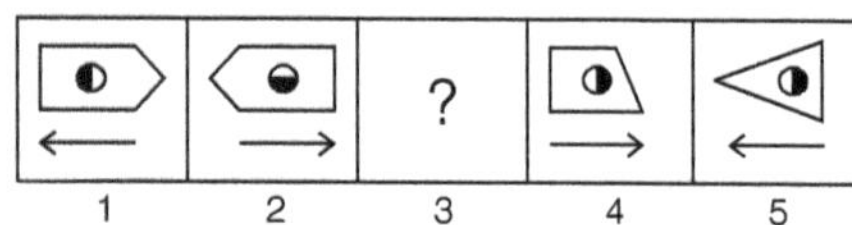

Answer Figures

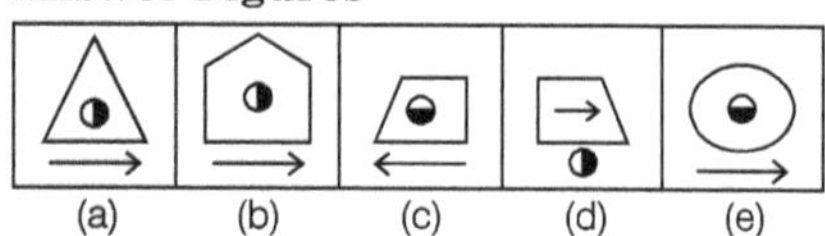

16. Problem Figures

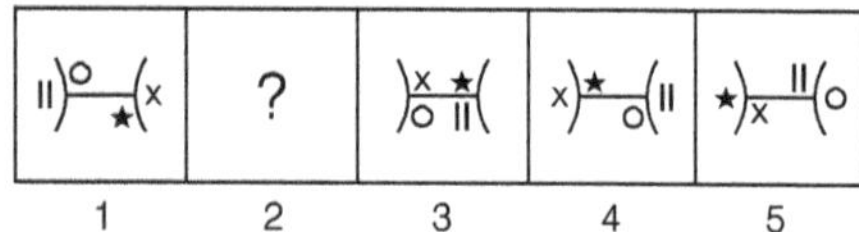

Answer Figures

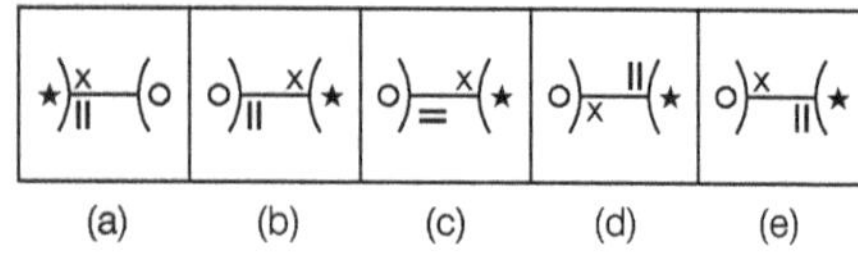

« SBI Clerk 2010

17. Problem Figures

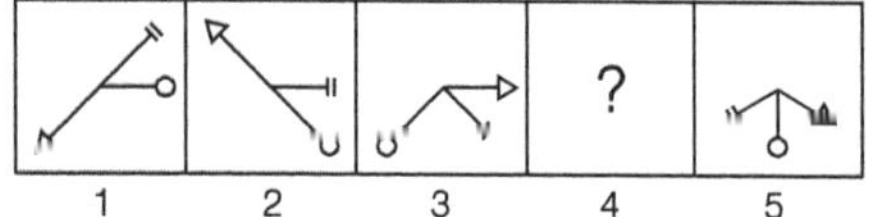

Answer Figures

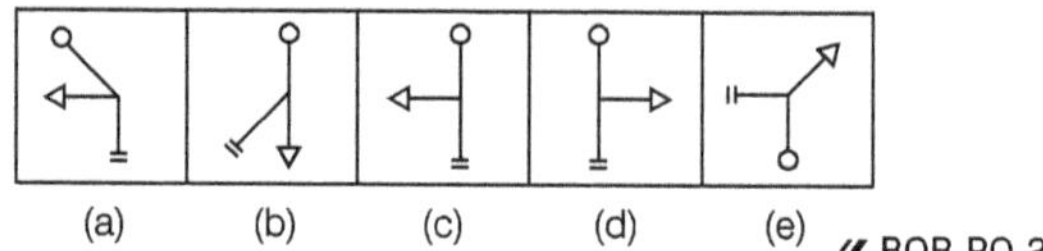

« BOB PO 2011

18. Problem Figures

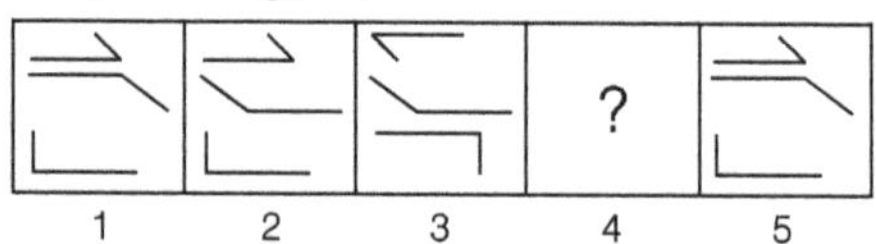

Answer Figures

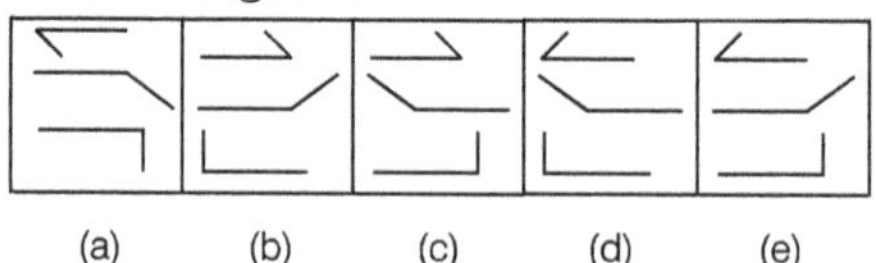

19. Problem Figures

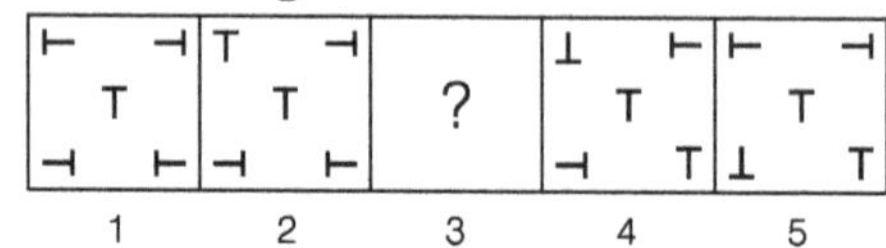

Answer Figures

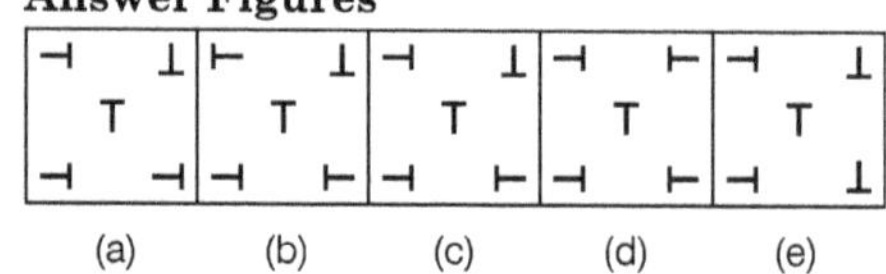

20. Problem Figures

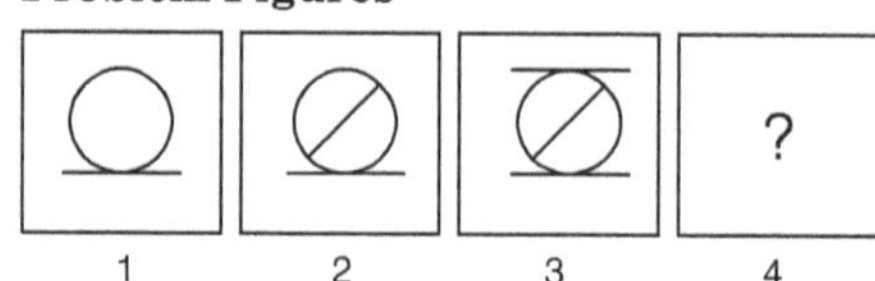

Answer Figures

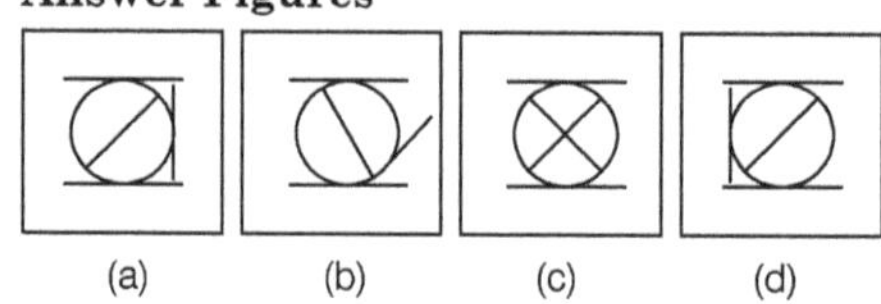

« SSC CPO 2018

21. Problem Figures

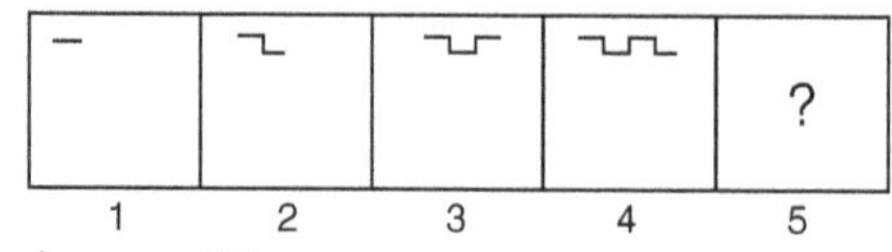

Answer Figures

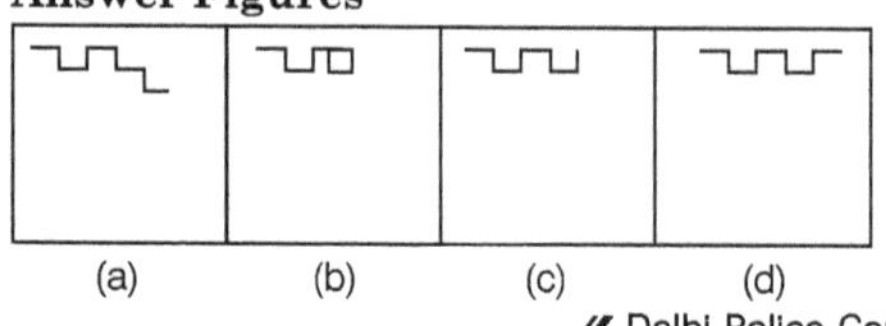

« Delhi Police Constable 2017

22. Problem Figures

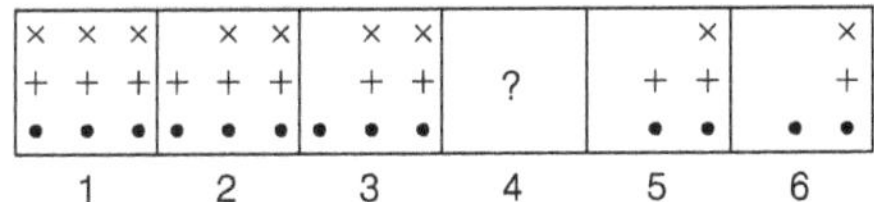

Answer Figures

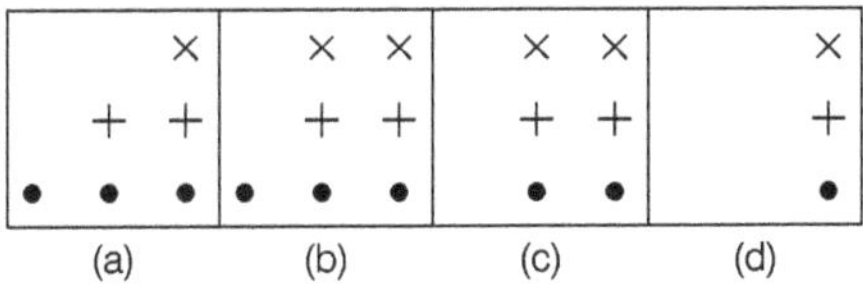

« RRB ALP 2018

23. Problem Figures

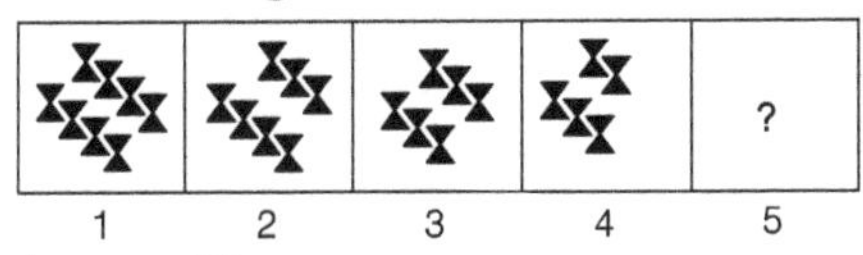

Answer Figures

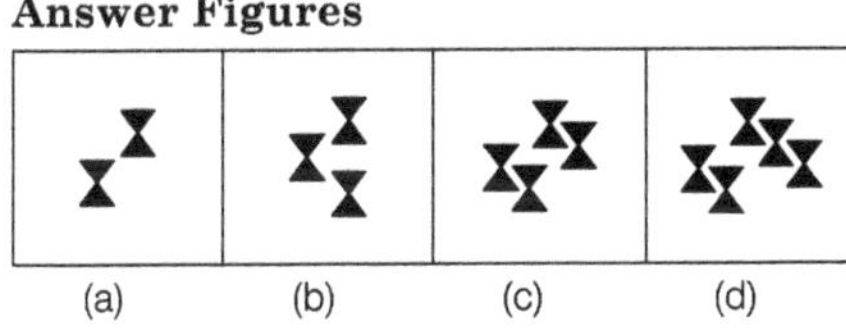

« RRB ALP 2018

24. Problem Figures

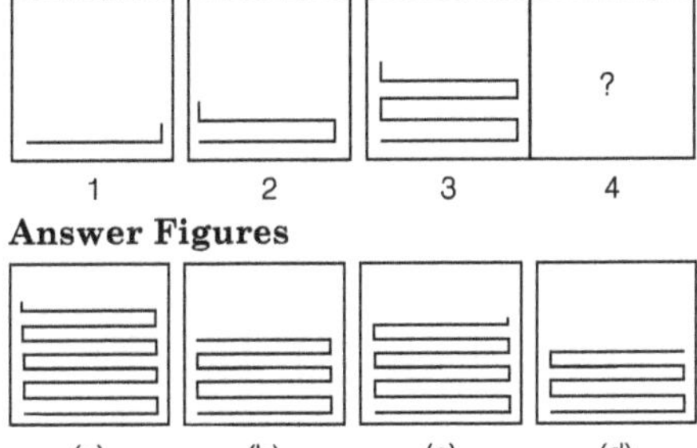

« UPSSSC Junior Assist. 2015

25. Problem Figures

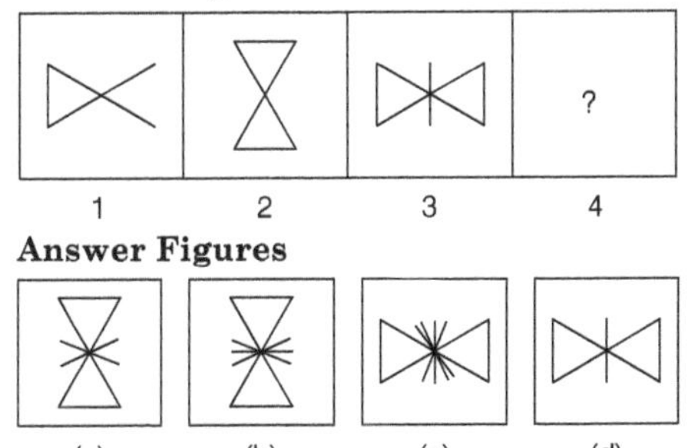

« SSC CGL 2009

26. Problem Figures

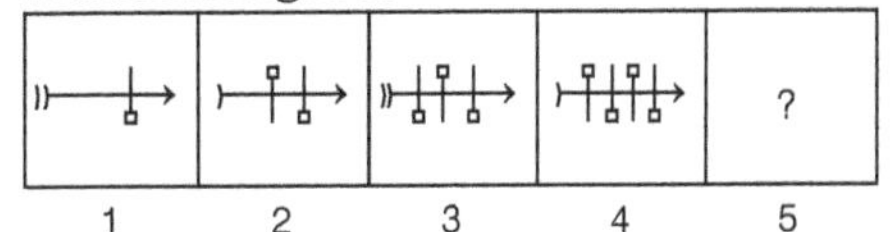

Answer Figures

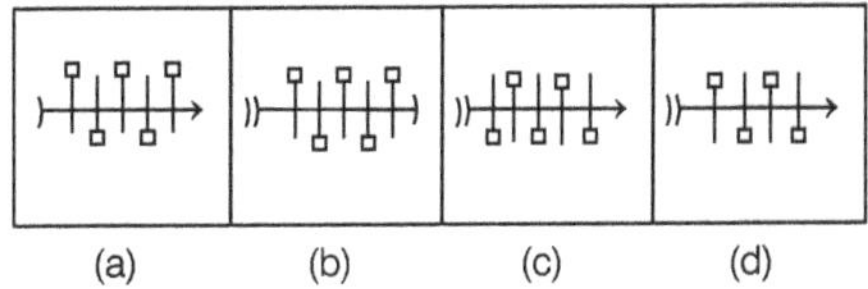

« Delhi Police Constable 2017

27. Problem Figures

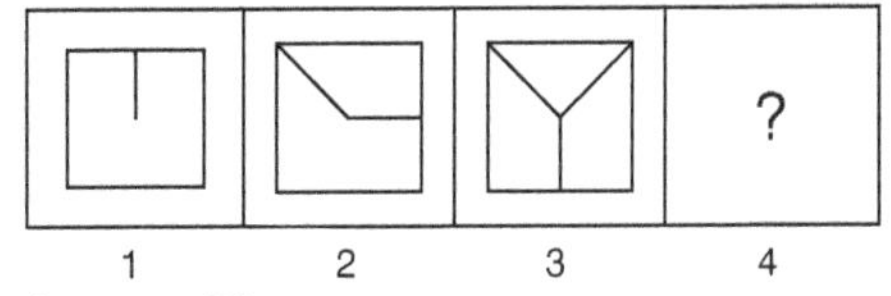

Answer Figures

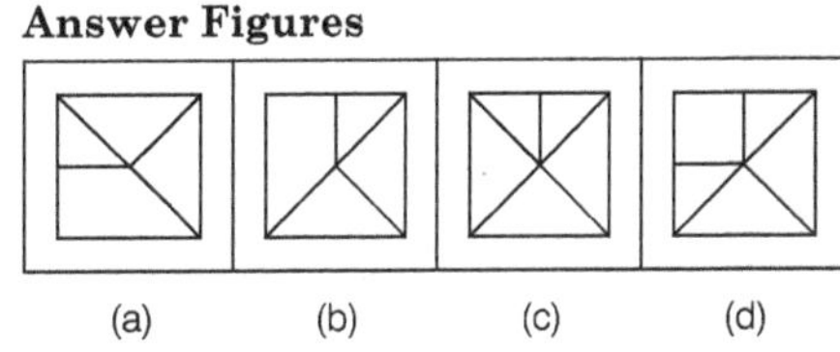

28. Problem Figures

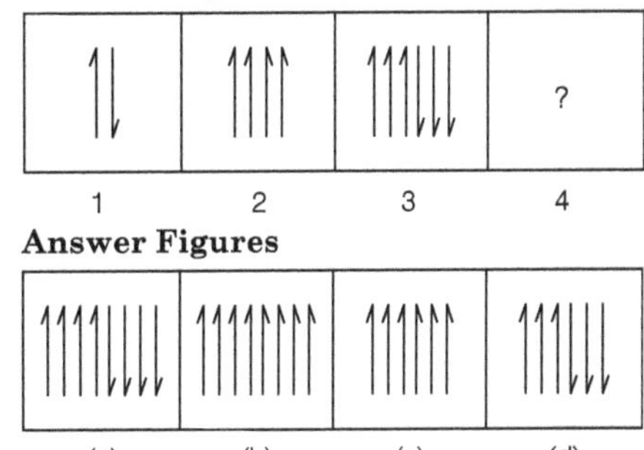

29. Problem Figures

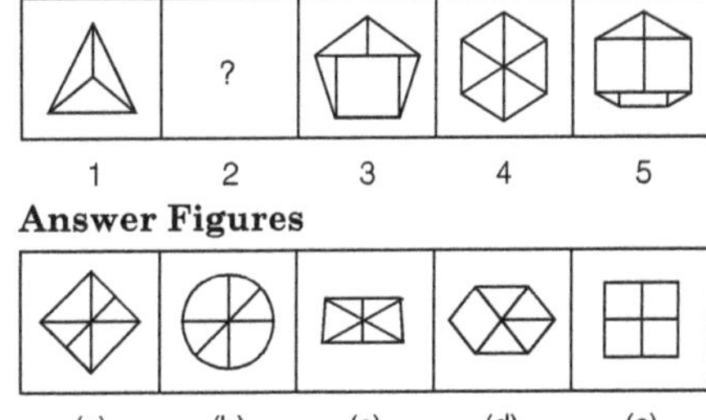

30. Problem Figures

Answer Figures

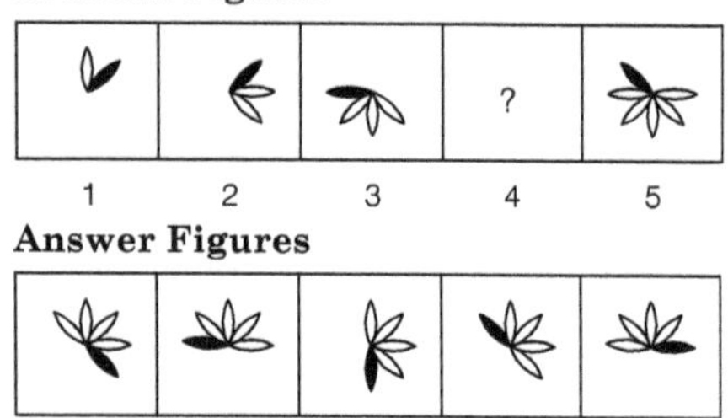

« Union Bank of India PO 2011, PNB Clerk 2008

31. Problem Figures

Answer Figures

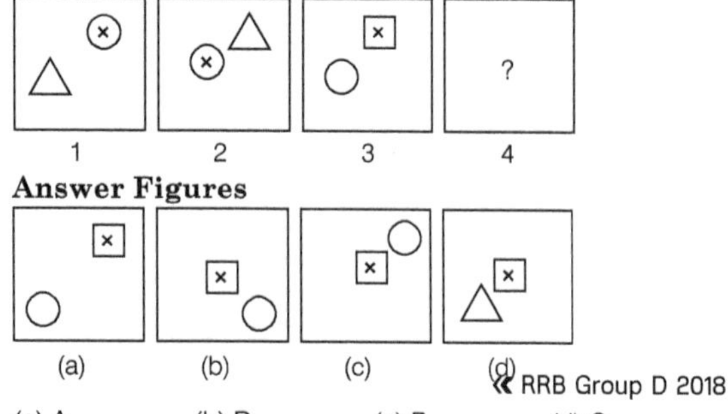

« RRB Group D 2018

(a) A (b) D (c) B (d) C

32. Problem Figures

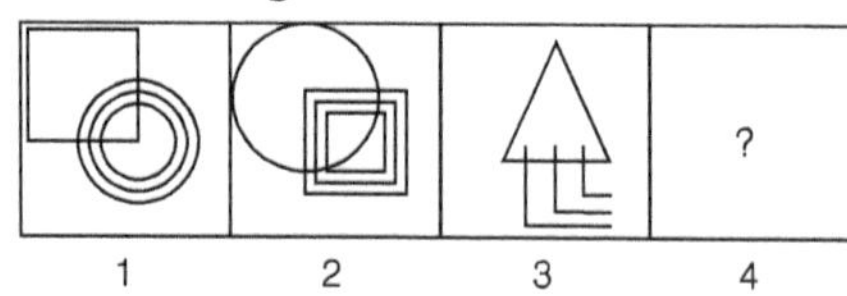

Answer Figures

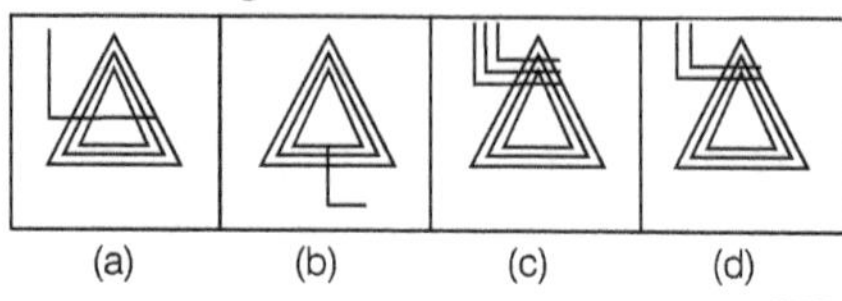

« RRB Group D 2018

33. Problem Figures

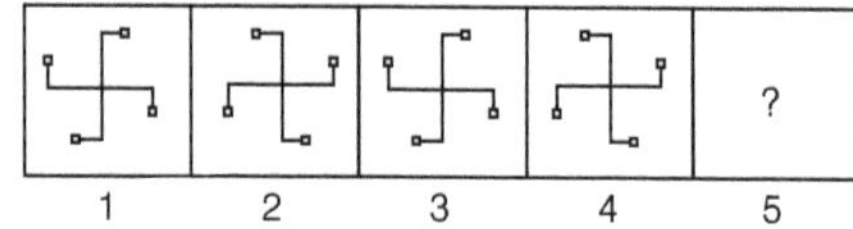

Answer Figures

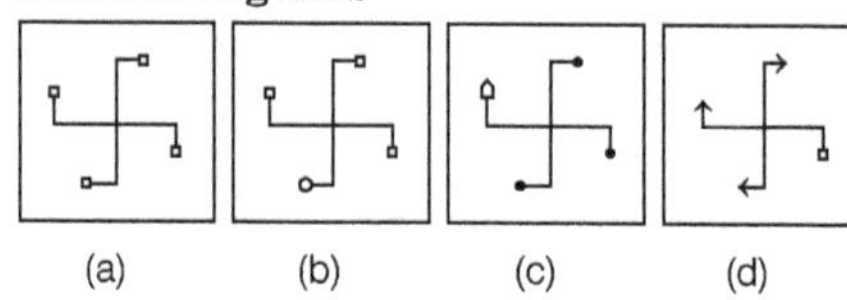

« Delhi Police Constable 2017

34. Problem Figures

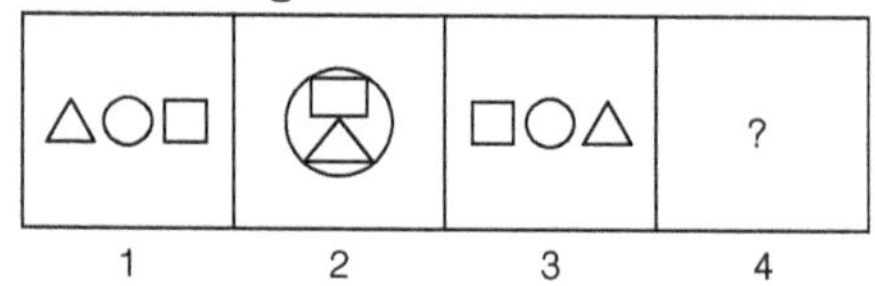

Answer Figures

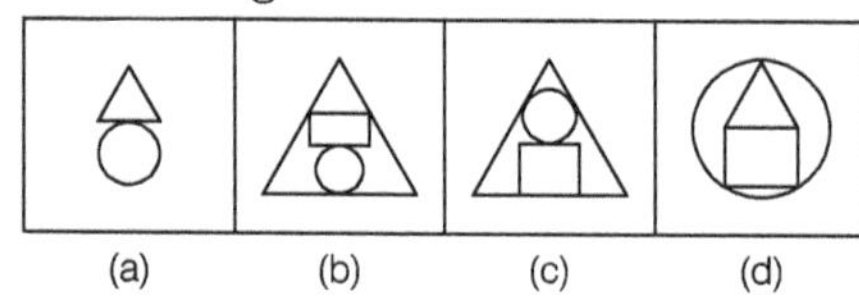

« RRB Group D 2018

35. Problem Figures

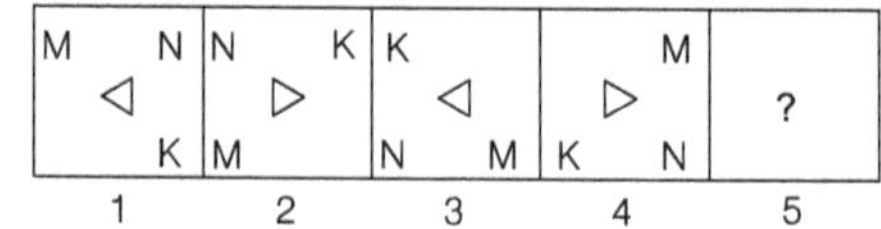

Answer Figures

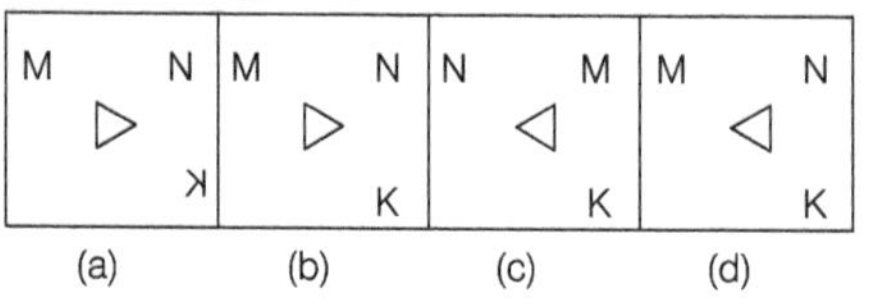

« SSC MTS 2019

36. Problem Figures

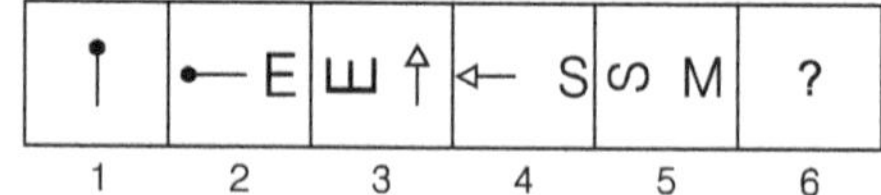

Answer Figures

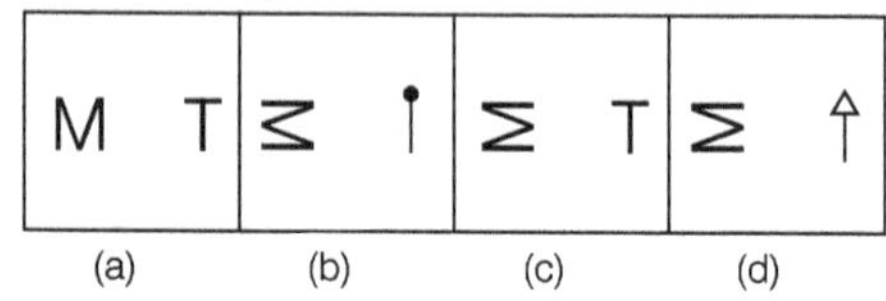

« DSSSB PRT 2016

37. Problem Figures

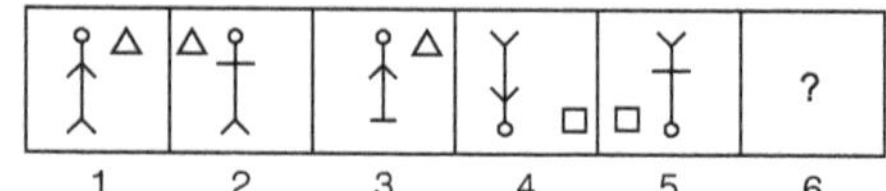

Answer Figures

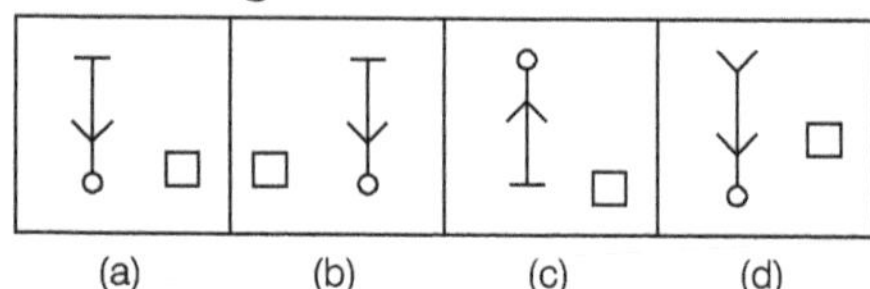

« DSSSB PRT 2016

38. Problem Figures

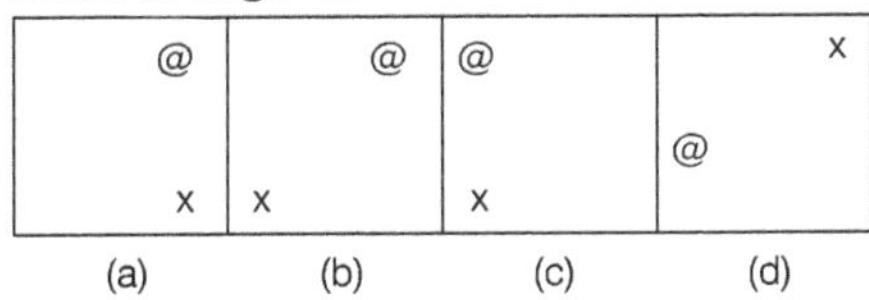

Answer Figures

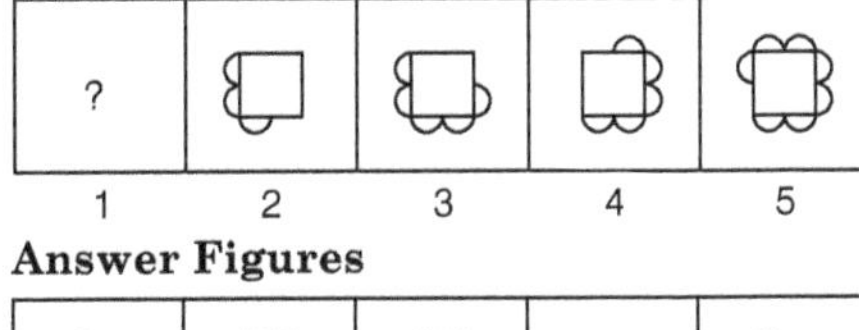

« SSC CPO 2019

39. Problem Figures

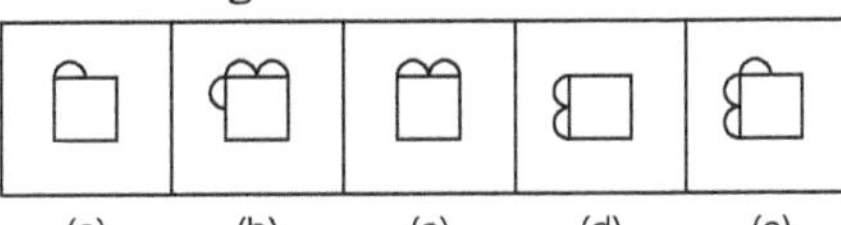

Answer Figures

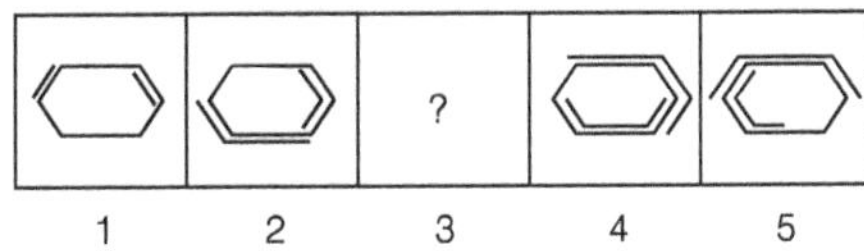

« Union Bank PO 2011,Canara Bank PO 2008

40. Problem Figures

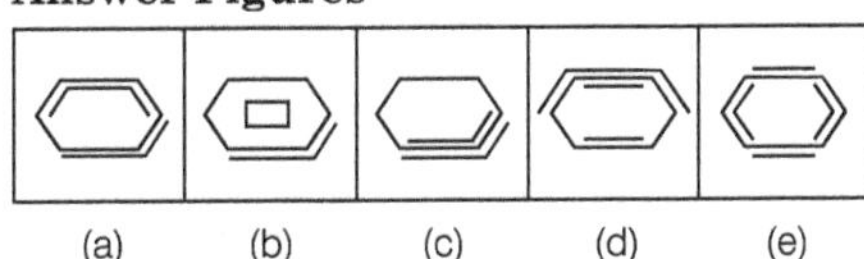

Answer Figures

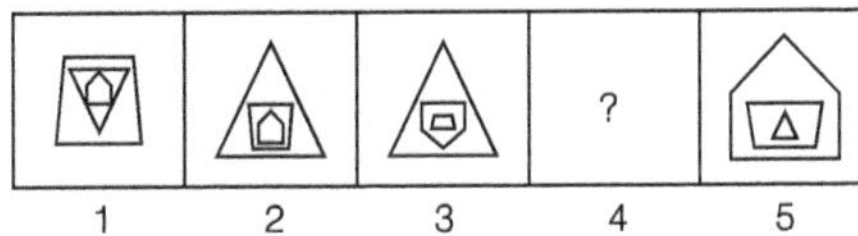

41. Problem Figures

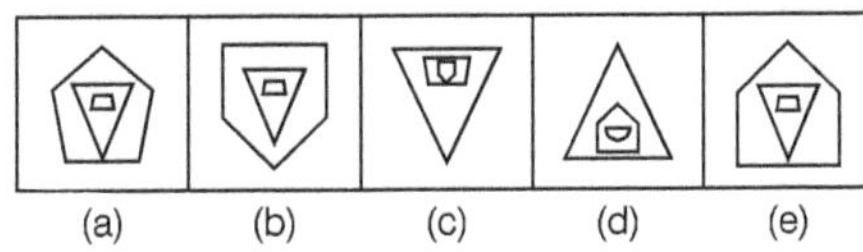

Answer Figures

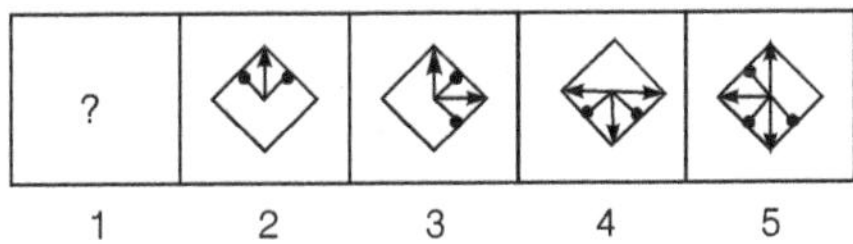

42. Problem Figures

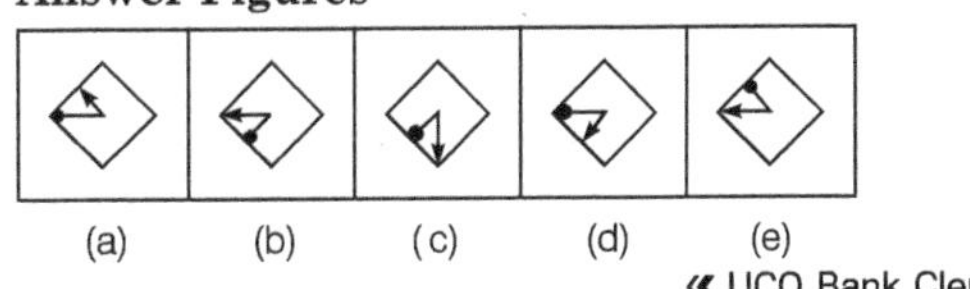

Answer Figures

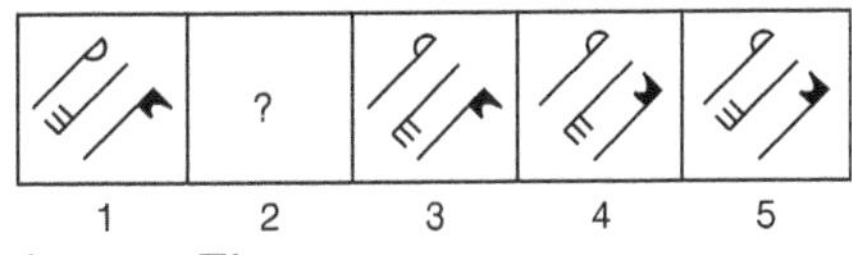

« UCO Bank Clerk 2010

43. Problem Figures

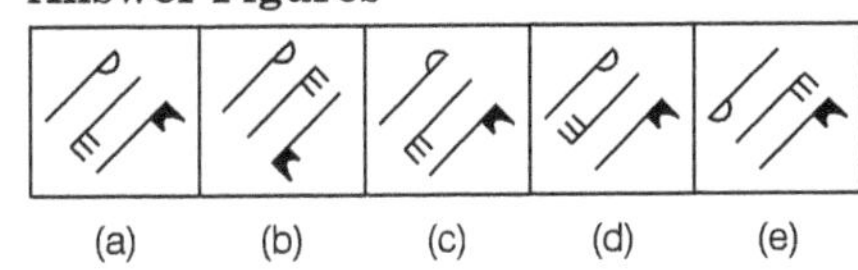

Answer Figures

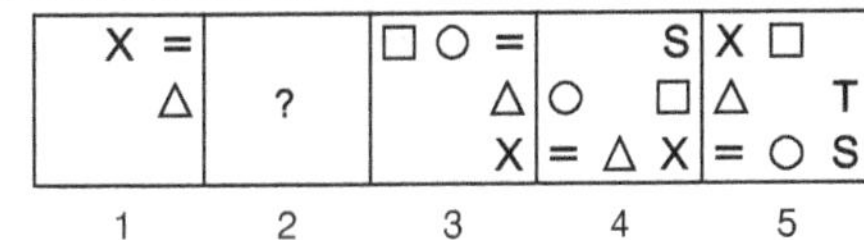

44. Problem Figures

X = Δ	?	□ ○ = Δ X	○ S □ = Δ X	X □ Δ T = ○ S
1	2	3	4	5

Answer Figures

Δ X = ○	X = Δ ○	○ Δ X =	= Δ X ○	○ = Δ X
(a)	(b)	(c)	(d)	(e)

45. Problem Figures

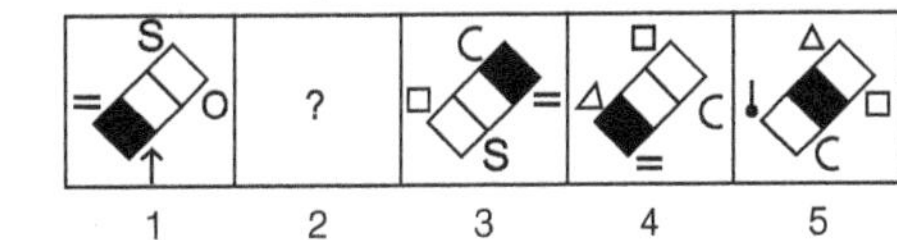

Answer Figures

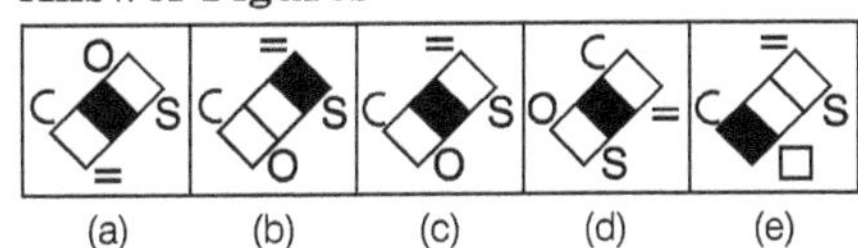

46. Problem Figures

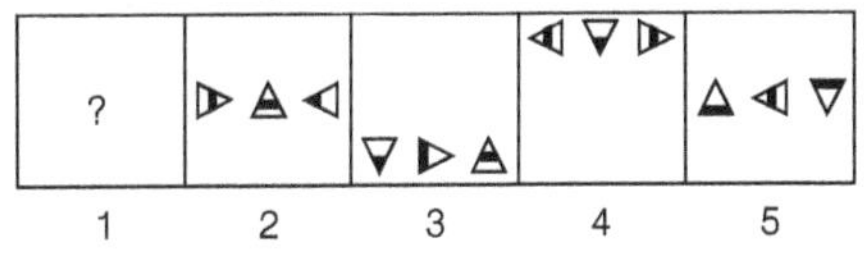

Answer Figures

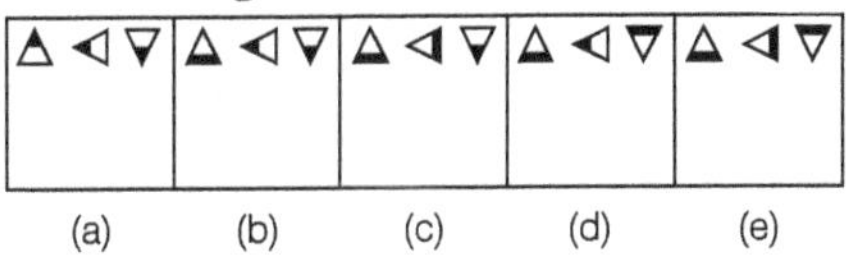

« OBC Clerk 2012

47. Problem Figures

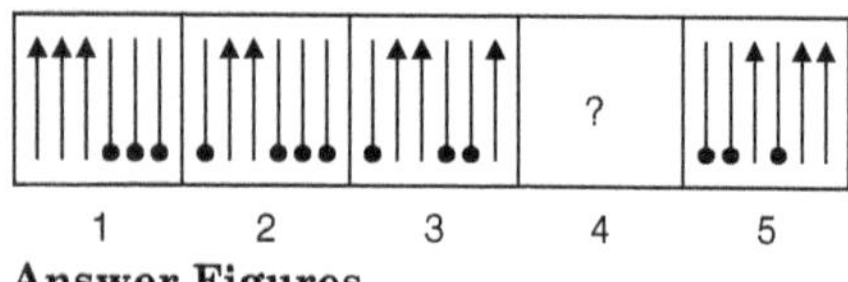

1 2 3 4 5

Answer Figures

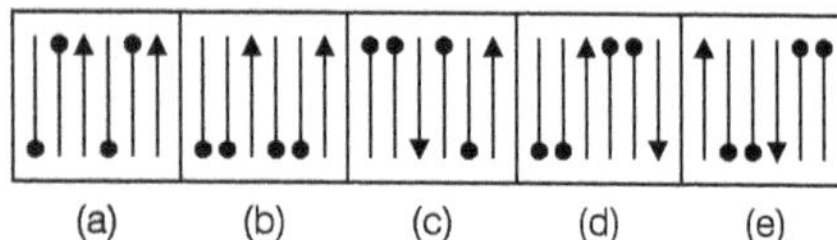

(a) (b) (c) (d) (e)

48. Problem Figures

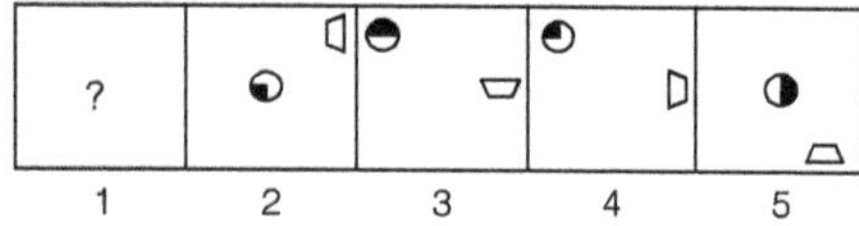

1 2 3 4 5

Answer Figures

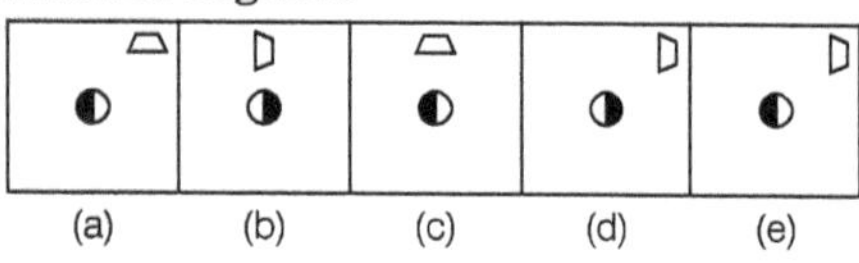

(a) (b) (c) (d) (e)

« Union Bank PO 2011, UCO Bank PO 2008

49. Problem Figures

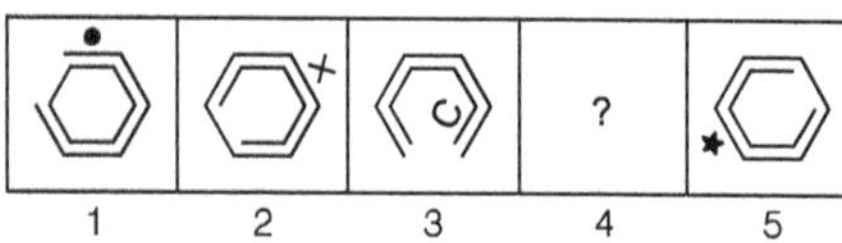

1 2 3 4 5

Answer Figures

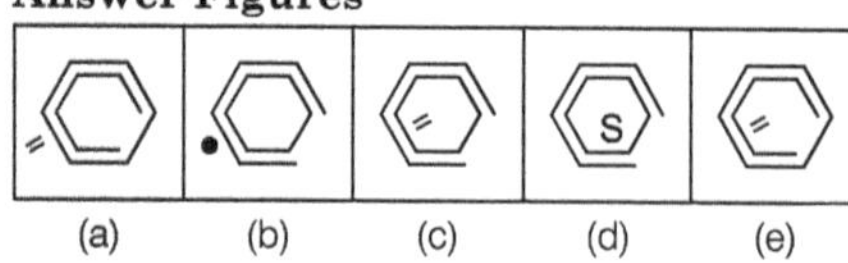

(a) (b) (c) (d) (e)

50. Problem Figures

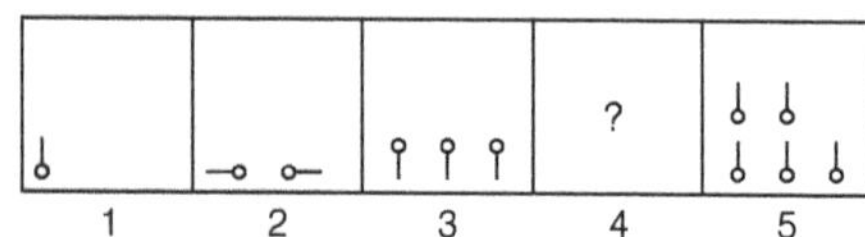

1 2 3 4 5

Answer Figures

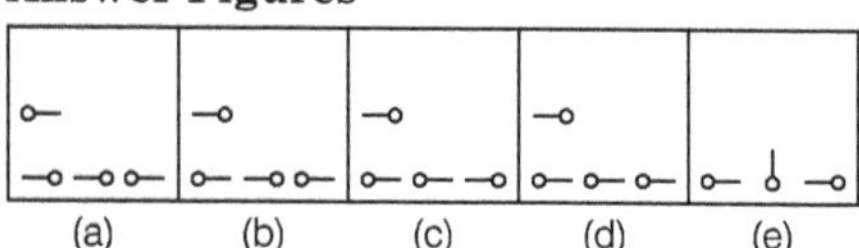

(a) (b) (c) (d) (e)

51. Problem Figures

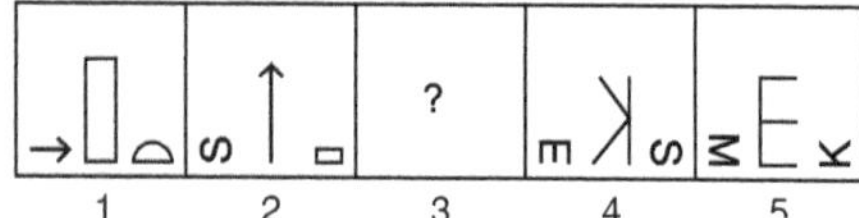

1 2 3 4 5

Answer Figures

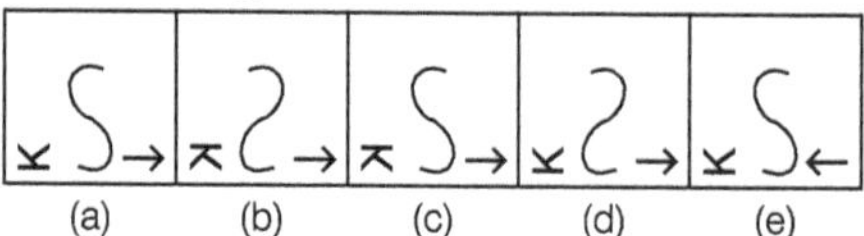

(a) (b) (c) (d) (e)

52. Problem Figures

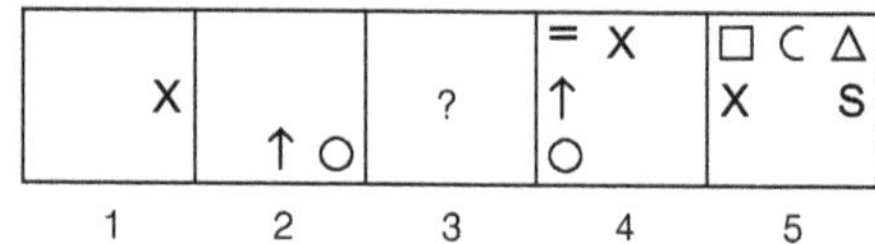

1 2 3 4 5

Answer Figures

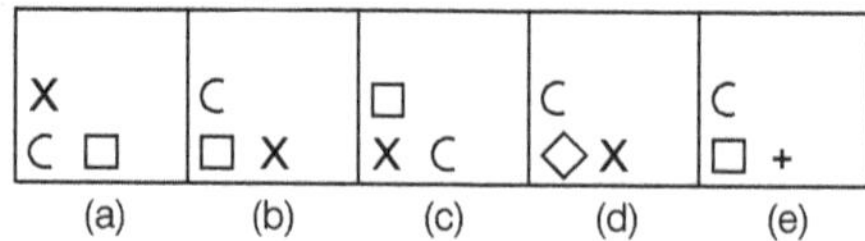

(a) (b) (c) (d) (e)

« UCO Bank 2008

53. Problem Figures

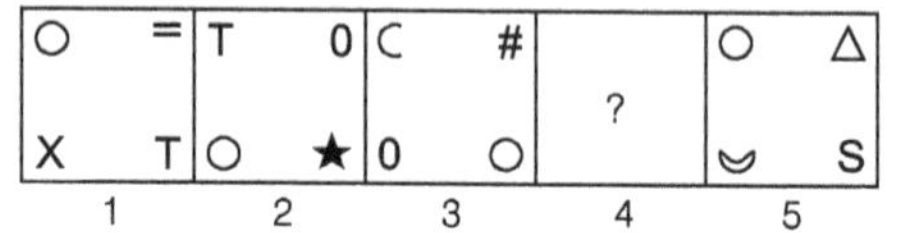

1 2 3 4 5

Answer Figures

(a)	(b)	(c)	(d)	(e)
O P	C O	P △	P O	O P
△ C	△ P	O C	△ C	C △

54. Problem Figures

1	2	3	4	5
□	O	=	?	T
=	X	T		O
O T X	T □ =	X O □		□ X =

Answer Figures

(a)	(b)	(c)	(d)	(e)
□	X	O	□	X
=	□	X	X	=
X T	O = T	T □ =	T = O	O □ T

55. Problem Figures

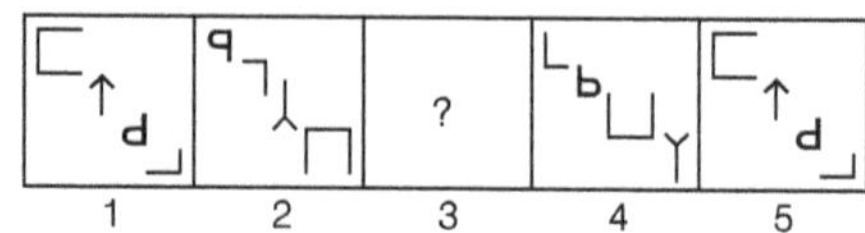

1 2 3 4 5

Answer Figures

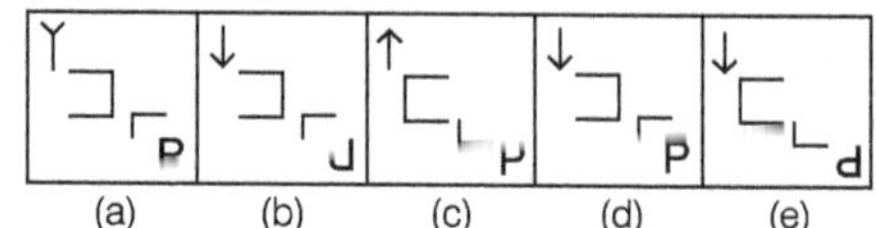

(a) (b) (c) (d) (e)

56. Problem Figures

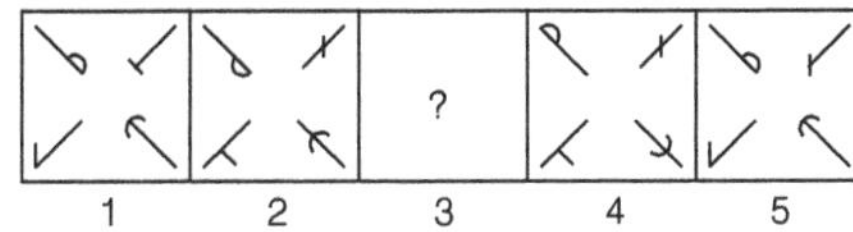

Answer Figures

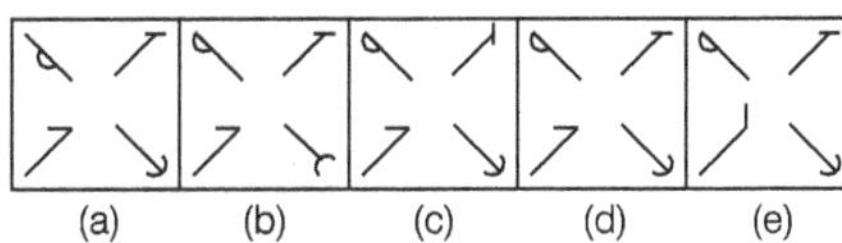

57. Problem Figures

1	2	3	4	5
Z ★ B T O	★ T O Z □	F □ ★ T Z	□ T Z F △	?

Answer Figures

(a)	(b)	(c)	(d)	(e)
P T □ △ F	□ △ Z T F	Z △ □ T F	P F □ △ T	P △ □ T F

« BOB PO 2011

58. Problem Figures

1	2	3	4	5
Z △ T D S	?	T D S F Z	A T D Z S	Z ★ T D S

Answer Figures

(a)	(b)	(c)	(d)	(e)
T Z S D P	T Z D S P	T Z S D P	T P D S Z	T Z D S P

« BOB PO 2011

59. Problem Figures

1	2	3	4	5
□ Z S O	★ Z O S	?	O = △ ★	= ⊠ △ ★

Answer Figures

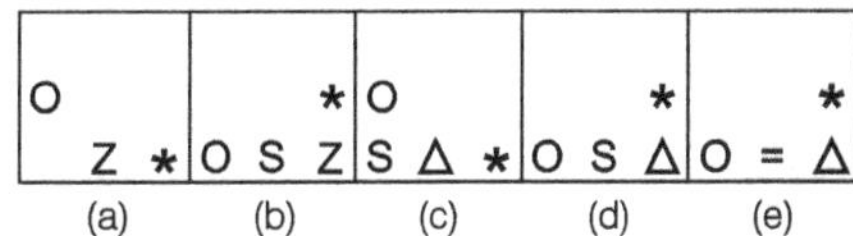

« Allahabad Bank PO 2008

60. Problem Figures

1	2	3	4	5
= O △ ↑ □	↑ △ □ = O	?	O □ △ = ↑	△ O □ ↑ =

Answer Figures

(a)	(b)	(c)	(d)	(e)
△ ↑ = O □	↑ = O △ □	O □ = △ ↑	O △ ↑ = □	O △ = □ ↑

61. Problem Figures

1	2	3	4	5
C = □ Z ★ △ O	= Z △ C □ O ★	?	= O ★ △ □ C Z	★ = □ C O Z △

Answer Figures

(a)	(b)	(c)	(d)	(e)
△ = □ ★ Z C O	△ = □ O Z C ★	Z = □ O △ ★ C	△ = □ O Z ★ C	Z □ = O △ ★ C

« CBI Clerk 2011

Answers / WITH EXPLANATIONS

1. (*a*) In each subsequent figure, the whole figure is rotated 90° anti-clockwise.

2. (*a*) In each successive figure, a line is increasing in inner shape and a line is decreasing in outer shape.

3. (*d*) Each successive figure is rotating 180° clockwise and after every two figures, the sides of the inner figure (triangle) is increasing by one. Hence, the figure shown in option (d) will complete the given series.

4. (*d*) The whole figure is rotated 90° clockwise in each step.

5. (*d*) In each successive figure, the large arrow inside the circle remains at the same position and the small arrow is rotating 90° in clockwise direction.

6. (*a*) In each step, the shaded portion is moving two steps in clockwise direction and the portion having '+' sign is moving two steps in anti-clockwise direction.

7. (*d*) The arrow rotates 45° clockwise in each successive step.

8. (*d*) The whole figure is rotated 90° anti-clockwise in each step and the element at the top becomes shaded.

9. (*d*) The semi-circle is rotating 45° in anti-clockwise direction and all the three small elements are changing their position in anti-clockwise direction in a cyclic manner.

10. (*a*) The '×' sign is moving from one block to other within the star in clockwise direction. The dot is moving from one block to the other outside the star in anti-clockwise direction. The triangle and square appear respectively in each alternate figure.

11. (*c*) The figure rotates 90° anti-clockwise in every successive step and the circle moves one block in clockwise direction.

12. (*a*) In each step, the symbols move in the sequence as shown below

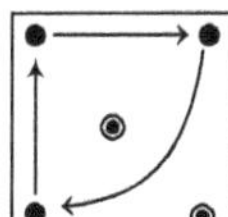

13. (*a*) The black circle, white circle and square, all three are moving in anti-clockwise direction. The triangle is moving from one corner to the other in clockwise direction and is also rotated 180° in each step.

14. (*e*) All the shaded portions rotate 90° in clockwise direction in each square except top right square in which the shaded portion rotates 90° anti-clockwise.

15. (*c*) From the problem figure (1) to (2), the main figure is reversed, the shaded portion rotates 90° anti-clockwise and the arrow is also reversed. The same process is repeated from problem figure (3) to (4).

16. (*b*) All the symbols shift one step in anti-clockwise direction.

17. (*c*) In each problem figure, design 'Δ' rotates 90°, 135°, 180° and 225° in clockwise direction. Design '=' rotates 45° in clockwise direction in each problem figure. Design ⚲ rotates 45°, 90°, 135° and 180° in clockwise direction.

18. (*a*) In one step, the middle element rotates through 180° and in the next step, the other two elements rotate through 180°. The two steps are repeated alternately.

19. (*d*) The middle sign does not change, the top left sign rotates 90° clockwise in each of the subsequent figures, the top right sign rotates 180° after every two figures, the bottom right sign rotates 90° clockwise after every third figure and the bottom left sign rotates 90° clockwise after every fourth figure.

20. (*c*) In each step one line is increasing inside the circle and outside the circle, alternately.

21. (*d*) In each subsequent figure, two lines are added and is therefore making a certain pattern like a chain.

22. (*c*) In figure (2), the first symbol of the first row is being disappeared, in figure (3), the first symbol of the second row being disappeared and this process continues.

23. (*a*) The number of given shapes in the box is decreased by one in every next figure.

24. (*a*) In the first figure there are two straight lines and with each successive figure, the number of lines are becoming twice of the previous one. Therefore, the number of straight lines will be two, four, eight and sixteen respectively.

25. (*a*) In each successive step, the whole design is rotating 90° and a line is also increasing in the subsequent figure.

26. (*c*) The number of lines given at the tail of arrow is decreasing and increasing alternatively and the number of lines attached with the square is increasing with 180° rotation every time.

27. (*a*) In every step, the whole figure is rotated 90° in clockwise direction and also a straight line is added in each step.

28. (*b*) In each successive step, both type of arrows increase by 1 and arrows on the right side are inverted vertically.

29. (*e*) The number of lines in each of the successive figures is increased by one and also the number of segments inside the figure is increased by one in subsequent figures.

30. (*b*) The whole figure rotates by 45°, 90°, 135°, 180°, ..., clockwise in subsequent steps. Every time a petal is added on the clockwise end and also the shaded petal changes side in subsequent steps.

31. (*c*) From first to second figure, the circle and triangle exchange their positions and get closer. Similarly, from third to fourth figure, the circle and square will exchange their positions and get closer.

32. (*a*) In problem figures, from first figure to second figure, square is replaced by circle and circles are replaced by the same number of squares. In the same way from third figure to fourth figure, lines will be replaced by same number of triangles and triangle will be replaced by lines.

33. (*a*) In the next figure, the mirror image of preceding figure is given or we can say that the figures are being repeated in alternate manner i.e. figures 2 and 4 are same, similarly figures 1, 3 and 5 will be same.

34. (*d*) In figure 2, the second shape of the figure 1 enlarges and the first and third figure go into this enlarged shape. Similarly for figure (4), the second shape of figure (3) will get enlarged and first and second shapes will go into this enlarged shape.

35. (*d*) In each step, the letters are moving from one corner to other in anti-clockwise direction and the triangle is rotating 180° in every next figure.

36. (*c*) In problem figures, the figure given in right side in the next block rotates 90° anti-clockwise, shifts to the left side and a new figure/shape is added on the right side.

37. (*a*) First three figures of the question figures follow a certain pattern. In the same way the last three figures will follow the same pattern. The geometrical shape i.e. triangle is moving from right to left and then left to right, similarly square will move from right to left and then left to right.

38. (*c*) In each step, the symbol '@' is moving from one corner to other in anticlockwise direction and the symbol 'x' is moving $1\frac{1}{2}$ side in anticlockwise direction.

39. (*b*) In every alternate step, the whole figure rotates 90° anti-clockwise and in alternate steps two arcs are added on the anti-clockwise side.

40. (*c*) Line segment outside the hexagon rotates anti-clockwise with an addition of one line after every second figure, the line segment inside the hexagon rotates clockwise with an addition of one line after every second figure.

41. (*e*) From problem figure (1) to (2), first and second figures interchange their positions and are reversed at the new positions and at the same time, the third figure remains unchanged. From problem figure (2) to (3), second and third figures interchange their positions and are reversed at the new positions and the figure (1) remains unchanged. The same process is repeated alternatively.

42. (*b*) In each step, the whole figure rotates by 90° clockwise and one element is added in each step alternately on clockwise and anti-clockwise end.

43. (*a*) From problem figure (1) to (2), the middle symbol is reversed, from figure (2) to (3), the upper symbol is reversed and from figure (3) to (4), the lower symbol is reversed and the same process is repeated in each of the successive figures.

44. (*d*) From problem figure (1) to (2), second symbol counting from anti-clockwise direction *i.e.*, = moves one side in anti-clockwise direction and is immediately followed by the third symbol *i.e.*, Δ and first symbol *i.e.*, X and a new symbol comes in the beginning of the series. The same process is repeated in the subsequent figures.

45. (*c*) All the symbols around the bar move in clockwise direction in such a way that one of the symbols is replaced by a new symbol as soon as it crosses the bar. The shaded portion moves one step from figure (1) to (2), (2) to (3) and then comes to the original position.

46. (*b*) In each step, the triangles rotate by 90° clockwise. The shading of the triangle changes alternately. The shadings of the middle and the left triangles change in each step in a set order i.e., in middle triangle from top to middle to bottom while in left triangle from bottom to middle to top.

47. (*b*) From problem figure (1) to (2), one arrow is replaced by another pin, from problem figure (2) to (3), one pin is replaced by one arrow. The same process is repeated in the subsequent steps.

48. (*a*) In each step, the quadrilateral rotates 90° anti-clockwise and shifts half step clockwise in alternate steps. Also, the circle is half shaded and one-fourth shaded alternately.

49. (*c*) In the first figure, outer part of the main figure has one line missing, in second figure, the inner part of the main figure has one line missing and in the third figure both the parts of the main figure have one line missing and is rotated anti-clockwise. Also, the outer symbol is replaced with new inner symbol and is rotated clockwise. This process will be repeated to obtain figure(4).

50. (*b*) One pin is added in each of the successive figures and the pins rotate anti-clockwise and clockwise in a set order.

51. (*a*) From problem figure (1) to (2), the figure at the bottom left position rotates 90° anti-clockwise, shifts in the middle and is enlarged. The middle figure rotates 90° clockwise, shifts to the right side and becomes small and a new symbol comes on the left side. The same process is repeated in the subsequent figures.

52. (*b*) Similar changes take place from problem figure (1) to (3) and from figure (3) to (5). From figure (1) to (3), the symbol moves one step clockwise and is preceded by two new symbols. Likewise, from figure (3) to (5), all the existing symbols move one side clockwise and are preceded by two new symbols.

53. (*d*) From problem figure (1) to (2), symbols change their positions as shown in the diagram and new symbols appear in place of • and the diagram, if rotated 90° anti-clockwise everytime, produces the changes in each of the subsequent figures.

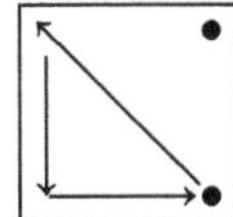

54. (*b*) Symbols change in each of the successive figures as shown in the two diagrams alternatively.

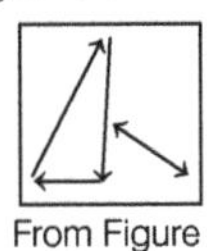

From Figure 1 to 2 3 to 4

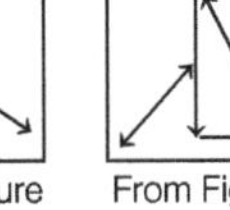

From Figure 2 to 3 4 to 5

55. (*d*) First, second, third and fourth symbols from the top become first, second, fourth and third from the bottom. The symbol in ⊓ shape rotates 90° clockwise in each successive figure. The P-shaped figure is first inverted and then reversed, alternatively.

The arrow head is inverted in each step.

56. (*d*) From problem figure (1) to (2), the top left symbol is reversed, line segment on the top right symbol moves half side and rotates 45°, line segment on the bottom left symbol moves half side and arc on the bottom right symbol moves half side. Similar changes occur from problem figure (3) to (4).

57. (*e*) The sequence of the problem figure (2) to (3) is

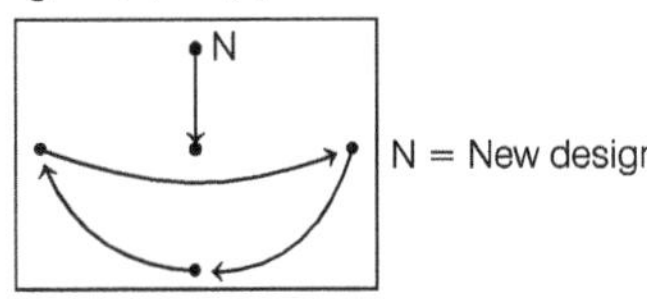

Similar rule follows from problem figure (4) to the answer figure.

58. (*b*) From problem figure (1) to (2) and (3) to (4) all designs move one place in clockwise direction and a new design comes in each subsequent problem figure.

59. (*d*) In alternate steps the elements shift one side and a half side clockwise while one of the elements beginning from the anti-clockwise end gets replaced by a new one in each step one by one.

60. (*a*) Symbols change place in subsequent figures in such a way that two symbols interchange positions whereas three symbols move in anti-clockwise direction as shown in the diagram. The order of arrangement is rotated 90° clockwise everytime to obtain successive changes in figures.

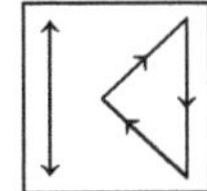

61. (*d*) All changes in problem figure (1) to (2) are given below

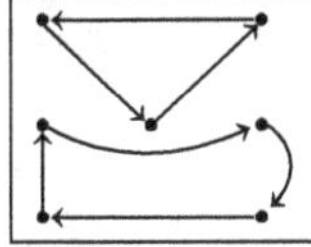

Similar rule follows from problem figure (3) to (4).

TYPE 03

Detection of Wrong Figure in the Series

In this type of questions, a series of seven figures is given. The series begins and ends with unnumbered figures. The other five figures, marked as (a, b, c, d and e), continue the series based on a certain rule or pattern.

However, one of these five figures does not fit into the series. A candidate is asked to find out that figure which does not follow the pattern and hence does not fit into the series. The number of that figure is the correct answer. This type of questions are explained in the following examples.

DIRECTIONS ~ (Example Nos. 31-34) *Each of the following questions consists of seven figures, out of which two figures at the ends are unmarked. One of the five marked figures* (a), (b), (c), (d) *and* (e) *does not fit into the series and is your answer.*

Ex 31

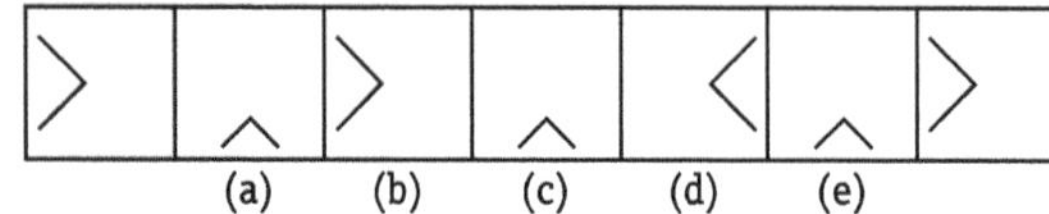

Solution (d) The figure rotates one step anti-clockwise and one step clockwise with increase and decrease in size alternatively in each of the successive figures. Following this pattern figure (d) does not fit into the series.

Ex 32

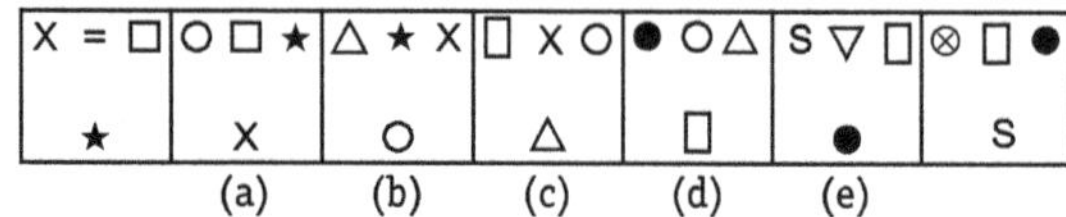

Solution (e) All the symbols change positions as shown in the figure below and every symbol in place of ★ is replaced by a new symbol one by one in each of the successive figures. Hence, figure (e) does not fit into the series.

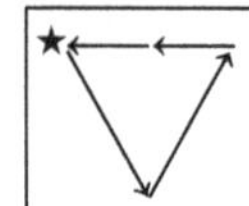

Ex 33

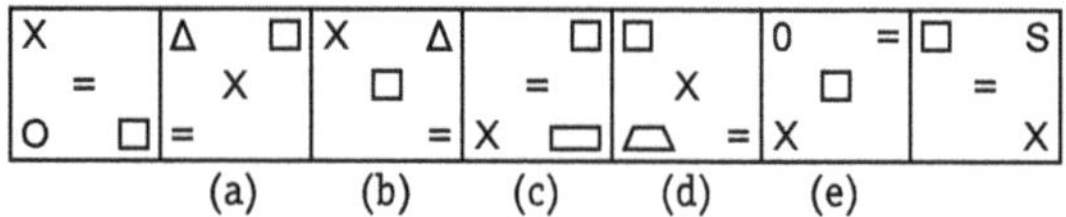

Solution (b) All the symbols change positions as shown in the figure below and every symbol in place of • is replaced by a new symbol. Subsequent figure is obtained by rotating this figure 90° clockwise everytime. Hence, figure (b) does not fit into the series.

Ex 34

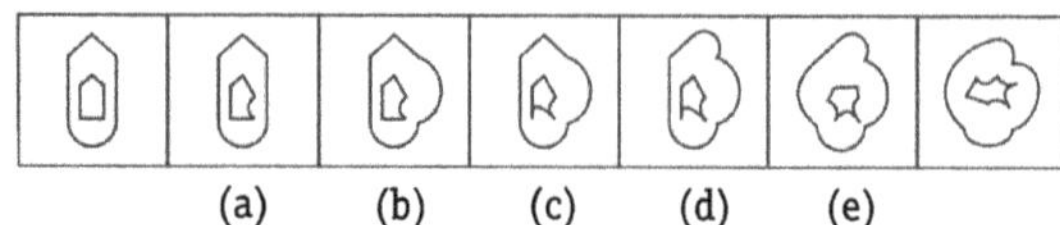

Solution (e) One side of inner and outer figure respectively is converted into arc one by one in each of the subsequent figures. Pattern figure (e) does not fit into the series.

Practice CORNER 1.3

DIRECTIONS ~(Q. Nos. 1-20) *Each of the following series consists of seven figures, two of which at the ends are unmarked. One of the five marked figures* (a), (b), (c), (d) *and* (e) *does not fit into the series. Find out that figure.*

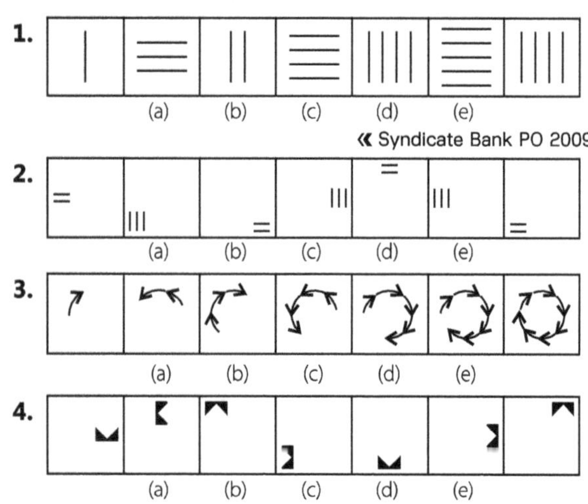

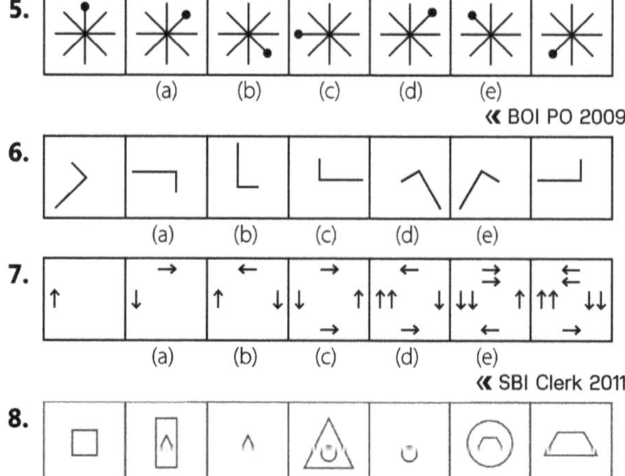

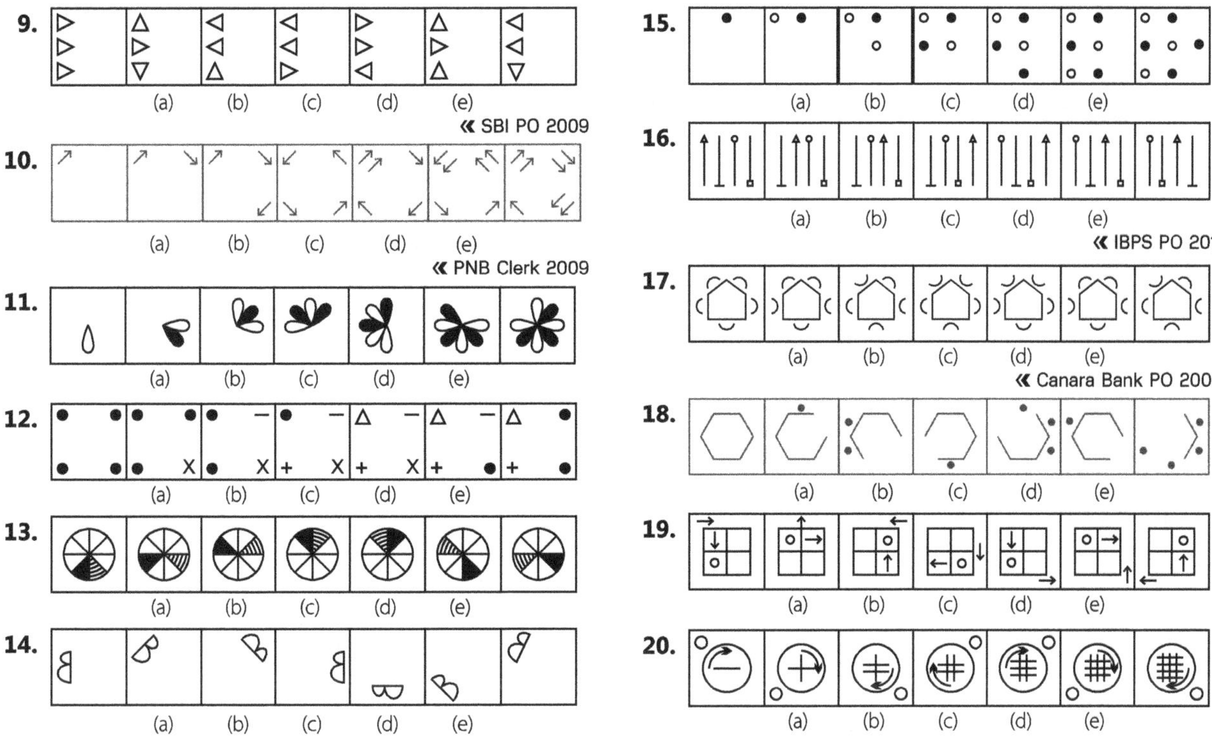

Answers / WITH EXPLANATIONS

1. (*d*) Two lines are added from first figure to (a) and one line is removed from figure (a) to (b), similarly two lines are added from figure (b) to (c) and one line is removed from figure (c) to (d).
   The same pattern continues for the other figures.
2. (*e*) One line is added and deleted alternatively and all the lines move half step and one step alternatively anti-clockwise after rotating 90°.
3. (*e*) One arrow is added in each of the subsequent figures and all existing arrows are reversed to make a certain pattern.
4. (*e*) Figure rotates 90° clockwise in each of the subsequent figures and moves 1 step and 1/2 step in anti-clockwise direction alternatively.
5. (*d*) The shaded circle moves 1/2 $1, 1\frac{1}{2}, 2, 2\frac{1}{2}$........ steps in clockwise directions in each of the subsequent figures.
6. (*a*) L-shaped figure rotates 90°, 45°, 90°, ... clockwise and is also reversed in subsequent each figures.
7. (*c*) One arrow is added in clockwise direction and other arrow(s) is/are reversed which is not followed in figure (c).
8. (*a*) In first step, the small figure becomes larger and a new figure, smaller in size, comes inside it. In second step, the outside larger figure is removed and this process continues.
9. (*c*) Upper triangle rotates 90° anti-clockwise, middle triangle rotates 180° after every two figures and the lower triangle rotates 90°, 180° clockwise alternatively in each of the successive figures.
10. (*a*) One arrow in clockwise direction is added in such a way that direction of the head of arrow is same as that of the other arrows and at the same time all the pre-existing arrows are inverted.
11. (*d*) The leaf rotates by 90° anti-clockwise and one shaded leaf and a blank leaf is added alternatively in each of the successive figures.
12. (*c*) In each of the subsequent figures, the circle is replaced by a new sign. When cycle completes, the circle starts reappearing in subsequent figures.
13. (*e*) The shaded portion moves half step clockwise and portion with lines moves half step anti-clockwise in each of the subsequent figures.
14. (*c*) In alternate steps, the whole figure rotates by 45° clockwise and 90° clockwise and gets inverted on its base.
15. (*b*) One blank and one shaded circle is added alternatively in each of the subsequent figures.
16. (*e*) The first arrow shifts its position by interchanging position with first, second, third and fourth arrows; and this process continues.
17. (*d*) In alternate steps, two and three alternate arcs get inverted.
18. (*d*) Sides of the polygon disappear in clockwise direction in an order 1, 2, 1, 3, 1, 4, ... and the number of shaded circles appear in anti-clockwise direction in an order 1, 2, 1, 3, 1, 4, ...
19. (*e*) Arrow outside the square moves half side and rotates 90° in anti-clockwise direction.
20. (*d*) Small circle moves one side anti-clockwise in each of the successive figures.

Master Exercise

DIRECTIONS ~(Q. Nos. 1 and 2) *In each of the following questions, a set of four figures marked as* 1, 2, 3 *and* 4 *forming a series is given. Out of these figures, the last one i.e., Figure* (4) *is missing. Identify from the four answer figures, marked as* (a), (b), (c) *and* (d) *the one which would replace the question mark (?) in Figure* (4), *so as to continue the series.*

1. Question Figures

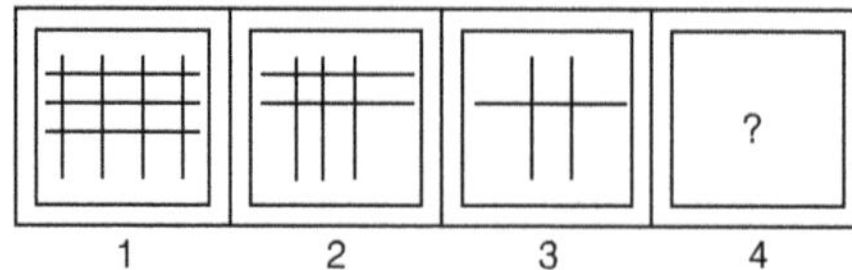

Answer Figures

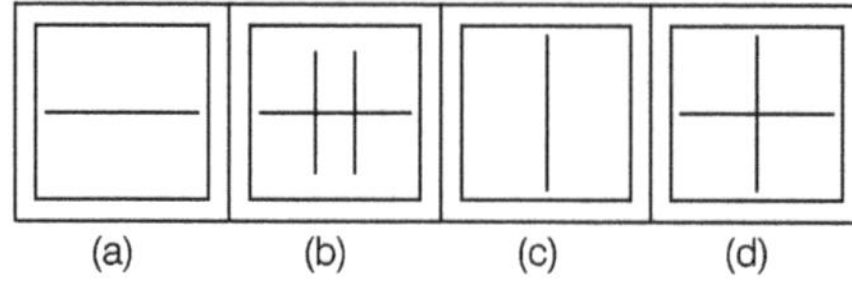

« SNAP 2012

2. Question Figures

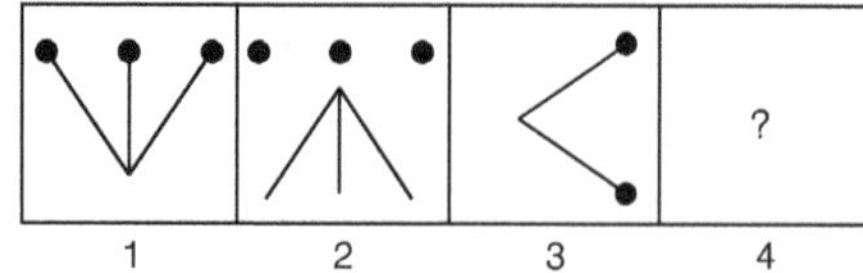

Answer Figures

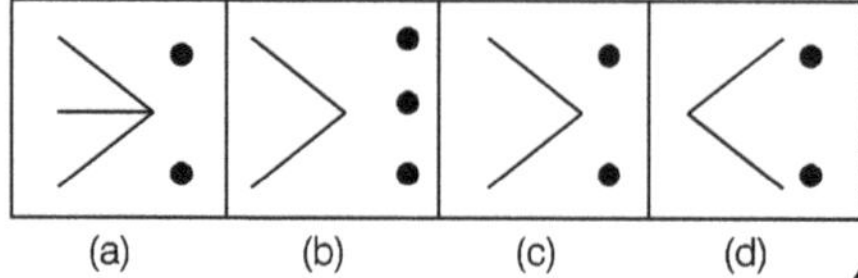

« SNAP 2012

DIRECTIONS ~ (Q. Nos. 3-6) *In each question, there are two sets of figures; first four figures named as question figures marked as* (1), (2), (3) *and* (4) *and next four figures named answer figures marked as* (a), (b), (c) *and* (d). *The question figures follow a particular sequence. In accordance with the same, which one of the four answer figures should appear as the fifth figure in the question figure?*

3. Question Figures

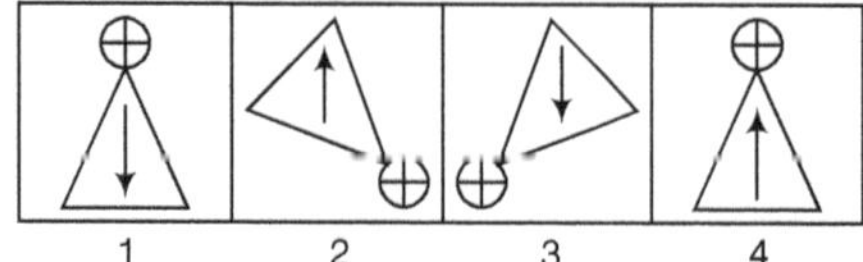

Answer Figures

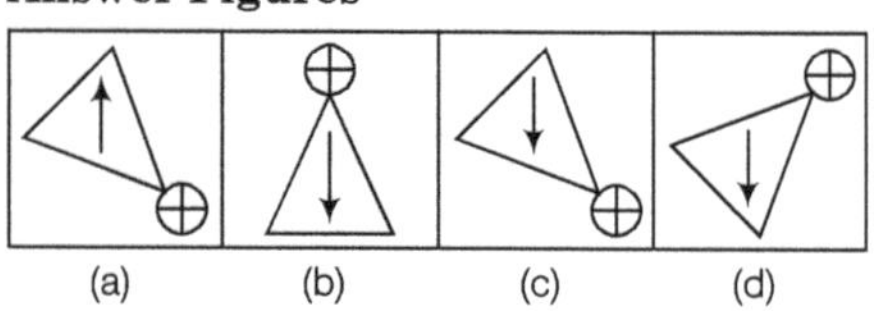

4. Question Figures

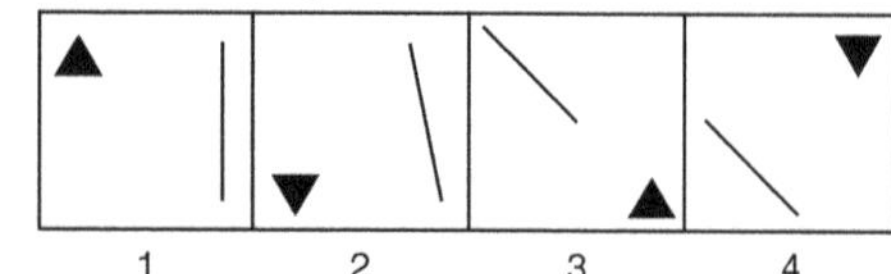

Answer Figures

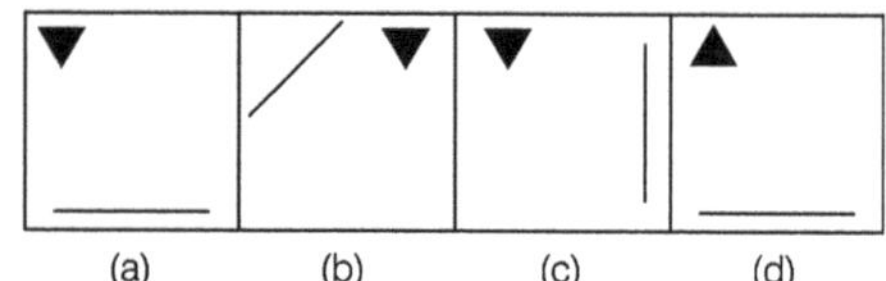

5. Question Figures

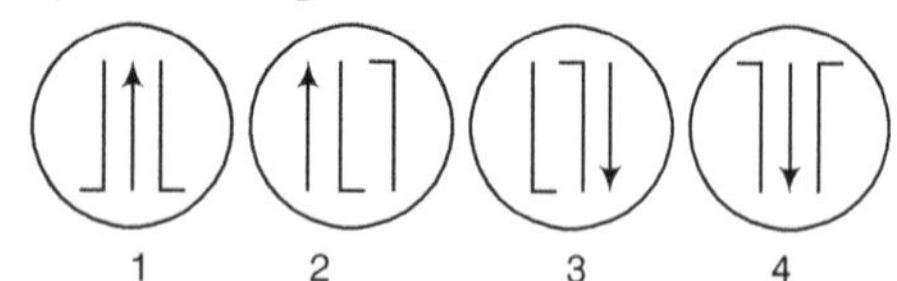

Answer Figures

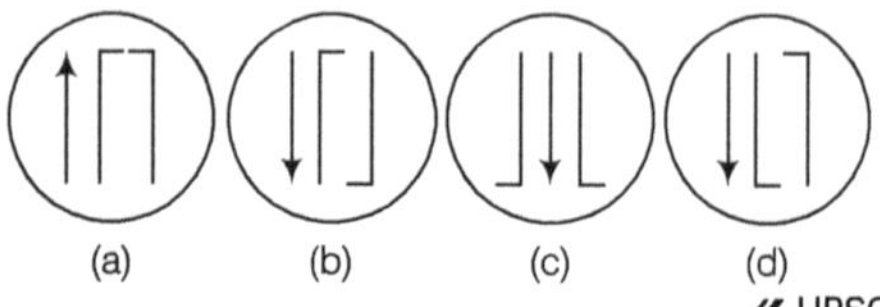

« UPSC CSAT 2013

6. Question Figures

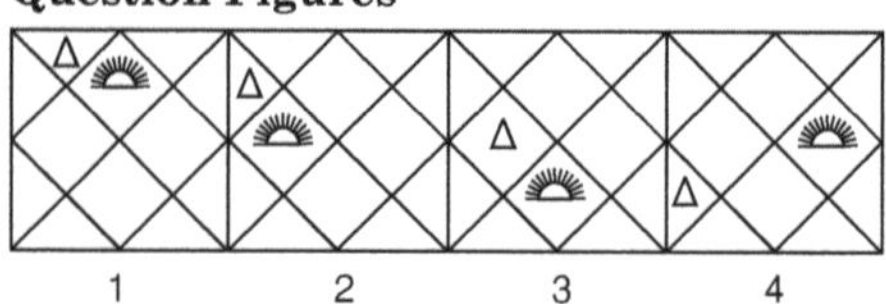

Answer Figures

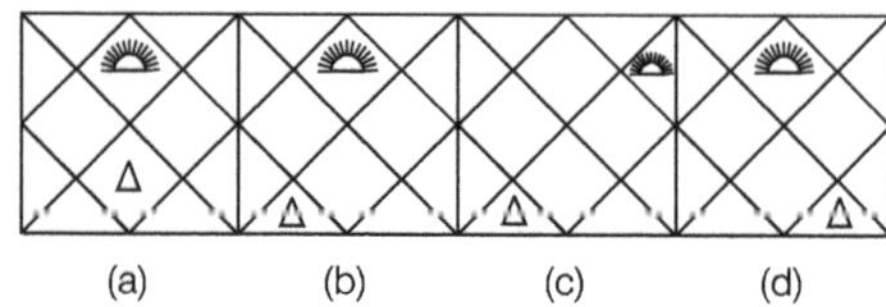

« UPSC CSAT 2013

7. Which pattern from the bottom line (a, b, c, d and e) is missing from the top line?

Question Figures

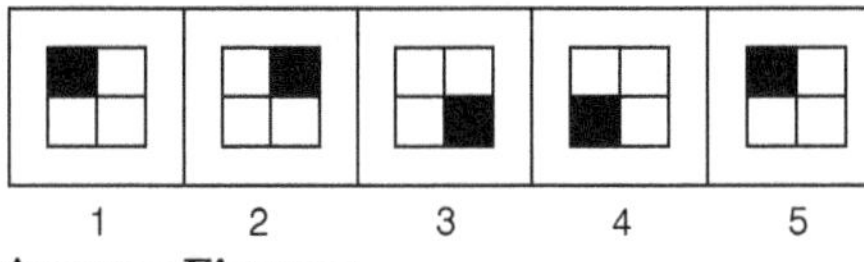

1 2 3 4 5

Answer Figures

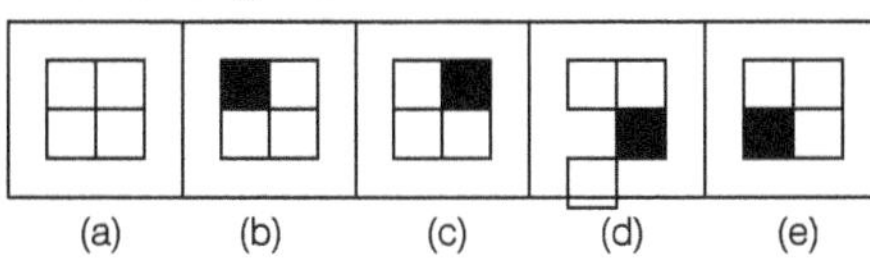

(a) (b) (c) (d) (e)

DIRECTIONS ~(Q. Nos. 8-68) *In each of the questions given below, which one of the four/five answer figures will come after the question figures on the right end, if the sequence is continued.*

8. Question Figures

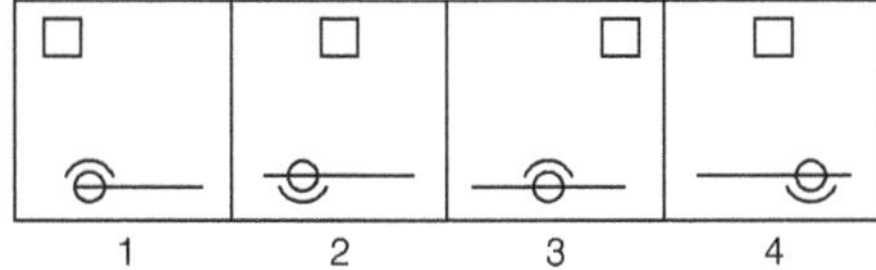

1 2 3 4

Answer Figures

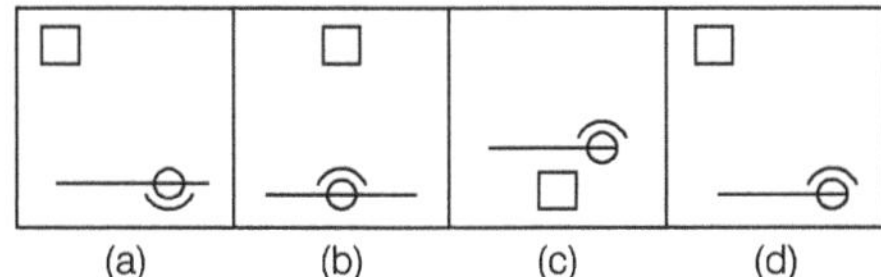

(a) (b) (c) (d)

« UP B.Ed 2010

9. Question Figures

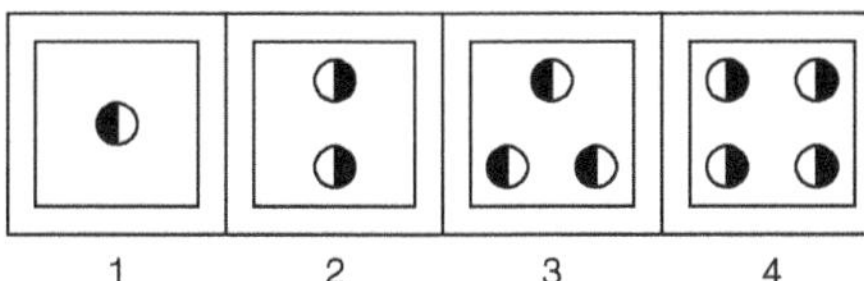

1 2 3 4

Answer Figures

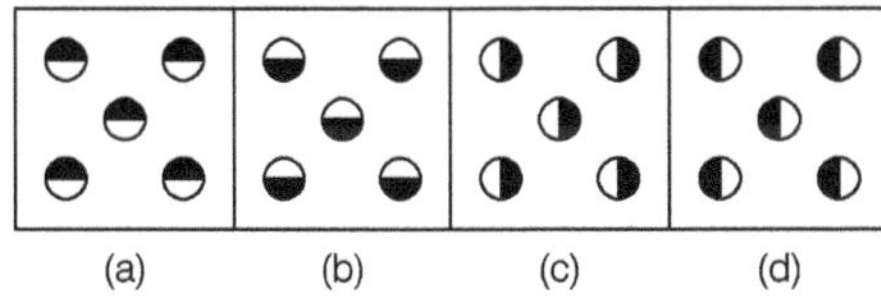

(a) (b) (c) (d)

10. Question Figures

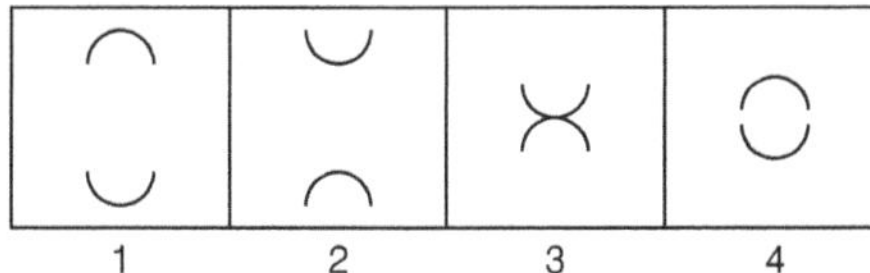

1 2 3 4

Answer Figures

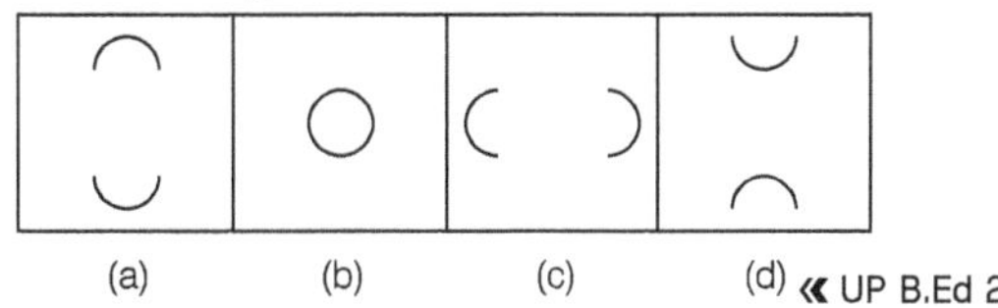

(a) (b) (c) (d) « UP B.Ed 2009

11. Question Figures

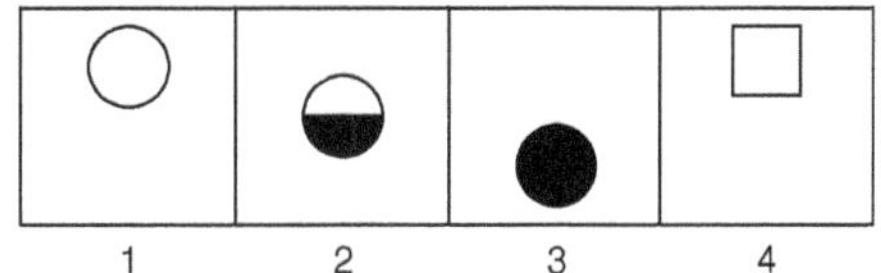

1 2 3 4

Answer Figures

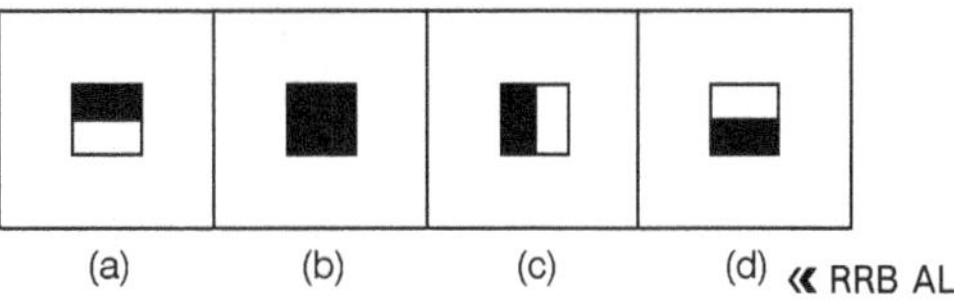

(a) (b) (c) (d) « RRB ALP 2010

12. Question Figures

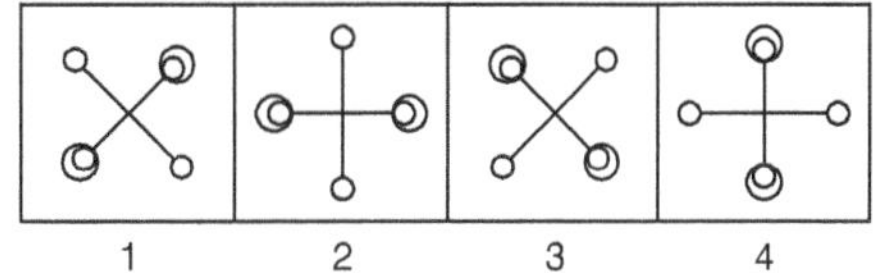

1 2 3 4

Answer Figures

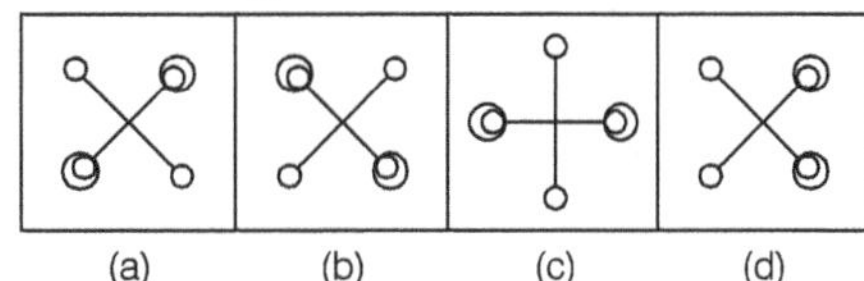

(a) (b) (c) (d)

13. Question Figures

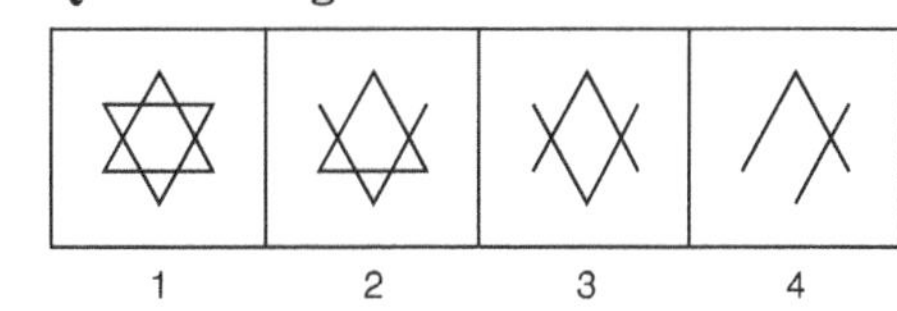

1 2 3 4

Answer Figures

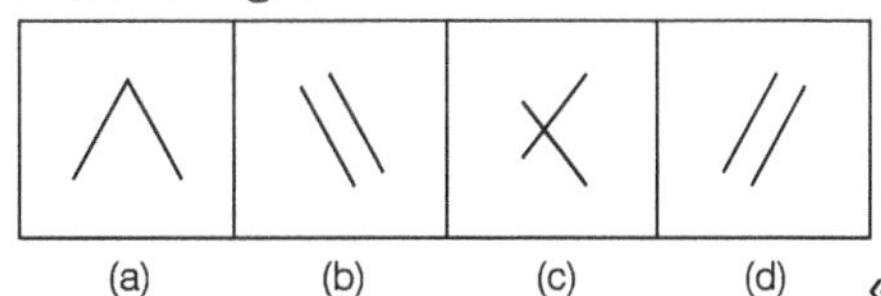

(a) (b) (c) (d) « MAT 2009

14. Question Figures

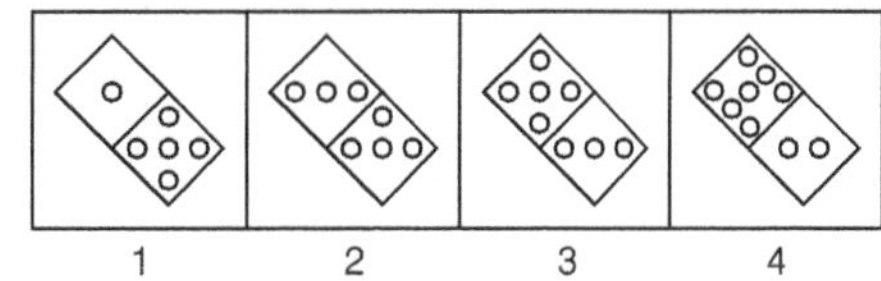

1 2 3 4

Answer Figures

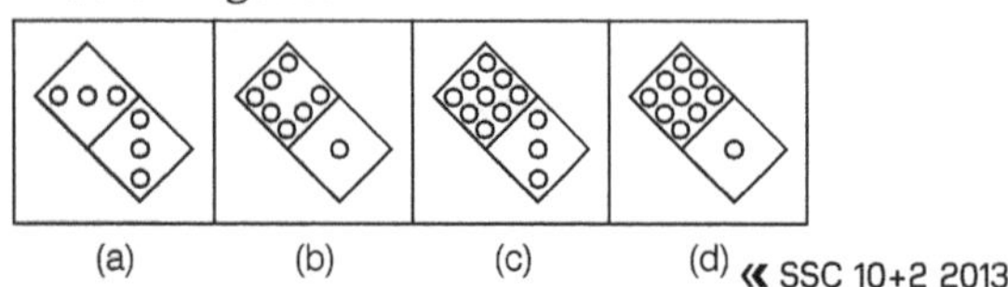

(a) (b) (c) (d) « SSC 10+2 2013

15. Question Figures

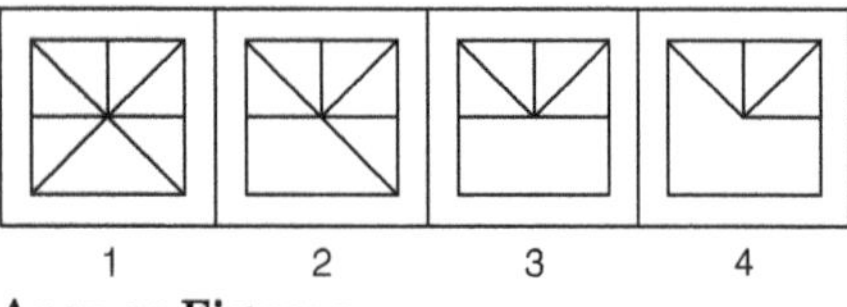

1 2 3 4

Answer Figures

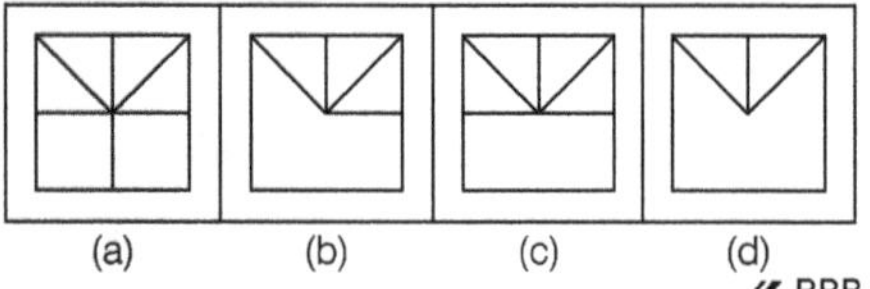

(a) (b) (c) (d)

« RRB TC/CC 2014

16. Question Figures

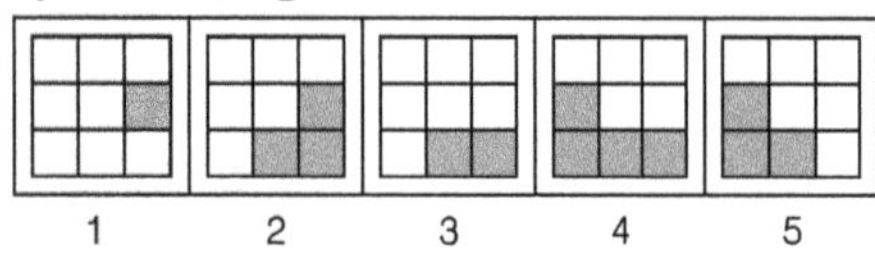

1 2 3 4 5

Answer Figures

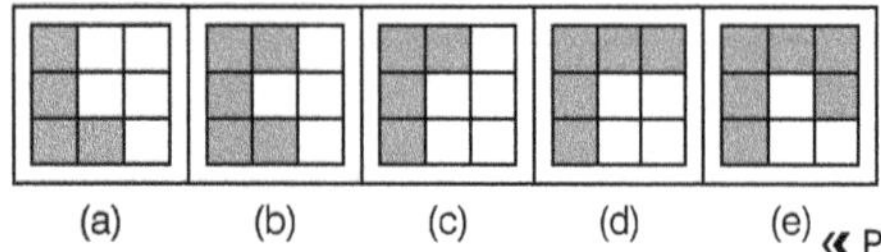

(a) (b) (c) (d) (e) « PNB PO 2011

17. Question Figures

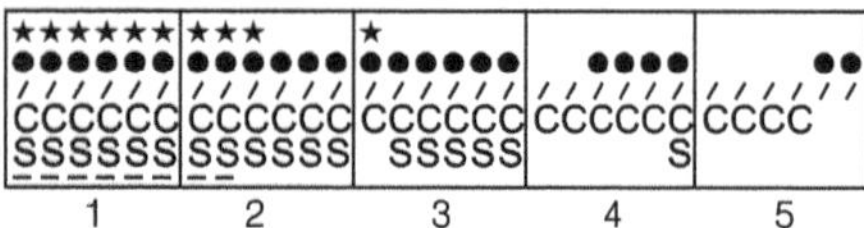

1 2 3 4 5

Answer Figures

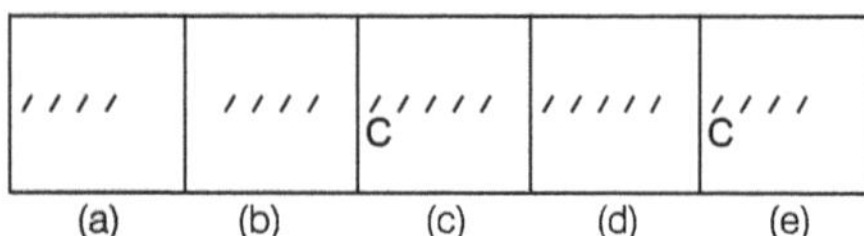

(a) (b) (c) (d) (e)

18. Question Figures

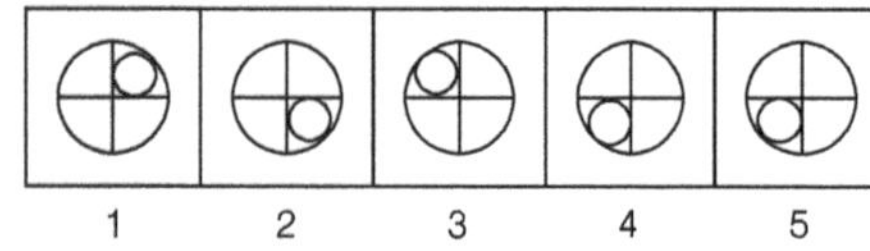

1 2 3 4 5

Answer Figures

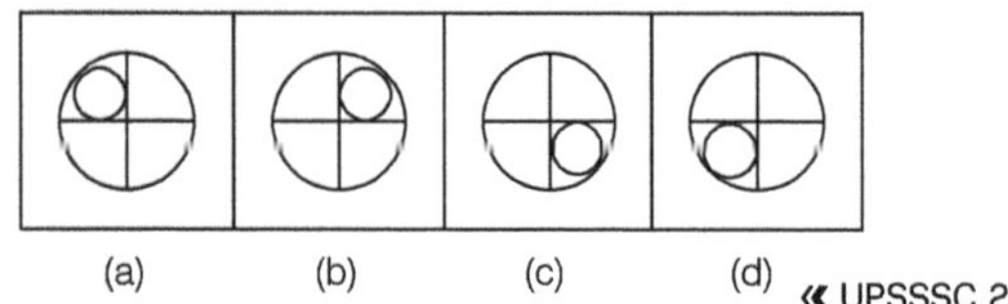

(a) (b) (c) (d) « UPSSSC 2016

19. Question Figures

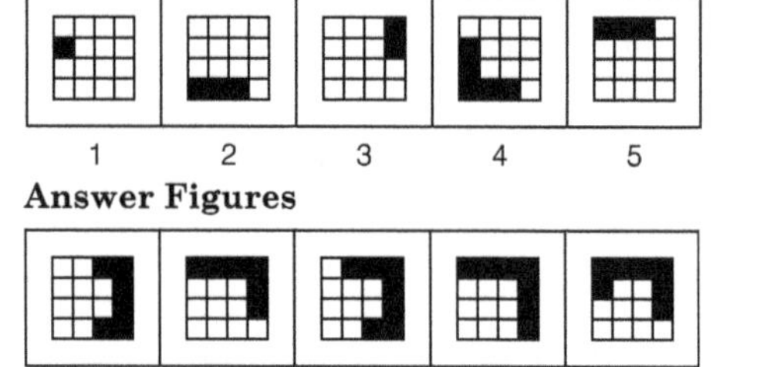

1 2 3 4 5

Answer Figures

(a) (b) (c) (d) (e)

« OBC PO 2010

20. Question Figures

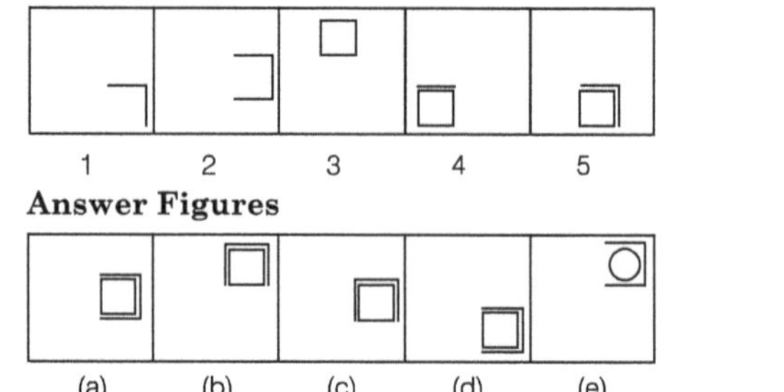

1 2 3 4 5

Answer Figures

(a) (b) (c) (d) (e)

« MHT MBA 2017

21. Question Figures

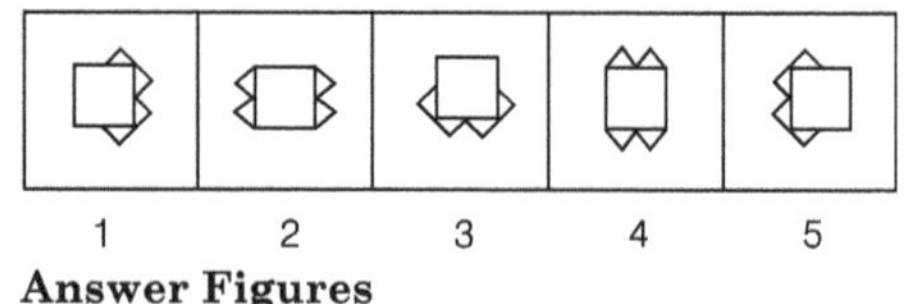

1 2 3 4 5

Answer Figures

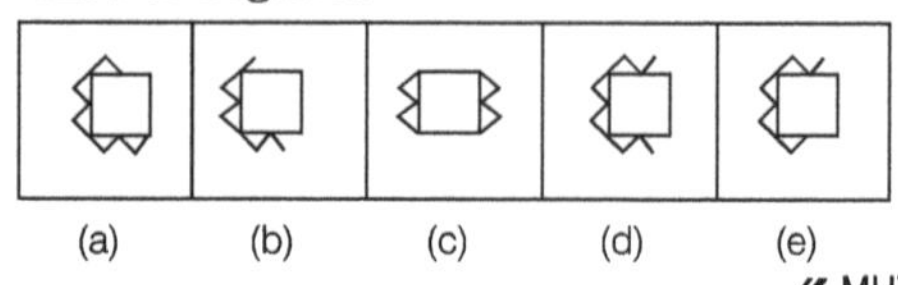

(a) (b) (c) (d) (e)

« MHT MBA 2017

22. Question Figures

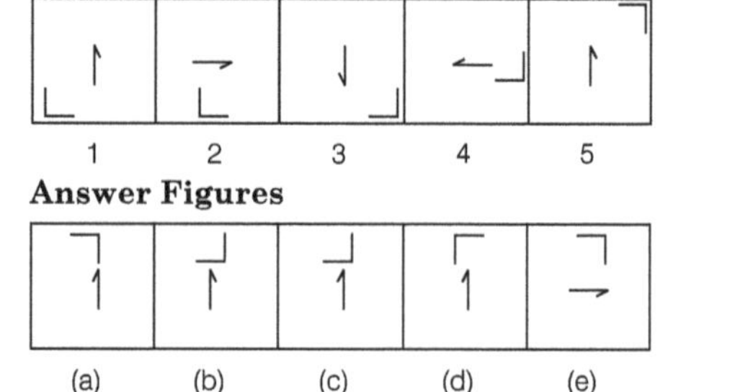

1 2 3 4 5

Answer Figures

(a) (b) (c) (d) (e)

« MHT MBA 2017

23. Question Figures

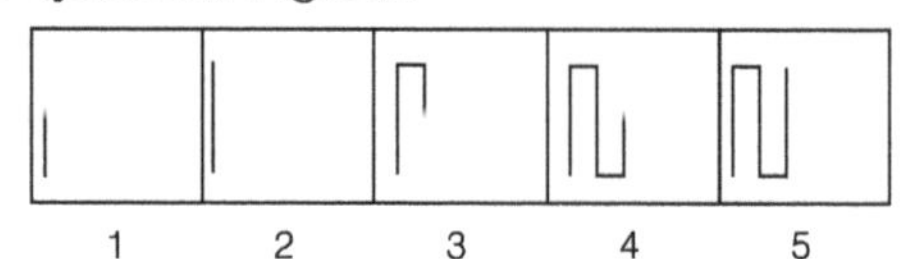

1 2 3 4 5

Answer Figures

(a) (b) (c) (d) (e)

« MHT MBA 2017

24. Question Figures

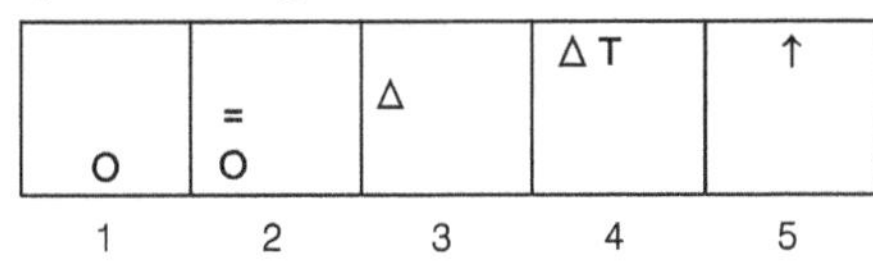

1 2 3 4 5

Answer Figures

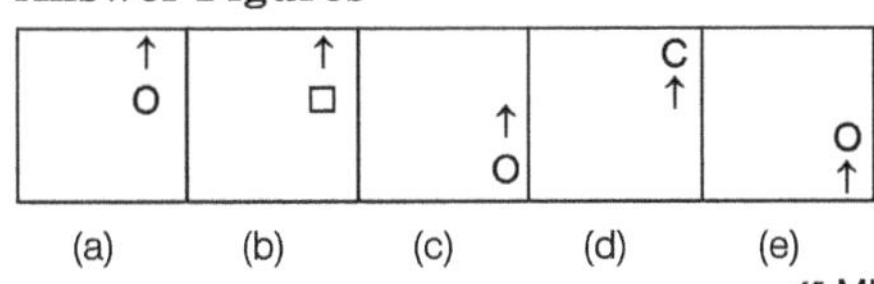

(a) (b) (c) (d) (e)

« MHT MBA 2017

25. Question Figures

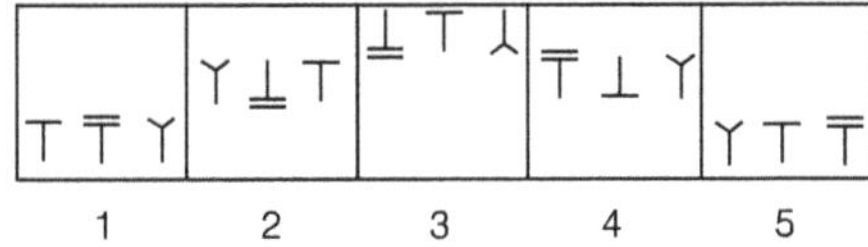

1 2 3 4 5

Answer Figures

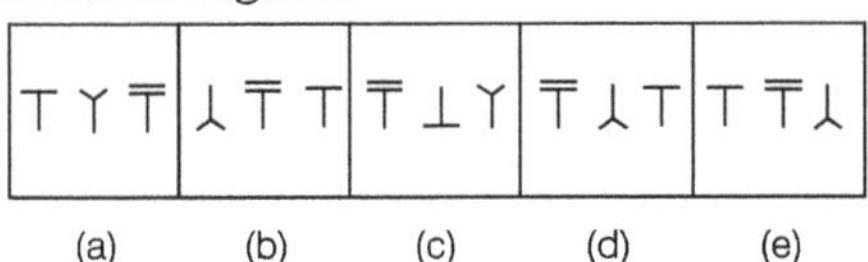

(a) (b) (c) (d) (e)

« MHT MBA 2017

26. Question Figures

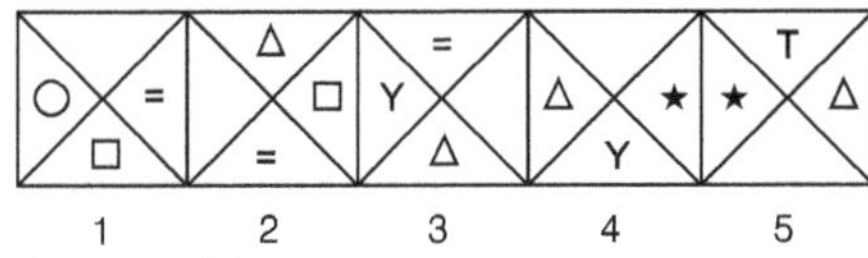

1 2 3 4 5

Answer Figures

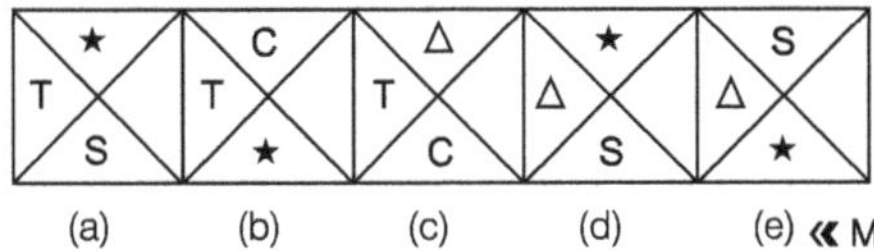

(a) (b) (c) (d) (e) « MHT MBA 2017

27. Question Figures

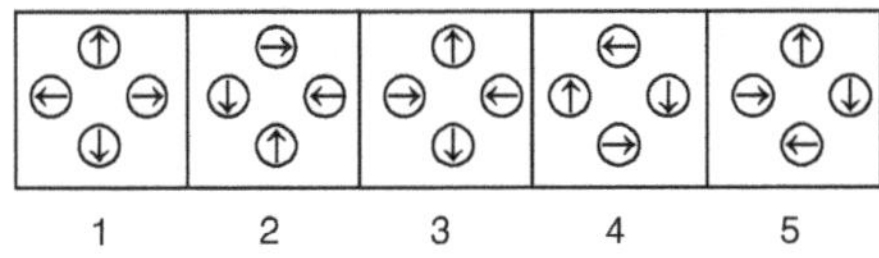

1 2 3 4 5

Answer Figures

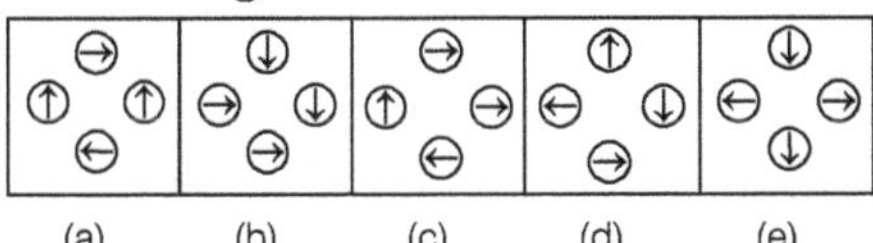

(a) (b) (c) (d) (e)

« MHT MBA 2017

28. Question Figures

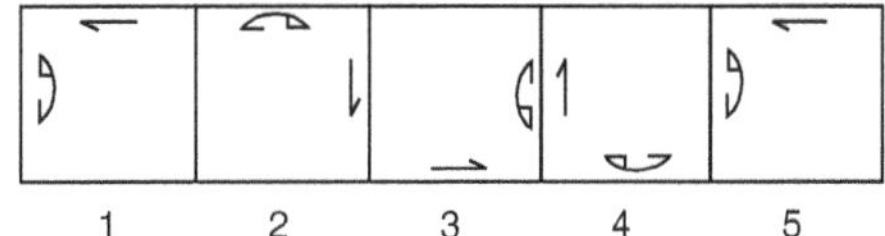

1 2 3 4 5

Answer Figures

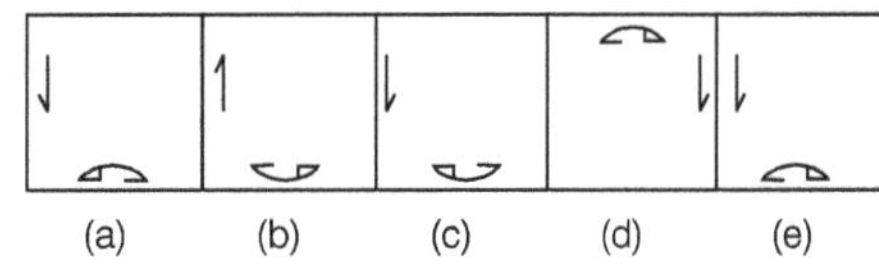

(a) (b) (c) (d) (e)

« MHT MBA 2017

29. Question Figures

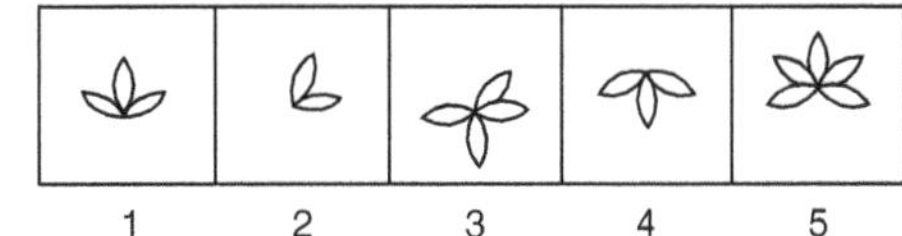

1 2 3 4 5

Answer Figures

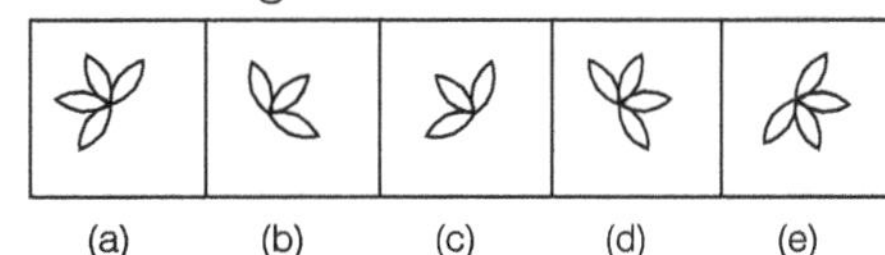

(a) (b) (c) (d) (e)

« SBI PO 2013

30. Question Figures

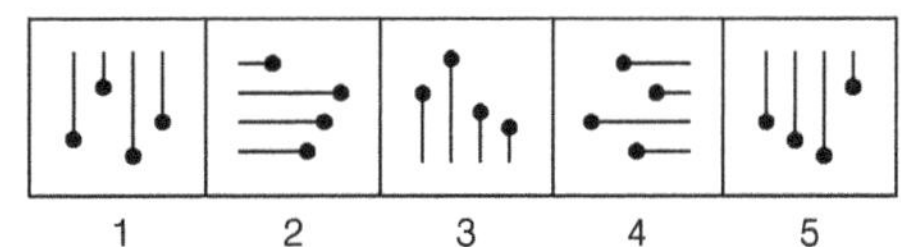

1 2 3 4 5

Answer Figures

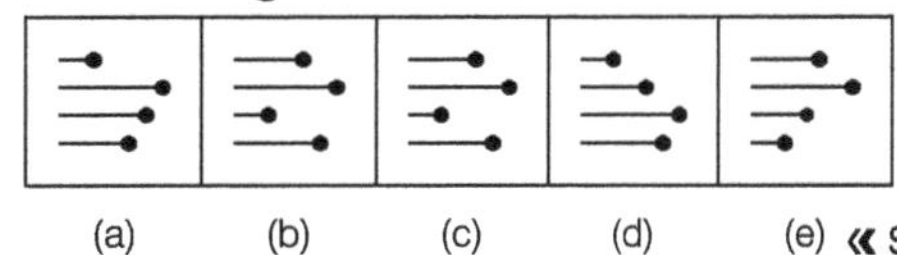

(a) (b) (c) (d) (e) « SBI PO 2010

31. Question Figures

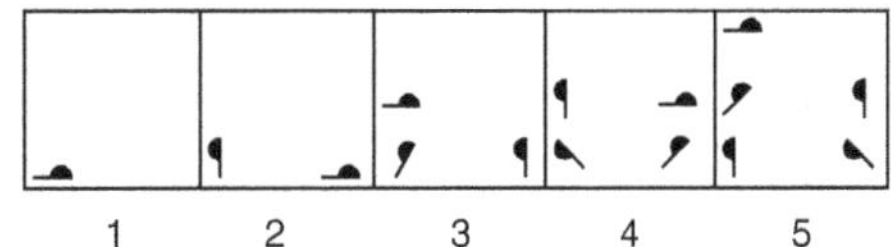

1 2 3 4 5

Answer Figures

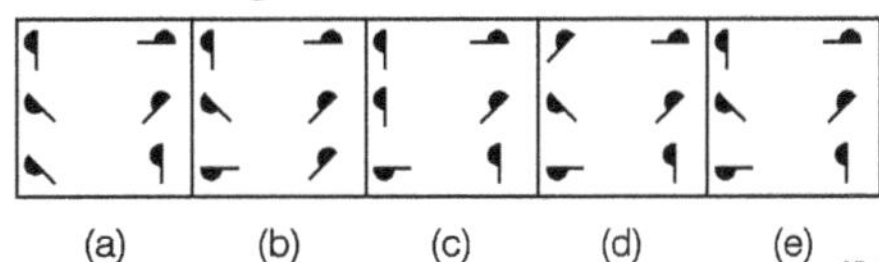

(a) (b) (c) (d) (e)

« CBI PO 2010

32. Question Figures

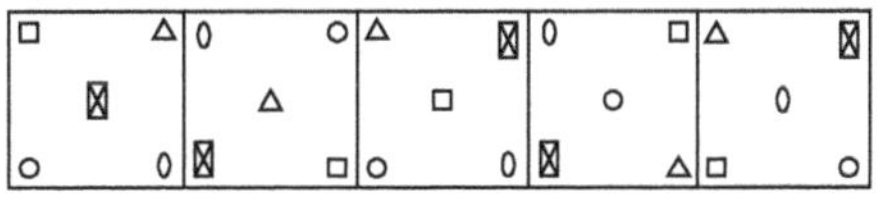

1 2 3 4 5

Answer Figures

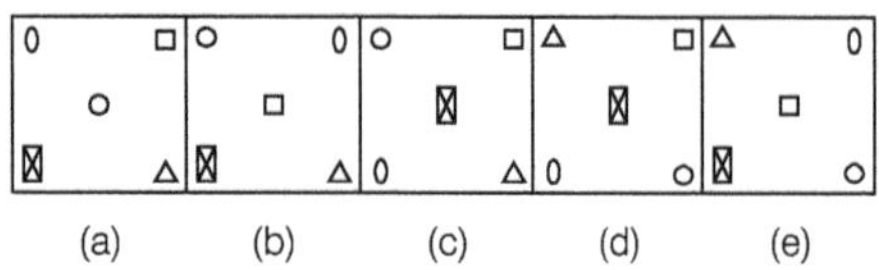

« IBPS Clerk 2011

33. Question Figures

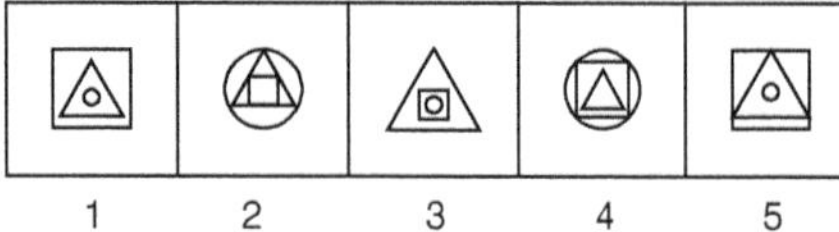

Answer Figures

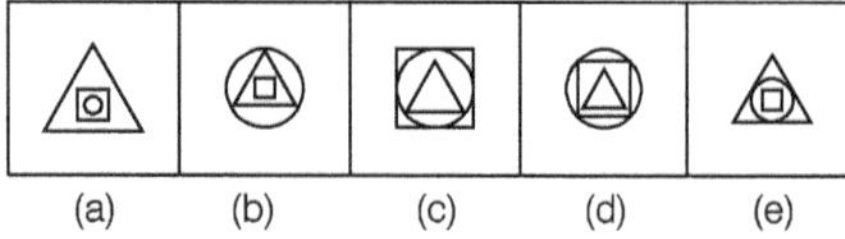

« CBI PO 2010

34. Question Figures

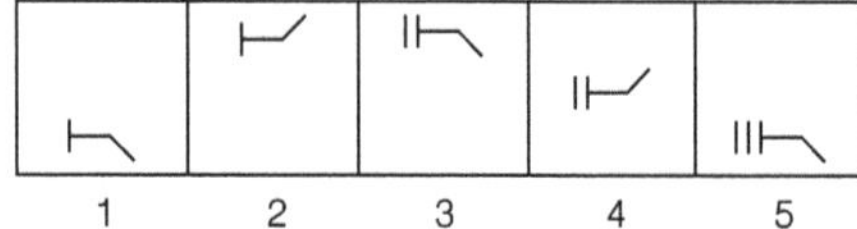

Answer Figures

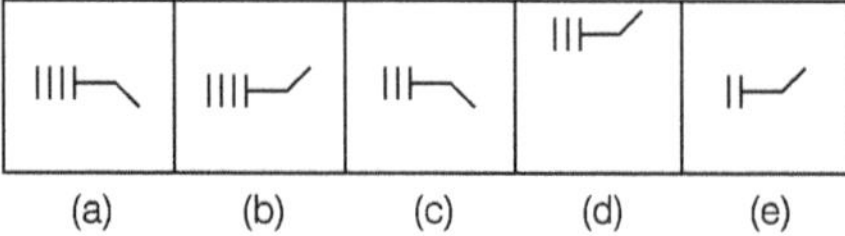

35. Question Figures

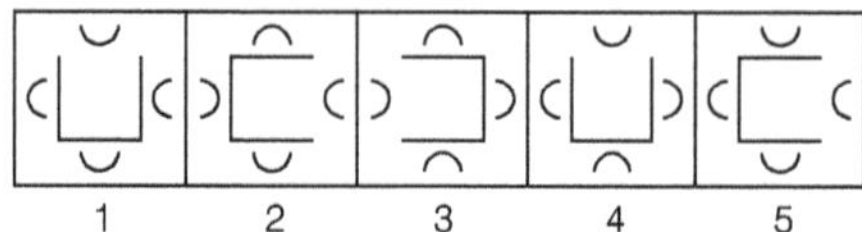

Answer Figures

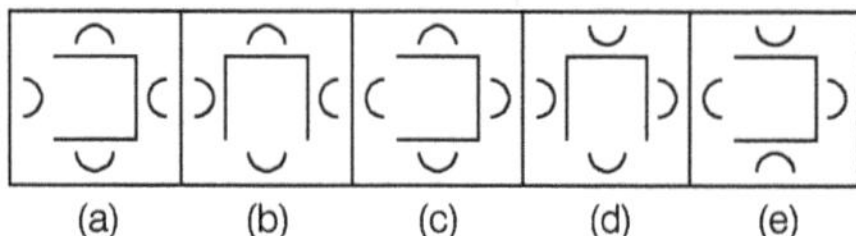

36. Question Figures

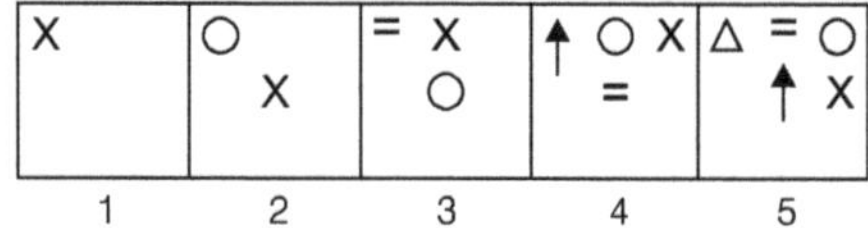

Answer Figures

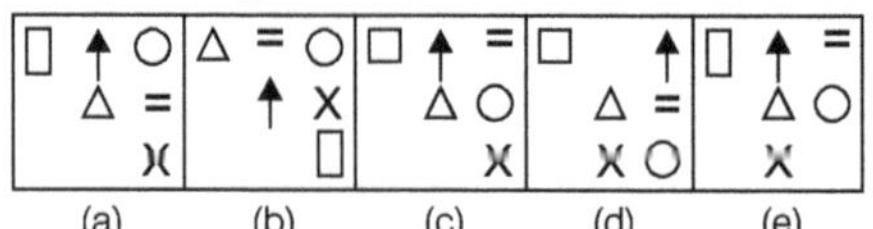

37. Question Figures

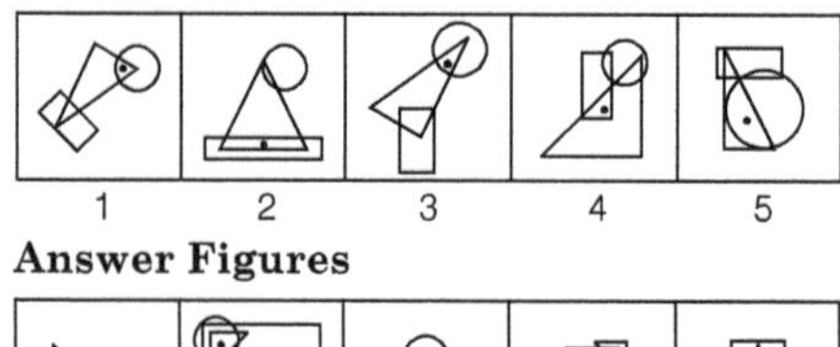

Answer Figures

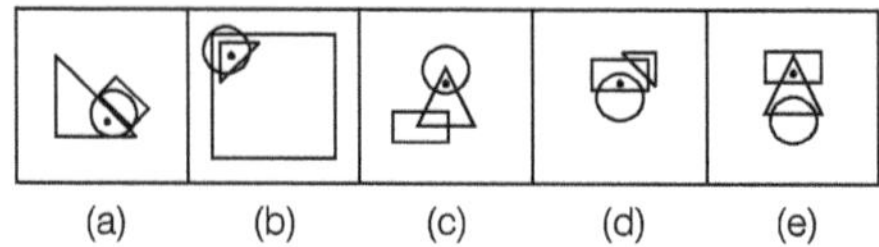

38. Question Figures

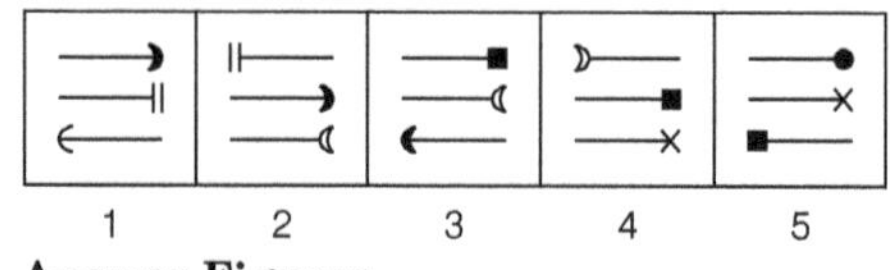

Answer Figures

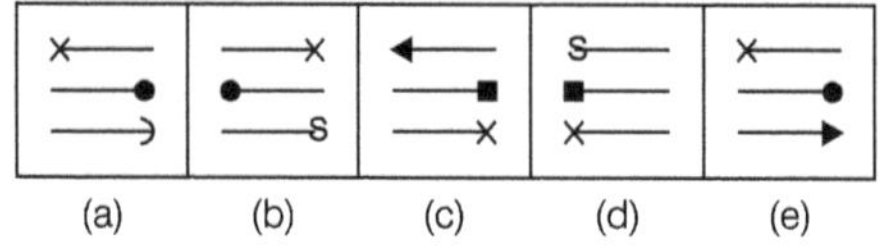

« OBC PO 2010

39. Question Figures

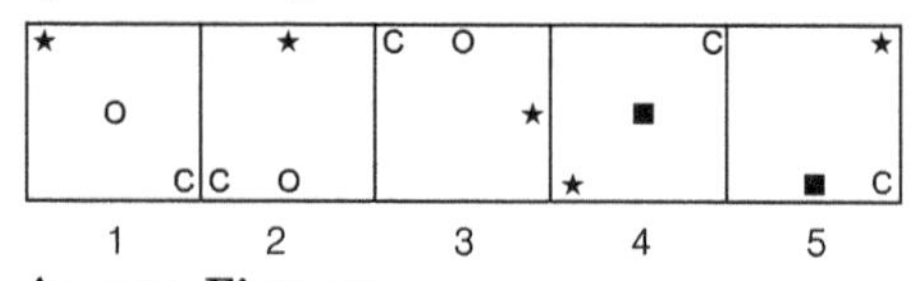

Answer Figures

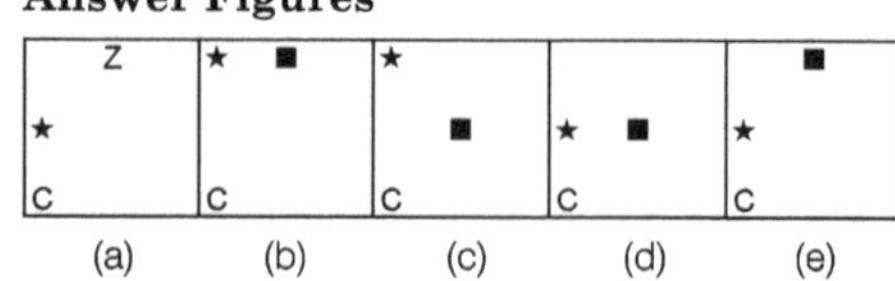

« PNB PO 2010

40. Question Figures

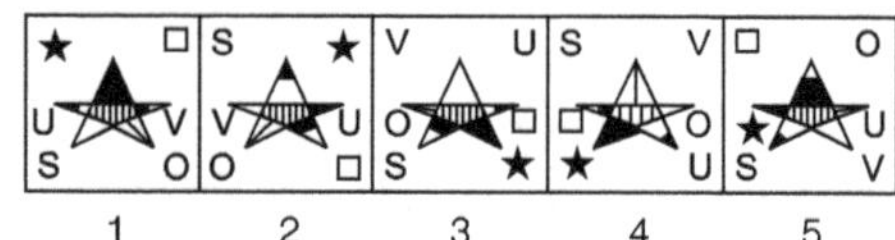

Answer Figures

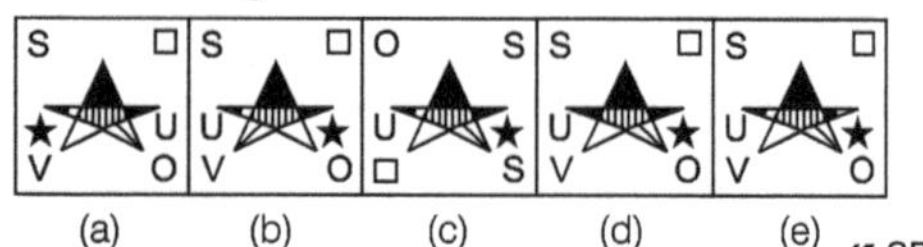

« SBI PO 2010

41. Question Figures

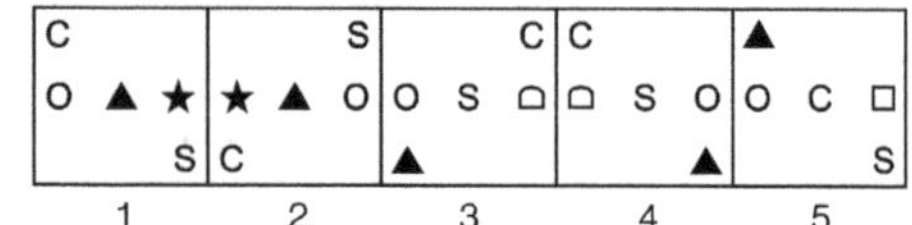

Answer Figures

(a)	(b)	(c)	(d)	(e)
S	▲	S	S	S
O C □	□ C O	□ ▲ ∨	O C ∨	□ C O
▲	S	C	▲	▲

« UBI PO 2010

42. Question Figures

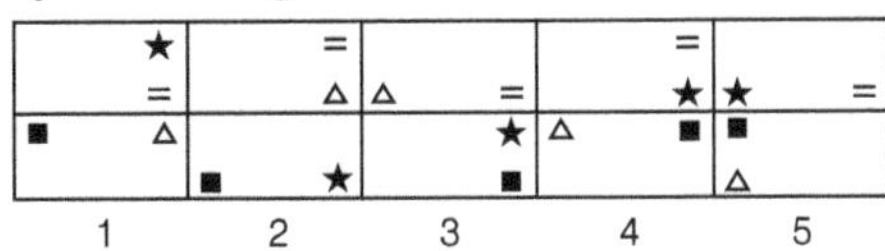

1 2 3 4 5

Answer Figures

(a)	(b)	(c)	(d)	(e)
★ Z	△ U	★ U	★ U	△ =
= S	Z S	■ S	■ S	Z O
O U	★ =	△ =	△ =	★ U
■ △	■ O	Z O	Z O	■ S

« UBI PO 2010

43. Question Figures

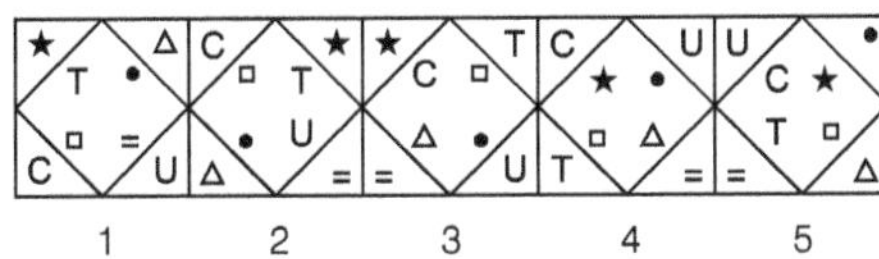

1 2 3 4 5

Answer Figures

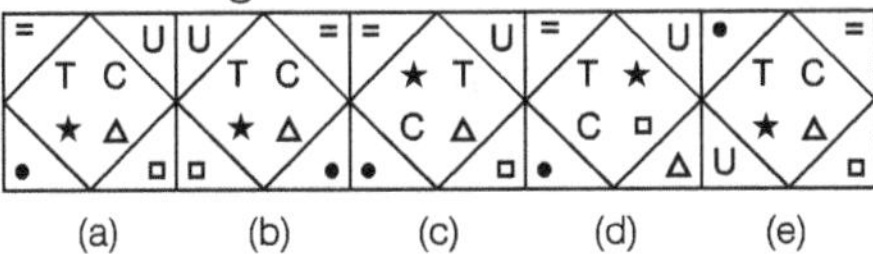

(a) (b) (c) (d) (e)

44. Question Figures

1	2	3	4	5
◇	Z	△	★	O
△ O D	◇ U O	O ◇ U	△ D ◇	◇ △ D
Z U ★	△ ★ D	★ D Z	O Z U	Z U ★

Answer Figures

(a)	(b)	(c)	(d)	(e)
◇	Z	Z	Z	Z
Z ★ △	D ◇ △	O D ★	O ★ △	O U △
O U D	U ★ O	◇ △ U	◇ D U	◇ ★ D

« IOB PO 2010

45. Question Figures

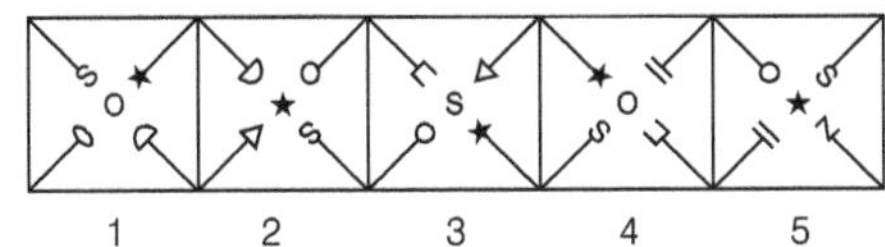

1 2 3 4 5

Answer Figures

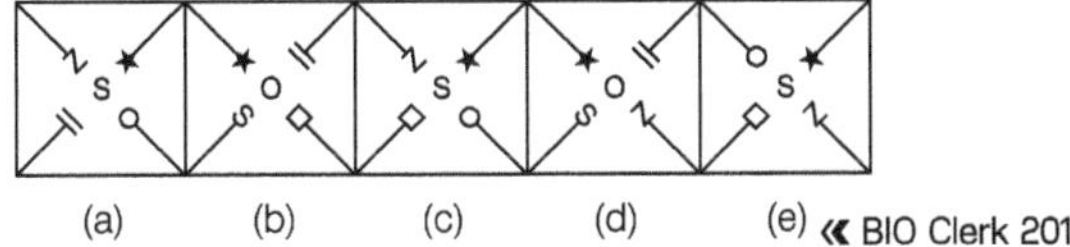

(a) (b) (c) (d) (e) « BIO Clerk 2010

46. Question Figures

1	2	3	4	5
C T S △ □	T C S □ △	△TCS□	T △ C □ S	□ C △ T S

Answer Figures

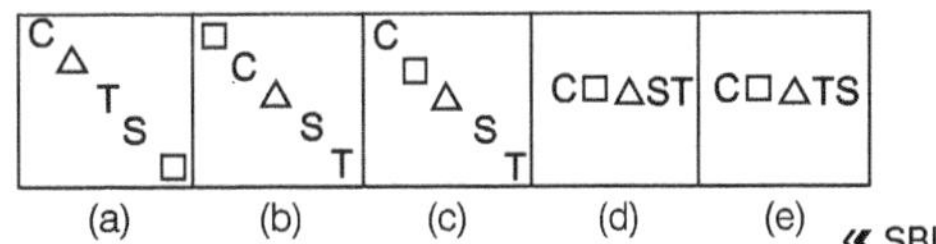

(a) (b) (c) (d) (e) « SBI PO 2013

47. Question Figures

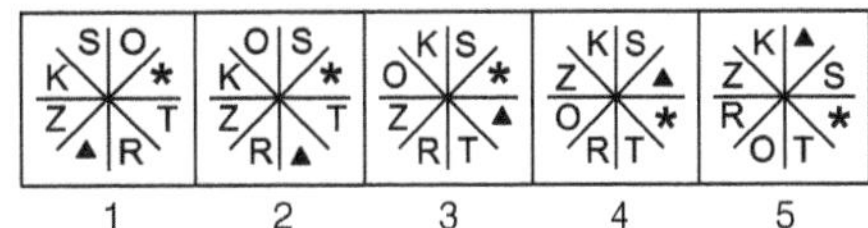

1 2 3 4 5

Answer Figures

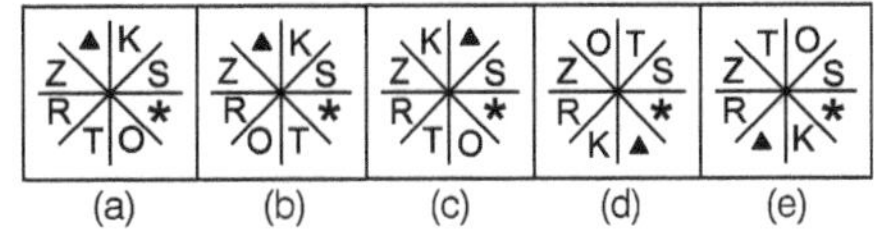

(a) (b) (c) (d) (e)

48. Question Figures

1	2	3	4	5
K = ★	Z = ★	△ Z ★	T Z ★	P T ★
Z S ●	△ K ●	T = ●	P △ ●	S Z ●
△ T P	T P S	P S K	S K =	K = △

Answer Figures

(a)	(b)	(c)	(d)	(e)
S T ★	S P ★	△ T ★	Z T R	S T ●
K P ●	K T ●	S Z ●	P △ ●	K P ★
= △ Z	= △ Z	P = K	S K =	= △ Z

49. Question Figures

1	2	3	4	5
=	V	△	T	★
O	△	V	★	T
□ V Z C ★	T C O = □	□ T C O =	Z O V △ □	□ Z O V △
△	Z	★	C	=
T	★	Z	=	C

Answer Figures

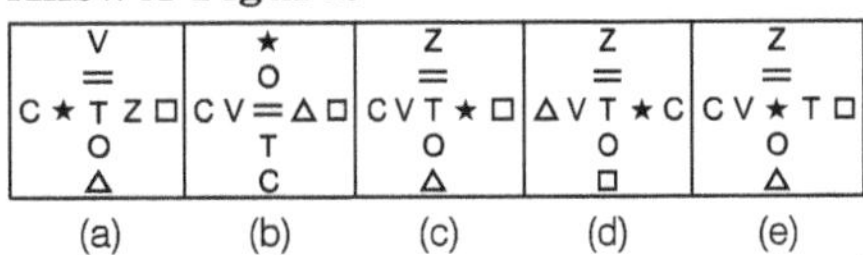

(a) (b) (c) (d) (e)

« PNB PO 2010

50. Question Figures

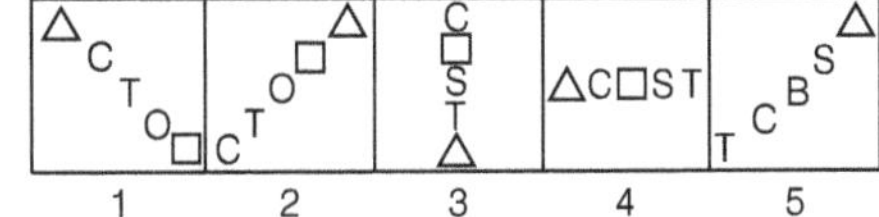

1 2 3 4 5

Answer Figures

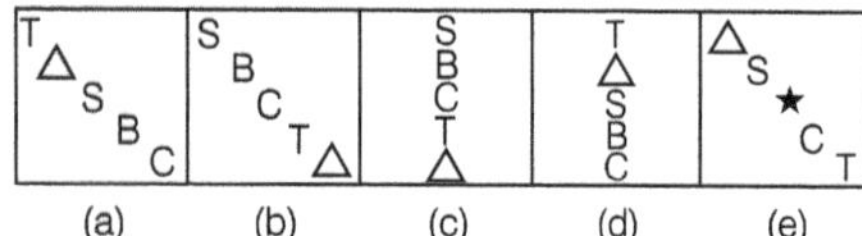

« IBPS PO 2012

51. Question Figures

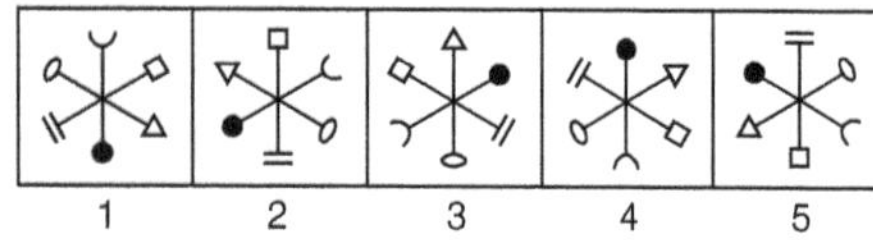

Answer Figures

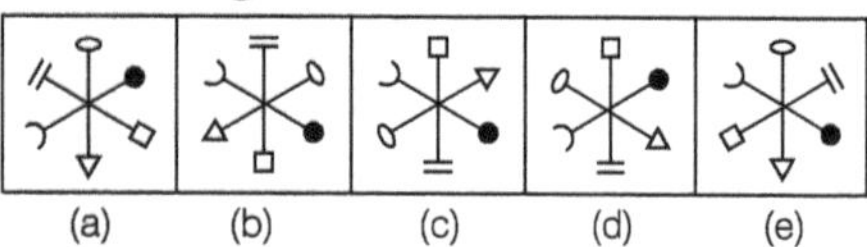

« CBI PO 2010

52. Question Figures

1	2	3	4	5
T □ O	A O △	3 A O	★ 3 B	3 □ K
A △	S □	K T	□ O	★ B
S L ★	K ★ T	△ □ ★	K △ T	△ T 6

Answer Figures

(a)	(b)	(c)	(d)	(e)
★ 8 □	★ K B	★ K B	★ B K	★ K B
△ K	△ □	△ □	△ □	3 □
P 6 3	T 6 3	C 6 3	C 6 3	Z 6 T

« IBPS PO 2012

53. Question Figures

1	2	3	4	5
● ★ ▲	C S ●	C	P	◪ Σ P
S	★	L	↑	◪
■	T	T ↑ □	□ L ■	■

Answer Figures

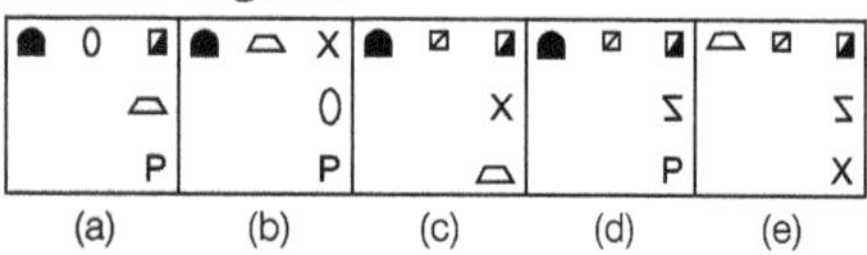

« UCO Bank PO 2010

54. Question Figures

1	2	3	4	5
O Z	△ D	D O	= △	△ D
D □ △	Z = O	△ Z =	O V D	= O V
= ★	★ □	V ↑	↑ Z	3 5

Answer Figures

(a)	(b)	(c)	(d)	(e)
V D	D V	D V	V =	V =
= 3 △	△ = O	△ = O	D 3 △	D 5 △
5 O	B C	5 3	5 O	3

« PNB PO 2010

55. Question Figures

1	2	3	4	5
↑	↗	→	↘	↓
△U○★D	U△★○Z	△UZ□★	U△O★□	O=U□★
⊣	↗	T	↖	⊢

Answer Figures

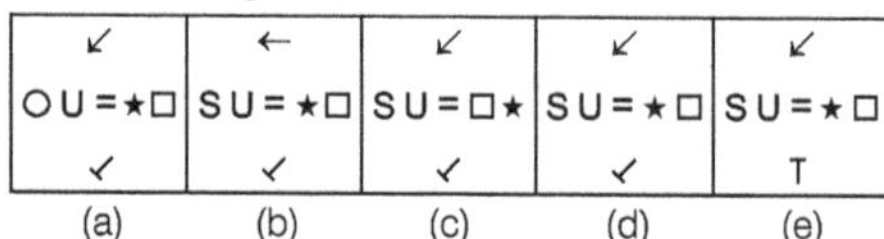

« UBI PO 2010

56. Question Figures

1	2	3	4	5
S = T	● T =	T ● ▲	S = ●	● S =
● ▲	C ★	S =	T ▲	C ★
C ★ ■	S ■ ▲	■ C ★	C ★ ■	T ■ ▲

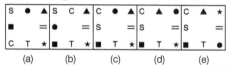

Answer Figures

(a)	(b)	(c)	(d)	(e)
S ● ▲	S C ▲	C ● ▲	C ▲ ●	C ▲ ★
■ =	● =	S =	S =	S =
C T ★	■ T ★	■ T ★	■ T ★	■ T ●

« IBPS Clerk 2011

57. Question Figures

1	2	3	4	5
S		↑	S O	O C S
T	T O	S	↑	T
↑ O C	S C ↑	C T O	T C	↑

Answer Figures

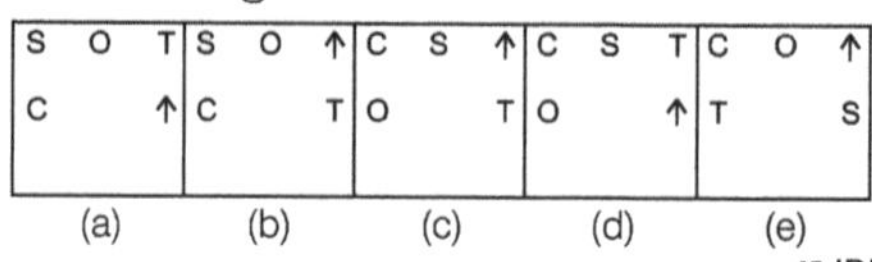

« IBPS Clerk 2011

58. Question Figures

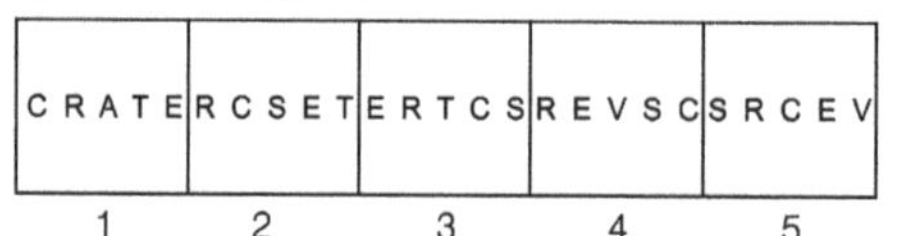

Answer Figures

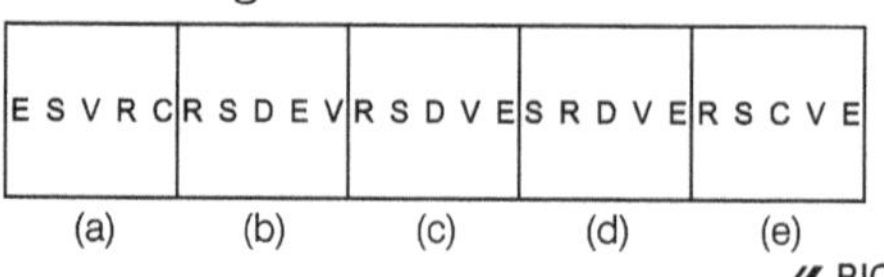

« BIO Clerk 2010

59. Question Figures

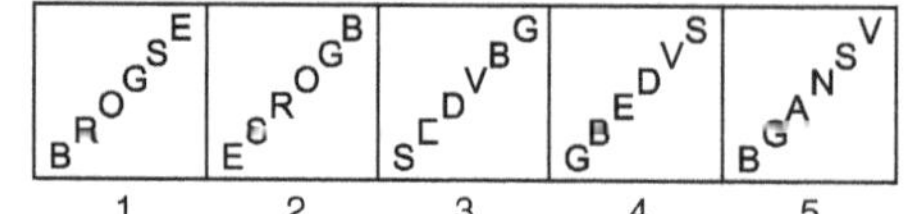

Answer Figures

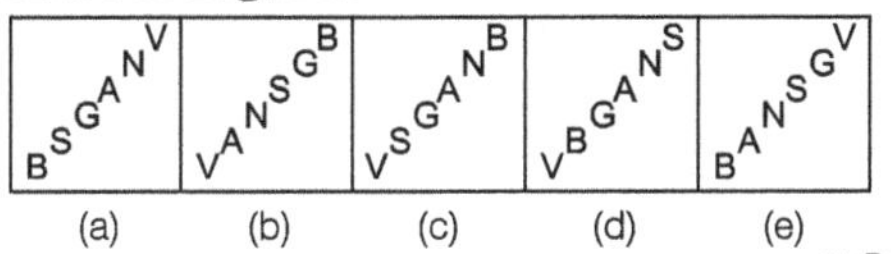

(a) (b) (c) (d) (e)

« BOB PO 2010

60. Question Figures

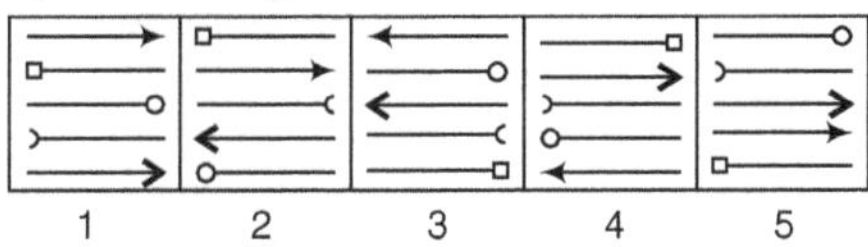

1 2 3 4 5

Answer Figures

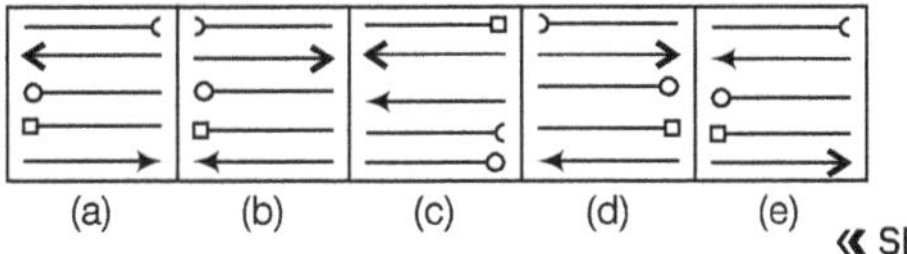

(a) (b) (c) (d) (e)

« SBI PO 2013

61. Question Figures

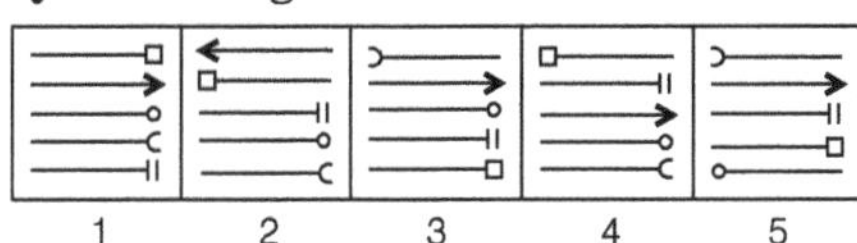

1 2 3 4 5

Answer Figures

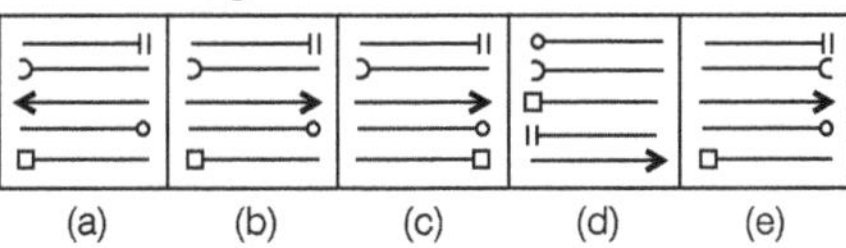

(a) (b) (c) (d) (e)

« IBPS PO 2012

62. Question Figures

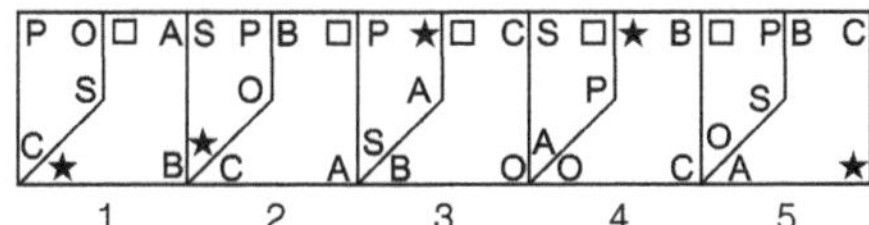

1 2 3 4 5

Answer Figures

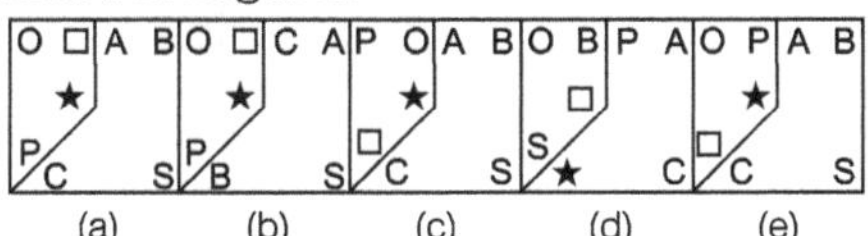

(a) (b) (c) (d) (e)

« IBPS PO 2012

63. Question Figures

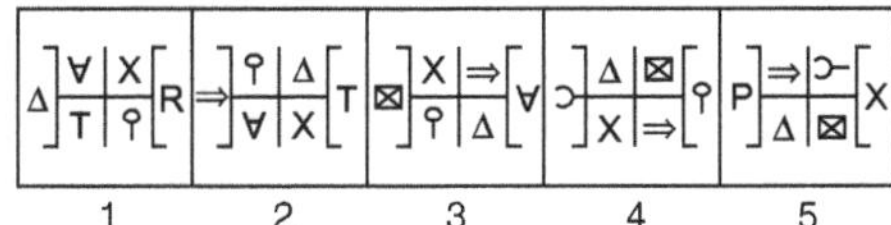

1 2 3 4 5

Answer Figures

(a) (b) (c) (d) (e)

64. Question Figures

1	2	3	4	5
M q B H	D N Y Z	q U X B	B q X U	F D Z Y
U D Z X	F M H V	D H M Z	V F Y N	H B U M
N F V Y	q U X B	F Y N V	D H M Z	q V N X

Answer Figures

(a)	(b)	(c)	(d)	(e)
q N V X	q V N X	q N V X	q V N X	q V N X
F U B Y	F U B Y	F B U Y	F B U M	F U B Y
H Z D M	H Z D M	H Z D M	H Z D Y	H D Z M

« Canara Bank PO 2011

65. Question Figures

1	2	3	4	5
⇒ ■ ⬠	B q ■	■ B q	X ⇒ B	B X ⇒
X P q	Y ⇒ ⬠	⬠ Y ⇒	P ■ q	q P ■
Y M B	M X P	P M X	M ⬠ Y	Y M ⬠

Answer Figures

(a)	(b)	(c)	(d)	(e)
⬠ ■ X	⇒ B X	⬠ X ⇒	Y M ⬠	⬠ ■ X
q B ⇒	■ q P	Y B ■	B X ⇒	Y B ⇒
Y M P	⬠ Y M	M q P	q P ■	M q P

66. Question Figures

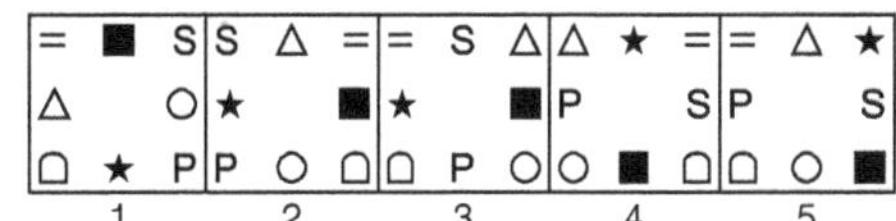

1 2 3 4 5

Answer Figures

(a)	(b)	(c)	(d)	(e)
= P ★	★ = △	★ S =	★ P =	⌂ P =
○ △	P S	△ ○	○ △	○ △
⌂ S ■	■ ⌂ ○	■ P ⌂	■ S ⌂	■ S ★

67. Question Figures

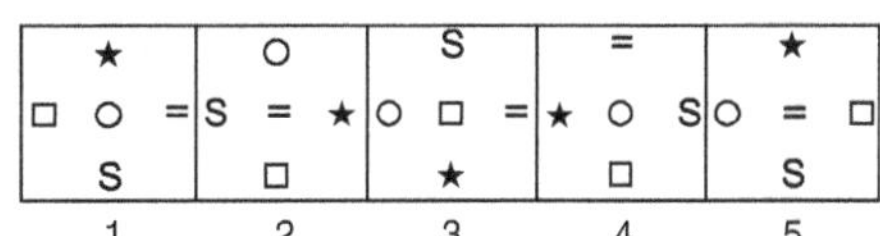

1 2 3 4 5

Answer Figures

(a)	(b)	(c)	(d)	(e)
=	□	=	○	=
S □ ★	S = ★	○ □ ★	= S ★	★ ○ S
○	○	S	□	□

« UBI PO 2010

68. Question Figures

1	2	3	4	5
×	★	×	H	×
o	c	⊣	□	△
c	=	□	c	★
=	□	c	★	□
□	×	★	×	H

Answer Figures

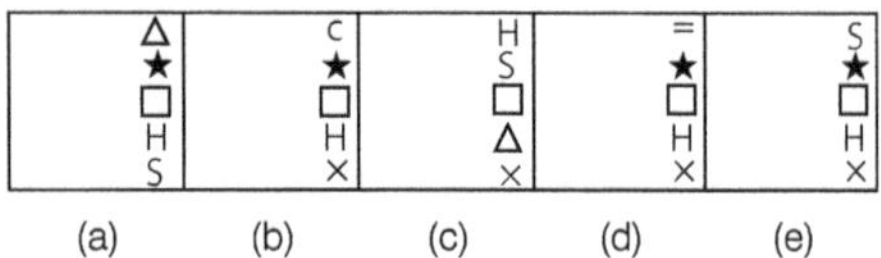

« IBPS PO 2011

69. Consider the following figures and answer the question given below.

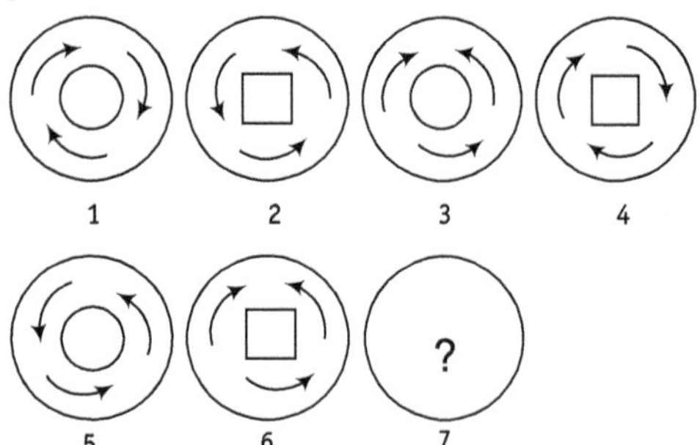

Which one of the following figures would logically come in the 7th position indicated above by a questions mark? « UPSC CSAT 2013

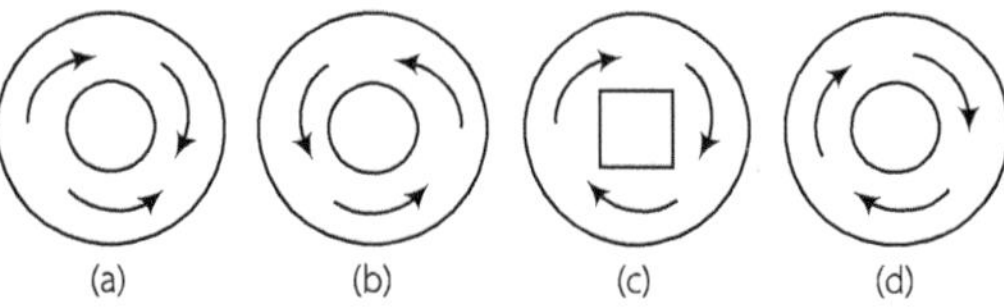

DIRECTIONS ~ (Q. Nos. 70-86) *In each of the questions given below, there are two sets of figures. The figures on the upper or left side are question figures marked by numbers* 1, 2, 3, 4 *and* 5 *and on the lower or right side there are answer figures marked by alphabets* a, b, c, d *and* e. *A series is established, if one of the five or four answer figures is placed in place of the sign ? in the question figures. The figure from answer figures which will replace the sign ? In question figures is your answer.*

70. Question Figures

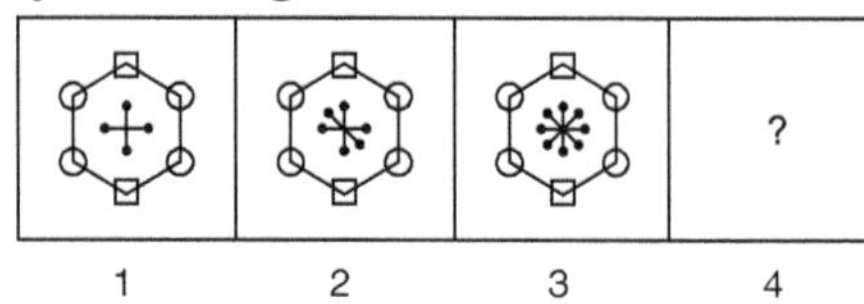

Answer Figures

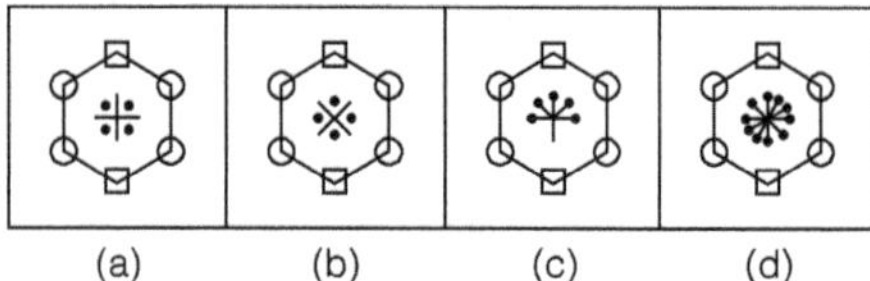

« SSC 10+2 2014

71. Question Figures

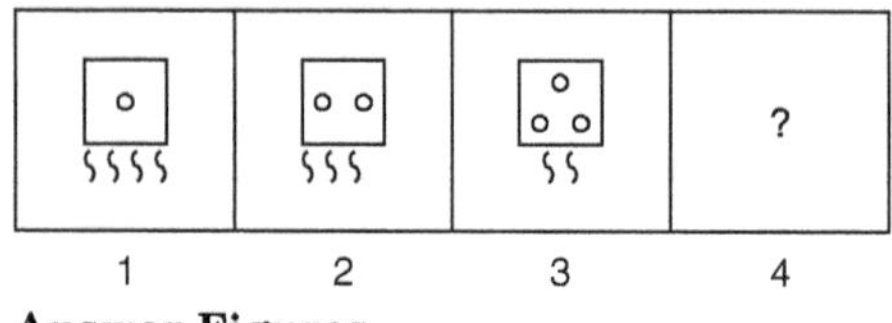

Answer Figures

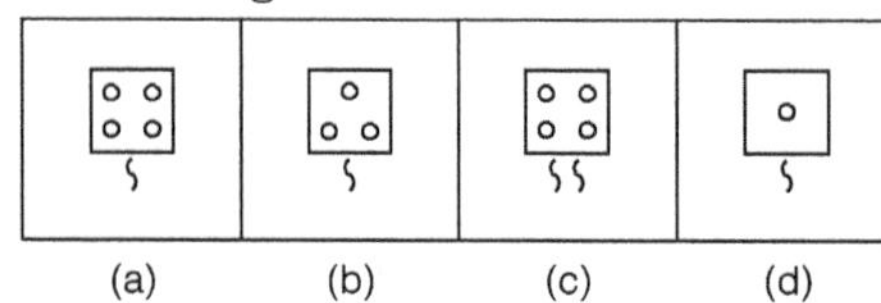

72. Question Figures

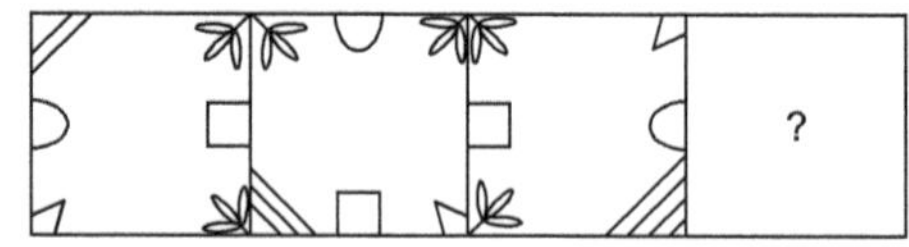

Answer Figures

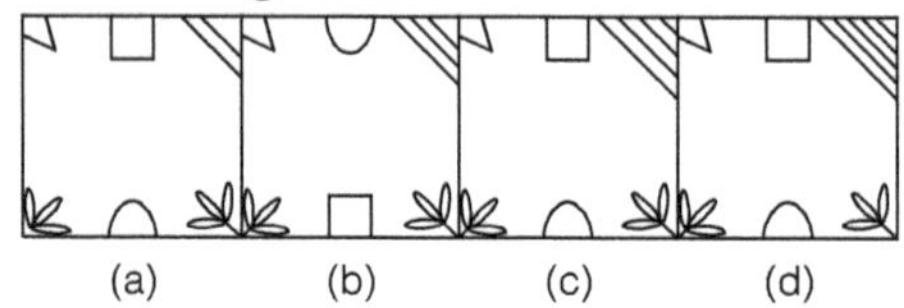

« Chhattisgarh Patwari 2019

73. Question Figures

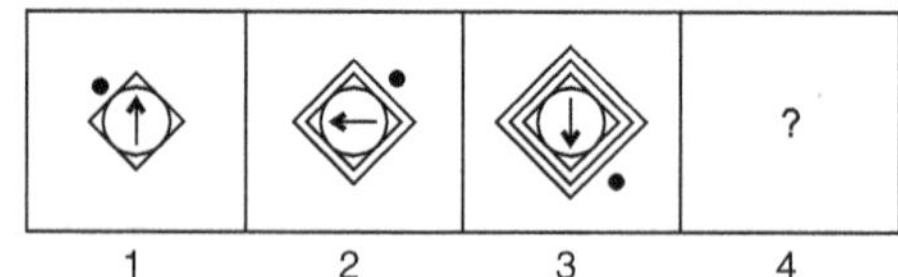

Answer Figures

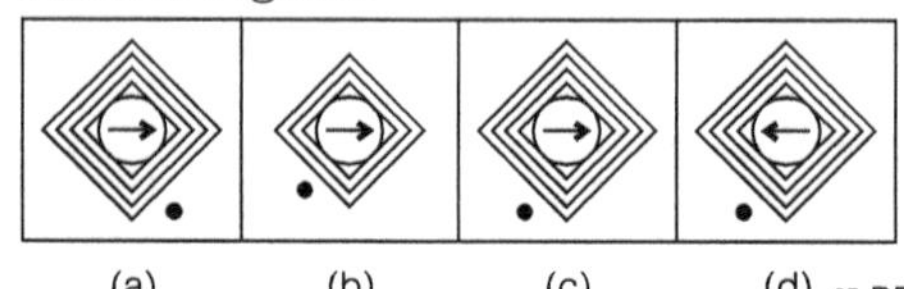

« RRB ALP 2010

74. Question Figures

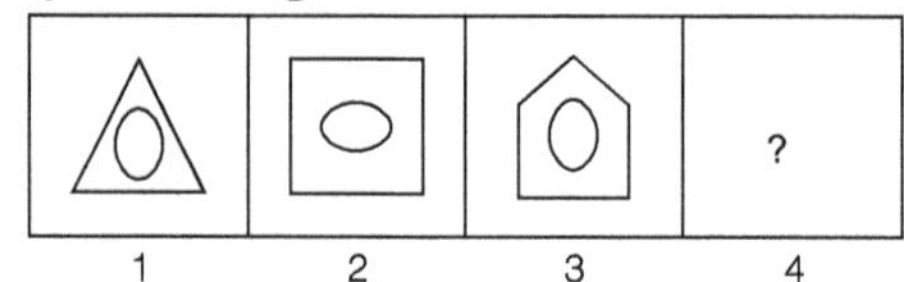

Answer Figures

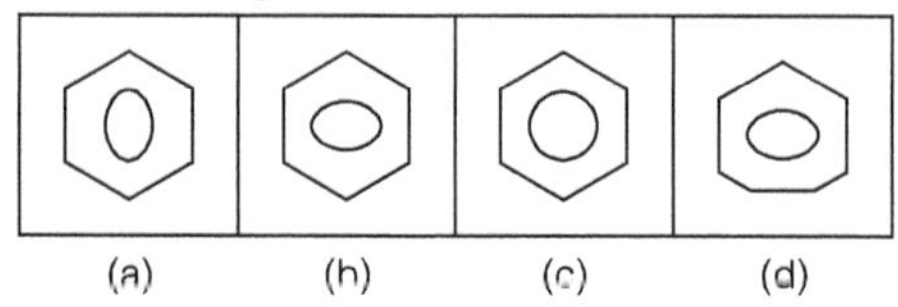

75. Question Figures

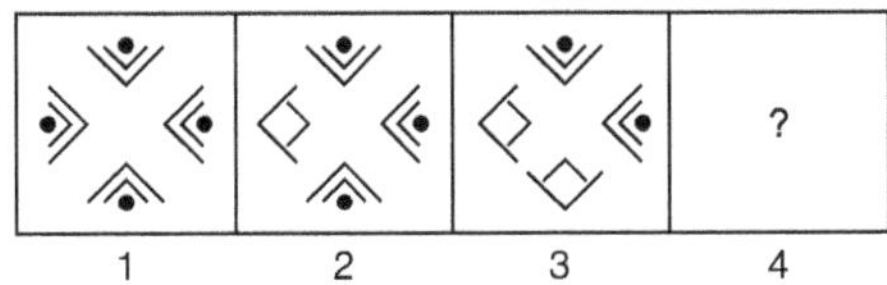

Answer Figures

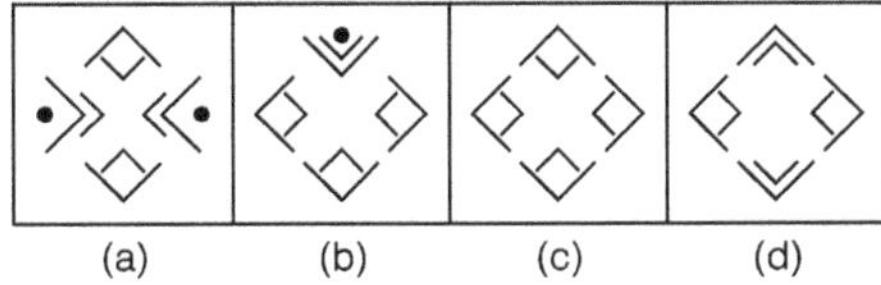

76. Question Figures

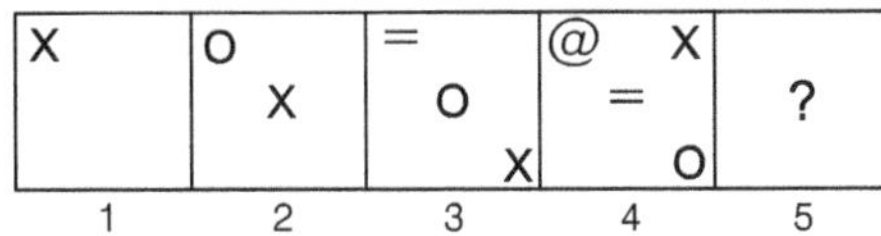

Answer Figures

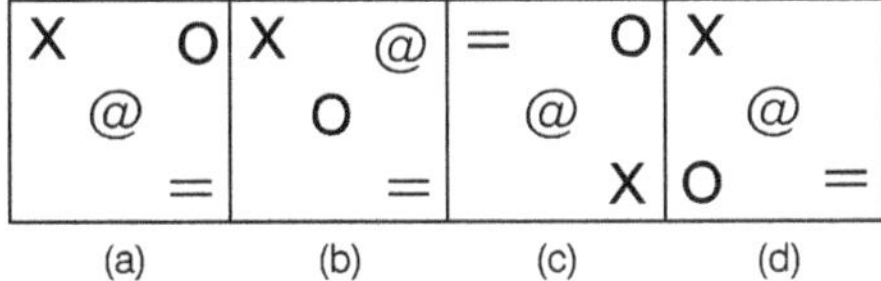

« SSC CPO 2019

77. Question Figures

Answer Figures

78. Question Figures

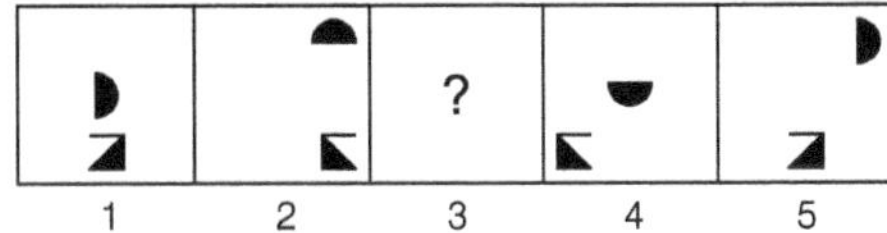

Answer Figures

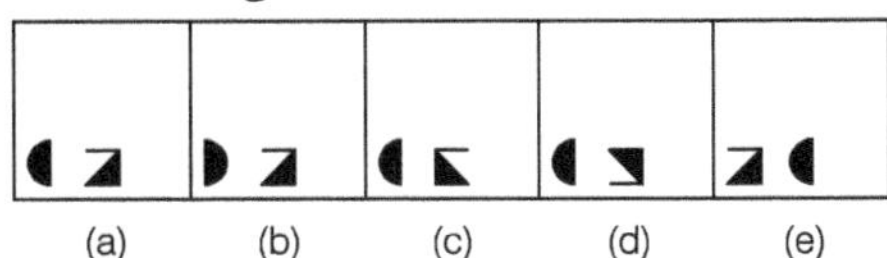

79. Question Figures

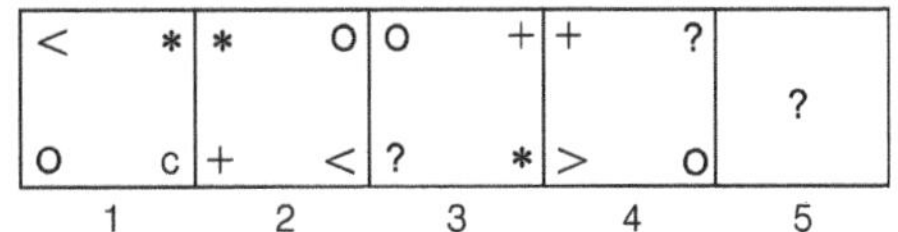

Answer Figures

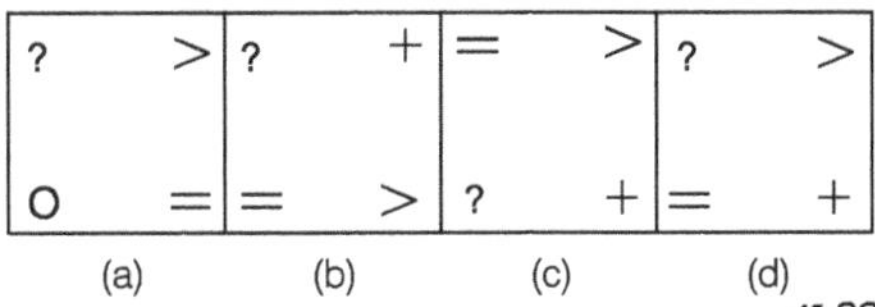

« SSC CPO 2019

80. Question Figures

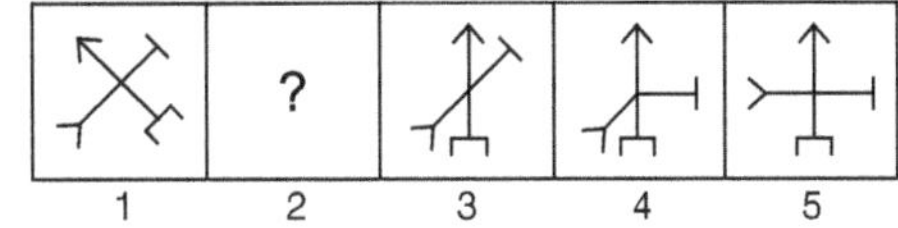

Answer Figures

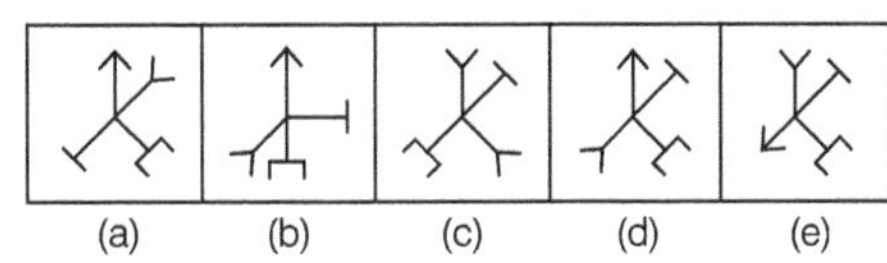

81. Question Figures

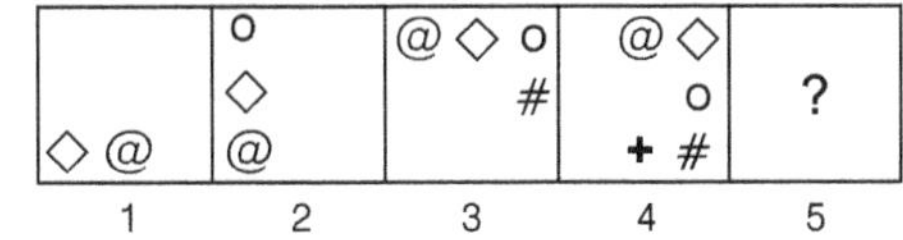

Answer Figures

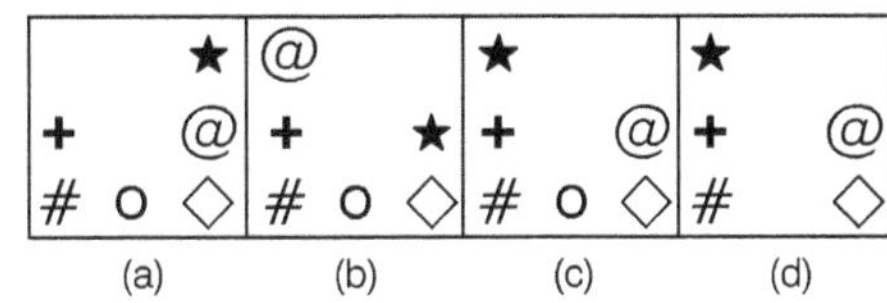

« SSC CGL 2019

82. Question Figures

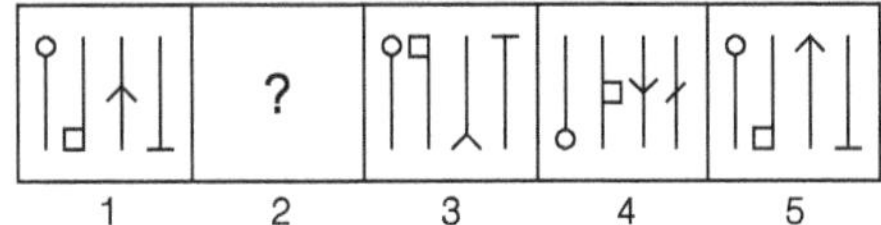

Answer Figures

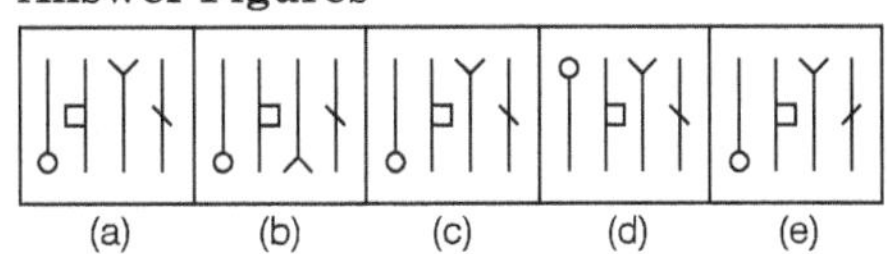

83. Question Figures

1	2	3	4	5
= S / C + / ★ O	S = / ★ O / C +	?	O ★ / + C / S =	+ C / O ★ / = S

Answer Figures

(a)	(b)	(c)	(d)	(e)
O ★ / = S / C +	★ O / S = / + C	O ★ / S = / + C	★ O / = S / + C	C + / S = / O ★

84. Question Figures

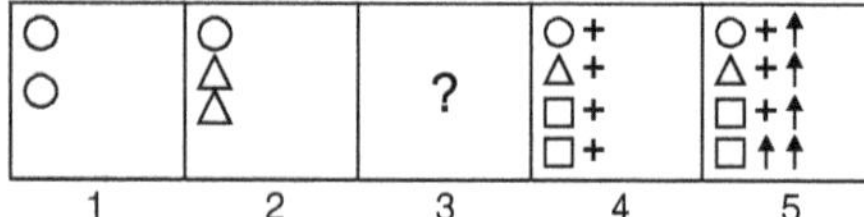

Answer Figures

(a)	(b)	(c)	(d)	(e)
O□ / △□ / △ / □	O□ / △ / △ / □	O / △ / □ / □	O□ / △ / □ / □	O□ / O□ / △ / △

85. Question Figures

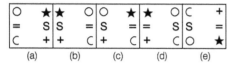

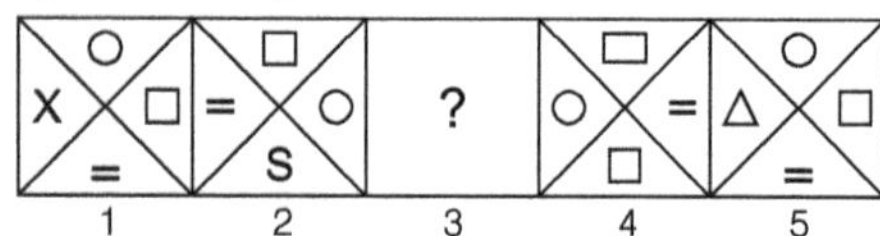

Answer Figures

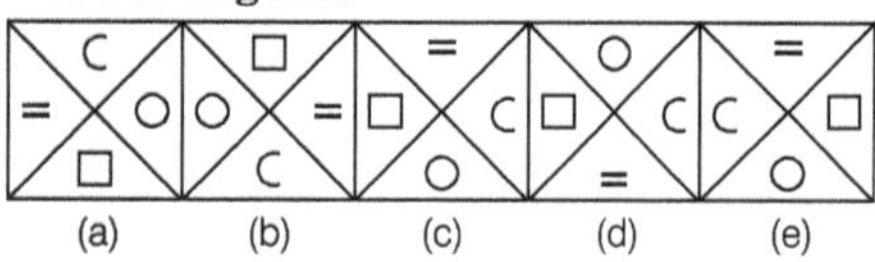

86. Question Figures

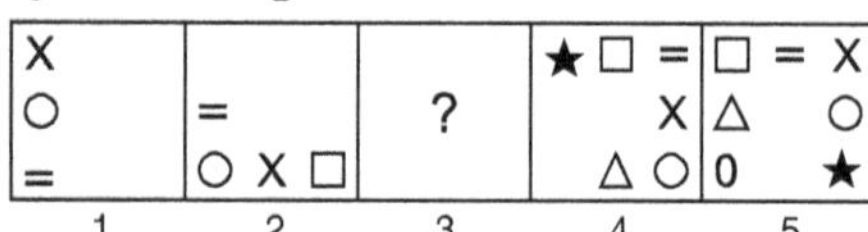

Answer Figures

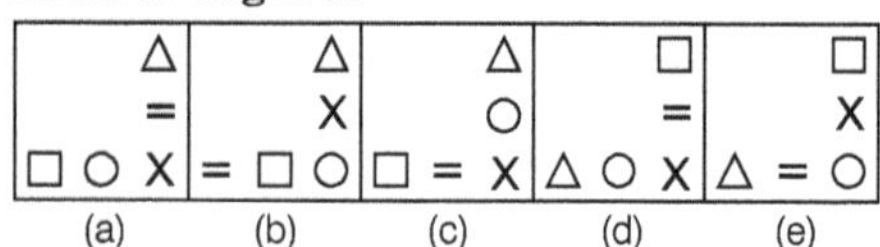

DIRECTIONS ~ (Q. Nos. 87-91) *Each of the following series consists of seven figures, two of which at the ends are unmarked. One of the five marked figures* (a), (b), (c), (d) *and* (e) *does not fit into the series. Find out that figure.*

87.

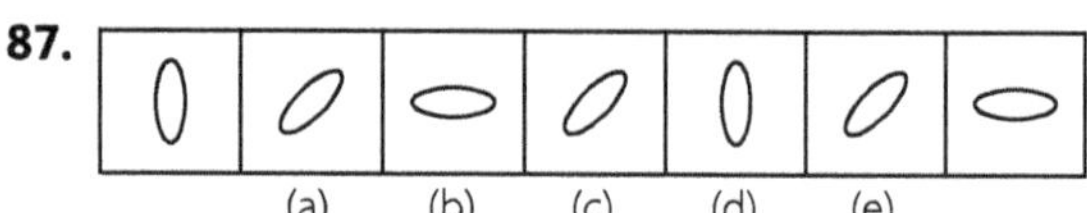

88.

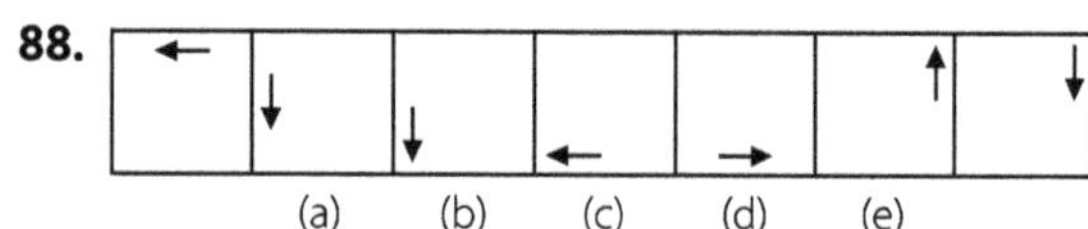

89.

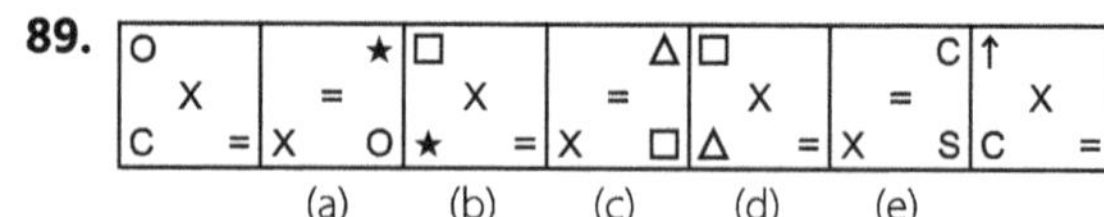

90.

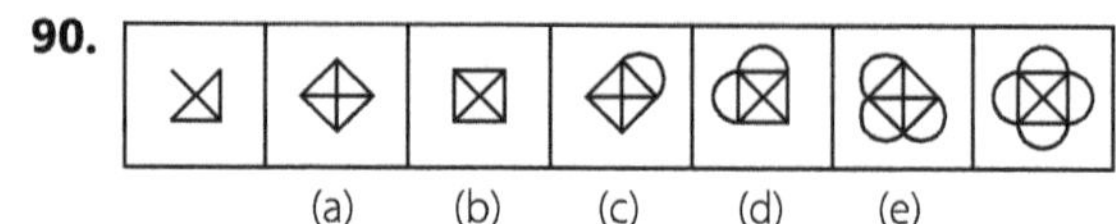

91.

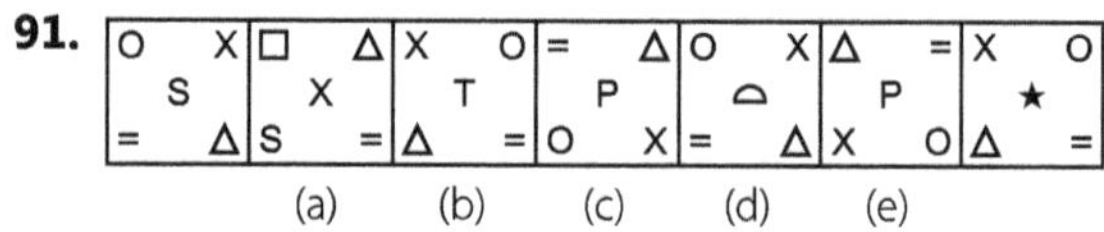

DIRECTIONS ~ (Q. Nos. 92 and 93) *In each of the following questions below, the figures follow a series/sequence. One and only one out of the five figures does not fit in the series/sequence. The number of that figure is your answer.* « IBPS PO 2012

92.

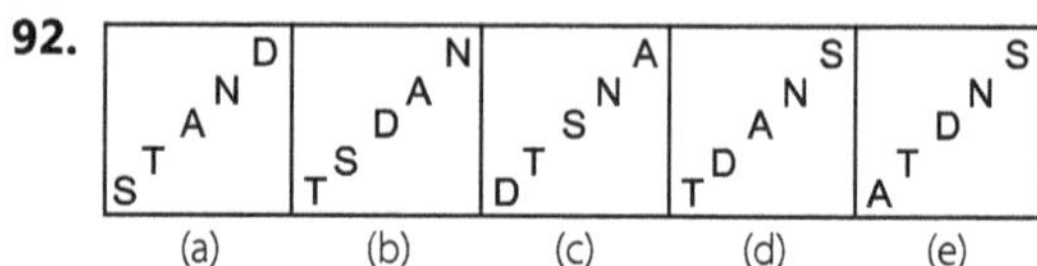

93.

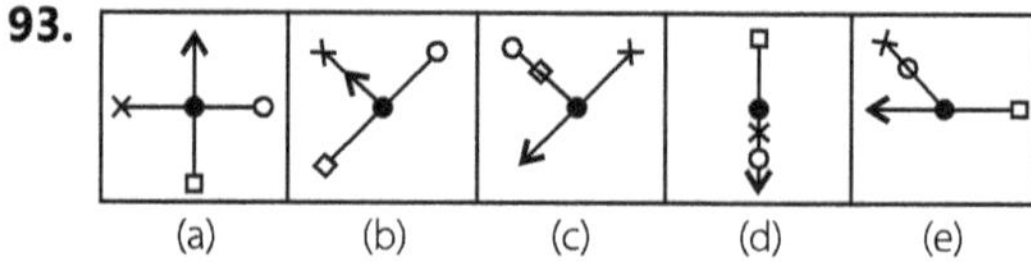

Answers / WITH EXPLANATIONS

1. (*c*) In the given arrangement, each time one vertical line and one horizontal line is removed to form the next figure.

2. (*c*) From figure (1) to (2), the black dots remain at the same place while the rest figure is rotated by 180°. Similarly, from figure (3) to (4), dots will remain at their places while the rest figure will be rotated by 180°.

3. (*c*) The problem figure (1) is same as problem figure (4) but with an inverted arrow. So, the answer figure must be same as problem figure (2) but with an inverted arrow.

4. (*d*) In the problem figures, the triangle is pointed towards up, followed by pointed towards down alternately. Also, the triangle moves one step anti-clockwise in each figure. So, in the answer figure triangle should point up and must be present at the top left corner. The straight line is rotating in anti-clockwise direction.

5. (*b*) In each step, the left most symbol gets shifted to the right most side and also gets inverted.

6. (*b*) The triangle is moving downwards in a zig-zag manner, while the movement of the semi-circle like element is anti-clockwise along the inner four squares.

7. (*c*) Shaded portion moves one block in clockwise direction in every successive step.

8. (*d*) In each of the successive figures initially the square is moving from left to right and then from right to left. The circle is moving from left to right and is also getting inverted vertically in each step.

9. (*d*) One circle is increasing in each step and also the circles are rotating 180° in each step.

10. (*a*) In the first step, both the arcs are inverted. In second step, the inverted arcs are joined together. In third step, the arcs are inverted again. Now, in fourth step they will be separated and moved away from each other.

11. (*d*) In each step, the circle is moving from top to middle and from middle to bottom. Also, it gets half-shaded (lower half) in first step and full shaded in second step. This process will be repeated for square also.

12. (*a*) In each successive figure, the design is rotating 45° in clockwise direction.

13. (*a*) In every successive figure, a line from both the triangles is removing.

14. (*d*) In every successive figure, two circles in the upper box are increasing and one circle in the lower box is decreasing.

15. (*d*) In first step, one line from left side is removed. In second step, one line from right side is removed. The process is repeated in the subsequent steps.

16. (*b*) From figure (1) to (2), two more boxes get shaded in clockwise direction, then from figure (2) to (3) one box at the anti-clockwise end gets unshaded. The same process is repeated.

17. (*d*) In every step 3, 2, 3 and 2 upper figures are deleted and 4,3,4 and 3 lower figures are deleted.

18. (*a*) The small circle is moving one part from first to second, two parts from second to third, three parts from third to fourth and so on.

19. (*c*) Darken part moves two steps and then becomes three parts, then moves three steps and becomes two, then moves four steps ahead and becomes five, then moves five steps ahead and becomes three darken parts.

20. (*a*) Here, the figure moves $\frac{1}{2}$ step, 1 step, $1\frac{1}{2}$ steps and then again $\frac{1}{2}$ step in anti-clockwise direction. Also every time a line is also added to the figure.

21. (*c*) Here, two patterns are going consecutively. In figures 1→3→5, figure moves 90° clockwise. In figure 2-4, figure moves 90° clockwise. So, figure 4 moves 90° clockwise to continue the sequence.

22. (*e*) The half arrow in the middle moves 90° clockwise. 'L' moves $\frac{1}{2}$ step in anti-clockwise direction and it rotates 90° anti-clockwise in each alternate figure.

23. (*d*) Here, in each figure one line, two lines and then three lines are added. This process is repeated from figure (4) onwards.

24. (*b*) There are two different series. One series contains one symbol and other series contains two symbols. In both the series, symbols move 1 step in clockwise direction and each time symbols are replaced by new symbols. The series having two elements contains one symbol same as the previous figure of one element series.

25. (*e*) Here, elements move from bottom to middle, middle to top, top to middle and then middle to bottom. This process repeats. Also, in first step, elements at both the ends interchange their positions and the remaining element gets inverted vertically. In next step, the element at left end shifts at the right end and also gets inverted vertically. In third step, all the three elements are inverted vertically. Now, this process is repeated from next step.

26. (*a*) In first step, the first and second symbols (counting in clockwise direction) interchange their positions and in the second step, the first and the third symbols interchange their positions. This goes on alternately. The remaining symbol moves to the vacant position and gets replaced by a new symbol in each step.

27. (*d*) All the arrows are pointing in four different directions.

28. (*d*) Both the elements move one step in clockwise direction. The half arrow rotates 90° anti-clockwise. The semi-circular gets laterally inverted in each successive steps.

29. (*d*) From figure (1) to (3), the figure is inverted and one leaf is added to one of its side. Also from figure (3) to (5), the figure is again inverted and one leaf is added to its other side. Same process follows from figure (2) to (4) and from figure (4) to the answer figure.

30. (*e*) Here, figure (1) is similar to (4) while figure (2) is similar to (5) except that the latter is 90° clockwise rotated form of the first. So, answer figure must be similar to figure (3) after 90° clockwise rotation.

31. (*e*) In each of the subsequent figure, one design is added in a set order and the designs rotate respectively 90° anti-clockwise and 45° clockwise alternately.

32. (*c*) The sequence of the problem figures is

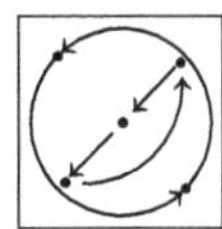

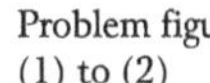
Problem figure (1) to (2)

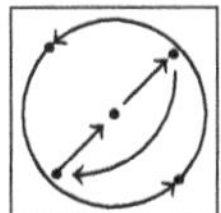
Problem figure (3) to (4)
figure (2) to (3)
figure (4) to (5)

Pattern of problem figure (1) to (2) will be repeated to obtain the answer figure.

33. (*b*) From problem figure (1) to (2) the innermost and outermost designs interchange their positions. Similar changes occur from problem figure (3) to (4) and from (5) to the answer figure.

34. (*d*) Main design in figure (5) is same as in figure (1), therefore, the main design for answer figure will be same as in figure (2). One line is added to the base of the main figure after every two figures.

35. (*a*) The central figure in figure (5) is same as in figure (2). Hence, it will be same in answer figure as it is in figure (3). The outer figures in figure (5) is same as in figure (1). Hence, in the answer figure, it will be same as it is in figure (2).

36. (*c*) In each of the successive figures, a new sign is formed at the top left position and the symbol it replaces comes in the middle.

The sign at the middle position comes at the middle top position and the sign at the midle top position comes to right top position. The same process is repeated in the successive figures.

37. (*e*) Figures change in such a way that dot lies in the space common to circle and triangle in one step and it lies in the space common to triangle and rectangle in next step. This process is repeated in the subsequent figures.

38. (*e*) The pattern is as follows

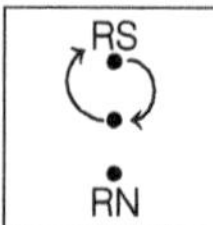

From figure (1) to (2) figure (3) to (4) and figure (5) to answer figure

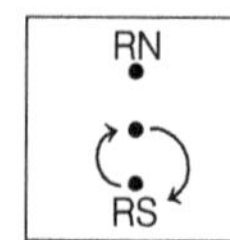

From figure (2) to (3) and figure (4) to (5)

RS = Reverse same design,
RN = Reverse new design.

39. (*e*) Diagram C moves clockwise 1 step in each figure, star moves in $\frac{1}{2}$,1,1$\frac{1}{2}$, 2 steps then it will move 2$\frac{1}{2}$ steps.

Remaining one diagram placed at middle moves from centre to bottom, bottom to top, top to centre and then again centre to bottom. This process continues for the successive steps.

40. (*e*) In the first step, the corner elements shift one step clockwise while the middle left and middle right elements interchange their places. In the next step, all the elements shift one step upwards in a cyclic order and the same process repeats. The shading of the main figure shifts one step clockwise in each step.

41. (*e*) In the first step, the corner elements shift one step anti-clockwise, the middle left and middle right elements interchange their places, while the central element remains at its place.

In the next step, the elements on the diagonal shift one step ahead diagonally, while the middle right goes to the middle left and the middle right is replaced by a new one. The same process repeats for successive steps.

42. (*e*) In the first step, the left column elements shift downwards in a cyclic order while the right column elements shift upward in a cyclic order. In the next step, the elements of the upper box shift clockwise while elements of the lower box shift anti-clockwise in a cyclic order. The process is repeated for successive steps.

43. (*a*) In question figures, for each of the subsequent figure, three outer corner elements shift one step in a cyclic order while the three corresponding inner elements also shift in the same way. The remaining one inner and outer elements interchange their places. This process repeats from figure (3) to (4) and (5) to answer figure.

44. (*e*) In the first step, the upper middle element shifts to the middle left, middle left to the lower left and then from lower left to the upper middle while the remaining four shift one step clockwise in a cyclic order. In the next step, the middle row elements shift from left to right in a cyclic order, while the remaining four elements shift one step clockwise. The same process repeats.

45. (*c*) In the sequence, the middle element is interchanged by one of the four surrounding elements and two of four surrounding elements interchange their places. Also a new element is replaces one of the surrounding elements everytime.

46. (*c*) In each subsequent figure, the series of symbols move 45° anti-clockwise. With reference to the position of symbols in the original series, from question figure (1) to (2) the upper two elements at corners interchange their positions. Also, the two elements at the lower end interchange their positions. From question figure (2) to (3), the lower most element gets shifted to the uppermost position in the series. Then, the whole process repeats.

47. (*a*) From figure 1 to 2 → S and O and ▲ and R interchange their places.

From figure 2 to 3 → K and O and ▲ and T interchange their places.

From figure 3 to 4 → O and Z and * and ▲ interchange their places.

From figure 4 to 5 → O and R and S and ▲ interchange their places.

Following the same pattern from figure 5 to 6 → O and T and K and ▲ will interchange their places.

48. (*a*) Changes of positions of elements from figure 1 to 2 is similar to the changes from figure 3 to 4. This pattern also follows from figure 5 to answer figure. Let us see the pattern

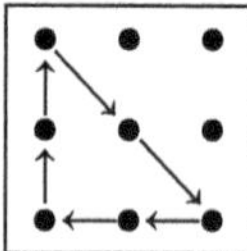

49. (*c*) The pattern of problem figures is

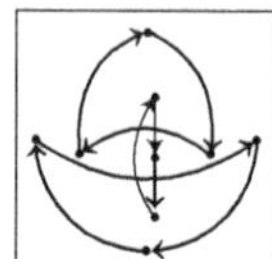

Problem figure (1) to (2),
Problem figure (3) to (4) and
Problem figure (5) to answer figure.

50. (*b*) In each step, the series rotates 90° and 45° anti-clockwise alternately. From figure (1) to (2), there is a cyclic movement among all the elements except top element of the series, From figure (2) to (3), the elements at both ends of the series interchange their places and the middle element is replaced by a new element.

51. (*e*) In each subsequent figure, one design is inverted and the other two designs rotate 45° clockwise and anti-clockwise, respectively.

52. (*c*) Changes from figure (1) to (2) takes place as shown in the diagram. (•) represents the element which is replaced by a new element. The same process is repeated for subsequent figures but the changing pattern is rotated 90° clockwise each time as shown below.

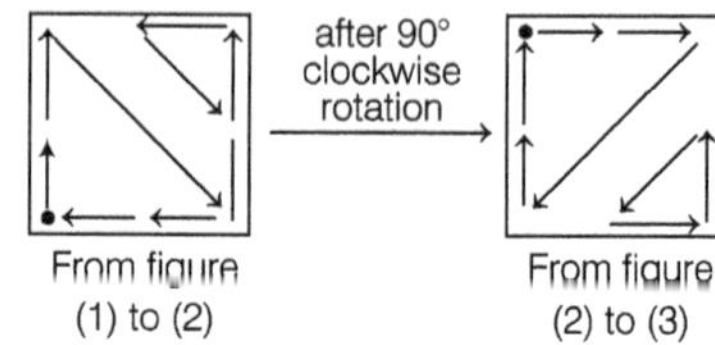

53. (*e*) In each step, elements shift one step clockwise. In the first step both the end elements are replaced by new ones while in the next step, the remaining three elements are replaced. The whole process repeats.

54. (*d*) In the first step, the upper left and the middle right elements interchange their places, so do the upper right and the middle left.

The remaining three elements shift one step clockwise. In the next step, the lower left and lower right elements are replaced by new ones, while the remaining five shift one step anti-clockwise in a cyclic order. The same process repeats for the subsequent steps.

55. (*d*) In each step, the upper middle elements rotates by 45° clockwise and the lower middle element rotates by 45° anti-clockwise. Among the middle row elements, the elements in two pairs interchange their places while the 5th element is replaced by a new one successively from the right to left, beginning from the right.

56. (*c*) The sequence of the problem figures is

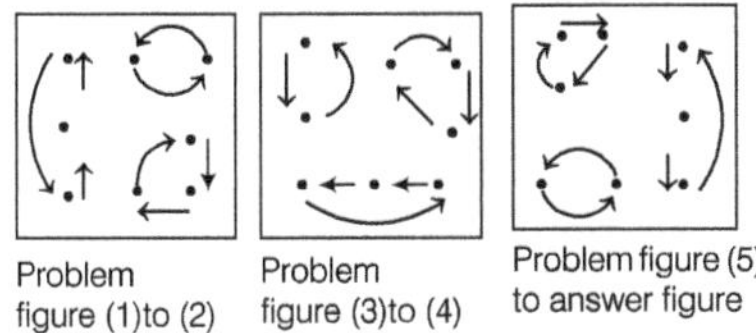

Problem figure (1)to (2) Problem figure (3)to (4) Problem figure (5) to answer figure

57. (*b*) The sequence of the problem figures is

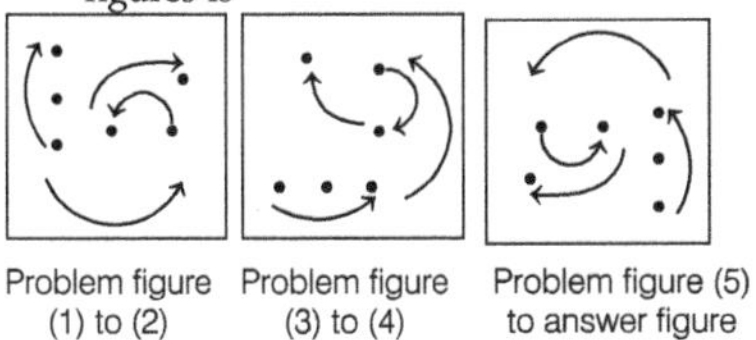

Problem figure (1) to (2) Problem figure (3) to (4) Problem figure (5) to answer figure

58. (*c*) From problem figure (1) to (2), first and second, fourth and fifth interchange places. Third design changes in a new design, similarly (3) ⇒ (4) and (5) ⇒ Answer figure.

59. (*c*) In the first step, the uppermost and the lowermost elements interchange their places while the remaining elements shift one step upwards in a cyclic order.

In the next step, the elements of the upper pair interchange their places. So do the elements of the lower pair while the two middle elements are replaced by new ones. These processes continue in the alternate manner.

60. (*a*) Change in positions of elements takes place as below

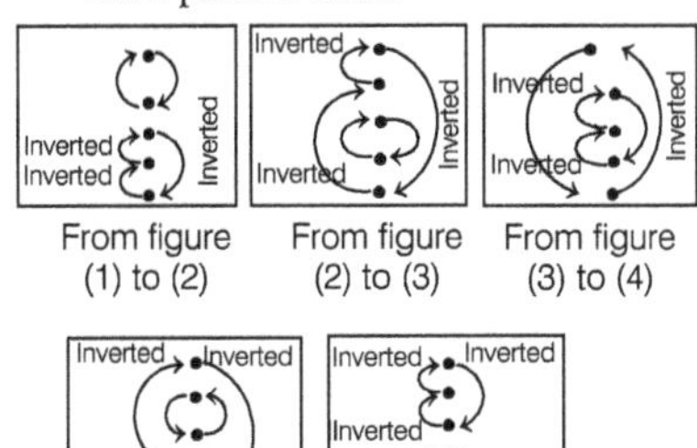

From figure (1) to (2) From figure (2) to (3) From figure (3) to (4)

From figure (4) to (5) From figure (5) to (answer figure)

61. (*b*) Changes in positions of elements take place as below

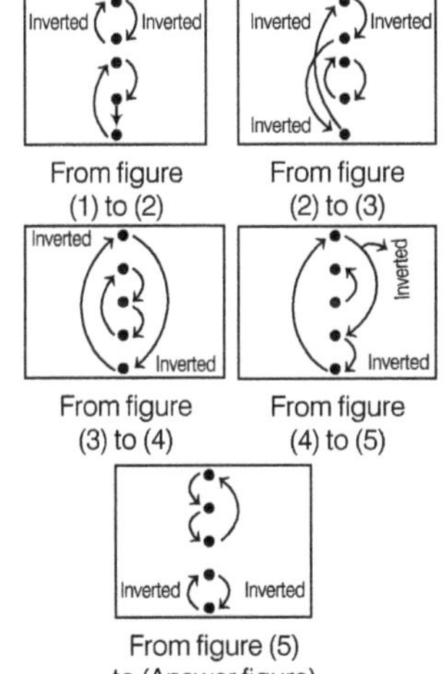

From figure (1) to (2) From figure (2) to (3)

From figure (3) to (4) From figure (4) to (5)

From figure (5) to (Answer figure)

62. (*a*) Changes in positions of elements take place as below

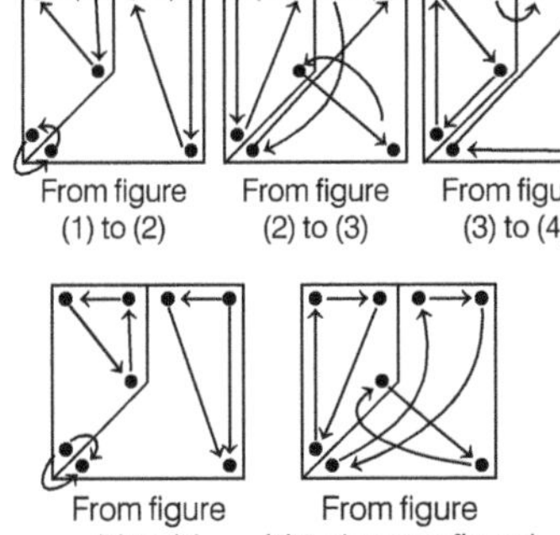

From figure (1) to (2) From figure (2) to (3) From figure (3) to (4)

From figure (4) to (5) From figure (5) to (answer figure)

63. (*d*) Elements moves from left to upper right → lower right → upper left → lower left → right position in subsequent steps. A new element appears in each step in the left base.

64. (*b*) Change from figure (4) to figure (5) is the same as change from figure (1) to (2). So, change from figure (5) to (answer figure) is the same as the change from figure (2) to (3).

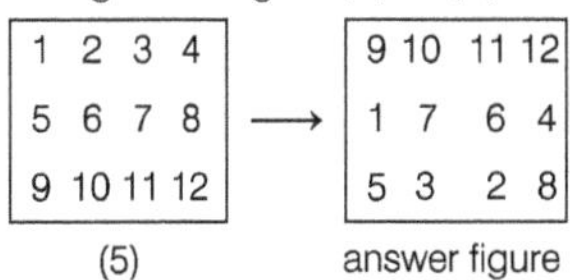

(5) answer figure

65. (*e*) Changes in position of elements from figure (1) to (2) = from figure (3) to (4) = from figure (5) to (answer figure).

Such changes take place as below

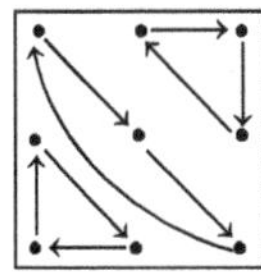

66. (*d*) Changes in positions of elements from figure 1 to 2 = from figure 3 to 4 = from figure 5 to answer figure. Let us see how the changes take place.

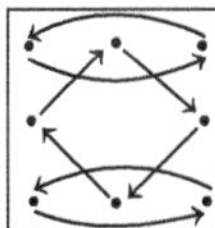

67. (*a*) In each step, two of the elements interchange their positions while the remaining three shift one step clockwise in a cyclic order. This movement itself shifts in clockwise order.

68. (*e*) In alternate steps, from (1) to (2), (3) to (4) and (5) to (6), the uppermost element goes to lowermost, the other elements shift one step upward and the element reaching the uppermost position is replaced by a new one.

69. (*d*) In the problem figures, there comes a circle and a square at the centre alternately. So, in the 7th figure, there must be a circle at the centre. Also, the direction of arrows is same in figure (1) and (4), (2) and (5), (3) and (6). So, the direction of arrows in figure (7) must be the same as in figure (4).

70. (*d*) In each of the successive figures two pins attached with the centre are increasing.

71. (*a*) In each of the successive figures, a small circle in the square is increasing and a design outside the square is decreasing.

72. (*d*) The designs at the corners are moving one step in anti-clockwise direction and the designs at the middle of the edges are moving one step in clockwise direction and also in each successive step, a line is increasing.

73. (*c*) In each successive figure, a square is increasing, the arrow is rotating 90° in anti-clockwise direction and the dot is moving from one side to the other in clockwise direction.

74. (*b*) In each successive figure, a line is increasing in the outer shape and the inner shape is rotating 90° in subsequent figures.

75. (*b*) In each step, a small design is inverted and this takes place in anti-clockwise direction. Also a dot is removed from the figure in each step.

76. (*a*) The elements are moving in following directions and in every step a new element appears at top left corner.

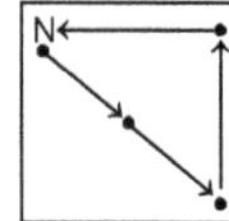

77. (*b*) The set of all four signs move from middle to right, right to left and then from left to middle. The upper two signs interchange their positions and lower two signs interchange positions and each of the signs is replaced by a new sign one by one in each of the successive figures.

78. (*a*) The shaded semi-circle moves along the diagonal and rotates 90° anti-clockwise and the other figure is same in problem figures (1), (3) and (5).

79. (*d*) In each step, the elements move as follow

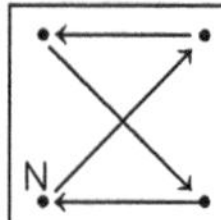

N = New element

80. (*d*) From problem figure (1) to (2), the upper half of one arrow rotates 45° clockwise, from figure (2) to (3), the lower half of the same arrow rotates 45° clockwise. From figure (3) to (4) and also from (4) to (5), the same process is repeated for the other arrow.

81. (*c*) The elements are moving 45° and 90° in clockwise direction alternatively and in each step a new element appears in the starting of the line of elements.

82. (*c*) The heads of the line move on the line in a set order.

83. (*b*) All the symbols interchange their positions with one another, as shown in the two diagrams, alternatively.

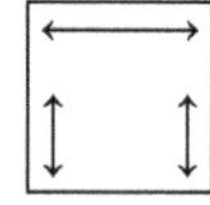

From figure (1) to (2) and (3) to (4)

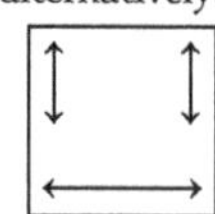

From figure (2) to (3) and (4) to (5)

84. (*d*) From problem figure (1) to (2), one circle is deleted and two triangles are added. From problem figure (2) to (3), one triangle is deleted and three squares are added.

From problem figure (3) to (4), one square is deleted and four plus are added. The same process continues for the subsequent steps.

85. (*c*) All the symbols interchange their positions with one another as shown in the two diagrams alternatively and a new symbol appears in place of previous symbol in each successive figure in anti-clockwise direction, starting from bottom position.

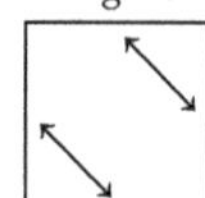

From figure (1) to (2)

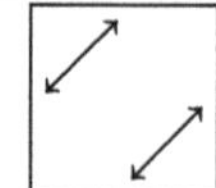

From figure (2) to (3)

86. (*a*) From problem figure (1) to (2), the symbols move half step in anti-clockwise direction and first and last symbols interchange positions. Also a new symbol is added in the beginning of the series. The same process is repeated in the successive figures.

87. (*c*) The figure rotates 45° clockwise in each of the successive figures.

88. (*b*) The arrow rotates 90°, 180° alternatively in the anti-clockwise direction.

89. (*d*) Symbols change their positions as shown in the two diagrams alternatively and the symbol in place of (•) is replaced by a new symbol.

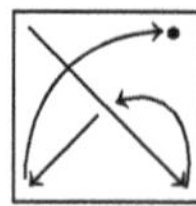

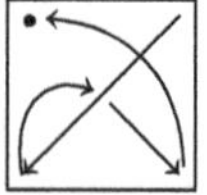

90. (*a*) The main figure rotates 45° anti-clockwise and one line/arc is added to the main figure.

91. (*a*) Four symbols at the corners interchange their positions as shown in the diagrams alternatively and symbols at the centre are converted into new symbols.

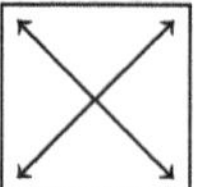

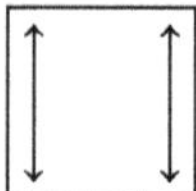

92. (*d*) Changes from figure (a) to (b) and from figure (b) to (c) are shown as below. The whole process repeats.

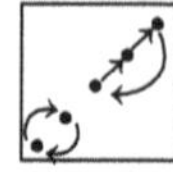

From figure (a) to (b)

From figure (b) to (c)

93. (*e*) Arrow rotates 45° anti-clockwise and 90° anti-clockwise, alternately.

CHAPTER / 02

Analogy

Analogy means similarity of relationship. If a pair of figures exhibits some kind of relationship on the basis of shape, size, rotation, interchange of elements, number of elements etc., and an another pair of figures exhibits the same kind of relationship, then the two pairs are said to be analogous to each other.

Basically, this chapter is all about identifying such logical patterns that establish a relationship between two given figures.

The basis for establishing relationship between the different figures are given below.

A. Number of Lines/ Elements

In this type of relationship, the number of lines / elements in first figure of a pair gets increased/decreased to obtain the second figure of the same pair.

***Ex* 01** Find the figure from the answer figures that will replace the question mark (?) from the problem figures.

Problem Figures

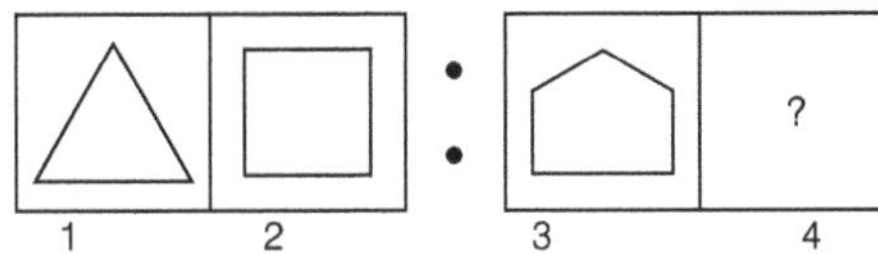

Answer Figures

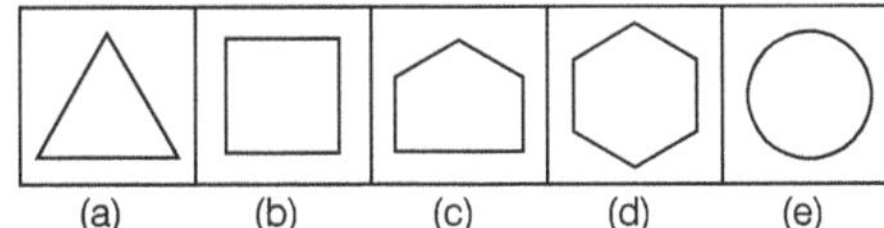

Solution (d) In the first pair of the problem figures, from first to the second figure one line is added. In the same manner in the second pair of figures, one line will be added from third figure to the fourth figure.

***Ex* 02** Find the figure from the answer figures that will replace the question mark (?) from the problem figures.

Problem Figures

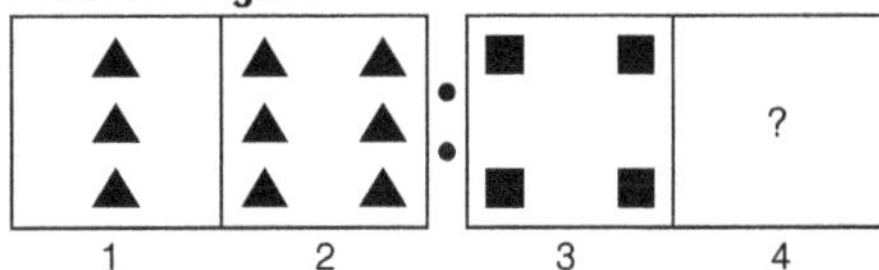

Answer Figures

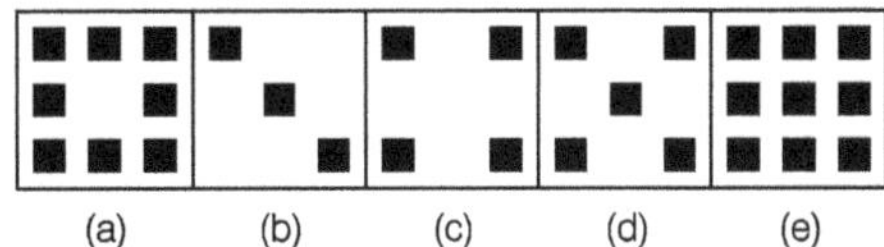

Solution (a) The triangles given in first figure of the first pair of problem figures gets doubled in second figure of the same pair.
Similarly, in second pair, the number of squares from third figure to the fourth figure will get doubled.

B. Size of Figures

In this type of relationship, the size of the first figure of a pair is changed to obtain the second figure of the same pair, i.e. the smaller figure becomes larger or the larger figure becomes smaller.

***Ex* 03** Find the figure from the answer figures that will replace the question mark (?) from the problem figures.

Problem Figures

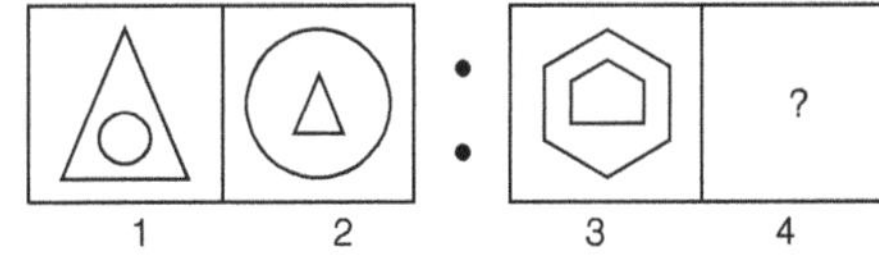

Answer Figures

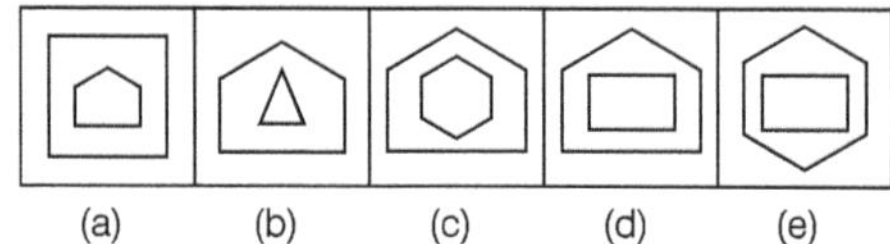

(a) (b) (c) (d) (e)

Solution (c) In the first pair of the problem figures from first to second figure, the large triangle becomes small and the small circle becomes large. In the same manner, from third to fourth figure, the large hexagon becomes small and the small pentagon becomes large.

C. Rotation of Figure

In this type of relationship, first figure of a pair rotates by a certain angle in clockwise or in anti-clockwise direction to obtain the second figure of the same pair.

***Ex* 04** Find the figure from the answer figures that will replace the question mark (?) from the problem figures.

Problem Figures

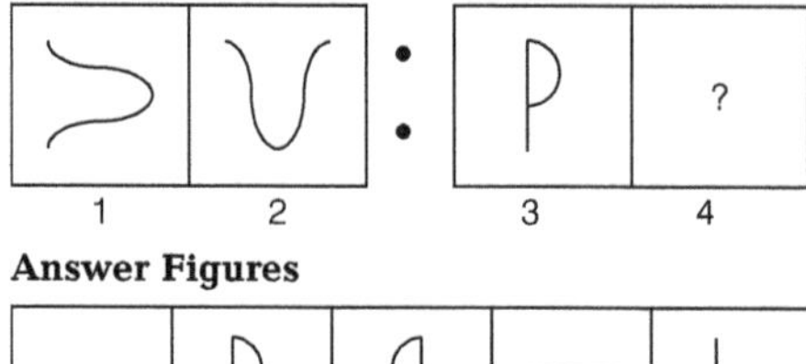

Answer Figures

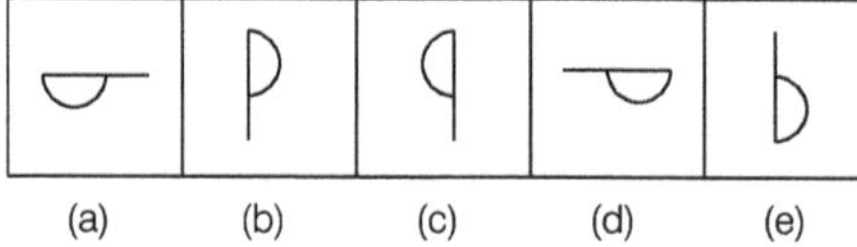

(a) (b) (c) (d) (e)

Solution (d) The first figure is rotated 90° clockwise to obtain the second figure. In the same manner, the third figure will be rotated 90° clockwise to obtain the answer figure.

D. Appearance of Figure

In this type of relationship, the changes occuring from one figure to the other are based on pattern of the figure or appearance of the design. In these changes, the portions of the design which were unshaded initially become shaded and the shaded portions become unshaded, after some changes.

***Ex* 05** Find the figure from the answer figures that will replace the question mark (?) from the problem figures.

Problem Figures

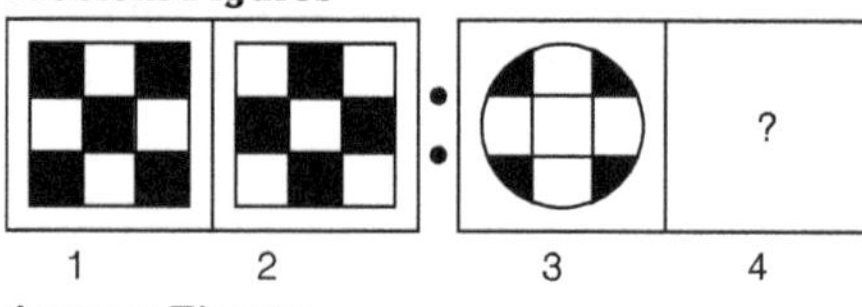

Answer Figures

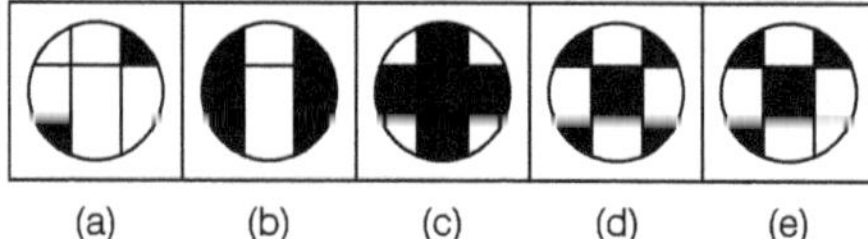

(a) (b) (c) (d) (e)

Solution (c) From first to second figure, the shaded portions become unshaded and unshaded portions become shaded. Similar changes will be followed from third to fourth figure.

E. Mirror/Water Image of Figure

In this type of relationship, the second figure is the mirror/water image of the first figure.

In mirror image, the object is laterally inverted. The Left Hand Side (LHS) and the Right Hand Side (RHS) of an object interchange their places while top and bottom remains at their respective positions.

The water image of an object is vertically inverted form of the real object in which LHS (Left Hand Side) and RHS (Right Hand Side) remain unchanged but the top and bottom of the object get interchanged.

***Ex* 06** Find the figure from the answer figures that will replace the question mark (?) from the problem figures.

Problem Figures

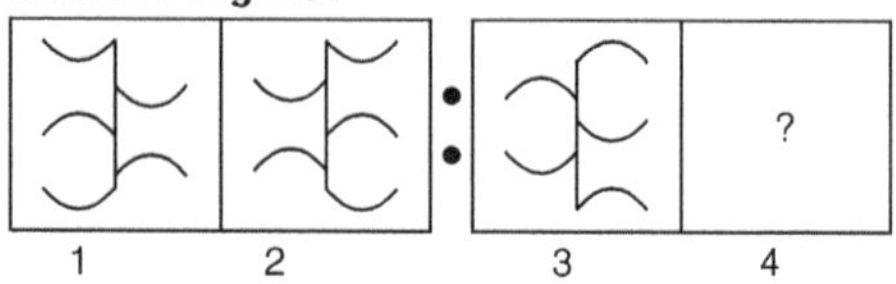

Answer Figures

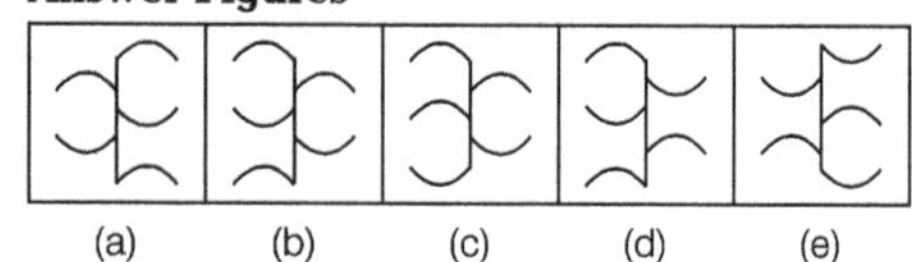

(a) (b) (c) (d) (e)

Solution (b) Here, the second figure is the mirror image of first figure. Similarly, the fourth figure will be the mirror image of the third figure.

***Ex* 07** Find the figure from the answer figures that will replace the question mark (?) from the problem figures.

Problem Figures

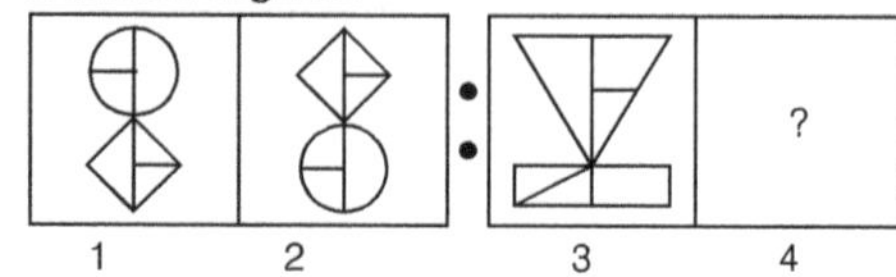

Answer Figures

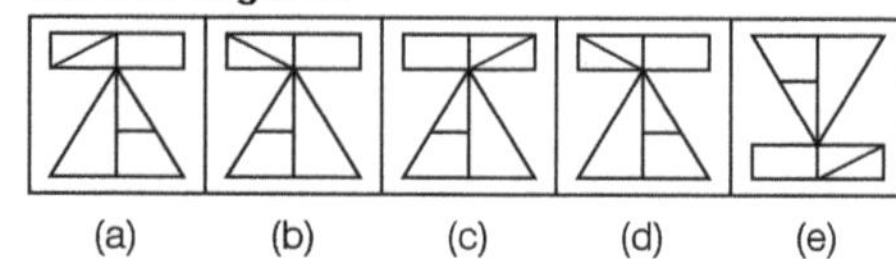

(a) (b) (c) (d) (e)

Solution (d) The second figure is the water image of the first figure. Similarly, the fourth figure will be the water image of the third figure as shown in option (d).

F. Interchanging Positions of the Figures

In this type of relationship, the figures inside the first figure of a pair interchange their places to obtain the second figure of the same pair.

***Ex* 08** Find the figure from the answer figures that will replace the question mark (?) from the problem figures.

Problem Figures

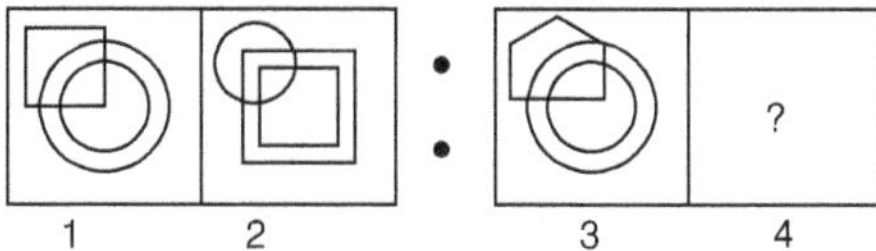

Answer Figures

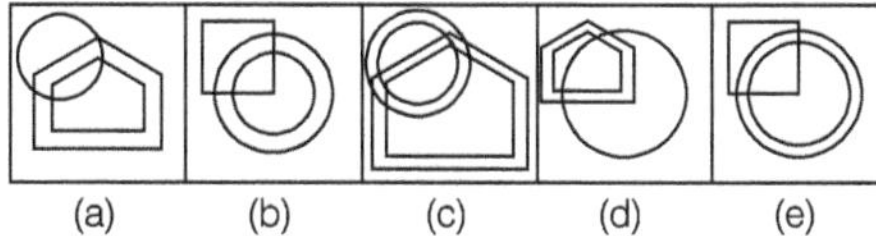

Solution (a) By the careful analysis of first pair of the problem figures, we find that from first to second figure, the upper and lower figures interchange their places, i.e. the upper figure becomes lower and the lower figure becomes upper.

Also, after interchanging the positions the upper figure becomes double at new position and lower figure becomes single at new position in second figure. Similar changes will be followed from third to the fourth figure.

G. Rearrangement of Symbols

In this type of relationship, the symbols of the first figure of a pair interchange their places with each other following a certain rule with or without producing a new symbol to obtain the second figure of the same pair.

***Ex* 09** Find the figure from the answer figures that will replace the question mark (?) from the problem figures.

Problem Figures

1	2	3	4
O	=	#	?
×	O	×	
=	×	÷	

Answer Figures

(a)	(b)	(c)	(d)	(e)
×	#	×	÷	÷
#	×	÷	#	×
+	+	#	×	#

Solution (d) Here, from first to second figure, each symbol moves one step downward and the lower most symbol becomes the topmost symbol. Similarly, from third to fourth figure, each symbol will move one step downward and the lowermost symbol will become the topmost symbol.

H. Based on Real Objects

In this type of relationship, objects belong to the real world given in a pair are related to each other in a certain way.

***Ex* 10** Find the figure from the answer figures that will replace the question mark (?) from the problem figures.

Problem Figures

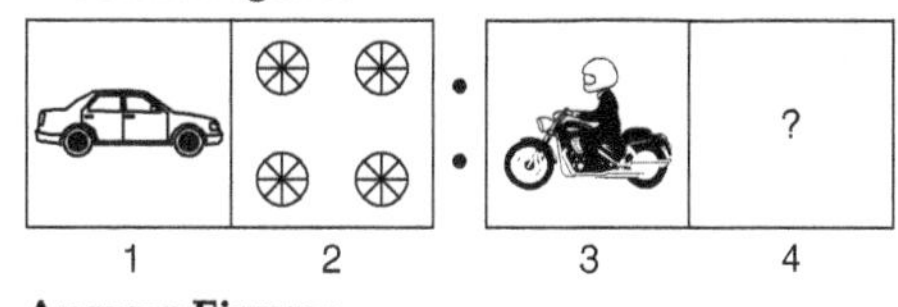

Answer Figures

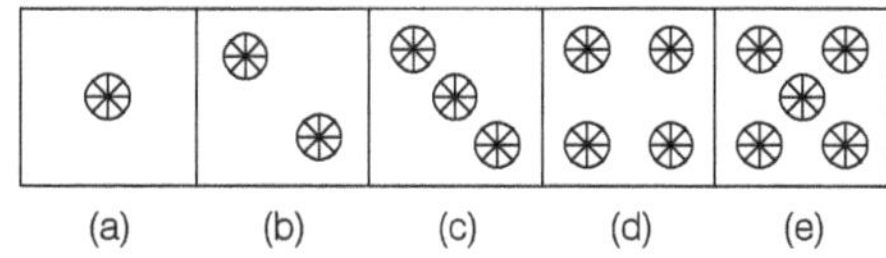

Solution (b) As, a car has four wheels. Similarly, a bike has two wheels. Hence, answer figure (b) will replace the question mark (?). Various types of problems based on analogy which are asked in exams are discussed below

TYPE 01

Finding the Missing Figure of a Similarly Related Pair

In this type of questions, a set of figures namely problem figures and four/five answer figures are given. The set of problem figures consists of two parts. The first part comprises of two figures which have some relationship between them on the basis of certain rule or pattern. The second part comprises one figure and a sign of '?'.

To solve this type of questions, candidates are required to identify the relationship between first two figures and then on the basis of this relationship, select one figure from the set of answer figures which replaces the sign of '?'. In this case always remember that it bears same relationship with the other figure as the first figure of the first part bears with second figure of the same part.

Following examples illustrate the methods to solve the questions based on finding the missing figure of a similarly related pair.

DIRECTIONS ~ (Example Nos. 11-19) *In the following questions, the first and second figure of the problem figures have certain relation between them and the same relation exists between the third figure and one of the four/five answer figures marked as* (a), (b), (c), (d)/(e). *Find that answer figure from the options that will replace (?) from problem figures.*

***Ex* 11 Problem Figures**

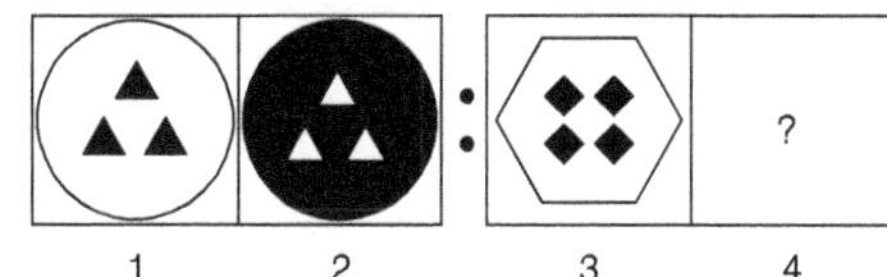

Answer Figures

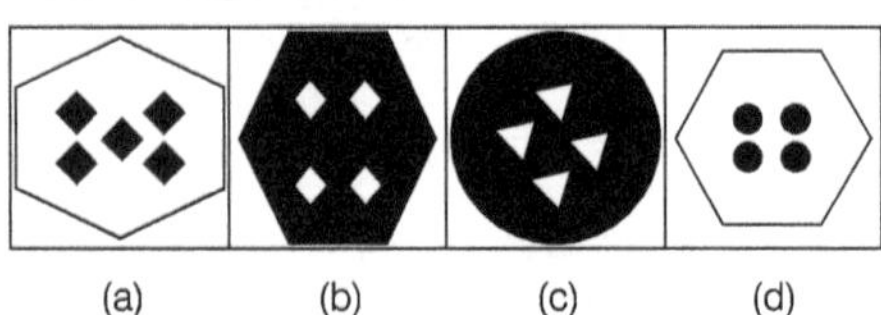

(a) (b) (c) (d)

« RRB Group D 2018

Solution (b) The shaded portions get unshaded and *vice-versa*. So, answer figure (b) is the correct figure, obtained from third figure.

Ex 12

Problem Figures

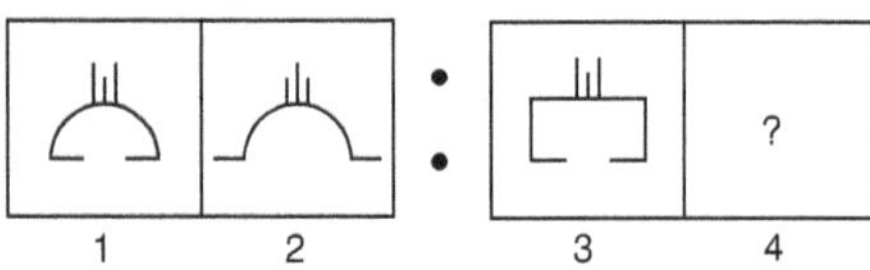

1 2 3 4

Answer Figures

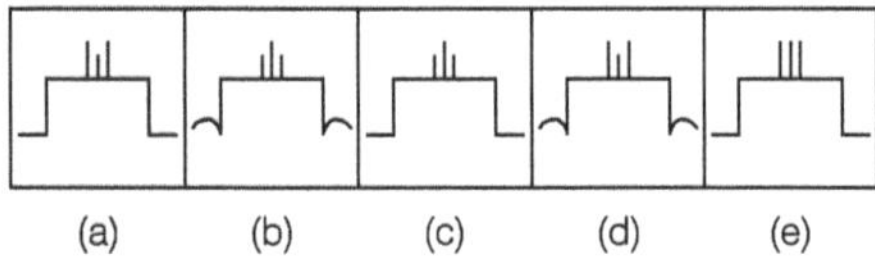

(a) (b) (c) (d) (e)

Solution (c) Line segments attached to the base of the first figure come outside and the line segments at the top interchange size to obtain the second figure.

Ex 13

Problem Figures

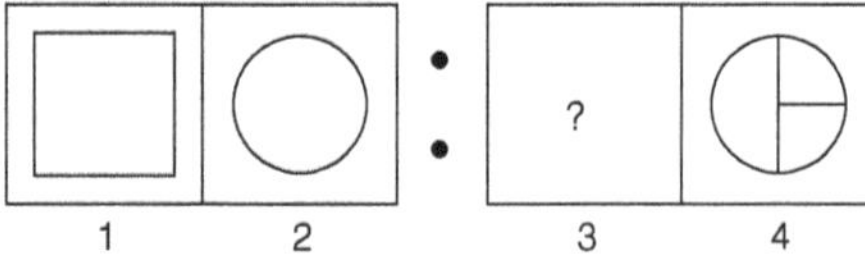

1 2 3 4

Answer Figures

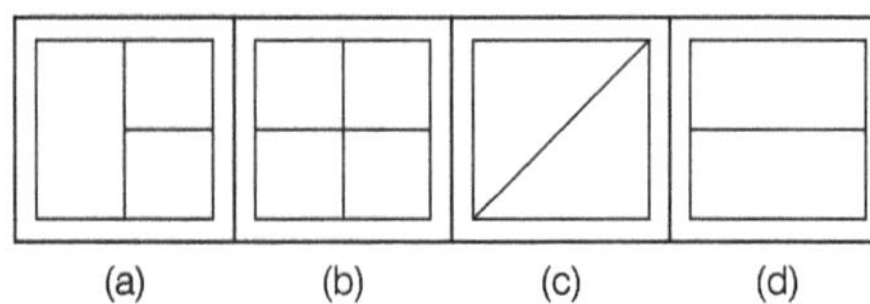

(a) (b) (c) (d)

« UPSSSC Junior Clerk 2016

Solution (a) As empty square is converted into an empty circle, in the similar way a square having some number of lines in a particular pattern will be converted into the circle having same number of lines in the same pattern.

Ex 14

Problem Figures

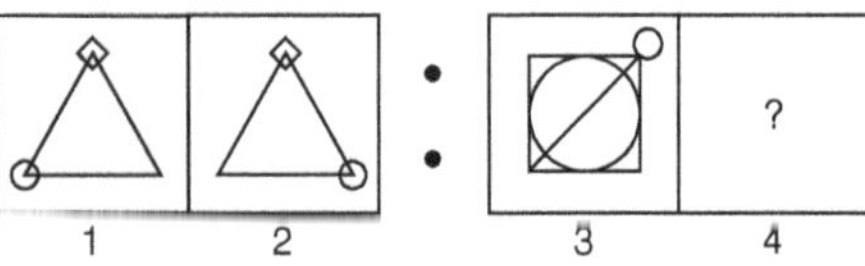

1 2 3 4

Answer Figures

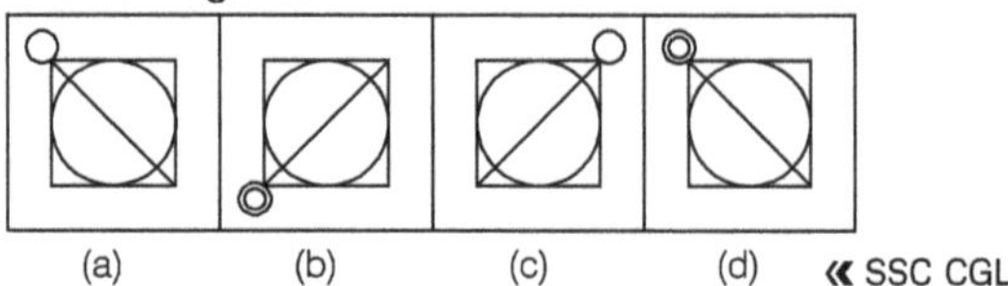

(a) (b) (c) (d) « SSC CGL 2006

Solution (a) Figure (2) is the mirror image of figure (1) when mirror is placed vertically. In the same way, the answer figure (a) is the mirror image of figure (3).

Ex 15 Problem Figures

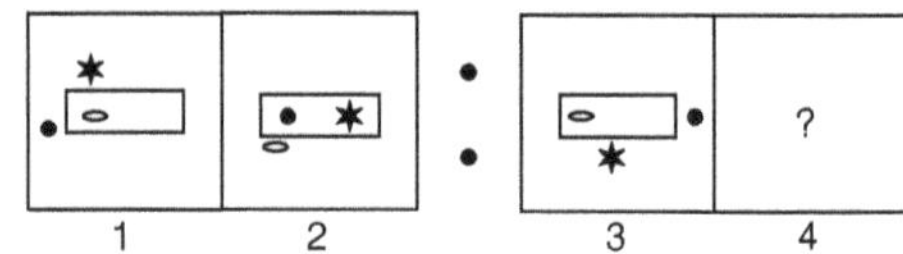

1 2 3 4

Answer Figures

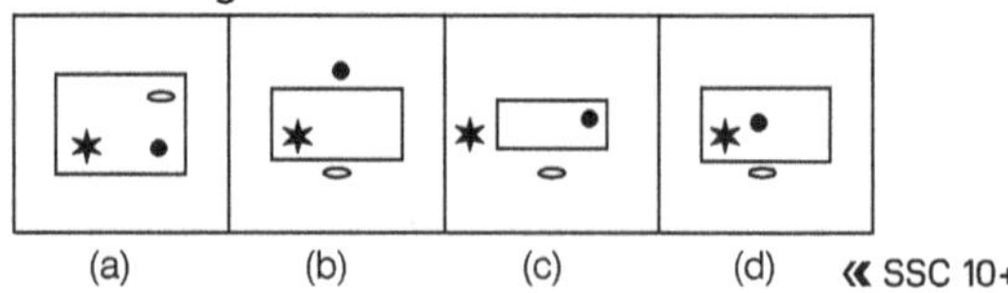

(a) (b) (c) (d) « SSC 10+2 2013

Solution (d) Here, the outer figures come inside the rectangle and the inner figure comes outside the rectangle.

Ex 16 Problem Figures

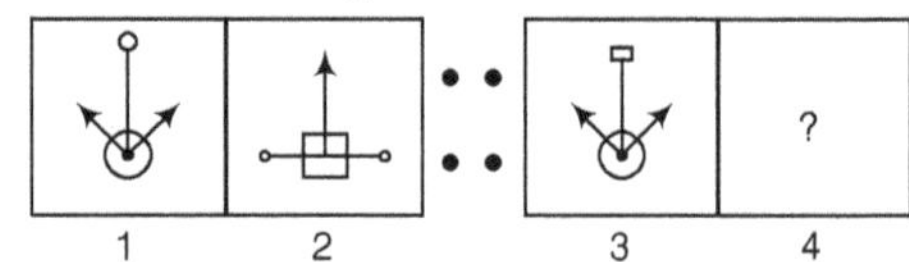

1 2 3 4

Answer Figures

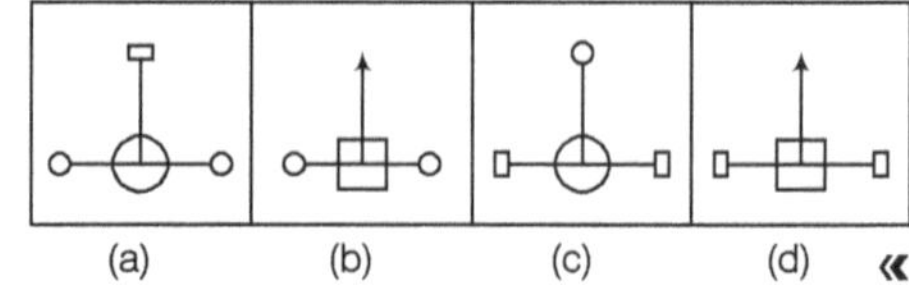

(a) (b) (c) (d) « SSC 10+2 2013

Solution (d) Here, bottom circle is replaced with square, both the side lines make an angle of 90° and the top part of both side lines is replaced with the top part of middle line and *vice-versa*.

Ex 17 Problem Figures

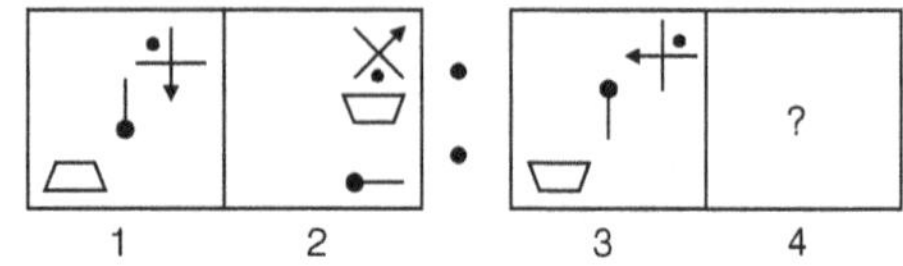

1 2 3 4

Answer Figures

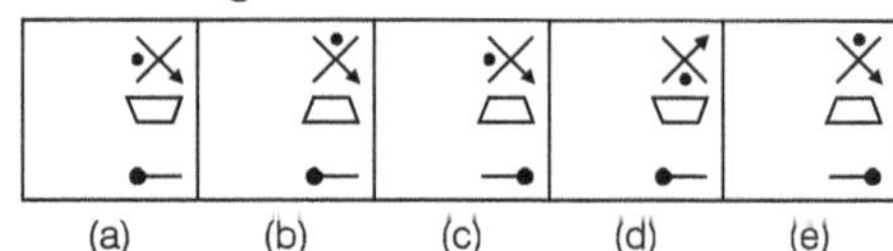

(a) (b) (c) (d) (e)

Solution (c) From problem figure (1) to (2), the pin rotates 90° clockwise, the trapezium is inverted and the third figure rotates 135° anti-clockwise. Similar changes will take place in figure (3) to obtain answer figure.

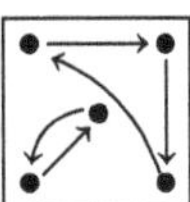

Ex 18

Problem Figures

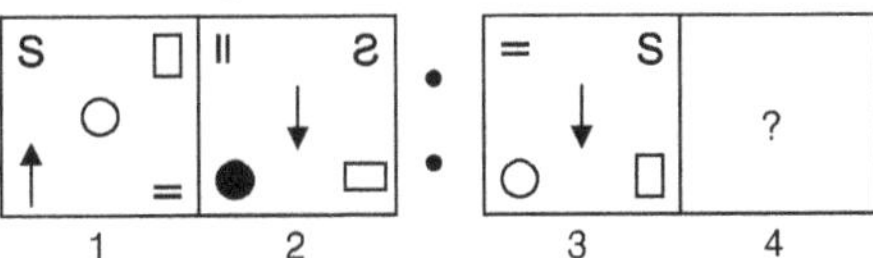

Answer Figures

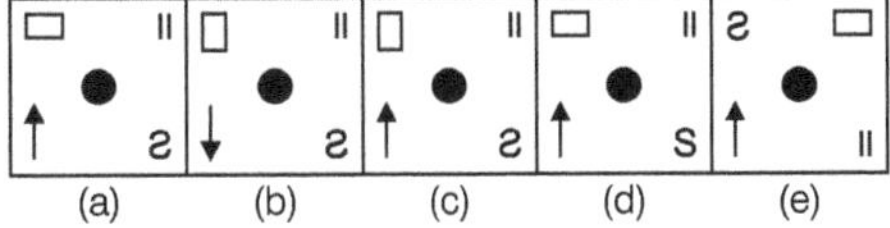

Solution (a) From problem figure (1) to (2), all the symbols change their positions as shown in the diagram in such a way that symbol S is reversed, rectangle rotates 90°, arrow is inverted, circle is shaded and the remaining symbol rotates 90°.

Ex 19

Problem Figures

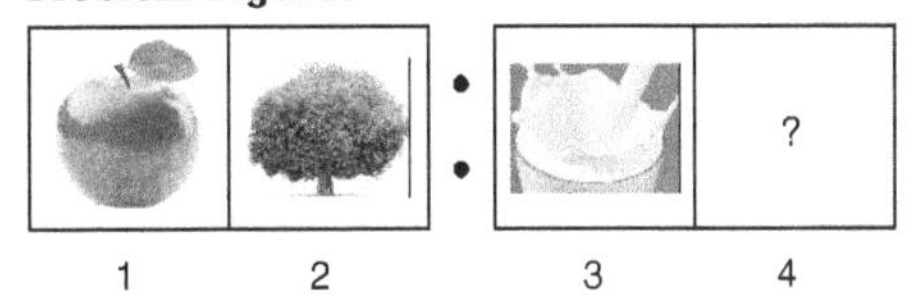

Answer Figures

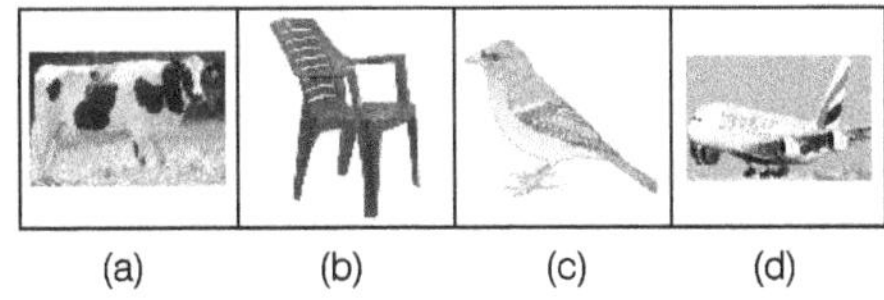

Solution (a) As, we get apple from tree. Similarly we get milk from cow.

Practice / CORNER 2.1

DIRECTIONS ~ (Q. Nos. 1-60) *The second figure in the first pair of the problem figures bears a certain relationship with the first figure. Similarly, one of the answer figures bears the same relationship with the first figure in the second pair of the problem figures. You have to select that figure from the set of answer figures which will replace the question mark (?)*

1. Problem Figures

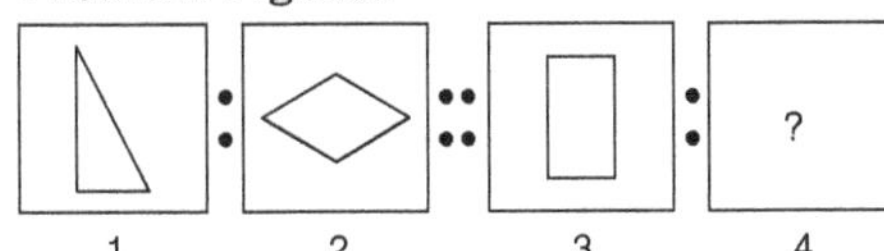

Answer Figures

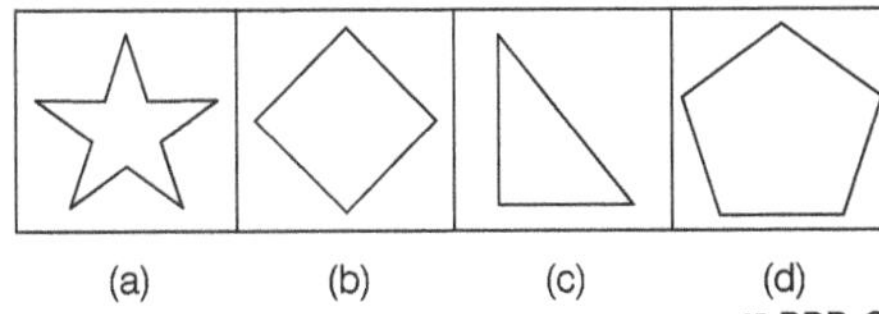

« RRB Group D 2018

2. Problem Figures

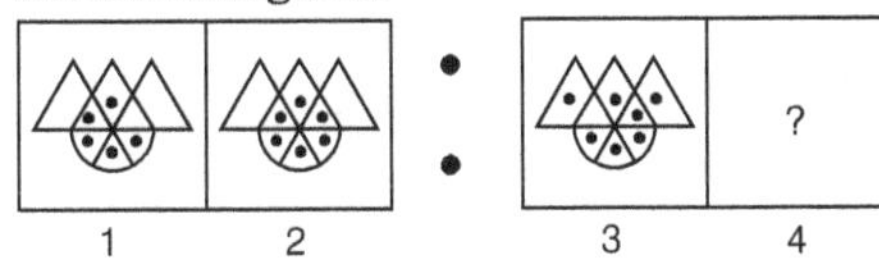

Answer Figures

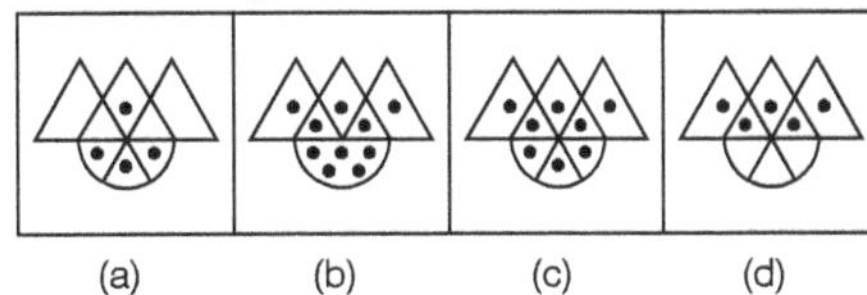

3. Problem Figures

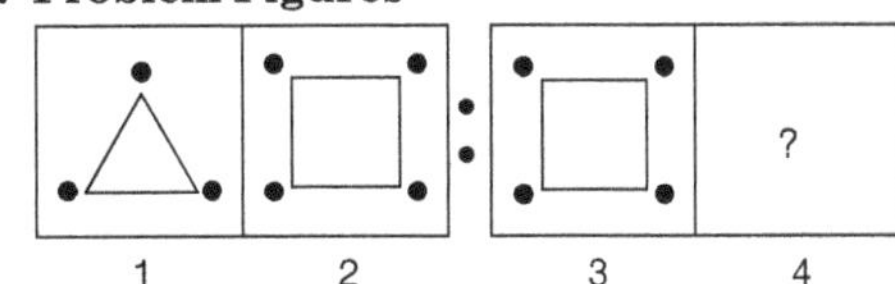

Answer Figures

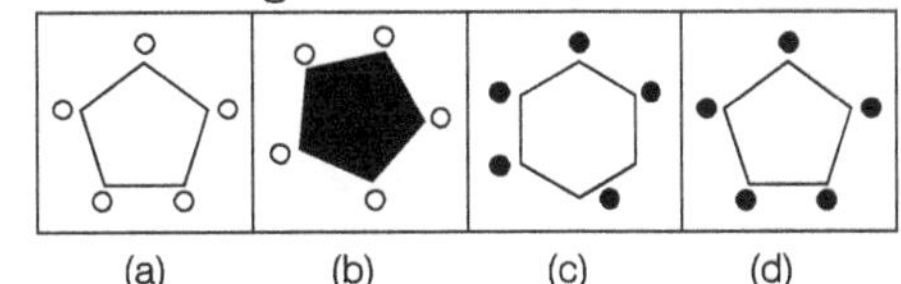

« RRB Group D 2018

4. Problem Figures

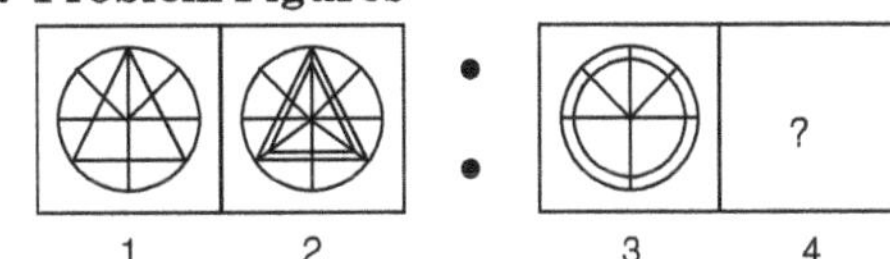

Answer Figures

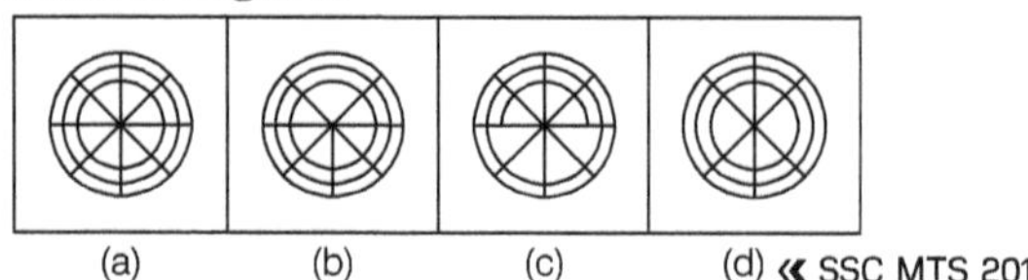

(a) (b) (c) (d) « SSC MTS 2012

5. Problem Figures

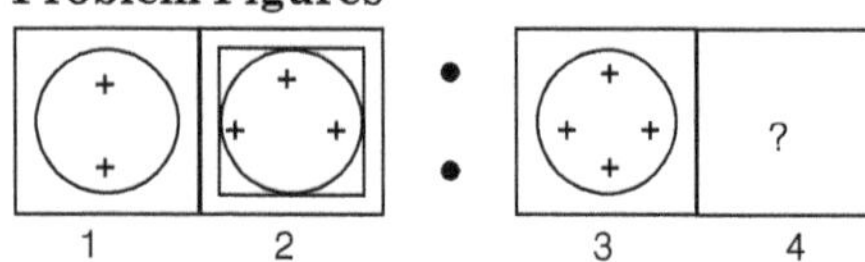

1 2 3 4

Answer Figures

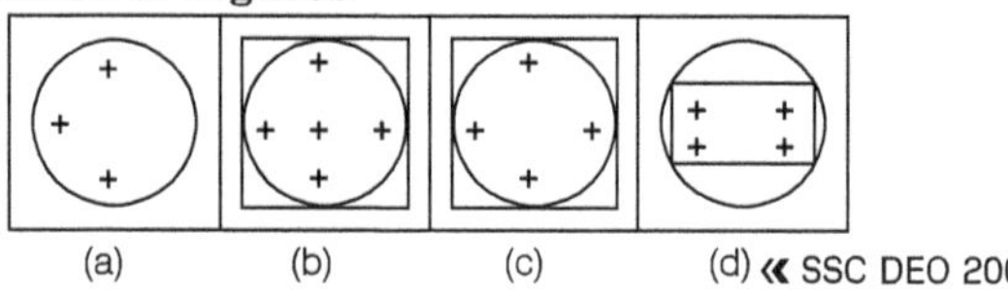

(a) (b) (c) (d) « SSC DEO 2008

6. Problem Figures

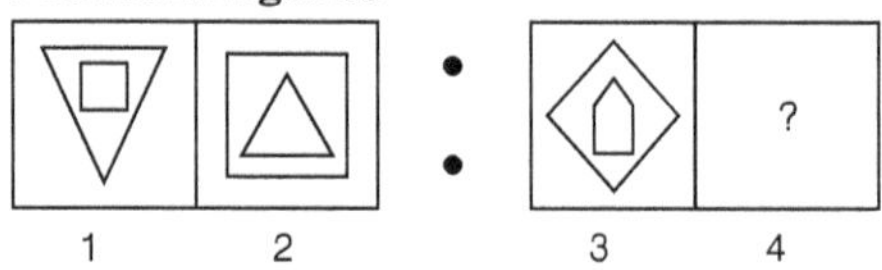

1 2 3 4

Answer Figures

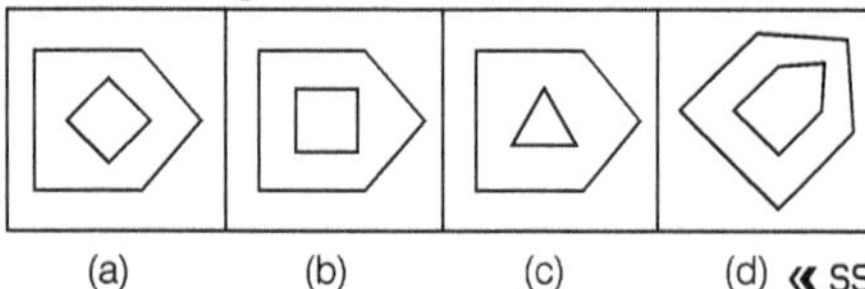

(a) (b) (c) (d) « SSC CGL 2008

7. Problem Figures

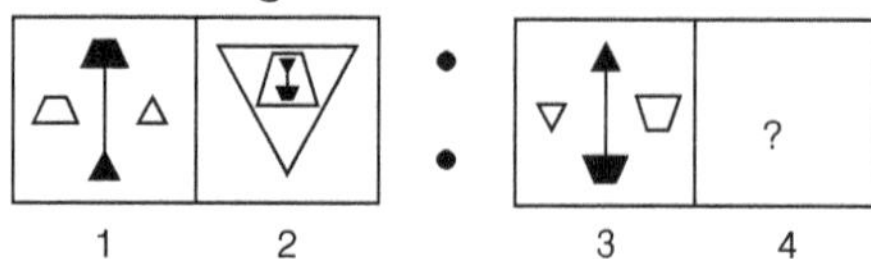

1 2 3 4

Answer Figures

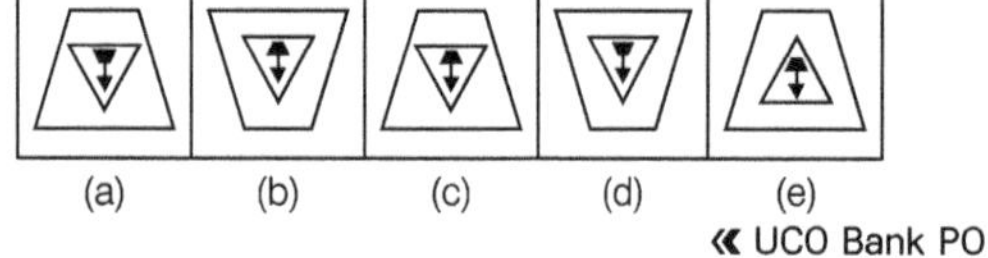

(a) (b) (c) (d) (e)

« UCO Bank PO 2009

8. Problem Figures

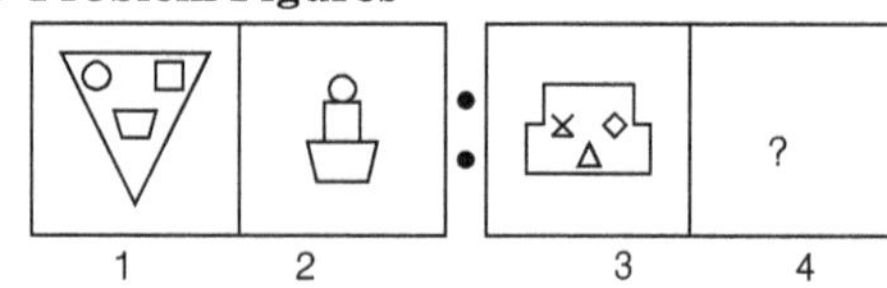

1 2 3 4

Answer Figures

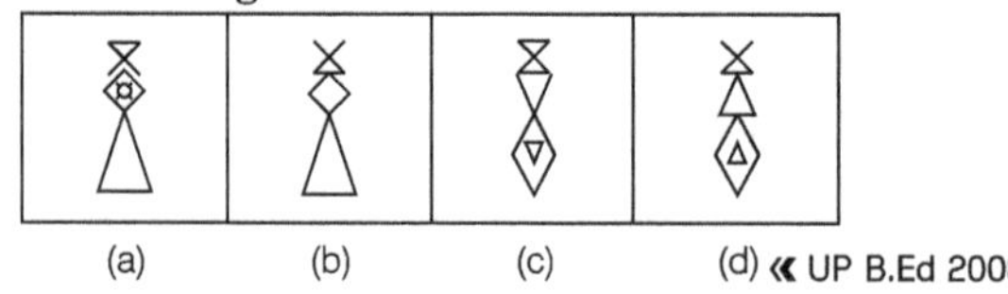

(a) (b) (c) (d) « UP B.Ed 2008

9. Problem Figures

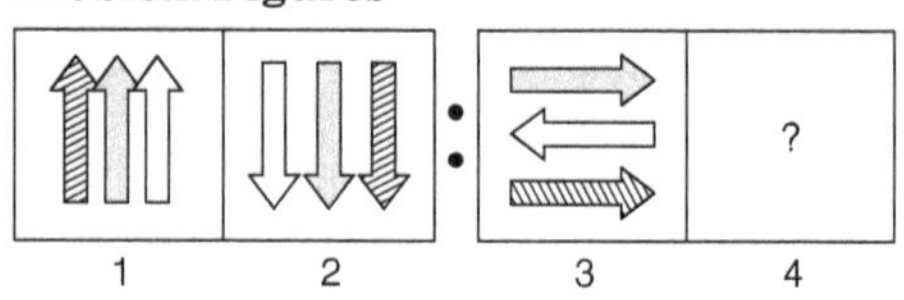

1 2 3 4

Answer Figures

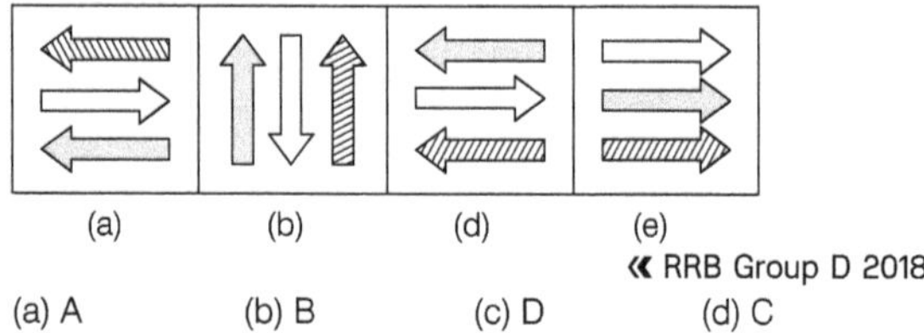

(a) (b) (d) (e)

« RRB Group D 2018

(a) A (b) B (c) D (d) C

10. Problem Figures

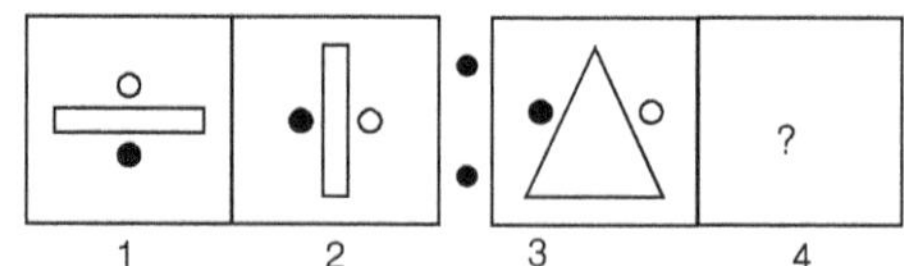

1 2 3 4

Answer Figures

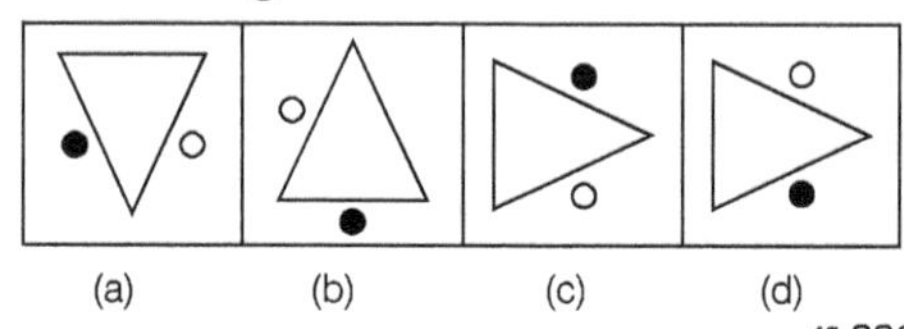

(a) (b) (c) (d)

« SSC CGL 2006

11. Problem Figures

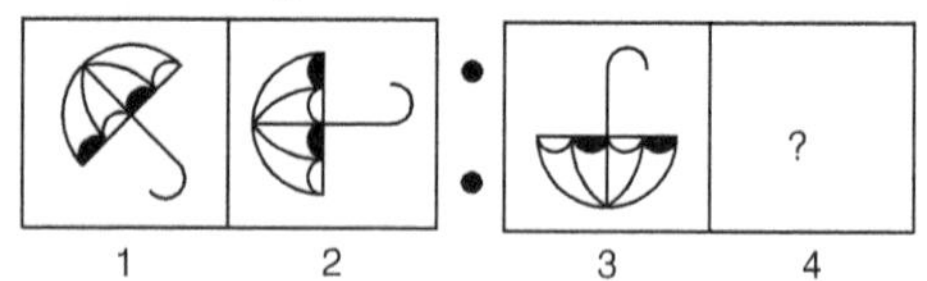

1 2 3 4

Answer Figures

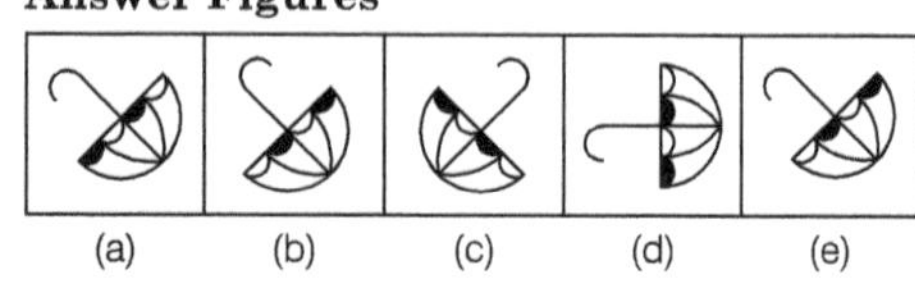

(a) (b) (c) (d) (e)

12. Problem Figures

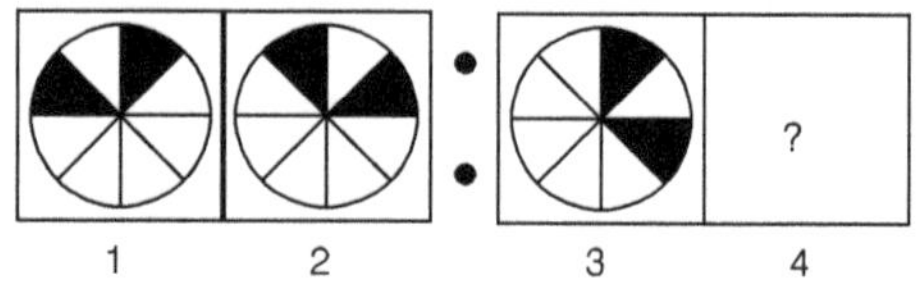

1 2 3 4

Answer Figures

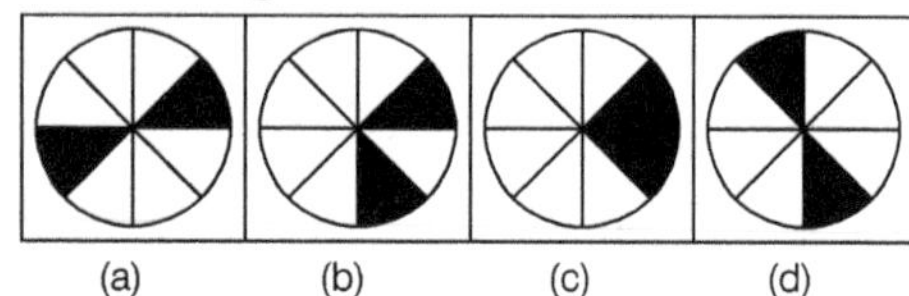

(a) (b) (c) (d)

13. Problem Figures

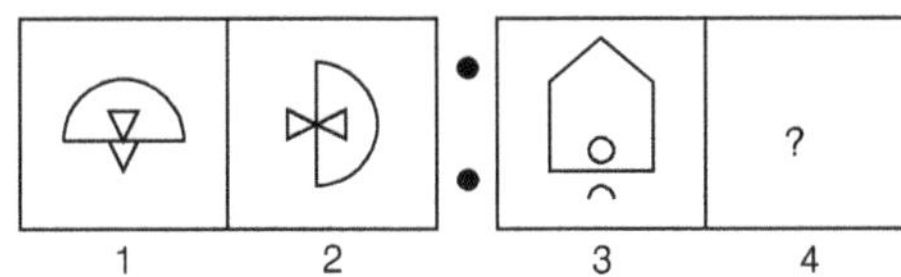

Answer Figures

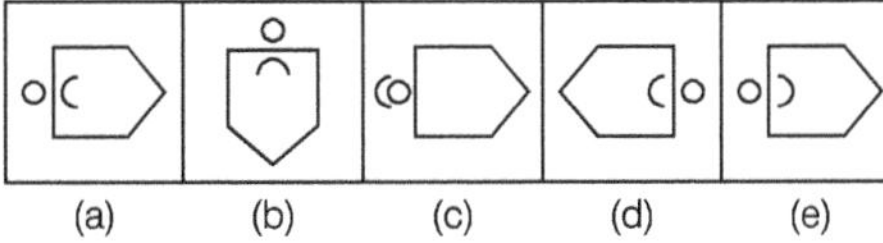

14. Problem Figures

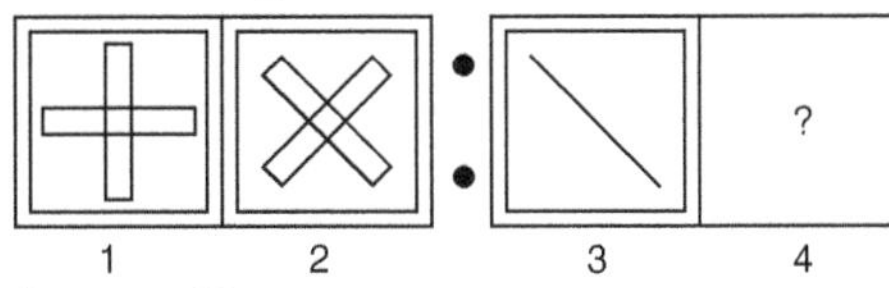

Answer Figures

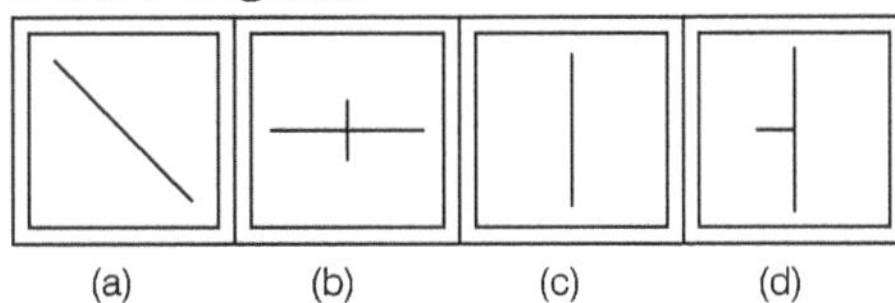

15. Problem Figures

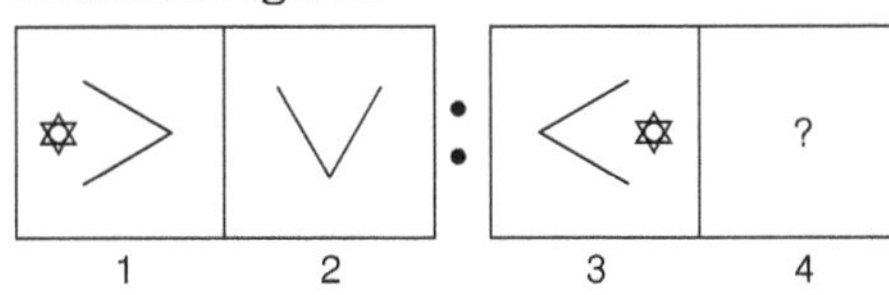

Answer Figures

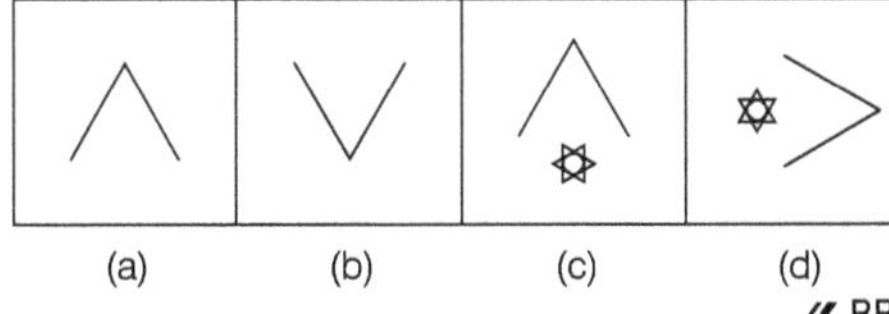

« RRB ASM 2011

16. Problem Figures

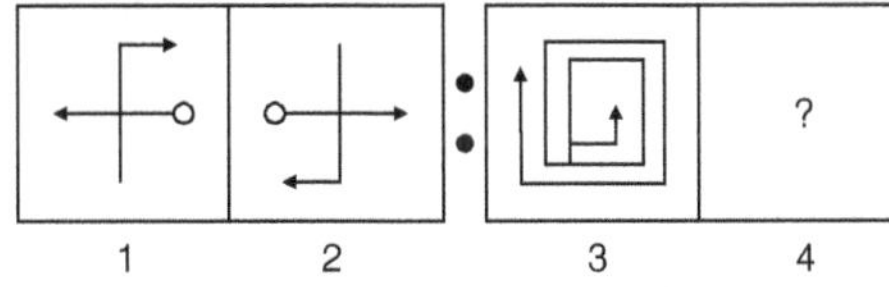

Answer Figures

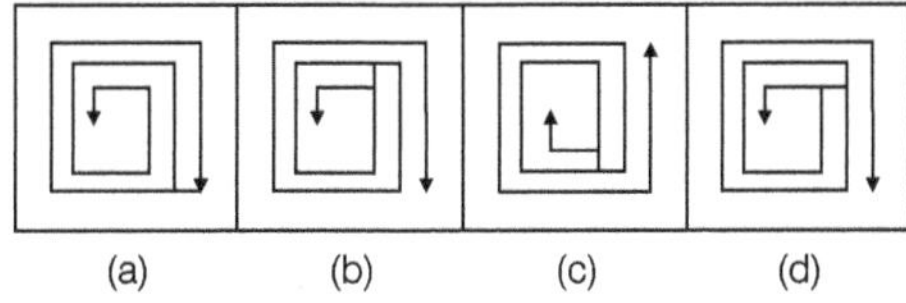

« UP B. Ed 2009

17. Problem Figures

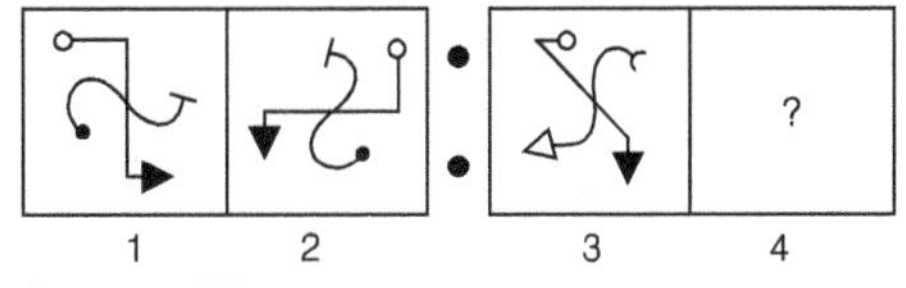

Answer Figures

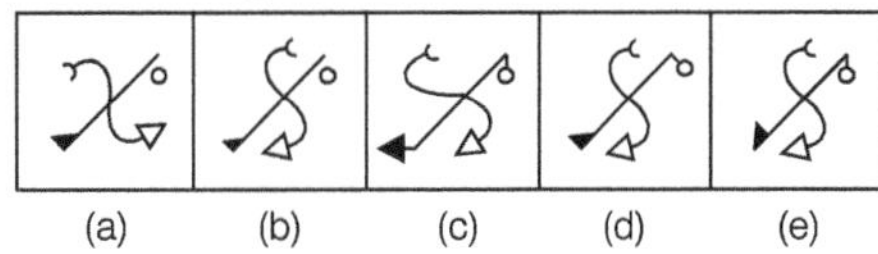

18. Problem Figures

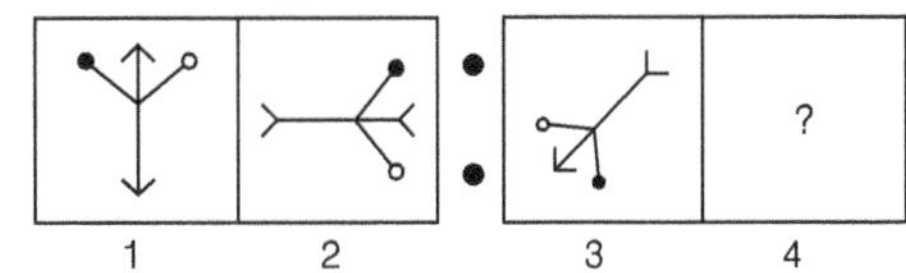

Answer Figures

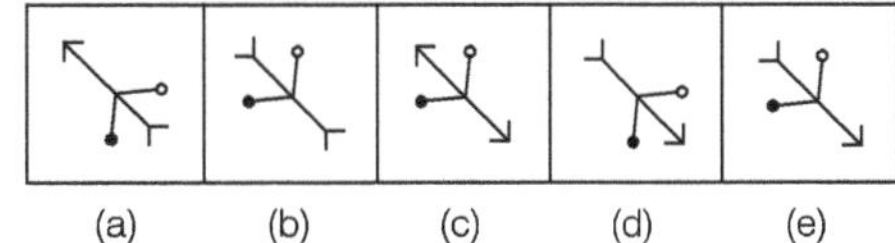

19. Problem Figures

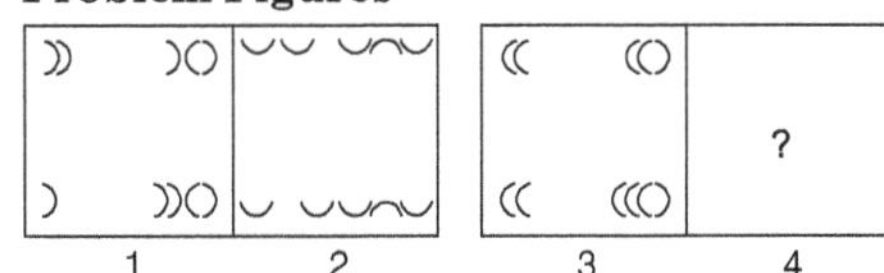

Answer Figures

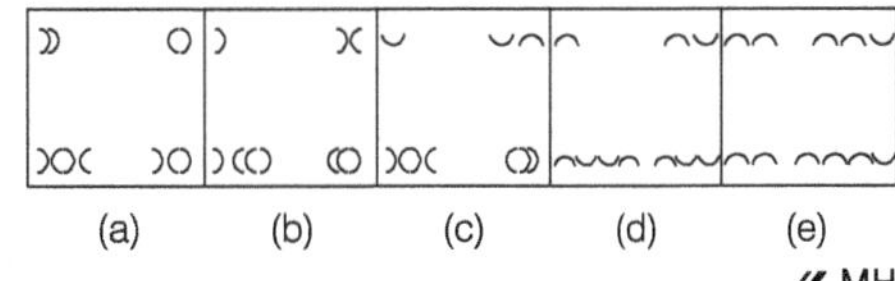

« MHT MBA 2017

20. Problem Figures

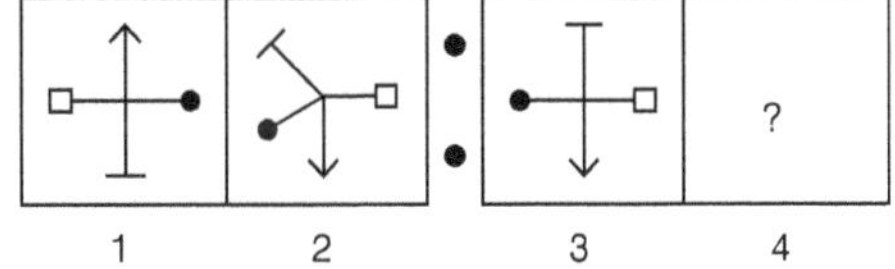

Answer Figures

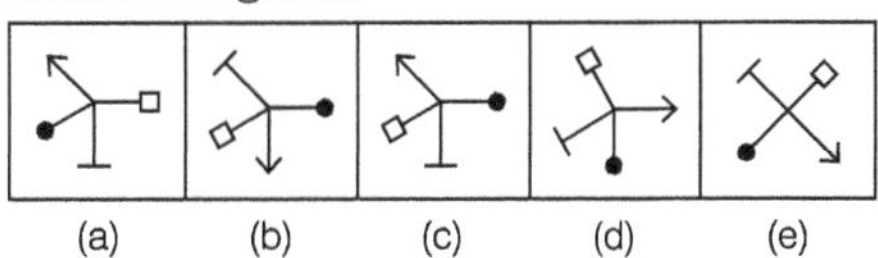

21. Problem Figures

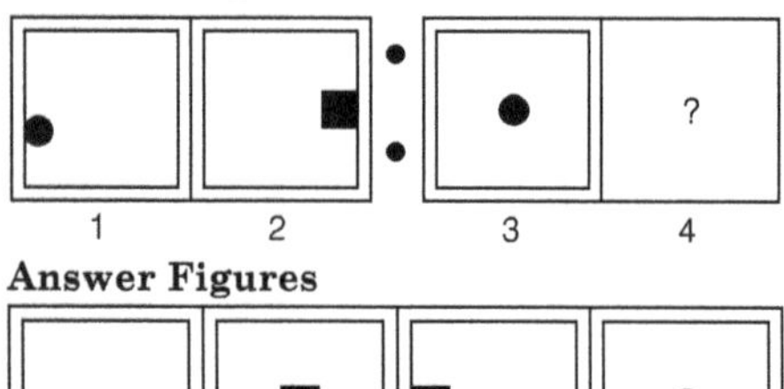

Answer Figures

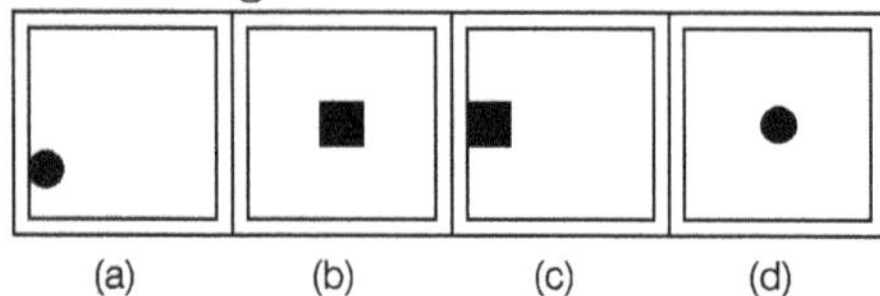

22. Problem Figures

Answer Figures

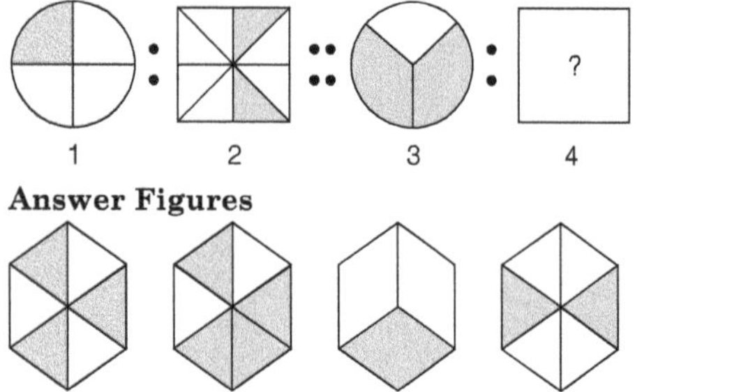

« UP Police Constable 2018

23. Problem Figures

Answer Figures

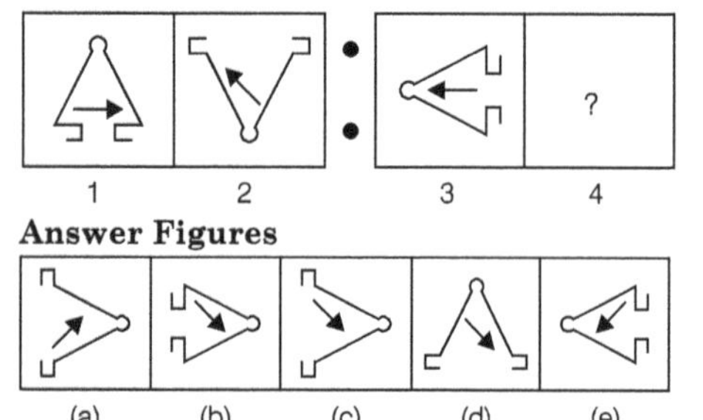

24. Problem Figures

Answer Figures

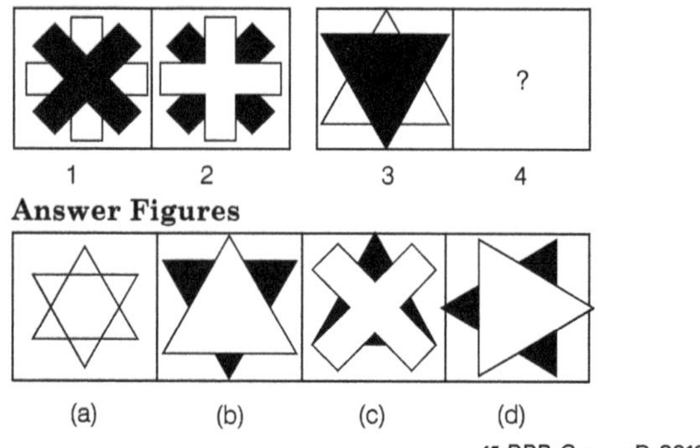

« RRB Group D 2018

(a) B (b) D (c) C (d) A

25. Problem Figures

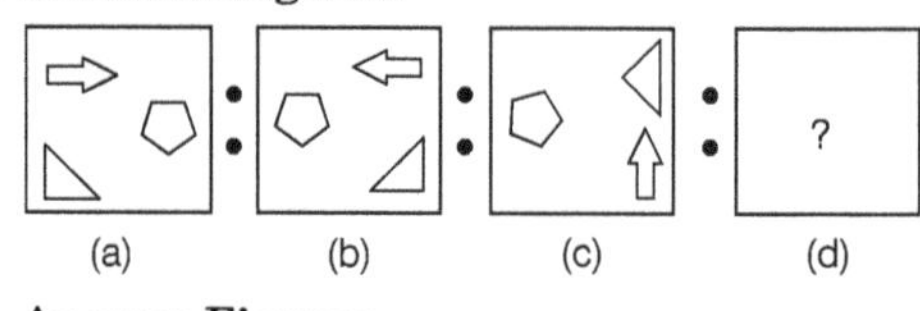

Answer Figures

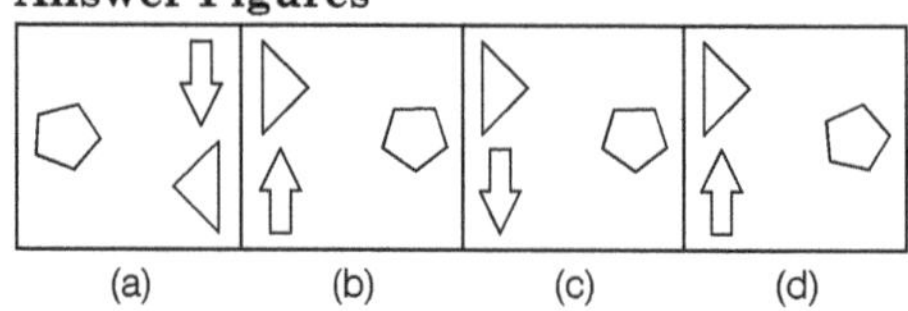

« UPSSSC Cane Supervisor 2019

26. Problem Figures

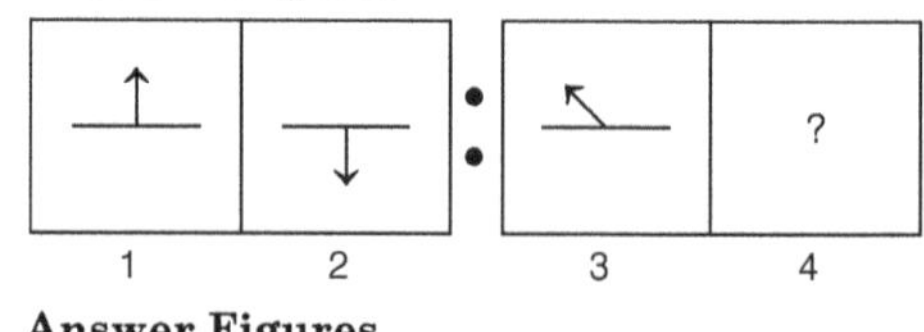

Answer Figures

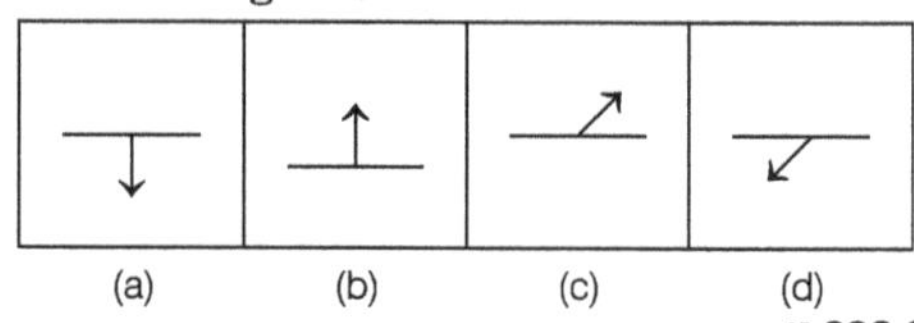

« SSC Steno 2007

27. Problem Figures

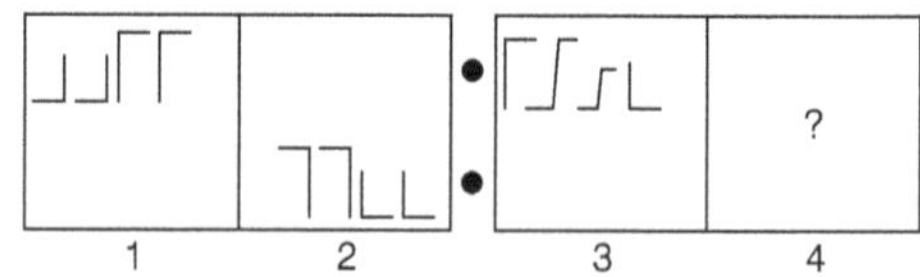

Answer Figures

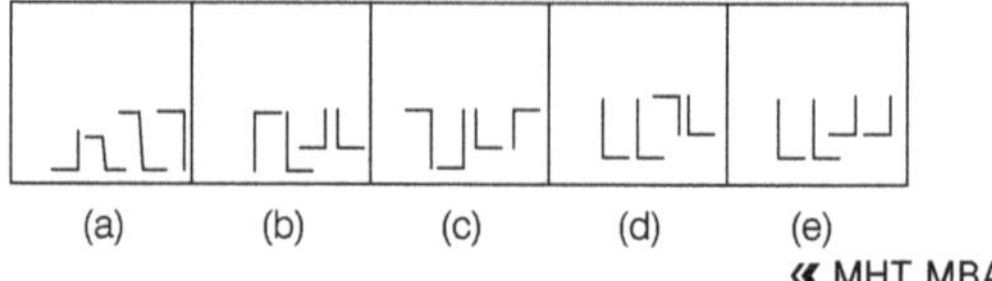

« MHT MBA 2017

28. Problem Figures

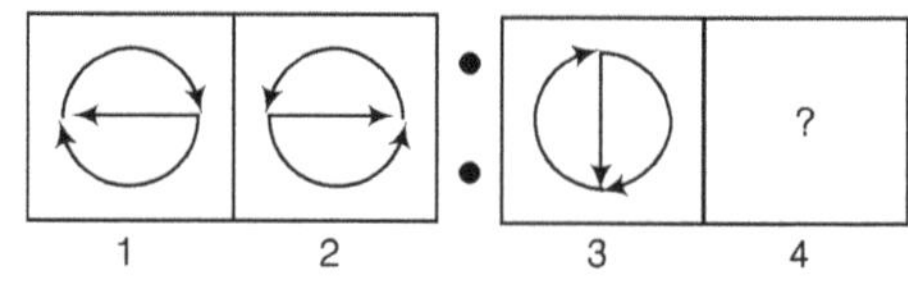

Answer Figures

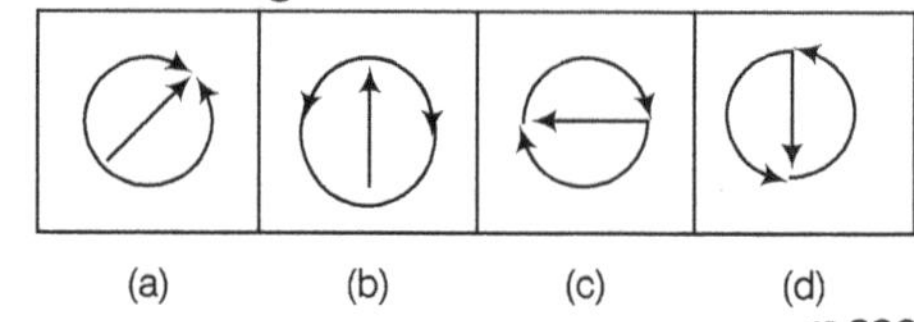

« SSC Steno 2012

29. Problem Figures

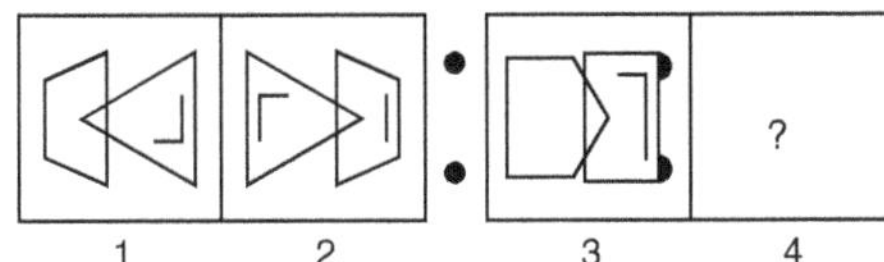

Answer Figures

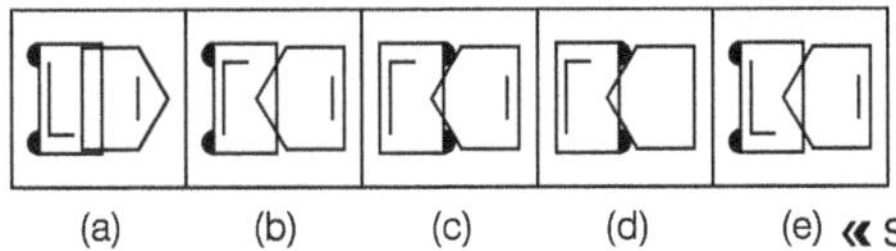

« SBI PO 2012

30. Problem Figures

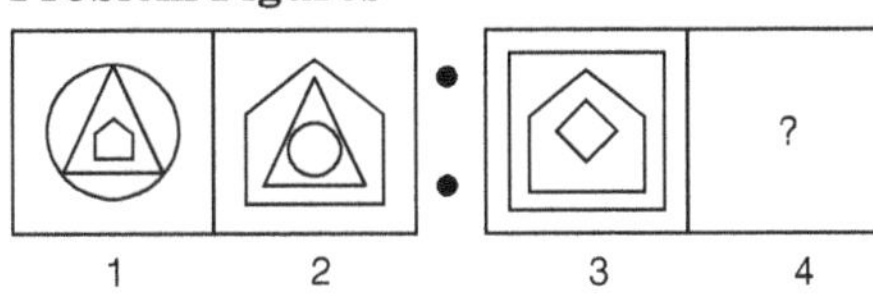

Answer Figures

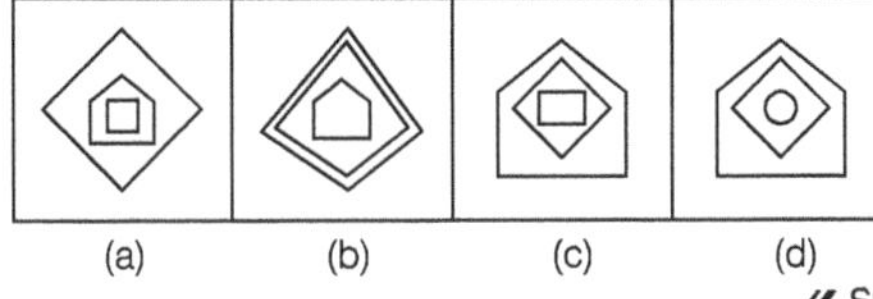

« SSC CGL 2012

31. Problem Figures

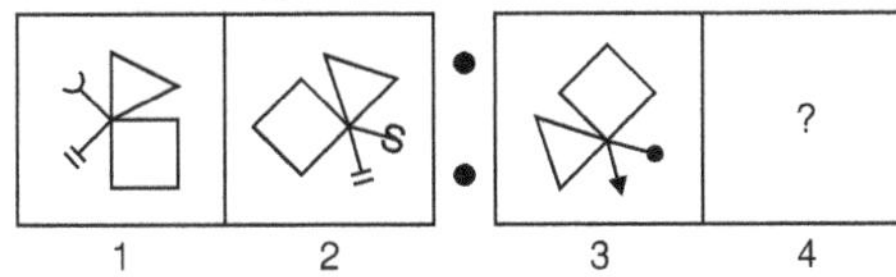

Answer Figures

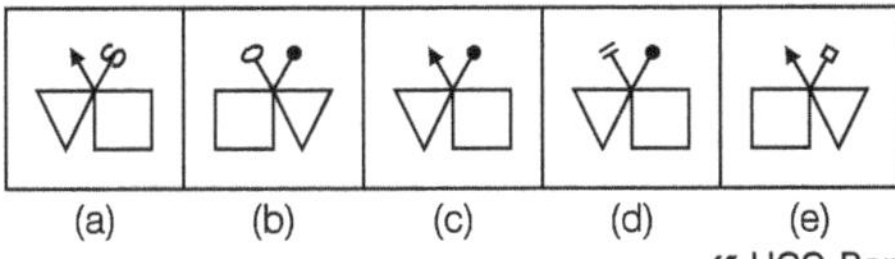

« UCO Bank PO 2009

32. Problem Figures

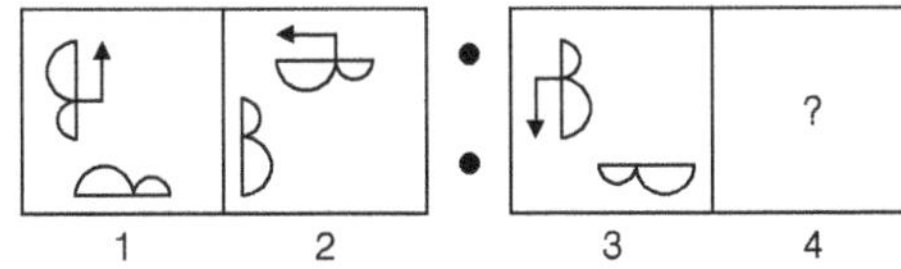

Answer Figures

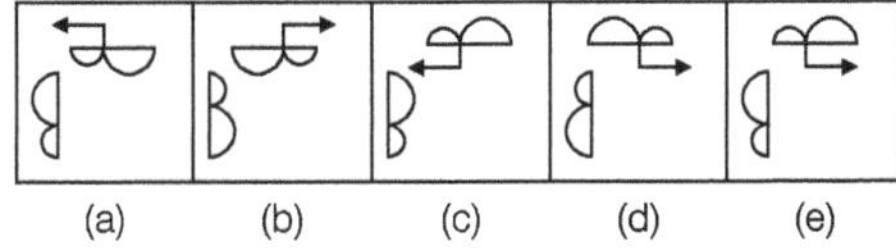

33. Problem Figures

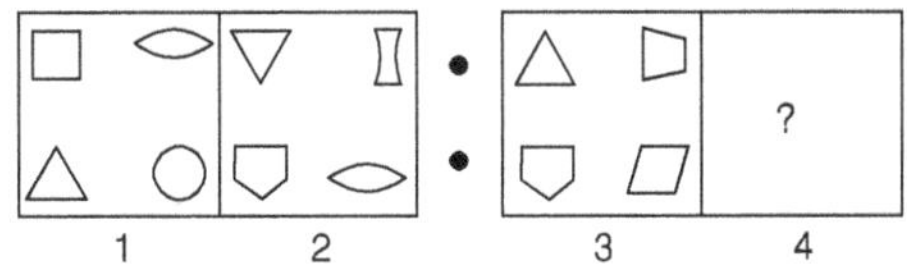

Answer Figures

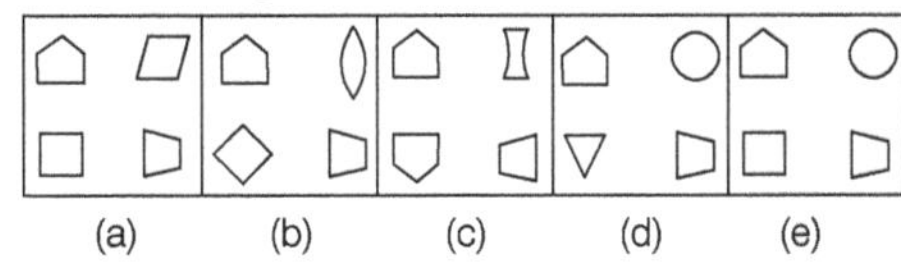

« MHT MBA 2017

34. Problem Figures

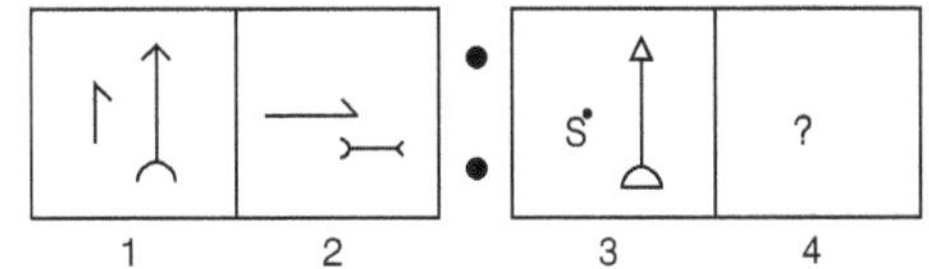

Answer Figures

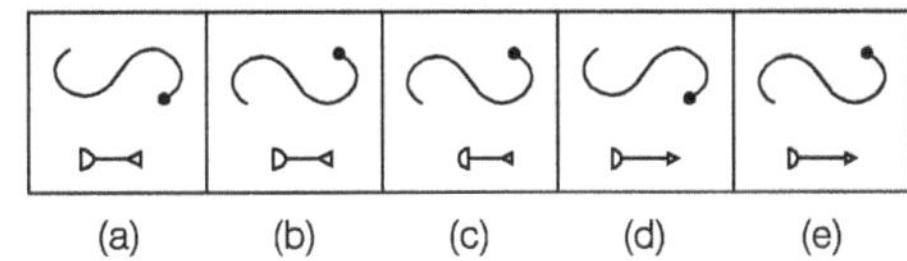

35. Problem Figures

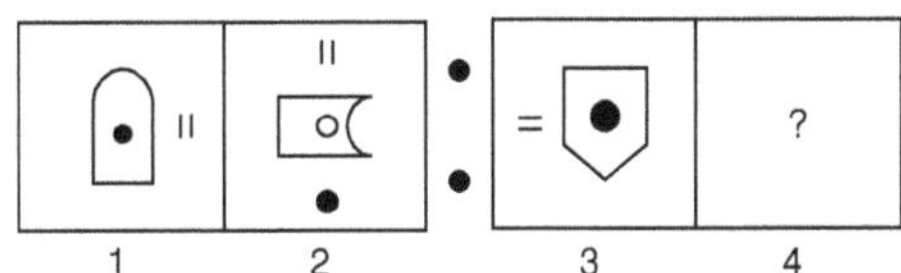

Answer Figures

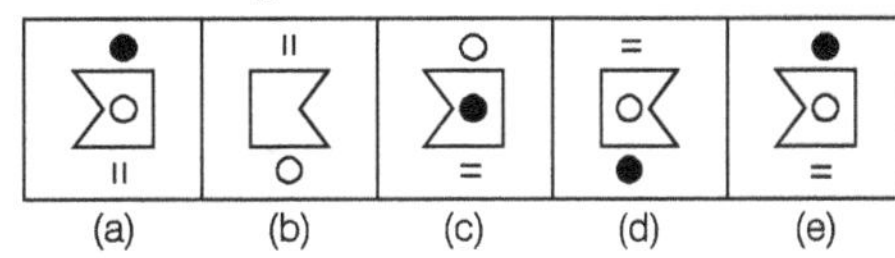

36. Problem Figures

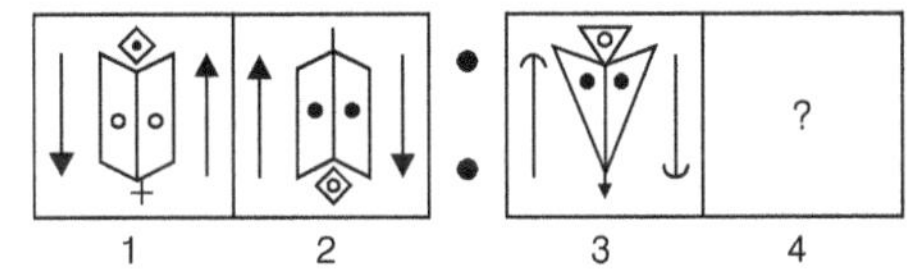

Answer Figures

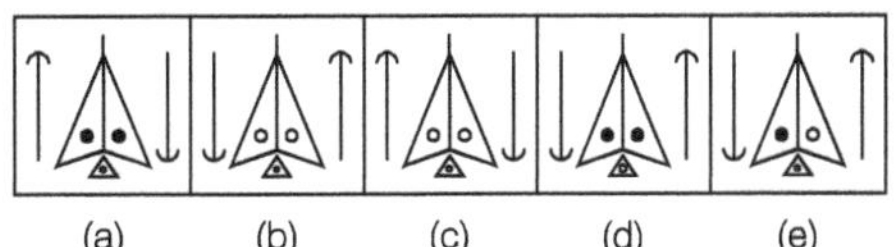

37. Problem Figures

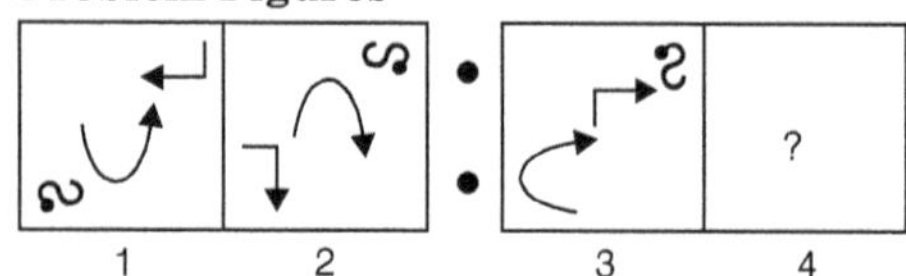

Answer Figures

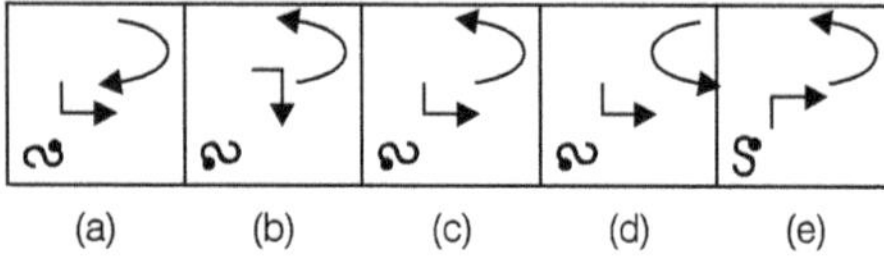

38. Problem Figures

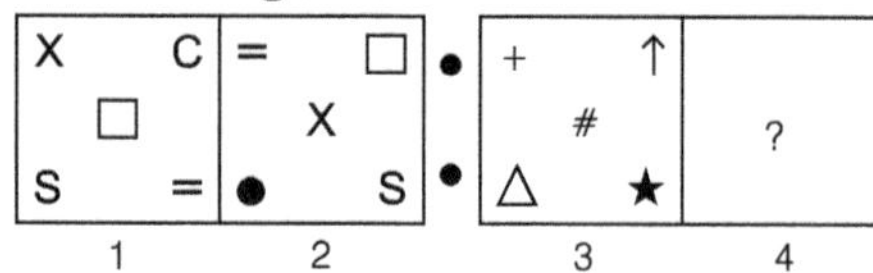

Answer Figures

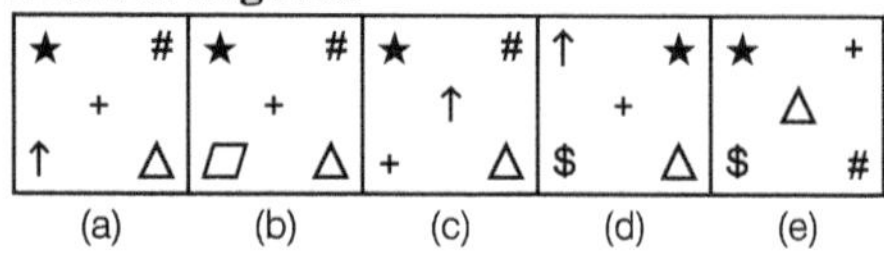

39. Problem Figures

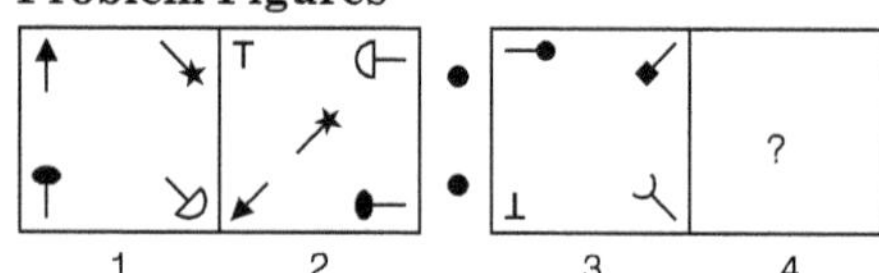

Answer Figures

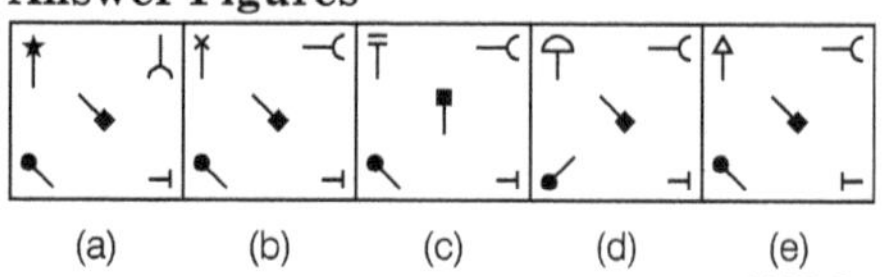

« UCO Bank PO 2009

40. Problem Figures

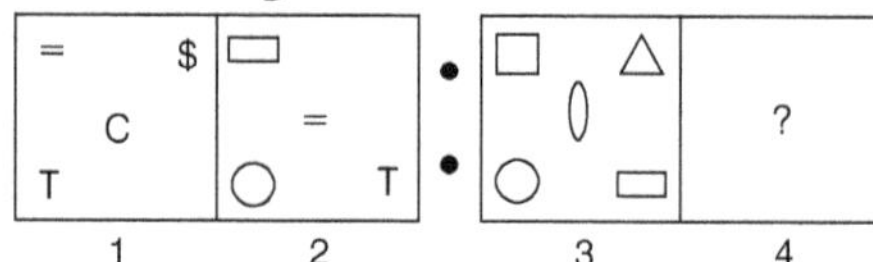

Answer Figures

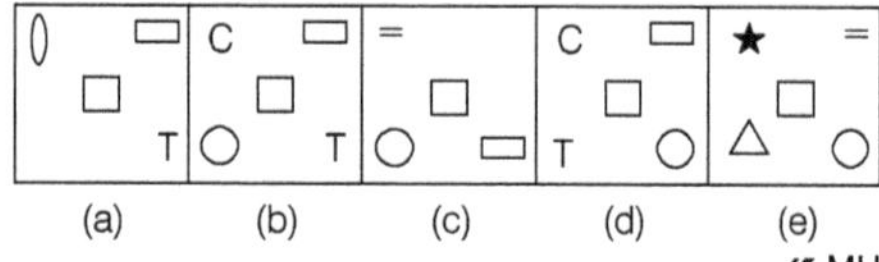

« MHT MBA 2017

41. Problem Figures

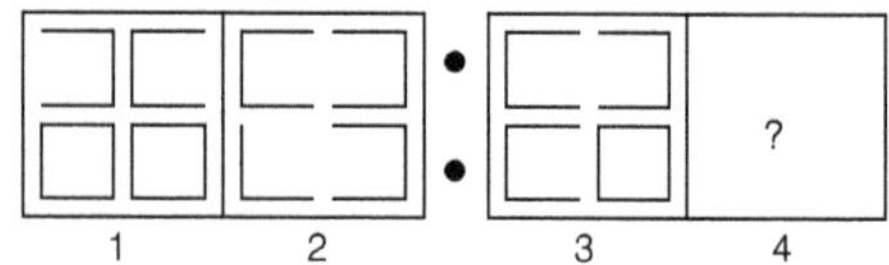

Answer Figures

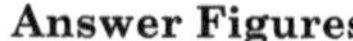

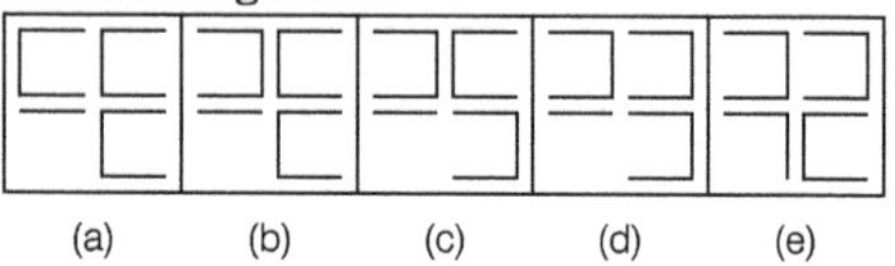

42. Problem Figures

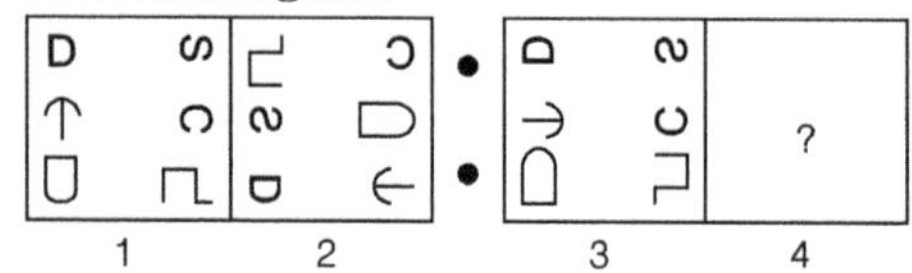

Answer Figures

43. Problem Figures

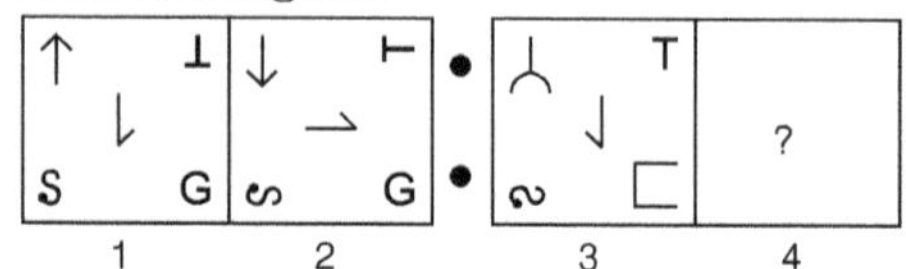

Answer Figures

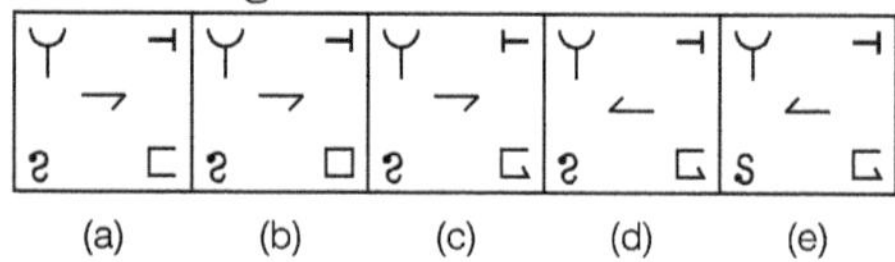

44. Problem Figures

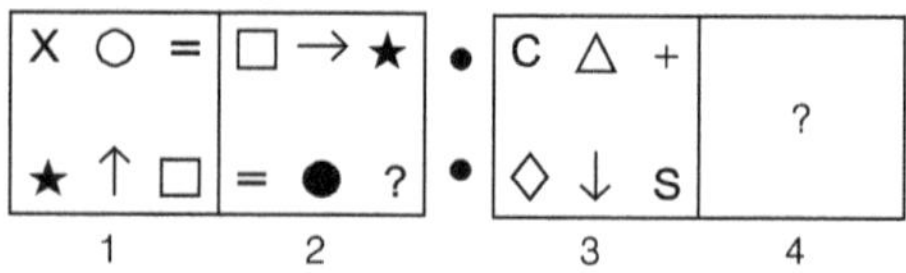

Answer Figures

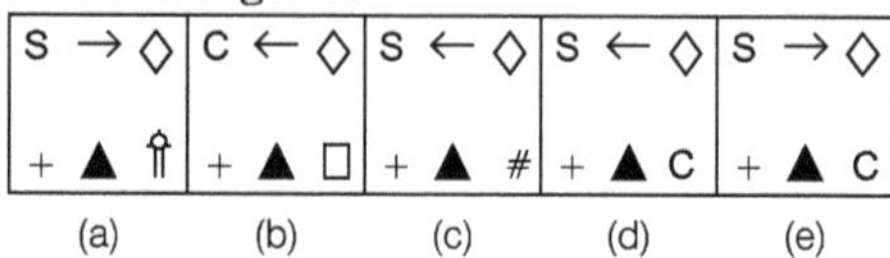

45. Problem Figures

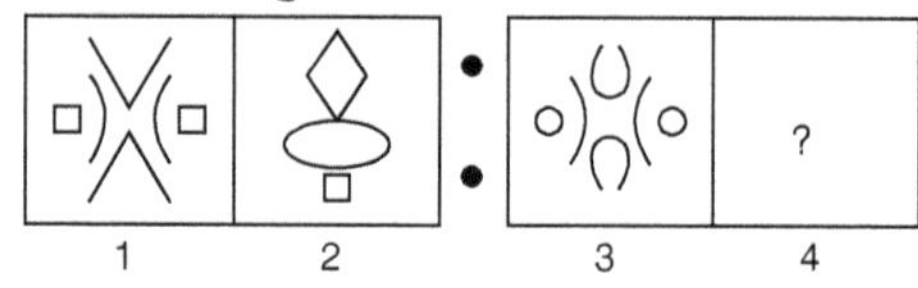

Answer Figures

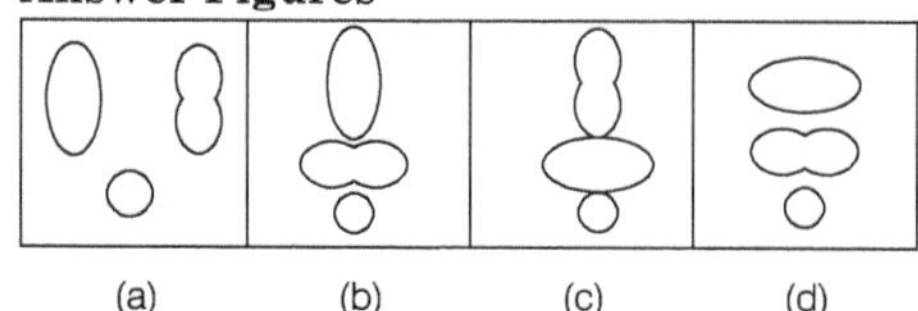

« SSC CGL 2011

46. Problem Figures

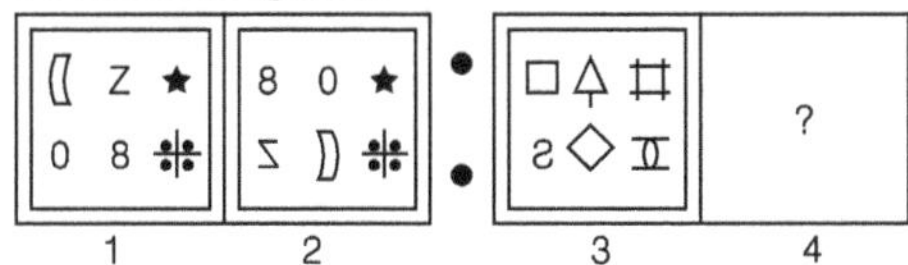

Answer Figures

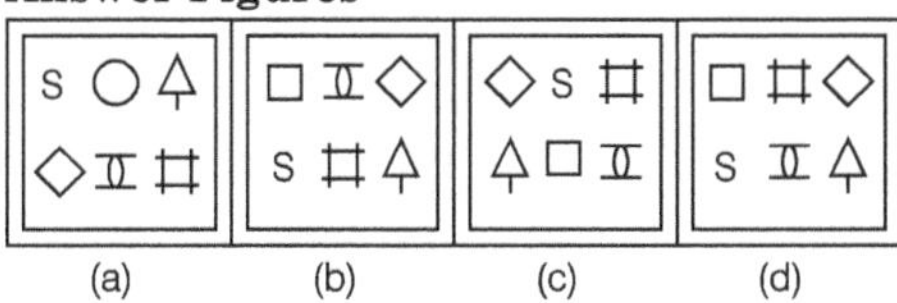

47. Problem Figures

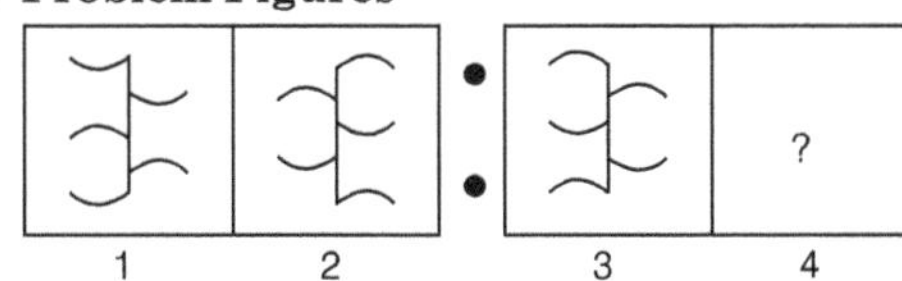

Answer Figures

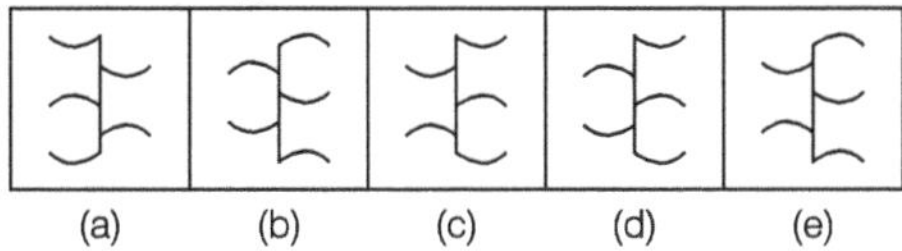

48. Problem Figures

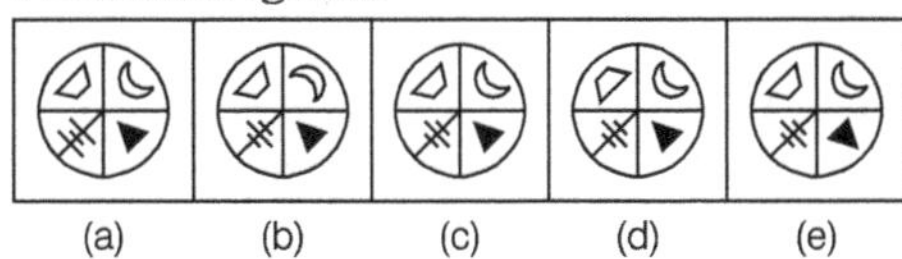

Answer Figures

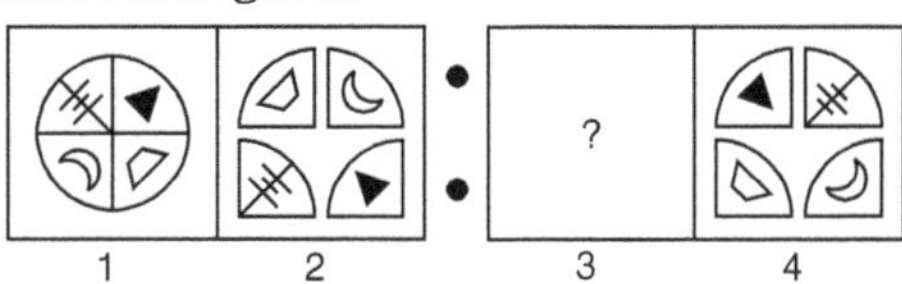

« UCO Bank PO 2008

49. Problem Figures

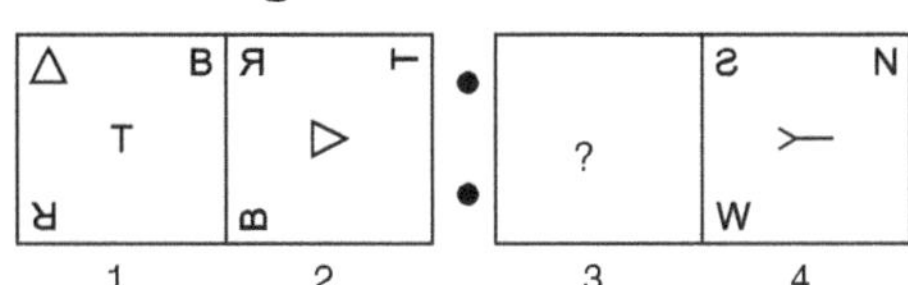

Answer Figures

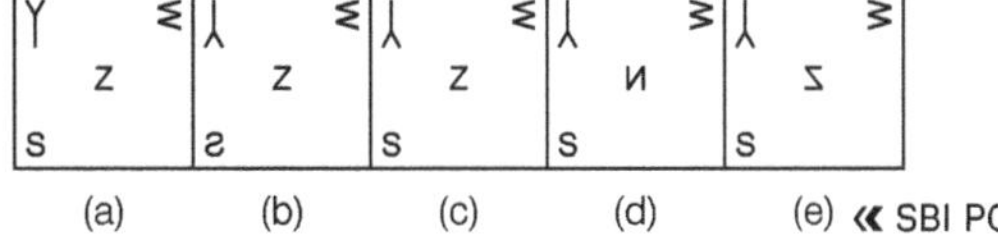

« SBI PO 2011

50. Problem Figures

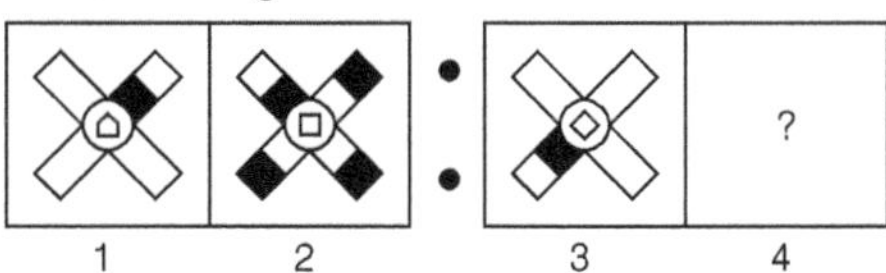

Answer Figures

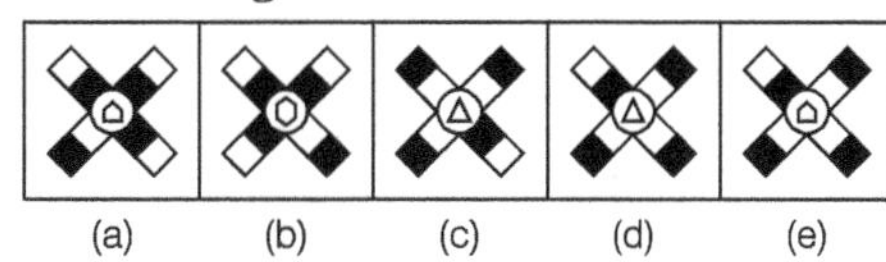

51. Problem Figures

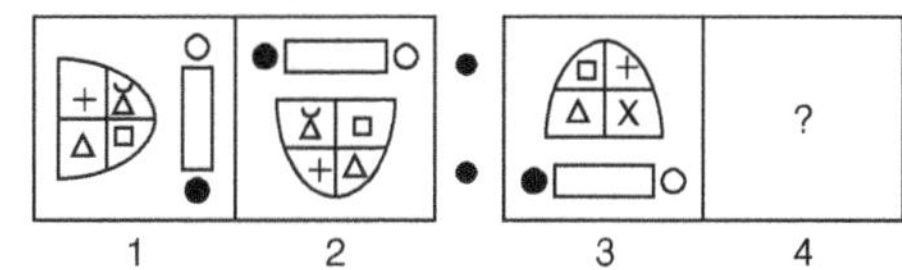

Answer Figures

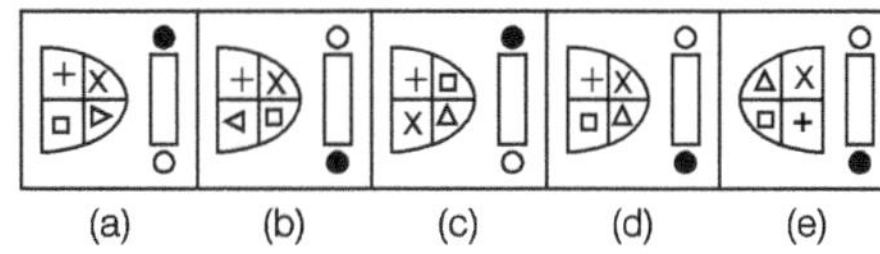

52. Problem Figures

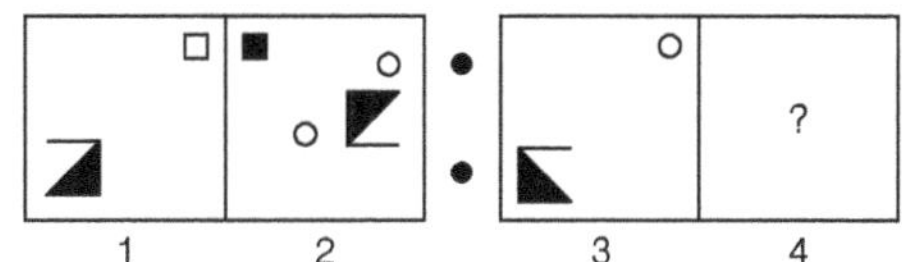

Answer Figures

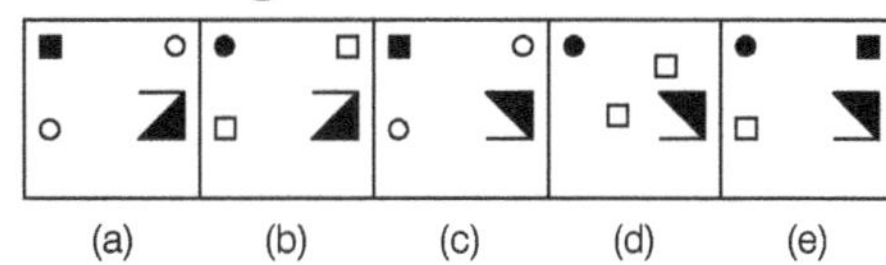

53. Problem Figures

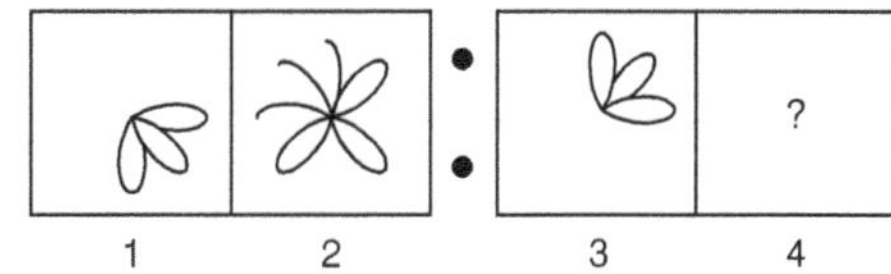

Answer Figures

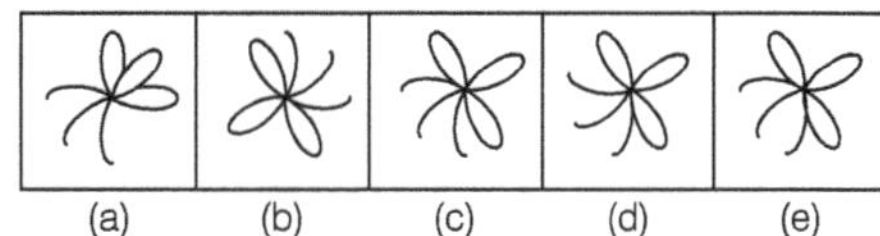

54. Problem Figures

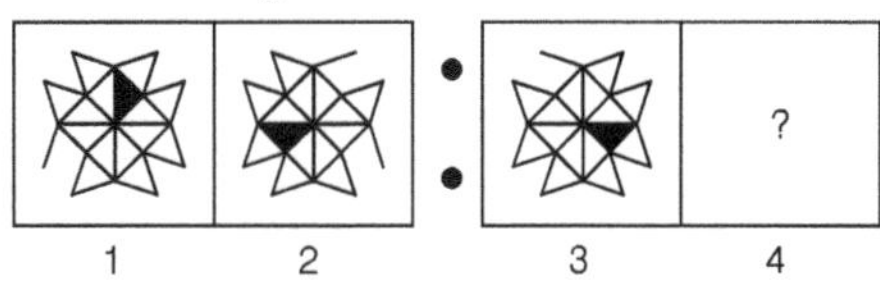

Answer Figures

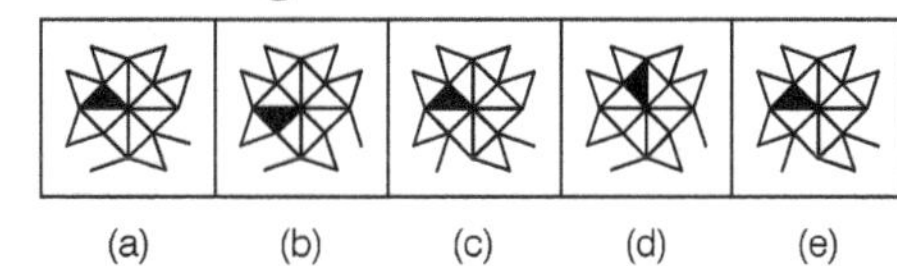

55. Problem Figures

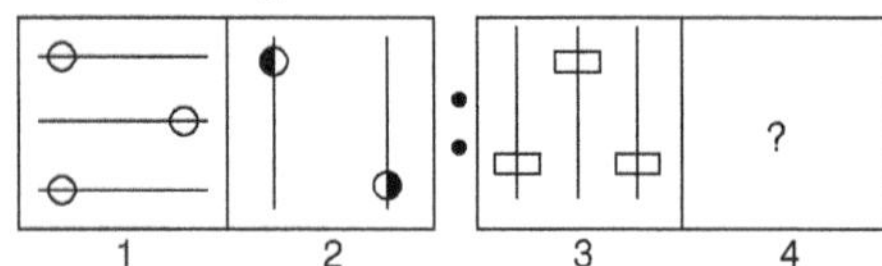

1 2 3 4

Answer Figures

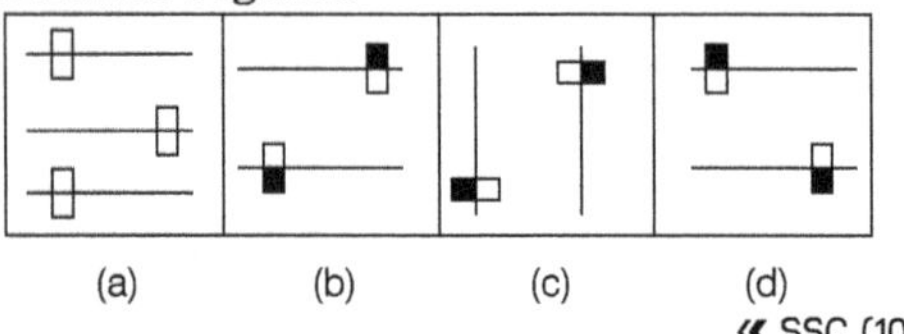

(a) (b) (c) (d)

« SSC (10 + 2) 2010

56. Problem Figures

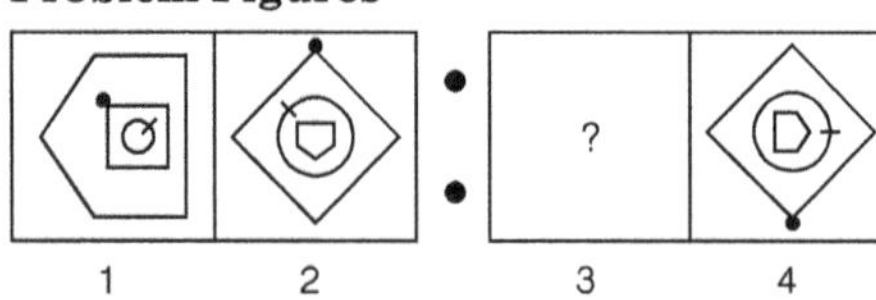

1 2 3 4

Answer Figures

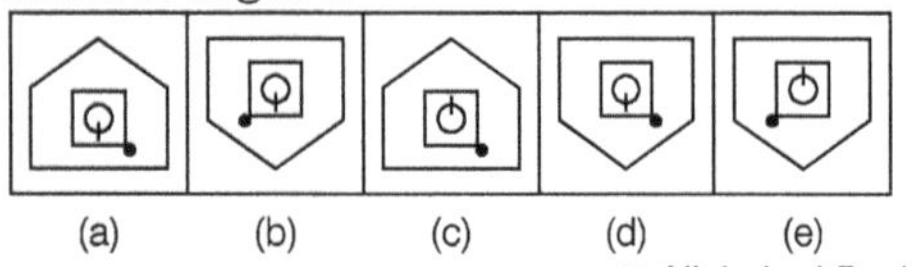

(a) (b) (c) (d) (e)

« Allahabad Bank PO 2008

57. Problem Figures

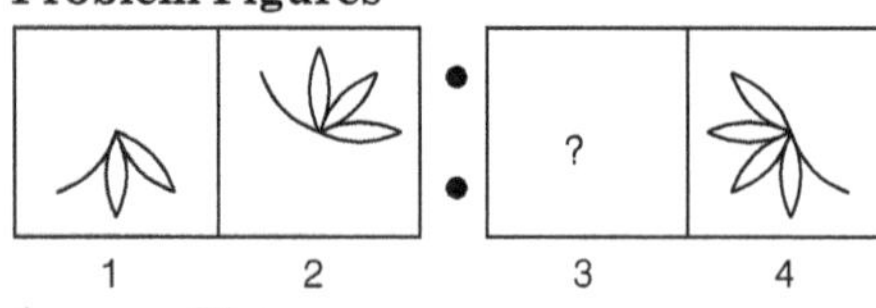

1 2 3 4

Answer Figures

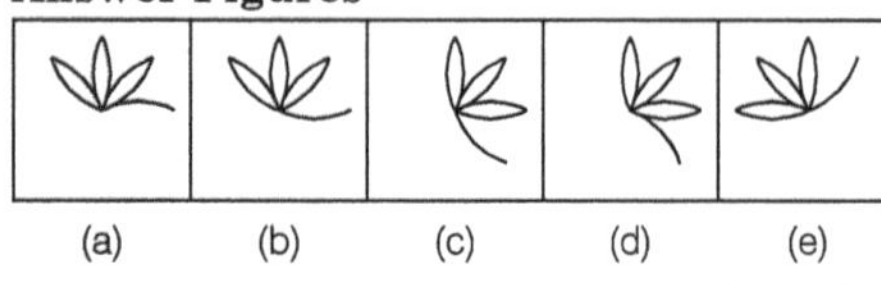

(a) (b) (c) (d) (e)

« Canara Bank PO 2008

58. Problem Figures

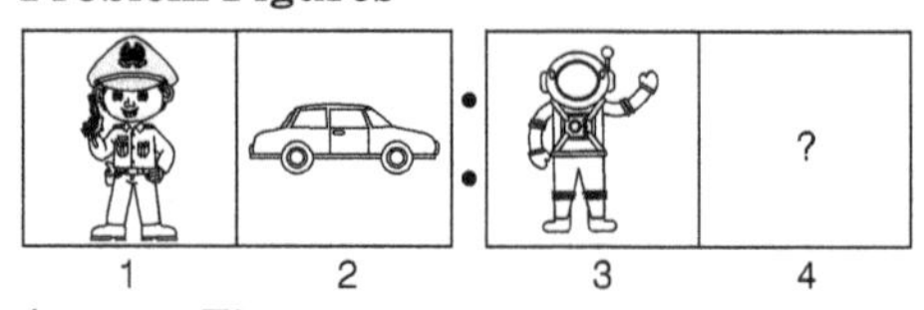

1 2 3 4

Answer Figures

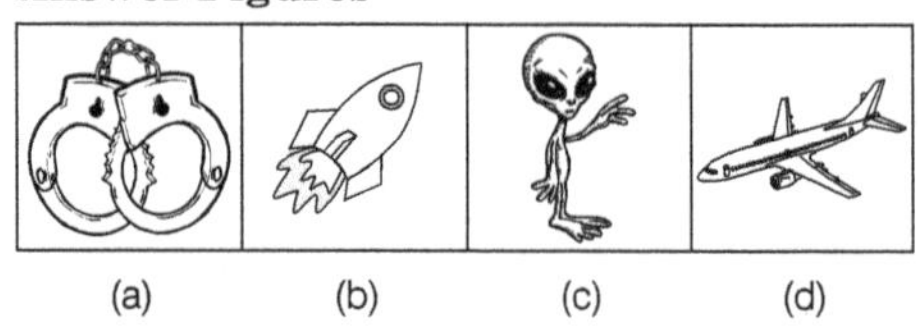

(a) (b) (c) (d)

59. Problem Figures

1 2 3 4

Answer Figures

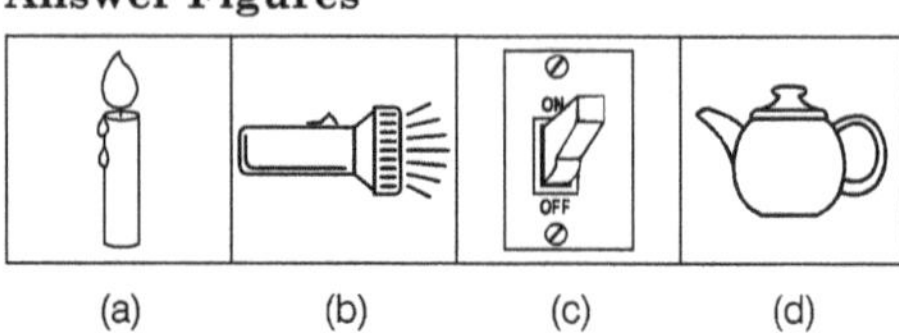

(a) (b) (c) (d)

60. Problem Figures

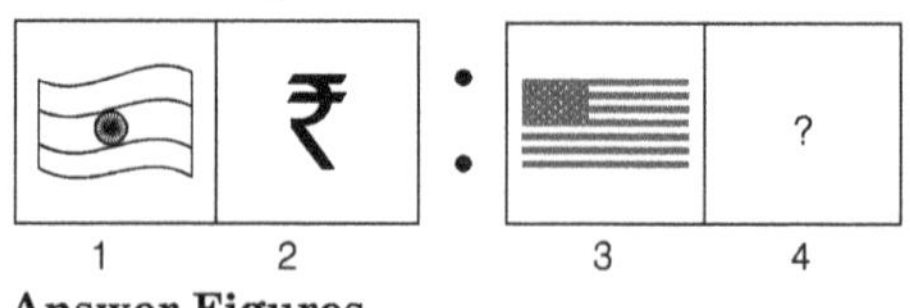

1 2 3 4

Answer Figures

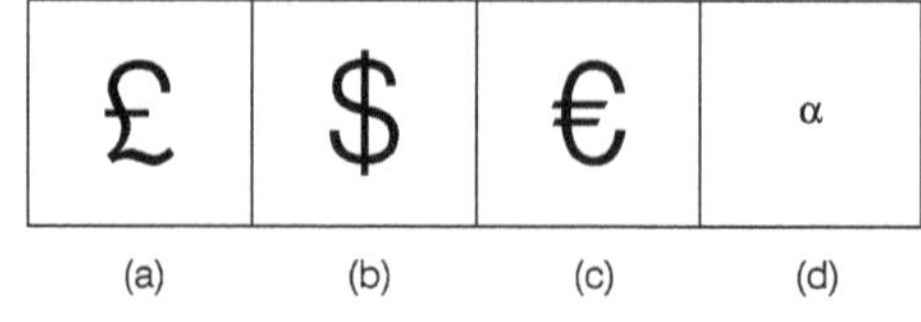

(a) (b) (c) (d)

Answers WITH EXPLANATIONS

1. (*d*) As, there are only three sides in first figure and it is increased by one, to obtain the second figure, having four sides. In the same way, the four sides given in the third figure will become five sides to obtain the answer figure.

2. (*c*) From first figure to second figure, one dot is added.

3. (*b*) From first to second figure, there is an increment of a side and a shaded dot.

4. (*a*) In the second figure, a small figure is added, same as that present inside the circle and two small lines are added in lower part of the figure.

5. (*b*) From first figure to second figure, both designs inside the circle move in clockwise direction and one same design appears in the middle of the two designs. Also, the circle is bounded by a square.

6. (*a*) From problem figure (1) to (2) both the designs interchange their positions and one design changes its direction.

7. (*c*) From problem figure (1) to (2), the right figure gets inverted and enlarged. The left one moves to the middle and the middle figure gets inverted and is reduced in size and becomes the innermost element.

8. (*b*) Outer figure is vanished and the remaining three inner figures get enlarged and combined vertically.

9. (*a*) Second figure is obtained by rotating the first figure at 180°. So the fourth figure will be obtained from the third figure in the same way.

10. (*c*) From first figure to second figure, the design rotates through 90° clockwise.

11. (*a*) The figure rotates 45° anti-clockwise, the handle of the umbrella is reversed, the black portion becomes white and the white portion becomes black.

12. (*b*) From first figure to the second figure, the shaded parts move one sector ahead in clockwise direction.

13. (*e*) The figure rotates through 90° clockwise. The inner figure is inverted and comes outside and the outer figure goes inside.

14. (*c*) From first figure to the second figure, the design rotates through 45° clockwise.

15. (*a*) As, figure (1) rotates 90° clockwise and star symbol is removed. In the same way, figure (3) will rotate 90° clockwise and star symbol will be removed to obtain the answer figure.

16. (*b*) As, figure (1) rotates 180° clockwise and is changed into figure (2). Similarly, figure (3) is changed into figure (b).

17. (*c*) Straight line portion of the figure rotates 90° clockwise and the curved line portion of the figure rotates 90° anti-clockwise.

18. (*e*) The figures rotate 90° clockwise and heads of the arrow are reversed.

19. (*e*) Here, each element rotates 90° clockwise.

20. (*c*) Bottom and right arms of the figure rotate through 135° clockwise while left and top arms of the figure rotate through 180°.

21. (*b*) From first figure to the second figure, the circle is changed into a square and it also shifts in the middle of the figure.

22. (*b*) In figure 1, only one portion is shaded and in figure 2, two portions are shaded.
Similarly, figure 3 has 2 shaded portions and figure 4 will have four shaded portions.

23. (*c*) The figure is inverted and bent lines on the base get reversed. The arrow inside the figure rotates through 135° anti-clockwise.

24. (*a*) Shaded portion goes behind and the unshaded portion comes up.

25. (*b*) Second figure is the mirror image of first figure.

26. (*d*) Second figure is the water image of the first figure.

27. (*a*) Here, all the elements get laterally inverted. Also, the row of elements comes down to the bottom right corner.

28. (*d*) Figure (2) is obtained by the lateral inversion of figure (1).

29. (*e*) From problem (1) to (2) , the whole figure gets laterally inverted and the L shaped figure rotates by 180°. Also, one line is added to the other figure.

30. (*a*) From problem figure 1 to 2, the inner most figure becomes outer most figure and the outer most figure becomes the inner most figure i.e. first and third figure get interchanged.

31. (*d*) From problem figure (1) to (2), the whole of the first figure gets inverted vertically, then rotates 45° clockwise and one of its small end elements is replaced by a new one.

32. (*e*) Both the figures move clockwise in such a way that the first figure moves one step and rotates by 90° anti-clockwise, the second figure moves half side, rotates by 90° anti-clockwise and is reversed.

33. (*b*) From figure (1) to figure (2), each element changes its position in the following manner.
(i) The element in the bottom left corner goes up and gets vertically inverted.
(ii) The element in the top left corner comes down and its side increases by 1.
(iii) The element in the top right corner comes down.
(iv) A new element is added in the top right corner.

34. (*b*) Small line rotates through 90° clockwise and is inverted and enlarged. Large arrow rotates through 90° clockwise, becomes smaller and the head of the arrow is reversed. Similar changes take place from problem figure (3) to (4).

35. (*e*) The whole figure rotates 90° clockwise and the outside portion of the figure is laterally inverted. Shaded dot comes outside the figure at the place of = and the sign of = moves to the opposite side after rotating 90° clockwise and a blank dot is formed inside the main figure.

36. (*b*) The entire figure along with arrows is vertically inverted, white dots become black and *vice-versa* and a line segment from the head of the figure is removed.

37. (*c*) Counting from top, the first figure rotates 90° anti-clockwise and comes at third position, second figure is reversed at the same position and third figure rotates 180° and after reversing it comes at the first position.

38. (*b*) From problem figure (1) to (2), all the symbols change positions as shown in the diagram and the symbol in place of * is replaced by a new symbol.

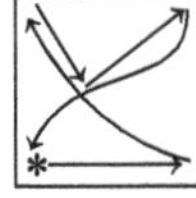

39. (*b*) From problem figure (1) to (2) , the upper left element rotates by 135° anti-clockwise and shifts to lower left. The lower left element rotates by 90° anti-clockwise and shifts to lower right. The lower right element rotates by 135° clockwise and shifts to upper right.
The upper right element rotates by 90° anti-clockwise and shifts to the centre.

40. (*d*) Here, the pattern is

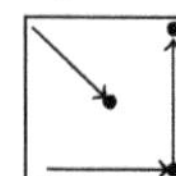

Also, two new elements are added in top left and bottom left corners.

41. (*c*) The upper two figures are reversed. The figure at the lower left position loses two sides and the figure at the lower right position loses one side.

42. (*d*) Change in the positions of the symbols takes place as shown in the diagram. Also, each of the symbols rotates in a specific order.

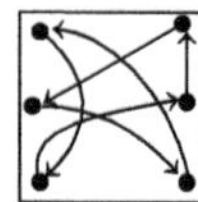

43. (*a*) Sign at the top left position is inverted, sign at top right position rotates 90° clockwise, sign at the bottom left position rotates 90° clockwise, sign at the central position rotates 90° anti-clockwise and the sign at bottom right position remains unchanged.

44. (*c*) All the symbols interchange their positions as shown in the diagram. Also, top middle symbol, when comes down gets shaded, below middle symbol, when goes up rotates 90° clockwise and the symbol in place of * is replaced by a new symbol.

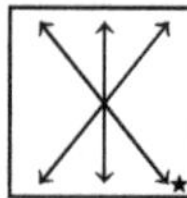

45. (*c*) Upper and lower designs get inverted vertically and then combined to form a design which comes at top. Two middle designs get inverted horizontally, then combined to form an ellipse shape. This shape comes in the middle after rotating through an angle of 90°.

One square is vanished and the other one comes below. In the same way, figure of option (c) forms from third figure.

46. (*c*) The following changes occur from first figure to the second figure with two symbols getting laterally inverted.

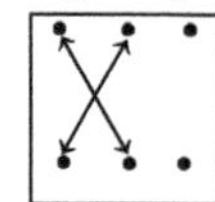

47. (*c*) The whole figure is first rotated by 180°, then the two arcs are reversed at the same positions.

48. (*c*) From problem figure (2) to (1) , the upper left part becomes the lower right; the lower right becomes the upper right; the upper right becomes the lower left, and the lower left becomes the upper left part and they join together to form a circle.

49. (*c*) From problem figure (2) to (1), every element rotates in certain manner and shifts by a fixed pattern as shown here.

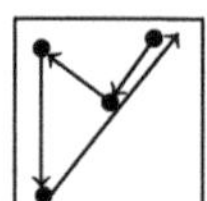

50. (*c*) The figure rotates 90° anti-clockwise and the upper portion of all the other three arms also become shaded. One side is reduced from the inner figure.

51. (*a*) Semi-circular figure rotates 90° clockwise and all the signs move two parts in anti-clockwise direction and all the shapes inside the semi-circular figure interchange cross-sectionally.

52. (*d*) From problem figure (1) to (2), larger figure rotates 180° in clockwise direction and moves one and half step in anti-clockwise direction. The smaller figure moves one step in anti-clockwise direction and becomes shaded and two new small figures are added.

53. (*c*) Both the leaves at the extreme ends get deviated by 45° and three half leaves are added on the back of the figure pointing in anti-clockwise direction.

54. (*d*) The shaded portion moves three portion anti-clockwise. One line is added to make the triangle near the shaded portion and two lines are removed from the triangles present on the border of the main figure.

55. (*b*) Upper pin is vanished, the remaining two pins of figure (1) rotate 90° clockwise and the outer half circles get shaded.

56. (*d*) From problem figure (2) to (1), the innermost element rotates by 90° clockwise and becomes the outermost element, the outermost element rotates by 45° anti-clockwise and becomes the middle one while the middle one rotates by 90° clockwise and becomes the innermost.

57. (*b*) From problem figure (2) to (1), the whole figure rotates by 90° clockwise. One and a half petals are lost from anti-clockwise side and a half petal is added to its clockwise side in the same manner as it was on the anti-clockwise side.

58. (*b*) As, police uses the car to chase a criminal. Similarly, Astronaut uses rocket to go in space.

59. (*a*) As, bulb in the lamp spreads the light. Similarly, flame of the candle spreads the light.

60. (*b*) As, the symbol of the currency of India is '₹'. Similarly, the symbol of the currency of USA is $.

TYPE 02

Finding a Pair of Similar Figures in Pattern to Original Pair

In these type of questions, an original pair of figures is given. The pair shows relationship between two sections containing different figures.

This pair is followed by five different pairs of figures as answer pairs. Candidates are required to select one pair out of these five pairs which shows the same relationship between two of its sections as shown by the original pair and this pair is the correct answer.

The following examples will help you to understand this type of questions

DIRECTIONS ~ (Example Nos. 20-25) *In each of the following questions, a related pair of figures is followed by five pairs of figures. Select the pair that has a relationship similar to that in the original pair. The best possible answer is to be selected from a group of fairly close choices.*

Ex 20 **Original Pair**

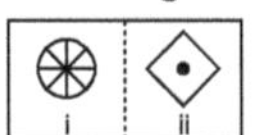

Answer Pairs

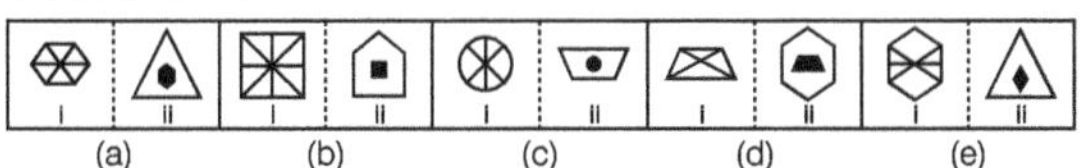

Solution (a) In the original pair, section (ii) contains a figure with as many sides as the number of lines inside the figure in section (i) and the figure in section (i) comes inside the figure of section (ii) after becoming smaller in size and shaded black.

Ex 21 **Original Pair**

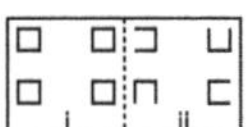

Answer Pairs

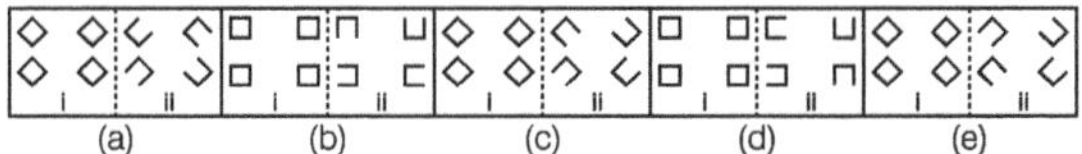

Solution (e) In the original pair, each of the squares in section (i) loses one of its sides sequentially in clockwise direction starting from any of the squares.

Ex 22 **Original Pair**

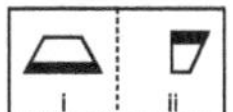

Answer Pairs

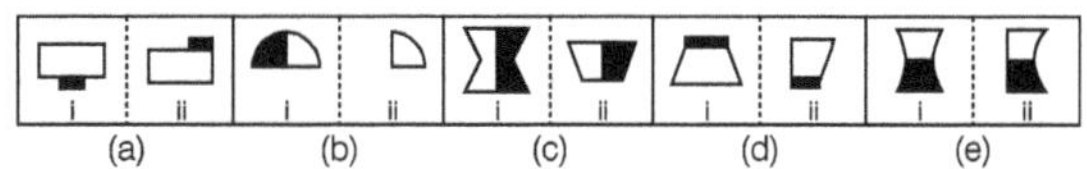

Solution (d) In the original pair, from section (i) to (ii), main figure is first divided into two halves, then the left half is deleted and the right half gets inverted.

Ex 23 **Original Pair**

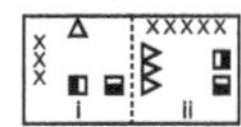

Answer Pairs

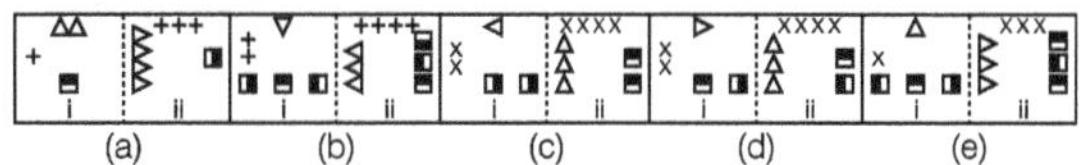

Solution (c) In the original pair, symbols on the left side move one side clockwise and are increased by two in number. The symbols at top positions move one side anti-clockwise and are increased by two in number. The symbols at bottom rotate through 90° anti-clockwise and are arranged along the line on right side.

Ex 24 **Original Pair**

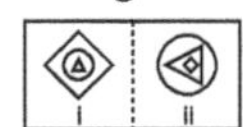

Answer Pairs

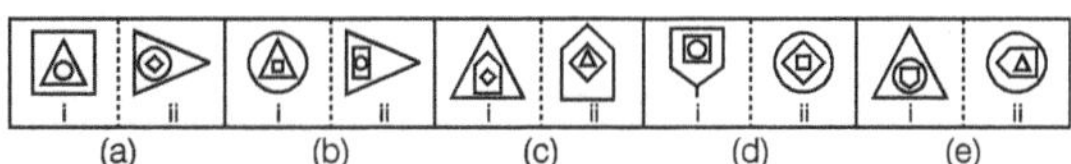

Solution (c) In the original pair, the innermost figure rotates through 90° anti-clockwise and comes in the middle, the outermost figure comes inside the main figure and the figure in the middle becomes the outermost figure.

Ex 25 **Original Pair**

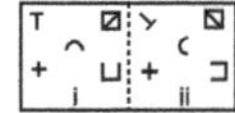

Answer Pairs

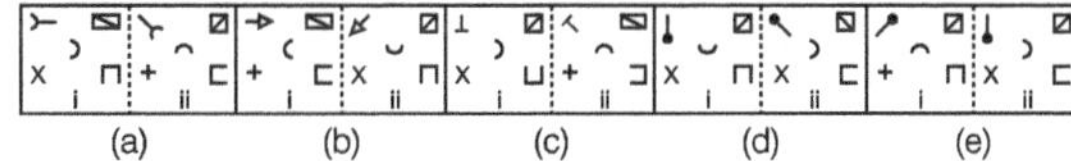

Solution (d) In the original pair, the symbols at the centre and bottom right positions rotate through 90° anti-clockwise, the symbols at top right and bottom left positions rotate through 90° clockwise and the symbol at the top left position rotates through 135° clockwise.

Practice CORNER 2.2

DIRECTIONS ~ (Q. Nos. 1-26) *In each of the following questions, a related pair of figures is followed by five numbered pairs of figures. Select the pair that has a relationship similar to that in the original pair. The best possible answer is to be selected from a group of fairly close choices.*

1. Original Pair

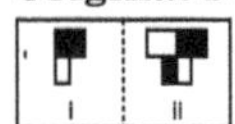

Answer Pairs

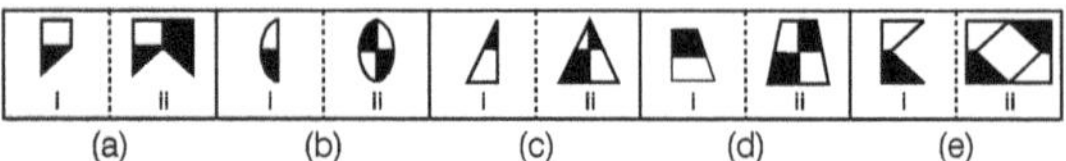

2. Original Pair

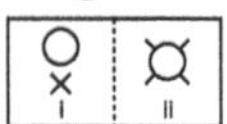

Answer Pairs

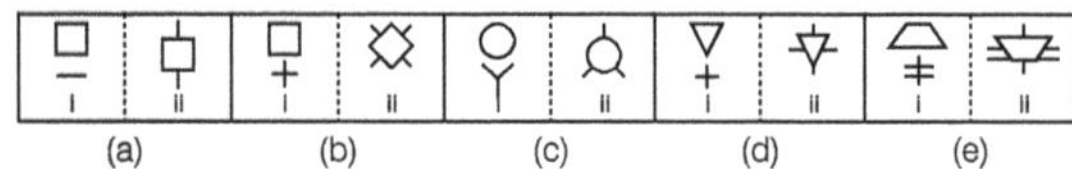

3. Original Pair

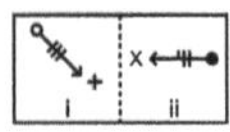

Answer Pairs

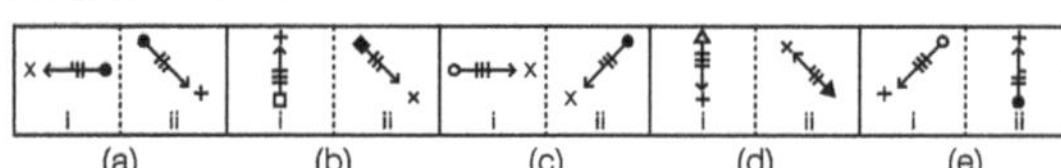

4. Original Pair

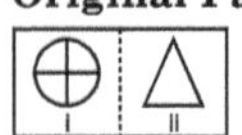

Answer Pairs

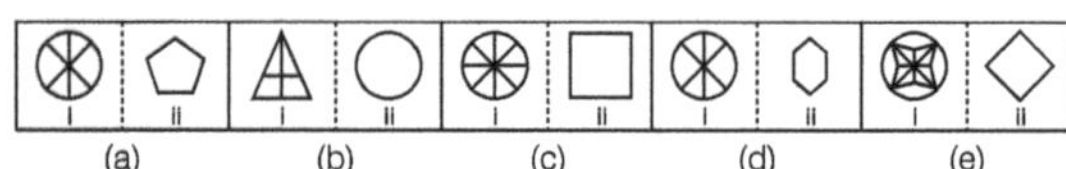

5. Original Pair

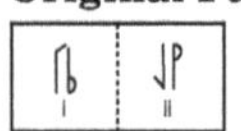

Answer Pairs

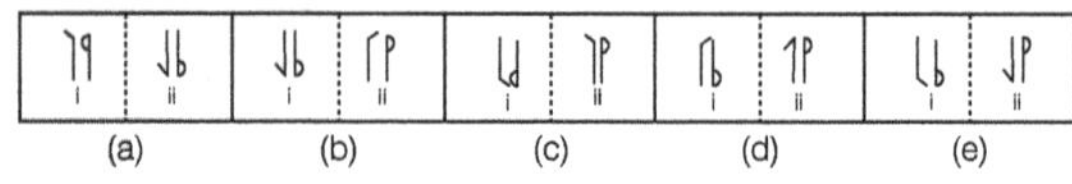

« MHT MBA 2017

6. Original Pair

Answer Pairs

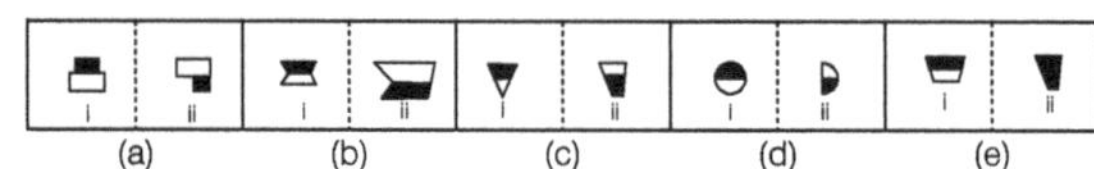

« MHT MBA 2017

7. Original Pair

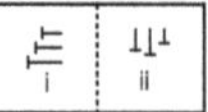

Answer Pairs

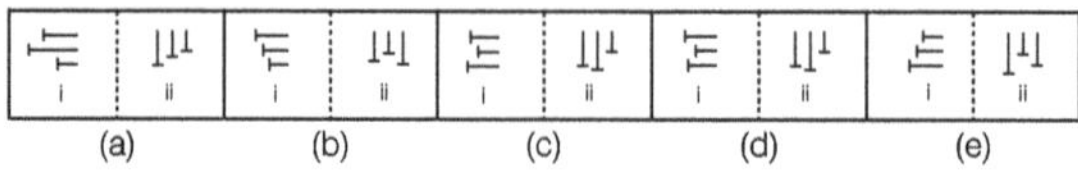

« MHT MBA 2017

8. Original Pair

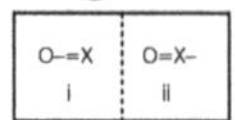

Answer Pairs

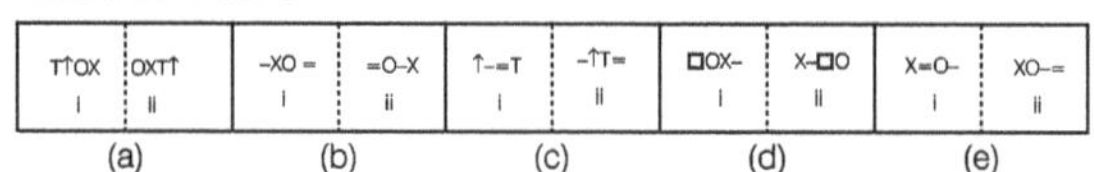

« MHT MBA 2017

9. Original Pair

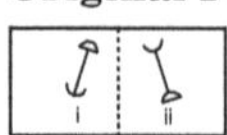

Answer Pairs

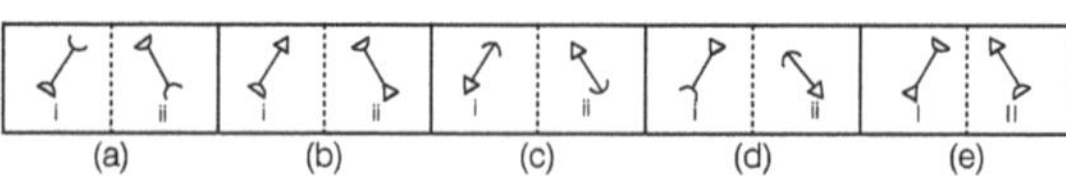

« MHT MBA 2017

10. Original Pair

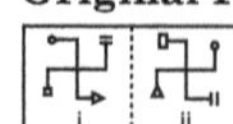

Answer Pairs

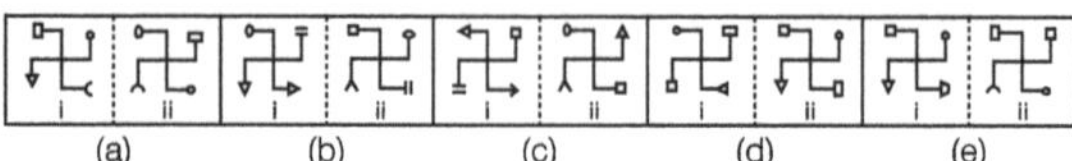

11. Original Pair

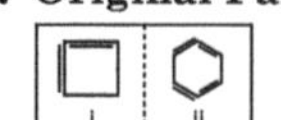

Answer Pairs

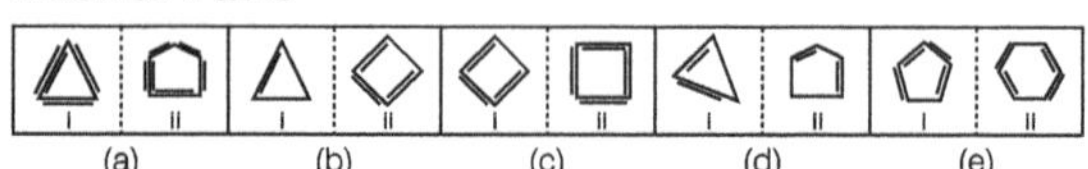

12. Original Pair

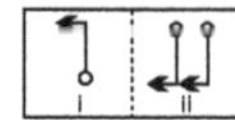

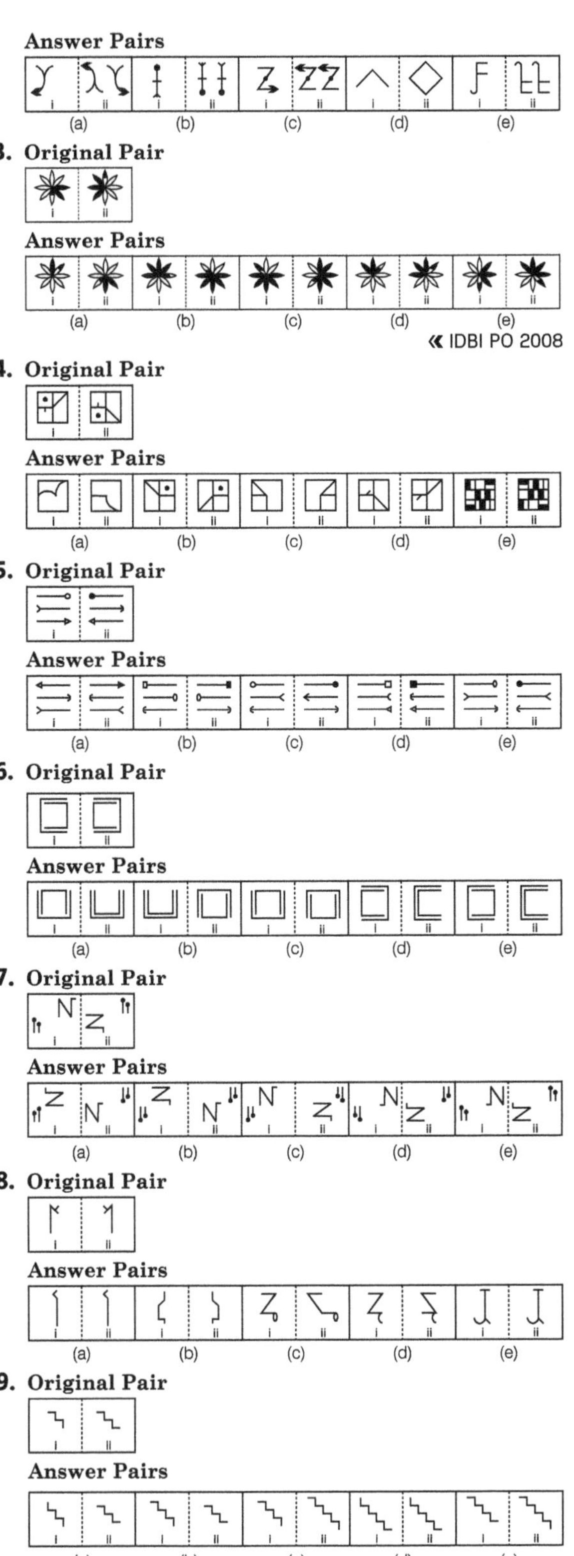
Answer Pairs
13. Original Pair
Answer Pairs
« IDBI PO 2008
14. Original Pair
Answer Pairs
15. Original Pair
Answer Pairs
16. Original Pair
Answer Pairs
17. Original Pair
Answer Pairs
18. Original Pair
Answer Pairs
19. Original Pair
Answer Pairs

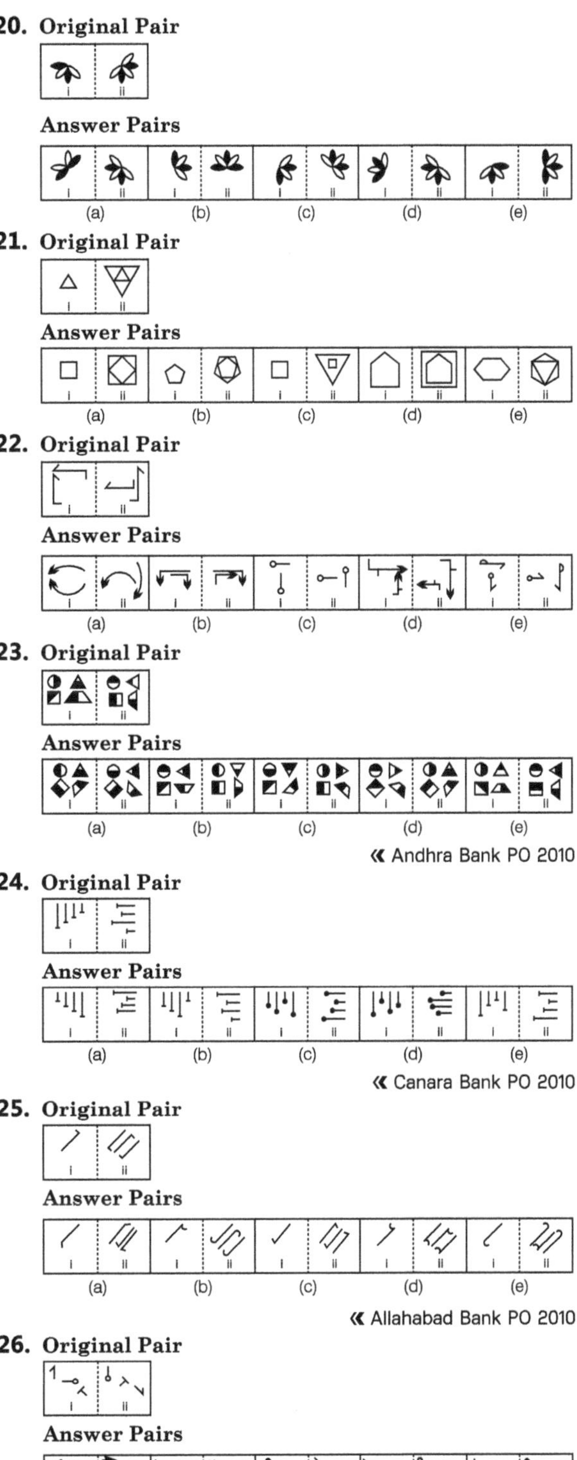
20. Original Pair
Answer Pairs
21. Original Pair
Answer Pairs
22. Original Pair
Answer Pairs
23. Original Pair
Answer Pairs
« Andhra Bank PO 2010
24. Original Pair
Answer Pairs
« Canara Bank PO 2010
25. Original Pair
Answer Pairs
« Allahabad Bank PO 2010
26. Original Pair
Answer Pairs
« OBC PO 2007

Answers / WITH EXPLANATIONS

1. (*d*) The mirror image of the figure is added to the LHS with a different shading.

2. (*d*) The line segments of the lower element are attached to the upper element.

3. (*d*) The arrow rotates through 135° clockwise in such a way that one line from bottom side of the arrow is deleted and shape on the back of it become shaded.

4. (*a*) The number of sides in the figure in section (ii) is one less than the number of radii in the circle present in section (i) of the original pair.

5. (*b*) Here, the first element gets vertically inverted and the half arrow moves 180° clockwise. Also, the second element gets vertically inverted.

6. (*b*) Here, the right half of the element is removed. Also, shaded portion gets unshaded and *vice-versa*. Among the given figures, only option figure (b) follows the similar pattern.

7. (*b*) Here, the figure gets rotated 90° anti-clockwise. Also, the element changes their position in clockwise manner as follows

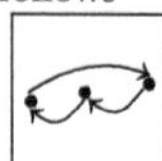

8. (*e*) Here, the pattern of movement of elements is as shown below.

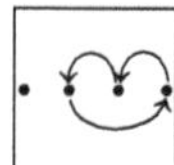

9. (*d*) Here, the line rotates 90° anti-clockwise and top and bottom elements interchange their positions. Among, the given figures, only option figure (d) follows the similar pattern.

10. (*c*) The figure rotates through 90° clockwise in such a way that symbols attached to the upper portion of the figure remain unchanged and symbols attached to the lower portion of the figure get replaced by new symbols.

11. (*a*) Section (ii) of the original pair contains a figure whose sides are two more than that of the figure in section (i) and the lines inside and outside of the main figure in section (ii) are two more than that of the lines in section (i).

12. (*e*) The main figure is the water image of (i), and appears in the a pair.

13. (*a*) The whole figure rotates by 180° clockwise and then one of its left petals is shaded and the shading of the half shaded petal is changed.

14. (*e*) Figure (ii) is the water image of figure (i).

15. (*c*) All the three arrows get laterally inverted in such a way that head of the top arrow gets shaded, the head of the middle arrow gets reversed and the head of the third arrow remains unchanged.

16. (*c*) Design in section (i) is rotated through 180° to obtain the design in section (ii).

17. (*e*) Both the main designs and pair of two small designs interchange their places where the main design rotates through 90° clockwise.

18. (*b*) The figure gets laterally inverted from section (i) to section (ii) of the original pair.

19. (*e*) One line segment is added to the existing figure from section (i) to section (ii) of the original pair.

20. (*c*) The main figure rotates through 90° anti-clockwise and a new white leaf is added at the clockwise end.

21. (*b*) The existing figure gets enlarged and inverted and the original figure gets inserted into it from section (i) to (ii).

22. (*e*) The lower figure rotates through 90° anti-clockwise and the upper figure rotates through 90° clockwise.

23. (*b*) The upper left, the upper right and the lower right element rotate by 90° anti-clockwise. The shading in lower left square rotates by 45° anti-clockwise while the shading of the upper right triangle gets changed.

24. (*c*) The whole figure rotates by 90° clockwise. The lower most remains static while the remaining three shift one step upwards in a cyclic order.

25. (*d*) The upper element of section (ii) is 180° rotated form of (i), the middle of section (ii) is obtained by reversing the arrow head of figure (i) while lower one is obtained by rotating the middle element through 180°.

26. (*a*) The upper element rotates by 135° clockwise and shifts to lower right. The middle element rotates 90° clockwise and shifts to upper left while the lower right element rotates 90° clockwise and shifts to the centre.

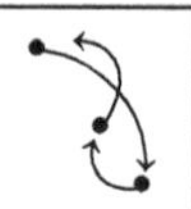

TYPE 03

Finding the Pair of Figures having Pattern other than the Original Pair

This type of analogy is just opposite in nature to the previous type of analogy (Type 02 Analogy). Unlike the previous one, in this type of questions, the candidates are required to select that pair of figures from answer pairs which does not bear the same relationship as shown by the original pair and the number denoted to that pair of figures is the correct answer.

Some examples are given below to explain this type of questions.

DIRECTIONS ~ (Example Nos. 26 and 27) *In each of the following questions, a related pair of figures (original pair) is followed by five numbered pairs of figures. Out of these five/four have relationship similar to that in the original pair. Only one pair of figures does not have similar relationship. Select that pair of figures which does not have a relationship similar to that in the original pair. That pair of figures is your answer.*

***Ex* 26 Original Pair**

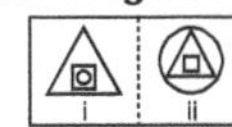

Answer Pairs

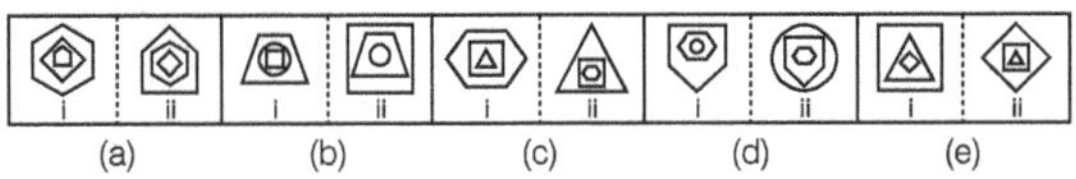

Solution (c) The innermost figure becomes the outermost figure, the outermost figure comes in the middle and the figure in the middle becomes the innermost figure. Pair (c) does not follow this pattern.

***Ex* 27 Original Pair**

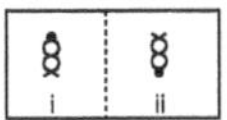

Answer Pairs

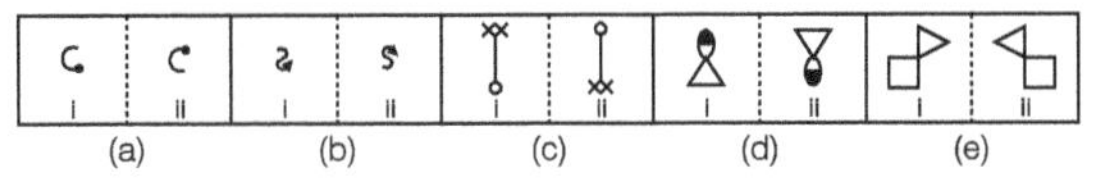

Solution (e) Section (ii) is the water image of section (i).

Practice / CORNER 2.3

DIRECTIONS ~ (Q. Nos. 1-24) *In each of the following questions, a related pair of figures (original pair) is followed by five numbered pairs of figures marked (a), (b), (c), (d) and (e). Out of these five/four have relationship similar to that in the original pair. Only one pair of figures does not have similar relationship. Select that pair of figures which does not have a relationship similar to that in the original pair. That pair of figures is your answer.*

1. Original Pair

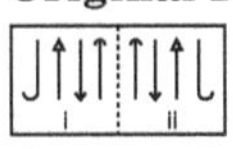

Answer Pairs

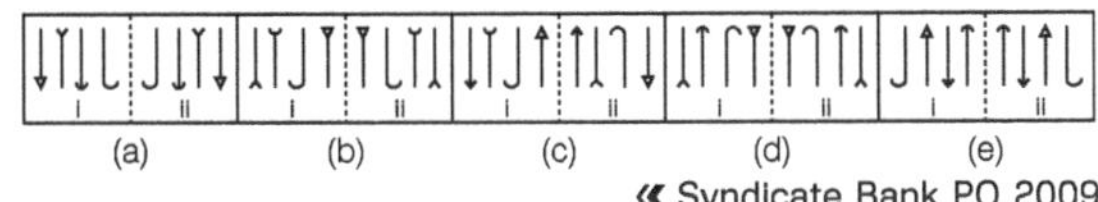

« Syndicate Bank PO 2009

2. Original Pair

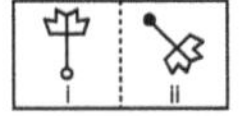

Answer Pairs

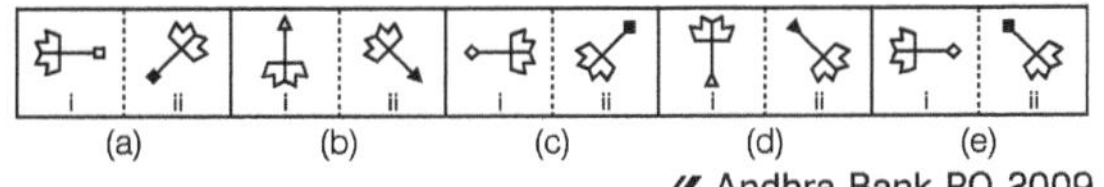

« Andhra Bank PO 2009

3. Original Pair

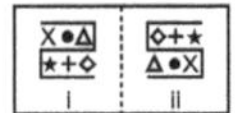

Answer Pairs

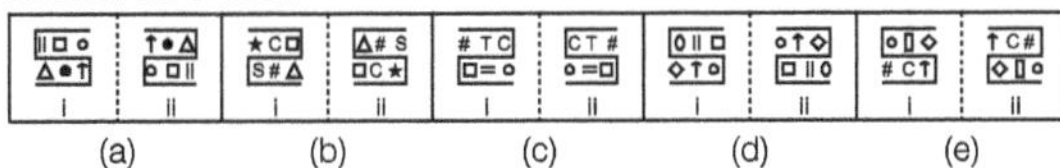

4. Original Pair

Answer Pairs

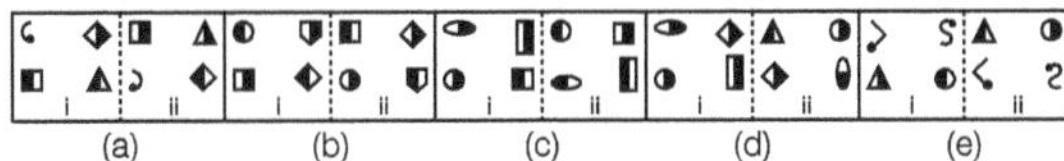

5. Original Pair

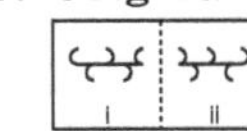

Answer Pairs

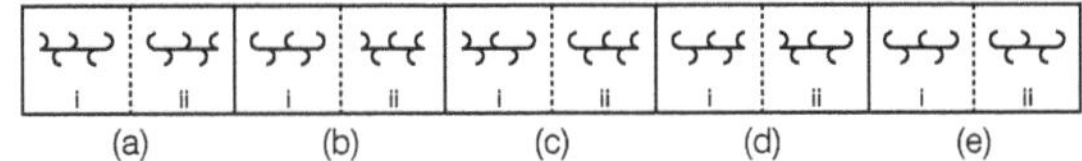

6. Original Pair

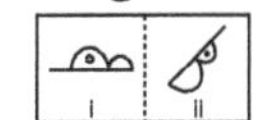

Answer Pairs

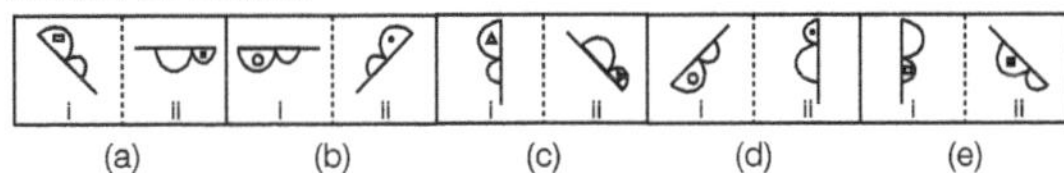

7. Original Pair

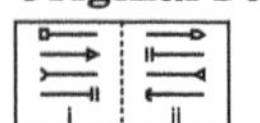

Answer Pairs

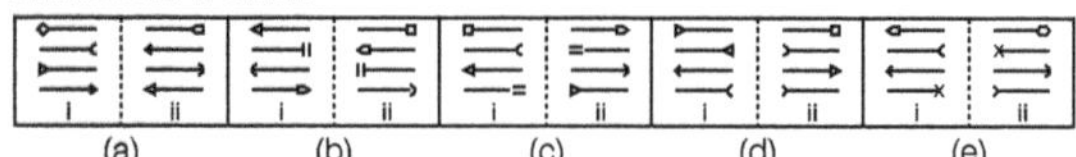

8. Original Pair

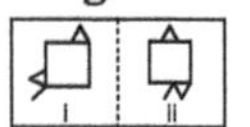

Answer Pairs

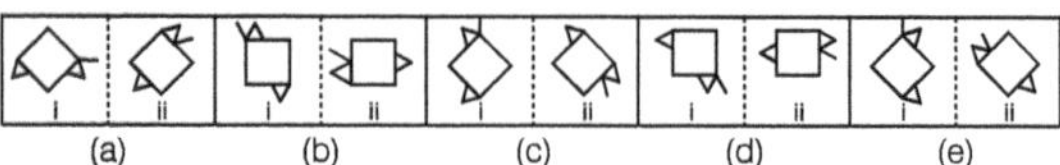

9. Original Pair

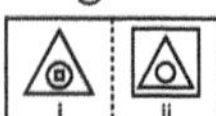

Answer Pairs

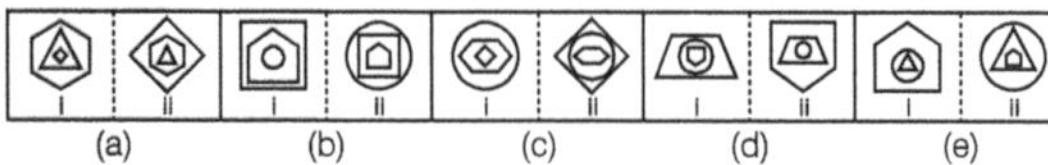

10. Original Pair

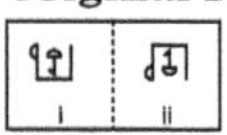

Answer Pairs

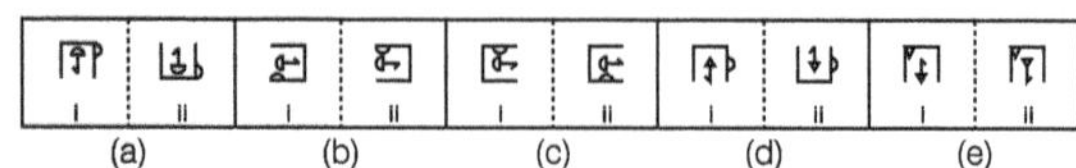

11. Original Pair

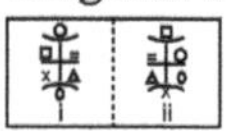

Answer Pairs

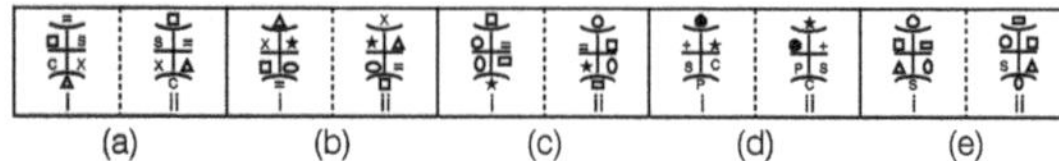

12. Original Pair

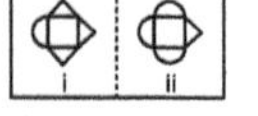

Answer Pairs

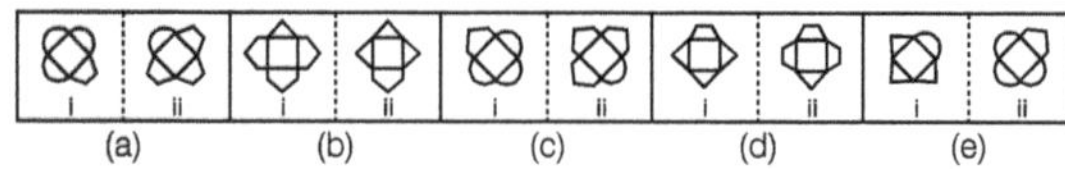

13. Original Pair

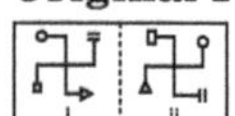

Answer Pairs

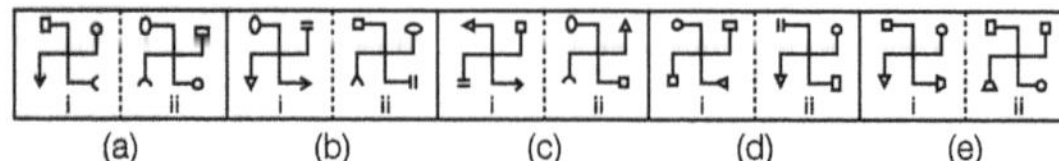

14. Original Pair

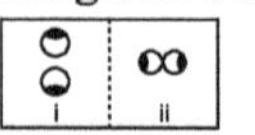

Answer Pairs

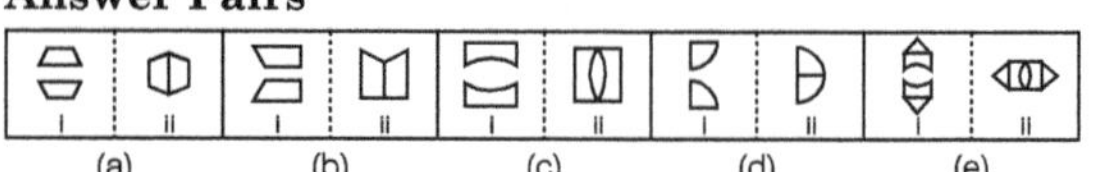

15. Original Pair

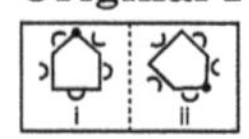

Answer Pairs

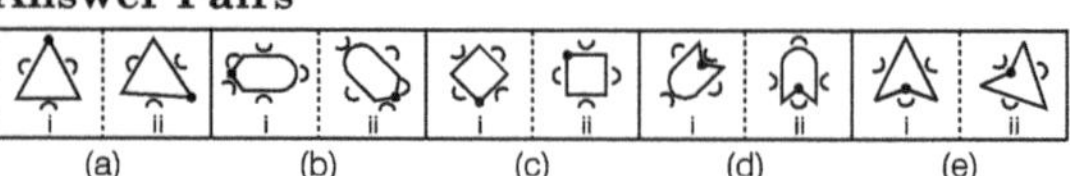

16. Original Pair

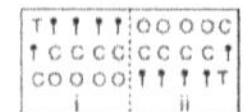

Answer Pairs

(a) (b) (c) (d) (e)

17. Original Pair

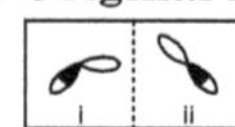

Answer Pairs

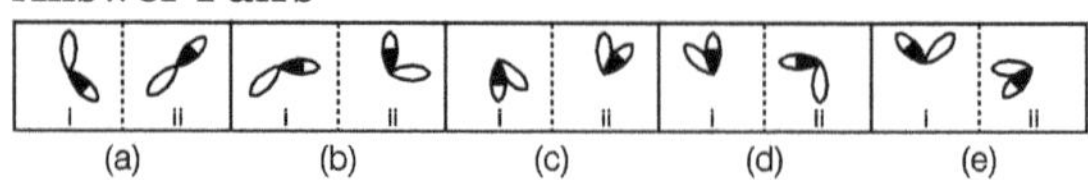

« Punjab & Sindh Bank PO 2009

18. Original Pair

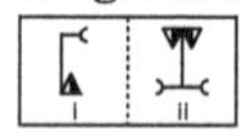

Answer Pairs

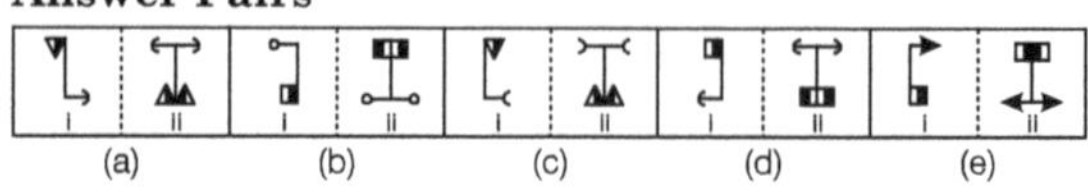

« BOB PO 2009

19. Original Pair

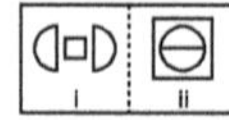

Answer Pairs

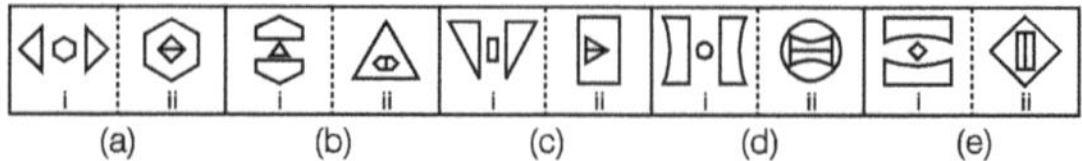

20. Original Pair

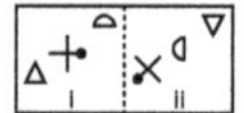

Answer Pairs

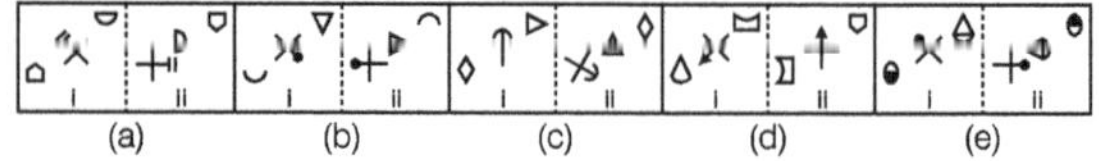

21. Original Pair

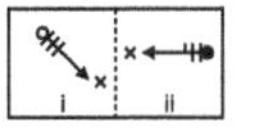

Answer Pairs

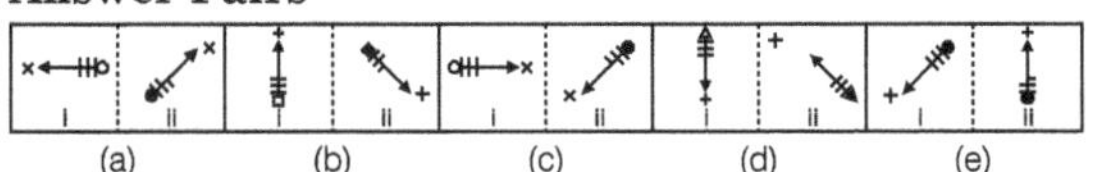

(a) (b) (c) (d) (e)

22. Original Pair

Answer Pairs

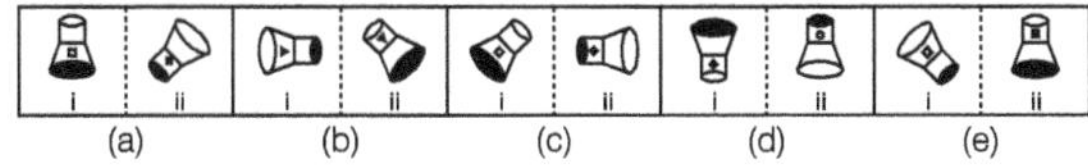

(a) (b) (c) (d) (e)

23. Original Pair

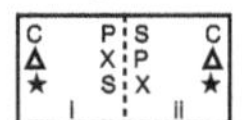

Answer Pairs

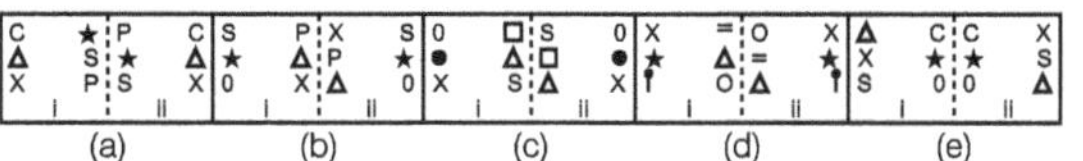

(a) (b) (c) (d) (e)

24. Original Pair

Answer Pairs

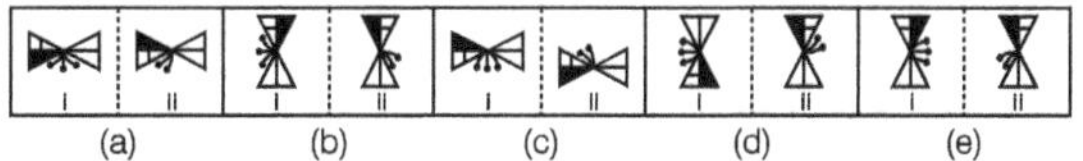

(a) (b) (c) (d) (e)

Answers / WITH EXPLANATIONS

1. (*c*) The first, second, third and fourth symbols, counting from left hand side become fourth, third, second and first symbols, respectively and one symbol is laterally reversed.

2. (*e*) The figure rotates through 135° clockwise in such a way that the head of the pin gets shaded.

3. (*b*) The main design gets reversed and all the symbols inside the design interchange their positions as shown in the diagram.

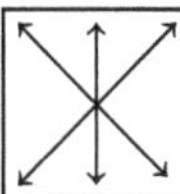

4. (*d*) The symbols interchange their positions from section (i) to (ii) as shown in the diagram in such a way that symbols get reversed at the new position.

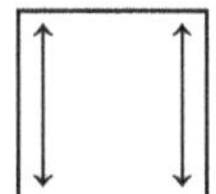

5. (*e*) All the arcs on the line get reversed except the arc present on the upper middle position.

6. (*b*) The main figure rotates through 45° anti-clockwise in such a way that it gets reversed at the new position, the extended line segment shifts to the opposite end and the circle inside the figure also shifts to the small semi-circle and gets shaded.

7. (*b*) The first, second, third and fourth arrows, counting from the top position become first, third, fourth and second arrows, respectively in such a way that one side is added to the head of the first arrow, the head of second and third arrows get reversed and first and fourth arrow get laterally inverted at the new position.

8. (*c*) Single triangle present on the boundary of the square moves half side anti-clockwise, the other triangle with a line attached to it moves one side in the anti-clockwise direction and gets reversed at the new position.

9. (*e*) The innermost figure becomes the outermost figure, the middle figure becomes the innermost figure and the outermost figure comes at the middle position.

10. (*e*) The main figure and the design inside it get inverted.

11. (*c*) All the symbols change their positions as shown in the diagram or we can say that the upper three elements and the lower three elements interchange positions in opposite directions.

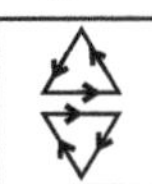

12. (*e*) Three triangles appearing on the boundary of the square are converted into a single triangle and the single semi-circle is converted into three semi-circles.

13. (*a*) The main figure rotates through 90° clockwise in such a way that both the designs appearing on the bottom ends of the figure are converted into new designs at the new positions.

14. (*d*) Both the figures rotate through 90° clockwise and appear along the straight line adjacent to each other.

15. (*b*) The main figure rotates through 135° clockwise in such a way that all the cups get reversed at the new positions.

16. (*a*) The symbols in the first and third rows interchange their positions and get rearranged at the new positions, symbols in the middle row also get rearranged in a particular way.

17. (*c*) The white leaf rotates through 135° anti-clockwise and half shaded leaf rotates through 90° anti-clockwise.

18. (*a*) The figure rotates through 180° and the shaded portion shifts to other side and an identical figure is attached to the pre-existing figure.

19. (*e*) From section (i) to section (ii), the small figure in between two figures gets enlarged and becomes the outer figure. The two similar figures get attached together and rotate through 90° anti-clockwise and come inside the outer figure.

20. (*d*) The figure at the bottom left position gets inverted and appears at the top right position, the figure in the middle rotates through 135° clockwise and occupies the bottom left position and the figure at the top right position rotates through 90° anti-clockwise and appears in the central position.

21. (*d*) The figure rotates through 135° clockwise in such a way that the circle at the back side of it gets shaded and one line segment appearing on the arrow is deleted.

22. (*d*) The main figure rotates through 135° anti-clockwise, whereas in figure (d), the figure rotates through 180°.

23. (*e*) All the signs change their positions in all the answer figures except figure (e), as shown in the diagram.

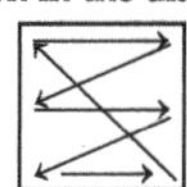

24. (*d*) From section (i) to section (ii) of the original figures, the shaded portion and line present on one side of the main figure interchange their positions and one pin appearing on the top of the figure is deleted.

TYPE 04

Selecting the Correct Set of Figures to Establish Analogy

In this type of questions, the problem figures constitute two figures with two other figures missing, one from each pair. Each missing figure is represented by the sign'?'.

The problem figures are followed by five pairs of answer figures marked as (a), (b), (c), (d) and (e). Candidates are required to select one pair from the answer pairs that will replace the '?' sign and establish a similar relation between figures (i) and (ii) and figures (iii) and (iv).

Examples given below will give a better idea about such type of questions.

DIRECTIONS ~ (Example Nos. 28-32) *In the following questions, find the best substitute from the answer figures which replaces the sign of question marks such that figure* (iii) *is related to figure* (iv) *in the same way as figure* (i) *relates to figure* (ii).

***Ex* 28 Problem Figures**

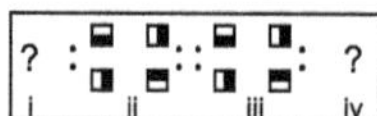

Answer Figures

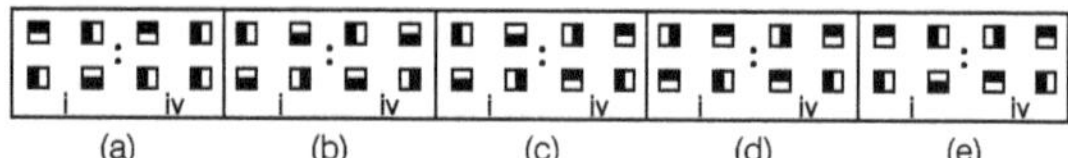

***Solution* (c)** From section (i) to section (ii) of the problem figures, all the squares rotate 90° anti-clockwise and the same process repeats from section (iii) to section (iv).

***Ex* 29 Problem Figures**

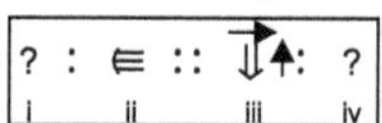

Answer Figures

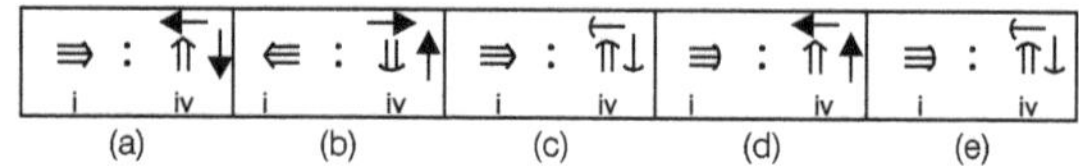

***Solution* (c)** Here, the main figure gets inverted in such a way that design on the head of the figure is changed into new design. The same process repeats from section (iii) to section (iv) of the problem figures.

***Ex* 30 Problem Figures**

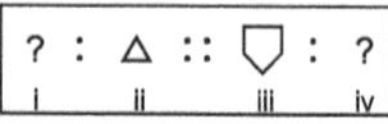

Answer Figures

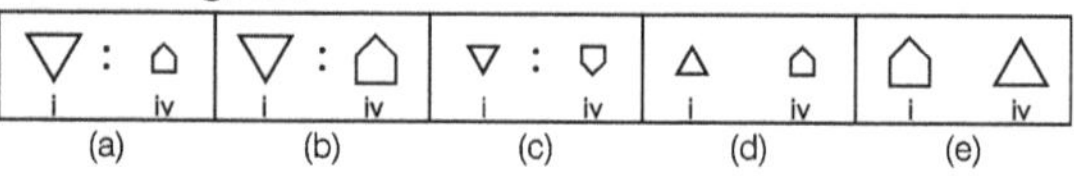

***Solution* (a)** From section (i) to section (ii) of the problem figures, the figure gets inverted and becomes small in size.

***Ex* 31 Problem Figures**

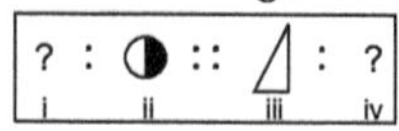

Answer Figures

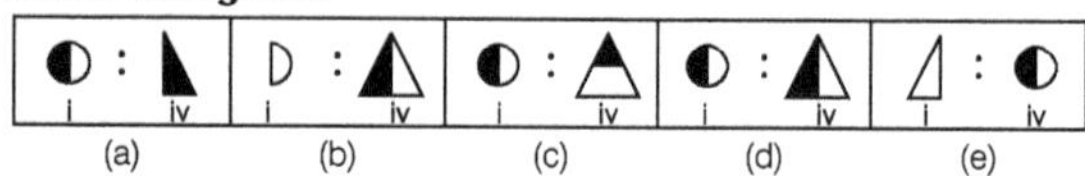

***Solution* (b)** From section (i) to section (ii) of the problem figures, an identical figure appears on the other side of the figure and existing figure gets shaded.

***Ex* 32 Problem Figures**

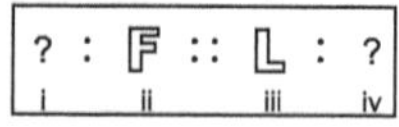

Answer Figures

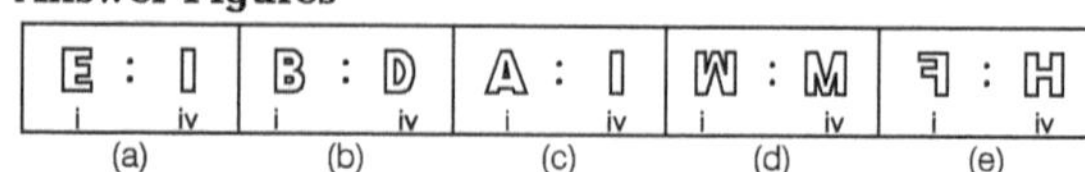

***Solution* (a)** One segment (lower) of the existing figure is removed from figure in section (i) to obtain the figure in section (ii).

Practice CORNER 2.4

DIRECTIONS ~ (Q. Nos. 1-18) *In each of the following questions, there are four figures* (i), (ii), (iii) *and* (iv) *which constitute the problem set and answer figures marked* as (a), (b), (c), (d) *and* (e) *each consisting of two figures marked* as (i) *and* (iv) *which constitute the answer set. Select a figure from the answer sets the contents of which best substitute* (?) *in the problem sets such that figure* (iii) *is related to figure* (iv) *in same way as figure* (i) *is related to figure* (ii).

1. Original Pair

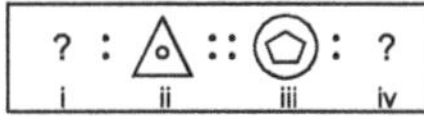

Answer Pairs

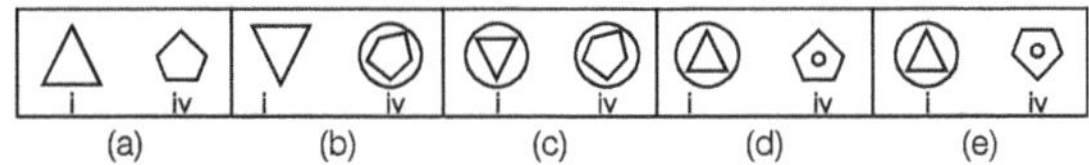

2. Original Pair

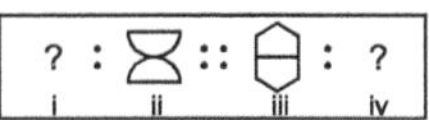

Answer Pairs

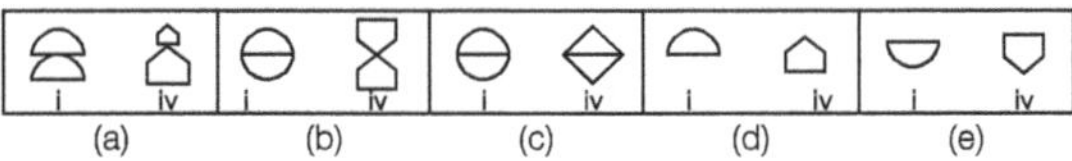

3. Original Pair

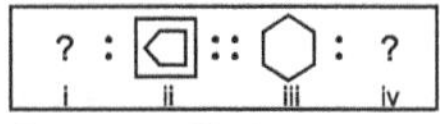

Answer Pairs

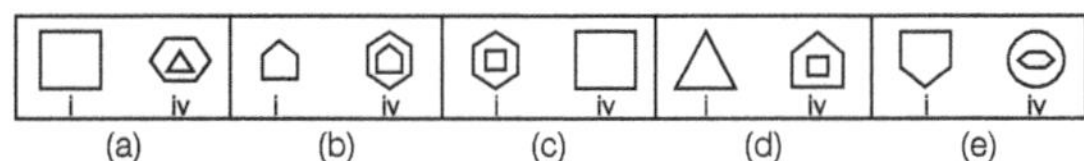

4. Original Pair

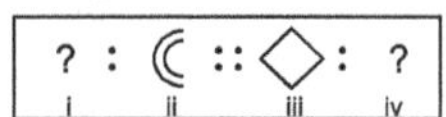

Answer Pairs

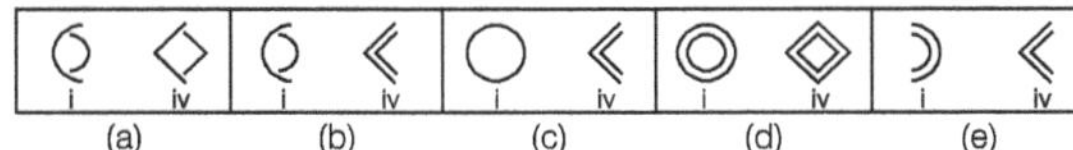

5. Original Pair

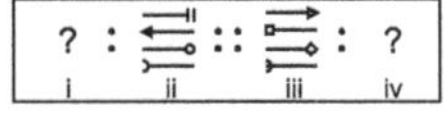

Answer Pairs

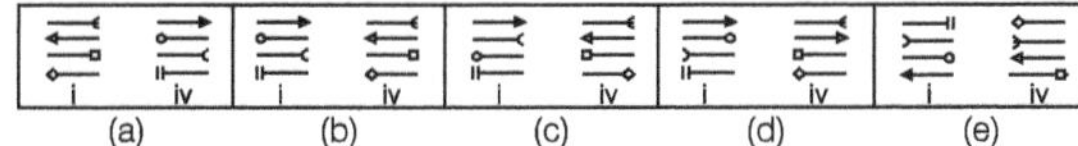

6. Original Pair

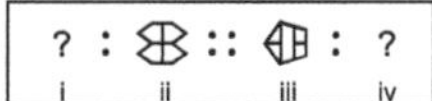

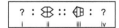

Answer Pairs

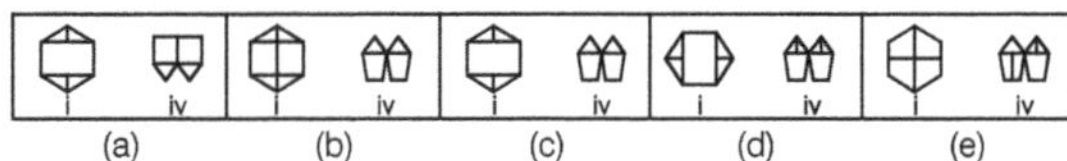

7. Original Pair

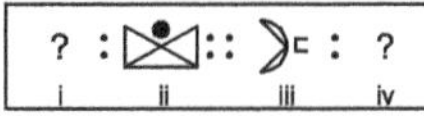

Answer Pairs

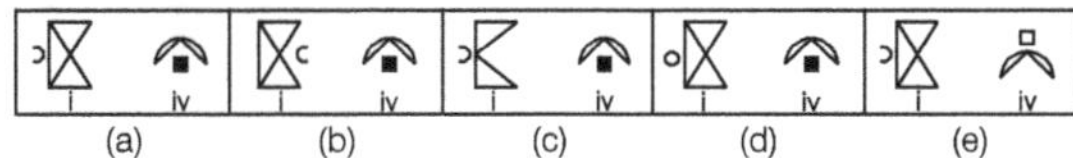

8. Original Pair

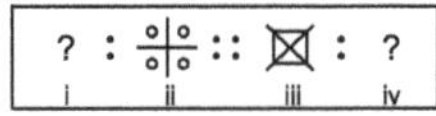

Answer Pairs

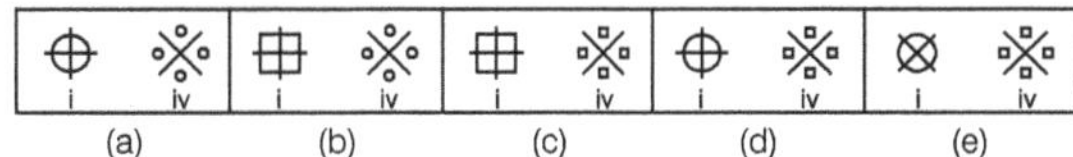

9. Original Pair

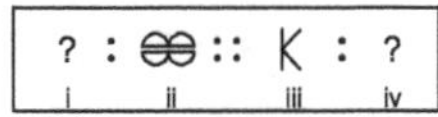

Answer Pairs

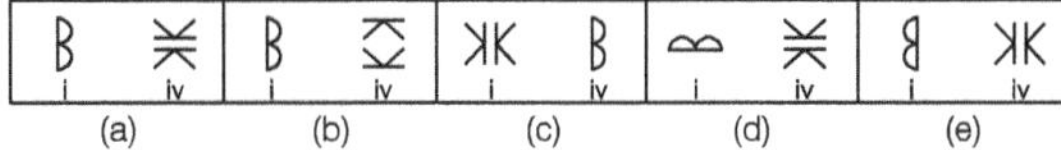

10. Original Pair

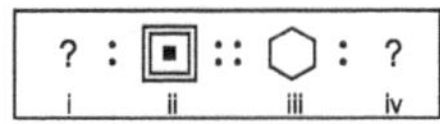

Answer Pairs

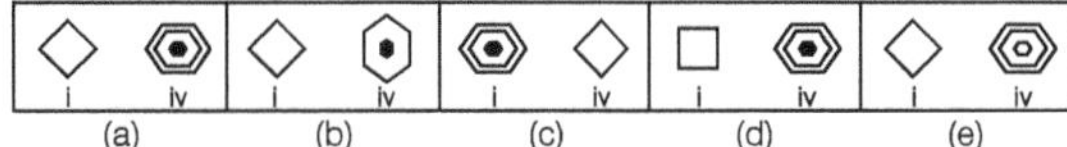

11. Original Pair

Answer Pairs

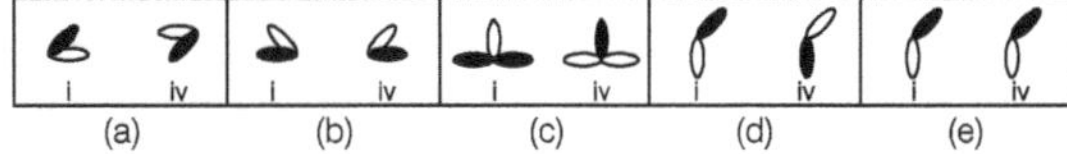

12. Original Pair

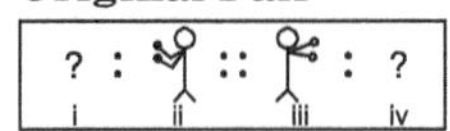

Answer Pairs

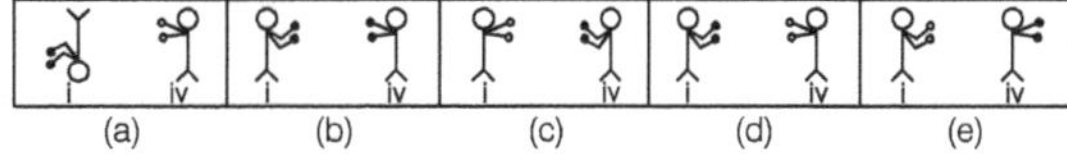

13. Original Pair

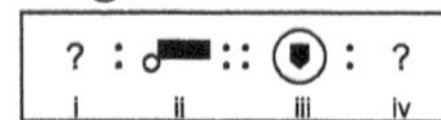

Answer Pairs

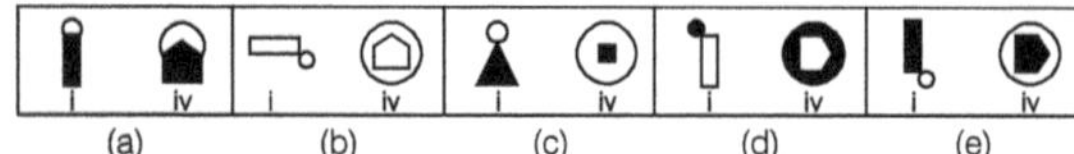

14. Original Pair

Answer Pairs

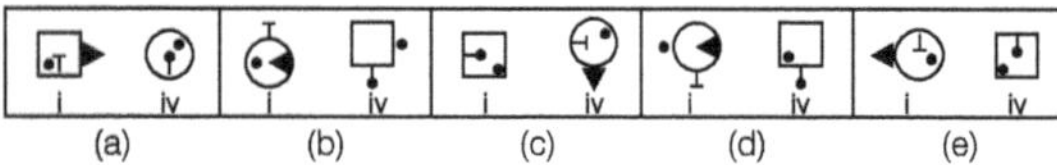

15. Original Pair

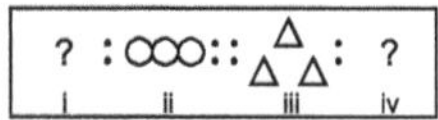

Answer Pairs

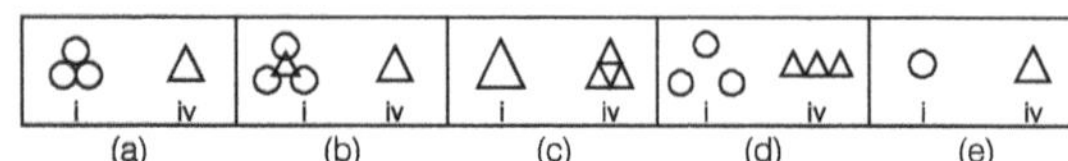

16. Original Pair

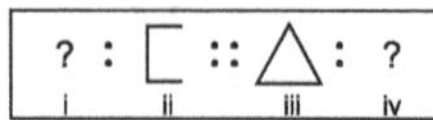

Answer Pairs

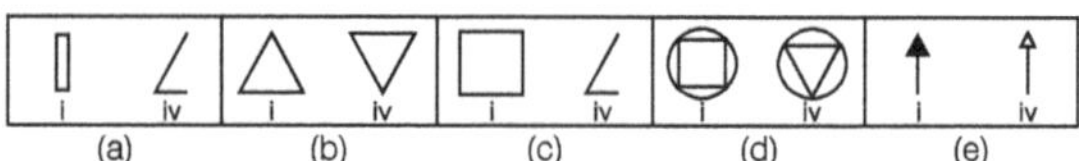

17. Original Pair

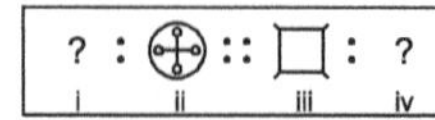

Answer Pairs

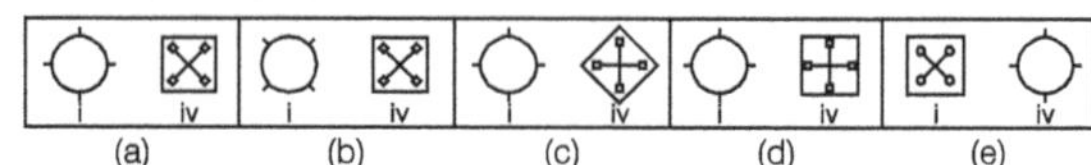

18. Original Pair

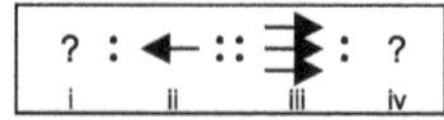

Answer Pairs

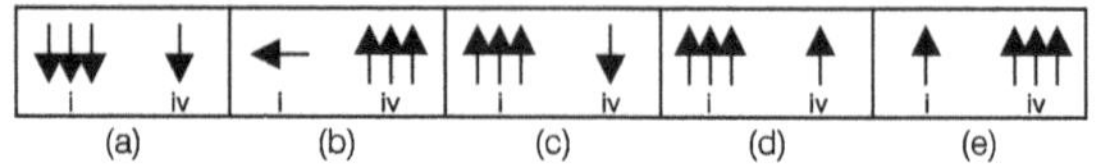

Answers WITH EXPLANATIONS

1. (*d*) Both the figures in a section interchange their positions.

2. (*b*) The upper and lower halves of the figure get inverted at their positions.

3. (*e*) The figure rotates through 90° clockwise and a new figure with number of sides one less than that of the original figure comes outside of it.

4. (*c*) The figure is divided into two halves through a vertical line and the right half comes inside the left half of the figure.

5. (*b*) The lowermost figure shifts to the uppermost position and all the other figures shift one step downwards in such a way that every figure is laterally reversed at the new position.

6. (*b*) The figure rotates through 90° clockwise in such a way that two parallel lines inside the figure are joined together and vertical line is removed and the resultant figure appears in pairs.

7. (*a*) The figure rotates through 90° anti-clockwise in such a way that the small figure is converted into a full one, it gets shaded and shifts to the opposite side of the figure.

8. (*d*) From section (i) to section (ii) of the problem figures, one fourth portion of the circle appeared in each quadrant (i) is converted into a full circle. The same process will be repeated from section (iii) to section (iv) of the problem figures.

9. (*a*) The figure rotates through 90° clockwise in such a way that an inverted identical figure appears on upper side of the original figure.

10. (*d*) The figure rotates through 90° clockwise and two similar concentric figures appear inside it in such a way that the innermost figure gets shaded.

11. (*e*) Black leaf and white leaf rotate through 90° anti-clockwise and clockwise, respectively.

12. (*d*) The figures from one section to the other are getting laterally inverted.

13. (*d*) The figure rotates through 90° anti-clockwise in such a way that the black shaded portion becomes white and the white portion becomes black shaded.

14. (*e*) The whole shaded design is rotated through 180° from one section to the other.

15. (*d*) From section (i) to section (ii), all the three figures get arranged in a straight line.

16. (*c*) From section (i) to section (ii) of the original figures, the right half of the figure is removed.

17. (*a*) From section (i) to section (ii) of the original figures, all the lines outside the main figure shift inside and join together and also four small figures identical to the main figure are attached to the ends of the lines.

18. (*d*) Two arrows, out of three arrows, are removed and the remaining arrow rotates through 90° anti-clockwise.

Master Exercise

DIRECTIONS ~ (Q. Nos. 1-46) *The second figure in the first pair of the problems figures bears a certain relationship with the first figure. Similarly, one of the answer figures bears the same relationship with the first figure in the second pair of the problem figures. You have to select that figure from the set of answer figures which will replace the question mark (?)?*

1. Problem Figures

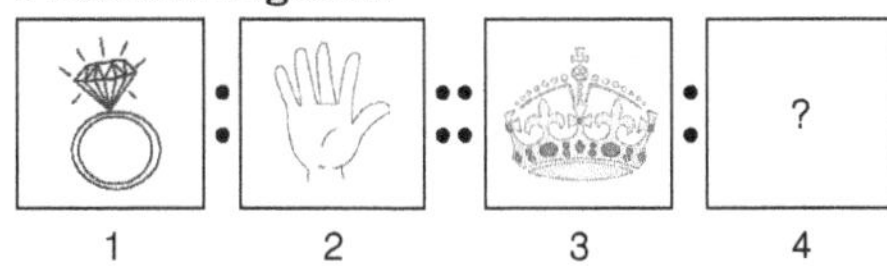

Answer Figures

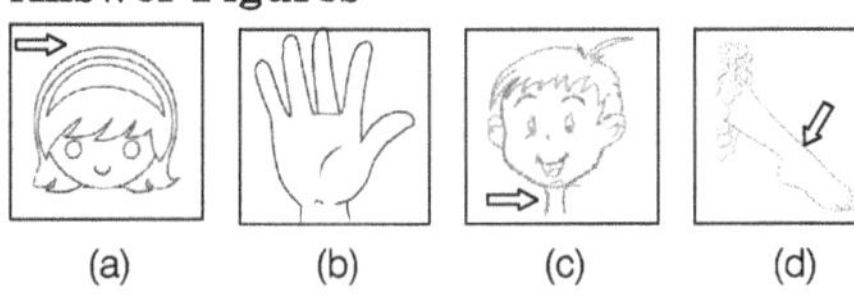

« RRB ALP 2018

2. Problem Figures

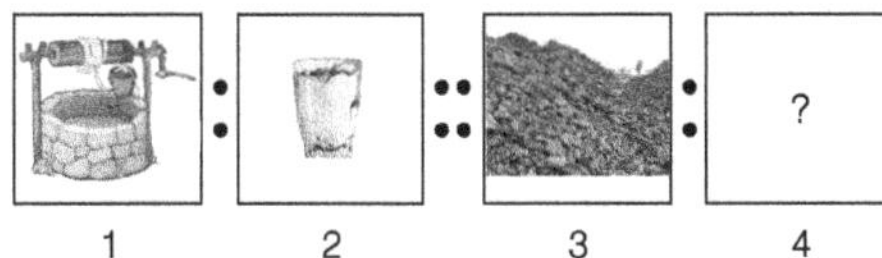

Answer Figures

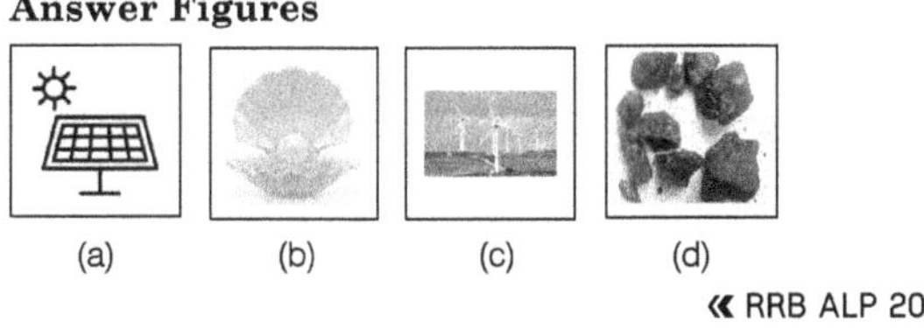

« RRB ALP 2018

3. Problem Figures

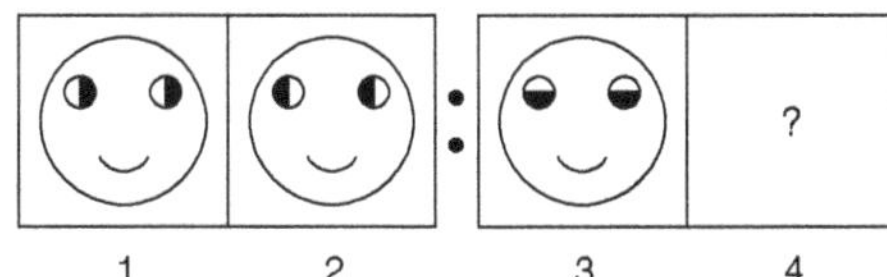

Answer Figures

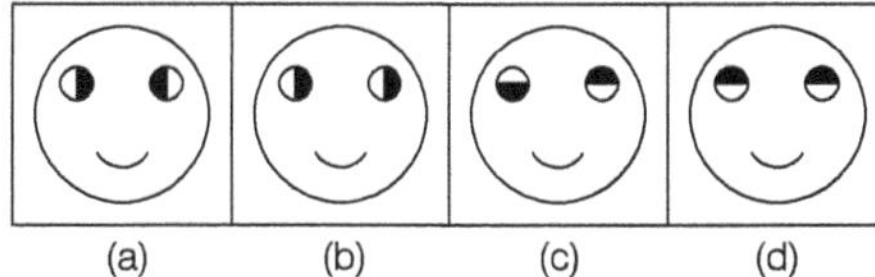

« UP Police Constable 2014

4. Problem Figures

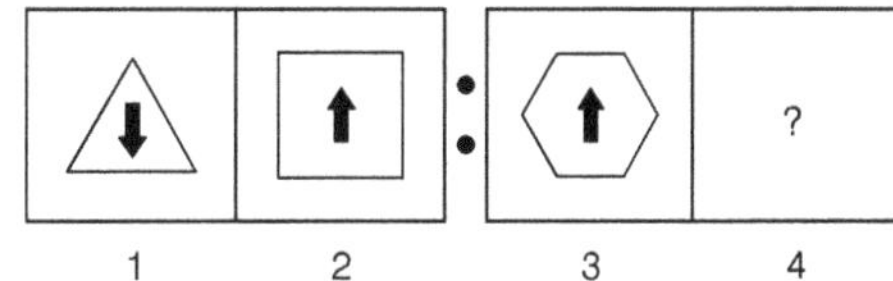

Answer Figures

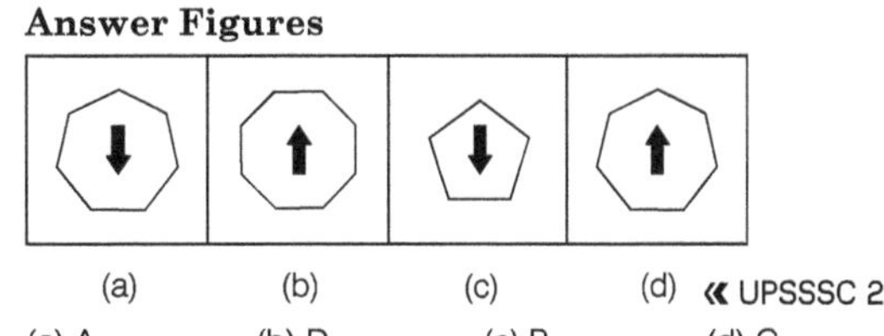

« UPSSSC 2018

(a) A (b) D (c) B (d) C

5. Problem Figures

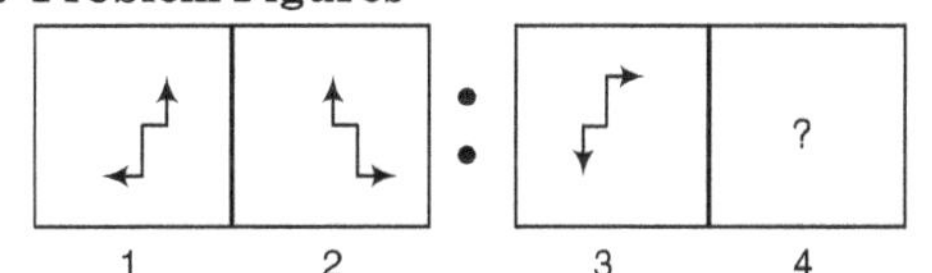

Answer Figures

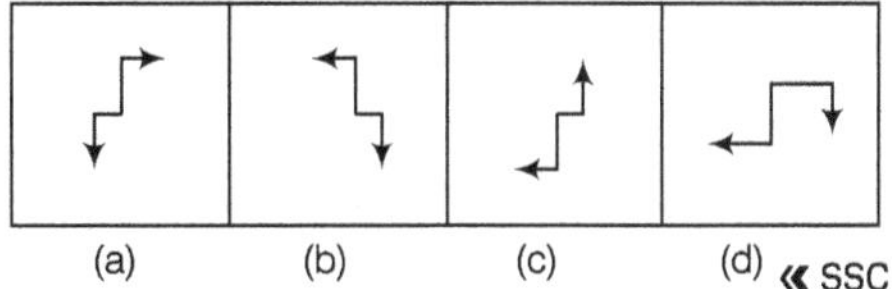

« SSC Steno 2011

6. Problem Figures

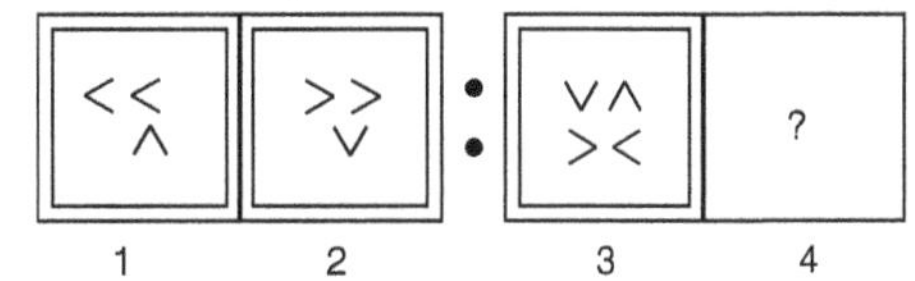

Answer Figures

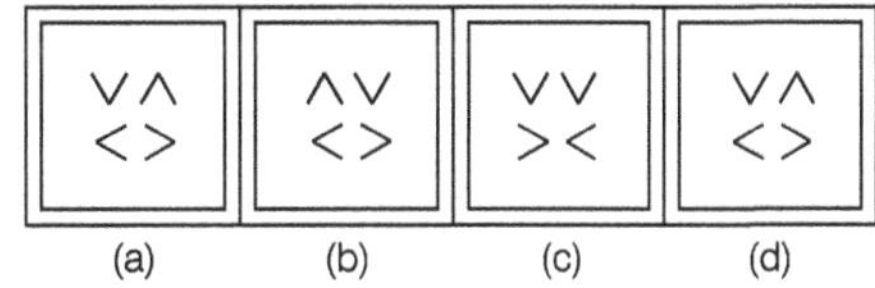

« SSC Steno 2011

7. Problem Figures

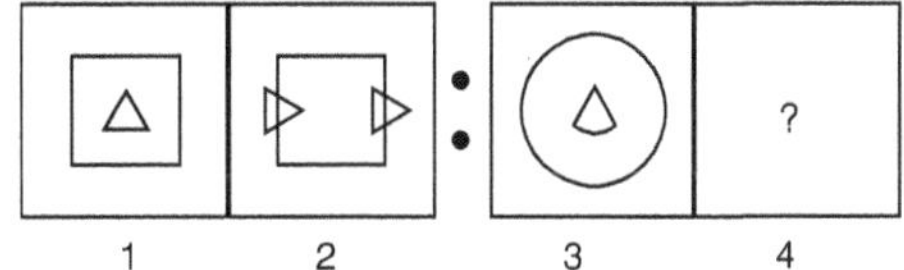

Answer Figures

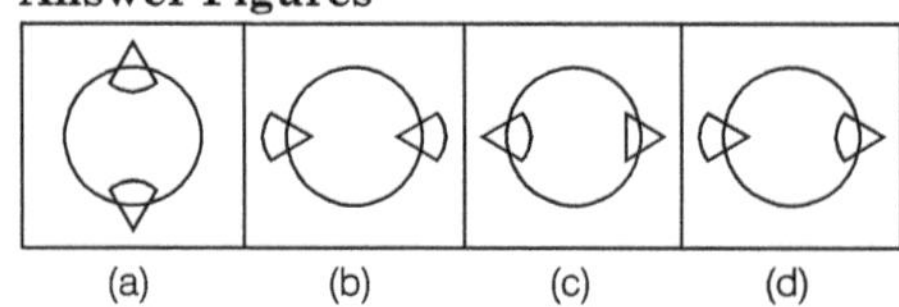

(a) (b) (c) (d)

8. Problem Figures

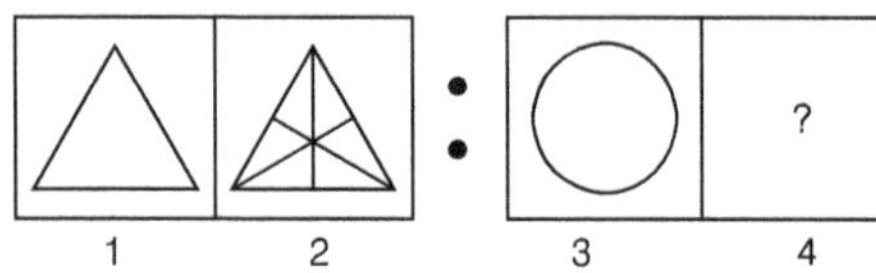

1 2 3 4

Answer Figures

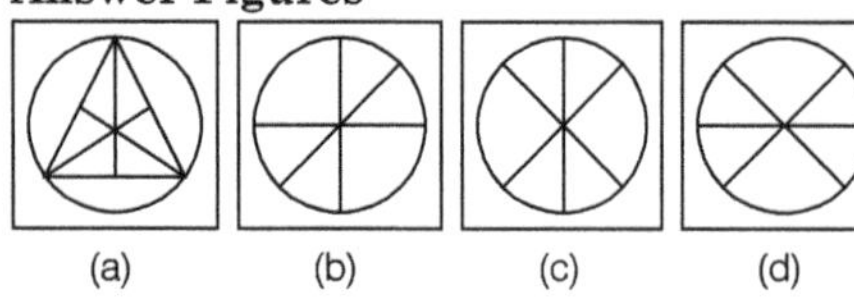

(a) (b) (c) (d)

9. Problem Figures

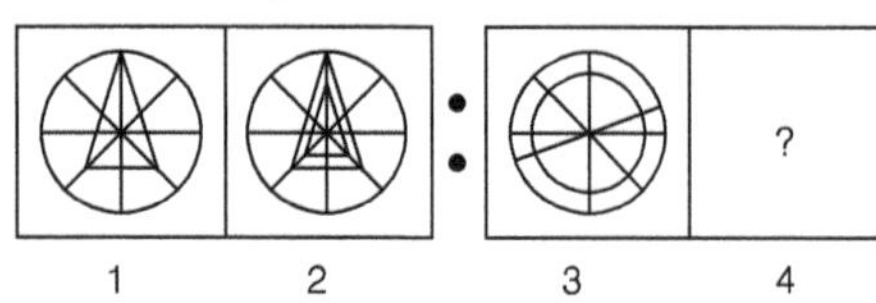

1 2 3 4

Answer Figures

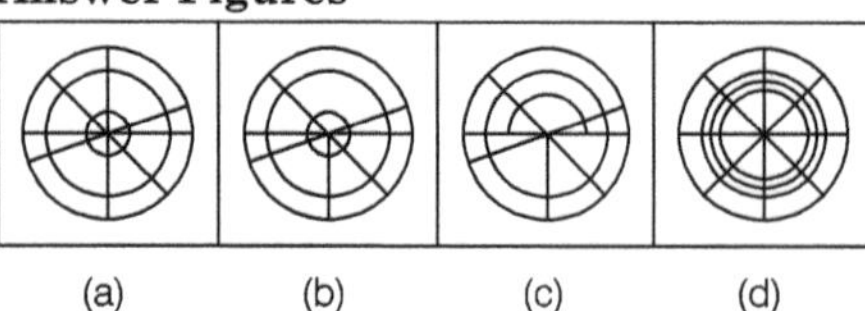

(a) (b) (c) (d)

« SSC CGL 2008

10. Problem Figures

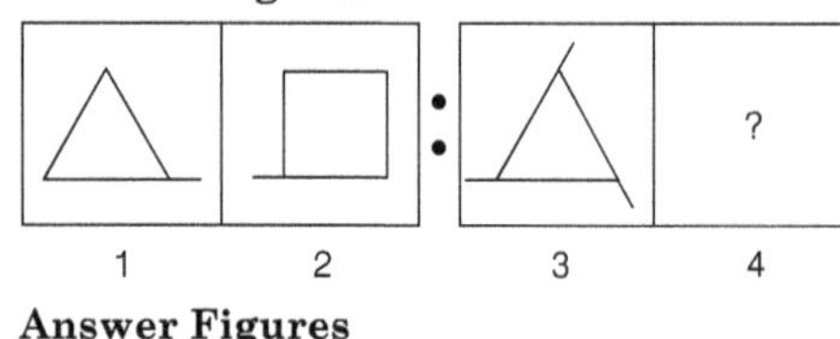

1 2 3 4

Answer Figures

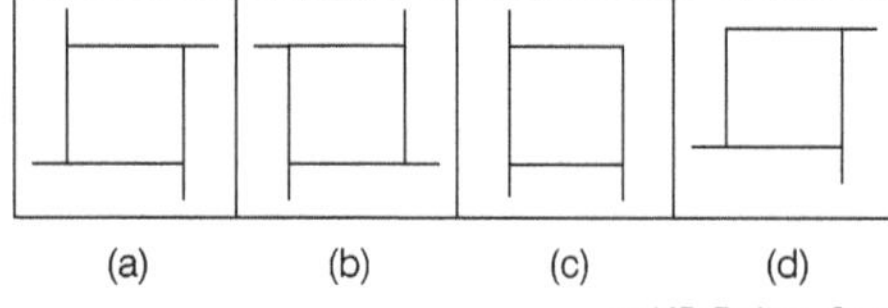

(a) (b) (c) (d)

« UP Police Constable 2014

11. Problem Figures

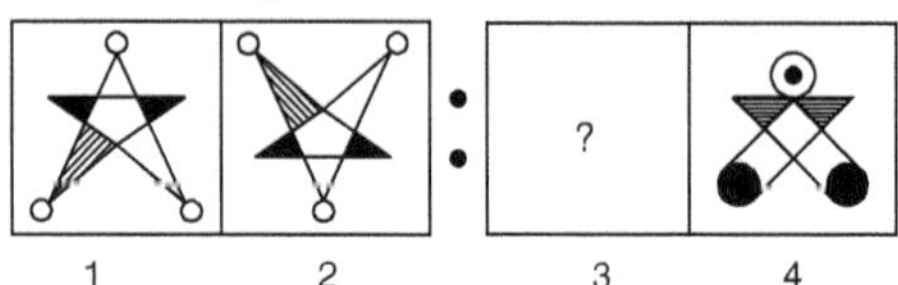

1 2 3 4

Answer Figures

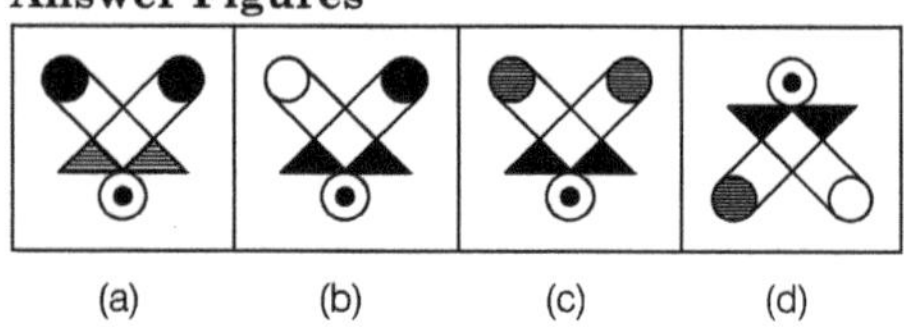

(a) (b) (c) (d)

12. Problem Figures

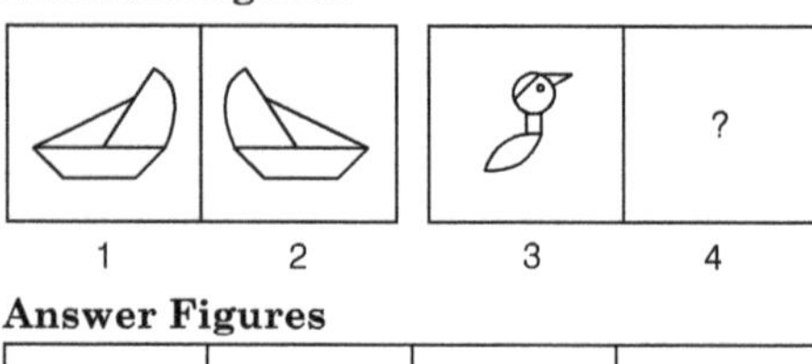

1 2 3 4

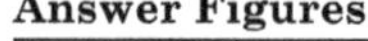

Answer Figures

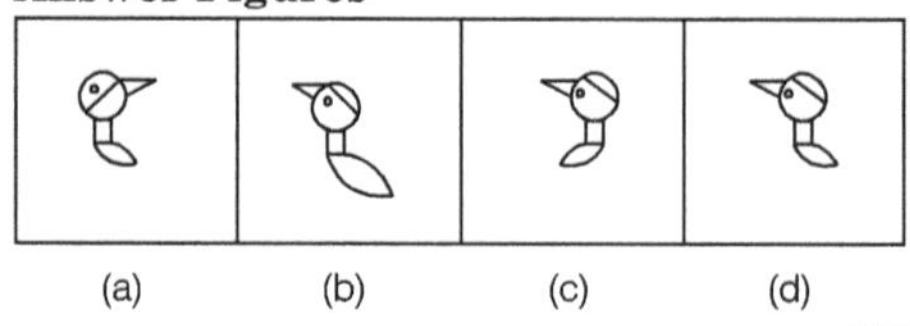

(a) (b) (c) (d)

« SSC CGL 2008

13. Problem Figures

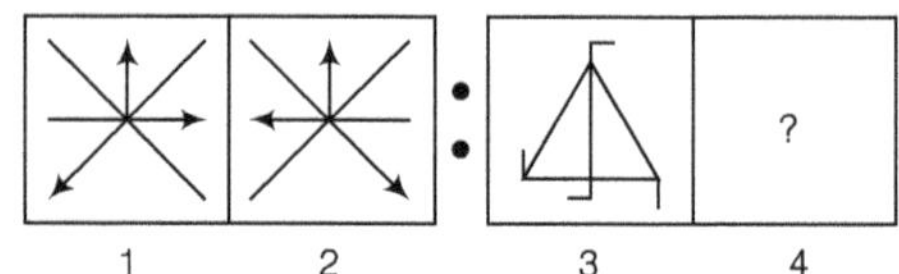

1 2 3 4

Answer Figures

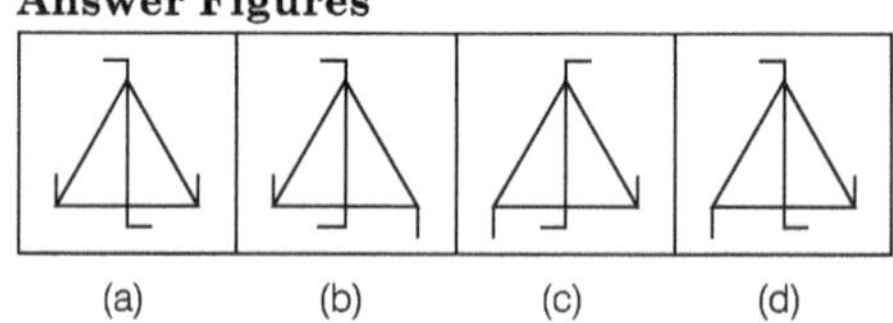

(a) (b) (c) (d)

« SSC CPO 2011

14. Problem Figures

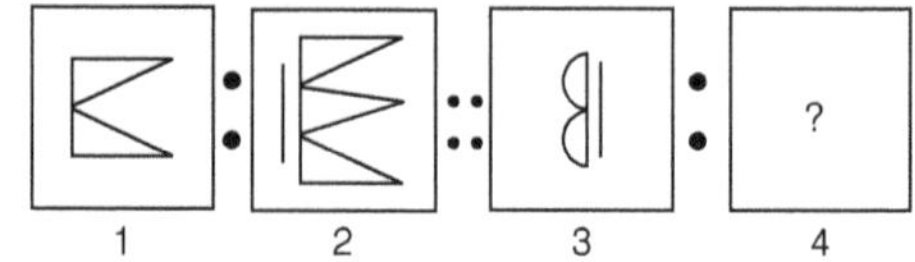

1 2 3 4

Answer Figures

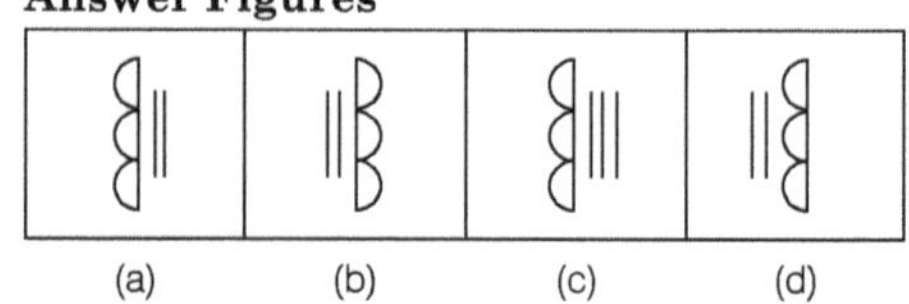

(a) (b) (c) (d)

« SSC CPO 2010

15. Problem Figures

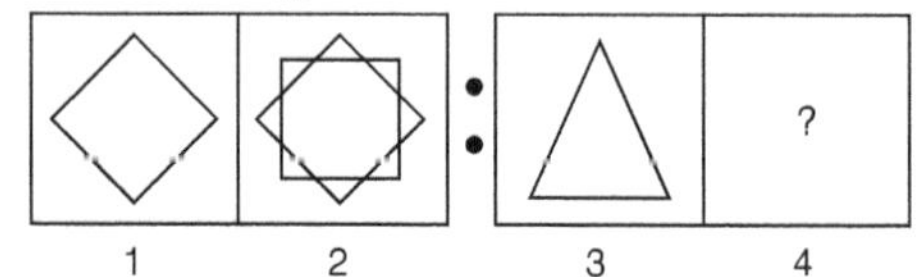

1 2 3 4

Answer Figures

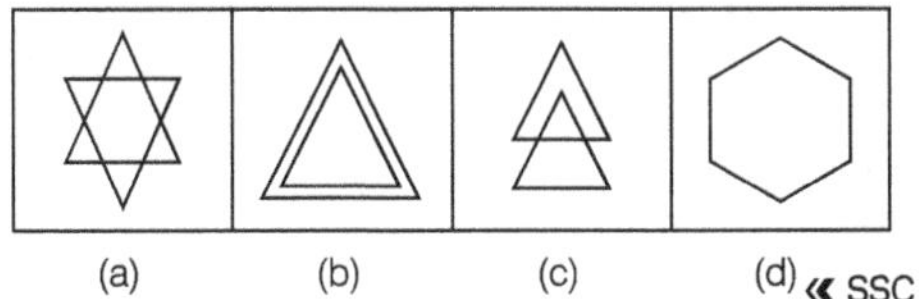

(a) (b) (c) (d) « SSC CPO 2009

16. Problem Figures

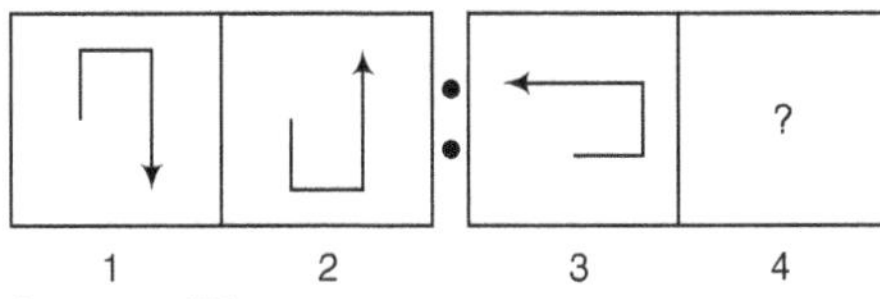

1 2 3 4

Answer Figures

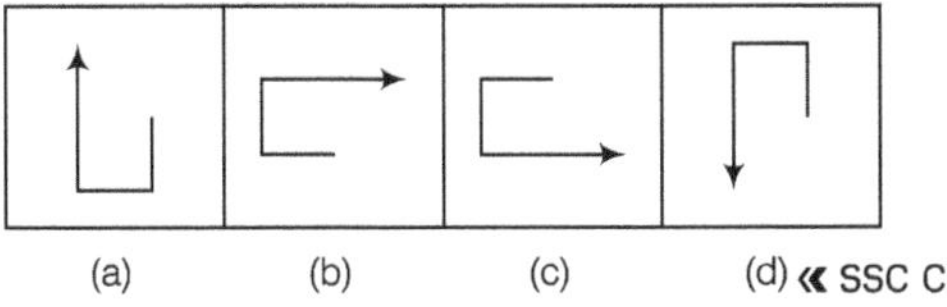

(a) (b) (c) (d) « SSC CPO 2010

17. Problem Figures

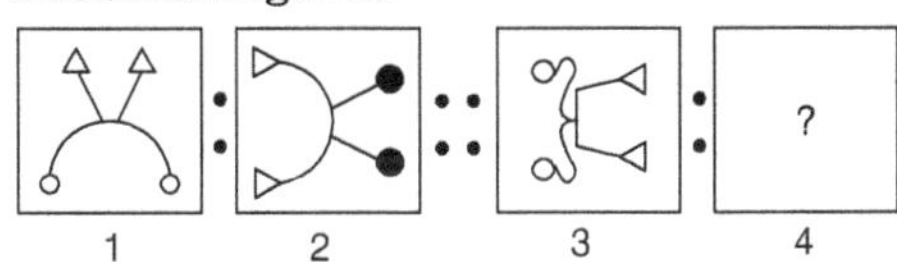

1 2 3 4

Answer Figures

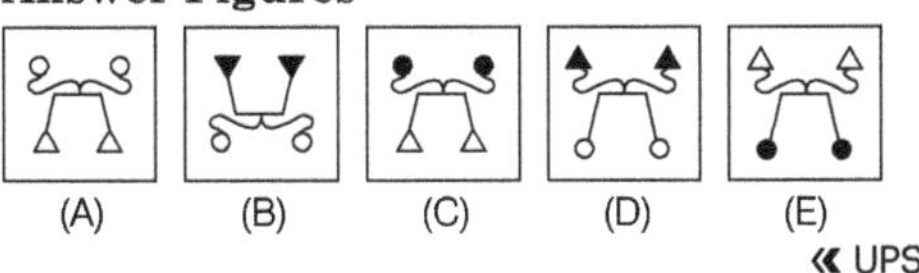

(A) (B) (C) (D) (E)

« UPSSSC 2018

(a) A (b) D (c) E (d) B

18. Problem Figures

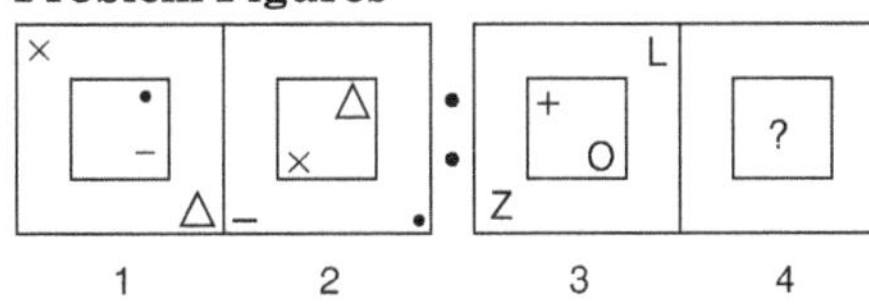

1 2 3 4

Answer Figures

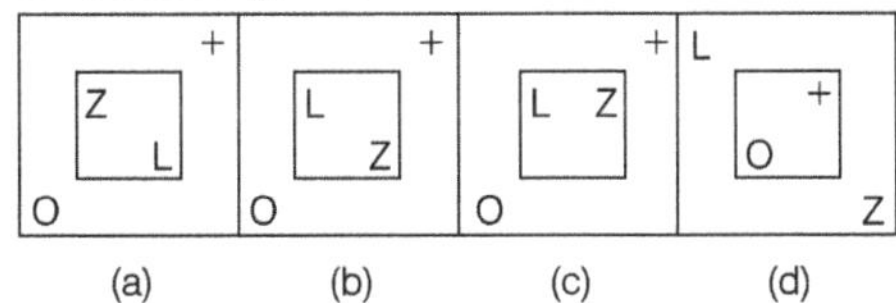

(a) (b) (c) (d)

« UP Police Constable 2018

19. Problem Figures

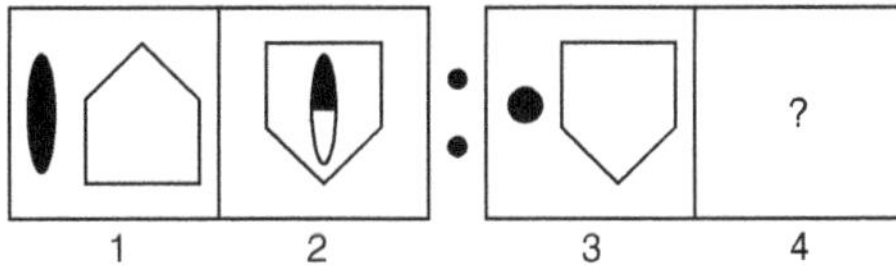

1 2 3 4

Answer Figures

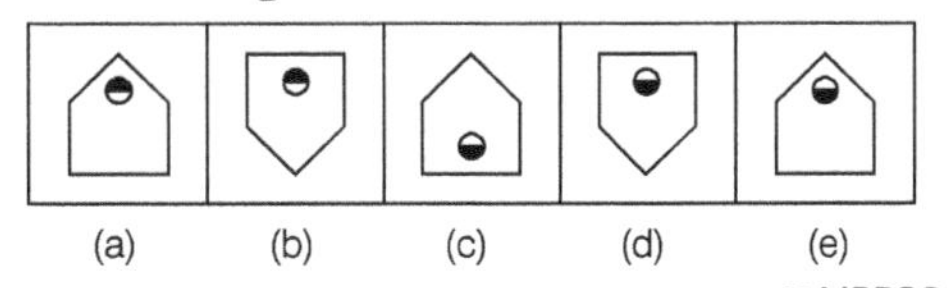

(a) (b) (c) (d) (e)

« MPPSC Pre 2018

20. Problem Figures

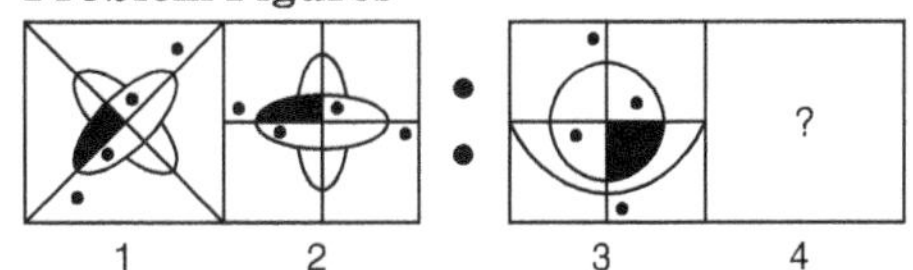

1 2 3 4

Answer Figures

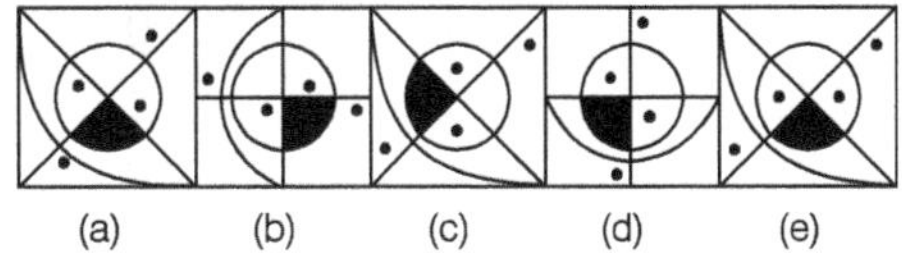

(a) (b) (c) (d) (e)

21. Problem Figures

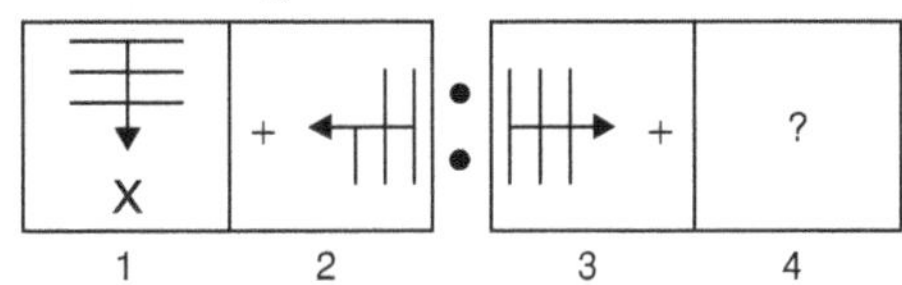

1 2 3 4

Answer Figures

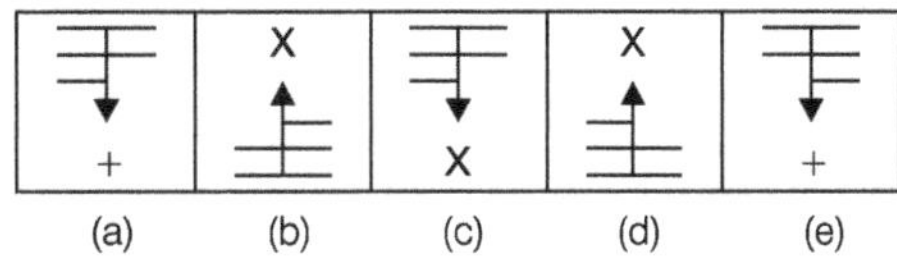

(a) (b) (c) (d) (e)

22. Problem Figures

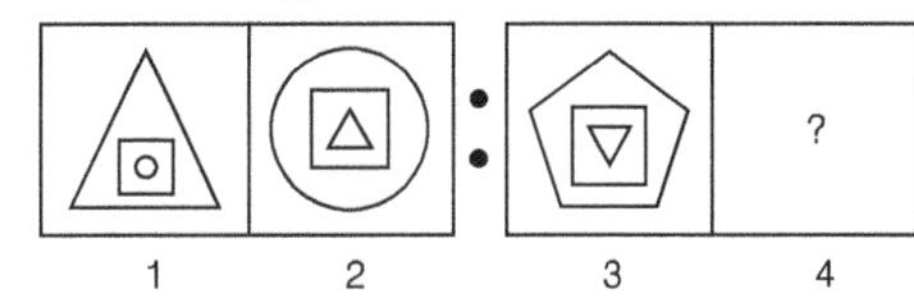

1 2 3 4

Answer Figures

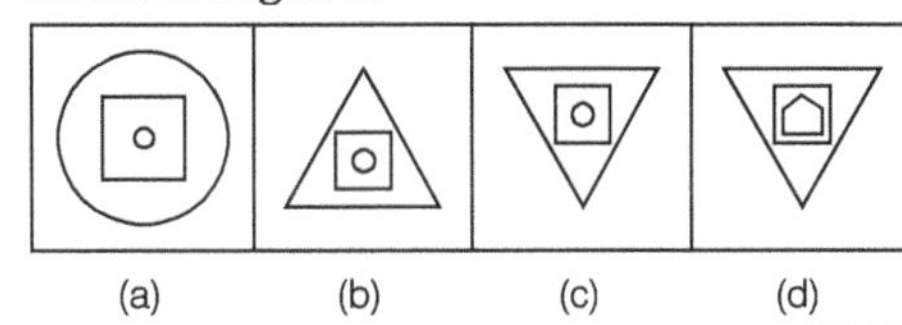

(a) (b) (c) (d)

« SSC Steno 2011

23. Problem Figures

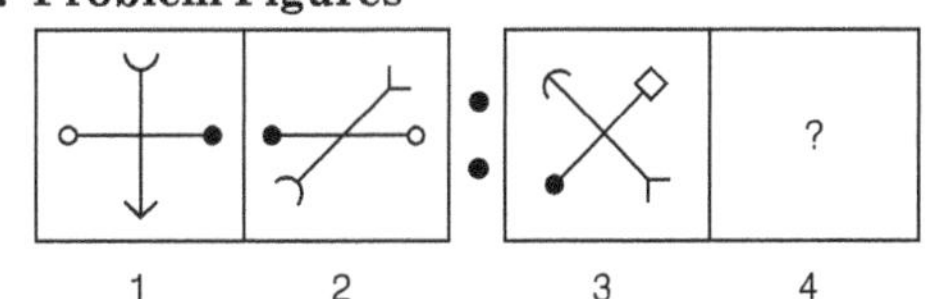

1 2 3 4

Answer Figures

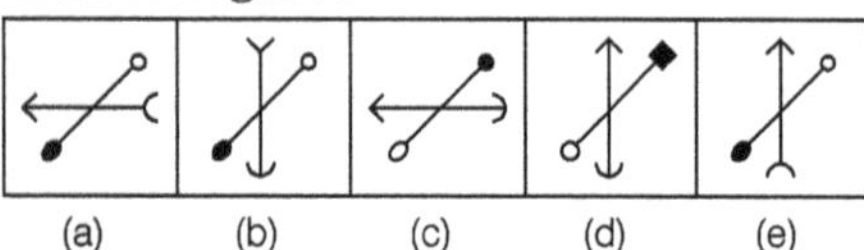

(a) (b) (c) (d) (e)

24. Problem Figures

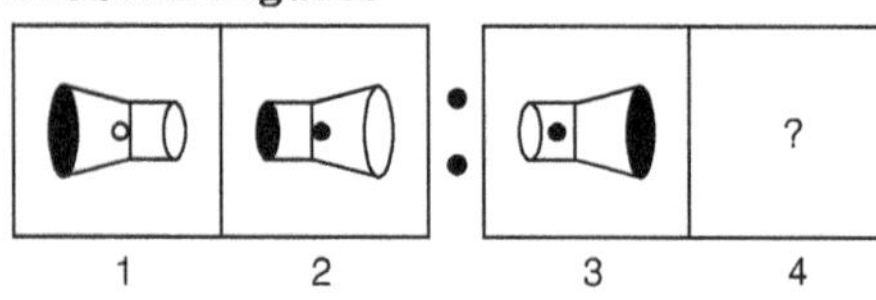

1 2 3 4

Answer Figures

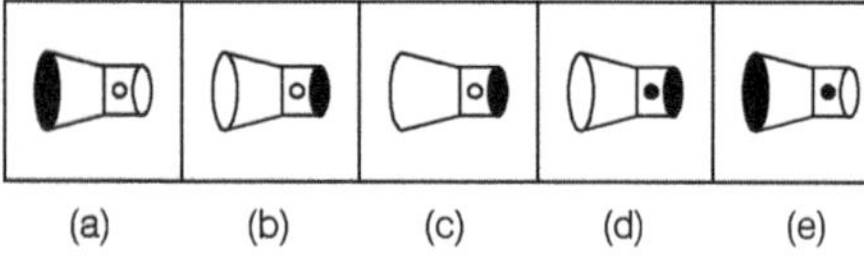

(a) (b) (c) (d) (e)

25. Problem Figures

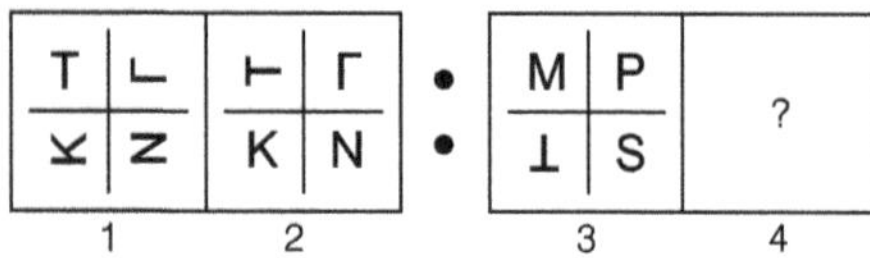

1 2 3 4

Answer Figures

(a) (b) (c) (d) (e)

26. Problem Figures

1 2 3 4

Answer Figures

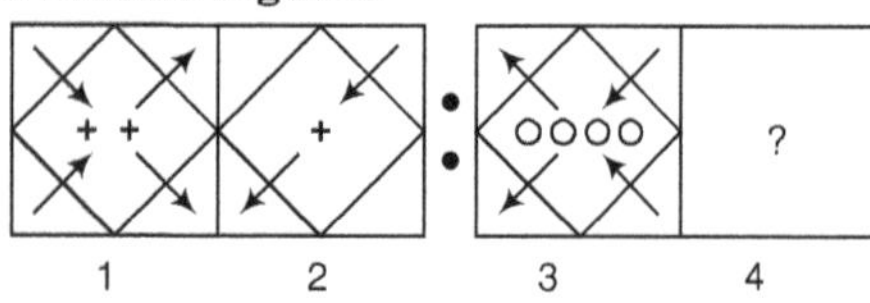

(a) (b) (c) (d)

27. Problem Figures

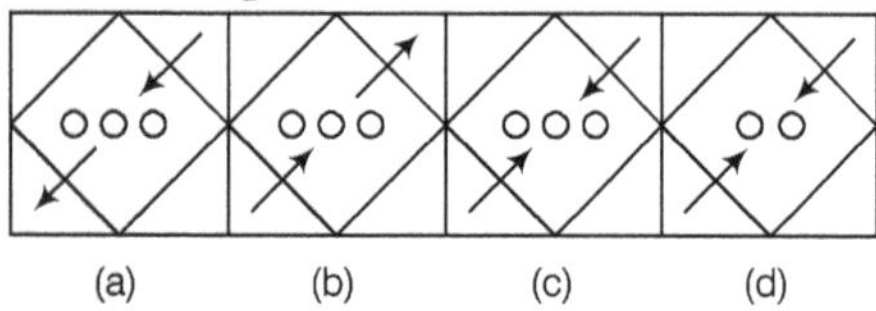

1 2 3 4

Answer Figures

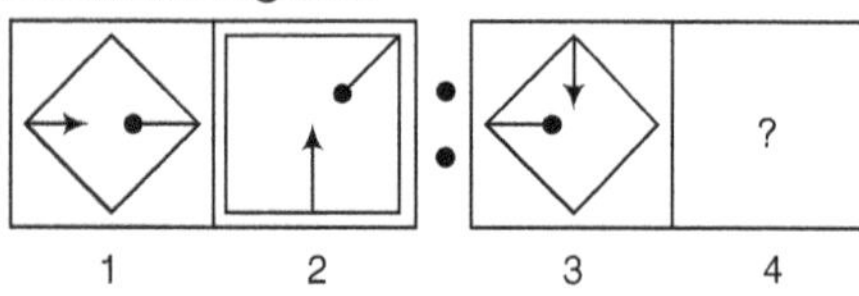

(a) (b) (c) (d) (e)

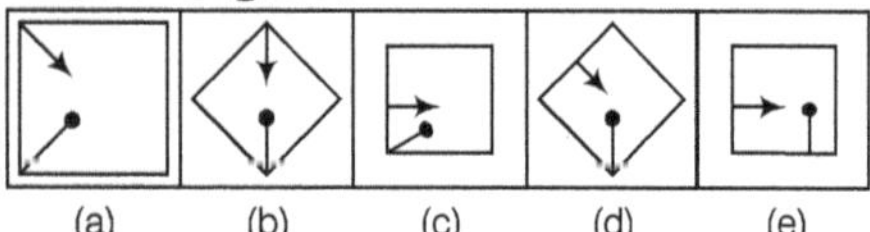

28. Problem Figures

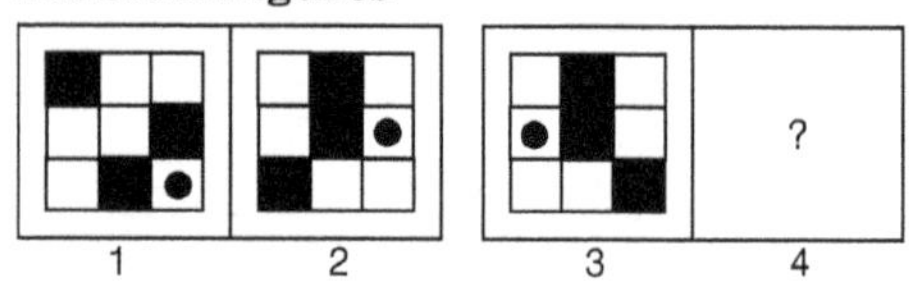

1 2 3 4

Answer Figures

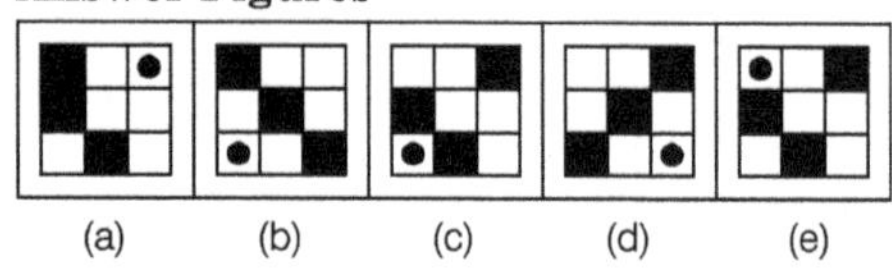

(a) (b) (c) (d) (e)

29. Problem Figures

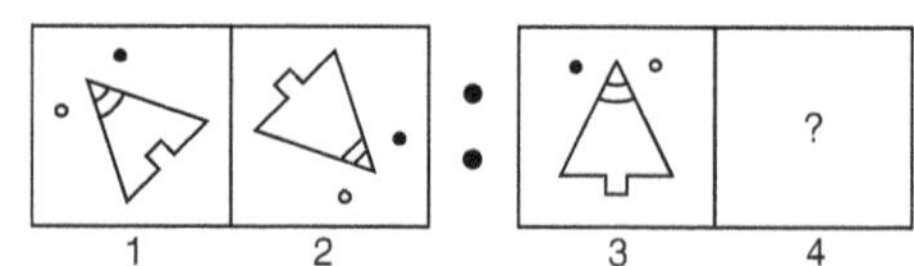

1 2 3 4

Answer Figures

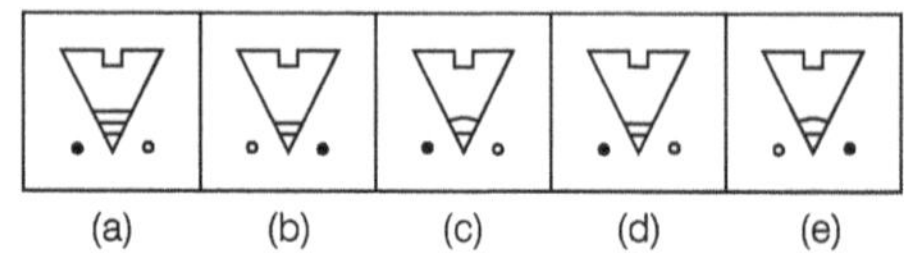

(a) (b) (c) (d) (e)

30. Problem Figures

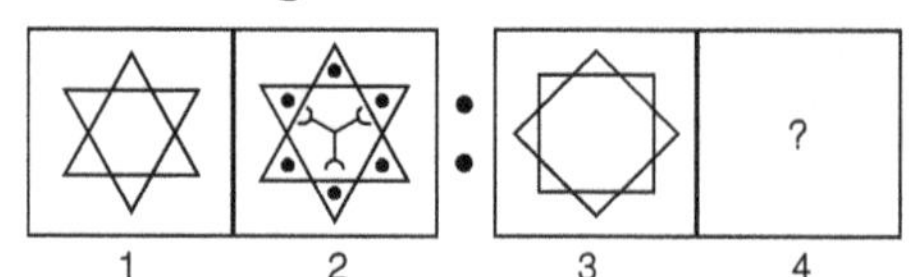

1 2 3 4

Answer Figures

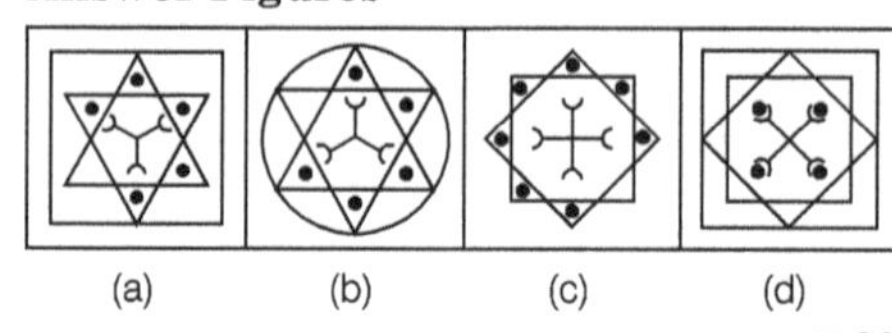

(a) (b) (c) (d)

« SSC CPO 2009

31. Problem Figures

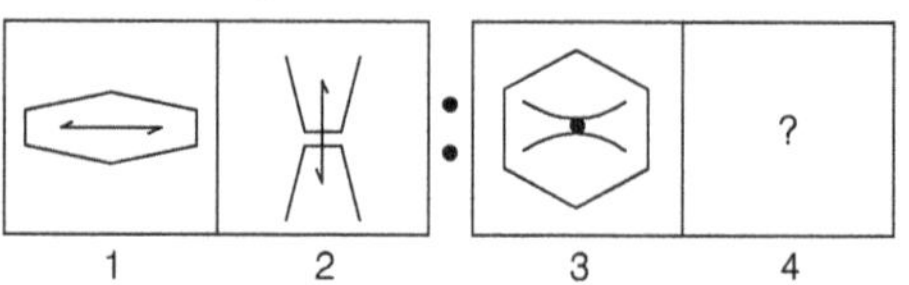

1 2 3 4

Answer Figures

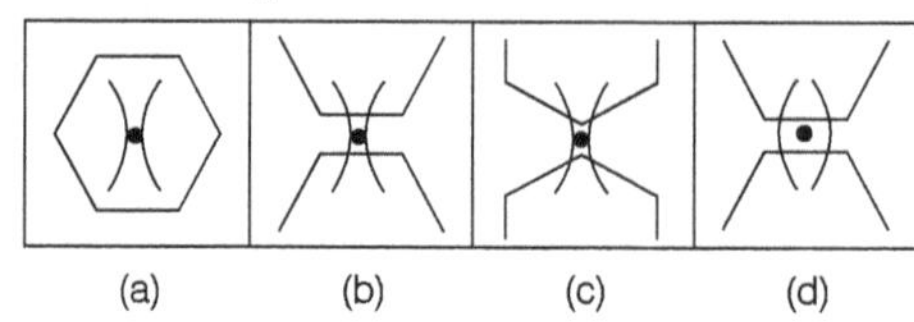

(a) (b) (c) (d)

« UP B. Ed 2014

32. Problem Figures

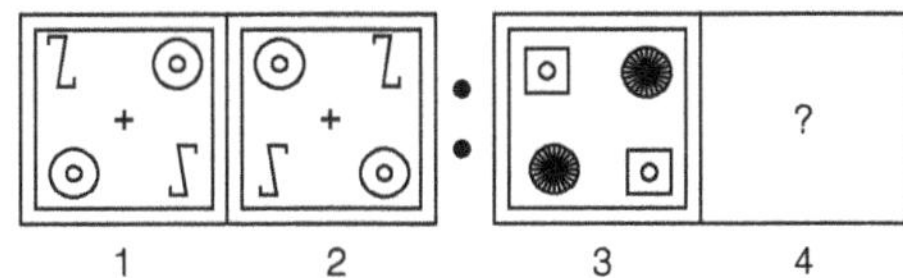

Answer Figures

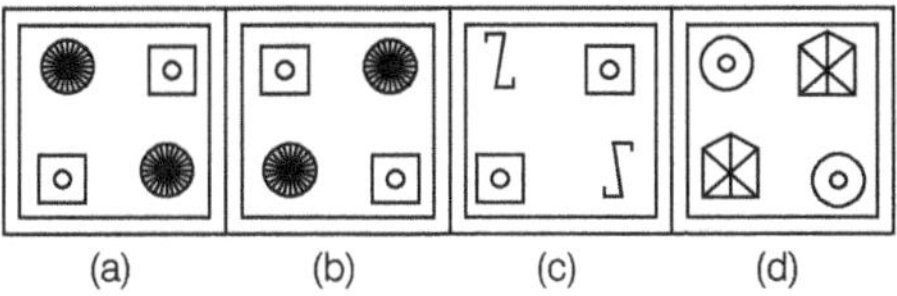

« SSC CPO 2010

33. Problem Figures

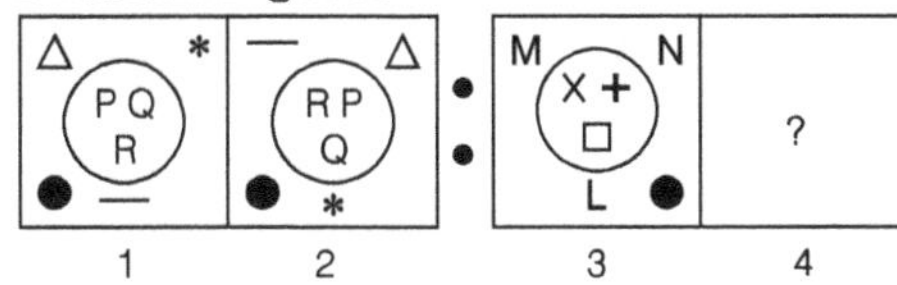

Answer Figures

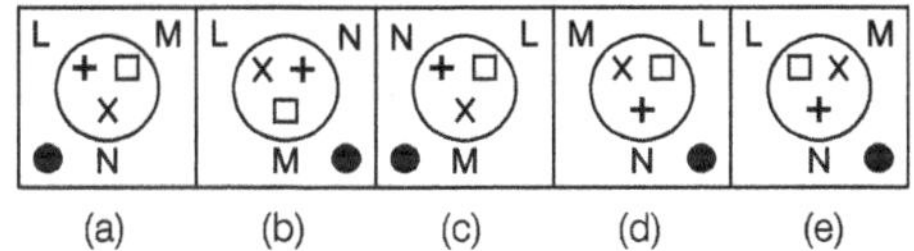

34. Problem Figures

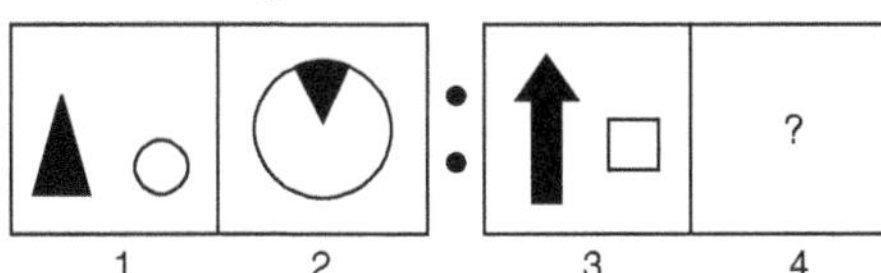

Answer Figures

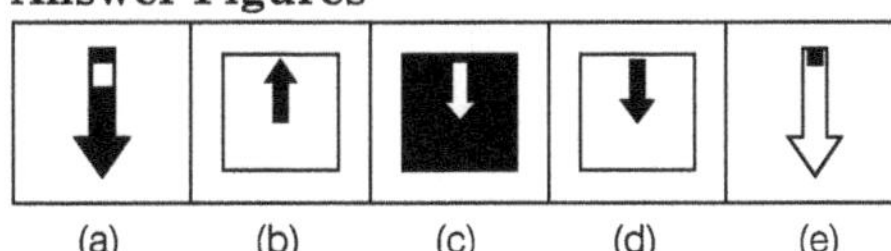

35. Problem Figures

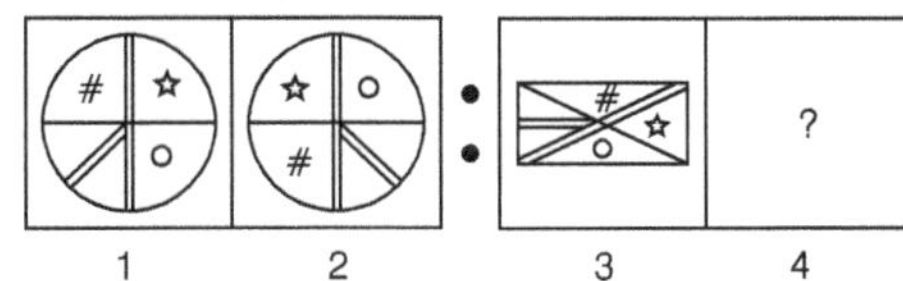

Answer Figures

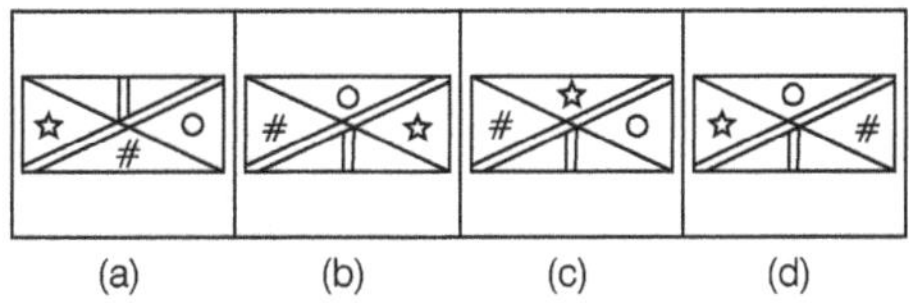

« SSC CPO 2010

36. Problem Figures

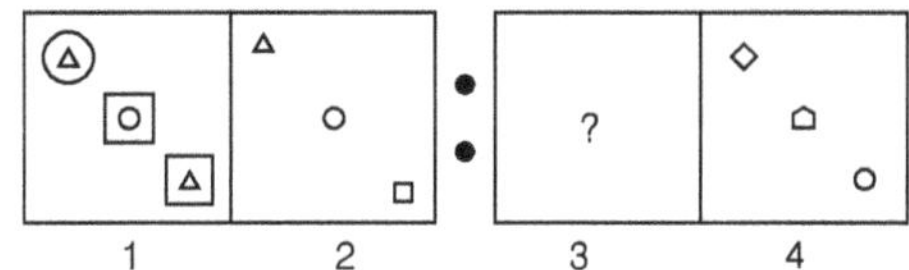

Answer Figures

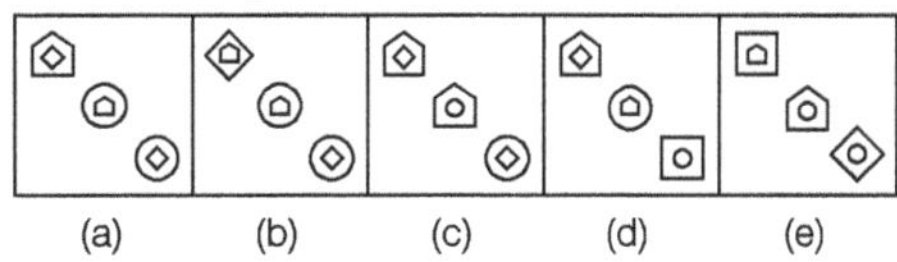

« IBPS PO 2011

37. Problem Figures

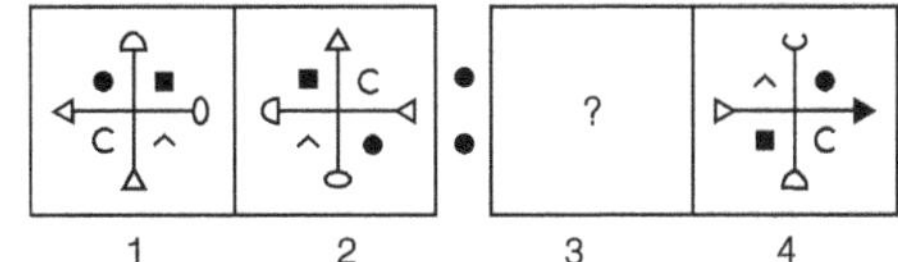

Answer Figures

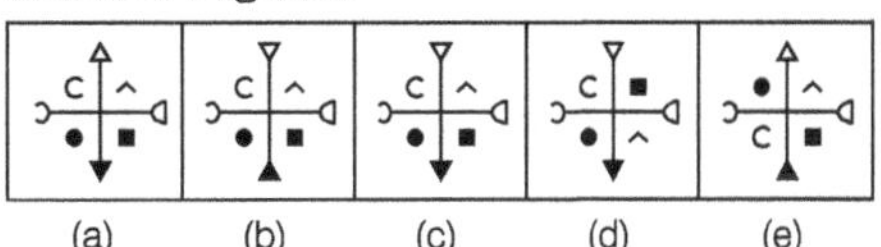

« IBPS PO 2011

38. Problem Figures

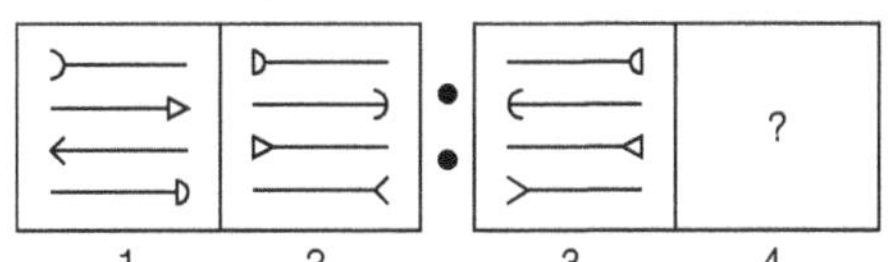

Answer Figures

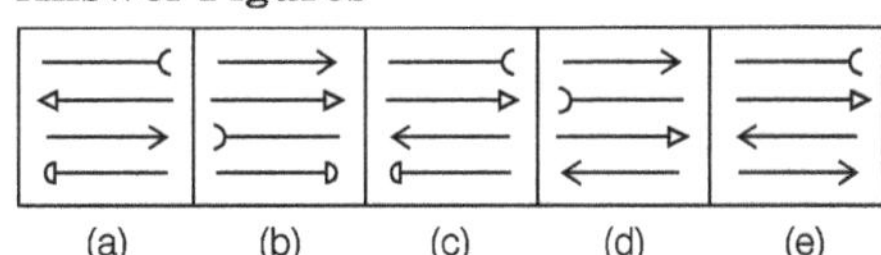

39. Problem Figures

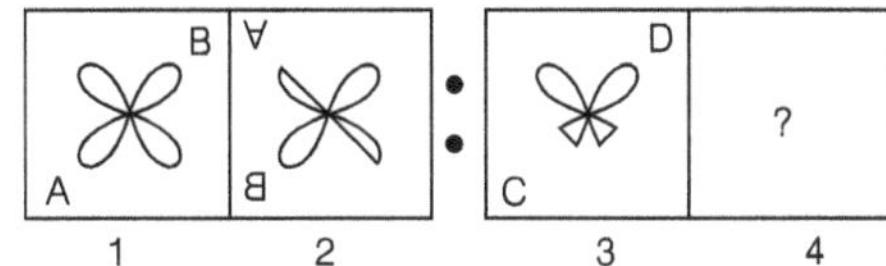

Answer Figures

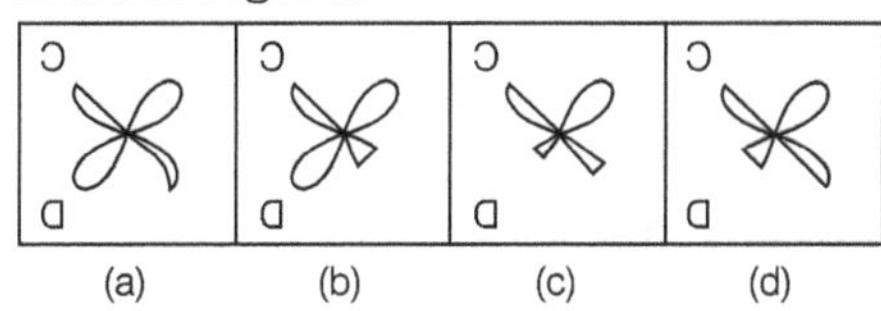

« SSC CGL 2008

40. Problem Figures

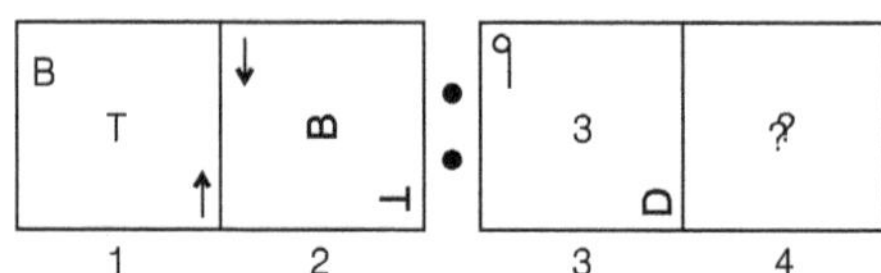

Answer Figures

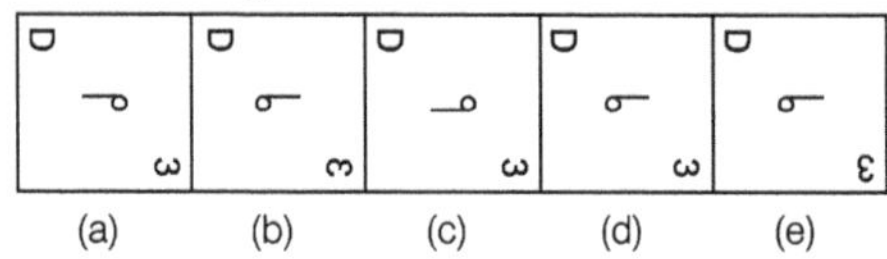

« MHA CET 2011

41. Problem Figures

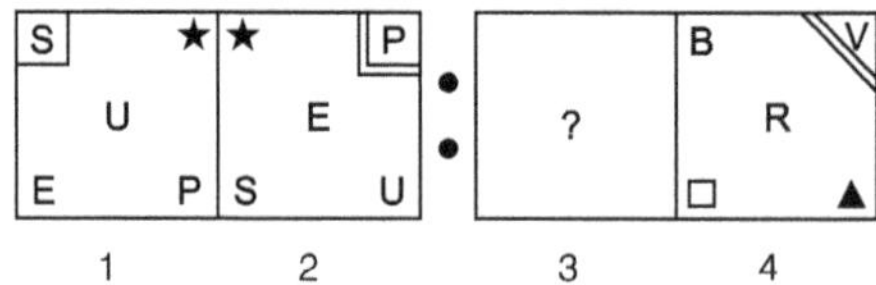

Answer Figures

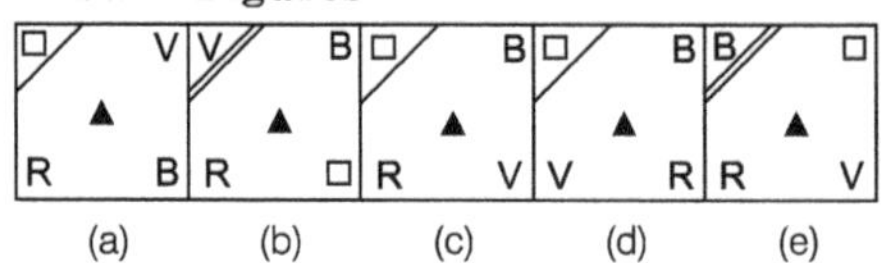

« MHA CET 2011

42. Problem Figures

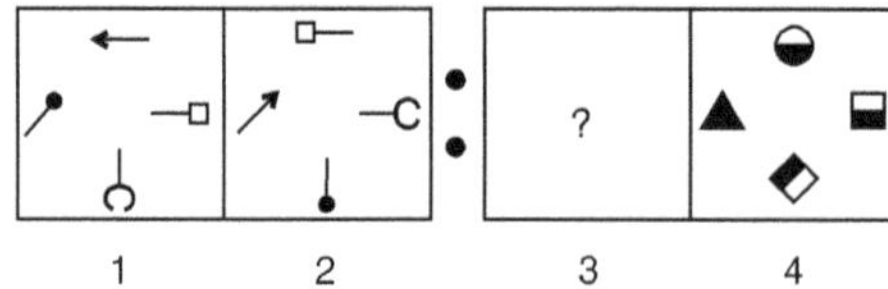

Answer Figures

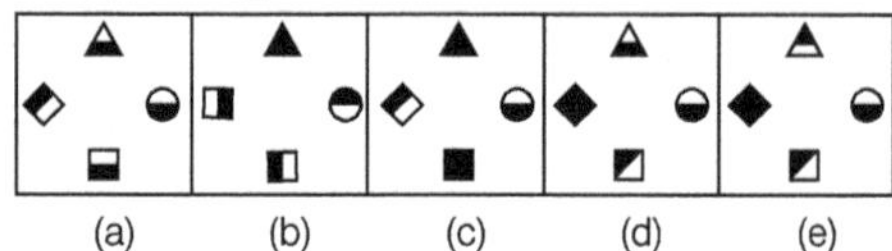

« MHA CET 2011

43. Problem Figures

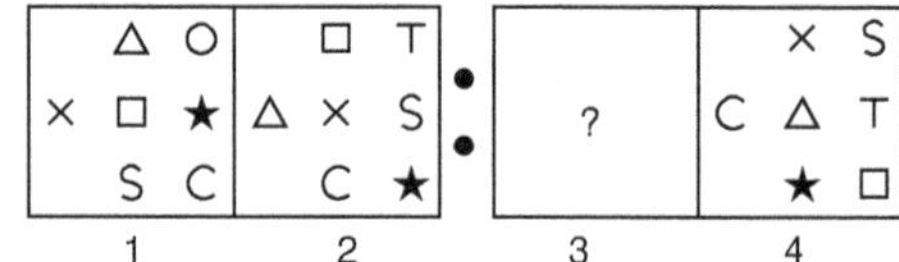

Answer Figures

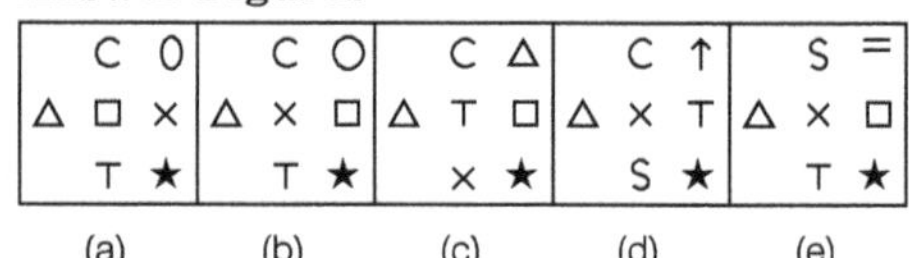

« IBPS PO 2011

44. Problem Figures

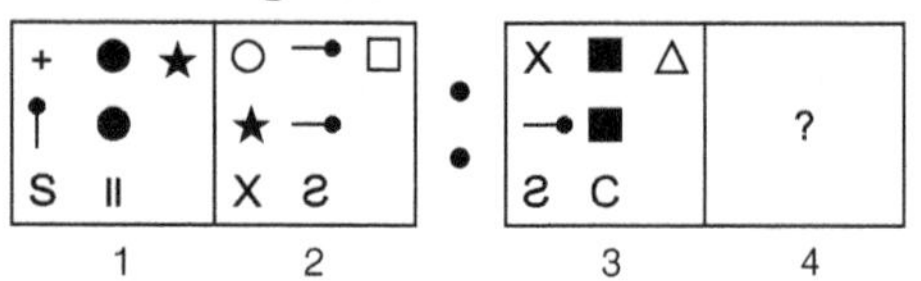

Answer Figures

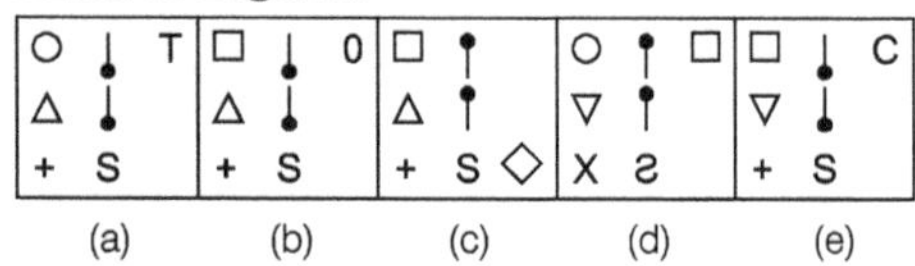

45. Problem Figures

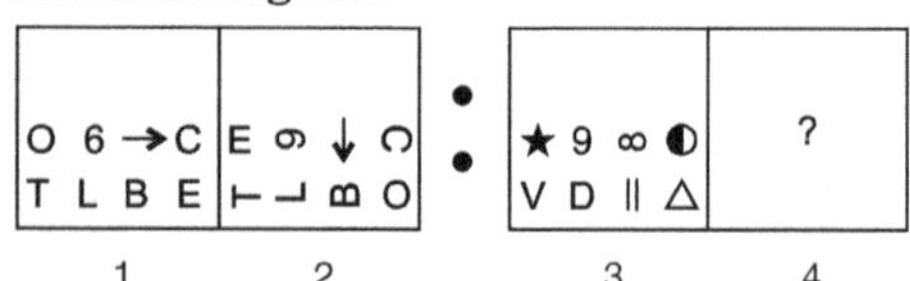

Answer Figures

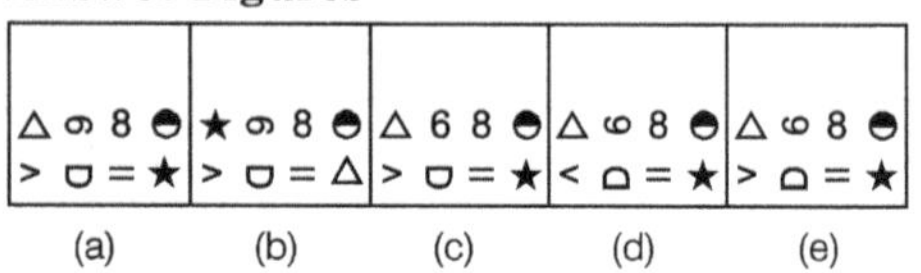

« MHA CET 2011

46. Problem Figures

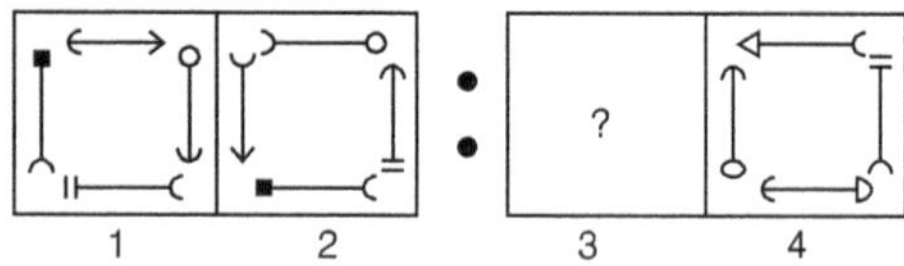

Answer Figures

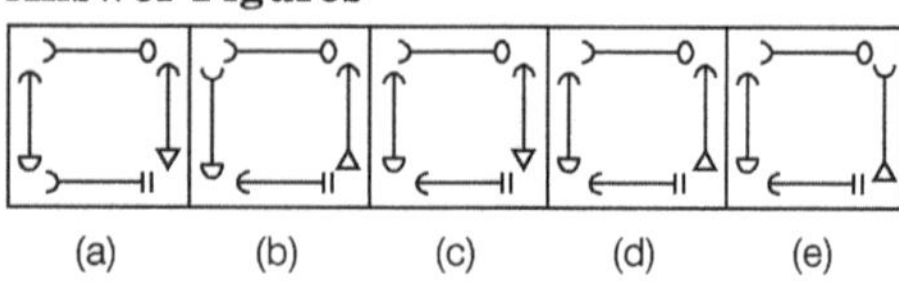

« IBPS PO 2011

DIRECTIONS ~(Q. Nos. 47-51) *In each of the following questions, a pair of problem figures is followed by five numbered pairs of figures. Select the pair that has a relationship similar to that in the problem figures. The best possible answer is to be selected from a group of fairly close choices.*

47. Problem Figures

Answer Figures

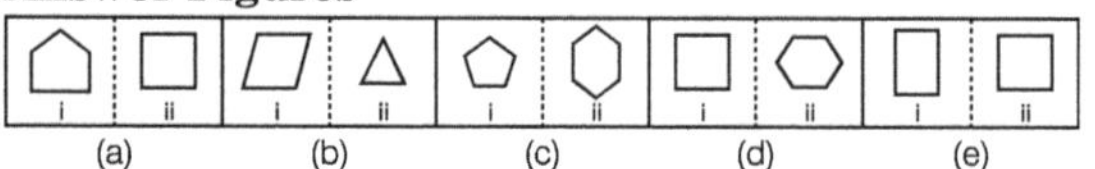

48. Problem Figures

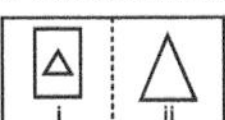

Answer Figures

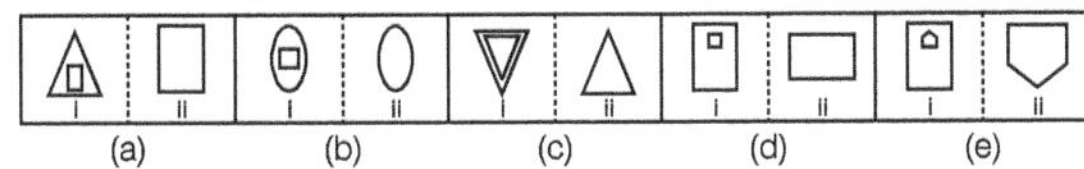

49. Problem Figures

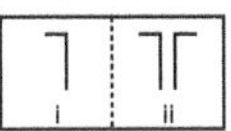

Answer Figures

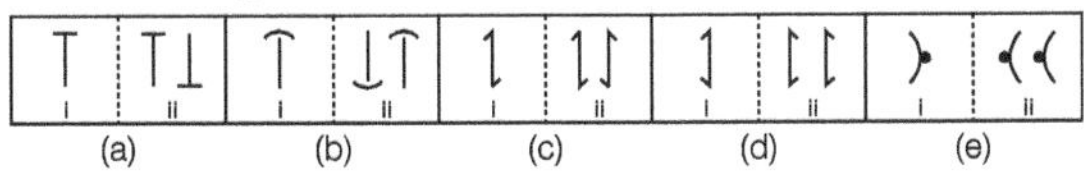

50. Problem Figures

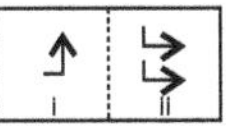

Answer Figures

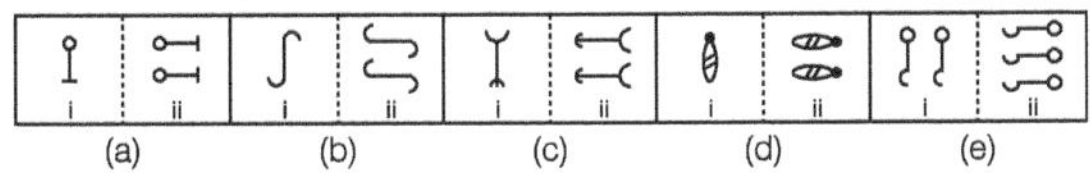

51. Problem Figures

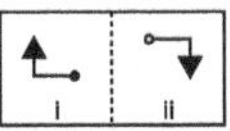

Answer Figures

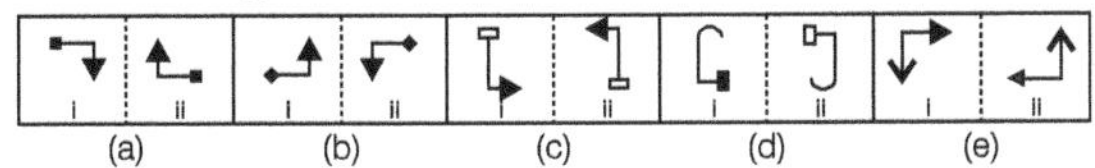

DIRECTIONS ~ (Q. Nos. 52-62) *In each of the following questions, a related pair of figures (problem figures) is followed by five numbered pairs of figures. Out of these five figures, four have relationship similar to that in the problem figures. Only one pair of figures does not have similar relationship. Select that pair of figures which does not have a similar relationship to that in the problem figures.*

52. Problem Figures

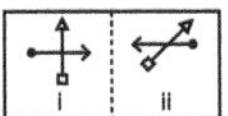

Answer Figures

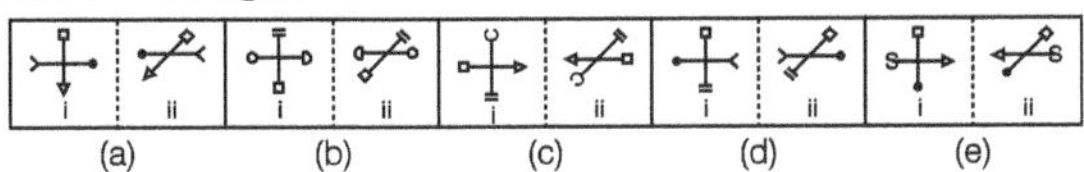

53. Problem Figures

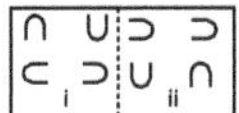

Answer Figures

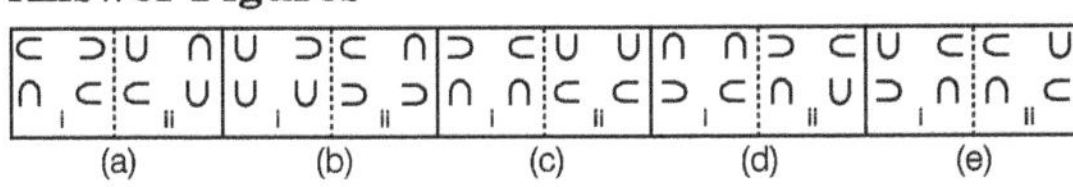

« Syndicate Bank PO 2009

54 Problem Figures

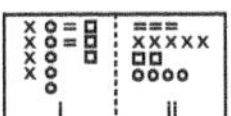

Answer Figures

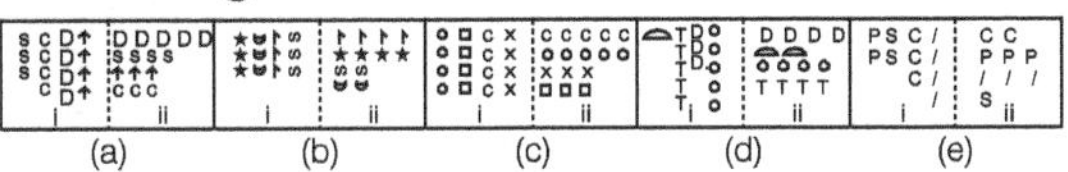

« UCO Bank PO 2009

55. Problem Figures

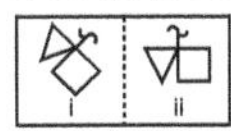

Answer Figures

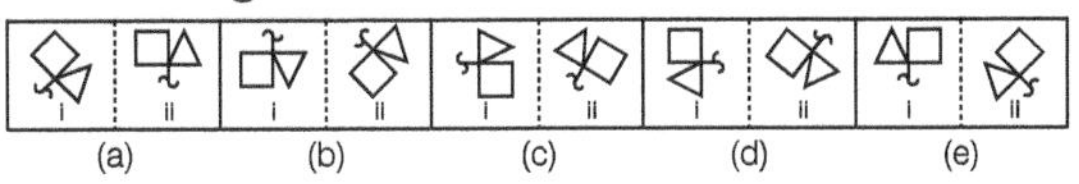

« Punjab & Sindh Bank PO 2009

56. Problem Figures

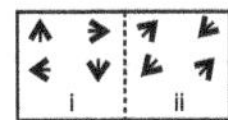

Answer Figures

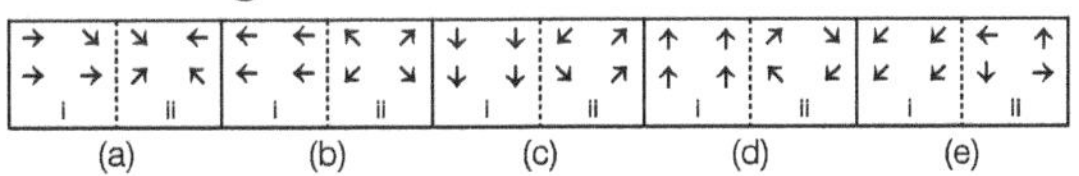

« BOB PO 2009

57. Problem Figures

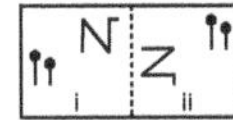

Answer Figures

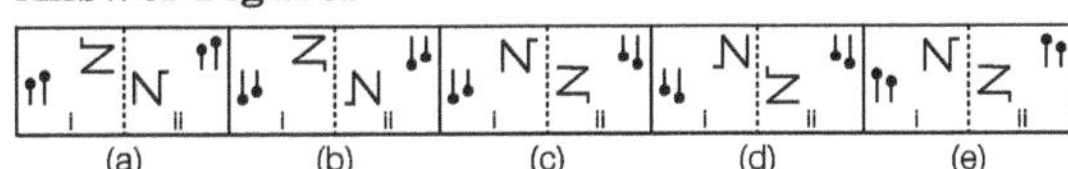

58. Problem Figures

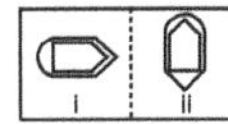

Answer Figures

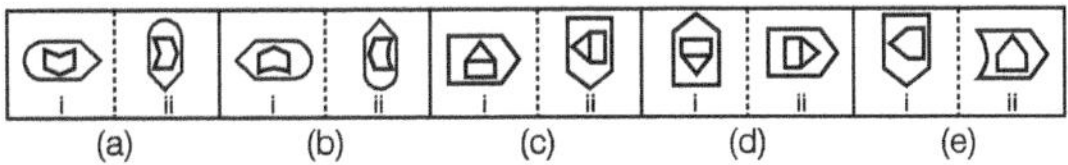

59. Problem Figures

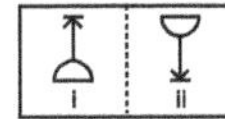

Answer Figures

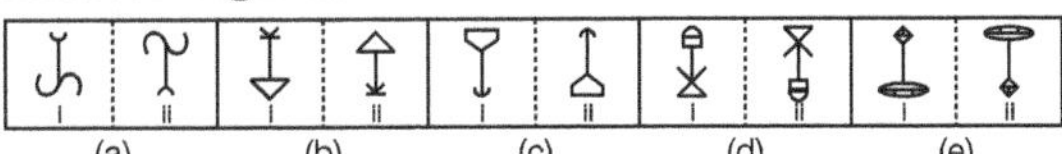

60. Problem Figures

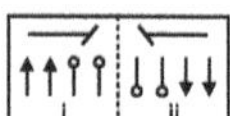

Answer Figures

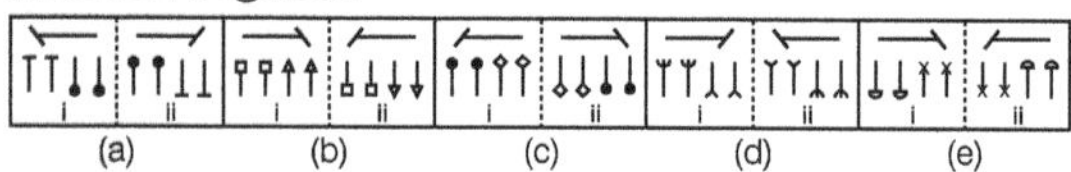

61. Problem Figures

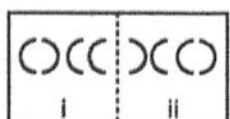

Answer Figures

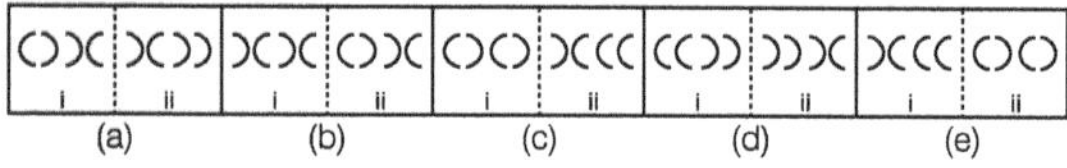

62. Problem Figures

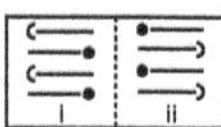

Answer Figures

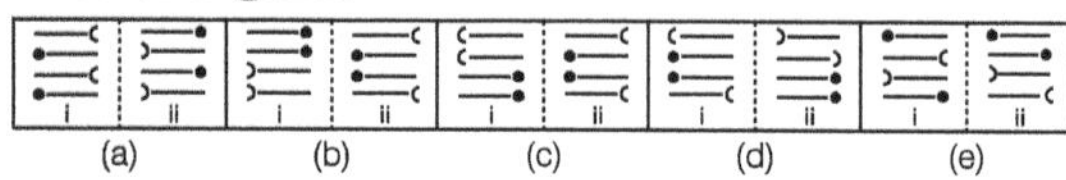

DIRECTIONS ~ (Q. Nos. 63-66) *In each of the following questions, a related pair of figures is followed by five numbered pairs of figures. Select the pair that has a relationship similar to that in the original pair. The best possible answer is to be selected from a group of fairly close choices.*

63. Original Pair

Answer Pairs

(a) (b) (c) (d) (e)

64. Original Pair

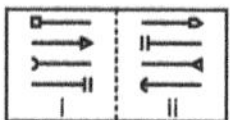

Answer Pairs

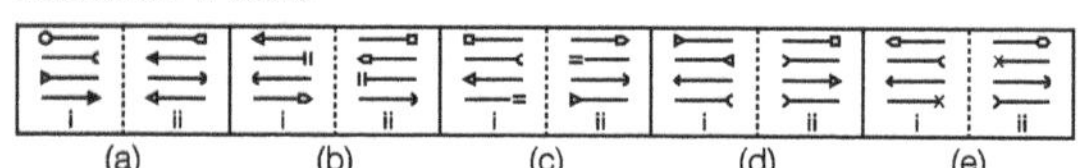

65. Original Pair

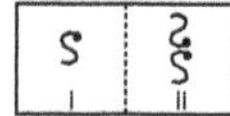

Answer Pairs

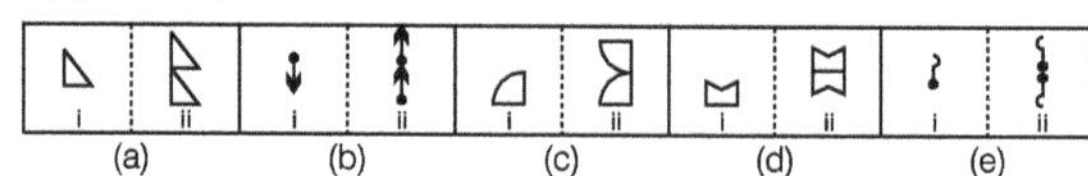

66. Original Pair

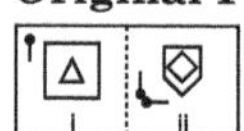

Answer Pairs

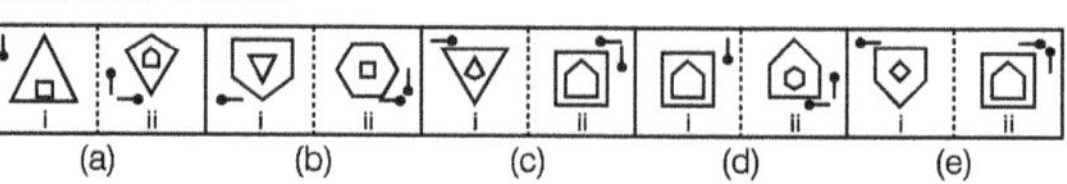

DIRECTIONS ~ (Q. Nos. 67-71) *In each of the following questions, a related pair of figures described as original pair is followed by five answer pairs marked as (a), (b), (c), (d) and (e). Out of these five pairs, four have a relationship similar to that in the original pair. Select that pair from answer pairs which does not have similar relationship as in the original pair.*

67. Original Pair

Answer Pairs

(a) (b) (c) (d) (e)

68. Original Pair

Answer Pairs

(a) (b) (c) (d) (e)

69. Original Pair

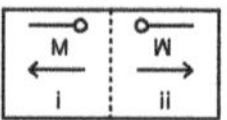

Answer Pairs

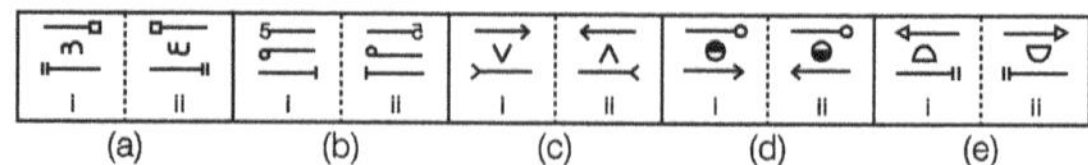

70. Original Pair

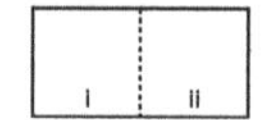

Answer Pairs

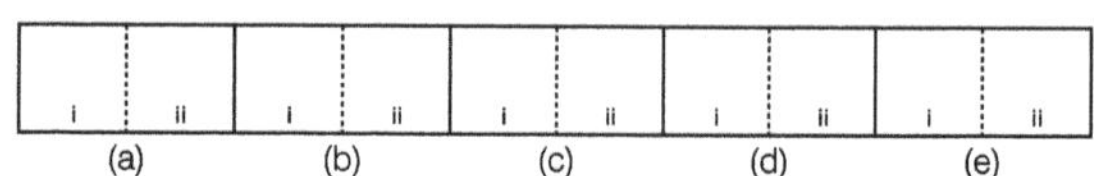

71. Original Pair

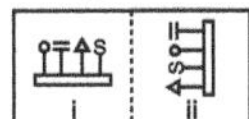

Answer Pairs

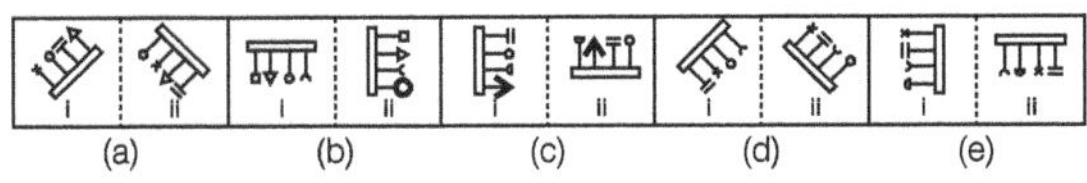

« Andhra Bank PO 2009

DIRECTIONS ~(Q. Nos. 72-75) *In the following questions, find the best substitute from the answer figures which replaces the sign of question marks such that figure* (iii) *is related to figure* (iv) *in the same way as figure* (i) *is related to figure* (ii).

72. Problem Figures

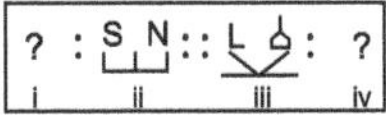

Answer Figures

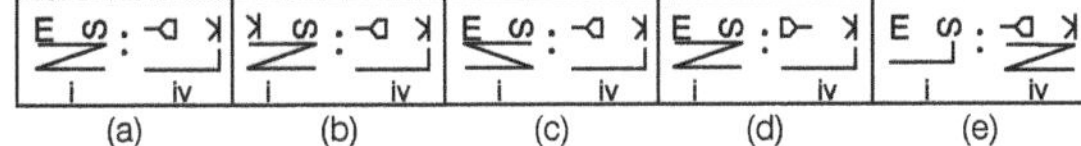

73. Problem Figures

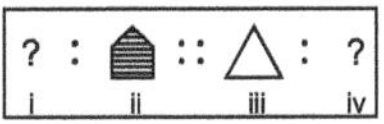

Answer Figures

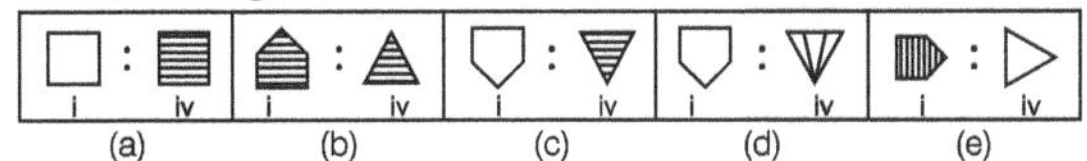

74. Problem Figures

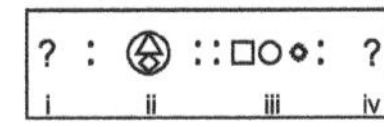

Answer Figures

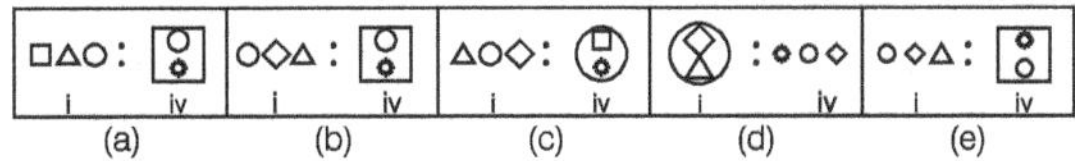

75. Problem Figures

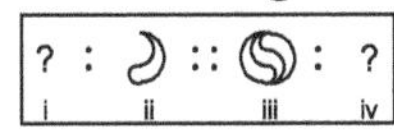

Answer Figures

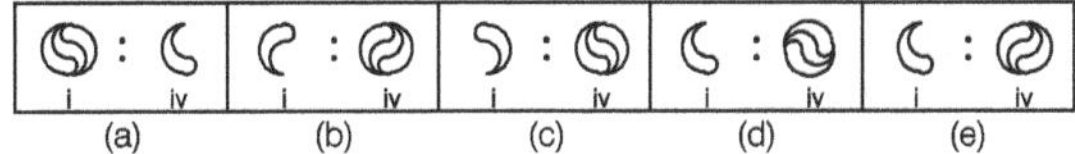

Answers / WITH EXPLANATIONS

1. (*a*) As, the ring is worn in finger. In the same way, the crown is worn on head.

2. (*d*) As, water is taken out from the well. In the same way, coals are taken out from the mine.

3. (*d*) As, from problem figures 1 to 2 the shaded portions of the small circles become unshaded and *vice-versa*. Similarly, answer figure (d) will be obtained from problem figure 3.

4. (*a*) From first figure to second figure there is an increment of one side in the outer figure and the inner sign is getting inverted.

5. (*b*) The second figure is the mirror image of the first figure.

6. (*b*) From first figure to second figure, all the designs are inverted.

7. (*d*) From first figure to second figure, the triangle rotates through 90° clockwise and moves to the side of square and a similar triangle appears on the opposite side.

8. (*c*) From first figure to the second figure, three line segments are added in a set pattern.

9. (*a*) From first figure to second figure one small triangle is added inside and rest of the figure is same. Similarly, small circle would be added from figure (3) to (4).

10. (*d*) Figure with three sides gets changed to a figure with four sides with the number of extended sides remaining same.

11. (*a*) The second figure in the first unit of problem figure can be obtained by rotating the first figure by 180° anti-clockwise.

12. (*b*) The second figure is mirror image of the first figure.

13. (*d*) The second figure is the mirror image of the first figure.

14. (*a*) From the first figure to the second figure,the number of figures attached to the vertical line increases by 1 and one outer line segment is added.

15. (*a*) From the first figure to the second figure, one similar figure is added in a set pattern.

16. (*b*) From the first figure to the second figure, the design is inverted.

17. (*b*) Whole figure rotates 90° clockwise, designs of circles and triangles interchange their positions and upper designs get shaded.

18. (*b*) From figure (1) to figure (2), following changes take place.

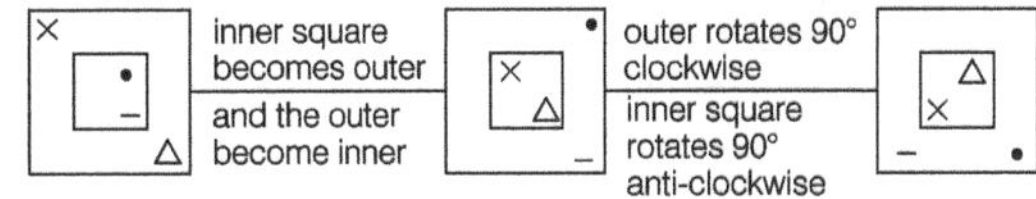

In the same way, figure of option (b) is formed from figure (3).

19. (*a*) The pentagon is inverted and the shaded figure adjacent to it comes inside the pentagon with the upper half shaded.

20. (*e*) The main figure rotates through 45° clockwise and dots outside the figure shift to the other side of the line.

21. (*c*) The main figure rotates through 90° clockwise and at the same time one of the lines of one side is deleted. The small sign moves one step clockwise and rotates through 45°.

22. (*d*) From the first figure to the second figure, the innermost and the outer most designs interchange their positions.

23. (*d*) The line with arrow rotates 135° anti-clockwise and its arrow head is reversed. At the other line, the black sign becomes white and white sign becomes black.

24. (*b*) The figure gets laterally inverted and the black shade shifts to the other side. The small circle inside the figure also gets shaded.

25. (*d*) Top left symbol rotates 90° anti-clockwise and the other three symbols rotate 90° in clockwise direction.

26. (*b*) From the first figure to the second figure, two arrows and one '+' sign are deleted and the remaining two arrows are inverted.

27. (*c*) From first figure to second figure, the main design rotates through 45° anti-clockwise and the arrow moves half step in anti-clockwise direction.

28. (*e*) The shaded portion on the middle and lower rows of the figure move one block to the left whereas the shaded portion on the upper row moves one block to the right. The dot inside the figure moves one block above.

29. (*d*) The main figure rotates through 180° and the pressed portion of the base is lifted outward and the two curved lines inside the figure become straight. Also, the two circles outside the main figure interchange their places.

30. (*c*) From first figure to second figure, one dot is added to every sector of the design and three line segments with curves are introduced in the center.

31. (*b*) The whole figure rotates 90° clockwise, the outer design is divided into two equal halves horizontally and both halves are reversed at the same position.

32. (*a*) From first figure to second figure, four designs move one step in the clockwise direction.

33. (*e*) All the letters inside the circle move one step clockwise. The symbol at the top left position moves one step clockwise, the symbol at the top right position moves one and half step clockwise and the symbol at the central bottom position also moves one and half step clockwise, as shown in the figure,

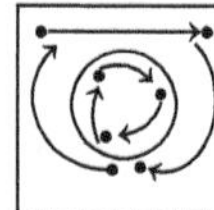

34. (*d*) The larger figure becomes small, gets inverted and occupies the top position inside the smaller figure which gets enlarged.

35. (*c*) From the first figure to the second figure, all the four smaller designs move one sector in anti-clockwise direction.

36. (*a*) From figure (2) to (1), upper and middle elements are encircled by the middle and lower elements respectively.

The lower element gets enlarged and an element similar to the upper element comes inside it.

37. (*c*) From figure (2) to (1), the vertical bar rotates by 90° anti-clockwise while the horizontal bar rotates by 90° clockwise.

The upper-left element goes to upper right, upper right to lower left, lower left to lower right, lower right to the upper left.

38. (*a*) First figure, from bottom, moves to the fourth position and is reversed. Its head is also reversed. Fourth figure comes at the third position and its head is also reversed.

The third figure comes at the second position and is reversed its head is also reversed second figure comes at the first position and its head and position get reversed.

39. (*c*) From the first figure to the second figure, the lower letter moves one step in clockwise direction and gets inverted.

The upper letter moves two steps clockwise and gets inverted. One side each of the two opposite petals becomes straight.

40. (*d*) From problem figure (1) to (2), upper design comes in middle position with 90° anti-clockwise rotation, middle design comes in lower side with 90° clockwise rotation and lower design comes in upper side with 180° rotation.

41. (*c*) The pattern from problem figure (2) to (1) is as follows.

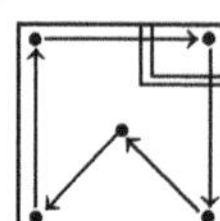

Similar rule is followed to obtain figure (3) from problem figure (4).

42. (*b*) From problem figure (2) to (1), each design moves one step in clockwise direction and rotates in a certain pattern. Similarly, answer figure (3) is obtained from problem figure (4).

43. (*b*) From figure (2) to (1), the changes in position of elements is given as follows

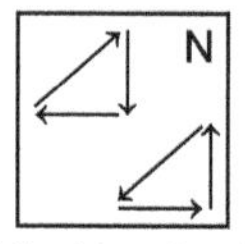

(N) = New Symbol

44. (*b*) Let us mark the position of symbols as follows,

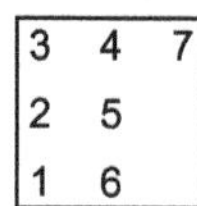

- The symbol at the first position is reversed and occupies sixth position.
- The symbol at the second position rotates 90° clockwise and occupies fourth and fifth positions.
- The symbol at the third position rotates 45° clockwise and occupies first position.
- The symbols at fourth and fifth positions are same and occupy third position but without shading and hence becomes white.
- The symbol at the sixth position occupies seventh position and is replaced by a new symbol.
- The symbol at the seventh position occupies the second position.

45. (*e*) The pattern of changes from problem figure (1) to (2) is as follows

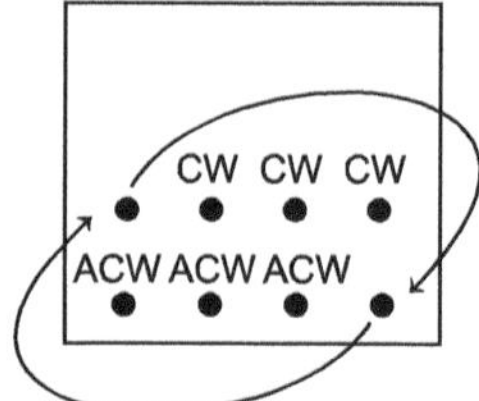

(CW) Clockwise = 90° clockwise rotation

(ACW) Anti-clockwise = 90° anti-clockwise rotation

Similar rule follows from problem figure (3) to figure (4).

46. (*c*) From figure (2) to (1), the upper and the left elements rotate by 90° anti-clockwise and shift to the right and upper positions respectively while one of their heads gets reversed. The lower element rotates 90° clockwise and goes to the left. The right element rotates 90° clockwise and one of its heads gets reversed and goes to the lower position.

47. (*c*) Figure in section (ii) has one side more than the figure in section (i) of the original pair.

48. (*a*) The inside figure gets enlarged while the outer figure is removed.

49. (*c*) The figure gets laterally reversed and appears with the pre-existing figure from section (i) to section (ii).

50. (*b*) The figure rotates through 90° clockwise and appears in pairs.

51. (*d*) The figures rotates through 180° in such a way that the black shaded portion becomes white.

52. (*c*) The pattern of problem figures is such that the vertical design rotates 45° in clockwise direction and horizontal design gets invaded with some upward movement.

53. (*a*) The upper left element rotates by 90° clockwise while the other three elements rotate by 90° anti-clockwise.

54. (*e*) The third column becomes first row, first column becomes second row, and both with the increment of one element while the fourth column becomes third row and the second column becomes fourth row and both with the decrement of one element.

55. (*d*) The whole figure rotates by 45° anti-clockwise while the element attached at the end gets inverted.

56. (*c*) The upper left element rotates by 45° clockwise and the lower left element rotates by 45° anti-clockwise. The upper right element rotates by 135° clockwise and the lower right element by 135° anti-clockwise.

57. (*c*) The main design rotates through 90° clockwise and shifts downwards. Also, both the pins shift to the other upward side.

58. (*e*) The outer figure rotates through 90° clockwise and the inner figure rotates through 90° anti-clockwise.

59. (*b*) Figure in section (ii) is the water image of the figure in section (i).

60. (*b*) The upper figure gets inverted, the pins and arrows get inverted and interchange their positions.

61. (*b*) All the semi-circles, except second from the right side, get reversed.

62. (*c*) The lowermost symbol becomes the uppermost symbol, when other symbol shift one step downwards. Also, each symbol gets reversed at the new position.

63. (*a*)

- The symbol at the top left position rotates through 180° and occupies the bottom right position.
- The symbol at the top right position gets inverted vertically and occupies the bottom left position.
- The symbol at the bottom right position rotates through 90° anti-clockwise and occupies the top left position.
- The figure at the bottom left position occupies the top right position in such a way that the number of sides of the figure is increased by one.

64. (*c*) The first, second, third and fourth arrows from the bottom become third, first, second and fourth arrows in such a way that the first arrow gets reversed, the head of the second and third arrows get reversed and the number of sides of the head of fourth arrow is increased by one.

65. (*c*) A water image is added on top of the existing figure from section (i) to section (ii) in the original pair.

66. (*b*) The pin rotates through 180° and shifts one-step anti-clockwise and a new pin with head joining towards the first pin appears and both the main figures are changed into new figures with one more side each.

67. (*c*) The symbols appearing in pairs shift to the upper row and appear in single whereas the symbols of the upper row shift downwards and appear in pairs.

68. (*b*) The pattern of change from section (i) to section (ii) is as follows.

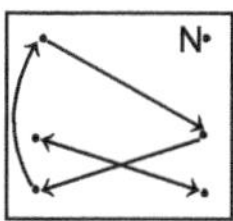

N = New symbol

69. (*d*) In the original pair of figures, from section (i) to section (ii), the first and last elements get laterally reversed at their places while the middle element gets vertically inverted.

70. (*a*)

1 2 3 4 5 → 4 5 2 1 3

(i) (ii)

The pattern of original figure is as follows. From section (i) to section (ii), the first element becomes fourth, second becomes third, third becomes last, fourth becomes first and fifth becomes second from top to bottom diagonally.

71. (*b*) The whole figure rotates by 90° anti-clockwise.The first and the third and the second and the fourth element interchange their positions.

72. (*a*) From section (i) to section (ii) of the problem figures, all the symbols rotate 90° anti-clockwise and move anti-clockwise to occupy next positions. Also, the sign that acquires the lower position gets enlarged and the signs that acquires upper position gets reduced in size.

73. (*c*) From section (i) to section (ii) of the problem figures, the existing figure gets inverted and parallel lines appear inside it.

74. (*e*) From section (i) to section (ii) of the problem figures, the leftmost figure becomes the outermost figure and the other two figures come inside it in such a way that the middle and the rightmost figures occupy lower and upper positions, respectively.

75. (*e*) From section (i) to section (ii) of the problem figures, the existing figure gets laterally inverted.

CHAPTER / 03

Classification

Classification is defined as the assorting of different items of a given group on the basis of certain common quality they possess and spotting the odd one out.

In these questions, four/five figures labelled as (a), (b), (c), (d)/(e) are given.

Three/Four of these four/five figures have common features/characteristics and hence are similar in a certain way but one of the figures does not have that common characteristics and hence does not fit with other figures. Select that figure which does not belong to the group and this figure is the required answer.

Let us consider an example

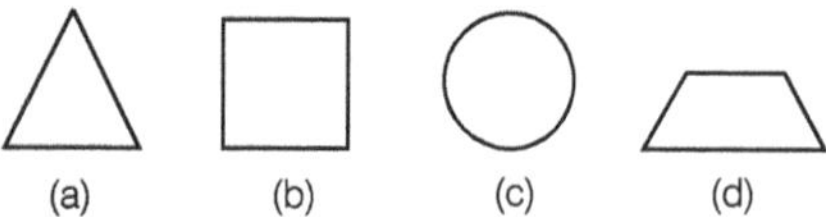

In all the figures given above, except circle, all others are formed with straight lines. Hence, circle does not fit into this group and is the odd one.

There are many criteria used for establishing the pattern or similarity between the figures which are given below.

Number of Elements or Lines

A group of figures may be classified on the basis of number of elements or lines present in figures. The figures can also be classified on the basis of even or odd number of lines or on the basis of elements present in figures. Classification can also be done on the basis of the ratio of number of lines and elements.

DIRECTIONS ~ (Example Nos. 1-5) *In the following questions, a group of four/five figures is given. Out of which three/four figures are similar to each other in a certain way and one is different from the others. Find the different/odd figure out.*

Ex 01

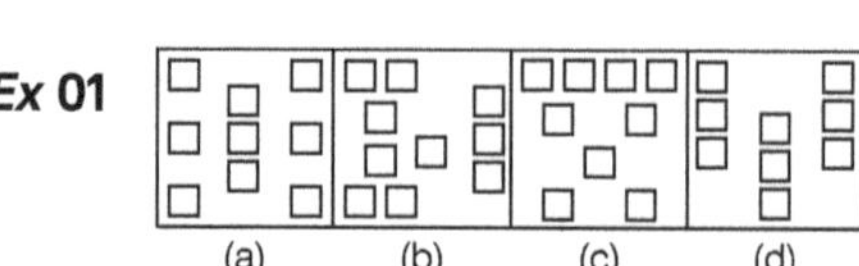

« RRB ALP 2018

Solution (b) Except figure (b), all other figures have 9 small squares, while figure (b) has 10 small squares.

Ex 02

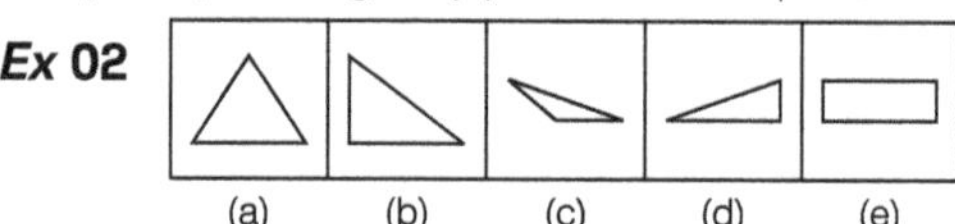

Solution (e) Except figure (e), all other figures have three sides but in figure (e) has four sides.

Ex 03

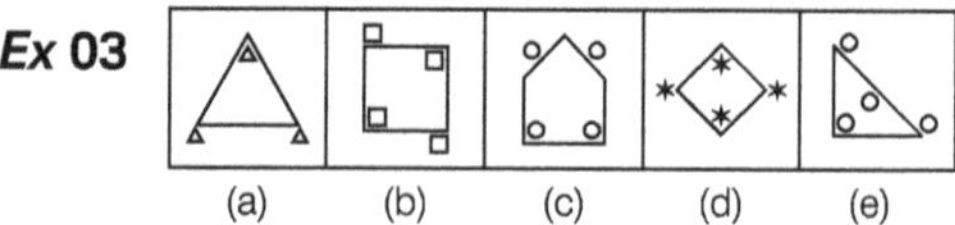

Solution (a) Except figure (a), all other figures have equal number of figures both inside and outside of the main figure.

Ex 04

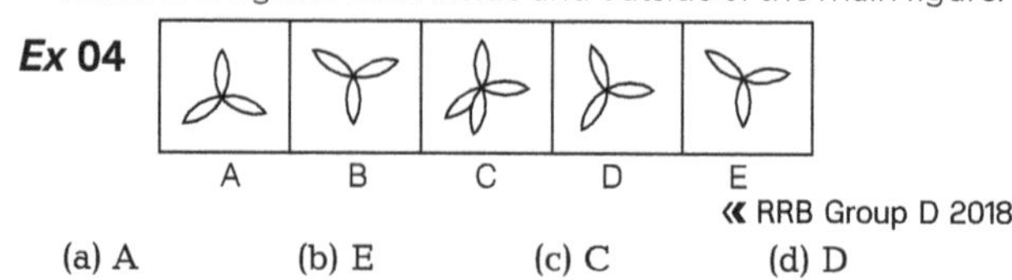

« RRB Group D 2018

(a) A (b) E (c) C (d) D

Solution (c) Except figure (c), rest of the figures have three leaves, whereas figure in option (c) has four leaves.

Ex 05

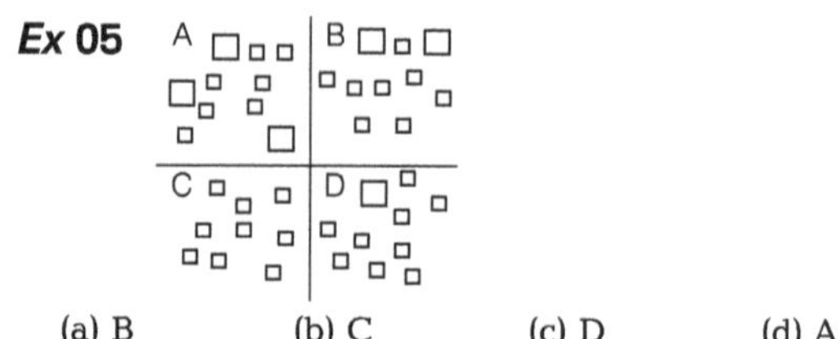

(a) B (b) C (c) D (d) A

Solution (b) Except figure (c) in all other figures, there are 10 elements (square) but in figure (c) there are only 9 elements (square).

Division of Figures

This type of classification is based on the equal or unequal division of figures or division of figures in some specified ratio or parts.

DIRECTIONS ~ (Example Nos. 6-8) *In the following questions, a group of four/five figures is given. Out of which three/four figures are similar to each other in a certain way and one is different from others. Find the odd figure out.*

Ex 06

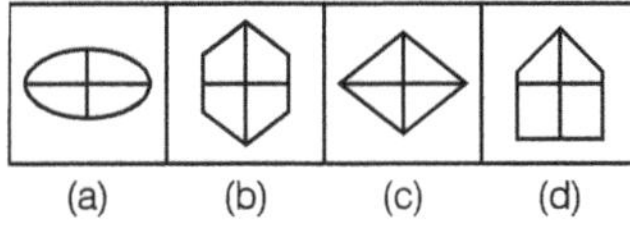

(a) (b) (c) (d) « SSC DEO 2009

Solution (d) Except figure (d), all the figures are divided into four equal parts.

Ex 07

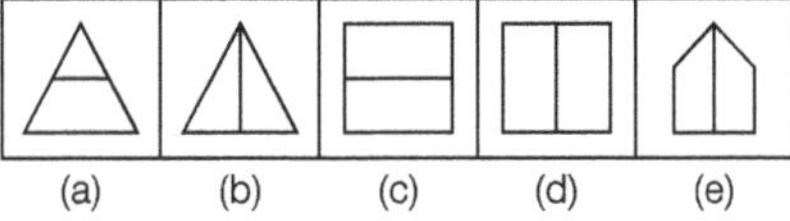

(a) (b) (c) (d) (e)

Solution (a) Except figure (a), all the other figures are divided into two equal parts.

Ex 08

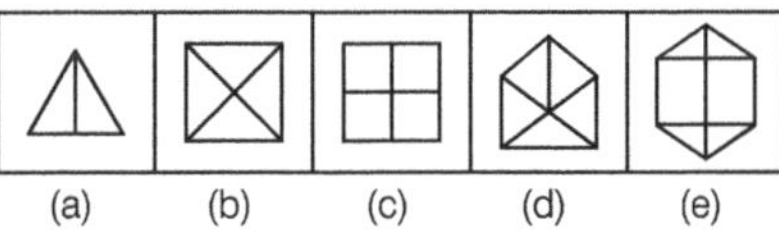

(a) (b) (c) (d) (e)

Solution (a) Except figure (a), all the other figures are divided in the way such that each figure contains as many parts as the number of sides in each figure.

Rotation of Same Figure

This is the most common type of classification. The similar figures are actually the rotated forms of the same figure in clockwise or in anti-clockwise direction.

The figure which comes out to be different from others is that figure which cannot be obtained by rotation of one of the other figures.

DIRECTIONS ~ (Example Nos. 9-11) *In the following questions, a group of four/five figures is given. Out of which three/four figures are similar to each other in a certain way and one is different from others. Find the odd figure out.*

Ex 09

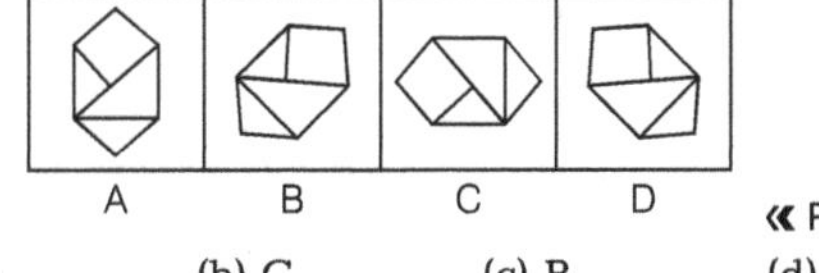

A B C D « RRB ALP 2018

(a) A (b) C (c) B (d) D

Solution (d) Except figure D, all the other figures are rotated form of the same figure. Hence, figure D is the odd one.

Ex 10

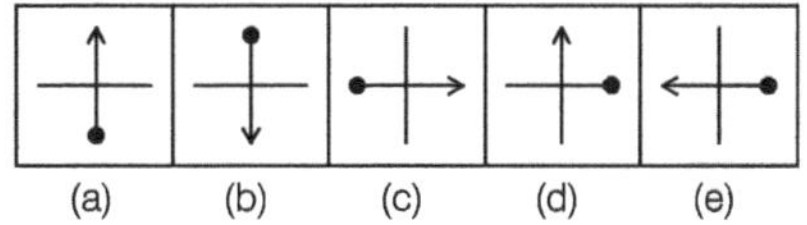

(a) (b) (c) (d) (e)

Solution (d) Except figure (d), all the other figures can be formed by rotating each other either clockwise or anti-clockwise.

Ex 11

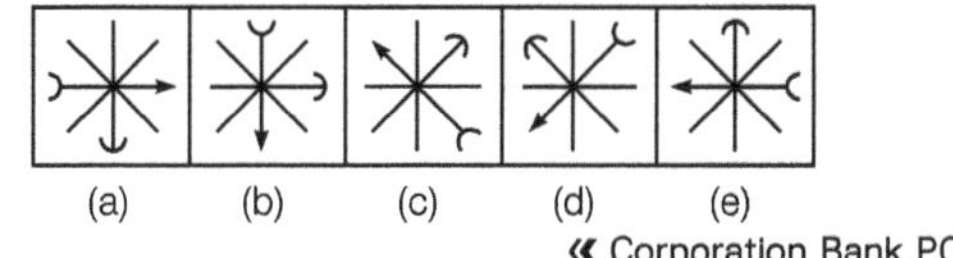

(a) (b) (c) (d) (e)

« Corporation Bank PO 2011

Solution (b) Except figure (b), all the other figures are rotated forms of the same figure.

Similarity of Figures

Classification on the basis of similarity of figures is done when orientation, shape, measure of angle or method of presentation of the group is same except for the odd figure.

DIRECTIONS ~ (Example Nos. 12-17) *In the following questions, a group of four/five figures is given. Out of which three/four figures are similar to each other in a certain way and one is different from others. Find the odd figure out.*

Ex 12

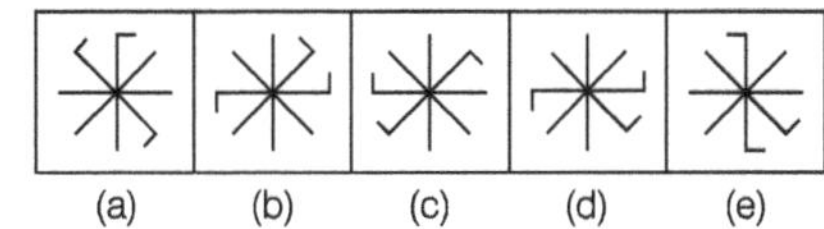

(a) (b) (c) (d) (e)

Solution (d) Let us consider the two adjacent bent lines as a pair. Then, in each figure except (d), there are two straight lines between the bent pair and the remaining bent line when the direction of bent is considered.

Ex 13

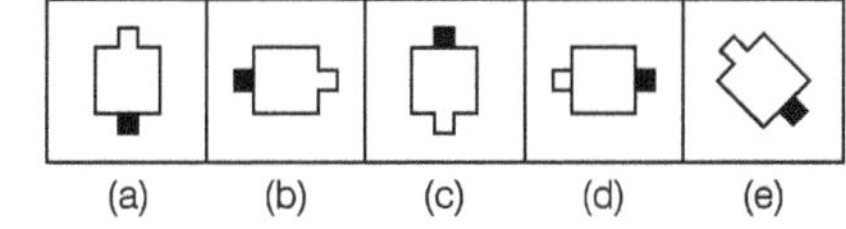

(a) (b) (c) (d) (e)

Solution (d) Except figure (d), in all the other figures, the embossed unshaded middle portion of the side of large square is open.

Ex 14

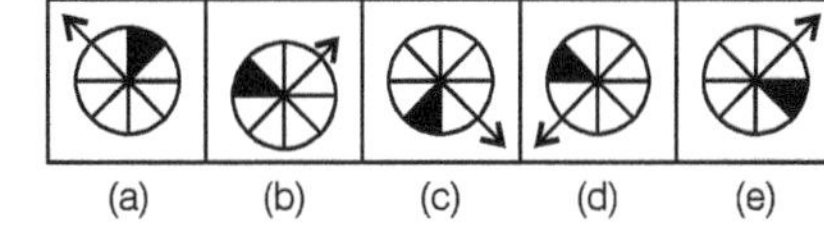

(a) (b) (c) (d) (e)

Solution (b) Except figure (b), in all the other figures, arrow is one step away from the shaded sector of the circle in anti-clockwise direction.

Ex 15

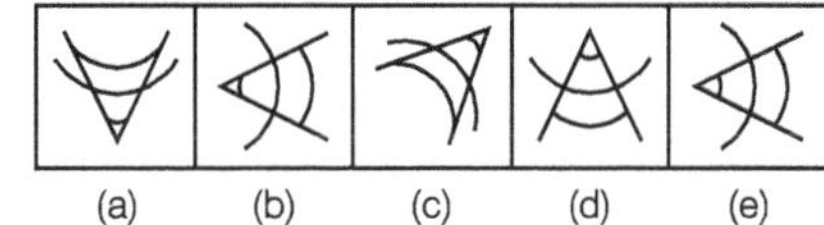

(a) (b) (c) (d) (e)

Solution ***(b)*** Except figure (b), in all the other figures, all the curved lines are in the same direction. In figure (b), the upper line has curve in opposite direction.

***Ex* 16**

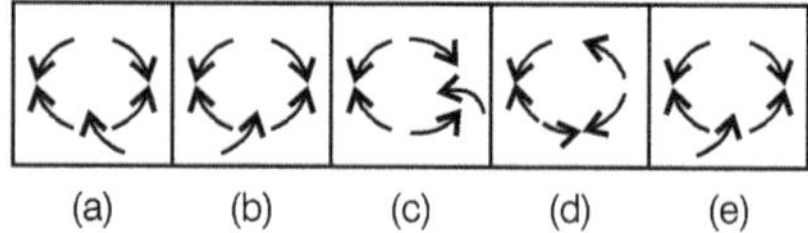

(a) (b) (c) (d) (e)

Solution ***(a)*** Except figure (a), in all the other figures, three arrows are in anti-clockwise direction and two arrows are in clockwise direction.

***Ex* 17**

(a)		(b)		(c)		(d)		(e)	
□	+	+	△	△	○	○	□	△	▽
○	△	□	○	×	▽	+	○	○	□
×	▽	▽	×	□	+	×	△	×	+

Solution ***(d)*** Except figure (d), all the other figures contain two triangles. Hence, it is different from the rest of the figures.

Relation between Elements of Figure

In this type of classification, the elements of the figure bear a certain relationship with each other except the odd figure. This relation can be based on the shape of elements, their presentation and their inversion.

DIRECTIONS ~ (Example Nos. 18-20) *In the following questions, a group of four/five figures is given. Out of which three/four figures are similar to each other in a certain way and one is different from others. Find the odd figure out.*

***Ex* 18**

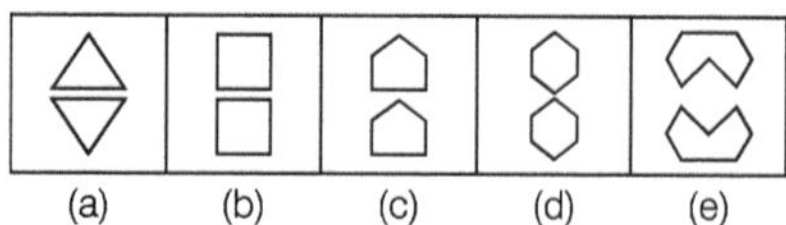

(a) (b) (c) (d) (e)

Solution ***(c)*** Except figure (c), in all the other figures, the bottom figure is the vertically inverted image of the top figure.

***Ex* 19**

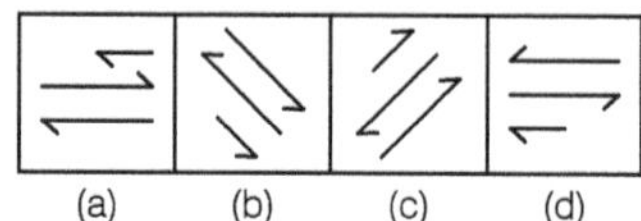

(a) (b) (c) (d) « SSC 10+2 2008

Solution ***(d)*** Two lines on the extreme ends of all the figures, except figure (d) have same direction of arrows. In figure (d), the direction of arrows at extreme ends is opposite.

***Ex* 20**

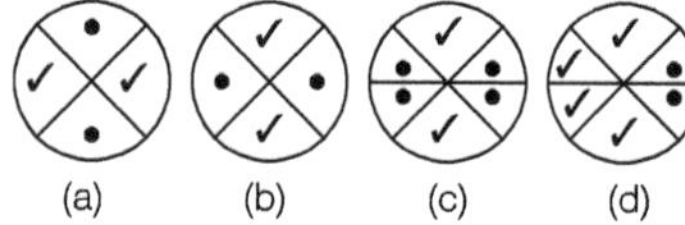

(a) (b) (c) (d)

« UP Police Constable 2018

Solution ***(d)*** Except figure (d), in all the other figures, elements in opposite sectors are same.

Interior-Exterior Consideration of Elements

A figure can be formed from two or more elements. It is likely that some elements may lie in interior of other elements while some may lie in the exterior of the other elements. This consideration can be used for the classification of elements within a group.

DIRECTIONS ~ (Example Nos. 21-23) *In the following questions, a group of four or five figures is given. Out of which three or four figures are similar to each other in a certain way and one is different from other. Find the odd figure out.*

***Ex* 21**

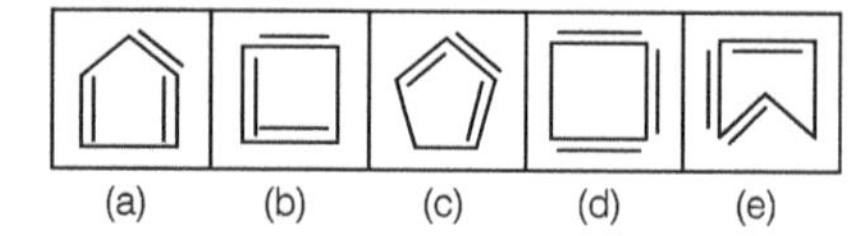

(a) (b) (c) (d) (e)

Solution ***(d)*** Only figure (d) does not contain any element present in the interior of the closed figure.

***Ex* 22**

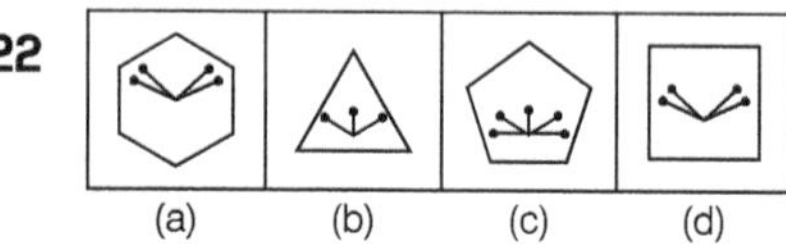

(a) (b) (c) (d)

« UP Police Constable 2018

Solution ***(a)*** Except figure (a), in all the other figures, the number of pins inside the geometrical figure is equal to the number of sides of the outer figure.

***Ex* 23**

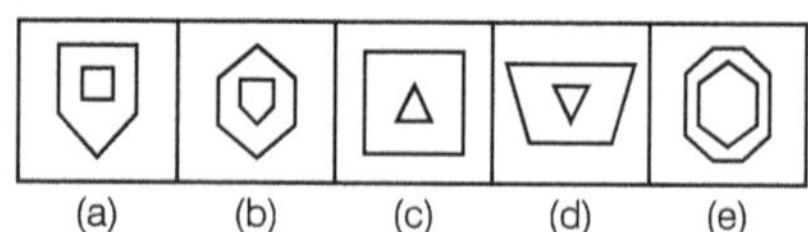

(a) (b) (c) (d) (e)

Solution ***(e)*** Except figure (e), in all the other figures, two concentric figures are arranged in such a way that the inner figure has one side less than the outer figure.

Based on Letter Shapes

This classification is based on shapes of different alphabets and how they are formed

(a) Letters made with straight lines

A, E, F, H, I, K, L, M, N, T, V, W, X, Y, Z

Letters made with one straight line = I

Letters made with two straight lines = L, T, V, X

Letters made with three straight lines = A, F, H, K, N, Y, Z

Letters made with four straight lines = E, M, W

(b) Letters made with curved lines = C, O, Q, U, S

(c) Letters made with the combination of straight and curved lines both = B, D, G, J, P, R

DIRECTIONS ~ (Example Nos. 24-25) *In the following questions, a group of four/five figures is given. Out of which three/four figures are similar to each other in a certain way and one is different from others. Find the different/odd figure out.*

Ex 24

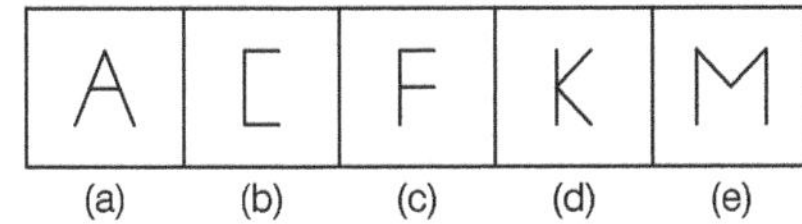

Solution (e) Except figure (e), all the other figures are made up of three straight lines but in option (e) four lines are involved.

Ex 25

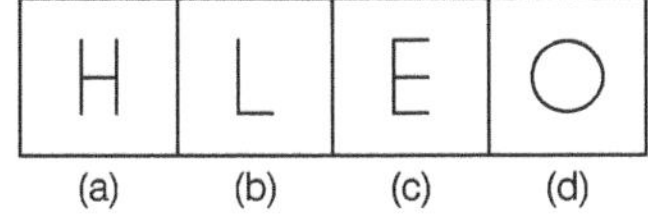

Solution (d) Except figure (d), all the other figures are made up of straight lines but figure (d) is made up of curved line.

Based on Real Objects

In this type of classification, the images of the objects that belong to the real world are given as alternatives. All the images except one have common meaning/features.

The candidate is required to choose the image which is different from others or does not have common feature as others or have different meaning from others.

DIRECTIONS ~ (Example Nos. 26 and 27) *In each of the following examples, choose the figure which is different from others.*

Ex 26

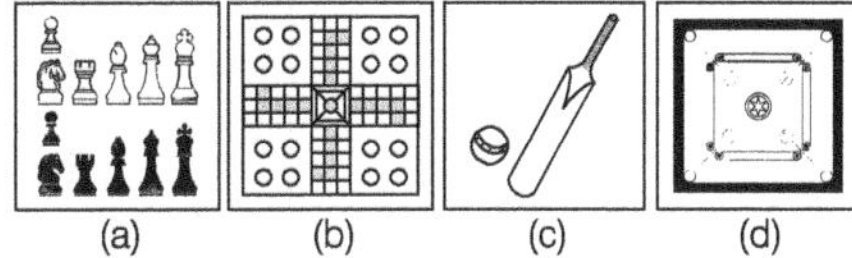

Solution (c) Except cricket, all the others are indoor games while cricket is an outdoor game.

Ex 27

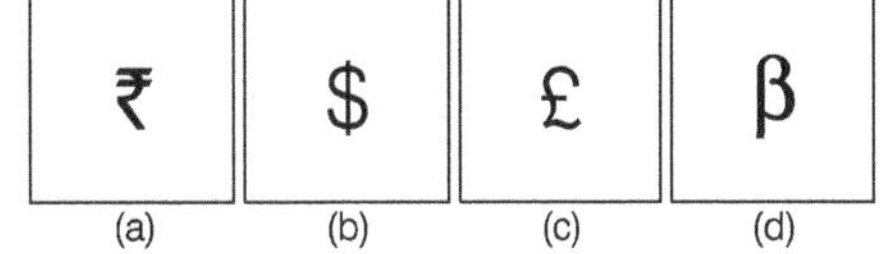

Solution (d) Except 'β' all the other symbols represent currencies of different nations.

₹ → Rupee (India)

$ → Dollar (USA)

£ → Pound (England)

Practice / CORNER

DIRECTIONS ~ (Q. Nos. 1-115) *In each of the following question, four/five figures are given. Three/four are similar in a certain way and so form a group. Find out which one of the figures does not belong to that group.*

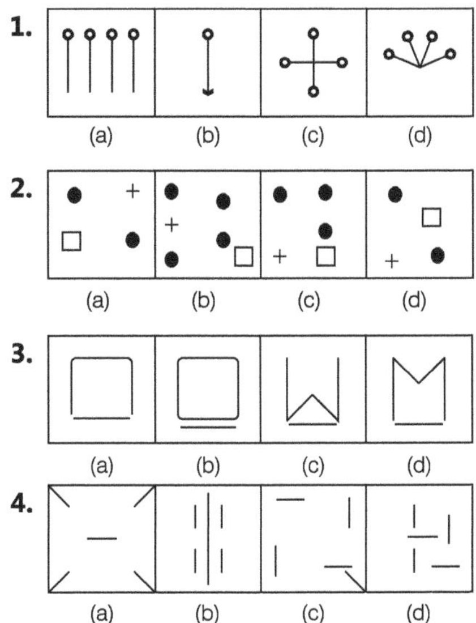

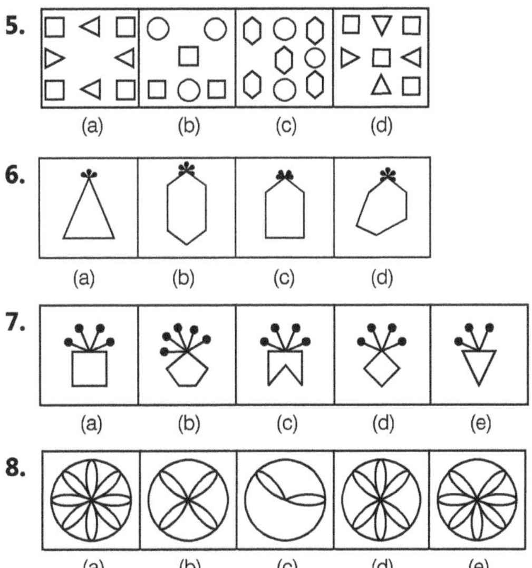

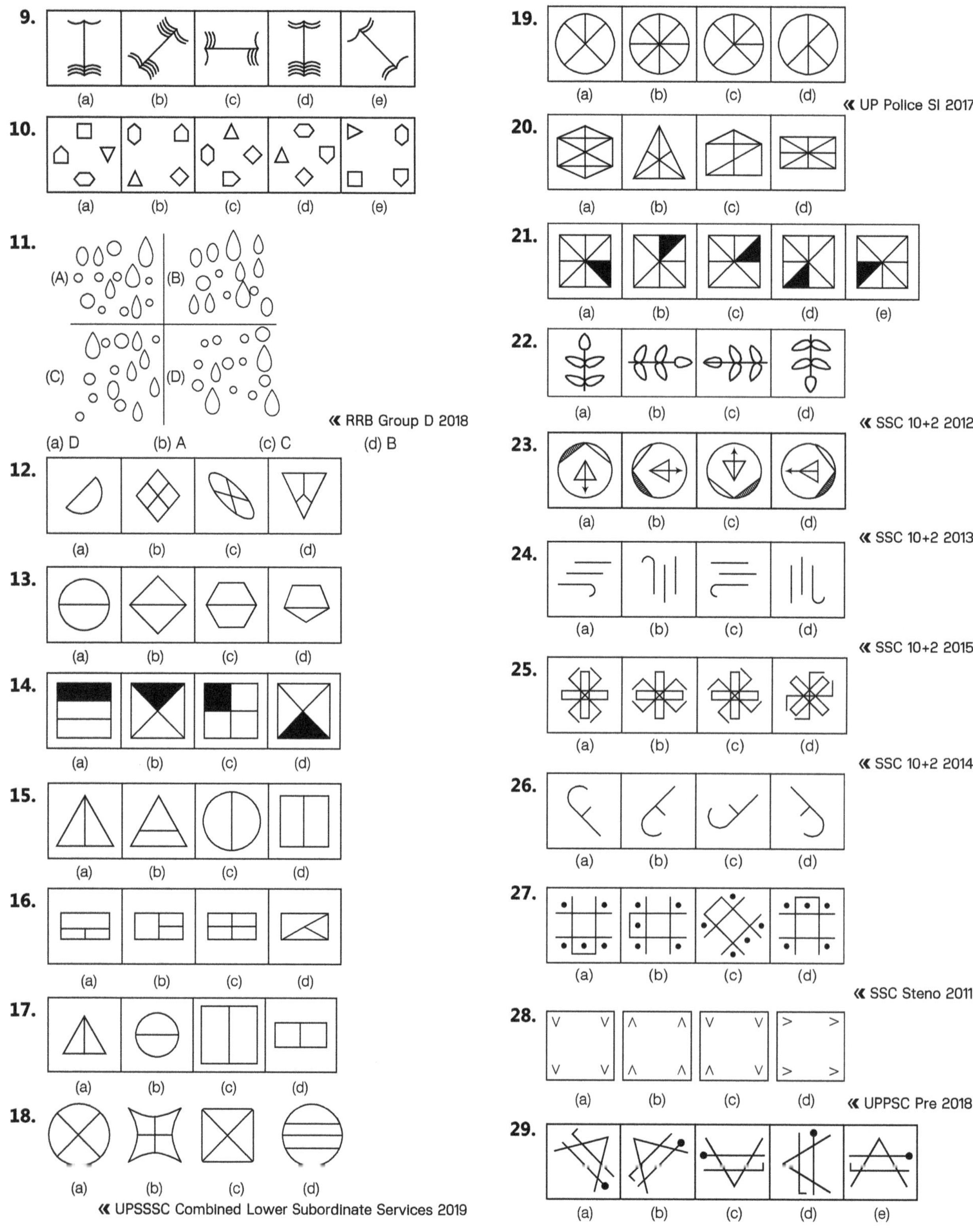
9.
(a) (b) (c) (d) (e)
10.
(a) (b) (c) (d) (e)
11.
(A) (B) (C) (D)
« RRB Group D 2018
(a) D (b) A (c) C (d) B
12.
(a) (b) (c) (d)
13.
(a) (b) (c) (d)
14.
(a) (b) (c) (d)
15.
(a) (b) (c) (d)
16.
(a) (b) (c) (d)
17.
(a) (b) (c) (d)
18.
(a) (b) (c) (d)
« UPSSSC Combined Lower Subordinate Services 2019
19.
(a) (b) (c) (d)
« UP Police SI 2017
20.
(a) (b) (c) (d)
21.
(a) (b) (c) (d) (e)
22.
(a) (b) (c) (d)
« SSC 10+2 2012
23.
(a) (b) (c) (d)
« SSC 10+2 2013
24.
(a) (b) (c) (d)
« SSC 10+2 2015
25.
(a) (b) (c) (d)
« SSC 10+2 2014
26.
(a) (b) (c) (d)
27.
(a) (b) (c) (d)
« SSC Steno 2011
28.
(a) (b) (c) (d)
« UPPSC Pre 2018
29.
(a) (b) (c) (d) (e)

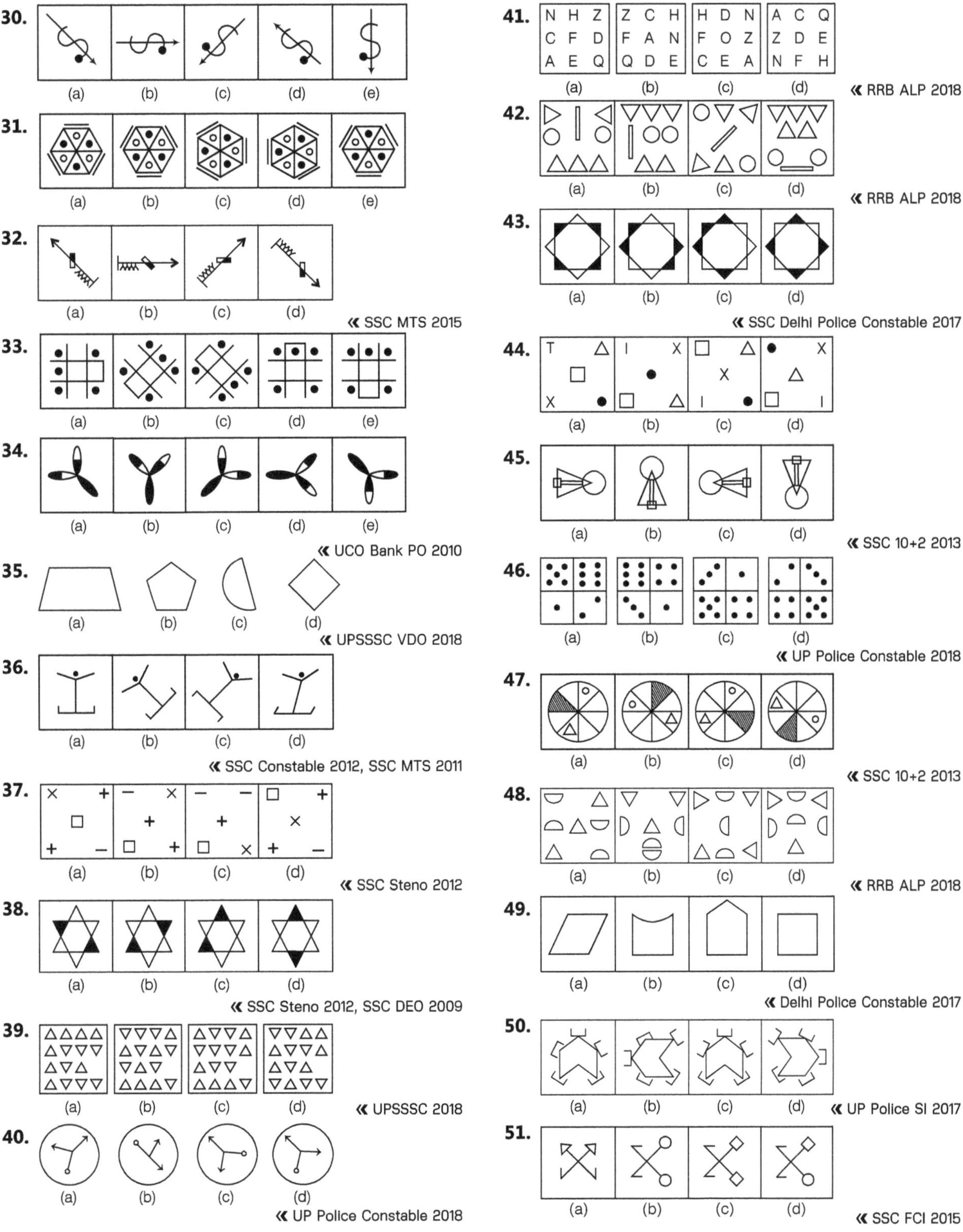
30.
(a) (b) (c) (d) (e)
31.
(a) (b) (c) (d) (e)
32.
(a) (b) (c) (d)
« SSC MTS 2015
33.
(a) (b) (c) (d) (e)
34.
(a) (b) (c) (d) (e)
« UCO Bank PO 2010
35.
(a) (b) (c) (d)
« UPSSSC VDO 2018
36.
(a) (b) (c) (d)
« SSC Constable 2012, SSC MTS 2011
37.
(a) (b) (c) (d)
« SSC Steno 2012
38.
(a) (b) (c) (d)
« SSC Steno 2012, SSC DEO 2009
39.
(a) (b) (c) (d)
« UPSSSC 2018
40.
(a) (b) (c) (d)
« UP Police Constable 2018
41.
N H Z
C F D
A E Q
Z C H
F A N
Q D E
H D N
F O Z
C E A
A C Q
Z D E
N F H
(a) (b) (c) (d)
« RRB ALP 2018
42.
(a) (b) (c) (d)
« RRB ALP 2018
43.
(a) (b) (c) (d)
« SSC Delhi Police Constable 2017
44.
T
X
I
X
X
I
X
I
(a) (b) (c) (d)
45.
(a) (b) (c) (d)
« SSC 10+2 2013
46.
(a) (b) (c) (d)
« UP Police Constable 2018
47.
(a) (b) (c) (d)
« SSC 10+2 2013
48.
(a) (b) (c) (d)
« RRB ALP 2018
49.
(a) (b) (c) (d)
« Delhi Police Constable 2017
50.
(a) (b) (c) (d)
« UP Police SI 2017
51.
(a) (b) (c) (d)
« SSC FCI 2015

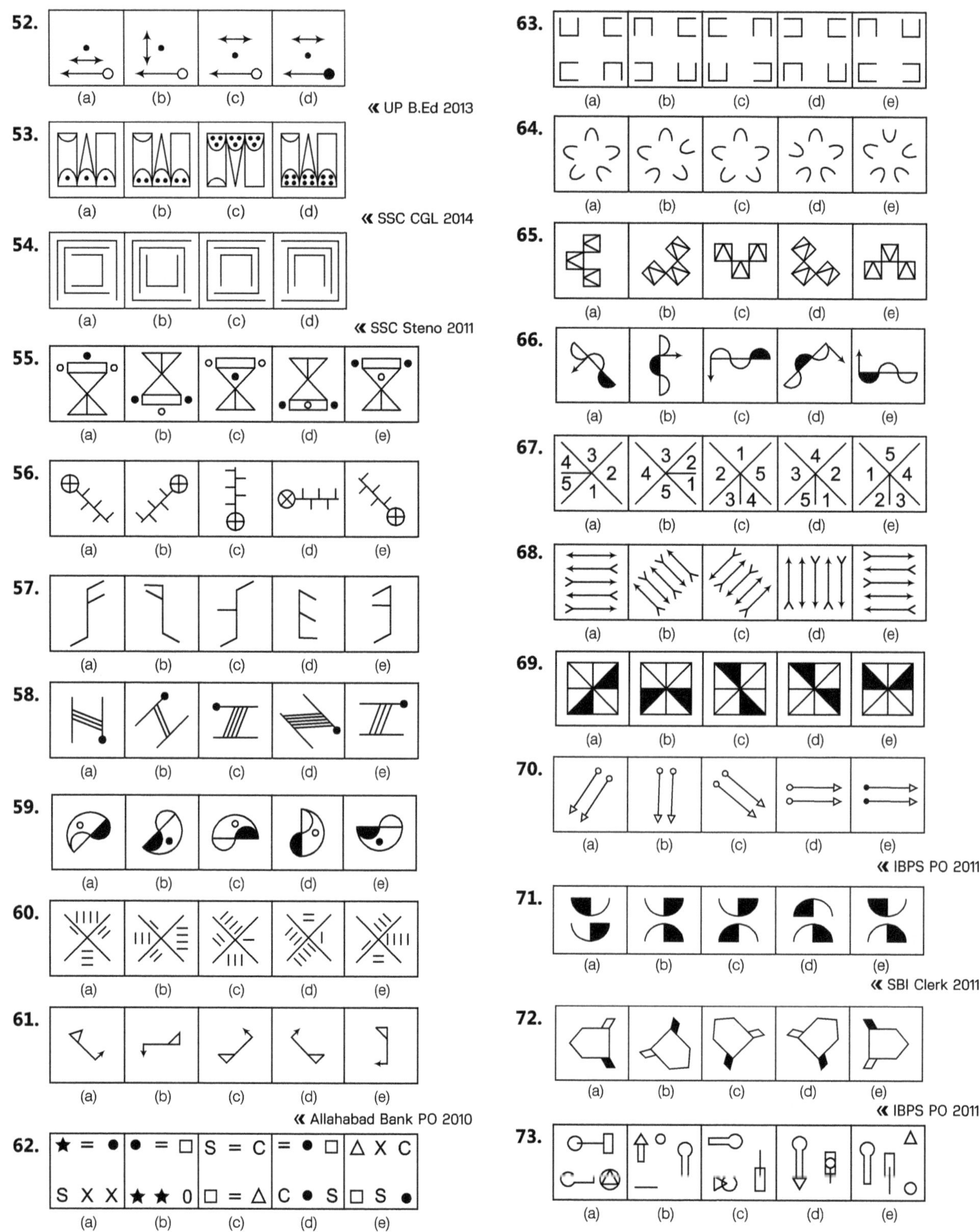
52.
(a) (b) (c) (d)
« UP B.Ed 2013
53.
(a) (b) (c) (d)
« SSC CGL 2014
54.
(a) (b) (c) (d)
« SSC Steno 2011
55.
(a) (b) (c) (d) (e)
56.
(a) (b) (c) (d) (e)
57.
(a) (b) (c) (d) (e)
58.
(a) (b) (c) (d) (e)
59.
(a) (b) (c) (d) (e)
60.
(a) (b) (c) (d) (e)
61.
(a) (b) (c) (d) (e)
« Allahabad Bank PO 2010
62.
★ = ● S X X
● = □ ★ ★ 0
S = C □ = △
= ● □ C ● S
△ X C □ S ●
(a) (b) (c) (d) (e)
63.
(a) (b) (c) (d) (e)
64.
(a) (b) (c) (d) (e)
65.
(a) (b) (c) (d) (e)
66.
(a) (b) (c) (d) (e)
67.
4 3 5 2 1
4 3 2 5 1
1 2 5 3 4
4 3 2 5 1
5 1 4 2 3
(a) (b) (c) (d) (e)
68.
(a) (b) (c) (d) (e)
69.
(a) (b) (c) (d) (e)
70.
(a) (b) (c) (d) (e)
« IBPS PO 2011
71.
(a) (b) (c) (d) (e)
« SBI Clerk 2011
72.
(a) (b) (c) (d) (e)
« IBPS PO 2011
73.
(a) (b) (c) (d) (e)

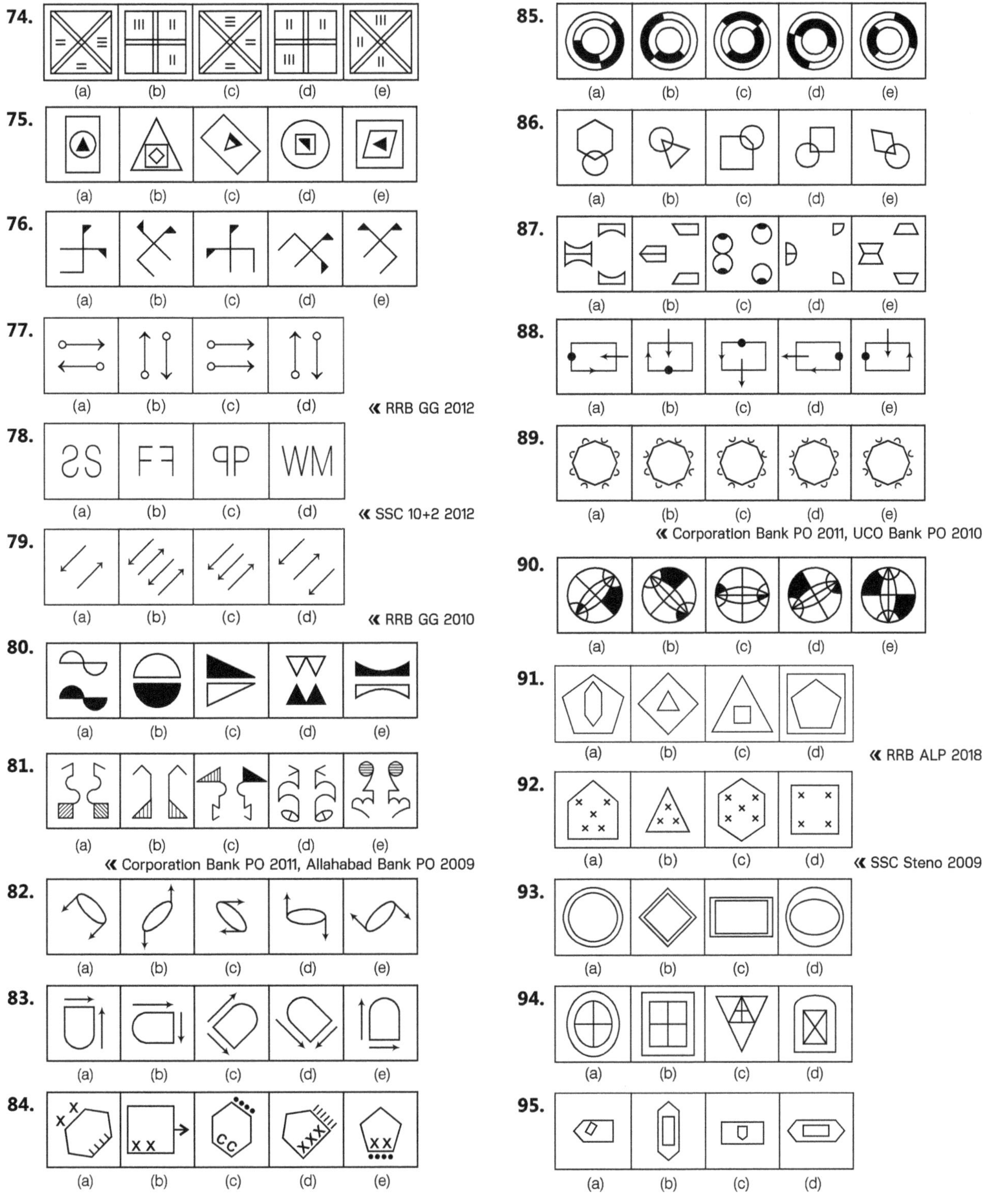

74.
75.
76.
77.
« RRB GG 2012
78.
« SSC 10+2 2012
79.
« RRB GG 2010
80.
81.
« Corporation Bank PO 2011, Allahabad Bank PO 2009
82.
83.
84.
85.
86.
87.
88.
89.
« Corporation Bank PO 2011, UCO Bank PO 2010
90.
91.
« RRB ALP 2018
92.
« SSC Steno 2009
93.
94.
95.

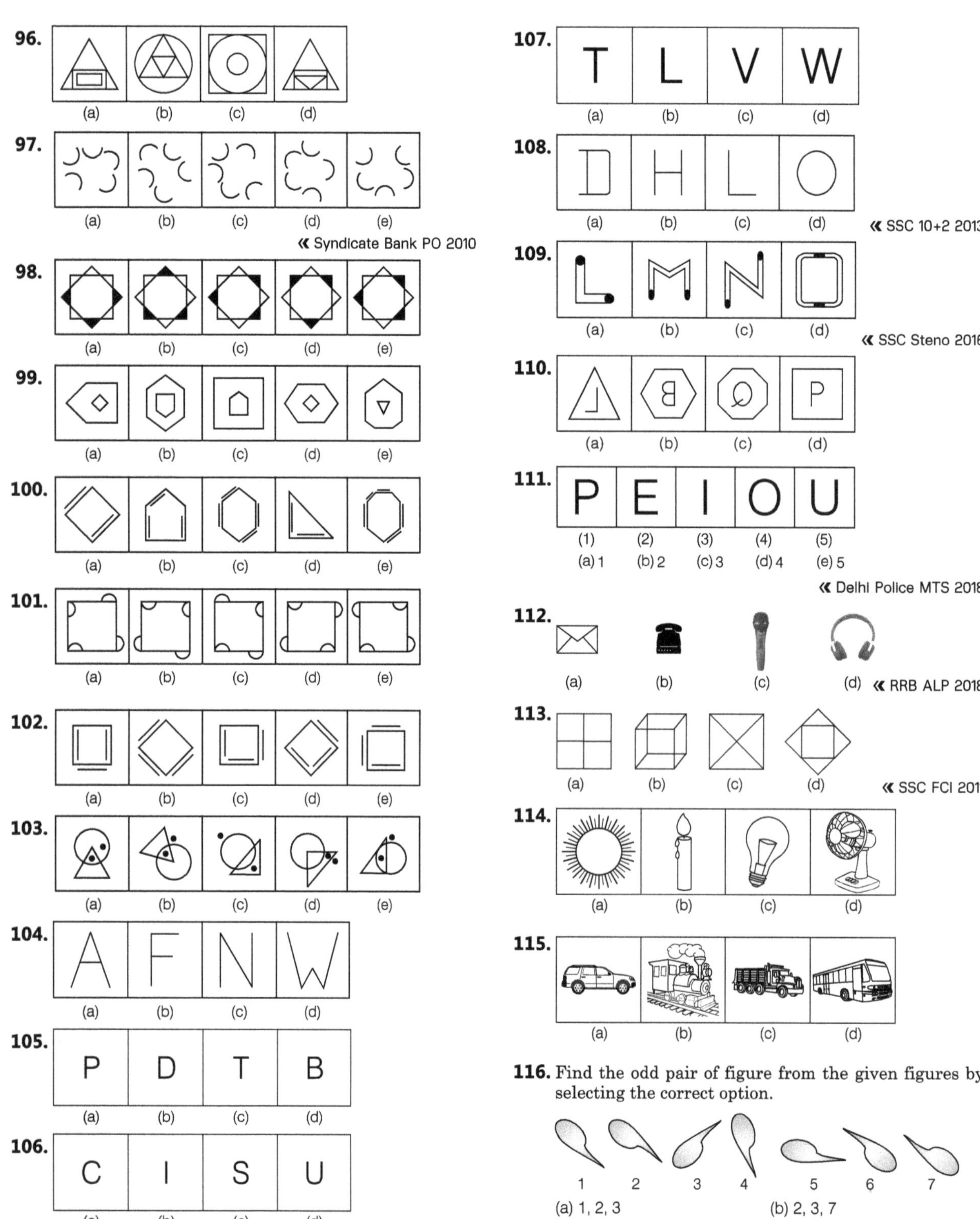
96. (a) (b) (c) (d)
97. (a) (b) (c) (d) (e)
« Syndicate Bank PO 2010
98. (a) (b) (c) (d) (e)
99. (a) (b) (c) (d) (e)
100. (a) (b) (c) (d) (e)
101. (a) (b) (c) (d) (e)
102. (a) (b) (c) (d) (e)
103. (a) (b) (c) (d) (e)
104. A F N W
(a) (b) (c) (d)
105. P D T B
(a) (b) (c) (d)
106. C I S U
(a) (b) (c) (d)
107. T L V W
(a) (b) (c) (d)
108. D H L O
(a) (b) (c) (d)
« SSC 10+2 2013
109. (a) (b) (c) (d)
« SSC Steno 2016
110. (a) (b) (c) (d)
111. P E I O U
(1) (2) (3) (4) (5)
(a) 1 (b) 2 (c) 3 (d) 4 (e) 5
« Delhi Police MTS 2018
112. (a) (b) (c) (d)
« RRB ALP 2018
113. (a) (b) (c) (d)
« SSC FCI 2011
114. (a) (b) (c) (d)
115. (a) (b) (c) (d)
116. Find the odd pair of figure from the given figures by selecting the correct option.
1 2 3 4 5 6 7
(a) 1, 2, 3 (b) 2, 3, 7
(c) 3, 7, 4 (d) 4, 1, 6

Answers WITH EXPLANATIONS

1. (*b*) Except figure (b), in all the other figures, there are four line segments and each line segment is attached with a small circle.

2. (*c*) Except figure (c), all the other figures have even number of shaded circles.

3. (*a*) Except figure (a), all the other figures have five sides.

4. (*b*) Except figure (b), in all the other figures, all the five segments are of equal length.

5. (*c*) Except figure (c), in all the other figures, two different shapes are equal in number.

6. (*a*) Except figure (a), in all the other figures, the number of pins at the top of the figure is one less than the number of sides of the geometrical figure.

7. (*c*) In all the other figures except (c), the number of pins at the top of the figure is equal to the number of sides of the geometrical figure.

8. (*e*) The number of leaves is odd in figure (e), whereas it is even in all the other figures.

9. (*e*) Only in figure (e), number of curves on either side of line is odd, whereas in all the other figures, it is even.

10. (*c*) In all the other figures except (c), all the four figures are arranged in anti-clockwise direction in ascending order of their sides.

11. (*d*) Except figure (B) in all the other figures, there are total 15 designs but in figure (B) there are only 14 designs in total.

12. (*a*) In all the other figures except (a), there is division of figures into several parts.

13. (*d*) Except figure (d), all the other figures are divided into two equal parts.

14. (*a*) In all the other figures, one-fourth part of the design is shaded, while in figure (a), only one-third part is shaded.

15. (*b*) Except figure (b), all the other figures are divided into two equal parts.

16. (*c*) Except figure (c), in all the other figures, the design has been divided into three parts.

17. (*b*) All figures have a vertical line dividing the figure equally, while figure (b) is divided by a horizontal line.

18. (*d*) Except figure (d), in all the others, the shape has been divided into four equal parts.

19. (*b*) The figure given in option (b) is divided into smaller parts of equal area whereas in rest of the figures, the area of the smaller parts is not equal.

20. (*c*) Except figure (c), in all the other figures, line segments divide the shape into equal parts.

21. (*a*) In all the other figures except (a), square is divided into seven parts and one part is shaded.

22. (*c*) Except figure (c), all the other figures have undivided leave on top of the line.

23. (*d*) Except figure (d), in all the other figures, the arrow in the triangle is drawn from the corner whereas in figure (d) the arrow is from one of the side.

24. (*a*) Except figure (a), design in all the other figures is same and can be obtained by rotating one-another.

25. (c) Except figure (c), design in all the other figures is same when rotated.

26. (*b*) Except figure (b), design in all the other figures is same when rotated anti-clockwise.

27. (*c*) Except figure (c), all the other figures are same when rotated 90° clockwise.

28. (*c*) Except figure (c), in all the other figures, all the four designs face the same direction respectively.

29. (*a*) In all the other figures except (a), the line is bent towards the pin.

30. (*d*) All the other figures, except figure (d), are rotated forms of same figure.

31. (*d*) In all the figures, except figure (d), the line is placed adjacent to the unshaded circle.

32. (*b*) Except figure (b), design in all the other figures is same when rotated.

33. (*d*) Except figure (d), all the other figures are same when rotated.

34. (*c*) All the other figures except (c), are the rotated forms of the same figure.

35. (*c*) Except figure (c), all the other shapes are made up of straight lines only.

36. (*c*) Except figure (c), all the other figures have their legs facing in upward direction.

37. (*c*) Except figure (c), all the other figures have two plus (+) and one minus (−) sign but in figure (c), it is *vice-versa*.

38. (*c*) In all figures except (c), the shaded portions lie opposite to each other.

39. (*a*) Figure given in option (a) has seven small triangles (∇) pointing downwards whereas in rest of the figures there are eight small triangles pointing downwards.

40. (*b*) In figure (b), the small circle and arrow are exactly opposite to each other, making an angle of 180° with each other whereas in rest of the figures, they are not opposite to each other.

41. (*c*) Figure given in option (c) has three vowels (O, E, A) whereas in rest of the figures there are two vowels (A, E).

42. (*c*) Except figure (c), all the other figures contain five triangles, two circles and one rectangle but in figure (c) there are four triangles only.

43. (*c*) Except figure (c), in rest of the figures, the shaded portions are opposite to each others.

44. (*a*) Except figure (a), in rest of the figures, the elements in the square are same, whereas in figure (a), element 'T' replaces element (I).

45. (*b*) Only in figure (b), pipe is present inside the square while it is absent in squares of the rest of the figures.

46. (*c*) Except figure (c), in rest of the figures, the number of dots in two small squares is even and number of dots in rest of the two small squares is odd.
Whereas in figure (c), three small squares have odd number of dots and one small square has even number of dots.

47. (*c*) In all the figures except figure (c), there is a blank portion between the shaded portion and the circle and triangle containing portion respectively.

48. (*c*) Except figure (c), all the other figures have 4 semicircle and 3 triangles.

49. (*b*) Except figure (b), all the other figures are made up of straight lines but in figure (b) there is a curved line.

50. (*c*) Except figure (c), in all the other figures, three small designs are facing towards the corners of the main figure but in figure (c) only two small designs are facing towards the corners of the main figure.

51. (*d*) Except figure (d), in all the other figures, designs attached to both the lines are same.

52. (*d*) Except figure (d), in all the other figures, the bottom arrow contains a white circle at one end.

53. (*c*) Except figure (c), all the other figures have same orientation whereas figure (c) is inverted figure.

54. (*d*) Except figure (d), in all other figures, the open shapes are in different directions.

55. (*d*) In all the other figures except (d), there is no small circle between the parallel lines.

56. (*c*) Only in figure (c), the cross inside the circle is directly attached with the main line segment.

57. (*a*) In all the other figures except (a), one of the small lines attached to the main line segment is perpendicular to it.

58. (*c*) In all the other figures except (c), transverse lines between the two parallel lines are inclined towards the dot.

59. (*c*) In all the other figures except (c), small semi-circle and dot inside the large semi-circle are identical. *i.e.,* either shaded or unshaded in similar manner.

60. (*d*) Only in figure (d), the lines are arranged in order (according to the number of times, the lines occur in anti-clockwise manner) while in all other figures, this order is not maintained.

61. (*b*) In all the figures, except figure (b), triangle is formed on the same side in which the arrow is directed. In figure (b), triangle and arrow are directed opposite to each other and hence, does not belong to this group.

62. (*e*) In all the other figures except (e), any two of the symbols are identical whereas in figure (e) all the symbols are different.

63. (*a*) In figure (a), two of the cups are placed in the same direction while in all the other figures, all the cups are placed in different directions.

64. (*c*) Only in figure (c), all the curves are positioned inside.

65. (*e*) In all the figures except (e), the orientation 'V' inside the squares are in the same direction.

66. (*a*) In all the other figures except (a), shaded portion is in the opposite direction of the arrow.

67. (*d*) In all the other figures except (d), the numbers from 1 to 5 are in a serial order.

68. (*b*) In figure (b), the double headed arrow (↔) is missing but it is present in all the other figures.

69. (*c*) In all other figures except (c), both the shaded portions have two and four blank portions between them whereas in figure (c) there are three blank portion between the two shaded portion.

70. (*e*)Except figure (e), all the other figures are completely same and are the different orientation of the same figure.

71. (*b*) Except figure (b), in all the other figures the opposite portion of both the shapes are shaded.

72. (*d*) Except figure (d), all the other figures are same when rotated.

73. (*a*) Figure (a) does not belong to the group as all the other figures contain same elements.

74. (*e*) In all figures except (e), the groups of lines are arranged anti-clockwise and the group of three lines is at the anti-clockwise end.

75. (*c*) In all the other figures except (c), there are three figures which are not identical to each other.

76. (*a*) In all the other figures except (a), shaded triangle and the line segment attached to straight line lie on the same side.

77. (*c*) Except figure (c), in all the other figures both the arrows are opposite to each other.

78. (*d*) Except figure (d), in all the other figures both the letters are mirror image of each other.

79. (*c*) Except figure (c), in all the other figures two adjacent arrows are opposite to each other.

80. (*a*) In all the other figures except figure (a), the lower figure is obtained by inverting the upper figure and shading it.

81. (*c*) Except figure (c), in all the other figures, the shading pattern is same, whereas in figure (c) one of the figure is dark shaded.

82. (*a*) In all the other figures except (a), both the arrows attached to the main figure are in opposite direction to each other.

83. (*b*) In all figures except (b), the two arrows are in opposite direction *i.e.,* one in clockwise direction and the other in anti-clockwise direction along the main figure.

84. (*e*) In all the other figures except (e), symbols inside and outside the figures are placed along the different sides of the figures.

85. (*e*) In all the other figures except (e), shaded portions of the circles are attached with each other at a point.

86. (*c*) In figure (c), circle intersects or covers three sides of the other figure whereas in all the other figures, it intersects or covers two sides of the other figure.

87. (*c*) In all the other figures except (c), if both the figures on the right hand side are first inverted and then joined together, then the figure on the left hand side is obtained.

88. (*e*) In all the other figures except figure (e), arrow and black dot are at the opposite sides but in figure (e), they are placed at the adjacent sides.

89. (*a*) In all the other figures except (a), equal number of arcs are facing inside and outside, respectively.

90. (*e*) Only in figure (e), both the shaded designs have the common base *i.e.,* the middle line.

91. (*b*) Except figure (b), in all the other figures number of lines in outer shape is one less than the number of lines in inner shape.

92. (*c*) Except figure (c), in all other figures the number of lines in the outer shape and the number of crosses are same respectively.

93. (*d*) Except figure (d), in all the other figures there are two similar designs.

94. (*d*) Except figure (d), in all other figures, the outer and inner figures are similar and there is a plus (+) sign in inner figure. While there is a cross in figure (d), the inner figure is not similar to the outer figure.

95. (*c*) Except figure (c), in all the other figures, the inner design consists of less number of sides than that of the outer design. But in option (c), the inner design has more sides than the outer design.

96. (*d*) Except figure (d), in all the other figures, the outer design encloses two similar shapes.

97. (*d*) In all the other figures except (d), three arcs face outside and two inside.

98. (*a*) Only in figure (a), the three adjacent vertices of the square are shaded.

99. (*c*) In all the other figures except (c), inner figure has less number of sides than the outer figure.

100. (*d*) In all the other figures except (d), the number of line segments along the boundary of the figure is two less than the number of sides of the respective figure.

101. (*c*) Only in figure (c) two semi-circles (one outer and one inner) are present on the same side of the square.

102. (*b*) Only in figure (b), all the line segments are outside the square.

103. (*a*) In all the other figures except (a), one dot is outside the figure while the other is inside the figure.

104. (*d*) Except figure (d), all the other designs are made up of three line segments, whereas figure (d) is made up of four line segments.

105. (*c*) Except 'T' all other letters are made up of straight and curved lines while letter 'T' is made up of only straight lines.

106. (*b*) Except I, all the other letters are made up of curved line while letter 'I' is made up of only straight lines.

107. (*d*) Except W, all other letters are made up of only two straight lines while letter 'W' is made up of four straight lines.

108. (*d*) Except figure (d), design in all the other figures is made up of straight lines but design in figure (d) is made up of curved line.

109. (*d*) Except figure (d), all the other figures contain open designs.

110. (*d*) Except figure (d) in all the other figures, the letter inside the figure is the mirror image of their respective capital letters of English alphabet.

111. (*a*) Except figure (1), all the others are vowels whereas P is a consonant.

112. (*d*) Except figure (d) all the others are used for sending the information while headphone is used for only receiving the information.

113. (*b*) Only figure (b) is a 3D image while all other figures are 2D image.

114. (*d*) Except fan, all other objects are different sources of light.

115. (*b*) Except Train, all others are four wheelers.

116. (*b*) Figures 2, 3 and 7 move in clockwise direction whereas figure number 1, 4, 5 and 6 move anti-clockwise direction.

CHAPTER / 04

Completion of Figures

Figure completion is a process of finding out the missing part of an incomplete figure.

Questions asked from this chapter are divided into two parts, a question figure and answer figures.

The question figure is incomplete as its one part (generally 1/4th part of the figure) is missing denoted by a question mark (?). Here, the candidate is required to choose a figure from the given answer figures that fits at the place of the question mark (?) in order to complete the design of the question figure.

Let us see some illustrative examples given below to have a better idea about the type of questions asked.

***Ex* 01** Which of the answer figures given below will complete the pattern of the question figure?

Question Figure **Answer Figures**

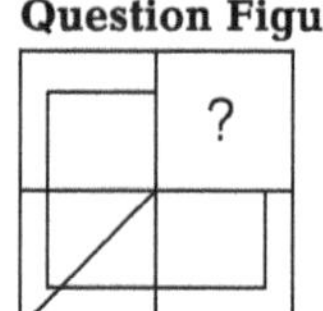

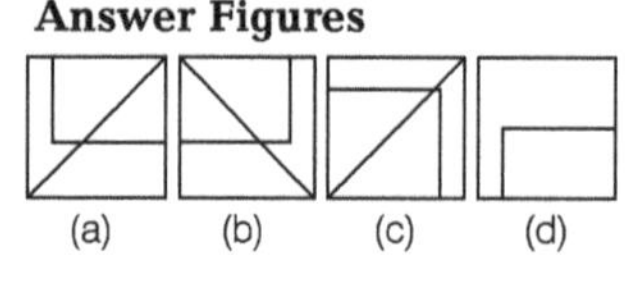

« SSC Steno 2019

***Solution* (c)** Here, the diagonally opposite parts have similar design. So, we can obtain the answer figure for the missing portion by rotating the question figure by 180°.

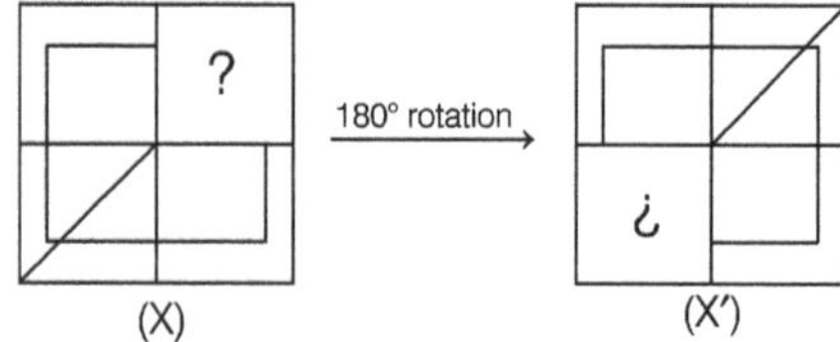

Now, on comparing figure (X) with (X′), we get

So, it is clear that the answer figure (c) will complete the question figure X, which will look like as shown in the following figure.

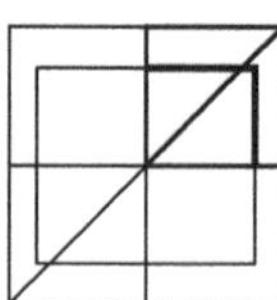

***Ex* 02** Which one of the answer figures will complete the given question figure? « SSC CGL 2016

Question Figure **Answer Figures**

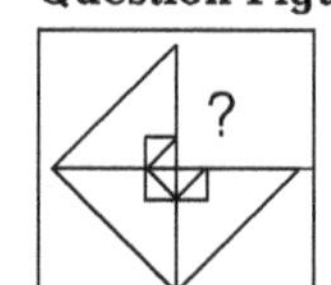

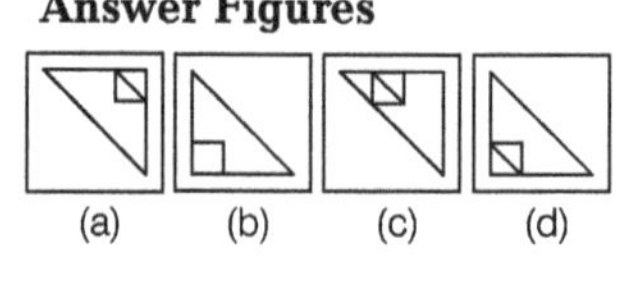

***Solution* (d)** Here, the diagonally opposite parts have similar design. So, we can obtain the answer figure for the missing portion by rotating the question figure by 180°.

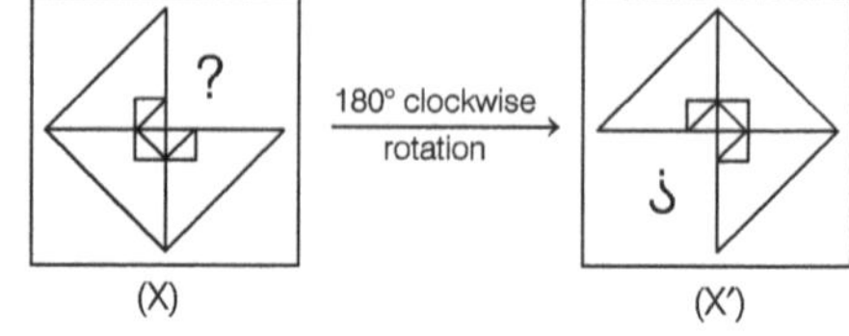

On comparing figures (X) and (X′), we get

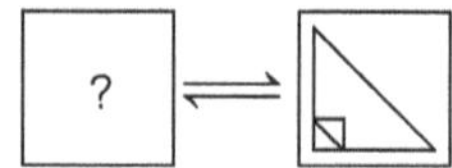

So, it is clear that the answer figure (d) will replace the (?) to make the question figure complete.

***Ex* 03** Identify the missing part of the question figure and select it from given answer figures.

Question Figure **Answer Figures**

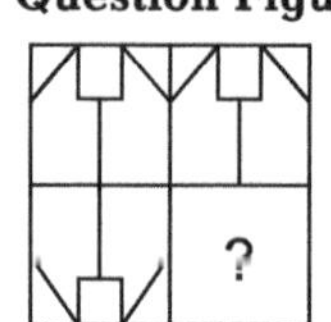

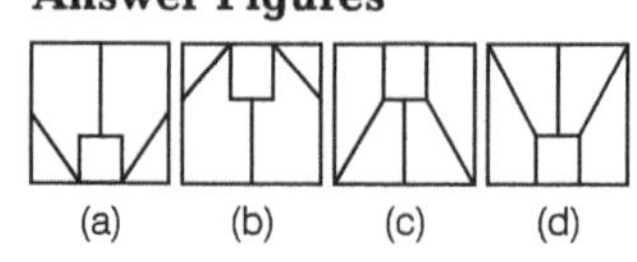

Solution (a) Here, the upper two parts i.e., (1) and (2) are same. Then, the missing part i.e. (3) will be same as part (4).

1	2
4	3

Hence, the answer figure (a) will replace the question mark (?).

Ex 04 **Which answer figure will complete the pattern in the given question figure?** « SSC CGL 2017

Question Figure **Answer Figures**

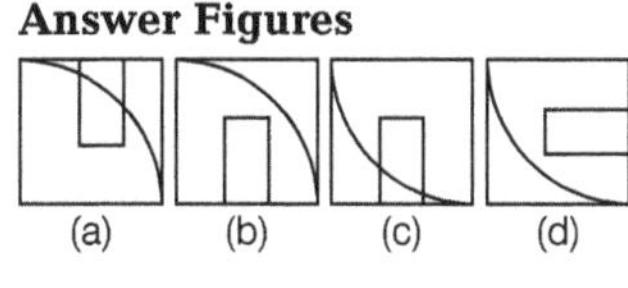

Solution (a) Let the figure is

1	2
4	3

Here, the upper two adjacent parts *i.e.*, (1) and (2) are laterally inverted form of each other. So, the missing part i.e., (4) will be the laterally inverted form of part (3). So, from the given answer figures, it is clear that the answer figure (a) is the laterally inverted form of (3) and hence figure (a) will replace the (?) to complete the pattern.

Ex 05 **A piece of paper is cut as shown in the following figure, in which a part of the picture is missing. From the given answer figures, select the appropriate part which is missing?** « UP Police SI 2017

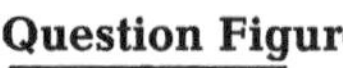

Question Figure **Answer Figures**

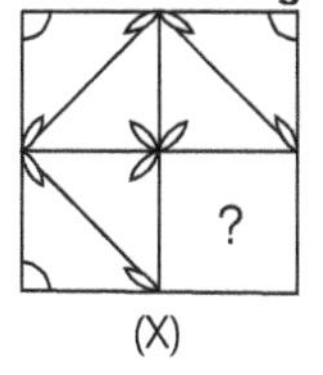

(X)

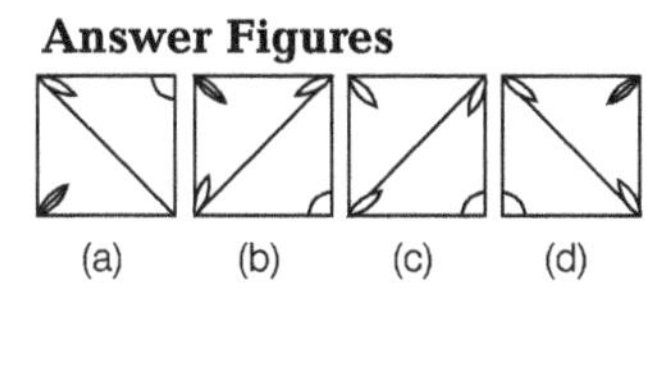

Solution (c) Here, all the three parts have similar design so, we can obtain the answer figure for the missing portion by rotating the question figure by 90° in clockwise direction.

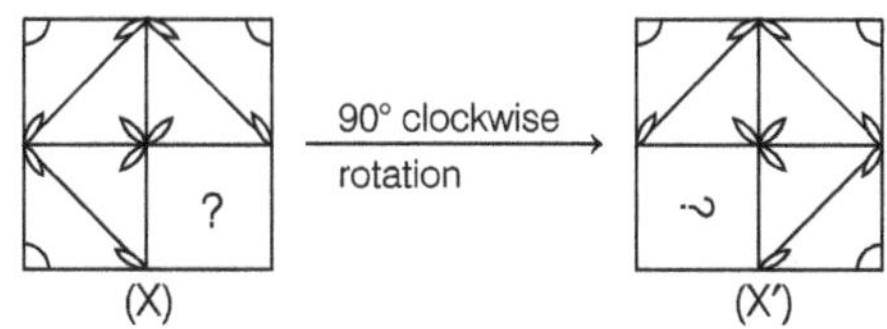

Now, on comparing figures (X) and (X′), we get

Now, it is clear that answer figure (c) will complete the question figure, which will look like as shown in the figure given below.

Ex 06 **Identify the missing part of the question figure and select it from given answer figures.**

Question Figure **Answer Figures**

(X)

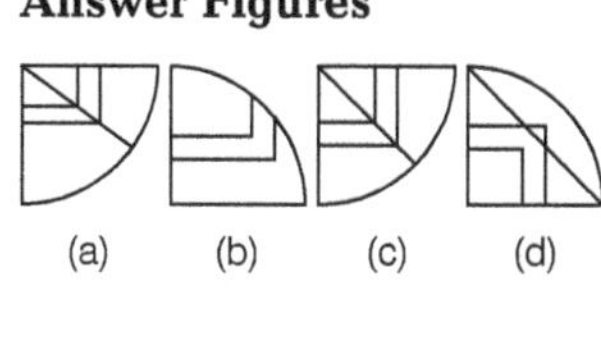

Solution (c) Here, all the three parts have similar design so, we can obtain the answer figure for the missing portion by rotating the question figure by 90° clockwise.

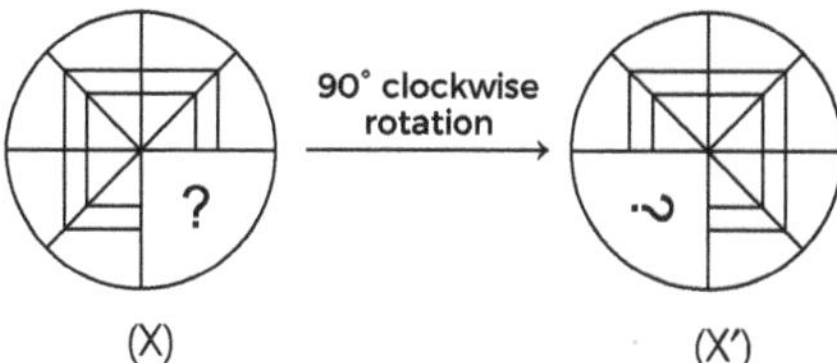

Now, on comparing figures (X) and (X′), we get

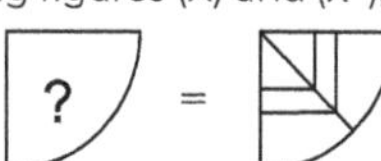

Now, it is clear that option (c) will fill the missing part of the question figure (X). After completion, the figure will look like as given below.

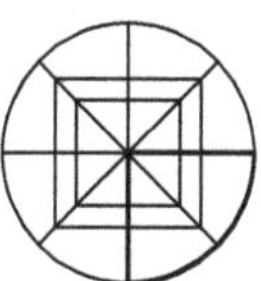

Ex 07 **Identify the missing part of the question figure and select it from the given answer figures.**

Question Figure **Answer Figures**

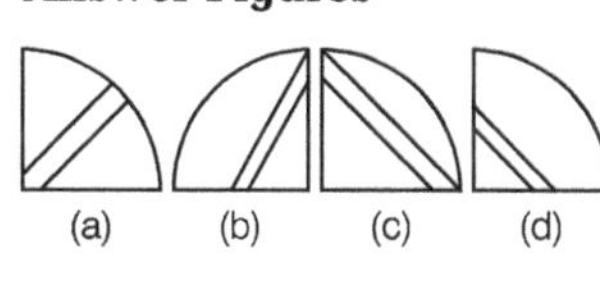

Solution (b) Here, we observe that the given pattern is of a double line triangle.

So, it is clear that the answer figure (b) will replace the (?) to complete the question figure as shown above.

Practice CORNER

DIRECTIONS ~ (Q. Nos. 1-84) *In each of the following questions, a part of the given question figure is missing. Find out from the given answer figures* (a), (b), (c) *and* (d), *that can replace the '?' to complete the question figure.*

Question Figure **Answer Figures**

1. ?

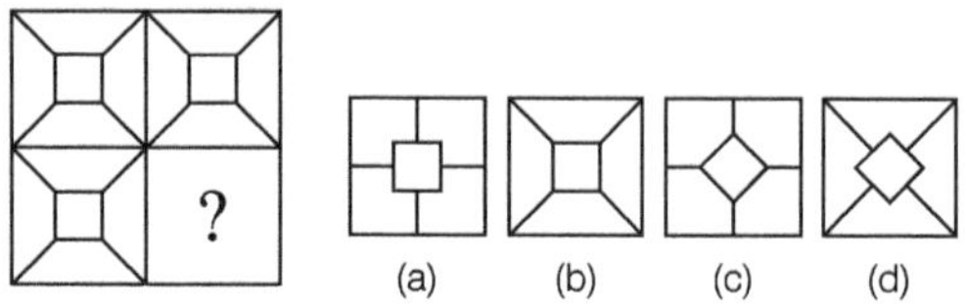

(a) (b) (c) (d)

2. ?

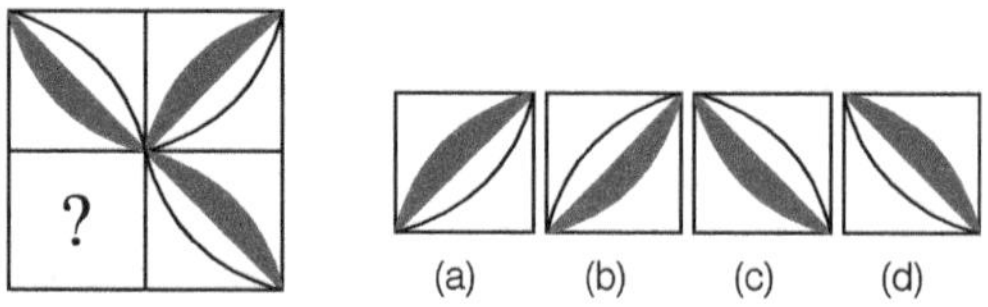

(a) (b) (c) (d)

« SSC Constable 2018

3. ?

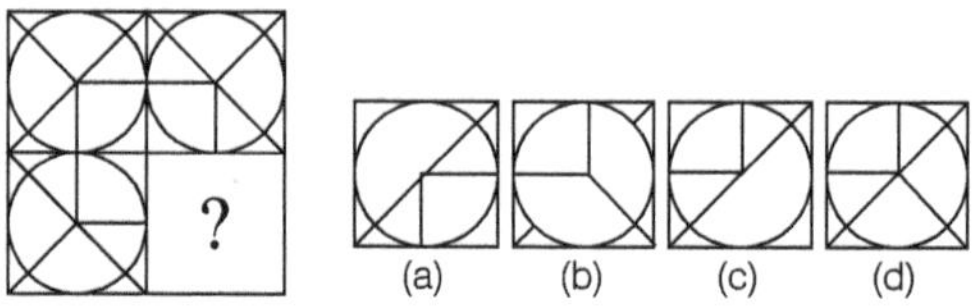

(a) (b) (c) (d)

« SSC CPO 2013

4. ?

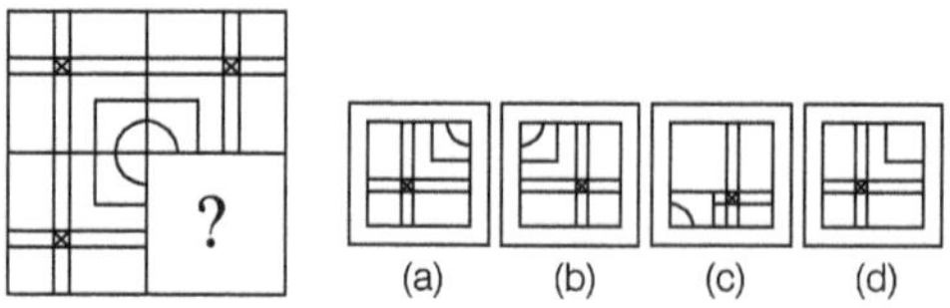

(a) (b) (c) (d)

« SSC Steno 2016

5. ?

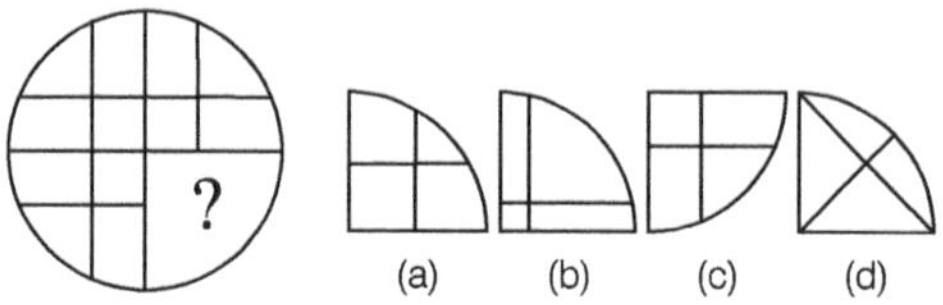

(a) (b) (c) (d)

« UP B.Ed 2011

6. ?

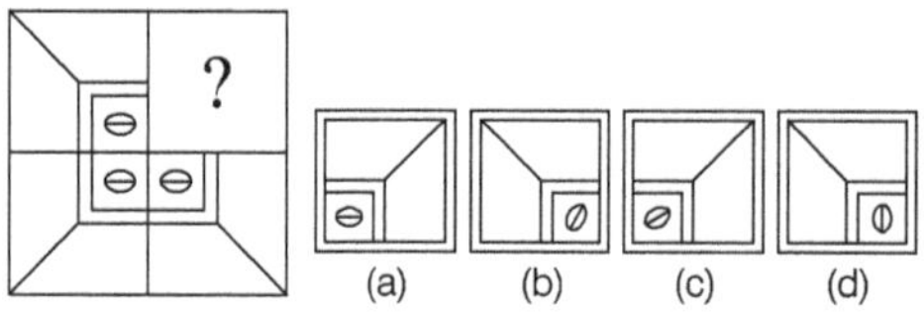

(a) (b) (c) (d)

« RRB JE 2019

7. ?

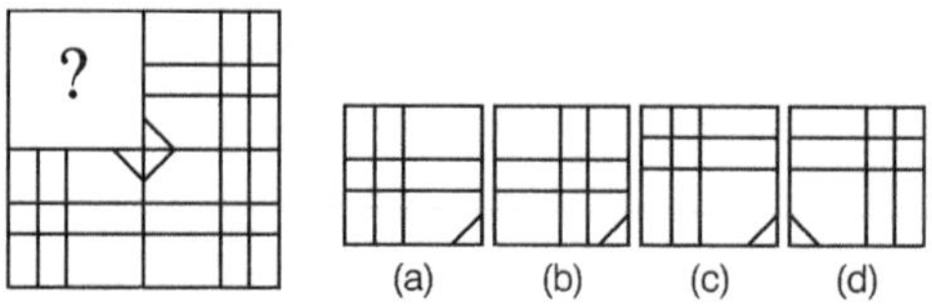

(a) (b) (c) (d)

Question Figure **Answer Figures**

8. ?

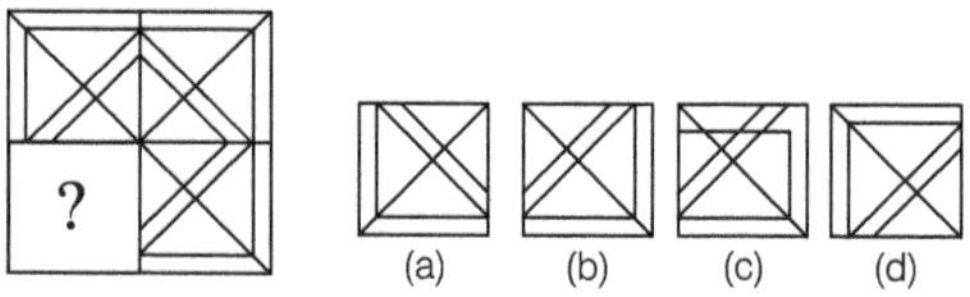

(a) (b) (c) (d)

« SSC MTS 2014

9. ?

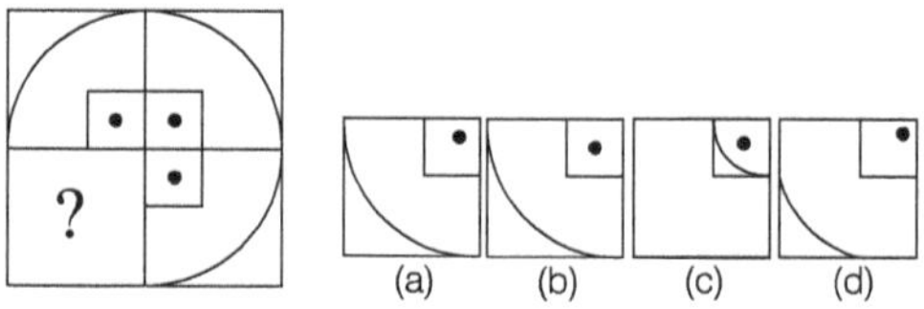

(a) (b) (c) (d)

« SSC MTS 2017

10. ?

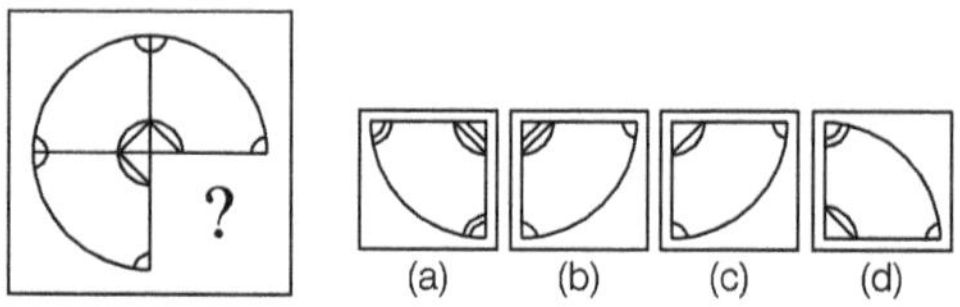

(a) (b) (c) (d)

« SSC Steno 2013

11. ?

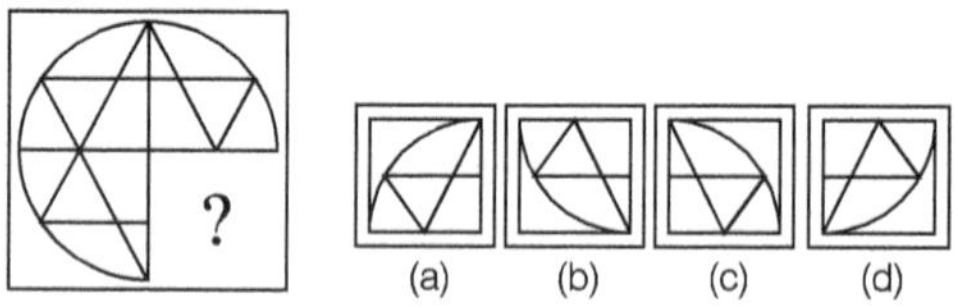

(a) (b) (c) (d)

« UPSSSC JA 2015

12. ?

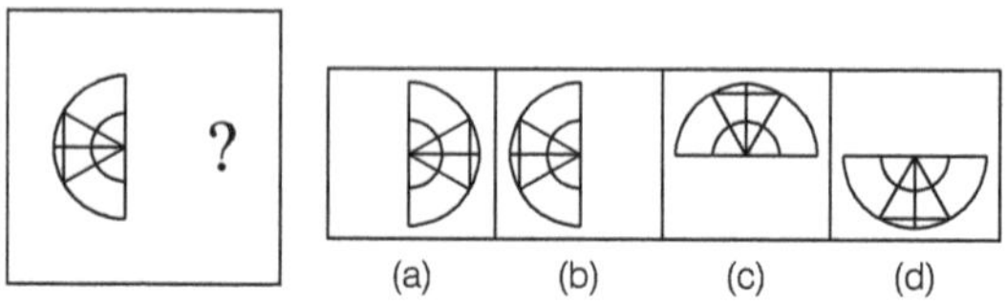

(a) (b) (c) (d)

« SSC FCI 2012

13. ?

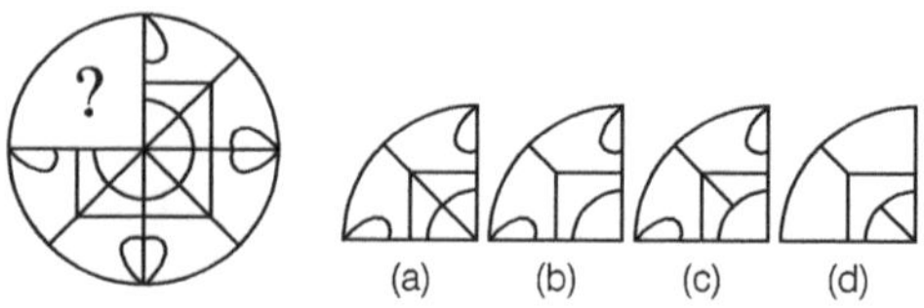

(a) (b) (c) (d)

14. ?

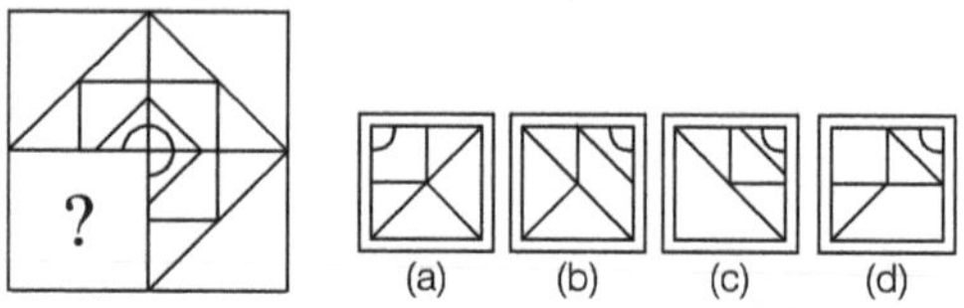

(a) (b) (c) (d)

« SSC Constable 2015

Question Figure

15. ?

Answer Figures

(a) (b) (c) (d)

16. ?

(a) (b) (c) (d)

17. ?

(a) (b) (c) (d)

18. ?

(a) (b) (c) (d)

19. ?

(a) (b) (c) (d)

« SSC MTS 2014

20. ?

(a) (b) (c) (d)

21. ?

(a) (b) (c) (d)

« SSC CPO 2008

22. ?

(a) (b) (c) (d)

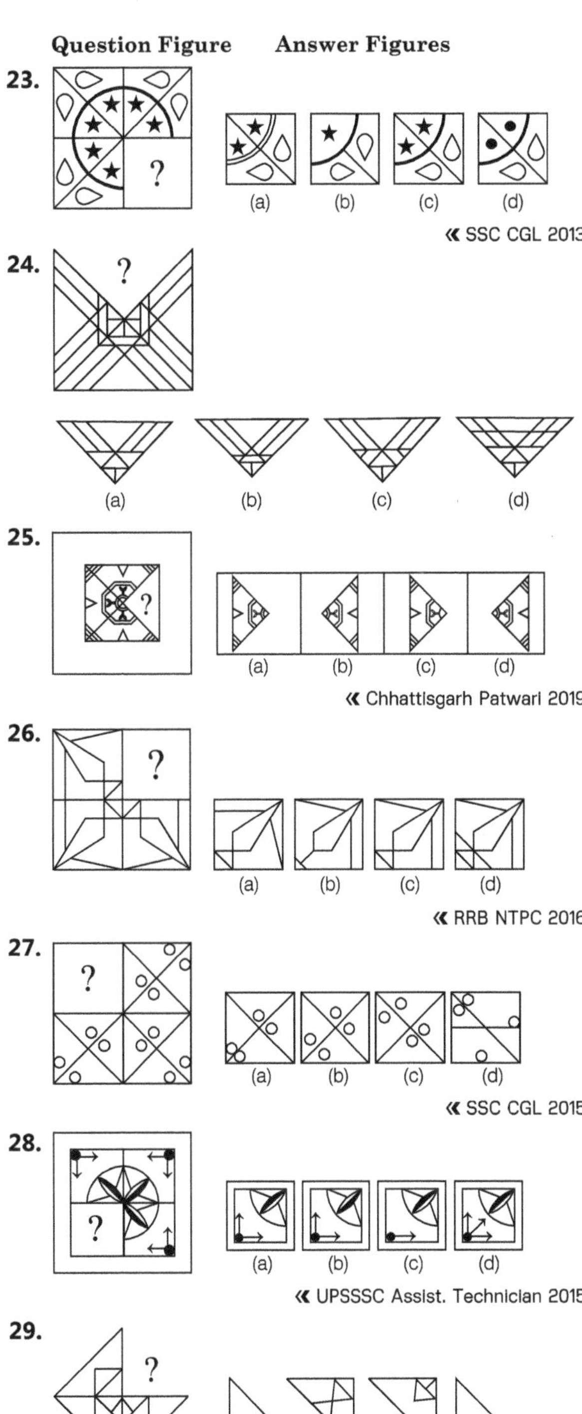

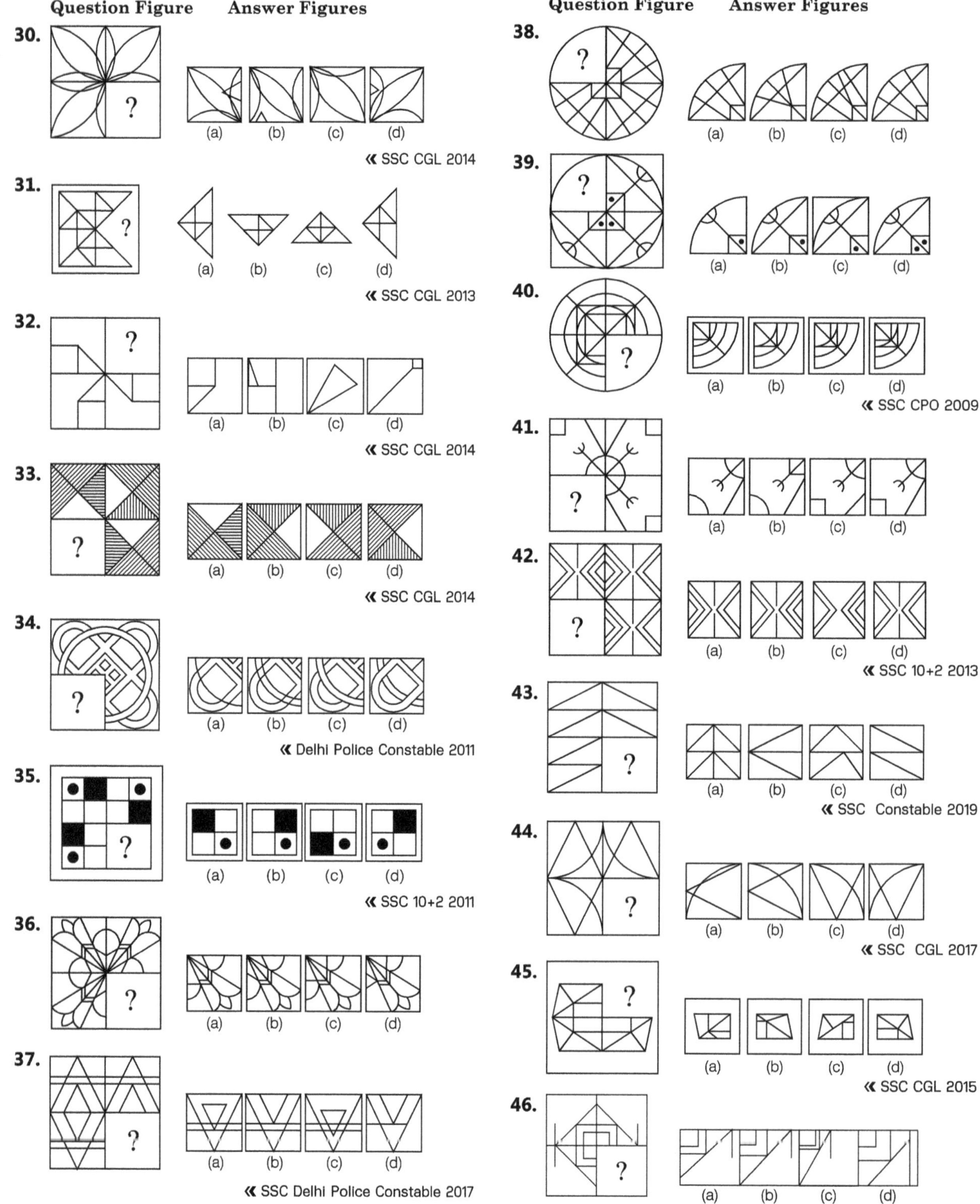
Question Figure
Answer Figures
30.
?
(a)
(b)
(c)
(d)
« SSC CGL 2014
31.
?
« SSC CGL 2013
32.
« SSC CGL 2014
33.
« SSC CGL 2014
34.
« Delhi Police Constable 2011
35.
« SSC 10+2 2011
36.
37.
« SSC Delhi Police Constable 2017
38.
39.
40.
« SSC CPO 2009
41.
42.
« SSC 10+2 2013
43.
« SSC Constable 2019
44.
« SSC CGL 2017
45.
« SSC CGL 2015
46.
« SSC Steno 2017

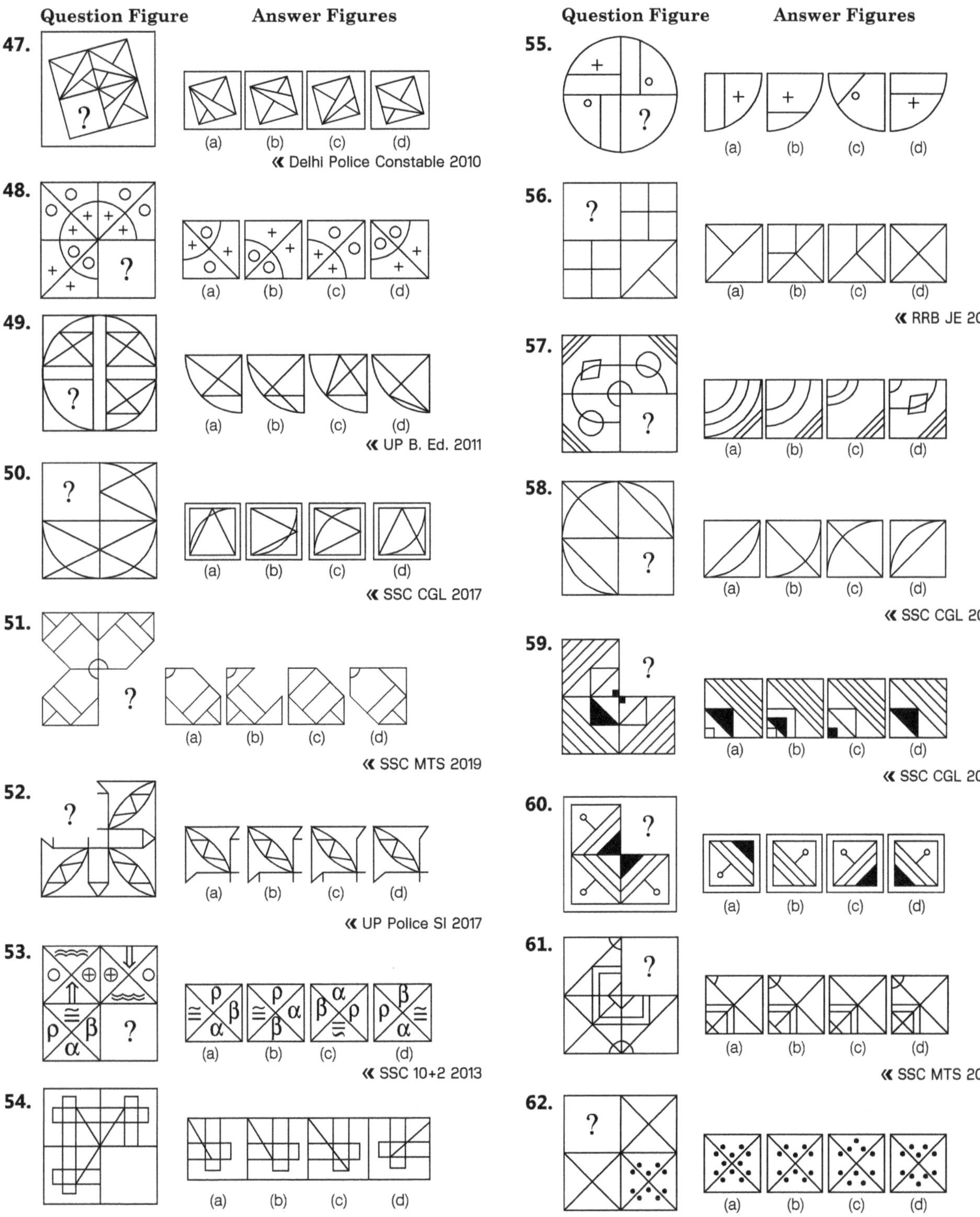
Question Figure
Answer Figures
47.
(a) (b) (c) (d)
« Delhi Police Constable 2010
48.
(a) (b) (c) (d)
49.
(a) (b) (c) (d)
« UP B. Ed. 2011
50.
(a) (b) (c) (d)
« SSC CGL 2017
51.
(a) (b) (c) (d)
« SSC MTS 2019
52.
(a) (b) (c) (d)
« UP Police SI 2017
53.
(a) (b) (c) (d)
« SSC 10+2 2013
54.
(a) (b) (c) (d)
« SSC MTS 2019
Question Figure
Answer Figures
55.
(a) (b) (c) (d)
56.
(a) (b) (c) (d)
« RRB JE 2019
57.
(a) (b) (c) (d)
58.
(a) (b) (c) (d)
« SSC CGL 2017
59.
(a) (b) (c) (d)
« SSC CGL 2016
60.
(a) (b) (c) (d)
61.
(a) (b) (c) (d)
« SSC MTS 2013
62.
(a) (b) (c) (d)
« UP B.Ed. 2010

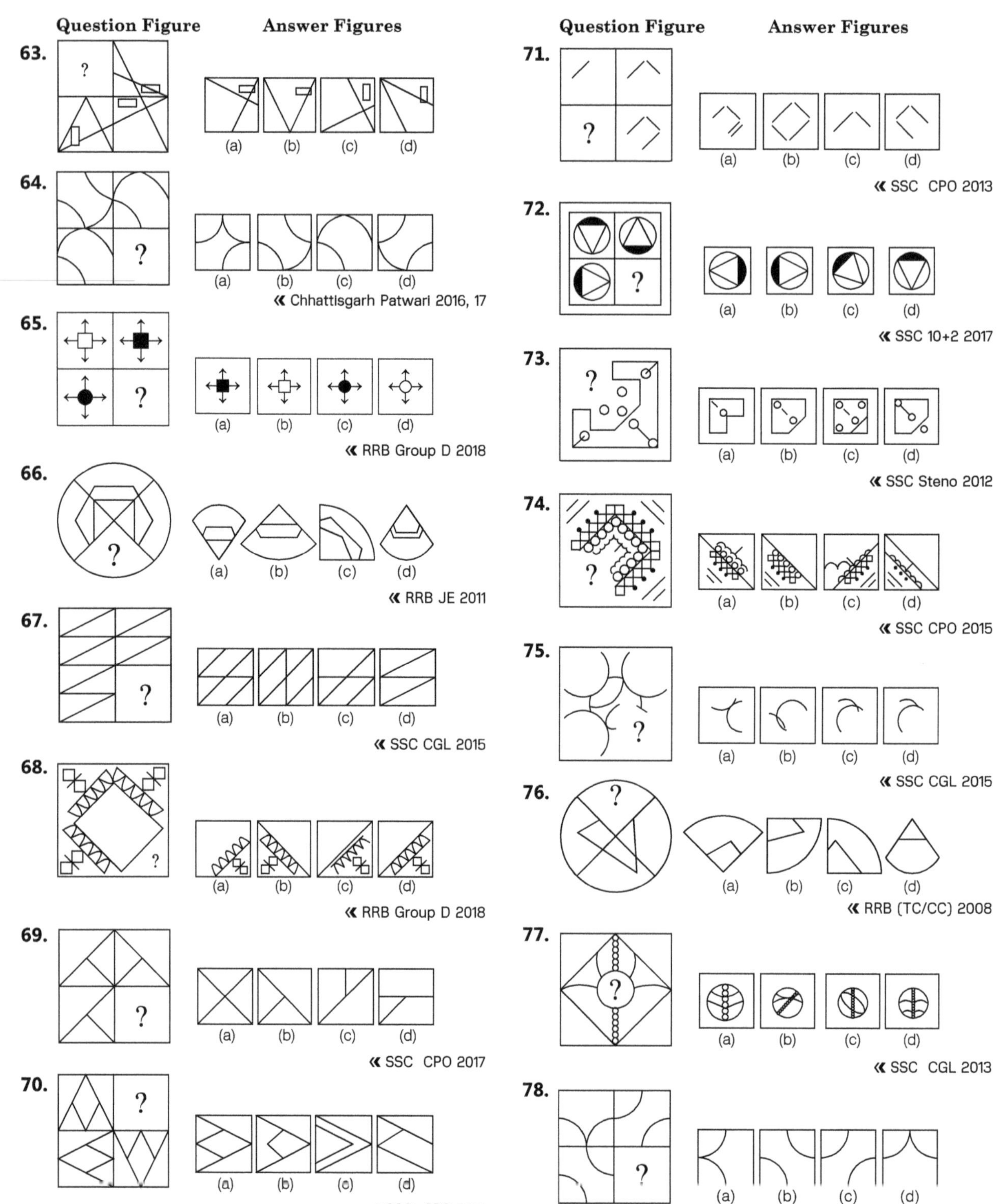
Question Figure
Answer Figures
63.
(a) (b) (c) (d)
64.
(a) (b) (c) (d)
« Chhattisgarh Patwari 2016, 17
65.
(a) (b) (c) (d)
« RRB Group D 2018
66.
(a) (b) (c) (d)
« RRB JE 2011
67.
(a) (b) (c) (d)
« SSC CGL 2015
68.
(a) (b) (c) (d)
« RRB Group D 2018
69.
(a) (b) (c) (d)
« SSC CPO 2017
70.
(a) (b) (c) (d)
« SSC CPO 2017
Question Figure
Answer Figures
71.
(a) (b) (c) (d)
« SSC CPO 2013
72.
(a) (b) (c) (d)
« SSC 10+2 2017
73.
(a) (b) (c) (d)
« SSC Steno 2012
74.
(a) (b) (c) (d)
« SSC CPO 2015
75.
(a) (b) (c) (d)
« SSC CGL 2015
76.
(a) (b) (c) (d)
« RRB (TC/CC) 2008
77.
(a) (b) (c) (d)
« SSC CGL 2013
78.
(a) (b) (c) (d)
« RRB ALP 2018

Question Figure Answer Figures

79. (a) (b) (c) (d)

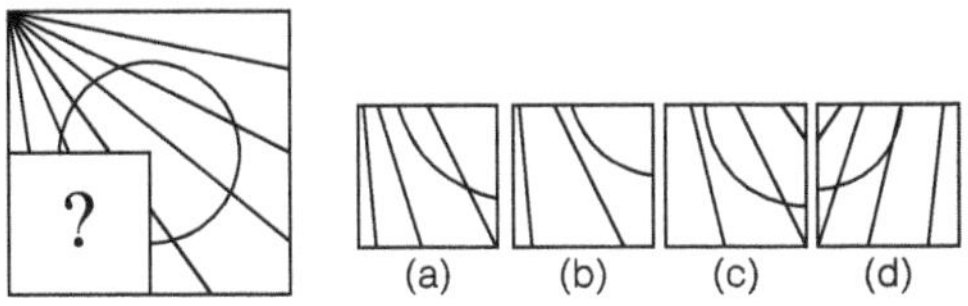

« SSC CGL 2015

80. (a) (b) (c) (d)

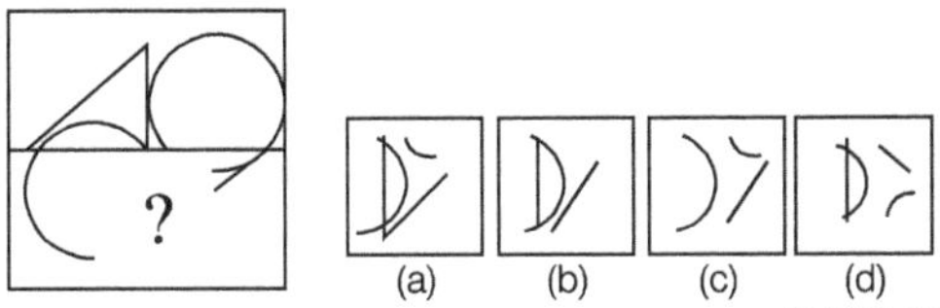

« SSC CGL 2015

81. (a) (b) (c) (d)

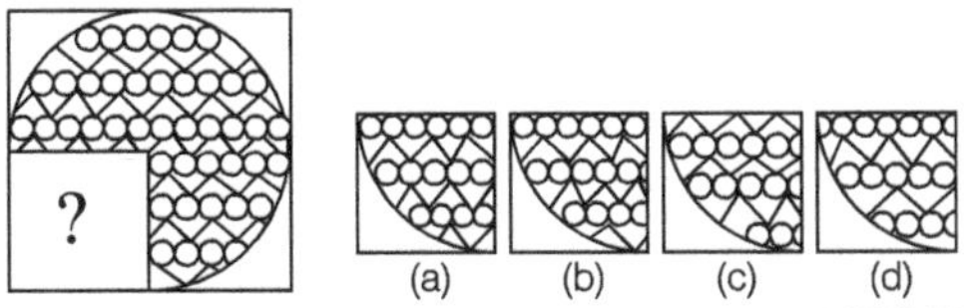

« SSC CGL 2014

Question Figure Answer Figures

82. (a) (b) (c) (d)

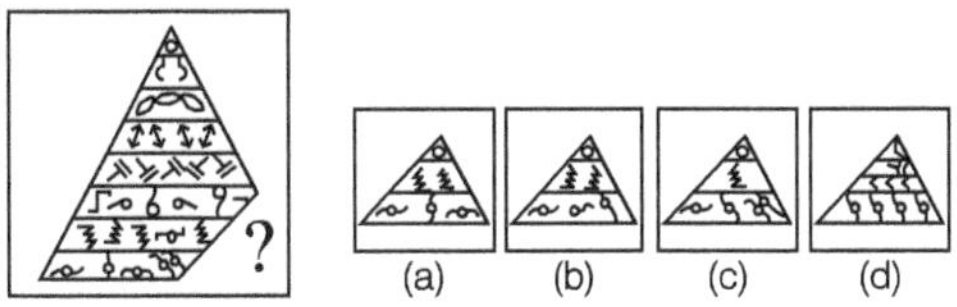

« SSC FCI 2012

83. (a) (b) (c) (d)

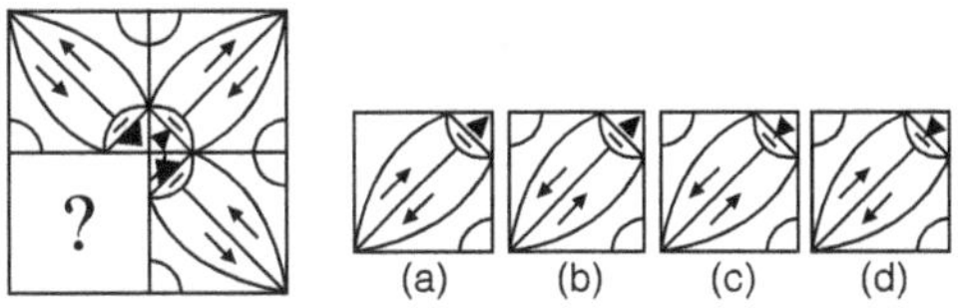

« SSC CGL 2008

84. (a) (b) (c) (d)

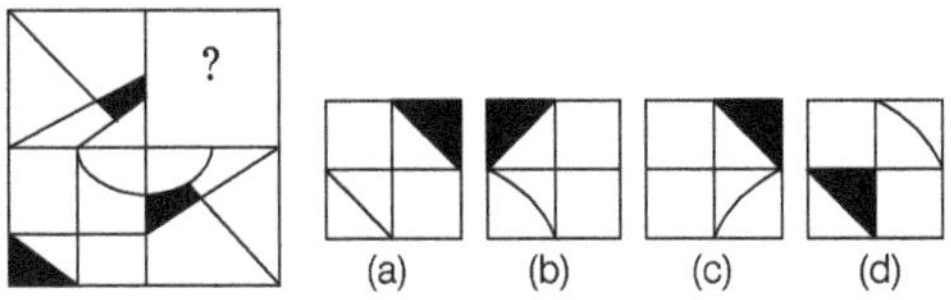

» Answers «

1. (b)	2. (b)	3. (d)	4. (b)	5. (c)	6. (a)	7. (a)	8. (a)	9. (b)	10. (c)
11. (d)	12. (a)	13. (a)	14. (c)	15. (d)	16. (d)	17. (a)	18. (b)	19. (d)	20. (a)
21. (d)	22. (c)	23. (c)	24. (b)	25. (d)	26. (c)	27. (c)	28. (a)	29. (a)	30. (c)
31. (a)	32. (a)	33. (b)	34. (c)	35. (c)	36. (b)	37. (b)	38. (a)	39. (b)	40. (d)
41. (d)	42. (b)	43. (d)	44. (d)	45. (d)	46. (a)	47. (b)	48. (d)	49. (a)	50. (c)
51. (a)	52. (b)	53. (c)	54. (b)	55. (d)	56. (a)	57. (d)	58. (b)	59. (d)	60. (b)
61. (b)	62. (b)	63. (a)	64. (b)	65. (d)	66. (b)	67. (d)	68. (a)	69. (b)	70. (a)
71. (b)	72. (a)	73. (d)	74. (a)	75. (d)	76. (a)	77. (a)	78. (a)	79. (c)	80. (c)
81. (a)	82. (a)	83. (d)	84. (a)						

CHAPTER / 05

Formation of Figures

The process of formation of a defined geometrical figure using the pieces of different designs is known as formation of figure.

This section of non-verbal reasoning deals with the problems related to the formation of geometrical figures like triangle, square, etc., by joining some pieces out of a group of pieces of different designs.

Different types of questions covered in this chapter are as follows.

TYPE 01

Based on Arrangement of the Figures

In this type of questions, a candidate is required to select a figure from the answer figures, that can be formed by arranging the pieces given in the question figure.

DIRECTIONS ~ (Example Nos. 1-4) *In each of the following questions, find a figure from the answer figures, that can be formed by joining the pieces given in the question figure.*

***Ex* 01**

Question Figure **Answer Figures**

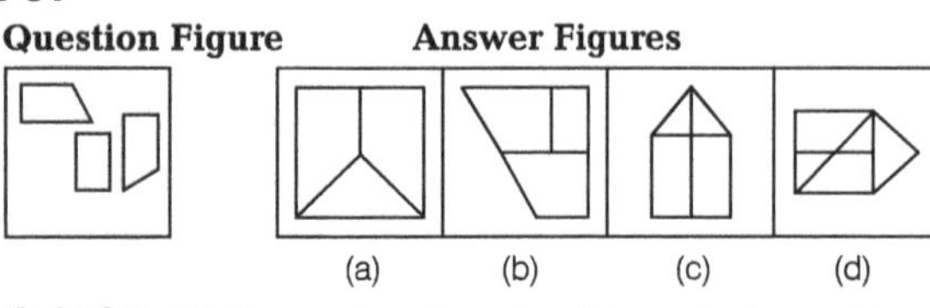

(a) (b) (c) (d)

***Solution* (b)** Figure given in option (b) can be formed by joining the pieces given in the question figure as shown below

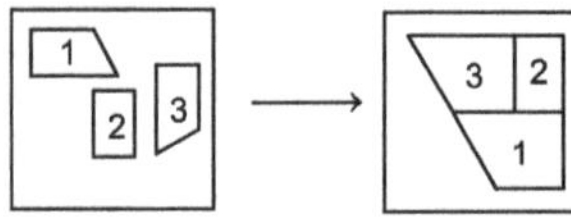

***Ex* 02** **Question Figure** **Answer Figures**

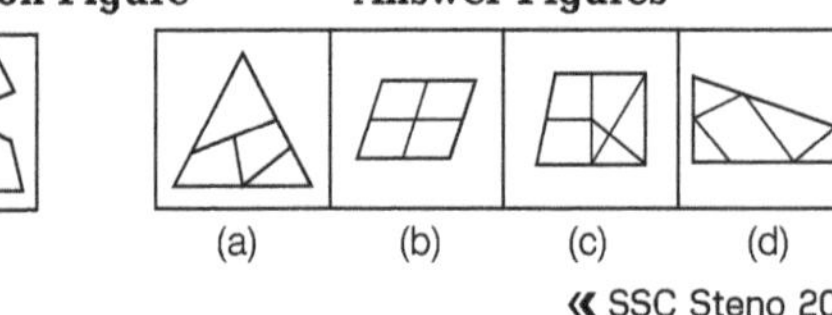

(a) (b) (c) (d)

« SSC Steno 2011

***Solution* (a)** Figure given in option (a) can be formed by joining the pieces given in the question figure as shown below

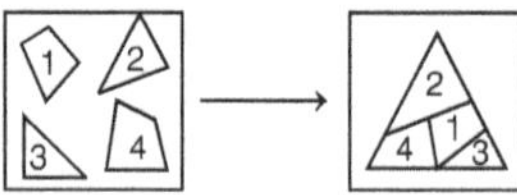

***Ex* 03** **Question Figure**

Answer Figures

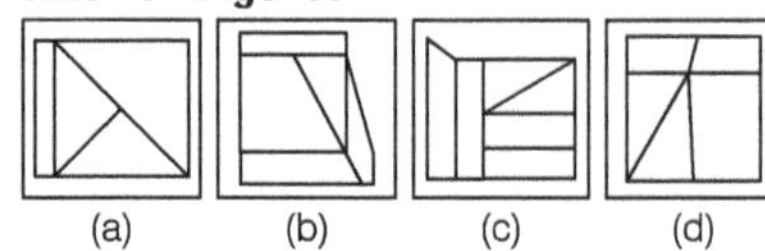

(a) (b) (c) (d)

***Solution* (b)** Figure given in option (b) can be formed by joining the pieces given in the question figure as shown below

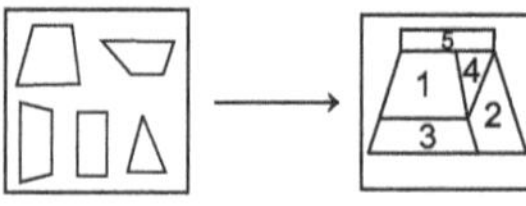

***Ex* 04**

Question Figure **Answer Figures**

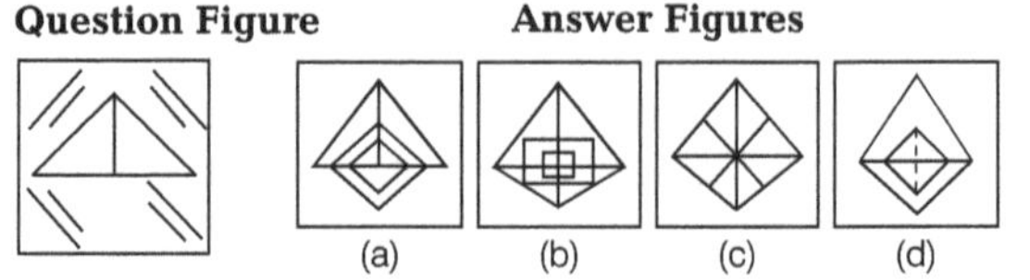

(a) (b) (c) (d)

« SSC Constable 2015

***Solution* (a)** Figure given in option (a) can be formed by joining the pieces given in the question figure as shown below

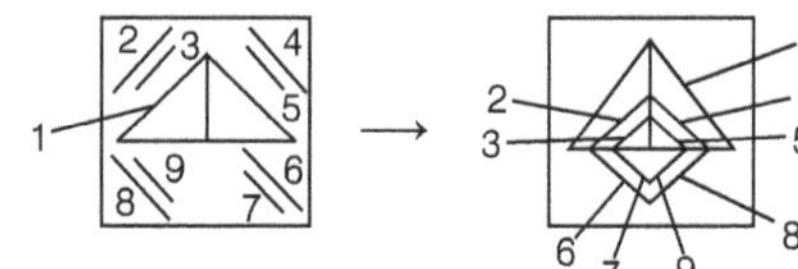

Practice CORNER 5.1

DIRECTIONS ~ (Q. Nos. 1-16) *In each of the following questions, find a figure from the answer figures that can be formed by joining the pieces given in the question figure.*

Question Figure Answer Figures

1. 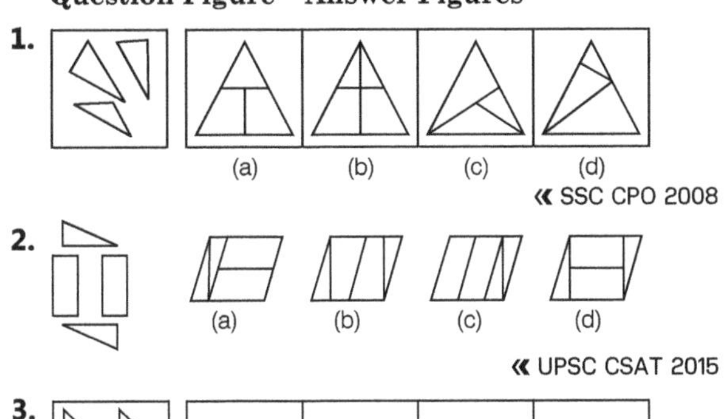

« SSC CPO 2008

2.

« UPSC CSAT 2015

3. 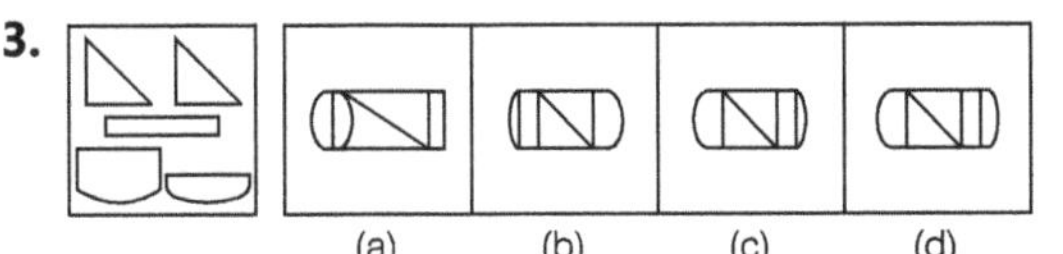

4. 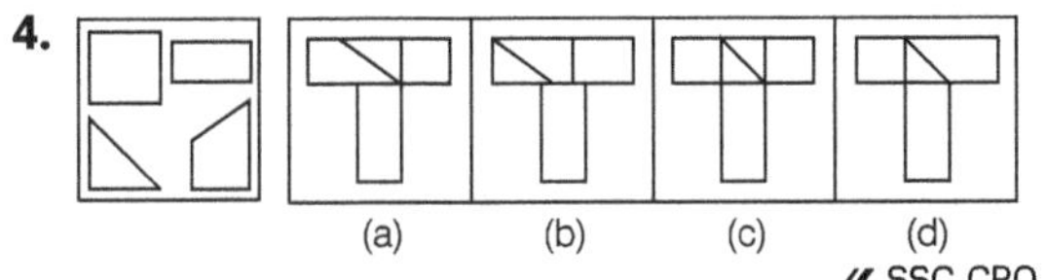

« SSC CPO 2019

5. 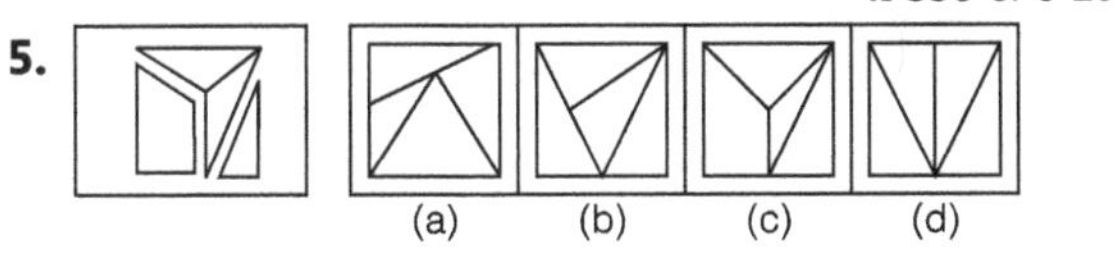

« SSC CGL 2015

6. 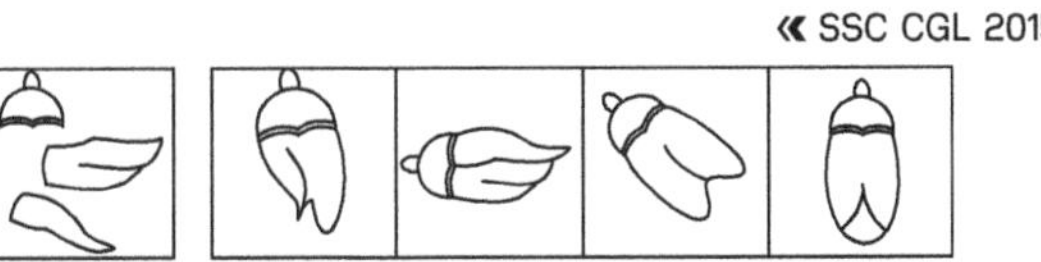

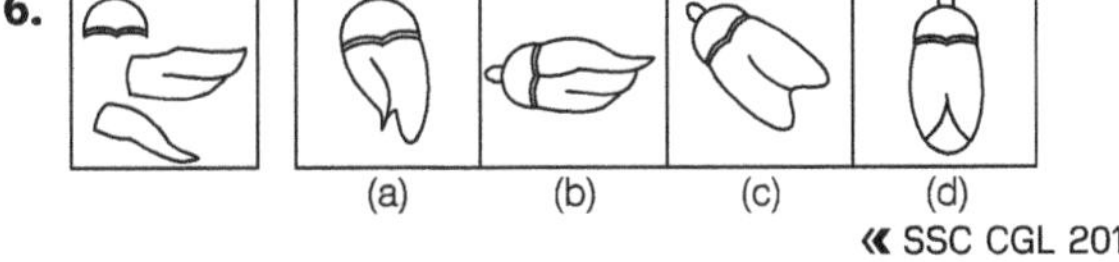

« SSC CGL 2015

7. 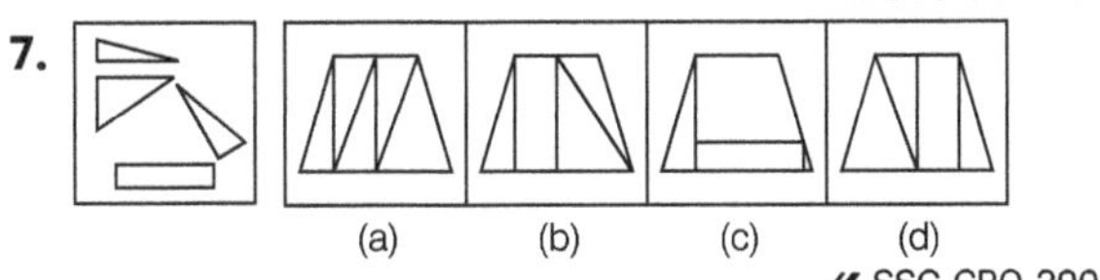

« SSC CPO 2008

8. 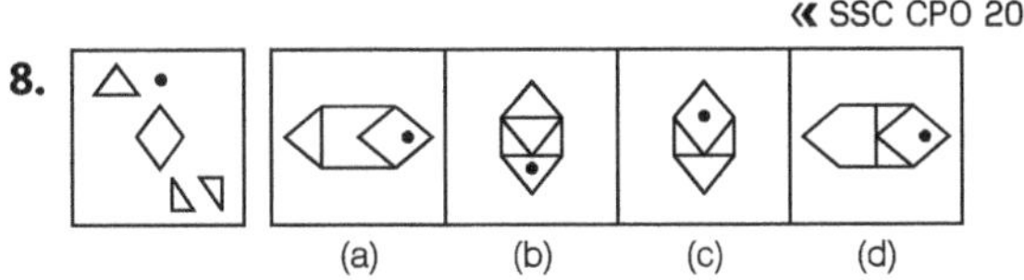

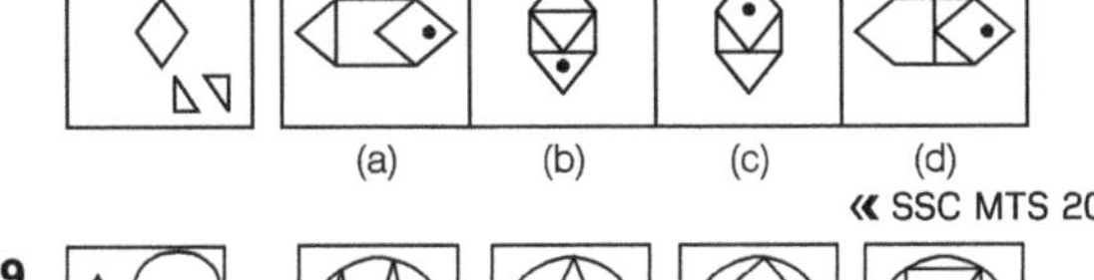

« SSC MTS 2019

9. 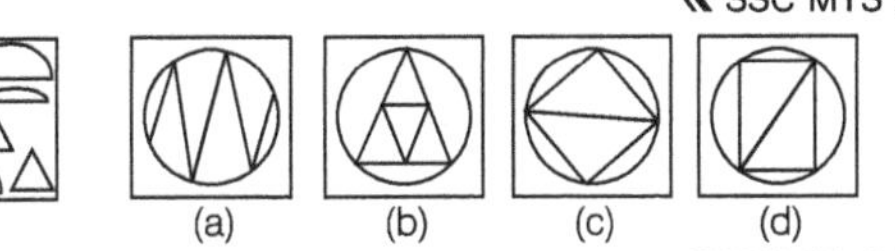

« SSC 10+2 2016

Question Figure Answer Figures

10. 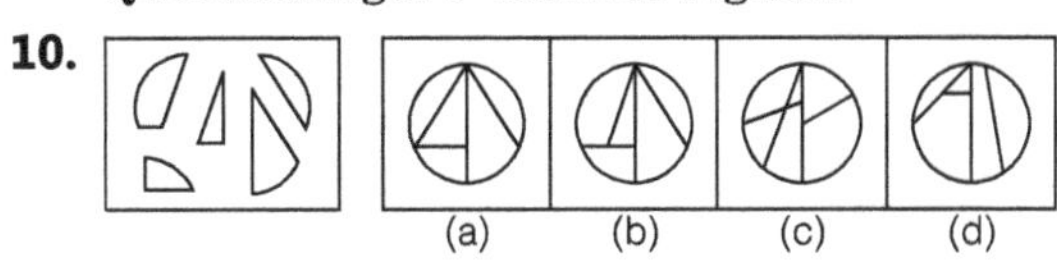

« UPSSSC Combined Exercise Trainer 2018

11. 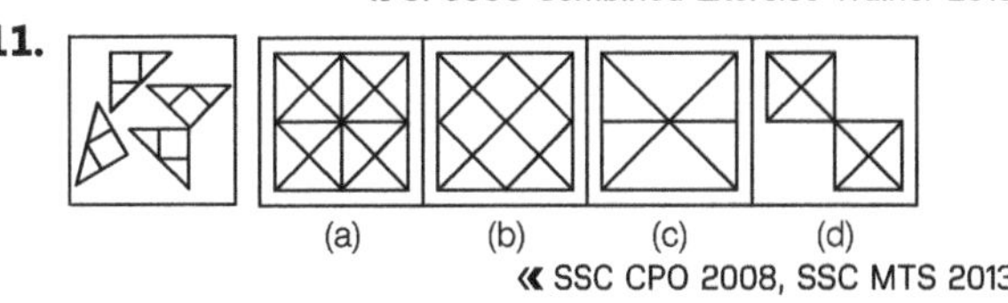

« SSC CPO 2008, SSC MTS 2013

12. 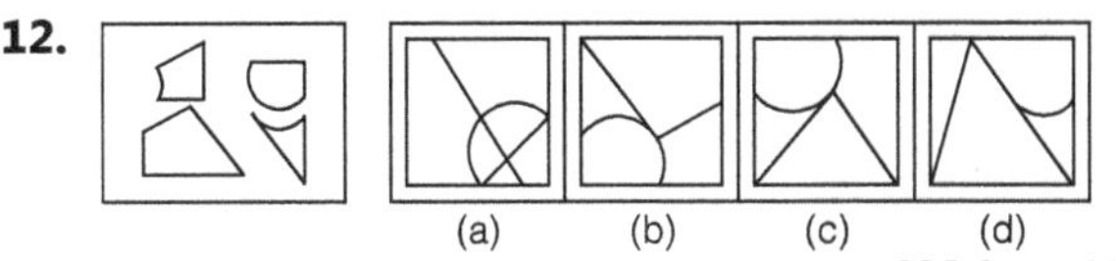

« SSC Steno 2011

13. 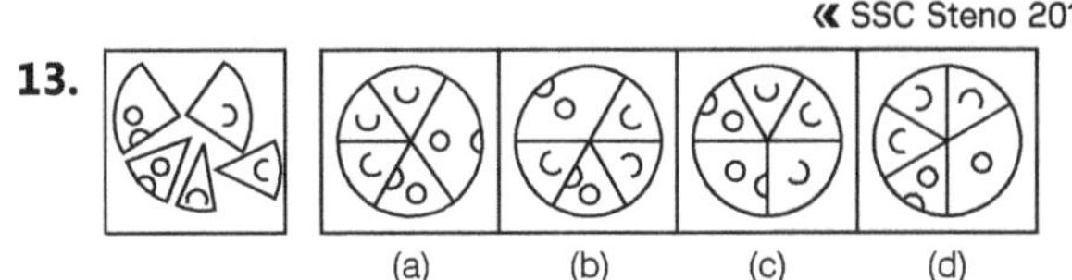

« SSC CGL 2009

14. 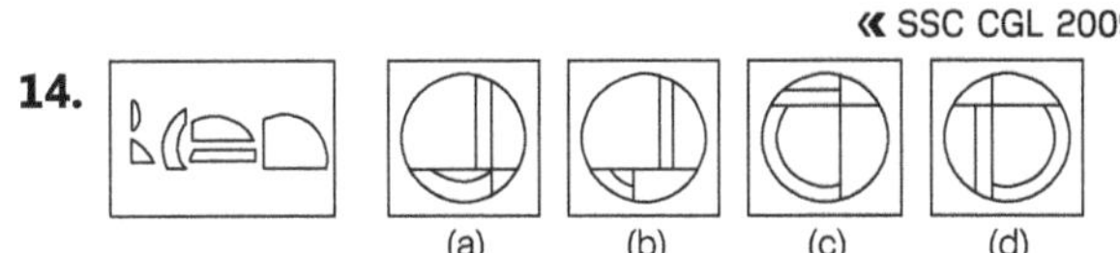

15. Question Figures

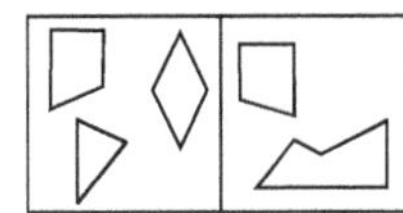

Answer Figures

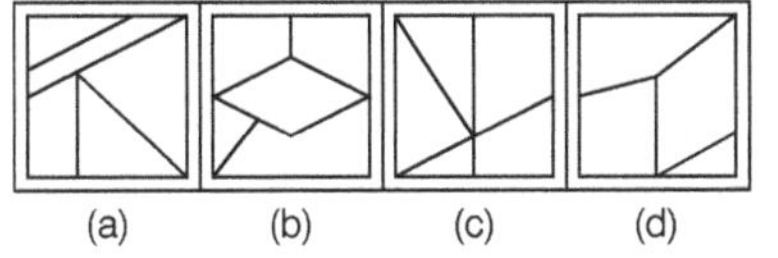

« SSC CGL 2014

16. Question Figures

« SSC DEO 2009

Answer Figures

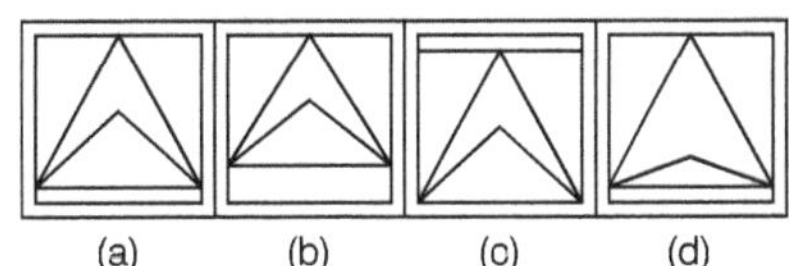

Answers WITH EXPLANATIONS

1. (c) Figure given in option (c) can be formed by joining the pieces given in the question figure.

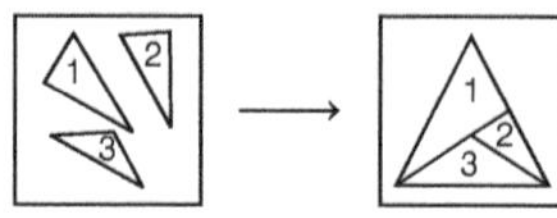

2. (d) Figure given in option (d) can be formed by joining the pieces given in the question figure.

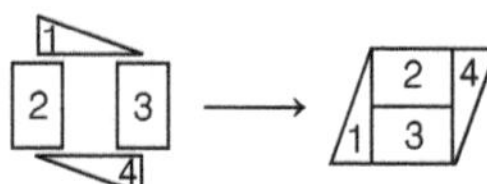

3. (d) Figure given in option (d) can be formed by joining the pieces given in the question figure.

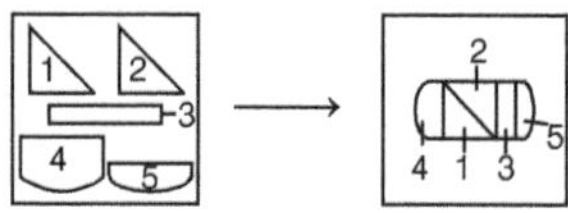

4. (d) Figure given in option (d) can be formed by joining the pieces given in the question figure.

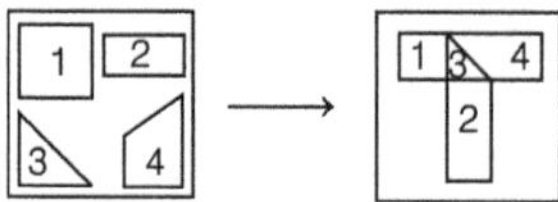

5. (c) Figure given in option (c) can be formed by joining the pieces given in the question figure.

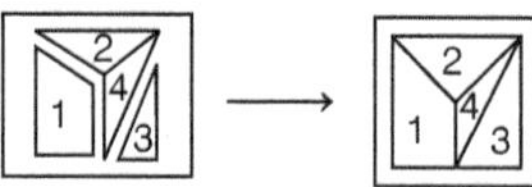

6. (b) Figure given in option (b) can be formed by joining the pieces given in the question figure.

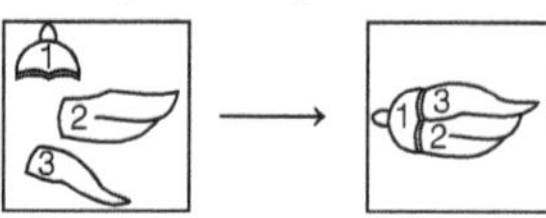

7. (b) Figure given in option (b) can be formed by joining the pieces given in the question figure.

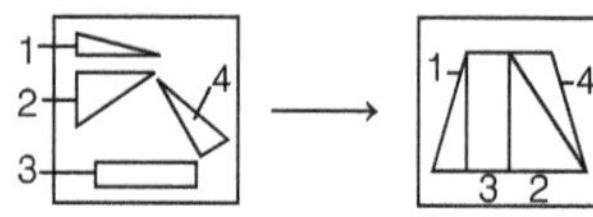

8. (c) Figure given in option (c) can be formed by joining the pieces given in the question figure.

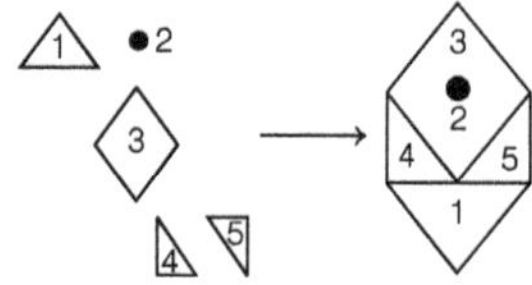

9. (b) Figure given in option (b) can be formed by joining the pieces given in the question figure.

10. (b) Figure given in option (b) can be formed by joining the pieces given in the question figure.

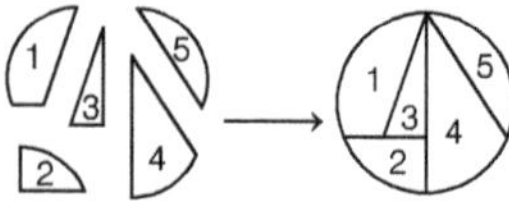

11. (b) Figure given in option (b) can be formed by joining the pieces given in the question figure.

12. (b) Figure given in option (b) can be formed by joining the pieces given in the question figure.

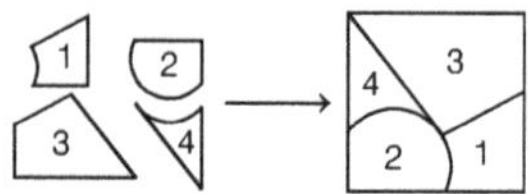

13. (c) Figure given in option (c) can be formed by joining the pieces given in the question figure.

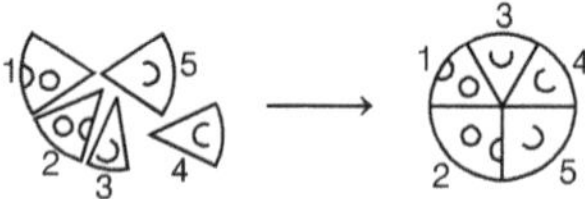

14. (a) Figure given in option (a) can be formed by joining the pieces given in the question figure.

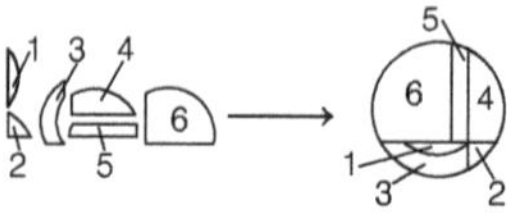

15. (b) Figure given in option (b) can be formed by joining the pieces given in the question figure.

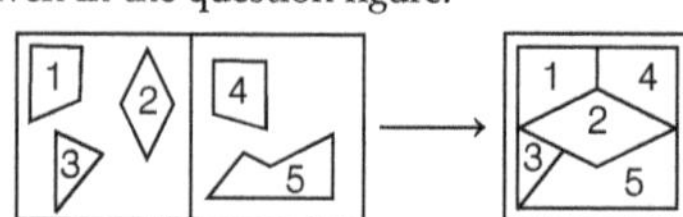

16. (b) Figure given in option (b) can be formed by joining the pieces given in the question figure.

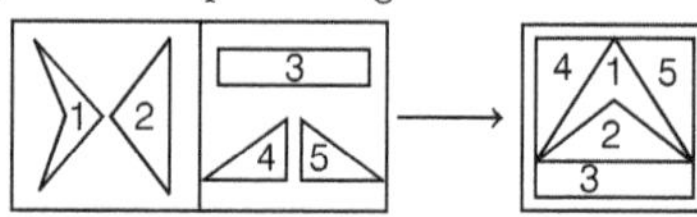

TYPE 02

Fragmentation of a Figure into Simple Parts

Such type of questions are just the reverse of type 01. In this type of questions, question figures are to be formed using the pieces given in one of the answer figures and the candidate is required to find out the correct answer figure.

Sometimes, pieces of boundary lines of the question figure are also given in the answer figure, then in this case, these pieces are also counted for the formation of question figure.

DIRECTIONS ~ (Example Nos. 5-8) *In each of the following questions, find the figure from the given answer figures, that can form the question figure.*

Ex 05

Question Figure **Answer Figures**

(a) (b) (c) (d)

Solution (c) The question figure can be formed by joining the pieces given in option (c) as shown below

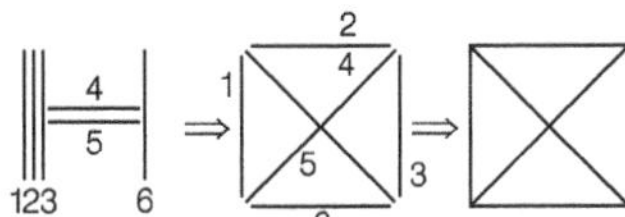

Ex 06

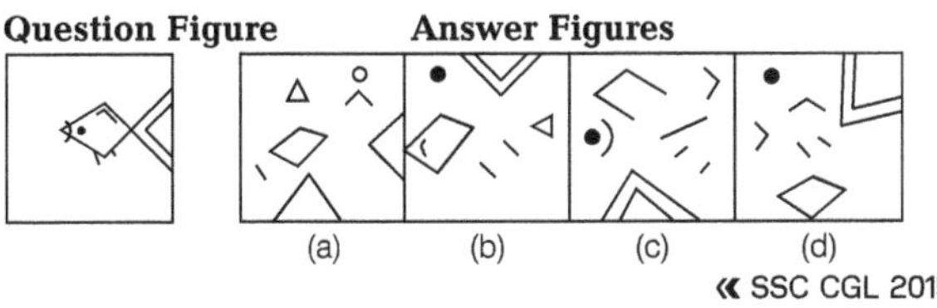

« SSC CGL 2015

Solution (c) The question figure can be formed by joining the pieces given in option (c) as shown below

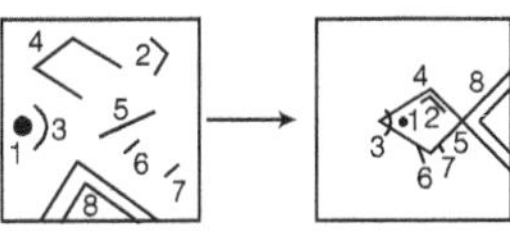

Ex 07

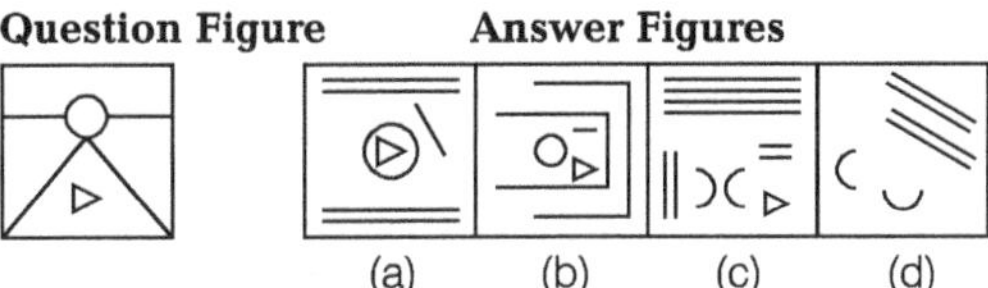

Solution (c) Here, the question figure can be formed by joining the pieces given in option (c) as shown below

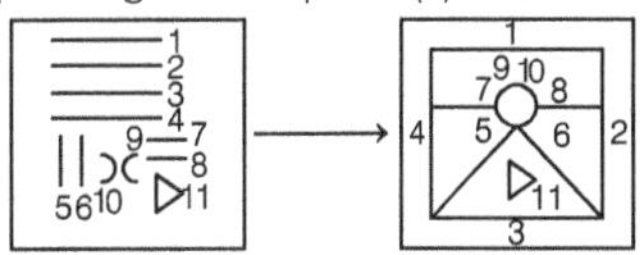

Ex 08

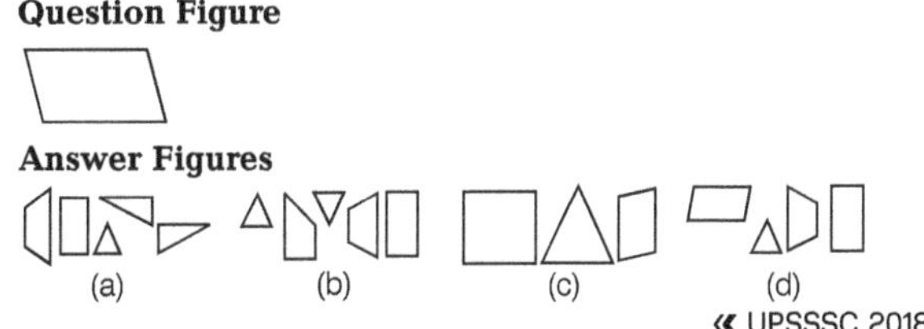

« UPSSSC 2018

Solution (a) The pieces given in answer figure (a) can be combined to make the question figure as shown below

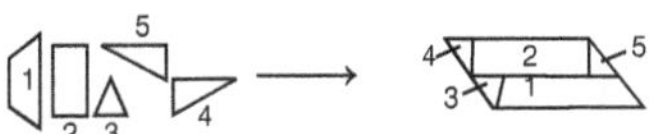

Chapter tip! In the questions based on figure formation, the number of elements given to form a figure must be equal to the number of elements present in the answer figure. This will help you to eliminate some of the option figures easily.

The size of pieces of figures present in the question figure and the size of pieces used to form a figure may vary but their shapes must have to be similar.

Practice / CORNER 5.2

DIRECTIONS ~ (Q. Nos. 1-16) *In each of the following questions, find the figure from the given answer figures, that can form the question figure.*

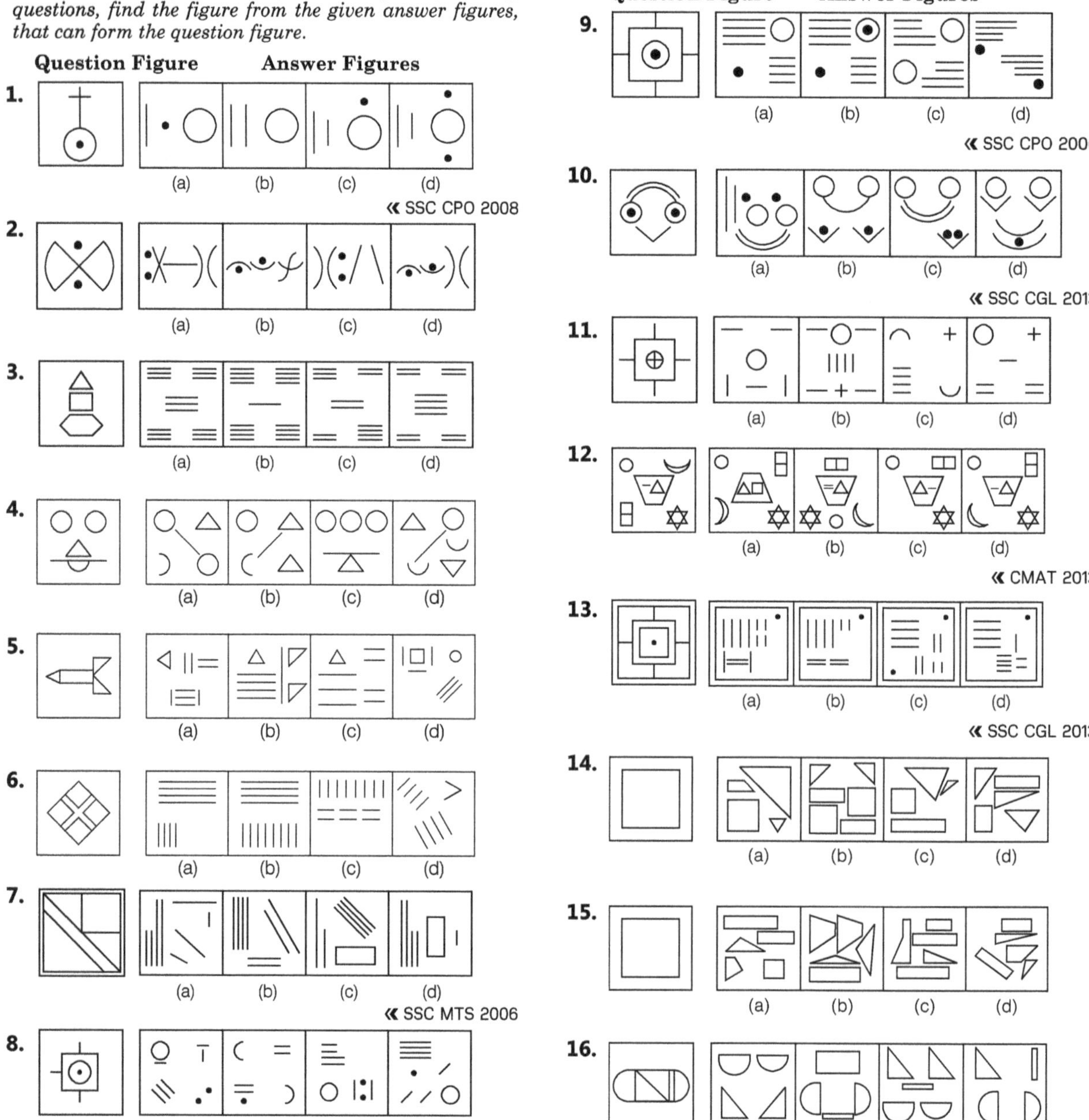

Answers WITH EXPLANATIONS

1. (c) The question figure can be formed by joining the pieces given in option (c).

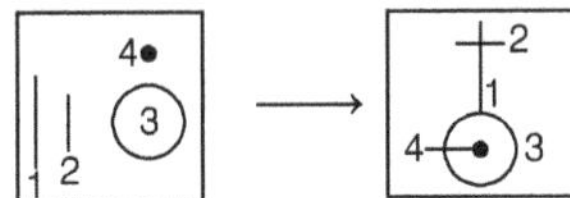

2. (c) The question figure can be formed by joining the pieces given in option (c).

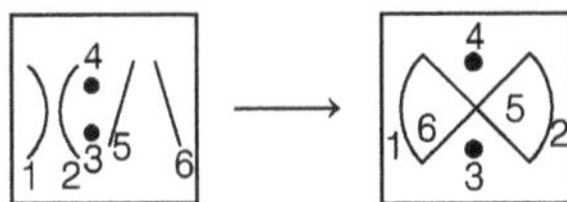

3. (c) The question figure can be formed by joining the pieces given in option (c).

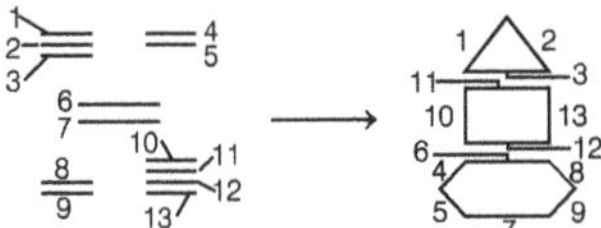

4. (a) The question figure can be formed by joining the pieces given in option (a).

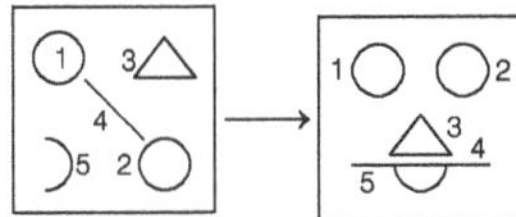

5. (c) The question figure can be formed by joining the pieces given in option (c).

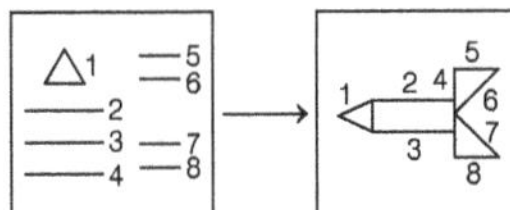

6. (b) The question figure can be formed by joining the pieces given in option (b).

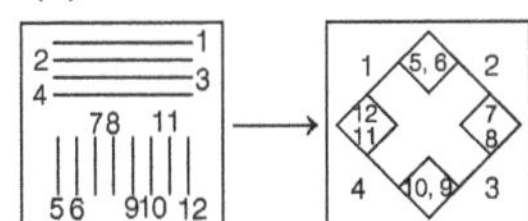

7. (b) The question figure can be formed by joining the pieces given in option (b).

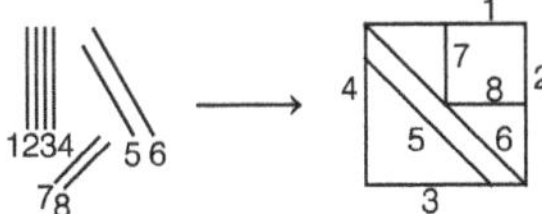

8. (d) The question figure can be formed by joining the pieces given in option (d).

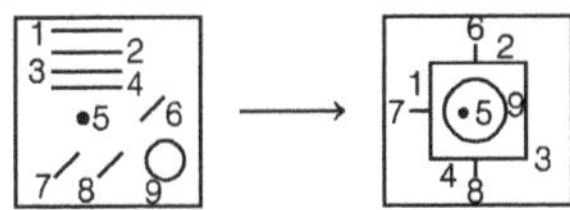

9. (a) The question figure can be formed by joining the pieces given in option (a).

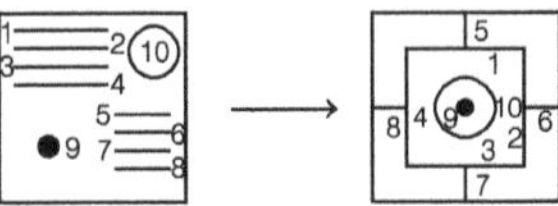

10. (c) The question figure can be formed by joining the pieces given in option (c).

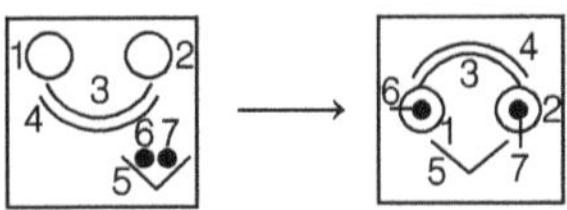

11. (b) The question figure can be formed by joining the pieces given in option (b).

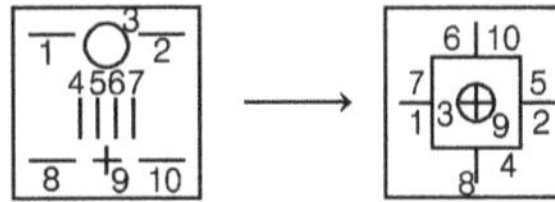

12. (d) The question figure can be formed by joining the pieces given in option (d).

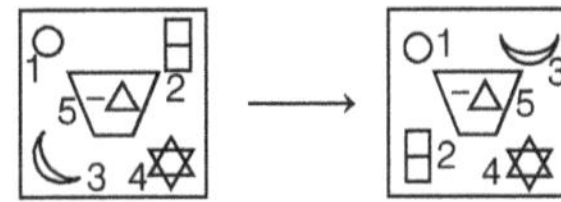

13. (a) The question figure can be formed by joining the pieces given in option (a).

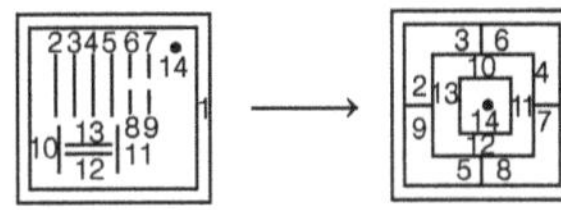

14. (b) The question figure can be formed by joining the pieces given in option (b).

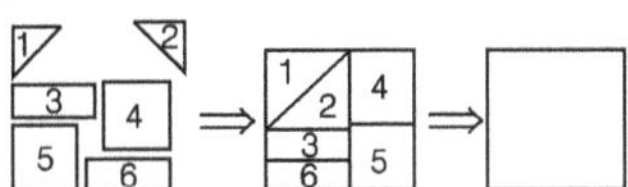

15. (b) The question figure can be formed by joining the pieces given in option (b).

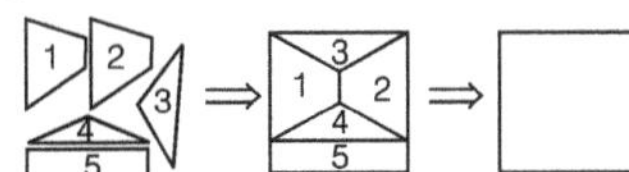

16. (c) The question figure can be formed by joining the pieces given in option (c).

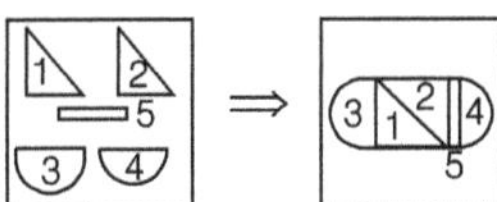

TYPE 03

Based on Formation of Triangle/Square

In this type of questions, a triangle (equilateral, isosceles etc.) or a square is to be formed by joining three figures out of a group of five figures of different designs.

A candidate is required to find out the correct combination of figures from the given alternative which can be joined to form the required figure.

To solve these type of questions, there is no fixed rule or method. These questions require a deep analysis of various elements (designs) present to form a figure and spatial analysis of the figure to be formed.

DIRECTIONS ~(Example Nos. 9-11) *In each of the following questions, five figures are given. Out of them, find the three figures that can be joined to form an equilateral triangle.*

Ex 09

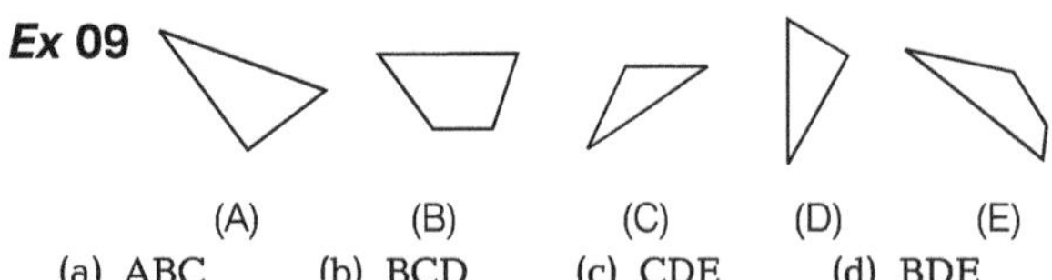

(a) ABC (b) BCD (c) CDE (d) BDE

Solution (c) An equilateral triangle has each angle equal to 60° and the lengths of all its three sides are also equal. Now, we cannot measure the exact value of angle and sides but we have to closely approximate these measures and values. So, keeping these points in mind, we first combine figure(s) E and C which will look like as

Now, the missing figure which can fit in the above figure is figure D. So, the complete figure is shown as

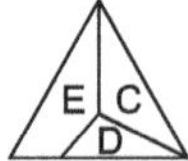

So, the correct group of figures is C, D and E.

Ex 10

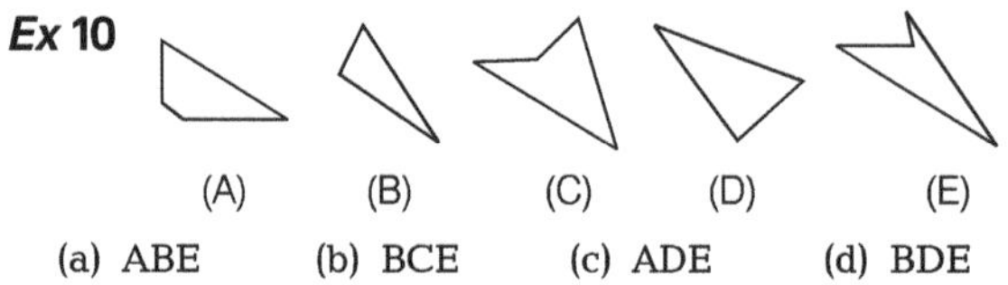

(a) ABE (b) BCE (c) ADE (d) BDE

Solution (c) As done in above example, we have to closely approximate the different measures. So, first we combine the figures (E) and (A) which will look like as

Now, the missing figure which will complete the above figure is figure (D). The complete figure will be as

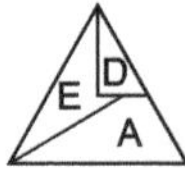

Ex 11

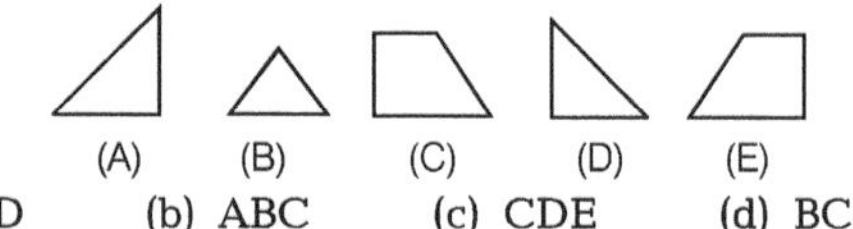

(a) BCD (b) ABC (c) CDE (d) BCE

Solution (d) Visualise two figures which on combining will give a part of an equilateral triangle. These figures are figures (E) and (C) which on combining will look like as shown below

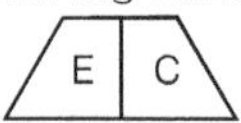

Now, the remaining figure which when combined with the above figure will give an equilateral triangle is figure B.

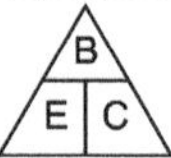

So, the complete figure will look like as

DIRECTIONS ~(Example Nos. 12 and 13) *In each of the following questions, a set of five figures marked as* (A), (B), (C), (D) *and* (E) *followed by four alternatives* (a), (b), (c) *and* (d) *are given. Select the alternative which contains those figures which, if fitted together, will form a complete square.*

Ex 12

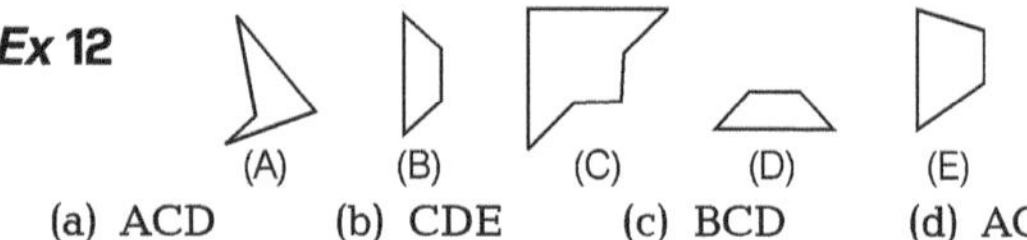

(a) ACD (b) CDE (c) BCD (d) ACE

Solution (c) The only figure with right angle is figure (C). If it is fitted with figure (B), the resultant figure will look like the below figure (X)

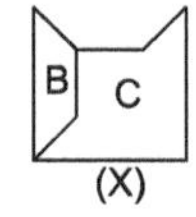

(X)

Now, when the figure (D) is fitted in figure (X), the resultant figure will be a square as shown in figure (Y)

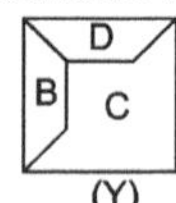

(Y)

Hence, combination of figures as presented by alternative (c) is the correct combination of figures to form a square.

Ex 13

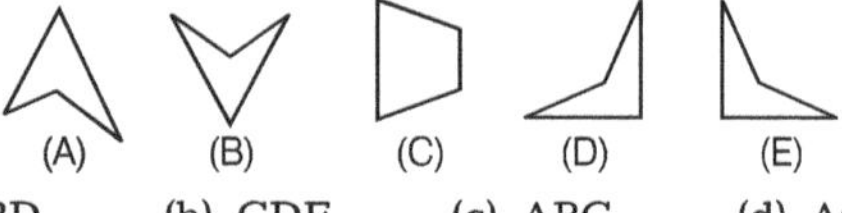

(a) ABD (b) CDE (c) ABC (d) ACE

Solution (d) If the figures (C) and (A) are fitted together, the resultant figure will look like the below figure (X)

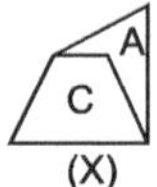

(X)

Now, if the figure (E) is fitted in figure (X), the resultant figure will be a square as shown in figure (Y).

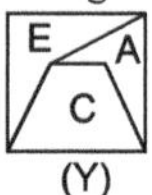

(Y)

Hence, combination of figures as presented by alternative (d) is the correct combination of figures to form a square.

Practice CORNER 5.3

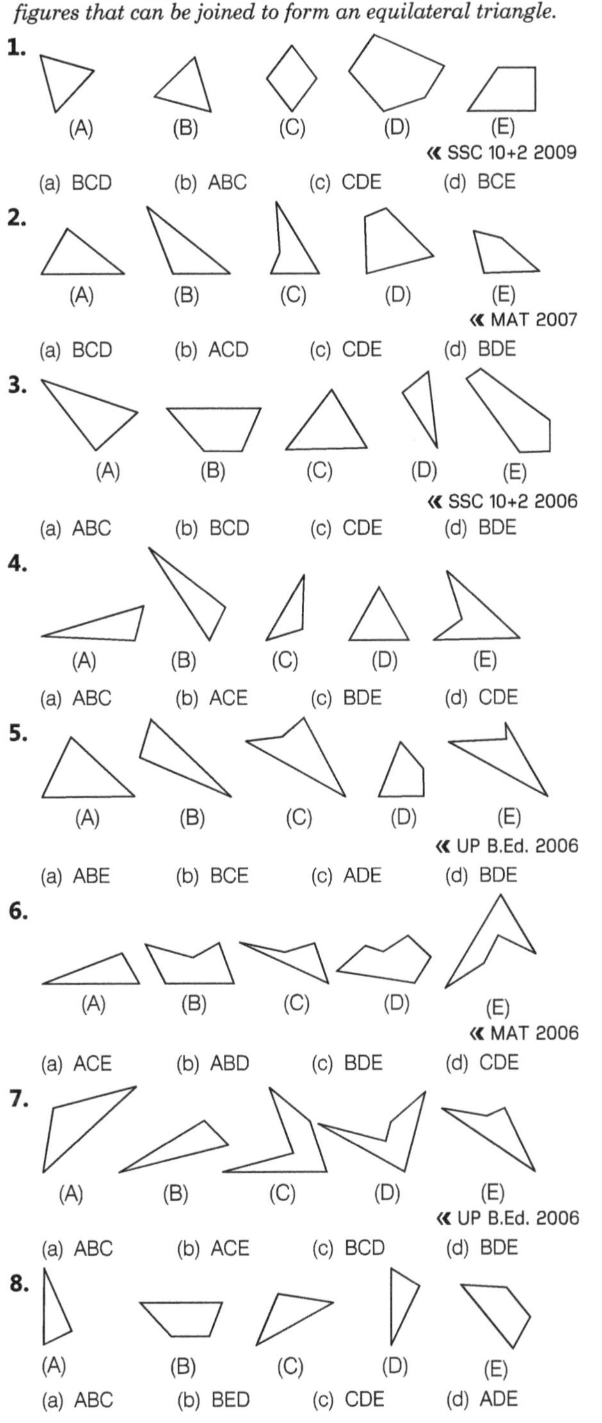

DIRECTIONS ~ (Q. Nos. 1-8) *In each of the following questions five figures are given. Out of them, find the three figures that can be joined to form an equilateral triangle.*

1.
« SSC 10+2 2009

(a) BCD (b) ABC (c) CDE (d) BCE

2.
« MAT 2007

(a) BCD (b) ACD (c) CDE (d) BDE

3.
« SSC 10+2 2006

(a) ABC (b) BCD (c) CDE (d) BDE

4.

(a) ABC (b) ACE (c) BDE (d) CDE

5.
« UP B.Ed. 2006

(a) ABE (b) BCE (c) ADE (d) BDE

6.
« MAT 2006

(a) ACE (b) ABD (c) BDE (d) CDE

7.
« UP B.Ed. 2006

(a) ABC (b) ACE (c) BCD (d) BDE

8.

(a) ABC (b) BED (c) CDE (d) ADE

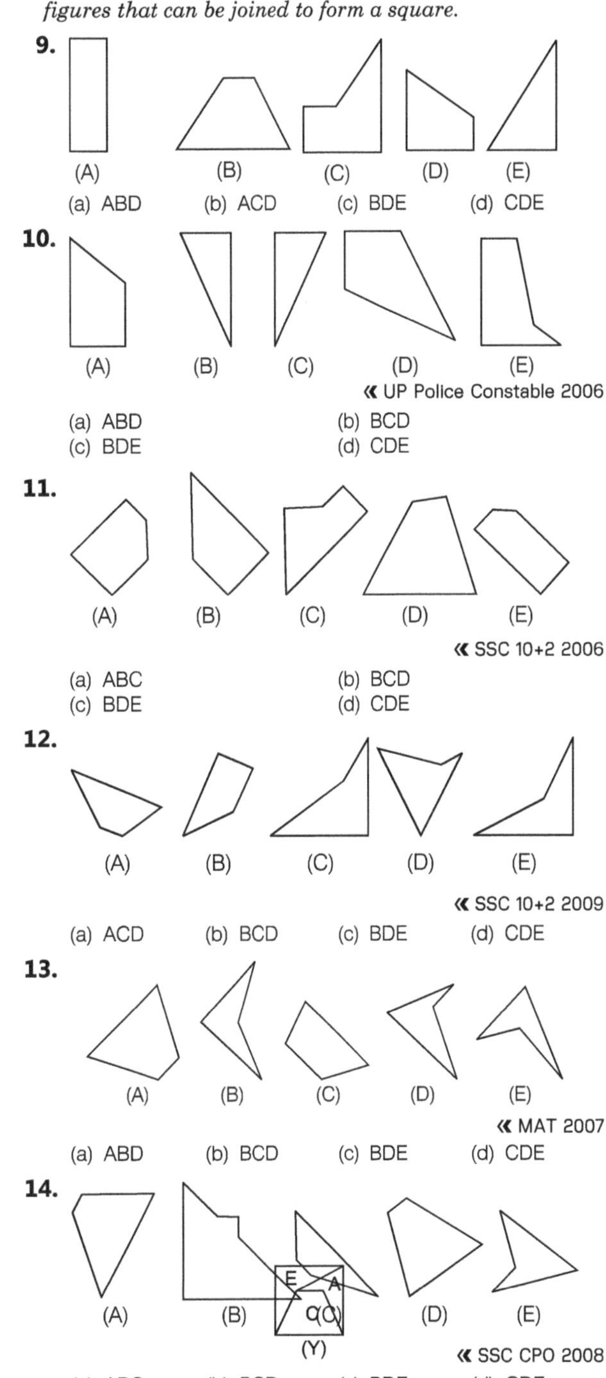

DIRECTIONS ~ (Q. Nos. 9-16) *In each of the following questions, five figures are given. Out of them, find the three figures that can be joined to form a square.*

9.

(a) ABD (b) ACD (c) BDE (d) CDE

10.
« UP Police Constable 2006

(a) ABD (b) BCD
(c) BDE (d) CDE

11.
« SSC 10+2 2006

(a) ABC (b) BCD
(c) BDE (d) CDE

12.
« SSC 10+2 2009

(a) ACD (b) BCD (c) BDE (d) CDE

13.
« MAT 2007

(a) ABD (b) BCD (c) BDE (d) CDE

14.
« SSC CPO 2008

(a) ABC (b) BCD (c) BDE (d) CDE

15.

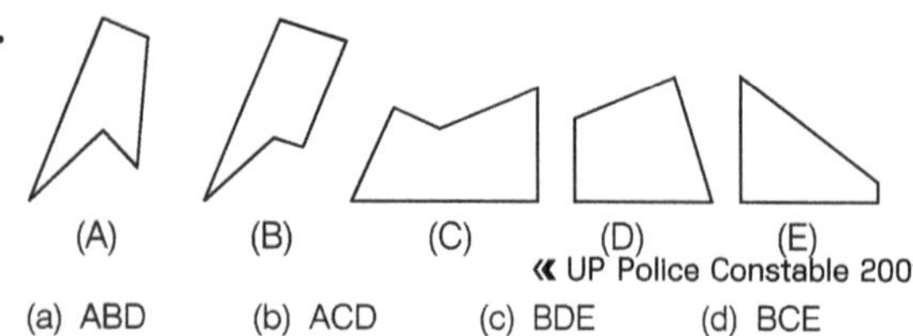

« UP Police Constable 2001

(a) ABD (b) ACD (c) BDE (d) BCE

16.

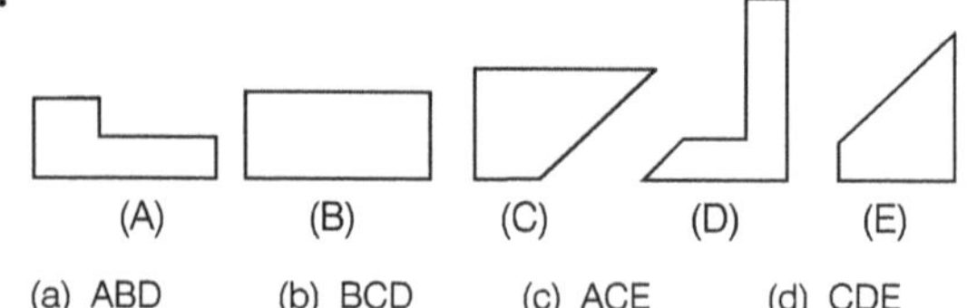

(a) ABD (b) BCD (c) ACE (d) CDE

Answers WITH EXPLANATIONS

1. (*b*) Figures A, B and C can be joined together to form an equilateral triangle.

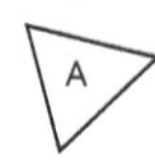
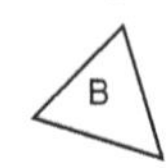
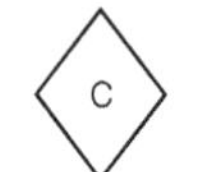
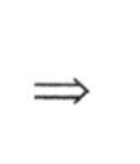
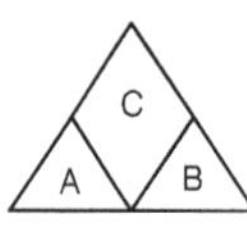

2. (*c*) Figures C, D and E can be joined together to form an equilateral triangle.

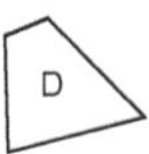
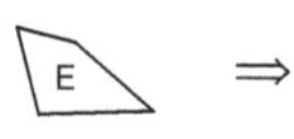
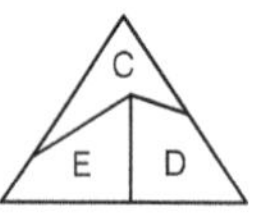

3. (*c*) Figures C, D and E can be joined together to form an equilateral triangle.

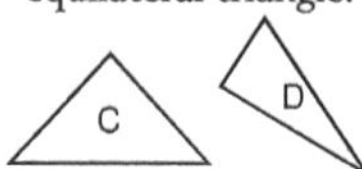
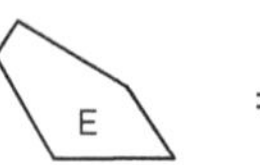

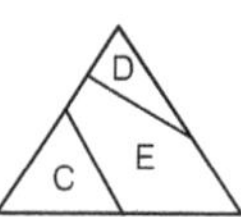

4. (*b*) Figures A, C and E can be joined together to form an equilateral triangle.

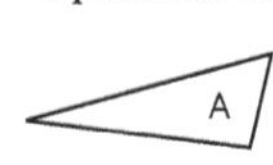
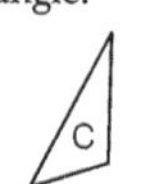
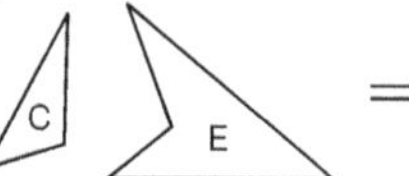
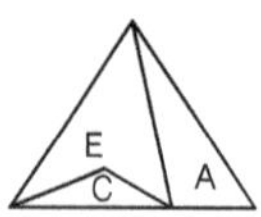

5. (*c*) Figures A, D and E can be joined together to form an equilateral triangle.

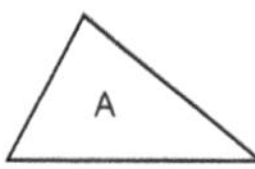

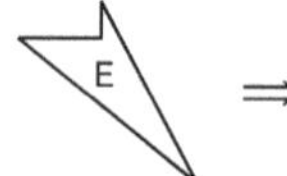

6. (*a*) Figures A, C and E can be joined together to form an equilateral triangle.

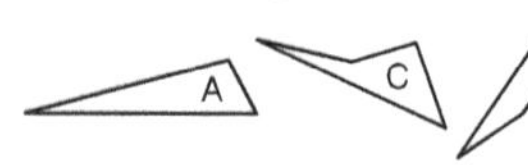

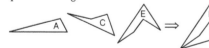

7. (*d*) Figures B, D and E can be joined together to form an equilateral triangle.

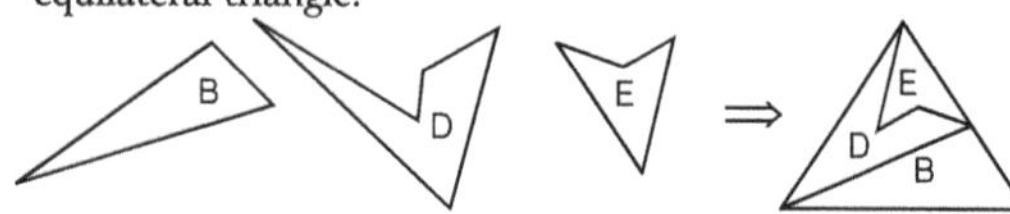

8. (*d*) Figures A, D and E can be joined together to form an equilateral triangle.

9. (*b*) Figures A, C and D can be joined together to form a square.

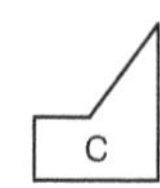

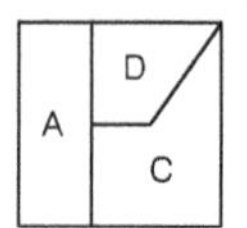

10. (*b*) Figures B, C and D can be joined together to form a square.

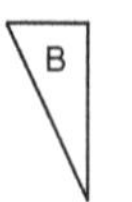

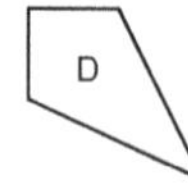
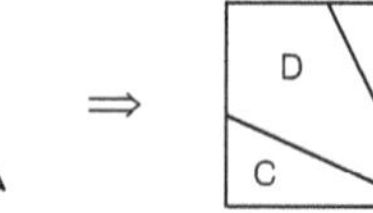
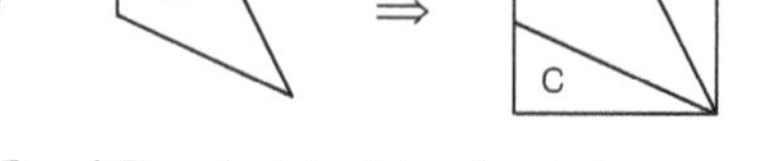

11. (*a*) Figures A, B and C can be joined together to form a square.

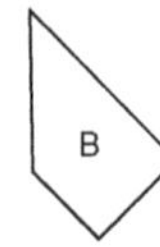
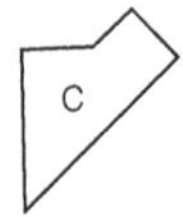
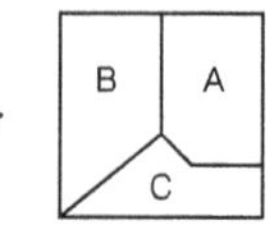

12. (*a*) Figures A, C and D can be joined together to form a square.

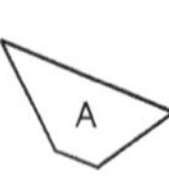
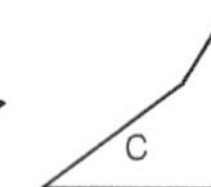

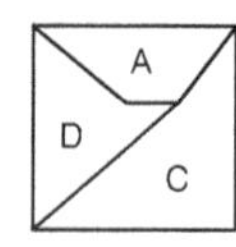

13. (*a*) Figures A, B and D can be joined together to form a square.

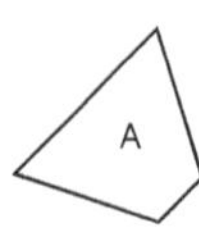

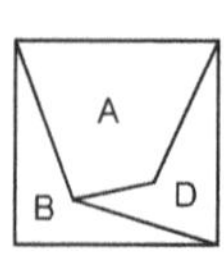

14. (*a*) Figures A, B and C can be joined together to form a square.

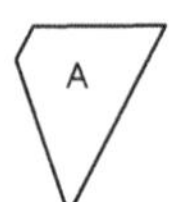
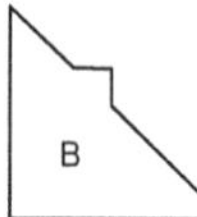
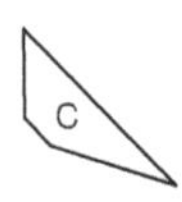
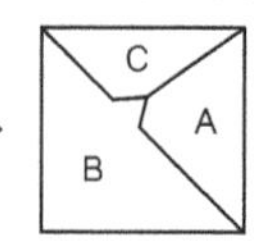

15. (*b*) Figures A, C and D can be joined together to form a square.

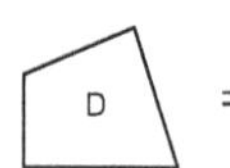
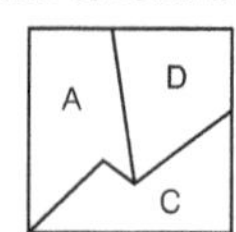

16. (*c*) Figures A, C and E can be joined together to form a square.

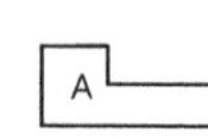
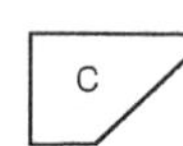
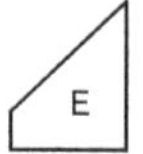
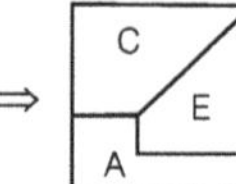

TYPE 04

Square Completion

Completion of an incomplete square given in question figure by joining it with one of the pieces given in the answer figures is known as square completion.

In questions based on square completion, a question figure which represents an incomplete square, is given. The candidate is required to choose the answer figure which is appropriate to make the square complete by joining it with the incomplete square given in the question figure.

DIRECTIONS ~ (Example Nos. 14-17) *In the following questions, a question figure followed by four answer figures is given. You have to choose that answer figure which on joining with the question figure will make a complete square.*

***Ex* 14**

Question Figure **Answer Figures**

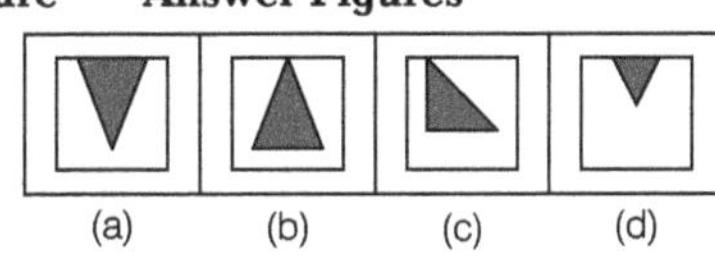

(a) (b) (c) (d)

Solution (a) Figure given in option (a) will fill the blank portion and make a complete square with the question figure. This is shown as below

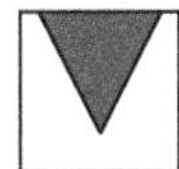

***Ex* 15** **Question Figure** **Answer Figures**

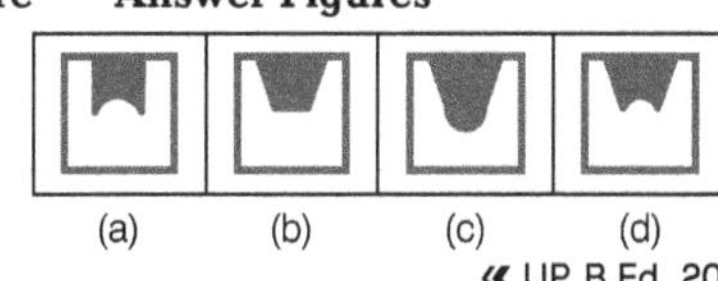

(a) (b) (c) (d)

« UP B.Ed. 2013

Solution (d) Figure given in option (d) will fill the blank portion and make a complete square with the question figure. This is shown as in side

***Ex* 16** **Question Figure** **Answer Figures**

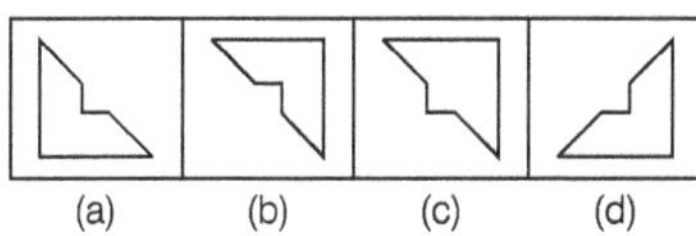

(a) (b) (c) (d)

Solution (c) Figure given in option (c) will make a complete square with the question figure. This is shown as in side

***Ex* 17**

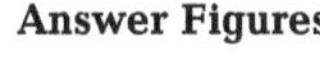

Question Figure **Answer Figures**

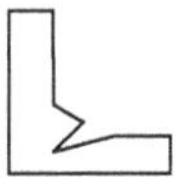

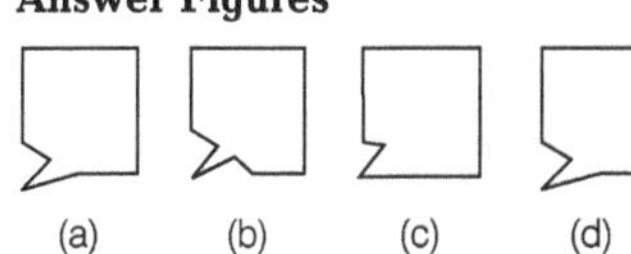

(a) (b) (c) (d)

Solution (a) Figure given in option (a) will fill the blank portion and make a complete square with the question figure. This is shown as below

Practice / CORNER 5.4

DIRECTIONS ~ (Q. Nos. 1-20) *In the following questions, choose the correct answer figure which will make a complete square on joining with the question figure will make a complete square.*

Question Figure **Answer Figures**

1. 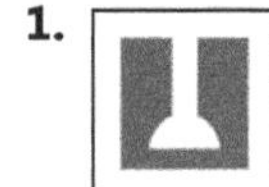

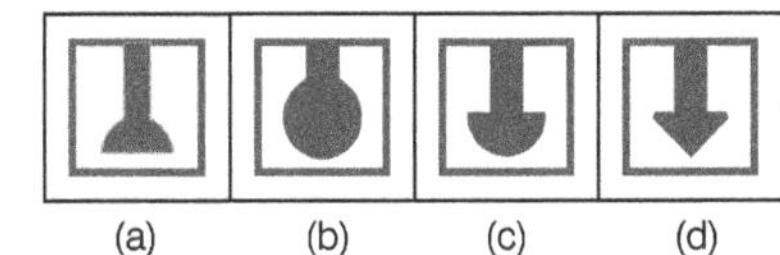

(a) (b) (c) (d)

« SSC CGL 2006

2. 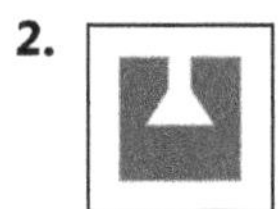

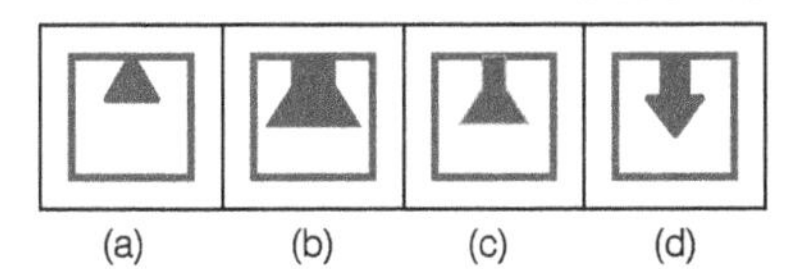

(a) (b) (c) (d)

Question Figure **Answer Figures**

3. 

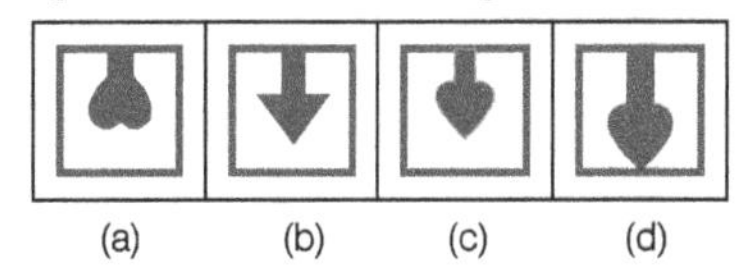

(a) (b) (c) (d)

4. 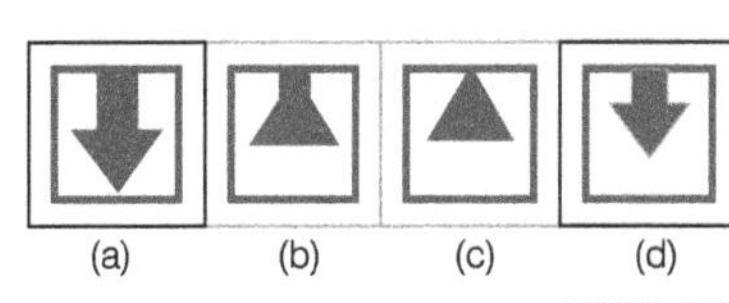

(a) (b) (c) (d)

« SSC CGL 2009

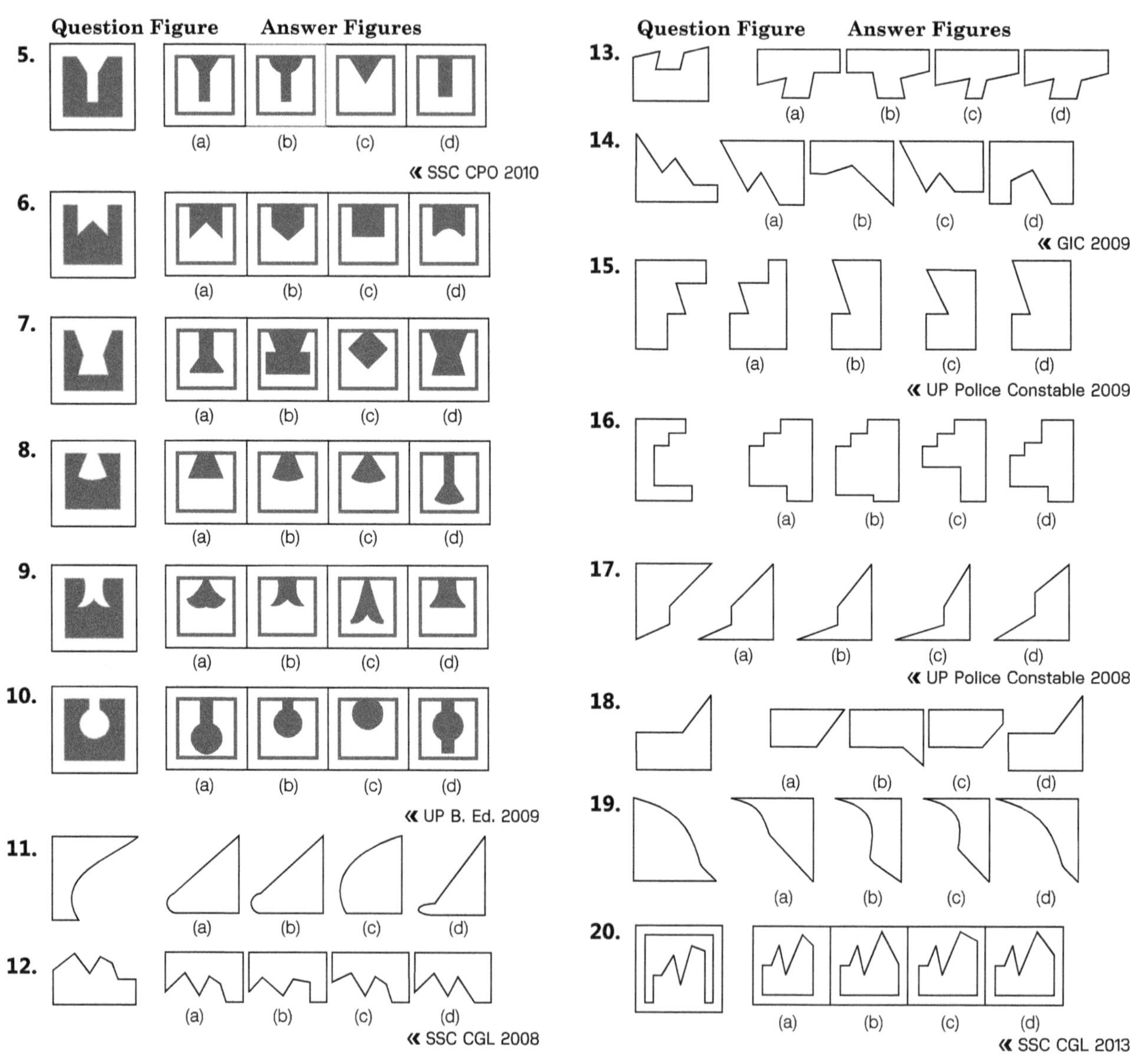

» Answers «

1. *(a)*	2. *(c)*	3. *(c)*	4. *(d)*	5. *(a)*	6. *(a)*	7. *(d)*	8. *(b)*	9. *(b)*	10. *(b)*
11. *(c)*	12. *(a)*	13. *(d)*	14. *(a)*	15. *(a)*	16. *(a)*	17. *(a)*	18. *(a)*	19. *(d)*	20. *(a)*

Master Exercise

DIRECTIONS ~ (Q. Nos. 1-12) *In each of the following questions find the figure from the answer figures, that can be formed by joining the pieces given in the question figure.*

Question Figure **Answer Figures**

1. (a) (b) (c) (d)

« SSC 10+2, DEO, LDC 2010

2. (a) (b) (c) (d)

« RRB Group D 2018

3. (a) (b) (c) (d)

« SSC CGL 2013

4. (a) (b) (c) (d)

« SSC CGL 2015

5. (a) (b) (c) (d)

« SSC FCI 2014

6. (a) (b) (c) (d)

« UP B. Ed. 2007

7. (a) (b) (c) (d)

« SSC CGL 2014

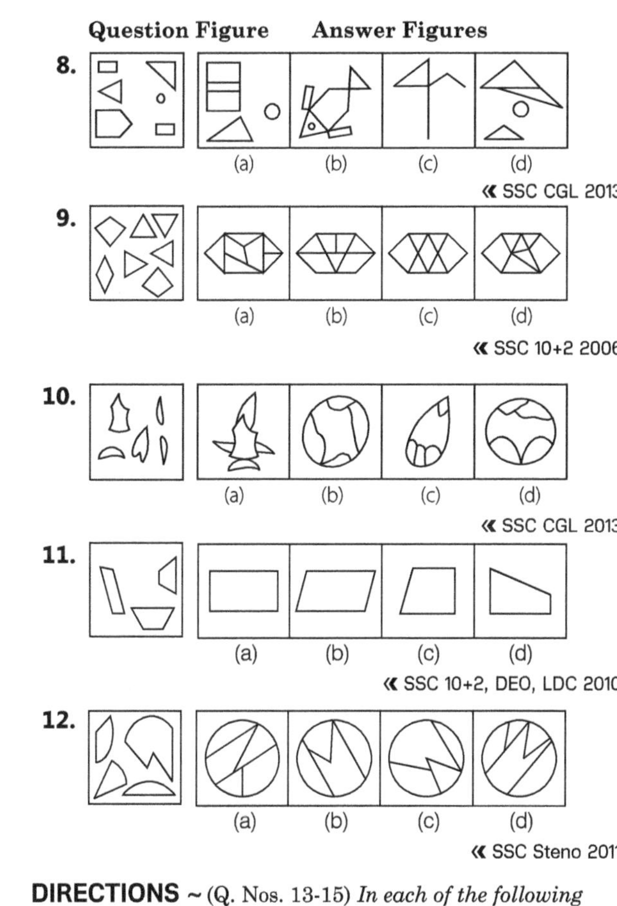

DIRECTIONS ~ (Q. Nos. 13-15) *In each of the following questions, from the four answer figures, find the figure that can form the figure given in the question figure.*

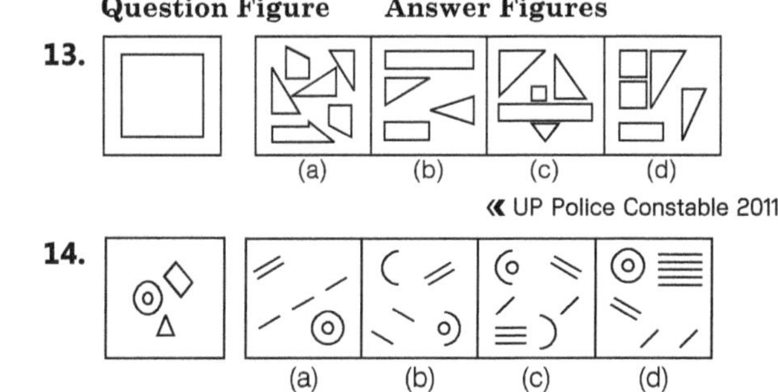

Question Figure **Answer Figures**

15.

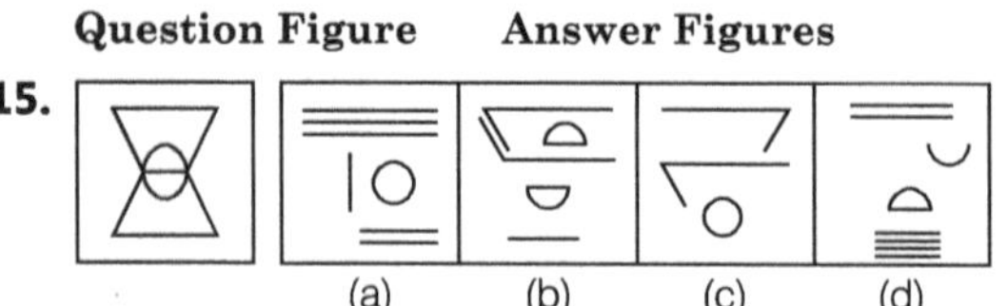

(a) (b) (c) (d)

DIRECTIONS ~ (Q. Nos. 16-18) *In each of the following questions, select that combination of figures which can be joined together to form an equilateral triangle.*

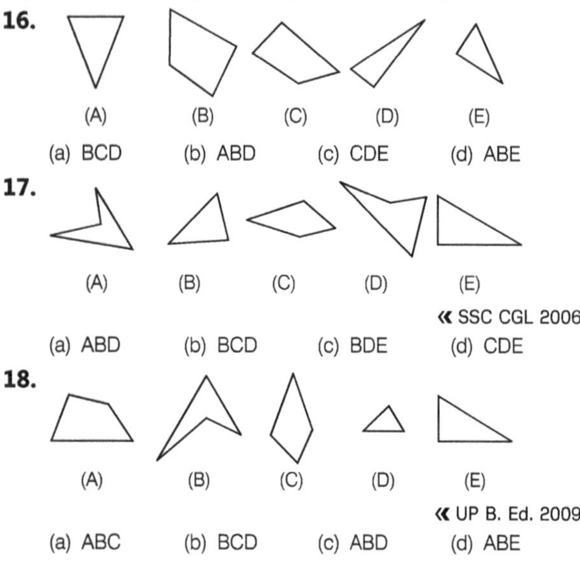

16. (A) (B) (C) (D) (E)

(a) BCD (b) ABD (c) CDE (d) ABE

17. (A) (B) (C) (D) (E)

« SSC CGL 2006

(a) ABD (b) BCD (c) BDE (d) CDE

18. (A) (B) (C) (D) (E)

« UP B. Ed. 2009

(a) ABC (b) BCD (c) ABD (d) ABE

DIRECTIONS ~ (Q. Nos. 19-23) *In each of the following question, select the alternative which represents the combination of figures which, if fitted together, will form a complete square.*

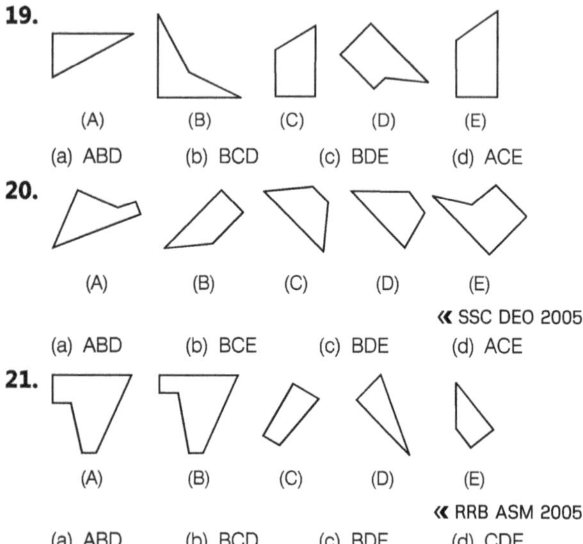

19. (A) (B) (C) (D) (E)

(a) ABD (b) BCD (c) BDE (d) ACE

20. (A) (B) (C) (D) (E)

« SSC DEO 2005

(a) ABD (b) BCE (c) BDE (d) ACE

21. (A) (B) (C) (D) (E)

« RRB ASM 2005

(a) ABD (b) BCD (c) BDE (d) CDE

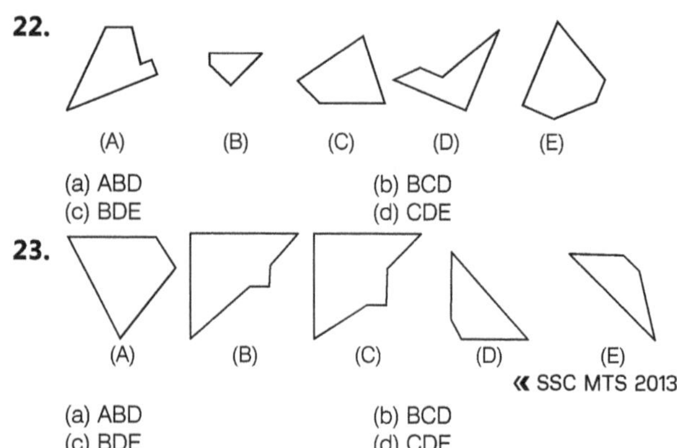

22. (A) (B) (C) (D) (E)

(a) ABD (b) BCD
(c) BDE (d) CDE

23. (A) (B) (C) (D) (E)

« SSC MTS 2013

(a) ABD (b) BCD
(c) BDE (d) CDE

DIRECTIONS ~ (Q. Nos. 24-48) *In the following questions, choose the correct answer figure which on joining with the question figure will make a complete square.*

Question Figure **Answer Figures**

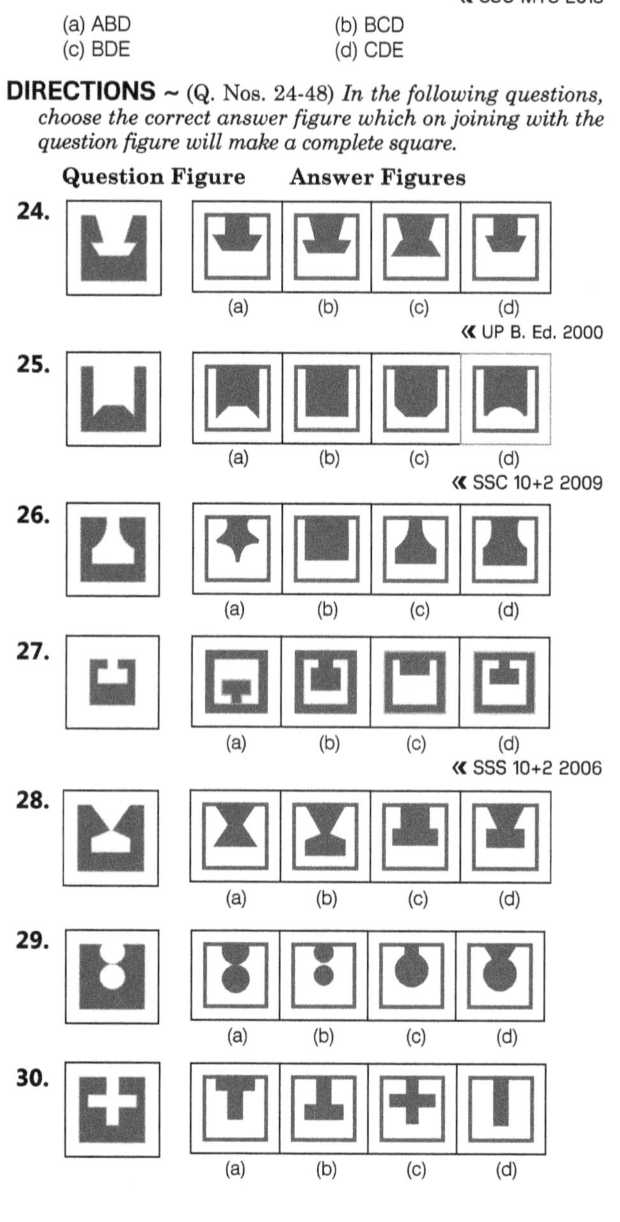

24. (a) (b) (c) (d)

« UP B. Ed. 2000

25. (a) (b) (c) (d)

« SSC 10+2 2009

26. (a) (b) (c) (d)

27. (a) (b) (c) (d)

« SSS 10+2 2006

28. (a) (b) (c) (d)

29. (a) (b) (c) (d)

30. (a) (b) (c) (d)

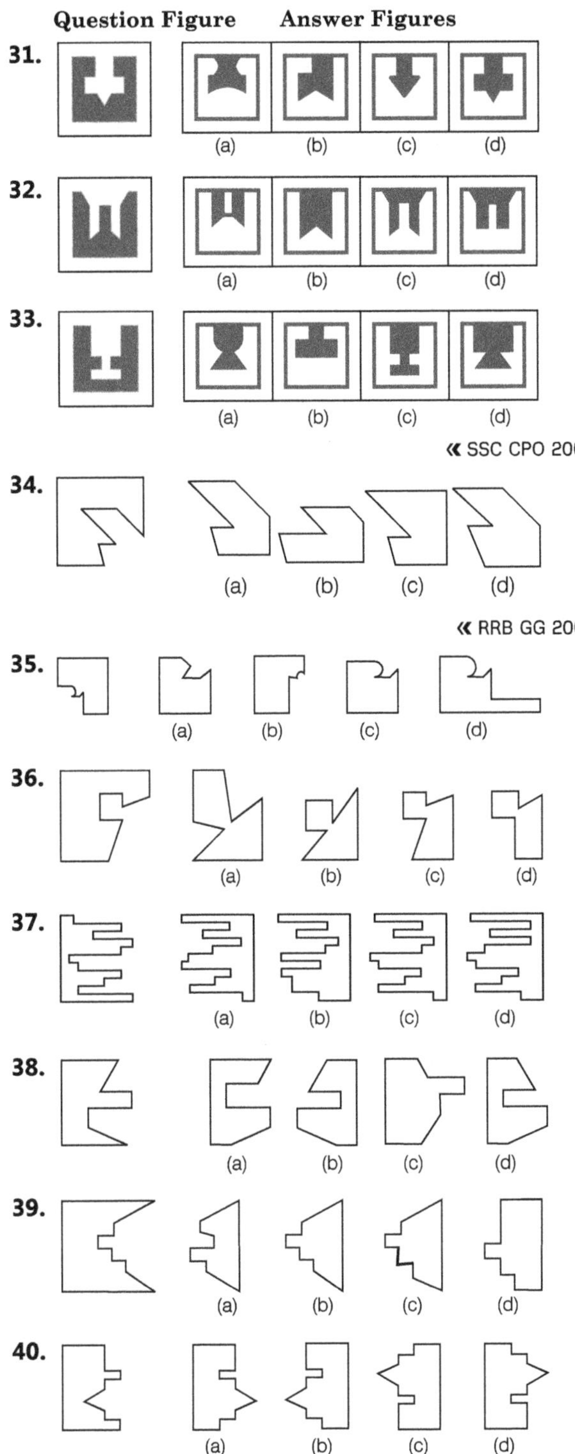

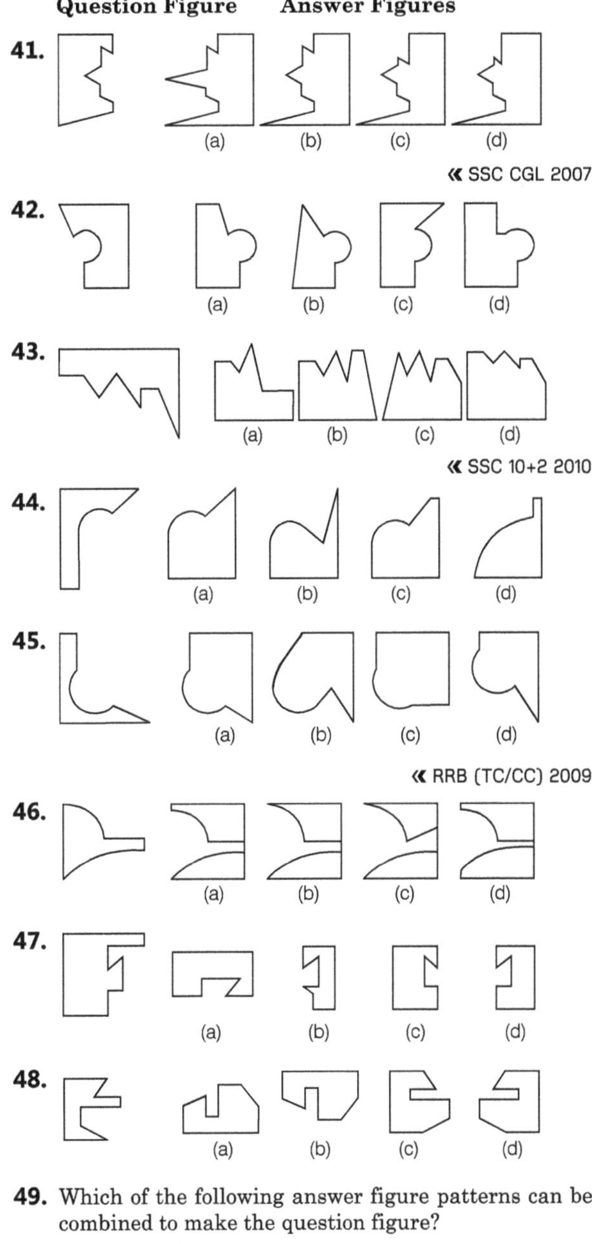

49. Which of the following answer figure patterns can be combined to make the question figure?

Question Figure

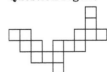

Answer Figures

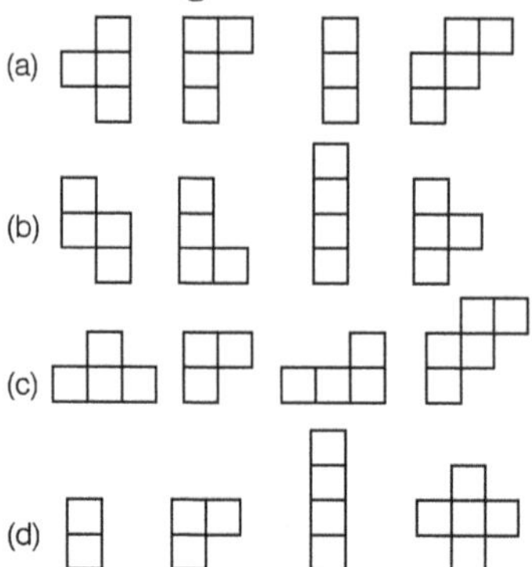

« UPSSSC 2018

50. A group of interconnected pieces is given. Suppose you were able to rotate the pieces, so that neighbouring sides aligned flatly, then find that figure from the answer figures that can be formed by joining the pieces given in the question figure.

Question Figure

Answer Figures

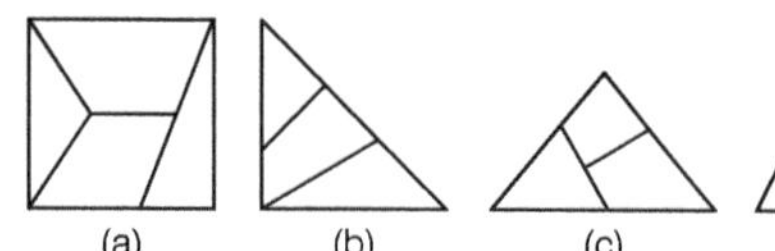

DIRECTIONS ~ (Q. Nos. 51-53) *Which of the following figures* (a), (b), (c) *and* (d), *when folded along the lines, will produce the given figure* (X)?

51.

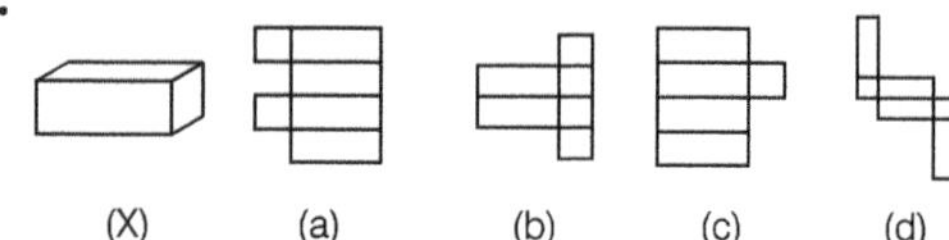

52.

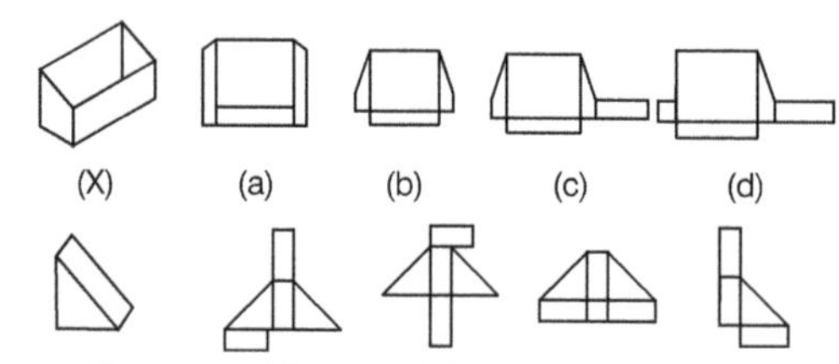

53.

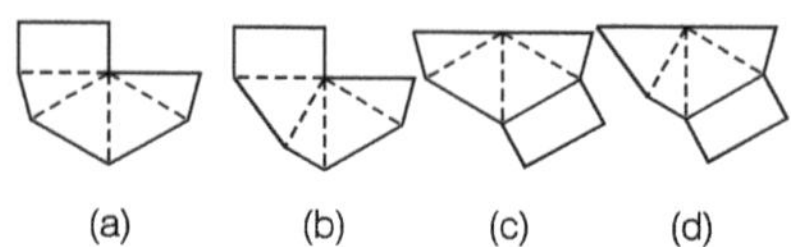

54. Which of the following figures shown below, when folded along the dotted lines, will form a pyramid shaped box with a rectangular base?

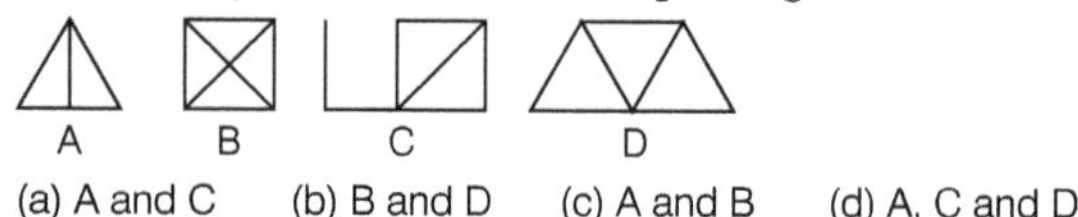

55. Which of the following figures can be drawn without lifting the pencil and without repeating a line?

A B C D

(a) A and C (b) B and D (c) A and B (d) A, C and D

Answers WITH EXPLANATIONS

1. (*a*) Figure given in option (a) can be formed by joining the pieces given in the question figure.

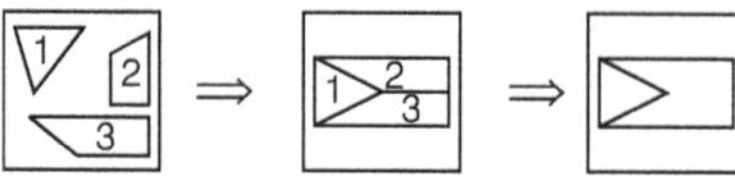

2. (c) Figure given in option (c) can be formed by joining the pieces given in the question figure.

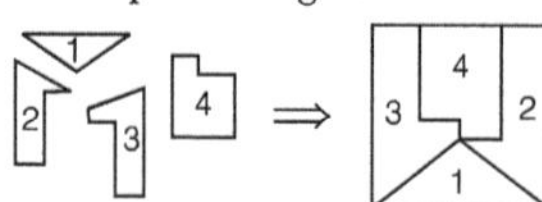

3. (*b*) Figure given in option (b) can be formed by joining the pieces given in the question figure.

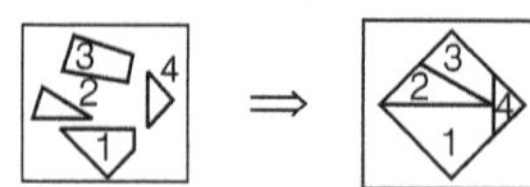

4. (*d*) Figure given in option (d) can be formed by joining the pieces given in the question figure.

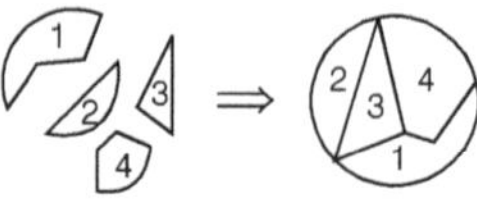

5. (*d*) Figure given in option (d) can be formed by joining the pieces given in the question figure.

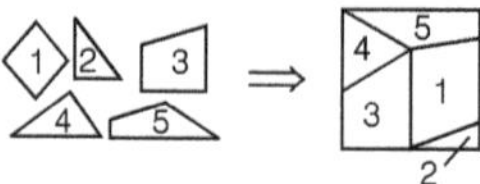

6. (c) Figure given in option (c) can be formed by joining the pieces given in the question figure.

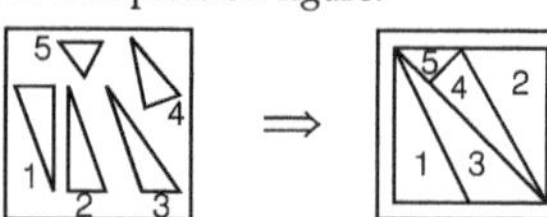

7. (c) Figure given in option (c) can be formed by joining the pieces given in the question figure.

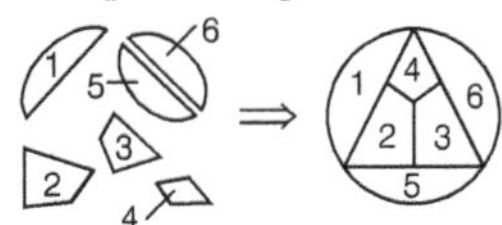

8. (b) Figure given in option (b) can be formed by joining the pieces given in the question figure.

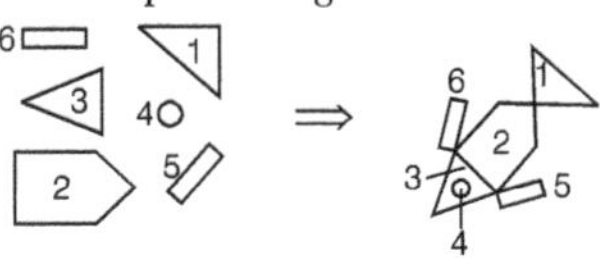

9. (c) Figure given in option (c) can be formed by joining the pieces given in the question figure.

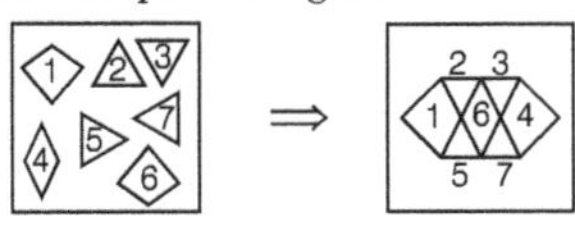

10. (a) Figure given in option (a) can be formed by joining the pieces given in the question figure.

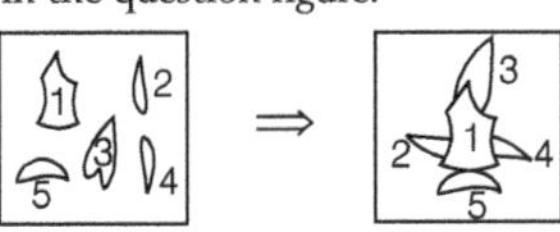

11. (b) Figure given in option (b) can be formed by joining the pieces given in the question figure.

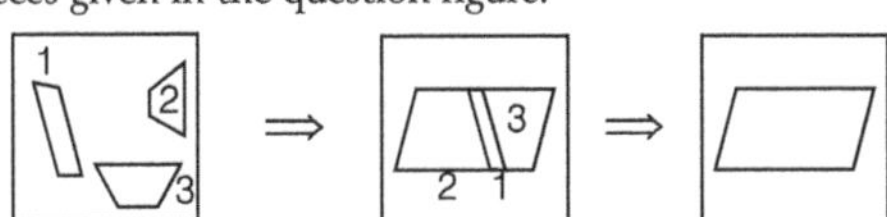

12. (c) Figure given in option (c) can be formed by joining the pieces given in the question figure.

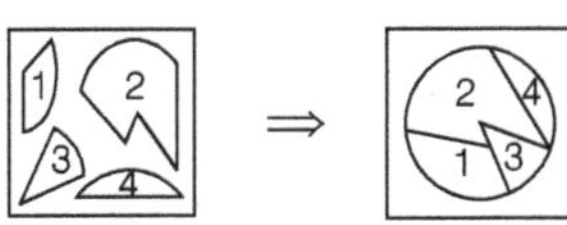

13. (a) Figure given in option (a) can be formed by joining the pieces given in the question figure.

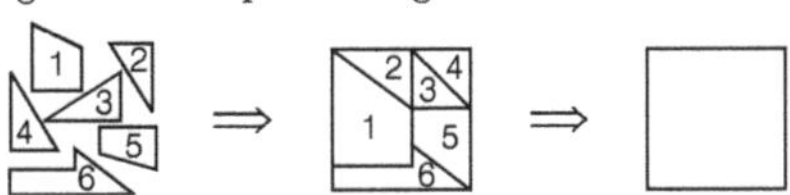

14. (c) Figure given in option (c) can be formed by joining the pieces given in the question figure.

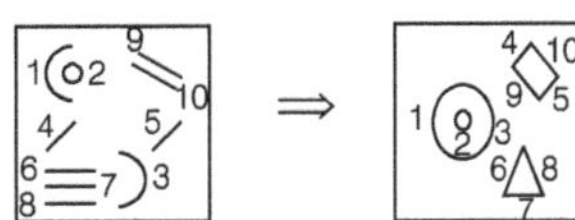

15. (d) Figure given in option (d) can be formed by joining the pieces given in the question figure.

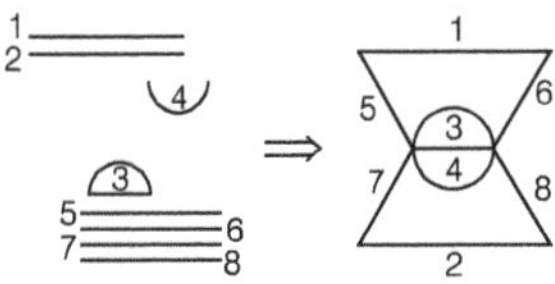

16. (d) Figures A, B and E can be joined together to form an equilateral triangle.

17. (b) Figures B, C and D can be joined together to form an equilateral triangle.

18. (b) Figures B, C and D can be joined together to form an equilateral triangle.

19. (d) Figures A, C and E can be joined together to form a square.

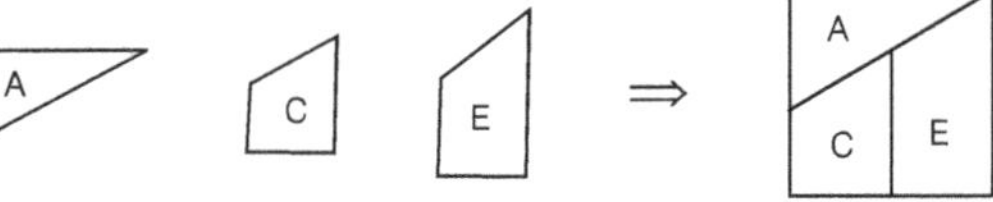

20. (b) Figures B, C and E can be joined together to form a square.

21. (b) Figures B, C and D can be joined together to form a square.

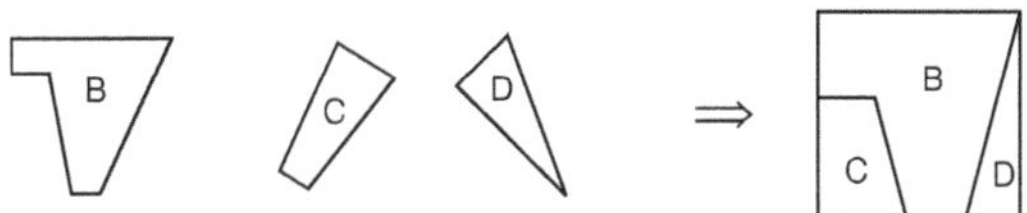

22. (c) Figures B, D and E can be joined together to form a square.

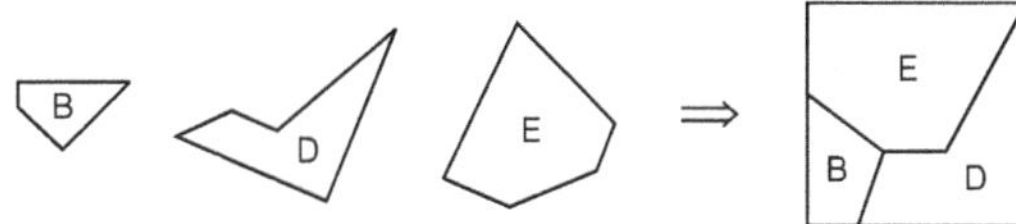

23. (*d*) Figures C, D and E can be joined together to form a square.

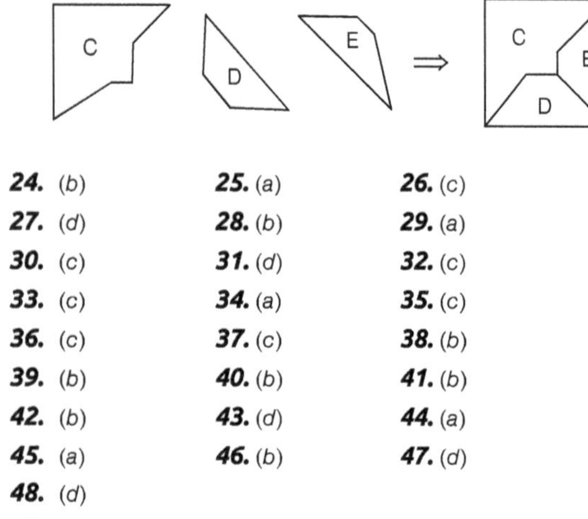

24. (*b*)	***25.*** (*a*)	***26.*** (*c*)
27. (*d*)	***28.*** (*b*)	***29.*** (*a*)
30. (*c*)	***31.*** (*d*)	***32.*** (*c*)
33. (*c*)	***34.*** (*a*)	***35.*** (*c*)
36. (*c*)	***37.*** (*c*)	***38.*** (*b*)
39. (*b*)	***40.*** (*b*)	***41.*** (*b*)
42. (*b*)	***43.*** (*d*)	***44.*** (*a*)
45. (*a*)	***46.*** (*b*)	***47.*** (*d*)
48. (*d*)		

49. (*c*) The patterns in answer figure (c) can be combined together to make the question figure as follows

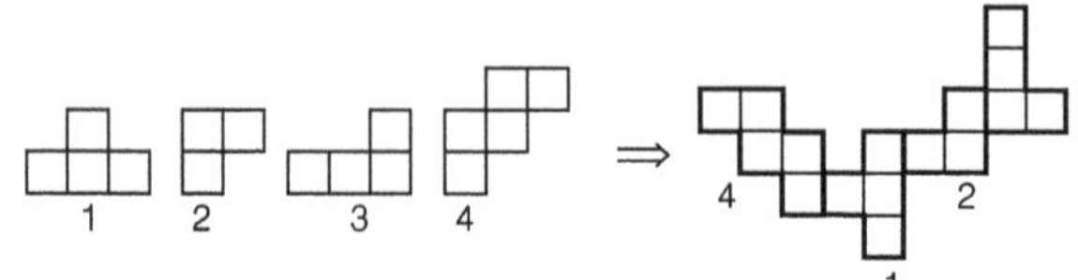

50. (*c*) Answer figure (c) can be formed by joining the pieces given the question figure.

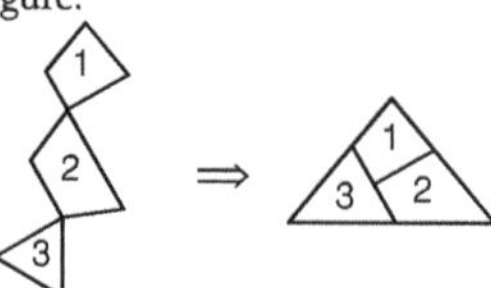

51. (*d*) The given figure (X) has six surfaces, in which 4 are rectangular and 2 are square shaped. The square shaped surfaces must be opposite to each other. Hence, option figure (d), when folded along the lines, will produce the given figure (X).

52. (*c*) The given figure (X) has 5 surfaces, in which '□' and '□' are opposite to each other.
Hence, option figure (c), when folded along the lines, will produce the given figure (X).

53. (*a*) The given figure (X) has 5 surfaces, in which 3 are rectangular and 2 are triangular shaped. Hence, option figure (a), when folded along the lines, will produce the given figure (X).

54. (*d*) The figure given in option (d), when folded along the dotted lines, will form a pyramid shaped box with a rectangular base as shown below

55. (*d*) Figure A, C and D can be drawn without lifting the pencil and without repeating a line as shown below

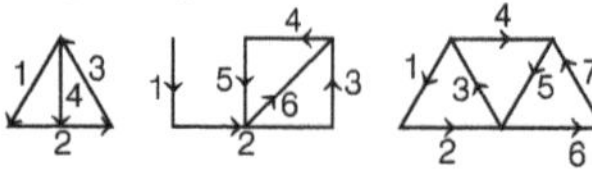

CHAPTER / 06

Embedded Figures

A figure is said to be embedded in an another figure when the first figure is hidden completely in the second figure. Questions based on embedded figures comprise of a question figure and four answer figures and it is asked to find the correct answer figure which is embedded in given question figure or the correct answer figure in which the given question figure is embedded.

Different types of questions covered in this chapter are as follows

TYPE 01

Question Figure Embedded in Answer Figure

In these questions, a question figure and four answer figures are given. The question figure is embedded in one of the answer figures. The candidate is required to find out that particular answer figure in which the question figure is embedded.

The following examples will give you a better idea about this type of questions.

DIRECTIONS ~ (Example Nos. 1-6) *In the following questions, a question figure and a set of four answer figures* (a), (b), (c) *and* (d) *are given. Find out that answer figure in which the question figure is embedded.*

***Ex* 01** **Question Figure** **Answer Figures**

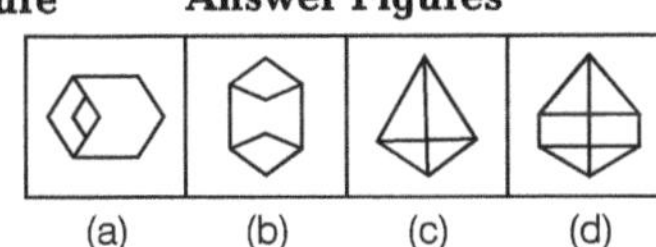

(a) (b) (c) (d)

« SSC 10+2 2010

Solution ***(b)*** Clearly, the question figure is embedded in answer figure (b). The portion which question figure occupies in the answer figure is shown in the below figure with dark lines.

***Ex* 02** **Question Figure** **Answer Figures**

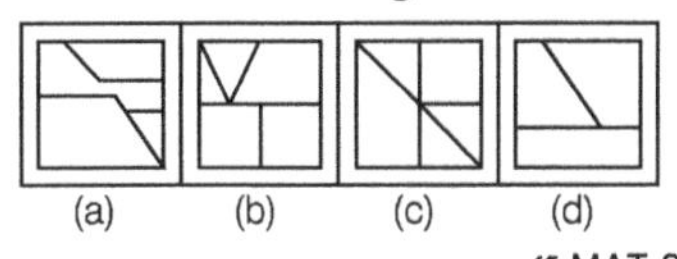

« MAT 2009

Solution ***(d)*** Clearly, the question figure is embedded in answer figure (d). The portion which question figure occupies in the answer figure is shown in the below figure with dark lines.

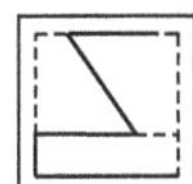

***Ex* 03** **Question Figure** **Answer Figures**

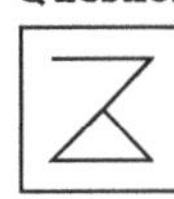

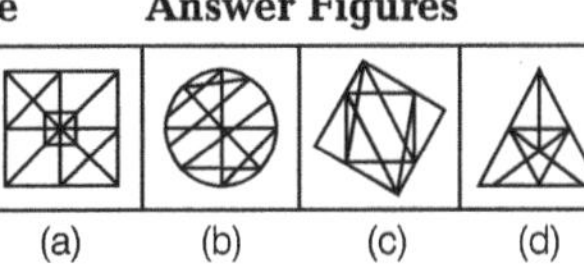

Solution ***(a)*** Clearly, the question figure is embedded in answer figure (a). The portion which question figure occupies in the answer figure is shown in the below figure with dark lines.

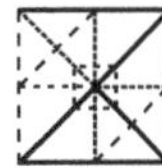

***Ex* 04** **Question Figure** **Answer Figures**

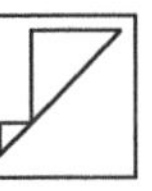

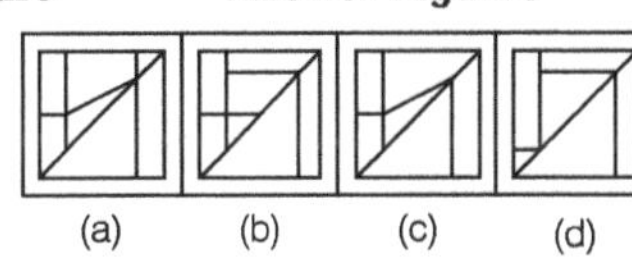

Solution ***(d)*** Clearly, the question figure is embedded in answer figure (d). The portion which question figure occupies in the answer figure is shown in the below figure with dark lines.

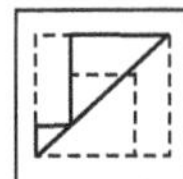

Ex 05 **Question Figure** **Answer Figures**

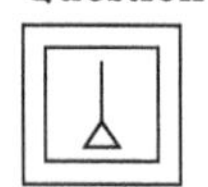

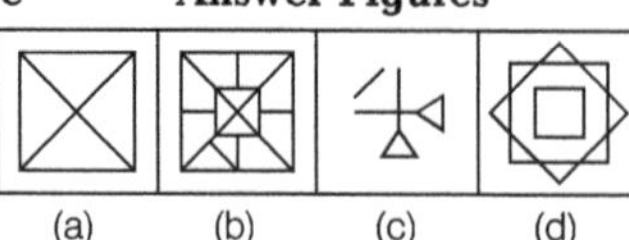

(a) (b) (c) (d)

« SSC CGL 2009

Solution (c) Clearly, the question figure is embedded in answer figure (c). Here, we have selected vertical image and not horizontal image because we give preference to the one which depicts the question figure embedded with least change in its orientation.

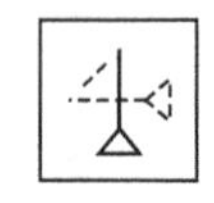

Ex 06 **Question Figure** **Answer Figures**

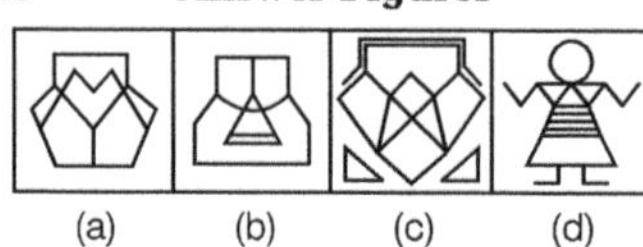

(a) (b) (c) (d)

« RRB ALP 2018, SSC Steno 2019

Solution (d) Clearly, the question figure is embedded in answer figure (d).

The portion which question figure occupies in the answer figure is shown in the below figure with dark lines.

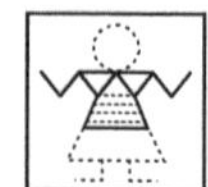

Chapter tip! There may be some questions in which the question figure is not directly embedded in any of the answer figures. In these type of questions, change the orientation of question figure to find the correct answer figure.

In some questions, the candidate will find the question figure embedded in two or more answer figures, then the most appropriate answer is that in which the question figure is embedded with least change in its orientation.

Practice CORNER 6.1

DIRECTIONS ~ (Q. Nos. 1-75) *In each of the following question(s), find the answer figure in which question figure is embedded.*

1. **Question Figure** **Answer Figures**

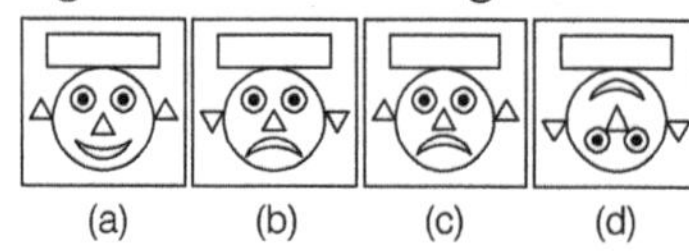

(a) (b) (c) (d)

« Delhi Police SI & ASI 2016

2.

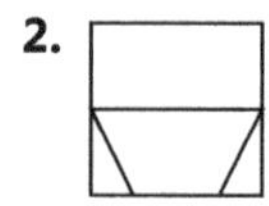

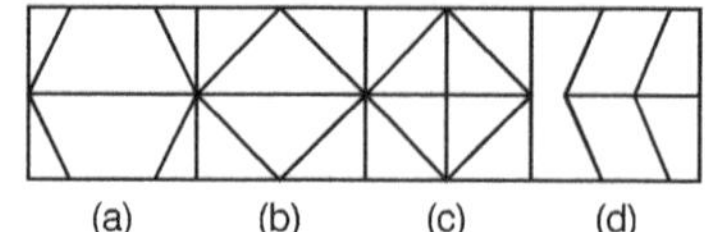

(a) (b) (c) (d)

« SSC LDC 2005, SSC Steno 2011

3.

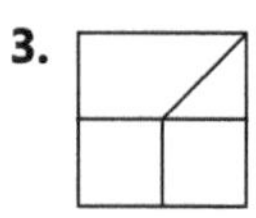

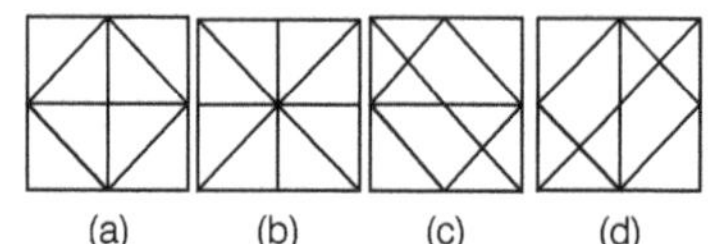

(a) (b) (c) (d)

« SSC MTS 2014

4.

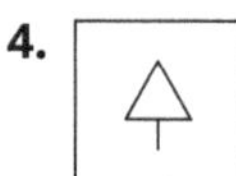

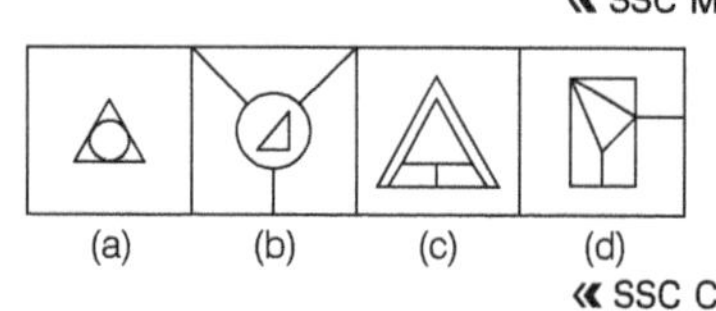

(a) (b) (c) (d)

« SSC CGL 2018

5. **Question Figure** **Answer Figures**

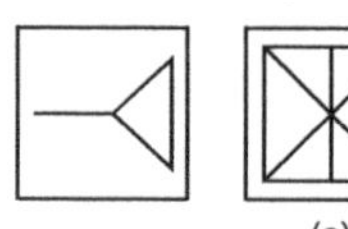

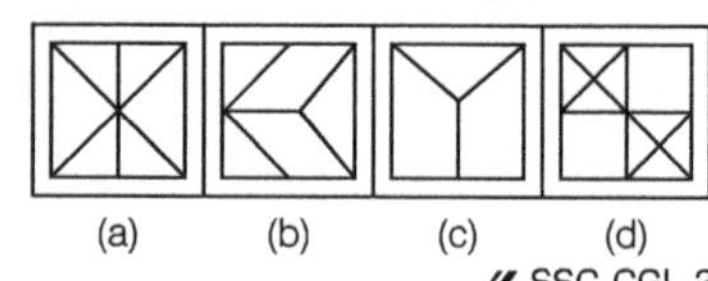

(a) (b) (c) (d)

« SSC CGL 2008, 2014

6.

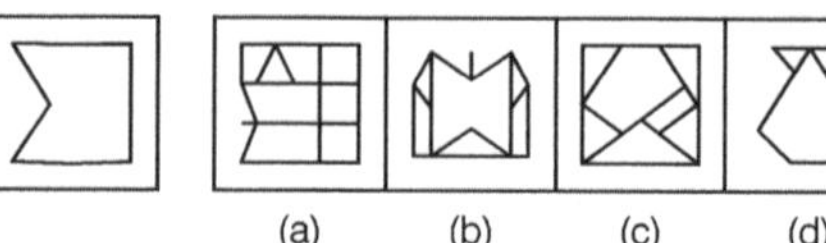

(a) (b) (c) (d)

7.

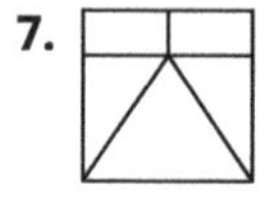

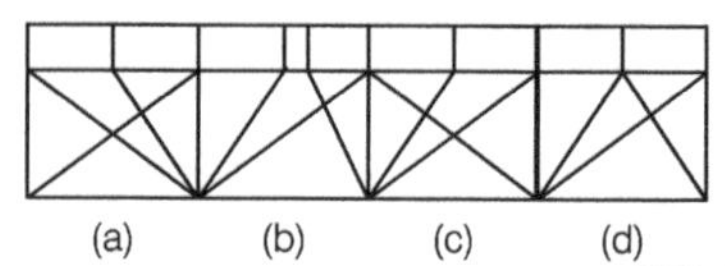

(a) (b) (c) (d)

« RRB ALP 2018

8.

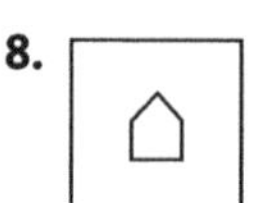

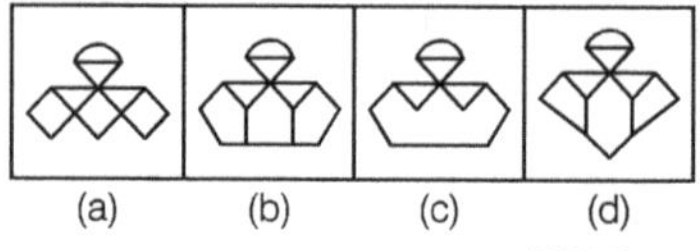

(a) (b) (c) (d)

« SSC Constable 2012

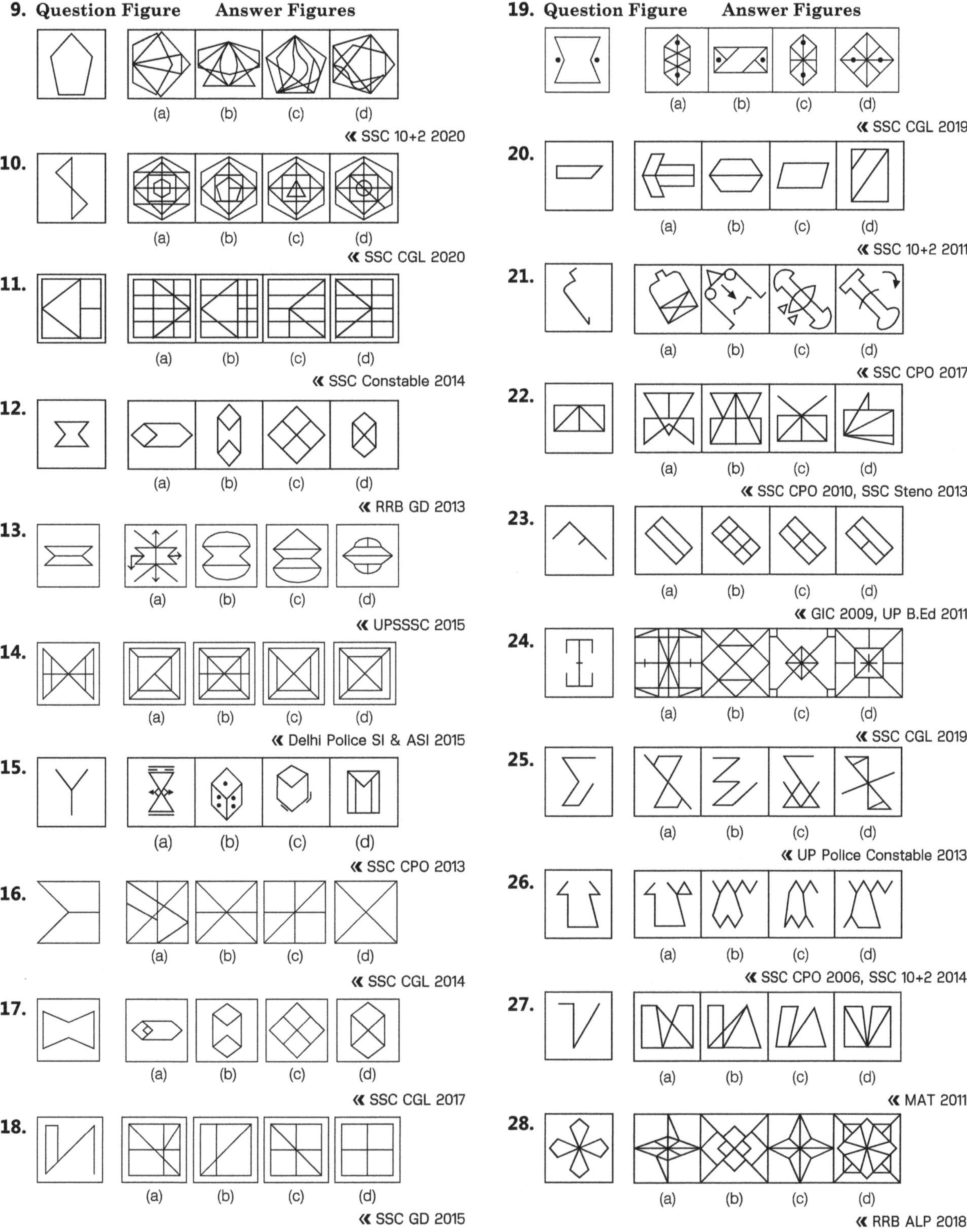
9. Question Figure Answer Figures
(a) (b) (c) (d)
« SSC 10+2 2020
10.
(a) (b) (c) (d)
« SSC CGL 2020
11.
(a) (b) (c) (d)
« SSC Constable 2014
12.
(a) (b) (c) (d)
« RRB GD 2013
13.
(a) (b) (c) (d)
« UPSSSC 2015
14.
(a) (b) (c) (d)
« Delhi Police SI & ASI 2015
15.
(a) (b) (c) (d)
« SSC CPO 2013
16.
(a) (b) (c) (d)
« SSC CGL 2014
17.
(a) (b) (c) (d)
« SSC CGL 2017
18.
(a) (b) (c) (d)
« SSC GD 2015
19. Question Figure Answer Figures
(a) (b) (c) (d)
« SSC CGL 2019
20.
(a) (b) (c) (d)
« SSC 10+2 2011
21.
(a) (b) (c) (d)
« SSC CPO 2017
22.
(a) (b) (c) (d)
« SSC CPO 2010, SSC Steno 2013
23.
(a) (b) (c) (d)
« GIC 2009, UP B.Ed 2011
24.
(a) (b) (c) (d)
« SSC CGL 2019
25.
(a) (b) (c) (d)
« UP Police Constable 2013
26.
(a) (b) (c) (d)
« SSC CPO 2006, SSC 10+2 2014
27.
(a) (b) (c) (d)
« MAT 2011
28.
(a) (b) (c) (d)
« RRB ALP 2018

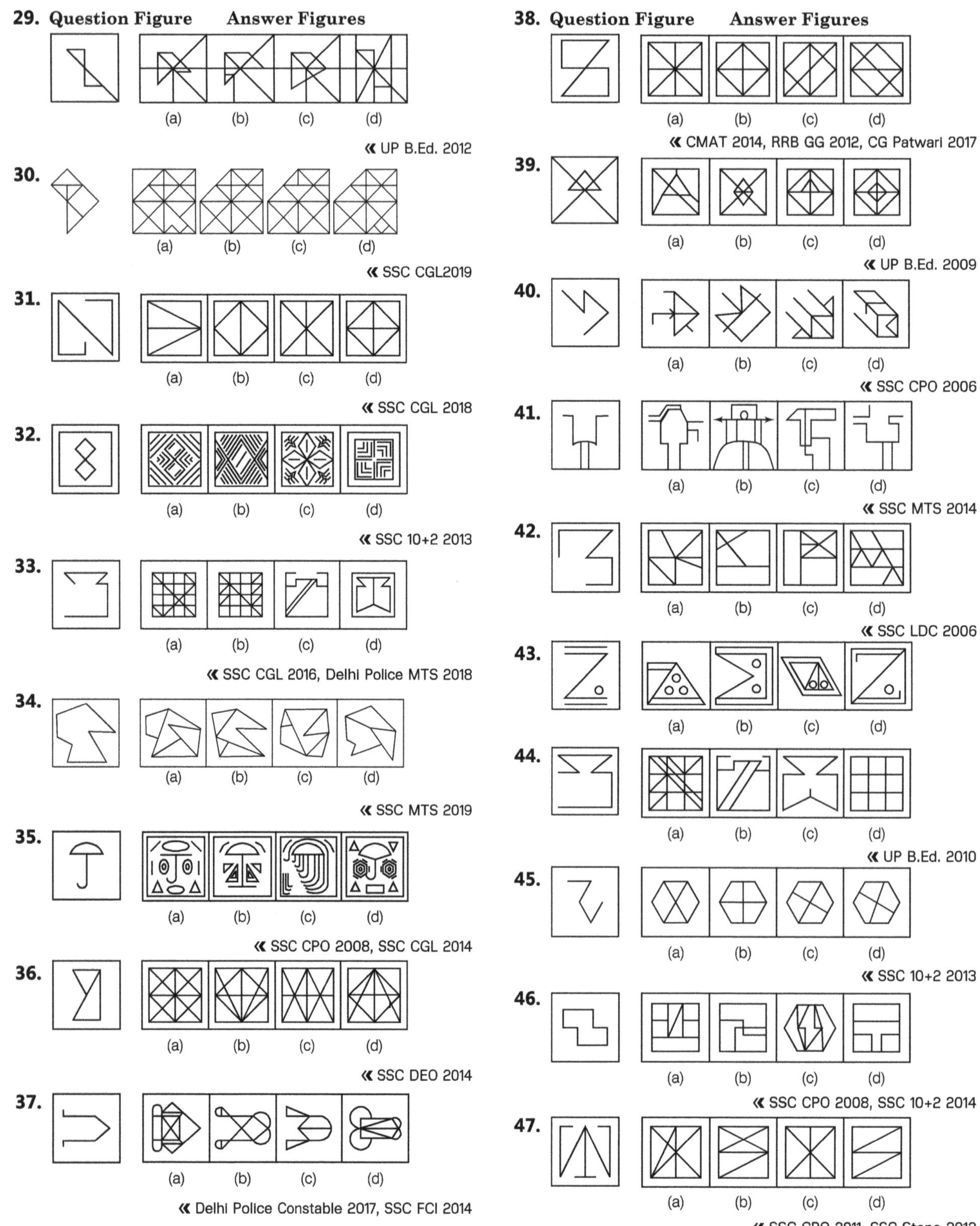
29. Question Figure Answer Figures
(a) (b) (c) (d)
« UP B.Ed. 2012
30.
(a) (b) (c) (d)
« SSC CGL2019
31.
(a) (b) (c) (d)
« SSC CGL 2018
32.
(a) (b) (c) (d)
« SSC 10+2 2013
33.
(a) (b) (c) (d)
« SSC CGL 2016, Delhi Police MTS 2018
34.
(a) (b) (c) (d)
« SSC MTS 2019
35.
(a) (b) (c) (d)
« SSC CPO 2008, SSC CGL 2014
36.
(a) (b) (c) (d)
« SSC DEO 2014
37.
(a) (b) (c) (d)
« Delhi Police Constable 2017, SSC FCI 2014
38. Question Figure Answer Figures
(a) (b) (c) (d)
« CMAT 2014, RRB GG 2012, CG Patwari 2017
39.
(a) (b) (c) (d)
« UP B.Ed. 2009
40.
(a) (b) (c) (d)
« SSC CPO 2006
41.
(a) (b) (c) (d)
« SSC MTS 2014
42.
(a) (b) (c) (d)
« SSC LDC 2006
43.
(a) (b) (c) (d)
44.
(a) (b) (c) (d)
« UP B.Ed. 2010
45.
(a) (b) (c) (d)
« SSC 10+2 2013
46.
(a) (b) (c) (d)
« SSC CPO 2008, SSC 10+2 2014
47.
(a) (b) (c) (d)
« SSC CPO 2011, SSC Steno 2012

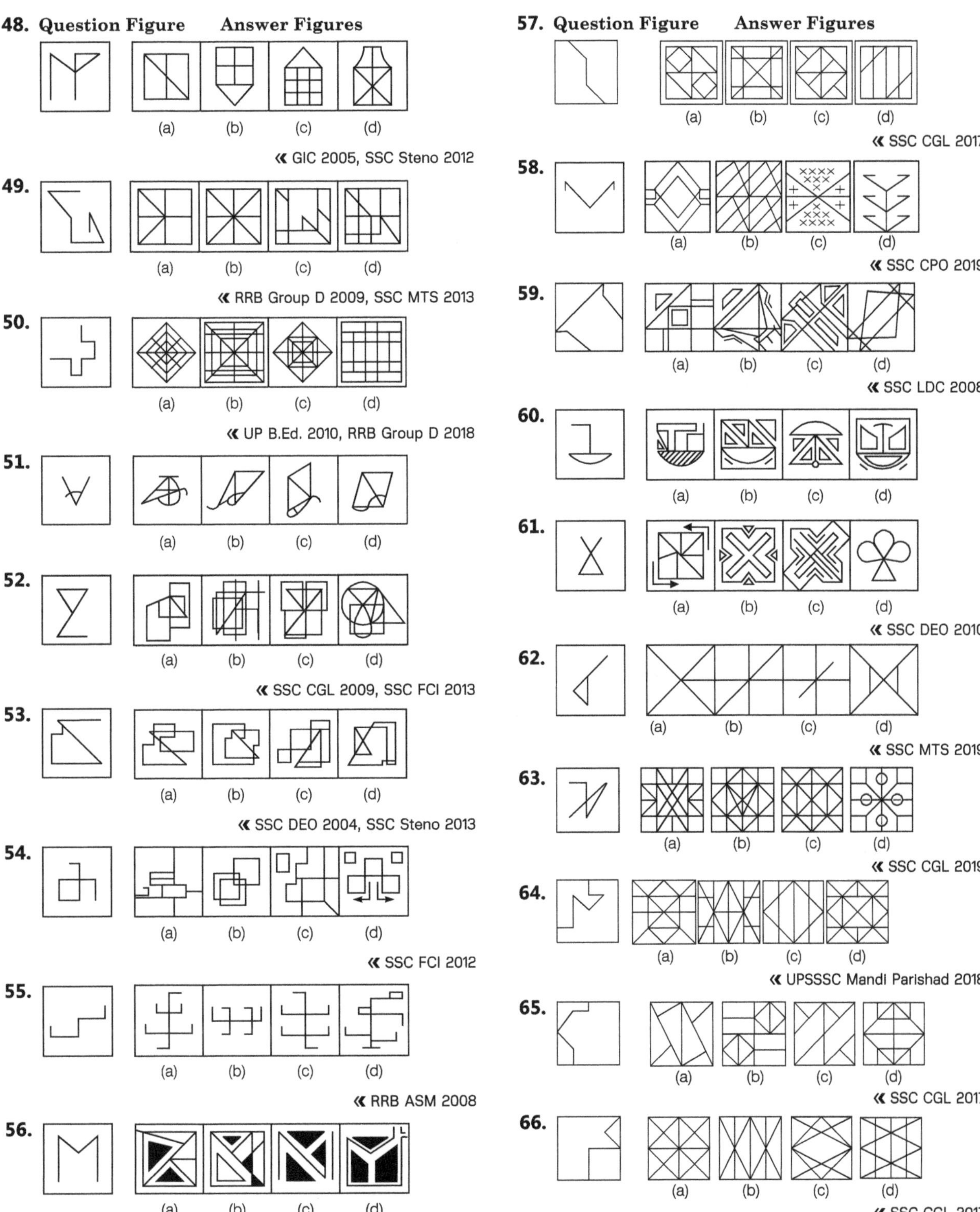
48. Question Figure Answer Figures
(a) (b) (c) (d)
« GIC 2005, SSC Steno 2012
49.
(a) (b) (c) (d)
« RRB Group D 2009, SSC MTS 2013
50.
(a) (b) (c) (d)
« UP B.Ed. 2010, RRB Group D 2018
51.
(a) (b) (c) (d)
52.
(a) (b) (c) (d)
« SSC CGL 2009, SSC FCI 2013
53.
(a) (b) (c) (d)
« SSC DEO 2004, SSC Steno 2013
54.
(a) (b) (c) (d)
« SSC FCI 2012
55.
(a) (b) (c) (d)
« RRB ASM 2008
56.
(a) (b) (c) (d)
57. Question Figure Answer Figures
(a) (b) (c) (d)
« SSC CGL 2017
58.
(a) (b) (c) (d)
« SSC CPO 2019
59.
(a) (b) (c) (d)
« SSC LDC 2008
60.
(a) (b) (c) (d)
61.
(a) (b) (c) (d)
« SSC DEO 2010
62.
(a) (b) (c) (d)
« SSC MTS 2019
63.
(a) (b) (c) (d)
« SSC CGL 2019
64.
(a) (b) (c) (d)
« UPSSSC Mandi Parishad 2018
65.
(a) (b) (c) (d)
« SSC CGL 2017
66.
(a) (b) (c) (d)
« SSC CGL 2017

67. **Question Figure** **Answer Figures**

(a) (b) (c) (d)

« SSC CGL 2017

68.

(a) (b) (c) (d)

« SSC CGL 2007

69.

(a) (b) (c) (d)

« SSC Constable 2019

70.

(a) (b) (c) (d)

71.

(a) (b) (c) (d)

« SSC 10+2 2013

72. **Question Figure** **Answer Figures**

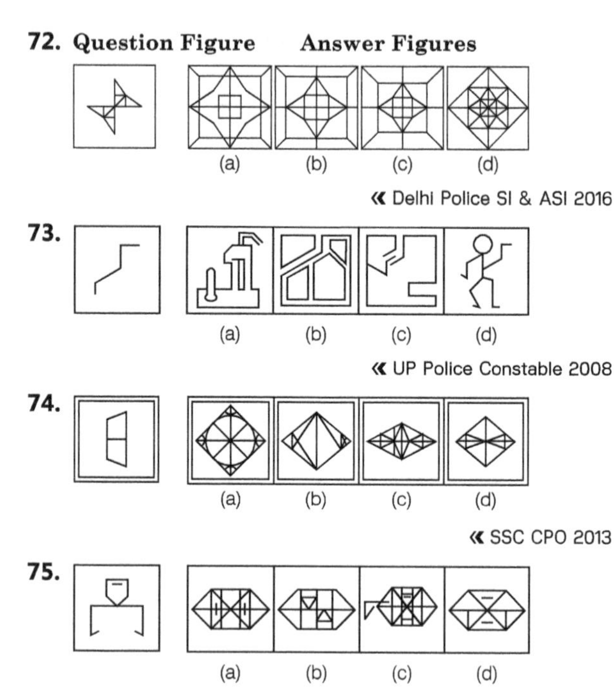

Answers WITH EXPLANATIONS

1. (*a*) The question figure is embedded in answer figure (a).

2. (*a*) The question figure is embedded in answer figure (a).

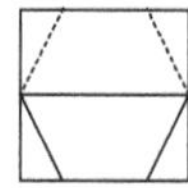

3. (*b*) The question figure is embedded in answer figure (b).

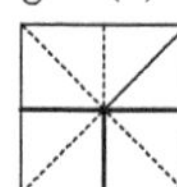

4. (*c*) The question figure is embedded in answer figure (c).

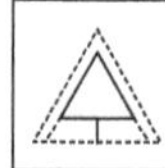

5. (*b*) The question figure is embedded in answer figure (b).

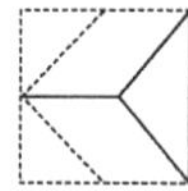

6. (*a*) The question figure is embedded in answer figure (a).

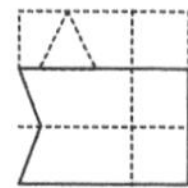

7. (*d*) The question figure is embedded in answer figure (d).

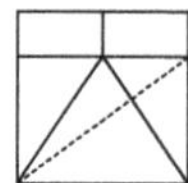

8. (*b*) The question figure is embedded in answer figure (b).

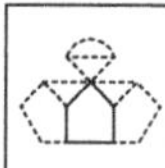

9. (*c*) The given question figure is embedded in answer figure (c).

10. (*d*) The given question figure is embedded in answer figure (d).

11. (*b*) The question figure is embedded in answer figure (b).

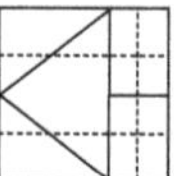

12. (*b*) The question figure is embedded in answer figure (b).

13. (*c*) The question figure is embedded in answer figure (c).

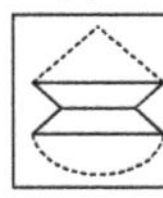

14. (*b*) The question figure is embedded in answer figure (b).

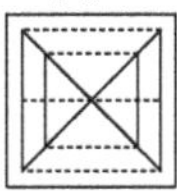

15. (*b*) The question figure is embedded in answer figure (b).

16. (*b*) The question figure is embedded in answer figure (b).

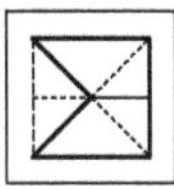

17. (*b*) The question figure is embedded in answer figure (b).

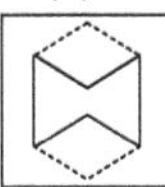

18. (*b*) The question figure is embedded in answer figure (b).

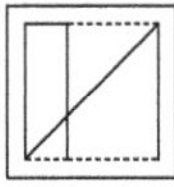

19. (*a*) The question figure is embedded in answer figure (a).

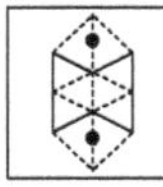

20. (*a*) The question figure is embedded in answer figure (a).

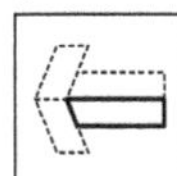

21. (*a*) The question figure is embedded in answer figure (a).

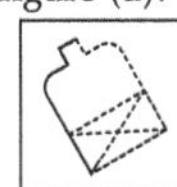

22. (*c*) The question figure is embedded in answer figure (c).

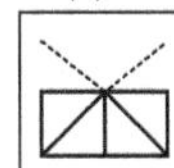

23. (*c*) The question figure is embedded in answer figure (c).

24. (*a*) The question figure is embedded in answer figure (a).

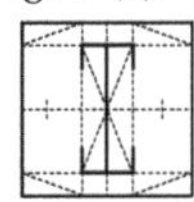

25. (*c*) The question figure is embedded in answer figure (c).

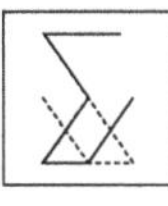

26. (*a*) The question figure is embedded in answer figure (a).

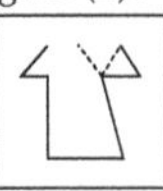

27. (*b*) The question figure is embedded in answer figure (b).

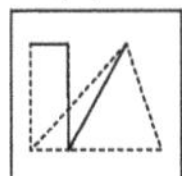

28. (*d*) The question figure is embedded in answer figure (d).

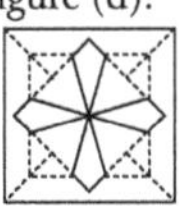

29. (*d*) The question figure is embedded in answer figure (d).

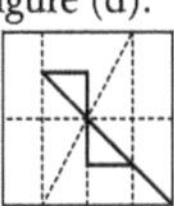

30. (*b*) The question figure is embedded in answer figure (b).

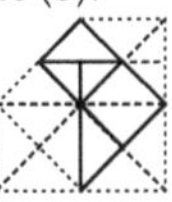

31. (*c*) The question figure is embedded in answer figure (c).

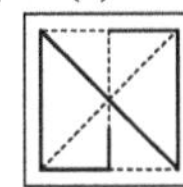

32. (*a*) The question figure is embedded in answer figure (a).

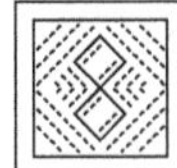

33. (*b*) The question figure is embedded in answer figure (b).

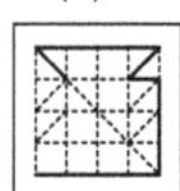

34. (*a*) The question figure is embedded in answer figure (a).

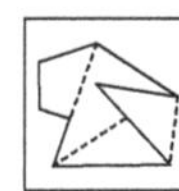

Given figure is embedded in option (a)

35. (*c*) The question figure is embedded in answer figure (c).

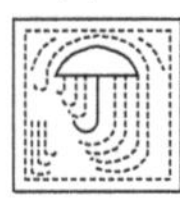

36. (*c*) The question figure is embedded in answer figure (c).

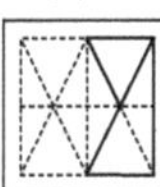

37. (*b*) The question figure is embedded in answer figure (b).

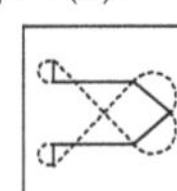

38. (*a*) The question figure is embedded in answer figure (a).

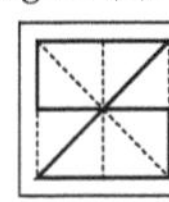

39. (*b*) The question figure is embedded in answer figure (b).

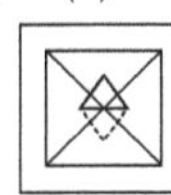

40. (*b*) The question figure is embedded in answer figure (b).

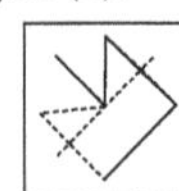

41. (*b*) The question figure is embedded in answer figure (b).

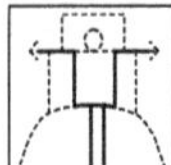

42. (*a*) The question figure is embedded in answer figure (a).

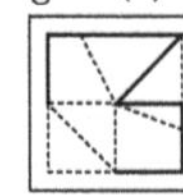

43. (*d*) The question figure is embedded in answer figure (d).

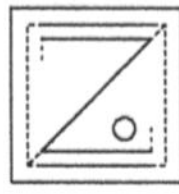

44. (*a*) The question figure is embedded in answer figure (a).

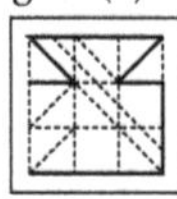

45. (*a*) The question figure is embedded in answer figure (a).

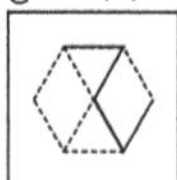

46. (*a*) The question figure is embedded in answer figure (a).

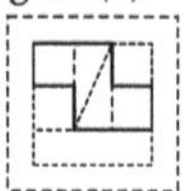

47. (*b*) The question figure is embedded in answer figure (b).

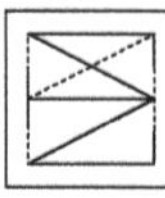

48. (*d*) The question figure is embedded in answer figure (d).

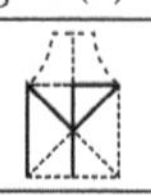

49. (*d*) The question figure is embedded in answer figure (d).

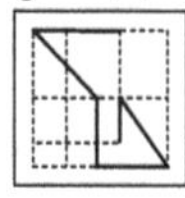

50. (*d*) The question figure is embedded in answer figure (d).

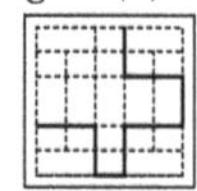

51. (*d*) The question figure is embedded in answer figure (d).

52. (*c*) The question figure is embedded in answer figure (c).

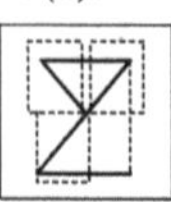

53. (*a*) The question figure is embedded in answer figure (a).

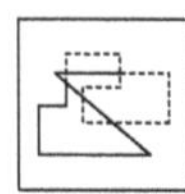

54. (*b*) The question figure is embedded in answer figure (b).

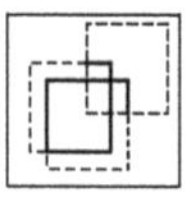

55. (*c*) The question figure is embedded in answer figure (c).

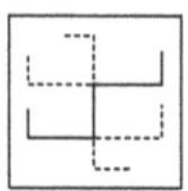

56. (*b*) The question figure is embedded in answer figure (b).

57. (*a*) The question figure is embedded in answer figure (a).

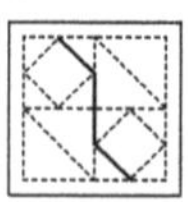

58. (*a*) The question figure is embedded in answer figure (a).

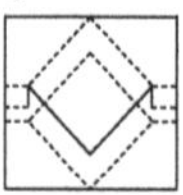

59. (*d*) The question figure is embedded in answer figure (d).

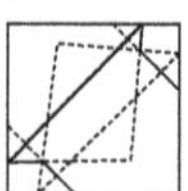

60. (*b*) The question figure is embedded in answer figure (b).

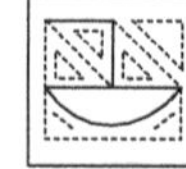

61. (*d*) The question figure is embedded in answer figure (d).

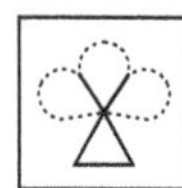

62. (*d*) The question figure is embedded in answer figure (d).

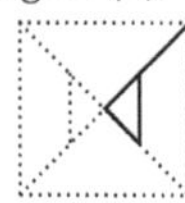

63. (*b*) The question figure is embedded in answer figure (b).

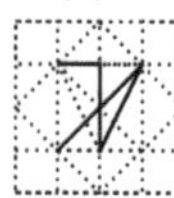

64. (*d*) The question figure is embedded in answer figure (d).

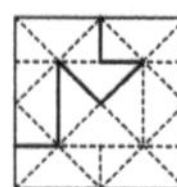

65. (*d*) The question figure is embedded in answer figure (d).

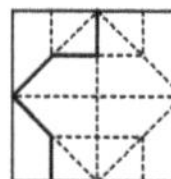

66. (*a*) The question figure is embedded in answer figure (a).

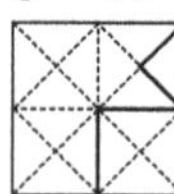

67. (*b*) The question figure is embedded in answer figure (b).

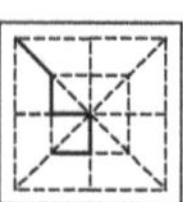

68. (*d*) The question figure is embedded in answer figure (d).

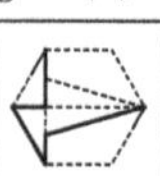

69. (*d*) The question figure is embedded in answer figure (d).

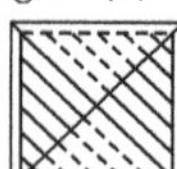

70. (*b*) The question figure is embedded in answer figure (b).

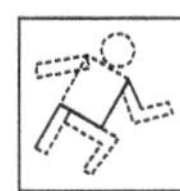

71. (*d*) The question figure is embedded in answer figure (d).

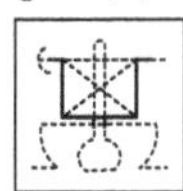

72. (*d*) The question figure is embedded in answer figure (d).

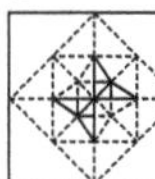

73. (*d*) The question figure is embedded in answer figure (d).

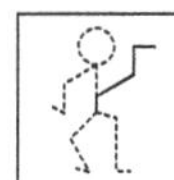

74. (*c*) The question figure is embedded in answer figure (c).

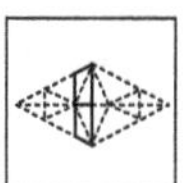

75. (*c*) The question figure, is embedded in answer figure (c).

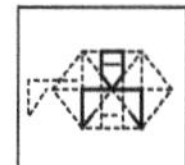

TYPE 02

Answer Figure Embedded in Question Figure

In these questions, a question figure and four answer figures (a), (b), (c) and (d) are given. Out of these answer figures, one figure is embedded in the question figure and a candidate is required to identify that particular answer figure.

The following examples will give you a better idea about such type of questions

DIRECTIONS ~ (Example Nos. 7-11) *In the following questions, a question figure is given with four answer figures* (a), (b), (c) *and* (d). *Find out that answer figure which is embedded in the question figure.*

***Ex* 07** **Question Figure** **Answer Figures**

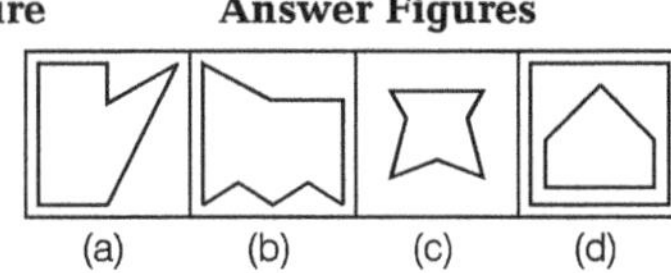

(a) (b) (c) (d)

« SSC MTS 2013

Solution **(a)** Clearly, answer figure (a) is embedded in question figure and shown in the below figure with dark lines.

***Ex* 08** **Question Figure** **Answer Figures**

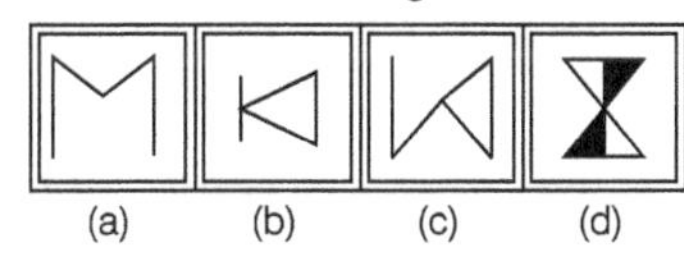

(a) (b) (c) (d)

Solution (a) Clearly, answer figure (a) is embedded in question figure and shown in the below figure with dark lines.

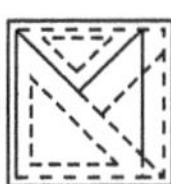

***Ex* 09**

Question Figure **Answer Figures**

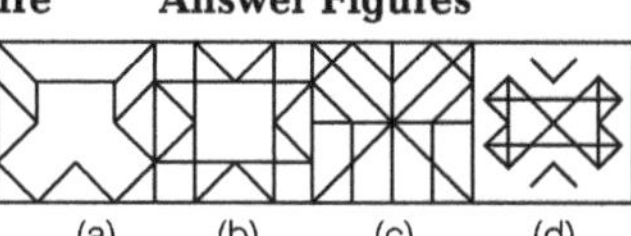

(a) (b) (c) (d)

Solution (b) Clearly, answer figure (b) is embedded in question figure and shown in the below figure with dark lines.

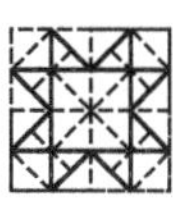

***Ex* 10**

Question Figure **Answer Figures**

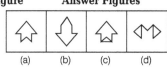

(a) (b) (c) (d)

« SSC Constable 2008

Solution **(a)** Clearly, answer figure (a) is embedded in question figure and shown in the below figure with dark lines.

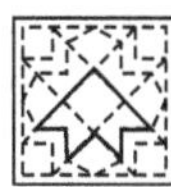

***Ex* 11**

Question Figure **Answer Figures**

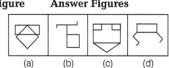

(a) (b) (c) (d)

Solution (d) Clearly, the answer figure (d) is embedded in question figure and shown in the below figure with dark lines.

Practice / CORNER 6.2

DIRECTIONS ~ (Q. Nos. 1-34) *In each of the following question, choose the answer figure which is embedded in the question figure.*

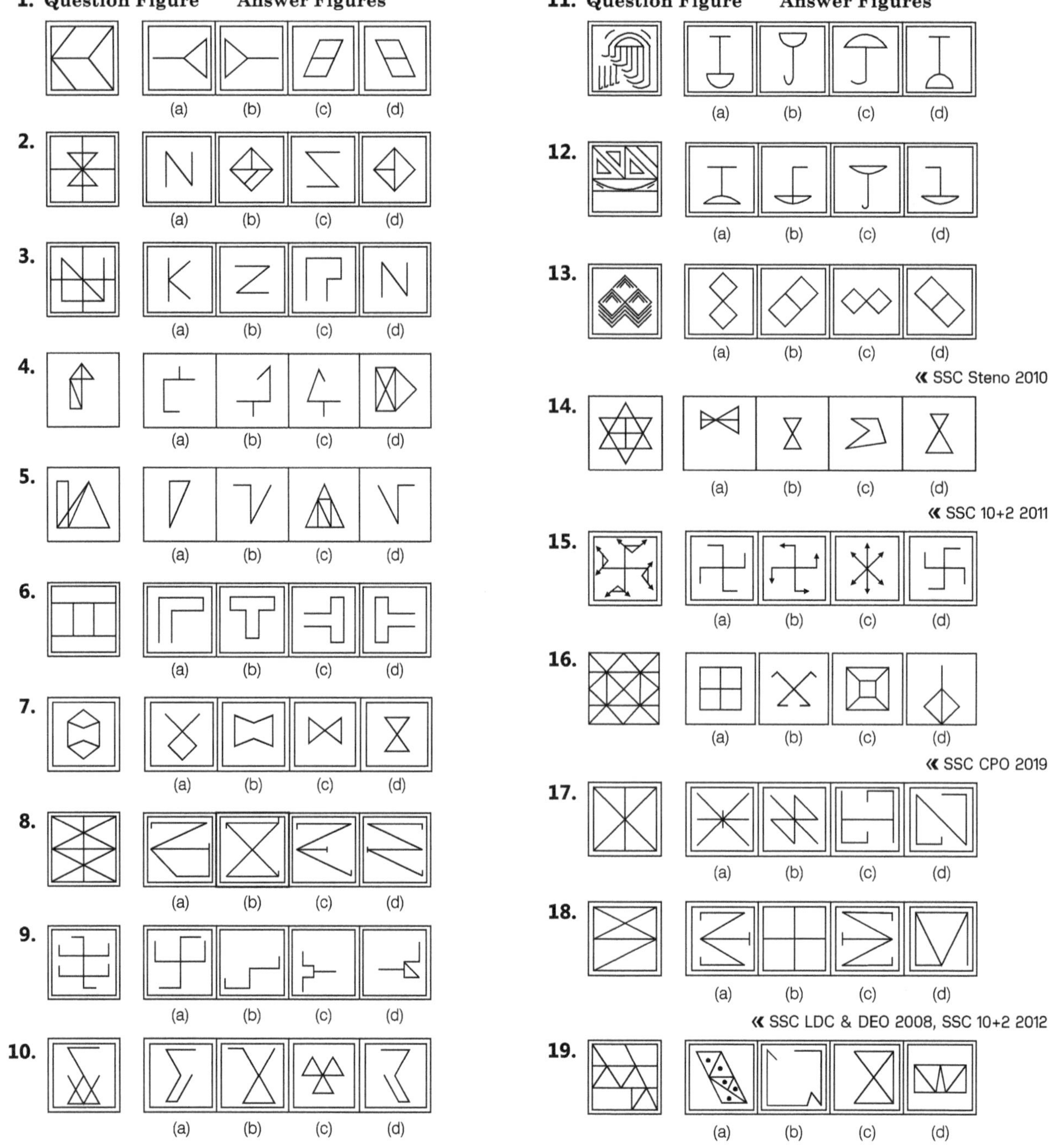

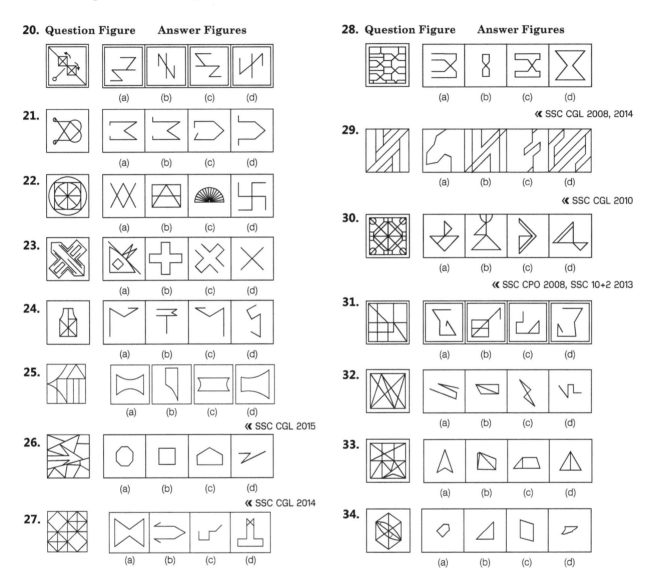

20. Question Figure Answer Figures

(a) (b) (c) (d)

21.

(a) (b) (c) (d)

22.

(a) (b) (c) (d)

23.

(a) (b) (c) (d)

24.

(a) (b) (c) (d)

25.

(a) (b) (c) (d)

« SSC CGL 2015

26.

(a) (b) (c) (d)

« SSC CGL 2014

27.

(a) (b) (c) (d)

« SSC CPO 2019

28. Question Figure Answer Figures

(a) (b) (c) (d)

« SSC CGL 2008, 2014

29.

(a) (b) (c) (d)

« SSC CGL 2010

30.

(a) (b) (c) (d)

« SSC CPO 2008, SSC 10+2 2013

31.

(a) (b) (c) (d)

32.

(a) (b) (c) (d)

33.

(a) (b) (c) (d)

34.

(a) (b) (c) (d)

« SSC MTS 2013

Answers WITH EXPLANATIONS

1. (*a*) The answer figure (a) is embedded in the question figure.

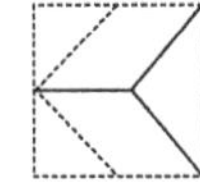

2. (*c*) The answer figure (c) is embedded in question figure.

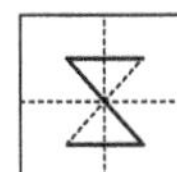

3. (*d*) The answer figure (d) is embedded in question figure.

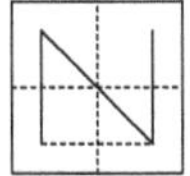

4. (*a*) The answer figure (a) is embedded in question figure.

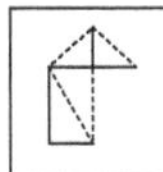

5. (*b*) The answer figure (b) is embedded in question figure.

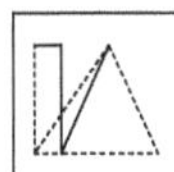

6. (*b*) The answer figure (b) is embedded in question figure.

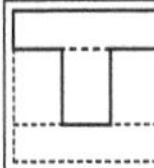

7. (*b*) The answer figure (b) is embedded in the question figure.

8. (*d*) The answer figure (d) is embedded in the question figure.

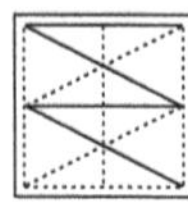

9. (*b*) The answer figure (b) is embedded in the question figure.

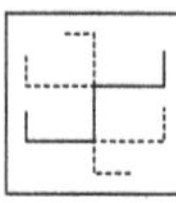

10. (*a*) The answer figure (a) is embedded in the question figure.

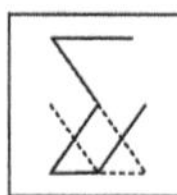

11. (*c*) The answer figure (c) is embedded in the question figure.

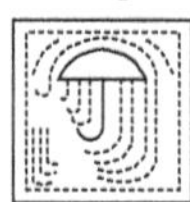

12. (*d*) The answer figure (d) is embedded in the question figure.

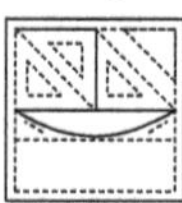

13. (*c*) The answer figure (c) is embedded in the question figure.

14. (*b*) The answer figure (b) is embedded in the question figure.

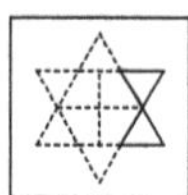

15. (*d*) The answer figure (d) is embedded in the question figure.

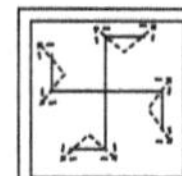

16. (*b*) The answer figure (b) is embedded in the question figure.

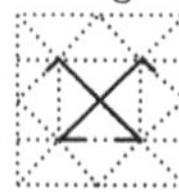

17. (*d*) The answer figure (d) is embedded in the question figure.

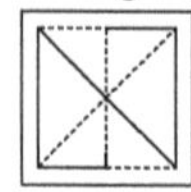

18. (*c*) The answer figure (c) is embedded in the question figure.

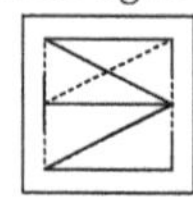

19. (*b*) The answer figure (b) is embedded in the question figure.

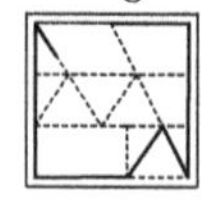

20. (*b*) The answer figure (b) is embedded in the question figure.

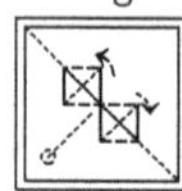

21. (*d*) The answer figure (d) is embedded in question figure.

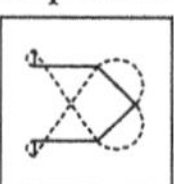

22. (*d*) The answer figure (d) is embedded in question figure.

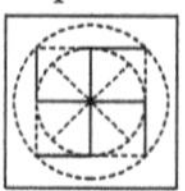

23. (*c*) The answer figure (c) is embedded in question figure.

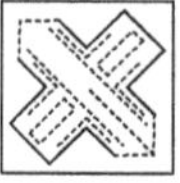

24. (*a*) The answer figure (a) is embedded in question figure.

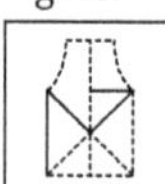

25. (*b*) The answer figure (b) is embedded in the question figure.

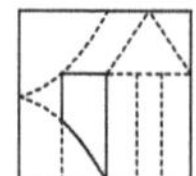

26. (*d*) The answer figure (d) is embedded in question figure.

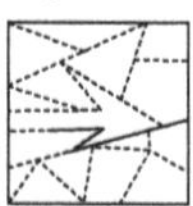

27. (*c*) The answer figure (c) is embedded in the question figure.

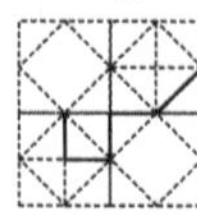

28. (*a*) The answer figure (a) is embedded in the question figure.

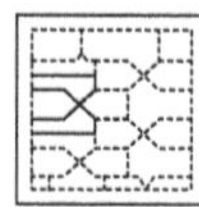

29. (*c*) The answer figure (c) is embedded in the question figure.

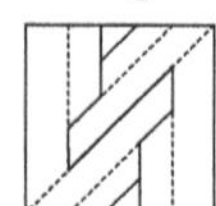

30. (*a*) The answer figure (a) is embedded in the question figure.

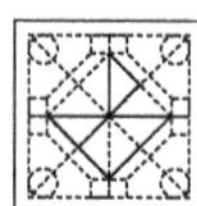

31. (*a*) The answer figure (a) is embedded in the question figure.

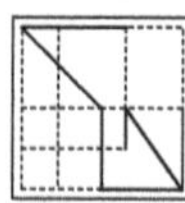

32. (*c*) The answer figure (c) is embedded in the question figure.

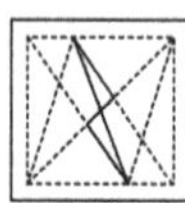

33. (*c*) The answer figure (c) is embedded in the question figure.

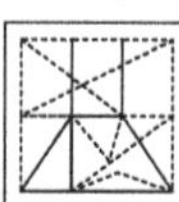

34. (*c*) The answer figure (c) is embedded in the question figure.

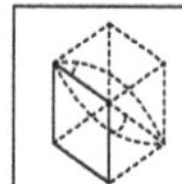

CHAPTER / 07

Counting of Figures

Counting of figures can be explained as the realisation of simple geometrical figures from a complex figure.

The figures which are asked for counting can be a straight line, triangle, square, rectangle, polygon etc.

To find the accurate answer for these questions, firstly, a candidate needs to find the required number of figures formed by individual section of the given figure, then the figure formed by combination of two figures and so on.

Different types of questions asked from this chapter are as follows

TYPE 01

Counting of Straight Lines and Triangles

In this type of questions, a candidate is required to find out the number of straight lines and triangles in the given figure.

A. Counting of Straight Lines

A **straight line** is defined by its length but it has no breadth. A line contains infinite points and hence can be extended infinitely in both directions.

Some types of straight lines are shown below

A. Horizontal line A———B B. Vertical line A | B

C. Slant line A/B A\B

Counting Method of Straight Line

Let us consider a line AB having a point C somewhere in between points A and B.

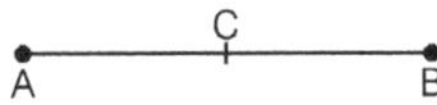

Then, on counting, it will be counted as one line i.e. AB and not as the two straight lines AC and CB.

Ex 01 How many straight lines are there in the figure given below?

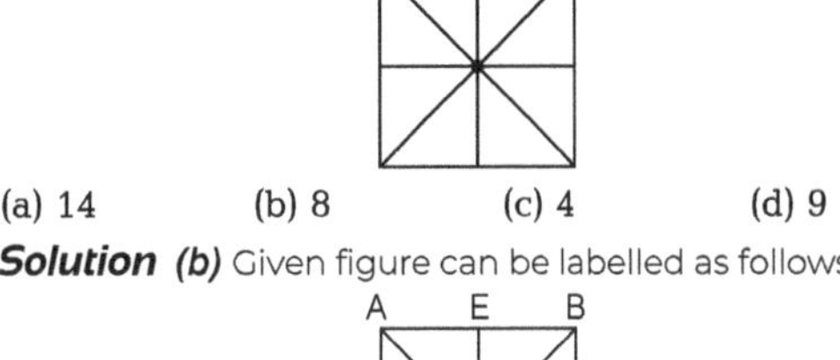

(a) 14 (b) 8 (c) 4 (d) 9

Solution **(b)** Given figure can be labelled as follows,

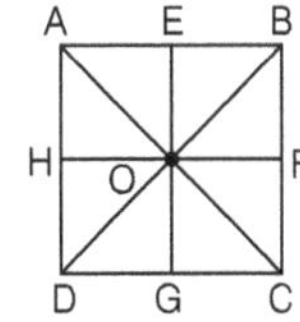

Horizontal lines = AB, HF, DC = 3

Vertical lines = AD, EG, BC = 3

Slant lines = AC, BD = 2

∴ Total number of lines = 3 + 3 + 2 = 8

Ex 02 Find the minimum number of straight lines required to make the given figure. « IB ACIO 2017

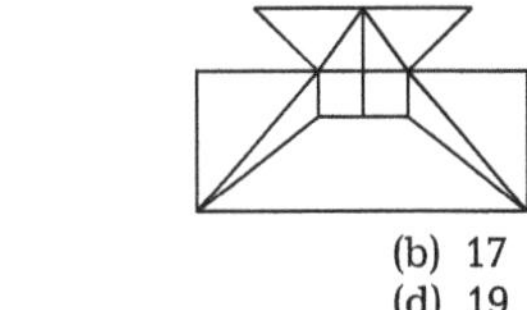

(a) 16 (b) 17
(c) 18 (d) 19

Solution **(b)** Given figure can be labelled as follows,

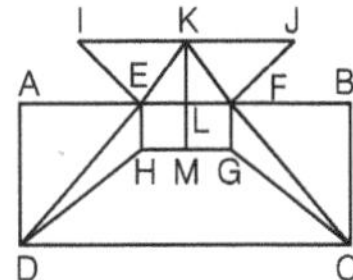

Horizontal lines = IJ, AB, HG, DC = 4

Vertical lines = AD, EH, KM, FG, BC = 5

Slant lines = DE, CF, IE, EK, JF, KF, DH, CG = 8

∴ Total number of lines = 4 + 5 + 8 = 17

B. Counting of Triangles

A **triangle** is a closed figure bounded by three sides. Here, ABC is a triangle.

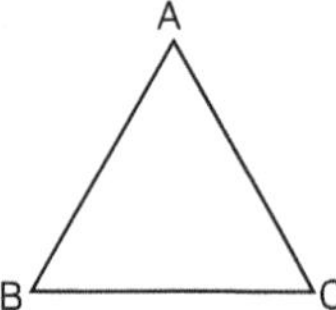

Counting Method of Triangle

- Single triangles are counted first.
- At the second step, those triangles are counted which are formed with the two triangles and further counting goes on in the same way *i.e.,* triangles formed with three, four, ... triangles are counted one after another.
- Largest triangle is counted at the final step.

Note *Counting can also be done in reverse order i.e., counting in order of largest to smallest.*

***Ex* 03** How many triangles are there in the given figure?

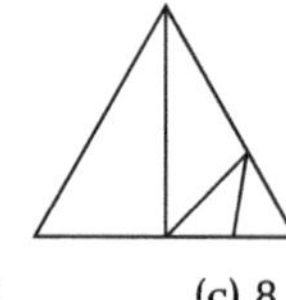

« SSC MTS 2017

(a) 5 (b) 7 (c) 8 (d) 9

Solution (b) Given figure can be labelled as follows,

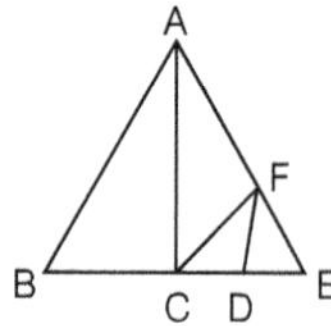

Single triangles = ΔABC, ΔAFC, ΔCFD, ΔDFE = 4

Triangles formed with two triangles

= ΔCFE (ΔCFD + ΔDFE) = 1

Triangles formed with three triangles

= ΔACE (ΔACF + ΔCFD + ΔDFE) = 1

Triangles formed with four triangles

= ΔABE(ΔABC + ΔAFC + ΔCFD + ΔDFE) = 1

∴ Total number of triangles = 4 + 1 + 1 + 1 = 7

***Ex* 04** Select the option that represents the number of triangles in the given figure. « RRB ALP 2018

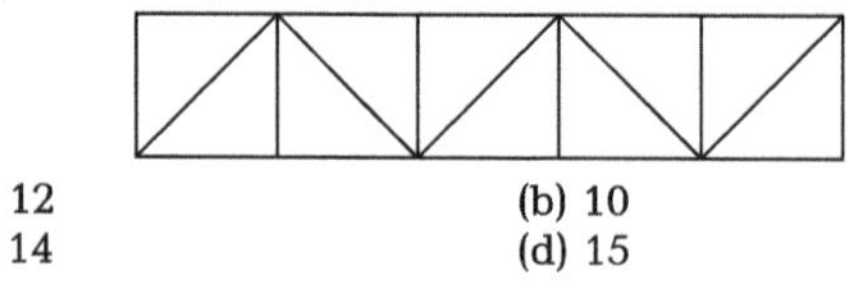

(a) 12 (b) 10
(c) 14 (d) 15

Solution (c) Given figure can be labelled as follows,

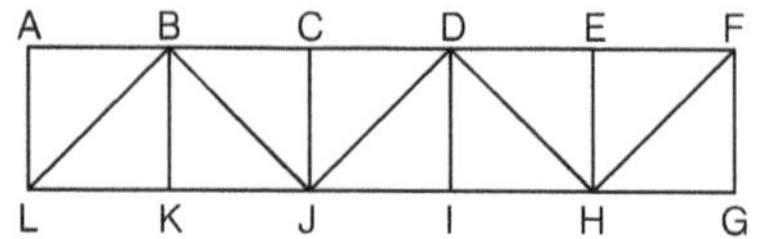

Single triangles = ΔABL, ΔBCJ, ΔCDJ, ΔDEH, ΔEFH, ΔGHF, ΔHID, ΔIJD, ΔJKB, ΔKLB = 10

Triangles formed with two triangles

= ΔLJB(ΔLBK + ΔBKJ), ΔJHD(ΔJDI + ΔDIH),
ΔFDH(ΔFEH + ΔDEH), ΔDBJ(ΔDCJ + ΔCBJ) = 4

∴ Total number of triangles = 10 + 4 = 14

***Ex* 05** How many triangles are there in the following figure?

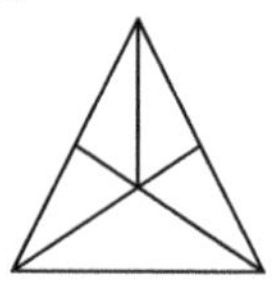

(a) 11 (b) 16
(c) 14 (d) 12

Solution (d) Given triangle is labelled as follows,

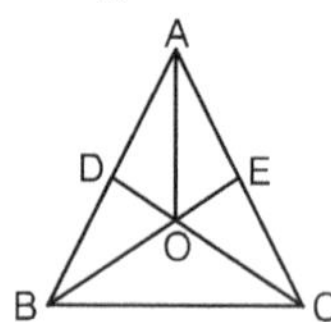

Single triangles = ΔAOD, ΔAOE, ΔCOE, ΔBOD, ΔBOC = 5

Triangles formed with two triangles

= ΔAOC (ΔAOE + ΔCOE), ΔAOB (ΔAOD + ΔBOD),
ΔBCD (ΔBOD + ΔBOC), ΔBCE (ΔBOC + ΔCOE) = 4

Triangles formed with three triangles

= ΔACD (ΔAOD + ΔAOE + ΔCOE),
ΔABE (ΔBOD + ΔAOD + ΔAOE) = 2

Largest triangle = ΔABC = 1

∴ Total number of triangles = 5 + 4 + 2 + 1 = 12

Practice /CORNER 7.1

1. How many triangles are there in the given figure? « SSC CGL 2020

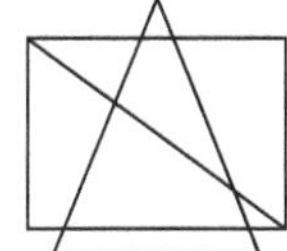

(a) 6 (b) 12 (c) 10 (d) 8

2. How many triangles are there in the following figure? « SSC 10 + 2 2020

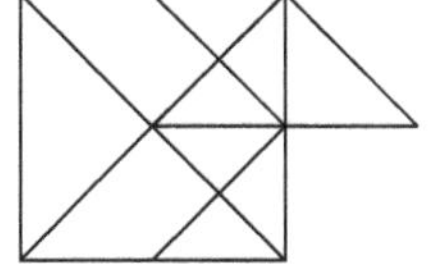

(a) 22 (b) 18 (c) 21 (d) 20

3. What is the minimum number of lines required to make the given image? « RRB ALP 2019

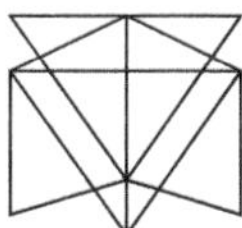

(a) 13 (b) 9 (c) 12 (d) 11

4. How many straight lines are there in the following figure? « SSC CPO 2009

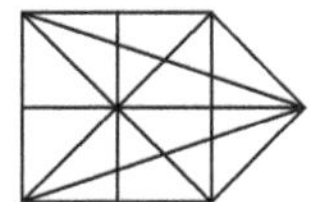

(a) 10 (b) 12 (c) 13 (d) 17

5. How many minimum number of straight lines are required to draw the following figure? « RRB Group D 2018

(a) 15 (b) 17 (c) 10 (d) 12

6. How many straight lines are there in the figure given below?

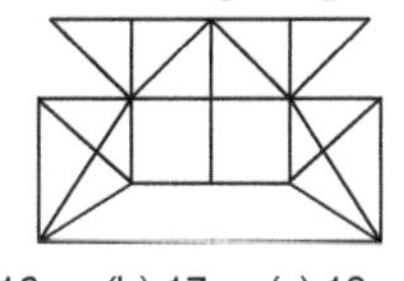

(a) 16 (b) 17 (c) 18 (d) 19

7. How many minimum number of straight lines are required to draw the following figure?

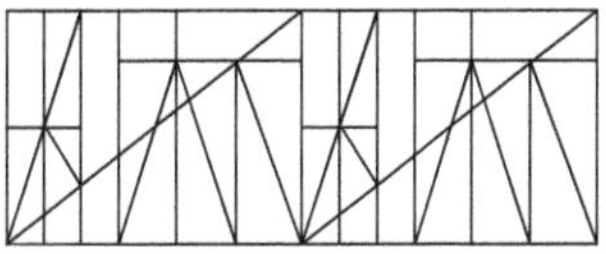

« RRB Group D 2018

(a) 36 (b) 55 (c) 31 (d) 28

8. Count the number of triangles in the following figure.

(a) 6 (b) 7 (c) 8 (d) 9

9. How many triangles are there in the figure given below?

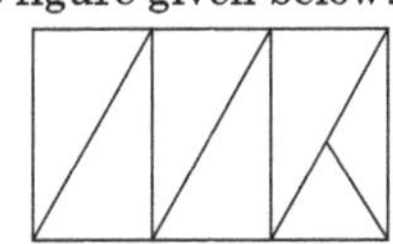

« UPSSSC Tubewell Operator 2018

(a) 8 (b) 10 (c) 12 (d) 7

10. How many triangles are there in the following figure?

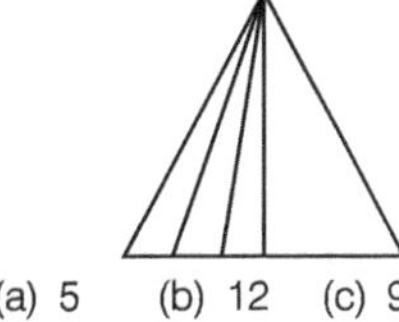

(a) 5 (b) 12 (c) 9 (d) 10

11. How many triangles are there in the figure given below? « SSC CGL 2013

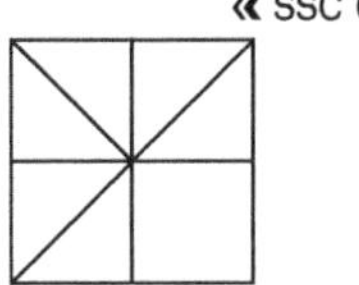

(a) 8 (b) 10 (c) 12 (d) 11

12. How many triangles are there in the figure given below? « SSC CPO 2017

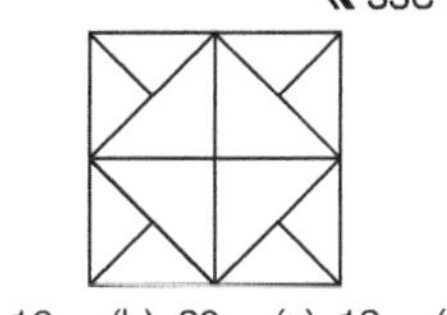

(a) 16 (b) 20 (c) 12 (d) 22

13. How many triangles are there in the following figure? « UK PSC 2016

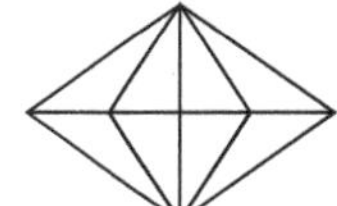

(a) 10 (b) 24 (c) 22 (d) 20

14. How many triangles are there in the following figures? « SSC CGL 2019

(a) 14 (b) 18 (c) 20 (d) 16

15. How many triangles are there in the figure given below? « RRB ALP 2018 ; SSC Steno 2008

(a) 5 (b) 6 (c) 8 (d) 10

16. How many triangles are there in the figure given below? « UPSSSC Lower Subordinate II 2018

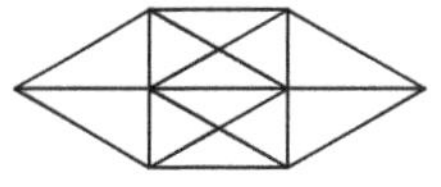

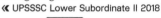

(a) 20 (b) 24 (c) 28 (d) 32

17. How many triangles are there in the following figure? « RRB Group D 2018

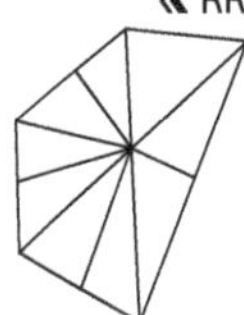

(a) 12 (b) 15 (c) 14 (d) 8

18. How many triangles are present in the given figure? « SSC CGL 2019

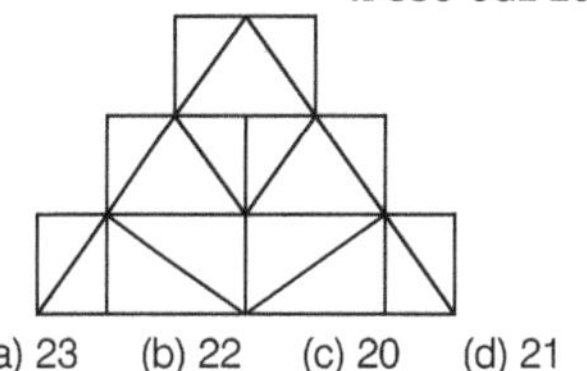

(a) 23 (b) 22 (c) 20 (d) 21

19. How many triangles are there in the given figure? « SSC CPO 2019

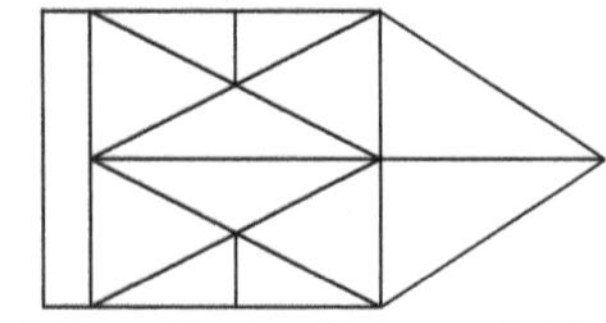

(a) 17 (b) 26 (c) 27 (d) 28

20. How many triangles are there in the following figure? « RRB NTPC 2016

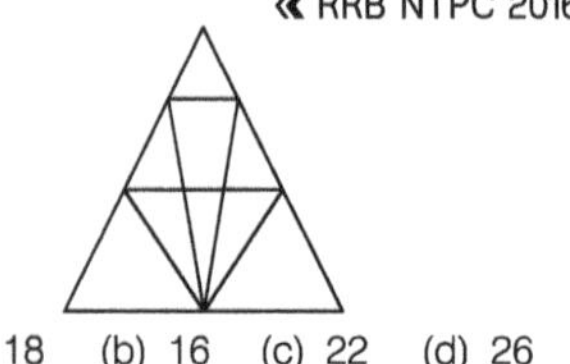

(a) 18 (b) 16 (c) 22 (d) 26

21. Find out the number of triangles in the given pattern. « SSC MTS 2013, Chhattisgarh Revenue Officer 2017

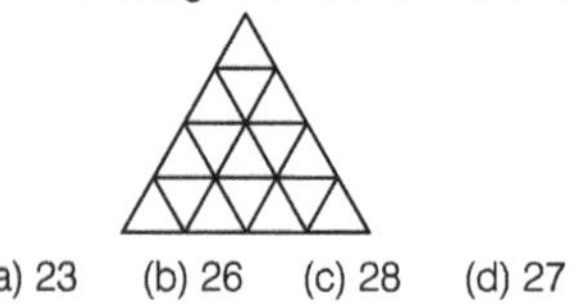

(a) 23 (b) 26 (c) 28 (d) 27

22. Find the number of triangles in the figure given below. « IB 2017

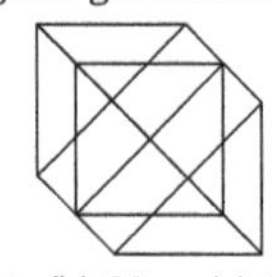

(a) 18 (b) 20 (c) 24 (d) 27

23. Find the number of triangles in the following figure. « SSC CGL 2017

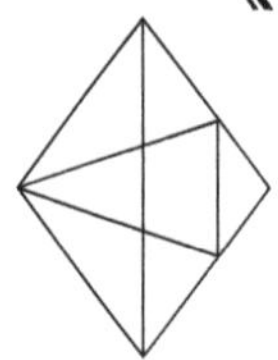

(a) 8 (b) 9
(c) 11 (d) 12

24. How many triangles are there in the following figure?

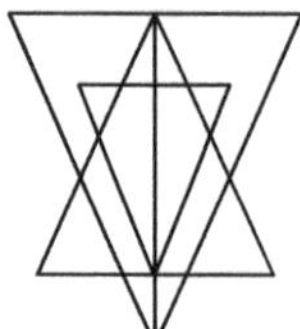

(a) 27 (b) 23
(c) 21 (d) 25

25. How many triangles are there in the figure given below?

(a) 22
(b) 24
(c) 26
(d) 28

26. How many triangles are there in the following figure? « SSC CPO 2019

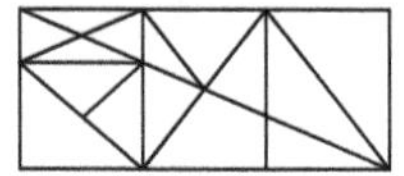

(a) 35 (b) 36 (c) 34 (d) 30

27. How many triangles are there in the following figure?

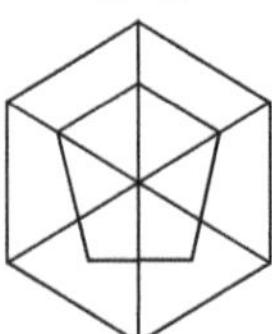

(a) 10 (b) 15 (c) 12 (d) 9

28. How many triangles are there in the following figure?

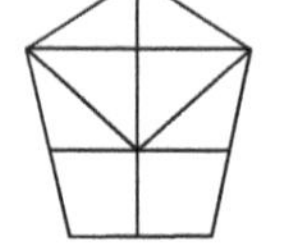

(a) 9 (b) 10 (c) 11 (d) 12

29. How many triangles are there in the figure shown below?

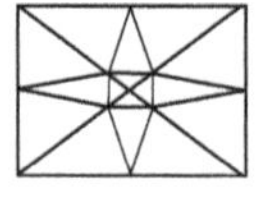

(a) 22 (b) 20
(c) 28 (d) 16

Answers WITH EXPLANATIONS

1. (*c*) Given figure can be labelled as follows,

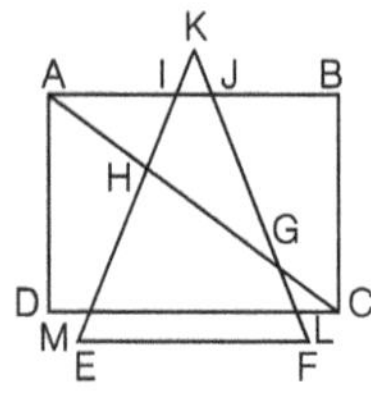

There are 10 triangles in the above figure

ΔADC, ΔABC, ΔIJK, ΔKEF, ΔAIH, ΔGLC, ΔMHC, ΔHKG, ΔAJG, ΔMKL.

2. (*d*) Given figure can be labelled as follows,

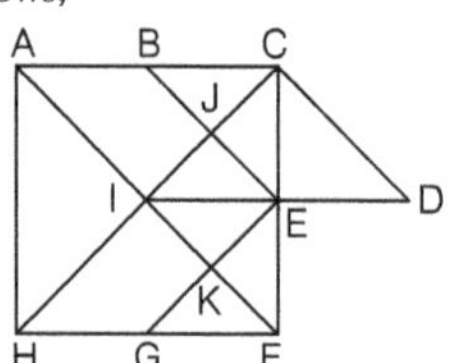

Above figure has following 20 triangles.

ΔAIH, ΔACI, ΔCIF, ΔFIH, ΔACF, ΔAHF, ΔACH, ΔHCF, ΔBCJ, ΔCJE, ΔEJI, ΔIEK, ΔEKF, ΔFKG, ΔBCE, ΔCEI, ΔIEF, ΔEFG, ΔCDE, ΔCID

3. (*a*) Given figure can be labelled as follows,

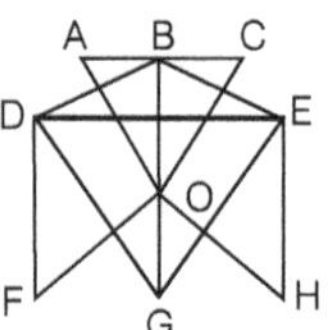

Horizontal lines = AC, DE = 2

Vertical lines = DF, BG, EH = 3

Slant lines
= AO, CO, OH, OF, DG, EG, BD, BE = 8

∴ Total number of lines = 2 + 3 + 8 = 13

4. (*b*) Given figure can be labelled as follows,

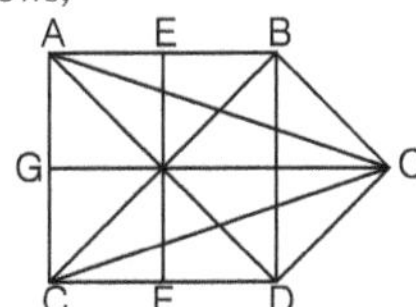

Horizontal lines = AB, GO, CD = 3
Vertical lines = AC, EF, BD = 3
Slant lines = BO, DO, AO, CO, AD, BC = 6
∴ Total number of lines = 3 + 3 + 6 = 12

5. (*a*) Given figure can be labelled as follows,

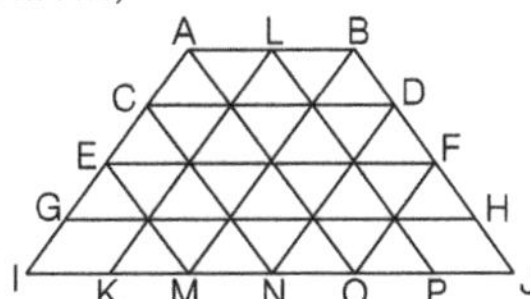

Horizontal lines = AB, CD, EF, GH, IJ = 5
Slant lines = AI, LK, BM, DN, FO, BJ, LP, AO, CN, EM = 10
∴ Total number of lines = 5 + 10 = 15

6. (*d*) Given figure can be labelled as follows,

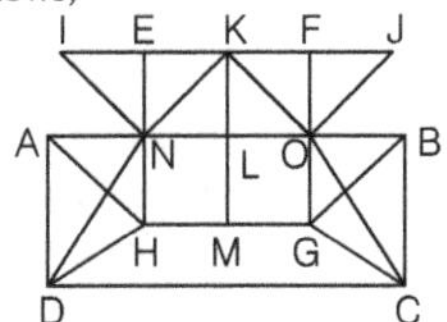

Horizontal lines = IJ, AB, DC, HG = 4
Vertical lines = AD, EH, KM, FG, BC = 5
Slant lines = IN, NK, KO, OJ, DH, CG, CO, DN, AH, BG = 10
∴ Total number of lines = 4 + 5 + 10 = 19

7. (*c*) Given figure can be labelled as follows,

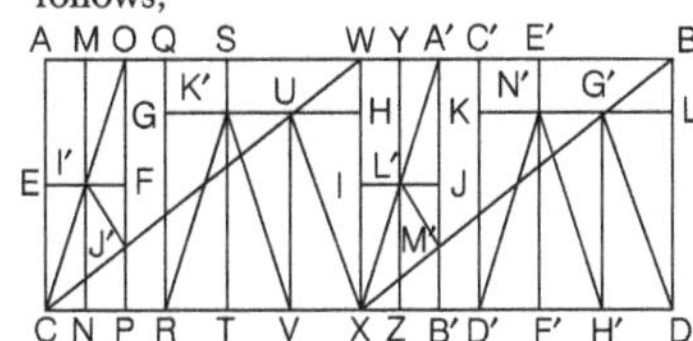

Horizontal lines = AB, CD, EF, GH, IJ, KL = 6
Vertical lines = AC, MN, OP, QR, ST, UV, WX, YZ, A′B′, C′D′, E′F′, G′H′, BD = 13
Slant lines = CO, I′J′, CW, RK′, K′V, UX, XA′, XB, L′M′, D′N′, N′H′, G′D = 12
∴ Total number of lines = 6 + 13 + 12 = 31

8. (*c*) Given figure can be labelled as follows,

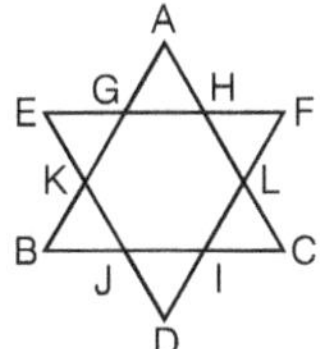

Single (or smallest) triangles = ΔGAH, ΔHFL, ΔLCI, ΔIDJ, ΔJBK, ΔKEG = 6
Largest triangles = ΔABC, ΔEFD = 2
∴ Total number of triangles = 6 + 2 = 8

9. (*a*) Given figure can be labelled as follows,

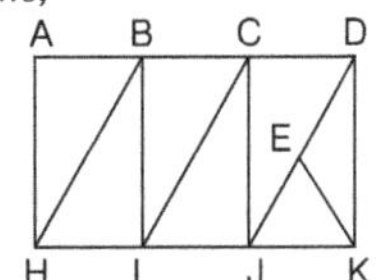

Single triangles = ΔHAB, ΔBHI, ΔIBC, ΔCIJ, ΔJCD, ΔJEK, ΔKED = 7
Triangles formed with two triangles = ΔDKJ
∴ Total triangles = 7 + 1 = 8

10. (*d*) Given figure can be labelled as follows,

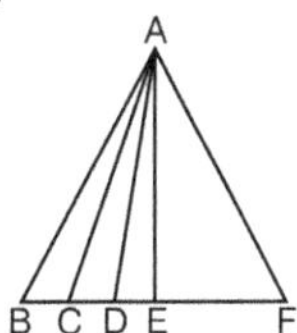

Single triangles = ΔABC, ΔACD, ΔADE, ΔAEF = 4
Triangles formed with two triangles = ΔABD, ΔACE, ΔADF = 3
Triangles formed with three triangles = ΔABE, ΔACF = 2
Triangles formed with more than three triangles = ΔABF = 1
∴ Total number of triangles = 4 + 3 + 2 + 1 = 10

11. (*b*) Given figure can be labelled as follows,

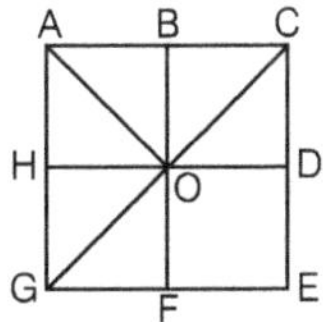

Single triangles = ΔBOC, ΔCOD, ΔFOG, ΔGOH, ΔHOA, ΔAOB = 6
Triangles formed with two small triangles = ΔAOG, ΔAOC = 2
Triangles formed with more than two geometrical figures = ΔACG, ΔEGC = 2
∴ Total number of triangles = 6 + 2 + 2 = 10

12. (*b*) Given figure can be labelled as follows,

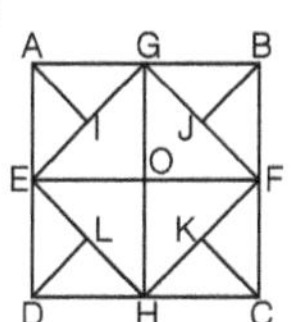

Single triangles = ΔAIE, ΔAIG, ΔGJB, ΔBJF, ΔELD, ΔDLH, ΔHKC, ΔKCF, ΔEGO, ΔGOF, ΔEOH, ΔHOF = 12
Triangles formed with two small triangles = ΔAEG, ΔGBF, ΔEDH, ΔHCF, ΔEGF, ΔEHF, ΔGEH, ΔGFH = 8
∴ Total number of triangles = 12 + 8 = 20

13. (*b*) Given figure can be labelled as follows,

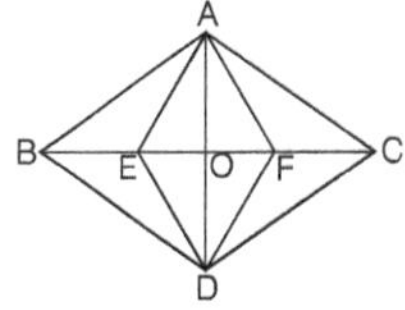

Single triangles = ΔABE, ΔAEO, ΔAOF, ΔAFC, ΔDEB, ΔDOE, ΔDFO, ΔDCF = 8
Triangles formed with two triangles = ΔABO, ΔAEF, ΔAOC, ΔBOD, ΔDEF, ΔDOC, ΔAED, ΔADF = 8
Triangles formed with three triangles = ΔABF, ΔAEC, ΔBDF, ΔEDC = 4
Triangles formed with more than three triangles = ΔABC, ΔBCD, ΔABD, ΔACD = 4
∴ Total number of triangles = 8 + 8 + 4 + 4 = 24

14. (*b*) Given figure can be labelled as follows,

Single triangles = ΔAIJ, ΔAJK, ΔEGI, ΔDGL, ΔLMB, ΔBMN, ΔNHC, ΔKFH = 8
Triangles formed with two triangles = ΔAIK, ΔLBN, ΔEJB, ΔAHB, ΔADM, ΔAMC, ΔFJB, ΔAGB = 8

Triangles formed with four or more triangles = ΔADC, ΔBEF = 2

∴ Total number of triangles

= 8 + 8 + 2 = 18

15. (*d*) Given figure can be labelled as follows,

Single triangles = ΔAJF, ΔBFG, ΔCGH, ΔDHI, ΔEIJ = 5

Triangles formed with two triangles = ΔAIC, ΔEHB, ΔEFC, ΔDJB, ΔDAG = 5

∴ Total number of triangles = 5 + 5 = 10

16. (*c*) Given figure can be labelled as follows,

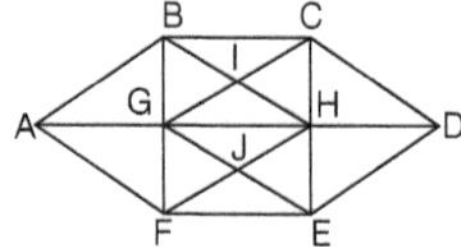

Single triangles = ΔAGB, ΔAGF, ΔBIC, ΔBIG, ΔIGH, ΔIHC, ΔCHD, ΔHDE, ΔEJH, ΔJHG, ΔJEF, ΔJFG = 12

Triangles formed with two triangles = ΔBCG, ΔBCH, ΔCHG, ΔHGB, ΔGHF, ΔGHE, ΔHEF, ΔEFG, ΔABF, ΔCDE = 10

Triangles formed with more than two triangles = ΔABH, ΔAFH, ΔCDG, ΔDEG, ΔBHF, ΔCGE = 6

∴ Total number of triangles = 12 + 10 + 6 = 28

17. (*b*) Given figure can be labelled as follows,

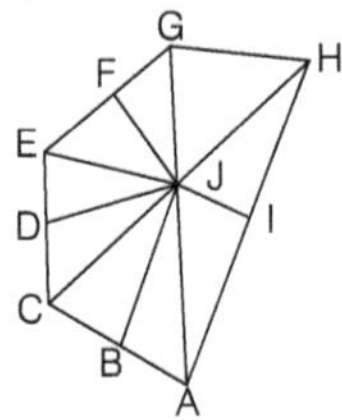

Single triangles = ΔAIJ, ΔAJB, ΔBJC, ΔCJD, ΔDJE, ΔEJF, ΔFJG, ΔGJH, ΔHJI = 9

Triangles formed with two triangles = ΔAJH, ΔAJC, ΔCJE, ΔEJG = 4

Triangles formed with three triangles = ΔAGH, ΔACH = 2

∴ Total number of triangles = 9 + 4 + 2 = 15

18. (*a*) Given figure can be labelled as follows

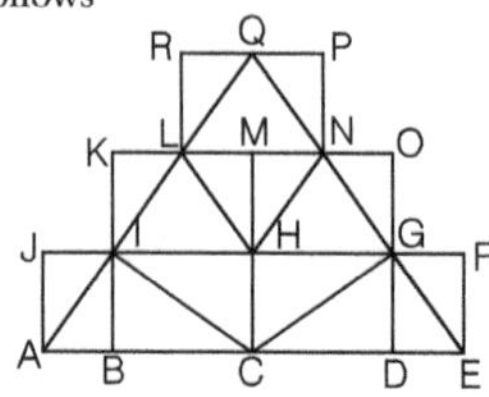

Single triangles = ΔJAI, ΔABI, ΔBIC, ΔIHC, ΔHCG, ΔGCD, ΔGDE, ΔGFE, ΔKIL, ΔILH, ΔLHM, ΔMHN, ΔHNG, ΔNOG, ΔRQL, ΔQLN, ΔQPN = 17

Triangles formed with two small triangles = ΔLNH, ΔICG, ΔAIC ΔCGH = 4

Triangles formed with more than two triangles = ΔIQG and ΔAQE = 2

∴ Total number of triangles = 17 + 4 + 2 = 23

19. (*c*) Given figure can be labelled as follows

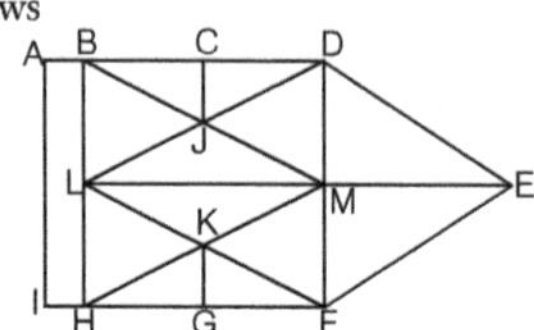

Single triangles = ΔBCJ, ΔDCJ, ΔBJL, ΔLJM, ΔDJM, ΔLMK, ΔMFK, ΔFGK, ΔGHK, ΔHKL, ΔDEM, ΔMEF = 12

Triangles formed with two small triangles = ΔBDJ, ΔBLM, ΔLDM, ΔLMF, ΔLMH, ΔHKF, ΔDEF = 7

Triangles formed with more than two triangles = ΔBDM, ΔBDL, ΔLHF, ΔMHF, ΔDLF, ΔBMH, ΔDLE, ΔFLE = 8

∴ Total number of triangles = 12 + 7 + 8 = 27

20. (*a*) Given figure can be labelled as follows,

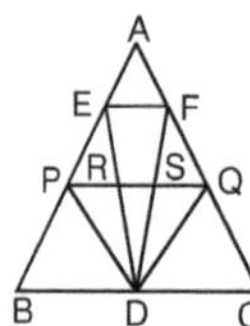

Single triangles = ΔAEF, ΔEPR, ΔFSQ, ΔPRD, ΔRSD, ΔSQD, ΔPBD, ΔQDC, ΔEFD = 9

Triangles formed with two triangles = ΔPSD, ΔRQD, ΔFDQ, ΔEDP = 4

Triangles formed with three or four triangles = ΔAPQ, ΔFDC, ΔBDE, ΔPQD = 4

Largest triangle = ΔABC = 1

∴ Total number of triangles = 9 + 4 + 4 + 1 = 18

21. (*d*) Given figure can be labelled as follows,

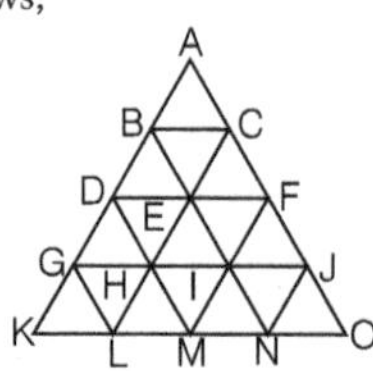

Single triangles = ΔABC, ΔBDE, ΔBCE, ΔCEF, ΔDGH, ΔDHE, ΔHEI, ΔEIF, ΔFIJ, ΔGKL, ΔGLH, ΔLHM, ΔHMI, ΔMIN, ΔINJ, ΔNJO = 16

Triangles formed with four triangles = ΔADF, ΔBGI, ΔCHJ, ΔDKM, ΔLEN, ΔMFO, ΔDFM = 7

Triangles formed with 9 triangles = ΔAGJ, ΔBKN, ΔCLO = 3

Largest triangle = ΔAKO

So, total number of triangles

= 16 + 7 + 3 + 1 = 27

22. (*c*) Given figure can be labelled as follows,

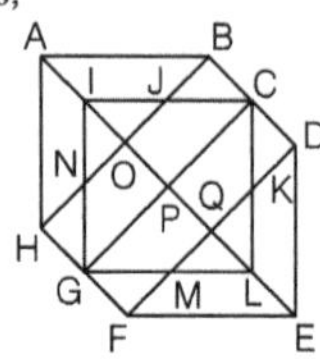

Single triangles = ΔBCJ, ΔCDK, ΔKLQ, ΔLMQ, ΔFGM, ΔGHN, ΔNOI, ΔIJO, ΔAOB, ΔDEQ, ΔFEQ, ΔAOH, ΔGIP, ΔCIP, ΔCLP, ΔGLP = 16

Triangles formed with two triangles ΔKLM, ΔNIJ = 2

Triangles formed with four or more triangles = ΔABH, ΔDEF, ΔICG, ΔCLG, ΔLGI, ΔICL = 6

∴ Total number of triangles

= 16 + 2 + 6 = 24

23. (*d*) Given figure can be labelled as follows,

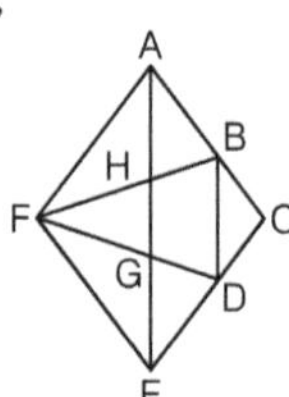

Single triangles

= ΔAFH, ΔAHB, ΔFGE, ΔDGE, ΔBCD, ΔBDF, ΔFHG = 7

Triangles formed with two or more triangles = ΔAFG, ΔAEC, ΔAFE, ΔDEF, ΔAFB = 5

∴ Total number of triangles

= 7 + 5 = 12

24. (*d*) Given figure can be labelled as follows,

Single triangles = ΔNGQ, ΔOHR, ΔPDO, ΔNDP, Δ JIC, ΔICK, ΔEMJ, ΔKLF, ΔRIF, ΔEQI, ΔPHI, ΔPGI = 12

Triangles formed with two triangles = ΔADM, ΔDBL, ΔDNO, ΔDQI, ΔDRI, ΔCJK, ΔGHI, ΔDEI, ΔDIF = 9

Triangles formed with three or more triangles = ΔADC, ΔDBC = 2

Largest triangles = ΔABC, ΔEDF = 2

∴ Total number of triangles

= 12 + 9 + 2 + 2 = 25

25. (*c*) Given figure can be labelled as follows,

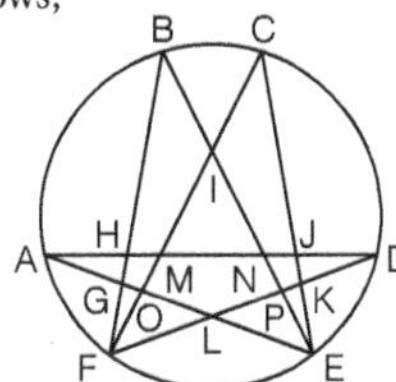

Single triangles = ΔAGH, ΔGFO, ΔLFO, ΔDJK, ΔEKP, ΔPEL, ΔIMN = 7

Triangles formed with two triangles = ΔGFL, ΔKEL, ΔAMO, ΔNDP, ΔBHN, ΔCMJ, ΔNEJ, ΔHFM, ΔIOE, ΔIFP, ΔBIF, ΔCEI, ΔANE, ΔFMD = 14

Triangles formed with more than two triangles = ΔFCK, ΔBGE, ΔADL, ΔBPF, ΔCOE = 5

∴ Total number of triangles

= 7 + 14 + 5 = 26

26. (*c*) Given figure can be labelled as follows,

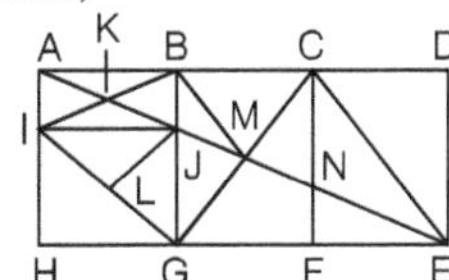

Single triangles = ΔAKB, ΔBKJ, ΔJKI, ΔIKA, ΔBJM, ΔJMG, ΔCMN, ΔCNE, ΔFNE, ΔCED, ΔBMC, ΔJLG, ΔJLI, ΔIHG = 14

Triangles formed with two triangles = ΔAIJ, ΔABJ, ΔAIB, ΔIJB, ΔIJG, ΔBMG, ΔCME, ΔGME, ΔCFG, ΔCFE = 10

Triangles formed with three triangles = ΔGJE, ΔBGC = 2

Triangles formed with four and more than four triangles = ΔABM, ΔAMC, ΔBIG, ΔCGE, ΔANC, ΔACE = 6

Largest triangles = ΔAED, ΔAHE = 2

∴ Total number of triangles

= 14 + 10 + 2 + 6 + 2 = 34

27. (a) Given figure can be labelled as follows,

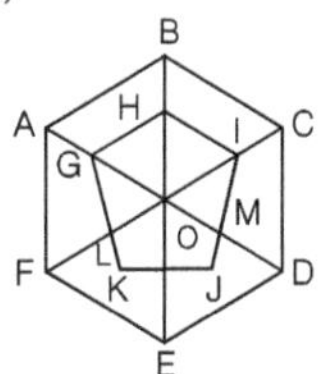

Single triangles = ΔGHO, ΔHIO, ΔIOM, ΔGOL, ΔEOD, ΔEOF = 6

Triangles formed with two triangles = ΔABO, ΔBCO, ΔCDO, ΔAOF = 4

∴ Total number of triangles

= 6 + 4 = 10

28. (*b*) Given figure can be labelled as follows,

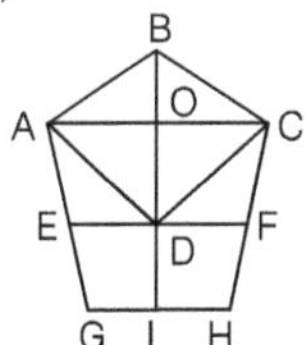

Single triangles = ΔABO, ΔOBC, ΔOCD, ΔOAD, ΔAED, ΔDFC = 6

Triangles formed with two triangles = ΔDAB, ΔABC, ΔBCD, ΔADC = 4

∴ Total number of triangles

= 6 + 4 = 10

29. (c) Given figure can be labelled as follows,

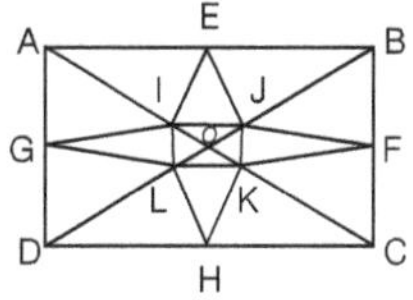

Single triangles

= ΔAIG, ΔAIE, ΔIEJ, ΔEJB, ΔJBF, ΔJFK, ΔFKC, ΔCKH, ΔKLH, ΔDLH, ΔGLD, ΔIGL, ΔIOJ, ΔJOK, ΔKOL, ΔIOL = 16

Triangles formed with two triangles = ΔLIJ, ΔIJK, ΔJKL, ΔIKL = 4

Triangles formed with three triangles = ΔAOD, ΔAOB, ΔBOC, ΔCOD = 4

Triangles formed with more than three triangles = ΔDBC, ΔCAB, ΔDBA, ΔADC = 4

∴ Total number of triangles

= 16 + 4 + 4 + 4 = 28

TYPE 02

Counting of Quadrilaterals and Polygons

In this type of questions, a candidate is required to find out the total number of quadrilaterals and polygons in the given figure. Now, let's understand the counting method of quadrilaterals and polygons, separately.

A. Quadrilaterals

A quadrilateral is a closed figure formed by joining four straight lines.

Different types of quadrilaterals are shown below

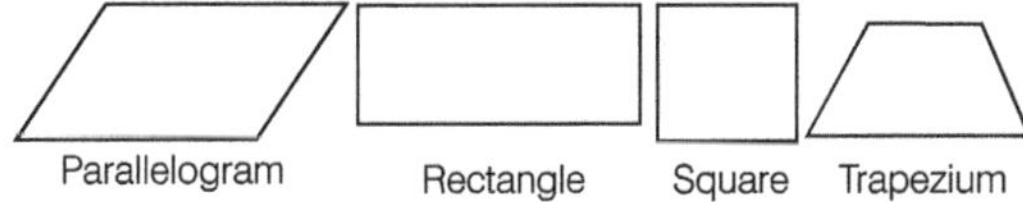

Note *The counting method of quadrilaterals is same as discussed for triangles i.e. Single quadrilaterals are counted first then quadrilaterals formed with combinations of two, three, four quadrilaterals and so on.*

Ex 06 How many parallelograms are there in the figure given below?

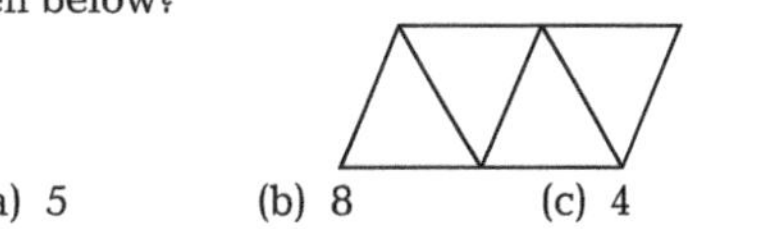

(a) 5 (b) 8 (c) 4 (d) 6

***Solution* (c)** Given figure can be labelled as follows,

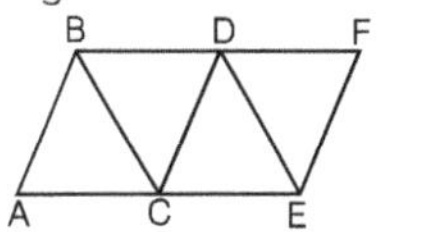

Single parallelograms = ▱CBDE, ▱ABDC, ▱CDFE = 3

Parallelograms formed with two parallelograms = ▱ABFE = 1

∴ Total number of parallelograms = 3 + 1 = 4

Ex 07 How many rectangles are there in the figure given below?

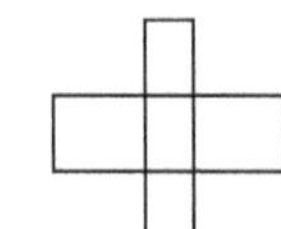

(a) 16 (b) 10 (c) 8 (d) 11

Solution (d) Given figure can be labelled as follows,

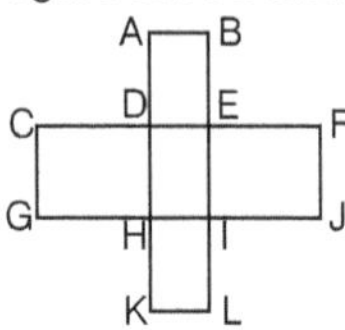

Single rectangles
= □ABED, □EFJI, □ILKH, □HGCD, □DEIH = 5

Rectangles formed with two rectangles
= □ABIH, □DELK, □CEIG, □DFJH = 4

Rectangles formed with three rectangles
= □ABLK, □CFJG = 2

∴ Total number of rectangles = 4 + 2 + 5 = 11

Chapter tip!

Formula for Counting of Rectangles and Parallelograms

Let r be the number of rows and c be the number of columns. Now, total number of rectangles or parallelograms

$$= [r + (r-1) + (r-2) + \ldots + 1] \times [c + (c-1) + (c-2) + \ldots + 1]$$

Note *This method is applicable only for those figures which are divided by rows and column into rectangles or parallelograms of equal areas.*

Examples 8 and 9 will make the above formula easy to understand

Ex 08 How many rectangles are there in the following figure?

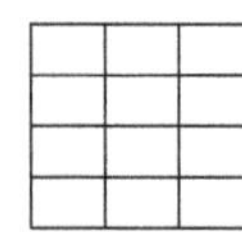

(a) 48 (b) 60 (c) 61 (d) 56

Solution (b) Total number of rectangles

$= (4 + 3 + 2 + 1) \times (3 + 2 + 1)$ [here, r = 4 and c = 3]

$= 10 \times 6 = 60$

Ex 09 How many parallelograms are there in the following figure?

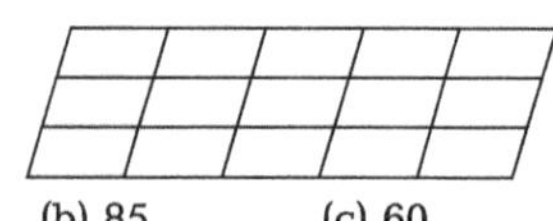

(a) 90 (b) 85 (c) 60 (d) 70

Solution (a) Total number of parallelograms

$= (3 + 2 + 1) \times (5 + 4 + 3 + 2 + 1)$ [here, r = 3 and c = 5]

$= 6 \times 15 = 90$

Ex 10 How many squares are there in the following figure?
« FCI UK Watchman 2018

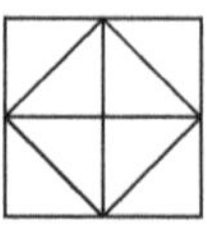

(a) 8 (b) 7 (c) 9 (d) 6

Solution (d) Given figure can be labelled as follows,

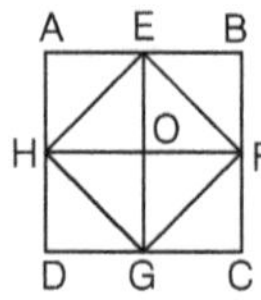

Single squares = □AHOE, □EOFB, □HDGO, □OGCF, □HGFE = 5

Square formed with five squares (the largest square)
= □ADCB = 1

∴ Total number of squares = 5 + 1 = 6

Chapter tip! **Formula for Counting of Squares**

Let r be the number of rows and c be the number of columns.

Now, total number of squares

$$= (r \times c) + \{(r-1) \times (c-1)\} + \{(r-2) \times (c-2)\} + \ldots$$

The terms are continued upto the term which is equal to zero (0).

Note *This method is applicable only for those figures which are divided by rows and columns into squares of equal area.*

Examples 11 and 12 will make the above formula easy to understand

Ex 11 How many squares are there in the following figure?
« MP Police 2017

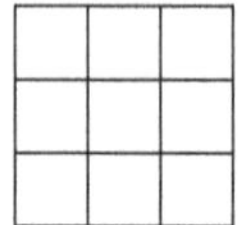

(a) 12 (b) 13 (c) 14 (d) 15

Solution (c) Total number of squares

$= (3 \times 3) + (2 \times 2) + (1 \times 1) + (0 \times 0)$ [here, r = 3 and c = 3]

$= 9 + 4 + 1 + 0 = 14$

Ex 12 How many squares are there in the following figure?

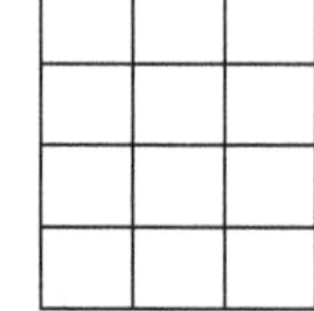

(a) 20 (b) 22 (c) 21 (d) 24

Solution (a) Total number of squares

$= (4 \times 3) + (3 \times 2) + (2 \times 1) + (1 \times 0)$ [here, r = 4 and c = 3]

$= 12 + 6 + 2 + 0 = 20$

Ex 13 How many trapeziums are there in the following figure?

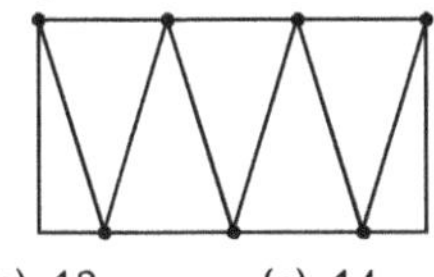

(a) 12 (b) 13 (c) 14 (d) 10

Solution (c) Given figure can be labelled as follows,

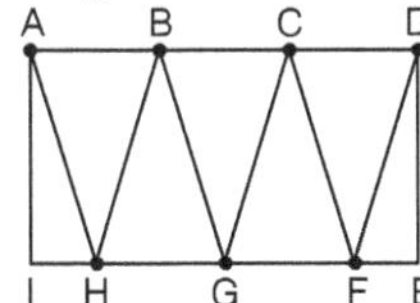

Smallest trapeziums = ABHI, CDEF = 2

Medium trapeziums = ABGI, ACGI, ACFI, ADFI, DCGE, DBGE, DBHE, DAHE, BCFH, AHGC, BGFD = 11

Largest trapeziums = AHFD = 1

∴ Total number of trapeziums = 2 + 11 + 1 = 14

B. Polygons

A polygon has more than four sides.

Polygons with five, six, seven, eight, nine and ten sides are called pentagon, hexagon, heptagon, octagon, no nagon and decagon respectively.

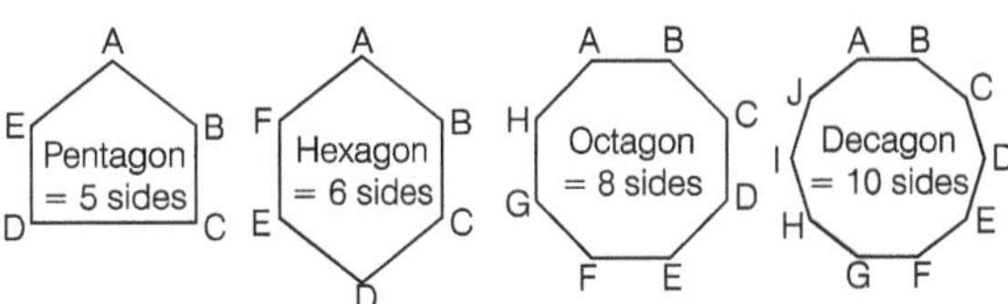

Note *The counting method of polygons is same as discussed for triangles and quadrilaterals.*

Ex 14 How many hexagons are there in the figure given below?

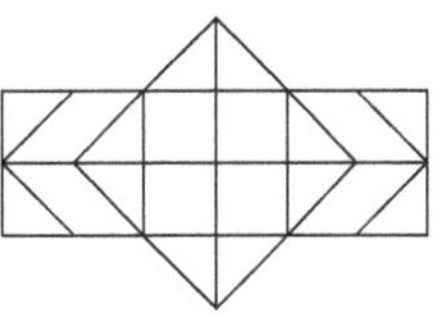

(a) 4 (b) 5
(c) 11 (d) 8

Solution (b) Given figure can be labelled as follows,

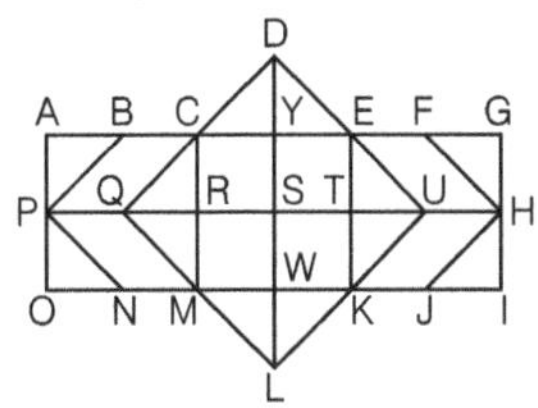

∴ Total hexagons = CDEKLM, CEUKMQ, CFHJMQ, BEUKNP, BFHJNP = 5

Practice / CORNER 7.2

1. How many parallelograms are there in the following figure? « SSC CPO 2008

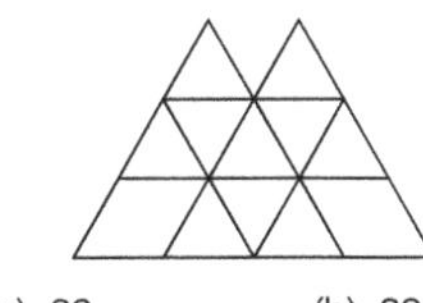

(a) 3 (b) 4
(c) 5 (d) 6

2. Count the number of parallelograms in the given figure?

(a) 23 (b) 22
(c) 21 (d) 18

3. Count the number of parallelograms in the given figure?

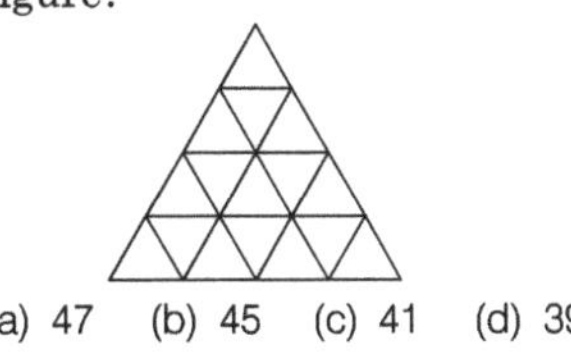

(a) 47 (b) 45 (c) 41 (d) 39

4. Count the number of parallelograms in the given figure?

(a) 8 (b) 11 (c) 12 (d) 15

5. How many rectangles are there in the figure given below? « RRB ALP 2009

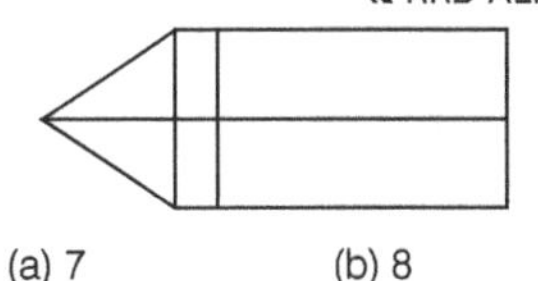

(a) 7 (b) 8
(c) 9 (d) 12

6. How many rectangles are there in the following figure? « SSC CPO 2009

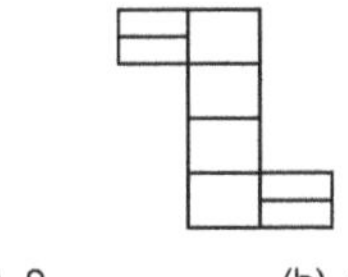

(a) 8 (b) 18
(c) 17 (d) 20

7. How many rectangles are there in the figure given below?

« UPSSSC 2015

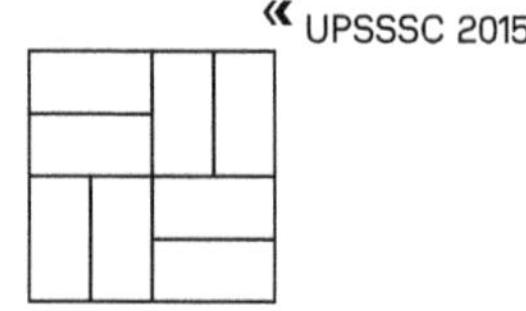

(a) 24 (b) 16 (c) 22 (d) 14

8. How many quadrilaterals are there in the figure given below?

« SSC FCI 2012

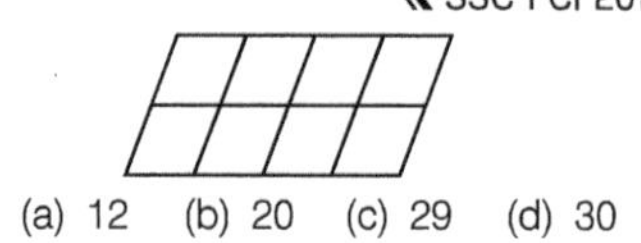

(a) 12 (b) 20 (c) 29 (d) 30

9. The number of squares in the figure is

« SSC Delhi Police & CAPF 2016

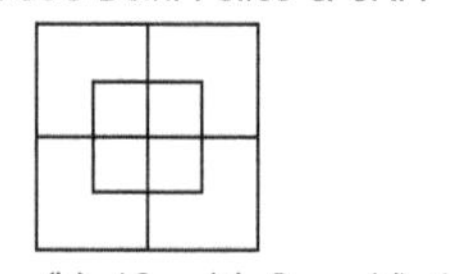

(a) 14 (b) 10 (c) 8 (d) 12

10. Count the number of squares in the figure given below.

« WBCS 2019

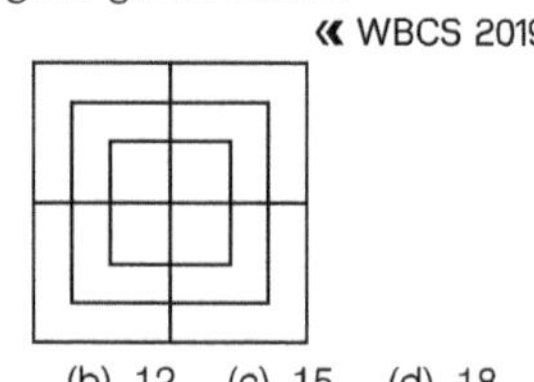

(a) 8 (b) 12 (c) 15 (d) 18

11. Count the number of squares in the given figure?

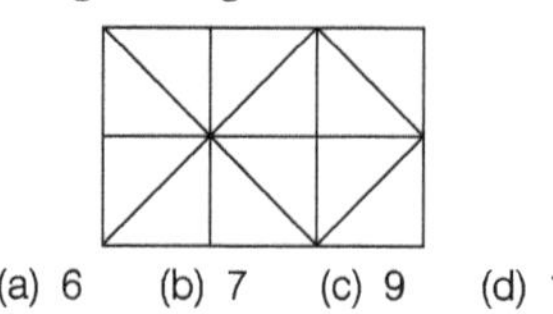

(a) 6 (b) 7 (c) 9 (d) 10

12. How many squares are there in the following figure?

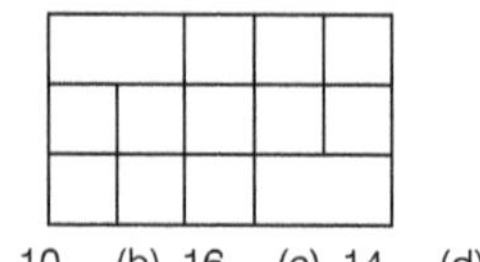

(a) 10 (b) 16 (c) 14 (d) 19

13. Count the number of squares in the given figure?

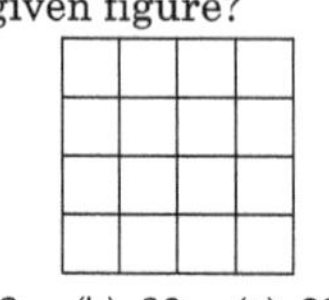

(a) 32 (b) 30 (c) 29 (d) 28

14. How many squares are there in this figure? « SSC 10+2 2012

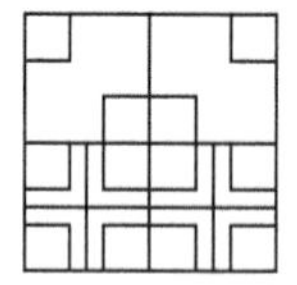

(a) 24 (b) 23 (c) 27 (d) 26

15. How many squares are there in this figure?

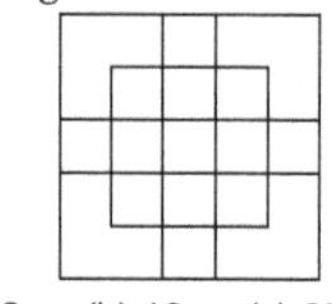

(a) 18 (b) 19 (c) 25 (d) 27

16. How many squares are there in the following figure?

« MP PSC 2018

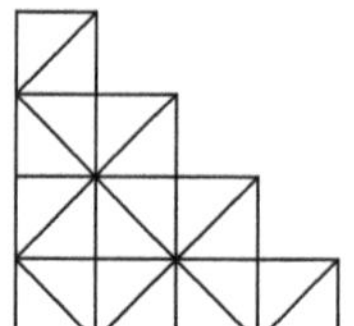

(a) 14 (b) 16
(c) 22 (d) 12

17. Count the number of squares in the given figures?

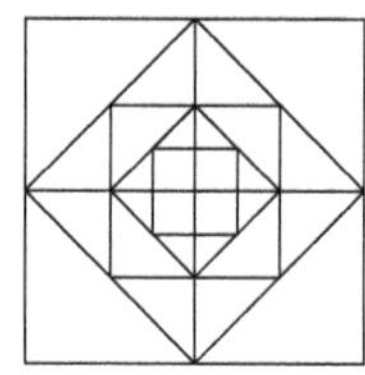

(a) 12 (b) 13
(c) 16 (d) 17

18. Find out the number of squares in the given pattern?

« SSC MTS 2013

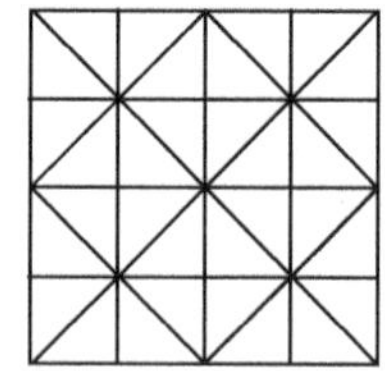

(a) 26 (b) 30
(c) 35 (d) 38

19. How many pentagons are there in the following figure?

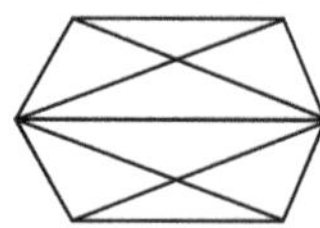

(a) 4 (b) 6
(c) 3 (d) 2

20. How many hexagons are there in the following figure?

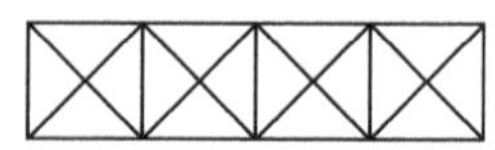

(a) 3 (b) 2
(c) 4 (d) 1

Answers / WITH EXPLANATIONS

1. (*d*) Given figure can be labelled as follows,

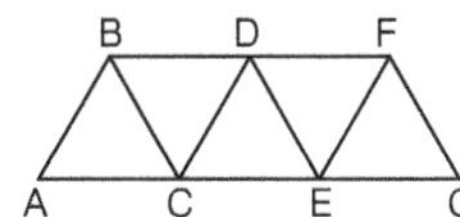

Single parallelograms = ▱ ABDC, ▱ DFEC, ▱ GFDE, ▱ DBCE = 4

Parallelograms formed with two parallelograms = ▱ ABFE, ▱ FBCG = 2

∴ Total number of parallelograms = 4 + 2 = 6

2. (*a*) Given figure can be labelled as

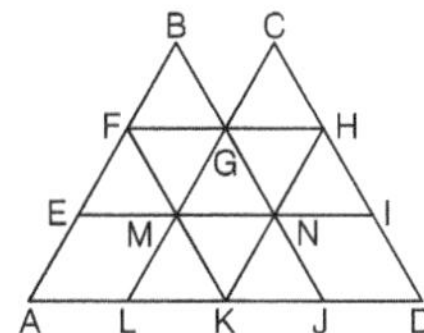

Simplest parallelogram EMLA and NIDJ = 2

Parallelogram formed with two components
= BFMG, CGNH, GMKN, FGME, GHNM, MNKL, FGNM, GHIN and MNJK = 9

Parallelogram formed with three components = FGLA, ENKA, GHDJ and MIDK = 4

Parallelogram formed with four components
= FGJK, GHKL, FBNK, CHKM EFHN and MFHI = 6

Parallelogram formed with seven components
= FHKA and FHDK = 2

∴ Total number of parallelograms
= 2 + 9 + 4 + 6 + 2 = 23

3. (*b*) Given figure can be labelled as

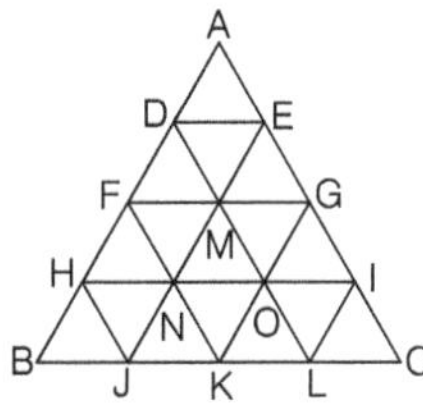

Parallelogram formed with two components = ADME, DFNM, EMOG, FHJN, MNKO, GOLI, HBJN, NJKO, OKLI, FHNM, MNOG, DFME, HJKN, NKLO, OLCI, FNOM, MOIG and DMGE. = 18

Parallelogram formed with four components = HOKB, NILJ, FGOH, HOLJ, NICK, FGIN, FMJB, DENH, MGKJ, MGCL, DEIO, FMLK, AENF, AGOD, DMJH, DOKF, EILM and EGKN = 18

Parallelogram formed with six components
= AEJH, DAIL, DECL, DEJB, HILB and HICJ = 6

Parallelogram formed with eight components = FGKB, FGCK and AGKF = 3

∴ Total number of parallelograms
= 18 + 18 + 6 + 3 = 45

4. (*d*) Given figure can be labelled as

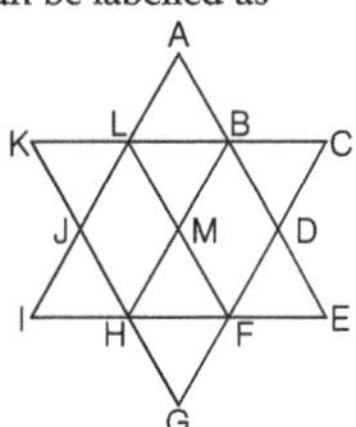

Simplest parallelogram = LMHJ and BDFM = 2

Parallelogram formed with two components = ABML and MFGH = 2

Parallelogram formed with three components = LBHI, LBEF, BDGH, DFLA, BCFH, KLFH, ABHJ and LFGJ = 8

Parallelogram formed with six components = LCFI, KBEH and ADGJ = 3

∴ Total number of parallelograms = 2 + 2 + 8 + 3 = 15

5. (*c*) Given figure can be labelled as follows,

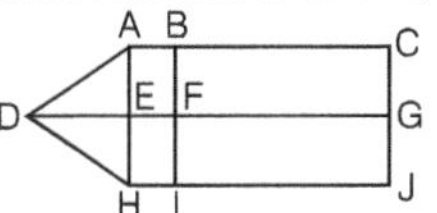

Single rectangles
= ▭ABFE, ▭EFIH, ▭BCGF, ▭FGJI = 4

Rectangles formed with two rectangles
= ▭ABIH, ▭AEGC, ▭EGJH, ▭BCJI = 4

Rectangles formed with four rectangles (or largest rectangle)
= ▭ ACJH = 1

∴ Total number of rectangles = 4 + 4 + 1 = 9

6. (*b*) Given figure can be labelled as follows,

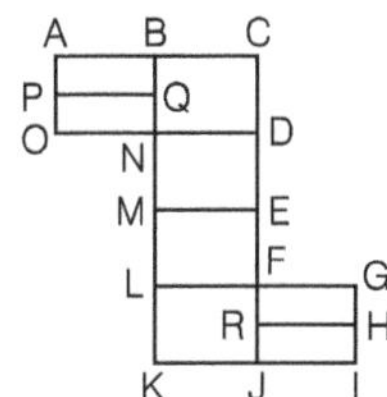

Single rectangles = ▭ABQP, ▭ PQNO, ▭ BCDN, ▭NDEM, ▭MEFL, ▭ LFJK, ▭FGHR, ▭RHIJ = 8

Rectangles formed with two rectangles = ▭ABNO, ▭BCEM, ▭ NDFL, ▭ MEJK, ▭FGIJ = 5

Rectangles formed with three or more rectangles
= ▭ACDO, ▭BCFL, ▭NDJK, ▭LGIK, ▭BCJK = 5

∴ Total number of rectangles = 8 + 5 + 5 = 18

7. (*b*) Given figure can be labelled as follows,

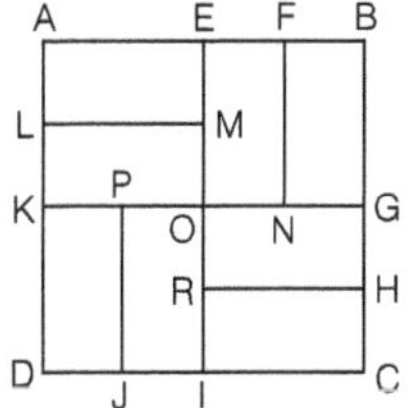

Single rectangles = ▭AEML, ▭LMOK, ▭EFNO, ▭FBGN, ▭OGHR, ▭RHCI, ▭POIJ, ▭KPJD = 8

Rectangles formed with three rectangles = ▭AFNK, ▭PGCJ, ▭LMID, ▭EBHR = 4

Rectangles formed with four rectangles = ▭ABGK, ▭KGCD, ▭AEID, ▭EBCI = 4

∴ Total number of rectangles = 8 + 4 + 4 = 16

8. (*d*) Given figure can be labelled as follows

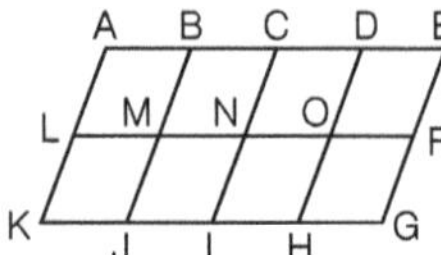

Single quadrilaterals = ▱ABML, ▱BCNM, ▱CDON, ▱DOFE, ▱LKJM, ▱MNIJ, ▱NIHO, ▱OFGH = 8

Quadrilaterals formed with two quadrilaterals = ▱ABJK, ▱BCIJ, ▱CDHI, ▱DEGH, ▱ACNL, ▱CEFN, ▱LNIK, ▱NFGI, ▱BDOM, ▱MOHJ = 10

Quadrilaterals formed with three quadrilaterals = ▱ADOL, ▱BEFM, ▱LOHK, ▱MFGJ = 4

Quadrilaterals formed with four quadrilaterals = ▱ACIK, ▱CEGI, ▱BDHJ, ▱AEFL, ▱LFGK = 5

Quadrilaterals formed with six or more quadrilaterals = ▱ADHK, ▱BEGJ, ▱AEGK = 3

∴ Total number of quadrilaterals = 8 + 10 + 4 + 5 + 3 = 30

Shortcut Method

Number of quadrilaterals

$= [r + (r-1) + (r-2) + \ldots\ldots] \times [c + (c-1) + (c-2) + \ldots\ldots]$ [∵ $r = 2$ and $c = 4$]

$= (2 + 1) \times (4 + 3 + 2 + 1) = 3 \times 10 = 30$

9. (*b*) Given figure can be labelled as follows,

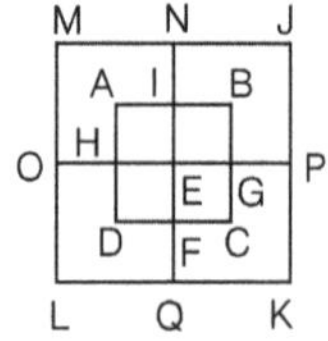

Single squares = □AIEH, □IBGE, □GCFE, □HEFD = 4

Squares formed with two squares = □MNEO, □NJPE, □PKQE, □EQLO = 4

Squares formed with four or more squares = □MJKL, □ABCD = 2

∴ Total number of squares = 4 + 4 + 2 = 10

10. (*c*) Given figure can be labelled as follows,

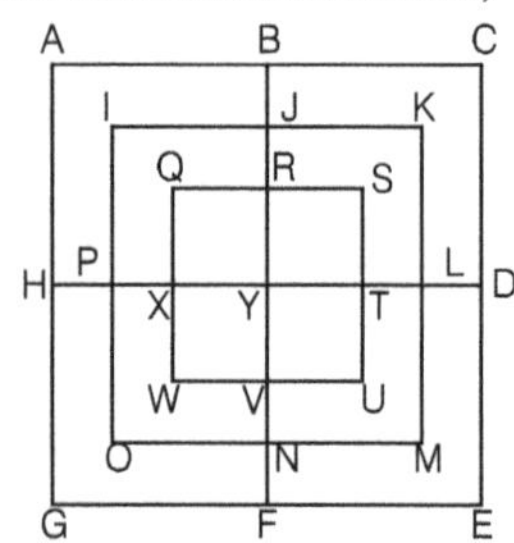

Single squares = □QRYX, □RSTY, □YTUV, □XYVW = 4

Squares formed with two squares = □IJYP, □JKLY, □YLMN, □PYNO, □ABYH, □BCDY, □YDEF, □HYFG = 8

Squares formed with four or more squares = □QSUW, □IKMO, □ACEG = 3

∴ Total number of squares = 4 + 8 + 3 = 15

11. (*c*) Given figure can be labelled as follows,

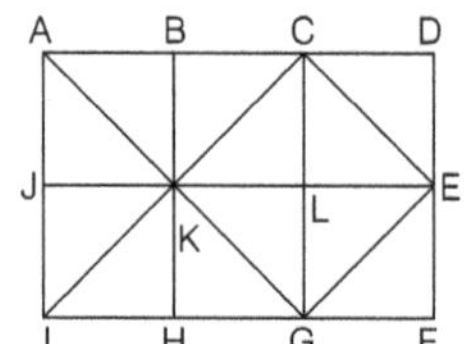

Squares formed with two components = ABKJ, BCLK, CDEL, LEFG, KLGH and JKHI = 6

Square formed with four components = CEGK = 1

Squares formed with eight components = ACGI and BDFH = 2

Total number of square = 6 + 1 + 2 = 9

12. (*d*) Given figure can be labelled as follows,

Single squares = □EFIH, □FGJI, □GBLJ, □JLMN, □JNOI, □IOPH, □HPRQ, □QRST, □SRUD, □RPVU, □POWV = 11

Squares formed with two squares and one rectangle = □AEPS, □ILCW = 2

Squares formed with four or more squares and one rectangle = □IWUQ, □EGNP, □FBMO, □HVDT, □AFWD, □EBCV = 6

∴ Total number of squares = 11 + 2 + 6 = 19

13. (*b*) Given figure can be labelled as follows,

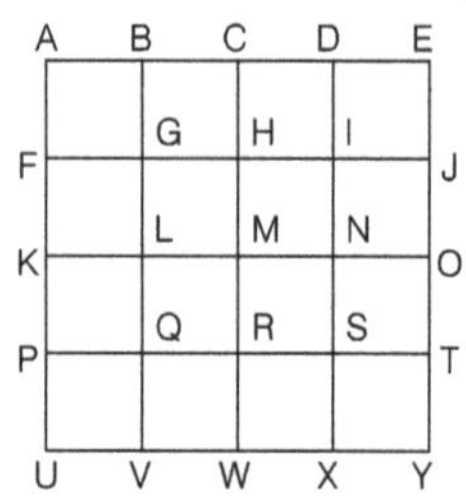

Simplest squares = ABGF, BCHG, CDIH, DEJI, FGLK, GHML, HINM, IJON, KLQP, LMRQ, MNSR, NOTS, PQVU, QRWV, RSXW and STYX = 16

Squares formed with four components = ACMK, BDNL, CEOM, FHRP, GISQ, HJTR, KMWU, LNXV and MOYW= 9

Squares formed with nine components

= ADSP, BETQ, FIXU and GJYV = 4

Squares formed with sixteen components = AEYU = 1

Total number of squares = 16 + 9 + 4 + 1 = 30

14. (*c*) Given figure can be labelled as follows,

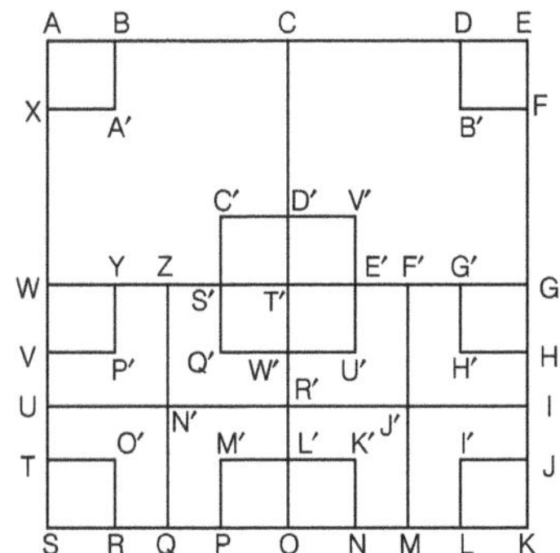

Single squares = □ ABA′X, □ DEFB′, □ G′GHH′, □ I′JKL, □ L′K′NO, □ M′L′OP, □ TO′RS, □ WYP′V, □ C′D′T′S′, □ D′V′E′T′, □ S′T′W′Q′, □ T′E′U′W′ = 12

Squares formed with two squares = □ WZN′U, □ ZT′R′N′ □ T′F′J′R′, □ F′GIJ′, □ J′IKM, □ R′J′MO, □ N′R′OQ, □ UN′QS = 8

Squares formed with three or more squares = □ ACT′W, □ CEGT′, □ T′GKO, □ WT′OS, □ ZF′MQ, □ C′V′U′Q′ □ AEKS = 7

∴ Total number of squares = 12 + 8 + 7 = 27

15. (*d*) Given figure can be labelled as follows,

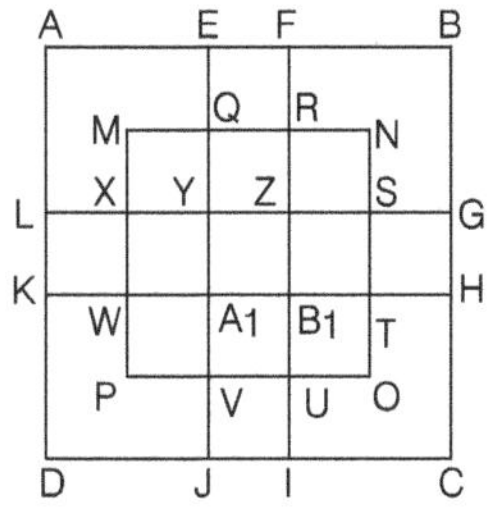

Single squares = □ EFRQ, □ MQYX, □ QRZY, □ RNSZ, □ LXWK, □ XYA$_1$W, □ YZB$_1$A$_1$, □ ZSTB$_1$, □ SGHT, □ WA$_1$VP, □ A$_1$B$_1$ UV, □ B$_1$ TOU and VUIJ = 13

Squares with two squares = □ AEYL, □ FBGZ, □ KA$_1$JD and □ B$_1$ HCI = 4

Squares with four squares = □ MRB$_1$W, □ QNTA$_1$, □ XZUP and □ YSOV = 4

Squares formed with seven squares □ AFB$_1$K, □ EBHA$_1$, □ LZID and □ YGCJ = 4

There is only one square composed of nine components i.e. □ MNOP

There is only one square composed of seventeen components i.e. □ ABCD

Total number of squares = 13 + 4 + 4 + 4 + 1 + 1 = 27

16. (*a*) Given figure can be labelled as follows,

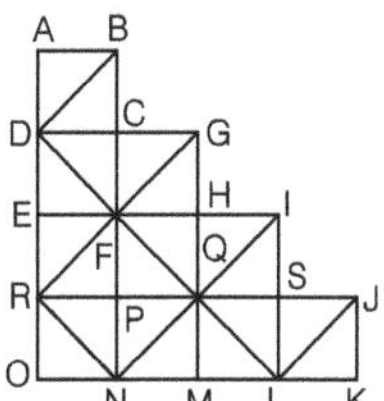

Single squares = □ ABCD, □ DCFE, □ CGHF, □ EFPR, □ FHQP, □ HISQ, □ RPNO, □ PQMN, □ QSLM, □ SJKL, □ RFQN = 11

Squares formed with four squares

= □ DGQR, □ EHMO, □ FILN = 3

∴ Total number of squares = 11 + 3 = 14

17. (*d*) Given figure can be labelled as follows,

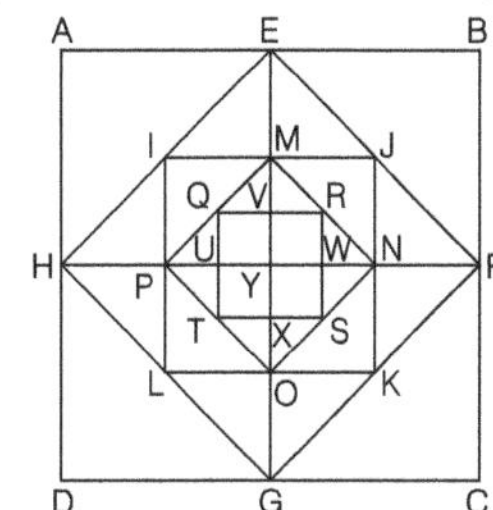

Single squares = □ QVYU, □ VRWY, □ YWSX and □ UYXT = 4

Square formed with two squares = □ IMYP, □ MJNY, □ YNKO, □ PYOL and □ QRST = 5

Squares formed with seven components = □ AEYH, □ EBFY, □ YFCG and □ HYGD = 4

The only square composed of twelve components = □ MNOP.

One square composed of sixteen components = □ IJKL

One square composed of twenty-four components = □ EFGH

One square which is composed of twenty-eight components = □ ABCD

Total number of squares = 4 + 5 + 4 + 1 + 1 + 1 + 1 = 17

18. (*c*) Given figure can be labelled as follows,

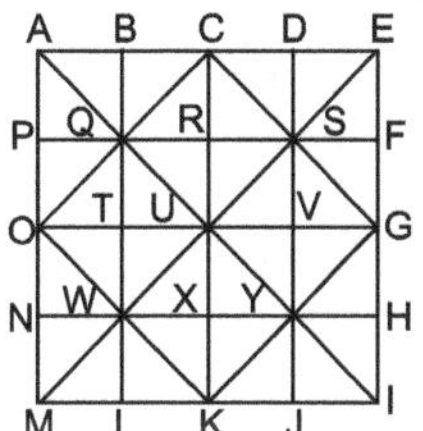

Single squares = □ ABQP, □ BCRQ, □ CDSR, □ DEFS, □ PQTO, □ QRUT, □ RSVU, □ SFGV, □ OTWN, □ TUXW, □ VYXU, □ VGHY, □ NWLM, □ WXKL, □ XYJK, □ YHIJ, □ QCSU, □ SGYU, □ YKWU, □ WOQU = 20

Squares formed with four small squares = □ ACUO, □ BDVT, □ CEGU, □ PRXN, □ QSYW, □ RFHX, □ OUKM, □ TVJL, □ UGIK, □ OCGK = 10

Squares formed with nine or more small squares = □ ADYN, □ BEHW, □ PSJM, □ QFIL, □ AEIM = 5

∴ Total number of squares = 20 + 10 + 5 = 35

19. (*b*) Given figures can be labelled as follows,

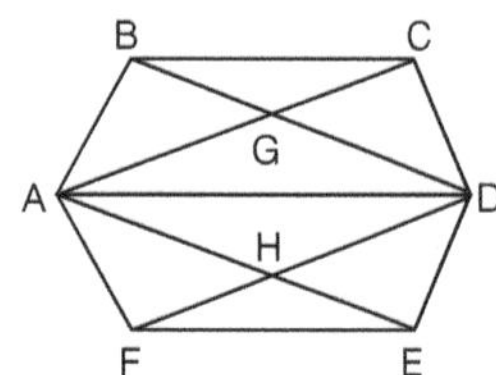

Total Pentagons = ABCDH, CBAED, GAFED,
BAFED, FDCBA, AFEDC = 6

20. (*a*) Given figures can be labelled as follows,

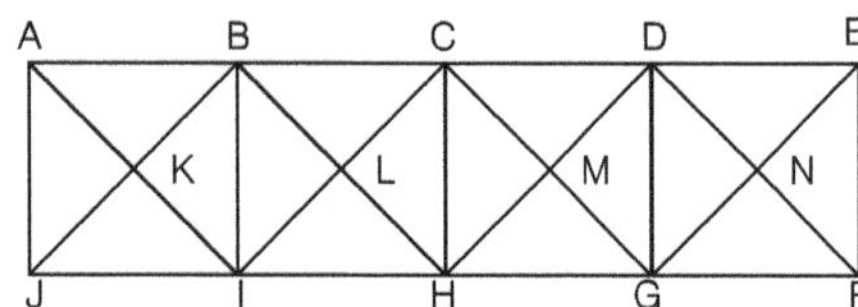

Smallest hexagons = KBCMHI, LCDNGH = 2
Largest hexagons = KBDNGI = 1
∴ Total number of hexagons = 2 + 1 = 3

TYPE 03

Counting of Circles and Colours

In this type of questions, a candidate is required to find the number of circles or colours in the given figure.

A. Counting of Circles

A circle is a round plane figure whose boundary consists of points equidistant from a fixed point called centre.

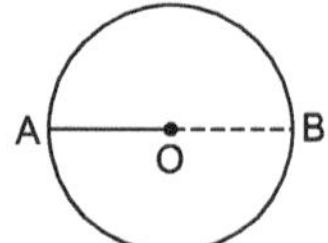

Counting Method of Circles

Counting of circles is done by numbering the circles one by one. The numeral that comes for the last circle is the required number of circles.

***Ex* 15** How many circles are there in the figure given below?

(a) 10 (b) 14 (c) 12 (d) 18

Solution (c) In the given question figure, we start counting the circles by numbering them as 1, 2 and so on and the last count is 12, which is the required number of circles as shown in the following figure.

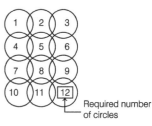

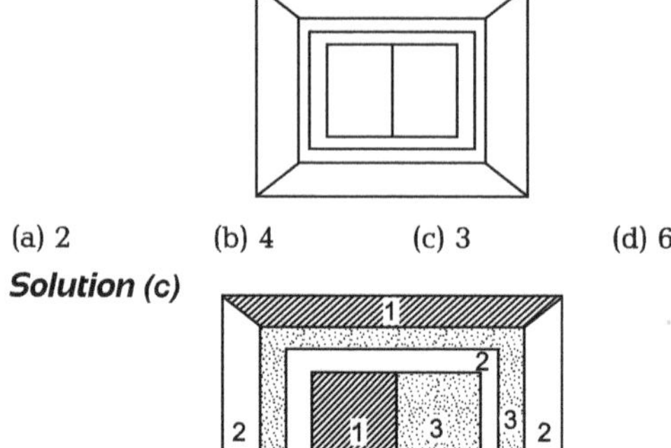

B. Counting of Colour

In this type of questions, a figure is given in which two adjacent areas cannot have the same colour. The candidate is required to find out the least number of colours to be used to fill the figure.

***Ex* 16** Consider the figure given below and find the least number of colours to be used to fill the figure, if no two adjacent areas can have the same colour?

(a) 2 (b) 4 (c) 3 (d) 6

Solution (c)

So, there are only 3 colours needed to fill the figure.

***Ex* 17** Consider the figure given below and answer the question that follows.

Find the least number of colours to be used to fill the figure, if no two adjacent areas can have the same colour.

(a) 3 (b) 4 (c) 5 (d) 6

Solution (a)

So, there are only three colours needed to fill the figure.

Practice CORNER 7.3

1. Find the total number of circles in following figure?
« RRB Group D 2017

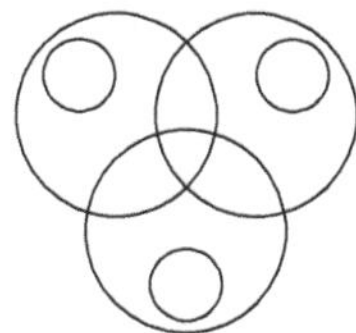

(a) 6 (b) 5 (c) 7 (d) 8

2. How many circles are there in the figure given below?

(a) 7 (b) 9 (c) 8 (d) 10

3. Count the number of circles in the figure given below?
« RRB Group D 2012

(a) 6 (b) 5 (c) 7 (d) 8

4. How many circles are there in the figure given below?

« UP B.Ed. 2012

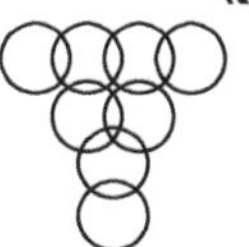

(a) 4 (b) 8 (c) 9 (d) 10

5. How many circles are there in the figure given below?

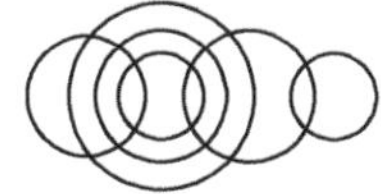

(a) 6 (b) 7 (c) 10 (d) 8

6. Find the total number of circles in the figure given below.
« SSC (DEO) 2012; LIC (ADO) 2007

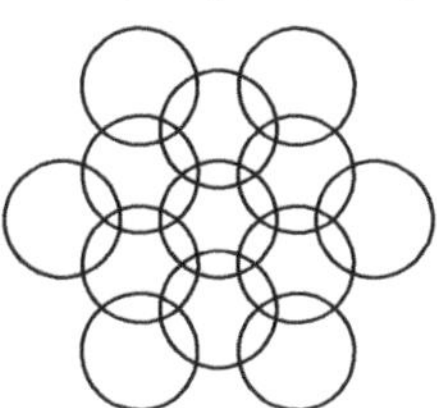

(a) 10 (b) 11
(c) 12 (d) 13

7. How many circles are there in this figure?

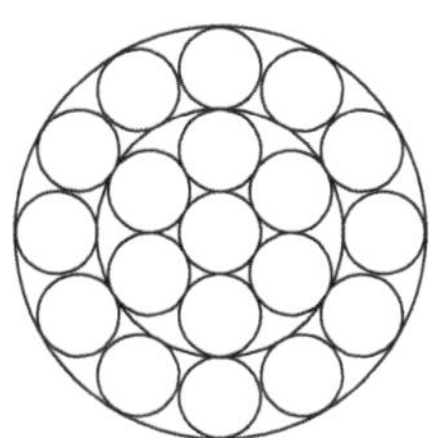

(a) 19 (b) 18
(c) 17 (d) 21

8. Find out the number of circles in the figure given below?

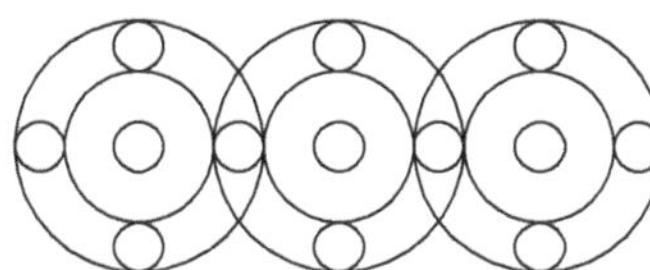

(a) 18
(b) 19
(c) 16
(d) 20

9. How many circles are there in the following figure?

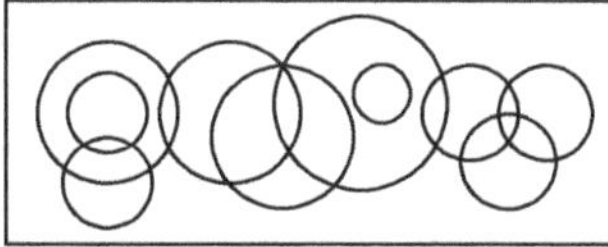

(a) 12 (b) 14
(c) 13 (d) 10

10. How many circles are there in the figure given below?

(a) 10 (b) 14 (c) 12 (d) 13

11. How many different sized circles appear below?

(a) 10 (b) 13 (c) 18 (d) 19

DIRECTIONS ~ (Q. Nos. 12-14) *If in the given figure, no two adjacent areas can have the same colour, find the least number of colours required to fill the figure/areas.*

12.

(a) 3 (b) 4 (c) 5 (d) 6

13.

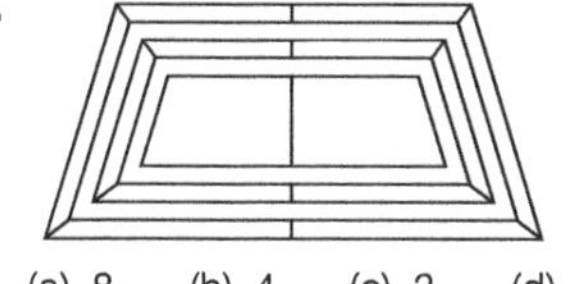

(a) 8 (b) 4 (c) 3 (d) 5

14.

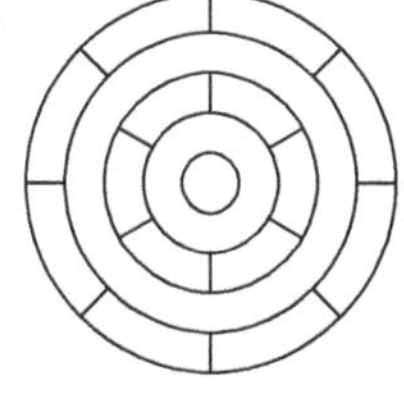

(a) 3 (b) 4
(c) 5 (d) 6

Answers / WITH EXPLANATIONS

1. (*a*)

Hence, the total number of circles = 6

2. (*a*)

∴ Total number of circles = 7

3. (*a*)

Total number of circles = 6

4. (*b*)

∴ Total number of circles = 8

5. (*a*)

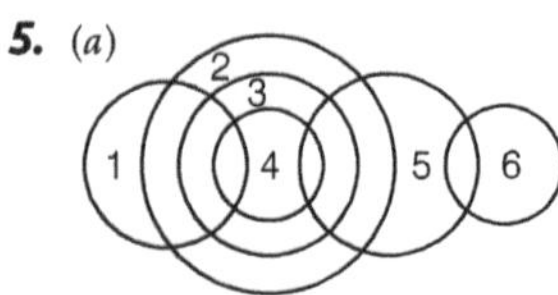

∴ Total number of circles = 6

6. (*d*)

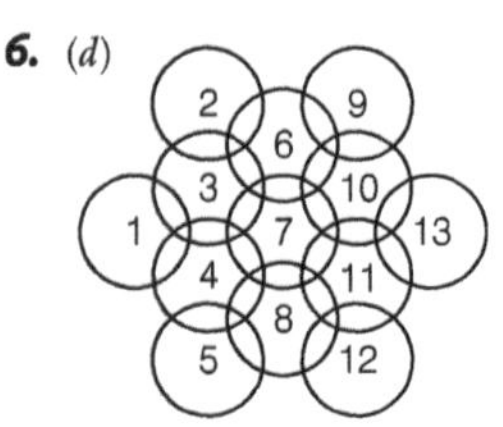

Total number of circles = 13

7. (*d*)

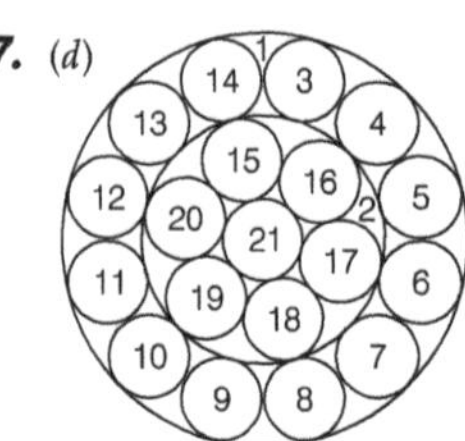

Total number of circles = 21

8. (*b*)

Total number of circles = 19

9. (*d*)

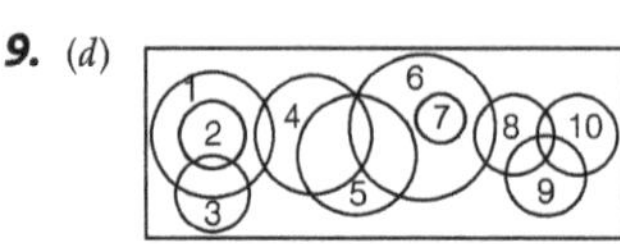

Total number of circles = 10

10. (*b*)

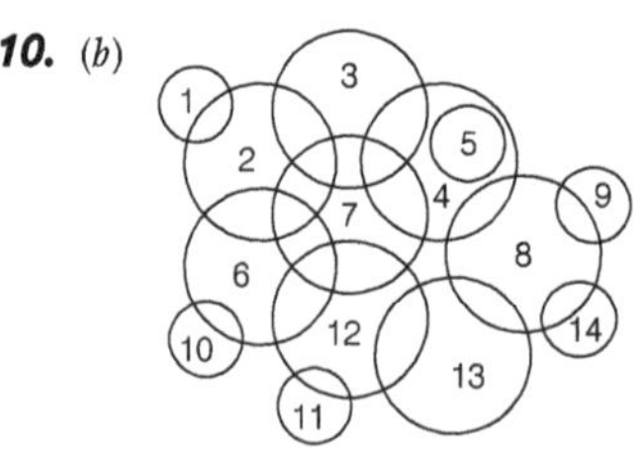

Hence, the total number of circles = 14

11. (*d*) On numbering the circles one by one *i.e.,*

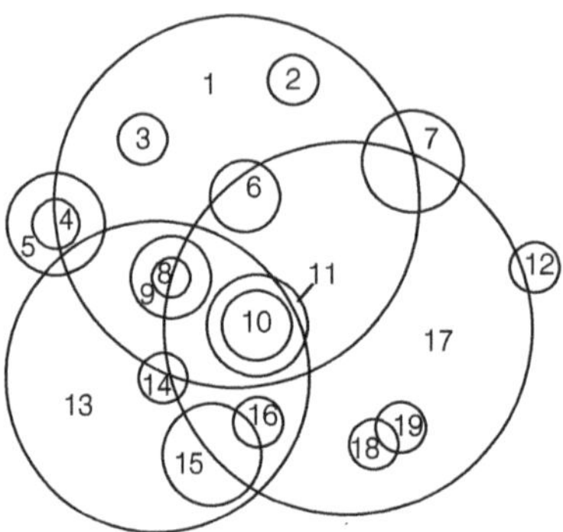

Total number of circles = 19

12. (*a*)

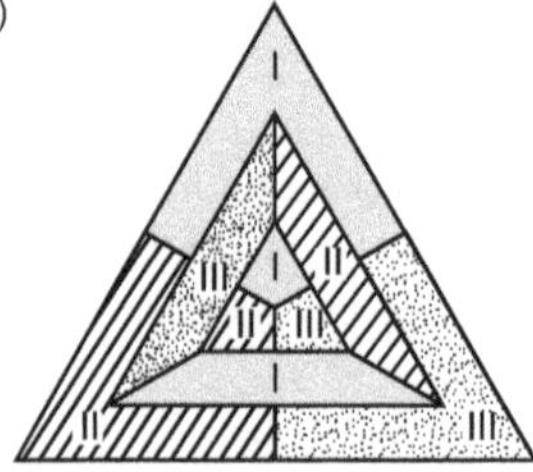

So, atleast three colours are needed to fill the figure such that no two adjacent areas can have the same colour.

13. (*c*)

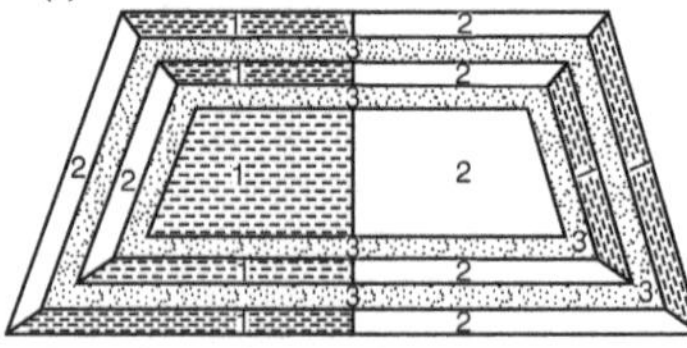

So, atleast three colours are needed to fill the figure based on trapezium.

14. (*a*)

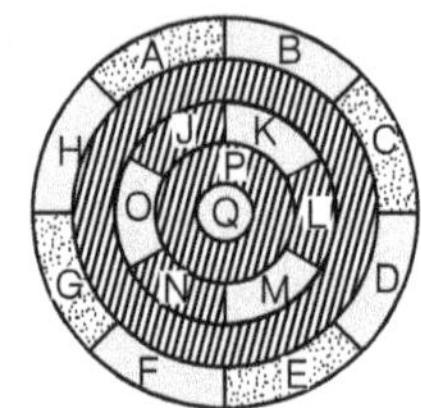

So, atleast three colours are needed to fill the figure such that no two adjacent areas can have the same colour.

The regions B, D, F and H can have the same colour (but different from colour 1) say colour 2.

The region I lies adjacent to each one of the regions A, B, C, D, E, F, G and H and therefore it should have a different colour say colour 3.

The regions J, L and N can have the same colour (different from colour 3) say colour 1.

The regions K, M and O can have the same colour (different from the colours 1 and 3). Thus, these regions will have colour 2.

The region P cannot have any of the colours 1 and 2 as it lies adjacent to each one of the regions J, K, L, M, N and O and so it will have colour 3.

The region Q can have any of the colours 1 or 2.

So, minimum number of colours required is 3.

Master Exercise

1. What is the number of straight lines in the following figure? « WBCS 2018

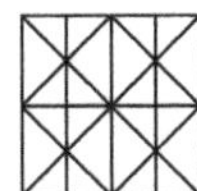

(a) 11 (b) 14 (c) 16 (d) 17

2. How many triangles are there in the figure given below? « SSC CGL 2016

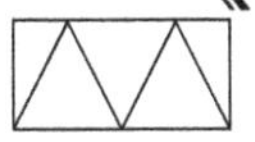

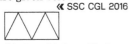

(a) 6 (b) 5 (c) 8 (d) 9

3. How many circles are there in the figure given below? « SSC CPO 2010

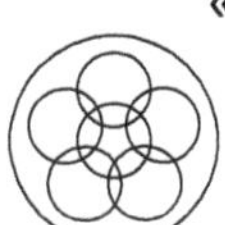

(a) 4 (b) 5 (c) 6 (d) 7

4. How many circles appear in the figure given below? « SSC CGL 2015

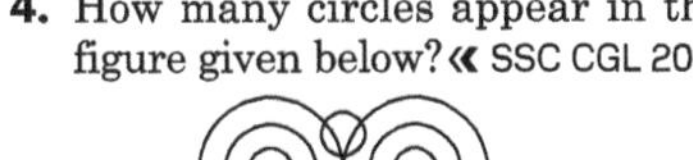

(a) 14 (b) 16
(c) 17 (d) 18

5. In the given figure, if the centres of all the circles are joined by horizontal and vertical lines, then find the number of squares that can be formed.

(a) 6 (b) 7 (c) 8 (d) 1

6. How many triangles are there in figure given below? « SSC CGL 2015

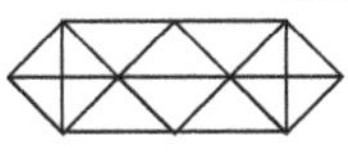

(a) 24 (b) 14
(c) 28 (d) 20

7. Find the number of triangles in the following figure. « UPPSC 2013

(a) 22 (b) 23 (c) 19 (d) 20

8. How many triangles are there in the following figure? « SSC Steno 2016

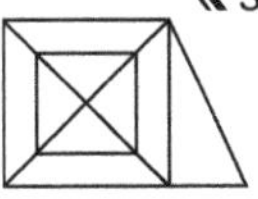

(a) 16 (b) 18 (c) 20 (d) 22

9. How many triangles and squares are there in the figure given below? « RRB ASM 2009, RPSC 2013

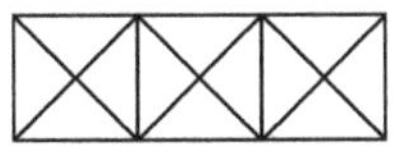

(a) 28 triangles, 5 squares
(b) 24 triangles, 4 squares
(c) 28 triangles, 4 squares
(d) 24 triangles, 5 squares

10. Find the number of triangles in the following figure. « RRB Group D 2018

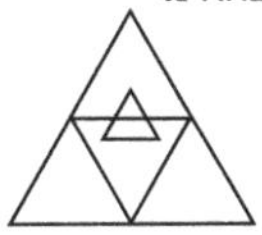

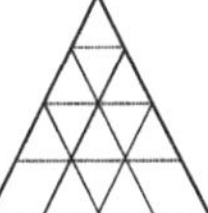

(a) 5 (b) 11 (c) 7 (d) 9

11. Consider the following figure and answer the question that follows

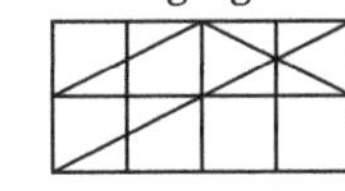

What is the total number of triangles in the above grid? « UPSSSC 2015

(a) 27 (b) 26 (c) 23 (d) 22

12. How many triangles are there in the following figure?

(a) 29 (b) 23
(c) 19 (d) None of these

DIRECTIONS ~ (Q. Nos. 13 and 14) *Following questions are based on figure given below.*

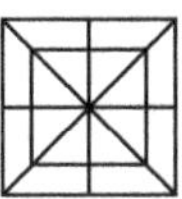

13. How many triangles are there in the figure?
(a) 16 (b) 24
(c) 28 (d) 32

14. Count the number of squares in the figure given above.
(a) 4 (b) 8
(c) 10 (d) 12

DIRECTIONS ~ (Q. Nos. 15-17) *Following questions are based on figure given below.* « CG PSC 2013, GIC 2009

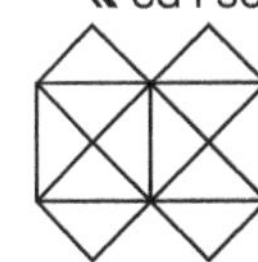

15. How many straight lines are there in the given figure?
(a) 11 (b) 13
(c) 15 (d) 21

16. How many triangles are there in the given figure?
(a) 12 (b) 16 (c) 20 (d) 22

17. How many squares are there in the given figure?
(a) 5 (b) 6 (c) 7 (d) 8

18. How many rectangles are there in the following figure? « SSC Delhi Police Constable 2017

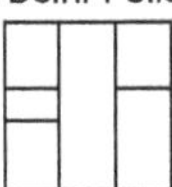

(a) 11 (b) 12 (c) 10 (d) 13

19. Find out the number of triangles in this figure. « SSC (CGL) 2014

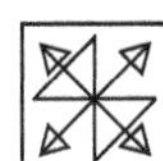

(a) 18 (b) 12
(c) 14 (d) 16

20. How many parallelograms are there in the figure given below?

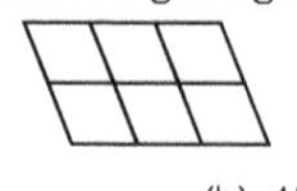

(a) 14 (b) 15
(c) 18 (d) 16

21. Count the number of squares in the following figure.

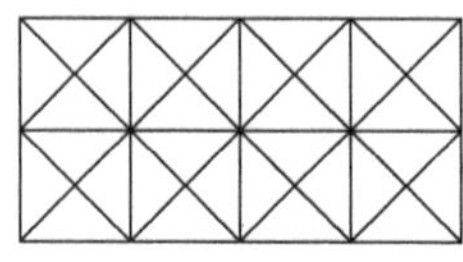

(a) 11 (b) 21
(c) 24 (d) 26

22. How many squares are there in the following figure?

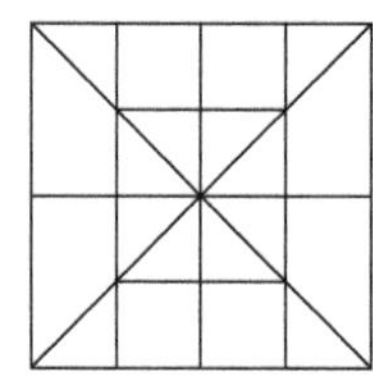

(a) 13 (b) 16
(c) 19 (d) 20

23. How many squares are there in the following figure?

(a) 22 (b) 20
(c) 18 (d) 14

24. How many triangles are there in the following figure? « RRB Group D 2018

(a) 21 (b) 27 (c) 23 (d) 19

25. Find the number of triangles in the following figure. « Delhi Police MTS 2018

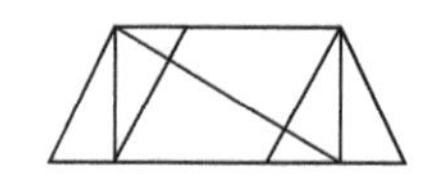

(a) 8 (b) 10
(c) 12 (d) 14

26. How many triangles are there in the following figure?

(a) 10 (b) 8 (c) 12 (d) 11

27. How many quadrilaterals are there in the figure given below?

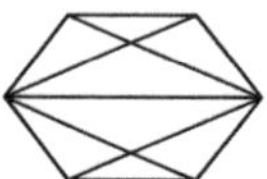

(a) 6 (b) 7 (c) 9 (d) 10

28. How many pentagons are there in the following figure?

(a) 16 (b) 13
(c) 11 (d) 10

29. How many hexagons are there in the following figure?

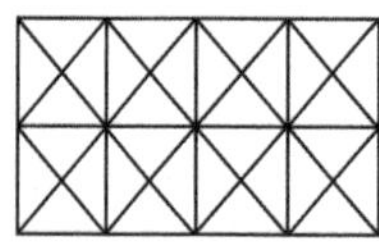

(a) 14 (b) 15
(c) 16 (d) 12

DIRECTIONS ~(Q. Nos. 30-31) *If in the given figure, no two adjacent area can have the same colour, find the least number of colours to be needed to fill the figure/areas.*

30.

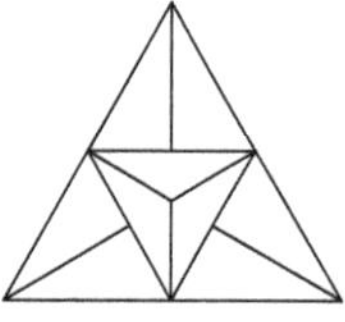

(a) 2 (b) 3 (c) 4 (d) 5

31.

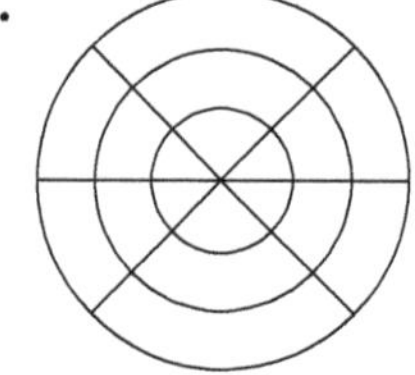

(a) 2 (b) 3 (c) 5 (d) 4

32. Consider the figure given below and answer the question that follows.

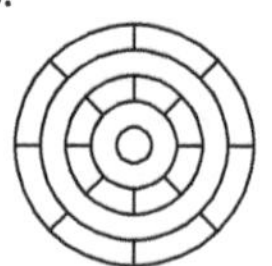

What is the minimum number of different colours required to paint the figure given above such that no two adjacent regions have the same colour? « UPSC CSAT 2011

(a) 3 (b) 4
(c) 5 (d) 6

33. Count the number of triangles in the figure given below.

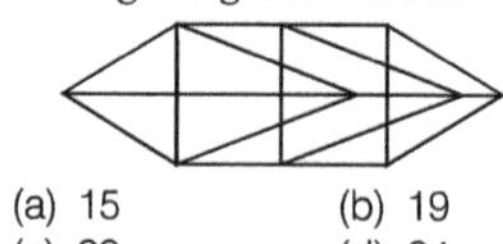

(a) 15 (b) 19
(c) 22 (d) 24

34. How many right angled triangles are there in this figure? « RRB Group D 2018

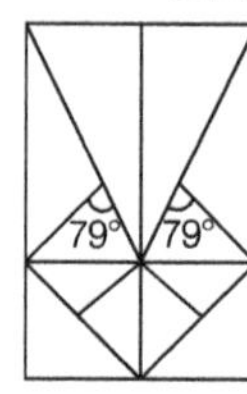

(a) 5 (b) 13 (c) 8 (d) 4

35. Consider the following three-dimensional figure. « UPSC Paper II 2018

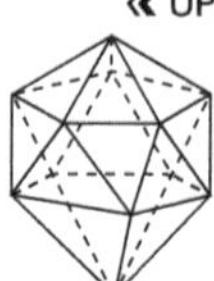

How many triangles does the above figure have?

(a) 18 (b) 20
(c) 22 (d) 24

36. How many triangles are there in the following figure? « RRB Group D 2018

(a) 31 (b) 34
(c) 30 (d) 29

Answers WITH EXPLANATIONS

1. *(b)* Given figure can be labelled as follows,

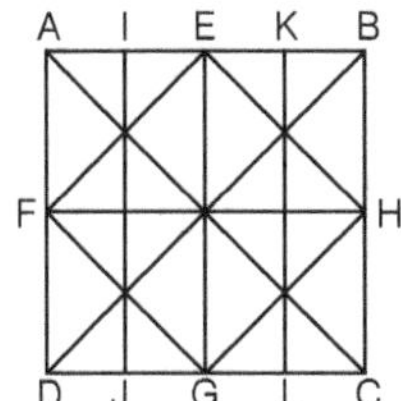

Horizontal Lines = AB, FH, DC = 3
Vertical Lines = AD, IJ, EG, KL, BC = 5
Slant Lines = AC, BD, EF, EH, FG, HG = 6
Therefore, total number of straight lines = 3 + 5 + 6 = 14

2. *(b)* Given figure can be labelled as follows,

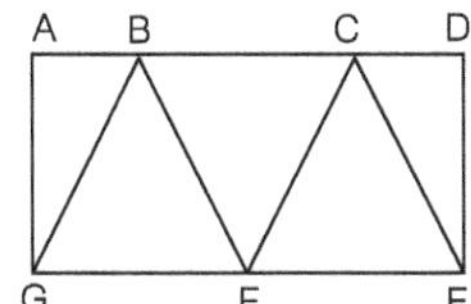

Triangles ΔABG, ΔBGF, ΔBFC, ΔCFE, ΔDCE = 5

3. *(d)* On numbering the circles one by one *i.e.,*

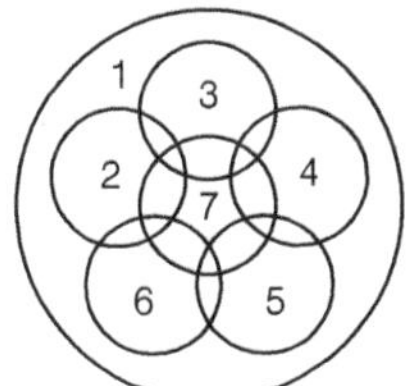

Hence, the total number of circles = 7

4. *(c)* On numbering the circles one by one *i.e.,*

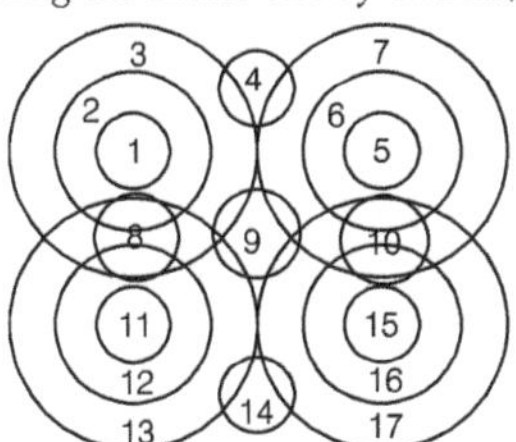

Hence, the total number of circles = 17

5. *(c)* We shall join the centres of all the circles by horizontal and vertical lines and then label the resulting figure as shown.

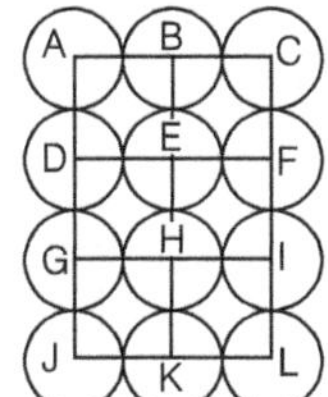

Single squares are □ ABED, □ BCFE, □ DEHG, □ EFIH, □ GHKJ and □ HILK i.e., 6 in number.

The squares composed of four squares are □ ACIG and □ DFLJ *i.e.,* 2 in number.
Thus, 6 + 2 = 8 squares will be formed.

6. *(c)* Given figure can be labelled as follows,

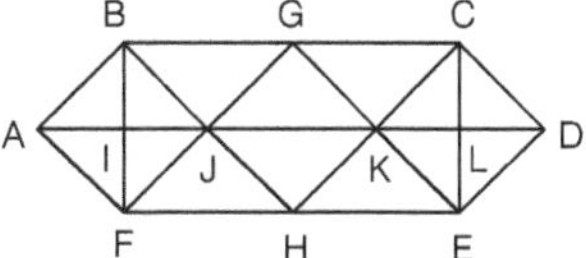

Single triangles = ΔABI, ΔAIF, ΔBIJ, ΔIJF, ΔBGJ, ΔGCK, ΔFJH, ΔHKE, ΔJGK, ΔJHK, ΔCKL, ΔKLE, ΔCDL, ΔLDE = 14

Triangles formed with two small triangles = ΔABF, ΔBJF, ΔABJ, ΔAFJ, ΔCDE, ΔCKE, ΔKCD, ΔKED= 8
Triangles formed from three small triangles = ΔBFG, ΔBFH, ΔGCE, ΔCEH = 4
Triangles formed from four small triangles = ΔBHC, ΔFGE = 2
∴ Total number of triangles = 14 + 8 + 4 + 2 = 28

7. *(a)* Given figure can be labelled as follows,

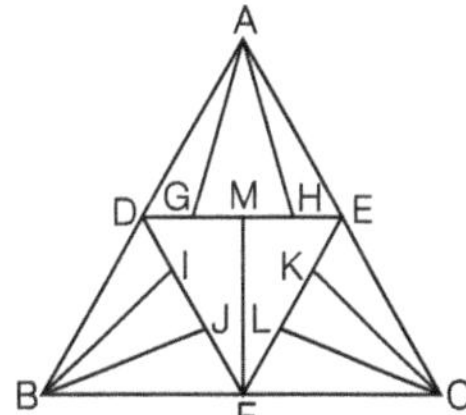

Single triangles = ΔADG, ΔAGH, ΔAHE, ΔDMF, ΔFME, ΔDIB, ΔIBJ, ΔJBF, ΔCFL, ΔCLK, ΔCKE = 11
Triangles formed with two triangles = ΔADH, ΔAGE, ΔDFE, ΔDBJ, ΔIBF, ΔECL, ΔCKF = 7
Triangles formed with three or more triangles = ΔADE, ΔBDF, ΔCFE, ΔABC = 4
∴ Total number of triangles $= 11 + 7 + 4 = 22$

8. *(b)* Given figure can be labelled as follows,

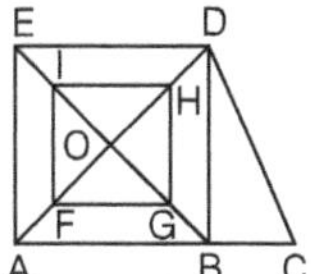

Single triangles = ΔFOI, ΔIOH, ΔHOG, ΔFOG, ΔDBC = 5
Triangles formed by one or more triangles
= ΔFHI, ΔIGH, ΔFHG, ΔGIF, ΔEDO, ΔDBO, ΔABO, ΔEAO, ΔEAD, ΔDEB, ΔBDA, ΔABE, ΔADC = 13
∴ Total number of triangles = 5 + 13 = 18

9. *(a)* Given figure can be labelled as follows,

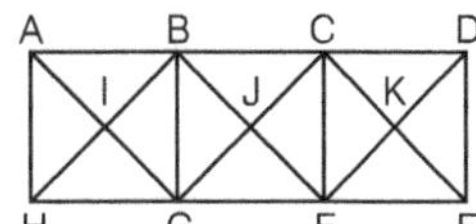

Single triangles = ΔABI, ΔBIG, ΔHIG, ΔAIH, ΔBJC, ΔBJG, ΔGJF, ΔCJF, ΔCKD, ΔCKF, ΔFKE, ΔDKE, = 12

Triangles formed with two triangles = ΔAHB, ΔHGB, ΔABG, ΔAHG, ΔBGC, ΔGFC, ΔBCF, ΔBGF, ΔCFE, ΔCDE, ΔCFD, ΔFED = 12

Triangles formed with three or more triangles = ΔHBF, ΔGCE, ΔAGC, ΔBFD = 4

∴ Total number of triangles = 12 + 12 + 4 = 28

Squares, □BIGJ, □CJFK, □ABGH, □BCFG, □CDEF

∴ Total number of squares = 5

10. *(c)* Given figure can be labelled as follows,

Single triangles = ΔAEF, ΔFDB, ΔECD, ΔFED, ΔJGK = 5

Triangles formed with one triangles = ΔHGI = 1

Triangles formed with four triangles = ΔABC = 1

∴ Total number of triangles = 5 + 1 + 1 = 7

11. *(c)* Given figure can be labelled as follows,

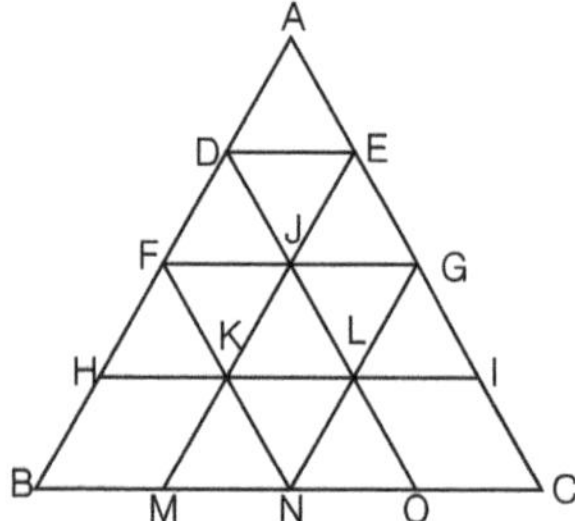

Single triangles = ΔADE, ΔDJE, ΔDJF, ΔEJG, ΔFKH, ΔFKJ, ΔJKL, ΔJLG, ΔGLI, ΔKMN, ΔKNL, ΔLNO = 12

Triangles formed with two triangles = ΔBFN, ΔNGC = 2

Triangles formed with four or more triangles = ΔAHI, ΔBDO, ΔMJO, ΔEKI, ΔFGN, ΔDHL, ΔMEC, ΔAFG, ΔABC = 9

∴ Total number of triangles = 12 + 2 + 9 = 23

12. *(d)* Given figure can be labelled as follows,

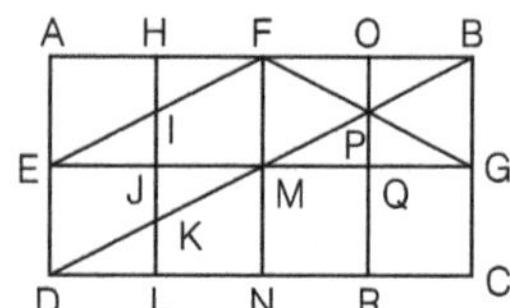

Single triangles = ΔEJI, ΔHFI, ΔFOP, ΔMPQ, ΔFPM, ΔPOB, ΔBPG, ΔJMK, ΔKLD, ΔPGQ = 10

Triangles formed with two triangles = ΔAFE, ΔFEM, ΔEMD, ΔDMN, ΔFBG, ΔMPG, ΔBMG, ΔFGM, ΔDNM, ΔFBM = 10

Triangles formed with three or more triangles = ΔDPR, ΔBKH, ΔEFG, ΔABD, ΔBDC = 5

∴ Total number of triangles

= 10 + 10 + 5 = 25

Solutions (Q. Nos. 13 and 14) Given figure can be labelled as follows,

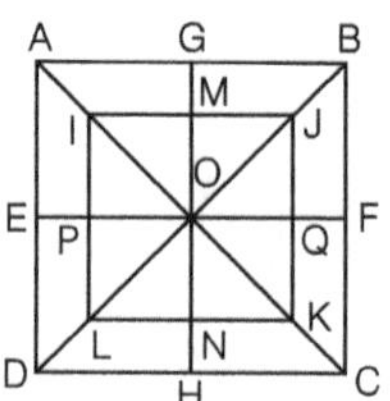

13. *(d)* Single triangles = ΔIMO, ΔIOP, ΔOLP, ΔONL, ΔONK, ΔKQO, ΔOQJ, ΔOMJ = 8

Triangles formed with one triangle = ΔAGO, ΔAOE, ΔGOB, ΔBOF, ΔEOD, ΔOHD, ΔOHC, ΔOFC = 8

Triangles formed with two triangles = ΔOLK, ΔJOK, ΔIOJ, ΔIOL = 4

Triangles formed with four or more triangles = ΔDOC, ΔBOC, ΔAOB, ΔAOD, ΔIKL, ΔIJK, ΔJIL, ΔJKL, ΔACD, ΔABC, ΔBAD, ΔBCD = 12

∴ Total number of triangles = 8 + 8 + 4 + 12 = 32

14. *(c)* Single squares = □IMOP, □MJQO, □OQKN, □ONLP = 4

Squares formed by two squares = □AGOE, □EOHD, □GBFO, □OFCH = 4

Squares formed by four or more squares = □IJKL, □ABCD = 2

∴ Total number of squares = 4 + 4 + 2 = 10

Solutions (Q. Nos. 15-17) Given figure can be labelled as follows,

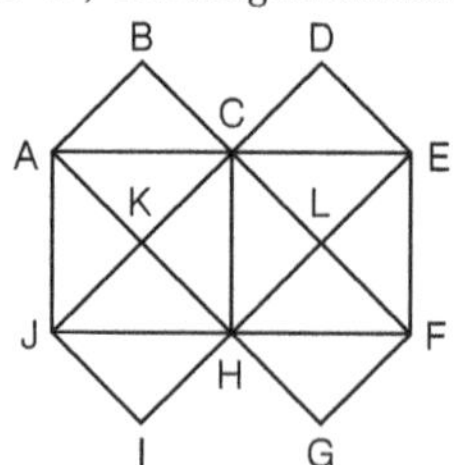

15. *(b)* Horizontal lines = AE, JF = 2

Vertical lines = AJ, CH, EF = 3

Slant lines = AB, JD, IE, GF, JI, AG, BF, DE = 8

∴ Total number of lines = 2 + 3 + 8 = 13

16. *(d)* Single triangles = ΔABC, ΔCDE, ΔAKC, ΔCLE, ΔAKJ, ΔCKH, ΔJKH, ΔJIH, ΔCLH, ΔLHF, ΔHFG, ΔELF = 12

Triangles formed with two triangles = ΔAJH, ΔACH, ΔAJC, ΔCHJ, ΔCHF, ΔCEF, ΔCHE, ΔEHF = 8

Triangles formed with four triangles = ΔJCF, ΔAHE = 2

∴ Total number of triangles = 12 + 8 + 2 = 22

17. *(c)* Squares = □ABCK, □CDEL, □ACHJ, □HIJK, □FGHL, □CEFH, □CLHK = 7

18. *(d)* Given figure can be labelled as follows,

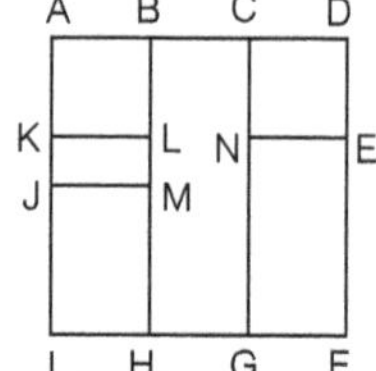

Single rectangles = ▭ ABLK, ▭ KLMJ, ▭ JMHI, ▭ BCGH, ▭ CDEN, ▭ NEFG = 6

Rectangles formed with two rectangles

= ▭ ABMJ, ▭ KLHI, ▭ CDFG = 3

Rectangles formed with three rectangles

= ▭ ABHI, ▭ BDFH = 2

Rectangles formed with four or more rectangles

= ▭ ACGI, ▭ ADFI = 2

∴ Total number of rectangles = 6 + 3 + 2 + 2 = 13

19. (*a*) Given figure can be labelled as follows,

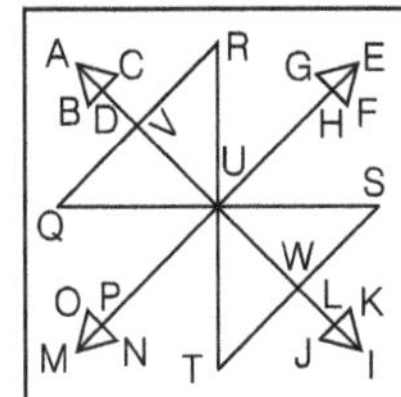

Single triangles = ΔABD, ΔACD, ΔGEH, ΔEHF, ΔLKI, ΔILJ, ΔMNP, ΔMOP, ΔQVU, ΔVUR, ΔUSW, ΔUWT = 12

Triangles formed with two triangles = ΔABC, ΔGFE, ΔJKI, ΔMPN, ΔQRU, ΔSTU = 6

∴ Total number of triangles = 12 + 6 = 18

20. (*c*) Given figure can be labelled as follows,

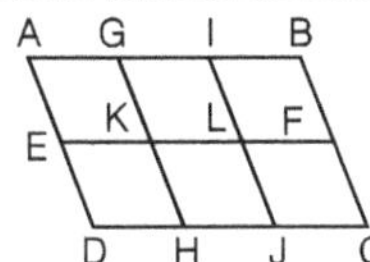

Single parallelograms = ▱ AGKE, ▱ GILK, ▱ IBFL, ▱ FLJC, ▱ LKHJ, ▱ KEDH = 6

Parallelograms formed with two parallelograms = ▱ AILE, ▱ GBFK, ▱ ELJD, ▱ KFCH, ▱ AGHD, ▱ GIJH, ▱ IBCJ = 7

Parallelograms formed with more than two parallelograms

= ▱ ABFE, ▱ EFCD, ▱ AIJD, ▱ GBCH, ▱ ABCD = 5

∴ Total number of parallelograms = 6 + 7 + 5 = 18

Shortcut Method

Number of parallelograms

$= [r + (r-1) + (r-2) + \ldots\ldots] \times [c + (c-1) + (c-2) + \ldots\ldots]$

$= (2 + 1) \times (3 + 2 + 1)$ $\quad [\because c = 3, r = 2]$

$= 3 \times 6 = 18$

21. (*c*) Given figure can be labelled as follows,

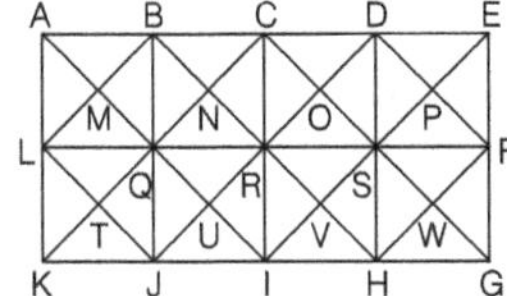

Squares formed with two components = □BNQM, □CORN, □DPSO, □MQTL, □NRUQ, □OSVR, □PFWS, □QUJT, □RVIU and □SWHV = 10

Squares formed with four components = □ABQL, □BCRQ, □CDSR, □DEFS, □LQJK, □QRIJ, □RSHI and □SFGH = 8

Squares formed with eight components = □BRJL, □CSIQ and □DFHR = 3

Squares formed with sixteen components = □ACIK, □BDHJ and □CEGI = 3.

∴ Total number of squares = 10 + 8 + 3 + 3 = 24

22. (*b*) Given figure can be labelled as follows,

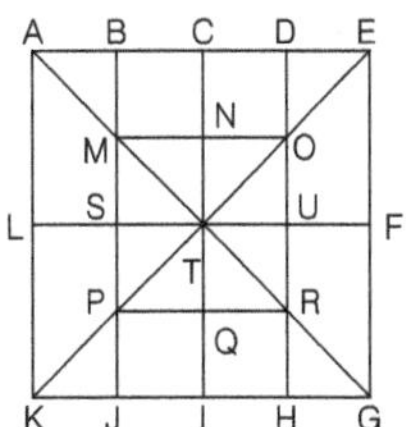

Single squares = □BCNM, □CDON, □PQIJ and □QRHI = 4

Square formed with two components

= □MNTS, □NOUT, □STQP and □TURQ = 4

Square formed with five components

= □ACTL, □CEFT, □TFGI and □LTIK = 4

Square formed with six components = □BDUS and □SUHJ = 2 Square formed with eight components = □MORP

Square formed with twenty components = □AEGK = 1

∴ Total number of squares = 4 + 4 + 4 + 4 + 2 + 1 + 1 = 16.

23. (*c*) Given figure can be labelled as follows,

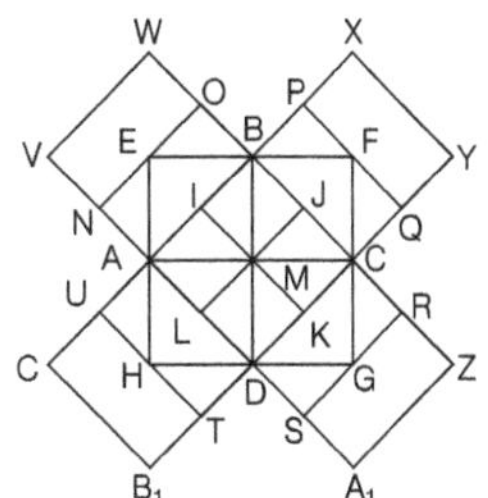

Squares formed with two components

= □BJMI, □CKMJ, □DLMK and □AIML = 4

Squares formed with three components

= □EBMA, □BFCM, □MCGD and □AMDH = 4

Squares formed with four components

= □VWBA, □XYCB, □ZA_1 DC and □B_1C_1AD = 4

Squares formed with seven components

= □NOJL, □PQKI, □RSLJ and □TUIK = 4

Square formed with eight components = □ABCD = 1

Square formed with twelve components = □EFGH = 1

∴ Total number squares in the figure

= 4 + 4 + 4 + 4 + 1 + 1 = 18

24. (*b*) Given figure can be labelled as follows,

Single triangles = ΔAGH, ΔHEI, ΔICJ, ΔKBL, ΔLFG, ΔGOL, ΔGOH, ΔJDM, ΔMDN, ΔNDK, ΔDLO, ΔDOH = 12

Triangles formed by two or more triangles

= ΔJDK, ΔJDN, ΔMDK, ΔLGH, ΔLHA, ΔDLH, ΔDLG, ΔDGH, ΔDGF, ΔDGE, ΔDHF, ΔLHF, ΔCMH, ΔABC, ΔDEF = 15

∴ Total number of triangles = 12 + 15 = 27

25. *(d)* Given figure can be labelled as follows,

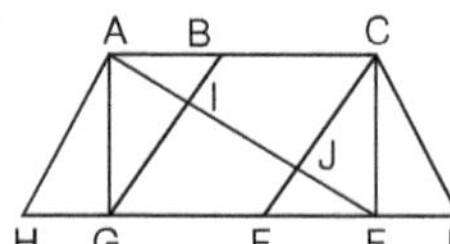

Single triangles = ΔAGH, ΔABI, ΔAIG, ΔCJE, ΔFJE, ΔCED = 6
Triangles formed with two triangles
= ΔABG, ΔCFE, ΔAGE, ΔAJC, ΔAEC, ΔEIG = 6
Triangles formed with three or more triangles
= ΔFCD, ΔAHE = 2
∴ Total number of triangles = 6 + 6 + 2 = 14

26. *(a)* Given figure can be labelled as follows,

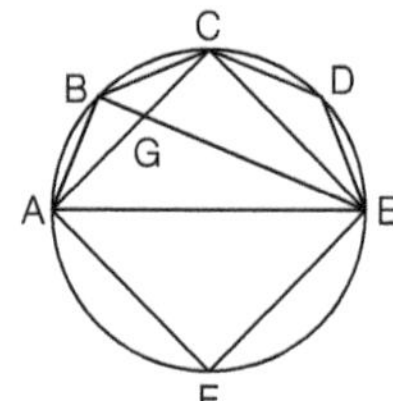

Single triangles
= ΔABG, ΔBGC, ΔCDE, ΔCGE, ΔAGE, ΔAEF = 6
Triangles formed with two triangles
= ΔABC, ΔACE, ΔABE, ΔBCE = 4
∴ Total number of triangles = 6 + 4 = 10

27. *(c)* Given figure can be labelled as follows,

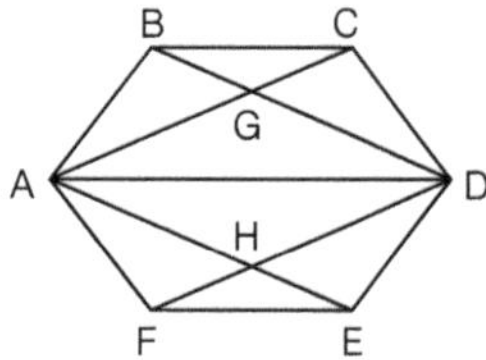

Quadrilaterals = □AGDH, □ BAFD, □CAED, □AGDF, □AGDE, □ABDH, □ACDH, □ACDF, □ABDE = 9

28. *(a)* Given figure can be labelled as follows,

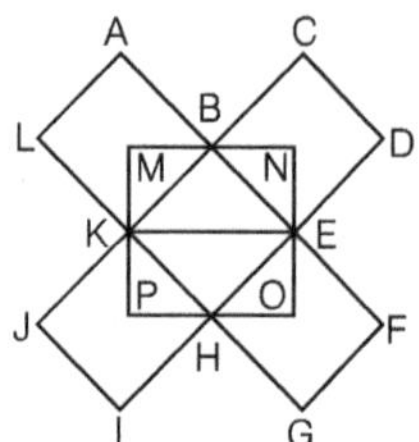

Smallest pentagons = KLABM, BCDEN, EFGHO, HIJKP = 4
Medium pentagons = KMBEH, BNEHK, EOHKB, HPKBE= 4
Largest pentagons = KMBFG, BNEIJ, EOHLA, HPKCD = 4
Pentagons in the middle of the figure = POEBK, ONBKH, MNEHK, MPHEB = 4
∴ Total number of pentagons
= 4 + 4 + 4 + 4 = 16

29. *(b)* Given figure can be labelled as follows,

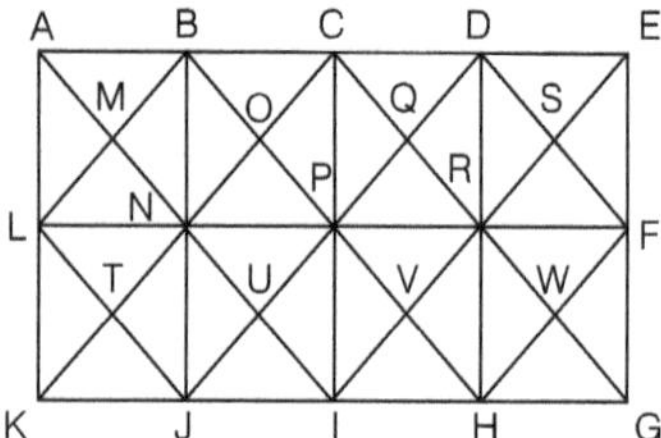

Smallest hexagons
= MBCQPN, OCDSRP, TNPVIJ, UPRWHI = 4
Medium hexagons
= KLBCPJ, JNCDRI, IPDEFH, GFDCPH, HRCBNI, IPBALJ, LBCRIJ, NCDFHI, MBDSRN, TNRWHJ = 10
Largest hexagons = LBDFHJ = 1
∴ Total hexagons = 4 + 10 + 1 = 15

30. *(b)*

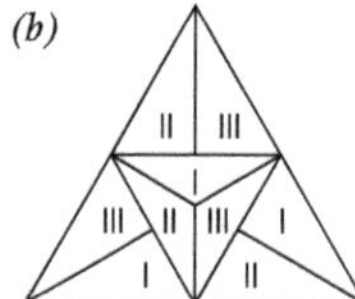

Hence, atleast three colours are needed.

31. *(a)*

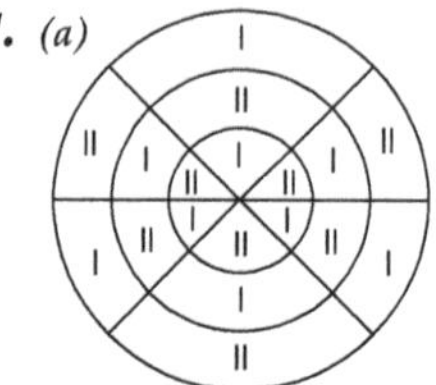

Hence, atleast two colour are needed.

32. *(a)*

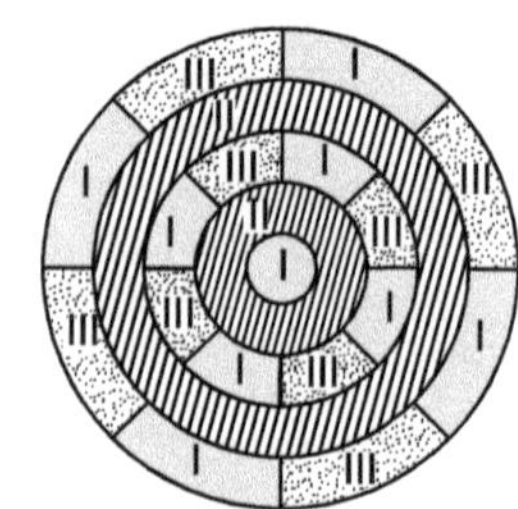

So, atleast 3 colours are needed to fill the figure such that no two adjacent regions have the same colour.

33. *(d)* Given figure can be labelled as follows,

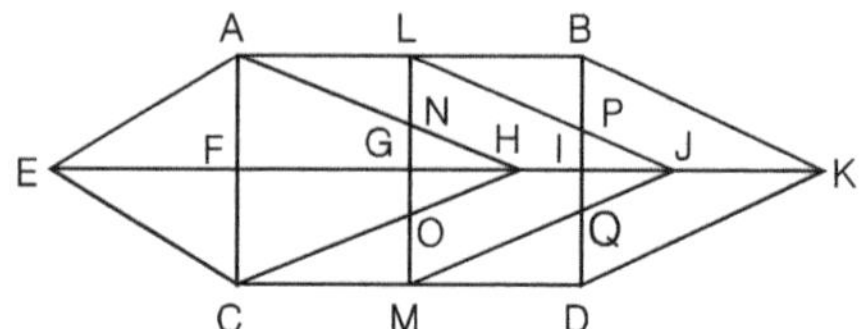

Single triangles = ΔAFE, ΔEFC, ΔALN, ΔCOM, ΔNHG, ΔGHO, ΔLBP, ΔMQD, ΔIPJ, ΔIJQ = 10

Triangles formed with two small triangles

= ΔAEC, ΔNOH, ΔGJM, ΔPQJ, ΔECH, ΔAEH, ΔLJG, ΔAFH, ΔCFH, ΔBIK, ΔDIK = 11

Triangles formed with three or four small triangles

= ΔAHC, ΔLMJ, ΔBDK = 3

∴ Total number of triangles = 10 + 11 + 3 = 24

34. (*b*) Given figure can be labelled as follows,

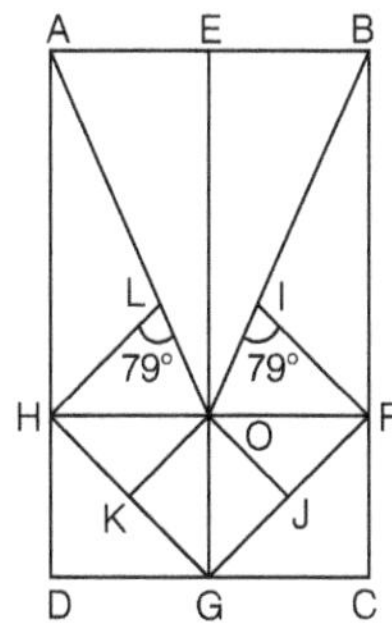

Right angled triangle is a triangle having one of its angle 90°.
Small right angled triangles = ΔHKO, ΔOJF, ΔGKO, ΔOJG, ΔAEO, ΔBEO, ΔHDG, ΔFCG = 8

Large right angled triangles = ΔAHO, ΔBFO, ΔHOG, ΔGOF, ΔHGF = 5

Hence, the total number of right angled triangles

= 8 + 5 = 13

35. (*b*) If we look at the given 3-dimensional figure. The top of the figure consists of 5 triangles in which 3 are visible, 2 in the back side.

Similarly at the bottom, it consists of 5 triangles.

In the middle portion, we can see 5 triangles in the front side and 5 triangles in the back side.

i.e., total 10 triangles

∴ Total number of triangles = 5 + 5 + 10 = 20

36. (*a*) Given figure can be labelled as follows,

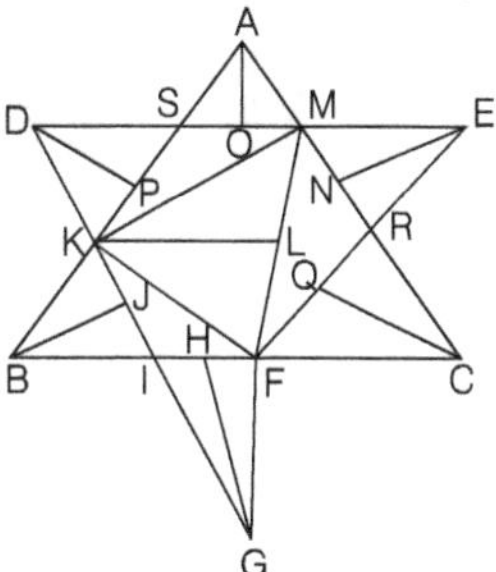

Single triangles = ΔASO, ΔAOM, ΔMEN, ΔENR, ΔQRC, ΔQCF, ΔFGH, ΔHGI, ΔIBJ, ΔBKJ, ΔDPK, ΔDPS, ΔSMK, ΔMFR, ΔFIK, ΔMKL, ΔKLF = 17

Triangles formed with two triangles

= Δ ASM, ΔMER, ΔRCF,ΔFGI, ΔIBK, ΔKDS, ΔMKF=7

Triangles formed with three triangles

= ΔAMK, ΔMEF, ΔMFC, ΔFGK, ΔKBF, ΔDKM = 6

Largest triangle = ΔABC = 1

∴ Total number of triangles = 17 + 7 + 6 + 1 = 31

CHAPTER / 08

Mirror Image

Mirror image is the image or the reflection of an object into a mirror when that object is placed near to or in front of it.

In case of standard form of mirror image i.e., when the mirror is placed vertically, the object gets laterally inverted. In other words, the Left Hand Side (LHS) and Right Hand Side (RHS) of the object interchange their places while top and bottom remain the same.

Let us see an example to get a better idea about the concept of mirror images

(i) (ii)

Here, fig. (ii) is the mirror image of fig. (i). On combining these two figures we get a triangle shaped which is symmetrical along an imaginary line which is used in place of the mirror.

Different types of questions which are asked in various exams, are as follows

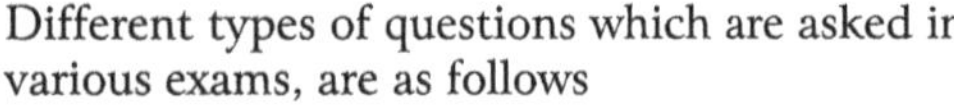

TYPE 01

Based on Vertical Mirror

In such questions, a vertical mirror is placed to the left or right of the object and standard form of mirror image is formed, where the Left Hand Side (LHS) and Right Hand Side (RHS) of the object interchange their places while top and bottom remain unchanged.

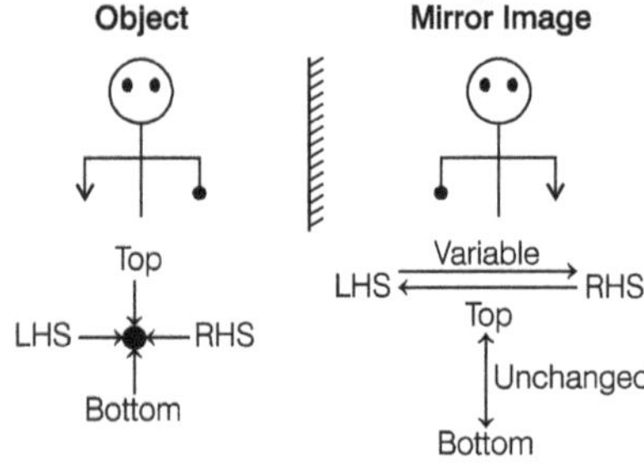

To get standard form of mirror image, the mirror is placed vertically to the left or right of the object and in both the cases, the image obtained is same.

Case I When the mirror is placed vertically to the right of the object

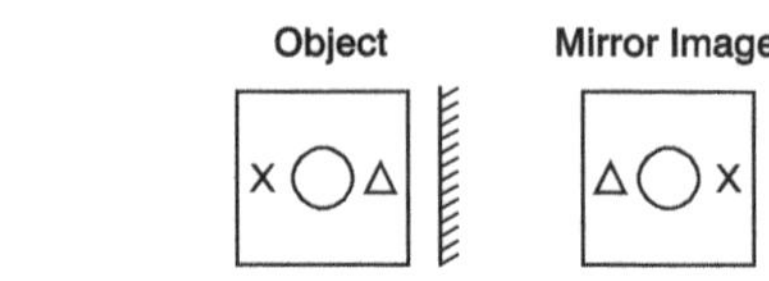

Case II When the mirror is placed vertically to the left of the object

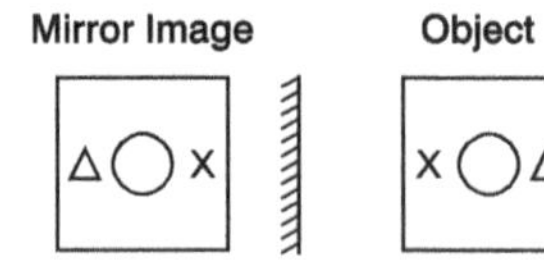

Note *In mirror image, if the position of mirror is not given, then always consider mirror to be placed vertically on right side. Also, the size of the mirror image of an object is similar to the original image of the object.*

You will get a better idea about the type of questions asked from the following examples.

DIRECTIONS ~ (Example Nos. 1-6) *In each of the following questions, choose the correct mirror image of the given figure from the four alternatives* (a), (b), (c) *and* (d), *when mirror is placed along the line* AB.

***Ex* 01**

Question Figure **Answer Figures**

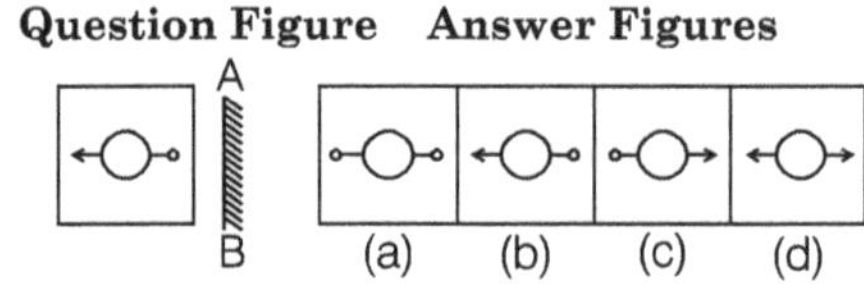

***Solution* (c)** Here, the mirror is placed vertically at AB on the RHS of the question figure. Hence, only the figure given in answer figure (c) will be obtained as the correct mirror image.

Ex 02 Question Figure Answer Figures

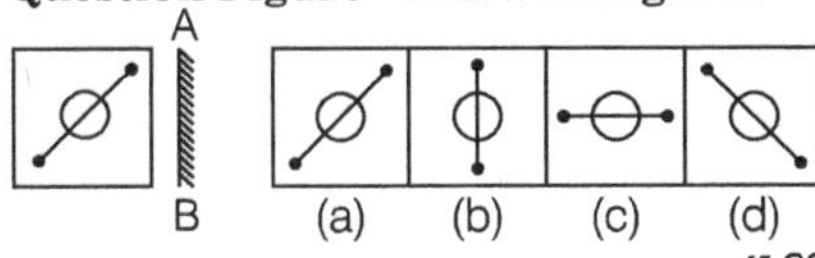

« SSC CPO 2009

Solution (d) Here, the mirror is placed vertically at AB on the RHS of the question figure. Hence, only the figure given in answer figure (d) will be obtained as the correct mirror image.

Ex 03 Question Figure Answer Figures

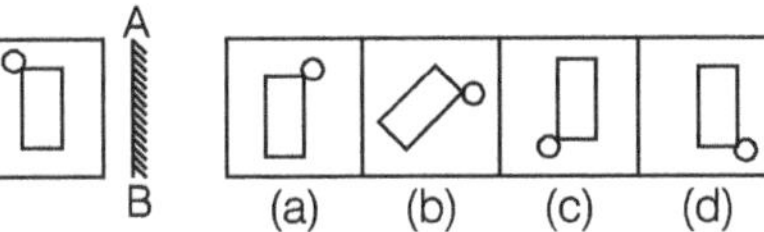

Solution (a) Here, the mirror is placed vertically at AB on the RHS of the question figure. Hence, only the figure given in answer figure (a) will be obtained as the correct mirror image.

Ex 04 Question Figure Answer Figures

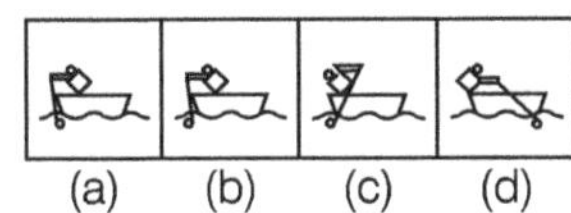

« SSC 10+2 2010

Solution (d) Here, the mirror is placed vertically at AB on the LHS of the question figure. Hence, only the figure given in answer figure (d) will be obtained as the correct mirror image.

Ex 05 Question Figure Answer Figures

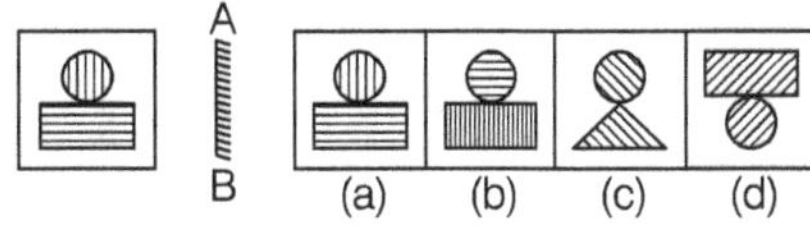

Solution (a) Here, the mirror is placed vertically at AB on the RHS of the question figure. Hence, only the figure given in answer figure (a) will be obtained as the correct mirror image.

Ex 06 Question Figure Answer Figures

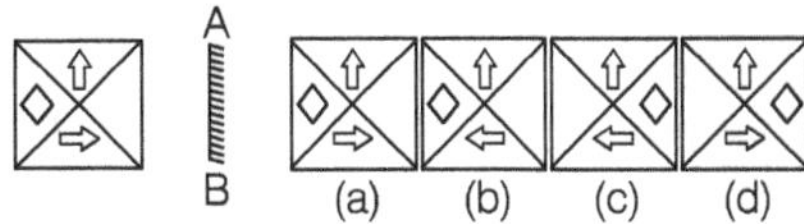

« SSC MTS 2019

Solution (c) Here, the mirror is placed vertically on the RHS of the question figure. Hence, only answer figure (c) will be obtained as the correct mirror image.

Practice CORNER 8.1

DIRECTIONS ~ (Q. Nos. 1-42) *In each of the following questions, choose the correct mirror image from the alternatives* (a), (b), (c) *and* (d), *when mirror is placed along the line* AB.

Question Figure Answer Figures

1.

(a) (b) (c) (d)

« SSC CGL 2019

2.

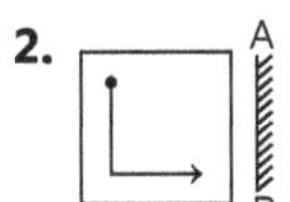

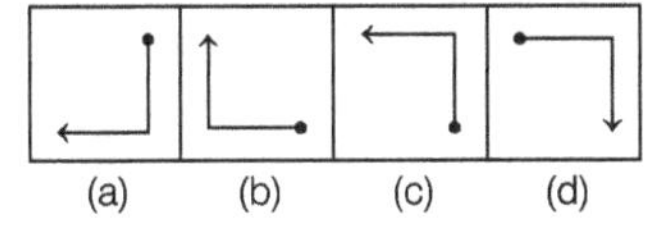

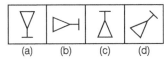

« SSC Constable 2015

3.

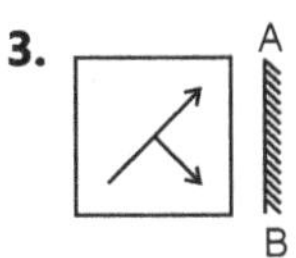

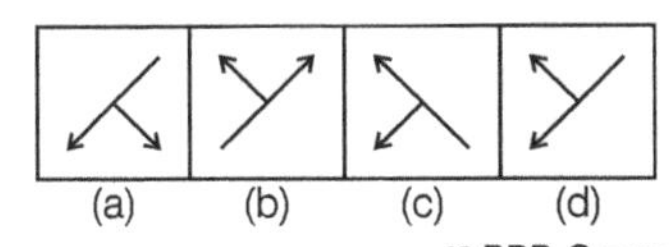

« RRB Group D 2018

Question Figure Answer Figures

4.

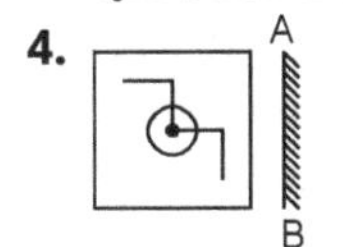

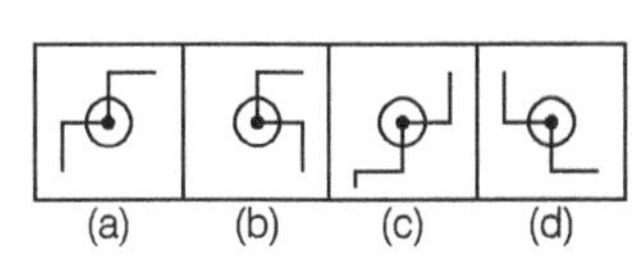

« RRB ALP 2018

5.

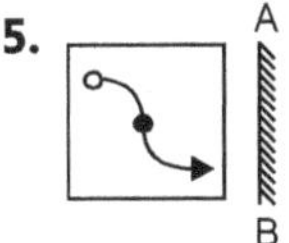

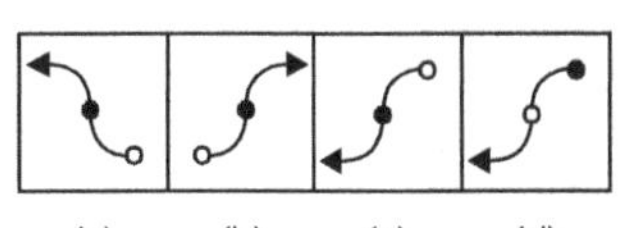

« FCI UK 2018

6.

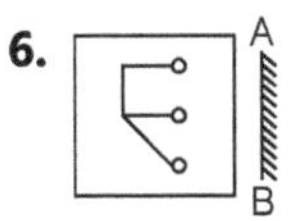

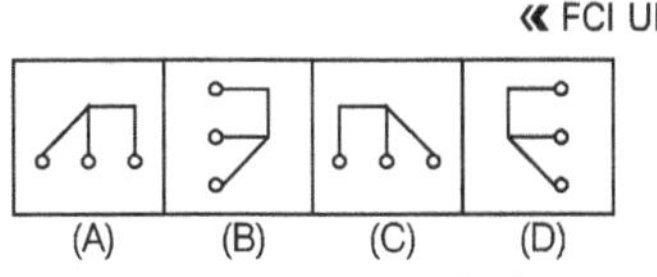

« RRB Group D 2018

(a) D (b) C (c) B (d) A

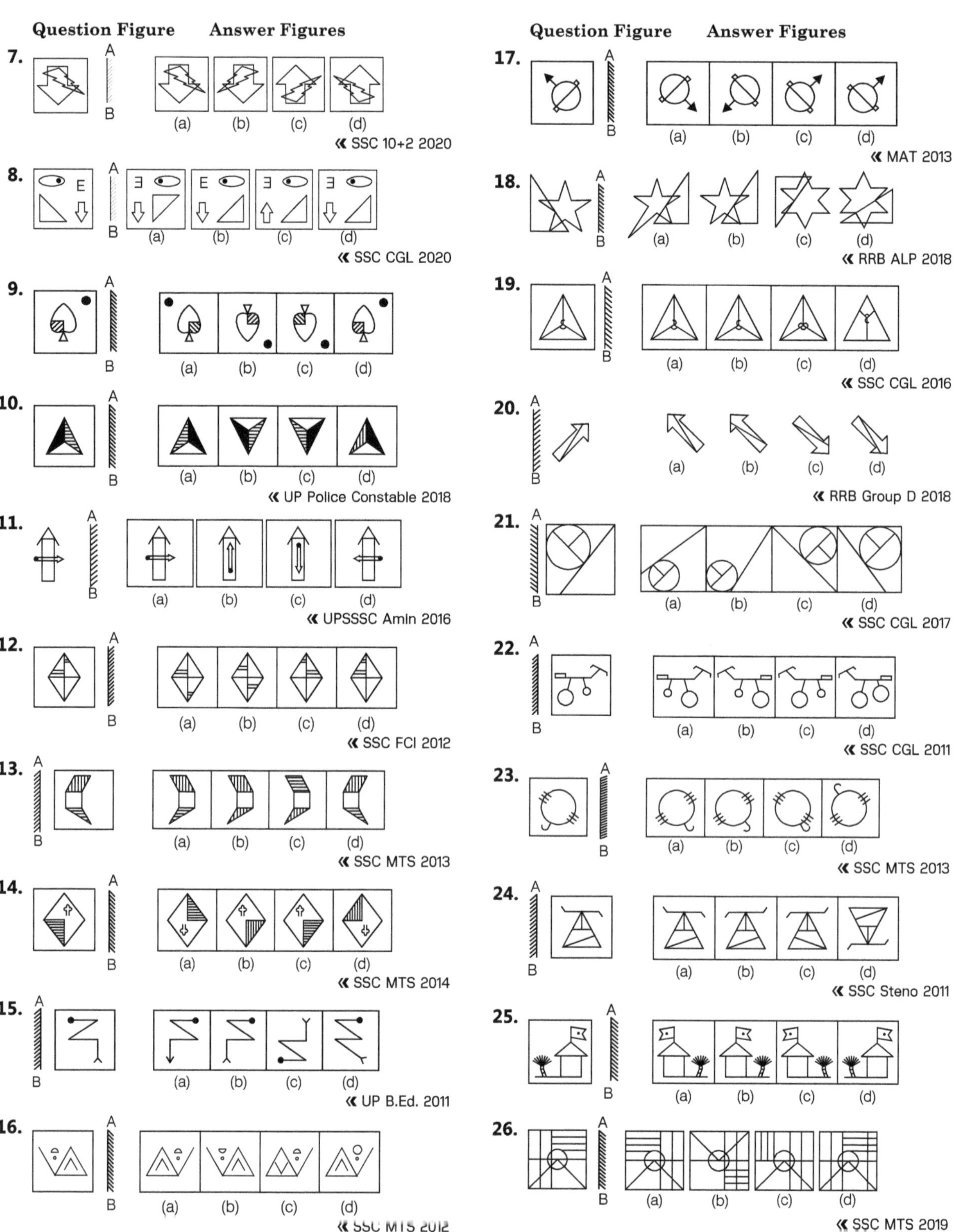
Question Figure
Answer Figures
7.
A
B
(a) (b) (c) (d)
« SSC 10+2 2020
8.
E
(a) (b) (c) (d)
« SSC CGL 2020
9.
(a) (b) (c) (d)
10.
(a) (b) (c) (d)
« UP Police Constable 2018
11.
(a) (b) (c) (d)
« UPSSSC Amin 2016
12.
(a) (b) (c) (d)
« SSC FCI 2012
13.
(a) (b) (c) (d)
« SSC MTS 2013
14.
(a) (b) (c) (d)
« SSC MTS 2014
15.
(a) (b) (c) (d)
« UP B.Ed. 2011
16.
(a) (b) (c) (d)
« SSC MTS 2012
Question Figure
Answer Figures
17.
(a) (b) (c) (d)
« MAT 2013
18.
(a) (b) (c) (d)
« RRB ALP 2018
19.
(a) (b) (c) (d)
« SSC CGL 2016
20.
(a) (b) (c) (d)
« RRB Group D 2018
21.
(a) (b) (c) (d)
« SSC CGL 2017
22.
(a) (b) (c) (d)
« SSC CGL 2011
23.
(a) (b) (c) (d)
« SSC MTS 2013
24.
(a) (b) (c) (d)
« SSC Steno 2011
25.
(a) (b) (c) (d)
26.
(a) (b) (c) (d)
« SSC MTS 2019

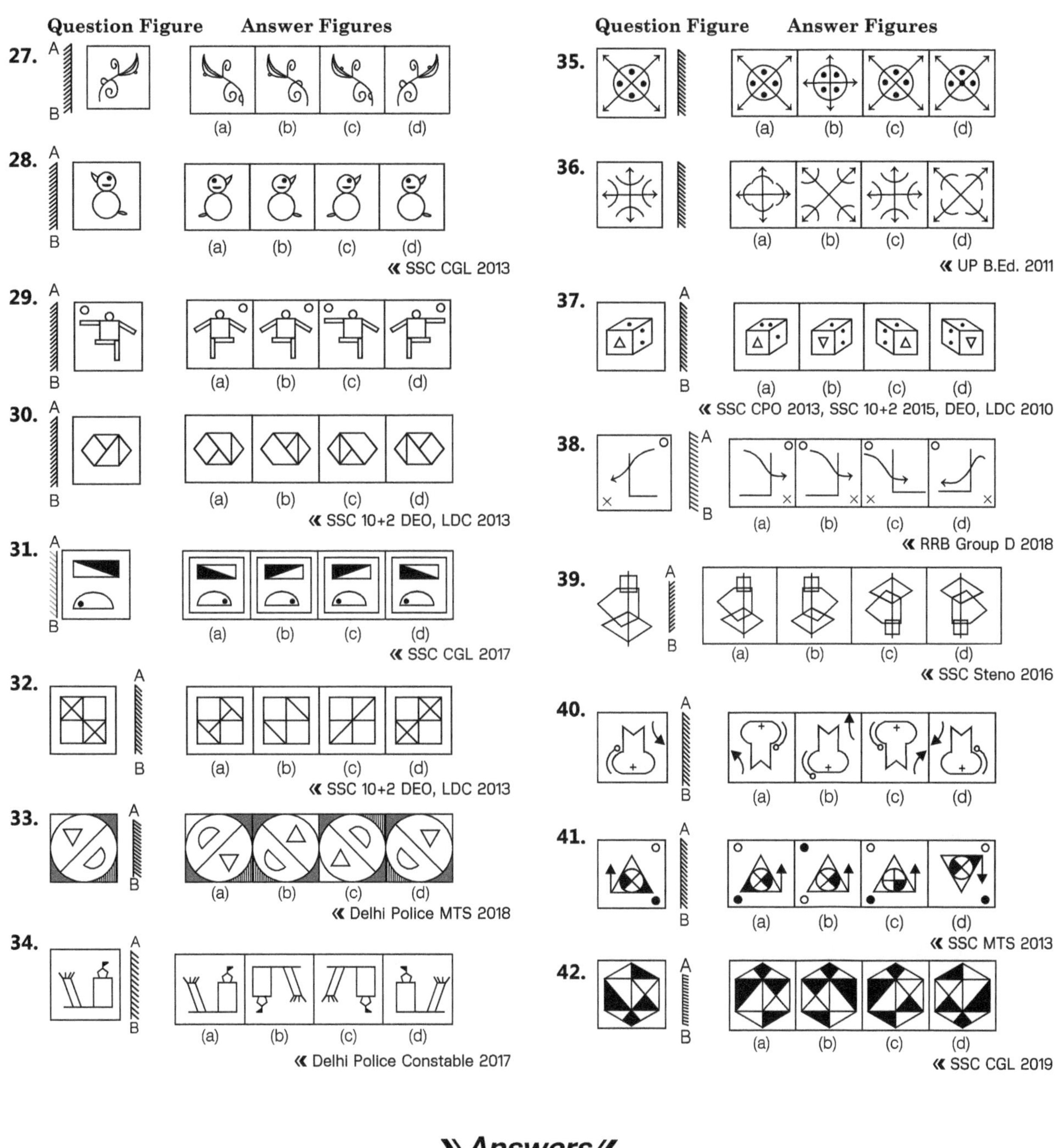

» Answers «

1. (b)	2. (a)	3. (c)	4. (a)	5. (c)	6. (c)	7. (b)	8. (d)	9. (a)	10. (a)
11. (d)	12. (c)	13. (a)	14. (c)	15. (b)	16. (a)	17. (c)	18. (b)	19. (a)	20. (a)
21. (d)	22. (b)	23. (a)	24. (c)	25. (a)	26. (a)	27. (b)	28. (a)	29. (d)	30. (d)
31. (b)	32. (d)	33. (d)	34. (d)	35. (a)	36. (c)	37. (c)	38. (b)	39. (b)	40. (d)
41. (a)	42. (d)								

TYPE 02

Based on Horizontal Mirror

In such questions, a horizontal mirror is placed at the top or at the bottom of the object and the image, so obtained is same as the water image. In this type of questions, LHS and RHS of the object remain unchanged while top and bottom of the object interchange their places.

Let us see the two cases as given below

Case I When mirror is placed horizontally at the top of the object

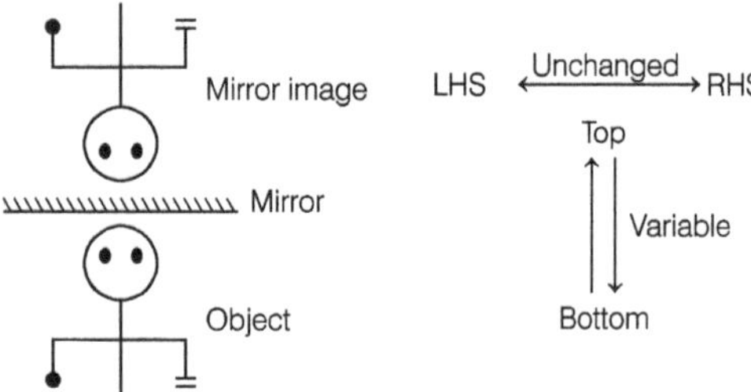

Case II When mirror is placed horizontally at the bottom of the object

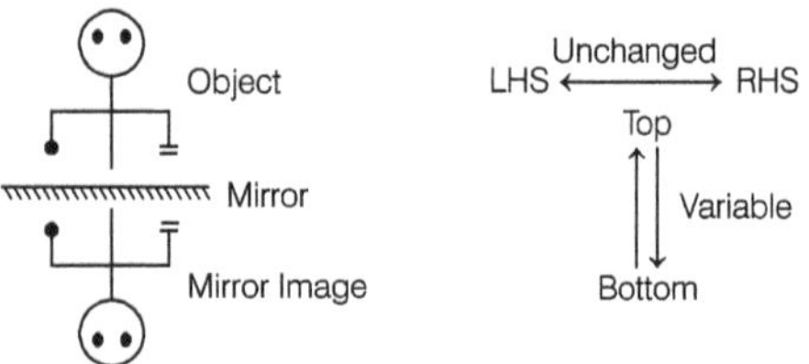

The following examples will give you a better idea about such type of questions

DIRECTIONS ~ (Example Nos. 7-9) *In each of the following questions, choose the correct mirror image from the alternatives* (a), (b), (c) *and* (d) *when mirror is placed along the line* AB.

Ex 07 **Question Figure** **Answer Figures**

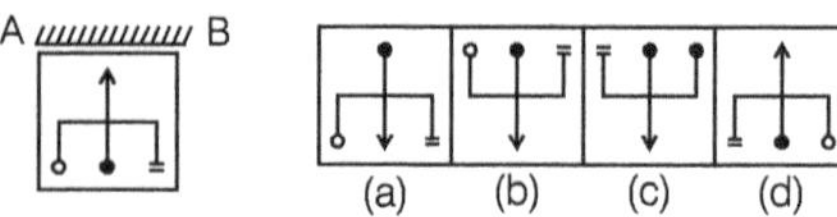

Solution (b) Here, the mirror is placed horizontally at AB on the top of the question figure. Hence, only answer figure (b) is the vertically inverted form of question figure in which top and bottom interchange places while LHS and RHS remain the same.

Ex 08 **Question Figure** **Answer Figures**

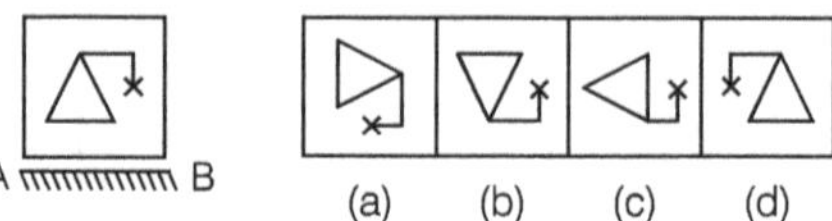

Solution (b) Here, the mirror is placed horizontally at AB on the bottom of the question figure. Hence, only answer figure (b) looks like the water image of the question figure. It means, option (b) is the vertically inverted form of question figure in which top and bottom interchange places while LHS and RHS remain the same.

Ex 09 **Question Figure** **Answer Figures**

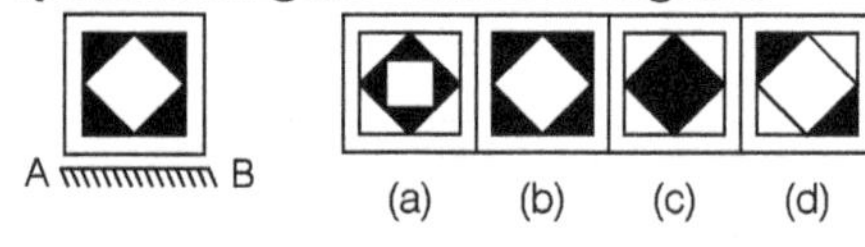

« SSC LDC & DEO 2009

Solution (b) Here, the mirror is placed horizontally at AB on the bottom of the question figure. Only answer figure (b) is the vertically inverted form of question figure in which top and bottom interchange places while LHS and RHS remain the same.

Practice CORNER 8.2

DIRECTIONS ~ (Q. Nos. 1-17) *In each of the following questions, choose the correct mirror image from the answer figures* (a), (b), (c) *and* (d), *when mirror is placed along the line* AB.

Question Figure **Answer Figures**

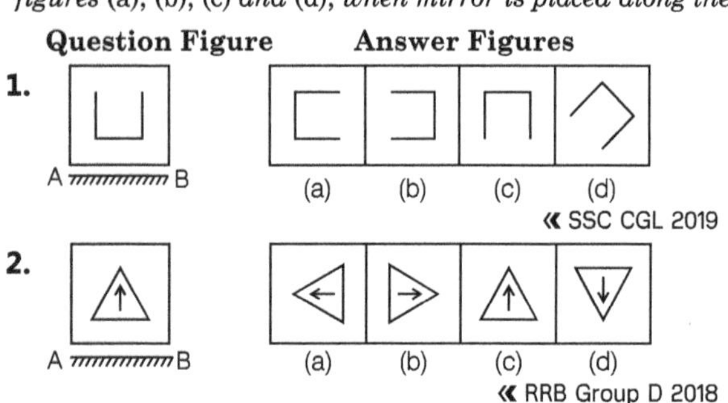

1. « SSC CGL 2019

2. « RRB Group D 2018

Question Figure **Answer Figures**

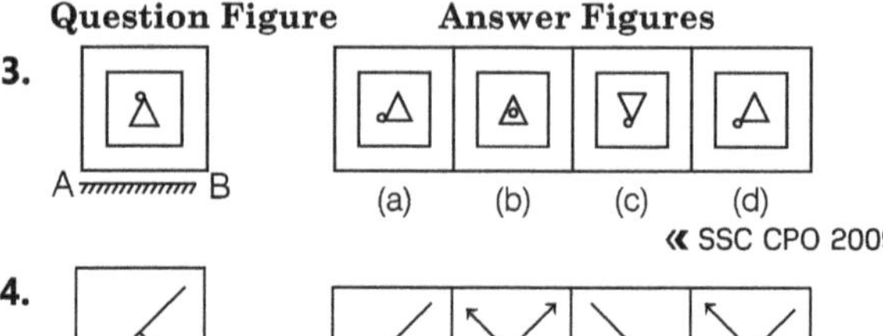

3. « SSC CPO 2009

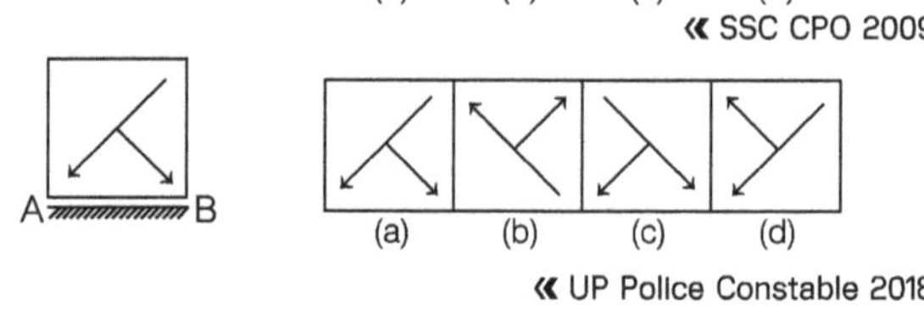

4. « UP Police Constable 2018

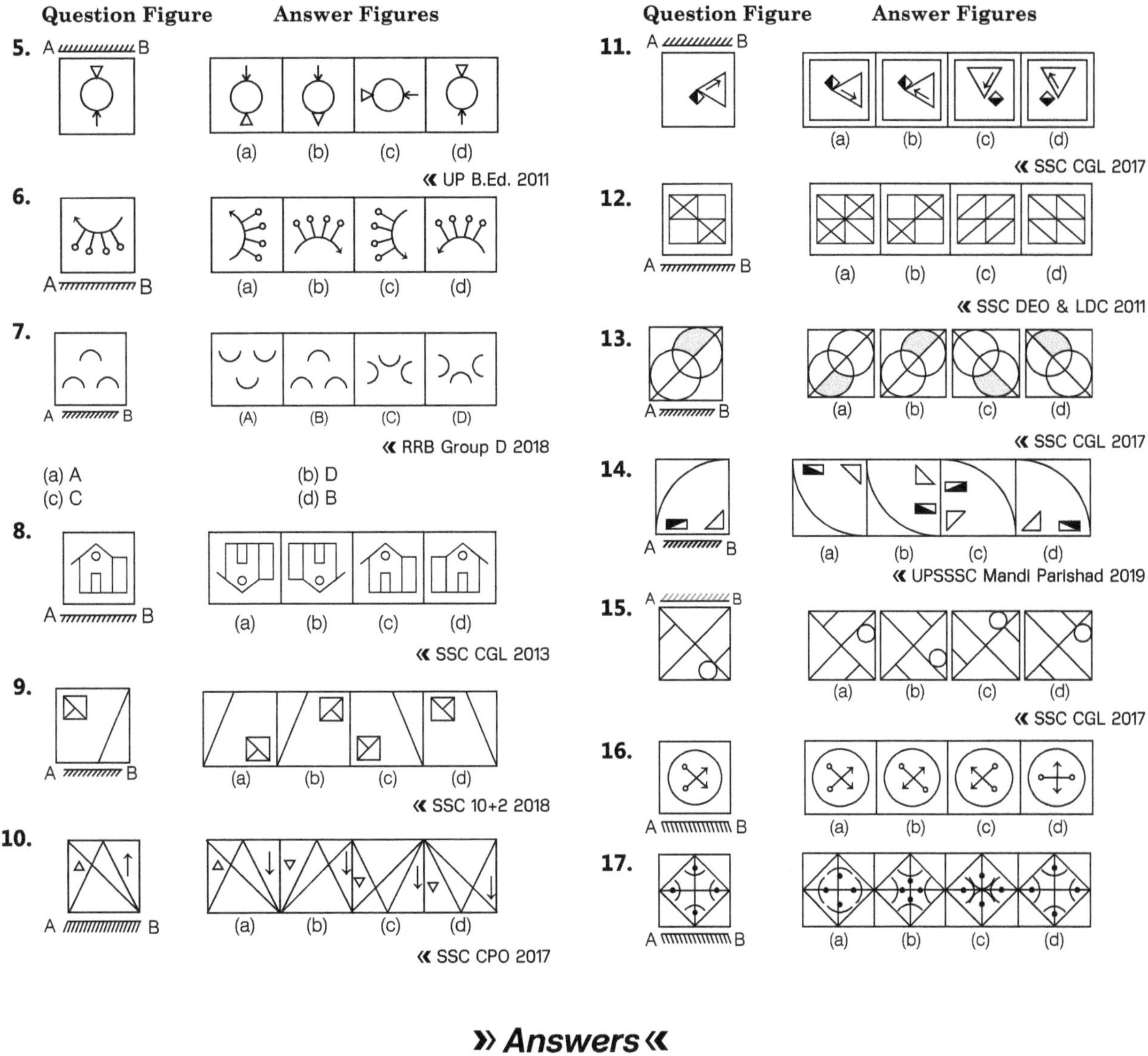

» Answers «

1. *(c)*	2. *(d)*	3. *(c)*	4. *(b)*	5. *(a)*	6. *(d)*	7. *(a)*	8. *(a)*	9. *(c)*	10. *(c)*
11. *(a)*	12. *(b)*	13. *(c)*	14. *(a)*	15. *(c)*	16. *(a)*	17. *(d)*			

TYPE 03

Mirror Image of Letters and Numbers

In such questions, a letter/number or a group of letters and/or numbers is given and the candidate is required to determine the mirror image of the letters and numbers according to the position of the mirror placed beside it.

The standard form of mirror image of letters and numbers 'in which the mirror is placed vertically' is given as below.

Mirror Images of Capital Letters

Letter	A	B	C	D	E	F	G	H	I	J	K	L	M
Mirror Image	A	ᗺ	Ɔ	ᗡ	Ǝ	ꟻ	Ꭾ	H	I	Ⴑ	ꓘ	⅃	M
Letter	N	O	P	Q	R	S	T	U	V	W	X	Y	Z
Mirror Image	И	O	ꟼ	Ϙ	Я	Ƨ	T	U	V	W	X	Y	Ƹ

- The capital letters which have the same mirror image are —
  A, H, I, M, O, T, U, V, W, X, Y

Mirror Images of Small Letters

Letter	a	b	c	d	e	f	g	h	i	j	k	l	m
Mirror Image	ɒ	d	ɔ	b	ɘ	ɟ	ǫ	ʜ	i	į	ʞ	l	m
Letter	n	o	p	q	r	s	t	u	v	w	x	y	z
Mirror Image	n	o	q	p	ɿ	ƨ	Ɉ	u	v	w	x	ʏ	ƹ

- The small letters which have the same mirror image are —
  i, l, o, v, w, x

Mirror Images of Numbers

Digit	1	2	3	4	5	6	7	8	9	0
Mirror Image	Ɩ	Ƨ	Ɛ	ᔭ	ट	ခ	Ꞁ	8	ɘ	0

- Numbers 0 and 8 have the same mirror image.

The following examples will give you a better idea about such type of questions

DIRECTIONS ~ (Example Nos. 10-14) *In each of the following questions, you are given a combination of letters and/or numbers followed by four alternatives* (a), (b), (c) *and* (d). *Choose the alternative which most closely resembles the mirror image (when mirror is placed vertically) of the given combination.*

***Ex* 10** FUN

(a) ИUF (b) ꟻUN (c) ИUꟻ (d) NUꟻ

***Solution* (c)** The correct mirror image is obtained as shown below

FUN | ИUꟻ

***Ex* 11** PRAYER

(a) ꟼЯAYƎЯ (b) ЯƎꟼAƎЯ (c) ЯƎYAЯꟼ (d) ꟼЯAYƎЯ

***Solution* (c)** The correct mirror image will be

PRAYER | ЯƎYAЯꟼ

***Ex* 12** 12698

(a) 1Ƨ698 (b) 8ɘခƧƖ (c) 12968 (d) 1Ƨ698

***Solution* (b)** The correct mirror image will be

12698 | 8ɘခƧƖ

***Ex* 13** R7MP « SSC CGL 2019

(a) ꟼMꞀЯ (b) ꟼM7Я (c) ЯꞀMꟼ (d) ꟼM7R

***Solution* (a)** The correct mirror image will be

R7MP | ꟼMꞀЯ

***Ex* 14** arihant

(a) ɒɿiʜɒnɈ (b) Ɉnɒniɿɒ (c) Ɉnʜ!ɿɒ (d) Ɉnɒʜiɿɒ

***Solution* (d)** The correct mirror image will be

arihant | Ɉnɒʜiɿɒ

DIRECTIONS ~ (Example Nos. 15 and 16) *In each of the following questions four alternatives are given. You have to select one alternative which exactly matches with the mirror image of the given word/combination of letters and numbers, when the mirror is placed horizontally at the bottom of the figure.*

***Ex* 15** TIGER

(a) ⊥IGEᗺ (b) ⊥I⅁Eᗺ (c) ITGEᗺ (d) ЯƎGIT

***Solution* (a)** The correct mirror image will be

TIGER
⊥IGEᗺ

***Ex* 16** boy29

(a) poʎƧ6 (b) poʎƧɘ (c) doʎƧɘ (d) poʎƧ6

***Solution* (d)** The correct mirror image will be

boy29
poʎƧ6

TYPE 04

Mirror Image of Clocks

In this type of questions, a candidate has to find the original positions of the hour hand and the minute hand of a clock from the positions of the hour hand and the minute hand as seen in a mirror. On the basis of time indicated by mirror image of the clock, we have to find the actual time in the clock.

These questions can also be solved by using the formula Actual time = 12 : 00 − Time in mirror.

The following examples will help you to understand the concept better.

***Ex* 17** A clock seen through a mirror shows quarter past three. What is the correct time shown by the clock?

(a) 9 : 45 (b) 9 : 15 (c) 8 : 45 (d) 3 : 15

***Solution* (c)**

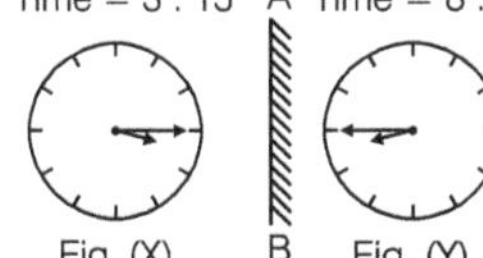

It is clear from figure (X) that if seen through a mirror the time indicated by clock is 3:15. When the mirror is placed vertically at AB, the mirror image *i.e.,* figure (Y) shows the actual time in the clock *i.e.,* (8 : 45).

Alternate method

Actual time = 12 : 00 – Time in mirror
= 12 : 00 – 3 : 15 = 8 : 45

***Ex* 18** A clock seen through a mirror shows quarter to three. What is the correct time shown by the clock?
(a) 8 : 15 (b) 9 : 12 (c) 8 : 17 (d) 9 : 15

***Solution* (d)**

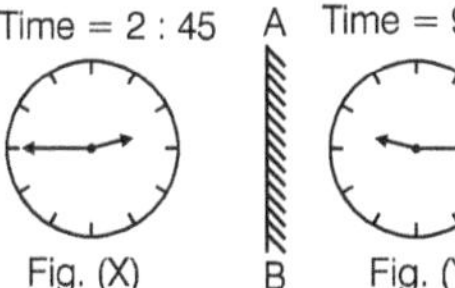

It is clear from figure (X) that if seen through a mirror the time indicated by clock is 2:45. When the mirror is placed vertically at AB, the mirror image *i.e.,* figure (Y) shows the actual time in the clock *i.e.,* (9 : 15).

Alternate method

Actual time = 12 : 00 –Time in mirror
= 12 : 00 – 2 : 45 = 9 : 15

Note *In case of words, letters and clocks, the mirror is always kept in standard form i.e., vertically to obtain the mirror image unless otherwise stated.*

Practice / CORNER 8.3

DIRECTIONS ~ (Q. Nos. 1-20) *In each of the following question, four alternatives are given. You have to select one alternative which exactly matches with the mirror image of the given word/number/combination of letters and numbers in the question when the mirror is placed vertically at the right of the given figure.*

1. SOLVED « SSC Steno 2019
(a) ᗡƎV⅃OƧ (b) ᗡƎ⅃VOS (c) ᗡƎVJOƧ (d) ᗡƎ⅃AOƧ

2. ARIHANT
(a) TͶAHIЯA (b) TNAHIRA (c) TARIHAN (d) AЯIHAͶT

3. INSOMNIA « SSC Constable 2019
(a) AIͶMOSͶI (b) AIͶMOƧNI (c) IͶƧOWͶIA (d) IͶƧOWͶIA

4. NIRMALA
(a) ALAMRIN (b) AJAMЯIͶ (c) NRILAMA (d) NIRMALA

5. FANTASY
(a) YƧATͶAꟻ (b) ꟻAͶTAƧY (c) YSATNAF (d) ꟻANTAƧY

6. RADIANT
(a) TͶAIDAЯ (b) TNAIDAЯ (c) TNAIDAR (d) TͶAIDAЯ

7. VINAYAKA
(a) VIͶAYAKA (b) AKAYANIV (c) AꓘAYAͶIV (d) AKAYAͶIV

8. FROWNING
(a) ᘜИIИWOЯꟻ (b) ᘜИIИWORꟻ (c) ᘜИIИMORꟻ (d) ᘜИIИMOЯꟻ

9. Alliance « SSC Steno 2019
(a) ɘɔnɐillA (b) ɘɔnɐillA (c) ɘɔnɐillA (d) ɘɔnɐillA

10. 13579 « SSC Steno 2019
(a) ⅃3ƧՐ9 (b) 9Ր5Ɛ⅃ (c) 9ՐƧƐ⅃ (d) ⅃ƐƧՐ9

11. 02468 « SSC Steno 2019
(a) 86ᔭS0 (b) 86ᔭ20 (c) 02ᔭ68 (d) 0Sᔭ68

12. 4291255 « UP B.Ed 2013
(a) ƧƧƨ1ϱƨᔭ (b) 55219ƨᔭ (c) 5ƧƨƐ924 (d) ƧƧ21924

13. 247596 « UP B.Ed 2015
(a) ƧƖƐϱƧᔭ (b) 21ϱƐᔭƧ (c) 21ϱƐᔭƧ (d) ∂ϱƧՐᔭƧ

14. 481988 «
(a) ᔭ81ϱ88 (b) 88ϱ18ᔭ (c) 88ϱ⅃8ᔭ (d) 88168ᔭ

15. DL3N469F
(a) DL3469FN (b) ꟻϱ6ᔭИƐ⅃ᗡ (c) ꟻ96ᔭИƐ⅃ᗡ (d) F964N3DL

16. KALINGA261B
(a) B162AGNILAK (b) 8ƖƐƧAᘜИI⅃Aꓘ (c) KAΓIИGA2ƏƖB (d) 8ƖϱƧAᘜИI⅃Aꓘ

17. graph « RRB GG 2015
(a) hparg (b) hqɒɿg (c) ɥqarg (d) ɥqɒɿϱ

18. investment « SSC 10+2 2015
(a) tnɘmtƨɘvni (b) tnɘmtƨɘvni (c) tnɘmtƨɘvni (d) tnɘmtsevni

19. between « SSC CGL 2015
(a) nɘɘwtɘd (b) neewtɘd (c) nɘɘwteb (d) nɘɘwtɘb

20. CAR27aug
(a) ɓuɒ72ЯAƆ (b) ɓuɒ72ЯAƆ (c) guaCAR27 (d) gua72RAC

DIRECTIONS ~ (Q. Nos. 21-25) *In each of the following questions four alternatives are given. You have to select one alternative which exactly matches with the mirror image of the given word/number/combination of letters and numbers, when the mirror is placed horizontally at the bottom of the figure.*

21. BOSTON
(a) BOƧꓕOИ (b) ꓭOSTOИ (c) ꓭOƧTOИ (d) BOƧTOИ

22. JACKAL
(a) ⅂ACKA⅃ (b) ⅂ⱯCKⱯ⅂ (c) JⱯCKⱯ⅃ (d) JⱯCKⱯ⅂

23. TOWN38
(a) TOMИ8Ɛ (b) ꓕOWN38 (c) ꓕOMИ38 (d) TOMИ8Ɛ

24. folm27
(a) folɯ7ㄥ (b) ɟolɯ7ㄥ (c) folm27 (d) ɟolɯS⅂

25. BOX78
(a) BOX⅂8 (b) BOX78 (c) ꓭOX87 (d) ꓭOX78

26. Looking into a mirror, the clock shows 9 : 30 as the time. The actual time is
(a) 2 : 30 (b) 3 : 30 (c) 4 : 30 (d) 6 : 30

27. When seen through a mirror, a clock shows 8 : 30. The correct time is
(a) 2 : 30 (b) 3 : 30
(c) 5 : 30 (d) 8 : 30

28. By looking in a mirror, it appears that it is 6 : 30 in the clock. What is the real time?
(a) 6 : 30 (b) 5 : 30
(c) 6 : 00 (d) 4 : 30

29. When seen through a mirror, a watch shows 12 : 15. The correct time is
(a) 12 : 30 (b) 1 : 15 (c) 12 : 45 (d) 11 : 45

30. Looking into a mirror, the clock shows 12 : 30 as the time. The actual time is
(a) 12 : 30 (b) 9 : 30 (c) 11 : 30 (d) 1 : 30

» Answers «

1. (c)	2. (a)	3. (b)	4. (b)	5. (a)	6. (b)	7. (c)	8. (a)	9. (d)	10. (c)
11. (a)	12. (a)	13. (d)	14. (b)	15. (b)	16. (d)	17. (d)	18. (a)	19. (a)	20. (b)
21. (a)	22. (b)	23. (c)	24. (d)	25. (a)	26. (a)	27. (b)	28. (b)	29. (d)	30. (c)

Answers / WITH EXPLANATIONS

26. *(a)* Time = 9 : 30 A Time = 2 : 30

Fig. (X) B Fig. (Y)

It is clear from figure (X) that if seen through a mirror, the time indicated by clock is 9 : 30. When the mirror is placed vertically at AB, its mirror image *i.e.,* figure (Y) shows the actual time in the clock *i.e.,* 2 : 30.

Alternate Method

Actual time = 12:00 –Time in mirror = 12:00 – 9 : 30 = 2 : 30

27. *(b)* Time = 8 : 30 A Time = 3 : 30

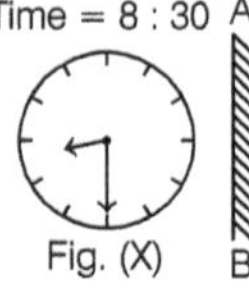
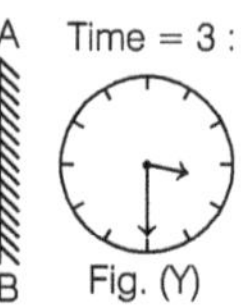

Fig. (X) B Fig. (Y)

It is clear from figure (X) that if seen through a mirror, the time indicated by clock is 8 : 30. When the mirror is placed vertically at AB, its mirror image *i.e.,* figure (Y) shows the actual time in the clock *i.e.,* 3 : 30.

Alternate Method

Actual time = 12:00 –Time in mirror = 12 : 00 – 8 : 30 = 3 : 30

28. *(b)* Time = 6 : 30 A Time = 5 : 30

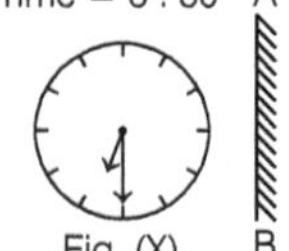

Fig. (X) B Fig. (Y)

It is clear from figure (X) that if seen through a mirror, the time indicated by the clock is 6 : 30. When the mirror is placed vertically at AB, its mirror image *i.e.,* figure (Y) shows the actual time in the clock *i.e.,* 5 : 30.

Alternate Method

Actual time = 12 : 00 –Time in mirror = 12 : 00 – 6 : 30 = 5 : 30

29. *(d)* Time = 12 : 15 A Time = 11 : 45

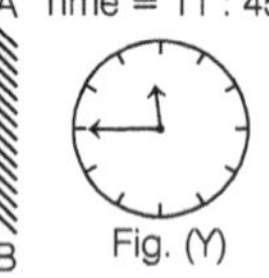

Fig. (X) B Fig. (Y)

It is clear from figure (X) that if seen through a mirror, the time indicated by clock is 12 : 15. When the mirror is placed vertically at AB, its mirror image *i.e.,* figure (Y) shows the actual time in the clock figure *i.e.,* 11 : 45.

Alternate Method

Actual time = 12 : 00 –Time in mirror = 12 : 00 –12 :15
= 12 : 00 –00 : 15= 11 : 45

30. *(c)* Time = 12 : 30 A Time = 11 : 30

Fig. (X) B Fig. (Y)

It is clear from figure (X) that if seen through a mirror, the time indicated by clock is 12 : 30. When the mirror is placed vertically at AB, its mirror image *i.e.,* figure (Y) shows the actual time in the clock *i.e.,* 11 : 30.

Alternate Method

Actual time = 12 : 00 – Time in mirror
= 12 : 00 – 12 : 30 or 12 : 00 – 00 : 30 = 11 : 30

Master Exercise

DIRECTIONS ~ (Q.Nos. 1-20) *In each of the following questions, choose the correct mirror image from the alternatives* (a), (b), (c) *and* (d), *when mirror is placed along the line* AB.

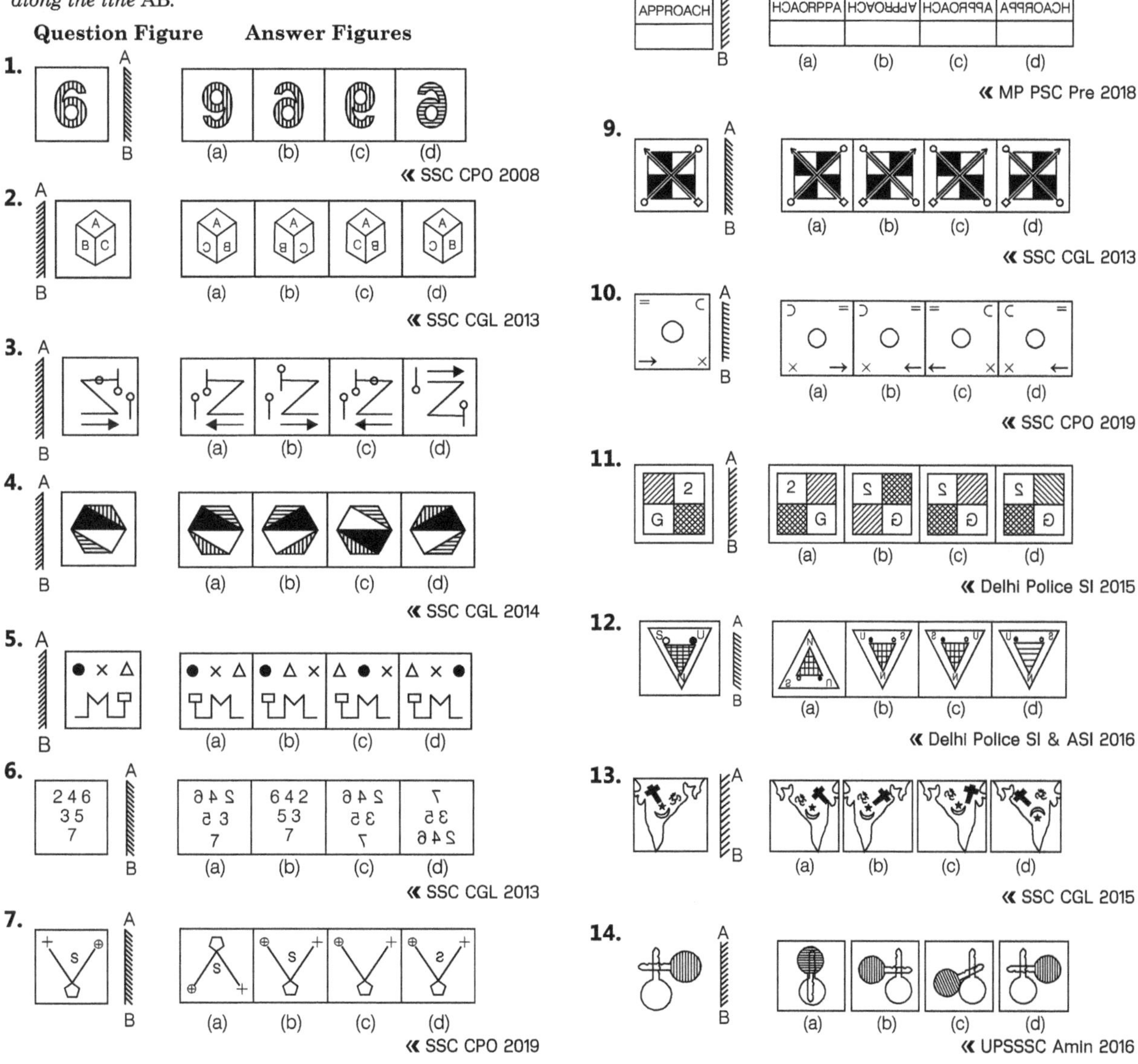

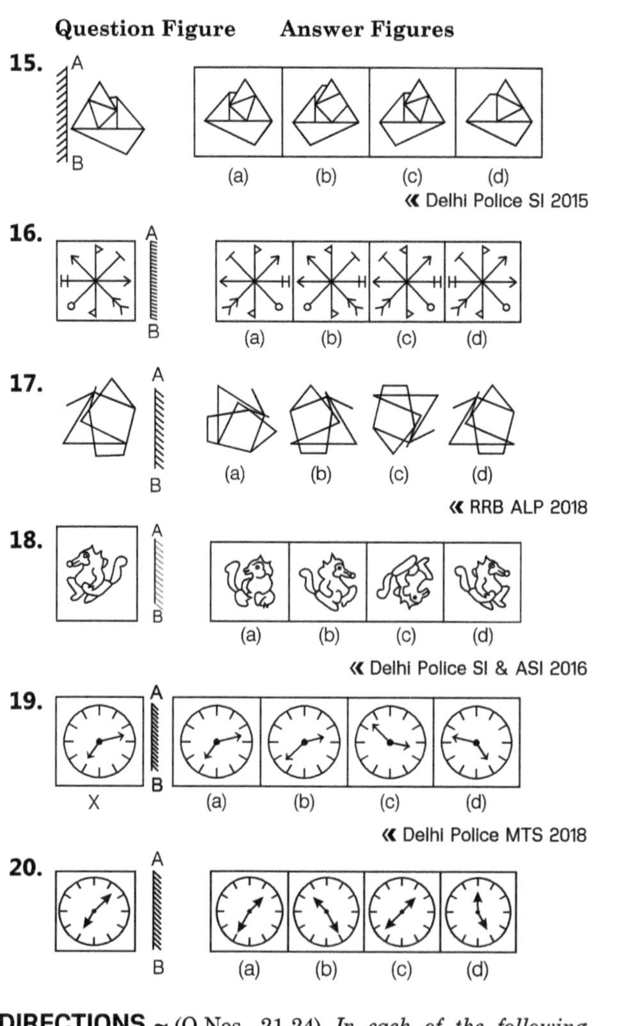

DIRECTIONS ~ (Q.Nos. 21-24) *In each of the following questions, choose the correct mirror image from the answer figure* (a), (b), (c) *and* (d), *when mirror is placed along the line* AB.

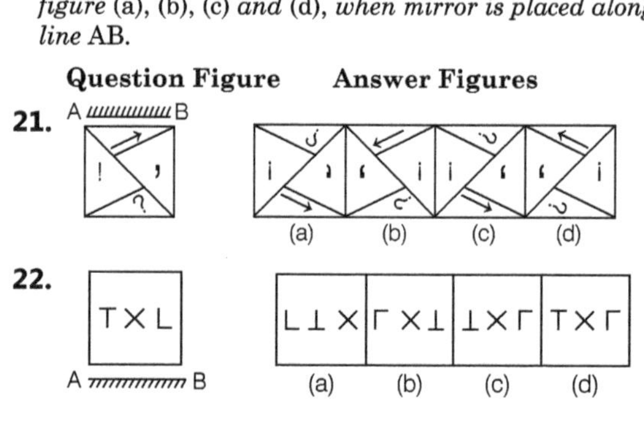

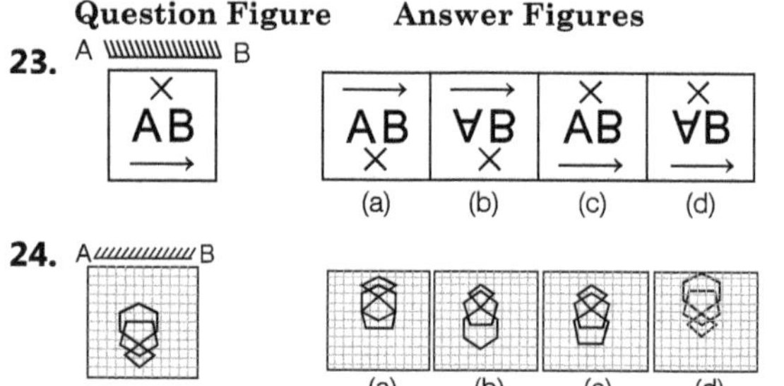

« SSC CGL 2017

25. If the given image is rotated 90° counter-clockwise and its mirror image is taken, with the mirror placed at the base of the image, the resultant structure will be

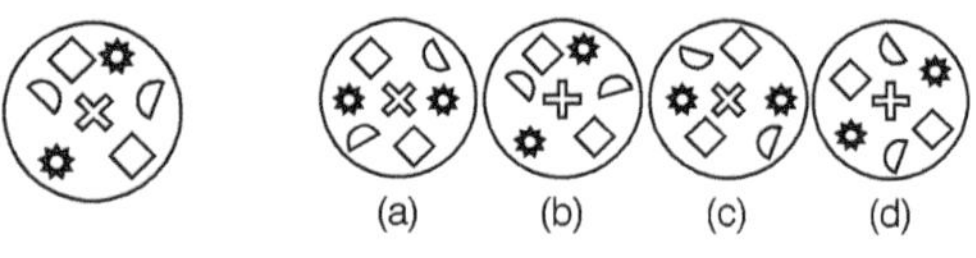

« UPSSSC VDO 2018

DIRECTIONS ~ (Q.Nos. 26-33) *In each of the following questions, four alternatives are given. You have to select one alternative which exactly matches with the mirror image of the given word/number/combination of letters and numbers in the question when the mirror is placed vertically at the right of the given figure.*

26. PRECARIOUS

(a) ƧUOIЯAƆƎЯԳ (b) SUOIRACERP
(c) SUOPRECARI (d) SPRECARIOU

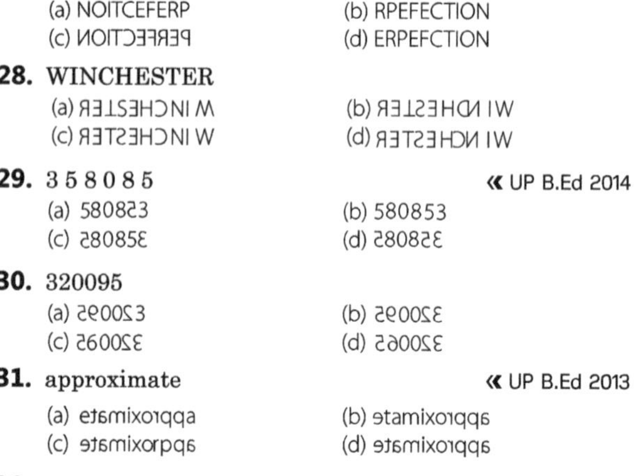

27. PERFECTION

(a) NOITCEFERP (b) RPEFECTION
(c) ИOITƆƎꟻЯƎԳ (d) ERPEFCTION

28. WINCHESTER

(a) ЯƎTƧƎHƆИIW (b) ЯƎTƧƎHƆИIW
(c) ЯƎTƧƎHƆИIW (d) ЯƎTƧƎHƆИIW

29. 3 5 8 0 8 5 « UP B.Ed 2014

(a) 58082Ɛ (b) 580853
(c) ƨ8085Ɛ (d) ƨ8082Ɛ

30. 320095

(a) ƨ900ƨ3 (b) ƨ900ƨƐ
(c) ƨ600ƨƐ (d) ƨ900ƨƐ

31. approximate « UP B.Ed 2013

(a) etamixorqqa (b) ɘtamixorqqɒ
(c) ɘtɒmixorpqɒ (d) ɘtɒmixorqqɒ

32. test5auto

(a) otuɒ5tset (b) otua5tset
(c) tset5uato (d) otuɒ5tset

33. NU56p7uR

(a) Ru7P65uN (b) RNu56p7u
(c) ЯuΓqƎƧUИ (d) ИuƧƎqΓuЯ

34. How many capital letters of English Alphabet appears same when seen through a mirror?

« UPSSSC Excise Constable 2016

(a) 9 (b) 10 (c) 11 (d) 12

35. When seen through a mirror, a watch shows 8 : 45. The correct time is

(a) 4 : 45 (b) 4 : 15
(c) 3 : 45 (d) 3 : 15

36. When seen through a mirror, a watch shows 5 : 15. The correct time is

(a) 6 : 15 (b) 7 : 15
(c) 6 : 45 (d) 7 : 45

» Answers «

1. (b)	2. (a)	3. (c)	4. (d)	5. (d)	6. (c)	7. (d)	8. (c)	9. (d)	10. (b)
11. (d)	12. (b)	13. (c)	14. (b)	15. (c)	16. (c)	17. (b)	18. (d)	19. (d)	20. (b)
21. (a)	22. (c)	23. (b)	24. (b)	25. (d)	26. (a)	27. (c)	28. (d)	29. (d)	30. (b)
31. (d)	32. (a)	33. (c)	34. (c)	35. (d)	36. (c)				

Answers WITH EXPLANATIONS

35. (d) Time = 8 : 45 A Time = 3 : 15

Fig. (X) B Fig. (Y)

It is clear from figure (X) that if seen through a mirror, the time indicated by clock is 8 : 45. When the mirror is placed vertically at AB, its mirror image *i.e.*, figure (Y) shows the actual time in the clock *i.e.*, 3 : 15.

Alternate Method

Actual time = 12 : 00 – Time in mirror
= 12 : 00 – 8 : 45 = 3 : 15

36. (c) Time = 5 : 15 A Time = 6 : 45

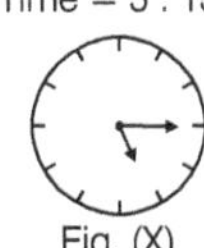

Fig. (X) B Fig. (Y)

It is clear from figure (X) that if seen through a mirror, the time indicated by clock is 5 : 15. When the mirror is placed vertically at AB, its mirror image *i.e.*, figure (Y) shows the actual time in the clock *i.e.*, 6 : 45.

Alternate Method

Actual time = 12 : 00 – Time in mirror
= 12 : 00 – 5 : 15 = 6 : 45

CHAPTER / 09

Water Image

The image formed by reflection of an object in water is called its water image. It is the vertically inverted form of the given object. The water image of the figure looks like its mirror image when the mirror is placed horizontally at its bottom.

Mostly the water image of a figure is different from the original figure which is because of the dissimilarity in the upper and lower half of the figure.

This can be better understood with the help of several different water images of figures which are given below

Example of water images which are different from their figures

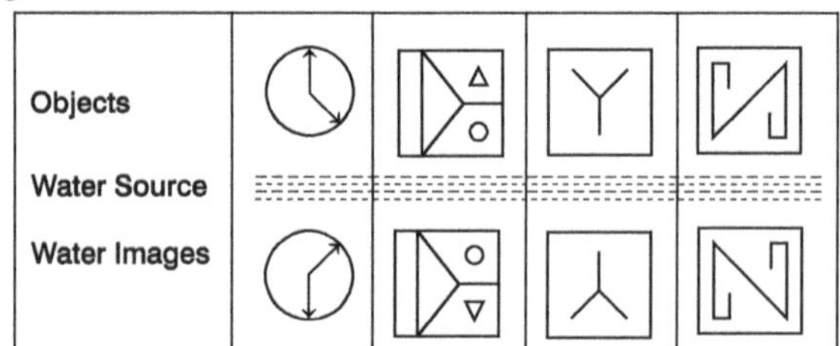

Sometimes the water image of figure is identical to the original figure. This is the case when the upper half of the figure is similar to the lower half of the figure but in opposite direction.

This can be better understood with the help of several identical water images of figures which are given below

Example of water images which are identical to their figures

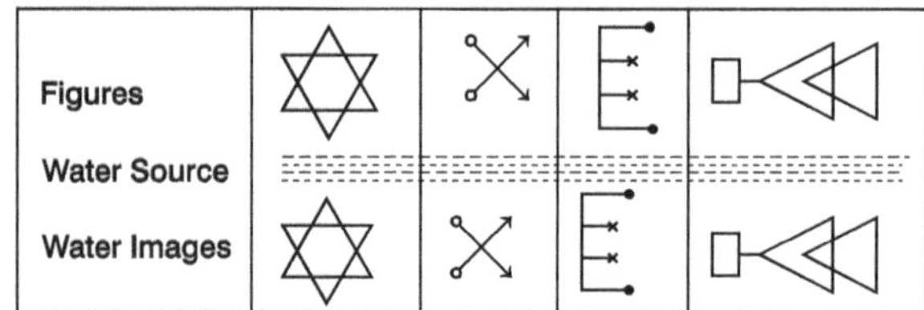

From the given examples, it is clear that in the water image, (LHS) and (RHS) remain unchanged while upper and lower parts get interchanged which means top becomes bottom and bottom becomes top.

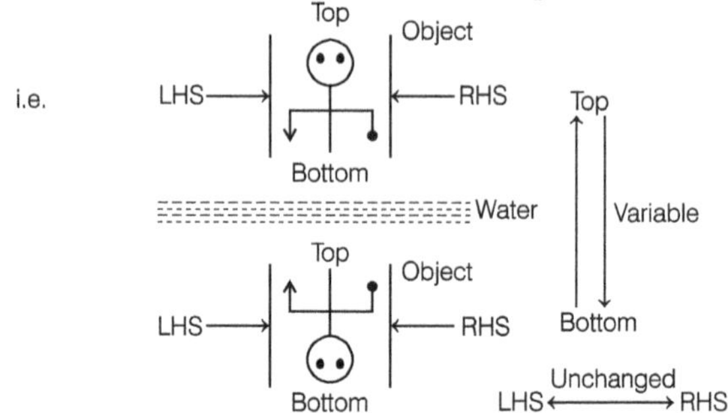

Different types of questions asked from this chapter are as follows

TYPE 01

Water Image of Figure/Symbol/Sign

In this type of questions, candidates are asked to find the water image of symbols, signs, figures, their combinations or any other pattern.

The following examples will give a better idea of the questions asked in exams.

DIRECTIONS ~ (Example Nos. 1-7) *Find the water image of the object given in the question figure denoted by* (A), *out of the figures given in the answer choices,* (a), (b), (c) *and* (d).

***Ex* 01** **Question Figure** **Answer Figures**

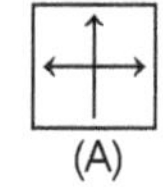
(A)

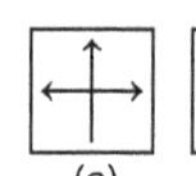
(a)

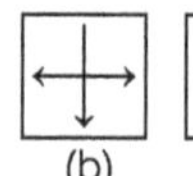
(b)

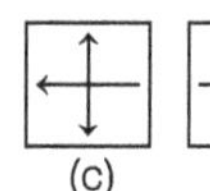
(c)

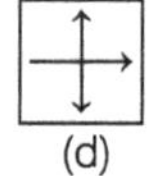
(d)

Solution (b) The figure in option (b) represents the correct water image of figure (A) as shown below

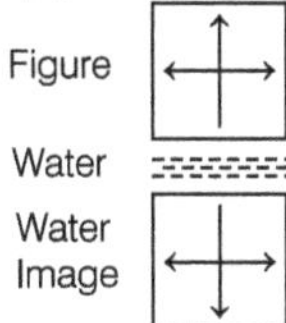

Ex 02 **Question Figure** **Answer Figures**

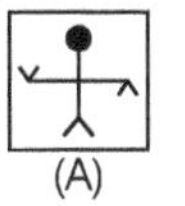

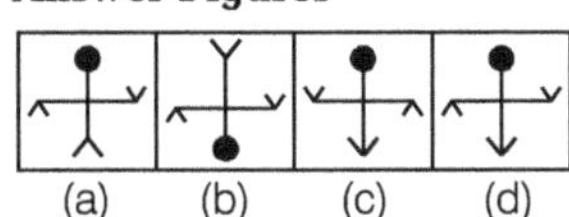

Solution (b) The figure in option (b) represents the correct water image of figure (A) as shown below

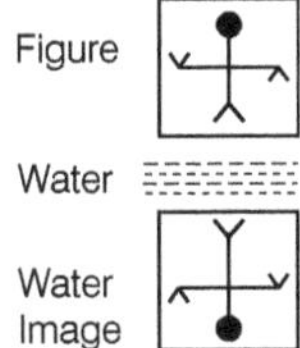

Ex 03 **Question Figure** **Answer Figures**

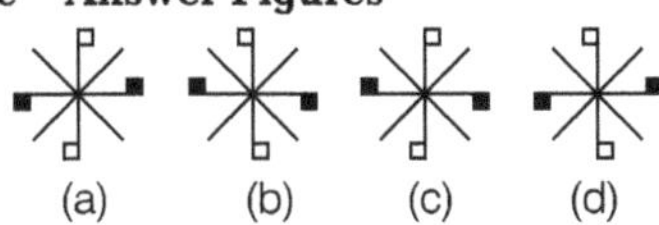

Solution (b) The figure in option (b) represents the correct water image of figure (A) as shown below

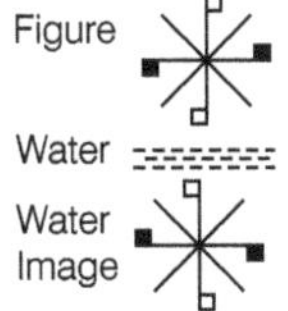

Ex 04 **Question Figure** **Answer Figures**

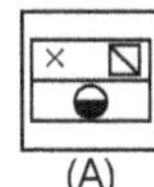

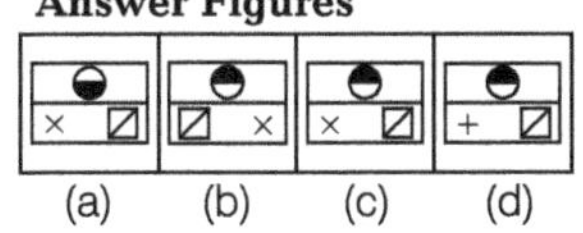

Solution (c) The figure in option (c) represents the correct water image of figure (A) as shown below

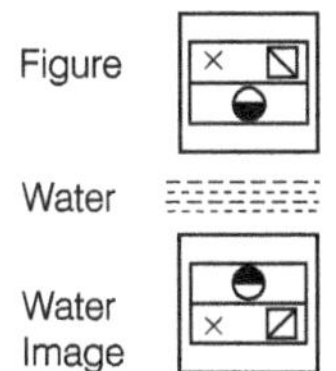

Ex 05 **Question Figure** **Answer Figures**

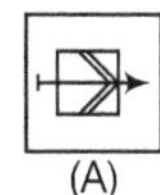

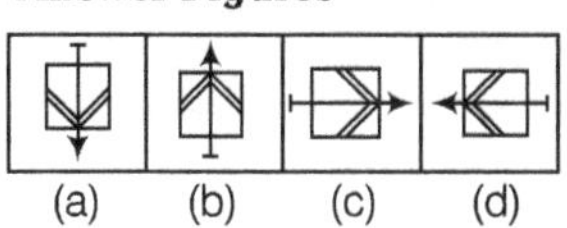

Solution (c) The figure in option (c) represents the correct water image of figure (A) as shown below

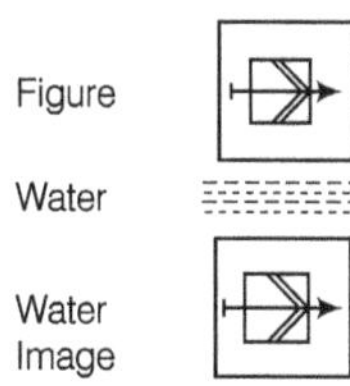

Ex 06 **Question Figure** **Answer Figures**

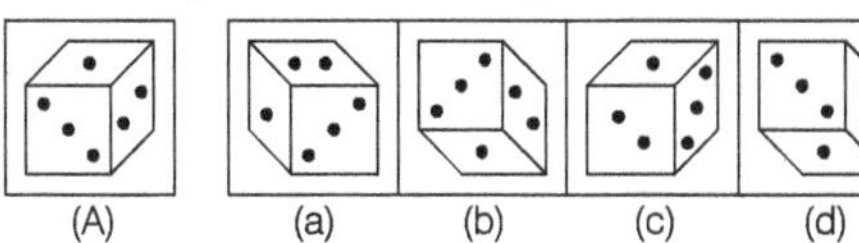

Solution (b) The figure in option (b) represents the correct water image of figure (A) as shown below

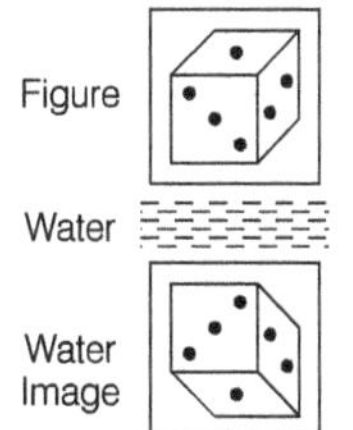

Ex 07 **Question Figure** **Answer Figures**

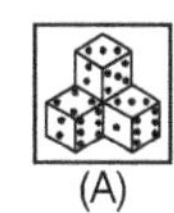

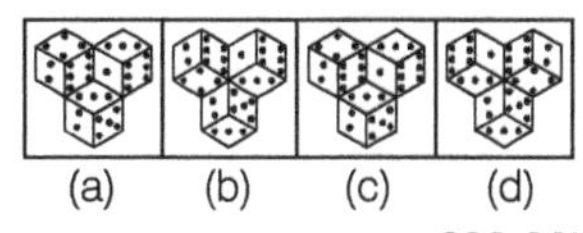

« SSC CGL 2010

Solution (b) The figure in option (b) represents the correct water image of figure (A) as shown below

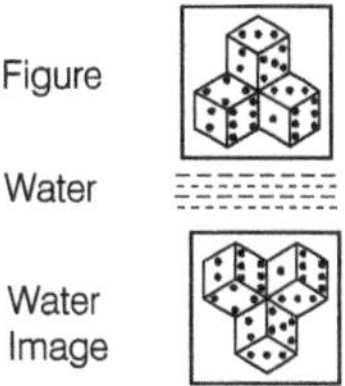

Practice CORNER 9.1

DIRECTIONS ~ (Q. Nos. 1-35) *Find the water image of the object given in the question figure denoted by (A) out of the figures given in the answer figures* (a), (b), (c) *and* (d).

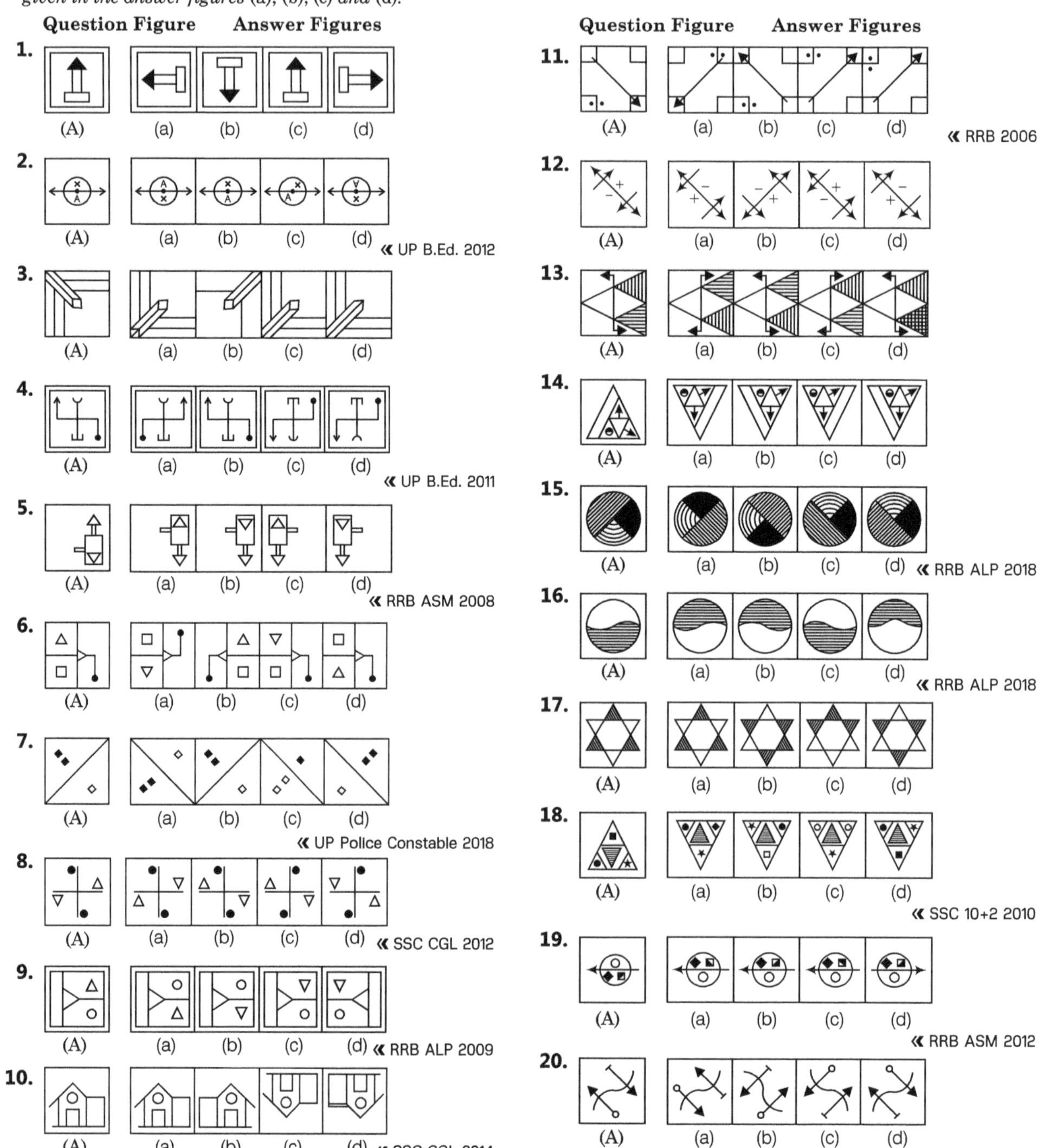

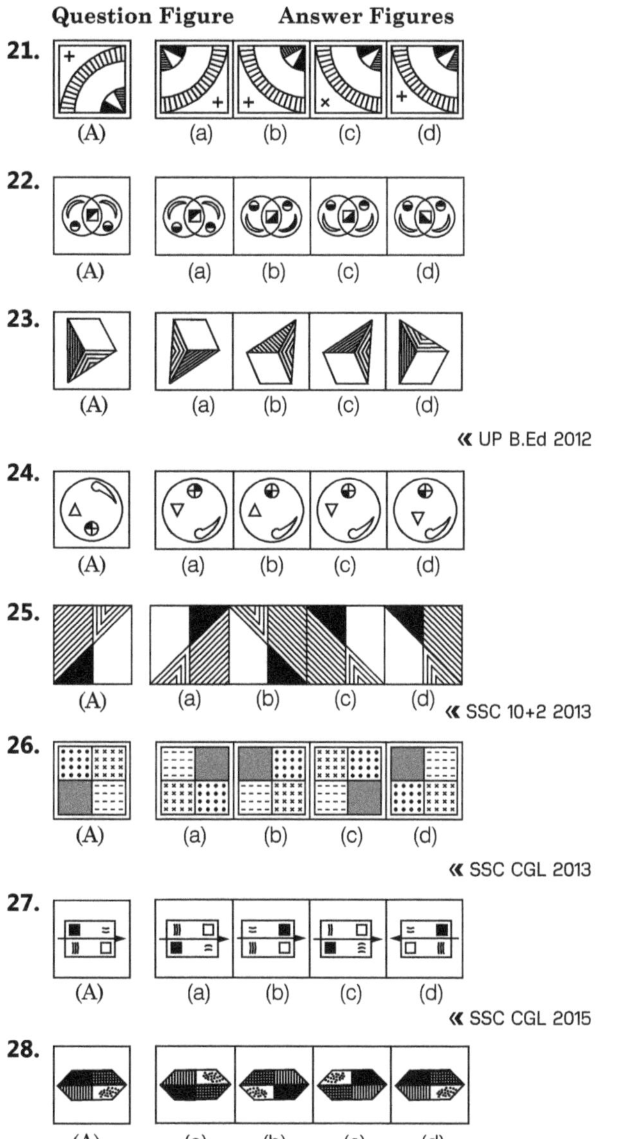

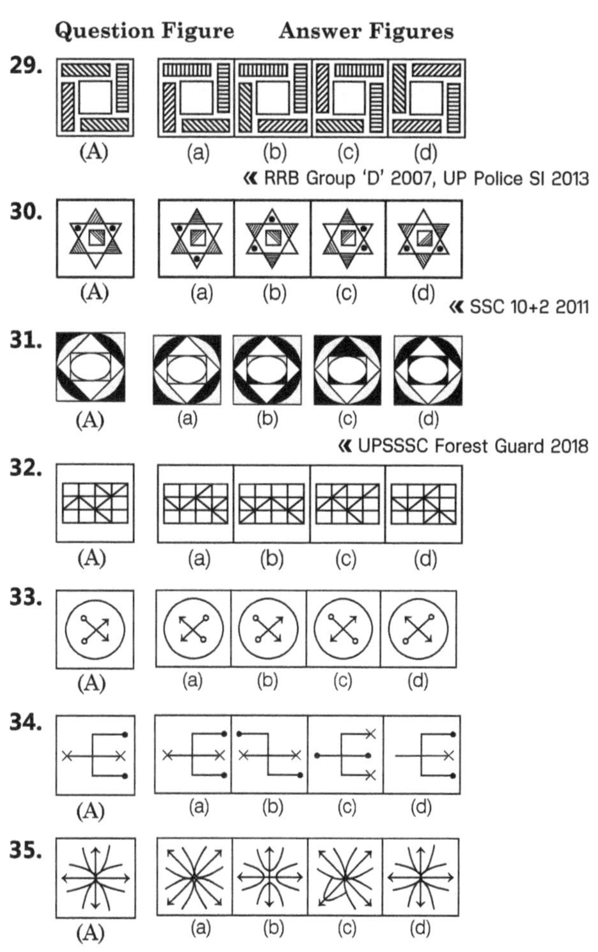

36. In the given figure, the pentagon is rotated 270° clockwise and the triangle is rotated 270° anti-clockwise and then the water image of the new figure is taken, what will be the final figure.

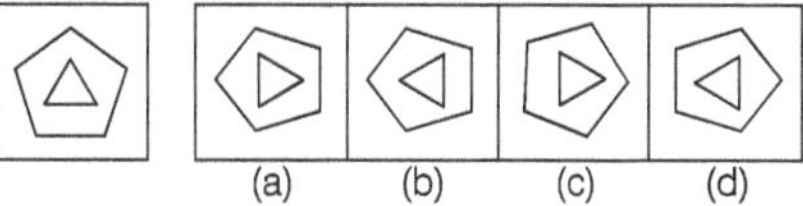

« UPSSSC Cane Supervisor 2019

» Answers «

1.(b)	2.(d)	3.(c)	4.(d)	5.(a)	6.(a)	7.(a)	8.(c)	9.(b)	10.(c)
11.(c)	12.(b)	13.(a)	14.(d)	15.(c)	16.(b)	17.(d)	18.(d)	19.(a)	20.(c)
21.(d)	22.(d)	23.(d)	24.(c)	25.(c)	26.(d)	27.(a)	28.(a)	29.(d)	30.(d)
31.(a)	32.(d)	33.(b)	34.(a)	35.(d)	36.(a)				

TYPE 02

Water Image of Letters and Numbers

In this type of questions candidates are required to find the water image of letters/numbers or their combination. For this candidates are required to learn how the letters and numbers get reflected in water and follow the same to solve the problems.

Water Images of Capital Letters

Letter	A	B	C	D	E	F	G	H	I	J	K	L	M
Water Image	∀	B	C	D	E	Ⅎ	⅁	H	I	ᒣ	K	Γ	W

Letter	N	O	P	Q	R	S	T	U	V	W	X	Y	Z
Water Image	И	O	b	Ó	ᴚ	Ƨ	⊥	∩	Λ	M	X	⅄	Ƶ

Note : The capital letters which have water images identical to the original letter are — C, D, E, H, I, O, X

Water Images of Small Letters

Letter	a	b	c	d	e	f	g	h	i	j	k	l	m
Water Image	ɐ	p	c	q	ə	ɟ	ɑ	ɥ	!	ɾ	k	l	ɯ

Letter	n	o	p	q	r	s	t	u	v	w	x	y	z
Water Image	u	o	b	d	ɹ	ƨ	ʇ	n	ʌ	ʍ	x	λ	ƹ

Note : The small letters which have water images identical to the original letter are — c, l, o, x.

Water Images of Digits

Digits	0	1	2	3	4	5	6	7	8	9
Water Image	0	Ɩ	Ƨ	3	ᔨ	ᘓ	e	ㄥ	8	ә

Note : Numbers 0, 3 and 8 have water images similar to the original numbers.

Now, some words with their water images are given below

Words	Water Image	Words	Water Image
IMAGINE	IW∀⅁IИE	PRACTICAL	bᴚ∀C⊥IC∀Γ
REGULAR	ᴚE⅁∩Γ∀ᴚ	OTHERS	O⊥HEᴚƧ
FORTUNE	ℲOᴚ⊥∩ИE	LANGUISH	Γ∀И⅁∩IƧH
ELASTIC	EΓ∀Ƨ⊥IC	FERVENT	ℲEᴚΛEИ⊥
IDENTITY	IDEИ⊥I⊥⅄	VERTICAL	ΛEᴚ⊥IC∀Γ
FURIOUS	Ⅎ∩ᴚIO∩Ƨ	FORMATION	ℲOᴚW∀⊥IOИ

The following examples will give a better idea about the types of questions asked in exams

DIRECTIONS ~ (Example Nos. 8-15) *In each of the following question, find the water image of the set of letters and/or digits given in the question figure out of the four answer choices* (a), (b), (c) *and* (d).

***Ex* 08** FROG

(a) ℲᴚO⅁ (b) GORF (c) ⅁OᴚℲ (d) ⅁ᴚOℲ

***Solution* (a)** The given word's reflection would be seen in the water as

FROG
ℲᴚO⅁

***Ex* 09** MOTIVE

(a) WOTIΛE (b) MO⊥IΛƎ (c) WO⊥IΛE (d) MO⊥IΛE

***Solution* (c)** The given word's reflection would be seen in the water as

MOTIVE
WO⊥IΛE

***Ex* 10** 189

(a) Ɩ8ә (b) ꓶ8ә (c) Ɩ86 (d) ꓶ86

***Solution* (a)** Reflection of the given number would be seen in the water as

189
Ɩ8ә

***Ex* 11** 13101989

(a) Ɩ3Ɩ0Ɩә89 (b) Ɩ3Ɩ0Ɩә8ә
(c) 1310Ɩә89 (d) Ɩ310198ә

***Solution* (b)** Reflection of the given number would be seen in the water as

13101989
Ɩ3Ɩ0Ɩә8ә

***Ex* 12** arihant

(a) ɐɹ!ɥɐuʇ (b) ɐɹ!ɥɐuʇ (c) ɐıɹμɐnt (d) ɐɹiɥɐuʇ

***Solution* (a)** Reflection of the given word would be seen in the water as

arihant
ɐɹ!ɥɐuʇ

***Ex* 13** 96FSH52

(a) әeℲƧHƧᘓ (b) әeℲƧH5Ƨ
(c) әeℲƧHᘓƧ (d) әeℲƧH25

***Solution* (c)** Reflection of the given group of letters and numbers would be seen in the water as

96FSH52
әeℲƧHᘓƧ

***Ex* 14** FOB128MU3

(a) FOBƖ28W∩3 (b) ℲOBƖƧ8W∩3
(c) ℲOBƖ 28W∩3 (d) ℲOBƖƧ8W∩3

***Solution* (d)** Reflection of the given group of letters and numbers would be seen in the water as

FOB128MU3
ℲO BƖƧ8W∩3

***Ex* 15** PQ8AF5BZ9

(a) bÓ8∀ℲᘓBƵә (b) bÓ8∀ℲᘓBƵ6
(c) bÓ8∀ꟻƧBZ9 (d) PQ8AFᘓBZe

***Solution* (a)** Reflection of the given group of letters and numbers would be seen in the water as

PQ8AF5BZ9
bÓ8∀ℲᘓBƵә

Practice CORNER 9.2

DIRECTIONS ~ (Q. Nos. 1-48) *In each of the following questions, a word or a number or mixed Alphabets-numbers word is given and followed by four alternatives* (a), (b), (c) *and* (d) *showing possible water images of that word or number. One out of these four alternatives shows the exact water image of that word or number. Choose the alternative which shows the correct water image of that word or number.*

1. FRUIT
(a) ꟻꓤUIT (b) ꟻꓤUIT
(c) TIUꓤꟻ (d) ꟻꓤUIT

2. EXPOSE
(a) ESOPXE (b) EXPOSE
(c) EXꓒOꙄE (d) EPOSXE

3. SURFACE
(a) ƎƆAꟻꓤUS (b) SUꓤꟻACE
(c) ꙄUꓤꟻAƆE (d) ꙄUꓤꟻACE

4. RADIANT
(a) TADIANR (b) TAᗡIAИR
(c) TNAIDAR (d) ꓤADIAИT

5. SARCASM
(a) ꙄAꓤCAꙄW (b) ꙄAꓤƆAꙄW
(c) WSAƆꓤAS (d) ꙄAꓤCAꙄW

6. MUNDANE
(a) EUNDANM (b) EUMDANM
(c) WUИDAИE (d) ƎИAᗡИUW

7. NUCLEAR
(a) ꓤAƎLCUИ (b) ИUCꓶEAꓤ
(c) ИUCLƎAꓤ (d) ИUCLEAꓤ

8. QUARREL
(a) ꝹUAꓤꓤƎꓶ (b) ꝹUAЯЯƎꓶ
(c) ꝹUAꓤꓤEꓶ (d) ꝹUAꓤꓤEꓶ

9. QUESTION
(a) ꝹUEꙄTIOИ (b) ꝹUEꙄTI OИ
(c) ꝹUƎꙄTION (d) NOITꙄƎUꝹ

10. DISCLOSE
(a) ƎSOꓶƆSIᗡ (b) DIꙄCꓶOꙄE
(c) ESOLCSID (d) ᗡIꙄCꓶOSE

11. ACOUSTIC
(a) ꓯƆOUꙄTIC (b) ꓯCOUꙄTIC
(c) ꓯCOUꙄTIC (d) ꓯCOUꙄTIC

12. TERMINATE
(a) ꓕEꓤMIИAƎꓕ (b) TEꓤMIИAꓕƎ
(c) ꓕEꓤMIИAꓕE (d) ꓕEꓤMIИAꓕƎ

13. DETERRENT
(a) ꓕИƎꓤꓤƎꓕƎᗡ (b) DEꓕEꓤꓤEИꓕ
(c) ᗡEꓕEꓤꓤEИꓕ (d) ᗡETEЯЯEИT

14. SUPERFLOUS
(a) SUPEꓤꟻꓶOUS (b) SUOꓶꟻꓤƎꓒUS
(c) ꙄUꓒEꓤꟻꓶOUꙄ (d) ꙄUꓒEꓤꟻꓶOUꙄ

15. PRECARIOUS
(a) ꓒꓤECAꓤIOUꙄ (b) PꓤECAꓤIOUꙄ
(c) SUORECARIP (d) ꙄUOIЯAƆƎЯꟼ

16. OBLITERATE
(a) OBꓶIꓕEꓤAꓕE (b) ƎTAЯƎTILBO
(c) OBꓶITƎꓤAꓕE (d) OBJITEꓤATE

17. 752398 « UP B.Ed 2015
(a) ⅂22398 (b) ⅂22368
(c) ⅂52368 (d) 722368

18. 521834 « UP B.Ed 2012
(a) 521834 (b) 528134
(c) 221834 (d) 521834

19. 213765 « SSC Steno 2012
(a) 213765 (b) 213765
(c) 567312 (d) 213765

20. 894058 « SSC 10+2 2013
(a) 894028 (b) 894058
(c) 894028 (d) 894058

21. 348796 « DSSSB PRT 2012
(a) 348796 (b) 348796
(c) 348796 (d) 348796

22. rise
(a) ɿise (b) esir
(c) ɿise (d) əsiɿ

23. train
(a) ɟɿain (b) ɟɿaiu
(c) niaɿt (d) ɟɿain

24. wrote « UP B.Ed 2014
(a) wɿotə (b) wɿotə
(c) wɿote (d) wɿotə

25. prize « SSC 10+2 2013
(a) bɿize (b) bɿize (c) bɿize (d) bɿize

26. first « SSC Steno 2012
(a) ɟiɿst (b) ɟiɿst (c) ɟiɿst (d) tsɿiɟ

27. bridge « SSC CGL 2013
(a) pɿiqɓe (b) pɿiqɓe
(c) pɿiqɓe (d) pɿipɓe

28. monday « UP B.Ed 2015
(a) yadnom (b) ʎɐpuom
(c) ʎɐpuow (d) woupɐʎ

29. success « UP B.Ed 2013

(a) succɘss (b) ƨuccess

(c) ƨuccess (d) ƨuccɘƨƨ

30. national

(a) ꓵɐtioual (b) ꓵɐtioual

(c) uɐtioual (d) ꓵɐtioual

31. D6Z7F4

(a) DɘZ٢ꟻ4 (b) ꓷɘZ٢ꟻ4

(c) DɘZ٢ꟻ4 (d) ꓷɘZ٢ꟻ4

32. 96FSH78

(a) ɘ9ꟻƧH78 (b) 69ꟻƧH78

(c) ɘɘꟻƧH٢8 (d) 69ꟻƧH8

33. U4P15B7

(a) ꓵ4ꟼ1ƧB٢ (b) ꓵ4d1ƧB٢

(c) ꓵ4ꟼ1ƧB٢ (d) ꓵ491ƧB٢

34. 5DOB6V2

(a) ƧꓷOBɘVƧ (b) ƧDOB9VƧ

(c) ƧꓷOB9VƧ (d) ƧDOBɘVƧ

35. UP15847

(a) ꓵꟼ1Ƨ84٢ (b) ꓵd1Ƨ84٢

(c) ꓵꟼ1Ƨ84٢ (d) ꓵd1Ƨ84٢

36. VAYU8436

(a) VAYꓵ84Ɛ9 (b) VAYꓵ84Ɛɘ

(c) VAYꓵ8439 (d) VAYꓵ84Ɛɘ

37. RAJ589D8

(a) ꓤAꓩƧ89D8 (b) ꓤAꓩƧ89D8

(c) ꓤAꓩƧ89D8 (d) ꓤAꓩƧ89D8

38. DL2CA34OO

(a) DꓶƧꓛA34OO (b) DꓶƧꓛA34OO

(c) DꓶƧꓛAƐ4OO (d) DꓶƧꓛAƐ4OO

39. 50JA32DEO6

(a) ƧOꓩAƐƧDEO9 (b) ƧOꓩAƐƧDEOɘ

(c) ƧOꓩAƐƧDEO9 (d) ƧOꓩAƐƧDEOɘ

40. GR98AP76ES

(a) ꓨꓤ68AꟼƖ9EƧ (b) ꓨꓤ98AꟼƖ9EƧ

(c) ꓨꓤ98AꟼƖɘEƧ (d) GRɘ8APƖ6ƎS

41. US91Q4M5W3

(a) ꓵƧ91Ọ4MƧWƐ (b) ꓵƧ91Ọ4MƧWƐ

(c) ꓵƧ91Ọ4MƧWƐ (d) ꓵƧ91Ọ4MƧWƐ

42.

(A)	(a)	(b)	(c)	(d)
ST	Ƨꓕ	ꓕS	TƧ	TS

43.

(A)	(a)	(b)	(c)	(d)
TOP	ꓕOꟼ	TOP	TOꟼ	ꓕOP

44.

(A)	(a)	(b)	(c)	(d)
109	10ɘ	109	109	10ɘ

45.

(A)	(a)	(b)	(c)	(d)
969	966	ɘ69	96ɘ	ɘ6ɘ

46.

(A)	(a)	(b)	(c)	(d)
53768	ƧƐ٢68	ƧƐ٢68	ƧƐ٢68	23768

47.

(A)	(a)	(b)	(c)	(d)
3DEX8	ƐDEX8	3DEX8	3ꓷEX8	3DƎX8

48.

(A)	(a)	(b)	(c)	(d)
8HEDI3	8HEDI3	8HƎDIƐ	8HEDIƐ	8HƎDIƐ

» Answers «

1. (b)	2. (c)	3. (d)	4. (d)	5. (d)	6. (c)	7. (d)	8. (d)	9. (a)	10. (b)
11. (b)	12. (c)	13. (b)	14. (d)	15. (a)	16. (a)	17. (b)	18. (a)	19. (d)	20. (c)
21. (c)	22. (a)	23. (b)	24. (c)	25. (b)	26. (c)	27. (b)	28. (d)	29. (d)	30. (d)
31. (c)	32. (c)	33. (c)	34. (d)	35. (a)	36. (b)	37. (a)	38. (a)	39. (b)	40. (c)
41. (d)	42. (a)	43. (a)	44. (a)	45. (d)	46. (a)	47. (b)	48. (a)		

CHAPTER / 10

Paper Folding and Cutting

The paper folding and cutting involves a process in which a transparent sheet is folded and then some cuts and folds are made. In the questions based on paper folding and cutting a few figures are given showing the way in which a piece is to be folded and then out from a particular section. The dotted line along which the paper is to be folded and the arrow indicates the direction of fold. Thus these figures indicate the sequence in which the paper is to be folded. The designs from the cut will appear on each one of the folds made on the paper. In questions based on paper folding and cutting it can be asked to find either the folded or unfolded pattern of the sheet.

Different types of questions asked from this chapter, are as follows.

TYPE 01

Paper Folding

Questions based on paper folding comprise of a question figure representing a transparent sheet and four or five answer figures. The transparent sheet contains some figural pattern and one or more dotted line/lines.

These dotted lines indicate the axis along which the paper is to be folded. A candidate is asked to choose the correct answer figure, which would resemble the design that appears on the transparent sheet after folding.

Let us consider an example,

DIRECTIONS ~ Find the pattern which will appear on the transparent sheet after it is folded along the dotted line.

Transparent Sheet **Answer Figures**

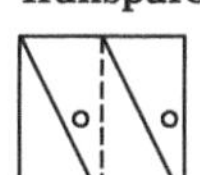

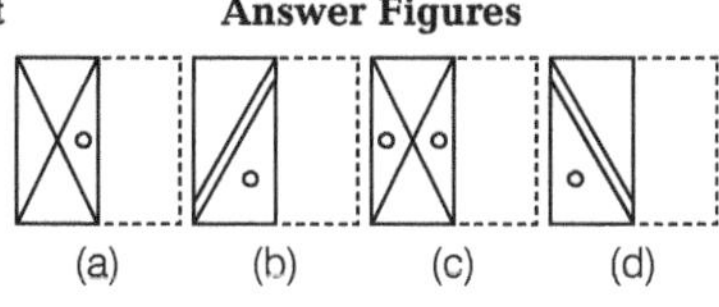

(a) (b) (c) (d)

Solution ***(c)*** The right half of the sheet will be folded along the dotted line, in such a way that its design will get superimposed on the design on left side of the transparent sheet.

Now, consider the right side *i.e.,*

If a mirror is kept on left side of this image/pattern, then it will look like as

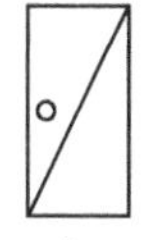

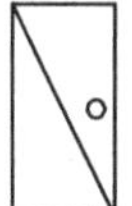

Mirror image Real image

To obtain the pattern after folding the transparent sheet, we should superimpose the mirror image of right half of sheet on the left half of the sheet.

So, the folded pattern will look like as

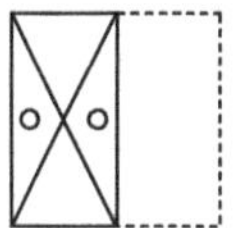

Hence, option (c) is the correct answer.

Let us see some more examples given below that will give a better idea about such type of problems ;

DIRECTIONS ~ (Example Nos. 1-7) *In each of the questions given below, a transparent sheet having some design on either side of dotted line is given. This figure is followed by four answer figures marked as (a), (b), (c) and (d). One out of these four alternatives is obtained by folding the transparent sheet along the dotted line. You are required to choose the correct option.*

***Ex* 01** Transparent Sheet Answer Figures

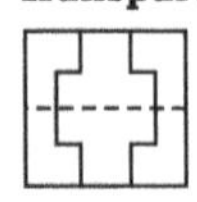

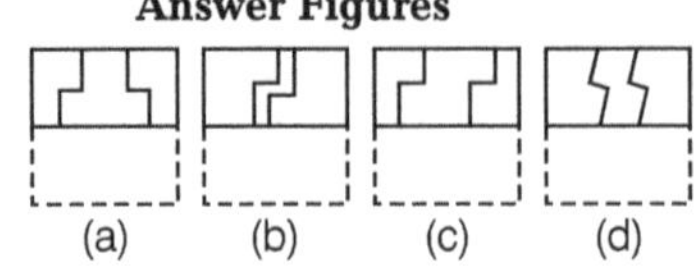

Solution (a) The lower half of the transparent sheet is folded along the dotted line and placed on the upper half of the transparent sheet.

The design on both the halves are identical. Hence, option (a) resembles the pattern formed when the transparent sheet is folded along the dotted line.

***Ex* 02** Transparent Sheet Answer Figures

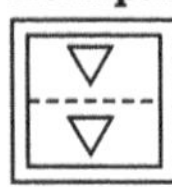

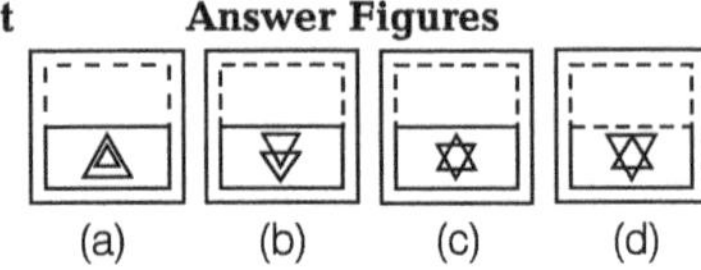

Solution (c) The upper half of the transparent sheet is folded along the dotted line and placed on the lower half of the sheet. The figure, thus obtained resembles the answer figure (c).

***Ex* 03** Transparent Sheet Answer Figures

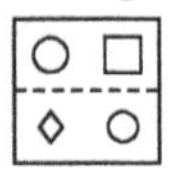

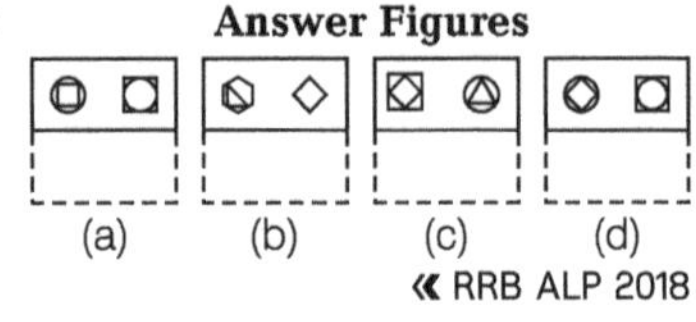

« RRB ALP 2018

Solution (d) It is clear that the lower half of the transparent sheet is folded along the dotted line and is placed on the upper half. The figure thus obtained resembles the figure as shown in option (d).

***Ex* 04** Transparent Sheet Answer Figures

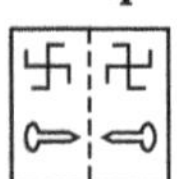

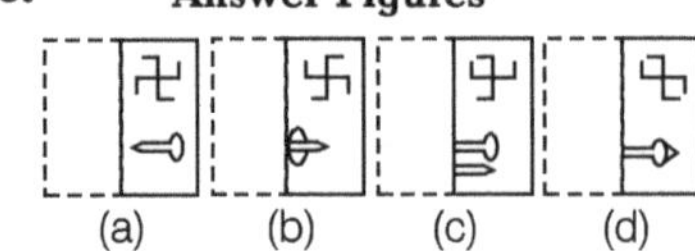

Solution (a) Clearly, the left half of the transparent sheet is folded along the dotted line and placed on the right half. The resultant figure, thus obtained resembles the option (a).

***Ex* 05**

Transparent Sheet Answer Figures

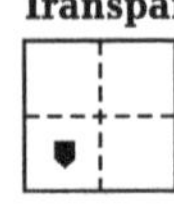

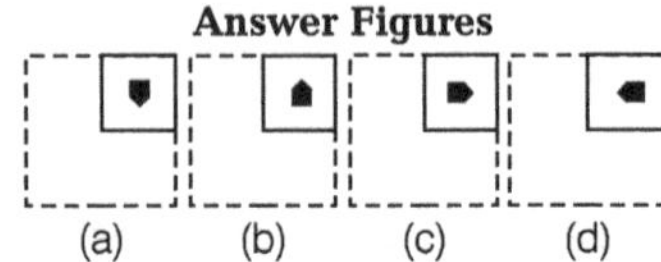

Solution (b) The lower half of the transparent sheet is folded along the dotted line and placed on the upper half of the sheet.

Then, the left half of the sheet is folded along the dotted line and placed on the right half of the sheet. The figure, thus obtained resembles the answer figure (b).

***Ex* 06**

Transparent Sheet Answer Figures

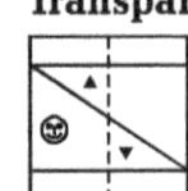

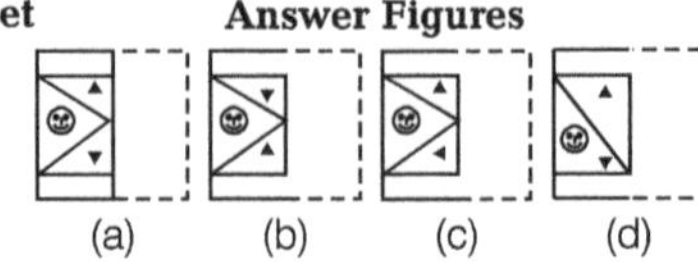

Solution (a) The right half of the sheet is folded along the dotted line and placed on the left half of the sheet. The figure, thus obtained resembles the answer figure (a).

***Ex* 07**

Transparent Sheet Answer Figures

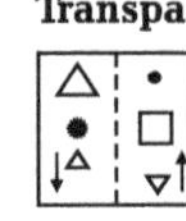

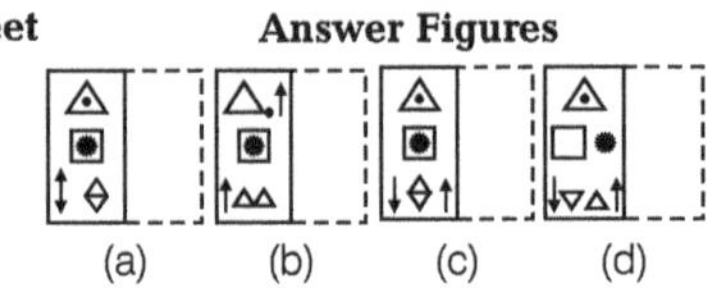

Solution (a) The right half of the transparent sheet is folded along the dotted line and placed on the left half of the sheet. The figure, thus obtained resembles the answer figure (a).

Practice CORNER 10.1

DIRECTIONS ~ (Q. Nos. 1-49) *In each of the following questions, a figure marked on transparent sheet is given and followed by four answer figures, one out of these four options resembles the figure, which is obtained by folding transparent sheet along the dotted line. This option is your answer.*

Transparent Sheet Answer Figures

1.

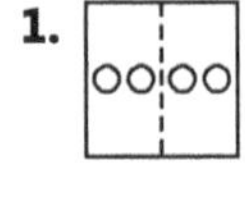

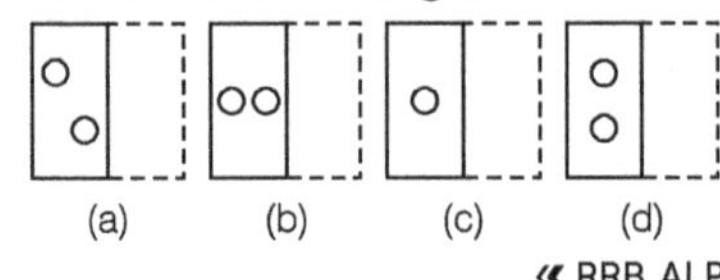

« RRB ALP 2019

2.

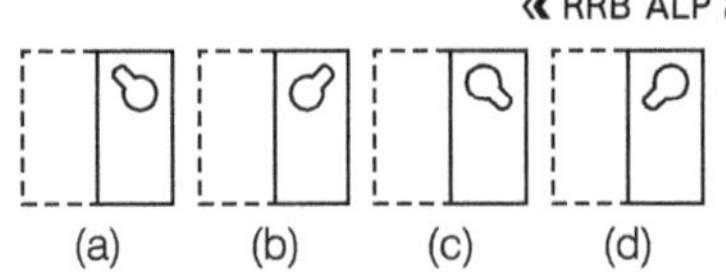

Transparent Sheet Answer Figures

3.

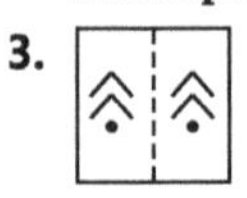

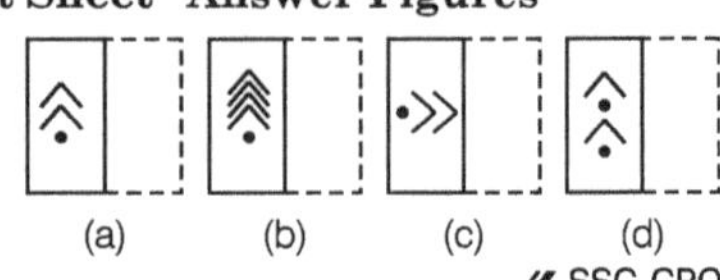

« SSC CPO 2012

4.

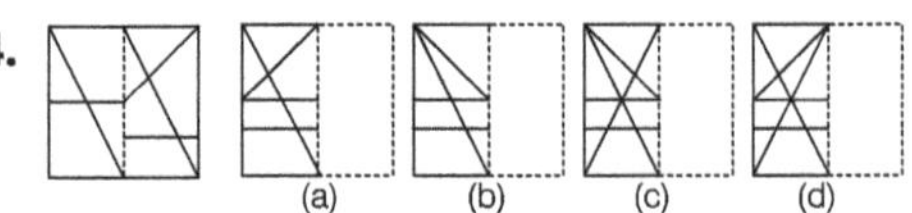

« SSC CGL 2020

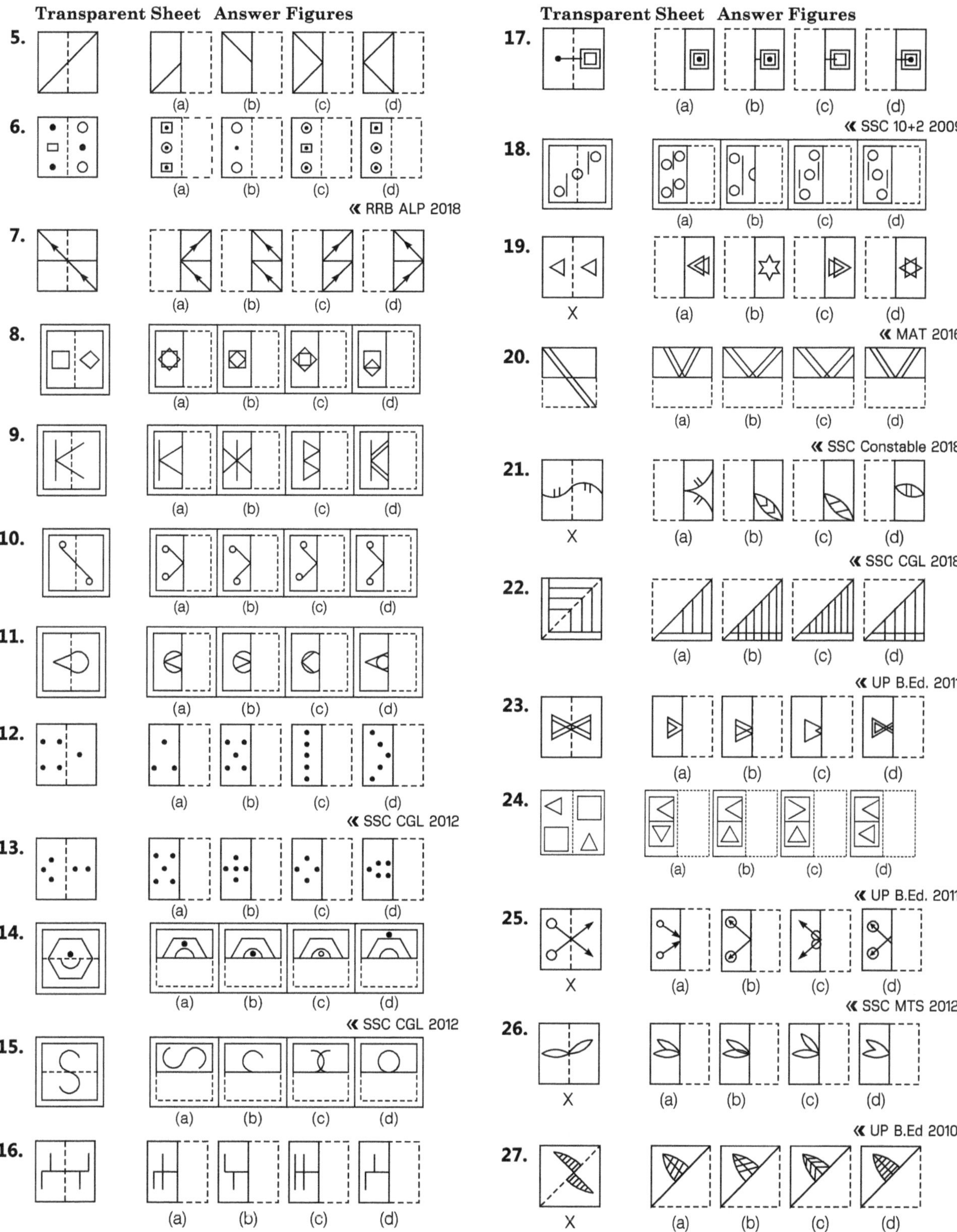
Transparent Sheet Answer Figures
5.
(a) (b) (c) (d)
6.
(a) (b) (c) (d)
« RRB ALP 2018
7.
(a) (b) (c) (d)
8.
(a) (b) (c) (d)
9.
(a) (b) (c) (d)
10.
(a) (b) (c) (d)
11.
(a) (b) (c) (d)
12.
(a) (b) (c) (d)
« SSC CGL 2012
13.
(a) (b) (c) (d)
14.
(a) (b) (c) (d)
« SSC CGL 2012
15.
(a) (b) (c) (d)
16.
(a) (b) (c) (d)
Transparent Sheet Answer Figures
17.
(a) (b) (c) (d)
« SSC 10+2 2009
18.
(a) (b) (c) (d)
19.
X
(a) (b) (c) (d)
« MAT 2016
20.
(a) (b) (c) (d)
« SSC Constable 2018
21.
X
(a) (b) (c) (d)
« SSC CGL 2018
22.
(a) (b) (c) (d)
« UP B.Ed. 2011
23.
(a) (b) (c) (d)
24.
(a) (b) (c) (d)
« UP B.Ed. 2011
25.
X
(a) (b) (c) (d)
« SSC MTS 2012
26.
X
(a) (b) (c) (d)
« UP B.Ed 2010
27.
X
(a) (b) (c) (d)

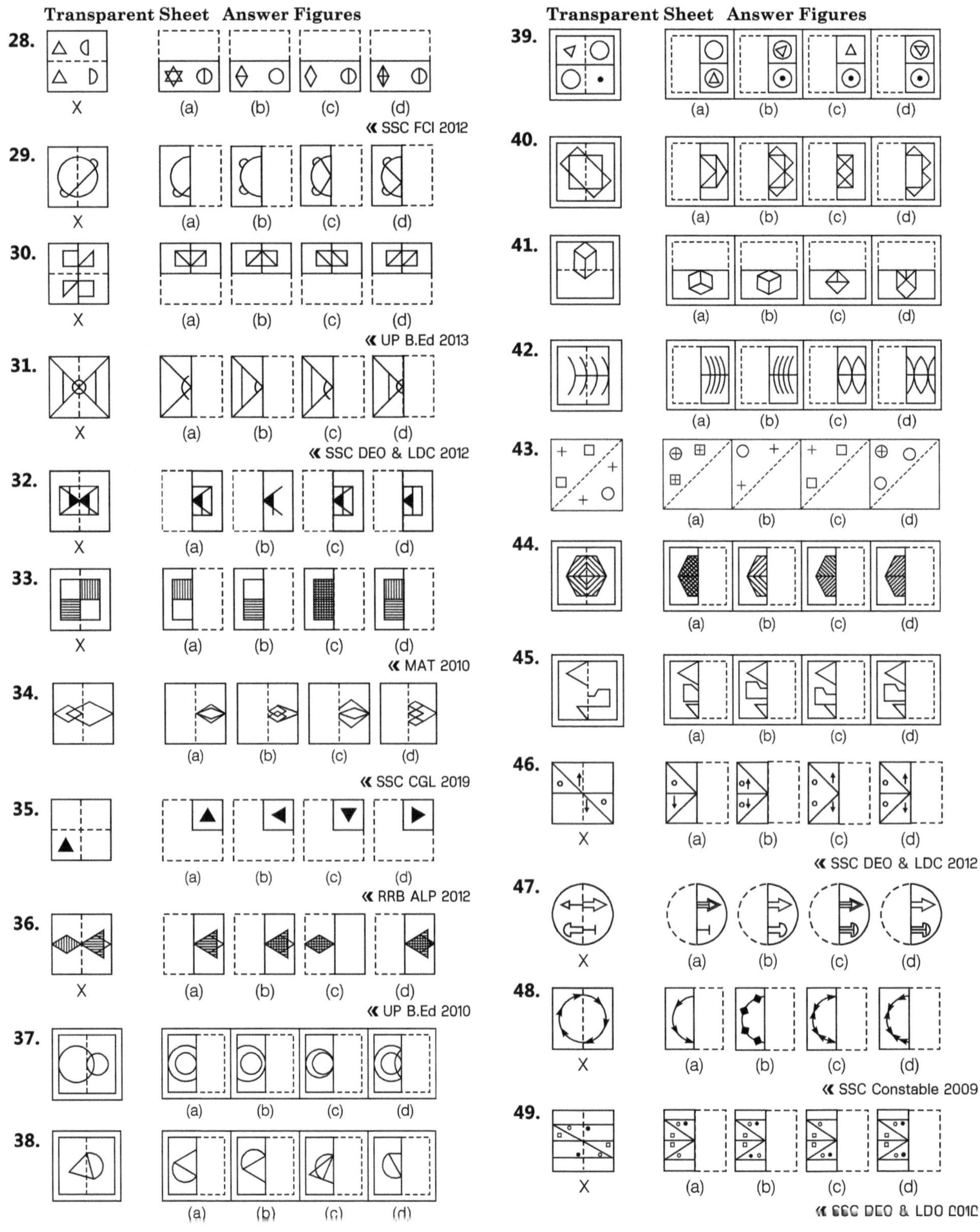
Transparent Sheet Answer Figures
28.
X
(a) (b) (c) (d)
« SSC FCI 2012
29.
30.
« UP B.Ed 2013
31.
« SSC DEO & LDC 2012
32.
33.
« MAT 2010
34.
35.
« SSC CGL 2019
« RRB ALP 2012
36.
« UP B.Ed 2010
37.
38.
Transparent Sheet Answer Figures
39.
40.
41.
42.
43.
44.
45.
46.
« SSC DEO & LDC 2012
47.
48.
« SSC Constable 2009
49.
« SSC DEO & LDC 2010

» Answers «

1. *(b)*	2. *(b)*	3. *(a)*	4. *(b)*	5. *(c)*	6. *(c)*	7. *(a)*	8. *(a)*	9. *(c)*	10. *(d)*
11. *(a)*	12. *(b)*	13. *(c)*	14. *(c)*	15. *(d)*	16. *(c)*	17. *(d)*	18. *(b)*	19. *(d)*	20. *(b)*
21. *(d)*	22. *(a)*	23. *(b)*	24. *(b)*	25. *(b)*	26. *(b)*	27. *(d)*	28. *(a)*	29. *(d)*	30. *(a)*
31. *(d)*	32. *(c)*	33. *(d)*	34. *(d)*	35. *(c)*	36. *(d)*	37. *(d)*	38. *(c)*	39. *(d)*	40. *(b)*
41. *(d)*	42. *(c)*	43. *(a)*	44. *(b)*	45. *(c)*	46. *(d)*	47. *(c)*	48. *(c)*	49. *(d)*	

TYPE 02

Paper Cutting

In questions based on paper cutting, one or more question figures showing the manner or process in which a piece of paper is folded and cut are given. The dotted line in the figures is the reference line along which the paper has to be folded and the arrow indicates the folding direction.

After folding, the paper is punched (cut) on a particular section. Such cuts may be based on several patterns. These patterns appear on the paper when the paper is unfolded after cutting. The candidates are required to see the question figure(s) carefully and then identify the unfolded paper having correct cutting pattern, out of the four answer choices.

Let us see some figures which are being folded, cut and then unfolded to have a basic idea about the concept of paper cutting

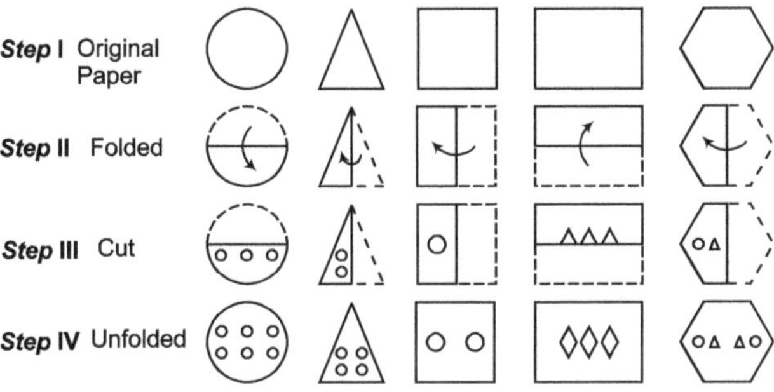

Note *(i) The above presentations depict fold punching (cutting). Questions based on paper cutting may involve multiple folds.*

(ii) The cuts that are shown in the above presentations may be made in any form.

Different types of questions asked in exams from paper cutting are as follows.

A. Selecting Unfolded Pattern of a Folded Punched Piece of Paper

In this type of questions, the order in which a paper is folded and then punched is depicted through a series of question figures or a single question figure. The objective is to select one of the figures among the four answer figures, which correctly shows the shape of the paper when it is unfolded.

The following examples will give you a better idea about such type of questions

***Ex* 08** A piece of paper is folded and cut as shown below in the question figures. From the given answer figures, indicate how it will appear when unfolded.
« SSC Steno 2013

Question Figures **Answer Figures**

X Y Z (a) (b) (c) (d)

Solution (a) It is clear that in figure (X), the paper has been folded from the upper half to the lower half. In figure (Y), the paper has been folded from left to right making it one fourth of the original size.

Now, as given in figure (Z), the cut is marked. The design of the cut will appear as in answer figure (a), when it is unfolded.

Hence, answer figure (a) represents the correct unfolded shape of the paper after the cut, as shown below.

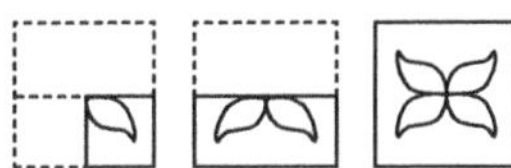

***Ex* 09** A circular piece of paper is folded and cut as shown below. How will it appear when unfolded? « SSC CPO 2018

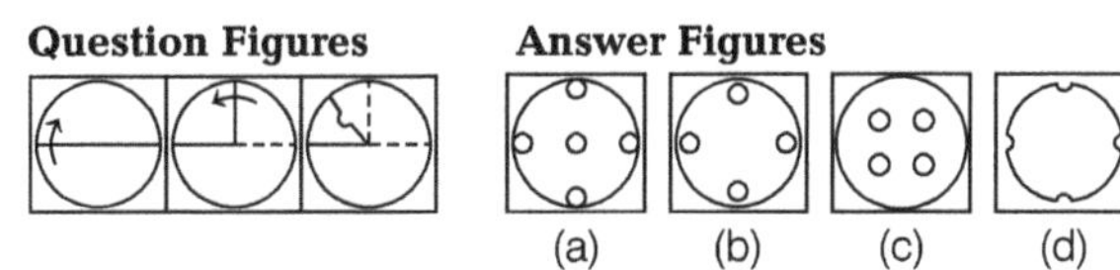

Solution (c) The paper has been folded from lower half to upper half and then from right half to the left half and then punched as shown. On being unfolded, it will appear as shown in option (c).

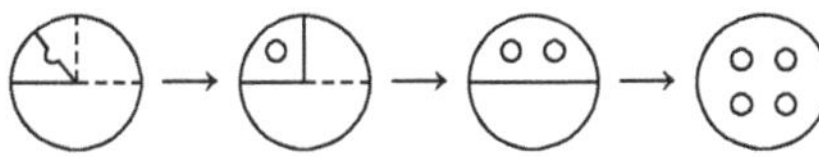

***Ex* 10** The three question figures marked X, Y and Z show the manner in which a piece of paper (P) is folded step by step and then cut. From the answer figures (a), (b), (c) and (d), select the one showing the unfolded pattern of the paper after the cut.

Question Figures

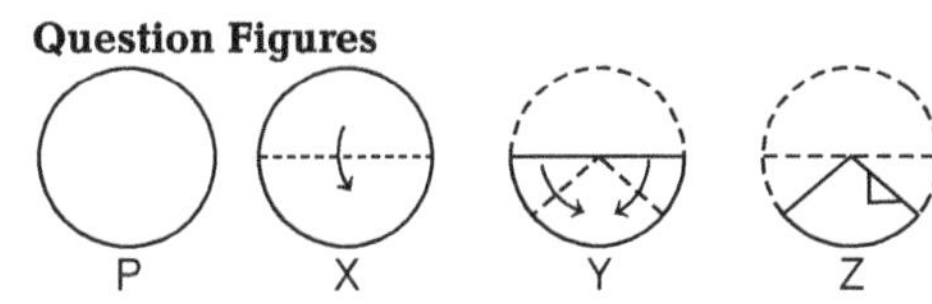

Answer Figures

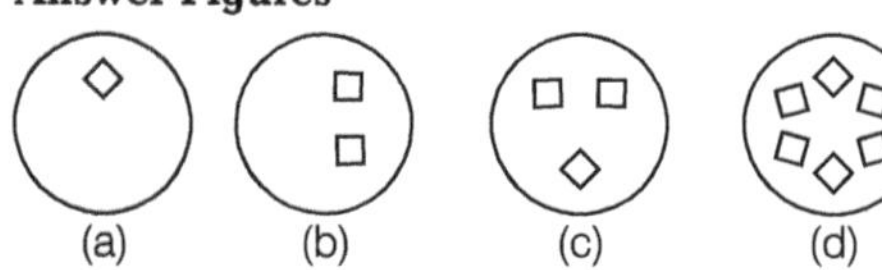

Solution (b) Figure (X) is the first step in which a circular piece of paper is folded from upper to the lower half along the diameter. In figure (Y), both the extreme ends of the figure (X) (after folding) have been folded to form a cone like shape and then as given in figure (Z), a cut has been made on the right side.

It is clear that this cut will result into two marks, one in the lower half and another in the upper half of the paper, when it is unfolded.

Answer figure (b) represents the unfolded shape of the paper after the cut, as shown below.

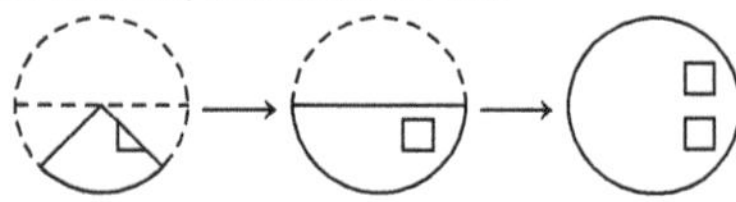

***Ex* 11** A piece of paper is folded and cut as shown below in the question figures. From the given answer figures, indicate how it will appear when unfolded? « SSC CGL 2014

Question Figures **Answer Figures**

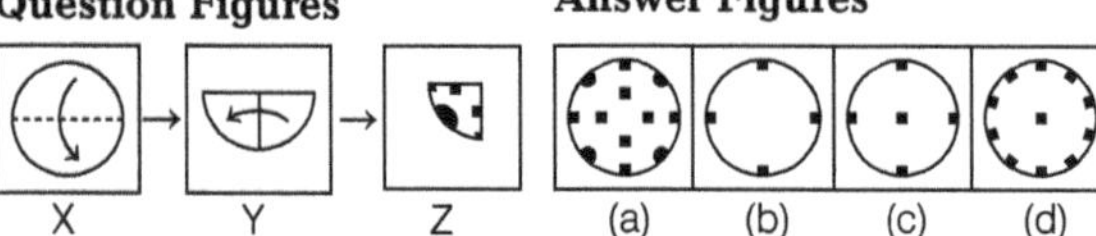

Solution (a) Figure (X) is the first step in which the circular piece of paper is folded from the upper to the lower half along the diameter. In figure (Y), the paper is folded from right to left.

Now, cuts have been made as shown in figure (Z). The design made by the cuts will appear as answer figure (a), when it is unfolded.

***Ex* 12** Select a figure from amongst the answer figures that would most closely resemble the sheet (X) when it is unfolded.

Question Figure **Answer Figures**

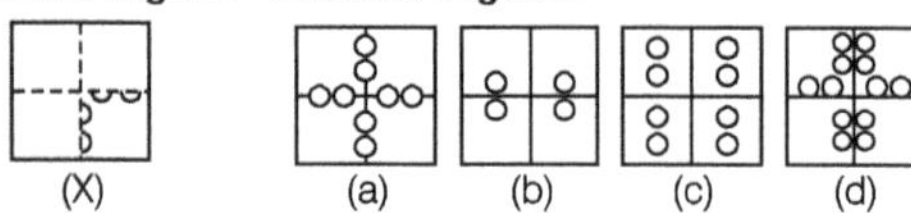

Solution (a) After careful observation of the question figure, we find that sheet (X) when unfolded will look like as answer figure (a), as shown below

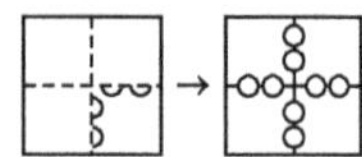

B. Selecting Folded and Punched Pattern Based on Unfolded Pattern

In such type of questions, a question figure is given which represents an unfolded piece of paper with several punches (cuts) made to it and along with the question figure, four answer figures representing differently folded and punched paper patterns are also given.

The candidate is required to analyse the answer figures to find out the correct folded and punched paper pattern for the given unfolded pattern.

Let us see the following examples to have an idea about this type of questions

DIRECTIONS ~ (Example Nos. 13-15) *A paper sheet is folded in a particular manner and several punches (cuts) are made on it. When unfolded, the paper sheet looks like the question figure (X). From the given options select the one that follows the manner in which the paper is folded and punched.*

***Ex* 13**

Question Figure **Answer Figures**

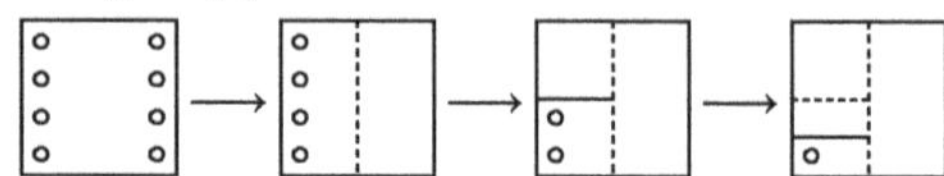

Solution (d) When we fold figure (X), then it looks like as answer figure (d).

***Ex* 14**

Question Figure **Answer Figures**

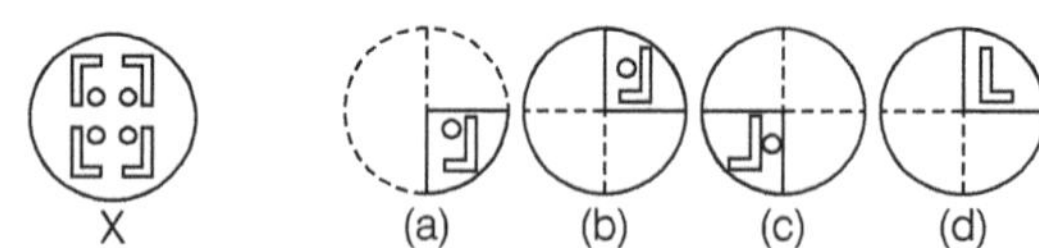

Solution (a) When we fold question figure (X), then it looks like as answer figure (a).

***Ex* 15**

Question Figure **Answer Figures**

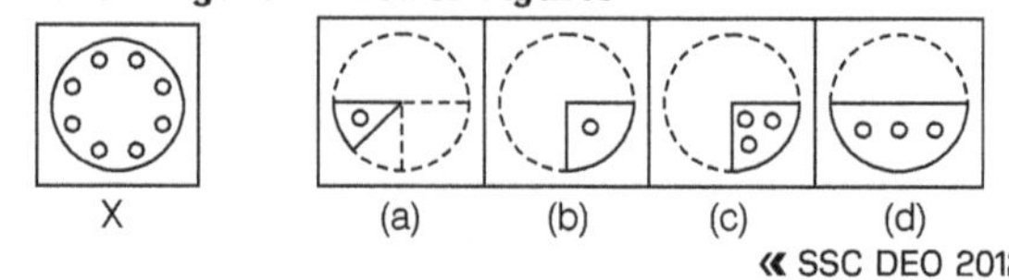

« SSC DEO 2012

Solution (a) When we fold the question figure (X) , then it looks like as answer figure (a).

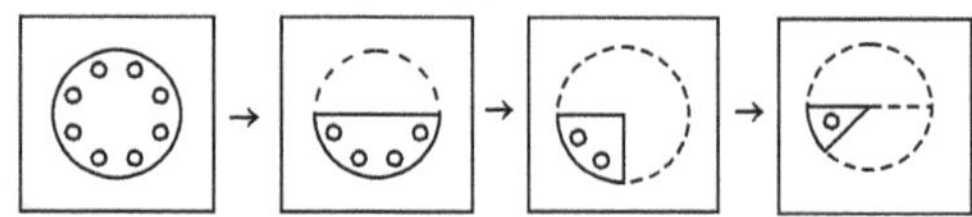

Practice / CORNER 10.2

DIRECTIONS ~ (Q. Nos. 1-68) *In each of the following questions, a transparent sheet is folded in the manner shown in the question figure(s). Select the figure out of the answer choices showing the unfolded pattern after the punches (cut).*

1. Question Figures

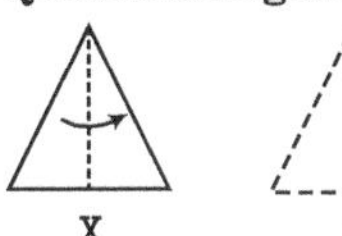
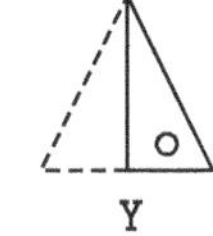

X Y « UP B.Ed 2010

Answer Figures

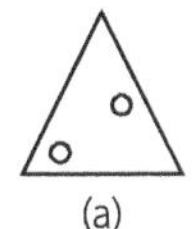
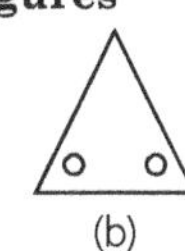
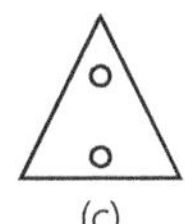
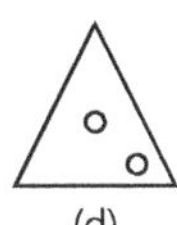

(a) (b) (c) (d)

2. Question Figures

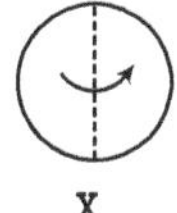
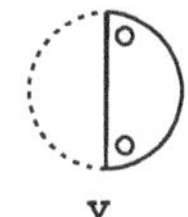
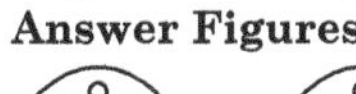

X Y « RRB Group D 2018

Answer Figures

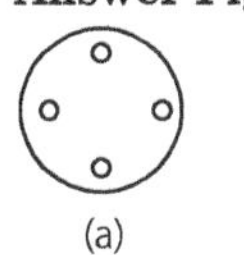
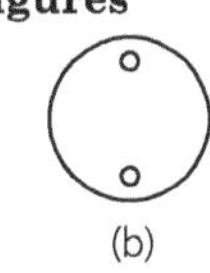
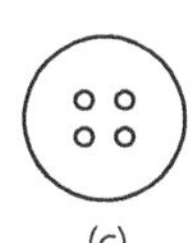
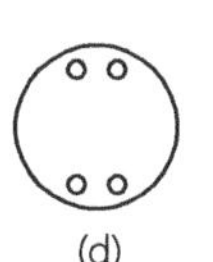

(a) (b) (c) (d)

3. Question Figures

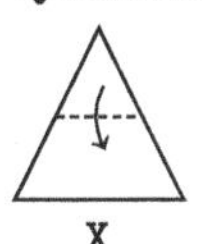
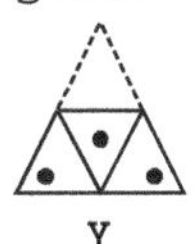

X Y « UP B.Ed. 2012

Answer figures

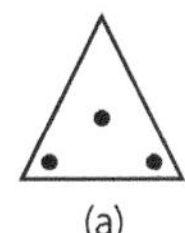
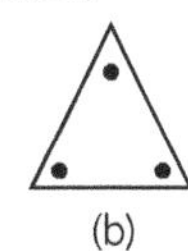
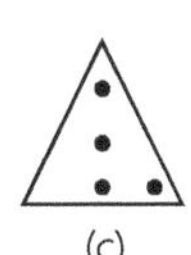
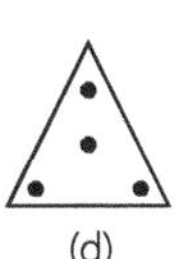

(a) (b) (c) (d)

4. Question Figures

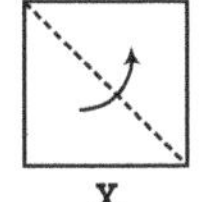
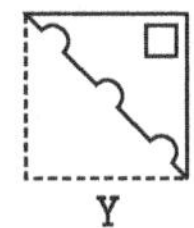

X Y

Answer Figures

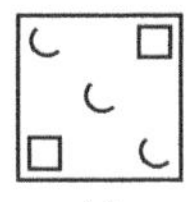
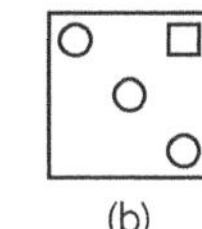
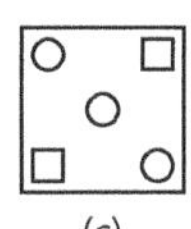
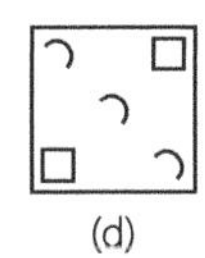

(a) (b) (c) (d)

5. Question Figures

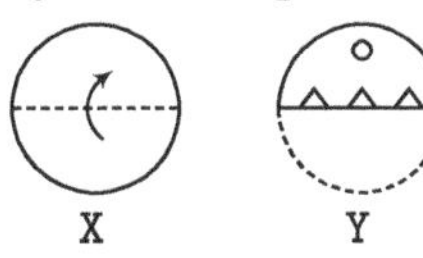

X Y « SSC 10+2 2012

Answer Figures

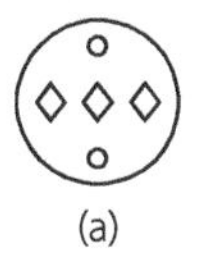
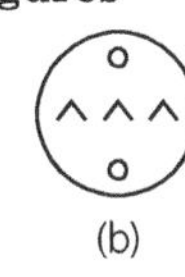
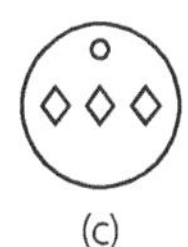
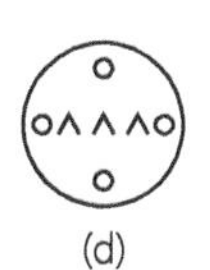

(a) (b) (c) (d)

6. Question Figures

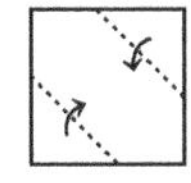
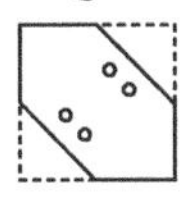

« UPSSSC Junior Assist. 2015

Answer Figures

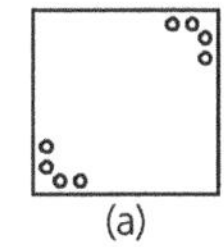
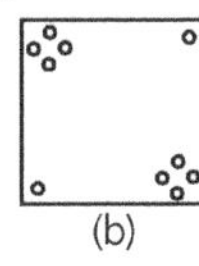
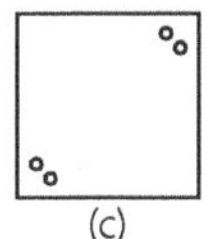
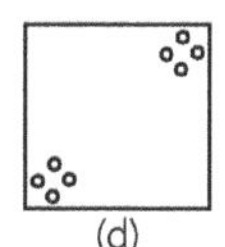

(a) (b) (c) (d)

7. Question Figures

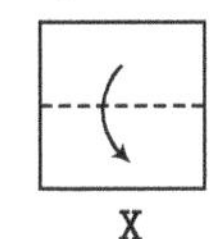
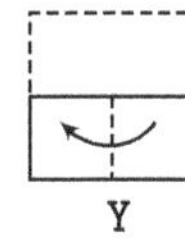
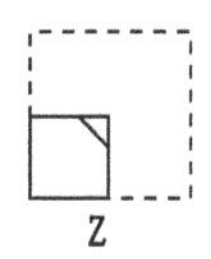

X Y Z « SSC CGL 2013

Answer figures

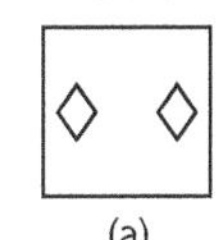
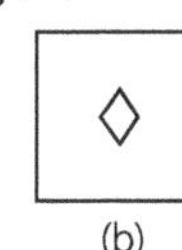
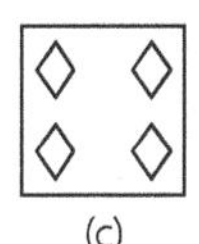
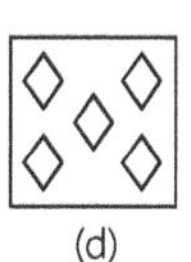

(a) (b) (c) (d)

8. Question Figures

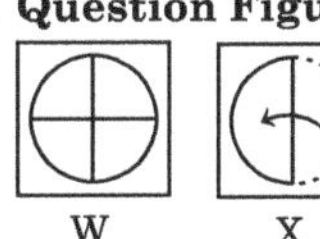
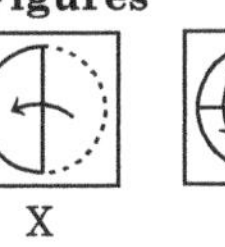
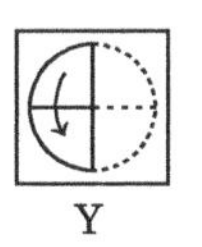
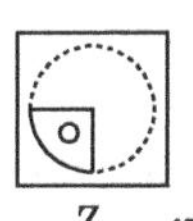

W X Y Z « SSC CGL 2018

Answer Figures

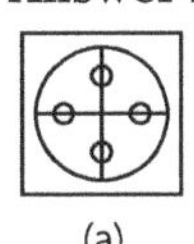
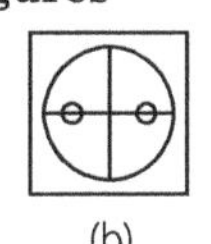
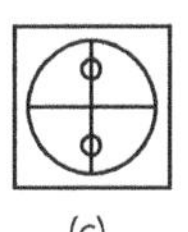
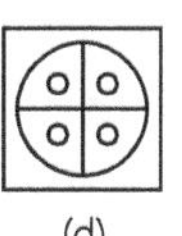

(a) (b) (c) (d)

9. Question Figures

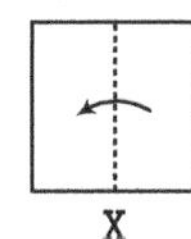
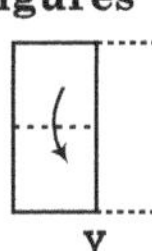
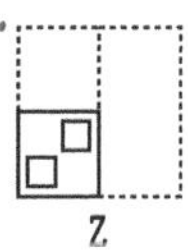

X Y Z « SSC CPO 2013

Answer Figures

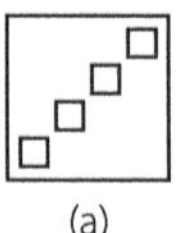
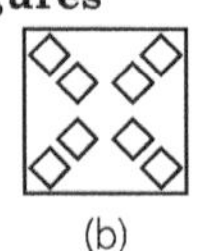
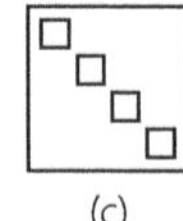
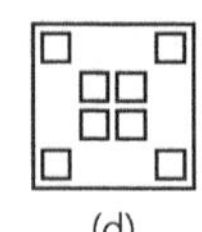

(a) (b) (c) (d)

10. Question Figures

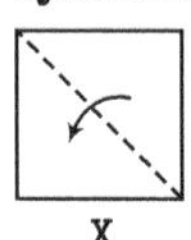
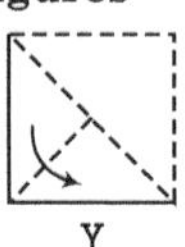

X Y Z

« Delhi Police SI, ASI 2016

Answer Figures

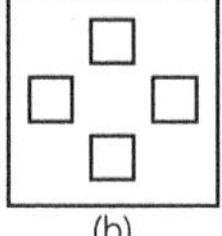
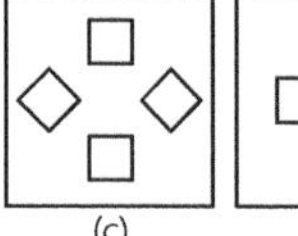
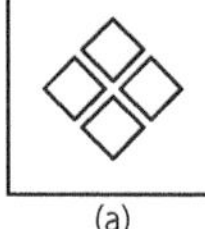
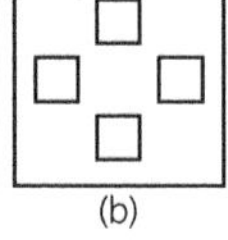
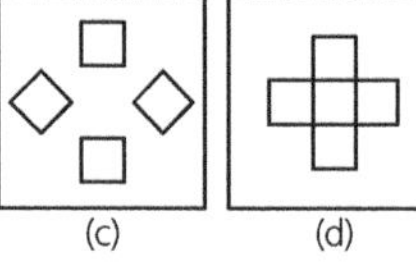

(a) (b) (c) (d)

11. Question Figures

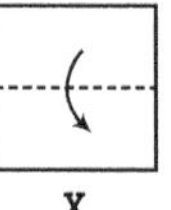
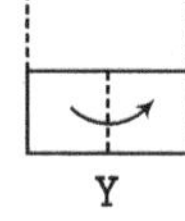
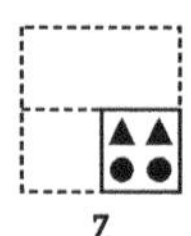

X Y Z

« MAT 2009

Answer Figures

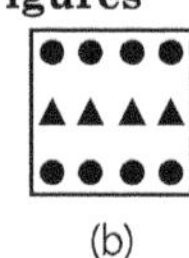
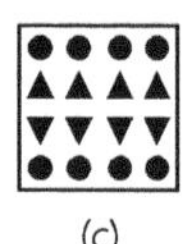
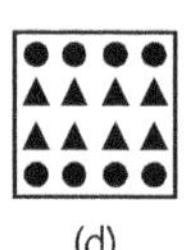

(a) (b) (c) (d)

12. Question Figures

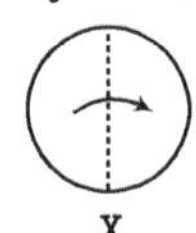
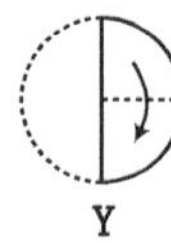
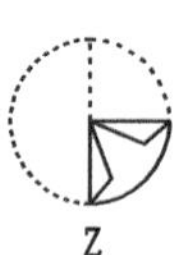

X Y Z

Answer Figures

(a) (b) (c) (d)

13. Question figures

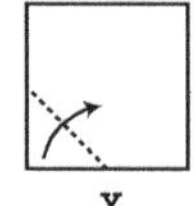
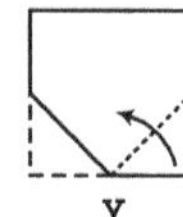
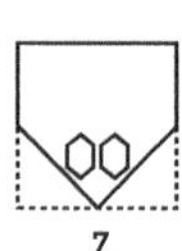

X Y Z

Answer Figures

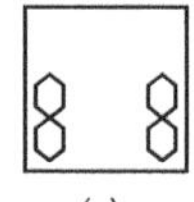
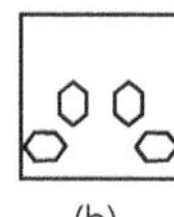
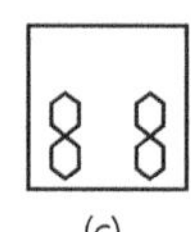
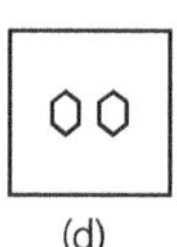

(a) (b) (c) (d)

14. Question Figures

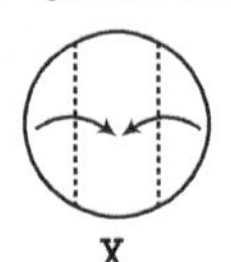
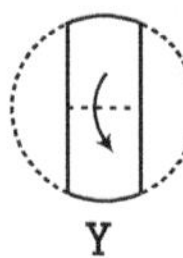
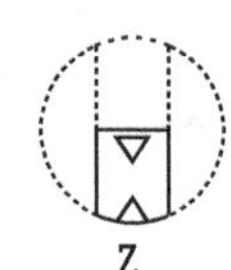

X Y Z

« SSC Constable 2019

Answer Figures

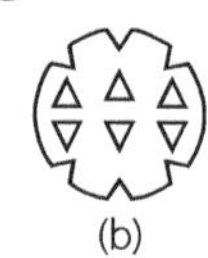

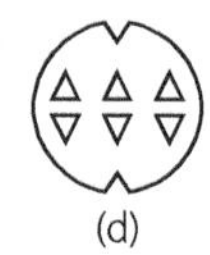

(a) (b) (c) (d)

15. Question Figures

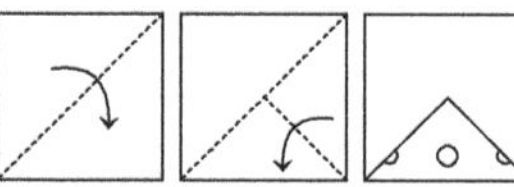

Answer Figures

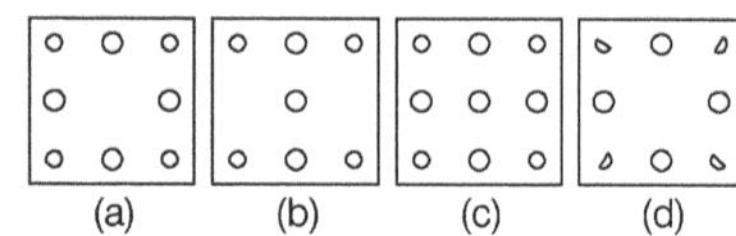

(a) (b) (c) (d)

16. Question Figures

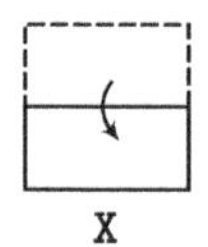
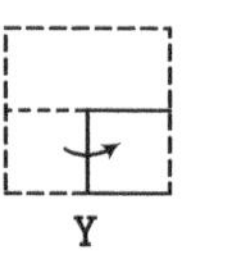
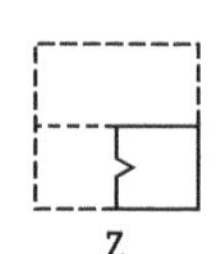

X Y Z

« SSC DEO 2011

Answer Figures

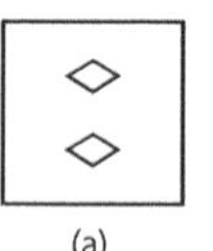
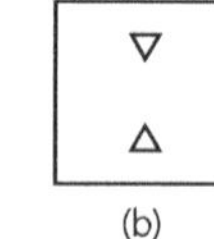
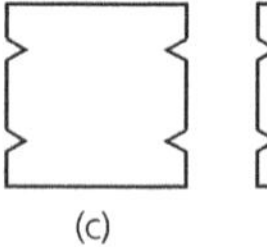
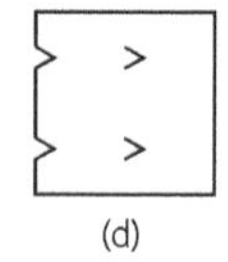

(a) (b) (c) (d)

17. Question Figures

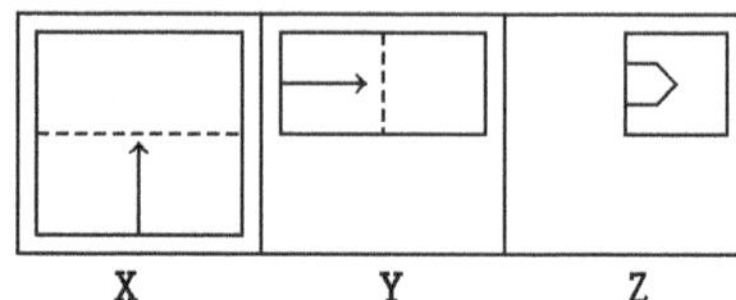

X Y Z

« SSC Steno 2016

Answer Figures

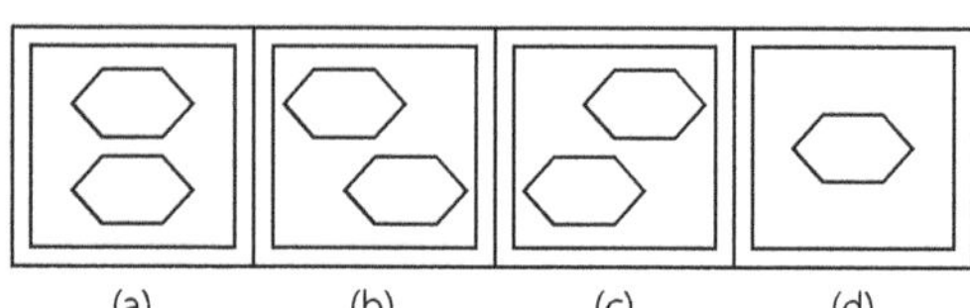

(a) (b) (c) (d)

18. Question Figures

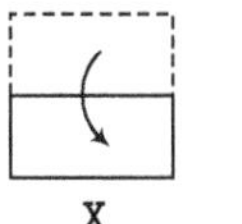
X

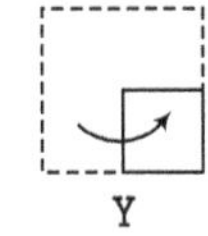
Y

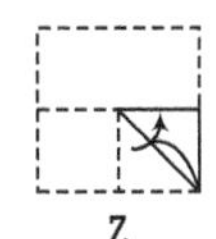
Z

« SSC MTS 2013

Answer Figures

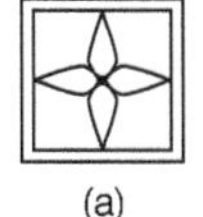
(a)

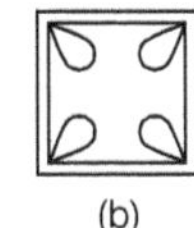
(b)

(c)

(d)

19. Question Figures

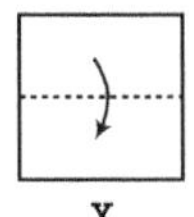
X

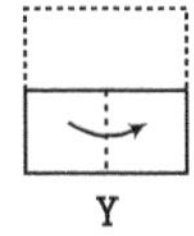
Y

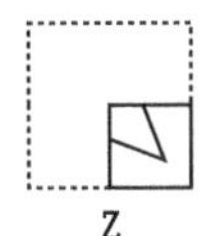
Z

Answer Figures

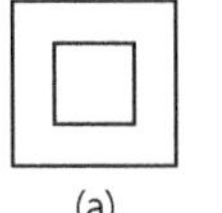
(a)

(b)

(c)

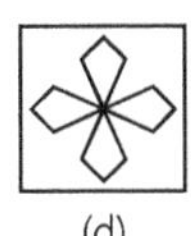
(d)

20. Question Figures

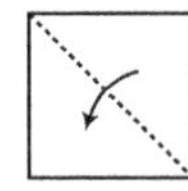
X

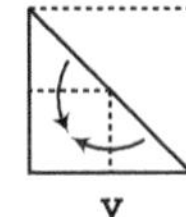
Y

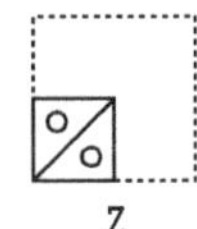
Z

« SSC CPO 2009

Answer Figures

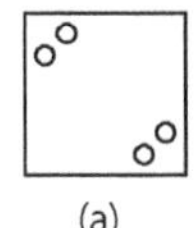
(a)

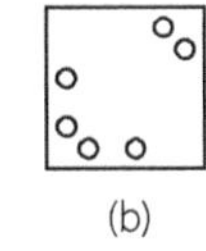
(b)

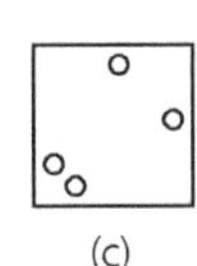
(c)

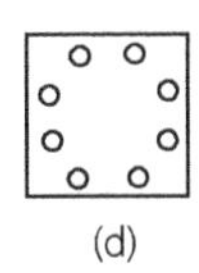
(d)

21. Question Figures

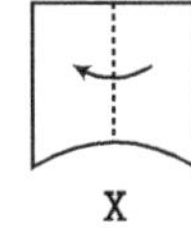
X

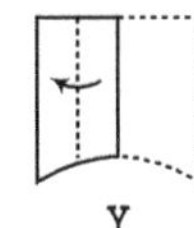
Y

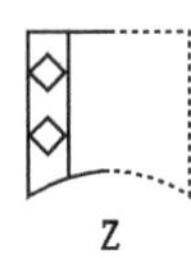
Z

Answer Figures

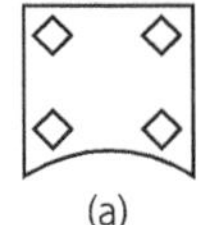
(a)

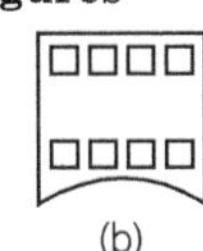
(b)

(c)

(d)

22. Question Figures

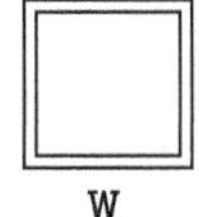
W

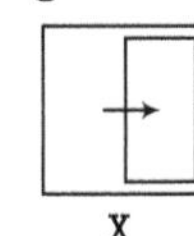
X

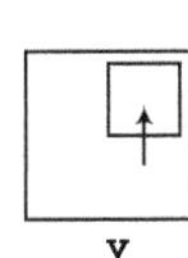
Y

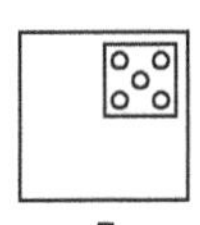
Z

« SSC 10+2 2012

Answer Figures

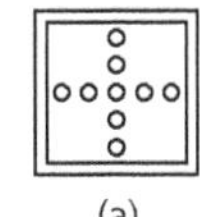
(a)

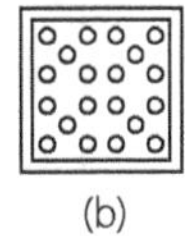
(b)

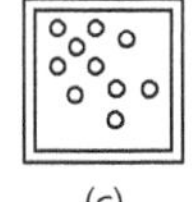
(c)

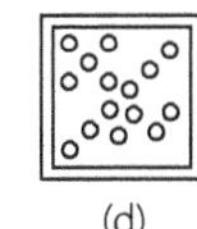
(d)

23. Question Figures

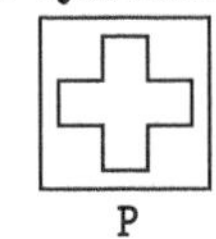
P

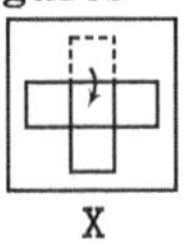
X

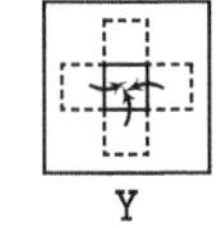
Y

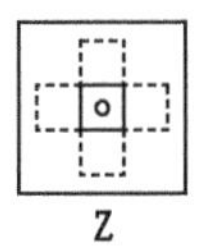
Z

« SSC FCI 2012

Answer Figures

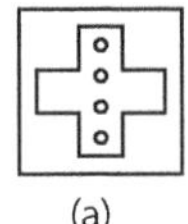
(a)

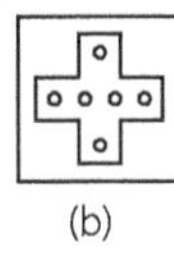
(b)

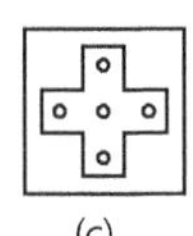
(c)

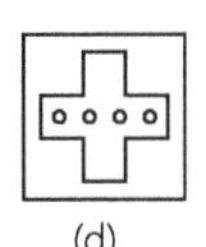
(d)

24. Question Figures

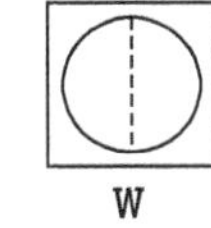
W

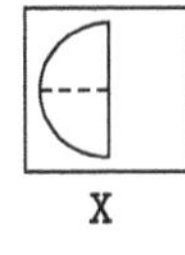
X

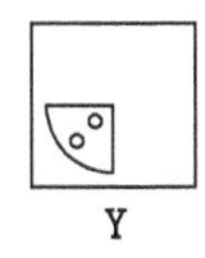
Y

« SSC DEO 2012

Answer Figures

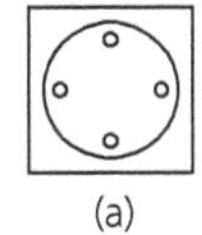
(a)

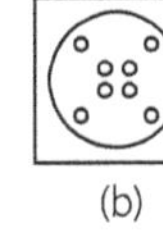
(b)

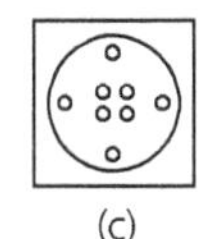
(c)

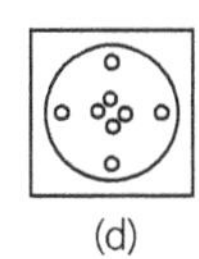
(d)

25. Question Figures

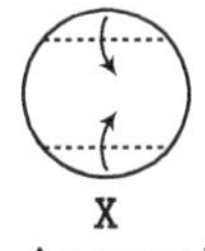
X

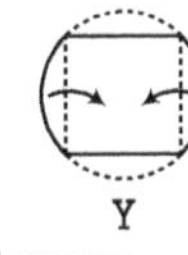
Y

Z

Answer Figures

(a)

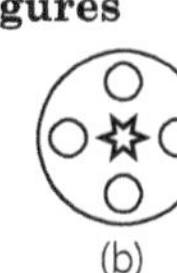
(b)

(c)

(d)

26. Question Figures

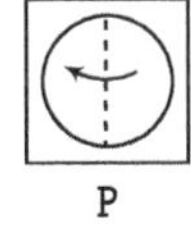
P

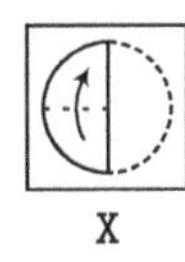
X

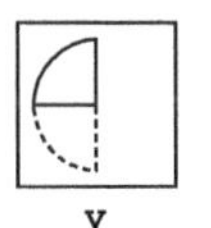
Y

Z

« SSC MTS 2013; SSC FCI 2012

Answer Figures

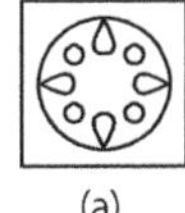
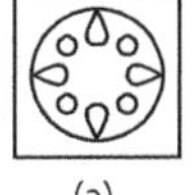
(a)

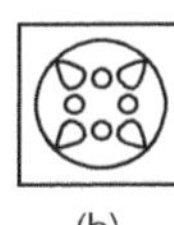
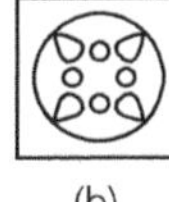
(b)

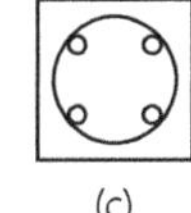
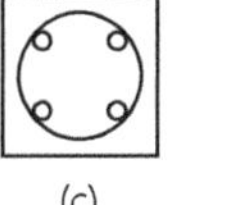
(c)

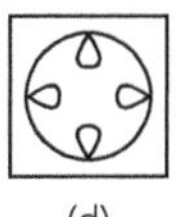
(d)

27. Question Figures

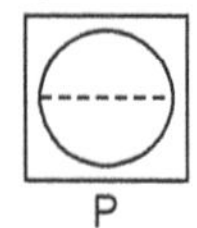
P
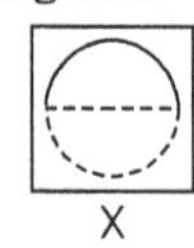
X
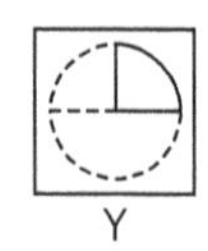
Y
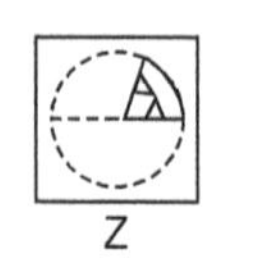
Z

« SSC CPO 2013

Answer Figures

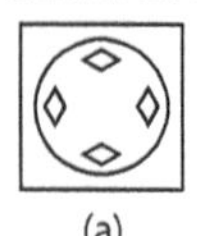
(a)
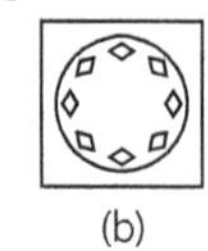
(b)
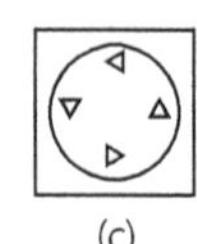
(c)
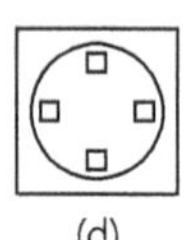
(d)

28. Question Figures

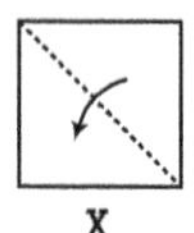
X
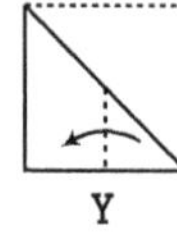
Y
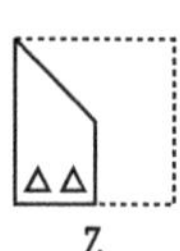
Z

Answer Figures

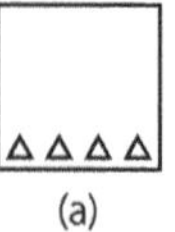
(a)
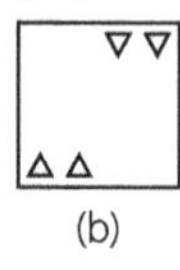
(b)
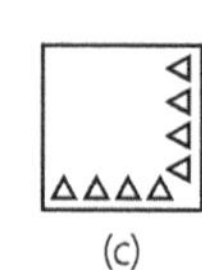
(c)
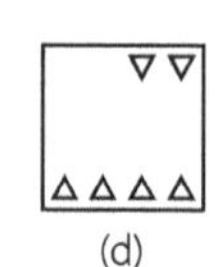
(d)

29. Question Figures

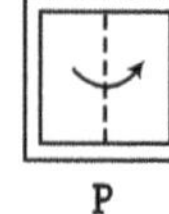
P
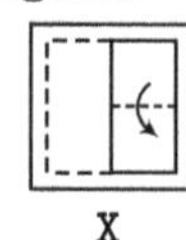
X
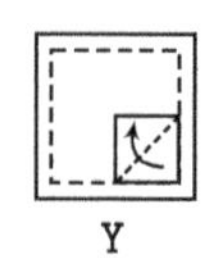
Y
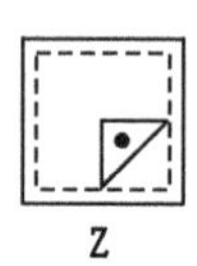
Z

« SSC MTS 2012

Answer Figures

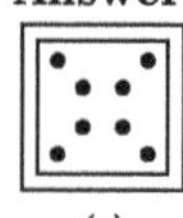
(a)
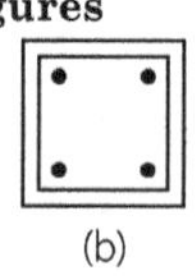
(b)
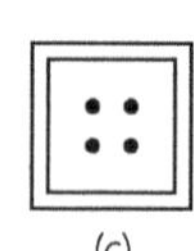
(c)
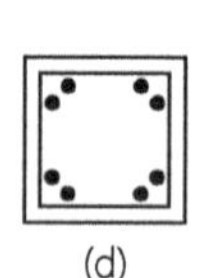
(d)

30. Question Figures

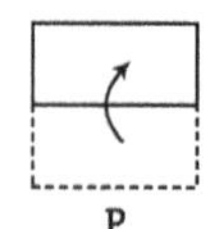
P
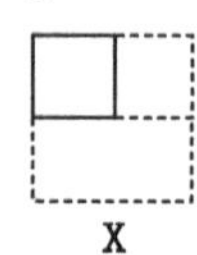
X
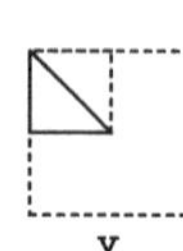
Y
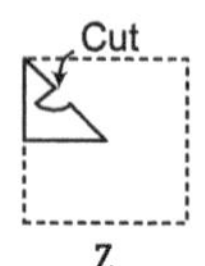

Z

« SSC MTS 2014

Answer Figures

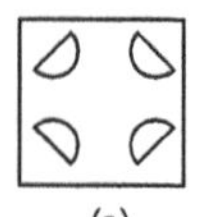
(a)
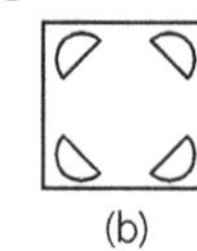
(b)
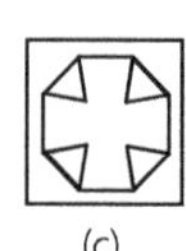
(c)
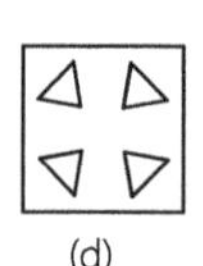
(d)

31. Question Figures

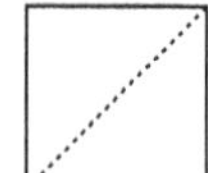
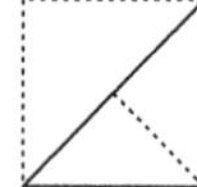
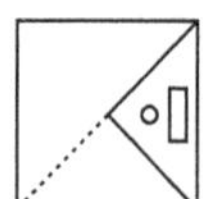

« SSC CGL 2019

Answer Figures

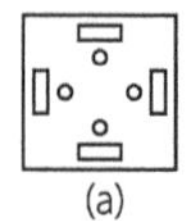
(a)
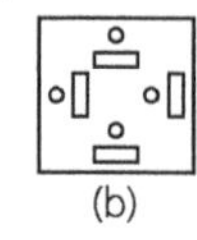
(b)
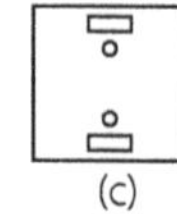
(c)
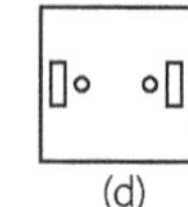
(d)

32. Question Figures

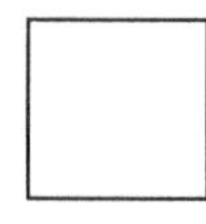
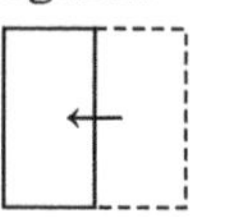
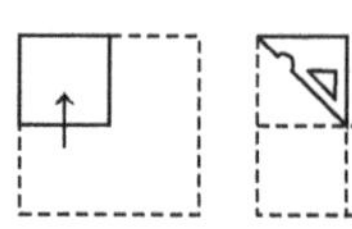

« UPSSSC Mandi Parishad 2018

Answer Figures

(a)
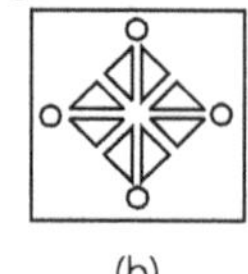
(b)
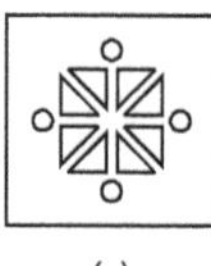
(c)
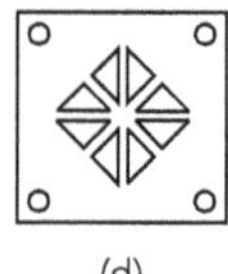
(d)

33. Question Figures

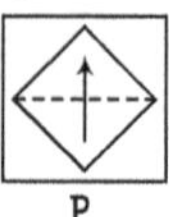
P
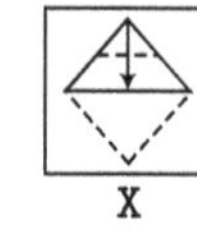
X
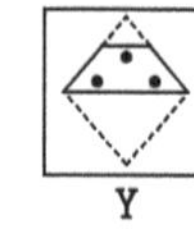
Y
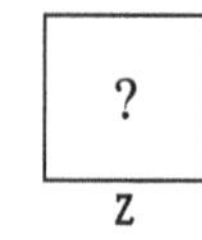

Z

« SSC 10+2 2013

Answer Figures

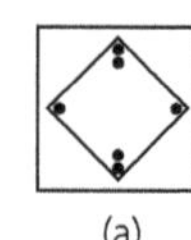
(a)
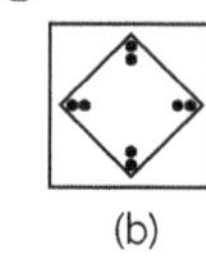
(b)
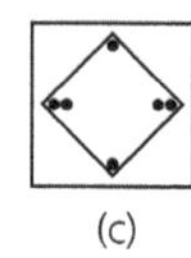
(c)
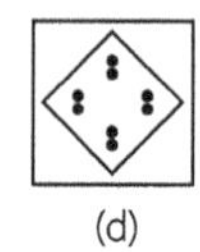
(d)

34. Question Figures

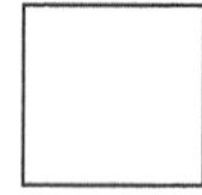
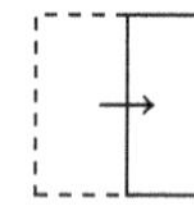
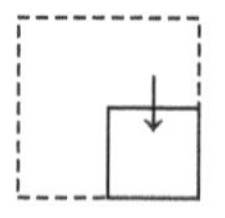
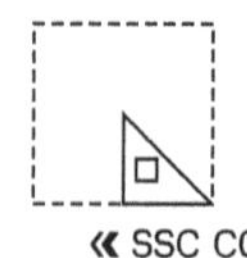

« SSC CGL 2017

Answer Figures

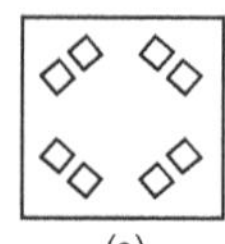
(a)
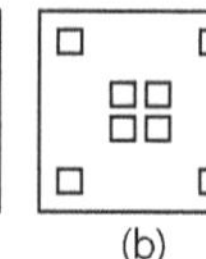
(b)
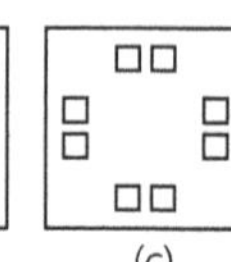
(c)
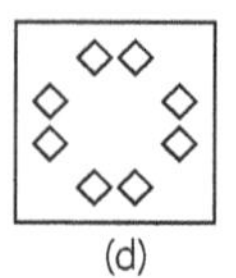
(d)

35. Question Figures

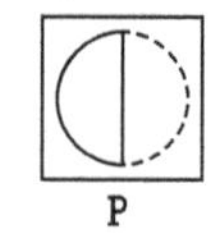
P
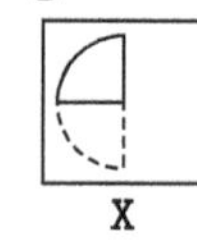
X
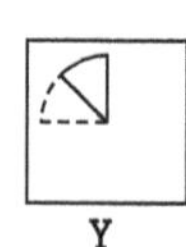
Y
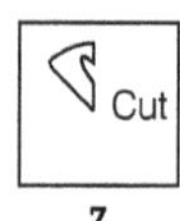

Z

« SSC MTS 2013

Answer Figures

(a)

(b)
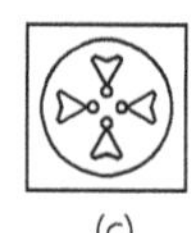
(c)
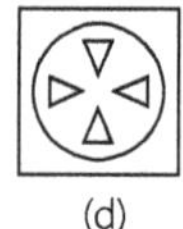
(d)

36. Question Figures

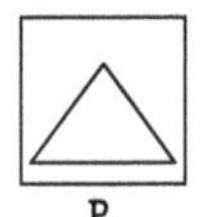
P

X

Y
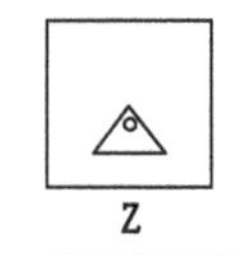
Z

« SSC MTS 2014

Answer Figure

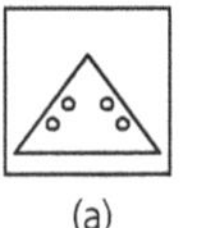
(a)
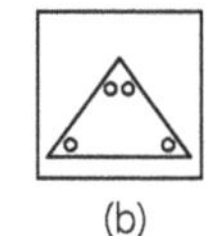
(b)
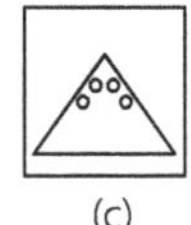
(c)
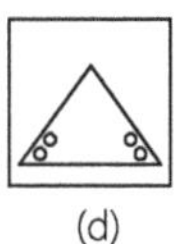
(d)

37. Question Figures

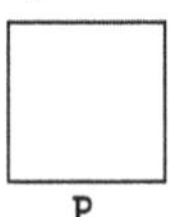
P
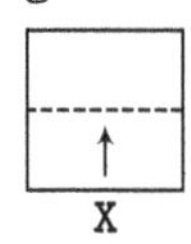
X
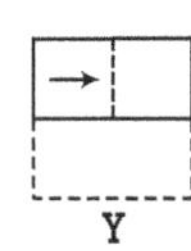
Y
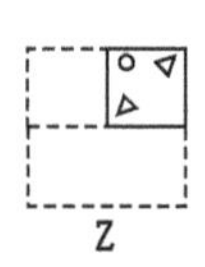
Z

« SSC 10+2 2013

Answer Figures

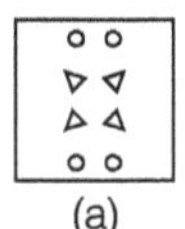
(a)
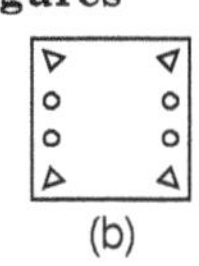
(b)
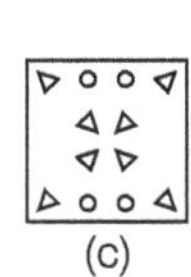
(c)
(d)

38. Question Figures

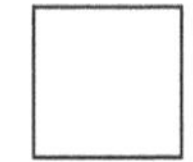
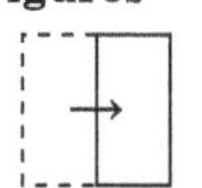
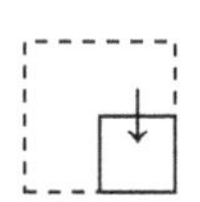

« SSC CGL 2017

Answer Figures

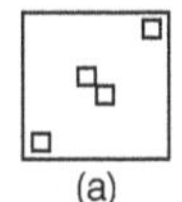
(a)
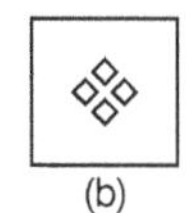
(b)
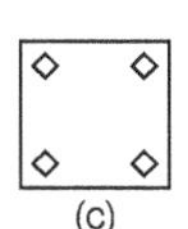
(c)
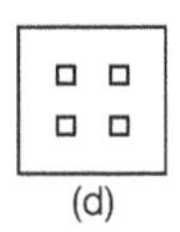
(d)

39. Question Figures

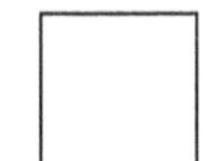
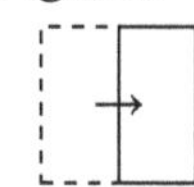
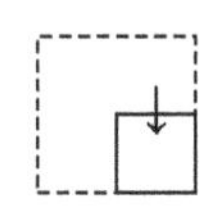

« SSC CGL 2017

Answer Figures

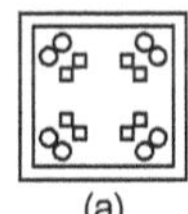
(a)
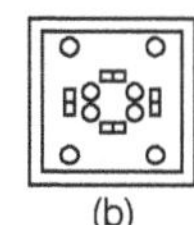
(b)
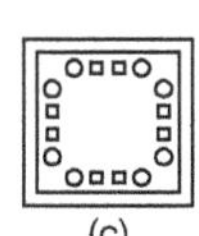
(c)
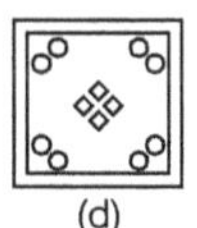
(d)

40. Question Figures

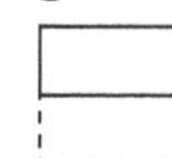
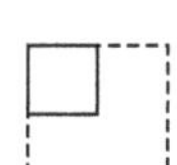

« SSC CGL 2017

Answer Figures

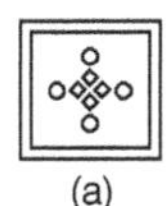
(a)
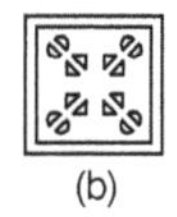
(b)
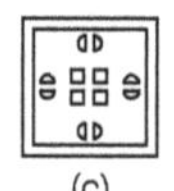
(c)
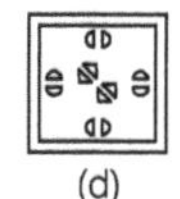
(d)

41. Question Figures

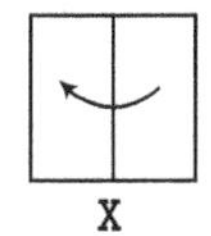
X
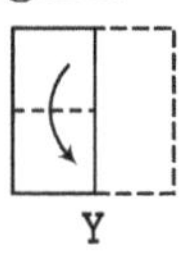
Y
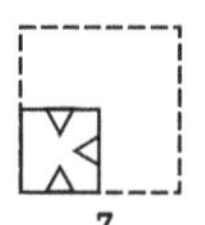
Z

« SSC Constable 2012

Answer Figures

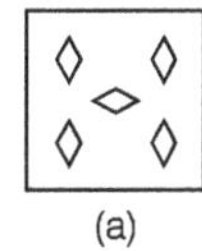
(a)
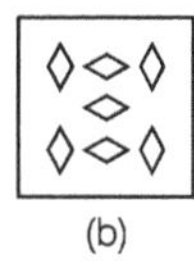
(b)

(c)

(d)

42. Question Figures

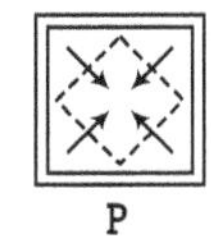
P
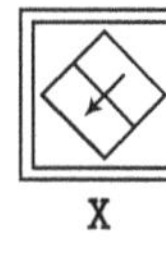
X

Y
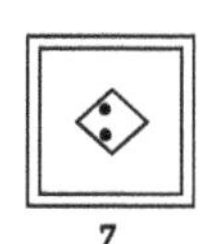
Z

Answer Figures

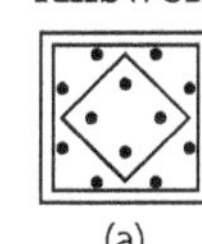
(a)
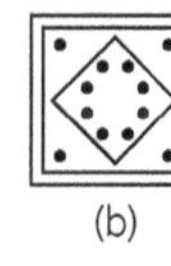
(b)
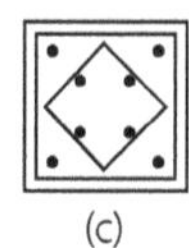
(c)
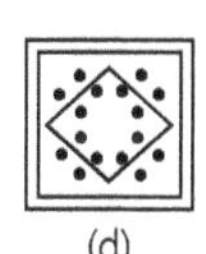
(d)

43. Question Figures

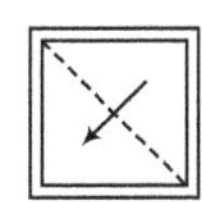
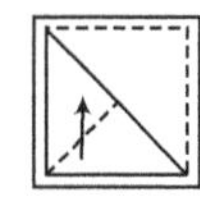
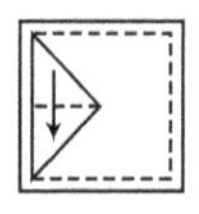
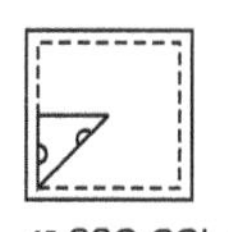

« SSC CGL 2013

Answer Figures

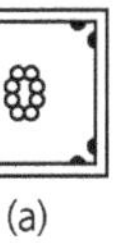
(a)

(b)
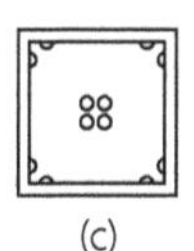
(c)
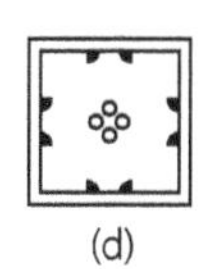
(d)

44. Question Figures

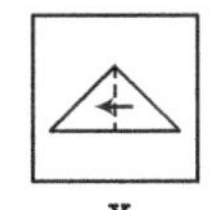
X

Y

Z

« SSC Steno 2012

Answer Figures

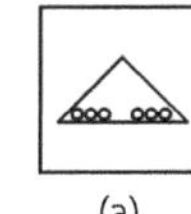
(a)
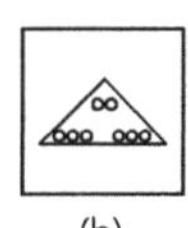
(b)
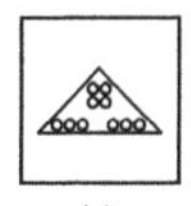
(c)

(d)

45. Question Figures

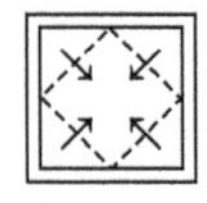 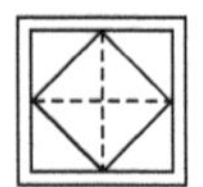 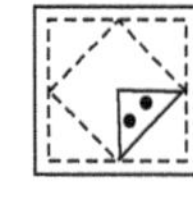

« SSC CGL 2017

Answer Figures

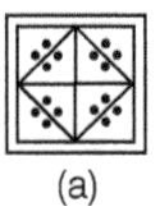 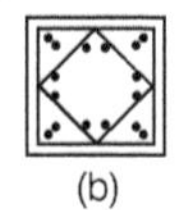 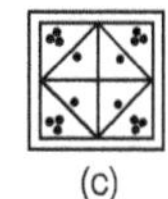 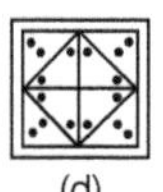

(a) (b) (c) (d)

46. Question Figures

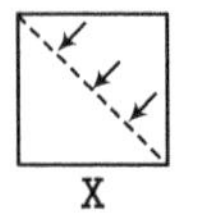 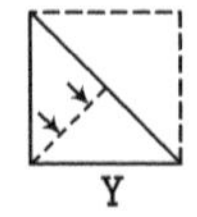 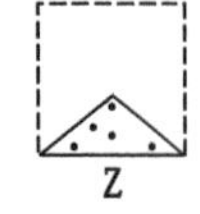

X Y Z

« SSC Steno 2012

Answer Figures

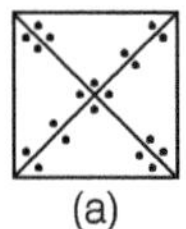 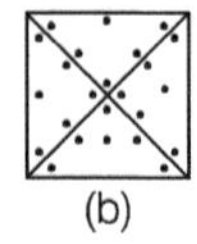 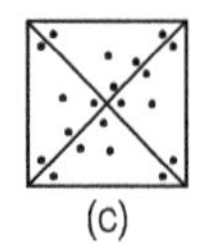 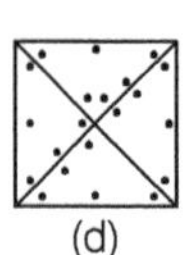

(a) (b) (c) (d)

47. Question Figures

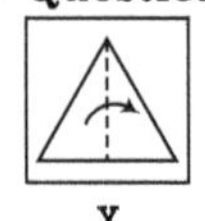  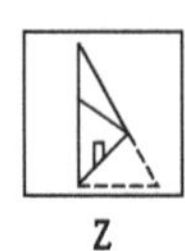

X Y Z

« SSC MTS 2013

Answer Figures

(a) (b) (c) (d)

48. Question Figures

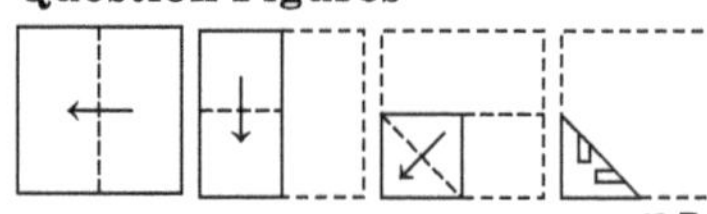

« Delhi Police SI, ASI 2016

Answer Figures

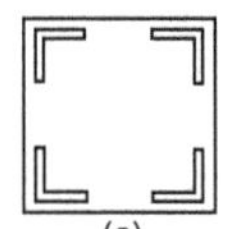  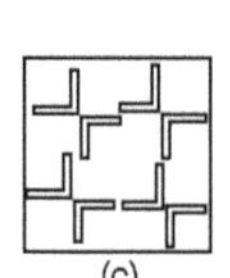 

(a) (b) (c) (d)

49. Question Figures

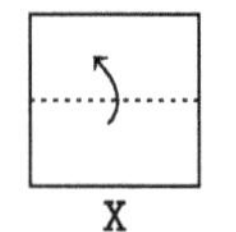 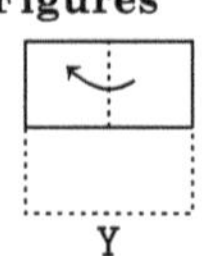 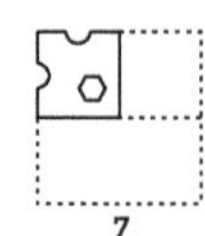

X Y Z

« SSC MTS 2019

Answer Figures

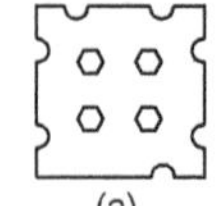 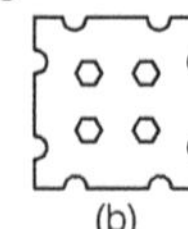 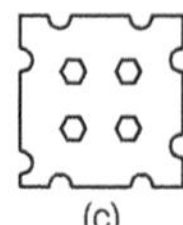 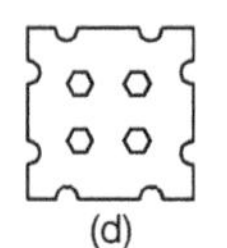

(a) (b) (c) (d)

50. Question Figures

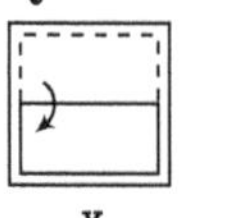 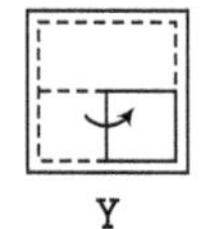 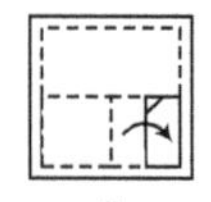

X Y Z

« SSC FCI 2012

Answer Figures

 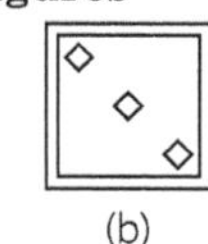  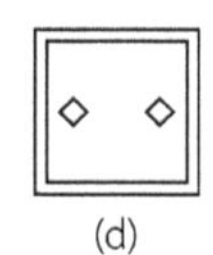

(a) (b) (c) (d)

51. Question Figures

 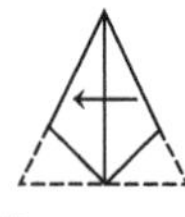 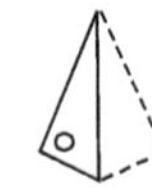

« SSC Constable 2015

Answer Figures

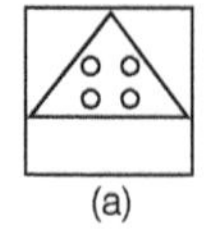 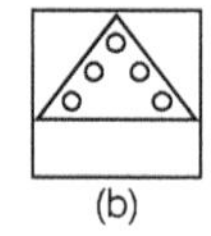 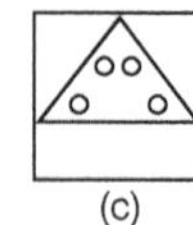 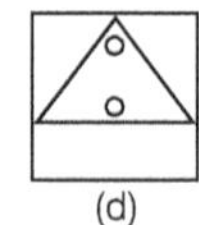

(a) (b) (c) (d)

52. Question Figures

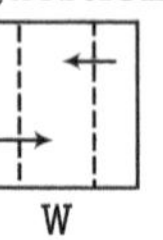 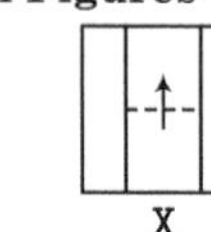 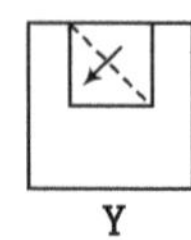 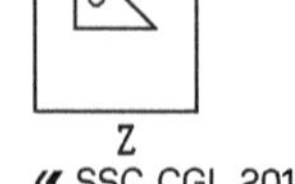

W X Y Z

« SSC CGL 2013

Answer Figures

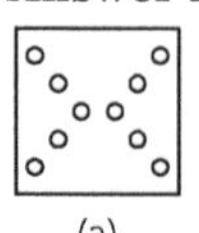 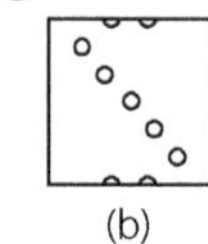 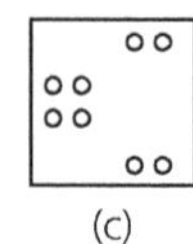 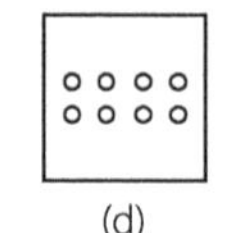

(a) (b) (c) (d)

53. Question Figures

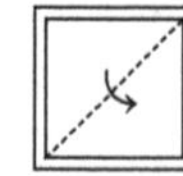 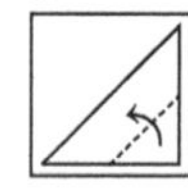 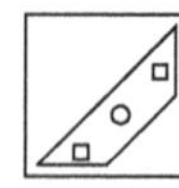

Answer Figures

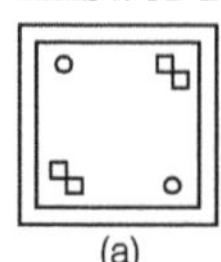 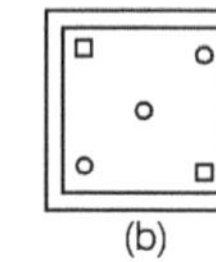  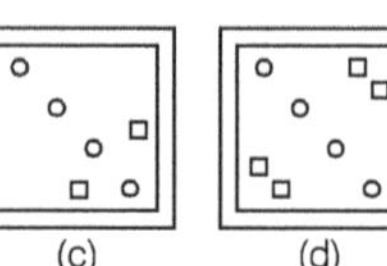

(a) (b) (c) (d)

54. Question Figures

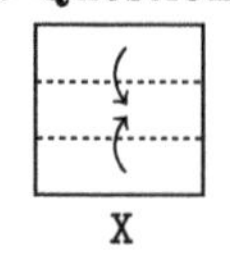 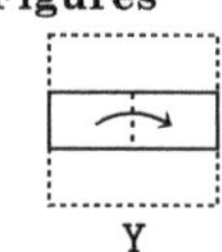 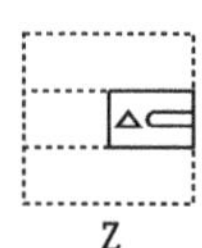

X Y Z

Answer Figures

  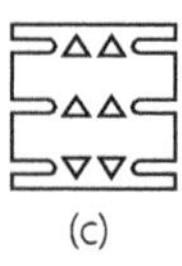 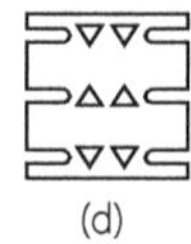

(a) (b) (c) (d)

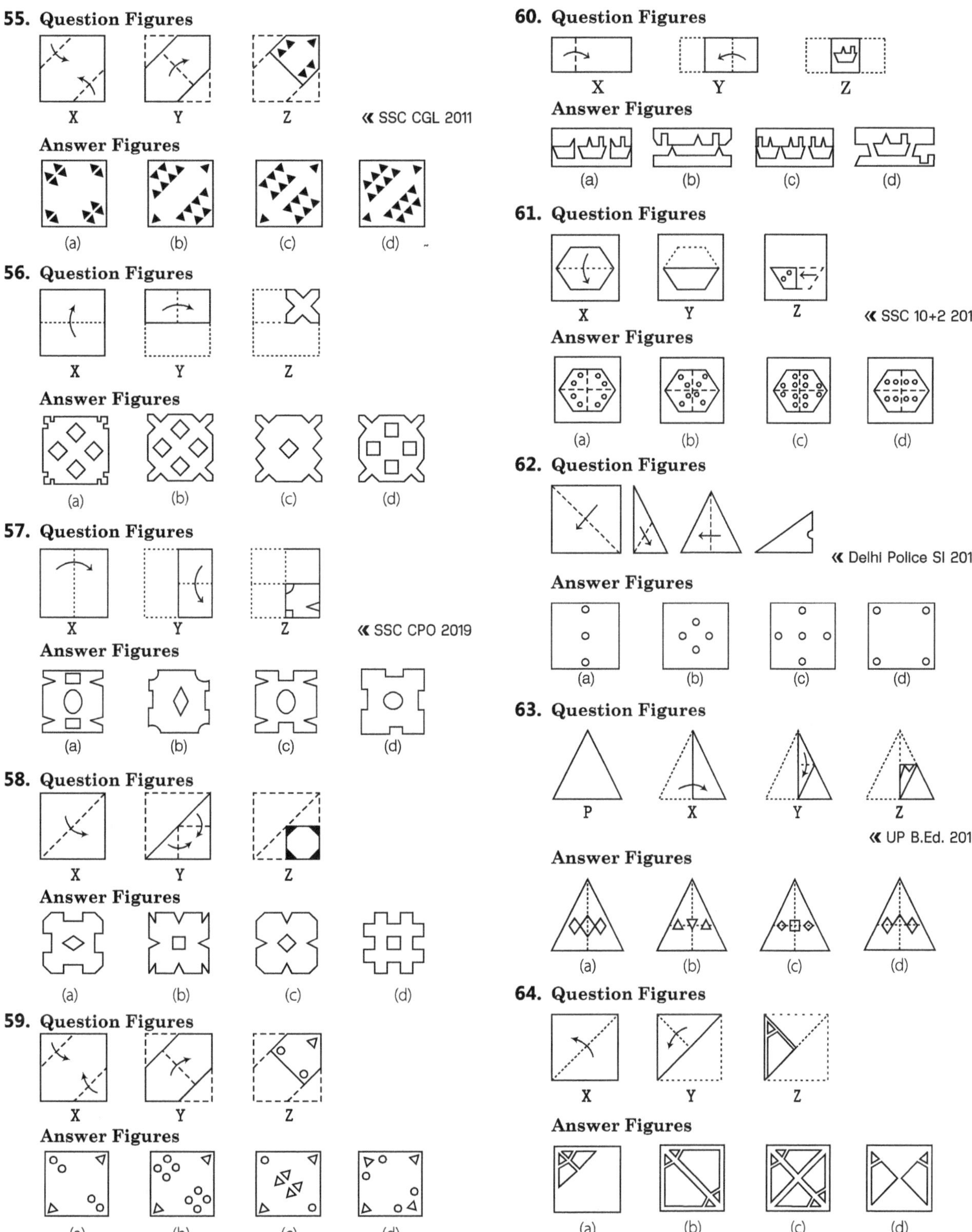
55. Question Figures
X
Y
Z
« SSC CGL 2011
Answer Figures
(a)
(b)
(c)
(d)
56. Question Figures
X
Y
Z
Answer Figures
(a)
(b)
(c)
(d)
57. Question Figures
X
Y
Z
« SSC CPO 2019
Answer Figures
(a)
(b)
(c)
(d)
58. Question Figures
X
Y
Z
Answer Figures
(a)
(b)
(c)
(d)
59. Question Figures
X
Y
Z
Answer Figures
(a)
(b)
(c)
(d)
60. Question Figures
X
Y
Z
Answer Figures
(a)
(b)
(c)
(d)
61. Question Figures
X
Y
Z
« SSC 10+2 2013
Answer Figures
(a)
(b)
(c)
(d)
62. Question Figures
« Delhi Police SI 2015
Answer Figures
(a)
(b)
(c)
(d)
63. Question Figures
P
X
Y
Z
« UP B.Ed. 2010
Answer Figures
(a)
(b)
(c)
(d)
64. Question Figures
X
Y
Z
Answer Figures
(a)
(b)
(c)
(d)

65. Question Figures

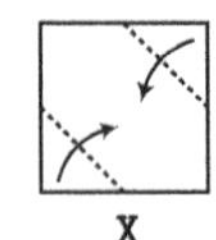 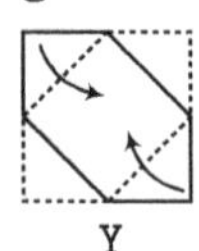 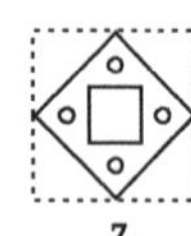

X Y Z

Answer Figures

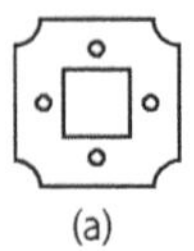   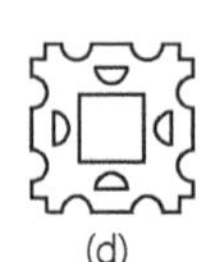

(a) (b) (c) (d)

66. Question Figures

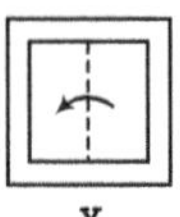 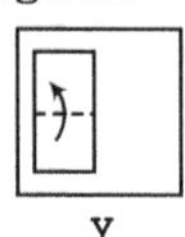 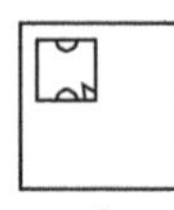

X Y Z « SSC CPO 2013

Answer Figures

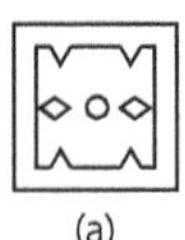 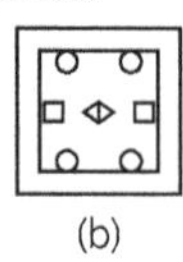 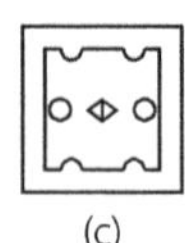 

(a) (b) (c) (d)

67. Question Figures

X Y Z

Answer Figures

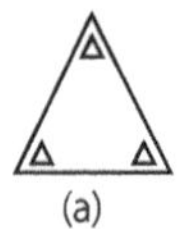 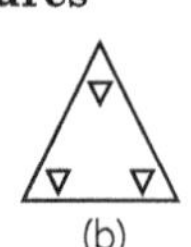  

(a) (b) (c) (d)

68. Question Figures

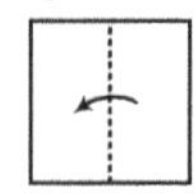 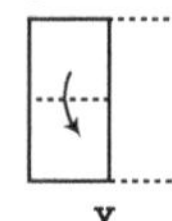 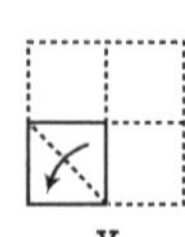 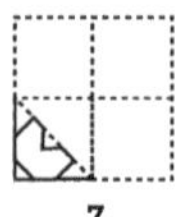

P X Y Z

Answer Figures

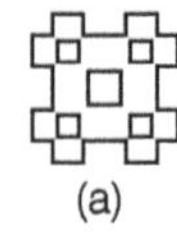   

(a) (b) (c) (d)

69. Suppose a square sheet of a paper is folded and creased. Then, a single ship of the scissor removes a corner of the fold as shown in the last step below. If the pattern is then unfolded, which square will it now resemble?

Question Figures

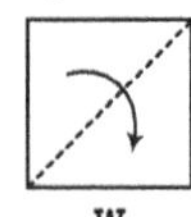 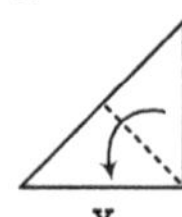  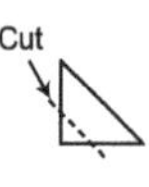

W X Y Z

Answer Figures

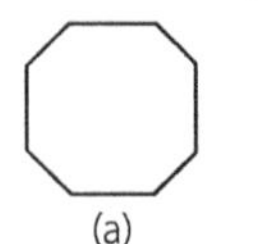 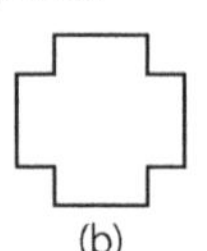  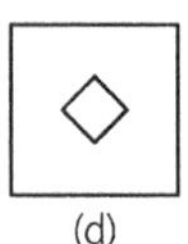

(a) (b) (c) (d)

DIRECTIONS ~ (Q. Nos. 70-80) *In each of the following questions, select a figure from amongst the answer figures that would most closely resemble the sheet (X) when it is unfolded.*

Question Figure **Answer Figures**

70. 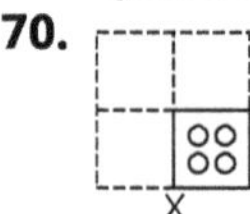 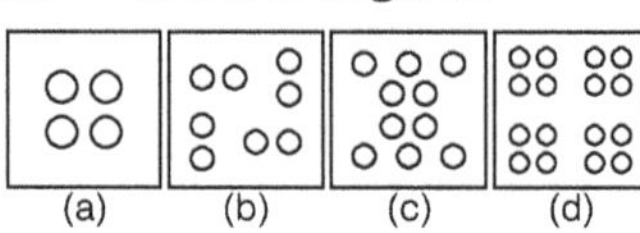

X (a) (b) (c) (d)

« SSC Steno 2017

71. 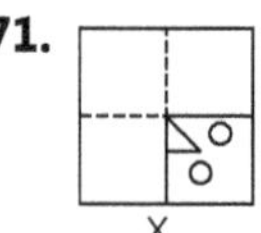 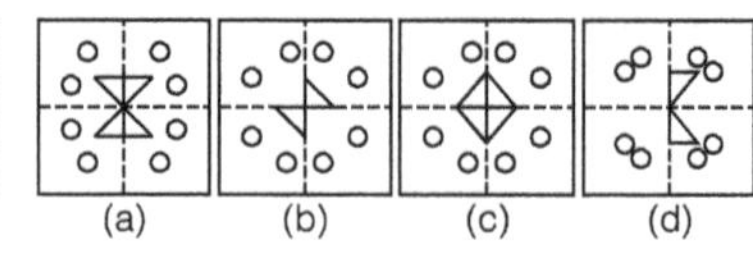

X (a) (b) (c) (d)

« SSC CGL 2015

72. 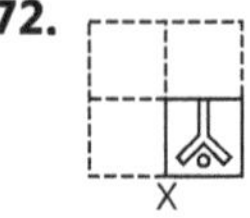 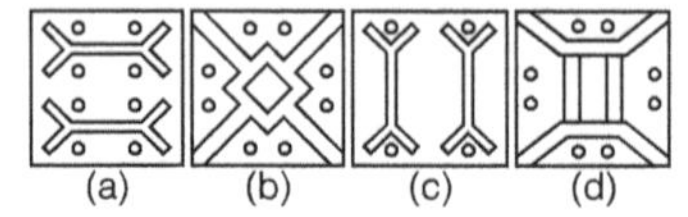

X (a) (b) (c) (d)

« UP B.Ed 2004

73. 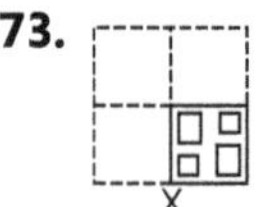 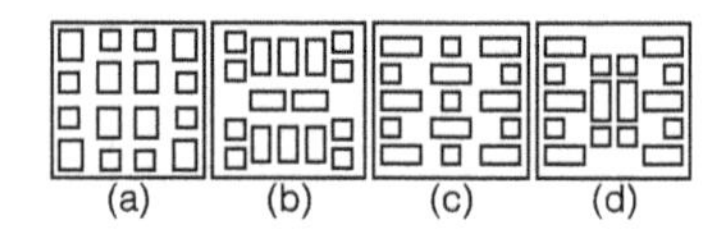

X (a) (b) (c) (d)

« SSC 10+2 2007

74. 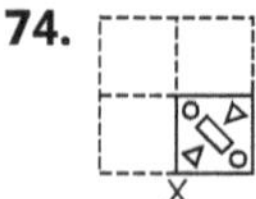 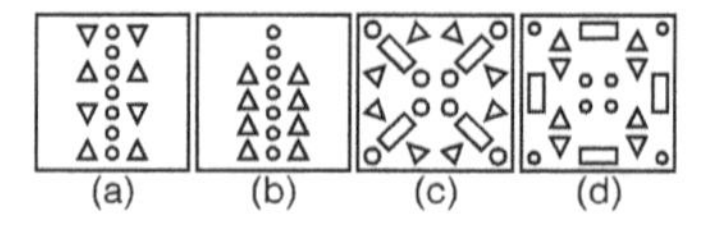

X (a) (b) (c) (d)

« SSC Steno 2007

75.  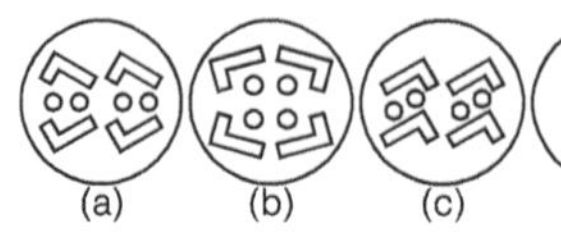

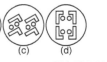

X (a) (b) (c) (d)

« SSC CPO 2007

76. 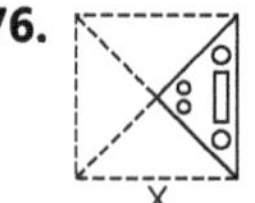 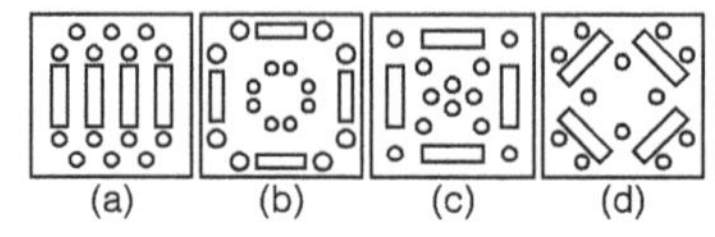

X (a) (b) (c) (d)

« SSC MTS 2003

77. 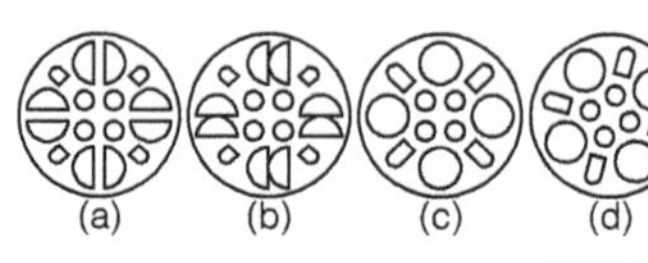

X (a) (b) (c) (d)

« UP B.Ed 2007

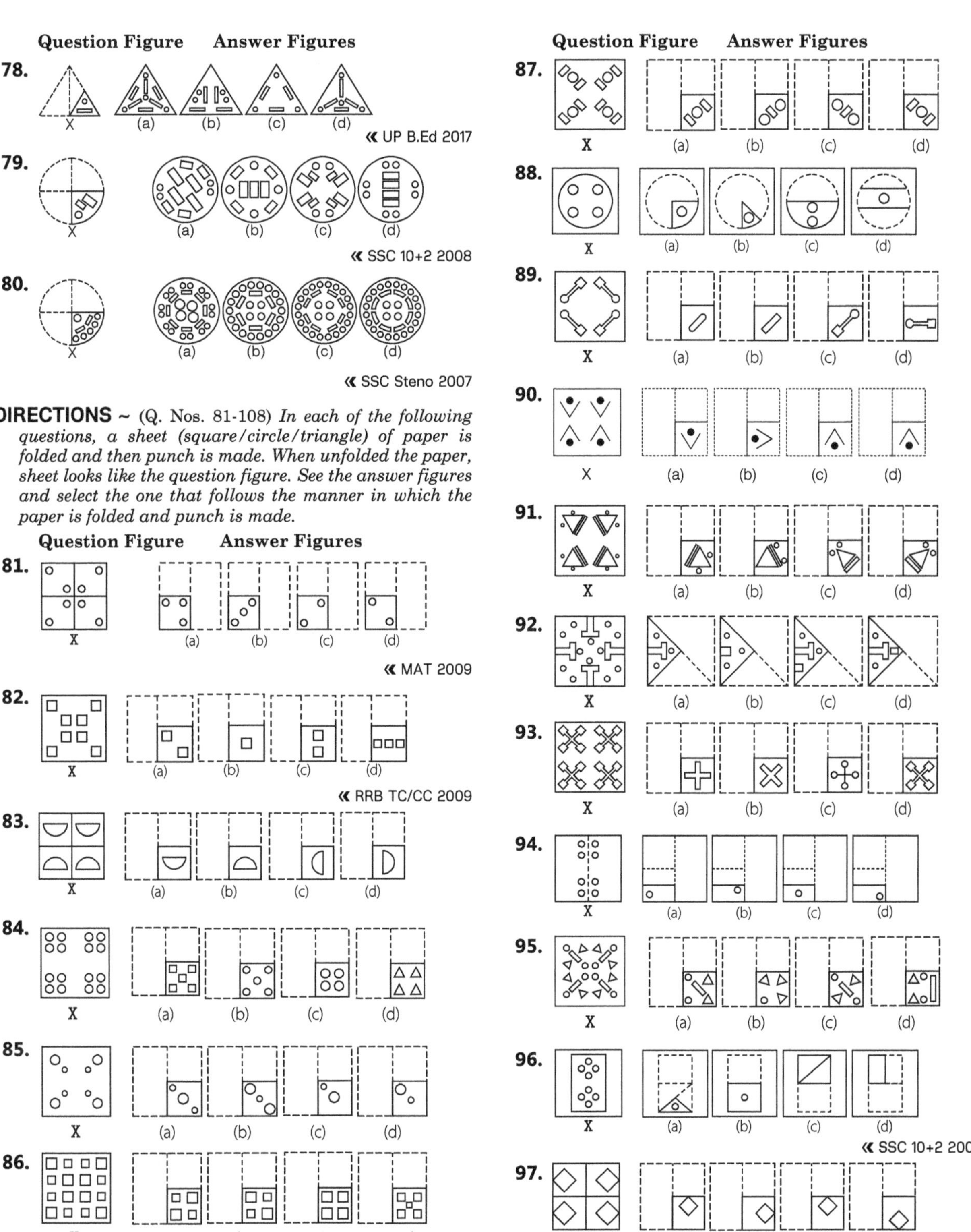

DIRECTIONS ~ (Q. Nos. 81-108) *In each of the following questions, a sheet (square/circle/triangle) of paper is folded and then punch is made. When unfolded the paper, sheet looks like the question figure. See the answer figures and select the one that follows the manner in which the paper is folded and punch is made.*

Question Figure **Answer Figures**

81. X (a) (b) (c) (d)

« MAT 2009

82. X (a) (b) (c) (d)

« RRB TC/CC 2009

83. X (a) (b) (c) (d)

84. X (a) (b) (c) (d)

85. X (a) (b) (c) (d)

86. X (a) (b) (c) (d)

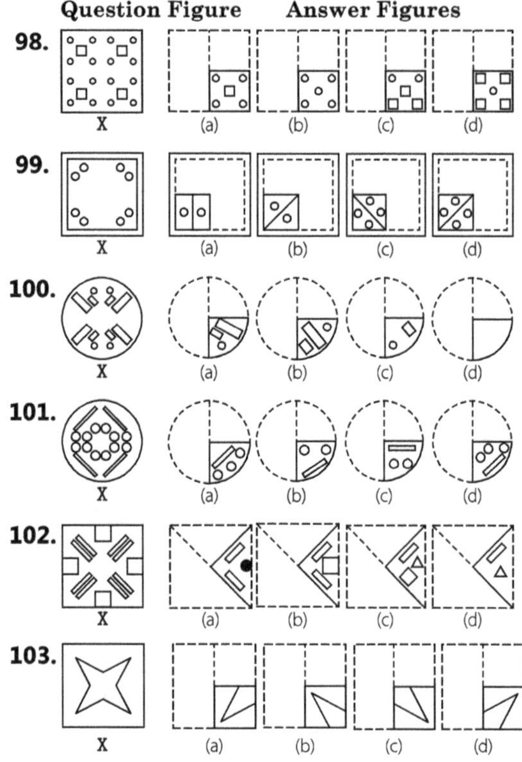

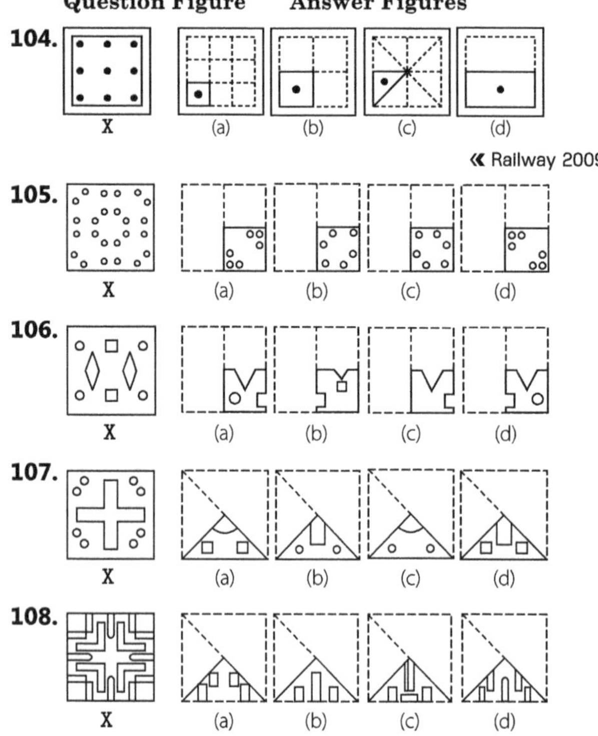

Answers WITH EXPLANATIONS

1. (*b*) After unfolding the last fold, the transparent sheet will look like the figure given in option (b).

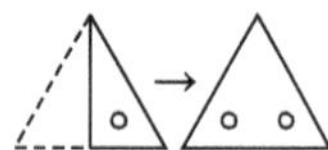

2. (*d*) After unfolding the last fold, the transparent sheet will look like the figure given in option (d).

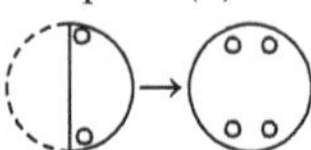

3. (*d*) After unfolding the last fold, the transparent sheet will look like the figure given in option (d).

4. (c) After unfolding the last fold, the transparent sheet will look like the figure given in option (c).

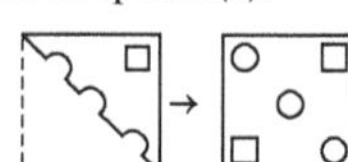

5. (*a*) After unfolding the last fold, the transparent sheet will look like the figure given in option (a).

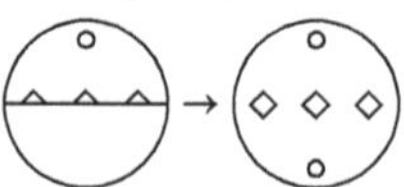

6. (*d*) After unfolding the last fold, the transparent sheet will look like the figure given in option (d).

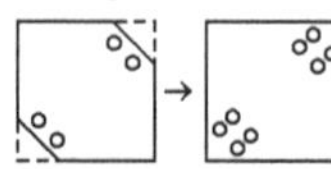

7. (*b*) After unfolding the last fold, the transparent sheet will look like the figure given in option (b).

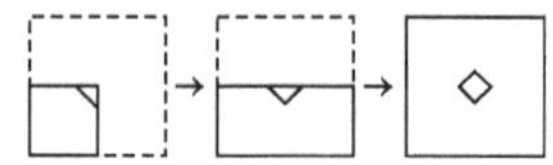

8. (*d*) After unfolding the last fold, the transparent sheet will look like the figure given in option (d).

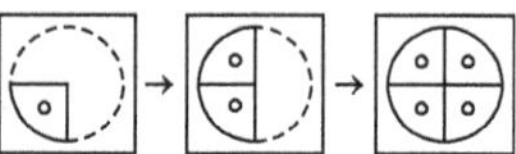

9. (*d*) After unfolding the last fold, the transparent sheet will look like the figure given in option (d).

10. (*b*) After unfolding the last fold, the transparent sheet will look like the figure given in option (b).

11. (*a*) After unfolding the last fold, the transparent sheet will look like the figure given in option (a).

12. (*b*) After unfolding the last fold, the transparent sheet will look like the figure given in option (b).

13. (*b*) After unfolding the last fold, the transparent sheet will look like the figure given in option (b).

14. (*d*) After unfolding the last fold, the transparent sheet will look like the figure given in option (d).

15. (*a*) After unfolding the last fold, the transparent sheet will look like the figure given in option (a).

16. (*a*) After unfolding the last fold, the transparent sheet will look like the figure given in option (a).

17. (*a*) After unfolding the last fold, the transparent sheet will look like the figure given in option (a).

18. (*b*) After unfolding the last fold, the transparent sheet will look like the figure given in option (b).

19. (*b*) After unfolding the last fold, the transparent sheet will look like the figure given in option (b).

20. (*d*) After unfolding the last fold, the transparent sheet will look like the figure given in option (d).

21. (*c*) After unfolding the last fold, the transparent sheet will look like the figure given in option (c).

22. (*b*) After unfolding the last fold, the transparent sheet will look like the figure given in option (b).

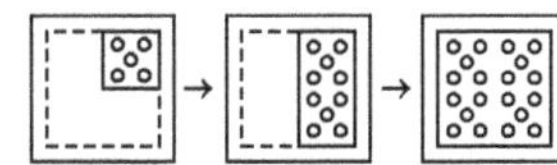

23. (*c*) After unfolding the last fold, the transparent sheet will look like the figure given in option (c).

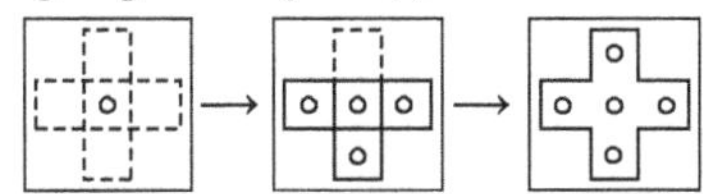

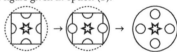

24. (*b*) After unfolding the last fold, the transparent sheet will look like the figure given in option (b).

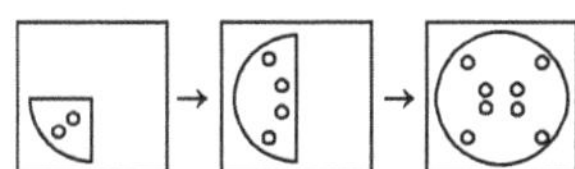

25. (*b*) After unfolding the last fold, the transparent sheet will look like the figure given in option (b).

26. (*d*) After unfolding the last fold, the transparent sheet will look like the figure given in option (d).

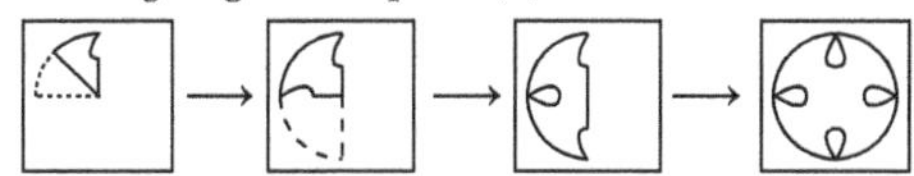

27. (*b*) After unfolding the last fold, the transparent sheet will look like the figure given in option (b).

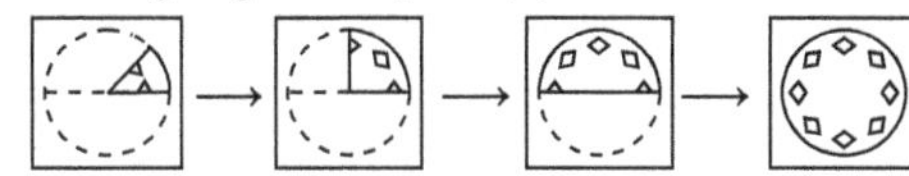

28. (*c*) After unfolding the last fold, the transparent sheet will look like the figure given in option (c).

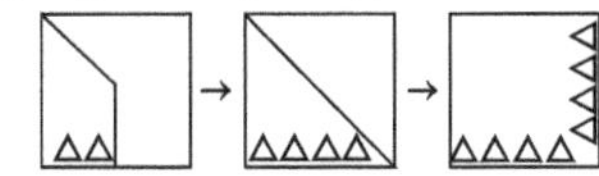

29. (*a*) After unfolding the last fold, the transparent sheet will look like the figure given option (a).

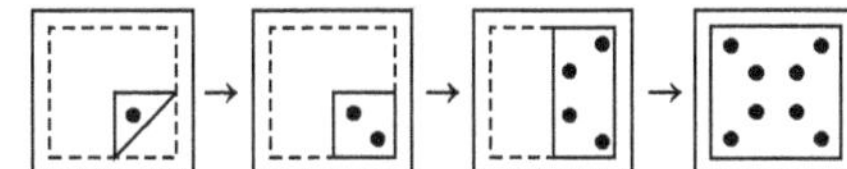

30. (a) After unfolding the last fold, the transparent sheet will look like the figure given in option (a).

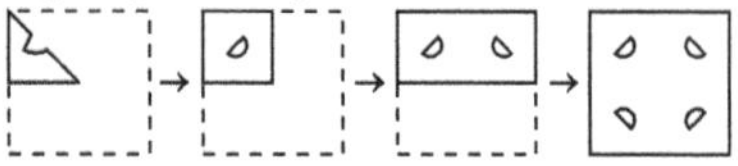

31. (a) After unfolding the last fold, the transparent sheet will look like the figure given in option (a).

32. (a) After unfolding the last fold, the transparent sheet will look like the figure given is option (a).

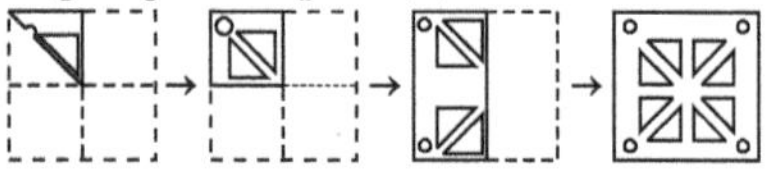

33. (d) After unfolding the last fold, the transparent sheet will look like the figure given in option (d).

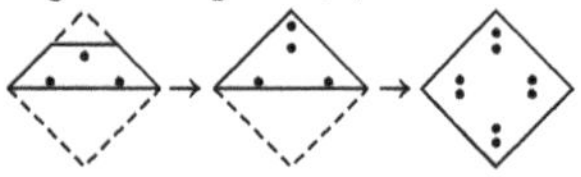

34. (c) After unfolding the last fold, the transparent sheet will look like the figure given in option (c).

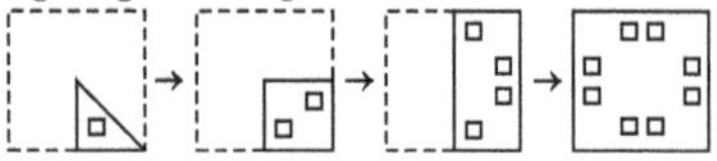

35. (a) After unfolding the last fold, the transparent sheet will look like the figure given in option (a).

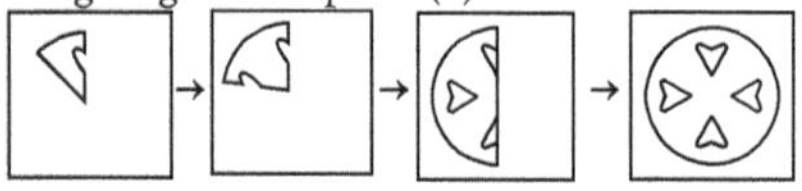

36. (a) After unfolding the last fold, the transparent sheet will look like the figure given in option (a).

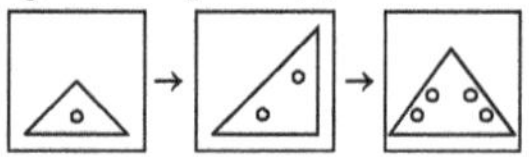

37. (c) After unfolding the last fold, the transparent sheet will look like the figure given in option (c).

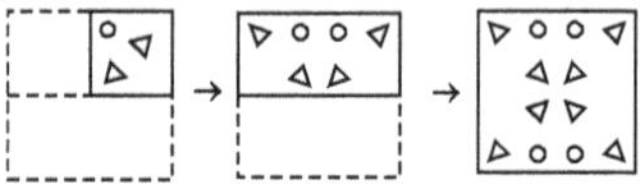

38. (d) After unfolding the last fold, the transparent sheet will look like the figure given in option (d).

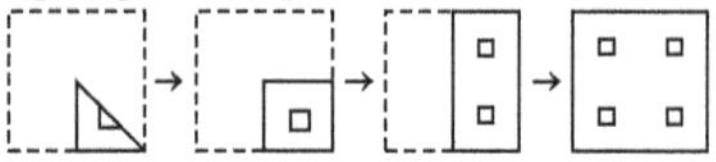

39. (a) After unfolding the last fold, the transparent sheet will look like the figure given in option (a).

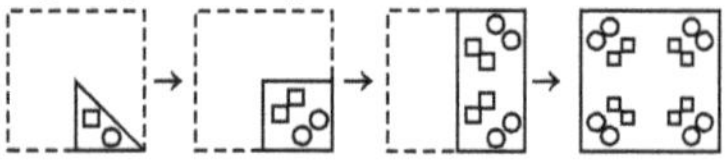

40. (c) After unfolding the last fold, the transparent sheet will look like the figure given in option (c).

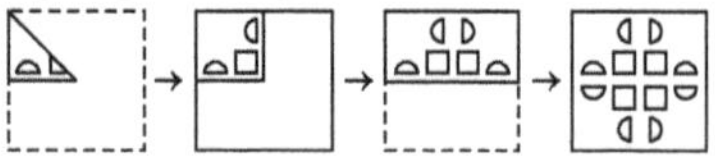

41. (c) After unfolding the last fold, the transparent sheet will look like the figure given in option (c)

42. (d) After unfolding the last fold, the transparent sheet will look like the figure given in option (d).

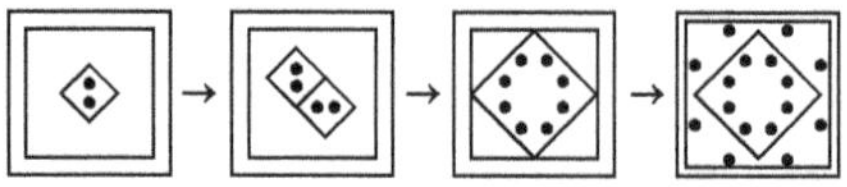

43. (c) After unfolding the last fold, the transparent sheet will look like the figure given in option (c).

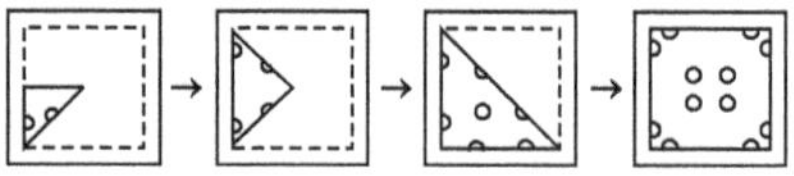

44. (d) After unfolding the last fold, the transparent sheet will look like the figure given in option (d).

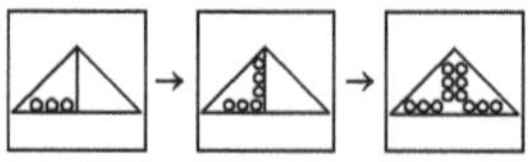

45. (a) After unfolding the last fold, the transparent sheet will look like the figure given in option (a).

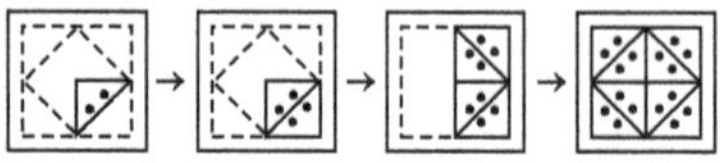

46. (c) After unfolding the last fold, the transparent sheet will look like the figure given in option (c).

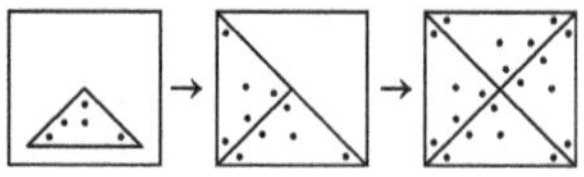

47. (d) After unfolding the last fold, the transparent sheet will look like the figure given in option (d).

48. (b) After unfolding the last fold, the transparent sheet will look like the figure given in option (b).

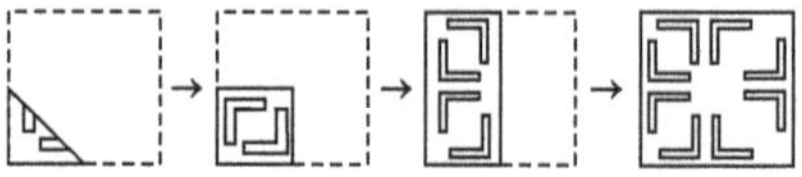

49. (b) After unfolding the last fold, the transparent sheet will look like the figure given in option (b).

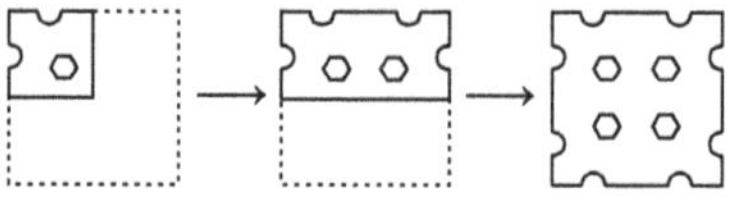

50. (d) After unfolding the last fold, the transparent sheet will look like the figure given in option (d).

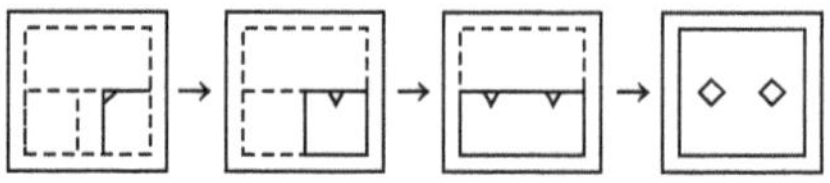

51. (c) After unfolding the last fold, the transparent sheet will look like the figure given in option (c).

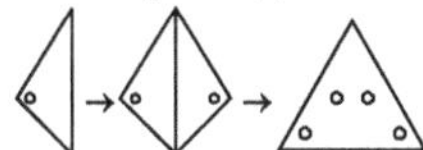

52. (c) After unfolding the last fold, the transparent sheet will look like the figure given in option (c).

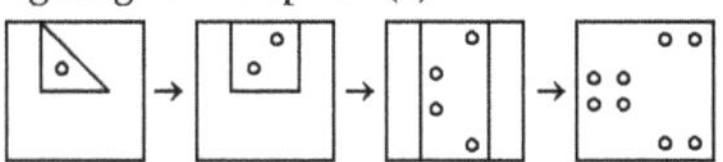

53. (d) After unfolding the last fold, the transparent sheet will look like the figure given in option (d).

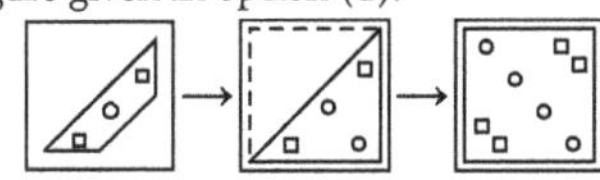

54. (d) After unfolding the last fold, the transparent sheet will look like the figure given in option (d).

55. (b) After unfolding the last fold, the transparent sheet will look like the figure given in option (b).

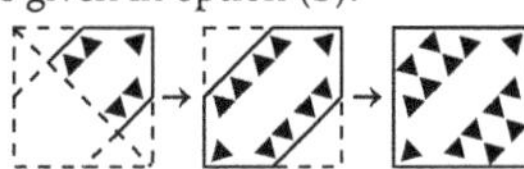

56. (b) After unfolding the last fold, the transparent sheet will look like the figure given in option (b).

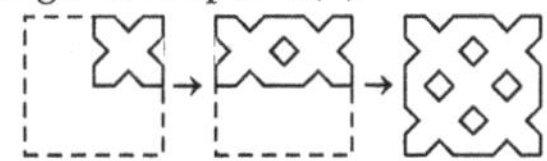

57. (c) After unfolding the last fold, the transparent sheet will look like the figure given in option (c).

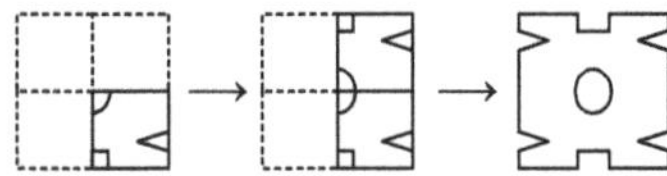

58. (c) After unfolding the last fold, the transparent sheet will look like the figure given in option (c).

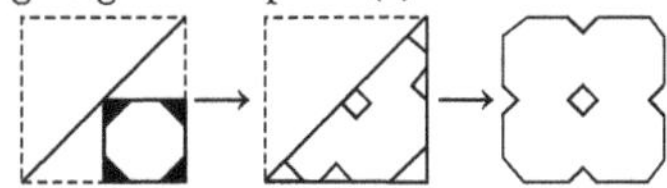

59. (b) After unfolding the last fold, the transparent sheet will look like the figure given in option (b).

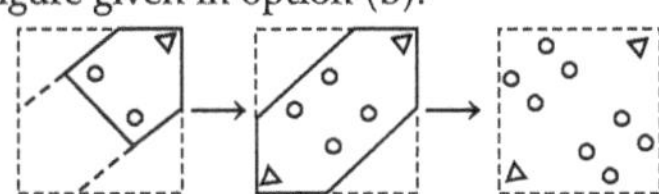

60. (c) After unfolding the last fold, the transparent sheet will look like the figure given in option (c).

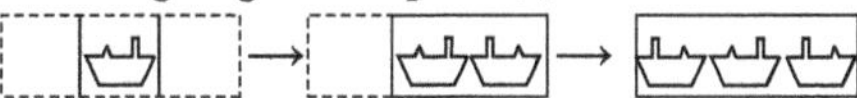

61. (b) After unfolding the last fold, the transparent sheet will look like the figure given in option (b).

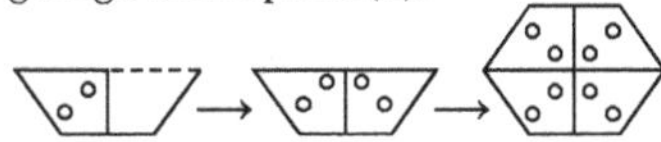

62. (b) After unfolding the last fold, the transparent sheet will look like the figure given in option (b).

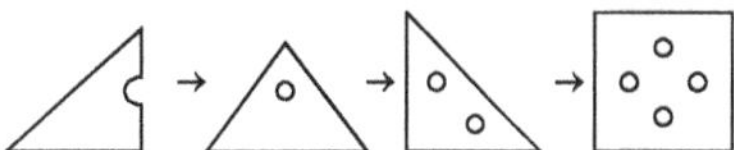

63. (a) After unfolding the last fold, the transparent sheet will look like the figure given in option (a).

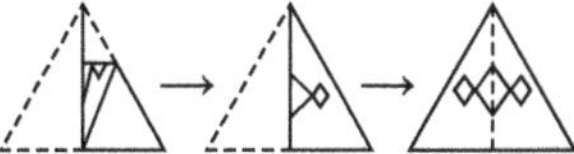

64. (b) After unfolding the last fold, the transparent sheet will look like the figure given in option (b).

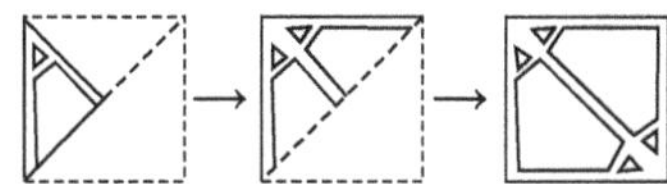

65. (c) After unfolding the last fold, the transparent sheet will look like the figure given in option (c).

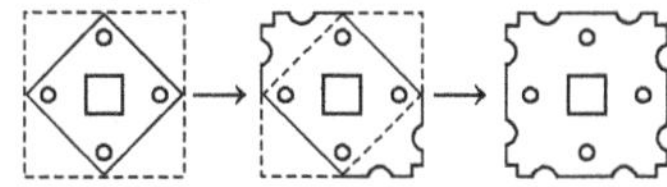

66. (d) After unfolding the last fold, the transparent sheet will look like the figure given in option (d).

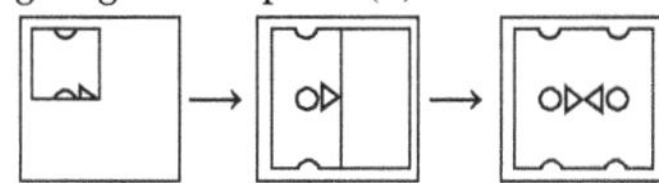

67. (c) After unfolding the last fold, the transparent sheet will look like the figure given in option (c).

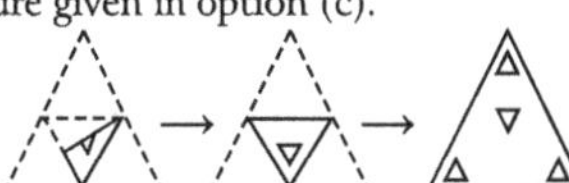

68. (c) After unfolding the last fold, the transparent sheet will look like the figure given in option (c).

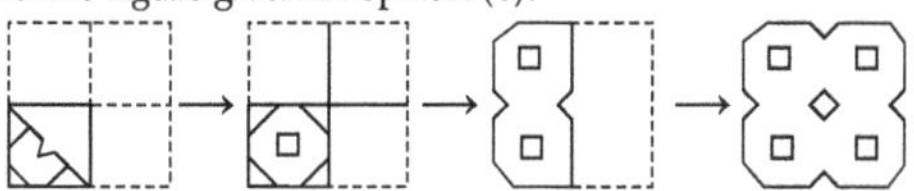

69. (c) After unfolding the last fold, the transparent sheet will look like the figure in option (c).

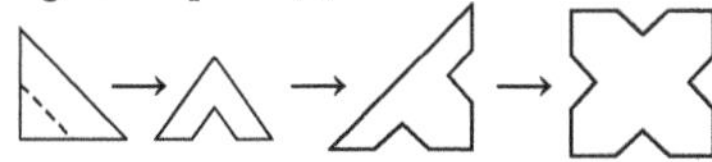

70. (d) The sheet (X) when unfolded will look like the answer figure (d).

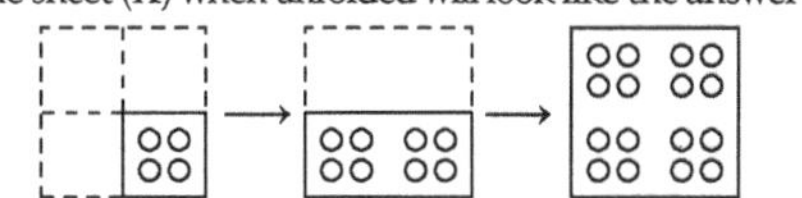

71. (a) The sheet (X) when unfolded will look like the answer figure (a).

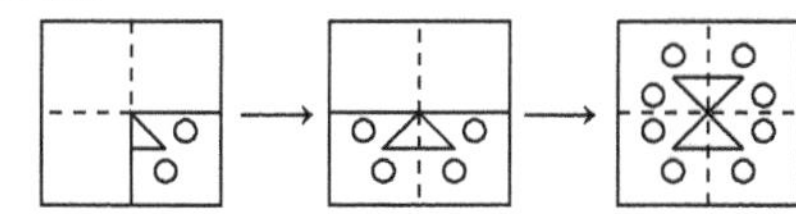

72. (c) The sheet (X) when unfolded will look like the answer figure (c).

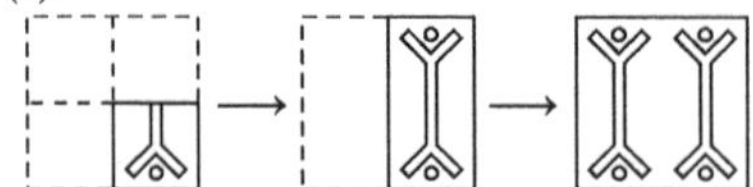

73. (a) The sheet (X) when unfolded will look like the answer figure (a).

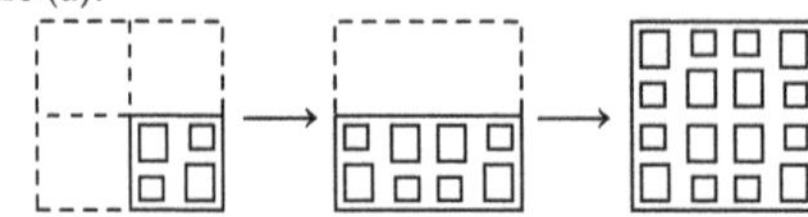

74. (c) The sheet (X) when unfolded will look like the answer figure (c).

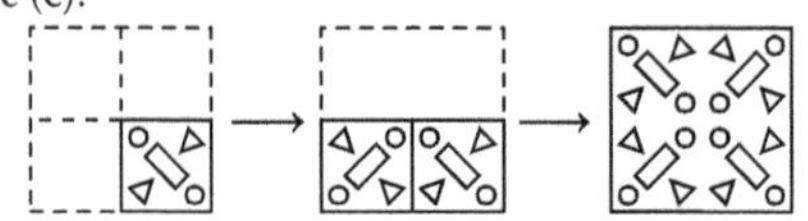

75. (d) The sheet (X) when unfolded will look like the answer figure (d).

76. (b) The sheet (X) when unfolded will look like the answer figure (b).

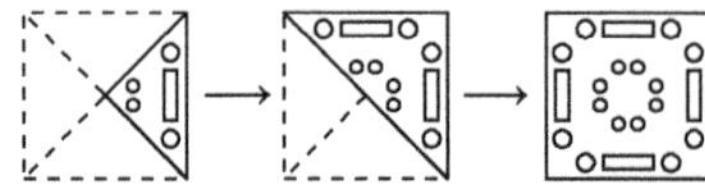

77. (c) The sheet (X) when unfolded will look like the answer figure (c).

78. (b) The sheet (X) when unfolded will look like the answer figure (b).

79. (c) The sheet (X) when unfolded will look like the answer figure (c).

80. (c) The sheet (X) when unfolded will look like the answer figure (c).

81. (c) When we fold question figure (X), then it looks like the answer figure (c).

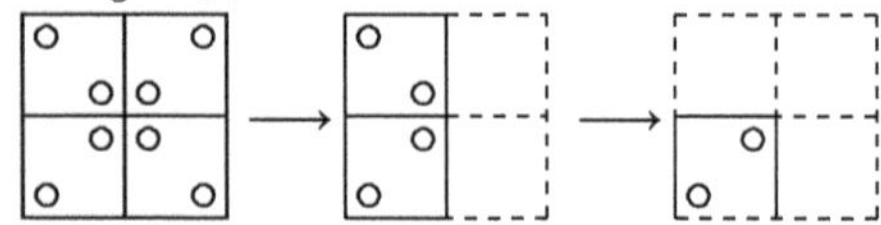

82. (a) When we fold question figure (X), then it looks like the answer figure (a).

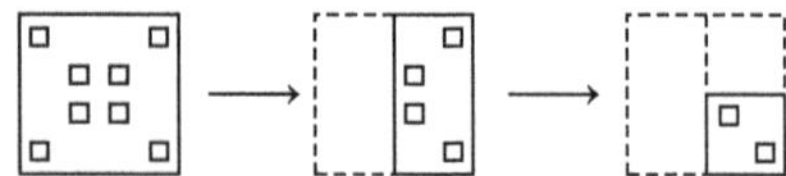

83. (b) When we fold question figure (X), then it looks like the answer figure (b).

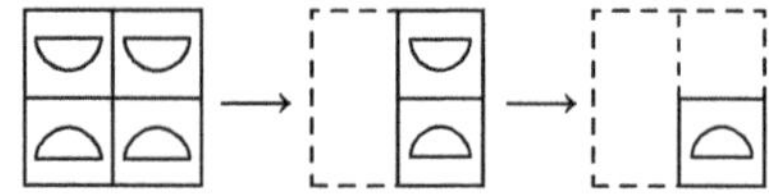

84. (c) When we fold question figure (X), then it looks like the answer figure (c).

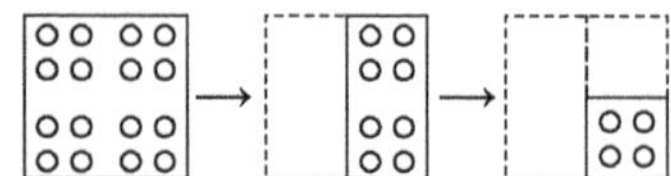

85. (c) When we fold question figure (X), then it looks like the answer figure (c).

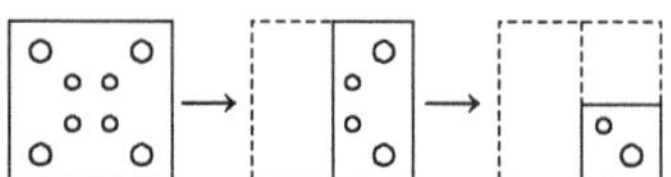

86. (b) When we fold question figure (X), then it looks like the answer figure (b).

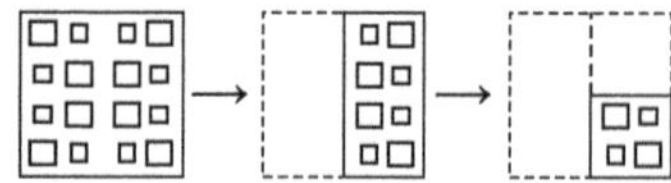

87. (d) When we fold question figure (X), then it looks like the answer figure (d).

88. (a) When we fold question figure (X), then it looks like the answer figure (a).

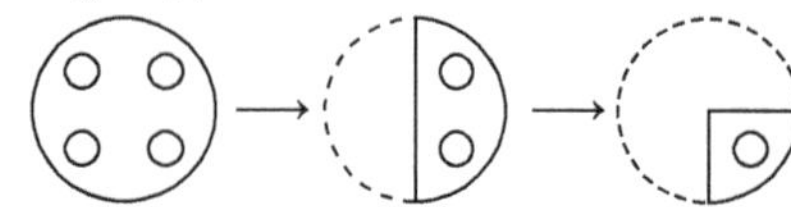

89. (c) When we fold question figure (X), then it looks like the answer figure (c).

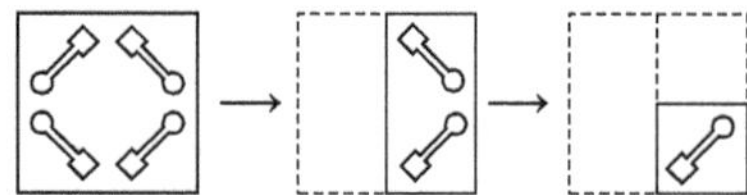

90. (*d*) When we fold question figure (X), then it looks like the answer figure (d).

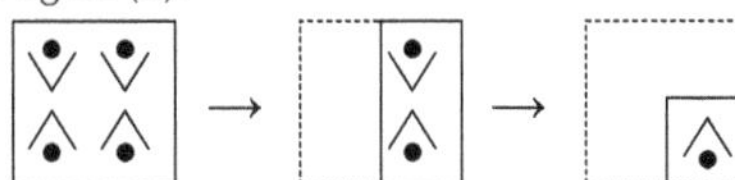

91. (*a*) When we fold question figure (X), then it looks like the answer figure (a).

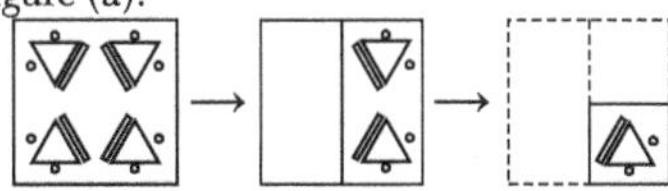

92. (*a*) When we fold question figure (X), then it looks like the answer figure (a).

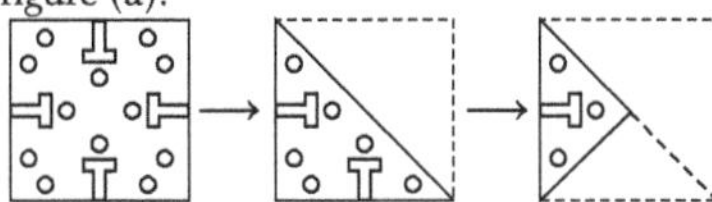

93. (*d*) When we fold question figure (X), then it looks like the answer figure (d).

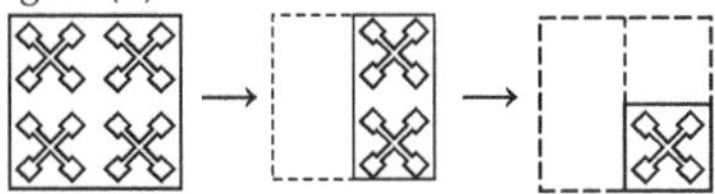

94. (*d*) When we fold question figure (X), then it looks like the answer figure (d).

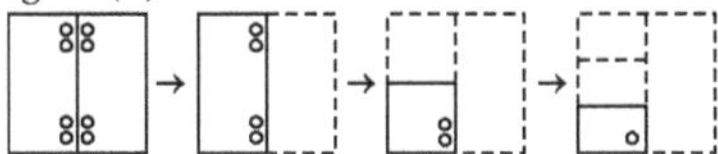

95. (*c*) When we fold question figure (X), then it looks like the answer figure (c).

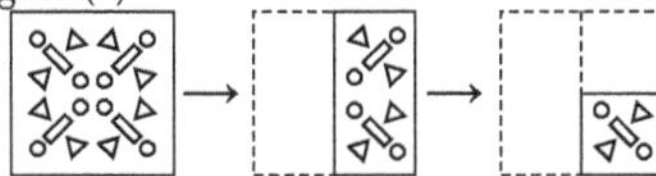

96. (*a*) When we fold question figure (X), then it looks like the answer figure (a).

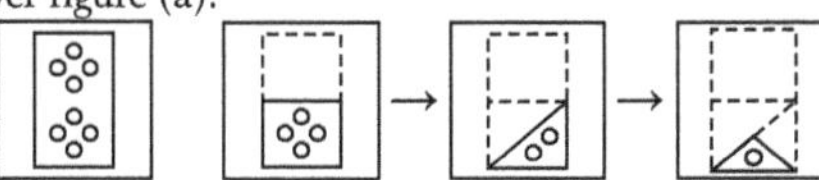

97. (*b*) When we fold question figure (X), then it looks like the answer figure (b).

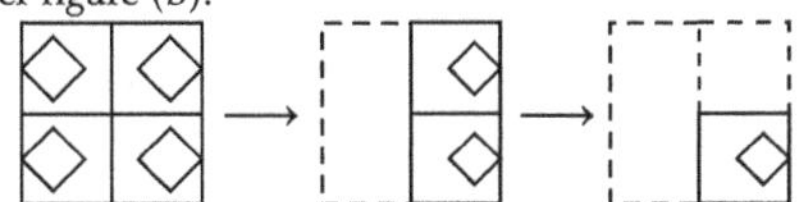

98. (*a*) When we fold question figure (X), then it looks like the answer figure (a).

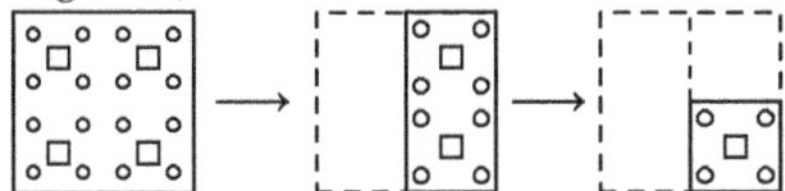

99. (*b*) When we fold question figure (X), then it looks like the answer figure (b).

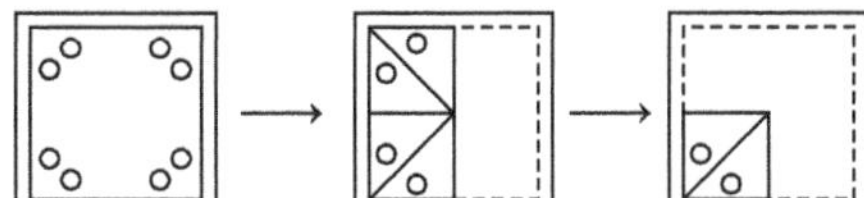

100. (*a*) When we fold question figure (X), then it looks like the answer figure (a).

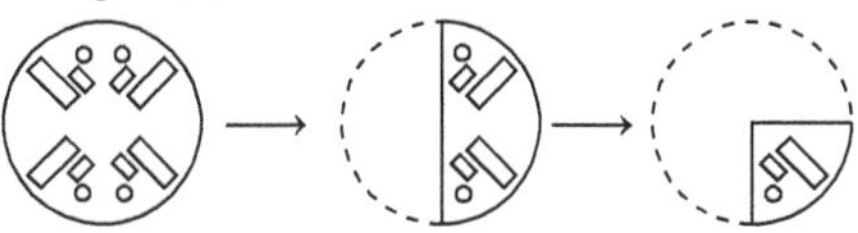

101. (*d*) When we fold question figure (X), then it looks like the answer figure (d).

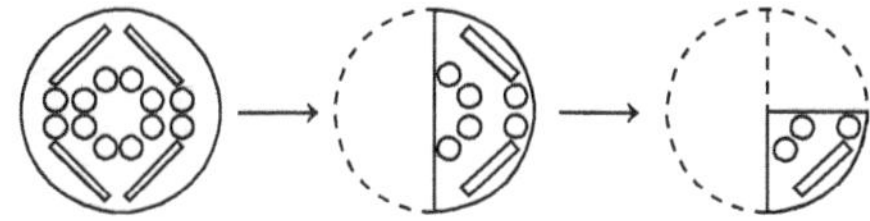

102. (*b*) When we fold question figure (X), then it looks like the answer figure (b).

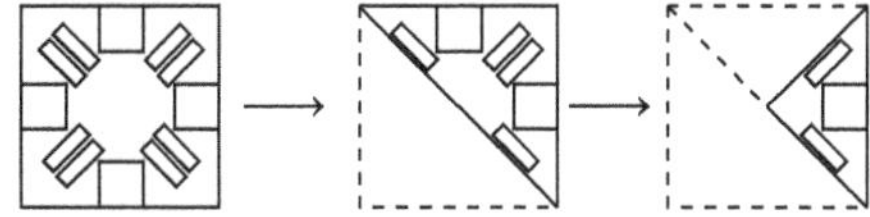

103. (*c*) When we fold question figure (X), then it looks like the answer figure (c).

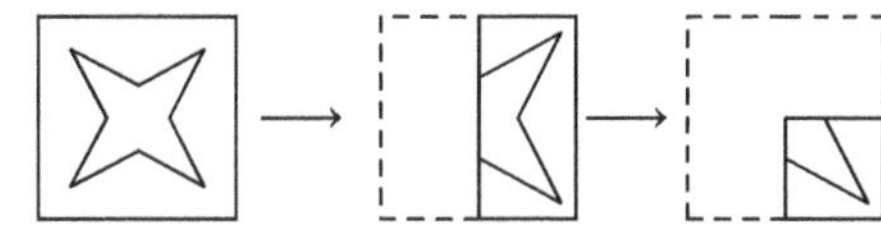

104. (*a*) When we fold question figure (X), then it looks like the answer figure (a).

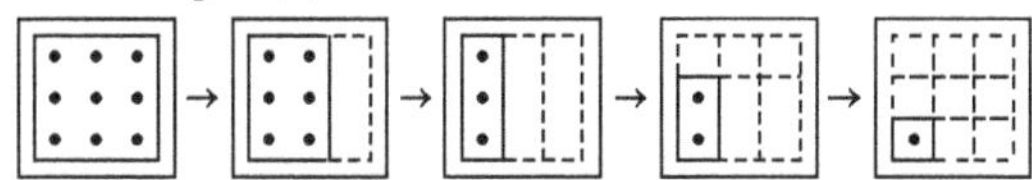

105. (*b*) When we fold question figure (X), then it looks like the answer figure (b).

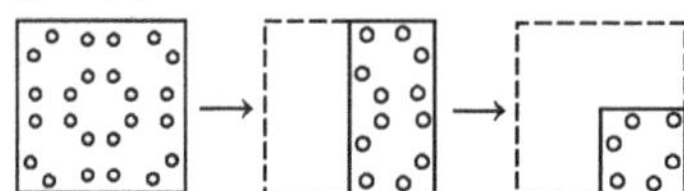

106. (*d*) When we fold question figure (X), then it looks like the answer figure (d).

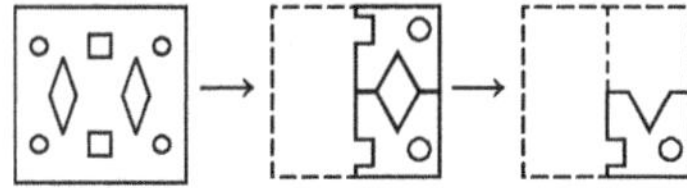

107. (*b*) When we fold question figure (X), then it looks like the answer figure (b).

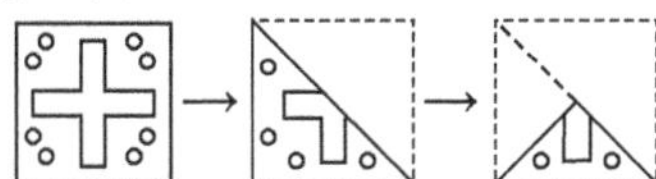

108. (*d*) When we fold question figure (X), then it looks like the answer figure (d).

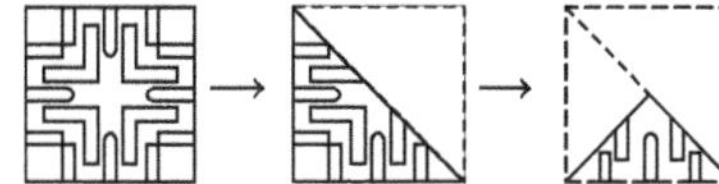

CHAPTER / 11

Similarity of Figures

When the given question figure is same or similar to one of the answer figures according to its appearance, features or position, then that answer figure is said to be a similar figure to the given question figure.

The basis of similarity in figures can be number of sides, circle, triangle, square, rectangle, arrow, pin etc.

In addition to this, the shape or orientation of figure is also a key feature of similarity in figures.

Different types of questions covered in this chapter are as follows

TYPE 01

Completely Similar Figure

In this type of questions, candidates are asked to find the figure which appears exactly the same as the given question figure without changing the orientation.

***Ex* 01** In the following question, a question figure and four answer figures are given. Choose the answer figure which is exactly the same as the question figure without changing the orientation.

Question Figure **Answer Figures**

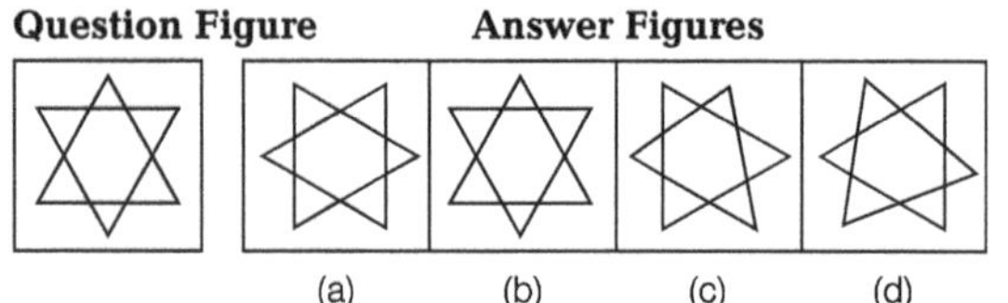

(a) (b) (c) (d)

Solution (b) The answer figure (b) is exactly the same as the question figure.

***Ex* 02** In the following question, a question figure and four answer figures are given. Choose the answer figure which is exactly the same as the question figure without changing the orientation.

Question Figure **Answer Figures**

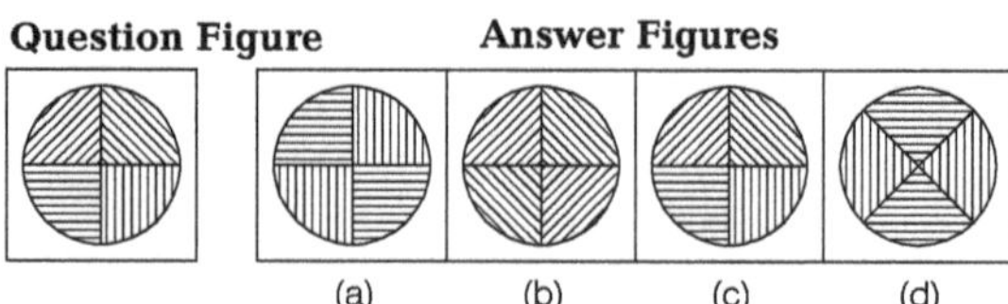

(a) (b) (c) (d)

Solution (c) The answer figure (c) is exactly the same as the question figure.

***Ex* 03** In the following question, a question figure and four answer figures are given. Choose the answer figure which is exactly the same as the question figure without changing the orientation.

Question Figure **Answer Figures**

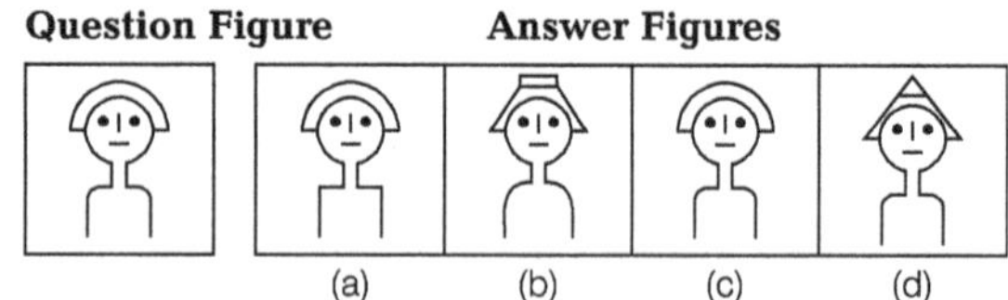

(a) (b) (c) (d)

Solution (c) The answer figure (c) is exactly the same as the question figure.

***Ex* 04** In the following question, a question figure and four answer figures are given. Choose the answer figure which is exactly the same as the question figure without changing the orientation. « SSC CPO 2015

Question Figure **Answer Figures**

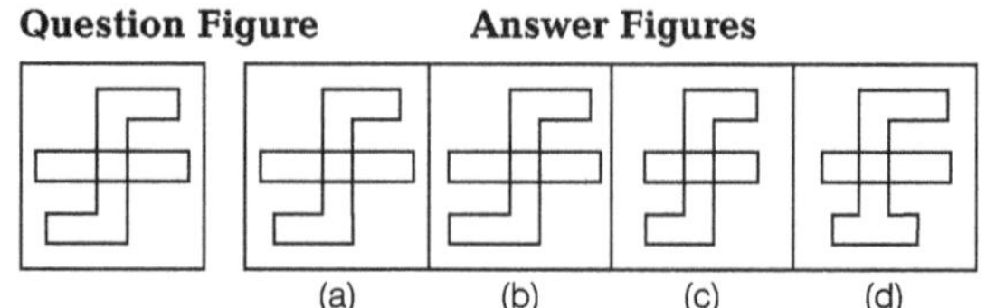

(a) (b) (c) (d)

Solution (a) After careful observation of the question figure we found that answer figure (a) is exactly the same as the question figure.

Practice / CORNER 11.1

DIRECTIONS ~ (Q. Nos. 1-20) *In each of the following questions, a question figure and four answer figures are given. Choose that answer figure, which is exactly the same as the question figure without changing the orientation.*

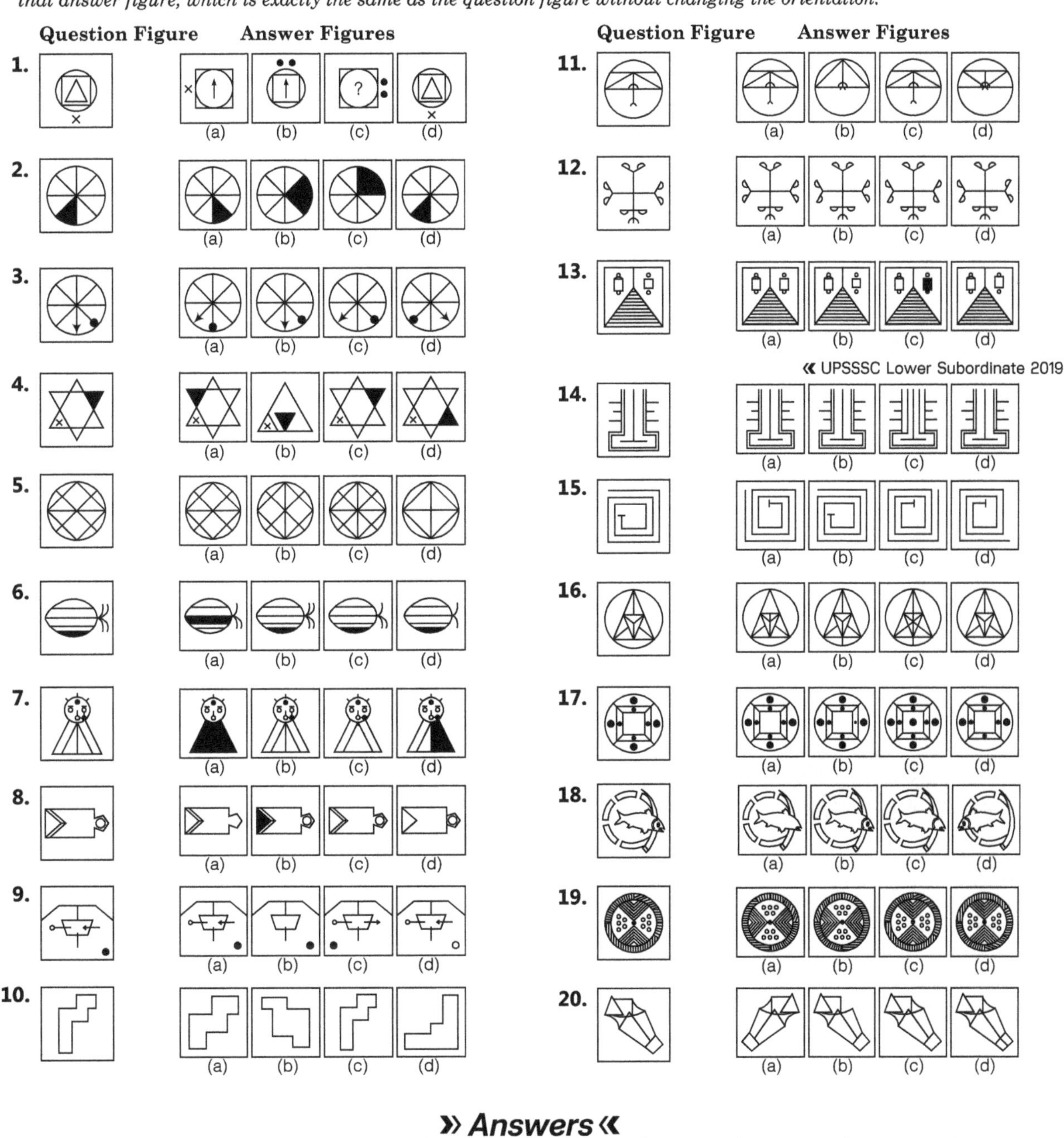

» Answers «

1. (d)	2. (d)	3. (b)	4. (c)	5. (a)	6. (b)	7. (b)	8. (c)	9. (a)	10. (c)
11. (c)	12. (a)	13. (b)	14. (a)	15. (b)	16. (d)	17. (a)	18. (b)	19. (c)	20. (c)

TYPE 02

Similar Figure on Changing the Direction/Figure Rotation

In this type of questions, candidates are required to find the figure from the answer figures which is exactly the same as the question figure without interchanging the designs. The answer figure is obtained by rotating the question figure through, 90°, 180°, 270°, ...

***Ex* 05** In the following question, a question figure and four answer figures are given. Choose the answer figure which is exactly the same as the question figure.

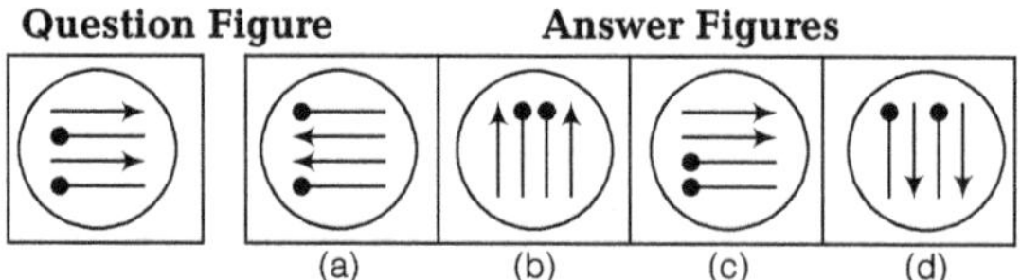

Solution (d) By rotating the question figure through 90° in clockwise direction, we will get the figure same as the answer figure (d).

***Ex* 06** In the following question, a question figure and four answer figures are given. Find the answer figure which is similar to the question figure, when the question figure is rotated through two places clockwise or anti-clockwise.

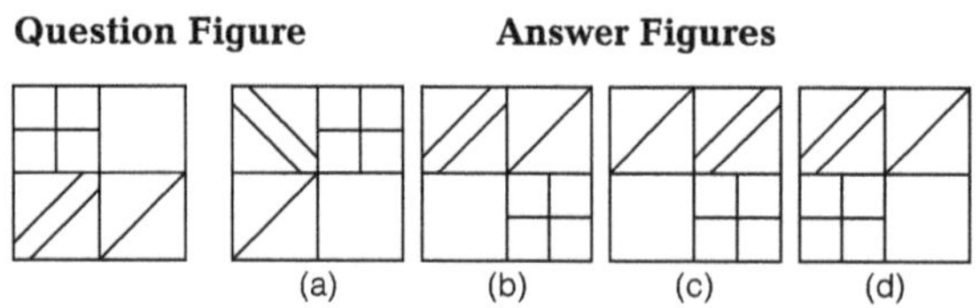

Solution (c) When the question figure rotates two places clockwise or anti-clockwise direction, then it is exactly in same as the answer figure (c).

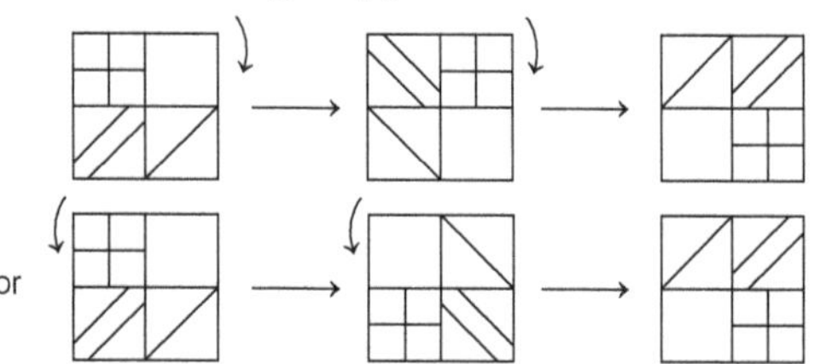

***Ex* 07** In the following question, a question figure and four answer figures are given. Find the answer figure which is similar to the question figure, when the question figure is rotated through three places (270°) clockwise.

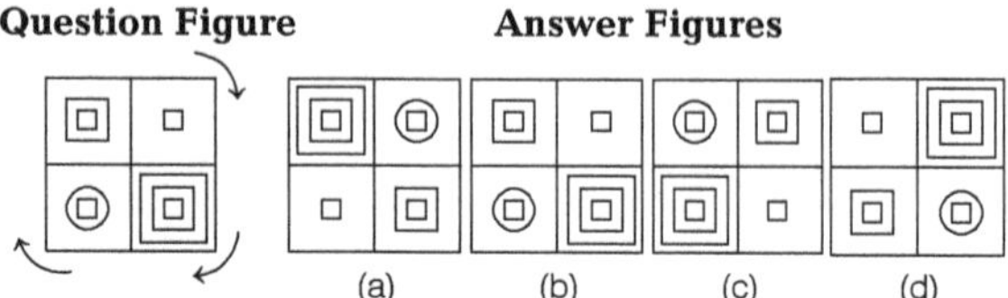

Solution (d) When the question figure rotates three places in clockwise direction, then it is exactly the same as the answer figure (d).

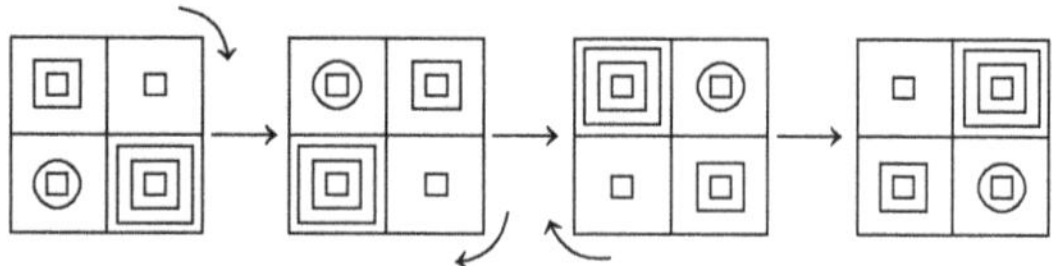

Practice /CORNER 11.2

DIRECTIONS ~ (Q. Nos. 1-10) *In each of the following questions, a question figure and four answer figures are given. Choose that answer figure, which is exactly the same as question figure.*

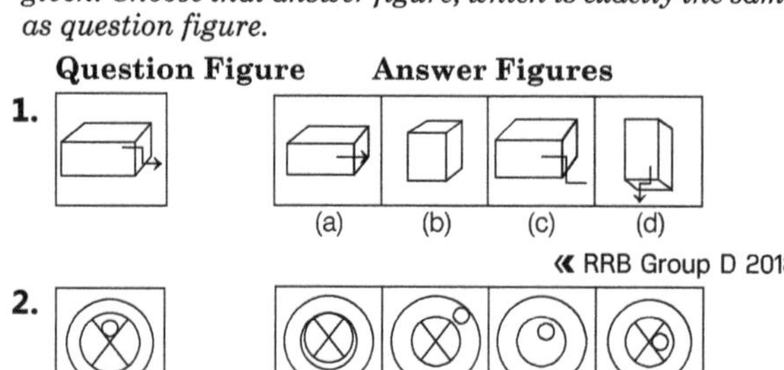

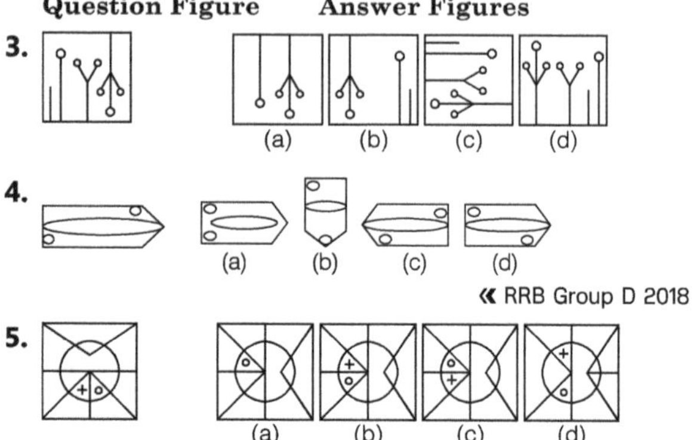

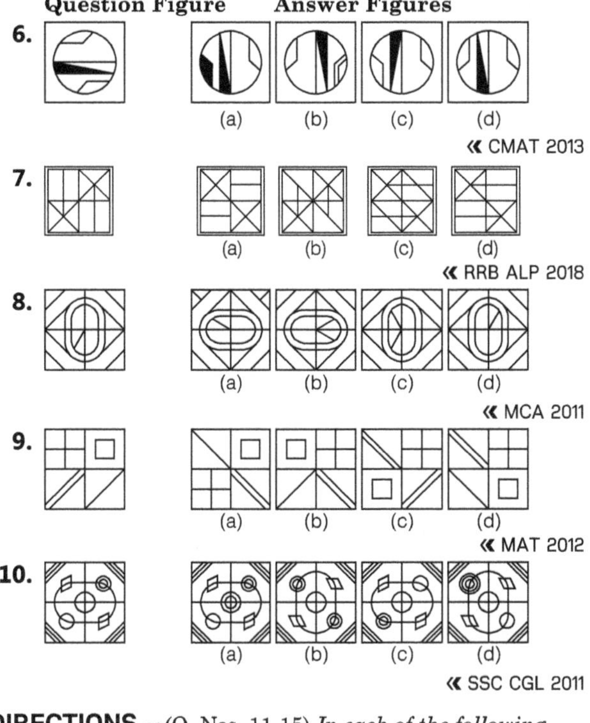

DIRECTIONS ~ (Q. Nos. 11-15) *In each of the following questions, a question figure and four answer figures are given. Find the answer figure which is similar to the question figure, when the question figure is rotated through one place (90°) clockwise.*

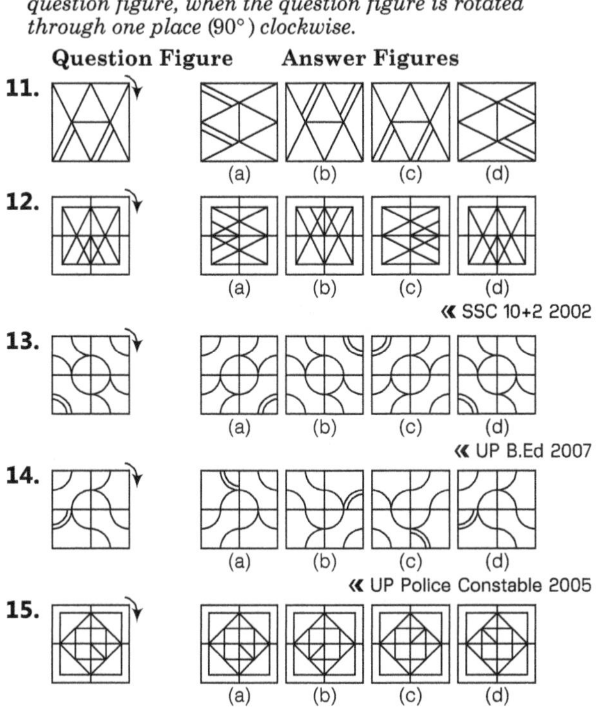

DIRECTIONS ~ (Q. Nos. 16-20) *In each of the following questions, a question figure and four answer figures are given. Find the answer figure which is similar to the question figure, when the question figure is rotated through two places (180°) clockwise.*

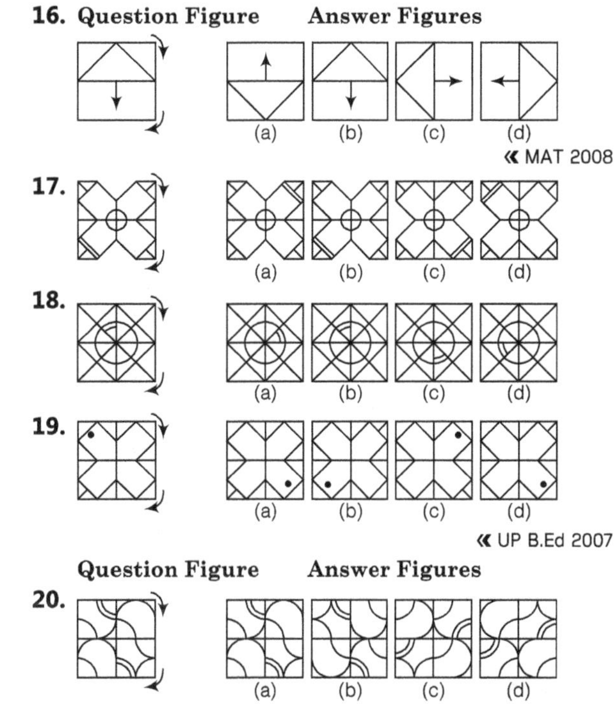

DIRECTIONS ~ (Q. Nos. 21-25) *In each of the following questions, a question figure and four answer figures are given. Find the answer figure which is similar to the question figure, when the question figure is rotated through three places (270°) clockwise.*

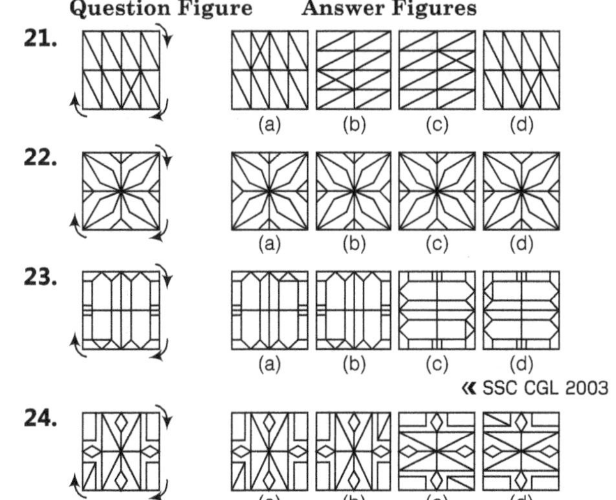

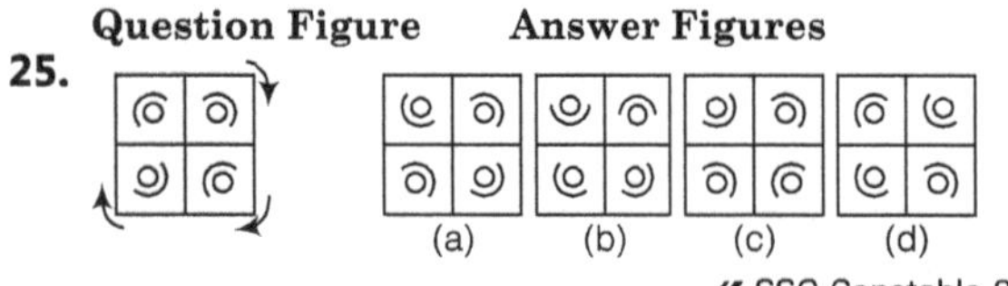

« SSC Constable 2005

DIRECTIONS ~ (Q. Nos. 26-30) *In each of the following questions, a question figure and four answer figures are given. Find the answer figure which is similar to the question figure, when the question figure is rotated through four places* (360°) *clockwise.*

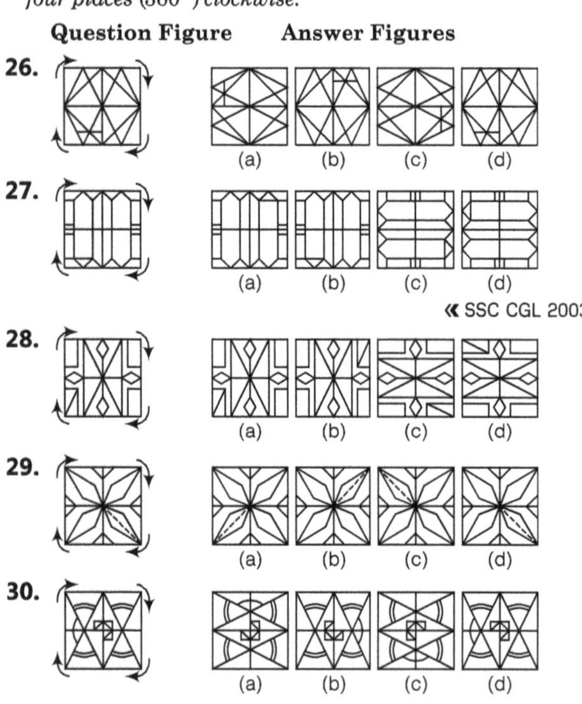

« SSC CGL 2003

DIRECTIONS ~ (Q. Nos. 31-35) *In each of the following questions, a question figure and four answer figures are given. Find the answer figure which is similar to the question figure, when the question figure is rotated through one place* (90°) *anti-clockwise.*

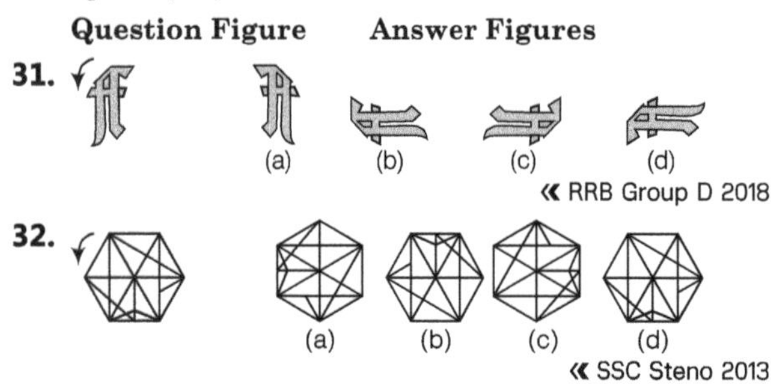

« RRB Group D 2018

« SSC Steno 2013

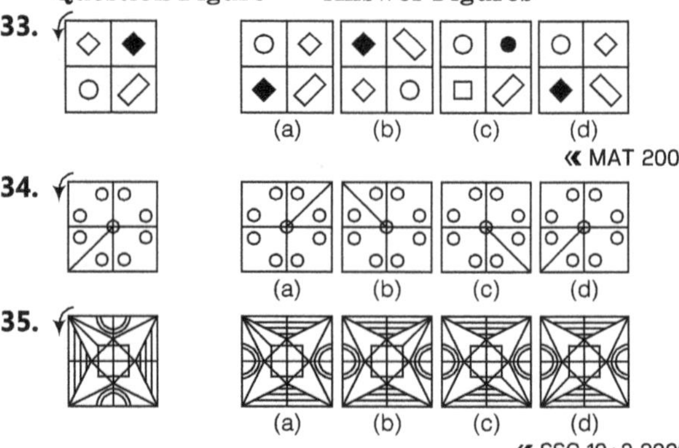

« MAT 2007

« SSC 10+2 2009

DIRECTIONS ~ (Q. Nos. 36-40) *In each of the following questions, a question figure and four answer figures are given. Find the answer figure which is similar to the question figure, when the question figure is rotated through two places* (180°) *anti-clockwise.*

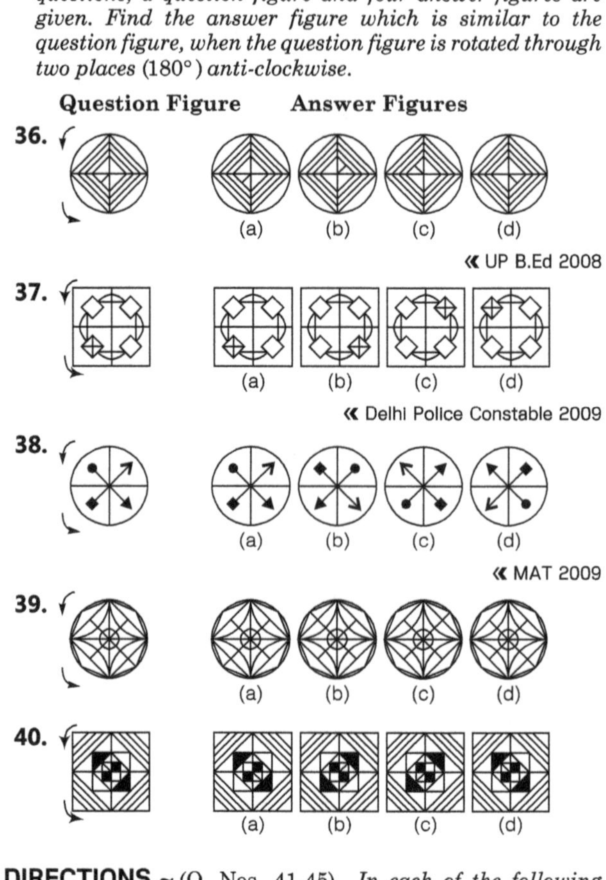

« UP B.Ed 2008

« Delhi Police Constable 2009

« MAT 2009

DIRECTIONS ~ (Q. Nos. 41-45) *In each of the following questions, a question figure and four answer figures are given. Find the answer figure which is similar to the question figure, when the question figure is rotated through three places* (270°) *anti-clockwise.*

Question Figure **Answer Figures**

41.

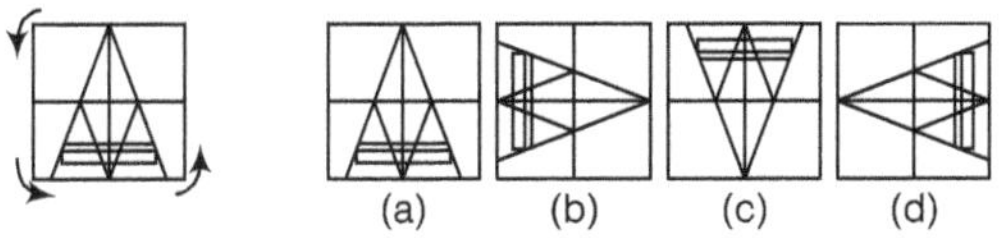

(a) (b) (c) (d)

« SSC 10+2 2005

42.

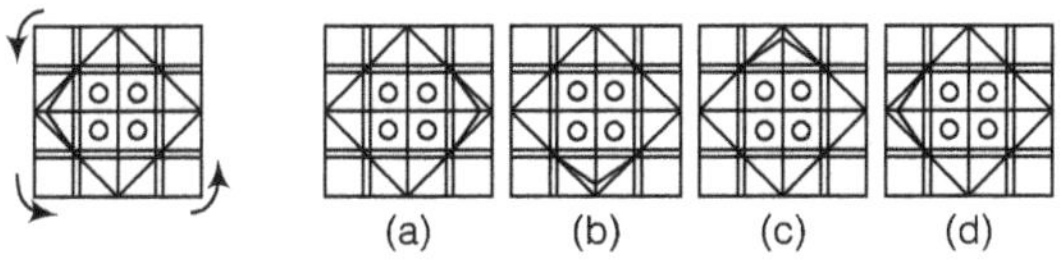

(a) (b) (c) (d)

« SSC Constable 2003

43.

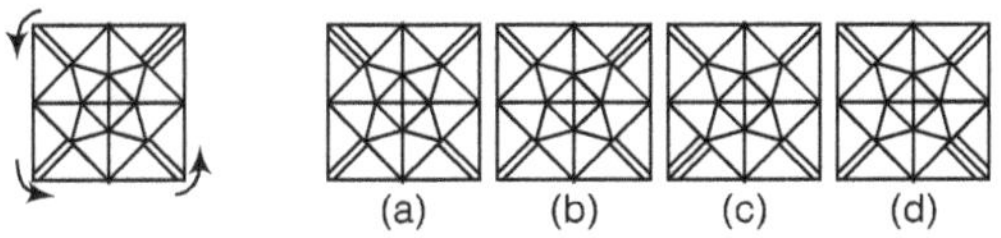

(a) (b) (c) (d)

« SSC 10+2 2005

44.

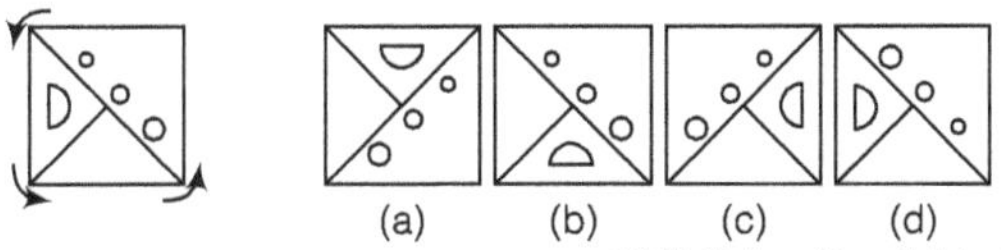

(a) (b) (c) (d)

« UP Police Constable 2009

45.

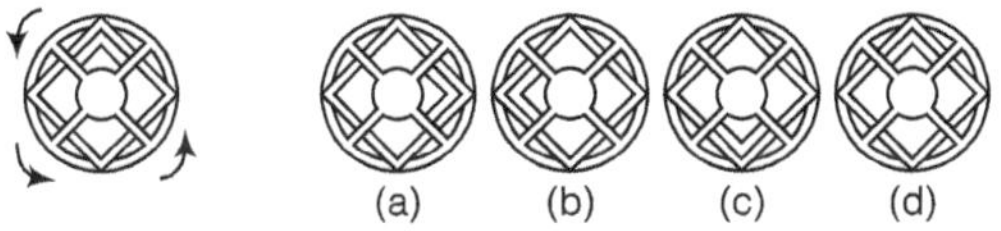

(a) (b) (c) (d)

DIRECTIONS ~ (Q. Nos. 46-50) *In each of the following questions, a question figure and four answer figures are given. Find the answer figure which is similar to the question figure, when the question figure is rotated through four places (360°) anti-clockwise.*

Question Figure **Answer Figures**

46.

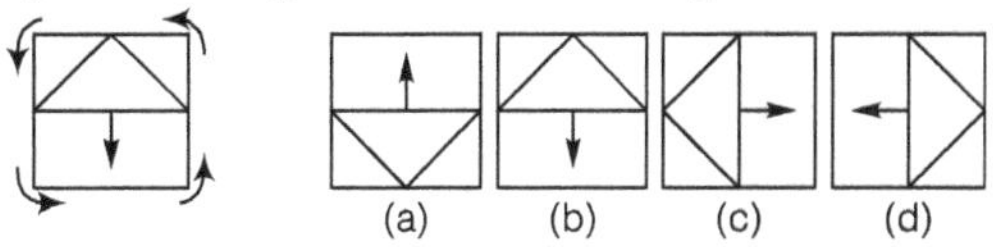

(a) (b) (c) (d)

47.

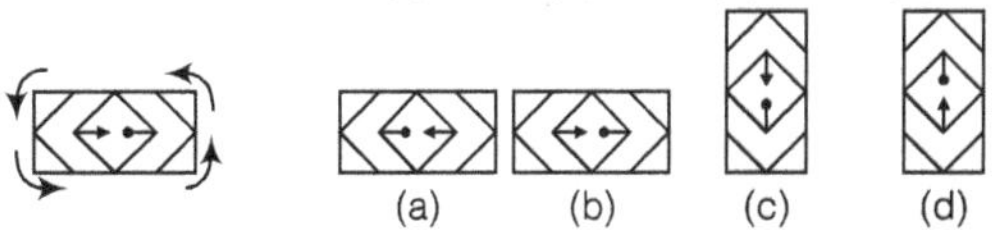

(a) (b) (c) (d)

48.

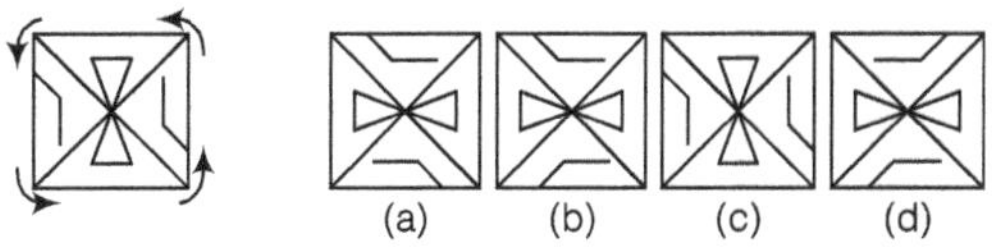

(a) (b) (c) (d)

49.

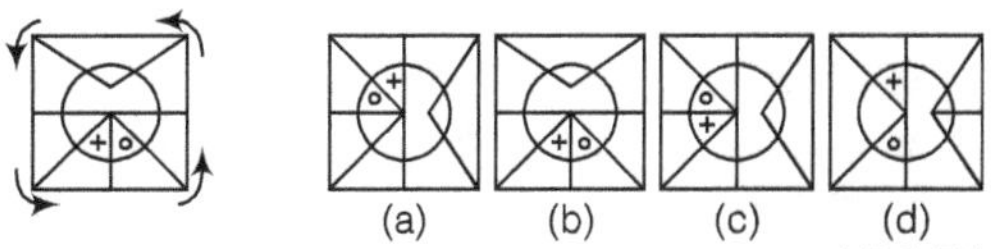

(a) (b) (c) (d)

« UP B.Ed 2005

50.

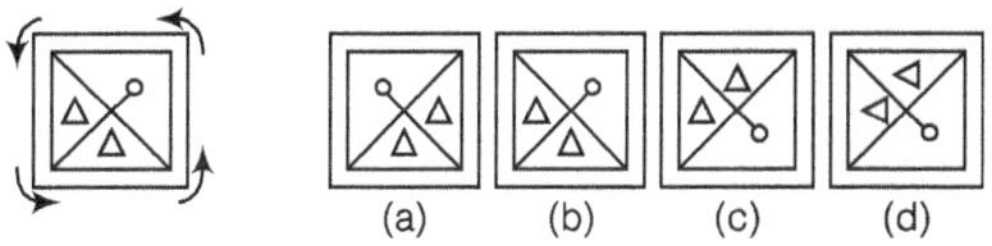

(a) (b) (c) (d)

» Answers «

1. (d)	2. (d)	3. (c)	4. (c)	5. (b)	6. (c)	7. (d)	8. (d)	9. (d)	10. (c)
11. (a)	12. (a)	13. (c)	14. (a)	15. (b)	16. (a)	17. (a)	18. (c)	19. (d)	20. (b)
21. (c)	22. (b)	23. (c)	24. (c)	25. (d)	26. (d)	27. (b)	28. (a)	29. (d)	30. (d)
31. (b)	32. (c)	33. (b)	34. (c)	35. (d)	36. (b)	37. (c)	38. (d)	39. (b)	40. (a)
41. (b)	42. (c)	43. (d)	44. (a)	45. (a)	46. (b)	47. (b)	48. (c)	49. (b)	50. (b)

TYPE 03

Completely Different Figure

In this type of questions, candidates are required to find the figure from the set of answer figures which is completely different from the given question figure or a figure which is not similar to the given question figure.

***Ex* 08** In the following question, a question figure and four answer figures are given. Choose the answer figure which is different from the given question figure.

Question Figure **Answer Figures**

(a) (b) (c) (d)

Solution (d) Answer figure (d) is not similar to the question figure.

***Ex* 09** In the following question, a question figure and four answer figures are given. Choose the answer figure which is not similar to the given question figure.

Question Figure **Answer Figures**

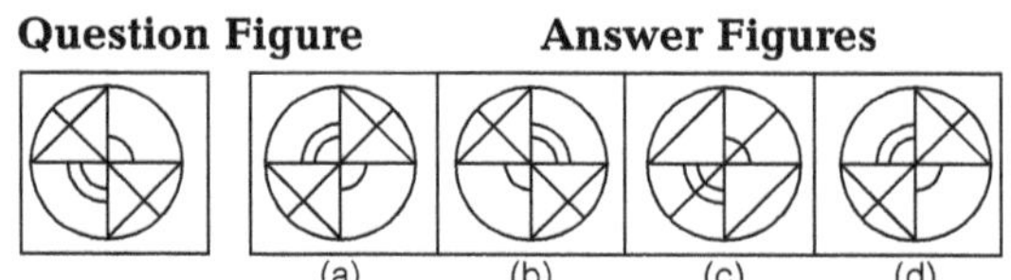

Solution (c) Answer figure (c) is not similar to the question figure.

Practice / CORNER 11.3

DIRECTIONS ~ (Q. Nos. 1-10) *In each of the following questions, a question figure and four answer figures are given. Find the answer figure which is not similar to the question figure.*

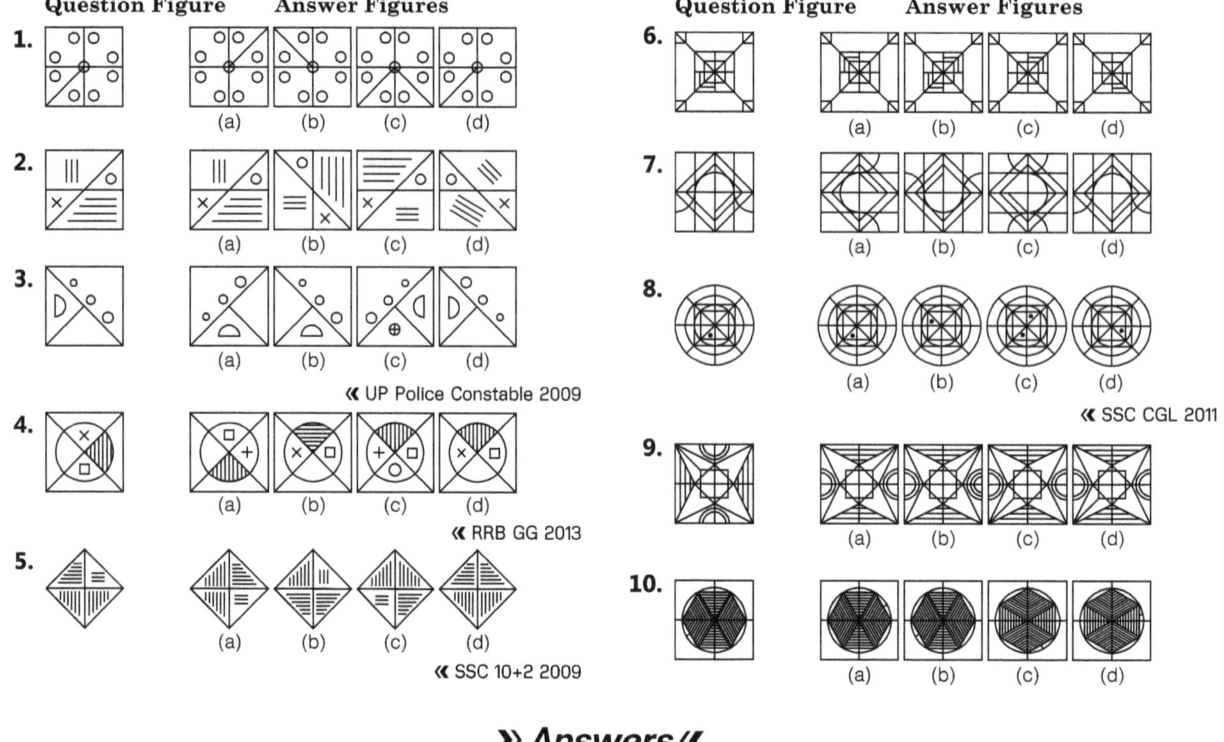

» *Answers* «

1. *(c)*	2. *(d)*	3. *(c)*	4. *(c)*	5. *(d)*	6. *(b)*	7. *(c)*	8. *(c)*	9. *(b)*	10. *(d)*

TYPE 04

Similar Figure on the Basis of Properties

In this type of questions one/two/three/four question figures and four or five answer figures are given. The candidates are required to find the figure from the set of answer figures which contains similar properties to that of the question figure(s).

***Ex* 10** In the following question, a question figure and four answer figures are given. Choose that answer figure which has similar properties to that of question figure.

Question Figure **Answer Figures**

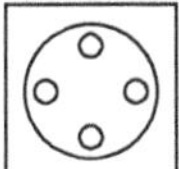

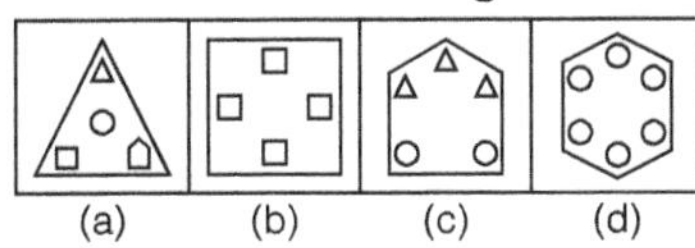

(a) (b) (c) (d)

Solution (b) As there are four small circles inside the big circle in the question figure, similarly four small squares inside the big square are given in the answer figure (b).

***Ex* 11** In the following question, four question figures and four answer figures are given. Choose that answer figure which has similar properties to that of the question figures.

Question Figures **Answer Figures**

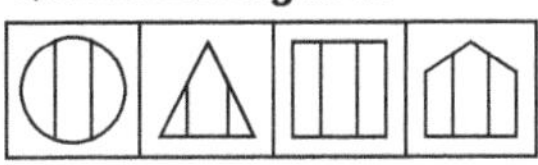

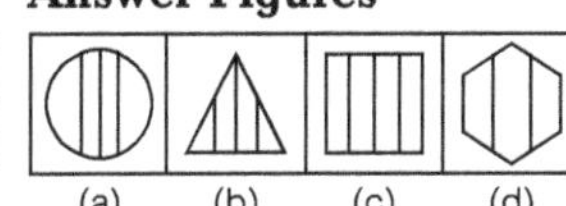

(a) (b) (c) (d)

Solution (d) Here, each question figure is divided into three parts.
Similarly, answer figure (d) is divided into three parts.

Practice / CORNER 11.4

DIRECTIONS ~(Q. Nos. 1-10) *In each of the following questions, one or more question figures and four answer figures are given. Choose the answer figure which has same properties to that of the question figure(s).*

Question Figure **Answer Figures**

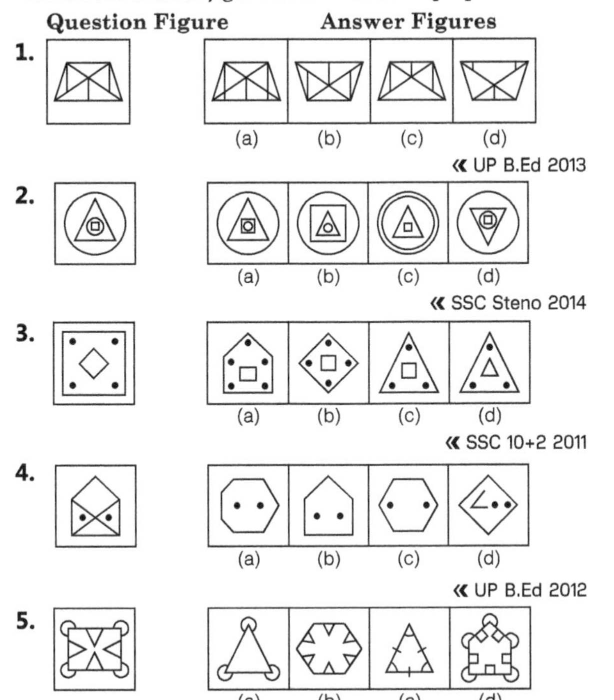

1. (a) (b) (c) (d) « UP B.Ed 2013

2. (a) (b) (c) (d) « SSC Steno 2014

3. (a) (b) (c) (d) « SSC 10+2 2011

4. (a) (b) (c) (d) « UP B.Ed 2012

5. (a) (b) (c) (d) « RRB ASM 2013

Question Figure **Answer Figures**

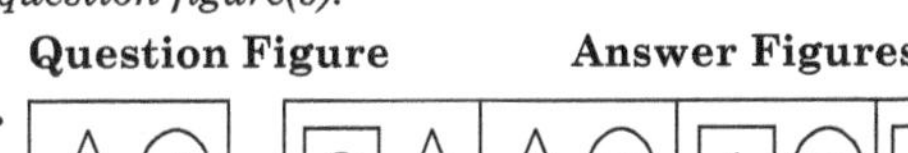

6.

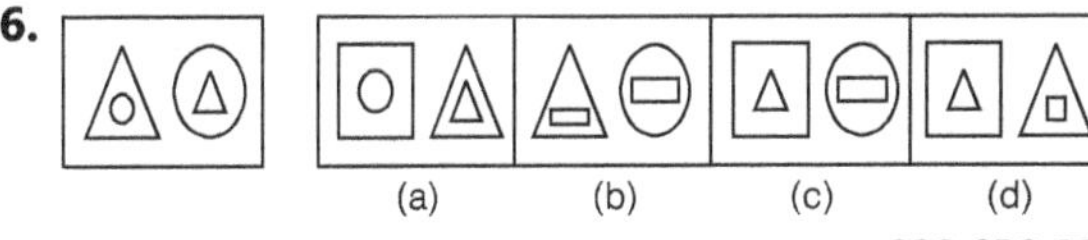

(a) (b) (c) (d) « SSC CPO 2010

7.

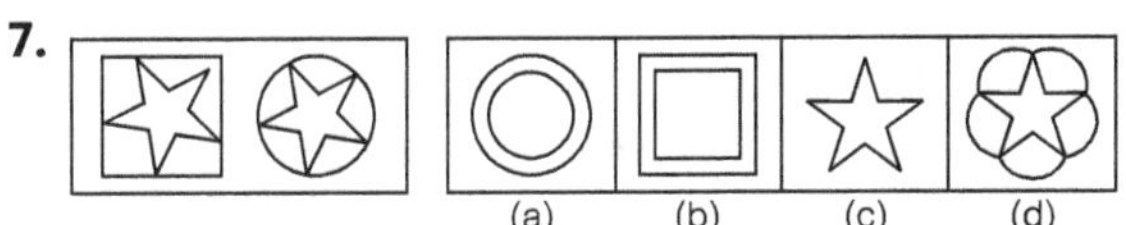

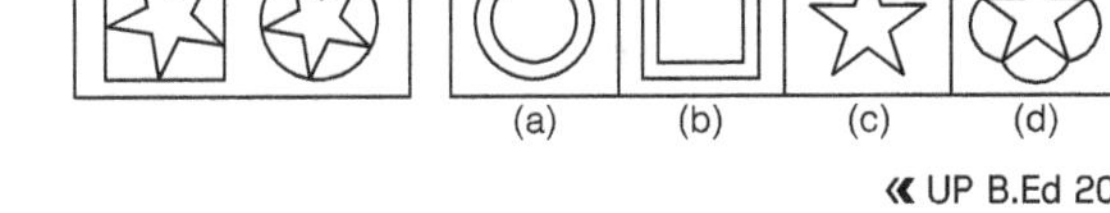

(a) (b) (c) (d) « UP B.Ed 2011

8.

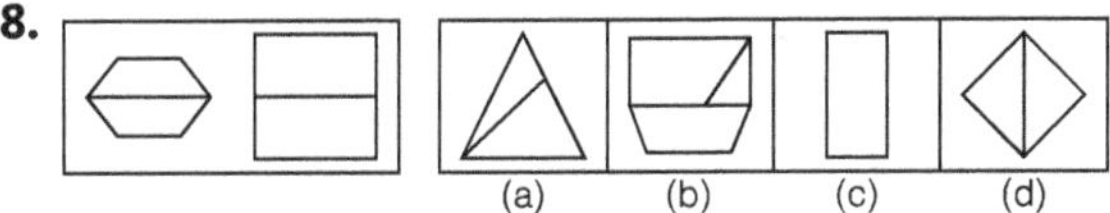

(a) (b) (c) (d) « MAT 2011

9.

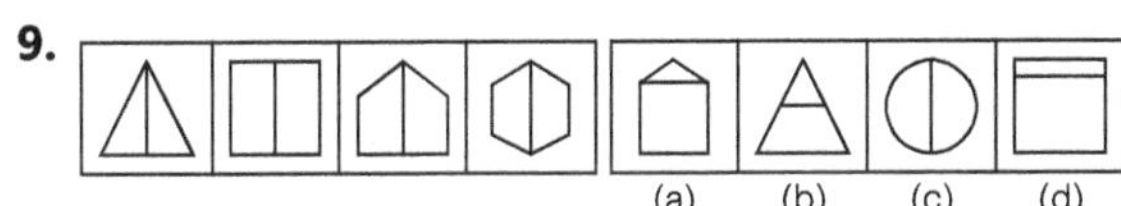

(a) (b) (c) (d) « RRB ASM 2010

10.

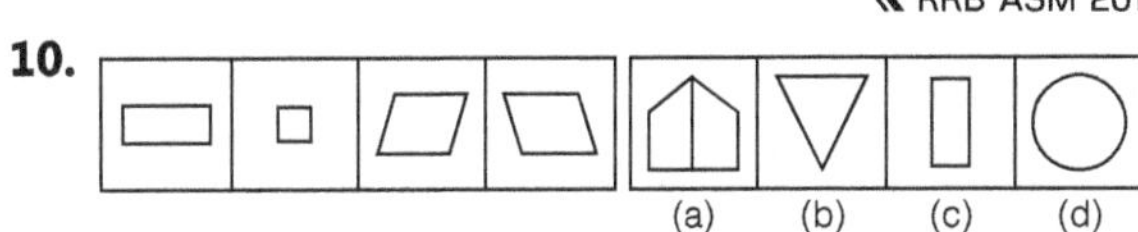

(a) (b) (c) (d) « SSC MTS 2012

» Answers «

1. (b)	2. (d)	3. (b)	4. (b)	5. (d)	6. (d)	7. (d)	8. (d)	9. (c)	10. (c)

TYPE 05

Similar Figure on the Basis of Elements

In this type of questions, a question figure containing many small figures of different designs, is given. In any of the given answer figures, all of the elements or designs of the question figure are present. The candidates are required to find that figure.

DIRECTIONS ~ (Example Nos. 12 and 13) *In each of the following questions, a question figure and four answer figures are given. In which of the answer figures all of the elements of question figure are present?*

Ex 12 **Question Figure** **Answer Figures**

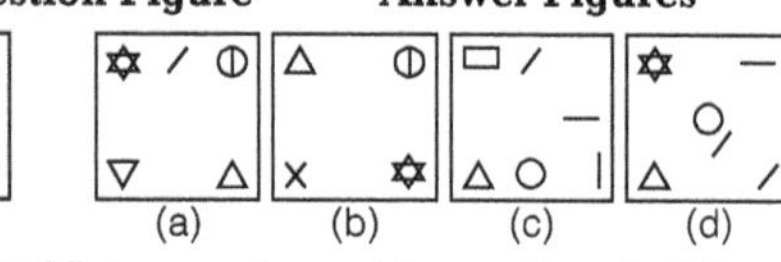

Solution (d) Answer figure (d) contains all of the elements given in the question figure.

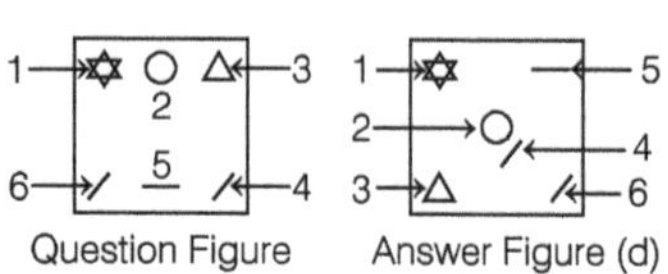

Question Figure Answer Figure (d)

Ex 13 **Question Figure** **Answer Figures**

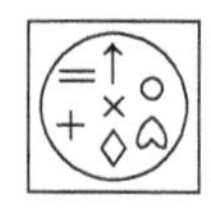

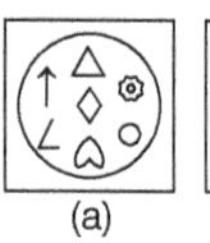

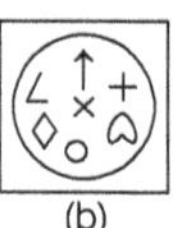

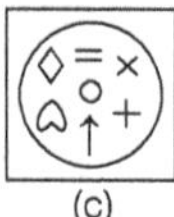

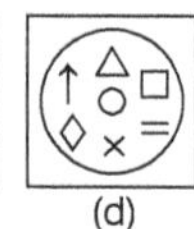

(a) (b) (c) (d)

« UPSSSC Amin 2016

Solution (c) Answer figure (c) contains all of the elements given in the question figure.

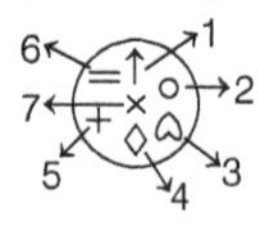

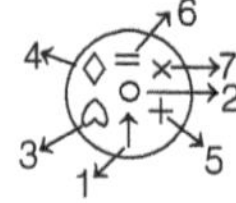

Question Figure Answer Figure (c)

Practice CORNER 11.5

DIRECTIONS ~ (Q. Nos. 1-10) *In each of the following questions, which of the answer figures contains almost all the elements of the question figure?*

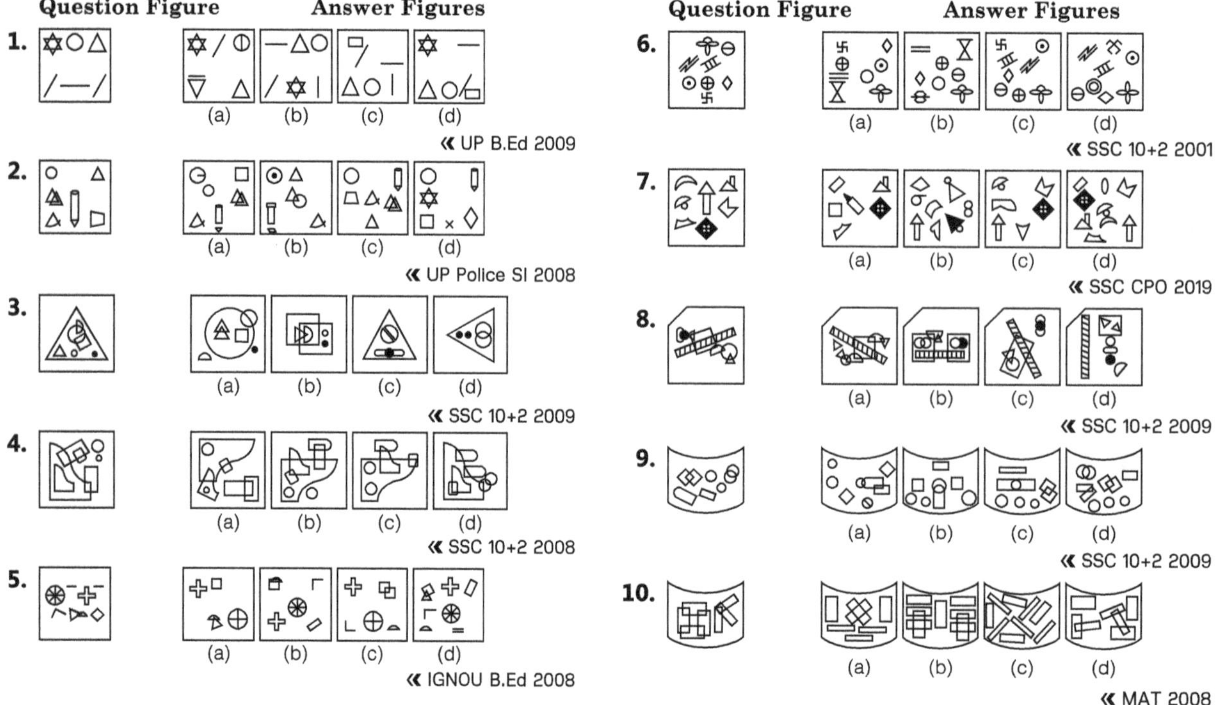

» Answers «

1. (b)	2. (c)	3. (a)	4. (a)	5. (d)	6. (c)	7. (d)	8. (d)	9. (b)	10. (a)

Master Exercise

DIRECTIONS ~(Q. Nos. 1-5) *In each of the following questions, choose that answer figure which is exactly the same as the question figure without changing the orientation.*

Question Figure **Answer Figures**

1. 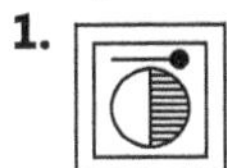 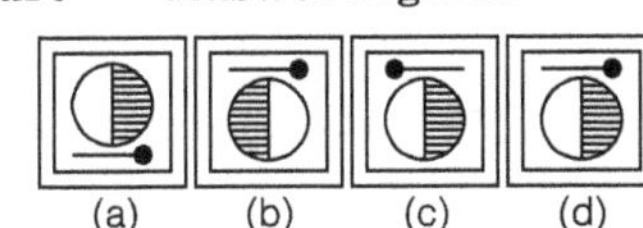

(a) (b) (c) (d)

« RRB ASM 2012

2. 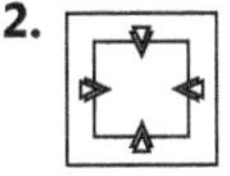 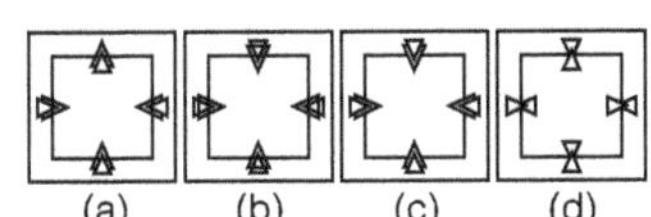

(a) (b) (c) (d)

3. 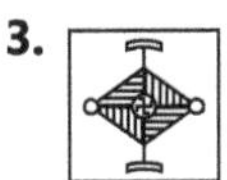 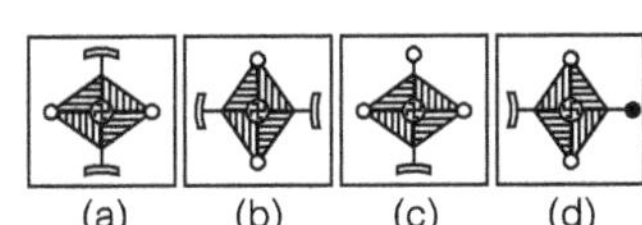

(a) (b) (c) (d)

« SSC CGL 2010

4.  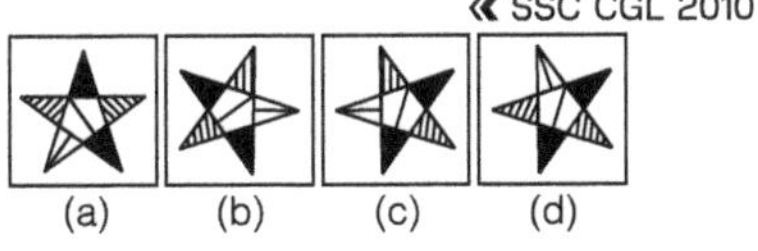

(a) (b) (c) (d)

5. 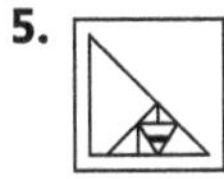 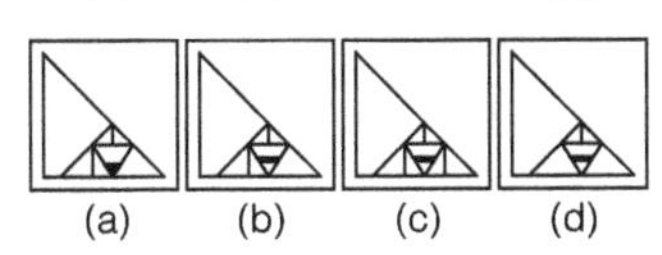

(a) (b) (c) (d)

« SSC CGL 2010

DIRECTIONS ~(Q.Nos.6-10) *In each of the following questions, choose that answer figure which is exactly the same as the question figure.*

Question Figure **Answer Figures**

6. 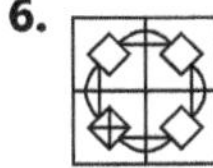 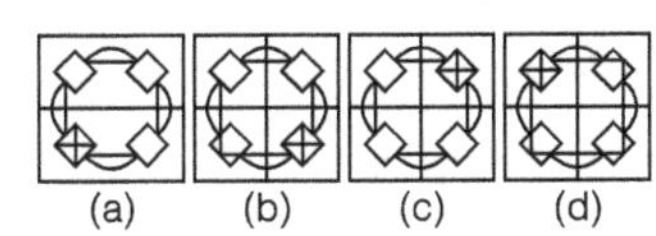

(a) (b) (c) (d)

« Delhi Police Constable 2013

7. 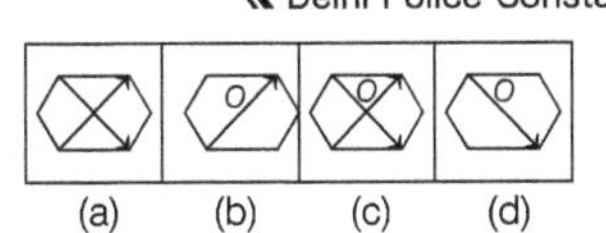

(a) (b) (c) (d)

« RRB Group D 2018

Question Figure **Answer Figures**

8.  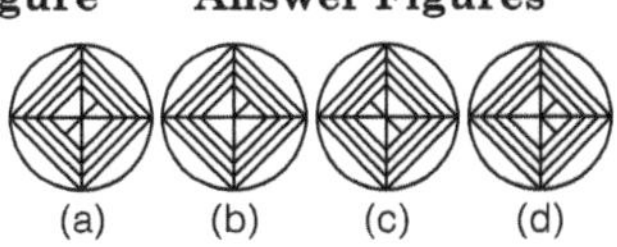

(a) (b) (c) (d)

« UP B.Ed 2012

9.  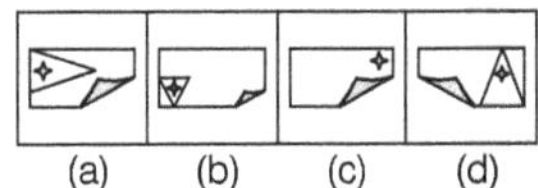

(a) (b) (c) (d)

« RRB Group D 2018

10.  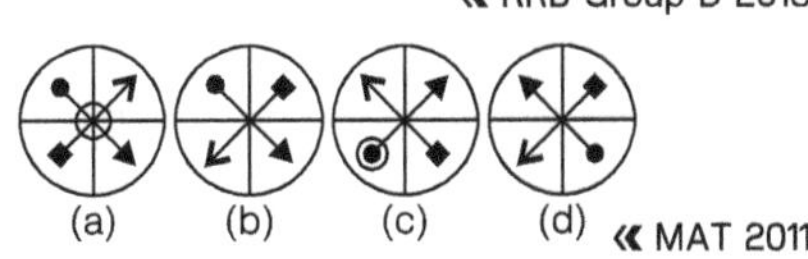

(a) (b) (c) (d) « MAT 2011

DIRECTIONS ~ (Q. Nos. 11 and 12) *In each of the following questions, choose that answer figure which is similar to the question figure, when the question figure is rotated through one place (90°) clockwise.*

Question Figure **Answer Figures**

11. 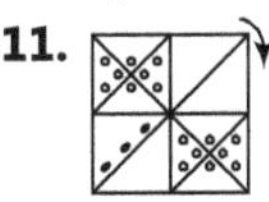 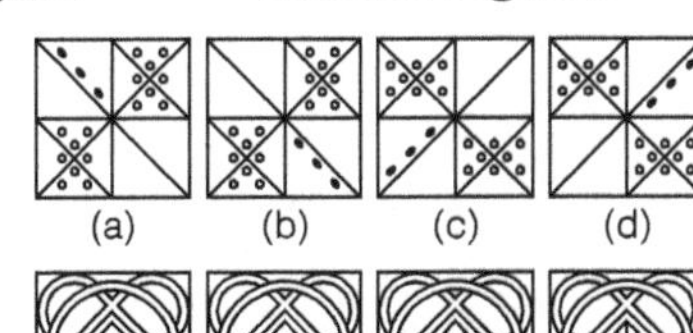

(a) (b) (c) (d)

12.  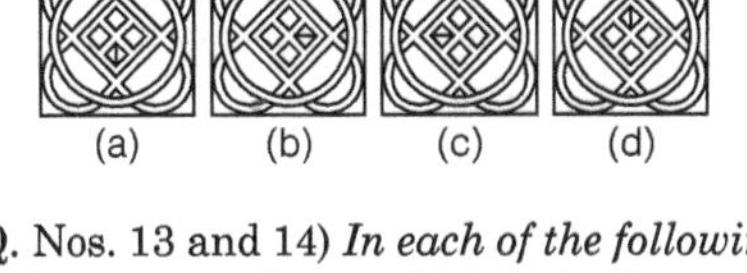

(a) (b) (c) (d)

DIRECTIONS ~ (Q. Nos. 13 and 14) *In each of the following questions, choose that answer figure which is similar to the question figure, when the question figure is rotated through one place (90°) anti-clockwise.*

Question Figure **Answer Figures**

13. 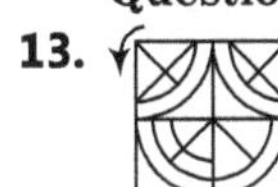 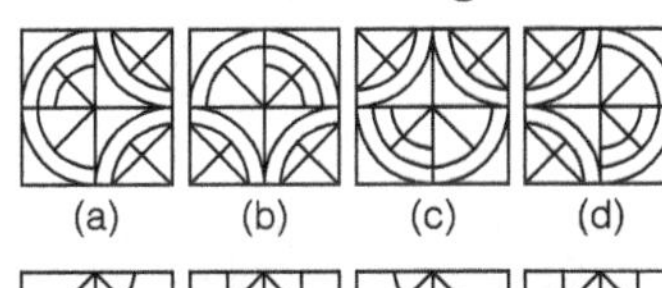

(a) (b) (c) (d)

14. 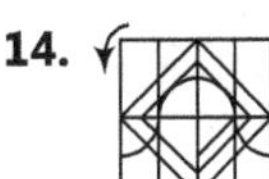 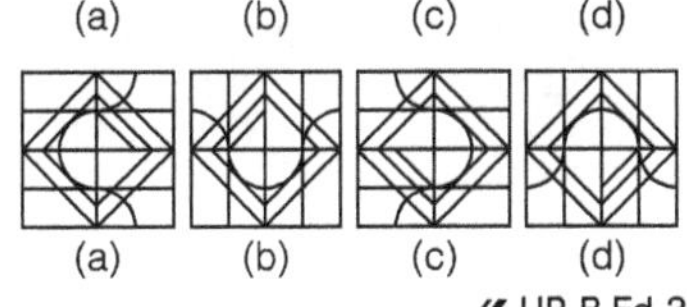

(a) (b) (c) (d)

« UP B.Ed 2003

DIRECTIONS ~(Q. Nos. 15 and 16) *In each of the following questions, choose that answer figure which is similar to the question figure, when the question figure is rotated through two places* (180°) *clockwise.*

Question Figure **Answer Figures**

15. (a) (b) (c) (d)

16. (a) (b) (c) (d)

DIRECTIONS ~ (Q. Nos. 17 and 18) *In each of the following questions, choose that answer figure which is similar to the question figure, when the question figure is rotated through two places* (180°) *anti-clockwise.*

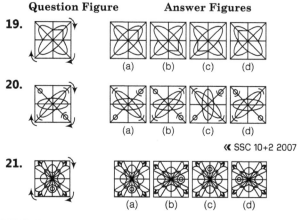

Question Figure **Answer Figures**

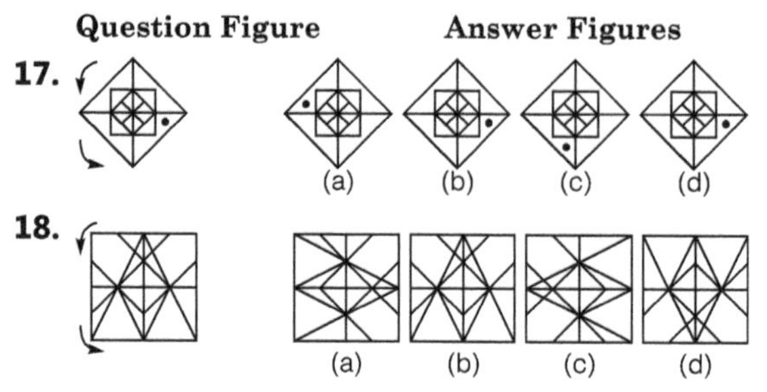

« UP B.Ed 2004

DIRECTIONS ~ (Q. Nos. 19-21) *In each of the following questions, choose that answer figure which is similar to the question figure, when the question figure is rotated through three places* (270°) *clockwise.*

Question Figure **Answer Figures**

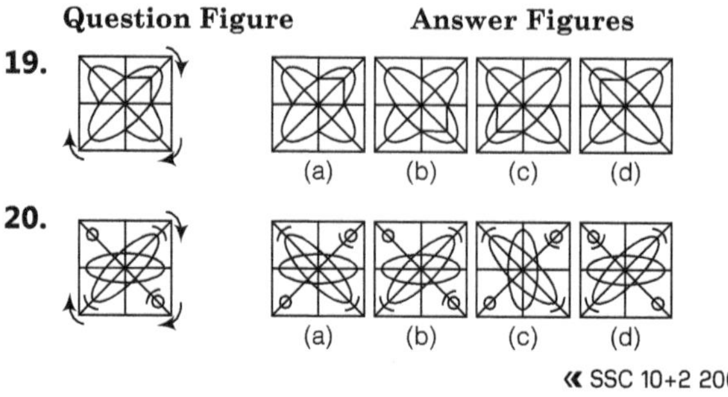

« SSC 10+2 2007

21. (a) (b) (c) (d)

DIRECTIONS ~(Q. Nos. 22 and 23) *In each of the following questions, choose that answer figure which is similar to the question figure, when the question figure is rotated through three places* (270°) *anti-clockwise.*

Question Figure **Answer Figures**

22. (a) (b) (c) (d)

23. (a) (b) (c) (d)

DIRECTIONS ~ (Q. Nos. 24 and 25) *In each of the following questions, choose that answer figure which is similar to the question figure, when the question figure is rotated through four places* (360°) *clockwise.*

Question Figure **Answer Figures**

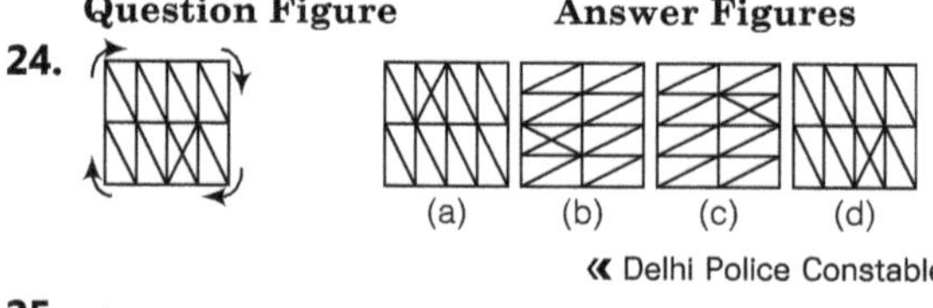

« Delhi Police Constable 2011

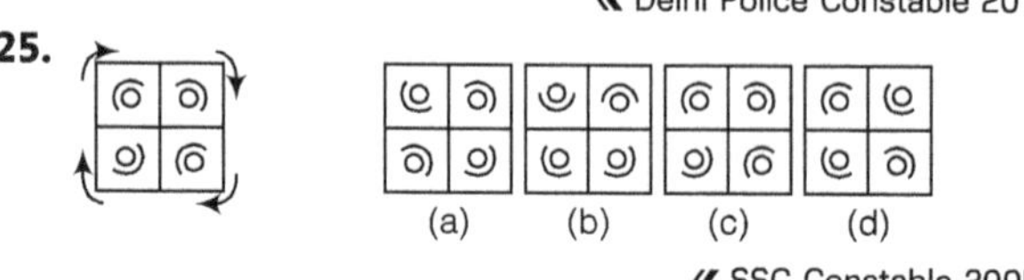

« SSC Constable 2005

DIRECTIONS ~ (Q. Nos. 26 and 27) *In each of the following questions, choose that answer figure which is similar to the question figure, when the question figure is rotated through four places* (360°) *anti-clockwise.*

Question Figure **Answer Figures**

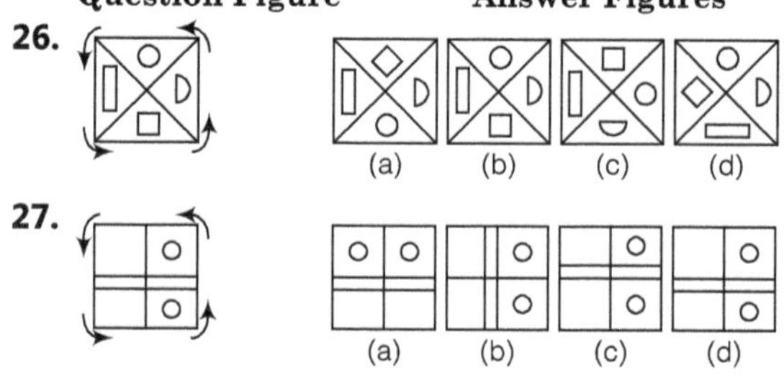

DIRECTIONS ~ (Q. Nos. 28-32) *In each of the following questions, choose that answer figure which is not similar to the question figure.*

Question Figure **Answer Figures**

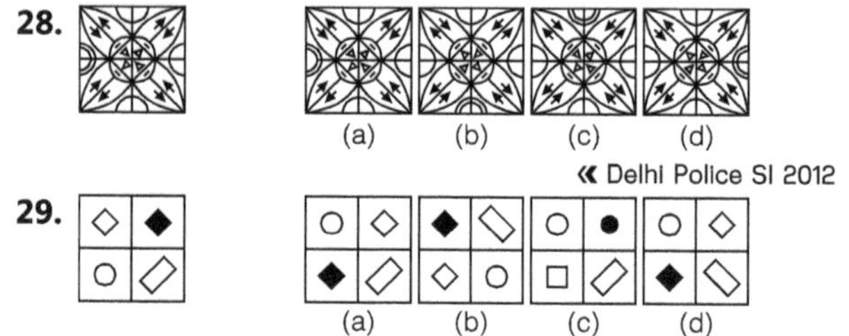

« Delhi Police SI 2012

« Delhi Police SI 2012

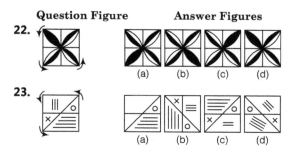

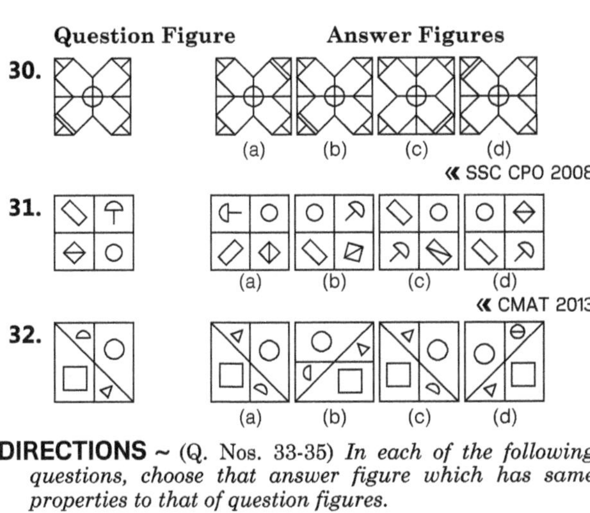

30. « SSC CPO 2008

31. « CMAT 2013

32.

DIRECTIONS ~ (Q. Nos. 33-35) *In each of the following questions, choose that answer figure which has same properties to that of question figures.*

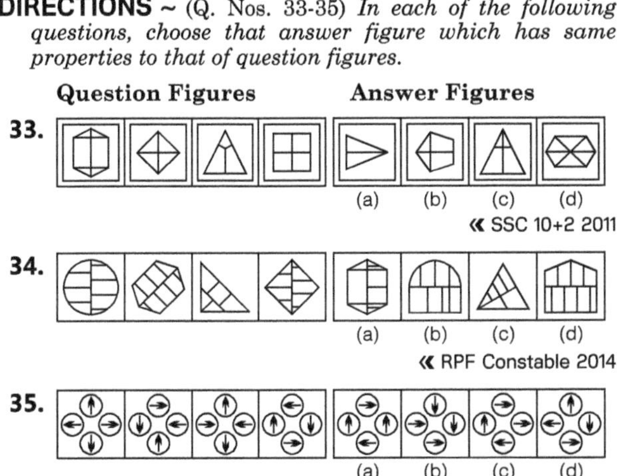

33. « SSC 10+2 2011

34. « RPF Constable 2014

35.

DIRECTIONS ~ (Q. Nos. 36-43) *In each of the following questions, choose that answer figure which is similar to the question figures.*

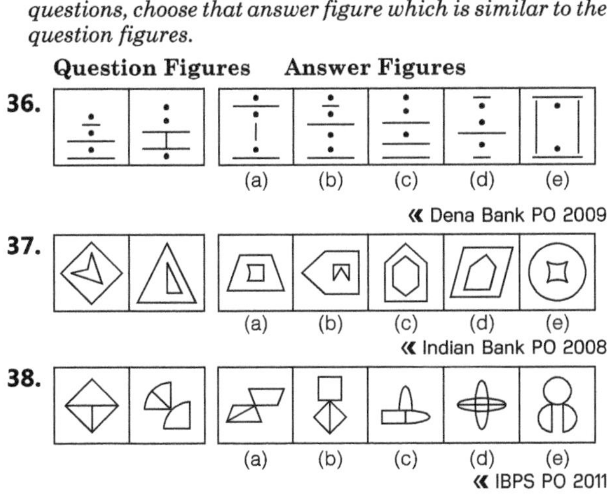

36. « Dena Bank PO 2009

37. « Indian Bank PO 2008

38. « IBPS PO 2011

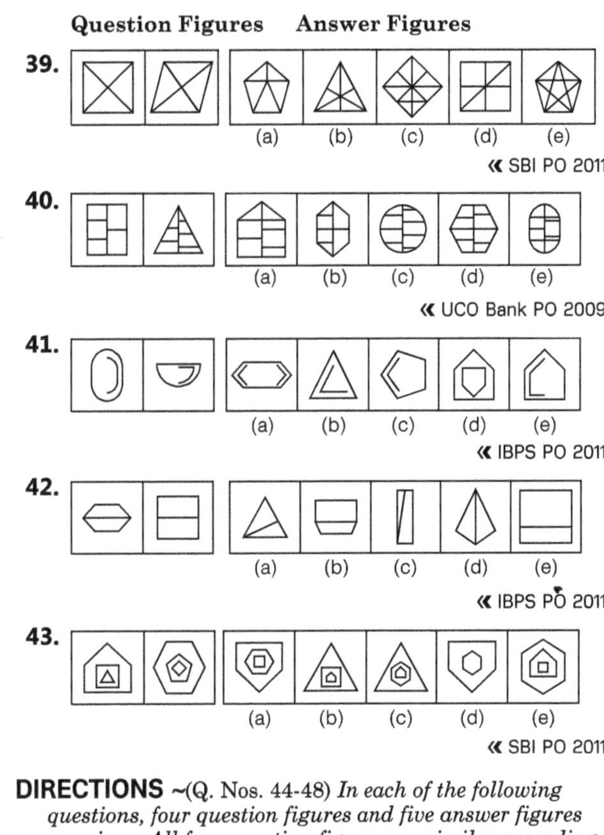

39. « SBI PO 2011

40. « UCO Bank PO 2009

41. « IBPS PO 2011

42. « IBPS PO 2011

43. « SBI PO 2011

DIRECTIONS ~(Q. Nos. 44-48) *In each of the following questions, four question figures and five answer figures are given. All four question figures are similar according to a certain property/feature. Choose that answer figure which is similar to the question figure following the same property/feature.*

44. Question Figures

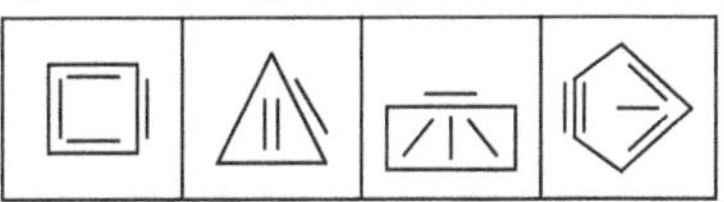

Answer Figures

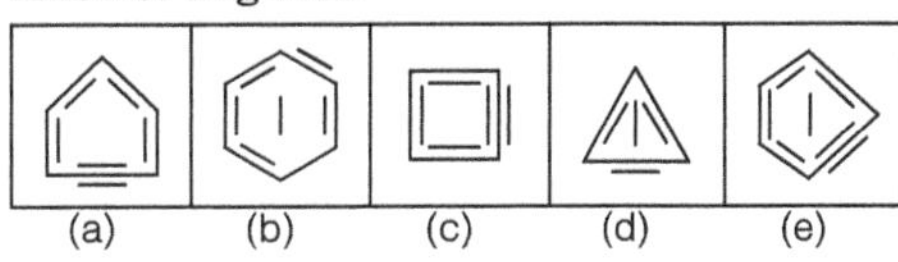

« IBPS PO 2011

45. Question Figures

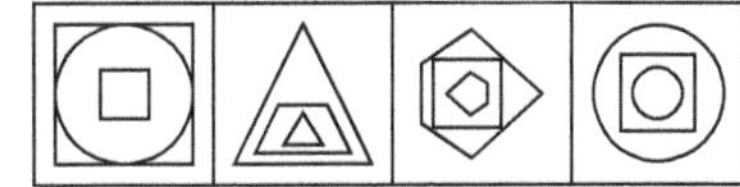

Answer Figures

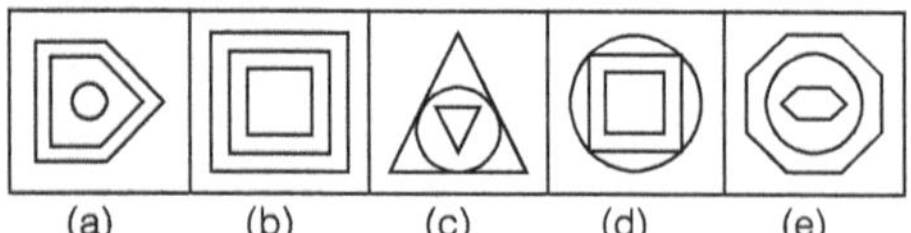

(a) (b) (c) (d) (e)

« IBPS PO 2011

46. Question Figures

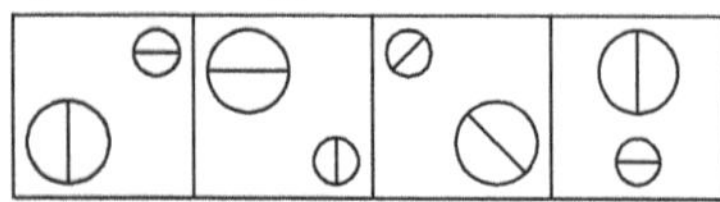

Answer Figures

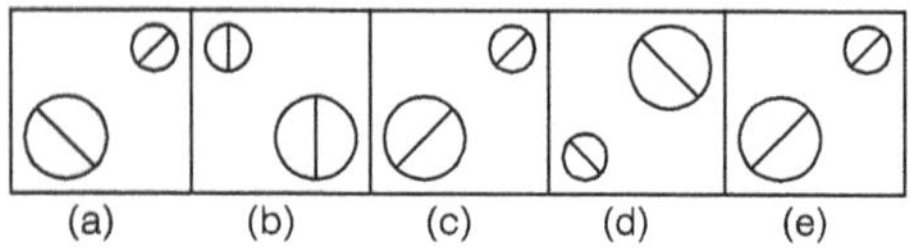

(a) (b) (c) (d) (e)

« SBI PO 2010

47. Question Figures

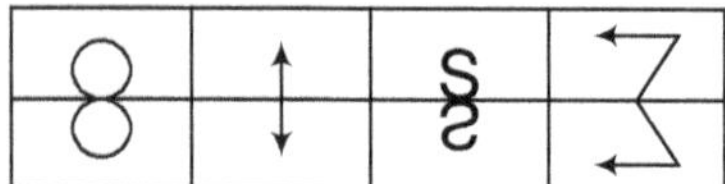

Answer Figures

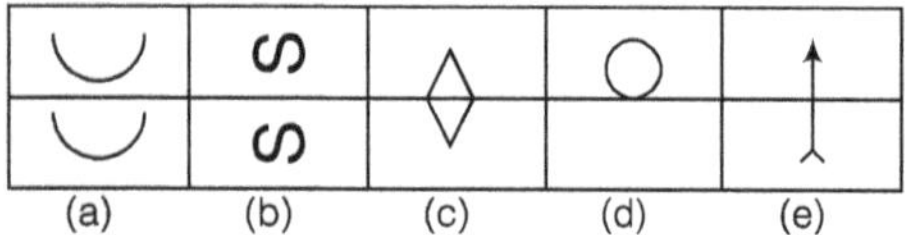

(a) (b) (c) (d) (e)

« IBPS PO 2011

48. Question Figures

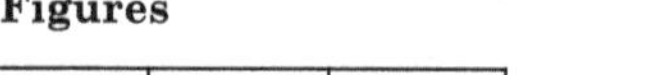

Answer Figures

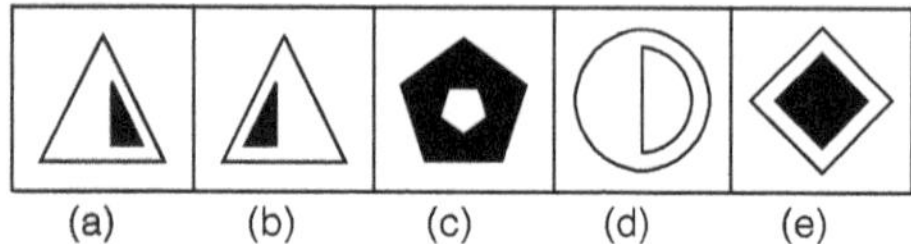

(a) (b) (c) (d) (e)

DIRECTIONS ~ (Q. Nos. 49-55) *In each of the following questions, which of the given answer figures contains almost all the elements/maximum elements of question figure.*

« SBI PO 2009

Question Figure **Answer Figures**

49. 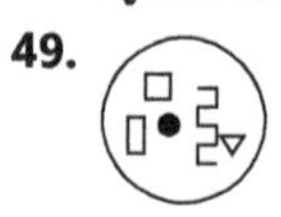

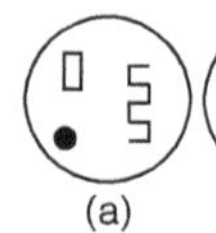
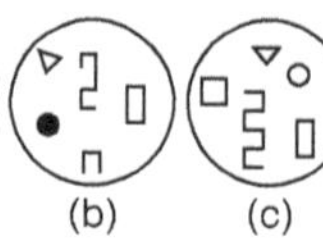
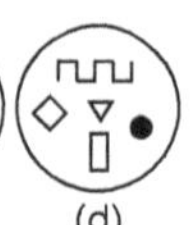

(a) (b) (c) (d)

« SSC CGL 2003

50. 

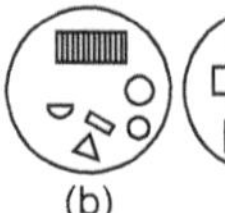
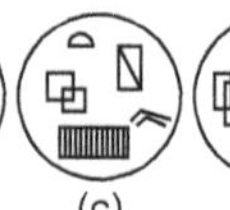
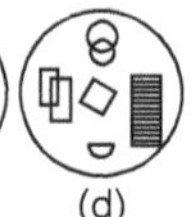

(a) (b) (c) (d)

51. 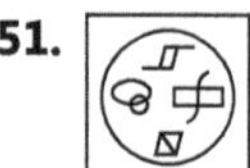

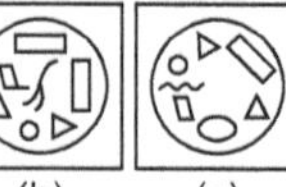

(a) (b) (c) (d)

« SSC CPO 2008

52. 

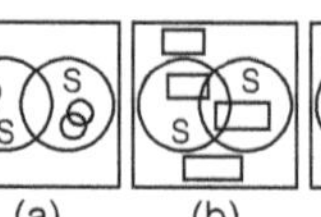
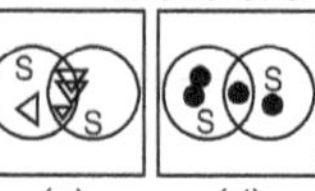

(a) (b) (c) (d)

« SSC 10+2 2009

53. 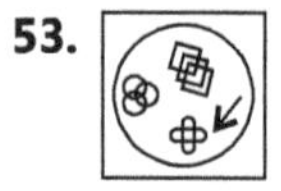

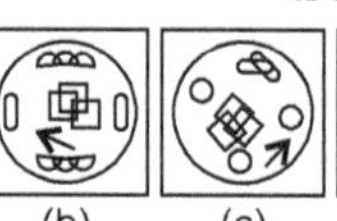
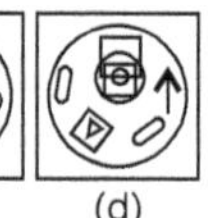

(a) (b) (c) (d)

« SSC CGL 2006

54. 

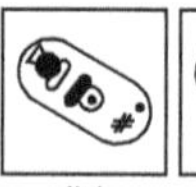
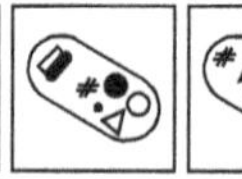

(a) (b) (c) (d)

« IGNOU B.Ed 2005

55. 

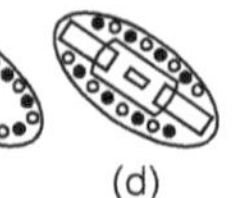

(a) (b) (c) (d)

« SSC 10+2 2009

» *Answers* «

1. *(d)*	2. *(c)*	3. *(a)*	4. *(a)*	5. *(b)*	6. *(c)*	7. *(c)*	8. *(b)*	9. *(d)*	10. *(d)*
11. *(a)*	12. *(c)*	13. *(d)*	14. *(a)*	15. *(c)*	16. *(a)*	17. *(a)*	18. *(d)*	19. *(d)*	20. *(c)*
21. *(b)*	22. *(c)*	23. *(b)*	24. *(d)*	25. *(c)*	26. *(b)*	27. *(d)*	28. *(a)*	29. *(c)*	30. *(c)*
31. *(c)*	32. *(d)*	33. *(d)*	34. *(d)*	35. *(d)*	36. *(a)*	37. *(b)*	38. *(b)*	39. *(e)*	40. *(c)*
41. *(e)*	42. *(d)*	43. *(e)*	44. *(b)*	45. *(c)*	46. *(a)*	47. *(c)*	48. *(e)*	49. *(d)*	50. *(a)*
51. *(a)*	52. *(b)*	53. *(c)*	54. *(b)*	55. *(c)*					

CHAPTER / 12

Grouping of Figures

Grouping of figures involves segregation of a given set of figures into different groups on the basis of some common characteristics.

In this type of questions, a set of figures or geometrical shapes are given. Candidates are required to analyse these figures and classify them into different groups based on one or more common characteristics, which the figures share with each other.

Grouping of figures can be done on the basis of their shape, orientation, number of elements and other such characteristics.

Some examples based on grouping of figures are as follows

DIRECTIONS ~ (Example Nos. 1-7) *In the following questions, group the figures into different classes on the basis of their orientation, shape etc.*

***Ex* 01**

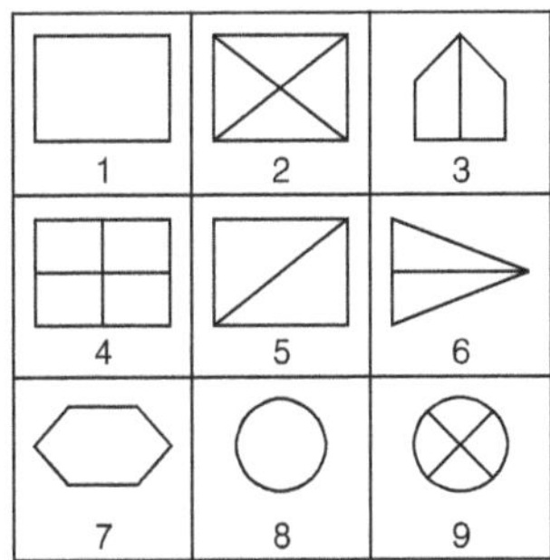

(a) (1, 2, 4), (3, 5, 6), (7, 8, 9) (b) (1, 7, 8), (3, 5, 6), (2, 4, 9)
(c) (1, 3, 4), (2, 8, 9), (5, 6, 7) (d) (1, 7, 8), (2, 3, 6), (4, 5, 9)

***Solution* (b)** Here, figures 1, 7 and 8 contain a simple geometrical shape. Figures 3, 5 and 6 contain a geometrical shape divided into two equal parts by a straight line. Figures 2, 4 and 9 contain a geometrical shape divided into four parts by two straight lines.

Thus, the given nine figures may be divided into three groups as (1, 7, 8), (3, 5, 6) and (2, 4, 9).

***Ex* 02**

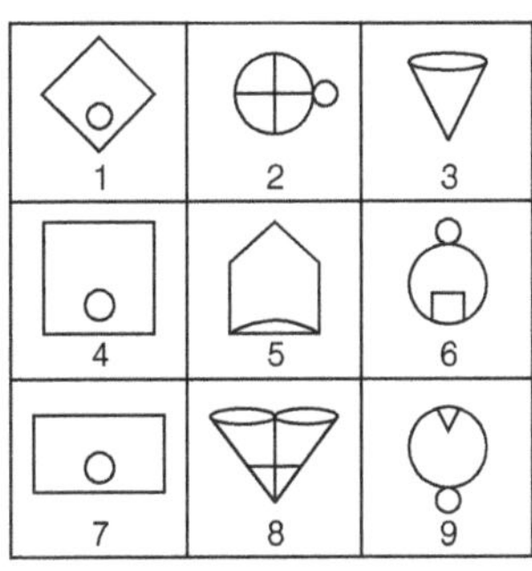

« RRB Group D 2018

(a) (1, 2, 4), (3, 5, 6), (8, 7, 9)
(b) (9, 7, 6), (5, 3, 1), (4, 8, 2)
(c) (2, 3, 4), (7, 6, 5), (9, 8, 1)
(d) (1, 4, 7), (2, 6, 9), (3, 5, 8)

***Solution* (d)** Here, figures 1, 4 and 7 comprise of a quadrilateral in which a circle is enclosed. Figures 2, 6 and 9 contain a smaller circle attached to a larger circle. Figures 3, 5 and 8 contain figure in which atleast one curve is present. Thus, the given nine figures may be divided into three groups as (1, 4, 7), (2, 6, 9) and (3, 5, 8).

***Ex* 03**

« SSC 10+2 2013

(a) (1, 2, 3), (4, 5, 6), (7, 8, 9) (b) (1, 3, 5), (2, 4, 6), (7, 8, 9)
(c) (1, 5, 9), (3, 6, 2), (4, 7, 8) (d) (1, 9, 7), (2, 8, 5), (3, 4, 6)

***Solution* (a)** Figures 1, 2 and 3 are made up of two straight lines.

Figures 4, 5 and 6 are made up of three straight lines.

Figures 7, 8, and 9 are made up of four straight lines.

***Ex* 04**

(a) (1, 5, 6), (2, 3, 4), (7, 8, 9)
(b) (1, 2, 4), (3, 5, 8), (6, 7, 9)
(c) (5, 6, 7), (1, 2, 4), (3, 8, 9)
(d) (1, 2, 4), (3, 5, 7), (6, 8, 9)

***Solution* (b)** Figures 1, 2 and 4 are made up of three straight lines.
Figures 3, 5 and 8 are made up of four straight lines.
Figures 6, 7, and 9 are made up of five straight lines.

***Ex* 05**

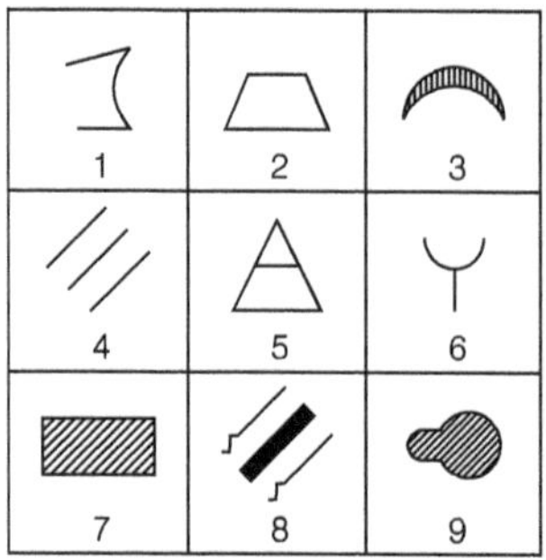

« SSC 10+2 2012

(a) (1, 3, 6), (4, 5, 8), (2, 7, 9)
(b) (2, 3, 9), (4, 5, 8), (1, 6, 7)
(c) (1, 6, 8), (3, 7, 9), (2, 4, 5)
(d) (3, 8, 9), (1, 2, 7), (4, 5, 6)

***Solution* (c)** Figures 1, 6 and 8 are made up of straight lines and curved lines.
Figures 3, 7 and 9 are shaded figures. Figures 2, 4 and 5 are made up of straight lines only.

***Ex* 06**

« SSC CGL 2014

(a) (1, 4, 7), (2, 5, 8), (3, 6, 9)
(b) (1, 4, 5), (2, 6, 8), (3, 7, 9)
(c) (1, 7, 9), (3, 6, 8), (2, 4, 6)
(d) (1, 6, 9), (2, 5, 8), (3, 4, 7)

***Solution* (a)** Here, figures 1, 4 and 7 form a group of figures in which one triangle is present at the base of figure and the figure as a whole looks like a flask. Figures 2, 5 and 8 are kettle shaped figures. Figures 3, 6 and 9 form a group of figures representing floral design.

***Ex* 07**

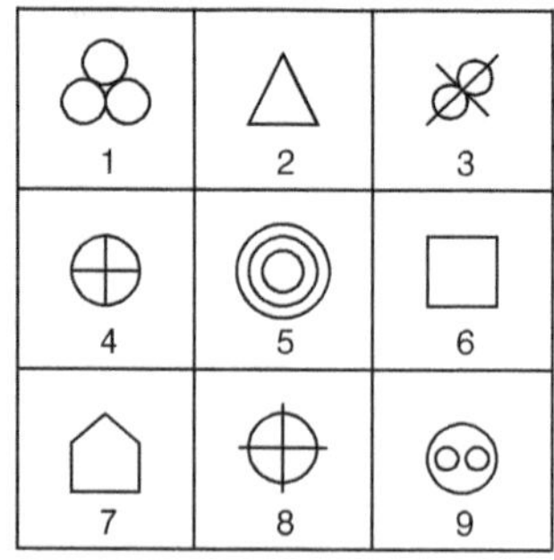

« SSC 10+2 2010

(a) (1, 2, 3); (4, 5, 6); (7, 8, 9)
(b) (3, 6, 9); (1, 5, 8); (2, 4, 7)
(c) (5, 6, 9); (4, 7, 8); (1, 2, 3)
(d) (1, 5, 9); (3, 4, 8); (2, 6, 7)

***Solution* (d)** Figures 1, 5 and 9 have three circles, figures 3, 4 and 8 are divided into four parts. Figures 2, 6 and 7 are simple geometrical figures.

***Ex* 08** Which of the following answer figures are similar to class 'I' figures?

Answer Figures

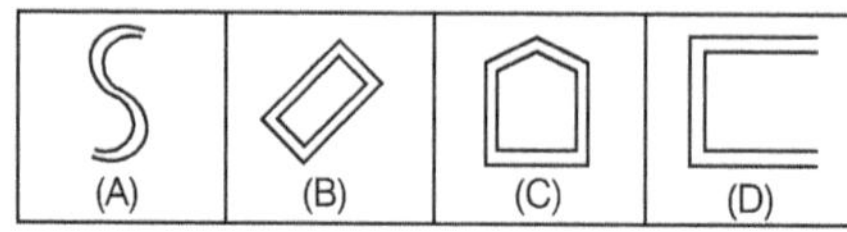

« SSC CGL 2004

(a) A and C
(b) A and B
(c) B and D
(d) B and C

***Solution* (d)** Each of the three class 'I' figures is composed of two similar and closed geometrical shapes one inside the other. Hence, answer figures 'B' and 'C' belong to class 'I'.

Practice CORNER

DIRECTIONS ~ (Q. Nos. 1-38) *In each of the following questions, group the given figures into different classes on the basis of their orientation, shape etc. and choose the correct option.*

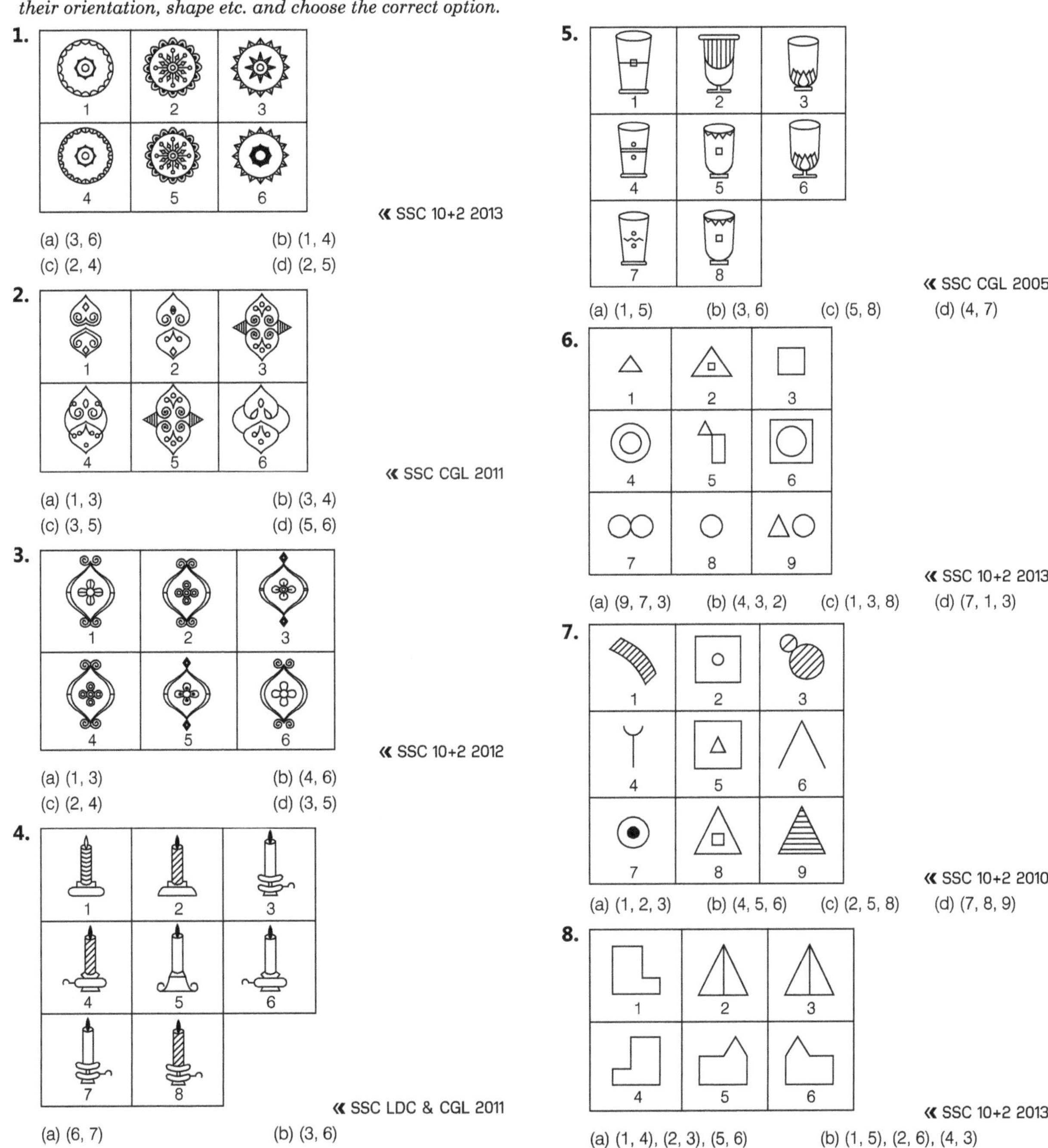

1. « SSC 10+2 2013

(a) (3, 6) (b) (1, 4)
(c) (2, 4) (d) (2, 5)

2. « SSC CGL 2011

(a) (1, 3) (b) (3, 4)
(c) (3, 5) (d) (5, 6)

3. « SSC 10+2 2012

(a) (1, 3) (b) (4, 6)
(c) (2, 4) (d) (3, 5)

4. « SSC LDC & CGL 2011

(a) (6, 7) (b) (3, 6)
(c) (3, 7) (d) (4, 8)

5. « SSC CGL 2005

(a) (1, 5) (b) (3, 6) (c) (5, 8) (d) (4, 7)

6. « SSC 10+2 2013

(a) (9, 7, 3) (b) (4, 3, 2) (c) (1, 3, 8) (d) (7, 1, 3)

7. « SSC 10+2 2010

(a) (1, 2, 3) (b) (4, 5, 6) (c) (2, 5, 8) (d) (7, 8, 9)

8. « SSC 10+2 2013

(a) (1, 4), (2, 3), (5, 6) (b) (1, 5), (2, 6), (4, 3)
(c) (1, 6), (2, 3), (4, 5) (d) (1, 2), (3, 6), (4, 5)

9.
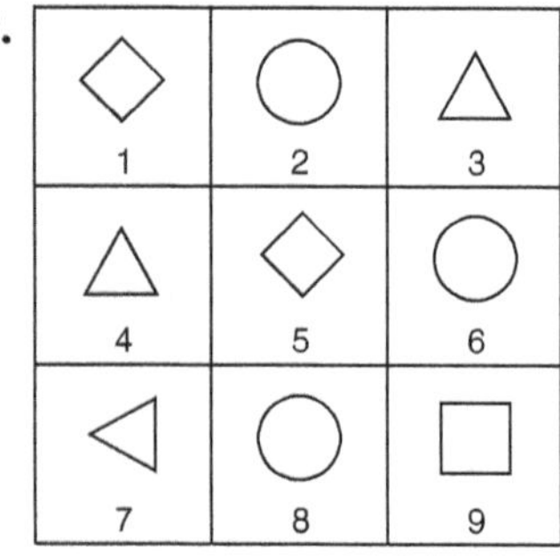

« SSC CPO 2010

(a) (1, 5, 9), (2, 4, 7), (3, 6, 8) (b) (2, 6, 8), (1, 5, 9), (3, 4, 7)
(c) (4, 3, 7), (2, 6, 9), (1, 5, 8) (d) (1, 2, 3), (4, 5, 6), (7, 8, 9)

10.
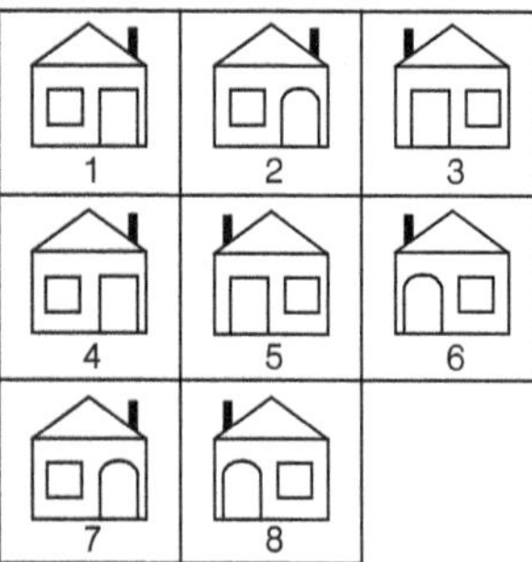

« SSC CPO 2011

(a) (1, 7), (2, 4), (3, 5), (6, 8) (b) (1, 4), (2, 7), (3, 5), (6, 8)
(c) (1, 3), (2, 7), (6, 8), (4, 5) (d) (1, 4), (3, 6), (3, 5), (7, 8)

11.
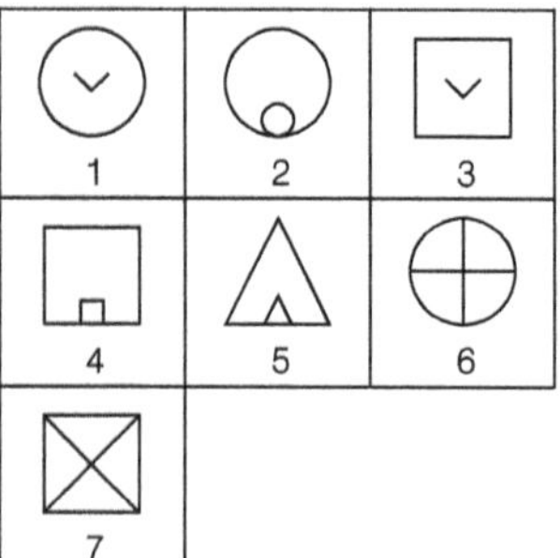

« SSC LDC 2009

(a) (1, 2, 6), (3, 4, 7), (5) (b) (1, 3), (2, 6), (4, 5, 7)
(c) (1, 2, 6, 7), (3), (4, 5) (d) (1, 3), (2, 4, 5), (6, 7)

12.
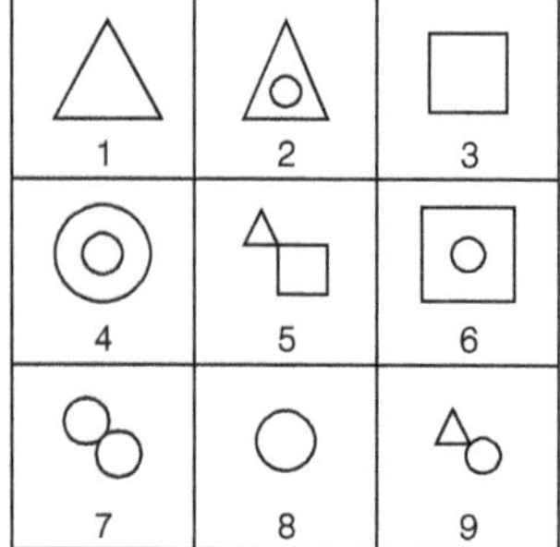

(a) (4, 7, 9), (2, 5, 8), (1, 3, 6) (b) (1, 3, 8), (2, 4, 6), (5, 7, 9)
(c) (1, 4, 6), (2, 3, 7), (5, 8, 9) (d) (3, 5, 4), (1, 6, 9), (2, 7, 8)

13.
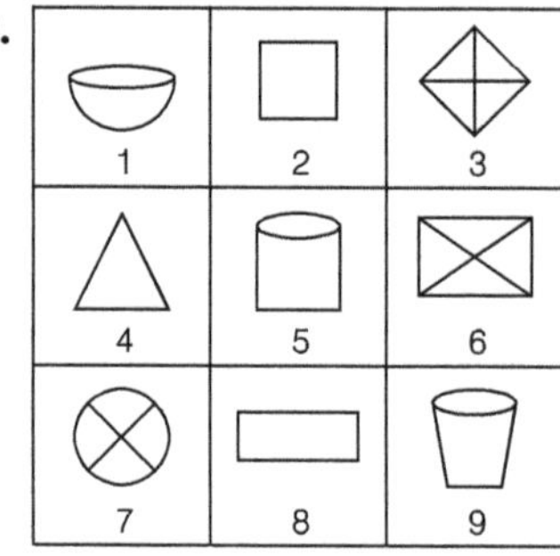

« UP B. Ed. 2008

(a) (1, 5, 9), (3, 6, 7), (2, 4, 8) (b) (2, 3, 6), (4, 8, 9), (1, 5, 7)
(c) (3, 6, 8), (2, 4, 9), (1, 5, 7) (d) (2, 5, 8), (1, 7, 9), (3, 4, 6)

14.
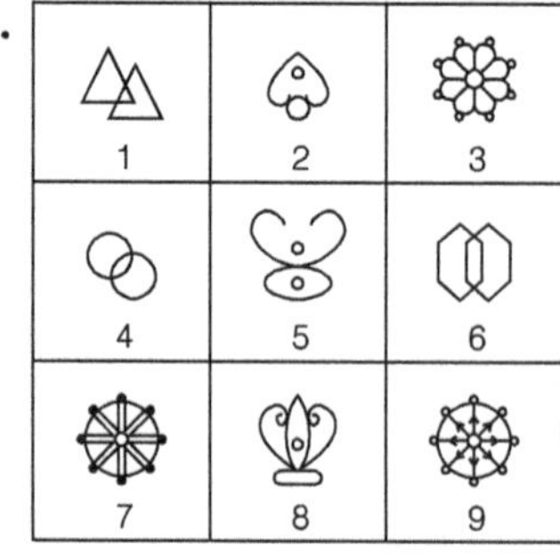

« LIC ADO 2009

(a) (1, 4, 8), (2, 5, 7), (3, 9, 6) (b) (1, 4, 6), (2, 5, 8), (3, 7, 9)
(c) (1, 4, 6), (2, 5, 7), (3, 8, 9) (d) (1, 2, 3), (4, 5, 6), (7, 8, 9)
(e) None of these

15.
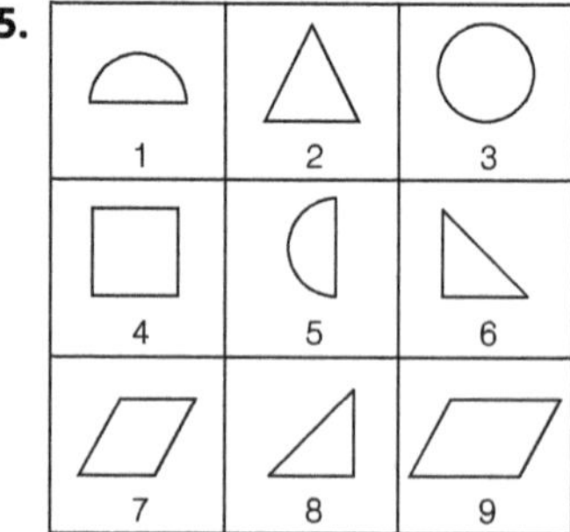

(a) (1, 3, 5), (2, 6, 9), (4, 7, 8) (b) (2, 3, 4), (5, 6, 8), (9, 1, 7)
(c) (1, 3, 5), (2, 6, 8), (4, 7, 9) (d) (3, 2, 4), (6, 5, 8), (7, 9, 1)

16.
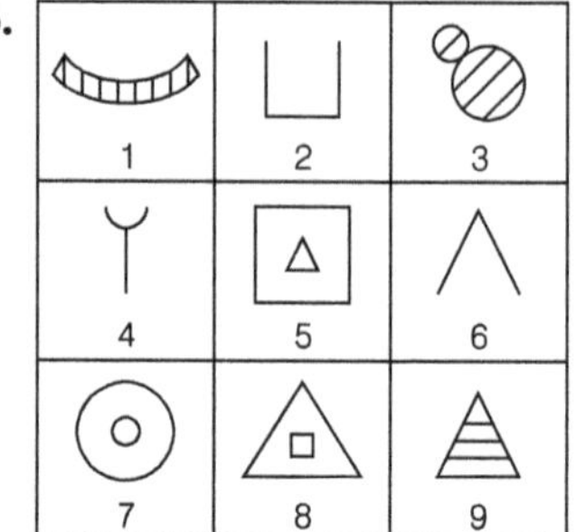

« RRB ALP 2018

(a) (1, 3, 9), (2, 4, 6), (5, 7, 8) (b) (3, 2, 1), (4, 6, 5), (9, 7, 8)
(c) (2, 4, 5), (9, 1, 3), (7, 8, 6) (d) (1, 5, 7), (2, 3, 9), (4, 6, 8)

17.

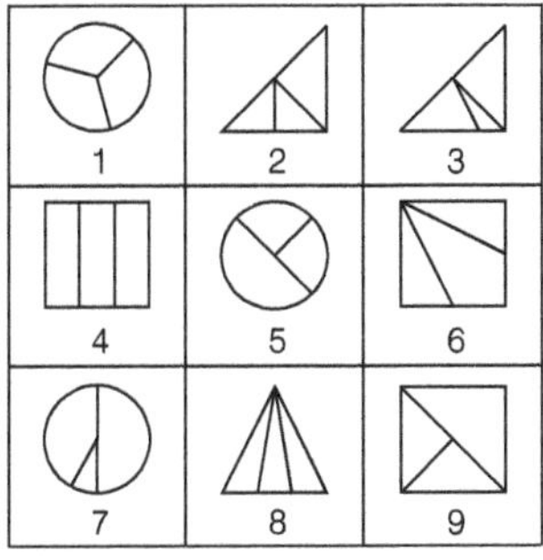

« MAT 2007

(a) (1, 5, 7), (2, 3, 8), (4, 6, 9) (b) (3, 7, 6), (1, 8, 4), (2, 5, 9)
(c) (1, 4, 9), (2, 5, 6), (3, 7, 8) (d) (1, 2, 6), (3, 4, 5), (7, 8, 9)

18.

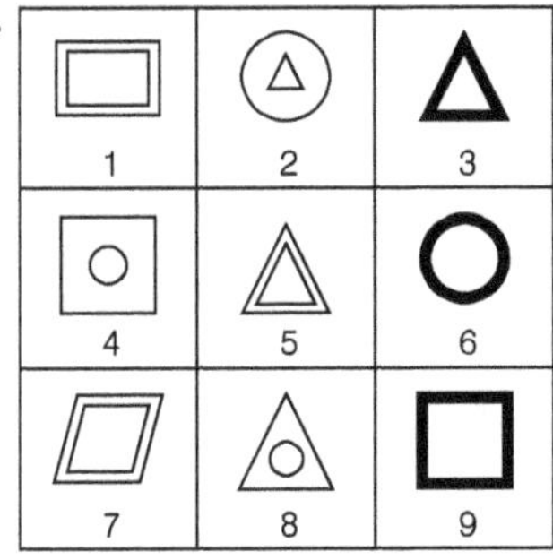

« SSC CGL 2004

(a) (1, 5, 7), (2, 4, 6), (3, 9, 8) (b) (1, 5, 7), (2, 4, 8), (3, 6, 9)
(c) (1, 5, 7), (4, 8, 9), (2, 3, 6) (d) (1, 5, 7), (3, 8, 9), (2, 4, 6)

19.

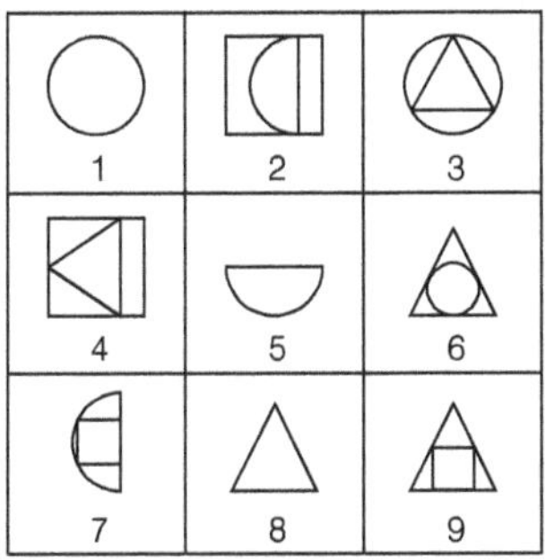

« SSC LDC 2009

(a) (1, 5, 8), (3, 4, 7), (2, 6, 9) (b) (1, 3, 6), (4, 5, 9), (2, 7, 8)
(c) (1, 3, 6), (2, 5, 7), (4, 8, 9) (d) (6, 7, 8), (1, 3, 7), (2, 4, 9)

20.

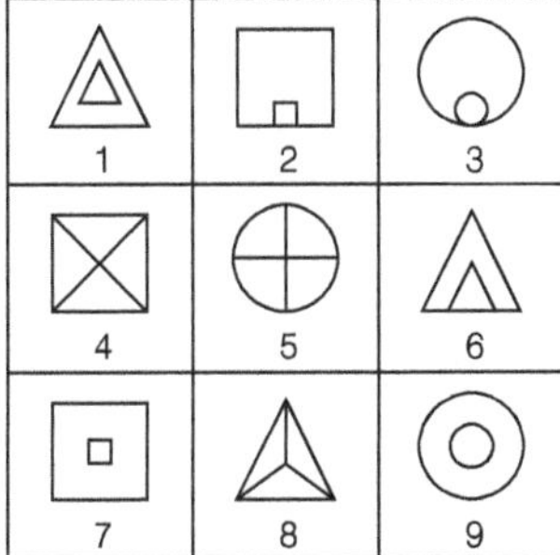

« UP (B. Ed) 2009

(a) (1, 7, 9), (2, 3, 6), (4, 5, 8) (b) (1, 2, 9), (3, 4, 6), (5, 7, 8)
(c) (1, 6, 8), (2, 4, 7), (3, 5, 9) (d) (1, 7, 8), (2, 9, 3), (6, 4, 5)

21.

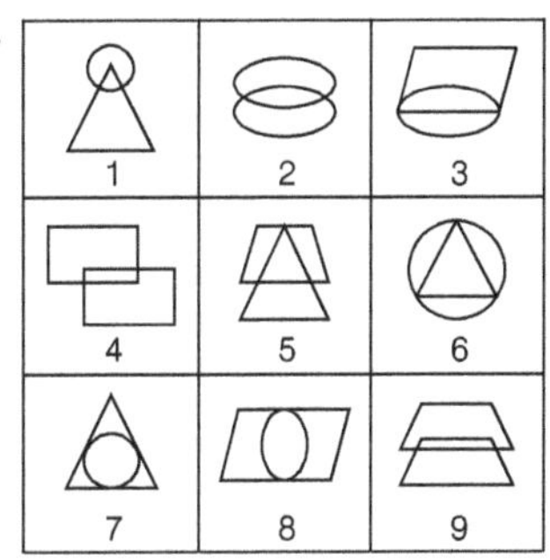

« SSC LDC 2008

(a) (1, 5, 9), (2, 7, 8), (3, 4, 6) (b) (2, 4, 9), (6, 7, 8), (1, 3, 5)
(c) (1, 5, 6), (4, 7, 8), (2, 3, 9) (d) (3, 7, 8), (4, 5, 9), (1, 2, 6)

22.

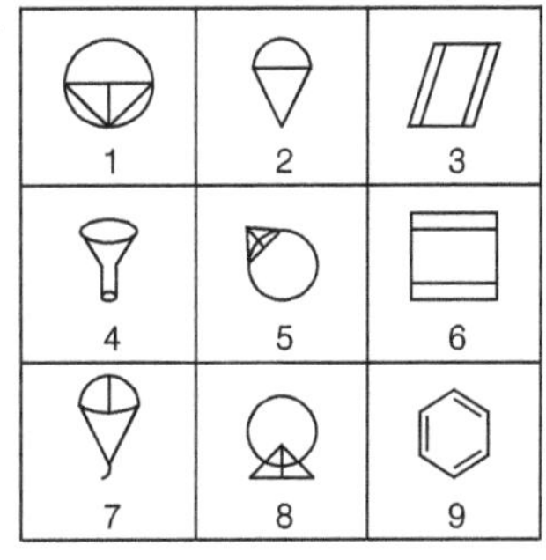

« SSC MTS 2013

(a) (1, 5, 8), (2, 6, 7), (3, 4, 9) (b) (1, 4, 9), (2, 3, 8), (5, 6, 7)
(c) (1, 7, 8), (2, 6, 9), (3, 4, 5) (d) (1, 5, 8), (2, 4, 7), (3, 6, 9)

23.

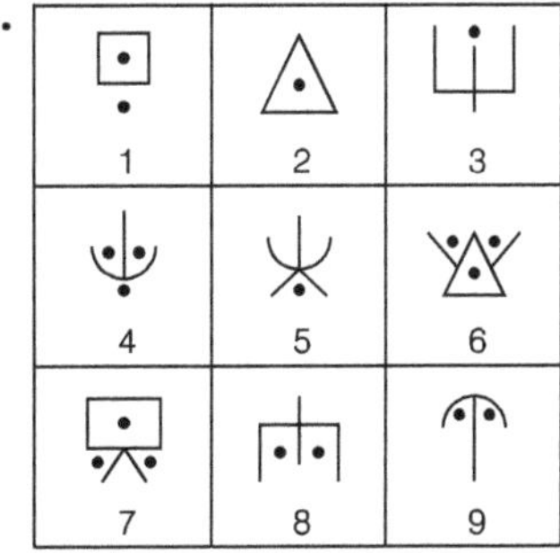

« SSC MTS 2012

(a) (1, 7, 8), (2, 5, 6), (3, 4, 9) (b) (1, 8, 9), (2, 3, 5), (4, 6, 7)
(c) (2, 3, 5), (1, 7, 8), (4, 6, 9) (d) (2, 6, 7), (1, 3, 4), (5, 8, 9)

24.

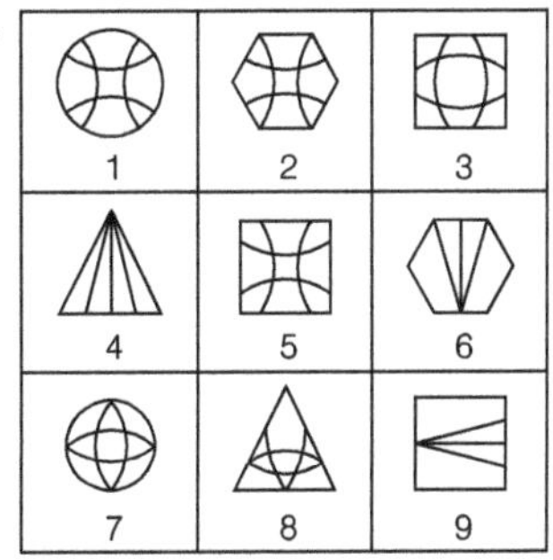

« RRB Group D 2018

(a) (1, 2, 5), (3, 7, 8), (4, 6, 9) (b) (1, 2, 7), (3, 6, 9), (4, 5, 8)
(c) (2, 3, 8), (4, 6, 9), (1, 5, 7) (d) (5, 6, 9), (1, 3, 4), (2, 7, 8)

25.

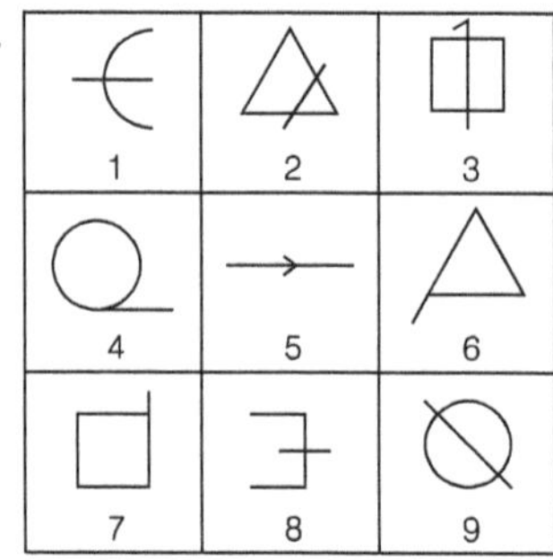

(a) (1, 5, 8), (2, 3, 9), (4, 6, 7) (b) (4, 8, 9), (1, 2, 5), (3, 6, 7)
(c) (2, 5, 9), (1, 3, 8), (2, 6, 7) (d) (1, 8, 9), (4, 6, 7), (2, 3, 5)

26.

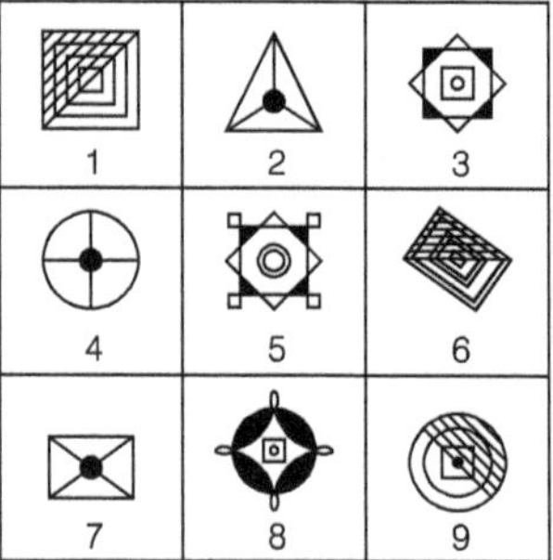

« SSC 10+2 2013

(a) (1, 6, 9), (2, 5, 7), (4, 8, 3) (b) (1, 6, 9), (2, 4, 8), (3, 5, 7)
(c) (1, 3, 5), (2, 6, 7), (4, 8, 9) (d) (1, 6, 9), (2, 4, 7), (3, 5, 8)

27.

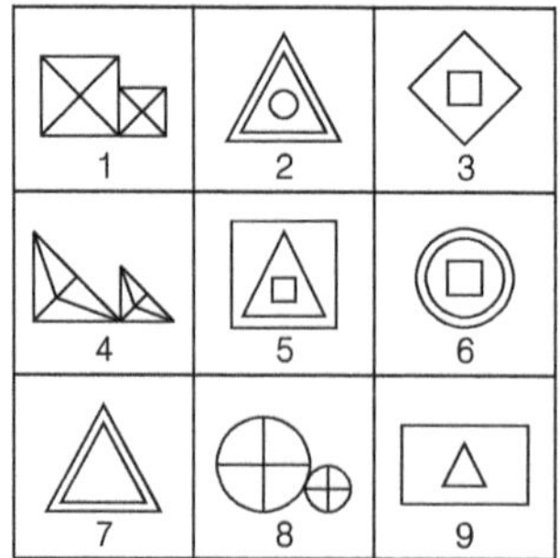

« SSC CGL 2010

(a) (1, 3, 7), (2, 4, 6), (5, 8, 9) (b) (1, 4, 6), (2, 5, 7), (3, 8, 9)
(c) (1, 4, 8), (2, 5, 6), (3, 7, 9) (d) (1, 4, 8), (2, 7, 9), (3, 5, 6)

28.

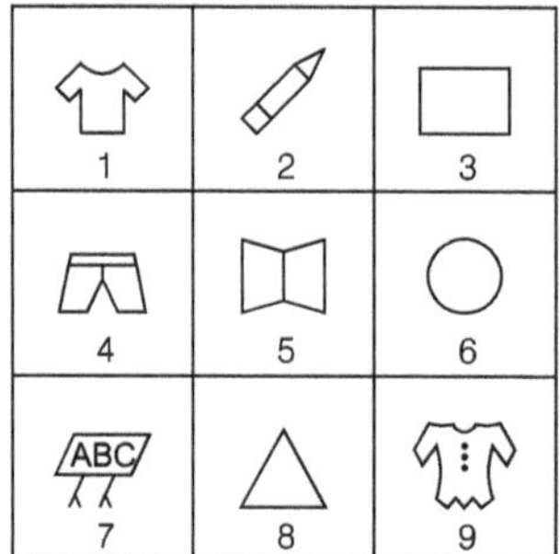

« SSC 10+2 2012

(a) (1, 4, 9), (2, 5, 7), (3, 6, 8) (b) (2, 3, 8), (4, 5, 7), (1, 6, 9)
(c) (5, 7, 9), (3, 4, 8), (2, 6, 1) (d) (1, 4, 9), (2, 3, 5), (6, 7, 8)

29.

« SSC Steno 2009

(a) (3, 4, 9), (5, 7, 8), (1, 2, 6) (b) (1, 5, 6), (2, 4, 8), (3, 7, 9)
(c) (4, 6, 8), (3, 5, 7), (1, 2, 9) (d) (1, 2, 7), (3, 5, 9), (4, 6, 8)

30.

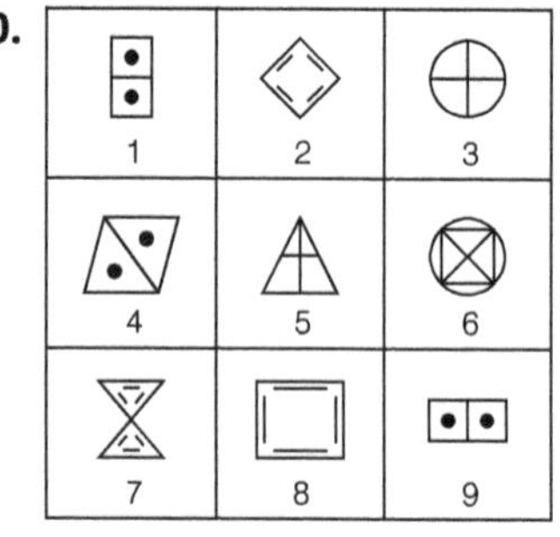

« SSC 10+2 2017

(a) (1, 4, 9), (2, 6, 8), (3, 5, 7) (b) (1, 2, 8), (3, 5, 7), (4, 6, 9)
(c) (2, 5, 8), (4, 6, 9), (1, 3, 7) (d) (1, 4, 9), (2, 7, 8), (3, 5, 6)

31.

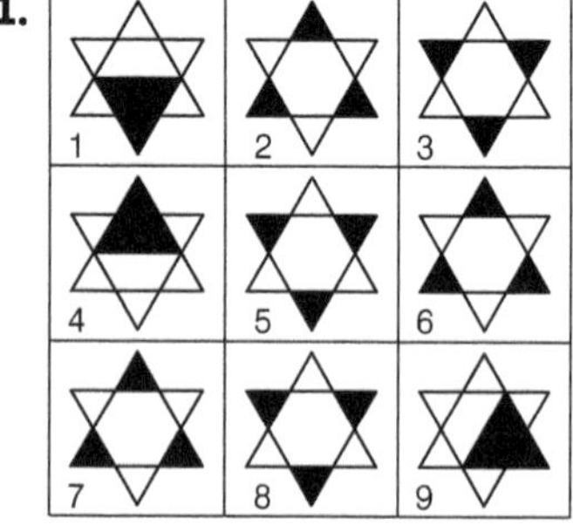

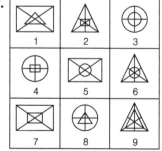

« UPSSSC Combined Lower Subordinate 2019

(a) (1, 4, 8), (2, 5, 7), (3, 6, 9) (b) (1, 5, 9), (2, 4, 7), (3, 6, 8)
(c) (1, 3, 8), (2, 5, 6), (4, 7, 9) (d) (1, 4, 9), (2, 6, 7), (3, 5, 8)

32.

« RRB ALP 2018

(a) (2, 4, 7), (1, 8, 9), (3, 5, 6) (b) (2, 6, 9), (1, 5, 7), (3, 4, 8)
(c) (2, 6, 7), (1, 5, 8), (3, 4, 9) (d) (2, 7, 8), (1, 5, 6), (3, 4, 9)

33.

« SSC 10+2 2013

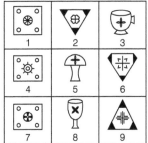

(a) (1, 4, 7), (3, 6, 9), (2, 5, 8) (b) (1, 4, 7), (2, 6, 9), (3, 5, 8)
(c) (1, 6, 9), (2, 4, 7), (3, 5, 8) (d) (1, 5, 7), (2, 6, 9), (3, 4, 8)

34.

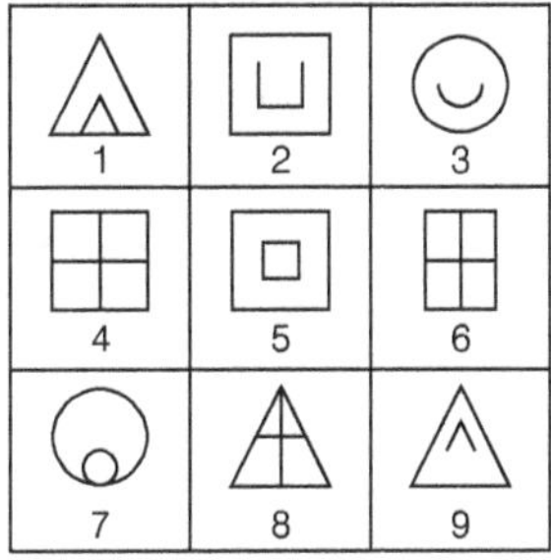

« SSC MTS 2012

(a) (1, 5, 7), (2, 3, 9), (4, 6, 8) (b) (1, 3, 9), (2, 4, 6), (5, 7, 8)
(c) (3, 4, 7), (2, 4, 9), (1, 6, 8) (d) (6, 7, 9), (1, 3, 4), (2, 4, 8)

35.

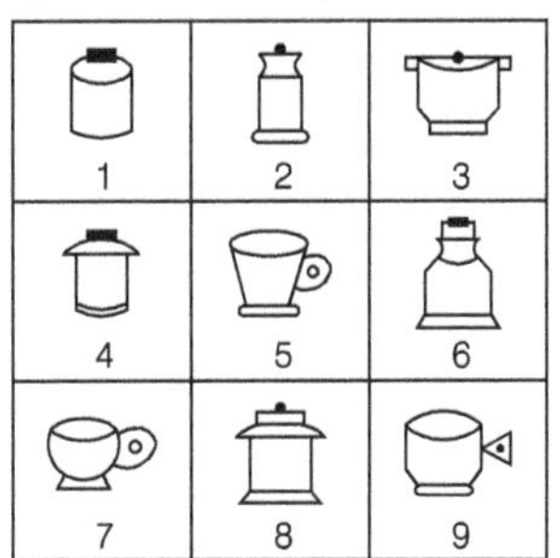

« SSC LDC 2009

(a) (1, 4, 6), (2, 3, 8), (5, 7, 9) (b) (2, 3, 8), (4, 5, 7), (1, 6, 9)
(c) (5, 7, 9), (3, 4, 8), (1, 6, 2) (d) (1, 4, 9), (2, 3, 5), (6, 7, 8)

36.

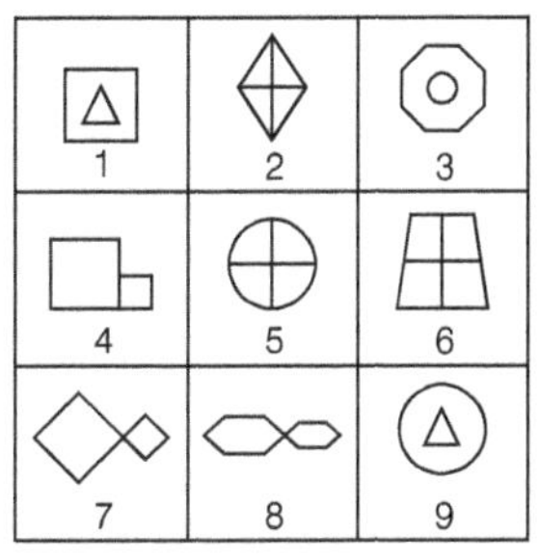

« RRB ALP 2018; SSC MTS 2012

(a) (1, 3, 9), (2, 5, 6), (4, 7, 8) (b) (1, 3, 9), (2, 7, 8), (4, 5, 6)
(c) (1, 2, 4), (3, 5, 7), (6, 8, 9) (d) (1, 3, 6), (2, 4, 8), (5, 7, 9)

37.

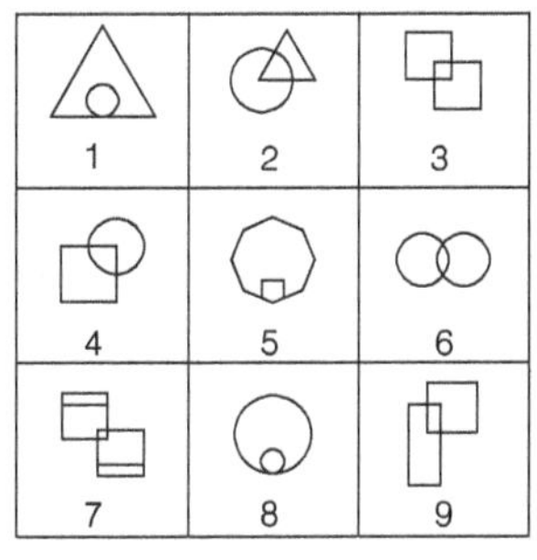

« RRB Group D 2018

(a) (1, 8, 5), (7, 6, 3), (4, 2, 9) (b) (1, 2, 8), (5, 6, 4), (3, 7, 9)
(c) (1, 8, 5), (5, 6, 3), (4, 7, 9) (d) (1, 2, 5), (8, 6, 4), (2, 7, 9)

38.

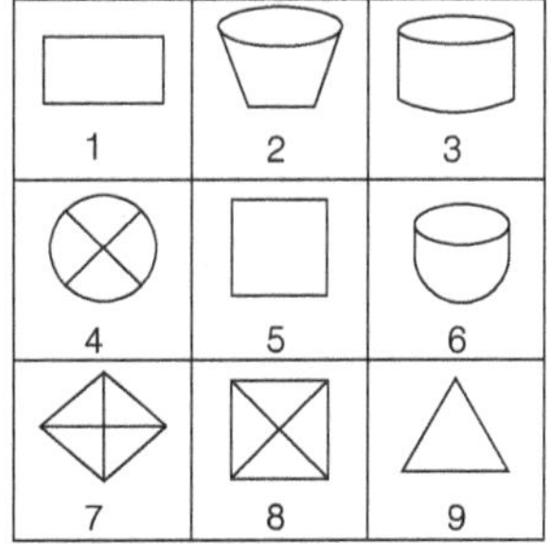

« RRB Group D 2018

(a) (1, 5, 9), (2, 3, 6), (4, 7, 8) (b) (1, 3, 9), (2, 4, 6), (5, 7, 8)
(c) (1, 2, 5), (3, 6, 7), (4, 8, 9) (d) (1, 5, 9), (2, 4, 6), (3, 5, 7)

Answers WITH EXPLANATIONS

1. (*d*) Figures 2 and 5 form a pair of same design.

2. (*c*) Figures 3 and 5 form a pair of same design.

3. (*c*) Figures 2 and 4 form a pair of same design.

4. (*c*) Figures 3 and 7 form a pair of same design.

5. (*c*) Figures 5 and 8 form a pair of identical figures.

6. (*c*) Figures 1, 3 and 8 form a group of figures which contain only one geometrical shape.

7. (*c*) Figures 2, 5 and 8 form a group of figures which are composed of two dissimilar figures, one inside the other.

8. (*a*) Figures (1, 4), (2, 3) and (5, 6) are groups of figures with similar shapes.

9. (*b*) Figures (2, 6, 8) are circles, figures (1, 5, 9) are quadrilaterals and figures (3, 4, 7) are triangles so these figures form a group of similar figures.

10. (*b*) Figures (1, 4), (2, 7), (3, 5) and (6, 8) are groups of identical figures.

11. (*d*) Figures 1 and 3 contain a V-shaped figure inside another figure.
Figures 2, 4 and 5 contain one figure placed inside a similar figure.
Figures 6 and 7 are divided into four equal parts by mutually perpendicular lines.

12. (*b*) Figures 1, 3 and 8 form a group of figures which contain only one geometrical figure.
Figures 2, 4 and 6 form a group of figures in which one figure is enclosed inside an another figure.
Figures 5, 7 and 9 form a group of figures in which two figures are attached to each other.

13. (*a*) Figures 1, 5 and 9 consist of cup-shaped figures.
Figures 3, 6 and 7 contain two straight lines dividing the figure into four parts.
Figures 2, 4 and 8 are simple geometrical figures.

14. (*b*) Figures 1, 4 and 6 contain two identical figures which intersect each other. Figures 2, 5 and 8 contain figures in which curves are present. Figures 3, 7 and 9 contain figures which represent circular design patterns.

15. (*c*) Figures 1, 3 and 5 are figures having partially or completely curved boundaries.
Figures 2, 6 and 8 are triangles.
Figures 4, 7 and 9 are quadrilaterals.

16. (*a*) Figures 1, 3 and 9 form a group of figures with shaded area. Figures 2, 4 and 6 are simple open figures.
Figures 5, 7 and 8 form a group of figures in which two figures are present, one inside the other.

17. (*b*) Figures 3, 7 and 6 form a group of figures which are divided into three unequal parts.
Figures 1, 8 and 4 form a group of figures which are divided into three equal parts.
Figures 2, 5 and 9 form a group of figures in which the figures are divided into three parts in such a way that one part is half and the other two parts are one-fourth of the original figure.

18. (*b*) Figures 1, 5 and 7 are composed of two similar figures, one inside the other. Figures 2, 4 and 8 contain a figure placed inside a dissimilar figure. Figures 3, 6 and 9 are figures with thick boundaries.

19. (*c*) Figures 1, 3 and 6 contain one complete circle each.
Figures 2, 5 and 7 contain one semi-circle each. Figures 4, 8 and 9 contain one triangle each.

20. (*a*) Figures 1, 7 and 9 contain two similar figures, one inside the other without touching each other.
Figures 2, 3 and 6 contain two similar figures one inside the other and both are touching each other.
Figures 4, 5 and 8 are divided into equal parts by straight lines passing through the centre.

21. (*b*) Figures 2, 4 and 9 consist of two similar figures intersecting each other. Figures 6, 7 and 8 consist of one figure enclosed inside the other.
Figures 1, 3 and 5 consist of two dissimilar figures intersecting each other.

22. (*d*) Figures 1, 5 and 8 form a group of figures in which a circle and a triangle (divided into two equal parts) are present in contact with each other.
Figures 2, 4 and 7 contain figures which have curved portions.
Figures 3, 6 and 9 form a group of figures formed by straight lines only.

23. (*b*) Figures 1, 8 and 9 form a group of figures in which two dots are present.
Figures 2, 3 and 5 form a group of figures in which one dot is present.
Figures 4, 6 and 7 form a group of figures in which three dots are present.

24. (*a*) Figures 1, 2 and 5 contain similar pattern enclosed inside different figures.
Figures 3, 7 and 8 contain similar pattern (different from that in figures 1, 2 and 5) enclosed inside different figures. Figures 4, 6 and 9 are figures enclosing a triangle with one median.

25. (*a*) Figures 1, 5 and 8 are open figures bisected by a straight line.
Figures 4, 6 and 7 are figures having an extended arm.
Figures 2, 3 and 9 are closed figures intersected by a line.

26. (*d*) Figures 1, 6 and 9 form a group of figures in which half of the figure is shaded.
Figures 2, 4 and 7 form a group of figures which are divided into equal parts and a dot is present at their centre.
Figures 3, 5 and 8 form a group of figures with similar design pattern.

27. (*c*) Figures 1, 4 and 8 contain similar figures both divided into four parts and attached to each other.
Figures 2, 5 and 6 contain three figures (two of which are similar) placed one inside the other.
Figures 3, 7 and 9 contain one figure inside the other which may or may not be similar.

28. (*a*) Figures 1, 4 and 9 form a group of clothes.
Figures 2, 5 and 7 form a group of study materials. Figures 3, 6 and 8 are simple geometrical shapes.

29. (*d*) Figures 1, 2 and 7 are simple closed figures.
Figures 3, 5 and 9 contain two dissimilar figures one inside the other.
Figures 4, 6 and 8 contain two different figures touching each other.

30. (*d*) Figures 1, 4 and 9 form a group of figures which are divided into two equal parts and each part contains one dot.
Figures 2, 7 and 8 form a group of figures in which lines equal to the number of lines present in the main figure are present inside the figure (one line parallel to each line).
Figures 3, 5 and 6 form a group of figures in which two straight lines mutually perpendicular to each other are present.

31. (*d*) In figures 1, 4 and 9 upper half of the triangle is shaded.
In figures 2, 6 and 7 corners of the triangles pointing upward is shaded.
In figures 3, 5 and 8 corners of the triangles pointing downwards is shaded.

32. (*b*) Figures 2, 6 and 9 contain triangles with three medians, each enclosing an another figure.
Figures 1, 5 and 7 contain rectangles with two diagonals, each enclosing an another figure. Figures 3, 4 and 8 contain circles with two diameters, each enclosing an another figure.

33. (*b*) Figures 1, 4 and 7 form a group of figures containing a square in which one smaller circle is present at each corner and one larger circle is present at the centre.
Figures 2, 6 and 9 form a group of figures which contain three shaded triangles at the corners and four similar designs at the centre of the figure. Figures 3, 5 and 8 form a group of figures in which the curved portion of the figure contains certain design.

34. (*a*) Figures 1, 5 and 7 contain two similar figures, one inside the other.
Figures 2, 3 and 9 form a group of figures enclosing similar incomplete (open) figure.
Figures 4, 6 and 8 contain two straight lines perpendicular to each other dividing the figure into four parts.

35. (*a*) Figures 1, 4 and 6 form a group of figures in which one shaded rectangle is present at the top of the figure.
Figures 2, 3 and 8 form a group of figures in which one shaded circle is present at the top of the figure.
Figures 5, 7 and 9 represent cup shaped figures.

36. (*a*) Figures 1, 3 and 9 contain a figure inside a different figure.
Figures 2, 5 and 6 are divided into four parts by mutually perpendicular lines. Figures 4, 7 and 8 contain two similar figures attached to each other.

37. (*a*) Clearly, figures 1, 8 and 5 comprise of a two geometrical figures, one completely inside the other. Figures 7, 6 and 3 have two similar intersecting figures. Figures 4, 2 and 9 have two different intersecting figures.

38. (*a*) Figures 1, 5 and 9 are made up of straight lines. Figures 2, 3 and 6 have figures in which upper portion is oval. Figures 4, 7 and 8 are divided into four equal parts.

CHAPTER / 13

Figure Matrix

Representation of figures/elements following a certain rule or pattern, either row-wise or column-wise in a matrix form is known as figure matrix.

Questions based on figure matrix generally have either a 2×2 or a 3×3 matrix. Each cell of this matrix contains a figure and there is a common pattern across each of the rows or columns.

A candidate is required to analyse each of the sets to find out the common pattern and then identify the missing figure from the set of given alternatives, so as to complete the given matrix.

The common pattern can be on the basis of number of elements, orientation of figure, addition or removal of elements etc.

For better understanding of this chapter, some examples are given below

DIRECTIONS ~ (Example Nos. 1-6) *In each of the following questions, find out the answer figure which completes the question figure matrix.*

***Ex* 01** **Question Figure** **Answer Figures**

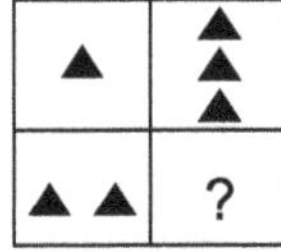

(a) (b) (c) (d)

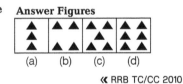

« RRB TC/CC 2010

Solution (d) In each row moving from left to right, the number of triangles in the second part is thrice the first part. So, in the missing figure there will be $2 \times 3 = 6$ triangles.

***Ex* 02** **Question Figure** **Answer Figures**

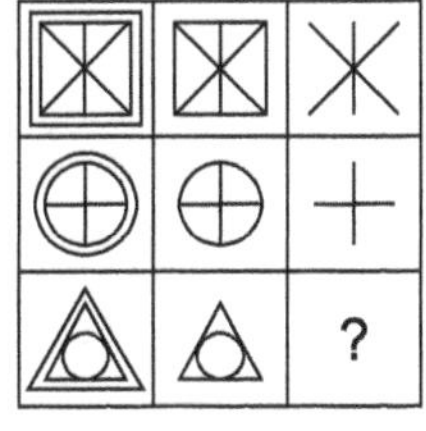

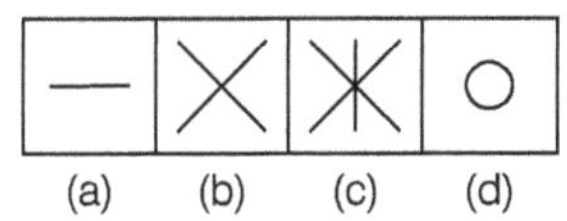

(a) (b) (c) (d)

Solution (d) In each row moving from left to right, the second figure is obtained by removing the outer most element of the first figure and the third figure is obtained by removing the outer most element of the second figure.

***Ex* 03**

Question Figure **Answer Figures**

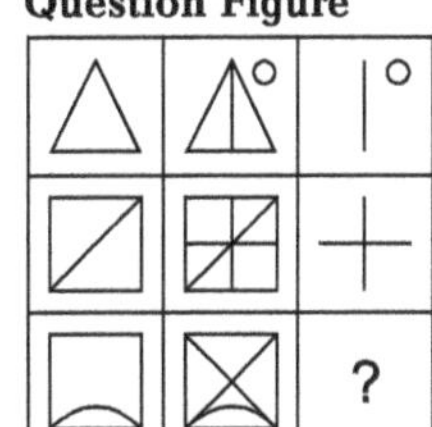

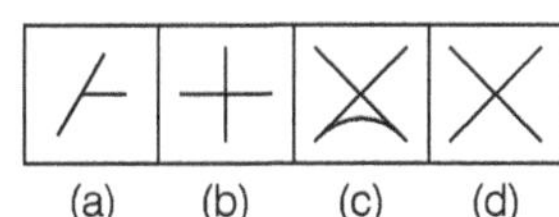

(a) (b) (c) (d)

« CMAT 2013

Solution (d) The third figure from the left in each row comprises of parts which are not common to the first two figures.

***Ex* 04**

Question Figure **Answer Figures**

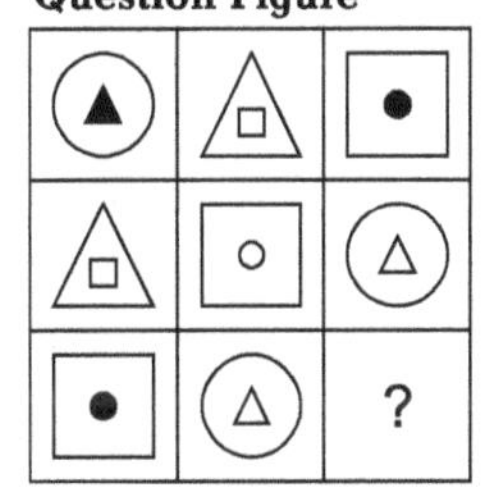

(a) (b) (c) (d)

« RRB ALP 2008

Solution (c) In each column and row, three types of figures , and are used and in figures at each corner of the matrix the internal geometrical figure is shaded.

Hence, the figure given in option (c) will replace the question mark.

Ex 05

Question Figure **Answer Figures**

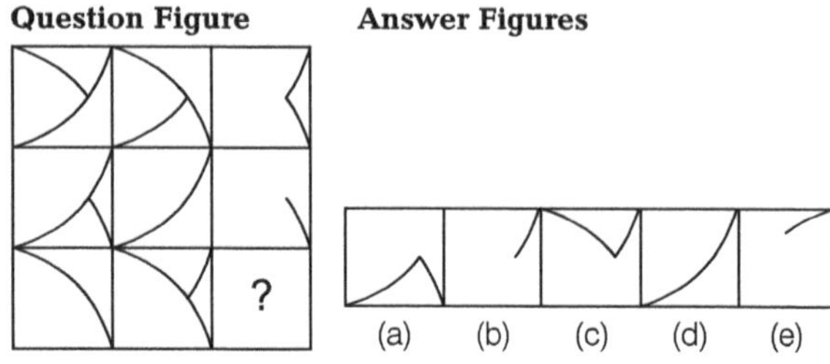

***Solution* (b)** In moving from left to right in each row or top to bottom in each column, the line/lines in the third figure is/are obtained by removing the common portion (line) of the first two figures.

Ex 06 **Question Figure** **Answer Figures**

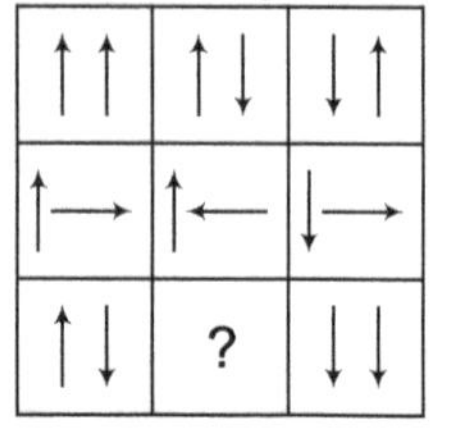

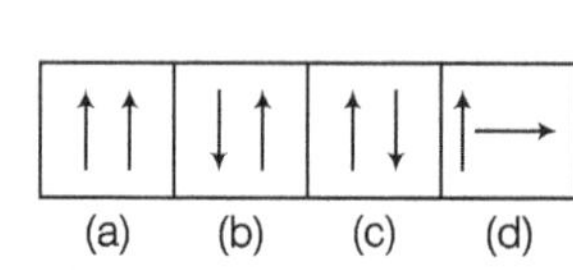

« UPSC CSAT 2014, UP B.Ed. 2008

***Solution* (a)** From left to right in each row to obtain the second figure, in first figure, the orientation of the first arrow remains unchanged but the second arrow gets inverted. While the arrows in the third figure are obtained by inverting both the arrows of the second figure.

Practice CORNER

DIRECTIONS ~(Q. Nos. 1-48) *In each of the following questions, find out the answer figure which completes the question figure matrix.*

Question Figure **Answer Figures**

1.

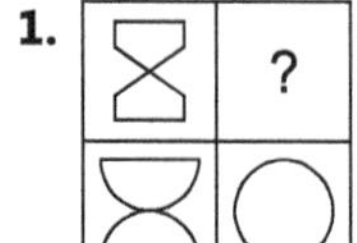

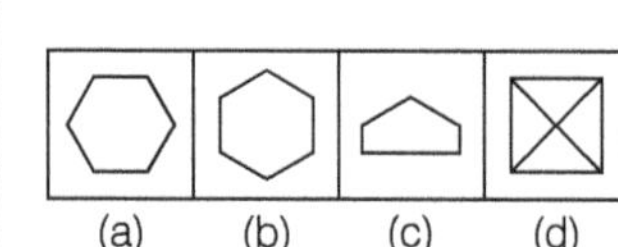

2.

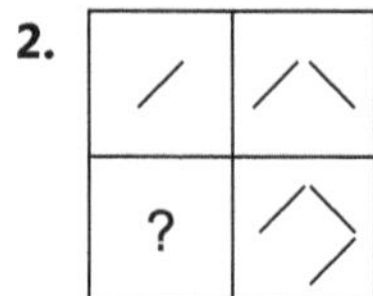

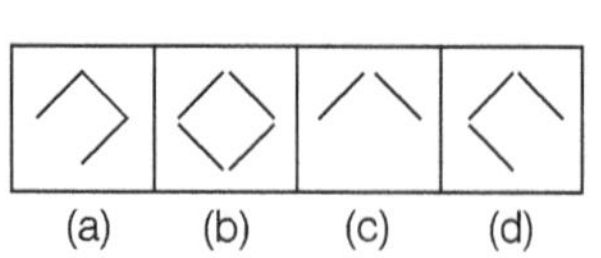

« SSC CGL 2008

3.

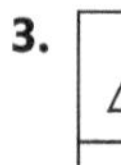

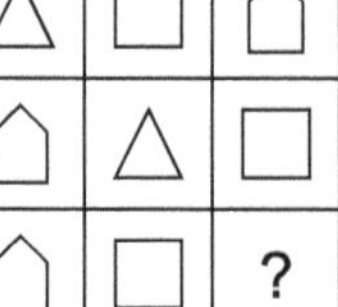

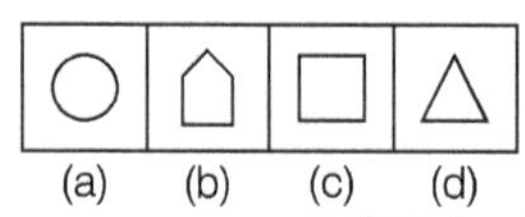

« UP Police SI 2009

4.

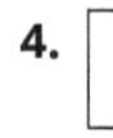

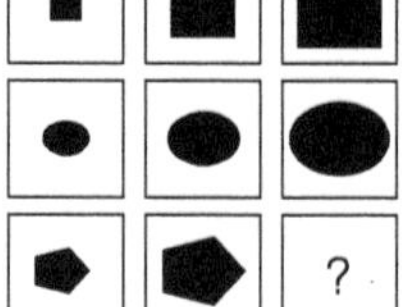

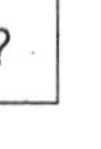

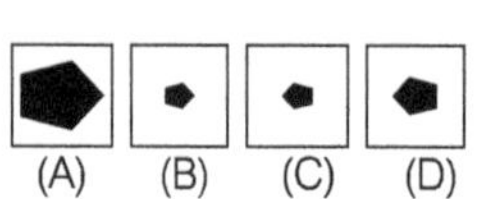

« UPSSSC 2018

(a) B (b) D (c) A (d) C

Question Figure **Answer Figures**

5.

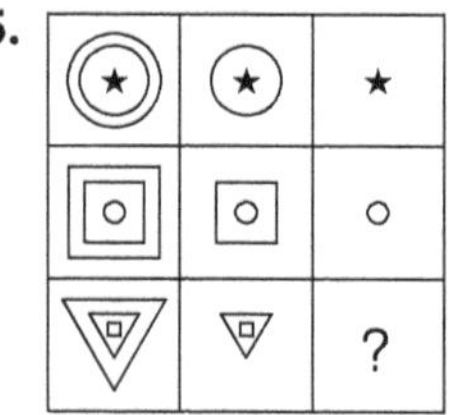

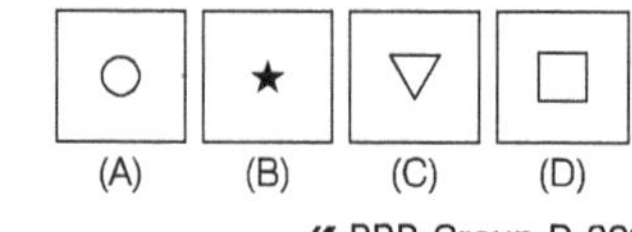

« RRB Group D 2018

(a) C (b) D
(c) B (d) A

6.

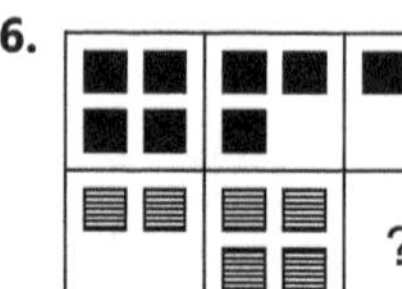

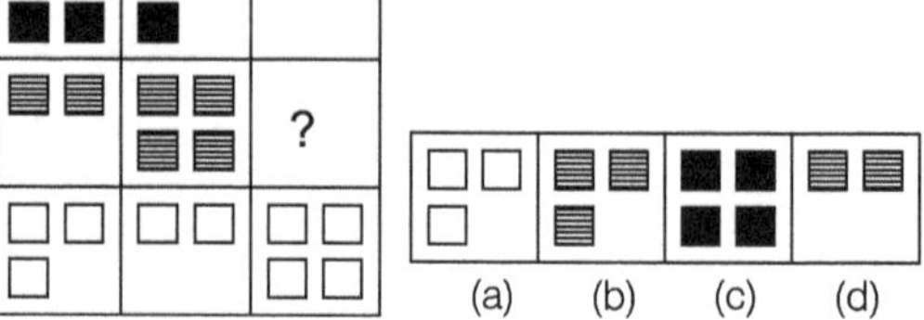

7.

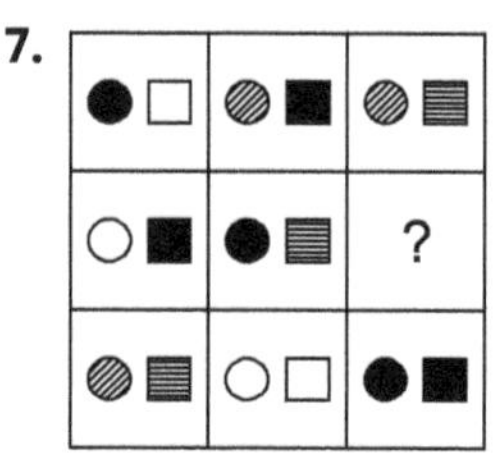

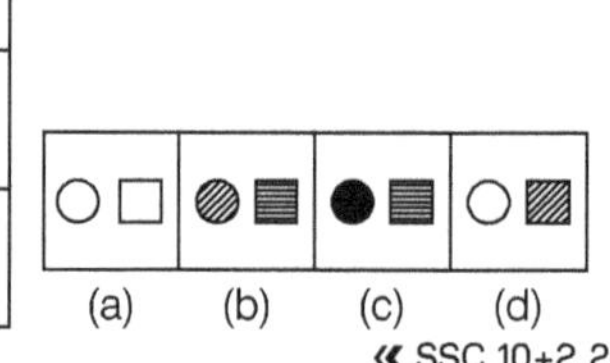

« SSC 10+2 2007

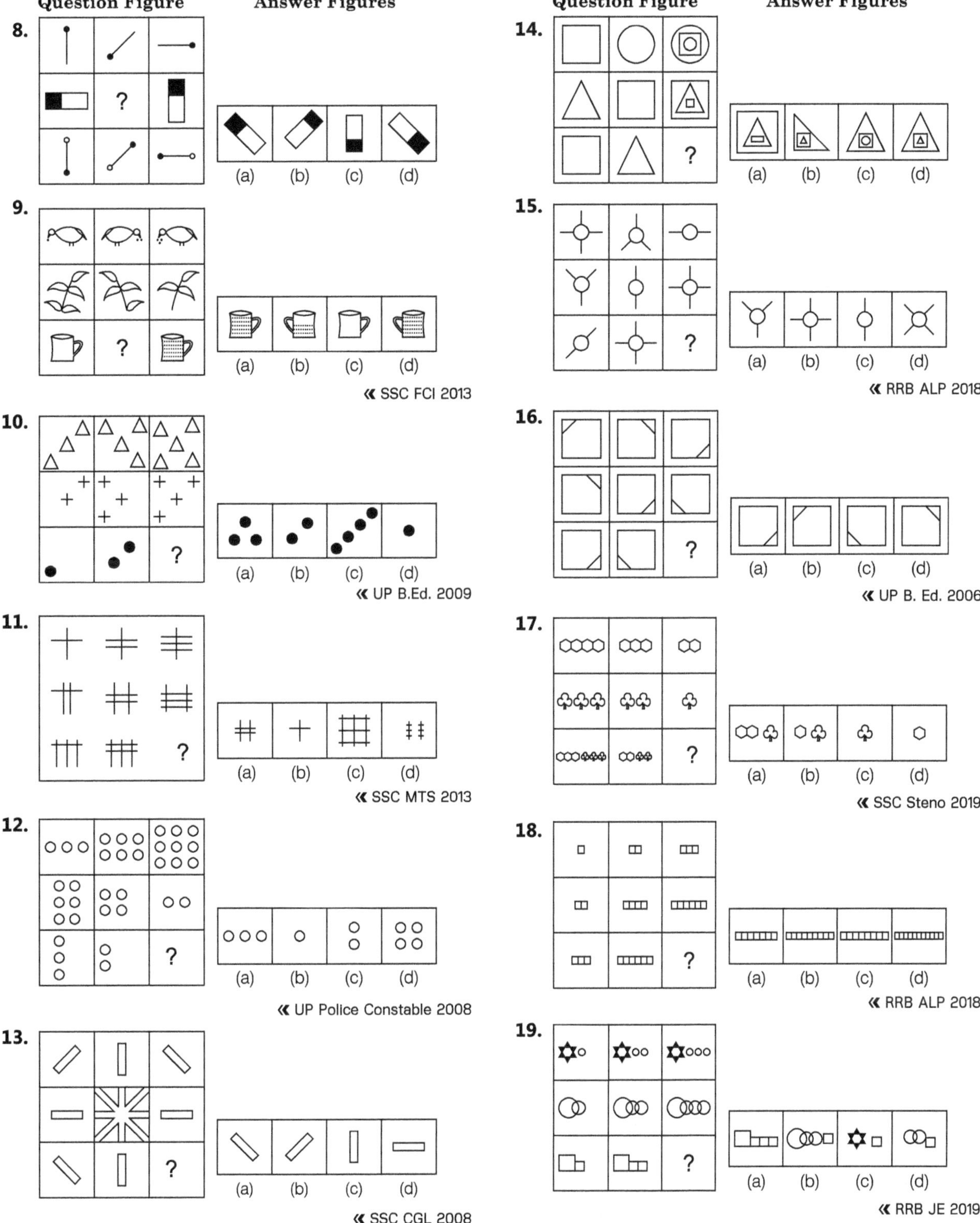
Question Figure
Answer Figures
8.
?
(a) (b) (c) (d)
9.
?
(a) (b) (c) (d)
« SSC FCI 2013
10.
?
(a) (b) (c) (d)
« UP B.Ed. 2009
11.
?
(a) (b) (c) (d)
« SSC MTS 2013
12.
?
(a) (b) (c) (d)
« UP Police Constable 2008
13.
?
(a) (b) (c) (d)
« SSC CGL 2008
Question Figure
Answer Figures
14.
?
(a) (b) (c) (d)
15.
?
(a) (b) (c) (d)
« RRB ALP 2018
16.
?
(a) (b) (c) (d)
« UP B. Ed. 2006
17.
?
(a) (b) (c) (d)
« SSC Steno 2019
18.
?
(a) (b) (c) (d)
« RRB ALP 2018
19.
?
(a) (b) (c) (d)
« RRB JE 2019

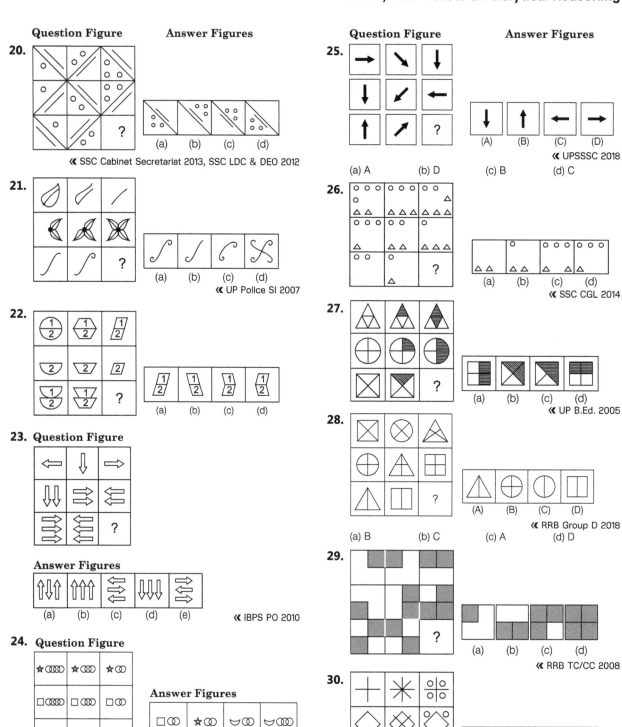

20. Question Figure Answer Figures

(a) (b) (c) (d)

« SSC Cabinet Secretariat 2013, SSC LDC & DEO 2012

21.

(a) (b) (c) (d)

« UP Police SI 2007

22.

(a) (b) (c) (d)

23. Question Figure

Answer Figures

(a) (b) (c) (d) (e)

« IBPS PO 2010

24. Question Figure

Answer Figures

(a) (b) (c) (d)

« RRB Group D 2018

25. Question Figure Answer Figures

(A) (B) (C) (D)

« UPSSSC 2018

(a) A (b) D (c) B (d) C

26.

(a) (b) (c) (d)

« SSC CGL 2014

27.

(a) (b) (c) (d)

« UP B.Ed. 2005

28.

(A) (B) (C) (D)

« RRB Group D 2018

(a) B (b) C (c) A (d) D

29.

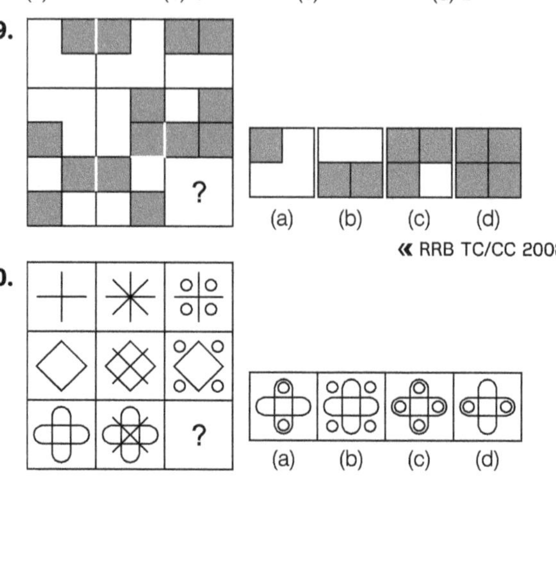

(a) (b) (c) (d)

« RRB TC/CC 2008

30.

(a) (b) (c) (d)

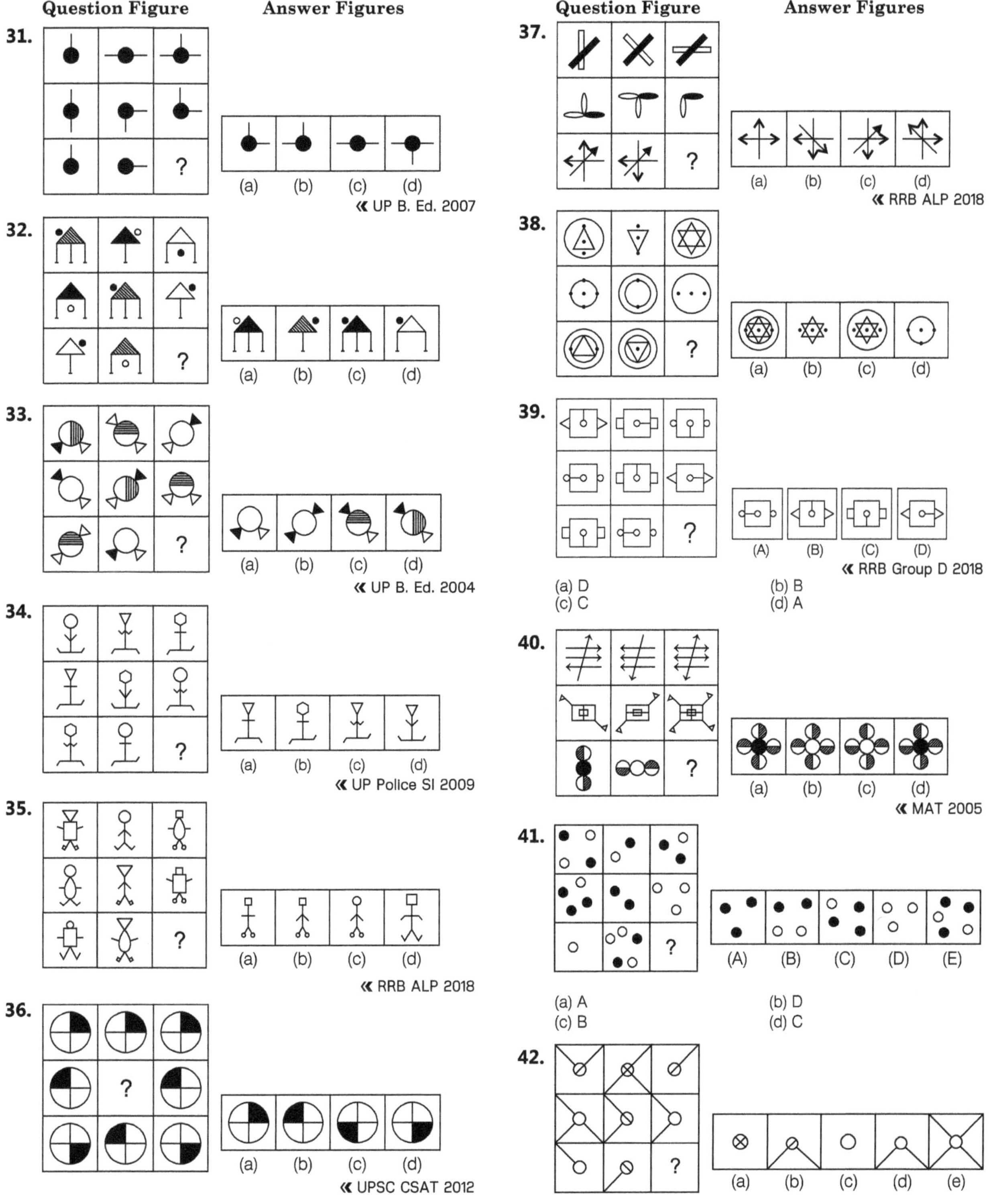
Question Figure
Answer Figures
31.
(a) (b) (c) (d)
« UP B. Ed. 2007
32.
(a) (b) (c) (d)
33.
(a) (b) (c) (d)
« UP B. Ed. 2004
34.
(a) (b) (c) (d)
« UP Police SI 2009
35.
(a) (b) (c) (d)
« RRB ALP 2018
36.
(a) (b) (c) (d)
« UPSC CSAT 2012
Question Figure
Answer Figures
37.
(a) (b) (c) (d)
« RRB ALP 2018
38.
(a) (b) (c) (d)
39.
(A) (B) (C) (D)
« RRB Group D 2018
(a) D
(b) B
(c) C
(d) A
40.
(a) (b) (c) (d)
« MAT 2005
41.
(A) (B) (C) (D) (E)
(a) A
(b) D
(c) B
(d) C
42.
(a) (b) (c) (d) (e)

43. Question Figure / Answer Figures

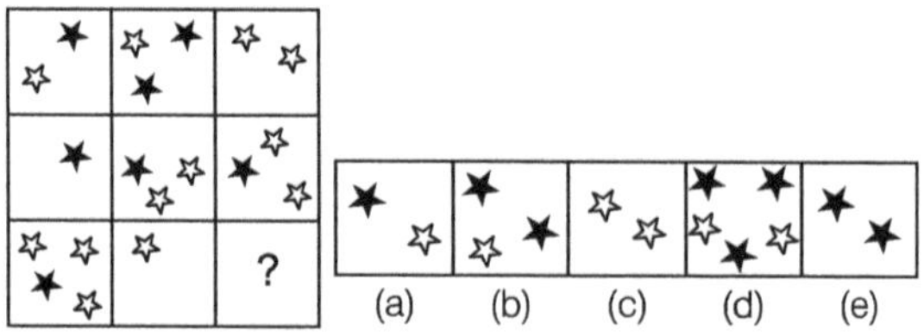

(a) (b) (c) (d) (e)

44. (a) (b) (c) (d) (e)

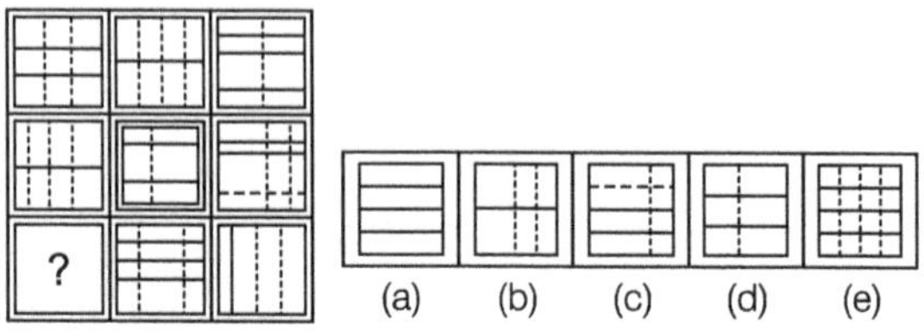

45. (a) (b) (c) (d) (e)

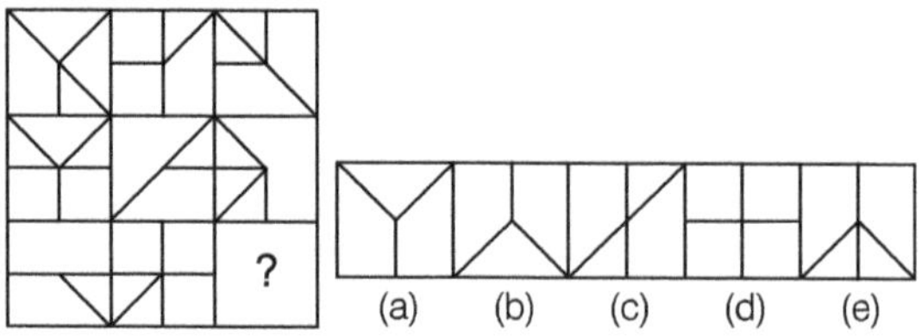

« CGPSC 2014

46. Question Figure / Answer Figures

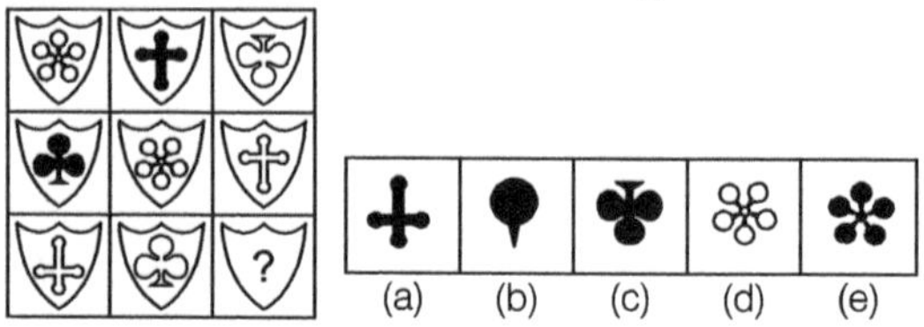

(a) (b) (c) (d) (e)

47. (a) (b) (c) (d)

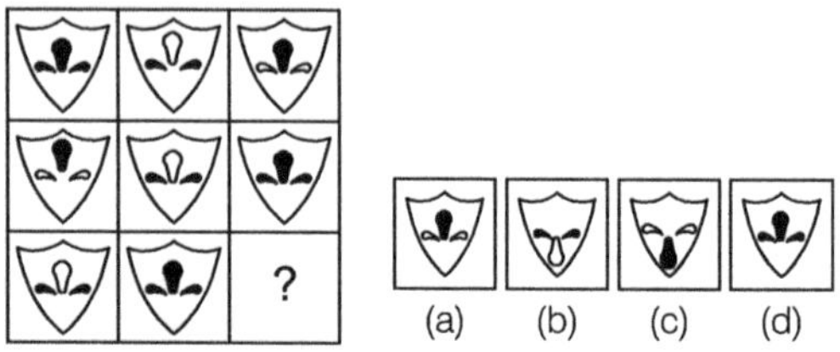

48. (A) (B) (C) (D)

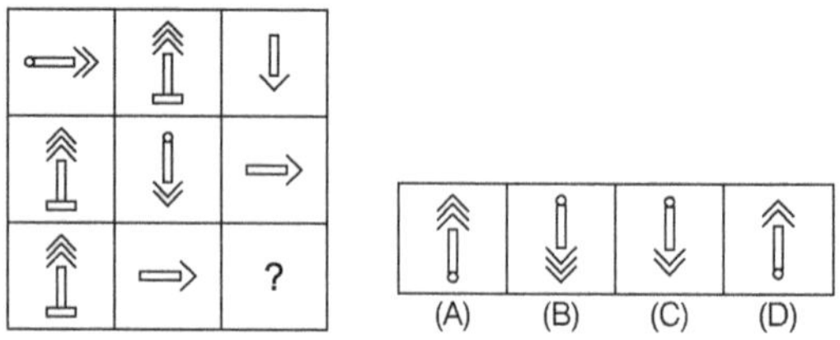

« RRB Group D 2018

(a) A (b) C (c) B (d) D

Answers WITH EXPLANATIONS

1. (*b*) The second figure in each row from left is obtained by joining the inverted lower half of first figure with its inverted upper half.

2. (*b*) Starting with the top left figure, one line is increasing in each figure while moving in clockwise direction. So, four lines will come in fourth part.

3. (*d*) In each row, all the three shapes *i.e.*, triangle, square and pentagon are present. So, triangle will replace the question mark.

4. (*c*) In each row moving from left to right, the size of the same figure is increasing. Hence, figure (A) will replace the question mark.

5. (*b*) In the given matrix in each row moving from left to right, the outer geometrical figure is getting eliminated in each step.

Hence, the figure (D) will replace the question mark.

6. (*b*) In each row, two, three and four similar squares are present. Hence, option figure (b) will replace the question mark.

7. (*a*) In each column, three figures with one circle and one square each are present in such a way that three different patterns of shading of both the circle and square are present in all columns.

8. (*d*) As we move from left to right in each row, the figure rotates through an angle of 135° anti-clockwise at each step.

9. (*b*) In each row, from left to right, figures are horizontally inverted and the number of elements are either increasing or decreasing.

10. (*a*) From left to right in each row, the number of elements is increasing by one.

11. (*c*) Moving from left to right in a row, the number of horizontal lines are increasing by one in each step.

12. (*b*) In each row from left to right, the ratio of the number of circles is 1:2:3 or 3:2:1.

13. (*b*) The central figure of the matrix is formed by combining rest of the figures.

14. (*d*) In each row, the second figure from left is placed inside the first figure and then this combination is again placed in the second figure to obtain the third figure.

15. (*a*) Each row of the matrix contains one circle with two lines, one with three lines and one with four lines.

16. (*b*) The line inside the square moves from one corner to another, clockwise, as we move from left to right in a row.

17. (*b*) Moving from left to right in each row, the number of each type of elements is decreasing by one in each step.

18. (*b*) In first row, the number of squares is increasing by one.

In second row, the number of squares is increasing by two and in third row, the number of squares is increasing by three while moving from left to right.

19. (*a*) In each row, the number of smaller figures increases by one at each step from left to right.

20. (*c*) On observing the figure in columnwise manner we notice that in first column the figure rotates 90° clockwise in each step. In second column, the figure rotates 90° anti-clockwise in each step.

Similarly, in third column, the figure rotates 90° clockwise in each step.

21. (*a*) Moving from left to right in each row, the number of elements is either increasing or decreasing. In the third row, the number of elements is increasing.

22. (*a*) Moving from top to bottom in each column, the third figure is obtained by placing the element marked as number '2', as it is and joining it with the inverted form of the element marked as number '1'.

23. (*d*) In each row, the arrows point in each of three directions left, right and down while the number of arrows remains same.

24. (*c*) Moving from left to right in each row, the left most symbol remains same and the number of the intersecting circles is decreasing by one. Hence, the figure (c) will replace the question mark.

25. (*b*) In each row moving from left to right, the arrow is rotating 45° in clockwise direction in each step.

26. (*a*) In each row as we move from left to right, the number of circles is decreasing by 1 and the number of triangles is increasing by 1.

27. (*b*) Moving from left to right, the first figure in each row is completely unshaded. The second one has one-fourth part shaded and the third one is half shaded, where the direction of shading for the last two figures in each row remains the same.

28. (*b*) In the given matrix, in each column three types of geometrical figures *i.e.* square, circle and triangle are used. Moreover in first row '×', in second row '+' and in third row '1' is used. Therefore, the figure (C) will replace the question mark.

29. (*d*) Moving from left to right in each row, the design of first and second figure is combined to obtain the design of the third figure.

30. (*b*) In each row as we move from first to the second figure, the figure gets intersected by two mutually perpendicular lines. In the next step, small circles appear at the ends of these lines and the lines disappear to give the third figure.

31. (*a*) The third figure from left in each row comprises of the lines which are not common to the first two figures.

32. (*c*) There are three types of triangular shadings, 3 positions of circles and 1 to 3 legs of triangle each of which is used only once in each row. Also, in each row two circles are shaded.

33. (*d*) In each row, the circle is unshaded in one of the figures, it has its upper part shaded in another figure and its RHS part shaded in the third figure. There are three positions of the two triangles, each of which is used only once in a row. Also, two of the figures in each row have one triangle shaded.

34. (*d*) There are three types of faces, 3 types of hands and 3 types of legs. Each type is used once in each row.

35. (*b*) There are three types of faces, 3 types of bodies, 3 types of hands and 3 types of legs, each of which is used only once in a row.

36. (*d*) In first and third columns, the black portion of middle image is diagonally opposite to that of lower image. Hence, middle image in second column must be same as given in option (d).

37. (*c*) In each row moving from left to right, the darkened part of each figure remains in the same direction while the remaining part of the figure rotates anti-clockwise.

38. (*b*) The third figure from left in each row comprises of parts which are not common to the first two figures.

39. (*b*) In each row, moving from left to right small squares,0 small circles and small triangles are getting attached to the bigger square. Each shape is used once in each row. Moreover the line attached to a circle in the bigger square is rotating 90° clockwise with each step. Hence, figure (B) will replace the question mark.

40. (*d*) In each row, both the common and uncommon parts of first two figures from left, combine together to obtain the third figure.

41. (*a*) Across each row and column, the total number (sum) of shaded and unshaded dots is five and four respectively.

42. (*c*) Moving from left to right in each row and top to bottom in each column, only portion which are common to the first two squares are carried forward to the third square.

43. (*e*) In each column and row, the number (sum) of shaded and unshaded stars is three and four respectively.

44. (*c*) Across each row the total number (sum) of continuous lines and hidden lines is six each.

45. (*e*) Moving left to right in each row and top to bottom in each column, only lines that are not common to the first two figures are carried forward to the final figure.

46. (*e*) Each row and column consists of three different elements out of which one is shaded.

47. (*a*) In each row, there are three types of shading pattern , and each occurring once. Therefore in third row, shading pattern will come at the place of question mark.

48. (*b*) The given matrix is made by using only three figures.

⟹, ⇑ and ⇓.

These three figures are given in three directions *i.e.* ↑, →, ↓ in each row.

Hence, in the third row the third figure will be ⇓.

CHAPTER / 14

Cube and Cuboid

A cube is a three-dimensional structure with three sides (length, width and height). Where all the sides are equal (length = width = height = a)

Cube

Cube is a three dimensional body whose length, breadth and height all are equal (a).

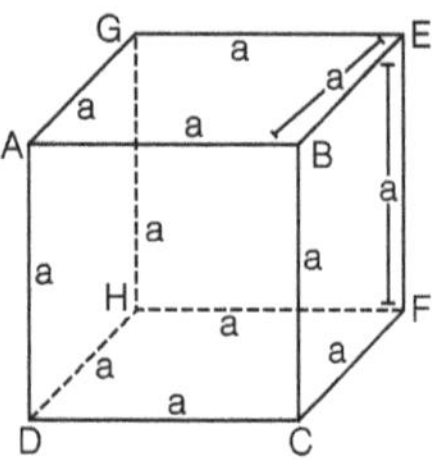

Surface/Faces

Every cube has six faces (front, back, right, left, top and bottom) out of which a maximum of 3 faces are visible at a time and the other 3 faces are invisible.

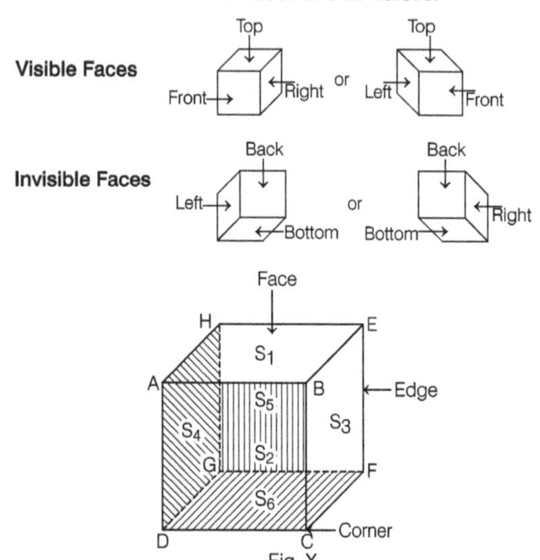

Fig. X

In the given figure (X), ABCD, BCFE, ABEH, ADGH, EFGH and CDGF are the six faces of the figure.

ABEH	⇒	S_1	Visible faces
ABCD	⇒	S_2	
BCFE	⇒	S_3	
ADGH	⇒	S_4	Invisible faces
EFGH	⇒	S_5	
CDGF	⇒	S_6	

ABCD	⇒	Front face	⇒	S_2	Faces opposite to each other
EFGH	⇒	Back face	⇒	S_5	
ABEH	⇒	Upper face	⇒	S_1	Faces opposite to each other
CDGF	⇒	Lower face	⇒	S_6	
BCFE	⇒	Right face	⇒	S_3	Faces opposite to each other
ADGH	⇒	Left face	⇒	S_4	

From the above facts it is clear that

(i) Every face has four adjacent faces and one opposite face.
(ii) Adjacent faces are connected to each other.
(iii) Two adjacent faces meet at a single side and three faces adjacent to each other meet at a single vertex.

Edges and Corners

Edges are the line segments where two faces meet and corners are the points where three edges meet.
A cube consists of 12 edges and 8 corners in which maximum 9 edges and 7 corners are visible at a time and rest edges and corners are not visible.

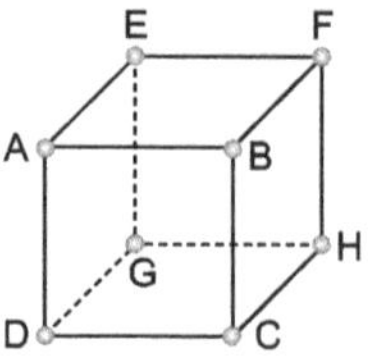

In the given cube,
Visible Edges 12 (AB, BC, CD, DA, AE, EF, FB, FH and CH)
Visible Corners 7 (A, B, C, D, E, F and H)
Invisible Edges 3 (GD, GH and GE)
Invisible Corner 1 (G)

Cuboid

A cuboid is a three-dimensional structure with three sides where all the sides are not equal. The three sides are the length, width and height. (All of its faces are rectangles)

Cuboid is also a three-dimensional body which possesses all the properties of a cube except equality of dimensions.

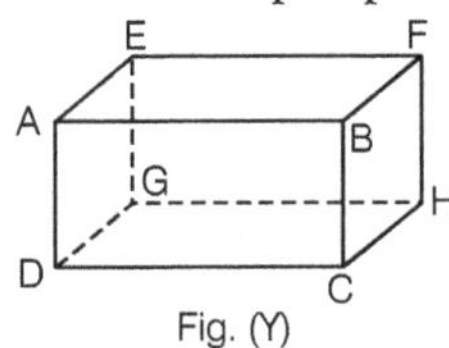

Fig. (Y)

It means a cuboid has

- 6 faces (3 are visible and 3 are hidden at a time)
  In the above figure (Y), three visible faces are ABCD, AEFB, BFHC and the invisible faces are AEGD, EFHG, CDGH.

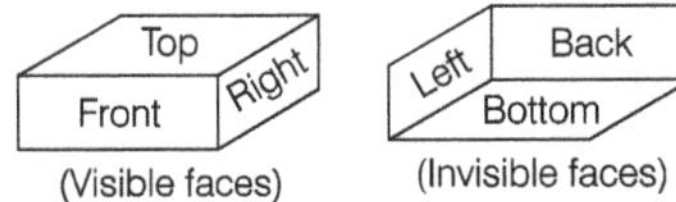

- 8 corners (only 7 are visible at a time)
  In the above figure (Y), visible corners are A, E, F, B, H, C, D and the invisible corner is G.
- 12 edges (only 9 are visible at a time)
  In the above figure (Y), visible edges are AE, EF, FB, BA, AD, DC, CB, FH, HC and the invisible edges are EG, GH, GD.
- Length, breadth and height all are not same.

Several types of questions asked from this chapter are as follows

TYPE 01

Cutting of a Cube or Cuboid

When we cut a rod in two equal parts, then we cut it only once. Similarly, if a rod is divided into three equal parts, then 2 cuts are made. For 4 equal parts 3 cuts are made and so on. *Let us see*

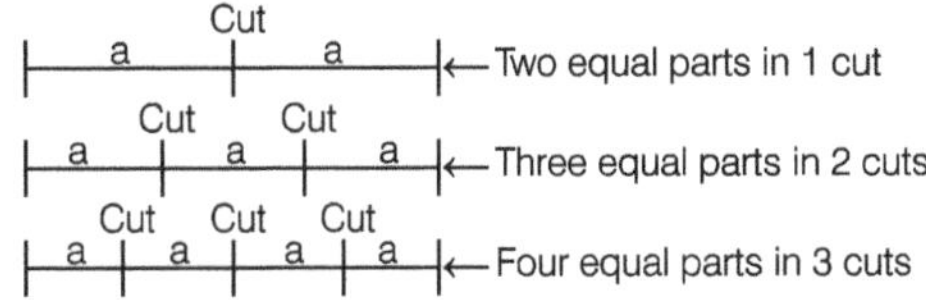

$\therefore$ For n equal parts, number of cuts $= (n - 1)$

Like a rod/stick, a cube can also be cut as per the rule given below If each edge of a cube = 8 cm and it has to be cut into smaller cubes having each edge of 2 cm as shown in figure, then Parts of each edge $(n) = \frac{8}{2} = 4$ and to divide the each edge into four parts, the cube will have to be cut into $(n - 1) = (4 - 1) = 3$ times from three sides.

Identification of smaller cubes when a larger cube is cut into smaller cubes

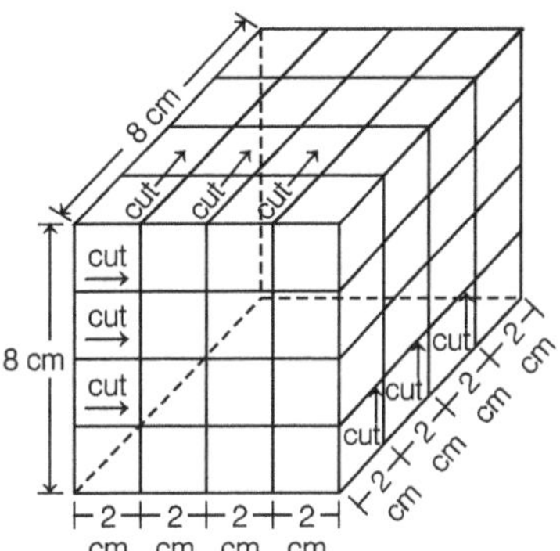

After cutting a cube, following type of smaller cubes are obtained

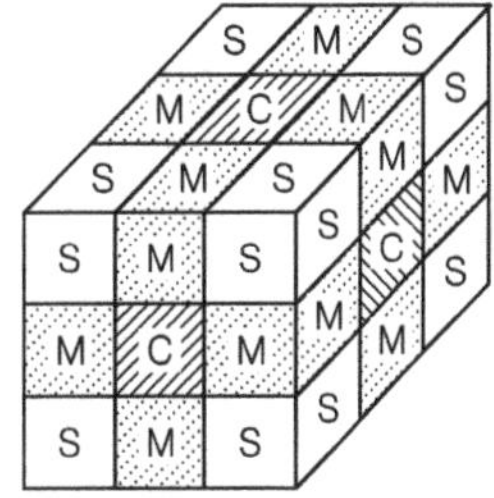

- Corner cubes = S (exist at each corner)
- Middle cubes = M (exist at the middle of each edge)
- Central cubes = C (exist at the middle of each face)
- Nuclear cube/Inner central cube = hidden and exist at the centre of the larger cube

Chapter tip! **Finding number of cubes when a larger cube is cut into smaller cubes**

If a larger cube is cut into smaller cubes of equal volume so that each edge is divided into n parts, then the formulae to calculate the number of different smaller cubes are given below

Number of smaller cubes so obtained $= (n)^3$

where, $n = \dfrac{\text{Edge of larger cube}}{\text{Edge of smaller cube}}$

- Number of inner central/nucleus cubes (N) $= (n - 2)^3$
- Number of central cubes (C) $= 6(n - 2)^2$
- Number of middle cubes (M) $= 12(n - 2)$
- Number of corner cubes (S) = 8
- When a big cube is cut into smaller cube,

  Required number of cuts $= \left[\dfrac{\text{Side of larger cube}}{\text{Side of smaller cube}} - 1\right] \times 3$

e.g., If a larger cube of 10 cm edge is cut into smaller cubes of equal volumes having each edge of 2 cm, then

$$n = \frac{\text{Edge of larger cube}}{\text{Edge of smaller cube}} = \frac{10}{2} = 5$$

Number of smaller cubes $= (n)^3 = (5)^3 = 125$

Number of inner central/nucleus cubes (N) $= (n-2)^3$

$= (5-2)^3 = 27$

Number of central cubes (C) $= 6(n-2)^2 = 6(5-2)^2 = 54$

Number of middle cubes (M) $= 12(n-2) = 12(5-2) = 36$

Number of corner cubes (S) $= 8$

***Ex* 01** A cube has each side 6 cm. In how many smaller cubes of side 1 cm each can it be divided? « SSC CPO 2010

(a) 36 (b) 12
(c) 18 (d) 216

***Solution* (d)** Each side of bigger cube will be divided into 6 parts

It means, $n = \frac{\text{Side of bigger cube}}{\text{Side of smaller cube}} = \frac{6}{1} = 6$

$\therefore$ Required number of smaller cubes $= (n)^3 = (6)^3 = 216$

***Ex* 02** A cube having 24 cm side is divided into 64 smaller cubes of equal volume. Find the side of smaller cubes?

(a) 5 cm (b) 6 cm
(c) 3 cm (d) 4 cm

***Solution* (b)** Here, number of smaller cubes

$= (n)^3 = 64 \Rightarrow n = \sqrt[3]{64} = 4$

$n = \frac{\text{Side of bigger cube}}{\text{Side of smaller cube}}$

$\Rightarrow \quad 4 = \frac{24}{\text{Side of smaller cube}}$

$\therefore$ Side of smaller cube $= \frac{24}{4} = 6$ cm

***Ex* 03** If a cube of 12 cm side is divided into smaller cubes of 3 cm side, then

(i) find the total number of smaller cubes.
(a) 16 (b) 64 (c) 128 (d) 32

(ii) find the total number of corner (vertex) cubes.
(a) 16 (b) 12 (c) 8 (d) 4

(iii) what is the total number of middle cubes?
(a) 8 (b) 16 (c) 24 (d) 32

(iv) what is the total number of central cubes?
(a) 45 (b) 9 (c) 15 (d) 24

(v) find the total number of inner central cubes?
(a) 18 (b) 9 (c) 8 (d) 81

Solution (i) *(b)* $n = \frac{\text{Side of bigger cube}}{\text{Side of smaller cube}} = \frac{12}{3} = 4$

$\therefore$ Total number of smaller cubes $= (n)^3 = (4)^3 = 64$

(ii) *(c)* As total number of corner cubes is always 8.

(iii) *(c)* Number of middle cubes

$= 12(n-2) = 12(4-2)$

$= 12 \times 2 = 24$

(iv) *(d)* Total number of central cubes

$= 6(n-2)^2 = 6(4-2)^2$

$= 6(2)^2 = 24$

(v) *(c)* Total number of inner central cubes

$= (n-2)^3 = (4-2)^3$

$= (2)^3 = 8$

***Ex* 04** How many times will a solid cube of 6 cm side be cut to obtain smaller cubes of 2 cm side?

(a) 2 (b) 6
(c) 4 (d) 8

***Solution.* (b)** Required number of cuts

$= \left[\frac{\text{Side of bigger cube}}{\text{Side of smaller cube}} - 1\right] \times 3 = \left[\frac{6}{2} - 1\right] \times 3$

$= [3-1] \times 3 = 2 \times 3 = 6$

Cutting of a Cuboid

When a cuboid is cut into smaller cubes of equal volume, then

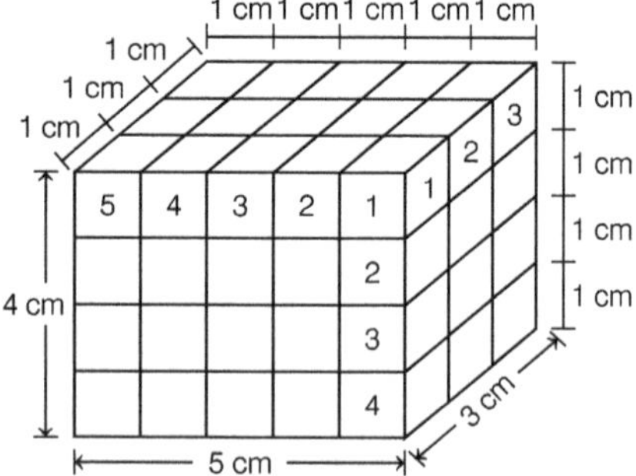

Total number of cubes $= \frac{\text{Volume of cuboid}}{\text{Volume of smaller cube}}$

$= \frac{\text{Length} \times \text{Breadth} \times \text{Height of cuboid}}{(\text{Side of smaller cube})^3}$

In the above cuboid,

Length = 5 cm

Breadth = 3 cm

Height = 4 cm

Then, total number of smaller cubes each having 1 cm side $= \frac{5 \times 3 \times 4}{(1)^3} = 60$

If NL = Segments cut on length
NB = Segments cut on breadth
NH = Segments cut on height
Then, the total number of smaller cubes = NL × NB × NH

***Ex* 05** If a cuboid with length = 10 cm, breadth = 8 cm and height = 8 cm is cut into smaller cubes of edge 2 cm each, then find the number of smaller cubes.

(a) 60 (b) 80
(c) 64 (d) 96

***Solution* (b)** Total number of smaller cubes

$= \frac{l \times b \times h}{(\text{Side of smaller cube})^3} = \frac{10 \times 8 \times 8}{(2)^3} = \frac{10 \times 8 \times 8}{8} = 80$

Or $\text{NL} = \frac{10}{2} = 5 \Rightarrow \text{NB} = \frac{8}{2} = 4 \Rightarrow \text{NH} = \frac{8}{2} = 4$

$\therefore$ Total number of smaller cubes $= 5 \times 4 \times 4 = 80$

Practice / CORNER 14.1

1. How many edges a cube/cuboid has? « UP B.Ed. 2012

(a) 4 (b) 12 (c) 16 (d) 10

2. A cube/cuboid has always. « MAT 2010

(a) 8 corners (b) 6 faces
(c) 12 edges (d) All of these

3. How many pair of opposite faces a cube/cuboid has? « MAT 2010

(a) 4 (b) 2
(c) 5 (d) None of these

4. How many adjacent faces, each face of a cube has? « RRB TC/CC 2010

(a) 2 (b) 4 (c) 6 (d) 8

5. How many faces are hidden in a cube? « UP B.Ed. 2012

(a) 4 (b) 1 (c) 2 (d) 3

6. How many edges are invisible in a cube?

(a) 5 (b) 4 (c) 2 (d) 3

7. How many hidden corners are there in a cube?

(a) 3 (b) 6 (c) 1 (d) 5

8. Which of the following statements is true?

(a) Length, breadth and height of cube are equal
(b) A cube is a three dimensional body
(c) A cube has 12 edges out of which only 9 are visible at a time
(d) All of the above

9. How many smaller cubes of 1 cm side can be formed with a solid cube of 3 cm side? « SSC CPO 2010

(a) 3 (b) 6 (c) 9 (d) 27

10. How many times will a solid cube of 4 cm side be cut to obtain smaller cubes of 2 cm side? « UP B.Ed. 2011

(a) 2 (b) 3 (c) 5 (d) 7

11. A solid cube is made by using 64 small cubes. In how many small cubes two sides are seen? « SSC 10+2 2010

(a) 24 (b) 32 (c) 40 (d) 42

12. A cube of 25 cm side is divided into 125 smaller cubes of equal volume. Find the side of smaller cubes.

(a) 2 cm (b) 3 cm
(c) 5 cm (d) 6 cm

DIRECTIONS ~ (Q. Nos. 13-19) *Read the following information carefully to answer the questions that follow.* « CMAT 2010

A cube of 3 cm side is divided into smaller cubes of side 1 cm.

13. How many times will it be cut to obtain smaller cubes?

(a) 2 (b) 4 (c) 6 (d) 8

14. Find the total number of smaller cubes.

(a) 3 (b) 9 (c) 27 (d) 81

15. Find the total number of corner (vertex) cubes.

(a) 4 (b) 6 (c) 8 (d) 10

16. What will be the total number of middle cubes?

(a) 6 (b) 12
(c) 18 (d) 24

17. Find the total number of central cubes.

(a) 3 (b) 6 (c) 8 (d) 12

18. What is the total number of inner central cubes?

(a) 1 (b) 2 (c) 3 (d) 4

19. In how many parts will each edge (side) of bigger cube be divided?

(a) 1 (b) 2 (c) 3 (d) 4

20. If a cuboid, having dimension $3 \times 2 \times 1$ cm, is cut into smaller cubes having dimension 1 cm, then the total number of smaller cubes obtained are

(a) 5 (b) 6 (c) 30 (d) 50

Answers / WITH EXPLANATIONS

1. (*b*) There are only 12 edges in a cube/cuboid.

2. (*d*) All the options are correct.

3. (*d*) A cube/cuboid has 3 pairs of opposite faces as it has 6 faces in total and each face has one opposite face.

4. (*b*) There are only 4 adjacent faces for each face of a cube.

5. (*d*) Hidden faces = 3

6. (*d*) A cube has 12 edges out of which 9 are visible

$\therefore$ Invisible edges $= 12 - 9 = 3$

7. (*c*) When a cube is seen from any direction, then at a time a maximum of only 7 corners are visible out of 8.

Hence, only 1 corner is hidden.

8. (*d*) All of the given statements are true.

9. (*d*) Required number of smaller cubes

$$= \frac{\text{Volume of bigger cube}}{\text{Volume of smaller cube}}$$

$$= \frac{(3)^3}{1^3} = (3)^3 = 27$$

10. (*b*) Required number of cuts

$$= \left(\frac{\text{Side of bigger cube}}{\text{Side of smaller cube}} - 1\right) \times 3$$

$$= \left(\frac{4}{2} - 1\right) \times 3 = (2 - 1) \times 3 = 3$$

11. (*a*)

Let, side of smaller cube = 1 cm

So, side of solid cube = 4

$$n = \frac{\text{Edge of larger cube}}{\text{Edge of smaller cube}} = \frac{4}{1} = 4$$

Number of cubes in which two sides are seen (middle cubes) $= 12(n-2)$

$= 12(4-2)$

$= 12(2) = 24$

$\therefore$ In 24 small cubes, two sides would be seen.

12. (*c*) $\frac{\text{Volume of bigger cube}}{\text{Volume of smaller cube}}$ = Number of smaller cubes

$$\Rightarrow \frac{25 \times 25 \times 25}{\text{Volume of smaller cube}} = 125$$

$\Rightarrow$ Volume of smaller cube

$$= \frac{25 \times 25 \times 25}{125} = 125$$

$\therefore$ Side of smaller cube

$$= \sqrt[3]{125} = 5 \text{ cm}$$

13. (*c*) Required number of cuts

$$= \left(\frac{\text{Side of bigger cube}}{\text{Side of smaller cube}} - 1\right) \times 3$$

$$= \left(\frac{3}{1} - 1\right) \times 3 = 2 \times 3 = 6$$

14. (*c*) Number of smaller cubes

$$= \frac{\text{Volume of bigger cube}}{\text{Volume of smaller cube}} = \frac{(3)^3}{(1)^3} = (3)^3 = 27$$

15. (*c*) Corner cubes are always 8.

16. (*b*) Number of middle cubes

$$= 12(n-2) = 12\left(\frac{3}{1} - 2\right) = 12 \times 1 = 12$$

17. (*b*) Number of central cubes $= 6(n-2)^2$

$$= 6 \times \left(\frac{3}{1} - 2\right)^2 = 6 \times 1 = 6$$

18. (*a*) Number of inner central cubes $= \left(\frac{3}{1} - 2\right)^3 = (3-2)^3 = 1$

19. (*c*) Required parts $= \frac{\text{Side of bigger cube}}{\text{Side of smaller cube}} = \frac{3}{1} = 3$

20. (*b*) Total number of smaller cubes

$$= \frac{\text{Volume of cuboid}}{\text{Volume of smaller cube}} = \frac{3 \times 2 \times 1}{1} = 6$$

TYPE 02

A Larger Cube/Cuboid is Painted and Cut

In such questions, a larger cube/cuboid is painted with one, two, three, four, five or maximum six different colours.

This larger cube/cuboid is then cut into smaller cubes of same or different dimensions and it is asked to determine the number of smaller cubes with one or more surfaces painted (with same or different colours).

1. Larger Cube Painted with a Single Colour

In this type, a larger cube is painted with single colour and then cuts are made to form smaller cubes.

e.g.

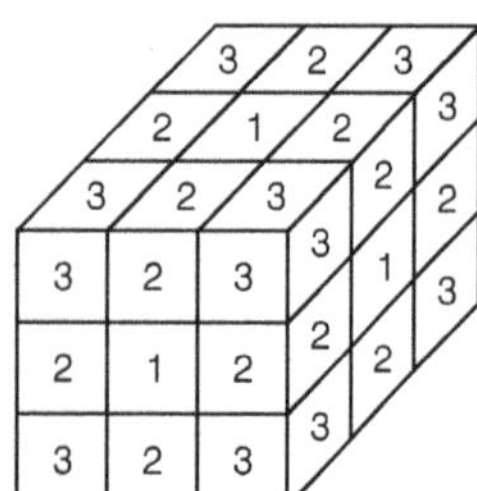

I. **Smaller cubes with one painted face**

Such cubes are **central cubes** and they are neither attached with any edge nor corners.

Let us see the given picture in which digit 1 represents such cubes. As digit 1 exits only once in each surface and there are 6 surfaces in a cube, hence number of smaller cubes having one surface painted must be 6.

If a cube is made up of n^3 smaller cubes, then

Number of smaller cubes having one face painted on each surface layer of cube $= (n-2)^2$

As a cube has 6 surfaces, therefore **number of smaller cubes in a larger cube having one face painted = $6(n-2)^2$**

e.g. In the given figure,

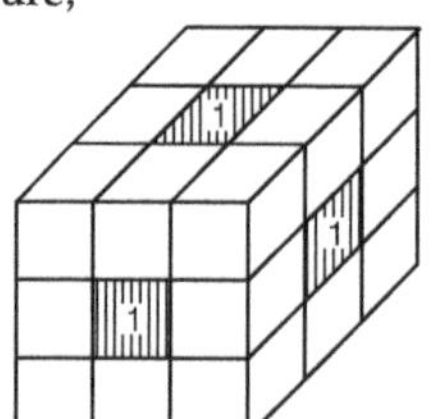

Each side of larger cube = 3 cm and each side of smaller cube = 1 cm

Then, $n = \frac{\text{Side of larger cube}}{\text{Side of smaller cubes}} = \frac{3}{1} = 3$

∴ Number of smaller cubes having one surface painted $= 6(n-2)^2 = 6(3-2)^2 = 6$

II. **Smaller cubes with two painted faces**

Such cubes are **middle cubes** and they are attached with edges (sides) as shown in the given figure by digit 2. As a cube has 12 edges, hence **number of smaller cubes having 2 surfaces painted in a larger cube = $12(n-2)$**

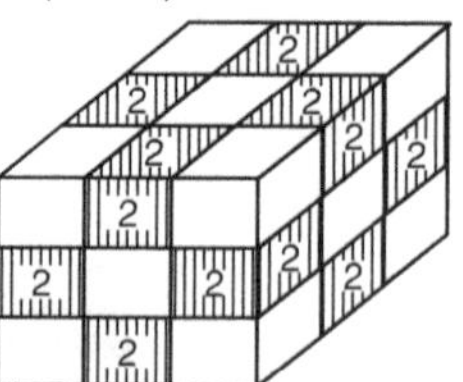

e.g. If $n = 3$, then

Number of such cubes $= 12(3-2) = 12 \times 1 = 12$

III. **Smaller cubes with three painted surfaces**

Such cubes are **corner cubes** which have been represented by digit 3 in the given figure. As a cube has 8 corners, hence **number of smaller cubes having 3 faces painted is always 8.**

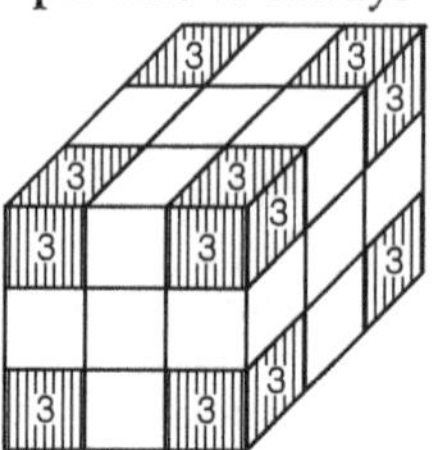

∴ Number of smaller cubes having three surfaces painted = 8

IV. Smaller cubes with no painted surfaces

Such cubes are **inner central or nucleus cubes** and they are invisible.

As we know, number of inner central or nucleus cubes = $(n-2)^3$ then

number of smaller cubes having no surface painted = $(n-2)^3$

e.g. If $n = 3$, then

Number of smaller cubes having no surface painted $= (n-2)^3 = (3-2)^3 = 1$

Chapter tip! Important Formulae

(i) Number of parts on an edge of the bigger cube after division $(n) = \dfrac{\text{Length of edge of bigger cube}}{\text{Length of edge of one smaller cube}}$

(ii) Total number of smaller cubes $= n^3$

(iii) Number of smaller cubes having one surface painted $= 6(n-2)^2$

(iv) Number of smaller cubes having two surfaces painted $= 12(n-2)$

(v) Number of smaller cubes having three surfaces painted $= 8$

(vi) Number of smaller cubes having no surface painted $= (n-2)^3$

(vii) Number of smaller cubes having four or more surfaces painted = 0

e.g. A cube of side 4 cm is painted black on all of its surfaces and then divided into various smaller cubes of side 1 cm each. The smaller cubes so obtained are separated. Then,

Total number of cubes so obtained $= \dfrac{4\times4\times4}{1\times1\times1} = 64$

Here, $n = \dfrac{\text{Side of bigger cube}}{\text{Side of a smaller cube}} = \dfrac{4}{1} = 4$

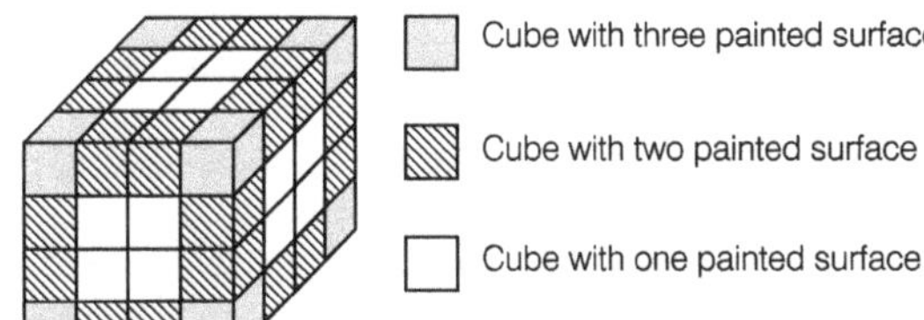

Note *Cube with no painted surfaces are always invisible.*

(i) Number of smaller cubes with three surfaces painted = 8

(ii) Number of smaller cubes with two surfaces painted $= (n-2)\times12 = (4-2)\times12 = 24$

(iii) Number of smaller cubes with one surface painted $= (n-2)^2\times6 = (4-2)^2\times6 = 4\times6 = 24$

(iv) Number of smaller cubes with no surface painted $= (n-2)^3 = (4-2)^3 = (2)^3 = 8$

Ex 06 All the surfaces of a cube of 15 cm side are painted with red colour and then it is cut into smaller cubes of 3 cm side. Then,

(i) How many smaller cubes are there having only one surface painted with red colour?
(a) 18 (b) 24 (c) 36 (d) 54

(ii) How many smaller cubes are there having two surfaces painted with red colour?
(a) 8 (b) 24 (c) 36 (d) 54

(iii) How many smaller cubes are there having only three surfaces painted with red colour?
(a) 8 (b) 24 (c) 36 (d) 54

(iv) How many smaller cubes are there having 4 or more faces painted with red colour?
(a) 0 (b) 8 (c) 36 (d) 81

(v) How many smaller cubes are there having no surfaces painted with red colour?
(a) 3 (b) 9 (c) 27 (d) 81

(vi) How many smaller cubes are obtained from larger cube?
(a) 5 (b) 25 (c) 75 (d) 125

Solution $n = \dfrac{\text{Side of bigger cube}}{\text{Side of smaller cube}} = \dfrac{15}{3} = 5$

(i) (*d*) Required number of smaller cubes $= 6(n-2)^2 = 6(5-2)^2 = 6\times9 = 54$

(ii) (*c*) Required number of cubes $= 12(n-2) = 12(5-2) = 12\times3 = 36$

(iii) (*a*) As cubes with three faces painted are always 8.

(iv) (*a*) As number of cubes with four or more faces painted is 0.

(v) (*c*) Required number of cubes $= (n-2)^3 = (5-2)^3 = (3)^3 = 27$

(vi) (*d*) Total number of smaller cubes $= (n)^3 = (5)^3 = 125$

Ex 07 A solid cube of 3 cm side, painted on all its faces, is cut into small cubes of 1 cm side. How many of the small cubes will have exactly two painted faces? « UPSC CSAT 2018
(a) 12 (b) 8 (c) 6 (d) 4

Solution (a) Number of smaller cubes having two faces painted $= 12(n-2) = 12(3-2)$ [$\because n = 3$]
$= 12$

Therefore, total number of cubes having two painted sides are 12.

2. When a Larger Cube is Painted with More Than One Colour

In this type, a larger cube is painted with more than one colour and then cuts are made to form smaller cubes.

I. Smaller cubes with one painted face

When it is asked to determine the number of smaller cubes with one face painted with a particular colour, then first and foremost task is to find the number of faces of the larger cube on which that particular colour is used. If this particular colour is L, then

Number of smaller cubes with one surface painted = $(n-2)^2$ × Number of faces painted with colour L.

II. Smaller cubes with two painted faces

The edges of a cube are connected with the smaller cubes having two painted faces. If larger cube is painted with more than one colour, then such cubes are obtained as below.

(i) **Smaller cubes having same colour on both the faces**

Such cubes are obtained when two faces of the larger cube having the same colour have an edge in common.

Hence, when the number of cubes with two faces painted with a particular colour is asked, then first and foremost task is to find the number of edges to which two faces (painted with a particular colour) of the larger cube are attached with.

Number of smaller cubes having both the faces painted with a particular colour $(x) = (n-2) \times$ Number of edges to which colour x is attached.

(ii) **Smaller cubes having different colours on both the faces**

Number of smaller cubes having a face painted with a particular colour R $= (n-2) \times$ Number of edges to which colour R is attached.

Number of smaller cubes having two faces painted with a colour (P) on one surface and another colour (Q) on another surface $= (n-2) \times$ Number of edges to which colours P and Q are attached together.

III. Smaller cubes with three painted faces

Such smaller cubes are always 8 in number. In this case three situations arise

(i) if all the three surfaces have same colour.
(ii) if all the three surfaces have different colours.
(iii) if one surface has one colour and two other surfaces have another colour.

For These Cases

If in a cube, one pair of opposite faces is painted with one colour (Red), another pair with second colour (Yellow) and third pair with third colour (Green), then no adjacent faces have same colour.

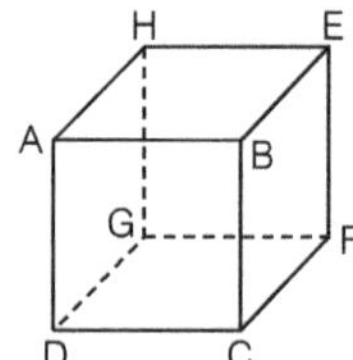

ABCD = EFGH = Red, BCFE = ADGH = Yellow
ABEH = CDGF = Green

If in a cube, one pair of adjacent faces is painted with one colour, another pair with second colour and the third pair with third colour, then no opposite faces have same colour.

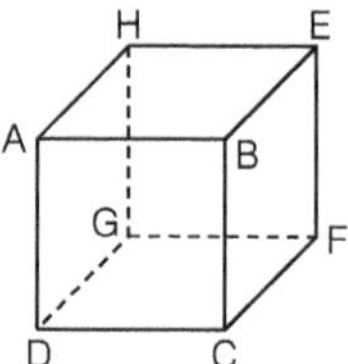

ABCD = BCFE = Red , EFGH = ABEH = Yellow
ADGH = CDGF = Green

Following cases will help you to grasp this concept in a better manner

<u>CASE I</u> If a cube is painted on all of its surfaces with different colours and then divided into various smaller cubes of equal size.

e.g. A cube of side 4 cm is painted black on one pair of opposite surfaces, blue on another pair of opposite surfaces and red on the remaining pair of opposite surfaces. The cube is now divided into smaller cubes of equal side of 1 cm each.

Then,

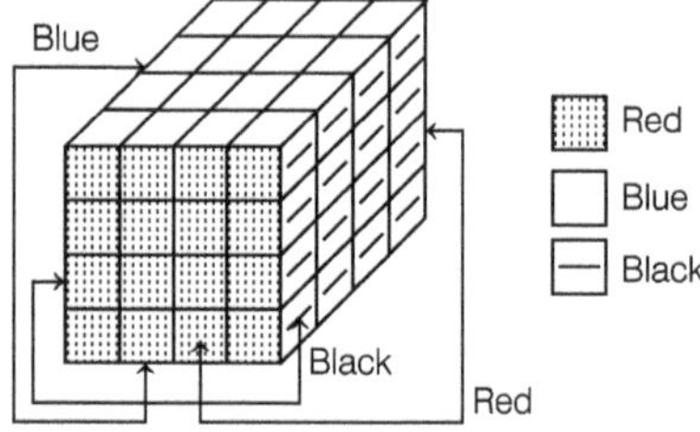

(i) Number of smaller cubes with three surfaces painted = 8 (these smaller cubes will have all the three surfaces painted with different colours—blue, black and red).

(ii) Number of smaller cubes with two surfaces painted = 24
   (a) Number of cubes with two surfaces painted with black and blue colours = 8
   (b) Number of cubes with two surfaces painted with blue and red colours = 8
   (c) Number of cubes with two surfaces painted with black and red colours = 8

(iii) Number of smaller cubes with one surface painted = 24 and out of these,
   (a) Number of cubes with one surface painted with black colour = 4 + 4 = 8
   (b) Number of cubes with one surface painted with blue colour = 4 + 4 = 8
   (c) Number of cubes with one surface painted with red colour = 4 + 4 = 8

Ex 08 Two adjacent faces of a solid cube are painted with red, opposite of these adjacent faces are painted with black while the remaining faces are painted with green colour and then this painted cube is cut into 64 smaller cubes. Solve the following questions based on this information.

(i) How many cubes have no surface painted?
(a) 2 (b) 4 (c) 8 (d) 16

(ii) How many cubes have only one surface painted?
(a) 18 (b) 24 (c) 36 (d) 48

(iii) How many cubes have two faces painted?
(a) 18 (b) 24 (c) 36 (d) 48

(iv) How many cubes have three faces painted?
(a) 8 (b) 16 (c) 24 (d) 32

(v) How many cubes have red colour on one face and black colour on the opposite face?
(a) 0 (b) 8 (c) 24 (d) 36

(vi) How many cubes have red or black colour on two adjacent faces?
(a) 2 (b) 4 (c) 6 (d) 8

Solution According to the given information,

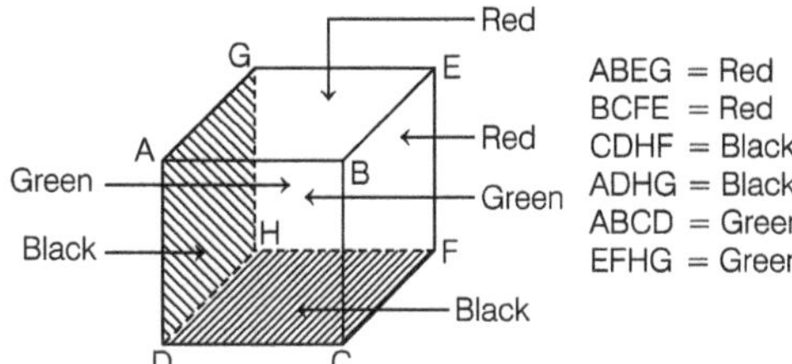

Total number of smaller cubes $= (n)^3 \Rightarrow 64 = (n)^3$

$\therefore \quad n = \sqrt[3]{64} = 4$

(i) ***(c)*** Number of smaller cubes having no faces painted $= (n-2)^3 = (4-2)^3 = (2)^3 = 8$

(ii) ***(b)*** Number of smaller cubes having one face painted $= 6(n-2)^2 = 6(4-2)^2 = 6 \times (2)^2 = 6 \times 4 = 24$

(iii) ***(b)*** Number of smaller cubes having two faces painted $= 12(n-2) = 12(4-2) = 12 \times 2 = 24$

(iv) ***(a)*** As cubes with three faces painted are 8.

(v) ***(a)*** As there are no such cubes.

(vi) ***(d)*** There are 8 cubes which have red or black colour on its adjacent faces *i.e.*, 4 cubes on edge BE and 4 cubes on edge DH.

CASE II If a cube is painted on its surfaces in such a way that one pair of opposite surfaces is left unpainted.

e.g. A cube of side 4 cm is painted red on one pair of opposite surfaces, green on another pair of opposite surfaces and one pair of opposite surfaces is left unpainted. Now, the cube is divided into 64 smaller cubes of side 1 cm each. Then,

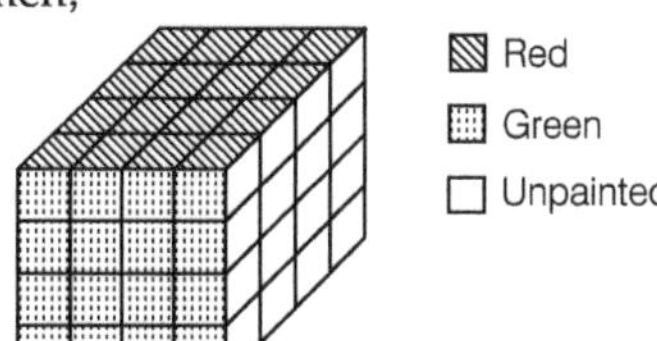

(i) Number of smaller cubes with three surfaces painted $= 0$
(because each smaller cube at the corner is attached to a surface which is unpainted).

(ii) Number of smaller cubes with two surfaces painted
= Number of cubes present at the corners + Number of middle cubes present at the 4 edges
$= 8 + (n-2) \times 4 \Rightarrow 8 + 8 = 16$

(iii) Number of smaller cubes with one surface painted
= Number of cubes present at the 8 edges + Number of cubes present at the four surfaces
$= (n-2) \times 8 + (n-2)^2 \times 4$
$= 2 \times 8 + 4 \times 4 \Rightarrow 16 + 16 = 32$

(iv) Number of smaller cubes with no side painted
= Number of central cubes on the two unpainted surfaces + Number of cubes present inside the cube
$= (n-2)^2 \times 2 + (n-2)^3$
$= 4 \times 2 + (2)^3 = 8 + 8 = 16$

CASE III If a cube is painted on its surfaces in such a way that one pair of adjacent surfaces is left unpainted.

e.g. A cube of side 4 cm is painted red on one pair of adjacent surfaces, green on another pair of other adjacent surfaces and two adjacent surfaces are left unpainted. Now, the cube is divided into 64 smaller cubes of side 1 cm each. Then,

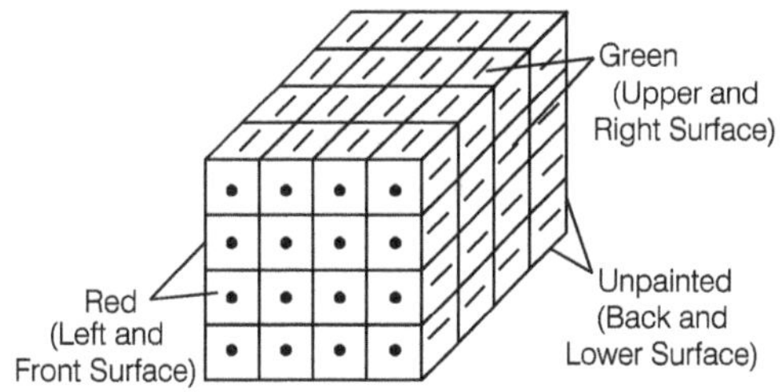

(i) Number of smaller cubes with three surfaces painted
= Number of smaller cubes at two corners = 2

(ii) Number of smaller cubes with two surfaces painted
= Number of smaller cubes at four corners + Number of smaller middle cubes at 5 edges
$= 4 + (n-2) \times 5 \Rightarrow 4 + 2 \times 5$
$= 4 + 10 = 14$

(iii) Number of smaller cubes with one surface painted
= Number of smaller central cubes at four surfaces + Number of smaller middle cubes at 6 edges + Number of smaller cubes at two corners
$= (n-2)^2 \times 4 + (n-2) \times 6 + 2$
$= 4 \times 4 + 2 \times 6 + 2$
$= 16 + 12 + 2 = 30$

(iv) Number of smaller cubes with no surface painted
= Number of smaller cubes present inside the larger cube + Number of central cubes at two surfaces + Number of middle cubes at one edge

$$= (n-2)^3 + (n-2)^2 \times 2 + (n-2)$$
$$= (2)^3 + (2)^2 \times 2 + 2$$
$$= 8 + 8 + 2$$
$$= 18$$

The cases discussed above will help you in solving questions based on painted cubes.

3. When a Cuboid is Painted and Cut

In this type, a cuboid is painted with one or more colours and then cut into smaller cubes.

If segments have been made on each side of the painted cuboid, then NL = Segments cut on length
NB = Segments cut on breadth
NH = Segments cut on height

Chapter tip! **Important Formulae**

(i) Number of smaller cubes having four or more faces painted = 0

(ii) Number of smaller cubes having 3 faces painted = 8

(iii) Number of smaller cubes having 2 faces painted
$$= 4(NL-2) + 4(NB-2) + 4(NH-2)$$
$$= 4[(NL-2) + (NB-2) + (NH-2)]$$

(iv) Number of smaller cubes having one face painted
$$= 2(NL-2)(NB-2) + 2(NB-2)(NH-2) + 2(NL-2)(NH-2)$$
$$= 2[(NL-2)(NB-2) + (NB-2)(NH-2) + (NL-2)(NH-2)]$$

(v) Number of smaller cubes having no faces painted
$$= (NL-2)(NB-2)(NH-2)$$

e.g. If in a painted cuboid, length = 20 cm, breadth = 18 cm and height = 16 cm and each smaller cube obtained after cutting this cuboid has volume = 8 cm^3, and the cubes so obtained are separated, then

(i) Side of each smaller cube = $\sqrt[3]{8} = 2$ cm

(ii) Number of segments on length (NL) = $\frac{20}{2} = 10$

Number of segments on breadth (NB) = $\frac{18}{2} = 9$

Number of segments on height (NH) = $\frac{16}{2} = 8$

(iii) Total number of smaller cubes = NL × NB × NH
$$= 10 \times 9 \times 8 = 720$$

(iv) Number of smaller cubes having four or more faces painted = 0

(v) Number of smaller cubes having 3 faces painted = 8

(vi) Number of smaller cubes having 2 faces painted
$$= 4(NL-2) + 4(NB-2) + 4(NH-2)$$
$$= 4(10-2) + 4(9-2) + 4(8-2)$$
$$= 4(8) + 4(7) + 4(6)$$
$$= 32 + 28 + 24 = 84$$

(vii) Number of smaller cubes having only one face painted
$$= 2(NL-2)(NB-2) + 2(NB-2)(NH-2) + 2(NL-2)(NH-2)$$
$$= 2(10-2)(9-2) + 2(9-2)(8-2) + 2(10-2)(8-2)$$
$$= (2 \times 8 \times 7) + (2 \times 7 \times 6) + (2 \times 8 \times 6)$$
$$= 112 + 84 + 96 = 292$$

(viii) Number of smaller cubes having no faces painted
$$= (NL-2)(NB-2)(NH-2)$$
$$= (10-2)(9-2)(8-2)$$
$$= 8 \times 7 \times 6 = 336$$

Practice / CORNER 14.2

1. A solid cube has been formed with 64 smaller cubes. How many smaller cubes are completely invisible? « SSC 10+2 2010
(a) 2 (b) 4 (c) 6 (d) 8

2. A cube has to be painted in such a way that there is no similar colour on adjacent faces. How many colours are needed for this?
(a) 3 (b) 4 (c) 6 (d) 2

3. All the faces of a cube are painted blue and then it is divided into 27 smaller cubes. How many smaller cubes have only one face painted? « UP B.Ed. 2012
(a) 0 (b) 6
(c) 8 (d) 18

4. A bigger cube of 3 inch side is formed by keeping together smaller cubes of 1 inch side. All the faces of this bigger cube is painted red. When the bigger cube is divided into original smaller cubes, then how many smaller cubes have two faces painted? « SSC 10+2 2010
(a) 4 (b) 8
(c) 12 (d) 0

5. All the faces of a cube having side 5 cm are painted green and then it is divided into smaller cubes of 1 cm side.
How many smaller cubes have three faces painted with green?
(a) 4 (b) 8 (c) 12 (d) 24

6. Six faces of a cube are painted as below
(i) Red opposite to black.
(ii) Green in between red and black.
(iii) Blue adjacent to white.
(iv) Brown adjacent to blue.
(v) Bottom face with red.
Find the colour opposite to brown. « SSC CGL 2010
(a) White (b) Red
(c) Green (d) Blue

7. A painted cube having 25 cm side is divided into smaller cube of 5 cm side. How many smaller cubes have atleast two faces painted?
(a) 40 (b) 44
(c) 48 (d) 50

8. A bigger solid cube is divided into 27 smaller cubes of equal volume. If two opposite faces of this bigger cube are painted with different colours and the remaining faces are left unpainted, then how many smaller cubes are obtained which have no faces painted?
(a) 1 (b) 9 (c) 27 (d) 36

9. A solid cube is formed with 27 smaller cubes. One pair of opposite faces of this cube is painted red, another pair is painted yellow and the third pair of opposite faces is painted white. How many smaller cubes are painted yellow and white only? « SSC CPO 2010
(a) 4 (b) 8 (c) 12 (d) 16

10. Pair of opposite faces of a solid cube having sides 3 cm are painted black, blue and yellow, respectively. After the painting this cube is divided into smaller cubes of side 1 cm. How many smaller cubes have only one face painted? « UP B.Ed. 2008
(a) 4 (b) 6 (c) 9 (d) 12

11. The following figure represents a wooden block of cube shape with 3 cm as its edge and all the faces of the cube are painted black. If the cube is cut along the dotted lines and 27 new cubes are formed with a volume of 1 cm^3 each. What will be the number of non-painted blocks? « UPSSSC Lower Subordinate 2016

(a) 1 (b) 3 (c) 6 (d) 9

12. A cube which is painted red on the outer surface is of 2 inches height, 2 inches wide and 2 inches across. If it is cut into one inch cubes as shown by dotted lines, then indicate the number of cubes which are painted red only on two sides? « SSC CGL 2013

(a) 8 (b) 0 (c) 4 (d) 6

DIRECTIONS ~ (Q. Nos. 13-16) *Read the following information carefully and answer the questions given below.*

A cube is coloured red on all of its faces. It is then cut into 64 smaller cubes of equal size. The smaller cubes so obtained are now separated.

13. How many smaller cubes have no face coloured?
(a) 24 (b) 16 (c) 8 (d) 10

14. How many smaller cubes will have atleast two surfaces painted with red colour?
(a) 4 (b) 8 (c) 32 (d) 24

15. How many smaller cubes have two surfaces painted with red colour?
(a) 24 (b) 8 (c) 12 (d) 20

16. How many smaller cubes have only 3 surfaces painted with red colour?
(a) 0 (b) 12 (c) 24 (d) 8

DIRECTIONS ~ (Q. Nos. 17-22) *Read the following information carefully and answer the questions given below.*

A cube is painted red on two adjacent surfaces and black on the surfaces opposite to the red surfaces and remaining faces with greens. Now, the cube is cut into 64 smaller cubes of equal size.

17. How many smaller cubes have only one surface painted?
(a) 8 (b) 16 (c) 24 (d) 32

18. How many smaller cubes will have no surface painted?
(a) 0 (b) 4 (c) 8 (d) 16

19. How many smaller cubes have less than three surfaces painted (either 1 or 2 surfaces painted)?
(a) 8 (b) 24 (c) 28 (d) 48

20. How many smaller cubes have three surfaces painted?
(a) 4 (b) 8 (c) 16 (d) 24

21. How many smaller cubes with two surfaces painted have one face green and one of the adjacent faces black or red?
(a) 8 (b) 16 (c) 24 (d) 28

22. How many smaller cubes have atleast one surface painted with green colour?
(a) 8 (b) 24 (c) 32 (d) 56

DIRECTIONS ~ (Q. Nos. 23-27) *Read the following information carefully and answer the questions given below.*

The outer border of width 1 cm of a cube with side 5 cm is painted yellow on each side and the remaining space enclosed by this 1 cm path is painted pink. This cube is now cut into 125 smaller cubes of each side 1 cm. The smaller cubes so obtained are now separated.

23. How many smaller cubes have all the surfaces uncoloured?
(a) 0 (b) 9 (c) 18 (d) 27

24. How many smaller cubes have three surfaces coloured yellow?
(a) 2 (b) 4 (c) 8 (d) 10

25. How many smaller cubes have atleast two surfaces coloured yellow?
(a) 24 (b) 44 (c) 48 (d) 96

26. How many smaller cubes have one face coloured pink and an adjacent face coloured yellow?
(a) 0 (b) 1 (c) 2 (d) 4

27. How many smaller cubes have atleast one face coloured?
(a) 27 (b) 98 (c) 48 (d) 121

DIRECTIONS ~ (Q. Nos. 28-32) *Read the following information carefully and answer the questions given below.* « LIC ADO 2010

There is a solid cuboid, two opposite faces of it are painted black, two opposite faces are painted red and the remaining faces are painted green. After painting, this cuboid is divided into 72 cubes so that 64 cubes of smaller size and 8 cubes of bigger size can be obtained. Bigger cubes have no face black.

28. How many cubes have only one face painted?
(a) 8 (b) 16 (c) 20 (d) 24
(e) None of these

29. How many cubes have only two faces painted?
(a) 8 (b) 16 (c) 24 (d) 32
(e) None of these

30. How many cubes have 3 faces painted?
(a) 0 (b) 4 (c) 8 (d) 24
(e) None of these

31. How many cubes have two or more faces painted?
(a) 16 (b) 32 (c) 48 (d) 40
(e) None of these

32. How many cubes have no faces painted?
(a) 4 (b) 8 (c) 16 (d) 32
(e) None of these

DIRECTIONS ~ (Q. Nos. 33-38) *Read the following information carefully and answer the questions given below.*

A solid cube has been painted yellow, blue and black on the pair of opposite surfaces. The cube is then cut into 36 smaller cubes such that 32 cubes are of the same size while 4 others are of bigger size. Also, no face of any of the bigger cube is painted blue.

33. How many cubes have atleast one face painted black?
(a) 20 (b) 8 (c) 16 (d) 32

34. How many cubes have only one face painted?
(a) 0 (b) 4 (c) 8 (d) 12

35. How many cubes have only two faces painted?
(a) 24 (b) 20 (c) 16 (d) 12

36. How many cubes have two or more faces painted?
(a) 36 (b) 20 (c) 28 (d) 24

37. How many cubes have only three faces painted?
(a) 8 (b) 4 (c) 2 (d) 0

38. How many painted cubes do not have any of their faces painted yellow?
(a) 0 (b) 4 (c) 8 (d) 16

DIRECTIONS ~ (Q. Nos. 39-41) *Study the following information carefully and answer the questions given below.* « CGPSC 2019

(i) A wooden cuboid has length 4 cm, breadth 3 cm and height 5 cm.
(ii) Opposite sides of 5 cm × 4 cm are coloured red.
(iii) Opposite sides of 4 cm × 3 cm are coloured blue.
(iv) Remaining two sides are coloured green.
(v) The cuboid is cut-off to divide into cubes of 1 cm × 1 cm × 1 cm.

39. How many cubes will have only one colour?
(a) 12 (b) 16 (c) 22 (d) 28

40. How many cubes will have all the three colours?
(a) 14 (b) 12 (c) 10 (d) 8

41. How many cube will have no colour?
(a) Nil (b) 6 (c) 4 (d) 2

Answers WITH EXPLANATIONS

1. (*d*) According to the given information,

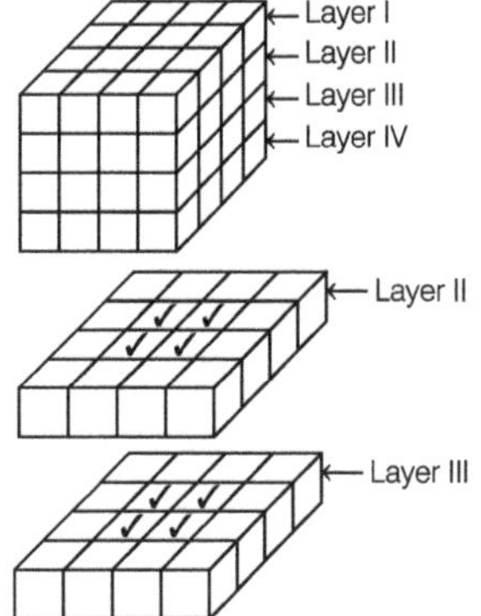

From the figures, it is clear that the number of invisible cubes
= 4 (in II layer) + 4 (in III layer) = 8

Or

Number of inner central cubes = $(n-2)^3 = (4-2)^3$
$= 2^3 = 8$ $[\because n = \sqrt[3]{64} = 4]$

2. (*a*) Clearly, when opposite faces are painted with different colours, then colours on adjacent faces will be different.

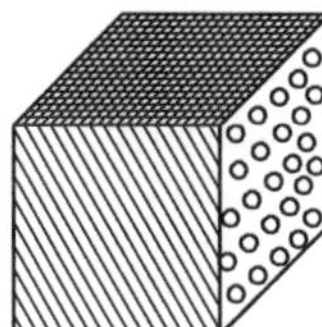

As we know that,
Number of pairs of opposite faces = 3
∴ Required number of colours = 3

3. (*b*) As we know that, when all the faces of a cube are painted with a single colour, then central cubes have only one face painted.
∴ Required number of central cubes = $6(n-2)^2$
$= 6(3-2)^2 = 6$ $[\because n = \sqrt[3]{27} = 3]$

4. (*c*) As we know that, when all the faces of a cube are painted with a single colour, then smaller cubes with only two faces painted are the middle cubes present at the edges.
∴ Number of middle cubes = $12(n-2) = 12(3-2)$
$= 12 \times 1 = 12$ [here, $n = 3$]

5. (*b*) Number of cubes having three faces painted
= Number of corner (vertex) cubes = 8

6. (*a*) Clearly, red is opposite to black, green is opposite to blue and brown is opposite to white.

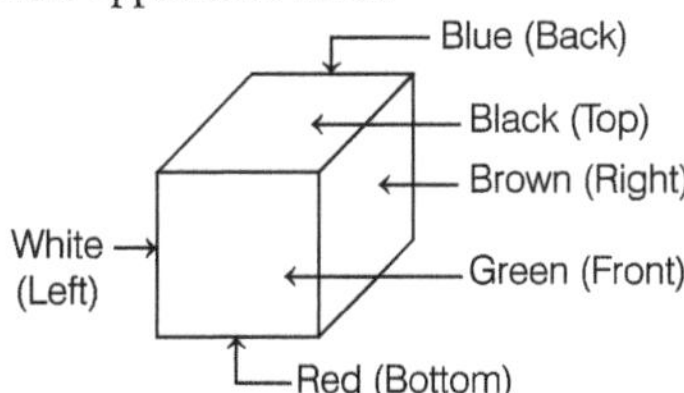

Hence, the colour opposite to brown is white.

7. (*b*) Number of smaller cubes having atleast two faces painted
= (Number of smaller cubes having 2 faces painted) + (Number of smaller cubes having 3 faces painted)
= (Number of middle cubes)+ (Number of corner cubes)
∴ Number of middle cubes
$= 12(n-2) = 12(5-2)$
$= 12 \times 3 = 36$ [here, $n = 25 \div 5 = 5$]

Number of corner (vertex) cubes = 8
∴ Required number of cubes = 36 + 8 = 44

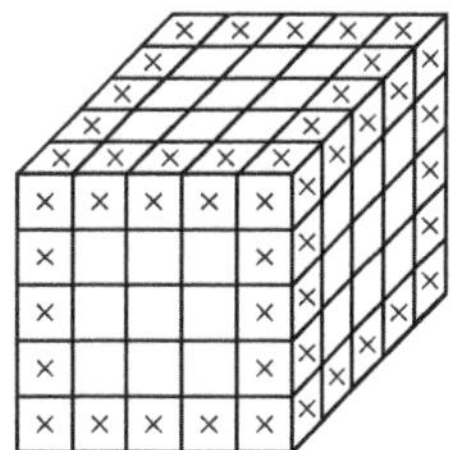

8. (*b*) According to the given information,

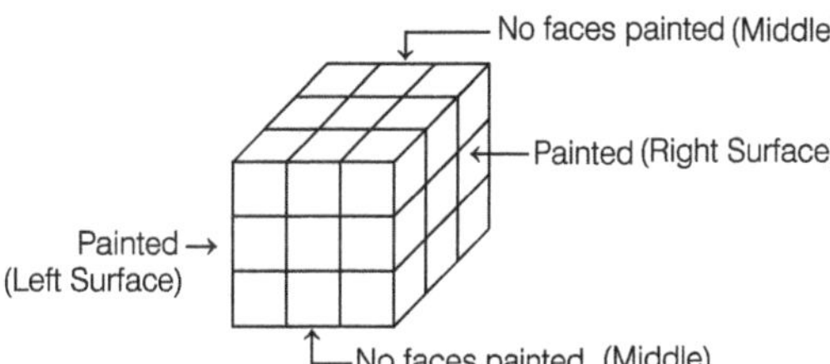

So, from above figure, it is clear that middle cubes are unpainted. Hence, 9 cubes are unpainted.

9. (*a*) According to the given information,

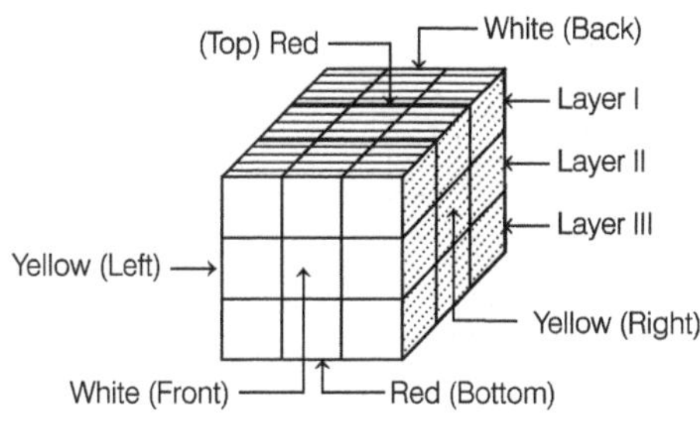

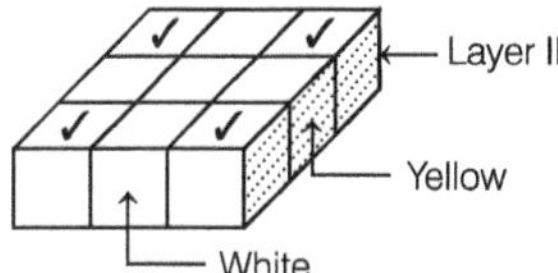

From the given figure, it is very much clear that the four corner cubes in the second layer have one face painted with white and one face painted with yellow.

10. (*b*) As we know that, the central cubes have only one face painted.

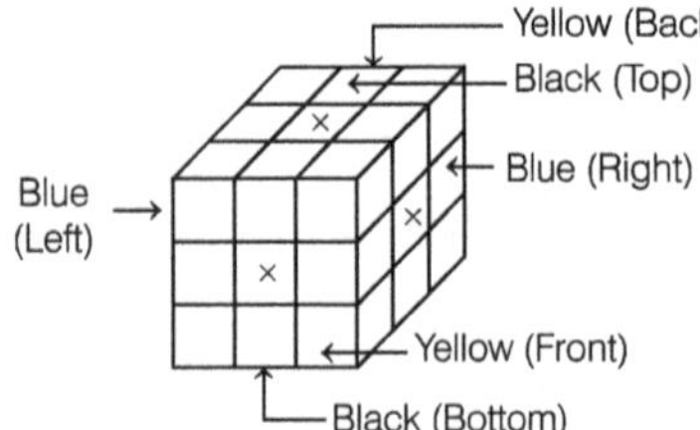

∴ Number of central cubes $= 6(n-2)^3$
$= 6(3-2)^2 = 6$ [here, $n = 3$]

11. (*a*) Here, $n = \dfrac{\text{Side of bigger cube}}{\text{Side of smaller cube}} = \dfrac{3}{1} = 3$

∴ Number of non-painted blocks $= (n-2)^3 = (3-2)^3 = 1$

12. (*b*)

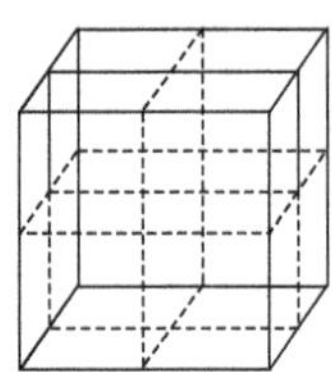

From the figure, there is no such cube which is painted red only on two sides.

13. (*c*) Number of smaller cubes with no surface painted
$= (n-2)^3 = (4-2)^3 = 8$ [$\because n = \sqrt[3]{64} = 4$]

14. (*c*) Number of smaller cubes with atleast two surfaces painted
= Number of cubes with three surfaces painted
+ Number of cubes with two surfaces painted
$= 8 + (n-2)\times 12 = 8 + (4-2)\times 12 = 8 + 24 = 32$

15. (*a*) Number of smaller cubes with two surfaces painted
$= (n-2)\times 12 = (4-2)\times 12 = 24$

16. (*d*) Number of smaller cubes with three surfaces painted = 8

Solutions (Q. Nos. 17-22) *According to the given information,*

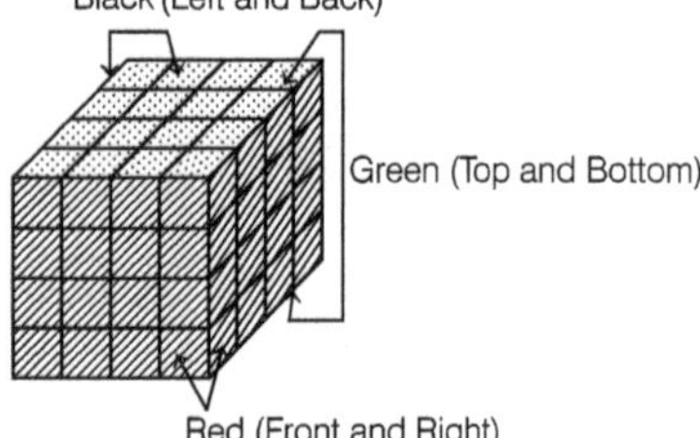

$n = \sqrt[3]{64} = 4$

17. (*c*) Since all the surfaces of the big cube are painted with some colour, therefore, number of smaller cubes with only one surface painted $= 6\times(n-2)^2 = 6\times(4-2)^2 = 24$

18. (*c*) Number of smaller cubes with no surface painted
$= (n-2)^3 = (2)^3 = 8$

19. (*d*) Number of smaller cubes with less than three surfaces painted = Number of cubes with two surfaces painted
+ Number of cubes with one surface painted
$= (n-2)\times 12 + (n-2)^2\times 6$
$= (4-2)\times 12 + (4-2)^2\times 6 = 24 + 24 = 48$

20. (*b*) Number of smaller cubes with three surfaces painted = 8

21. (*b*) Green colour is on the top and bottom surfaces of the cube. Hence, two surfaces painted with one surface green and another black or red will be present on the edges on the top and bottom surfaces.

∴ Required number of cubes $= (n-2)\times 8 = 16$

22. (*c*) All the smaller cubes present on the top and bottom of the bigger cube have green colour on atleast one of the surfaces.

∴ Required number of cubes = 16 + 16 = 32

Solutions (Q. Nos. 23-27) *According to the given information,*

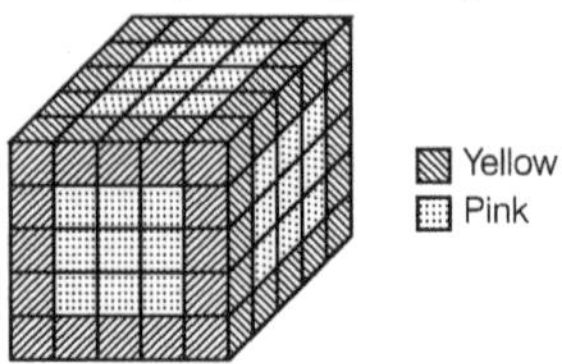

$n = \sqrt[3]{125} = 5$

23. (*d*) Smaller cubes with no surface painted will be present inside the cube

∴ Required cubes $= (n-2)^3 = (5-2)^3 = (3)^3 = 27$

24. (*c*) Smaller cubes with three surfaces coloured yellow will be present at the corners and their number is 8.

25. (*b*) Number of smaller cubes with atleast two surfaces coloured yellow = Number of cubes with three surfaces coloured yellow + Number of cubes with two surfaces painted yellow
$= 8 + (n-2)\times 12 = 8 + 3\times 12 = 44$

26. (*a*) No such smaller cubes are present in the bigger cube.

27. (*b*) Number of cubes with atleast one face coloured = Number of cubes with three surfaces coloured + Number of cubes with two surfaces coloured + Number of cubes with one surface coloured $= 8 + 12(n-2) + 6(n-2)^2 = 8 + 36 + 54 = 98$

Solutions (Q. Nos. 28-32) *According to the given information,*

Red ⇒ Top, Bottom, Black ⇒ Front, Back
Green ⇒ Left, Right, Total cubes = 72
Small cubes = 64, Big cubes = 8

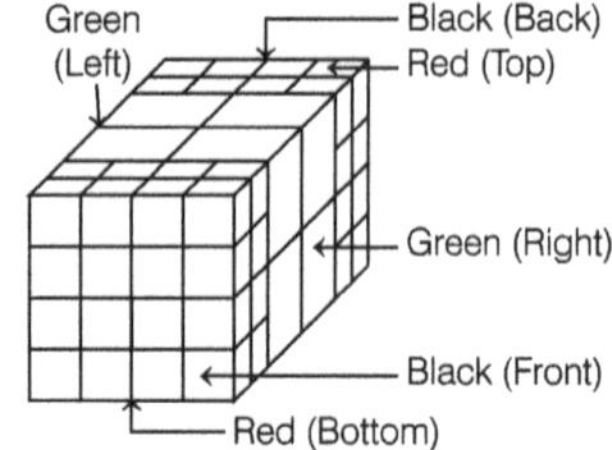

28. (*d*) Number of cubes having only one face painted
= Number of central cubes = 24

29. (*d*) Number of cubes having only two faces painted
= Number of middle cubes = 32

30. (*c*) Number of cubes having three surfaces painted
= Number of corner (vertex) cubes = 8

31. (*d*) Number of cubes having two or more faces painted
= Number of cubes having 2 faces painted
+ Number of cubes having 3 faces painted
= 32 + 8 = 40

32. (*b*) Number of cubes having no faces painted
= Total number of cubes
− Number of cubes with atleast one face painted
= 72 − (24 + 32 + 8) = 8

Solutions (Q. Nos. 33-38) *According to the given information,*

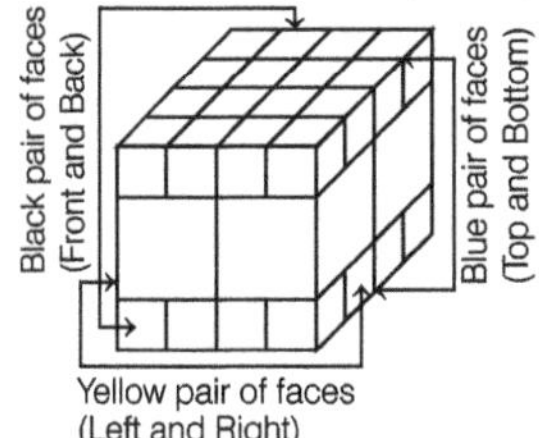

33. (*a*) Number of cubes having atleast one face painted with black colour = 16 smaller cubes + 4 bigger cubes = 20

34. (*c*) Only one face painted cubes will be four on each of the two faces (top and bottom). Hence, there are total 8 cubes.

35. (*b*) Number of cubes having only two faces painted
= 2 each on 8 edges and 1 each on 4 edges = 16 + 4 = 20

36. (*c*) Number of cubes with two or more faces painted
= Number of cubes with three faces painted
+ Number of cubes with two faces painted = 8 + 20 = 28

37. (*a*) Three faces painted cubes will be present on the corners and their number is 8.

38. (*d*) Number of cubes with no face painted yellow = 16 (8 each from top and bottom).

Solutions (Q. Nos. 39-41) *According to the given information,*

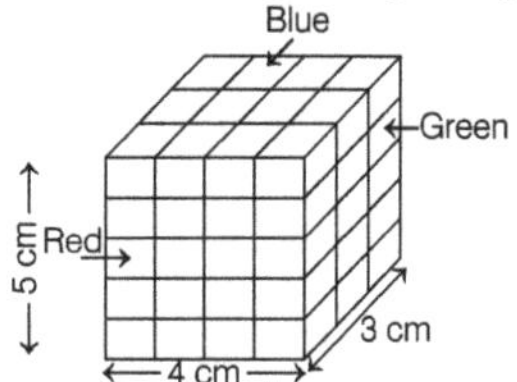

39. (*c*) Number of one coloured cubes on the side
$5 \text{ cm} \times 4 \text{ cm} = 2(5-2)(4-2) = 2 \times 3 \times 2 = 12$
Similarly, number of one coloured cubes on $4 \text{ cm} \times 3 \text{ cm}$ side
$= 2 \times (4-2)(3-2) \text{ cm} = 2 \times 2 \times 1 = 4$
Number of one coloured cubes on $5 \text{ cm} \times 3 \text{ cm}$ side
$= 2(5-2) \times (3-2) = 2 \times 3 \times 1 = 6$
$\therefore$ Total number of required cubes $= 12 + 4 + 6 = 22$

40. (*d*) Number of cubes of all the three colours = 8 (corners of the cube)

41. (*b*) Number of cubes with no colour $= (5-2)(4-2)(3-2)$
$= 3 \times 2 \times 1 = 6$

TYPE 03

Counting of Blocks

In this type of questions, the candidates are asked to count the number of cubes (or blocks/cuboids) in a given figure. The procedure to count the number of cubes (or blocks/cuboids) is described with the help of the following illustrations (example).

***Ex* 09** Count the number of cubes in the given figure.

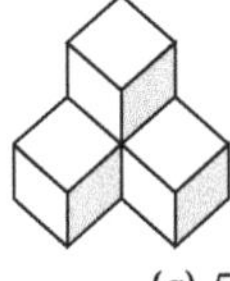

(a) 3 (b) 4 (c) 5 (d) 6

Solution (b) It is clear from the figure, 1 column contains 2 cubes and 2 columns contain 1 cube each.

$\therefore$ Total number of cubes $= (1 \times 2) + (2 \times 1) = 2 + 2 = 4$

***Ex* 10** Count the number of cubes in the given figure.

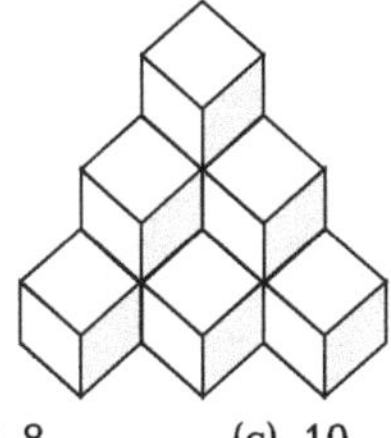

(a) 6 (b) 8 (c) 10 (d) 12

Solution (c) Clearly, in the figure, 1 column contains 3 cubes, 2 columns contains 2 cubes each and 3 columns contains 1 cube each.

$\therefore$ Total number of cubes $= (1 \times 3) + (2 \times 2) + (3 \times 1)$
$= 3 + 4 + 3 = 10$

***Ex* 11** Count the number of cubes in the given figure.

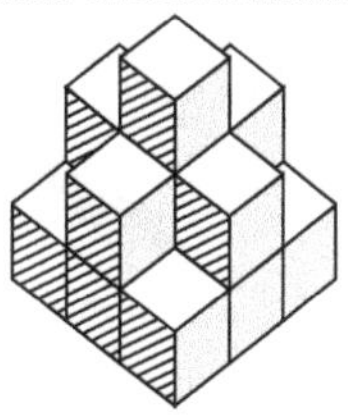

(a) 8 (b) 9 (c) 12 (d) 15

Solution (d) From the given question figure, it is clear that
4 corner columns containing 1 cube each.
1 column containing 3 cubes.
4 columns containing 2 cubes each.
$\therefore$ Total cubes $= (4 \times 1) + (1 \times 3) + (4 \times 2)$
$= 4 + 3 + 8 = 15$

***Ex* 12** How many cubes are there in the following figure?
« LIC ADO 2011

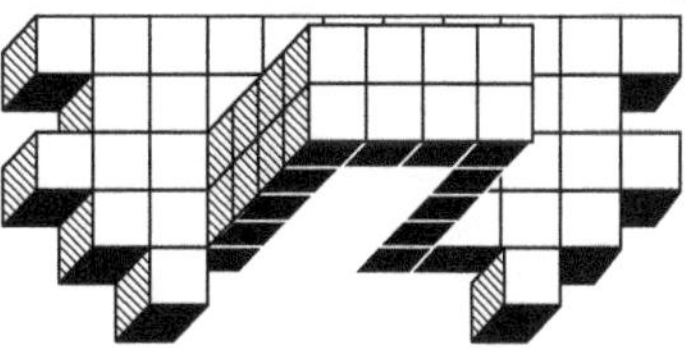

(a) 48 (b) 58 (c) 68 (d) 78
(e) None of these

Solution (b) From the given figure, it is clear that
4 columns containing 5 cubes each.
38 columns containing 1 cube each.
$\therefore$ Total cubes $= (4 \times 5) + (38 \times 1) = 20 + 38 = 58$

Practice CORNER 14.3

1. How many cubes are there in this diagram? « SSC 10+2 2012

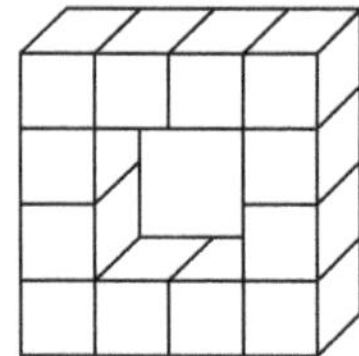

(a) 16 (b) 12 (c) 10 (d) 8

2. Count the number of blocks in the given figure.

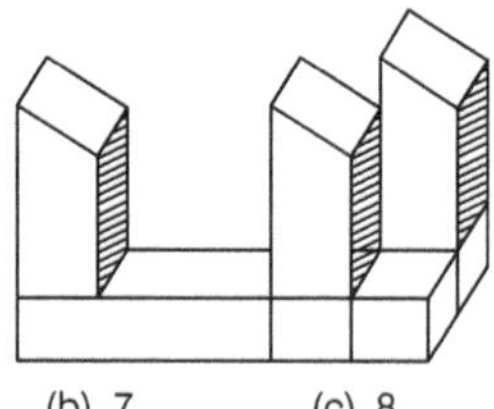

(a) 6 (b) 7 (c) 8 (d) 9

3. How many blocks are there in the below figure? « SSC 10+2 2009

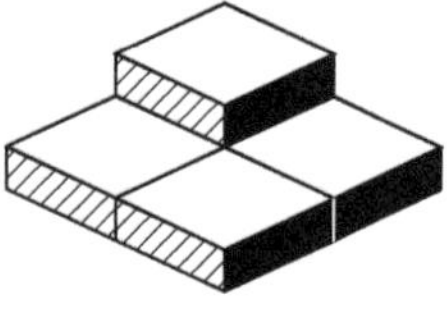

(a) 3 (b) 4 (c) 5 (d) 6

4. How many blocks are there in the below figure? « SSC 10+2 2008

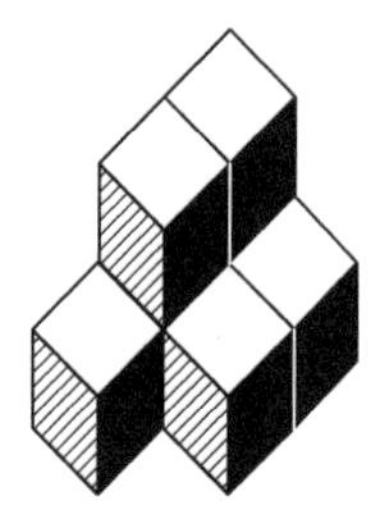

(a) 3 (b) 5 (c) 7 (d) 13

5. How many blocks are there in the below figure? « SSC 10+2 2011

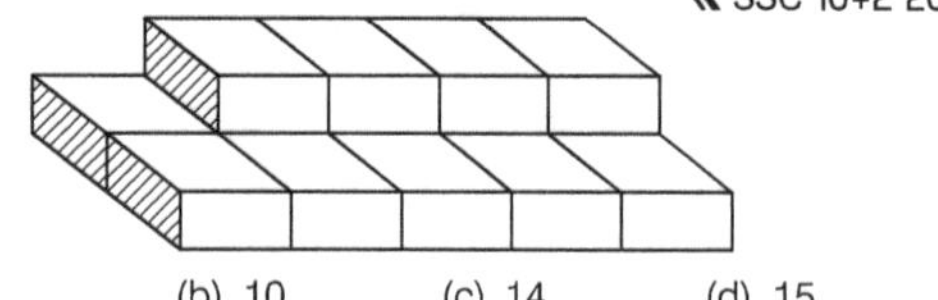

(a) 5 (b) 10 (c) 14 (d) 15

6. How many faces are there in the given three-dimensional model? « SSC CPO 2015

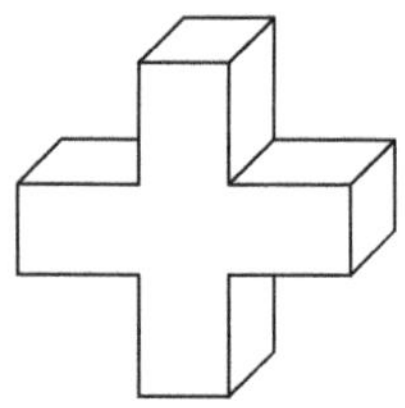

(a) 18 (b) 14
(c) 16 (d) 12

7. How many cubes are there in the group? « SSC CGL 2013

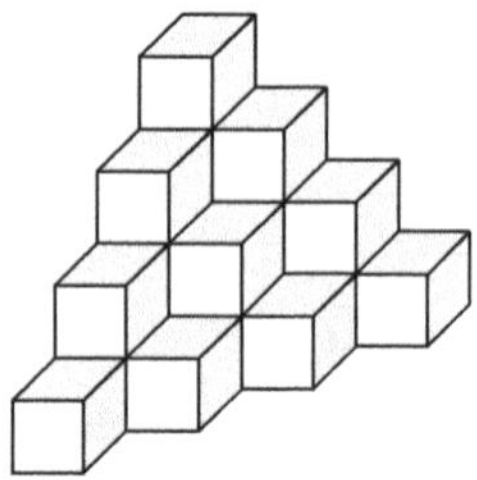

(a) 10 (b) 16
(c) 18 (d) 20

8. Count the number of cubes in the given figure. « IGNOU B.Ed. 2010

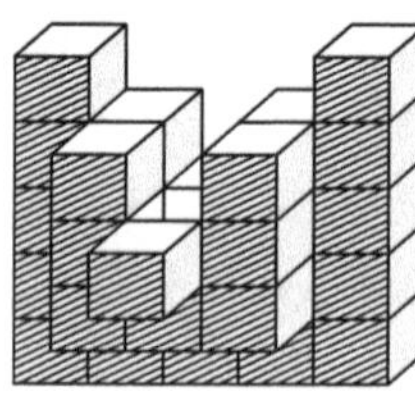

(a) 25 (b) 30
(c) 35 (d) 40

9. How many cubes are there in this figure? « SSC DEO & LDC 2012

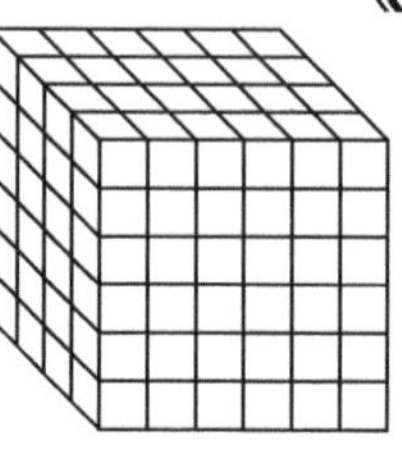

(a) 69 (b) 180
(c) 144 (d) 84

10. How many cubes are there in below figure?
« UP B.Ed 2009

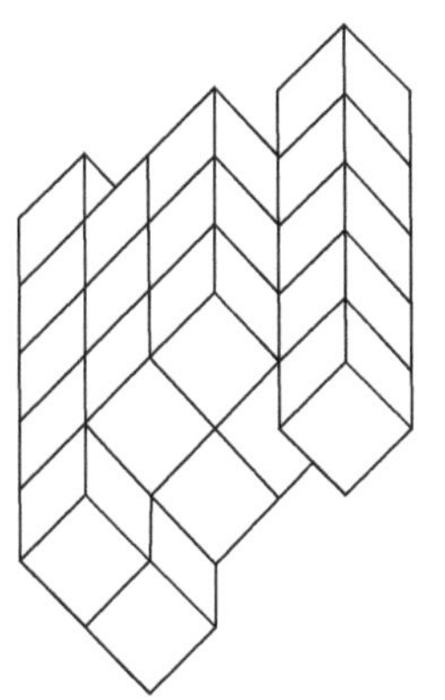

(a) 24 (b) 25 (c) 26 (d) 27

11. How many cubes are there in the following figure?

« CAT 2009

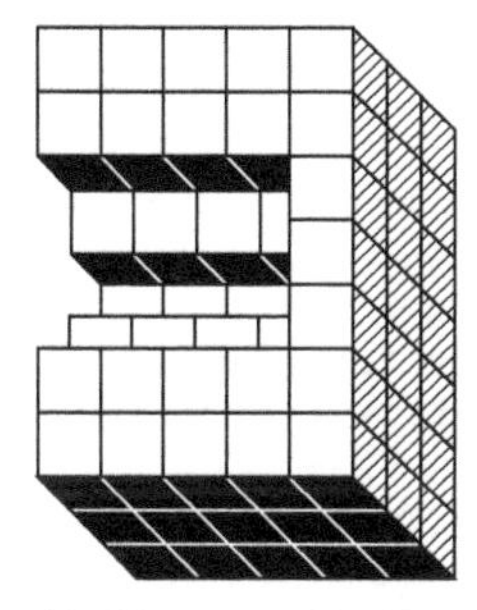

(a) 88 (b) 89 (c) 90 (d) 91

12. How many cubes are there in the following figure?
« MAT 2008

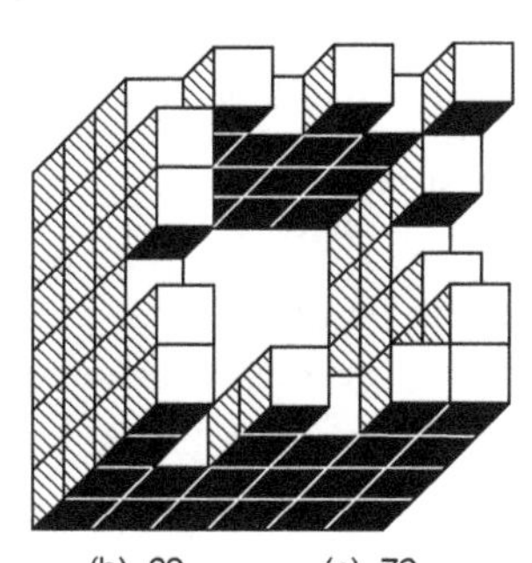

(a) 59 (b) 69 (c) 79 (d) 89

13. How many cubes are there in the following figure?
« IGNOU B.Ed 2011

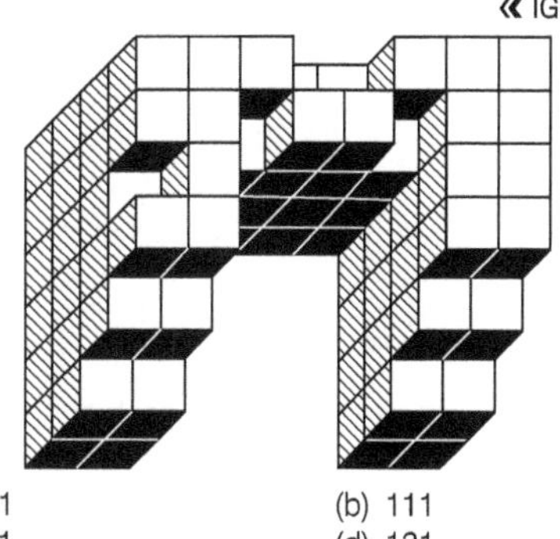

(a) 101 (b) 111
(c) 121 (d) 131

14. How many cubes are there in the following figure?

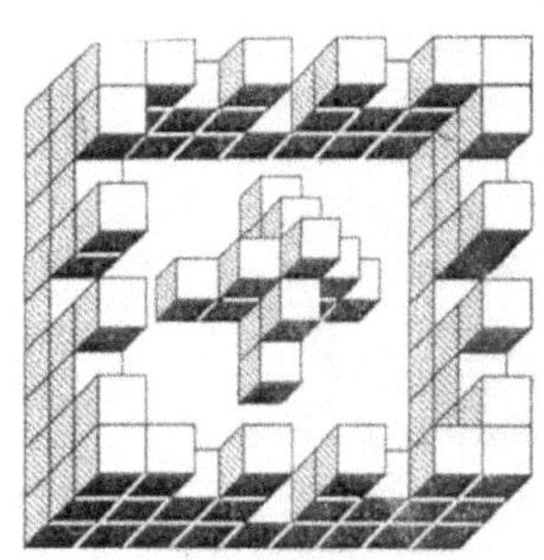

(a) 89 (b) 91
(c) 95 (d) 99

15. How many cubes are there in the following figure?

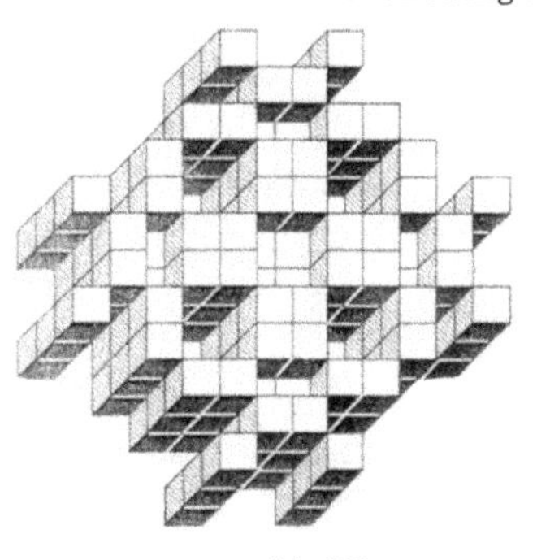

(a) 144 (b) 150
(c) 158 (d) 168

Answers / WITH EXPLANATIONS

1. (*b*) According to the given information,

So, there are 12 cubes in the given figure, which are illustrated above.

2. (*b*) It is clear from the figure, that there are four blocks in the lower part close to the ground. Also, there are 3 blocks standing over the lower layer of blocks.
Thus, there are $4+3=7$ blocks in the given figure.

3. (*c*) From the given question figure, it is clear that
1 column contains 2 blocks
3 columns contain 1 block each.
$\therefore$ Total blocks $=(1\times2)+(3\times1)=2+3=5$

4. (*c*) From the given question figure, it is clear that
2 columns contain 2 blocks each.
3 columns contain 1 block each.
$\therefore$ Total blocks $=(2\times2)+(3\times1)=4+3=7$

5. (*c*) From the given question figure, it is clear that
4 columns contain 2 blocks each.
6 columns contain 1 block each
$\therefore$ Total blocks $=(4\times2)+(6\times1)=8+6=14$

6. (*b*) According to the given information,

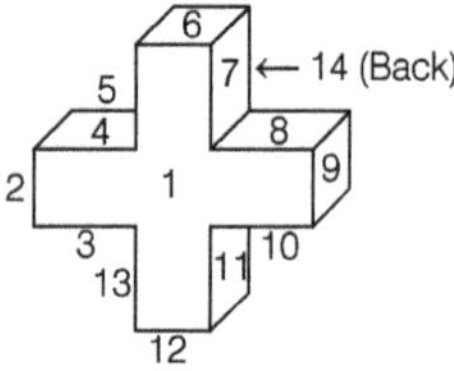

Clearly, the above figure has 14 faces.

7. (*d*) From the given question figure, it is clear that
1 column contain 4 cubes.
2 columns contain 3 cubes each.
3 columns contain 2 cubes each.
4 columns contain 1 cube each.
$\therefore$ Total cubes $=(1\times4)+(2\times3)+(3\times2)+(4\times1)$
$=4+6+6+4=20$

8. (*b*) From the given question figure, it is clear that
13 rows contain 1 cube each.
7 rows contain 2 cubes each.
1 row contain 3 cubes.
$\therefore$ Total cubes $=(13\times1)+(7\times2)+(1\times3)$
$=13+14+3=30$

9. (*c*) Total number of cubes $=6\times6\times4=144$

10. (*d*) From the given question figure, it is clear that
3 columns contain 5 cubes each.
4 columns contain 3 cubes each.
$\therefore$ Total cubes $=(3\times5)+(4\times3)=15+12=27$

11. (*b*) From the given figure, it is clear that
23 columns contain 3 cubes each.
8 columns contain 2 cubes each.
4 columns contain 1 cube each.
$\therefore$ Total cubes $=(23\times3)+(8\times2)+(4\times1)$
$=69+16+4=89$

12. (*b*) From the given figure, it is clear that
11 columns contain 4 cubes each.
7 columns contain 3 cubes each.
2 columns contain 2 cubes each.
$\therefore$ Total cubes $=(11\times4)+(7\times3)+(2\times2)$
$=44+21+4=69$

13. (*b*) From the given figure, it is clear that
19 columns contain 4 cubes each.
9 columns contain 3 cubes each.
4 columns contain 2 cubes each.
$\therefore$ Total cubes $=(19\times4)+(9\times3)+(4\times2)$
$=76+27+8=111$

14. (*c*) From the given question figure, it is clear that 21 columns contain 3 cubes each.
12 columns contain 2 cubes each.
8 columns contain 1 cube each.
$\therefore$ Total cubes $=(21\times3)+(12\times2)+(8\times1)$
$=63+24+8=95$

15. (*d*) From the given question figure, it is clear that
48 columns contain 3 cubes each.
12 columns contain 2 cubes each.
$\therefore$ Total cubes $=(48\times3)+(12\times2)$
$=144+24=168$

Master Exercise

1. The cube given below has been painted by three different colours. The opposite surfaces have been painted by the same colour. Next, the cube has been cut into 27 equal parts. How many such small cubes will be there whose only one surface is painted?

« SSC SAS 2006

(a) 4 (b) 6 (c) 8 (d) 12

2. Wooden little cubes each with an edge of one inch are put together to form a solid cube with an edge of three inches. This big cube is then painted red all over the outside. When the big cube is broken-up into the original little ones, how many cubes will be without paint? « SSC DEO & LDC 2010

(a) 0 (b) 1 (c) 3 (d) 4

3. In a solid cube made up of 27 small cubes, two opposite sides are painted red, two opposite sides yellow and two other sides white. How many small cubes have the colours yellow and white alone in them? « SSC 10+2 2010

(a) 4 (b) 8 (c) 12 (d) 16

4. A solid cube of 4 inches has been painted red, green, and black on pair of opposite faces. It has been cut into one inch cubes. How many cubes have only one face painted that too only red? « SSC LDC 2011

(a) 4 (b) 8 (c) 18 (d) 24

5. A solid red coloured cube is painted yellow on all sides. The cube is cut into 125 equal cubes. How many cubes will have 3 sides yellow? « SSC DEO & LDC 2012

(a) 10 (b) 4
(c) 8 (d) 12

DIRECTIONS ~ (Q. Nos. 6-10) *Read the following information carefully and answer the questions given below.*

A cube of 4 cm has been painted on its surfaces in such a way that two opposite surfaces have been painted blue and two adjacent surfaces have been painted red. Two remaining surfaces have been left unpainted. Now, the cube is cut into smaller cubes of side 1 cm each.

6. How many cubes will have no side painted?

(a) 18 (b) 16
(c) 22 (d) 8

7. How many cubes will have atleast red colour on its surfaces?

(a) 20 (b) 22
(c) 28 (d) 32

8. How many cubes will have atleast blue colour on its surfaces?

(a) 20 (b) 8 (c) 24 (d) 32

9. How many cubes will have only two surfaces painted with red and blue colours, respectively?

(a) 8 (b) 12
(c) 24 (d) 30

10. How many cubes have three surfaces coloured?

(a) 3 (b) 4 (c) 2 (d) 16

DIRECTIONS ~ (Q. Nos. 11-20) *Read the following information carefully and answer the questions given below.* « MAT 2009

Two adjacent faces of a solid cube have been painted red and the faces just opposite to the red painted faces have been painted black while the remaining faces have been painted green. After painting this cube has been divided into 64 smaller cubes.

11. How many cubes have only one face painted?

(a) 12 (b) 16
(c) 20 (d) 24

12. How many cubes have only two faces painted?

(a) 20 (b) 24
(c) 32 (d) 48

13. How many cubes have three surface painted?

(a) 4 (b) 6 (c) 8 (d) 12

14. How many cubes have four faces painted?

(a) 0 (b) 2 (c) 8 (d) 12

15. How many cubes have no faces painted?

(a) 4 (b) 6 (c) 8 (d) 12

16. How many cubes have atleast one face painted in red?

(a) 20 (b) 16 (c) 28 (d) 32

17. How many cubes have one or two faces painted but they have no three faces painted?

(a) 16 (b) 32
(c) 48 (d) 60

18. How many cubes have one face painted in green and have black or red colour on the face just adjacent to green face?

(a) 12 (b) 16 (c) 20 (d) 24

19. How many cubes have two adjacent faces painted red or black?

(a) 2 (b) 4 (c) 6 (d) 8

20. How many cubes have black colour at the face which is just opposite to the face having red colour?

(a) 0 (b) 8 (c) 12 (d) 24

21. A solid cube is painted yellow, blue and black such that opposite faces are of same colour. The cube is then cut into 36 cubes of two different sizes such that 32 cubes are small and the other four cubes are big. None of the faces of the bigger cubes is painted blue. How many cubes have only one face painted? « UPSC (CSAT) 2019

(a) 4 (b) 6
(c) 8 (d) 10

DIRECTIONS ~ (Q. Nos. 22-24) *Read the following instructions carefully and answer the questions given below.*

I. There is a rectangular wooden block of length 4 cm, height 3 cm and breadth 3 cm.
II. The two opposite surfaces of 4 cm × 3 cm are painted yellow on the outside.
III. The other two opposite surfaces of 4 cm × 3 cm are painted red on the outside.
IV. The remaining two surfaces of 3 cm × 3 cm are painted green on the outside.
V. Now the block is cut in such a way that cubes of 1 cm × 1 cm × 1 cm are created.

22. How many cubes will have only one colour?

(a) 10 (b) 12
(c) 14 (d) 18

23. How many cubes will have no colour?

(a) 1 (b) 2
(c) 4 (d) 8

24. How many cubes will have any two colours?

(a) 32 (b) 24
(c) 16 (d) 12

DIRECTIONS ~ (Q. Nos. 25-29) *Read the following information carefully and answer the questions given below.*

A cuboid of dimensions (6 cm× 4 cm× 1 cm) is painted black on both the surfaces of dimensions (4 cm× 1 cm), green on the surfaces of dimensions (6 cm× 4 cm) and red on the surfaces of dimensions (6 cm × 1 cm). Now, the block is divided into various smaller cubes of side 1 cm each. The smaller cubes so obtained are separated.

25. How many cubes will have atleast two colours?

(a) 16 (b) 12 (c) 10 (d) 8

26. How many cubes will be formed?

(a) 6 (b) 12 (c) 16 (d) 24

27. If cubes having only black as well as green colour painted faces are removed, then how many cubes will be left?

(a) 4 (b) 8 (c) 16 (d) 20

28. How many cubes will have 4 coloured sides and 2 sides without colour?

(a) 8 (b) 4 (c) 16 (d) 10

29. How many cubes will have two sides with green colour and remaining sides without any colour?

(a) 12 (b) 10
(c) 8 (d) 4

DIRECTIONS ~ (Q. Nos. 30-39) *Read the following information carefully and answer the questions given below.*

91 small cubes of same size are arranged in two cubes of sides 4 cm and 3 cm each. The bigger cube is coloured red on two opposite faces, white on two adjacent faces and blue on the remaining faces while the smaller one is coloured white on two opposite faces, blue on two adjacent faces and red on the remaining faces. Taking both the cubes into consideration, answer the following questions based on the above information.

30. How many smaller cubes are not coloured on any of faces?

(a) 1 (b) 4
(c) 8 (d) 9

31. How many cubes are coloured red, white and blue on one face each?

(a) 4 (b) 8
(c) 12 (d) 16

32. Leaving out uncoloured cubes, how many cubes are there without any red face?

(a) 36 (b) 40
(c) 42 (d) None of these

33. How many cubes have atleast one red face?

(a) 35 (b) 44
(c) 45 (d) 47

34. How many cubes have one face white and one face red and no face blue?

(a) 8 (b) 10
(c) 12 (d) 15

35. How many cubes are coloured blue, red or white on two faces each and not coloured on any other face?

(a) 6 (b) 7
(c) 18 (d) 10

36. How many cubes are coloured red, white or blue on one face each and have no other coloured face?

(a) 8 (b) 22 (c) 30 (d) 40

37. How many cubes are coloured blue on atleast one face?

(a) 41 (b) 43
(c) 45 (d) 47

38. How many cubes have atleast one white face?

(a) 40 (b) 44
(c) 46 (d) 48

39. How many cubes are coloured on two faces only?

(a) 24 (b) 28
(c) 32 (d) 36

40. A cube has six faces each of a different colour. The red face is opposite to black. The green face is in between red and black. The blue face is adjacent to white and brown face is adjacent to blue. The four colours adjacent to green are « UP PSC 2013

(a) red, black, brown and white
(b) red, black, brown and blue
(c) red, black, blue and white
(d) red, brown, blue and white

41. If the stack of blocks pictured here looks same from all four directions, what is the maximum number of blocks that could be used to build it, based on what you can see from this angle?

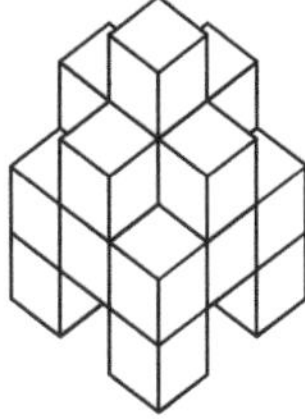

(a) 16 (b) 18 (c) 19 (d) 21

42. A $6 \times 6 \times 6$ cube is formed by gluing 216 wooden blocks of $1 \times 1 \times 1$ dimensions together. If the cube is kept on a table, what is the maximum number of blocks of $1 \times 1 \times 1$ dimensions that you can see from any angle at any one time? (If you can see even one face of a block of $1 \times 1 \times 1$ dimensions, then count it.)

(a) 46 (b) 86 (c) 91 (d) 126

43. What is the fewest number of blocks you need to add to make this shape into a cube?

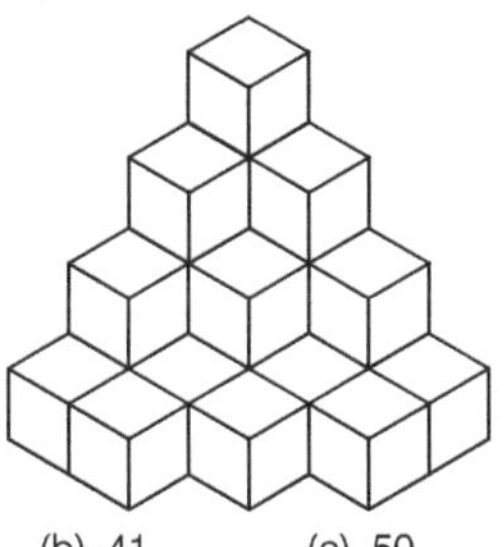

(a) 30 (b) 41 (c) 50 (d) 51

44. How many cubes are there in the following figure?

« CAT 2011

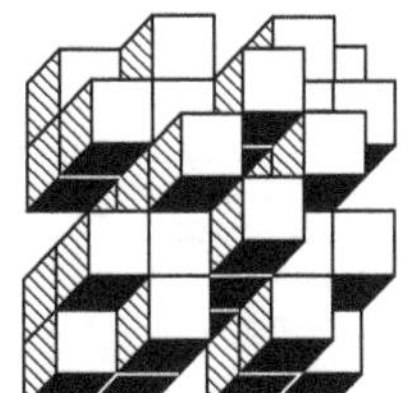

(a) 38 (b) 40 (c) 42 (d) 45

45. How many cubes are there in the following figure?

« MAT 2011

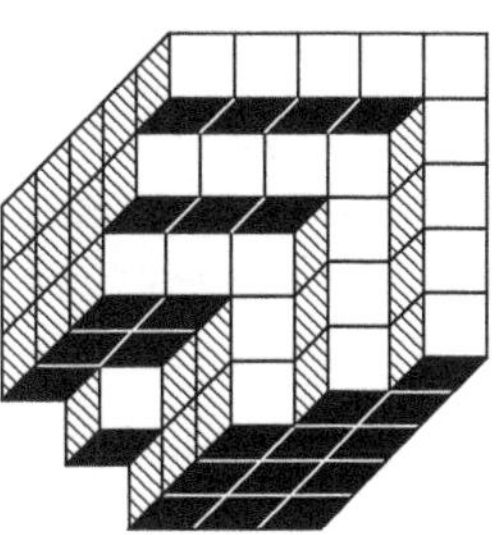

(a) 87 (b) 88
(c) 89 (d) 90

46. How many cubes are there in the following figure?

« CMAT 2011

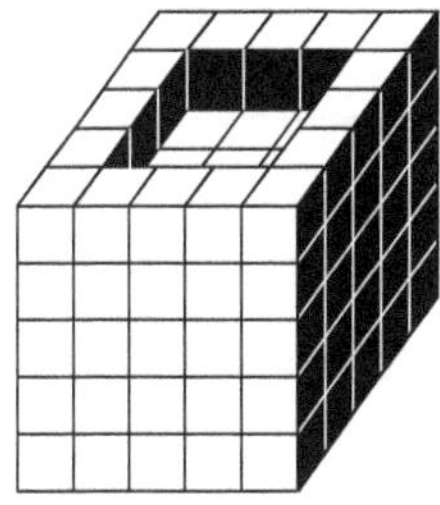

(a) 125 (b) 120
(c) 116 (d) 112

47. How many cubes are there in the following figure?

« MAT 2010

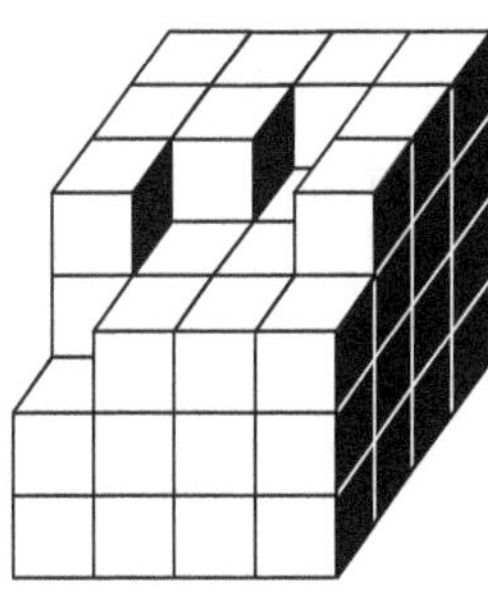

(a) 54 (b) 55
(c) 56 (d) 58

Answers / WITH EXPLANATIONS

1. (*b*) The central cube of each face will have only one face painted. Thus, there are six such cubes.

Or

Number of smaller cubes having one surface painted

$$= 6(n-2)^2 = 6(3-2)^2 = 6$$

2. (*b*) Here, $n = \frac{3}{1} = 3$

$\therefore$ Number of cubes with no painted face

$$= (n-2)^3$$
$$= (3-2)^3 = 1$$

3. (*a*) According to the given information,

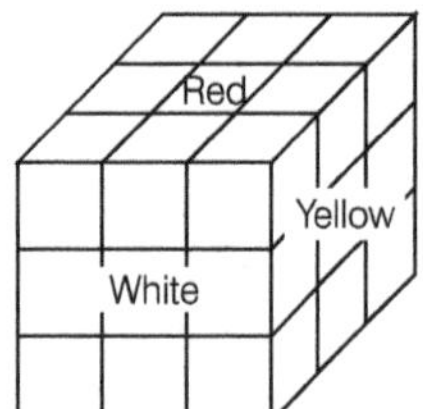

The cubes of middle row will have no red colour ⇒ 9 Cubes

The central cube will have no colour.

Now, out of 8 cubes, 4 cubes have both yellow and white colour.

4. (*b*) According to the given information,

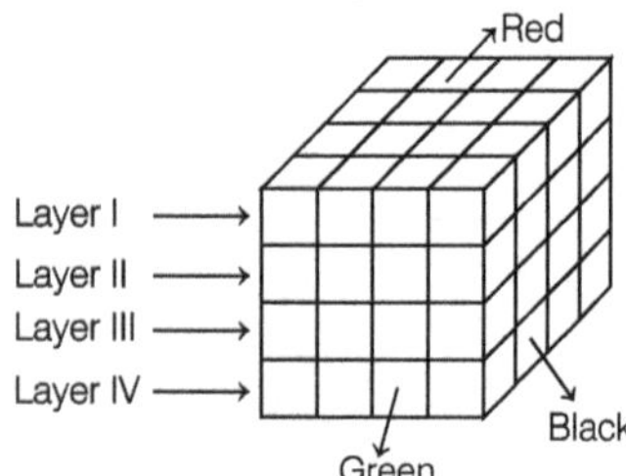

There are four cubes in Layer I and four cubes in Layer IV which have only one face painted red and all the other faces are not painted at all. Thus, there are eight such cubes.

5. (*c*) According to the given information,

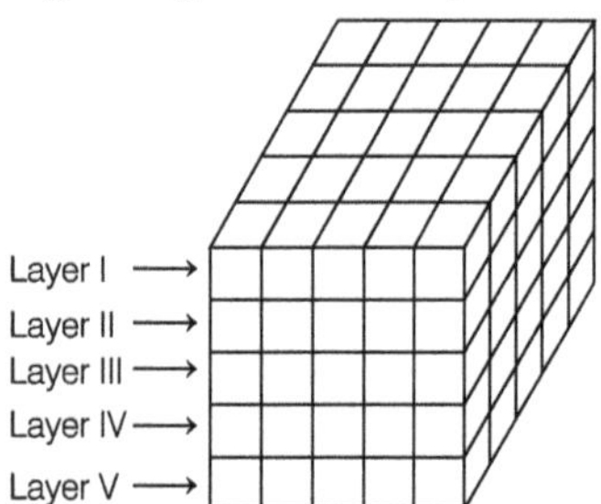

In layer I, the nine central cubes have only one face painted, four cubes at the corner have three faces painted and the remaining 12 cubes have two faces painted.

In each of the layers II, III and IV, the nine central cubes have no face painted, the four cubes at the corner have two faces painted and the remaining 12 cubes have one face painted.

In layer V, the nine central cubes have only one face painted, the four cubes at the corner have three faces painted and the remaining 12 cubes have two faces painted.

Thus, the number of cubes having three faces painted (from layer I and layer V) = 4 + 4 = 8

Solutions (Q. Nos. 6-10) *According to the given information,*

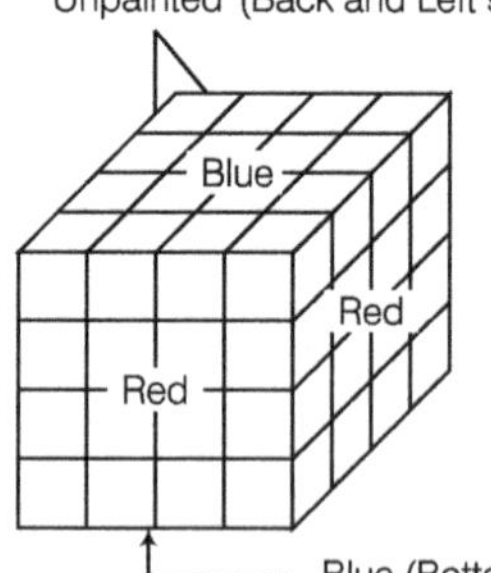

6. (*a*) Number of smaller cubes which are unpainted = 8 cubes from inside + 10 cubes from two adjacent unpainted surfaces = 18 cubes

7. (*c*) 28 cubes from two adjacent surfaces painted red will have atleast red colour on their surfaces.

8. (*d*) 32 cubes from two opposite surfaces painted blue will have atleast one surface painted blue.

9. (*b*) 12 cubes present on the four edges common to blue and red surfaces will have two surfaces painted one with red colour and the other with blue colour.

10. (*c*) Only 2 cubes from the two corners will have three surfaces painted.

Solutions (Q. Nos. 11-20) *According to the given information,*

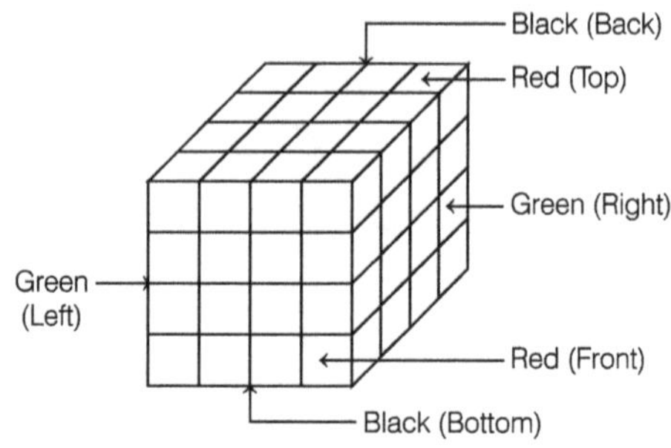

Red : Top, Front
Black : Back, Bottom
Green : Left, Right
Total cubes = 64

$\therefore \quad n = \sqrt[3]{64} = 4$

11. (*d*) Number of cubes having one face painted = Number of central cubes = $6(n-2)^2 = 6(4-2)^2 = 6 \times 4 = 24$

12. (*b*) Number of cubes having two faces painted = Number of middle cubes = $12(n-2)$

$$= 12(4-2) = 12 \times 2 = 24$$

13. (*c*) Three faces painted cubes are always 8.

14. (*a*) It is clear from the figure that cubes having four faces painted = 0

15. (*c*) Required cubes = Inner central cubes

$$= (n-2)^3 = (4-2)^3 = 8$$

16. (*c*) Number of cubes having atleast one face painted in red
= Number of cubes having one face painted in red
+ Number of cubes having two faces painted in red
= 24 + 4 = 28

17. (*c*) Number of cubes having one or two faces painted
= Number of cubes having one face painted + Number of cubes having two faces painted = 24 + 24 = 48

18. (*b*) Required number of cubes = (Number of cubes painted in green + black) + (Number of cubes painted in green + red)
= $(4 \times 2) + (4 \times 2) = 8 + 8 = 16$

19. (*b*) Required number of cubes = Number of cubes painted in red on two adjacent faces + Number of cubes painted in black on two adjacent faces = 2 + 2 = 4

20. (*a*) It is clear from the figure that required number of cubes are zero in the given case.

21. (*c*) According to question, on cutting the cube

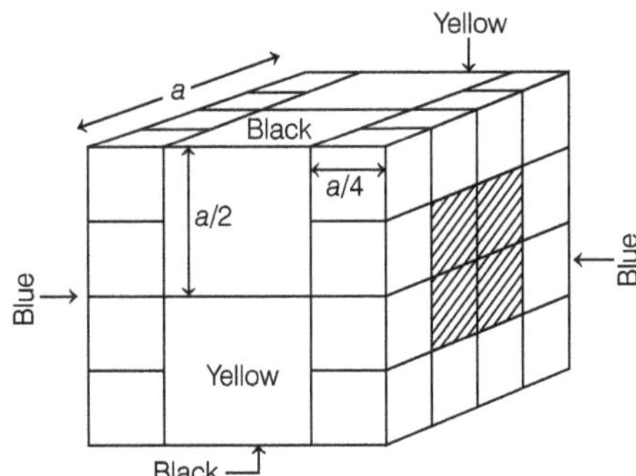

It is clear from the above figure that number of cubes with one face painted = 4 + 4 = 8

Solutions (Q. Nos. 22-24) *According to the given information,*

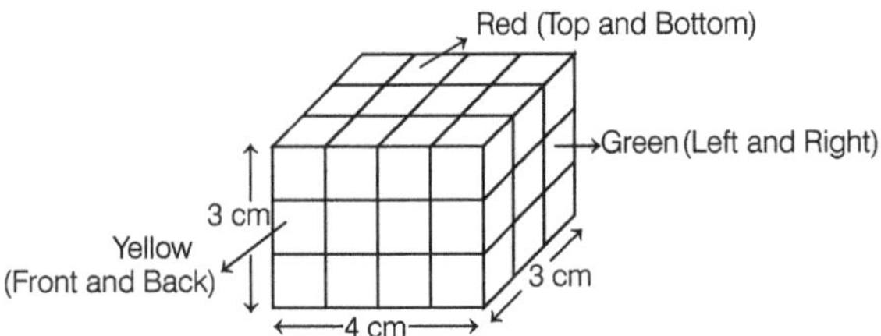

22. (*a*) The total number of cubes having only one colour

$$= (2 \times 4) + (1 \times 2)$$
$$= 8 + 2 = 10$$

23. (*b*) The total number of cubes having no colour = $2 \times 1 = 2$

24. (*c*) The total number of cubes have any two colours

$$= (4 \times 2) + (8 \times 1)$$
$$= (8 + 8) = 16$$

Solutions (Q. Nos. 25-29) *According to the given information,*

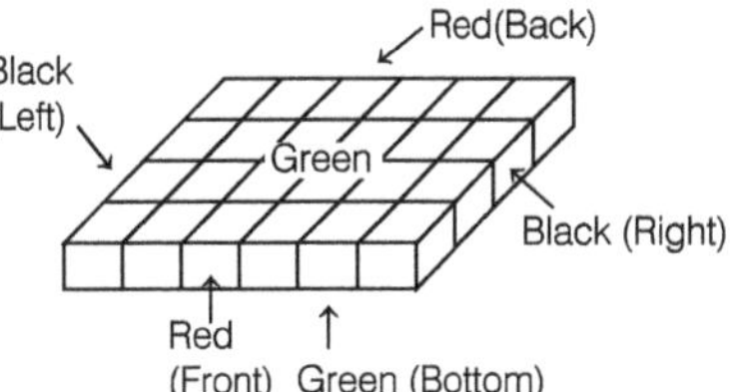

25. (*a*) All the 16 cubes present on the boundary of this block will have atleast two colours.

26. (*d*) $6 \times 4 = 24$ smaller cubes will be formed.

27. (*c*) A total of 16 cubes will be left, if cubes with black as well as green colours are removed.

28. (*b*) All the 4 cubes present at the corners will have four faces painted and two faces unpainted.

29. (*c*) 8 cubes from the upper and lower surfaces surrounded by 1 cm boundary will have two surfaces painted and remaining unpainted.

Solutions (Q. Nos. 30-39) *According to the given information,*

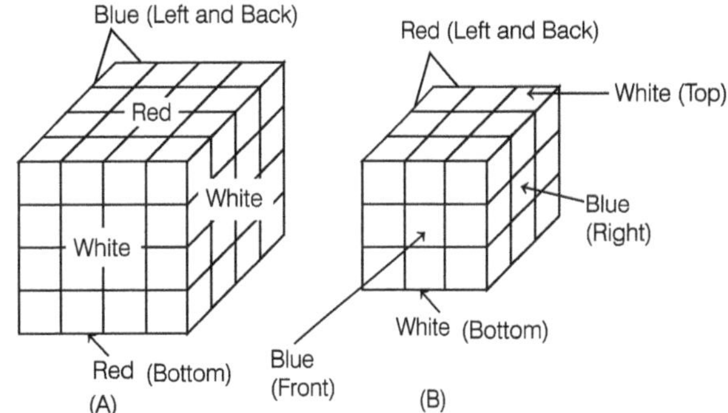

30. (*d*) 8 smaller cubes from cube (A) and 1 smaller cube from cube (B) will have none of its surfaces painted *i.e.,* a total of 9 cubes will have none of its surface painted.

31. (*a*) 4 smaller cubes each from cubes (A) and (B) will have red, white and blue colours on one face each.

32. (*d*) 24 cubes from (A) and 11 cubes from (B) will not have red colours on any of their faces.
i.e. a total of 35 cubes will have none of red face.

33. (*d*) 32 smaller cubes from (A) and 15 smaller cubes from (B) will have atleast one face red.
i.e. a total of 47 cubes have atleast one red face.

34. (*c*) 8 smaller cubes from (A) and 4 smaller cubes from (B) *i.e.,* a total 12 cubes will have one face white and one face red and no face blue.

35. (*c*) 12 smaller cubes from (A) and 6 smaller cubes from (B) *i.e.,* a total of 18 cubes are coloured blue, red or white on two faces each and not coloured on any of other faces.

36. (*b*) 16 smaller cubes from (A) and 6 smaller cubes from (B) *i.e.,* a total of 22 cubes are coloured red, white or blue on one face each and have no other face coloured.

37. (*b*) 28 cubes from (A) and 15 cubes from (B) are coloured blue on atleast one of their faces.
i.e. a total of 43 cubes are coloured blue on atleast one face.

38. (*c*) 28 cubes from (A) and 18 cubes from (B) are coloured blue on atleast one of their faces.

i.e. a total of 46 cubes have atleast one white face.

39. (*d*) $(n-2)\times 12 = (4-2)\times 12 = 24$ cubes from (A) and $(n-2)\times 12 = (3-2)\times 12 = 12$ cubes from (B) *i.e.*, total 36 cubes are coloured on two faces only.

40. (*a*) According to the given information,

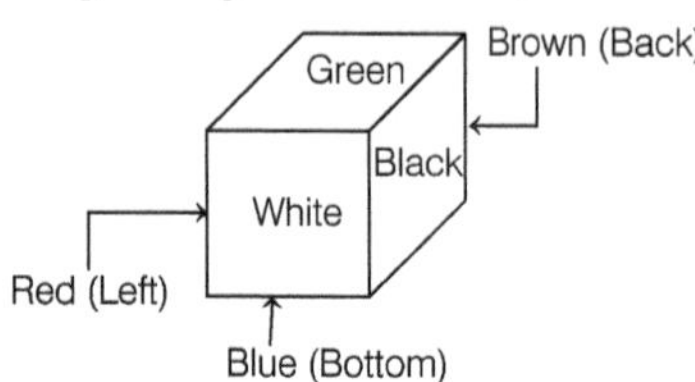

Clearly, the four colours adjacent to green are red, black, brown and white.

41. (*c*) There are four layers from the top to bottom.
1st layer has 1 block
2nd layer has 5 blocks
3rd layer has 3 rows of 3 blocks each
4th layer has 4 blocks
$\therefore$ Total blocks $= 1 + 5 + 3 \times 3 + 4$
$= 10 + 9 = 19$ blocks

42. (*c*) 91 cubes

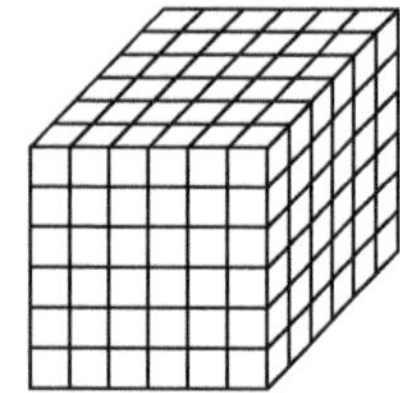

Method I

You can see three faces at once. You can see only one face of 25 blocks on each of the three faces, for a total of 75 blocks. You can see two faces of 5 blocks along each of the three edges visible, for a total of 15 blocks. Finally, you can see three sides of the one corner block that is facing you. The total number of blocks you can see is $75 + 15 + 1 = 91$.

Method II

If you remove all of the blocks you can see, you are left with a $5\times5\times5$ cube that you cannot see. There are $6\times6\times6 = 216$ blocks in all and you cannot see $5\times5\times5 = 125$ of them. So, you can see $216 - 125 = 91$ blocks.

43. (*b*) The bottom layer requires 3 blocks, so that it can be turned into 4×4 block. Second layer from bottom will need 10 blocks similarly, third layer from bottom and top layer requires 13 blocks and 15 blocks respectively.

$\therefore$ Total blocks required $= 3 + 10 + 13 + 15 = 41$ blocks

Alternate Method

From bottom layer we can see that the cube that will be formed will have $4\times4\times4$ dimensions.
$\therefore$ Total number of smaller cubes in $4\times4\times4$ larger cube $= 64$
$\therefore$ Cubes shown in the given figure $= 1 + 3 + 6 + 13 = 23$
$\therefore$ Total number of smaller cubes/blocks needed $= 64 - 23 = 41$

44. (*b*) From the given figure, it is clear that
4 columns contain 3 cubes each
12 columns contain 2 cubes each
4 columns contain 1 cube each
$\therefore$ Total number of cubes $= (4\times3)+(12\times2)+(4\times1)$
$= 12 + 24 + 4 = 40$

45. (*c*) From the given figure, it is clear that
9 columns contain 5 cubes each.
7 columns contain 4 cubes each.
5 columns contain 3 cubes each.
1 column contains 1 cube.
$\therefore$ Total number of cubes $= (9\times5)+(7\times4)+(5\times3)+(1\times1)$
$= 45 + 28 + 15 + 1 = 89$

46. (*c*) From the given figure, it is clear that
16 columns contain 5 cubes each.
9 columns contain 4 cubes each.
$\therefore$ Total number of cubes
$= (16\times5)+(9\times4) = 80 + 36 = 116$

47. (*c*) From the given figure, it is clear that
9 columns contain 4 cubes each.
6 columns contain 3 cubes each.
1 column contains 2 cubes.
$\therefore$ Total number of cubes $= (9\times4)+(6\times3)+(1\times2)$
$= 36 + 18 + 2 = 56$

CHAPTER / 15

Dice

Dice are cubical or cuboidal shape objects containing numbers /figures/symbols/ dots embedded on their surfaces.

Die/Dice is/are a three-dimensional figure with each of its six surfaces/faces showing different numbers/letters/ colours etc. It has 8 corners and 12 edges (sides).

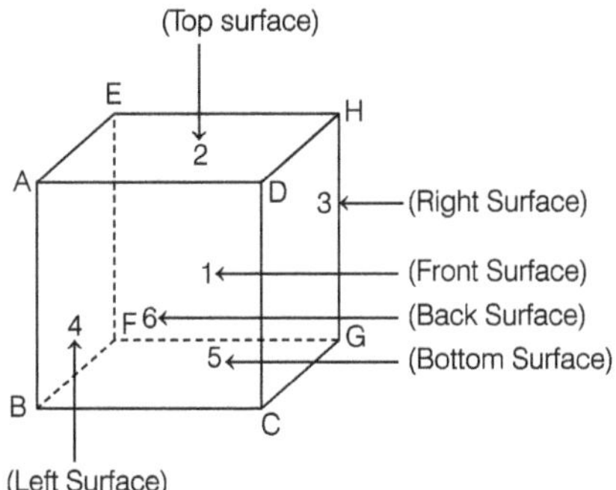

In the above dice,

Sides/Edges	=	AE, EH, HD, AD, BF, FG, GC, BC, AB, DC, HG and EF (12)
Vertices/ Corners	=	A, B, C, D, E, F, G and H (8)
Faces/ Surfaces	=	AEHD, DHGC, AEFB, BCGF, ABCD and EFGH (6)

Every face has four adjacent faces and one opposite face. The opposite faces are discussed below

ADCB ⇒ Front face ⎤ faces opposite
EHGF ⇒ Back face ⎦ to each other
AEHD ⇒ Upper face ⎤ faces opposite
BFGC ⇒ Lower face ⎦ to each other
DHGC ⇒ Right face ⎤ faces opposite
AEFB ⇒ Left face ⎦ to each other

Note *Only 3 sides of a cube are visible at a time (known as "Joint Sides") and these sides can never be on the opposite side of each other.*

Types of Dice

Dice having digits/number of dots from 1 to 6 on its surfaces can be divided into two types

1. Standard Dice

When the sum of digits/number of dots on opposite faces is equal to 7, then the dice is called standard dice. In other words, we can say that, when the sum of digits/number of dots on adjacent faces is not equal to 7, then the die is called standard die.

Let us see,

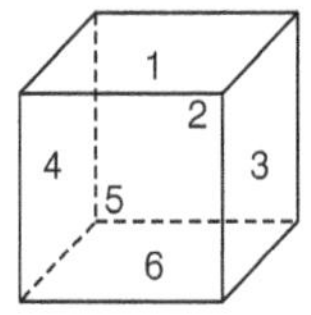

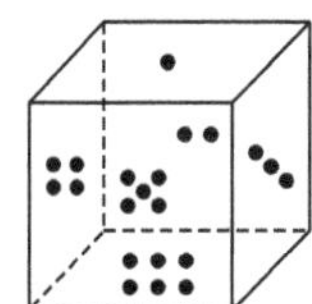

Sum of the opposite faces,

$$1+6=7, 4+3=7, 2+5=7, 5+2=7,$$
$$3+4=7, 6+1=7$$

Sum of the adjacent faces,

$1+2=3$, $2+1=3$, $3+1=4$, $4+1=5$, $5+1=6$, $6+2=8$, $1+3=4$, $2+3=5$, $3+2=5$, $4+2=6$,$5+3=8$, $6+3=9$, $1+4=5$, $2+4=6$, $3+5=8$,$4+5=9$, $5+4=9$, $6+4=10$, $1+5=6$, $2+6=8$, $3+6=9$, $4+6=10$,$5+6=11$, $6+5=11$

If digits/dots 1 to 6 are marked on the surface of a dice, then in standard dice,

Face/Surface	Opposite Face/Surface	Adjacent Faces/Surfaces
1	6	2, 3, 4, 5
2	5	1, 3, 4, 6
3	4	1, 2, 5, 6
4	3	1, 2, 5, 6
5	2	1, 3, 4, 6
6	1	2, 3, 4, 5

2. General Dice

When the sum of digits/number of dots on opposite faces is not equal to 7, then the dice is called general dice. In other words, we can say that, when the sum of digits/number of dots on adjacent faces is equal to 7, then the dice is called a general dice.

Let us see

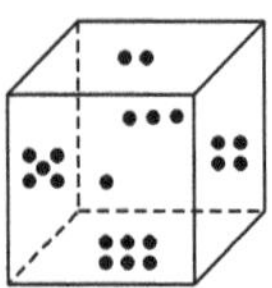

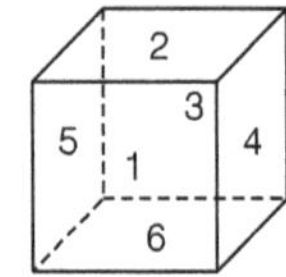

Sum of the opposite faces

$1+3=4,\ \ 4+5=9,\ \ 2+6=8,$

$5+4=9,\ \ 3+1=4,\ \ 6+2=8$

Sum of the adjacent faces

$1+2=3,\ \ 2+1=3,\ \ 3+2=5,\ \ 4+1=5,\ \ 5+1=6,$

$\boxed{6+1=7,}\ 1+4=5,\ \ 2+3=5,\ \ \boxed{3+4=7,}\ \ 4+2=6,$

$\boxed{5+2=7,}\ 6+3=9,\ \ 1+5=6,\ \ 2+4=6,\ \ 3+5=8,$

$\boxed{4+3=7,}\ 5+3=8,\ \ 6+4=10,\ \boxed{1+6=7,}\ \ \boxed{2+5=7,}$

$3+6=9,\ \ 4+6=10,5+6=11,\ \ 6+5=11$

If digits/dots 1 to 6 are marked on the surface of a dice, then in general dice

Face/Surface	Opposite Faces/Surfaces	Adjacent Faces/Surfaces
1	2/3/4/5	6 or 2/3/4/5
2	1/3/4/6	5 or 1/3/4/6
3	1/2/5/6	4 or 1/2/5/6
4	1/2/5/6	3 or 1/2/5/6
5	1/3/4/6	2 or 1/3/4/6
6	2/3/4/5	1 or 2/3/4/5

Certain Basic Rules

Methods to Find Digits/Dots/Words/Letters /Figures/Symbols at Opposite Faces of a Dice

There are 6 faces in the dice and every face has a opposite face.

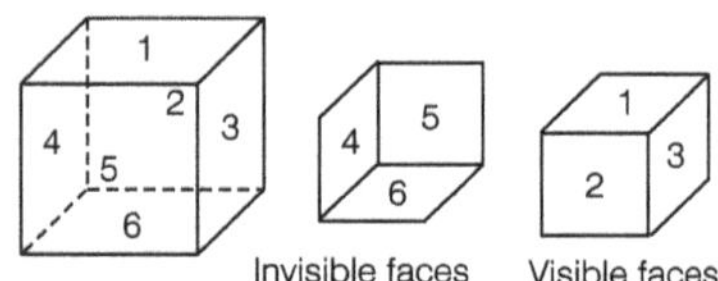

Invisible faces   Visible faces

A. When Single Position of a Dice is Given

If only one position of a dice is given in the question, the candidates are required to find out whether the given dice is a standard dice or general dice.

CASE I When the given dice is a standard dice,

As we know that, in a standard dice, the sum of the digits/number of dots on opposite faces is equal to 7.

Hence, in a standard dice, the opposite faces are as follows

1 and 6 or 6 and 1 are opposite faces.

2 and 5 or 5 and 2 are opposite faces.

3 and 4 or 4 and 3 are opposite faces.

Ex 01 What will be the digit on the opposite face of the particular face having digit 4 in the dice given below?

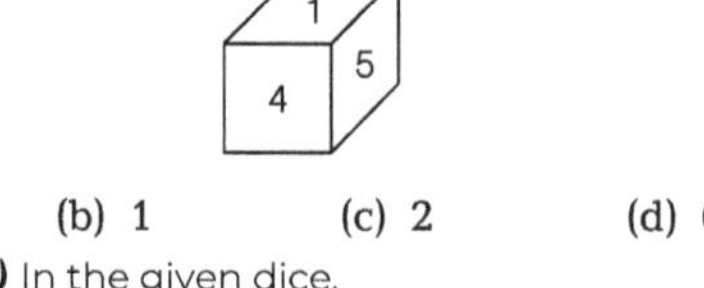

(a) 3 (b) 1 (c) 2 (d) 6

Solution (a) In the given dice,

$$1+4=5 \Rightarrow 1+5=6 \Rightarrow 4+5=9$$

Clearly, the sum of the digits on the adjacent faces is not equal to 7. Hence, the given dice is a standard dice. As sum of the digits on opposite faces of a standard dice is 7. Hence, the face opposite to the face having digit 4 will have the digit 3.

$$4+3=7$$

CASE II When the given dice is a general dice

As we know that, in a general dice sum of the digits at any of the two adjacent faces is equal to 7.

Let us consider a dice

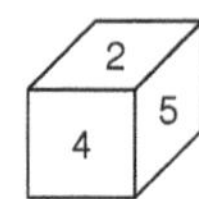

Now, the above dice is a general dice as sum of numbers on any of the two adjacent faces is 7 i.e. $2+5=7$.

Now, number opposite to 5 can be 1, 3 or 6. 2 cannot be on the opposite face of 5 as it is adjacent to 5. So, the correct group of numbers opposite to 5 is 1/3/6.

Ex 02 What digit will take place at the face opposite to the face having digit 2?

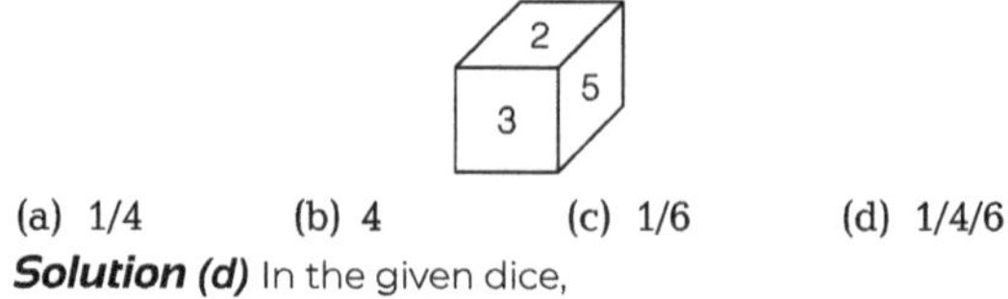

(a) 1/4 (b) 4 (c) 1/6 (d) 1/4/6

Solution (d) In the given dice,

$$2+5=7 \text{ (adjacent faces digits sum)}$$

Hence, the given dice is not a standard dice as in a standard dice, sum of the digits of any two adjacent faces cannot be 7. Infact, this situation is related to general dice. Hence, this problem will be solved on the basis of a general dice.

As 5 and 3 are the adjacent faces of 2 therefore the faces opposite to 2 can be 1 or 4 or 6 ⇒ 1/4/6.

B. When Two Positions of a Single Dice are Given

CASE I Digits are different in both positions as follows;

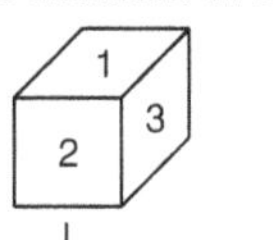
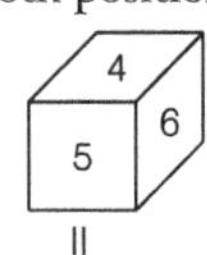

In both the positions of given dice, all the digits are different from one another. In such case any digit in position I can be opposite to any of the three digits in position II and *vice-versa* as given below

1 can be opposite to 4/5/6.
2 can be opposite to 4/5/6.
3 can be opposite to 4/5/6.
4 can be opposite to 1/2/3.
5 can be opposite to 1/2/3.
6 can be opposite to 1/2/3.

***Ex* 03** In the two positions of a given dice as shown below, what digit comes at the face opposite to the face having digit 2?

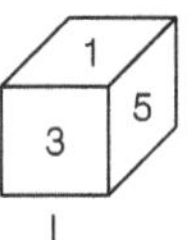
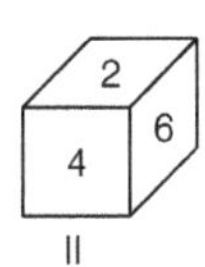

(a) 1/5/6 (b) 1/3/4 (c) 1/3/5 (d) 1/4/6

Solution (c) As all the digits given in both the positions (I and II) are different from one another. So, any of the digits 1, 3 and 5 can be opposite to digit 2.

CASE II When one digit is common in both the positions and the common digit is at the same face as follo follows

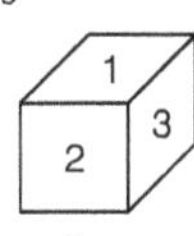
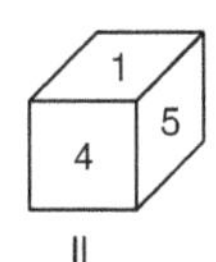

In this case, except the common digit, the digits on the other faces are opposite to each other and the face opposite to the common digit will have that digit which is invisible.

Hence,
1 and 6 are opposite.
2 and 4 are opposite.
3 and 5 are opposite.

***Ex* 04** What digit will be on the face opposite to face having digit 1 in the two positions of a single dice given below?

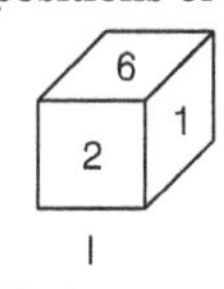
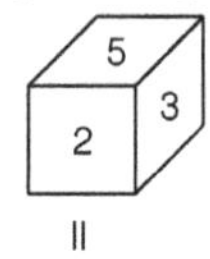

(a) 5 (b) 4 (c) 3 (d) 2

Solution (c) In both the positions of dice, common digit 2 is on the same face. In position I, right face has digit 1 while in position II, right face has digit 3. Therefore, 1 and 3 are on opposite faces.

CASE III When the common digit is on different faces as follows; one digit is common in both positions but not at same faces as follows

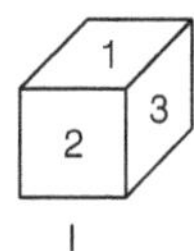
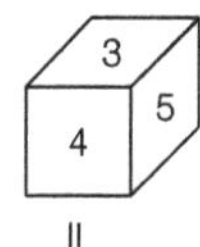

In this case, we form two different orders of the digits from both positions of dice in clockwise direction starting from the common digit.

In both the orders, the digits written after the common digit are opposite to each other.

Let us see the changed order of digits. The position II is given in the position III, when digits move clockwise.

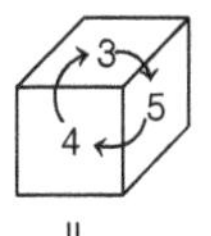
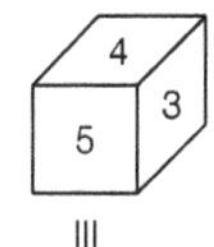

Writing digits of position I (clockwise)
Writing digits of position II (clockwise)

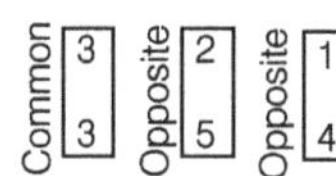

Clearly, in this case
1 and 4 are opposite.
2 and 5 are opposite.
Hence, 3 and 6 are opposite.

***Ex* 05** In the following question, two positions of a single dice are given. Find the face which is opposite to the face having digit 6.

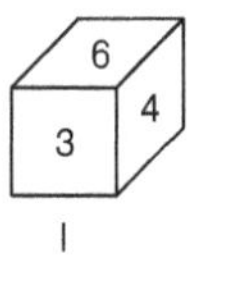
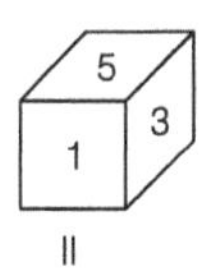

(a) 1 (b) 5
(c) 3 (d) 2

Solution (a) In this problem, common digit 3 is at different faces.
Writing the digits of position I, (clockwise)
Writing the digits of position II, (clockwise)
Clearly, 6 and 1 are opposite to each other

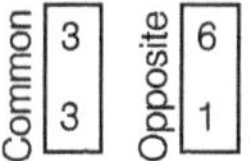

CASE IV When two digits are common in both the positions as follows

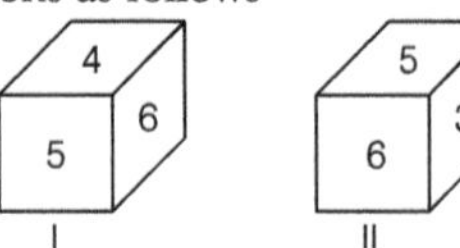

In this case,

(i) There is a probability of two digits on the faces opposite to the faces having common digits which are invisible.

(ii) Uncommon digits in each dice are opposite to each other.

Hence, for the figures, given in the Case IV, the following conditions will be true

1 and 5/6 are opposite faces.
2 and 5/6 are opposite faces.
3 and 4 are opposite faces.
6 and 1/2 are opposite faces.

***Ex* 06** In the following question the two positions of a single dice are given. Find the digit on the face which is opposite to the face having digit 2.

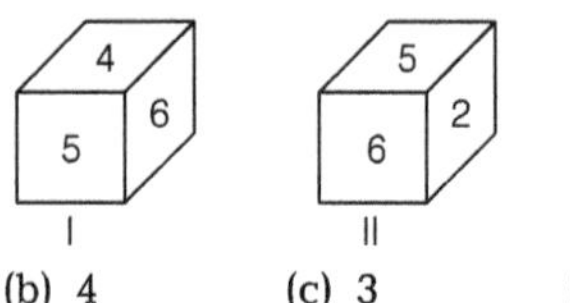

(a) 6 (b) 4 (c) 3 (d) 1

***Solution* (b)** As in this case, 5 and 6 are common digits while 4 and 2 are uncommon. As the rule given in case IV, here uncommon digits will be opposite to each other. Hence, 4 will definitely be opposite to digit 2.

C. When Three or Four Positions of a Single Dice are Given

In this case, first of all, position of that dice is considered which shows the particular digit about which the question is asked and at the same time any of the remaining positions of the dice is taken to get two positions of the same dice. Finally the given question is solved by applying two position rules.

The following example will give a better idea about solving the problems under this category.

***Ex* 07** In the following question, three positions of the same dice are given. What will be the digit on the face opposite to the face having digit 1?

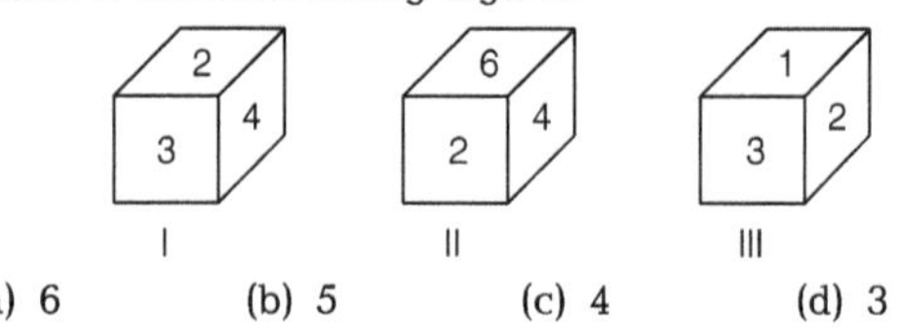

(a) 6 (b) 5 (c) 4 (d) 3

***Solution* (c)** In the given question, the correct solution can be found out by two methods.

Method I

Taking positions I and III, 2 and 3 are common.
So, 4 will be opposite to 1. (from case IV)

Method II

Taking positions II and III, only one digit i.e. 2 is common.
Now, writing digits of dice position II (clockwise)
writing digits of dice position III (clockwise)

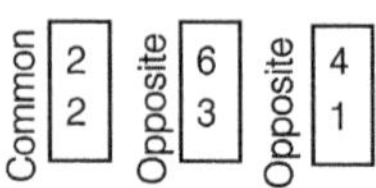

Clearly, 4 will be opposite to 1.

Surfaces of Unfolded Dice

In an unfolded dice all six faces of the dice are shown. The following figure is an unfolded form of a dice.

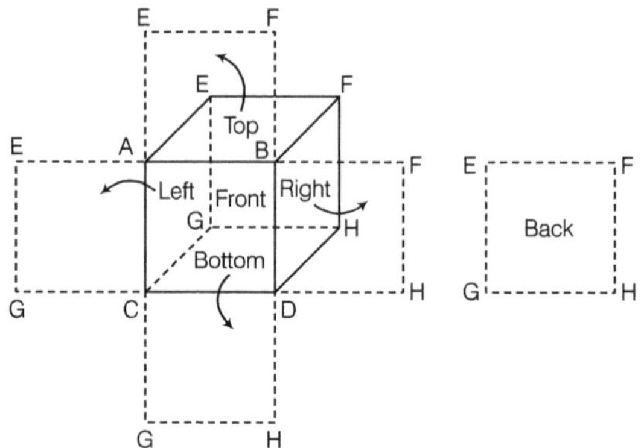

This dice has been unfolded by supposing front as base. The unfolded form of the dice looks like as the figure given below

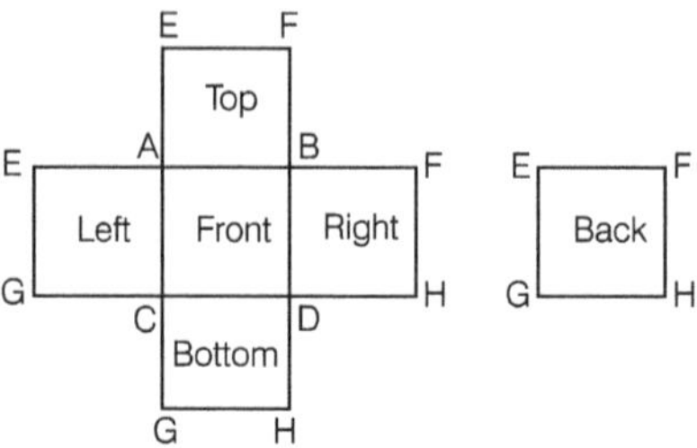

The back face (the face opposite to front face) to be shown separately, can be added to remaining four faces as each face is attached to four other faces. Except front face, the back face is also attached to four other faces.

If the unfolded form of a dice attached with the back face has to be presented, then following four presentations can be possible

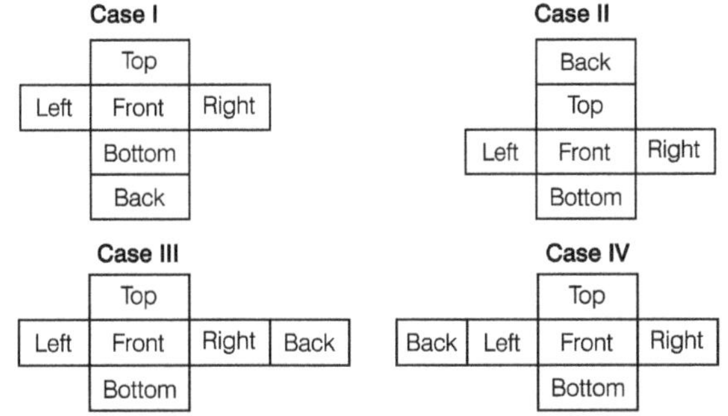

Opposite Faces of Unfolded Dice

- Top and bottom faces are opposite to each other.
- Left and right faces are opposite to each other.
- Front and back faces are opposite to each other.

If the top, bottom, left, right, front and back faces of a dice are denoted by letters/digits/symbols then opposite faces are as below

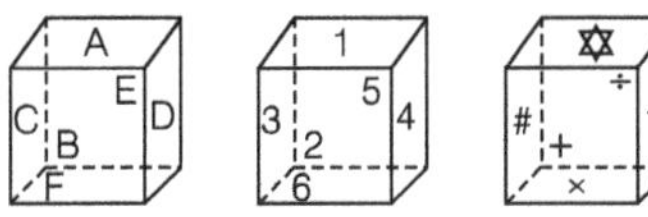

In the form of words		In the form of letters		In the form of digits		In the form of symbols	
Face	Opposite face	Face	Opposite face	Face	Opposite face	Face	Opposite face
Top	Bottom	A	F	1	6	✡	×
Bottom	Top	F	A	6	1	×	✡
Front	Back	B	E	2	5	+	÷
Back	Front	E	B	5	2	÷	+
Left	Right	C	D	3	4	#	−
Right	Left	D	C	4	3	−	#

The unfolded form of above letters/digits/symbols with respect to the unfolded patterns of dice can be shown as

CASE I

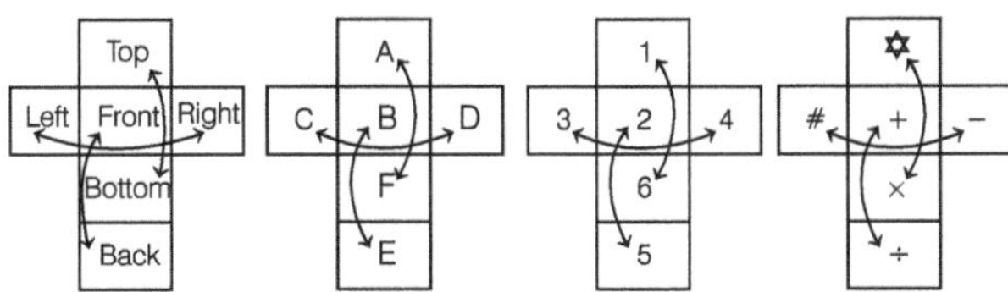

CASE II

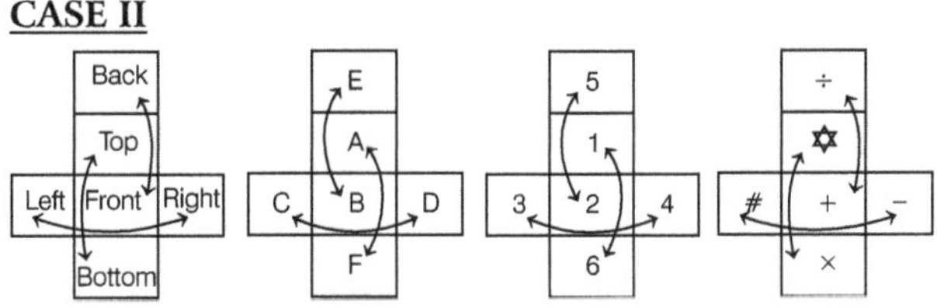

CASE III

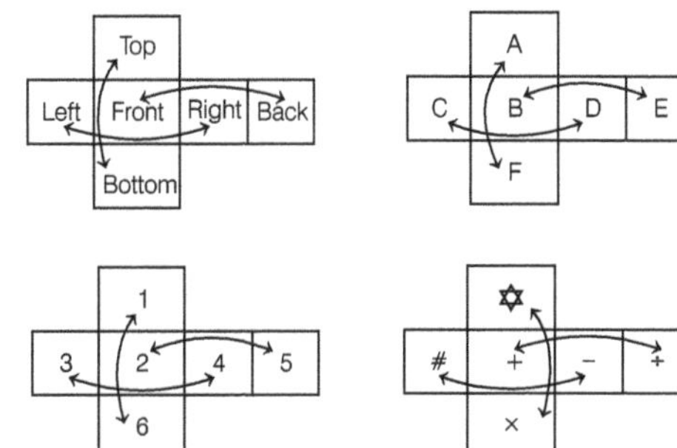

CASE IV

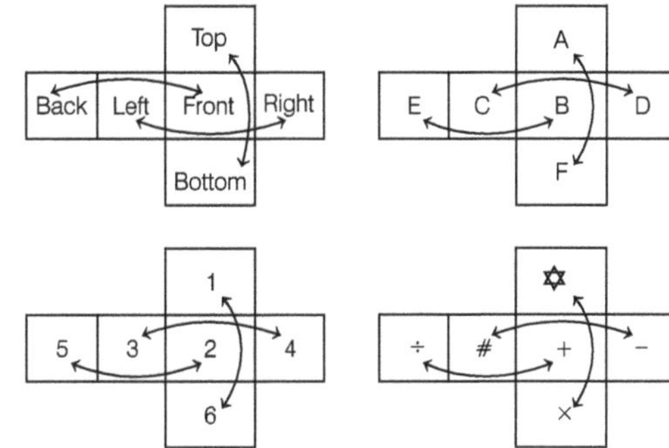

How to Mark Unfolded Faces with Digits?

If the unfolded faces of any dice is marked with digits/numbers, then any question based on dice can be solved very easily. Two positions of a dice are given below. With the help of these positions of the dice, the unfolded faces have been marked by the digits.

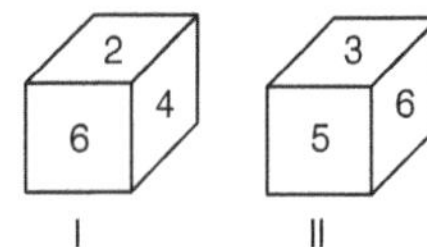

Note *Atleast two positions of a dice must be given to fill the unfolded faces.*

Now, we will form the following unfolded figure with the help of the mentioned positions of dice.

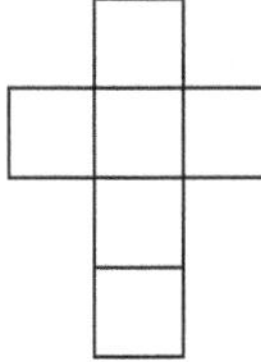

Now, the common digit (6) in both the positions will be written at the second face from the top which is between left and right faces.

Let us see

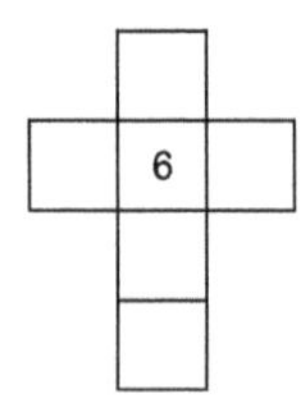

Now, going anti-clockwise direction from the common digit 6 of position I, we will get digit '4' first and after that, we will get digit 2.

Let us see

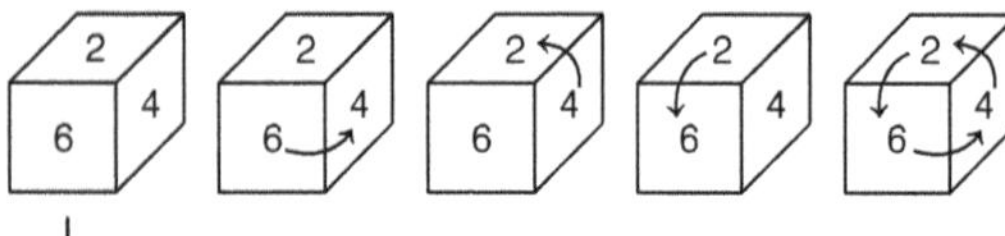

At the unfolded faces, 4 and 2 will be written in the following way

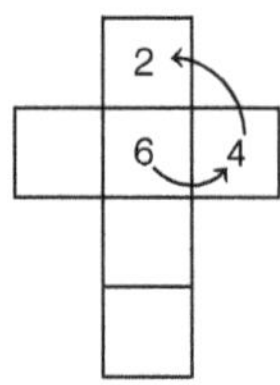

Again, going towards anti-clockwise direction from the common digit 6 of position II, we will get digit 3 first and after that we will get digit 5.

Let us see

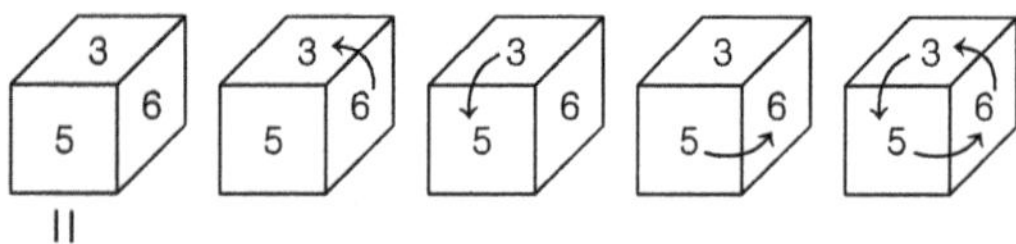

At the unfolded faces, 3 and 5 will be written in the following way

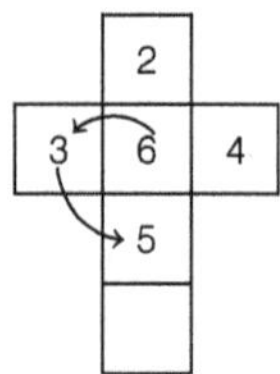

Now, the remaining blank face is filled up with the hidden digit 1 and now all the unfolded faces will look like as shown below

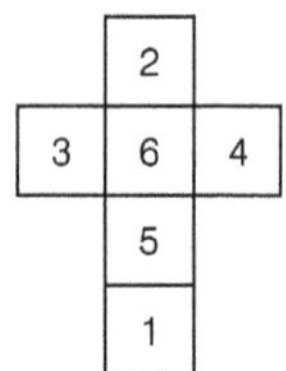

Some unfolded patterns of a dice are given below

Unfolded Faces	Opposite Faces
	1 and 6 are opposite to each other 2 and 5 are opposite to each other 3 and 4 are opposite to each other
	1 and 6 are opposite to each other 2 and 5 are opposite to each other 3 and 4 are opposite to each other
	1 and 6 are opposite to each other 2 and 5 are opposite to each other 3 and 4 are opposite to each other
	1 and 6 are opposite to each other 2 and 5 are opposite to each other 3 and 4 are opposite to each other
	1 and 6 are opposite to each other 2 and 5 are opposite to each other + − = × and 3 are opposite to each other
	1 and 6 are opposite to each other 2 and 5 are opposite to each other 3 and − + × = are opposite to each other
	1 and 6 are opposite to each other 2 and 5 are opposite to each other = + and − × are opposite to each other
	1 and 6 are opposite to each other 2 and 5 are opposite to each other 3 and + − are opposite to each other

Methods to Find Digits/Dots/Figures/ Symbols at the Blank Face

Basically, there are two methods :
1. Right angle method
2. Anti-clockwise method

The two methods mentioned above can be understood by the given example;

e.g. In the following example, three positions of a single dice are given below.

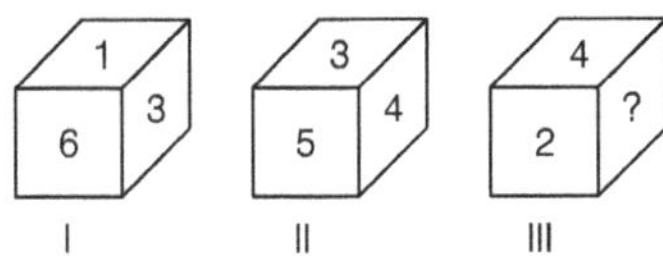

To find (?), firstly we take positions I and II of the given dice as these two positions have a common digit 3.
Now, the unfolded figure will be as shown below

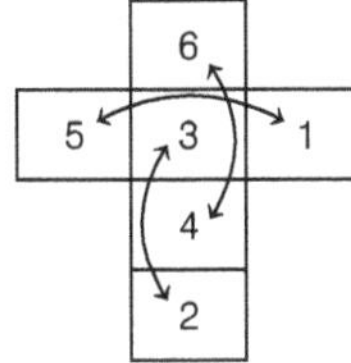

From the above figure, it is clear that,

1 and 5 are opposite faces.
2 and 3 are opposite faces.
4 and 6 are opposite faces.

1. Right Angle Method

Face having digit 1 in the unfolded figure is pushed beside the face having digit 2 in the following way

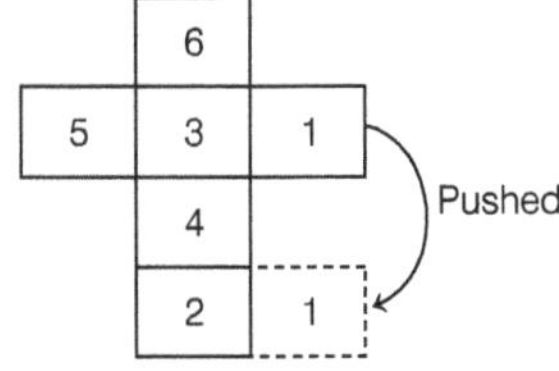

Now, compare the position III with right angle and unfolded figure obtained after pushing,

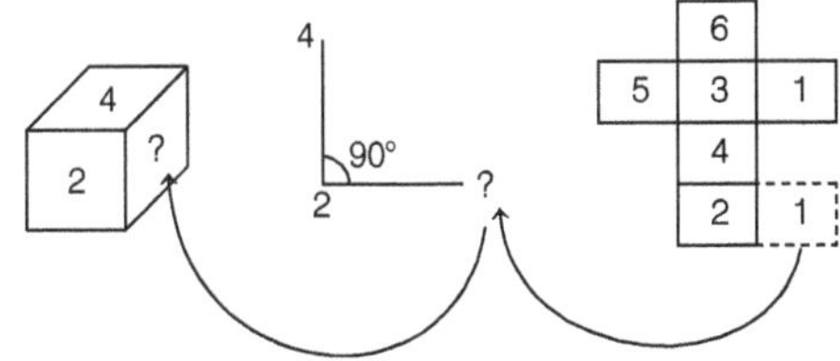

∴ ? = 1

How to Push Unfolded Faces?

Consider the following unfolded figure

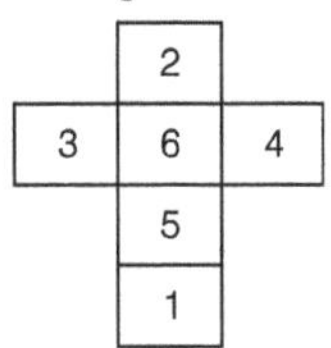

- Now, faces can be pushed as below

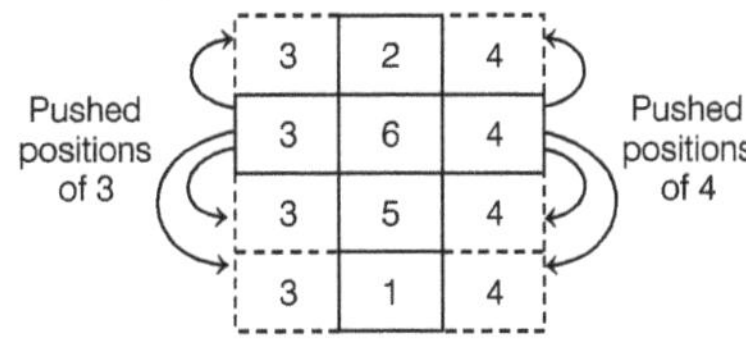

As any face of a dice is attached with other four faces, therefore any face can be pushed towards its adjacent faces. For the faces having digits 3 and 4, the faces having digits 2, 6, 5 and 1 are adjacent faces.

- Similarly, faces having digits 2 and 5 can be pushed as below

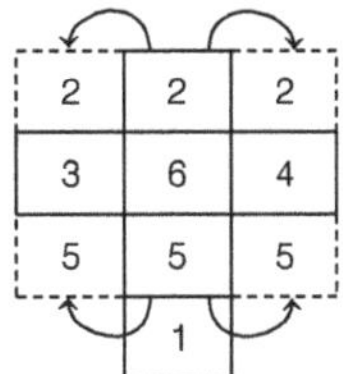

- Again, face having digit 1 can be pushed as given below

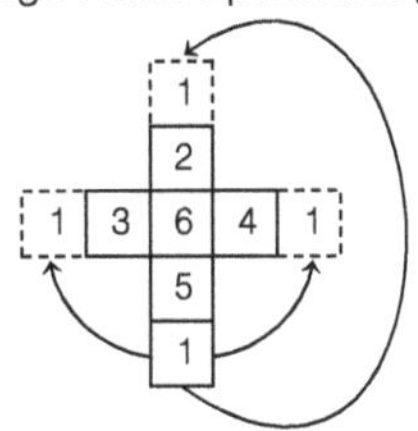

2. Anti-clockwise Method

Compare position III of a dice with unfolded figure obtained by pushing and go anti-clockwise from the face having digit 2 as shown in figures given below

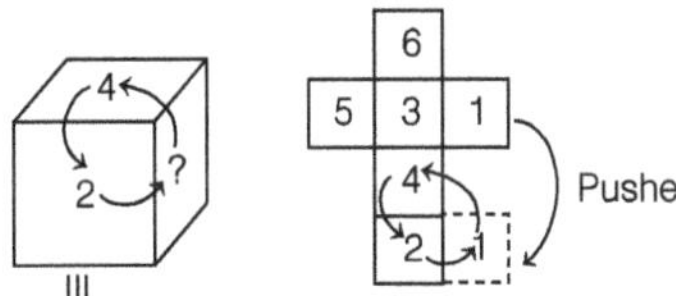

From the above figures

Position III of dice	2	?	4
Pushed unfolded figure	2	1	4

∴ ? = 1

Different types of questions asked from this chapter are as follows

TYPE 01

Finding Digit/Dot /Letter /Colour on the Opposite Face of Any Particular Face

In this type of questions, figure(s) of dice is/are given and the candidates are asked about the opposite digit/dot/letter/colour of a particular face.

***Ex* 08** Find the digit at the face opposite to the face having digit 6 in the given dice.

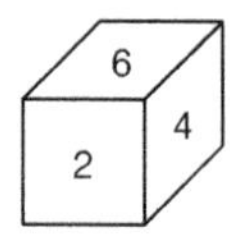

(a) 1 (b) 3 (c) 5 (d) 1/3

Solution (a) According to the question,

$$6+2=8,\ 2+4=6,\ 4+6=10$$

Here, the sum of digits on adjacent faces is not 7.

So, the given dice is a standard dice.

∴ Digit opposite to 6 is 1. [∵ 6 + 1 = 7]

***Ex* 09** In the following question, two positions of a single dice are given. Find the digit at the face opposite to the face having digit 1.

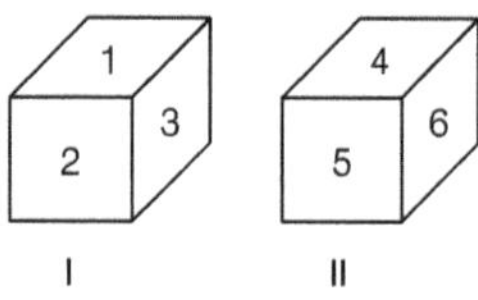

(a) 4 (b) 5
(c) 6 (d) 4/5/6

Solution (d) As in position I, 1 is at the top and 2 and 3 are the adjacent faces of 1, also there is no any common digit in positions I and II. Hence, 1 may have any one of the digits given in position II at its opposite face. It means 1 may have 4 or 5 or 6 at its opposite face.

***Ex* 10** In the following question, two positions of a single dice are given. Find the number of dots at the face opposite to the face having 3 dots.

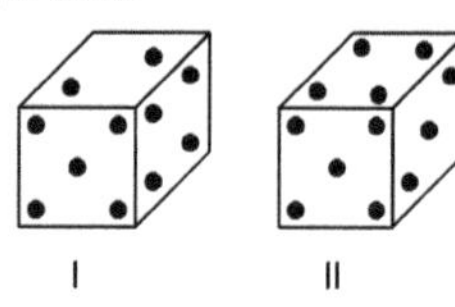

(a) 1 (b) 2
(c) 5 (d) 6

Solution (b) Common dots in positions I and II = 4 and 5

Hence uncommon digits will be opposite to each other.

∴ Face opposite to the face having 3 dots
= Face having 2 dots

***Ex* 11** On the basis of the given two positions of single dice, find the letter at the face opposite to the face having letter A.

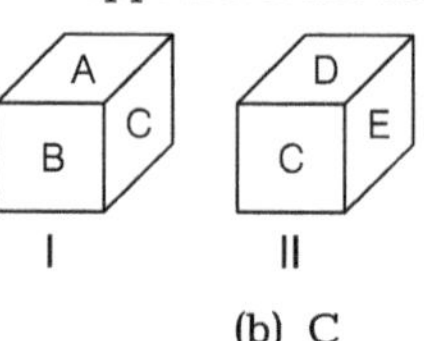

(a) B (b) C
(c) E (d) D

Solution (c) Common letter = C (on different faces)

From position I, (clockwise)

From position II, (clockwise)

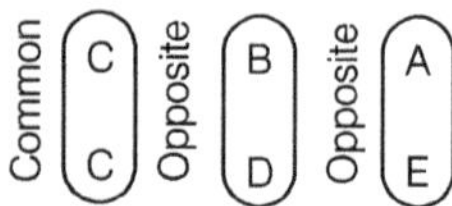

Clearly, E is opposite to A.

***Ex* 12** Six faces of a block have been painted with green, yellow, red, black, pink and white. Two positions of this block are given below. If the pink colour be at the top, then which colour will be at the bottom? « MAT 2009

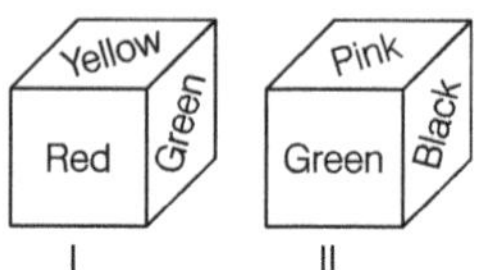

(a) Blue (b) Green
(c) Yellow (d) Red

Solution (d) From both the positions I and II,

Common colour = green (at different faces)

From position I, (clockwise),

From position II, (clockwise),

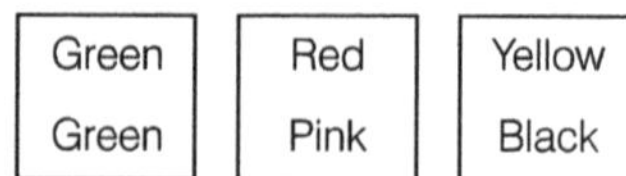

Clearly, red colour is opposite to pink. It means red will be at the bottom, if pink is at the top.

***Ex* 13** Two positions of a cube are shown below. What will come at the face opposite to the face having '&' ?
« SSC CPO 2017

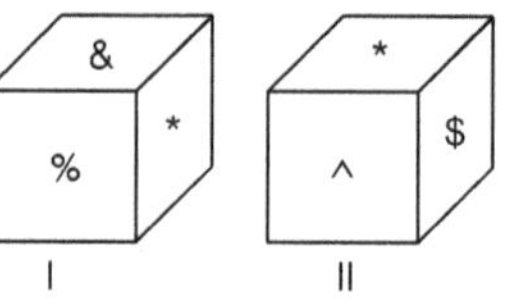

(a) ∧ (b) %
(c) $ (d) None of these

Solution (a) From both the positions I and II,
Common symbol = * (on different faces)
From position I, (clockwise)
From position II, (clockwise)

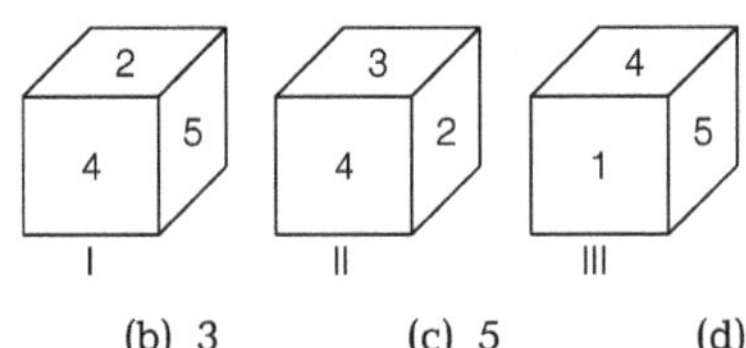

Clearly, '^' is opposite to '&'.

Ex 14 **From the given three positions of a single dice, find the digit at the face opposite to the face having digit 4.** « SSC CGL 2008

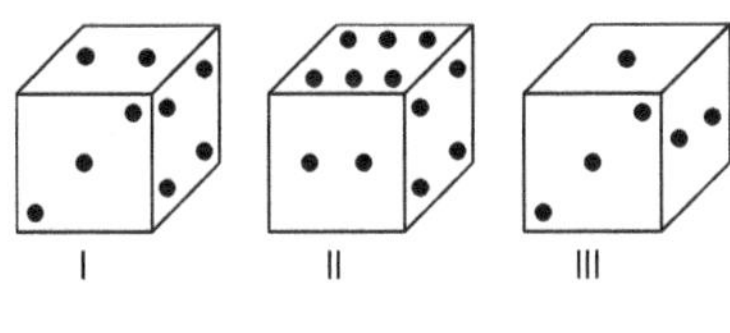

(a) 1 (b) 3 (c) 5 (d) 6

Solution (d) From all the three positions of the dice, adjacent faces of 4 = 1, 2, 3 and 5.

Remaining digit = 6

∴ It is clear that, the digit opposite to 4 is 6.

Ex 15 **From the given three positions of a single dice, find the number of dots at the face opposite to the face having 3 dots.**

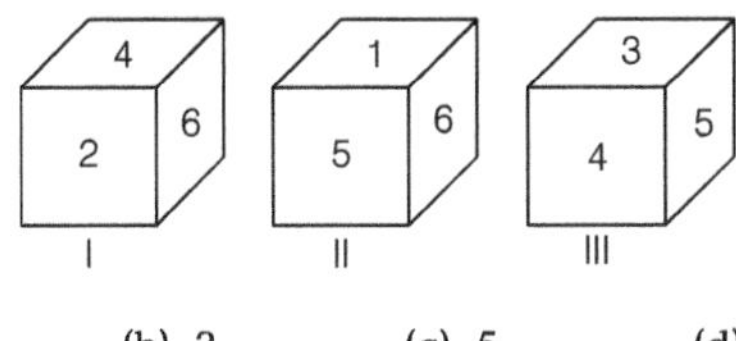

(a) 2 (b) 4 (c) 5 (d) 6

Solution (d) From positions I and II, common dots = 2 and 4 (at the common right face)

So, the face opposite to face having 3 dots will be the face having 6 dots.

Ex 16 **Three different positions of a dice are shown below. Find the number opposite to '2'.** « SSC CPO 2019

(a) 1 (b) 3 (c) 5 (d) 6

Solution (c) From figure second and third, adjacent numbers of 5 are 1, 6, 4 and 3. So, the remaining number 2 is opposite to 5.

Ex 17 **Four positions of a dice are given below. Which letter will be opposite to D?** « SSC CGL 2013

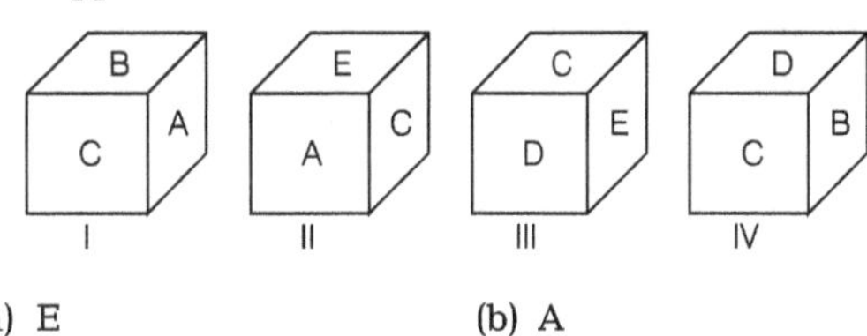

(a) E (b) A
(c) B (d) C

Solution (b) From figures I and III, dice can be shown as

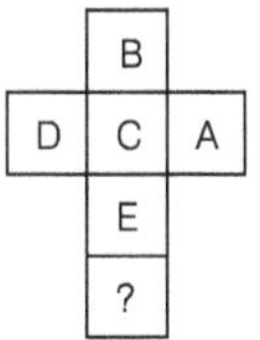

So, from the unfolded dice, it is clear that the letter opposite to D is A.

Ex 18 **From the given four positions of a single dice, find the number of dots at the face opposite to the face having 2 dots.** « Delhi Police MTS 2018

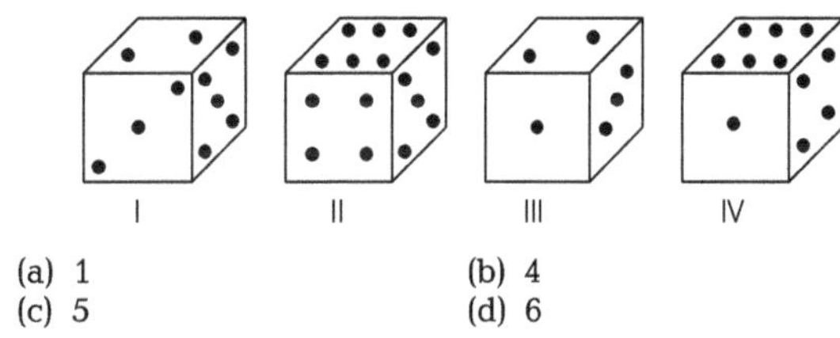

(a) 1 (b) 4
(c) 5 (d) 6

Solution (d) From positions I and II,
Common dots = 5 (at the same (Right) face)

So, face opposite to the face having 2 dots will be the face having 6 dots.

Ex 19 **From the given four positions of a single dice, find the colour at the face opposite to the face having red colour.**

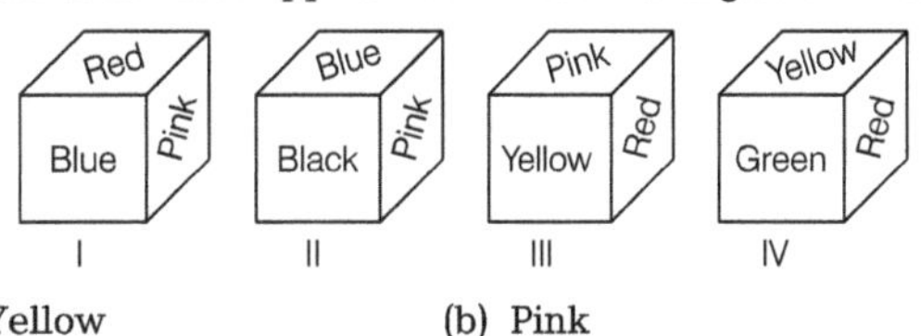

(a) Yellow (b) Pink
(c) Green (d) Black

Solution (d) From the given four positions of a single block, faces adjacent to face having red colour = blue, pink, yellow, green

Clearly, black is opposite to red.

Practice / CORNER 15.1

1. Find the digit at the face opposite to the face having digit 2 in the dice given below.

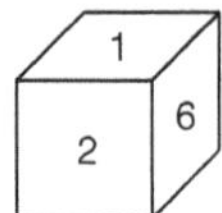

(a) 3/4 (b) 3/5 (c) 4/5 (d) 3/4/5

2. Find the digit at the face opposite to the face having digit 1 in the given dice. « UP B.Ed. 2011

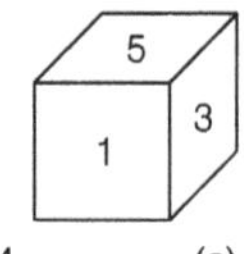

(a) 2 (b) 4 (c) 6 (d) 3

3. Find the digit at the face opposite to the face having digit 3 in the given dice. « UP B.Ed. 2012

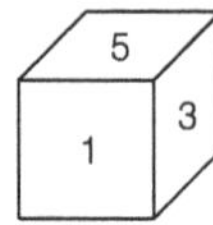

(a) 2 (b) 4 (c) 6 (d) 3

4. Find the digit at the face opposite to the face having digit 5 in the given dice. « MAT 2010

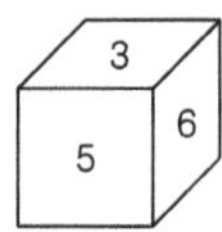

(a) 1 (b) 2
(c) 1/4 (d) 1/2/4

5. Find the digit at the face opposite to the face having digit 4 in the given dice. « UP B.Ed. 2012

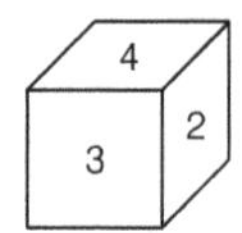

(a) 1 (b) 5 (c) 6 (d) 1/5/6

6. Where is the invisible number in the two positions of the same cube? « SSC CGL 2008

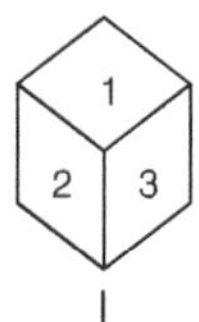

(a) Opposite of 2 (b) Opposite of 3
(c) Opposite of 4 (d) Opposite of 6

7. Which number will appear on the face opposite to 1? « SSC 10+2 2012

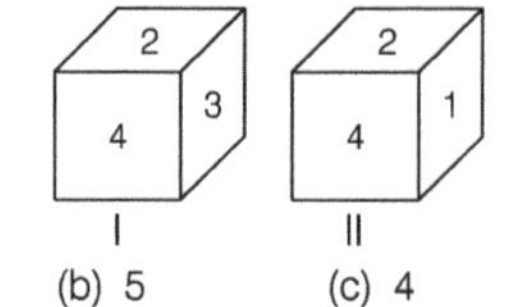

(a) 6 (b) 5 (c) 4 (d) 3

8. From the given two positions of a single dice, find the digit at the face opposite to the face having digit 4. « UP B.Ed. 2012

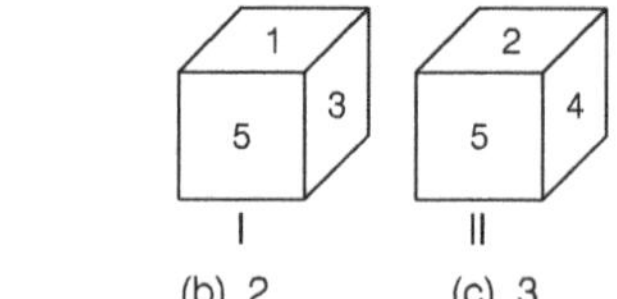

(a) 1 (b) 2 (c) 3 (d) 4

9. Two positions of a dice are shown. Find the number of the dots on the face opposite the face bearing 3 dots. « WBCS 2020

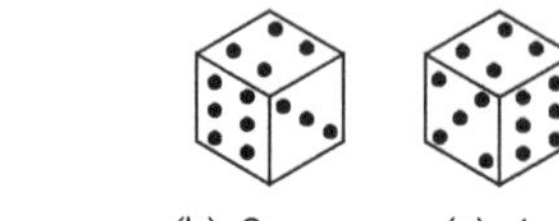

(a) 1 (b) 2 (c) 4 (d) 5

10. Two positions of a dice are shown. When 4 is at the bottom, what number will be on the top? « FCI (Watchman) 2018

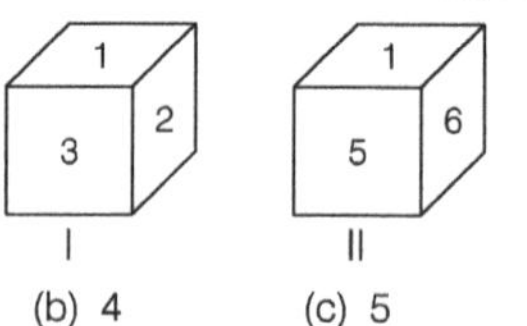

(a) 2 (b) 4 (c) 5 (d) 1

11. Two positions of a dice are shown as below. If the number 6 is exactly opposite to number 4, then which number is exactly opposite to number 3? « UPSSSC Combined Lower Subordinate Services 2019

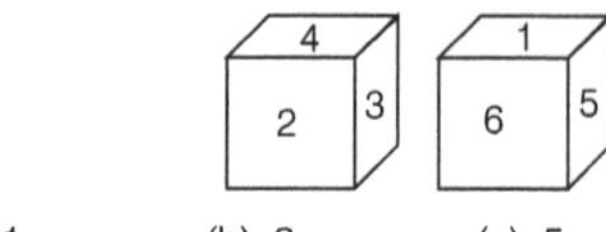

(a) 1 (b) 2 (c) 5 (d) 6

12. Two positions of a dice are shown below. If the top face has three dots, then how many dots are there at bottom face? « SSC CGL 2015

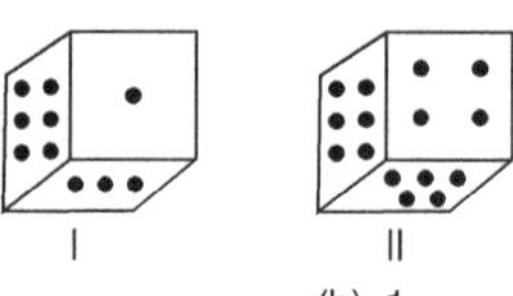

(a) 5 (b) 1
(c) 4 (d) 2

13. From the given two positions of a single dice, find the letter at the face opposite to the face having letter V. « SSC FCI 2008

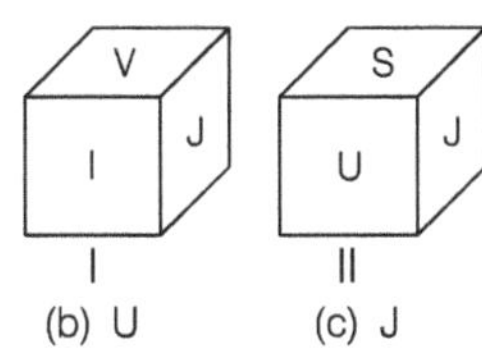

(a) S (b) U (c) J (d) I

14. Two positions of a dice are shown below. How many dots will appear on the face opposite to the face containing 5 dots? « Delhi Police MTS 2018

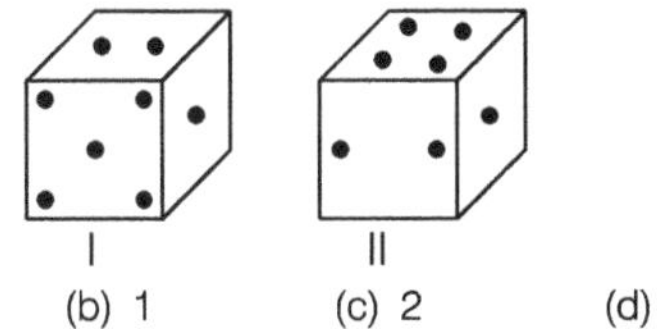

(a) 3 (b) 1 (c) 2 (d) 4

15. From the given two positions of a single dice, find the figure at the face opposite to the face having figure of ϕ. « MAT 2012

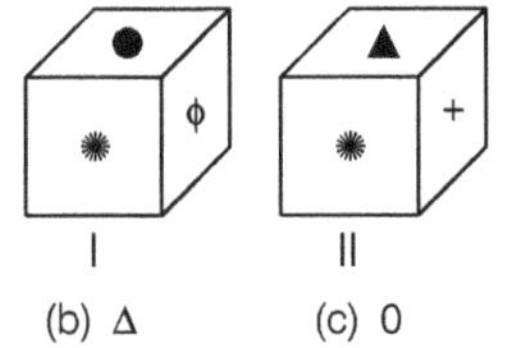

(a) ✺ (b) Δ (c) 0 (d) +

16. From the given two positions of a single dice, find the number of dots at the bottom face, if the top face has 3 dots. « MAT 2010

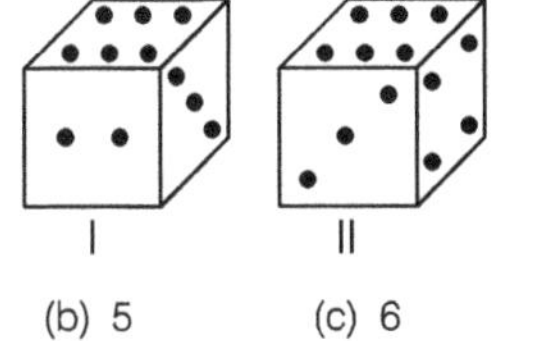

(a) 1 (b) 5 (c) 6 (d) 1/5

17. Six faces of a block have been painted with green, blue, white, yellow, black and pink. Two positions of this block is given below. If the black colour be at top, then which colour will be at the bottom?

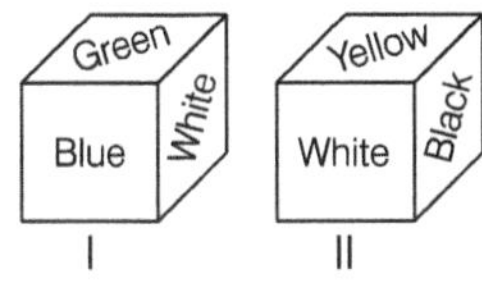

(a) Green (b) Blue (c) Yellow (d) White

18. From the given blocks when 10 is at the bottom, which number will be at the top? « SSC CGL 2013

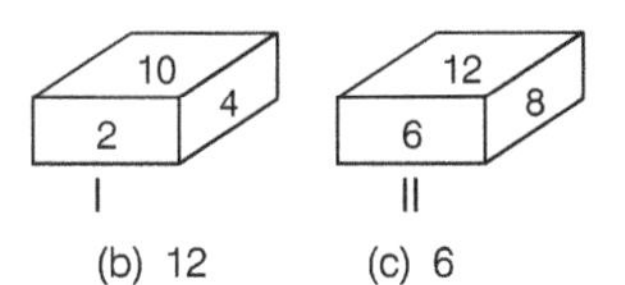

(a) 8 (b) 12 (c) 6 (d) 4

19. Three position of a cube are given. Based on them find out which number exists opposite of number 2 in a given cube? « SSC CPO 2017

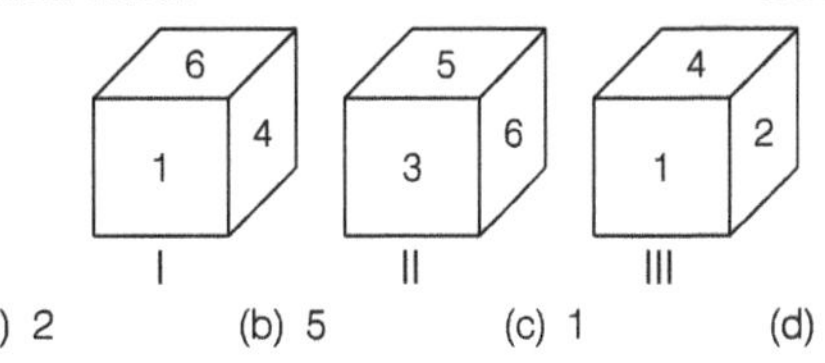

(a) 2 (b) 5 (c) 1 (d) 6

20. Three different positions of the same dice are shown below. Which number is on the face opposite the face with 1? « UPSSSC Combined Lower Subordinate Services 2019

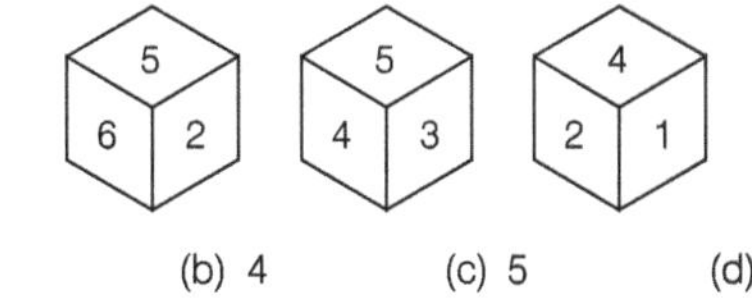

(a) 3 (b) 4 (c) 5 (d) 6

21. Three positions of a cube are shown below. What will come opposite to face containing 'α'? « SSC Delhi Police Constable 2017

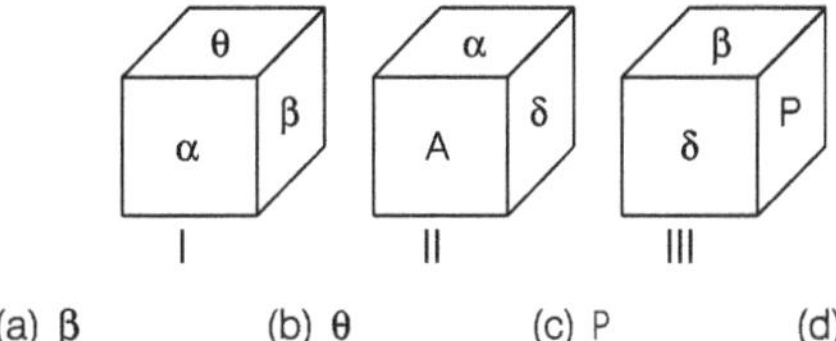

(a) β (b) θ (c) P (d) A

22. How many dots will appear on the surface opposite to the surface having 6 dots? « SSC CPO 2009

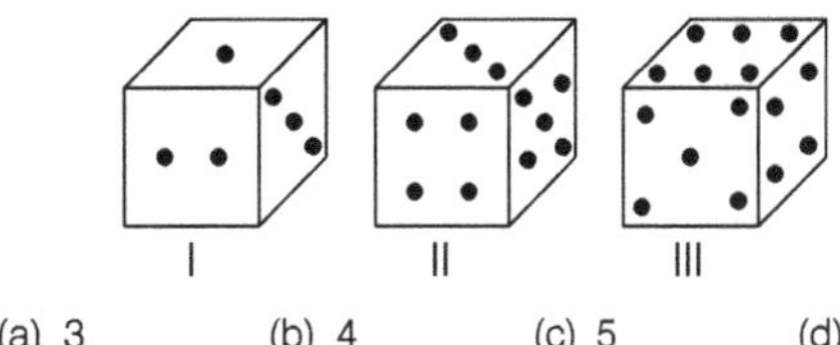

(a) 3 (b) 4 (c) 5 (d) 2

23. From the given three positions of a single dice, find the number of dots at the face opposite to the face having 1 dot.

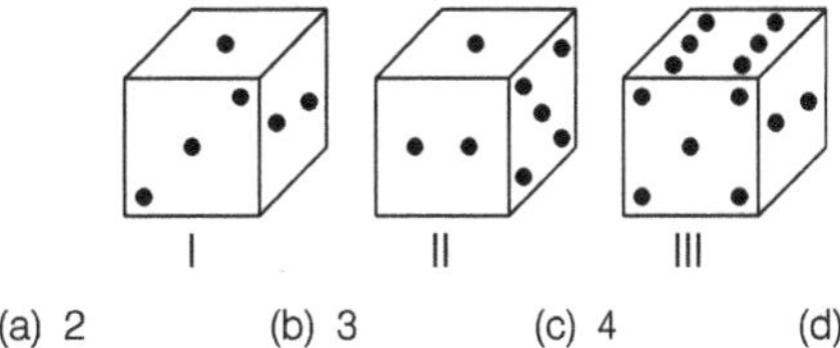

(a) 2 (b) 3 (c) 4 (d) 6

24. By using the following figures, find that if B is at the top, then which letter will be at the bottom? « CG Patwari 2019

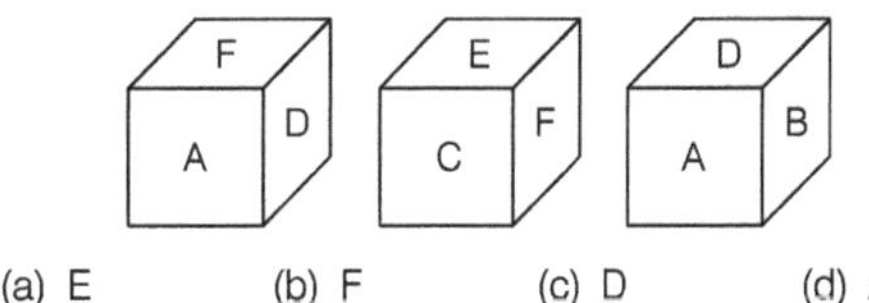

(a) E (b) F (c) D (d) A

25. Three views of a cube following a particular motion are given below. « UPSC CSAT 2012

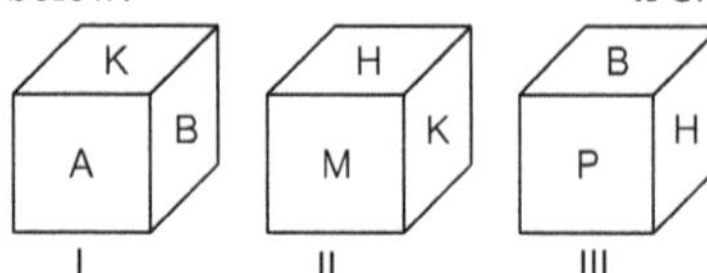

What is the letter opposite to A?

(a) H (b) P (c) B (d) M

26. From the given three positions of a single dice, find the letter at the face opposite to the face having letter Q. « MAT 2011

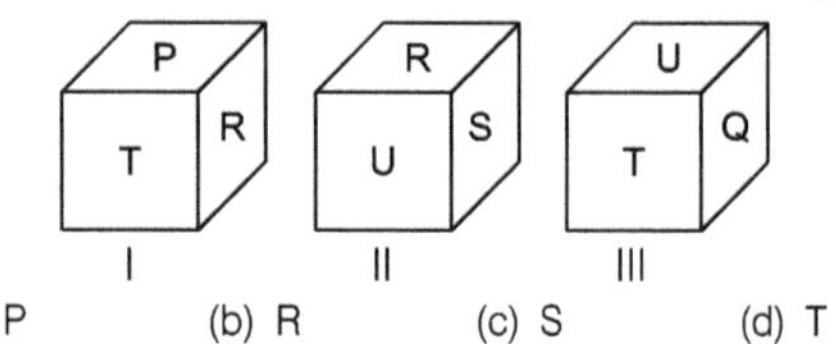

(a) P (b) R (c) S (d) T

27. From the given three positions of a single dice, find the number of dots at the face opposite to the face having 5 dots. « RRB ASM 2010

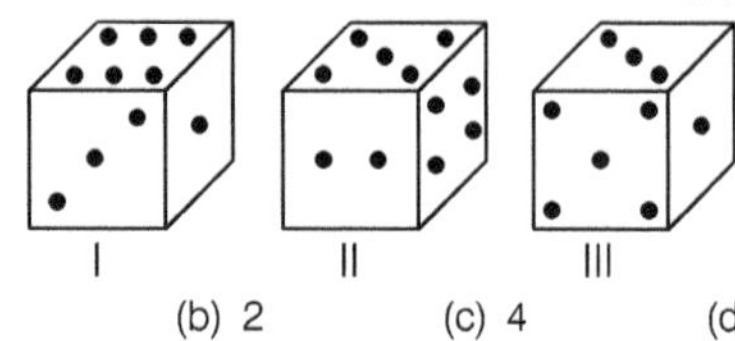

(a) 1 (b) 2 (c) 4 (d) 6

28. Four positions of a cube are shown below. Identify the number at the bottom when the number at the top is 6? « SSC CPO 2016

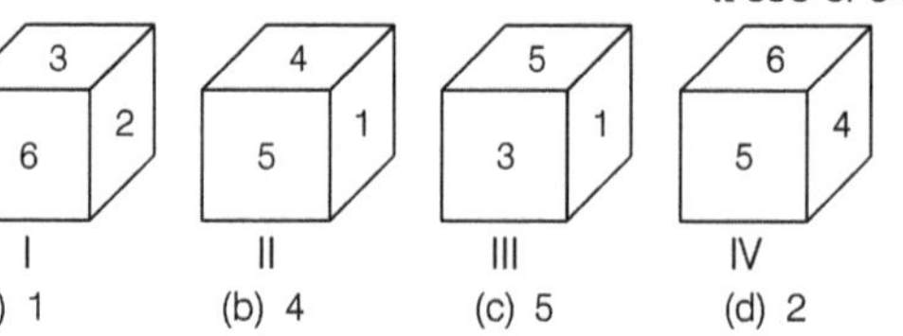

(a) 1 (b) 4 (c) 5 (d) 2

29. From the given four positions of a single dice, find the digit at the face opposite to the face having digit 6.

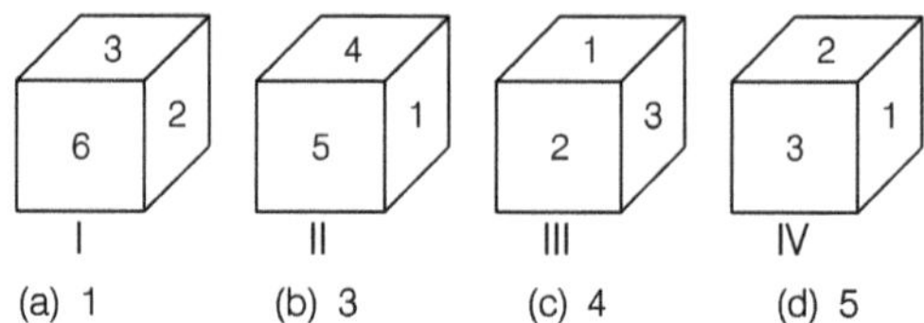

(a) 1 (b) 3 (c) 4 (d) 5

30. Four positions of a dice are shown below. Identify the number at the bottom if top is 2. « UPSSSC (AMIN) 2016

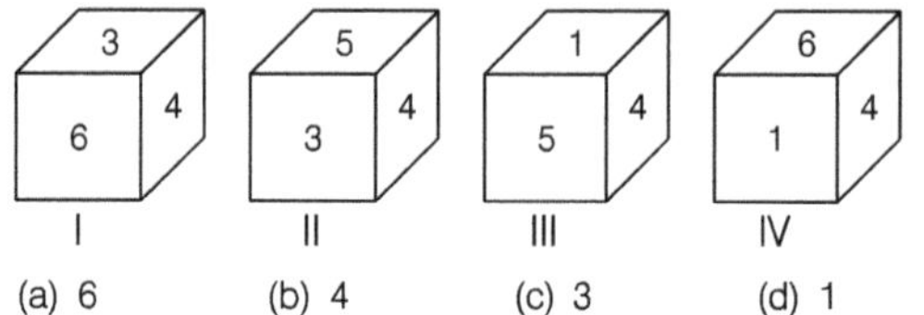

(a) 6 (b) 4 (c) 3 (d) 1

31. A dice is thrown four times and its different positions are shown below. What number is opposite to face showing 2? « SSC CPO 2013

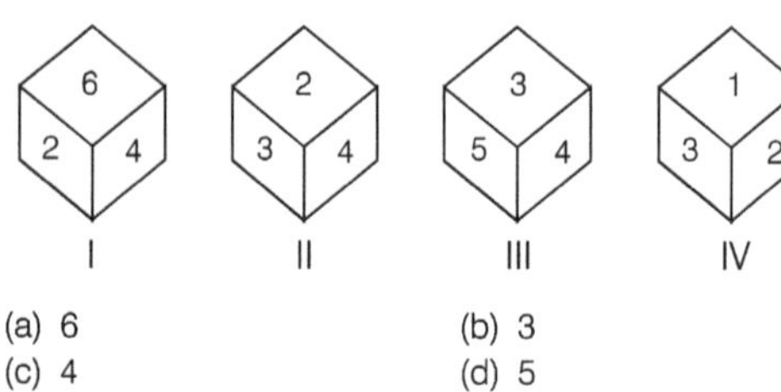

(a) 6 (b) 3
(c) 4 (d) 5

32. From the given four positions of a single dice, find the number of dots at the face opposite to the face having 1 dot.

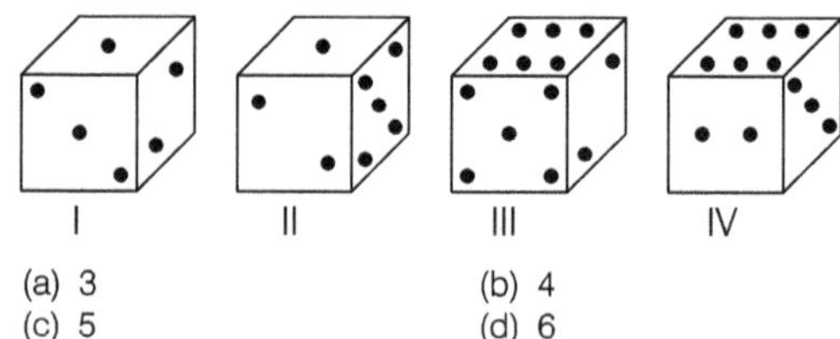

(a) 3 (b) 4
(c) 5 (d) 6

33. From the given four positions of a single dice, find the number of dots at the face opposite to the face having 3 dots.

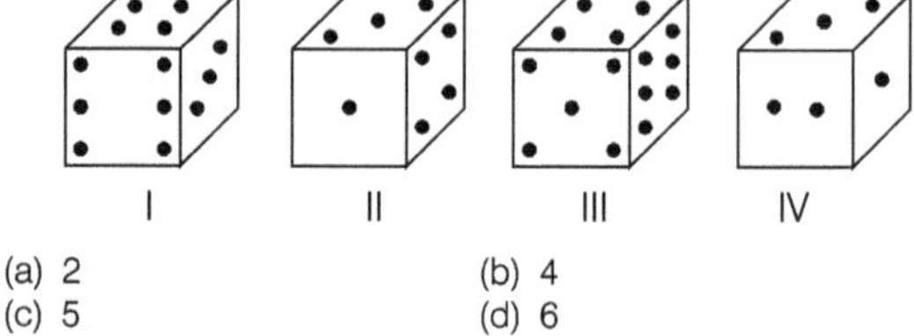

(a) 2 (b) 4
(c) 5 (d) 6

34. From the given four positions of a single dice, find the letter at the face opposite to the face having letter D.

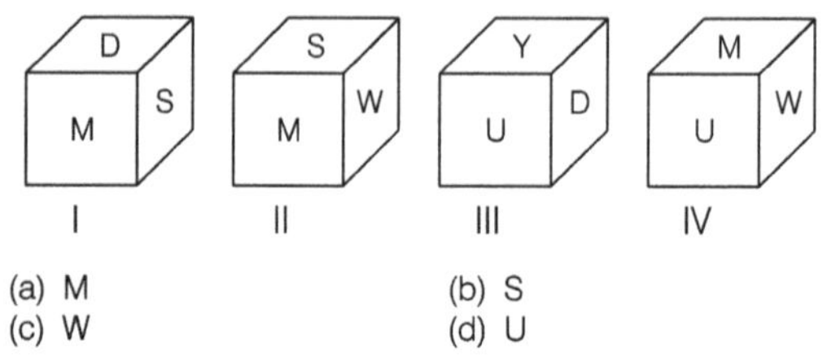

(a) M (b) S
(c) W (d) U

35. From the given four positions of a single dice, find the colour at the face opposite to the face having green colour. « SSC DEO 2008

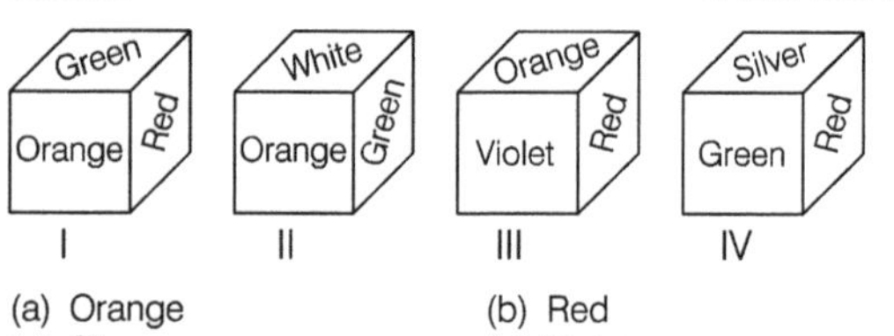

(a) Orange (b) Red
(c) Silver (d) Violet

36. A dice has numbers 1, 2, 3, 4, 5 and 6 on its faces. Four positions of dice are shown below. The number on the face opposite to the number 3, is « CG PSC 2013

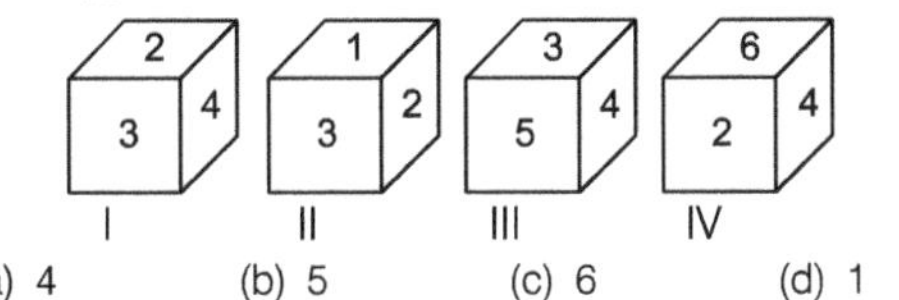

(a) 4 (b) 5 (c) 6 (d) 1 (e) 2

37. Four positions of the same dice are shown. Select the number that will be on the face opposite to the one shown '3'. « SSC CGL 2019

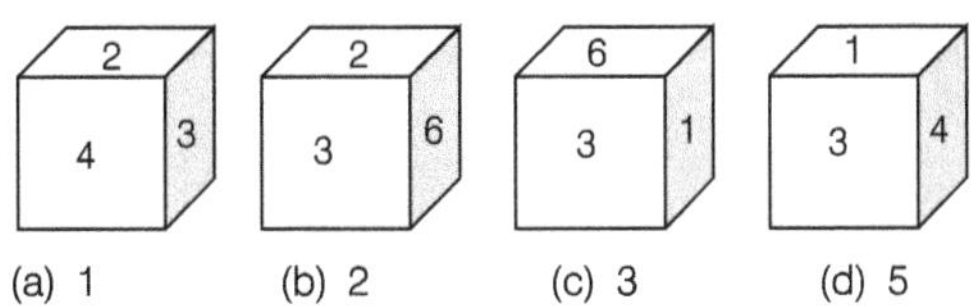

(a) 1 (b) 2 (c) 3 (d) 5

38. From the given four positions of a single dice, find the number of dots at the face opposite to the face having 4 dots. « SSC 10+2 2010

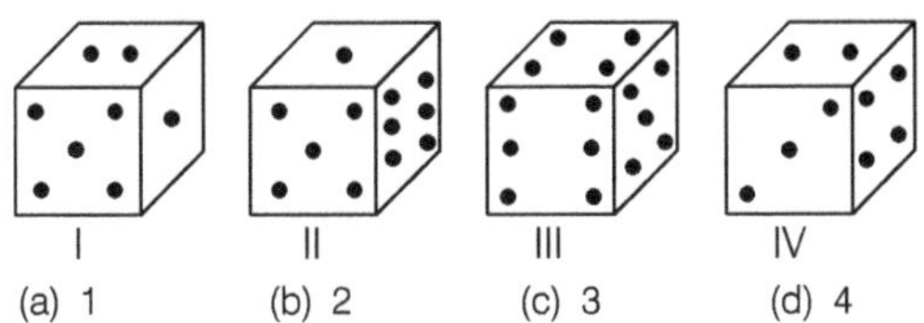

(a) 1 (b) 2 (c) 3 (d) 4

39. What is the letter opposite to 'e' in the following sequence of diagrams? « Chhattisgarh Revenue Inspector 2017

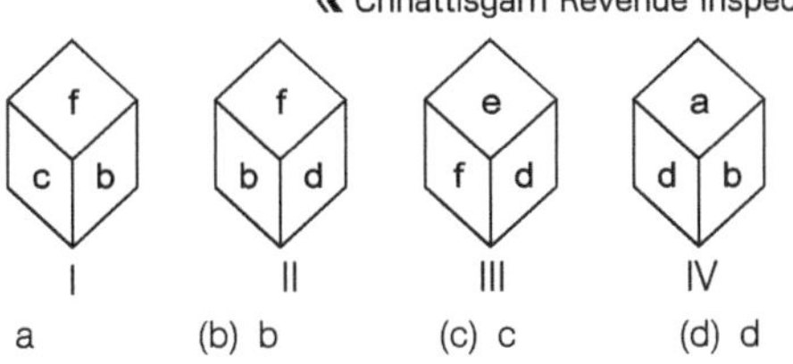

(a) a (b) b (c) c (d) d

40. Given below are 4 pictures of a cube

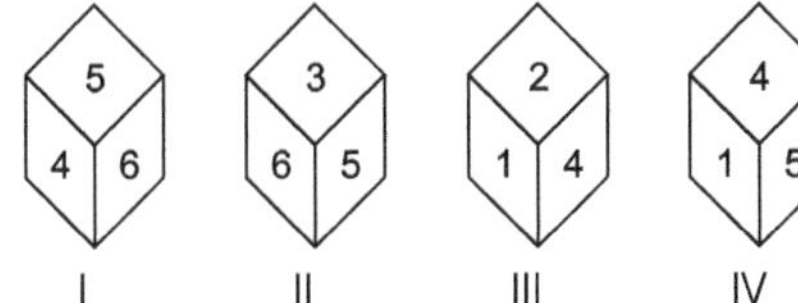

Which number is on the face opposite to 3? « MAT 2016, SNAP 2013

(a) 1 (b) 2 (c) 4 (d) 5

41. Four positions of a dice are given below. Find the digit which is opposite to 3? « SSC 10+2 2012

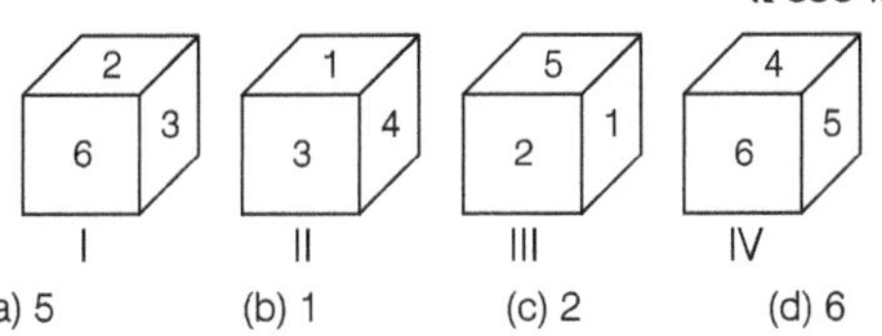

(a) 5 (b) 1 (c) 2 (d) 6

42. Four positions of dice are given below. Which letter will be opposite to D? « SSC MTS 2013

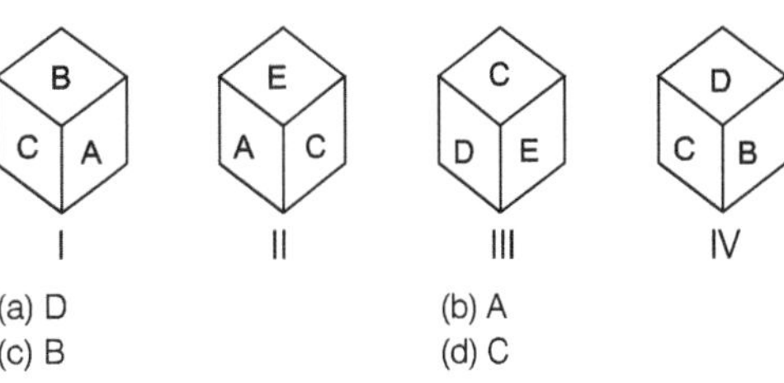

(a) D (b) A
(c) B (d) C

43. A cube has six numbers marked 1, 2, 3, 4,5 and 6 on its faces. Three views of the cube are shown below

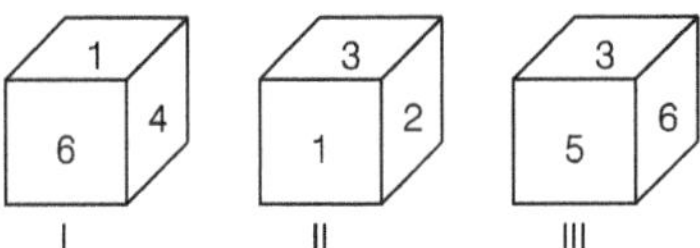

What possible numbers can exist on the two faces marked A and B, respectively? « UPSC CSAT 2013

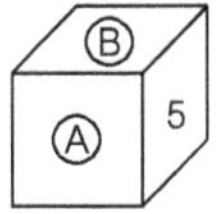

(a) 2 and 3 (b) 6 and 1
(c) 1 and 4 (d) 3 and 1

DIRECTIONS ~ (Q. Nos. 44 and 45) Rotated positions of a single solid are shown below. The various faces of the solid are marked with different symbols like dots, cross and line. Answer the questions that follow the given figures.

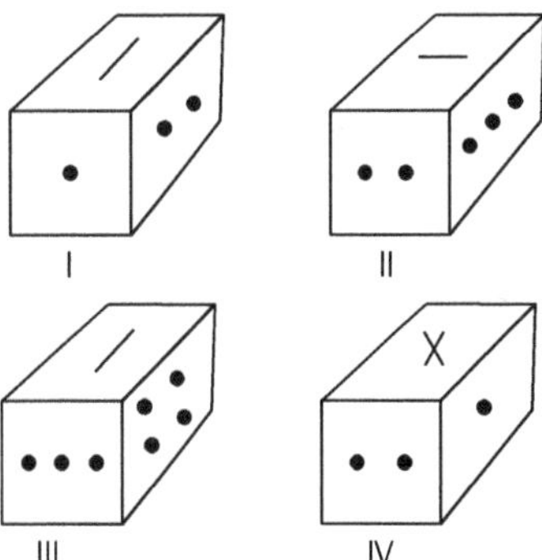

« UPSC Civil Services 2018

44. What is the symbol on the face opposite to that containing a single dot?

(a) Four dots
(b) Three dots
(c) Two dots
(d) Cross

45. What is the symbol on the face opposite to that containing two dots?

(a) Single dot (b) Three dots
(c) Four dots (d) Line

Answers WITH EXPLANATIONS

1. (*d*) According to the question,

$$1 + 2 = 3$$
$$2 + 6 = 8$$
$$\boxed{6 + 1} = 7$$

Clearly, it is not a standard dice.

∴ Digit at the opposite face of 2 = 3 or 4 or 5

2. (*c*) According to the question,

$$5 + 1 = 6$$
$$1 + 3 = 4$$
$$3 + 5 = 8$$

Clearly, it is a standard dice.

∴ Digit at the face opposite to 1 = 7 − 1 = 6

3. (*b*) According to the question,

$$5 + 1 = 6$$
$$1 + 3 = 4$$
$$3 + 5 = 8$$

Clearly, it is a standard dice.

∴ Digit at the face opposite to 3 = 7 − 3 = 4

4. (*b*) According to the question,

$$3 + 5 = 8$$
$$5 + 6 = 11$$
$$6 + 3 = 9$$

Clearly, it is a standard dice.

∴ Digit at the face opposite to 5 = 7 − 5 = 2

5. (*d*) According to the question,

$$\boxed{4 + 3} = 7$$
$$4 + 2 = 6$$
$$3 + 2 = 5$$

Clearly, it is not a standard dice.

∴ Digit opposite to 4 = 1 or 5 or 6

6. (*a*) The invisible number is 4 and it is opposite to the number 2.

	3	
6	2	1
	5	
	4	

7. (*d*) From positions I and II, common numbers are 2 and 4.
So, opposite side of 1 is 3.

8. (*c*) In both the positions, common digit 5 is at same face (front face).
So, digit 3 at the side face in position I will be opposite to the side face having digit 4 in position II.

9. (*d*) From the given positions, common dots 4 and 6. So, the face opposite to face bearing 3 dots will be the face bearing 5 dots.

10. (*d*) In positions I and II, 1 is at the top and 2, 3, 5 and 6 are the adjacent faces. So, 4 is opposite number of 1. Hence, when 4 is at the bottom, 1 will be on the top.

11. (*a*) According to the rule of dice, moving in clockwise direction

$$4 \longrightarrow \boxed{3} \longrightarrow 2$$
$$6 \longrightarrow \boxed{1} \longrightarrow 5$$

∴ '1' will be opposite to 3.

12. (*a*) In both the positions, 6 dots are common at the same (left) face. So, face having 5 dots will be opposite to the face having 3 dots.

13. (*a*) Common letter = J (at the same (right) face)
Clearly, S is opposite to V.

14. (*d*) From positions I and II,
Common dots = 1 and 2
Hence, face containing 5 dots will be opposite to the face containing 4 dots.

15. (*d*) From both the positions I and II,
Common figure = ✱ (at the same face)
Clearly, + is opposite to ϕ.

16. (*d*) From both the positions I and II,
Common dots = 3 and 6.
Hence, 1/5 dots will be opposite to 3 dots.
Clearly, 1/5 dots will be at the bottom face, if 3 dots are at the top face.

17. (*a*) From positions I and II, Common colour = White (at different faces)

From position I, (clockwise)	White	Blue	Green
From position II, (clockwise)	White	Yellow	Black

Clearly, green is opposite to black. It means green is at the bottom, if black is at the top.

18. (*b*) From the two views of blocks it is clear that when 10 is at the bottom, number 12 will be at the top.

19. (*d*) In positions I and III,
Common numbers = 1 and 4
∴ Number opposite to 2 = 6

20. (*c*) From the given positions, adjacent numbers of 5 are 6, 2, 4 and 3. So, the remaining number 1 is opposite to 5.

21. (*c*) In this problem, common symbol β is at different faces.

	common	opposite	opposite
Writing the symbols of position I, (clockwise)	β	α	θ
Writing the symbols of position III, (clockwise)	β	P	δ

Clearly, α and P are opposite to each other.

22. (*a*) From the figures II and III, it is clear that the two surfaces are common to both figures *i.e.*, 4 and 5.
So, the surfaces left contains 3 and 6 dots, which are opposite to each other.

23. (*d*) From positions II and III, Common dots = 2 and 5
So, the face opposite to the face having 1 dot will be the face having 6 dots.

24. (*b*) From figures first and third, common letters are A and D. So, if B is at the top, then F will be at the bottom.

25. (*a*) From positions I and III, Common letter = B

From position I, (clockwise)	B	A	K
From position III, (clockwise)	B	H	P

Clearly, A is opposite to H.

26. (*b*) From positions I and III,
Common letter = T (at the same face)
Clearly, R is opposite to Q.
Hence, option (b) is correct.

27. (*d*) From positions I and III,
Common dots = 1 and 3
Clearly, 6 dots is opposite to 5 dots.
Hence, option (d) is correct.

28. (*a*) From positions I and IV adjacent faces of 6 contain numbers = 3, 2, 5, 4
Hence, the number at the bottom when 6 is at the top = 1

29. (*a*) From positions I and III,
Common digits = 2 and 3
∴ Digit opposite to 6 = 1

30. (*b*) From positions first and third, adjacent faces of number 4 = 6, 3, 1 and 5
So, if 2 is at the top, then 4 will be at the bottom.

31. (*d*) It is quite clear from the positions I and IV that except 5, all numbers (6, 4, 3 and 1) are on adjacent faces of 2. Hence, 5 and 2 are opposite to each other.

32. (*d*) From positions II and III, two dots are at common face (right surface).
So, face opposite to the face having 1 dot will be the face having 6 dots.

33. (*c*) From positions I, II and IV,
Adjacent faces of the face having 3 dots = 1, 2, 4 and 6
So, face opposite to the face having 3 dots will be the face having 5 dots.

34. (*c*) From, positions I and II,
Common letters = M and S
Clearly, W is opposite to D.

35. (*d*) From the given four positions of a single dice, faces adjacent to face having green colour = Orange, red, white, silver
Clearly, violet is opposite to green.

36. (*c*) From positions I and IV,
Common digits = 2 and 4
Clearly, 3 is opposite to 6. Hence, option (c) is correct.

37. (*d*) From the given positions, adjacent numbers of 3 are 4, 2, 6 and 1. So, the remaining number 5 will be on the face opposite to the one showing 3.

38. (*a*) From positions I and IV,
Common dots = 2 (at the same face)
Clearly, 1 dot is opposite to 4 dots.

39. (*b*) In positions II and III,
Common letters = f and d
∴ Letter opposite to e = b

40. (*c*) From figures (I), (III) and (IV), we conclude that 5, 6, 1 and 2 lie adjacent to 4. Hence, 3 must lie opposite to 4 and *vice-versa*.

41. (*a*) From positions II and IV, common digit = 4
From position II (clockwise) 4 3 1
From position IV (clockwise) 4 5 6
So, number 3 is opposite to numbers 5.

42. (*b*) From positions I and IV,
Common letters = C and B
Clearly, D is opposite to A.

43. (*a*) From positions I and II, common letter = 1
From position I, (Clockwise) 1 4 6
From position II, (Clockwise) 1 3 2
Looking at the first two figures we see that 2 is opposite to 6 and 3 is opposite to 4. The third figure tells us that 5 is opposite to 1. Thus, the numbers A and B, which are adjacent to 5 could be any of the following four, 6 and 4, 4 and 2, 2 and 3, and 3 and 6. Out of these only 2 and 3 are given in a option, so (a) is the right answer.

44. (*b*) If we look at figures (I) and (II), we can observe that figure (II) is the result of rotating figure (I) clockwise, and thus single dot moves side and the three dots i.e. opposite of single dot face of cube comes to the visible side.

45. (*c*) Figure (III) is formed by rotating figure (II) clockwise, thus cube face with four dots which is opposite to two dots face, comes to the visible side. Hence, option (c) is correct answer.

TYPE 02

Questions Related to Unfolded Dice

In this type of questions, a figure of unfolded dice with design/symbols/signs/figure etc. is given and candidates are required to pick a dice (which can be formed with the given unfolded dice) out of the given options.

DIRECTIONS ~ (Example Nos. 20-25) *In the questions given below an unfolded dice is given in the left side while in the right side, four answer choices are given in the form of a a complete dice. You are required to select the correct answer choice which is formed by folding the unfolded dice.*

Ex 20

Question Figure **Answer Figures**

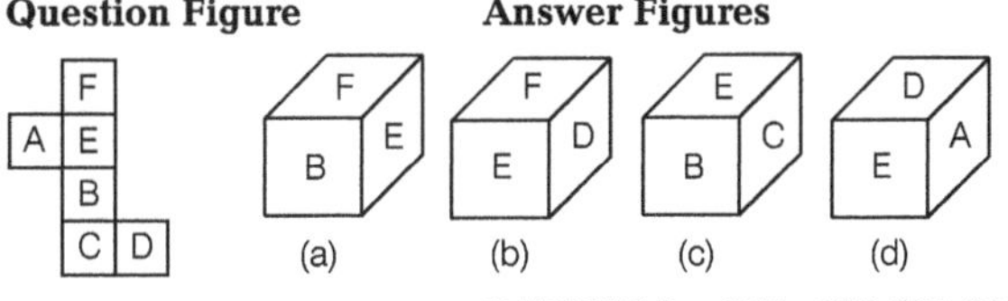

« UPSSSC Pre 2015 , SSC CGL 2013

Solution (b) According to the question,

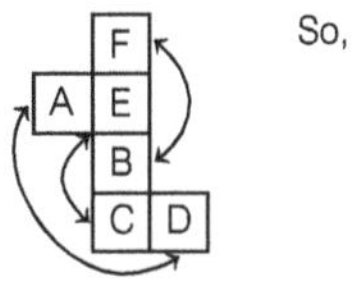

So, A is opposite to D

F is opposite to B

E is opposite to C

In figure (a), B and F are adjacent to each other, in figure (c), E and C are adjacent to each other and in figure (d), D and A are adjacent to each other. So, these cubes are not possible to be formed. Clearly, option (b) is correct answer because when unfolded cube will be folded, only the cube in figure (b) can be formed.

Ex 21

Question Figure **Answer Figures**

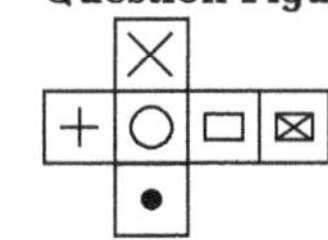

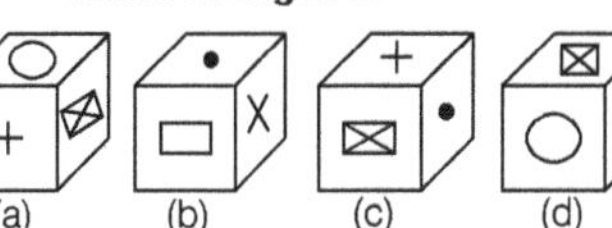

***Solution* (c)** According to the question,

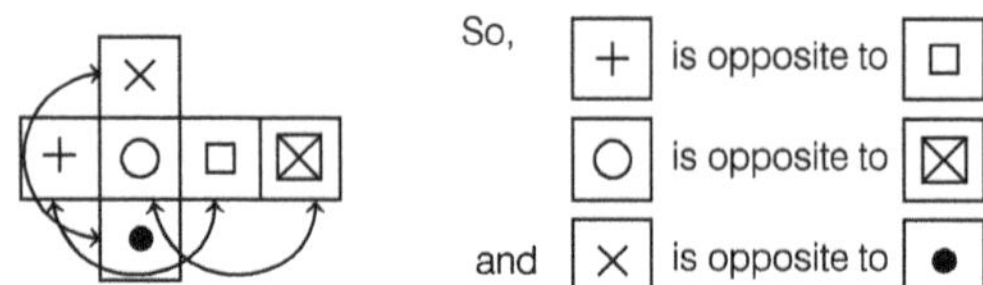

In figures (a) and (d), 'O' and ⊠ are shown adjacent to each other. In figure (b), '•' and 'x' are shown adjacent to each other. So, these cubes are not possile to be formed.

Hence, only the cube in figure (c) can be formed from the given question figure.

***Ex* 22 Question Figure** **Answer Figures**

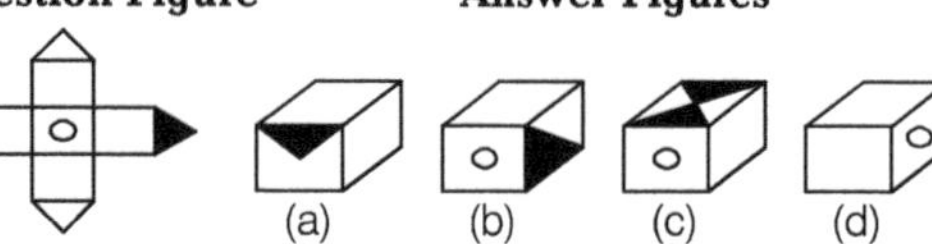

***Solution* (d)** According to the question,

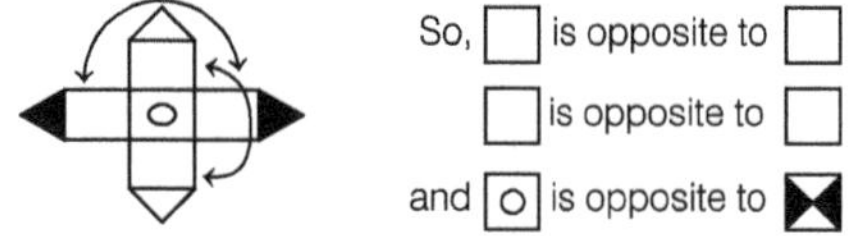

After the observation of unfolded figure, we find that option (d) is correct answer.

***Ex* 23 Question Figure** **Answer Figures**

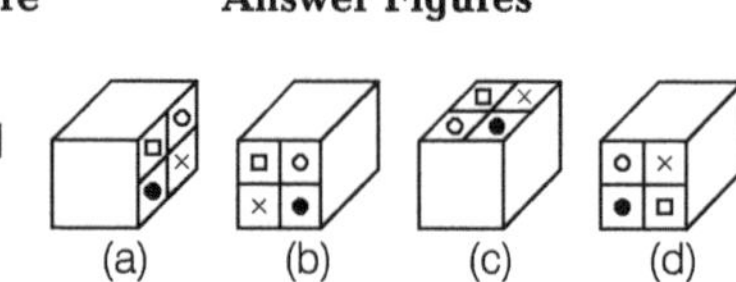

***Solution* (a)** According to the figure,

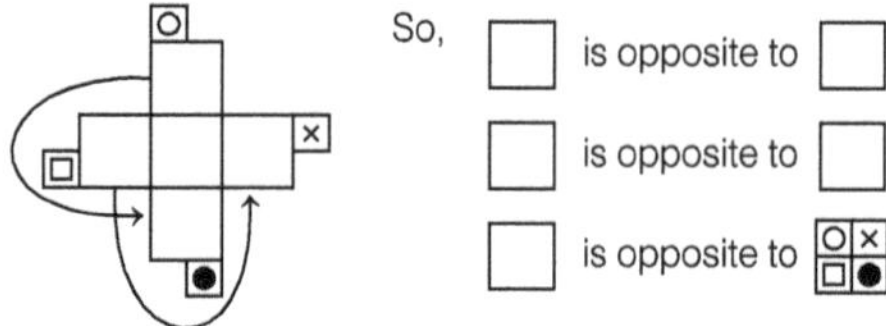

Hence, only option (a) is correct, which gives the exact sequence of symbols opposite to the blank face of cube.

***Ex* 24 Question Figure** **Answer Figures**

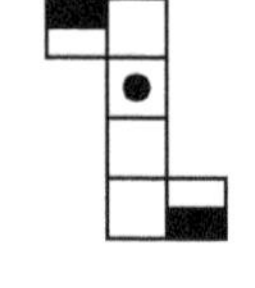

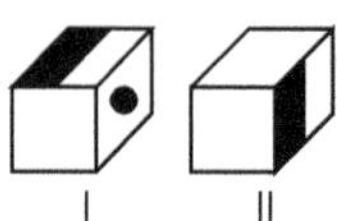

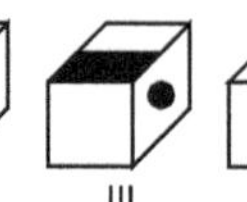

(a) I and II
(b) II and III
(c) I, II and III
(d) I, II, III and IV

***Solution* (d)** According to unfolded dice,

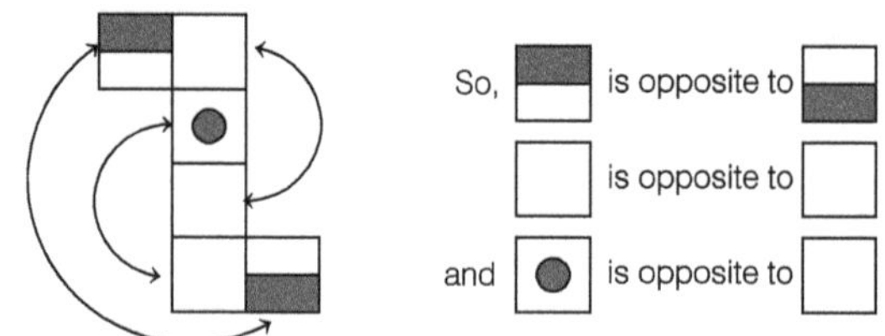

Clearly, all the cubes I, II, III and IV can be formed.

***Ex* 25 Question Figure** **Answer Figures**

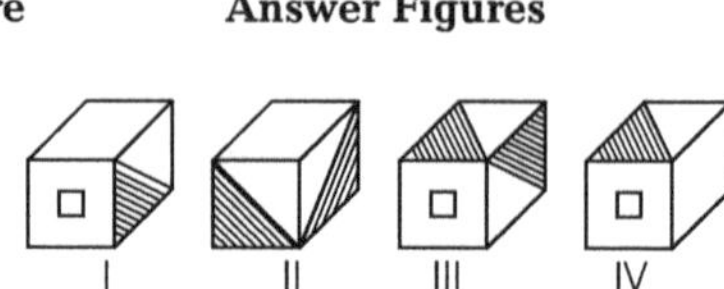

(a) I and II
(b) III and IV
(c) I and IV
(d) I, II, III and IV

***Solution* (c)** According to the given figure,

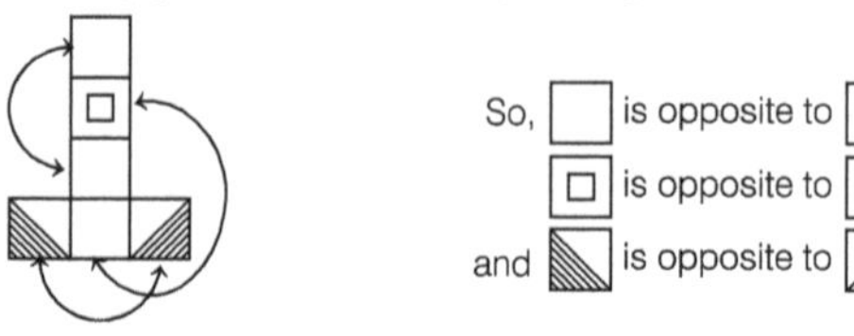

Hence, option (c) has the correct cubes, which can be formed when unfolded figure will be folded.

Practice CORNER 15.2

1. If the given figure is folded to form a cube, then which symbol will be opposite to the symbol '+'?
« SSC CPO 2019

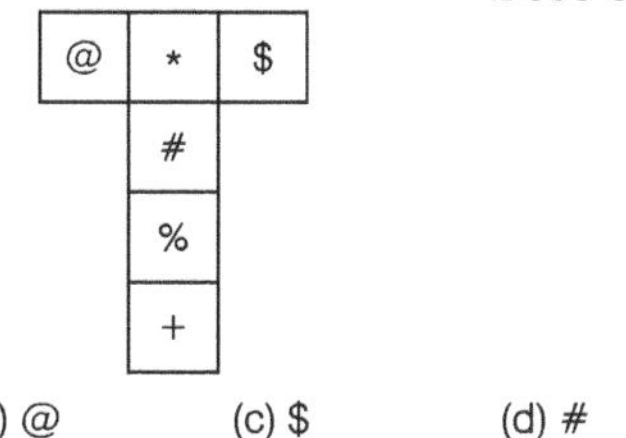

(a) % (b) @ (c) $ (d) #

2. In the following figure, if the base of the cube is the shaded part and face 1 is in front of you, then which will be the opposite face of it ?
« SSC 10+2 2006

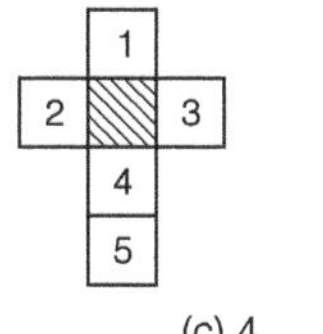

(a) 2 (b) 3 (c) 4 (d) 5

3. If a cube is formed from the following figure, then which face will be opposite to the face having 3 dots?
« SSC FCI 2011

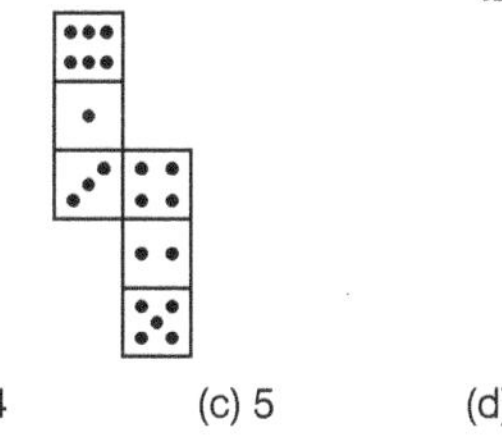

(a) 2 (b) 4 (c) 5 (d) 6

4. If a cube is made from the following figure, then which lettered face will be opposite to the face F?
« IGNOU B.Ed 2010

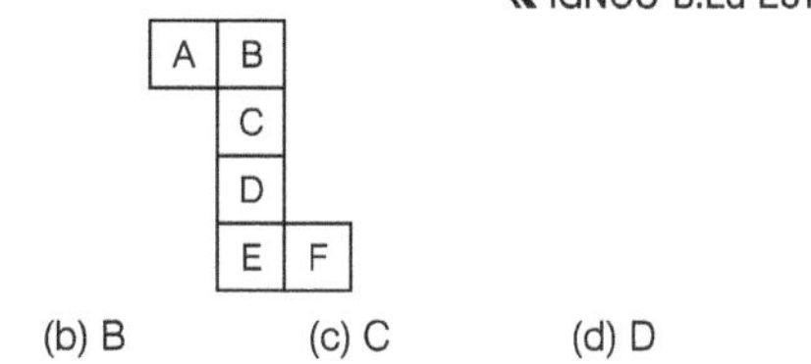

(a) A (b) B (c) C (d) D

DIRECTIONS ~ (Q. Nos. 5-37) *In each question given below, an unfolded dice is given in the left side while in the right side, four answer choices are given in the form of complete dice. You are required to select the correct answer choice(s) which is/are formed by folding the unfolded dice.*

Question Figure **Answer Figures**

5.

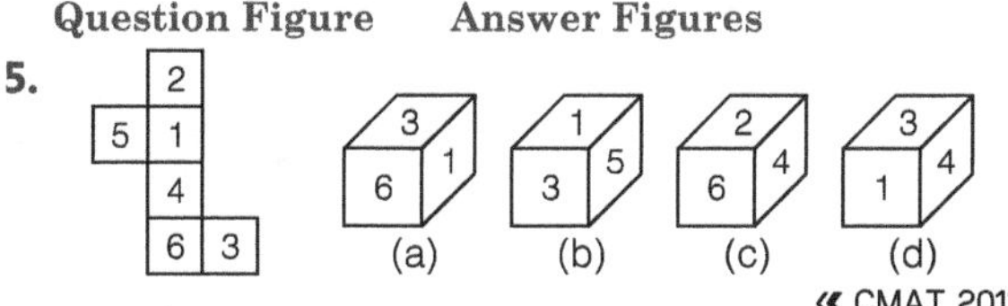

« CMAT 2013

Question Figure **Answer Figures**

6. **7.** **8.**

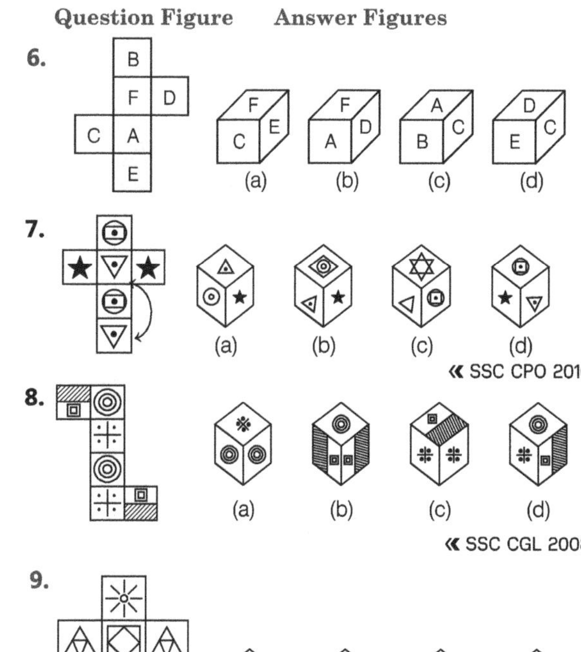

« SSC CPO 2010

« SSC CGL 2008

9. **10.** **11.** **12.**

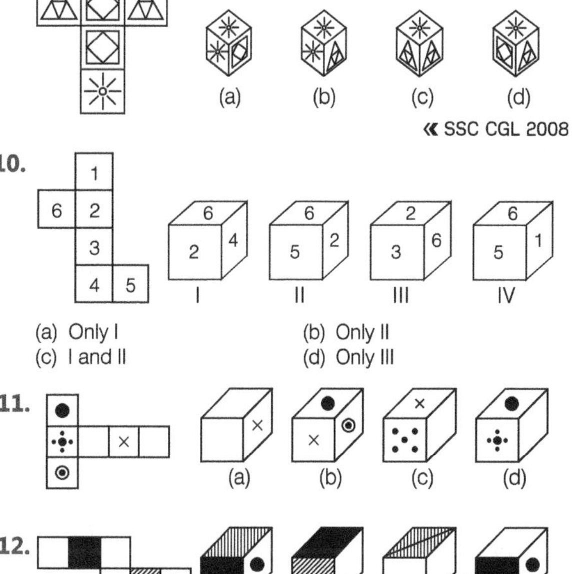

« SSC CGL 2008

(a) Only I (b) Only II
(c) I and II (d) Only III

13.

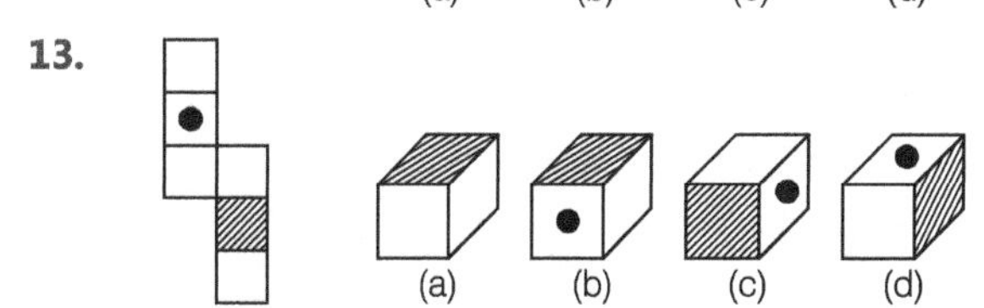

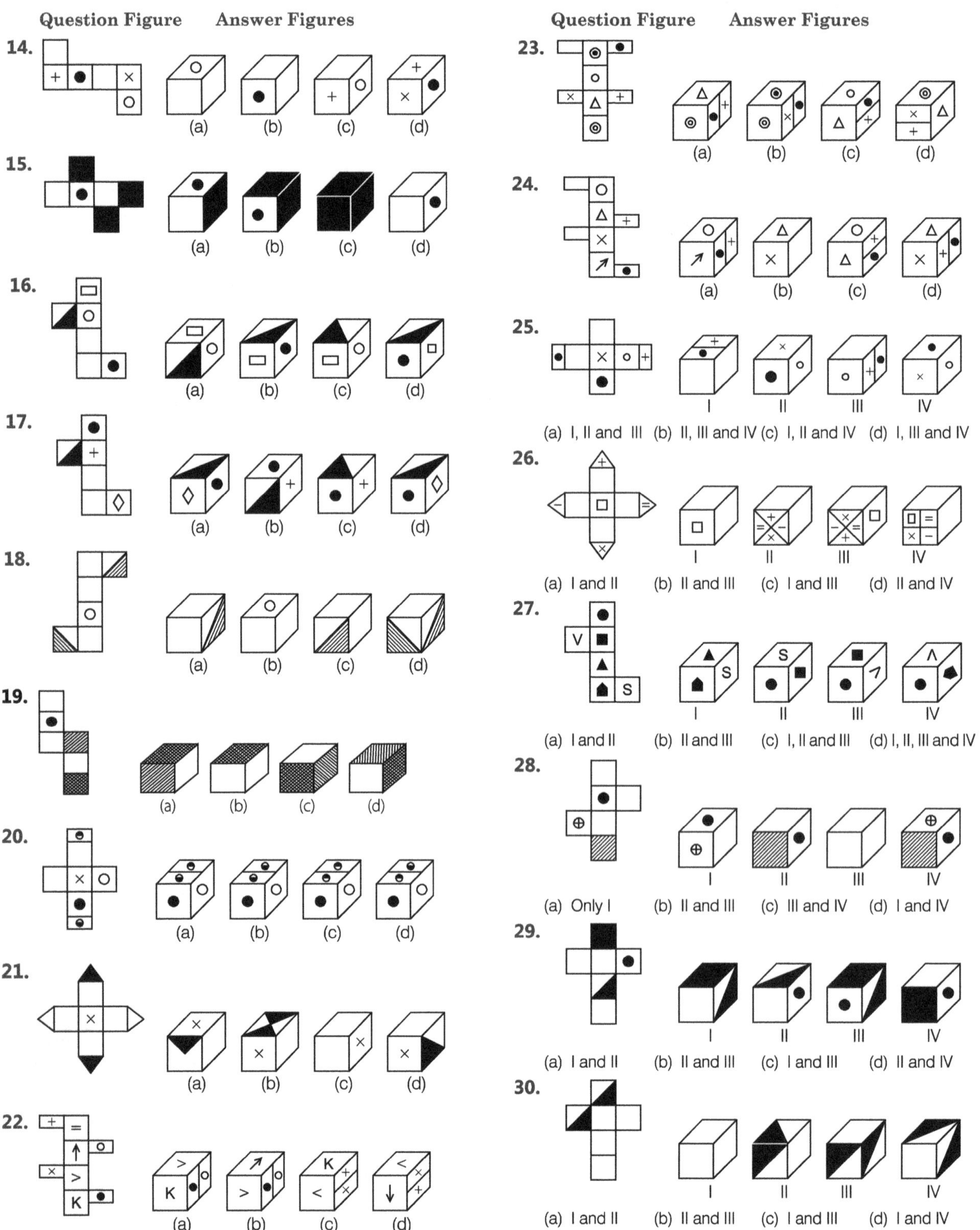
Question Figure Answer Figures
14. (a) (b) (c) (d)
15. (a) (b) (c) (d)
16. (a) (b) (c) (d)
17. (a) (b) (c) (d)
18. (a) (b) (c) (d)
19. (a) (b) (c) (d)
20. (a) (b) (c) (d)
21. (a) (b) (c) (d)
22. (a) (b) (c) (d)
Question Figure Answer Figures
23. (a) (b) (c) (d)
24. (a) (b) (c) (d)
25. I II III IV
(a) I, II and III (b) II, III and IV (c) I, II and IV (d) I, III and IV
26. I II III IV
(a) I and II (b) II and III (c) I and III (d) II and IV
27. I II III IV
(a) I and II (b) II and III (c) I, II and III (d) I, II, III and IV
28. I II III IV
(a) Only I (b) II and III (c) III and IV (d) I and IV
29. I II III IV
(a) I and II (b) II and III (c) I and III (d) II and IV
30. I II III IV
(a) I and II (b) II and III (c) I and III (d) I and IV

Question Figure **Answer Figures**

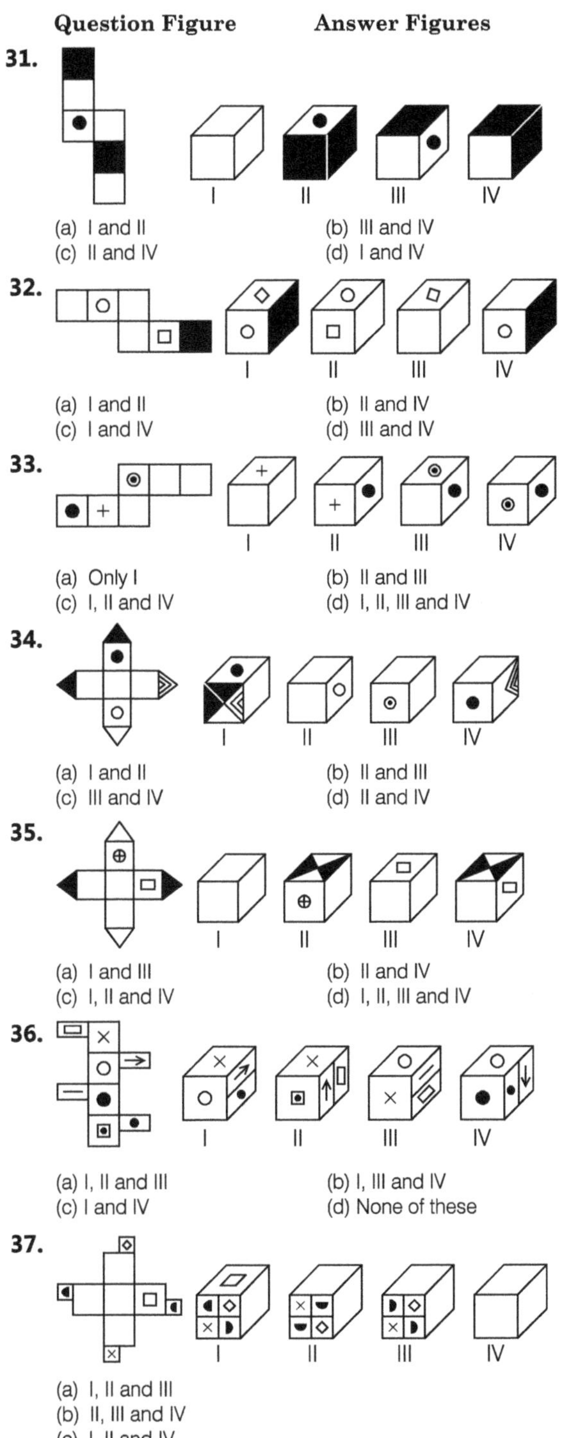

31. I II III IV

(a) I and II (b) III and IV
(c) II and IV (d) I and IV

32. I II III IV

(a) I and II (b) II and IV
(c) I and IV (d) III and IV

33. I II III IV

(a) Only I (b) II and III
(c) I, II and IV (d) I, II, III and IV

34. I II III IV

(a) I and II (b) II and III
(c) III and IV (d) II and IV

35. I II III IV

(a) I and III (b) II and IV
(c) I, II and IV (d) I, II, III and IV

36. I II III IV

(a) I, II and III (b) I, III and IV
(c) I and IV (d) None of these

37. I II III IV

(a) I, II and III
(b) II, III and IV
(c) I, II and IV
(d) I, III and IV

DIRECTIONS ~ (Q. Nos. 38-43) *Which of the following cube in the answer figures cannot be made based on the unfolded cube in the question figure?*

Question Figure **Answer Figures**

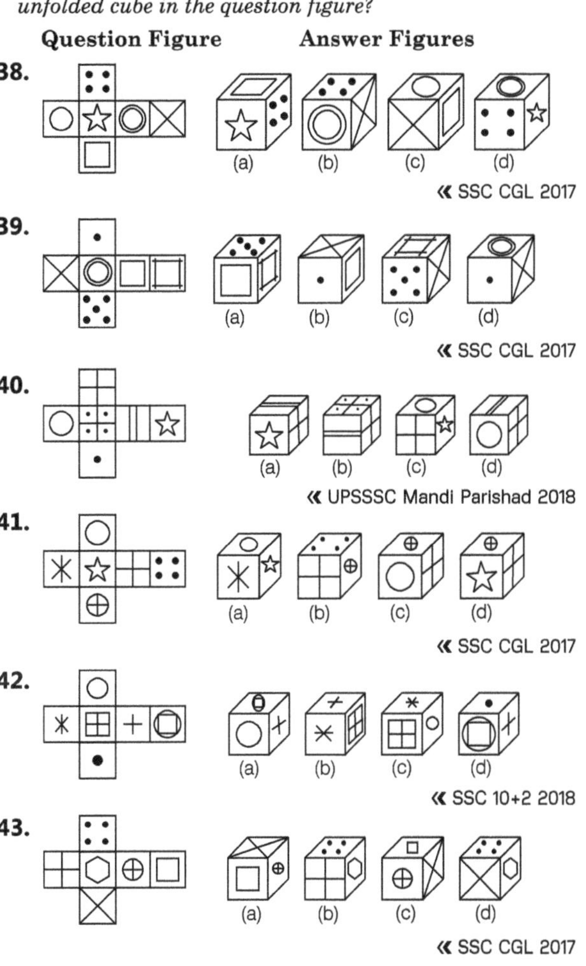

38. (a) (b) (c) (d)

« SSC CGL 2017

39. (a) (b) (c) (d)

« SSC CGL 2017

40. (a) (b) (c) (d)

« UPSSSC Mandi Parishad 2018

41. (a) (b) (c) (d)

« SSC CGL 2017

42. (a) (b) (c) (d)

« SSC 10+2 2018

43. (a) (b) (c) (d)

« SSC CGL 2017

44. Three views of the same cube are given. All the faces of the cube are numbered from 1 to 6. Select one figure which will result when the cube is unfolded.

« SSC CGL 2013

Question Figures

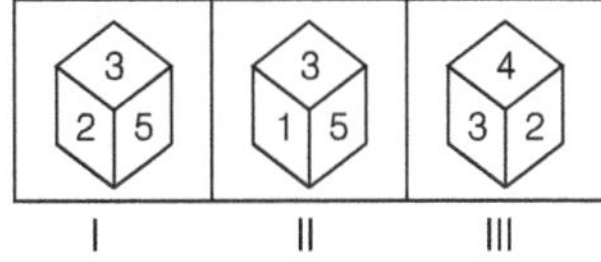

Answers Figures

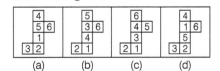

(a) 4, 5 6, 1, 3 2
(b) 5, 3 6, 4, 2 1
(c) 6, 4 5, 3, 2 1
(d) 4, 1 6, 5, 3 2

Answers WITH EXPLANATIONS

1. (*d*) According to the question,

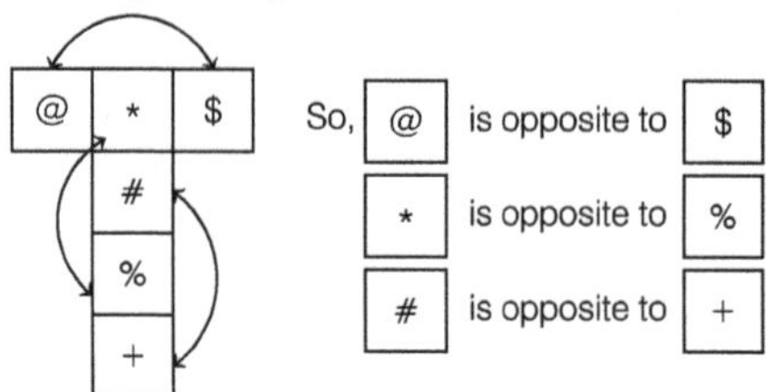

@
*
$
#
%
+
So, @ is opposite to $
* is opposite to %
# is opposite to +

Hence, the face having symbol '#' will be opposite to the face having symbol '+'.

2. (*c*) According to the question,

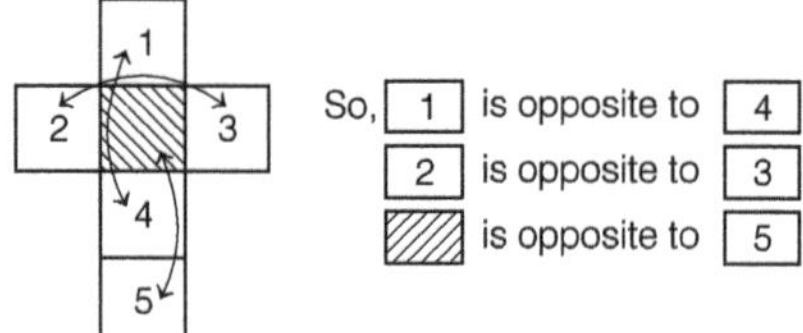

1
2
3
4
5
So, 1 is opposite to 4
2 is opposite to 3
is opposite to 5

Hence, 1 will be opposite to 4.

3. (*d*) According to the question,

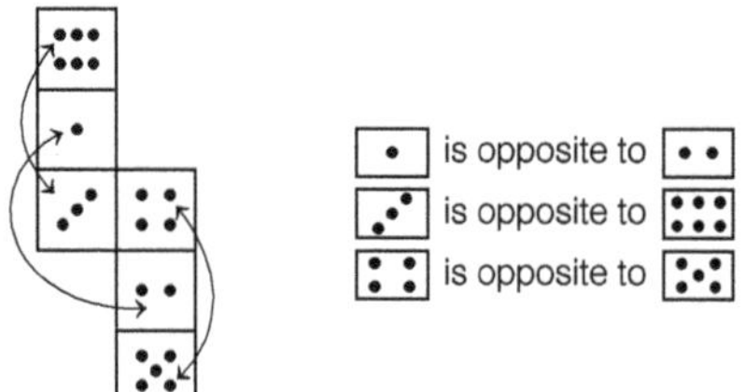

is opposite to
is opposite to
is opposite to

Hence, the face having 6 dots will be opposite to the face having 3 dots.

4. (*a*) According to the question,

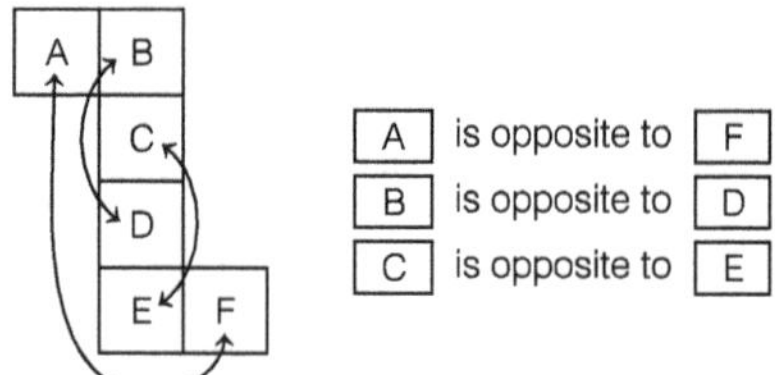

A
B
C
D
E
F
A is opposite to F
B is opposite to D
C is opposite to E

Hence, the face having letter A will be opposite to the face having letter F.

5. (*d*) According to the question.

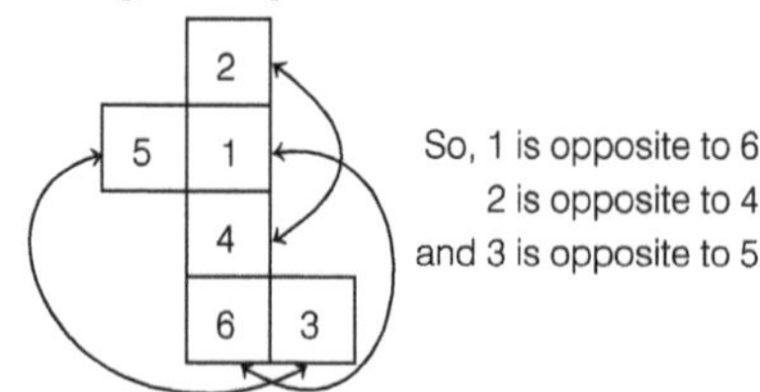

2
5
1
4
6
3
So, 1 is opposite to 6
2 is opposite to 4
and 3 is opposite to 5

Hence, only the cube in option (d) is correct.

6. (*b*) According to the question,

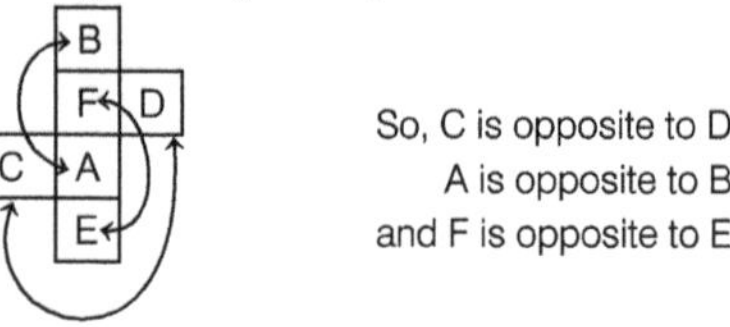

B
F
D
C
A
E
So, C is opposite to D
A is opposite to B
and F is opposite to E

Hence, only the cube in option (b) is correct.

7. (*d*) According to the question,

So, is opposite to
is opposite to
and is opposite to

Hence, only the cube in option (d) is correct.

8. (*d*) According to the question,

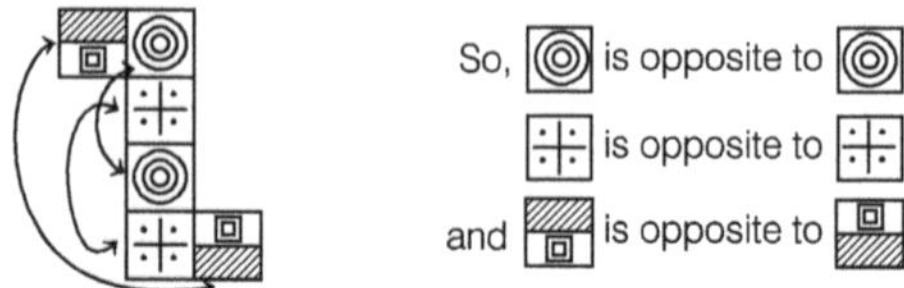

So, is opposite to
is opposite to
and is opposite to

Hence, only the cube in option (d) is correct.

9. (*d*) According to the question,

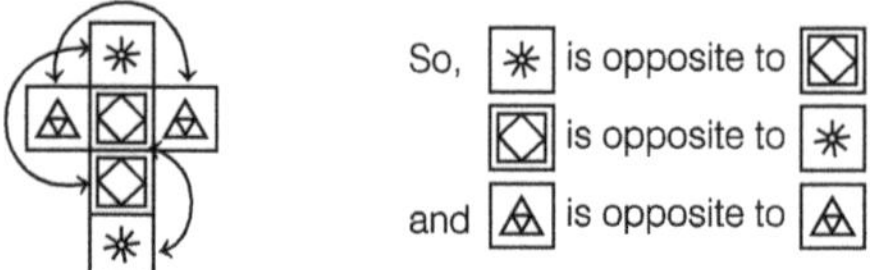

So, is opposite to
is opposite to
and is opposite to

Hence, only the cube in option (d) is correct.

10. (*d*) According to the question,

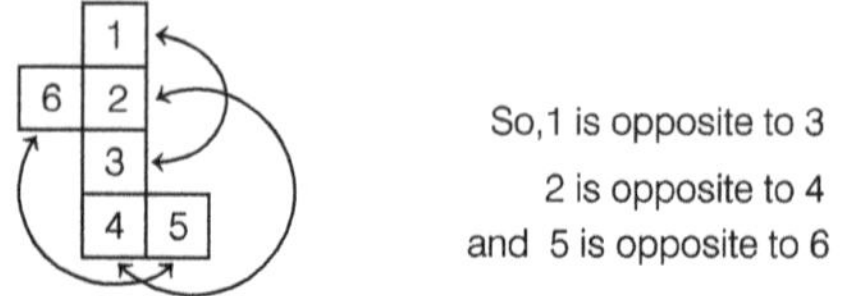

1
6
2
3
4
5
So,1 is opposite to 3
2 is opposite to 4
and 5 is opposite to 6

Hence, only the cube in option (d) is correct.

11. (*d*) According to the question,

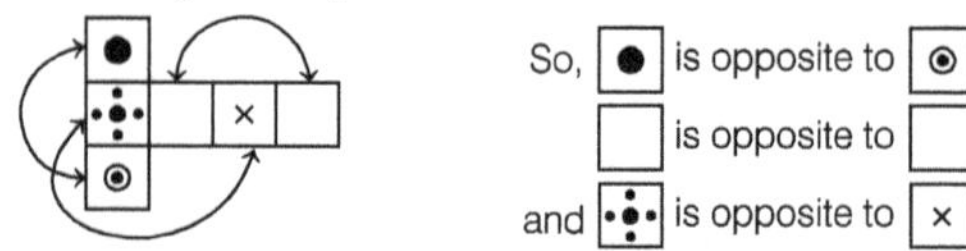

×
So, is opposite to
is opposite to
and is opposite to ×

Hence, only the cube in option (d) is correct.

12. (*d*) According to the question,

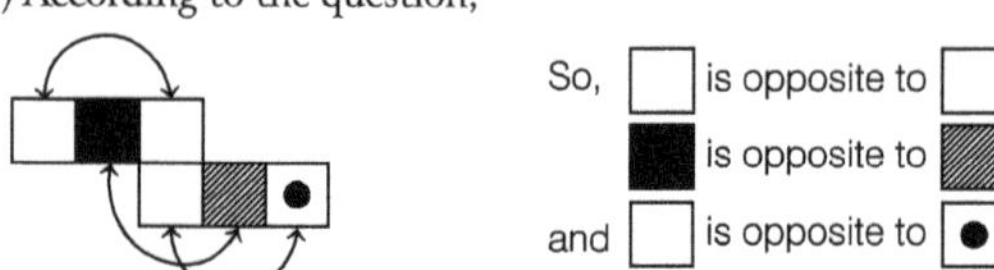

So, is opposite to
is opposite to
and is opposite to

Hence, only the cube in option (d) is correct.

13. (*a*) According to the question,

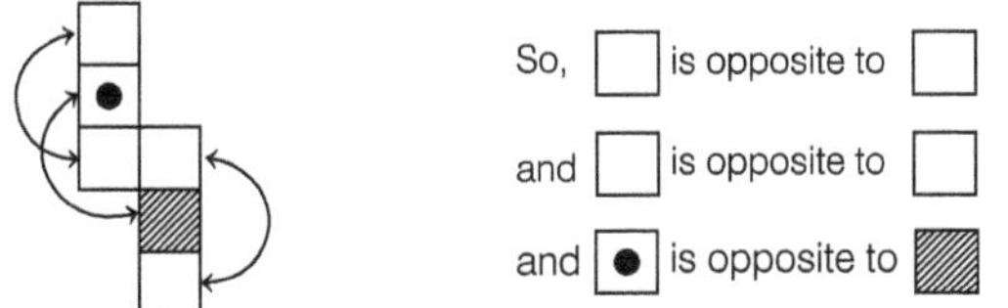

Hence, only the cube in option (a) is correct.

14. (*b*) According to the question,

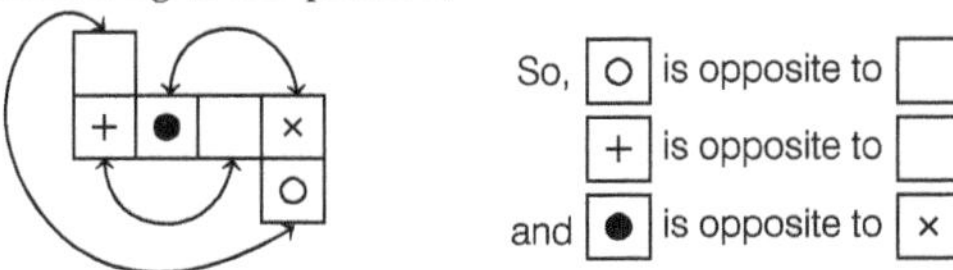

Hence, only the cube in option (b) is the correct answer.

15. (*a*) According to the question,

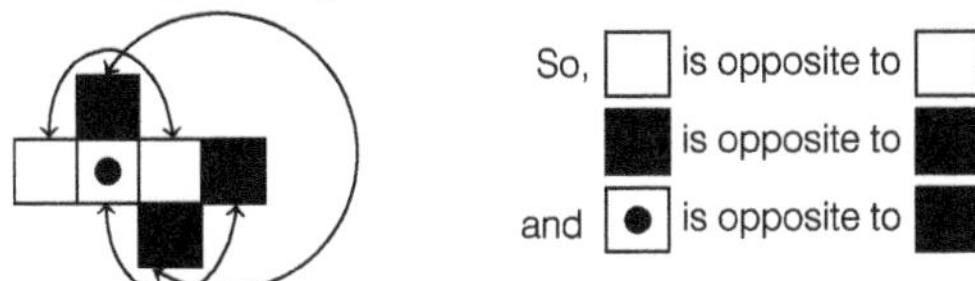

Hence, only the cube in option (a) is correct.

16. (*a*) According to the question,

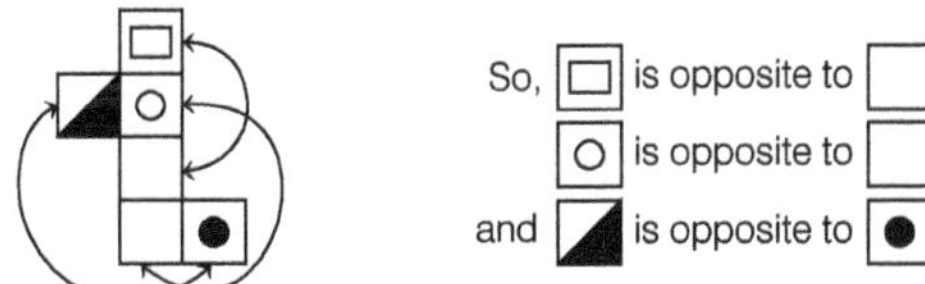

Hence, only the cube in option (a) is correct.

17. (*b*) According to the question,

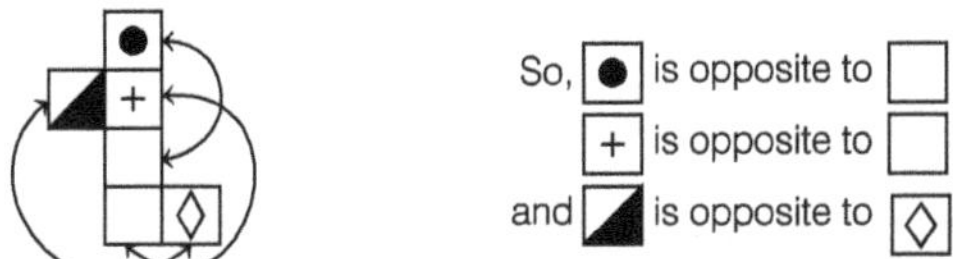

Hence, only the cube in option (b) is correct.

18. (*a*) According to the question,

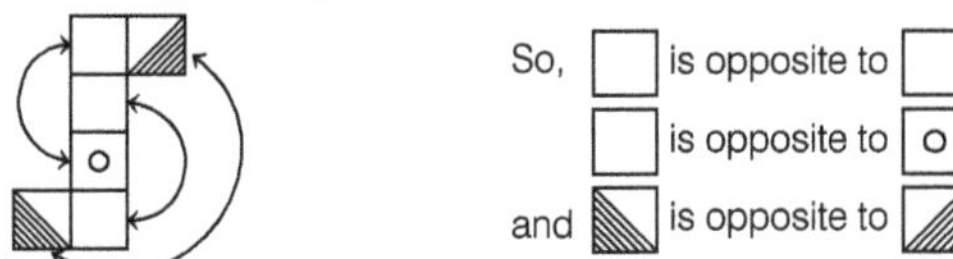

Hence, only the cube in option (a) is correct.

19. (*b*) According to the question,

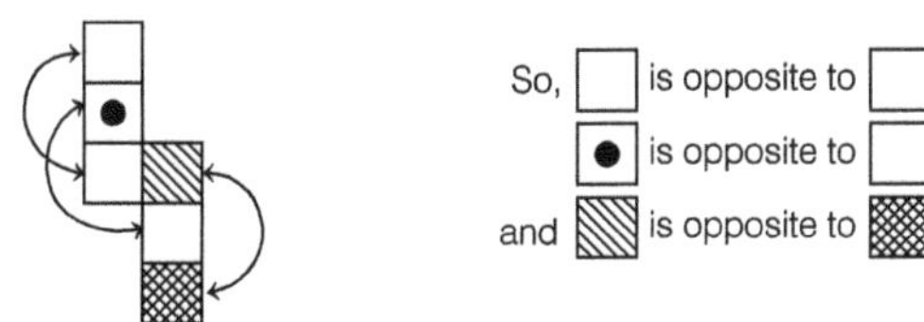

Hence, only the cube in option (b) is correct.

20. (*d*) According to the question,

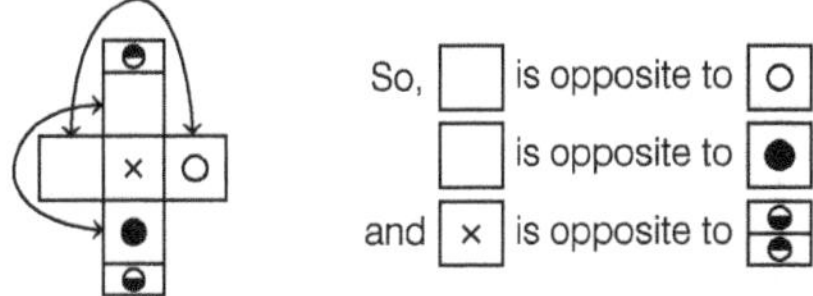

Hence, only the cube in option (d) is correct.

21. (*c*) According to the question,

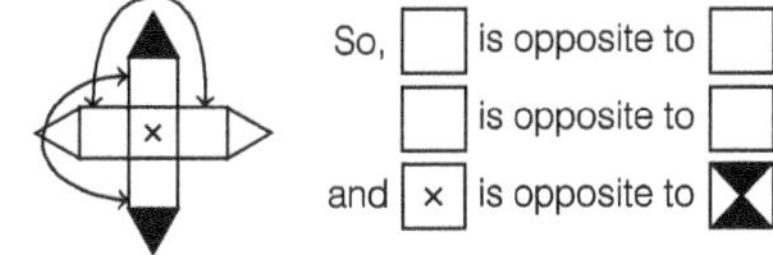

Hence, only the cube in option (c) is correct.

22. (*b*) According to the question,

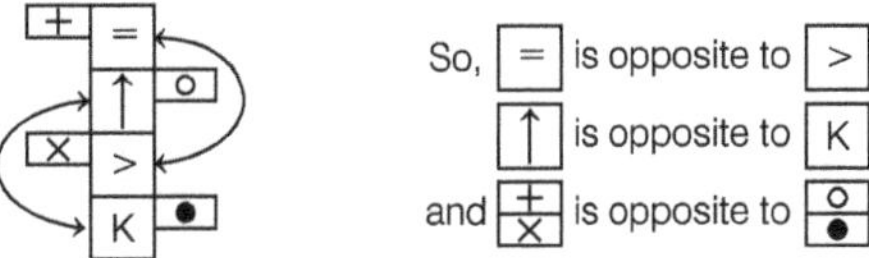

Hence, only the cube in option (b) is correct.

23. (*a*) According to the question,

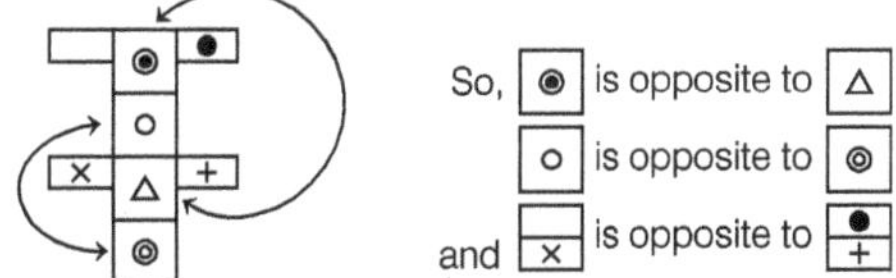

Hence, only the cube in option (a) is correct.

24. (*d*) According to the question,

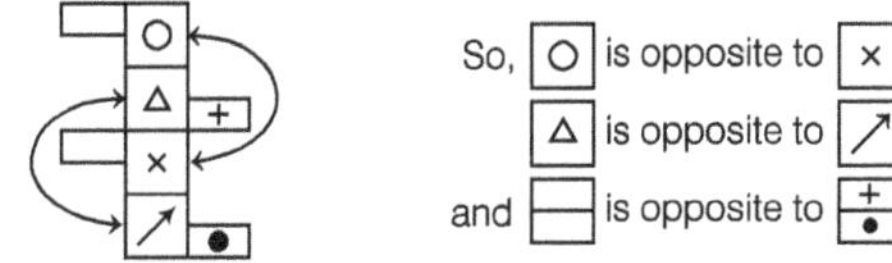

Hence, only the cube in option (d) is correct.

25. (*a*) According to the question,

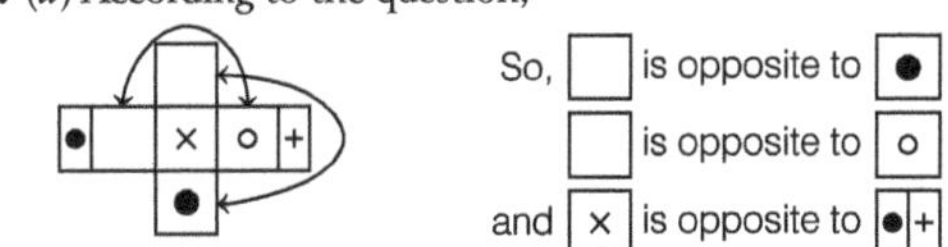

Hence, only the cubes in option (a) is correct.

26. (*a*) According to the question,

So, is opposite to
is opposite to
and is opposite to

Hence, only the cubes in option (a) is correct.

27. (*d*) According to the question,

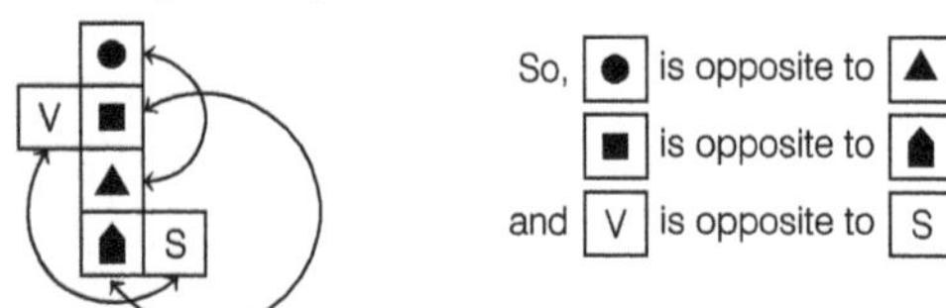

Hence, only the cubes in option (d) is correct.

28. (*a*) According to the question,

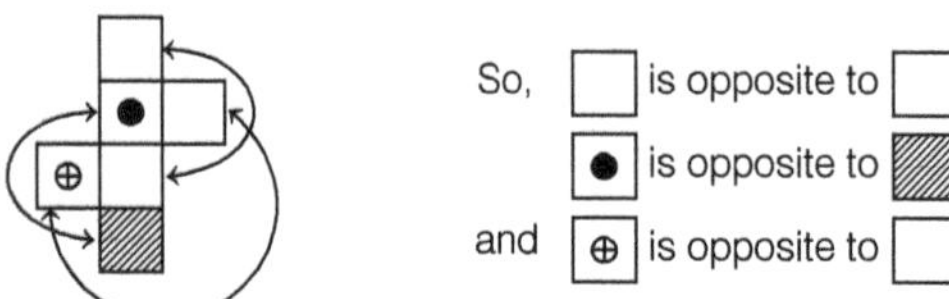

Hence, only the cube in option (a) is correct.

29. (*d*) According to the question,

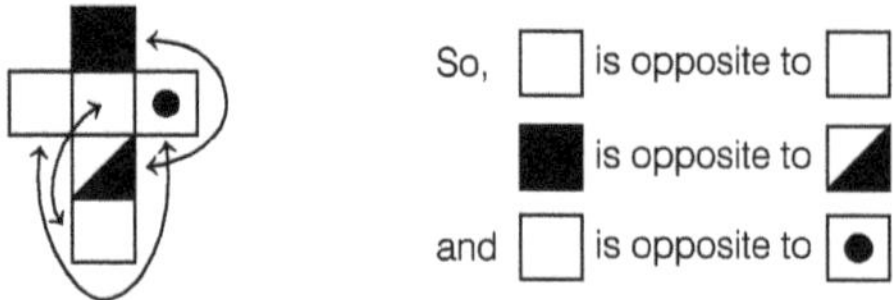

Hence, only the cubes in option (d) is correct.

30. (*d*) According to the question,

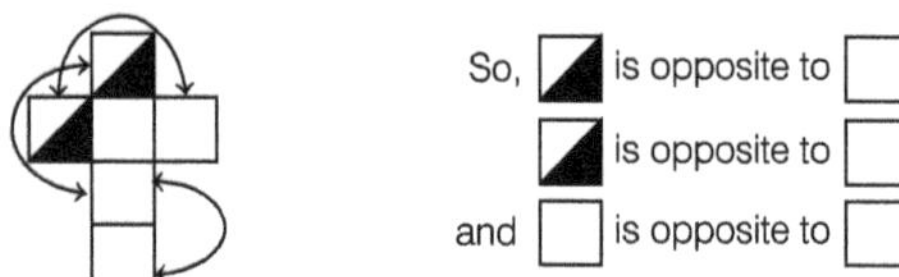

Hence, only the cubes in option (d) is correct.

31. (*b*) According to the question,

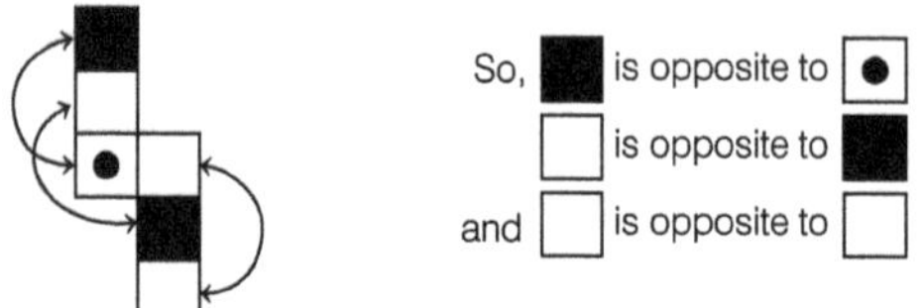

Clearly, only cubes III and IV can be formed when unfolded cube is folded.

32. (*d*) According to the question,

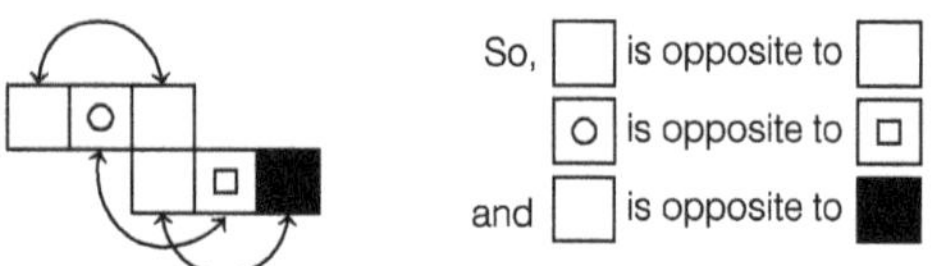

So, figures III and IV can be formed.
Hence, option (d) is correct.

33. (*d*) According to the question,

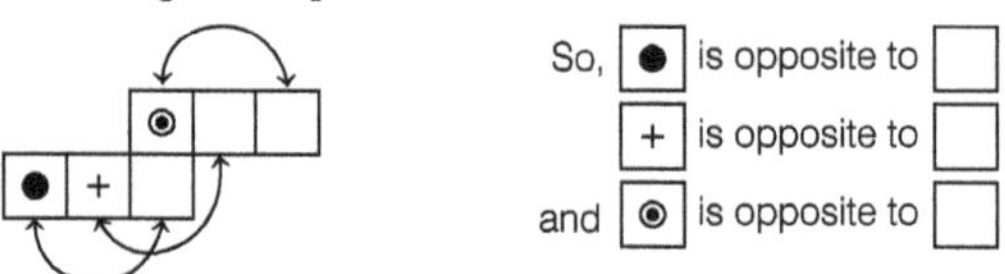

So, all the cube figures can be formed.
Hence, option (d) is correct.

34. (*a*) According to the question,

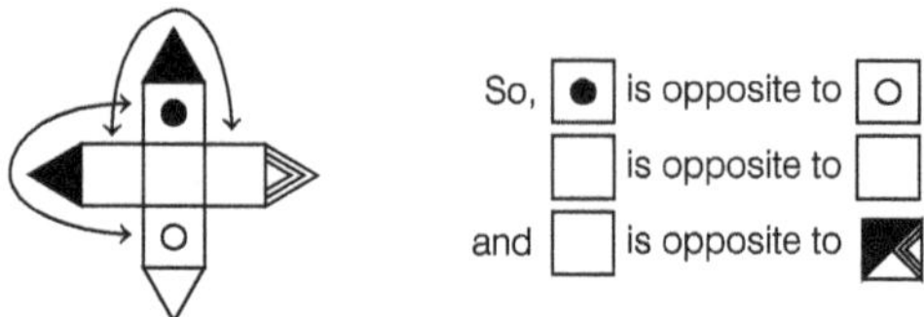

So, cube figures I and II can be formed.
Hence, option (a) is correct.

35. (*d*) According to the question,

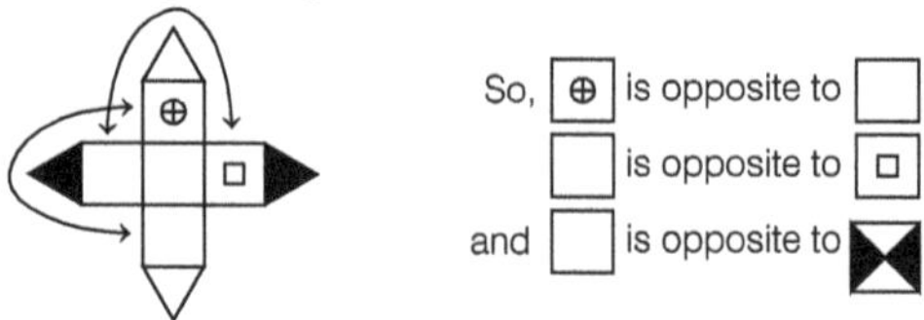

So, all the cube figures can be formed. Hence, option (d) is correct.

36. (*b*) According to the question,

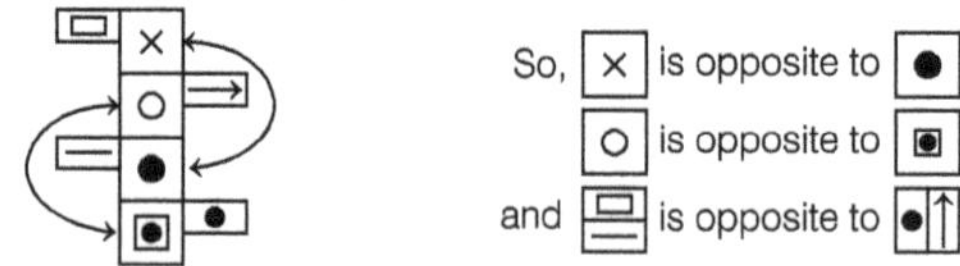

So, figures I, III and IV can be formed, Hence, option (b) is correct.

37. (*b*) According to the question,

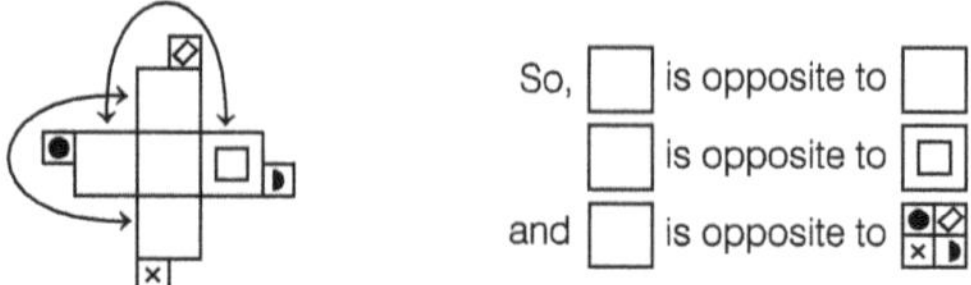

So, figure II, III and IV can be formed.
Hence, option (b) is correct.

38. (*a*) According to the question,

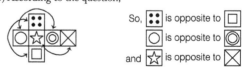

So, is opposite to
is opposite to
and is opposite to

Option figure (a) cannot be made as in this figure and are adjacent to each other.

39. (*b*) According to the question,

So, is opposite to
is opposite to
and is opposite to

Option figure (b) cannot be made as in this figure and are adjacent to each other.

40. (*d*) According to the question,

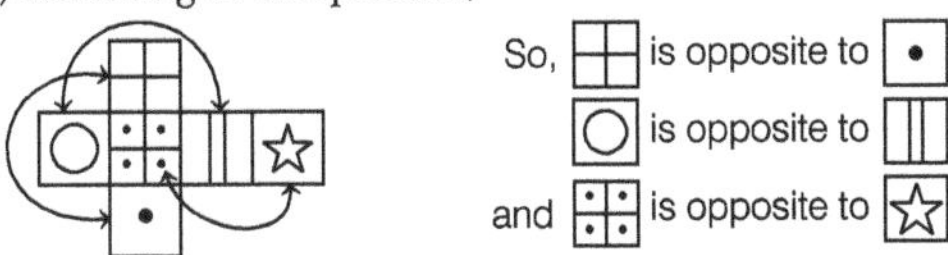

Answer figure (d) cannot be made as in this figure and are adjacent to each other.

41. (*c*) According to the question,

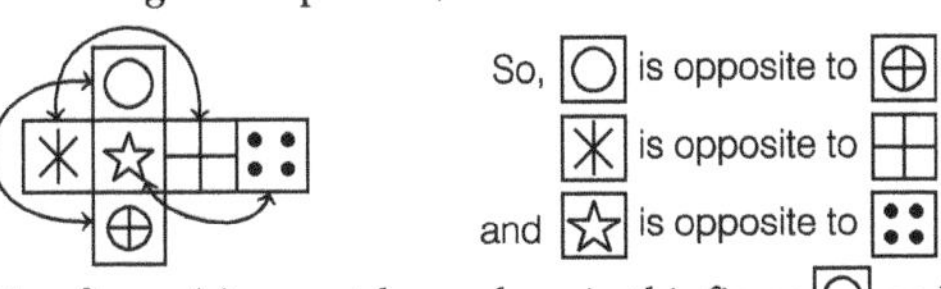

Option figure (c) cannot be made as in this figure and are adjacent to each other.

42. (*b*) According to the question,

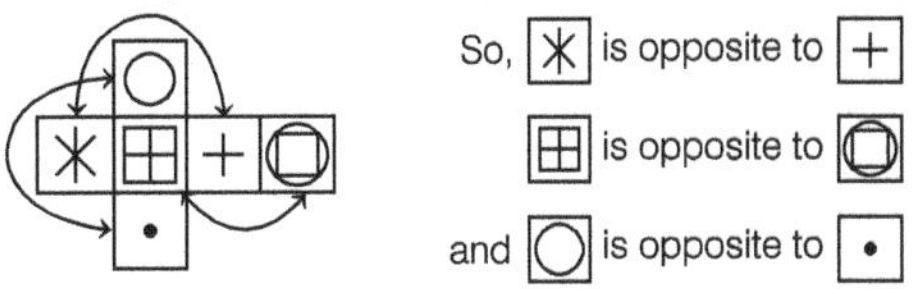

Cube given in answer figure (b) cannot be made from the given unfolded cube.
Hence, the cube in option (b) is correct.

43. (*d*) According to the question,

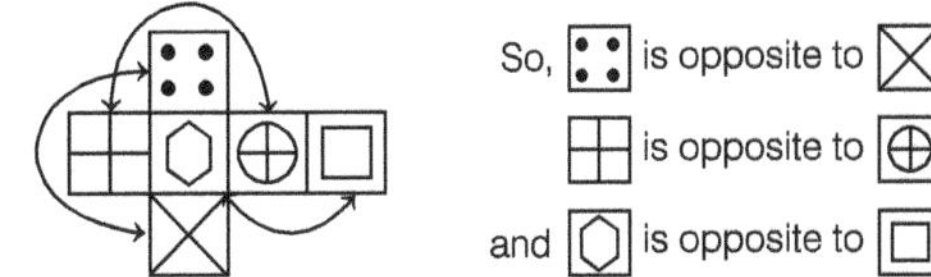

Cube given in answer figure (d) cannot be made from the given unfolded cube.
Hence, only the cube in option (d) is correct.

44. (*d*) If we fold the figure (a) the number 2 will lie opposite to (5).
If we fold the figure (b) the number (1) will lie opposite to (3).
If we fold the figure (c) the number (2) will lie opposite to (5).
Therefore, answer figure (d) is correct.

CHAPTER / 16

Dot Situation

Dot situation relates to an activity in which candidates have to find a common characteristic between a dot placed in between a group of geometrical figures and area enclosed by the same group of figures.

This chapter deals with the questions in which a group of geometrical figures with a dot is given. Candidates are asked to find which amongst the given options, is similar to the given group of figures.

The correct answer figure is the one which contains an area common to the shapes that have been marked by the dot in the question figure.

Let us see some illustrative examples given below to have a better idea about the type of questions asked:

DIRECTIONS ~ (Example Nos. 1-3) *In the following questions, one or more dots are placed in the question figure. The figure is followed by four alternatives marked as* (a), (b), (c) *and* (d). *One out of these four options contains region(s) common to the circle, square and triangle, similar to that marked by the dot in question figure. Choose that figure.*

Ex 01

Question Figure **Answer Figures**

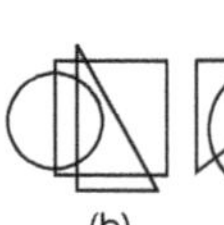

(a) (b) (c) (d)

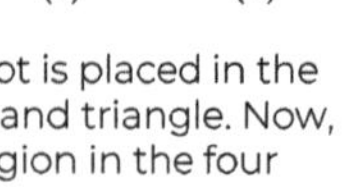

Solution (c) In question figure, the dot is placed in the region which is common to the circle and triangle. Now, we have to search similar common region in the four options.

Only in figure (c), we find such a region which is common to the circle and triangle and is shown by the shaded portion in the figure given below.

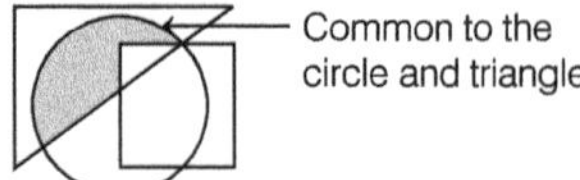

Ex 02

Question Figure **Answer Figures**

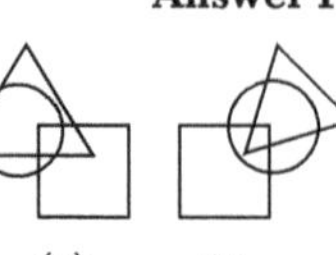

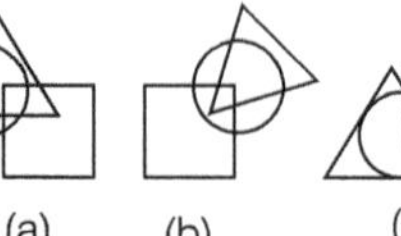
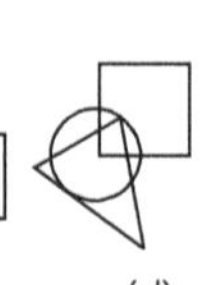

(a) (b) (c) (d)

Solution (a) In question figure, one dot is placed in the region which is common to the circle and triangle and the other dot is placed in the region which is common to the triangle and square.

Out of all the answer figures, only answer figure (a) possesses a region which is common to the circle and triangle and a region which is common to the triangle and square.

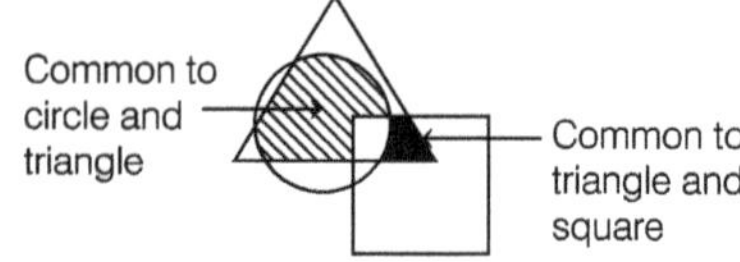

Ex 03

Question Figure **Answer Figures**

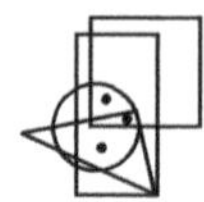
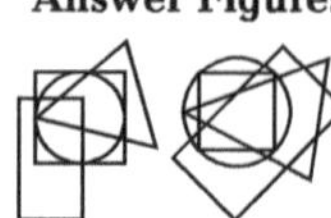

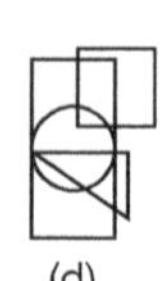

(a) (b) (c) (d)

« Hotel Mgmt 2005

Solution (b) One of the three dots is placed in the region which is common to the circle, rectangle and triangle; another dot is placed in the region which is common to the triangle, circle, rectangle and square and the third dot is placed in the region which is common to the circle, rectangle and square.

These three characteristics shown by three dots are found in figure (b). It possesses region which is common to the circle, rectangle and triangle, a region which is common to the triangle circle, rectangle and square and a region which is common to the circle, rectangle and square.

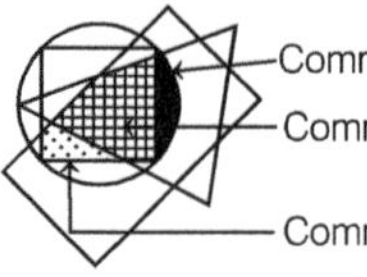

Ex 04

To which pentagon below can a dot be added so that it meets the same conditions as in the pentagon above?

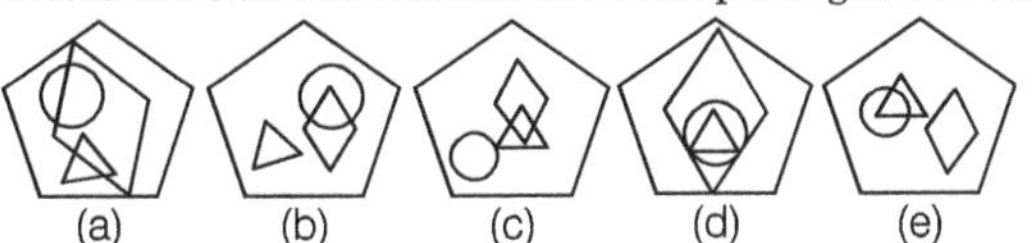

Solution (e) The dot appears in the region common to circle and triangle. This characteristics is found in figure (e) as shown below

Common to circle and triangle

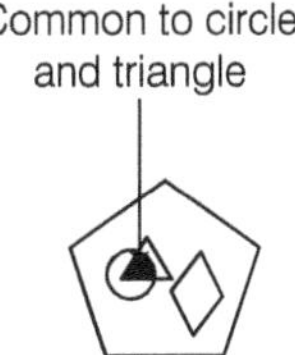

Practice / CORNER

DIRECTIONS ~ (Q. Nos. 1-32) *In the following questions, one or more dots is/are placed in the question figure. This figure is followed by four alternatives* (a), (b), (c) *and* (d). *One out of these four options contains region(s) common to circle, square and triangle, similar to that marked by the dot in question figure. Choose that figure.*

Question Figure **Answer Figures**

1. (a) (b) (c) (d)

« UP B.Ed 2009

2. (a) (b) (c) (d)

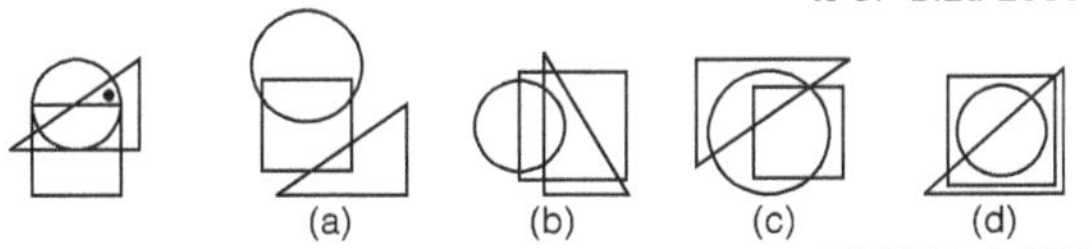

« SSC 10+2 2011

3. (a) (b) (c) (d)

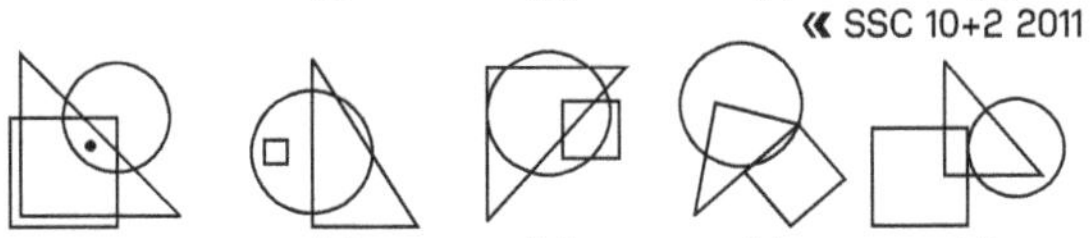

« UP B.Ed 2010

4. (a) (b) (c) (d)

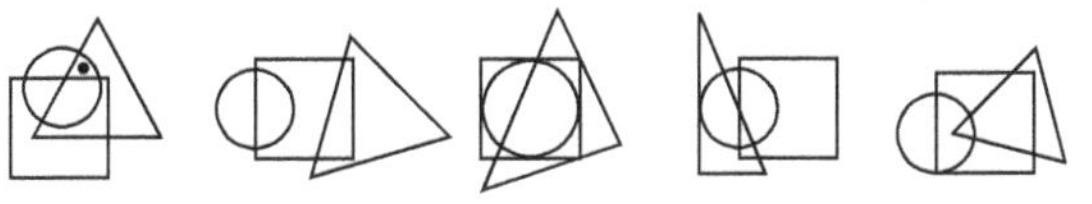

5. (a) (b) (c) (d)

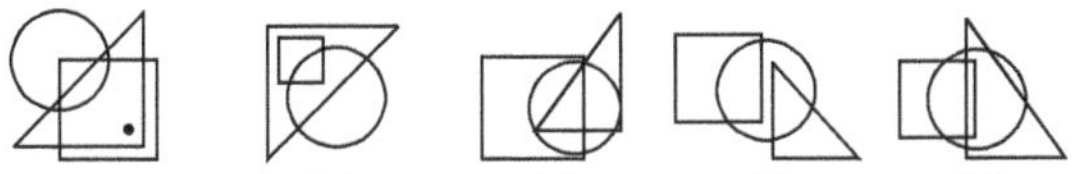

« SSC 10+2 2010

6. (a) (b) (c) (d)

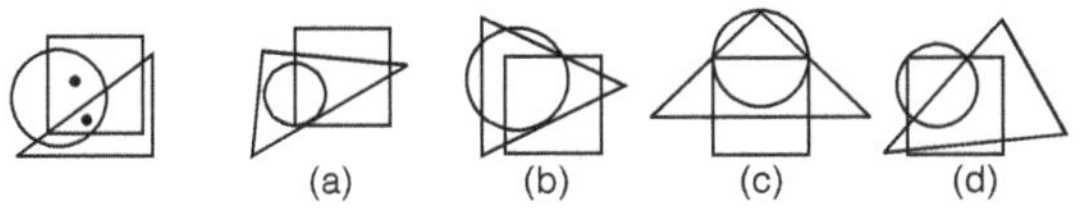

7. (a) (b) (c) (d)

Question Figure **Answer Figures**

8. (a) (b) (c) (d)

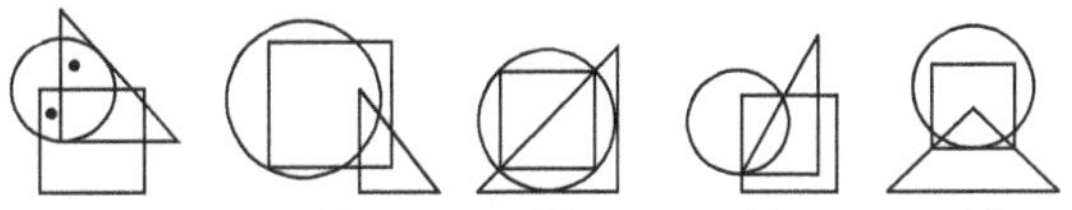

« SSC 10+2 2013

9. (a) (b) (c) (d)

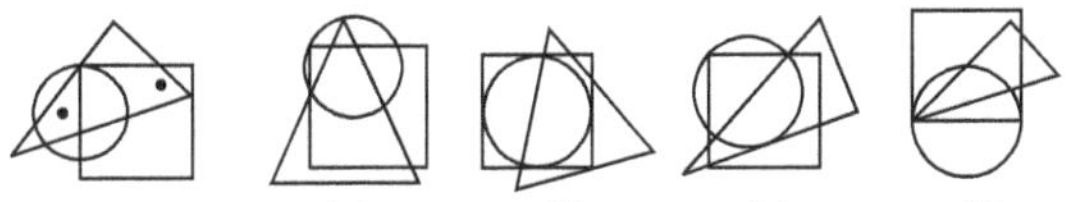

« UP B.Ed 2010

10. (a) (b) (c) (d)

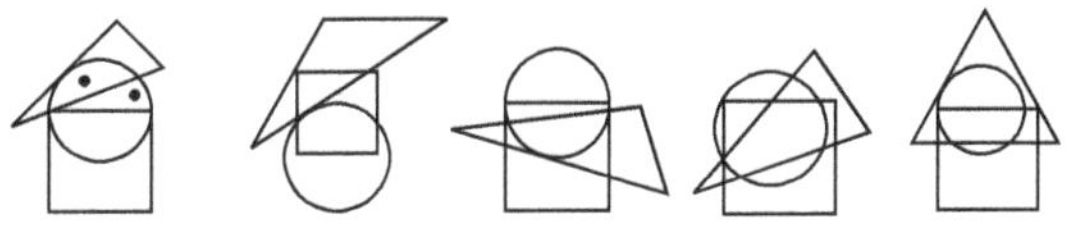

« SSC CGL 2006

11. (a) (b) (c) (d)

12. (a) (b) (c) (d)

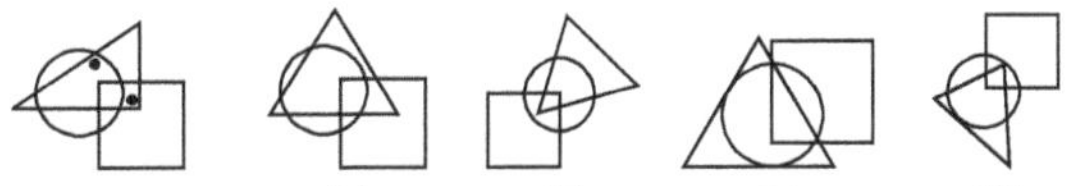

« SSC CGL 2006

13. (a) (b) (c) (d)

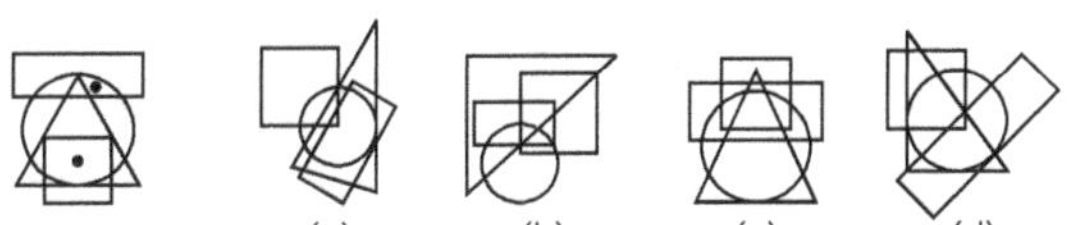

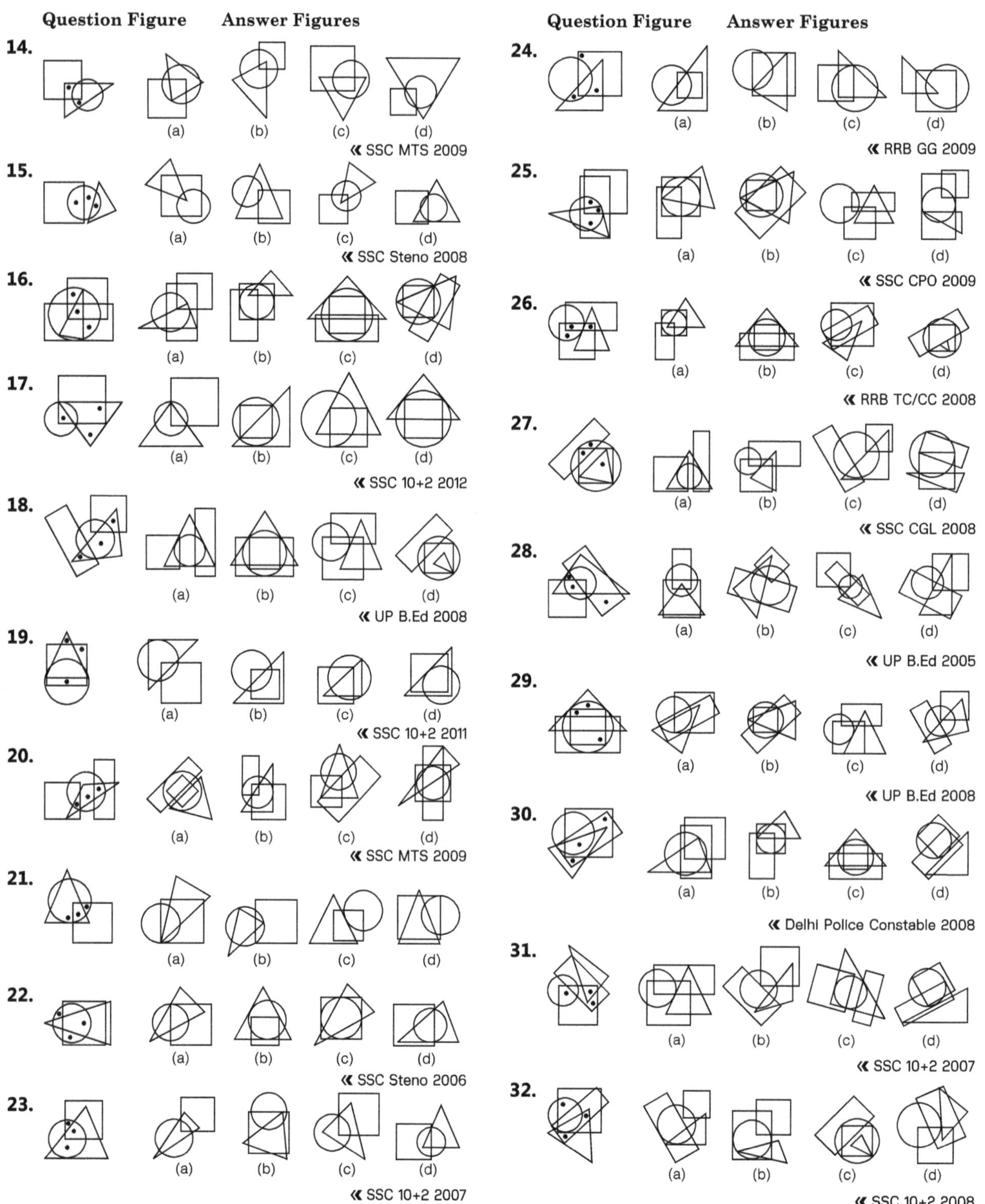
Question Figure
Answer Figures
14.
(a) (b) (c) (d)
« SSC MTS 2009
15.
(a) (b) (c) (d)
« SSC Steno 2008
16.
(a) (b) (c) (d)
17.
(a) (b) (c) (d)
« SSC 10+2 2012
18.
(a) (b) (c) (d)
« UP B.Ed 2008
19.
(a) (b) (c) (d)
« SSC 10+2 2011
20.
(a) (b) (c) (d)
« SSC MTS 2009
21.
(a) (b) (c) (d)
22.
(a) (b) (c) (d)
« SSC Steno 2006
23.
(a) (b) (c) (d)
« SSC 10+2 2007
Question Figure
Answer Figures
24.
(a) (b) (c) (d)
« RRB GG 2009
25.
(a) (b) (c) (d)
« SSC CPO 2009
26.
(a) (b) (c) (d)
« RRB TC/CC 2008
27.
(a) (b) (c) (d)
« SSC CGL 2008
28.
(a) (b) (c) (d)
« UP B.Ed 2005
29.
(a) (b) (c) (d)
« UP B.Ed 2008
30.
(a) (b) (c) (d)
« Delhi Police Constable 2008
31.
(a) (b) (c) (d)
« SSC 10+2 2007
32.
(a) (b) (c) (d)
« SSC 10+2 2008

DIRECTIONS ~ (Q. Nos. 33-36) *In the following questions, to which hexagon below can a dot be added, so that both dots then meet the same conditions as the two dots in the hexagon above?*

33. Question Figure **Answer Figures**

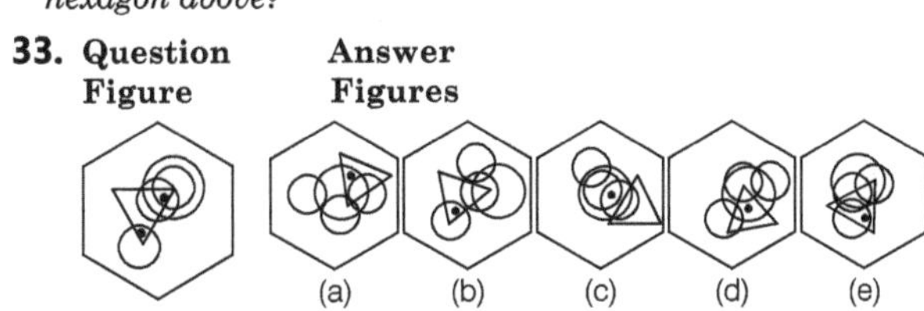

34. Question Figure **Answer Figures**

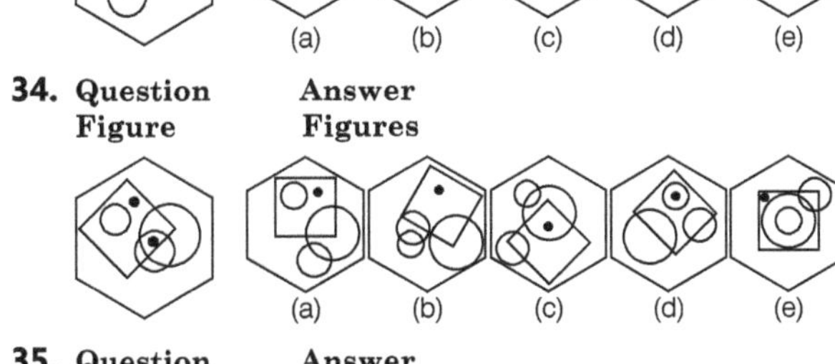

35. Question Figure **Answer Figures**

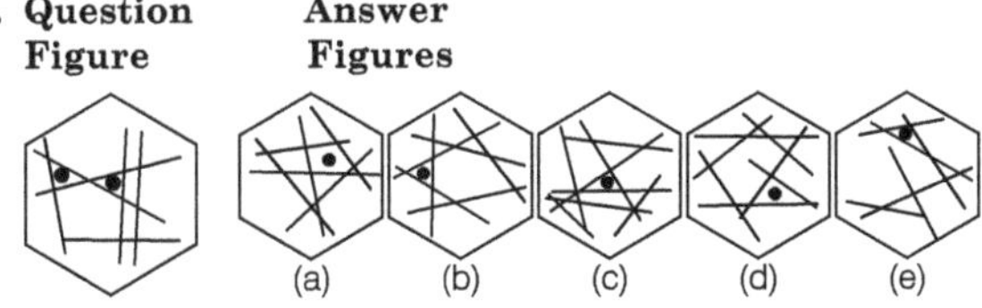

36. Question Figure **Answer Figures**

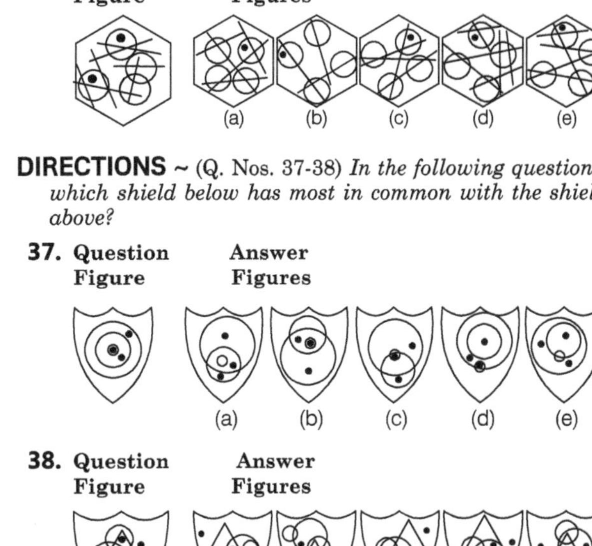

DIRECTIONS ~ (Q. Nos. 37-38) *In the following questions, which shield below has most in common with the shield above?*

37. Question Figure **Answer Figures**

38. Question Figure **Answer Figures**

Answers / WITH EXPLANATIONS

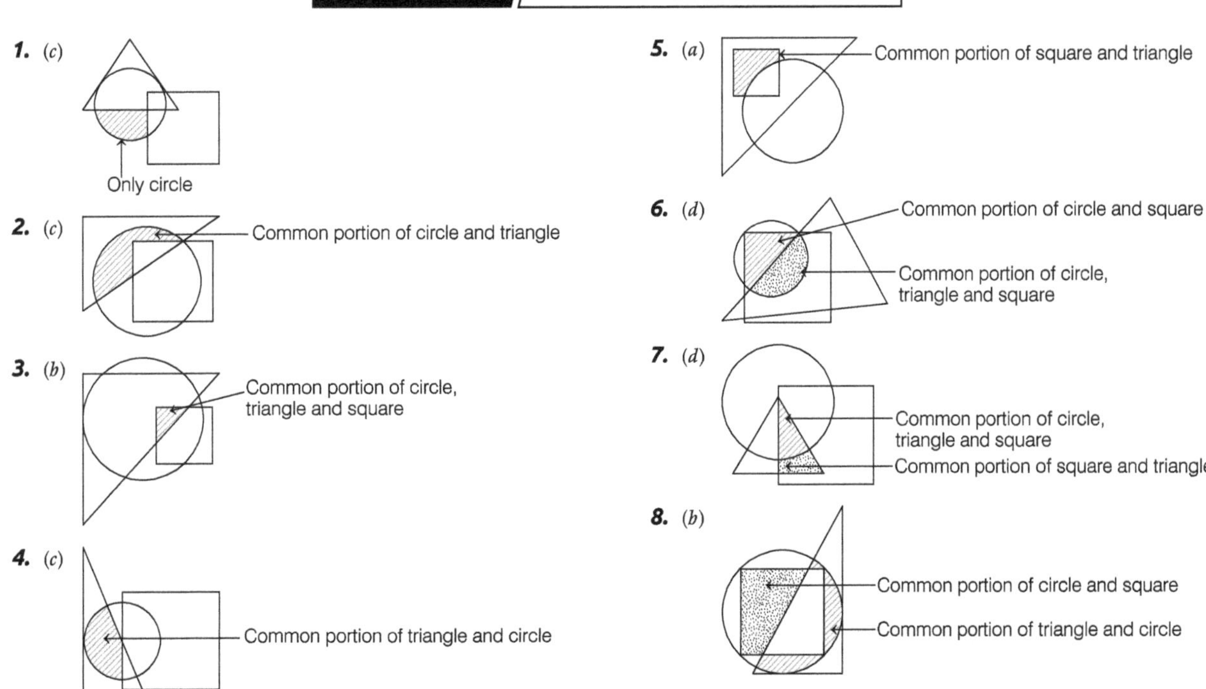

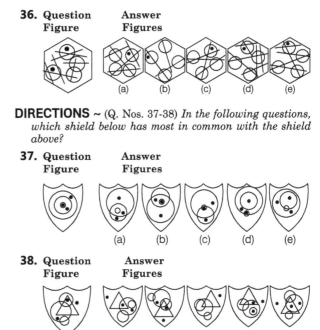

9. (*a*)

Common portion of triangle and circle

Common portion of triangle and square

10. (*c*)

Only circle

Common portion of triangle and circle

11. (*b*)

Common portion of circle and square

Common portion of triangle and square

12. (*a*)

Common portion of circle and triangle

Common portion of triangle and square

13. (*d*)

Common portion of circle, triangle and square

Common portion of rectangle and circle

14. (*c*)

Common portion of square and triangle

Common portion of circle and triangle

15. (*c*)

Common portion of triangle and circle

Only circle

Common portion of circle and square

16. (*d*)

Common portion of square and circle

Common portion of circle, triangle, square and rectangle

Common portion of rectangle and circle

17. (*c*)

Only triangle

Common portion of square and triangle

Common portion of circle and square

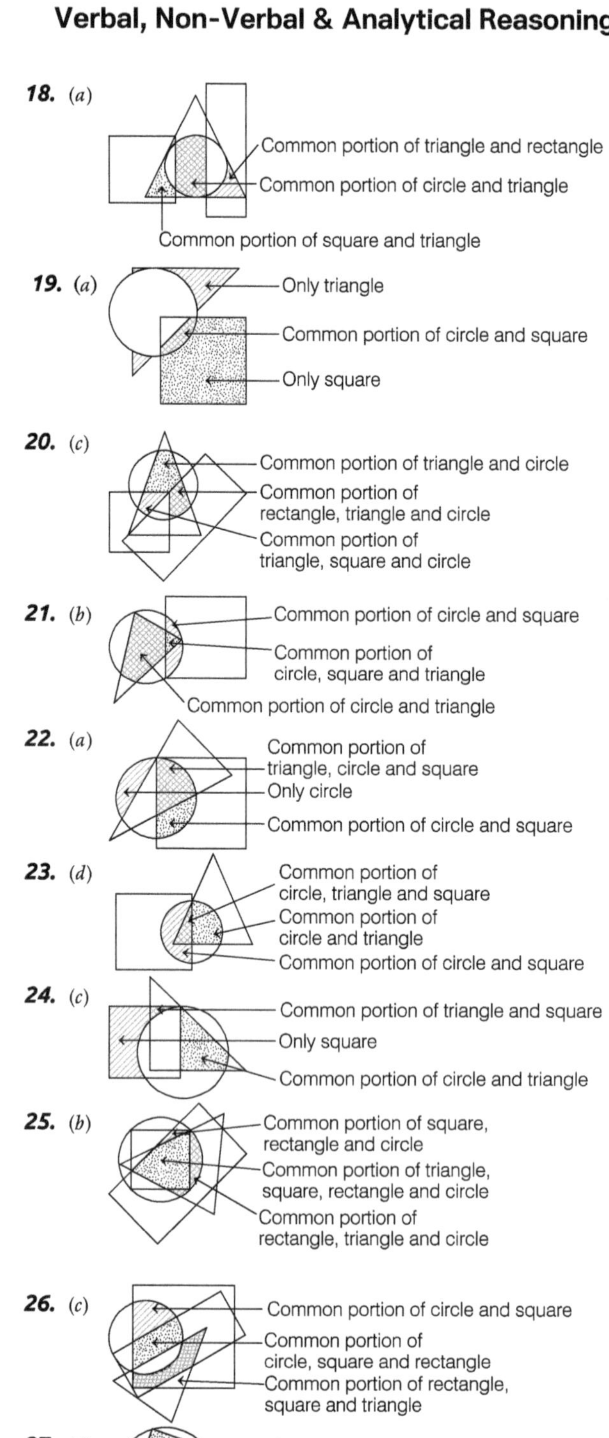

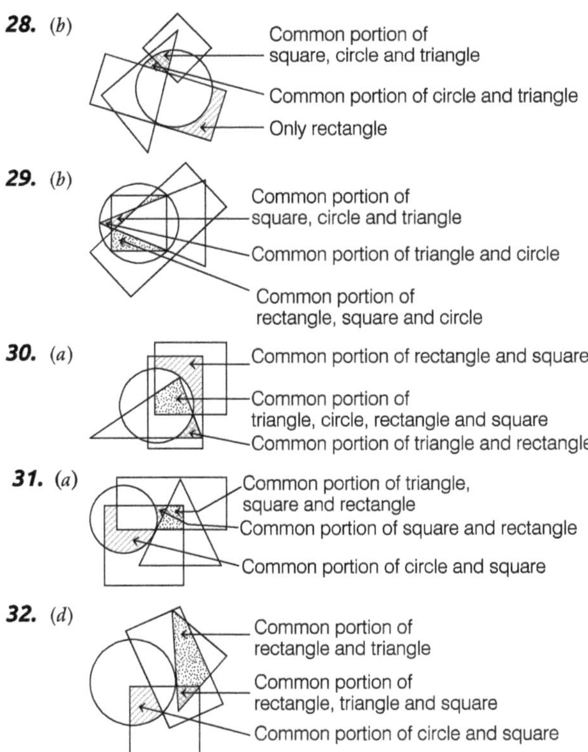

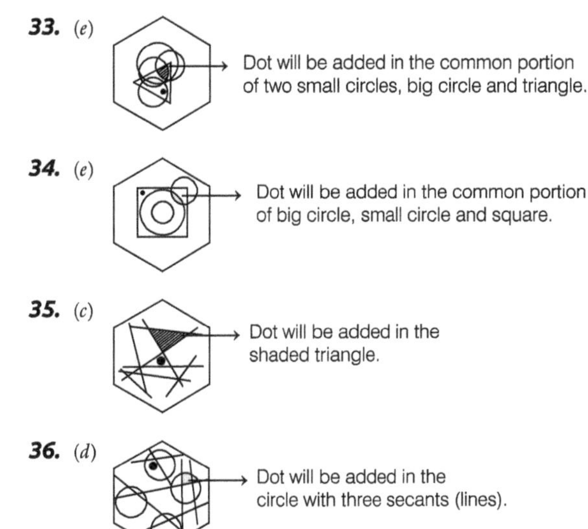

33. (e)
Dot will be added in the common portion of two small circles, big circle and triangle.
34. (e)
Dot will be added in the common portion of big circle, small circle and square.
35. (c)
Dot will be added in the shaded triangle.
36. (d)
Dot will be added in the circle with three secants (lines).

37. (*b*) It contains one dot in one circle, one dot in two circles and one dot in three circles.

38. (*b*) The given figure has three circles of different sizes, one triangle, one dot out on its own, one dot in the larger circle only and the other dot in the middle sized circle and triangle.

A New Approach to

REASONING

ANALYTICAL REASONING

CHAPTER / 01

Syllogism

The word syllogism is derived from the Greek word "Syllogismos" which means "Conclusion, inference or deduction". These deductions are based on propositions (premise).

'Syllogism' checks basic aptitude and ability of a candidate to derive inferences from given statements using step by step methods of solving problems.

Proposition

A **proposition** or **premise** is grammatical sentence comprising of four components

- Quantifier
- Subject
- Copula
- Predicate

Let us consider the following sentences,

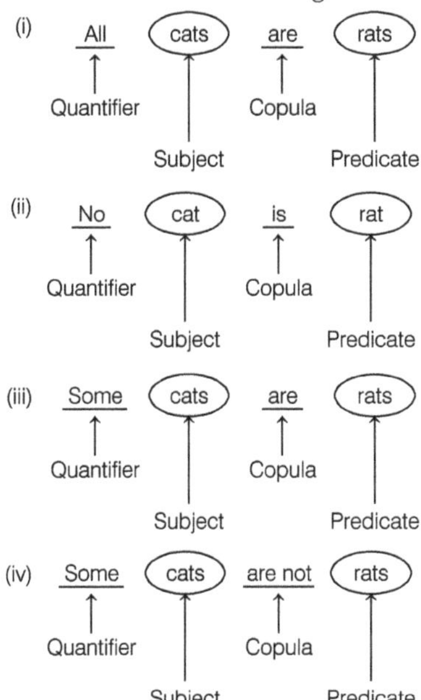

In all the sentences mentioned above, a **relation** is established between **subject** and **predicate** with the help of **quantifier** and **copula**.

Components of Proposition

- **Quantifier** The words 'All', 'No' and 'Some' are called quantifiers as they specify a quantity.
  Keep in mind that 'All' and 'No' are universal quantifiers because they refer to each and every object of a certain set.
  'Some' is a particular quantifier as it refers to atleast one existing object in a certain set.
- **Subject (S)** A subject is that part of a proposition about which something is said.
- **Copula (C)** It is that part of a proposition that denotes the relation between subject and predicate.
- **Predicate (P)** It is that part of a proposition which is affirmed detail about that subject.

Important Terms Used in Syllogism

To find a logical deduction from two statements there should be three terms present. Those three terms are

1. **Major term** It is the predicate of the conclusion and is denoted by 'P' (for predicate).
2. **Minor term** It is the subject of the conclusion and is denoted by 'S' (for subject).
3. **Middle term** It is the term common to both the statements and is denoted by 'M' (for middle).
   The middle term should not appear in the conclusion.

e.g. **Statements**

All ships are buses.

All cars are ships.

Conclusion All cars are buses.

Here, 'buses' is the predicate of the conclusion. Therefore, it is major term, P. 'Cars' is the subject of the conclusion. Therefore, it is the minor term, S. 'Ships' is the term common to both the statements. Therefore, it is the middle term, M.

Major and Minor Statements

The 'major statement' is that in which the middle term is the subject and the 'minor statement' is that in which the middle term is the predicate.

e.g. **Statements**

All dogs are cats.

All cats are white.

Here, the middle term 'cats' is the subject of second statement.

So, it is the major statement and the middle term, 'cats' is the predicate of first statement. So, it is the minor statement.

Classification of Proposition

A proposition can mainly be divided into three categories

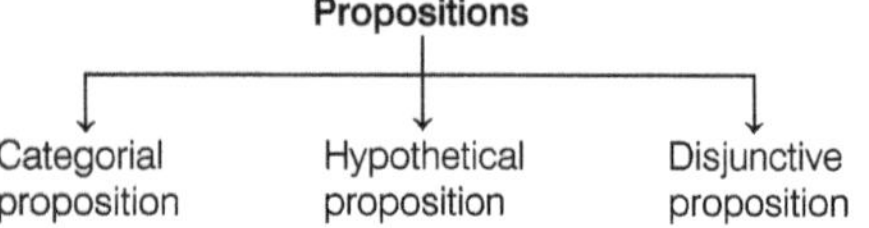

(i) **Categorical Proposition** In categorical proposition, there exists a relationship between the subject and the predicate without any condition. It means predicate is either affirmation or denial of the subject unconditionally.

e.g., I. All cups are plates. II. No girl is boy.

(ii) **Hypothetical Proposition** In a hypothetical proposition, relationship between subject and predicate is asserted conditionally.

e.g., I. If it rains, he will not come.

II. If he comes, I will accompany him.

(iii) **Disjunctive Proposition** In a disjunctive proposition, the assertion is of alteration.

e.g., I. Either he is honest or he is loyal.

II. Either he is educated or he is illiterate.

Keeping in view with the existing pattern of Syllogism in competitive examinations, we are concerned only with the categorical type of proposition.

Types of Categorical Proposition

Propositions have been classified on the basis of quality and quantity. Quality denotes whether the proposition is affirmative or negative in nature. Quantity denotes whether the proposition is universal or particular.

Types of proposition can be understood by the following diagram

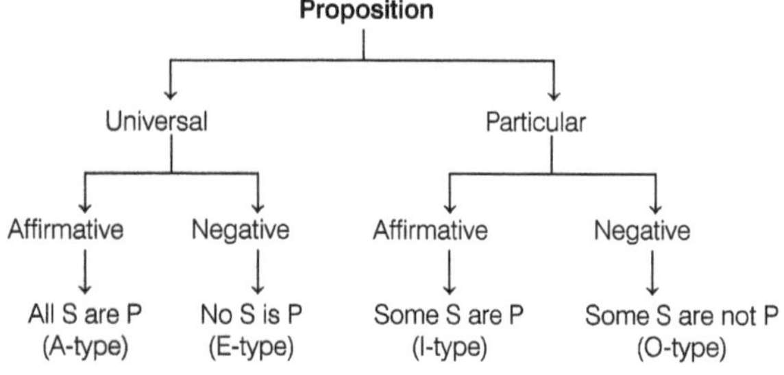

From the above diagram, following things are very much clear

(i) Universal propositions, Either

(a) completely include the subject (A-type)

or (b) completely exclude the subject (E-type)

(ii) Particular propositions, Either

(a) partly include the subject (I-type)

or (b) partly exclude the subject (O-type)

Now, we can summarize the four standard types of propositions (premises) as below

Type	Proposition	Quantity	Quality
A	All A are B	Universal	Affirmative
E	No A is B	Universal	Negative
I	Some A are B	Particular	Affirmative
O	Some A are not B	Particular	Negative

To draw valid inferences from the statements, the candidate is required to have a clear understanding of A, E, I, O relationships.

Venn Diagram Representation

(i) **A-Type** (All S are P)	Either [P ⊃ S] All S are P (Some P are S) Or [SP] All P are S
(ii) **E-Type** (No S are P)	[S] [P] No P are S
(iii) **I-Type** (Some S are P)	Either, [S ∩ P] Some P are S (Some S are not P) Or [S ⊃ P] Some S are P (All P are S) Or [P ⊃ S] Some P are S (All S are P)
(iv) **O-Type** (Some S are not P)	Either, [S ∩ P] Some S are not P (Some S are P) Or [S ⊃ P] Some S are not P (All P are S) Or [S] [P] Some S are not P (No S are P)

Hidden Propositions

The type of propositions we have discussed earlier are of standard nature but there are propositions which do not appear in standard format and yet can be classified under any of the four types.

Let us now discuss the type of such propositions

I. A-Type Propositions

(i) All positive propositions beginning with 'every', 'each' and 'any' are A-type propositions. *e.g.,*
   (a) Every cot is mat ⇒ All cots are mats.
   (b) Each of students of class V has passed.
      ⇒ All students of class V have passed.
   (c) Anyone can do this job.
      ⇒ All (men) can do this job.

(ii) A positive sentence with a particular person as its subject is always an A-type proposition. e.g.,

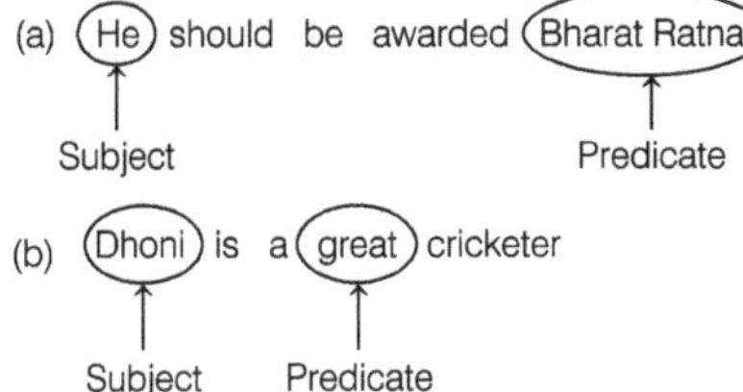

(iii) A sentence with a definite exception is A-type. e.g.,

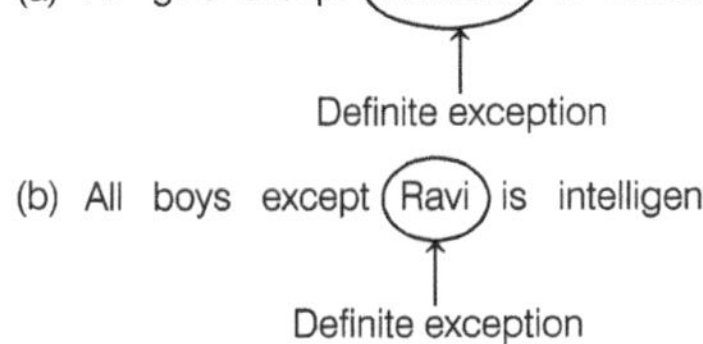

II. E-Type Propositions

(i) All negative sentences beginning with 'no one', 'none', 'not a single' etc., are E-type propositions.
   e.g., (a) Not a single student could answer the question.
   (b) No one can cross the river.

(ii) A negative sentence with a very definite exception is also of E-type proposition.
   e.g.,

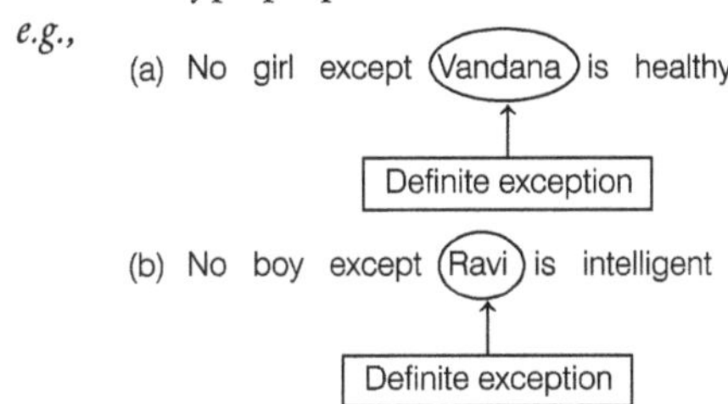

(iii) When an interrogative sentence is used to make an assertion, This could be reduced to an E-type proposition.
   e.g., Is there any person who can scale Mount Everest? ⇒ None can climb Mount Everest.

(iv) A negative sentence with a particular person as its subject is E-type proposition.
   e.g.,

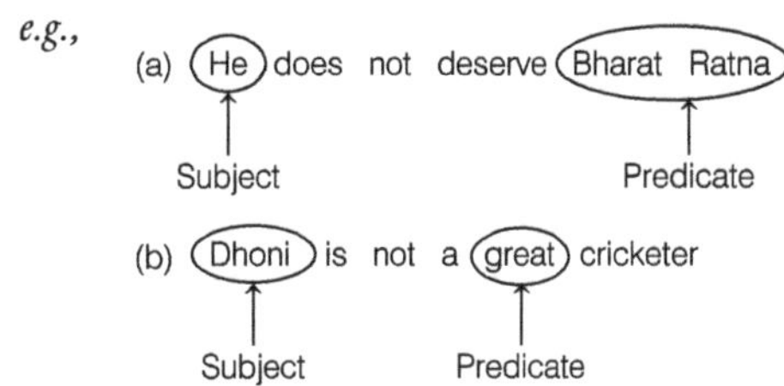

III. I-Type Propositions

(i) Positive propositions beginning with words such as 'most', 'a few', 'mostly', 'generally', 'almost', 'frequently' and 'often' are to be reduced to the I-type propositions.
   e.g., (a) Almost all the fruits have been sold.
      ⇒ Some fruits have been sold.
   (b) Most of the students will qualify in the examination.
      ⇒ Some of the students will qualify in the examination.
   (c) Girls are frequently physically weak.
      ⇒ Some girls are physically weak.

(ii) Negative propositions beginning with words such as 'few', 'seldom', 'hardly', 'scarcely', 'rarely', 'little' etc. are to be reduced to I-type propositions.
   e.g., (a) Seldom players do not take rest.
      ⇒ Some players take rest.
   (b) Few priests do not tell a lie.
      ⇒ Some priests tell a lie.
   (c) Rarely IT professionals do not get a good job.
      ⇒ Some IT professionals get a good job.

(iii) A positive sentence with an exception which is not definite, is reduced to an I-type proposition.
   e.g.,

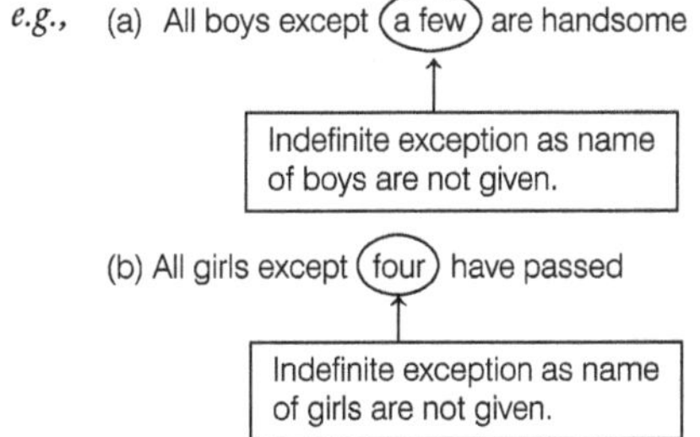

IV. O-Type Propositions

(i) All negative propositions beginning with words such as 'all', 'every', 'any', 'each' etc. are to be reduced to O-type propositions.
   e.g., (a) All innocents are not guilty.
      ⇒ Some innocents are not guilty.
   (b) All that glitters is not gold.
      ⇒ Some glittering objects are not gold.
   (c) Everyone is not present.
      ⇒ Some are not present.

(ii) Negative propositions with words as 'most', 'a few', 'mostly, 'generally', 'almost', 'frequently' are to be reduced to the O-type propositions.

e.g., (a) Girls are usually not physically weak.
⇒ Some girls are not physically weak.
(b) Priests are not frequently thiefs.
⇒ Some priests are not thiefs.
(c) Almost all the questions cannot be solved.
⇒ Some questions cannot be solved.

(iii) Positive propositions with starting words such as 'few', 'seldom', 'hardly', 'scarcely', 'rarely', 'little', etc., are to be reduced to the O-type propositions.

e.g., (a) Few girls are intelligent.
⇒ Some girls are not intelligent
(b) Seldom are innocents guilty.
⇒ Some innocent are not guilty.

(iv) A negative sentence with an exception, which is not definite is to be reduced to the O-type propositions.

e.g., 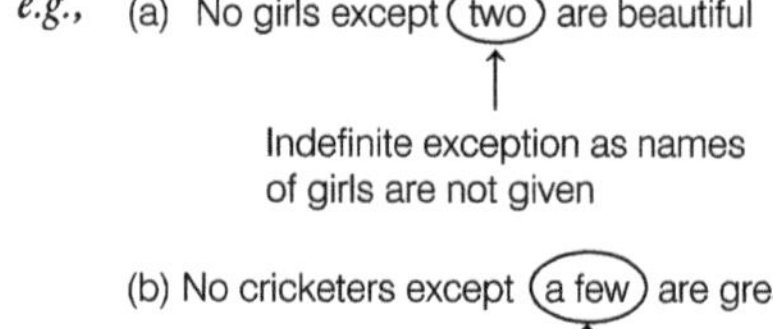

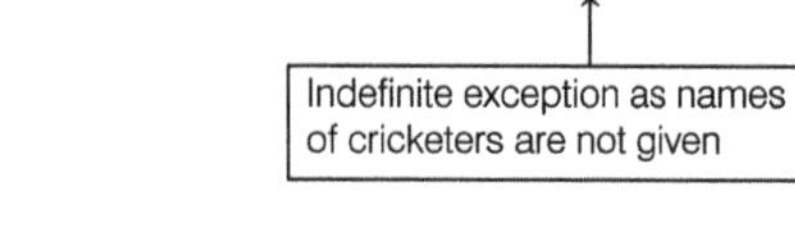

Exclusive Propositions

Such propositions start with 'only', 'alone', 'none but', 'none else but' etc., and they can be reduced to either A or E or I-type.

e.g., Only graduates are officers.

None graduate is officer.	(E-type)
All officers are graduates.	(A-type)
Some graduates are officers.	(I-type)

Inference

Inference is a logical conclusion derived from premises or statements known or assumed to be true.

Types of Inferences

Inferences drawn from statements can be of two types

1. **Immediate Inference** When an inference is drawn from a single statement, then that inference is known as an immediate inference.
   e.g., **Statement** All books are pages.
   Conclusion Some pages are books.
   In the above example, a conclusion is drawn from a single statement and does not require the second statement to be referred, hence the inference is called an immediate inference.
2. **Mediate Inference** In mediate inference, conclusion is drawn from two given statements.
   e.g., **Statements** All dogs are cats.
   All cats are black.
   Conclusion All dogs are black.

In the above example, conclusion is drawn from the two statements or in other words, both the statements are required to draw the conclusion. Hence, the above conclusion is known as mediate inference.

Method to Draw Immediate Inferences

There are various methods to draw immediate inferences like **conversion, obversion, contraposition**, etc. Keeping in view the nature of questions asked in various competitive examinations, we are required to study only two methods, **implications** and **conversion.**

(i) **Implications** (of a given proposition) Below we shall discuss the implications of all the four types of propositions. While drawing a conclusion through implication, **subject remains the subject and predicate remains the predicate.**

A-Type ***All boys are blue.***

From the above A-type proposition, it is very clear that if all boys are blue, then some boys will definitely be blue because **some is a part of all.** Hence, from A-type proposition, we can draw I-type conclusion (through implication).

E-Type ***No cars are buses.***

If no cars are buses, it clearly means that some cars are not buses. Hence, from E-type proposition, O-type conclusion (through implication) can be drawn.

I-Type ***Some chairs are tables.***

From the above I-type proposition, we can not draw any valid conclusion (through implication).

O-Type ***Some A are not B.***

From the above O-type proposition, we can not draw any valid inference (through implication). On first look, it appears that if some A are not B, then conclusion that some A are B must be true but the possibility of this conclusion being true can be over ruled with the help of following example.

Case I	A= {a, b, c} and B= {d, e, f}
Case II	A= {a, b, c} and B= {b, c, d}

The above two cases show the relationship between A and B given by O-type proposition "Some A are not B". Now, in case I, none of the element of set A is the element of set B. Hence, conclusion "Some A are B" cannot be valid. However, in case II, elements b and c are common to both sets A and B. Hence, here conclusion "Some A are B" is valid. But for any conclusion to be true, it should be true for all the cases. Hence, conclusion "Some A are B" is not a valid conclusion drawn from an O-type proposition.

All the results derived for **immediate inference** through **implication** can be presented in the table as below

Types of propositions	Proposition	Types of inferences	Inference
A	All S are P	I	Some S are P
E	No S is P	O	Some S are not P
I	Some S are P	—	—
O	Some S are not P	—	—

(ii) **Conversion** Conversion is other way of getting immediate inferences. Unlike implication, in case of conversion, **subject becomes predicate and predicate becomes subject.** *Let us see*

- **Conversion of A-type**

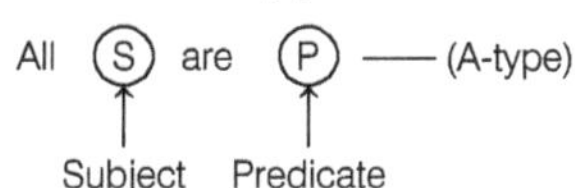

After conversion, it becomes

Clearly, A gets converted into I-type.

- **Conversion of E-type**

No (S) is (P) — (E-type)

Subject Predicate

After conversion, it becomes

No (P) is (S) — (E-type)

Subject Predicate

Clearly, E gets converted into E-type.

- **Conversion of I-type**

Some (S) are (P) — (I-type)

Subject Predicate

After, conversion, it becomes

Some (P) are (S) — (I-type)

Subject Predicate

Clearly, I gets converted into I-type.

- **Conversion of O-type**

  O-type of propositions cannot be converted.

Now, we can make a conversion table as below

Types of propositions	Gets converted into
A	I
E	E
I	I
O	Never gets converted

Chapter tip!

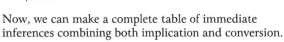

- In implication, subject and predicate do not interchange their places.
- In conversion, subject and predicate interchange their places.

Now, we can make a complete table of immediate inferences combining both implication and conversion.

Immediate Inference Table

Types of Propositions	Format of Proposition	Valid immediate inference	Types of immediate inferences	Method
A	All S are P	Some S are P	I	Implication
		Some P are S	I	Conversion
E	No S is P	Some S are not P	O	Implication
		No P is S	E	Conversion
I	Some S are P	No valid inference	—	Implication
		Some P are S	I	Conversion
O	Some S are not P	No valid inference	—	Implication
		No valid inference	—	Conversion

Venn Diagram Representation of Immediate Inferences

Immediate inferences drawn from each type of propositions (A, E, I, O), as given in the above table, are based on the different rules (implication and conversion) as discussed above.

The same inferences can also be drawn with the help of Venn-diagrams but one of the important point to be noted while drawing inference from Venn-diagrams is that all possibilities of Venn diagrams should be taken into account. Let us discuss each type of proposition in relation to the pictorial representation.

1. A-Type – All S are P

It is clear from the A-type of proposition that all S are contained in P. Therefore, circle representing S will be either inside or equal to circle representing P.

However, in both the cases, conclusions (Some P are S) and (Some S are P) are true. This case can be understood clearly by taking two sets in all possible ways.

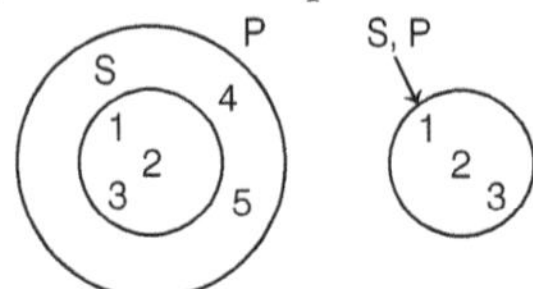

(i) S = {1,2,3}, P = {1, 2, 3, 4, 5}
(ii) S = {1, 2, 3}, P = {1, 2, 3}

The above cases show the all the possibilities of two sets S and P showing the relationship between each other as represented by the proposition. All S are P, now in both the cases we see that set {2, 3} is the part of set S and also of set P. Hence, it is clear that inference (Some S are P) is true from this relationship. Likewise set {2, 3} is the part of set P and also of set S.

Therefore, it is also clear that inference (Some P are S) is true. Inference (Some P are not S) is not valid because it is true from case (i) but false from case (ii). Inference (All P are S) is not valid because it is true from case (ii) and false from case (i).

2. E-Type – No S is P

There is only one possibility of Venn diagram representation of E-type proposition.

The relationship can also be shown by two sets S = {1, 2, 3} and P = {4, 5, 6}. From these two sets, we see that set {2, 3} is the part of set S but not of set P.

It implies that inference (Some S are not P) is true. Similarly, set {5, 6} is the part of set P but not of set S. This means that inference (some P are not S) is true.

Therefore, on the basis of E-type proposition, we can draw following immediate inferences.

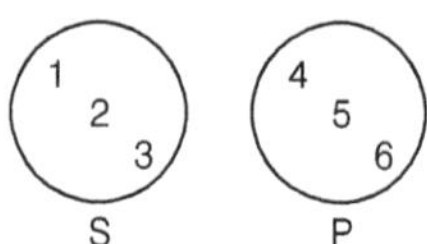

(i) No P is S
(ii) Some S are not P
(iii) Some P are not S

Any other immediate inference drawn from E-type proposition is not valid.

3. I-Type – Some S are P

This proposition gives rise to many possible representations of Venn diagrams and hence most of the inferences drawn therefrom are invalid and doubtful.

This relationship can be shown by following sets and respective Venn diagrams.

(i) S = {1,2,3,4}, P = {3,4,5,6}

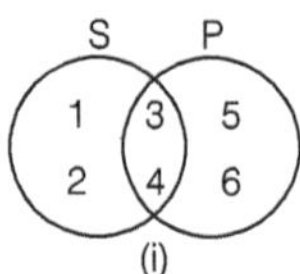

(i)

Set {3, 4} is the part of set S as well as set P, hence some S are P.

(ii) S = {1, 2, 3, 4}, P = {1, 2}

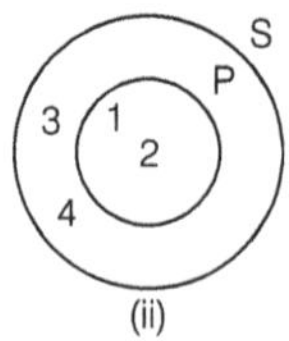

(ii)

Set {1, 2} is the part of set S as well as set P, hence some S are P.

(iii) S = {1, 2}, P = {1, 2, 3, 4}

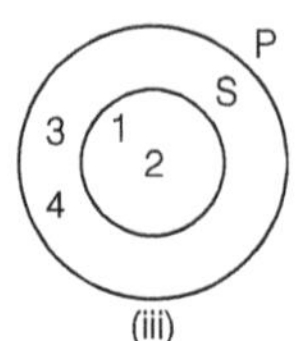

(iii)

Set {2} is the part of set S as well as set P, hence some S are P.

(iv) S = {1, 2, 3}, P = {1, 2, 3}

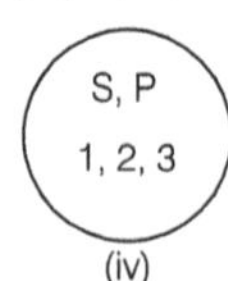

(iv)

Set {1, 2} is the part of set S as well as set P, hence some S are P.

The above four combinations of sets and respective diagrams show the relationship between S and P as represented by I-type proposition. From all the possible combinations, it is clear that inference (Some P are S) is true.

Inference (Some S are not P) is true from combinations (i) and (ii) but it is not true from combinations (iii) and (iv). Therefore, inference (Some S are not P) is not a valid inference drawn from the above proposition.

4. O-Type – Some S are not P

From this proposition, no immediate inference can be drawn. Let us discuss this proposition in the light of Venn-diagram representation.

(i) S = {1, 2, 3, 4}, P = {3, 4, 5, 6}

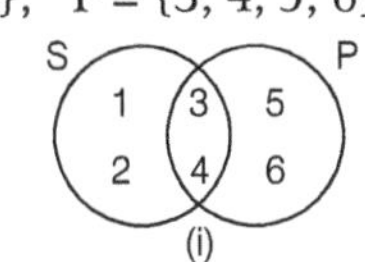

(i)

Set {1, 2} is the part of set S but not of set P, hence this shows the relationship represented by the proposition 'Some S are not P'.

(ii) S = {1, 2, 3}, P = {4, 5, 6}

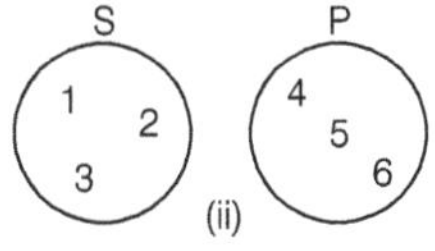

(ii)

Set {2, 3} is the part of set S but not of set P, hence this shows the relation represented by the proposition 'Some S are not P'.

(iii) S = {1, 2, 3, 4, 5}, P = {4, 5}

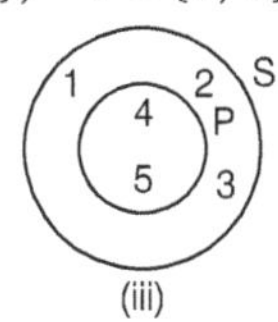

(iii)

Set {1, 2, 3} is the part of set S but not set P, hence denotes proposition 'Some S are not P'.

On the basis of all possible combinations showing relationship between S and P, no valid inference can be drawn.

Inference (some S are P) is true from combinations (i) and (iii) but not true for combination (ii), hence it is invalid inference. Inference (some P are not S) is true from combination (i) and (ii) but not true for combination (iii). Hence, it is also invalid inference.

Method to Draw Mediate Inferences

Mediate inference can be drawn only if,

- there are two statements/propositions.
- there is a common term in the given two statements.
- the common term is predicate of the first statement and subject of the second statement.

To draw a Mediate Inference the following conclusion table is used,

Mediate Inference Table

Proposition I	Proposition II	Type of conclusion
A	A	A
A	E	E
E	A	O^R
E	I	O^R
I	A	I
I	E	O

- Apart from 6 pairs of propositions given in the conclusion table no other pair will give any conclusion.
- The conclusion/inference drawn out of two propositions is itself a proposition and its subject is the subject of first statement while its predicate is predicate of the second statement. The common term gets disappeared.
- O^R means, the conclusion is of O-type but is in reverse order. In this case, the subject of the inference/conclusion is the predicate of the second statement and the predicate of the inference or conclusion is the subject of the first statement.
- The mediate inference table gives correct inference/conclusion if and only if the two statements are in proper alignment.

Alignment

Two statements are said to be aligned if and only if

- common term must be the predicate of the first statement
- common term must be the subject of the second statement

In other words, we can say that a pair of statements will be aligned, if predicate of the first statement is the subject of the second or subject of the second sentence is the predicate of the first.

Let us see the following pairs of statements

(i) All cats are (rats)
All (rats) are dogs } ⟶ Aligned pair

In the above pair, common term = rats

The common term (rats) is the predicate of the first statement and subject of the second statement. Hence, the above pair is aligned.

(ii) Some (bats) are chairs
Some cars are (bats) } ⟶ Non-aligned pair

In this case, common term = bats

The common term (bats) is not the predicate of the first statements and subject of the second statement. Hence, the given pair is not properly aligned.

Process of Alignment

1. **By changing order of sentences**

Let us consider the following pair of statements

I. Some (bats) are chairs
II. Some cats are (bats) } → Non-aligned pair

To make the above pair aligned, we change the order of the two sentences by putting Statement II in place of Statement I and Statement I in place of Statement II as given below

I. Some cats are bats
II. Some bats are chairs } → Aligned pair

2. **By converting one of the sentences**

   Let us consider the following pair of statements

   I. All (bats) are chairs
   II. Some (bats) are cats } → Non-aligned pair

   Here, we convert Statement I to make the pair aligned.

   I. Some chairs are (bats)
   II. Some (bats) are cats } → Aligned pair

3. **By changing the order of statements and then converting one of the sentences**

   ***Step* 1** Let us consider the following pair of statements

   I. All (bats) are chairs
   II. All (bats) are cats } → Non-aligned pair

   Let us change the order as below

   I. All (bats) are chairs
   II. All (bats) are cats

   ***Step* 2** Do conversion for II and aligned pair takes the form as below

   II. Some cats are (bats)
   I. All (bats) are chairs } → Aligned pair

Hence, it is clear that alignment is done as per the requirement and nature of sentences.

Rule of Alignment (IEA)

While aligning the priority should be given in the following order

$$\xrightarrow{\text{I E A}}$$

i.e., I is converted before E and A.
E is converted before A.
A is converted at the end.

It means

- if I and E-type of statements are given, then I will be converted before E.
- if E and A-type of statements are given, then E will be converted before A.
- if I and A-type of statements are given, then I will be converted before A.

Finally we are in a position to draw **mediate inferences**. The method to draw such inferences consists of two main steps as below

***Step* 1** Aligning the pair of sentences if required

***Step* 2** Using mediate inference table

Let us solve some examples

e.g., **Statements** I. All cats are lions.
II. All lions are tigers.

***Step* 1** No need of alignment as the statements are already aligned. (Common term (lions) is predicate of 1st and subject of 2nd.)

***Step* 2** Use of mediate inference table

I. All cats are lions. (A-type)
II. All lions are tigers. (A-type)

From the mediate inference table

A + A = A-type of conclusion

∴ Valid conclusion = All cats are tigers.

e.g., **Statements** I. Some books are papers.
II. No copies are papers.

***Step* 1** Statements are not aligned as common term (papers) is the predicate of both the sentences. Hence, alignment is needed here. Statement I is I-type while Statement II is E-type.

Therefore, according to IEA rule, Statement I gets converted 1st, then interchanges its position with II to be aligned with it. After alignment, both the statements are written as below

I. No copies are papers.
II. Some papers are books.

***Step* 2** Use of mediate inference table

I. No copies are papers. (E-type)
II. Some papers are books. (I-type)

From the mediate inference table E + I = O^R– type of conclusion

∴ Valid conclusion
= Some books are not copies.

Method to Solve Problems

We have learnt deriving immediate and mediate inference separately but now we have come to the actual format of the questions in which the conclusion part may include

- only immediate inferences.
- only mediate inferences.
- both immediate and mediate inferences.

Therefore, while solving actual questions of syllogism we must check, if the given conclusions are immediate or mediate or both.

Let us consider the example

Statements I. Some dogs are pens.
II. All pens are pots.

Conclusions I. Some dogs are pots.
II. Some pens are pots.
III. All pots are pens.

(a) Only I follows (b) Only II follows
(c) Only III follows (d) Both I and II follow
(e) None of these

Solving Process

***Step* 1** Check the immediate inferences

Conclusion I is not the immediate inference of any of the two statements. Let us see

Statement I Some dogs are pens. (I-type)

↓

Immediate inference (by conversion I into I)

↓

Some pens are dogs. (I-type)

Clearly, Conclusion II is not the immediate inference of Statement I.

Statement II (A-type)

All pens are pots.

↓

Immediate inference

Some pens are pots. (I-type) (By implication A into I) | Some poets are pens. (I-type) (by conversion A into I)

- Clearly, Conclusion I is not the immediate inference of Statement II.
- Conclusion II is the immediate inference of Statement II (It is an immediate inference by implication.) which is already clear from above diagram. Hence, **this conclusion is valid.**
- Conclusion III definitely cannot be the immediate inference of any of the two statements because both I and A-type of statements produce an immediate inference in the form of I-type of proposition but Conclusion III is A-type proposition.

Decision of *Step* 1 Conclusion II follows.

***Step* 2** Check the mediate inferences.

- As Conclusion II has already been declared valid at step 1, we will check now Conclusions I and III.
- Conclusion I is mediate inference of the given statements. *Let us see*

I. Some dogs are pens (I-type)

II. All pens are pots (A-type)

From the table of mediate inference I + A = I-type of conclusions

∴ Valid conclusion = Some dogs are pots = Conclusion I

- Conclusion III cannot be the valid mediate inference of given statements as I and A-type statements can give only I-type of mediate inference.

Decision of Step 2 Conclusion I follows.

***Step* 3**

- Checking through conversion/implication of valid conclusions.
- At this stage only Conclusion III remains to be checked as Conclusion I and Conclusion II have already declared valid.
- Conclusion III will be invalid at step 3 also as valid Conclusions I and II both are I-type and I-type proposition produce I-type statement after conversion but Conclusion III is A-type. Further, no valid conclusion is possible through the implication of I-type of proposition.

Decision of Step 3 Conclusion III is invalid at step 3.

***Step* 4** Check mediate inferences derived from given statements and valid conclusions.

At this stage, again Conclusion III remains to be checked. Let us see

Statement I Some dogs are pens. (I-type)
Conclusion I Some dogs are pots. (I-type)

I + I = No conclusion possible

Again, **Statement I** Some dogs are pens. (I-type)
Conclusion II Some pens are pots. (I-type)

I + I = No conclusion possible

Again, **Statement II** All pens are pots. (A-type)
Conclusion I Some dogs are pots. (I-type)

A + I = No conclusion possible

Again, **Statement II** All pens are pots. (A-type)
Conclusion II Some pens are pots. (I-type)

A + I = No conclusion possible

Further, conclusion is also not possible because subject and predicate of both Statement II and Conclusion II are same.

Decision of Step 4 Conclusion III is invalid.

As Conclusions I and II are declared valid after the four steps mentioned above we can select option (d) (both I and II follow) as our answer.

On the basis of all the four steps mentioned above we can firmly say that valid conclusions are

- immediate inference and their conversion/implication
- mediate inferences and their conversion/implication
- mediate inferences derived from each of the given statement + each of the valid conclusion.

Let us find the total valid conclusions from pair of statements given below

Statements I. Some dogs are pens.
II. All pens are pots.

Conclusions I. Some pens are dogs.
II. Some pens are pots.
III. Some pots are pens.
IV. Some dogs are pots.
V. Some pots are dogs.

Explanations

- Conclusion I is the conversion of Statement I.
- Conclusion II is the implication of Statement II.
- Conclusion III is the conversion of Statement II.
- Conclusion IV is the mediate inference of Statements I and II.
- Conclusion V is the conversion of Conclusion IV.

Note *In the actual question, the conclusion part may include all/some/none of the valid conclusions.*

Complementary Pair of Conclusions ('Either-or' Situation)

In drawing mediate inference from given statements, students are required to be more attentive to select complementary pair of conclusions where neither of the conclusions is definitely true but a combination of both makes a complementary pair.

Let us consider the example

Statements Some cars are scooters.
Some scooters are buses.

Conclusions I. Some cars are buses.
II. No cars are buses.

Solution Both the statements are properly aligned, therefore fulfil the first requirement but both the statements are of I-type and as per table for immediate inference, a combination I + I does not produce any valid mediate inference. Hence, no mediate inference can be drawn.

It is important to note here, that Conclusion I "Some cars are buses" is not valid because there is a possibility of "No cars are buses". Likewise, Conclusion II "No cars are buses" is invalid because there is a possibility of "Some cars are buses".

In other words, both the conclusions are invalid individually. However, we can say that either of Conclusion I or II is true. Hence, here, both the conclusions make a complementary pair of conclusions.

A complementary pair of conclusions must follow the following two conditions

I. Both of them must have the same subject and the same predicate.

II. They are any one of three types of pairs.
(a) I-O type (b) A-O type (c) I-E type

The following examples show the complementary pairs.

e.g., 1. (i) All trees are green. (A-type)
(ii) Some trees are not green. (O-type)
2. (i) Some trees are green. (I-type)
(ii) Some trees are not green. (O-type)
3. (i) Some trees are green. (I-type)
(ii) No trees are green. (E-type)

All the three pairs of conclusions comply with the two conditions given above to form a complementary pair, hence form a complementary pair.

The following examples show the pairs which do not form a complementary pair.

e.g., 1. (i) All trees are green. (A-type)
(ii) Some green are not trees. (O-type)
2. (i) All trees are green. (A-type)
(ii) No trees are green. (E-type)

Though the first pair is A O-type pair, yet it does not form a complementary pair because subject and predicate of both the propositions are not the same.

Second pair is not a complementary pair because A-E type proposition does not form a complementary pair.

Finally, we can combine all the approaches and steps together to prepare a summarized stepwise approach for solving problems. Such as

***Step* 1** is the aligning of statements if required.

***Step* 2** is the checking of immediate inferences.

***Step* 3** is the checking of mediate inferences using mediate inference table.

***Step* 4** is the checking of conversion/implication of valid conclusions.

***Step* 5** is the checking of mediate inferences derived from the combination of each given statement and each valid conclusion.

***Step* 6** is the checking of complementary pair of conclusions.

Note *The above solving method of Syllogism is called* ***Analytical Method****.*

Method To Solve Problems Through Venn Diagram

***Step* 1** Drawing standard representation for each statement separately.

Point to be noted that standard representation means a representation which is most common and usually sufficient way to denote the statement.

Let us see the standard representation of all the four standard types of proposition

Types of propositions	Standard representation
All S are P (A-type)	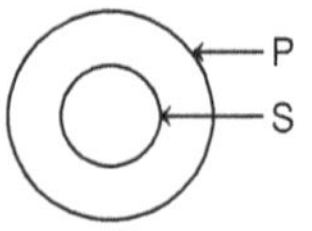 P, S
No S is P(E-type)	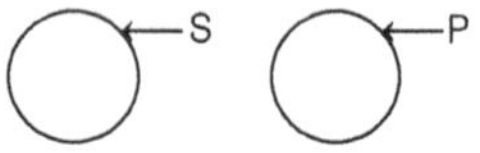 S, P
Some S are P (I-type)	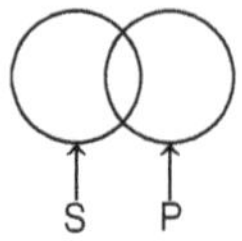 S, P
Some S are not P (O-type)	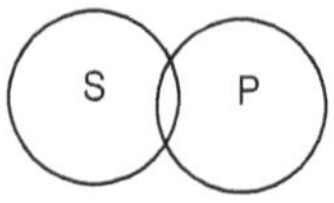 S, P

Let us consider the following pair of statements

Statements I. Some tigers are winners.
II. Some winners are ladies.

Standard representation for Statement I

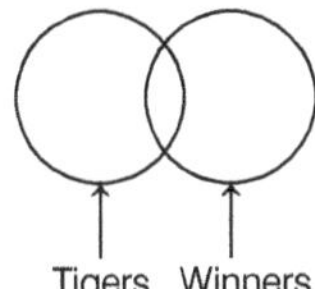

Standard representation for Statement II

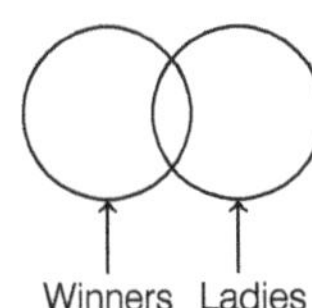

***Step* 2** Combining the representations (drawn in Step 1) in all possible ways. *Let us see*

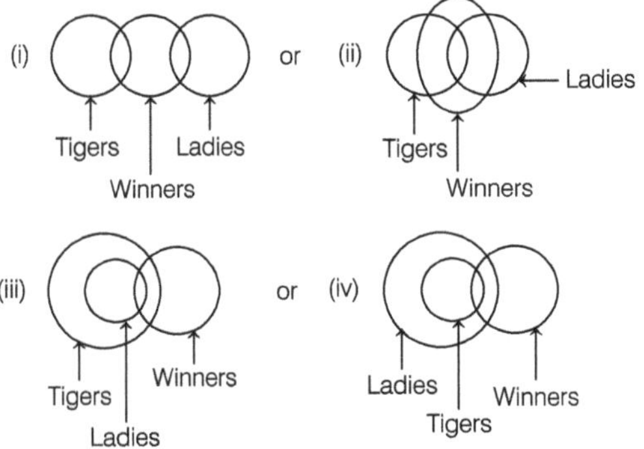

***Step* 3** Making interpretations from the combined figures obtained from Step 2.

Point to be noted that any given conclusion will be true if and only if it is supported by all the combined figures and no combined figure contradicts it.

Let us consider over two conclusions

X. Some winners are tigers.

Y. Some tigers are ladies.

- **Conclusion** X (Some winners are tigers) is a valid conclusion as it is supported by all the combined figures (i), (ii), (iii) and (iv) represented in Step 2.
- **Conclusion** Y (Some tigers are ladies) is an invalid conclusion at it is rejected by figure (i) represented in Step 2.

***Step* 4** Checking the complementary pair of conclusions.

e.g., The following conclusions form a complementary pair for the statements given in Step 1

A. Some tigers are ladies.

B. Some tigers are not ladies.

Conclusion A (Some tigers are ladies) is invalid because of the rejection by combined figure (i) obtained from Step 2.

Conclusion B (Some tigers are not ladies) is invalid because of the rejection by combined figures (ii), (iii) and (iv) obtained from Step 2.

- Conclusions A and B both have same subject – tigers
- Conclusions A and B both have same predicate – ladies

  Hence, Conclusions A and B form complementary pair.

Avoiding Confusion While Selecting Complementary Pair

On some occasions, a pair of conclusions may be complementary but it may not appear so. Let us see the following pair of propositions

I. Some bikes are hangers.

II. Some hangers are not bikes.

In this case,

I. Subject of 1st statement = bikes

II. Predicate of 1st statement = hangers

III. Subject of 2nd statement = hangers

IV. Predicate of 2nd statement = bikes

Clearly, both statements have different subject and predicate. Hence, both the statements do not appear to be complementary but if we convert the first sentence from

I. 'Some bikes are hangers'.

II. 'Some hangers are bikes'.

Then, the two statements have the same subject and predicate now and they take the form as under

Some hangers are bikes
Some hangers are not bikes } → Complementary pair

Possibility Cases in Syllogism and Solving them using Venn Diagrams

In syllogism, when there is no exact conclusion for the given statements, then possibility case arises.

If conclusion is **false** in one diagram and **true** in another diagram, then the conclusion is deduced as **partially true**. In this case, partially true is considered as true.

Statements Some walls are roads.
All roads are floors.

Conclusions

I. All roads being walls is a possibility.

II. All walls being floors is a possibility.

Solution All possible diagrams are as follows

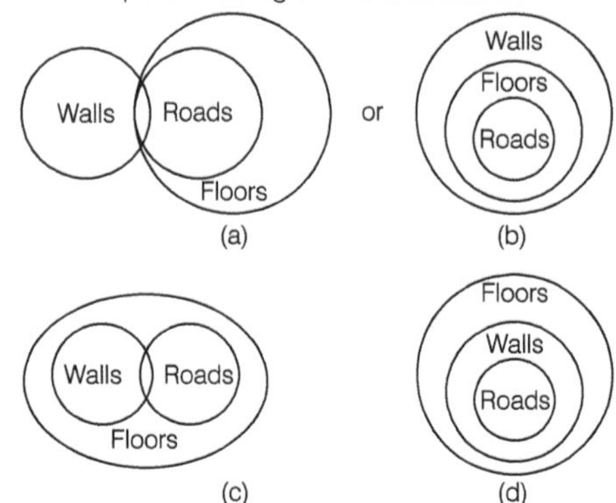

Here, the Conclusion I, i.e. 'All roads being walls is a possibility', is true in the diagrams (b) and (d). And, the Conclusion II, i.e. 'All walls being floors is a possibility', is true in the diagrams (c) and (d). Hence, both the conclusion follow.

Generally, there are three types of questions can be asked in various competitive examination which is as follows

TYPE 01

Two Statements and Two Conclusions

In this type of questions, two statements and two conclusions are given. The candidate is required to check the validity of the given conclusions on the basis of the given statements.

DIRECTIONS ~ (Example Nos. 1-5) *In the questions below are given two statements followed by two conclusions. You have to take the two given statements to be true even if they seem to be at variance from commonly known facts and decide which of the conclusion(s) logically follow(s) from the two given statements.*

Give answer

(a) If only Conclusion I follows
(b) If only Conclusion II follows
(c) If either Conclusion I or II follows
(d) If both Conclusions I and II follow

***Ex* 01 Statements** Some dogs are cats.
All cats are pigs.

Conclusions I. Some cats are dogs.
II. Some dogs are pigs.

Solution (d) According to the question,

Dogs
Pigs
Cats

Conclusions

I. Some cats are dogs. (✓) II. Some dogs are pigs. (✓)

Solution by using mediate and immediate inference table Some dogs are cats. (I-type) All cats are pigs. (A-type)
I + A = I-type of conclusion = Some dogs are pigs = Conclusion II

Again, Some dogs are cats $\xrightarrow{\text{Conversion}}$ Some cats are dogs = Conclusion I

Clearly, Conclusions I and II both follow.

***Ex* 02 Statements** Some players are singers.
All singers are tall.

Conclusions I. Some players are tall.
II. All players are tall.

Solution (a)

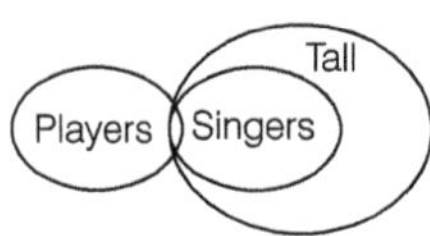

Conclusions I. Some players are tall. (✓)
II. All players are tall. (✗)

***Ex* 03 Statements** All stones are water.
Some water are clean.

Conclusions I. Some water are stones.
II. All clean are water.

Solution (a) According to the given statements,

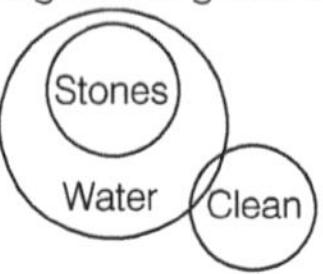

Conclusions I. Some water are stones. (✓)
II. All clean are water. (✗)

***Ex* 04 Statements** All tables are books.
All pens are books. « SSC MTS 2019

Conclusions I. Some tables are pens.
II. Some books are pens.

Solution (b) According to the given statements,

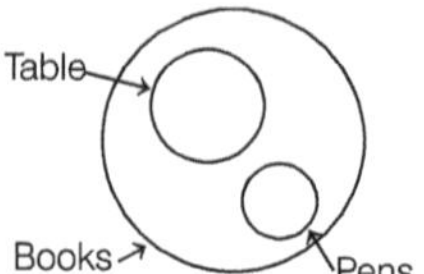

Conclusions I. All tables are books. (✗)
II. All pens are books. (✓)
Only Conclusion II is true.

***Ex* 05 Statements** Some books are cars.
Some cars are dogs.
« SSC Stenographer 2019

Conclusions I. Some dogs are cars.
II. Some cars are books.

Solution (d) According to the statements,

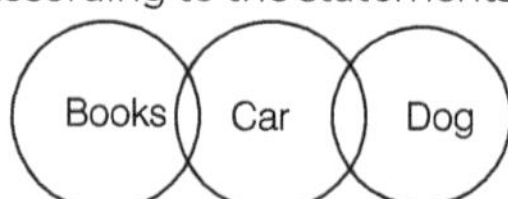

Conclusions I. Some dogs are cars. (✓)
II. Some cars are books. (✓)

Ex 06 Consider the following statements followed by two conclusions.

Statements Some men are great.
Some men are wise. « UPSC 2015

Conclusions I. Men are either great or wise.
II. Some men are neither great nor wise.

Which one of the following is correct?
(a) Only Conclusion I is valid.
(b) Only Conclusion II is valid.
(c) Both the conclusions are valid.
(d) Neither of the conclusions is valid.

Solution **(d)** According to the statements

Conclusions I. Men are either great or wise. (✗)
II. Some men are neither great nor wise. (✗)
So, neither of the conclusions is valid.

DIRECTIONS ~ (Example Nos. 7 and 8) *In each of the questions below. Some statements are given followed by conclusions/group of conclusions numbered* I *and* II. *You have to assume all the statements to be true even if they seem to be at variance from the commonly known facts and then decide which of the given two conclusions logically follows from the information given in the statements.* « LIC (AAO) 2019

Ex 07 Statements Only a few books are reading.
All readings are general.

Conclusions I. All books are general.
II. Some general are reading.

(a) If only Conclusion II follows
(b) If neither I nor II follows
(c) If both Conclusions I and II follow
(d) If only Conclusion I follows
(e) If either Conclusion I or II follows

Solution **(a)** According to the given statements,

General
Book
Reading

Conclusions I. All books are general. (✗)
II. Some general are reading. (✓)
Hence, only Conclusion II follows.

Ex 08 Statements Only a few woods are trees.
Only a few woods are stems.

Conclusions I. Some stems are trees is a possibility.
II. Some stems are tree.

(a) If only Conclusion II follows
(b) If neither I nor II follows
(c) If both Conclusions I and II follow
(d) If only Conclusion I follows
(e) If either Conclusion I or II follows

Solution **(d)** According to the given statements,

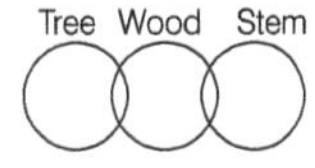

Conclusions I. Some stems are trees is a possibility. (✓)
II. Some stems are tree. (✗)
Hence, only Conclusion I follows.

Practice / CORNER 1.1

DIRECTIONS ~ (Q. Nos. 1-26) *In each of the questions below are given two statements followed by two conclusions numbered I and II. You have to take the two given statements to be true even if they seem to be at variance from commonly known facts and decide which of the given conclusion(s) logically follow(s) from the two given statements, disregarding commonly known facts.*

Give answer
(a) If only Conclusion I follows
(b) If only Conclusion II follows
(c) If either I or II follows
(d) If neither I nor II follows
(e) If both I and II follow

1. Statements All cars are balls.
All balls are tables.
Conclusions
I. Some tables are balls. II. Some tables are cars.

2. Statements Some rats are cats.
All cats are bats.
Conclusions
I. No rats are cats. II. Some rats are bats.

3. Statements Some exams are tests.
No exam is a question.
Conclusions
I. No question is a test. II. Some tests are exams.

4. Statements All greens are yellows.
No yellows are black. « IBPS RRB Office Assistant 2020
Conclusions
I. No greens are black. II. Some greens are black.

5. Statements No colour is a paint.
No paint is a brush. « SBI (Clerk) 2012
Conclusions
I. No colour is a brush. II. All brushes are colours.

6. Statements All stars are planets.
All planets are galaxies. « SBI (Clerk) 2012

Conclusions

I. All galaxies are planets.
II. All stars are galaxies.

7. Statements Some schools are factories.
All factories are shops.

Conclusions

I. All shops are factories.
II. Some shops are schools.

8. Statements No house is an apartment.
Some apartments are bungalows. « UCO Bank (Clerk) 2011

Conclusions

I. No house is a bungalow.
II. All bungalows being houses is a possibility.

9. Statements All plants are animals.
All insects are plants. « UCO Bank (Clerk) 2011

Conclusions

I. All insects being animals is a possibility.
II. There is a possibility that some animals are neither insects nor plants.

10. Statements All pens are ink.
No ink is an eraser. « UCO Bank (Clerk) 2011

Conclusions

I. No pen is an eraser.
II. Some erasers are pens.

11. Statements All DSLR are lenses.
Some camera are DSLR.

Conclusions

I. All camera is lenses.
II. Some lenses are camera.

12. Statements Some books are pen.
Some pens are pencil. « IBPS Clerk 2018

Conclusions

I. No book is pencil.
II. All pencils are books.

13. Statements Some cities are towns.
Some villages are cities.

Conclusions

I. Atleast some villages are towns.
II. No village is a town.

14. Statements Some sands are particles.
Some particles are glasses. « SBI (PO) 2015

Conclusions

I. Some glasses are definitely not particles.
II. Some glasses being sands is a possibility.

15. Statements Some trees are plants.
All bushes are plants. « IBPS (PO) 2012

Conclusions

I. Atleast some trees are bushes.
II. Some trees are definitely not bushes.

16. Statements All Bottles are glasses.
No cup is a glass. « SBI (Clerk) 2012

Conclusions

I. No bottle is a cup.
II. Atleast some glasses are bottles.

17. Statements No bangle is an earrings.
Some earrings are rings. « RBI (Grade 'B') 2012

Conclusions

I. No ring is a bangle.
II. Some rings are definitely not earrings.

18. Statements All exams are tests.
No test is a question. « RBI (Grade 'B') 2012

Conclusions

I. Atleast some exams are questions.
II. No exam is a question.

19. Statements All rivers are lakes.
All lakes are oceans. « RBI (Grade 'B') 2012

Conclusions

I. All rivers are oceans.
II. Atleast some oceans are lakes.

20. Statements Some banks are colleges.
All colleges are schools. « RBI (Grade 'B') 2012

Conclusions

I. Atleast some banks are schools.
II. All schools are colleges.

21. Statements Some exams are tests.
No exam is a question. « IBPS (PO) 2012

Conclusions

I. No question is a test.
II. Some tests are definitely not exams.

22. Statements Some wires are fires.
All fires are tyres. « SBI (Clerk) 2012

Conclusions

I. Atleast some tyres are wires.
II. Some fires are definitely not wires.

23. Statements No toffee is coffee.
No sweet is toffee. « SBI (Clerk) 2012

Conclusions

I. No coffee is sweet.
II. All sweets are coffee.

24. Statements Only a few numbers are palindrome.
No digits are palindrome. « IBPS (PO) 2019

Conclusions

I. Some digits are numbers.
II. All numbers can never be digits.

25. Statements Only a few A is B.
No B is C. « IBPS (PO) 2019

Conclusions
I. All A can never be C.
II. All C can never be A.

26. Statements Only a few strong is tough.
Only a few tough is dark. « IBPS (PO) 2019

Conclusions
I. Some strong is not dark.
II. No tough is strong.

DIRECTIONS ~(Q. Nos. 27-38) *Two statements are given below followed by two Conclusions* I *and* II. *You have to consider the two statements to be true even if they seem to be at variance with commonly known facts. You have to decide which of the conclusions, if any, follow from the given statements.*

Give answer
(a) Only I follows (b) Only II follows
(c) Both I and II follow (d) Neither I nor II follows

27. Statements All flowers are leaves.
Some flowers are plants. « SSC CGL 2017

Conclusions
I. Some leaves are plants.
II. Some plants are flowers.

28. Statements Some apples are red.
All red are oranges. « SSC CGL 2017

Conclusions
I. No oranges are apples.
II. Some apples are oranges.

29. Statements All beans are meat.
All breads are meat. « SSC (10+2) 2020

Conclusions
I. Some beans are breads.
II. Some breads are beans.

30. Statements
No quadrilaterals are polygons.
All polygons are rhombuses. « RRB ALP 2018

Conclusions
I. Some rhombuses are quadrilaterals.
II. Some rhombuses are polygons.

31. Statements All candles are lanterns.
All lanterns are bulbs. « MP Police Constable Cadre 2017

Conclusions
I. All lanterns are candles.
II. All bulbs are candle.

32. Statements All kerchiefs are towels.
All towels are blankets. « MP Police Constable Cadre 2017

Conclusions
I. All kerchiefs are blankets.
II. All blankets are towels.

33. Statements Some interviews are exams.
All exams are tests. « MP Police Constable Cadre 2017

Conclusions
I. All tests are exams.
II. Some tests are interviews.

34. Statements All good hockey players are in the Indian hockey team.
'X' is not a good hockey player. « CLAT 2014

Conclusions
I. 'X' is not in the Indian hockey team.
II. 'X' wants to be in the Indian hockey team.

35. Statements Some scales are pencils.
Some erasers are pencils. « SSC (Multitasking) 2014

Conclusions
I. Some pencils are erasers.
II. Some pencils are scales.

36. Statements All word files are excel files.
No excel file is a power point presentation.

Conclusions « MP Police Constable Cadre 2017
I. No word file is a power point presentation.
II. Some excel files are word files.

37. Statements All cats are dogs.
All cats are black. « UPSC CSAT 2020

Conclusions
I. All dogs are black.
II. Some dogs are not black.

38. Statements Some jaguars are cheetahs.
Some cheetahs are leopards. « RRB Group D 2018

Conclusions
I. No leopards is a jaguar.
II. Some jaguars are leopards.

39. Study the following statements carefully and decide which of the given conclusions follows.

Statements Some bulbs are LEDs.
Some LEDs are tubelights.

Conclusions « SSC CAPFs 2019
I. Some tubelights are bulbs.
II. No tubelight is a bulb.
(a) Only I (b) Only II (c) Either I or II (d) Both follow

Answers / WITH EXPLANATIONS

1. (*e*) **Method I**

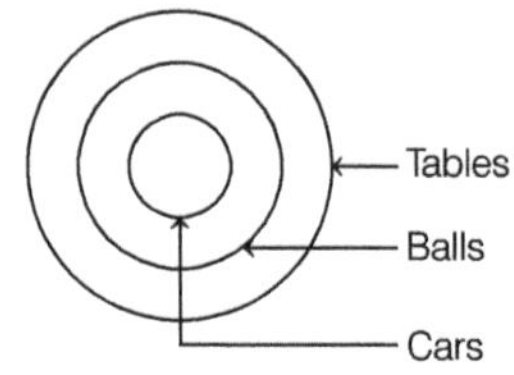

Conclusions I. Some tables are balls. (✓)

II. Some tables are cars. (✓)

Method II Solutions by using mediate and immediate inference table.

All cars are balls. (A-type)
All balls are tables. (A-type)
A + A = A-type conclusion = All cares are tables.

All cars are tables $\xrightarrow{\text{Conversion}}$ Some tables are cars = Conclusion II

All balls are tables $\xrightarrow{\text{Conversion}}$ Some tables are balls = Conclusion I

Hence, both Conclusions I and II follow.

2. (*b*) **Method I**

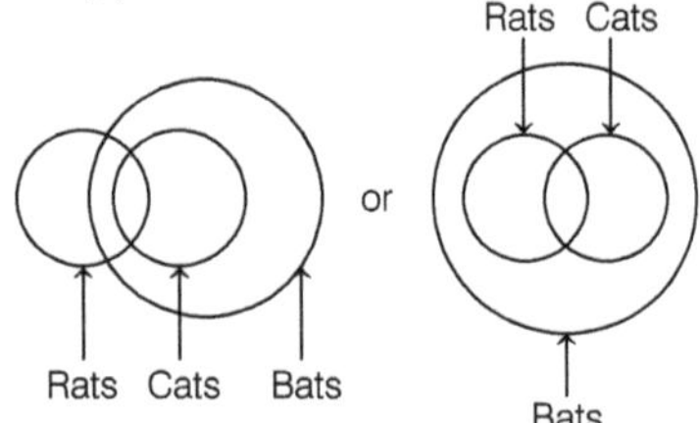

Conclusions I. No rats are cats. (✗)

II. Some rats are bats. (✓)

Method II Some rats are cats. (I-type)
All cats are bats. (A-type)

I + A = I-type conclusion
Some rats are bats = Conclusion II
No rats are cats is invalid because.
Some rats are cats (Statement I).
So, only Conclusion II follows.

3. (*b*) **Methods I**

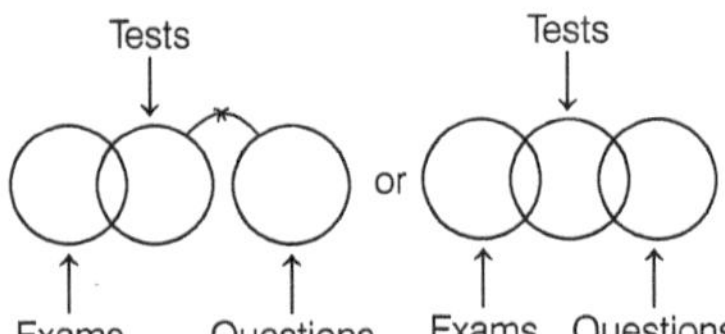

Conclusions

I. No question is a test. (✗)
II. Some tests are exams. (✓)

Method II Some exams are tests. (I-type)
No exam is a question. (E-type)

First we align the statements by following IEA Rule.

Some exams are tests $\xrightarrow{\text{Conversion}}$ Some tests are exams.

Some tests are exams. (I-types)
No exam is a question. (E-type)
Statement I = Conclusion II
I + E = O-type conclusion
i.e., some tests are not questions.
Hence, Conclusion I does not follows.
So, only Conclusion II follows.

4. (*a*)

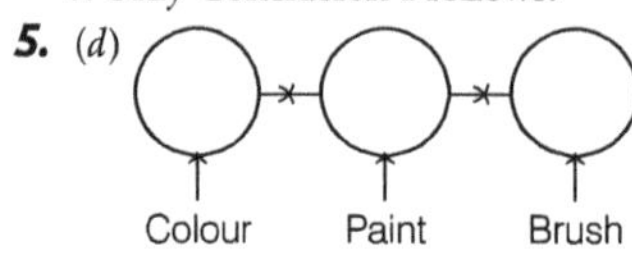

Conclusions I. (✓) II. (✗)

∴ Only Conclusion I follows.

5. (*d*)

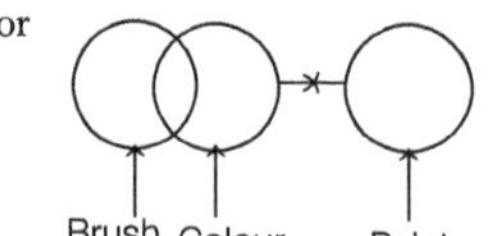

or

Conclusions

I. No colour is a brush. (✗)
II. All brushes are colours. (✗)

6. (*b*)

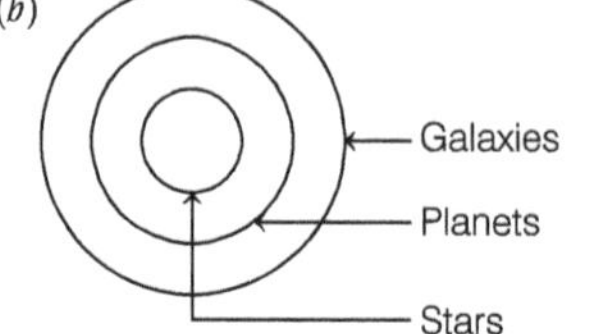

Conclusions

I. All galaxies are planets. (✗)
II. All stars are galaxies. (✓)

7. (*b*)

Conclusions

I. All shops are factories. (✗)
II. Some shops are schools. (✓)

8. (*d*)

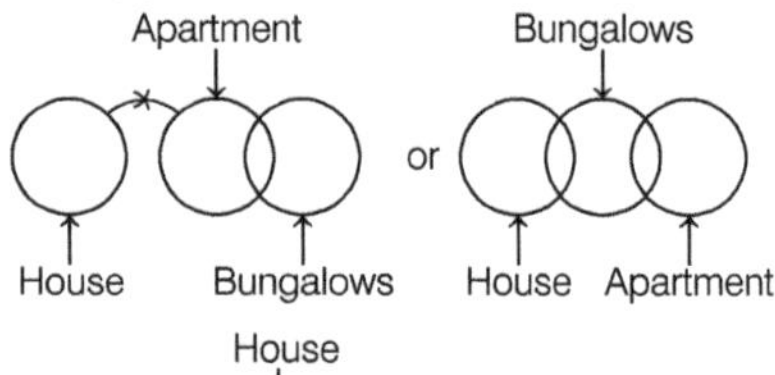

or

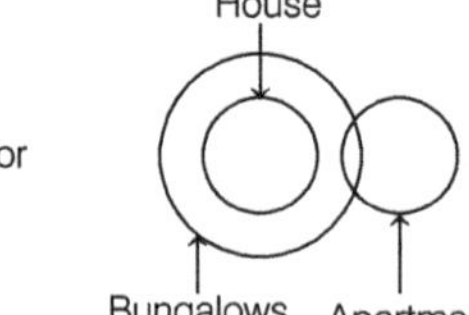

Conclusions

I. No house is a bungalow. (✗)
II. All bungalows being houses is a possibility. (✗)

9. (*b*)

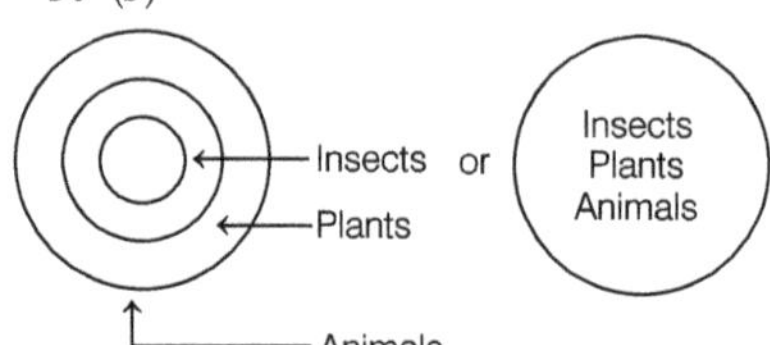

Conclusions

I. All insects being animals is a possibility. (✗)
II. There is a possibility that some animals are neither insects nor plant. (✓)

10. (*a*)

Ink
Pens
Eraser

Conclusions

I. No pen is an eraser. (✓)
II. Some erasers are pens. (✗)

11. (*b*)

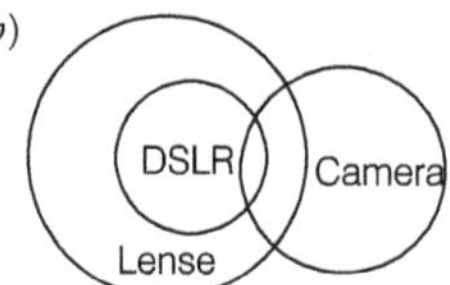

Conclusions

I. All camera is lenses. (✗)
II. Some lenses are camera. (✓)

12. (*d*) According to the statements,

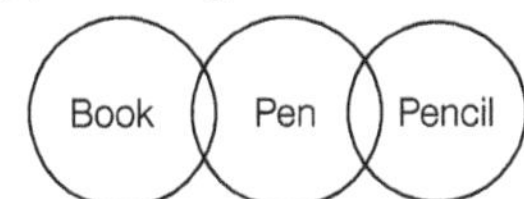

Conclusions I. No book is pencil. (✗)
II. All pencils are book. (✗)

13. (*c*)

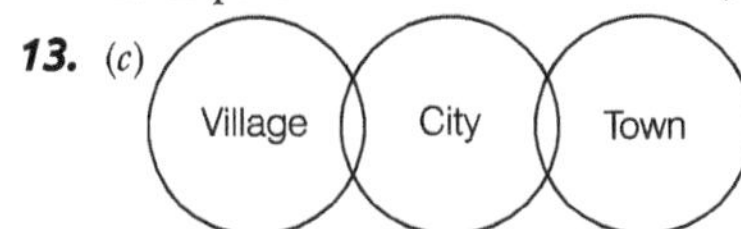

Complementary pair (E-I)
∴ Either I or II follows.

14. (*b*)

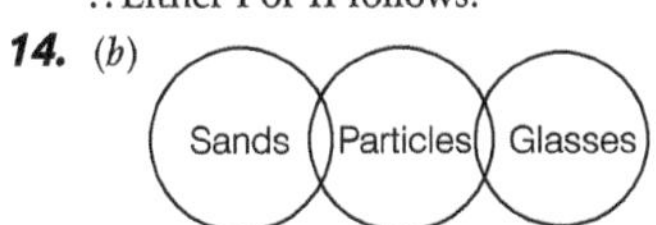

Conclusions I. Some glasses are definitely not particles. (✗)
II. Some glasses being sands is a possibility. (✓)

15. (*c*)

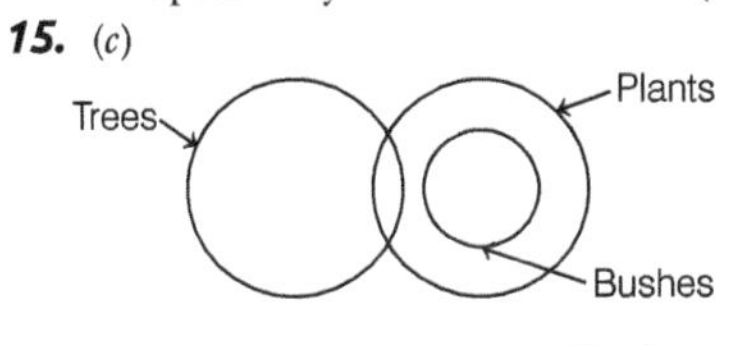

or

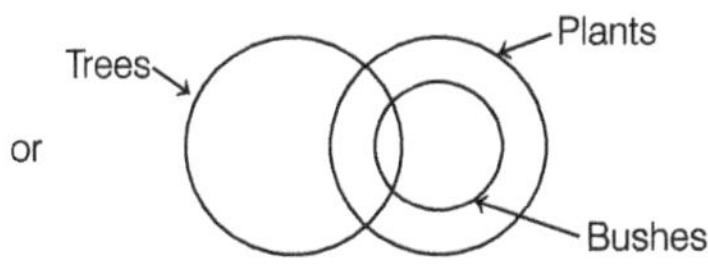

Conclusions I. Atleast some trees are bushes. (✗)
II. Some trees are definitely not bushes. (✗)

Complementary pair (I-O)
∴ Either I or II follows.

16. (*e*)

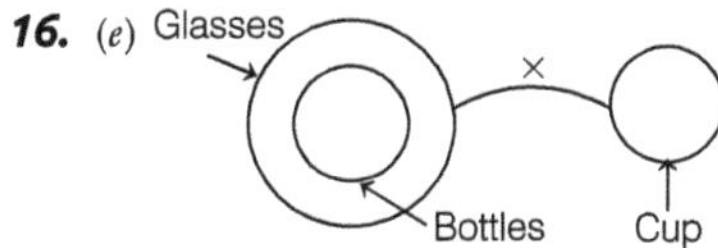

Conclusions I. No bottle is a cup(✓)
II. Atleast some glasses are bottles. (✓)

17. (*d*)

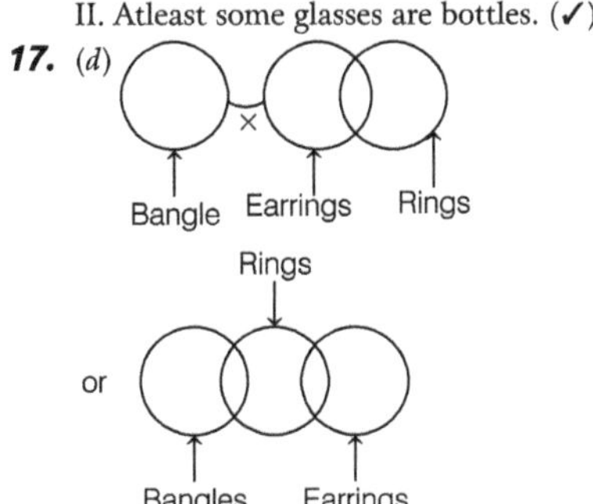

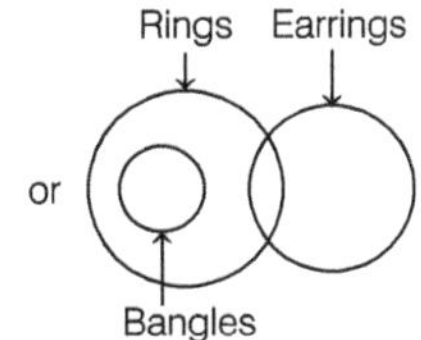

Conclusions
I. No ring is a bangle. (✗)
II. Some rings are definitely not earrings. (✗)

18. (*b*)

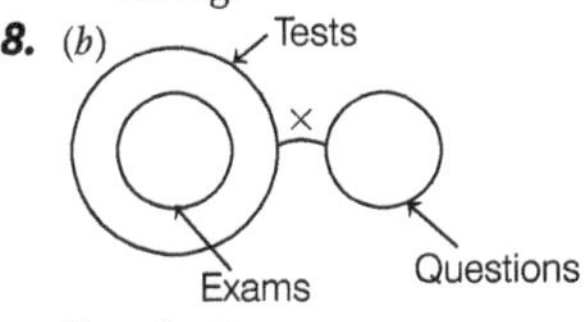

Conclusions
I. Atleast some exams are questions. (✗)
II. No exam is a question. (✓)

19. (*e*)

Oceans
Lakes
Rivers

Conclusions
I. All rivers are oceans. (✓)
II. Some oceans are lakes. (✓)

20. (*a*)

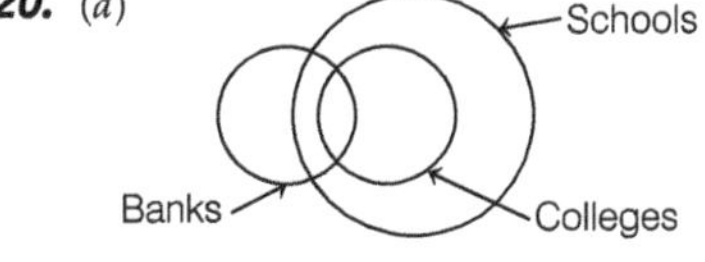

or

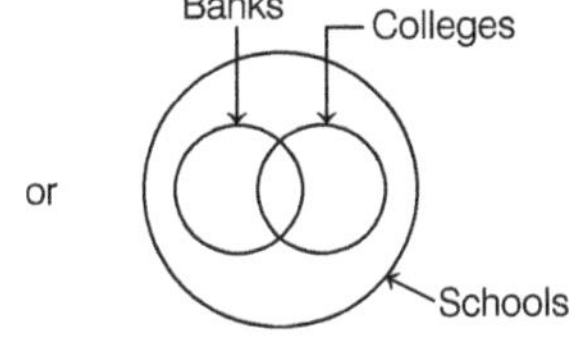

Conclusions
I. Atleast some banks are schools. (✓)
II. All schools are colleges. (✗)

21. (*d*)

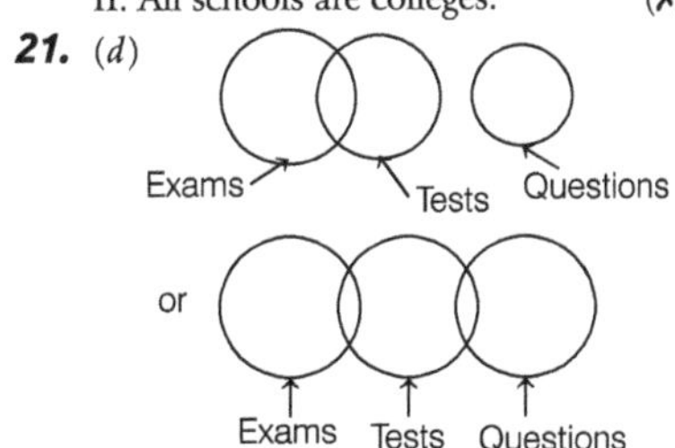

Conclusions
I. No question is a test. (✗)
II. Some tests are definitely not exams. (✗)

22. (*a*)

Tyres Wires Fires or Wires Fires Tyres

Conclusions
I. Atleast some tyres are wires. (✓)
II. Some fires are definitely not wires. (✗)

23. (*d*) **Method I**

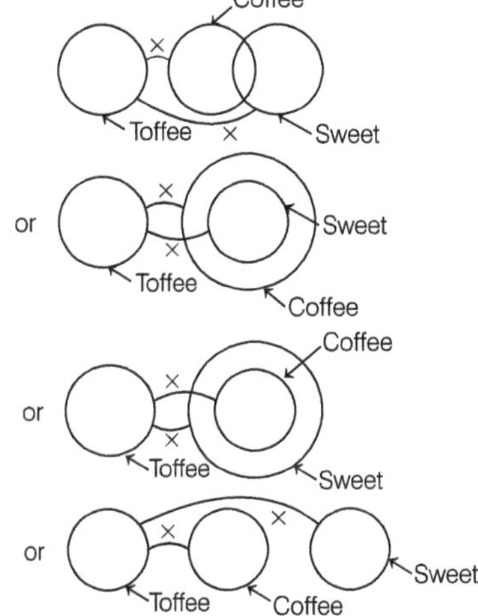

Conclusions
I. No coffee is sweet. (✗)
II. All sweets are coffee. (✗)

Method II
No toffee is coffee. (E-type)
No sweet is toffee. (E-type)
E + E = Invalid conclusion
From Conclusion I,
No coffee is sweet $\xrightarrow{\text{Conversion}}$ No sweet is coffee.
No sweet is coffee. (E-type)
All sweets are coffee. (A-type)
Since, they have same subject and predicate they does not form complementary pair.
Hence, neither of the conclusion follows.

24. (*b*) According to the given statements,

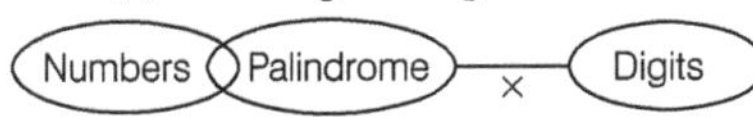

Conclusions
I. Some digits are numbers. (✗)
II. All numbers can never be digits. (✓)

25. (*a*) According to the given statements,

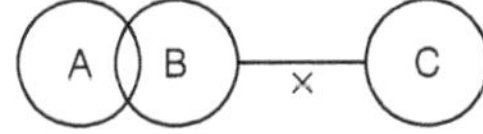

Conclusions
I. All A can never be C. (✓)
II. All C can never be A. (✗)

26. (*d*) As per question,

Conclusions
I. Some strong is not dark. (✗)
II. No tough is strong. (✗)

27. (*c*)

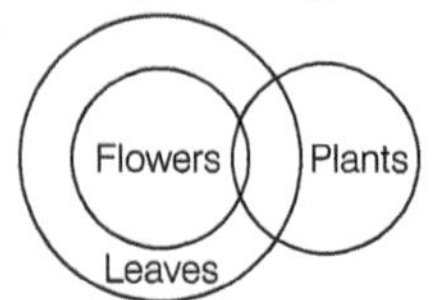

Conclusions
I. Some leaves are plants. (✓)
II. Some plants are flowers. (✓)

28. (*b*)

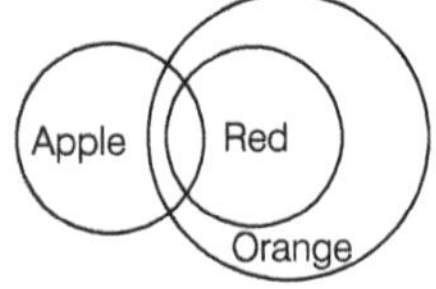

Conclusions
I. No oranges are apples. (✗)
II. Some apples are oranges. (✓)

29. (*d*) From the given statements,

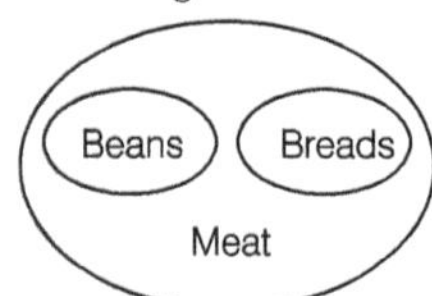

Conclusions I. (✗) II. (✓)

Hence, neither conclusion I nor II follows.

30. (*b*)

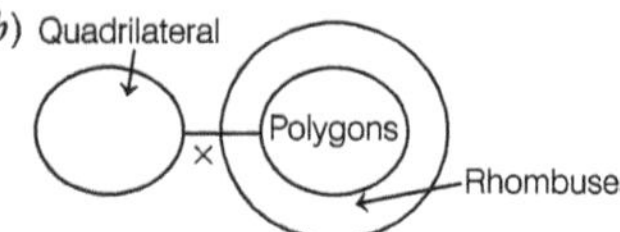

Conclusions
I. Some rhombuses are quadrilaterals. (✗)
II. Some rhombuses are polygons. (✓)

31. (*d*) According to the statements,

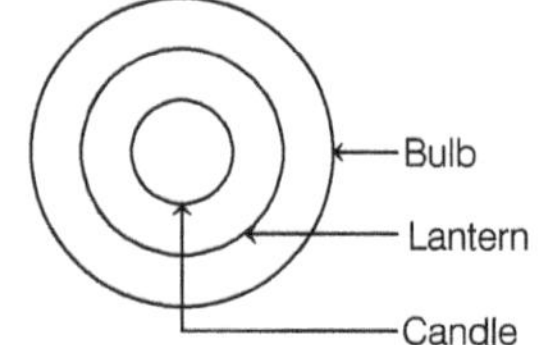

Conclusions
I. All lanterns are candles. (✗)
II. All bulbs are candles. (✗)

32. (*a*) According to the statements,

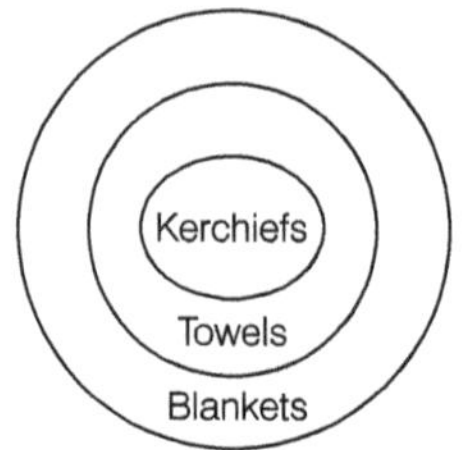

Conclusions
I. All kerchiefs are blankets. (✓)
II. All blankets are towels. (✗)

33. (*b*) According to the statements,

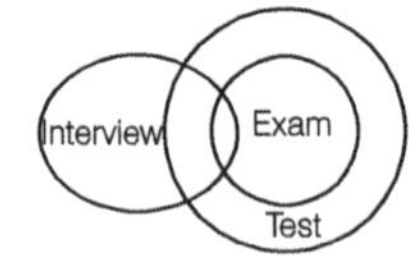

Conclusions I. All tests are exams. (✗)
II. Some tests are interviews. (✓)

34. (*d*)

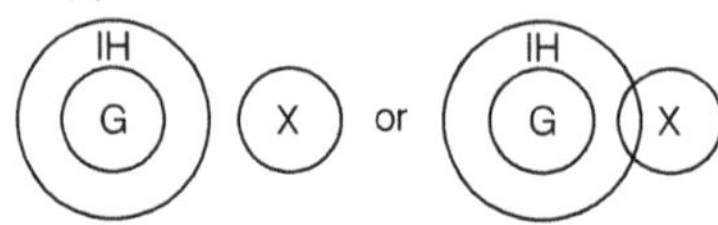

G : Good Hockey Players
IH : People in Indian Hockey Team

Conclusions I. 'X' is not in the Indian Hockey Team. (✗)
II. 'X' wants to be in the Indian Hockey Team. (✗)

35. (*c*)

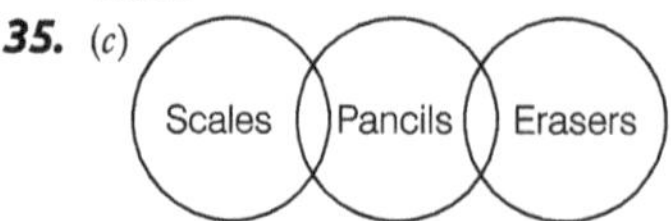

Conclusions
I. Some pencils are erasers. (✓)
II. Some pencils are scales. (✓)

36. (*c*) According to the statements,

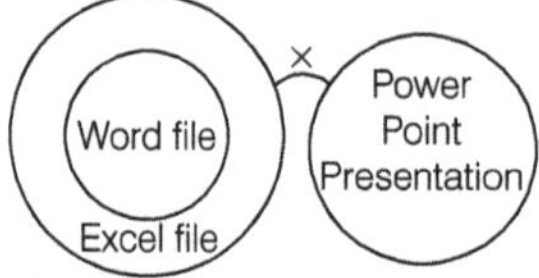

Conclusions
I. No word file is a power point presentation. (✓)
II. Some excel files are word files. (✓)

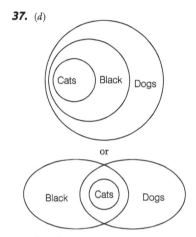

37. (*d*)

Cats Black Dogs

or

Black Cats Dogs

Conclusions
I. (✗) II. (✗)
∴ Neither Conclusion I nor II follows.

38. (*d*) According to the statements,

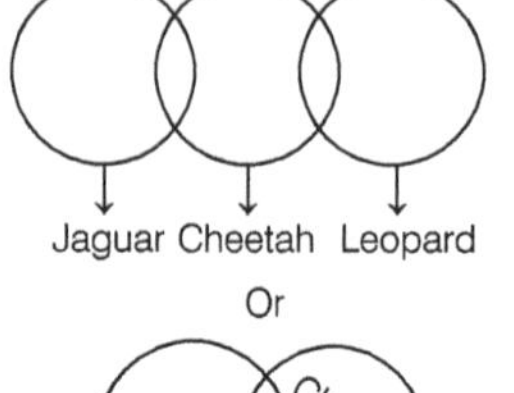

Or

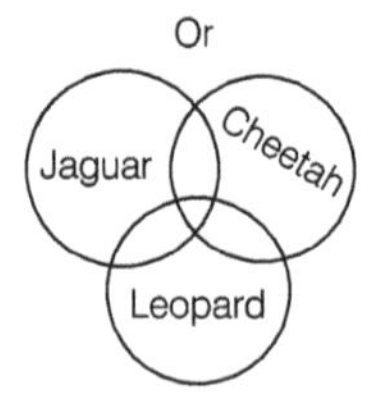

Conclusions
I. No leopards is a jaguar. (✗)
II. Some jaguars are leopards. (✗)

39. (*c*)

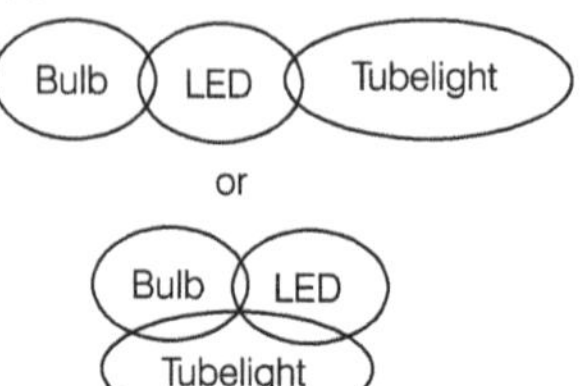

Conclusions
I. Some tubelights are bulb. (✗) (May be true)
II. No tubelight is a bulb. (✗) (May be true)
∴ Either I or II is follows.

TYPE 02

Three Statements and Two or More Conclusions

In this type of questions, three statements and some conclusions are given. The candidate is required to check the validity of the conclusions on the basis of given statements.

DIRECTION ~(Example No. 9) *In the question below are given three statements followed by two conclusions numbered* I *and* II. *You have to take the two given statements to be true even if they seem to be at variance from commonly known facts and decide which of the given conclusion(s) logically follow (s) from the three given statements.*

Give answer

(a) If only Conclusion I follows
(b) If only Conclusion II follows
(c) If either Conclusion I or II follows
(d) If neither Conclusion I nor II follows
(e) If both Conclusions I and II follow

***Ex* 9 Statements** All label are packets.
All mobiles are cables.
Some mobiles are packets. « IBPS Clerk 2018

Conclusions I. Some label is mobile.
II. Some cables are label.

Solution (d) According to the statements,

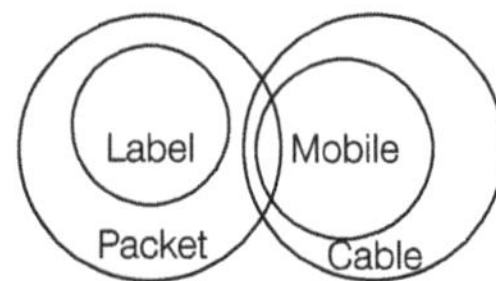

Conclusions I. Some label is mobile. (✗)
II. Some cables are label. (✗)

DIRECTIONS ~(Example Nos. 10-12) *In each of the questions below. Some statements are given followed by conclusions/ group of conclusions. You have to assume all the statements to be true even if they seem to be at variance from the commonly known facts and then decide which of the given conclusions logically follow from the information given in the statements.*
« RBI Office Assistant 2020

(a) If only Conclusion I follows (b) If only Conclusion II follows
(c) If either I or II follows (d) If neither I nor II follows
(e) If both I and II follow

***Ex* 10 Statements** All numbers are digits.
All digits are fraction.
No fraction is multiply.

Conclusions I. All multiply can be digit.
II. Some fraction is number.

Solution (b) According to the statements,

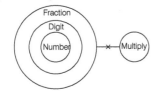

Conclusions I. All multiply can be digit. (✗)
II. Some fraction is number. (✓)

***Ex* 11 Statements** No words are letters.
Some letters are alphabet.
Only a few alphabets are sentence.

Conclusions I. Some alphabets are not word.
II. Some sentence can be word.

Solution (e) According to the statements,

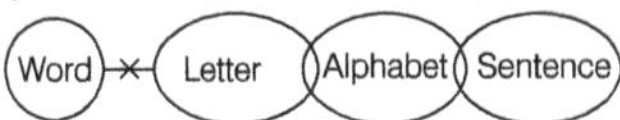

Conclusions I. Some alphabets are not word. (✓)
II. Some sentence can be word. (✓)

***Ex* 12 Statements** Only a few river is lake.
Some lake is mountain.
All mountain is hill.

Conclusions I. Some rivers can be mountain.
II. Some lakes can be hill.

Solution (e) According to the statements,

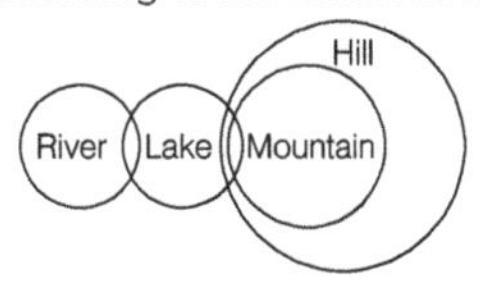

Conclusions I. Some rivers can be mountain. (✓)
II. Some lakes can be hill. (✓)

DIRECTION ~(Example No. 13) *In the question below are given three statements followed by four conclusions numbered* I, II, III *and* IV. *You have to take the three given statements to be true even if they seem to be at variance from commonly known facts and decide which of the given conclusion(s) logically follow (s) from the three given statements.*

Give answer

(a) If only Conclusion III follows
(b) If either Conclusions I or IV and III follow
(c) If only Conclusion II follows
(d) If only Conclusion IV follows

***Ex* 13 Statements** Some doors are windows.
All windows are black.
Some black are brown.

Conclusions I. Some windows are brown.
II. All doors are black.
III. Some doors are black.
IV. No window is brown.

Solution (b)

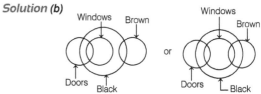

Conclusions

I. Some windows are brown. (✗)
II. All doors are black. (✗)
III. Some doors are black. (✓)
IV. No window is brown. (✓)

Complementary pair (I-E)

Practice CORNER 1.2

DIRECTIONS ~ (Q. Nos. 1-36) *In each of the questions below are given three statements followed by two conclusions numbered* I *and* II. *You have to take the given statements to be true even if they seem to be at variance from commonly known facts and decide which of the given conclusion(s) logically follow(s) from the three given statements.*

Give answer

(a) If only Conclusion I follows
(b) If only Conclusion II follows
(c) If either Conclusion I or II follows
(d) If neither Conclusion I nor II follows
(e) If both Conclusions I and II follow

1. Statements
All numbers are digits.
All digits are fraction.
No fraction is multiply. « RBI Office Asst. 2020

Conclusions
I. All multiply can be digit.
II. Some fraction is number.

2. Statements
All benches are parks.
No park is a tree.
All trees are swings. « SBI Clerical Cadre 2016

Conclusions
I. All benches being swings is a possibility.
II. No tree is a bench.

3. Statements
No words are letters.
Some letters are alphabet.
Only a few alphabets are sentence. « RBI Office Asst. 2020

Conclusions
I. Some alphabets are not word.
II. Some sentence can be word.

4. Statements
Only a few river is lake.
Some lake is mountain.
All mountain is hill. « RBI Office Asst. 2020

Conclusions
I. Some rivers can be mountain.
II. Some lakes can be hill.

5. Statements
No table is wood.
Some woods are chairs.
All chairs are stones. « IBPS (PO) 2012

Conclusions
I. No stone is table.
II. Some stones are woods.

6. Statements
Only a few stick is glue. No glue is paint. Only a few paint is carpet. « SBI Clerk 2020

Conclusions I. Some carpet is not glue.
II. All stick can be paint.

7. Statements Only a few paper is pencil. Some pencil is pen. Only a few eraser is pen. « SBI Clerk 2020

Conclusions I. Some eraser is not pen.
II. All pen can be pencil.

8. Statements Only a few apple is grapes. All grapes is guava. Some guava is fruit. « SBI Clerk 2020

Conclusions I. Some grapes is fruit.
II. All fruits can be apple.

9. Statements All desk is table. All table is chair. Some chair is wood. « SBI Clerk 2020

Conclusions I. Some wood is desk.
II. No wood is desk.

10. Statements No apple is fruit. All fruits is guava. All apple is grapes. « SBI Clerk 2020

Conclusions I. Some grapes is guava.
II. All guava can be apple.

11. Statements Some movies are films.
No film is a show.
All shows are pictures. « SBI PO 2015

Conclusions
I. At least some pictures are films.
II. No show is a movie.

12. Statements Some actors are singers.
All singers are dancers.
Some dancers are players. « SBI PO 2015

Conclusions
I. All actors being dancers is a possibility.
II. All dancers are singers.

13. Statements Some actors are singers.
All singers are dancers.
Some dancers are players. « SBI PO 2015

Conclusions
I. At least some dancers are actors.
II. No player is an actor.

DIRECTIONS ~ (Q. Nos. 14 and 15)

Statements All forces are energies.
All energies are powers.
No power is heat. « IBPS (PO) 2012

14. Conclusions I. Some forces are definitely not powers.
II. No heat is force.

15. Conclusions I. No energy is heat.
II. Some forces being heat is a possibility.

DIRECTIONS ~ (Q. Nos. 16 and 17)

Statements No note is a coin.
Some coins are metals.
All plastics are notes. « IBPS (PO) 2012

16. Conclusions
I. No coin is plastic.
II. All plastics being metals is a possibility.

17. Conclusions
I. No metal is plastic.
II. All notes are plastics.

18. Statements All jungles are parks. « LIC AAO 2019
All parks are lake.
Only a few lakes are rivers.
Conclusions
I. All jungles are lakes.
II. Some rivers are parks is a possibility.

19. Statements No centeres are venues. « LIC AAO 2019
All places are venues.
No places are laboratory.
Conclusions
I. No places are centres.
II. No centre are laboratory.

20. Statements Some guns are steel. « LIC AAO 2019
All steels are iron.
All iron is silver.
Conclusions
I. All guns are silver.
II. Some guns are not silver.

21. Statements Only a few home is picnic.
No picnic is mystery. « IBPS Clerk (Pre) 2019
All mystery is real.
Conclusions
I. Some mystery are not picnic.
II. All home being picnic is a possibility.

22. Statements No network is dull. « IBPS Clerk (Pre) 2019
Only a few dull is fast.
All fast is memory.
Conclusions
I. Some memory are definitely not network.
II. Some dull are not network.

23. Statements All tennis is football.« IBPS Clerk (Pre) 2019
All football is basketball.
No basketball is cricket.
Conclusions
I. No football is cricket.
II. All tennis is basketball.

24. Statements Only a few palace is home. All home is office. No office is building. « IBPS RRB PO 2019
Conclusions
I. All palace is home is a possibility.
II. Some palace is building.

25. Statements All men is women. Some child is women. No men is boy. « IBPS RRB PO 2019
Conclusions
I. Some men is child.
II. No men is child.

26. Statements No professor is student. Only a few student is lecturer. All lecturer is principal.
Conclusions « IBPS RRB PO 2019
I. All professor is principal is a possibility.
II. All student is lecturer is a possibility.

27. Statements Only a few palace is home. All home is office. No office is building. « IBPS RRB PO 2019
Conclusions
I. Some home is building.
II. No home is building.

28. Statements No professor is student. Only a few student is lecturer. All lecturer is principal.
Conclusions « IBPS RRB PO 2019
I. Some student is principal.
II. Some lecturer is professor.

29. Statements « IBPS PO 2019
Some nature are beauty.
Only a few world are wonder.
All wonder are beauty.
Conclusions
I. All beauty can be world.
II. All world being nature is a possibility.

30. Statements All plants are tree. « IBPS PO 2019
Only a few tree are ship.
No ship is bike.
Conclusions
I. Some plants are not bike.
II. All plant can never be ship.

31. Statements All chairs are sofas.
Only a few sofas are beds.
No beds are curtains.
Conclusions « IBPS RRB Office Assistant 2020
I. Some sofas are not beds.
II. Some sofas are not curtains.

32. Statements Only a few coffee are tea.
All tea is drinks. « IBPS RRB Office Assistant 2020
Only a few drinks are cold drinks.

Conclusions
I. Some tea is not cold drinks.
II. No coffee are drinks.

33. Statements All flowers are trees.
Only a few trees are gardens.
No gardens are lawns.

Conclusions « IBPS RRB Office Assistant 2020
I. All lawns can never be trees.
II. Some flowers can be gardens.

34. Statements No party is gathering. All summary are gathering. Only a few gathering are committee.

Conclusions « SBI Clerk 2019
I. Some committee can be summary.
II. Some party can be committee.

35. Statements No market is home. Only a few home are room. Only a few room is vance. « SBI Clerk 2019

Conclusions
I. Some home are vance.
II. Some market can never be room.

36. Statements Some ball are garden. All garden are trade. Only a few trade are pump. « SBI Clerk 2019

Conclusions
I. Some ball are pump.
II. Some garden can be pump.

DIRECTIONS ~ (Q. Nos. 37-56) *In each of the questions below are given three statements followed by three conclusions numbered* I, II *and* III. *You have to take the given statements to be true even, if they seems to be at variance with commonly known facts. Read all the conclusions and then decide which of the given conclusions logically follows from the given statements disregarding commonly known facts.*

37. Statements Some rats are cats. « UPSC CSAT 2019
Some cats are dogs.
No dog is a cow.

Conclusions
I. No cow is a cat. II. No dog is a rat.
III. Some cats are rats.

Which of the above conclusions is/are drawn from the statements.
(a) I, II and III (b) I and II
(c) Only III (d) II and III

38. Statements Some carrots are brinjals.
Some brinjals are apples.
All apples are bananas. « Dena Bank (PO) 2010

Conclusions
I. Some apples are carrots.
II. Some bananas are brinjals.
III. Some bananas are carrots.
(a) Only I follows
(b) Only II follows
(c) Only III follows
(d) Either II or III follows
(e) None of these

39. Statements All keys are locks.
All locks are bangles.
All bangles are cars. « Dena Bank (PO) 2010

Conclusions
I. Some cars are locks.
II. Some bangles are keys.
III. Some cars are keys.
(a) Only I follows (b) I and II follow
(c) I and III follow (d) II and III follow
(e) All I, II and III follow

40. Statements All fruits are leaves.
Some leaves are trees.
No tree is house. « Dena Bank (PO) 2010

Conclusions
I. Some houses are fruits.
II. Some trees are fruits.
III. No house is a fruit.
(a) Only I follows (b) Only II follows
(c) Only III follows (d) Either I or III follows
(e) None follows

41. Statements All tables are mirrors.
Some mirrors are chairs.
All chairs are glasses. « Dena Bank (PO) 2010

Conclusions
I. Some glasses are mirrors.
II. Some chairs are tables.
III. Some mirrors are tables.
(a) I and II follow
(b) II and III follow
(c) I and III follow
(d) All I, II and III follow
(e) None of these

42. Statements All calculators are boxes.
All boxes are taps.
Some taps are machines. « Dena Bank (PO) 2010

Conclusions
I. Some machines are boxes.
II. Some taps are calculators.
III. Some boxes are calculators.
(a) I and II follow
(b) I and III follow
(c) II and III follow
(d) All I, II and III follow
(e) None of these

43. Statements Some books are papers.
Some papers are desks.
Some desks are chairs. « UCO Bank (PO) 2008

Conclusions
I. Some books are desks.
II. Some papers are chairs.
III. Some books are chairs.
(a) None follows (b) Only I follows
(c) Only II follows (d) Only III follows
(e) I and II follow

44. **Statements** Some pots are buckets.
All buckets are tubs.
All tubs are drums. « UCO Bank (PO) 2008

Conclusions
I. Some drums are pots.
II. All tubs are buckets.
III. Some drums are buckets.
(a) I and II follows (b) I and III follow
(c) II and III follow (d) All follow
(e) None of these

45. **Statements** All pins are bags.
All chalks are bags.
All needles are bags.

Conclusions
I. Some needles are pins.
II. Some chalks are needles.
III. No needle is pin. « UCO Bank (PO) 2008
(a) Only I follows
(b) Only III follows
(c) Either I or III follows
(d) Either I or III and II follow
(e) None of the above

46. **Statements** Some buses are trucks.
Some trucks are boats.
No boat is jeep. « UCO Bank (PO) 2008

Conclusions
I. Some jeeps are buses.
II. Some boats are buses.
III. Some jeeps are trucks.
(a) None follows (b) Only I follows
(c) Only II follows (d) Only III follows
(e) II and III follow

47. **Statements** All flowers are trees.
All trees are jungles.
No jungle is hill. « Andhra Bank (PO) 2008

Conclusions
I. No flower is hill. II. No tree is hill.
III. Some jungles are flowers.
(a) None follows (b) I and II follow
(c) I and III follow (d) II and III follow
(e) All I, II and III follow

48. **Statements** Some uniforms are covers.
All covers are papers.
All papers are bags. « CMAT 2013

Conclusions
I. All covers are bags.
II. Some bags are covers, papers and uniforms.
III. Some uniforms are not papers.
(a) Only I follows
(b) I and II follow
(c) Only III follow
(d) All I, II and III follow

49. **Statements** All buildings are mirrors.
Some mirrors are pens.
No pen is paper. « Syndicate Bank (PO) 2009, CMAT 2013

Conclusions
I. Some papers are buildings.
II. Some pens are buildings.
III. Some papers are mirrors.
(a) None follows (b) Only I follows
(c) Only II follows (d) Only III follows
(e) II and III follow

50. **Statements** Some books are trees.
All trees are roads.
All roads are wheels. « Syndicate Bank (PO) 2009

Conclusions
I. Some wheels are books.
II. Some roads are books.
III. Some wheels are trees.
(a) I and II follow (b) II and III follow
(c) I and III follow (d) All follow
(e) None of these

51. **Statements** All stones are rivers.
All rivers are cars.
Some cars are trains. « IDBI Bank (PO) 2009

Conclusions
I. Some trains are stones.
II. Some cars are stones.
III. Some trains are rivers.
(a) None follows (b) Only I follows
(c) Only II follows (d) Only III follows
(e) II and III follow

52. **Statements** Some bags are plates.
Some plates are chairs.
All chairs are tables. « Allahabad Bank (PO) 2009

Conclusions
I. Some tables are plates.
II. Some chairs are bags.
III. No chair is bag.
(a) Only I follows
(b) Either II or III follows
(c) I and either II or III follow
(d) Only III follows
(e) None of the above

53. **Statements** All desks are rooms.
Some rooms are halls.
All halls are leaves. « Allahabad Bank (PO) 2009

Conclusions
I. Some leaves are desks.
II. Some halls are desks.
III. Some leaves are rooms.

(a) None follows
(b) Only I follows
(c) Only II follows
(d) Only III follows
(e) II and III follow

54. Statements Some doors are windows.
Some windows are lamps.
All lamps are candles. « Andhra Bank (PO) 2009

Conclusions
I. Some candles are doors.
II. Some candles are windows.
III. Some lamps are doors.

(a) Only I follows
(b) Only II follows
(c) Only III follows
(d) I and II follow
(e) None of these

55. Statements Some towns are villages.
Some villages are lanes.
Some lanes are hamlets. « Andhra Bank (PO) 2009

Conclusions
I. Some hamlets are villages.
II. Some lanes are towns.
III. Some hamlets are towns.

(a) None follows
(b) Only I follows
(c) Only II follows
(d) Only III follows
(e) I and II follow

56. Statements Some towns are villages.
Some villages are lanes.
Some lanes are hamlets. « Andhra Bank (PO) 2009

Conclusions
I. Some hamlets are villages.
II. Some lanes are towns.
III. Some hamlets are towns.

(a) Only III follows
(b) Only I follows
(c) Only II follows
(d) None follows
(e) I and III follow

DIRECTIONS ~ (Q. Nos. 57-67) *In each of the questions below are given three statements followed by four conclusions numbered* I, II, III *and* IV. *You have to take the given statements to be true even, if they seem to be at variance from commonly known facts. Read all the conclusions and then decide which of the given conclusion(s) logically follow(s) from the given statements disregarding commonly known facts.*

57. Statements Some dogs are rats. « CMAT 2013
All rats are trees.
Some trees are not dogs.

Conclusions
I. Some trees are dogs.
II. All dogs are trees.
III. All rats are dogs.
IV. No tree is dog.

(a) None follows
(b) Only I follows
(c) I and II follow
(d) II and III follow

58. Statements Some bricks are gates.
Some gates are roofs.
All tyres are bricks. « MP Police SI 2017

Conclusions
I. Some tyres are gates.
II. No gate is tyre.

(a) If neither Conclusion I nor II follows
(b) If only Conclusion II follows
(c) If only Conclusion I follows
(d) If either Conclusion I or II follows

59. Statements All bricks are flowers.
Some houses are flowers.
All pens are houses.

Conclusions
I. Some houses are bricks.
II. Some pens are flowers.
III. Some flowers are bricks.
IV. No pen is flower.

(a) Either II or IV and III follow
(b) Either II or IV and I follow
(c) Either I or III and IV follow
(d) None follows
(e) All follow

60. Statements All rocks are balls.
Some balls are rings.
All rings are stones. « UCO Bank (PO) 2008

Conclusions
I. Some stones are rocks.
II. Some rings are rocks.
III. Some balls are rocks.
IV. No stone is rock.

(a) I and III follow
(b) III and IV follow
(c) Either I or IV and III follow
(d) Either I or IV follows
(e) None of the above

61. Statements All books are papers.
All pencils are papers.
All tables are papers. « UCO Bank (PO) 2008

Conclusions
I. Some books are pencils.
II. Some pencils are tables.
III. Some tables are books.
IV. Some papers are tables.

(a) Only I follows
(b) Only II follows
(c) Only III follows
(d) Only IV follows
(e) None of these

62. Statements Some desks are mirrors.
Some mirrors are combs.
Some combs are pins. « UCO Bank (PO) 2008

Conclusions
I. Some pins are desks.
II. Some combs are desks.
III. Some pins are mirrors.
IV. Some pins are either desks or mirrors.

(a) None follows
(b) Only II follows
(c) Only I follows
(d) Only IV follows
(e) Only III follows

63. Statements All blades are hammers.
All hammers are rods.
All rods are buckets. « UCO Bank (PO) 2008

Conclusions
I. Some buckets are hammers.
II. Some rods are blades.
III. All hammers are buckets.
IV. All blades are rods.

(a) I and II follow (b) II and III follow
(c) I, II and III follow (d) II, III and IV follow
(e) All follow

64. Statements All trees are chairs.
No chair is flower.
Some flowers are bangles. « UCO Bank (PO) 2008

Conclusions
I. No tree is bangle.
II. No chair is bangle.
III. Some flowers are trees.
IV. Some bangles are trees.

(a) None follows
(b) Either I or IV follows
(c) Either II or III follows
(d) I and II follow
(e) III and IV follow

65. Statements Some boys are girls.
No men are cycles.
All girls are men.

Conclusions
I. Some boys are men.
II. Some boys are cycles.
III. Some boys are not cycles.
IV. No cycle is girl.

(a) I and III follow
(b) III and IV follow
(c) II and IV follow
(d) II, III and IV follow
(e) I, III and IV follow

66. Statements Some motors are books.
Some scooters are motors.
All girls are scooters.

Conclusions
I. Some girls are motors.
II. Some girls are books.
III. Some scooters are girls.
IV. No girl is a book.

(a) I and III follow
(b) II and III follow
(c) I and II follow
(d) I, II and III follow
(e) Either II or IV and III follow

67. Statements All dogs are rats.
All rats are crows.
All crows are parrots.

Conclusions
I. All dogs are parrots.
II. Some parrots are dogs.
III. Some crows are dogs.
IV. All rats are dogs.

(a) I and II follow
(b) I, II and III follow
(c) Either II or IV follow
(d) Either I or II and III follow

Answers / WITH EXPLANATIONS

1. (*b*) According to the statements,

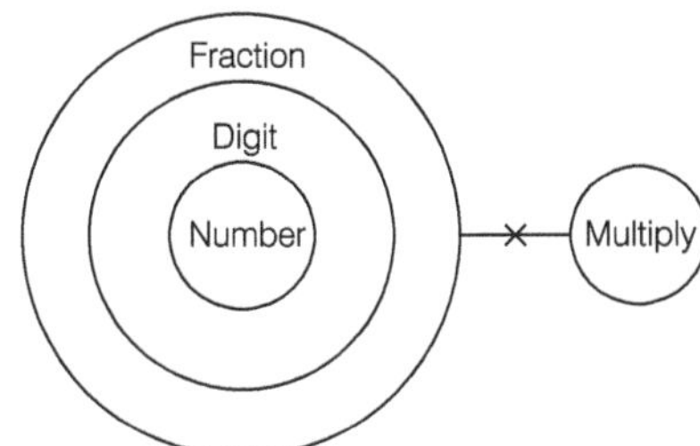

Conclusions I. (✗) II. (✓)

2. (*e*)

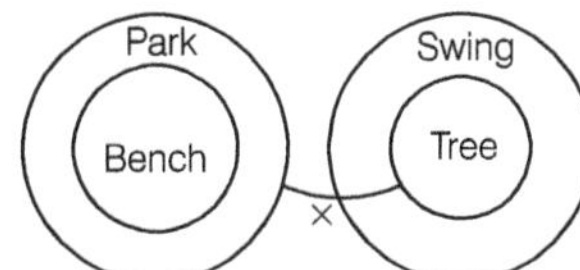

Conclusions
I. All benches being swings is a possibility (✓)
II. No tree is bench. (✓)

3. (*e*) **According to the statements,**

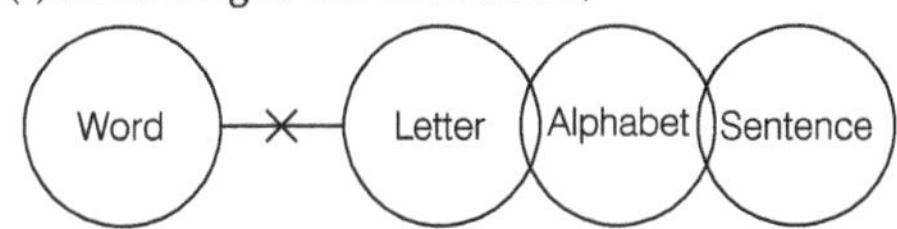

Conclusions I. (✓) II. (✓)

4. (*e*) According to the statements,

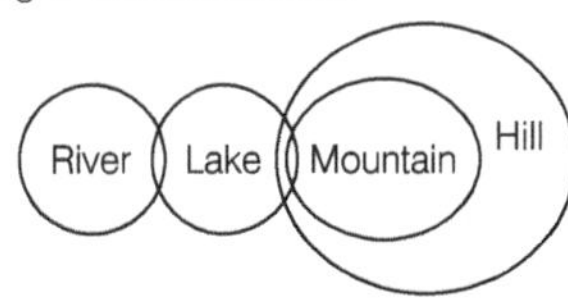

Conclusions I. (✓) II. (✓)

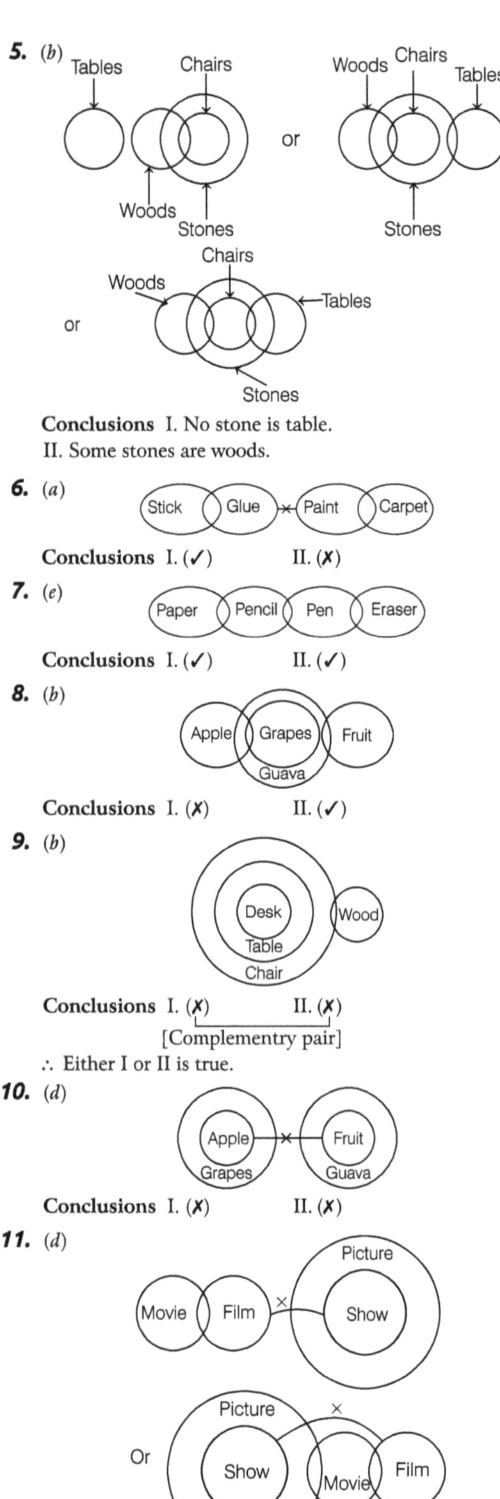

5. (*b*)

Conclusions I. No stone is table. (✗)
II. Some stones are woods. (✓)

6. (*a*)

Conclusions I. (✓) II. (✗)

7. (*e*)

Conclusions I. (✓) II. (✓)

8. (*b*)

Conclusions I. (✗) II. (✓)

9. (*b*)

Conclusions I. (✗) II. (✗)
[Complementry pair]
∴ Either I or II is true.

10. (*d*)

Conclusions I. (✗) II. (✗)

11. (*d*)

Conclusions I. At least some pictures are film. (✗)
II. No show is a movie. (✗)

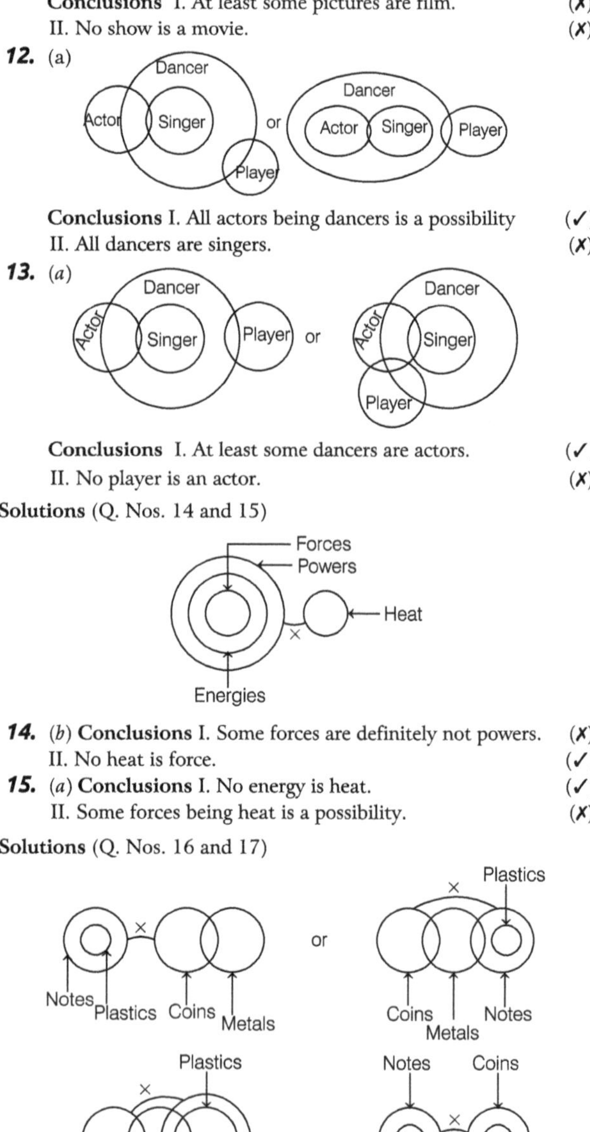

12. (a)

Conclusions I. All actors being dancers is a possibility (✓)
II. All dancers are singers. (✗)

13. (*a*)

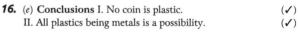

Conclusions I. At least some dancers are actors. (✓)
II. No player is an actor. (✗)

Solutions (Q. Nos. 14 and 15)

14. (*b*) **Conclusions** I. Some forces are definitely not powers. (✗)
II. No heat is force. (✓)

15. (*a*) **Conclusions** I. No energy is heat. (✓)
II. Some forces being heat is a possibility. (✗)

Solutions (Q. Nos. 16 and 17)

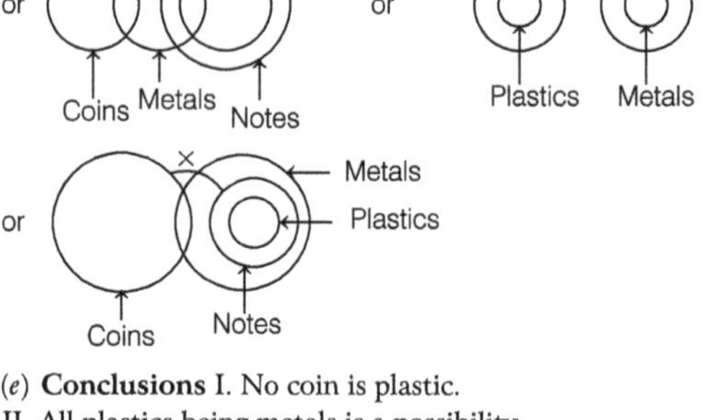

16. (*e*) **Conclusions** I. No coin is plastic. (✓)
II. All plastics being metals is a possibility. (✓)

17. (*d*) **Conclusions** I. No metal is plastic. (✗)
II. All notes are plastics. (✗)

18. (*e*) According to the given statements,

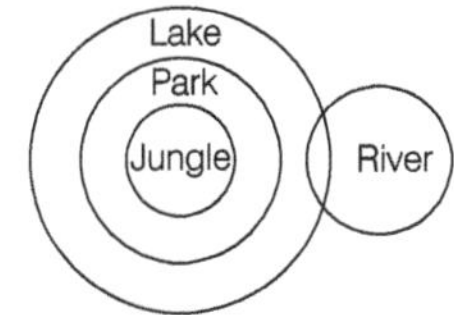

Conclusions I. All jungles are lakes. (✓)
II. Some rivers are parks is a possibility. (✓)
Hence, both conclusions follow.

19. (*a*) According to the given statements,

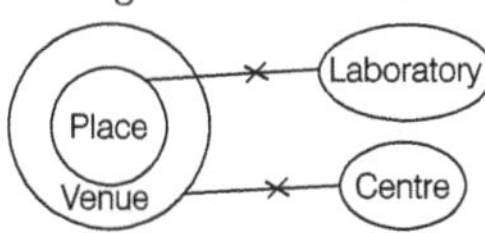

Conclusions I. No places are centres. (✓)
II. No centre are laboratory. (✗)
Hence, only conclusion I follows.

20. (*c*) According to the given statements

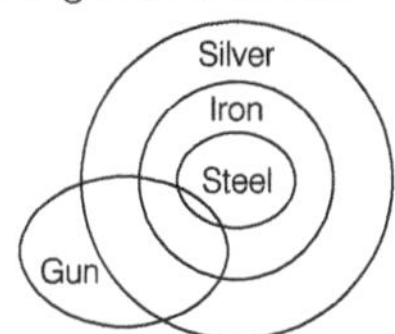

Conclusions I. All guns are silver. (May be true)
II. Some guns are not silver. (May be true)
Hence, either Conclusion I or II follows.

21. (*a*) As per question,

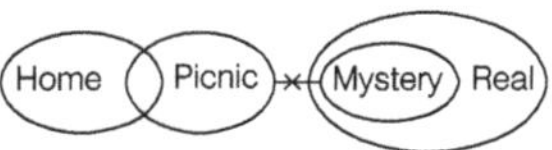

Conclusions
I. Some mystery are not picnic. (✓)
II. All home being picnic is a possibility. (✗)

22. (*e*) As per question,

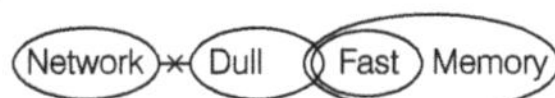

Conclusions
I. Some memory are definitely not network (✓)
II. Some dull are not network (✓)

23. (*e*) As per question,

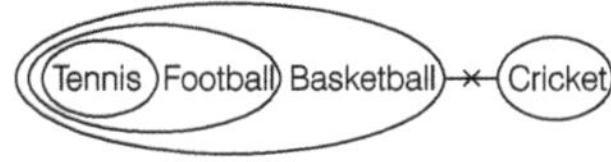

Conclusions
I. No football is cricket. (✓)
II. All tennis is basketball. (✓)

24. (*d*) As per question,

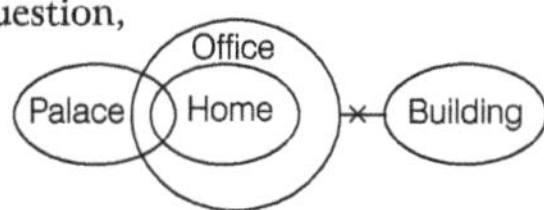

Conclusions
I. All palace is home is a possibility. (✗)
II. Some palace is building. (✗)

25. (*c*) As per question,

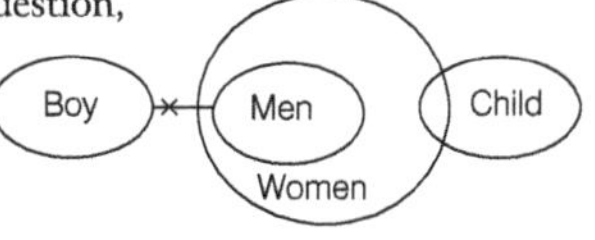

Conclusions
I. Some men is child. (May be true) (✗)
II. No men is child. (May be true) (✗)
∴ Either I or II follows.

26. (*a*) As per question,

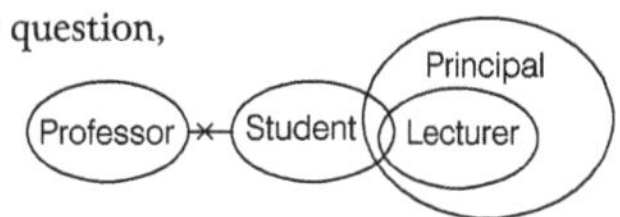

Conclusions
I. All professor is principal is a possibility. (✓)
II. All student is lecturer is a possibility. (✗)

27. (*b*) As per question,

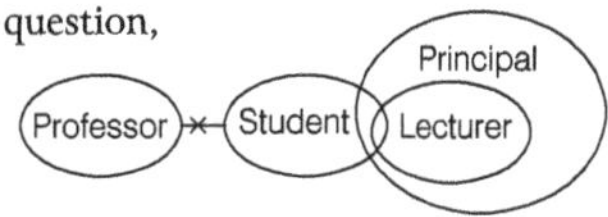

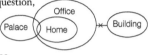

Conclusions
I. Some home is building. (✗)
II. No home is building. (✓)

28. (*a*) As per question,

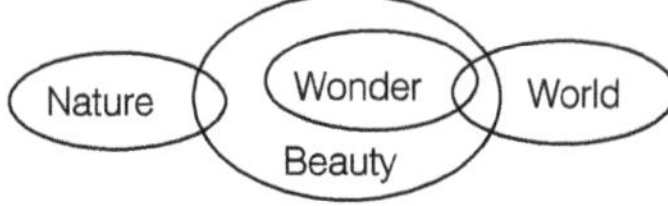

Conclusions
I. Some student is principal. (✓)
II. Some lecturer is professor. (✗)

29. (*e*) According to the given statements,

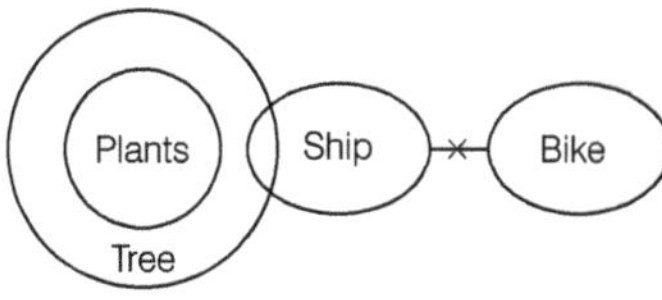

Conclusions
I. All beauty can be world. (✓)
II. All world being nature is a possibility. (✓)

30. (*d*) According to the given statements,

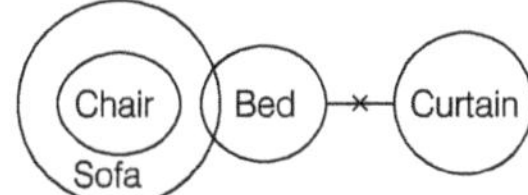

Conclusions
I. Some plants are not bike. (✗)
II. All plant can never be ship. (✗)

31. (*e*) According to the statement,

Chair Bed Curtain Sofa

Conclusions
I. Some sofas are not beds. (✓)
II. Some sofas are not curtains. (✓)
Hence, both Conclusions follow.

32. (*d*) According to the statement,

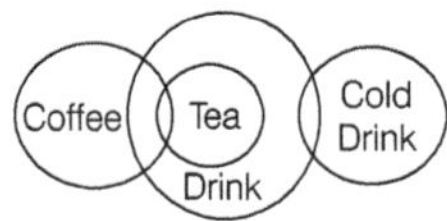

Conclusions
I. Some tea is not cold drinks. (✗)
II. No coffee are drinks. (✗)
Neither Conclusion I nor II follows.

33. (*b*) According to the statement,

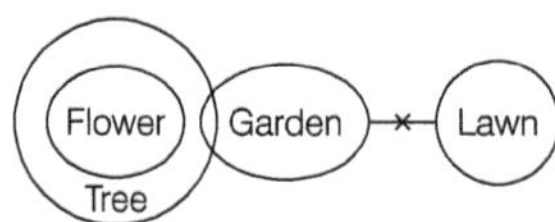

Conclusions
I. All lawns can never be trees. (✗)
II. Some flowers can be gardens. (✓)
Only Conclusion II follows.

34. (*e*) According to the given statements,

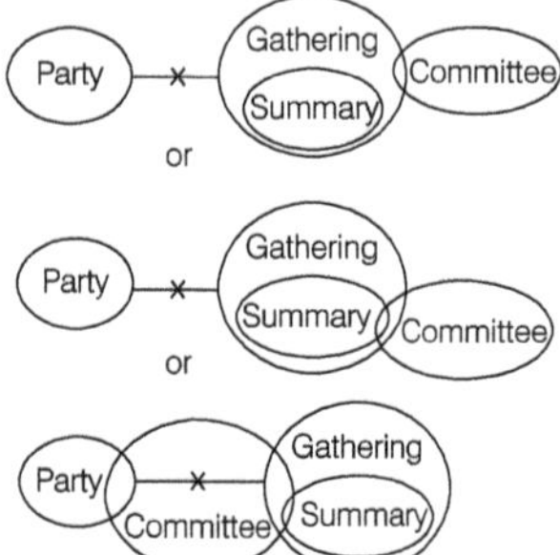

Conclusions
I. Some committee can be summary. (✓)
II. Some party can be committee. (✓)
Hence, both conclusions follow.

35. (*d*) According to the given statements,

Conclusions
I. Some home are vance. (✗)
II. Some market can never be Room. (✗)
Hence, neither Conclusion I nor II follows.

36. (*b*) According to the given statements,

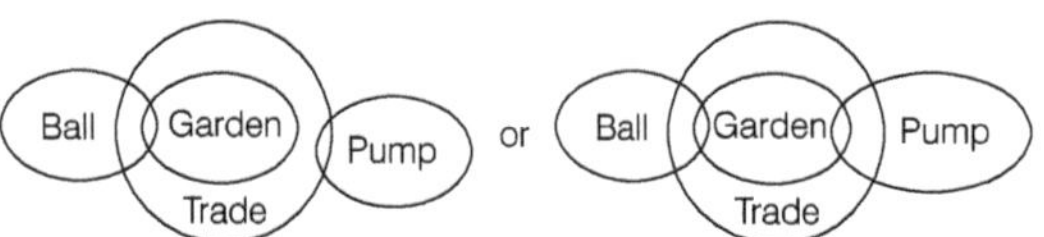

Conclusions
I. Some ball are pump. (✗)
II. Some garden can be pump. (✓)
Hence, only Conclusion II follows.

37. (*c*) According to the statements,

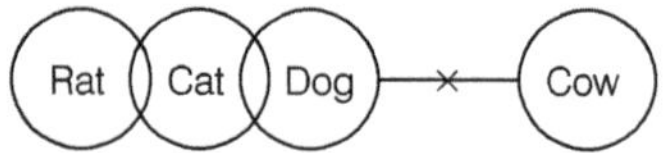

Conclusions
I. No cow is a cat. (✗)
II. No dog is a rat. (✗)
III. Some cats are rats. (✓)

38. (*b*) According to the statement,

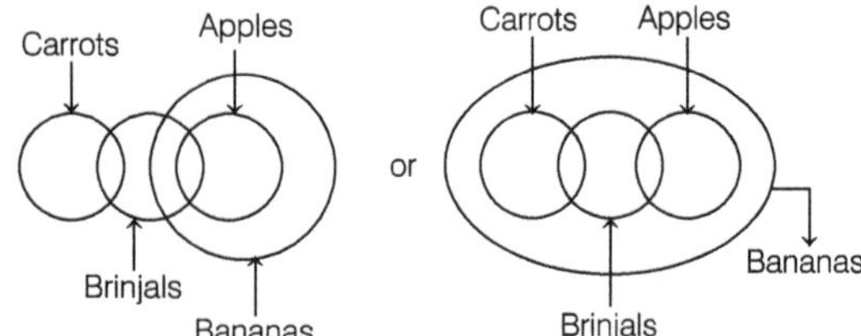

Conclusions I. Some apples are carrots. (✗)
II. Some bananas are brinjals. (✓)
III. Some bananas are carrots. (✗)

39. (*e*) According to the statement,

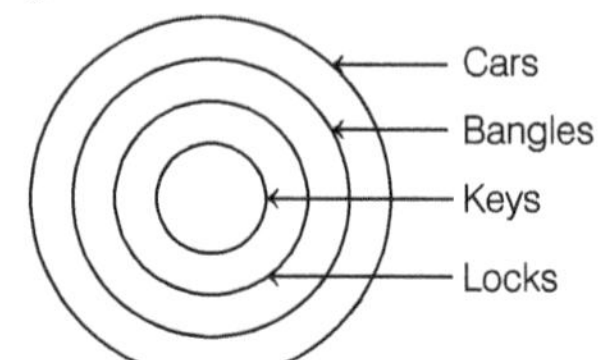

Conclusions I. Some cars are locks. (✓)
II. Some bangles are keys. (✓)
III. Some cars are keys. (✓)

40. (*d*) According to the statement,

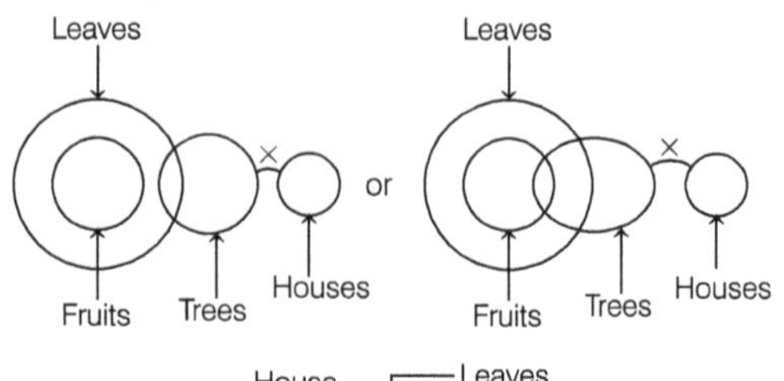

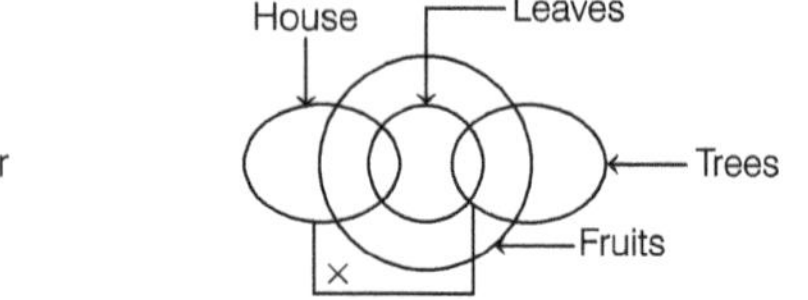

Conclusions I. Some houses are fruits. (✗)
II. Some trees are fruits. (✗)
III. No house is a fruit. (✗)
I and III make a complementary pair (I-E).
∴ Either I or III follows.

41. (*c*) According to the statement,

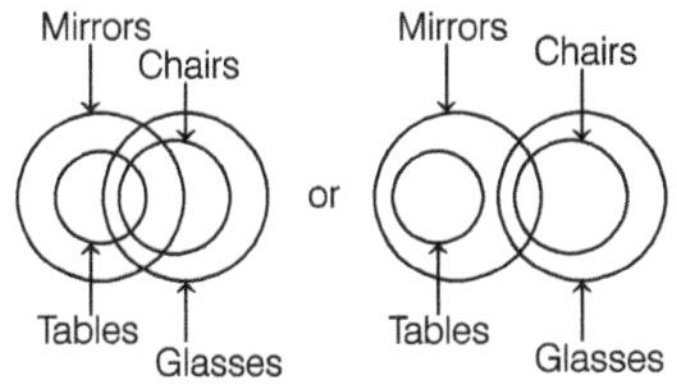

Conclusions I. Some glasses are mirrors. (✓)
II. Some chairs are tables. (✗)
III. Some mirrors are tables. (✓)

42. (*c*) According to the statement,

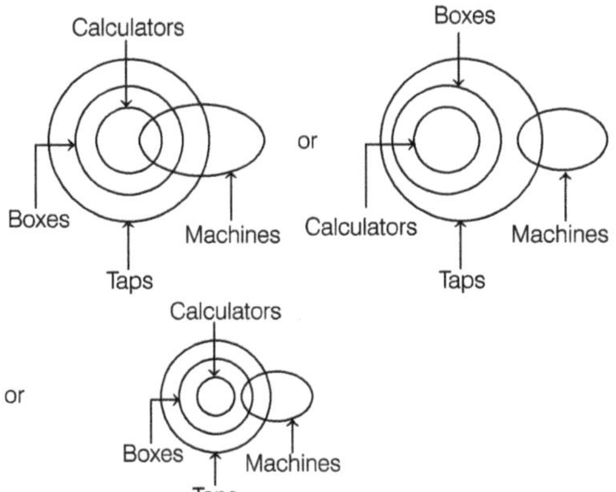

Conclusions I. Some machines are boxes. (✗)
II. Some taps are calculators. (✓)
III. Some boxes are calculators. (✓)

43. (*a*) According to the statement,

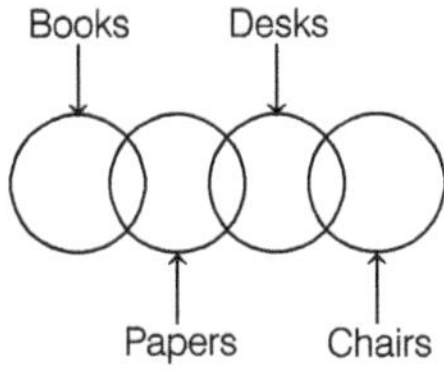

Conclusions I. Some books are desks. (✗)
II. Some papers are chairs. (✗)
III. Some books are chairs. (✗)

44. (*b*) According to the statement,

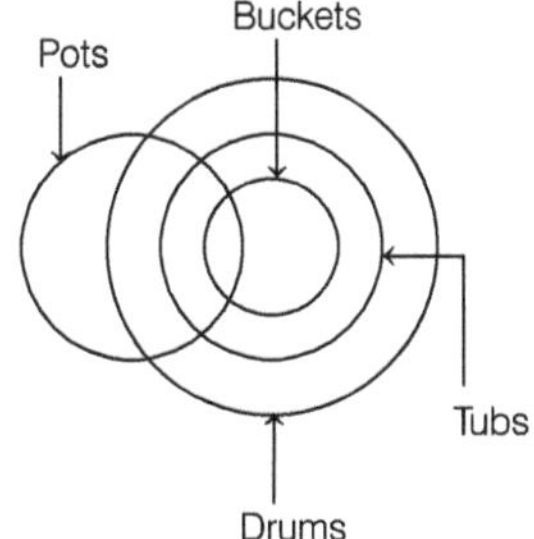

Conclusions I. Some drums are pots. (✓)
II. All tubs are buckets. (✗)
III. Some drums are buckets. (✓)

45. (*c*) According to the statement,

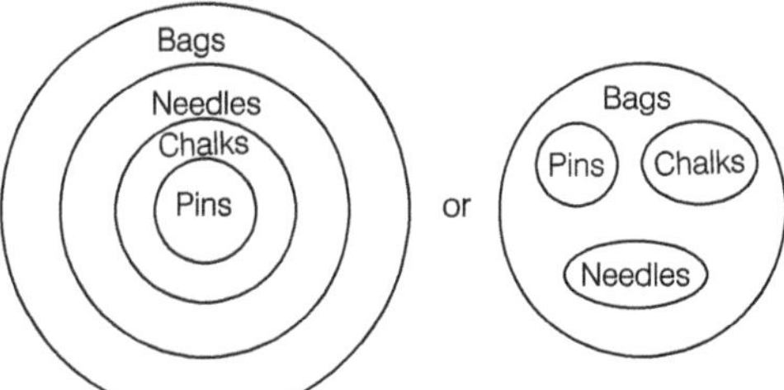

Conclusions I. Some needles are pins. (✗)
II. Some chalks are needles. (✗)
III. No needle is a pin (✗)
I and III make a complimentary pair (I-E).
∴ Either I or III follows.

46. (*a*) According to the statement,

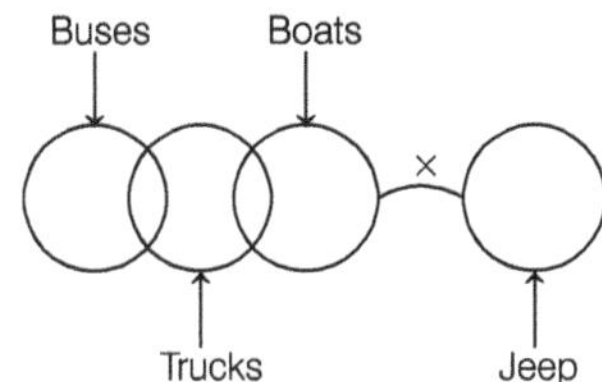

Conclusions I. Some jeeps are buses. (✗)
II. Some boats are buses. (✗)
III. Some jeeps are trucks. (✗)

47. (*e*) According to the statement,

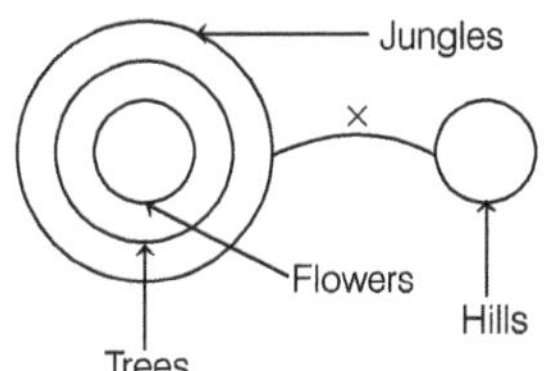

Conclusions I. No flower is hill. (✓)
II. No tree is hill. (✓)
III. Some jungles are flowers. (✓)

48. (*b*) According to the statement,

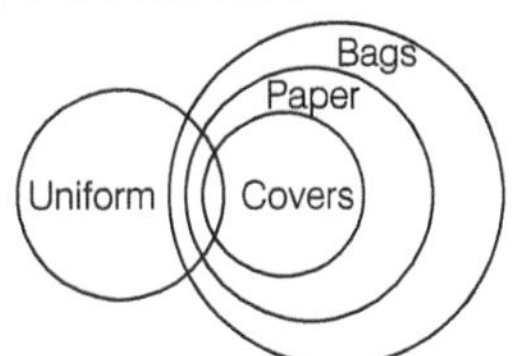

Conclusions I. All covers are bags. (✓)
II. Some bags are covers, papers and uniforms. (✓)
III. Some uniforms are not papers. (✗)

49. (*a*) According to the statement,

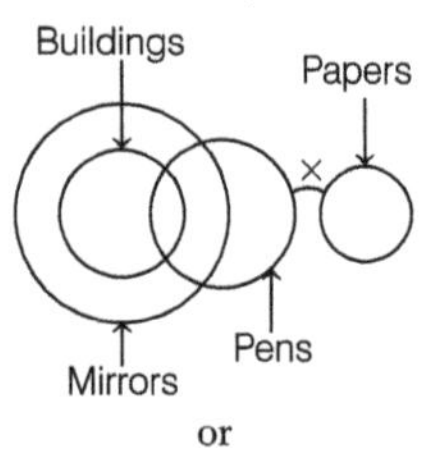

or

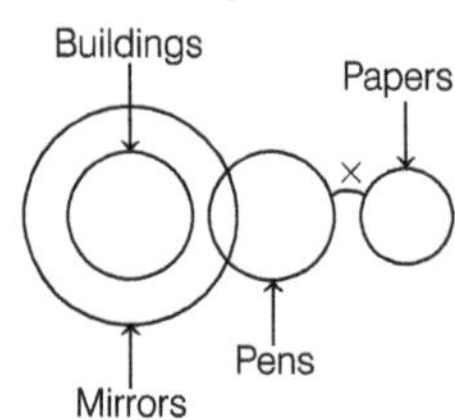

Conclusions I. Some papers are buildings. (✗)
II. Some pens are buildings. (✗)
III. Some papers are mirrors. (✗)

50. (*d*) According to the statement,

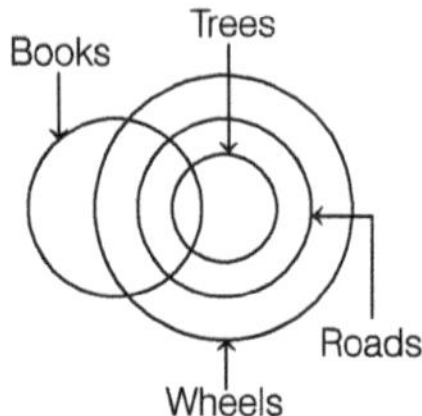

Conclusions I. Some wheels are books. (✓)
II. Some roads are books. (✓)
III. Some wheels are trees. (✓)

51. (*c*) According to the statement,

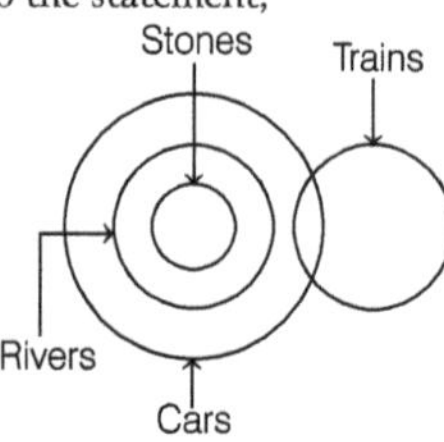

Conclusions I. Some trains are stones. (✗)
II. Some cars are stones. (✓)
III. Some trains are rivers. (✗)

52. (*c*) According to the statement,

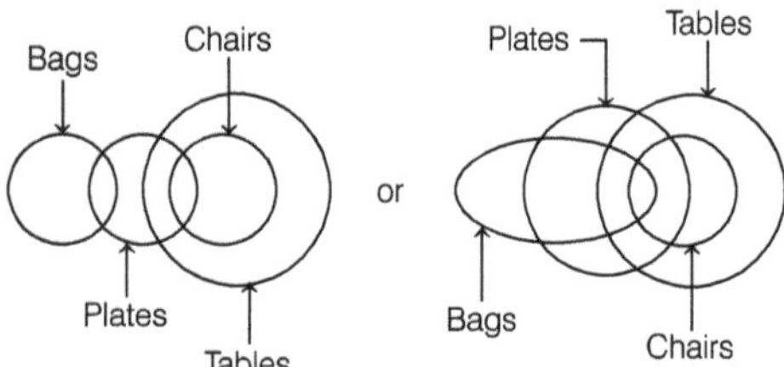

Conclusions I. Some tables are plates. (✓)
II. Some chairs are bags. (✗)
III. No chair is bag. (✗)
II and III make a complementary pair (I-E).

53. (*d*) According to the statement,

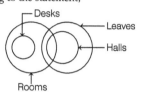

Conclusions I. Some leaves are desks. (✗)
II. Some halls are desks. (✗)
III. Some leaves are rooms. (✓)

54. (*b*) According to the statement,

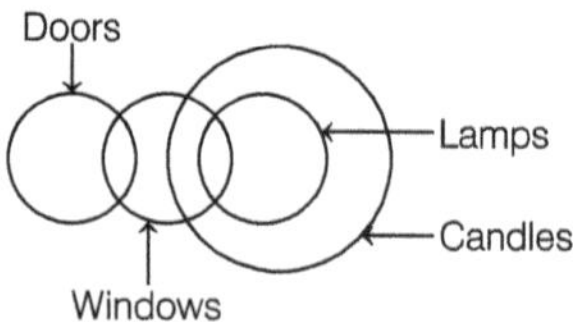

Conclusions I. Some candles are doors. (✗)
II. Some candles are windows. (✓)
III. Some lamps are doors. (✗)

55. (*a*) According to the statement,

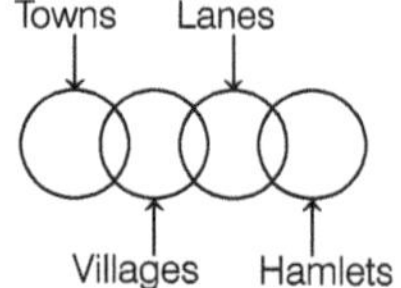

Conclusions I. Some hamlets are villages. (✗)
II. Some lanes are towns. (✗)
III. Some hamlets are towns. (✗)

56. (*d*) According to the statement,

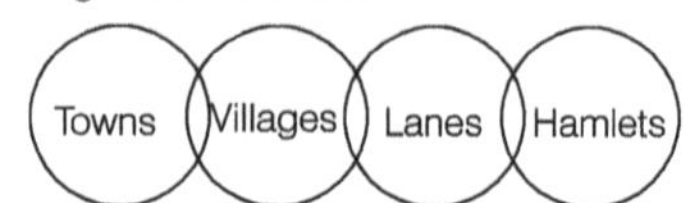

Conclusions I. Some hamlets are villages. (✗)
II. Some lanes are towns. (✗)
III. Some hamlets are towns. (✗)

57. (*b*) According to the statement,

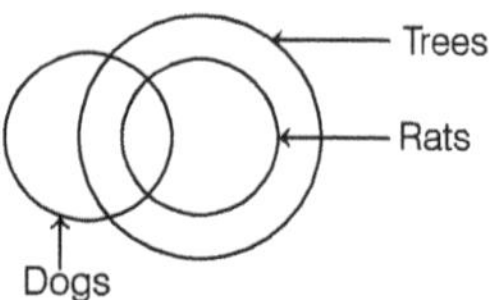

Conclusions I. Some trees are dogs. (✓)
II. All dogs are trees. (✗)
III. All rats are dogs. (✗)
IV. No tree is dog. (✗)

58. (*d*) According to the statements,

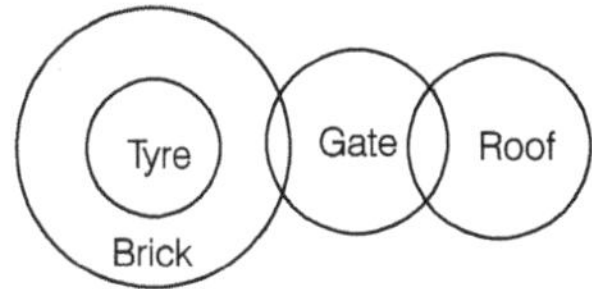

Conclusions I. Some tyres are gates. (✗)
II. No gate is tyre. (✗)
Complementary pair (I-E).

59. (*a*) **Method I**

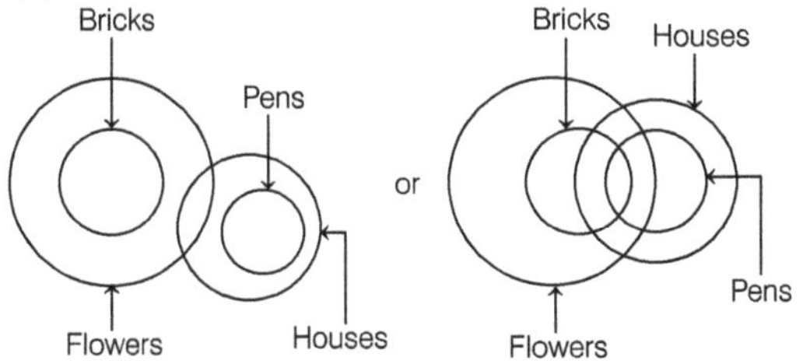

Conclusions I. Some houses are bricks. (✗)
II. Some pens are flowers. (✗)
III. Some flowers are bricks. (✓)
IV. No pen is flower. (✗)
II and IV make a complementary pair (I-E).

Method II

All bricks are flowers.
Some houses are flowers.
All pens are houses.
Aligning the above statements using IEA rule.
All bricks are flowers. (A-type)
Some flowers are houses. (I-type)
Some houses are persons. (I-type)
From Statements 1 and 2,
A + I = Not a valid conclusion
Hence, Conclusion I does not follow.
From Statements 2 and 3,
I + I = Not a valid conclusion
So, Conclusion II does not follow from Statement 1.
All bricks are flowers $\xrightarrow{\text{Conversion}}$
Some flowers are bricks = Conclusion III
Conclusion II and IV are invalid.
But Conclusions II and IV have both subject and predicate same, hence form (I–E) complementary pair.
Hence, either II or IV and III follow.

60. (*c*) According to the statements,

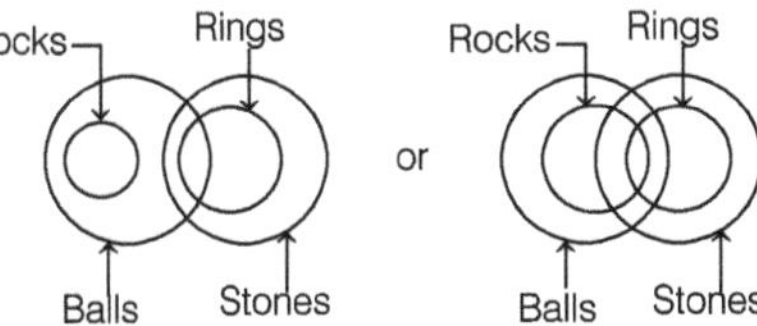

Conclusions I. Some stones are rocks. (✗)
II. Some rings are rocks. (✗)
III. Some balls are rocks. (✓)
IV. No stone is rock. (✗)
I and IV form a complementary pair (I-E).

61. (*d*) According to the statements,

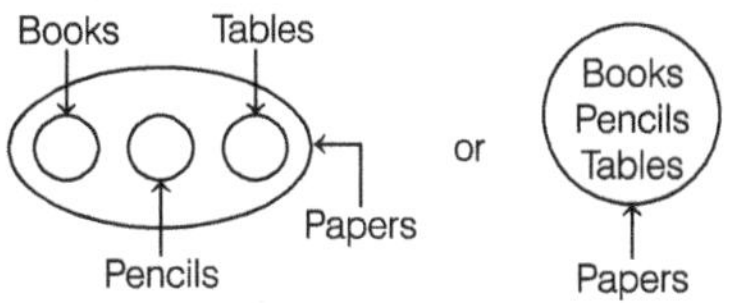

Conclusions I. Some books are pencils. (✗)
II. Some pencils are tables. (✗)
III. Some tables are books. (✗)
IV. Some papers are tables. (✓)

62. (*a*) According to the statements,

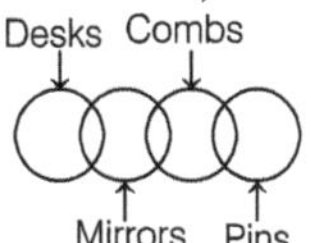

Conclusions I. Some pins are desks. (✗)
II. Some combs are desks. (✗)
III. Some pins are mirrors. (✗)
IV. Some pins are either desks or mirrors. (✗)

63. (*e*) According to the statements,

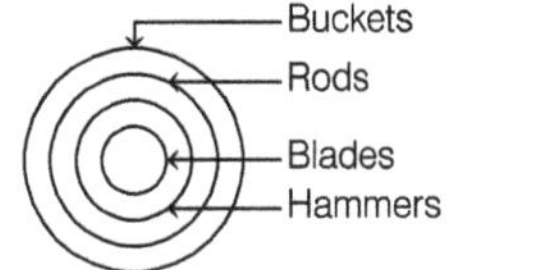

Conclusions I. Some buckets are hammers. (✓)
II. Some rods are blades. (✓)
III. All hammers are buckets. (✓)
IV. All blades are rods. (✓)

64. (*b*) According to the statements,

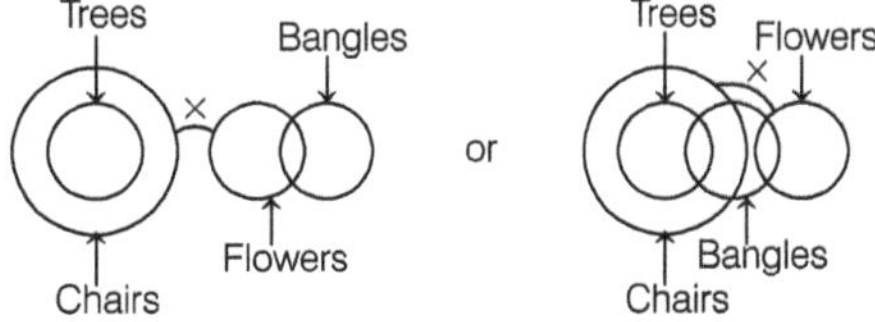

Conclusions
I. No tree is bangle. (✗)
II. No chair is bangle. (✗)
III. Some flowers are trees. (✗)
IV. Some bangles are trees. (✗)
I and IV make a complementary pair (E-I).

65. (*e*) According to the statements,

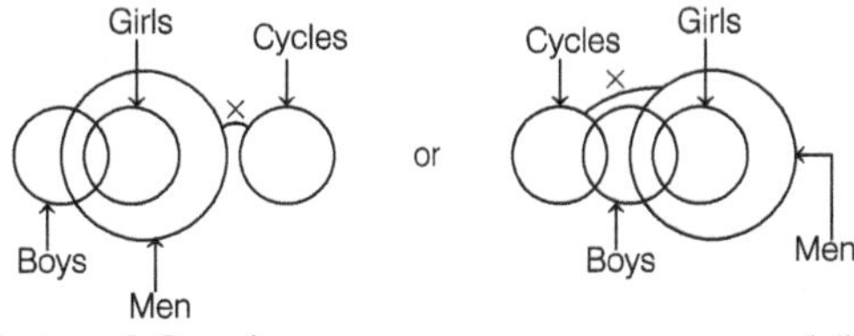

Conclusions I. Some boys are men. (✓)
II. Some boys are cycles. (✗)
III. Some boys are not cycles. (✓)
IV. No cycle is girl. (✓)

66. (e) **Method I**

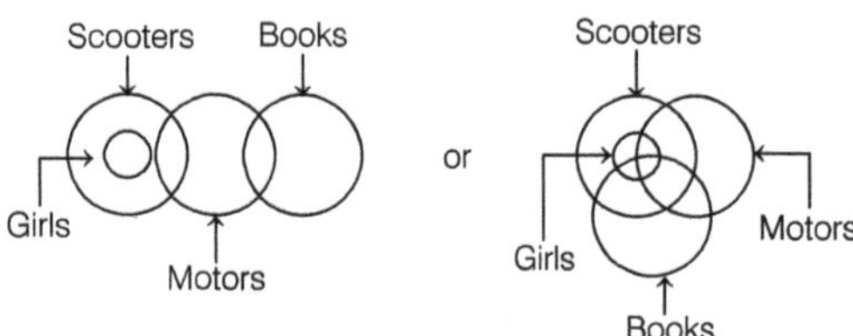

Conclusions I. Some girls are motors. (✗)
II. Some girls are books. (✗)
III. Some scooters are girls. (✓)
IV. No girl is book. (✗)

II and IV make a complementary pair (I-E).

Method II Some motors are books.
Some scooters are motors.
All girls are scooters.
Aligning the above statement by using IEA rule.
All girls are scooters. (A-type)
Some scooters are motors. (I-type)
Some motors are books. (I-type)

From Statements 1 and 2,
A + I = Not a valid conclusion
Hence, Conclusion I does not follow.
From Statements 1, 2 and 3,
$\underbrace{A + I}_{\text{Invalid}} + I$ = Not a valid conclusion
Hence, Conclusion II does not follow.
From Statement 1,
All girls are scooter $\xrightarrow{\text{Conversion}}$ Some scooter are girls.

Conclusion III
Hence, Conclusion III follows.
Conclusion IV is invalid.
But Conclusions II and IV have same subject and predicate and hence form (I-E) complementary pair.
So, either II or IV and III follow.

67. (b)

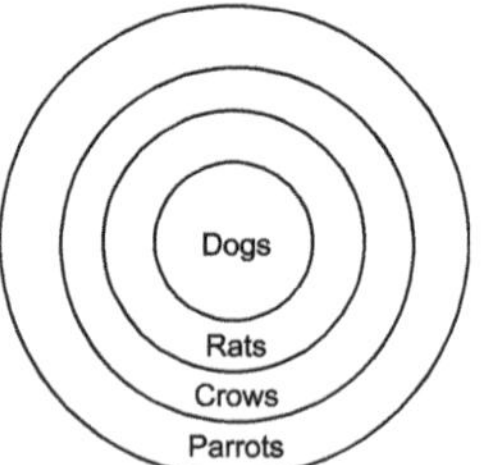

Conclusions I. All dogs are parrots. (✓)
II. Some parrots are dogs. (✓)
III. Some crows are dogs. (✓)
IV. All rats are dogs. (✗)

TYPE 03

Four Statements and Two or More Conclusions

In this type of questions, four statements and some conclusions are given and the candidates are required to check the validity of the conclusions on the basis of the given statements.

DIRECTION ~ (Example No.14) *In the question below are given four statements followed by two Conclusions I and II. You have to take the given statements to be true even if they seem to be at variance from commonly known facts. Read all the conclusions and then decide which of the given conclusion(s) logically follow(s) from given statements disregarding commonly known facts.*

***Ex* 14 Statements** All jaguar are cheetah.
All cheetah are leopard.
All leopards are panthers.
All panthers are cats.

Conclusions I. Some cats are cheetah. « RRBs Group D 2018
II. Some panthers are cheetah.

(a) Both Conclusions I and II follow
(b) Only Conclusion II follows
(c) Only Conclusion I follows
(d) Either Conclusion I or II follows

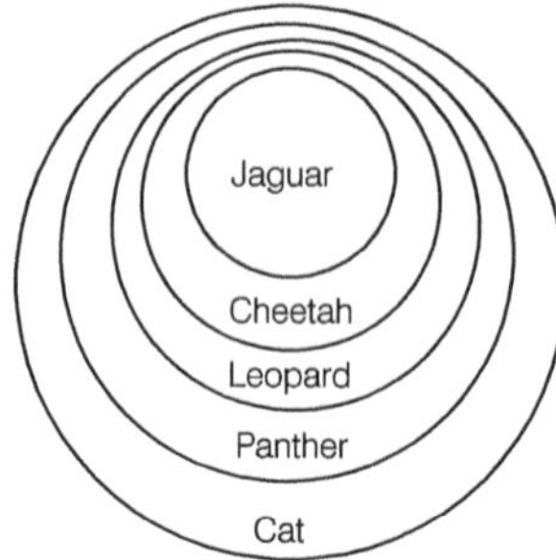

Solution **(a)** According to statements,

Conclusions I. Some cats are cheetah. (✓)
II. Some panthers are cheetah. (✓)

DIRECTION ~ (Example No.15) *In the question below are given four statements followed by three Conclusions I, II and III. You have to take the given statements to be true even if they seem to be at variance from commonly known facts. Read all the conclusions and then decide which of the given conclusion(s) logically follow(s) from given statements disregarding commonly known facts.*

***Ex* 15 Statements** All lions are tigers.
All tigers are leopards.
Some leopards are wolves.
No wolves is elephant.

Conclusions I. No elephant is lion.
II. Some wolves are lions.
III. Some leopards are lions.

(a) Only I follows (b) Only II follows
(c) Only III follows (d) I and II follow

***Solution* (c)**

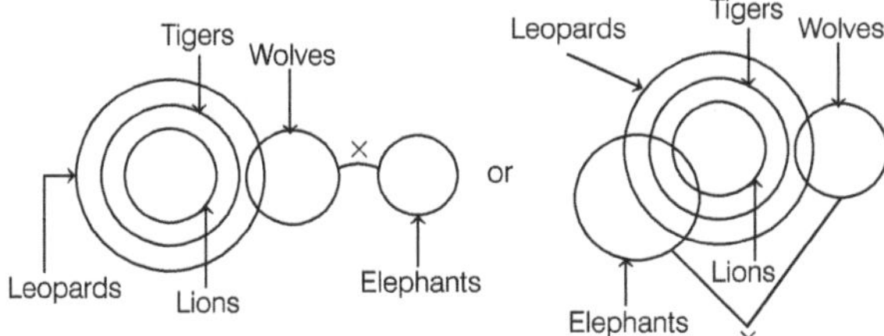

Conclusions

I. No elephant is lion. (✗)
II. Some wolves are lions. (✗)
III. Some leopards are lions. (✓)

DIRECTION ~(Example No. 16) *In the question below are given four statements followed by four Conclusions I, II, III and VI. You have to take the given statements to be true even if they seem to be at variance from commonly known facts. Read all the conclusions and then decide which of the given conclusion(s) logically follow(s) from given statements disregarding commonly known facts.*

***Ex* 16 Statements** Some roses are flowers.
Some flowers are buds.
All buds are leaves.
All leaves are plants. « IDBI (PO) 2013

Conclusions I. Some plants are flowers.
II. Some roses are buds.
III. No leaves are roses.
IV. No roses are buds.

(a) Only I follows
(b) I and II follow
(c) I and either II or IV follow
(d) Either II or IV follows

***Solution* (c)**

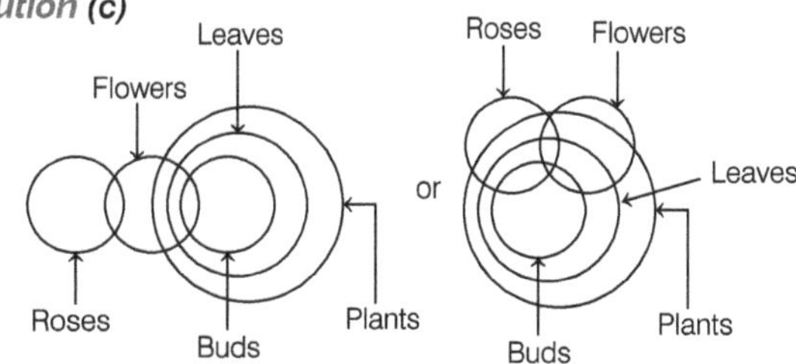

Conclusions I. Some plants are flowers. (✓)
II. Some roses are buds. (✗)
III. No leaves are roses. (✗)
IV. No roses are buds. (✗)
II and IV make a complementary pair (I-E).

Practice / CORNER 1.3

DIRECTIONS ~ (Q. Nos. 1-12) *In each question below are four statements followed by two conclusions numbered I and II. You have to take the four given statements to be true even if they seem to be at variance with commonly known facts and then decide which of the given conclusions logically follows from the four statements disregarding commonly known facts.*

Give answer

(a) If only Conclusion I follows
(b) If only Conclusion II follows
(c) If either Conclusion I or II follows
(d) If neither Conclusion I nor II follows
(e) If both Conclusions I and II follow

1. Statements Some apples are orange.
Some orange are pineapples.
Some pineapples are not coconuts.
Some coconuts are black forests.

Conclusions « SBI (PO) 2015
I. Some apples are pineapples.
II. Some pineapples are coconuts.

2. Statements Some apples are orange.
Some orange are pineapples.
Some pineapples are not coconuts.
Some coconuts are black forests.

Conclusions « SBI (PO) 2015
I. Some orange being black forests is a possibility.
II. Some pineapples being coconuts is a possibility.

3. Statements All mobiles is tablets.
All tablets is smartphones.
All smartphones is laptops.
All laptops is computers. « SBI (PO) 2015

Conclusions
I. Some tablets are laptops.
II. Some laptops are not tablets.

4. Statements All mobiles is tablets.
All tablets is smartphones.
All smartphones is laptops.
All laptops is computers. « SBI (PO) 2015

Conclusions
I. All computers being mobiles is a possibility.
II. All tablets being computers is a possibility.

5. Statements No U is L.
No L is K.
Some N are Z.
Some Z are magic. « SBI (PO) 2015

Conclusions
I. No U is Z.
II. All Z being L is a possibility.

6. Statements All pictures are paintings.
All paintings are photographs.
Some photographs are designs.
Some designs are movies.

Conclusions « Andhra Bank (PO) 2008
I. Some paintings are designs.
II. Some photographs are movies.

7. Statements Some tablets are capsules.
All capsules are syrups.
Some syrups are medicines.
All medicines are powders.

Conclusions « Andhra Bank (PO) 2008
I. Some syrups are powders.
II. Some syrups are tablets.

8. Statements All jungles are trees.
All trees are roads.
All roads are houses.
All houses are buildings. « LIC (ADO) 2007

Conclusions
I. All trees are houses.
II. Some buildings are roads.

9. Statements All cups are bowls.
All bowls are trays.
Some trays are plates.
No plate is spoon. « NIACL 2014

Conclusions
I. Some bowls are plates.
II. Some cups are spoons.

10. Statements All books are pens.
Some pens are desks.
Some desks are chairs.
Some chairs are tables. « NIACL 2014

Conclusions
I. Some tables are desks.
II. Some chairs are pens.

11. Statements All bangles are rings.
All rings are bracelets.
Some bracelets are jewels.
Some jewels are stones. « LIC (ADO) 2007

Conclusions
I. Some stones are bangles.
II. Some jewels are rings.

12. Statements All trousers are pants.
Some pants are shirts.
All shirts are buttons.
Some buttons are threads.

Conclusions « LIC (ADO) 2007
I. Some threads are pants.
II. Some buttons are trousers.

DIRECTIONS ~ (Q. Nos. 13-28) *In each of the questions below are given four statements followed by three conclusions numbered* I, II, *and* III. *You have to take the given statements to be true even, if they seem to be at variance with commonly known facts. Read all the conclusion(s) and then decide which of the given conclusions logically follow(s) from the given statements disregarding commonly known facts.*

13. Statements All flowers are books.
All books are carpets.
Some carpets are keys.
Some keys are locks. « IDBI Executive 2018

Conclusions
I. Some keys are books.
II. Some keys are flowers.
III. Some locks are books.

(a) Only I follows (b) Only II follows
(c) Only III follows (d) None follows
(e) All follow

14. Statements All boxes are cups.
All chairs are cups.
All cups are mirrors.
All tables are mirrors.

Conclusions « IDBI Executive 2018
I. Some tables are chairs.
II. Some mirrors are boxes.
III. Some mirrors are chairs.

(a) Only I follows (b) Only II follows
(c) Only III follows (d) All follow
(e) I and II follow

15. Statements Some pins are needles.
All needles are ropes.
Some ropes are buckets.
All buckets are trees. « IDBI Executive 2018

Conclusions
I. Some buckets are pins.
II. Some ropes are pins.
III. No bucket is pin.

(a) Only I follows (b) Only II follows
(c) Only III follows (d) None follows
(e) Either I or III and II follow

16. Statements Some shoes are socks.
All socks are towels.
All towels are bedsheets.
No bedsheet is blanket.

Conclusions « IDBI Bank (PO) 2008

I. No towel is blanket.
II. Some shoes are towels.
III. Some shoes are bedsheets.

(a) I and II follow (b) II and III follow
(c) I and III follow (d) All follow
(e) None of these

17. Statements Some fruits are flowers.
Some flowers are buds.
No bud is leaf.
All leaves are plants.

Conclusions « IDBI Bank (PO) 2008

I. No plant is bud.
II. Some plants are flowers.
III. Some buds are fruits.

(a) None follows (b) Only I follows
(c) II and III follow (d) Only III follows
(e) None of these

18. Statements Some pearls are gems.
Some gems are diamonds.
All diamonds are rings.
All rings are bangles.

Conclusions « Punjab & Sindh Bank (PO) 2008

I. Some bangles are rings.
II. All rings are diamonds.
III. All diamonds are bangles.

(a) Only I follows (b) I and II follow
(c) I and III follow (d) All follow
(e) None of these

19. Statements All chairs are tables.
All tables are telephones.
All telephones are cell phones.
No cell phone is computer.

Conclusions « Punjab & Sindh Bank (PO) 2008

I. All cell phones are tables.
II. Some chairs are computers.
III. No chair is computer.

(a) Only I follows
(b) Only II follows
(c) Only III follows
(d) Either II or III follows
(e) None of the above

20. Statements Some rocks are hills.
All hills are mountains.
All mountains are rivers.
No river is canal.

Conclusions « Punjab & Sindh Bank (PO) 2008

I. All rocks are rivers.
II. Some hills are canals.
III. Some rivers are canals.

(a) Only I follows (b) II and III follow
(c) I and III follow (d) Only II follows
(e) None follows

21. Statements Some books are files.
All files are balls.
All balls are plates.
No plate is glass.

Conclusions « Punjab & Sindh Bank (Clerk) 2011

I. No glass is plate.
II. Some balls are books.
III. All plates are balls.

(a) Only I follows (b) I and III follow
(c) I and II follow (d) None follows
(e) All follow

22. Statements All pens are cats.
All cats are rats.
All rats are snakes.
All snakes are foxes.

Conclusions « Punjab & Sindh Bank (Clerk) 2011

I. Some snakes are cats.
II. All snakes are rats.
III. Some cats are pens.

(a) None follows (b) All follow
(c) Only II follows (d) I and III follow
(e) None of these

23. Statements Some shirts are pants.
All pants are caps.
All caps are ties.
No tie is socks. « UBI (PO) 2010

Conclusions

I. No cap is socks.
II. Some pants are shirts.
III. All caps are pants.

(a) I and II follow
(b) Only II follows
(c) Only III follows
(d) None follows
(e) All follow

24. Statements All boxes are foxes.
All foxes are schools.
No school is college.
All colleges are markets. « UBI (PO) 2010

Conclusions

I. No fox is college.
II. No college is school.
III. No box is fox.

(a) Only I follows (b) Only III follows
(c) I and II follow (d) None follows
(e) All follow

25. Statements Some leaves are flowers.
No flower is fruit.
Some fruits are branches.
Some branches are stems

Conclusions « OBC (PO) 2007

I. Some leaves are stems.
II. All leaves are either stems or fruits.
III. All stems are either branches or fruits.

(a) Only I follows (b) II and III follow
(c) Only III follows (d) All follow
(e) None follows

26. Statements Some caps are umbrellas.
Some umbrellas are raincoats.
All raincoats are trousers.
All trousers are jackets. « OBC (PO) 2007

Conclusions
I. Some raincoats are caps.
II. Some trousers are umbrellas.
III. All raincoats are jackets.
(a) None follows (b) I and II follow
(c) II and III follow (d) I and III follow
(e) None of these

27. Statements Some fans are coolers.
Some coolers are machines.
Some machines are computers.
All computers are televisions.

Conclusions « OBC (PO) 2007
I. Some televisions are machines.
II. Some machines are fans.
III. No machine is a fan.
(a) None follows
(b) Only I follows
(c) Only either II or III follows
(d) Only I and either II or III follow
(e) All follow

28. Statements All keys are staplers.
All staplers are blades.
Some blades are erasers.
Some erasers are sharpeners.

Conclusions « OBC (PO) 2007
I. Some sharpeners are keys.
II. All keys are blades.
III. Some erasers are keys.
(a) I and II follow (b) Only I follows
(c) Only II follows (d) All follow
(e) None of these

DIRECTIONS ~ (Q. Nos. 29-43) *In each of the questions below are given four statements followed by four conclusions numbered* I, II, III *and* IV. *You have to take the given statements to be true even if they seem to be at variance with commonly known facts. Read all the conclusions and then decide which of the given conclusion (s) logically follow (s) from the given statements disregarding commonly known facts.*

29. Statements Some trains are cars.
All cars are branches.
All branches are nets.
Some nets are dresses.
« Syndicate Bank (PO) 2010

Conclusions
I. Some dresses are cars.
II. Some nets are trains.
III. Some branches are trains.
IV. Some dresses are trains.
(a) I and III follow
(b) II and III follow
(c) I and IV follow
(d) II, III and IV follow
(e) None of these

30. Statements Some pencils are kites.
Some kites are desks.
All desks are jungles.
All jungles are mountains.

Conclusions « Syndicate Bank (PO) 2010
I. Some mountains are pencils.
II. Some jungles are pencils.
III. Some mountains are desks.
IV. Some jungles are kites.
(a) I and III follow (b) I, II and III follow
(c) III and IV follow (d) II, III and IV follow
(e) None of these

31. Statements All papers are clips.
Some clips are boards.
Some boards are lanes.
All lanes are roads.

Conclusions « Syndicate Bank (PO) 2010
I. Some roads are boards.
II. Some lanes are clips.
III. Some boards are papers.
IV. Some roads are clips.
(a) I and II follow (b) I and III follow
(c) I, II and III follow (d) II, III and IV follow
(e) None of these

32. Statements All birds are horses.
All horses are tigers.
Some tigers are lions.
Some lions are monkeys. « PNB (PO) 2010

Conclusions
I. Some tigers are horses.
II. Some monkeys are birds.
III. Some tigers are birds.
IV. Some monkeys are horses.
(a) I and III follow
(b) I, II and III follow
(c) II, III and IV follow
(d) All I, II, III and IV follow
(e) None of these

33. Statements Some benches are walls.
All walls are houses.
Some houses are jungles.
All jungles are roads. « PNB (PO) 2010

Conclusions
I. Some roads are benches.
II. Some jungles are walls.
III. Some houses are benches.
IV. Some roads are houses.
(a) I and II follow (b) I and III follow
(c) III and IV follow (d) II, III and IV follow
(e) None of these

34. Statements Some sticks are lamps.
Some flowers are lamps.
Some lamps are dresses.
All dresses are shirts. « PNB (PO) 2010

Conclusions
I. Some shirts are sticks.
II. Some shirts are flowers.
III. Some flowers are sticks.
IV. Some dresses are sticks.
(a) None follows (b) Only I follows
(c) Only II follows (d) Only III follows
(e) Only IV follows

35. Statements Some baskets are glasses.
All glasses are pots.
Some pots are plates.
All plates are cups.

Conclusions
I. No glasses are pots.
II. All glasses are baskets.
III. Atleast some pots are baskets.
IV. Some plates being glasses is a possibility.
(a) III and IV follow (b) Only IV follows
(c) I and II follow (d) None follows
(e) All follow

36. Statements All potatos are onions.
All onions are grapes.
Some grapes are mangoes.
All mangoes are brinjals.

Conclusions
I. Potatos are grapes.
II. Some brinjals being potatos is a possibility.
III. Each potato is grape.
IV. Some potatos are definitely onions.
(a) All follow (b) None follows
(c) Only IV follows (d) Follow II, III and IV
(e) Only I follows

37. Statements All bats are cats.
No cat is rat.
All rats are tigers.
Some tigers are fighters.

Conclusions
I. Some tigers are cats.
II. Atleast some fighters being rats is a possibility.
III. Atleast some cats are definitely bats.
IV. None of the fighters is rat.
(a) All follow (b) None follows
(c) Only III follows (d) I, II and IV follow
(e) II and III follow

38. Statements All snakes are eagles.
Some eagles are rabbits.
All rabbits are birds.
Some birds are animals.

Conclusions « UCO Bank (PO) 2009
I. Some animals are snakes.
II. Some birds are snakes.
III. Some birds are eagles.
IV. All birds are rabbits.
(a) None follows (b) Only II follows
(c) Only III follows (d) Both II and III follow
(e) None of these

39. Statements Some cameras are calculators.
Some calculators are diaries.
All notebooks are diaries.
All diaries are computers.

Conclusions « UCO Bank (PO) 2009
I. Some notebooks are calculators.
II. Some calculators are computers.
III. All notebooks are computers.
IV. Some diaries are cameras.
(a) None follows
(b) Only II follows
(c) Only III follows
(d) Both II and III follow
(e) None of the above

40. Statements Some books are journals.
All journals are papers.
Some papers are cards.
All cards are boards.

Conclusions « IDBI Bank (PO) 2009
I. Some papers are books.
II. Some papers are boards.
III. Some boards are journals.
IV. Some boards are books.
(a) I and II follow (b) Only I follows
(c) I, II and III follow (d) All follow
(e) None of the above

41. Statements Some grapes are apples.
Some apples are bananas.
All bananas are guavas.
No guava is pomegranate.

Conclusions « IDBI Bank (PO) 2009
I. No grapes are pomegranates.
II. Some guavas are grapes.
III. Some guavas are apples.
IV. No bananas are pomegranates.
(a) None follows (b) II and III follow
(c) Either I or III follows (d) Both III and IV follow
(e) None of the above

42. Statements Some doors are walls.
All walls are floors.
All floors are rooms.
Some rooms are windows.

Conclusions « IDBI Bank (PO) 2009
I. All walls are rooms.
II. Some rooms are doors.
III. Some rooms are walls.
IV. Some floors are doors.
(a) None follows (b) I and II follow
(c) II and III follow (d) II, III and IV follow
(e) All follow

43. Statements Some men are girls.
Some girls are foolish.
All foolish are mads.
Some mads are bads.

Conclusions
I. Some girls are definitely mads.
II. Most of the mads are foolish.
III. At least some girls are men.
IV. All foolish except few are girls.
(a) None follows (b) Only I follows
(c) Only II follows (d) All follow
(e) II and III follow

Answers WITH EXPLANATIONS

Solutions (Q.Nos. 1 and 2)

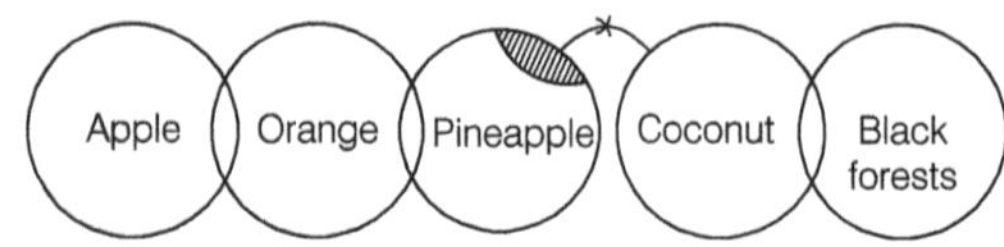

1. (*d*) **Conclusions**
   I. Some apples are pineapples. (✗)
   II. Some pineapples are coconuts. (✗)
2. (*e*) **Conclusions**
   I. Some orange being black forests is a possibility. (✓)
   II. Some pineapples being coconuts is a possibility. (✓)

Solutions (Q.Nos. 3 and 4)

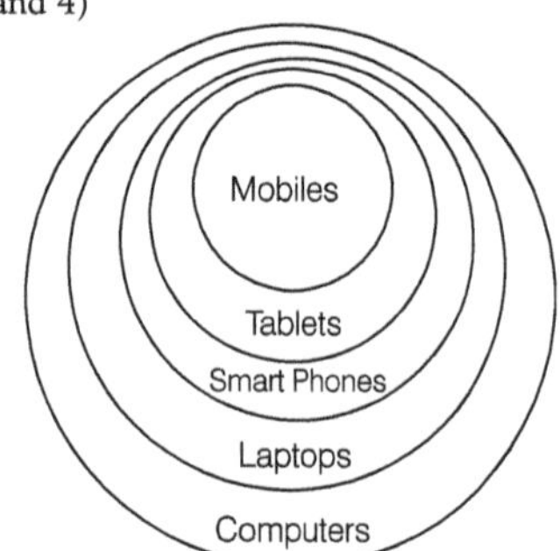

3. (*a*) **Conclusions** I. Some tablets are laptops. (✓)
   II. Some laptops are not tablets. (✗)
4. (*a*) **Conclusions**
   I. All computers being mobiles is a possibility (✓)
   II. All tablets being computers is a possibility. (✗)
5. (*b*)

Conclusions
I. No U is Z . (✗)
II. All Z being L is a possibility. (✓)

6. (*d*)

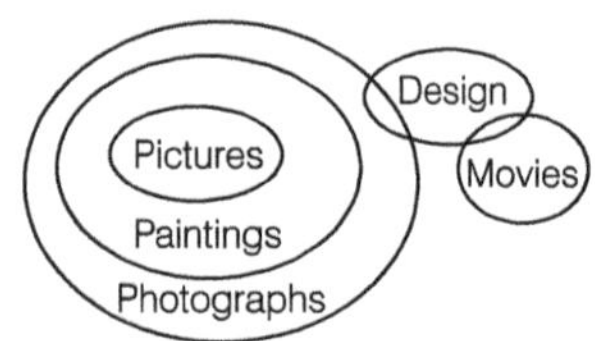

Conclusions
I. Some paintings are designs. (✗)
II. Some photographs are movies. (✗)

7. (*e*)

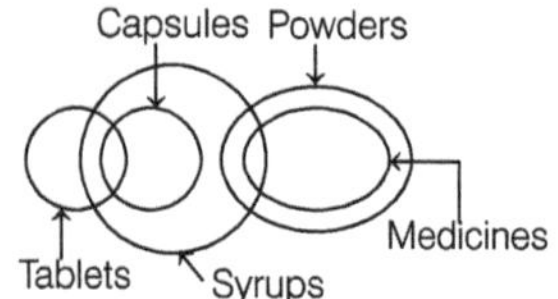

Conclusions
I. Some syrups are powders. (✓)
II. Some syrups are tablets. (✓)

8. (*e*)

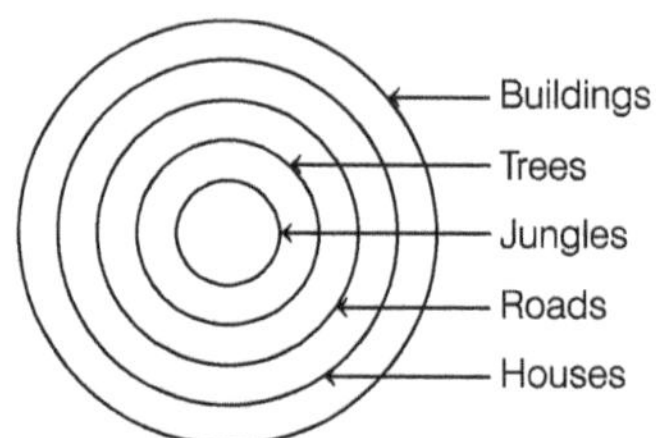

Conclusions
I. All trees are houses. (✓)
II. Some buildings are roads. (✓)

9. (*d*)

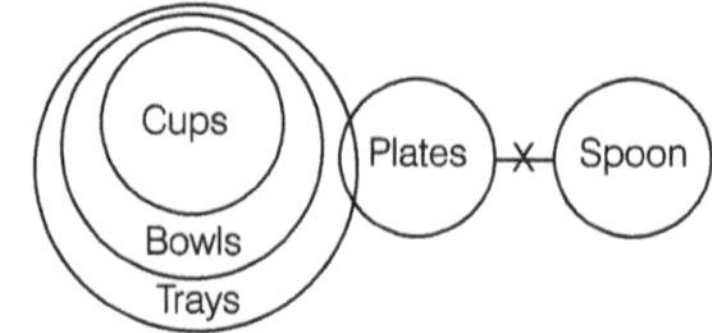

Conclusions
I. Some bowls are plates. (✗)
II. Some cups are spoons. (✗)

10. (*d*)

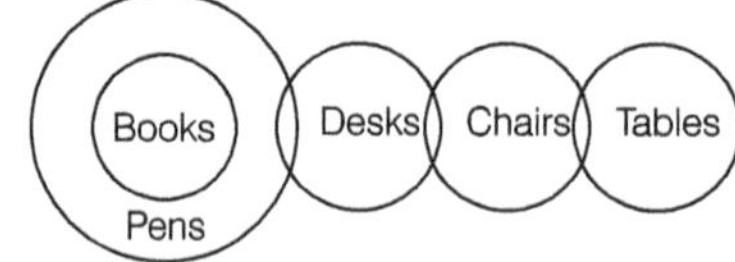

Conclusions I. Some tables are desks. (✗)
II. Some chairs are pens. (✗)

11. (*d*)

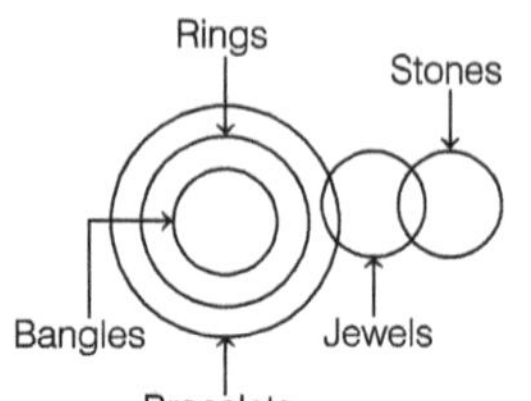

Conclusions I. Some stones are bangles. (✗)
II. Some jewels are rings. (✗)

12. (*d*)

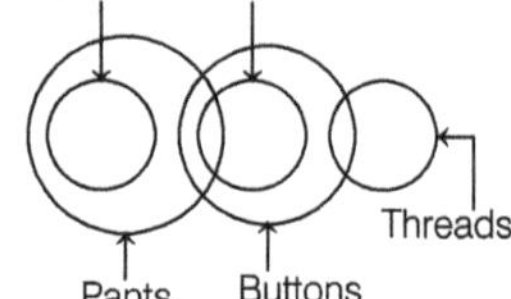

Conclusions I. Some threads are pants. (✗)
II. Some buttons are trousers. (✗)

13. (*d*)

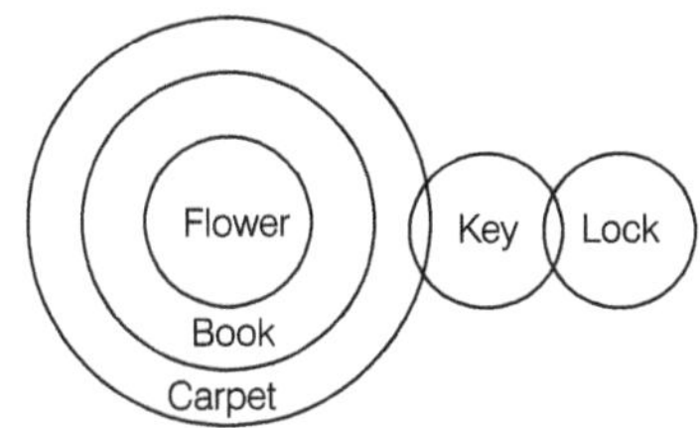

Conclusions

I. Some keys are books. (✗)
II. Some keys are flowers. (✗)
III. Some locks are books. (✗)

14. (*e*)

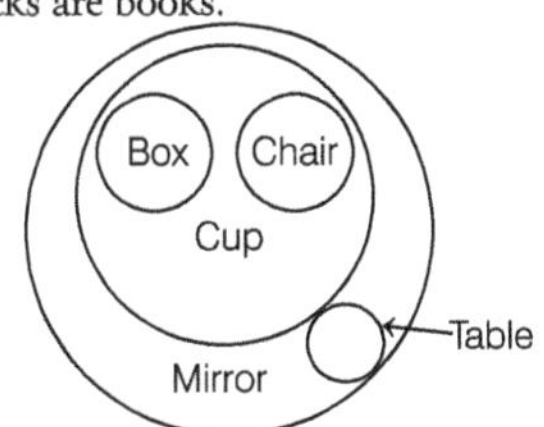

Conclusions

I. Some tables are chairs. (✓)
II. Some mirrors are boxes. (✓)
III. Some mirrors are chairs. (✗)

15. (*e*)

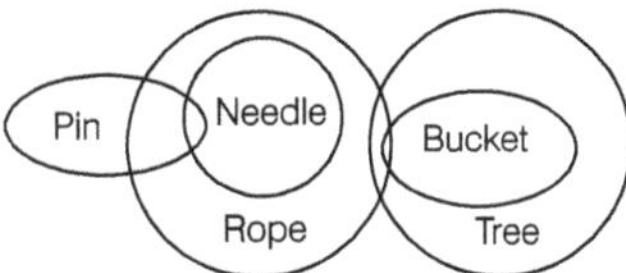

Conclusions I. Some buckets are pins. (✗)
II. Some ropes are pin. (✓)
III. No bucket is pin. (✗)

I and III make a complementary pair (I-E).

16. (*d*)

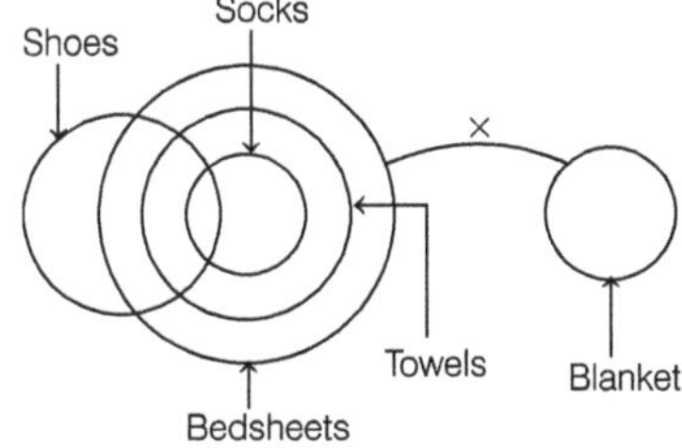

Conclusions

I. No towel is blanket. (✓)
II. Some shoes are towels. (✓)
III. Some shoes are bedsheets. (✓)

17. (*a*)

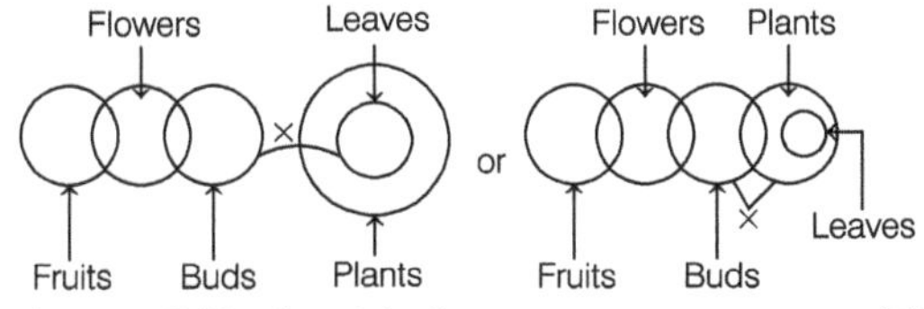

Conclusions I. No plant is bud. (✗)
II. Some plants are flowers. (✗)
III. Some buds are fruits. (✗)

18. (*c*)

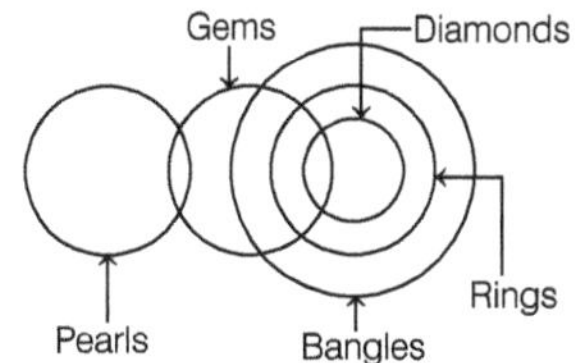

Conclusions I. Some bangles are rings. (✓)
II. All rings are diamonds. (✗)
III. All diamonds are bangles. (✓)

19. (*c*)

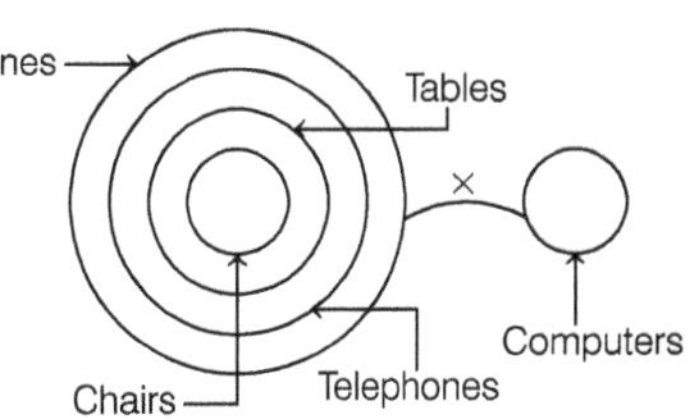

Conclusions

I. All cell phones are tables. (✗)
II. Some chairs are computers. (✗)
III. No chair is computer. (✓)

20. (*e*)

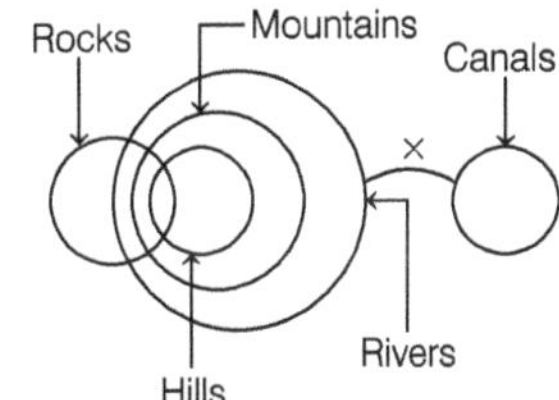

Conclusions I. All rocks are rivers. (✗)
II. Some hills are canals. (✗)
III. Some rivers are canals. (✗)

21. (*c*)

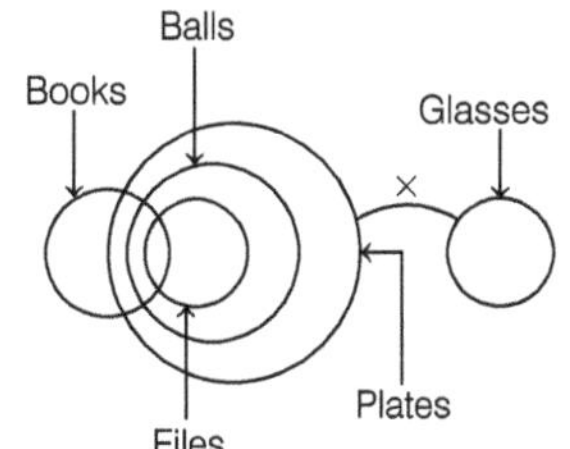

Conclusions I. No glass is plate. (✓)
II. Some balls are books. (✓)
III. All plates are balls. (✗)

22. (*d*)

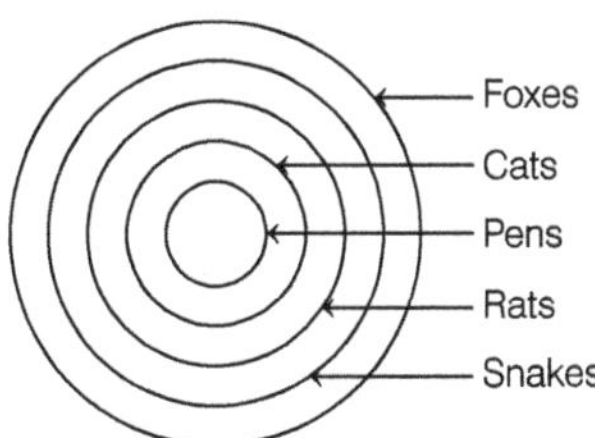

Conclusions
I. Some snakes are cats. (✓)
II. All snakes are rats. (✗)
III. Some cats are pens. (✓)

23. (*a*)

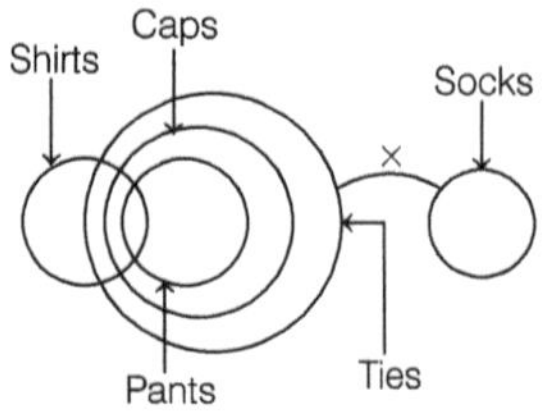

Shirts, Caps, Socks, Pants, Ties

Conclusions
I. No cap is socks. (✓)
II. Some pants are shirts. (✓)
III. All caps are pants. (✗)

24. (*c*)

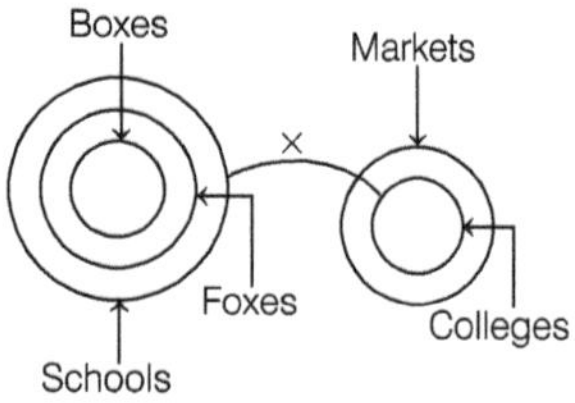

Boxes, Markets, Foxes, Colleges, Schools

Conclusions I. No fox is college. (✓)
II. No college is school. (✓)
III. No box is fox. (✗)

25. (*e*)

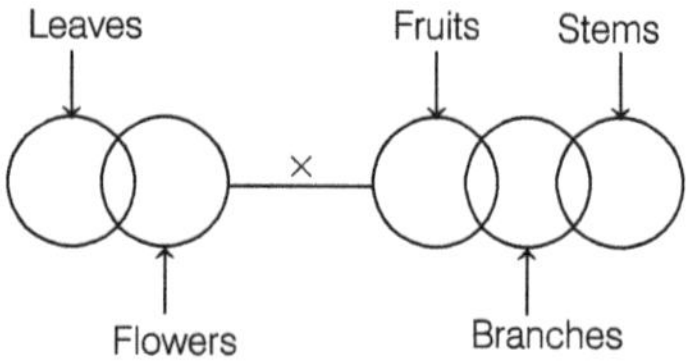

Leaves, Fruits, Stems, Flowers, Branches

Conclusions
I. Some leaves are stems. (✗)
II. All leaves are either stems or fruits. (✗)
III. All stems are either branches or fruits. (✗)

26. (*c*)

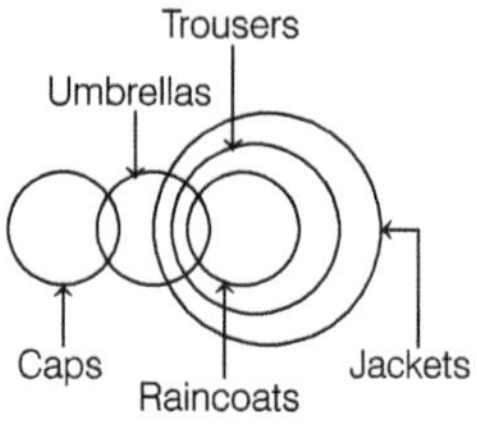

Trousers, Umbrellas, Caps, Raincoats, Jackets

Conclusions
I. Some raincoats are caps. (✗)
II. Some trousers are umbrellas. (✓)
III. All raincoats are jackets. (✓)

27. (*d*)

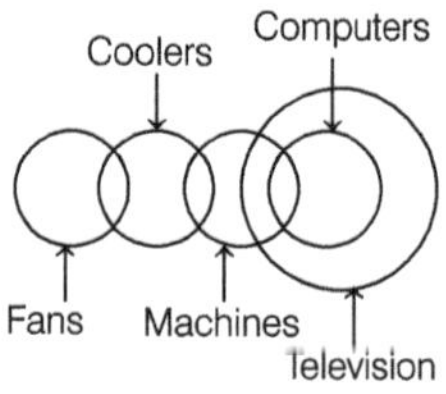

Coolers, Computers, Fans, Machines, Television

Conclusions
I. Some televisions are machines. (✓)
II. Some machines are fans. (✗)
III. No machine is fan. (✗)
II and III make a complementary pair (I-E).

28. (*c*)

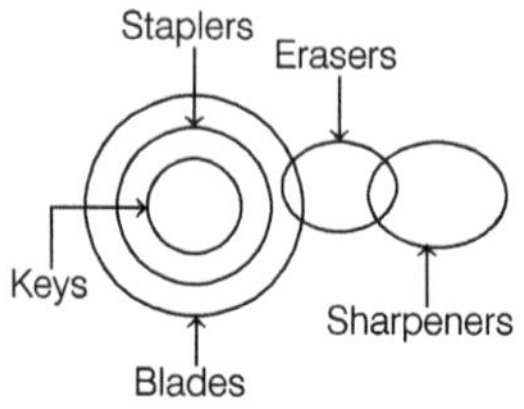

Staplers, Erasers, Keys, Sharpeners, Blades

Conclusions I. Some sharpeners are keys. (✗)
II. All keys are blades. (✓)
III. Some erasers are keys. (✗)

29. (*b*)

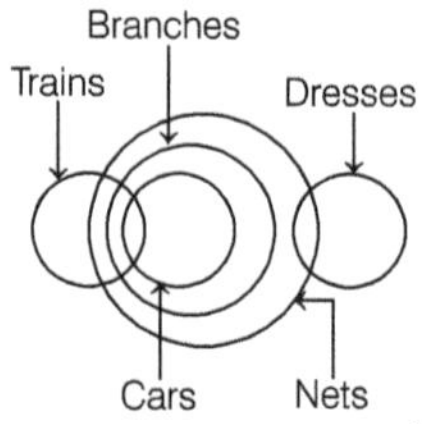

Branches, Trains, Dresses, Cars, Nets

Conclusions I. Some dresses are cars. (✗)
II. Some nets are trains. (✓)
III. Some branches are trains. (✓)
IV. Some dresses are trains. (✗)

30. (*c*) **Method I**

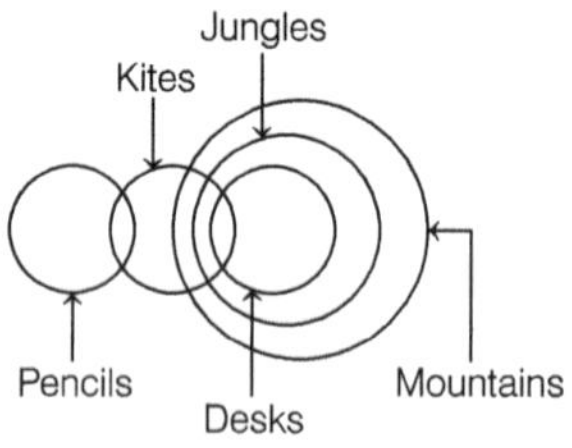

Jungles, Kites, Pencils, Desks, Mountains

Conclusions I. Some mountains are pencils. (✗)
II. Some jungles are pencils. (✗)
III. Some mountains are desks. (✓)
IV. Some jungles are kites. (✓)

Method II
Some pencils are kites. (I-type)
Some kites are desks. (I-types)
All desks are jungles. (A-type)
All jungles are mountains. (A-type)
From Statements 1, 2, 3 and 4,

$$[\underbrace{(I + I)}_{\text{Invalid}} + A] + A = \text{Not a valid conclusion}$$

Hence, Conclusion I does not follow.
From Statements 1, 2 and 3,

$$\underbrace{(I + I)}_{\text{Invalid}} + A = \text{Not a valid conclusion}$$

Hence, Conclusion II does not follow.
From Statements 3 and 4,

$$A + A = \text{A-type conclusion}$$

All desks are mountains $\xrightarrow{\text{Conversion}}$ Some mountains are desks.
Conclusion III follows.
From Statements 2 and 3,
I + A = I-type conclusion
Some kits are jungles ⇒ Some jungles are kites = Conclusion IV
So, Conclusions III and IV follow.

31. (*e*)

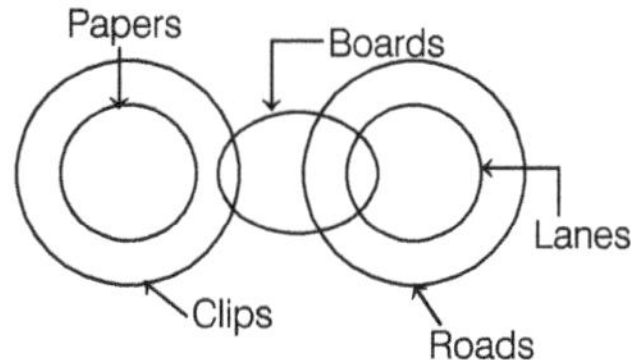

Conclusions

I. Some roads are boards. (✓)
II. Some lanes are clips. (✗)
III. Some boards are papers. (✗)
IV. Some roads are clips. (✗)

32. (*a*)

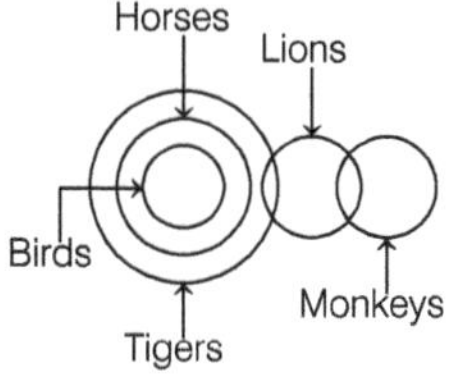

Conclusions

I. Some tigers are horses. (✓)
II. Some monkeys are birds. (✗)
III. Some tigers are birds. (✓)
IV. Some monkeys are horses. (✗)

33. (*c*)

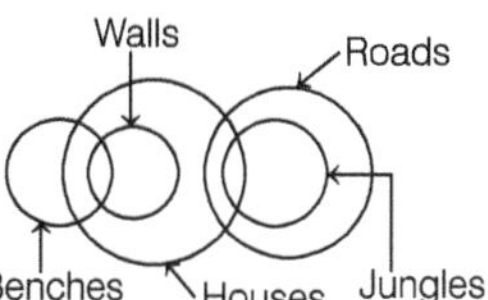

Conclusions

I. Some roads are benches. (✗)
II. Some jungles are walls. (✗)
III. Some houses are benches. (✓)
IV. Some roads are houses. (✓)

34. (*a*)

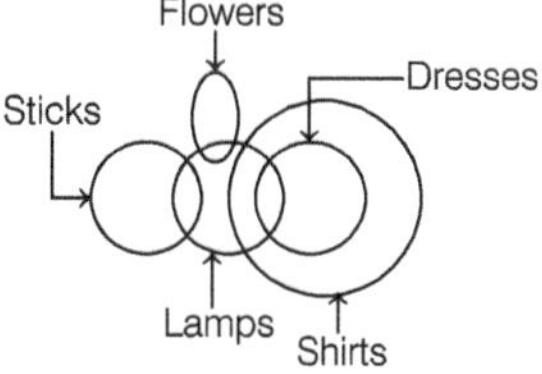

Conclusions

I. Some shirts are sticks. (✗)
II. Some shirts are flowers. (✗)
III. Some flowers are sticks. (✗)
IV. Some dresses are sticks. (✗)

35. (*a*)

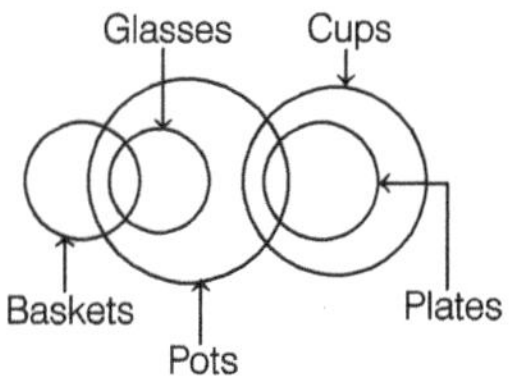

Conclusions

I. No glasses are pots. (✗)
II. All glasses are baskets. (✗)
III. Atleast some pots are baskets. (✓)
IV. Some plates being glasses is a possibility. (✓)

36. (*a*)

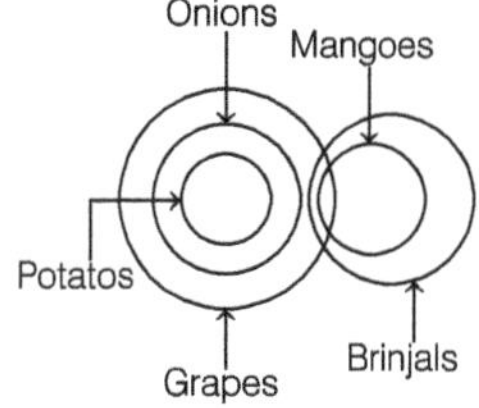

Conclusions

I. Potatos are grapes. (✓)
II. Some brinjals being potatos is a possibility. (✓)
III. Each potato is grape. (✓)
IV. Some potatos are definitely onions. (✓)

37. (*e*)

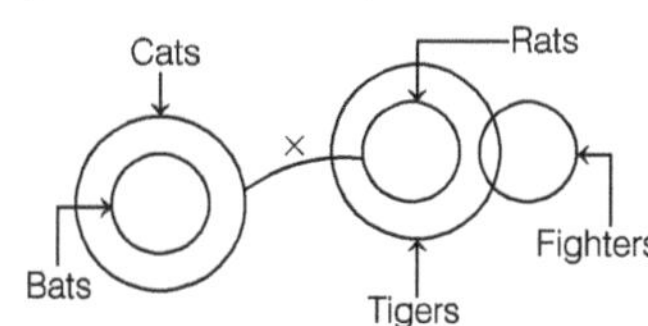

Conclusions

I. Some tigers are cats. (✗)
II. Atleast some fighters being rats is a possibility. (✓)
III. Atleast some cats are definitely bats. (✓)
IV. None of the fighters is rat. (✗)

38. (*c*)

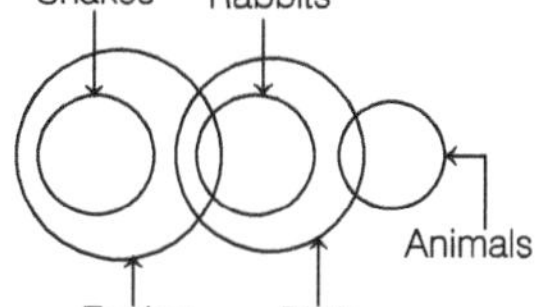

Conclusions I. Some animals are snakes. (✗)
II. Some birds are snakes. (✗)
III. Some birds are eagles. (✓)
IV. All birds are rabbits. (✗)

39. (*d*) **Method I**

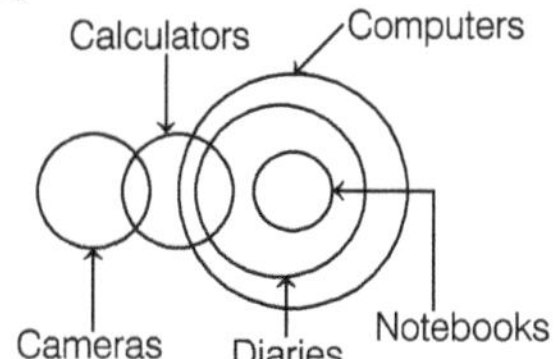

Conclusions

I. Some notebooks are calculators. (✗)
II. Some calculators are computers. (✓)
III. All notebooks are computers. (✓)
IV. Some diaries are cameras. (✗)

Method II

Some cameras are calculators. (I-type)
Some calculators are diaries. (I-type)
All notebooks are diaries. (A-type)
All diaries are computers. (A-type)
From Statement 2 and aligning by IEA Rule,
All notebooks are diaries. (A-type)
Some diaries are calculators. (I-type)
A + I = Not a valid conclusion.
Hence, Conclusion I does not follow.
From Statements 2 and 4,
Some calculators are diaries. (I-type)
All diaries are computers. (A-type)
I + A = I-type conclusion
∴ Some calculators are computers = Conclusion II
From Statements 3 and 4,
A + A = A-type conclusion
All notebooks are computers = Conclusion III
From Statements 1 and 2,
I + I = Not a valid conclusion
∴ Conclusion IV is not valid.
Hence, Conclusions II and III follow.

40. (*a*)

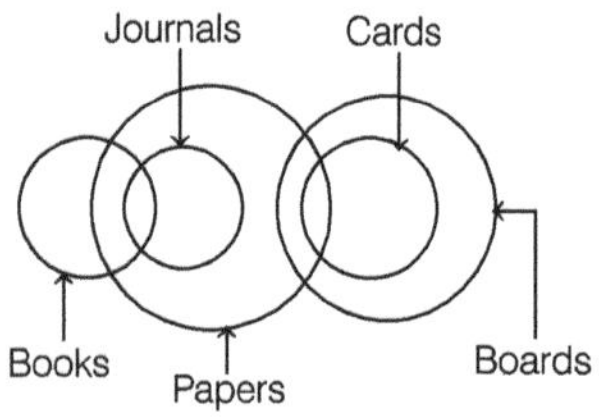

Conclusions

I. Some papers are books. (✓)
II. Some papers are boards. (✓)
III. Some boards are journals. (✗)
IV. Some boards are books. (✗)

41. (*d*)

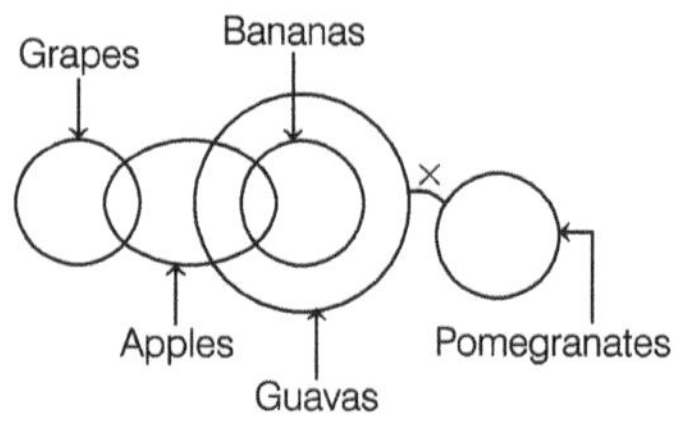

Conclusions I. No grapes are pomegranates. (✗)
II. Some guavas are grapes. (✗)
III. Some guavas are apples. (✓)
IV. No bananas are pomegranates. (✓)

42. (*e*)

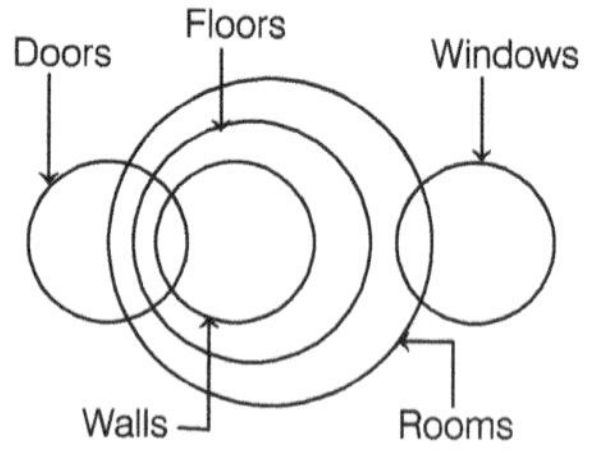

Conclusions I. All walls are rooms. (✓)
II. Some rooms are doors. (✓)
III. Some rooms are walls. (✓)
IV. Some floors are doors. (✓)

43. (*d*)

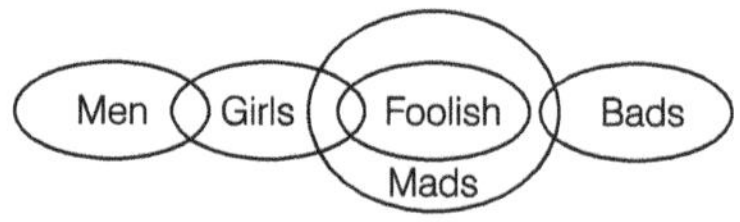

Conclusions I. Some girls are definitely mads. (✓)
II. Most of the mads are foolish. (✓)
III. Atleast some girls are men. (✓)
IV. All foolish except few are girls. (✓)

Master Exercise

1. Read the given statements and conclusions carefully. Assuming that the information given in the statements is true, even if it appears to be at variance with commonly known facts, decide which of the given conclusions logically follow(s) from the statements.

Statements All dogs are lions. « SSC CGL 2020
No elephant is a lion.

Conclusions
I. No dog is an elephant.
II. No lion is a dog.
III. Some elephants are dogs.
(a) Conclusions II and III follow
(b) Only Conclusion II follow
(c) Conclusions I and III follow
(d) Only Conclusion I follows

2. Study the following statements carefully and decide which of the conclusions logically follows disregarding the commonly known facts.

Statements All aeroplanes are trains.
Some trains are chairs. « SSC Stenographer 2016

Conclusions
I. Some aeroplanes are chairs.
II. Some chairs are aeroplanes.
III. Some chairs are trains.
IV. Some trains are aeroplanes.
(a) None follows (b) I and II follow
(c) II and III follow (d) III and IV follow

3. Given the following premises:
I. Every human beings are mortals.
II. All men are human beings.

Which of the following is the appropriate conclusion to be drawn? « CGPSC 2016
(a) All men are mortals
(b) All mortals are men
(c) All human beings are men
(d) All mortals are human beings
(e) None of the above

DIRECTIONS ~ (Q. Nos. 4-16) *In the questions below are given two statements followed by two conclusions. You have to take the given statements to be true even if they seem to be at variance from commonly known facts and decide which of the conclusion(s) logically follows from the two given statements.*

Give answer
(a) If only Conclusion I follows
(b) If only Conclusion II follows
(c) If both Conclusions I and II follow
(d) If neither Conclusion I nor II follows

4. Statements All clouds are fog.
All fog are white. « SSC CGL 2017

Conclusions
I. Some white are clouds.
II. Some fog are clouds.

5. Statements All poets are daydreamers.
All painters are daydreamers.

Conclusions « SSC CGL 2015
I. All painters are poets.
II. Some daydreamers are not painters.

6. Statements Some men are good.
Some men are wise. « SSC CGL 2015

Conclusions
I. Some wise men are good.
II. Some good men are wise.

7. Statements Some wagons are buggies.
All wagons are carts. « RRBs ALP 2019

Conclusion
I. All buggies are carts.
II. Some carts are buggies.

8. Statements Some radiologists are physicians.
All radiologists are cardiologists. « CMAT 2015

Conclusions
I. Some cardiologists are physicians.
II. All physicians are cardiologists.

9. Statements Some camels are ships.
No ship is a boat. « SSC (10+2) 2017

Conclusions
I. Some ships are camels.
II. Some camels are not boats.

10. Statements No squares are rectangles.
All rectangles are triangles. « SSC CGL 2017

Conclusions
I. Some triangles are squares.
II. Some triangles are rectangles.

11. Statements
1. All women are girls.
2. Some girls are painters.

Conclusions « SSC (GD) 2018
I. All girls are women.
II. Some women are painters.

12. Statements All apples are oranges.
Some oranges are papayas.

Conclusions « SSC (Steno) 2016

I. Some apples are papayas.
II. Some papayas are apples.

13. Statements All sticks are canes.
Some wands are sticks.

Conclusions « SSC (10+2) 2018

I. Some canes are wands.
II. No wands are canes.

14. Statements Some pencils are sticks.
All sticks are trees.

Conclusions « UPSSSC VDO 2018

I. All sticks are pencils.
II. All pencils are trees.

15. Statements All leaves are green.
Some leaves are hard.

Conclusions « SSC Delhi Police Constable 2017

I. Some hard are green.
II. All green are leaves.

16. Statements All pink are doors.
All male are doors.

Conclusions « SSC Delhi Police Constable 2017

I. Some males are pink.
II. All doors are pink.

17. Study the following statement carefully and decide which of the conclusions logically follows disregarding the commonly known facts.

Statements

I. All politicians are honest person.
II. All honest persons are fair.

Conclusions « UGC NET 2018

I. Some honest persons are politicians.
II. No honest person is politician.
III. Some fair persons are politicians.
IV. All fair persons are politicians.

(a) II and IV (b) I and III
(c) I, II and IV (d) II and III

DIRECTIONS ~ (Q. Nos. 18-20) *In each question/set of questions below are two/three statements followed by two conclusions numbered* I *and* II. *You have to take the two/three given statements to be true even if they seem to be at variance from commonly known facts and then decide which of the given conclusions logically follows from the given statements disregarding commonly known facts.*

Give answer

(a) If only Conclusion I follows
(b) If only Conclusion II follows
(c) If either Conclusion I or II follows
(d) If neither Conclusion I nor II follows
(e) If both Conclusions I and II follow

18. Statements All kings are queens.
Some queens are rulers.

Conclusions « Bihar Keshtriya (GBO) 2012

I. No ruler is a king.
II. All rulers being king is a possibility.

19. Statements Some lights are rays.
All rays are optics.

Conclusions « Bihar Keshtriya (GBO) 2012

I. Some lights are definitely not optics.
II. Some rays are definitely not lights.

20. Statements All vacancies are jobs.
Some jobs are occupations.

Conclusions « IBPS (PO) 2012

I. All vacancies are occupations.
II. All occupations being vacancies is a possibility.

DIRECTIONS ~(Q. Nos. 21 and 22) *Each question comprises two statements (numbered as* I *and* II*). You have to take the statements as true even, if they seem to be at variance with commonly known facts. Read all the conclusions and then decide which of the given conclusions/derivations logically follow from the given statements, disregarding commonly known facts.*

21. Statements

I. All contracts are agreements.
II. All agreements are accepted offers. « CLAT 2014

Which of the following derivations is correct?

(a) All accepted offers are contracts
(b) All agreements are contracts
(c) All contracts are accepted offers
(d) None of the above

22. Statements

I. Some beautiful women are actresses.
II. All actresses are good dancers. « CLAT 2014

Which of the following derivations is correct?

(a) Some beautiful women are good dancers
(b) All good dancers are actresses.
(c) Both (a) and (b) follow
(d) None of the above

DIRECTIONS ~ (Q. Nos. 23-26) *In each question below are given two statements numbered* I *and* II. *You have to take the two given statements as true even if they seem to be at variance with commonly known facts. Read all the conclusions and then decide which of the given conclusions and then decide which of the given conclusions logically follow from the given statements, disregarding commonly known facts.*

23. Statements

I. All vegetables have gravy.
II. All lunch has vegetable. « CLAT 2013

(a) All lunch has gravy (b) All gravy has lunch
(c) Both (a) and (b) follow (d) None of these

24. Statements
I. Some blue are green.
II. Pink is green. « CLAT 2013
(a) Some blue is pink
(b) Some green is pink
(c) Either 'a' or 'b' follows
(d) Some pink are blue

25. Statements
I. All boys are tall.
II. All Punjabi are tall. « CLAT 2013
(a) All boys are Punjabi (b) Some boys are Punjabi
(c) Both of these (d) None of these

26. Statements
I. Some red are yellow.
II. No yellow is green. « CG PSC 2013

Conclusions
I. Some yellow are red.
II. Some green are red.
III. Some red are not green.
IV. All green are red.
(a) II and III follow (b) I and II follow
(c) Either III or IV follows (d) Only I follows

DIRECTIONS ~ (Q. Nos 27-66) *Two/three statements are given below followed by two conclusions I and II. You have to consider the two/three statements to be true even if they seem to be at variance with commonly known facts. You have to decide which of the conclusions, if any follow from the given statements.*

Give answer
(a) Only I follows
(b) Only II follows
(c) Both I and II follow
(d) Neither I nor II follow
(e) Either I or II follows

27. Statements All rats are cats.
No cow is cat.
All dogs are cows. « NIACL 2014

Conclusions
I. No dog is rat.
II. No dog is cat.

28. Statements All trains are buses.
All buses are jeeps.
All jeeps are aeroplanes. « SBI (Clerk) 2016

Conclusions
I. Some buses are not aeroplanes.
II. All jeeps are trains.

29. Statements Some parties are celebrations.
All celebrations are occasions.
No occasion is a festival.

Conclusions « SBI (Clerk) 2016
I. No celebration is a festival.
II. Some occasions are parties.

30. Statements All shores are beaches.
Some beaches are coasts.
All banks are coasts.

Conclusions « SBI (Clerk) 2016
I. Some banks are beaches.
II. No banks is a shore.

31. Statements All locks are keys.
All keys are doors.
Some doors are windows.
Some windows are floors.

Conclusions « NIACL 2014
I. Some keys are windows.
II. No floor is door.

32. Statements No banks is a locker.
All banks are stores.
No store is a panel.

Conclusions « IBPS PO/MT 2015
I. No store is a locker.
II. No panel is a bank.

33. Statements Some strikes are hits.
No strike is a raid.
All attacks are raids.

Conclusions « IBPS PO/MT 2015
I. Some hits are definitely not raids.
II. All hits being strikes is a possibility.

34. Statements Some equations are formulae.
All equations are terms.
All terms are symbols.

Conclusions « IBPS PO/MT 2015
I. All equations are symbols.
II. No symbol is a formula.

35. Statements Some strikes are hits.
No strike is a raid.
All attacks are raids.

Conclusions « IBPS PO/MT 2015
I. No attacks is a strike.
II. All attacks being hits is a possibility.

36. Statements Some stands are racks.
No rack is a box.
All boxes are cartons.

Conclusions « LIC (AAO) 2016
I. All stands can never be boxes.
II. All racks being cartons is a possibility.

37. Statements All kittens are turtles.
Some turtles are puppies.

Conclusions « LIC (AAO) 2016
I. At least some puppies are kittens.
II. No puppy is a kitten.

38. Statements All papers are mills.
All mills are factories.

Conclusions « LIC (AAO) 2016

I. All mills are papers.
II. All papers are factories.

39. Statements No perfume is a fragrance.
Some perfumes are deodorants.
All deodorants are cologne.

Conclusions « LIC (AAO) 2016

I. At least some perfumes are colognes.
II. No fragrance is a deodorant.

40. Statements No perfume is a fragrance.
Some perfumes are deodorants.
All deodorants are cologne.

Conclusions « LIC (AAO) 2016

I. At least some deodorants are not fragrances.
II. All fragrance being colognes is a possibility.

41. Statements Some roads are houses.
Some houses are bungalows.
No bungalow is an apartment.

Conclusions « NABARD Grade A & B 2016

I. All roads being apartments is a possibility.
II. No apartment is a house.

42. Statements All guests are hosts.
Some guests are relatives.
All relatives are friends.

Conclusions « NABARD Grade A & B 2016

I. All guests are friends.
II. No host being friends is a possibility.

43. Statements Some shops are outlets.
Some outlets are factories.
All factories are industries.

Conclusions « NABARD Grade A & B 2016

I. At least some shops are factories.
II. At least some outlets are industries.

44. Statements Some roads are houses.
Some houses are bungalows.
No bungalow is an apartment.

Conclusions « NABARD Grade A & B 2016

I. Some houses are definitely not apartments.
II. At least some roads are bungalows.

45. Statements All certainties are beliefs.
Some beliefs are fears.

Conclusions « NABARD Grade A & B 2016

I. At least some fears are certainties.
II. No fear is a certainty.

46. Statements Some ratios are percent.
All percent are fractions.
No fractions is a section.

Conclusions « IBPS RRB Officer Grade B 2017

I. No section is a percent.
II. All ratios beings fractions is a possibility.

47. Statements All metals are plastics.
All plastics are ores.
Some ores are wood.

Conclusions « IBPS RRB Officer Grade B 2017

I. All wood being metals is a possibility.
II. No ore is a metal.

48. Statements Some ratios are percent.
All percent are fractions.
No fraction is a section.
« IBPS RRB Officer Grade B 2017

Conclusions

I. All sections being ratios is a possibility.
II. At least some fractions are ratios.

49. Statements All metals are plastics.
All plastics are ores.
Some ores are wood.

Conclusions « IBPS RRB Officer Grade B 2017

I. At least some metals are wood.
II. All plastics being wood is a possibility.

50. Statements Some sketches are paintings.
All paintings are drawings.
Some drawings are letters.

Conclusions « RBI Assistant 2017

I. All sketches can never be drawings.
II. No painting is a letter.

51. Statements All cubes are spheres.
Some spheres are triangles.

Conclusions « RBI Assistant 2017

I. No cube is a triangle. II. All spheres are cubes.

52. Statements Some juices are drinks.
All drinks are snacks.
No snack is cookie.

Conclusions « RBI Assistant 2017

I. All juices can never be cookies.
II. At least some juices are snacks.

53. Statements Some juices are drinks.
All drinks are snacks.
No snack is cookie.

Conclusions « RBI Assistant 2017

I. No drink is a cookie.
II. At least some juices are cookies.

54. Statements All packets are envelopes.
No envelope is a gift.
Some gifts are boxes.

Conclusions « IBPS PO/MT 2017

I. All envelopes are packets.
II. All boxes can never be envelopes.

55. Statements All diaries are novels.
All novels are biographies.
Some biographies are scripts.

Conclusions « IBPS PO/MT 2017

I. At least some diaries are scripts.
II. No diary is a script.

56. Statements Some days are months.
Some months are weeks.

Conclusions « IBPS PO/MT 2017

I. Some weeks are days.
II. No week is a day.

57. Statements All packets are envelopes.
No envelop is a gift.
Some gifts are boxes. « IBPS PO/MT 2017

Conclusions

I. All packets being boxes is possibility.
II. No packet is a gift.

58. Statements All diaries are novels.
All novels are biographies.
Some biographies are scripts.

Conclusions « IBPS PO/MT 2017

I. All diaries are biographies.
II. Some scripts are definitely not novels.

59. Statements All circles are triangles.
Some triangles are rectangles.
All rectangles are squares.

Conclusions « IBPS PO/MT 2016

I. All rectangles being triangles is a possibility.
II. All circles being square is a possibility.

60. Statements Some chairs are tables.
Some bed are tables.
No furniture is bed.

Conclusions « IBPS PO/MT 2016

I. All chairs being furniture is a possibility.
II. Some tables are not bed is a possibility.

61. Statements All circles are triangles.
Some triangles are rectangles.
All rectangles are squares.

Conclusions « IBPS PO/MT 2016

I. Some triangles are not rectangles.
II. No square is a circle.

62. Statements All arts are theatre.
Some arts are drama.

Conclusions « IBPS PO/MT 2016

I. All drama being theatre is a possibility.
II. Some dramas are theatre.

63. Statements Some chairs are table.
Some bed are tables.
No furniture are bed.

Conclusions « IBPS PO/MT 2016

I. Some tables are not furniture.
II. All tables being furniture is a possibility.

64. Statements Some dares are dream.
All dreams are real.
No real is fake.

Conclusions « IBPS Clerk 2017

I. Some dreams are fake.
II. All dreams are not fake.

65. Statements No rain is game.
Some games are chain.
No chain is lane.

Conclusions « IBPS Clerk 2017

I. Some chains are not rain.
II. Some games are lane.

66. Statements Some movies are tickets.
No ticket is popcorn.
Some popcorn is burger.

Conclusions « IBPS Clerk 2017

I. Some movies are burger.
II. Some burgers are not movies.

DIRECTIONS ~(Q. Nos 67-71) *In the questions below are given few statements followed by few conclusions. You have to take the given statements to be true even if they seem to be at variance with the commonly known facts and then decide which of the given conclusions logically follows from the given statements, disregarding commonly known facts.*

67. Statements All Indians are Americans.
All Americans are Pakistanis.
No Britisher is Americans.

Conclusions « MP Police Sub-Inspector 2017

I. All Indians are Pakistani.
II. Some Pakistani are Britisher.
III. No Indian is Britisher.

(a) Only I and III follow
(b) All follow
(c) Only III follows
(d) Only II follows

68. Statements All aids are devices.
No device is a tool.
All tools are machines.
Some machines are electronics.

Conclusions « MHT MBA 2017

(a) Some aids are definitely not electronics
(b) No tool is an electronic
(c) All aids are machines
(d) All electronics can never be devices
(e) All electronics being aids is a possibility

69. Statements Some evidences are files.
No file is document.
All documents are papers.
Some documents are copies.

Conclusions « MHT MBA 2017

(a) All papers being files is a possibility
(b) Some evidences are documents
(c) Some files being copies is a possibility
(d) No evidence is a paper
(e) All copies are papers

70. Statements Some villages are towns.
Some towns are huts.
All huts are rivers.
Some rivers are tents.

Conclusions « IDBI Executive 2018

I. Some tents are towns.
II. Some rivers are towns.
III. Some huts are villages.

(a) Only I follows (b) Only II follows
(c) Only III follows (d) I and II follow
(e) None of these

71. Statements All hotels are buses.
Some buses are cars.
All cars are trams.
Some trams are clouds.

Conclusions « IDBI Executive 2018

I. Some trams are buses.
II. Some trams are hotels.
III. Some clouds are cars.

(a) Only I follows (b) Only II follows
(c) Only III follows (d) I and II follow
(e) None of the above

DIRECTIONS ~ (Q. Nos. 72-76) *Some statements are given followed by some conclusions. You have to consider the statements to be true even if they seem to be at variance from commonly known facts. You have to decide which of the following conclusions follow from the given statements.* « IBPS Clerk Mains 2019

72. Statements Some dolls are barbie.
Some barbie are famous.
All famous are player.
No famous is actor.
Some actors are barbie.

Conclusions

(i) Some barbie are not actors.
(ii) Some barbie are players.
(iii) Some players are famous.

(a) Only (i) follow
(b) Only (ii) and (iii) follow
(c) Only (i) and (ii) follow
(d) All follow
(e) None of these

73. Statements All cats are dogs.
Some dogs are not cows.
No cow is a rat.
Some rats are dogs.
No rat is horse.

Conclusions

I. All cats are horses.
II. Some dogs being cows is a possibility.
III. All cats being cows is a possibility.

(a) Only I follow
(b) Only II and III follow
(c) Only I and II follow
(d) All follow
(e) None of the above

74. Statements All bags are books.
Some books are pencils.
No pencils are boxes.

Conclusions

I. Some books are not boxes.
II. Some books being boxes is a possibility.
III. Some bags are not boxes.

(a) Only I follow
(b) Only II and III follow
(c) Only I and II follow
(d) All follow
(e) None of the above

75. Statements All good are bad.
All bad are best.
All best are worst.
Some worst is fair.
No best is normal.
Some normal are worst.

Conclusions

I. All fair being normal is a possibility.
II. Some best are fair.
III. Some normal being good is a possibility.

(a) Only I follow
(b) Only II and III follow
(c) Only I and III follow
(d) All follow
(e) None of the above

76. Statements All eyes are legs.
No eyes are nose.
All noses are hands.
Some hands are legs.
No legs are ears.

Conclusions

I. Some hands are ears.
II. Some hands are not nose.
III. Some hands are not ears.

(a) Only I follow
(b) Either I or II and III follow
(c) Either I or III and II follow
(d) All follow
(e) None of the above

DIRECTIONS ~ (Q. Nos. 77 and 78) *Each question given below consists of five or six statements followed by options consisting of three statements put together in a specific order. Choose the option which indicates a valid argument containing logically related statements that is, where the third statement is a conclusion drawn from the preceding two statements.* « CMAT 2014

77. A : All synopses are poets.
B : Some synopses are mentors.
C : Some X are not mentors.
D : All X are poets.
E : All synopses are mentors.
F : All synopses are X.
(a) ACB (b) AEC
(c) FEC (d) DFA

78. A : All heroines are pretty.
B : Some heroines are popular.
C : Sweta is pretty.
D : Sweta is a popular heroine.
E : Some popular heroines are pretty.
(a) ABE (b) ACD
(c) DCA (d) EDC

DIRECTIONS ~ (Q. Nos. 79 and 80) *Each of the following questions has four statements. Three are logically correct. Some of which may look factually absurd. Ignore this absurdity and look to the logical corrections. Choose the statement which is wrong or doubtful.* « AFCAT 2014

79. (a) Birds fly in the air. Trees are birds. Therefore trees fly in the air.
(b) Some boys steal. All who steal are naughty. All naughty are honest. Therefore, some boys are honest.
(c) All girls like dance. Some girls are Indians. All Indians are artists. Therefore, some artists like dance.
(d) All liars are not thieves. All thieves are criminals. Therefore, all liars are criminals.

80. (a) All books can read. Some pencils are books. All pencils are clever. Therefore, some clevers can read.
(b) Some who fail are stupid. Some criminals are stupid. Therefore, all criminals fill.
(c) Some liars are thieves. All thieves are criminals. Therefore, some liars are criminals.
(d) All that is green is black. Trees are green. Therefore, trees are black.

DIRECTIONS ~ (Q. Nos. 81 and 82) *In each group of questions below are two conclusions followed by five set of statements. You have to choose the correct set of statements that logically satisfies given conclusions. Given statements to be true even if they seem to be at variance from commonly known facts.*

81. Conclusion Some enjoy is not comedy. Some fun are circus.
(a) **Statement** Some joke is enjoy. No enjoy is fun. Some fun is circus. Some joke are comedy.
(b) **Statement** Some joke is enjoy. Some enjoy are circus. All circus are fun. All comedy are not fun.
(c) **Statement** All comedy is circus. some joke are circus. all joke is fun. No enjoy is fun.
(d) **Statement** No circus is joke. Some joke are fun. Some fun is circus. Some enjoy are comedy.
(e) **Statement** All fun is circus. No circus is comedy. Some joke are comedy. some joke is enjoy.

82. Conclusion Some students are teachers. Some principal are not students.
(a) **Statement** No school is study. Some teachers is students. Some teachers is study. Some school are principal.
(b) **Statement** No study is school. All Teachers is students. Some teachers is study. Some school are principal.
(c) **Statement** All students is teachers. Some teachers is school. Some study are principal. Some school is study.
(d) **Statement** Some teachers is students. No teachers is school. Some school is study. Some school are principal.
(e) **Statement** All students is teachers. Some teachers is study. No students is school. Some school are principal.

DIRECTIONS ~ (Q. Nos. 83 and 84) *In each group of questions below are two conclusions followed by five set of statements. You have to choose the correct set of statements that logically satisfies given conclusions. Given statements to be true even if they seem to be at variance from commonly known facts.*

83. Conclusions
Some reds being black is a possibility.
Some blue being red is a possibility.

Statements
I. All black are pink. Some red are pink. No blue is red.
II. All black are pink. No red is pink. All blue are black.
III. Some black are pink. Some red are pink. No blue is red.
IV. Some black are pink. Some red are pink. No pink is blue.
V. Some black are pink. Some red are pink. All blues are black.
(a) Only Statement I
(b) Both Statements IV and V
(c) Only Statement IV
(d) Both Statements II and III
(e) Only Statement V

84. Conclusions
At least some caps being pens is a possibility.
Some copies are caps.
Statements
I. All caps are copies. All caps are papers. No cap is a pen.
II. All caps are copies. Some caps are papers. No paper is a pen.
III. Some caps are copies. Some caps are papers. No cap is a pen.
IV. Some caps are copies. All copies are papers. No cap is a pen.
V. All caps are copies. Some caps are papers. No paper is a pen.
(a) Only Statement I
(b) Only Statement V
(c) Only Statement III
(d) Both Statements III and V
(e) Both Statements II and IV

DIRECTIONS ~ (Q. Nos. 85-87) *In each of the questions below. Some statements are given followed by conclusions/group of conclusions. You have to assume all the statements to be true even if they seem to be at variance from the commonly known facts and then decide which of the given conclusions logically does not follows from the information given in the statements.*

85. Statements All plastic is rubber.
Some plastic is teflon.
Some teflon is cotton.
All cotton is woolen.

Conclusions

(a) All rubber is plastic.
(b) No plastic is woolen is a possibility.
(c) All teflon can be woolen.
(d) Some teflon is rubber.
(e) Some woolen is teflon.

86. Statements Some air is ball.
No ball is cat.
Some cat is dog.
All dog is egg.

Conclusions

(a) Some dogs are not ball
(b) All egg can be ball
(c) All air is egg is a possibility
(d) Some egg are not ball
(e) Some air is dog is a possibility.

87. Statements All watch is clock.
All clock is table.
No watch is pen.
No clock is chair.

Conclusions

(a) Some table can be chair.
(b) Some table are watch.
(c) No watch is chair.
(d) Some table is not pen.
(e) No pen is chair.

DIRECTIONS ~ (Q. Nos. 88-90) *In each question below are given some statements followed by some conclusions numbered* I, II, III *and* IV. *You have to take the given statements to be true even if they seem to be at variance with commonly known facts. Read all the conclusions and then decide which of the given conclusions definitely does not logically follow from the given statements, disregarding commonly known facts.*

88. Statements All puma are reebok.
All adidas are reebok.
Some adidas are woodland.

Conclusions

I. No puma is adidas.
II. Some reebok being woodland is a possibility.
III. Some reebok are puma.
IV. Some reebok are adidas.

(a) Only II does not follow
(b) Only I and III do not follow
(c) All follow except III
(d) Only I and II do not follow
(e) All follow except I

89. Statements Some pepsi are cocacola.
No cocacola is a mirinda.
All mirinda are dew.

Conclusions

I. Some cocacola not being mirinda is a possibility.
II. Some dew are not cocacola.
III. All pepsi are mirinda.
IV. Some pepsi can be dew.

(a) Only I and II do not follow
(b) Only III and IV do not follow
(c) Only III does not follow
(d) All follow except IV
(e) None of these

90. Statements Some tibbet are china.
All china are nepal.
No nepal is bhutan.

Conclusions

I. Some bhutans are not tibbet.
II. All tibbet being nepal is a possibility.
III. At least some bhutans are nepal.
IV. All china can be nepal.

(a) II and IV do not follow
(b) I and IV do not follow
(c) I and III does not follow
(d) II and III do not follow
(e) None of these

DIRECTIONS ~ (Q. Nos. 91-93) *In the following questions, the symbols #, @ $ and © are used with following meanings as illustrated below. Study the following information and answer the given questions. In each of the questions given below statements are followed by some conclusions. You have to take the given statements to be even if they seem to be at variance from commonly known facts. Read all the conclusions and then decide which of the given conclusions logically does not follows from the given statements disregarding commonly known facts.*

P#Q–All P is Q.

P@Q–Some Q is P.

P©Q–No P is Q.

P$Q–Some P is not Q.

91. Statements Rubber © Pencil # Eraser @ Scale # Copy $ Book

Conclusions

(a) Eraser $ Rubber
(b) Eraser @ Pencil
(c) Eraser @ Copy
(d) Scale @ Eraser
(e) Rubber $ Book

92. Statements Air @ Car # Drive $ Exit © Ride @ Air

Conclusions

(a) Drive @ Air (b) Air $ Exit
(c) Car @ Ride (d) Car @ Drive
(e) Exit $ Ride

93. Statements Rat @ Cat # Dog © Fish @ Goat $ Hen

Conclusions

(a) Cat © Fish (b) Goat @ Fish
(c) Rat @ Dog (d) Rat $ Fish
(e) Fish $ Hen

DIRECTIONS ~ (Q. Nos. 94-96) *In the following questions, the symbols *, +, – and / are used with the following meanings as illustrated below. Study the following information and answer the given questions. In each of the questions given below statements are followed by some conclusions. You have to take the given statements to be true even if they seem to be at variance from commonly known facts. Read all the conclusions and then decide which of the given conclusions logically does not follows from the given statements disregarding commonly known facts.*

A*B–All A is B.
A+B–Some B is A.
A/B–No B is A.
A–B–Some A is not B.
?–Possibility case

Note : *If ? is placed after any of the symbols mentioned above then it will be considered as possibility case of the symbol. E.g. A+?B means some B being A is a possibility.*

94. Statements road/traffic/light*crossing

Conclusions

(a) road+?light (b) road+?crossing
(c) traffic*?crossing (d) crossing–light
(e) crossing–traffic

95. Statements pen+eraser*paper;pen*pencil

Conclusions

(a) pencil*?paper (b) paper+pencil
(c) paper+?pencil (d) pencil+eraser
(e) paper+pen

96. Statements mall+plaza*market-complex

Conclusions

(a) mall–complex (b) complex+?market
(c) market+plaza (d) mall+market
(e) plaza–?complex

Answers / WITH EXPLANATIONS

1. (*d*) According to the statements,

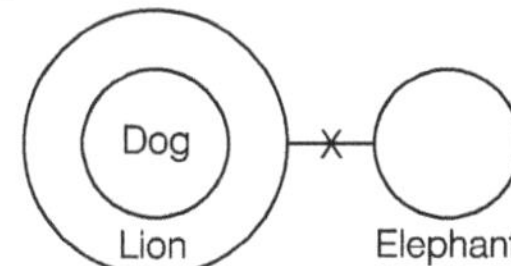

Conclusion

I. No dog is an elephant. (✓)
II. No lion is a dog. (✗)
III. Some elephants are dogs. (✗)

2. (*d*) According to the statements,

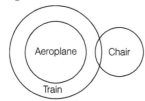

So, only Conclusions III and IV follow.

3. (*a*) According to the statements,

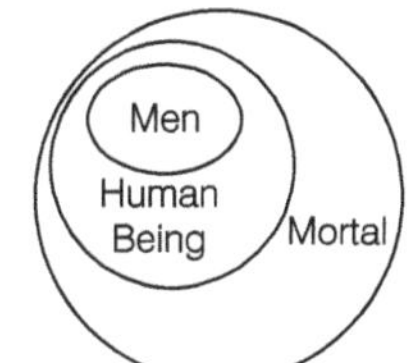

It can be concluded that all men are mortals.

4. (*c*) According to the statements,

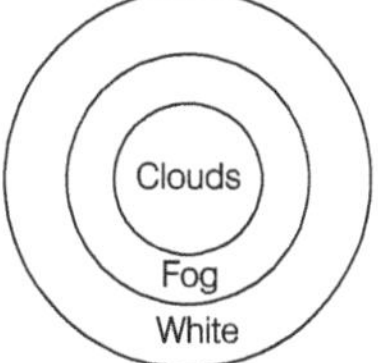

Conclusions

I. Some white are clouds. (✓)
II. Some fog are clouds. (✓)

5. (*d*) According to the statements,

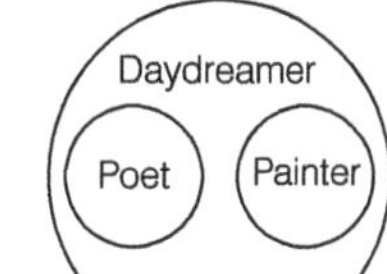

Conclusions

I. All painters are poets. (✗)
II. Some day dreamers are not painters. (✗)

6. (*d*) According to the statements,

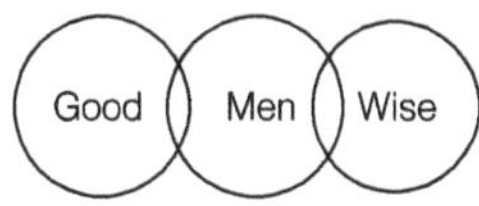

Conclusions

I. Some wise men are good. (✗)
II. Some good men are wise. (✗)

7. (*b*) According to the statements,

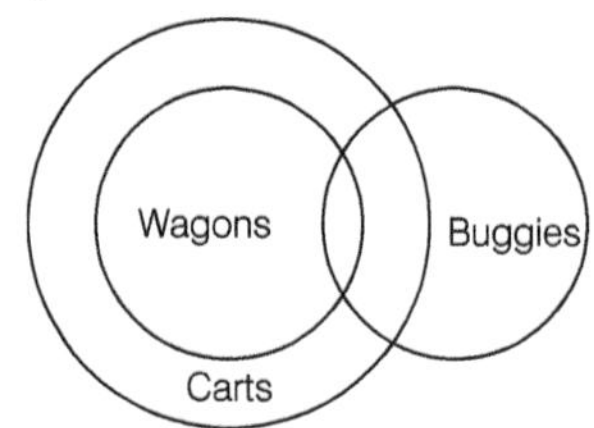

Conclusions
I. All buggies are carts. (✗)
II. Some carts are buggies. (✓)

8. (*a*) According to the statements,

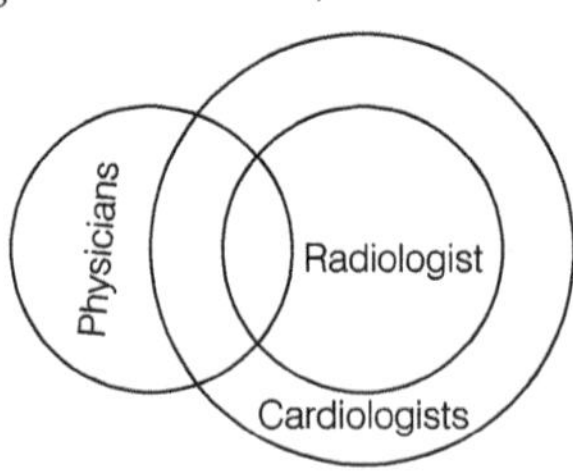

Conclusions
I. Some cardiologists are physicians. (✓)
II. All physicians are cardiologists. (✗)

9. (*c*) According to the statements,

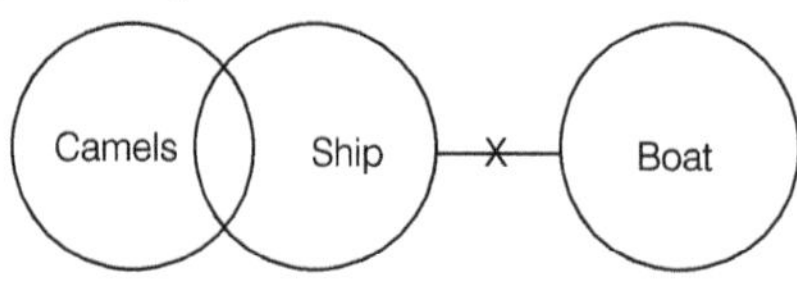

Conclusions
I. Some ships are camels. (✓)
II. Some camels are not boat. (✓)

10. (*b*) According to the statements,

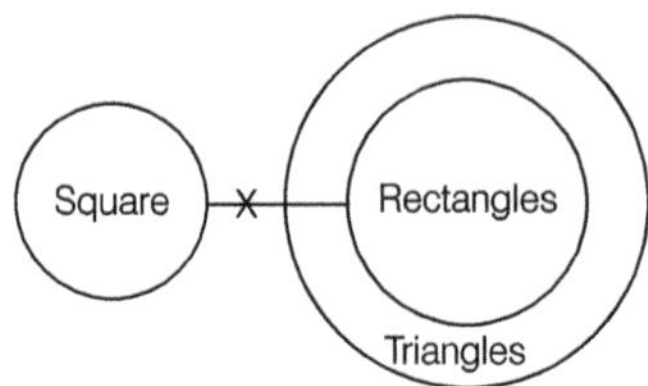

Conclusions
I. Some triangles are squares. (✗)
II. Some triangles are rectangles. (✓)

11. (*d*) According to the statements,

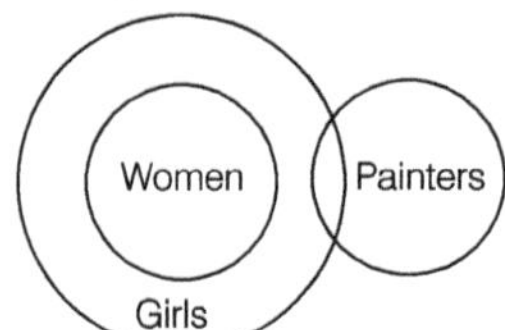

Conclusions
I. All girls are women. (✗)
II. Some women are painters. (✗)

12. (*d*) According to the question,

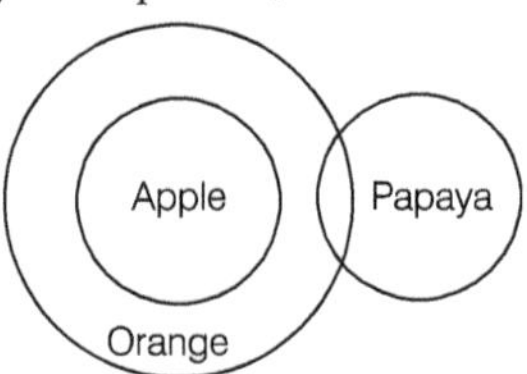

Conclusions I. Some apples are papayas. (✗)
II. Some papayas are apples. (✗)

13. (*a*) According to the question,

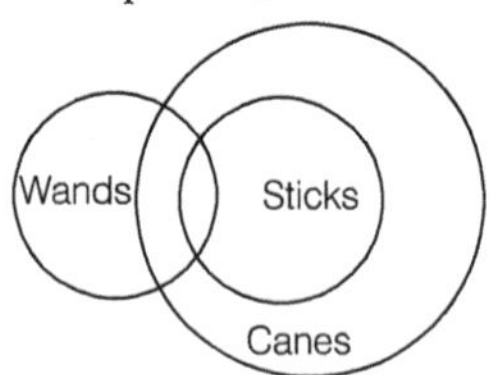

Conclusions I. Some canes are wands. (✓)
II. No wands are canes. (✗)

14. (*d*) According to the statements,

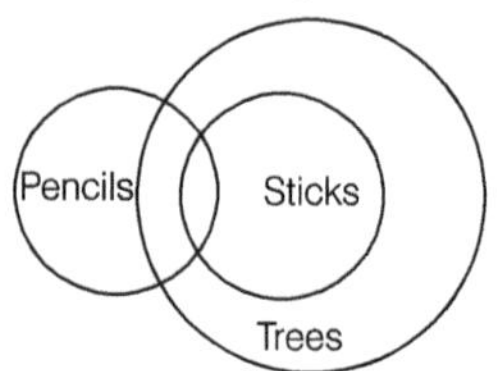

Conclusions
I. All sticks are pencils. (✗)
II. All pencils are trees. (✗)

15. (*a*) According to the statements,

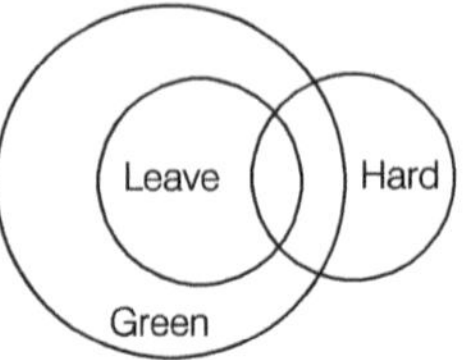

Conclusions
I. Some hard are green. (✓)
II. All green are leaves. (✗)

16. (*d*) According to the statements,

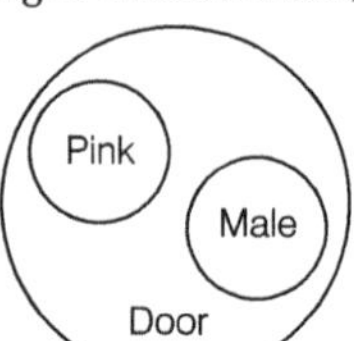

Conclusions I. Some males are pink. (✗)
II. All doors are pink. (✗)

17. (*b*) According to the statements,

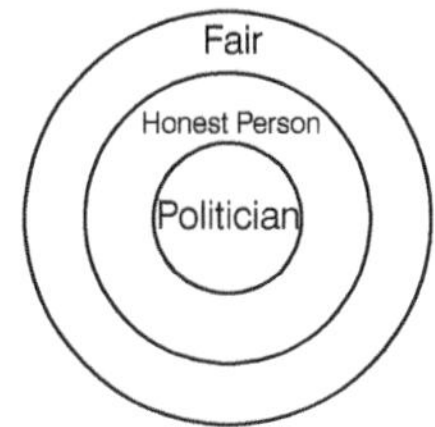

Conclusions

I. Some honest persons are politician. (✓)
II. No honest person is politician. (✗)
III. Some fair persons are politicians. (✓)
IV.4 All fair persons are politicians. (✗)

18. (*b*) According to the statements,

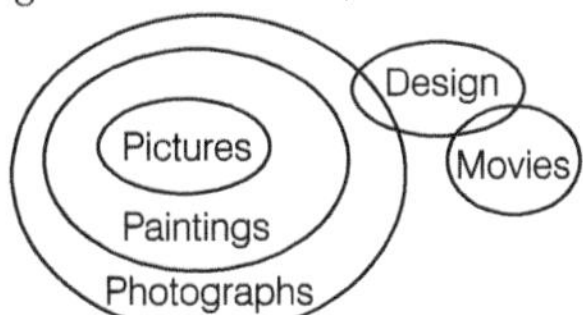

Conclusions

I. No ruler is a king. (✗)
II. All rulers being king is a possibility. (✓)

19. (*d*) According to the statements,

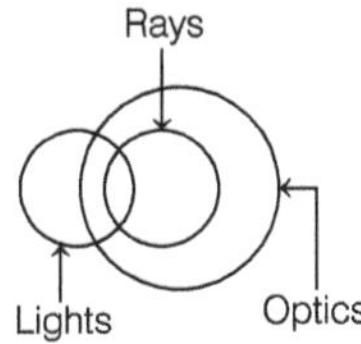

Conclusions

I. Some lights are definitely not optics. (✗)
II. Some rays are definitely not lights. (✗)

20. (*b*) According to the statements,

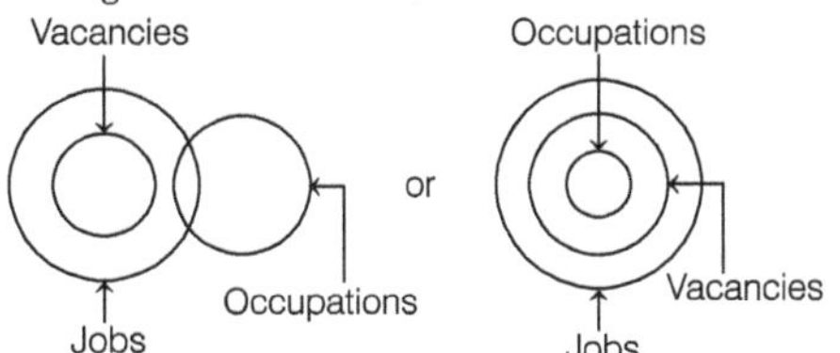

Conclusions

I. All vacancies are occupations. (✗)
II. All occupations being vacancies is a possibility. (✓)

21. (*c*) According to the statements,

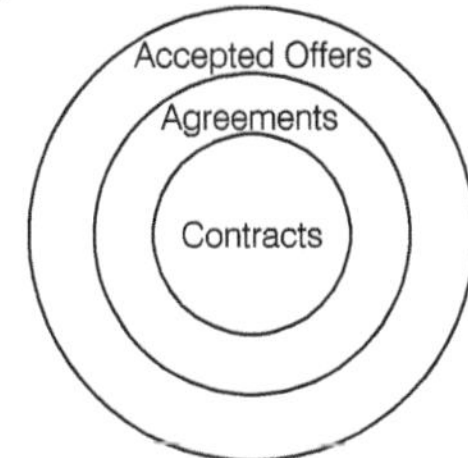

So, all contracts are accepted offers is the correct.

22. (*a*) According to the statements,

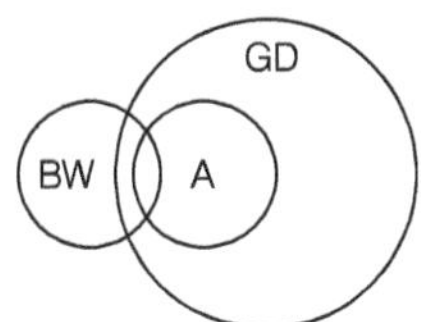

BW : Beautiful Women
A : Actresses
GD : Good Dancers

Some beautiful women are good dancers but there are some good dancers who are not actresses.

23. (*a*) According to the statements,

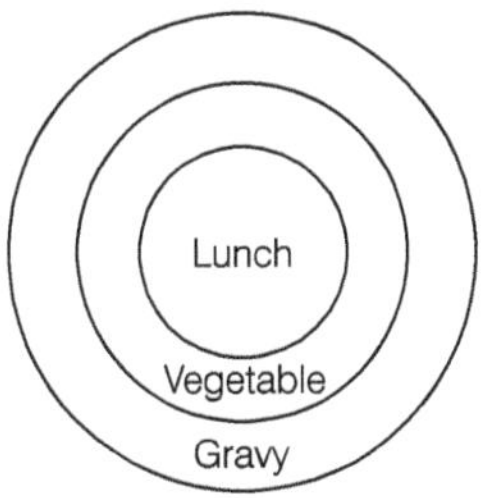

Conclusions

I. All lunch has gravy. (✓)
II. All lunch has vegetable. (✗)

24. (*b*) According to the statements,

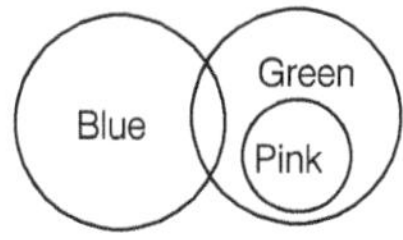

Conclusions

I. Some blue is pink. (✗)
II. Some green is pink. (✓)
III. Some pink are blue. (✗)

25. (*d*) According to the statements,

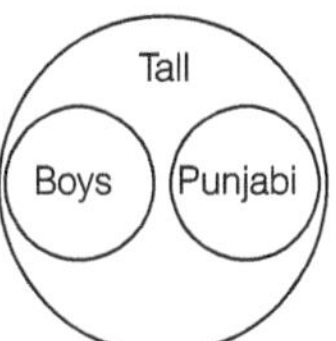

Conclusions

I. All boys are Punjabi. (✗)
II. Some boys are Punjabi. (✗)

26. (*d*) According to the statements,

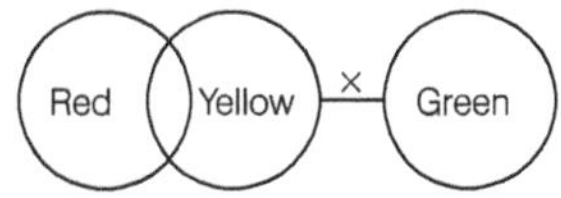

Conclusions

I. Some yellow are red. (✓)
II. Some green are red. (✗)
III. Some red are not green. (✗)
IV. All green are red. (✗)

27. (*c*) According to the statements,

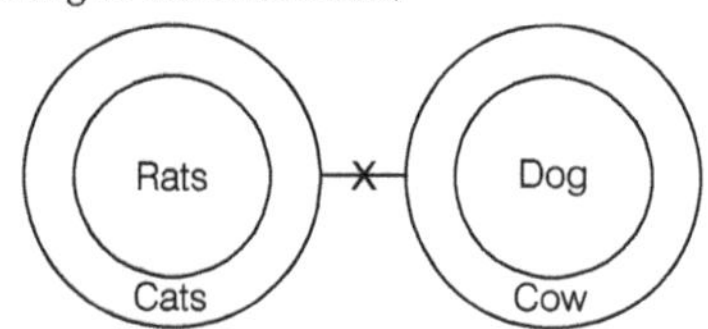

Conclusions I. No dog is rat. (✓)
II. No dog is cat. (✓)

28. (*d*) According to the statements,

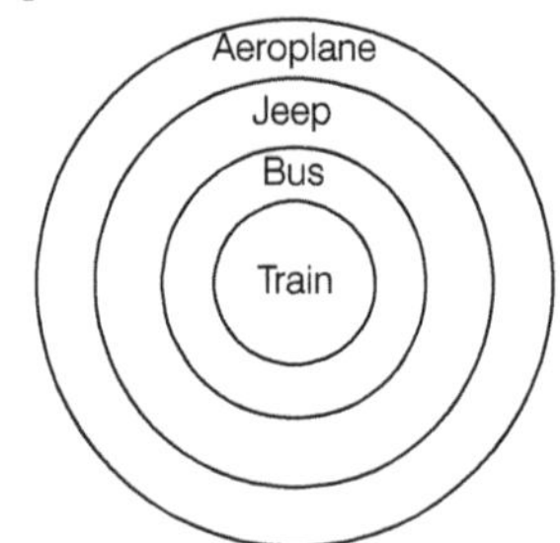

Conclusions
I. Some buses are not aeroplanes. (✗)
II. All jeeps are trains. (✗)

29. (*c*) According to the statements,

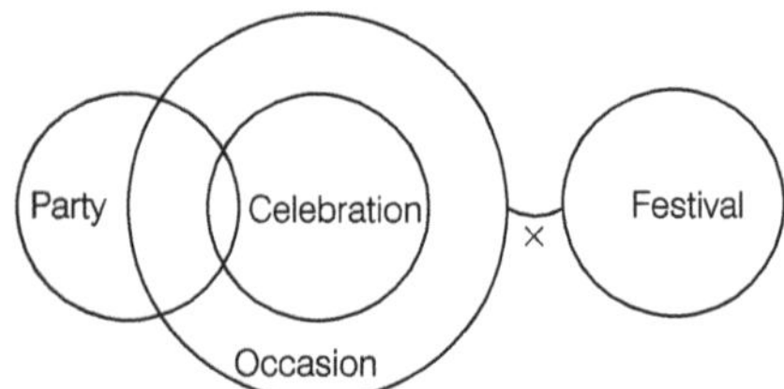

Conclusions
I. No celebration is a festival. (✓)
II. Some occasions are parties. (✓)

30. (*d*) According to the statements,

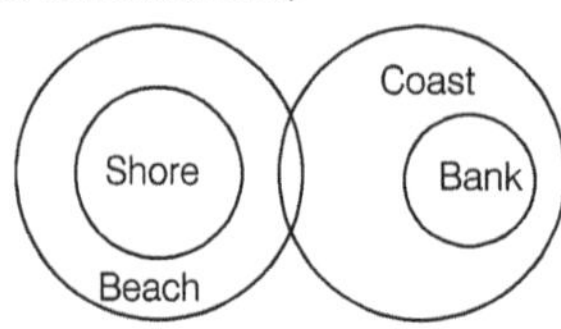

Conclusions
I. Some banks are beaches. (✗)
II. No banks is a shore. (✗)

31. (*d*) According to the statements,

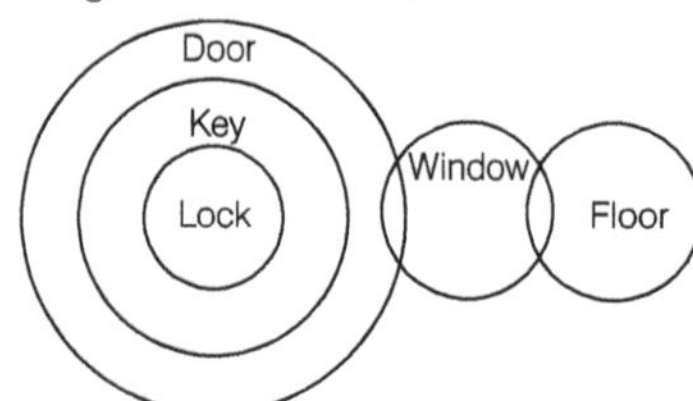

Conclusions
I. Some keys are windows. (✗)
II. No floor is door. (✗)

32. (*b*) According to the statements,

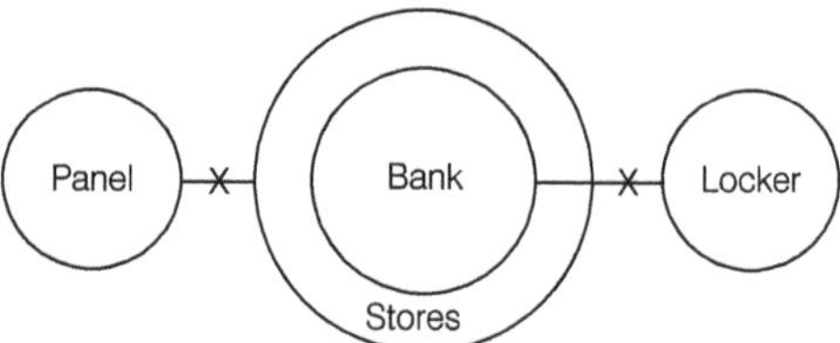

Conclusions
I. No store is a locker. (✗)
II. No panel is a bank. (✓)

33. (*c*) According to the statements,

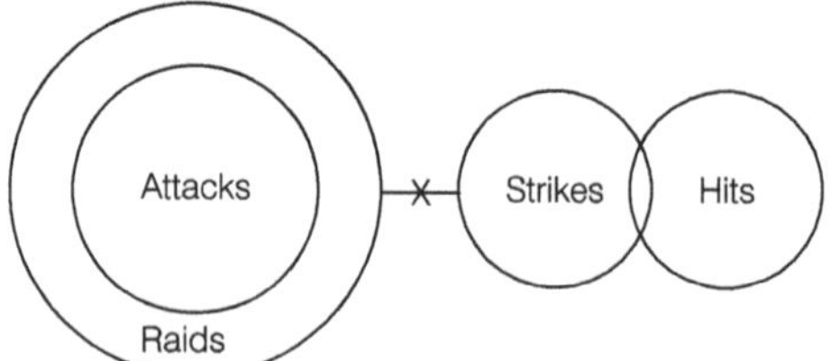

Conclusions
I. Some hits are definitely not raids. (✓)
II. All hits being strikes is a possibility. (✓)

34. (*a*) According to the statements,

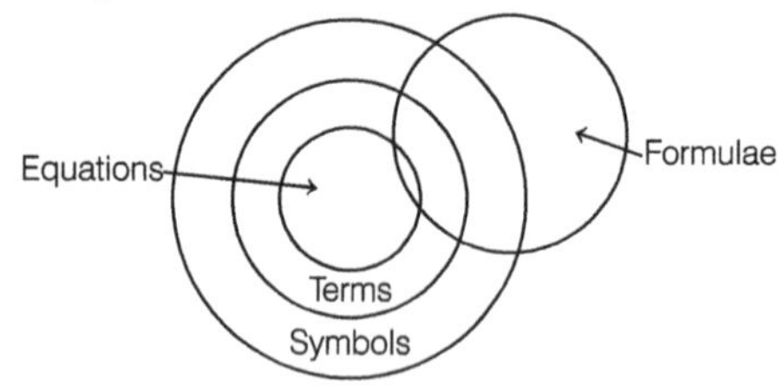

Conclusions
I. All equations are symbols. (✓)
II. No symbol is a formula. (✗)

35. (*c*) According to the statements,

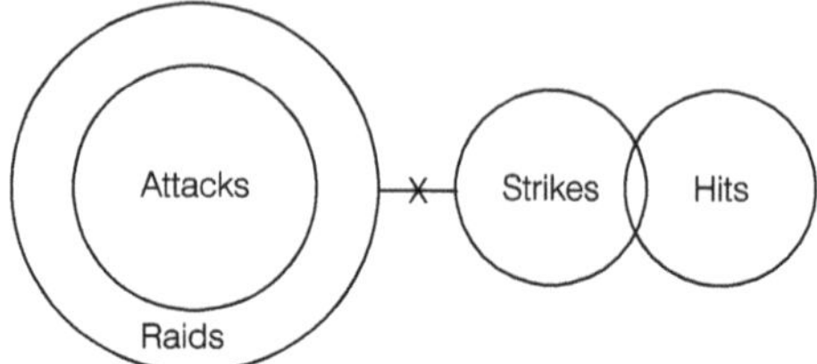

Conclusions
I. No attacks is a strike. (✓)
II. All attacks being hits is a possibility. (✓)

36. (*c*) According to the statements,

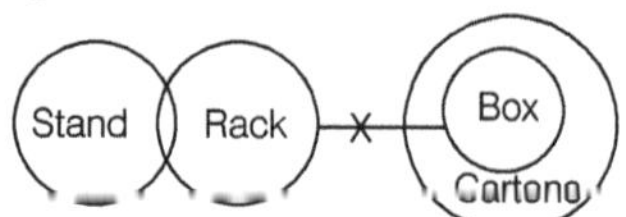

Conclusions

I. All stands can never be boxes. (✓)

II. All racks being cartons is a possibility. (✓)

37. (*e*) According to the statements,

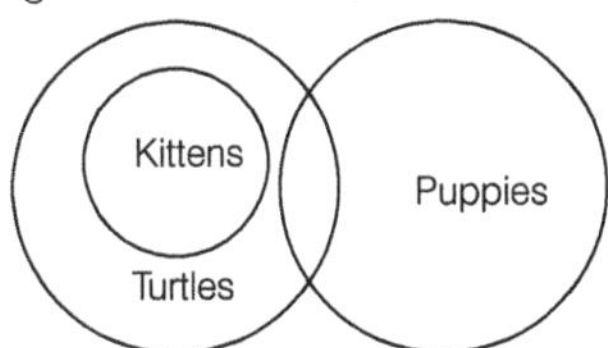

Conclusions

I. At least some puppies are kittens. (✗) (Complementry pair)

II. No puppy is a kitten. (✗) (Complementry pair)

38. (*b*) According to the statements,

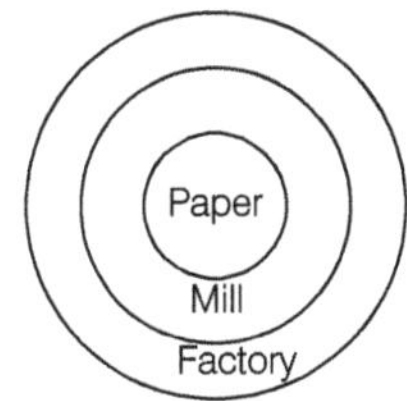

Conclusions

I. All mills are papers. (✗)

II. All papers are factories. (✓)

39. (*a*) According to the statements,

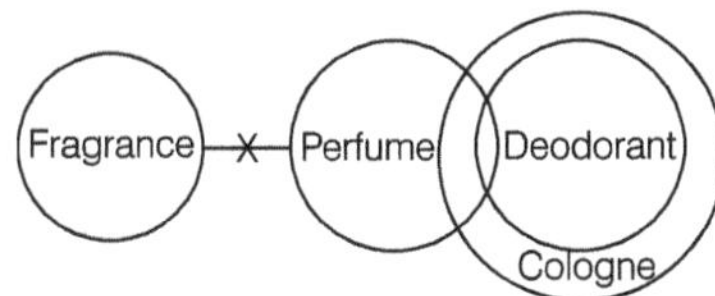

Conclusions

I. At least some perfumes are colognes. (✓)

II. No fragrance is a deodorant. (✗)

40. (*c*) According to the statements,

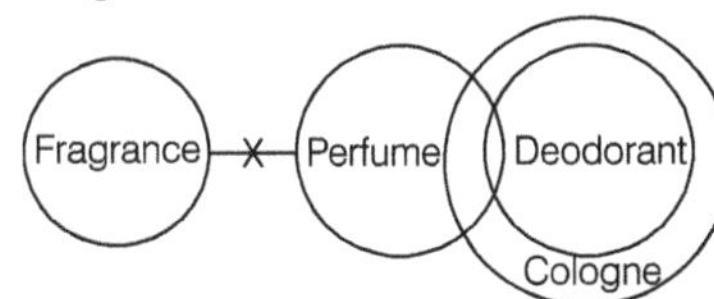

Conclusions

I. At least some deodorants are not fragrances. (✓)

II. All fragrance being colognes is a possibility. (✓)

41. (*a*) According to the statements,

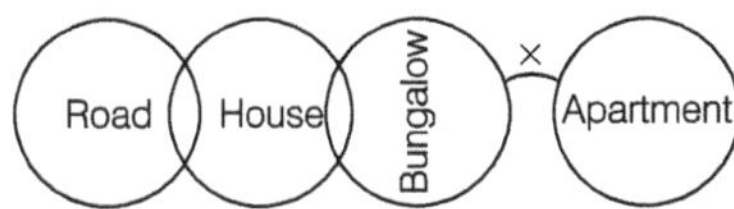

Conclusions

I. All roads being apartments is a possibility. (✓)

II. No apartment is a house. (✗)

42. (*d*) According to the statements,

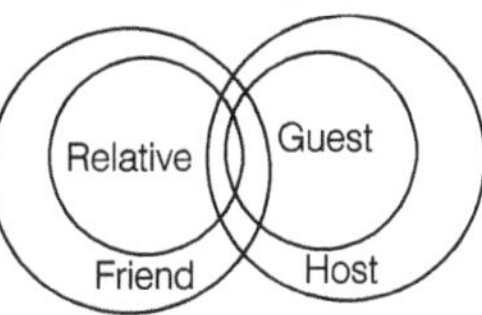

Conclusions

I. All guests are friends. (✗)

II. No host being friends is a possibility. (✗)

43. (*b*) According to the statements,

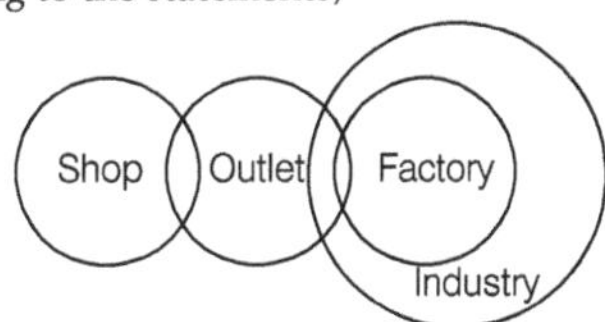

Conclusions

I. At least some shops are factories. (✗)

II. At least some outlets are industries. (✓)

44. (*a*) According to the statements,

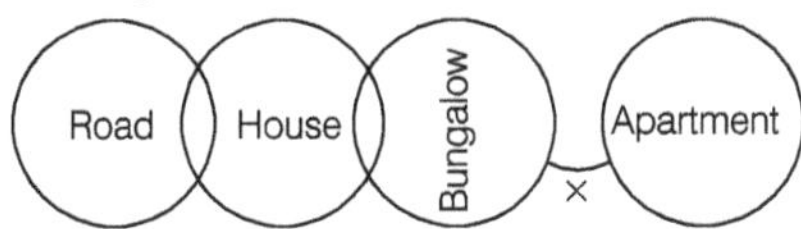

Conclusions I. Some houses are definitely not apartments. (✓)

II. At least some roads are bungalows. (✗)

45. (*e*) According to the statements,

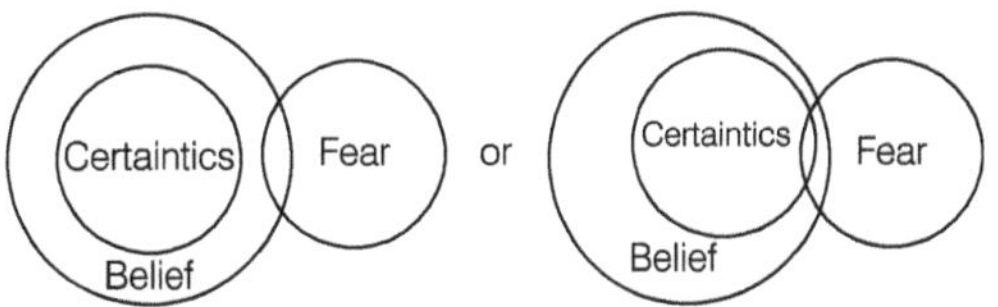

Conclusions

I. At least some fears are certainties. (✓)] Complemantry pair

II. No fear is a certainty. (✗)]

46. (*c*) According to the statements,

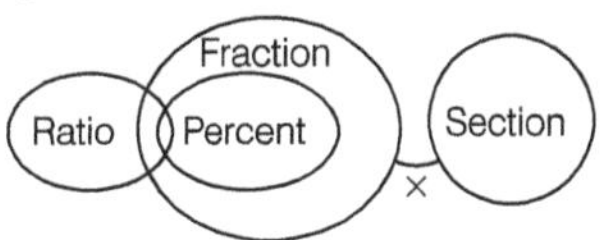

Conclusions

I. No section is a percent. (✓)

II. All ratios being fractions is a possibility. (✓)

47. (*a*) According to the statements,

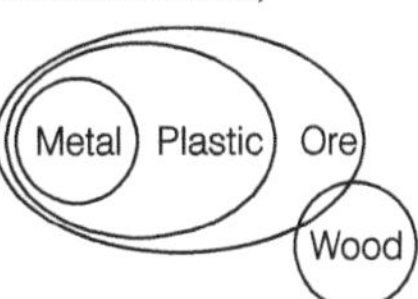

Conclusions

I. All wood being metals is a possibility. (✓)

II. No ore is a metal. (✗)

48. (*c*) According to the statements,

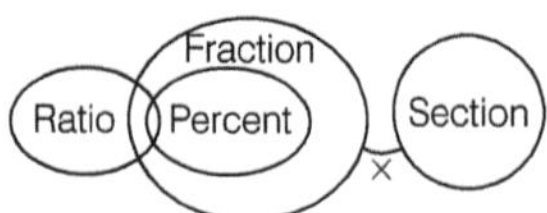

Conclusions

I. All sections being ratios is a possibility. (✓)

II. At least some fractions are ratios. (✓)

49. (*b*) According to the statements,

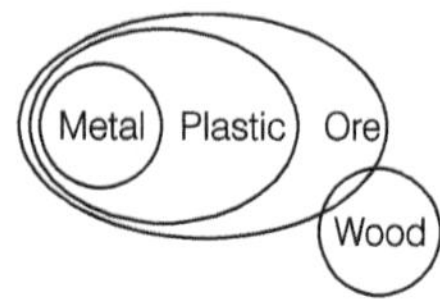

Conclusions

I. At least some metals are wood. (✗)

II. All plastics being wood is a possibility. (✓)

50. (*d*) According to the statements,

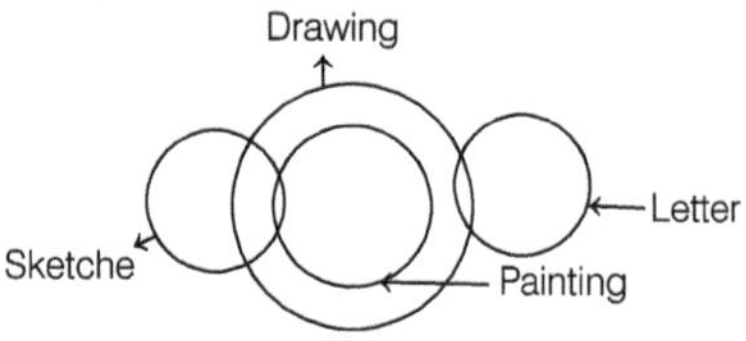

Conclusions

I. All sketches can never be drawings. (✗)

II. No painting is a letter. (✗)

51. (*d*) According to the statements,

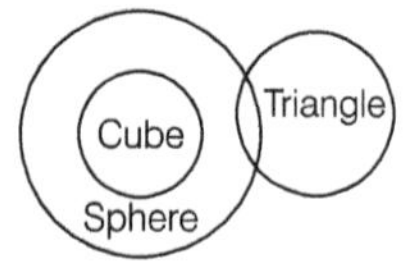

Conclusions

I. No cube is a triangle. (✗)

II. All spheres are cubes. (✗)

52. (*c*) According to the statements,

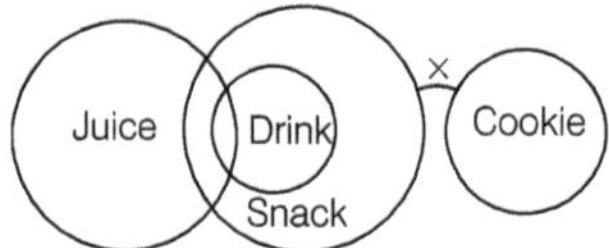

Conclusions

I. All juices can never be cookies. (✓)

II. At least some juices are snacks. (✓)

53. (*a*) According to the statements,

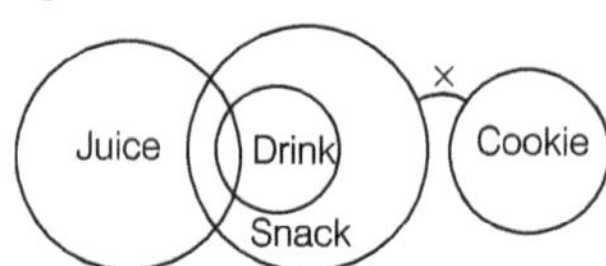

Conclusions

I. No drink is a cookie. (✓)

II. At least some juices are cookies. (✗)

54. (*b*) According to the statements,

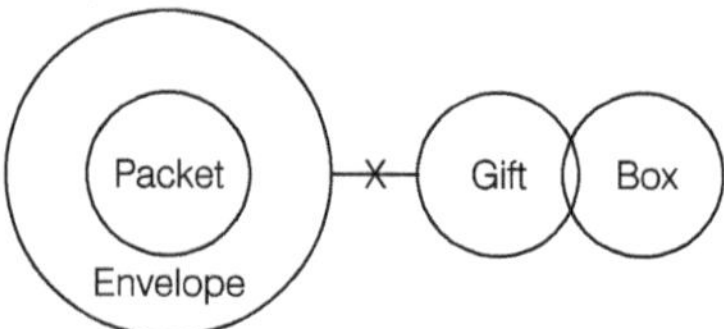

Conclusions

I. All envelopes are packets. (✗)

II. All boxes can never be envelopes. (✓)

55. (*e*) According to the statements,

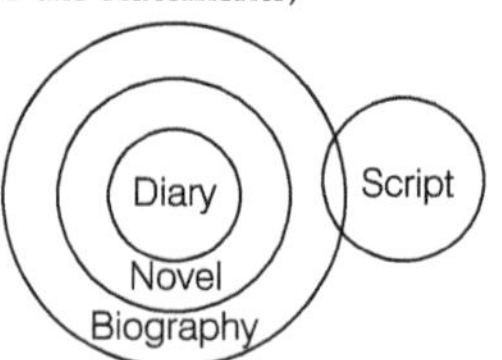

Conclusions

I. At least some diaries are scripts. (✗) (Complementry pair)

II. No diary is a script. (✗) (Complementry pair)

56. (*e*) According to the statements,

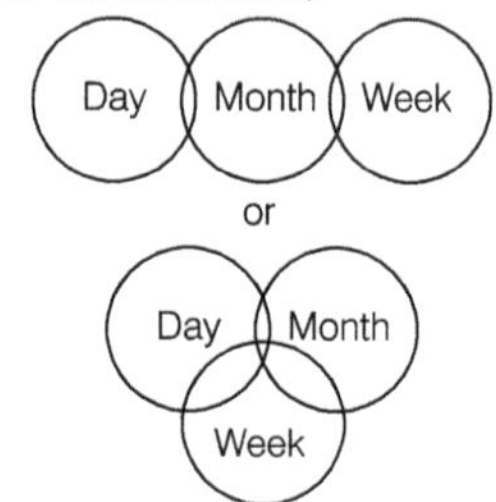

Conclusions

I. Some weeks are days. (✗) (Complementry pair)

II. No week is a day. (✗) (Complementry pair)

57. (*c*) According to the statements,

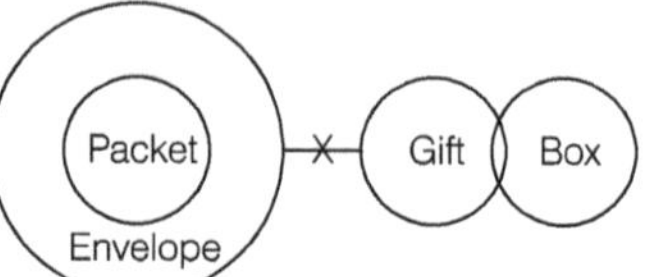

Conclusions

I. All packets being boxes is a possibility. (✓)

II. No packet is a gift. (✓)

58. (*a*) According to the statements,

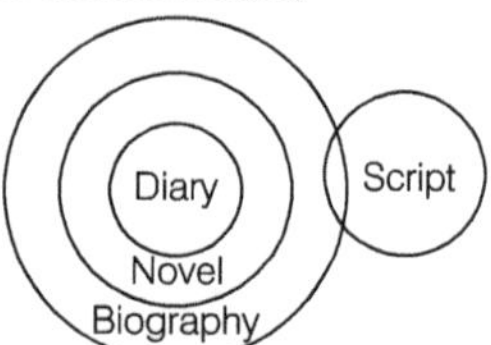

Conclusions

I. All diaries are biographies. (✓)

II. Some scripts are definitely not novels. (✗)

59. (*c*) According to the statements,

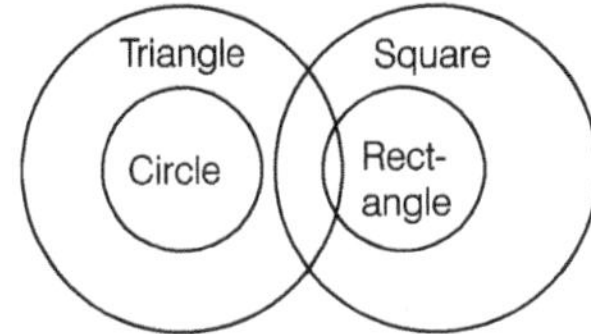

Conclusions
I. All rectangles being triangles is a possibility. (✓)
II. All circles being square is a possibility. (✓)

60. (*c*) According to the statements,

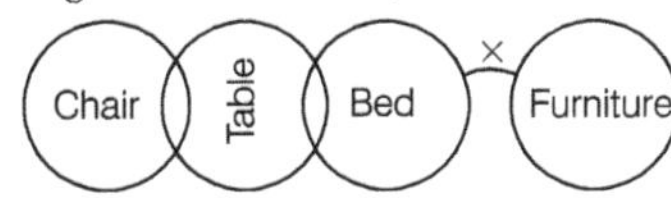

Conclusions
I. All chairs being furniture is a possibility. (✓)
II. Some tables are not bed is a possibility. (✓)

61. (*d*) According to the statements,

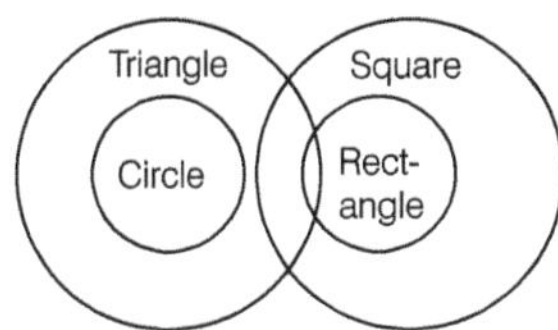

Conclusions I. Some triangles are not rectangles. (✗)
II. No square is a circle. (✗)

62. (*c*) According to the statements,

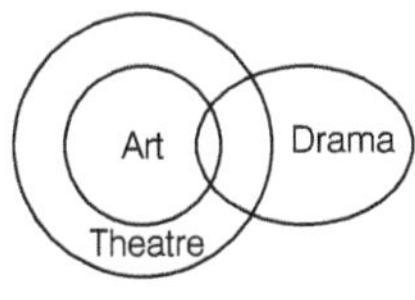

Conclusions
I. All drama being theatre is a possibility. (✓)
II. Some dramas are theatre. (✓)

63. (*a*) According to the statements,

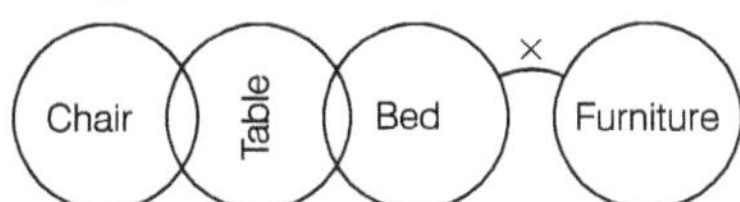

Conclusions
I. Some tables are not furniture. (✓)
II. All tables being furniture is a possibility. (✗)

64. (*b*) According to the statements,

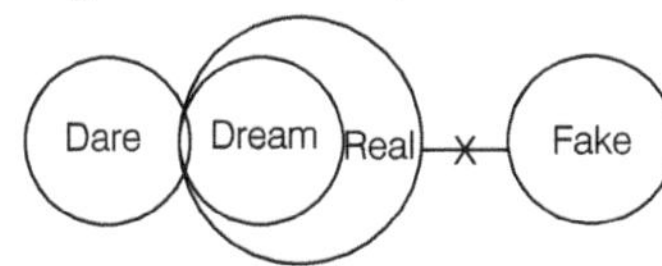

Conclusions
I. Some dreams are fake. (✗)
II. All dreams are not fake. (✓)

65. (*a*) According to the statements,

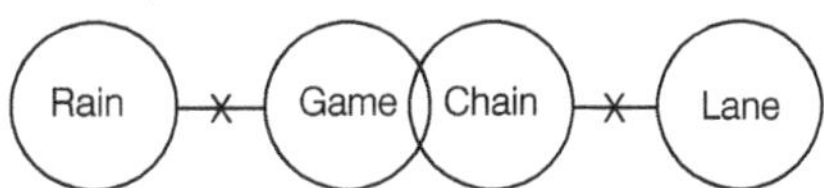

Conclusions
I. Some chains are not rain. (✓)
II. Some games are lane. (✗)

66. (*e*) According to the statements,

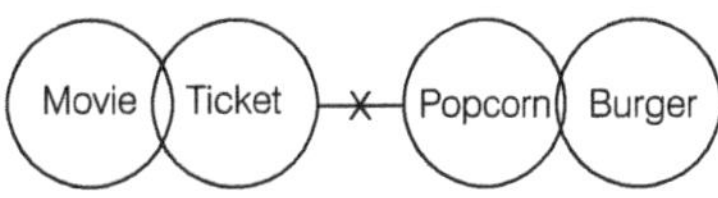

Conclusions
I. Some movies are burger. (✗)
II. Some burgers are not movies. (✗)
Complementary pair

67. (*a*) According to the statements,

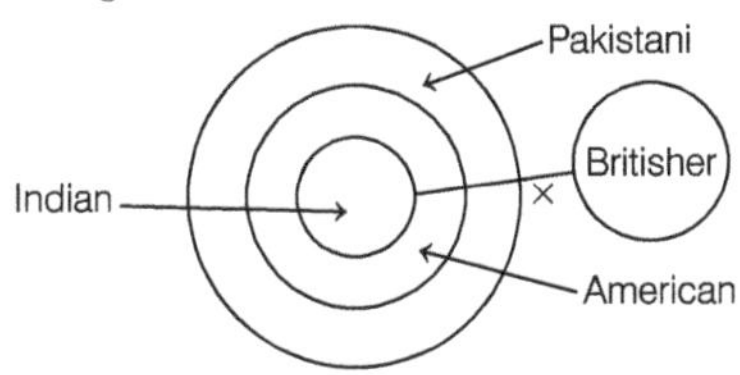

Conclusions
I. All Indians are Pakistani. (✓)
II. Some Pakistani are Britisher. (✗)
III. No Indian is Britisher. (✓)

68. (*e*) According to the statements,

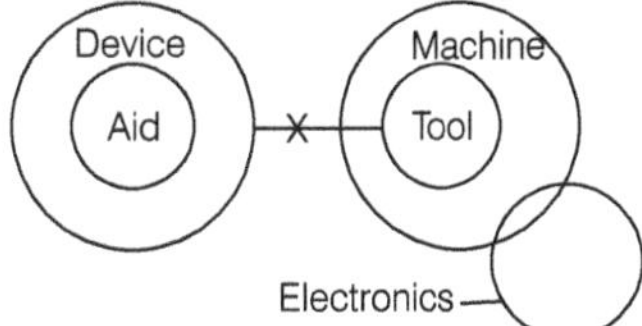

All electronics being aids is a possibility.

69. (*c*)

Some files being copies is a possibility is true.

70. (*b*) According to the statements,

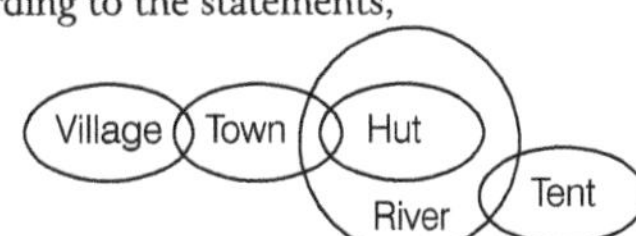

Conclusions
I. Some tents are towns. (✗)
II. Some rivers are towns. (✓)
III. Some hunts are villages. (✗)

71. (*a*) According to the statements,

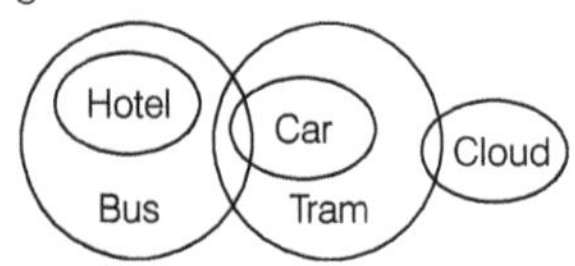

Conclusions
I. Some trams are buses. (✓)
II. Some trams are hotels. (✗)
III. Some clouds are cars. (✗)

72. (*d*)

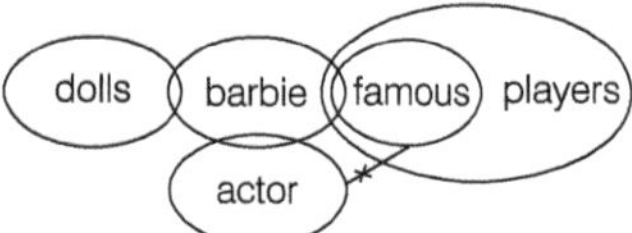

Conclusions
I. Some barbie are not actors. (✓)
II. Some barbie are players. (✓)
III. Some players are famous. (✓)

73. (*b*)

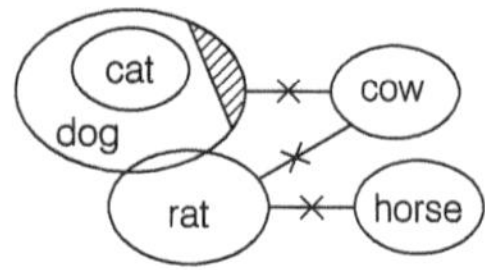

Conclusions
I. All cats are horses. (✗)
II. Some dogs being cows is a possibility. (✓)
III. All cats being cows is a possibility. (✓)

74. (*c*)

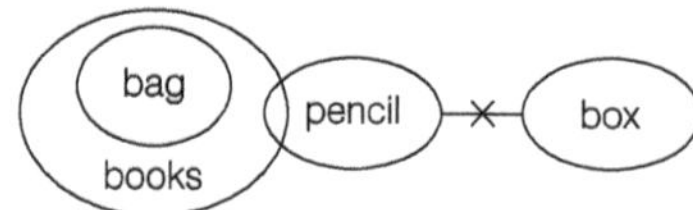

Conclusions
I. Some books are not boxes. (✓)
II. Some books being boxes is a possibility. (✓)
III. Some bags are not boxes. (✗)

75. (*a*)

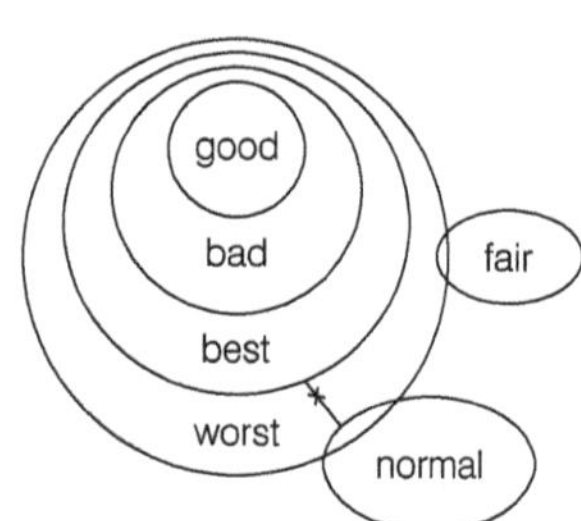

Conclusions
I. All fair being normal is a possibility. (✓)
II. Some best are fair. (✗)
III. Some normal being good is a possibility. (✗)

76. (*e*)

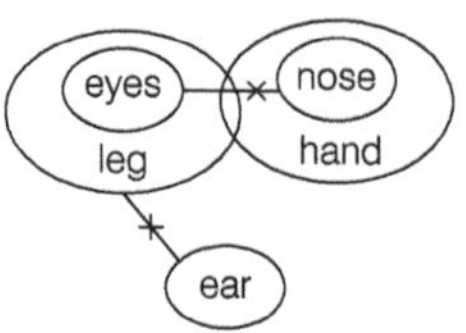

Conclusions
I. Some hands are ears. (✗)
II. Some hands are not nose. (✗)
III. Some hands are not ears. (✓)

77. (*d*)

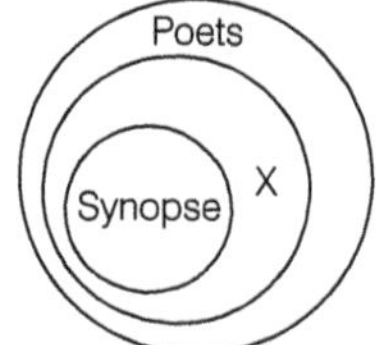

It is clearly shown from the above figure that DFA is correct argument.
D - All X are poets.
F-All synopses are X.
A-All synopses are poets.

78. (*a*)

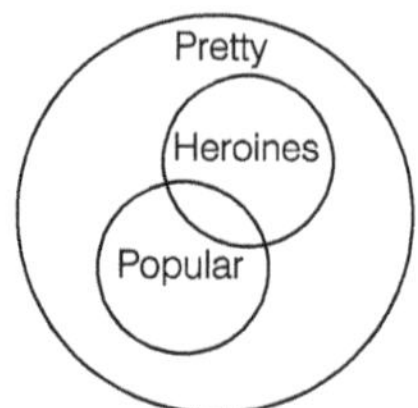

It is clear from the above figure that ABE is valid argument.
A - All heroines are pretty.
B - Some heroines are popular.
E - Some popular girls are pretty.

79. (*d*) From option (a),

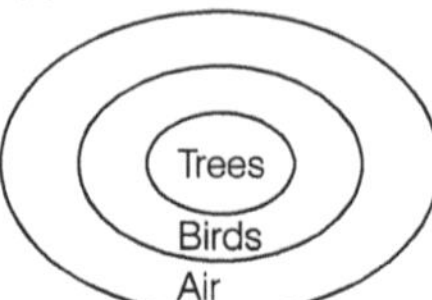

Clearly, trees fly in the air.
From option (b),

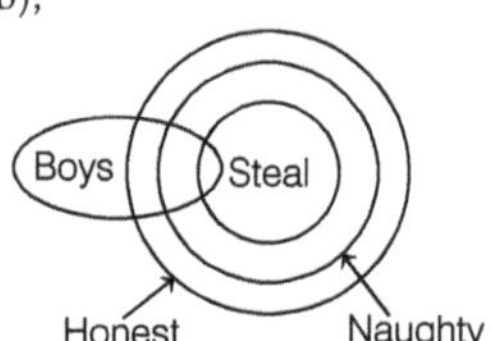

Clearly, some boys are honest.
From option (c),

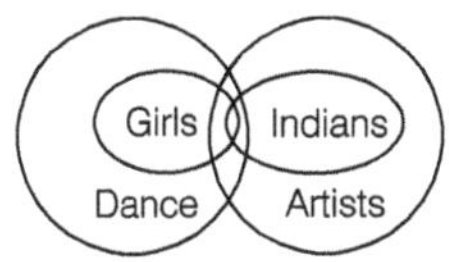

Clearly, some artists like dance.
From option (d),

Here, it is not true that 'all liars are criminals'.

80. (*b*) From option (a),

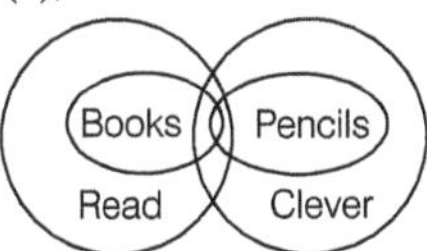

Clearly, some clevers can read.
From option (b),

Clearly, it is not true that 'all criminals fail'.
From option (c),

Clearly, some liars are criminals.
From option (d),

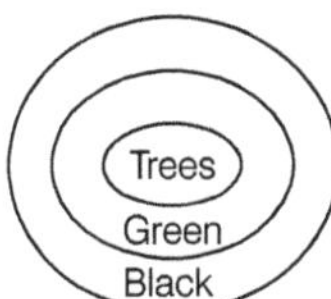

Clearly, trees are black.

81. (*b*) From option (b),

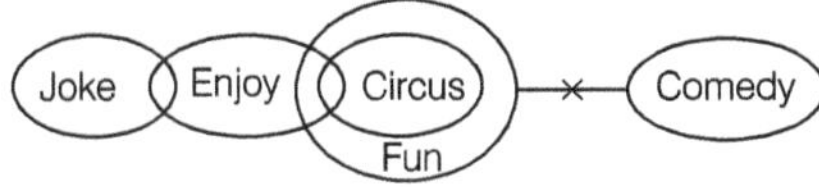

Conclusions

I. Some enjoy is not comedy. (✓)
II. Some fun are circus. (✓)

82. (*e*) From option (c),

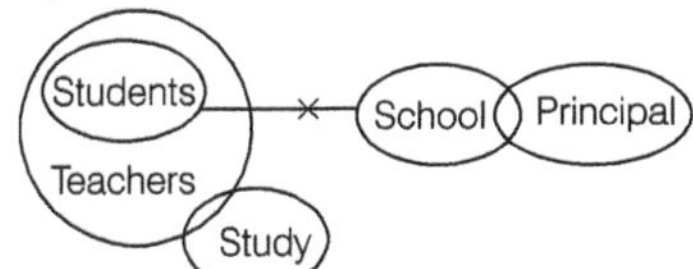

Conclusions

I. Some students are teachers. (✓)
II. Some principal are not students. (✓)

83. (*b*) From Statement IV,

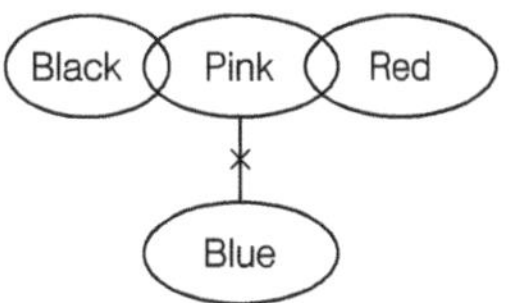

From Statement V,

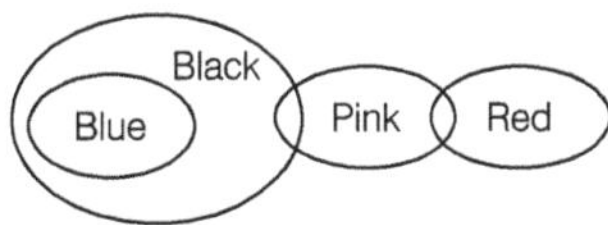

Conclusions

I. Some reds being black is a possibility. (✓)
II. Some blue being red is a possibility. (✓)

84. (*b*) From Statement V,

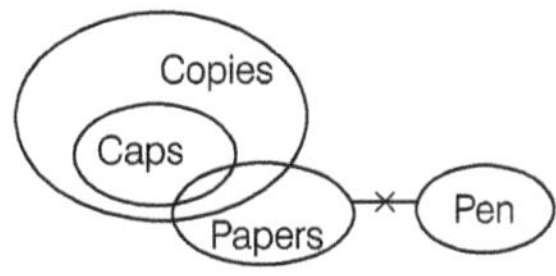

Conclusions

I. At least some caps being pens is a possibility. (✓)
II. Some copies are caps. (✓)

85. (*a*)

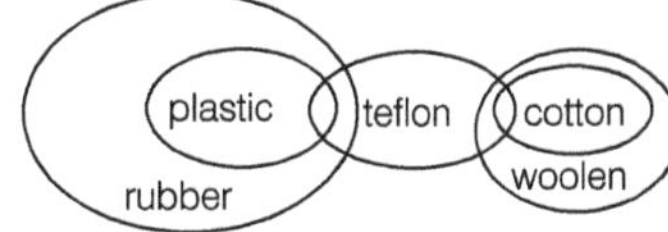

Here, conclusion (a) does not follow as some rubber is definitely plastic but nothing can be said about all rubber being plastic.

86. (*b*)

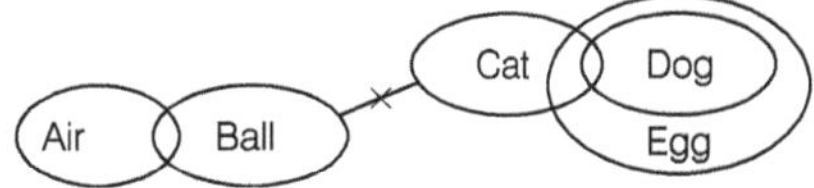

Here, conclusion (b) does not follows as some part of egg is cat and no cat is ball. Therefore, all egg cannot be ball.

87. (*e*)

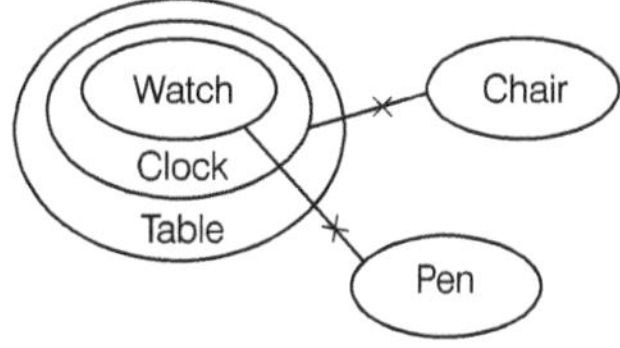

Here, conclusion (e) does not follow as there is no direct relation between the elements pen and chair. Therefore, we cannot conclude that no pen is chair.

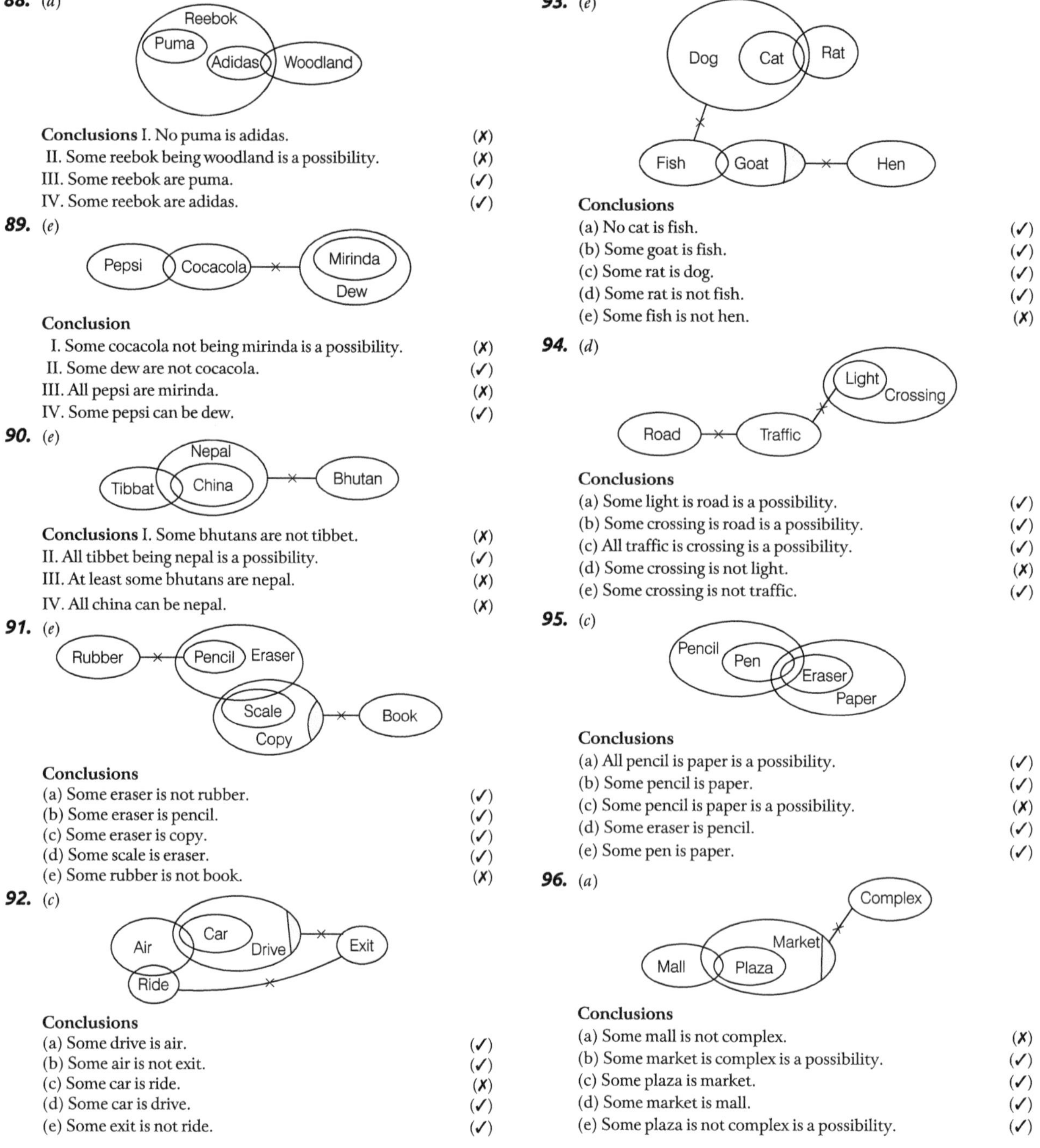

88. (*d*)

Conclusions I. No puma is adidas. (✗)
II. Some reebok being woodland is a possibility. (✗)
III. Some reebok are puma. (✓)
IV. Some reebok are adidas. (✓)

89. (*e*)

Conclusion
I. Some cocacola not being mirinda is a possibility. (✗)
II. Some dew are not cocacola. (✓)
III. All pepsi are mirinda. (✗)
IV. Some pepsi can be dew. (✓)

90. (*e*)

Conclusions I. Some bhutans are not tibbet. (✗)
II. All tibbet being nepal is a possibility. (✓)
III. At least some bhutans are nepal. (✗)
IV. All china can be nepal. (✗)

91. (*e*)

Conclusions
(a) Some eraser is not rubber. (✓)
(b) Some eraser is pencil. (✓)
(c) Some eraser is copy. (✓)
(d) Some scale is eraser. (✓)
(e) Some rubber is not book. (✗)

92. (*c*)

Conclusions
(a) Some drive is air. (✓)
(b) Some air is not exit. (✓)
(c) Some car is ride. (✗)
(d) Some car is drive. (✓)
(e) Some exit is not ride. (✓)

93. (*e*)

Conclusions
(a) No cat is fish. (✓)
(b) Some goat is fish. (✓)
(c) Some rat is dog. (✓)
(d) Some rat is not fish. (✓)
(e) Some fish is not hen. (✗)

94. (*d*)

Conclusions
(a) Some light is road is a possibility. (✓)
(b) Some crossing is road is a possibility. (✓)
(c) All traffic is crossing is a possibility. (✓)
(d) Some crossing is not light. (✗)
(e) Some crossing is not traffic. (✓)

95. (*c*)

Conclusions
(a) All pencil is paper is a possibility. (✓)
(b) Some pencil is paper. (✓)
(c) Some pencil is paper is a possibility. (✗)
(d) Some eraser is pencil. (✓)
(e) Some pen is paper. (✓)

96. (*a*)

Conclusions
(a) Some mall is not complex. (✗)
(b) Some market is complex is a possibility. (✓)
(c) Some plaza is market. (✓)
(d) Some market is mall. (✓)
(e) Some plaza is not complex is a possibility. (✓)

CHAPTER / 02

Statement and Conclusions

Statement A Statement is a group of words arranged to form a meaningful sentence.

Conclusion A Conclusion is a judgement or decision reached after consideration about the given statement.

How to Reach to the Conclusion A conclusion is an opinion or decision that is formed after a period of thought or research on some facts or sentence stated by someone. A consequent effect has always to be analysed before reaching to the final result or conclusion of a given premise. This requires a very systematic and logical approach.

To reach to a conclusion, think only about the information given in the statement. There is no need to use, assume anything else or add any further or extra information from outside but **established facts cannot be denied like the Sun always rises in the East, a day consists of 24 h etc.**

e.g., **Statement** Indian President is elected through secret ballot.

Conclusion Indian President is not the supreme officer of India.

Here, the statement gives us the information that the President of India is elected through a secret ballot which is absolutely true. Now, the conclusion given *i.e.,* Indian President is not the supreme officer of India cannot be concluded from the statement, so it seems to be invalid. Also, according to the constitution it is an established fact that President is the supreme head or officer of India. Hence, the given conclusion goes against the established fact, so it is invalid.

Chapter tip!

- If statement is formed with two or more sentences, then there should be no mutual contradiction in sentences.
- Statements and conclusion should not go against established facts and prevailing notions of truth.
- If definitive words like all, always, atleast, only, exactly and so on are used, then such words may make the conclusion invalid or ambiguous.
- Always read very carefully and try to find key words as they play an important role in analysing valid and invalid conclusions.
- If the conclusion is justified with a stated example, then the conclusion is invalid.

These are several types of questions that are asked from this section in different exams. So, here we have classified the problems in two types which are explained below

TYPE 01

One Statement and Two Conclusions Based Problems

In this type of questions, a statement is given followed by two conclusions. The candidate is required to find out which of conclusions follows the given statement and select the correct option accordingly.

Following examples will give a better understanding about the type of questions asked

DIRECTIONS ~ (Example Nos. 1-8) *Each of these questions has a statement followed by two Conclusions I and II. Consider the statement and the following conclusions. Decide which of the conclusion follows from the statement.*

Give answer

(a) If Conclusion I follows
(b) If Conclusion II follows
(c) If either Conclusion I or II follows
(d) If neither Conclusion I nor II follows

***Ex* 01** **Statement** Power consumption in every family has been doubled during the last five years. « MAT 2018

Conclusions

I. There is a lot of development in the society.
II. Power rates have become cheaper.

Solution (a) Only Conclusion I follows as increase in consumption of power shows development. Also, nothing is mentioned in the statement regarding the power rates.

***Ex* 02** **Statement** A friend in need is a friend indeed. « SSC (CGL) 2013

Conclusions

I. All are friends in good times.
II. Enemies in bad times are not friends.

Solution (d) A friend who offers help in time of need is a true friend. The use of term 'all' in Conclusion I makes it invalid. Conclusion II does not express the inherent meaning of the statement. Therefore, neither Conclusion I nor II follows.

***Ex* 03** **Statement** Vegetable prices are soaring in the market. « RRB Group D 2018

Conclusions

I. Vegetables are becoming a rare commodity.
II. People cannot eat vegetables.

Solution (d) Both the conclusions are not related to the statement. Hence, neither I nor II follows.

***Ex* 04** **Statement** Industries destroy the natural resources.

Conclusions

I. All natural resources are destroyed by industries.
II. No industries, no environmental pollution. « SSC (10+2) 2008

Solution (d) None of the conclusions follows the statement. It is erroneous to assume that all natural resources are destroyed by industries. Similarly, there are other factors which pollute environment.

***Ex* 05** **Statement** Parents are prepared to pay any price for an elite education to their children. « MAT 2013

Conclusions

I. All parents these days are very well off.
II. Parents have an obsessive passion for perfect development of their children through good schooling.

Solution (b) It may be concluded from the statement that since parents want a perfect development of their children through good schooling, therefore they are prepared to pay any price for a good education but the statement does not give sense of the parents being very well off. Hence, only Conclusion II follows.

***Ex* 06** **Statement** To participate in a long and a complete debate, a person should be very intelligent, because intelligent people are talkative and boring.

Conclusions « RRB Group D 2018

I. All intelligent people are boring.
II. All intelligent people are capable of handling long and complex debates.

Solution (b) Conclusion I doesn't follow as we can not say that all intelligent people are boring.

Conclusion II can be clearly concluded from the statement that intelligent people are capable of handling long and complex debates.

***Ex* 07** **Statement** The Prime Minister has made clear that his government will make concerted effort for the upliftment of poor farmers and announced an annual pension for them. « SSC (CPO) 2019

Conclusions

I. Government understands that the condition of poor farmers needs immediate attention.
II. No benefits are announced for other sections of society.

Solution (a) The action taken by the government indicates that the government understands the condition of poor farmers and they need immediate attention. Conclusion II is not related to the given statement. Hence, only Conclusion I follows.

***Ex* 08** **Statement** In India, emphasis should be given more to agriculture engineering and technology rather than on basic and pure science.

Conclusions

I. India has achieved sufficient development in the field of basic and pure science.
II. In the past, the production sector of economy was neglected.

Solution (d) The extent of the development in the field of basic and pure science cannot be ascertained from the statement. Similarly,the production sector of economy was neglected in the past cannot be concluded. Hence, none of the conclusions follows from the statement.

Practice / CORNER 2.1

DIRECTIONS ~ (Q. Nos. 1-19) *Each of these questions has a statement followed by two Conclusions* I *and* II. *Consider the statement and the following conclusions. Decide which of the conclusion follows from the statement.*

Give answer
(a) If Conclusion I follows
(b) If Conclusion II follows
(c) If both Conclusion I and II follow
(d) If neither Conclusion I nor II follows

1. Statement Ram and Shyam always get first and second ranks in class. « UPSSSC VDO 2018

Conclusions
I. Ram always gets the first rank while Shyam gets the second rank.
II. The competition between Ram and Shyam is as tough as nails.

2. Statement This world is neither good nor evil; each man manufactures as world for himself. « MAT 2018

Conclusions
I. Some people find this world quite good.
II. Some people find this world quite bad.

3. Statement Morning Walk is good for health. « MAT 2014, NIFT (UG) 2014

Conclusions
I. Most of the healthy people go for morning walk.
II. Evening walk is not good for health.

4. Statement Animals live on oxygen. « SSC (Cabinet Secretariat) 2013

Conclusions
I. Plants do not live on oxygen.
II. Anything that needs oxygen is bound to be animal.

5. Statement Only white colour vehicles should be allowed in India for promoting peace. « SSC (MTS) 2019

Conclusions
I. Blue colour vehicles promote peace.
II. White colour vehicles promote peace.

6. Statement India's economy is depending mainly on forests. « NIFT (PG) 2014, MAT 2013

Conclusions
I. Trees should be preserved to improve Indian economy.
II. India wants only maintenance of forests to improve economic conditions.

7. Statement "On October 2, let us pledge to make the country free of single-use plastic."– Prime Minister of India « SSC (CPO) 2019

Conclusions
I. All Indians should reduce and then completely eliminate the consumption of single-use plastic like packaged drinking water.
II. India is going to be completely plastic free on October 2.

8. Statement A room with flowers looks beautiful. « SSC (FCI) 2012

Conclusions
I. Flowers are grown for decoration of rooms.
II. Room without flowers looks ugly.

9. Statement Fortune favours the brave.

Conclusions « NIFT (PG) 2014
I. Risks are necessary for success.
II. Cowards die many times before their death.

10. Statement A man must be wise to be a good wrangler. Good wranglers are talkative and boring. « MAT 2014

Conclusions
I. All the wise-persons are boring.
II. All the wise-persons are good wranglers.

11. Statement Fruits and vegetables grown at home are far more healthy as compared to those fetched from markets, as those are kept under artificial refrigeration and preservation to make them look fresh. « RRB Group D 2018

Conclusions
I. Fruits and vegetables in the market are kept under artificial refrigeration and preservation.
II. Fruits and vegetables grown at home are more healthy.

12. Statement The best way to escape from a problem is to solve it. « NIFT (PG & UG) 2014, MAT 2013

Conclusions
I. Your life will be dull if you don't face a problem.
II. To escape from problems, you should always have some solution with you.

13. Statement A neurotic is a non-stupid person who behaves stupidly. « NIFT (PG) 2014

Conclusions
I. Neuroticism and stupidity go hand in hand.
II. Normal persons behave intelligently.

14. Statement The best evidence of India's glorious past is the growing popularity of Ayurvedic medicines in the West. « NIFT (PG) 2014

Conclusions
I. Ayurvedic medicines are not popular in India.
II. Allopathic medicines are more popular in India.

15. Statement Financial security makes people better and happier and has a good influence on their personality. « Delhi Police Inspector 2016

Conclusions
I. People who earn enough money are happier.
II. To have a good personality people should be economically sound.

16. Statement Religions provide the means for attaining eternal peace. People should follow these means. « SSC (FCI) 2012

Conclusions
I. Religions ensure prosperous life.
II. Religions help people to eradicate poverty.

17. Statement The National Skill Development committee conducted an assessment among their trainers and found the performance below mandatory level. « UPSSSC Junior Assistant 2020

Conclusions
I. The committee should immediately organise remedial courses and training to improve standards.
II. The committee should terminate poor performers and hire new trainers.

18. Statement According to the education minister, the students will have the option of skipping the board examination for class X from this academic year to ease some pressure on them.

Conclusions
I. Class X board examination was compulsory till the last academic year.
II. Students were traumatized by the pressure created by these board exams.

19. Statement Domestic demand has been increasing faster than the production of indigenous crude oil.

Conclusions
I. Crude oil must be imported.
II. Domestic demand should be reduced.

DIRECTIONS ~ (Q. Nos. 20-33) *In each of the questions given below, there is a statement followed by two conclusions numbered I and II. You have to assume everything in the statement to be true, then consider the two conclusions together and decide which of them logically follows from the information given in the statement.*

Give answer
(a) If only Conclusion I follows
(b) If only Conclusion II follows
(c) If either I or II follows
(d) If neither I nor II follows
(e) If both I and II follow

20. Statement Unemployment is one of the main reason for the poverty of the country. « Canara Bank (PO) 2009

Conclusions
I. To end poverty, it is required to create employment opportunities.
II. All the people in the country are unemployed.

21. Statement Prostitution is also one of the main reason of AIDS. « UCO Bank (PO) 2011

Conclusions
I. AIDS is an incurable disease.
II. AIDS cannot be completely controlled by banning prostitution only.

22. Statement The nation 'X' faced the increased international opposition due to its decision of performing eight nuclear explosions.

Conclusions
I. The citizens of the nation have favoured the decision.
II. Some powerful nations do not want that others may become powerful.

23. Statement The Chief Minister emphasised the point that the Government will try its best for the development of farmers and rural poor.

Conclusions
I. The former Government had not tried seriously for the development of these people.
II. This Government will not try seriously for the development of urban poor.

24. Statement The majority of Indian labourers belong to unorganised sector and most of them earn very low.

Conclusions
I. The labourers belonging to organised sector have better benefits and stability.
II. Some labourers belonging to unorganised sector have regular and certain income.

25. Statement The multinational fast food chains have started their operation in India after facing many problems but association of farmers are ready for competition.

Conclusions
I. Association of farmers are not supporting modernisation.
II. Association of Farmers are not ready for competition with the multinational companies.

26. Statement In deserts, camels are indispensable for people to travel from one place to another.

Conclusions « SBI (PO) 2009
I. Camels are the only cheapest mode of transport available in deserts.
II. There are plenty of camels in deserts.

27. Statement He emphasised the need to replace the present training programme by other methods which will bring out the real merit of the managers.

Conclusions
I. It is important to bring out the real merit of the managers.
II. The present training programme does not bring out the real merit of the managers.

28. Statement The greatest need in India today is not for sophisticated gadgets but for programmes which will provide employment to a large number of people.

Conclusions
I. There is an adequate number of sophisticated gadgets in India.
II. Emphasis is being laid on procuring sophisticated gadgets.

29. Statement In case of the outstanding candidates, the condition of previous experience of social work may be waived by the Admission Committee for MA (social work).

Conclusions
I. Some of the students for MA (social work) will have previous experience of social work.
II. Some of the students for MA (social work) will not have previous experience of social work.

30. Statement It is almost impossible to survive and prosper in this world without sacrificing Ethics and Morality.

Conclusions

I. World appreciates some concepts but may not uphold it.
II. Concept of Ethics and Morality are not practicable in life.

31. Statement The persons who were on the waiting list could finally get berth reservation in Rajdhani Express. « UCO Bank (PO) 2008

Conclusions

I. Wait listed passengers generally find it difficult to get berth reservation in Rajdhani Express.
II. The number of berth available in the Rajdhani Express is small.

32. Statement Crime is a function of the criminal's biological make up and his family relations.

Conclusions

I. The incidence of crime is higher in identical twins than in fraternal twins.
II. Families in which parents lack in warmth and affection fail to build a moral conscience in the children.

« PNB (PO) 2009

33. Statement Fashion is a form of ugliness, so is tolerable that we have to alter it every six months.

Conclusions

I. Fashion designers do not understand people's mind very well.
II. People by and large are highly susceptible to novelty.

« PNB (PO) 2008

Answers / WITH EXPLANATIONS

1. (*b*) From the given statement, only Conclusion II follows because in statement, it is not mentioned that who one comes first or who comes second.

2. (*c*) Both the conclusions follow, as it is mentioned in the statement that each man manufactures a world for himself. So, some people may find it quite good and some may find it quite bad.

3. (*d*) Neither I nor II follows as it can't be concluded that most of the healthy people go for morning walk. Evening walk is not good for health, can't be concluded from the statement.

4. (*d*) None of the conclusions follows. 'Animals live on oxygen' does not imply that other things do not need oxygen.

5. (*b*) In the given statement, it is mentioned that 'white colour vehicle should be allowed to promote peace,' from this we can concluded that white colour vehicles promote peace. Only Conclusion II follows.

6. (*a*) Conclusion I follows because trees are a part of forest and India's economy depends mainly on forest. Conclusion II is not correlated with the statement. So, it does not follow. Hence, Statement I follows.

7. (*a*) The statement given by PM indicates that all Indians eliminate should reduce and then completely the consumption of single use plastic. But we cannot say that India is going to be completely plastic free on October 2. Hence, only Conclusion I follows.

8. (*d*) Neither of the conclusions is true. A room may look beautiful with other decorative items also.

9. (*a*) According to the statement, only those who tackle situation bravely achieve success. So, Conclusion I follows, however Conclusion II is ambiguous with concern to the given statement and so does not follow.

10. (*d*) According to the statement, good wranglers are wise-men. But it doesn't mean that all wise-men are good wranglers. So, neither I nor II follows.

11. (*c*) Both conclusions follow as both are clearly stated in the statement.

12. (*b*) The given statement does not tell anything about life. It only tells about problems and the way to escape from them. Hence, Conclusion II follows.

13. (*a*) It is mentioned in the statement that a neurotic is a person who behaves stupidly. So, Conclusion I follows. The behaviour of normal persons cannot be deduced from the given statement. So, Conclusion II does not follow.

14. (*d*) The popularity of Ayurvedic or Allopathic medicines in India is not being talked about in the statement. So, neither I nor II follows.

15. (*d*) Neither I nor II follows and only earning money doesn't ensure happiness and good personality also comes from behaviour and moral ethics, money just has a good influence on personality.

16. (*d*) None of the conclusions is correct. Nothing is given about the prosperous life and poverty.

17. (*a*) From the given statement it is clear that the committee should immediately organise remedial courses and training to improve standards.

18. (*a*) It is clear from the given statement that only Conclusion I follows.

19. (*b*) The domestic demand of crude oil should be decreased.

20. (*a*) Conclusion I is valid because if unemployment is the main reason behind poverty, then creating employment opportunities is the need to end poverty. Conclusion II is invalid because of the presence of word 'all'.

21. (*b*) Prostitution is not the only reason of AIDS. It is one of the main reasons of this disease. Hence, banning only prostitution cannot work 100% to control this disease. It means other factors must be considered also. Therefore, II is a valid conclusion. Conclusion I is invalid as it has not been discussed in the statement that AIDS is curable or not.

22. (*b*) Nuclear explosion is not the result of the favour by the citizens. Hence, Conclusion I does not follow. However, increase in the international opposition is due to the fact that some powerful nations don't want that others may become powerful.

23. (*d*) From the commitment of the present Government, it cannot be concluded that former Government did not do anything serious about the development nor does it mean that present Government will not do anything for the development of other sectors, hence none of the conclusion follows.

24. (*b*) It is given in the statement that most of the labourers belonging to unorganised sector earn very low and uncertain income, it means that there are some labourers who earn regular and certain income.
Hence, Conclusion II definitely follows from the statement.

25. (*d*) Conclusion I is totally unrelated to the statement and Conclusion II is contrary to the statement. Hence, none of the conclusions follows.

26. (*d*) None follows as the given statement merely says that camels are very useful for deserts. It does not state whether they are cheap or available in large number.

27. (*e*) Both the conclusions follow from the statement. Conclusion I is the direct result of the statement. Conclusion II follows because in the given statement, there is a need to replace the present system with a new one.

28. (*d*) The statement says that greatest need in India is not for sophisticated gadgets but for programmes but this does not mean that there is an adequate number of sophisticated gadgets. Secondly, there is a need for programmes but it cannot be concluded that emphasis is being laid on procuring sophisticated gadgets. Hence, none of the conclusions follows.

29. (*e*) Both the conclusions follow. The waiver is incorporated because some of the students for MA will not have previous experience and some of the students will have previous experience of social work.

30. (*e*) Conclusions I and II convey almost the same meaning that principles related to Ethics and Morality seem to be good but are not practicable in real life. Hence, both the conclusions follow.

31. (*a*) Conclusion I is a valid conclusion as the use of word 'could' implies a difficulty in obtaining reservation but Conclusion II is invalid as it is not certain.

32. (*d*) Both I and II are invalid as statement itself is vague and ambiguous which is unable to make proper connectivity with the given conclusions.

33. (*d*) Both I and II are invalid because they lack proper connectivity with the given statement.

TYPE 02

More Than one Statements and Two/Three/Four Conclusions

In this type of questions, more then two statements are given followed by some conclusions. Candidates are required to choose the conclusion which follows the given statement.

DIRECTIONS ~ (Example Nos. 9-12) *Which of the conclusions can be drawn from the given statements.*

***Ex* 9** **Statement** All the students in my class are intelligent. Kaushik is not intelligent. « SSC (10+2) 2013

(a) Some students are not intelligent
(b) Non-intelligent are not students
(c) Kaushik is not a student of my class
(d) All other than Kaushik are intelligent

Solution (c) As all the students in my class are intelligent and Kaushik is not intelligent, so Kaushik is not a student of my class.

***Ex* 10** **Statement** All guilty politicians were arrested. Ranjan and Kamlesh were among those arrested.

(a) All politicians are guilty
(b) All arrested people are politicians
(c) Ranjan and Kamlesh were not politicians
(d) Ranjan and Kamlesh were guilty

Solution (d) It is given in the statement that Ranjan and Kamlesh were arrested and all those who arrested were guilty. Therefore, Ranjan and Kamlesh were guilty.

***Ex* 11** **Statement** Many business offices located in buildings having two to eight floors. If a building has more than three floors, it has a lift.

(a) All floors may be reached by lifts
(b) Only floors above the third floor have lifts
(c) Fifth floor has lifts
(d) Second floors do not have lifts

Solution (c) It is given in the question that if a building has more then three floors. It has a lift. Therefore, it is clear that fifth floor has lifts.

***Ex* 12** **Statements**

A. Karan Johar is a good director.
B. Directors are intelligent. « CLAT 2013

(a) All intelligent are directors
(b) Karan Johar is intelligent
(c) Both (a) and (b)
(d) None of the above

Solution (b) As directors are intelligent and Karan Johar is good director, so Karan Joahar is intelligent.

DIRECTIONS ~ (Examples Nos. 13-14) *In the following questions, two statements are given followed by two Conclusions I and II. You have to consider the statements to be true even if they seem to be at variance from commonly known facts. You have to decide which of the given conclusions, if any, follow from the given statements. Indicate your answer.*

***Ex* 13** **Statements**

A. AIDS is a killer disease.
B. It is easy to prevent AIDS than to treat it.

Conclusions

I. AIDS prevention is very expensive.
II. People will not cooperate for AIDS prevention.

(a) Only Conclusion I follows
(b) Only Conclusion II follows
(c) Neither Conclusion I nor II follows
(d) Both Conclusions I and II follow

Solution (c) None of the conclusions follows. If one takes precaution, he/she may prevent it. But it does not imply that AIDS prevention is very expensive.

***Ex* 14** **Statements**

A. People who live in the big city crowd into jammed trains or buses.
B. They cross the street in competition with high powered motorcars.

Conclusions

I. Travelling is very difficult for city people.
II. Traffic jam is inevitable in big cities.
(a) Only Conclusion I follows
(b) Only Conclusion II follows
(c) Neither Conclusion I nor II follows
(d) Both Conclusion I and II follow

Solution (a) From both the statements, it is clear that people who live in city face problems in travelling. Therefore, only Conclusion I follows.

***Ex* 15 Statements** The Union health ministry has made Aadhaar a compulsory document for tuberculosis patients to be able to avail treatment under the government's Revised National Tuberculosis Control Programme (RNTCP).

Conclusions « IBPS Clerk (Mains) 2018

I. A person cannot take treatment of TB without aadhaar card.
II. Patients suffering from TB will be unable to get benefits under a central government secheme till they produce their Aadhaar card.
III. An individual eligible to receive the benefit under the scheme, is hereby, required to furnish proof of possession of Aadhaar number or undergo aadhaar authentication.
IV. The World Health Organisation (WHO) recently said that tuberculosis epidemic in India was "larger" than what had been previously estimated.

Which of the following could be the inference of the given statement?
(a) Only II
(b) I and III
(c) II and III
(d) Only I
(e) None of these

Solution (c)

I. Cannot be infered from the given statement because Aadhaar card is compulsory to avail treatment under the government's Revised National Tuberculosis Control Programme (RNTCP).
II. Can be infered from the given statement as Aadhaar card is compulsory to get benefits under a Central Government scheme.
III. Can be infered from the given statement.
IV. Cannot be infered as this statement is not directly related to the given statement.

Hence, II and III could be the inference of the given statement.

Practice / CORNER 2.2

DIRECTIONS ~ (Q. Nos. 1-10) *In each of the following questions, two statements are given followed by two Conclusions I and II. You have to consider the two statements to be true even if they seem to be at variance from commonly known facts. You have to decide which of the given conclusions, if any follow from the given statements.*

1. Statements

A. No teacher comes to the school on a bicycle.
B. Anand comes to the school on a bicycle.
« SSC (CPO) 2012

Conclusions

I. Anand is not a teacher.
II. Anand is a student.
(a) Conclusion I alone can be drawn
(b) Conclusion II alone can be drawn
(c) Both conclusions can be drawn
(d) Both conclusions cannot be drawn

2. Statement

A. Most of the 64 number buses go to my office.
B. This is 64 number bus. « SSC (CGL) 2008

Conclusions

I. This bus goes to my office.
II. This bus does not go to my office.
(a) Conclusion I and II both can be drawn
(b) Conclusion II alone can be drawn
(c) Conclusion I alone can be drawn
(d) Conclusions I and II both cannot be drawn

3. Statements

A. All students are boys.
B. No boy is dull.

Conclusions « CGPSC Pre 2017

I. No student is dull.
II. There are no girls in the class.
(a) Only I is inferred
(b) Only II is inferred
(c) Both I and II are inferred
(d) Either I or II is inferred
(e) Neither I nor II is inferred

4. Statements

A. All employees except one or two are slow and inactive.
B. All employees are old man.

Conclusions « CGPSC Pre 2017

I. Some employees are efficient.
II. Some old man are good employees.
(a) Only I is inferred
(b) Only II is inferred
(c) Both I and II are inferred
(d) Either I or II is inferred
(e) Neither I nor II is inferred

5. Statements

A. The constitution assures the fundamental rights.
B. Parliament has right to amend the constitution.
« SSC (CGL) 2013

Conclusions

I. Parliament included fundamental rights in the constitution.

II. Parliament did not assure the fundamental rights.

(a) Only Conclusion I follows
(b) Only Conclusion II follows
(c) Both Conclusion I and II follow
(d) None of the above

6. Statements

A. In comparision with 2 decades ago, India is producing more two wheelers.

B. The quality of such vehicles has also been improved.

Conclusions

I. We are exporting two wheelers.

II. Our two wheeler industries have done commendable progress.

(a) Only Conclusion II can be drawn
(b) Only Conclusion I can be drawn
(c) Neither Conclusion I nor II can be drawn
(d) Both the Conclusions I and II can be drawn

7. Statements

A. Education is a process of lighting.

B. Mind requires light to enlighten the core of cognitive aspect. « SSC (10+2) 2013

Conclusions

I. Education is a light which removes the darkness of mind.

II. Education is a static process for mind.

(a) Only Conclusion I follows
(b) Only Conclusion II follows
(c) Both Conclusions I and II follow
(d) Neither Conclusion I nor II follows

8. Statements

A. Best performance in Olympics fetches a gold medal.

B. Player 'X' got gold medal but later was found to be using a prohibited drug.

Conclusions

I. 'X' should be allowed to keep the gold medal.

II. Gold medal should be withdrawn and given to the next person.

(a) Only Conclusion II follows
(b) Neither Conclusion I nor II follow
(c) Both Conclusions I and II follow
(d) Only Conclusion I follows

9. Statements

A. Science has brought the gadgets of happiness, prosperity and wealth.

B. Science has not solved the problems of overpopulation.

Conclusions « SSC (CGL) 2007

I. Overpopulation is due to unscientific thinking.

II. Science has not helped world peace.

(a) Only Conclusion I follows
(b) Only Conclusion II follows
(c) Both Conclusions I and II follow
(d) Neither Conclusions I and II do not follow

10. Statements

A. Conflicts in mind create tension

B. Resolution of conflict leads to good mental health.

Conclusions

I. One becomes very hefty and strong by resolving one's conflicts.

II. Freedom from conflict leads to good mental health.

(a) Only Conclusion I follows
(b) Only Conclusion II follows
(c) Neither Conclusion I nor II follows
(d) Both Conclusions I and II follow

DIRECTIONS ~ (Q. Nos. 11-13) *In the following questions, two statements are given followed by four conclusions (a), (b), (c) and (d). You have to consider the statements to be true even if they seem to be at variance from commonly known facts. You have to decide which of the given conclusions, if any, follow from the given statements.*

11. Statements « SSC (CGL) 2013

I. Ravi has five pens.

II. No one else in the class has five pens.

Conclusions

(a) All students in the class have pens
(b) All students in the class have five pens each
(c) Some of the students have more than five pens
(d) Only one student in the class has exactly five pens

12. Statements

A. All the students in my class are intelligent.

B. Rashmi is not intelligent.

(a) Rashmi should do hard labour
(b) Rashmi is not the student of my class
(c) Some students are not intelligent
(d) Rashmi is a sports person

13. Statements

A. There are monks among those who are felicitated for remarkable social service.

B. Jitananda and Vidyananda are among those felicitated.

Conclusions

(a) Jitananda and Vidyananda did remarkable social service
(b) All monks do social service
(c) Jitananda and Vidyananda are not monks
(d) All monks are felicitated

14. Examine the following statements

I. Only those who have a pair of binoculars can become the members of the birdwatcher's club.

II. Some members of the birdwatcher's club have cameras.

III. Those members who have cameras cannot photo-contests.

Which of the following conclusions can be drawn from the above statements?

(a) All those who have a pair of binoculars are members of the birdwatcher's club
(b) All members of the birdwatcher's club have a pair of binoculars
(c) All those who take part in photo-contests are members of the birdwatcher's club
(d) No conclusion can be drawn

15. Examine the following statements

I. None but students are members of the club.
II. Some members of the club are married persons.
III. All married persons are invited for dance.

Which one of the following conclusions can be drawn from the above statements?

(a) All students are invited for dance
(b) All married students of the club, are invited for dance
(c) All members of the club are married persons
(d) None of the above

16. Examine the following statements

I. I watch TV only if I am bored.
II. I am never bored when I have my brother's company.
III. Whenever I go to the theater I take my brother along.

Which one of the following condusigris is valid in the context of the above statements?

(a) If I am bored, I watch TV
(b) If I am bored, I seek my brother's company
(c) If I am not with my brother, then I watch TV
(d) If I am not bored, I do not watch TV

17. Consider the following statements

I. All artists are whimsical.
II. Some artists are drug addicts.
III. Frustrated people are prone to become drug addicts

From the above three statements it may concluded that

(a) artists are frustrated
(b) some drug addicts are whimsical
(c) all frustrated people are drug addicts
(d) whimsical people are generally frustrated

18. Consider the following three statements

I. Only students can participate in the race.
II. Some participants in the race are girls.
III. All girl participants in the race are invited for coaching.

Which one of the following conclusions can be drawn from the above statements?

(a) All participants in the race are invited for coaching
(b) All students are invited for coaching
(c) All participants in the race are students
(d) None of the above

19. A research study recorded that the number of unemployed educated youth was equal to the number of unemployed uneducated youth. It was concluded by the researchers that being educated does not enhance the probability of being employed.

Which of the following information would be required to validate the above conclusion? « IIFT 2013

(a) The number of unemployed educated and uneducated people in other age groups
(b) The number of organisations employing youth
(c) The percentage of unemployment in educated youth versus percentage of unemployment in uneducated youth
(d) The percentage increase in number of educated youth versus last year

20. During the last summer vacation, Ankit went to a summer camp where he took part in hiking, swimming and boating. This summer, he is looking forward to a music camp where he hopes to sing, dance and learn to play the guitar.

Based on the above information, four conclusions, as given below, have been made.

Which one of these logically follows from the information given above?

(a) Ankit's parents want him to play the guitar
(b) Ankit prefers music to outdoor activities
(c) Ankit goes to some type of camp every summer
(d) Ankit likes to sing and dance

21. Ten new TV shows started in January, 5 sitcoms, 3 drama and 2 news magazines. By April only seven of the new shows were still on, five of them being sitcoms.

Based on the above information, four conclusions, as given below, have been made. Which one of these logically follows from the information given above?

(a) Only one news magazine show is still on
(b) Only one of the drama shows is still on
(c) At least one discontinued show was a drama
(d) Viewers prefer sitcoms over drama

22. All existing and upcoming hotels within a 5 km radius of national parks and sanctuaries in India will have to pay 30% of their annual turnover as tax to the government. « IBPS (PO) Mains 2019

Which of the following statements can be inferred from the facts/information given in the above statement?

(a) The tax collected from the hotels will be used for the betterment of these national parks and sanctuaries
(b) Hotels which are sponsored by the government will not have to pay any tax even if these are located within the 5 km radius of such wildlife hotspots
(c) The ecosystem of the national parks and sanctuaries is adversely affected even if the hotels are located outside the 5 km radius
(d) Government allows the construction of hotels within 5 km radius of national parks and sanctuaries
(e) Such a step is taken by the environment ministry to boost eco-tourism and perk up revenue collection of state governments

DIRECTION ~ (Q. No. 23) *Study the following information in which a statement is followed by five conclusions, read carefully and answer the question below.*
« IBPS Clerk (Mains) 2019

Other than being an essential source of water for Indian agriculture, the monsoon plays a critical role in flushing out pollutants over Asia. However, recently increased pollution - particularly from coal burning - could potentially weaken this ability of the monsoon.

23. Which of the following can be deduced from the given statement?

(a) The annual average rainfall has remained the same because the frequency of heavy downpours increased in the past two decades.

(b) As the climate gets warmer and frequency of rains reduces, such spurts in coarse particles making breathing difficult will become a new normal and the government is not waking up to the alarm.

(c) Both the periodicity and duration of dry spells in the country were rising as total rainfall events in a year had fallen even though the average rainfall in a year has not changed much, a direct consequence of climate change.

(d) The unusually high concentration of particulate matter in the last few days in India clearly shows that air pollution is emerging as a big problem.

(e) The air quality in the region deteriorated because of dust storms in western India, particularly Rajasthan

Answers / WITH EXPLANATIONS

1. (*a*) Anand comes on a bicycle which is not used by any teacher. Hence, Anand cannot be a teacher. Therefore, I is valid. II is not valid because if Anand is not a teacher, he is either a student or a staff member.

2. (*d*) Presence of word 'most' in the statement makes both I and II ambiguous. Hence, none of I and II can be drawn.

3. (*a*) Nothing can be concluded about girls. Hence, only Conclusion I can be inferred.

4. (*c*) Both I and II can be inferred as some employees are efficient and some old man are good employees.

5. (*d*) From the above two statements, it is not clear whether the parliament can assure the fundamental rights or not.

6. (*a*) I is invalid as export is not the subject of discussion in the given statement. II is a valid conclusion because there has been increase in production of two wheelers with improved qualities.

7. (*a*) Only Conclusion I follows.

8. (*a*) If a player is found guilty of doping, his medal is confiscated. Therefore, only Conclusion II follows.

9. (*d*) Neither Conclusion I nor II follows. Only scientific gadgets do not ensure prosperity and happiness. It only make our work easier. Overpopulation is a result of several factors. Therefore, only unscientific thinking cannot be held responsible for overpopulation.

10. (*b*) The second statement clearly corroborates the Conclusion II.

11. (*d*) From both the statements it is clear that only Ravi has five pens in the class. Therefore, only Conclusion (d) follows.

12. (*b*) If all the students in a particular class are intelligent and Rashmi is not intelligent, then it means Rashmi is not the student of that particular class.

13. (*a*) From both the statements it is clear that Conclusion I is true.

14. (*b*) Only those who have binoculars can be a part of birdwatcher's club, hence all the members of birdwatcher's club will have binoculars for sure. But all those who have binoculars may not be part of birdwatcher's club.

15. (*b*) It is given that all married persons are invited for the dance and some members of the club are married persons. So, all married students of the club are invited for the dance.

16. (*d*) The pre-condition for watching TV is to get bored. So, If I am not bored, I do not watch TV. So, option (d) is correct.

17. (*b*) All artists are whimsical and some of the artists are drug addicts. Thus, all those artists who are drug addicts are also whimsical. Hence, some drug addicts are whimsical.

18. (*c*) From Statement I, it can be concluded that 'All participants in the race are students'. Since, it is given in Statement III that 'All girl participants in the race are invited for coaching'. So options (a) and (b) cannot be concluded. Hence, answer is option (c).

19. (*c*) Option (c) is required to validate the conclusion stated in the given passage.

20. (*c*) No reasons are specified in the question for going to different camps. As, Ankit has been going to different camps since the past two year, so it can be said that he goes to some type of camp every summer.

21. (*c*) No reason is provided for discontinuation of any programme. Hence, option (d) is not correct. Three shows were discontinued. As no sitcoms shows were discontinued, they must be either drama or news magazine.

Now, there were only two news magazines. So, atleast one discontinued show was a drama. Hence, option (c) is correct.

22. (*a*) Option (a) seems to be the only logic behind the imposition of tax in such specific areas.

23. (*d*) Only statement (d) can be deduced from the given statement as by burning the coal the concentration of its particles is increased which lead to excessive amount of air pollution.

Master Exercise

DIRECTIONS ~ (Q. Nos. 1-3) *In the following questions, two statements are given followed by four conclusions (a), (b), (c) and (d). You have to consider the statements to be true even if they seem to be at variance from commonly known facts. You have to decide which of the given conclusions, if any, follow from the given statements.*

1. Statement This book can help because all good books help.

Conclusions

(a) This is not a good book
(b) This is a good book
(c) No good book help
(d) Some good books help

2. Statement To pass the examination one must work hard. « CMAT 2013

Conclusions

(a) Examination is related with hard work
(b) All those who work hard pass
(c) Examination causes some anxiety and those who work hard overcome it
(d) Without hard work, one does not pass

3. Statement Most dresses in that shop are expensive. « SSC (CPO) 2006

Conclusions

(a) Some dresses in that shop are expensive
(b) There are cheap dresses also in that shop
(c) Handloom dresses in that shop are cheap
(d) There are no cheap dresses available in that shop

DIRECTIONS ~ (Q.Nos. 4-6) *In the questions below one statement is followed by two conclusions. Examine the logical applications of the conclusions and decide which of the answer choices is correct.*

Give answer

(a) If I is inferred
(b) If II is inferred
(c) If both I and II are inferred
(d) If either I or II is inferred
(e) if neither I nor II is inferred

4. Statements « CGPSC Pre 2016

A. Sunlight is a very good source of energy.
B. There is a great need for solar energy.

Conclusions

I. Energy can also be obtained from other sources.
II. Coal is a very good source of energy.

5. Statements

A. Intelligent people have great insight.
B. Anil is able to see through things very quickly.

Conclusions

I. Anil is intelligent.
II. Anil has great insight.

6. Statement

Homeopathic medicines are now popular only in India. « CGPSC Pre 2017

Conclusions

I. Homeopathic medicines are popular in the West.
II. Homeopathic medicines are not popular in the West.

7. What do you conclude from the following two statements? « SSC (10+2) 2008

I. Hybrid plants are resistant to fungus.
II. Fungal infection reduces the life of plants

(a) For a long life-span grow hybrid plants
(b) Fungus attacks hybrid plants
(c) Yield is more in hybrid plants
(d) All plants are hybrid plants

8. Consider the following statements

The Third World War, if it ever starts, will end very quickly with the possible end of civilisation. It is only the misuse of nuclear power which will trigger it.

Based on the above statement, which one of the following inferences is correct? « CSAT 2012

(a) Nuclear power will be used in the Third World War
(b) There will be no civilisation left after the Third World War
(c) The growth of nuclear power will destroy civilisation in the long run
(d) The Third World War will not take place

DIRECTIONS ~ (Q. Nos. 9-17) *In each of these questions, a statement is given followed by two conclusions numbered* I *and* II. *You have to assume everything in the statement to be true and then consider the two conclusions together to decide which of them logically follows beyond a reasonable doubt from the information given in the statement.*

Give answer

(a) If only Conclusion I follows
(b) If only Conclusion II follows
(c) If both the Conclusions I and II follow
(d) If neither Conclusion I nor II follows

9. **Statement** Most Indians are aware that they have a great heritage, but few would include science in it.

Conclusions « SSC (CGL) April 2014

I. Many Indians consider science to have made Indian heritage great.
II. Many Indians are not aware that India has a great scientific heritage.

10. **Statements** Leaders are human beings. All human beings need rest. « SSC (Steno) 2013

Conclusions

I. All human beings are not leaders.
II. Leaders need rest.

11. **Statement** A loss making company has won a ₹ 5 crore contract in a low-price bidding system.

Conclusions « UPSSSC Mandi Parishad 2018

I. The company will make a profit this year as it has won a large contract.
II. A low-price bidding system leaves no scope of a high profit margin.

12. **Statement** Reacting to the news of suicides by the farmers, the Prime Minister stated that his government will make every possible effort for the upliftment of poor farmers and farmhands.

Conclusions

I. Only farmers are attempting suicides due to poverty and debt.
II. No serious effort has been made till now for the upliftment of any section of society.

13. **Statement** Workers feel highly motivated when they get sense of involvement by participating in the management of companies. « MAT 2018

Conclusions

I. Workers should be motivated to produce more.
II. Workers should be allowed to participate in the management of companies.

14. **Statement** All organised person find time for entertainment. Mahesh in spite his busy schedule, find time for entertainment. « SSC Steno Grade C & D 2019

Conclusions

I. Mahesh is organised person.
II. Mahesh is an actor.

15. **Statement** The employer said to the daily wage workers, "There will no extra time given to the person, to complete the work who started late".

Conclusions « RRB Group D 2018

I. Daily wage workers hope to complete the alloted work till the end of the day.
II. The employer is addressing those workers who come late.

16. **Statement** Government has spoiled many top ranking financial institutions by appointing bureaucrats as directors of these institutions. « CLAT 2015

Conclusions

I. Government should appoint directors of the financial institutes taking into consideration the expertise of the person in the area of finance.
II. The director of the financial institute should have expertise commensurate with the financial work carried out by the institute.

17. **Statement** In japan, the incidence of stomach cancer is very high, while that of bowel cancer is very low. But Japanese immigrate to Hawaii, this is reversed-the rate of bowel cancer increases but the rate of stomach cancer is reduced in the next generation. All this is related to nutrition-the diets of Japanese in Hawaii are different than those in Japan. « CLAT 2015

Conclusions

I. The same diet as in Hawaii should be propagated in Japan also.
II. Bowel cancer is less severe than stomach cancer.

DIRECTIONS ~ (Q. Nos. 18-26) *In each of the questions below is given a statement followed by two conclusions numbered I and II. You have to assume everything in the statement to be true, then consider the two conclusions together and decide which of them logically follows beyond a reasonable doubt from the information given in the statement.*

Give answer

(a) If only Conclusion I follows
(b) If only Conclusion II follows
(c) If either Conclusion I or II follows
(d) If neither Conclusion I nor II follows
(e) If both Conclusions I and II follow

18. **Statement** To cultivate interest in reading, the school has made it compulsory from June, 1996 for each student to read two books per week and submit a weekly report on the books.

Conclusions

I. Interest in reading can be created by force.
II. Some students eventually will develop interest in reading.

19. **Statement** While presenting a stage show recently, the famous actor declared that he has a practice of either taking full payment or none for his stage shows.

Conclusions

I. The actor has taken full payment for his recent stage show.
II. The actor did not take any money for his recent stage show.

20. **Statement** From the next academic year, students will have the option of dropping Mathematics and Science for their school leaving certificate examination.

Conclusions

I. Students, who are weak in Science and Mathematics, will be benefitted.
II. Earlier students did not have the choice of continuing their education without taking these subjects.

21. **Statement** As far as the rate of literacy is concerned, there is hardly any difference between the States of Kerala and Paschim Bengal, but one is ahead of the other in respect of the percentage of population employed.

Conclusions

I. Unemployment is more is Kerala than in Paschim Bengal.

II. Paschim Bengal has higher unemployment than Kerala.

22. Statement Until our country achieves Economic equality and Political freedom, Democracy would be meaningless.

Conclusions

I. Political freedom and Democracy go hand in hand.

II. Economic equality leads to real Political freedom and Democracy.

23. Statement From all available cutural records, it is evident that even in ancient India, both the masters and disciples valued not the quantity but the quality of knowledge.

Conclusions

I. Giving importance to quantity of knowledge is meaningless.

II. There was an identity of educational values between teachers and students in ancient India.

24. Statement In a one day cricket match, the total runs made by a team were 200, out of which 160 runs were made by spinners.

Conclusions

I. 80% of the team consists of spinners.

II. The opening batsmen were spinners.

25. Statement Inspite of the claim of Government, of terrorism being under check, their nefarious activities still continue.

Conclusions

I. The terrorists have not come to an understanding with the Government.

II. The Government has been constantly telling a lie.

26. Statement Computer advertisements now fill magazine pages but the real computer revolution in India is taking place quietly and is a likely organisation of Government.

Conclusions

I. Both the Central and State Government are computerising rapidly.

II. The Government does not fill the magazine pages with its computer advertisements.

27. A Statement is given followed by three Conclusions I, II and III. You have to consider the statement to be true even if it seems to be at variance from commonly known facts. You have to decide which of the given conclusions, if any, follows from the given statement.

Statement Comic books contain pictures.

Conclusions « SSC (Constable) 2013

I. All books contain pictures.

II. Books may or may not contain pictures.

III. Books other than the comic books do not contain pictures.

(a) Only Conclusion I follows
(b) Only Conclusion II follows
(c) Only Conclusion III follows
(d) Neither Conclusion I nor II follows

28. Statement Most of the mobile phones in that shop are costly.

(a) Some of the mobile phones in that shop are costly
(b) Mobile phone of brand X are costly in that shop
(c) None of the mobile phones in that shop is cheap
(d) Some of the mobile phones in that shop are cheap
(e) None of the above

29. Consider the following statements

I. All X-brand cars parked here are white.

II. Some of them have radial tyres.

III. All X-brand cars manufactured after 1986 have radial tyres.

IV. All cars are not X-brand.

Which one of the following conclusions can be drawn from the above statements? « CSAT 2012

(a) Only white cars are parked here
(b) Some white X-brand cars with radial tyres are parked here
(c) Cars other than X-brand cannot have radial tyres
(d) Most of the X-brand cars are manufactured before 1986

Answers WITH EXPLANATIONS

1. (*b*) This is a good book can be concluded from the given statement.

2. (*d*) Without hard word, one does not pass can be concluded.

3. (*b*) Most dresses are expensive means some are cheap also.

4. (*a*) Nothing about coal is said in the statement. As sunlight is good source of energy, it can be inferred that there are other sources of energy also.

5. (*c*) Since, Anil is able to see through things quickly, he has great insight and hence he is intelligent.

6. (*b*) Only Conclusion II is inferred because it is clearly stated that Homeopathic medicines are popular only in India, which means that they are not popular in the west.

7. (*a*) Clearly, Conclusions I follows. Hybrid plants are resistant to fungus and hence the life-span of hybrid plants is greater.

8. (*a*) There is a possibility of end of civilisation with the use of nuclear power which will be used in Third World War which if starts ever.

9. (*b*) From the given statement, only Conclusion II follows.

10. (*b*) From the given statements, 'Leaders are human beings' and 'All human beings a need rest' Hence, 'Leaders need rest' follows.

11. (*d*) Neither Conclusion I nor II follows as just winning contract doesn't ensure profit and this is also not necessary that a low price bidding system leaves no scope for high margin.

12. (*d*) Both the conclusions are not related to the statement Hence, neither I nor II follows.

13. (*b*) Only Conclusion II follows. As the workers feel motived when they get sense of involvement by participating in the management of companies, so they should be allowed to participate.

14. (*a*) Only Conclusion I follows as it can be clearly concluded from the statement.
Conclusion II is vague.

15. (*d*) Neither I nor II follows as both are assumptions not conclusions.

16. (*c*) Conclusion I follows as appointments should be made considering the expertise of the person in the area of finance.
Conclusion II also follows as the director should have expertise commensurate with the financial work carried out by the institute.

17. (*d*) Conclusion I doesn't follow as propagating the same diet in Japan as in Hawaii doesn't mitigate the risk of cancer.
Conclusion II also doesn't follow as nothing is said about the severity of cancer of any type in the statement. Hence, neither I nor II follows.

18. (*b*) Interest in reading cannot be inculcated by force. Hence, Conclusion I does not follow. However, compulsory reading will develop a gradual inclination towards reading.
Hence, Conclusion II follows.

19. (*c*) As given in the condition in the statement, the actor will either take the full payment for his show or will not take any money for the same. Hence, either of the conclusions follows.

20. (*e*) Both the conclusions follow. Since the option is available from next year, it implies that this option was not available earlier. Secondly, students who are weak in Mathematics and Science will be benefitted.

21. (*c*) It is not given in the statement that which of the two states has more unemployment problem. Therefore, it may be either Kerala or Paschim Bengal.

22. (*a*) As in the given statement, Economic equality and political freedom are related with Democracy, so Conclusion I follows from the statement but Economic equality and Political freedom are not related with each other. Hence, Conclusion II does not follow.

23. (*b*) Only Conclusion II follows, since both the teachers and students valued the quality of knowledge. So, it can be concluded that there existed an identity of educational values between teachers and students in ancient India.

24. (*d*) Team may consist of the number of spinners more or less than that given in Conclusion I. Hence, Conclusion I does not follow. Secondly, it is not known from the statement that opening batsman were spinners. Hence, Conclusion II does not follow.

25. (*a*) Since killing still continues, the terrorists may not have come to an understanding with the Government.

26. (*a*) It is given in the statement that computer revolution is taking place quietly and is a likely organisation of the Government which means that computerisation is being done rapidly. Hence, I is valid and II is invalid.

27. (*b*) Only Conclusion II follows. Comic books and some other books may contain pictures. Some books do not contain pictures.

28. (*d*) From the given statement, the conclusion 'some of the mobile phones in that shop are cheap' follows.

29. (*b*) All X-brand cars parked here are white and some of them have radial tyres. Hence, some white X-brand cars parked here have radial tyres.

CHAPTER / 03

Statement and Arguments

An argument is a statement or series of statements in which a certain point of view is put forth, expressing different opinions for or against something.

In this type of questions, a statement concerned with an issue is given, followed by certain arguments in favour or against that statement. You have to identify the logical correct arguments.

Generally, both the arguments are contrary to each other and refer to the positive and negative results of the action as mentioned in the statement issue.

Arguments can be of two types

- **Strong Argument** An argument is called strong, if it touches the practical and real aspect of the situation as described in the statement. It is backed up by reasons and facts related to the situation.
- **Weak Argument** An argument is called weak, if it is not directly related to the given statement and it does not address all the points put forward in the given statement. A weak argument is of minor importance or may be related to trival aspect of the statement.

Points to be Taken Into Consideration while Choosing a Strong Argument

- A strong argument should give the realistic diagnosis of the situation described in the statement.
- A strong argument should give the deep analysis of the topic dealt within the statement.
- A strong argument should relate with the statement and be supported up by facts or established notions.
- There should be consistency and conformity in arguments with the prevailing ideas and truth.
- A strong argument should not be mere reiteration of the situation given in the statement.
- Arguments should not be based on assumption.
- The argument should be specific, not generalised.
- The argument should not be ambiguous.
- There should not be material fallacy in the argument i.e. there should not be a fallacy of composition, division, equivocation or amphibology uncritical analogy.

TYPE 01

Two Arguments Based Questions

In the following type of questions, a statement is followed by two arguments and a candidate is asked to examine the strength of both the arguments.

Examples given below will give a better idea about the type of questions asked in exam

DIRECTIONS ~ (Example Nos. 1-3) *Study the following instructions carefully and then answer the questions that follow. In making decisions about important questions, it is desirable to be able to distinguish between 'strong' and 'weak' arguments so far as they relate to the questions. 'Weak' arguments may not be directly related to the question and may be of minor importance or may be related to the trivial aspect of the question. Each question below is followed by two arguments numbered I and II. You have to decide which of the arguments is a 'strong' argument and which is a 'weak' argument?*

Give answer

(a) If only Argument I is strong
(b) If only Argument II is strong
(c) If either I or II is strong
(d) If both I and II are strong

***Ex* 1** **Statement** Should computer knowledge be made compulsory for all school students? « UP Police SI 2017

Arguments

I. Yes, India is aiming at digitialising its villages and starting computer education at school level will facilitate this.

II. Yes, this will help the youth to be better equipped to seek jobs as computer knowledge is considered as an essential skill.

Solution **(d)** Argument I is strong as for digitalisation, computer education is necessary and providing computer education at school level will facilitates this.

Argument II is also strong because computer knowledge have become prerequisite in almost every kind of job.

So, computer knowledge will be an added skill for job seekers.

Hence, both arguments are strong.

***Ex* 2** **Statement** Should the provision to dissolve the assembly prematurely be amended? « MP PSC 2017

Arguments

I. Yes, on many occasions the provision has been used by ruling governments to fulfil vested interests.

II. No, to fulfil the constitutional obligations and norms, it sometimes becomes the need of the hour to dissolve the assemly prematurely.

Solution **(c)** Either Argument I or II is strong because many times ruling government misuse it while sometimes dissolving the assembly becomes the need of the hour.

***Ex* 3** **Statement** Should a child from a not-so-affluent family in India be allowed to follow his / her passion? « UP Police Constable 2018

Arguments

I. Yes, these days if a child is allowed to pursue her / his interests, she / he can excel in it, even financially.

II. No, even today our country does not have a strong social security system and establishing oneself in unconventional fields is time consuming and can be financially taxing.

Solution **(a)** Argument I is strong as now a days there are ocean of opportunities available in diverse fields. If a child has a passion, then he/she can excel in any field of his/her interest and can become financially independent also.

Argument II is weak as lack of social security system, should not hinder the growth of a child. This type of idea is deteremental to the expansion of talent and will only on society a regressive one.

DIRECTIONS ~ (Example Nos. 4-7) *Study the following instructions carefully and then answer the questions that follow. In making decisions about important questions, it is desirable to be able to distinguish between 'strong' and 'weak' arguments so far as they relate to the questions. 'Weak' arguments may not be directly related to the question and may be of minor importance or may be related to the trivial aspect of the question. Each question below is followed by two arguments numbered* I *and* II. *You have to decide which of the arguments is a 'strong' argument and which is a 'weak' argument?*

Give answer

(a) If only Argument I is strong.

(b) If only Argument II is strong.

(c) If either I or II is strong.

(d) If neither I nor II is strong.

(e) If both I and II are strong.

***Ex* 4** **Statement** Should parents in India. In future be forced to opt for only one child as against two or many at present?

Arguments

I. Yes, this is the only way to check the ever increasing population of India.

II. No, this type of pressure tactic is not adopted by any other country in the world. « UCO Bank (PO) 2008

Solution **(d)** Argument I is weak because it is superfluous. It does not go into the reason for population control. Argument II is an argument by example and hence, it is weak.

***Ex* 5** **Statement** Should the sex determination test during pregnancy be completely banned?

Arguments

I. Yes, this leads to indiscriminate female foeticide and eventually will lead to social imbalance.

II. No, people have a right to know about their unborn child. « UCO Bank (PO) 2008

Solution **(a)** Argument I is strong as female foeticide is undesirable. Argument II is weak. Which right are we talking about? Right to know the gender of the unborn child ? No. Parents can wait till the child's birth.

***Ex* 6** **Statement** Should all the slums in big cities be demolished and the people living in such slums be relocated outside the city limits?

Arguments

I. No, all these people will lose their home and livelihood and hence, they should not be relocated.

II. Yes, the big cities need more and more spaces to carry out development activites and hence, these slums should be removed. « Syndicate Bank (PO) 2008

Solution **(e)** Argument I is strong on humanitarian grounds. Argument II is strong on economic grounds.

***Ex* 7** **Statement** Should there be a complete ban on mining coal in India?

Arguments

I. Yes, the present stock coal will not last long, if we continue mining at the present rate.

II. No, we do not have alternate energy source of sufficient quantity.

Solution **(b)** Argument I is a weak argument as it is not relevant to 'complete ban.' Argument II is strong as banning in such a scenario will lead us into great trouble.

Practice CORNER 3.1

DIRECTIONS ~ (Q. Nos. 1-18) *In making decisions about important questions, it is desirable to be able to distinguish between 'strong' arguments and 'weak' arguments. 'Strong' arguments are those which are both important and directly related to the question. 'Weak' arguments are those which are of minor importance and also may not be directly related to the question or may be related to a trivial aspect of the question. Each question below is followed by two arguments numbered I and II. You have to decide which of the arguments is a 'strong' argument and which is a 'weak' argument?*

Give answer

(a) If only Argument I is strong.
(b) If only Argument II is strong.
(c) If both I and II are strong.
(d) If neither I nor II is strong.

1. **Statement** Should school education be made free in India? « OPSC 2018

Arguments

I. Yes, this is the only way to improve the level of literacy.

II. No, it will add to the already heavy burden on the exchequer.

2. **Statement** Should young entrepreneurs be encouraged?

Arguments « RRB Group D 2018

I. Yes, they will help in the industrial development of the country.

II. Yes, they will reduce the burden on the employment market.

3. **Statement** Should there be complete ban on manufacture of fire crackers in India?

Arguments « NIFT (UG) 2013

I. No, this will render thousands of workers jobless.

II. Yes, the fire cracker manufacturers use child labour to a large extent.

4. **Statement** Luxury hotels should be banned in India.

Arguments

I. Yes, these places are turning into operating centers for international criminals.

II. No. well off foreign tourists won't be able to find a suitable place to stay.

5. **Statement** Should educational institutes allow their students to join student unions that are sponsored by political parties?

Arguments

I. No, the decision will politicise the educational environment of their institute.

II. Yes, the decision will help students nurture their talent and develop into future political leaders.

6. **Statement** Should the government shut down all government organisations to arrest the misuse of funds?

Arguments

I. Yes, public funds will be saved by shutting down government organisations.

II. No, services from the government organisations cannot be handed over to the private institutions.

7. **Statement** Are 21st century teenagers under stress?

Arguments « RRB Group D 2018

I. Yes, teenagers perception is that they are expected to be successful or good at everything. Failure has somehow gone from being viewed as a learning opportunity to being clearly unacceptable.

II. No, stress is a relative perception that can be managed with proper guidance.

8. **Statement** Should only reputed NGO's be authorised to distribute the commodities to the public under the programme of Public Distribution System (PDS)?

Arguments « MPPSC 2018

I. Yes, the move will be helpful to implement the programme more effectively and will keep a tab on various problems like black marketing of the commodities supplied under PDS.

II. Yes, NGO's have helped government on many occasions.

9. **Statement** Should one year of army training be compulsory for all Indian citizens?

Arguments « SSC CGL 2017

I. No, the costs of training will be prohibitive and one year of labour will be lost.

II. Yes, army training helps make better citizens.

10. **Statement** Should parents invest as much in educating their daughters as much as they spend on educating their sons?

Arguments « UP Police Constable 2018

I. No, almost all data points to the fact that boys are way more intelligent than girls.

II. No, though girls may be intelligent, parents have to keep money aside for their marriages.

11. **Statement** Should the government sell major part of its stake in all the profit making public sector undertakings?

Arguments « MPPSC 2018

I. No, government should not give up its control of these undertaking as these are profit making organisations.

II. Yes, this will help government reduce the quantum of huge budgetary deficit and argument its resources.

12. Statement Should the private compaines be allowed to operate passenger train services in India?

Arguments « MPPSC 2018

I. Yes, this will improve the quality of service in Indian Railways as it will have to face severe competition.

II. No, the private companies may not agree to operate in the non-profitable sectors.

13. Statement Should advertisements be banned on television?

Arguments « RRB ALP 2018

I. Yes, advertisement are immoral.

II. No, advertisement bring in revenue which helps reduce cost for viewers.

14. Statement Should all the electricity state boards be privatised in India?

Arguments « MPPSC 2018

I. No, this will increase the grievances of the people.

II. Yes, it will check the growing menace of power theft which has resulted in annual pilferage of a huge amount.

15. Statement Should children be prevented completely from watching the television?

Arguments « NIFT (UG) 2012

I. No, we get vital information regarding education through television.

II. Yes, it hampers the study of children.

16. Statement Should medical entrance test be made compulsory? « UP Police SI 2017

Arguments

I. Yes, we have to ensure high quality of medical education to meet the demands of rapidly advancing medical field.

II. No, this will keep medical education out of the reach of large number of rural and urban deprived children.

17. Statement Should a cricket team have more than one captain during a match?

Arguments « UP Police Constable 2018

I. No, one needs to make decisions on the spot and there won't be time to resolve conflicting ideas between the captains on the field if such a scenario emerges.

II. Yes, it is always better to have more brains coming to an understanding before taking a decision.

18. Statement Should speed breakers on roads be outlawed?

Arguments « UPSSSC Mandi Parishad 2018

I. No, speed breakers are a simple way to reduce vehicle speed.

II. Yes, some people fail to see the speed breakers at night.

DIRECTIONS ~ (Q. Nos. 19-65) *In making decisions about important questions, it is desirable to be able to distinguish between 'strong' arguments and 'weak' arguments. 'Strong' arguments are those which are both important and directly related to the question. 'Weak' arguments are those which are of minor importance and also may not be directly related to the question or may be related to a trivial aspect of the question. Each question below is followed by two arguments numbered I and II. You have to decide which of the arguments is a 'strong' argument and which is a 'weak' argument?*

Give answer

(a) If only Argument I is strong.
(b) If only Argument II is strong.
(c) If either I or II is strong.
(d) If neither I nor II is strong.
(e) If both I and II are strong.

19. Statement Should there be uniforms for students in the colleges in India like they are in the schools?

Arguments « Syndicate Bank (PO) 2008

I. Yes, this will improve the ambience of the colleges as all the students will be decently dressed.

II. No, college students should not be regimented and they should be free to choose their clothes while coming to college.

20. Statement Should the sale of all the toys made in China be banned in India?

Arguments « Andhra Bank (PO) 2009

I. Yes, these are very cheap and hence, will put the local toy manufacturers out of business.

II. No, Indian toys are of much better quality and their sale will not be affected.

21. Statement Should there be no examination upto Std IX in all the schools in India?

Arguments « Andhra Bank (PO) 2009

I. No, students need to go through the process of giving examinations right from young age.

II. Yes, this will help students to think laterally and achieve their creative pursuits.

22. Statement Should there be only a uniform rate of income tax irrespective of the level of income?

Arguments « SBI (PO) 2009

I. Yes, this will substantially reduce the work of the officials of the income tax department.

II. No, this will reduce government tax collection to a large extent.

23. Statement Should the sale of tobacco products be restricted to only a few outlets in each city/town?

Arguments « SBI (PO) 2009

I. Yes, this will substantially reduce consumption of tobacco products.

II. No, those who want to purchase tobacco products should get them at convenient locations.

24. Statement Should small states be formed out of bigger states in India?

Arguments

I. Yes, there will be greater administrative convenience.

II. No, it will jeopardise the national integration.

25. Statement Should all the government owned educational institutions be given to private sector?

Arguments

I. Yes, there will be upgradation of educational standard in these institutions.

II. No, the educational standard of these institutions will decrease.

26. Statement Should the organisations like the UNO be abolished?

Arguments

I. Yes, the cold war is going to an end, so there is no role of such organisations.

II. No, in the absence of these organisations, there will be a World War.

27. Statement Should we impart sex education in schools?

Arguments

I. Yes, all the progressive nations do so.

II. No, we cannot impart it in a co-educational school.

28. Statement Should there be a ban on product advertisements ?

Arguments

I. No, it is an age of advertising. unless your advertisement is better than that of your other competitors, the products will not be sold.

II. Yes, the money spent on advertising is very huge and it inflates the cost of the products.

29. Statement Should the government levy tax on agricultural income also?

Arguments

I. Yes, that is the only way to fill Government's coffer.

II. No, 80% of our population live in rural areas.

30. Statement Should graduation be made minimum educational qualification for entry level jobs in any public sector organisation?

Arguments « Canara Bank (PO) 2007

I. Yes, graduates always perform better than non-graduates by virtue of their higher level of education.

II. No, there are quite a few people who cannot afford to remain unemployed till the completion of graduation and are capable of performing equally well as the graduate candidates.

31. Statement Should the examination bodies for all university examinations permit the use of calculators?

Arguments « Canara Bank (PO) 2007

I. No, it is necessary for the students to know the methods of manual calculation to make their concepts clear.

II. Yes, manual calculations are no more required with extensive use of computers in all fields.

32. Statement Should the knowledge of Hindi languages be made compulsory for all the employees of public sector organisations?

Arguments « UCO Bank (PO) 2007

I. Yes, it is necessary for dealing with people from the educationally backward strata of the society.

II. No, It is not necessary for every employee to have the knowledge of Hindi language.

33. Statement Should it be made compulsory for all the private sector organisations to reserve quota for socially backward classes?

Arguments « IBPS (PO) 2011

I. No, the private sector should not be governed by the Government rules.

II. Yes, private sector organisations should also contribute in upliftment of socially backward classes.

34. Statement Should the women be advised not to travel alone at night in view of the increasing incidences of rape and sexual abuse?

Arguments « IBPS (PO) 2011

I. No, instead the government should take measures to control such incidences.

II. Yes, it is difficult even for the police department to control such cases.

35. Statement Are the fabulous prices demanded by the art dealers for the original paintings of old masters justified?

Arguments

I. Yes, those are unattainable antique pieces of art, hence, worth their price for the collectors of art.

II. No, modern painters can paint as well, if not better than them and for much less price.

36. Statement Should the public sector undertakings be allowed to adopt hire-and-fire policy?

Arguments « IDBI Executive 2018

I. Yes, as this will help the public sector undertaking to get rid of non-performing employees and will also help to reward the performing employees.

II. No, the management may not be able to implement the policy in an unbiased manner and the employees will suffer due to the high-handedness of the management.

37. Statement Should India make efforts to harness solar energy to fulfil its energy requirement?

Arguments « CG PSC 2013

I. Yes, most of the energy sources used at present are exhaustible.

II. No, harnessing solar energy requires a lot of capital, which India lacks in.

38. Statement Should the major part of school examinations be made objective type?

Arguments « Andhra Bank (PO) 2007

I. No, objective type examination does not test the students ability to express.

II. Yes, this is the best method of assessing one's ability and knowledge.

39. Statement Should government service in rural areas be made compulsary atleast for two years after completion of graduation for the students of medicine? « Andhra Bank (PO) 2007

Arguments

I. Yes, it is everyone's duty to serve the people in rural areas and contribute to their upliftment.

II. No, it cannot be applied only to the medicine students, since anyways they are contributing during their studies and particularly in the period of internship.

40. Statement Should all the factories in the cities be shifted to the outskirts, far away from the main city?

Arguments « Canara Bank (PO) 2007

I. Yes, this is an essential Step for controlling pollution in the city.

II. No, such a Step will lead to lot of inconvenience to the employees of the factories and their families as well.

41. Statement Should the practice of rewarding high scorers be stopped to handle frustration among the moderate scorers? « UCO Bank (PO) 2007

Arguments

I. No, it is necessary to motivate the high scorers and reward is one of the best ways of motivating.

II. Yes, too much appreciation for high scores affects the moderate students adversely at times leading to extreme situations.

42. Statement Should there be a total ban on use of plastic bags? « UCO Bank (PO) 2007

Arguments

I. No, instead the thickness of plastic bags, which can be used without much damage to the environment, should be specified.

II. Yes, use of plastic bags causes various problems like water pollution and water logging and hence, it is necessary to ban it.

43. Statement Should there be a complete ban on sale of soft drinks within the premises of all the schools in India?

Arguments

I. Yes, this will considerably decrease the consumption of such drinks by the school children as these contain harmful chemicals.

II. No, the authorities do not have right to impose such restriction in a democratic country.

44. Statement Should there be a complete ban on use of chemical pesticides in the agricultural fields?

Arguments

I. No, the crops will get damaged by the pests as almost each crop is attacked by pests during its life cycle.

II. Yes, this pollutes the environment and also contaminates ground water, instead biological pesticides should be used.

45. Statement Should English be the medium of instruction for higher education in India?

Arguments

I. Yes, even in advanced countries like UK and USA, the medium of instruction is English for higher education.

II. Yes, English is much widely spoken language in the world today.

46. Statement Should religion be taught in our schools?

Arguments

I. No, ours is a secular state.

II. Yes, teaching religion helps inculcate moral values among children.

47. Statement Is India going to have elections in near future?

Arguments

I. Yes, some of the political parties are creating a situation that demands elections.

II. No, our Prime Minister is a strong man, has a good support and will complete his term.

48. Statement Does President's rule in a State improve law and order in the disturbed areas?

Arguments

I. Yes, the Chief Minister does not know how to cope with the deteriorating conditions of law and order.

II. President rule is better than rule by State Government.

49. Statement Can the young enjoy the old movies?

Arguments

I. Yes, the movies of these days have no proper story.

II. No, the old movies lack the glamour and fastness of modern movies.

50. Statement Should adulteration in food stuff be considered serious crime?

Arguments

I. Yes, the stuff may cause ill health and sometimes result in the death of the poor victims.

II. No, the things that are mixed with food stuff are not really poisonous.

51. Statement Should private sector be permitted to operate telephone services?

Arguments

I. Yes, they are operating in advanced Western countries.

II. No, it is risky to put them in private hands.

52. **Statement** Should so much of money be spent on games and sports?

Arguments

I. Yes, we are a rich nation and can easily spare any amount of money for games and sports.

II. No, our teams are unable to put up a good show in international competitions.

53. **Statement** Are educational institutions responsible for unrest among the youth?

Arguments

I. Yes, there is no discipline in educational institutions.

II. No, there is no disciplinary problem in educational institutions.

54. **Statement** Should coal engines be replaced by electric engines in trains?

Arguments

I. Yes, coal engines cause a lot of pollution.

II. No, India does not produce enough electricity to fulfil even the domestic needs.

55. **Statement** Do discussions lead to solutions of disputes?

Arguments

I. Yes, all the pros and cons are weighted in their proper perspectives and the right solution is reached.

II. No, no one is really convinced.

56. **Statement** Is the verdict of a judge always just and the right one?

Arguments

I. Yes, the judges are very learned and intelligent.

II. No, tricky lawyer and false evidence often twist the case and mislead the judge.

57. **Statement** Is investment of money in insurance policies a wise step?

Arguments

I. Yes, it ensures security and covers risks.

II. No, by the time the policy matures, the value of money falls down considerably.

58. **Statement** Should one close relative of a retiring government employee be given a job in government in India? « IDBI Executive 2018

Arguments

I. Yes, where else will the relative get a job like this?

II. No, it will close doors of government service to competent and needy youth.

59. **Statement** Should cottage industries be encouraged in rural areas?

Arguments

I. Yes, rural people are creative.

II. Yes, this would help to solve the problem of unemployment to some extent.

60. **Statement** Do commoners, who marry distinguished persons, have a happy life?

Arguments

I. Yes, they get so much honour and respect.

II. No, their spouse and in laws don't respect them sufficiently and treat them with contempt.

61. **Statement** Should little children be loaded with such heavy school bags?

Arguments

I. Yes, a heavy bag means more knowledge.

II. No, heavy school bags spoil the posture of the children.

62. **Statement** Do children adopted from poor families love their new rich parents like their own poor ones?

Arguments

I. Yes, because they are loved, cared for and provided with comforts of life.

II. No, because in the criminal world, they become selfish and hard boiled.

63. **Statement** Should the term of the elected members of Parliament be reduced to two years in India?

Arguments « IDBI Executive 2018

I. Yes, even otherwise the election are generally held every alternate year in India.

II. No, every round of Parliament election needs huge amount of money and It's a national waste.

64. **Statement** Should competitive examinations for selecting candidates for job consist through objective test only?

Arguments

I. Yes, the assessment of objective test is reliable.

II. No, the number of questions to be answered is always very large.

65. **Statement** Should strikes in the field of education be banned?

Arguments

I. Yes, it is against professional ethics.

II. Yes, it affects the students adversely.

DIRECTION (Q. No. 66) *In the following question, a statement is given followed by two statements numbered as* I *and* II. *You have to read both the statements and decide which of them strengthens or weakens the statements.* « IBPS Clerk (Mains) 2018

66. The company A used to outsource its recruitment process for some years but this year the company has decided to conduct the recruitment process within the organisation.

I. The employees who have been working in the organisation are aware of that hard work is required to work in the company.

II. The company has decided to appoint three new persons in its senior level authority for the smooth recruitment process.

(a) Both I and II strengthens
(b) I strengthen while II weakens
(c) II strengthens while I is neutral
(d) Statement I and Statement II is neutral
(e) Both I and II weakens

Answers WITH EXPLANATIONS

1. (*b*) Argument I is not strong because word 'only' makes the argument weak as it is not the only real and practical solution to improve the level of literacy. Argument II is strong as it describes the practical problem which may arise out of the decision of making education free in India.

2. (*c*) It is very clear that encouragement to the young entrepreneurs will open up the fields for setting up of new industries. Therefore, it will help in industrial development. Consequently, more job opportunities will be created. Thus, both the arguments are strong.

3. (*c*) Both the arguments refer to the practical consequences of the action mentioned in the statement and hence, are strong.

4. (*b*) The luxury hotels are symbols of country's development and a place for staying the affluent foreign tourists. So, Argument II is a strong one. Argument I is a weak argument because there is no strong evidence that international crime operates from luxury hotels. Moreover banning will not eliminate the crime instead making stringent laws and impleting them will be desirable step.

5. (*c*) Both the arguments are strong, as educational institutes think about educational environment. But at the same time talent of students should also be nurtured.

6. (*b*) Only Argument II is strong as services from the government organisation cannot be handed over to private institutions.

7. (*c*) Both the arguments are strong, teenager of 21st century are expected to be successful and they do not accept failures which in turn gives birth to stress. But stress is also a relative perception and can be managed with proper guidance.

8. (*a*) Argument I is strong because it will reduce the problem of black marketing of commodities supplied under PDS. Argument II is not strong because it is not directly related with the statement.

9. (*a*) As per the statement, if one year of army training be compulsory for all Indian citizens, then it is not so beneficial because the cost of training will be prohibitive and one year of labour will be lost. It is not necessary to join army to be a better citizen.

10. (*d*) Argument I is weak, as it is totally gender biased and absurd.
Argument II is also weak, as it is a socially regressive mindset. Educating girls will make them more stronger both socially and financially.
∴ Both the arguments are weak.

11. (*b*) Argument II is strong because the organisations are profit making, so government can reduce budgetary deficit by selling its stake in the organisation.

12. (*a*) Argument I is strong because competition increases the quality of service. From the statement, it is not clear that railways is a non-profitable sector and private companies are also operating in non-profitable sectors. So, Argument II is not strong.

13. (*b*) Argument I is weak because not every advertisement is immoral.
Argument II is strong as advertisement bring in revenue which helps reduce cost for viewers.

14. (*b*) Argument I is not strong because it does not tell that why the grievances of people will increase. Argument II is strong because it will reduce the power theft which has resulted in annual pilfenge of a huge amount.

15. (*a*) No, children should not be prevented completely from watching the television because we get vital information regarding education through television and it does not hamper the study of children, if it is watched in limits. So, Argument I is strong, while Argument II is weak.

16. (*a*) Argument I is strong because to ensure quality of medical education with advancing medical field, we need more and more competent and knowledgable people. Hence for this medical test should be made compulsary.
Argument I is weak as making medical entrance test compulsary doesn't deprive rural and urban children out of education. Infact it promotes students to work hard and gain more and more knowledge.

17. (*a*) Argument I is strong because if there will be only one captain, then the descision will be quick otherwise conflicting ideas will only lead to ambiguous situations.
Argument II is weak, as having one captain doesn't forbid him to consult other members of his team. He can take advice and suggestions from his team members.

18. (*a*) Argument I is strong as speed breakers reduces speed.
Argument II is weak as people fails to see speed breakers because of the absence of proper lighting. Road lighting should be improved instead of eliminating speed breakers.

19. (*e*) Argument I is strong as improved ambience is desirable. Argument II is strong because segmentation of adults is undesirable.

20. (*c*) Both are strong but both cannot be true at the same time. The sale will either be affected (as I says) or not be affected (as II says). Hence, either is strong.

21. (*e*) Argument I is strong as school is the ground where we prepare the students for the future battles of life. Argument II is strong as examinations kill our creativity, turning us all into mere clerks.

22. (*b*) Argument I is weak because reduction of work load of IT officials is not too desirable a motive.
Argument II is strong as reduced tax collection will have a bad impact on state activities.

23. (*a*) Argument I is strong as reduced tobacco consumption is desirable.
Argument II is weak as such convenience is not desirable.

24. (*e*) Arguments I and II both are strong as there will be greater administrative convenience by forming small states out of bigger states in India. Secondly, it may also lead to a danger to the national integration.

25. (*a*) Private sector is supposed to be more disciplined and efficient than the government sector. Hence, I is strong. II is rubbish.

26. (*b*) An organisation like UNO is meant to maintain peace all over and will always serve to prevent conflicts between countries. So, its role never ends. Hence, Argument I does not hold. Also, lack of such an organisation may in future lead to increased mutual conflicts and international wars, on account of lack of a common platform for mutual discussions. So, Argument II holds.

27. (*d*) The culture of India is very much different from that of the western countries. So whatever is liked there may not be necessarily regarded good here. Moreover, children need not such type of education but they are adults who should be imparted sex education. Knowledge of sex in real sense is not an innate process. So, both the arguments are ambiguous and not supported by a clear cut logic. Hence, both are weak.

28. (*e*) It is a known fact that unless you create awareness through advertisements, about your product, you lag behind from your competitors. Also, heavy cost on advertisements adds to your product. Hence, both the arguments are strong.

29. (*d*) Arguments I and II both are weak, the argument that government's coffer can be filled only with the tax on agriculture is totally irrelevant. Secondly, it cannot be said that all the 80% rural population are poor.

30. (*d*) Argument I is not necessarily true. Hence, it is weak. Argument II deviates from the core issue. Hence, it is also weak.

31. (*c*) Methods of manual calculations are necessary for individuals. Hence, they should be encouraged. Thus, Argument I is strong. Argument II is also strong in its way but since I and II contradict each other, we go for the choice (c).

32. (*a*) Argument I is strong because in public sector organizations, there are some people who are not well educated. Hence, with Hindi language, it will be possible to deal with them. Hence, only Argument I is strong.

33. (*a*) For all the private sector organisations to reserve quota for socially backward classes is not necessary. All the people should get the chance for job. Hence, only Argument I is strong.

34. (*d*) Argument I does not establish proper relation with the statement. Argument II may be an opinion and has not been discussed in the given statement. Hence, I and II both are weak.

35. (*a*) Argument I is strong. Fabulous prices for old master piece are demanded because of their originality and innovative hard efforts.

36. (*a*) Argument I is strong as hire and fire policy will help public sector enterprise to get rid of non performing employes.
Argument II is ambiguous. Hence weak.

37. (*a*) Argument I is strong *i.e.*, India should make efforts to harness solar energy to fulfill its energy requirement because most of the energy sources used at present are exhaustible. Argument II is weak.

38. (*a*) Argument I is strong as the ability to express gives groundness to one's education. Argument II is weak because to call a method 'the best' without giving any reason is a simplistic assertion.

39. (*d*) Argument I is weak because it is not true. You cannot sweep 'everyone' with the same brush. Argument II is ambiguous. It first says, 'it cannot be applied only to the medicine students'. But remaining part of the argument has got nothing to do with this only.

40. (*a*) Argument I is strong because pollution control is highly desirable. Argument II is weak.

41. (*a*) Argument I is strong as motivation is desirable action. Argument II is weak as it is superfluous. It is simply restating the question.

42. (*e*) Argument I is strong as it takes a wise, reconciliatory approach to the problem. Argument II is also strong as water pollution, etc. may severally harm mankind.

43. (*a*) Argument I is strong because soft drinks contain some harmful chemicals which are harmful to school children. But Argument II is not strong because we should and can ban wrong things in a democracy.

44. (*e*) Arguments I and II, both are strong. If there is ban on the use of pesticides, the whole crop will be damaged by pests and if there is no ban on the use of pesticides, then it will pollute the environment.

45. (*b*) Anything successful in other countries may not succeed in India. However, since English is much widely spoken language in the world today and hence, should be adopted, is a strong idea. Hence, Argument II is the strong argument.

46. (*b*) The first argument is not related directly to the statement. But second argument that teaching religion helps to inculcate moral values among children is strong. Hence, the Argument II is strong.

47. (*d*) None of the arguments is strong.

48. (*d*) Both the arguments are weak. Argument I is weak as it is totally hypothetical. Argument II is irrelevant.

49. (*d*) Both the arguments are weak.

50. (*a*) Argument I is strong because adulteration may cause ill health and death of poor victims.

51. (*d*) None of the arguments is strong. Argument I is weak because if it is operating successfully in Western Countries, it may not necessarily succeed in India *i.e.*, based on example. Argument II is irrelevant.

52. (*d*) None of the arguments is strong. Spending money just because of being rich is not a valid reason. Argument II is weak because it is absolutely illogical that just because of poor performance in international competitions, we should not finance games and sports.

53. (*d*) None of the argument strongly and logically supports the statement.

54. (*e*) Both the arguments are logical and directly related to the statement and hence, are strong arguments.

55. (*a*) Argument I is strong as it provides a clear logic and is directly related to statement. Argument II is without logic and hence, is a weak argument.

56. (*b*) Verdict of judge depends on evidences and pleading of advocate, hence Argument I is weak. Argument II is strong as false evidence can mislead the judge.

57. (*a*) Argument I is strong because insurance is meant to cover the risk and promotes savings. Argument II lacks clear logic.

58. (*b*) Argument I is weak as it is absurd. Any educated and hard working person should get job according to his/her capability. Argument II is strong as giving jobs to their relatives will leads to nepotism and favoritism and will close the door for competent and hard working youth.

59. (*b*) Argument II is strong as cottage industries will definitely solve the problem of unemployment in rural areas. Argument I is not logical.

60. (*d*) Both the arguments are not strong because both the arguments do not contain any logic.

61. (*d*) None of the arguments is strong. Argument I is weak because heavy bag is not related at all with more knowledge. Argument II is weak because heavy bag is also not related with the posture of the children.

62. (*a*) If poor children are loved, cared for and provided with comforts of life, they will definitely respond strongly and positively in terms of respect to their parents. Argument II is not strong.

63. (*e*) Both the arguments are strong as concluding elections every alternate year will be very impractical.
Huge amount of money is also masted in the process of election and it is a national waste.

64. (*a*) The second argument that the number of questions to be answered is always very large is very generalised. But the first argument that the assessment of objective test is reliable is a strong argument.

65. (*b*) Argument II is strong. Strike is against the professional ethics is weak argument, but it affects the students adversely, is strong one.

66. (*c*) I is not related to the recruitment process, so I is neutral. II strengthen the statement as the decision to appoint three new persons in its senior level authority for the smooth recruitment process strengthen the recruitment process.

TYPE 02

Three or More Arguments Based Questions

In this type, the questions consist of a statement followed by three or more arguments. These arguments are based on some stated facts or any other aspect to support the statement.

A candidate is asked to check the strength of these arguments and accordingly choose the answer.

Examples given below will give a better idea about such type of questions

DIRECTIONS ~(Example Nos. 8-9) *Each question below is followed by three arguments numbered* I, II *and* III. *You have to decide which of the arguments is a 'strong' argument and which is a 'weak' argument.*

***Ex* 8 Statement** Should there be a complete ban on celebration of various 'days' in colleges'?

Arguments

I. No, there is nothing wrong in celebrating the days and enjoying once in a while.

II. Yes, children are giving more importance to such celebrations than the studies.

III. No, this type of celebration gives opportunity for children to express their feelings.

(a) I and II are strong
(b) II and III are strong
(c) Only III is strong
(d) Only II is strong
(e) None of these

Solution ***(b)*** Argument I is vague because it lacks a proper reason. Arguments II and III are strong as they provide a proper answer to the question. Argument II explains the correct reason for putting a ban on such days. Also, during these days the children can express their feelings, so III is also correct.

***Ex* 9 Statement** Should the minimum age of marriage for boys be brought down to 18 yr?

Arguments

I. No, an 18 yr old boy is not capable of taking responsibility to start a family.

II. Yes, since the minimum age for marriage for girls is 18 yr, the same should be applicable for boys as well.

III. No, the boys should be allowed to marry only after they become self-dependent.

(a) Only I is strong
(b) Only II is strong
(c) Only III is strong
(d) Only either I or II is strong
(e) None of these

Solution ***(a)*** Only Argument I holds strong to support the statement. Argument II shows the comparison between girls and boys, so it is weak and also Argument III is vague.

DIRECTION ~(Example No. 10) *In the question below, a statement is given followed by four arguments. You have to decide which of the following Argument(s) is strong and which is 'weak'.*

***Ex* 10 Statement** Should the consumption of aerated drinks be banned in India?

Arguments

I. Yes, this is the only way to reduce the risk of exposing people to some diseases.

II. No, each individual should have right to choose what he wants.

III. No, there is no confirmed evidence that such products have adverse effects on human body.

IV. Yes, it is banned in many other countries also.

(a) Only I is strong
(b) I and II are strong
(c) Only III is strong
(d) I and IV are strong
(e) All are strong

Solution ***(c)*** Argument I is not strong due to the word 'only'. Argument II is not strong because it is baseless and Argument III is strong because there is no confirmed evidence that such products have adverse effects on human body. What other countries are doing, we should not follow that blindly. So, Argument IV is not strong.

Practice / CORNER 3.2

DIRECTIONS ~(Q. Nos. 1-24) *In making decisions about important questions, it is desirable to be able to distinguish between 'strong' arguments and 'weak' arguments. 'Strong' arguments must be both important and directly related to the question. 'Weak' arguments may not be directly related to the question and may be of minor importance or may be related to the trivial aspects of the question. Each question below is followed by three arguments numbered* I, II *and* III. *You have to decide which of the arguments is a 'strong' argument and which is a 'weak' argument?*

1. Statement Should smoking cigarettes and drinking alcohol by the actors be completely banned in the movies in India?

Arguments

I. Yes, this will significantly reduce the trend of smoking cigarettes and drinking alcohol among the youth in India.

II. No, there should be no such ban on the creative pursuits of the filmmaker.

III. No, the films portray the society and hence such scenes should be an integral part of the movie, if the storyline demands so. « UCO Bank (PO) 2008

(a) None is strong (b) I and II are strong
(c) II and III are strong (d) I and III are strong
(e) All are strong

2. Statement Should sale of vital human organs be made legal in India?

Arguments

I. No, it goes against our culture.
II. No, this will lead to unhealthy practices.
III. Yes, this will bring an end to the illegal trading of human organs. « Canara Bank (PO) 2008

(a) None is strong (b) I and II are strong
(c) Only III is strong (d) II and III are strong
(e) All are strong

3. Statement Should the conscription of citizens for defence services be made compulsory in India?

Arguments

I. Yes, this is the only way to tackle the serious shortage of manpower in defence services.
II. No, instead the compensation package be made comparable to other job sectors to attract people to join defence services.
III. Yes, many other countries have made this compulsory. « Andhra Bank (PO) 2008

(a) Only I is strong (b) Only II is strong
(c) I and II are strong (d) Either I or II is strong
(e) None of the above

4. Statement Should the salary and perquisites of public sector undertaking employees be made equivalent to those in the private sector?

Arguments

I. Yes, this will help the public sector undertaking to attract and retain competent workforce.
II. No, public sector undertakings cannot afford to pay salaries to the level of private sector.
III. Yes, otherwise the public sector undertakings will not be able to compete with the private sector organisations. « Syndicate Bank (PO) 2008

(a) None is strong (b) Only III is strong
(c) Only I is strong (d) Only II is strong
(e) I and III are strong

5. Statement Should the Government order closure of all educational institutions for a month to avoid fast spreading of the contagious viral infection?

Arguments

I. No, the closure of educational institutions alone is not the solution for curbing the spread of the viral infection.
II. No, students will visit crowded places like malls, markets, play grounds etc in more numbers and spread the disease, as they will have a lot of spare time at their disposal.
III. Yes, young persons are more prone to get affected by the viral infection and hence, they should remain indoors. « Syndicate Bank (PO) 2009

(a) None is strong (b) Only I is strong
(c) Only III is strong (d) I and II are strong
(e) All are strong

6. Statement Should the Government ban export of all types of foodgrains for the next one year to tide over the unpredicted drought situation in the country?

Arguments

I. Yes, there is no other way to provide food to its citizens during the year.
II. No, the Government does not have its jurisdiction over private exporters for banning export.
III. Yes, the Government should not allow the exporters to export foodgrains and procure all the foodgrains held by such exporters and make it available for home consumption.

(a) I and II are strong (b) II and III are strong
(c) I and III are strong (d) All are strong
(e) None of these

7. Statement Should there be a limit on drawing ground water for irrigation purposes in India?

Arguments

I. No, irrigation is of prime importance for food production in India and it is heavily dependent on ground water in many parts of the country.
II. Yes, water tables have gone down to alarmingly low levels in some parts of the country where irrigation is primarily dependent on ground water, which may lead to serious environmental consequences.
III. Yes, India just cannot afford to draw groundwater any further as the international agencies have cautioned India against it.

(a) I and II are strong (b) II and III are strong
(c) I and III are strong (d) All are strong
(e) None of these

8. Statement Should there be a complete ban on setting up thermal power plants in India?

Arguments « UCO Bank (PO) 2010

I. Yes, this is the only way to control further addition to environmental pollution.
II. No, there is a huge shortage of electricity in most parts of the country and hence, generation of electricity needs to be augmented.
III. No, many developed countries continue to set up thermal power plants in their countries.

(a) None is strong (b) Only I is strong
(c) Only II is strong (d) Only III is strong
(e) Either I or II is strong

9. Statement Should there be a restriction on the construction of high rise buildings in big cities in India?

Arguments « UCO Bank (PO) 2010

I. No, big cities in India do not have adequate open land plots to accommodate the growing population.
II. Yes, only the builders and developers benefit from the construction of high-rise buildings.
III. Yes, the government should first provide adequate infrastructural facilities to the existing buildings before allowing the construction of new high-rise buildings.

(a) Only II is strong (b) Only III is strong
(c) I and III are strong (d) Only I is strong
(e) None of the above

10. Statement Should road repair work in big cities be carried out only late at night?

Arguments

I. No, this way the work will never get completed.

II. No, there will be unnecessary use of electricity.

III. Yes, the commuters will face a lot of problems due to repair work during the day. « Canara Bank (PO) 2010

(a) None is strong (b) Only I is strong
(c) Only III is strong (d) I and III are strong
(e) I and II are strong

11. Statement Should all the deemed universities be derecognised and attached to any of the Central or state universities in India?

Arguments

I. Yes, many of these deemed universities do not conform to the required standards of a full-fledged university and hence, the level of education is compromised with.

II. No, these Deemed Universities have been able to introduce innovative courses suitable to the requirement of various industries as they are free from strict Government controls.

III. Yes, many such universities are basically money spinning activities and education takes a backseat in these institutions. « Canara Bank (PO) 2010

(a) I and II are strong (b) II and III are strong
(c) I and III are strong (d) All are strong
(e) None of the above

12. Statement Should the Government impose restrictions on access to sensitive information to the journalists to avoid the media hype?

Arguments

I. Yes, the media creates hype and publishes distorted information at times.

II. No, journalists should have an access to all the information as media is the best source to expose the malfunction sin the society.

III. Yes, at times it leads to harassment of those who are affected and alleged to be involved in the crisis.

(a) All I, II and III are strong
(b) I and II are strong
(c) II and III are strong
(d) Only II is strong
(e) None is strong

13. Statement Should the Government introduce a system of obtaining bond from students for working in India before sanctioning education loan for higher studies?

Arguments

I. No, this is not a workable solution and will obstruct the development of young talent in the country.

II. Yes, this is the only way to ensure use of the talent of our country for the development of the country and not only an individual.

III. No, this step will be too harsh.

(a) Only I is strong (b) Only II is strong
(c) Only I and II are strong (d) None is strong
(e) None of these

14. Statement Should there be only few banks in place of numerous smaller banks in India?

Arguments « SBI (PO) 2012

I. Yes, This will help secure the investor's money as these big banks will be able to withstand intermittent market related shocks.

II. No, A large number of people will lose their jobs as after the merger many employees will be redundant.

III. Yes, This will help consolidate the entire banking industry and will lead to healthy competition.

(a) None is strong
(b) Only I and II are strong
(c) Only II and III are strong
(d) Only I and III are strong
(e) All are strong

15. Statement Should there be a complete ban on registration of new cars for a few months in the big cities in India?

Arguments

I. Yes, this will significantly reduce the number of cars on the already overcrowded roads of the big cities in India.

II. Yes, the existing car owners will be very happy as they will face less traffic snarls in peak hours.

III. No, this is highly discriminatory against those who decide to buy cars now and hence should not be enforced.

(a) Only I is strong (b) I and III are strong
(c) Only III is strong (d) All are strong
(e) None of these

16. Statement Should there be a complete ban on genetically modified imported seeds?

Arguments

I. Yes, this will boost the demand of domestically developed seeds.

II. No, this is the only way to increase production substantially.

III. Yes, genetically modified products will adversely affect the health of those who consume these products.

(a) I and II are strong (b) Only II is strong
(c) II and III are strong (d) I and III are strong
(e) All are strong

17. Statement Should there be a complete ban on Indian professionals seeking jobs elsewhere after getting their education in India?

Arguments

I. Yes, this is the only way to sustain present rate of technological development in India.

II. No, the Indians settled abroad send huge amount of foreign exchange and this constitutes a significant part of foreign exchange reserve.

III. No, the practical knowledge gained by Indians by working in other countries help India to develop its economy.

(a) None is strong (b) All are strong
(c) I and II are strong (d) Only III is strong
(e) II and III are strong

18. **Statement** Should there be a common syllabus for all subjects in graduate courses in all the universities across the country?

Arguments

I. Yes, this is the only way to spring in uniformity in the education system in the country.

II. Yes, it will help standardise the quality of graduation certificates being given by different universities in the country.

III. No, each university should have the autonomy to decide its syllabus based on the specific requirement of the university. « RBI (Grade 'B') 2009

(a) None is strong (b) Only I is strong
(c) Only II is strong (d) I and II are strong
(e) II and III are strong

19. **Statement** Should all those students who failed in one or two subjects in HSC be allowed to take admission in degree courses and continue their study, subject to their successfully passing in the supplementary examination?

Arguments

I. Yes, this will help the students to complete their education without a break of one year.

II. Yes, this is a forward looking strategy to help the students and motivate them for higher studies.

III. No, such students do not choose to continue their studies without having passed in all the subjects in HSC.

(a) Only I is strong
(b) Only II is strong
(c) Only III is strong
(d) Either II or III and I are strong
(e) None of the above

20. **Statement** Should all the students graduating in any discipline desirous of pursuing post-graduation of the subjects of their choice be allowed to enroll in the post-graduate courses?

Arguments

I. Yes, the students are the best judge of their capabilities and there should not be restriction for joining post-graduate courses.

II. No, the students need to study relevant subjects in graduate courses to enroll in post-graduate courses and the students must fulfill such conditions.

III. No, there are not enough institutes offering post-graduate courses which can accommodate all the graduates desirous of seeking post-graduate education of their own choice.

(a) All are strong (b) I and II are strong
(c) II and III are strong (d) I and III are strong
(e) None of these

21. **Statement** Should admission to all professional courses be made on the basis of past academic performance rather than through entrance tests?

Arguments

I. Yes, it will be beneficial for those candidates who are unable to bear the expenses of entrance tests.

II. Yes, many deserving candidates securing high marks in their qualifying academic examinations do not perform well on such entrance tests.

III. No, the standard of examinations and assessment conducted by different boards and universities are not comparable and hence there is a need to conduct entrance tests to calibrate them on a common yardstick.

(a) I and II are strong (b) II and III are strong
(c) I and III are strong (d) III is strong
(e) All are strong

22. **Statement** Should 'literacy' be the minimum criterion for becoming a voter in India?

Arguments

I. No, mere literacy is no guarantee of political maturity of an individual.

II. Yes, illiterate people are less likely to make politically wiser decisions of voting for a right candidate or party.

III. No, voting is the constitutional right of every citizen.

(a) None is strong (b) I and II are strong
(c) III is strong (d) II and III are strong
(e) All are strong

23. **Statement** Should the public sector undertakings be allowed to adopt hire and fire policy?

Arguments

I. Yes, this will help the public sector undertakings to get rid of non-performing employees and reward the performing employees.

II. No, this will give an unjust handle to the management and they may use it indiscriminately.

III. Yes, this will help increase the level of efficiency of these organisation and these will become profitable establishments.

(a) None is strong (b) I and II are strong
(c) II and III are strong (d) I and III are strong
(e) All are strong

24. **Statement** Should all the indirect taxes in India be combined into a single tax on all commodities?

Arguments

I. Yes, this will considerably simplify the tax collection mechanism and the cost of collecting tax will also reduce.

II. Yes, the manufacturers and traders will be benefited by this which in turn will boost tax collections.

III. No, no other country has adopted such system.

(a) None is strong (b) I and III are strong
(c) Only II is strong (d) II and III are strong
(e) None of these

DIRECTIONS ~ (Q. Nos. 25-31) *In making decisions about important questions, it is desirable to be able to distinguish between 'strong' arguments and 'weak' arguments. 'Strong' arguments must be both important and directly related to the question. 'Weak' arguments may not be directly related to the question and may be of minor importance or may be related to the trivial aspects of the question. Each question below is followed by four arguments numbered* I, II, III *and* IV. *You have to decide which of the arguments is a 'strong' argument and which is a 'weak' argument?*

25. Statement Should the rule of wearing helmet for both driver and pillion rider while driving a motor bike be enforced strictly?

Arguments

I. Yes, it is a rule and should be followed strictly by all.
II. No, each individual knows how to protect his own life and it should be left to this discretion.
III. No, it does not ensure safety as only the head is protected and rest of the body is not.
IV. Yes, it is a necessity as head, being the most sensitive organ, is protected by the helmet.

(a) None is strong
(b) I and III are strong
(c) I and IV are strong
(d) II and IV are strong
(e) All are strong

26. Statement Should all the management institutes in the country be brought under government control?

Arguments

I. No, the government does not have adequate resources to run such institutes effectively.
II. No, each institute should be given freedom to function on its own.
III. Yes, this will enable to have standarised education for all the students.
IV. Yes, only then the quality of education would be improved.

(a) None is strong
(b) I, II and III are strong
(c) I and II are strong
(d) All are strong
(e) Only III is strong

27. Statement Is it necessary that education should be job oriented?

Arguments

I. Yes, the aim of education is to prepare persons for eaone may take up agriculture where education is not rning.
II. Yes, educated person should stand on his own feet after completion of education.
III. No, education should be for sake of knowledge only.
IV. No, necessary. « SSC (CGL) 2011

(a) I and II arguments are strong
(b) III and IV arguments are strong
(c) Only I argument is strong
(d) I and III arguments are strong

28. Statement Should all the school teachers be debarred from giving private tuitions?

Arguments « Syndicate Bank (PO) 2009

I. No, the needy students will be deprived of the expertise of these teachers.
II. Yes, this is an injustice to the unemployed educated people who can earn their living by giving tuitions.
III. Yes, only then the quality of teaching in schools will improve.
IV. Yes, now salary of these teachers is reasonable.

(a) I and III are strong
(b) I, II and III are strong
(c) III and IV are strong
(d) II, III and IV are strong
(e) None of these

29. Statement Should people with educational qualification higher than the optimum requirements be debarred from seeking jobs?

Arguments

I. No, it will further aggravate the problem of educated unemployment.
II. Yes, it creates complexes among employees and affects the work adversely.
III. No, this goes against the basic rights of the individuals.
IV. Yes, this will increase productivity. « PNB (PO) 2006

(a) I and III are strong
(b) All are strong
(c) II and IV are strong
(d) Only III is strong
(e) None of these

30. Statement Should class IV children have Board examination?

Arguments

I. Yes, this will motivate the children to study and get higher marks and thus more knowledge can be imbibed at a younger age.
II. No, the children will be forced to study and won't enjoy the process.
III. Yes, in today's competitive world the children need to be prepared right from the beginning to face such difficult examinations.
IV. No, this will add pressure on tender aged children and leave very little time for them to play.

« Allahabad Bank (PO) 2004

(a) All are strong
(b) I, II and IV are strong
(c) II, III and IV are strong
(d) I and III are strong
(e) I and IV are strong

31. Statement The Captain Amarinder Singh-led government in Punjab has announced free education for girls in government schools and colleges from Nursery to PhD. « IBPS Clerk (Mains) 2019

Arguments

I. Good social welfare law. It is initially for girls as they are comparatively disadvantaged. Hopefully it will soon be followed by free education for everyone.

II. It is gender biased as if a poor or average person wants to educate his son for higher education he has to pay higher bills. If you are introducing a law/scheme/bills under no circumstance it should not favour any particular gender, if they are really concerned about education.

III. Do not differentiate a poor or average person on gender. A poor boy or man should also get free education as well.

Which of the following argument holds strong for the given statement?

(a) Only II (b) Only III
(c) II and III (d) I and II
(e) All of these

DIRECTION (Q. No. 32) *Read the following information carefully and answer the given question.* « SBI (PO) 2013

Despite repeated announcements that mobile phones are not allowed in the examination hall, three students were caught with their mobile phones.

A. Mobile phones now-a-days have a lot of features and it is easy to cheat with their help.

B. The invigilator must immediately confiscate the mobile phones and ask the students to leave the exam hall immediately.

C. Mobile phones are very expensive and leaving them in bags outside the exam hall is not safe.

D. There have been incidents where students who left the exam hall early stole the mobile phones kept in the bags of the students who were writing the exam.

32. Which of the following among A, B, C and D may be a strong argument in favour of the three students who were caught with the mobile phone?

(a) Only A
(b) Both A and B
(c) Both C and D
(d) Only C
(e) Both B and D

DIRECTION ~ (Q. No. 33) *Read the following statements carefully and answer the given questions.* « IBPS (PO) 2014

33. Cocoas and chocolate products have been used as medicine in many cultures for centuries. Chocolate is made from plants which means it contains many of the health benefits of leafy vegetables.

Which of the following statements weakens the above arguments?

A. Dark chocolate contains a large number of antioxidants which slow downs the aging process.

B. A small study revealed that regular intake of chocolate increase insulin sensitivity thus, lowering the chances of diabetes.

C. Green leafy vegetables have flavonoids which protect skin from UV rays.

D. Chocolates have 3 types of fats one out of which increase the cholesterol level.

E. Cocoas increases blood flow to the retina thus giving a boost to vision.

(a) Only D
(b) A and E
(c) Only C
(d) None of the given statements
(e) Both C and D

DIRECTION ~ (Q. No. 34) *Read the following information carefully and answer the given question.* « SBI (PO) 2013

The convenience of online shopping is what I like best about it. Where else can you shop even at mid-night wearing your night suit? You do not have to wait in a line or wait till the shop assistant is ready to help you with your purchases. It is a much better experience as compared to going to a retail store. —A consumer's view

34. Which of the following can be a strong argument in favour of retail store owners?

(a) Online shopping portals offer a great deal of discounts which retail stores offer only during the sale season
(b) One can compare a variety of products online which cannot be done at retail stores
(c) Many online shopping portals offer the 'cash on delivery' feature which is for those who are sceptical about online payments
(d) Many consumers prefer shopping at retail stores which are nearer to their houses
(e) In online shopping the customer may be deceived as he cannot touch the product he is paying for

35. Read the given information and answer the question.

Company Z and company F launched similar high end cars last year. However, six months later it was found that the popularity of car manufactured by company Z sky-rocketed while the sales of the one manufactured by company F did not pick up at all. Manager X: "The only reason our car did not succeed was the price of the car. Had our car been priced at a little lower value, the sales of our cars would also have been as good as the one manufactured by company Z".

Which of the following weakens the statement of manager X? « NABARD Asst. Manager 2016

(a) Experts have suggested that there is always a segment of population which reviews the car after it has been launched and purchases it only after a certain amount of time has passed after the launch
(b) A few potential buyers had a problem with the fact that the only two air bags while the one manufactured by company F had six
(c) In the past two years, all cars launched by company F were of mediocre quality and needed frequent repairs and maintenance thus tarnishing the name of the company to a great extent
(d) The car launched by company F is available in limited colours, although the owners can request for the colour of their choice
(e) A few other cars launched by company F several years ago had been priced lower than most other cars in the market and they worked very well

Answers / WITH EXPLANATIONS

1. (*d*) Argument I is strong because such a reduction in trend will be a desirable consequence. Argument II is weak as it silent as to what effect the ban will have on the creative pursuits. III is strong as a ban will take away from the power of the portrayal.

2. (*a*) Argument I is weak because talking of culture is irrelevant in this case. Argument II is weak because it is simplistic. We are not told what these 'unhealthy practices' will be. Argument III is weak because it is superfluous.

3. (*e*) Argument I is weak because it is not true. Look at the alternative given in II. Argument II is also not strong because instead of getting into the reason, it provides an alternative. Argument III is simplistic and hence weak. It is argument by example.

4. (*e*) Competent work force is desirable. Hence, Argument I is strong. Argument II does not appear to be true for all PSUs. And even it is true, an argument that takes recourse in helplessness seems to fall short on merit. Argument III is strong as competition is desirable.

5. (*c*) Argument I is weak as it merely tries to evade the issue. Argument II may turn out to be true but it is based on a negative mind set, may be it's mere of an assumption. Hence, II is weak. Argument III gets into the reason and is therefore strong.

6. (*e*) Argument I is weak as it is not true. Argument II is also weak on the same grounds. Argument III is strong as it elaborates on how banning exports would help tackle the drought situation.

7. (*a*) Argument I is strong as it addresses the problem of food scarcity. Argument II is strong as environment is a very important issue. Argument III is weak as 'the caution' part is neither convincing nor mature.

8. (*c*) Argument I is weak because of the use of only Argument II is strong as the country's power need cannot be ignored. Argument III is weak because it is the argument based on example.

9. (*c*) Argument I is strong as space constraints do play a crucial role. Argument II is false as the buyers also benefit in terms of cost and greenery. Argument III is strong as merely constructing new buildings does not make sense. First adequate infrastructural facilities should be provided to the existing buildings.

10. (*c*) Argument I is not true for all roads : work is often done in phases and meets completion.
Argument II is weak : such use of electricity cannot be termed 'unnecessary.' Argument III is strong as it shows concern for commuters.

11. (*e*) Only Argument II is strong, Arguments I and III are weak as 'All' cannot be punished for the fault of 'many.'

12. (*a*) Argument I is strong because at times media can be responsible for creating hype of a distorted information.
Also, Journalists plays an important role in exposing the malfunctioning of the society, so Argument II is also strong. Argument III is strong because it some times leads to harassment of affected person. So, all three statement are strong.

13. (*a*) Only Argument I holds strong because this is definitely not the solution. Arguments II and III are weak arguments.

14. (*a*) All arguments stated do not strongly support the statement because if there are few banks in place of several small banks, then security for investor cannot be ensured. Also, it cannot help to consolidate the entire banking industry.

15. (*c*) Arguments I and II do not provide a strong enough reason for putting up a complete ban on registration of new cars because this is highly discriminatory against the new buyers. So, Argument III is strong argument because it opposes the statement with a strong reason.

16. (*d*) If there is complete ban on genetically modified seeds, it will boost the demand of domestically developed seeds, so Argument I is strong. Argument II is not strong due to the word 'only'. Argument III is strong because genetically modified products will adversely affect the health of those who consume these products.

17. (*a*) In context of Jobs none of the given statement is giving a valid justification in favor or against the statement. None of them is strong enough. Hence, option (a) is correct.

18. (*e*) In Argument I the use of key word only makes it weak. If there is common syllabus for graduation across the universities, then this will standardise the quality of graduation certificates, which is desirable, hence Argument II is strong. Argument III is also strong as specific requirement and autonomy of the university cannot be overlooked.

19. (*d*) Argument I is definitely strong as this will help a student to avoid one year gap that could occur in his studies. Argument II and III are both correct and hold strong but they contradict each other, so only one can be true.

20. (*e*) Students should take subject of their interest at graduate level. At post-graduate level only interest is not the factor to take subjects. So, Argument I is not strong but II is strong because at post-graduate level, students must fulfill the essential conditions.

21. (*d*) Only Argument III is strong because the standard of examinations and assessment conducted by different boards and universities are not comparable and entrance tests help calibrate them on a common yardstick.

22. (*e*) It cannot be said that a literate person has all round knowledge of politics. So, Argument I is strong. Illiterate person can easily be misled on various factors but voting is also a constitutional right of every citizen. So, Arguments II and III are also strong.

23. (*d*) In 'hire and fire' policy, performing employees are rewarded while non-performing employees are shown the door. This increases the level of efficiency and profitability. So, Arguments I and III are strong while Argument II is not.

24. (*e*) Arguments I and II are strong because a single tax will simplify the tax collection mechanism and manufactures and traders will be benefited by it.
What other countries are doing, we should not adopt that blindly. So, Argument III is not strong.

25. (*c*) Arguments I and IV are strong because the rule of wearing helmet for both driver and pillion rider while driving a motor bike should be followed strightly by all. It protects our head which is the most sensitive organ of human body.

26. (*a*) As, these kind of institutes are semi government, they work under government but are not questionable by government. So, none of the arguments has strong reasons to support or to oppose the given statements.

27. (*d*) Arguments I and III are strong. Education is meant for both knowledge and securing a job.

28. (*e*) The lust of earning private tuitions reduces the efforts and devotion of the teachers towards the students in schools. So, if tuitions are banned, students can benefit from their teacher's knowledge in the school itself. So, Argument III holds strong while I does not. However, a person cannot be barred from earning more just because he already has a good salary. So, Argument IV is vague. Further, the unemployed people thriving on tutions can survive with the school teachers holding tuitions too, if they are capable enough to guide the students well. So, argument II also does not hold strong.

29. (*d*) Only Argument III is strong because we can seek any job for which we qualify and stopping an individual from doing this will go against the basic rights of the individual.

30. (*c*) Argument I is not strong as board exams do not provide any criterion to gain more knowledge but they certainly provide a competitive environment to prepare a child to face such exams. Also, it would add an extra burden and pressure on tender aged children and will leave them with less time to play and enjoy. So, Arguments II, III and IV are strong.

31. (*c*) Argument I does not hold strong because this initiative is for girls to get benefited initially but it is not like that education will be free for everyone. Argument II holds strong because a law/scheme/bill should not favour any particular gender. If they are really concerned about education, the scheme should be for the one who really need it.
Argument III also holds strong because the people should not be differentiated on the basis of gender. The poor people should get the benefits.
Hence, Arguments II and III are strong.

32. (*c*) The strong arguments are C and D. As, mobile phones are very expensive and leaving them in bags outside the exam hall is not safe. And there have been incidents where students who left the exam hall early stole the mobile phones kept in the bags of the students who were writing the exam.

33. (*a*) Chocolates have three types of fats, one out of which increase level of cholestrol weakens the arguments because it shows negative quality of chocolates.
Hence, only statement D weakens the given argument.

34. (*e*) We know that, in online shopping the customer cannot touch the product he is paying for.

35. (*e*) Option (c) weakens the statement of manager X.

CHAPTER / 04

Statement and Assumptions

Statement is an information or a fact related to any general subject.

Assumption is said to be hidden because it is generally assumed, supposed and taken for granted.

When we analyse assumption, we find that when one says or writes something, he does not put everything into words and leaves some part unsaid or unwritten. Why does he do so? He does so because he takes this unsaid part for granted.

In other words, he thinks this unsaid part will be understood without saying and there is no need to put this (unsaid part) into words.

e.g. **Statement** "Buy different products from our shop and get 20% discount". An advertisement.

From the above advertisement we can assume following points

(i) People want to get discount.
(ii) The advertisement is given to earn more.
(iii) Generally people read advertisement.
(iv) The advertisement is given to attract more people.

Except the above assumptions we can assume more. But the main assumption behind the advertisement is to attract more people to earn more.

Conditions for Invalidity of Assumptions

1. An assumption is said to be invalid, if it has no connection with the given statement.

   e.g.,

   (i) **Statement** Hard labour is required to be perfect in Mathematics.

   Invalid Assumption Hard labour is not required for subjects other than Mathematics.

   Reason Nothing has been said in the statement about other subjects.

   (ii) **Statement** "Get the house painted before Diwali", Ranjana tells her husband Aashutosh.

   Invalid Assumption Aashutosh does not need to do what Ranjana says.

   Reason Infact, somebody says anything to anybody with the assumption that he would be listened to. Hence, the given assumption is invalid as it has no connection with the given statement.

2. An assumption becomes invalid, if it is a restatement of the given statement in different words.

   e.g., **Statement** Of all the books published by Arihant Publication, book 'A' has the largest sale.

   Invalid Assumption No other book published by Arihant Publication has as high a sale as book 'A'.

   Reason It is clear that the given assumption is not implicit in the given statement. It is a different form of given statement *i.e.,* a restatement.

3. If the given assumption is an obversion of given statement, then the assumption is said to be invalid. In fact, obversion is a slightly different case of restating the same fact.

   In it, out of subject, verb and predicate, any two are changed into negative which changes the appearance of the sentence without changing its meaning.

   e.g., **Statement** Beauty is lovable.

   Invalid Assumptions

   I. Ugliness is hateable.
   II. Ugliness is not lovable.
   III. Beauty is not hateable.

4. When we study the chapter of syllogism, we find that we convert given statements to get immediate inferences. There are three standard cases of conversion.

Let us see

(i) All X are Y $\xrightarrow{\text{Gets converted into}}$ Some Y are X.

(ii) Some X are Y $\xrightarrow{\text{Gets converted into}}$ Some Y are X.

(iii) No X are Y $\xrightarrow{\text{Gets converted into}}$ No Y are X.

Point to be noted that the given assumptions will be invalid, if they are such conversions.

e.g.,

(i) **Statement** Some cats are dogs.
Invalid Assumption Some dogs are cats.

(ii) **Statement** Some politicians harm the society by distorting facts.
Invalid Assumption Some of those who distorts facts and harm society are politicians.

5. An assumption is said to be invalid, if it is an inference derivable from the given statement. Remember that an assumption is something on which the statement is based while an inference of a statement is based upon the statement.

e.g., **Statement** Sanjeev went to Kolkata on 15th February and Babita went 4 days after him.

Invalid Assumption Babita went Kolkata on 19th February.

6. Sometimes a given assumption appears to be probably correct but is declared invalid as it makes too far fetched reasoning or long drawn conclusions.

e.g., **Statement** All teaching should be done in religious spirit because religious instruction leads to a curiosity for knowledge.

Invalid Assumption Curious persons are good persons.

Reason It is too long drawn to come to the conclusion that religious instructions lead to curiousity and religious people are generally good and therefore curious persons must be good.

Use of Specific Words

1. **Definitive words case** Let us consider some of the keywords like 'only', 'best', 'certainly', 'strongest', 'all' etc. Such words put a greater degree of emphasis on the sentence, they give a certain type of exclusiveness to the sentence which reduces the range or scope of the sentence. Point to be noted that all these words have some kind of certainty associated with them.

e.g. **Statement** Government should take every effort to boost sugar import as its crisis has worsened.

Assumptions

I. Imports are the best solution to avert the sugar crisis.

II. Imports are a reasonably good solution to avert the sugar crisis.

III. Import are the only solution to overcome the sugar crisis.

IV. The sugar crisis will definitely be averted by boosting imports.

V. The sugar crisis will probably be averted by boosting imports.

Solution Valid Assumptions—II and V.
Invalid Assumptions I, III, and IV. Point to be noted that I, III and IV are invalid because of the use of definitive words (best, only and definitely).

2. **Cases of conjunction** If a statement has two clauses and the given clauses are linked by a conjunction, then the nature of conjunction helps in detecting assumptions. Such conjunction may be 'as', 'because', 'so', 'hence', 'therefore', 'despite', 'in spite of', 'even', 'after', 'although', 'as a result of' etc.

e.g. **Statement** You will find improvement in your logical ability after reading a reasoning book published by Arihant Publication.

Valid Assumption A reasoning book may help in improving logical ability.

Solution In the given statement the conjunction is 'after' which helps us is reaching the conclusion that the given assumption is hidden or implicit in the given statement.

Rules Related to Assumptions

1. If A says something to B, it means A assumes that B will hear what he (A) says.

Reason When we say something, we expect we will be heared. Without expecting so, there is no purpose of saying anything to anyone.

e.g., **Statement** 'A book of reasoning published from Arihant Publication will help you a lot in preparing for Bank PO exams', Vandana Advises Aarti.

Valid Assumption Aarti will pay attention towards Vandana's advice.

2. Any form of advertisements are given by assuming that people will respond to such materials.

Reason The purpose of such materials is getting response from targeted mass. Therefore, without assuming response from targeted mass, any kind of advertisement is of no use.

e.g., **Statement** A new approach to reasoning, a magical book by Arihant Publication that gives exclusive materials on reasoning-an advertisement.

Valid Assumption The advertisement have some effect on those who read it.

3. Any form of public interest notice/official notice is assumed to be paid attention to.

Reason The purpose of such notice is to benefit the people/organisation and its ignorance may be harmful. Therefore, it is the duty of authorities to issue such notices.

e.g., **Statement** The civic authorities have advised the residents in the area to use mosquito repellents or sleep inside nets as large number of people are suffering from malaria.

Valid Assumption People will pay attention to such notice.

4. If an appeal is made, it is assumed that the appeal will get response.

   Reason An appeal is made only when we expect a desired result from it. Why will we make an appeal when we do not expect a positive response? Therefore, we make an appeal with a thinking that the desired purpose will be fulfilled through it.

   e.g., **Statement** Donate money, clothes and food items for the victims of earthquake, an appeal.

   Valid Assumption The appeal will have some effect on people.

5. A single statement can have more than one assumptions.

   e.g. **Statement** 'A book of reasoning published by Arihant Publication will help you a lot in preparing for Bank PO exams', Vandana advices Aarti.

   Valid Assumptions

   (i) Aarti will pay attention towards Vandana's advice.

   (ii) Vandana knows the quality of reasoning book published from Arihant Publication.

Chapter tip!

- Assumption should be a general statement.
- The meaning of assumption should be embedded in the statement.
- **Assumption** is always indefinite and positive.
- Some words like only, each, any, every, all question indicating words (why, what), answer indicating words (therefore), definitely, but, certainly exist in the assumption that assumption will always be explicit (false).
- Some words like some, to large extent, many, much exist in the assumption that assumption will always be implicit (True).
- Any assumption is talking about the social welfare (positive), govt. policies that assumption will always be implicit (True).
- Any assumption that is conveying the notice, appeal that assumption will always be implicit (True).
- Any assumption that is talking about the social welfare (Positive), government policies that assumption will always be implicit (True).
- If any assumption is talking about past and future that assumption will always be explicit (False).
- If any assumption showing the word like suggestion, order, request that will always be implicit. (True)
- Restatement is never implicit.
- Assumption should not be more expandable in comparison to statement.
- Statement and assumption should be logical to each other.
- Assumption should not be a conclusion on the basis of statement.

Mainly two types of questions are asked from Statement and Assumptions, which are discussed as under

TYPE 01

One Statement and Two Assumptions Based Problems

In this type of problems, a statement is given which is followed by two assumptions. The candidate is required to analyse the given statement and then decide which of the given assumptions is implicit in the statement.

DIRECTIONS ~(Example Nos. 1-12) *In each of the questions below is given a statement followed by assumptions numbered* I *and* II. *Consider the statement and decide which of the given assumptions is implicit.*

Give answer

(a) If only Assumption I is implicit
(b) If only Assumption II is implicit
(c) If both I and II are implicit
(d) If neither I nor II is implicit

***Ex* 01** **Statement** Get your child examined by a specialist doctor, X tells Y.

Assumptions

I. Y will not listen what X tells to him.
II. Y will hear X's advice.

Solution (b) We advise someone with the assumption that our advice will be listened to. Why will we advise someone with a thinking that our advice will not be heard? While saying something, we go with a positive frame of mind that the targeted people will hear and pay attention towards our point of view. Hence, II is a valid assumption but I is not.

***Ex* 02** **Statement** Patient's condition would improve after this operation.

Assumptions

I. The patient can be operated upon in this condition.
II. The patient cannot be operated upon in this condition.

Solution (a) It is very much implied in the statement that the patient is in a position to be operated upon. Therefore, Assumption I is implicit.

***Ex* 03** **Statement** It is faster to travel by air to Delhi from Patna.

Assumptions

I. Patna and Delhi are connected by air.
II. There are no other means of transport available to Delhi from Patna.

Solution (a) The given statement advises to travel by air between Delhi and Patna. Hence, no doubts, I is implicit. II is the contrary to the given statement. 'It is faster to travel by air' does mean that other means of transport, slower than air transport, are available. Therefore, II is not implicit.

Ex 04 **Statement** The book published by Arihant Publication is intended to guide the layman to study reasoning in the absence of a teacher.

Assumptions

I. Reasoning can be learnt with the help of a book.

II. A teacher of reasoning may not be available to everyone.

Solution (c) It is given in the statement that the book intends to teach reasoning which implies that I is a valid assumption. Further, the statement says that the book is intended to teach reasoning in the absence of a teacher. This means that the absence of a teacher is a possibility. Hence, II is also valid.

Ex 05 **Statement** Buy pure milk of company 'X', an advertisement in a newspaper.

Assumptions

I. No other company supplies pure milk.

II. People read advertisements.

Solution (b) I is definitely not mentioned in the advertisement. II is implicit, otherwise company 'X' would not have given the advertisement.

Ex 06 **Statement** The boy is too clever to fail in the examination.

Assumptions

I. The boy is appearing in a competitive examination.

II. Very clever boys do not fail in the examination.

Solution (b) Assumption I is not valid as it has no connection at all with the given statement. Statement does not specifically say about competitive examination. But II is valid because the statement says that the boy would not fail (effect) because he is very clever (cause). Obviously, it is assumed that very clever boys do not fail.

Ex 07 **Statement** The best evidence of India's glorious past is the growing popularity of Ayurvedic medicines in West.

Assumptions

I. Ayurvedic medicines are not popular in India.

II. Allopathic medicines are more popular in India.

Solution (d) The statement given in the question states only about the place which Ayurvedic medicine had occupied in the past on account of its increasing popularity in West and this signifies neither non-popularity of Ayurvedic medicines in India nor speaks of popularity of Allopathic medicines. Hence, none of the assumptions is implicit in the statement.

Ex 08 **Statement** Most of the classical dance themes are based on stories of Gods and Avatars.

Assumptions

I. Classical arts maintain their heritage by sticking to traditions.

II. New themes are not interesting.

Solution (a) Stories of Gods and Avatars carry the reflection of our tradition. Therefore, the statement implies that the classical arts endeavor to maintain their heritage by sticking to traditions. Hence, Assumption I is clearly implicit. But it is not given anywhere in the statement that new themes are not interesting. Therefore, Assumption II is not implicit.

Ex 09 **Statement** The anti-reservation movement was taken up by all the states.

Assumptions

I. If one state starts a movement, it is customary for the other states to follow it.

II. A major portion of the youths and employees all over the country were not in favour of reservation.

Solution (b) The anti-reservation movement could get acceptability by all the states only because major portion of the youths and employees were not in favour of reservation. Our statement is not based on the assumption that it becomes customary for the other states to follow a movement started by one state. Therefore, only Assumption II is implicit.

Ex 10 **Statement** "If you want to give any advertisement, give it in newspaper 'X' "– A tells B.

Assumptions

I. B wants to publicise his products.

II. Newspaper 'X' has a wide circulation.

Solution (b) The word 'if' in the statement implies that B may or may not be willing to publicise his products. Statement further suggests that advertisement should be given in newspaper 'X'. This means that 'X' will help advertise better. In other words, newspaper 'X' has a wide circulation. So, only Assumption II is implicit.

Ex 11 **Statement** Aim for the stars, you will at least land on the Moon.

Assumptions

I. People aim for the stars because they are bigger than the Moon.

II. Astronomers aim for stars and land on the Moon.

Solution (d) The given statement is a proverb which talks about the positive attitude towards life.

But none of the assumptions follow the statement.

Hence, none of them follow the statement.

Ex 12 **Statement** Of all the cars manufactured in India, 'A' brand has the largest sale.

Assumptions

I. The sale of all the cars manufactured in India is known.

II. The manufacturing of no other cars in India is as large as 'A' brand.

Solution (a) Unless the sale of all cars manufactured in India was known, the statement could not have been made. Hence, I is a valid assumption.

II is not implicit as we do not know about manufacturing, we know only about sales. 'A' brand has the largest sale but it may not be the largest manufacturer of cars. May be 'B' company manufactures more cars than 'A' does but it exports all its cars. In that case 'B' is a bigger manufacturer but its sale in India would be lesser than that of 'A'.

Practice CORNER 4.1

DIRECTIONS ~ (Q. Nos. 1-12) *In each of the questions below, is given a statement followed by two assumptions numbered* I *and* II. *An assumption is something supposed or taken for granted. You have to consider the statement and the assumptions and decide which of the assumption(s) is/are implicit in the statement.*

Give answer

(a) If only Assumption I is implicit
(b) If only Assumption II is implicit
(c) If either I or II is implicit
(d) If neither I nor II is implicit
(e) If both I and II are implicit

1. Statement Want to be a PO? Solve sample paper published by Arihant Publication, A tells B.

Assumptions

I. B will hear A's advice.
II. A knows about Arihant Publication.

2. Statement The next meeting of the governing body of the Arihant Publication will be held after one year.

Assumptions

I. There will be no meeting before one year.
II. Arihant Publication will remain in function after one year.

3. Statement Please do not lean out of the running bus, a notice in a tourist bus.

Assumptions

I. Leaning out of running bus is dangerous.
II. The passengers are likely to pay attention to this notice.

4. Statement 'A' computer, the largest selling name with the largest range, an advertisement.

Assumptions

I. 'A' computer is the only one with the wide variations.
II. There is a demand for computers in the market.

5. Statement The Government has decided to provide monetary relief to the farmers in the drought hit areas. « Andhra Bank (PO) 2007

Assumptions

I. The farmers of the affected areas may accept the Government relief.
II. The Government machinery may be able to reach the affected farmers to provide relief.

6. Statement Even with the increase in the number of sugar factories in India, we still continue to import sugar.

Assumptions

I. The consumption of sugar per capita has increased in India.
II. Many of the factories are not in a position to produce sugar to their fullest capacity.

7. Statement "You must learn to refer to a dictionary, if you want to become a good writer". A advises B.

Assumptions

I. Only writers refer to the dictionary.
II. All writers, good or bad, refer to the dictionary.

8. Statement If it does not rain throughout this month, most farmers would be in trouble this year.

Assumptions

I. Timely rain is essential for farming.
II. Most of the farmers are generally dependent on rains.

9. Statement Food poisoning due to the consumption of liquor is very common in rural areas.

Assumptions

I. There are more illegal and unauthorised shops selling liquor in villages and rural areas.
II. The ratio of people drinking liquor in villages is much more than that in towns.

10. Statement The leader of the main opposition party asserted that the call for chakka jam turned out to be a great success in the entire state.

Assumptions

I. The people in future will support the main opposition party.
II. People probably are convinced about the reason behind the chakka jam strike call.

11. Statement Government aided schools should have uniformity in charging various fees.

Assumptions

I. The Government's subsidy comes from money collected by way of taxes from people.
II. The Government, while giving subsidy, may have stipulated certain uniform conditions regarding fees.

12. Statement Please consult before making any decision on exports from the company.

Assumptions

I. You may take a wrong decision, if you don't consult me.
II. It is important to take a right decision.

DIRECTIONS ~ (Q. Nos. 13-32) *Each of these questions, given below consists of a statement followed by two assumptions numbered as* I *and* II. *Decide which of the assumption (s) is /are implicit from the statement and then decide which of the answer is correct.*

Give answer

(a) If only Assumption I is implicit
(b) If only Assumption II is implicit
(c) If neither Assumption I nor II is implicit
(d) If both Assumptions I and II are implicit

13. Statement Warning : Smoking is injurious to health. « UP Police SI 2017

Assumptions

I. Non smoking promotes health.
II. Really, this warning is not necessary.

14. Statement Most people who stop smoking gain weight.
Assumptions « NIFT (UG) 2013
I. If one stops smoking, one will gain weight.
II. If one does not stop smoking, one will not gain weight.

15. Statement Good teachers develop good students.
Assumptions « UP Police SI 2017
I. Strict teachers give quality education.
II. Students like knowledgeable teacher.

16. Statement Unemployment allowance should be given to all unemployed Indian youths above 18 yr of age.
Assumptions « RPSC 2013
I. There are unemployed youths in India who need monetary support.
II. The Government has sufficient funds to provide allowance to all the unemployed youth.

17. Statement Postal rates have been increased to meet the deficit. « NIFT (UG) 2013
Assumptions
I. The present rates are very low.
II. If the rates are not increased, the deficit cannot be met.

18. Statement Now a days harassment of women in public is increasing day by day. « UP Police SI 2017
Assumptions
I. Easy access to media such as internet results in the corruption of the minds of the youth.
II. Moral education is not properly imparted in the school and college levels.

19. Statement Only dead fish go with the flow.
Assumptions « UPSSSC VDO 2018
I. Fish that are alive will never go with the flow.
II. One must have individuality in thinking and making decisions.

20. Statement "To keep myself up-to-date, I always listen to prime time news on television", A candidate tells the interview board. « RRB 2009
Assumptions
I. The candidate does not read newspaper.
II. Recent news are broadcast only on television.

21. Statement The government has instructed all the private schools in the city to maintain the current fees for atleast two more years. « UP Police SI 2017
Assumptions
I. The authorities of private schools may not follow the government instruction as they are not dependent on government funds.
II. The parents of the students of private schools of the city may still be eager to pay higher fees.

22. Statement The new educational policy envisages major modifications in the education system.
« SSC (CPO) 2007
Assumptions
I. Present educational system is inconsistent with national needs.
II. Present educational system needs changes.

23. Statement Politicians become rich by the votes of the people. « SSC (CGL) 2010
Assumptions
I. People vote to make politicians rich.
II. Politicians become rich by their virtue.

24. Statement He is too industrious to be poor.
« SSC (Steno) 2010
Assumptions
I. Very industrious people also can be poor.
II. Very lazy people can also be rich.

25. Statement If people are intelligent they should be creative. « SSC (CGL) 2013
Assumptions
I. Creativity and intelligence are related.
II. Creative people are intelligent.

26. Statement Inculcate saving habit in your school going child.
Assumptions
I. Saving habit is expected.
II. Good habits should be inculcated from the childhood.

27. Statement The root cause of all social evils is love for wealth.
Assumptions
I. Wealth gives power and makes selfish.
II. All those who love wealth are anti-social.

28. Statement The human body produces Vitamin D when exposed to sunlight. « RRB ALP 2018
Assumptions
I. The human body have Vitamin D even if it is not consumed via food.
II. A large portion of the global population suffers from Vitamin D deficiency.

29. Statement During an exam, an invigilator said, "if anyone tries to copy, I will cancel their exam".
Assumptions « RRB ALP 2018
I. Some students copy during exams.
II. Students will not copy during exams.

30. Statement The attendance of students of public schools has increased by 20% after the introduction of the mid-day meal scheme.
Assumptions « UPSSSC (Mandi Parishad) 2018
I. A meal is an added incentive to go to school.
II. Attendance at public schools was below 100% before introduction of the mid-day meal scheme.

31. Statement Rich people are more prone to have heart attacks. « SSC (10+2) 2011
Assumptions
I. Most of the deaths among rich people are due to heart attacks.
II. Poor people do not have heart attacks.

32. Statement The municipal authority has decided to demolish the old bridge on a bus road for constructing a new flyover. « UP Police SI 2017

Assumptions

I. The traffic department may be able to divert movement of vehicles through alternate roads.
II. The people travelling in the nearby areas may demonstrate to protest against the authority's decision.

DIRECTIONS ~(Q. Nos. 33-59) In each question below is given a statement followed by two assumptions numbered I and II. An assumption is something supposed or taken for granted. You have to consider the statement and the following assumptions and decide which of the assumption(s) is/are implicit in the statement.

Give answer

(a) If only Assumption I is implicit
(b) If only Assumption II is implicit
(c) If either Assumption I or II is implicit
(d) If neither Assumption I nor II is implicit
(e) If both Assumptions I and II are implicit

33. Statement "We need to appoint more teachers", principal informs the school staff.

Assumptions « Andhara Bank (PO) 2009

I. Teachers are available.
II. Present teachers are not good.

34. Statement "Those who are appearing for this examination for the first time, should be helped in filling up the forms", an instruction to the invigilating staff.

Assumptions

I. The form is somewhat complicated.
II. Candidates can appear more than once for this examination.

35. Statement Be humble even after gaining victory.

Assumptions

I. Many people are humble after gaining victory.
II. Generally people are not humble.

36. Statement The income tax rules need to be amended so that there is more incentive for the people to declare their actual wealth.

Assumptions

I. The income tax rules are not proper.
II. Some people do not declare their actual wealth.

37. Statement "Considering that his ministry contains many hawala-tainted ministers, the Prime Minister has a moral obligation to resign", a politician.

Assumptions

I. The politician is not close to the Prime Minister.
II. The politician would like to inculcate moral principles in politics.

38. Statement In case of any difficulty about this case, you may contact our company's lawyer.

Assumptions

I. Each company has a lawyer of his own.
II. The company's lawyer is thoroughly briefed about this case.

39. Statement I can take you quickly from Kanpur to Lucknow by my car but then you must pay me double the normal charges.

Assumptions

I. Normally, it will take more time to reach Lucknow from Kanpur.
II. People want to reach quickly but they will not pay extra money for it.

40. Statement It is dangerous to lean out of a running train.

Assumptions

I. All those who lean out of a train run the risk of being hurt.
II. Generally, people don't like to get hurt.

41. Statement "Buy pure and natural honey of company 'X', an advertisement in a newspaper."

Assumptions

I. No other company supplies pure and natural honey.
II. People read advertisement.

42. Statement The target of a fiscal deficit of 5% of GDP could not be met because of major shortfall in revenue collection.

Assumptions

I. Shortfall in revenue collection leads to an increase in fiscal deficit.
II. Shortfall in revenue collection leads to a decrease in fiscal deficit.

43. Statement The impact of economic sanctions on economy, that is already so weak, could be devastating.

Assumptions

I. Economic sanctions impact only a weak economy.
II. The impact of economic sanctions varies from economy to economy.

44. Statement "Exercise is necessary to maintain good health", the advertisement.

Assumptions

I. Exercise is a pre-requisite for good health.
II. Such advertisements have some effect on people.

45. Statement The railway authorities have decided to increase the freight charges by 10% in view of the possibility of incurring losses in the current financial year.

Assumptions

I. The volume of freight during the remaining period may remain same.
II. The amount so obtained may set off a part or total of the estimated deficit.

46. Statement Subodh wrote to his brother at Bengaluru to collect personally the Application form from the university for the post graduation course in Mathematics.

Assumptions

I. The university may issue Application form to a person other than the prospective student.
II. Subodh's brother may receive the letter well before the last date of collecting the Application form.

47. Statement "Private property, trespassers will be prosecuted", a notice on a plot of land.

Assumptions

I. The passerby may read the notice and may not trespass.
II. The people are scared of prosecution.

48. Statement All the students of a school were instructed by the principal to reach school atleast 15 min before the stipulated time for the coming month. « Andhra Bank (PO) 2007

Assumptions

I. The parents of the students of the school may protest against the principal's instruction.
II. The parents may request the principal to withdraw the instruction.

49. Statement Every year doctors, scientists and engineers migrate from India for greener pastures.

Assumptions

I. Brain-drain has affected India adversely.
II. Better scales and better standards of living act as a bait to lure them.

50. Statement The Government is making efforts to boost tourism in Jammu and Kashmir.

Assumptions

I. Tourism in Jammu and Kashmir dropped during last couple of years.
II. Special discount in the railway fare has been announced.

51. Statement If you don't get desired response to your fund raising campaign through the routine advertisements, appeal to the public's regional sentiments.

Assumptions

I. It is desirable to adopt alternative strategy in case the response to the first fund raising strategy is lukewarm.
II. People contribute in terms of money, if proper appeals are made.

52. Statement If you don't get desired response to your fund raising campaigns through the routine advertisements, appeal to the public's regional sentiments.

Assumptions

I. People in general nurture regional sentiments.
II. Nobody bothers to read advertisements in the newspaper.

53. Statement Government should deploy army to rehabilitate the people displaced due to earthquake.

Assumptions

I. Army can be used for purposes other than war also.
II. Only army can rehabilitate the displaced victims of earthquake.

54. Statement The municipal authority blocked movement of traffic in and around the temple on the main festival day.

Assumptions

I. Very large number of devotees may visit the temple on the main festival day.
II. People travelling to the areas near the temple may postpone their journey by a day unless they have very urgent work in the areas.

55. Statement The police in India have to cope with tremendous stress and strain, while maintaining security and order.

Assumptions

I. In other countries, the police don't have to undergo stress and strain while doing their duties.
II. The police are expected to do their duties without stress and stain.

56. Statement If children are to manage our world in future, then they need to be equipped to do so.

Assumptions

I. The world has always educated children.
II. It is possible to educate children.

57. Statement The cotton crop continues to be poor even after the introduction of improved variety of cotton seeds.

Assumptions

I. The yield of cotton was expected to increase after introduction of improved variety of seeds.
II. The yield of cotton was adequate before the introduction of new variety of seeds.

58. Statement No budgetary provision for the purpose of appointing additional faculty would be made in the context of Institute's changed financial priorities.

Assumptions

I. Appointment of faculty requires funds.
II. There are areas other than appointment of faculty which require more financial attention.

59. Statement Theoretical education does not bring in economic advancement and it lends to a steady loss of confidence and money in the country.

Assumptions

I. There is close relationship between development of confidence and economic development.
II. Theoretical education makes priceless contribution for development of confidence.

DIRECTIONS ~ (Q. Nos. 60-63) *Each of these questions has a statement followed by two assumptions numbered* I *and* II. *An assumption is something supposed or taken for granted. Consider the statement and the following assumptions.*

Give answer

(a) If Assumption I is implicit
(b) If Assumption II is implicit
(c) If either Assumption I or II is implicit
(d) If neither Assumption I nor II is implicit

60. Statement The KLM company has decided go for tax-free and taxable bonds to raise its resources.

Assumptions « NIFT (UG) 2012

I. The KLM company has already explored other sources to raise money.
II. The products of KLM company have little competition in the market.

61. Statement It is felt that when the airline is facing stiff competition coupled with a precarious financial position, the top level posts should be kept open for outside professionals rather than internal candidates.

Assumptions « NIFT (UG) 2012

I. Internal candidates aspire only for getting promotions, without much contribution.
II. Experienced professionals are more likely to handle the problems of the airline.

62. Statement Lack of stimulation in the first four five years of life can have adverse consequences.

« NIFT (UG) 2012

Assumptions

I. A great part of the development of observed intelligence occurs in the earliest years of life.

II. 50% of the measurable intelligence at the age of 17 is already predictable by the age of four.

63. Statement Take this 'oven' home and you can prepare very tasty dishes which you were unable to prepare earlier-an advertisement of X brand oven.

Assumptions « NIFT (UG) 2012

I. The user knows the recipes of tasty dishes but does not have the proper oven to cook.

II. Only 'X' brand oven can cook very tasty dishes.

DIRECTIONS ~ (Q. Nos. 64-68) *In each question below is given a statement followed by two assumptions numbered* I *and* II. *An assumption is something supposed or taken for granted. You have to consider the statement and the following assumptions and decide which of the assumption(s) is/are implicit in the statement.*

Give answer « NABARD (PO) 2010

(a) If only Assumption I is implicit
(b) If only Assumption II is implicit
(c) If either Assumption I or II is implicit
(d) If neither Assumption I nor II is implicit
(e) If both Assumptions I and II are implicit

64. Statement A leading university has begun a practice of displaying results only on the Internet rather than on the main notice boards.

Assumptions

I. All the students enrolled with the university have access to Internet at home.

II. Most of the students referred to the result displayed on both the internet as well as the notice boards earlier.

65. Statement In order to replenish the nutrients in the soil, it is important to grow different types of crops every alternate season.

Assumptions

I. A crop can never be grown for the second time in the same field.

II. If a different crop is grown in the successive season, no additional nutrients such as fertilizers are required to be added to the soil.

66. Statement If farmers want to improve their yield, they must use organic fertilizers in place of chemical fertilizers.

Assumptions

I. Chemical fertilizers have certain ill effects on health.

II. Chemical fertilizers do not produce as much yield as the organic fertilizers.

67. Statement Store eatables in the deep freeze in order to preserve these for a long time.

Assumptions

I. Food material remains eatable even after deep freezing for a long time.

II. It is not possible to store any eatable at room temperature even for a shorter period of time.

68. Statement A leading NGO has decided to open a library containing books and newspapers of all major publishers in a remote village.

Assumptions

I. All other nearby villages already have similar libraries.

II. There is adequate number of literate people in the village.

DIRECTIONS ~ (Q. Nos. 69-73) *In each question below, is given a statement followed by two assumptions numbered* I *and* II. *An assumption is something supposed or taken for granted. You have to consider the statement and the following assumptions and decide which of the assumptions is implicit in the statement.*

Give answer « Syndicate Bank (PO) 2010

(a) If only Assumption I is implicit
(b) If only Assumption II is implicit
(c) If either Assumption I or II is implicit
(d) If neither Assumption I nor II is implicit
(e) If both Assumptions I and II are implicit

69. Statement Banks should always check financial status before lending money to a client.

Assumptions

I. Checking before lending would give a true picture of the client's financial status.

II. Clients sometimes may not present the correct picture of their ability to repay loan amount to the bank.

70. Statement The Government has decided to run all commercial vehicles on bio-fuels in order to save the depleting fossil fuel reserves.

Assumptions

I. It is possible to switch over from fossil fuels to bio-fuels for vehicles.

II. Sufficient amount of bio-fuel can be produced in the country to run all commercial vehicles.

71. Statement To save the environment, enforce total ban on illegal mining throughout the country.

Assumptions

I. Mining which is done legally does not cause any harm to the environment.

II. Mining is one of the factors responsible for environmental degradation.

72. Statement Give adequate job related training to the employees before assigning them full-fledged work.

Assumptions

I. Training helps in boosting the performance of employees.

II. Employees have no skill sets before training is provided to them.

73. Statement Take a ferry or a boat instead of a bus to reach the Kravi islands faster.

Assumptions

I. The islands being in remote location are not easily accessible.

II. Ferries and boats are available to travel to Kravi islands.

DIRECTIONS ~ (Q. Nos. 74-78) *In each question below, is given a statement followed by two assumptions numbered* I *and* II. *An assumption is something supposed or taken for granted. You have to consider the statement and the following assumptions and decide which of the assumption (s) is / are implicit in the statement.*

Give answer « Punjab & Sindh Bank (PO) 2010

(a) If only Assumption I is implicit
(b) If only Assumption II is implicit
(c) If either Assumption I or II is implicit
(d) If neither Assumption I nor II is implicit
(e) If both Assumptions I and II are implicit

74. Statement A very large number of people stood in the queue for buying tickets for the one day international cricket match scheduled to be played in the city on the next day.

Assumptions

I. No other one day international cricket match may be played in the city for the next six months.
II. Majority of those who stood in the queue may be able to get ticket for the one day international cricket match.

75. Statement The highway police authority put up large boards at regular intervals indicating the speed limit and dangers of over speeding on the highways.

Assumptions

I. Most of the motorists may drive their vehicles within the speed limit on the highways.
II. Motorists generally ignore such cautions and over speed on the highways.

76. Statement The employees association urged its members to stay away from the annual function as many of their demands were not met by the management.

Assumptions

I. Majority of the members of the association may not attend the function.
II. The management may cancel the annual function.

77. Statement The sarpanch of the village called a meeting of all the heads of families to discuss the problem of acute shortage of drinking water in the village.

Assumptions

I. The sarpanch had earlier called such meetings to discuss about various problems.
II. Most of the heads of families may attend the meeting called by the sarpanch.

78. Statement The municipal corporation advised all the people living in the shanties along the beaches to move to higher places during monsoon.

Assumptions

I. Many people living in the shanties may leave the city and relocate themselves elsewhere in the state.
II. Majority of the people living in the shanties along the beach may try to relocate to higher places during monsoon.

DIRECTIONS ~(Q. Nos. 79-83) *In each question below is given a statement followed by two assumptions numbered* I *and* II. *An assumption is something supposed or taken for granted. You have to consider the statement and the following assumptions and decide which of the assumption(s) is/are implicit in the statement.*

Give answer « Canara Bank (PO) 2009

(a) If only Assumption I is implicit
(b) If only Assumption II is implicit
(c) If either Assumption I or II is implicit
(d) If neither Assumption I nor II is implicit
(e) If both Assumptions I and II are implicit

79. Statement Even though the number of sugar factories is increasing at a fast rate in India, we still continue to import it from other countries.

Assumptions

I. Even the increased number of factories may not be able to meet the demand of sugar in India.
II. The demand for sugar may increase substantially in future.

80. Statement The Government announced a heavy compensation package for all the victims of the terrorist attacks.

Assumptions

I. Such incidents of terror may not occur in near future.
II. Compensation may mitigate the anger among the citizens against the current Government.

81. Statement Many organisations have switched over to online mode of examinations.

Assumptions

I. Candidates from all parts of the country may be well versed using computers.
II. Online mode of examinations helps in recruiting more capable personnel.

82. Statement Government has decided to relocate all the factories from the city with immediate effect to reduce pollution.

Assumptions

I. Pollution in the city is being caused only because of the factories existing there.
II. People may be able to manage travelling daily to the relocated factories.

83. Statement Gambling through lotteries is banned by the Central Government in all the states with immediate effect.

Assumptions

I. This may save innocent citizens from getting cheated of their hard earned money.
II. The citizens may not gamble in any other way, if the lotteries are banned.

DIRECTIONS ~(Q. Nos. 84-87) *In each of the questions below, a statement is followed by two assumptions numbered* I *and* II. *Consider the statement and the assumptions given to decide which of the assumption(s) is/are implicit in the statement.* « MAT 2006

Give answer

(a) If only Assumption I is implicit
(b) If either Assumption I or II is implicit
(c) If only Assumption II is implicit
(d) If neither Assumption I nor II is implicit

84. **Statement** Like a mad man, I decided to follow him.
Assumptions
I. I am not a mad man. II. I am a mad man.

85. **Statement** If it is easy to become an engineer I do not want to be an engineer.
Assumptions
I. An individual aspires to be a professional.
II. One desires to achieve a thing which is hard earned.

86. **Statement** All the employees are notified that the organisation will provide transport facilities at half the cost from the nearby railway station to the office except for those who have been provided with travelling allowance.
Assumptions
I. Most of the employees will travel by the office transport.
II. Those who are provided with travelling allowance will not read such notice.

87. **Statement** An advertisement of a bank "Want to open a bank account! Just dial our 'home service' and we will come at your doorsteps".
Assumptions
I. There is a section of people who require such service at their home.
II. Now-a-days banking has become very competitive.

DIRECTIONS ~(Q. Nos. 88-96) *In each question below is given a statement followed by two assumptions numbered* I *and* II. *An assumption is something supposed or taken for granted. You have to consider the statement and the following assumptions and decide which of the assumption(s) is/are implicit in the statement.*

Give answer
(a) If only Assumption I is implicit
(b) If only Assumption II is implicit
(c) If either Assumption I or II is implicit
(d) If neither Assumption I nor II is implicit
(e) If both Assumptions I and II are implicit

88. **Statement** It is surprising that India beat Australia even after follow on. It happens 2nd time in the history of test cricket.
Assumptions
I. Winning after follow on is possible.
II. India cannot repeat such victory again.

89. **Statement** "We must appoint more subordinate officers on our office staff", the manager said to the chairman.
Assumptions
I. Subordinate officers are available.
II. The present office staff is inefficient.

90. **Statement** The Government has decided to hold the employers responsible for deducting tax at source for all its employees.
Assumptions
I. The employee may still not arrange to deduct tax at source for its employees.
II. The employees may not allow the employers to deduct tax at source.

91. **Statement** The X-airlines has decided to increase the passenger fare by 15% with immediate effect.
Assumptions
I. The demand for seats of X-airlines may remain unchanged even after the hike of the fare.
II. Other airline companies may also hike the passenger fares.

92. **Statement** "Our bank provides all your banking requirements in one location", an advertisement of a bank.
Assumptions
I. Customers prefer to carry out all banking transactions at one place.
II. People may get attracted by the advertisement and carry out their transactions with the bank.

93. **Statement** Imprisonment for 27 yr made Nelson Mandela the President.
Assumptions
I. Only who will be imprisoned for 27 yr will become the President.
II. To become the President, imprisonment is a qualification.

94. **Statement** There has been a remarkable increase in the air traffic in India during the past few years.
Assumptions
I. Travelling by air has become a status symbol now.
II. Large number of people are able to afford air travel now.

95. **Statement** Read this book to get detailed and most comprehensive information on this issue.
Assumptions
I. The person who wants this information can read.
II. There are other books available on this issue.

96. **Statement** Let us announce attractive incentives for better performance.
Assumptions
I. Incentives schemes don't work in long run.
II. The performance can be improved.

DIRECTIONS ~ (Q. Nos. 97-101) *In each question below is given a statement followed by two assumptions numbered* I *and* II. *An assumption is something supposed or taken for granted. You have to consider the statement and the following assumptions and decide which of the assumption(s) is/are implicit in the statement.*

Give answer « Corporation Bank (PO) 2010
(a) If only Assumption I is implicit
(b) If only Assumption II is implicit
(c) If either Assumption I or II is implicit
(d) If neither Assumption I nor II is implicit
(e) If both Assumptions I and II are implicit

97. **Statement** The largest domestic airlines corporation has announced new summer schedules in which more number of flights in trunk routes are introduced.
Assumptions
I. More number of passengers may travel by this airlines corporation during summer months in trunk routes.
II. Other airlines companies may also increase the number of flights in all the sectors.

98. Statement The chairman of the company decided to hold a grand function to celebrate silver jubilee during the next weekend and invited a large number of guests.

Assumptions

I. The company officials may be able to make all the necessary preparations for the silver jubilee celebration.

II. Majority of the guests invited by the chairman may attend the function.

99. Statement The largest computer manufacturing company slashed the prices of most of the desktop models by about 15% with immediate effect.

Assumptions

I. The company may incur heavy losses due to reduction in prices of the desktop.

II. The sales of desktop manufactured by the company may increase in near future.

100. Statement The school authority decided to rent out the school premises during weekends and holidays for organising various functions to augment its resources.

Assumptions

I. The parents of the school students may protest against decision of the school authority.

II. There may not be enough demand for hiring the school premises for organising functions.

101. Statement The local civic body has urged all the residents to voluntarily reduce consumption of potable water by about 30% to tide over the water crisis.

Assumptions

I. Many residents may reduce consumption of potable water.

II. Many activists may welcome the civic body's move and spread awareness among residents.

DIRECTIONS ~ (Q. Nos. 102-106) *In each question below, is given a statement followed by two assumptions numbered* I *and* II. *An assumption is something supposed or taken for granted. You have to consider the statement and the following assumptions and decide which of the assumption(s) is/are implicit in the statement.*

Give answer « BOM (PO) 2009

(a) If only Assumption I is implicit
(b) If only Assumption II is implicit
(c) If either Assumption I or II is implicit
(d) If neither Assumption I nor II is implicit
(e) If both Assumptions I and II are implicit

102. Statement Mohan requested his mother to arrange for food for about thirty persons as he invited all his friends to celebrate his birthday.

Assumptions

I. Most of Mohan's friends may come to his house on his birthday.

II. There may not be more than thirty who may attend Mohan's birthday party.

103. Statement A very large number of aspiring students applied for admission to the professional courses run by the renowned college in town.

Assumptions

I. All the applicants may be able to get admission to the college.

II. The admission process adopted by the renowned college may be fair to all the applicants.

104. Statement The state administration banned gathering of more than fifty people at any place during the visit of foreign dignitaries to the city.

Assumptions

I. People may avoid gathering at any place in the city during the period of visit of foreign dignitaries.

II. Many people may ignore the prohibitory orders and gather to get a glimpse of the dignitaries.

105. Statement The Government decided to levy a toll tax of ₹ 100 for every vehicle using the superhighway connecting the two big cities of the state.

Assumptions

I. Majority of the vehicles travelling between these two cities may not use the superhighway.

II. The Government may not be able to recover the cost incured for constructing the superhighway from the toll tax collection.

106. Statement The teachers of all the degree colleges went on an indefinite strike in protest against the Government's decision to postpone the pay revision to next year.

Assumptions

I. The Government may suspend all the striking teachers.

II. The Government may revise the pay of the college teachers in the current year.

DIRECTIONS ~ (Q. Nos. 107-110) *In each question below is given a statement followed by two assumptions numbered I and II. An assumption is something supposed or taken for granted. You have to consider the statement and the following assumptions and decide which of the assumption(s) is/are implicit in the statement.*

Give answer « Andhra Bank (Clerk) 2009

(a) If only Assumption I is implicit
(b) If only Assumption II is implicit
(c) If either Assumption I or Assumption II is implicit
(d) If neither Assumption I nor Assumption II is implicit
(e) If both Assumptions I and II are implicit

107. Statement The railway authority has rescheduled the departure time of many long-distance trains and put up the revised timing on its website.

Assumptions

I. The passengers may note the change in departure times from the website.

II. The passengers may be able to notice the change and board their respective trains before departure.

108. Statement The school authority has decided to give five grace marks in English to all the students of standard IX as the performance of these students in English was below expectation.

Assumptions

I. Majority of the students of standard IX may still fail in English even after giving grace marks.

II. Majority of the students of standard IX may now pass in English after giving grace marks.

109. Statement The civic administration has asked the residents of the dilapidated buildings to move out as these buildings will be demolished within the next thirty days.

Assumptions

I. The civic administration may be able to demolish these buildings as per schedule.

II. The residents of these buildings may vacate and stay elsewhere.

110. Statement The captain of the school football team selected only fourteen players to play all the eight matches of the interschool football competition.

Assumptions

I. There may be adequate number of football players for all the matches.

II. The captain may be able to play in all the matches.

DIRECTIONS ~ (Q. Nos. 111-113) *In each question below is given a statement followed by two assumptions numbered I and II. An assumption is something supposed or taken for granted. You have to consider the statement and the following assumptions and decide which of the assumption(s) is/are implicit in the statement.*

Give answer « Andhra Bank (PO) 2009

(a) If only Assumption I is implicit
(b) If only Assumption II is implicit
(c) If either Assumption I or II is implicit
(d) If neither Assumption I nor II is implicit
(e) If both Assumptions I and II are implicit

111. Statement Many people fell ill after consuming meal at a wedding reception and were rushed to the nearby Government and private hospitals.

Assumptions

I. The relatives of the affected people may refuse to take them to the Government hospitals.

II. The nearby hospitals may be able to attend to all the affected people.

112. Statement The Government has recently announced an incentive package for setting up new business ventures in the rural areas and promised uninterrupted power supply to all the units.

Assumptions

I. The Government may be able to supply adequate power to all such units.

II. People living in the rural areas may welcome the Government decision.

113. Statement The municipal authority blocked movement of traffic in and around the temple on the main festival day.

Assumptions

I. Very large number of devotees may visit the temple on the main festival day.

II. People travelling to the areas near the temple may postpone their journey by a day unless they have very urgent work in that area.

DIRECTIONS ~ (Q. Nos. 114-118) *In each question below is given a statement followed by two assumptions numbered I and II. An assumption is something supposed or taken for granted. You have to consider the statement and the following assumptions and decide which of the assumption(s) is/are implicit in the statement.*

Give answer « BOI (PO) 2008

(a) If only Assumption I is implicit
(b) If only Assumption II is implicit
(c) If either Assumption I or II is implicit
(d) If neither Assumption I nor II is implicit
(e) If both Assumptions I and II are implicit

114. Statement The General Administration Department has issued a circular to all the employees informing them that hence forth the employees can avail their lunch break at any of the half hour slots between 1 : 00 pm and 2 : 30 pm.

Assumptions

I. The employees may welcome the decision and avail lunch break at different time slots.

II. There may not be any break in the work of the organisation as the employees will have their lunch break at different time slots.

115. Statement The Government has decided against reduction of prices of petroleum products though there is a significant drop in the crude oil prices in the international market.

Assumptions

I. The prices of crude oil in the international market may again increase in the near future.

II. The present price difference of petroleum products will help the government to with stand any possible price rise in future.

116. Statement The Government has made an appeal to all the citizens to honestly pay income tax and file returns reflecting the true income level to help the Government to carry out development activities.

Assumptions

I. People may now start paying more taxes in response to the appeal.

II. The total income tax collection may considerably increase in the near future.

117. Statement The State Government has decided to appoint four thousand primary school teachers during the next financial year.

Assumptions

I. There are enough schools in the state to accommodate four thousand additional primary school teachers.

II. The eligible candidates may not be interested to apply as the Government may not finally appoint such a large number of primary school teachers.

118. Statement The school authority has decided to increase the number of students in each classroom to seventy from the next academic session to bridge the gap between income and expenditure to a larger extent.

Assumptions

I. The income generated by way of fees of the additional students will be sufficient enough to bridge the gap.

II. The school will get all the additional students in each class from the next academic session.

Answers WITH EXPLANATIONS

1. (*e*) Assumption I is implicit as we say something to anybody with the assumption that we will be listened to. Assumption II is implicit because without knowing about a particular publishers, how can we suggest some one to solve/study its sample papers.
2. (*b*) Assumption I is invalid because it has no connection with the given statement. The statement clearly says about meeting of governing body and not about any other meeting. Assumption II is valid as only those bodies that are functional hold meetings. So, if it is announced that next meeting will be held after one year, the announcers must be assuming that the institute will remain functional after one year.
3. (*e*) 'Do not lean out' implies that this act can be dangerous. Hence, Assumption I is implicit. The purpose of a notice is getting response from targeted mass. Therefore, without assuming response from targeted mass, there will be no such notice. Clearly, Assumption II is also valid.
4. (*b*) Assumption I is not implicit because of the word 'only'. 'A' computer has the largest range. But this does not mean that it is the only brand to have a wide range. In case of Assumption II, it is a truth that if computers are being advertised, a demand for them must be existing. Hence, Assumption II is implicit.
5. (*e*) It is the plan of the Government to provide a relief to the farmers. It means the Government must be assuming that the plan can be executed. Infact the objective cannot be fulfilled without Assumptions I and II. Hence, both I and II are implicit.
6. (*a*) **Assumption I** is implicit as it is this that makes us import sugar in spite of the increase in the number of sugar factories.
   Assumption II is invalid because 'future' is beyond the scope of given statement.
7. (*d*) It does not follow from the statement that only writers and no body else refers to the dictionary. Also, nothing is mentioned about bed writers. So, neither I nor II is implicit.
8. (*e*) Since the statement speaks of the essentiality and requirement of rain for farmers, hence both the assumptions are implicit in the statement.
9. (*a*) The statement is talking about food poisoning due to liquor so the number of people consuming liquor in towns or villages is not the main concern here.
   So, only **Assumption I** follows.
10. (*b*) Since, the chakka jam call was accepted by and large in the entire state, it is very likely that people are convinced about the reasons behind the chakka jam strike call. However, it is not necessary that people will support the main opposition party in future without any strong and valid reasons.
11. (*b*) Assumption I is not related with the statement, hence it is not implicit in the statement. Assumption II is implicit as it gives the solid base for the fact defined in the statement.
12. (*e*) It is directed in the statement that consultation is necessary before making any decision on the export. It is, therefore, assumed that person directed may take a wrong decision. Secondly, it is assumed in the light of the statement that it is important to take a right decision.
13. (*a*) Smoking is injurious to health means that non-smoking promotes health and yes, this warning is necessary for various public places, therefore Assumption I is implicit.
14. (*c*) Most of the people who stop smoking have gained weight, that does not mean that if one quits smoking, he/she will surely gain weight or non-smokers cannot gain weight. So, neither Assumption I nor II is implicit.
15. (*d*) Neither I nor II is implicit as the assumptions have no link with the statement.
16. (*a*) Assumption I that Indian unemployed youths need monetary support is the solid base for providing allowances to all the unemployed youths. However, Assumption II that the Government has sufficient funds does not give valid reason. Hence, only Assumption I is implicit.
17. (*d*) On the basis of statement, it is not certain that present rates are very low. We cannot say that increasing the rates is the only way to meet the deficit. Hence, none of the assumptions is implicit.
18. (*b*) Only Assumption II is implicit as increasing cases of harassment of women in public is due to the lack of moral education in people.
19. (*b*) The given statement is a proverb which talks about the thoughts of individual ones.
    Hence, Assumption II follows the statement.
20. (*c*) Assumption I is not implicit as the candidates listening to news on the television does not mean that he does not read newspaper. Assumption II is also invalid because of the word 'only'. The word 'only' disconnect Assumption II from he given statement.
21. (*c*) The government has taken that step after analysing many facts and parents never want to pay more fees. So, neither Assumption I nor II is implicit.
22. (*d*) Both the assumptions are implicit in the statement. Major modifications in the educational system imply that the existing educational system was not serving the purpose very well and there was need to modify it.
23. (*c*) The statement implies that politicians win elections by the votes of people. Therefore, neither of the assumptions is implicit in the statement.
24. (*c*) None of the assumptions is implicit in the statement. The statement implies that industrious people are rich.
25. (*a*) Only Assumption I is valid. It is clear that creativity and intelligence are related.
    Assumption II is not an assumption at all. It is mere restatement of the given statement.
26. (*d*) Clearly, both the assumptions are implicit in the statement.
27. (*a*) Only Assumption I is implicit in the statement. Power and selfishness are root cause of social evils.
28. (*a*) It is clear from the statement that food is not the only source of vitamin D in the human body. It can also be produced by exposing body to sunlight. Therefore, I is implicit. Assumption II is not implicit, as nothing is mentioned about deficiency of vitamin D in the statement.
    Therefore, only Assumption I follows.
29. (*d*) It is clearly assumed that some students copy during exams otherwise. there is no need for the invigilator to issue warning.
    Hence, Assumption I is implicit.
    It is also assumed that students will not copy after the issue of warning Hence, Assumption II is also implicit.
30. (*a*) Assumption I is implicit, as it is clearly mentioned in the statement that attendance has increased by 20% after the introduction of mid-day meal scheme.

But nothing is mentioned about the percentage of attendance.
Hence, Assumption II is not implicit.

31. (*c*) None of the statements is implicit in the statement. Rich people are more prone to have heart attacks. It does not imply that most of the deaths caused among rich people are due to heart attack. Again, the statement does not imply that poor people do not have heart attacks.

32. (*a*) Assumption I is implicit diversion would be necessary when the construction is going on. Assumption II is not implicit as negative reactions are not assumed.

33. (*a*) School requires more teachers. It is assumed in the light of statement that teachers are available but it cannot be said that present staff of teachers is not good. Hence, only Assumption I is implicit.

34. (*e*) It is given in the statement that those who are appearing for the first time in the examination should be helped in filling up the form. The statement is totally based on the assumption that form is somewhat complicated and secondly, candidates can appear more than once in the examination. Hence, both the assumptions are implicit.

35. (*d*) The statement says a man should be humble even after being victorious. This implies that people are usually not humble after victory. Assumption I is just opposite to it, hence is not implicit. Assumption II generalises the statement. Generally, people may be humble, the point is if they are humble or not after victory. Hence, none follows.

36. (*b*) It is given in the statement that income tax rules need to be amended to tempt people to declare their actual wealth. It does not mean that income tax rules are not proper. Proper in what respect is not clear. However, Assumption II describes the reasons for such amendment of income tax rules. Hence, only Assumption II is implicit.

37. (*b*) In his opinion, the politician basically intends to point towards moral principles of politics,. Hence, Assumption II is implicit. Politician may or may not be close to the Prime Minister. So, Assumption I is not implicit.

38. (*b*) It is not necessary that every company has a lawyer. So, Assumption I is not implicit. Since it is advised in the statement that for any difficulty about the case, consult company's lawyer, its therefore assumed that company's lawyer is throughly briefed about the case. Hence, Assumption II is implicit.

39. (*a*) From the word 'quickly' in the statement, it is clearly assumed that normally it will take more time to reach Lucknow from Kanpur. However, it cannot be said whether people will pay extra money for reaching quickly or not. Hence, only Assumption I is implicit in the statement.

40. (*a*) Instruction in the statement is based on the assumption that those who lean out of a train carry the risk of being hurt. It is not inferred from the statement that people don't like to get hurt. Hence, Assumption I is implicit.

41. (*b*) Honey produced by company 'X' is being recommended because of its quality, not because of the fact that no other company supplies pure and natural honey. Since, advertisement recommends it, hence it is assumed that people read advertisements.

42. (*a*) Clearly, the statement is based on the assumption that shortfall in revenue collection leads to an increase in fiscal deficit. Hence, Assumption I is implicit.

43. (*b*) Economic sanctions may also affect a strong economy, hence, it is assumed in the light of statement that impact of economic sanctions varies from economy to economy. Hence, Assumption II is implicit.

44. (*e*) It is clearly given in the statement that exercise is necessary to maintain good health, which means that exercise is pre-requisite for good health. Secondly, an advertisement gives this advice. Hence, it is supposed that such advertisements have some effect on people.

45. (*b*) Nothing can be said about the volume of freight during the remaining period. So, Assumption I is not implicit in the statement. Secondly, it is given in the statement that fare has been increased in view of the possibility of incurring losses *i.e.*, to meet the probable deficit. Hence, Assumption II is implicit in the statement.

46. (*e*) Subodh has written to his brother to collect the form from the university. It is, therefore assumed that university may issue form to other person also and it is also supposed that his brother may receive the letter well before the last date of collecting the Application form.

47. (*e*) Any notice is displayed assuming that it will get desired response from targeted mass. Hence, Assumption I is implicit. Assumption II is also implicit as the notice threatens any trespassers to be prosecuted.

48. (*d*) Point to be noted that, if a person instructs an individual or a group of people, the former assumes that the latter will abide by it. The principal must be assuming the same. Hence, Assumption I is not implicit. Again, Assumption II is no implicit as it has no connection with the given statement.

49. (*b*) The statement is based on the assumption that lucrative offers tempt the scientists to migrate abroad. Hence, only Assumption II is implicit.

50. (*a*) The Government is making efforts to boost tourism in Jammu and Kashmir on the assumption that tourism in Jammu and Kashmir dropped during last couple of years. Therefore, Assumption I is implicit in the statement.

51. (*e*) It is advised in the statement to appeal to the people's regional sentiments, if the desired response to fund raising campaign is not achieved. It is therefore assumed that it is desirable to adopt alternative strategy in case the response to the first fund raising strategy is lukewarm. At the same time, it is also assumed that people contribute in terms of money. Hence, both the assumptions are implicit in the statement.

52. (*a*) It is assumed in the light of statement that people nurture regional sentiments. Assumption II is not implicit because fund raising is also expected from appeal through advertisements.

53. (*a*) It is given in the statement that the Government should be deployed to rehabilitate people which means that army can be used for purposes other than war. Hence, Assumption I is implicit. The word 'only' makes the assumption baseless.

54. (*e*) It is expected that large number of devotees may visit the temple on main festival day. So, municipal authority is blocking the movement of traffic in that area. So, Assumption I is implicit. People travelling to that areas may postpone their journey because of blocked movement. So, Assumption II is also implicit.

55. (*d*) Statement does not compare Indian police with the police of any other country, hence, Assumption I is not implicit in the statement. Secondly, it is not proper to assume in the light of statement that police are expected to do their duties without stress and strain. Hence, none of the assumptions is implicit.

56. (*d*) None of the assumptions is implicit in the statement.

57. (*a*) Improved variety of cotton seeds has been used in anticipation of good crop. Hence, Assumption I is implicit in the statement. Clearly, Assumption II is not implicit in the statement.

58. (*e*) It is clear that appointment of faculty requires funds, that is why it has been stated that no budgetary provisions will be made. Secondly, budget has been restricted to be invested in other areas. Hence, both the assumptions are implicit.

59. (*d*) Neither I nor II is implicit in the statement. The statement does not indicate that confidence and economic development are related.

60. (*a*) Only Assumption I follows.

61. (*b*) Experienced professionals are more likely to handle the professional hurdles.

62. (*b*) Assumption II is implicit.

63. (*d*) To cook good food there is no need to have a good oven or any other materialistic things. The only thing you need is skill.

64. (*d*) Assumption I is invalid as the assumption is that the students have access to the internet. But it is not necessary that they have this access at home. Further, past practice may not have been borne in mind while switching over to internet only display. Hence, Assumption II is also invalid.

65. (*d*) Assumption I is not implicit as it has no connection with the given statement. The need to grow different types of crops is talked about precisely because there is a likelihood of farmers growing the same crop again and again unless instructed. Further, growing different types of crops is important but not sufficient. Therefore, Assumption II is also not valid.

66. (*b*) Assumption I is invalid as the given statement does not focus on health. The sentence 'If farmers want to improve their yield' proves that Assumption II is hidden in the given statement because the word 'improve' itself hints towards the increase of production. Hence, Assumption II is implicit.

67. (*a*) Assumption I must be valid because only then does the storage make sense. Further, the statement has nothing to do with "a shorter period of time".
Hence, Assumption II is invalid.

68. (*b*) Assumption I is not implicit as it has no relation with the given statement. The statement does not give any information about other villages. Further literacy is necessary for a library to be functional. Hence, II is implicit.

69. (*a*) Assumption I is implicit in the norm prescribed in the statement. This is the reason why checking is being advised. However, II is vague. If cross checking is what the speaker has in mind, II would become implicit.

70. (*a*) Assumption I is implicit. The reason is that if the Government has taken such a decision, it must have assumed that its implementation would be possible. Assumption II is not implicit because on the basis of given statement it cannot be said with surety that sufficient amount of bio-fuel can be produced in the country. It is possible that the Government has import on its mind for the said purpose.

71. (*b*) Assumption I is invalid because it is not implied that legal mining does not harm and illegal mining does all harm.
It is only implied that illegal mining is more harmful for the environment. This happens because in illegal mining norms are flouted with impurity. Only a look on Assumption II gives the idea that it is very much implied in the given statement.

72. (*a*) No doubts, Assumption I is implicit in the need for training but what happens in case of II? It takes things to an extreme with the phrase "no skill sets". Hence Assumption II is an invalid assumption.

73. (*b*) Assumption I is not implicit as there may be several reasons for the preference being stated (taking a ferry or a boat). Assumption II is very much valid because we ask someone to employ a means only when we assume the availability of that particular means.

74. (*b*) Assumption I is not implicit as people may like to see this particular match even if other matches are played in near future. Again, when we start in a queue, we hope to get ticket. Hence, Assumption II is implicit.

75. (*a*) Boards have been put with the assumption that it will get desired response from the motorists. Hence, Assumption I is implicit. Assumption II is not implicit because it negates the desired response from the boards put up.

76. (*a*) Employee association urged so because it assumed that members would respond positively. Hence, I is implicit. II is not implicit as it may not be there in the association's mind.

77. (*b*) I is invalid as there is no indication of an earlier meeting. II is implicit in the call for the meeting.

78. (*b*) The corporation has not advised the people to leave the city. Hence, I is not implicit. II is implicit as any advice is given with the assumption that it will be listened to and then listeners will do what the advice suggests.

79. (*a*) Assumption I is implicit as it is this that makes us import sugar in spite of the increase in the number of sugar factories. Assumption II is invalid because "future" is beyond the scope of given statement.

80. (*b*) Assumption I is not implicit as it has no connection with the given statement. Infact compensation cannot be a solution to terrorist attack. Assumption II is implicit because compensation is a way of sympathising with the victims.

81. (*a*) Assumption I is implicit because only then switching over to online mode makes sense. But in case of Assumption II, the switching over may have been prompted by economic factors or those of convenience. Hence, II is not implicit.

82. (*b*) Assumption I is invalid because of the world 'only'. Assumption II is implicit as without considering this factor the relocation of factories would not make sense.

83. (*a*) It is a fact that Government's moves are generally aimed at protecting the interests of the masses. Hence, I is implicit. II is invalid because "any other way" suggests that there might be other means of gambling which have not been considered detrimental for the people.

84. (*a*) If I say that I do something madly, that does not mean that I am actually mad. Infact, it means that I was out of senses while doing that act but otherwise, I am fine. A mad man will definitely not say that "I chased him like a mad man". Hence, I is implicit but II is not.

85. (*c*) **Statement** says that if any task is easy he don't want to do it.
Assumption I says about the nature of job so it is not implicit but Assumption II. follows the statement. Hence, option (c) is correct

86. (*a*) I is implicit as any notification is given with the assumption that targeted people will respond according to the want of such the notification. II is not implicit as notification has been given for all employees and hence all are expected to read it.

87. (*c*) Assumption I is not related to the statement. So, it is not implicit but Assumption II is implicit because banking has become very competitive, so bank officers are trying to earn goodwill of public by giving them good service.

88. (*a*) Assumption I is implicit as if it had not been possible India would not have won after follow on. Further, the word 'surprising' tells that winning after follow on is very difficult and this is the reason it happens only 2nd time. But if it is possible, we cannot say that India will not repeat such victory again. Hence, Assumption II is invalid.

89. (*a*) Here, the manager stresses the need to appoint more subordinate officers. It does mean that present staff is not efficient. In fact, he wants to say that work is much more than the working capacity of present staff strength. Hence, Assumption II is invalid. But Assumption I is implicit because without assuming the availability of subordinate officers, the manager would not have said so.

90. (*d*) Any decision is taken assuming that it will be useful. Hence, none of the assumptions is implicit in the statement.

91. (*a*) The 'X'-airlines has decided to increase the fares assuming that it will not affect its business adversely. Therefore, Assumption I is implicit in the statement. Other airlines may or may not follow this pursuit.

92. (*e*) Both the assumptions are implicit in the statement. The point which is highlighted in any advertisement is liked by people.

93. (*d*) The given statement does not mean imprisonment is necessary. Nelson Mandela's dedicated service to the nation and his struggle for freedom, despite so many hardships won him the desired public appeal to be elected the President. Hence, neither I nor II is implicit.

94. (*b*) The given statement hints that in recent years, the number of people travelling by air has increased. This implies that large number of travellers can now afford air travel. Hence, only II is a valid assumption.

95. (*a*) It is assumed that the person instructed is capable of reading the book. However, we cannot say anything about the other sources of information. Hence, the Assumption I is implicit.

96. (*b*) As in the given statement, incentive is meant for better performance, it is, therefore assumed that incentive will improve the performance.

97. (*a*) The increase would make no sense without passengers. Hence, Assumption I is implicit. Assumption II may be a probable reason but not a necessary one for the increase. Hence, II is invalid.

98. (*e*) We do not hold a function without being ready for the preparation. Hence, Assumption I is a valid assumption. Assumption II is also valid as when you invite someone, you assume that he will come.

99. (*b*) Assumption I is invalid because it has no relation with the statement. Assumption II is implicit as prices have been slashed with assumption that sales will increase, thus leading to profit.

100. (*d*) Both assumptions are negative and hence, invalid.

101. (*a*) Assumption I is implicit as a request is made to the people with assumption that they would comply. Assumption II is beyond the scope of statement because it takes into account the activists. Hence, II is invalid.

102. (*a*) Assumption I is implicit because without this assumption Mohan would not have said to prepare food for almost all his friends. Assumption II is invalid as about 30 implies "nearly 30, may be a few less, may be a few more."

103. (*b*) The word "All" makes I invalid but II is implicit as applicants assume a fair selection process.

104. (*a*) When an order is passed, it is assumed that people will comply with it. Hence, Assumption I is valid. II is not implicit as such an assumption makes the given statement invalid because of its negativity.

105. (*d*) Assumption I is irrelevant while II is contrary to the assumption being made.

106. (*b*) Assumption II is implicit because when workers go on a strike, they assume a positive response. Assumption I is negative to the given statement and hence becomes invalid.

107. (*e*) Assumptions I and II must be valid otherwise the given statement makes no sense.

108. (*b*) Assumption I is contrary to the statement hence, it becomes invalid. Assumption II is implicit as grace marks are given with the assumption that adding these marks would lead to a positive result.

109. (*e*) Both are positive statements and are in accordance with the given statement.

110. (*a*) Assumption I is implicit; otherwise more players would have been selected. Further, even without captain, there will be sufficient number of players.

111. (*b*) Assumption I is invalid and has no connection with the given statement. Assumption II is implicit as if people go to nearby hospitals, they assume that those hospitals will be able to attend to all affected people.

112. (*e*) If someone make a promise, he assumes that he would be able to fulfil it. Hence, Assumption I is valid. Again, since the business ventures are planned to be setup in rural areas, Assumption II must be implicit.

113. (*e*) Assumption I is implicit as the municipal corporation takes this action in expectation of large number of devotees. Assumption II is also valid because whenever we plan something, we assume that conditions will be favourable enough.

114. (*e*) A decision is taken if it is felt that the decision would be an acceptance among most of the people. Hence, Assumption I is implicit. Assumption II is also implicit as the reason behind need.

115. (*d*) It is not necessary that the price rise be there in the mind of Government while taking the decision. Infact the truth is that our petroleum companies are running losses even after the drop in international price. Hence, both are invalid assumptions.

116. (*e*) Assumptions I and II both are implicit because both are imminent positive outcomes assumed.

117. (*a*) Such decisions as given in the statement are taken only after taking the existing vacancies into consideration. So, only Assumption I is implicit while II is not.

118. (*e*) Assumption I is implicit because when a decision is made, it is assumed to be effective. Further, Assumption II is also implicit as it is assumed that the stipulated target will be met.

TYPE 02

One Statement and Three or More Assumptions Based Problems

This type is very much similar to the type I. The only difference is that such problems have three or more assumptions in place of two.

DIRECTIONS ~ (Example Nos. 13-16) *In each of the examples below, is given a statement followed by three assumptions numbered I, II and III. An assumption is something supposed or taken for granted, you have to consider the statement and the assumptions and decide which of the assumption(s) is/are implicit in the statement.*

***Ex* 13** **Statement** Dhoni is the best captain of the Indian cricket history so far, Tendulkar to a news reporter.

Assumptions

I. Other captains were worst.

II. India will not get better captain than Dhoni in future.

III. Tendulkar knows the captainship quality of Dhoni.

(a) Only Assumption I is implicit
(b) Only Assumption II is implicit
(c) Only Assumption III is implicit
(d) None is implicit

Solution ***(c)*** Assumption I is not implicit as it has no connection with the given statement. Dhoni is the best does not mean others were worst. Assumption II is also not implicit because of the phrase 'so far' which indicates that Tendulkar's assessment is for past and present scenario and not for the future. There may be a possibility that India would get better captain than Dhoni in future. But Assumption III is a valid assumption. Without knowing the captainship quality of Dhoni, Tendulkar will not say him best.

***Ex* 14** **Statement** Go and vote out the congress from your constituency, Anna Hazare in his address to the people of Hisar.

Assumptions

I. Anna wants congress defeat in Hisar election.

II. Anna is supporting BJP.

III. People will ignore what Anna said.

(a) Both Assumptions II and III are implicit
(b) Only Assumption III is implicit
(c) Both Assumptions I and II are implicit
(d) Only Assumption I is implicit

Solution ***(d)*** I is implicit in 'vote out the congress'. II is not implicit as nothing has been said about BJP directly or indirectly. Infact, II has no connection with the given statement. Again, III is invalid assumption as saying something to an individual or a group does mean assuming desired response. Infact, we cannot address a mass with an assumption that we will be ignored for what we say.

***Ex* 15** **Statement** Prakash decided to get the railway reservation in April for the journey he wants to make in July to Mumbai.

Assumptions

I. The railways issue reservation three months in advance.

II. There are more than one train to Mumbai.

III. There will be vacancy in the desired class.

(a) Both Assumptions II and III are implicit
(b) Only Assumption I is implicit
(c) All Assumptions are implicit
(d) Both Assumptions I and II are implicit

Solution ***(b)*** In the statement, it is given that Prakash has decided to get reservation three months in advance. This clearly implies that there exists a provision for getting seat/berth reservations three months in advance. Hence, Assumption I is implicit. But nothing in the statement has been given about number of trains and availability of seats in desired class. Hence, Assumptions II and III do not follow.

***Ex* 16** **Statement** Radha wrote second letter to her father after two months as she did not receive any reply to the first letter.

Assumptions

I. Radha's father did not receive the letter.

II. The letter generally reaches within a week.

III. Her father promptly sends reply to her letters.

(a) Both Assumptions II and III are implicit
(b) Only Assumption III is implicit
(c) None Assumption is implicit
(d) Both Assumption I and III are implicit

Solution ***(b)*** It cannot be said definitely that Radha's father did not receive the letter and there may be other reasons for not responding to the letter immediately. Time limit for letter has not been given anywhere in the statement. Hence, Assumptions I and II are not implicit. Since her father use to respond her promptly, therefore after having waited, she had written to her father again. Hence, Assumption III is implicit.

DIRECTION ~(Example No. 17) *A statement is given followed by four assumptions (a), (b), (c) and (d). You have to consider the statement to be true, even if it seems to be variance from commonly known facts. You are to decide which of the given assumptions can definitely be drawn from the given statement. Indicate your answer.*

« SSC (CGL) 2008

***Ex* 17** **Statement** Television has a strong influence in the development of young children.

Assumptions

(a) Children watching TV should be controlled by the parents
(b) Young Children should not be allowed to watch TV programmes
(c) Television affects the academic progress of the young children
(d) While developing TV programmes, educational, developmental and moral aspects of children should be taken care of

Solution ***(d)*** Clearly, assumption (d) is valid. It is mentioned that television has a strong influence in the young children's development. Therefore, while developing TV programmes, educational developmental and moral aspects of children should be taken care of.

Practice / CORNER 4.2

DIRECTIONS ~ (Q. Nos. 1-29) *In each of the questions below, is given a statement followed by three assumptions numbered* I, II *and* III. *An assumption is something supposed or taken for granted, you have to consider the statement and the assumptions and decide which of the assumption(s) is/are implicit in the statement.*

1. Statement Fast Track Objective Arithmetic published by 'Arihant Publication' can do wonders for those preparing for objective competitive exams, an advertisement in newspaper 'X'.

Assumptions

I. Arithmetic is asked in objective competitive exams.
II. Fast Track Objective Arithmetic is the only book on Arithmetic published by Arihant Publication.
III. People read newspaper 'X'.

(a) Only Assumption III is implicit
(b) Only Assumption I is implicit
(c) Only Assumption II is implicit
(d) I and III are implicit

2. Statement Read the instructions before playing the game. « RRB Group D 2018

Assumptions

I. A game is being played.
II. No blind person is playing the game.
III. All the players are literate.

(a) Only I follows (b) All follow
(c) None follows (d) I and III follow

3. Statement "If Mr 'X' does not mend his ways, I will call the police".

Assumptions

I. Mr. 'X' may mend his ways.
II. The police may help me.
III. Mr 'X' was my friend in past.

(a) I and II are implicit (b) II and III are implicit
(c) I and III are implicit (d) All are implicit

4. Statement You should not drink. You must take care of your health, Ramesh tells his friend Ravi.

Assumptions

I. Ravi will heed to Ramesh's advice.
II. Ramesh knows the ill effects of drinking.
III. Drinking is not good for health.

(a) II and III are implicit
(b) None is implicit
(c) All are implicit
(d) I and III are implicit

5. Statement 'Smoking is injurious to health', A warning printed on the cigarette packets. « MAT 2005

Assumptions

I. People read printed matter on a cigarette packet.
II. People take careful note of a warning.
III. Non-smoking promotes health.

(a) Only I is implicit (b) I and II are implicit
(c) Only II is implicit (d) All are implicit

6. Statement The company has decided to increase the price of all its products to tackle the precarious financial position. « NIFT (PG) 2013

Assumptions

I. The company may be able to wipe out the entire losses incurred earlier by this decision.
II. The buyer may continue to buy its products even after the increase.
III. The company has adequate resources to continue production for few more months.

(a) None is implicit (b) II and III are implicit
(c) I and III are implicit (d) Only II is implicit

7. Statement The State Government has unilaterally increased octroi by 5% on all commodities entering into the State without seeking approval of the Central Government.

Assumptions

I. The State Government may be able to implement its decision.
II. The Central Government may agree to support the State Government's decision.
III. The State Government may be able to earn considerable amount through the additional octroi.

(a) All are implicit (b) I and II are implicit
(c) None is implicit (d) II and III are implicit

8. Statement The Central Government has directed the State Government to reduce the Government expenditure in view of the serious resource crunch and it may not be able to sanction every additional grant to the states for the next six months.

Assumptions

I. The State Government is totally dependent on the Central Government for its expenditure.
II. The Central Government has reviewed the expenditure account of the State Government.
III. The State Government will abide by the directives.

(a) II and III are implicit (b) All are implicit
(c) None is implicit (d) Only III is implicit

9. Statement "To make a company commercially viable there is an urgent need to prune the staff strength and borrow money from the financial institutions.", opinion of a consultant.

Assumptions

I. The financial institutions lend money for such proposals.
II. The product of the company has a potential market.
III. The employees of the company are inefficient.

(a) II and III are implicit (b) All are implicit
(c) None is implicit (d) I and II are implicit

10. Statement "Buy 'Y' TV for better sound quality.", an advertisement.

Assumptions

I. 'Y' TV is the only TV in the market.
II. 'Y' TV is the costliest.

III. People generally ignore such advertisements.
(a) Only I is implicit (b) Only II is implicit
(c) Only III is implicit (d) None is implicit

11. Statement "Look at her audacity Madhu has not replied to my letter", A tells B.

Assumptions

I. Madhu received his letter.
II. Madhu did not receive his letter.
III. The letter was sent by post.
(a) Only I is implicit (b) Only II is implicit
(c) Only III is implicit (d) All are implicit

12. Statement She had the ability to be a very good singer but she could not explore herself in that direction, A tells B about D.

Assumptions

I. D is a male. II. D is a female.
III. A and B are close friends.
(a) Only III is implicit (b) I and III are implicit
(c) Only II is implicit (d) None is implicit

13. Statement "Use 'Nova' cold cream for fair complexion.", an advertisement.

Assumptions

I. People like to use cream for fair complexion.
II. People are easily fooled.
III. People respond to the advertisements.
(a) Only I is implicit (b) Only II is implicit
(c) I and III are implicit (d) I and II are implicit

14. Statement "Since no university has responded to our proposal, we shall not depute any faculty member on the course this year."

Assumptions

I. The proposal has been received by the universities.
II. The proposal had also indicated financial provision.
III. The proposal was unanimously approved by the State Government also.
(a) Only I is implicit (b) Only III is implicit
(c) None is implicit (d) I and III are implicit

15. Statement "We must introduce objective type tests to reform improve our examination system for admission to MBA", the chairman of the admission committee tells the committee.

Assumptions

I. The admission at present is directly through interview.
II. The admission committee is desirous of improving the admission exams.
III. The chairman himself is an MBA.
(a) Only I is implicit (b) Only II is implicit
(c) I and II are implicit (d) I and III are implicit

16. Statement The electricity company informed the consumers through a notice that those who did not pay their bills by the due date would be charged penalty for every day of default. « CG PSC 2013

Assumptions

I. Money collected as penalty would compensate for the losses incurred due to delay in making payments of the bills.
II. People generally read notice.
III. Majority of people would pay their bills by the due date to avoid penalty.
(a) All are implicit (b) Only I is implicit
(c) None is implicit (d) I and II are implicit
(e) II and III are implicit

17. Statement "In our report published last week, the name of the author was miss-spelt. We regret the error", a magazine editor.

Assumptions

I. The name of the author was not easy to spell.
II. Publishing correct name of authors is not as important as the quality of the article.
III. Publishing correct name of authors is desirable.
(a) Only I is implicit (b) II is implicit
(c) Only III is implicit (d) I and III are implicit

18. Statement "Wanted a two bedroom flat for immediate possession", an advertisement.

Assumptions

I. Flats are available in the court area.
II. Some people will respond to the advertisement.
III. It is a practice to give such an advertisement.
(a) None is implicit (b) I and II are implicit
(c) Only II is implicit (d) All are implicit

19. Statement A group of friends decided to go for a picnic to Avon during the next holiday season to avoid crowd of people.

Assumptions

I. Generally many people don't go to Avon.
II. People prefer other spots to Avon.
III. Many people know about Avon.
(a) All are implicit (b) Only II is implicit
(c) I and II are implicit (d) I and III are implicit

20. Statement The telephone company informed the subscribers through a notification that those who don't pay their bills by the due date will be charged penalty for every defaulting day.

Assumptions

I. Majority of the people may pay their bills by the due date to avoid penalty.
II. The money collected as penalty may settle off the losses due to the delayed payments.
III. People generally pay heed to such notices.
(a) None is implicit
(b) I and III are implicit
(c) Only II is implicit
(d) II and III are implicit

21. Statement Considering the tickets sold during the last seven days, the circus authorities decided to continue the show for another fortnight which includes two weekends.

Assumptions

I. People may not turn up on week days.
II. The average number of people who will be visiting circus will be more or less same as that of the last seven days.
III. There may not be enough response at other places.
(a) None is implicit (b) Only II is implicit
(c) I and II are implicit (d) All are implicit

22. Statement "Slogans against smoking in office should be put on the notice board", An employee in an office suggests.

Assumptions

I. The employee felt that his suggestion will be considered.
II. People smoke in the office.
III. Some people will stop smoking in the office after reading the slogans.

(a) None is implicit
(b) I and III are implicit
(c) I and II are implicit
(d) Only I is implicit

23. Statement Unable to manage with the present salary, Tarun joined another company.

Assumptions

I. The new company has better work environment.
II. The present company offers moderate pay package.
III. The new company offers higher salary to all its employees.

(a) All are implicit
(b) None is implicit
(c) Only II is implicit
(d) II and III are implicit

24. Statement The municipal corporation has given permission for holding fun fairs in the local football ground during the holiday season. « Hotel Mgmt 2009

Assumptions

I. The local residents may protest against the corporation's decision.
II. Many people may not participate in the fun fair.
III. Only children are allowed to take part in the fun fair.

(a) None is implicit (b) All are implicit
(c) Only III is implicit (d) I and II are implicit

25. Statement "Buy pure and natural honey of company 'X', an advertisement in a newspaper.

Assumptions

I. Artificial honey can be prepared.
II. People do not mind paying more for pure honey.
III. No other company supplies pure honey.

(a) Only I is implicit (b) I and II are implicit
(c) I and III are implicit (d) All are implicit

26. Statement Railway authority has started internet booking facility of long distance trains and also delivering the tickets at the doorstep through courier service at a little extra cost.

Assumptions

I. Many customers may now book their tickets through internet, resulting into less crowd at ticket booking office.
II. Most of the customers may still buy their railway tickets at the booking counters.
III. People will ignore this facility.

(a) Only III is implicit (b) II and III are implicit
(c) None is implicit (d) None of these

27. Statement " 'Z' TV is the only TV which gives the viewers chance to watch two programmes simultaneously", an advertisement.

Assumptions

I. Sale of 'Z' TV may increase because of the advertisement.
II. Some people may be influenced by the advertisement and buy 'Z' TV.
III. The sale of 'Z' TV may be on the downward trend.

(a) None is implicit
(b) II and III are implicit
(c) I and II are implicit
(d) All are implicit

28. Statement The company has recently announced series of incentives to the employees who are punctual and sincere.

Assumptions

I. Those who are not punctual at present may get motivated by the announcement.
II. The productivity of the company may increase.
III. The profit earned by the company may be more than the amount to be spent for the incentive programmes.

(a) None is implicit
(b) All are implicit
(c) II and III are implicit
(d) I and II are implicit

29. Statement In a recently held all-India conference, the session on Brand Management in India surprisingly attracted a large number of participants and also received excellent media coverage in the leading newspapers. « JMET 2011

Assumptions

I. Nobody expected such an encouraging response to Brand Management.
II. Brands are not managed properly in India.
III. The Media is always very positive towards Brands.

(a) Only I (b) Both I and II
(c) Both I and III (d) I, II and III

DIRECTIONS ~ (Q. Nos. 30-38) *In each question below, is given a statement followed by three assumptions numbered* I, II *and* III. *An assumption is something supposed or taken for granted, you have to consider the statement and the assumptions and decide which of the assumption(s) is/are implicit in the statement.*

30. Statement "Do not lean out of the moving train", a warning in the railway compartment.

Assumptions

I. Such warning will have some effect.
II. Leaning out of a moving train is dangerous.
III. It is the duty of railway authorities to take care of passengers' safety.

(a) I and II are implicit
(b) II and III are implicit
(c) Only II is implicit
(d) I and III are implicit
(e) All are implicit

31. Statement Training must be given to all the employees for increasing productivity and profitability.

Assumptions

I. Training is an essential component of productivity.
II. Employees cannot function effectively without proper training.
III. Profitability and productivity are supplementary to each other.

(a) None is implicit (b) All are implicit
(c) Only III is implicit (d) I and II are implicit
(e) I and III are implicit

32. Statement The situation of this area still continues to be tense and out of control. People are requested to be in their homes only.

Assumptions

I. There had been some serious incidents.
II. People will not go to the office.
III. Normality will its be restored shortly.

(a) All are implicit (b) None is implicit
(c) Only I is implicit (d) I and III are implicit
(e) I and II are implicit

33. Statement "If you are a first class graduate with atleast 65% marks, you are eligible to apply for the post of officer in our organisation." an advertisement for recruitment of officers.

Assumptions

I. There may be adequate number of applicants who will fulfil the stipulated educational qualifications.
II. Those graduates who have secured less than 65% marks may not perform well in the job.
III. Those candidates who have secured 65% or more marks in graduation are likely to perform well on the job.

(a) All are implicit (b) I and II are implicit
(c) II and III are implicit (d) I and III are implicit
(e) None of these

34. Statement "X Chocolate is an ideal gift for someone you love", an advertisement.

Assumptions

I. People generally give gifts to loved ones.
II. Such advertisements generally influence people.
III. Chocolate can be considered as a gift item.

(a) I and II are implicit
(b) I and III are implicit
(c) All are implicit
(d) II and III are implicit
(e) None of these

35. Statement Prabodh wrote a second letter to his mother after a month as he did not receive any reply to the first letter.

Assumptions

I. Prabodh's mother did not receive the letter.
II. The letter generally reaches within a fortnight.
III. His mother promptly sends reply to his letters.

(a) II and III are implicit
(b) I and II are implicit
(c) Only III is implicit
(d) I and III are implicit
(e) None of these

36. Statement "I want to present a novel written by Prem Chand to Amar on his birthday", A tells B.

Assumptions

I. Amar does not have any novel written by Prem Chand.
II. Novel is an acceptable gift for birthday.
III. A will be invited by Amar on his birthday.

(a) I and II are implicit
(b) I and III are implicit
(c) Only II is implicit
(d) All are implicit
(e) None of these

37. Statement "The employees' association has appealed to the manager of company 'S' to introduce written examination for clerical cadre recruitment to prevent selection of incompetent persons."

Assumptions

I. So, far the company 'S' used to select candidates without conducting a written examination.
II. A written examination can help to identify competent persons.
III. At higher level, written examination may not be of much use.

(a) I and II are implicit (b) Only I is implicit
(c) Only II is implicit (d) All are implicit
(e) None of the above

38. Statement The residents of the locality wrote a letter to the corporation requesting to restore normal in the supply of drinking water immediately as the supply at present is just not adequate.

Assumptions

I. The corporation may not take any action on the letter.
II. The municipality has enough water to meet the demand.
III. The water supply to the area was adequate in the past.

(a) I and II are implicit (b) II and III are implicit
(c) Only II is implicit (d) Only III is implicit
(e) None of the above

DIRECTIONS ~(Q. Nos. 39-42) *In each of the questions below, is given a statement followed by three assumptions numbered* I, II *and* III. *An assumption is something supposed or taken for granted, you have to consider the statement and the assumptions and decide which of the assumption(s) is/are implicit in the statement.*

« Andhra Bank (PO) 2007

39. Statement "If you have obtained 75% or more marks in X standard, your admission to our coaching class for XII standard is guaranteed", an advertisement.

Assumptions

I. Bright students generally do not opt for attending coaching classes.
II. The coaching class has adequate capacity to accomodate all such students.
III. The advertisement will be ignored.

(a) Only II is implicit (b) Only III is implicit
(c) None is implicit (d) Only I is implicit
(e) All are implicit

40. Statement "Television 'P', the neighbour's envy the owner's pride", a TV advertisement.

Assumptions

I. Catchy slogans appeal to people.
II. People are envious of their neighbour's superior possessions.
III. People want to be annoyed by their neighbours.

(a) I and II are implicit (b) Only III is implicit
(c) I and III are implicit (d) All are implicit
(e) None of these

41. Statement There is a big boom in drug business and a number of Jhuggi-Jhopari dwellers in Delhi can be seen pedaling with small pouches of smack and brown sugar.

Assumptions

I. Drug addiction is increasing in the country, specially in the capital.
II. All the big dons involved in the smuggling of drugs live in Jhuggi-Jhopari areas.
III. Most of the Jhuggi-Jhopari dwellers would do anything for money.

(a) Only I is implicit
(b) Only II is implicit
(c) Only III is implicit
(d) I and III are implicit
(e) None is implicit

42. Statement The school authority decided to open a summer school this year in the school compound for the students in the age group of 7-14 yr.

Assumptions

I. All the students will attend the summer school.
II. All the parents will prefer to remain in city than going out of town for enabling their children to attend the summer school.
III. Those who cannot afford to go out of the station, will send their children to summer school.

(a) Only II is implicit (b) II and III are implicit
(c) None is implicit (d) All are implicit
(e) Only III is implicit

DIRECTION (Q. No. 43) *Study the following information carefully and answer the question asked.*

The principal of St. Mary school organised extra classes for week students of X class and the concerned teachers are getting paid extra amount for the classes. But the average salary of teachers more or less remains the same.

43. Which of the following can be assumed from the given statement? « IBPS Clerk Main 2018

I. The students of class X of school Y will score more marks than students of St. Mary school.
II. Students of class X are not serious about exams.
III. Extra classes arranged by the principal for students of class X will help the students to score well in exams.

(a) Both I and II (b) Both II and III
(c) Only II (d) Only III
(e) None of these

DIRECTIONS ~ (Q. Nos. 44-48) *In each question below is given a statement followed by three Assumptions I, II and III. An assumption is something supposed or taken for granted. You have to consider the statement and the following assumption(s) is/are implicit in the statement.*
« SBI (PO) 2010

44. Statement The police authority cordoned off the entire locality for the entire day and stopped all vehicular movement for the visit of a top functionary of the government in view of the threat perception and advised all the residents in the area to limit their movement outside their dwellings.

Which of the following assumption(s) is/are implicit in the above statement?

I. The police personnel may not be able to control the vehicular movement in the locality and may seek help from the armed forces.
II. People living in the locality may move out of their houses for the day to avoid inconvenience.
III. The Government functionary may request the police authority to lift the ban on the movement of residents of the locality outside their dwellings.

(a) None is implicit
(b) Only I is implicit
(c) Only II is implicit
(d) Only III is implicit
(e) II and III are implicit

45. Statement The apex body controlling universities in the country has decided to revise the syllabus of all the technical courses to make them focused towards the present needs of the industry, thereby making the technical graduates more employable than they are at present.

Which of the following assumption(s) is/are implicit in the above statement?

I. Technical college affiliated to different universities may not welcome the apex body's decision and may continue with the same syllabus as at present.
II. The industry may welcome the decision of the apex body and scale up their hiring from these colleges.
III. The Government may not allow the apex body to implement its decision in all the colleges as it may lead to chaos.

(a) None is implicit (b) Only I is implicit
(c) Only II is implicit (d) Only III is implicit
(e) II and III are implicit

46. Statement Government has urged all the citizens to use electronic media for carrying out their daily activities, whenever possible, instead of using paper as the manufacture of paper requires the cutting down of a large number of trees causing severe damage to the ecosystem.

Which of the following assumption(s) is/are implicit in the above statement?

I. Most people may be capable of using electronic media to carry out various routines.
II. Most people may have access to electronic media for carrying out their daily routine activities.

III. People at large may reject the Government's appeal and continue using paper as before.

(a) Only I is implicit (b) Only II is implicit
(c) I and II are implicit (d) Only III is implicit
(e) None of the above

47. Statement The Government has decided to auction construction of highways to private entities in several blocks across the country on build-operate-transfer basis.

Which of the following assumption(s) is/are implicit in the above statement?

I. An adequate number of private entities may not respond to the Government's auction notification.
II. Many private entities in the country are capable of constructing highways within a reasonable time.
III. The Government's proposal of build- operate-transfer may financially benefit the private entities.

(a) I and II are implicit (b) II and III are implicit
(c) Only II is implicit (d) I and III are implicit
(e) None of the above

48. Statement The airlines have requested all their bonafide passengers to check the status of flight operations before leaving their homes as heavy fog is causing immense problems to normal flight operations.

Which of the following assumption(s) is/are implicit in the above statement?

I. Majority of the air passengers may check the flights status before starting their journey to the airport.
II. The Government may take serious objection to the notice issued by the airline company.
III. Majority of the passengers may cancel their tickets and postpone their journey till the situation become normal.

(a) None is implicit (b) Only I is implicit
(c) Only II is implicit (d) Only III is implicit
(e) I and III are implicit

DIRECTION ~(Q. No. 49) *A statement followed by four assumptions numbered* I, II, III *and* IV *are given. An assumption is something supposed or taken for granted. You have to consider the statement and the following assumptions and decide which of the assumptions is implicit in the statement then decide which of the answers (a), (b), (c) or (d) is correct.* « JMET 2009

49. Statement The companies that showed relatively high import orientation in India were not the ones that benefited the most from Government interventions during the heydays of import substitution.

Assumptions

I. High import companies do not need Government support.
II. Low import companies received more Government support.
III. Import oriented companies are affected by Government prices.
IV. Exporting of goods get affected by Government .

(a) Only I (b) Only III
(c) Both II and IV (d) All four

DIRECTION ~(Q. No. 50) *Read the following information carefully and answer the given question.*

Pets are not allowed in the park premises-A notice put up at the park entrance by the authority that is responsible for maintenance of the park.

50. Which of the following can be an assumption according the the given information? (An assumption is something that is supposed or taken for granted).

(a) Atleast some people who visit the park have pets
(b) This is the only park which does not allow pets
(c) People who ignored this notice were fined
(d) There are more than one entrances to the park
(e) Many people have now stopped visiting the park

51. Choose an option that is a valid assumption for the below statement. « UPSSSC Combined Lower Subordinate 2019

Statement The ministry of railways introduces additional holiday special trains and also adds extra coaches to existing trains during vacations.

(a) During vacations, kids love to travel by trains instead of aeroplanes
(b) Passenger traffic in trains significantly increases during vacations.
(c) People need change and like to see new trains during vacations.
(d) Engine drivers like to work for more hours during vacations.

52. Installing scrubbers in smokestacks and switching to cleaner-burning fuel are the two methods available to Northern Power for reducing harmful emissions from its plants. Scrubbers will reduce harmful emissions more than cleaner-burning fuels will. Therefore, by installing stallmg scrubbers, Northern power will be doing the most that can be done to reduce harmful emissions from its plants.

Which of the following is an assumption on which the argument depends? « IBPS PO Mains 2019

(a) Switching to cleaner-burning fuel will not be more expensive than installing scrubbers
(b) Northern Power can choose from among various Kinds of scrubbers, some of which are more effective than others
(c) Northern Power is not necessarily committed to reducing harmful emissions from its plants
(d) Harmful emissions from Northern Power's plants cannot be reduced more by using both methods together than by the installation of scrubbers alone
(e) Aside from harmful emissions from the smokestacks of its plants, the activities of Northern Power do not cause significant air pollution.

Answers WITH EXPLANATIONS

1. (*d*) Assumption I is implicit as the advertisement suggests to read the given book for objective competitive exams. Assumption II is invalid because it has no relation with the given statement. Assumption III will be implicit because only then the advertisement makes sense.

2. (*b*) Since, the instructions are about playing a game. Therefore, it is clear that a game is being played. Hence, I follows.

Since, the instructions are meant to be read by the players, therefore it is clear that players are literate and not blind.

Hence, all follow.

3. (*a*) 'If he does not mend his ways' implies that there is a possibility for him to mend his ways. Hence, Assumption I is implicit. Further, the person is depending upon the police, if he finds it necessary. It means the person must be assuming that police will help him. Hence, Assumption II is also implicit. Assumption III is nothing to do with the given statement.

4. (*c*) Anybody advises anyone with the assumption that his advice will get proper attention from the one who hears it. Without assuming so, giving advice makes no sense. Hence, Assumption I is implicit.
Assumption II is implicit because if one discusses about the merits or demerits of a thing, then he assumes that he knows about it.
Assumption III is very much valid, otherwise the statement becomes meaningless.

5. (*c*) There is a special warning in printed form to caution people against the ill effects of smoking. Hence, Assumption II is implicit but I is not. Further, 'smoking is injurious to health' does not mean non-smoking promotes health. Therefore, Assumption III has no connection with the given statement. Hence, Assumption III is not implicit.

6. (*a*) None of the assumptions is implicit in the statement.
Assumption I is not implicit because the word 'entire' makes the assumption doubtful.
Assumption II is not implicit because neither we know the quality of the product nor the market for this product. Assumption III is not implicit because we cannot say anything about the quantity of resources of the company.

7. (*a*) State Government's decision to increase octroi by 5% is based on the assumption that the State Government is competent enough to implement the decision and also get the consent of the Central Government. The hike is in view of earning additional amount.

8. (*a*) The use of the word 'totally' makes the assumption doubtful. It is given that the Central Government has directed the State Government to reduce its expenditure account and also the State Government will abide by the directives.

9. (*d*) Consultant in his opinion emphasises the need for mobilising the staff and raising the funds. This means that the product of the company has a potential market and also that the financial institutions provide money for such proposals.

10. (*d*) Assumption I is invalid because of the word 'only'. Assumption II has also no connection with the given statement. So, Assumption II also becomes invalid. In case of III, we can say that an advertisement is given to get desired response and not to be ignored. Hence, Assumption III again is an invalid assumption.

11. (*a*) Assumption I is implicit as A has categorically stated that Madhu has not replied to his letter, it means that she has received his letter.
Assumption II is invalid because of the correctness of Assumptions I and III are not implicit as it has no relation with the given statement.

12. (*c*) Assumption II is implicit because the word 'she' has been used for D. Assumption I is not implicit because of the correctness of II while III is not implicit as we cannot conclude on the basis of given statement that A and B are close friends.

13. (*c*) Advertisement is issued assuming that product is used by people for various uses. Secondly, advertisements are used for publicity because people respond to the advertisements.

Hence, Assumptions I and III are implicit. However, we cannot say that people are easily fooled. Hence, Assumption II is not implicit.

14. (*a*) Statement contains the reaction of the department over the silent view taken by the university on their proposal for some course. It is, therefore assumed that university has received the proposal.

15. (*b*) The present method of admission is not known from the statement. Secondly, it is not necessary that Chairman is an MBA.

However, it is clear that intention behind introducing the objective type test is to reform the system of examination.

16. (*e*) The given statement is based on the assumptions that consumer generally read notice. Otherwise what is the use of giving notice, so it is implicit.

It is definitely assumed by the company that people will read notice and pay the bill to avoid penalty. Hence, III is also implicit.

17. (*c*) It is only said in the statement that author's name was miss spelt and that is regretted. It would not be proper to draw assumptions such as I or II. Only Assumption III is implicit.

18. (*c*) Advertisement has been given assuming that some people will respond to the advertisement. Hence, only Assumption II is implicit. However, Assumptions I and III are doubtful.

19. (*c*) It is given in the statement that friends have decided to go for picnic to avoid crowd. This implies that many people don't go to Avon. Hence, I and II are implicit. Now, we cannot say that reason for the Avon being non-crowdy is people's unacquaintance with this spot. It may be due to other reasons also.

20. (*b*) It cannot be definitely said that for what purpose the money collected as penalty will be used. However, Assumptions I and III are in tune with the statement and hence implicit in the statement.

21. (*b*) The response of the public to the circus shows during the last seven days is reasonably good. It is, therefore assumed by the authorities to get the similar responses during the extended days. Hence, Assumption II is implicit.

22. (*c*) Assumptions I and II are clearly implicit in the statement. Assumption III represents the consequent effect for which nothing can be said definitely.

23. (*c*) Tarun has left the company due to the meagre salary. Hence, Assumption II is implicit. However, we cannot say anything about the work environment and salary of all other employees from this statement.

24. (*a*) The step taken by municipal corporation aims at providing good entertainment for local residents during the holidays. No doubts, the municipal corporation must be assuming that local residents will take part in it to enjoy.

Assumptions I and II go against this assumption and hence they are not valid. Assumption III is also not implicit because of the word 'only'.

25. (*a*) The word 'natural' has been mentioned in the statement and that part of the statement is 'natural and pure honey'.

It does mean that artificial honey can be made. Hence, Assumption I is implicit. Assumption II is not implicit as no comparison is made of the prices of natural and artificial honey. Assumption III is again invalid as it has no relation with the given statement.

26. (*d*) Assumption I is implicit as the initiative taken by the railway authority has been aimed at making the service customer friendly. But Assumption II is not implicit because it may or may not be an assumption. Assumption III is not implicit, because if railway authority assumes that people will ignore this facility, then why would it start it.

27. (*c*) The advertisement as described in the statement is meant to influence the buyers and thus increasing sale of the television. Hence, Assumptions I and II, both are implicit.

28. (*d*) Incentives for the punctuality and sincerity will work as a motivation force.

This will definitely increase the productivity of the company. However, profitability cannot be predicted definitely as it depends on other factors.

29. (*a*) Since, the response was 'surprising'. So, I is implicit. Nothing about the real management of service sector can be deduced from the statement.

So, II is not implicit. Also, the statement talks of the media's response to only a particular session on service sector and not all in general. So, III is also not implicit.

30. (*e*) Assumptions I and II are implicit because the warning against leaning out suggests one to be careful are against the dangers involved.

No doubts that ensuring the passengers safety is the responsibility of railway authorities and hence III is also a valid assumption.

31. (*d*) Training has been necessitated in the statement, *i.e.*, it is related to the efficiency and effectiveness of an employee.

Therefore, both the Assumptions I and II are implicit in the statement.

32. (*e*) The situation is tense, it means that some serious incident has occurred. Hence, Assumption I is implicit. Secondly, it is given that situation still continues to be tense and people have been requested to be inside home. Hence, Assumption II is implicit. Assumption III is rubbish and has no relation with the given statement. Hence, III is an invalid assumption.

33. (*c*) Assumptions II and III are implicit. According to II, those who have secured less than 65% marks may not perform well in the job and according to Assumption III those who have secured 65% or more marks are likely to perform well.

Hence, those with atleast 65% marks are eligible to apply for the post.

34. (*c*) The statement implies that gifts are given for loved ones. It is also assumed that such advertisements generally influence people. Since, chocolate has been recommended in the advertisement, hence it is an ideal gift. Therefore, all the assumptions are implicit.

35. (*c*) Prabodh wrote the second letter to his mother only when he did not receive the reply from his mother. This fact implies that his mother promptly sends reply to his letters. Hence, only Assumption III is implicit.

36. (*e*) 'A' wants to present a book on B's birthday. It means that book is an acceptable gift and also Assumption III is implicit.

But we do not have this combination as our alternative.

37. (*a*) Assumption I is implicit because there is a demand for introduction of written examination.

Assumption II is also implicit as it is said in the statement that written exam will prevent the selection of incompetent persons.

38. (*b*) Assumption II and III are implicit because without these assumptions the statement does not make any sense.

Assumption I is contrary to what is the purpose of the statement. Hence, I is an invalid assumption.

39. (*a*) Assumption I is invalid as it goes against the given statement. Further, without assuming II, such advertisement makes no sense. Hence, Assumption II is implicit. Assumption III again is an invalid assumption because any advertisement is given with the assumption of getting desired response and not for being ignored.

40. (*a*) This advertisement does not make any sense without assuming Assumptions I and II. Hence, I and II are implicit.

Assumption III is rubbish, it has actually no connection with the given statement. Hence, it is an invalid assumption.

41. (*d*) The given statement tells of boom in drug business and cites examples from the capital city. This makes Assumption I a valid assumption. Again, it is given that most Jhuggi-Jhopari dwellers are seen to indulge in transactions of drug pouches.

This implies that they give in to their lust for money quite easily and get involved in illegal activities for the same.

Hence, Assumption III is very much valid. But Assumption II is not implicit as II has no connection with the given statement.

42. (*c*) The use of the word 'all' in Assumptions I and II makes the assumptions doubtful and also we cannot say that those, who cannot afford to go out of the station, will send their children to summer school. Hence, none of the assumptions is implicit.

43. (*d*) Only Statement III can be assumed from the given information. As, from the given information it can be assumed that extra classes arranged by the principal will help the students of class X to score well in exams.

44. (*a*) All the given assumptions are contrary to the given statement and hence, they all are invalid.

45. (*c*) Assumption II is implicit because whenever such a decision is taken, the assumptions are that it would be welcomed and allowed to implement. Assumptions I and III will be invalid for the same reason.

46. (*c*) The urging of the Government makes sense only when Assumptions I and II are implicit.

47. (*b*) The decision to auction assumes response to it. Hence, Assumption I is not implicit. Assumption II is implicit as unless the private entities are capable, the decision would make no sense.

Further, without financial benefit, private entities would not turn up for the auction. Hence, Assumption III is implicit.

48. (*b*) To make the request meaningful I must be a valid assumption. Hence, Assumption I is implicit. In case of II, Government is out of the picture. Hence, Assumption II is not implicit. Assumption III also invalid as the case may be only of delay, not of cancellation of flight.

49. (*b*) Only Assumption III follows.

50. (*a*) From the statement, it can be said that at least some people who visit the park have pets.

51. (*b*) Assumption (b) is valid as number of passengers during vacation increases. Hence, Ministry of railways introduces new special trains and increases the number of coaches.

52. (*d*) The argument assumes that both cannot be used at the same time. If this were true. then Northern Power would not be doing everything it can, thus the argument falls apart.

CHAPTER / 05

Course of Action

A course of action is a guideline or administrative step initiated to improve or solve the problem based on the information provided in the question.

In daily life, a person faces problems with his work, travel, administration, society, friends and family etc. These problems are needed to be solve and the way of acting or dealing to solve these problems or situations is called the correct course of action.

A course of action is considered appropriate or acceptable only when it completely or partially solves the problem, otherwise not.

The problem or situation may vary in different circumstances and so its solution will vary. So, a careful analysis of the problem is required to reach the correct course of action.

There can be two types of problems as discussed below

1. Simple Problem

These problems can be solved by simple action and there is no need of planned, accelerated and solid action to get rid of such problems. In fact, such problems need a slight improvement to be cured and this slight improvement can be made by putting a simple effort.

e.g., If you get tired after 2-3 hours work, then your tiredness is a simple problem for you and you can solve this problem *i.e.,* refresh yourself by having a cup of tea or by taking a glass of juice or by any other simple means. Similarly, other simple problems like indiscipline, noise etc., can be solved by simple and easy action.

2. Complex Problem

In this type of problems, due to larger intensity, a planned, accelerated and solid action is required to get rid of it. In other words, a simple action or effort is useless in this case and a perfect strategy is needed to take an accelerated solid action.

e.g., If a major train accident takes place, it comes under the category of complex problems and to control this unwanted situation a rescue operation with proper planning must be started to prevent possible increase in casualties.

Conditions for the Correctness of 'Course of Action'

A 'course of action' will be correct, if

(i) it solves or reduces or minimises the problem.

(ii) suggested solution is a practical one.

How to determine whether a 'course of action' solves/reduces/minimises a problem?

A. On the basis of established facts we can check the validity of a given course of action *i.e.,* whether the suggested solution solves/reduces/minimises the problem or not. An established fact may be scientifically established or universally or socially acknowledged.

Let us see the following example;

Statement A 10 yr old boy was caught in a bus while attempting to steal the wallet of a person.

Courses of Action

I. The boy should be handed over to child welfare society. *(correct)*

II. The boy should be beaten severely. *(incorrect)*

Solution It is a socially established fact that child criminals should be made to mend their ways instead of being treated as punishable wretches. Hence, the Course of Action I is correct one as the child welfare society can make the boy mend his ways.

B. If a solution suggested by 'course of action' seems to be correct on the basis of our experiences, then the given 'course of action' will solve/reduce/ minimise the problem otherwise the suggested solution is incorrect.

Let us see the following example;

Statement Casteism has become a base for our life and that too, to the alarming extent.

Course of Action Strict legislation must be passed to promote intercaste marriages. *(incorrect)*

Solution Applying our past experiences, if we think over the suggested solution by the given 'course of action', we come to our conclusion very easily. Our previous experiences tell that legislation has been useless in the case of dowry. Casteism is equally deep rooted problem of our society.

So, if legislation has been proved failure for dowry cases, then how can one expect that it can do wonders in case of casteism. Hence, on the basis of our past experiences, the given course of action is incorrect.

Let us see another example;

Statement Female foeticide is still a major problem of our country.

Course of Action Efforts should be made to eradicate illiteracy among women. *(correct)*

Solution Our previous experiences tell that so many social problems can be solved by making people aware through literacy or by any other means. Hence, the given course of action is correct.

C. Sometimes a new problem may come our way and we do not have any previous experience about it. In this case, our logical and reasoning ability help us in deciding the validity of solution suggested by the given course of action.

Let us see the following example;

Statement The police has failed to protect the elderly citizens of the society as 10 old persons were killed in different areas in the last two days.

Courses of Action

I. Police and youth should be asked to take special care of old people. *(correct)*

II. Government should bring a legislation against killing of elderly people. *(incorrect)*

Solution Our logic says that I is correct as we must take care of those who are likely to get affected by this new problem. II is a proper course of action, yet it is invalid because our logical sense says that punishment for murderers is already in our legislation.

D. In some cases, the validity of the solution suggested by the given course of action is decided on the basis of prevailing notions of truth. In other words, we can say that sometimes, as per the societal norms, it is determined whether a particular course of action solves/ reduces/minimises the given problem or not.

Let us see the following example

Statement Balwant got angry and beat his son severely.

Course of Action Balwant should be publicly caned. *(incorrect)*

Solution No doubts, caning would be an accepted punishment for medieval periods but today public-beating is not acceptable at all. Even for the most serious offences our societal norms do not allow such kind of punishment.

Following flow chart will give a step-by-step method for checking correctness of a course of action

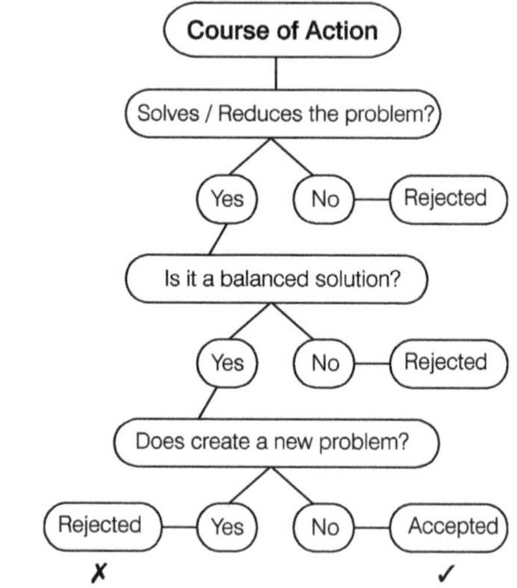

Chapter tip!

- Don't make your individual perception and act according to the rules of any organisation.
- Course of action should be a practical solution to the problem.
- Course of action should be a balanced solution.
- It should not create any further problems.
- The course of action should be taken according to the gravity of the problem and unnecessary harsh or strict action should be avoided as this becomes sometimes unparliamentary or unconstitutional which can only aggravate the problem rather than reducing it.
- The course of action should be feasible, practical and administrative in nature and must touch the aspects of common situations.
- In most of the cases, a situation has more than one course of action. But they are never exclusive to each other. So, our answer should be always 'both follow' and not 'either of them follows'.
- If the course of action and problems are properly balanced and if the course of action is also feasible than that action can be followed.

Mainly two types of questions are asked from this section, which are discussed as under

TYPE 01

Based on Two Courses of Action

In this type of questions, a statement is given followed by two courses of action numbered I and II. The candidate is required to understand the statement, analyse the problem or policy it mentions and then decide which of the courses of action logically follows.

Following examples will give a better understanding about this chapter.

DIRECTIONS ~ (Example Nos. 1-3) *In each of the questions below is given a statement followed by two courses of action numbered I and II. A course of an action is a step or an administrative decision to be taken for improvement, follow up or further action in regard to the problem, policy etc. On the basis of the information given in the statement you have to assume everything in the statement to be true and then decide which of the two given courses of action logically follow(s).*

Give answer

(a) If only I follows (b) If only II follows
(c) If either I or II follows (d) If neither I nor II follows
(e) If both I and II follow

***Ex* 01** **Statement** A recent study shows that children below five, die in the cities of the developing countries mainly from diarrhoea and parasitic intestinal worms.

Courses of Action

I. Government of the developing countries should take adequate measures to improve the hygienic conditions in the cities.

II. Children below five years in the cities of the developing countries need to be kept under constant medication.

Solution (e) If Government concentrates to improve the hygienic condition in the cities, it may definitely reduce the impact of problem and this course of action appears to be feasible also. hence, this course of action follows. A constant medication is another practical feasible step, which would help minimise the cases of death due to diarrhoea and intestinal worms. Therefore, course of action II also follows.

***Ex* 02** **Statement** Many villages face flood fury every year in the monsoon. « CGPSC Pre 2017

Courses of Action

I. Timely evacuation of the people is necessary.

II. The government should take measures to control floods by building dams etc.

Solution (b) I is not feasible. II follows because building dams to control floods is a permanent solution for the perennial flood problem.

***Ex* 03** **Statement** Cell phone users have found that tariff plans are not as attractive as promoted by telecom companies and complained to regulatory authority about the same. « SCRA 2013, UCO Bank (PO) 2009

Courses of Action

I. The regulatory authority should direct telecom companies to be transparent on the tariff structure of all plans.

II. The Government should restrict the number of telecom companies operating in the country.

Solution (a) Being 'not as attractive as promoted' is clear case of hiding things. Hence, transparency is the action to the problem and I follows.

II goes against the spirit of free market and is not relevant to the problem either.

Practice / CORNER 5.1

DIRECTIONS ~ (Q. Nos. 1-7) *Each question contains one statement and two Courses of action I and II. Assuming the statements to be true, decide which of the two courses of action most logically follows.*

Give answer

(a) If only I follows (b) If only II follows
(c) If either I or II follows (d) If neither I nor II follows

1. Statement Due to heavy rain in Bangalore, the normal lives of the citizens are paralysed. « RRB ALP 2018

Courses of Action

I. Government should take measures to help people and avoid life and property destruction.

II. Government should provide free treatment in all the hospitals of Bangalore.

2. Statement Majority of the students have failed in one paper in the first semester examination. « CMAT 2013

Courses of Action

I. All those student who failed should be asked to drop out of the course.

II. The faculty teaching the paper should be asked to resign.

3. Statement The manufacturing companies in Tamil Nadu are facing acute power shortage. « RRB ALP 2018

Courses of Action

I. Government should take steps to solve the power crisis.

II. Government should shut down manufacturing companies to save power.

4. Statement A man wants to get admission in a certain unique elite club. « UPSSSC Mandi Parishad 2018

Courses of Action

I. Find and complete the procedure to get entry into the club.

II. Get admission into another club.

5. Statement The pollution and air quality in Delhi is beyond the acceptable level.

This is due to industrial and automobile exhaustion.

Courses of Action « RRB ALP 2018

I. Automobiles should be divided into groups to be run only on odd and even days, respectively.

II. The government should stop the registration of new factories and vehicles.

6. Statement School dropout rate is very high in the rural areas as children support their parents in income earning activities. « CLAT 2013

Courses of Action

I. Public awareness programme on primary education should be expanded immediately to educate parents.

II. Compensation should be given to rural families.

7. Statement The Central Bureau of Investigations (CBI) receives the complaint of an officer taking bribe to do the duty he is supposed to.

Courses of Action

I. CBI should try to catch the officer red-handed and then take a strict action against him.

II. CBI should wait for some more complaints about the officer to be sure about the matter.

DIRECTIONS ~ (Q. Nos. 8-54) *In each of the questions below is given a statement followed by two courses of action. Course of action is a step for administrative decision to be taken for improvement, follow-up or further action in regard to the problem, policy etc. On the basis of the information given in the statement, you have to assume everything in the statement to be true, then decide which of the given suggested courses of action is/are logically worth pursuing.*

Give answer

(a) If only I follows
(b) If only II follows
(c) If either I or II follows
(d) If neither I nor II follows
(e) If both I and II follow

8. Statement The younger people do not look after their elders. « CGPSC Pre 2017

Courses of Action

I. Legal action should be taken.

II. Old age homes should be opened.

9. Statement The police harass the common man.

Courses of Action « CGPSC Pre 2017

I. The government should take firm steps against the erring policeman.

II. The police force should be educated for public dealing.

10. Statement While laying pipelines by one of the utility companies a huge fire broke out due to damage done to the pipeline.

Courses of Action

I. All the licences of the utility company should immediately be suspended pending enquiry into the incident.

II. People residing in the area should be advised to stay indoors to avoid burn injuries.

11. Statement There has been large number of internet hacking in the recent months creating panic among the internet users.

Courses of Action

I. The Government machinery should make an all out effort to check those who are responsible and put them behind bars.

II. The internet users should be advised to stay away from using internet till the culprits are caught.

12. Statement People see tax as a burden and thus devise ways to underpay or avoid it altogether. « SBI Clerk Mains 2016

Courses of Action

I. Government should educate and inform citizens about the ways in which taxes help in development of the nation.

II. Tax rates should be increased so that the under-recovery in collection is compensated.

13. Statement A very large number of students have failed in the final high school examinations due to wrong questions in one of the subjects.

Courses of Action

I. All the students who have failed in that subject should be allowed to take supplementary examination.

II. All those who are responsible for the error should be suspended and an enquiry should be initiated to find out the facts.

14. Statement Exporters in the capital are alleging that commercial banks are violating a Reserve Bank of India directive to operate a post shipment export credit denominated in foreign currency at international rates from January this year. « IBPS Clerk Mains 2017

Courses of Action

I. The officers concerned in the commercial banks are to be suspended.

II. The RBI should be asked to stop giving such directives to commercial banks.

15. Statement There has been an unprecedented increase in the number of requests for berths in most of the long distance trains during the current holiday season.

Courses of Action

I. The railway authority should immediately increase the capacity in each of these trains by attaching additional coaches.

II. The people seeking accommodation should be advised to make their travel plan after the holiday.

16. Statement As many as ten coaches of a passenger train have derailed and blocked both pairs of the railway tracks.

Courses of Action

I. The railway authorities should immediately send men and equipment to the spot to clear the railway tracks.

II. All the trains running in both directions should be diverted to other routes.

17. Statement Two persons, while on their daily walks in the jogger's park were killed by unidentified miscreants early in the morning.

Courses of Action

I. The police authority should deploy police constables near the jogger's park to prevent such criminal acts in future.

II. The citizens of the locality should go for early morning walks in groups to avoid such attacks. « BOI (PO) 2010

18. Statement Many school children died in few accidents caused due to poor maintenance of school buses during the last few months.

Courses of Action

I. The Government should set up an expert group to inspect the condition of school buses to avoid such accidents.

II. The Government should suspend the licence of all the school buses till these buses are properly checked. « BOI (PO) 2010

19. Statement A huge tidal wave swept away many fishing boats and hutments of the fishermen living along the coastline.

Courses of Action

I. The fisherman should henceforth be restrained from constructing their huts along the coast line.

II. The local administration should send a team of officials to assess the extent of damage and suggest remedial measures.

« Corporation Bank (PO) 2010

20. Statement Prices of essential commodities have risen alarmingly due to prolonged transport strike.

Courses of Action

I. The transporter's association should be ordered by the Government to immediately withdraw strike call or else they will face severe consequences.

II. The Government should take help of military vehicles to restore supply of essential goods to the city.

21. Statement A large number of students studying in vernacular medium have not passed the Xth standard final examination.

Courses of Action

I. The Government should immediately review the situation and initiate measures to improve it.

II. All the teachers of these schools should be issued notices to improve performance of the students.

22. Statement A large number of invitees who attended the marriage function fell ill due to food poisoning and were rushed to various hospitals located in the area.

« Corporation Bank (PO) 2010

Courses of Action

I. The Government should ban such marriage functions till further notice.

II. The local hospitals should be advised by the Government to provide best services to the affected people.

23. Statement Researchers are feeling agitated as libraries are not well equipped to provide the right information to the right users at the right time in the required format. Even the users are not aware about the various services available for them.

Courses of Action

I. All the information available in the libraries should be computerised to provide faster services to the users.

II. Library staff should be trained in computer operations.

24. Statement Two local passenger trains collided while running in opposite directions on the same track as the signalling system failed for a short period.

« SBI (PO) 2009

Courses of Action

I. The services of the motormen of the trains should immediately be terminated.

II. The Government should immediately constitute a task force to review the functioning of the signalling system.

25. Statement Almost 90% of the flights of one of the private airline company were cancelled for the fourth consecutive day as the pilots refused to join their duties in protest against sacking of two of their colleagues by the airline management. « SBI (PO) 2009

Courses of Action

I. The management of the airline company should be ordered by the Government to immediately reinstate the sacked pilots to end the crisis.

II. The Government should immediately take steps to end the impasse between the management and the pilots to help the helpless passengers.

26. Statement A major part of the local market in the city was gutted due to a short circuit causing extensive damage to goods and property. « SBI (PO) 2009

Courses of Action

I. The Government should issue strict guidelines for all establishments regarding installation and maintenance of electrical fittings.

II. The Government should relocate all the markets to the outskirts of the city.

27. Statement Air export volume has increased substantially over the past decade causing backlogs and difficulties for air cargo agents because of increased demand for space and service.

Courses of Action

I. Airlines and air cargo agents should jointly work out a solution to combat the problem.

II. The reasons for the increase in the volume of air export should be found out.

28. Statement The world conference of 'Education for All' took place in 1990. Members who attended conference endorsed the frame-work of action for meeting the basic learning needs of all children.

Courses of Action

I. India should suitably implement the action points of this conference.

II. India should also immediately organise this type of conference.

29. Statement Drinking water supply to many parts of the town has been disrupted due to loss of water because of leakage in pipes supplying water.

« Andhra Bank (PO) 2009

Courses of Action

I. The Government should order an enquiry into the matter.

II. The civic body should set up a fact finding team to assess the damage and take effective steps.

30. Statement A number of school children in the local schools have fallen ill after the consumption of their subsidised tiffin provided by the school authority.

« SCRA 2013, PNB (PO) 2011

Courses of Action

I. The tiffin facility of all schools should be discontinued with immediate effect.

II. The Government should implement a system to certify the quality of tiffin provided by the school.

31. Statement Heavy rains hit the state during October, just before the State Assembly elections and caused heavy damage to standing crops in most parts of the state. « SCRA 2013, PNB (PO) 2011

Courses of Action

I. Elections should be postponed to give candidates the opportunity to campaign.

II. The Government should announce a relief package for those who are affected.

32. Statement An increasing number of graduates produced by Indian universities are unemployable.

Courses of Action « PNB (PO) 2011

I. Colleges and institutes of higher learning should be given greater autonomy to decide the course content.

II. World class foreign universities should be encouraged to set up campuses in India.

33. Statement Although the Indian economy is still heavily dependent on agriculture, its share in global agricultural trade is less than the share of agricultural exports to total exports.

Courses of Action

I. Efforts should be made to increase our agricultural production.

II. The exports of non-agricultural commodities should be reduced.

34. Statement There is no motivation among today's generation to join the armed forces owing to frequent transfers to risky areas. Perhaps they are not aware of the good side of it. « SBI Clerk Mains 2016

Courses of Action

I. Short term internship should be introduced at high school level to give students a peek into the adventurous life of the forces and provide a more realistic job purview.

II. The salary level of the defence forces should be increased with immediate effect.

35. Statement The Government has decided not to provide financial support to voluntary organisations from next five years plan and has communicated that all such organisations should raise funds to meet their financial needs.

Courses of Action

I. Voluntary organisations should collaborate with foreign agencies.

II. They should explore other sources of financial support.

36. Statement The experts group on technical education has stressed that computer education should be provided to children from primary school itself. It should be implemented in urban and rural schools, simultaneously.

Courses of Action

I. Government should issue instructions to all schools for computer education.

II. Atleast one teacher of each school should be trained in computer operations for teaching children.

37. Statement The dolphin population in India has been decreasing sharply over the past few years. « UCO Bank (PO) 2009

Courses of Action

I. Dolphins should be declared an endangered species and bred in aquariums or protected areas.

II. Locals should be enlisted to protect dolphins.

38. Statement The chairman stressed the need for making education system more flexible and regretted that the curriculum has not been revised in keeping with the pace of the changes taking place.

Courses of Action

I. Curriculum should be reviewed and revised periodically.

II. System of education should be made more flexible.

39. Statement Reports of steep and continued decline in the inflows into the Gobindsagar reservoir of the Bhakra Dam, coupled with a depleted stock of steam coal with the thermal power plants in the North, may lead to a serious power crisis in the region.

Courses of Action

I. The supply of steam coal to the thermal power plants needs to be immediately stepped up by the Government.

II. The Government should set up hydraulic power plants on other rivers in the region.

40. Statement The police department has come under a cloud with recent revelations that atleast two senior police officers are suspected to have been involved in the illegal sale of a large quantity of weapons from the state police armoury.

Courses of Action

I. A thorough investigation should be ordered by the State Government to find out all those who are involved into the illegal sale of arms.

II. State police armoury should be kept under Central Government control.

41. Statement A large part of the locality was flooded as the main pipe supplying drinking water bursted while the workers of a utility company were laying cables in the area. « Canara Bank (PO) 2010

Courses of Action

I. The civic authority should immediately arrange to repair the damage and stop loss of water.

II. The civic authority should seek an explanation and compensation from the utility company for the damage caused by them.

42. Statement Millions of pilgrims are expected to take a dip in the Ganga at the holy place during the next fortnight. « Canara Bank (PO) 2010

Courses of Action

I. The Government should restrict the number of pilgrims who can take dip each day during the fortnight.

II. The Government should deploy an adequate number of security personnel to maintain law and order during the next fortnight at the holy place.

43. Statement The rate of inflation has reached its highest in last twenty years and there is no sign of it softening in the coming months. « Canara Bank (PO) 2010

Courses of Action

I. The Government should initiate steps like reducing Government taxes on essential commodities with immediate effect.

II. Farmers should be asked by the Government to sell their products at lower prices.

44. Statement The State Government has decided to declare 'Kala Azar' as a notifiable disease under the Epidemic Act. Under the Epidemic Act, 1897, family members or neighbours of the patient are liable to be punished in case they did not inform the State Authorities.

Courses of Action

I. Efforts should be made to efficiently implement the Act.

II. The cases of punishment should be propagated through mass media, so that more people become aware of the stern action.

45. Statement Every year, at the beginning or at the end of the monsoon, we have some cases of conjuctivitis, but this year, it seems to be a major epidemic, witnessed after nearly four years.

Courses of Action

I. Precautionary measures should be taken after every four years to check the epidemic.

II. People should be advised to drink boiled water during the monsoon season.

46. Statement The committee has criticised the institute for its failure to implement a dozen of regular programmes despite an increase in the staff strength and not drawing up a firm action plan for studies and researches.

Courses of Action

I. The broad objectives of the institute should be redefined to implement a practical action plan.

II. The institute should give a report on reasons for not having implemented the planned programmes.

47. Statement It is reported that vitamins and minerals in vegetables and fruits are beneficial for human body. Medicines do not have the same effect on human body.

Courses of Action

I. People should be encouraged to take fresh fruits and vegetables to meet human body's requirement of vitamins and minerals.

II. The sale of medicines of vitamins and minerals should be banned.

48. Statement Many pilgrims died in a stampede while boarding a private ferry to the holy place on the first day of the ten day long festival. « IDBI Bank (PO) 2010

Courses of Action

I. The Government should immediately cancel the licences of all the private ferry operators with immediate effect.

II. The Government should deploy an adequate number of its personnel to guide pilgrims on their journey to the holy place.

49. Statement Some students of the local college were caught travelling in the train without purchasing valid tickets. « Syndicate Bank (PO) 2010

Courses of Action

I. The parents of these students should be informed about the incident and requested to counsel their wards.

II. These students should be put behind bars for travelling without bonafide credentials.

50. Statement Cases of road accidents are increasing constantly, particularly in the urban areas. « NABARD 2008

Courses of Action

I. Transport Authorities in the urban areas should impose stringent norms for maintenance of vehicles.

II. Traffic police should severely punish those found to be violating traffic rules.

51. Statement Despite good economic progress of the country, significant number of under-nourished children has been observed in the rural parts of the country. « NABARD 2008

Courses of Action

I. Government should increase Wealth Tax/ Income Tax and use that money for upliftment of the deprived class.

II. Government should introduce schemes like free meals in primary schools and make primary education compulsory.

52. Statement There has been a spurt of robbery and house breaking incidents in one locality during the past fortnight. « OBC (PO) 2008

Courses of Action

I. The local police station personnel should start patrolling the locality at regular intervals.

II. The residents in the locality should be asked by the police authority not to leave their houses during the night.

53. Statement The local college principal has ordered that all the students must strictly adhere to the dress code stipulated by college authority in the admission brochure. « BOI (PO) 2008

Courses of Action

I. Those students who are found to violate the dress code should be terminated from the college.

II. Those students who are found to violate the dress code for the first time should be reprimanded and be warned against further violation.

54. Statement The railway have decided to repair the main tracks within the city on the following Sunday and have decided to suspend operations for the whole day. « BOI (PO) 2008

Courses of Action

I. The railway authority should issue public notification well in advance to case inconvenience to the passengers.

II. All the long distance trains entering the city during the repair hours should be terminated outside the city limit.

Answers // WITH EXPLANATIONS

1. (*a*) I is the immediate course of action, helping people and preventing life and property destruction is the major step to mitigate the problem. Hence, only I follows.

2. (*d*) The failure of majority of students hints at there being some lack on the part of the teaching faculty, which needs to be removed by constant efforts. So, none of the given courses of action follows.

3. (*a*) Shutting down manufacturing industries would be a detrimental step for the economy, hence not feasible.
Only course of action I follows because government should take steps to solve the power crisis.

4. (*a*) I follows, if man wants to take admission in a certain unique elite club, then he must find and complete the procedure to get entry into the club.

5. (*d*) Neither of the two are the permanent solutions. They are temporary in nature. Hence, neither I nor II follows.

6. (*a*) Only Course of action I can follow as increasing the public awareness will educate the parents of importance of education and thus the dropout rate will decrease.

7. (*a*) Only Course of action I follows as CBI should try to catch the officer red-handed and then take a strict action against him.

8. (*a*) Opening old age homes are not permanent solution. Taking legal actions is the most feasible course of action. Hence, I follows.

9. (*e*) Both the course of actions follow as the culprit should be brought to book and police force should be educated for public dealing.

10. (*b*) It is an accident and hence suspending licence of other utilities for this happening is not a right course of action. However, instructions should be given to the people to remain inside their houses.

11. (*a*) Internet users should not suffer on account of certain individuals who indulge in internet tracking. However, such wrong doers ought to be penalised so that there are no hassles in the use of internet. Hence, only Course of action I is appropriate.

12. (*a*) II is not a feasible step. I is necessary as only education can aware the citizen about the benefits of paying taxes.
Hence, only II follows.

13. (*e*) Both the courses of action are suitable for pursuing. A large number of students failed without committing any mistake. Therefore, they should be allowed to take supplementary examinations. Also, the responsible persons should be punished.

14. (*d*) The statement mentions that the commercial banks violent a directive issued by the RBI. The remedy is only to make the banks implement the act. So, none of the course of action follows.

15. (*a*) People cannot be deprived of going to a certain destination merely for lack of berths. Instead it is the duty of the railway authority to accommodate all the booking by all means. Hence, only I follows.

16. (*e*) Both the courses of action are appropriate.

17. (*e*) To avoid such mishappening, deploying police constables can be of help. Also, if people go in groups, then such incidents can be avoided.

18. (*a*) The Government should set up an expert group to inspect the condition of school buses to avoid such accidents while II is impractical.

19. (*e*) Fishermen should, hence forth be restrained from constructing their huts along the coast line and also a team of officials should be sent to inspect the situation.

20. (*b*) Every establishment/institution has the legal right to protest by way of strike. However, Course of action II is the right course of action.

21. (*e*) Both courses of action are suitable for pursuing.

22. (*d*) Neither I nor II follows. Marriage functions could not be banned. Also, it is the duty of hospitals to provide best services and Government advice is not required.

23. (*e*) Computerisation will definitely help the users to take best available information available in the library. Also, training to the staff in computer operations can further add to betterment of services to the users. Hence, both are feasible and therefore right courses of action.

24. (*b*) Motormen should not be made the scapegoat for the failure of the signalling system.

25. (*b*) If the Government goes for I, it would impinge on the autonomy of the private sector.
Hence, only II follows.

26. (*a*) I follows as a measure of caution. But II won't solve the problem and poor electrical fittings would wreak havoc where ever the market be.

27. (*a*) The problem faced by the airlines and cargo agents is the non-availability of cargo space. Therefore, right course of action is to combat the problem.

28. (*a*) Implementation of such action plans as framed by the conference is a right course of action as it will give an immediate and effective impact on the standard of education for the children.

29. (*b*) The first course of action does not match the scale of the problem. The problem is not so big as to merit a Government enquiry. It is enough that the civic body takes action and hence, II follows.

30. (*b*) Course of action I does not follows due to the words All and immediate. Course of action II follows because a system should be implemented to certify the quality of tiffin provided.

31. (*e*) I follows because holding the elections at this juncture would render the exercise meaningless. II follows for 'heavy damage'.

32. (*d*) None focuses on the real reason of unemployability.

33. (*a*) Only by increasing our agricultural production, we can have a better position in international agricultural trade. Reduction in non-agricultural commodities will further worsen our position. So, only I is the right course of action.

34. (*a*) I is the only feasible course of action as short term internship at high school level will give students a peek into the adventurous life of the forces and motivate them towards it.

35. (*b*) Obviously, if Government has decided to stop financial support to voluntary organisations, these organisations should find other sources of financial support. Hence, II is valid.

36. (*e*) Both are the right courses of action for effective implementation of computer education at primary level in urban and rural schools.

37. (*e*) Both courses of action are protecting dolphins and definitely, the population of dolphins will increase.

38. (*e*) Statement speaks of inadequacies of the education system and emphasises the need for flexibility and revision. Hence, both the actions are right courses of action to update the curriculum.

39. (*a*) Statement points out the crisis faced by the power plants and one of the crisis is depletion of stock of steam coal with the thermal power plants in the North. Therefore, it is the right course of action to supply the steam coal to the thermal power plants. Secondly, since the water inflow into the Gobindsagar has declined, setting up of another hydraulic power plant will be futile.

40. (*a*) Keeping the State police armoury under the supervision of Central Government control is not the right course of action to bring the guilty to the book. However, an investigation may help to reveal those involved into the illegal acts. Hence, only action I is the right course of action.

41. (*e*) I is advisable in the short term while II in the long term.

42. (*b*) I is a resitive issue and not feasible. II will help take care of the rush.

43. (*d*) Going for I and II will create other problems.

44. (*e*) It is given in the statement that 'Kala Azar' has been declared as notifiable disease. Since, it is a good effort by the Government, hence effort should be made to implement the Act. Moreover, a deterrent in the form of punishment will ensure effective implementation of the Act.

45. (*b*) It is not necessary that such an epidemic occurs after four years. Hence, Course of action I is not the right course of action. Secondly, prevention during monsoon season is the right step to face the problem of conjuctivitis. So, Course of action II is the right course of action.

46. (*e*) The efficiency of the institute can be boosted up by redefining the institute's objectives laid down for this purpose and by way of finding the reasons for the failure. Hence, both the actions are right courses.

47. (*a*) According to the statement, the suitable Course of action is I. People should be encouraged to take fresh fruits and vegetables instead of medicines to meet human body's requirement of vitamins and minerals.

48. (*b*) I is an insensible action. But II will be helpful in preventing such accidents.

49. (*a*) We should remember that the culprits are mere students. Going for II instead of I would make sense only if it is a repeated act.

50. (*b*) Poor maintenance of vehicles may lead to pollution, but is seldom a cause of accident. Hence, I does not follow. But II follows as violation of traffic rules is the chief cause of accidents.

51. (*e*) Both I and II follow, because providing nourishment to children needs money. Also, making primary education compulsory is a step forward to tackle the problem of under-nourishment.

52. (*a*) I follows, because the patrolling would create a fear among the robbers and act as a deterrent. II does not follow, because it is not feasible.

53. (*b*) Going for I is an extreme action and should be resorted to only when the students fail to behave themselves after repeated warnings like the one given in II.

54. (*e*) Both I and II follow. I follows because such an advance notice makes the passengers mentally prepared, II follows as an inevitable course of action.

TYPE 02

Based on Three or More Courses of Action

In this type of questions, a statement is given followed by three or more courses of action. The candidate is required to assess the given situation and take the administrative decision(s) with regard to the given problem and provide the requisite course of action to be taken to lesson the extremities of the problem.

DIRECTIONS ~(Example Nos. 4 and 5) *A statement is given followed by three courses of action. A course of action is taken for improvement, follow-up etc. Read the statement carefully and pick the correct answer choice.*

***Ex* 04** **Statement** The meteorological department has predicted that this year, the rainfall will be 20% below normal in a particular state. « UPSSSC Mandi Parishad 2019

Courses of Action

I. Increase tax on water usage by 100%.

II. Reduce water allocated to swimming pools and resorts.

III. The government should reduce electricity generation and purchase 1,00,000 water tankers.

(a) Only I follows
(b) Only II follows
(c) Only III follows
(d) II and III follow

***Solution* (b)** Since, rainfall is below normal, then government must cut down the wastage of water, hence water allocated to swimming pools and resorts must be reduced. Therefore, only II follows.

***Ex* 05** **Statement** Many political activists have decided to stage demonstrations and block traffic movement in the city during peak hours to protest against the steep rise in prices of essential commodities. « Canara Bank (PO) 2010

Courses of Action

I. The Government should immediately ban all forms of agitations in the country.

II. The police authority of the city should deploy additional forces all over the city to help traffic movement in the city.

III. The state administration should carry out preventive arrests of the known criminals staying in the city.

(a) Only I
(b) Only II
(c) Only III
(d) Both I and II
(e) None of these

***Solution* (b)** I is not feasible in a democracy. III does not follow because the problem is not concerned with 'criminals'. II is the only course of action the authorities can resort to.

Practice / CORNER 5.2

DIRECTIONS ~ (Q. Nos. 1-39) *In each of the questions below is given a statement followed by three courses of action numbered I, II and III. A course of action is a step or administrative decision to be taken for improvement, follow-up or further action in regard to the problem, policy, etc. On the basis of information given in the statement, you have to assume everything in the statement to be true and then decide which of the three given suggested courses of action logically follows. Then, decide which of the alternatives (a), (b), (c), (d) or (e) is correct.*

1. Statement There is significant increase in the number of patients affected by some disease in a city.

Courses of Action « CGPSC 2014

I. This problem should be raised in the Municipal Corporation of the city.

II. This problem should be raised in the Parliament.

III. Hospitals in the city should be equipped properly for the treatment of patients.

Which of the following course(s) of action logically follows (follow)?

(a) I and II follow (b) Only III follows
(c) I and III follow (d) All follow
(e) None of these

2. Statement Faced with a serious resource crunch and a depressing overall economic scenario, the state 'X' is unlikely to achieve the targeted per cent compound annual growth rate during the 10th plan.

Courses of Action

I. The target growth should be reduced for the next plan.

II. The reasons for the failures should be studied.

III. The state 'X's performance should be compared with that of other states.

(a) Only I follows (b) Both I and III follow
(c) Both II and III follow (d) None follows

3. Statement Over 27000 bonded labourers identified and freed are still awaiting rehabilitation.

Courses of Action

I. More cases of bonded labourers should be identified.

II. Till the proper rehabilitation facilities are available, the bonded labourers should not be freed.

III. The impediments in the way of speedy and proper rehabilitation of bonded labourers should be removed.

(a) Only I follows
(b) Only II follows
(c) Only III follows
(d) Both II and III follow

4. Statement Higher disposal costs encourage those who produce waste to look for cheaper ways to get rid of it.

Courses of Action

I. The disposal costs should be made higher.

II. The disposal costs should be brought down.

III. A committee should be set up to study the details in this respect.

(a) Only I follows (b) Only II follows
(c) Either I or II follows (d) Both II and III follow

5. Statement If the faculty members also join the strike, there is going to be a serious problem.

Courses of Action

I. The faculty members should be persuaded not to go on strike.

II. Those faculty members who join the strike should be suspended.

III. The management should not worry about such small things.

(a) Only I follows (b) Only II follows
(c) Both II and III follow (d) None follows

6. Statement According to the officials, paucity of funds with the organisation has led to the pathetic condition of this brilliant architectural structure.

Courses of Action

I. A new architectural structure for the building should be designed.

II. The reasons for the poor condition of the structure should be found out.

III. Grant should be given to improve the condition of the structure.

(a) Only I follows (b) Only II follows
(c) Only III follows (d) Both II and III follow

7. Statement In the Teacher's Day function, Shri Sharma, a State Awardee and a retired Principal, had questioned the celebration of Teacher's Day in today's materialistic world.

Courses of Action

I. The expenditure of Teacher's Day celebration should be reduced.

II. More funds should be allocated for the celebration of Teacher's Day.

III. The role and responsibilities of teachers should be seen in today's perspective.

(a) All follow (b) None follows
(c) Either I or II follows (d) Only III follows

8. Statement The members belonging to two local clubs occasionally fight with each other on the main road and block traffic movement. « SBI (PO) 2009

Courses of Action

I. The local police station should immediately deploy police personnel round the clock on the main road.

II. Those involved in fighting should be identified and put behind bars.

III. The local administration should disband the management of the two clubs with immediate effect.

(a) Both I and II follow (b) Both II and III follow
(c) Both I and III follow (d) All follow

9. Statement Many students of the local school fell ill for the fourth time in a row in the last six months after consuming food prepared by the school canteen.

Courses of Action « SBI (PO) 2009

I. The school management should immediately terminate the contract of the canteen and ask for compensation.

II. The school management should advise all the students not a eat food articles from the canteen.

III. The owner of the canteen should immediately be arrested for negligence.

(a) None follows (b) Only II follows
(c) Only III follows (d) Both I and II follow
(e) Both II and III follow

10. Statement A blast was triggered off injuring many, when the night shift workers at an ordinance factory were handling 'fox signalling explosive'.

Courses of Action

I. The factory management should train its staff as regards to the safety aspects of handling such explosive materials.

II. The service of the supervisor incharge of the night shift should be terminated immediately.

III. The factory should immediately stop carrying out such exercises at night.

(a) None follows (b) All follow
(c) Only I follows (d) Both I and II follow
(e) None of these

11. Statement A major railway accident involving a mail train was averted due to the presence of mind of one signal man at a wayside cabin.

Courses of Action

I. The railway track for atleast 50 km should be cleared off any traffic ahead of all the mail trains.

II. The railway signalling systems should immediately be made automatic.

III. The signal man should be rewarded so as to encourage others.

(a) All follow
(b) None follows
(c) Both I and II follow
(d) Both II and III follow
(e) None of these

12. Statement Cholera broke out recently in most of the cities killing a large number of people and affecting hundreds of households.

Courses of Action

I. An enquiry should be initiated to identify the cause of the catastrophe.

II. The civic administration should make the general public aware of, through mass media, the preventive measures to be adopted in such a situation.

III. The para-military forces should be called into help the civic administration.

(a) None follows (b) Only II follows
(c) Both I and II follow (d) All follow

13. Statement A large number of tribal inhabitants are found to have been suffering from various diseases due to exposure to radioactive waste near the uranium mine.

Courses of Action

I. The Government should immediately close down the mine.

II. The Government should immediately take steps to save local people from exposure to radioactive waste.

III. The tribals should be rehabilitated at a safer place.

(a) Both II and III follow
(b) Both I and II follow
(c) Both I and III follow
(d) Only III follows

14. Statement Many school buses have fitted CNG kit without observing the safety guidelines properly. This results into some instances of these buses catching fire due to short circuit and endangering the lives of the school children. « UCO Bank (PO) 2008

Courses of Action

I. The regional transport authority should immediately carry out checks of all the school buses fitted with CNG kit.

II. The management of all the schools should stop hiring buses fitted with CNG kit.

III. The Government should issue a notification banning school buses for the use of CNG kit.

(a) Only I follows (b) Only II follows
(c) Only III follows (d) Both I and III follow
(e) None of these

15. Statement Every year thousands of eligible students do not get admission in colleges, both in urban and rural areas, after passing their school leaving certificate examination.

Courses of Action

I. More colleges should be set up in both urban and rural areas.

II. The number of schools in both urban and rural areas should be reduced.

III. More schools should offer vocational courses to equip students for taking up their vocation after completing their school education.

(a) Only I follows (b) Both II and III follow
(c) All follow (d) Both I and III follow

16. Statement Any further increase in pollution level in the city, by way of industrial effluent and automobile exhaustion, would pose a severe threat to the inhabitants.

Courses of Action

I. All the factories in the city should be immediately closed down.

II. The automobiles should not be allowed to ply on the road for more than four hours a day.

III. The Government should restrict the issue of fresh licenses to factories and automobiles.

(a) Only III follows (b) All follow
(c) Only II follows (d) None follows

17. Statement India's pre-eminent position in the world black pepper production and trade is in danger as some of the countries, which recently started production of the 'king of the spices' crop from Indian root stocks, are farming better by adopting modern cultivation practices.

Courses of Action

I. India should immediately stop supplying root stocks of black pepper to other countries.

II. India should adopt modern technology for cultivating black pepper to compete in the international market.

III. India should reduce the price of its black pepper to remain competitive in the world market.

(a) All follow (b) Only II follows
(c) Only I follows (d) Only III follows

18. Statement A large private bank has decided to retrench one-third of its employees in view of the huge losses incurred by it during the past three quarters.

« Canara Bank (PO) 2010

Courses of Action

I. The Government should issue a notification to general public to immediately stop all transactions with the bank.

II. The Government should direct the bank to refrain from retrenching its employees.

III. The Government should ask the central bank of the country to initiate an enquiry into the bank's activities and submit its report.

(a) None follows (b) Only I follows
(c) Only II follows (d) Only III follows
(e) Both I and II follow

19. Statement Incessant rain for the past several days has posed the problem of overflowing and flood as the river bed is full of silt and mud.

Courses of Action

I. The people residing near the rivers should be shifted to a safer place.

II. The people should be made aware about the immediate danger over radio/television.

III. The silt and mud from the river bed should be cleared immediately after the receding of the water level.

(a) Both I and II follow
(b) Both II and III follow
(c) Both I and III follow
(d) All follow

20. Statement In the city, over 75% of the people are living in slums and sub standard houses, which is a reflection on the housing and urban development policies of the Government.

Courses of Action

I. There should be a separate department looking after housing and urban development.

II. The policies in regard to urban housing should be reviewed.

III. The policies regarding rural housing should also be reviewed, so that such problems could be avoided in rural areas.

(a) Only I follows
(b) Only II follows
(c) Both II and III follow
(d) Either II or III follows

21. Statement Lack of coordination between the university, its colleges and various authorities has resulted in students ousted from one college seeking migration to another.

Courses of Action

I. If a student is ousted from a college, the information should be sent to all the other colleges of university.

II. The admissions to all the colleges of the universities should be handled by the university directly.

III. A separate section should be made for taking strict action against students indulging in anti-social activities.

(a) Only I follows (b) Only II follows
(c) Only III follows (d) Both I and III follow

22. Statement The institute has fixed for the investors a validity period of one year for transfer forms for some of its listed schemes.

Courses of Action

I. The institute should consult investors before fixing the duration of validity period.

II. The investors should be duly informed about the validity period.

III. List of schemes covered under this validity period should be communicated.

(a) All follow (b) Both I and II follow
(c) Both I and III follow (d) Both II and III follow

23. Statement Without the active cooperation between the proprietor and the employees of the mill, it cannot remain a profitable concern for long.

Courses of Action

I. The mill should be closed down.

II. The workers should be asked to cooperate with the owners.

III. The owner should be asked to cooperate with the employees.

(a) Both I and II follow (b) None follows
(c) All follow (d) Both II and III follow

24. Statement Some strains of mosquito have become resistant to chloroquine, the widely used medicine for malaria patients.

Courses of Action

I. Selling of chloroquine should be stopped.

II. Researchers should develop a new medicine for patients affected by such mosquitos.

III. All the patients suffering from malaria should be checked for identification of causal mosquito.

(a) None follows (b) Both I and II follow
(c) Both II and III follow (d) All follow

25. Statement In one of the accidents on a railway level crossing, fifty people died when a bus carrying them collided with a running train.

Courses of Action

I. The train driver should immediately be suspended.
II. The driver of the bus should be tried in court for negligence on his part.
III. The railways authorities should be asked to man all its level crossings.

(a) None follows
(b) Only III follows
(c) Both I and II follow
(d) All follow

26. Statement There was a spurt in criminal activities in the city during the recent festival season.

Courses of Action

I. The police should immediately investigate into the causes of this increase.
II. In future the police should take adequate precautions to avoid recurrence of such a situation during festivals.
III. The known criminals should be arrested before any such reason.

(a) None follows
(b) Both II and III follow
(c) Both I and II follow
(d) All follow

27. Statement A mass mortality of shrimps in ponds on entire Andhra coast has recently been reported due to the presence of a virus.

Courses of Action

I. The water of the ponds affected should immediately be treated for identifying the nature of the virus.
II. The catching of shrimps from the ponds should temporarily be stopped.
III. The fishermen should be asked to watch for the onset of such phenomenon in nature.

(a) Only I follows
(b) All follow
(c) Both I and II follow
(d) Both II and III follow

28. Statement The weather bureau has through a recent bulletin forecast heavy rainfall during the next week which may cause water logging in several parts of the city.

Courses of Action

I. The bulletin should be given wide publicity through the mass media.
II. The civic authority should keep in readiness the pumping system for removal of water from these parts.
III. The people should be advised to stay indoors during period.

(a) None follows
(b) Only II follows
(c) Both I and II follow
(d) Both II and III follow

29. Statement The world will have to feed more than a billion people in the next century, of whom half will be in Asia and will eat rice as their staple food.

Courses of Action

I. More funds should immediately be allocated for rice research to help ensure adequate supplies.
II. The people in Asia should be encouraged to change their food habits.
III. The rice should be grown in countries outside Asia to meet the demand.

(a) Both I and II follow
(b) All follow
(c) Both II and III follow
(d) Both I and III follow

30. Statement Occurrences of natural calamities have now increased as compared to the situation five years ago.

Courses of Action

I. Government should always be ready with the action plan for disaster management.
II. Government should not permit development activities which are likely to cause harm to nature.
III. Government should appoint a committee of environmentalists and scientists to work out plans to handle various calamities.

(a) Both I and II follow
(b) Both I and III follow
(c) Both II and III follow
(d) All follow
(e) None of the above

31. Statement Despite increasing BPO jobs in our country, a large number of educated youth are unemployed.

Courses of Action

I. Government should give unemployment allowance to all unemployed youth.
II. Government should introduce various schemes in different areas that will generate employment opportunities.
III. Efforts should be made by the society and the Government to encourage the youth for vocational education.

(a) Both I and II follow
(b) Both II and III follow
(c) Both I and III follow
(d) Only II follows
(e) None of the above

32. Statement Cases of asthama sufferers have been rising, particularly in the big cities.

Courses of Action

I. Civic authorities should ensure adequate supply of medicines at normal rates.
II. Civic authorities need to control the air pollution caused due to emission from vehicles.
III. Act of tree-cutting without permission should be severely punished.

(a) Both I and II follow
(b) Both II and III follow
(c) Only III follows
(d) Only II follows
(e) None of the above

33. Statement Many students at school and degree level are not able to master the subjects even if they have passed out with high scores.

Courses of Action

I. Education boards should examine and revise the examination system to tap the real talent.

II. Examination system at all levels should be so designed as to discourage rote learning.

III. Difficulty level of the examination papers should be significantly increased.

(a) Only I follows
(b) Only II follows
(c) Both I and II follow
(d) Either I or II follows
(e) None of these

34. Statement A large number of management institutes are mushrooming all over the country and not all the MBA's coming out are worth it.

Courses of Action

I. The Government should follow stringent norms for granting permission to the management institutes.

II. The students while taking admission should examine the market value for the degree, they are going to get.

III. The employers should make MBA as an essential qualification only for the positions where it is genuinely essential.

(a) Only I follows
(b) Only II follows
(c) Both I and II follow
(d) All follow
(e) None of the above

35. Statement Many people in the locality have fallen sick and admitted in the local hospital after consuming sweets served during a community meal.

Courses of Action « SBI (PO) 2010

I. The police should immediately arrest all the people responsible for making the sweets.

II. The people admitted in the local hospital should immediately be shifted to bigger hospitals.

III. The local food and drug authority should investigate to find out the cause of the sickness and take necessary action.

(a) Both I and III follow
(b) Both II and III follow
(c) Only III follows
(d) All follow
(e) None follows

36. Statement Many management institutes in the city have enrolled a large number of students for management courses which are not recognised either by the local university or by the department of technical education. « SBI (PO) 2010

Courses of Action

I. All these management institutes should immediately be derecognised by the university and the department of technical education.

II. All these management institutes should be asked to refund fees to all such students and enroll them only for recognised courses.

III. All such students should be advised to switch over to the recognised courses in other institutes.

(a) Only I follows
(b) Only II follows
(c) Only III follows
(d) Both II and III follow
(e) None of the above

37. Statement Large number of students have failed in the recently held SSC final examination due to their performance in the English language paper.

Courses of Action

I. The Government should immediately issue a circular to all the schools to appoint competent English language teachers.

II. The Government should immediately instruct all the schools to send their English language teachers for refresher courses to be conducted by the Government.

III. The Government should instruct the examining body to lower the difficulty level of the English language paper in the future examinations.

(a) None follows
(b) Only I follows
(c) Only III follows
(d) Both I and II follow
(e) All follow

38. Statement Every year during monsoon quite a few people get drowned and die while swimming in the sea on various beaches in the city.

Courses of Action

I. The civic administration should deploy atleast two life guards on each of the beaches during monsoon.

II. The civic administration should make arrangements to caution people whole swimming in the sea during monsoon.

III. The civic administration should put up prominent sign posts near the treacherous parts of the beaches advising people not to venture into the sea in the monsoon season.

(a) Both I and II follow
(b) Both II and III follow
(c) Both I and III follow
(d) All follow
(e) None of the above

39. Statement It is feared by the experts that there may be deficient rainfall in many parts of the country due to weak monsoon.

Courses of Action

I. The Government should immediately set up a committee of experts to study the amount of rainfall in various parts of the country.

II. The Government should make arrangements for providing relief supplies to the areas affected due to poor monsoon.

III. The farmers in the affected areas should be advised to switch over to crops requiring less water during the Kharif season.

(a) Only I follows
(b) Only II follows
(c) Only III follows
(d) Both I and III follow
(e) None of the above

DIRECTION ~(Q. No. 40) *Read the following information carefully and answer the given question.*

Despite repeated announcements that mobile phones were not allowed in the examination hall, three students were caught with their mobile phones. « SBI (PO) 2013

A. Mobile phones now-a-days have a lot of features and it is easy to cheat with their help.

B. The invigilator must immediately confiscate the mobile phones and ask the students to leave the exam hall immediately.

C. Mobile phones are very expensive and leaving them in bags outside the exam hall is not safe.

D. There have been incidents where students who left the exam hall early stole the mobile phones kept in the bags of the students who were writting the exam.

E. The school authorities must ask the students to leave their phones in the custody of the invigilator before the exam in order to avoid thefts of mobile phones.

F. None of the other students were carrying their phones in the exam hall.

40. Which of the following among A, B, D and F can be an immediate course of action for the invigilator?

(a) Only B
(b) Both A and D
(c) Only A
(d) Both D and F
(e) Only F

41. Read the following information carefully and answer the question which follows. « SBI Associate (PO) 2015

Most students from State X prefer to move base to other States for higher education. The government of the State is concerned about this problem as these students might not come back even after completing their education.

Which of the following statements may be a course of action to deal with this problem?

(a) The Government should set-up well equipped State of the Art universities which will provide quality education
(b) The Government should not give much importance to this problem as there is high density of population per square km in the State
(c) Scholarships should be declared for those students who perform well in tenth and twelfth standard examinations
(d) All the colleges and universities should be asked to emphasise the importance of higher education and benefits of studying in their institute should also be highlighted
(e) The Government should make education free for all people of the State

42. Statement The prices of vegetables and other food articles have decreased in the recent months raising hope among policy planners that the RBI's (Reserve Bank of India) tight grip on supply of liquid money in the market for controlling inflation may be eased. « IBPS (SO) 2012

Which of the following may be a possible action of the above situation?

(a) The Reserve Bank of India may not reduce its key interest rates in near future
(b) The government may step in and make certain concessions to the common people on various issues
(c) The Reserve Bank of India may consider lowering certain rates to bring in more liquidity in the market
(d) The RBI may wait for atleast another year before taking any step
(e) The RBI may collect more data from the market and wait for another four months to ensure that they take the correct step

43. Statement A severe cyclonic storm hit the Eastern coastline last month resulting in huge loss of life and property on the entire East coast and the government had to disburse a considerable amount for relief activities through the district administration machineries. « IBPS (SO) 2012

Which of the following may possibly be a follow up measure to be taken up by the government?

(a) The government may setup a task force to review the post relief scenario in all districts and also to confirm proper and user receipt of the relief supplies
(b) The government may setup a committee for proper disbursement of relief supplies in future
(c) The government may empower the District Magistrates to make all future disbursements of relief
(d) The government may send relief supplies to the affected people in future only after proper assessment of the damage caused by such calamities
(e) The government may not need to activate any follow up measure

Answers WITH EXPLANATIONS

1. (c) Only I and III follow because raising the problem in Municipal corporation will divert the attention of the administration of the city towards the problem.
Equipping the hospitals to tackle with the problem is also imperative.

2. (c) Courses of action II and III are worth pursuing the problem as defined in the statement. Reasons for failure should be studied and performance of the affected state should be compared with that of other states.

3. (c) Only Course of action III provides a feasible and effective solution to combat the problem, that impediments in the way of speedy and proper rehabilitation should be removed. Courses of action I and II are not effective courses.

4. (d) Courses of action II and III are feasible and effective to combat the problem.

5. (a) The best way to prevent faculty members to go on strike is to persuade them. Hence, Course of action I is the right course of action.

6. (c) Condition of the architectural structure can be improved by way of adequate finance. Hence, Course of action III, that grant should be given to improve the condition of the structure, is the right course of action.

7. (d) In the statement, celebration of Teacher's Day in today's materialistic world is in question which means that the role and responsibilities of teachers should be seen in today's perspective. Hence, Course of action III is the right course of action.

8. (c) A proper course of action would be serving notices to these clubs to behave themselves. Even police personnel may be deployed but only during the sensitive hours.

9. (a) Courses of action I and III would be too harsh; II is absurd. Efforts should be made to supervise the quality of the food prepared by the canteen.

10. (d) Course of action I is the right course of action because training to the staff as to the safety aspects of handling explosive material will reduce the chances of such accidents in future. Course of action II is also a right course as it will work as a deterrent to check any negligence in such work.

11. (a) Courses of action I and II will directly improve the working condition of railways. Course of action III though, not directly related with improving railway traffic conditions but will encourage other signal men to be more watchful on their duties, which in turn, will reduce the probability of accidents.

12. (d) All the courses of action provide the feasible and effective solutions for the problem discussed in the statement. Hence, all the courses of action are correct.

13. (a) Course of action I is not practical one, hence does not follow. Courses of action II and III are right courses and deal with the problem positively and effectively.

14. (a) As safety guidelines are not observed by many school buses, so, regional transport authority should carry out checks of all the buses fitted with CNG kit. So, course of action I follows. CNG is a pollution free fuel and its course are more than petrol and diesel so, it should be encouraged but with safety norms. So, course of action II and III do not follow.

15. (d) The statement describes the problem of admission in colleges faced by students. Both the courses of action I and III are the right steps towards providing solution of this problem.

16. (a) The existing industrial units and automobiles ought to be checked for pollution level and fitted with proper equipments to minimise the same. Restricting their operation is no solution. So neither I nor II follows. Besides, fresh licences ought to be given only to those vehicles or factories which operate at the optimum emission level. So, only III follows.

17. (b) Only better quality can put India back in the competitive field of black pepper production. So, India should go for modern technology for cultivating black pepper to compete in the present international market.

18. (d) Course of action I would be an extreme step. Course of action II is not within the Government's preview. Course of action III is advisable when there is retrenchment on such a large scale.

19. (d) All actions given are right course(s) of action following problem caused by the incessant rain for the past several days because each of the courses will provide relief to the victims.

20. (b) The statement speaks of the failure of housing and urban development policies of the Government, hence the policies in regard to urban housing should be reviewed.

21. (a) Only Course of action I is the right course of action which says that, if a student is ousted from a college, the information should be sent to all the other colleges of university. This is the way by which coordination between the university and the colleges can be maintained.

22. (d) The investors should be informed about the validity period, and the list of schemes covered under this validity period should be communicated so that the investors can be benefited from this facility.

23. (d) It is given in the statement that cooperation between the proprietor and the employees is required for profit making reasons. It is therefore, required that both employees and proprietor should cooperate with each other.

24. (c) It is given in the statement that chloroquine has become ineffective for malaria patients. Therefore, researchers should develop a new medicine for the patients and all the patients suffering from malaria should be checked for identification of the causal mosquito.

25. (b) The problem discussed in the statement is not regarding the current accident, but to do something to avert such mishaps. Accidents at railways crossings can be averted by deploying men to regulate traffic and installing barriers to check traffic movement when a train passes by. Hence, only III follows.

26. (c) I and II Courses of action logically follow because it is necessary for police to investigate into the causes and to avoid the recurrence of such situations, police should take adequate precautions.

27. (b) All courses of action logically follow. First of all, the water in ponds should be treated to identify the nature of the virus. Since the problem is being faced, so the catching of the shrimps from the ponds should be temporarily stopped. Also, the fisherman should be asked to watch for the onset of such phenomenon in nature.

28. (d) II and III Courses of action logically follow because for such time the pumping system for removal of water should be kept ready and the people should be advised to stay indoor during the period.

29. (*d*) I and III Courses of action logically follow. Since, in the next century the increased population will have to be fed more rice, hence, it is necessary to allocate more funds for rice research to help ensure adequate supplies. Besides, the rice should be grown in countries outside Asia to meet the demand.

30. (*d*) If the Government is not ready with the action plan for disaster management, then it is not possible to remove distress, hence Course of action I is appropriate. If the Government permits development activities which are likely to cause harm to nature, then natural calamities will increase, hence, II follows. If the Government appoints a committee of environmentalists and scientists and takes action accordingly, then it will be beneficial. Hence, Course of action III is appropriate.

31. (*b*) If the Government gives allowances to all the unemployed youths, then there will be great loss of money and they will not think for their future. Hence, I does not follow. II follows because various schemes in different areas will reduce the unemployment. If the Government and society introduce vocational education, it will also reduce unemployment. Hence, Course of action III follows.

32. (*a*) Civic authorities should ensure adequate supply of medicines at normal rates. By this we can control asthama. Hence, course of action I follows. Pollution is caused due to emission of fumes from vehicles. Due to this, problem in breathing is caused and asthama spreads.

Hence, controlling pollution is necessary. Hence, II follows but Course of action III is not related to the statement.

33. (*c*) Course of action I follows because on examining the examination system, the defects of the education system can be removed.

Course of action II also follows because the system of education should be so designed as to discourage rote learning. But Course of action III does not follow because it is of no use.

34. (*c*) It is necessary for the Government to follow stringent norms for granting permission to the management institutes. For the students too, it is necessary to examine the market value of the degree while taking admissions. But course of action III is not related to the statement. Hence, Courses of action I and II are appropriate.

35. (*c*) Only III follows. After finding the cause of the sickness, necessary action should be taken.

36. (*a*) The prime and effective course of action is derecognisation of such institutes by the university. Hence, the Course of action I is appropriate.

37. (*d*) To improve the standard in English language, the Courses of action I and II are necessary.

38. (*d*) In order to save the people from getting drowned, all the courses of action are necessary.

39. (*b*) Only, the Course of action II is appropriate because providing relief supplies to the affected areas is necessary.

40. (*a*) The immediate course of action for the invigilator is that he must immediately confiscate the mobile phones and ask the students to leave the exam hall immediately.

41. (*d*) When the students get to know the benefits of studying in college and universities of their own State, then they will think twice before going outside the State for higher education. Hence, correct action will be option (d).

42. (*e*) From the given statement, the RBI may collect more data from the market and wait for another four months to ensure that they take the correct step for controlling inflation.

43. (*b*) Option (b) may be a follow up measure as it will help in proper disbursement of relief supplies.

CHAPTER / 06

Assertion and Reason

Assertion is a strong and forceful statement or claim an opinion/a fact/a comment/made in regard with a thing, element for its use and effects. Reason means a fact, event or statement that provides an explanation to the assertion.

In the questions based on Assertion and Reason, two statements are given. Out of these two statements, one is the Assertion (A) and other is the Reason (R).

The candidate is required to analyse whether the reason is an optimum and correct explanation of the assertion.

Some times both assertion and reason are correctly stated facts but the reason does not correctly explain the assertion.

So, different possibilities can exist between these two statements and accordingly the correct answer is marked from the given alternatives.

The examples given below will give you a better idea about 'Assertion and Reason'.

DIRECTIONS ~ (Example Nos. 1-5) *Choose the correct alternative from the following options for the Assertion* (A) *and Reason* (R) *given below.*

Give answer

(a) If both 'A' and 'R' are true and 'R' is the correct explanation of 'A'
(b) If both 'A' and 'R' are true but 'R' is not the correct explanation of 'A'
(c) If 'A' is true but 'R' is false
(d) If 'A' is false but 'R' is true

***Ex* 01 Assertion** (A) Silver is not used to make wires.
Reason (R) Silver is a bad conductor.

Solution (c) Besides a good conductor of electricity, silver is not used to make electric wires because it is expensive. Hence, Assertion is true but Reason is false.

***Ex* 02 Assertion** (A) India celebrates its Independence Day on 15th August.

Reason (R) India became independent on 15th August, 1947. « MAT 2018

Solution (a) Both the assertion and reason are true and the reason is correct explanation of assertion.

As, India became independent on 15th August, 1947, so its Independence Day is celebrated every year on 15th August.

***Ex* 03 Assertion** (A) A body weighs less when immersed in water.
Reason (R) Newton's law explains the above phenomenon. « MAT 2013

Solution (c) A is true and R is false. Newton's law discusses about the force, while a body weighs less when immersed in water because of buoyancy.

***Ex* 04 Assertion** (A) We feel colder on mountains than on plains.
Reason (R) Temperature decreases with altitude. « NIFT (UG) 2014

Solution (a) Both A and R are true and R is the correct explanation of A. Above the sea level, temperature decreases with an increase in altitude which makes mountain peaks colder.

***Ex* 05 Assertion** (A) The colour of light with the shortest wavelength is violet.
Reason (R) One can notice this colour of light on one end of the rainbow which has seven colours of different wavelengths. « MAT 2011

Solution (b) Both A and R are true but R is not the correct explanation of A.

***Ex* 06** An Assertion (A) and Reason (R) are given below.
Assertion (A) Leakages in household gas cylinders can be detected.
Reason (R) LPG has a strong smell.
Choose the correct option. « RRB NTPC 2016

(a) Both A and R are true and R is the correct explanation of A
(b) Both A and R are true and R is not the correct explanation of A
(c) Both A and R are false
(d) A is true but R is false

Solution (a) LPG contains ethyl mercaptan which has strong smell. Because of this, smell leakages in household gas cylinders can be detected.

***Ex* 07** In the following question, there are two statements labelled as Assertion (A) and Reason (R).
Assertion (A) Autism is a developmental disability.
Reason (R) Heredity and lower development of brain are the causes of the Autism. « SSC (CGL) 2014

(a) 'A' is false and 'R' is true (b) Both 'A' and 'R' are false
(c) Both 'A' and 'R' are true (d) 'A' is true and 'R' is false

Solution (c) Both A and R are true. Autism is caused by Heredity and lower development of brain.

Master Exercise

DIRECTIONS ~ (Q.Nos. 1-35) *Choose the correct alternative from the following options for the Assertion* (A) *and Reason* (R) *given below.*

Give answer

(a) If both 'A' and 'R' are true and 'R' is the correct explanation of 'A'
(b) If both 'A' and 'R' are true but 'R' is not the correct explanation of 'A'
(c) If 'A' is true but 'R' is false
(d) If 'A' is false but 'R' is true

1. **Assertion** (A) India is a democratic country. « MAT 2018
Reason (R) People elect their own representatives who form the government.

2. **Assertion** (A) In India, 2nd October, is observed as 'Martyr's Day'. « MAT 2018
Reason (R) Pt. Nehru was the first Prime Minister of India.

3. **Assertion** (A) Copper is used to make electrical wires. « MAT 2018
Reason (R) Copper is a good conductor of electricity.

4. **Assertion** (A) Methane gas released by some industries lends to global warming. « UPSSSC Mandi Parishad 2018
Reason (R) Methane is a heavy gas and it settles in the lower regions of the atmosphere.

5. **Assertion** (A) Railway tracks are longer during the day than at night. « UPSSSC Mandi Parishad 2018
Reason (R) Days are hotter and metal expands due to heat.

6. **Assertion** (A) Rainwater harvesting reduces soil erosion.
Reason (R) Rainwater harvesting is not important for conservation of water. « RRB NTPC 2016

7. **Assertion** (A) The steam engine was invented by James Watt. « CMAT 2016
Reason (R) There was a problem of taking out water from flooded mines.

8. **Assertion** (A) Inside the Earth, metals are present in molten state. « CMAT 2016
Reason (R) Earth absorbs the Sun's rays.

9. **Assertion** (A) The escape velocity from the surface of the moon is less than that from the Earth's surface.
Reason (R) The Moon has no atmosphere. « MAT 2011

10. **Assertion** (A) The British sovereignty continued to exist in India.
Reason (R) The British sovereign appointed the last Governor-General of free India. « MAT 2004

11. **Assertion** (A) Increase in carbon dioxide would melt polar ice. « NIFT (UG) 2014
Reason (R) Global temperature would rise.

12. **Assertion** (A) We prefer to wear white clothes in winter.
Reason (R) White clothes are good reflectors of heat. « RRB NTPC 2016

13. **Assertion** (A) Forest cutting is undesirable from the point of view of soil erosion.
Reason (R) Cutting of forests reduces the interception of rain water. « MAT 2008

14. **Assertion** (A) Most of the Himalayan rivers are perennial.
Reason (R) They are fed by melting snow. « MAT 2008

15. **Assertion** (A) Ashoka pillars have retained their gloss on their surface.
Reason (R) Moisture laden winds do not blow in the areas where it is located. « MAT 2008

16. **Assertion** (A) Graphite is slippery and used as a lubricant.
Reason (R) Graphite has free electrons. « NIFT (PG) 2014

17. **Assertion** (A) India's 'Republic Day' falls on 26th January.
Reason (R) Constitution of India, declaring India as a 'Republic', came into force on 26th January 1950. « MAT 2013

18. **Assertion** (A) India is a democracy.
Reason (R) India is a developing country. « MAT 2013

19. **Assertion** (A) In India, the judiciary is independent of the executive.
Reason (R) Judiciary favours the government and helps in the implementation of its plans. « NIFT (PG) 2014

20. **Assertion** (A) Carbon monoxide when inhaled causes death.
Reason (R) Carbon monoxide combines with hemoglobin. « NIFT (PG) 2014

21. **Assertion** (A) India is a secular country.
Reason (R) Indian people can practice any faith they like. « MAT 2013

22. **Assertion** (A) Tamil Nadu gets most of the rainfall in winter.
Reason (R) Tamil Nadu gets rainfall from retreating monsoons. « NIFT (PG) 2014

23. **Assertion** (A) Clothes are not washed properly in hard water.
Reason (R) Hard water contains many minerals. « NIFT (PG) 2014

24. **Assertion** (A) The common value of all religion should be taught to the children in our schools.
Reason (R) Yes, it will help in calculating moral values amongst the children of our country. « MAT 2014

25. **Assertion** (A) Indira Gandhi was the Prime Minister of India for many years.
Reason (R) Indira Gandhi was the daughter of Jawaharlal Nehru. « MAT 2014

26. **Assertion** (A) India is a 'sovereign' country.
Reason (R) Policies of India are decided by USA. « MAT 2014

27. **Assertion** (A) Mahatma Gandhi is considered as 'Father of the nation' in India.
Reason (R) Mahatma Gandhi was the first Governor General of Independent India. « MAT 2014

28. **Assertion** (A) 'DNA' Finger Printing has become an important test to establish paternity and identify of criminal of rape cases.
Reason (R) Small samples such as hair, dried blood and semen are adequate for DNA analysis. « MAT 2014

29. **Assertion** (A) Too much work causes stress.
Reason (R) It disturbs the body balance between its capacity and the demand. « MAT 2012

30. **Assertion** (A) Good performance at work causes satisfaction.
Reason (R) Job satisfaction results in good performance. « MAT 2012

31. **Assertion** (A) Social integration at workplace is necessary.
Reason (R) There are many backward classes in society. « MAT 2012

32. **Assertion** (A) An apple a day keeps the doctor away.
Reason (R) Apple are very costly. « MAT 2012

33. **Assertion** (A) Perennial rivers mostly originate from the Himalayas.
Reason (R) The fountains in the Himalayas feed the rivers. « RRB NTPC 2016

34. **Assertion** (A) In the ordinary fire extinguisher, carbon dioxide is generated by the chemical reaction of sodium bicarbonate and dilute sulphuric acid.
Reason (R) Carbon dioxide can be used to extinguish fire. « MAT 2011

35. **Assertion** (A) All machines suffer a loss of efficiency due to the frictional force acting on any moving member of that machine.
Reason (R) The frictional force can be reduced by providing a thin film of lubricant between any two mating parts. « MAT 2011

DIRECTIONS ~ (Q. Nos. 36-64) *In each of the following questions, there are two statements labelled as Assertion* (A) *and Reason* (R).

Give answer
(a) If both 'A' and 'R' are true and 'R' is the correct explanation of 'A'
(b) If both 'A' and 'R' are true but 'R' is not the correct explanation of 'A'
(c) If 'A' is true but 'R' is false
(d) If 'A' is false but 'R' is true
(e) If both 'A' and 'R' are false

36. **Assertion** (A) Salt is added to cook food at higher altitudes.
Reason (R) Temperature is lower at higher altitudes.

37. **Assertion** (A) Indian President is the head of the state.
Reason (R) Indian Parliament consists of the President, Lok Sabha and Rajya Sabha.

38. **Assertion** (A) Aurangzeb failed in his Deccan policy.
Reason (R) He could not follow the policy of appeasement.

39. **Assertion** (A) Land breeze blows during night.
Reason (R) Land gets heated up quickly.

40. **Assertion** (A) We feel comfortable in hot and humid climate.
Reason (R) Sweat evaporates faster in humid climate.

41. **Assertion** (A) Bulb filament is made of titanium.
Reason (R) The filament should have low melting point.

42. **Assertion** (A) Ventilators are provided near the roof.
Reason (R) Conduction takes place better near the roof.

43. **Assertion** (A) Uttar Pradesh is called the 'Sugar Bowl' of India.
Reason (R) Uttar Pradesh is the leading sugarcane producer.

44. **Assertion** (A) Venus is placed distant from Sun as compared to Mercury, yet it is the hottest planet.
Reason (R) Immense carbon dioxide in the atmosphere of Venus creates a green house effect.

45. **Assertion** (A) Pluto is the coldest planet.
Reason (R) It receives slanty rays of the Sun.

46. **Assertion** (A) Baking soda creates acidity in the stomach.
Reason (R) Baking soda is alkaline.

47. **Assertion** (A) There is rainbow in the sky only after rains.
Reason (R) Water drops suspended in the air break up Sun's rays into seven colours.

48. **Assertion** (A) Mohammad-bin-Tughlaq is called the 'wisest fool'.
Reason (R) He had wise plans but implemented them foolishly.

49. **Assertion** (A) DDT has now-a-days lost its use as an insecticide.
Reason (R) DDT is harmful to man.

50. **Assertion** (A) Buddha left home after his marriage.
Reason (R) He wished to be free of all worldly ties and become an ascetic.

51. **Assertion** (A) Carbon dioxide turns lime water milky.
Reason (R) Carbon dioxide sullies the water.

52. **Assertion** (A) Red-green colour blindness occurs with more frequency in males than in females.
Reason (R) Females have two 'X' chromosomes and males have one.

53. **Assertion** (A) Food materials should not be soaked in water for a long time.
Reason (R) Washing leads to loss of vitamin A and vitamin D from the food stuff.

54. **Assertion** (A) Pressure cookers are fitted with ebonite handles.
Reason (R) Ebonite is a strong conductor of heat.

55. **Assertion** (A) Earth is the only planet known to have life.
Reason (R) Earth has an atmosphere which is a mixture of oxygen, nitrogen and carbon dioxide.

56. **Assertion** (A) Leaves of plants are green.
Reason (R) Plants contain chromoplasts, the green pigment.

57. **Assertion** (A) There is no vaccine for AIDS.
Reason (R) The AIDS virus changes its genetic code.

58. **Assertion** (A) In India, females have higher life expectancy than the males.
Reason (R) Females receive a better diet.

59. **Assertion** (A) Unpolished rice should be eaten.
Reason (R) Polished rice lacks vitamin B.

60. **Assertion** (A) A salt water fish drinks sea water whereas a fresh water fish never drinks water.
Reason (R) A salt water fish is hypertonic to its environment while a fresh water fish is not hypertonic to its environment.

61. **Assertion** (A) River Narmada flows westward.
Reason (R) Narmada falls into the Bay of Bengal.

62. **Assertion** (A) Himalayas once laid under the sea.
Reason (R) Fossils of marine creatures are traced on the Himalayas.

63. **Assertion** (A) Eskimos reside in igloos.
Reason (R) No other material except snow is available.

64. **Assertion** (A) India celebrates its Independence day on 15th August, 1947.
Reason (R) India become independent on 15th August 1947.

Answers / WITH EXPLANATIONS

1. (*a*) Both the assertion and reason are true and the reason is correct explanation of assertion. India, being a democracy, it is a government run by the representatives elected by its people.

2. (*d*) Assertion is false as 2nd October is observed as International Day of non-violence. But the reason is true.

3. (*a*) Both the assertion and reason are true and the reason is correct explanation of assertion. As, we use copper to make electrical wires because it is a good conductor of electricity.

4. (*a*) Since, assertion given says methane released is playing a role to cause global warming and reason given correctly explains the assertion as methane setteled in tropopause and stratosphere. Breaking down methane molecule into carbon dioxide in water and causes green house effect and desinteration of ozone layer respectively. Hence, both A and R true are and R is the correct explanation of A.

5. (*a*) Assertion bears the fact of thermal expansions in metal. There is small increment in the dimensions of metalic substances when slowly treated with heat. Hence, both A and R true and R is the correct explanation of A.

6. (*c*) A is true, but R is false one of the main reason of rainwater harvesting is conserve water for future.

7. (*a*) The problem of pumping out water from the flooded mines required the need of a self-working engine which led James Watt to invent the same.

8. (*c*) Inside the Earth, the high temperature and pressure keep the metals in molten state. The Earth reflects the Sun's rays rather than absorbing them.

9. (*b*) We know that the escape velocity depends on the value of G (Universal gravitational constant) and M (Mass of body). The escape velocity from the surface of the Moon is less than from the Earth's surface because the value of G and M are less than that of Earth. So, both A and R are true but R is not the correct explanation of A.

10. (*d*) India drafted its own constitution and formed its own government after gaining independence. Hence, A is false but R is true.

11. (*a*) The carbon dioxide envelope in Earth's atmosphere traps the heat. With increase in the proportion of carbon dioxide, the global temperature would rise, thus causing the polar ice to melt.

12. (*d*) We prefer to wear dark clothes in winter as they absorb the heat and keep the body warm. However, white clothes are good reflectors of heat and are worn in summer.

13. (*a*) It is true that the forest cutting is undesirable from the point of view of soil erosion and cutting of forests reduces the interception of rain water. So, R is complete explanation of A.

14. (*a*) Most Himalayan rivers are perennial as they are fed by melting snow throughout the year. Therefore, R is the correct explanation of A.

15. (*c*) Because of superior quality material being used, Ashoka pillars have retained their gloss on their surfaces. Hence, R is completely false.

16. (*b*) Graphite possesses a layer structure with two successive layers held by weak forces. Because of such weak forces these layers are able to slide over one another. Therefore, graphite is slippery and because of this property, it is used as lubricant.

17. (*a*) Constitution of India, declaring India as a 'Republic', came into force on 26 January 1950. So, we celebrate Republic day on 26 January. Hence, R correctly explains A.

18. (*b*) India is a democracy and India is a developing country both statements are true but India is a developing country does not explain that India is a democracy. Hence, both A and R are true but R is not correct explanation of A.

19. (*c*) A is true but R is false. As in India, the judiciary is completely independent of the executive the government has no interference in the judicial affairs.

20. (*a*) Both A and R are true and R is the correct explanation of A. As, carbon monoxide combines with the hemoglobin when it is inhaled, if forms carboxy hemoglobin compound which inhibits the transport of oxygen.

21. (*a*) Both A and R are true and R is the correct explanation of A. Since India is a secular country, people of India can practice any faith they like.

22. (*a*) Both A and R are true and R is the correct explanation of A as, rainfall in Tamil Nadu is caused by the retreating which occurs in winter.

23. (*b*) Both A and R are true but R is not the correct explanation of A. Clothes are not washed properly in hard water because it does not form lather with soap. However, it is true that hard water contains many minerals.

24. (*a*) Both A and R are true and R is the correct explanation of A. As, Teaching common values of all religion should be taught to the children in our schools will help in calculating moral values amongst the children of our country.

25. (*b*) Indira Gandhi was the Prime Minister of India for many years but she was the daughter of Jawaharlal Nehru is not related to the first one. Hence, both A and R are true but R is not the correct explanation of A.

26. (*c*) A is true and R is false. As, India is a 'sovereign' country, policies of India are not decided by USA.

27. (*c*) A is true and R is false. As, Mahatma Gandhi is considered as 'Father of the nation' in India but he was not the first Governor General Independent India.

28. (*a*) Both A and R are true and R explains of A. As, DNA fingerprinting or DNA profiling, any of several similar techniques for analysing and compairing DNA from seprate sources, used especially in law enforcement to identify suspects from hair, blood, semen, or other biological materials found at the scene of a violent crime.

It depends on the fact that no two people, save identical twins, have exactly the same DNA sequence and that although only limited segment's of a persons DNA are scrutinized in the procedure, those segments will be statistically unique.

29. (*a*) Too much work causes stress because it disturbs the body balance between its capacity and the demand. Hence, both A and R are true and R is the correct explanation of A.

30. (*c*) 'Good performance at work causes satisfaction' is definitely true but it cannot be determined whether job satisfaction results in good performance or not. Hence, A is true but R is false.

31. (*b*) 'Social integration at workplace is necessary' is definitely true but the reason given is not a correct explanation for this social integration. Hence, both A and R are true but R is not the correct explanation of A.

32. (*c*) 'An apple a day keeps the doctor away' is definitely true but the statement R may or may not be true. Hence, A is true but R is false.

33. (*c*) A is true, but R is false Perennial rivers usually originate from mountainous snowy regions or glaciers.

34. (*a*) Both A and R are true and R is the correct explanation of A.

35. (*b*) As, frictional force is always act in the direction opposite to the applied force, so all the machines suffer a loss of efficiency. Hence, both A and R are true but R is not the correct explanation of A.

36. (*b*) As pressure decreases at higher altitudes, water boils much below 100°C, so that the food does not get sufficient heat for being cooked. Salt increases the boiling point of water.

37. (*b*) Both A and R are true. Indian President is the constitutional or titular head of the executive, the real power being vested in the Council of Ministers.

38. (*a*) R explains A as Aurangzeb failed in his Deccan policy mainly due to political and religions intolerance.

39. (*b*) Land gets heated up quickly and also cools quicker than sea at night so that cool wind called the land breeze blows from land to sea.

40. (*e*) We do not feel comfortable in hot and humid climate as in hot weather, body sweats more but this sweat does not evaporates easily because of high humidity.

41. (*e*) Filament of a bulb is made of tungsten as it can be drawn into very thin metal wires that have a high melting point.

42. (*c*) Air, upon heating, rises and so can be thrown out of a room through high ventilators. This is the reason why ventilators are provided near the roof.

43. (*a*) Uttar Pradesh is the leading sugarcane producer of India and this is the reason why this state is called 'Sugar Bowl' of India.

44. (*a*) 97% of Venus atmosphere comprises of carbon dioxide that traps the incoming solar energy very efficiently.

45. (*c*) Pluto is the coldest planet, as Pluto being farthest from the Sun, hardly gets the Sun's rays.

46. (*d*) Being alkaline, baking soda neutralizes the acidity in the stomach.

47. (*a*) Water droplets act like prisms. Sun's rays falling on water droplets undergo dispersion, producing spectrum.

48. (*a*) He is known as wisest fool because of good plans and bad implementation which is clearly pointed out is a reason.

Hence, R correctly explains A.

49. (*b*) Insects have developed immunity against DDT. This is the reason why DDT has lost its use as an insecticide. Further, it is very much true that DDT is harmful to man.

50. (*a*) Buddha left home after his marriage as he wished to free himself of all worldly ties to become an ascetic.

51. (*c*) Carbon dioxide reacts with lime water *i.e.,* calcium hydroxide to form milky precipitate of calcium carbonate.

52. (*a*) 'X' chromosome is responsible for Red-Green colour blindness. Because female have two X chromosome and male have only one. So, Red-Green colour blindness occurs with more frequency in males than in females. Hence, R correctly explains A.

53. (*c*) Soaking food materials in water for long time leads to loss of water soluble vitamin B and vitamin C.

54. (*c*) Ebonite is a bad conductor of heat. It does not heat up. This is the reason why handles of pressure cookers are made of ebonite.

55. (*b*) Earth has presence of water which is the sustainer of life on it.

56. (*c*) Leaves contain green pigment-chlorophyll. This is the reason behind their being green. Plants contain chromoplasts but they are not green pigments.

57. (*a*) Infact a vaccine contains the inactivated germs of the disease. But the AIDS virus changes its genetic code and no vaccine has been invented for so far.

58. (*e*) Because of high birth rate and negligence, females have lower life expectancy than males in India. Although a better diet is a requirement for females, they do not receive that.

59. (*a*) Unpolished rice should be eaten as the husk of unpolished rice contains vitamin B1, the deficiency of which causes the disease Beri-Beri.

60. (*a*) Assertion is true, and this happens because a salt water fish is hypertonic to its environment while a fresh water fish is not hypertonic to its environment.

61. (*c*) River Narmada flows westward and drains into the Arabian sea.

62. (*a*) Himalayas are the young fold mountains which at one time are believed to lie inside the Tethys sea. This is evident from the recovery of fossils of marine creatures on its peak.

63. (*c*) Eskimos live in snow houses called igloos as such houses are warm inside.

64. (*a*) India became independent on 15th August 1947, so it celebrates independence day on 15th August.

CHAPTER / 07

Cause and Effects

It is a fundamental property of nature that events do not just happen; they happen because there was a cause behind them. These causes are the conditions under which these events happen.

The necessary condition for an event to occur is a cause which supplements an event to occur.

For a cause to be valid it must be either sufficient or necessary.

1. **Necessary Condition** is one that must be satisfied for the occurrence of an event.
2. **Sufficient Condition** for an event to take place is that condition under whose presence event must occur.

e.g., For life to exist on earth, we require (a) air (b) water (c) food.

Condition (a), (b) and (c) together makes sufficient conditions for life to exist on earth but individually they are necessary condition for life to exist on earth.

Therefore, we can say that there may be more than one necessary conditions for the occurrence of an event and all those necessary conditions must be included in the sufficient conditions.

Different Types of Causes

Immediate Cause It immediately precedes the effect. In other words immediate causes are the most proximate in time, to the effect.

e.g. I slapped Rohan after that he slapped me. Here, the immediate cause is "I slapped Rohan".

Principal Cause It is the most important reason behind the effect. The immediate cause can be the principal cause and *vice versa.*

e.g. Rohit fails in annual exam because he does not study. Here, the principal cause is "he does not study".

Common Cause Two effects given in two statements may be caused by a third unmentioned event which may be called the common cause of the given events.

e.g. **Statement 1** Global warming is increasing.

Statement 2 The glaciers are melting. Here, the common cause will be the amount of carbon dioxide is increasing.

Mainly two types of questions are asked from Cause and Effects, which are discussed as under.

TYPE 01

Two Statements Based Questions

In this type of questions, two statements are given and the student has to identify whether they are independent causes or effects of independents causes or a common cause etc., and accordingly have to select the answer options.

Following examples will give a better understanding about the types of questions asked

DIRECTIONS ~ (Example Nos. 1-5) *In each of these questions, two Statements* I *and* II *are given. These may have a cause and effect relationship or may have independent causes or be the effects of independent causes.*

Give answer

(a) If Statement I is the causes and Statement II is its effect

(b) If Statement II is the cause and Statement I is its effect

(c) If both Statements I and II are effects of independent causes

(d) If both Statements I and II are effects of some common cause

Ex 01

I. The Times of India has reported today that water of Ganga at Varanasi contains level of pollutant much higher than the permissible limit.

II. The people living in the area are to be shifted to another area to avoid a catastrophic situation.

« NIFT (PS) 2015

Solution (d) Both are the effects of common cause i.e. water of Ganga at Varanasi contains higher level of pollutant.

Ex 02

I. The Government has planned to make arrangements for supply of safe drinking water from Tehri Dam.

II. The Ganga water at Kanpur is not even fit for bathing as it contains very high level of pollutants.

« NIFT (PS) 2015

***Solution* (b)** Statement II is the cause i.e. Water of Ganga is not even fit for bathing and Statement I is its effect because Government is taking necessary action for the occurred problem.

Ex 03

I. The internet users of the country have been advised to stay alert while using internet till the hackers are caught.

II. The Government machinery will make an all out effort to catch those who are responsible for hacking and put in place a sound internet security system for all its websites. « NIFT (PS) 2015

***Solution* (d)** Both the statements are the effects of common cause i.e. hackers are active.

Ex 04

I. The prices of petroleum products dropped marginally last week.

II. The State Government reduced the tax on petroleum products last week. « MAT 2013

***Solution* (b)** State Government reduced the tax on petroleum products last week, that is why the price of petroleum products dropped marginally, so Statement II is the cause and Statement I is the effect.

Ex 05

I. Many people visited the religious place during the weekend.

II. Few people visited the religious place during the week days. « MAT 2013

***Solution* (d)** People visit religious places for peace and other religious activities. So, the cause remains the same despite of the effect that they visit on different days. Thus, both statements are effects of independent causes.

DIRECTIONS ~ (Example Nos. 6-7) *Below in the questions are given two statements A and B. These statements may be either independent causes or may be effects of independent causes or a common cause. One of these statements may be the effect of the other statement. Read both the statements and decide which of the following answer choices correctly depicts the relationship between these two statements.*

Give answer

(a) If Statement A is the cause and Statement B is the effect
(b) If Statement B is the cause and Statement A is the effect
(c) If both the Statements A and B are independent causes
(d) If both the Statements A and B are effects of independent causes
(e) If both the Statements A and B are effects of common cause

Ex 06

A. The government has made the rules for the disposal of waste and other chemicals from the industries more stringent to keep a check on pollution level in the atmosphere.

B. Complex reaction of chemicals, such as sulphur dioxide and nitrogen oxide emitted from power plants, industries and automobiles escalate the level of particulate matter in the atmosphere. « MHT MBA 2017

***Solution* (b)** Clearly, due to the escalation in the level of particulate matter in the atmosphere the government has mandate to keep a check on pollution level in the atmosphere. Hence, Statement B is the cause and Statement A is its effect.

Ex 07

A. There is increase in water level of all water tanks supplying drinking water to the city during the last fortnight.

B. Most of the trains were cancelled last week due to water logging on the tracks.

***Solution* (e)** The problems discussed in both the statements are clearly the result of heavy rain in the area. Hence, A and B both are effects of common cause. Therefore, option (e) is correct.

Practice / CORNER 7.1

DIRECTIONS ~(Q. Nos. 1-50) *Below in each question are given two Statements A and B. These statements may be either independent causes or may be effects of independent causes or of a common cause. One of these statements may be the effect of the other statement. Read both the statements and decide which of the following answer choices correctly depicts the relationship between these two statements.*

Give answer

(a) If Statement A is the cause and Statement B is its effect
(b) If Statement B is the cause and Statement A is its effect
(c) If both statements are independent causes
(d) If both statements are effects of independent causes
(e) If both statements are effects of some common cause

1. **Statement A** Ahmed is a healthy boy.
Statement B His mother is very particular about the food he eats.

2. **Statement A** The average day temperature of the city has increased by about 2 degrees in the current year over the average of past ten years.
Statement B More people living in rural areas of the state have started migrating to the urban areas in comparison with the earlier year. « SBI (PO) 2010

3. **Statement A** Most of the shopkeepers in the locality closed their shops for the second continuous day.
Statement B Two groups of people living in the locality have been fighting with each other with bricks and stones, forcing people to stay indoors. « SBI (PO) 2010

4. **Statement A** The Government has decided to increase the prices of LPG cylinders with immediate effect.

Statement B The Government has decided to increase the prices of Kerosine with immediate effect.

« BOI (PO) 2010

5. **Statement A** Party 'X' won clear majority in the recently held state assembly elections.

Statement B Of late, there was unrest in public and also among the members of the ruling party of the state. « BOI (PO) 2007

6. **Statement A** There has been an increase in the underground water level column at all places in Delhi due to the last year's monsoon rains.

Statement B Many trains had to be cancelled last year due to water-logging on the railway tracks.

« IBPS Clerk (Mains) 2017

7. **Statement A** The prices of sugar had risen very sharply in Indian markets last year.

Statement B The Government imported large quantities of sugar as per trade agreements with other countries last year. « IBPS Clerk (Mains) 2017

8. **Statement A** The prices of petrol and diesel in the domestic market have remained unchanged for the past few months.

Statement B The crude oil prices in the international market have gone up substantially in the last few months.

9. **Statement A** It is the bounden duty of each member of the civil society to control the air pollution by contributing their best in this endeavour to safeguard the health of their countrymen.

Statement B The alarming air pollution in our country is causing asthma cases to constantly multiply.

10. **Statement A** The Government has recently fixed the fees for professional courses offered by the unaided institutions which are much lower than the fees charged last year.

Statement B The parents of the aspiring students launched a severe agitation last year protesting against the high fees charged by the unaided institutions.

11. **Statement A** Despite giving their best performance, more than 100 employees of XYZ Pvt. Ltd. have been laid off.

Statement B More than 40% employees of XYZ Pvt. Ltd. who have crossed the age of 50 yrs have been asked to take voluntary retirement from their services.

« Andhra Bank (PO) 2016

12. **Statement A** As per the statistics, there has been a rise in the number of electric cars in country 'Y' this year.

Statement B The oil prices have fallen strongly in country. 'Y' this year and are estimated to stay low for at least two years for now and not decrease further.

« New India Assurance Company Ltd (AO) 2015

13. **Statement A** Staff members of the university decided to go on strike in protest during the examinations.

Statement B The university administration made all the arrangements for smooth conduct of examination with the help of outsiders. « BOI (PO) 2007

14. **Statement A** In the university examination, overall performance of students from college 'X' was better than that of students from college 'Y'.

Statement B Majority of the students depend upon coaching classes for university examinations.

« SBI (PO) 2007

15. **Statement A** The Government of state 'X' decided to ban working of women in night shifts and also in late evening hours.

Statement B The percentage of working women has a significant rise in the last one decade. « SBI (PO) 2007

16. **Statement A** Frequent robberies in jewellery shops were recorded in distant suburbs of the city.

Statement B Shop owners in the city and suburbs demanded improvement in security situation from the police authorities. « SBI (PO) 2007

17. **Statement A** The staff of airport authorities called off the strike they were observing in protest against privatisation.

Statement B The staff of airport authorities went on strike, anticipating a threat to their jobs.

18. **Statement A** The university authority has decided to conduct all terminal examinations in March/April every year to enable them to declare results in time.

Statement B There has been considerable delay in declaring results in the past due to shortage of teachers evaluating the answer sheets of the examination conducted by the university.

19. **Statement A** Government has decided to distribute part of the foodgrain stock through Public Distribution System to people below poverty line.

Statement B There has been bumper kharif crop for the last two seasons. « Andhra Bank (Clerk) 2009

20. **Statement A** Most of the students enrolled themselves for the educational tour scheduled for next month.

Statement B The school authority cancelled the educational tour scheduled for next month.

« Andhra Bank (Clerk) 2009

21. **Statement A** The prices of fruits have dropped substantially during the last few days.

Statement B The prices of foodgrains have increased substantially during the last few days.

« Andhra Bank (PO) 2009

22. **Statement A** The road traffic between the two towns in the state has been disrupted since last week.

Statement B The rail traffic between the two towns in the state has been disrupted since last week.

« Andhra Bank (PO) 2009

23. Statement A Heavy showers are expected in the city area during the next forty-eight hours.

Statement B The inter-club cricket tournament scheduled for the week was called off.
« Andhra Bank (PO) 2009

24. Statement A The prices of vegetables have been increased considerably during the summer.

Statement B There is tremendous increase in the temperature during this summer there by damaging crops greatly.

25. Statement A The private medical colleges have increased the tution fees in the current year by 200% over the last year's fee to meet the expenses.

Statement B The Government medical colleges have not increased their fees inspite of price evaluation.

26. Statement A The police authority has recently caught a group of house breakers.

Statement B The citizens group in the locality have started night vigil in the area.

27. Statement A Huge tidal waves wrecked the vast coastline early in the morning killing thousands of people.

Statement B Large number of people gathered along the coastline to enjoy the spectacular view of sunrise.
« PNB (PO) 2008

28. Statement A The Government has suspended several police officers in the city.

Statement B Five persons carrying huge quantity of illicit liquor were apprehended by police.
« PNB (PO) 2008

29. Statement A The traffic police removed the signal post at the intersection of two roads in a quiet locality.

Statement B There have been many accidents at the intersection involving vehicles moving at high speed.
« PNB (PO) 2008

30. Statement A The local steel company has taken over the task of development and maintenance of the civic roads in the town.

Statement B The local civic body requested the corporate bodies to help them maintain the civic facilities. « PNB (PO) 2008

31. Statement A Majority of the students in the college expressed their opinion against the college authority's decision to break away from the university and become autonomous.

Statement B The university authority has expressed its inability to provide grants to its constituent colleges. « PNB (PO) 2008

32. Statement A Worldwide recession has created uncertainity in job market.

Statement B Many people are opting for change from private sector to public sector. « MHA-CET 2009

33. Statement A A large number of employees could not report to the duty on time.

Statement B Police had laid down barricades on the road to trap the miscreants. « MHA-CET 2009

34. Statement A There was a huge crowd of buyers at various shopping outlets in the city.

Statement B Prices of most of the commodities have gone up substantially in the recent past.
« MHA-CET 2009

35. Statement A There has been constant rise in the number of immigrants to the metropolis for last many years.

Statement B The infrastructure of the metropolis is struggling to take care of its increasing population.
« MHA-CET 2009

36. Statement A This year, the Government has decided to procure foodgrains earlier than the stipulated date.

Statement B This year, the farmers have decided to sell their crops to private traders. « IRMA 2006

37. Statement A The farmers have decided against selling their Kharif crops to the Government agencies.

Statement B The Government has reduced the procurement-price of Kharif crops starting from last month to the next six months.

38. Statement A The Reserve Bank of India has recently put restrictions on few small banks in the country.

Statement B The small banks in the private and cooperative sector in India are not in a position to withstand the competitions of the bigger in the public sector.

39. Statement A The Government has marginally increased the procurement price of wheat for the current crop.

Statement B The current wheat crop is expected to be 20% more than the previous wheat crop.
« Andhra Bank (PO) 2010

40. Statement A The braking system of the tourist bus carrying 40 passengers failed while negotiating a stiff climb on a hilly road.

Statement B The tourist bus fell into the gorge killing at least ten passengers and seriously injuring all the remaining. « IPPB PO (Mains) 2017

41. Statement A The state Government has decided to boost English language education in all the schools from the next academic year.

Statement B The level of English language of the school students of the State is comparatively lower than that of the neighbouring states.
« IPPB PO (Mains) 2017

42. Statement A The municipal authority demolished the tea stall located on the footpath on the busy road.

Statement B A large number of people have been taking their evening tea at the tea stall located on the footpath on the main road, blocking pedestrian movement. « PNB (PO) 2010

43. **Statement A** Majority of the students left the local school as the school building was in a dilapidated condition.

Statement B The school authority decided to close down the school immediately and shift the remaining students to a make shift school.

44. **Statement A** There has been mass recruitment of IT professionals by Indian IT companies.

Statement B Many developed countries are increasingly outsourcing IT related functions to India and China. « UBI (PO) 2009

45. **Statement A** Many farmers have given up jute cultivation as it is no longer economically viable.

Statement B The textile ministry has proposed a hike in the Minimum Support Price of jute. « UBI (PO) 2009

46. **Statement A** The Government is considering changes in the Land Acquisition Act.

Statement B Several large infrastructure development projects have been stalled due to unavailability of land. « UBI (PO) 2009

47. **Statement A** The Government is considering the possibility of involving private sector companies in highway construction projects.

Statement B The implementation of many highway projects undertaken by Government agencies is behind schedule in various states.
« Punjab & Sindh Bank (PO) 2009

48. **Statement A** The price of aircraft fuel has risen during the past few months.

Statement B Many passenger airlines in India have been forced to cut their air fares by about 10%.
« Punjab & Sindh Bank (PO) 2009

49. **Statement A** The life today is too fast, demanding and full of variety in all aspects which at times leads to stressful situation.

Statement B Number of suicide cases among teenagers is on increase.

50. **Statement A** The bank has provided a link on its website to obtain feedback from customers.

Statement B Customers have been complaining about poor services in the bank's branches.
« Punjab & Sindh Bank (PO) 2009

DIRECTIONS ~ (Q. Nos. 51-53) *In each of the following questions two statements* I *and* II *are given. They may or may not be cause and effect relationship between the two statements.* « NIFT (PG) 2012

Give answer

(a) If Statement I is the cause and Statement II is its effect
(b) If Statement II is the cause and Statement I is its effect
(c) If both the Statements are independent causes
(d) If both the Statements are independent effects

51. **Statement I** School education has been made free for children of poor families.

Statement II Literacy rate among poor is steadily growing.

52. **Statement I** Hallmarking of gold jewellery has been made compulsory.

Statement II Many persons do not prefer to buy hall marked jewellery.

53. **Statement I** Many vegetarians are suffering stomach ailments.

Statement II Many dead fish were found near the lake shor.

DIRECTIONS ~(Q. Nos. 54-58) *In each of these questions, two Statements* I *and* II *are given. These may have a cause and effect relationship or may have independent causes or be the effects of independent cause.* « MAT 2013

Give answer

(a) If Statement I is the cause and Statement II is its effect
(b) If Statement II is the cause and Statement I is its effect
(c) If both Statements I and II are effects of independent causes
(d) If both Statements I and II are effects of some common cause

54. **Statement I** There is sharp decline in the production of oil seeds this year.

Statement II The Government has decided to increase the import quantum of edible oil.

55. **Statement I** Large number of people living in the low-lying areas have been evacuated during the last few days to safer places.

Statement II The Government has rushed in relief supplies to the people living in the affected areas.

56. **Statement I** International Agency for Research on Cancer (IARC) —an arm of the World Health Organisation (WHO)—will meet in France to take a call on bitumen, the black, oily material used to make roads to be banned as probably carcenogenic, *i.e.*, causing cancer to humans.

Statement II IARC has asked experts from across the globe to submit data from their research studies conducted on bitumen so as to help it to come to some conclusion.

57. **Statement I** In a survey conducted recently in America, almost 70% of Americans said they find it easier to care for their cars than their personal health. 40% of them said they would be more likely to address their issues with their car than their health .

Statement II Base on the above survey, the national campaign network for men's health launched this awareness through Abbott Laboratories to encourage men to visit their doctors more often to enjoy better health.

58. **Statement I** The local cooperative credit society has decided to stop giving loans to farmers with immediate effect.

Statement II A large number of credit society members have withdrawn major parts of their deposits from the credit society.

DIRECTIONS ~ (Q. Nos. 59 and 60) *In each of these questions, two Statements* I *and* II *are provided. These may have a cause and effect relationship or may have some common cause or be the effects of independent causes.*

Give answer

(a) If Statement I is the cause and Statement II is the effect
(b) If Statement II is the cause and Statement I is its effect
(c) If both statements are effects of independent causes
(d) If both statements are effects of some common cause

59. **Statement I** Six months after Glaxo Smith Kline (GSK) consumer healthcare India brought in its global oral care brand Sensodyne to the Indian market, Sensodyne has garnered a 10% share of the sensitive toothpaste market.

Statement II GSK has not only invested heavily in the advertising and promotion of the brand but has contacted 15000 dentists in two months and in keen on building on the sensodyne equity.

60. **Statement I** A mobile phone, if kept on during an air flight, can actually disrupt the plane's electronic systems and eventually lead to crash; a study has reveald. Older planes are most at risk to mobiles, Laptops and iPads.

Statement II One case involved a Boeing 747 flying at a height of 4500 feet whose pilot disengaged by itself. When the flight attendants went through the cabin, they found four passengers using their cell phones. Once these were switched off, the flight carried on without any problem.

DIRECTIONS ~ (Q. Nos. 61-66) *In each question, two Statements* A *and* B *are provided. These may have a cause and effect relationship or may have independent causes.*

Give answer

(a) If the Statement A is the cause and Statement B is its effect
(b) If the Statement B is the cause and Statements A is its effect
(c) If both statements are effects of independent causes
(d) If both statements are effects of some common cause

61. **Statement A** Sri Lankan skipper Kumar Sangakara justified his decision to step down from the captaincy of the ODI and T20 teams by saying, 'I will be 37 by the next World Cup and I can't be sure of my place in the team. It is better that Sri Lanka is now led by a player who will be at the peak of his career during that tournament'

Statement B Remarkably, unlike most skippers whose individual performance drops after assuming the leadership role, Sangakara has actually batted better as captain in all three formats of the game. « MAT 2012

62. **Statement A** India is ranked fifth most powerful country in the world, next to US, China, Russia and Japan, in the hierarchy of top 50 nations, identified on the basis of their GDP, as per national security index.

Statement B The assessment is based on defence capability, economic strength, effective population, technological capability and energy security of top 50 countries. « MAT 2012

63. **Statement A** The prices of 'silver' have gone up from ₹27000 per kg to ₹50000 per kg in almost a year's time.

Statement B Indian jewellers are receiving a lot of demand for the silver ornaments from American and European clients. « MAT 2012

64. **Statement A** There is an alarming increase in the number of young unemployed MBA's this year in comparison to the last year's figures.

Statement B Nearly one lakh applications were received against a recruitment call given by a private bank for only ten vacant posts. « MAT 2012

65. **Statement A** Many people visits the religious places on week days and weekends to pray to Mother Durga in Navratras.

Statement B Many religious people go on fasting during Navratras to seek the blessings of Mother Durga. « MAT 2012

66. **Statement A** Indian women don't believe in donating blood. According to the first ever data bank on gender distribution of blood donors, India has only 6% blood donations by women. The rest 94% were male donors.

Statement B Just twenty five countries in the world collect more than 40% of their blood supplies from female donors, these include Australia, US, Thailand, Switzerland, Portugal, New Zealand, Mongolia, Zimbabwe, etc. « MAT 2018

Answers / WITH EXPLANATIONS

1. (*b*) Since, Ahmed's mother take care of what he eats, Ahmed has a good health.

2. (*d*) Both statements are effects of independent causes.

3. (*b*) The fighting has led to the closure of the shops.

4. (*e*) It seems the price of Petroleum has increased in general. Alternatively, subsidies may have been reduced, again a cause common to both the statements.

5. (*e*) It can be safely assumed that party 'X' was earlier in the opposition and has benefitted from anti-incumbancy. But A and B are consequences of a common cause, *i.e.*, bad governance by the ruling party.

6. (*e*) Clearly, both the statements are the effects of some common cause.

7. (*a*) Statement I is the cause and Statement II is its effect.

8. (*d*) Since, in one part of word prices are same and in other parts prices are shooting up. So, Statement I and II both are the effect of independent causes.

9. (*b*) Statement II is cause and Statement I is effect.

10. (*b*) Closing the schools for a week and the parents with drawing their words from the local schools are independent issues, which must have been triggered by different individual causes. Thus, Statement II is cause and Statement I is its effect.

11. (*e*) Both the statements are effects of some common cause.

12. (*b*) Electric cars does not depend on the prices of oil, so both the Statements I and II are effects of independent causes.

13. (*a*) Since, the staff members have gone on strike, the help of outsiders has been sought.

14. (*d*) A seems to have happened as X is a better college. B seems to be the result of the falling standard of teaching in colleges.

15. (*d*) A might have happened because harassment of woman is on the rise while B seems to be the result of a change in gender role perception.

16. (*a*) The robberies have led to a demand of improvement in security situation.

17. (*d*) Clearly, calling of the strike and going on strike are events that may not be backed by the same cause. Therefore, they must have been effects triggered by separate independent causes.

18. (*c*) Both statements are independent causes.

19. (*b*) The bumper crop has led to the largesse shown by the Government. Thus, Statement II is the cause and Statement I is its effect.

20. (*c*) A happened so that students could see more of the world. B happened so that the school may attend to other important task. So, both statements are independent causes.

21. (*d*) A has happened because of increased supply of fruits. B has happened because of decreased supply of foodgrains. So, both are effects of independent causes.

22. (*e*) A and B both seem to have a common cause, agitation on a large scale.

23. (*a*) The fear of rain has led to the tournament being called off.

24. (*b*) Clearly, damage to crops due to high temperature may have resulted in a short supply of vegetables and an increase in their prices.

25. (*c*) The increase in the fees of the private colleges and there being no increase in the same in Government colleges seem to be policy matters undertaken by the individual decisive boards at the two levels.

26. (*e*) Both the statements A and B are clearly backed by a common cause, which is clearly an increase in the number of thefts in the locality.

27. (*e*) It appears some special cosmic phenomenon has led to both A and B.

28. (*d*) A certainly cannot be the effect of B, if we believe in an ethical world. A is the effect of bad policing and B of good policing.

29. (*a*) The removal of the signal post has led to the accident.

30. (*b*) A has been done in response to B.

31. (*c*) It is obvious from given statements that both are independent causes of action.

32. (*a*) Many people are opting for change from private sector to public sector because worldwide recession has created uncertainly in the job market. It is considered that public sector jobs are more certain than the private sector jobs. So, Statements A is the cause while Statements B is the effect.

33. (*b*) A large number of employees could not report to the duty on time because police had laid down barricades on the road to drop the miscreants. So, Statement B is the cause while Statement A is its effect.

34. (*d*) Both Statements A and B are effects of independent causes.

35. (*a*) Clearly, A is the cause and B is the effect.

36. (*b*) Government has decided to procure foodgrain earlier than the stipulated data because farmers are planning to sell their crops to private traders. So, Statement B is the cause and Statement A is its effect.

37. (*b*) The reduction in procurement price of crops must have instigated the farmers not to sell their produce to Government agencies.

38. (*b*) The inability of the small banks to compete with the bigger ones shall not ensure security and good service to the customers, which is an essential concomitant that has to be looked into by the RBI. It seems to be a remedial step for the same.

39. (*a*) The Government initiative has led to greater wheat cultivation.

40. (*a*) Brake failure led to the accident.

41. (*b*) Since the level is lower, the Government has decided to boost English language education.

42. (*b*) Since pendestrian movement was getting blocked, the authority demolished the tea stall.

43. (*e*) Dilapidated condition of the school is the common cause.

44. (*b*) The outsourcing has led to creation of jobs in IT in India.

45. (*a*) Seeing the farmers getting discouraged, the Government has taken this step.

46. (*b*) Since the projects have been stalled, the Government is considering an amendment.

47. (*b*) The inability of Government has led it to explore the private sector.

48. (*d*) A is usually the effect of hike in global petroleum prices. B is usually the effect of competition in aviation.

49. (*d*) Both statements are effects of independent causes.

50. (*b*) The surge in complaints has led the banks to receive them in an electronic mode.

51. (*a*) Statement II is the effect of Statement I.

52. (*b*) Since many people have reservations about buying hallmarked jewellery, therefore it has been made compulsory.

53. (*d*) Statement I and Statement II are not related to each other and seem to be effects of different causes.

54. (*a*) A sharp decline in oil seed production is bound to reduce oil supply and import of oil is the only means to restore the essential supply.

55. (*d*) Both statements are effects of some common cause as these are measures taken by Government.

56. (*d*) Since, both Statements I and II are effects of some common cause *i.e.*, bitumen causing cancer to humans.

57. (*a*) Here, Statement I is the cause and Statement II is its effect *i.e.*, after the survey is conducted, then based on that survey, national campaign network for men's health launched its awareness.

58. (*b*) Here, Statement II is the cause and Statement I is its effect *i.e.*, since a large number of members have withdrawn major amount of deposits from the credit society, so the credit society has decided to stop giving loans to farmers with immediate effect.

59. (*d*) Both the Statements I and II are effects of some common cause.

60. (*a*) Statement I is the cause and Statements II is its effect.

61. (*c*) Both statements are effects of independent causes.

62. (*b*) Statement B is the cause and Statement A is its effect because India's rank as the fifth most powerful county is based on its defence capability, economic strength, effective population, technological capability and energy security among top 50 countries.

63. (*c*) The prices of 'silver' going up from ₹ 27000 per kg to over ₹ 50000 per kg and Indian jewellers receiving a lot of demand for the silver ornaments from American and European clients are effects of independent causes.

64. (*a*) Statement A is the cause and Statement B is its effect.

65. (*d*) 'Blessing of Mother Durga' is a common cause between two statements.
Hence, both the statements are effects of some common cause.

66. (*c*) Both statements are effects of an independent cause.

TYPE 02

Based on Selection of Logically Related Cause or Effect

In such type of questions, a cause or effect is given followed by 4 or 5 options. The student has to choose the correct effect or cause from the options which suits the given statement most.

Given examples will help understand such type of questions better.

***Ex* 08 Cause** Two wings of a building complex in a residential area collapsed.

Which of the following is the possible effect of the cause mentioned above?

I. Most of the flats of such residential wings were vacant from long time.
II. A flat owner got done some major repairing works and in this process a main part got collapsed.
III. Residents of the other wings in the complex were said to vacate their flats immediately.

(a) Only I (b) Only II
(c) Only III (d) Both II and III
(e) None of these

***Solution* (c)** Because of the collapse of certain wings, the residents of other wings may be said to vacate their flats, so that the residents of other wings could be safe from possible danger. Hence, option (c) is correct.

***Ex* 09 Effect** Cost of Petroleum products has been increased almost 20% in last two months.

Which of the following may be the possible cause of the effect mentioned above?

(a) The cost of vegetables and other food items has been increased by more than 30%
(b) Union of truck owners has decided to increase carriage about 20% with immediate effect
(c) In last couple of weeks, the cost of crude oil in the international market has been increased immensely
(d) People have decided to protest against the inertia of government towards essential commodities
(e) None of the above

***Solution* (c)** It is the obvious reason for the given effect.

***Ex* 10 Effect** The prices of food grains and vegetables have increased by about 30% in the past three months.

Which of the folllowing can be a probable cause of the above effect? « CG PSC 2013

(a) The farmers have decided to change their farming style
(b) The prices of other products have increased more than 30%
(c) The number of farmers has reduced
(d) Occupation of farming has not been viewed as a reputed work
(e) None of the above

***Solution* (b)** The prices of foodgrains and vegetables have increased by about 30% due to increase of more than 30% in the price of other products, because farmers will need 30% more funding for purchasing other products.

Practice CORNER 7.2

1. **Cause** The Government has recently increased its taxes on Petrol and diesel by about 10%.

   Which of the following can be a possible effect of the above cause? « CBI (PO) 2010

   (a) The Petroleum companies will reduce the prices of petrol and diesel by about 10%
   (b) The Petroleum companies will increase the price of petrol and diesel by about 10%
   (c) The Petroleum companies will increase the prices of petrol and diesel by about 5%
   (d) The petrol pumps will stop selling petrol and diesel till the taxes are rolled back by the Government
   (e) None of the above

2. **Effect** Majority of the employees of the ailing organisation opted for voluntary retirement scheme and left the organisation with all their retirement benefits within a fortnight of launching the scheme.

   Which of the following can be a probable cause of the above effect? « IOB (PO) 2010

   (a) The company has been making huge losses for the past 5 yr and is unable to pay salary to its employees in time
   (b) The management of the company made huge personal gains through unlawful activities
   (c) One of the competitons of the company went bankrupt last year
   (d) The company owns large tracts of land in the state which will fetch huge sum of its owners
   (e) None of the above

3. **Effect** Atleast 20 school children were seriously injured while going for a school picnic during the weekend.

   Which of the following can be a probable cause of the above effect? « RBI (Grade 'B') 2009

   (a) The teacher accompanying the school children fell ill during the journey
   (b) The bus in which the children were travelling met with an accident while taking turn on the main highway
   (c) The driver of the bus in which the children were travelling did not report after the break at the halting place on their journey
   (d) The school authority banned all school picnics for the next six months with immediate effect
   (e) None of the above

4. **Cause** Government has recently decided to hike the procurement price of paddy for the rabi crops.

   Which of the following will be a possible effect of the above cause? « RBI (Grade 'B') 2009

   (a) The farmers may be encouraged to cultivate paddy for the rabi season
   (b) The farmers may switch over to other cash crops in their paddy fields
   (c) There was a drop in production of paddy during Kharif season
   (d) Government may not increase the procurement price of paddy during the next Kharif season
   (e) Government will buy paddy from the open market during the next few months

5. **Cause** A severe cyclonic storm swept away most part of the state during the last two days.

   Which of the following cannot be a possible effect of the above cause? « PNB (PO) 2009

   (a) Heavy rainfall was reported in most part of the state during the last two days
   (b) Many people were rendered homeless as their houses were flown away
   (c) The communication system of the state was severely affected and continues to be out of gear
   (d) Government has ordered that all the offices and schools should be kept open
   (e) All above are possible effects

6. **Cause** It has been reported by some important news papers that current year monsoon can be lower than desired level as in so many part of the country it is not raining as it is required.

   Which of the following can be a possible effect of above mentioned situation? « UBI (PO) 2011

   (a) People from less rain affected area can be displaced towards urban area
   (b) Government can help the farmers of these areas with money package
   (c) Government can declare these areas as drought regions
   (d) People can blame Government for this situation and they can protest for not getting sufficient water for agriculture
   (e) None of the above

7. **Effect** It has been reported in recent years that so many seats remain vacant in the engineering colleges of the country, at the end of admission session.

   Which of the following can be possible cause for the effect mentioned above? « IBPS (PO) 2011

   (a) Because of the bad state of economy in the recent years, there has been dearth of jobs for engineering graduates
   (b) Students have always given a priority to 3 yr engineering course in stead of 4 yr
   (c) Government has decided to give professional training to all qualified engineering graduates on Government expenditure
   (d) The success rate of engineering graduates has always been very poor
   (e) None of the above

8. **Cause** To make available banking services to all citizens Government has decided to give directions to banks for opening of new branches so that one branch of any bank must be available for villages having population 1000 or more or for group of villages having population less than 1000.

Which of the following can be the possible effect of the cause mentioned above in the passage?

(a) All the banks will follow the directives of Government
(b) No bank will follow the directives of the Government
(c) Banks will incur great loss
(d) Only public sector banks will follow the directives of the Government

9. Effect Most of the final year students of the management institution have opted specialisation in finance.

Which of the following can be a possible cause of the effect mentioned in the above passage?

(a) Last year, students with other specialisation got better proposals for jobs than those specialised in HR
(b) Management institution gives specialisation in finance only to the final year students
(c) Last year, students with specialisation in finance got most of the beneficial proposals in comparison to those specialised in marketing or HR
(d) Management institution apart from already giving specialisation in marketing and HR, has afflate started specialisation in finance
(e) None of the above

DIRECTION ~ (Q.No. 10) *Study the following information carefully and answer the question given below.*

The principal of St. Mary school organised extra classes for week students of X class and the concerned teachers are getting paid extra amount for the classes. But the average salary of teachers more or less remains the same.

10. What can be the reason behind the average of the salary remain same of teachers?

I. Student of class X attend the extra class two or three days in a week although the teachers provide the class regularly.
II. Teachers started taking more holidays after the commencement of the extra classes.
III. Teachers are already working overtime for checking and preparing homework for students on daily basis. « IBPS Clerk Mains 2018

(a) Both I and II (b) Both II and III
(c) Only II (d) Only III
(e) None of these

11. Effect During the last six months the sale of four wheelers has come down in comparison to the sale of four wheelers last year for the same period.

Which of the following can be the possible cause for the effect mentioned above?

I. Government has increased the excise duty on the four wheelers from the beginning of this year.
II. Cost of petrol has increased immensely during the last eight months.
III. Interest rates on car and home loans has been increasing from last seven months. « IBPS (PO) 2011

(a) I, II and III (b) Both I and II
(c) Both II and III (d) Only II
(e) Only I

12. Cause School authority has increased the tution fee excessively from the current academic session.

Which of the following can be possible effect of the cause mentioned in the above passage?

I. Parents of the students of this school will get their child admitted in other schools.
II. No new student will get admission in this academic session.
III. Parents of the students of this school will contact the school authority for the roll back of the increased fee.

(a) None (b) Only II
(c) Only III (d) Only I
(e) Both II and III

13. Cause There has been incessant rain during the last 48 h.

Which of the following can be a possible effect for the cause mentioned in the above statement?

I. Transport system of the city has completely failed from last 48 h.
II. There is flood like situation in most down town areas of the city.
III. So many slum dwellers have been shifted to municipal schools.

(a) Both I and II (b) Both II and III
(c) Both I and III (d) I, II and III

14. Statement Most part of the boundary walls of the local school collapsed completely last night.

Which of the following can be a possible consequence of the facts stated in the above statement? « OBC (PO) 2010

I. The local school authority will close down the school till the boundary walls are erected.
II. The Government will levy penalty to the school management for their negligence.
III. The management of the school will erect temporary fences till the boundary walls are erected.

(a) Only I (b) Only II
(c) Both II and III (d) Both I and III
(e) None of these

15. Statement The prices of foodgrains and other essential commodities have decreased for the second consecutive week.

Which of the following can be possible consequence of the facts stated in the above statement? « OBC (PO) 2010

I. The consumer price index will come down considerably.
II. People will increases their purchase of quantity of essential commodities and foodgrains.
III. Government will increase its taxes on essential commodities and foodgrains.

(a) Both I and II (b) Both II and III
(c) Both I and III (d) All I, II and III
(e) None of these

16. Statement Many students were caught while using unfair means during the final examinations by the special team of the university.

Which of the following can be a possible consequence of the facts stated in the above statement? « OBC (PO) 2010

I. The teacher responsible for invigilation in all such examination halls in where the students were caught are to be suspended from their services.
II. All those students who were caught while using unfair means are to be debarred from appearing in these examinations for a year.
III. The college should be blacklisted by the university for holding final examinations atleast for a year.

(a) Only I (b) Only II
(c) Only III (d) Both II and III
(e) None of these

17. Cause All the major rivers in the state have been flowing way over the danger level for the past few weeks.

Which of the following is/are possible effect(s) of the above cause? « Canara Bank (PO) 2007

I. Many villages situated near the riverbanks are submerged, forcing the residents to flee.
II. Government has decided to provide alternate shelter to all the affected villagers residing near the river banks.
III. The entire state has been put on high flood alert.

(a) Only I (b) Both I and II
(c) Both II and III (d) All I, II and III
(e) None of these

18. Effect Government has allowed all the airlines to charge additional amount as peak time congestion charges for the flights landing between 6 : 00 a m and 10 : 00 am.

Which of the following is a probable cause of the above effect? « Canara Bank (PO) 2007

(a) All the airline companies had threatened to suspend their services during peak hours
(b) The Government has increased its tax for peak time flights
(c) The aircrafts are routinely put on hold over the airports while landing during peak time, causing extra fuel consumption
(d) The airline companies can now charge unlimited additional charge for peak time flights
(e) None of the above

19. If two objects (or events) are correlated by cause and effect in such a manner that A causes B, it is argued that B also causes A. For example, high debts in a country causes slow growth, therefore slow growth in a country will definitely lead to increase in debts.

Which of the following examples fall in line with the condition presented above?

(a) Better health leads to higher incomes, therefore people with higher incomes definitely have better health.
(b) We never vote because politicians never do what our group wants, therefore politicians are paying more need to us in order to make us vote.
(c) Higher the intake of high calorie diet, higher is the risk of coronary heart diseases, therefore people who have coronary heart disease definitely consume high calorie diets.
(d) Company A generates higher profits in the year in which its client generates higher profits, therefore the Company A generates higher profits, will definitely make higher profits as well.
(e) A windmill rotates faster when more wind is observed, therefore more winds will be caused if the windmill is rotating faster.

Answers WITH EXPLANATIONS

1. (*e*) Companies may hike the price to cover the loss because of the increased tax. But increase in price is totally the matter of company, we cannot make any guesses about it.

2. (*a*) It should be the obvious cause for the given effect.

3. (*b*) We often hear of accidents leading to such injuries.

4. (*a*) The decision of hiking the procurement price of a crop may encourage the farmers to cultivate it.

5. (*d*) In such a catalcysmic scenario, the Government is likely to order the closure of offices and schools.

6. (*c*) Option (b) is also possible but its possibility can only be after declaring the areas as drought regions.

7. (*a*) It is the obvious possible cause.

8. (*a*) Government's directive is followed on priority basis.

9. (*c*) It is the obvious possible cause.

10. (*b*) Both Statements II and III can be the reason behind the average of the salary remain same of teachers.

11. (*a*) All may be the possible causes.

12. (*c*) Only III can be the possible effect.

13. (*d*) I, II and III, all the three can be the possible effects.

14. (*c*) Both II and III can be a possible consequence.

15. (*a*) I and II can be possible consequences.

16. (*d*) II and III can be possible consequence. It will be a tosh if all such teachers who invigilate, in all such examinations are suspended.

17. (*d*) All I, II and III are possible effects.

18. (*c*) Option (c) seems to be a probable cause.

19. (*c*) Except (c), all others do not follow the condition presented in the question.

CHAPTER / 08

Passage and Conclusions

It is a combination of an information based passage followed by some conclusions based on that, which are to be checked according to a given set of directions.

This section demands a thorough reading of a passage with a clear understanding of the subject and then judging the truth of certain pre-given statements based upon candidates vision of understanding but that should match the questioner's vision of understanding too. This process can be made simpler by using the correct way of logical interpretation of the passage.

This section deals with the questions in which unusual patterns of conclusions are inferred on the basis of a passage. Such conclusions are unusual as they are different from other type of conclusions which are based on the statements (as in case of syllogism).

Infact, other type of conclusions are definite *i.e.,* they are either definitely true or definitely false but here in the passage based conclusions, probability factor is also taken into consideration.

It means apart from definite conclusion, (either definitely true or false), these passage based conclusions have scope for probability of truthfulness or falsity. This is the reason why these conclusions may be definitely true or definitely false or probably true or probably false.

Explanation of all these four types of conclusions will give a better idea about how to draw such inference

1. Definitely True

Such inferences are either directly given in the passage or are drawn on the basis of given information in the passage and logical analysis. They should prove to be 100% true.

See the following example

Passage 1

What to say about the greatness of the great Sachin Tendulkar. He does not need any introduction as more than 30 thousand international runs, 100 international centuries and 23 yr of long career inspite of so many serious injuries speak volume for him. The time when his colleagues like Rahul Dravid and Saurav Ganguli have called it a day, Sachin is still on his job.

Conclusions

I. Sachin has played international cricket for more than 20 yr.

II. Sachin has played with Rahul Dravid and Saurav Ganguli in the past.

Solution

(i) Conclusion I is definitely true from the sentence given in the passage '23 yr of long career'.

(ii) Conclusion II is definitely true because of the presence of word colleague. As Rahul Dravid and Saurav Ganguli have been the colleagues of Sachin, hence, he must have played with them in the past.

2. Definitely False

Such inferences either directly deny the facts given in the passage or by logical analysis, they prove to be 100% false.

See the following example

Passage 2

A worrying feature of Indian urbanisation has been its tendency to increase pressure on the inner cities. The first results of the 2001 census suggest that the density of population in urban areas is within manageable limits, with most cities, including Greater Mumbai, being well below the 23000 per square m mark, set by Kolkata but within several of the older cities, the walled areas have high densities which exert pressure on the outdated amenities in these areas, a pressure that is accentuated by the poor maintenance of housing as well as other assets in the inner cities. The inner cities were designed for a pattern of urban life far removed from what exists today. The makers of narrow winding lanes could hardly have anticipated modern transportation. « UCO Bank (PO) 2010

Conclusions

I. The density of population in the inner city of Greater Mumbai is the highest in India.

II. At the time of planning the cities in the past, the use of bigger roads was envisaged by the planners.

Solution

(i) It is given in the passage that as per 2001 census, density of population in the inner city of Greater Mumbai is within manageable limits.
Hence, conclusion is definitely false as it contradicts the information given in the passage.

(ii) It is clear from the last line of the passage.

3. Probably True

The word probable means that there are chances of occuring or not occuring of an event. This option is available for testing a conclusion when it is not definitely true. In other words, it does not follow the statement directly. It is to be noted here that a conclusion is not definitely true because there exists little chance for its being wrong as well. Therefore, there is every possibility of its swing towards truthfulness.

See the following example

Passage 3

After the victory in the last two test series, Mahendra Singh Dhoni has become the most successful Indian captain in terms of test wins surpassing the former best Saurav Ganguli. No doubts, India will record another victory in the upcoming test series against Australia, if Dhoni gets a chance to captain the Indian side again against the Kangaroos. Further, Dhoni needs only two runs to complete his 4000 test runs, cricket lovers hope that his dream also be fulfilled against Australia.

Conclusions

I. Dhoni will definitely be the Indian captain against Australia in the upcoming test series.

II. Dhoni will complete 4000 test runs in his next test match.

Solution

(i) Conclusion I is probably true as Dhoni's past performances as an Indian captain make a fair chance for his being captain in the upcoming test series against Australia. However, the captain has not been declared so for, hence, it cannot be definitely said that he will certainly get the captaincy.
No doubts, his past record is fabulous but some other factors may play a vital role behind his not being the captain. *e.g.*, Because of some personal reasons, Dhoni may keep himself out of the captaincy but inspite of all these facts, the conclusion derived has greater swing towards probability of being true.

(ii) Conclusion II will be probably true as Dhoni has to score only 2 runs to complete his 4000 test runs. As 2 runs is a very little score to complete 4000 test runs, hence, the chances are bright.. Therefore, conclusion derived has greater swing towards probability of being true.

4. Probably False

This is similar to the one applied in the case of probably true. Whenever, the conclusion is not definitely false it is so because there exists little chance of its being true. In such cases, the conclusion is said to be probably false. Here, the swing seems to be towards falsity and the conclusion is termed probably false.

See the following example

Passage 4

Now the question of the freedom of the press becomes an important question in view of the fact that the press vast potentialities for both good and evil. The press is as much a passion rouser as it is a peacemaker. In the days of discords and dissensions, it bars the door to reconciliation or atleast the quarrel is prolonged beyond its limits. Knowledge is not always good and sometimes ignorance is bliss.

Conclusion Knowledge is good.

Solution Though the conclusion contradicts the statement of the passage that knowledge is not always good, yet the conclusion cannot be taken for as definitely false.

The use of word 'always' in the statement reduces the chance of the conclusion being definitely true and there is an apparent swing towards falsity. Hence, the given conclusion is probably false.

5. Data Inadequate

Data inadequate is one of the answer options given in the question. It means the candidate doesn't have enough information to arrive at a conclusion.

See the following example

Passage 5

There is more bad news on food front. It now appears certain that there will be a shortfall of about 9 million tonnes in the food production in the current Kharif season, which in turn means 5 million tonnes less than the production achieved in the last Kharif season. However, rice procurement may only be partially affected, since Paschim Bangal and Andhra Pradesh have had sufficient rainfall while Punjab, the major contributor to the central pool, is less dependent on rainfall. Still the overall availability of rice may go down by more than 4 million tonne. There may be worse news ahead.

« IDBI Bank (PO) 2008

Conclusion Last year, there was deficit production of rice by 5 million tonnes.

Solution It is only given in the passage that this year, there is 5 million tonnes less production than the last season

Chapter tip!

There are certain words which helps us in finding whether the given statement is definitely true, probably true, definitely false or probably false; words such as all, some, none, never, must be, might be, will be, would be, sometimes, always, inspite of, despite of, because of, nevertheless, usually, similarly, exactly, probably, etc.

e.g.,

- The rise of crude oil prices usually results in rise of petrol prices in India.
- The rise of crude oil prices always results in rise of petrol prices in India.

From Statement 1 We infer that when the crude oil prices are increased, then petrol prices in India may remain same or may increase. This can be inferred by the key word 'usually' that means not always.

From Statement 2 We infer that when crude oil prices are increased, then petrol prices also increase in India.

This can be inferred by the key word 'always'.

The following examples will give you a better idea about the questions asked.

DIRECTIONS ~(Example Nos. 1-3) *Below is given a passage followed by several possible inferences which can be drawn from the facts stated in the passage. You have to examine each inference separately in the context of the passage and decide upon its degree of truth or falsity.*

Give answer « NIFT (PG) 2013

(a) If the inference is definitely true, *i.e.*, it properly follows from the statement of facts given

(b) If the inference is probably true though not definitely true in the light of the facts given

(c) If the data is inadequate , i.e., from the facts given you cannot say whether the inference is likely to be true or false

(d) If the inference is definitely false, *i.e.*, it cannot possibly be drawn from the facts given or it contradicts the given facts

Urban lifestyles, fast foods, changing diet patterns, lack of exercise, obesity and smoking are responsible for increase in the incidence of diabetes, heart attacks and cancer. Research has also shown, that modern cooking oils have an unhealthy ratio of harmful fatty acids to essential fatty acids, which contribute to free radical attacks and increase insulin resistance.

Ghee, coconut oil and mustard oil have a healthy ratio of fatty acids. Their use in rural India, coupled with a traditional high fiber diet and physical exercise, probably account for the lower incidence of diabetes and heart attacks in the rural population, the study reveals.

***Ex* 01** Rural people should not migrate to urban cities, if they value their health.

***Ex* 02** Most of the rural population is healthy and free of diseases.

***Ex* 03** The increase in diseases like diabetes, heart attacks etc is controllable by taking proper measures.

Solutions (Example Nos. 1-3)

1. (*b*) From the above facts, it is probably true, that rural people should not migrate to urban cities, as there the way and standard of living is different from that of rural areas, so it will be hard for them to adjust but it is not definitely true as with time they can adjust.

2. (*a*) It is definitely true that most of the people from rural areas are healthy because of their diet and regular exercise, it properly follows from the facts of paragraph given.

3. (*b*) The statement is probably true but from the facts given in paragraph, it cannot be deduced that it is definitely true.

DIRECTIONS ~(Example Nos. 4 and 5) *A passage is given followed by some inferences. You have to examine each inference separately in the context of the passage and decide upon its degree of truth or falsity.* « CG PSC 2013

Give answer

(a) If you think the inference is 'definitely true'

(b) If you think the inference is 'probably true'

(c) If the data given is inadequate

(d) If you think the inference is 'probably false'

(e) If the inference is 'definitely false'

The water resources of our country are very much underutilised. The main reason of this underutilisation is the lack of capital and technology. A large portion of our water resources is wasted due to floods and unwise use of water for irrigation as well as domestic purposes. We can make full use of our water resources by building dams on river and by adopting policy of awareness among people not to waste water.

***Ex* 04** Conservation of water resources is possible through wise use of water.

***Ex* 05** Technology does not have any effect on uses of water utilisation.

Solutions (Example Nos. 4 and 5)

4. (*a*) It has been reported in the passage that conservation of water resources is possible through wise use of water, so the inference is definitely true.

5. (e) In the given passage, technology, is considered crucial for water utilzation. So, the inference technology does not have any effect on uses of water utilization is definitely false.

DIRECTIONS ~ (Example Nos. 6-10) *Below is given a passage followed by several possible inferences which can be drawn from the facts stated in the passage. You have to examine each inference separately in the context of the passage and decide upon its degree of truth or falsity.*

Give answer

(a) If the inference is definitely true, *i.e.*, it properly follows from the facts given

(b) If the inference is probably true though not definitely true in the light of the facts given

(c) If the data is inadequate , i.e., from the facts given you cannot say whether the inference is likely to be true or false

(d) If the inference is definitely false, *i.e.*, it cannot possibly be drawn from the facts given or it contradicts the given facts

In an era of globalisation, we need to find appropriate tools to confront the challenges facing agriculture. Commodity future markets can play a major role in addressing some of these challenges.

In order to improve agricultural productivity, we need to encourage private investment including that from individual farmers and reasonable returns for agriculture produce is a prerequisite for this.

The price appreciation in agriculture commodities has failed to match the increase in price of inputs of the price rise of other commodities, indicating deteriorating terms of trade for agriculture. Our spot markets are fragmented and being dominated by a large chain of intermediaries can hardly ensure a fair return for the farmers. Spot transactions, being mostly offline, lack audit trail.

Different prices for the same commodity in different parts of the country give rise to arbitrage opportunities for traders. Further, driven by the need for immediate cash, most farmers engage in distress sale after harvest when supply exceeds demand and price is at its lowest.

***Ex* 06** Private funding in agricultural activity will significantly improve productivity.

***Ex* 07** Traders are largely benefited due to distress sale of agriculture produces.

***Ex* 08** Prices of agricultural produces are comparable throughout the country.

***Ex* 09** The prices of agricultural produce do not generate expected return at present.

***Ex* 10** Traders are at a disadvantage for lack of organised trade practices of agricultural produces.

Solutions (Example Nos. 6-10)

6. (*b*) A measure suggested is likely to be true.

7. (*a*) If farmers stand to lose in distress sale, then traders are obviously the gainers.

8. (*d*) The passage says that there are different prices for the same commodity in different parts of the country.

9. (*a*) It is obvious from the third sentence.

10. (*d*) It is the farmers who are being hurt; traders are benefiting from the lack of organised trade practices.

***Ex* 11** When people have access to health care, they live healthier lives and miss work less, allowing them to contribute more to the economy. A March 2014 study by researchers at the Universities of Colorado and Pennsylvania showed that workers with health insurance miss an average of 4.7 fewer work days than employees without health insurance. According to an Institute of Medicine report, the US economy loses \$65-\$130 billion annually as a result of diminished worker productivity, due to poor health and premature deaths, among the uninsured. In a Jan 14, 2016 speech, World Bank President Jim Yong Kim stated that all nations should provide a right to health care "to help foster economic growth". Which of the following statements can be inferred from the passage? « SBI (PO) 2017

(a) Countries which provide health care to its citizens might have more hardworking citizens than those which don't

(b) Countries which provide health care to its citizens are richer than those which don't

(c) Provision of health care increases the chances of better economic productivity

(d) If health care is provided to citizens, they are bound to be more productive economically

(e) Countries which provide health care to its citizens are economically productive than those which don't

Solution (c) Option (a) cannot be inferred from the passage, as the passage provides us comparative data about the level of hard work done by citizens of countries that provide health care, and of those that don't.

Option (b) cannot be inferred from the passage, as the passage does not draw any comparison between the wealth of countries that provide health care to its citizens and those that don't.

Option (c) is the right answer, as the passage gives us sufficient information from which we may be able to justifiably infer this option.

Option (d) cannot be inferred from the passage, as we cannot assume that provision of health care is the only factor upon which the economic productivity depends. Thus, we cannot conclude that providing health care is bound to make citizens more productive.

Option (e) is eliminated, as we are not given any information that compares economic productivity of countries that provide health care, and of those which don't. Which makes it possible for infer option (e).

Master Exercise

DIRECTIONS ~ (Q. Nos. 1-62) *Questions in the form of inferences/ conclusions are based on the passages given below. Each passage is followed by five inferences. You are required to examine each inference separately in the context of the passage and decide upon its degree of truth or falsity.*

Give answer

(a) If the inference is definitely true, *i.e.*, it properly follows from the statement of facts given

(b) If the inference is probably true though not definitely true in the light of the facts given

(c) If the data are inadequate *i.e.*, from the facts given you cannot say whether the inference is likely to be true or false

(d) If the inference is probably false though not definitely false in the light of the facts given

(e) If the inference is definitely false *i.e.*, it cannot possibly be drawn from the facts given or it contradicts the given facts

Passage 1

Asia has become the growth centre of the world economy in recent years. Within the region, India and South Korea are the third and fourth largest economies after China and Japan. Though the Asian growth stories mainly revolve around India and China, South Korea has remained a key player for these countries as one of their major trading and investment partners. South Korea adopted outward oriented economic policies with the beginning of its first five-year economic development plan in 1962, which resulted in high growth and the integration of the Korean economy with the rest of the world.

Subsequently, high and consistent economic growth made South Korea one of the high-income economies in Asia. South Korea is still growing at a faster rate compared to other developed economies. India on the other hand adopted an import substitution policy, since its independence until the early 1990. Since, then India has introduced wide ranging economic policy reforms and is moving towards market driven economy. This has resulted in consistent high economic growth over the last one and half a decades. « SBI (PO) 2010

1. Only Korean economy is considered as robust by the international community.

2. Japan's economic growth over the last decade is the highest in Asia.

3. The Korean economy is traditionally different than the Indian economy in its approach.

4. The economic growth of India prior to 1990s was much higher than the present growth rate.

5. India and China together are considered to be the driving force of the Asian economy.

Passage 2

The first time I saw The Wizard of Oz, the story bewitched me. The second time I saw the Wizard of Oz, the special effects amazed me. The third time I saw The Wizard of Oz, the photography dazzled me. Have you ever seen a movie twice, three times? You notice subtleties and hear sounds you completely missed the first time around.

It's the same on the phone. Because your business conversations are more consequential than movies, you should listen to them two, may be three times, often we have no clear idea of what really happened in our phone conversation until we hear it again. You'll find shadings more significant than the colour of toto's collar and more scare crows than you imagined who 'haven't got a brain!'

How do you listen to your important business conversation again? Simply legally and ethically tape record them. I call the technique of recording and analysing your business conversations for subtleties. « PNB (PO) 2010

6. The movie 'The Wizard of Oz' will help improve business conversation.

7. For most, if they watch a movie more than once, different aspects in different order, like special effects, photography, story, music etc., would impress in a better way.

8. The tips are given for understanding business conversation.

9. The advice is being given to the sales team.

10. The author watches most movies more than twice.

Passage 3

Urban services have not expanded fast enough to cope with urban expansion. Low investment allocations have tended to be underspent. Both public (*e.g.*, Water and sewage) and private (*e.g.*, Low income area housing) infrastructure quality has declined. The impact of the environment in which children live and the supporting services available to them when they fall ill, seems clear. The decline in average food availability and the rise in absolute poverty, point in the same unsatisfactory directions. « IDBI Bank (PO) 2010

11. There is nothing to boast about urban services.

12. The public transport system is in the hand of private sector.

13. Birth rate is higher in urban areas as compared to rural areas.

14. Low cost urban housing is on the priority.

15. The environment around plays a important role on the health status.

Passage 4

There is some controversy about the percentage of population below the poverty line in India. The criteria for the poverty line is basis on person's nutritional requirement in terms of calories.

It is assumed that the minimum nutritional requirement per person per day in rural areas is 2400 calories whereas it is 2200 calories in urban areas. If the household is unable to bear the expenditure for this level of nutrition, it is categorised as below the poverty line. There is also a view that alongwith calories, the amount of protein intake be treated as a criterion as it is related to physical energy, mental alertness and resistance to infection.

« SBI (PO) 2010

16. Many Indians, who are below the poverty line, get necessary amount of proteins.

17. People living above the poverty line are less likely to suffer from infections.

18. India's poverty alleviation programmes can only succeed after reaching agreement about the poverty line.

19. People in urban areas are less physically weak compared to people in rural areas.

20. In other countries, there is no controversy about defining the poverty line.

Passage 5

A radical new surgery procedure launched not long ago in India, is holding out fresh hope for patients of cardiac myopathy or enlargement of the heart. The technique new in India, allows patients to go home two weeks after the operation to lead a near normal sedentary life.

Cardiac myopathy is a condition that has a variety of causative factors. An attack from one of the 20 indentified viruses, parasite infection, long term alcohol abuse and blood pressure could bring it on and in rare cases, it could follow child birth and is even known to run in families. The condition is marked by an increase in the size of heart's chambers and a decrease in the efficiency of pumping. « BOI (PO) 2009

21. The cardiac myopathy slows down the heartbeat.

22. Cardiac myopathy is hereditary.

23. Earlier, the patients suffering from the cardiac myopathy were required to travel abroad for such operations.

24. The new technique was never tried in India in the past.

25. The efficiency of the heart is inversely proportional to the size of the heart.

Passage 6

The latest data to show that the overall power situation has gotten worse, with the ratio for peak-load shortages now the highest in a decade. In absolute terms, the power deficit has hit record levels and seems almost certain to further deteriorate without real reforms on the ground. Even as aggressive technical and commercial losses in the power system remain much high at over a third of total generation, pan India capacity addition is now well below target

A shortage of equipment and skills is blamed for the marked slowdown in augmenting power capacity but the dearth of resources can only be relative. Infact, the real bane of the sector is continuing revenue leakage in the state power utilities and unacceptably high aggregate technical and commercial losses, much of it plain theft of electricity. Given, the preponderance of state utilities in power supply, the fact that they remain very much in red does affect investor comfort and return funds flow.

« SBI (PO) 2008

26. Indian power generation is largely controlled by private sector.

27. Reform in power sector in India has not yet attained its desired level.

28. Indian power sector is yet to attain status comparable to developed countries.

29. Power theft is one of the major components of revenue losses in power sector.

30. Aggregate technical and commercial loss is much less than 30% of the total power generation.

Passage 7

Domestic steel industry has been going through challenging times with raw material prices rising unabated and Government trying to cap final product (steel) prices in order to keep inflation under check. Notably, the Government has taken several measures in the past six months to keep a check on steel prices. which contribute around 3.63% of WPI. Now, after holding prices for three months the battle between the Government and steel players has erupted again. With the anticipation of players increasing prices very soon, Government is trying to counter this with the imposition of a price band on steel products. Imposition of price band may unfairly treat the domestic steel industry as global steel prices are ruling at 30% premium to domestic prices. Global prices have increased by 50% to 60% in 2008 as compared to just 20% rise in the domestic market.

« Syndicate Bank (PO) 2008

31. Some countries in the Western World have fixed a price band for steel products in their domestic markets.

32. Government move to fix a price band of steel prices may adversely affect the steel manufacturing units in India.

33. Price of steel is an integral part of the Wholesale Price Index (WPI) of India.

34. There has been a decline in the rate of inflation in recent months in India.

35. In recent past, the increase of steel prices in the international market is much lower than that in the domestic market.

Passage 8

Data available from the National Institute of Nutrition (NIN) compares, separately for boys and girls, the average height recorded during 1979 with the 10 States covered by the period 1974-79 at different ages in the average for the NNMB survey. The 1979 height turns out to be neither uniformly higher nor uniformly lower than the 1974-79 average highest at ages 3, 5 and 9 in most of the States.

However, the comparison at age 13 is more meaningful as it represents the cumulative result of childhood growth. At the age of 13 yr, the average height recorded for boys in 1979 is lower than the average for 1974-79 in only one State, Karnataka. For girls at this age, the average hight recorded in 1979 turns out to be lower than the 1974-79 average in four States Andhra Pradesh, Gujarat, Madhya Pradesh and Uttar Pradesh. In all other States, the 1979 average was greater than or equal to the 1974-79 average. « UCO Bank (PO) 2010

36. There are only two institutes NIN and NNMB which have collected data on average height.

37. The data from Karnataka was collected by both NIN and NNMB.

38. In Karnataka, the average age recorded in 1979 for both boys and girls was lower than that for 1974-79.

39. More States indicated higher average in 1979 as compared to that of 1974-79.

40. Both the institutes NIN and NNMB collected data from 10 States only.

41. Separate statistics for boys and girls help understand the data in a better way.

42. There may be large differences in the height of boys and girls from 2nd and 5th year.

Passage 9

Doordarshan has undoubtedly helped popularise yoga among the people especially city dwellers but performing various 'asanas' without adequate instructions could be hazardous, according to a renowned 'yoga expert' who has conducted hundreds of yoga shivirs (camps).

He says several people, who tried to learn yoga through the programme of Doordarshan, have come to him complaining of pain in different parts of their body. He explains that the asanas involve a complicated but scientific technique of breathing which controls the flow of oxygen in various parts of the body under calculated stress. « BOI (PO) 2009

43. TV programmes on yoga have successfully replaced personal guidance by 'yoga experts'.

44. Yoga exercises (asanas) are quite safe for any person.

45. Many TV viewers of yoga programmes are unable to master the scientific technique of breathing while performing 'asanas'.

46. Uncontrolled flow of oxygen in parts of the body causes pain in those parts.

47. Quite a large number of 'yoga experts' are available.

Passage 10

The most empirical argument in favour of prayer is that it relieves the mind of tension, which is the natural concomitant of a life of hurry and worry.It neutralises mental repressions and purifies the subconsciousness. It releases an extra amount of hope and energy and thus enables a person to face life squarely. Life is not all sweetness, enjoyment and success, it is drudgery, pain and failure too. « UBI (PO) 2008

48. Prayer is an important part of all religions.

49. People are interested in finding out effects of prayer.

50. Subconsciousness plays no role in our life.

51. There are some arguments for the benefits of prayer, which can be tested.

52. Prayer, by direct miracles, removes hurdles and difficulties from our life.

Passage 11

Between 2002-03 and 2006-07 Indian economy grew annually at 8.7% led by the services sector at 9% per year. In 1990, India's share of services at 40% of GDP was consistent with its per capita income for low income country. By 2001, its share of one-half of the GDP was higher by five percentage points, compared to the average for low income countries.

Economic reforms that energized the private corporate sector and technological changes that opened up new vistas in telecommunications, IT and outsourcing are believed to be responsible for the impressive performance. However, the services led growth remains a puzzle at a low per capita income, with 55% of the workforce still engaged in agriculture and when agriculture decelerated and industry stagnated defying a styled fact in Economics. « UCO Bank (PO) 2009

53. Share of services sector in India's GDP crossed the halfway mark in early 2000.

54. India has now emerged as a high per capita income country.

55. Growth in India's services sector post 2005 is more than 9%.

56. In early nineties, the share of services sector in GDP for low per capita income group of countries was about 40%.

57. Less than half of total workforce is engaged in agricultural sector in India.

Passage 12

In its most ambitious bid ever to house 6 crore slum dwellers and realize the vision of a slumfree India, the Government is rolling out a massive plan to build 50 lakh dwelling units in five years across 400 towns and cities.

The programme could free up thousands of acres of valuable Government land across the country and generate crores worth of business for real estate developers. Proliferation of slums has had an adverse impact on the GDP growth for years.

Slum dwellers are characterised by low productivity and susceptible to poor health conditions. The Government believes that better housing facilities will address social issues and also have a multiplier effect and serve as an economic stimulus. « PNB (PO) 2009

58. Health and sanitary conditions in slums are far below the acceptable norm of human habitat in Indian cities and towns.

59. Cities and towns of developed countries are free from slums.

60. Per capita income of slum dwellers is significantly lower than those living in better housing facilities.

61. Majority of the slums in cities and towns in India are on prime private properties.

62. Development of land occupied by slums in cities of India will not have any effect on the common public.

DIRECTIONS ~ (Q. Nos. 63-97) *Each of these questions has a statement based on the preceding passage. Evaluate each statement.*

Give answer

(a) If the statement is a major objective in making the decision; one of the goals sought by the decision maker

(b) If the statement is a major factor in making the decision; an aspect of the problem, specifically mentioned in the passage, which fundamentally affects and/or determines the decision

(c) If the statement is a minor factor in making the decision; a less important element bearing on or affecting a major factor, rather than a major objective directly

(d) If the statement is a major Assumption in making the decision; a projection or supposition arrived at by the decision maker before considering the factor and alternative

Passage 13

Morgan Stanley on Monday became the second large global giant to exit India's crowded and barely profitable mutual fund industry when it agreed to sell its business to HDFC, the country's biggest mutual fund manager. HDFC Mutual Fund (MF), with assets of ₹ 1.03 lakh crore, agreed to buy all eight schemes of Morgan Stanley with combined assets of ₹ 3290 crore.

The purchase is expected to help the fund widen the gap with Reliance, the second biggest mutual fund house and consolidate its position at the top of the industry. Reliance has assets worth ₹ 93249 crore. Morgan was the first global giant to launch a mutual fund in India in 1994 after liberalisation but its performance in the country has been rather lacklustre.

Its asset size is small by international and Indian standards and like Fidelity it has been unable to keep pace with the growth of Indian mutual funds such as HDFC MF, Reliance MF, ICICI Pru, UTI MF and Birla Sunlife which between them control over 50% of the industry' size. The fund posted losses in both 2011 and 2012. The mutual fund and insurance industry must go through consolidation.

Small funds are not viable and more people are beginning to sense that.

The opportunity cropped up as Morgan Stanley approached us, Chairman HDFC told. Tough business conditions are forcing many Asset Management Companies (AMCs) to either rope in strategic partners or exit the business completely. India has about 44 mutual fund houses with numerous schemes and they compete for investors money in the main cities of Mumbai and Delhi.

The proportion of small savers investing in these schemes is not very high and the funds depend upon cash rich companies and high net worth individuals for a bulk of their investments. The consolidation in the industry is likely to continue as industry faces tough times we believe only those companies can survive which have a strong distribution reach, said CEO of mutual fund AMC who did not want to be identified. « NIFT (PG) 2014

63. The purchase is expected to help the fund widen the gap with Reliance.

64. The asset size of Morgan Stanley is small by international and Indian Standards.

65. Small funds are not viable and more and more people are beginning to sense that.

66. Only those companies can survive which have a strong distribution reach.

67. Asset management companies are facing tough business conditions.

Passage 14

ING Groep NV, the biggest Dutch financial services company, is said to be seeking a buyer for its 43% stake in, ING Vysya Bank, as the prospects of limited purpose banking in India and tough competition in retail market make it rethink its local strategy, five people familiar with the thinking said. ING, which has been selling assets across the Asian region and some in Europe itself to repay the Dutch Government for bailing it out from the 2008 credit crisis, may exit the domestic banking business comprising retail, corporate and treasury, to focus on corporate banking. they said.

The group, which also has to bolster capital to meet the Basel III regulations, may get atleast $ 600 million at current market prices, or even more for the stake depending on the transaction There is no certainty that a deal will happen.

Although ING Vysya may be an attractive asset for every private sector bank because of its clean books, 575 branches and loyal customer. Kotak Mahindra Bank seems to be best placed to benefit from the acquisition of ING Vysya, say analysis. It is a very good business and it (ING Vysya) provides Kotak the opportunity to scale up, said chief mentor BMR and Associates, an advisory firm.

Although Kotak's market value is about six times that of ING Vysya, Kotak's loan assets is about ₹ 50539 crore, compared with ING's ₹ 33575 crore regulatory filings show ING's ₹ 40000 crore of deposits, of which a third is low cost and its customer loyalty may be the most attractive part. But Kotak said it is not negotiating for a takeover. 'We have not been approached for purchase of shares of ING Group in ING, Vysya Bank, said a Kotak Mahindra Group spokesman in an e-mail response.

'We have had no negotiations with officials of ING, Vysya Bank on this matter.' For Kotak, it might make sense to go for a stock-swap deal, since it could achieve twin objectives of the management, said one of the persons familiar with the thinking.

There will be no cash outflow and at the same time help founder Uday Kotak to reduce his stake in the bank to meet regulations.

The Reserve Bank of India last June directed Uday Kotak to lower his stake in the bank to 10% over the next eight years. It is at 44% now, filings show International banks in India are redrawing their strategy as the industry goes through tough capital requirements after the credit crisis. Institutions such as

JP Morgan Chase and Co have decided to remain a corporate and investment banking company in India and others such as Barclays are moving toward that, shedding retail, the Reserve Bank of India's decision to possibly mandate local incorporation many lead to further changes. « NIFT (PG) 2014

68. ING Groep NV, the biggest Dutch financial services company perceives that there is tough competition in retail market.

69. ING will focus on corporate banking.

70. The group may get atleast $ 600 million at current market price.

71. ING Vysya has 575 branches.

72. The industry in India is going through tough requirements after the credit crisis.

Passage 15

The railroads was not the first institution to impose regularity on society or to draw attenion to the importance of precise time keeping. For as long as merchants have set out their wars at day break and communal festivities have been celebrated, people have been in rough agreement with their neighbours as to the time of day. The value of tradition is today mor apparent than ever.

Were it not for public acceptance of a single yardstick of time, social life would be unbearably chaotic. The massive daily transfer of goods. Services and information would proceed in fits and starts, the very fabric of modern society would begin to unravel. « NIFT (PG) 2014

73. An accepted way of measuring time is essential for the smooth functioning of society.

74. In modern society we must make more time for our neighbour's.

75. Society judges people by the time at which they conduct certain activities.

76. The Phrase 'this tradition' in the passage refers to people's agreement on the measurement of time.

77. Railroad supports precise time keeping.

Passage 16

McLeod Russel India Ltd (MRIL) is keen to make further acquisitions in Rwanda where it already has a presence. "Rwanda is on our scanner now", sources said. MRIL, which had bought into a Government-owned tea oufit in the African country in 2010, has so far had a good experience, according to sources. Following a privatization drive in Rwanda, the Government had divested 60% of its stake in this estate while retaining 30%. The remaining 10% has been given to a workers, cooperative. "This is as per the divestment policy of the Government." At present, two more tea estates-Mulundi and Saggasa have been put on the block for which bids have been invited by the Government.

MRIL may bid for these two estates after getting a nod from its board. The Gisovu tea estate in Rwanda, which was bought earlier this year, contributed 2 million kg out of the 23 million kg tea crop that McLeod Russel reaped out of its overseas estates in Vietnam, Rwanda and Uganda. "Production increases were recorded from our tea estates in all these three countries," say sources.

The company's overseas foray started with acquisition of the Phu Ben Tea Company in Vietnam in 2008-09. From a production level of 4.5 million kg, Phu Ben now produces around 5 million kg.

The B M Khaitan group company believes that the only way to grow is through acquisition and since 2005 it has made quite a few acquisitions within the country. In 2010, it completed its acquisition of the Ugandan tea company, Rwenzi Tea Investments Ltd, from James Finlay International Holdings Ltd. of the UK through its wholly-owned subsidiary Borelli Tea Holdings (UK), the outfit through which McLeod Russel makes its overseas acquisitions.

MRIL, which makes its acquisitions through a mix of debt and internal accruals, currently has reserves of around ₹ 900 crore. "Our debts are set to decline to ₹ 260 crore by 31 March, 2012, from ₹ 316 crore at end-March 2011 and we have enough liquidity to fund any future acquisition," sources said.

« NIFT (PG) 2012

78. The privatisation drive by the Government of Rwanda.

79. The company's belief that the only way to grow is through acquisitions.

80. The debts of MRIL are set to decline in the coming months.

81. The board of MRIL, will give its permission to bid for two more tea estates in Rwanda.

82. Making further acquisitions in Rwanda.

Passage 17

A slowing economy, rising fuel prices and high taxes hit Indian aviation in 2012. Strikes at Air India and a bleeding Kingfisher added to the heat because foreign airlines would not pick up stakes in cash-strapped Indian carriers unless steps are taken to stem high costs of aviation operations in India, International Air Transport Association (IATA) chief Tony Tyler said, No, I don't think it (allowing foreign airlines to invest in Indian carriers) is a game changer but it is a good thing, said Tyler in but it will not solve the problems of Indian aviation. It is a step in the right direction but not the panacea that some believe it is', 'As long as high taxes prevail, high airport costs and congestion and poorly developed air navigation (services) means more congestion, high cost of operations exist, you are not going to get a lot of people to invest in airlines,' the director-general and CEO of IATA said.

Observing that there were restrictions on investing in airlines around the world, which was 'a problem for the industry', Tyler said "any move that we see in liberalising is a good thing. 'But unless conditions in India are improved for airlines, you are not going to see a flood of foreign carriers coming into the industry. Because foreign capital needs a return just as anywhere else." he added. « NIFT (PG) 2013

83. Foreign capital should be invested in Indian aviation.

84. There is a slowing Indian economy.

85. There were strikes at Air India.

86. Foreign airlines would pick up stakes in Indian carriers,

87. There is a poorly developed air navigation leading to more congestion.

Passage 18

Wipro Consumer Care and Lighting, part of Wipro, plans to enter body lotions and shampoo categories with its flagship brand Santoor. "While the category is highly competitive, there is a lot of headroom to grow as penetration level is significantly lower in India compared to other markets," according to the president at Wipro Consumer Care.

The company started test marketing, the hair care and body lotion products recently. Wipro Consumer, which recorded a 17% increase in its revenues in the third quarter and ended December at ₹ 1028 crore, also expects hall of its total sales to come from international business with the addition of Singapore-based FMCG firm LD Waxsons.

At present international operations contribute 40-45% to its revenues, Wipro Consumer acquired LD Waxsons for about $144 million (approx ₹ 775 crore). During the third quarter, its Indonesia and Vietnam businesses grew 26% and 24%, respectively, while China and middle East grew by 32%.The Santoor brand has been growing over 20% in the last few quarters. It is the third largest soap brand in the country after Hindustan Unilever's Lifeboy and Lux and has market leadership in South and Western India. Last month, it became the top brand in states such as Maharashtra , Karnataka and Gujarat.

However, it's a huge task for Wipro to replicate a similar feat in the ₹ 4500 crore shampoo market, where HUL is by far the leader with over 50% market share. Also, margins have moderated in the past on account of promotions and ad spends, says a recent report by JP Morgan. Hence, companies such as Proctor and Gamble and L'Oreal are introducing various premium products like hair treatments, serums, hair masks, hair conditioners to help support margin profile for their hair care portfolio. « NIFT (PG) 2013

88. Expanding in the body lotion and shampoo category is easier due to low penetration levels in India.

89. Santoor is an established brand in certain markets and hence, it will be easier to grow.

90. Margins in the shampoo market decreasing due to increasing promotion and ad spends.

91. Ensuring growth in international markets through the Waxsons acquisition.

92. Significant growth in the international businesses of the company.

Passage 19

The Union Commerce and Industry Minister on Friday unveiled a new corporate logo for the National Textile Corporation (NTC), reflecting the new face of the state-owned enterprise as part of the plans to make it a world-class textile company.

"The Government is committed to making NTC a world-class eco-friendly integrated textile company and flag bearer of the sector. The ongoing revival-cum-modernization programme and new corporate and brand identity launch by NTC is aimed at achieving this goal", he said at a function organised for the purpose.

He said NTC was a key player in the textile sector and its recent moves would definitely transform it into an integrated company capable of addressing the needs of the nation. NTC had made a turn-around within a short span to emerge as a debt-free company with a highly competitive revival strategy, he added. He also launched two new look retail stores of NTC-one in Delhi and another in Coimbatore, Tamil Nadu via satellite link up. This is a part of revamping of NTC's 93 stores to reflect the company's new face across the country.

Speaking on the occasion, the Textile Secretary said the revamp and modernization steps taken by NTC in the recent past in view of the changing times and consumer aspirations of modern India would help in instilling confidence in the minds of all stakeholders. The NTC Chairman and Managing Director said the new corporate logo reflected the new face of NTC to the world. It had been designed as free flowing fabric, indicating the new aspirations and changing aspirations of India.

Apart from re-branding, NTC had developed a new marketing and corporate strategy that included revamping of all NTC stores and setting up of new stores, he said. The internal marketing programme to employees and key customers includes undertaking a complete programme to bring the new vision and culture to its employees. Respective mill managers would be conducting a smaller unveiling ceremony of the new logo along with the NTC anthom at all the mills. Besides, all the employees would be given a small commemorative badge of the new logo. « NIFT (PG) 2012

93. Making NTC a world-class integrated textile company and the leader of the Indian textile industry.

94. The new corporate logo of NTC reflects its new face to the world.

95. The highly competitive revival strategy that helped make NTC debt-free.

96. The recent modernisation steps taken by NTC would instill confidence in the minds of all stakeholders.

97. Implementing a programme to bring the new vision and culture to the employees of NTC.

98. Read the following information carefully and answer the given question.

One of the main reasons behind the lack of applicants for teachers training/degree programmes is that teachers have not experienced any improvement in working conditions and their salaries have not kept pace with salaries in other professions.

« SBI Clerk (Mains) 2016

Which of the following can be inferred from the given paragraph?

(a) No direct relationship can be established between the work conditions of a particular profession and preference for it amongst the qualified candidates

(b) Number of applicants for teachers training programmes will improve, if the salaries in other professions are reduced

(c) Training programmes for other profesions are not as good as teachers training programmes

(d) Very high entrance exam is also one of the reasons behind plunging number of applicants for teachers training programmes

(e) In the years to come, the schools would face a crunch in terms of availability of qualified teachers, if the salaries and working conditions of teachers do not improve

99. Read the given information and answer the question.

The MB Road near highway has an average of one pothole or patched piece of asphalt for every yards of road. The primary reason for the condition of the road is not age, weather or rush hour traffic. It's 18-wheeler trucks. These heavy trucks roar down this route that was never meant to carry weights above 40 tonnes. While regular traffic on the road averages 2 tonnes in terms of weight per vehicle, the average weight per 18-wheeler truck is 35 times this weight.

Which of the following can be concluded from the given information? « NABARD Asst. Manager (Grade A) 2016

A. The highway close to the MB Road can definitely carry atleast 35 times more number of vehicles than that possible on MB road.
B. 18-wheeler trucks which are 30 tonnes lighter will not cause harm to the mentioned road.
C. Restricting small vehicles while permitting only 18-wheeler trucks may reduce harm caused to the road.
D. A road is constructed considering the type of vehicles plying on it.

(a) Only C (b) A and C
(c) B and D (d) A and D
(e) None of those given as options

100. During the SARS days, about 23500 doctors who had treated SARS sufferers died and about 23670 doctors who had not engaged in treatment for SARS sufferers died. On the basis of those figures, it can be concluded that it was not much more dangerous to participate in SARS treatment during the SARS day than it was not to participate in SARS treatment.

Which of the following would reveal most clearly the absurdity of the conclusion drawn above?
« MHT CET MBA 2014

(a) Counting deaths among doctors who had participated in SARS treatment in addition to deaths among doctors who had not participated is SARS treatment
(b) Expressing the difference between the numbers of deaths among doctors who had treated SARS sufferers and doctors who had treated SARS sufferers and doctors who had not treated SARS suffers as a percentage of the total number of deaths
(c) Separating deaths caused by accidents during the treatment to SARS suffers from deaths caused by infect of SARS suffers
(d) Comparing darth rates per thousand members of each group rather than comparing total numbers of deaths
(e) None of the above

DIRECTION ~ (Q. No. 101) *Read the following paragraph carefully and answer the question which follows.*
« UPSC CSAT 2020

In India, over the last decade or so, labour has been departing agriculture, but is only going to construction and unregistered manufacturing which are not markedly better jobs. Sevices, where labour tends to be most productive, are not generating the additional jobs the country needs. India will need 24 million or so jobs over the next decade. The new sector, e-commerce, can at best close only half the jobs gap. Only those sectors that drive domestic demand such as health and education can comfortably fill the other half.

101. Which one of the following is best implied in the passage?

(a) Strong measures need to be taken to reduce the rural to urban migration of labour
(b) The working condition in construction and unregistered manufacturing needs to be improved
(c) Service sector has been reducing the problem of unemployment
(d) Increased social sector spending is imperative for large-scale job creation

DIRECTION ~(Q. No. 102) *Read the following paragraph and answer the questions which follows.* « UPSC CSAT 2020

One of the biggest ironies around water is that it comes from rivers and other wetlands. Yet it is seen as divorced from them. While water is used as a resource, public policy does not always grasp that it is a part of the natural ecosystem. Efforts at engineering water systems are thus efforts at augmenting water supply rather than strengthening the capacities of ecological systems.

102. Which one of the following is the most logical and rational inference that can be made from the above passage?

(a) Rivers and other wetlands should be protected under Ramsar Convention
(b) Engineering water systems should be modernised and further augmented
(c) Wetlands need to be rainforced as your more than just open sources of water
(d) Water supply should not be free of cost so as to prevent its misuse or overuse

103. Find the best conclusion of the passage.

Now-a-days, people are so busy in their work that they do not take care of their health. A lot of diseases like diabetes, arthritis, heart attack, blood pressure are increasing due to unhealthy lifestyle. People do not find time to exercise. Stress is continuously increasing. The fast food is quick, easy and tastes better but it is not healthy. Habits like smoking and drinking alcohol have many side effects. Polluted city environment has also negative impact on the health of citizens. To live happy and healthy life; it is important to take care of oneself. « SNAP 2014

(a) Now-a-days everybody smokes and drinks
(b) Diseases are increasing only because of pollution
(c) People are happy and stress free because their life is too busy
(d) Current city environment, life style and habits are affecting health of citizens

DIRECTIONS ~ (Q. Nos. 104-106) *Study the following information carefully and answer the questions given below.* « SBI (PO) 2017

The centre reportedly wants to continue providing subsidies to consumers for cooking gas and kerosene for five more years. This is no-good news form the point of view of in the fiscal deficit. Mounting subventions for subsidies means diversion of savings by the government from investment to consumption, raising the cost of capital in the process. The government must cut expenditure on subsidies to create more fiscal space for investments in both physical and social infrastructure. It should outline a plan for comprehensive reform in major subsidies including petroleum, food and fertilisers and set goal posts.

104. Which of the following is a conclusion which can be drawn from the fact stated in the given paragraph?
(a) Subsidy provided by the government under various heads to the citizen increases the cost of capital
(b) Government is unable to withdraw subsidies provided to various items
(c) Government subsidy on kerosene is purely a political decision
(d) Government does not have enough resources to continue providing subsidy on petroleum products
(e) None of the above

105. Which of the following is an assumption which is implicit in the facts stated in the given paragraph?
(a) People in India may not be able to pay more of petroleum products
(b) Many people in India are rich enough to buy petroleum products at market cost
(c) Government may not be able to create more infrastructure facilities if the present level of subsidy continues for a longer time
(d) Government of India has sought assistance from international financial organisations for its infrastructural projects
(e) None of the above

106. Which of the following is an inference which can be made from the facts stated in the given paragraph?
(a) India's fiscal deficit is negligible in comparison to other emerging economies in the world
(b) Subsidy on food and fertilisers are essential for the growth of Indian economy
(c) Reform in financial sector will weaken India's position in the international arena
(d) Gradual withdrawl of subsidy is essential for effectively managing fiscal deficit in India
(e) None of the above

DIRECTIONS ~ (Q. Nos. 107-109) *Study the following information carefully and answer the questions that follow.*

Poverty measurement is an unsettled issue, both conceptual and methodological. Since, poverty is a process as well as an outcome; many come out of it while others may be falling into it. The net effect of these two parallel processes is a proportion commonly identified as the 'head count ratio' but these ratios hide the fundamental dynamism that characterises poverty in practice.

The most recent poverty re-estimates by an expert group has also missed the crucial dynamism. In a study conducted on 13000 households which represented the entire country in 1993-94 and again on 2004-05, it was found that in the ten-year period 18.2% rural population moved out of poverty whereas another 22.1% fell into it over this period. This net increase of about four percentage points was seen to have a considerable variation across states and regions.

107. Which of the following is an assumption which is implicit in the facts stated in the above paragraph?
(a) It may not be possible to have an accurate poverty measurement in India
(b) Level of poverty in India is static over the years
(c) Researchers avoid making conclusions on poverty measurement data in India
(d) Government of India has a mechanism to measure level of poverty effectively and accurately
(e) None of the above

108. Which of the following is a conclusion which can be drawn from the facts stated in the above paragraph?
(a) Accurate estimates of number of people living below poverty line in India is possible to be made
(b) Many expert groups in India are not interested to measure poverty objectively
(c) Process of poverty measurement needs to take into account various factors to tackle its dynamic nature
(d) People living below poverty line remain in that position for a very long time
(e) None of the above

109. Which of the following is an inference which can be made from the facts stated in the above paragraph?
(a) Poverty measurement tools in India are outdated
(b) Increase in number of persons falling into poverty varies considerably across the country over a period of time
(c) Government of India has stopped measuring poverty related studies
(d) People living in rural areas are more susceptible to fall into poverty over the time
(e) None of the above

Answers / WITH EXPLANATIONS

1. (*e*) China, India and Japan also have robust economies.

2. (*b*) It is clear from the second line of last passage.

3. (*a*) South Korea adopted "outward oriented economic policies," while India continued with "import substitution policy".

4. (*e*) It is obvious from the last sentence of the passage.

5. (*b*) The Asian growth stories mainly revolve around India and China.

6. (*e*) The movie has been used just as a example of how repeated interactions aquaint us with a fuller meaning.

7. (*b*) Could even have been 'definitely true' except that question number 8 below is a sure shot.

8. (*a*) Properly follows the statement of facts given.

9. (*c*) It could be given to any individual or any business team.

10. (*d*) Note the line in "Have you ever seen ... ?" (4th line in first paragraph).

11. (*a*) It is clearly mentioned in the opening lines of the passage that urban services have deteriorated due to meager finances and related supports.

12. (*c*) It is not mentioned anywhere in the passage that public transport system is in the hands of private sector.

13. (*c*) Data regarding comparative birth rate are not given in the passage. Hence, data is inadequate.

14. (*b*) It is given in the passage that private infrastructure quality *i.e.*, low income area housing has declined. Therefore, it is very likely that low cost urban housing gets priority.

15. (*a*) This is clearly given in the passage that environment plays an important role on the health status. Hence, conclusion definitely follows from the passage.

16. (*c*) Data given in the passage is inadequate.

17. (*b*) It is given in the last line of the passage that protein is related to resistance to infections. Since, people above poverty line may get sufficient amount of protein intake and so are less likely to suffer from infections.

18. (*c*) Nothing has been discussed in the passage regarding agreement about poverty line.

19. (*b*) It is probably true because calorie requirement per person in the urban areas is less than that of the rural areas.

20. (*c*) Nothing has been given in the passage regarding the poverty line in the other countries.

21. (*b*) Conclusion is probably true because it is given in the last line that cardiac myopathy is a result of enlargement of heart's chamber and decrease in the efficiency of pumping.

22. (*a*) Conclusion is definitely true as it is given in the passage that cardiac myopathy could follow child birth.

23. (*c*) Data given in the passage is inadequate to analyse this conclusion as nothing has been given regarding the facility available for this disease earlier in India.

24. (*a*) Opening line of the passage reads "a radical new surgical procedure launched not long ago is holding fresh hopes". *i.e.*, this surgery has not been used in India earlier.

25. (*a*) Conclusion is definitely true from the last line of the passage that the condition is marked by an increase in the size of heart's chamber and a decrease in efficiency of pumping.

26. (*e*) The passage talks of "preponderance of state utilities" in power supply.

27. (*a*) The passage clearly says that there has been no "real reforms on the ground".

28. (*b*) Seems true on the basis of the grim scenario of the power sector painted in the passage.

29. (*a*) Just go through the second last sentence.

30. (*e*) They are "over a third of total generation".

31. (*d*) Such a scenario is unlikely when "global steel prices are ruling at 30% premium to domestic prices".

32. (*a*) This move will only worsen the "challenging times".

33. (*a*) Obvious from the first two sentences.

34. (*d*) This is unlikely given the Government's dogged efforts to keep steel prices and inflation under control.

35. (*e*) Read the last sentence.

36. (*c*) It is not given in the passage that there are only two institutes. There can also be more than two institutes. So, data are inadequate.

37. (*a*) It is given in the passage that data from Karnataka were collected by both the institutes. So, the conclusion is definitely true.

38. (*e*) The last line of the passage indicates that the height of girls is not lower in Karnataka.

39. (*a*) It is very clear from the last line of the passage.

40. (*c*) It is not given in the passage that institutes NIN and NNMB collected data from 10 States only.

41. (*b*) Conclusion seems to be probably true is it can be inferred from the passage that separate statistics certainly help.

42. (*b*) Conclusion is probably true as it is clearly given in the passage that at the age of 2, 5 and 9 comparative heights neither turn out to be uniformly higher nor lower.

43. (*e*) Definitely false. It is given in the passage that persons doing asanas complain of pains.
Hence, it is definitely false to say that TV programmes on yoga have successfully replaced personal guidance by the yoga expert.

44. (*e*) It is given in the passage that without adequate instructions, yoga could be hazardous.

Hence, the conclusion is definitely false.

45. (*a*) It is given in the passage that 'asanas' involve scientific technique of breathing which is the main reason for many complaints of pain.

46. (*b*) Conclusion is probably true because uncontrolled flow of oxygen in various parts of body causes pain in these parts.

47. (*c*) Data is inadequate, as it is not given in the passage that quite a large number of yoga experts are available.

48. (*c*) Data is not adequate, as it has not been given anywhere in the passage whether prayer forms an important part of all religions or not.

49. (*e*) Conclusion is definitely false, because effects of prayer are arguable as per opening line of the passage.

50. (*e*) Conclusion is definitely false, because it has been given in the passage that prayer purifies the subconsciousness. Hence, subconscious has a role in our life.

51. (*a*) Conclusion is definitely true, as it has been given in the opening line of the passage.

52. (*e*) Conclusion is definitely false because as in the given passage, prayer has an indirect impact on the life of human beings.

53. (*c*) There is nothing in the passage which determines the share of services sector precisely "in early 2000".

54. (*e*) The passage clearly says that in the Indian context, the services led growth remains a puzzle at a low per capita income.

55. (*b*) Probably true from the first sentence of the passage.

56. (*b*) Deduced from the second sentence of the passage.

57. (*e*) 55% is engaged in agriculture.

58. (*a*) Obvious from the passage.

59. (*c*) There is no explanation about developed countries in the passage.

60. (*a*) Since slum dwellers are characterized by low productivity.

61. (*b*) Probably true from the passage.

62. (*e*) Conclusion is definitely false.

63. (*c*) Statement is a minor factor in making the decision as it is not mentioned further in the passage any where.

64. (*b*) Statement is a major factor in making the decision as it shows a causal dependency with the consequence.

65. (*b*) Statement is a major factor in making the decision as it is mentioned in passage.

66. (*d*) Statement is a major assumption in making the decision as it includes the personal view.

67. (*b*) Statement is a major factor in making decision as it is mentioned in passage with facts and figures.

68. (*d*) Statement is major assumption in making the decision as it is not firmly presented paragraph anywhere.

69. (*a*) Statement is a major objective in making the decision as it is clear in passage.

70. (*d*) Sentence is a major assumption in making the decision as it based on future prospects.

71. (*b*) Sentence is a major factor in making the decision as its aspect is clearly depicted in passage.

72. (*b*) Sentence is a major factor in making the decision as it is clearly mentioned in passage.

73. (*a*) Statement is a major objective in making the decision one of the goals sought by the decision maker.

74. (*c*) Statement is a minor factor in making the decision, a less important element bearing on or affecting a major factor rather than a major objective directly.

75. (*c*) This statement is minor factor in making the decision.

76. (*a*) The phrase, this tradition, refers to the preceding clause 'people have been in rough agreement with their neighbours as to the time of day' means people don't have enough time for social activities.

77. (*d*) This statement is major assumption made in the passage.

78. (*a*) The decision is major decision that drove the Government of Rawanda towards disinvestment of 60%.

79. (*d*) The belief of a company is an assumption. It has assumed that, through acquisition only, we can achieve the growth and development.

80. (*d*) The assumption of decline in debt of MRIL has been made.

81. (*a*) It is a major decision as the company is increasing it's production.

82. (*c*) A statement is a minor factor in making decisions as the current acquisitions are enough to further invest and is a economically feasible event.

83. (*a*) It is the major objective as foreign capital will help the Indian aviation to come out of the crisis, that it is facing right know.

84. (*b*) The slowing down of the economy is a major factor for decision make to make the decision, an aspect of the problem

85. (*b*) Strikes at Air India is also a major factor for the decision maker to reach to the decision an important aspect of the problem.

86. (*c*) It is a minor factor that foreign airlines would pick up states in Indian carries as compared to others, it will help the Indian aviation to grow, but other factors are more important.

87. (*d*) Poorly developed air navigation leading to more congestion is the major assumption as, this is the primary problem before which any factors or objective is considered. This has played a major role for the current situation of the Indian aviation.

88. (*d*) Expanding in the body lotion and shampoo category is easier due to low pentration level in India is a major assumption for the decision maker before considering any aspect.

89. (*a*) It is the major objective because the ultimate aim is to grow and as it has already established brand of santoor, which will help it to grow.

90. (*c*) It is a minor factor for the decision maker, as if its market grows, then he can spend easily on ads etc.

91. (*b*) As the decision maker has ensured its growth in international market, so it is a major factor for the decision maker to reach to that decision to expand its business in India.

92. (*b*) Significant growth in international market is also a major factor for the decision maker to reach that decision to expand its business in India in other producs and aspects.

93. (*a*) This is because the NTC to be made worldclass is a goal that will change the view of textile industry.

94. (*d*) This is because when the new logo of NTC was formulated it was assumed that some targets will be achieved through this step.

95. (*a*) Because the review of competitive strategy helped them to achieve the goal of making the industry debt free.

96. (*d*) The steps are taken assuming the future results to be achieved.

97. (*d*) The programme has been implemented assuming the new vision will be coming with cultural innovations that will benefit the employees of NTC.

98. (*e*) Clearly, conclusion (e) can be inferred from the given statement.

99. (*c*) A road is constructed considering the type of vehicles plying on it and 18-wheeler trucks which are 30 tonnes lighter will not cause harm to the mentioned road.

100. (*d*) Most logically such comparison should reveal mortality rate per thousand doctors indulged in SARS treatment and not indulged in treatment.

101. (*d*) It is implied from the passage that social sector spending such as health and education sector spending should be increased for large scale job creation.

As the service sector can close only half of the job gap prevailing in the country, the other half can be comfortably filled by social sectors such as health and education.

102. (*c*) It is seen in the passage that through water from wetlands and rivers is used a resource but policy does not recognise it as a part of natural ecosystem.

To strengthen capacities of the ecological systems, there is a need to recognise the wetlands as more than just open sources of water.
If they are considered as a part of the natural ecosystem, only then their capacity can be increased.

103. (*d*) The conclusion that can be drawn from the paragraph most appropriately and correct is option (d).

104. (*a*) From the passage, it can be concluded that subsidy provided by the government under various heads to the citizen increases the cost of capital.

105. (*c*) From the passage, it can be assumed that government may not be able to create more infrastructure facilities if the present level of subsidy continue for a longer time.

106. (*d*) From the passage, it is clear that gradual withdrawl of subsidy is essential for effectively managing fiscal deficit in India.

107. (*a*) From the passage, it is clear that accurate poverty measurement is not possible in India.

108. (*c*) From the passage it can be concluded that to tackle the dynamic nature of poverty, process of its measurement needs to be taken into account.

109. (*b*) From the passage it can be concluded that the increase in number of persons falling into poverty varies considerably across the country over a period of time.

Lightning Source UK Ltd.
Milton Keynes UK
UKHW030637060223
416537UK00015B/3022